WITHDRAWN

D1597409

The Oxford Handbook of Substance Use
and Substance Use Disorders

OXFORD LIBRARY OF PSYCHOLOGY

EDITOR-IN-CHIEF

Peter E. Nathan

AREA EDITORS:

Clinical Psychology

David H. Barlow

Cognitive Neuroscience

Kevin N. Ochsner and Stephen M. Kosslyn

Cognitive Psychology

Daniel Reisberg

Counseling Psychology

Elizabeth M. Altmaier and Jo-Ida C. Hansen

Developmental Psychology

Philip David Zelazo

Health Psychology

Howard S. Friedman

History of Psychology

David B. Baker

Methods and Measurement

Todd D. Little

Neuropsychology

Kenneth M. Adams

Organizational Psychology

Steve W. J. Kozlowski

Personality and Social Psychology

Kay Deaux and Mark Snyder

MONTGOMERY COLLEGE
GERMANTOWN CAMPUS LIBRARY
GERMANTOWN, MARYLAND

OXFORD LIBRARY OF PSYCHOLOGY

Editor in Chief PETER E. NATHAN

The Oxford Handbook of Substance Use and Substance Use Disorders

Volume 2

Edited By

Kenneth J. Sher

OXFORD
UNIVERSITY PRESS

3301756

SEP 2 0 2016

OXFORD
UNIVERSITY PRESS

Oxford University Press is a department of the University of Oxford. It furthers
the University's objective of excellence in research, scholarship, and education
by publishing worldwide.Oxford is a registered trade mark of Oxford University
Press in the UK and certain other countries.

Published in the United States of America by Oxford University Press
198 Madison Avenue, New York, NY 10016, United States of America.

© Oxford University Press 2016

All rights reserved. No part of this publication may be reproduced, stored in
a retrieval system, or transmitted, in any form or by any means, without the
prior permission in writing of Oxford University Press, or as expressly permitted
by law, by license, or under terms agreed with the appropriate reproduction
rights organization. Inquiries concerning reproduction outside the scope of the
above should be sent to the Rights Department, Oxford University Press, at the
address above.

You must not circulate this work in any other form
and you must impose this same condition on any acquirer.

Library of Congress Cataloging-in-Publication Data
Names: Sher, Kenneth J., editor.
Title: Oxford library of psychology / edited by Kenneth J. Sher.
Description: Oxford ; New York : Oxford University Press, [2016] |
Series: Oxford library of psychology | Includes bibliographical references and index. |
Description based on print version record and CIP data provided
   by publisher; resource not viewed.
Identifiers: LCCN 2016020729 (print) | LCCN 2016018961 (ebook) |
ISBN 978–0–19–537974–7 (hardback, combined volume) |
ISBN 978–0–19–938169–2 (ebook, v. 1) | ISBN 978–0–19–938167–8 (hardback, v. 1) |
ISBN 978–0–19–938172–2 (ebook, v. 2) | ISBN 978–0–19–938170–8 (hardback, v. 2)
Subjects: LCSH: Substance abuse. | BISAC: PSYCHOLOGY / Clinical Psychology.
Classification: LCC RC564 (print) | LCC RC564 .O96 2016 (ebook) | DDC
   362.29—dc23
LC record available at https://lccn.loc.gov/2016020729

9 8 7 6 5 4 3 2 1
Printed by Sheridan Books, Inc., United States of America

SHORT CONTENTS

The *Oxford Library of Psychology*, a landmark series of handbooks, is published by Oxford University Press, one of the world's oldest and most highly respected publishers, with a tradition of publishing significant books in psychology. The ambitious goal of the *Oxford Library of Psychology* is nothing less than to span a vibrant, wide-ranging field and, in so doing, to fill a clear market need.

Encompassing a comprehensive set of handbooks, organized hierarchically, the *Library* incorporates volumes at different levels, each designed to meet a distinct need. At one level are a set of handbooks designed broadly to survey the major subfields of psychology; at another are numerous handbooks that cover important current focal research and scholarly areas of psychology in depth and detail. Planned as a reflection of the dynamism of psychology, the *Library* will grow and expand as psychology itself develops, thereby highlighting significant new research that will impact on the field. Adding to its accessibility and ease of use, the *Library* will be published in print and, later on, electronically.

The *Library* surveys psychology's principal subfields with a set of handbooks that capture the current status and future prospects of those major subdisciplines. This initial set includes handbooks of social and personality psychology, clinical psychology, counseling psychology, school psychology, educational psychology, industrial and organizational psychology, cognitive psychology, cognitive neuroscience, methods and measurements, history, neuropsychology, personality assessment, developmental psychology, and more. Each handbook undertakes to review one of psychology's major subdisciplines with breadth, comprehensiveness, and exemplary scholarship. In addition to these broadly-conceived volumes, the *Library* also includes a large number of handbooks designed to explore in depth more specialized areas of scholarship and research, such as stress, health and coping, anxiety and related disorders, cognitive development, or child and adolescent assessment. In contrast to the broad coverage of the subfield handbooks, each of these latter volumes focuses on an especially productive, more highly focused line of scholarship and research. Whether at the broadest or most specific level, however, all of the *Library* handbooks offer synthetic coverage that reviews and evaluates the relevant past and present research and anticipates research in the future. Each handbook in the *Library* includes introductory and concluding chapters written by its editor to provide a roadmap to the handbook's table of contents and to offer informed anticipations of significant future developments in that field.

An undertaking of this scope calls for handbook editors and chapter authors who are established scholars in the areas about which they write. Many of the nation's and world's most productive and best-respected psychologists have agreed to edit *Library* handbooks or write authoritative chapters in their areas of expertise.

For whom has the *Oxford Library of Psychology* been written? Because of its breadth, depth, and accessibility, the *Library* serves a diverse audience, including graduate students in psychology and their faculty mentors, scholars, researchers, and practitioners in psychology and related fields. Each will find in the *Library* the information they seek on the subfield or focal area of psychology in which they work or are interested.

Befitting its commitment to accessibility, each handbook includes a comprehensive index, as well as extensive references to help guide research. And because the *Library* was designed from its inception as an online as well as a print resource, its structure and contents will be readily and rationally searchable online. Further, once the *Library* is released online, the handbooks will be regularly and thoroughly updated.

In summary, the *Oxford Library of Psychology* will grow organically to provide a thoroughly informed perspective on the field of psychology, one that reflects both psychology's dynamism and its increasing interdisciplinarity. Once published electronically, the *Library* is also destined to become a uniquely valuable interactive tool, with extended search and browsing capabilities. As you begin to consult this handbook, we sincerely hope you will share our enthusiasm for the more than 500-year tradition of Oxford University Press for excellence, innovation, and quality, as exemplified by the *Oxford Library of Psychology.*

Peter E. Nathan
Editor-in-Chief
Oxford Library of Psychology

Kenneth J. Sher

Kenneth J. Sher, PhD, is Curators' Distinguished Professor of Psychological Sciences at the University of Missouri. He received his undergraduate degree from Antioch College (1975), his PhD in clinical psychology from Indiana University (1980), and his clinical internship training at Brown University (1981). His primary areas of research focus on etiological processes in the development of alcohol dependence, factors that affect the course of drinking and alcohol use disorders throughout adulthood, longitudinal research methodology, psychiatric comorbidity, and nosology. At the University of Missouri he has directed the predoctoral and postdoctoral training program in alcohol studies, and his research has been continually funded by the National Institute on Alcohol Abuse and Alcoholism for more than 30 years. A Fellow of the American Association for Advancement of Science, the Association for Psychological Science, and the American Psychological Association, his research contributions have been recognized by professional societies including the Research Society on Alcoholism (where he was awarded the Young Investigator Award, the Distinguished Researcher Award, and the G. Alan Marlatt Mentoring Award) and the American Psychological Association (the Distinguished Scientific Contribution Award from the Division on Addictions and a Presidential Citation), as well as by the University of Missouri (the Chancellor's Award for Research and Creativity and the President's Award for Research and Creativity) and the National Institutes of Health (a MERIT Award and a Senior Scientist and Mentoring Award). Throughout his career, he has been heavily involved in service to professional societies (e.g., he is current president-elect of the Research Society on Alcoholism and serves on the American Psychological Association's Policy and Planning Board and Council of Representatives). He also has a long history of service to scholarly publications, serving as an associate/field editor for both disciplinary journals (*Clinical Psychological Science, Journal of Abnormal Psychology, Psychological Bulletin*), and specialty journals (*The Journal of Studies on Alcohol and Drugs, and Alcoholism: Clinical and Experimental Research*). His current work is focused on attempting to define the "core" of addiction and developing methods to improve the diagnosis of alcohol use disorders.

CONTRIBUTORS

Genevieve M. Ames
Pacific Institute for Research and Evaluation
Oakland, California

James C. Anthony
Michigan State University
Lansing, Michigan

Lindsay L. Barber
Ohio Department of Public Safety
Columbus, Ohio

David A. Barondess
Michigan State University
Lansing, Michigan

Alissa D. Bazinet
Oregon Health & Science University
Portland, Oregon

Iris Beltran
Children's Hospital
Los Angeles, California

Sanjiv V. Bhave
University of Colorado
Denver, Colorado

Warren K. Bickel
Virginia Tech Carilion
Research Institute
Roanoke, Virginia

Kaitlin Bountress
Medical University of South Carolina
Charleston, South Carolina

Whitney C. Brown
University of Buffalo
The State University of New York
Buffalo, New York

Raul Caetano
University of Texas Southwestern
Medical Center
Dallas, Texas

Laurie Chassin
Arizona State University
Tempe, Arizona

Tammy A. Chung
University of Pittsburgh School
of Medicine
Pittsburgh, Pennsylvania

Patricia J. Conrod
Université de Montréal
Montréal, Quebec, Canada

M. Lynne Cooper
University of Missouri
Columbia, Missouri

John C. Crabbe
Oregon Health and Science University
Portland, Oregon

Elizabeth J. D'Amico
RAND Corporation
Santa Monica, California

Jack Darkes
University of South Florida
Tampa, Florida

Louisa Degenhardt
UNSW Australia
Sydney, Australia

Frances K. Del Boca
University of Connecticut Health Center
Farmington, Connecticut

Karen J. Derefinko
University of Tennessee Health
Science Center
Memphis, Tennessee

Jaye L. Derrick
University at Buffalo
The State University of New York
Buffalo, New York

Robert E. Drake
Dartmouth Medical School
Hanover, New Hampshire

James C. Fell
Pacific Institute for Research and Evaluation
Calverton, Maryland

Matt Field
University of Liverpool
Liverpool, United Kingdom

Michael T. French
University of Miami
Miami, Florida

Ian R. Gizer
University of Missouri
Columbia, Missouri

Valerie V. Grant
Gormand & Garland Psychological
Services
Dartmouth, Nova Scotia, Canada

Joel W. Grube
Pacific Institute for Research
and Evaluation
Oakland, California

Paul J. Gruenewald
Pacific Institute for Research
and Evaluation
Oakland, California

Wayne Hall
University of Queensland
Brisbane, Queensland, Australia

Moira Haller
VA San Diego Health Care System
San Diego, California

Elizabeth Handley
Mt. Hope Family Center
University of Rochester
Rochester, New York

R. Adron Harris
University of Texas
Austin, Texas

Jennifer E. Hettema
University of New Mexico
Albuquerque, New Mexico

Harold D. Holder
Prevention Research Center
Oakland, California

Avram J. Holmes
Yale University
New Haven, Connecticut

Keith Humphreys
Stanford University
Stanford, California

William G. Iacono
University of Minnesota
Minneapolis, Minnesota

Karen S. Ingersoll
University of Virginia
Charlottesville, Virginia

Kristina M. Jackson
Brown University
Providence, Rhode Island

Seungmin Jahng
Sungkyunkwan University
Seoul, South Korea

Keith Klostermann
Medaille College
Buffalo, New York

George F. Koob
National Institute on Alcohol Abuse
and Alcoholism
Rockville, Maryland

Emmanuel Kuntsche
Swiss Institute for the Prevention of
Alcohol and Drug Problems
Lausanne, Switzerland

S. Janet Kuramoto-Crawford
Centers for Disease Control and Prevention
Washington, DC

James W. Langenbucher
Rutgers University
Piscataway, New Jersey

Elizabeth A. LaScala
Prevention Research Center
Oakland, California

Matthew R. Lee
University of Missouri
Columbia, Missouri

Anna Lembke
Stanford University
Stanford, California

Kenneth E. Leonard
University at Buffalo
The State University of New York
Buffalo, New York

Ash Levitt
University at Buffalo
The State University of New York
Buffalo, New York

Andrew K. Littlefield
Texas Tech University
Lubbock, Texas

Catalina Lopez-Quintero
Michigan State University
Lansing, Michigan

Clare J. Mackie
King's College London, Strand
London, United Kingdom

James MacKillop
McMaster University
Hamilton, Ontario, Canada

Jennifer L. Maggs
The Pennsylvania State University
University Park, Pennsylvania

Christopher S. Martin
University of Pittsburgh School of Medicine
Pittsburgh, Pennsylvania

Julie Maslowsky
University of Texas
Austin, Texas

Lindsay M. McCracken
US Trust
New York, New York

Mandy L. McCracken
National Institute on Drug Abuse
Baltimore, Maryland

Christy McKinney
University of Washington
Seattle, Washington

Kristin D. McLaughlin
University of Missouri
Columbia, Missouri

Bonnie McRee
University of Connecticut Health Center
Farmington, Connecticut

Roland S. Moore
Pacific Institute for Research
and Evaluation
Oakland, California

E. Terry Mueller
Virginia Tech Carilion Research Institute
Roanoke, Virginia

Kim T. Mueser
Boston University
Boston, Massachusetts

Douglas L. Noordsy
Dartmouth Medical School
Hanover, New Hampshire

Marlene Oscar-Berman
Boston University
Boston, Massachusetts

Karen Chan Osilla
RAND Corporation
Santa Monica, California

Megan E. Patrick
University of Michigan
Ann Arbor, Michigan

William E. Pelham Jr.
Florida International University
Miami, Florida

Tamara J. Phillips
Oregon Health and Science
University
Portland, Oregon

Megan M. Pinkston-Camp
Brown University
Providence, Rhode Island

Svetlana Popova
University of Toronto
Toronto, Ontario, Canada

Ioana Popovici
Nova Southeastern University
Fort Lauderdale, Florida

Mirjana Radovanovic
University Psychiatric Hospital
Ljubljana, Slovenia

Jürgen Rehm
University of Toronto
Toronto, Ontario, Canada

Edward P. Riley
San Diego State
San Diego, California

Damaris J. Rohsenow
Brown University
Providence, Rhode Island

Cristel Antonia Russell
American University
Washington, DC

Dale W. Russell
Uniformed Services University
Bethesda, Maryland

Jennifer M. Russo
University of Virginia
Charlottesville, Virginia

Carolyn E. Sartor
Yale University School of Medicine
New Haven, Connecticut

Lauren Schaefer
University of South Florida
Tampa, Florida

John E. Schulenberg
University of Michigan
Ann Arbor, Michigan

Kenneth J. Sher
  University of Missouri
  Columbia, Missouri
Saul Shiffman
  University of Pittsburgh
  Pittsburgh, Pennsylvania
Lawrence D. Snell
  Colorado Neurological Institute
  Denver, Colorado
Marika B. Solhan
  Boston University
  Boston, Massachusetts
Lindsay Squeglia
  Medical University of South Carolina
  Charleston, South Carolina
Alan W. Stacy
  Claremont Graduate University
  Claremont, California
Michael C. Stallings
  University of Colorado
  Boulder, Colorado
Stefanie A. Stern
  RAND Corporation
  Santa Monica, California
Sherry H. Stewart
  Dalhousie University
  Halifax, Nova Scotia, Canada
Chiara Stone
  UNSW Australia
  Sydney, Australia
Robert M. Swift
  Brown University
  Providence, Rhode Island
Boris Tabakoff
  University of Colorado
  Denver, Colorado
Laszlo Takacs
  BioSystems International
  Paris, France
Susan F. Tapert
  University of California
  San Diego, California
Rachel L. Tomko
  Medical Center of South Carolina
  Charleston, South Carolina

Andrew J. Treno (deceased)
  Pacific Institute for Research and
    Evaluation
  Oakland, California
Timothy J. Trull
  University of Missouri
  Columbia, Missouri
Erin C. Tully
  Georgia State University
  Atlanta, Georgia
Trinity A. Urban
  Massachusetts General Hospital
  Boston, Massachusetts
Alvaro Vergés
  Pontificia Universidad Católica
    de Chile
  Santiago, Chile
Robert B. Voas
  Pacific Institute for Research
    and Evaluation
  Calverton, Maryland
Christopher C. Wagner
  Virginia Commonwealth University
  Richmond, Virginia
Helene Raskin White
  Rutgers, The State University
    of New Jersey
  Piscataway, New Jersey
Reinout W. Wiers
  University of Amsterdam
  Amsterdam, Netherlands
Holly C. Wilcox
  Johns Hopkins University
  Baltimore, Maryland
Scott Wolf
  Huge
  Brooklyn, New York
Richard Yi
  University of Maryland
  College Park, Maryland
Kelly C. Young-Wolff
  Kaiser Permanente Division
    of Research
  Oakland, California

CONTENTS

Volume 1

The Oxford Handbook of Substance Use
and Substance Use Disorders

Introduction and Overview

Kenneth J. Sher *and* Alvaro Vergés

Abstract

Substance use and substance use disorders (SUDs) have been documented in a number of cultures since the beginnings of recorded time and represent major societal concerns in the present day. The chapters in this *Handbook* review a number of different areas of inquiry into the fundamental nature of substance use and SUDs, their features, their causes, their consequences, their course, their treatment, and their prevention. It is clear that understanding these various aspects of substance use and SUDs requires a multidisciplinary perspective that considers the pharmacology of drugs of abuse, genetic variation in these acute and chronic effects, and psychological processes in the context of the interpersonal and cultural contexts. This chapter provides a general overview of most (but not all) of the topics covered in the *Handbook*, guiding the reader to the relevant chapters that address each topic in more detail.

Key Words: substance use, substance use disorders, etiology, course, assessment, treatment, prevention

Substance use has been a human activity for much of recorded history. According to Escohotado (1999), references to poppy plants appear in Sumerian tablets dating back more than 4,000 years ago, and the word referring to them was synonymous with "to enjoy"; moreover, remains of hemp fibers dating back 6,000 years have been found in China. Archaeological findings suggest that alcoholic beverages were produced as long ago as 7000–5000 BC (Crocq, 2007). Indeed, the origins of substance use likely have deep evolutionary roots. As Keller (1979) provocatively suggested, "It is hard to understand why the human liver should be endowed with enough alcohol dehydrogenase, the enzyme that catalyzes the first step in the oxidation of alcohol and does not seem to have very much else to do, to metabolize a quart of whisky a day unless alcohol was amply present in the dietary [*sic*] of man, or of his ancestors, in remote evolutionary time" (p. 2822). Comparative biologists have speculated that sensory biases may have developed in response to ethanol plumes emanating from ripening fruit that may have helped our mammalian forebears localize food sources and pair nutritional reward with the psychoactive effects of alcohol (Dudley, 2004). From this perspective, there is an intimate evolutionary relationship between the roots of drug-seeking and more general aspects of human behavior.

Although religious and medical use of psychoactive substances has generally been controlled and associated with relatively little harm, recreational use has been related to significant problems, including epidemics of alcohol use in England and opium use in China (Heyman, 2009; Westermeyer, 2005). However, the magnitude of problems derived from substance misuse at the current time is likely to be larger than ever before due to chemical alterations that make substances more potent, changes in routes of administration that produce faster and potentially more harmful effects, and economic and geopolitical factors that facilitate the spread of substances throughout the world (Vetulani, 2001; Westermeyer, 1988).

The modern study of substance use and substance use disorders (SUDs) is highly multidisciplinary, involving basic and applied research in numerous behavioral, social, and biomedical disciplines. This is because the use and consequences of psychoactive substances are influenced by a range of factors from the molecular to the cultural, traversing almost every conceivable level of causal explanation with no single discipline holding a monopoly on the key to understanding who uses psychoactive substances, why they use them, how it affects them, and what to do about it. Perhaps the greatest challenge to those interested in understanding substance use and SUDs is how to integrate these different factors into comprehensive explanatory models that can form the basis of a more rational approach to assessment, treatment, prevention, and social policy. Indeed, it is difficult to imagine any area of study that brings together more disciplines with a common interest than the study of substance use and SUDs.

As just noted, the origin of current-day substance-related problems has its roots in human prehistory, and substance use has been a prominent feature of many geographically and culturally diverse societies throughout recorded history. Consequently, there is much to learn from scholarship in evolution, history, and anthropology (see, e.g., Dietler, 2006). The role of intoxicants in day-to-day life has been of central concern to many religions and spiritual traditions, where the use of some substances (at least in some situations) has been explicitly promoted, proscribed, or both. Beyond intoxication itself, compulsive use of substances and the related concept of addiction raises basic philosophical, religious, and legal questions concerning the nature of "free will" (e.g., Foddy & Savulescu, 2010). More than 25 years ago, this question was echoed in the halls of the US Supreme Court, where a central issue was whether addiction should be considered a form of "willful misconduct" or a "disease" in an administrative determination of the basis of making a ruling (Taylor, 1988).

Although this Handbook is primarily concerned with behavioral and biomedical approaches to understanding substance use and SUDs from a scientific perspective, it would be myopic to fail to acknowledge that portraying the motivations and contexts for substance use and SUDs has long been an important focus of literature, theater, and film. Many of these portrayals are considered major artistic accomplishments in how they reveal the mind of the addict and the consequences of his or her behavior. It has not gone unnoticed that many of the creators of these artistic works have themselves been afflicted by alcohol and drug problems, often of a severe nature (e.g., Laing, 2014). Thus, for the minority of readers who have had little personal or professional experience with individuals affected by psychoactive substances, there is an immense lay literature (both biographical and fictional) and filmography (e.g., Internet Movie Data Base, 2012) offering sensitive, graphic, and insightful portrayals of the contexts of use, the behavior of users, and the myriad consequences of substance use and addiction.

Impact of Substance Use and SUDs

Martin, Chung, and Langenbucher (Chapter 2, Vol. 1) summarize some of the historical and cultural variation in substance use, as well as the history of classification attempts of substance-related problems. As these authors describe, over the past 200 years, there has been considerable change in how substance use and associated problems have been construed along with related changes in formal diagnostic criteria used by clinicians, researchers, and public health officials.

Substance use and SUDs are associated with a number of negative consequences, including health, behavioral, social, and economic outcomes. Indeed, much of this Handbook is directly concerned with the medical, psychological, and social consequences of substance use, which are considerable. McGinnis and Foege (1999) estimated that 591,000 deaths and 40,338,000 illnesses and injuries are attributable to substance use each year in the United States, and projections of future consequences of substance use are even more pessimistic, with worldwide tobacco-attributable deaths estimated at 6.4 million in 2015 and 8.3 million in 2030, in spite of the slight decrease in use reported in high-income countries (Mathers & Loncar, 2006). Even for alcohol, which has potential health benefits when consumed in moderation in some subpopulations (particularly middle-aged men), the net effect of its use is negative across regions of the world (Rehm et al., 2009). A review of the epidemiological literature showed that problem or dependent users of illicit drugs, alcohol, and tobacco have been estimated to be 0.3–0.9%, 1.2%, and 26% of the population 15 years or older, respectively, worldwide, with corresponding 0.4%, 3.8%, and 8.7% attributable deaths, and 0.9%, 4.5%, and 3.7% attributable disability-adjusted life years (DALYs; a composite metric that captures both premature mortality and disability; Degenhardt & Hall, 2012). Recent results from the Global Burden of Disease Study 2010 indicate that tobacco, alcohol, and drug use are ranked 2, 3, and 19, respectively, among all risk factors for global disease burden in the world, and all of them increased their ranking from the study conducted in 1990 (Lim et al., 2013). In addition, drug use disorders (DUDs) are ranked 12, 31, and 58 and alcohol use disorders (AUDs) are ranked 15, 35, and 55 among all causes of years lived with disability, DALYs, and causes of years of life lost, respectively, in the same study (Lozano et al., 2012; Murray et al., 2012; Vos et al., 2013). The physical and mental health consequences of alcohol, tobacco, and illicit drug use are reviewed by Popova and Rehm (Chapter 10, Vol. 2) and by Degenhardt, Hall, and Bucello (Chapter 3, Vol. 1). As highlighted by Popova and Rehm, identifying causal mechanisms is not always straightforward using existing methodologies. Other chapters focus on more specific health-related consequences of substance use and SUDs. For example, Kuramoto and Wilcox (Chapter 11, Vol. 2) review the evidence of an association between SUDs and intentional injuries, emphasizing suicide and intimate partner violence. The implications of this research for the prevention of intentional injuries in the population diagnosed with SUDs are also presented. Oscar-Berman, Urban, and Holmes (Chapter 9, Vol. 2) review the neurobehavioral consequences of AUDs, describing the contextual factors that influence this association as well as the possibility of recovery after achieving abstinence.

Substance Use and SUDs in the Context of Development

In recent decades, it has become increasingly accepted that one needs to consider developmental factors when studying both the acute effects of substances as well as the lingering consequences of use (either due to passive exposure during fetal development or voluntary use through self-administration). Indeed, the epidemiology of substance use and SUDs shows dramatic age gradients in characterizing the onset of use and disorder, as well as some age differences in course (e.g., persistence, escalation, desistance, recurrence; Vergés et al., 2012, 2013). Bazinet, Squeglia, Riley, and Tapert (Chapter 8, Vol. 2) review the effects of drugs, either through prenatal exposure or through adolescent substance use, on development, highlighting similarities and differences across types of drugs and the importance of

considering development for understanding durable effects of drug exposures. Jackson and Sartor (Chapter 4, Vol. 1) review the course of substance use and SUDs, noting the large range of variability in course and how some of this variability is related to stage of development. Many other chapters in this *Handbook* addressing social influences, intimate relations, personality, and psychopathology also emphasize the importance of a developmental perspective in understanding substance use and its consequences.

Etiology

The etiology of substance use and addictive behaviors is complex and involves multiple factors including genetic, neurobiological, psychopharmacological, personality-related, and environmental (see Sher, Grekin, & Williams, 2005, for a discussion focused on alcohol use and AUD).

Genetic Vulnerability

The existence of significant genetic influences on SUDs has been firmly established in adoption studies (Cadoret, Yates, Troughton, Woodworth, & Stewart, 1995; Cloninger, Bohman, & Sigvardsson, 1981; Goodwin, Schulsinger, Hermansen, Guze, & Winokur, 1973) that show strong effects of biological parents independent of being reared with them. Moreover, classical twin studies (Agrawal & Lynskey, 2006, 2008; Heath, 1995; Lessov et al., 2004) that compare concordance of substance-related phenotypes between monozygotic ("identical") and dizygotic ("fraternal") twins consistently show significant genetic contribution for SUDs, including alcohol dependence (with heritability estimates ranging between 50% and 60%; Knopik et al., 2004; Prescott & Kendler, 1999; True et al., 1999), nicotine dependence (with heritability estimates ranging between 50% and 70%; Kendler et al., 1999; Lessov et al., 2004; Maes et al., 2004; True et al., 1999), and cannabis dependence (with heritability estimates ranging between 30% and 80%; Agrawal & Lynskey, 2006; Lynskey et al., 2012; Verweij et al., 2010). The studies that investigate other illicit drugs yield similar heritability estimates (Kendler, Aggen, Tambs, & Reichborn-Kjennerud, 2006; Kendler, Karkowski, Neale, & Prescott, 2000; Tsuang et al., 1996). Although the new era of molecular genetics has moved the focus from establishing the importance of genetic factors to identifying specific genes that are important in SUD etiology (Dick, Rose, & Kaprio, 2006; Wang, Kapoor, & Goate, 2012), these twin and adoption studies remain useful in demonstrating (1) common genetic influences on SUDs and comorbid conditions, (2) substance-specific influences, and (3) the importance of Gene × Environment (G×E) interaction in the absence of knowledge of specific genes involved (e.g., Kendler, Jacobson, Prescott, & Neale, 2003; Kendler, Myers, & Prescott, 2007).

In recent years, there have been increasing numbers of molecular genetic studies seeking to identify specific genes that confer risk. Probably the major success in the case of AUDs has been the identification of ALDH2 and ADH1B as genes that influence the metabolism of alcohol. Polymorphisms in these genes, mostly found among Asians, are associated with an unpleasant flushing response to alcohol intake, thus protecting against the development of alcohol dependence. Luczak, Glatt, and Wall (2006) reviewed these findings and conducted a meta-analysis suggesting that the association of the two variants and alcohol dependence varies depending on the characteristics of the studies and the samples used. Perhaps more relevant for understanding genetic influences in individuals of European descent, a number of genes associated with central brain neurotransmitter systems have been found to be associated with alcohol dependence. For example, γ-aminobutyric acid (GABA) is a neurotransmitter involved in many of the anxiolytic and sedative effects of alcohol, and GABA receptors are involved in alcohol tolerance. Recent studies have established associations between GABA$_A$ receptor genes (esp. GABRA2) and AUDs across human and animal studies (Dick & Beirut, 2006), although the specificity of this finding for alcohol-related phenotypes is far from clear. In the case of nicotine, genes encoding for nicotinic acetylcholine receptor (nAChR) subunits have been found to be robustly associated with nicotine use and dependence. For instance, Saccone et al. (2007) reported results from a study identifying a number of genetic variants—mainly nicotinic receptor genes—that might influence nicotine dependence. Moreover, recent genome-wide association meta-analyses have confirmed an association of nAChR subunits with heavy smoking (Furberg et al., 2010; Liu et al., 2010; Thorgeirsson et al., 2010).

At present, a number of large-scale genome-wide association studies are under way that will likely reveal additional genes that are associated with the SUD (or closely related) phenotypes. However, as is true for all psychological disorders (Kendler, 2005, 2006), it seems unlikely that any single gene will reveal more than a small bivariate association with SUDs given the long and complex causal chain between gene action and the manifestation of substance-related pathology (Kendler, 2005, 2006; Sher, 1991), the likely etiological heterogeneity of drug-seeking and SUDs, and the failure of genome-wide scans to identify strong single-gene effects on complex disorders (Goldstein, 2009; Wang et al., 2012). Stallings, Gizer, and Young-Wolff (Chapter 7, Vol. 1) provide a systematic overview of both the genetic epidemiology literature demonstrating the strong influence of genetic factors in SUDs as well as past and current strategies designed to identify specific genes and how they operate. With respect to identifying specific genes, their review highlights the arguably disappointing findings to date but also the new directions genetic research is taking. This includes focusing more on endophenotypes that are proximally closer to gene effects, a strategy being employed in psychiatric genetics more generally (e.g., Cannon & Keller, 2006). As Stallings et al. suggest, in the case of substance use and SUDs, such endophenotypes might be grouped into those related to general externalizing psychopathology (e.g., deficits in self-regulation, variability in reward-seeking, lack of sensitivity to punishment), to drug sensitivity and drug metabolism, and to the development of addiction. Indeed, recent data from twin studies (Kendler, Aggen, Prescott, Crabbe, & Neale, 2012) suggest the value of deconstructing the SUD or dependence syndrome in order to identify subgroups of symptoms that are associated with distinct genetic factors. Not only were different symptoms of alcohol dependence related to different genetic factors, but these dissociable genetic factors were differentially associated with external correlates. It seems likely that greater resolution of the various endophenotypes comprising SUDs in general and for specific substances will aid in genetic analyses, as well as help to map the underlying architecture of individual differences in drug-seeking, drug effects, and the development of dependence.

Indeed, such an approach to deconstructing the phenomena and syndromes observed in humans aids in creating consilience with genetic animal models in which many (though clearly not all) features of the human condition can be effectively modeled and their neurobiology more effectively explored. Crabbe and Phillips (Chapter 8, Vol. 1) highlight the extraordinary range of animal models that can be employed to gain insight into drug-seeking, dependence, and treatment response in humans. They note, importantly, that a key obstacle to effective animal models of various human behaviors and characteristics is not necessarily the intrinsic translatability of the construct from humans to other species but the often poorly defined and operationalized nature of the target construct in humans. From this perspective, cross-translations of human and animal behaviors will not only improve the generalizability of animal models to humans, but will also aid in refining our behavioral and clinical constructs in those suffering from SUDs.

Neurobiology

There has been an impressive increase in our understanding of the neural basis of addictive behaviors during the past decades. One influential perspective regarding neural changes produced by drug use is the theory of incentive sensitization (Robinson & Berridge, 1993, 2001). According to this theory, craving is the result of a hypersensitization of the dopamine system that increases the incentive salience of drugs and drug-associated stimuli. Importantly, this incentive salience ("wanting") can diverge from the pleasurable effects of drugs ("liking"), so that craving can be experienced even in the absence of any expected positive experience.

A related perspective on changes associated with the chronic use of various drugs of abuse is termed *allostasis* (i.e., adaptive homeostatic changes that occur in response to repeated drug challenges; e.g., Koob & Le Moal, 2001, 2008). According to this notion, an organism responds to drug challenges by producing counterdirectional (i.e., homeostatic) responses that increase over time. Thus, addiction is conceptualized as an allostatic state in the brain reward system in which apparent reward function stability is achieved by changes in the reward and stress system neurocircuitry. Allostasis explains the phenomenon of *acquired tolerance*—the tendency for a given dose of a drug to elicit progressively less response over time—in a way similar to that proposed by Solomon and Corbit (1974) in their opponent-process theory and Siegel and colleagues (e.g., Siegel, Baptista, Kim, McDonald, & Weise-Kelly, 2000) in their Pavlovian account of tolerance development. However, the allostatic perspective goes further than these theories by specifically positing that repeated homeostatic challenges present an adaptive burden and result in a shift of a hedonic "set point" in the direction of the opponent process. Theoretically, such a process could explain intermediate- to long-term deviations in tonic emotional levels, resulting in a more depressed, irritable, and/or anxious

substance-dependent person. These allostatic, chronic adaptations are believed to be mediated by the hypothalamic-pituitary axis (HPA) via effects of corticotrophin-releasing factor (CRF; Koob & Le Moal, 2001, 2008).

Whereas most theories of the neural basis of addictive behavior are concerned with the late stages of compulsive use, the influential model proposed by Everitt and Robbins (2005) tries to explain the transition from initial to compulsive use of addictive substances. According to this model, this change is paralleled by a transition from prefrontal to striatal control of behavior, as well as a progression from ventral to more dorsal domains of the striatum (Everitt et al., 2008; Everitt & Robbins, 2005, 2013). These various theories of addiction highlight the advances in neurobiology that have taken place with respect to understanding addiction, but they also highlight the persistent lack of consensus, even at the neurobiological level, as to what forms the "core" or "essence" of addiction.

Clearly, we cannot understand how various substances of abuse work acutely and produce long-term adaptations without understanding the neuropharmacology of drug actions and the neural circuitry they act on. McCracken, McCracken, and Harris (Chapter 5, Vol. 1) provide a description of acute and chronic drug effects at the molecular level and highlight similarities and differences across different substances of abuse. Koob's (Chapter 6, Vol. 1)review extends McCracken et al.'s review by highlighting motivational changes that accompany these neuroadaptations and by providing a conceptual framework for understanding how "normal" use can lead to addiction and compulsive drug-seeking. It is also important to recognize that substance users frequently use multiple substances, often simultaneously. As described by Anthony, Barondess, Radovanovic, and Lopez-Quintero (Chapter 2, Vol. 2), such polydrug use opens up additional complexities in understanding the nature of acute and chronic effects of psychoactive substances.

Personality

Although the concept of an "addictive personality," understood as a specific configuration of personality traits that is uniquely associated with addictive behaviors, has been disregarded in current conceptualizations of SUD etiology, the notion that certain personality characteristics confer increased risk to addictive behaviors is also embraced by most scholars (see Littlefield & Sher, 2010). For instance, Elkins King, McGue, and Iacono (2006) reported findings from the Minnesota Twin Family Study showing that both low constraint and negative emotionality prospectively predict the onset of nicotine, alcohol, and illicit drug disorders during a 3-year follow-up. Moreover, changes in personality during adolescence and emerging and young adulthood have been found to be associated with changes in substance use and related problems (King, Fleming, Monahan, & Catalano, 2011; Littlefield, Sher, & Wood, 2009, 2010; Littlefield, Vergés, Wood, & Sher, 2012), and personality changes have been documented during the course of SUD treatment (Blonigen, Timko, Finney, Moos, & Moos, 2011; Littlefield et al., 2015).

The personality-related construct that has received more attention in recent years is impulsivity (broadly defined as "a predisposition toward rapid, unplanned reactions to internal or external stimuli without regard to the negative consequences of these reactions to the impulsive individual or to others"; Moeller, Barratt, Dougherty, Schmitz, & Swann, 2001, p. 1784), which is considered a vulnerability factor that might constitute a useful endophenotype (Verdejo-García, Lawrence, & Clark, 2008). Indeed, Slutske et al. (2002) found that behavioral undercontrol (a broad trait that includes measures of impulsivity) accounted for 40% of the genetic variation in alcohol dependence, suggesting that common genetic factors that underlie both behavioral undercontrol and alcohol dependence could be identified. More recently, different specific facets of impulsivity have been identified (Cyders et al., 2007; Whiteside & Lynam, 2001) and linked with substance use and SUDs. In a meta-analysis of the association of these facets and alcohol use, Coskunpinar, Dir, and Cyders (2013) found that impulsivity facets differentially predict alcohol use outcomes such as drinking quantity, drinking problems, and alcohol dependence, thus highlighting the importance of considering narrow, homogenous personality constructs when investigating the personality–substance use associations (Smith, McCarthy, & Zapolski, 2009).

The literature on personality and SUDs is reviewed by Littlefield and Sher (Chapter 10, Vol. 1) in this *Handbook* and presents the different pathways through which personality traits can influence the development and course of SUDs. As mentioned in that chapter, one of those pathways involves the mediating role of expectancies and motives, which are briefly discussed in the next section.

Expectancies and Motives

Although we can view the neurobiology of drug effects as providing an essential framework for understanding substance use and SUDs, research with humans has shown that there is considerable variability in the beliefs that individuals hold with respect to the anticipated effects of various substances (i.e., outcome expectancies) and the reasons they provide for using substances. Although the two concepts (i.e., expectancies and motives) are intimately linked, they are clearly dissociable, and one may hold very specific expectancies for the effects of a given substance (e.g., alcohol makes me more sociable) but not necessarily use the substance for sociability reasons. We can envision both explicit substance expectancies and self-reported substance use motives as reflecting a bridge between the underlying neurobiology of substance effects and patterns of drug-seeking. However, it is clear that the cognitive representations that people construct with respect to how various substances will make them feel and why they engage in drug-seeking behavior represents more than direct pharmacological experiences with substances and is conditioned by a range of individual and environmental factors.

Elaborating a bit more, expectancies can be defined as beliefs that people have about the affective, cognitive, and behavioral effects of using a substance (Goldman, Brown, & Christiansen, 1987; Jones, Corbin, & Fromme, 2001). Goldman, Del Boca, and Darkes (1999) suggest that outcome expectancies can be categorized along three basic dimensions: (1) positive versus negative expected outcomes (e.g., increased sociability versus increased aggressiveness), (2) positive versus negative reinforcement (e.g., social facilitation versus tension reduction), and (3) arousal versus sedation (e.g., stimulant versus depressant effects). Associations have been consistently found in cross-sectional studies between expectancies and both substance use and substance-related problems among children (Anderson et al., 2005), adolescents (Fromme & D'Amico, 2000; Grube & Agostinelli, 1999), college students (Brandon & Baker, 1991; Christiansen, Vik, & Jarchow, 2002; Jaffe & Kilbey, 1994; Read, Wood, Lejuez, Palfai, & Slack, 2004; Schafer & Brown, 1991), and adults (Jaffe & Kilbey, 1994; Pastor & Evans, 2003), and an early meta-analysis showed that expectancies account for 12% of the variance in alcohol use (McCarthy & Smith, 1996). With respect to alcohol, outcome expectancies tend to develop in childhood (Anderson et al., 2005; Christiansen, Goldman, & Inn, 1982; Miller, Smith, & Goldman, 1990), strengthen during adolescence (Aas, Leigh, Anderssen, & Jakobsen, 1998; Sayer & Willett, 1998; Smith, Goldman, Greenbaum, & Christiansen, 1995), and weaken during early adulthood (presumably following extended experience with drugs; Sher, Wood, Wood, & Raskin, 1996). Moreover, several prospective studies demonstrate that expectancies uniquely predict future use over extended time periods (Patrick, Wray-Lake, Finlay, & Maggs, 2010; Sher et al., 1996; Smith et al., 1995; Stacy, Newcomb, & Bentler, 1991). Although the outcome expectancy literature is not as extensive for other substances as it is for alcohol, research suggests that they are also important correlates for other forms of substance use, including marijuana and cocaine (e.g., Galen & Henderson, 1999; Schafer & Brown, 1991) and tobacco products including smokeless tobacco (Gottlieb, Cohen, Demarree, Treloar, & McCarthy, 2013), electronic cigarettes (Hendricks et al., 2015), and combustible cigarettes (Wetter et al., 1994).

In recent years, there has been increasing interest in implicit cognitive processes and how they relate to substance involvement (Wiers & Stacy, 2006). In contrast to explicit outcome expectancies that are assessed by self-report questionnaires and assume that these expectancies are conscious, implicit expectancies are assessed by any of a variety of behavioral tasks that are assumed to be automatic and largely unconscious. Both of these levels of cognition are thought to act in concert in "dual-process" models. Dual-process models posit that both more reflective explicit and more reflexive, automatic implicit cognitive processes influence behavior (e.g., Fazio & Towles-Schwen, 1999). Implicit alcohol-related cognitions (e.g., implicit alcohol expectancies) are thought to represent individual differences in memory associations between substance-related cues, outcomes, and behavior (Thush et al., 2008). These implicit cognitions might explain why some individuals use drugs in spite of knowing about their negative consequences (Stacy & Wiers, 2010). Dual-process models of addiction also posit that controlled self-regulatory processes interact with both implicit and explicit expectancies (e.g., Thush et al., 2008; but see Littlefield, Vergés, McCarthy, & Sher, 2011). In Wiers, Field, and Stacy's chapter (Chapter 9, Vol. 1), the recent explosion of research on implicit processes using diverse experimental procedures is reviewed and the potential for implicit processes to serve as a bridge between addiction-related neural processes and overt behavior is highlighted. Additionally, this recent work provides a foundation for novel treatment approaches that directly target impulsive processes rather than the reflective processes targeted by most existing psychosocial treatments.

Individuals report a range of motives for consuming substances, and factor analyses of self-reported reasons for drinking reliably yield a multidimensional, four-factor structure (Cooper, 1994) that can be described as: (1) social motives (e.g., "to be sociable"), (2) enhancement motives (e.g., "to get high," "because it's fun"), (3) coping motives (e.g., "to forget your worries," "because it helps when you feel depressed or nervous"), and (4) conformity motives (e.g., "to fit in"). An additional factor labeled as expansion (e.g., "to understand things differently," "to expand my awareness") has been reported among marijuana users (Simons, Correia, Carey, & Borsari, 1998), and individuals may endorse different motives for different substances (Simons, Correia, & Carey, 2000). Cooper, Kuntsche, Levitt, Barber, and Wolf (Chapter 11, Vol. 1) describe similarities and differences in self-reported motives across substances and provide a conceptual framework for understanding the motivational basis of diverse forms of substance use in humans.

Notably, enhancement and coping motives (but not social or conformity motives) are strongly associated with drinking, heavy drinking, and drinking problems in both adolescents and adults (Cooper, 1994; Cooper, Frone, Russell, & Mudar, 1995). Although it has been proposed that enhancement and coping drinkers constitute two distinct clusters of individuals, the case is far from clear, with recent analyses suggesting that motives are better conceptualized as dimensional constructs (Littlefield, Vergés, Rosinski, Steinley, & Sher, 2013), at least in nonclinical samples. That is, individuals vary in their overall profiles of motives for using a specific substance but do not necessarily "specialize" in using a substance for one specific reason.

A growing body of literature indicates that there is an intimate relation between personality traits and motives for substance use. As one example, extraversion and sensation-seeking tend to correlate with enhancement motives, and the personality trait of neuroticism tends to correlate with coping motives (Kuntsche, Knibbe, Gmel, & Engels, 2006). Furthermore, changes in coping motives appear to mediate the relation between both changes in impulsivity and neuroticism with alcohol-related problems (Littlefield et al., 2010). These findings point to somewhat specific motivational pathways arising from individual differences in temperamental/personality traits and, thus, link broad dispositional traits to etiology via these pathways.

Environmental Influences

The potential environmental influences that might play a role in the development of substance use and SUDs are extremely diverse and difficult to categorize. For example, although it is well known that alcohol and other substance use during pregnancy has deleterious effects on the fetus (i.e., fetal alcohol spectrum disorders; see Kodituwakku, 2007, for a review), its effect on the substance use of the offspring is less clear. Baer, Sampson, Barr, Connor, and Streissguth (2003) reported results from a prospective study following the offspring of 500 women in prenatal care. They found that prenatal alcohol exposure predicted alcohol dependence at age 21 even after adjusting for a number of covariates including family history of alcoholism.

Both parental styles and peer use have been found to be associated with substance use during adolescence. For instance, Adalbjarnardottir and Hafsteinsson (2001) conducted a longitudinal study over 3 years and found that adolescents who perceived their parents as being more neglectful at age 14 were more likely to try hashish and amphetamines and to engage in heavy drinking by age 17, compared with adolescents who perceived their parents as being authoritative. Similar results were reported in a sample of adolescents from six different European countries in which both indulgent and authoritative parenting styles were found to be protective against the development of substance use (Calafat, García, Juan, Becoña, & Fernández-Hermida, 2014). Chassin et al. (Chapter 13, Vol. 1) review familial factors influencing substance use and SUDs, going beyond the role played by parents to consider also the influences of siblings and the broader family system. With regard to the influence of peers, Curran, Stice, and Chassin (1997) reported results from a prospective study of adolescents who were asked about their own and their peer's alcohol use. Results suggested bidirectional effects, such that adolescent use predicted increases in peer use, and peer use predicted increases in adolescent use. The association between peer's alcohol use and one's own alcohol use has been found to be influenced by both genetic and environmental factors, the relative contribution of which changes throughout development (Edwards, Maes, Prescott, & Kendler, 2015; also see Leung, Toumbourou, & Hemphill, 2014). The developmental changes in peer influences

are further examined in the chapter by Patrick, Schulenberg, Maggs, and Maslowsky (Chapter 15, Vol. 1), focusing on the processes of selection into substance-using groups and socialization by peers who introduce the use of substances.

Another powerful environmental influence on addictive behaviors comes from social roles such as marital status and employment. In fact, role incompatibility (Yamaguchi & Kandel, 1985) and social control (Umberson, 1987) theories have been proposed to account for the fact that involvement in adult roles is associated with decreases in substance use. Dick et al. (2006) investigated the association of marital status and both the gene GABRA2 and alcohol dependence. They found evidence of both gene–environment correlation and gene–environment interaction in the prediction of alcohol dependence. In addition, Head, Stansfeld, and Siegrist (2004) investigated the association between work environment and alcohol dependence, finding that a work environment characterized by effort–reward imbalance predicts future alcohol dependence. More recently, Vergés et al. (2012, 2013) examined the influence of role transitions on the course of SUDs, finding that the effect of changes in marital status, parenthood, and employment might vary over the life span. Derrick and Leonard (Chapter 16, Vol. 1) review the effect of marital status and quality of the relationship on substance use, as well as the effects of substance use in marital processes. In addition, Ames and Moore (Chapter 17, Vol. 1) review the epidemiology of substance use by occupations, as well as the rates of use in the workplace and the military, considering the consequences associated with consumption on the job.

The role of the media in decreasing or increasing the prevalence of health-related behaviors in the population (particularly in children and adolescents) has been discussed for decades, and it will likely continue to be a matter of concern for both researchers and public health practitioners in the future. For instance, Primack, Colditz, Pang, and Jackson (2015) examined YouTube videos that portrayed alcohol intoxication and found a more frequent presence of humor and attractiveness than of negative consequences. Russell, Russell, and Grube (Chapter 19, Vol. 1) summarize the evidence linking social marketing through the media with substance use and related behaviors, with special attention paid to the emergence of new media forms. A final environmental factor on addictions can be found in the role of culture in the transmission of social values. In a review of the literature, Eckersley (2005) argued that the individualism and materialism characteristic of Western culture can affect well-being and lead to an increase in the prevalence of substance use and SUDs.

Defining the Phenotype

Research on substance use needs to distinguish the different phenomena that underlie consumption. For instance, a broad distinction can be made between licit and illicit substances, although the nonprescribed use of medication can lie somewhere in between. In addition, a discussion of substance-related problems needs to distinguish the acute and chronic effects of the substance, which each require different intervention approaches. Here, we focus on the distinction between substance-related problems and problematic patterns of consumption.

Substance Use Disorders

The *Diagnostic and Statistical Manual of Mental Disorders*, version 5 (DSM-5; American Psychiatric Association, 2013) integrates the two classes of SUDs used in previous versions of the DSM—substance dependence and substance abuse—into a single category. SUD is defined in the DSM-5 as a maladaptive pattern of use characterized by 2 (or more) of 11 symptoms (see Martin et al., Chapter 2, Vol. 1, Table 1 for a listing of DSM-IV and DSM-5 symptoms).

The abuse/dependence distinction made its debut in the DSM-III (American Psychiatric Association, 1980), reflecting, in part, the distinction introduced by Edwards and Gross (1976) between the alcohol dependence syndrome and alcohol-related disabilities. Unlike Edwards and Gross's conceptualization of the dependence syndrome and alcohol-related disabilities as distinct but related dimensions, the categorical diagnostic approach embraced by the DSM viewed abuse and dependence as mutually exclusive categories, with a dependence diagnosis representing the more severe condition and precluding the ostensibly less severe abuse diagnosis.

Despite the seemingly widespread acceptance of the abuse/dependence distinction since its introduction, accumulating data challenged the validity of this distinction. For example, item-response theory (IRT)-based analyses that conceptualize diagnostic criteria as indicators of a latent trait of SUD indicate that some dependence criteria (e.g., tolerance, impaired control) are prevalent and thus statistically "less severe" than are some abuse

criteria, which are comparatively rare (e.g., legal difficulties; Kahler & Strong, 2006; Langenbucher et al., 2004; Saha, Chou, & Grant, 2006). These results are inconsistent with the notion that abuse is a less severe condition than dependence. Moreover, although some early factor analyses suggested that abuse and dependence items formed statistically distinct (albeit highly correlated) factors (e.g., Hasin, Muthén, Wisnicki, & Grant, 1994; Muthén, Grant, & Hasin, 1993), more recent data further suggest either unifactorial solutions (e.g., Martin, Chung, Kirisci, & Langenbucher, 2006; Proudfoot, Baillie, & Teeson, 2006) or two factors that do not clearly map onto abuse and dependence (e.g., Harford & Muthén, 2001). Two additional types of findings have been cited as support for the validity of the abuse/dependence distinction: (1) dependence is more persistent than abuse (e.g., Schuckit, Smith, & Landi, 2000), and (2) dependence is more highly comorbid with other Axis I and Axis II disorders than is abuse (e.g., Hasin, Stinson, Ogburn, & Grant, 2007). However, Vergés, Steinley, Trull, and Sher (2010) examined the extent to which the DSM-IV diagnostic algorithm (3 of 7 dependence criteria for a diagnosis of dependence; 1 of 4 abuse criteria for a diagnosis of abuse) produces this pattern of findings independent of which symptoms are in the two criterion sets and found that much of the putative support for the validity of the abuse/dependence distinction is an artifact of the diagnostic algorithm and not attributable to the specific criteria sets assigned to the abuse and dependence diagnoses.

The new DSM-5 (American Psychiatric Association, 2013) abandons the abuse/dependence distinction in favor of a single SUD diagnosis that includes in its criteria set symptoms of both DSM-IV abuse and dependence (American Psychiatric Association, 2000). Major changes include the inclusion of craving (long considered a hallmark symptom of dependence but not included in DSM-IV) and the dropping of legal problems (a DSM-IV abuse symptom that has proved problematic in a number of respects). Under DSM-5, only 2 of the 11 symptoms are required to make a diagnosis, leading to concern that the new criteria are too liberal and will yield artificially high prevalence rates and excessive heterogeneity (Martin, Steinley, Vergés, & Sher, 2011). In addition, a number of critics (e.g., Martin, Sher, & Chung, 2011) do not believe that one of the most prevalent symptoms of SUD—hazardous use—should be included as a diagnostic criterion at all because it fails to resolve substance-specificity (i.e., repeated heedless use that could reflect little more than incautious behavior that is simply being manifested by use of the substance but is not specific to it) and is associated with large changes in prevalence rates even when seemingly minor changes in assessment are applied (Vergés, Littlefield, & Sher, 2011). Other recent challenges to the validity of DSM-5 include the seemingly high prevalence rates and questionable specificity leading some scholars to propose revised criteria (Wakefield & Schmitz, 2015). Thus, whereas the notion of what constitutes SUD continues to evolve with successive revisions of diagnostic manuals, providing sensible refinements based upon accumulating data (e.g., Hasin et al., 2013), there is still considerable debate over the fundamental nature of the disorder and how to operationalize it.

Substance Consumption

It is important to note that current DSM-related diagnostic criteria for SUDs fail to include direct measures of consumption despite health concerns based on consumption patterns. For example, the US government has recently, and for the first time, provided safe alcohol drinking guidelines as part of its Dietary Guidelines for Americans, 2005 (US Department of Agriculture and US Department of Health and Human Services, 2005). These guidelines discourage levels of consumption that exceed two drinks per day for men and one drink per day for women. Surveys of representative samples of adults estimate that, among past-year drinkers 18 years of age and older, 46% of men and 32% of adult women in the United States exceed these safe drinking levels and are appropriate targets for interventions (Dawson, Grant, & Li, 2005).

In addition, there has been increasing concern in recent years over drinking patterns associated with high levels of consumption on drinking days (i.e., "binge" drinking). The National Institute on Alcohol Abuse and Alcoholism (2004) defined binge drinking as "a pattern of drinking alcohol that brings blood alcohol concentration (BAC) to 0.08 gram percent or above. For the typical adult, this pattern roughly corresponds to consuming 5 or more drinks (male), or 4 or more drinks (female), in about 2 hours," noting that such patterns represent significant risk for the drinker and society. These consumption-based limits have not been included in formal diagnostic algorithms although psychometric analyses suggest that their inclusion would be useful in measuring a latent construct of AUD that has better lower-end resolution than the DSM-IV (see Hasin, Hatzenbuehler, Keyes, & Ogburn, 2006; Saha, Stinson, & Grant, 2007). However, cutoffs such as the four- or five-drink criterion

for binge drinking fail to consider individual differences in ethanol metabolism and body weight among adults, and this problem may be magnified when applied to children and adolescents. For example, Donovan (2009) estimates that children 9–13 years of age drinking four or five drinks over 2 hours would have BACs approximately 2–3 times the legal limit of .08%.

When we move away from alcohol to consider other substances, it is more difficult to quantify consumption. Although there is a high degree of consistency in the nicotine content of specific cigarette brands, variations in smoking topography behavior result in considerable variability in nicotine delivered to the smoker (Hammond, Fong, Cummings, & Hyland, 2005). Moreover, there is considerable variability in the purity and potency of most illicit drugs (e.g., Parrott, 2004) and most surveys and assessment devices typically assess frequency of consumption and/or route of administration (although dosages can be more easily obtained when considering nonmedical use of prescription medications).

Assessment

The assessment of substance use and SUDs includes several different areas and goals, and these require different assessment instruments. For instance, the instruments used to screen for addictive behaviors in the general population are different from those used to assess the severity of substance-related problems in clinical populations (see Tucker, Murphy, & Kertesz, 2010, for a review).

Diagnostic Interviews

Several diagnostic interviews have been used to assess SUDs and other disorders as defined by the DSM-IV. These include the Diagnostic Interview Schedule Version IV (DIS-IV; Robins, Cottler, Bucholz, & Compton, 1996), the Composite International Diagnostic Interview (WHO CIDI—Version 3.0; Kessler & Ustün, 2004), the Alcohol Use Disorder and Associated Disabilities Interview Schedule-IV (AUDADIS-IV; Grant & Dawson, 2000), the Semi-Structured Assessment for the Genetics of Alcoholism (SSAGA; Bucholz et al., 1994), and the Structured Clinical Interview for DSM-IV (SCID; First, Spitzer, Gibbon, & Williams, 2002). These and other instruments have recently been or are currently being adapted for DSM-5.

Despite the high reliability associated with these interviews, a number of practical drawbacks exist, such as the personnel and time required for data gathering, leading researchers and clinicians to employ other assessments, such as questionnaires.

Assessment of Consumption

Substance use questionnaires account for the variation in consumption styles by focusing on both frequency and quantity of consumption on a given occasion. More extensive assessments of drinking behavior, such as "graduated frequency" approaches (in which individuals are queried as to how often they use varying numbers of substances/occasions [1–2 drinks, 3–4 drinks, 5–6 drinks, etc.], Greenfield, 2000) are often employed in order to have sufficient data to measure intraindividual variability in consumption patterns, although these approaches have been criticized due to their potential for overestimation of consumption (Poikolainen, Podkeltnova, & Alho, 2002). Another strategy used in the assessment of alcohol use is to measure typical quantity/frequency with supplementation using measures of heavy drinking, such as the 5/4 criteria (five drinks on an occasion for men and four drinks on an occasion for women) promoted by Wechsler and Austin (1998) as a measure of "binge drinking." Although this distinction appears somewhat crude, evidence suggests that this measure roughly corresponds to the NIAAA's (2004) aforementioned definition of a "binge" episode as drinking that yields a BAC of .08% or more.

The timeline follow-back interview (TLFB; Robinson, Sobell, Sobell, & Leo, 2014; Sobell & Sobell, 1992, 2000, 2003) is a method that obtains detailed retrospective assessments of substance use. Although originally used for assessing alcohol use patterns, the methodology is easily extended to assessing illicit substances (e.g., Fals-Stewart, O'Farrell, Freitas, McFarlin, & Rutigliano, 2000; Robinson et al., 2014). By utilizing a calendar and memory aids to enhance recall (e.g., key dates that serve as anchors for reporting use), individuals provide retrospective estimates of their daily consumption over a specified time period that can vary up to 12 months from the interview date. The TLFB has been shown to have good psychometric characteristics with a variety of groups and can be flexibly scored to provide a range of measures relevant to substance use and abstention patterns (Sobell, Brown, Leo, & Sobell, 1996). The chapter by Del Boca, Darkes, and McRee (Chapter 15, Vol. 2) describes multiple self-report measures of substance use and related constructs, with recommendations for the optimal selection of instruments. In addition, the chapter presents a model of the question-answering process to help structure the assessment situation in a way that promotes accurate responding.

Daily Diary and Ecological Momentary Assessment Approaches

Most questionnaire-based assessments of use are cross-sectional and rely on retrospective reports. Cross-sectional, retrospective data suffer from several shortcomings, including potential reporting bias and the inability to address questions about the temporal order of cause-and-effect relationships. Although some approaches, such as retrospective time-line follow-back assessments (Sobell & Sobell, 2003) and prospective panel studies resolve these issues to some degree, they fail to address shorter term, dynamic associations between substance use and other variables of interest. To address these issues, daily diary and ecological momentary assessment (EMA) methodologies have been developed. Participants in daily diary studies are instructed to record events or feelings that occurred during the day on structured nightly recording forms (Carney, Tennen, Affleck, Del Boca, & Kranzler, 1998), by providing daily reports via the Internet (e.g., Park, Armeli, & Tennen, 2004), or interactive voice response via telephone (Collins, Kashdan, & Gollnisch, 2003; Perrine, Mundt, Searles, & Lester, 1995). In EMA studies, however, participants are prompted several times per day to record substance use and other variables of interest in real time on handheld computers. Thus, daily diary and EMA studies allow researchers to examine continually changing behaviors while utilizing naturalistic conditions and minimizing retrospective bias. In many clinical and research contexts, such assessments are burdensome, but the value of obtaining real-time or near real-time data is increasingly recognized (Piasecki, Hufford, Solhan, & Trull, 2007; Shiffman et al., 2002). Shiffman (Chapter 16, Vol. 2) reviews the literature on EMA and its applications to substance use research and examines issues related to study design and data analysis.

Direct assessment of substances use in humans should also be noted. These approaches typically involve direct assessment of the substance itself (in blood, urine, expired air, or hair), its metabolites, or its effects on a range of physiological processes influenced by the drug. Snell, Bhave, Takacs, and Tabakoff (Chapter 14, Vol. 2) note that, in recent years, ways to monitor substance use directly in the "real world" using noninvasive sensors that can detect a substance's presence in sweat or breath have been developed. At present, it seems highly likely that these types of sensors will be increasingly adopted by individuals interested in monitoring their health via "smart" wearable devices that can store or transmit these data for personal, medical, and research purposes. However, such enabling technologies introduce new challenges with respect to safeguarding individual privacy of health-related information (e.g., Safavi & Shukur, 2014).

Prevention

Prevention efforts can be categorized into universal, selective, and indicated prevention (Mrazek & Haggerty, 1994). Universal prevention strategies seek to address an entire population (e.g., all adults in a community). Selective prevention strategies target subsets of the entire population who are thought to be at risk for problematic substance involvement (e.g., individuals with a family history of SUDs). Indicated prevention efforts are designed to prevent the onset of a full-blown disorder in individuals who indicate early signs of SUD (e.g., mandated college students involved in problematic drinking). In this section, we focus on the first two approaches. Indicated prevention will be covered together with other treatment approaches.

Universal Prevention Approaches

Most public policies on substance use are conceived and instituted with the express purpose of universally reducing consumption and related injuries and harms, either via penalties (sanctions) for risky behavior (e.g., drunk driving) or inducements (e.g., monetary appropriations) to support education and prevention efforts. Although supply control for illicit drugs (aimed at reducing access to drugs by interfering with the activities of drug suppliers) has been shown to have limited effectiveness (Strang et al., 2012), policies concerning the price/taxation of alcohol and tobacco appear to be particularly effective. For example, a report of 112 studies on alcohol tax showed a consistent moderately strong association between higher taxes on alcohol and lower heavy drinking rates (Wagenaar, Salois, & Komro, 2009).

School-based approaches are usually aimed at educating elementary school youths and adolescents about the ill effects of alcohol and drugs and how to resist peer pressure to use. School-based approaches can be affect-based (i.e., focused on self-esteem and self-efficacy), skills-based (i.e., focused on

interpersonal interactions), or knowledge-based (i.e., educating students about drugs and their effects), or a combination of the three (Tobler, 1986). Abstinence-only approaches that emphasize a "just say no" ideology toward alcohol consumption typically rely on education alone. Despite millions of dollars spent on programs that emphasize zero-tolerance approaches, such as Drug Abuse Resistance Education (D.A.R.E.), a consensus of empirical studies indicate that these approaches fail to reduce alcohol use and related consequences (Lynam et al., 1999; Moskowitz, 1989). Such programs do, however, successfully increase children's overall knowledge of drugs. Moreover, interventions that also incorporate skills training (e.g., Project ALERT) have been shown to reduce some hard drug use and also improve self-efficacy and general decision-making (Faggiano et al., 2008; Faggiano, Minozzi, Versino, & Buscemi, 2014), although some promising findings have not been replicated by independent researchers (Pierre, Osgood, Mincemoyer, Kaltreider, & Kauh, 2005).

Selective Approaches

Selective approaches are common in college populations, which have characteristically high binge drinking rates. Social norms marketing (where information is disseminated to correct misperceptions regarding peer drinking behavior) and "expectancy challenge" interventions (that focus on perceptions of alcohol's effects and provides accurate information) are two approaches that appear to have garnered empirical support (Cruz & Dunn, 2003; Perkins, Haines, & Rice, 2005), although results are somewhat mixed (Wechsler et al., 2003). A recent meta-analysis of randomized trials of preventive interventions for college students reported evidence of their overall efficacy, highlighting the utility of specific interventions, including personalized feedback and expectancy challenge (Scott-Sheldon, Carey, Elliott, Garey, & Carey, 2014). With regard to more structured programs, Marlatt et al. (1998) reported findings from a randomized trial evaluating the Brief Alcohol Screening and Intervention for College Students (BASICS) program, an intervention targeting at-risk college students. Results showed that the BASICS group had greater decreases in alcohol use and fewer alcohol-related problems at 2-year follow-up. Fromme and Corbin (2004) investigated the effect of the Lifestyle Management Class program among voluntary and mandated college students. Results at 6-month follow-up suggested that the intervention reduced the frequency of driving after drinking, although reductions in heavy alcohol use were not significant.

D'Amico, Chan-Osilla, and Stern (Chapter 23, Vol. 2) review the rationale and efficacy of school-based prevention and intervention programs for adolescent alcohol and other drug use, highlighting the opportunities and challenges presented when working in this setting. Gruenewald, Treno, Holder, and LaScala (Chapter 18, Vol. 1) review the community-based (defined as programs that affect specific components of community systems) prevention literature, highlighting the breadth of preventive efforts throughout the world.

Treatment

Depending on the nature and extent of excessive consumption, physical dependence, and substance-related problems, a variety of treatment approaches to address these problems may be relevant. National studies investigating the effectiveness of treatment under conditions of normal clinical practice have yielded generally positive results. The Drug Abuse Treatment Outcome Study (DATOS), conducted in the United States, investigated the effectiveness of outpatient methadone (OMT), long-term residential (LTR), outpatient drug-free (ODF), and short-term inpatient (STI) programs from 11 cities across the country. Hubbard, Craddock, Flynn, Anderson, and Etheridge (1997) reported 1-year follow-up outcomes indicating that rates of drug use and related problems tend to decrease significantly at follow-up and that better results arc evidenced among clients who stay in treatment for a longer period. The National Treatment Outcome Research Study (NTORS), conducted in the United Kingdom, investigated the effectiveness of specialist in-patient, residential rehabilitation, methadone maintenance, and methadone reduction programs. Gossop, Marsden, Stewart, and Kidd (2003) reported 4- to 5-year follow-up outcomes, showing significant reductions in consumption of several substances, psychological health problems, and crime, although no reductions in crack cocaine and alcohol use were found. Similar positive results were reported in the Australian Treatment Outcome Study (ATOS; Teesson et al., 2008), suggesting that treatment for SUDs is generally effective.

These positive findings have led researchers to try to understand the processes that take place during treatment. A good example of these efforts is provided by the Texas Christian University model of treatment processes, which depicts the key processes associated with better retention and treatment outcomes (Simpson, 2001, 2004). Interestingly, this model has been expanded to incorporate organizational variables that influence treatment outcome as well as the adoption of empirically supported innovations (Simpson, 2002; Simpson & Flynn, 2007).

Brief Interventions

Brief interventions, which can be as short as 10–15 minutes (e.g., Fleming et al., 2000, 2002), are often used in primary care settings with individuals who have low levels of dependence and/or are unwilling to pursue more intensive treatment regimens. These interventions often involve motivational approaches designed to encourage substance users to consider changing their behavior (Miller & Rollnick, 2013; Wilk, Jensen, & Havighurst, 1997). Typically, the role of the clinician is to help the drinker set drinking goals, agree on a plan to reduce or stop consumption, and provide advice and educational materials. Follow-up sessions are scheduled to monitor progress and renegotiate drinking goals and strategies. Brief interventions can be administered by a wide variety of providers in a range of treatment modalities and are relatively less expensive than extended treatment (Heather, 1986).

Meta-analyses of controlled trials indicate that brief interventions reduce alcohol consumption and drinking-related outcomes (when compared to individuals who do not receive treatment) and appear to be as effective as extended treatment conditions (Moyer, Finney, Swearingen, & Vergun, 2002; Neighbors, Larimer, Lostutter, & Woods, 2006; Wilk et al., 1997). Furthermore, these approaches appear to result in significant cost savings compared to the utilization of other health care services. Additionally, recent studies indicate that brief, motivational interventions delivered in an emergency room setting have been shown to reduce alcohol consumption, alcohol-related negative consequences, and recidivism, including among trauma patients (Bombardier & Rimmele, 1999; Gentilello, Ebel, Wickizer, Salkever, & Rivara, 2005; Monti et al., 1999). Thus, such brief motivational interventions are considered as a "best-practice" recommendation in the United States (Neighbors et al., 2006). Hettema, Wagner, Ingersoll, & Russo (Chapter 17, Vol. 2) review the rationale and evidence base of brief interventions and motivational interviewing across multiple settings. Special attention is paid to the organizing frameworks (presented in the form of acronyms) that are used to define and disseminate brief interventions.

Cognitive-Behavioral Approaches

Although numerous cognitive-behavioral interventions to treat SUDs have been developed and assessed, a predominant model of cognitive-behavioral therapy is based on the work of Marlatt (Marlatt & Donovan, 2005; Marlatt & Gordon, 1985) regarding the relapse process. Marlatt's cognitive-behavioral model of relapse centers on high-risk situations and the individual's response in that situation (see Witkiewitz & Marlatt, 2004). Under this model, individuals who lack confidence to deal with the situation and/or lack an effective coping response are more likely to be tempted to drink. It is thought that the decision to use or not use is then mediated by the individual's outcome expectancies for the initial effects of using the substance (Jones et al., 2001). This model provides the basis for relapse prevention interventions that are designed to prevent and manage relapse by identifying potential high-risk situations for relapse and challenging the individual's expectations for the perceived positive effects of a substance (Witkiewitz & Marlatt, 2004). A meta-analysis conducted by Irvin, Bowers, Dunn, and Wang (1999) suggested that relapse prevention was a successful intervention for substance use and for improving psychosocial adjustment.

A related component of cognitive-behavioral therapy (CBT) is social skills training (Monti & O'Leary, 1999). This approach assumes that increasing the repertoire of coping skills will reduce the stress of high-risk situations and provide alternatives to drinking. Techniques include assertiveness training and role-playing skills related to alcohol refusal. Several studies suggest that social skills training is effective in reducing substance use (see Chambless & Ollendick, 2001).

Based on the notion that substance-related cues (e.g., the sight and smell of tobacco) can trigger a relapse for dependent individuals, cue-exposure therapy repeatedly exposes patients to those cues while preventing consumption, with the desired outcome of reducing or eliminating urges to drink in response to cues (Monti & Rohsenow, 1999). Cue-exposure is listed as a probably efficacious treatment for SUDs (Chambless & Ollendick, 2001), although some researchers have questioned the effectiveness of cue-exposure for treating SUDs as currently conducted, suggesting procedural improvements based on animal extinction research

(Conklin & Tiffany, 2002; see also Siegel & Ramos, 2002).

Another approach that is also based on learning theory is contingency management (CM). CM involves the application of reinforcement principles to arrange reinforcing or punishing consequences in order to promote positive behavior change (Higgins, Silverman, & Heil, 2008). Dutra et al. (2008; see also Prendergast, Podus, Finney, Greenwell, & Roll, 2006) conducted a meta-analysis of CBT treatments for illicit DUDs and found that CM had the highest effect size and lowest drop-out rate. The combination of CM and cognitive behavioral therapy was found to be promising but only included two studies. The chapter by Rohsenow and Pinkston-Camp (Chapter 18, Vol. 2) summarizes the rationale for these and other cognitive-behavioral approaches (including, e.g., acceptance and commitment therapy) and reviews the evidence for their efficacy in the treatment of alcohol, tobacco, and drug use disorders.

Marital and Family Approaches

SUDs often manifest themselves in the context of the family and have considerable consequences for spouses and other family members who often try to exert interpersonal influence over the drinker (Epstein & McCrady, 1998; Orford, Velleman, Natera, Templeton, & Copello, 2013). Consequently, it is not surprising that a number of interventions involve couples and the family unit.

At the couples' level, the most extensively studied approach is behavioral couples therapy (BCT). In addition to sharing many features of traditional cognitive-behavioral treatment for the user, BCT also targets partners' coping with substance use situations, reinforcing abstinence, and improving the dyadic relationship. A recent meta-analysis of BCT in SUDs (Powers, Vedel, & Emmelkamp, 2008) demonstrated that this treatment approach was more effective than control treatments in improving relationship satisfaction as well as substance-related outcomes. Interestingly, the comparatively stronger salutary effect of BCT on substance-related outcomes was not evident immediately after treatment when all treatments fared well but, instead, the couples' treatment effect strengthened relative to control treatments over time. This suggests that the improved interpersonal relationships fostered better substance-related outcomes. Importantly, there was no relation between the number of sessions and outcomes, suggesting that BCT could be delivered as a relatively brief treatment.

A number of treatment approaches that target the entire family and larger social networks have also been developed (Copello, Velleman, & Templeton, 2005). Arguably the most systematically studied of these, the community reinforcement and family training approach (Smith & Meyers, 2004) is an extension of the community reinforcement approach (CRA; Sisson & Azrin, 1986). Under this approach, a friend or family member (e.g., spouse) either provides or removes agreed reinforcers (e.g., television access) to reward periods of abstinence and punish use for the targeted individual. Furthermore, the agreed-upon friend/family member may also encourage the dependent individual to enter treatment and supervise the use of disulfiram. Several studies suggest that CRA is an effective treatment for substance abuse and dependence (Carr, 2009; Chambless & Ollendick, 2001; Luty, 2006). Klostermann (Chapter 19, Vol. 2) presents these and other (e.g., multisystemic family therapy) marital and family therapy approaches for the prevention of, initiation of change in, and active treatment of SUDs.

Pharmacotherapy

Increasing knowledge about the mechanism of action of different drugs and the neurobiological vulnerability to addiction has led to the development of several pharmacological interventions. Acamprosate and naltrexone are the most common pharmacotherapies for alcohol dependence. The Combined Pharmacotherapies and Behavioral Interventions (COMBINE) Study was designed to test the efficacy of naltrexone, acamprosate, a combined behavioral intervention (CBI), and their combination in a randomized multisite study of alcohol treatment. Anton et al. (2006) reported 1-year follow-up results indicating that medical management plus naltrexone produced positive outcomes similar to those for medical management plus CBI, whereas acamprosate was not better than placebo. However, Maisel, Blodgett, Wilbourne, Humphreys, and Finney (2013) reported findings from a meta-analysis suggesting that acamprosate and naltrexone might lead to different results depending on the outcome variable and the conditions of treatment. In particular, in accordance with their respective presumed mechanism of action, acamprosate had larger effect sizes associated with abstinence, whereas naltrexone had larger effect sizes associated with reduced heavy drinking. In addition, acamprosate had larger effect sizes when detoxification was required before treatment, and naltrexone had larger effect sizes when abstinence was required before treatment.

Bupropion SR and varenicline are the two US Food and Drug Administration (FDA)-approved medications for the treatment of nicotine dependence that do not involve nicotine replacement. Gonzales et al. (2006; see also Jorenby et al., 2006, for an identically designed study conducted at a different center) reported results from a double-blind, placebo-controlled study comparing bupropion and varenicline. They found that although bupropion was associated with more continuous abstinence rates than placebo, varenicline was more efficacious than both bupropion and placebo and was also associated with lower craving, withdrawal, and smoking satisfaction.

Several medications have been shown to be effective for the treatment of opioid dependence. Buprenorphine alone and in combination with naloxone (used to decrease the potential of buprenorphine for abuse) has been found to be efficacious, and the possibility of prescribing it in an office-based setting has the potential to increase availability of treatment. Fudala et al. (2003) conducted a randomized, placebo-controlled trial together with an open-label study to obtain safety data and concluded that both buprenorphine alone and in combination with naloxone were associated with lower rates of opioid use and craving.

Although several pharmacotherapies have been proposed for the treatment of cocaine dependence, results of clinical trials have been disappointing. De Lima, Soares, Reisser, and Farrell (2002) reported results from a meta-analysis of 45 trials investigating the efficacy of different medications in which no evidence of efficacy was found, regardless of the type of drug or dose used. However, recent advances in the development of a vaccine-based treatment for cocaine have shown promising results (Kosten et al., 2014; Martell et al., 2009) Swift (Chapter 21, Vol. 2) reviews the mechanisms of action and therapeutic use (both during and after detoxification) of several medications.

Self-help Organizations and Recovery

Perhaps no other class of disorders is more associated with self-help organizations as a major "treatment" modality than SUDs. The very nature of self-help organizations limits the types of randomized controlled trials used to evaluate other treatment modalities, at least with the fidelity as practiced in the community, as reviewed by Lembke and Humphreys (Chapter 20, Vol. 2).

However, randomized studies in which individuals are referred to Alcoholics Anonymous or provided support and guidance to facilitate involvement with 12-step programs show empirical support for the effectiveness of Alcoholics Anonymous with respect to a range of outcomes, and, in general, these appear to be roughly equivalent to those associated with professionally administered behavioral treatments and may be particularly effective when abstinence as an outcome is considered (Humphrey & Moos, 2007) and for those who are most severely dependent (Moos & Timko, 2008).

Although the effectiveness of self-help groups not employing a 12-step approach has not been as extensively studied, as reviewed by Lembke and Humphreys (Chapter 20, Vol. 2) in this handbook, studies of those affiliated with Moderation Management, which does not necessarily promote an abstinence goal, show that members frequently consume alcohol at immoderate levels. Lembke and Humphreys note that the shape of support communities is undergoing rapid change in the age of social media and that, over time, we will have a clearer indication of the relative benefits and effectiveness of online versus face-to-face self-help groups.

The Scope of the Study of Substance Use and SUDs

This brief overview selectively highlights the scope of research on substance use and SUDs. In the two volumes that follow, all of these issues are examined in greater detail, as well as some topics not explicitly mentioned here, especially in the areas of comorbidity and consequences, which we briefly highlight in the concluding chapter of this *Handbook*. However, it should be clear, even from this brief overview that substance use and its complications have been an important part of diverse societies for millennia and that such use has been both vilified and prized, both between and across cultures and historical periods. The distinctions among mere use, excessive use, and clearly problematic use are important ones, although the acceptability of any of these are highly culturally determined. A range of causal factors have been implicated in all stages of progression from experimentation to compulsive use or addiction, and there is currently a lack of consensus as to what factors are most critical. Such knowledge is essential for developing the most effective policies and approaches for preventing and treating the myriad harms associated with substance use and SUDs.

References

Aas, H., Leigh, B., Anderssen, N., & Jakobsen, R. (1998). Two-year longitudinal study of alcohol expectancies and drinking among Norwegian adolescents. *Addiction, 93*, 373–384.

Adalbjarnardottir, S., & Hafsteinsson, L. G. (2001). Adolescents' perceived parenting styles and their substance use: Concurrent and longitudinal analyses. *Journal of Research on Adolescence, 11*(4), 401–423.

Agrawal, A., & Lynskey, M. T. (2006). The genetic epidemiology of cannabis use, abuse and dependence. *Addiction, 101*(6), 801–812.

Agrawal, A., & Lynskey, M. T. (2008). Are there genetic influences on addiction: Evidence from family, adoption and twin studies. *Addiction, 103*(7), 1069–1081.

American Psychiatric Association. (1980). *Diagnostic and statistical manual of mental disorders* (3rd ed.). Washington, DC: Author.

American Psychiatric Association. (2000). *Diagnostic and statistical manual of mental disorders* (4th ed., Text Rev.). Washington, DC: Author.

American Psychiatric Association. (2013). *Diagnostic and statistical manual of mental disorders* (5th ed.). Washington, DC: Author.

Ames, G., & Moore, R. S. (2016). Substance use in specific settings: The workplace and the military. In K. J. Sher (Eds.), *The Oxford handbook of substance use and substance use disorders.* (Vol. 1, pp. 579–599). New York: Oxford University Press. doi:10.1093/oxfordhb/9780199381678.013.014

Anderson, K. G., Smith, G. T., McCarthy, D. M., Fischer, S. F, Fister, S., Grodin, D. . . . Hill, K. K. (2005). Elementary school drinking: The role of temperament and learning. *Psychology of Addictive Behaviors, 19*, 21–27.

Anthony, J. Barondess, D. A., Radovanovic, & M., Lopez-Quintero, C. (2016). Polydrug use: Research topics and issues. In K. J. Sher (Ed.), *The Oxford handbook of substance use and substance use disorders* (Vol. 2, pp. 29–59). New York: Oxford University Press.

Anton, R. F., O'Malley, S. S., Ciraulo, D. A., Cisler, R. A., Couper, D., Donovan, D. M., . . . Zweben, A. (2006). Combined pharmacotherapies and behavioral interventions for alcohol dependence: The COMBINE study: A randomized controlled trial. *Journal of the American Medical Association, 295*(17), 2003–2017.

Baer, J. S., Sampson, P. D., Barr, H. M., Connor, P. D., & Streissguth, A. P. (2003). A 21-year longitudinal analysis of the effects of prenatal alcohol exposure on young adult drinking. *Archives of General Psychiatry, 60*(4), 377–385.

Bazinet, A. D., Squeglia, L, Riley, E., & Tapert, S. F. (2016). Effects of drug exposure on development. In K. J. Sher (Ed.), *The Oxford handbook of substance use and substance use disorders* (Vol. 2, pp. 215–254) New York: Oxford University Press.

Blonigen, D. M., Timko, C., Finney, J. W., Moos, B. S., & Moos, R. H. (2011). Alcoholics Anonymous attendance, decreases in impulsivity and drinking and psychosocial outcomes over 16 years: Moderated-mediation from a developmental perspective. *Addiction, 106*(12), 2167–2177.

Bombardier, C. H., & Rimmele, C. T. (1999). Motivational interviewing to prevent alcohol abuse after traumatic brain injury: A case series. *Rehabilitation Psychology, 44*, 52–67.

Brandon, T. H., & Baker, T. B. (1991). The Smoking Consequences Questionnaire: The subjective expected utility of smoking in college students. *Psychological Assessment, 3*(3), 484–491.

Bucholz, K. K., Cadoret, R., Cloninger, C. R., Dinwiddie, S. H., Hesselbrock, V. M., Nurnberger, J. I., . . . Schuckit, M. A. (1994). A new, semi-structured psychiatric interview for use in genetic linkage studies: A report on the reliability of the SSAGA. *Journal of Studies on Alcohol and Drugs, 55*(2), 149–158.

Cadoret, R. J., Yates W. R., Troughton E., Woodworth G., & Stewart M. A. (1995). Adoption study demonstrating two genetic pathways to drug abuse. *Archives of General Psychiatry, 52*, 42–52.

Calafat, A., García, F., Juan, M., Becoña, E., & Fernández-Hermida, J. R. (2016). Which parenting style is more protective against adolescent substance use? Evidence within the European context. *Drug and Alcohol Dependence, 138*, 185–192.

Cannon, T. D., & Keller, M. C. (2006). Endophenotypes in the genetic analyses of mental disorders. *Annual Review of Clinical Psychology*, 2, 267–290.

Carney, M. A., Tennen, H., Affleck, G., Del Boca, F. K., & Kranzler, H. R. (1998). Levels and patterns of alcohol consumption using timeline follow-back, daily diaries and real-time "electronic interviews." *Journal of Studies on Alcohol, 59*, 447–454.

Carr, A. A. (2009). The effectiveness of family therapy and systemic interventions for adult-focused problems. *Journal of Family Therapy, 31*, 46–74.

Chambless, D. L., & Ollendick, T. H. (2001). Empirically supported psychological interventions: Controversies and evidence. *Annual Review of Psychology, 52*, 685–716.

Chassin, L., Haller, M., Lee, M., Handley, E., Bountress, K., & Beltran, E. (2016). Familial factors influencing offspring substance use and dependence. In K. J. Sher (Eds.), *The Oxford handbook of substance use and substance use disorders* (Vol. 1, pp. 449–482). New York: Oxford University Press. doi:10.1093/oxfordhb/9780199381678.013.008

Christiansen, B, Goldman, M., & Inn, A. (1982). Development of alcohol-related expectancies in adolescents: Separating pharmacological from social-learning influences. *Journal of Consulting and Clinical Psychology, 50*, 336–344.

Christiansen, M., Vik, P. W., & Jarchow, A. (2002). College student heavy drinking in social contexts versus alone. *Addictive Behaviors, 27*(3), 393–404.

Cloninger, C. R., Bohman, M., & Sigvardsson, S. (1981). Inheritance of alcohol abuse: Cross-fostering analysis of adopted men. *Archives of General Psychiatry, 38*, 861–868.

Collins, R. L., Kashdan, T. B., & Gollnisch, G. (2003). The feasibility of using cellular phones to collect ecological momentary assessment data: Application to alcohol consumption, *Experimental and Clinical Psychopharmacology, 11*, 73–78.

Conklin, C. A., & Tiffany, S. T. (2002). Applying extinction research and theory to cue-exposure addiction treatments. *Addiction, 97*, 155–167.

Cooper, M. L. (1994). Motivations for alcohol use among adolescents: Development and validation of a four-factor model. *Psychological Assessment, 6*, 117–128.

Cooper, M. L., Frone, M. R., Russell, M., & Mudar, P. (1995). Drinking to regulate positive and negative emotions: A motivational model of alcohol use. *Journal of Personality and Social Psychology, 69*, 990–1005.

Cooper, M. L., Kuntsche, E., Levitt, A. Barber, L. L. Wolf, S. (2016). Motivational models of substance use: A review of theory and research on motives for using alcohol, marijuana, and tobacco. In K. J. Sher (Ed.), *The Oxford handbook of substance use and substance use disorders* (Vol. 1, pp. 375–421). New York: Oxford University Press.

Copello, A. G., Velleman, R. D., & Templeton, L. J. (2005). Family interventions in the treatment of alcohol and drug problems. *Drug and Alcohol Review, 24*(4), 369–385.

Coskunpinar, A., Dir, A. L., & Cyders, M. A. (2013). Multidimensionality in impulsivity and alcohol use: A meta-analysis using the UPPS model of impulsivity. *Alcoholism: Clinical and Experimental Research, 37*(9), 1441–1450.

Crabbe, J. C., & Phillips, T. J. (2014). Genetic Animal Models. In K. J. Sher (Ed.), *The Oxford handbook of substance use and substance use disorders* (Vol. 1., pp. 273–308). New York: Oxford University Press. doi:10.1093/oxfordhb/9780199381678.013.003

Crocq, M. A. (2007). Historical and cultural aspects of man's relationship with addictive drugs. *Dialogues in Clinical Neuroscience, 9*(4), 355–361.

Cruz, I. Y., & Dunn, M. E. (2003). Lowering risk for early alcohol use by challenging alcohol expectancies in elementary school children. *Journal of Consulting and Clinical Psychology, 71*, 493–503.

Curran, P. J., Stice, E., & Chassin, L. (1997). The relation between adolescent alcohol use and peer alcohol use: A longitudinal random coefficients model. *Journal of Consulting and Clinical Psychology, 65*(1), 130–140.

Cyders, M. A., Smith, G. T., Spillane, N. S., Fischer, S., Annus, A. M., & Peterson, C. (2007). Integration of impulsivity and positive mood to predict risky behavior: Development and validation of a measure of positive urgency. *Psychological Assessment, 19*(1), 107–118.

D'Amico, E. J., Chan-Osilla, K., & Stern, S. A. (2014). Prevention and Intervention in the School Setting. In K. J. Sher (Ed.), *The Oxford handbook of substance use and substance use disorders* (Vol. 2, pp. 675–724). New York: Oxford University Press.

Dawson, D. A., Grant, B. F., & Li, T. K. (2005). Quantifying the risks associated with exceeding recommended drinking limits. *Alcoholism: Clinical and Experimental Research, 29*, 902–908.

Degenhardt, L., & Hall, W. (2012). Extent of illicit drug use and dependence, and their contribution to the global burden of disease. *Lancet, 379*(9810), 55–70.

Degenhardt, L., Hall, W., & Bucello, C. (2014). Illicit drugs: Patterns of use, dependence, and contribution to disease burden in developed countries. In K. J. Sher (Ed.), *The Oxford handbook of substance use and substance use disorders* (Vol. 1, pp. 50–66). New York: Oxford University Press. doi:10.1093/oxfordhb/9780199381708.013.16

Del Boca, F. K., Darkes, J., & McRee, B. (2014). Self-report assessments of psychoactive substance use and dependence. In K. J. Sher (Ed.), *The Oxford handbook of substance use and substance use disorders* (Vol. 2, pp. 430–465). New York: Oxford University Press. doi:10.1093/oxfordhb/9780199381708.013.005

De Lima, M. S., Soares, B. G. D. O., Reisser, A. A. P., & Farrell, M. (2002). Pharmacological treatment of cocaine dependence: A systematic review. *Addiction, 97*(8), 931–949.

Derrick, J. L., & Leonard, K. E. (2014). Substance use in committed relationships. In K. J. Sher (Eds.), *The Oxford handbook of substance use and substance use disorders* (Vol. 1, pp. 549–578). New York: Oxford University Press. doi:10.1093/oxfordhb/9780199381678.013.012

Dick, D. M., Agrawal, A., Schuckit, M. A., Bierut, L., Hinrichs, A., Fox, L., . . . Begleiter, H. (2006). Marital status, alcohol dependence, and GABRA2: Evidence for gene-environment correlation and interaction. *Journal of Studies on Alcohol and Drugs, 67*(2), 185–194.

Dick, D. M., & Beirut, L. J. (2006). The genetics of alcohol dependence. *Current Psychiatry Reports, 8,* 151–157.

Dick, D. M., Rose, R. J., & Kaprio, J. (2006). The next challenge for psychiatric genetics: Characterizing the risk associated with identified genes. *Annals of Clinical Psychiatry, 18,* 223–231.

Dietler, M. (2006). Alcohol: Anthropological/archaeological perspectives. *Annual Review of Anthropology, 35,* 229–249.

Donovan, J. E. (2009). Estimated blood alcohol concentrations for child and adolescent drinking and their implications for screening instruments. *Pediatrics, 123*(6), e975–e981.

Dudley, R. (2004). Ethanol, fruit ripening, and the historical origins of human alcoholism in primate frugivory. *Integrative and Comparative Biology, 44,* 315–323.

Dutra, L., Stathopoulou, G., Basden, S., Leyro, T., Powers, M., & Otto, M. (2008). A meta-analytic review of psychosocial interventions for substance use disorders. *American Journal of Psychiatry, 165*(2), 179–187.

Eckersley, R. M. (2005). "Cultural fraud": The role of culture in drug abuse. *Drug and Alcohol Review, 24*(2), 157–163.

Edwards, A. C., Maes, H. H., Prescott, C. A., & Kendler, K. S. (2015). Multiple mechanisms influencing the relationship between alcohol consumption and peer alcohol use. *Alcoholism: Clinical and Experimental Research, 39,* 324–332.

Edwards, G., & Gross, M. (1976). Alcohol dependence: Provisional description of a clinical syndrome. *British Medical Journal, 1,* 1058–1061.

Elkins, I. J., King, S. M., McGue, M., & Iacono, W. G. (2006). Personality traits and the development of nicotine, alcohol, and illicit drug disorders: Prospective links from adolescence to young adulthood. *Journal of Abnormal Psychology, 115*(1), 26–39.

Epstein, E. E., & McCrady, B. S. (1998). Behavioral couples treatment of alcohol and drug use disorders: Current status and innovations. *Clinical Psychology Review, 18,* 689–711.

Escohotado, A. (1999). *A brief history of drugs: From the Stone Age to the Stoned Age.* Rochester, VT: Park Street Press.

Everitt, B. J., Belin, D., Economidou, D., Pelloux, Y., Dalley, J. W., & Robbins, T. W. (2008). Neural mechanisms underlying the vulnerability to develop compulsive drug-seeking habits and addiction. *Philosophical Transactions of the Royal Society B: Biological Sciences, 363*(1507), 3125–3135.

Everitt, B. J., & Robbins, T. W. (2005). Neural systems of reinforcement for drug addiction: From actions to habits to compulsion. *Nature Neuroscience, 8,* 1481–1489. doi:10.1038/nn1579

Everitt, B. J., & Robbins, T. W. (2013). From the ventral to the dorsal striatum: Devolving views of their roles in drug addiction. *Neuroscience & Biobehavioral Reviews, 37*(9), 1946–1954.

Faggiano, F., Minozzi, S., Versino, E., Buscemi, D. (2014) Universal school-based prevention for illicit drug use. *Cochrane Database of Systematic Reviews,* Issue 12. Art. No.: CD003020. doi: 10.1002/14651858.CD003020.pub3

Faggiano, F., Vigna-Taglianti, F. D., Versino, E., Zambon, A., Borraccino, A., & Lemma, P. (2008). School-based prevention for illicit drugs use: A systematic review. *Preventive Medicine, 46,* 385–396.

Fals-Stewart, W., O'Farrell, T. J., Freitas, T. T., McFarlin, S. K., & Rutigliano, P. (2000). The timeline followback reports of psychoactive substance use by drug-abusing patients: Psychometric properties. *Journal of Consulting and Clinical Psychology, 68*(1), 134.

Fazio, R. H., & Towles-Schwen, T. (1999). The MODE model of attitude–behavior processes. In S. Chaiken & Y. Trope (Eds.), *Dual-process theories in social psychology* (pp. 97–116). New York: Guilford.

First, M. B., Spitzer, R. L., Gibbon, M., & Williams, J. B. W. (2002). *Structured clinical interview for DSM-IV Axis I disorders, research version, non-patient edition (SCID-I/NP).* New York: Biometrics Research, New York State Psychiatric Institute.

Fleming, M. F., Mundt, M. P., French, M. T., Manwell, L. B., Stauffacher, E. A., & Barry, K. L. (2000). Benefit-cost analysis of brief physician advice with problem drinkers in primary care settings. *Medical Care, 38*(1), 7–18.

Fleming, M. F., Mundt, M. P., French, M. T., Manwell, L. B., Stauffacher, E. A., & Barry, K. L. (2002). Brief physician advice for problem drinkers: Long-term efficacy and benefit-cost analysis. *Alcoholism: Clinical and Experimental Research, 26*(1), 36–43.

Foddy, B., & Savulescu, J. (2010). A liberal account of addiction. *Philosophy, Psychiatry, & Psychology, 17*(1), 1–22.

Fromme, K., & Corbin, W. (2004). Prevention of heavy drinking and associated negative consequences among mandated and voluntary college students. *Journal of Consulting and Clinical Psychology, 72*(6), 1038–1049.

Fromme, K., & D'Amico, E. J. (2000). Measuring adolescent alcohol outcome expectancies. *Psychology of Addictive Behaviors, 14,* 206–212.

Fudala, P. J., Bridge, T. P., Herbert, S., Williford, W. O., Chiang, C. N., Jones, K., . . . Tusel, D. (2003). Office-based treatment of opiate addiction with a sublingual-tablet formulation of buprenorphine and naloxone. *New England Journal of Medicine, 349*(10), 949–958.

Furberg, H., Kim, Y., Dackor, J., Boerwinkle, E., Franceschini, N., Ardissino, D., . . . Canova, C. (2010). Genome-wide meta-analyses identify multiple loci associated with smoking behavior. *Nature Genetics, 42*(5), 441–447.

Galen, L. W., & Henderson, M. J. (1999). Validation of cocaine and marijuana effect expectancies in a treatment setting. *Addictive Behaviors, 24*(5), 719–724.

Gentilello, L. M., Ebel, B. E., Wickizer, T. M., Salkever, D. S., & Rivara, F. P. (2005). Alcohol interventions for trauma patients treated in emergency departments and hospitals: A cost benefit analysis. *Annals of Surgery, 241*(4), 541–550.

Goldman, M. S., Brown, S. A., & Christiansen, B. A. (1987). Expectancy theory: Thinking about drinking. In H. T. Blane & K. E. Leonard (Eds.), *Psychological theories of drinking and alcoholism* (pp. 181–226). New York: Guilford.

Goldman, M. S., Del Boca, F. K., & Darkes, J. (1999). Alcohol expectancy theory: The application of cognitive neuroscience. In H. T. Blane & K. E. Leonard (Eds.), *Psychological theories of drinking and alcoholism* (pp. 203–246). New York: Guilford.

Goldstein, D. B. (2009). Common genetic variation and human traits. *New England Journal of Medicine, 360,* 1696–1698.

Gonzales, D., Rennard, S. I., Nides, M., Oncken, C., Azoulay, S., Billing, C. B., . . . Reeves, K. R. (2006). Varenicline, an α4β2 nicotinic acetylcholine receptor partial agonist, vs sustained-release bupropion and placebo for smoking cessation. *Journal of the American Medical Association, 296*(1), 47–55.

Goodwin, D. W., Schulsinger, F., Hermansen, L., Guze, S. B., & Winokur, G. (1973). Alcohol problems in adoptees raised apart from alcoholic biological parents. *Archives of General Psychiatry 28*, 238–243.

Gossop, M., Marsden, J., Stewart, D., & Kidd, T. (2003). The National Treatment Outcome Research Study (NTORS): 4–5 year follow-up results. *Addiction, 98*(3), 291–303.

Gottlieb, J. C., Cohen, L. M., DeMarree, K. G., Treloar, H. R., & McCarthy, D. M. (2013). The development and psychometric evaluation of the Smokeless Tobacco Expectancies Scale (STES). *Psychological Assessment, 25*(3), 997.

Grant, B. F., & Dawson, D. (2000). The Alcohol Use Disorder and Associated Disabilities Interview Schedule-IV (AUDADIS-IV). Rockville, MD: National Institute on Alcohol Abuse and Alcoholism.

Greenfield, T. K. (2000). Ways of measuring drinking patterns and the difference they make: Experience with graduated frequencies. *Journal of Substance Abuse, 12*, 33–49.

Grube, J. W., & Agostinelli, G. E. (1999). Perceived consequences and adolescent drinking: Nonlinear and interactive models of alcohol expectancies. *Psychology of Addictive Behaviors, 13*(4), 303–312.

Gruenewald, P. J., Treno, A. J., Holder, H. D., & LaScala, E. A. (2016). Community-based approaches to the prevention of substance use-related problems. In K. J. Sher (Ed.), *The Oxford handbook of substance use and substance use disorders* (Vol. 1, pp. 600–624). New York: Oxford University Press. doi:10.1093/oxfordhb/9780199381678.013.005

Hammond, D., Fong, G. T., Cummings, K. M., & Hyland, A. (2005). Smoking topography, brand switching, and nicotine delivery: Results from an in vivo study. *Cancer Epidemiology Biomarkers & Prevention, 14*(6), 1370–1375.

Harford, T. C., & Muthén, B. O. (2001). The dimensionality of alcohol abuse and dependence: A multivariate analysis of *DSM–IV* symptom items in the National Longitudinal Survey of Youth. *Journal of Studies on Alcohol, 62*, 150–157.

Hasin, D., Hatzenbuehler, M. L., Keyes, K., & Ogburn, E. (2006). Substance use disorders: Diagnostic and Statistical Manual of Mental Disorders (DSM-IV) and International Classification of Diseases (ICD-10). *Addiction, 101*(s1), 59–75.

Hasin, D. S., Muthén, B., Wisnicki, K. S., & Grant, B. (1994). Validity of the bi-axial dependence concept: A test in the US general population. *Addiction, 89*, 573–579.

Hasin, D. S., O'Brien, C. P., Auriacombe, M., Borges, G., Bucholz, K., Budney, A., . . . & Grant, B. F. (2013). DSM-5 criteria for substance use disorders: Recommendations and rationale. *American Journal of Psychiatry, 170*(8), 834–851.

Hasin, D. S., Stinson, F. S., Ogburn, E., & Grant, B. F. (2007). Prevalence, correlates, disability, and comorbidity of *DSM–IV* alcohol abuse and dependence in the United States: Results from the National Epidemiologic Survey on Alcohol and Related Conditions. *Archives of General Psychiatry, 64*, 830–842.

Head, J., Stansfeld, S. A., & Siegrist, J. (2004). The psychosocial work environment and alcohol dependence: A prospective study. *Occupational and Environmental Medicine, 61*(3), 219–224.

Heath, A. C. (1995). Genetic influences on alcoholism risk: A review of adoption and twin studies. *Alcohol Health & Research World, 19*, 166–171.

Heather, N. (1986). Minimal treatment intervention for problem drinkers. In G. Edwards (Ed.), *Current issues in clinical psychology* (Vol. 4, pp. 171–186). London: Plenum.

Hendricks, P. S., Cases, M. G., Thorne, C. B., Cheong, J., Harrington, K. F., Kohler, C. L., & Bailey, W. C. (2015). Hospitalized smokers' expectancies for electronic cigarettes versus tobacco cigarettes. *Addictive Behaviors, 41*, 106–111.

Hettema, J., Wagner, C. C., Ingersoll, K. S., & Russo, J. M. (2016). Brief interventions and motivational interviewing. In K. J. Sher (Ed.), *The Oxford handbook of substance use and substance use disorders* (Vol. 2, pp. 513–530). New York: Oxford University Press. doi:10.1093/oxfordhb/9780199381708.013.007

Heyman, G. M. (2009). *Addiction: A disorder of choice.* Harvard University Press.

Higgins, S. T., Silverman, K., & Heil, S. H. (2008). *Contingency management in substance abuse treatment.* New York: Guilford.

Hubbard, R. L., Craddock, S. G., Flynn, P. M., Anderson, J., & Etheridge, R. M. (1997). Overview of 1-year follow-up outcomes in the Drug Abuse Treatment Outcome Study (DATOS). *Psychology of Addictive Behaviors, 11*(4), 261–278.

Humphreys, K., & Moos, R. H. (2007). Encouraging posttreatment self-help group involvement to reduce demand for continuing care services: Two-year clinical and utilization outcomes. *Alcoholism: Clinical and Experimental Research, 31*, 64–68.

Internet Movie Data Base. (2012, Nov). Top 70 movies about alcohol and drugs. Retrieved from http://www.imdb.com/list/ls050657088/.

Irvin, J. E., Bowers, C. A., Dunn, M. E., & Wang, M. C. (1999). Efficacy of relapse prevention: A meta-analytic review. *Journal of Consulting and Clinical Psychology, 67*, 563–570.

Jackson, K. M., & Sartor, C. E. (2016). The natural course of substance use and dependence. In K. J. Sher (Ed.), *The Oxford handbook of substance use and substance use disorders* (Vol. 1, pp. 67–132). New York: Oxford University Press. doi:10.1093/oxfordhb/9780199381708.013.007

Jaffe, A. J., & Kilbey, M. M. (1994). The Cocaine Expectancy Questionnaire (CEQ): Construction and predictive utility. *Psychological Assessment, 6*(1), 18–26.

Jones, B. T., Corbin, W., & Fromme, K. (2001). A review of expectancy theory and alcohol consumption. *Addiction, 96*, 57–72.

Jorenby, D. E., Hays, J. T., Rigotti, N. A., Azoulay, S., Watsky, E. J., Williams, K. E., . . . Reeves, K. R. (2006). Efficacy of varenicline, an α4β2 nicotinic acetylcholine receptor partial agonist, vs placebo or sustained-release bupropion for smoking cessation. *Journal of the American Medical Association, 296*, 56–63.

Kahler, C. W., & Strong, D. R. (2006). A Rasch model analysis of DSM-IV Alcohol abuse and dependence items in the National Epidemiological Survey on Alcohol and Related Conditions. *Alcoholism: Clinical & Experimental Research, 30*, 1165–1175.

Keller, M. (1979). A historical overview of alcohol and alcoholism. *Cancer Research, 39*, 2822–2829.

Kendler, K. S. (2005). Psychiatric genetics: A methodologic critique. *American Journal of Psychiatry, 162*, 3–11.

Kendler, K. S. (2006). Reflections on the relationship between psychiatric genetics and psychiatric nosology. *American Journal of Psychiatry, 163*, 1138–1146.

Kendler, K. S., Aggen, S. H., Prescott, C. A., Crabbe, J., & Neale, M. C. (2012). Evidence for multiple genetic factors underlying the DSM-IV criteria for alcohol dependence. *Molecular Psychiatry, 17*, 1306–1315.

Kendler, K. S., Aggen, S. H., Tambs, K., & Reichborn-Kjennerud, T. (2006). Illicit psychoactive substance use, abuse and dependence in a population-based sample of Norwegian twins. *Psychological Medicine, 36*(7), 955–962.

Kendler, K. S., Jacobson, K. C., Prescott, C. A., & Neale, M. C. (2003). Specificity of genetic and environmental risk factors for use and abuse/dependence of cannabis, cocaine, hallucinogens, sedatives, stimulants, and opiates in male twins. *American Journal of Psychiatry, 160*(4), 687–695.

Kendler, K. S., Karkowski, L. M., Neale, M. C., & Prescott, C. A. (2000). Illicit psychoactive substance use, heavy use, abuse, and dependence in a US population-based sample of male twins. *Archives of General Psychiatry, 57*(3), 261–269.

Kendler, K. S., Myers, J., & Prescott, C. A. (2007). Specificity of genetic and environmental risk factors for symptoms of cannabis, cocaine, alcohol, caffeine, and nicotine dependence. *Archives of General Psychiatry, 64*(11), 1313.

Kendler, K. S., Neale, M. C., Sullivan, P., Corey, L. A., Gardner, C. O., & Prescott, C. A. (1999). A population-based twin study in women of smoking initiation and nicotine dependence. *Psychological Medicine, 29*(02), 299–308.

Kessler, R. C., & Ustün, T. B. (2004). The World Mental Health (WMH) Survey Initiative Version of the World Health Organization (WHO) Composite International Diagnostic Interview (CIDI). *International Journal of Methods in Psychiatric Research, 13*, 93–121.

King, K. M., Fleming, C. B., Monahan, K. C., & Catalano, R. F. (2011). Changes in self-control problems and attention problems during middle school predict alcohol, tobacco, and marijuana use during high school. *Psychology of Addictive Behaviors, 25*(1), 69–79.

Klostermann, K. (2016). Marital and family approaches. In K. J. Sher (Ed.), *The Oxford handbook of substance use and substance use disorders* (Vol. 2, pp. 567–581). New York: Oxford University Press. doi:10.1093/oxfordhb/9780199381708.013.11

Knopik, V. S., Heath, A. C., Madden, P. A., Bucholz, K. K., Slutske, W. S., Nelson, E. C., ... Martin, N. G. (2004). Genetic effects on alcohol dependence risk: Re-evaluating the importance of psychiatric and other heritable risk factors. *Psychological Medicine, 34*(08), 1519–1530.

Kodituwakku, P. W. (2007). Defining the behavioral phenotype in children with fetal alcohol spectrum disorders: A review. *Neuroscience & Biobehavioral Reviews, 31*(2), 192–201.

Koob, G. (2016). The neurobiology of reward and stress and its relevance for understanding drug seeking and dependence symptomatology. In K. J. Sher (Ed.), *The Oxford handbook of substance use and substance use disorders* (Vol. 1, pp. 166–191). New York: Oxford University Press. doi:10.1093/oxfordhb/9780199381678.013.013

Koob, G. F., & Le Moal, M. (2001). Drug addiction, dysregulation of reward and allostasis. *Neuropsychopharmacology, 24*, 97–127.

Koob, G. F., & Le Moal, M. (2008). Addiction and the brain antireward system. *Annual Review of Psychology, 59*, 29–53.

Kosten, T. R., Domingo, C. B., Shorter, D., Orson, F., Green, C., Somoza, E., ... Kampman, K. (2014). Vaccine for cocaine dependence: A randomized double-blind placebo-controlled efficacy trial. *Drug and Alcohol Dependence, 140*, 42–47.

Kuntsche, E., Knibbe, R., Gmel, G., & Engels, R. (2006). Who drinks and why? A review of socio-demographic, personality, and contextual issues behind the drinking motives in young people. *Addictive Behaviors, 31*(10), 1844–1857.

Kuramoto, S. J., & Wilcox, H. C. (2016). Substance use disorders and intentional injury. In K. J. Sher (Ed.), *The Oxford handbook of substance use and substance use disorders* (Vol. 2, pp. 322–346) New York: Oxford University Press. doi:10.1093/oxfordhb/9780199381708.013.002

Laing, O. (2014). *The trip to Echo Spring: On writers and drinking*. New York: Picador.

Langenbucher, J. W., Labouvie, E., Martin, C. S., Sanjuan, P. M., Bavly, L., Kirisci, L., & Chung, T. (2004). An application of item response theory analysis to alcohol, cannabis, and cocaine criteria in DSM-IV. *Journal of Abnormal Psychology, 113*(1), 72–80.

Lembke, A., & Humphreys, K. (2016). Self-help organizations for substance use disorders. In K. J. Sher (Ed.), *The Oxford handbook of substance use and substance use disorders* (Vol. 2, pp. 582–593). New York: Oxford University Press. doi:10.1093/oxfordhb/9780199381708.013.16

Lessov, C. N., Martin, N. G., Statham, D. J., Todorov, A. A., Slutske, W. S., Bucholz, K. K., ... Madden, P. A. (2004). Defining nicotine dependence for genetic research: Evidence from Australian twins. *Psychological Medicine, 34*(5), 865–879.

Leung, R. K., Toumbourou, J. W., & Hemphill, S. A. (2014). The effect of peer influence and selection processes on adolescent alcohol use: A systematic review of longitudinal studies. *Health Psychology Review, 8*(4), 426–457.

Lim, S. S., Vos, T., Flaxman, A. D., Danaei, G., Shibuya, K., Adair-Rohani, H., ... Degenhardt, L. (2013). A comparative risk assessment of burden of disease and injury attributable to 67 risk factors and risk factor clusters in 21 regions, 1990–2010: A systematic analysis for the Global Burden of Disease Study 2010. *Lancet, 380*(9859), 2224–2260.

Littlefield, A. K., & Sher, K. J. (2010). The multiple, distinct ways that personality contributes to alcohol use disorders. *Social and Personality Psychology Compass, 4*(9), 767–782.

Littlefield, A. K., & Sher, K. J. (2016). Personality and substance use disorders. In K. J. Sher (Eds.), *The Oxford handbook of substance use and substance use disorders* (Vol. 1, pp. 351–374). New York: Oxford University Press. doi:10.1093/oxfordhb/9780199381678.013.006

Littlefield, A. K., Sher, K. J., & Wood, P. K. (2009). Is "maturing out" of problematic alcohol involvement related to personality change? *Journal of Abnormal Psychology, 118*(2), 360–374.

Littlefield, A. K., Sher, K. J., & Wood, P. K. (2010). Do changes in drinking motives mediate the relation between personality change and the "maturing out" of alcohol problems? *Journal of Abnormal Psychology, 119*, 93–105.

Littlefield, A. K., Stevens, A. K., Cunningham, S., Jones, R. E., King, K. M., Schumacher, J. A., & Coffey, S. F. (2015). Stability and change in multi-method measures of impulsivity across residential addictions treatment. *Addictive Behaviors, 42*, 126–129.

Littlefield, A. K., Vergés, A., McCarthy, D. M., & Sher, K. J. (2011). Interactions between self-reported alcohol outcome expectancies and cognitive functioning in the prediction of alcohol use and associated problems: A further examination. *Psychology of Addictive Behaviors, 25*(3), 542–546.

Littlefield, A. K., Vergés, A., Rosinski, J. M., Steinley, D., & Sher, K. J. (2013). Motivational typologies of drinkers: Do enhancement and coping drinkers form two distinct groups? *Addiction, 108*(3), 497–503.

Littlefield, A. K., Vergés, A., Wood, P. K., & Sher, K. J. (2012). Transactional models between personality and alcohol involvement: A further examination. *Journal of Abnormal Psychology, 121*(3), 778–783.

Liu, J. Z., Tozzi, F., Waterworth, D. M., Pillai, S. G., Muglia, P., Middleton, L., . . . Satler, L. (2010). Meta-analysis and imputation refines the association of 15q25 with smoking quantity. *Nature Genetics, 42*, 436–440.

Lozano, R., Naghavi, M., Foreman, K., Lim, S., Shibuya, K., Aboyans, V., . . . Dabhadkar, K. C. (2012). Global and regional mortality from 235 causes of death for 20 age groups in 1990 and 2010: A systematic analysis for the Global Burden of Disease Study 2010. *Lancet, 380*(9859), 2095–2128.

Luczak, S. E., Glatt, S. J., & Wall, T. L. (2006). Meta-analyses of ALDH2 and ADH1B with alcohol dependence in Asians. *Psychological Bulletin, 132*, 607–612.

Luty, J. (2006). What works in alcohol use disorders. *Advances in Psychiatric Treatment, 12*, 13–22.

Lynam, D. R., Milich, R., Zimmerman, R., Novak, S. P., Logan, T. K., Martin, C., . . . Clayton, R. (1999). Project DARE: No effects at 10-year follow-up. *Journal of Consulting and Clinical Psychology, 67*, 590–593.

Lynskey, M. T., Agrawal, A., Henders, A., Nelson, E. C., Madden, P. A., & Martin, N. G. (2012). An Australian twin study of cannabis and other illicit drug use and misuse, and other psychopathology. *Twin Research and Human Genetics, 15*(05), 631–641.

Maes, H. H., Sullivan, P. F., Bulik, C. M., Neale, M. C., Prescott, C. A., Eaves, L. J., & Kendler, K. S. (2004). A twin study of genetic and environmental influences on tobacco initiation, regular tobacco use and nicotine dependence. *Psychological Medicine, 34*(07), 1251–1261.

Maisel, N. C., Blodgett, J. C., Wilbourne, P. L., Humphreys, K., & Finney, J. W. (2013). Meta-analysis of naltrexone and acamprosate for treating alcohol use disorders: When are these medications most helpful? *Addiction, 108*(2), 275–293.

Marlatt, G. A., Baer, J. S., Kivlahan, D. R., Dimeff, L. A., Larimer, M. E., Quigley, L. A., . . . Williams, E. (1998). Screening and brief intervention for high-risk college student drinkers: Results from a 2-year follow-up assessment. *Journal of Consulting and Clinical Psychology, 66*(4), 604–615.

Marlatt, G. A., & Donovan, D. M. (Eds.). (2005). *Relapse prevention: Maintenance strategies in the treatment of addictive behaviors.* New York: Guilford.

Marlatt, G. A., & Gordon, J. R. (1985). *Relapse prevention: Maintenance strategies in the treatment of addictive behaviors.* New York: Guilford.

Martell, B. A., Orson, F. M., Poling, J., Mitchell, E., Rossen, R. D., Gardner, T., & Kosten, T. R. (2009). Cocaine vaccine for the treatment of cocaine dependence in methadone-maintained patients: A randomized, double-blind, placebo-controlled efficacy trial. *Archives of General Psychiatry, 66*(10), 1116–1123.

Martin, C. S., Chung, T., Kirisci, L., & Langenbucher, J. W. (2006). Item response theory analysis of diagnostic criteria for alcohol and cannabis use disorders in adolescents: Implications for *DSM–V. Journal of Abnormal Psychology, 115*, 807–814.

Martin, C. S., Chung, T., & Langenbucher, J. W. (2014). Historical and cultural perspectives on substance use and substance use disorders. In K. J. Sher (Eds.), *The Oxford handbook of substance use and substance use disorders* (Vol. 1, pp. 29–49). New York: Oxford University Press. doi:10.1093/oxfordhb/9780199381678.013.001

Martin, C. S., Sher, K. J., & Chung, T. (2011). Hazardous use should not be a diagnostic criterion for substance use disorders in DSM-5. *Journal of Studies on Alcohol and Drugs, 72*, 685–686.

Martin, C. S., Steinley, D. L., Vergés, A., & Sher, K. J. (2011). The proposed 2/11 symptom algorithm for DSM-5 substance-use disorders is too lenient. *Psychological Medicine, 41*, 2008–2010.

Mathers, C. D., & Loncar, D. (2006). Projections of global mortality and burden of disease from 2002 to 2030. *PLoS Medicine, 3*, e442.

McCarthy, D. M., & Smith, G. T. (1996, June). *Meta-analysis of alcohol expectancy.* Paper presented at the annual meeting of the Research Society on Alcoholism, Washington, DC.

McCracken, L. M., McCracken, M. L., & Harris, R. A. (2014). Mechanisms of action of different drugs of abuse. In K. J. Sher (Ed.), *The Oxford handbook of substance use and substance use disorders* (Vol. 1, pp. 135–165). New York: Oxford University Press. doi:10.1093/oxfordhb/9780199381708.013.010

McGinnis, J. M., & Foege, W. H. (1999). Mortality and morbidity attributable to use of addictive substances in the United States. *Proceedings of the Association of American Physicians, 111*(2), 109–118.

Miller, P. M., Smith, G. T., & Goldman, M. S. (1990). Emergence of alcohol expectancies in childhood: A possible critical period. *Journal of Studies on Alcohol, 51*, 343–349.

Miller, W. R., & Rollnick, S. (2013). *Motivational interviewing: Helping people change,* 3rd ed. New York: Guilford.

Moeller, F. G., Barratt, E. S., Dougherty, D. M., Schmitz, J. M., & Swann, A. C. (2001). Psychiatric aspects of impulsivity. *American Journal of Psychiatry, 158*(11), 1783–1793.

Monti, P. M., Colby, S. M., Barnett, N. P., Spirito, A., Rohsenow, D. J., Myers, M., . . . Lewander, W. (1999). Brief intervention for harm reduction with alcohol-positive older adolescents in a hospital emergency department. *Journal of Consulting and Clinical Psychology, 67*(6), 989–994.

Monti, P. M., & O'Leary, T. A. (1999). Coping and social skills training for alcohol and cocaine dependence. *Psychiatric Clinics of North America, 22*(2) 447–470.

Monti, P. M., & Rohsenow, D. J. (1999). Coping-skills training and cue-exposure therapy in the treatment of alcoholism. *Alcohol Research and Health, 23*, 107–115.

Moos, R. H., & Timko, C. (2008). Outcome research on 12-step and other self-help programs. In Galanter & H. D. Kleber (Eds.), *Textbook of substance abuse treatment* (4th ed., pp. 511–521). Washington, DC: American Psychiatric Press.

Moskowitz, J. M. (1989). The primary prevention of alcohol problems: A critical review of the research literature. *Journal of Studies on Alcohol, 50*, 54–88.

Moyer, A., Finney, J. W., Swearingen, C. E., & Vergun, P. (2002). Brief interventions for alcohol problems: A meta-analytic review of controlled investigations in treatment-seeking and non-treatment seeking populations. *Addiction, 97*, 279–292.

Mrazek, P. J., & Haggerty, R. J. (Eds.). (1994). *Reducing risks for mental disorders: Frontiers for preventive intervention research.* Washington, DC: National Academy Press.

Murray, C. J., Vos, T., Lozano, R., Naghavi, M., Flaxman, A. D., Michaud, C., . . . Brooker, S. (2012). Disability-adjusted life years (DALYs) for 291 diseases and injuries in 21 regions, 1990–2010: A systematic analysis for the Global Burden of Disease Study 2010. *Lancet, 380*(9859), 2197–2223.

Muthén, B. O., Grant, B., & Hasin, D. (1993). The dimensionality of alcohol abuse and dependence: Factor analysis of DSM-III-R and proposed DSM-IV criteria in the 1988 National Health Interview Survey. *Addiction*, 88, 1079–1090.

National Institute on Alcohol Abuse and Alcoholism. (2004). NIAAA Council Approves Definition of Binge Drinking, NIAAA Newsletter, No. 3. National Institute on Alcohol Abuse and Alcoholism, Bethesda, MD.

Neighbors, C., Larimer, M. E., Lostutter, T. W., & Woods, B. A. (2006). Harm reduction and individually focused alcohol prevention. *International Journal of Drug Policy*, 17(4), 304–309.

Orford, J., Velleman, R., Natera, G., Templeton, L., & Copello, A. (2013). Addiction in the family is a major but neglected contributor to the global burden of adult ill-health. *Social Science & Medicine*, 78, 70–77.

Oscar-Berman, M., Urban, T. A., & Holmes, A. J. (2016). Effects of alcoholism on neurological function and disease in adulthood. In K. J. Sher (Ed.), *The Oxford handbook of substance use and substance use disorders* (Vol. 2, pp. 255–272) New York: Oxford University Press. doi:10.1093/oxfordhb/9780199381708.013.22

Park, C. L., Armeli, S., & Tennen, H. (2004). Appraisal-coping goodness of fit: A daily internet study. *Personality and Social Psychology Bulletin*, 30(5), 558–569.

Parrott, A. C. (2004). Is ecstasy MDMA? A review of the proportion of ecstasy tablets containing MDMA, their dosage levels, and the changing perceptions of purity. *Psychopharmacology*, 173, 234–241.

Pastor, A. D., & Evans, S. M. (2003). Alcohol outcome expectancies and risk for alcohol use problems in women with and without a family history of alcoholism. *Drug and Alcohol Dependence*, 70, 201–214.

Patrick, M. E., Schulenberg, J. E., Maggs, J., & Maslowsky, J. (2016). Substance use and peers during adolescence and the transition to adulthood: Selection, socialization, and development. In K. J. Sher (Eds.), *The Oxford handbook of substance use and substance use disorders* (Vol. 1, pp. 526–548). New York: Oxford University Press. doi:10.1093/oxfordhb/9780199381678.013.004

Patrick, M. E., Wray-Lake, L., Finlay, A. K., & Maggs, J. L. (2010). The long arm of expectancies: Adolescent alcohol expectancies predict adult alcohol use. *Alcohol & Alcoholism*, 45, 17–24.

Perkins, H. W., Haines, M. P., & Rice, R. (2005). Misperceiving the college drinking norm and related problems: A nationwide study of exposure to prevention information, perceived norms and student alcohol misuse. *Journal of Studies on Alcohol*, 66, 470–478.

Perrine, M. W., Mundt, J. C., Searles, J. S., & Lester, L. S. (1995). Validation of daily self-reported alcohol consumption using interactive voice response (IVR) technology. *Journal of Studies on Alcohol*, 56, 487–490.

Piasecki, T. M., Hufford, M. R., Solhan, M., & Trull, T. J. (2007). Assessing clients in their natural environments with electronic diaries: Rationale, benefits, limitations, and barriers. *Psychological Assessment*, 19, 25–43.

Pierre, T. L. S., Osgood, D. W., Mincemoyer, C. C., Kaltreider, D. L., & Kauh, T. J. (2005). Results of an independent evaluation of Project ALERT delivered in schools by cooperative extension. *Prevention Science*, 6, 305–317.

Poikolainen, K., Podkeltnova, & Alho, H. (2002). Accuracy of quantity-frequency and graduated frequency questionnaires in measuring alcohol intake: Comparison with daily diary and commonly used laboratory markers. *Alcohol & Alcoholism*, 37, 573–576.

Popova, S., & Rehm, J. (2016). Substance involvement and physical health: Unintentional injury, organ-specific diseases including cancer, and infectious diseases. In K. J. Sher (Ed.), *The Oxford handbook of substance use and substance use disorders* (Vol. 2, pp. 273–321). New York: Oxford University Press. doi:10.1093/oxfordhb/9780199381708.013.13

Powers, M. B., Vedel, E., & Emmelkamp, P. (2008). Behavioral couples therapy (BCT) for alcohol and drug use disorders: A meta-analysis. *Clinical Psychology Review 28*, 952–962.

Prendergast, M., Podus, D., Finney, J., Greenwell, L., & Roll, J. (2006). Contingency management for treatment of substance use disorders: A meta-analysis. *Addiction*, 101, 1546–1560.

Prescott, C. A., & Kendler, K. S. (1999). Genetic and environmental contributions to alcohol abuse and dependence in a population-based sample of male twins. *American Journal of Psychiatry*, 156(1), 34–40.

Primack, B. A., Colditz, J. B., Pang, K. C., & Jackson, K. M. (2015). Portrayal of alcohol intoxication on YouTube. *Alcoholism: Clinical and Experimental Research*, 39(3), 496–503.

Proudfoot, H., Baillie, A. J., & Teesson, M. (2006). The structure of alcohol dependence in the community. *Drug and Alcohol Dependence*, 81(1), 21–26.

Read, J. P, Wood, M. D., Lejuez, C. W., Palfai, T. P., & Slack, M. (2004). Gender, alcohol consumption and differing alcohol expectancy dimensions in college drinkers. *Experimental and Clinical Psychopharmacology*, 12, 298–308.

Rehm, J., Mathers, C., Popova, S., Thavorncharoensap, M., Teerawattananon, Y., & Patra, J. (2009). Alcohol and Global Health 1 Global burden of disease and injury and economic cost attributable to alcohol use and alcohol-use disorders. *Lancet*, 373(9682), 2223–2233.

Robins, L., Cottler, L., Bucholz, K., & Compton, W. (1996). *Diagnostic Interview Schedule, fourth version (DIS-IV)*. St. Louis, MO: Washington University.

Robinson, S. M., Sobell, L. C., Sobell, M. B., & Leo, G. I. (2014). Reliability of the Timeline Followback for cocaine, cannabis, and cigarette use. *Psychology of Addictive Behaviors*, 28(1), 154–162.

Robinson, T. E., & Berridge, K. C. (1993). The neural basis of drug craving: An incentive-sensitization theory of addiction. *Brain Research Reviews*, 18(3), 247–291.

Robinson, T. E., & Berridge, K. C. (2001). Incentive-sensitization and addiction. *Addiction*, 96(1), 103–114.

Rohsenow, D. J., & Pinkston-Camp, M. M. (2016). Cognitive-behavioral approaches. In K. J. Sher (Ed.), *The Oxford handbook of substance use and substance use disorders* (Vol. 2, pp. 531–566). New York: Oxford University Press. doi:10.1093/oxfordhb/9780199381708.013.010

Russell, C. A., Russell, D. W., & Grube, J. W. (2016). Substance use and media. In K. J. Sher (Eds.), *The Oxford handbook of substance use and substance use disorders* (Vol. 1, pp. 625–650). New York: Oxford University Press. doi:10.1093/oxfordhb/9780199381678.013.19

Saccone, S. F., Hinrichs, A. L., Saccone, N. L., Chase, G. A., Konvicka, K., Madden, P. A., . . . Bierut, L. J. (2007). Cholinergic nicotinic receptor genes implicated in a nicotine dependence association study targeting 348 candidate genes with 3713 SNPs. *Human Molecular Genetics*, 16(1), 36–49.

Safavi, S., & Shukur, Z. (2014). Conceptual privacy framework for health information on wearable device. *PloS One*, *9*(12), e114306.

Saha, T. D., Chou, S. P., & Grant, B. F. (2006). Toward an alcohol use disorder continuum using item response theory: Results from the National Epidemiologic Survey on Alcohol and Related Conditions. *Psychological Medicine*, *36*(7), 931–942.

Saha, T. D., Stinson, F. S., & Grant, B. F. (2007). The role of alcohol consumption in future classifications of alcohol use disorders. *Drug and Alcohol Dependence*, *89*, 82–92.

Sayer, A, & Willett, J. (1998). A cross-domain model for growth in adolescent alcohol expectancies. *Multivariate Behavioral Research*, *33*, 509–543.

Schafer, J., & Brown, S. A. (1991). Marijuana and cocaine effect expectancies and drug use patterns. *Journal of Consulting and Clinical Psychology*, *59*(4), 558–565.

Schuckit, M. A., Smith, T. L., & Landi, N. A. (2000). The 5-year clinical course of high-functioning men with *DSM–IV* alcohol abuse or dependence. *American Journal of Psychiatry*, *157*, 2028–2035.

Scott-Sheldon, L. A., Carey, K. B., Elliott, J. C., Garey, L., & Carey, M. P. (2014). Efficacy of alcohol interventions for first-year college students: A meta-analytic review of randomized controlled trials. *Journal of Consulting and Clinical Psychology*, *82*(2), 177–188.

Sher, K. J. (1991). *Children of alcoholics: A critical appraisal of theory and research*. A volume in the John D. and Catherine T. MacArthur Foundation Series on Mental Health and Development. Chicago: University of Chicago Press.

Sher, K. J., Grekin, E. R., & Williams, N. A. (2005). The development of alcohol use disorders. *Annual Review of Clinical Psychology*, *1*, 493–523.

Sher, K. J., Wood, M., Wood, P., & Raskin, G. (1996). Alcohol outcome expectancies and alcohol use: A latent variable cross-lagged panel study. *Journal of Abnormal Psychology*, *105*, 561–574.

Shiffman, S. (2016). Ecological monetary assessment. In K. J. Sher (Ed.), *The Oxford handbook of substance use and substance use disorders* (Vol. 2, pp. 466–510). New York: Oxford University Press. doi:10.1093/oxfordhb/9780199381708.013.1

Shiffman, S., Gwaltney, C. J., Balabanis, M. H., Liu, K. S., Paty, J. A., Kassel, J. D., ... Gnys, M. (2002). Immediate antecedents of cigarette smoking: An analysis from ecological momentary assessment. *Journal of Abnormal Psychology*, *111*(4), 531–545.

Siegel, S., Baptista, M. A., Kim, J. A., McDonald, R. V., & Weise-Kelly L. (2000). Pavlovian psychopharmacology: The associative basis of tolerance. *Experimental and Clinical Psychopharmacology*, *8*, 276–293.

Siegel, S., & Ramos, B. (2002). Applying laboratory research: Drug anticipation and the treatment of drug addiction. *Experimental and Clinical Psychopharmacology*, *10*, 162–183.

Simons, J., Correia, C. J., & Carey, K. B. (2000). A comparison of motives for marijuana and alcohol use among experienced users. *Addictive Behaviors*, *25*(1), 153–160.

Simons, J., Correia, C. J., Carey, K. B., & Borsari, B. E. (1998). Validating a five-factor marijuana motives measure: Relations with use, problems, and alcohol motives. *Journal of Counseling Psychology*, *45*(3), 265–273.

Simpson, D. D. (2001). Modeling treatment process and outcomes. *Addiction*, *96*, 207–211.

Simpson, D. D. (2002). A conceptual framework for transferring research to practice. *Journal of Substance Abuse Treatment*, *22*(4), 171–182.

Simpson, D. D. (2004). A conceptual framework for drug treatment process and outcomes. *Journal of Substance Abuse Treatment*, *27*, 99–121.

Simpson, D. D., & Flynn, P. M. (2007). Moving innovations into treatment: A stage-based approach to program change. *Journal of Substance Abuse Treatment*, *33*(2), 111–120.

Sisson, R. W., & Azrin, N. H. (1986). Family-member involvement to initiate and promote treatment of problem drinkers. *Journal of Behavior Therapy and Experimental Psychiatry*, *17*, 15–21.

Slutske, W. S., Heath, A. C., Madden, P. A., Bucholz, K. K., Statham, D. J., & Martin, N. G. (2002). Personality and the genetic risk for alcohol dependence. *Journal of Abnormal Psychology*, *111*(1), 124–133.

Smith, G., Goldman, M., Greenbaum, P., & Christiansen, B. (1995). Expectancy for social facilitation from drinking: The divergent paths of high expectancy and low expectancy adolescents. *Journal of Abnormal Psychology*, *104*, 32–40.

Smith, G. T., McCarthy, D. M., & Zapolski, T. C. (2009). On the value of homogeneous constructs for construct validation, theory testing, and the description of psychopathology. *Psychological Assessment*, *21*(3), 272–284.

Smith, J. E., & Meyers, R. J. (2004). *Motivating substance abusers to enter treatment: Working with family members*. New York: Guilford.

Snell, L. D., Bhave, S. V., Takacs, L., & Tabakoff, B. (2016). Biological markers of substance use: Focus on the objective assessment of alcohol exposure. In K. J. Sher (Ed.), *The Oxford handbook of substance use and substance use disorders* (Vol. 2, pp. 393–429). New York: Oxford University Press.

Sobell, L. C., Brown, J., Leo, G. I., & Sobell, M. B. (1996). The reliability of the Alcohol Timeline Followback when administered by telephone and by computer. *Drug and Alcohol Dependence*, *42*(1), 49–54.

Sobell, L. C., & Sobell, M. B. (1992). Timeline follow-back: A technique for assessing self-reported alcohol consumption. In R. Z. Litten & J. P. Allen (Eds.), *Measuring alcohol consumption: psychosocial and biochemical methods* (pp. 41–72). Totowa, NY: Humana.

Sobell, L. C., & Sobell, M. B. (2000). Alcohol Timeline Followback (TLFB). In American Psychiatric Association (Ed.), *Handbook of psychiatric measures* (pp. 477–479). Washington, DC: American Psychiatric Association.

Sobell, L. C., & Sobell, M. B. (2003). Alcohol consumption measures. In P. Allen & V. B. Wilson (Eds.), *Assessing alcohol problems: A guide for clinicians and researchers* (2nd ed., pp. 75–99). Bethesda, MD: National Institute on Alcohol Abuse and Alcoholism.

Solomon, R. L., & Corbit, J. D. (1974). An opponent-process theory of motivation: I. Temporal dynamics of affect. *Psychological Review*, *81*, 119–145.

Stacy, A., Newcomb, M., & Bentler, P. (1991). Cognitive motivation and drug use: A 9-year longitudinal study. *Journal of Abnormal Psychology*, *100*, 502–515.

Stacy, A. W., & Wiers, R. W. (2010). Implicit cognition and addiction: A tool for explaining paradoxical behavior. *Annual Review of Clinical Psychology*, *6*, 551–575.

Stallings, M. C., Gizer, I. R., & Young-Wolff, K. C. (2016). Genetic epidemiology and molecular genetics. In K. J. Sher (Ed.), *The Oxford handbook of substance use and substance use disorders* (Vol. 1, pp. 192–272). New York: Oxford University Press. doi:10.1093/oxfordhb/9780199381678.013.002

Strang, J., Babor, T., Caulkins, J., Fischer, B., Foxcroft, D., & Humphreys, K. (2012). Drug policy and the public good: Evidence for effective interventions. *Lancet, 379*(9810), 71–83.

Swift, R. M. (2016). Pharmacotherapy of substance use, craving, and acute abstinence syndromes. In K. J. Sher (Ed.), *The Oxford handbook of substance use and substance use disorders* (Vol. 2, pp. 594–618). New York: Oxford University Press.

Taylor, S. T. (1988, April 21). VA's denial of benefits to alcoholics is upheld. *The New York Times*. Retrieved from http://www.nytimes.com/1988/04/21/us/va-s-denial-of-benefits-to-alcoholics-is-upheld.html

Teesson, M., Mills, K., Ross, J., Darke, S., Williamson, A., & Havard, A. (2008). The impact of treatment on 3 years' outcome for heroin dependence: Findings from the Australian Treatment Outcome Study (ATOS). *Addiction, 103*, 80–88.

Thorgeirsson, T. E., Gudbjartsson, D. F., Surakka, I., Vink, J. M., Amin, N., Geller, F., ... Laitinen, J. (2010). Sequence variants at CHRNB3-CHRNA6 and CYP2A6 affect smoking behavior. *Nature Genetics, 42*, 448–453.

Thush, C., Wiers, R. W., Ames, S. L., Grenard, J. L., Sussman, S., & Stacy, A. W. (2008). Interactions between implicit and explicit cognition and working memory capacity in the prediction of alcohol use in at-risk adolescents. *Drug and Alcohol Dependence, 94*(1), 116–124.

Tobler, N. S. (1986). Meta-analysis of 143 adolescent drug prevention programs: Quantitative outcome results of program participants compared to a control or comparison group. *Journal of Drug Issues, 16*, 537–567.

True, W. R., Xian, H., Scherrer, J. F., Madden, P. A., Bucholz, K. K., Heath, A. C., ... Tsuang, M. (1999). Common genetic vulnerability for nicotine and alcohol dependence in men. *Archives of General Psychiatry, 56*(7), 655–661.

Tsuang, M. T., Lyons, M. J., Eisen, S. A., Goldberg, J., True, W., Lin, N., ... Eaves, L. (1996). Genetic influences on DSM-III-R drug abuse and dependence: A study of 3,372 twin pairs. *American Journal of Medical Genetics, 67*(5), 473–477.

Tucker, J. A., Murphy, J. G., & Kertesz, S. G. (2010). Substance use disorders. In M. M. Antony & D. H. Barlow (Eds.), *Handbook of assessment and treatment planning for psychological disorders* (2nd ed., pp. 529–605). New York: Guilford.

Umberson, D. (1987). Family status and health behaviors: Social control as a dimension of social integration. *Journal of Health and Social Behavior, 28*, 306–319.

US Department of Agriculture and US Department of Health and Human Services (2005). *Dietary guidelines for Americans, 2005, 6th ed.* Washington, DC: US Government Printing Office.

Verdejo-García, A., Lawrence, A. J., & Clark, L. (2008). Impulsivity as a vulnerability marker for substance-use disorders: Review of findings from high-risk research, problem gamblers and genetic association studies. *Neuroscience & Biobehavioral Reviews, 32*(4), 777–810.

Vergés, A., Haeny, A. M., Jackson, K. M., Bucholz, K. K., Grant, J. D., Trull, T. J., ... Sher, K. J. (2013). Refining the notion of maturing out: Results from the National Epidemiologic Survey on Alcohol and Related Conditions. *American Journal of Public Health, 103*(12), e67–e73.

Vergés, A., Jackson, K. M., Bucholz, K. K., Grant, J. D., Trull, T. J., Wood, P. K., & Sher, K. J. (2012). Deconstructing the age-prevalence curve of alcohol dependence: Why "maturing out" is only a small piece of the puzzle. *Journal of Abnormal Psychology, 121*(2), 511–523.

Vergés, A., Littlefield, A. K., & Sher, K. J. (2011). Did lifetime rates of alcohol use disorders increase by 67% in 10 years? A comparison of NLAES and NESARC. *Journal of Abnormal Psychology, 120*(4), 868–877.

Vergés, A., Steinley, D., Trull, T. J., & Sher, K. J. (2010). It's the algorithm! Why differential rates of chronicity and comorbidity are not evidence for the validity of the abuse-dependence distinction. *Journal of Abnormal Psychology, 119*(4), 650–661.

Verweij, K. J., Zietsch, B. P., Lynskey, M. T., Medland, S. E., Neale, M. C., Martin, N. G., ... Vink, J. M. (2010). Genetic and environmental influences on cannabis use initiation and problematic use: A meta-analysis of twin studies. *Addiction, 105*(3), 417–430.

Vetulani, J. (2001). Drug addiction. Part I. Psychoactive substances in the past and presence. *Polish Journal of Pharmacology, 53*, 201–214.

Vos, T., Flaxman, A. D., Naghavi, M., Lozano, R., Michaud, C., Ezzati, M., ... Brooks, P. (2013). Years lived with disability (YLDs) for 1160 sequelae of 289 diseases and injuries 1990–2010: A systematic analysis for the Global Burden of Disease Study 2010. *Lancet, 380*(9859), 2163–2196.

Wagenaar, A. C., Salois, M. J., & Komro, K. A. (2009). Effects of beverage alcohol price and tax levels on drinking: A meta-analysis of 1,003 estimates from 112 studies. *Addiction, 104*, 179–190.

Wakefield, J. C., & Schmitz, M. F. (2015). The harmful dysfunction model of alcohol use disorder: Revised criteria to improve the validity of diagnosis and prevalence estimates. *Addiction, 110*(6), 931–942.

Wang, J. C., Kapoor, M., & Goate, A. M. (2012). The genetics of substance dependence. *Annual Review of Genomics and Human Genetics, 13*, 241–261.

Wechsler, H., & Austin S. B. (1998). Binge drinking: The five/four measure. *Journal of Studies on Alcohol, 59*, 122–123.

Wechsler, H., Nelson, T. F., Lee, J. E., Seibring, M., Lewis, C., & Keeling, R. P. (2003). Perception and reality: A national evaluation of social norms marketing interventions to reduce college students' heavy alcohol use. *Journal of Studies on Alcohol, 64*, 484–494.

Westermeyer, J. (1988). The pursuit of intoxication: Our 100 century-old romance with psychoactive substances. *American Journal on Drug and Alcohol Abuse, 14*, 175–187.

Westermeyer, J. (2005). Historical and social context of psychoactive substance use disorders. In Frances, R. J., Miller, S. I., & Mack, A. H. (Eds.), *Clinical textbook of addictive disorders* (pp. 16–34). New York: Guilford.

Wetter, D. W., Smith, S. S., Kenford, S. L., Jorenby, D. E., Fiore, M. C., Hurt, R. D., ... Baker, T. B. (1994). Smoking outcome expectancies: Factor structure, predictive validity, and discriminant validity. *Journal of Abnormal Psychology, 103*(4), 801.

Whiteside, S. P., & Lynam, D. R. (2001). The five factor model and impulsivity: Using a structural model of personality to understand impulsivity. *Personality and Individual Differences, 30*(4), 669–689.

Wiers, R. W., Field, M., & Stacy, A. W. (2016). Passion's slave? Conscious and unconscious cognitive processes in alcohol and drug abuse. In K. J. Sher (Ed.), *The Oxford handbook of substance use and substance use disorders* (Vol. 1, pp. 311–350). doi:10.1093/oxfordhb/9780199381678.013.009

Wiers, R. W., & Stacy, A. W. (Eds.). (2006). *Handbook of implicit cognition and addiction*. Thousand Oaks, CA: Sage.

Wilk, A. I., Jensen, N. M., & Havighurst, T. C. (1997). Meta-analysis of randomized control trials addressing brief interventions in heavy alcohol drinkers. *Journal of General Internal Medicine, 12*, 274–283.

Witkiewitz, K., & Marlatt, G. A. (2004). Relapse prevention for alcohol and drug problems: That was Zen, this is Tao. *American Psychologist, 59*, 224–235.

Yamaguchi, K., & Kandel, D. B. (1985). On the resolution of role incompatibility: A life event history analysis of family roles and marijuana use. *American Journal of Sociology*, 1284–1325.

PART I

Psychiatric Comorbidity

Polydrug Use: Research Topics and Issues

James C. Anthony, David A. Barondess, Mirjana Radovanovic, *and* Catalina Lopez-Quintero

Abstract

This chapter reviews selected research topics and issues in relation to research on polydrug use. It includes a review of the history of the concept of polydrug use and often-referenced terminological confusion in this area of public health research. A pharmacoepidemiological perspective on responses to drug compounds taken in combination is presented, with coverage of sometimes misunderstood concepts such as interaction, antagonism, and synergy. The distinction is made between a description of subgroup variation in responses to a drug and drug–drug interactions for which there is an underlying pharmacological or toxicological theory to guide the research. Finally, there is a selective review of published evidence on population studies of polydrug use, with an emphasis upon investigations with epidemiologically defined populations under study. This review is organized in relation to five main rubrics of epidemiology, and includes topics, issues, and directions for future research on patterns of polydrug use.

Key Words: polydrug, multiple substance use, alcohol, cannabis, prevention, etiology, epidemiology, interaction, antagonism, synergy

(Redacted material from Grateful Dead song about Sweet Jane's polydrug use.)

polydrug, *adj*. Of, relating to, or involving several drugs together;

esp. (of abuse) involving several drugs. Cf. polypharmacy *n*.

1971 Times 13 May 5/2

The committee says a cult of 'poly drug' abusers is emerging in Scotland.

—*(In Oxford English Dictionary online, "Polydrug," 2006)*

Introduction

Immunologist and Nobel Laureate Sir Peter Medawar (1967) noted Aristotle's description of politics as "the art of the possible" and declared science to be "the art of the soluble." In most branches of the applied public health and biomedical sciences, there is no clear separation between these "arts." Research on human consumption of internationally regulated psychoactive drug compounds is no exception. An interesting fact is offered as evidence of the interpenetration of politics and science in this field of study. Namely, in published clinical research articles on humans who consume these compounds, mostly produced by American research teams, there is a real choice between three pertinent adjectives: illicit, illegal, and unlawful. Nonetheless, the odds are overwhelming that scientists in this area, including American scientists, will choose the term "illicit" even though in conventional American usage this term "carries moral overtones < [as in] illicit love affairs> in addition to the basic sense of all three: 'not in accordance with or sanctioned by law'" (Garner, 2000).

Political considerations also were present in the first stirrings of formal public health research on the topic of "polydrug" use. Here are the background details as told by Robert L. Dupont, a former director of the National Institute on Drug Abuse in the United States (hereinafter, U.S.), during an after-dinner speech that was converted into a published essay during the mid-1970s:

> Let me begin by describing the word "polydrug." I confess my involvement with the first official use of the word. It is a federal political term, rather than a scientific term, which captures some important ideas. Despite its utility, it is difficult to relate to the word in a scholarly or scientific way. This word became big in the field about 2½ years ago [c. 1971-73]. That was the time when the federal government's drug abuse response appeared to be preoccupied with the heroin problem. There was also a quite separate federal concern with the alcohol problem, but there was a growing recognition that there were drug problems that were distinct from either the alcohol problem or the heroin problem. It was this concern with these other drug problems that led to the coining of the term "polydrug." A tremendous bureaucratic shoving and tugging went on within the federal establishment at that time about how to react to this concept. Many budgeteers feared that we were talking about some overwhelming new drug problem that would break the federal budget. Others worried that the new interest in the polydrug problem signaled the premature end of the federal antiheroin efforts. Some treatment experts doubted that we knew how to treat polydrug abuse.
>
> *(Dupont, 1976, p. 311).*

Implicit in Dupont's description of these origins of research on polydrug use in the U.S. is the notion that the concept of "polydrug" in those days was broad enough to encompass the use of a single drug, such as cannabis, provided the drug was not heroin. Indeed, the first major research project on "polydrug abuse" was based upon this definition, such that "cannabis only" users were counted in the tally of "polydrug abusers" but heroin users were not counted (Wesson, Carlin, Adams, & Beschner, 1978). About the same time, once the National Institute on Drug Abuse (NIDA) had supported scientists Lloyd Johnston and James Sample to conduct an early review of definitions for this term, Sample chose to focus on the use of more than one drug,

unless the victim happened to qualify as a "regular" heroin user. He wrote: "At the risk of adding still another definition to the long list, I will use the term polydrug abuse to mean the use of more than one drug, excluding heroin, which are used simultaneously and with a frequency of use of at least once per month. Regular use of heroin, regardless of how many other drugs are also used, will not be classified as polydrug use (Sample, 1977, p. 19). Needless to say, with this interpenetration of political, moral, and scientific issues, and given the field's sustained failure to distinguish between mere use of a drug and "abuse" of that drug, it might be true that one's scientific reputation could be tarnished by becoming involved in these matters. With definitions of basic terms wandering far afield from the *Oxford English Dictionary* (OED) definition given above, it certainly is true that the task of reviewing and synthesizing the available published evidence on the topic of "polydrug use" now represents somewhat of a Herculean effort. Instead, a review of selected research topics and issues is presented, in lieu of a more comprehensive literature review. Readers interested in a complete review must look elsewhere. Works cited in this essay represent selective starting points, highlights, and points of reference for new investigators interested in research issues and gaps in evidence that might be filled sooner rather than later.

For the purposes of this essay, and for research in general, the OED definition of "polydrug" serves well. In the coverage of salient polydrug research topics, the concept of a "polydrug user" would not include individuals whose psychoactive drug experience is limited to one and only one drug (such as "cannabis only"), but the polydrug concept is broad enough to encompass anyone who has used heroin as well as at least one other psychoactive drug compound, including tobacco, alcohol, and the inhalant drugs such as glue or gases, as well as "internationally regulated drugs" (IRD) such as lysergic acid diethylamide (LSD). Here and in all our science articles and essays, we quite deliberately are going to avoid the adjective "illicit" in order to avoid dragging morals into the science.

When necessary, a creation of subsets in the fashion recommended more than 40 years ago by a World Health Organization Expert Committee is advocated, which urged the scientific community to jettison the stigma-laden term "drug addiction" and to put into its place the term "drug dependence" of this type or that type (World Health Organization, 1965)—notwithstanding the recent DSM-5 word choice of the American Psychiatric Association (APA), which apparently made a deliberate choice of a stigma-laden term when alternatives were available (APA, 2013). Another decision made by the APA DSM-5 task panel was to jettison diagnostic codes 304.8 and 304.9, which are used in the *International Classification of Diseases* for "unspecified drug dependence" (i.e., when combinations of drug compounds contributed to the dependence syndrome) and in relation to DSM-IV-TR "polysubstance dependence" (APA, 2000). Interested readers may wish to consult Rosenthal & Levounis (2011) for background information about polysubstance dependence and the transitions from DSM-IV-TR to DSM-5. As it happens, there are no more than a few clinical research articles on polysubstance dependence and other polydrug use disorders (e.g., Kedea et al., 2007; Martinotti et al., 2009), and our literature review turned up no epidemiological estimates for population prevalence or rates of polysubstance dependence.

For this reason, the essay relates primarily to "polydrug use of the alcohol-tobacco-cannabis type" or "A+T+C polydrug use." This turns out to be one of the more prevalent combinations observed when the use of multiple drug compounds has been studied in clinical and population contexts and when the tobacco product is counted, quite appropriately, as a drug compound (e.g., see Dierker et al., 2006, as well as estimates presented in this essay). The A+T+C combination can be distinguished from other combinations such as "polydrug use of the heroin-cocaine or 'speedball' type," which has at times been a favored combination for regular heroin users (e.g., see Ersine, 1933; Leri, Bruneau, & Stewart, 2003; Malow, West, Corrigan, Pena, & Lott, 1992).

The "polydrug" concept used here also will encompass serendipitously identified combinations of interest to drug users (e.g., pentazocine and tripelennamine, also known as "T's and Blues," as described by Showalter, 1980). There also are deliberately designed combinations such as pentazocine-naloxone and other opioid agonist-antagonist products developed to thwart extra-medical (EM) drug-taking (i.e., outside the boundaries of prescribed or approved indications for use), as reviewed not too long ago by Fudala and Johnson (2006) and by Helm, Trescot, Colson, Sehgal, and Silverman (2008).

During this essay's review of issues, patterns of sequential polydrug use will be addressed (e.g., see O'Brien, Comment, Liang, & Anthony, 2012; Wagner & Anthony, 2002), as well as patterns of concurrent and simultaneous polydrug use (e.g., see Earleywine & Newcomb, 1997; Martin, Clifford, & Clapper 1992; McCabe, Cranford, Morales, & Young, 2006). Most of the essay material has been drawn from epidemiological studies pertinent to polydrug use, following an outline of research topics and issues in relation to the five main rubrics of epidemiology, described elsewhere. Some of the ideas and short phrases in this essay originally appeared in other essays for which these five rubrics have been used in outline form in relation to topics other than polydrug use (e.g., see Anthony, 2010a; Anthony & Van Etten, 1998).

Polydrug or Multiple Drug Use: A Pharmacoepidemiological Perspective

For most epidemiologists, a phenomenon of polydrug or multiple drug use can be understood as a subset of a more general problem of multiple possibly toxic exposures, any one of which might combine with others to produce effects more (or less) than values observed under the circumstances of just one exposure. This orientation to the problem invokes a theoretical perspective and research approach that is attuned to the possibility of subgroup variation in effect estimates, and possibly one or another form of toxicological or pharmacological interactions. Here, there is a deliberate distinction between "subgroup variation" versus "interaction," and as explained below, with the expectation of pharmacological, toxicological, or other biological theory in epidemiological research guiding the hypothesized "interactions."

The pharmacoepidemiological perspective outlined in this essay section is one that can be used to understand the degree to which population subgroups characterized by the alcohol-tobacco polydrug combination might experience adverse health responses, such as one of the oral cancers, at greater rates than do other subgroups with consumption of alcohol only or tobacco only. This perspective also can be useful in guiding research on overdose deaths attributable to polydrug combinations, but the resulting inferences can be made complex when the specific identities and doses of the drugs are unknown or have been misclassified, as has been discovered in research on the amphetamine derivative drugs such as methylenedioxymethamphetamine (MDMA, or ecstasy; Byard, Gilbert, James, & Lokan, 1998).

To help orient the readers to this pharmacoepidemiological perspective, Figure 2.1 was created (reprinted within this essay with the author's permission). The figure has two complementary panels; it is advantageous to study Figure 2.1A before turning to Figure 2.1B. Both panels are framed in relation to a hypothetical combination of "Drug A" and "Drug B" as in a comparative trial or epidemiological "cohort" or "prospective" study, with follow-up assessments to discover what might happen to subgroups exposed to the combination compared to

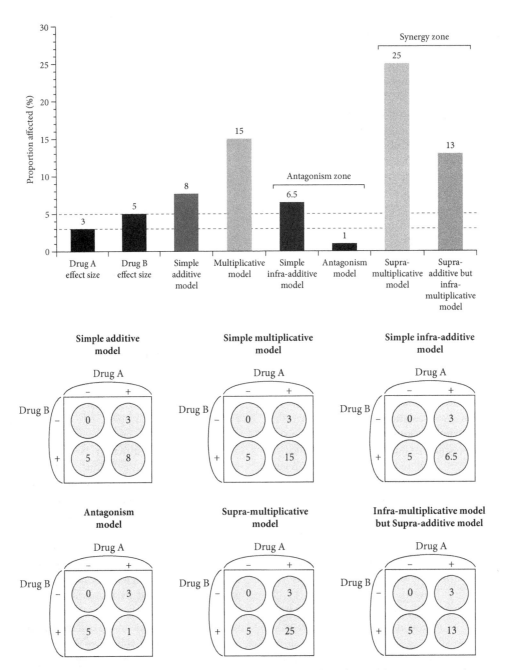

Figure 2.1. (A) Pharmacoepidemiological models of Drug A and Drug B independent effects and drug interactions indicating zones of synergism and antagonism. (B) Pharmacoepidemiological Additive and Multiplicative Models of Drug A and Drug B interactions.

what might happen to subgroups exposed to one drug only, all other determining influences of the response held constant in the research design or analysis approach (e.g., via randomization, matching, stratification, statistical modeling of covariates).

Consider the y-axis for Figure 2.1A, which is labeled "Proportion Affected" by which the occurrence of some clinically or socially significant response of interest is estimated, after population subgroups self-administer or allow themselves to be exposed to Drug A or B, singly, or in the A-B polydrug combination. Under the best of circumstances, this "proportion affected" has a person-time reference, either implicitly (as in an "attack rate" or "cumulative incidence proportion" for some specific interval of time, such as hours or days after drug consumption) or explicitly (as in a person-hours, person-days, or other person-time formulation as is required for a proper time-to-event or survival analysis). As shown at the far left of the figure, with the time interval set implicitly or explicitly in this hypothetical example, a clinically or socially significant response is detected for 3% of individuals in the subgroup exposed to Drug A in the absence of Drug B, and working rightward in the figure, this response is detected for 5% of individuals in the subgroup exposed to Drug B in the absence of Drug A. This same combination is shown in the upper left corner of Figure 2.1B, with the "proportion affected" shown in each cell for the subgroups exposed to Drug A by itself, Drug B by itself, and the doubly exposed combination of Drugs A and B, compared with a reference condition of neither Drug A nor Drug B, with an expectation of no response whatsoever when there is double nonexposure (i.e., exposure to neither Drug A nor Drug B for the subgroups represented in that cell of the table). This type of data pattern, with a zero response in the doubly nonexposed subgroup, is observed in some research contexts (e.g., the study of "death due to drug overdose"), but in many research contexts, there is a nonzero "background" level of response even in the doubly nonexposed subgroup (e.g., because the causal determinants of the response are not limited to the two exposures under study). When there is a nonzero "background" response in the doubly nonexposed subgroup, the arithmetic for studying "subgroup variation" or "interaction" requires a small adaptation, but the concepts and logic still apply as outlined below.

As shown in the third bar of Figure 2.1A, under a "Simple Additive Model" of the combined effects of Drug A and Drug B, the expected value is 8% [(3 + 5)%], more or less, within the limits of sampling or other error not entirely under the control of the research team. The same value of 8% is shown for the doubly exposed condition (A + B) in the "++ corner" of Figure 2.1B.

All of the remaining bars in Figure 2.1A and the drawings in Figure 2.1B represent departures from this "Simple Additive Model" of one type or another. One possibility is a "Simple Multiplicative Model," and under this model the proportion affected would be 15% [(3* 5)%]. All of Figure 2.1A's bars to the right of this "Simple Multiplicative Model" represent departures both from the "Simple Additive Model" and the "Simple Multiplicative Model," the first one of which is a "Simple Infra-Additive (but Not Multiplicative) Model" according to which the proportion affected would be in less than the 8% value from simple addition. Next in line is an "Antagonism Model" such that the proportion affected among those doubly exposed is less than has been observed when there is exposure to either Drug A only or Drug B only (as illustrated by the 1% value represented by the height of the "Antagonism Model" bar, with the idea that a strict definition of antagonism requires this magnitude of combined effect). That is, an "Antagonism Model" can be defined to require an observed response to the drug combination that is less than the response observed to either drug exposure considered separately. Nonetheless, in some research, the label "antagonism" has been used to describe observed relationships that have been labeled as "Simple Infra-Additive," and for this reason the pair of these bars have been marked with a bracket labeled "Antagonism Zone."

The last two bars of Figure 2.1A convey expectations under the "Supra-Multiplicative Model" and also the "Supra-Additive but Infra-Multiplicative Model," with a bracket labeled "Synergy Zone" because there is an advantage gained by restricting the term "synergy" to combinations that evoke supra-multiplicative responses—in this instance, values of greater than 15% (i.e., the 15% value observed for the "Simple Multiplicative Model"). Nonetheless, in some instances, the term "synergy" has been defined quite loosely to encompass any response of a supra-additive character. Under this very liberal (and, to the authors' opinions, incorrect) definition of "synergy," the 13% response under the "Supra-Additive But Infra-Multiplicative Model" would qualify as a evidence of Drug A-B synergy. Research trainees are encouraged to reserve the term "synergy" for supra-multiplicative point estimates in the "synergy zone" and to describe "supra-additive but infra-multiplicative" point estimates with a very clear but not particularly jazzy adjective: "supra-additive." In consequence, the jazziest adjective "synergistic" is reserved for truly jazzy results—i.e., supra-supra-additive effects.

In the first paragraph of this section, Figure 2.1A, patterns were described in terms of sub-group variation in effects, and referenced "possible" inter-actions between Drugs A and B. Here, on one hand, the general problem is framed as one of asking whether the study of a response to the condition of double exposure (i.e., A and B combined) is based upon a theory of how Drug A might modify the effect of Drug B, or how Drug B might modify the effect of Drug A (e.g., a pharmacological theory of agonist-antagonist interaction with receptor system substrates), for which the concept of "interaction" clearly is applicable. On the other hand, when there is no guiding theory about the underlying mecha-nisms at play, it would seem to be more sensible to speak of "subgroup variation" in the effect of Drug A across levels of Drug B exposure, or in the effect of Drug B across levels of Drug A exposure, reserving the concept of "interaction" for theory-grounded research on these topics. Most of the best introduc-tory texts in epidemiology and pharmacology try to keep the concept of "interaction" in reserve for the special occasions when there is an underlying theory to guide the study of observed patterns of responses when exposures occur singly or in combination with one another. If there is no theory, the concept of "subgroup variation" in the effect estimates can serve well. The concept of "subgroup variation" also serves well when the only available evidence is of mere "statistical interaction"—i.e., a departure from what might be expected by simply adding together the sum of effects, or by multiplying them. "Subgroup variation" can arise in any given sample by chance alone, or by completely unpredicted cir-cumstances, and this would give rise to a "statistical interaction" without any theory-based expectation. In our proposed glossary of terms for polydrug use, that kind of evidence would be put in the category of "subgroup variation," but it will not be claimed that it deserves to be called evidence of "interac-tion." With these important conceptual distinctions and an initial glossary of terms in mind, it becomes possible to move on to the other research topics and issues of the essay.

The mechanisms involved in the pharma-cological interaction between alcohol, tobacco, psychotropic medications, and internationally regulated drugs (IRD) include pharmacodynamic mechanisms in which one compound modulates the pharmacological effect of another (additively, synergistically, or antagonistically), typically by act-ing in the same receptor, via second messenger or related molecular or biochemical sites, or via phar-macokinetic mechanisms in which the concentra-tion of one compound is altered by the presence of another compound in the system. Common pharmacokinetic mechanisms described in poly-drug use context include: alterations in the hepatic metabolism, particularly involving cytochrome P450 (CYP) enzymes; alterations in the glucuroni-dation effects on the transporter P-glycoprotein (P-gp); and alterations in the absorption and production of pharmacologically active metabo-lites (Karan, McCance-Katz, & Zajicek, 2009). A detailed description of these mechanisms is beyond the scope of any essay on the epidemiology of polydrug use, but some examples of these interac-tions might be mentioned: (a) co-administration of Δ9-tetrahydrocannabinol and nicotine attenuating the somatic expression and dysphoric signs of nico-tine withdrawal in preclinical animal research, pos-sibly due to interaction between the cannabinoids and cholinergic neurotransmission with nicotine receptor involvement (Balerio, Aso, Berrendero, Murtra, & Maldonado, 2004); (b) concurrent use of cannabis and high methadone doses found to be followed by lower 24-hour plasma (R)-methadone and (S)-methadone concentrations/dose, possibly as a consequence of CYP1A2 isoenzyme induc-tion leading to increased metabolism of metha-done, or the inhibition of P-gp by cannabinoids (Hallinan et al., 2009); (c) co-administration of buprenorphine and cocaine, followed by decreased buprenophine concentrations, possibly when cocaine induces CYP, possibly involving P-gp, or perhaps diminished sublingual absorption of buprenorphine due to vasoconstriction caused by cocaine (McCance-Katz, Rainey, & Moody, 2010); and (d) ethanol-associated decline in cocaine clear-ance via inhibition of cocaine hydrolysis toward benzoylecgonine and ecgonine methyl ester by enzyme carboxylesterase 1 (hCE1) (i.e., a shift in the hydrolysis pathway to transesterification is thought to generate an active metabolite, cocaeth-ylene (Laizure, Mandrell, Gades, & Parker, 2003; Parker & Laizure, 2010); and (e) co-administration of hydromorphone ER and ethanol increasing peak plasma concentrations of hydromorphone (Walden, Nicholls, Smith, & Tucker, 2007). These examples are offered as theory-driven substrates for polydrug research in the domain of "interactions" as opposed to mere subgroup variations.

The Five Main Rubrics of Epidemiology

The rest of this essay is organized in relation to five main rubrics of epidemiology and public health research that the authors and others have found to provide a useful outline when the task is to consider past, present, and future research challenges in relation to specified responses of clinical, social, and public health significance. More detailed descriptions of the rubrics and their utility in review of evidence appear in primary sources on epidemiological research (e.g., see Anthony & Van Etten, 1998; Anthony, 2010a). Nonetheless, this essay represents the first time the rubrics concept has been applied to the subject matter of polydrug use.

In general, the first two rubrics or subheadings address relatively basic research topics that tend to preoccupy workers in epidemiology until (a) resources become available to press onward toward more complex and ultimately more interesting subject-matter, or (b) boredom from simple challenges sets in. The last three rubrics call upon higher levels of mastery of epidemiological concepts, principles, and research approaches, along with challenges and puzzles that might keep one's mind occupied for many years, the most rewarding of which is the production of definitive evidence about mass population public health techniques or programs that can change population health parameters, with beneficial effects for 100s, 1000s, 10,000s, or even millions at a time (i.e., more than might be gained by treating one sick patient at a time).

As initially explained elsewhere (Anthony & Van Etten, 1998), the first main rubric concerns epidemiological evidence about "Quantity" and the main research question posed under this rubric is "How many are becoming affected?" or related questions such as "How many now are affected?" or "How many ever have become affected?" where the response of interest generally is either one or more causes of death or the occurrence of some disease or illness, some other health-related condition of interest (e.g., disablement), or a health-affecting exposure of interest (e.g., one of the various types of polydrug use). It may be of special note that the current projects to reestimate the global burdens of disease have made a point to look into the disease burdens as might be caused by exposure to tobacco (i.e., without

reference to concomitant exposures or "alone"), or alcohol ("alone") or cannabis ("alone"). From this renaissance of the "Global Burden of Disease Project" (GBD) a new set of summary estimates for the world population should be expected, but the overall conclusions about rank-ordering of these drug exposures are not apt to be much different from the original GBD estimates, in which tobacco smoking was counted in the top-rank as a preventable cause of disease burdens. By comparison, heavy or hazardous drinking and associated alcohol dependence syndromes were counted after tobacco with respect to global disease burden, and cannabis use was counted as making much less of a contribution. It is this type of work that preoccupies public health scientists working under the rubric of "Quantity" when the population of interest is global, as in Mathers and Loncar (2006).

The rubric of "Quantity" also can be pertinent when the goal is to quantify the disease burden for more narrowly defined nation-state or substate populations, as when a public health official has responsibility for the health of a geopolitically defined subset of the world population. As such, when the U.S. Department of Health and Human Services reports on prevalence estimates from the National Surveys on Drug Use and Health, these overall estimates for the population as a whole might be regarded as evidence under the rubric of Quantity—prior to any stratification by subgroups of the population. Once stratification occurs, the evidence falls under the rubric of Location, as would be the case when epidemiologists look for disease occurrence in specifically identifiable population subgroups characterized by family background (e.g., historically disadvantaged minority groups), occupation (e.g., the military), place of residence or institutional affiliation (e.g., homeless, inmates of prisons, persons admitted to drug treatment programs, college dormitory residents, and school-attending students).

There is somewhat more complexity and more challenge when the work shifts to this second rubric of epidemiology, called "Location" because the main research questions can be framed as variations on a common theme: "Where, within populations of interest, are we more (or less) likely to find subgroups of people becoming cases, with subgroups defined in terms of characteristics of time (season, decade, century), place (e.g., in dry or wet places, hot or cold, across national or other geopolitical boundaries), and person (e.g., birth year, sex, race-ethnicity, family history of disease, lifestyle)?" Note that epidemiologists who seek to answer questions about how many are becoming or have become affected often concurrently seek to answer questions about where affected individuals are more or less likely to be found within the population or population group under study. As illustrated later in the essay, there are many papers on "the prevalence and correlates" of polydrug use of one type or another, with the term "prevalence" referring to the evidence about quantity and the term "correlates" referring to evidence about location within subgroups defined by characteristics of person, place or time.

Epidemiological evidence under the "Location" rubric includes trend data that mark off the interval from 1976 to about 1982 as peak years in "America's 2nd cocaine epidemic," at least with respect to risk of becoming a new cocaine user in North America during the 20th century (given that America's 1st cocaine epidemic occurred early in the 20th century; Anthony, 1992). By making comparisons of similar data across national boundaries, it is possible to observe that peak values for cocaine were not seen in Chile of South America until the 1990s. Moreover, there has been negligible consumption of cocaine hydrochloride powder or crack-cocaine among the inhabitants of the coca-producing regions of Colombia, Peru, and Bolivia, even in the areas where coca leaf cultivation and chewing are quite common (Caris, Anthony, Rios-Bedoya, & Anthony, 2009). Here, when there has been no more than limited research work under the rubric of "Location," it can be declared that these epidemiological patterns exist, but it would be impossible to answer questions about "why" these patterns exist, "how" they came about (e.g., in terms of biological, interpersonal, sociocultural, or economic processes), or whether these patterns help to make choices about prevention programs or drug control policies. To answer the "why?" "how?" and "what can be done?" questions, an epidemiologist's attention must be re-focused on the next three rubrics, as described below. Answers to these more complex questions of "why?" and "how?" and "what can be done?" require mastery of substantially more difficult concepts, principles, and research approaches than what is required to answer questions about quantity and location.

In complement with what it is understood about the occurrence of drug taking in relation to locational parameters of time and place, most readers of this essay (especially psychologists, psychiatrists, and behavioral scientists) will have considerable acquaintance with associations that link the occurrence of drug taking with characteristics of subgroups or individual differences, such as a general male excess in observed prevalence of Internationally Regulated Drug (IRD) use (i.e., when internationally regulated drugs are used to get high or for other "EM" reasons). There also have been fairly distinctive patterns that appear in research on drug-taking across birth cohort or stages of child, adolescent, and adult development, and patterns in relation to personality traits such as risk-taking or harm-avoidance, or in relation to family history, such as excess occurrence of alcohol dependence among subgroups with a dense family history of alcohol dependence during prior generations. These patterns of association, often conveyed with the term "risk factor" but better described as either "correlates" or "suspected causes," may be said to account for almost all of the epidemiological findings on polydrug use that have been published during the past 50 years, with no more than a handful of exceptions. For the most part, this research has helped to describe the epidemiological patterns as they exist, but it has not helped to answer the "why?" question, the "how?" question, or the "what might be done to prevent or control?" question as focused on polydrug use.

Whereas research under the first two rubrics has a decidedly "descriptive" character, it is under the rubric of "Causes" that the epidemiologist seeks to answer questions about what accounts for some people becoming affected while others are spared, and these questions require some degree of mastery of the apparatus of causal inference. In consequence, the research approaches required to answer questions about "why?," the "how?," and the "what can be done?" tend to be substantially more challenging to master and to be more complex than the approaches used when estimating prevalence or when studying mere correlates ("risk factors"). As noted previously in this essay, these are difficult questions and because they are difficult to answer there is not much definitive evidence on the causes of polydrug use, the causal processes or mechanisms leading to polydrug exposures, or effective approaches for their prevention and control.

Under the rubric of "Mechanisms" there is a shift in attention from the "why?" questions about causes, to "how?" questions about linked states and processes that lead up to an exposure, a health condition, and the aftermath of the health condition. As explained elsewhere (e.g., Anthony

& Van Etten, 1998; Anthony, 2010b), the earliest public health research under this rubric included longitudinal observational studies of the "natural history" of disease under conditions of no effective treatment interventions. This rubric concerning "Mechanisms" also encompasses some of the research on comorbidity patterns (e.g., co-occurrence of drug use and general medical or psychiatric conditions), especially when the comorbidity research team ultimately seeks to understand which conditions come first and account for the occurrence of later conditions. Whereas there is no formally declared research on the "natural history" of polydrug use, there is research on the sequencing of drug compounds across time, with a building up of drug experience to form a polydrug use pattern, akin to comorbidity research on sequences of psychiatric and behavioral disturbances (e.g., see Degenhardt et al., 2010; O'Brien et al., 2012). This rubric also subsumes research on complications that are hypothesized to follow the exposure under study or the health condition of interest, including studies of overdose emergencies and deaths in the context of polydrug research, as well as disease states or illnesses that occur more frequently among subgroups of individuals who consume drug combinations compared with those who use just one of the drugs in the combination. Other illustrations of polydrug research of this type will be provided in the next sections of the essay. It will be seen that some limited evidence on mechanisms can be gained from cross-sectional studies, but for the most part, research on mechanisms and the "how" questions require longitudinal designs with repeated measures. Moreover, at times, formal randomized experimentation will be required to answer these questions about mechanisms.

There is some limited polydrug research of a longitudinal character; and virtually none on randomized experimental designs used to probe formally into theories of mechanisms that lead up to polydrug use or its complications. This gap will be addressed when the essay turns to a section on directions for future research.

The final rubric concerns "prevention and control," and as mentioned previously, most epidemiologists studying polydrug use patterns would be delighted to produce definitive evidence that would lead toward prevention or effective control of polydrug use or its complications. The main research question under this rubric can be expressed simply as "What can be done?" and in the domain of public health work the question is re-expressed as "What

can be done to prevent or delay onset, control, or otherwise reduce associated suffering and death?" In the domain of polydrug use, there is a small amount of published evidence on this topic, but more is needed. This is another topic that will be discussed in the later sections of this essay, including the section on future directions in research.

Illustrations of Polydrug Research Under Each Rubric

There are no studies that provide a complete global view of polydrug use and its consequences, although a recent article has worked in that direction via research on alcohol, tobacco, cannabis, and cocaine as separable drug compounds in multiple regions and countries of the world, using the same general methodological survey research approach in each jurisdiction under study (Degenhardt et al., 2008). One very clear implication of this reach toward a global view of the use of these drugs is that in many countries (e.g., in Asia) there must be insubstantial burdens associated with the types of polydrug use that involve cocaine, cannabis, and other IRD. In these countries, there are very low prevalence estimates for use of cocaine and for use of cannabis, considered separately. By way of contrast, in other places such as the U.S., New Zealand, and several countries of Western Europe, the published estimates on these separate drug compounds or products indicate that there must be tangible occurrences of polydrug use, at least for the alcohol-cannabis combination. This conclusion is based on the marginal proportions estimated with respect to the use of these two drugs in the community, considered one by one.

For example, in New Zealand, by age 21, a projected 55–60% of the adult population has consumed both alcohol and cannabis, even if there were not shared influences that account for co-occurrence of alcohol and cannabis use with a greater than chance frequency. This projection, based upon chance co-occurrence, is achieved by deriving a simple product: the New Zealand estimate for the cumulative occurrence of alcohol use by age 21 multiplied by the corresponding estimate for cannabis use. One of the directions for future research on polydrug use will be to make more direct estimates of the co-occurrence of various types of polydrug use in the countries now participating in this global mental health surveys project, and to extend the project to include more countries in the regions now represented in the published work by

Degenhardt and colleagues. These co-occurrence estimates should be relatively easy to produce, and to compare with the projections based on chance co-occurrence. A more difficult challenge for the future will be to produce definitive evidence on the causes or processes that lead to a greater than chance co-occurrence, whenever an excess has been observed.

The work by Degenhardt and colleagues is unusual in that most studies of the prevalence and correlates of polydrug use under the first two rubrics (Quantity and Location) do not attempt to characterize the experience of all community-dwelling or household-dwelling adult population members in multiple countries. It is more typical to find surveys of the general population of individual countries, or coordinated multi-country surveys of school-attending youths. For example, the current situation in the United States is such that at least one national survey is conducted annually, producing prevalence estimates of the type shown in Figure 2.2, which are based upon analyses completed by the authors for the present essay. These estimates are based upon data from the public use data files of the National Survey of Drug Use and Health (NSDUH), with fieldwork during 2006 and with a nationally representative sample of community-dwelling U.S. residents aged 12 years and older. For this analysis, the population prevalence proportions for each type of individual drug

or polydrug use were estimated, formed by considering the EM use in the past year prior to the survey of alcohol, tobacco, cannabis, and "other" drugs (including inhalants as well as internationally regulated psychoactive drug compounds such as cocaine, morphine, and the benzodiazepines). The NSDUH assessments were conducted privately within the dwelling units from which each participant was sampled by rigorous probability sampling methods. In general, the assessment data are self-reports elicited via audio-enhanced computer-assisted self-interviews.

As shown in Figure 2.2, based on fairly recent NSDUH data on the U.S. population under study, about 25% had not engaged in alcohol, tobacco, cannabis, or other EM drug use during the year prior to the date of survey assessment in 2006. An estimated 33% had consumed alcohol during that year, but had not used another of the other drug compounds. The corresponding estimate for "tobacco only" was just over 5%, and the estimated prevalence value for "cannabis only" is too small to estimate with any degree of statistical precision; it can only be said that it is a rather small subgroup that uses cannabis and only cannabis. The estimate for polydrug use of the alcohol-tobacco type (A+T, without cannabis or other drugs) was just under 20%, and the next largest estimates involve the combination of alcohol, tobacco, and cannabis (A+T+C, all three in the prior year, 3–5%), as

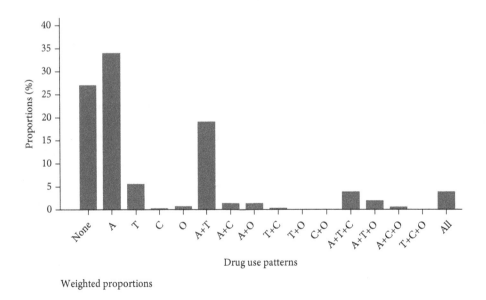

Weighted proportions

Figure 2.2. Alcohol, tobacco, and internationally regulated drug use. National Survey on Drug Use and Health, 2006.

Note. A, alcohol; T, tobacco; C, cannabis; A + T, alcohol + tobacco; A + C, alcohol + cannabis; A + O, alcohol + other; T + C, tobacco + cannabis; T + O, tobacco + other; C + O, cannabis + other; A + T + C, alcohol + tobacco + cannabis; A + T + O, alcohol + tobacco + other; A + C + O, alcohol + cannabis + other; T + C + O, tobacco + cannabis + other; All, alcohol + tobacco + cannabis + other.

well as the combination of all four in the prior year ("All," 3–5%). As has been noted for the "cannabis only" group, there were several other quite rare types of polydrug use, including several combinations that often interest polydrug researchers: alcohol, tobacco, and other drugs; tobacco and cannabis (without alcohol or other drugs); tobacco and other drugs; cannabis and other drugs. Of course, given that the size of the U.S. population under study was not too distant from 200 million individuals, a 1% prevalence estimate for polydrug use of the "alcohol, cannabis, and other drug" type (without tobacco smoking) translates into least at 2 million individuals with this pattern of polydrug use. Suppose that just 1% of these Alcohol + Cannabis + Other (A+C+O) polydrug users have need for treatment in order to avoid complications of this EM pattern of drug taking. With that conservative value of 1%, there would be 20,000 individuals in need of such treatment in the United States. Health care costs associated with effective treatment might well be at the $1000 level per A+C+O polydrug user, or larger. At the conservative value of $1000 per case, $20 million would be required for effective health care in response to this condition every year.

The authors anticipate that this example is an adequate demonstration of the power of relatively simple epidemiological estimates gathered under the rubric of "Quantity" as well as the potential utility of such estimates in the "political arithmetic" required to plan, to set priorities for public health programs, and to formulate policies to prevent or control polydrug use patterns associated with substantial health and social consequences. One important direction for future research along these lines is to devise improved estimates of prevalence and to make more complete projections of health care costs as might be required for effective treatment of the various polydrug use patterns with clinically significant health or social complications, with an eye toward the possibility that in the polydrug domain of public health work it would be found that an ounce of prevention might be better than a pound of cure.

As noted in the prior section of this essay, it is typical for public health scientists to produce evidence under the rubric of Location at the same time they are producing estimates under the rubric of Quantity. To illustrate, also using NSDUH data from 2006, estimates for population subgroups of males and females in each of four age strata (12–17, 18–25, 26–34, and 35+ years; Figure 2.3) were produced, in order to illustrate the focus of research under the "Location" rubric, which seeks a description of population experience, but offers no probing test of theory or explanation about what accounts for the observed patterns. For the most part, these descriptive studies raise more questions than they settle, but they have the advantage of highlighting male-female differences as well as age-related differences in the occurrence of polydrug types. For example, there is a general similarity in the prevalence estimates for single drug and polydrug use types between males and females aged 12–17 years old (Figure 2.3A), with the possible exception of the "A+T" combination (in the absence of both cannabis and other drug use), for which there is an apparent slight excess prevalence among males. A tangible occurrence of the "other drug only" category is noteworthy for both males and females in the 12- to 17-year-old age group. This is an epidemiological detail not directly central to the issue of polydrug use, but it is indirectly pertinent in that some polydrug research is based on a concept of lifetime co-occurrence patterns. That is, this essay's general polydrug definition requires neither simultaneous nor concurrent use of two or more drugs (i.e., "concurrent" within some specified interval such as a year), in contrast to the ideas of "concurrent" and "simultaneous" polydrug use that have been advocated by some research teams (e.g., see Earleywine & Newcomb, 1997; McCabe et al., 2006). When this lifetime perspective is taken in later years, a tangible proportion of this year's 12- to 17-year-olds qualify as polydrug users. In later years, these individuals would be expected to have already have engaged in EM use of these "other drugs" (often prescription opioids and stimulants in this epoch), even if they did not engage in alcohol, tobacco, or cannabis use in this most recent year prior to the date of assessment.

Among 18- to 25-year-olds (Figure 2.3B), the great majority of males and females have engaged in at least one form of single or polydrug use during the prior year, but there is a slight female excess among those in the "none" category and in the "alcohol only" category, which has a complement in the observed a male excess for several of the other single and polydrug types. For example, the male excess prevalence for the A+T polydrug combination appears in this age stratum, just as it was found among 12- to 17-year-olds. In addition, there is a male excess for other polydrug combinations, in particular the "A+T+C" combination and the "All" four drug compound" combination.

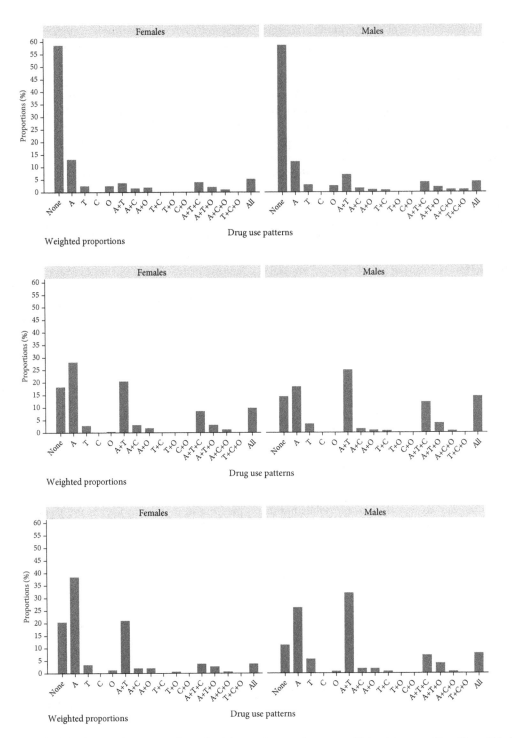

Figure 2.3. Alcohol, tobacco, and internationally regulated drug use by sex and age group. National Survey on Drug Use and Health, 2006. (A) Alcohol, tobacco, and internationally regulated drug use among US females and males 12 to 17 years old. National Survey on Drug Use and Health, 2006. (B) Alcohol, tobacco, and internationally regulated drug use among US females and males 18 to 25 years old. National Survey on Drug Use and Health, 2006. (C) Alcohol, tobacco, and internationally regulated drug use among US females and males 26 to 34 years old. National Survey on Drug Use and Health, 2006. (D) Alcohol, tobacco, and internationally regulated drug use among US females and males 35+ years old. National Survey on Drug Use and Health, 2006.

Note. A, alcohol; T, tobacco; C, cannabis; O, other; A+T, alcohol + tobacco; A+C, alcohol + cannabis; A+O, alcohol + other; T+C, tobacco + cannabis; T+O, tobacco + other; C+O, cannabis + other; A+T+C, alcohol + tobacco + cannabis; A+T+O, alcohol + tobacco + other; A+C+O, alcohol + cannabis + other; T+C+O, tobacco + cannabis + other; All, alcohol + tobacco + cannabis + other.

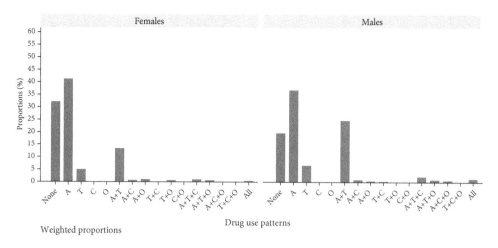

Figure 2.3. Continued

Comparison of the polydrug experience of 26- to 34-year-olds in 2006 (Figure 2.3C) with the experiences of the younger age groups of the population in that same year raises questions about the sources of these age, period, and cohort variations, which cannot be disentangled in cross-sectional data from a single year, and which can even be difficult to disentangle in cross-sectional data across multiple years. To illustrate, consider that among the 18- to 25-year-olds, there is a tangible prevalence of polydrug use of "all" drug compounds represented for both males and females, but the prevalence estimates for the 26- to 34-year-olds are at lower levels for both males and females. This variation across age strata in cross-sectional data from 1 year might reflect differences in a relatively constant age-developmental pattern (e.g., "maturing out" of cannabis and "other" drug use as individuals traverse from one younger adult age stratum to the next older stratum), or might be differences that are not age-developmental per se but are linked to the experience of the various birth cohorts represented within each age group. In order to account for the observed variation, one must move from research work under the rubric of "Location" onward toward research under the rubric of "Causes," with gathering of repeated cross-sectional or longitudinal data that have the resolving power needed to sort out the alternative explanations (e.g., as illustrated in Fabio et al., 2006). A similar approach must be applied to understand the sources of variation that account for the markedly different prevalence estimates for polydrug use observed for the oldest age group under study—i.e., those age 35 years and older in 2006 (Figure 2.3D). Here, the age stratum is broad and encompasses a large number of diverse birth cohorts, including some individuals who lived through the alcohol prohibition and temperance movement eras, as well as some who lived through the Vietnam and Haight-Ashbury "counter-cultural revolution" era. These experiences almost certainly account for some of the observed differences when contrasting their polydrug experiences with those of the younger age groups. In addition, to the extent that drinking and other drug use behaviors tend to decline in age-developmental patterns, these sources of variation are at play, in addition to any distinctive cohort or period "effects."

Against a background of these basic male-female and age-related variations, it must be mentioned that work under the rubric of "Location" almost always has involved the study of racial and more recently race-ethnicity variations in the occurrence of health conditions. Polydrug use patterns are no exceptions. As noted elsewhere, this tradition most likely can be traced in part to the fact that a person's age, sex, and race or race-ethnicity are recorded routinely on death certificates and in medical records once standardized certification and record-keeping systems are in place—that is, these sometimes are the only data elements made available when the research is based upon certificate and record review, as opposed to the in-person assessments of the type conducted for national surveys of drug use and health. A more subtle explanation for this tradition is that age, sex, and race, for the most part, are not responsive to the health characteristics or disease processes experienced by an individual. As such, they are truly "independent" or "exogenous" variables in any conceptual model that seeks to account for variations in health and disease. In contrast, one's educational status, occupational standing, income, and even marital status might be responsive to the drug-taking or health status of an individual. As such, variables of this type are not truly "independent" or "exogenous" and they do not meet the assumptions of the relatively simple research approaches that must be mastered for work under the rubric of "Location" (e.g., stratified analyses, age-adjustment).

Figure 2.4 conveys NSDUH estimates for various race-ethnicity subgroups of the U.S. population in 2006. What is noteworthy is that roughly 80% of the non-Hispanic White subgroup had engaged in EM alcohol, tobacco, or other drug use during the year prior to assessment, and the "alcohol only" subgroup is the most frequently observed drug use pattern. In contrast, nonusers are in the majority for all of the other race-ethnicity groups shown (e.g., roughly 40% of non-Hispanic Blacks and non-Hispanic Asians had no recent EM drug use, compared with roughly 20% of non-Hispanic Whites). "Alcohol only" and the "A+T" polydrug type were observed to be relatively common patterns in all of the subgroups. The next most common patterns were "tobacco only," "A+T+C" and "All" four compound combinations.

Here again, these are descriptions pertinent to polydrug research at the national level, but under the rubric of "Location" the data do not have the resolving power to answer questions about why or how it happens that there might be race or race-ethnicity variations in the patterns of EM polydrug types or single drug compounds. Answers to the "why?" and "how?" questions require the more probing types of research approaches that are harnessed under Rubrics 3-5.

Location

Before turning to selected examples under the rubric of "Causes," readers of the essay may appreciate some observations based upon the published literature of research articles on the occurrence and correlates of polydrug use, where "occurrence" refers primarily to "prevalence" proportions that convey how many, in a study population, are users or have become users (i.e., cumulative to the date of assessment). The notion of studying polydrug use "incidence" rates does not seem to have developed deep roots in population research on this topic (i.e.,

the probability of becoming a new polydrug user, expressed per unit of person-time explicitly, or with time expressed implicitly as in an annual incidence rate or in an "attack rate" with a fixed interval for all persons at risk of becoming a polydrug user).

Because it would be possible to fill a monograph-length volume with the published findings on polydrug use as it has been investigated in cross-sectional epidemiological research, a comprehensive review of estimates for prevalence and correlates of polydrug use in this essay will not be attempted. Indeed, three separate polydrug research monographs could be written on the findings of each of the three American research teams studying this subject: (a) Lloyd Johnston and colleagues at the University of Michigan, who since the mid-1970s have had the monopoly for NIDA-sponsored annual surveys of school-attending youths as part of the Monitoring the Future (MTF) project in the U.S.; (b) Joseph Gfroerer and colleagues, first at NIDA and now at SAMHSA, who have tended the now-annual National Surveys on Drug Use and Health (formerly National Household Survey on Drug Abuse, NSDUH/NHSDA) in the U.S.; and (c) Bridget Grant and colleagues affiliated with the National Institute on Alcohol and Alcoholism's series of U.S. national household surveys conducted over the past 15–20 years (NLAES/NESARC). Regrettably, the contributions from the MTF and NSDUH/NHSDA research teams on polydrug research to peer reviewed scientific literature have been more limited than the contributions of the NESARC team; it has been only the NLAES/NESARC team that has emphasized publication of its work in the peer-reviewed literature (e.g., see Huang et al., 2006). In some instances, other scholars have reviewed and synthesized these findings on selected issues, such as timing of onset of alcohol and other drug use (e.g., see Martin, 2008) by using the public domain versions of the various survey data. Unfortunately, these studies have primarily focused on single drugs as opposed to polydrug research issues, and without the benefit of longitudinal data that now lie fallow and for the most part unexamined. A scholarly review of the MTF and NHSDA/NSDUH estimates on the topic of polydrug use and potential future use of the data is beyond the scope of this essay.

Next steps for others who wish to make a contribution to the synthesis of these many years of epidemiological "findings" on polydrug use patterns and trends over time must include the creation of a coherent theoretical framework to guide

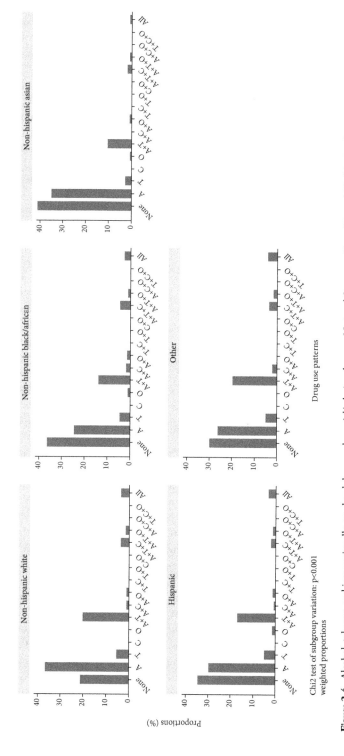

Figure 2.4. Alcohol, tobacco, and internationally regulated drug use by racial/ethnic subgroup. National Survey on Drug Use and Health, 2006.

Note: A, alcohol; T, tobacco; C, cannabis; A + T, alcohol + tobacco; A + C, alcohol + cannabis; A + O, alcohol + other; T + C, tobacco + cannabis; T + O, tobacco + other; C + O, cannabis + other; A + T + C, alcohol + tobacco + cannabis; A + T + O, alcohol + tobacco + other; A + C + O, alcohol + cannabis + other; T + C + O, tobacco + cannabis + other; All, alcohol + tobacco + cannabis + other.

the synthesis in order to avoid a cumbersome piling up of "particularistic factoids" that might be pertinent in one place for a time, but with no broad generalizability. In this reach for theory, there is no need for a grand theory, but it most likely will be useful to forge a middle ground in a position that lies between the grand theory and an operations research approach that often has guided massive epidemiological enterprises. Over the past decade, the MTF and NSDUH research teams have generally taken an atheoretical perspective and have not forged any theory-based positions that might guide their work, as illustrated in this excerpt from that work:

> In recent decades, there has been a good deal of measurement (some more theoretically guided, some less so) as well as a good deal of relational analysis; this activity has contributed importantly to the further development and refinement of theory. We see our own research, past and future, as providing valuable ingredients for this ongoing process as we and others continue gradually to advance theory relating to drug use (some of our recent work in terms of advancing a developmental perspective—e.g., Schulenberg & Maggs, 2002; Schulenberg, Maggs, & O'Malley, 2003—is described later when considering Objective 6). But, to repeat the point, we did not think it appropriate to have premised such a large and ongoing research endeavor, with its many varied research purposes, on any single theoretical position (Johnston, O'Malley, Schulenberg, & Bachman, 2006, p. 9).

In the polydrug research arena, it is not clear that there is much more value to be gained in the year-in and year-out piling up of mountains of data in a research enterprise that has contributed little more than the particularistic fact that in the U.S. the alcohol-tobacco combination is the most prevalent polydrug type, and after that, it is the A+T+C polydrug type, with other drugs typically coming onboard later in the sequence. In the authors' view, it is time to develop a broad consensus about theory-driven polydrug research that can replace or create a new structure for what may have become the public health–university–research institute version of Eisenhower's military-industrial complex. This kind of enterprise requires guidance by a set of competing theories, with deliberate efforts to forge a consensus about concepts and definitional issues that always endure without resolution until they are disciplined by the thrust and parry of alternative conceptual models.

What now is needed in the U.S., where there has been more than three decades to build mountains of "particularistic factoids" on polydrug research, may not be what is needed elsewhere. Indeed, a capacity to turn the American research enterprise in the direction of theory-testing was developed part and parcel with years of experience in the MTF, NSHDA/NSDUH, and NLAES/NESARC research enterprise, as well as concurrent "programs" of research such as the Epidemiologic Catchment Area Program and the National Comorbidity Surveys research program. Similar programs have evolved in Europe, such as the European School Survey Project on Alcohol and Other Drugs (ESPAD), guided in part by the American experiences in this domain of research (e.g., see United Nations Office on Drugs and Crime, 2003), and there are recent similar developments in the "observatory" work created by the Organization of American States (Organization of American States, 2011)

In other countries and regions of the world, where most of the world's inhabitants live, there is good reason to conduct school, household, and community surveys of the type that have become commonplace each year in the Americas and in parts of Western Europe and Oceania, but perhaps these initiatives should be more than "observatory" initiatives akin to star-gazing. In these parts of the globe, it is useful and sometimes theory-challenging to have the benefit of empiricism-grounded particularistic factoids, but why not extend the work into the realms of theory and public health practice by taking a more experimental, theory-testing, and intervention research-oriented approach? By way of illustration, it is possible to draw attention to a recently published important contribution to the peer-reviewed polydrug research literature from Taiwan. Drawing from a Taiwanese series of national school surveys with a cross-sectional design akin to that used in the MTF surveys, W.J. Chen's research team (2009) not only estimated prevalence proportions for single drugs and drug combinations, but also provided estimates of cumulative incidence proportions (akin to "attack rates") to express the risk of becoming a drug user. Here, the logic for extracting incidence data from cross-sectional survey data on age or recency of first drug use is one that has been used in a number of prior epidemiological studies, including the work of C.Y. Chen and colleagues, which suggested polydrug use might increase the risk of a rapid transition from initial cannabis smoking to onset of a cannabis dependence syndrome (Chen, O'Brien, & Anthony, 2005). More to the point, what makes this study in Taiwan particularly interesting is a departure from American, western European, and Oceania contexts such that the first illegal drugs used by these youths in Taiwan were not compounds in the cannabis family. Instead, they were MDMA and ketamine, with cannabis in the third rank and rarely the first illegal drug compound in sequence after onset of use of legal drugs such as alcohol, tobacco, or betel nut. In addition, it is of interest that betel nut chewing had started for some youths early in the middle school years or even during childhood, often at the same age as tobacco use, consistent with patterns observed for betel nut and tobacco consumption among children and adolescents of the Federated States of Micronesia in the western Pacific region. As noted by Chen et al. (2009), the "gateway" pattern that has received so much attention in North American studies may not hold for contexts such as those encountered in Taiwan, the rest of China, and South Asia or Africa, where most of the world's inhabitants live.

The "particularistic factoid" that betel nut chewing, with tobacco, is a very early onset form of legal drug use, and may prove to be the world's most prevalent polydrug use type among children and adolescents is something that never could be predicted from a research enterprise based in the Americas, western Europe, Australia, or New Zealand (where almost all of the polydrug survey research has been done), and it would not have been predicted by any theory grounded in published evidence from these areas. Betel nut chewing is not even mentioned in the United Nations recently published recommendations and guidelines for school surveys, which for the most part are based upon experiences in the Americas and Western Europe (United Nations Office on Drugs and Crime, 2003).

Accordingly, it is possible to anticipate that future polydrug research of the 21st century under the rubrics of "Quantity" and "Location" will benefit from a greater emphasis on theory-testing and challenges to existing theory, and a reduced emphasis upon annual research projects that produce little more than the "particularistic factoids" of disease surveillance in the more established market economies of the Americas, western Europe, Australia, and New Zealand. Nonetheless, in parts of the world where there is no strong tradition of particularistic field research on various types of polydrug use, there is good reason to build up a base of polydrug research experience and expertise, as has been done in the more established market economies. Elsewhere, a first approach might involve occasional repetitions of epidemiological field surveys of community populations, perhaps with an initial focus upon school-attending youths because there generally is a lower level of complexity of methodological challenges when one completes a school survey (once problems of parental consent have been addressed to the satisfaction of committees for the protection of children in research). Several peer-reviewed journals, such as "Substance Use and Misuse" and "Drug and Alcohol Dependence" continue to give priority to contributions of basic epidemiological findings from the emerging market economies and other parts of the world where there has been no strong tradition of epidemiological field studies on polydrug use. These journals also have been receptive to hypothesis—and theory-challenging epidemiological studies from all countries of origin. Understandably, over the years, the anonymous reviewers for these peer-reviewed journals have become less enthusiastic about articles from field surveys that describe "particularistic factoids" concerning previously reported facets of single drug and polydrug use patterns in school or community populations, even when the research approach is of the highest caliber. One useful approach may be to design each surveillance project with a deliberate effort to test a hypothesis or theory that is thought out in advance, before the data are gathered, in order to ensure that any published report on the surveillance project can include at least one contribution of theoretical importance, as has been illustrated recently by Caris and colleagues (2009), who studied social maladaptation and behavioral problems in association with use of smoked tobacco, cannabis, and coca paste products.

Causes

Turning to polydrug research under the rubric of "Causes," one can see lines of research that have more theory in the substrates (i.e., more theory than one sees in evidence under the rubrics of Quantity and Location). During the early decades of the 21st century, prior investments in behavioral genetics and genomics research fostered a renaissance of thinking about inherited susceptibility traits that might account for observed variations in polydrug use patterns and types, with intergenerational transmission of the genetically mediated variety (i.e., via protein expression of genes singly or in combination with one another), or in combination with experiential characteristics of the host or environmental context (e.g., see Wei, Anthony, & Lu, 2012, or Anthony, 2010b). Before considering a few examples from these lines of behavior genetics and genomics research, and related polydrug research topics and issues, it may be a comfort to some behavioral and social scientists to know that the sources of variation in the underlying susceptibility traits can be investigated quite usefully without the apparatus of twin or genomics research.

The first example offered here is the work of Morral and colleagues (2002a), whose quantitative acumen allowed them to challenge the idea that the observed "gateway" sequence (e.g., alcohol-tobacco-cannabis-cocaine) was anything more than an expression of a generalized underlying frailty. In a very clever reanalysis of previously gathered survey data on age of starting to use each of multiple drug compounds, they harnessed a random effects regression model for multivariate time-to-event data, and found that an individual-level frailty or susceptibility component of their model could account for the observed "gateway" sequence. There are some concerns about this modeling approach, including an inability to examine the nature and statistical moments of the underlying frailty/susceptibility distribution, but this is not to gainsay that research team's effort to push thinking about the "gateway" sequence to an entirely new and theoretically interesting level (Anthony, 2002; Morral, McCaffrey, & Paddock, 2002a, 2002b). Several of the important next steps in this line of research involve (a) parameterizing the underlying frailty now captured by the "random effects" intercept in the conceptual and statistical model built by Morral and colleagues, (b) creating an allowance for "violations" of the modal sequences, as recently discussed by Degenhardt and colleagues (2009), and (c) possibly developing a "random slopes" complement to the "random intercept" model. Because it is unlikely that these steps can be achieved via analyses of cross-sectional sample data on retrospectively recalled age at first use of each drug, a longitudinal design almost certainly will be required, and the intervals between assessments are apt to require a more fine-grained approach than is permitted by the year-to-year discreteness of age of onset data such as now are available in most longitudinal studies of drug use (e.g., the Add Health longitudinal research project tapped by Vaughn, Beaver, Delisi, Perron, & Schelbe, 2009, discussed in greater detail below). Moreover, it would be imprudent to undertake this type of ambitious large-sample longitudinal research project without specification of a theoretical model for what might be exerting an influence on the latent constructs captured in the "random effects" components of these models.

Working on the statistical side of the problem, it might be advantageous to look into application of the "recurrent time-to-event models" of the type developed by Wang and Chiang (2002) and Luo, Wang, and Huang (2010). In this formulation, the onset of the use of each drug in the polydrug sequence might be modeled parsimoniously as an example of a recurrence of the same event, based on a theoretical formulation that the first drug encountered and the sequence of drugs have much to do with exposure opportunities at the individual-level or "street-level" availability at the group context level (e.g., see Chen et al., 2009), and less to do with individual-level frailty or susceptibility traits. An alternative specification might involve formulation of two latent constructs, one construct for legal or widely available drugs such as alcohol and tobacco (or betel nut!), and one construct for illegal drugs, representing a less parsimonious approach, but a model that might fit the data better than others. At a more complex level, it might be necessary to re-specify the model with time to first use of each drug in a multivariate discrete-time approach, with each drug deserving its own time-to-event slope—more akin to what was done in the random effects model applied by Morral and colleagues (2002a).

As for specification of what might account for variation in the frailty or susceptibility trait or traits, there already is an initial theoretical model for human polydrug use that integrates genetic information about two facets of dopaminergic system processing with information about endophenotypes (e.g., neurocognitive skills) and experiential circumstances of "hosts" of varying susceptibility (e.g., maternal withdrawal, level of affiliation with deviant peers), which might be regarded as aspects of a socially shared environmental context (e.g., maternal withdrawal as experienced by siblings within the same family), but which often are presumed to be experiential characteristics because they generally are measured at the individual level. The first pioneering empirical test of this theoretical model might best be characterized by the term "exploratory structural equation modeling," and there are some peculiarities in this research approach (e.g., discarding information about one randomly chosen twin in a twin pair rather than making use of information from both twins). Nevertheless, the research team deserves congratulations for its formulation of an interesting and plausible theoretical model that allows gene–environment interplay outside the context of preclinical animal lab research (Vaughn et al., 2009). This pioneering work serves as an excellent foundation upon which to build future tests of the team's "final" model and to extend that model for new insights into the determinants of susceptibility traits that help account for polydrug use patterns.

This selective review of research on the causes of polydrug use would be incomplete without reference to (a) twin studies in which the richness of experience of both twins has helped to shed light on polydrug use of various types, especially pairs of drug compounds such as nicotine or tobacco and cannabis, and (b) the work of molecular genetics laboratory researchers whose efforts draw upon the strengths of the preclinical animal lab research as well as the clinical and community population research. In this domain, recent work by the K.S. Kendler lab is of special interest because it has fostered an integration of these two often-separate lines of twin and molecular genetics research, with resulting insights into a possible male-female difference in a suspected causal linkage from susceptibility traits measured in relation to cannabinoid receptor genes expressed in the human brain (previously associated with polydrug use and dependence) to the development of dependence upon tobacco products, as measured by the Fagerstrom Test for Nicotine Dependence (Chen et al., 2008). Related lines of twin research on a cannabis-tobacco connection, as recently reported from the Andrew Heath–Patricia Madden lab, are provocative, and all will require replication, but they deserve the attention of polydrug researchers who wish to contribute more definitive evidence to the understanding of the causes of polydrug use and associated hazards.

For example, working in the Heath-Madden line of research, Sartor and colleagues (2009) formulated their polydrug response variables in terms of the timing of onset for alcohol, tobacco, and cannabis use in the tradition of Morral et al. (2002a). In the lab's subset of African American female twins, they found the timing of initiation of these drugs to be linked more to genetic sources of variation, and only modestly to sources of variation in the shared environment—in contrast to what has been reported in prior studies of primarily Caucasian samples of women, which used a somewhat different formulation of the phenotypic polydrug response variables. Agrawal and colleagues (2009), of the same lab but with a different and more general sample of female twins, found that the simultaneous onset of tobacco and cannabis smoking could be traced entirely to shared environmental influences, with no more than modest or no influence from underlying genetic susceptibility traits. Their discussion of findings will be very useful in the formulation of future models of gene–environment interplay in polydrug research. The researchers also found that co-occurring and simultaneous cannabis-tobacco use could be associated with greater levels of cannabis involvement and that particularly simultaneous use could be associated with higher rates of DSM-IV cannabis abuse. Broadening the model developed by Vaughan and colleagues (2009), they synthesize lines of research on twin-shared beliefs, intentions, and experiences (e.g., prodrug beliefs, intentions to use in the future, drug exposure opportunities), as well as facets of the socially shared environment (home, peer group, neighborhood, school, broader community). Their view also incorporates smoking of blunts (cannabis rolled in tobacco wrappers, especially the tobacco leaf shell from commercially available cigars), which apparently was not measured in the twin study, but has figured prominently in sociological and ethnographic research descriptions of polydrug use of the tobacco-cannabis type (e.g., see Golub, Johnson, & Dunlap, 2006; Sifaneck, Johnson, & Dunlap, 2005), and more recently, polydrug use research that involves EM use of prescription medicines such as the opioid analgesics (e.g., see Bardhi, Sifaneck, Johnson, & Dunlap, 2007).

As these lines of research on the causes of polydrug use continue, there should be pressure to create a more ambitious theoretical synthesis of concepts, principles, and ideas from the pre-clinical animal laboratory, human molecular genetics labs, twin research, and other behavioral and social science research traditions that already have enriched this domain of polydrug research. Interested readers from biological backgrounds will be especially interested in the polydrug research contributed by preclinical researchers, followed by human clinical and community studies. In addition to what has been cited above, the work of George Uhl's lab should be of interest, due to its coverage of both animal and human models (e.g., see Johnson et al., 2008; Uhl et al., 2008a). Uhl's recent collaborative research on the pharmacogenomics of smoking cessation success also should be of interest to scientists who study the etiology of polydrug use when tobacco is one of the drugs involved (e.g., see Uhl et al., 2008b; Uhl, Drgon, Johnson, & Rose, 2009). For reasons explained in the next essay sections on mechanisms, prevention and control, an extended line of longitudinal research built upon pharmacogenomically informative smoking cessation experiments may promote acceleration in the production of increasingly definitive evidence on causal linkages that subserve tobacco-involvement in polydrug use. Similar acceleration might be achieved via extension of current lines of experimentation that seek to prevent polydrug use via prevention or delay of early onset tobacco smoking or cannabis smoking, but much larger population samples would be required for that type of progress. This topic and related issues also will be covered in the coverage of "mechanisms," and later in the section on "prevention and control" of polydrug use.

Mechanisms

As has been conveyed in the last several paragraphs, the rubric of "Causes" has an etiological focus upon "Why?" questions such as "What accounts for some population subgroups becoming cases while others are spared?" In contrast, the rubric of "Mechanisms" is distinguished by its focus on process and the "How?" questions, especially the processes thought to be unfolding in a "natural" order as observed by clinicians sitting by patients suffering from one or another syndrome of unknown etiology (e.g., see Van Etten & Anthony, 1998, on the early origins of "natural history" research in medicine and epidemiology). In the realm of polydrug research, there were early clinical observations that patients incarcerated for "narcotics" problems often had been started down that pathway when patent medicine vendors had sold them a "headache" or "neurasthenia" remedy laced with "alcoholic stimulants" or "tincture of opium" or "extract of the coca leaf plant" (Terry & Pellens, 1929). These early observations were followed by more systematic research that was largely sociological and social psychological in orientation, with an element of ethnography, and often with heavy reliance upon retrospection. For example, a classic monograph entitled "The Road to H," (Chein, Gerard, Lee, & Rosenfield, 1964) described processes that the research team thought might lead up to and through initial heroin use and habitual heroin use, which often involved prior or concomitant use of other drugs (i.e., polydrug use), sometimes in the context of gangs of the type displayed in the musical "West Side Story": " . . . use of heroin among gangs is by no means rare, and the smoking of marijuana is extremely common. The general attitude seems to be that it's okay to use heroin "as long as you make sure you don't get hooked" (Chein, 1980, p. 79).

It was in this tradition of research that the first epidemiological studies of polydrug use emerged and included a focus on the marijuana-heroin circumstances characterized as "common" by Chein and colleagues. For example, almost 30 years ago, Denise Kandel, perhaps the most prominent contributor to this literature, wrote:

> Retrospective studies of the drug histories of heroin addicts, in which marijuana use was found to characterize every respondent, gave rise to the controversial "stepping stone" theory of drug addiction in which use of marijuana was assumed inevitably to lead to the use of hard drugs, especially heroin. The theory is problematic . . ., and with rare exceptions, few investigators today accept it (Kandel, 1980, p. 120).

Informed readers already will know that Professor Kandel substituted a "gateway" metaphor in place of the "stepping stone" metaphor, and ultimately traced essentially stochastic rather than deterministic processes from one drug to the next, as conveyed in the title of her 1993 article: "From beer to crack—developmental patterns of drug involvement" (Kandel & Yamaguchi, 1993). Like flies to honey, many research teams were drawn to this metaphor, and this statement includes one of this essay's authors (J.C.A.), who has tried to convert the descriptive gateway metaphor into a more understandable and theory-driven process, particularly in relation to a "mechanism" involving drug exposure opportunities' akin to the "agent exposure opportunity" mechanisms that help account for variations in the epidemiology of communicable diseases (e.g., see Wagner & Anthony, 2002). Another noteworthy example is the work of Jackson et al. (2008), who provide an exceptionally thorough literature review, and whose research is noteworthy for two reasons. First, because it makes use of the Monitoring the Future (MTF) longitudinal data not yet being made available to investigators outside the MTF research team, and second, because it represents one of the limited number of peer-reviewed research articles to have been published by the MTF team since the origins of the MTF more than 30 years ago. Thanks to the thorough literature reviews that appear elsewhere, it is not important for the present essay to be detailed in coverage here, except to note that Morral and colleagues are not alone in their skepticism about the gateway description of sequences in polydrug involvement. Many, but not all, of the contrary points of view are based on one or another formulation of the idea, already mentioned in relation to the work of Morral and colleagues, that there might be an underlying susceptibility trait or frailty that accounts for the observed sequencing patterns (Jackson, Sher, & Schulenberg, 2008; Morral et al., 2002a; Peele & Brodsky, 1997). Notably, Irons, McGue, Iacono, and Oetting (2007) made clever use of the genetically informative Mendelian randomization design to test facets of the gateway sequence in a sample of Asian probands, and found evidence contrary to the predicted sequence. Clearly, this is a line of research in which there are open research questions. The comments with respect to next steps in locational and etiological research offer some of the authors' ideas about how the field might accelerate progress in relation to these still-open research issues. Namely, basic descriptive empirical data are still needed from parts of the world other than the established market economies that already have produced an overabundance of particularistic factoids on this topic, and the field will require longitudinal tests and formal experimentation in order to produce definitive evidence on this aspect of the polydrug research agenda.

As noted in the introduction to the rubrics, research on "mechanisms" also includes comorbidity research and studies of the consequences of health conditions. Polydrug researchers have been quite active at this interface. In recent work on comorbidity patterns, Wittchen and colleagues (2009) integrated patterns of polydrug use with information about psychiatric disturbances and other life circumstances in order to shed light on latent classes of cannabis-involved youths in their longitudinal study of youths in Germany. It is useful to contrast the methodological approach of the Wittchen lab with that used by Agrawal, Lynskey, Madden, Bucholz, and Heath (2007), who also harnessed the latent class approach in the study of a U.S. epidemiological sample and evoked classes of single and multiple drug users. In the comorbidity research from the Wittchen lab, the data were longitudinal and the manifest indicators of underlying latent classes were not restricted to drug use variables. Instead, the variables entered into the latent class analysis (LCA) were mental disorders thought to co-occur with drug use disorders (e.g., major depression), cannabis use related problems, cannabis use disorders (CUD), and alcohol plus other drug use disorders. With this approach, the best fitting LCA model included four latent classes described by the research team as "Unproblematic CU" (60% of the sample); "Primary alcohol use disorders" (14%), "Delinquent cannabis/alcohol disorders" (14%), "Delinquent cannabis/alcohol

DSM-IV-abuse" (18%), and "CUD with multiple problems" (8-9%).

In contrast to the Wittchen approach to comorbidity, Agrawal et al. (2007) studied patterns in the NESARC cross-sectional sample of adults in the U.S. to investigate how the occurrence of psychiatric disorders such as major depression might be related to latent classes defined solely by drug involvement and drug use disorders. They found five latent classes: no DSM-IV abuse or dependence (93%); cannabis abuse or dependence only (6%), a polydrug class that included stimulant and hallucinogen abuse or dependence (<1%), a class of individuals with EM prescription drug abuse or dependence (<1%), and a class of individuals qualifying for many different abuse and dependence diagnoses ("poly dependence" <1%). In this study, major depression and nicotine dependence were associated most strongly with those in the poly dependence class.

These two peer-reviewed articles illustrate how far the study of polydrug use and comorbidity has progressed by this point in the 21st century, and demonstrate two alternative approaches when research teams attempt to seek order in their longitudinal or cross-sectional data on polydrug use, drug use disorders, and other psychiatric disturbances. In one approach, the data are longitudinal, and the "other psychiatric disturbances" are allowed to participate in the formation of latent classes. In the other approach, the data are cross-sectional, and the "other psychiatric disturbances" are not made part of the latent class structure. Instead, the odds of psychiatric disturbance are expressed as a function of membership in the polydrug classes evoked using LCA. What comes to mind is a research approach that involves holding a crystal or kaleidoscope and turning it round and round. If this metaphor is correct, then this area of comorbidity research may be another opportunity for consensus development within the field with respect to definitions, conceptualization, principles of research approach, and interpretation based upon theoretical models specified in advance. Otherwise, there will be no possibilities for meta-analyses or other informed syntheses of interesting research from different parts of the world.

Some of the issues in the domain of polydrug research have been organized as tests of hypotheses about suspected hazards of single drug or polydrug use, with an appeal to concepts of subgroup variation or "interaction" introduced early in this essay. Some of the least complex of these tests have involved a question about rapid transitions from first use of a drug until appearance of clinically diagnosable syndromes of dependence on the drug. This work sometimes has considered whether a background of alcohol or other drug dependence might influence occurrence of particularly hazardous forms of drug taking. In these studies, there are issues of sequencing of drugs, but not in the formulation seen for the gateway studies. Instead, histories of prior drug involvement are allowed to compete with other variables in an effort to account for variation in the consequences of drug use. That is, this is polydrug research on mechanisms in which the background of polydrug use is a suspected determinant of hazards in the form of drug dependence.

In one early example, Chen and colleagues (2005) analyzed public use data from the U.S. NSDUH surveys and found that transitions from onset of cannabis use to fully formed cannabis dependence occurred more rapidly when there was a background of polydrug use as evaluated in relation to the lifetime history (i.e., use of three or more drugs prior to onset of cannabis smoking). Consistent with the cannabis work by Chen et al. (2005), but studying EM use of prescription stimulants and illegal stimulants (e.g., injectable methamphetamine), O'Brien & Anthony (2009) found that the *absence* of prior EM drug use signaled a *reduced* risk of rapid transition from onset of EM stimulant use to onset of fully formed syndromes of DSM-IV stimulant dependence; independently, recent-onset stimulant users with a prior history of alcohol dependence were more likely to develop stimulant dependence quite rapidly. More recently, Behrendt, Wittchen, Höfler, Lieb, and Beesdo (2009), with longitudinal data from Germany, also have studied rapid transitions from onset of cannabis use to dependence. The use of alcohol and tobacco also were studied, but pre-cannabis onsets of alcohol and tobacco use were not studied as determinants of the rapid cannabis transition. Instead, Behrendt and colleagues studied rapid transition from first alcohol use to alcohol dependence, and then separately, the rapid transition from first tobacco use to tobacco dependence.

With the exception of the work by O'Brien & Anthony (2009), the studies investigating rapid onset of drug dependence after first use of a drug have not generally allowed a prior history of alcohol dependence or heavy drinking to participate as explanatory variables in the model of rapid transition from cannabis or tobacco initiation until

onset of dependence upon these smoked drugs. The idea that drinking might shape later progression to dependence is quite plausible and has support in both animal [e.g. cross-tolerance to Δ^9-tetrahydrocannabinol has been observed in ethanol pretreated mice (da Silva, Morato, & Takahashi, 2001)] and human clinical observations [e.g. alcohol ingestion increases after acute nicotine administration (Barrett, Tichauer, Leyton, & Pihl, 2006)]. Evidence from twin studies in Colorado (Palmer et al., 2009) and Missouri (agrawal et al., 2009) suggest that concurrent and simultaneous alcohol or tobacco use among cannabis users might increase risk to develop cannabis use disorders. Moreover, in comorbidity research, there are tangible associations (cross-sectionally and retrospectively) linking dependencies on alcohol, tobacco, and cannabis, with evidence from studies too numerous to mention here. A similar circumstance is faced in relation to prior nicotine exposure (in preclinical research labs) and tobacco smoking and dependence (in clinical research on humans). That is, here also there is support in the background theory and in some (but not all) of the evidence from pre-clinical and both clinical and community studies of a cross-sectional or retrospective character.

There also now are the pharmacogenomically informed smoking cessation experiments mentioned in the essay's section on the rubric of "Causes." As signaled in that section, it should be possible to gain more definitive evidence about sequences of polydrug use and the causal importance of prior exposure to drugs in humans if the future pharmacogenomically informed smoking cessation trials are extended via longitudinal follow-up. Via these extensions it should be possible to test experimentally whether success in the smoking cessation enterprise has been followed by reduced risks of initiation into other forms of psychoactive drug use. If feasible with respect to the experiment's sample size or length of follow-up intervals, this approach would make it possible to study a possibly reduced risk of dependence upon these other drugs. Interested readers are referred to the work of the Uhl lab and their collaborators at Duke University and elsewhere, who have been pioneers in the pharmacogenomically informed smoking cessation research domain, who are experienced in polydrug dependence research issues, but who have not yet had the opportunity or resources to extend these smoking cessation experiments along the lines just sketched (Uhl et al., 2008b, 2009).

A model for this type of extended follow-up after a smoking oriented prevention trial can be found in the work of the Botvin and Kellam research groups. For example, the Kellam group found evidence consistent with early success in prevention or delay of tobacco smoking among males in the prevention research sample, with long-term follow-up evidence of later reduced involvement in some (but not all) drugs included in the polydrug types. Other research teams have produced similar findings, which may represent the strongest and most definitive current evidence that there is something of causal importance in the linkage from earlier tobacco smoking and later involvement with other drugs in that polydrug sequence (e.g., see Botvin, Baker, Dusenbury, Botvin, & Diaz, 1995; Furr-Holden, Ialongo, Anthony, Petras, & Kellam, 2004; Kellam & Anthony, 1998; Storr, Ialongo, Kellam, & Anthony, 2002).

However, the evidence from this type of long-term follow-up of prevention program participants can be mixed, and not all follow-up data are consistent with a pattern of earlier success with one drug (typically tobacco or alcohol) followed by success with other drugs (typically cannabis). Interested readers will find a growing set of useful examples to counterbalance any successes in this domain of research on polydrug use issues (e.g., see Bell, Ellickson, & Harrison, 1993; Hawkins, Kosterman, Catalano, Hill, & Abbot, 2008; Hornik & Jacobsohn, 2008; Komro et al., 2008).

The resulting balance of evidence, at present, might be interpreted to be one that is consistent with the idea that there is no need to probe into the intricate mechanisms of the "gateway" sequence, as suggested by Wagner and Anthony (2002). Rather, it could be an underlying susceptibility trait or traits that can account for the observed sequencing. Interventions directed toward the common susceptibility traits are now indicated, with randomized trials to confirm this theory. The authors of this essay advocate an alternative position, that the jury still is out, and that there may be opportunities to probe more carefully into the theory that early success in a tobacco or alcohol prevention/delay program may account for later reduced risk of other drug involvement. Hopefully, the necessary investments will be made to bring closure to what remains as an open polydrug issue for research that makes use of prevention experiments in order to shed light on causal mechanism theories that generally have been probed only with research designs having an observational and nonexperimental character.

A final issue for polydrug research under the rubric of "mechanisms" involves the risk of death, which might be occurring with excess frequency among polydrug users compared with users of single drugs. As with the gateway, comorbidity, and drug dependence risk issues just covered, this research problem was grouped here under the heading of "mechanisms" rather than under the rubric of "causes" because the underlying conceptual model is one in which there might be an underlying susceptibility trait or traits or perhaps environmental circumstances, or an interplay of both, accounting for excess mortality when a superficial analysis would suggest otherwise. Regrettably, most of the inquiries into polydrug use and risk of dying do not have measurements capable of holding constant the underlying background features in the linkage of states and processes that lead up toward any observed excess risk of dying. Consequently, public health researchers who have made important descriptive contributions in this area should be honored. Nonetheless, these lines of research cannot be complete and the evidence will not be definitive until there is more careful consideration in future research of the background linkages. Interested readers may wish to consider any one or more of several recently published articles on these polydrug topics (e.g., Coffin et al., 2003; Hall et al., 2008; Martyres, Clode, & Burns, 2004; Shah, Lathrop, Reichard, & Landen, 2008). Gruenewald, Freisthler, Remer, LaScala, and Treno (2006) have offered exceptionally well-argued discussions in favor of building models that allow environmental and contextual influences to play a role in the mechanisms underlying alcohol-associated excess risk of harm (e.g., otherwise attributed to alcohol-induced violence). In brief, an underlying susceptibility toward violence may lead someone to go to a bar to start a fight, and where a drink can be had along the way, but it also may be true that neighborhoods with a high density of bars that tolerate violence account for some of the excess risk of violence now attributed to drinking. In this analysis, it is useful to keep in mind a distinction between "causes of cases" (operating at the individual level, whether they are individual-level susceptibilities, or behavioral outcomes such as polydrug use) and "causes of incidence" (operating upon individuals at the level of social groups, neighborhoods, and community, and that generally have been ignored in research on polydrug use). This important distinction between "causes of cases" and "causes of incidence" is one of the especially useful contributions of the late Professor Geoffrey Rose (2001).

This distinction often is forgotten in the work of researchers who adopt the "high risk" paradigms in order to shed light on what are presumed to be the most important sources of variation in population health—namely, the "individual differences" that account for observed variations in polydrug use outcomes.

Prevention and Control

Under the rubric of "prevention and control," it must be said that most public health researchers and epidemiologists would give an arm (if not a leg) to be able to discover a public health intervention in the form of a mass action that might prevent disease or other ill-health outcomes in the lives of 100s or even 1000s of individuals. This is the goal that draws most public health researchers and epidemiologists to this field, in contrast with the goal of treating and succeeding with one patient at a time.

The goal of effective mass action prevention and control can be elusive. As noted above, in the domain of prevention of polydrug use, the published research now shows more or less a balance of evidence, neither supporting nor rejecting the claim that preventive interventions that make a tangible difference can be undertaken. For example, the research of the Botvin and Kellam groups represents promising work, but it needs to be replicated in the hands of others before the evidence of beneficial intervention impact is regarded as definitive.

Substantially more demonstrable success has been achieved in the domain of "control" research, where "control" refers to (a) shortening duration, (b) reducing ancillary disablement, impairment, and handibap, or (c) reducing risk of death from this specific condition. Although not generally grouped under the heading of polydrug research, it is the authors' belief that the published work on the combinations of naloxone, an opioid antagonist, with pentazocine and buprenorphine, should be studied by polydrug researchers in an effort to understand how combinations of drugs can yield different effects compared to each drug studied individually (e.g., see Fudala & Johnson, 2006; Helm et al., 2008), as outlined in this essay's coverage of subgroup variation and interaction of drug combinations.

Nonetheless, it is important to note that there is remarkably little research on how the treatment of one drug problem might help, exacerbate, or even provoke problems with some other drug. Readers should take note of important exceptions to this general rule, as can be seen in the work of Katz, Goldberg, Smith, and Trick (2008), whose findings suggest that patients might be willing to change multiple drug use patterns all at once. Whether this evidence is generally true remains to be seen, and progress on this research front almost certainly will prove to be important work of public health significance. For example, Hurt and colleagues (1996) found excess risk of tobacco-attributable mortality in patients treated for alcohol problems in a well-studied cohort of patients. Agosti and Levin (2009) suggest that remission from alcohol and other drug use disorders actually might increase the likelihood of tobacco smoking cessation among young adults who developed nicotine dependence. One suspects that an especially complex process is at play, and that a general pattern might be that down-regulation of one psychoactive drug-taking pattern might be followed by up-regulation of some other psychoactive drug-taking pattern in a form of sequential "polydrug use" that has been studied in some but not many research projects. Polydrug scientists interested in producing definitive evidence about this facet of "prevention and control" research now have many opportunities to make forward progress on this research front, concomitant with the many randomized trials of new drug dependence medications and therapies that generally now are targeting one drug dependence problem at a time.

Future Directions for Research and Conclusions

This essay offers suggestions about future directions for research, part and parcel with a review of research issues and examples from published work. In this section, the main goal simply is to highlight some especially pertinent issues, the first one of which involves development of a consensus among scientists that will convert the term "polydrug use" from a political term into a more scientifically useful term. As it has been signaled in this essay, the most functional definitions for the term "polydrug use" will come from researchers who agree to test hypotheses and theories, and who can formulate a definition of terms in relation to these more challenging facets of public health research. The alternatives, which would include handing the definitional problem over to scientists interested only in descriptive research and surveillance, are options that most likely will not lead to forward progress in this domain.

As noted previously in the essay, it is possible to take a lifetime perspective when studying polydrug use, allowing each drug to be considered in a developmental sequence, with the possibility that the combination of early Drug A with later Drug B might yield a response that is quantitatively different from what is seen with Drug A and Drug B individually. Alternately, as outlined by Earleywine and Newcomb (1997) and by McCabe and colleagues (2006), there are distinctions to be made by considering whether Drug A and Drug B are taken simultaneously (i.e., at the very same time) or concurrently (within some time interval in the recent past).

Readers with imagination will perceive that the study of concurrent and simultaneous polydrug use requires more careful and detailed questioning approaches, compared with the more superficial lifetime history approach. Nonetheless, there is much to be gained by studying outcomes of polydrug use in relation to these three quite different conceptual models for the combinations of pairs of drug compounds (and for combinations of more than pairs of drug compounds). A longitudinal study in which the research team specifies all three approaches (lifetime, concurrent, and simultaneous) in relation to hypotheses or theories about outcomes, and compares the results, which might depend upon which approach is chosen is highly expected.

The authors' position on future research about the "Quantity" and "Location" rubrics already has been made quite clear. In countries and jurisdictions already well characterized, we need little more in the form of prevalence estimates from field surveys. More is needed from parts of the world that have not yet had evidence reaching the peer-reviewed journal literature. Meta-analyses will be especially useful when the data have been gathered over many years, as in the MTF and NHSDA/NSDUH research, but these MTF and NSDUH surveillance projects may have outlived their usefulness as surveillance activities. It is possible that the resources for the MTF and NSDUH should be re-positioned in the hands of scientists who can test theories of importance and produce definitive evidence of a lasting value, in addition to producing particularistic factoids that satisfy politicians and the public appetite for answers to questions about how many high school seniors are smoking cannabis in a specific year. This essay's authors take a clear position about research under the rubrics of "Causes" and "Mechanisms" and "Prevention/Control": there has not yet been enough of it—a situation that is due in part to an overemphasis upon bland surveillance activities. Hopefully, this essay provides encouragement to new

polydrug researchers who can mount observational and experimental tests of causal hypotheses, and who have an interest and capacity to conduct longitudinal studies and experimental trials to answer questions about mechanisms, prevention, and control. It should go without saying that some of these research projects necessarily should involve treatment and intervention research, and there is much to be done in research on the agonist-antagonist combination products now being used to help reduce population-level harms secondary to drug use.

As an example, clinical and epidemiological studies among polydrug users tend simplify drug use experiences by focusing on a primary or specific IRD used, and attributing any drug-use related problem(s) to this primary or specific compound. Ignoring the pharmacologic implications of concurrent or simultaneous use of multiple compounds (Kenna, Mello, Nielsen, Schiesl, & Swift, 2007), the agency and intentionality of polydrug use (Schensul, Convey, Burkholder, 2005) or the fluctuating course of IRD use among users of multiple compounds in treatment (Brecht, Huang, Evans, & Hser, 2008) might potentially bias the understanding of the magnitude of the effect of a compound, or mask the effectiveness of treatment interventions. Research addressing these complexities is needed, particularly in regards to the measurement of the timing, doses, intentionality, and variations over time of the polydrug use experience. Experience Sampling Methods (ESM) [also known as Ecological Momentary Assessment methods (EMA)], and context-aware experience sampling techniques (Intille et al, 2003) provide ways to address many of these issues, as when polydrug use research participants can characterize their polydrug use patterns as they are occurring, as well as cognitive, emotional, social and environmental circumstances in which such polydrug use occurs (e.g., the user's mood, craving, or withdrawal state, drug availability, environmental cues or social pressure, as illustrated in Moskowitz & Young, 2006; Shiffman, 2009). The few studies on polydrug use employing EMA methods indicate that individuals in treatment for a primary drug often use other drugs (e.g., estimated prevalence of 14-15% for nicotine treatment patients and 44-45% for opioid treatment patients; Serre, et al., 2012) and that simultaneous polydrug use might increase the appraisals of pleasure and craving for the drugs used (Piasecki, et al., 2011). Empirical evidence also suggests that rates of compliance using these methods vary between 50% to over 90% according to the intensity of assessments, the number and type of drugs used and populations studied (Serre et al. 2012; Shiffman, 2009). Of course, one concern is that there might be reactivity of EMA methods (Serre et al. 2012; Shiffman, 2009); more evidence on this topic is needed for users of drugs other than nicotine and alcohol and users with different degrees of use.

In conclusion, the organization of scientific research on psychoactive drug compounds has tended to be compound-specific, such that a research lab or group has staked out its domain of research in relation to a compound or in relation to a pharmacological class of related compounds. As seen in the evidence of this essay, human consumption of psychoactive drug compounds does not generally follow these neat patterns. Rather, it is more typical for humans to consume drug compounds that can be sorted into different pharmacological classes (e.g., alcohol, tobacco, cannabis). In consequence, the organization of scientific research has not followed the contours of human experience.

Now is the time for public health scientists of the future to make their research follow the contours of human experience as has been learned from multiple drug surveillance projects. Where the human experience can be localized to one drug at a time, it makes good sense to organize the research as it has been organized. But where the human experience has the character of "polydrug use" it makes more sense to study antecedents, suspected correlates and causes, and consequence of drug-taking in the polydrug mode, allowing Drug A to combine with Drug B with the types of relationships that have been outlined in Figures 2.1A and 2.1B of this essay. It is expected that "polydrug research" of the next four decades will be more productive of definitive evidence than the polydrug research of the prior 40 years, if it is guided by what is already known about humans and their involvement with psychoactive drug compounds. To date, polydrug use has been the rule, rather than the exception—notwithstanding a general focus in research on one drug at a time.

Acknowledgments

The authors wish to thank the support of a NIDA Senior Scientist Award (K05DA015799) to J. Anthony, a NIDA Research Training Award (T32DA021129) to D. Barondess, and support from Michigan State University (to M. Radovanovic and C. Lopez-Quintero). The authors also wish to thank Mr. Brian Fairman for research assistance during preparation of this chapter.

Appendix: Glossary

• Addition: Situation in which, within the limits of the dose-response curve, the effect produced by the agents is the algebraic sum of their independent actions (Mitchell, 1986).

• Antagonism: Situation in which the effect is less than the algebraic sum of their individual effects (Mitchell, C., 1986).

• Concurrent polydrug use: Use of more than one drug in the same time period (e.g., a month a year) but not necessarily at the same time (Martin et al., 1992).

• Cross-tolerance: Occurs when tolerance to the repeated use of a specific drug in a given category is generalized to other drugs in that same structural and mechanistic category (Karan, McCance-Katz, & Zajicek, 2009).

• Ecological Momentary Assessment (EMA): Technique in which a research participant can report on symptoms, affect, behavior and cognitions close in time to experience, and these reports are obtained many times over the course of a study. Also known as, Experience Sampling Method (ESM) and context-aware experience sampling techniques (Moskowitz & Young, 2006).

• Extramedical use: Use of a medication without a prescription, in a greater quantity or for a longer period than prescribed, or for the experience or feelings elicited.

• Illegal: Anything against the law, even the civil law (Garner, 2000).

• Illicit: Anything against the law that carries moral overtones (Garner, 2000).

• Interaction: Interdependent operation of two or more exposures that cause or prevent the occurrence of an outcome given an underlying theory to guide the study of observed patterns of responses.

• Internationally regulated drugs: Compounds controlled by a government that could be illegal or legal in certain circumstances or environments.

• Polydrug use: Of, relating to, or involving several drugs together; *esp.* (of abuse) involving several drugs (OED).

• Simple infra-additive: Situation in which the combined effects are smaller than the simple algebraic sum of the individual effects.

- Simultaneous polydrug use: Co-ingestion of different drugs at the same time (e.g., Martin et al., 1992).
- Statistical interaction: Departure from what might be expected by simply adding together the sum of effects, or by multiplying them.
- Supra-multiplicative: Situation in which the combined effects are greater than that expected from a multiplicative model.
- Supra-additive but infra-multiplicative: Situation in which the combined effects are greater than the algebraic sum of the individual effects but smaller than those expected from a multiplicative model.
- Subgroup variation: Variation that arise in any given sample by chance alone, or by completely unpredicted circumstances. Mere statistical interaction can be also defined as subgroup variation.
- Supra-additive: Situation in which the combined effects are greater than the algebraic sum of the individual effects.
- Synergism: Our preference is to be restrictive when using the terms 'synergism' and 'synergy' such that we refer to 'supra-additivity', while 'synergy' criteria are met when the combination is not only supra-additive but also at least multiplicative (Greco et al., 1995).

Note

1. reds = American slang for secobarbital, a barbiturate compound, in a red capsule.

References

Agosti, V., & Levin, F. R. (2009). Does remission from alcohol and drug use disorders increase the likelihood of smoking cessation among nicotine dependent young adults? *Social Psychiatry and Psychiatric Epidemiology, 44*(2), 120–124. doi: 10.1007/s00127-008-0407-0

Agrawal, A., Lynskey, M. T., Madden, P. A. F., Bucholz, K. K., & Heath, A. C. (2007). A latent class analysis of illicit drug abuse/dependence: Results from the National Epidemiological Survey on Alcohol and Related Conditions. *Addiction (Abingdon, England), 102*(1), 94–104. doi: 10.1111/j.1360-0443.2006.01630.x

Agrawal, A., Lynskey, M. T., Madden, P. A. F., Pergadia, M. L., Bucholz, K. K., & Heath, A. C. (2009). Simultaneous cannabis and tobacco use and cannabis-related outcomes in young women. *Drug and Alcohol Dependence, 101*(1-2), 8–12. doi: 10.1016/j.drugalcdep.2008.10.019

American Psychiatric Association, APA. (2000). *The Diagnostic and Statistical Manual of Mental Disorders, Fourth Edition, Text Revision (DSM-IV-TR)*. Washington, DC: American Psychiatric Publishing.

American Psychiatric Association, APA. (2013). *The Diagnostic and Statistical Manual of Mental Disorders, Fifth Edition (DSM-5)*. Washington, DC: American Psychiatric Publishing.

Anthony, J. C. (2002). Death of the "stepping-stone" hypothesis and the "gateway" model? Comments on Morral et al. *Addiction (Abingdon, England), 97*(12), 1505–1507. doi: 10.1046/j.1360-0443.2002.00287.x

Anthony, J. C. (2010a). Epidemiology and etiology hand in hand. In L. M. Scheier (Ed.), *Handbook of drug use etiology: Theories, methods, and empirical findings* (pp. 113–124). Washington, DC: American Psychological Association.

Anthony, J. C. (2010b). Novel phenotype issues raised in cross-national epidemiological research on drug dependence. *Annals of the New York Academy of Sciences, 1187*, 353–369. doi: 10.1111/j.1749-6632.2009.05419.x

Anthony, J. C., & Van Etten, M. L. (1998). Epidemiology and its rubrics. In Bellack A, Hersen M (eds), *Comprehensive clinical psychology* (pp. 355–390). Oxford, UK: Elservier Science Publication.

Anthony, J. C. (1992). *Epidemiological research on cocaine use in the USA*. Proceedings of the CIBA Foundation Symposium 166, Cocaine: Scientific and Social Dimensions; London, England. John Wiley and Sons: Chichester. pp 20–39.

Balerio, G. N., Aso, E., Berrendero, F., Murtra, P., & Maldonado, R. (2004). Delta9-tetrahydrocannabinol decreases somatic and motivational manifestations of nicotine withdrawal in mice. *European Journal of Neuroscience, 20*(10), 2737–2748.

Barrett, S. P., Tichauer, M., Leyton, M., & Pihl, R. O. (2006). Nicotine increases alcohol self-administration in non-dependent male smokers. *Drug and Alcohol Dependence, 81*(2), 197–204. doi: 10.1016/j.drugalcdep.2005.06.009

Bardhi, F., Sifaneck, S. J., Johnson, B. D., & Dunlap, E. (2007). Pills, thrills and bellyaches: Case studies of prescription pill use and misuse among marijuana/blunt smoking middle class young women. *Contemporary Drug Problems, 34*(1), 53–101.

Behrendt, S., Wittchen, H.-U., Höfler, M., Lieb, R., & Beesdo, K. (2009). Transitions from first substance use to substance use disorders in adolescence: Is early onset associated with a rapid escalation? *Drug and Alcohol Dependence, 99*(1–3), 68–78. doi: 10.1016/j.drugalcdep.2008.06.014

Bell, R. M., Ellickson, P. L., & Harrison, E. R. (1993). Do drug prevention effects persist into high school? How project ALERT did with ninth graders. *Preventive Medicine, 22*(4), 463–483. doi: 10.1006/pmed.1993.1038

Botvin, G. J., Baker, E., Dusenbury, L., Botvin, E. M., & Diaz, T. (1995). Long-term follow-up results of a randomized drug abuse prevention trial in a white middle-class population. *JAMA, 273*(14), 1106–1112. doi: 10.1001/jama.1995.03520380042033

Brecht, M.-L., Huang, D., Evans, E., & Hser, Y.-I. (2008). Polydrug use and implications for longitudinal research: Ten-year trajectories for heroin, cocaine, and methamphetamine users. *Drug and Alcohol Dependence, 96*(3), 193–201. doi: 10.1016/j.drugalcdep.2008.01.021

Byard, R. W., Gilbert, J., James, R., & Lokan, R. J. (1998). Amphetamine derivative fatalities in South Australia: Is "Ecstasy" the culprit? *The American Journal of Forensic Medicine and Pathology, 19*(3), 261–265.

Caris, L., Anthony, C. B., Ríos-Bedoya, C. F., & Anthony, J. C. (2009). Behavioral problems and the occurrence of tobacco, cannabis, and coca paste smoking in Chile: Evidence based on multivariate response models for school survey data. *Drug and Alcohol Dependence, 104*(1–2), 50–55. doi: 10.1016/j.drugalcdep.2009.03.010

Chein, I. (1980). Psychological, social, and epidemiological factors in juvenile drug use. In D. J. Ettieri, M. Sayers, & H. Wallenstein Pearson (Eds.), *NIDA research monograph, 30* (p. 76). Washington, DC: Department of Health and Human Services.

Chein, I., Gerard, D. L., Lee, R. S., & Rosenfield, E. (1964). *The road to H: Narcotics, delinquency, and social policy.* New York: Basic Books.

Chen, C.-Y., O'Brien, M. S., & Anthony, J. C. (2005). Who becomes cannabis dependent soon after onset of use? Epidemiological evidence from the United States: 2000-2001. *Drug and Alcohol Dependence, 79*(1), 11–22. doi: 10.1016/j.drugalcdep.2004.11.014

Chen, W. J., Fu, T.-C., Ting, T.-T., Huang, W.-L., Tang, G.-M., Hsiao, C. K., & Chen, C.-Y. (2009). Use of ecstasy and other psychoactive substances among school-attending adolescents in Taiwan: National surveys 2004-2006. *BMC Public Health, 9*(27). doi: 10.1186/1471-2458-9-27

Chen, X., Williamson, V. S., An, S.-S., Hettema, J. M., Aggen, S. H., Neale, M. C., & Kendler, K. S. (2008). Cannabinoid receptor 1 gene association with nicotine dependence. *Archives of General Psychiatry, 65*(7), 816–824. doi: 10.1001/archpsyc.65.7.816

Coffin, P. O., Galea, S., Ahern, J., Leon, A. C., Vlahov, D., & Tardiff, K. (2003). Opiates, cocaine and alcohol combinations in accidental drug overdose deaths in New York City, 1990-1998. *Addiction (Abingdon, England), 98*(6), 739–747. doi: 10.1046/j.1360-0443.2003.00376.x

da Silva, G. E., Morato, G. S., & Takahashi, R. cN. (2001). Rapid tolerance to Delta(9)-tetrahydrocannabinol and cross-tolerance between ethanol and Delta(9)-tetrahydrocannabinol in mice. *European Journal Pharmacology, 431*(2), 201–207.

Degenhardt, L., Chiu, W. T., Conway, K., et al. (2009). Does the "gateway" matter? Associations between the order of drug use initiation and the development of drug dependence in the National Comorbidity Study Replication. *Psychological Medicine, 39*(1), 157–167. doi: 10.1017/S0033291708003425

Degenhardt, L., Chiu, W.-T., Sampson, N., Kessler, R. C., Anthony, J. C., Angermeyer, M., Bruffaerts, R., et al. (2008). Toward a global view of alcohol, tobacco, cannabis, and cocaine use: Findings from the WHO World Mental Health Surveys. *PLoS Medicine, 5*(7), e141. doi: 10.1371/journal.pmed.0050141

Degenhardt, L., Dierker, L., Chiu, W. T., Medina-Mora, M. E., Neumark, Y., Sampson, N., Alonso, J., et al. (2010). Evaluating the drug use "gateway" theory using cross-national data: consistency and associations of the order of initiation of drug use among participants in the WHO World Mental Health Surveys. *Drug and Alcohol Dependence, 108*(1-2), 84–97. doi: 10.1016/j.drugalcdep.2009.12.001

Dierker, L., Lloyd-Richardson, E., Stolar, M., Flay, B., Tiffany, S., Collins, L., Bailey, S., et al. (2006). The proximal association between smoking and alcohol use among first year college students. *Drug and Alcohol Dependence, 81*(1), 1–9. doi: 10.1016/j.drugalcdep.2005.05.012

DuPont, R. L. (1976). Polydrug abuse and the maturing National Drug Abuse Data Base. *Annals of the New York Academy of Sciences, 281*(1 Interactions), 311–320. doi: 10.1111/j.1749-6632.1976.tb27941.x

Earleywine, M., & Newcomb, M. D. (1997). Concurrent versus simultaneous polydrug use: Prevalence, correlates, discriminant validity, and prospective effects on health outcomes. *Experimental and Clinical Psychopharmacology, 5*(4), 353–364. doi: 10.1016/S0014-2999(01)01449-2

Ersine, N. (1933). *Underworld and prison slang.* Upland, IN: Freese & Son.

Fabio, A., Loeber, R., Balasubramani, G. K., Roth, J., Fu, W., & Farrington, D. P. (2006). Why some generations are more violent than others: Assessment of age, period, and cohort effects. *American Journal of Epidemiology, 164*(2), 151–160. doi: 10.1093/aje/kwj172

Fudala, P. J., & Johnson, R. E. (2006). Development of opioid formulations with limited diversion and abuse potential. *Drug and Alcohol Dependence, 83 Suppl 1*, S40–S47. doi: 10.1016/j.drugalcdep.2006.01.016

Furr-Holden, C. D. M., Ialongo, N. S., Anthony, J. C., Petras, H., & Kellam, S. G. (2004). Developmentally inspired drug prevention: middle school outcomes in a school-based randomized prevention trial. *Drug and Alcohol Dependence, 73*(2), 149–158. doi: 10.1016/j.drugalcdep.2003.10.002

Garcia, J., Weir, B., Lesh, P. & Hunter, R. (1970). Truckin'. On American Beauty [CD]. Burbank, CA: Warner Bros. Records.

Garner, B. A. (2000). *The Oxford Dictionary of American Usage and Style.* New York: Oxford University Press.

Golub, A., Johnson, B. D., & Dunlap, E. (2006). The growth in marijuana use among American youths during the 1990s and the extent of blunt smoking. *Journal of Ethnicity in Substance Abuse, 4*(3–4), 1–21. doi: 10.1300/J233v04n03_01

Greco, W. R., Bravo, G., & Parsons, J. C. (1995). The search for synergy: A critical review from a response surface perspective. *Pharmacol Rev, 47*(2):331–385. PMID: 7568331

Gruenewald, P. J., Freisthler, B., Remer, L., Lascala, E. A., & Treno, A. (2006). Ecological models of alcohol outlets and violent assaults: Crime potentials and geospatial analysis. *Addiction (Abingdon, England), 101*(5), 666–677. doi: 10.1111/j.1360-0443.2006.01405.x

Hall, A. J., Logan, J. E., Toblin, R. L., Kaplan, J. A., Kraner, J. C., Bixler, D., Crosby, A. E., et al. (2008). Patterns of abuse among unintentional pharmaceutical overdose fatalities. *JAMA, 300*(22), 2613–2620. doi: 10.1001/jama.2008.802

Hallinan, R., Crettol, S., Agho, K., Attia, J., Besson, J., Croquette-Krokar, M.......Eap, C. B. (2009). Cannabis and benzodiazepines as determinants of methadone trough plasma concentration variability in maintenance treatment: A transnational study. *European Journal of Clinical Pharmacology, 65*(11), 1113–1120.

Hawkins, J. D., Kosterman, R., Catalano, R. F., Hill, K. G., & Abbott, R. D. (2008). Effects of social development intervention in childhood 15 years later. *Archives of Pediatrics & Adolescent Medicine, 162*(12), 1133–1141. doi: 10.1001/archpedi.162.12.1133

Helm, S., Trescot, A. M., Colson, J., Sehgal, N., & Silverman, S. (2008). Opioid antagonists, partial agonists, and agonists/antagonists: The role of office-based detoxification. *Pain Physician, 11*(2), 225–235.

Hornik, R., & Jacobsohn, L. (2008). The best laid plans: Disappointments of the National Youth Anti-Drug Media Campaign. *LDI Issue Brief, 14*(2), 1–4.

Huang, B., Dawson, D. A., Stinson, F. S., Hasin, D. S., Ruan, W. J., Saha, T. D., Smith, S. M., et al. (2006). Prevalence, correlates, and comorbidity of nonmedical prescription drug use and drug use disorders in the

United States: Results of the National Epidemiologic Survey on Alcohol and Related Conditions. *The Journal of Clinical Psychiatry, 67*(7), 1062–1073. doi: 10.4088/JCP.v67n0708

Hurt, R. D., Offord, K. P., Croghan, I. T., Gomez-Dahl, L., Kottke, T. E., Morse, R. M., & Melton, L. J. (1996). Mortality following inpatient addictions treatment. Role of tobacco use in a community-based cohort. *JAMA, 275*(14), 1097–1103. doi: 10.1001/jama.1996.03530380039029

Intille, S., Tapia, E., Rondoni, J., Beaudin, J., Kukla, C., Agarwal, S., Bao, L., & Larson, K. (2003). Tools for studying behavior and technology in natural settings. In A. K. Dey, A. Schmidt, & J. F. McCarthy (Eds.), *UbiComp 2003: Ubiquitous computing* (pp. 157–174). Berlin/Heidelberg: Springer.

Irons, D. E., McGue, M., Iacono, W. G., & Oetting, W. S. (2007). Mendelian randomization: A novel test of the gateway hypothesis and models of gene-environment interplay. *Development and Psychopathology, 19*(4), 1181–1195. doi: 10.1017/S0954579407000612

Jackson, K. M., Sher, K. J., & Schulenberg, J. E. (2008). Conjoint developmental trajectories of young adult substance use. *Alcoholism, Clinical and Experimental Research, 32*(5), 723–737. doi: 10.1111/j.1530-0277.2008.00643.x

Johnson, C., Drgon, T., Liu, Q.-R., Zhang, P.-W., Walther, D., Li, C.-Y., Anthony, J. C., et al. (2008). Genome wide association for substance dependence: convergent results from epidemiologic and research volunteer samples. *BMC Medical Genetics, 9*(113). doi: 10.1186/1471-2350-9-113

Johnston, L. D., O'Malley, P. M., Schulenberg, J., & Bachman, J. G. (2006). The aims and objectives of the Monitoring the Future study and progress toward fulfilling them. *Monitoring the Future Occasional Paper*, 65. Retrieved from http://www.monitoringthefuture.org/pubs/occpapers/occ65.pdf

Kandel, D. B. (1980). Developmental stages in adolescent drug involvement. In D.J. Ettieri, M. Sayers, & H. Wallenstein Pearson (Eds.), *NIDA research monograph, 30* (p. 120). Washington, DC: Department of Health and Human Services.

Kandel, D., & Yamaguchi, K. (1993). From beer to crack: Developmental patterns of drug involvement. *American Journal of Public Health, 83*(6), 851–855.

Karan, L. D., McCance-Katz, E., & Zajicek, A. (2009) Pharmacokinetic and pharmacodynamic principles. In R. K. Ries, R. Ries, S. C. Miller, & D. A.Fiellin (Eds.), *Principles of addiction medicine* (pp. 67–84). Philadelphia: Wolters Kluwer Lippincott Williams & Wilkins.

Katz, A., Goldberg, D., Smith, J., & Trick, W. E. (2008). Tobacco, alcohol, and drug use among hospital patients: Concurrent use and willingness to change. *Journal of Hospital Medicine, 3*(5), 369–375. doi: 10.1002/jhm.358

Kedea, S., Sell, M. A., & Relyea, G. (2007). Mono- versus polydrug abuse patterns among publicly funded clients. *Substance Abuse Treatment, Prevention, and Policy, 2*(2007), 33. doi: 10.1186/1747-597X-2-33. http://www.substance-abusepolicy.com/content/2/1/33

Kellam, S. G., & Anthony, J. C. (1998). Targeting early antecedents to prevent tobacco smoking: Findings from an epidemiologically based randomized field trial. *American Journal of Public Health, 88*(10), 1490–1495. doi: 10.2105/AJPH.88.10.1490

Kenna, G. A., Mello, P., Nielsen, D. M., Schiesl, A., & Swift, R. M. (2007). Pharmacotherapy of dual substance abuse and dependence. *CNS Drugs, 21*(3), 213–237. doi: 10.2165/00023210-200721030-00003

Komro, K. A., Perry, C. L., Veblen-Mortenson, S., Farbakhsh, K., Toomey, T. L., Stigler, M. H., Jones-Webb, R., et al. (2008). Outcomes from a randomized controlled trial of a multi-component alcohol use preventive intervention for urban youth: Project Northland Chicago. *Addiction (Abingdon, England), 103*(4), 606–618. doi: 10.1111/j.1360-0443.2007.02110.x

Laizure, S. C., Mandrell, T., Gades, N. M., & Parker, R. B. (2003). Cocaethylene metabolism and interaction with cocaine and ethanol: Role of carboxylesterases. *Drug Metabolism Disposition, 31*(1), 16–20.

Leri, F., Bruneau, J., & Stewart, J. (2003). Understanding polydrug use: Review of heroin and cocaine co-use. *Addiction (Abingdon, England), 98*(1), 7–22. doi: 10.1046/j.1360-0443.2003.00236.x

Luo, X., Wang, M.-C., & Huang, C.-Y. (2010). A comparison of various rate functions of a recurrent event process in the presence of a terminal event. *Statistical Methods in Medical Research, 19*(2), 167–182. doi: 10.1177/0962280208090220

Malow, R. M., West, J. A., Corrigan, S. A., Pena, J. M., & Lott, W. C. (1992). Cocaine and speedball users: differences in psychopathology. *Journal of Substance Abuse Treatment, 9*(4), 287–291. doi: 10.1016/0740-5472(92)90021-F

Martin, C. S. (2008). Timing of alcohol and other drug use. *Alcohol Research & Health, 31*(2), 96–99.

Martin, C. S., Clifford, P. R., & Clapper, R. L. (1992). Patterns and predictors of simultaneous and concurrent use of alcohol, tobacco, marijuana, and hallucinogens in first-year college students. *Journal of Substance Abuse, 4*(3), 319–326. doi: 10.1016/0899-3289(92)90039-Z

Martinotti, G., Carli, V., Tedeschi, D., Di Giannantonio, M., Roy, A., Janin, L., & Sarchiapone, M. (2009). Mono- and polysubstance dependent subjects differ on social factors, childhood trauma, personality, suicidal behavior, and comorbid Axis I diagnoses. *Addictive Behaviors, 34*(9): 790–793. doi: 10.1016/j.addbeh.2009.04.012

Martyres, R. F., Clode, D., & Burns, J. M. (2004). Seeking drugs or seeking help? Escalating "doctor shopping" by young heroin users before fatal overdose. *The Medical Journal of Australia, 180*(5), 211–214.

Mathers, C. D., & Loncar, D. (2006). Projections of global mortality and burden of disease from 2002 to 2030. *PLoS Medicine, 3*(11), e442. doi: 10.1371/journal.pmed.0030442

McCabe, S. E., Cranford, J. A., Morales, M., & Young, A. (2006). Simultaneous and concurrent polydrug use of alcohol and prescription drugs: Prevalence, correlates, and consequences. *Journal of Studies on Alcohol, 67*(4), 529–537.

McCance-Katz, E. F., Rainey, P. M., & Moody, D. E. (2010). Effect of cocaine use on buprenorphine pharmacokinetics in humans. *American Journal of Addictions, 19*(1), 38–46.

Medawar, P. B. (1967). *The art of soluble*. London: Methuen.

Mitchell, C. (1986). Statistical analysis of drug interactions. In M. Braude & H. Ginzburg (Eds.), *NIDA Research Monograph 68* (p. 41–64). Washington, DC: Department of Health and Human Services.

Morral, A. R., McCaffrey, D. F., & Paddock, S. M. (2002a). Reassessing the marijuana gateway effect. *Addiction (Abingdon, England), 97*(12), 1493–1504. doi: 10.1046/j.1360-0443.2002.00280.x

Morral, A. R., McCafrey, D. F., & Paddock, S. M. (2002b). Evidence does not favor marijuana gateway effects over a common-factor interpretation of drug use initiation: Responses to Anthony, Kenkel & Mathios and Lynskey. *Addiction (Abingdon, England)*, *97*(12), 1509–1510. doi: 10.1046/j.1360-0443.2002.00297.x

Moskowitz, D. S., & Young, S. N. (2006). Ecological momentary assessment: What it is and why it is a method of the future in clinical psychopharmacology. *Journal of Psychiatry & Neuroscience*, *31*(1), 13–20.

O'Brien, M. S., & Anthony, J. C. (2009). Extra-medical stimulant dependence among recent initiates. *Drug and Alcohol Dependence*, *104*(1–2), 147–155. doi: 10.1016/j.drugalcdep.2009.04.016

O'Brien, M. S., Comment, L. A., Liang, K. Y., & Anthony, J. C. (2012). Does cannabis onset trigger cocaine onset? A case-crossover approach. *International Journal of Methods in Psychiatric Research*, *21*(1), 66–75. doi: 10.1002/mpr.359

Organization of American States (OAS). (2011). *Hemispheric Report Evaluation of Progress in Drug Control: Fifth Evaluation Round.* Multilateral Evaluation Mechanism Inter-American Drug Abuse Control Commission (CICAD) and Secretariat for Multidimensional Security (SMS).

Palmer, R. H. C., Young, S. E., Hopfer, C. J., Corley, R. P., Stallings, M. C., Crowley, T. J., & Hewitt, J. K. (2009). Developmental epidemiology of drug use and abuse in adolescence and young adulthood: Evidence of generalized risk. *Drug and Alcohol Dependence*, *102*(1), 78–87.

Parker, R. B., Casey Laizure, S. (2010). The effect of ethanol on oral cocaine pharmacokinetics reveals an unrecognized class of ethanol-mediated drug interactions. *Drug Metab Dispos*, *38*(2), 317–322.

Peele, S., & Brodsky, A. (1997). Gateway to nowhere: How alcohol came to be scapegoated for drug abuse. *Addiction Research & Theory*, *5*(5), 419–425. doi: 10.3109/16066359709004356

Piasecki, T. M., Jahng, S., Wood, P. K., Robertson, B. M., Epler, A. J., Cronk, N. J, ... Sher, K. J. (2011). The subjective effects of alcohol–tobacco co-use: An ecological momentary assessment investigation. *Journal of Abnormal Psychology*, *120*(3), 557–571. doi: 10.1037/a0023033

Polydrug. (2006). *Oxford English Dictionary online.* Retrieved from http://dictionary.oed.com

Rose, G. (2001). Sick individuals and sick populations. 1985. *Bulletin of the World Health Organization*, *79*(10), 990–996.

Rosenthal, R. N., & Levounis, P. (2011). 11. Polydrug substance use, abuse, and dependence. In R. J. Frances, A. H. Mack, & K. Brady (Eds.), *Clinical textbook of addictive disorders* (pp. 245–270). New York: Guilford Press.

Sample, C. J. (1977). The epidemiology of drug abuse: Current issues. Concept of polydrug use. *NIDA research monograph*, *10*, 19–31. Retrieved from http://www.ncbi.nlm.nih.gov/pubmed/405601

Sartor, C. E., Agrawal, A., Lynskey, M. T., Bucholz, K. K., Madden, P. A. F., & Heath, A. C. (2009). Common genetic influences on the timing of first use for alcohol, cigarettes, and cannabis in young African-American women. *Drug and Alcohol Dependence*, *102*(1–3), 49–55. doi: 10.1016/j.drugalcdep.2008.12.013

Schensul, J. J., Convey, M., & Burkholder, G. (2005). Challenges in measuring concurrency, agency and intentionality in polydrug research. *Addictive Behaviors*, *30*(3), 571–574. doi: 10.1016/j.addbeh.2004.05.022

Schulenberg, J. E., & Maggs, J. L. (2002). A developmental perspective on alcohol use and heavy drinking during adolescence and the transition to young adulthood. *Journal of Studies on Alcohol*, *14*, 54–70.

Schulenberg, J. E., and Maggs, J. L., & O'Malley, P. M. (2003). How and why the understanding of developmental continuity and discontinuity is important: The sample case of long-term consequences of adolescent substance use. In J. T. Mortimer & M. J. Shanahan (Eds.), *Handbook of the life course* (pp. 413–436). New York: Plenum Press.

Serre, F., Fatseas, M., Debrabant, R., Alexandre, J. M., Auriacombe, M., & Swendsen, J. (2012). Ecological momentary assessment in alcohol, tobacco, cannabis and opiate dependence: A comparison of feasibility and validity. *Drug and Alcohol Dependence*, *126*(1–2), 118–123. doi: 10.1016/j.drugalcdep.2012.04.025

Shah, N. G., Lathrop, S. L., Reichard, R. R., & Landen, M. G. (2008). Unintentional drug overdose death trends in New Mexico, USA, 1990-2005: Combinations of heroin, cocaine, prescription opioids and alcohol. *Addiction (Abingdon, England)*, *103*(1), 126–136. doi: 10.1111/j.1360-0443.2007.02054.x

Shiffman, S. (2009). Ecological momentary assessment (EMA) in studies of substance use. *Psychological Assessment*, *21*(4), 486–497. doi: 10.1037/a0017074

Showalter, C. V. (1980). T's and blues. Abuse of pentazocine and tripelennamine. *JAMA*, *244*(11), 1224–1225. doi: 10.1001/jama.1978.03280430026008.

Sifaneck, S. J., Johnson, B. D., & Dunlap, E. (2005). Cigars-for-blunts: Choice of tobacco products by blunt smokers. *Journal of Ethnicity in Substance Abuse*, *4*(3–4), 23–42. doi: 10.1300/J233v04n03_02

Storr, C. L., Ialongo, N. S., Kellam, S. G., & Anthony, J. C. (2002). A randomized controlled trial of two primary school intervention strategies to prevent early onset tobacco smoking. *Drug and Alcohol Dependence*, *66*(1), 51–60. doi: 10.1016/S0376-8716(01)00184-3

Terry, C. E., & Pellens, M. (1929). The opium problem. *The American Journal of the Medical Sciences*, *177*(3), 432.

Uhl, G. R., Drgon, T., Johnson, C., & Rose, J. E. (2009). Nicotine abstinence genotyping: Assessing the impact on smoking cessation clinical trials. *The Pharmacogenomics Journal*, *9*(2), 111–115. doi: 10.1038/tpj.2008.10

Uhl, G. R., Drgon, T., Johnson, C., Fatusin, O. O., Liu, Q.-R., Contoreggi, C., Li, C.-Y., et al. (2008a). "Higher order" addiction molecular genetics: Convergent data from genome-wide association in humans and mice. *Biochemical Pharmacology*, *75*(1), 98–111. doi: 10.1016/j.bcp.2007.06.042

Uhl, G. R., Liu, Q.-R., Drgon, T., Johnson, C., Walther, D., Rose, J. E., David, S. P., et al. (2008b). Molecular genetics of successful smoking cessation: Convergent genome-wide association study results. *Archives of General Psychiatry*, *65*(6), 683–693. doi: 10.1001/archpsyc.65.6.683

United Nations Office on Drugs and Crime. (2003). *Conducting school surveys on drug abuse: Global Assessment Programme on Drug Abuse: Toolkit Module 3.* Retrieved from http://www.unodc.org/pdf/iran/links/UNODC/gap_toolkit_module3.pdf

Vaughn, M. G., Beaver, K. M., DeLisi, M., Perron, B. E., & Schelbe, L. (2009). Gene-environment interplay and the importance of self-control in predicting polydrug use and substance-related problems. *Addictive Behaviors, 34*(1), 112–116. doi: 10.1016/j.addbeh.2008.08.011

Wagner, F. A., & Anthony, J. C. (2002). Into the world of illegal drug use: Exposure opportunity and other mechanisms linking the use of alcohol, tobacco, marijuana, and cocaine. *American Journal of Epidemiology, 155*(10), 918–925.

Walden, M., Nicholls, F. A., Smith, K. J., & Tucker, G. T. (2007). The effect of ethanol on the release of opioids from oral prolonged-release preparations. *Drug Development and Industrial Pharmacy, 33*(10), 1101–1111.

Wang, M.-C., & Chiang, C.-T. (2002). Non-parametric methods for recurrent event data with informative and non-informative censorings. *Statistics in Medicine, 21*(3), 445–456. doi: 10.1002/sim.1029

Wei, C., Anthony, J. C., & Lu, Q. (2012). Genome-environmental risk assessment of cocaine dependence. *Frontiers in Genetics, 3*(83), 1–7. doi: 10.3389/fgene.2012.00083

Wesson, D. R., Carlin, A. S., Adams, K. M., & Beschner, G. (Eds.). (1978). *Polydrug abuse: The results of a national collaborative study.* San Francisco: Academic Press.

Wittchen, H.-U., Behrendt, S., Höfler, M., Perkonigg, A., Rehm, J., Lieb, R., & Beesdo, K. (2009). A typology of cannabis-related problems among individuals with repeated illegal drug use in the first three decades of life: Evidence for heterogeneity and different treatment needs. *Drug and Alcohol Dependence, 102*(1-3), 151–157. doi: 10.1016/j.drugalcdep.2009.02.012

World Health Organization. (1965). *WHO Expert Committee on Dependence-Producing Drugs* (No. 14). Geneva, Switzerland: World Health Organization.

ADHD and Substance Use

Karen J. Derefinko *and* William E. Pelham Jr.

Abstract

This chapter discusses the current understanding of relations between attention deficit hyperactivity disorder (ADHD) and substance use. Children with ADHD are at risk for problems in substance use; evidence suggests that the relations between ADHD and substance use may differ across age groups, gender, and comorbid conditions. Important issues regarding appropriate assessment and developmental trajectories may play a role in how these differences are understood. In comorbid substance use and ADHD, significant overlap in genetic, neurobiological, and trait factors suggests that ADHD and substance use share a common etiology, although factors influencing the phenotypic expression of these factors continue to play an important role in how comorbidity is expressed. Finally, treatment of these comorbid conditions is discussed, both in terms of the issues surrounding medication for ADHD in the context of substance abuse and potential nonmedication treatments that address both substance use and ADHD symptoms through cognitive behavioral strategies.

Key Words: ADHD, substance use, inattention, impulsivity

Attention deficit hyperactivity disorder (ADHD) is among the most widely diagnosed disorders in mental health settings for children (Barkley, 2006). In general population studies prior to 2000, 3–5% of children met diagnostic criteria (Bauermeister et al., 2003; Feehan, McGee, & Williams, 1993; Jensen et al., 1999; Pelham, Gnagy, Greenslade, & Milich, 1992; Shaffer et al., 1996) and this figure is sometimes higher. The prevalence has increased substantially since these studies. A 2005 report from the Centers for Disease Control (CDC) indicated that, in the United States in 2003, 7.8% of 4- to 17-year-olds (~ 4.4 million children) had been diagnosed with ADHD, and in a later report, the CDC reported a national prevalence of 9%, with higher rates for low-income populations (11%) and in the South and Midwest (10%) (Akinbami, Liu, Pastor, & Reuben, 2011). In childhood, this very common disorder is characterized by developmentally inappropriate levels of inattention, impulsivity, and hyperactivity and clinically significant impairment

in closely associated areas of functioning (e.g., academic performance, social functioning). Although the diagnostic criteria for ADHD in the *Diagnostic and Statistical Manuals of Mental Disorders* (DSMs) were developed for children, research has clearly indicated the likelihood of symptom persistence and/or impairment into adolescence and adulthood for the majority of children with ADHD (Barkley, Fischer, Smallish, & Fletcher, 2002; Faraone et al., 2006; Mannuzza, Klein, Abikoff, & Moulton, 2004; Molina et al., 2009). In response to the evolving awareness that the disorder persists, DSM-5 (American Psychiatric Association, 2013) includes modified language in the symptom list that makes the symptoms applicable to adolescents and adults. In addition, in response to data documenting that the symptom cutpoints for children were too stringent for older adolescents and adults (Sibley et al., 2012*a*; 2012*b*), DSM-5 requires five rather than six symptoms of either inattention or hyperactivity/impulsivity to meet diagnostic criteria. One other change made in the most recent DSM definition is that the maximum age of onset was increased from age 7 to age 12. A recent national survey reported a prevalence rate for ADHD in adults at 4.4% (Kessler et al., 2006), but this would be expected to increase given the increases in prevalence for children noted earlier and these changes in diagnostic criteria.

Many studies and reviews have documented that individuals with ADHD are at risk for increased substance use, abuse, and experimentation (Barkley, Fischer, Smallish, & Fletcher, 2004; Burke, Loeber, & Lahey, 2001; Charach, Yeung, Climans, & Lillie, 2011; Faraone et al., 2007; Gittelman, Mannuzza, Shenker, & Bonagura, 1985; Hartsough & Lambert, 1987; Lee, Humphreys, Flory, Liu, & Glass, 2011; Molina & Pelham, 2014; Molina, Flory et al., 2007; Molina & Pelham, 2003; Molina, Smith, & Pelham, 1999; Sibley, Pelham, Molina, Kipp, Gnagy, Meinzer, Ross & Lahey, 2014a; Wilson & Levin, 2005). Among individuals with adult ADHD, rates of substance use disorders (SUDs) approach 40% (Biederman et al., 1995; Kalbag & Levin, 2005), a rate that is significantly higher than for individuals in the general population (Kessler et al., 2006). Much of the basis for this research has been that the defining characteristics of ADHD (e.g., impulsivity) and associated characteristics (e.g., conduct problems, school-related difficulties, poor parenting, neuropsychological deficits) have long been associated with risk for development of substance abuse (Iacono, Malone, & McGue, 2008; Pelham & Lang, 1993; Sher, 1991; Sher, Grekin & Williams, 2005; Tarter et al., 1999; Zucker, 2006).

Although some discrepancies exist, much of the literature in this area suggests that individuals with ADHD have high rates of substance use across a wide range of substances, including illicit drugs (e.g., marijuana, cocaine), alcohol, and cigarettes (Arias et al., 2008; Charach et al., 2011; Hartsough & Lambert, 1987; Gittelman et al., 1985; Lee et al., 2011; Molina & Pelham, 2003; Molina et al., 2013; Szobot et al., 2007). In addition to higher rates of general use, those with ADHD are at risk for early onset of substance use behaviors and disorders (Arias et al., 2008; Milberger, Biederman, Faraone, Chen, & Jones, 1997; Molina & Pelham, 2003), as well as higher rates of frequency, amount, and variation in the substances used (Arias et al., 2008; Kessler et al., 2006; Lee et al., 2011; Sibley et al., 2014a).

With a rich research base documenting this relation, much attention has turned to exploring this relation in more specific ways, including across age groups (Biederman et al., 1995; Szobot et al., 2007), gender (Abrantes, Strong, Ramsey, Lewinsohn, & Brown, 2005; Hinshaw, Owens, Sami, & Fargeon, 2006; Lee & Hinshaw, 2006), comorbid externalizing disorders (Biederman et al., 1995; Elkins, McGue, & Iacono, 2007; Flory, Milich, Lynam, Leukefeld, & Clayton, 2003; Iacono et al., 2008; Jester et al., 2005; Sibley et al., 2014a), and across the ADHD symptoms themselves (Molina & Pelham, 2003) in the hopes that these lines of research will provide a better understanding of why these conditions coexist. Thus far, many factors have been associated with the codevelopment of these disorders, including several predispositional characteristics (Esposito-Smythers, Spirito, Rizzo, McGeary, & Knopik, 2009; Masse & Tremblay, 1997) and the interplay between preexisting characteristics and environmental factors known to elevate the risk for SUD (Molina et al., 1999; 2012). Extant literature suggests that the strong association between disorders warrants identification and concurrent treatment programs that address the multiple sources of dysfunction (Spencer, 2009; Sullivan & Rudnik-Levin, 2001).

Prevalence
Variation Across Substances

Individuals with ADHD are likely to use many types of licit and illicit substances, including tobacco, alcohol, marijuana, and hard drugs. Notably, relations between substance use and ADHD often depend on comorbid conduct problems (Biederman et al., 1997; Bussing, Mason, Bell, Porter, & Garvan, 2010; Crowley & Riggs 1995; Disney, Elkins, McGue, & Iacono, 1999; Elkins et al., 2007; Flory et al., 2003; Greenbaum, Prange, Friedman, & Silver, 1991; Sibley et al., 2014a; Wilens, Biederman, & Spencer, 1996), a subject addressed later in this chapter (see the section "Comorbid Externalizing Disorders"). However, there is a substantial evidence base documenting relations between specific substances and ADHD that provides a good starting point for understanding this broad area.

There is considerable research documenting the relation between ADHD and tobacco use and dependence across age groups (Biederman, Monuteaux, Mick, Wilens et al., 2006; Blase et al., 2009; Kollins, McClernon, & Fuemmeler, 2005; Lee et al., 2011; Milberger et al., 1997; Molina et al., 1999; Pomerleau, Downey, Stelson, & Pomerleau, 1995; Sibley et al., 2014a; Tercyak, Lerman, & Audrain,

2002; Upadhyaya & Carpenter, 2008; Whalen, Jamner, Henker, Delfino, & Lozano, 2002), with a number of studies finding that, for those with ADHD, tobacco use starts earlier than other types of substance use (Biederman et al., 2006; Kollins et al., 2005; Kuperman et al., 2001; Molina & Pelham, 2003) and has a tendency to result in heavy use (Wilens et al., 2007) and adult nicotine dependence disorders (Lambert & Hartsough, 1998).

High rates of alcohol use, abuse, and dependence have also been documented in individuals with ADHD starting from adolescence (Abrantes et al., 2005; Kuperman et al., 2001; Molina, Flory et al., 2007) and ranging to college students (Blase et al., 2009; Upadhyaya & Carpenter, 2008) and adults (Biederman, Wilens, Mick, Faraone, & Spencer, 1998; Biederman, Monuteaux, Mick, Wilens et al., 2006; Knop et al., 2009). Although initiation of alcohol use and frequency of alcohol use are not always increased in adults with ADHD (Barkley, Murphy, & Kwasnik, 1996; Lee et al., 2011; Molina, Pelham et al., 2007), some have found that the severity or amount is often elevated in those with ADHD versus comparison individuals (Barkley, Murphy, DuPaul, & Bush, 2002), as well as the frequency of heavy alcohol use occasions (Abrantes et al., 2005) and the presence of alcohol use dependence or disorders (Lee et al., 2011). As noted by Zucker, Donovan, Masten, Mattson, and Moss (2008), although the behavioral dysregulation and disinhibition of ADHD are likely to contribute to the development of alcohol use, factors specifically associated with emotional regulation may also play an important role in the development of alcohol use disorders (AUDs).

There is less research on and consensus regarding other illicit substance use. Some studies report elevated risk for ADHD samples (Biederman et al., 2006; Molina & Pelham, 2003), but other studies indicate that ADHD is related to other illicit substance use almost exclusively in the context of other externalizing behavior, such as conduct disorder (CD), oppositional defiant disorder (ODD), or antisocial personality disorder (August et al., 2006; Elkins et al., 2007; Flory & Lynam, 2003; Kuperman et al., 2001; Mannuzza, Gittelman-Klein, Bessler, Malloy, & LaPadula, 1993; Mannuzza, Klein, Bessler, Malloy, & LaPadula, 1998). Among illicit substances, cocaine use has been found to relate to ADHD in adolescents and young adults (Lambert & Hartsough, 1998; Murphy & Barkley, 1996; Wilens et al., 2007), as has stimulant use in a variety

of samples (Lambert & Hartsough, 1998; Wilens et al., 2007), including female offenders (Rösler, Retz, Yaqoobi, Berg, & Retz-Junginger, 2008).

Interestingly, although many studies have examined the link between childhood ADHD and adolescent substance use in general terms, relatively few have investigated the link specific to marijuana use (Charach et al., 2011). Instead, marijuana is often included in broader categories such as "illicit drugs," "nonalcohol drugs," and "hard drugs," or it is grouped into substance abuse or dependence disorder (e.g., Biederman et al., 1997; 2006; Gittelman et al., 1985; Lynskey & Furgesson, 1995; Molina et al., 1999). For those studies that specifically identify marijuana use, some have found concurrent relations between ADHD and marijuana use independently of comorbid conduct problems in adolescents (Abrantes et al., 2005; Derefinko, MacLean, Pelham, Molina, & Gnagy, 2011; Fergusson & Boden, 2008; Sibley et al., 2014a), and rates of marijuana use have been found to be elevated in college students with ADHD (Blase et al., 2009; Upadhyaya & Carpenter, 2008), although some studies of concurrent associations in adolescents have found no relations (Rohde, Biederman, Busnello, Zimmerman, & Schmitz, 1999). Interestingly, longitudinal work to date generally does not appear to indicate that ADHD is predictive of earlier marijuana initiation (Barkley et al., 2004; Elkins et al., 2007; Lambert & Hartsough, 1998; Molina & Pelham, 2003), although some studies have found that childhood ADHD is related to adolescent and adult use and frequency of use (Derefinko, MacLean, Graziano, Molina, Gnagy, Pelham, 2011; Derefinko, MacLean, Pelham et al., 2011; Lee et al., 2011; Sibley et al., 2014a) and one reported that early cigarette smoking differentially predicted elevated frequency of use in children with ADHD versus comparison children.

Age

As noted by Molina and Pelham (2003), much of the longitudinal research on childhood ADHD and later substance use/SUD has been conducted secondary to the initial goal of studying the long-term course of ADHD. Consequently, the detailed substance use assessment that is common in longitudinal studies of substance use has been missing in longitudinal studies of childhood ADHD. The result may be missed group differences in substance use behaviors prognostic of later abuse or dependence. In addition, several methodological limitations have been noted in existing studies. First, diagnosing substance abuse or dependence in adolescence, when rates of disorder have not yet reached their peak, can miss emerging problems (e.g., Biederman et al., 1997; Mannuzza et al., 1991) that may be more appropriately measured as continuous variables. Second, for substances widely experimented with in adolescence (e.g., alcohol, cigarettes, marijuana), analysis of frequency or quantity of use, including heavy use, rather than any use over the lifetime or dependence, is more important and relevant toward development of later problematic use. Finally, age of first substance use is also a well-established predictor of later problematic substance use (Grant & Dawson, 1997; Robins & Przybeck, 1985) that has not been sufficiently included in ADHD studies.

Because of the early presentation of symptoms in ADHD and the complex interaction of factors that influence substance use, the impulsivity and hyperactivity associated with ADHD always appears at earlier ages than substance use behaviors. Some studies have found that, for those with ADHD, substance use is likely to begin at earlier ages than for comparison individuals (Arias et al., 2008; Elkins et al., 2007; Molina & Pelham, 2003; Sibley et al., 2014a), particularly for tobacco products (Kuperman et al., 2001; Milberger et al., 1997; Molina & Pelham, 2001). In fact, some have argued that trends in substance use suggest a developmental progression reminiscent of the "gateway hypothesis" (Kandel, 2002) in which nicotine serves as a catalyst for future alcohol and illicit drug abuse or dependence for those with ADHD (Biederman et al., 2006; Sibley et al., 2014a). Notably there are other potential causes for this trend, including the availability of specific substances and increasing conduct, social, and academic deficits also associated with ADHD and substance use problems.

Not surprisingly, longitudinal research has found that the association between ADHD and substance use increases from early to late adolescence (Kessler, Adler et al., 2005; Kessler, Berglund et al., 2005; Kessler et al., 2006; Mannuzza et al., 1998; Molina, Pelham et al., 2007), but relations into adulthood are less clear (Lambert & Hartsough, 1998; Sullivan & Rudnick-Levin, 2001). Some researchers have reported stability in the relation (Glass & Flory, 2012 Sullivan & Rudnick-Levin, 2001), whereas others have found nonsignificant relations between ADHD and substance use in early adulthood (Fischer, Barkley, Smallish, & Fletcher, 2002), particularly for alcohol use (Claude & Firestone, 1995; Lambert &

Hartsough, 1998; Mannuzza et al., 1993; Molina, Pelham et al., 2007).

Ambiguous relations have been explained in several ways, including the possibility of a severe, adult "typology" of the disorder. ADHD symptoms typically persist into adulthood, and it is estimated that 11–30% of children with ADHD continue to meet criteria for ADHD as adults (Weiss, Hechman, & Weiss, 1999). A larger percentage show evidence of persistence of symptoms, at least by parent report (Molina et al., 2009; Sibley et al., 2012a; 2012b). Disney, Elkins, McGue, and Iacono (1999) have argued that those whose ADHD symptoms persist into adulthood may represent a more severe typology of the disorder, one that is associated with antisocial behavior. This suggests that the relation between ADHD and substance use in adulthood may be driven by comorbid conduct problems rather than by specific ADHD symptoms (Barkley et al., 2004). Some research has supported the argument that adult-persistent ADHD is a severe presentation; Sullivan and Rudnick-Levin found that among adults with persistent ADHD, as many as 50% may meet criteria for SUD (2001). Similarly, in the Pittsburgh ADHD Longitudinal Study (Molina & Pelham, 2003; Molina et al., 2007), both persistence of ADHD symptoms and presence of concurrent CD or antisocial personality predicted increased alcohol use. Notably, childhood (vs. adolescent or adulthood) symptoms of ODD and CD did not predict later substance use. Sibley et al. (2012a,b) found that early ADHD drove the growth of CD, and both ADHD and CD symptoms resulting from ADHD were related to indices of later problematic alcohol, tobacco, and marijuana use.

There is also evidence that the relation between ADHD and substance use in adulthood is confounded by age-specific and reporting issues (Molina, Pelham et al., 2007). First, because problematic drinking and substance use is prevalent among young adults in general (Substance Abuse and Mental Health Services Administration [SAMHSA], 2003), individuals with ADHD may not appear impaired when compared with non-ADHD individuals in this age group. In addition, there is evidence that suggests individuals with ADHD are not adequate reporters of their symptomatology as adults, both due to changes in presentation of ADHD symptoms over time (Barkley, Murphy, & Fischer, 2008) and underreporting of the severity of symptoms (Kooij et al., 2008; Sibley et al., 2012a; 2012b). These findings suggest that

ADHD assessments in adulthood might not be adequately identifying those with ADHD impairment (Barkley & Brown, 2008), thereby masking true relations to substance use.

Gender

It is important to note several factors that influence gender effects on the relation between substance use and ADHD. First, ADHD is much less common in females, with sex ratios of community samples ranging from 2:1 to 4:1 and typically even higher in referred samples (e.g., American Psychiatric Association, 2000; Carlson, Tamm, & Gaub, 1997; Lahey et al., 1994). Thus, females with ADHD are poorly represented in research, leading to smaller sample sizes, lower power to detect significant effects, and fewer studies from which to draw conclusions. Second, because girls with ADHD often present with fewer behavioral problems than boys with ADHD (Barkley, 2006), this leads to differential referral conditions, with only the more severe cases of girls with ADHD presenting in clinical settings and research. Aside from these issues, there is reason to believe that females with ADHD would be at high risk for substance use, given that females with ADHD often present with higher rates of internalizing problems (Bagwell, Molina, Kashdan, Pelham, & Hoza, 2006), a factor known to covary with substance use, particularly alcohol use (Hasin, Stinson, Ogburn, & Grant, 2007). On the other hand, boys with ADHD have higher rates of conduct problems (Barkley, 2006), a factor also associated with higher rates of substance use, suggesting that males and females with ADHD might both be at risk for substance use but for different reasons.

In studies that investigate relations in females only, there is emerging evidence of a relation between ADHD and substance use. For instance, Rösler, Retz, Yaqoobi, and Retz-Junginger (2008) found that, among female prisoners, the prevalence of lifetime amphetamine use disorders was nearly twice that of comparison inmates (63.6% vs. 31.3%), and prevalence of any SUD was also significantly higher among those with ADHD (81.8% vs. 47.0%). Similarly, Hinshaw and colleagues (2006) investigated the relation in a prospective study of girls in the community and found that, over a 5-year span, girls with ADHD continued to be at increased risk for SUDs than comparison girls without an ADHD diagnosis. Interestingly, Babinski and colleagues (2011a) found that adolescent girls originally referred in childhood for ADHD did not

have significantly more substance use than adolescent girls without ADHD, although the sample size in this study was relatively small.

With regard to direct comparisons of gender effects, some studies have found no differences across gender. Elkins, McGue, and Iacono (2007) explored interaction terms to determine whether the relation differed across gender in community adolescents and found no significant effects, suggesting that, regardless of gender, those with ADHD are at increased risk for substance use and abuse. Similarly, Flory, Milich, Lynam, Leukefeld, and Clayton (2003) found that gender did not influence relations between hyperactive/impulsive symptoms and substance use in a community sample of young adults.

Other studies report differential relations across gender. Abrantes and colleagues (2005) reported that in a population of adolescent inpatients ADHD was related to substance use frequency in males, but not females, although the relatively small sample was comprised only of adolescent smokers. In a longitudinal design, Babinski et al. (2011b) found that among ADHD clinic-referred boys and girls, rates of adult substance use among ADHD females were lower than ADHD males and comparable to comparison females for cigarettes and alcohol but elevated for marijuana. In contrast, Disney and colleagues (1999) reported that in a sample of adolescent males and females, odds ratios were higher in females with ADHD than in males with ADHD for nicotine dependence, cannabis abuse/dependence, and any SUD, suggesting that ADHD may put girls at slightly greater risk for these problems than boys. Interestingly, there is evidence documenting sexually dimorphic patterns of amphetamine-induced striatal dopamine release (Munro et al., 2006; Riccardi et al., 2006), which may imply divergence in substance abuse vulnerability across the sexes, although current findings do not yet provide clear answers.

Comorbid Externalizing Disorders

Perhaps the most widely studied comorbid disorders in both the ADHD and substance use areas are CD and ODD. ADHD and CD/ODD are highly comorbid; almost three-quarters of children with ADHD also meet criteria for CD or ODD (Biederman, Munir, & Knee, 1987; Biederman, Newcorn, & Sprich 1991; Szatmari, Offord, & Boyle, 1989), and few children with CD/ODD do not also meet criteria for ADHD (e.g., Pelham et al., 1992). Thus, the comorbidity between ADHD and

CD/ODD must be taken into account to understand the relation between ADHD and substance use. Several studies have found that CD or ODD symptoms account for a significant portion of the variance in SUDs, thereby reducing the relation between substance use and ADHD to nonsignificance (Barkley, Fischer, Edelbrock, & Smallish, 1990; Biederman et al., 1997; Bussing et al., 2010; Crowley & Riggs 1995; Disney et al., 1999; Elkins et al., 2007; Greenbaum et al., 1991; Loeber, Stouthamer-Loeber, & White, 1999; Wilens et al., 1996). These findings suggest that the relation between ADHD and substance use may be spurious (Flory et al., 2003), existing only due to the relation between ADHD and CD.

Others argue that the interaction of ADHD and CD may represent not simply a comorbid condition, but a particularly virulent form of disorder that increases risk for extremely adverse outcomes, such as antisocial behavior and psychopathy (Flory et al., 2003; Lynam, 1996). Molina, Smith, and Pelham (1999) found significant interactive effects of ADHD and CD on substance use; adolescents with both current ADHD and current CD reported more use of tobacco, alcohol, and other drugs than did individuals with either ADHD or CD alone. Furthermore, Flory et al. (2003) found that, in a community sample, young adults with

high self-reported levels of both ADHD and CD symptoms had the highest levels of marijuana dependence symptoms and hard drug use and dependence symptoms when compared with hyperactive/impulsive-only or conduct problem-only groups. However, others have found that symptoms of ADHD are, in fact, valuable predictors of substance use when assessed appropriately (Elkins et al., 2007). In fact, Elkins and colleagues (2007) assert that categorical assessments of ADHD may make relations between ADHD and later substance use unclear, and they call for a dimensional assessment of symptoms to better understand early contributions.

It is possible that, in addition to assessment issues, longitudinal course may cloud true relations. For example, in the Collaborative Study on the Genetics of Alcoholism, adolescent alcohol dependence was higher among children with ADHD, and all but one of the ADHD-AUD cases had CD, but the developmental sequencing clearly indicated that ADHD preceded the other conditions; onset of ADHD occurred before the development of CD, and CD before AUD (Kuperman et al., 2001). This interpretation is consistent with developmental models of deviance proneness (e.g., Iacono et al., 2008; Sher, 1991 [see Figure 3.1; Zucker, 2006) and is represented in findings that characteristics

Model of alcoholism vulnerability, Sher (1991)

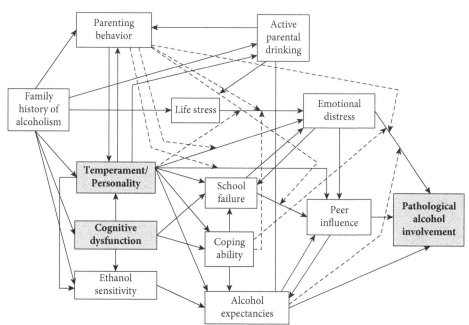

Figure 3.1. Risk pathways to alcohol use disorders among children of alcoholics.
Reprinted with permission from Sher, 1991.

of ADHD, such as problems with inhibitory control and impulsivity, are important predictors of risk for many forms of delinquent and antisocial behaviors in adolescence and adulthood, including substance use and SUDs (Moffit, 1993; Newman & Wallace, 1993; White et al., 1994). Indeed, Patterson, DeGarmo, and Knutson (2000) have argued that ADHD and CD are not comorbid but are instead two different points on the same developmental continuum; behaviors that are manifested as ADHD symptoms at early ages are exhibited as behaviors characterized as CD at later ages. Molina and Pelham (2003) and Molina, Flory et al. (2007) found that *childhood* measures of ODD/CD were not reliable predictors of later SUD in an ADHD sample, whereas *concurrent measures in adolescence and adulthood were strongly associated with substance use.* Similarly, Sibley et al. (2014a) modeled growth in ADHD and CD from age 4 to age 18 in a clinical sample recruited for ADHD, as well as in a typical comparison group, as they related to substance use outcomes in adolescence. They found that growth in ADHD over time accounted for most of the growth in CD; consequently, adolescent substance use (marijuana, cigarettes, alcohol) was accounted for by both ADHD and CD through both direct and indirect paths.

Furthermore, as noted by Lynam, Hoyle, and Newman (2006), prediction analyses utilizing highly collinear variables should be conducted with caution because this can lead to misguided conclusions about true relations. In this case, given the high rates of comorbidity, conduct problems and ADHD share considerable variance (Hinshaw, 1987; Pelham, Fabiano, & Massetti, 2005; Waschbusch, 2002). Thus, residual relations between ADHD or conduct problems and substance use rest primarily on the variance in conduct problems and ADHD that is independent of the commonalities shared by the two (e.g., impulsivity). Factor analyses suggest that ODD/CD and ADHD represent correlated but distinct factors (Pillow, Pelham, Hoza, Molina, & Stultz, 1998). However, the nature of the unique ODD/CD variance associated with the ODD/CD–substance use relation (when ADHD is controlled) is unclear. It is possible that the incremental variance provided by measures of CD/ODD is tapping a construct closely linked with substance use (e.g., rule violations), or it may simply represent more proximal symptom assessment. As suggested by Lynam and colleagues (Lynam et al., 2006), regression analyses utilizing correlated predictors should be conducted with great care to theory. In the current example, longitudinal evidence that ADHD precedes multiple forms of later behavior problems suggests that statistical models should take this linear progression into account, as Sibley et al. (2014a) demonstrated.

Inattention Versus Hyperactivity/Impulsivity

Several studies have examined relations between the underlying dimensions of ADHD and substance use, and findings suggest that the two ADHD dimensions may predict dissimilar outcomes. For instance, Elkins and colleagues (2007) found that, over the course of early to late adolescence, hyperactive/impulsive symptoms of ADHD predicted initiation of all types of substance use, including nicotine dependence and cannabis abuse/dependence over time, whereas inattention predicted alcohol initiation and nicotine dependence. Abrantes et al. (2005) found that ADHD inattention symptoms, but not hyperactivity/impulsivity symptoms, were associated with marijuana and nicotine dependence in inpatient adolescent smokers. In a sample of clinic-referred boys, Burke, Loeber, and Lahey (2001) found that adolescent inattention was associated with a greater risk for concurrent tobacco use, whereas adolescent hyperactivity-impulsivity was associated with alcohol use. Similarly, Burke, Loeber, White, Stouthamer-Loeber, and Pardini (2007) found that inattention, but not hyperactivity/impulsivity, significantly predicted adolescent tobacco use and young adult daily tobacco use. Although Molina, Smith, and Pelham (1999) found that impulsivity/hyperactivity symptoms were associated with cigarette use and alcohol use in a cross-sectional sample of adolescents, later longitudinal work by Molina and Pelham (2003) suggested that inattention was associated with multiple forms of substance use, including illicit substance use onset, age of first cigarette, severity of alcohol use, alcohol problems, marijuana use, marijuana problems, and the number of cigarettes smoked in a sample of community adolescents.

The ambiguity in these results may suggest differential relations between different forms of substance use and different ADHD symptoms, or it may speak to the issue of how symptoms of impulsivity and inattention are conceptualized and assessed, both in the DSM-5 and in measures of ADHD. Although impulsivity is widely associated with substance use (White, 1999), the DSM-IV and DSM-5 criteria for the hyperactive/impulsive dimension of ADHD contain only three impulsivity items of the nine on the list (American Psychiatric Association, 2000; 2013), suggesting that the content of this dimension (and the measures that are based on it) is not assessing impulsivity broadly. Furthermore, assessments of the different dimensions of ADHD largely depend on the setting in which assessments take place and the context in which behavior is observed (Milich & Landau, 1988), as well as on the person reporting on symptoms. Teacher ratings, the most commonly used format for making ADHD diagnoses and ratings in studies, reflect behaviors that teachers notice in the classroom (e.g., violations of classroom rules). Psychologists then infer that those behaviors are caused by putatively independent underlying constructs (i.e., inattention, impulsivity). In the few studies that have included teacher ratings and laboratory assessments of impulsivity and inattention, the teacher ratings account for all of the variance in prediction (White et al., 1994). Furthermore, a child might fail to complete his assignments due to either an inability to sustain attention on his primary assignment or poor impulse control that causes him to switch away from the primary task; the DSM labels failure to complete assignments a symptom of inattention. Such blurring of the distinction between symptoms of inattention and impulsivity suggests that inconsistencies among the just mentioned studies could reflect a problem in measurement rather than valid findings related to substance abuse vulnerability. What conceptualization and assessment issues mean in terms of substance use research is not wholly clear, although it is necessary to consider this possibility when interpreting differential relations across dimensions of ADHD. The ways in which dimensions are assessed may influence relations not because of true differences, but because measures are not providing adequate assessments of the putative cognitive deficits associated with ADHD.

Why ADHD and SUD Are Linked

There are several hypotheses regarding the cause for comorbidity between ADHD and substance use. Among these include genetic, neurobiological, trait, and prenatal risk factors; self-medication of ADHD symptoms; priming effects of stimulant medication use; and environmental risk factors. Although evidence exists for each of these proposed areas, it is likely that combinations of factors interact to produce conditions ripe for substance use propensity.

Genetic Risk Factors

Evidence from twin, family, and adoption studies strongly suggests a common etiology for ADHD and SUDs (Iacono et al., 2008; Steinhausen, Göbel, & Nestler, 1984; Wilens et al., 1995). Children whose parents meet criteria for SUDs are at higher risk for developing inattention, impulsivity, aggressiveness, and elevated rates of both ADHD and SUDs (Clark, Cornelius, Wood, & Vanyukov, 2004; Steinhausen et al., 1984; Wilens, Biederman, Kiely, Bredin, & Spencer, 1995). In addition, among children diagnosed with ADHD, there is evidence that parental drug use predicts adolescent drug use (Biederman, Faraone, Monuteaux, & Feighner, 2000). These findings suggest that characteristics of parental substance use increase the likelihood for children developing symptoms of ADHD, as well as potential comorbid substance use problems.

Specific genes are linked to both ADHD and substance use and abuse (Blum et al., 1990; Faraone et al., 2005; Laucht, Becker, Blomeyer, & Schmidt, 2007; McClernon & Kollins, 2008). Although discrete relations are difficult to replicate due to likely polygenic and variable expression of risk factors, genes associated with the transmission of dopamine have captured considerable attention (Swanson et al., 2000). Importantly, variation in dopaminergic genes may affect dependence rates across substances, including alcohol, marijuana, and cocaine (Hiroi & Agatsuma; 2005; Kreek, Nielsen, Butelman, & LaForge, 2005; Persico, Bird, Gabbay, & Uhl, 1996). For instance, studies have found a relation between the DRD4 gene and substance use (Laucht et al., 2007) and the DRD2 polymorphism and substance use (Bidwell et al., 2012; Blum et al., 1990). Similarly, some studies have found relations between dopamine transporter genes and ADHD (Faraone et al., 2005; Nyman et al., 2007; Todd et al., 2005). In fact, the ADHD-DRD4 association has become one of the most replicated findings in psychiatric genetics (Collier, Curran, & Asherson, 2000; Faraone, Doyle, Mick, & Biederman, 2001). However, more recent research has suggested that the characteristic of impulsivity, not the diagnosis of ADHD, is related to substance use and dopaminergic dysfunction (Esposito-Smythers et al., 2009).

Neurobiological Risk Factors

As noted by Iacono, Malone, and McGue (2008), electroencephalogram (EEG) research suggests that attenuation of the P300 event-related potential has been associated with externalizing disorders and deviance (Iacono & McGue, 2006), substance use

(Yoon, Iacono, Malone, & McGue, 2006), and parental substance use (Hill, Yuan, & Locke, 1999), and this attenuated wave is predictive of later SUDs (Carlson, McLarnon, & Iacono, 2007). However, as Iacono et al. (2008) note, nonspecific indicators of brain activity, such as P300 waveforms, are difficult to link with specific processes or genes, suggesting that other measures of brain activity may elucidate important mechanisms.

Results from positron emission tomography (PET) and single photon emission tomography (SPECT) studies show some similarities in brain activity for those with ADHD and SUDs. ADHD imaging studies implicate dopaminergic (DA) system dysfunction across many components of the neurotransmitter system, including transporters, receptors, and synthesis of DA (Arnsten, 2006; Cheon et al., 2003; Dougherty et al., 1999; Krause, Dresel, Krause, Kung, & Tatsch, 2000; Larisch et al., 2006; Swanson et al., 2007; Volkow, Wang, Newcorn, Telang et al., 2007, Volkow, Wang et al., 2009). In addition, structural and functional abnormalities have been identified in several brain regions in individuals with ADHD, including the prefrontal-striatal and parietal areas (Ernst & Zametkin, 1995) and the dopamine reward pathway (i.e., ventral caudate, accumbens, and midbrain regions; Volkow, Wang et al., 2009), all areas associated with the synthesis and messaging of dopamine.

Trait Risk Factors

In addition to genetic contributions and neurobiological predisposition, several heritable personality traits are associated with substance use and abuse (see White, 1999, for a review). Importantly, those personality characteristics known to be associated with ADHD are also those implicated in substance use, suggesting that traits may assist in the understanding of the relation between ADHD and substance use (Iacono et al., 2008; Molina & Pelham, 2014).

As noted by White (1999), a significant portion of the research on characteristics associated with ADHD has focused on traits of extraversion and impulsivity (Barkley, 1997; Nigg, 2000). Barkley (1997) has suggested that, as a result of executive neuropsychological functions related to impulsivity and extraversion, individuals with ADHD seek external stimulation through increased activity and sensory experiences. Indeed, research investigating relations between sensation-seeking and impulsivity traits and ADHD has been supportive of this hypothesis (Braaten & Rosen, 1997; Miller,

Derefinko, Lynam, Milich, & Fillmore, 2010; Shaw & Giambra, 1993), and both impulsivity and sensation seeking have been widely associated with substance use and abuse (Donohew et al., 1999; Kotov, Gamez, Schmidt, & Watson, 2010), suggesting that these traits may underlie the association between ADHD and SUD. Sher, Grekin, and Williams (2005) have emphasized the role that executive dysfunction plays as a risk factor for development of SUD, as have Iacono, Malone, and McGue (2008). Variously defined on a number of laboratory tasks of cognition (planning, attention, shifting focus) and neurobiological measures (e.g., P300), which Iacono, Malone and McGue have labeled as endophenotypes, the role of these constructs in development is not well understood, but they are reliable premorbid characteristics of both ADHD and SUD. In support, research examining traits of impulsivity and sensation seeking through behavioral tasks has also found relations to both substance use (Kollins, 2003; Nigg et al., 2004) and ADHD (Carr, Nigg, & Henderson, 2006; Derefinko et al., 2008; Epstein, Johnson, Varia, & Conners, 2001; Lijffijt, Kenemans, Verbaten, & van Engeland, 2005; Logan & Irwin; 2000; Nigg, 2005).

Another trait often investigated in the ADHD literature is the trait domain of neuroticism or emotional lability (Molina & Pelham, 2014; White, 1999). Although relations between ADHD and measures of neuroticism have been found (Braaten & Rosen, 1997; Shea & Fisher, 1996), due to the overlap between measures of neuroticism and impulsivity, it remains unclear whether relations are indicative of emotional lability per se. The same may be true for positive relations between neuroticism and substance use; although some studies find a positive relation (Anderson, Tapert, Moadab, Crowley, & Brown, 2007; Sintov, Kendler, Walsh, Patterson, & Prescott, 2009), recent large meta-analytic work suggests that the relation may not be as resilient as that found for impulsivity (Kotov et al., 2010).

A related issue is how underlying trait factors impact the effects of substances. Emerging work suggests that individuals with high levels of impulsivity and sensation seeking may be at risk for heightened impairment from alcohol based on inhibitory failures on a cued go/no-go laboratory task (Fillmore, Blackburn, & Harrison, 2008), and the same appears to be true for individuals with ADHD (Weafer, Fillmore, & Milich, 2009). This suggests that impulsive and sensation-seeking individuals who are at risk for substance use and abuse might exhibit an increased sensitivity to the disinhibiting effects of alcohol. This disinhibitory sensitization to alcohol could thereby compound the risk for engagement in other types of problematic behavior during intoxication, such as aggression, risky sexual activity, driving under the influence, and driving accidents (Jonah, 1997; Weafer, Camarillo, Fillmore, Milich, & Marczinski, 2008; Wechsler, Lee, Kuo, & Lee, 2000), thereby creating an increasingly dangerous environment that could serve to foster future substance use.

Prenatal Risk Factors

Although difficult to disentangle from other conditions that impact prenatal health, prenatal exposure to substances has been found to be a factor in later development of ADHD (Mayes & Bornstein 1997; Schmitz et al., 2006; Weinberg, 1997; Weissman, Warner, Wickramaratne, & Kandel, 1999). Prenatal exposure to nicotine and alcohol has been associated with the development of ADHD (see Linnet et al., 2003, for a review; Mick, Biederman, Faraone, Sayer, & Kleinman, 2002; Milberger, Biederman, Faraone, Chen, & Jones, 1996). In their review, Linnet and colleagues (2003) found that in case–control studies that controlled for parental and sibling ADHD, children of mothers who smoked during pregnancy were four times more likely to develop ADHD (Mick et al., 2002; Milberger et al., 1996; Milberger, Biederman, Faraone, & Jones, 1998), and a majority of longitudinal studies supported relations between prenatal nicotine exposure and disruptive behavior as well (Fried, Watkinson, & Gray, 1992; O'Connor, Heron, Golding, Beveridge, & Glover, 2002).

Although findings are less consistent, a number of studies support a relation between prenatal alcohol exposure and inattentive/impulsive symptoms (see Linnet et al., 2003, for a review; Brown et al., 1991; Delaney-Black et al., 2000; Mick et al., 2002; Streissguth, Barr, Sampson, & Bookstein, 1994). Knopik and colleagues (2006) found that there was an increased risk for ADHD diagnosis in children prenatally exposed to alcohol, even after controlling for prenatal nicotine exposure, which remained a significant predictor of ADHD in offspring.

Cocaine exposure during the prenatal period has been associated with impulsivity, inattention, and language irregularities (Mayes & Bornstein 1997; Morrow et al., 2009). Interestingly, in a case–control study conducted by Morrow and colleagues (2009), prenatal cocaine exposure predicted ADHD in offspring, but not other mood or disruptive disorders, suggesting that there may be something specific to cocaine exposure that contributes to ADHD risk.

As noted by Wilson and Levin (2005), prenatal substance use is often related to a number of other conditions that are known to impact infant development, both pre- and postnatally. Conditions that covary with maternal substance use may include economic disadvantage, exposure to multiple substances of abuse, premature birth, and poor parenting skills, thereby making it difficult to determine specific relations (Wasserman et al., 1998). In addition, although early exposure (prenatal or otherwise) to substances is associated with the development of SUDs (Kandel, 2002), it is notable that disruptive behavior disorders in themselves are risk factors for substance use, thereby suggesting that it may be inattentive/impulsive behavior and aggressive behaviors, rather than substance exposure, that is responsible for this relation (Loney, Kramer, & Salisbury, 2002).

Self-Medication

Some have argued that individuals with ADHD use substances in an attempt to alleviate symptoms of ADHD. Specifically, individuals with ADHD may knowingly or unknowingly attempt to increase focus and attention through stimulant or tobacco use. This hypothesis is supported in part by numerous research studies documenting the relation between ADHD and tobacco use and dependence (Blase et al., 2009; Tercyak et al., 2002; Upadhyaya & Carpenter, 2008). In addition, other work has suggested that, for those with ADHD, tobacco dependence persists into adulthood, often at rates twice as high as non-ADHD comparison individuals (Lambert & Hartsough, 1998). Importantly, Lambert and Hartsough (1998) investigated rates of smoking and other substance use for adults with and without histories of stimulant medication use; a higher percentage of individuals who were stimulant medication naïve were smokers as adults, although those who had a history of stimulant medication for at least a year were more likely to be daily smokers. Similarly, Whalen, Jamner, Henker, Gehricke, and King (2003) found that for adults with ADHD, those who were being treated with stimulant medication were less likely to smoke than those who were not being treated. In contrast, a more recent study and a meta-analysis failed to show a link between smoking and stimulant treatment (Groenman et al., 2013; Humphreys, Eng, & Lee, 2013).

The link between smoking and self-medication is tenable, given that, similar to methylphenidate, nicotine serves as a stimulant for the dopamine transporter of the striatum (Krause et al., 2002). Furthermore, investigations support the benefits of nicotine use for the treatment of impairments associated with ADHD (Levin et al., 1996). For instance, Potter and Newhouse (2004; 2008) demonstrated that acute nicotine improves behavioral inhibition, stop signal reaction time, delay of reward tolerance, and recognition memory in nonsmoking young adults and adolescents with ADHD. Poltavski and Petros (2006) found that, for adults with ADHD, transdermal nicotine administration reduced errors of commission on Conners's Continuous Performance Test, but no effects were found on other cognitive tests. In addition to tobacco findings, studies from the cocaine literature appear to tentatively support a self-medication hypothesis (Collins, Levin, Foltin, Kleber, & Evans, 2006; Lambert & Hartsough, 1998; Murphy & Barkley, 1996; Wilens et al., 2007), although more work would be required to establish whether individuals with ADHD are using cocaine explicitly for this purpose.

In further support of a self-medication hypothesis, imaging research suggests that individuals with ADHD have deficient dopaminergic activity in the caudate (Volkow, Wang, Newcorn, Telang et al., 2007) and ventral striatum (Volkow, Wang, Newcorn, Fowler et al., 2007), conditions commonly associated with methylphenidate liking and substance use (Elkins et al., 2007; Volkow, Wang, Newcorn, Telang et al., 2007). Furthermore, Bidwell et al. (2012) found that polymorphisms in the DRD2 gene interacted with ADHD symptoms to predict initial pleasant reactions to nicotine.

Effect of Childhood Pharmacotherapy on Later Substance Use

A controversial area has been the question of what impact treatment with stimulants in childhood may have on later SUD in ADHD individuals. In a seminal paper, Biederman, Wilens, Mick, Spencer, and Faraone (1999) argued that teens with ADHD medicated as children were less likely to abuse substances in adolescence than were previously unmedicated teens with ADHD. However, there were numerous methodological problems with this paper, and, in a follow-up study, Biederman et al. (2008) wrote that these early findings did not hold; they found no relationship between childhood pharmacotherapy and later substance use. Although a few other studies have reported similar results,

the bulk of studies have failed to find an association between childhood treatment with stimulants and later substance use (Humphreys et al., 2013; Molina et al., 2013), and other research suggests that stimulant use may, in fact, increase rates of substance use, such as tobacco (Rush et al., 2005). It would be surprising if stimulants had a beneficial effect in this domain because there is no evidence of a beneficial long-term effect of stimulant pharmacotherapy in any other domain of functioning in which ADHD individuals typically suffer impairment (e.g., Molina et al., 2009). Because these other domains (e.g., peer relations, academic functioning, family relationships) are thought to mediate later substance use, absence of an effect on them would suggest that there will be no subsequent effect on substance use.

Conversely, others have proposed that individuals with ADHD who have previously been treated with stimulant medication have increased substance use propensity, indicating that stimulant medication may have the adverse effect of awakening the physiological appetite for specific substances such as tobacco, cocaine, and other stimulants (Brandon, Marinelli, Baker, & White, 2001; Lambert & Hartsough, 1998; Robinson & Berridge, 1993; 2000). Animal models have found that behavioral sensitization to other substances, such as cocaine, can occur after stimulant use (Horger, Giles, & Schenk, 1992), suggesting that previously medicated individuals with ADHD may be at increased risk for developing later substance dependence.

Volkow, Fowler, Wang, Baler, and Telang (2009) describe the effects of chronic substance use on the dopaminergic transmitter system in humans, whereby stimulant, nicotine, or opiate use produces changes in the structure of cells in areas of the brain associated with motivation, reward, judgment, and the inhibitory control of behavior (Robinson & Kolb, 2004). Indeed, research has demonstrated that individuals who are addicted to a wide variety of substances (including methamphetamine) show significant reductions in D2DA receptor availability in the striatum that continues to persist months after detoxification (Fehr et al., 2008; Martinez et al., 2004; 2005; 2007; Volkow, Wang, Newcorn, Telang et al., 2007), and the administration of methylphenidate results in significantly lower dopaminergic activity for individuals with a history of cocaine or alcohol use than for those without such a history (Martinez et al., 2007; Volkow et al., 1997), suggesting that chronic stimulant use has the effect of reducing dopaminergic activity and potentially increasing the individual's craving for dopamine-enhancing substances.

In support of this notion, some studies indicate that individuals with ADHD and a history of stimulant medication use may be at increased risk of smoking relative to others without a medication history (Biederman, Faraone et al., 1999; Lambert, 2002). Lambert (2002) investigated the effects of stimulant medication use on adult smoking and found that a significantly greater percentage of stimulant-treated individuals with ADHD reported regular smoking relative to untreated controls. Laboratory findings also reflect this longitudinal finding; both d-amphetamine and methylphenidate have been found to increase smoking (Chait & Griffiths, 1983; Cousins, Stamat, & deWit, 2001; Rush et al., 2005; Tidey, O'Neill, & Higgins, 2000).

Results from both sides of the argument make this issue difficult to disentangle. Research in the animal literature has found that the developmental timing of amphetamine exposure in rats may be predictive of later reinforcing properties of cocaine; rats exposed to amphetamine early in development were less likely to find cocaine reinforcing than were those exposed to amphetamine later in development (Carlezon, Mague, & Andersen, 2003). Furthermore, Augustyniak, Kourrich, Rezazadeh, Stewart, and Arvanitogiannis (2006) showed that prepubertal spontaneous hypertensive rats exposed to methylphenidate hydrochloride showed decreased sensitivity to incentive properties of cocaine in adulthood, although more recent research indicates that continuity of administration may be an important factor in this relation (Griggs, Weir, Wayman, & Koeltzow, 2010).

Coupling animal research with previous findings from the human literature, it appears as though there may exist a specific developmentally beneficial ADHD intervention period, after which stimulant medication interventions for ADHD cease to become preventative in terms of substance use (Carlezon et al., 2003). However, aside from specific psychophysiological explanations, it may simply be the case that early and successful intervention practices (be they medication or other valid forms of treatment) have the effect of decreasing risk of conduct problems in general, including substance use (Groenman et al., 2013; Klein, 2002; Wilens et al., 2008). At minimum, the difficulties of extrapolating animal findings to humans remains problematic, and longitudinal studies of humans are still needed to examine this issue more accurately.

Environment

The environmental influences associated with ADHD place those with this diagnosis at risk for substance use independently of and in conjunction with heritable risk factors (Iacono et al., 2008). Environmental risk factors that have been identified for SUD and for ADHD are similar, including parenting/family factors, school functioning, and peer relationships as prominent influences (Flory, Malone, & Lamis, 2011; Iacono et al., 2008; Molina et al., 2009; 2012; Pelham et al., 2005; Sher et al., 2005; Zucker, 2006).

Many children with ADHD experience what is known as the "double whammy" of (1) inheriting a propensity for these conditions from parents with ADHD and substance use problems and (2) being raised by parents who have ADHD and substance use problems. These parental characteristics interact with child misbehavior to influence parents' parenting styles, as well as their alcohol consumption, which in turn exacerbate child misbehavior and putatively later substance use in their offspring (Lang, Pelham, Atkeson, & Murphy, 1999; Pelham et al., 1997). It is therefore necessary to consider these factors in tandem with the heritable factors with which they interact. Thus, the children who inherit behaviorally disruptive disorders and substance use risk are also likely to be raised in less stable family environments with poor modeling, explicit deviant behavior, fewer resources, and poor parenting known to exacerbate the development of deviant behavior in children (Johnston & Chronis, in press; Molina & Pelham, 2014).

Aside from these issues, the factors associated with impulsivity have direct consequences on environmental conditions. It is clear that the core symptoms of ADHD (inattention, impulsivity, and hyperactivity), associated features of ADHD (parental impulsivity and substance use, deviant peer groups), and functional impairments of those with ADHD (poor academic achievement) converge to increase risk for substance use. Longitudinal work has documented that adolescents with ADHD may have increased vulnerability to deviant peer socialization effects because relations between deviant peer affiliation and alcohol use are stronger for those with ADHD (Marshal, Molina, & Pelham, 2003). This follows directly from the fact that children and adolescents with ADHD have severely disturbed peer relationships (Pelham & Bender, 1982) that set the occasion for association with deviant peers. Molina and colleagues (1999) and Molina and Pelham (2003) have hypothesized that early-presenting inattentive symptoms of ADHD may increase substance use through subsequent environmental influences, such as poor academic achievement, deviant peer group associations, and peer difficulties, known risk factors for substance use and abuse (Hawkins, Catalano, & Miller, 1992). For instance, Molina and colleagues have demonstrated that teacher ratings of inattention symptoms in adolescence were more strongly correlated with academic grade-point average than were ratings of impulsivity-hyperactivity and ODD (Molina, Smith, & Pelham, 2001) and that lower reading scores in childhood prospectively predicted AUD in adolescence (Molina & Pelham, 2001). Furthermore, Flory and colleagues (2011) found that the relation between childhood ADHD and cigarette smoking in adolescence was mediated by school adjustment, suggesting that the environmental influence of ADHD greatly contributes to substance use outcomes.

Tarter and colleagues (1999) suggest that, for children with ADHD, early deficits in behavioral regulation likely promote subsequent maladaptive social interactions, which likely promote delinquent peer groups, higher impulsivity, poor or disrupted familial relationships, poor academic functioning, and substance use (see also Iacono et al., 2008; Sher et al., 2005; Zucker, 2006). As argued by Tarter et al., it is likely that characteristics associated with ADHD, such as inattention and impulsivity, interfere in multiple ways significantly with adolescents' propensity for long-term drug use. Furthermore, children of alcoholics are known for their higher positive expectations of alcohol's effects (Brown, 1999; Reese, Chassin, & Molina, 1994), as are adolescents with ADHD (Derefinko, MacLean, Pelham et al., 2011), thus suggesting that expectancies influenced by substance-using family members or peers may have a strong impact on propensity for those with ADHD.

Along with other factors, the importance of parental involvement has also begun to be explored as a key factor of substance use. Molina et al. (2012) evaluated the development of heavy alcohol use in teens with ADHD along with a number of moderating and mediating risk factors including parental monitoring, peer relationships, delinquency, symptom persistence, and grade point average (GPA).

They found that teens with ADHD whose parents were poor monitors of the teens' whereabouts had elevated growth in heavy alcohol use compared to non-ADHD controls. Furthermore, those who were poorly monitored by parents had a propensity for multiple areas of dysfunction included as mediators in analyses, including social impairment, symptoms of ADHD, and lower GPAs. These multiple areas of dysfunction were able to predict alcohol use growth factors, as well as delinquency, a factor also associated with alcohol use. This paper illustrates the importance of measuring those environmental factors that are known to influence development of substance use in normative populations in ADHD samples, to assess whether common risk factors work in similar ways for those with and without ADHD.

Treatment

Because ADHD is associated with inattention, impulsivity, conduct problems, early onset of substance use, and more severe substance use and outcomes, it is not surprising that treatment of both conditions concurrently presents a number of problems for clinicians. Common issues for those with comorbid ADHD and substance use include poor treatment adherence, lack of treatment progress, impaired achievement of treatment goals, and high rates of relapse (Carroll & Rounsaville, 1993; Levin et al., 2004; Wilens, Biederman, Mick, Faraone, & Spencer, 1997; Wise, Cuffe, & Fischer, 2001). In addition, stimulant medication, generally the first course of treatment for symptoms of ADHD (Smith, Barkley, & Shapiro, 2006), is often not considered an option for those with comorbid substance use problems due to abuse potential and the perceived dangers of stimulant administration in those with co-occurring substance abuse. It is often recommended that patients attain sobriety before beginning a course of stimulant medication, although this prerequisite is an unrealistic expectation and its necessity has not been well studied. Although behavioral treatment for ADHD is a well-established, effective strategy at reducing impairment associated with ADHD symptoms (Evans, Owens, & Bunford, 2013; Fabiano et al., 2009; Pelham & Fabiano, 2008), there is less evidence for its effectiveness in adolescents with ADHD (Sibley et al., 2014b), and the use of this type of treatment for co-occurring SUDs has promise but remains understudied (Schubiner et al., 2002; Stanger, Budney, Kamon, & Thostensen, 2009).

Medication

Schubiner (2005) reviewed the area of treatment for co-occurring ADHD and SUDs, including more recent evidence of the use of stimulant medication treatments. As noted by Schubiner (2005), one of the primary concerns regarding the prescription of stimulant medications to reduce ADHD symptoms in those with comorbid SUDs is the potential for abuse. However, although some have reported that a number of college students have used prescription stimulants recreationally (Babcock & Byrne, 2000), it is unlikely that the typical oral administration of stimulant medication creates the rapid euphoric "high" commonly associated with drugs of abuse, such as cocaine (Volkow et al., 1998).

Given this conclusion, researchers have conducted trials of methylphenidate for individuals with ADHD and comorbid substance abuse problems (Castaneda, Levy, Hardy, & Trujillo, 2000; Grabowski et al., 1997; 2001; Levin, Evans, McDowell, & Kleber, 1998; Roache, Grabowski, Schmitz, Creson, & Rhoades, 2000; Schubiner et al., 2002). Schubiner et al. (2002) conducted the first randomized control study of methylphenidate use in cocaine abusers with comorbid ADHD. Although few adverse effects were found (e.g., drug craving, adverse physiological effects), suggesting relative safety of stimulant treatment in this group, few benefits were found with regard to the actual reduction of self-reported DSM-IV ADHD symptoms or urine screens for cocaine use. Subsequent randomized research by Szobot and colleagues (2007) found that a long-acting formulation of methylphenidate decreased self-reported symptoms of ADHD but was unrelated to self-reported substance use, again suggesting that prescribed methylphenidate does not appear to decrease substance use.

Alternatives to stimulant medications are available for treatment of ADHD symptoms, although results for individuals with comorbid ADHD and substance use are not necessarily promising (Thurstone, Riggs, Salomonsen-Sautel, & Mikulicn-Gilbertson, 2010). A randomized controlled trial of atomoxetine produced no improvements in ADHD or substance use symptoms (Thurstone et al., 2010). Open trials with bupropion (Riggs, Leon, Mikulich, & Pottle, 1998; Solhkhah et al., 2005) and a randomized controlled trial with pemoline (Riggs, Hall, Mikulich-Gilbertson, Lohman, & Kayser, 2004) indicate some efficacy in reducing ADHD symptoms but little change in substance use, suggesting that these alternatives function much the same as methylphenidate in ADHD treatment efficacy in substance-using populations. The most recent study is a large, multisite test of sustained-release methylphenidate (Concerta) for teens with ADHD and SUD and concurrently receiving cognitive behavioral therapy (CBT) for SUD (Riggs et al., 2011). Results were consistent with previous smaller studies: methylphenidate did not reduce SUD (use in past 30 days) compared to placebo. All participants showed significant improvement in substance use, presumably as a result of the CBT, although no control for CBT was employed. Surprisingly, compared to placebo, methylphenidate did not have a significant effect on ADHD symptoms, although the outcome measure was self-report, which is insensitive in ADHD samples. Thus, the main conclusion that can be drawn from this study is that concurrent methylphenidate does not facilitate treatment for SUD in teens with ADHD and SUD, and it may also not be effective for ADHD symptoms.

Nonpharmacologic Interventions

The emphasis in research has been on the use of medications to treat ADHD and comorbid SUD, and there are few studies that have addressed psychosocial approaches in this comorbid population. This is surprising, given that (1) psychosocial approaches are the most widely employed approach in practice to treat adolescent substance use, (2) the majority of SUD adolescents have a comorbid psychiatric disorder, (3) comorbid psychiatric disorders influence SUD treatment outcome, and (4) the environmental influences that must be addressed in treatment are common across many of the comorbidities and SUD (Brown & Abrantes, 2006; Waldron & Turner, 2008; Williams, Chang, & Addiction Centre Adolescent Research Group, 2000; Winters, 1999).

Several interventions for teens with SUD are well established (Waldron & Turner, 2008). These consist primarily of CBT approaches (e.g., Waldron, Slesnick, Brody, Turner, & Peterson, 2001) and family approaches (e.g., Liddle, Dakog, Diamond, Barrett, & Tejeda, 2001), but other approaches, such as 12-step-based community programs show promise (Waldron & Turner, 2008). Unfortunately, controlled evaluations of how comorbid ADHD affects the effectiveness of these studies are lacking. Typical studies that have examined efficacy in comorbid disorders conduct secondary analyses to see if comorbid psychiatric diagnosis moderates outcome. Findings are mixed except for the consensus that comorbid psychiatric disorders are associated with poorer adherence and worse outcomes (Stanger et al., 2009; Waldron & Turner, 2008; Winters, 1999). To our knowledge, to date, only a single study (Riggs et al., 2011) has been conducted with participants preselected to have both ADHD and SUD. We reviewed earlier the outcomes regarding pharmacological intervention. The results suggest that CBT is an effective treatment for SUD in a population of teens with ADHD—there was a highly significant reduction in past-month substance use for the participants. However, both groups received CBT, so there is no control for other variables that might have produced improvements over time. This study is also the only one that combined an established intervention for ADHD—methylphenidate—with an established intervention for SUD—CBT. This conjoint approach to intervention, targeting both the underlying psychiatric comorbidity and the SUD, is routinely recommended but rarely studied. As discussed earlier, this strategy was ineffective in the Riggs et al. (2010) study; concurrent medication did not have any impact on change over time/presumed response to CBT.

Because psychosocial interventions for teens with ADHD (Smith et al., 2006) are similar to the CBT approach employed by Riggs (Waldron et al., 2001), it would not be surprising if CBT for SUD was effective in teens with comorbid ADHD, but controlled studies are needed. Furthermore, there is considerable support for family-based programming for treating substance use in adolescents; these programs seek to change teen–parent relationships and parenting strategies (Liddle et al., 2001; Waldron et al., 2001). Contemporary family strategies are generally based on work that has found basic parenting strategies effective at reducing initiation of substance use (Wolchik et al., 2002). In addition, family involvement in treatment has been found to reduce delinquent behaviors that co-occur with substance use as well (Chassin, Knight, Vargas-Chanes, Losoya, & Naranjo, 2009).

How well CBT and family therapy will work in individuals with ADHD awaits further research. In general, CBT approaches, although apparently helpful with adults with ADHD (Safren, 2006), have been consistently ineffective in children with ADHD (Pelham & Fabiano, 2008). Whether this approach will be effective in adolescents with ADHD remains to be explored. Studies that have employed family therapy programs with adolescents with ADHD (Barkley, Edwards, Laneri, Fletcher, & Metevia, 2001; Barkley, Guevremont, Anastopoulos, & Fletcher, 1992,) have shown that, despite symptom reductions, family therapy programs demonstrate rather poor reliable magnitude of change (between 5% and 30% across studies).

The psychosocial approach that is solidly evidence-based with children with ADHD involves behavioral parent training, school-based intervention, and peer-relationship focused intervention, all of which are contingency management-based approaches (Evans et al., 2013; Fabiano et al., 2009; Pelham & Fabiano, 2008; Sibley et al., 2014*b*). Notably, these interventions focus on parenting, peer relations, and school functioning, the three domains that are key risk factors for the development of adolescent substance use and other adverse outcomes of adolescence and adulthood (e.g., Pelham & Fabiano, 2008; Sher et al., 2005).

Contingency management approaches are gaining credence as effective components of behavioral treatments that target adult substance use (Higgins, Silverman, & Heil, 2008; Petry & Simic, 2002). These treatments involve providing increasing incentives for documented substance abstinence. Stanger, Budney, Kamon and Thostensen (2009) conducted a randomized trial of contingency management for abstinence for marijuana-abusing adolescents, which included incentives for negative regularly scheduled drug tests and a family-based component for parents that provided instruction on limit-setting, contingency management, and relationship skills. More than half of the participants had diagnoses of ADHD, ODD, or CD. The adolescents receiving this treatment were abstinent for longer periods of time during treatment, were more likely to achieve 10 or more weeks of abstinence, and had lower scores on measures of externalizing problems than comparison adolescents. This suggests that effective SUD treatments (CBT, family therapy, contingent incentives for abstinence) that include traditional contingency management strategies that are employed in the ADHD treatment literature (e.g., behavioral parent training) may be effective for individuals with both ADHD and SUDs. The sample size was insufficient to analyze the impact of the intervention as a function of comorbid ADHD, but the results were promising. At the same time, the beneficial effects dissipated at endpoint and follow-up points. This study represents a positive initial step, but additional research will be necessary to document maintenance of beneficial treatment effects, as well as documented benefits for teens with ADHD/SUD of an intervention that combines the well-established treatments for ADHD and SUD in teens.

Furthermore, it has been suggested that strategies for substance use treatment are more effective if they follow "best practice" treatment duration guidelines put forth by the National Institute on Drug Abuse (NIDA, 2006). Chassin and colleagues

(2009) investigated the NIDA (2006) principles of drug treatment for criminal justice populations, which suggest that treatment must last long enough to produce stable changes over time, by studying treatment outcome effects of existing substance use programs. Only treatments that lasted for at least 90 days were successful in reducing marijuana use, which suggests that duration/intensity of treatment should be considered as programs are further developed and evaluated. Winters (1999) argued that SUD in a psychiatric teen population is a particularly severe disorder that requires intensive and sustained intervention if substance abuse desistance is desired. The same argument has been made for ADHD, given the chronic nature of the disorder and its poor long-term outcome (Pelham & Fabiano, 2008).

Importantly, some intensive intervention programs for ADHD are beginning to include substance use prevention components; Sibley et al. (2011) recently reported positive results for teens with ADHD from an intensive (40 day) Summer Treatment Program for Adolescents (STP-A) that had been modified from a well-validated, effective summer program intervention for children with ADHD (Pelham et al., 2010). The STP-A program includes a prevention component for substance use (Botvin, Baker, Dusenbury, Botvin, & Diaz, 1995), parent training, academic skills training, social skills training, and vocational skills training. Although the STP-A has been applied to teens with ADHD but without SUD to date, combining this approach with interventions for SUD might yield a useful intervention focused on comorbid teens with ADHD and SUD.

Finally, it is noteworthy that studies of dopaminergic functioning in individuals with substance use have led to the consideration of reward-focused strategies for the treatment of drug addiction that might be particularly important for individuals with comorbid ADHD (Volkow, Fowler et al., 2009). For instance, Volkow, Fowler, and colleagues (2009) suggest that treatment should be focused on decreasing the reward value of the drug of choice, increasing reward value of nondrug reinforcers, weakening conditioned drug behaviors, and strengthening frontal inhibitory and executive control. A series of laboratory studies have addressed the effects of incentive, methylphenidate, and their combination on these cognitive processes in children with ADHD and demonstrate positive effects that may underlie response to behavioral interventions and combined treatments in treatment (e.g.,

Rosch et al., 2015; Shiels et al., 2009; Strand et al., 2012). Volkow and colleagues argue that only through the use of salient alternative rewards will individuals with ADHD be able to resist the reinforcing effects of substances (e.g., Stanger et al., 2009) and be able to continue this resistance into the future. Integration of such strategies into combined ADHD- and SUD-focused interventions is clearly warranted.

Conclusion

The relationship between ADHD and substance use is well documented. Understanding the relation in terms of variation across substances of abuse, age, gender, comorbid externalizing behavior, symptoms of ADHD, and risk factors provides necessary understanding of how the relationship is expressed. We can draw several conclusions. As reviewed herein, ADHD is related to elevated use of a wide variety of substances (Charach et al., 2011; Lee et al., 2011; Molina & Pelham, 2014). Notably, for those with ADHD, tobacco use starts early and often develops into heavy use and dependence. Similarly, there is evidence for early use, increased average amounts used, and more heavy-use incidents of alcohol, partially moderated by parental monitoring and other psychosocial risk factors. Those with ADHD are also prone to other drugs of abuse, including marijuana use. Less is known about ADHD and SUD in females, but preliminary studies suggest the relationship may also exist albeit less extensively and severely in females with ADHD.

Conclusions regarding relations across age generally follow developmental models of deviance (Iacono et al., 2008; Molina & Pelham, 2014; Sher, 1991; Sher et al., 2005; Zucker, 2006), with the onset of ADHD preceding the environmental and psychiatric risk factors that in turn set the stage for substance use (e.g., Sibley et al., 2014a). Thus, children with ADHD have disturbed peer relationships from an early age, as well as poor academic performance in school; furthermore, their parents have dysfunctional parenting styles—all three domains that set the occasion for the continuation of peer problems (affiliation with deviant peers), academic dysfunction (drop out), and poor parenting (ineffective monitoring) that give rise to development of substance use in adolescents. Also important to the understanding of age relations is the ability of individuals to adequately report on their symptoms and impairment (Molina & Pelham, 2014).

The presence of comorbid externalizing behavior has been widely studied with regard to ADHD and substance use, with some concluding that those with both ADHD and conduct problems are at increased risk for more severe substance use issues, and others suggesting that conduct problems, rather than ADHD, are responsible for positive associations with substance use. However, it is important to note that early presenting characteristics of ADHD are important predictors of risk for many forms of delinquent and antisocial behaviors in adolescence and adulthood, including substance use and SUDs (Iacono et al., 2008; Moffit, 1993; Sher et al., 2005; Sibley et al., 2014a; Zucker, 2006), suggesting that later conduct problems and substance use are related developmental outcomes of individuals with the core symptoms of ADHD and years of ADHD-related impairments.

Common underlying factors of ADHD and substance use abound and strongly suggest similar etiology or propensity. Genetic work suggests that parental substance use is a common risk factor (Beiderman et al., 2000; Clark et al., 2004), as are genes associated with the transmission of dopamine (Blum et al., 1990; Laucht et al., 2007; Swanson et al., 2000). Imaging studies support a dopaminergic link between disorders, with various studies finding decreased activity in brain areas associated with the synthesis and messaging of dopamine (Arnsten, 2006; Cheon et al., 2003; Swanson et al., 2007; Volkow, Wang et al., 2009). In addition, trait risk factors of impulsivity, sensation seeking, executive dysfunctions, and neurobiological endophenotypes are common among those with ADHD and substance use. The trait of impulsivity may be an indicator of heightened sensitivity to specific substances, such as alcohol. Finally, prenatal exposure to a wide variety of substances has been linked with impulsivity and ADHD characteristics, although there are many environmental factors that interact with exposure to produce risk.

The question of whether individuals with ADHD use substances to self-medicate remains unclear. It is possible that individuals with ADHD are taking substances to alleviate symptoms of inattention or to increase feelings of relaxation; there is evidence that nicotine serves as a stimulant for the dopamine transporter of the striatum, much like methylphenidate (Krause et al., 2002). It has been speculated that individuals with ADHD take substances in adulthood as a result of medication with stimulants during childhood. However, current longitudinal research has not supported the idea that previous stimulant medication prescribed

in childhood has a direct impact on substance use in later stages of development.

Important to the development of comorbid ADHD and substance use is the presence of adverse environmental conditions that undoubtedly contribute to multiple areas of risk. Similar to models of substance vulnerability (Sher, 1991), individuals with ADHD may experience compounding factors that drive them toward later substance use. Specifically, core symptoms of ADHD contribute to the development of parental substance use, poor parenting, poor academic achievement, and deviant peer groups—all factors known to be associated with substance use. The few studies that have examined these in ADHD samples have shown that they indeed moderate the development of substance use (e.g., Molina et al., 2012).

A handful of studies have examined whether ADHD-focused pharmacotherapy in adolescents with both ADHD and SUD improves the substance use outcomes, and they have uniformly failed to provide evidence of benefit (Humphreys et al., 2013). Although psychosocial treatments are the most widely used and evidence-based for SUD in adolescence and are widely used and evidence-based for ADHD as well, there have been no studies directly evaluating the benefit of effective psychosocial treatments for SUD (CBT, family therapy) on adolescents with ADHD. Studies that have examined sample characteristics in a post hoc manner have suggested that comorbid externalizing disorders give rise to reductions in treatment efficacy for teens with SUD.

No programs have been specifically developed for the treatment of these co-occurring conditions. However, there is promise in strategies that employ contingency management, as this is common practice in both ADHD and substance use treatment designs and can be included in the CBT and family therapy approaches that are effective for SUD in adolescence. One of the commonalities shared by SUD and ADHD in adolescence is persistence of disorder and the need for intensive interventions delivered across multiple settings with multiple targets for extended periods of time. Thus, the treatment of these co-occurring disorders would do well to provide an intensive, multisystemic, and highly structured system that takes into account the chronic nature of both ADHD and SUDs.

Future Directions

Despite considerable achievements in this area, future work would do well to focus on several remaining issues. First, the majority of work has investigated the relation between nicotine and ADHD; relatively fewer studies have explored risk for other types of substance abuse (Charach et al., 2011; Lee et al., 2011). This is important, given the nature of the risk factors associated with both ADHD and escalation into polydrug use. Poor parental monitoring, access to substances, peer/familial approval of substance use, and lack of participation in adult responsibilities have all been associated with escalation in drug use and variability in substances used (Brown & Abrantes, 2006); it is therefore likely that individuals with ADHD are at risk for polydrug use and greater SUD severity than are those without ADHD, although research has only just begun to explore the extent of this possibility.

Second, the longitudinal work exploring relations between ADHD and substance use relies on small, independent samples in which power to detect effects is small. In fact, the largest (and uniquely so) sample sizes include the Pittsburgh ADHD Longitudinal Study (PALS; N = 516; Molina et al., 2012) and the Multimodal Treatment Study of Children with ADHD (MTA; N = 579; Molina et al., 2013), rather small samples when compared with other epidemiological research. Because of the potential for type I error, researchers should consider combining samples to get a more accurate picture of cross-drug heterogeneity and risk factors for individuals with ADHD. This strategy was employed successfully by Duncan and colleagues (2007) in the education field, in which multiple existing longitudinal studies were integrated to examine the relationship between early childhood characteristics and later achievement. In addition, treatment studies that investigate relations typically utilize samples of convenience (e.g., post hoc analyses of psychiatric comorbidities that happen to be found in samples selected for substance abuse). Although a good starting point, these samples with relatively small Ns for any given comorbid condition are often not ideal for studying treatment for one particular comorbid condition. For the present purposes, samples that are selected a priori to include large groups of ADHD, SUD, and comorbid groups (e.g., Riggs et al., 2011) could more powerfully address relevant questions than existing studies.

Third, new prevention and intervention programs have a wealth of information that can be drawn on to create, in effect, programs tailored for this specific at-risk population. For instance, correlates of ADHD known to be risk factors for substance use/abuse, such as reward dependence, executive functioning deficits, and impulsivity, could be used as effective areas of intervention (Volkow, Fowler et al., 2009). Additionally, aside from traditional treatment considerations, tailoring prevention and treatment to a group of individuals likely to value novel and exciting stimuli may make treatment more engaging, which may increase both motivation and value of treatment among the adolescents themselves (Zimmerman et al., 2007).

Finally, due to the chronic nature and refractoriness of ADHD and SUDs, it is clear that treatments need to be sustained for longer periods than that characterizing research to date. Proposed treatments would do well to consider both intensity and duration of treatment programs, as well as the fidelity with which they are implemented in practice, to ensure that gains are not only achieved but sustainable for individuals who face pervasive, chronic issues. Others have commented on the need for adaptations of substance use treatment programs for populations with concomitant mental health problems (Brown & Abrantes, 2006), and it is likely that successful programs would take into account the treatment research from both the substance use and the ADHD literature to develop ideal prevention and intervention practices.

Acknowledgments

This work was supported by grants DA12414, DA05605, F31 DA017546 from the National Institute on Drug Abuse and, additionally, AA11873 from the National Institute on Alcohol Abuse and Alcoholism. The work was also supported in part by AA00202, AA08746, AA12342, AA0626, and grants from the National Institute of Mental Health (MH12010, MH4815, MH47390, MH45576, MH50467, MH53554, MH069614) and Institute of Education Sciences (IESLO3000665A, IESR324B060045).

References

Abrantes, A. M., Strong, D. R., Ramsey, S. E., Lewinsohn, P. M., & Brown, R. A. (2005). Substance use disorder characteristics and externalizing problems among inpatient adolescent smokers. *Journal of Psychoactive Drugs, 37,* 391–399.

Akinbami, L., Liu, X., Pastor, P., & Reuben, M. (2011). *Attention deficit hyperactivity disorder among children aged 5–17 years in the United States, 1998–2009* (Data Brief No. 70). Atlanta, GA: CDC, National Center for Health Statistics.

American Psychiatric Association. (2000). *Diagnostic and statistical manual of mental disorders-text revision* (4th ed.). Washington, DC: Author.

American Psychiatric Association. (2013). *Diagnostic and statistical manual of mental disorders* (5th ed.). Washington, DC: Author.

Anderson, K. G., Tapert, S. F., Moadab, I., Crowley, T. J., & Brown, S. A. (2007). Personality risk profile for conduct disorder and substance use disorders in youth. *Addictive Behaviors, 32*(10), 2377–2382.

Arias, A. J., Gelernter, J., Chan, G., Weiss, R. D., Brady, K. T., Farrer, L., et al. (2008). Correlates of co-occurring ADHD in drug-dependent subjects: Prevalence and features of substance dependence and psychiatric disorders. *Addictive Behaviors, 33*, 1199–1207.

Arnsten, A. F. (2006). Fundamentals of attention-deficit/ hyperactivity disorder: Circuits and pathways. *Journal of Clinical Psychiatry, 67*(Suppl. 8), 7–12.

August, G. J., Winters, K. C., Realmuto, G. M., Fahnhorst, T., Botzet, A., & Lee, S. (2006). Prospective study of adolescent drug use among community samples of ADHD and Non-ADHD participants. *Journal of the American Academy of Child and Adolescent Psychiatry, 45*(7), 824–832.

Augustyniak, P. N., Kourrich, S., Rezazadeh, S. M., Stewart, J., & Arvanitogiannis, A. (2006). Differential behavioral and neurochemical effects of cocaine after early exposure to methylphenidate in an animal model of attention deficit hyperactivity disorder. *Behavioural Brain Research, 167*(2), 379–382.

Babcock, Q., & Byrne, T. (2000). Student perceptions of methylphenidate abuse at a public liberal arts college. *Journal of American College Health, 49*, 143–145.

Babinski, D. E., Pelham, W. E., Molina, B. S. G., Waschbusch, D. A., Gnagy, E. M., Yu, J., et al. (2011*a*). Late adolescent and young adult outcomes of girls diagnosed with ADHD in childhood: An exploratory investigation. *Journal of Attention Disorders, 15*, 204–214.

Babinski, D. E., Pelham, W. E., Molina, B. S. G., Waschbusch, D. A., Gnagy, E. M., Yu, J., et al. (2011*b*). Women with childhood ADHD: Comparisons by diagnostic group and gender. *Journal of Psychopathology and Behavioral Assessment, 33*, 420–429.

Bagwell, C. L., Molina, B. S. G., Kashdan, T. B., Pelham, W. E., & Hoza, B. (2006). Anxiety and mood disorders in adolescents with childhood attention-deficit/hyperactivity disorder. *Journal of Emotional and Behavioral Disorders, 14*, 178–187.

Barkley, R. A. (1997). Behavioral inhibition, sustained attention, and executive functions: Constructing a unifying theory of ADHD. *Psychological Bulletin, 121*, 65–94.

Barkley, R. A. (2006). Attention-Deficit/Hyperactivity Disorder. In D. A. Wolfe & E. J. Mash (Eds.), *Behavioral and emotional disorders in adolescents: Nature, assessment, and treatment* (pp. 91–152). New York: Guilford.

Barkley, R. A., & Brown, T. E. (2008). Unrecognized attention-deficit/hyperactivity disorder in adults presenting with other psychiatric disorders. *CNS Spectrums, 13*(11), 977–984.

Barkley, R. A., Edwards, G., Laneri, M., Fletcher, K., & Metevia, L. (2001). The efficacy of problem-solving communication training alone, behavior management training alone, and their combination for parent-adolescent conflict in teenagers with ADHD and ODD, *Journal of Consulting and Clinical Psychology, 69*, 926–941.

Barkley, R. A., Fischer, M., Edelbrock, C. S., & Smallish, L. (1990). The adolescent outcome of hyperactive children diagnosed by research criteria: I. An 8-year prospective longitudinal study. *Journal of the American Academy of Child and Adolescent Psychiatry, 29*, 546–557.

Barkley, R. A., Fischer, M., Smallish, L., & Fletcher, K. (2002). The persistence of attention-deficit/hyperactivity disorder into young adulthood as a function of reporting source and definition of disorder. *Journal of Abnormal Psychology, 111*(2), 279–289.

Barkley, R. A., Fischer, M., Smallish, L., & Fletcher, K. (2004). Young adult follow-up of hyperactive children: Antisocial activities and drug use. *Journal of Child Psychology and Psychiatry, 45*(2), 195–211.

Barkley, R. A., Guevremont, D. G., Anastopoulos, A. D., & Fletcher, K. F. (1992). A comparison of three family therapy programs for treating family conflicts in adolescents with attention deficit hyperactivity disorder. *Journal of Consulting and Clinical Psychology, 60*, 450–462.

Barkley, R. A., Murphy, K. R., Dupaul, G. J., & Bush, T. (2002). Driving in young adults with attention deficit hyperactivity disorder: Knowledge, performance, adverse outcomes, and the role of executive functioning. *Journal of the International Neuropsychological Society, 8*(5), 655–672.

Barkley, R. A., Murphy, K. R., & Fischer, M. (2008). *ADHD in adults: What the science says.* New York: Guilford.

Barkley, R. A., Murphy, K., & Kwasnik, D. (1996). Psychological adjustment and adaptive impairments in young adults with ADHD. *Journal of Attention Disorders, 1*(1), 41–54.

Bauermeister, J. J., Canino, G., Bravo, M., Ramírez, R., Jensen, P. S., Chavez, L., et al. (2003). Stimulant and psychosocial treatment of ADHD in Latino/Hispanic children. *Journal of the American Academy of Child & Adolescent Psychiatry, 42*(7), 851–855.

Bidwell, L., Garrett, M., McClernon, J., Fuemmeler, B., Williams, R., Ashley-Koch, A., et al. (2012). A preliminary analysis of interactions between genotype, retrospective ADHD symptoms, and initial reactions to smoking in a sample of young adults. *Nicotine and Tobacco Research, 14*(2), 229–233.

Biederman, J., Faraone, S. V., Mick, E., Williamson, S., Wilens, T. E., Spencer, T. J., et al. (1999). Clinical correlates of ADHD in females: Findings from a large group of girls ascertained from pediatric and psychiatric referral sources. *Journal of the American Academy of Child and Adolescent Psychiatry, 38*(8), 966–975.

Biederman, J., Faraone, S. V., Monuteaux, M. C., & Feighner, J. A. (2000). Patterns of alcohol and drug use in adolescents can be predicted by parental substance use disorders. *Pediatrics, 106*, 792–797.

Biederman, J., Monuteaux, M. C., Mick, E., Wilens, T. E., Fontanella, J. A., Poetzl, K. M., et al. (2006). Is cigarette smoking a gateway to alcohol and illicit drug use disorders? A study of youths with and without attention deficit hyperactivity disorder. *Biological Psychiatry, 59*(3), 258–264.

Biederman, J., Monuteaux, M. C., Spencer, T., Wilens, T. E., MacPherson, H. A., & Faraone, S. V. (2008). Stimulant therapy and risk for subsequent substance use disorders in male adults with ADHD: A naturalistic controlled 10-year follow-up study. *American Journal of Psychiatry, 165*, 597–603.

Biederman, J., Munir, K., & Knee, D. (1987). Conduct and oppositional disorder in clinically referred children with attention deficit disorder: A controlled family study. *Journal of the American Academy of Child and Adolescent Psychiatry, 26*(5), 724–727.

Biederman, J., Newcom, J., & Sprich, S. (1991). Comorbidity of attention deficit hyperactivity disorder with conduct, depressive, anxiety, and other disorders. *American Journal of Psychiatry, 148,* 564–577.

Biederman, J., Wilens, T. E., Mick, E., Faraone, S. V., & Spencer, T. (1998). Does attention-deficit hyperactivity disorder impact the developmental course of drug and alcohol abuse and dependence? *Biological Psychiatry, 44*(4), 269–273.

Biederman, J., Wilens, T., Mick, E., Faraone, S. V., Weber, W., Curtis, S., et al. (1997). Is ADHD a risk factor for psychoactive substance use disorders? Findings from a four-year prospective follow-up study. *Journal of the American Academy of Child and Adolescent Psychiatry, 36,* 21–29.

Biederman, J., Wilens, T., Mick, E., Milberger, S., Spencer, T. J., & Faraone, S. V. (1995). Psychoactive substance use disorders in adults with attention deficit hyperactivity disorder (ADHD): Effects of ADHD and psychiatric comorbidity. *American Journal of Psychiatry, 152*(11), 1652–1658.

Biederman, J., Wilens, T., Mick, E., Spencer, T., & Faraone, S. V. (1999). Pharmacotherapy of Attention-deficit/Hyperactivity Disorder reduces risk for substance use disorder. *Pediatrics, 104*(2), e20.

Blase, S. L., Gilbert, A. N., Anastopoulos, A. D., Costello, E. J., Hoyle, R. H., Swartzwelder, H., et al. (2009). Self-reported ADHD and adjustment in college: Cross-sectional and longitudinal findings. *Journal of Attention Disorders, 13*(3), 297–309.

Blum, K., Noble, E. P., Sheridan, P. J., Montgomery, A., Ritchie, T., Jagadeeswaran, P., et al. (1990). Allelic association of human dopamine D2 receptor gene in alcoholism. *Journal of the American Medical Association, 263*(15), 2055–2060.

Botvin, G. J., Baker, E., Dusenbury, L. D., Botvin, E. M., & Diaz, T. (1995). Long-term follow-up results of a randomized drug abuse prevention trial in a White middle-class population. *Journal of the American Medical Association, 273,* 1106–1112.

Braaten, E. B., & Rosen, L. A. (1997). Emotional reactions in adults with symptoms of attention deficit hyperactivity disorder. *Personality and Individual Differences, 22,* 355–361.

Brandon, C. L., Marinelli, M., Baker, L. K., & White, F. J. (2001). Enhanced reactivity and vulnerability to cocaine following methylphenidate treatment in adolescent rats. *Neuropsychopharmacology, 25,* 651–661.

Brown, R. T., Coles, C. D., Smith, I. E., Platzman, K. A., Silverstein, J., Erickson, S., et al. (1991). Effects of prenatal alcohol exposure at school age, II: Attention and behavior. *Neurotoxicology and Teratology, 13,* 369–376.

Brown, S. A. (1999). Treatment of adolescent alcohol problems. In National Institute on Alcohol Abuse and Alcoholism Extramural Advisory Board (Eds.), *Treatment* (pp. 1–26). Bethesda, MD: National Institute on Alcohol Abuse and Alcoholism.

Brown, S. A., & Abrantes, A. M. (2006). Substance use disorders. In D. A. Wolfe & E. J. Mash (Eds.), *Behavioral and emotional disorders in adolescents: Nature, assessment, and treatment* (pp. 226–256). New York: Guilford.

Burke, J. D., Loeber, R., & Lahey B. B. (2001). Which aspects of ADHD are associated with tobacco use in early adolescence? *Journal of Child Psychology and Psychiatry, 42*(4), 493–502.

Burke, J. D., Loeber, R., White, H. R., Stouthamer-Loeber, M., & Pardini, D. A. (2007). Inattention as a key predictor of tobacco use in adolescence. *Journal of Abnormal Psychology, 116*(2), 249–259.

Bussing, R., Mason, D. M., Bell, L., Porter, P., & Garvan, C. (2010). Adolescent outcomes of childhood attention-deficit/ hyperactivity disorder in a diverse community sample. *Journal of the American Academy of Child & Adolescent Psychiatry, 49*(6), 595–605.

Carlezon, W. A., Mague, S. D., & Anderson, S. L. (2003). Enduring behavioral effects of early exposure to methylphenidate in rats. *Biological Psychiatry, 54*(12), 1330–1337.

Carlson, C. L., Tamm, L., & Gaub, M. (1997). Gender differences in children with ADHD, ODD, and co-occurring ADHD/ODD identified in a school population. *Journal of the American Academy of Child & Adolescent Psychiatry, 36*(12), 1706–1714.

Carlson, S. R., McLarnon, M. E., & Iacono, W. G. (2007). P300 amplitude, externalizing psychopathology, and earlier- versus later-onset substance-use disorder. *Journal of Abnormal Psychology, 116,* 565–577.

Carr, L. A., Nigg, J. T., & Henderson, J. M. (2006). Attentional versus motor inhibition in adults with attention deficit hyperactivity disorder. *Neuropsychology, 20,* 430–441.

Carroll, K. M., & Rounsaville, B. J. (1993). History and significance of childhood attention deficit disorder in treatment-seeking cocaine abusers. *Comprehensive Psychiatry, 34,* 75–82.

Castaneda, R., Levy, R., Hardy, M., & Trujillo, M. (2000). Long-acting stimulants for the treatment of attention-deficit disorder in cocaine-dependent adults. *Psychiatric Services, 51*(2), 169–171.

Chait, L. D., & Griffiths, R. R. (1983). Effects of caffeine on cigarette smoking behavior and subjective response. *Clinical Pharmacology and Therapeutics, 34,* 612–622.

Charach, A., Yeung, E., Climans, T., & Lillie, E. (2011). Childhood attention-deficit/hyperactivity disorder and future substance use disorders: Comparative meta-analyses. *Journal of the American Academy of Child and Adolescent Psychiatry, 50*(1), 9–21.

Chassin, L., Knight, G., Vargas-Chanes, D., Losoya, S. H., & Naranjo, D. (2009). Substance use treatment outcomes in a sample of male serious juvenile offenders. *Journal of Substance Abuse Treatment, 36*(2), 183–194.

Cheon, K. A., Ryu, Y. H., Kim, Y. K., Namkoong, K., Kim, C. H., & Lee, J. D. (2003). Dopamine transporter density in the basal ganglia assessed with [123I]IPT SPET in children with attention deficit hyperactivity disorder. *European Journal of Nuclear Medicine and Molecular Imaging, 30,* 306–311.

Clark, D. B., Cornelius, J., Wood, D. S., & Vanyukov, M. (2004). Psychopathology risk transmission in children of parents with substance use disorders. *American Journal of Psychiatry, 161,* 685–691.

Claude, D., & Firestone, P. (1995). The development of ADHD boys: A 12-year follow-up. *Canadian Journal of Behavioural Science, 27*(2), 226–249.

Collier, D., Curran, S., & Asherson, P. (2000). Mission: Not possible? Candidate gene studies in child psychiatric disorders. *Molecular Psychiatry, 5,* 457–460.

Collins, S. L., Levin, F. R., Foltin, R. W., Kleber, H. D., & Evans, S. M. (2006). Response to cocaine, alone and in combination with methylphenidate, in cocaine abusers with ADHD. *Drug and Alcohol Dependence, 82*(2), 158–167.

Cousins, M. S., Stamat, H. M., & de Wit, H. (2001). Acute doses of d-amphetamine and bupropion increase cigarette smoking. *Psychopharmacology, 157*(3), 243–253.

Crowley, T. J., & Riggs, P. D. (1995). Adolescent substance use disorder with conduct disorder and comorbid conditions. In E. Rahdert & D. Czechowicz (Eds.), *Adolescent drug abuse: Clinical assessment and therapeutic interventions*. NIDA Research Monograph 156. Rockville, Maryland; National Institute on Drug Abuse.

Delaney-Black, V., Covington, C., Templin, T., Ager, J., Nordstrom-Klee, B., Martier, S., et al. (2000). Teacher assessed behavior of children prenatally exposed to cocaine. *Pediatrics, 106*, 782–1729.

Derefinko, K. J., MacLean, M. G., Graziano, P. A., Molina, B. S. G., Gnagy, E. M., & Pelham, W. E. (2011, June). *Childhood ADHD and adult marijuana use*. Poster session presented at the national conference of the College on Problems of Drug Dependence.

Derefinko, K. J., MacLean, M. G., Pelham, W. E., Molina, B. S. G., & Gnagy, E. M. (2011). *The relationship between childhood ADHD and adolescent marijuana use*. Manuscript submitted for publication.

Derefinko, K. J., Adams, Z. W., Milich, R., Fillmore, M. T., Lorch, E. P. & Lynam, D. R. (2008). Response style differences in the inattentive and combined subtypes of attention-deficit/hyperactivity disorder. *Journal of Abnormal Child Psychology, 36*, 745–758.

Disney, E. R., Elkins, I. J., McGue M., & Iacono W. G. (1999). Effects of ADHD, conduct disorder, and gender on substance use and abuse in adolescence. *American Journal of Psychiatry, 156*, 1515–1521.

Donohew, R. L., Hoyle, R. H., Clayton, R. R., Skinner, W. F., Colon, S. E., & Rice, R. E. (1999). Sensation seeking and drug use by adolescents and their friends: Models for marijuana and alcohol. *Journal of Studies on Alcohol, 60*(5), 622–631.

Dougherty, D. D., Bonab, A. A., Spencer, T. J., Rauch, S. L., Madras, B. K., & Fischman, A. J. (1999). Dopamine transporter density in patients with attention deficit hyperactivity disorder. *Lancet, 354*, 2132–2133.

Duncan, G., Dowsett, C., Classens, A., Magnuson, K., Huston, A., Klebanov, P., et al. (2007). School readiness and later achievement. *Developmental Psychology, 43*, 1428–1446.

Elkins, I. J., McGue, M., & Iacono, W. G. (2007). Prospective effects of attention-deficit/hyperactivity disorder, conduct disorder, and sex on adolescent substance use and abuse. *Archives of General Psychiatry, 64*(10), 1145–1152.

Epstein, J. N., Johnson, D. E., Varia, I. M., & Conners, C. K. (2001): Neuropsychological assessment of response inhibition in adults with ADHD. *Journal of Clinical and Experimental Neuropsychology, 23*, 362–371.

Ernst, M., & Zametkin, A. (1995). The interface of genetics, neuroimaging, and neurochemistry in attention-deficit hyperactivity disorder. In F. E. Bloom & D. J. Kupfer (Eds.), *Psychopharmacology: The fourth generation of progress* (pp. 1643–1652). New York: Raven Press.

Esposito-Smythers, C., Spirito, A., Rizzo, C., McGeary, J. E., & Knopik, V. S. (2009). Associations of the DRD2 TaqIA polymorphism with impulsivity and substance use: Preliminary results from a clinical sample of adolescents. *Pharmacology, Biochemistry and Behavior, 93*(3), 306–312.

Evans, S., Owens, J., & Bunford, N. (2013). Evidence-based psychosocial treatments for children and adolescents with ADHD. *Journal of Clinical Child and Adolescent Psychology*, 1–25.

Fabiano, G. A., Pelham, W. E., Coles, E. K., Gnagy, E. M., Chronis-Tuscano, A., & O'Connor, B. C. (2009). A meta-analysis of behavioral treatments for attention-deficit/hyperactivity disorder. *Clinical Psychology Review, 29*, 129–140.

Faraone, S. V., Biederman, J., Spencer, T., Mick, E., Murray, K., Petty, C., et al. (2006). Diagnosing adult attention deficit hyperactivity disorder: Are late onset and subthreshold diagnoses valid? *American Journal of Psychiatry, 163*(10), 1720–1729.

Faraone, S. V., Doyle, A. E., Mick, E., & Biederman, J. (2001). Meta-analysis of the association between the 7-repeat allele of the dopamine D_4 receptor gene and attention deficit hyperactivity disorder. *American Journal of Psychiatry, 158*(7), 1052–1057.

Faraone, S. V., Perlis, R. H., Doyle, A. E., Smoller, J. W., Goralnick, J. J., Holmgren, M. A., et al. (2005). Molecular genetics of attention-deficit/hyperactivity disorder. *Biological Psychiatry, 57*, 1313–1323.

Faraone, S. V., Wilens, T. E., Petty, C., Antshel, K., Spencer, T., & Biederman, J. (2007). Substance use among ADHD adults: Implications of late onset and subthreshold diagnoses. *American Journal on Addictions, 16*, 24–34.

Feehan, M., McGee, R., & Williams, S. M. (1993). Mental health disorders from age 15 to age 18 years. *Journal of the American Academy of Child & Adolescent Psychiatry, 32*(6), 1118–1126.

Fehr, C., Yakushev, I., Hohmann, N., Buchholz, H., Landvogt, C., Deckers, H., et al. (2008). Association of low striatal dopamine D2 receptor availability with nicotine dependence similar to that seen with other drugs of abuse. *American Journal of Psychiatry, 165*, 507–514.

Fergusson, D. M., & Boden, J. M. (2008). Cannabis use and adult ADHD symptoms. *Drug and Alcohol Dependence, 95*(1–2), 90–96.

Fillmore, M. T., Blackburn, J. S., & Harrison, E. L. R. (2008). Acute disinhibiting effects of alcohol as a factor in risky driving behavior. *Drug and Alcohol Dependence, 95*(1–2), 97–106.

Fischer, M., Barkley, R. A., Smallish, L., & Fletcher, K. (2002). Young adult follow-up of hyperactive children: Self-reported psychiatric disorders, comorbidity, and the role of childhood conduct problems and teen CD. *Journal of Abnormal Child Psychology, 30*(5), 463–475.

Flory, K., & Lynam, D. R. (2003). The relation between attention deficit hyperactivity disorder and substance abuse: What role does conduct disorder play? *Clinical Child and Family Psychology Review, 6*(1), 1–16.

Flory, K., Malone, P. S., & Lamis, D. A. (2011). Childhood ADHD symptoms and risk for cigarette smoking during adolescence: School adjustment as a potential mediator. *Psychology of Addictive Behaviors, 25*(2), 320–329.

Flory, K., Milich, R., Lynam, D. R., Leukefeld, C., & Clayton, R. (2003). Relation between childhood disruptive behavior disorders and substance use and dependence symptoms in young adulthood: Individuals with symptoms of attention-deficit/hyperactivity disorder are uniquely at risk. *Psychology of Addictive Behaviors, 17*(2), 151–158.

Fried, P. A., Watkinson, B., & Gray, R. (1992). A follow-up study of attentional behavior in 6-year-old children exposed prenatally to marihuana, cigarettes, and alcohol. *Neurotoxicology and Teratology, 14*, 299–311.

Gittelman, R., Mannuzza, S., Shenker, R., & Bonagura, N. (1985). Hyperactive boys almost grown up: I. Psychiatric status. *Archives of General Psychiatry, 42*, 937–947.

Glass, K. & Flory, K. (2012). Are symptoms of ADHD related to substance use among college students? *Psychology of Addictive Behavior, 26*(1), 124-32.

Grabowski, J., Roache, J. D., Schmitz, J., Rhoades, H., Creson, D., & Korszun, A. (1997). Replacement medication for cocaine dependence: Methylphenidate. *Journal of Clinical Psychopharmacology, 17*, 485–488.

Grabowski, J., Rhoades, H., Schmitz, J., Stotts, A., Daruzska, L. A., Creson, D., et al. (2001). Dextroamphetamine for cocaine-dependence treatment: A double-blind randomized clinical trial. *Journal of Clinical Psychopharmacology, 21*, 522–526.

Grant, B. F., & Dawson, D. A. (1997). Age at onset of alcohol use and its association with DSM-IV alcohol abuse and dependence: Results from the National Longitudinal Epidemiologic Survey. *Journal of Substance Abuse, 9*, 103–110.

Greenbaum, P. E., Prange, M. E., Friedman, R. M., & Silver, S. E. (1991). Substance abuse prevalence and comorbidity with other psychiatric disorders among adolescents with severe emotional disturbances. *Journal of the American Academy of Child and Adolescent Psychiatry, 30*(4), 575–583.

Griggs, R., Weir, C., Wayman, W., & Koeltzow, T. E. (2010). Intermittent methylphenidate during adolescent development produces locomotor hyperactivity and an enhanced response to cocaine compared to continuous treatment in rats. *Pharmacology, Biochemistry and Behavior, 96*(2), 166–174.

Groenman, A., Oosterlaan, J., Rommelse, N., Franke, B., Greven, C., Hoekstra, P., et al. (2013). Stimulant treatment for attention-deficit hyperactivity disorder and risk of developing substance use disorder. *British Journal of Psychiatry, 203*, 112–119.

Hartsough, C. S., & Lambert, N. M. (1987). Pattern and progression of drug use among hyperactives and controls: A prospective short-term longitudinal study. *Journal of Child Psychology and Psychiatry, 28*(4), 543–553.

Hasin, D. S., Stinson, F. S., Ogburn, E., & Grant, B. F. (2007). Prevalence, correlates, disability, and comorbidity of DSM-IV alcohol abuse and dependence in the United States: Results from the National Epidemiologic Survey on Alcohol and Related Conditions. *Archives of General Psychiatry, 64*(7), 830–842.

Hawkins, J., Catalano, R., & Miller, J. (1992). Risk and protective factors for alcohol and other drug problems in early adolescence and early adulthood: Implications for substance abuse prevention. *Psychological Bulletin, 112*, 64–105.

Higgins, S. T., Silverman, K., & Heil, S. H. (2008). *Contingency management in substance abuse treatment.* New York: Guilford.

Hill, S. Y., Yuan, H., & Locke, J. (1999). Path analysis of P300 amplitude of individuals from families at high and low risk for developing alcoholism. *Biological Psychiatry, 45*, 346–359.

Hinshaw, S. P. (1987). On the distinction between attentional deficits/hyperactivity and conduct problems/aggression in child psychopathology. *Psychological Bulletin, 101*, 443–463.

Hinshaw, S. P., Owens, E. B., Sami, N., & Fargeon, S. (2006). Prospective follow-up of girls with attention-deficit/hyperactivity disorder into adolescence: Evidence for continuing cross-domain impairment. *Journal of Consulting and Clinical Psychology, 74*, 489–499.

Hiroi, N., & Agatsuma, S. (2005). Genetic susceptibility to substance dependence. *Molecular Psychiatry, 10*, 336–344.

Horger, B. A., Giles, M. K., & Schenk, S. (1992). Preexposure to amphetamine and nicotine predisposes rats to self-administer a low dose of cocaine. *Psychopharmacology, 107*(2–3), 271–276.

Humphreys, K. L., Eng, T., & Lee. S. S. (2013). Stimulant medication and substance use outcomes a meta-analysis. *Journal of the American Medical Association Psychiatry, 70*, 740–749.

Iacono, W. G., Malone, S. M., & McGue, M. (2008). Behavioral disinhibition and the development of early-onset addiction: Common and specific influences. *Annual Review of Clinical Psychology, 4*, 325–348.

Iacono, W. G., & McGue, M. (2006). Association between P3 event-related brain potential amplitude and adolescent problem behavior. *Psychophysiology, 43*, 465–469.

Jester, J. M., Nigg, J. T., Adams, K., Fitzgerald, H. E., Puttler, L. I., Wong, M. M., et al. (2005). Inattention/hyperactivity and aggression from early childhood to adolescence: Heterogeneity of trajectories and differential influence of family environment characteristics. *Development and Psychopathology, 17*, 99–125.

Jensen, P. S., Kettle, L., Roper, M. T., Sloan, M. T., Dulcan, M. K., Hoven, C., et al. (1999). Are stimulants overprescribed? Treatment of ADHD in four U. S. communities. *Journal of the American Academy of Child & Adolescent Psychiatry, 38*(7), 797–804.

Johnston, C., & Chronis-Tuscano, A. M. (2014). Families of children with ADHD. In R. A. Barkley (Ed.), *Attention-deficit/hyperactivity disorder: A handbook for diagnosis and treatment* (4th ed.). New York: Guilford.

Jonah, B. A. (1997). Sensation seeking and risky driving: A review and synthesis of the literature. *Accident Analysis & Prevention, 29*(5), 651–665.

Kalbag, A. S., & Levin, F. R. (2005). Adult ADHD and substance abuse: Diagnostic and treatment issues. *Substance Use and Misuse, 40*(13-14), 1955–1981.

Kandel, D. B. (2002). *Stages and pathways of drug involvement: Examining the gateway hypothesis.* New York: Cambridge University Press.

Kessler, R. C., Adler, L., Barkley, R., Biederman, J., Conners, C. K., Demler, O., et al. (2006). The prevalence and correlates of adult ADHD in the United States: Results from the National Comorbidity Survey Replication. *American Journal of Psychiatry, 163*(4), 716–723.

Kessler, R. C., Adler, L. A., Barkley, R., Biederman, J., Conners, C. K., Faraone, S. V., et al. (2005). Patterns and predictors of Attention-Deficit/Hyperactivity Disorder persistence into adulthood: Results from the National Comorbidity Survey Replication. *Biological Psychiatry, 57*(11), 1442–1451.

Kessler, R. C., Berglund, P., Demler, O., Jin, R., Merikangas, K. R., & Walters, E. E. (2005). Lifetime prevalence and age-of-onset distributions of DSM-IV disorders in the National Comorbidity Survey Replication. *Archives of General Psychiatry, 62*(6), 593–602.

Klein, R. G. (2002). Alcohol, stimulants, nicotine, and other drugs in ADHD. In P. S. Jensen & J. R. Cooper (Eds.), *Attention-deficit/hyperactivity disorder: State of the science/best practices* (pp. 16–1–16–17). Kingston, NJ: Civic Research Institute.

Knop, J., Penick, E. C., Nickel, E. J., Mortensen, E. L., Sullivan, M. A., Murtaza, S., et al. (2009). Childhood ADHD and conduct disorder as independent predictors of male alcohol dependence at age 40. *Journal of Studies on Alcohol and Drugs, 70*(2), 169–177.

Knopik, V. S., Heath, A. C., Jacob, T., Slutske, W. S., Bucholz, K. K., Madden, P. A. F., et al. (2006). Maternal alcohol use disorder and offspring ADHD: Disentangling genetic and environmental effects using a children-of-twins design. *Psychological Medicine, 36*(10), 1461–1471.

Kollins, S. H. (2003). Comparing the abuse potential of methylphenidate versus other stimulants: A review of available evidence and relevance to the ADHD patient. *Journal of Clinical Psychiatry, 64*(11), 14–18.

Kollins, S. H., McClernon, F. J., & Fuemmeler, B. F. (2005). Association between smoking and attention-deficit/hyperactivity disorder symptoms in a population-based sample of young adults. *Archives of General Psychiatry, 62*(10), 1142–1147.

Kooij, J. J. S., Boonstra, A. M., Swinkels, S. H. N., Bekker, E. M., de Noord, I., & Buitelaar, J. K. (2008). Reliability, validity, and utility of instruments for self-report and informant report concerning symptoms of ADHD in adult patients. *Journal of Attention Disorders, 11*(4), 445–458.

Kotov, R., Gamez, W., Schmidt, F., & Watson, D. (2010). Linking "big" personality traits to anxiety, depressive, and substance use disorders: A meta-analysis. *Psychological Bulletin, 136*(5), 768–821.

Krause, K. H., Dresel, S. H., Krause, J., Kung, H. F., & Tatsch, K. (2000). Increased striatal dopamine transporter in adult patients with attention deficit hyperactivity disorder: Effects of methylphenidate as measured by single photon emission computed tomography. *Neuroscience Letters, 285*, 107–110.

Krause, K. H., Dresel, S. H., Krause, J., Kung, H. F., Tatsch, K., & Ackenheil, M. (2002). Stimulant-like action of nicotine on striatal dopamine transporter in the brain of adults with attention deficit hyperactivity disorder. *International Journal of Neuropsychopharmacology, 5*(2), 111–113.

Kreek, M. J., Nielsen, C. A., Butelman, E. R., & LaForge, K. S. (2005). Genetic influences on impulsivity, risk taking, stress responsivity and vulnerability to drug abuse and addiction. *Nature Neuroscience, 8*(11), 1450–1457.

Kuperman, S., Schlosser, S. S., Kramer, J. R., Bucholz, K., Hesselbrock, V., Reich, T., et al. (2001). Developmental sequence from disruptive behavior diagnosis to adolescent alcohol dependence. *American Journal of Psychiatry, 158*(12), 2022–2026.

Lahey, B. B., Applegate, B., McBurnett, K., Biederman, J., Greenhill, L., Hynd, G. W., et al. (1994). DSM-IV field trials for attention deficit hyperactivity disorder in children and adolescents. *American Journal of Psychiatry, 151*(11), 1673–1685.

Lambert, N. M. (2002). Stimulant treatment as a risk factor for nicotine use and substance abuse. In P. S. Jensen & J. R. Cooper (Eds.), *Attention deficit hyperactivity disorder: State of science: Best practices* (pp. 18–1—18–24). Kingston, NJ: Civic Research Institute.

Lambert, N. M., & Hartsough, C. S. (1998). Prospective study of tobacco smoking and substance dependencies among samples of ADHD and non-ADHD participants. *Journal of Learning Disabilities, 31*, 533-544.

Lang, A. R., Pelham, W. E., Atkeson, B. M., & Murphy, D. A. (1999). Effects of alcohol intoxication on parenting behavior in interactions with child confederates exhibiting normal or deviant behaviors. *Journal of Abnormal Child Psychology, 27*, 177–189.

Larisch, R., Sitte, W., Antke, C., Nikolaus, S., Franz, M., Tress, W., et al. (2006). Striatal dopamine transporter density in drug naive patients with attention-deficit/hyperactivity disorder. *Nuclear Medicine Communications, 27*, 267–270.

Laucht, M., Becker, K., Blomeyer, D., & Schmidt, M. (2007). Novelty seeking involved in mediating the association between the dopamine D4 Receptor Gene Exon III polymorphism and heavy drinking in male adolescents: Results from a high-risk community sample. *Biological Psychiatry, 61*(1), 87–92.

Lee, S. S., & Hinshaw, S. P. (2006). Predictors of adolescent functioning in girls with Attention Deficit Hyperactivity Disorder (ADHD): The role of childhood ADHD, conduct problems, and peer status. *Journal of Clinical Child and Adolescent Psychology, 35*(3), 356–368.

Lee, S. S., Humphreys, K. L., Liu, R., Flory, K., & Glass, K. (2011). Prospective association of childhood attention-deficit/hyperactivity disorder (ADHD) and substance use and abuse/dependence: A meta-analytic review. *Clinical Psychology Review, 31*, 328–341.

Levin, E. D., Conners, C. K., Sparrow, E., Hinton, S. C., Erhardt, D., Meck, W. H., et al. (1996). Nicotine effects on adults with attention-deficit/hyperactivity disorder. *Psychopharmacology, 123*, 55–63.

Levin, F. R., Evans, S. M., McDowell, D. M., & Kleber, H. D. (1998). Methylphenidate treatment for cocaine abusers with adult attention-deficit hyperactivity disorder: A pilot study. *Journal of Clinical Psychiatry, 59*, 300–305.

Levin, F. R., Evans, S. M., Vosburg, S. K., Horton, T., Brooks, D., & Ng, J. (2004). Impact of attention-deficit hyperactivity disorder and other psychopathology on treatment retention among cocaine abusers in a therapeutic community. *Addictive Behavior, 29*, 1875–1882.

Liddle, H. A., Dakog, G. A., Diamond, G. S., Barrett, K., & Tejeda, M. (2001). Multidimensional family therapy for adolescent substance abuse: Results of a randomized clinical trial. *American Journal of Drug and Alcohol Abuse, 27*, 651–687.

Lijffijt, M., Kenemans, L., Verbaten, M. N., & van Engeland, H. (2005). A meta-analytic review of stopping performance in attention-deficit/hyperactivity disorder: Deficient inhibitory motor control? *Journal of Abnormal Psychology, 114*(2), 216–222.

Linnet, K. M., Dalsgaard, S., Obel, C., Wisborg, K., Henriksen, T. B., Rodriguez, A., et al. (2003). Maternal lifestyle factors in pregnancy risk of attention deficit hyperactivity disorder and associated behaviors: Review of the current evidence. *American Journal of Psychiatry, 160*(6), 1028–1040.

Loeber, R., Stouthamer-Loeber, M., & White, H. R. (1999). Developmental aspects of delinquency and internalizing problems and their association with persistent juvenile substance use between ages 7 and 18. *Journal of Clinical Child Psychology, 28*(3), 322–332.

Logan, G. D., & Irwin, D. E. (2000). Don't look! Don't touch! Inhibitory control of eye and hand movements. *Psychonomic Bulletin and Review, 7*, 107–112.

Loney, J., Kramer, J. R., & Salisbury, H. (2002). Medicated versus unmedicated children—Adult involvement with legal and illegal drugs. In P. S. Jensen & J. R. Cooper (Eds.), *Attention-deficit/hyperactivity disorder: State of the science/best practices* (pp. 17–1–17–16). Kingston, NJ: Civic Research Institute.

Lynam, D. R. (1996). Early identification of chronic offenders: Who is the fledgling psychopath? *Psychological Bulletin, 120*(2), 209–234.

Lynam, D. R., Hoyle, R. H., & Newman, J. P. (2006). The perils of partialling: Cautionary tales from aggression and psychopathy. *Assessment, 13*(3), 328–341.

Lynskey, M. T., & Fergusson, D. M. (1995). Childhood conduct problems, attention deficit behaviors, and adolescent alcohol, tobacco, and illicit drug use. *Journal of Abnormal Child Psychology, 23*, 281–302.

Mannuzza, S., Gittelman-Klein, R., Bessler, A., Malloy, P., & LaPadula, M. (1993). Adult outcome of hyperactive boys: Educational achievement, occupational rank, and psychiatric status. *Archives of General Psychiatry, 50*, 565–576.

Mannuzza, S., Klein, R. G., Abikoff, H., & Moulton, J. L. (2004). Significance of childhood conduct problems to later development of Conduct Disorder among children with ADHD: A prospective follow-up study. *Journal of Abnormal Child Psychology, 32*(5), 565–573.

Mannuzza, S., Klein, R., Bessler, A., Malloy, P., & LaPadula, M. (1998). Adult psychiatric status of hyperactive boys grown up. *American Journal of Psychiatry, 155*, 493–498.

Mannuzza, S., Klein, R. G., Bonagura, N., Malloy, P., Giampino, T. L., & Addalli, K. A. (1991). Hyperactive boys almost grown up: V. Replication of psychiatric status. *Archives of General Psychiatry, 48*, 77–83.

Marshal, M. P., Molina, B., & Pelham, W. E. (2003). Deviant peer affiliation as a risk factor for substance use in adolescents with childhood ADHD. *Psychology of Addictive Behaviors, 17*, 293–302.

Martinez, D., Broft, A., Foltin, R. W., Slifstein, M., Hwang, D., Huang, Y., et al. (2004). Cocaine dependence and D2 receptor availability in the functional subdivisions of the striatum: Relationship with cocaine-seeking behavior. *Neuropsychopharmacology, 29*, 1190–1202.

Martinez, D., Gil, R., Slifstein, M., Hwang, D., Huang, Y., Perez, A., et al. (2005). Alcohol dependence is associated with blunted dopamine transmission in the ventral striatum. *Biological Psychiatry, 58*, 779–786.

Martinez, D., Narendran, R., Foltin, R. W., Slifstein, M., Hwang, D., Broft, A., et al. (2007). Amphetamine-induced dopamine release: Markedly blunted in cocaine dependence and predictive of the choice to self-administer cocaine. *American Journal of Psychiatry, 164*, 622–629.

Masse, L. C., & Tremblay, R. E. (1997). Behavior of boys in kindergarten and the onset of substance use during adolescence. *Archives of General Psychiatry, 54*, 62–68.

Mayes, L. C., & Bornstein, M. H. (1997). The development of children exposed to cocaine. In S. S. Luthar, J. A. Burack, D. Cicchetti, & J. Weisz (Eds.), *Developmental psychopathology* (pp. 166–188). New York: Cambridge University Press.

McClernon, F., & Kollins, S. (2008). ADHD and smoking: From genes to brain to behavior. *Annals of the New York Academy of Sciences, 1141*, 131–147.

Mick, E., Biederman, J., Faraone, S. V., Sayer, J., & Kleinman, S. (2002). Case-control study of attention-deficit hyperactivity disorder and maternal smoking, alcohol use, and drug use during pregnancy. *Journal of the American Academy of Child and Adolescent Psychiatry, 41*, 378–385.

Milberger, S., Biederman, J., Faraone, S. V., Chen, L., & Jones, J. (1996). Is maternal smoking during pregnancy a risk factor for attention deficit hyperactivity disorder in children? *American Journal of Psychiatry, 153*, 1138–1142.

Milberger, S., Biederman, J., Faraone, S. V., Chen, L., & Jones, J. (1997). ADHD is associated with early initiation of cigarette smoking in children and adolescents. *Journal of Academic Child Adolescent Psychiatry, 36*, 37–44.

Milberger, S., Biederman, J., Faraone, S. V., & Jones, J. (1998). Further evidence of an association between maternal smoking during pregnancy and attention deficit hyperactivity disorder: Findings from a high-risk sample of siblings. *Journal of Clinical Child Psychology, 27*, 352–358.

Milich, R., & Landau, S. (1988). Teacher ratings of inattention/overactivity and aggression: Cross-validation with classroom observations. *Journal of Clinical Child Psychology, 17*(1), 92–97.

Miller, D. J., Derefinko, K. J., Lynam, D. R., Milich, R., & Fillmore, M. T. (2010). Impulsivity and attention deficit-hyperactivity disorder: Subtype classification using the UPPS Impulsive Behavior Scale. *Journal of Psychopathology and Behavioral Assessment, 32*(3), 323–332.

Moffitt, T. E. (1993). Adolescence-limited and life-course-persistent antisocial behavior: A developmental taxonomy. *Psychological Review, 100*(4), 674–701.

Molina, B., & Pelham, W. E. (2001). Substance use, substance abuse, and LD among adolescents with a childhood history of ADHD. *Journal of Learning Disabilities, 34*, 333–342.

Molina, B. S., Pelham, W. E., Cheong, J., Marshal, M. P., Gnagy, E. M., & Curran, P. J. (2012). Childhood attention-deficit/hyperactivity disorder (ADHD) and growth in adolescent alcohol use: The roles of functional impairments, ADHD symptom persistence, and parental knowledge. *Journal of Abnormal Psychology, 121*, 922–935.

Molina, B. S. G. (2011). Delinquency and substance use in ADHD: Adolescent and young adult outcomes in developmental context. In S. W. Evans & B. Hoza (Eds.), *Treating Attention deficit hyperactivity disorder: Assessment and intervention in developmental context* (19:1-52)). Kingston, NJ: Civic Research Institute.

Molina, B. S. G., Flory, K., Hinshaw, S. P., Greiner, A. R., Arnold, L. E., Swanson, J. M., et al. (2007). Delinquent behavior and emerging substance use in the MTA at 36 months: Prevalence, course, and treatment effects. *Journal of the American Academy of Child and Adolescent Psychiatry, 46*(8), 1028–1040.

Molina, B. S. G., Hinshaw, S. P., Arnold, L. E., Swanson, J. M., et al. (2013). Adolescent substance use in the multimodal treatment study of attention-deficit/hyperactivity disorder (ADHD) (MTA) as a function of childhood ADHD, random assignment to childhood treatments, and subsequent medication. *Journal of the American Academy of Child and Adolescent Psychiatry, 52*, 250–263.

Molina, B. S. G., Hinshaw, S. P., Swanson, J. M., Arnold, L. E., Vitiello, B., Jensen, P. J., et al. (2009). The MTA at 8 years: Prospective follow-up of children treated for combined-type ADHD in a multisite study. *Journal of the American Academy of Child and Adolescent Psychiatry, 48*, 484–500.

Molina, B. S. G., & Pelham, W. E. (2003). Childhood predictors of adolescent substance use in a longitudinal study of children with ADHD. *Journal of Abnormal Psychology, 112*, 497–507.

Molina, B. S. G., & Pelham, W. E. (2014). Attention deficit/ hyperactivity disorder and risk of substance use disorder: Developmental considerations, potential pathways, and opportunities for research. *Annual Review of Clinical Psychology, 10*, 607-640.

Molina, B. S. G., Pelham, W. E., Gnagy, E. M., Thompson, A. L., & Marshal, M. P. (2007). Attention-deficit/hyperactivity disorder risk for heavy drinking and alcohol use disorder is age specific. *Alcoholism: Clinical and Experimental Research, 31*(4), 643–654.

Molina, B. S. G., Smith, B. H., & Pelham, W. E. (1999). Interactive effects of attention deficit hyperactivity disorder and conduct disorder on early adolescent substance use. *Psychology of Addictive Behaviors, 13*, 348–358.

Molina, B. S. G., Smith, B. H., & Pelham, W. E. (2001). Factor structure and criterion validity of secondary school teacher ratings of ADHD and ODD. *Journal of Abnormal Child Psychology, 29*(1), 71–82.

Morrow, C. E., Accornero, V. H., Xue, L., Manjunath, S., Culbertson, J. L., Anthony, J. C., et al. (2009). Estimated risk of developing selected DSM-IV disorders among 5-year-old children with prenatal cocaine exposure. *Journal of Child and Family Studies, 18*, 356–364.

Munro, C. A., McCaul, M. E., Wong, D. F., Oswald, L. M., Zhou, Y., Brasic, J., et al. (2006). Sex differences in striatal dopamine release in healthy adults. *Biological Psychiatry, 59*(10), 966–974.

Murphy, K., & Barkley, R. A. (1996). Attention deficit hyperactivity disorder in adults: Comorbidity and adaptive impairments. *Comprehensive Psychiatry, 37*, 393–401.

National Institute on Drug Abuse (NIDA). (2006). *Principles of drug abuse treatment for criminal justice populations: A research-based guide* (NIH Publication No. 06-5316). Washington, DC: US Government Printing Office.

Newman, J. P., & Wallace, J. F. (1993). Diverse pathways to deficient self-regulation: Implications for disinhibitory psychopathology in children. *Clinical Psychology Review, Special Issue: Disinhibition disorders in childhood, 13*(8), 699–720.

Nigg, J. T. (2000). On inhibition/disinhibition in developmental psychopathology: Views from cognitive and personality psychology and a working inhibition taxonomy. *Psychological Bulletin, 126*, 220–246.

Nigg, J. T. (2005). Attention, task difficulty, and ADHD. *British Journal of Developmental Psychology, 23*, 513–516.

Nigg, J. T., Glass, J. M., Wong, M. M., Poon, E., Jester, J. M., et al. (2004). Neuropsychological executive functioning in children at elevated risk for alcoholism: Findings in early adolescence. *Journal of Abnormal Psychology, 113*, 302–314.

Nyman, E. S., Ogdie, M. N., Loukola, A., Varilo, T., Taanila, A., Hurtig, T., et al. (2007). ADHD candidate gene study in a population-based birth cohort: Association with DBH and DRD2. *Journal of the American Academy of Child and Adolescent Psychiatry, 46*, 1614–1621.

O'Connor, T. G., Heron, J., Golding, J., Beveridge, M., & Glover, V. (2002). Maternal antenatal anxiety and children's behavioural/emotional problems at 4 years: Report from the Avon Longitudinal Study of Parents and Children. *British Journal of Psychiatry, 180*, 502–508.

Patterson, G. R., DeGarmo, D. S., & Knutson, N. (2000). Hyperactive and antisocial behaviors: Comorbid or two points in the same process? *Development and Psychopathology, 12*, 91–106.

Pelham, W., & Lang, A. (1993). Parental alcohol consumption and deviant child behavior: Laboratory studies of reciprocal effects. *Clinical Psychology Review, 13*(8), 763–784.

Pelham, W. E., & Bender, M. E. (1982). Peer relationships in hyperactive children: Description and treatment. In K. Gadow & I. Bialer (Eds.), *Advances in learning and behavioral disabilities* (Vol. 1, pp. 366–436). Greenwich, CT: JAI.

Pelham, W. E., & Fabiano, G. A. (2008). Evidence-based psychosocial treatment for attention deficit/hyperactivity disorder: An update. *Journal of Clinical Child and Adolescent Psychology, 37*(1), 185–214.

Pelham, W. E., Fabiano, G. A., & Massetti, G. M. (2005). Evidence-based assessment of attention deficit hyperactivity disorder in children and adolescents. *Journal of Clinical Child and Adolescent Psychology, 34*(3), 449–476.

Pelham, W. E., Gnagy, E. M., Greiner, A. R., Waschbusch, D. A., Fabiano, G. A., & Burrows-MacLean, L. (2010). Summer treatment programs for attention-deficit/hyperactivity disorder. In Weisz, J. R., & Kazdin, A. E. (Eds.), *Evidence-based psychotherapies for children and adolescents* (2nd ed., pp. 277–292). New York: Guilford.

Pelham, W. E., Jr., Gnagy, E., Greenslade, K. E., & Milich, R. (1992). Teacher ratings of DSM–III–R symptoms for the disruptive behavior disorders. *Journal of the American Academy of Child and Adolescent Psychiatry, 31*, 210–218.

Pelham, W. E., Lang, A. R., Atkeson, B., Murphy, D. A., Gnagy, E. M., et al. (1997). Effects of deviant child behavior on parental distress and alcohol consumption in laboratory interactions. *Journal of Abnormal Child Psychology, 25*, 413–424.

Persico, A. M., Bird, G., Gabbay, F. H., & Uhl, G. R. (1996). D2 dopamine receptor gene TaqI A1 and B1 restriction fragment length polymorphisms: Enhanced frequencies in psychostimulant-preferring polysubstance abusers. *Biological Psychiatry, 40*, 776–784.

Petry, N. M., & Simic, F. (2002). Recent advances in the dissemination of contingency management techniques: Clinical and research perspectives. *Journal of Substance Abuse Treatment, 23*, 81–86.

Pillow, D. R., Pelham, W. E., Hoza, B. Molina, B. S. G., & Stultz, C. H. (1998). Confirmatory factor analyses examining attention deficit hyperactivity disorder symptoms and other childhood disruptive behaviors. *Journal of Abnormal Child Psychology, 26*(4), 293–309.

Poltavski, D. V., & Petros, T. (2006). Effects of transdermal nicotine on attention in adult non-smokers with and without attentional deficits. *Physiology & Behavior, 87*(3), 614–624.

Pomerleau, O. F., Downey, K. K., Stelson, F. W., & Pomerleau, C. S. (1995). Cigarette smoking in adult patients diagnosed with attention deficit hyperactivity disorder. *Journal of Substance Abuse, 7*(3), 373–378.

Potter, A. S., & Newhouse, P. A. (2004). Effects of acute nicotine on behavioral inhibition in adolescents with attention-deficit/ hyperactivity disorder. *Psychopharmacology, 176*, 182–194.

Potter, A. S., & Newhouse, P. A. (2008). Acute nicotine improves cognitive deficits in young adults with attention-deficit/ hyperactivity disorder. *Pharmacology, Biochemistry and Behavior, 88*(4), 407–417.

Reese, F., Chassin, L., & Molina, B. S. G. (1994). Alcohol expectancies in early adolescents, predicting drinking behavior from alcohol expectancies and parental alcoholism. *Journal of Studies on Alcohol, 55*, 276–284.

Riccardi, P., Zald, D., Li, R., Park, S., Ansari, M. S., Dawant, B., et al. (2006). Sex differences in amphetamine-induced displacement of [¹⁸F]Fallypride in striatal and extrastriatal regions: A PET study. *American Journal of Psychiatry, 163*(9), 1639–1641.

Riggs, P. D., Hall, S. K., Mikulich-Gilbertson, S. K., Lohman, M., & Kayser, A. (2004). A randomized controlled trial of pemoline for attention-deficit/hyperactivity disorder in substance-abusing adolescents. *Journal of the American Academy of Child & Adolescent Psychiatry, 43*(4), 420–429.

Riggs, P. D., Leon, S. L., Mikulich, S. K., & Pottle, L. C. (1998). An open trial of bupropion for ADHD in adolescents with substance use disorders and conduct disorder. *Journal of the American Academy of Child and Adolescent Psychiatry, 37,* 1271–1278.

Riggs, P. D., Winhusen, T., Davies, R. D., Leimberger, J. D., Mikulich-Gilbertson, S., Klein, C., . . . & Liu, D. (2011). Randomized controlled trial of osmotic-release methylphenidate with cognitive-behavioral therapy in adolescents with attention-deficit/hyperactivity disorder and substance use disorders. *Journal of the American Academy of Child & Adolescent Psychiatry, 50,* 903–914.

Roache, J. D., Grabowski, J., Schmitz, J. M., Creson, D. L., & Rhoades, H. M. (2000). Laboratory measures of methylphenidate effects in cocaine-dependent patients receiving treatment. *Journal of Clinical Psychopharmacology, 20,* 61–68.

Robins, L. N., & Pryzbeck, T. R. (1985). *Age of onset of drug use as a factor in drug and other disorders* (NIDA Research Monograph, No. 56, pp. 178–192). Washington, DC: National Institute on Drug Abuse.

Robinson, T. E., & Berridge, K. C. (1993). The neural basis of drug craving: An incentive sensitization theory of addiction. *Brain Research Reviews, 18,* 247–291.

Robinson, T. E., & Berridge, K. C. (2000). The psychology and neurobiology of addiction: An incentive–sensitization view. *Addiction, 95,* S91–S117.

Robinson, T. E., & Kolb, B. (2004). Structural plasticity associated with exposure to drugs of abuse. *Neuropharmacology, 47*(Suppl. 1), 33–46.

Rohde L. A., Biederman J., Busnello E. A., Zimmermann H., & Schmitz M. (1999). ADHD in a school sample of Brazilian adolescents: A study of prevalence, comorbid conditions and impairments. *Journal of the American Academy of Child and Adolescent Psychiatry, 38,* 716–722.

Rosch, K., Fosco, W., Pelham, W. Waxmonsky, J., Bubnik, M., & Hawk, L (2015). Reinforcement and stimulant medication ameliorate deficient response inhibition in children with attention-deficit/hyperactivity disorder.

Rösler, M., Retz, W., Yaqoobi, K., Burg, E., & Retz-Junginger, P. (2008). Attention deficit/hyperactivity disorder in female offenders: Prevalence, psychiatric comorbidity and psychosocial implications. *European Archives of Psychiatry and Clinical Neuroscience, 259,* 98–105.

Rush, C. R., Higgins, S. T., Vansickel, A. R., Stoops, W. W., Lile, J. A., & Glaser, P. E. A. (2005). Methylphenidate increases cigarette smoking. *Psychopharmacology, 181,* 781–789.

Safren, S. A. (2006). Cognitive-behavioral approaches to ADHD treatment in adulthood. *Journal of Clinical Psychiatry, 67*(Suppl. 8), 46–50.

Schmitz, M., Denardin, D., Silva, T. L., Pianca, T., Hutz, M. H., Faraone, S., et al. (2006). Smoking during pregnancy and attention-deficit/hyperactivity disorder, predominantly inattentive type: A case-control study. *Journal of the American Academy of Child and Adolescent Psychiatry, 45*(11), 1338–1345.

Schubiner, H. (2005). Substance abuse in patients with attention-deficit hyperactivity disorder: Therapeutic implications. *CNS Drugs, 19*(8), 643–655.

Schubiner, H., Downey, K. K., Arfken, C. L., Johanson, C., Schuster, C. R., Lockhart, N., et al. (2002). Double-blind placebo-controlled trial of methylphenidate in the treatment of adult ADHD patients with comorbid cocaine dependence. *Experimental Clinical Psychopharmacology, 10*(3), 286–294.

Shaffer, D., Fisher, D., Dulcan, M. K., Davies, M., Piacentini, J., Schwab- Stone, M. E., et al. (1996). The NIMH Diagnostic Interview Schedule for Children version 2.3 (DISC-2.3): Description, acceptability, prevalence rates, and performance in the MECA study. *Journal of the American Academy of Child and Adolescent Psychiatry, 35,* 865–877.

Shaw, G. A., & Giambra, L. M. (1993). Task unrelated thoughts of college students diagnosed as hyperactive in childhood. *Developmental Neuropsychology, 9,* 17–30.

Shea, T., & Fisher, B. E. (1996). Self ratings of mood levels and mood variability as predictors of Junior I-6 impulsivity and ADHD classroom behaviors. *Personality and Individual Differences, 20,* 209–214.

Sher, K. J. (1991). *Children of alcoholics: A critical appraisal of theory and research.* The John D. and Catherine T. MacArthur Foundation series on mental health and development. Chicago, IL: University of Chicago.

Sher, K. J., Grekin, E. R., & Williams, N. A. (2005). The development of alcohol use disorders. *Annual Review of Clinical Psychology, 1*(1), 493–523.

Shiels, K., Hawk, L., Reynolds, B., Mazzullo, R., Rhodes, J., Pelham, W., Waxmonsky, J., & Gangloff, B. (2009). The effects of methylphenidate in discounting of delayed rewards in ADHD. *Experimental and clinical psychopharmacology, 17*(5), 291–301.

Sibley, M. H., Kuriyan, A. B., Evans, S. W., Waxmonsky, J. G., & Smith, B. H. (2014*b*). Pharmacological and psychosocial treatments for ADHD in adolescents: An updated systematic review of the literature. *Clinical Psychology Review, 34,* 218–232.

Sibley, M. H., Pelham, W. E., Evans, S. W., Gnagy, E. M., Ross, J. M., & Greiner, A. R. (2011). Evaluation of a summer treatment program for adolescents with attention deficit/ hyperactivity disorder. *Cognitive and Behavioral Practice, 18,* 530–544.

Sibley, M. H., Pelham, W. E., Jr., Molina, B. S., Gnagy, E. M., Waschbusch, D. A., et al. (2012*a*). Diagnosing ADHD in adolescence. *Journal of Consulting and Clinical Psychology, 80,* 139–150.

Sibley, M. H., Pelham, W. E., Molina, B. S., Gnagy, E. M., Waxmonsky, J. G., et al. (2012*b*). When diagnosing ADHD in young adults emphasize informant reports, DSM items, and impairment. *Journal of Consulting and Clinical Psychology, 80,* 1052–1061.

Sibley, M. H. Pelham, W. E., Molina, B. S. G., Kipp, H., Gnagy, E. M., Meinzer, M., Ross, J. M. Lahey, B. B. (2014*a*). The role of early childhood ADHD and subsequent CD in the initiation and escalation of adolescent cigarette, alcohol, and marijuana use. *Journal of Abnormal Psychology, 123,* 362–374.

Sintov, N. D., Kendler, K. S., Walsh, D., Patterson, D. G., & Prescott, C. A. (2009). Predictors of illicit substance dependence among individuals with alcohol dependence. *Journal of Studies on Alcohol and Drugs, 70*(2), 269–278.

Smith, B., Barkley, R., & Shapiro, C. (2006). Attention-deficit/ hyperactivity disorder. Treatment of childhood disorders. In E. J. Mash & R. A. Barkley (Eds.), *Treatment of childhood disorders* (3rd. ed., pp. 65–136). New York: Guilford.

Solhkhah, R., Wilens, T. E., Daly, J., Prince, J. B., Van Patten, S. L., & Biederman, J. (2005). Bupropion SR for the treatment of substance abusing outpatient adolescents with attention-deficit/hyperactivity disorder and mood disorders. *Journal of Child and Adolescent Psychopharmacology, 15,* 777–786.

Spencer, T. J. (2009). Issues in the management of patients with complex ADHD symptoms. *Journal of Pediatrics, 154*(5, Suppl.), S4–S12.

Stanger, C., Budney, A. J., Kamon, J. L., & Thostensen, J. (2009). A randomized trial of contingency management for adolescent marijuana abuse and dependence. *Drug and Alcohol Dependence, 105*(3), 240–247.

Steinhausen, H., Göbel, D., & Nestler, V. (1984). Psychopathology in the offspring of alcoholic parents. *Journal of the American Academy of Child Psychiatry, 23*(4), 465–471.

Strand, M., Hawk, L., Bubnik, M., Shiels, K., Pelham, W., & Waxmonsky, J. (2012). Improving working memory in children with ADHD: The separate and combined effects of incentives and stimulant medication. *Journal of Abnormal Child Psychology, 40,* 1193–1207.

Streissguth, A. P., Barr, H. M., Sampson, P. D., & Bookstein, F. L. (1994). Prenatal alcohol and offspring development: The first fourteen years. *Drug and Alcohol Dependence, 36,* 89–99.

Substance Abuse and Mental Health Services Administration (SAMHSA). (2003). *Overview of findings from the 2002 National Survey on Drug Use and Health.* Rockville, MD: Author.

Sullivan, M. A., & Rudnik-Levin, F. (2001). Attention deficit/ hyperactivity disorder and substance abuse: Diagnostic and therapeutic considerations. *Annals of the New York Academy of Sciences, 931,* 251–270.

Swanson, J. M., Flodman, P., Kennedy, J., Spence, M. A., Moyzis, R., Schuck, S., et al. (2000). Dopamine genes and ADHD. *Neuroscience and Biobehavioral Reviews, 24*(1), 21–25.

Swanson, J. M., Kinsbourne, M., Nigg, J., Lanphear, B., Stefanatos, G. A., Volkow, N., et al. (2007). Etiologic subtypes of attention-deficit/hyperactivity disorder: Brain imaging, molecular genetic and environmental factors and the dopamine hypothesis. *Neuropsychology Review, 17,* 39–59.

Szatmari, P., Offord, D. R., & Boyle, M. (1989). Ontario Child Health Study: Prevalence of attention deficit disorder with hyperactivity. *Journal of Child Psychology and Psychiatry, 30,* 219–230.

Szobot, C. M., Rohde, L. A., Bukstein, O., Molina, B. S. G., Martins, C., Ruaro, P., et al. (2007). Is attention-deficit/ hyperactivity disorder associated with illicit substance use disorders in male adolescents? A community-based case-control study. *Addiction, 102,* 1122–1130.

Tarter, R., Vanyukov, M., Giancola, P., Dawes, M., Blackson, T., Mezzich, A., et al. (1999). Etiology of early age onset substance use disorder; a maturational perspective. *Developmental Psychopathology, 11,* 657–683.

Tercyak, K. P., Lerman, C., & Audrain, J. (2002). Association of attention-deficit/hyperactivity disorder symptoms with levels of cigarette smoking in a community sample of adolescents.

Journal of the American Academy of Child and Adolescent Psychiatry, 41(7), 799–805.

Thurstone, C., Riggs, P. D., Salomonsen-Sautel, S., & Mikulicn-Gilbertson, S. K. (2010). Randomized, controlled trial of atomoxetine for attention-deficit/hyperactivity disorder in adolescents with substance use disorder. *Journal of the American Academy of Child & Adolescent Psychiatry, 49*(6), 573–582.

Tidey, J. W., O'Neill, S. C., & Higgins, S. T. (2000). d-Amphetamine increases choice of cigarette smoking over monetary reinforcement. *Psychopharmacology, 153,* 85–92.

Todd, R. D., Huang, H., Smalley, S. L., Nelson, S. F., Willcutt, E. G., Pennington, B. F., et al. (2005). Collaborative analysis of DRD4 and DAT genotypes in population-defined ADHD subtypes. *Journal of Child Psychology and Psychiatry, 46,* 1067–1073.

Upadhyaya, H. P., & Carpenter, M. J. (2008). Is attention deficit hyperactivity disorder (ADHD) symptom severity associated with tobacco use? *American Journal on Addictions, 17*(3), 195–198.

Volkow, N. D., Fowler, J. S., Wang, G. J., Baler, R., & Telang, F. (2009). Imaging dopamine's role in drug abuse and addiction. *Neuropharmacology, 56,* 3–8.

Volkow, N. D., Wang, G. J., Fowler, J. S., Gatley, S. J., Logan, J., Ding, Y., et al. (1998). Dopamine transporter occupancies in the human brain induced by therapeutic doses of oral methylphenidate. *American Journal of Psychiatry, 155,* 1325–1331.

Volkow, N. D., Wang, G. J., Fowler, J. S., Logan, J., Gatley, S. J., Hitzemann, R., et al. (1997). Decreased striatal dopaminergic responsiveness in detoxified cocaine-dependent subjects. *Nature, 386,* 830–833.

Volkow, N. D., Wang, G. J., Kollins, S. H., Wigal, T. L., Newcorn, J. H., Telang, F., et al. (2009). Evaluating dopamine reward pathway in ADHD: Clinical implications. *Journal of the American Medical Association, 302*(10), 1084–1091.

Volkow, N. D., Wang, G. J., Newcorn, J., Fowler, J. S., Telang, F., Solanto, J. L., et al. (2007). Brain dopamine transporter levels in treatment and drug naive adults with ADHD. *Neuroimage, 34,* 1182–1190.

Volkow, N. D., Wang, G. J., Newcorn, J., Telang, F., Solanto, M. V., Fowler, J. S., et al. (2007). Depressed dopamine activity in caudate and preliminary evidence of limbic involvement in adults with attention-deficit/hyperactivity disorder. *Archives of General Psychiatry, 64,* 932–940.

Waldron, H. B., Slesnick, N., Brody, J. L., Turner, C. W., & Peterson, T. R. (2001). Treatment outcomes for adolescent substance abuse at 4- and 7- month assessments. *Journal of Consulting and Clinical Psychology, 69,* 802–813.

Waldron, H. B., & Turner, C. W. (2008). Evidence-based psychosocial treatments for adolescent substance abuse. *Journal of Clinical Child and Adolescent Psychology, 37*(1), 238–261.

Waschbusch, D. A. (2002). A meta-analytic examination of comorbid hyperactive–impulsive–attention problems and conduct problems. *Psychological Bulletin, 128,* 118–150.

Wasserman, G. A., Kline, J. K., Bateman, D. A., Chiriboga, C., Lumey, L. H., Friedlander, H., et al. (1998). Prenatal cocaine exposure and school age intelligence. *Drug and Alcohol Dependence, 50,* 203–210.

Weafer, J., Camarillo, D., Fillmore, M. T., Milich, R., & Marczinski, C. A. (2008). Simulated driving performance of adults with ADHD: Comparisons with alcohol intoxication. *Experimental and Clinical Psychopharmacology, 16,* 251–263.

Weafer, J., Fillmore, M. T., & Milich, R. (2009). Increased sensitivity to the disinhibiting effects of alcohol in adults with ADHD. *Experimental and Clinical Psychopharmacology, 17*, 113–121.

Wechsler, H., Lee, J. E., Kuo, M., & Lee, H. (2000). College binge drinking in the 1990s: A continuing problem: Results of the Harvard School of Public Health 1999 College Alcohol Study. *Journal of American College Health, 48*(5), 199–210.

Weinberg, N. Z. (1997). Cognitive and behavioral deficits associated with parental alcohol use. *Journal of the American Academy of Child and Adolescent Psychiatry, 36*, 1177–1186.

Weiss, M., Hechtman, L. T., & Weiss, G. (1999). *ADHD in adulthood.* Baltimore, MD: Johns Hopkins University Press.

Weissman, M. M., Warner, V., Wickramaratne, P. J., & Kandel, D. B. (1999). Maternal smoking during pregnancy and psychopathology in offspring followed to adulthood. *Journal of the American Academy of Child and Adolescent Psychiatry, 38*, 892–899.

Whalen, C. K., Jamner, L. D., Henker, B., Delfino, R. J., & Lozano, J. M. (2002). The ADHD spectrum and everyday life: Experience sampling of adolescent moods, activities, smoking, and drinking. *Child Development, 73*(1), 209–227.

Whalen, C. K., Jamner, L. D., Henker, B., Gehricke, J., & King, P. S. (2003). Is there a link between adolescent cigarette smoking and pharmacotherapy for ADHD? *Psychology of Addictive Behaviors, 17*(4), 332–335.

White, J. D. (1999). Personality, temperament and ADHD: A review of the literature. *Personality and Individual Differences, 27*(4), 589–598.

White, J. L., Moffitt, T. E., Caspi, A., Bartusch, D. J., Needles, D. J., & Stouthamer-Loeber, M. (1994). Measuring impulsivity and examining its relationship to delinquency. *Journal of Abnormal Psychology, 103*(2), 192–205.

Wilens, T. E., Adamson, J., Monuteaux, M. C., Faraone, S. V., Schillinger, M., Westerberg, D., et al. (2008). Effect of prior stimulant treatment for attention-deficit/hyperactivity disorder on subsequent risk for cigarette smoking and alcohol and drug use disorders in adolescents. *Archives of Pediatric and Adolescent Medicine, 162*(10), 916–921.

Wilens, T. E., Adamson, J., Sgambati, S., Whitley, J., Santry, A., Monuteaux, M. C., et al. (2007). Do individuals with ADHD self-medicate with cigarettes and substances of abuse? Results from a controlled family study of ADHD. *American Journal on Addictions, 16*(Suppl. 1), 14–21.

Wilens, T. E., Biederman, J., Kiely, K., Bredin, E., & Spencer, T. J. (1995). Pilot study of behavioral and emotional disturbances in the high-risk children of parents with opioid

dependence. *Journal of the American Academy of Child & Adolescent Psychiatry, 34*(6), 779–785.

Wilens, T. E., Biederman, J., Mick, M. E., Faraone, S. V., & Spencer, T. (1997). Attention deficit hyperactivity disorder (ADHD) is associated with early onset of substance use disorders. *Journal of Nervous and Mental Disease, 185*, 475–482.

Wilens, T. E., Biederman, J., & Spencer, T. J. (1996). Attention-deficit hyperactivity disorder and the psychoactive substance use disorders. *Child and Adolescent Psychiatric Clinics of North America, 5*(1), 73–91.

Williams, R. J., Chang, S. Y., & Addiction Centre Adolescent Research Group. (2000). A comprehensive and comparative review of adolescent substance abuse treatment outcome. *Clinical Psychology: Science and Practice, 7*, 138–166.

Wilson, J. J., & Levin, F. R. (2005). Attention-deficit/hyperactivity disorder and early-onset substance use disorders. *Journal of Child and Adolescent Psychopharmacology, 15*(5), 751–763.

Winters, K. C. (1999). Treating adolescents with substance use disorders: An overview of practice issues and treatment outcome. *Substance Abuse, 20*(4), 203–225.

Wise, B. K., Cuffe, S. P., & Fischer, T. (2001). Dual diagnosis and successful participation of adolescents in substance abuse treatment. *Journal of Substance Abuse Treatment, 21*, 161–165.

Wolchik, S. A., Sandler, I. N., Millsap, R. E., Plummer, B. A., Greene, S. M., Anderson, E. R., et al. (2002). Six-year follow-up of preventive interventions for children of divorce. A randomized controlled trial. *Journal of the American Medical Association, 288*(15), 1874–1881.

Yoon, H. H., Iacono, W. G., Malone, S. M., & McGue, M. (2006). Using the brain P300 response to identify novel phenotypes reflecting genetic vulnerability for adolescent substance misuse. *Addictive Behaviors, 31*, 1067–1087.

Zimmerman, R. S., Palmgreen, P. M., Noar, S. M., Lustria, M. L., Lu, H. Y., & Lee Horosewski, M. (2007). Effects of a televised two-city safer sex mass media campaign targeting high-sensation-seeking and impulsive-decision-making young adults. *Health Education and Behavior, 34*, 810–826.

Zucker, R. A. (2006). The developmental behavior genetics of drug involvement: Overview and comments. *Behavioral Genetics, 36*, 616–625.

Zucker, R. A., Donovan, J. E., Masten, A. S., Mattson, M. E., & Moss, H. B. (2008). Early developmental processes and the continuity of risk for underage drinking and problem drinking. *Pediatrics, 121*(Suppl. 4), S252–S272.

Serious Mental Illness

Kim T. Mueser, Douglas L. Noordsy, *and* Robert E. Drake

Abstract

The high comorbidity between substance use disorders and serious mental illnesses is a significant challenge to traditional treatment systems that have historically treated psychiatric and substance use disorders with different providers and agencies. Defining characteristics of serious mental illness include difficulty with work, performing in school or parenting, social difficulties, and problems caring for oneself. Common serious psychiatric disorders include schizophrenia, schizoaffective disorder, bipolar disorder, and severe major depression, posttraumatic stress disorder, and borderline personality disorder. The epidemiology of substance use disorders in serious mental illness is reviewed, including prevalence, correlates, and onset and course of the disorder. The clinical consequences of substance use disorders in this population are devastating for every possible aspect of the illness. Common factors may increase vulnerability to both substance abuse and psychiatric disorders. The principles of treating co-occurring disorders are based on modern integrated methods, as well as research on the effectiveness of integrated treatment.

Key Words: comorbidity, dual diagnosis, dual disorder, severe mental illness, schizophrenia, schizoaffective disorder, bipolar disorder, integrated treatment, stages of change, stages of treatment

Introduction

Serious mental illnesses (also sometimes referred to as *severe mental illness*) are psychiatric disorders that prevent individuals from achieving typical age appropriate goals for functioning for extended periods of time (Corrigan, Mueser, Bond, Drake, & Solomon, 2008). Serious mental illnesses most often interfere with the ability of individuals to function at work, in school, or parenting or result in difficulty taking care of oneself, living independently, and limiting the person's capacity to participate in and enjoy close relationships with others (Parabiaghi, Bonetto, Ruggeri, Lasalvia, & Leese, 2006; Ruggeri, Leese, Thornicroft, Bisoffi, & Tansella, 2000; Schinnar, Rothbard, Kanter, & Jung, 1990). When the negative effects of the psychiatric illness on these areas of functioning are sustained over a significant period of time, such as 6 months or more, family members often play a role in helping individuals get their basic needs met, and the person often becomes eligible for disability income, such as Social Security Supplemental Income or a Social Security Disability Income in the United States.

The most common diagnosis among persons with a serious psychiatric disorder include schizophrenia-spectrum disorders (schizophreniform disorder, schizophrenia, schizoaffective disorder, schizotypal personality disorder) (Siever, Kalus, & Keefe, 1993), bipolar disorder, and severe treatment-refractory major depression (Goldman, 1984). Although the preponderance of people with a mental illness have schizophrenia-spectrum or major mood disorders, severe anxiety disorders such as posttraumatic stress disorder (Friedman & Rosenheck, 1996) and obsessive compulsive disorder (Goodman, Rudorfer, & Maser, 2000) can also result in significant disability. In addition, some individuals with borderline personality disorder (Lieb, Zanarini, Schmahl, Linehan, & Bohus, 2004) have a sufficiently severe course of disorder to be included in the broad category of serious mental illness. Although serious mental illness includes a broad range of possible diagnosis, the present essay will focus primarily on individuals with schizophrenia and major mood disorders.

Epidemiology

In this section, we review the prevalence of substance use disorders in people with a mental illness, including patterns of abuse. We then describe correlates of substance use disorders in this population that can facilitate the identification of who is most likely to develop or have such a disorder. We then discuss the onset and natural course of substance use disorders in people with a serious mental illness.

Prevalence

There are a variety of methodological challenges associated with determining the prevalence of substance use disorders in persons with a serious mental illness, such as the optimal place to conduct the assessment, the instruments used to evaluate each disorder, and the sources of information tapped (Drake, Rosenberg, & Mueser, 1996; Galanter, Castaneda, & Ferman, 1988). The optimal way of determining the comorbidity of two disorders is to conduct a community-based survey and to evaluate the degree of co-occurrence of the two disorders within that sample. Community-based surveys provide more accurate estimates of comorbidity than do surveys of clinical populations (e.g., individuals in a clinic or hospital who are receiving treatment for an illness) because in clinical samples each disorder increases the chances of propelling a person into treatment, resulting in systematic overestimation of comorbidity (Berkson, 1949). However, serious mental illnesses such as schizophrenia and bipolar disorder have relatively low prevalence rates in the general population (Kessler et al., 2005; Kessler, Rubinow, Holmes, Abelson, & Zhao, 1997; Robins & Regier, 1991), making it difficult or impossible to assess enough people to accurately evaluate rates of comorbidity based solely on community surveys.

Multiple epidemiologic studies document the high rate of substance use problems in people with a serious mental illness, with 40–50% rates of lifetime substance use disorder in people with a serious mental illness, compared with rates of approximately 15% in the general population (Kessler et al., 1996;

Petrakis, Rosenheck, & Desai, 2011; Regier et al., 1990). These high rates of co-occurring substance use disorders in people with a mental illness are consistent with the limited number of other epidemiologic surveys that have examined comorbidity of substance abuse and serious mental illness (Jablensky et al., 1999).

In contrast to the limited number of community-based epidemiologic surveys conducted, multiple studies have been published examining the rates of substance use disorders in clinical samples of individuals with a serious mental illness (Dixon, 1999; Maslin et al., 2001; Mueser, Yarnold, & Bellack, 1992; Mueser et al., 1990, 2000; Kavanagh et al., 2004; Weaver et al., 2003). Most of these studies have been conducted at either mental health centers serving persons with a serious mental illness or inpatient psychiatric settings where acute exacerbations of psychiatric disorders are treated. Across the broad range of studies conducted in clinical settings, the general finding is that approximately 50–60% of persons with a serious psychiatric disorder develop a substance use disorder, either abuse or dependence, at some point during their life. Furthermore, research also indicates that current or recent substance use disorders (e.g., within the past 6 months) are present in 25–35% of persons with a serious mental disorder (Mueser, Bennett, & Kushner, 1995).

While approximately one-half of people with a serious mental illness have a substance use disorder at some point in their lives, rates of comorbidity are even higher when assessments are conducted in certain settings. For example, rates of substance abuse tend to be higher in people with a serious mental illness who are homeless (Caton et al., 1995; Caton, Shrout, Eagle, Opler, & Felix, 1994; Folsom et al., 2005; Susser, Struening, & Conover, 1989), incarcerated (Edens, Peters, & Hills, 1997; McCabe et al., 2012; Peters, Kearns, Murrin, & Dolente, 1992), or who present for treatment in an emergency department (Barbee, Clark, Craqanzano, Heintz, & Kehoe, 1989; Barry et al., 2006). Rates of comorbidity are inflated in the settings because, as discussed below, substance abuse often has negative effects on housing, involvement in the criminal justice system, and symptom stabilization.

Across most studies of comorbidity, alcohol is the most frequently abused substance (Cuffel, 1996; Kavanagh et al., 2004). Depending on the time and location, either cannabis or cocaine is most often the second most frequently abused substance (Mueser et al., 1992; Mueser et al., 1990). As in the general population (Heyman, 2013), the primary determinant of which substances are most likely to be abused by people with a serious mental illness is the availability of that substance in the individual's community and social group. Although some individuals with a serious mental illness show a clear preference for one type of substance over another, polysubstance abuse is more often the norm (Chen et al., 1992; Lecomte et al., 2013), with individuals changing their pattern of substance use depending on the market availability.

Correlates of Substance Use Disorder

Most of the demographic characteristics that are related to substance use disorders in the general population show similar relationships among persons with a serious mental illness (Bahorik, Newhill, & Eack, 2013; Dixon, Haas, Weiden, Sweeney, & Frances, 1991; Kavanagh et al., 2004; Montross et al., 2005; Mueser et al., 1990, 1992, 2000). Men are more likely to have a substance use disorder than women, as are younger individuals compared with older ones. Interestingly, the relationship between age and substance use disorder is also true for lifetime substance use disorder; that is, younger individuals are more likely than older individuals to have a lifetime history of substance use disorder. This may be surprising considering that older people by definition have had more time to develop a substance use disorder than younger individuals. It is likely that the effects of substance abuse on increased mortality in people with a serious mental illness due to factors such as increased suicidality (Bartels, Drake, & McHugo, 1992; Gut-Fayand et al., 2001) and risk of infectious diseases (Rosenberg et al., 2001) results in people with co-occurring disorders being less likely represented in older samples of persons with a psychiatric disorder.

Race has been found to be related to the type of substance use disorder but not to overall rates of substance use disorder in people with a serious mental illness (Montross et al., 2005; Mueser, Essock, Drake, Wolfe, & Frisman, 2001). These differences appear to reflect the variations in the availability of substances to different racial groups rather than differences in preference for specific types of substances. For example, a study by Mueser et al. (1990) in Philadelphia in the early to mid 1980s found that African Americans were more likely to abuse cannabis than were white individuals, whereas in a subsequent study, when cocaine had overtaken cannabis as the most available and most commonly used substance in the inner city of Philadelphia, African

Americans were more likely to abuse cocaine than were white persons (Mueser et al., 1992).

Educational level is related to drug use disorders among people with a serious mental illness, but not alcohol use disorder, similar to the general population. Individuals with a drug use disorder are more likely to have dropped out of school before obtaining a high school diploma than persons without a drug use disorder. Marital status is also related to substance use disorders in persons with a serious mental illness, with those who are single are more likely to have a co-occurring substance use disorder.

A family history of substance use disorder is a well established predictor of substance use problems in the general population (Knopik et al., 2004). Similarly, among persons with a serious mental illness, family history of substance use disorder increases the likelihood that the individual will develop a substance use disorder (Gershon et al., 1988; Noordsy, Drake, Biesanz, & McHugo, 1994). However, as discussed in the later section on etiology, people with a serious mental illness do not in general have higher rates of substance abuse among their family members. Thus, family history of substance abuse may account for some comorbidity in the serious mental illness population but does not explain the high rates of co-occurring disorders.

An important indicator of vulnerability to substance use disorders in people with a serious mental illness is the presence of conduct disorder in childhood and antisocial personality disorder in adulthood. Among people with the serious mental illness, conduct disorder and antisocial personality disorder are associated with significantly higher rates of substance use disorder (Hodgins, Tiihonen, & Ross, 2005; Mueser et al., 1999; Tengström, Hodgins, Grann, Långström, & Kullgren, 2004). Furthermore, among individuals with co-occurring disorders, conduct disorder and antisocial personality disorder are associated with a more severe substance use disorder, including an earlier age of onset of substance use disorder, a more rapid progression to dependence, higher levels of polysubstance abuse, and more severe consequences of use in domains such as social adjustment, involvement in the criminal justice system, and symptomatology (Mueser et al., 1997, 2006, 2012). Later, we consider the evidence of whether antisocial personality disorder in people with a serious mental illness can explain some of the excess comorbidity with substance use disorders.

A somewhat counterintuitive finding for people with schizophrenia is that in studies conducted in the United States, individuals with good premorbid social functioning tend to be *more* likely to develop a drug use disorder than do people with poor premorbid social functioning (Arndt, Tyrrell, Flaum, & Andreasen, 1992; Cohen & Klein, 1970; Salyers & Mueser, 2001; Serper et al., 1995). Premorbid social functioning refers to the quality of an individual's social relationships before he or she developed a psychiatric illness, as reflected by behaviors such as having close friends and having had a sexually intimate relationship. Good premorbid social functioning in schizophrenia is a robust predictor of a better social and symptomatic course and outcome of the disorder (Zigler & Glick, 1986). The finding that good premorbid functioning increases the chances of an individual with schizophrenia developing a drug use disorder may be explained by the fact that in settings where drug use is common, it most often occurs in social situations (Addington & Duchak, 1997; Dixon et al., 1991; Mueser, Nishith, Tracy, DeGirolamo, & Molinaro, 1995), and people are most likely to be introduced to drugs in such settings; individuals with poor premorbid social functioning may be less likely to be introduced to drugs due to their diminished social contacts, and thus less likely to develop drug use disorders. In countries where drug use is less common and not normative behavior, such as Norway, opposite relationships have been reported, with poor premorbid social functioning associated with higher rates of drug abuse in people with a serious mental illness (Ringen et al., 2008, 2013).

Onset and Course

There is no clear pattern in the relative onset of a serious mental illness and substance use disorder (Hambrecht & Häfner, 1996; Silver & Abboud, 1994). For some individuals, the substance use disorder precedes the onset of the serious mental illness, while for others it follows it. However, efforts to establish a clear order of onset are often thwarted by memory biases, and the tendency for the age of onset of the two disorders appears to be relatively close (e.g., within a year).

Once a substance use disorder has developed in someone with a serious mental illness, in the absence of integrated treatment the course tends to be a chronic and relapsing one for both disorders (Cuffel & Chase, 1994; Kozaric-Kovacic, Folnegovic-Smalc, Folnegovic, & Marusic, 1995; Schmidt, Hesse, & Lykke, 2011; Xie et al., 2006, 2009). As in the general population (Hser, Hoffman, Grella, & Anglin, 2001; Hser, Anglin, &

Powers, 1993; Vaillant, 2002), persistence of substance abuse is associated with premature mortality (Xie, Drake, & McHugo, 2009). Conversely, remission of substance abuse is associated with improved clinical and psychosocial functioning in areas such as competitive work (McHugo et al., 2012).

Consequences of Substance Use Disorders

Substance abuse is associated with a broad-range negative effect in people with a serious mental illness (Drake, O'Neal, & Wallach, 2008). One of the most consistent findings has been that substance use disorders frequently provoke symptom relapses and rehospitalizations (Drake, Osher, & Wallach, 1989; Min, Biegel, & Johnsen, 2005). There are several ways in which substance use can trigger relapses and hospitalizations. Some substances have a direct effect on neurobiological mechanisms believed to be responsible for the core psychopathology of specific disorders. For example, stimulant drugs such as cocaine and amphetamines can increase dopaminergic turnover in the brain, which is believed to be a major contributing factor in schizophrenia. For this reason, even very modest amounts of stimulant usage can trigger relapses in people with schizophrenia (Shaner et al., 1995). Substance use in people with a serious mental illness is frequently accompanied by nonadherence to prescribed medications and dropout from treatment, which can lead to relapses (Miller et al., 2009; Miner, Rosenthal, Hellerstein, & Muenz, 1997; Weiss, Smith, Hull, Piper, & Hubbert, 2002). Medication nonadherence may be related to a variety of factors, including concerns about potential interactions between psychiatric medications and substances, attempts to enhance the effects of the substances, or medication side effects (Potvin, Blanchet, & Stip, 2009; Salyers & Mueser, 2001). Last, as discussed later, substance use disorders can have dramatic negative effects on the quality of individuals' lives (Drake, Brunette, & Mueser, 1998; Pollack, Cramer, & Varner, 2000), resulting in high levels of stress and trauma. Since stress is well known to contribute to relapses in people with a mental illness (Myin-Germeys et al., 2001; Nuechterlein & Dawson, 1984), substance abuse related stress may represent another contributing factor to relapse.

Increased severity of depression is the most consistent clinical correlate of substance use disorders in serious mental illness (Potvin, Sepehry, & Stip, 2007). The directional relationship between depression and substance use disorder in people with a serious mental illness is unclear, with bidirectional effects most plausible. Some substances, such as alcohol, act as central nervous system depressants, while the negative effects of all substances on life functioning can naturally lead to depression as a consequence of these losses. At the same time, many individuals report using substances in an attempt to temporarily escape negative feelings such as depression (Carey & Carey, 1995; Test, Wallish, Allness, & Ripp, 1989), which may lead to a vicious cycle of substance use worsening depression and increased depression leading to more severe substance abuse.

Substance abuse can have negative effects on close relationships (Drake et al., 1998), especially on families (Dixon, McNary, & Lehman, 1995; Kashner et al., 1991; Salyers & Mueser, 2001), whom many people with a serious mental illness depend on for getting their basic needs met. Substance abuse can contribute to family conflict because it can lead to stealing and aggression (Räsänen et al., 1998), and frustration on the part of relatives who are more likely to perceive psychiatric symptoms in a loved one with co-occurring disorders as under the person's control than the same symptoms in a relative with only a serious mental illness (Niv, Lopez, Glynn, & Mueser, 2007).

Family involvement in the lives of people with a co-occurring disorder is associated with a better course and higher likelihood of remission of the substance use disorder than similar people who are not involved with their families (Clark, 2001). However, the stress inherent to maintaining a close relationship with a person with co-occurring disorders and can result in overwhelming the ability of the family to maintain supports for the person, resulting in a loss of family involvement. A common result of this loss of support is housing instability and homelessness (Caton et al., 1994).

Substance abuse is a major factor contributing to the growing rate of incarcerated individuals with a serious mental illness (McCabe et al., 2012; Teplin, 1994). Substance abuse can contribute to legal problems in people with a serious mental illness in a variety of ways. Simple possession or minor sales of illegal drugs are common legal problems. A high sensitivity of people with a serious mental illness to the effects of alcohol and drugs can lead to disorderly conduct, bizarre behavior, or other socially inappropriate behaviors that trigger public complaints and arrests (Drake & Wallach, 1993). The disinhibiting effects of substances such as alcohol can lead to aggression, resulting in arrests. Furthermore, the poor social judgment that frequently characterized as serious mental illness often

results in people getting caught using or possessing substances by law enforcement officials. Finally, people may engage in illegal behaviors such as prostitution, theft, or armed robbery in order to support their habit, leading to arrest and incarceration (Mueser et al., 2006).

People with co-occurring disorders are more prone to both violence and victimization than people with only a serious mental illness (Räsänen et al., 1998; Teplin, McClelland, Abram, & Weiner, 2005). While some of the violence in people with co-occurring disorders may be attributed to the presence of antisocial personality disorder (Hodgins, Hiscoke, & Freese, 2002; Hodgins, Toupin, & Côté, 1996), the disinhibiting effects of some substances and frustration related to chaotic and disruptive effects of substance abuse on their lives can be other factors contributing to aggression. Victimization is a common consequence of substance abuse both in the general population (Dansky et al., 1996) and among people with a serious mental illness (Gearon & Bellack, 1999; Walsh et al., 2003). Vulnerability to victimization can be increased by substance use in several ways. People may be less able to defend themselves from other people when they are under the influence of drugs or alcohol. People may also be more likely to be victimized by virtue of spending time with other people who have active substance use disorders and who are more likely to take advantage of vulnerable others. Additionally, individuals may engage in high-risk interpersonal behaviors such as prostitution or exchanging sex for drugs in order to support their substance use habit, increasing their vulnerability to victimization.

A final consequence of substance abuse in people with a serious mental illness is medical problems. People with a serious mental illness have increased rates of infectious diseases such as HIV, sexually transmitted diseases, and especially hepatitis C, with drug abuse as the most important factor contributing to this medical comorbidity (Meade et al., 2009; Rosenberg et al., 2001; Susser et al., 1998). Substance use disorders can also interfere with the management of chronic medical disorders that occur at increased rates in people with a serious mental illness, such as diabetes.

Models of Comorbidity

Almost all the data on the prevalence of substance use disorders in serious mental illness are drawn from clinical samples of people in treatment, including most of data from the Epidemiologic Catchment Area study (Regier et al., 1990).

According to *Berkson's fallacy* (Berkson, 1949), estimates of comorbidity are inflated when samples are obtained from treatment settings, as opposed to the general population, because either disorder increases the likelihood that individuals will receive treatment. As a result, most estimates of comorbidity are probably inflated by sampling bias. However, it is unlikely that this factor is sufficient to explain the high rates observed.

Many explanations have been proposed for the increased risk of substance use disorders in people with a serious mental illness. Four general models of increased comorbidity include: secondary psychiatric disorder models, secondary substance use disorder models, common factor models, and bidirectional models. According to *secondary psychiatric disorder models*, substance use precipitates mental illness in individuals who would otherwise not develop these disorders. *Secondary substance use disorder models* propose that serious mental illness increases the person's chances of developing a substance use disorder. Different models may account for comorbidity in individual patients, and more than one model may apply for a given individual over time, or in relation to different substances.

Secondary Psychiatric Illness Models

The theory that substance abuse can lead to serious mental illness has focused primarily on stimulants, hallucinogens, and cannabis because of their psychotomimetic effects (Krystal et al., 2005). In contrast, there is a general consensus that alcohol misuse does not cause schizophrenia or bipolar disorder, and some debate as to whether it can mask their onset (Goodwin & Jamison, 2007; Hambrecht & Häfner, 1996). The fact that alcohol misuse is not considered to be a cause of secondary serious mental illness limits the potential significance of secondary psychiatric models, given the high prevalence of alcohol use disorder in serious mental illness.

Models proposing that psychotomimetic drug misuse can lead to long-term psychotic disorders build on the catecholamine hypothesis of schizophrenia or affective disorders (Bunney & Davis, 1965). Animal research has shown that repeated or continuous stimulant administration can lead to increased sensitivity of response, or *behavioral sensitization*. Similarly, increased electrophysiological and behavioral responses can be induced by repeated electrical stimulation or stimulant administration, referred to as *kindling*. Behavioral sensitization and kindling due to substance use have been suggested as mechanisms by which drug misuse

may precipitate serious mental illness (Lieberman, Kinon, & Loebel, 1990; O'Daly, Joyce, Stephan, Murray, & Shergill, 2011; Strakowski, McElroy, Keck, & West, 1996).

McLellan et al. (1979) followed 51 male veterans with at least yearly hospitalizations for drug misuse over a 6-year period. Although there were no differences in psychiatric symptoms initially, by end point 5 of 11 stimulant users had developed psychosis, and 8 of 14 depressant users had developed severe depression. However, if substance type predicted psychiatric diagnosis, then different diagnostic groups would tend to misuse different types of substances, which is not the case for serious mental illness (Cuffel, 1996; Kavanagh et al., 2004; Mueser et al., 1992, 2000; Regier et al., 1990).

Several studies have compared people who develop long-term serious mental illness following drug abuse with similar people without substance use disorders. Most of this research has failed to find consistent differences between these groups. Furthermore, there are no consistent differences between people with co-occurring disorders whose substance use disorder developed before versus after the mental illness (Tsuang, Simpson, & Kronfol, 1982; Vardy & Kay, 1983).

Andréasson et al. (1987) reported a large 15-year prospective follow-up study of young men conscripted into the Swedish army. There was a strong association between history of cannabis use at conscription and later diagnosis of schizophrenia, which was reduced when other variables were controlled but nevertheless remained elevated. No associations were found between other drug use and later development of schizophrenia. Subsequent analyses indicated that the cannabis users who developed schizophrenia had a more rapid onset of illness characterized by positive symptoms, which the authors interpreted as supporting an etiologically distinct subgroup (Allebeck, Adamsson, Engström, & Rydberg, 1993; Andréasson, Allebeck, & Rydberg, 1989). Since this study, several other population-based studies have demonstrated a relationship between cannabis use and the development of schizophrenia, controlling for possible confounders (Arseneault et al., 2002; Fergusson, Horwood, & Swain-Campbell, 2003; Hall & Degenhardt, 2008; Henquet et al., 2005; van Os et al., 2002). The relationship between cannabis use and schizophrenia is dose dependent, is stronger for earlier cannabis use but persists with continued use, and is not modified by other drug use (Kuepper et al., 2011; McGrath et al., 2010). However, cannabis use may interact with the environment to increase risk of psychosis. The effects of cannabis use on the onset of psychosis appear to be stronger in individuals born in urban settings (Kuepper, van Os, Wittchen, & Henquet, 2011) and those exposed to childhood maltreatment (Houston, Murphy, Shevlin, & Adamson, 2011; Konings et al., 2012).

Although evidence suggests that cannabis use may precipitate the onset of psychosis (Evins, Green, Kane & Murray, 2013), some data are inconsistent with the causal role that cannabis is hypothesized to play. If cannabis use induced schizophrenia in people who would not otherwise develop it, one would expect increases in the prevalence of schizophrenia in settings where cannabis use has increased. Two studies that examined this in birth cohorts in Australia between 1940 and 1979 (Degenhardt, Hall, & Lynskey, 2003), and in the United Kingdom from 1996 to 2005 (Frisher, Crome, Martino, & Croft, 2009), failed to find such an association.

While support for a simple causal role for cannabis use in schizophrenia is inconclusive, evidence is stronger that substance use can precipitate psychiatric disorders in vulnerable individuals (Gururajan, Manning, Klug, & van den Buuse, 2012). Both people whose schizophrenia was preceded by substance use disorder and those with only schizophrenia have stronger family histories of schizophrenia than people with only a substance use disorder (Tsuang et al., 1982; Vardy & Kay, 1983). Also, cannabis and other drug abuse is associated with an earlier age of schizophrenia onset (Large, Sharma, Compton, Slade, & Nielssen, 2011; Mueser et al., 1990; Salyers & Mueser, 2001; Tsuang et al., 1982) and heavier use following the onset of psychosis (Di Forti et al., 2009). Caspi and colleagues (2005) reported that adolescent cannabis use elevated risk for subsequent schizophreniform disorder but only among those with a genetic marker for schizophrenia risk. This version of the hypothesis is consistent with the stress-vulnerability model of schizophrenia (Bramness et al., 2013; Zubin & Spring, 1977), in which substance use may trigger the psychotic disorder in people who are vulnerable because of genetic or neurodevelopmental risk, but in the model substance abuse serves as just one of many potential influences.

In bipolar disorder, people whose alcohol use disorder came first have been found to have a *later* age of onset of bipolar disorder than those whose alcoholism came second (Strakowski et al., 1996). Furthermore, lower familial rates of bipolar disorder have been found in people whose alcoholism

antedated their bipolar disorder (DelBello et al., 1999), as well as fewer affective episodes and a more rapid recovery, compared with those whose bipolar disorder came first (Winokur et al., 1995). These findings suggest that alcohol misuse may precipitate first episodes of mania in some persons who might not otherwise develop the disorder, or may have developed it at a later age (Strakowski & DelBello, 2000).

Secondary Substance Use Disorder Models

A variety of different models posit that serious mental illness increases individuals' vulnerability to developing a substance use disorder, including *alleviation of symptoms/dysphoria, multiple risk factors, supersensitivity,* and *brain reward circuitry dysfunction.*

Alleviation of symptoms/dysphoria model. The term *self-medication* to refer to people's use of substances to alleviate psychiatric symptoms or other negative mood states (Khantzian, 1997) has been used in so many different ways that there is little consensus in the scientific community as to its meaning. To avoid confusion, we adopt the alternative term *alleviation of symptoms/dysphoria model* for this broad set of explanations for high rates of substance use disorders in people with a serious mental illness. One version of this model is that substances are selected by the individual based on their specific effects on symptoms. Although research indicates that people are aware of their initial psychological reactions to substances (Mueser, Nishith et al., 1995), there is little evidence for substance selection related to specific diagnoses or internal states. Self-report studies find that people with co-occurring disorders report that alcohol and other substances alleviate social problems, insomnia, depression, and other problems across diagnoses (Addington & Duchak, 1997; Carey & Carey, 1995; Laudet, Magura, Vogel, & Knight, 2004) but rarely report that specific substances alleviate specific symptoms (Dixon et al., 1991; Noordsy et al., 1991). Studies of clinical epidemiology show that individuals with a serious mental illness use the same substances as others in society but at higher rates (Cuffel, 1996), substance selection is not related to diagnosis (Mueser et al., 1992; Mueser et al., 1990; Mueser et al., 2000; Regier et al., 1990), and substance selection is related to availability and market forces (Mueser et al., 1992).

Another more general version of this model is that people with a serious mental illness are prone to using substances in response to distress. In support of this, research shows that people with a serious mental illness often experience dysphoria (Birchwood, Mason, MacMillian, & Healy, 1993), and self-reports of people with co-occurring disorders indicate that the alleviation of unpleasant feelings is a common motive for using substances (Addington & Duchak, 1997; Carey & Carey, 1995; Laudet et al., 2004; O'Hare et al., 2011). Furthermore, there is some evidence that people with co-occurring disorders have higher levels of dysphoria and depression than those with a serious mental illness alone (Blanchard et al., 1999; Brunette, Mueser, Xie, & Drake, 1997; Hambrecht & Häfner, 2000; Potvin et al., 2007).

Multiple risk factors model. Possible indirect mechanisms involve a variety of risk factors related to serious mental illness, such as social isolation, poor interpersonal skills, poor cognitive skills, school and vocational failure, poverty, lack of adult role responsibilities, lack of structured daily activities, association with substance-using subgroups, and living in neighborhoods with high rates of drug availability (Anthony, 1991; Berman & Noble, 1993; Jones, Guth, Lewis, & Murray, 1994). This model is consistent with Kandel's work demonstrating that achievement of adult social roles and responsibilities was associated with discontinuation of substance use among young adults (role incompatibility theory; Kandel & Raveis, 1989). Little research has addressed multiple risk factor models, but self-reports regarding reasons for use are consistent with the identified factors (Warner et al., 1994).

Supersensitivity model. This model is an elaboration of the stress-vulnerability model for schizophrenia, which proposes that environmental stress interacts with psychobiological vulnerability to precipitate the onset of serious mental illness or to trigger relapses. Because vulnerability is defined in terms of increased biological sensitivity to stress, it may also apply to the effects of alcohol and drugs. This sensitivity may render people with a serious mental illness more likely to experience negative consequences from using relatively small amounts of substances.

A number of avenues of research provide support for this model. First, people with co-occurring disorders tend to misuse lower quantities of substances than those with primary substance use disorders (Lehman, Myers, Corty, & Thompson, 1994) and are less likely than primary substance use disorder populations to develop physical dependence (Corse, Hirschinger, & Zanis, 1995). Second, in pharmacological "challenge" tests, people with a serious mental illness are highly sensitive to low doses of amphetamine and cannabis that produce minimal responses in controls (D'Souza et al., 2005; Lieberman, Kane, & Alvir, 1987). Third, people with a serious mental illness often report negative clinical effects such as symptom relapses following use of small quantities of alcohol or drugs (Knudsen & Vilmar, 1984; Treffert, 1978). Fourth, Drake and Wallach (1993) reported that fewer than five percent of people with a serious mental illness were able to sustain symptom-free drinking over time without negative consequences, in marked contrast to approximately 50% of the general population who drink alcohol over time without developing a disorder, suggesting increased sensitivity to the effects of alcohol. Similarly, Harrison et al. (2008) reported in a naturalistic follow-up of first-episode schizophrenia clients that rates of problematic drinking and marijuana abuse or dependence dropped approximately in half over 14 months after the initial episode, suggesting some reduced tolerance to the effects of alcohol and cannabis.

Brain Reward Circuitry Dysfunction Model. A number of authors have noted overlap in the neural circuitry putatively involved in both substance use disorder and schizophrenia (Chambers, Krystal, & Self, 2001; Green, Zimmet, Strous, & Schildkraut, 1999; Lettfuss, Seeger-Armbruster, & von Ameln-Mayerhofer, 2013). This has led to a model that theorizes that biological vulnerability to substance use disorder is inherent to the neurobiology of schizophrenia. Substances of abuse activate dopaminergic mesocorticolimbic tracts involved in reward, and repeated use increases sensitivity to substance effects (Redish, 2004; Robinson & Berridge, 1993). The reward circuit regulates repetition of behavior. People with schizophrenia appear to have a dysregulation of this circuit, which results in blunted responses to rewarding stimuli (Chambers & Self, 2002; Chau, Roth, & Green, 2004). The hypothesis suggests that people with schizophrenia are vulnerable to substance use disorders because substances of abuse directly stimulate this circuit, creating relatively greater reward response. Similar reward circuitry dysfunction hypotheses have been put forward to explain the etiology of substance use disorder in other contexts (Blum et al., 2000; Volkow, Fowler, & Wang, 2003). The reward dysfunction argument is consistent with research showing that abused substances can increase dopaminergic turnover in reward circuitry in both animals (Wise, 1998) and humans (Boileau et al., 2003; O'Leary et al., 2000), as well as data indicating abnormal reward circuitry responsiveness to drug cues in people with primary substance use disorders (Wexler et al., 2001).

Several areas of research have provided indirect support for the hypothesis in schizophrenia. For example, people with schizophrenia do not show the normal increase in P300 event-related potential amplitude to stimuli associated with monetary reward (Brecher & Begleiter, 1983), have abnormal hedonic and brain activation responses to odors (Crespo-Facorro et al., 2001), and have structural and functional brain abnormalities in their reward circuitry, including frontal lobe subregions, striatum, amygdala, and hippocampus (Shenton, Dickey, Frumin, & McCarley, 2001). This model has been primarily been applied to schizophrenia.

Common Factor Models

Common factor models posit that high rates of comorbidity are the result of shared vulnerabilities to both disorders. To the extent that specific factors can independently increase the risk of developing both disorders, increased comorbidity can be explained. Two risk factors have been studied: genetics and antisocial personality disorder. Other factors have been identified but less thoroughly evaluated as reasons for increased rates of comorbidity, including socioeconomic status and cognitive impairment.

Genetic Factors

Family history and twin studies provide strong evidence that genetic factors contribute to the development of schizophrenia, bipolar disorder, and substance use disorder, although single, common genetic causes of these disorders are unknown. The question is whether genetic vulnerability to one disorder also increases risk for another disorder. Research shows that people with comorbid disorders are more likely to have relatives with a substance use disorder than similar people with only a serious mental illness (Gershon et al., 1988; Noordsy et al., 1994; Tsuang et al., 1982). These findings suggest that genetic vulnerability to substance use disorders plays a role in the development of some cases of comorbid substance use and serious mental disorders.

However, do such genetic factors account for *increased* comorbidity via susceptibility to both disorders? Research examining the rate of substance use disorders in the relatives of people with a mental illness and the rate of serious mental illness in relatives of people with a substance use disorder addresses this question. If shared genetic vulnerability to both serious mental illness and substance use disorder accounts for increased comorbidity, higher rates of the other disorder would be expected in the relatives of persons with one of the disorders. There are at least two possible sources of shared genetic vulnerability in families. First, within individual family members, genetic vulnerability to one disorder could also be associated with increased vulnerability to another disorder, with offspring at increased risk to developing both disorders from the genetic contribution of that individual parent. Second, if family members with one disorder were more likely to mate with individuals with the other disorder than would be expected by chance alone (i.e., cross-trait *assortative mating*), the offspring would be at increased risk to developing comorbid disorders, due to the genetic contributions from each parent.

Research provides evidence against a simple genetic model. Several studies indicate that genetic risk to schizophrenia or bipolar disorder is not associated with an increased risk of substance use disorder in relatives, or vice versa (Gershon et al., 1988; Maier, Lichtermann, Minges, Delmo, & Heun, 1995; Tsuang et al., 1982). These findings suggest that shared genetic factors do not account for increased rates of comorbid substance use disorder in serious mental illness.

Genetic models of the relationship between co-occurring serious mental illness and substance use disorder are more complex. For example, Caspi et al. (2005) reported that a genetic variation in the *COMT* gene moderated the effect of adolescent cannabis use on the later development of psychotic symptoms or schizophrenia. Adult cannabis use did not have the same effect, highlighting that the effect of substance use on the developing brain may be different and more deleterious than the effect of substances on adult brains. This research also exemplifies that genetic risk for co-occurring disorders may be enacted via gene–environment interactions, whereby substance abuse acts as an environmental stressor on the developing brain.

Genetic susceptibility for these disorders is not simple; rather, it accumulates across a multitude of genes regulating various aspects of brain function. One line of research has examined variations of the DRD3 gene that encodes for the dopamine D3 receptor. D3 receptors are expressed in the mesocorticolimbic dopaminergic system and are increased in postmortem studies of schizophrenia. The D3 receptor is highly expressed in the nucleus accumbens, where reward, including substance-induced reward, is mediated. The D3 receptor modulates dopamine movement in this structure when substances are used. Although studies have been mixed, some research has shown that homozygosity in a polymorphism in the DRD3 gene was associated with co-occurring addiction in schizophrenia (Krebs et al., 1998).

Antisocial Personality Disorder

Another possible common factor that has been the focus of recent research is antisocial personality disorder. Extensive research has shown that antisocial personality disorder and its childhood precursor, conduct disorder, are strongly related to substance use disorder (Kessler et al., 1997; Regier et al., 1990). In addition, similar associations have been reported between antisocial personality disorder and serious mental illness. Specifically, symptoms of conduct disorder in childhood, such as repeated fighting, truancy, and lying, have been found to be predictive of the later development of schizophrenia (Asarnow, 1988; Cannon et al., 1993; Robins, 1966) and, to a lesser extent, bipolar disorder (Carlson & Weintraub, 1993; Robins, 1966). Furthermore, increased rates of antisocial personality disorder have been reported in both schizophrenia and bipolar disorder (Bland, Newman, & Orn, 1987; Hodgins et al., 1996; Jackson, Whiteside, Bates, Rudd, & Edwards, 1991).

The strong associations between conduct disorder, antisocial personality disorder, and substance use disorders and the increased prevalence of antisocial personality disorder in persons with a mental illness suggest a role for antisocial personality disorder as a common factor underlying increased comorbidity. More direct support is provided by evidence people with a serious mental illness and past conduct disorder or antisocial personality disorder are more likely to have comorbid substance use disorder than are similar people without antisocial personality disorder (Hodgins et al., 2002, 2005; Mueser et al., 1999). Finally, among persons with co-occurring disorders, the additional diagnosis of conduct disorder or antisocial personality disorder (Mueser et al., 1997, 2006, 2012) is associated with a more severe course of substance use disorder and a stronger family history of substance use disorder, consistent with research on antisocial personality disorder in persons with primary substance use disorder (Alterman & Cacciola, 1991).

Thus, moderately strong evidence suggests that antisocial personality disorder is a common factor that may contribute to the increased rate of substance use disorders in a subset of people with a serious mental illness. Further work is needed to evaluate the role of temperament and to rule out other common factors related to antisocial personality disorder that could account for its relationships with substance use disorder and serious mental illness.

Bidirectional Models

Bidirectional models suggest that ongoing interactions between serious mental illness and substance use disorder account for increased rates of comorbidity. For example, substance abuse could trigger serious mental illness in a biologically vulnerable individual, which is subsequently maintained by continued substance use due to socially learned cognitive factors, such as beliefs, expectancies, and motives for substance use (Graham, 1998). Consistent with this model, there is evidence both that substance use disorder worsens the course of serious mental illness, and that worsening symptoms are related to higher substance use (Hides, Dawe, Kavanagh, & Young, 2006). Despite the intuitive appeal of bidirectional models, research has not demonstrated that bidirectional interactions lead to greater comorbidity.

Treatment

Traditionally, treatments for co-occurring disorders have typically employed either parallel or sequential treatment approaches (Polcin, 1992). In a *parallel treatment approach*, mental illness treatment and substance abuse treatment are provided at the same time by different clinicians who are usually working for different agencies. In the *sequential treatment approach*, an attempt is made to first stabilize or reduce the problems associated with one disorder before then turning attention to the other disorder. There are a variety of problems associated with both of these approaches.

A major problem with parallel treatment for people with a serious mental illness is that these individuals frequently do not follow through on referrals for treatment of their substance use disorder at other agencies. Awareness of one's substance use disorder and motivation to treat it is often very limited in people with a serious mental illness (DiClemente, Nidecker, & Bellack, 2008). Furthermore, many substance abuse treatment agencies have eligibility criteria for services that exclude people with a serious mental illness from treatment. An additional problem with parallel treatment is that clinicians working for different agencies often fail to coordinate treatment. In some cases, the failure in communication can lead to mixed messages or inconsistent treatment approaches taken by mental health clinicians and substance abuse treatment clinicians. The most common outcome of parallel treatment approaches has been that individuals with the co-occurring disorder do not receive treatments for both disorders, either because they fail to initially engage in treatment or because they drop out from treatment early.

Sequential treatment approaches are based on the assumption that if attention is focused on treating the most problematic disorder, often conceptualized as the "primary" disorder, then that the second disorder will be more readily treated and in some cases may remit on its own without additional treatment. The fundamental problem with sequential treatment approaches is that they fail to take into account the interactive nature of serious psychiatric and substance use disorders. As the severity of the mental illness increases vulnerability to substance abuse, and substance abuse in turn worsens the psychiatric disorder, the ability to successfully treat one disorder without attending to the other is very limited. For example, attempting to successfully treat and stabilize a person with bipolar disorder who is actively abusing alcohol without attending to his substance abuse is an extremely difficult task. Similarly, efforts to curb cocaine abuse in someone with schizophrenia without attending to her psychiatric disorder are usually doomed to failure.

By the late 1980s and early 1990s, there was a growing consensus in the field, bolstered by literature reviews (Ridgely, Goldman, & Talbott, 1986; Ridgely, Goldman, & Willenbring, 1990), that traditional parallel and sequential approaches to treating co-occurring substance use and serious psychiatric disorders were ineffective. Consistent problems associated with the ability to actually deliver both types of treatment to individuals were a major impediment but not the only limitation of these approaches. The failure of existing treatment models led to the conclusion that effective treatment of co-occurring disorders at a minimum requires the integrated treatment of both disorders. Since that time, a variety of integrated treatment programs for co-occurring disorders have been articulated (Carey, 1996; Drake, Antosca, Noordsy, Bartels, & Osher, 1991; Graham et al., 2004; Minkoff, 1989; Mueser, Noordsy, Drake, & Fox, 2003; Ziedonis & Fisher,

1994), and at least some form of integrated treatment is now broadly accepted as a standard of care.

Integrated treatment is defined as treatment of both the psychiatric and substance use disorders at the same time, by the same clinician or team of clinicians, in which those clinicians assume the responsibility of integrating the treatments for the two disorders. The integration of the treatment for both disorders is a natural byproduct of treating both disorders at the same time by the same clinicians. Motives for using substances are often related to an individual's serious mental illness, such use to facilitate socialization, as a type of recreation, or as a coping strategy for problematic symptoms. Integrated treatment that takes into account these types of motives, and seeks to provide individuals with better skills or other opportunities for getting their basic needs met, can treat both disorders simultaneously (Mueser et al., 2003). For example, people can be taught more effective social skills for getting their socialization needs met in ways other than spending time with people using substances (Bellack, Mueser, Gingerich, & Agresta, 2004), they can be engaged in supported employment that can both improve their economic standing and give them something meaningful to do other than using substances (Becker & Drake, 2003), and they can learn more effective coping strategies for dealing with distressing symptoms such as hallucinations, depression, and sleep problems (Gingerich & Mueser, 2010).

In addition to the integration of mental health and substance abuse treatment, a number of principles of effective integrated treatment programs have emerged in recent years. While not every program adheres to every principle, there is growing evidence supporting the importance of each of the principles. These principles are described next.

Comprehensive Assessment

Effective treatment needs to be guided by systematic and thorough assessments. Comprehensive assessment can be broken down into four steps, including detection, classification, functional assessment, and functional or contextual analysis.

Detection. One of the most common problems in the treatment of co-occurring disorders in persons with a serious mental illness is the failure to detect substance use disorders when they are present. People usually do not volunteer information about their substance use, and even when asked they often minimize or deny use altogether. Mental health agencies serving persons with a serious psychiatric disorders are notoriously poor at detecting substance use disorders, and historically only a small percentage of people with active substance use disorders have had their disorders noted in their charts. When attempting to detect a substance use disorder in people with a serious mental illness, the goal is to "cast a wide net" in order to identify as many possible cases, and to conduct subsequent assessments to establish which individuals have actual substance use disorders and require treatment.

Several strategies can be useful for detecting substance abuse in people with a serious mental illness. Several self-report screening instruments specially developed for persons with a serious mental illness have demonstrated satisfactory sensitivity to substance use disorders (Hides et al., 2009; Ley, Jeffery, Shaw, & Weaver, 2007; Rosenberg et al., 1998), while some screens developed for the general population have also shown good sensitivity, such as the Alcohol Use Identification Test, the Drug Abuse Screening Test, and the Michigan Alcoholism Screening Test (Bennett, 2009). Routine use of these screening instruments on all people with a serious mental illness can facilitate the detection of substance use disorders. Educating clinicians about the effects of substance abuse on serious mental illness can also heighten their clinical acumen in identifying substance use disorders. For example, frequent relapses, money problems, housing difficulties, and social problems can all indicate the presence of a covert substance use disorder. In addition, clinicians can benefit from being educated about the increased sensitivity to the effects of drugs and alcohol in people with a serious mental illness. Many clinicians assume that unless an individual uses large quantities of drugs or alcohol, the person cannot have a substance use disorder. However, as previously reviewed, even moderate amounts of substance use can trigger negative consequences in people with a serious mental illness.

Classification. Individuals who have been screened for having a probable substance use disorder need additional assessment to determine whether they meet diagnostic criteria for a substance use disorder. Diagnostic evaluations of substance use disorders are most effective when they take into account multiple sources of information, including client self-reports, observations of clinicians, reports from collaterals such as family members, and reviews of records, including toxicology screens. Structured diagnostic assessments such as the Structured Clinical Interview for DSM-5 (First, Williams, Karg, & Spitzer, 2015) can be useful for classifying substance use disorders but can also be time consuming to administer.

An alternative is to use clinician-based rating scales such as the Alcohol Use Scale and the Drug Use Scale (Drake et al., 1990; Mueser et al., 2003). Both of these scales prompts clinicians to review the diagnostic criteria for substance use disorder and then to summarize the information pertaining to the worst 1-month period over the past 6 months on a 5-point rating scale corresponding to: 1 = no substance use over the past 6 months, 2 = substance use without impairment, 3 = substance abuse, 4 = substance dependence, and 5 = severe dependence with institutionalization (e.g., either multiple hospitalizations or incarcerations due to substance abuse). Several other clinician administered instruments have been developed to facilitate the diagnosis of substance use disorders in people with a serious mental illness (Bennett, 2009).

Functional assessment. A functional assessment is aimed at gathering detailed information about the nature of the person's substance use, as well as gaining an understanding of their social and psychological functioning, and interactions with substance use (Mueser et al., 2003). Important information about substance use includes the type of substances that are used, the frequency and quantities with which they are used, situations in which use is most likely to occur, and the consequences of use, both positive and negative. The Timeline Follow-Back is a useful instrument for gaining information about an individual's pattern of substance abuse over the past six months (Sobell & Sobell, 1992). The Timeline Follow-Back has been adapted for persons with a serious mental illness (Mueser et al., 2003) found to be both reliable and valid in this population (Carey, Carey, Maisto, & Henson, 2004; DeMarce, Burden, Lash, Stephens, & Grambow, 2007). It is useful to supplement this assessment with questions that probe individuals' motives or expectancies for substance use, such as use to facilitate socialization, coping with symptoms, or as a recreational activity.

The assessment of psychosocial and psychological functioning can also inform treatment planning. Assessments should cover a broad range of domains of functioning affected by serious mental illness, including social relationships (e.g., relationships with non-using peers), role functioning (e.g., work, school, parenting), symptoms, housing, health, and satisfaction with life.

Functional or contextual analysis. Once information has been gathered about the individual's specific substance use behaviors and their functioning in different life domains, a functional or contextual analysis is conducted to identify the critical factors that contribute to or maintain the person's use of substances. The primary assumption underlying any functional analysis is that the problem behavior (i.e., substance abuse) is maintained by specific desired outcomes (Goldiamond, 1974; Lindsley, 1964). The positive effects of using substances are often immediate and outweigh the long-term negative consequences. If the specific functions of the substance use can be identified, treatment can focus on addressing the maintaining factors such as providing alternative social outlets or teaching more effective coping skills for dealing with symptoms.

Motivation Based Treatment

People with co-occurring disorders vary in their motivation to work on their substance use problems. In order for treatment to the maximally effective, it must take into account the individual's desire to change, and customize treatment accordingly. A useful heuristic for conceptualizing the change process was developed by Prochaska and DiClemmenti (1984) in their trans-theoretical model of change. According to this model, humans change health-related behaviors by progressing through a series of five discrete steps. People begin in the *precontemplation phase*, in which they are not even thinking about change. Second, they move onto the *contemplation stage*, in which change is being considered. Third, when individuals decide to change they move into the *preparation phase*, when plans for change are undertaken. Fourth, people enter the *action phase* when actual behavioral change takes place. Fifth, when change has successfully occurred, people enter the *maintenance phase*, in which the goal is to keep the change and avoid slipping back into old habits.

The stages of change model was adapted by Osher and Kofoed (1989) to the *stages of treatment model*, which describes a similar series of stages that people with serious psychiatric and substance use disorders go through during the process of receiving integrated treatment for their co-occurring disorders. Each stage describes a motivational state of the person with respect to their willingness and desire to work on their substance use problems. Based on this motivational state, a treatment goal can be established for that stage, with multiple treatment options possible at each stage (Mueser et al., 2003).

The first stage of treatment is *engagement*. At this point in treatment the individual does not have a therapeutic alliance with the clinician providing integrated treatment and is not seeing the person on a regular basis. A therapeutic relationship is assumed to be critical to effective treatment of co-occurring disorders, and therefore the goal of this stage is to establish a therapeutic relationship (or working alliance), which is defined as seeing the person on a regular basis. Strategies such as assertive outreach into the community providing practical assistance, helping to resolve a crisis, or providing support to the person's social network (e.g., family members) can all facilitate establishing a therapeutic relationship. Efforts to enlighten the person about his or her substance use problems are postponed until the next stage.

When a working alliance has been established, and the person is seeing the clinician on a regular basis but continuing to abuse substances, the person enters the *persuasion stage*. During this stage the person is not yet committed to working on his or her substance use problems, but the presence of a therapeutic relationship makes it possible to talk openly about substance use. The goal of this stage is to help the client become more aware of the effects of substance use on them, to instill hope for change, and to begin working with the person on addressing their problematic use. A variety of strategies can be used to instill motivation for working on substance use problems. One commonly used approach is motivational interviewing (Miller & Rollnick, 2012), in which an emphasis is placed on helping the client develop personal goals and then exploring how substance use interferes with achieving those goals (Bellack, Bennet, & Gearon, 2007; Carey, Leontieva, Dimmock, Maisto, & Batki, 2007; Mueser et al., 2003). By supporting clients' self-efficacy for achieving personally meaningful goals, and taking steps towards those goals, insight into the interference caused by substance use develops naturally, which is followed by motivation to work on substance use problems. Other strategies are useful at the persuasion stage, such as educating people about the interactions between their psychiatric disorder and their substance use, structuring the individual's time to reduce opportunities to use substances, and group interventions designed to explore the effects of substance use on people's lives in a nonjudgmental atmosphere that encourages honest self-disclosure and exploration (Mueser & Noordsy, 1996). Attempts to actually change the individual's substance use behavior are not undertaken at this stage because motivation to change is assumed to be a prerequisite for benefiting from behavioral change strategies.

When motivation to reduce substance use or become abstinent has been established, as indicated by a reduction in substance use or repeated efforts to reduce, the person enters the *active stage of treatment*. During this stage, the shared focus of work is on helping the individual further reduce using, and preferably obtain abstinence. A wide range of strategies can be used to achieve the goal of active treatment, including social skills training for dealing with offers to use substances, teaching coping skills to manage urges to use substances or deal with symptoms that have previously precipitated substance, peer support groups (e.g., Alcoholics Anonymous, Dual Recovery Anonymous), and using family and other social supports to increase time spent with others who do not use substances.

When the person has achieved sustained abstinence or has not met criteria for a substance use disorder for at least 6 months, he or she enters the *relapse prevention stage*. At this stage, the goals of treatment are to maintain an awareness that a relapse could occur, and to extend the recovery to other areas of functioning, such as social relationships, role functioning, health, or independent living. During this stage, relapse prevention plans are developed and shared with members of the treatment team and other supportive individuals. The increased focus on the other life domains during the relapse prevention stage is based on the assumption that the better the individual's functioning and satisfaction with life, the less vulnerable he or she will be to relapse of their substance use disorder.

The stages of treatment concept helps clinicians optimize their selection of treatment by matching the intervention to the client's level of motivation. It also provides insight into the nature of two common problems experienced by clinicians treating individuals with co-occurring disorders. First, it is common for clinicians to attempt to educate or persuade people that they have substance use problem during their initial meetings of the person. A common consequence of these efforts is that the person feels misunderstood, not cared for, and drops out of treatment because the clinician has offered nothing of value to him or her. The problem is that the person with co-occurring disorders is in the engagement stage of treatment, where priority should be placed on developing a working relationship, whereas the clinician is providing a persuasion-stage intervention that assumes such a therapeutic relationship already exists.

A second common problem occurs when the person has a therapeutic relationship with the clinician but has not yet begun to reduce using substances, and the clinician tries to teach the person how to refuse offers to use substances or avoid other "high-risk situations" for substance use (i.e., an active treatment stage intervention). These efforts usually prove to be unsuccessful, because the client is not yet motivated to reduce his or her use of substances, and therefore to apply the skills the clinician is teaching. In this scenario, the person is in the persuasion stage of treatment, but the clinician is providing an intervention that is geared to the active stage of treatment stage, when the client has demonstrated some motivation to cut down or stop using substances. The clinician's time would be better spent using interventions designed to increase the person's awareness and motivation to work on his or her substance use problems.

Comprehensive Treatment

The treatment of substance use disorders in people with a serious mental illness needs to address the broad range of functional domains affected by both disorders. Reducing or eliminating substance abuse alone will only produce marginal improvements in the quality of life experienced by many people with a serious mental illness. Furthermore, the ability to successfully treat substance abuse often depends on being able to simultaneously address other areas of functioning that may contribute to substance use. Important domains that require treatment include psychiatric symptoms and illness self-management, housing, social relationships, health, role functioning, and leisure and recreational activities. For example, individuals with unstable housing or who are homeless benefit from supported housing irrespective of the client's substance abuse (McHugo et al., 2004; Tsemberis, Gulcur, & Nakae, 2004). Helping an individual find stable housing facilitates the therapeutic relationship, and creates new opportunities for bringing substance abuse into focus by reducing the individual's constant exposure to cues to use substances while on the street.

Harm Reduction

Harm reduction involves minimizing the most negative and costly consequences of substance use, while accepting the fact that the person is continuing to use (Denning, 2000). Most people with co-occurring disorders are not willing to endorse abstinence as an initial treatment goal even, after they recognize they recognize that they have a substance use problem. Harm reduction efforts provide the opportunity for the clinician to reduce some of the most injurious consequences of the person's substance use, which can facilitate the development of a therapeutic relationship without requiring the person to endorse abstinence as their goal. The notion of "allowing the client to hit rock bottom" is not acceptable for people with a serious mental illness, for whom "rock bottom" is all too often death. Harm reduction strategies, similar to gradual reduction of substance use, opens the door for many people to changing their substance use behaviors, which in the long run often leads to the person recognizing the value of endorsing abstinence as a goal. Examples of harm reduction strategies include providing clean needles for injection drug users, identifying places where the person can use substances where they are less likely to be victimized, teaching safe sex practices (e.g., requesting a partner to use a condom), and shifting from the use of more harmful substances to less harmful ones such as substituting marijuana for cocaine or amphetamine abuse).

Cognitive-Behavioral Therapy Strategies

Cognitive-behavioral strategies include a broad range of clinical interventions that are based on theories of learning and the role of cognition in mediating emotional reactions to events. The field of cognitive-behavioral therapy has flourished over the last several decades, and integrated treatment programs for co-occurring disorders frequently use cognitive-behavioral interventions to teach new skills or more adaptive functioning. *Social skills training* is used in many integrated treatment programs with the dual focus on teaching more effective skills for dealing with social situations involving substance use (e.g., substance refusal skills), and teaching interpersonal skills for developing rewarding relationships with people who do not use substances (e.g., conversational skills, friendship and dating skills) (Bellack et al., 2007; Mueser & Noordsy, 1996).

Many programs use cognitive-behavioral strategies for *coping skills training* for dealing with cravings to use substances or to manage symptoms that increase susceptibility to substance use (e.g., depression, hallucinations, sleep problems) (Barrowclough et al., 2009; Mueser & Noordsy, 1996; Weiss & Connery, 2011). *Relapse prevention training* is another cognitive-behavioral approach often used with people with co-occurring disorders (Fox et al., 2010). *Cognitive restructuring* involves teaching

people how to identify and challenge inaccurate thoughts or beliefs that underlying negative emotional reactions to events. Cognitive restructuring is used in some treatment programs for co-occurring disorders to help people challenge thoughts and beliefs related to negative feelings or psychotic symptoms that lead to substance use (Barrowclough et al., 2009; Graham et al., 2004). A final example of a cognitive-behavioral strategy used in some integrated programs for co-occurring disorders is contingent reinforcement. *Contingent reinforcement* involves rewarding people with money, goods, or access to something else of value for changes in desired behaviors, such as abstinence. Contingent reinforcement for abstinence from drugs has been shown to be a powerful intervention in people with a primary addiction (Higgins et al., 2003). Successful applications of contingent reinforcement for abstinence from drugs have shown promising effects for people with co-occurring disorders (Ries et al., 2004; Sigmon & Higgins, 2006).

Long-term Perspective

For many individuals, a serious mental illness is a chronic relapsing disorder. Similarly, for some, co-occurring substance use disorders can also be chronic and relapsing (Xie et al., 2010). Considering the often persistent nature of co-occurring disorders, it is not realistic to impose time constraints on treatment programs for this population. Integrated treatment programs are usually cognizant of the long-term treatment needs of most people, and provide necessary services on a time unlimited basis. Long-term studies of integrated treatment for co-occurring disorders indicate that there is gradual improvement over the years, with many people experiencing sustained remissions of their substance use disorder only after receiving several years of treatment (Drake, McHugo, Xie, Packard, & Helmstetter, 2006; McHugo et al., 2012.

Research
Psychosocial Interventions

The research literature on integrated treatment of co-occurring disorders has been periodically reviewed over the past several years (Brunette, Mueser, & Drake, 2004; Chow et al., 2013; Donald, Dower, & Kavanagh, 2005; Drake, Mercer-McFadden, Mueser, McHugo, & Bond, 1998; Drake, Mueser, Brunette, & McHugo, 2004; Drake et al., 2008; Kavanagh & Mueser, 2007; Ley, 2003; Mueser, Drake, Sigmon, & Brunette, 2005). One of the most comprehensive reviews was conducted by Drake et al. (2008), which identified 45 unique studies of psychosocial treatment, including 22 randomized controlled trials and 23 quasi-experimental studies. The findings of that review, combined with other reviews, clarify several aspects of integrated treatment, and suggest several conclusions, as described next.

First, the research literature supports combining mental health and substance abuse treatments in what has been termed integrated treatment more strongly as additional research emerges. The total number of studies of integrated treatments is increasing dramatically, and the most recent studies are often the most methodologically sound (Kavanagh & Mueser, 2007). Two important caveats regarding integrated treatment warrant mention. Integrated treatments could be more effective than parallel or sequential treatments merely because few people with co-occurring disorders in the United States receive any interventions for both disorders (Substance Abuse and Mental Health Services Administration, 2006). In addition, integrated treatment subsumes widely diverse interventions, ranging from individual counseling to hospitalization. Thus, there is a need for greater specificity than the integrated versus non-integrated distinction.

Second, the most consistent evidence regarding interventions that reduce substance abuse in this population involves two types of interventions: group interventions and residential interventions. Drake et al. (2008) identified eight controlled studies of group interventions. All but one showed positive effects on substance use outcomes and often on other outcomes as well. These studies used a range of interventions, but most involved group counseling for at least six months. All included education, peer support, and a focus on managing mental and substance use disorders concurrently. The recent studies were methodologically the most rigorous. Bellack, Bennett, Gearon, Brown, and Yang (2006) used a highly specified, multiintervention approach (including cognitive-behavioral, skills training, and contingency management) for people with schizophrenia and drug use disorders (not alcoholism) and found positive outcomes in several areas. Weiss et al. (2000, 2007, 2009) used a cognitive-behavioral intervention for people with bipolar disorder plus substance use disorder and found positive substance use outcomes. The consistency of positive findings in relation to different models of long-term group counseling suggests the possibility that peer group support is the active component of these interventions.

Residential interventions typically include a program of treatment and support within a full-time, monitored residence. Brunette, Mueser, and Drake (2004) identified several relevant studies. Among these studies, the long-term programs consistently show positive outcomes on substance use and on other outcomes. However, the studies of residential interventions almost entirely employed quasi-experimental designs, which limit scientific inference. Residential interventions are unique because they typically serve homeless persons with co-occurring disorders who have not responded to less intensive outpatient interventions. Thus, residential treatment is the only evidence-based intervention for treatment non-responders.

Third, individual counseling, case management, and supported employment have been studied extensively with people with co-occurring disorders and show consistent impacts on outcomes other than substance use. Several studies of brief individual counseling based on motivational approaches (Miller & Rollnick, 2012) produced inconsistent results on substance use reduction but appear to be important in the engagement process. One long-term study by Barrowclough and colleagues (2001), which included 9 months of motivational interviewing and cognitive behavioral treatment combined with family intervention, documented numerous positive results at post-treatment, but most of the beneficial effects had disappeared by 18 months (Haddock et al., 2003). A larger trial of the motivational interviewing and cognitive-behavioral therapy showed modest effects on reduction of substance abuse severity (Barrowclough et al., 2010).

Case management interventions refer to intensive, team-based, multidisciplinary, outreach-oriented, clinically coordinated services, usually involving the model assertive community treatment (Stein & Test, 1980). Case management studies have produced inconsistent results on substance use outcomes, but they have shown consistent positive outcomes on other domains, such as increasing engagement, decreasing hospital use, increasing community tenure, and improving quality of life, which are the traditional outcomes associated with case management (Mueser, Bond, Drake, & Resnick, 1998). The outcomes may be even more positive for more complex subgroups, such as those who also have antisocial behaviors (Frisman et al., 2009). Thus, case management is effective for people with co-occurring disorders, but a specific substance abuse intervention probably needs to be included to impact substance use outcomes.

Supported employment has been used successfully with people with co-occurring disorders in several studies (Bond, Drake, & Becker, 2008; Campbell, Bond, & Drake, 2009; Mueser, Campbell, & Drake, 2011). In most studies the presence of a substance use disorder has been uncorrelated with work outcomes, suggesting that people with co-occurring disorders do as well as single diagnosis individuals in finding and keeping jobs. Employment may also have an effect on their long-term recovery (Bush, Drake, Xie, McHugo, & Haslett, 2009; Xie et al., 2009). One study did find that addiction was a negative predictor, perhaps because it included many people who had no work goals (Lehman et al., 2002).

Fourth, two types of interventions, contingency management and legal interventions, are emerging in the literature in recent years (Drake et al., 2008). Both have shown some promising findings, but the specific approaches and the research are too limited to draw firm conclusions at this point.

Fifth, at the time of the review (Drake et al., 2008), very little research had been conducted on family intervention, aside from one promising trial that combined family psychoeducation with individual-based motivational interviewing and cognitive behavioral therapy (Haddock et al., 2003). Two recent randomized controlled trials of family programs suggest some beneficial effects and the need for more work in this area. One trial compared a brief (3-month) family psychoeducational approach to a more comprehensive family program, including psychoeducation and training in communication and problem-solving skills delivered over 18 months, in clients with a serious mental illness and co-occurring substance use disorder (Mueser et al., 2013). Clients in both family programs showed significant and comparable improvements in substance abuse over 3 years, while those in the comprehensive program improved more in overall symptoms and psychotic symptoms and tended to improve more in overall functioning than those in the brief family psychoeducation program. Relatives in the comprehensive program also improved more in knowledge about co-occurring disorders and mental health functioning but did not differ in family burden, compared with those in the psychoeducation program. The other trial compared the effects of training the parents of offspring with recent-onset schizophrenia and cannabis use disorder on motivational interviewing and communication skills with routine family support (Smeerdijk et al., 2012). The clients of parents who received the motivational interviewing and communication skills training had significantly greater reductions in cannabis use over treatment and at follow-up than those who parents received routine support, although there were no differences between the groups in overall functioning.

Finally, two commonly used interventions were found to have little or no research base (Drake et al., 2008): intensive outpatient interventions and inpatient interventions. More research is needed in each of these areas.

Pharmacological Interventions

Pharmacological interventions have been studied extensively in people with co-occurring disorders, but there is a paucity of randomized controlled trials and of solid findings. We review here the evidence for people with schizophrenia-spectrum disorders.

Many uncontrolled reports and theoretical articles suggest that the atypical antipsychotic medications are superior to the typical antipsychotic medications (Green, Noordsy, Brunette, & O'Keefe, 2008). However, the findings from several randomized controlled studies show mixed findings and do not support these optimistic conclusions (Brown, Garza, & Carmody, 2008; Sayers et al., 2005; Smelson et al., 2002, 2004, 2006). For example, Sayers et al. (2005) compared olanzapine and haloperidol for people with schizophrenia and cocaine abuse and found no differences in negative urines and greater craving in the olanzapine group.

The most compelling data involve clozapine, which has been linked to reduced substance use in multiple naturalistic studies. Clozapine uniquely brings together mild D2 blockade, modest serotonin-2 antagonism (releasing dopamine) and modest α_2 antagonism (releasing norepinephrine) (Green et al., 2008). Each of these actions has been linked to restoring normalized transmission in the mesocorticolimbic circuit in animal models of schizophrenia, which may improve signaling in the brain reward system (see earlier section on brain reward dysfunction) (Svensson et al., 1995). One small randomized controlled trial in people with schizophrenia and cannabis use disorder reported significantly greater reductions in cannabis use for clients who were randomly assigned to switch to clozapine compared with remaining on their other antipsychotic medication (Brunette et al., 2011). Other randomized controlled trials of clozapine for co-occurring disorders are currently under way.

The use of medications for alcoholism in schizophrenia is somewhat more positive. In one small randomized controlled trial, Petrakis et al. (2004) found that naltrexone was helpful in controlling alcohol use in people with a psychotic-spectrum disorder and co-occurring alcohol use disorder. In a second trial, Petrakis, Nich, and Ralevski (2006) found that naltrexone and disulfiram were similarly effective in reducing alcohol use among people with psychotic-spectrum disorders and alcoholism. Mueser, Noordsy, Fox, and Wolfe (2003) found that naturalistic disulfiram treatment among patients with schizophrenia and mood disorders in case management services was associated with substantial periods of remission of alcoholism and reduced hospital days, without significant psychiatric complications.

Thus, the medication literature on co-occurring disorders is long on speculation and short on data. Drake and Wallach (2008) argue that the biases of industry, government research agencies, and professionals have produced a disproportionate attention to the least effective interventions and relative neglect of interventions, such as self-help groups, that are proliferating around the country.

Future Directions

Current research is limited by numerous factors: lack of standardization, absence of fidelity assessments, diversity of participants, varying lengths of intervention, short-term follow-ups, diversity of outcomes, and inconsistency of measures. The resulting heterogeneity limits comparability of studies, the potential for meta-analysis, and the strength of inferential validity. Methodological consistency will facilitate comparability and progress. McHugo and colleagues (2006) have also argued for greater ecological validity: studies that reflect the real world context of decision making by clients and practitioners.

Addiction is clearly a long-term disorder (McLellan, Lewis, O'Brien, & Kleber, 2000), yet research continues to focus on short-term outcomes. As Vaillant (2002) points out, however, brief episodes of abstinence—the key outcome for most research studies—appear to have no impact on the long-term course of recovery from addiction. Prospective long-term follow-ups may tell us more about the behaviors, supports, and interventions that lead to recovery. As one example, Alverson et al. (2000) studied ethnographically a small group of people with co-occurring disorders intensively over 3 years and identified four variables associated

with recovery: safe housing, employment, friends who were not substance abusers, and on-going involvement in some type of treatment or self-help program focused on abstinence. These findings are remarkably similar to Vaillant's (2002) longitudinal research on alcoholism.

The few existing long-term studies show that most people with a serious mental disorders recover from substance use disorders gradually, over months and years, and in stages (Drake et al., 2006; Drake, Xie, McHugo, & Shumway, 2004; Drake et al., 2016; McHugo, Drake, Burton, & Ackerson, 1995; Xie, Drake, & McHugo, 2006; Xie, McHugo, Helmstetter, & Drake, 2005). Models identifying stages of treatment and stages of change are clinically relevant because different interventions are effective at different stages of the recovery process (Carey, 1996; McGovern & Wrisley, 2005; Ziedonis & Trudeau, 1997).

In all intervention studies, people with co-occurring disorders respond variably to a particular intervention or program. If diagnosis is not a strong predictor of treatment response, perhaps we should search for other ways of identifying subgroups for future intervention studies (Mueser et al., 1999). Xie et al. (2006, 2009) have recently used latent class trajectory analysis to identify four subgroups: one group of rapid and stable responders, a second group of rapid but unstable responders, a third group of slow but steady responders, and a fourth group of complete nonresponders. These groups are characterized by severity of substance use disorder, use of services, and other factors. Should evidence supporting neurobiological models such as brain reward circuit dysfunction grow, they may prove useful in subdividing groups of individuals, developing specific interventions, and predicting treatment response.

Although some people with co-occurring disorders respond rapidly to integrated treatment, others respond slowly or not at all. The field needs to develop guidelines for sequenced or stepped-care approaches, with less intensive and expensive interventions offered first, and more intensive and expensive interventions contingent on earlier response (Carey, 1996; Kay-Lambkin, Baker, & Lewin, 2004; McHugo et al., 2006).

As the field moves toward the development guidelines and algorithms for the treatment of co-occurring disorders, there is also a need for evidence-based approaches to changing systems of care and implementing integrated treatments (Brunette et al., 2008; Drake, Essock, & Bond,

2009). Current research supports starting with early adopters, critical roles of different stakeholder groups, and the length and timing of clinical training are relatively clear (Bond, Drake, Rapp, McHugo, & Xie, 2009).

Evidence-based medicine requires that both clients and practitioners have access to current scientific information on treatments, effectiveness, side effects, and individualized risks (Drake, Rosenberg, Teague, Bartels, & Torrey, 2003). The World-Wide Web provides efficient, available, and continuously modifiable ways to convey such information, but researchers need to find ways to incorporate critical information into decision supports within electronic medical records, decision aids, patient portals, and procedures for shared decision-making (Adams & Drake, 2006).

Finally, we note that biomedical solutions to socioeconomic problems are rarely effective. The problem of co-occurrence of substance use disorder with mental illness is at least in part a sociological phenomenon reflecting the society's extrusion of people with a serious mental illness from safe neighborhoods and protected living arrangements that limit access to substances of abuse. Safe housing programs and hospitalization are increasingly unavailable to people with the most severe disorders. As a result, they have to reside in settings rife with drugs and alcohol, and increasingly they are shunted to jails and prisons. The current psychiatric emphasis on neurobiology is apparent in clinical approaches, journal articles, and research institutes. Nevertheless, substance abuse and dependence, particularly among people with co-occurring disorders, are strongly influenced by socioenvironmental factors (Drake, Wallach, Alverson, & Mueser, 2002). It has been clear for years that many of these individuals are able to be abstinent in some settings but not in others (Bartels & Drake, 1996). Future research needs to attend to social and environmental context. Co-occurring disorders may be related to the socioeconomic phenomena of weathering (Geronimus, 1992) and allostatic loading (McEwen & Seeman, 1999) more than medical phenomena. American culture and many European cultures tend to value personal autonomy and independence at the expense of community, which may limit studies of protected housing arrangements, even though some individuals clearly express a preference for living with others who are pursuing recovery and clearly do better in such settings (Drake, Wallach, & McGovern, 2005).

References

Adams, J. R., & Drake, R. E. (2006). Shared decision-making and evidence-based practice. *Community Mental Health Journal, 42,* 87–105.

Addington, J., & Duchak, V. (1997). Reasons for substance use in schizophrenia. *Acta Psychiatrica Scandinavica, 96,* 329–333.

Allebeck, P., Adamsson, C., Engström, A., & Rydberg, U. (1993). Cannabis and schizophrenia: A longitudinal study of cases treated in Stockholm County. *Acta Psychiatrica Scandinavica, 88,* 21–24.

Alterman, A. I., & Cacciola, J. S. (1991). The antisocial personality disorder diagnosis in substance abusers: Problems and issues. *Journal of Nervous and Mental Disease, 179,* 167–175.

Alverson, H., Alverson, M., & Drake, R. E. (2000). An ethnographic study of the longitudinal course of substance abuse among people with severe mental illness. *Community Mental Health Journal, 36,* 557–569.

Andréasson, S., Allebeck, P., Engström, A., & Rydberg, U. (1987). Cannabis and schizophrenia: A longitudinal study of Swedish conscripts. *The Lancet, December 26,* 1483–1486.

Andréasson, S., Allebeck, P., & Rydberg, U. (1989). Schizophrenia in users and nonusers of cannabis: A longitudinal study in Stockholm County. *Acta Psychiatrica Scandinavica, 79,* 505–510.

Anthony, J. C. (1991). Epidemiology of drug dependence and illicit drug use. *Current Opinion in Psychiatry, 4,* 435–439.

Arndt, S., Tyrrell, G., Flaum, M., & Andreasen, N. C. (1992). Comorbidity of substance abuse and schizophrenia: The role of pre-morbid adjustment. *Psychological Medicine, 22,* 379–388.

Arseneault, L., Cannon, M., Poulton, R., Murray, R., Caspi, A., & Moffitt, T. E. (2002). Cannabis use in adolescence and risk for adult psychosis: longitudinal prospective study. *British Medical Journal, 325,* 1212–1213.

Asarnow, J. R. (1988). Children at risk for schizophrenia: Converging lines of evidence. *Schizophrenia Bulletin, 14,* 613–631.

Bahorik, A. L., Newhill, C. E., & Eack, S. M. (2013). Characterizing the longitudinal patterns of substance use among individuals diagnosed with serious mental illness after psychiatric hospitalization. *Addiction, 108,* 1259–69.

Barbee, J. G., Clark, P. D., Craqanzano, M. S., Heintz, G. C., & Kehoe, C. E. (1989). Alcohol and substance abuse among schizophrenic patients presenting to an emergency service. *Journal of Nervous and Mental Disease, 177,* 400–407.

Barrowclough, C., Haddock, G., Beardmore, R., Conrod, P., Craig, T., Davies, L., . . . Wykes, T. (2009). Evaluating integrated MI and CBT for people with psychosis and substance misuse: Recruitment, retention and sample characteristics of the MIDAS trial. *Addictive Behaviors, 34,* 859–866.

Barrowclough, C., Haddock, G., Tarrier, N., Lewis, S., Moring, J., O'Brien, R., . . . McGovern, J. (2001). Randomized controlled trial of motivational interviewing, cognitive behavior therapy, and family intervention for patients with comorbid schizophrenia and substance use disorders. *American Journal of Psychiatry, 158,* 1706–1713.

Barrowclough, C., Haddock, G., Wykes, W., Beardmore, R., Conrod, P., Craig, T., . . . Tarrier, N. (2010). Integrated motivational interviewing and cognitive behavioural therapy for people with psychosis and comorbid substance misuse: Randomised controlled trial. *British Medical Journal, 341,* c6325.

Barry, K. L., Milner, K., Blow, F. C., Impens, A., Welsh, D., & Amash, J. (2006). Screening psychiatric emergency department patients with major mental illnesses for at-risk drinking. *Psychiatric Services, 57*, 1039–1042.

Bartels, S. J., & Drake, R. E. (1996). A pilot study of residential treatment for dual diagnoses. *Journal of Nervous and Mental Disease, 184*, 379–381.

Bartels, S. J., Drake, R. E., & McHugo, G. (1992). Alcohol use, depression, and suicidal behavior in schizophrenia. *American Journal of Psychiatry, 149*(3), 394–395.

Becker, D. R., & Drake, R. E. (2003). *A working life for people with severe mental illness.* New York: Oxford University Press.

Bellack, A. S., Bennet, M. E., & Gearon, J. S. (2007). *Behavioral treatment for substance abuse in people with serious and persistent mental illness: A handbook for mental health professionals.* New York: Taylor and Francis.

Bellack, A. S., Bennet, M. E., Gearon, J. S., Brown, C. H., & Yang, Y. (2006). A randomized clinical trial of a new behavioral treatment for drug abuse in people with severe and persistent mental illness. *Archives of General Psychiatry, 63*, 426–432.

Bellack, A. S., Mueser, K. T., Gingerich, S., & Agresta, J. (2004). *Social skills training for schizophrenia: A step-by-step guide* (2nd ed.). New York: Guilford Press.

Bennett, M. E. (2009). Assessment of substance use and substance use disorders in schizophrenia. *Clinical Schizophrenia & Related Psychoses, 3*(2), 50–63.

Berkson, J. (1949). Limitations of the application of four-fold tables to hospital data. *Biological Bulletin, 2*, 47–53.

Berman, S. M., & Noble, E. P. (1993). Childhood antecedents of substance misuse. *Current Opinion in Psychiatry, 6*, 382–387.

Birchwood, M., Mason, R., MacMillian, F., & Healy, J. (1993). Depression, demoralization and control over psychotic illness: A comparison and non-depressed patients with a chronic psychosis. *Psychological Medicine, 23*, 387–395.

Blanchard, J. J.J., Squires, D., Henry, T., Horan, W. P., Bogenschutz, M., Lauriello, J., & Bustillo, J. (1999). Examining an affect regulation model of substance abuse in schizophrenia: The role of traits and coping. *Journal of Nervous and Mental Disease, 187*, 72–79.

Bland, R. C., Newman, S. C., & Orn, H. (1987). Schizophrenia: Lifetime comorbidity in a community sample. *Acta Psychiatrica Scandinavica, 75*, 383–391.

Blum, K., Braverman, E. R., Holder, J. M., Lubar, J. F., Monastra, V. J., Miller, D., . . . Comings, D. E. (2000). Reward deficiency syndrome: A biogenetic model for the diagnosis and treatment of impulsive, addictive, and compulsive behaviors. *Journal of Psychoactive Drugs, 32*(Suppl I–IV), 1–112.

Boileau, I., Assaad, J. M., Pihl, R. O., Benkelfat, C., Leyton, M., Tremblay, R. E., & Dagher, A. (2003). Alcohol promotes dopamine release in the human nucleus accumbens. *Synapse, 49*, 226–231.

Bond, G. R., Drake, R. E., & Becker, D. R. (2008). An update on randomized controlled trials of evidence-based supported employment. *Psychiatric Rehabilitation Journal, 31*, 280–290.

Bond, G. R., Drake, R. E., Rapp, C. A., McHugo, G. J., & Xie, H. (2009). Individualization and quality improvement: Two new scales to complement measurement of program fidelity. *Administration and Policy in Mental Health, 36*, 349–355.

Bramness, J. G., Gundersen, Ø. H., Guterstam, J., Rognli, E. B., Konstenius, M., Løberg, E. M., . . . Franck, J. (2013). Amphetamine-induced psychosis: A separate diagnostic entity or primary psychosis triggered in the vulnerable? *BMC Psychiatry, 12*, 221.

Brecher, M., & Begleiter, H. (1983). Event-related brain potentials to high-incentive stimuli in unmedicated schizophrenic patients. *Biological Psychiatry, 18*, 661–674.

Brown, E. S., Garza, M., & Carmody, T. J. (2008). A randomized, double-blind, placebo-controlled add-on trial of quetiapine in outpatients with bipolar disorder and alcohol use disorders. *Journal of Clinical Psychiatry, 69*, 701–705.

Brunette, M. F., Asher, D., Whitley, R., Lutz, W. J., Wieder, B. L., Jones, A. M., & McHugo, G. J. (2008). Implementation of integrated dual disorders treatment: A qualitative analysis of facilitators and barriers. *Psychiatric Services, 59*, 989–995.

Brunette, M. F., Dawson, R., O'Keefe, C. D., Narasimhan, M., Noordsy, D. L., Wojcik, J., & Green, A. I. (2011). A randomized trial of clozapine versus other antipsychotics for cannabis use disorder in patients with schizophrenia. *Journal of Dual Diagnosis, 7*, 50–63.

Brunette, M. F., Mueser, K. T., & Drake, R. E. (2004). A review of research on residential programs for people with severe mental illness and co-occurring substance use disorders. *Drug and Alcohol Review, 23*, 471–481.

Brunette, M. F., Mueser, K. T., Xie, H., & Drake, R. E. (1997). Relationships between symptoms of schizophrenia and substance abuse. *Journal of Nervous and Mental Disease, 185*, 13–20.

Bunney, W. E., Jr., & Davis, J. (1965). Norepinephrine in depressive reactions. *Archives of General Psychiatry, 13*, 483–494.

Bush, P., Drake, R. E., Xie, H., McHugo, G. J., & Haslett, W. (2009). The long-term impact of employment on mental health service use and costs. *Psychiatric Services, 60*, 1024–1031.

Campbell, K., Bond, G. R., & Drake, R. E. (2009). Who benefits from supported employment? *Schizophrenia Bulletin, 37*, 370–380.

Cannon, T. D., Mednick, S. A., Parnas, J., Schulsinger, F., Praestholm, J., & Vestergaard, A. (1993). Developmental brain abnormalities in the offspring of schizophrenic mothers. *Archives of General Psychiatry, 50*, 551–564.

Carey, K. B. (1996). Treatment of co-occurring substance abuse and major mental illness. In R. E. Drake & K. T. Mueser (Eds.), *Dual diagnosis of major mental illness and substance abuse: Volume 2: Recent research and clinical implications* (Vol. 70, pp. 19–31). San Francisco: Jossey-Bass Publishers.

Carey, K. B., & Carey, M. P. (1995). Reasons for drinking among psychiatric outpatients: Relationship to drinking patterns. *Psychology of Addictive Behaviors, 9*, 251–257.

Carey, K. B., Carey, M. P., Maisto, S. A., & Henson, J. M. (2004). Temporal stability of the Timeline Followback Interview for alcohol and drug use with psychiatric outpatients. *Journal of Studies on Alcohol, 65*, 774–781.

Carey, K. B., Leontieva, L., Dimmock, J., Maisto, S. A., & Batki, S. L. (2007). Adapting motivational interviewing interventions for comorbid schizophrenia and alcohol use disorders. *Clinical Psychology and Psychotherapy, 14*, 39–57.

Carlson, G. A., & Weintraub, S. (1993). Childhood behavior problems and bipolar disorder—relationship or coincidence? *Journal of Affective Disorders, 28*, 143–153.

Caspi, A., Moffitt, T. E., Cannon, M., McClay, J., Murray, R., Harrington, H., . . . Craig, I. W. (2005). Moderation of the effect of adolescent-onset cannabis use on adult psychosis by a functional polymorphism in the catechol-O-methyltransferase gene: Longitudinal evidence of a gene

X environment interaction. *Biological Psychiatry, 57,* 1117–1127.

Caton, C. L., Shrout, P. E., Eagle, P. F., Opler, L. A., Felix, A. F., & Dominguez, B. (1994). Risk factors for homelessness among schizophrenic men: A case-control study. *American Journal of Public Health, 84,* 265–270.

Caton, C. L. M., Shrout, P. E., Dominguez, B., Eagle, P. F., Opler, L. A., & Cournos, F. (1995). Risk factors for homelessness among women with schizophrenia. *American Journal of Public Health, 85,* 1153–1156.

Caton, C. L. M., Shrout, P. E., Eagle, P. F., Opler, L. A., & Felix, A. (1994). Correlates of codisorders in homeless and never homeless indigent schizophrenic men. *Psychological Medicine, 24,* 681–688.

Chambers, R. A., Krystal, J. H., & Self, D. W. (2001). A neurobiological basis for substance abuse comorbidity in schizophrenia. *Biological Psychiatry, 50,* 71–83.

Chambers, R. A., & Self, D. W. (2002). Motivational responses to natural and drug rewards in rats with neonatal ventral hippocampal lesions: an animal model of dual diagnosis schizophrenia. *Neuropsychopharmacology, 27,* 889–905.

Chau, D. T., Roth, R. M., & Green, A. I. (2004). The neural circuitry of reward and its relevance to psychiatric disorders. *Current Psychiatry Reports, 6,* 391–399.

Chen, C., Balogh, M., Bathija, J., Howanitz, E., Plutchik, R., & Conte, H. R. (1992). Substance abuse among psychiatric inpatients. *Comprehensive Psychiatry, 33,* 60–64.

Chow, C. M., Wieman, D., Cichocki, B., Qvicklund, H., & Hiersteiner, D. (2013). Mission impossible: Treating serious mental illness and substance use co-occurring disorder with integrated treatment: A meta-analysis. *Mental Health and Substance Use, 6,* 150–68.

Clark, R. E. (2001). Family support and substance use outcomes for persons with mental illness and substance use disorders. *Schizophrenia Bulletin, 27,* 93–101.

Cohen, M., & Klein, D. F. (1970). Drug abuse in a young psychiatric population. *American Journal of Orthopsychiatry, 40,* 448–455.

Corrigan, P. W., Mueser, K. T., Bond, G. R., Drake, R. E., & Solomon, P. (2008). *The principles and practice of psychiatric rehabilitation: An empirical approach.* New York: Guilford Press.

Corse, S. J., Hirschinger, N. B., & Zanis, D. (1995). The use of the Addiction Severity Index with people with severe mental illness. *Psychiatric Rehabilitation Journal, 19,* 9–18.

Crespo-Facorro, B., Paradiso, S., Andreasen, N. C., O'Leary, D. S., Watkins, G. L., Ponto, L. L.L., & Hichwa, R. D. (2001). Neural mechanisms of anhedonia in schizophrenia; a PET study of response to unpleasant and pleasant odors. *Journal of the American Medical Association, 286,* 427–435.

Cuffel, B., & Chase, P. (1994). Remission and relapse of substance use disorders in schizophrenia: Results from a one year prospective study. *Journal of Nervous and Mental Disease, 182,* 704–708.

Cuffel, B. J. (1996). Comorbid substance use disorder: Prevalence, patterns of use, and course. In R. E. Drake & K. T. Mueser (Eds.), *Dual diagnosis of major mental illness and substance abuse: Volume 2: Recent research and clinical implications. New directions in mental health services* (Vol. 70, pp. 93–105). San Francisco: Jossey-Bass.

D'Souza, D. C., Abi-Saab, W. M., Madonick, S., Forselius-Bielen, K., Doersch, A., Braley, G., ... & Krystal, J. H. (2005). Delta-9-tetrahydrocannabinol effects in schizophrenia: Implications for cognition, psychosis, and addiction. *Biological Psychiatry, 57,* 594–608.

Dansky, B. S., Brady, K. T., Saladin, M. E., Killeen, T., Becker, S., & Roitzsch, J. C. (1996). Victimization and PTSD in individuals with substance use disorders: Gender and racial differences. *The American Journal of Drug and Alcohol Abuse, 22,* 75–93.

Degenhardt, L., Hall, W., & Lynskey, M. (2003). Testing hypotheses about the relationship between cannabis use and psychosis. *Drug and Alcohol Dependence, 71,* 37–48.

DelBello, M. P., Strakowski, S. M., Sax, K. W., McElroy, S. L., Keck, P. E. J., ... Kmetz, G. F. (1999). Effects of familial rates of affective illness and substance abuse on rates of substance abuse in patients with first-episode mania. *Journal of Affective Disorders, 56,* 55–60.

DeMarce, J. M., Burden, J. L., Lash, S. J., Stephens, R. S., & Grambow, S. C. (2007). Convergent validity of the Timeline Followback for persons with comorbid psychiatric disorders engaged in residential substance use treatment. *Addictive Behaviors, 32,* 1582–1592.

Denning, P. (2000). *Practicing harm reduction psychotherapy: An alternative approach to addictions.* New York: Guilford Publications.

DiClemente, C. C., Nidecker, M., & Bellack, A. S. (2008). Motivation and the stages of change among individuals with severe mental illness and substance abuse disorders. *Journal of Substance Abuse Treatment, 34,* 25–35.

Di Forti, M., Morgan, C., Dazzan, P., Pariante, P., Mondelli, V., Marques, T. R., Handley, R., Luzi, S., Russo, M., Paparelli, A., Butt, A., Stilo, S. A., Wiffen, B., Powell, J., & Murray, R. M. (2009). High-potency cannabis and the risk of psychosis. *British Journal of Psychiatry, 195,* 488–91.

Dixon, L. B., (1999). Dual diagnosis of substance abuse in schizophrenia: Prevalence and impact on outcomes. *Schizophrenia Research, 35*(Suppl), S93–S100.

Dixon, L., Haas, G., Weiden, P. J., Sweeney, J., & Frances, A. J. (1991). Drug abuse in schizophrenic patients: Clinical correlates and reasons for use. *American Journal of Psychiatry, 148,* 224–230.

Dixon, L., McNary, S., & Lehman, A. (1995). Substance abuse and family relationships of persons with severe mental illness. *American Journal of Psychiatry, 152,* 456–458.

Donald, M., Dower, J., & Kavanagh, D. J. (2005). Integrated versus non-integrated management and care for clients with co-occurring mental health and substance use disorders: A qualitative systematic review of randomised controlled trials. *Social Science & Medicine, 61,* 1371–1383.

Drake, R. E., Antosca, L. M., Noordsy, D. L., Bartels, S. J., & Osher, F. C. (1991). New Hampshire's specialized services for the dually diagnosed. In K. Minkoff & R. E. Drake (Eds.), *Dual diagnosis of major mental illness and substance disorder: New directions for mental health services* (Vol. 50, pp. 57–67). San Francisco: Jossey-Bass.

Drake, R. E., Brunette, M. F., & Mueser, K. T. (1998). Substance use disorder and social functioning in schizophrenia. In K. T. Mueser & N. Tarrier (Eds.), *Handbook of social functioning in schizophrenia* (pp. 280–289). Boston, MA: Allyn & Bacon.

Drake, R. E., Essock, S. M., & Bond, G. R. (2009). Implementing evidence-based practices for the treatment of schizophrenia patients. *Schizophrenia Bulletin, 35,* 704–713.

Drake, R. E., Luciano, A., Mueser, K. T., Covell, N. H., Essock, S. M., Xie, H., & McHugo, G. J. (2016). Longitudinal course of clients with co-occurring schizophrenia-spectrum and substance use disorders in urban mental health centers: A seven-year prospective study. *Schizophrenia Bulletin, 42*, 202–211.

Drake, R. E., McHugo, G. J., Xie, H., Fox, M., Packard, J., & Helmstetter, B. (2006). Ten-year recovery outcomes for clients with co-occurring schizophrenia and substance use disorders. *Schizophrenia Bulletin, 32*, 464–473.

Drake, R. E., Mercer-McFadden, C., Mueser, K. T., McHugo, G. J., & Bond, G. R. (1998). Review of integrated mental health and substance abuse treatment for patients with dual disorders. *Schizophrenia Bulletin, 24*, 589–608.

Drake, R. E., Mueser, K. T., Brunette, M. F., & McHugo, G. J. (2004). A review of treatments for clients with severe mental illness and co-occurring substance use disorder. *Psychiatric Rehabilitation Journal, 27*, 360–374.

Drake, R. E., O'Neal, E., & Wallach, M. A. (2008). A systematic review of psychosocial interventions for people with co-occurring severe mental and substance use disorders. *Journal of Substance Abuse Treatment, 34*, 123–138.

Drake, R. E., Osher, F. C., Noordsy, D. L., Hurlbut, S. C., Teague, G. B., & Beaudett, M. S. (1990). Diagnosis of alcohol use disorders in schizophrenia. *Schizophrenia Bulletin, 16*, 57–67.

Drake, R. E., Osher, F. C., & Wallach, M. A. (1989). Alcohol use and abuse in schizophrenia: A prospective community study. *Journal of Nervous and Mental Disease, 177*, 408–414.

Drake, R. E., Rosenberg, S. D., & Mueser, K. T. (1996). Assessing substance use disorder in persons with severe mental illness. In R. E. Drake & K. T. Mueser (Eds.), *Dual diagnosis of major mental illness and substance abuse: Volume 2: Recent research and clinical implications. New directions for mental health services* (Vol. 70, pp. 3–17). San Francisco: Jossey-Bass.

Drake, R. E., Rosenberg, S. D., Teague, G. B., Bartels, S. J., & Torrey, W. C. (2003). Fundamental principles of evidence-based medicine applied to mental health care. *Psychiatric Clinics of North America, 26*, 811–820.

Drake, R. E., & Wallach, M. A. (1993). Moderate drinking among people with severe mental illness. *Hospital and Community Psychiatry, 44*, 780–782.

Drake, R. E., & Wallach, M. A. (2008). Conceptual models of treatment for co-occurring substance use. *Alcohol and Substance Use: Dual Diagnosis, 1*, 189–193.

Drake, R. E., Wallach, M. A., & McGovern, M. P. (2005). Future directions in preventing relapse to substance abuse among clients with severe mental illnesses. *Psychiatric Services, 56*, 1297–1302.

Drake, R. E., Wallach, W. A., Alverson, H. S., & Mueser, K. T. (2002). Psychosocial aspects of substance abuse by clients with severe mental illness. *Journal of Nervous and Mental Disease, 190*, 100–106.

Drake, R. E., Xie, H., McHugo, G. J., & Shumway, M. (2004). Three-year outcomes of long-term patients with co-occurring bipolar and substance use disorders. *Biological Psychiatry, 56*, 749–756.

Edens, J. F., Peters, R. H., & Hills, H. A. (1997). Treating prison inmates with co-occurring disorders: An integrative review of existing programs. *Behavioral Sciences and the Law, 15*, 439–457.

Evins, A. E., Green, A. I., Kane, J. M., & Murray, R. M. S. (2013). Does using marijuana increase the risk for developing schizophrenia? *Journal of Clinical Psychiatry, 74*, e08.

Fergusson, D. M., Horwood, L. J., & Swain-Campbell, N. R. (2003). Cannabis dependence and psychotic symptoms in young people. *Psychological Medicine, 33*, 15–21.

First, M. B., Williams, J. B. W., Karg, R. S., & Spitzer, R. L. (2015). *Structured Clinical Interview for DSM-5 Disorders: Clinician Version*. Washington, DC: American Psychiatric Press.

Folsom, D. P., Hawthorne, W., Lindamer, L., Gilmer, T., Bailey, A., Golshan, S., Garcia, P., Unützer, J., Hough, R., & Jeste, D. V. (2005). Prevalence and risk factors for homelessness and utilization of mental health services among 10,340 patients with serious mental illness in a large public mental health system. *American Journal of Psychiatry, 162*, 370–76.

Fox, M. B., Drake, R. E., Mueser, K. T., Brunette, M. F., Becker, D. R., McGovern, M. P., ... Acquilano, S. C. (2010). *Integrated dual disorders treatment manual: Best practices, skills, and resources for successful client care*. Center City, MN: Hazelden.

Friedman, M. J., & Rosenheck, R. A. (1996). PTSD as a persistent mental illness. In S. Soreff (Ed.), *The seriously and persistently mentally ill: The state-of-the-art treatment handbook* (pp. 369–389). Seattle: Hogrefe & Huber.

Frisher, M., Crome, I., Martino, O., & Croft, P. (2009). Assessing the impact of cannabis use on trends in diagnosed schizophrenia in the United Kingdom from 1996 to 2005. *Schizophrenia Research, 113*, 123–128.

Frisman, L. K., Mueser, K. T., Covell, N. H., Lin, H.-J., Crocker, A., Drake, R. E., & Essock, S. M. (2009). Use of integrated dual disorder treatment via assertive comunity treatment versus clinical case management for persons with co-occurring disorders and antisocial personality disorder. *Journal of Nervous and Mental Disease, 197*, 822–828.

Galanter, M., Castaneda, R., & Ferman, J. (1988). Substance abuse among general psychiatric patients: Place of presentation, diagnosis and treatment. *American Journal of Drug and Alcohol Abuse, 14*, 211–235.

Gearon, J. S., & Bellack, A. S. (1999). Women with schizophrenia and co-occurring substance use disorders: An increased risk for violent victimization and HIV. *Community Mental Health Journal, 35*, 401–419.

Geronimus, A. T. (1992). The weathering hypothesis and the health of African-American women and children: Evidence and speculations. *Ethnicity and Disease, 2*, 207–221.

Gershon, E. S., DeLisi, L. E., Hamovit, J., Nurnberger, J. I., Maxwell, M. E., Schreiber, J., ... Guroff, J. J.J. (1988). A controlled family study of chronic psychoses: Schizophrenia and schizoaffective disorder. *Archives of General Psychiatry, 45*, 328–336.

Gingerich, S., & Mueser, K. T. (2010). *Illness management and recovery implementation resource kit* (Revised ed.). Rockville, MD: Center for Mental Health Services, Substance Abuse and Mental Health Services Administration.

Goldiamond, I. (1974). Toward a constructional approach to social problems: Ethical and constitutional problems raised by applied behavioral analysis. *Behaviorism, 2*, 1–85.

Goldman, H. H. (1984). The chronically mentally ill: Who are they? Where are they? In M. Mirabi (Ed.), *The chronically mentally ill: Research and services* (pp. 33–44). New York: Spectrum Publications.

Goodman, W. K., Rudorfer, M. V., & Maser, J. D. (2000). *Obsessive-compulsive disorder: Contemporary issues in treatment*. Mahwah, NJ: Lawrence Erlbaum Associates.

Goodwin, F. K., & Jamison, K. R. (2007). *Manic depressive illness* (2nd ed.). New York: Oxford University Press.

Graham, H. L. (1998). The role of dysfunctional beliefs in individual who experience psychosis and use substances: Implications for cognitive therapy and medication adherence. *Behavioural and Cognitive Psychotherapy, 26,* 193–207.

Graham, H. L., Copello, A., Birchwood, M. J., Mueser, K. T., Orford, J., McGovern, D., ... Georgion, G. (2004). *Cognitive-behavioural integrated treatment (C-BIT): A treatment manual for substance misuse in people with severe mental health problems.* Chichester, England: John Wiley & Sons.

Green, A. I., Noordsy, D. L., Brunette, M. F., & O'Keefe, C. D. (2008). Substance abuse and schizophrenia: Pharmacotherapeutic intervention. *Journal of Substance Abuse Treatment, 34,* 61–71.

Green, A. I., Zimmet, S. V., Strous, R. D., & Schildkraut, J. J.J. (1999). Clozapine for comorbid substance use disorder and schizophrenia: Do patients with schizophrenia have a reward-deficiency syndrome that can be ameliorated by clozapine? *Harvard Review of Psychiatry, 6,* 287–296.

Gururajan, A., Manning, E. E., Klug, M., & van den Buuse, M. (2012). Drugs of abuse and increased risk of psychosis development. *Australian & New Zealand Journal of Psychiatry, 46,* 1120–35.

Gut-Fayand, A., Dervaux, A., Olié, J.-P., Lôo, H., Poirier, M.-F., & Krebs, M.-O. (2001). Substance abuse and suicidality in schizophrenia: A common risk factor linked to impulsivity. *Psychiatry Research, 102,* 65–72.

Haddock, G., Barrowclough, C., Tarrier, N., Moring, J., O'Brien, R., Schofield, N., ... Lewis, S. (2003). Cognitive-behavioural therapy and motivational intervention for schizophrenia and substance misuse: 18-Month outcomes of a randomised controlled trial. *British Journal of Psychiatry, 183,* 418–426.

Hall, W., & Degenhardt, L. (2008). Cannabis use and the risk of developing a psychotic disorder. *World Psychiatry, 7,* 68–71.

Hambrecht, M., & Häfner, H. (1996). Substance abuse and the onset of schizophrenia. *Biological Psychiatry, 40,* 1155–1163.

Hambrecht, M., & Häfner, H. (2000). Cannabis, vulnerability, and the onset of schizophrenia: An epidemiological perspective. *Australian and New Zealand Journal of Psychiatry, 34,* 468–475.

Harrison, I., Joyce, E. M., Mutsatsa, S. H., Hutton, S. B., Huddy, V., Kapasi, M., & Barnes, T. R. E. (2008). Naturalistic follow-up of co-morbid substance use in schizophrenia: The West London first-episode study. *Psychological Medicine, 38,* 79–88.

Henquet, C., Krabbendam, L., Spauwen, J., Kaplan, C., Lieb, R., Wittchen, H. U., & van Os, J. (2005). Prospective cohort study of cannabis use, predisposition for psychosis, and psychotic symptoms in young people. *British Medical Journal, 330,* 11.

Heyman, G. M. (2013). Quitting drugs: Quantitative and qualitative features. *Annual Review of Clinical Psychology, 9,* 29–59.

Hides, L., Cotton, S. M., Berger, G., Gleeson, J., O'Donnell, C., Proffitt, T., ... Lubman, D. I. (2009). The reliability and validity of the Alcohol, Smoking and Substance Involvement Screening Test (ASSIST) in first-episode psychosis. *Addictive Behaviors, 34,* 821–825.

Hides, L., Dawe, S., Kavanagh, D. J., & Young, R. M. (2006). A prospective study of psychotic symptom and cannabis relapse

in recent onset psychosis. *British Journal of Psychiatry, 189,* 137–143.

Higgins, S. T., Sigmon, S. C., Wong, C. J., Heil, S. H., Badger, G. J., Donham, R., ... Anthony, S. (2003). Community reinforcement therapy for cocaine-dependent outpatients. *Archives of General Psychiatry, 60,* 1043–1052.

Hodgins, S., Hiscoke, U. L., & Freese, R. (2002). The antecedents of aggressive behavior among men with schizophrenia: A prospective investigation of patients in community treatment. *Behavioral Sciences & the Law, 21,* 523–546.

Hodgins, S., Tiihonen, J., & Ross, D. (2005). The consequences of conduct disorder for males who develop schizophrenia: Associations with criminality, aggressive behavior, substance use, and psychiatric services. *Schizophrenia Research, 78,* 323–335.

Hodgins, S., Toupin, J., & Côté, G. (1996). Schizophrenia and antisocial personality disorder: A criminal combination. In L. B. Schlesinger (Ed.), *Explorations in criminal psychopathology: Clinical syndromes with forensic implications* (pp. 217–237). Springfield, IL: Charles C Thomas.

Houston, J. E., Murphy, J., Shevlin, M., & Adamson, G. (2011). Cannabis use and psychosis: Re-visiting the role of childhood trauma. *Psychological Medicine, 41,* 2339–48.

Hser, Y.-I., Hoffman, V., Grella, C. E., & Anglin, D. (2001). A 33-year follow-up of narcotics addicts. *Archives of General Psychiatry, 58,* 503–508.

Hser, Y. I., Anglin, D., & Powers, K. (1993). A 24-year follow-up of California narcotics addicts. *Archives of General Psychiatry, 50,* 577–584.

Jablensky, A., McGrath, J., Herrman, H., Castle, D., Gureje, O., Morgan, V., & Korten, A. (1999). *People living with psychotic illness: An Australian Study 1997-1998.* Canberra, Australia: Commonwealth of Australia.

Jackson, H. J., Whiteside, H. L., Bates, G. W., Rudd, R. P., & Edwards, J. (1991). Diagnosing personality disorders in psychiatric inpatients. *Acta Psychiatrica Scandinavica, 83,* 206–213.

Jones, P., Guth, C., Lewis, S., & Murray, R. (1994). Low intelligence and poor educational achievement precede early onset schizophrenic psychosis. In A. S. David & J. C. Cutting (Eds.), *The neuropsychology of schizophrenia* (pp. 131–144). Brighton, England: Lawrence Erlbaum.

Kandel, D. B., & Raveis, V. H. (1989). Cessation of illicit drug use in young adulthood. *Archives of General Psychiatry, 46,* 109–16.

Kashner, M., Rader, L., Rodell, D., Beck, C., Rodell, L., & Muller, K. (1991). Family characteristics, substance abuse, and hospitalization patterns of patients with schizophrenia. *Hospital and Community Psychiatry, 42,* 195–197.

Kavanagh, D. J., & Mueser, K. T. (2007). Current evidence on integrated treatment for serious mental disorder and substance misuse. *Journal of the Norwegian Psychological Association, 5,* 618–637.

Kavanagh, D. J., Waghorn, G., Jenner, L., Chant, D. C., Carr, V., Evans, M., ... McGrath, J. J.J. (2004). Demographic and clinical correlates of comorbid substance use disorders in psychosis: Multivariate analyses from an epidemiological sample. *Schizophrenia Research, 66,* 115–124.

Kay-Lambkin, F. J., Baker, A. L., & Lewin, T. J. (2004). The 'co-morbidity roundabout': A framework to guide assessment and intervention strategies and engineer change among people with co-morbid problems. *Drug and Alcohol Review*, *23*, 407–423.

Kessler, R. C., Bergland, P., Demler, O., Jin, R., Merikangas, K. R., & Walters, E. E. (2005). Lifetime prevalence and age-of-onset distributions of DSM-IV disorders in the National Comorbidity Survey Replication. *Archives of General Psychiatry*, *62*, 593–602.

Kessler, R. C., Crum, R. M., Warner, L. A., Nelson, C. B., Schulenberg, J., & Anthony, J. C. (1997). Lifetime co-occurrence of DSM-III-R alcohol abuse and dependence with other psychiatric disorders in the National Comorbidity Survey. *Archives of General Psychiatry*, *54*, 313–321.

Kessler, R. C., Nelson, C. B., McGonagle, K. A., Edlund, M. J., Frank, R. G., & Leaf, P. J. (1996). The epidemiology of co-occurring addictive and mental disorders: Implications for prevention and service utilization. *American Journal of Orthopsychiatry*, *66*, 17–31.

Kessler, R. C., Rubinow, D. R., Holmes, C., Abelson, J. M., & Zhao, S. (1997). The epidemiology of DSM-III-R bipolar I disorder in a general population survey. *Psychological Medicine*, *27*, 1079–1089.

Khantzian, E. J. (1997). The self-medication hypothesis of substance use disorders: A reconsideration and recent applications. *Harvard Review of Psychiatry*, *4*, 231–244.

Knopik, V. S., Heath, A. C., Madden, P. A. F., Bucholz, K. K., Slutske, W. S., Nelson, E. C., . . . Martin, N. G. (2004). Genetic effects on alcohol dependence risk: Re-evaluating the importance of psychiatric and other heritable risk factors. *Psychological Medicine*, *34*, 1519–1530.

Knudsen, P., & Vilmar, T. (1984). Cannabis and neuroleptic agents in schizophrenia. *Acta Psychiatrica Scandinavica*, *69*, 162–174.

Konings, M., Stefanis, N., Kuepper, R., de Graaf, R., Have, M. T., van Os, J., . . . Henquet, C. (2012). Replication in two independent population-based samples that childhood maltreatment and cannabis use synergistically impact on psychosis risk. *Psychological Medicine*, *42*, 149–59.

Kozaric-Kovacic, D., Folnegovic-Smalc, V., Folnegovic, Z., & Marusic, A. (1995). Influence of alcoholism on the prognosis of schizophrenic patients. *Journal of Studies on Alcohol*, *56*, 622–627.

Krebs, M. O., Sautel, F., Bourdel, M. C., Sokoloff, P., Schwartz, J. C., Olie, J. P., . . . Poirier, M. F. (1998). Dopamine D3 receptor gene variants and substance abuse in schizophrenia. *Molecular Psychiatry*, *3*, 337–341.

Krystal, J. H., Perry, E. B., Gueorguieva, R., Belger, A., Madonick, S. H., Abi-Dargham, A., . . . D'Souza, D. C. (2005). Comparative and interactive human psychopharmacologic effects of ketamine and amphetamine. *Archives of General Psychiatry*, *62*, 985–995.

Kuepper, R., van Os, J., Lieb, R., Wittchen, H. U., Höfler, M., & Henquet, C. (2011). Continued cannabis use and risk of incidence and persistence of psychotic symptoms: 10 Year follow-up cohort study. *British Medical Journal*, *342*, d738.

Kuepper, R., van Os, J., Wittchen, H.-U., & Henquet, C. (2011). Do cannabis and urbanicity co-participate in causing psychosis? Evidence from a 10-year follow-up cohort study. *Psychological Medicine*, *41*, 2121–29.

Large, M., Sharma, S., Compton, M. T., Slade, T., & Nielssen, O. (2011). Cannabis use and earlier onset of psychosis: A systematic meta-analysis. *Archives of General Psychiatry*, *68*, 555–561.

Laudet, A. B., Magura, S., Vogel, H. S., & Knight, E. L. (2004). Perceived reasons for substance misuse among persons with a psychiatric disorder. *American Journal of Orthopsychiatry*, *74*, 365–375.

Lecomte, T., Paquin, K., Mueser, K. T., MacEwan, W., Goldner, E., Thornton, A. E., . . . Honer, W. G. (2013). Relationships among depression, PTSD, methamphetamine abuse, and psychosis. *Journal of Dual Diagnosis*, *9*, 115–22.

Lehman, A. F., Goldberg, R., Dixon, L. B., McNary, S., Postrado, L., Hackman, A., & McDonnell, K. (2002). Improving employment outcomes for persons with severe mental illnesses. *Archives of General Psychiatry*, *59*, 165–172.

Lehman, A. F., Myers, C. P., Corty, E., & Thompson, J. W. (1994). Prevalence and patterns of "dual diagnosis" among psychiatric inpatients. *Comprehensive Psychiatry*, *35*, 106–112.

Lettfuss, N. Y., Seeger-Armbruster, S., & von Ameln-Mayerhofer, A. (2013). Is behavioral sensitization to 3,4-methylenedioxymethamphetamine (MDMA) mediated in part by cholinergic receptors? *Behavioural Brain Research*, *244*, 116–19.

Ley, A., Jeffery, D., Shaw, S., & Weaver, T. (2007). Development of a brief screen for substance misuse amongst people with severe mental health problems living in the community. *Journal of Mental Health*, *16*, 679–690.

Ley, A. J. (2003). Cochrane review of treatment outcome studies and its implications for future developments. In H. L. Graham & A. Copello & M. J. Birchwood & K. T. Mueser (Eds.), *Substance misuse in psychosis: Approaches to treatment and service delivery* (pp. 349–365). Chichester, England: John Wiley & Sons.

Lieb, K., Zanarini, M. C., Schmahl, C., Linehan, M. M., & Bohus, M. (2004). Borderline personality disorder. *Lancet*, *364*, 453–461.

Lieberman, J. A., Kane, J. M., & Alvir, J. (1987). Provocative tests with psychostimulant drugs in schizophrenia. *Psychopharmacology*, *91*, 415–433.

Lieberman, J. A., Kinon, B. J., & Loebel, A. D. (1990). Dopaminergic mechanisms in idiopathic and drug-induced psychoses. *Schizophrenia Bulletin*, *16*, 97–110.

Lindsley, O. R. (1964). Direct measurement and prosthesis of retarded behavior. *Journal of Education*, *147*, 304–312.

Maier, W., Lichtermann, D., Minges, J., Delmo, C., & Heun, R. (1995). The relationship between bipolar disorder and alcoholism: A controlled family study. *Psychological Medicine*, *25*, 787–796.

Maslin, J., Graham, H. L., Cawley, M., Birchwood, M., Georgiou, G., McGovern, D., . . . Orford, J. (2001). Combined severe mental health and substance use problems: What are the training and support needs of staff working with this client group? *Journal of Mental Health*, *10*, 131–140.

McCabe, P. J., Christopher, P. P., Druhn, N., Roy-Bujnowski, K. M., Grudzinskas, A. J., & Fisher, W. H. (2012). Arrest types and co-occurring disorders in persons with schizophrenia or related psychoses. *Journal of Behavioral Health Services and Research*, 1–13.

McEwen, B. S., & Seeman, T. (1999). Protecting and damaging effects of mediators of stress: Elaborating and testing the concepts of allostasis and allostatic load. *Annals of the New York Academies of Science*, *896*, 30–47.

McGovern, M. P., & Wrisley, B. R. (2005). Relapse of substance use disorder and its prevention among persons with co-occurring disorders. *Psychiatric Services*, *56*, 1270–1273.

McGrath, J. J., Scott, J., Varghese, D., Degenhardt, L., Hayatbakhsh, M. R., Alati, R., ... Najman, J. M. (2010). Association between cannabis use and psychosis-related outcomes using sibling pair analysis in a cohort of young adults. *Archives of General Psychiatry, 67*, 440–447.

McHugo, G. J., Bebout, R. R., Harris, M., Cleghorn, S., Herring, G., Xie, H., ... Drake, R. E. (2004). A randomized controlled trial of integrated versus parallel housing services for homeless adults with severe mental illness. *Schizophrenia Bulletin, 30*, 969–982.

McHugo, G. J., Drake, R. E., Brunette, M. F., Xie, H., Essock, S. M., & Green, A. I. (2006). Enhancing validity in co-occurring disorders treatment research. *Schizophrenia Bulletin, 32*, 655–665.

McHugo, G. J., Drake, R. E., Burton, H. L., & Ackerson, T. H. (1995). A scale for assessing the stage of substance abuse treatment in persons with severe mental illness. *Journal of Nervous and Mental Disease, 183*, 762–767.

McHugo, G. J., Drake, R. E., Xie, H., & Bond, G. R. (2012). A 10-year study of steady employment and non-vocational outcomes among people with serious mental illness and co-occurring substance use disorders. *Schizophrenia Research, 138*, 233–39.

McLellan, A. T., Lewis, D. C., O'Brien, C. P., & Kleber, H. D. (2000). Drug dependence, a chronic medical illness: Implications for treatment, insurance, and outcomes evaluation. *JAMA, 284*, 1689–1695.

McLellan, T. A., Woody, G. E., & O'Brien, C. P. (1979). Development of psychiatric illness in drug abusers: Possible role of drug preference. *New England Journal of Medicine, 301*(24), 1310–1314.

Meade, C. S., Kershaw, T. S., Hansen, N. B., & Sikkema, K. J. (2009). Long-term correlates of childhood abuse among adults with severe mental illness: Adult victimization, substance abuse, and HIV sexual risk behavior. *AIDS Behavior, 13*, 207–16.

Miller, R., Ream, G., McCormack, J., Gunduz-Bruce, H., Sevy, S., & Robinson, D. (2009). A prospective study of cannabis use as a risk factor for non-adherence and treatment dropout in first-episode schizophrenia. *Schizophrenia Research, 113*, 138–144.

Miller, W. R., & Rollnick, S. (2012). *Motivational interviewing: Preparing people for change.* (3rd ed.). New York: Guilford Press.

Min, M. O., Biegel, D. E., & Johnsen, J. A. (2005). Predictors of psychiatric hospitalization for adults with co-occurring substance and mental disorders as compared to adults with mental illness only. *Psychiatric Rehabilitation Journal, 29*, 114–121.

Miner, C. R., Rosenthal, R. N., Hellerstein, D. J., & Muenz, L. R. (1997). Prediction of compliance with outpatient referral in patients with schizophrenia and psychoactive substance use disorders. *Archives of General Psychiatry, 54*, 706–712.

Minkoff, K. (1989). An integrated treatment model for dual diagnosis of psychosis and addiction. *Hospital and Community Psychiatry, 40*, 1031–1036.

Montross, L. P., Barrio, C., Yamada, A.-M., Lindarner, L., Golshan, S., Garcia, P., ... Jeste, D. V. (2005). Tri-ethnic variations of co-morbid substance and alcohol use disorders in schizophrenia. *Schizophrenia Research, 79*, 297–305.

Mueser, K. T., Bennett, M., & Kushner, M. G. (1995). Epidemiology of substance abuse among persons with chronic mental disorders. In A. F. Lehman & L. Dixon (Eds.), *Double jeopardy: Chronic mental illness and substance abuse* (pp. 9–25). New York: Harwood Academic Publishers.

Mueser, K. T., Bond, G. R., Drake, R. E., & Resnick, S. G. (1998). Models of community care for severe mental illness: A review of research on case management. *Schizophrenia Bulletin, 24*, 37–74.

Mueser, K. T., Campbell, K., & Drake, R. E. (2011). The effectiveness of supported employment in people with dual disorders. *Journal of Dual Diagnosis, 7*, 90–102.

Mueser, K. T., Crocker, A. G., Frisman, L. B., Drake, R. E., Covell, N. H., & Essock, S. M. (2006). Conduct disorder and antisocial personality disorder in persons with severe psychiatric and substance use disorders. *Schizophrenia Bulletin, 32*, 626–636.

Mueser, K. T., Drake, R. E., Ackerson, T. H., Alterman, A. I., Miles, K. M., & Noordsy, D. L. (1997). Antisocial personality disorder, conduct disorder, and substance abuse in schizophrenia. *Journal of Abnormal Psychology, 106*, 473–477.

Mueser, K. T., Drake, R. E., Sigmon, S. C., & Brunette, M. F. (2005). Psychosocial interventions for adults with severe mental illnesses and co-occurring substance use disorders: A review of specific interventions. *Journal of Dual Diagnosis, 1*, 57–82.

Mueser, K. T., Essock, S. M., Drake, R. E., Wolfe, R. S., & Frisman, L. (2001). Rural and urban differences in dually diagnosed patients: Implications for service needs. *Schizophrenia Research, 48*, 93–107.

Mueser, K. T., Glynn, S. M., Cather, C., Xie, H., Zarate, R., Smith, M. F., ... Feldman, J. (2013). A randomized controlled trial of family intervention for co-occurring substance use and severe psychiatric disorders. *Schizophrenia Bulletin, 39*, 658–72.

Mueser, K. T., Gottlieb, J. D., Cather, C., Glynn, S. M., Zarate, R., Smith, L. F., Clark, R. E., &... Wolfe, R. (2012). Antisocial personality disorder in people with co-occurring severe mental illness and substance use disorders: Clinical, functional, and family relationship correlates. *Psychosis, 4*, 52–62.

Mueser, K. T., Nishith, P., Tracy, J. I., DeGirolamo, J., & Molinaro, M. (1995). Expectations and motives for substance use in schizophrenia. *Schizophrenia Bulletin, 21*, 367–378.

Mueser, K. T., & Noordsy, D. L. (1996). Group treatment for dually diagnosed clients. In R. E. Drake & K. T. Mueser (Eds.), *Dual diagnosis of major mental illness and substance abuse: Volume 2: Recent research and clinical implications* (Vol. 70, pp. 33–51). San Francisco: Jossey-Bass.

Mueser, K. T., Noordsy, D. L., Drake, R. E., & Fox, L. (2003). *Integrated treatment for dual disorders: A guide to effective practice.* New York: Guilford Press.

Mueser, K. T., Noordsy, D. L., Fox, L., & Wolfe, R. (2003). Disulfiram treatment for alcoholism in severe mental illness. *American Journal on Addictions, 12*, 242–52.

Mueser, K. T., Rosenberg, S. D., Drake, R. E., Miles, K. M., Wolford, G., Vidaver, R., & Carrieri, K. (1999). Conduct disorder, antisocial personality disorder, and substance use disorders in schizophrenia and major affective disorders. *Journal of Studies on Alcohol, 60*, 278–284.

Mueser, K. T., Yarnold, P. R., & Bellack, A. S. (1992). Diagnostic and demographic correlates of substance abuse in schizophrenia and major affective disorder. *Acta Psychiatrica Scandinavica, 85*, 48–55.

Mueser, K. T., Yarnold, P. R., Levinson, D. F., Singh, H., Bellack, A. S., Kee, K., ... Yadalam, K. G. (1990). Prevalence of substance abuse in schizophrenia: Demographic and clinical correlates. *Schizophrenia Bulletin, 16*, 31–56.

Mueser, K. T., Yarnold, P. R., Rosenberg, S. D., Swett, C., Miles, K. M., & Hill, D. (2000). Substance use disorder in hospitalized severely mentally ill psychiatric patients: Prevalence, correlates, and subgroups. *Schizophrenia Bulletin, 26*, 179–192.

Myin-Germeys, I., van Os, J., Schwartz, J. E., Stone, A. A., & Delespaul, P. S. (2001). Emotional reactivity to daily life stress in psychosis. *Archives of General Psychiatry, 58*, 1137–44.

Niv, N., Lopez, S. R., Glynn, S. M., & Mueser, K. T. (2007). The role of substance use in families, attributions and affective reactions to their relative with severe mental illness. *Journal Nervous and Mental Disease, 195*, 307–314.

Noordsy, D. L., Drake, R. E., Biesanz, J. C., & McHugo, G. J. (1994). Family history of alcoholism in schizophrenia. *Journal of Nervous and Mental Disease, 186*, 651–655.

Noordsy, D. L., Drake, R. E., Teague, G. B., Osher, F. C., Hurlbut, S. C., Beaudett, M. S., & Paskus, T. S. (1991). Subjective experiences related to alcohol abuse among schizophrenics. *Journal of Nervous and Mental Disease, 179*, 410–414.

Nuechterlein, K. H., & Dawson, M. E. (1984). A heuristic vulnerability/stress model of schizophrenic episodes. *Schizophrenia Bulletin, 10*, 300–312.

O'Daly, O. G., Joyce, D., Stephan, K. E., Murray, R. M., & Shergill, S. S. (2011). Functional magnetic resonance imaging investigation of the amphetamine sensitization model of schizophrenia in healthy male volunteers. *Archives of General Psychiatry, 68*, 545–554.

O'Hare, T., & Sherrer, M. (2011). Drinking motives as mediators between PTSD symptom severity and alcohol consumption in persons with severe mental illnesses. *Addictive Behaviors, 36*, 465–69.

O'Leary, D. S., Block, R. I., Flaum, M., Schultz, S. K., Boles Ponto, L. L.L., Watkins, G. L., ... Hichwa, R. D. (2000). Acute marijuana effects of rCBF and cognition: A PET study. *Neuroreport, 11*, 3835–3841.

Osher, F. C., & Kofoed, L. L.L. (1989). Treatment of patients with psychiatric and psychoactive substance use disorders. *Hospital and Community Psychiatry, 40*, 1025–1030.

Parabiaghi, A., Bonetto, C., Ruggeri, M., Lasalvia, A., & Leese, M. (2006). Severe and persistent mental illness: a useful definition for prioritizing community-based mental health service interventions. *Social Psychiatry and Psychiatric Epidemiology, 41*, 457–563.

Peters, R. H., Kearns, W. D., Murrin, M. R., & Dolente, A. S. (1992). Psychopathology and mental health needs among drug-involved inmates. *Journal of Prison and Jail Health, 111*, 3–25.

Petrakis, I. L., Nich, C., & Ralevski, E. (2006). Psychotic spectrum disorders and alcohol abuse: a review of pharmacotherapeutic strategies and a report on the effectiveness of naltrexone and disulfiram. *Schizophrenia Bulletin, 32*, 644–654.

Petrakis, I. L., O'Malley, S. S., Rounsaville, B., Poling, J., McHugh-Strong, C., & Krystal, J. H. (2004). Naltrexone augmentation of neuroleptic treatment in alcohol abusing patients with schizophrenia. *Psychopharmacology, 172*, 291–297.

Petrakis, I. L., Rosenheck, R., & Desai, R. (2011). Substance use comorbidity among Veterans with posttraumatic stress disorder and other psychiatric illness. *American Journal on Addictions, 20*, 185–189.

Polcin, D. L. (1992). Issues in the treatment of dual diagnosis clients who have chronic mental illness. *Professional Psychology: Research and Practice, 23*, 30–37.

Pollack, L. E., Cramer, R. D., & Varner, R. V. (2000). Psychosocial functioning of people with substance abuse and bipolar disorders. *Substance Abuse, 21*, 193–203.

Potvin, S., Blanchet, P., & Stip, E. (2009). Substance abuse is associated with increased extrapyramidal symptoms in schizophrenia: A meta-analysis. *Schizophrenia Research, 113*, 181–188.

Potvin, S., Sepehry, A. A., & Stip, E. (2007). Meta-analysis of depressive symptoms in dual-diagnosis schizophrenia. *Australian and New Zealand Journal of Psychiatry, 41*, 792–799.

Prochaska, J. O., & DiClemente, C. C. (1984). *The Transtheoretical Approach: Crossing the Traditional Boundaries of Therapy*. Homewood, IL: Dow-Jones/Irwin.

Räsänen, P., Tiihonen, J., Isohanni, M., Rantakallio, P., Lehtonen, J., & Moring, J. (1998). Schizophrenia, alcohol abuse, and violent behavior: A 26-year followup study of an unselected birth cohort. *Schizophrenia Bulletin, 24*, 437–441.

Redish, A. D. (2004). Addiction as a computational process gone awry. *Science, 306*, 1944–47.

Regier, D. A., Farmer, M. E., Rae, D. S., Locke, B. Z., Keith, S. J., Judd, L. L.L., & Goodwin, F. K. (1990). Comorbidity of mental disorders with alcohol and other drug abuse: Results from the Epidemiologic Catchment Area (ECA) study. *Journal of the American Medical Association, 264*, 2511–2518.

Ridgely, M. S., Goldman, H. H., & Talbott, J. A. (1986). *Chronically mentally ill young adults with substance abuse problems: A review of the literature and creation of a research agenda*. Baltimore, MD: University of Maryland Mental Health Policy Studies Center.

Ridgely, M. S., Goldman, H. H., & Willenbring, M. (1990). Barriers to the care of persons with dual diagnoses: Organizational and financing issues. *Schizophrenia Bulletin, 16*, 123–132.

Ries, R. K., Dyck, D. G., Short, R., Srebnik, D., Fisher, A., & Comtois, K. A. (2004). Outcomes of managing disability benefits among patients with substance dependence and severe mental illness. *Psychiatric Services, 55*, 445–447.

Ringen, P. A., Melle, I., Berg, A. O., Agartz, I., Spigset, O., Simonsen, C., ... Andreassen, O. A. (2013). Cannabis use and premorbid functioning as predictors of poorer neurocognition in schizophrenia spectrum disorder. *Schizophrenia Research, 143*, 84–9.

Ringen, P. A., Melle, I., Birkenaes, A. B., Engh, J. A., Faerden, A., Vaskinn, A., ... Andreassen, O. A. (2008). The level of illicit drug use is related to symptoms and premorbid functioning in severe mental illness. *Acta Psychiatrica Scandinavica, 118*, 297–304.

Robins, L. N. (1966). *Deviant children grown up*. Huntington, NY: Robert E. Krieger.

Robins, L. N., & Regier, D. A. (1991). *Psychiatric disorders in America: The Epidemiologic Catchment Area Study*. New York: The Free Press.

Rosenberg, S. D., Drake, R. E., Wolford, G. L., Mueser, K. T., Oxman, T. E., Vidaver, R. M., ... Luckoor, R. (1998). The Dartmouth Assessment of Lifestyle Instrument (DALI): A substance use disorder screen for people with severe mental illness. *American Journal of Psychiatry, 155*, 232–238.

Rosenberg, S. D., Goodman, L. A., Osher, F. C., Swartz, M., Essock, S. M., Butterfield, M. I., . . . Salyers, M. P. (2001). Prevalence of HIV, hepatitis B and hepatitis C in people with severe mental illness. *American Journal of Public Health*, *91*, 31–37.

Ruggeri, M., Leese, M., Thornicroft, G., Bisoffi, G., & Tansella, M. (2000). Definition and prevalence of severe and persistent mental illness. *British Journal of Psychiatry*, *176*, 149–155.

Salyers, M. P., & Mueser, K. T. (2001). Social functioning, psychopathology, and medication side effects in relation to substance use and abuse in schizophrenia. *Schizophrenia Research*, *48*, 109–123.

Sayers, S. L., Campbell, E. C., Kondrich, J., Mann, S. C., Cornish, J., O'Brien, C., & Caroff, S. N. (2005). Cocaine abuse in schizophrenic patients treated with olanzapine versus haloperidol. *Journal of Nervous and Mental Disease*, *193*, 379–386.

Schinnar, A. P., Rothbard, A. B., Kanter, R., & Jung, Y. S. (1990). An empirical literature review of definitions of severe and persistent mental illness. *American Journal Psychiatry*, *147*, 1602–1608.

Schmidt, L. M., Hesse, M., & Lykke, J. (2011). The impact of substance use disorders on the course of schizophrenia—A 15-year follow-up study. *Schizophrenia Research*, *130*, 228–33.

Serper, M. R., Alpert, M., Richardson, N. A., Dickson, S., Allen, M. H., & Werner, A. (1995). Clinical effects of recent cocaine use on patients with acute schizophrenia. *American Journal of Psychiatry*, *152*, 1464–1469.

Shaner, A., Eckman, T. A., Roberts, L. J., Wilkins, J. N., Tucker, D. E., Tsuang, J. W., & Mintz, J. (1995). Disability income, cocaine use, and repeated hospitalization among schizophrenic cocaine abusers. *The New England Journal of Medicine*, *333*, 777–783.

Shenton, M. E., Dickey, C. C., Frumin, M., & McCarley, R. W. (2001). A review of MRI findings in schizophrenia. *Schizophrenia Research*, *49*, 1–52.

Siever, L. J., Kalus, O. F., & Keefe, R. S. (1993). The boundaries of schizophrenia. *Psychiatric Clinics of North America*, *16*, 217–244.

Sigmon, S. C., & Higgins, S. T. (2006). Voucher-based contingent reinforcement of marijuana abstinence among individuals with serious mental illness. *Journal of Substance Abuse Treatment*, *30*, 291–295.

Silver, H., & Abboud, E. (1994). Drug abuse in schizophrenia: Comparison of patients who began drug abuse before their first admission with those who began abusing drugs after their first admission. *Schizophrenia Research*, *13*, 57–63.

Smeerdijk, M., Keet, R., Dekker, N., van Raaij, B., Krikke, M., Koeter, M., . . . Linszen, D. H. (2012). Motivational interviewing and interaction skills training for parents to change cannabis use in young adults with recent-onset schizophrenia: A randomized controlled trial. *Psychological Medicine*, *42*, 1627–36.

Smelson, D. A., Losonczy, M. F., Davis, C. W., Kaune, M., Williams, J., & Ziedonis, D. (2002). Risperidone decreases craving and relapses in individuals with schizophrenia and cocaine dependence. *Canadian Journal of Psychiatry*, *47*, 671–675.

Smelson, D. A., Williams, J., Ziedonis, D., Sussner, B. D., Losonczy, M. F., Engelhart, C., & Kaune, M. (2004). A double-blind placebo-controlled pilot study of risperidone for decreasing cue-elicited craving in recently withdrawn cocaine dependent patients. *Journal of Substance Abuse Treatment*, 45–49.

Smelson, D. A., Ziedonis, D., Williams, J., Losonczy, M. F., Williams, J., Steinberg, M. L., & Kaune, M. (2006). The efficacy of olanzapine for decreasing cue-elicited craving in individuals with schizophrenia and cocaine dependence: A preliminary report. *Journal of Clinical Psychopharmacology*, *26*, 9–12.

Sobell, L. C., & Sobell, M. B. (1992). Timeline Follow-Back: A technique for assessing self-reported alcohol consumption. In R. Z. Litten & J. Allen (Eds.), *Measuring alcohol consumption: Psychosocial and biological methods* (pp. 41–72). Totowa, NJ: Humana Press.

Stein, L. I., & Test, M. A. (1980). Alternatives to mental hospital treatment: Conceptual, model, treatment program and clinical evaluation. *Archives of General Psychiatry*, *37*, 392–397.

Strakowski, S. M., & DelBello, M. P. (2000). The co-occurrence of bipolar and substance use disorders. *Clinical Psychology Review*, *20*, 191–206.

Strakowski, S. M., McElroy, S. L., Keck, P. E. J., & West, S. A. (1996). The effects of antecedent substance abuse on the development of first-episode mania. *Journal of Psychiatric Research*, *30*, 59–68.

Substance Abuse and Mental Health Services Administration. (2006). Results from the 2005 National Survey on Drug Use and Health: National findings. Rockville, MD: DHHS.

Susser, E., Struening, E. L., & Conover, S. (1989). Psychiatric problems in homeless men: Lifetime psychosis, substance use, and current distress in new arrivals at New York City shelters. *Archives of General Psychiatry*, *46*, 845–850.

Susser, E., Valencia, E., Berkman, A., Sohler, N., Conover, S., Torres, J., . . . Miller, S. (1998). Human immunodeficiency virus sexual risk reduction in homeless men with mental illness. *Archives of General Psychiatry*, *55*, 266–272.

Svensson, T. H., Mathe, J. M., Andersson, J. L., Nomikos, G. G., Hildebrand, B. E., & Marcus, M. (1995). Mode of action of atypical neuroleptics in relation to the phencyclidine model of schizophrenia: Role of 5-HT2 receptor and alpha 1-adrenoceptor antagonism. *Journal of Clinical Psychopharmacology*, *15* (*1 Suppl. 1*), 11S–18S.

Tengström, A., Hodgins, S., Grann, M., Långström, N., & Kullgren, G. (2004). Schizophrenia and criminal offending: The role of psychopathy and substance misuse. *Criminal Justice and Behavior*, *31*, 1–25.

Teplin, L. A. (1994). Psychiatric and substance abuse disorders among male urban jail detainees. *American Journal of Public Health*, *84*, 290–293.

Teplin, L. A., McClelland, G. M., Abram, K. M., & Weiner, D. A. (2005). Crime victimization in adults with severe mental illness. *Archives of General Psychiatry*, *62*, 911–921.

Test, M. A., Wallish, L. S., Allness, D. G., & Ripp, K. (1989). Substance use in young adults with schizophrenic disorders. *Schizophrenia Bulletin*, *15*, 465–476.

Treffert, D. A. (1978). Marijuana use in schizophrenia: A clear hazard. *American Journal of Psychiatry*, *135*, 1213–1215.

Tsemberis, S., Gulcur, L., & Nakae, M. (2004). Housing first, consumer choice, and harm reduction for homeless individuals with a dual diagnosis. *American Journal of Public Health*, *94*, 651–656.

Tsuang, M. T., Simpson, J. C., & Kronfol, Z. (1982). Subtypes of drug abuse with psychosis. *Archives of General Psychiatry*, *39*, 141–147.

Vaillant, G. E. (2002). *The natural history of alcoholism* (2nd ed.). Cambridge, MA: Harvard University Press.

van Os, J., Bak, M., Hanssen, M., Vijl, R. V., de Graaf, R., & Verdoux, H. (2002). Cannabis use and psychosis: A longitudinal population-based study. *American Journal of Epidemiology, 156,* 319–327.

Vardy, M. M., & Kay, S. R. (1983). LSD psychosis or LSD-induced schizophrenia? A multimethod inquiry. *Archives of General Psychiatry, 40,* 877–883.

Volkow, N. D., Fowler, J. S., & Wang, G. J. (2003). The addicted human brain: Insights from imaging studies. *Journal of Clinical Investigation, 111,* 1444–1451.

Walsh, E., Moran, P., Scott, C., McKenzie, K., Burns, T., Creed, F., Tyrer, P., Murray, R. M., & Fahy, T. (2003). Prevalence of violent victimisation in severe mental illness. *British Journal of Psychiatry, 183,* 233–38.

Warner, R., Taylor, D., Wright, J., Sloat, A., Springett, G., Amold, S., & Weinberg, H. (1994). Substance use among the mentally ill: Prevalence, reasons for use and effects on illness. *American Journal of Orthopsychiatry, 64,* 30–39.

Weaver, T., Madden, P., Charles, V., Stimson, G., Renton, A., Tyrer, P., . . . Ford, C. (2003). Comorbidity of substance misuse and mental illness in community mental health and substance misuse services. *British Journal of Psychiatry, 183,* 304–313.

Weiss, K. A., Smith, T. E., Hull, J. W., Piper, A. C., & Hubbert, J. D. (2002). Predictors of risk of nonadherence in outpatients with schizophrenia and other psychotic disorders. *Schizophrenia Bulletin, 28,* 341–349.

Weiss, R. D., & Connery, H. S. (2011). *Integrated group therapy for bipolar disorder and substance abuse.* New York: Guilford Press.

Weiss, R. D., Griffin, M. L., Greenfield, S. F., Najavits, L. M., Wyner, D., Soto, J. A., & Hennen, J. A. (2000). Group therapy for patients with bipolar and substance dependence: Results of a pilot study. *Journal of Clinical Psychiatry, 61,* 361–367.

Weiss, R. D., Griffin, M. L., Jaffee, W. B., Bender, R. E., Graff, F. S., Gallop, R. J., & Fitzmaurice, G. M. (2009). A "community-friendly" version of Integrated Group Therapy for patients with bipolar disorder and substance dependence: A randomized controlled trial. *Drug and Alcohol Dependence, 104,* 212–219.

Weiss, R. D., Griffin, M. L., Kolodziej, M. E., Greenfield, S. F., Najavits, L. M., Daley, D. C., . . . & Hennnen, J. A. (2007). A randomized trial of integrated group therapy versus group drug counseling for patients with bipolar disorder and substance dependence. *American Journal of Psychiatry, 164,* 100–107.

Wexler, B. E., Gottschalk, C. H., Fulbright, R. K., Prohovnik, I., Lacadie, C. M., Rounsaville, B. J., & Gore, J. C. (2001). Functional magnetic resonance imaging of cocaine craving. *American Journal of Psychiatry, 158,* 85–96.

Winokur, G., Coryell, W., Akiskal, H. S., Maser, J. D., Keller, M. B., Endicott, J., & Mueller, T. (1995). Alcoholism in manic-depressive (bipolar) illness: Familial illness, course of illness, and the primary-secondary distinction. *American Journal of Psychiatry, 152,* 365–372.

Wise, R. A. (1998). Drug-activation of brain reward pathways. *Drug and Alcohol Dependence, 51,* 13–22.

Xie, H., Drake, R. E., & McHugo, G. J. (2006). Are there distinctive trajectory groups in substance abuse remission over 10 years? An application of the group-based modeling approach. *Administration and Policy in Mental Health, 33,* 423–432.

Xie, H., Drake, R. E., & McHugo, G. J. (2009). The 10-year course of substance use disorder among patients with severe mental illness: An analysis of latent class trajectory groups. *Psychiatric Services, 60,* 804–811.

Xie, H., Drake, R. E., McHugo, G. J., Xie, L., & Mohandas, A. (2010). The 10-year course of remission, abstinence, and recovery in dual diagnosis. *Journal of Substance Abuse Treatment, 39,* 132–40.

Xie, H., McHugo, G. J., Helmstetter, B. S., & Drake, R. E. (2005). Three-year recovery outcomes for long-term patients with co-occurring schizophrenic and substance use disorders. *Schizophrenia Research, 75,* 337–348.

Ziedonis, D., & Fisher, W. (1994). Assessment and treatment of comorbid substance abuse in individuals with schizophrenia. *Psychiatric Annals, 24,* 477–483.

Ziedonis, D. M., & Trudeau, K. (1997). Motivation to quit using substances among individuals with schizophrenia: Implications for a motivation-based treatment model. *Schizophrenia Bulletin, 23,* 229–238.

Zigler, E., & Glick, M. (1986). *A developmental approach to adult psychopathology.* New York: John Wiley & Sons.

Zubin, J., & Spring, B. (1977). Vulnerability: A new view of schizophrenia. *Journal of Abnormal Psychology, 86,* 103–126.

Substance Use Disorders and Personality Disorders

Timothy J. Trull, Marika B. Solhan, Whitney C. Brown, Rachel L. Tomko, Lauren Schaefer, Kristin D. McLaughlin, *and* Seungmin Jahng

Abstract

Personality disorders (PDs) and substance use disorders (SUDs) frequently co-occur both in the general population and in clinical settings. The authors review the recent literature that documents high comorbidity between these two classes of disorders, discuss possible mechanisms of comorbidity, and describe the clinical implications of this comorbidity. Although most attention on comorbidity between PDs and SUDs has focused on antisocial personality disorder (ASPD) and borderline personality disorder (BPD), it is also clear that other PDs (in particular, paranoid, avoidant, and obsessive compulsive PD) are prevalent among those suffering from SUDs. The effect of SUD on PD expression appears to be one of exacerbating PD symptomatology and, in turn, contributing to chronicity. This has important treatment implications in that clinicians must keep in mind the challenges present when planning and implementing treatment for those with both SUD and PD.

Key Words: personality disorders, substance use disorders, comorbidity, antisocial personality disorder, borderline personality disorder

Substance use disorders (SUDs), specifically substance abuse and substance dependence, are among the most prevalent psychological disorders in North America and in many other societies (American Psychiatric Association [APA], 2000, 2013; Ball, 2005; Helzer & Canino, 1992). According to the *Diagnostic and Statistical Manual of Mental Disorders* (DSM-IV-TR; APA, 2000), both substance abuse and substance dependence refer to "a maladaptive pattern of substance use, leading to clinically significant impairment or distress." *Substance dependence* is considered to be a more severe condition in which the individual has difficulty controlling use and/or is physically or psychologically dependent on the substance, whereas *substance abuse* is a residual category reserved for problematic or hazardous use in the absence of dependence. In DSM-5 (APA, 2013), these categories have been collapsed into one labeled *substance use disorder*. To obtain an SUD diagnosis, one must meet at least two of the 11 criteria. Many of the same criteria from DSM-IV-TR are still included, and DSM-5 reintroduced the craving criterion as well.

SUDs are prevalent, even among the general population. Recently, one of the largest epidemiological studies assessing mental illness and its correlates was completed in the United States, the National Epidemiological Survey on Alcohol and Related Conditions (NESARC). The NESARC is a nationally representative, face-to-face survey that evaluated mental health in the civilian, noninstitutionalized population of the United States (Grant, Moore, Shepard, & Kaplan, 2003) conducted over two waves of data collection. The NESARC epidemiological study estimated that the Wave 1 12-month prevalence rate for any DSM-IV alcohol use disorder (AUD) is 8.5% (alcohol abuse 4.7%; alcohol dependence 3.8%) and for any DSM-IV drug use disorder (DUD), excluding nicotine dependence, 2.0% (drug abuse 1.4%; drug dependence 0.6%)

(Grant, Stinson et al., 2004). The corresponding NESARC Wave 1 lifetime prevalence rates for alcohol use abuse/dependence (17.8%/12.5%) and drug use abuse/dependence (7.7%/2.6%) are markedly higher, indicating the extent of substance use problems in the United States.

Personality Disorders

In recent years, there has been increasing recognition of extensive comorbidity between SUDs and personality disorders (PDs). In DSM-IV-TR (APA, 2000), a PD is defined as "an enduring pattern of inner experience and behavior that deviates markedly from the expectations of the individual's culture, is pervasive and inflexible, has an onset in adolescence or early adulthood, is stable over time, and leads to distress or impairment" (p. 685). DSM-IV describes ten PDs grouped into three clusters based on similarity of symptoms: Cluster A, which includes three "odd/eccentric" PDs (paranoid PD, schizoid PD, and schizotypal PD); Cluster B, which includes four "dramatic/emotional" PDs (antisocial PD [ASPD], borderline PD [BPD], histrionic PD, and narcissistic PD); and Cluster C, which includes three "anxious/fearful" PDs (avoidant PD, dependent PD, and obsessive-compulsive PD). In DSM-5 (APA, 2013), the same PDs using the same criteria sets are included.

Major areas of functioning that are disrupted in those with PDs include *cognitive* (the way one perceives oneself, others, and events), *affective or emotional* (the intensity, range, lability, and expression of emotional experience), *interpersonal* (the quality of interpersonal relationships), and *impulse control* (acting without reflection or appropriate constraint; APA, 2000; 2013). These same areas of functioning often prove problematic in those with SUDs. For example, those with AUD are prone to experience negative affect, experience difficulties in romantic or family relationships, and exhibit difficulty controlling drinking in situations that call for restraint.

Therefore, it should come as no surprise that both researchers and clinicians have taken note of the overlap and comorbidity between these two classes of disorders. The overall purpose of this chapter is to examine in some detail the comorbidity between SUDs, including alcohol and drugs other than tobacco, to provide models for understanding this comorbidity and to discuss the implications of this comorbidity.

How Prevalent Are Personality Disorders?

Before we evaluate the comorbidity of these disorders in both general and clinical populations, it is useful to briefly discuss the prevalence of PDs in the general population. It may be somewhat surprising to know that until very recently no large-scale epidemiological studies of the full range of PDs in representative populations existed. Rather, previous studies either focused on only one or two PDs (typically ASPD) or used nonclinical samples that were convenient but not necessarily representative of the population. In this chapter, we focus primarily on the NESARC study because it represents the largest epidemiological study to date that used structured interviews to establish the full range of SUDs and PDs.

The NESARC study presents a unique opportunity to assess the comorbidity rates of PDs and SUDs in a representative population sample, sampling approximately 40,000 individuals. However, we must first present a major caveat concerning the original NESARC method of diagnosing PDs. In the NESARC study, PD features were assessed in two waves, separated by approximately 3 years (Wave 1: 2001–2002 and Wave 2: 2004–2005). Initial reports from the NESARC indicated very high prevalence rates for the PDs. For example, seven PDs were assessed at Wave 1, and it was reported that the prevalence rate for *any* of these PD diagnoses was approximately 15% (Grant, Stinson et al., 2004). Even with the exclusion of an additional three PDs that were assessed at Wave 2, this estimate is much larger than previous prevalence estimates of PDs in the general population (Coid, Yang, Tyrer, Roberts, & Ullrich, 2006; Lenzenweger, Lane, Loranger, & Kessler, 2007). One potential explanation for these high rates is the NESARC investigators' decision to require extreme distress, impairment, or dysfunction for *only one* of the requisite endorsed PD items in order for a diagnosis to be assigned (see Grant, Hasin et al., 2004). Given the general criteria for PD presented in the DSM-IV-TR, it is of interest to determine the effect of requiring distress or impairment for each NESARC PD symptom in order for that symptom to count toward a diagnosis.

DSM-IV-TR (and now DSM-5) states that only "when personality traits are inflexible and maladaptive and cause significant functional impairment or subjective distress do they constitute Personality Disorders" (APA, 2000, p. 686). Furthermore, such consideration of significant distress or impairment is built into the General Diagnostic Criteria for a Personality Disorder (APA, 2000, 2013). Personality traits or behaviors are judged maladaptive (i.e., indicative of PD) *only* if these traits or behaviors cause significant distress or impairment. Most see this as a very important addition to the nomenclature (e.g., Livesley, 1998; 2003).

For this reason, we recalculated the rates of PDs in the NESARC sample, requiring that each PD symptom be accompanied by significant distress or impairment (Trull, Jahng, Tomko, Wood, & Sher, 2010). Table 5.1 presents prevalence rates of PDs in the NESARC study using (1) the original method of determining the presence of a PD diagnosis ("NESARC"), which only requires at least one symptom to be associated with distress or impairment; and (2) an alternative method ("NESARC-REVISED") that diagnoses a PD only if all symptoms counting toward the diagnosis are associated with distress or impairment. For comparison, Table 5.1 also presents prevalence estimates obtained from recent nationally representative studies conducted in Great Britain (Coid et al., 2006) and in the United States (NCS-R; Lenzenweger et al., 2007).

As expected, prevalence rates of PDs using our revised method of diagnosis (NESARC-REVISED) were lower than those reported previously, sometimes markedly so. For example, prevalence of *any* PD diagnosis decreased from 21.52% to 9.12%. Although all prevalence rate differences were significant for individual PD diagnoses (except for antisocial personality disorder [ASPD] in which no separate impairment/distress questions were asked), the largest drops in rates occurred for schizoid (3.13% to 0.57%), schizotypal (3.93% to 0.62%), histrionic (1.84% to 0.27%), narcissistic (6.18% to 0.96%), and obsessive compulsive (7.88% to 0.91%) PDs.

Table 5.1 also reveals that the rates using the original NESARC scoring for PDs were generally much higher than estimates from the Great Britain (Coid et al., 2006) and NCS-R (Lenzenweger et al., 2007) studies, sometimes dramatically so. From these studies, the overall estimate of any PD was 10.1% and 9.1%, respectively. In contrast to the original NESARC calculations, the NESARC-REVISED

Table 5.1. Prevalence Estimates of *Diagnostic and Statistical Manual of Mental Disorders* (DSM-IV) Personality Disorders from Representative National Samples.

Personality Disorder	Great Britain*	NCS-R**	NESARC	NESARC-Revised
Any PD	10.1[a]	9.1[b]	21.5	9.1
Any Cluster A	1.6	5.7	7.1	2.1
Paranoid	0.7	–	4.4	1.9
Schizoid	0.8	–	3.1	0.6
Schizotypal	0.1	–	3.9	0.6
Any Cluster B	1.2	1.5	9.7	5.5
Antisocial	0.6	0.6	3.8	3.8
Borderline	0.7	1.4	5.9	2.7
Histrionic	–	–	1.8	0.3
Narcissistic	–	–	6.2	1.0
Any Cluster C	1.6	6.0	8.1	2.3
Avoidant	0.8	–	2.4	1.2
Dependent	0.1	–	0.5	0.3
Obsessive-compulsive	1.9	–	7.9	1.9

[a] Includes PD-NOS.
[b] Includes PD-NOS; NCS-R prevalence rates estimates were not available for some individual PD categories due to low base rates in subsample from which estimates were projected.
* Rates from Coid et al. (2006).
** Rates from Lenzenweger et al. (2007).

method of determining PD diagnoses resulted in an overall prevalence rate of PDs (9.1%) that was much closer to the estimates from the Great Britain and NCS-R studies.

Comorbidity Studies
Comorbidity of SUDs and PDs in NESARC

For these reasons, we adopted this revised procedure for diagnosing PDs in the NESARC data set; overdiagnosing the PDs using the original scoring method might introduce a significant bias in calculating comorbidity estimates. There are two ways to examine comorbidity, depending on the perspective of the index diagnosis. Given this volume's focus on SUDs, we first present the rate of PDs in those with SUDs. In addition, we focus on diagnoses of past year (12-month) substance dependence for alcohol and for drugs. We do this so that comparisons with comorbidity rate estimates obtained from clinical samples (discussed later) can be made easily because 12-month or current SUD diagnoses are most frequently reported.

Based on the NESARC-revised PD diagnoses, among those with *past-year alcohol dependence*, the following rates of PDs were found: any PD (27.1%), paranoid (7.8%), schizoid (1.7%), schizotypal (2.8%), antisocial (18.8%), borderline (12.8%), histrionic (1.8%), narcissistic (4.2%), avoidant (4.3%), dependent (1.3%), and obsessive compulsive (5.1%). Among those with *past-year drug dependence*, the following rates of PDs were found: any PD (54.4 %), paranoid (19.7%), schizoid (5.6%), schizotypal (8.6%), antisocial (40.2%), borderline (27.8%), histrionic (7.4%), narcissistic (10.3%), avoidant (14.2%), dependent (7.3%), and obsessive compulsive (10.6%).

It is also instructive to consider the rates of different substance dependence diagnoses in those with PD diagnoses. These rates, for example, might be of primary interest as nonclinical comparison data for those who study or treat patients from general outpatient clinics or clinics that focus on the treatment of PDs. Overall, the rate of 12-month alcohol dependence and 12-month drug dependence, respectively, in those with *any PD* was 13.0% and 5.0%. The following rates of past-year alcohol dependence and drug dependence, respectively, were found for each PD: paranoid (15.7%; 6.5%), schizoid (11.5%; 6.1%), schizotypal (19.6%; 11.4%), antisocial (19.2%; 6.8%), borderline (20.6%; 8.3%), histrionic (25.5%; 17.4%), narcissistic (19.3%; 8.8%), avoidant (14.2%; 7.7%),

dependent (18.5%; 17.1%), and obsessive compulsive (10.2%; 3.5%).

Evaluating Comorbidity Rates Between SUDs and PDs in Clinical Samples

Previous reviews of PD and SUD comorbidity are based on studies published before 2000 (e.g., Trull, Sher, Minks-Brown, Durbin, & Burr, 2000). To obtain a current estimate of the extent of the comorbidity between SUDs and PDs in clinical samples, we conducted a comprehensive literature search of published articles in peer-reviewed, English-language journals that appeared in 2000–2013, inclusive. The search used the PsycINFO and PubMed databases and included substance use keywords (e.g., *substance abuse, dependence, alcohol*) for each PD. In order to be included in this review, we required each study (a) to use structured interviews to diagnose PDs in adults, (b) to use structured interviews to diagnose SUDs *or* to sample adult participants currently in treatment for SUDs, (c) to diagnose both PDs and SUDs according to DSM-IV criteria, and (d) to provide summary statistics such that comorbidity rates could be computed. Furthermore, we required that at least part of the sample must be treatment-seeking in those cases that combined clinical and community participants. In the event that multiple articles reported data on the same samples or a subsample of participants, the article with the largest sample size was included in the review. The other articles with smaller subsets of this largest sample were excluded from the review to avoid "double counting" such data.

It is important to note that the studies we review here used DSM-IV(-TR) definitions of SUD, which included both abuse and dependence syndromes. As noted earlier, the new DSM-5 collapses these into one SUD category.

Each table presents the relevant study citation, the type of sample (inpatient, outpatient), how diagnoses were established and the diagnostic system used, the number of participants in the index group, data on the age of participants, percentage of the index group that was female, and the comorbidity rate of interest. Please note that some studies appear in multiple tables because data were available for several types of comorbidity rates. Furthermore, each table focuses on either an SUD or a PD index sample and reports the number of participants within each study with this disorder (*N*). Each table then also provides the number of

Table 5.2. Prevalence of Comorbid Antisocial Personality Disorder (ASPD) in Individuals with Substance Use Disorder (SUD).

Reference	Sample	Diagnostic Instrument	N with SUD	% Female	Mean Age (SD)	N with ASPD (%)
Anthenelli, Maxwell, Geracioti Jr., & Hauger (2001)	Outpatient (alcohol dependence-L)	Alcohol Research Center Intake Interview for DSM-IV	67	0	40.3 (8.3)	31 (46.0)
Assanangkornchai, Saunders, & Conigrave (2000)	Outpatient/Community (alcohol dependence-C)	AUDADIS (Alcohol Experiences Section); ICD-10	91	0	41.0 (11.8)	27 (29.0)
Ball, 2007; Ball & Cecero, 2001	Outpatient (opioid dependence-C, L	SCID I/P; SCID-II	78	54.0 of those with a PD	37.4 (5.9) of those with a PD	29 (37.2)
Becker, Añez, Paris, & Grilo, 2010	Outpatient (AUD-L, SUD-L)	Admission; S-DIPD-IV	130	31.0	37.4 (10.5)	17 (13.0)
Bottlender, Preuss, & Soyka, 2006	Inpatient (alcohol dependence-L)	SSAGA; SCID-II (German)	237	18.1	42.0 (–)	46 (19.5)
Chiang, Chan, Chang, Sun, Chen, & Chen, 2007	Outpatient (heroin abuse-C)	MINI	155	20.6	30.8 (7.7)	60 (39.7)
Darke, Williamson, Ross, Teesson, & Lynskey, 2004	Community (heroin user sample); Clinical (heroin dependence treatment; heroin abuse/dependent-C)	Diagnostic Interview Schedule (DIS) –Modified	615	34.0	29.3 (7.8)	440 (71.5)
DeMarce, Lash, Parker, Burke, & Brambow, 2013	Outpatient	SCID-I; SCID-II	183	0.04	50.1 (8.3)	39 (21.3)
Easton et al., 2012	Outpatient (cannabis dependence-C)	SCID	136	–	21.29 (1.9)	60 (44.0)
Easton, Weinberger, & McKee, 2008	Forensic/Outpatient (alcohol dependence-C)	SCID-I	85	0	38 (–)	20 (23.5)
Echeburua, De Medina, & Aizpiri, 2007	Outpatient (alcohol dependence-C)	SCID-I; International Personality Disorders Examination (IPDE)[b]	158	34.8	43.4	11 (7.0)

Falck, Wang, Siegal, & Carlson, 2004	Community (crack-cocaine abuse/dependence-L)	DIS	313	40.6	37.8 (–)	75 (24.0)
Fals-Stewart, Golden, & Schumacher, 2003	Outpatient (substance abuse -C)	SCID-I; SCID-II (ASPD module only)	149	0	36.1 (8.2)	57 (38.0) with SUD
Fenton et al., 2012	Community (NESARC)	AUDADIS-IV	613	32.5	–	57 (9.3)
Ford et al., 2009	Community (cocaine dependence-L)	SSADDA;	898	49.8	38.74 (7.5)	123 (14.3)
Fotiadou, Livaditis, Manou, Kaniotou, Samakouri, Tzavaras, & Xeniitidis, 2004	Forensic (opiate abuse/dependence-L)	Mini International Neuropsychiatric Interview (MINI) - 5	33	0	36 (–)	17 (51.5)
Goudriaan, Oosterlaan, Beurs, & van den Brink, 2006	Outpatient (abstinent alcohol dependence-L)	DIS-Dutch Version	48	22.9	42.7 (8.3)c	1 (2.1)
Grella et al., 2008	Incarcerated (Substance Use Disorders-L)	SCID-II	280	35.0	34.8 (–)	118 (42.1)
Gustavson et al., 2007	Forensic (early onset substance abuse/dependence-L)	SCID-I; SCID-II	31	8.0	30 (median) 17-76 (range)	22 (71.0)
Havens et al., 2007	Outpatient (injecting drug users-C)	SCID-I; SCID-II	162	32.1	38 (median)	37 (22.8)
Helmus, Downey, Arfken, Henderson, & Schuster, 2001	Community (opioid-dependent subjects-C)	SCID-I; SCID-II	68	36.3	41.4 (7.2)	17 (25.4)
Himmerich et al., 2004	Clinical (alcohol dependence & abuse-L)	SCID-I; SCID-II	191	23	44 (9.9)	11 (5.8)
Johann, Bobbe, Putzhammer, & Wodarz, 2003	Inpatient (alcohol dependent-C)	Composite International Diagnostic Interview-Substance Abuse Module; SCID-II	282	17	43.1 (–)	72 (25.5)
Jones, Johnson, Bigelow, & Strain, 2004	Inpatient & outpatient (opioid or cocaine dependence- C)	SCID-I; SCID-II	259	40.9	35.6	69 (26.6)

(continued)

Table 5.2. Continued

Reference	Sample	Diagnostic Instrument	N with SUD	% Female	Mean Age (SD)	N with ASPD (%)
Kidorf et al., 2004	Community (opioid dependence-C)	SCID-I; SCID-II	389	34.8	38.3 (–)	142 (36.5)
Ladd & Petry, 2003	Outpatient (cocaine abuse and dependence-C)	SCID-I; SCID-II	174	47.7 (estimated)	35.7 (estimated)	61 (35.1)
Lenzenweger et al., 2007[c]	Community (over sampled for psychiatric disorders) (any SUD- C)	CIDI- NCS-R interview (DSM-IV); Portions of IPDE (DSM-IV)	assessed 214	–	–	7 (3.2)
Lin et al., 2004	Forensic (methamphetamine abuse-L)	Diagnostic Interview for Genetic Studies (Chinese)	351	44.6	26.8 (7.0)	24 (7.4)
Mellentin, Skøt, Teasdale, & Habekost, 2013	Outpatient	Admission to methadone maintenance program; MINI;	46	15.1 – of those with a PD	36.8 (8.6) - of those with a PD	16 (34.7)
Messina, Farabee, & Rawson, 2003	Inpatient (cocaine dependence-L)	SCID-I; SCID-II	108	29	43 (–)	48 (44.0)
Mills, Teeson, Darke, & Ross, 2007[d]	Community/Clinical (heroin dependence-L)	DIS-Antisocial Module	309	38.0	–	210 (68.0)
Miranda et al., 2009	Community (alcohol dependence)	SCID-I; SCID-II	39	0.0	26.1 (6.0)	17 (43.6)
Mitchell, Brown, & Rush, 2007	Outpatient	MINI	65 (alcohol dependence-C) 36 (cocaine dependence-C) 65 (alcohol & cocaine dependence-C)	41.0	36.2 (8.8)	24 (37.5) with AUD 19 (52.8) with CUD 39 (60.0) with SUD
Modestin, Matutat, & Wurmle, 2001	Inpatient (opioid dependence-L)	SCID-II	100	0	–	23 (23.0)
Moeller et al., 2002	Inpatient & outpatient (cocaine dependence-C)	SCID-I; SCID-II	49	16.32	35.5 (–)	19 (38.8)

Paim Kessler et al., 2012	Inpatient & outpatient (psychoactive substance abuse)	Admission; MINI-Plus	290	–	–	43 (14.8)
Preuss, Koller, Bondy, Bahlmann, & Soyka, 2001	Inpatient (alcohol dependence)	SCID-II	135	20.7	41.8 (8.8)	25 (16.6)
Putkonen, Kotilainen, Joyal, & Tuhonen, 2004	Forensic (substance abuse disorders)	SCID-I; SCID-II	65	0	43.6 (11.5)	40 (61.5)
Ralevski, Ball, Nich, Limoncelli, & Petrakis, 2007	Clinical (alcohol dependent-C)	SCID-I; SCID-II	254	3.0	–	95 (42.0)
Reback, Kamien, & Amass, 2007	Community (amphetamine, cocaine, hallucinogen/PCP, marijuana, sedative, opioid) C, L	SCID-I; SCID-II	20	0	37 (6.1)	8 (43.0)
Ross et al., 2005	Community/Outpatient (heroin dependent-L)	DIS-Antisocial Module	825	35.0	29.5 (7.8)	594 (72.0)
Schmitz et al., 2000	Outpatient (cocaine dependent-C)	SCID-I; SCID-II—Antisocial, Borderline, and Dependent Modules	151	32.5	36.1 (6.6)	32 (21.2)
Tang, Kranzler, Gelernter, Farrer, & Cubells, 2007	Community (cocaine dependence-L)	Semi-Structured Assessment for Drug Dependence and Alcoholism	243	41.0	39.5 (7.8)	44 (18.1)
Van Emmerik-van Oortmerssen et al., 2014	Inpatients & outpatients	Admission; MINI-Plus; SCID-II	1205	26.5	–	263 (22.0)
Vergara-Moragues, González-Saiz, Lozano, & García, 2013	Inpatients	Admission; PRISM	218	8.7	–	46 (21.19)
Weizman, Gelkopf, Melamed, Adelson, & Bleich, 2003	Outpatient (benzodiazepine dependence)	SCID-I module for benzodiazepine dependence; SCID-II	66	–	–	33 (50.0)
Wilens et al., 2005	Outpatient /Community	SCID-I; SCID-II	39	–	43.7	10 (25.6)

(continued)

Table 5.2. Continued

Reference	Sample	Diagnostic Instrument	N with SUD	% Female	Mean Age (SD)	N with ASPD (%)
Wu & Howard, 2007	Community (inhalant users– L)	AUDADIS-IV (DSM-IV)[a]	664	29.2	–	213 (32.1)
Zikos, Gill, & Charney, 2010	Inpatients	SCID-I; SCID-II	138	33.0	44 (9.7)	8 (5.0)
Zimmerman et al., 2005	Outpatient (alcohol use disorder–C)	SCID-I, SCID-II	85	–	–	9 (10.6)

C, current diagnosis; L, lifetime diagnosis

[a] Alcohol Use Disorders and Associated Disabilities Interview Schedule (Grant et al. 1995).

[b] International Personality Disorders Examination

[c] For alcohol dependent sample.

[d] a subsample of Darke, Williamson, Ross, Teesson, & Lynskey (2004). Lenzenweger et al. (2007) provides predicted prevalence rates extrapolated from a smaller sample (n = 214). SSAGA, Semi-Structured Assessment for the Genetics of Alcoholism (Bucholz et al. 1994; Hesselbrock et al. 1999).

[e] Lenzenweger et al. (2007) provides predicted prevalence rates extrapolated from a smaller sample (n = 214) NCS-R, National Comorbidity Survey Replication NESARC, National Epidemiologic Survey on Alcohol and Related Conditions.

these individuals who were also diagnosed with the other, comorbid disorder (*n*). So, for example, Table 5.2 reports studies with samples that included participants with an SUD (*N*) and the number of those individuals who were also diagnosed with comorbid ASPD (*n*).

We present these data, first, for ASPD (Tables 5.2 and 5.3) and BPD (Tables 5.4 and 5.5), given the prevalence of these PDs in the general population, as well as the relatively larger literature on SUD comorbidity with these PDs.

Antisocial Personality Disorder and SUDs

ASPD has been studied extensively for three decades, and much more is currently known about comorbidity between SUDs and ASPD than with other PDs. The comorbidity between ASPD and SUDs has been evaluated in past major epidemiological studies such as the Epidemiological Catchment Area study (ECA; Regier, Narrow, & Rae, 1990) and the National Comorbidity Survey (NCS; Kessler et al., 1994). As we noted earlier (using NESARC data), the comorbidity between ASPD and SUDs in the general population is among the highest of all the DSM-IV PDs.

ASPD continues to be an important focus in the literature on SUDs. Overall, across relevant studies, ASPD appears highly comorbid with broadly defined SUDs (i.e., combining abuse and dependence across substances; see Table 5.2). In our review, studies of clinical samples only reported comorbidity estimates ranging from 2.1% to 60.0% (weighted mean = 24.8%), those for combined clinical/community samples reported comorbidity estimates ranging from 25.6% to 72.0% (weighted mean = 68.2%), and those for forensic samples reported comorbidity estimates ranging from 7.4% to 71.0% (weighted mean = 28.5%).

Many of the studies reviewed, however, examined specific SUDs and not SUDs in general. The SUDs most often targeted were alcohol, opiate, and cocaine use disorders. SUDs rarely studied included cannabis, hallucinogens, or inhalants. Notably, ASPD appeared to be highly comorbid within those diagnosed with *heroin use disorder*. For example, two studies by Darke et al. (2004) and Ross et al. (2005) reported rates of 71.5% and 72.0%, respectively. However, ASPD comorbidity rates were more often studied among opiate users, broadly. Of the clinical samples that assessed *opiate use disorders*, comorbidity rates ranged from 23.0% to 72.0%, with a weighted mean of 59.51% of

those with opiate use disorders having the ASPD diagnosis. ASPD was also diagnosed often in those with cocaine use disorders. The comorbidity rates for ASPD in those with *cocaine use disorder* in clinical samples ranged from 21.2% and 52.8%, with a weighted average of 23.54%. Last, ASPD tended to be slightly less comorbid with AUDs. The rates of comorbidity in clinical samples ranged from 2.1% to 46.0%, with a weighted average of 21.79%.

Fewer investigators have studied the rates of comorbid SUDs *in those with ASPD* (see Table 5.3). The majority of these data were obtained from forensic samples. Also, as may be expected given the gender distribution in most forensic settings, very few of these individuals were women. In fact, only one study by Ralevski, Ball, Nich, Limoncelli, and Petrakis (2007) included any women participants (3% of the sample). Regardless, SUDs in general were found to be highly comorbid with ASPD (weighted average = 63.21%), with sample estimates ranging from 20.3% to 100%. Most often reported was comorbidity with AUD, with a weighted average of 68.00% that was computed from studies with rates of 45.05% and 77% comorbidity (Lu, Lin, Lee, Ko, & Shih, 2003; Moran & Hodgens, 2004).

Borderline Personality Disorder and SUDs

BPD is the most commonly diagnosed PD in clinical settings (Widiger & Trull, 1993), and, as noted in Table 5.1, the prevalence of BPD in the general population rivals that of ASPD. BPD is frequently comorbid with a range of both Axis I and other (i.e., non-BPD) PDs (Gunderson, 2001), and this extensive comorbidity is consistent with the view that BPD represents a level of personality organization/dysfunction that cuts across existing diagnostic categories (Kernberg, 1984; Millon, 1981).

Table 5.4 presents the rates of comorbid BPD among individuals with SUDs. The comorbidity rates presented in these studies ranged from 0% to 51.0%. Across all studies in Table 5.4, 15.5% of individuals with SUD diagnoses also met diagnostic criteria for BPD. Among studies specifically reporting AUD prevalence rates, 16.5% of individuals with an AUD diagnosis (abuse or dependence) also received a BPD diagnosis. Among individuals with a DUD diagnosis (abuse or dependence), 41.9% also met diagnostic criteria for BPD. Finally, several studies in Table 5.4 focused exclusively on inpatient or outpatient populations. Among individuals in outpatient

Table 5.3. Prevalence of Comorbid Substance Use Disorder (SUD) in Individuals with Antisocial Personality Disorder (ASPD).

Reference	Sample	Diagnostic Instrument	N with ASPD	% Female	Mean Age (SD)	N with SUD (%)
Goodwin & Hamilton, 2003	Community	WHO Composite International Diagnostic Interview (CIDI)	261	0	15–54 (range)	165 (63.2) with AUD 125 (47.9) with SUD
Lu, Lin, Lee, Ko, & Shinh, 2003	Forensic	Modified Chinese version of the Schedule of Affective Disorder and Schizophrenia-lifetime	91	0	–	41 (45.05) with AUD
Moran & Hodgens, 2004	Clinical/forensic[a]	SCID-I; SCID-II	232	0	(8.0)	39 (77.0) with AUD 33 (65.0) with DUD
Putkonen, Kotilainen, Joyal, & Tuhonen, 2004	Clinical/forensic	SCID-I; SCID-II	88	0	–	88 (100.0) with SUD
Ralevski, Ball, Nich, Limoncelli, & Petrakis, 2007	Clinical	SCID-I; SCID-II	95	3	–	64 (67.7) with CUD 19 (20.3) with OUD

[a] All had schizophrenia spectrum disorders. CUD, cocaine use disorder; OUD, opiate use disorder.

treatment, 32.7% of those with an SUD diagnosis also received a BPD diagnosis. This compares to 22.1% of inpatients with an SUD diagnosis that also met criteria for BPD.

Table 5.5 presents the rates of comorbid SUDs among individuals with BPD. Generally, very high comorbidity rates of SUDs are found within a borderline personality disordered population, ranging from 28.0% to 86.9%. Across all studies reviewed, 58.9% of those with BPD also received one or more SUD diagnoses. Within the studies in Table 5.5 that specified individuals with AUD, 48.1% of those with BPD also received an AUD diagnosis. Finally, 45.9% of those with BPD also received a DUD diagnosis.

These rates can be compared to findings from a previous review of SUD-BPD comorbidity rates in the 1987–1997 literature conducted by Trull and colleagues (2000). Trull and colleagues found higher rates of BPD within an SUD population (27.4% compared to 15.5% in the current review). However, the previous review found lower rates of BPD within specific AUD and DUD populations (14.3% and 16.8% to 18.5%, respectively, compared to 16.5% and 41.9% in the current review). In addition, Trull and colleagues (2000) found that 57.4% of individuals with BPD also met criteria for one or more SUDs, while the current review found a similar comorbidity rate (58.9%). When distinguishing between individuals with BPD meeting criteria for either AUDs or DUDs, Trull and colleagues (2000) found that 48.8% of individuals with BPD also had an AUD and 38.0% of individuals with BPD also had a DUD. These rates compare to 48.1% of individuals with BPD with an AUD and 45.9% of individuals with BPD with a DUD in the current review.

Other Personality Disorders Among Persons with SUDs

Although ASPD and BPD are the most prevalent personality disorders among those with SUDs, moderate comorbidity exists between other PDs and SUDs. Our review revealed that

Table 5.4. Prevalence of Comorbid Borderline Personality Disorder (BPD) in Individuals with Substance Use Disorder (SUD).

Reference	Sample	Diagnostic Instrument	N with SUD	% Female	Mean Age (SD)	N with BPD (%)
Anestis, Gratz, Bagge, & Tull, 2012	Inpatient	SCID-I/P; DIPD-IV	176	35.8	36.12 (10.3)	53 (30.1)
Ball, 2007; Ball & Cicero, 2001	Outpatient (opioid dependence)	Admission to methadone maintenance program; SCID-II	78	54.0 (of those with PDs)	37.4 (5.9)	23 (29.5)
Bardeen et al., 2014	Inpatient (cocaine dependence)	Admission; DIPD-IV	58	45%	44.5 (6.6)	22 (38.0)
Becker, Añez, Paris, & Grilo, 2010	Outpatient (AUD-L, SUD-L)	Admission; S-DIPD-IV	130	31.0	37.4 (10.5)	39 (30.0)
Bornovalova et al., 2008	Inpatient	SCID	76	32.9	42.2 (8.2)	24 (31.6)
Bottlender, Preuss, & Soyka, 2006	Inpatient (alcohol dependence)	SSAGA SCID-II	237	18.1	42.0 (–)	42 (17.9)
Chapman & Cellucci, 2007	Incarcerated	Triage Assessment for Addictive Disorders SCID-II	58 with alcohol dependence 73 with drug dependence	100	–	14 (24.1) of AUD 21 (28.8) of DUD
DeMarce, Lash, Parker, Burke, & Brambow, 2013	Outpatient	SCID-I; SCID-II	183	0.04	50.1 (8.3)	16 (8.7)
Dunsieth et al., 2004	Residential (sex offenders without paraphilias)	SCID	26	0.0	39.0 (6.1)	4 (15.4)
Grella et al., 2008	Incarcerated	SCID-II (PD)	280	35.0	34.8 (–)	37 (13.2)
Echeburua et al., 2005	Outpatient (alcohol dependence, no other SUDs)	SCID-I IPDE	30	0.0	–	0 (0.0)
Echeburua, et al., 2007	Outpatient (alcohol dependence)	SCID-I IPDE	158	34.8	43.4 (–)	8 (5.1)
Fenton et al., 2012	Community (NESARC)	AUDADIS-IV	613	32.5	–	138 (22.5)

(*continued*)

Table 5.4. Continued

Reference	Sample	Diagnostic Instrument	N with SUD	% Female	Mean Age (SD)	N with BPD (%)
Gratz & Tull, 2010	Inpatient	Admission; SCID-IV; DIPD-IV	61	46.0	44.45 (7.05)	24 (39.0)
Hasin et al., 2006	Inpatient & outpatient	PRISM-IV	285	46.0	36.3 (8.8)	56 (19.5)
Modestin et al., 2001	Inpatient (opioid dependence)	Admission; SCID-II	100	0.0	29.7 (–)	51 (51.0)
Palmer et al., 2003	Outpatient (opioid dependent)	SCID	107	53.0	43.1 (6.6)	40 (37.4)
Preuss et al., 2001	Inpatient (alcohol dependent)	SCID	135	20.7	41.8 (8.8)	23 (17.0)
Ralevski et al., 2007	Outpatient (alcohol dependent)	SCID	225	2.7	47.0 (–)	68 (30.2)
Ross et al., 2003	Inpatient	SCID	100	19.0	37.1 (9.3)	39 (39.0)
Ross et al., 2005	Outpatient, residential, community (heroin dependent)	CIDI	825	35.0	29.5 (7.8)	388 (47.0)
Rubio et al., 2007	Inpatient, outpatient (alcohol dependent)	SCID	247	0.0	40.3 (–)	29 (11.7)
Schmitz et al., 2000	Outpatient, residential, community (cocaine dependent)	SCID	151	32.5	36.1	29 (19.2)
Torrens et al., 2004	Inpatient & outpatient	SCID	105	31.0	33.3 (7.7)	7 (6.7)
Torrens et al., 2004	Inpatient & outpatient	PRISM-IV	105	31.0	33.3 (7.7)	12 (11.4)
Tull, Gratz, & Weiss, 2011	Inpatient	DIPD-IV; SCID-I/P	94	44.7	36.0 (10.1)	31 (33.0)
van Emmerik-van Oortmerssen et al., 2014	Inpatients & Outpatients	Admission; MINI-Plus; SCID-II	1198	–	–	172 (14.4)
Vergara-Moragues, González-Saiz, Lozano, & García, 2013	Inpatients	Admission; PRISM	218	8.7	–	30 (13.8)
Zikos, Gill, & Charney, 2010	Inpatients	SCID-I; SCID-II	138	33.0	44 (9.7)	19 (13.0)
Zimmerman et al., 2005	Outpatient	SCID-I SIDP-IV	85	–	–	15 (17.6)

NR denotes studies in which the raw count of individuals with BPD was not provided.
CIDI, Composite International Diagnostic Interview; IPDE, International Personality Disorder Examination; PRISM, Psychiatric Research Interview for Substance and Mental Disorders; SCID, Structured Clinical Interview for DSM-IV Disorders; SIDP-IV, Structured Interview for DSM-IV Personality; SSAGA, Semi-Structured Assessment for the Genetics of Alcoholism

Table 5.5. Prevalence of Comorbid Substance Use Disorder (SUD) in Individuals with Borderline Personality Disorder (BPD).

Reference	Sample	Diagnostic Instrument	N with BPD	% Female	Mean Age (SD)	N with SUD (%)
Asnaani et al., 2007	Outpatient	SCID SIDP-IV	237	72.6	31.6 (8.6)	105 (44.3) with DUD
Barone, Fossati, & Guiducci, 2011	Outpatients and inpatients	SCID; SCID-I	140	61.0	32.39 (9.5)	40 (29.0) with SUD 40 (29.0) with AUD
Baschnagel et al., 2013	Community	SIDP-IV; CDIS; MINI	51	80.0 of those with SUD	38.0 (9.9) of those with SUD	35 (69.0)
Chapman & Cellucci, 2007	Incarcerated	Triage Assessment for Addictive Disorders; SCID-II	50	100	–	14 (28.0) with AUD 21 (42.0) with DUD
Chen et al., 2007	Outpatient	SCID-I; SCID-II & IPDE	184	100	31.0 (8.0)	82 (44.6)
Comtois et al., 2003	Outpatient	SCID-I PDE	29	76.0	–	25 (86.2)[a]
Johnson et al., 2003	Outpatient	SCID-I DIPD-IV	240	72.9	31.9 (–)	157 (65.4)
McCormick et al., 2007	Inpatient, outpatient, community	SCID-I SIDP-IV	163	84.7	31.0 (–)	82 (50.3) with AUD 77 (47.2) with DUD
Riihimäki, Vuorilehto, & Isometsä, 2013	Outpatient	SCID-I/P; SCID-II	35	86.0	37.3 (13.7)	10 (29.0)
Tadić et al., 2009	Inpatient	M-CIDI; SCID-I; SCID-II	169	70.0	32.9 (9.1)	115 (68.0) Lifetime SUD 47 (28.0) Current SUD
Tomko, Trull, Wood, & Sher, 2014	Community (NESARC-Revised)	AUDADIS-IV	1,030	57.3	41.8	805 (78.2)[a]
Walter et al., 2009	Inpatients /outpatients	SCID-I/P; DIPD-IV	175	75.0	32.1 (7.8)	91 (52.0) AUD 96 (54.9) DUD
Wedig et al., 2012	Inpatients	SCID-I; DIPD-R; DIB-R	290	80.3	26.9 (5.8)	180 (62.1) with SUD
Welch & Linehan, 2002	Outpatient	SCID-I; PDE/SCID-II	122	100	31.0 (–)	47 (35.5) with DUD
Widom, Czaja, & Paris, 2009	Community	DIPD-R; DIB-R; DIS-III-R	112	–	–	70 (62.7) with AUD 62 (55.5) with DUD
Zanarini et al., 2009	Inpatients	SCID-I; DIPD-R	341	78.6	27.7 (6.9)	182 (53.4) with AUD 158 (46.3) with DUD

[a] Lifetime (not current) SUD rates were reported. All other rates reflect current diagnoses.

DIPD, Diagnostic Interview for DSM-IV Personality Disorders; IPDE, International Personality Disorder Examination; PDE, Personality Disorder Examination; SCID, Structured Clinical Interview for DSM-IV Disorders; SIDP-IV, Structured Interview for DSM-IV Personality; DIB-R, Revised Diagnostic Interview for Borderlines; DIS-III-R, National Institute of Mental Health Diagnostic Interview Schedule, Revised; CIDI, Composite International Diagnostic Interview; CDIS, Diagnostic Interview Schedule-Computerized for DSM-IV

45.3% of substance use disordered inpatients (range, 16.6–74.0%) and 45.2% of substance use disordered outpatients (range, 28.6–78.0%) meet criteria for any PD (see Table 5.6). The literature reporting percentages based on PD cluster also suggests that although Cluster B PDs are most prevalent among drug use disordered inpatients or outpatients (38.2% vs. 15.2% in Cluster A and vs. 15.3% in Cluster C), the differences between clusters are less apparent among individuals with an AUD. In fact, individuals with an AUD were more likely to have a comorbid Cluster C PD (30.2%) than a Cluster A (20.8%) or Cluster B (27.8%) diagnosis (Tables 5.7–5.9).

Some studies also reported comorbidity rates for individual PDs, in addition to those for ASPD and BPD. These are also presented in Tables 5.7–5.9. Cluster A PDs are characterized by odd or eccentric features such as suspiciousness toward others (paranoid PD), odd or peculiar beliefs and behaviors (schizotypal PD), and lack of desire for close relationships and emotional detachment (schizoid PD; APA, 2013). Interestingly, paranoid PD is one of the most common PDs among outpatients and inpatients with an SUD (after ASPD and BPD) according to our review literature and previous research reviews (Cacciola, Alterman, McKay, & Rutherford, 2001; Verheul, 2001). An estimated 13.0% of individuals with SUD have comorbid paranoid PD. Studies report a wide range of prevalence rates of paranoid PD among outpatients and inpatients with an AUD, ranging from 7.0% to 23%, and with a weighted average prevalence rate of 15.8%. Schizotypal PD is much less common among those with SUD, particularly among those with an AUD. Extensive research has been done examining a link between drug use and schizotypal traits (Dumas et al., 2002; Earleywine, 2006; Schiffman, Nakamura, Earleywine, & LaBrie, 2005). However, few studies have looked at the relationship between drug use and schizotypal PD in a clinic population. Studies suggest a 3.4% rate of schizotypal PD among those with SUD and a 3.8% prevalence rate among those with an AUD. Of those with an AUD, 5.1% of individuals have comorbid schizoid PD, whereas 4.3% of individuals with any SUD have comorbid schizoid PD.

Cluster B PDs share dramatic, emotional, and erratic features (APA, 2013). The studies that report comorbidity rates between Cluster B disorders and SUDs in substance abusing clinical populations are shown in Table 5.8. In addition to ASPD and BPD, the Cluster B PDs include narcissistic PD, characterized by patterns of grandiosity, a need for excessive admiration, preoccupations with fantasies of unlimited success or power, and arrogant or haughty behaviors; and histrionic PD, characterized by self-dramatization and the need to be the center of attention (APA, 2013). In the current review, narcissistic PD was present in 7.6% of individuals with any SUD and in 5.1% of those individuals with an AUD. Histrionic PD was present in 6.1% of individuals with any SUD and in 2.8% of those with an AUD.

Those with Cluster C PDs (shown in Table 5.9) are often characterized as anxious or fearful (APA, 2013). These personality disorders include avoidant, dependent, and obsessive-compulsive PD. Features of avoidant personality disorder include feelings of inadequacy, extreme sensitivity to negative evaluation, and social inhibition in a variety of situations (APA, 2013). By taking the weighted means of the reviewed samples, approximately 11.0% of those with any SUD and 9.6% of individuals with an AUD received an avoidant PD diagnosis. According to the DSM-5 (APA, 2013), dependent PD is one of the most frequently diagnosed PDs in mental health settings. Defining features of dependent PD include an extreme need to be cared for and fear of separation (APA, 2013). The rate of dependent PD among those with any SUD was 7.1% and among those with an AUD was 6.9%. Obsessive-compulsive PD is characterized by a preoccupation with perfectionism, orderliness, and excessive devotion to work or productivity at the expense of friendships or leisure time (APA, 2013). Studies indicate that 14.7% of individuals with any SUD and 20.0% of individuals with an AUD also have obsessive compulsive PD, the latter rate being higher than previous reviews have found (Ball, 2005; Verheul, 2001).

Substance Use Disorders Among Persons with Other PDs

Verheul (2001) suggests that individuals with PDs may have different motives for using substances. For example, Verheul proposes that those with a diagnosis of schizotypal, dependent, and avoidant PDs may be motivated to use substances (particularly alcohol, heroin, or benzodiazepines) to reduce stress or to "self-medicate." In addition, Verheul suggests that those with narcissistic or histrionic PD are more sensitive to the rewards associated with using substances and tend to use substances because they find them positively

Table 5.6. Prevalence of Any Personality Disorder in Individuals with Substance Use Disorder (SUD).

Reference	Sample	Diagnostic Instrument	N with SUD	% Female	Mean Age (SD)	N with Any PD (%)
Ball, 2007; Ball & Cecero, 2001	Outpatient (opioid dependent-C, L)	SCID I/P; SCID-II	78	54.0 -of those with a PD	37.4 (5.9) (those with a PD)	41 (52.6)
Bottlender, Preuss, & Soyka, 2006	Inpatient (alcohol dependent-C)	SSAGA; SCID-II (German)	237	18.1	42.0 (–)	175 (74.0)[a]
Carra, Scioli, Monti, & Marinoni, 2006	Outpatient (opioid or cocaine dependent-C, L)	SCID I (Italian); SCID-II (Italian)	148	19.0	31.9 (–)	65 (43.9)
Echeburua, De Medina, & Aizpiri, 2005	Outpatient (alcohol dependent; excluded for other SUDs-C)	SCID-I; IPDE	30	0.0	–	12 (40.0)
Echeburua, De Medina, & Aizpiri, 2007	Outpatient (alcohol dependent- C)	SCID-I; IPDE	158	34.8	43.4 (–)	70 (44.3)
Jansson, Hesse, & Fridell, 2008	Residential (mandated treatment; drug/ alcohol abuse- C)	Admission; SCID-II	132	100.0	–	103 (78.0)[a]
Jones et al., 2004	Outpatient or brief residential + outpatient (opioid or cocaine dependent- C)	SCID-I; SCID-II	259	40.9	35.6 (–)	74 (28.6)
Karterud, Arefjord, Andresen, & Pedersen, 2009	Inpatient	MINI; SCID-II	253	57.7	–	42 (16.6)
Lenzenweger et al., 2007[b]	Community-NCS-R; oversampled for psychiatric disorders (any SUD- C)	CIDI-NCS-R interview; Portions of IPDE	Assessed 214	–	–	– (28.5)
Modestin, Matutat, & Wurmle, 2001	Inpatient (opioid dependent- C)	Admission; SCID-II	100	0.0	29.7 (–)	67 (67.0)
Trathen et al., 2007	Outpatient (any SUD-C)	Admission; COSMIC interview	50	–	–	16 (31.1)
Vergara-Moragues, González-Saiz, Lozano, & García, 2013	Inpatients	Admission; PRISM	218	8.7	–	64 (29.4)

(*continued*)

Table 5.6. Continued

Reference	Sample	Diagnostic Instrument	N with SUD	% Female	Mean Age (SD)	N with Any PD (%)
Zikos, Gill, & Charney, 2010	Inpatients	SCID-I; SCID-II	138	33.0	44 (9.7)	81 (59.0)
Zimmerman et al., 2005	Outpatient (AUD-C)	SCID-I; SIDP-IV	85	–	–	44 (51.8)

[a] Includes Depressive and Negativistic PDs
[b] Lenzenweger et al. (2007) provides predicted prevalence rates extrapolated from a smaller sample (n = 214)
C, current diagnosis, L, lifetime diagnosis
SSAGA, Semi-Structured Assessment for the Genetics of Alcoholism; NCS-R, National Comorbidity Survey Replication; NESARC, National Epidemiologic Survey on Alcohol and Related Conditions; COSMIC interview, semi-structured interview from COSMIC Study (Weaver, 2003); CIDI, Composite International Diagnostic Interview; IPDE, International Personality Disorder Examination; SCID, Structured Clinical Interview for DSM-IV Disorders; SIDP-IV, Structured Interview for DSM-IV Personality; AUDADIS-IV, Alcohol Use Disorders and Associated Disabilities Interview Schedule

reinforcing. Rates of substance abuse (especially drug abuse) in samples with PDs other than ASPD and BPD are less frequently reported. Table 5.10 presents these estimates obtained from our review. Due to the relatively small number of studies, however, generalizations to other samples should be made with caution.

Zimmerman, Rothschild, and Chelminski (2005) report that 11.3% of those diagnosed with a PD in their outpatient sample also had a comorbid AUD. Within this sample, 2.8% of those with paranoid PD had a comorbid AUD diagnosis. Comorbidity studies using outpatient samples suggest moderate co-occurrence between schizotypal PD and SUDs. The studies reviewed indicate that a range from 20.0% (Zimmerman et al., 2005) to 47.7% (McGlashan et al., 2000) of individuals with schizotypal PD in outpatient samples also have an AUD. Also, 41.9% of participants with schizotypal PD in McGlashan and colleagues' study met diagnostic criteria for a DUD. Very little research has examined the comorbidity between schizoid PD and SUDs in clinical samples; the one study we reviewed reported that not one of the 12 individuals with a schizoid diagnosis had a comorbid AUD (Zimmerman et al., 2005).

Among Cluster B disorders, histrionic PD and narcissistic PDs show slightly elevated rates of comorbid alcohol use when compared to many of the other PDs. According to Zimmerman and colleagues (2005), 22.2% of individuals diagnosed with histrionic PD in an outpatient sample had an AUD, and a 25% comorbidity rate was found among with those with narcissistic PD.

Concerning Cluster C PDs, 27.9% of people diagnosed with avoidant PD also had a comorbid AUD (McGlashan et al., 2000; Zimmerman et al., 2005). McGlashan and colleagues reported that 32.5% of those diagnosed with avoidant PD in their sample also had a DUD. Zimmerman and colleagues (2005) found a 25% prevalence rate of AUDs in their outpatient sample of dependent PD participants. However, the sample only consisted of 12 individuals with this PD. Finally, 21.9% of those with obsessive-compulsive PD were diagnosed with alcohol abuse or dependence (range 6.7% to 29.4%), and McGlashan and colleagues' reported that 25.7% of those with obsessive-compulsive PD also had a comorbid drug abuse or dependence diagnosis.

Models of SUD and PD Comorbidity

Up to this point, we have provided empirical data on the rates of comorbidity found between SUDs and PDs. However, how do we understand these comorbidity rates, and are there reasons that some PDs are more highly comorbid with SUDs than other PDs? The observation that two conditions co-occur frequently within individuals raises multiple possibilities (Sher, Trull, Bartholow, & Vieth, 1999; Trull et al., 2000). First, the association between PDs and SUDs may be artifactual because of measurement or design confounds. For example, substance use problems are considered to be one example of impulsivity in the criteria set for ASPD and for BPD, thus ensuring some degree of overlap between these two PDs and SUD diagnoses. Similarly, a number of antisocial behaviors that reflect social deviance, impulsivity, and aggressiveness can be substance-related (e.g., drug possession, driving while intoxicated, substance-related violence). Fortunately, this has been recognized by a number of investigators, and

Table 5.7. Prevalence of Comorbid Cluster A Personality Disorders in Individuals with Substance Use Disorder.

Reference	Sample	Diagnostic Instrument	N with SUD	% Female	Mean Age (SD)	N with Paranoid PD (%)	N with Schizoid PD (%)	N with Schizotypal PD (%)	N with Any Cluster A PD (%)
Ball, 2007; Ball & Cecero, 2001	Outpatient (opioid dependent-C, L)	SCID I/P; SCID-II	78	54.0 -of those with a PD	37.4 (5.9) (those with a PD)	5 (6.4)	3 (3.9)	3 (3.9)	–
Bottlender, Preuss, & Soyka, 2006	Inpatient (alcohol dependent-C)	SSAGA; SCID-II (German)	237	18.1	42.0 (–)	55 (23.0)	18 (7.4)	6 (2.6)	66 (27.8)
Carra, Scioli, Monti, & Marinoni, 2006	Outpatient (opioid or cocaine dependent-C, L)	SCID I (Italian); SCID-II (Italian)	148	19.0	31.9 (–)	–	–	–	8 (5.4)
Dunsieth et al., 2004	Residential (sex offenders without paraphilias-any SUDs-L)	SCID I/P; SCID-II	26	0.0	39.0 (6.1)	4 (15.4)	1 (3.8)	0 (0.0)	–
Echeburua, De Medina, & Aizpiri, 2005	Outpatient (alcohol dependent; excluded for other SUDs-C)	SCID-I; IPDE	30	0.0	–	3 (10.0)	1 (3.3)	1 (3.3)	–
Echeburua, De Medina, & Aizpiri, 2007	Outpatient (alcohol dependent- C)	SCID-I; IPDE	158	34.8	43.4 (–)	11 (7.0)	4 (2.5)	1 (0.6)	–
Grant, Stinson, et al., 2004	Community- NESARC (alcohol abuse/ dependence-C)	AUDADIS-IV	3327	–	–	339 (10.2)	170 (5.1)	–	–

(continued)

Table 5.7. Continued

Reference	Sample	Diagnostic Instrument	N with SUD	% Female	Mean Age (SD)	N with Paranoid PD (%)	N with Schizoid PD (%)	N with Schizotypal PD (%)	N with Any Cluster A PD (%)
Grant, Stinson, et al., 2004[b]	Community-NESARC (drug abuse/dependence-C)	AUDADIS-IV	777	–	–	145 (18.6)	96 (12.3)	–	–
Karterud, Arefjord, Andresen, & Pedersen, 2009	Inpatient	MINI; SCID-II	253	57.7	–	–	–	–	45 (17.8)
Lenzenweger et al., 2007[a]	Community- NCS-R; oversampled for psychiatric disorders (any SUD- C)	CIDI-NCS-R interview; Portions of IPDE	Assessed 214	–	–	–	–	–	– (9.4)
Modestin, Matutat, & Wurmle, 2001	Inpatient (opioid dependent- C)	Admission; SCID-II	100	0.0	29.7 (–)	14 (14.0)	4 (4.0)	12 (12.0)	23 (23.0)
Wu & Howard, 2007[b]	Community- NESARC (inhalant users-L)	AUDADIS-IV	664	29.2	–	87 (13.1)	50 (7.5)	–	–
Zimmerman et al., 2005	Outpatient (AUD-C)	SCID-I; SIDP-IV	85	–	–	1 (1.2)	0 (0.0)	1 (1.2)	1 (1.2)

[a] Lenzenweger et al. (2007) provides predicted prevalence rates extrapolated from a smaller sample (n =214).

[b] Use the same sample.

C, current diagnosis; L, lifetime diagnosis.

SSAGA, Semi-Structured Assessment for the Genetics of Alcoholism; NCS-R, National Comorbidity Survey Replication; NESARC, National Epidemiologic Survey on Alcohol and Related Conditions; CIDI, Composite International Diagnostic Interview; IPDE, International Personality Disorder Examination; SCID, Structured Clinical Interview for DSM-IV Disorders; SIDP-IV, Structured Interview for DSM-IV Personality; AUDADIS-IV, Alcohol Use Disorders and Associated Disabilities Interview Schedule.

Table 5.8. Prevalence of Other Comorbid Cluster B Personality Disorders in Individuals with Substance Use Disorder (SUD).

Reference	Sample	Diagnostic Instrument	N with SUD	% Female	Mean Age (SD)	N with Histrionic PD (%)	N with Narcissistic PD (%)	N with Any Cluster B PD (%)
Albein-Urios, Martínez-Gonzalez, Lozano-Rojas, & Verdejo-Garcia, 2014	Outpatient (cocaine dependent- C)	SCID-I; IPDE	107	36.4 of those with a PD	33.43 (7.20) of those with a PD	8 (7.5)	1 (0.9)	22 (20.5)
Ball, 2007; Ball & Cecero, 2001	Outpatient (opioid dependent-C, L)	SCID I/P; SCID-II	78	54.0 of those with a PD	37.4 (5.9) (those with a PD)	0 (0.0)	2 (2.5)	–
Bottlender, Preuss, & Soyka, 2006	Inpatient (alcohol dependent-C)	SSAGA; SCID-II (German)	237	18.1	42.0 (–)	7 (3.0)	19 (7.9)	89 (37.6)
Carra, Scioli, Monti, & Marinoni, 2006	Outpatient (opioid or cocaine dependent-C, L)	SCID I (Italian); SCID-II (Italian)	148	19.0	31.9 (–)	–	–	52 (35.1)
Dunsieth et al., 2004	Residential (sex offenders without paraphilias-any SUDs-L)	SCID I/P; SCID-II	26	0.0	39.0 (6.1)	0 (0.0)	6 (23.1)	–
Echeburua, De Medina, & Aizpiri, 2005	Outpatient (alcohol dependent; excluded for other SUDs-C)	SCID-I; IPDE	30	0.0	–	0 (0.0)	1 (3.3)	1 (3.3)
Echeburua, De Medina, & Aizpiri, 2007	Outpatient (alcohol dependent-C)	SCID-I; IPDE	158	34.8	43.4 (–)	8 (5.1)	10 (6.3)	30 (19.0)
Grant, Stinson, et al., 2004	Community- NESARC (alcohol abuse/dependence-C)	AUDADIS-IV	3327	–	–	210 (6.3)	–	–
Grant, Stinson, et al., 2004c	Community- NESARC (drug abuse/dependence-C)	AUDADIS-IV	777	–	–	92 (11.8)	–	–
Karterud, Arefjord, Andresen, & Pedersen, 2009	Inpatient	MINI; SCID-II	253	57.7	–	–	–	108 (42.7)

(continued)

Table 5.8. Continued

Reference	Sample	Diagnostic Instrument	N with SUD	% Female	Mean Age (SD)	N with Histrionic PD (%)	N with Narcissistic PD (%)	N with Any Cluster B[a] PD (%)
Lenzenweger et al., 2007[b]	Community- NCS-R; oversampled for psychiatric disorders (any SUD- C)	CIDI-NCS-R interview; Portions of IPDE	Assessed 214	–	–	–	–	– (8.2)
Modestin, Matutat, & Wurmle, 2001	Inpatient (opioid dependent- C)	Admission; SCID-II	100	0.0	29.7 (–)	12 (12.0)	2 (2.0)	59 (59.0)
Wu & Howard, 2007[c]	Community- NESARC (inhalant users-L)	AUDADIS-IV	664	29.2	–	50 (7.6)	–	–
Zikos, Gill, & Charney, 2010	Inpatients	SCID-I; SCID-II	138	33.0	44 (9.7)	–	–	44 (32.0)
Zimmerman et al., 2005	Outpatient (AUD-C)	SCID-I; SIDP-IV	85	–	–	2 (2.4)	5 (5.9)	22 (25.9)

[a] Includes BPD and ASPD.
[b] Lenzenweger et al. (2007) provides predicted prevalence rates extrapolated from a smaller sample (n = 214).
[c] Uses the same sample.

C, current diagnosis; L, lifetime diagnosis.

SSAGA, Semi-Structured Assessment for the Genetics of Alcoholism; NCS-R, National Comorbidity Survey Replication; NESARC, National Epidemiologic Survey on Alcohol and Related Conditions; CIDI, Composite International Diagnostic Interview; IPDE, International Personality Disorder Examination; SCID, Structured Clinical Interview for DSM-IV Disorders; SCID-I/P, Structured Clinical Interview for DSM-IV Axis I Disorders/Patient Edition; SIDP-IV, Structured Interview for DSM-IV Personality; AUDADIS-IV, Alcohol Use Disorders and Associated Disabilities Interview Schedule.

Table 5.9. Prevalence of Comorbid Cluster C Personality Disorders in Individuals with Substance Use Disorder (SUD).

Reference	Sample	Diagnostic Instrument	N with SUD	% female	Mean Age (SD)	N with Avoidant PD (%)	N with Dependent PD (%)	N with OCPD (%)	N with Any Cluster C PD (%)
Albein-Urios, Martinez-Gonzalez, Lozano-Rojas, & Verdejo-Garcia, 2014	Outpatient (cocaine dependent- C)	SCID-I; IPDE	107	0.0 - of those with a PD	33.57 (5.80) - of those with a PD	10 (9.3)	–	5 (4.6)	15 (14.0)
Ball, 2007; Ball & Cecero, 2001	Outpatient (opioid dependent-C, L)	SCID I/P; SCID-II	78	54.0 –of those with a PD	37.4 (5.9) (those with a PD)	23 (29.5)	13 (17.1)	3 (3.9)	–
Bottlender, Preuss, & Soyka, 2006	Inpatient (alcohol dependent-C)	SSAGA; SCID-II (German)	237	18.1	42.0 (–)	35 (14.9)	17 (7.0)	75 (31.6)	95 (40.1)[a]
Carra, Scioli, Monti, & Marinoni, 2006	Outpatient (opioid or cocaine dependent-C, L)	SCID I (Italian); SCID-II (Italian)	148	19.0	31.9 (–)	–	–	–	5 (3.4)
Dunsieth et al., 2004	Residential (sex offenders without paraphilias-any SUDs-L)	SCID I/P; SCID-II	26	0.0	39.0 (6.1)	1 (3.8)	0 (0.0)	4 (15.4)	–
Echeburua, De Medina, & Aizpiri, 2005	Outpatient (alcohol dependent; excluded for other SUDs-C)	SCID-I; IPDE	30	0.0	–	1 (3.3)	4 (13.3)	3 (10.0)	8 (26.6)
Echeburua, De Medina, & Aizpiri, 2007	Outpatient (alcohol dependent- C)	SCID-I; IPDE	158	34.8	43.4 (–)	4 (2.5)	11 (7.0)	19 (12.0)	34 (21.5)
Grant, Stinson, et al., 2004	Community- NESARC (alcohol abuse/dependence-C)	AUDADIS-IV	3327	–	–	150 (4.5)	43 (1.3)	403 (12.1)	–

(continued)

Table 5.9. Continued

Reference	Sample	Diagnostic Instrument	N with SUD	% female	Mean Age (SD)	N with Avoidant PD (%)	N with Dependent PD (%)	N with OCPD (%)	N with Any Cluster C PD (%)
Grant, Stinson, et al., 2004[c]	Community- NESARC (drug abuse/dependence-C)	AUDADIS-IV	777	–	–	78 (10.1)	36 (4.6)	131 (16.9)	–
Karterud, Arefjord, Andresen, & Pedersen, 2009	Inpatient	MINI; SCID-II	253	57.7	–	–	–	–	58 (22.9)
Lenzenweger et al., 2007[b]	Community- NCS-R; oversampled for psychiatric disorders (any SUD- C)	CIDI-NCS-R interview; Portions of IPDE	Assessed 214	–	–	–	–	–	– (10.2)
Loas et al., 2002	Inpatient/Outpatient (any SUD-C)	MINI (French)	414	34.5	27.2 (8.6)	–	122 (29.5)	–	–
Modestin, Matutat, & Wurmle, 2001	Inpatient (opioid dependent- C)	Admission; SCID-II	100	0.0	29.7 (–)	7 (7.0)	3 (3.0)	7 (7.0)	15 (15.0)
Wu & Howard, 2007[c]	Community- NESARC (inhalant users-L)	AUDADIS-IV	664	29.2	–	52 (7.8)	14 (2.1)	114 (17.2)	–
Zimmerman et al., 2005	Outpatient (AUD-C)	SCID-I; SIDP-IV	85	–	–	9 (10.6)	3 (3.5)	5 (5.9)	17 (20.0)

[a] Includes Depressive and Negativistic PDs.

[b] Lenzenweger et al. (2007) provides predicted prevalence rates extrapolated from a smaller sample (n = 214).

[c] Use the same sample.

C, current diagnosis; L, lifetime diagnosis.

SSAGA, Semi-Structured Assessment for the Genetics of Alcoholism; NCS-R, National Comorbidity Survey Replication; NESARC, National Epidemiologic Survey on Alcohol and Related Conditions; MINI, Mini International Neuropsychiatric Interview; CIDI, Composite International Diagnostic Interview; IPDE, International Personality Disorder Examination; SCID, Structured Clinical Interview for DSM-IV Disorders; SIDP-IV, Structured Interview for DSM-IV Personality; AUDADIS-IV, Alcohol Use Disorders and Associated Disabilities Interview Schedule.

Table 5.10. Prevalence of Comorbid Substance Use Disorder (SUD) in Individuals with Personality Disorders.

Reference	Sample	Diagnostic Instrument	N with PD	% Female	Mean Age (SD)	N with any SUD (%)	N with drug use disorder (%)	N with alcohol use disorder (%)
Lenzenweger et al., 2007[a]	Community- NCS-R; over sampled for psychiatric disorders (any PD)	CIDI- NCS-R interview; Portions of IPDE	Assessed 214	–	–	– (22.6)	–(5.6)	–(10.9)
McGlashan et al., 2000	Outpatient (schizotypal PD)	SCID-I; DIPD-IV	86	–	–	–	36 (41.9)	41 (47.7)
McGlashan et al., 2000	Outpatient (avoidant PD)	SCID-I; DIPD-IV	157	–	–	–	51 (32.5)	70 (44.6)
McGlashan et al., 2000	Outpatient (OCPD)	SCID-I; DIPD-IV	153	–	–	–	39 (25.7)	45 (29.4)
Stinson et al., 2008	Community-NESARC (narcissistic PD)	AUDADIS-IV	2148	37.2	–	872 (40.6)	200 (9.3)	466 (21.7)
Walter et al., 2009	Inpatients/ Outpatients (schizotypal, avoidant, or obsessive compulsive PD)	SCID-I/P; DIPD-IV	396	60.0	32.7 (8.3)	–	121 (30.6)	152 (38.4)
Zimmerman et al., 2005	Outpatient (any PD)	SCID-I; SIDP-IV	391	61.4	37.0 (12.2)	–	–	44 (11.3)

[a] Lenzenweger et al. (2007) provides predicted prevalence rates extrapolated from a smaller sample (*n* = 214).

NCS-R, National Comorbidity Survey Replication; NESARC, National Epidemiologic Survey on Alcohol and Related Conditions; CIDI, Composite International Diagnostic Interview; IPDE, International Personality Disorder Examination; SCID, Structured Clinical Interview for DSM-IV Disorders; SIDP-IV, Structured Interview for DSM-IV Personality; AUDADIS-IV, Alcohol Use Disorders and Associated Disabilities Interview Schedule; DIPD-IV, Diagnostic Interview for DSM-IV Personality Disorders; Structured Clinical Interview for DSM-IV Axis I Disorders/Patient Edition; OCPD, obsessive compulsive personality disorder.

significant comorbidity between PDs and SUDs remains even when substance use problems were not considered in the diagnosis of the PD (e.g., Grande, Wolf, Schubert, Patterson, & Brocco, 1984; Grilo et al., 1997).

Concerning design confounds, most studies of this comorbidity are cross-sectional and many are conducted on patients who are either currently in or recently ending an active phase of their SUD. Substance use can contribute to problems of affective instability, impulsivity, and interpersonal problems, for example, all of which are core features of BPD (Trull et al., 2000). Although many studies attempt to circumvent this potential confound by having patients report only those PD traits that were present when not using substances, the reliability and validity of these retrospective reports remain unclear.

Another possibility is that an unmeasured third variable related to both PDs and SUDs is responsible for their association in a given study. A third variable such as age (both sets of disorders are more common among younger individuals) is not etiologically important, in the causal sense. In contrast, a third variable like childhood trauma (especially physical and sexual abuse) or a common genetic diathesis is etiologically important. In this case, the two disorders may co-occur at greater than chance frequency because they share common risk factors.

Another important class of comorbidity explanations to consider is that SUDs cause or lead to PD (or vice versa). In other words, one condition may be the consequence of the other. For example, chronic excessive alcohol consumption may result in serotonin depletion (e.g., Ballenger, Goodwin, Major, & Brown, 1979) that, in turn, can lead to impulsive, self-destructive behavior. Presumably, individuals with a neurobiological vulnerability to BPD might be especially susceptible to these neuropharmacological sequelae of substance abuse. Alternatively, SUDs are defined, in part, by the consequences of substance use (e.g., loss of important relationships, Legal problems no longer in DSM-5; APA, 2000; 2013). Substance-related life events may represent critical stressors for the individual vulnerable to BPD. On the other hand, individuals with BPD might turn to psychoactive substances in order to "self-medicate" affective disturbance or to cope with feelings of emptiness or abandonment (e.g., Dulit, Fyer, Haas, Sullivan, & Frances, 1990); in this case, BPD might influence the development of SUD.

Understanding the Association between PDs and SUDs: Theoretical Models

Aside from understanding the comorbidity of PDs and SUDs from a methodological perspective, there are theoretical reasons for this co-occurrence. Because PDs, by definition, involve maladaptive personality traits, research on the interface between personality and substance use and abuse can inform theories of the comorbidity of these conditions. Reviews of major personality factors suggest three major models of etiology for alcoholism and SUDs, including pharmacological vulnerability, affect regulation, and deviance proneness (Sher, 1991; Sher & Trull, 1994; Sher at al., 1999). These models highlight the interplay between factors that appear to be associated with and give rise to both PDs and SUDs. In addition, these models are not mutually exclusive; each may be at least partially responsible for the observed comorbidity pattern. We briefly review each model's relevance to AUD, but note that these models also apply to other SUDs as well.

PHARMACOLOGICAL VULNERABILITY

This model evolved from the observation that there are individual differences in the effects of alcohol, especially the relation between personality and alcohol sensitivity (Sher et al., 1999). The most consistent findings in this area include the association between the personality trait of impulsivity/disinhibition and the stress-reducing properties of alcohol (e.g., Levenson, Oyama, & Meek, 1987; Sher & Levenson, 1982) and that individual differences in reactions to alcohol have been shown to prospectively predict alcohol problems (Schuckit & Smith, 1996; Volavka et al., 1996).

Impulsivity/disinhibition is a central feature of several PDs, but especially antisocial, borderline, and histrionic PDs (APA, 2013). To the extent that impulsivity is present, this may serve as a risk factor for both PDs and SUDs, given that disinhibited individuals may subjectively experience more stress reduction (reinforcement) when using alcohol or other drugs. Aside from enhancing the stress-reducing properties of substances, impulsivity may influence the decision to use psychoactive substances, as well as their continued use (or overuse) in those situations in which many would discontinue substance use.

Several behavioral genetic studies support the connection between the personality trait of impulsivity and substance use and abuse. Following up on the earlier finding that most of the overlap between conduct disorder and alcohol dependence was due to common genetic risk factors (Slutske et al., 1998), Slutske et al. (2002) examined whether the personality trait of impulsivity/behavioral under-control accounted for the shared genetic risk common to alcohol dependence and conduct disorder. Results from a large twin sample suggested that this personality trait accounted for about 90% of the common genetic risk for these two disorders. More recently, Iacono, Malone, and McGue (2008) have summarized and integrated findings suggesting that SUDs and disorders characterized by behavioral disinhibition/impulsivity share a common underlying genetic diathesis. Furthermore, they speculate that this liability is expressed through neural mechanisms related to cognitive control and sensitivity to reward, for example. SUDs may develop over time depending on the interaction between genetic liability and environmental risks.

NEGATIVE AFFECT REGULATION

A number of psychological motives or reasons for substance use have been identified. Alcohol use motives, personality traits, and alcohol use problems are interrelated in the literature. There is evidence suggesting that these motives may partially mediate the relationship between personality traits and alcohol problems (Sher et al., 1999). For example, Cooper, Frone, Russell, and Mudar (1995) reported that negative emotionality/neuroticism was related to the motive "drinking to cope," and this motive partially mediated the effects of negative emotionality/neuroticism on drinking. Tragesser, Sher, Trull, and Park (2007) found that coping motives related to both impulsivity and negative emotionality (major personality traits underlying PDs) were associated with problematic drinking. Enhancement motives (i.e., drinking in order to increase positive affect) mediated the relationship between Cluster B PD traits and problematic drinking.

Negative reinforcement theories of SUDs suggest that individuals are motivated to use substances in order to alleviate negative affect or aversive states (e.g., Conger, 1956; Baker, Piper, McCarthy, Majeskie, & Fiore, 2004). The psychopharmacological properties of alcohol and other substances may provide some temporary relief. In addition, the belief that these substances will alleviate negative affective states may be powerful motivation for consumption. Although almost all PDs can be characterized by high levels of negative affect, individuals

with certain PDs (e.g., borderline) may be especially vulnerable to this effect, given that affective lability and emotion dysregulation are core features (Trull et al., 2008).

DEVIANCE PRONENESS

This model posits that constitutional factors (temperamental traits, especially those related to impulsivity/disinhibition) may interact in a transactional way (i.e., influence reciprocally) with deficits in parental control, leading to problems in socialization (Sher et al., 1999). In turn, deficits in socialization are associated with a host of problems, including poor academic performance, delinquent behavior, and substance abuse (Sher, 1991). Thus, impulsivity/disinhibition, although perhaps quite distal from outcome, can contribute to a process leading to SUD.

Given that impulsivity/disinhibition is a major feature, it should not be surprising that those with ASPD and BPD may engage in a variety of behaviors that violate social norms (e.g., shoplifting, financial irresponsibility, excessive promiscuity; APA, 2013). In addition, BPD and ASPD, a disorder characterized by a disregard for and violation of the rights of others (APA, 2013), frequently co-occur (Trull et al., 2000). Data we presented earlier on the comorbidity between PDs and SUD are also consistent with this impulsivity–social deviance link. Furthermore, indirectly supporting the influence of deficient parenting or lack of parental control in the development of these PDs, there is evidence suggesting family conflict and communication problems in the families of probands diagnosed with BPD (e.g., Zanarini & Frankenburg, 1997). However, it should be noted that most of the studies implicating an adverse family environment in BPD patients have relied solely on patients' self-report and have assessed patients in adulthood (Nigg, Lohr, Westen, Gold, & Silk, 1992; Laporte & Guttman, 2007).

Finally, it must be recognized that poor parental control and family problems may be a consequence of BPD. It is likely that the impulsive behaviors and extreme negative affective episodes characteristic of BPD contribute to a stressful family atmosphere (e.g., Gunderson et al., 2006; Hoffman, Fruzetti, & Buteau, 2007).

Treatment Implications

Understanding the nature and extent of this comorbidity between SUDs and PDs is important for researchers seeking to characterize the etiology of both PDs and SUDs and for clinicians hoping to optimize treatment programs and develop a better understanding of prognostic factors concerning recovery and relapse. In the treatment community, there is increasing recognition of the need to address comorbid SUD in the treatment of PDs (e.g., Ball, 2005; Verheul, van den Bosch, & Ball, 2005). Individuals with an SUD who also have one or more PDs show greater severity in their substance use symptoms, experience more severe levels of psychopathology in general, and have more employment and legal problems (e.g., Ball, 2005; Jansson, Hesse, & Fridell, 2008). Concerning psychotherapy for substance use problems, they are more likely to relapse, have a worse treatment outcome, and are more likely to be hospitalized (Ball, 2005).

In addition to these correlates of SUD–PD comorbidity, it is also important to consider how comorbid PD symptoms may affect treatment approaches (Ball, 2005; Verheul et al., 2005). For example, Ball (2005) notes that individuals with both SUD and PD are more likely to exhibit resistant or provocative behaviors during treatment, to exhibit higher levels of impulsivity and acting out, to experience affective instability, to be less able to form quality interpersonal bonds (including that with the therapist), and to experience difficulty complying with treatment. Such difficulties seem to call for a more structured, supportive, and intensive treatment approach, with frequent contacts by the therapist (e.g., Bornovalova & Daughters, 2007).

Certain structured therapies for SUD–PD comorbid clients have preliminary empirical support. For example, dialectical behavior therapy (DBT), an empirically supported treatment for BPD, also has been shown to be effective with individuals with comorbid substance dependence (Harned et al., 2008). Additionally, DBT has been modified specifically for use with substance abusing populations (Dimeff & Linehan, 2008). Dynamic deconstructive psychotherapy (DPP), a psychodynamic treatment for alcohol-dependent clients with comorbid BPD, has been shown to be more effective than treatment as usual (Gregory et al., 2008). Furthermore, behavioral techniques have been shown to improve attendance and treatment compliance in opioid-dependent clients with comorbid ASPD (Neufeld et al., 2008).

Pharmacotherapy may be a promising treatment option for individuals with both an AUD and a PD (Ralevski et al., 2007). Ralevski and colleagues (2007) conducted a clinical trial testing naltrexone and naltrexone plus disulfiram. The findings suggested that the medications were equally effective at reducing drinking in individuals with AUD alone and in individuals with BPD or ASPD in addition to AUD. However, the medications were significantly worse at reducing cravings for those with a comorbid PD than for those with AUD alone.

Conclusion and Future Directions

We have shown that PDs frequently co-occur with SUDs, and these relations hold in both clinical populations and the general population. This comorbidity can be understood in a number of ways. For example, the SUD–PD comorbidity may be a function of common etiological processes, with early expression of impaired impulse control and affective dysregulation in these conditions. These findings suggest that SUDs and especially ASPD and BPD are related disorders that share commonalities in their determinants and in their expression. Future research is needed to identify common biomarkers or endophenotypes that can help lead us to a better understanding of the shared genetic vulnerabilities that influence the expression of these disorders.

Many would not be surprised to hear that both ASPD and BPD are highly comorbid with SUDs. However, it was also interesting to find that (in both population-based and clinical samples) paranoid, avoidant, and obsessive-compulsive PDs are fairly prevalent in both SUD and AUD. How do we understand this relationship? One common feature underlying these three PDs is negative affectivity. In paranoid PD, this is typically manifested as the experience and expression of anger, as well as verbally lashing out at others. Those with avoidant PD experience intense negative affects, including anxiety and dysphoria. Finally, those with obsessive-compulsive PD, although seeming constrained on the surface, are prone to experience strong frustration, disappointment, and anger, as well as depression. Therefore, the negative affect regulation model for substance abuse and dependence seems most applicable to the observed comorbidity for these three PDs.

The question of whether SUDs are a cause or consequence of PDs cannot be answered definitely by our review of the existing research. However, because common genetic, personality, and early environmental influences predate overt substance use, it seems unlikely that PDs are simply secondary to SUD. The effect of SUD on PD expression appears to be one of exacerbating PD symptomatology and, in turn, contributing to chronicity. This has important treatment implications in that clinicians must keep in mind the challenges present when planning and implementing treatment for those with both SUD and PD. It may be the case that variations on existing treatments or even new treatments are needed for this comorbid condition.

References

Albein-Urios, N., Martinez-Gonzalez, J. M., Lozano-Rojas, O., & Verdejo-Garcia, A. (2014). Executive functions in cocaine-dependent patients with cluster B and cluster C personality disorders. *Neuropsychology, 28*(1), 84–90.

American Psychiatric Association. (2000). *Diagnostic and statistical manual of mental disorders* (4th ed., rev.). Washington, DC: Author.

American Psychiatric Association. (2013). *Diagnostic and statistical manual of mental disorders* (5th ed.). Arlington, VA: American Psychiatric Publishing.

Anestis, M. D., Gratz, K. L., Bagge, C. L., & Tull, M. T. (2012). The interactive role of distress tolerance and borderline personality disorder in suicide attempts among substance users in residential treatment. *Comprehensive Psychiatry, 53*(8), 1208–1216.

Anthenelli, R. M., Maxwell, R. A., Geracioti, T. D., & Hauger, R. (2001). Stress hormone dysregulation at rest and after serotonergic stimulation among alcohol-dependent men with extended abstinence and controls. *Alcoholism: Clinical and Experimental Research, 25*, 692–703.

Asnaani, A., Chelminski, I., Young, D., & Zimmerman, M. (2007). Heterogeneity of borderline personality disorder: Do the number of criteria met make a difference? *Journal of Personality Disorders, 21*, 615–625.

Assanangkornchai, S., Saunders, J. B, & Conigrave, K. M. (2000). Patterns of drinking in Thai men. *Alcohol & Alcoholism, 35*, 263–269.

Baker, T. B., Piper, M .E., McCarthy, D. E., Majeskie, M. R., & Fiore, M. C. (2004). Addiction motivation reformulated: An affective processing model of negative reinforcement. *Psychological Review, 111*, 33–51. DOI: 10.1037/0033-295X.111.1.33

Ball, S. A. (2007). Comparing individual therapies for personality disordered opioid dependent patients. *Journal of Personality Disorders, 21*, 305–321.

Ball, S. A. (2005). Personality traits, problems, and disorders: Clinical applications to substance use disorders. *Journal of Research in Personality, 39*, 84–102.

Ball, S. A., & Cecero, J. J. (2001). Addicted patients with personality disorders: Traits, schemas, and presenting problems. *Journal of Personality Disorders, 15*, 72–83.

Ballenger, J. C., Goodwin, F. K., Major, L. F., & Brown, G. L. (1979). Alcohol and central serotonin metabolism in men. *Archives of General Psychiatry, 36*, 224–227.

Bardeen, J. R., Dixon-Gordon, K. L., Tull, M. T., Lyons, J. A., & Gratz, K. L. (2014). An investigation of the relationship between borderline personality disorder and cocaine-related attentional bias following trauma cue exposure: The moderating role of gender. *Comprehensive Psychiatry, 55*(1), 113–122.

Barone, L., Fossati, A., & Guiducci, V. (2011). Attachment mental states and inferred pathways of development in borderline personality disorder: A study using the Adult Attachment Interview. *Attachment & Human Development, 13*(5), 451–469.

Baschnagel, J. S., Coffey, S. F., Hawk, L. W., Jr., Schumacher, J. A., & Holloman, G. (2013). Psychophysiological assessment of emotional processing in patients with borderline personality disorder with and without comorbid substance use. *Personality Disorders: Theory, Research, and Treatment, 4*(3), 203.

Becker, D. F., Añez, L. M., Paris, M., & Grilo, C. M. (2010). Exploratory factor analysis of borderline personality disorder criteria in monolingual Hispanic outpatients with substance use disorders. *Psychiatry Research, 178*(2), 305–308.

Bornovalova, M. A., & Daughters, S. B. (2007). How does Dialectical Behavior Therapy facilitate treatment retention among individuals with comorbid borderline personality disorder and substance use disorders? *Clinical Psychology Review, 27*, 923–943.

Bornovalova, M. A., Gratz, K. L., Daughters, S. B., Nick, B., Delany-Brumsey, A., Lynch, T. R., et al. (2008). A multimodal assessment of the relationship between emotion dysregulation and borderline personality disorder among inner-city substance users in residential treatment. *Journal of Psychiatric Research, 42*, 717–726.

Bottlender, M., Preuss, U. W., & Soyka, M. (2006). Association of personality disorders with Type A and Type B alcoholics. *European Archives of Psychiatry and Clinical Neuroscience, 256*, 55–61.

Bucholz, K., Cadoret, R., Cloninger, C., Dinwiddie, S., Hesselbrock, V., Nurnberger, J., . . . , Schuckit, M. (1994). A new, semistructured psychiatric interview for use in genetic linkage studies. A report on the reliability of the SSAGA. *Journal of Studies on Alcohol, 55*, 149–158.

Cacciola, J. S., Alterman, A. I., McKay, J. R., & Rutherford, M. J. (2001). Psychiatric comorbidity in patients with substance abuse disorders: Do not forget Axis II disorders. *Psychiatric Annals, 31*, 321–331.

Carra, G., Scioli, R., Monti, M. C., & Marinoni, A. (2006). Severity profiles of substance-abusing patients in Italian community addiction facilities: Influence of psychiatric concurrent disorders. *European Addiction Research, 12*, 96–101.

Chapman, A. L., & Cellucci, T. (2007). The role of antisocial and borderline personality features in substance dependence among incarcerated females. *Addictive Behaviors, 32*, 1131–1145.

Chen, E. Y., Brown, M. Z., Lo, T. T. Y., & Linehan, M. M. (2007). Sexually transmitted disease rates and high-risk sexual behaviors in borderline personality disorder versus borderline personality disorder with substance use disorder. *Journal of Nervous and Mental Disease, 195*, 125–129.

Chiang, S. Chan, H. Chang, Y. Sun, H. Chen, W., & Chen, C. (2007). Psychiatric comorbidity and gender differences among treatment seeking heroin abusers in Taiwan. *Psychiatry and Clinical Neurosciences, 61*, 105–111.

Coid, J., Yang, M., Tyrer, P., Roberts, A., & Ullrich, S. (2006). Prevalence and correlates of personality disorder in Great Britain. *British Journal of Psychiatry, 188*, 423–431.

Comtois, K. A., Russo, J., Snowden, M., Srebnik, D., Ries, R., & Roy-Byrne, P. (2003). Factors associated with high use of public mental health services by persons with borderline personality disorder. *Psychiatric Services, 54*, 1149–1154.

Conger, J. J. (1956). Reinforcement theory and the dynamics of alcoholism. *Quarterly Journal of Studies on Alcohol, 17,* 296–305.

Cooper, M. L., Frone, M. R., Russell, M., & Mudar, P. (1995). Drinking to regulate positive and negative emotions: A motivational model of alcohol use. *Journal of Personality and Social Psychology, 69,* 990–1005.

Darke, S., Williamson, A., Ross, J., Teesson, M., & Lynskey, M. (2004). Borderline personality disorder, antisocial personality disorder, and risk-taking among heroin users: Findings from the Australian Treatment Outcome Study (ATOS). *Drug and Alcohol Dependence, 74,* 77–83.

DeMarce, J. M., Lash, S. J., Parker, J. D., Burke, R. S., & Grambow, S. C. (2013). Validity of the structured clinical interview for DSM-IV among veterans seeking treatment for substance use disorders. *International Journal of Mental Health and Addiction, 11*(5), 546–556.

Dimeff, L. A., & Linehan, M. M. (2008). Dialectical Behavior Therapy for Substance Abusers. *Addiction Science & Clinical Practice, 4,* 39–47.

Dulit, R. A., Fyer, M. R., Haas, G. L., Sullivan, T., & Frances, A. J. (1990). Substance use in borderline personality disorder. *American Journal of Psychiatry, 147,* 1002–1007.

Dumas, P., Saoud, M., Bouafia, S., Gutknecht, C., Ecochard, R., Dale´ry, J., et al. (2002). Cannabis use correlates with schizotypal personality traits in healthy students. *Psychiatry Research, 109,* 27–35.

Dunsieth, N. W., Nelson, E. B., Brusman-Lovins, L. A., Holcomb, J. L., Beckman, D., Welge, J. A., et al. (2004). Psychiatric and legal features of 113 men convicted of sexual offenses. *Journal of Clinical Psychiatry, 65,* 293–300.

Earleywine, M. (2006). Schizotypy, marijuana, and differential item functioning. *Human Psychopharmacology, 21,* 455–461.

Easton, C. J., Oberleitner, L. M., Scott, M. C., Crowley, M. J., Babuscio, T. A., & Carroll, K. M. (2012). Differences in treatment outcome among Marijuana-dependent young adults with and without antisocial personality disorder. *American Journal of Drug and Alcohol Abuse, 38*(4), 305–313.

Easton, C. J., Weinberger, A. H., & McKee, S. A. (2008). Cigarette smoking and intimate partner violence among men referred to substance abuse treatment. *American Journal of Drug and Alcohol Abuse, 34,* 39–46.

Echeburua, E., De Medina, R. B., & Aizpiri, J. (2005). Alcoholism and personality disorders: An exploratory study. *Alcohol & Alcoholism, 40,* 323–326.

Echeburua, E., De Medina, R. B., & Aizpiri, J. (2007). Comorbidity of alcohol dependence and personality disorders: A comparative study. *Alcohol & Alcoholism, 42,* 618–622.

Falck, R. S., Wang, J., Siegal, H. A., & Carlson, R. G. (2004). The prevalence of psychiatric disorder among a community sample of crack cocaine users: An exploratory study with practical implications. *Journal of Nervous and Mental Disease, 192,* 503–507.

Fals-Stewart, W., Golden, J., & Schumacher, J. A. (2003). Intimate partner violence and substance use: A longitudinal day-to-day examination. *Addictive Behaviors, 28,* 1555–1574.

Fenton, M. C., Keyes, K., Geier, T., Greenstein, E., Skodol, A., Krueger, B., ... Hasin, D. S. (2012). Psychiatric comorbidity and the persistence of drug use disorders in the United States. *Addiction, 107*(3), 599–609.

Ford, J. D., Gelernter, J., DeVoe, J. S., Zhang, W., Weiss, R. D., Brady, K., ... Kranzler, H. R. (2009). Association of psychiatric and substance use disorder comorbidity with cocaine dependence severity and treatment utilization in cocaine-dependent individuals. *Drug and Alcohol Dependence, 99*(1), 193–203.

Fotiadou, M., Livaditis, M., Manou, I., Kaniotou, E., Samakouri, M., Tzavaras, N., et al. (2004). Self-reported substance misuses in Greek male prisoners. *European Addiction Research, 10,* 56–60.

Goodwin, R. D., & Hamilton, S. P. (2003). Lifetime comorbidity of antisocial personality disorder and anxiety disorders among adults in the community. *Psychiatry Research, 117,* 159–166.

Goudriaan, A. E, Oosteriaan, J., de Beurs, E., & van den Brink, W. (2006). Neurocognitive functions in pathological gambling: A comparison with alcohol dependence, Tourette syndrome and normal controls. *Addiction, 101,* 534–547.

Grande, T. P., Wolf, A. W., Schubert, D. S., Patterson, M. B., & Brocco, K. (1984). Associations among alcoholism, drug abuse, and antisocial personality: A review of literature. *Psychological Reports, 55,* 455–474.

Grant, B. F., Harford, T. C., Dawson, D. A., Chou, P. S., & Pickering, R. P. (1995). The Alcohol Use Disorder and Associated Disabilities Interview Schedule (AUDADIS): Reliability of alcohol and drug modules in a general population sample. *Drug Alcohol Depend, 39,* 37–44.

Grant, B. F., Hasin, D. S., Chou, S. P., Stinson, F. S., & Dawson, D. A. (2004). Nicotine dependence and psychiatric disorders in the United States. *Archives of General Psychiatry, 61,* 1107–1115.

Grant, B. F., Moore, T. C., Shepard, J., & Kaplan, K. (2003). *Source and accuracy statement: Wave 1 National epidemiologic survey on alcohol abuse and related conditions (NESARC).* Bethesda, MD: National Institute on Alcohol Abuse and Alcoholism. (http://niaaa.census.gov/pdfs/source_and_accuracy_statement.pdf)

Grant, B. F., Stinson, F. S., Dawson, D. A., Chou, S. P. Ruan, W. J., & Pickering, R. P. (2004). Co-occurrence of 12-month alcohol and drug use disorders and personality disorders in the United States. *Archives of General Psychiatry, 61,* 361–368.

Gratz, K. L., & Tull, M. T. (2010). The relationship between emotion dysregulation and deliberate self-harm among inpatients with substance use disorders. *Cognitive Therapy and Research, 34*(6), 544–553.

Gregory, R. J., Virk, S., Chlebowski, S., Kang, D., Remen, A. L., Soderberg, M. G., et al. (2008). A controlled trial of psychodynamic psychotherapy for co-occurring borderline personality disorder and alcohol use disorder. *Psychotherapy: Theory, Research, Practice, Training, 45,* 28–41.

Grella, C. E., Greenwell, L., Prendergast, M., Sacks, S., & Melnick, G. (2008). Diagnostic profiles of offenders in substance abuse treatment programs. *Behavioral Sciences and the Law, 26,* 369–388.

Grilo, C. M., Martino, S., Walker, M. L., Becker, D. F., Edell, W. S., & McGlashan, T. H. (1997). Controlled study of psychiatric comorbidity in psychiatrically hospitalized young adults with substance use disorders. *American Journal of Psychiatry, 154,* 1305–1307.

Gunderson, J. G. (2001). *Borderline personality disorder: A clinical guide.* Washington, DC: American Psychiatric Press.

Gunderson, J. G., Daversa, M. T., Grilo, C. M., McGlashan, T. H., Zanarini, M. C., Shea, M. T., Skodol, A. E., Yen, S., & Sanislow, C. A. (2006). Predictors of two year outcome for patients with borderline personality disorder. *American Journal of Psychiatry, 163*, 822–826.

Gustavson, C., Stahlberg, O., Shodin, A., Forsman, A., Nilsson, T., & Anckarsater, H. (2007). Age at onset of substance abuse: A crucial covariate of psychopathic traits and aggression in adult offenders. *Psychiatry Research, 153*, 195–198.

Harned, M. S., Chapman, A. L., Dexter-Mazza, E. T., Murray, A., Comtois, K. A., & Linehan, M. M. (2008). Treating co-occurring axis I disorders in recurrently suicidal women with borderline personality disorder: A 2-year randomized trial of dialectical behavior therapy versus community treatment by experts. *Journal of Consulting and Clinical Psychology, 76*, 1068–1075.

Hasin, D., Samet, S., Nunes, E., Meydan, J., Matseoane, K., & Waxman, R. (2006). Diagnosis of comorbid psychiatric disorders in substance users assessed with the Psychiatric Research Interview for Substance and Mental Disorders for DSM-IV. *American Journal of Psychiatry, 163*, 689–696.

Havens, J. R., Cornelius, L. J., Ricketts, E. P., Latkin, C. A., Bishai, D., Lloyd, J. J., et al. (2007). The effect of a case management intervention on drug treatment entry among treatment-seeking injection drug users with and without comorbid antisocial personality disorder. *Journal of Urban Health: Bulletin of the New York Academy of Science, 84*, 267–271.

Helmus, T. C., Downey, K. K., Arfken, C. L., Henderson, M. J., & Schuster, C. R. (2001). Novelty seeking as a predictor of treatment retention for heroin dependent cocaine users. *Drug and Alcohol Dependence, 61*, 287–295.

Helzer, J. E., & Canino, G. J. (1992). Comparative analysis of alcoholism in ten cultural regions. In J. E. Helzer & G. J. Canino (Eds.), *Alcoholism in North America, Europe, and Asia* (pp. 289–308). New York: Oxford University Press.

Hesselbrock, M., Easton, C., Bucholz, K. K., Schuckit, M., & Hesselbrock, V. (1999). A validity study of the SSAGA-a comparison with the SCAN. *Addiction, 94*(9), 1361–1370.

Himmerich, H., Muller, M. J., Anghelescu, I., Klawe, C. Scheurich, A., & Szegedi, A. (2004). Antisocial personality disorder and its correlate in the Michigan alcoholism screening test. *German Journal of Psychiatry, 7*, 14–19.

Hoffman, P. D., Fruzzetti, A. E., & Buteau, E. (2007). Understanding and engaging families: An education, skills, and support program for relatives impacted by borderline personality disorder. *Journal of Mental Health, 16*, 69–82.

Iacono, W. G., Malone, S. M., & McGue, M. (2008). Behavioral disinhibition and the development of early-onset addiction: Common and specific influences. *Annual Review of Clinical Psychology, 4*, 325–348.

Jansson, I., Hesse, M., & Fridell, M. (2008). Personality disorder features as predictors of symptoms five years post-treatment. *American Journal on Addictions, 17*, 172–175.

Johann, M., Bobbe, G., Putzhammer, A., & Wodarz, N. (2003). Comorbidity of alcohol dependence with attention-deficit hyperactivity disorder: Differences in phenotype with increased severity of the substance disorder, but not in genotype (Serotonin transporter and 5-hydroxytryptamine-2c receptor). *Alcoholism: Clinical and Experimental Research, 27*, 1527–1534.

Johnson, D. M., Shea, M. T., Yen, S., Battle, C. L., Zlotnick, C., Sanislow, C. A., et al. (2003). Gender differences in borderline personality disorder: Findings from the Collaborative Longitudinal Personality Disorders Study. *Comprehensive Psychiatry, 44*, 284–292.

Jones, H. E., Johnson, R. E., Bigelow, G. E., & Strain, E. C. (2004). Differences at treatment entry between opioid-dependent and cocaine dependent males and females. *Addictive Disorders and Their Treatment, 3*, 110–121.

Karterud, S., Arefjord, N., Andresen, N. E., & Pedersen, G. (2009). Substance use disorders among personality disordered patients admitted for day hospital treatment. Implications for service developments. *Nordic Journal of Psychiatry, 63*(1), 57–63.

Kernberg, O. (1984). *Severe personality disorders.* New Haven, CT: Yale University Press.

Kessler, R. C., McGonagle, K. A., Zhao, S., Nelson, C. B., Hughes, M., Eshleman, S., et al. (1994). Lifetime and 12-month prevalence of DSM-III-R psychiatric disorders in the United States: Results from the National Comorbidity Survey. *Archives of General Psychiatry, 51*, 8–19.

Kidorf, M., Disney, E. R., King, V. L., Neufeld, K., Beilenson, P. L., & Brooner, R. K. (2004). Prevalence of psychiatric and substance use disorders in opioid abusers in a community syringe exchange program. *Drug and Alcohol Dependence, 74*, 115–122.

Ladd, G. T., & Petry, N. M. (2003). Antisocial personality in treatment-seeking cocaine abusers: Psychosocial functioning and HIV risk. *Journal of Substance Abuse Treatment, 24*, 323–330.

Laporte, L., & Guttman, H. (2007). Recollections of parental bonding among women with borderline personality disorder as compared with women with anorexia nervosa and a control group. *Australian Journal of Psychology, 59*(3), 132–139.

Lenzenweger, M. F., Lane, M. C., Loranger, A. W., & Kessler, R. C. (2007). DSM-IV personality disorders in the national comorbidity survey replication. *Biological Psychiatry, 62*, 553–564.

Levenson, R. W., Oyama, O. N., & Meek, P. S. (1987). Greater reinforcement from alcohol for those at risk: Parental risk, personality risk, and gender. *Journal of Abnormal Psychology, 96*, 242–253.

Lin, S., Ball, D., Hsiao, C., Chiang, Y., Ree, S., & Chen, C. (2004). Psychiatric comorbidity and gender differences of persons incarcerated for methamphetamine abuse in Taiwan. *Psychiatry and Clinical Neurosciences, 58*, 206–212.

Livesley, W. J. (1998). Suggestions for a framework for an empirically based classification of personality disorder. *Canadian Journal of Psychiatry, 43*, 137–147.

Livesley, W. J. (2003). Diagnostic dilemmas in classifying personality disorder. In K. A. Phillips, M. B. First, & H. A. Pincus (Eds.), *Advancing DSM. Dilemmas in psychiatric diagnosis* (pp. 153–190). Washington, DC: American Psychiatric Association.

Loas, G., Atger, F., Perdereau, F., Verrier, A., Guelfi, J., Halfon, H., et al. (2002). Comorbidity of dependent personality disorder and separation anxiety disorder in addictive disorders and in healthy subjects. *Psychopathology, 35*, 249–253.

Lu, R., Lin, W., Lee, J., Ko, H., & Shih, J. (2003). Neither antisocial personality disorder nor antisocial alcoholism is associated with the MAO-A gene in Han Chinese males. *Alcoholism: Clinical Experimental Research, 27,* 889–893.

McCormick, B., Blum, N., Hansel, R., Franklin, J. A., St. John, D., Pfohl, B., et al. (2007). Relationship of sex to symptom severity, psychiatric comorbidity, and health care utilization in 163 subjects with borderline personality disorder. *Comprehensive Psychiatry, 48,* 406–412.

McGlashan, T. H., Grilo, C. M., Skodol, A. E., Gunderson, J. G., Shea, M. T., Morey, L. C., et al. (2000). The collaborative longitudinal personality disorders study: Baseline Axis I/II and II/II diagnostic co-occurrence. *Acta Psychiatrica Scandinavica, 102,* 256–264.

Messina, N., Farabee, D., & Rawson, R. (2003). Treatment responsivity of cocaine-dependent patients with antisocial personality disorder to cognitive-behavioral and contingency management interventions. *Journal of Counseling and Clinical Psychology, 71,* 320–329.

Mellentin, A. I., Skøt, L., Teasdale, T. W., & Habekost, T. (2013). Conscious knowledge influences decision-making differently in substance abusers with and without co-morbid antisocial personality disorder. *Scandinavian Journal of Psychology, 54*(4), 292–299.

Millon, T. (1981). *Disorders of personality: DSM-III Axis II.* New York: Wiley.

Mills, K., Teesson, M., Darke, S., & Ross, J. (2007). Reliability of self-reported trauma exposure among people with heroin dependence: A longitudinal investigation. *Journal of Traumatic Stress, 20,* 313–323.

Miranda, R., Jr., MacKillop, J., Meyerson, L. A., Justus, A., & Lovallo, W. R. (2009). Influence of antisocial and psychopathic traits on decision-making biases in alcoholics. *Alcoholism: Clinical and Experimental Research, 33*(5), 817–825.

Mitchell, J. D., Brown, E. S., & Rush, A. J. (2007). Comorbid disorders in patients with bipolar disorder and concomitant substance dependence. *Journal of Affective Disorders, 102,* 281–287.

Modestin, J., Matutat, B., & Wurmle, O. (2001). Antecedents of opioid dependence and personality disorder: Attention-deficit/hyperactivity disorder and conduct disorder. *European Archives of Psychiatry and Clinical Neuroscience, 251,* 42–47.

Moeller, F. G., Dougherty, D. M., Barratt, E. S., Oderinde, V., Mathias, C. W., Harper, R. A., et al. (2002). Increased impulsivity in cocaine dependent subjects independent of antisocial personality disorder and aggression. *Drug and Alcohol Dependence, 68,* 105–111.

Moran, P., & Hodgins, S. (2004). The correlates of comorbid antisocial personality disorder in schizophrenia. *Schizophrenia Bulletin, 30,* 791–802.

Neufeld, K. J, Kidorf, M. S., Kolodner, K., King, V. L., Clark, M., & Brooner, R. K. (2008). A behavioral treatment for opioid-dependent patients with antisocial personality. *Journal of Substance Abuse Treatment, 34,* 101–111.

Nigg, J. T., Lohr, N. E., Westen, D., Gold, L. J., & Silk, K. R. (1992). Malevolent object representations in borderline personality disorder and major depression. *Journal of Abnormal Psychology, 10,* 61–67.

Paim Kessler, F. H., Barbosa Terra, M., Faller, S., Ravy Stolf, A., Carolina Peuker, A., Benzano, D., & Pechansky, F. (2012). Crack users show high rates of antisocial personality disorder, engagement in illegal activities and other psychosocial problems. *American Journal on Addictions, 21*(4), 370–380.

Palmer, N. B., Salcedo, J., Miller, A. L., Winiarski, M., & Arno, P. (2003). Psychiatric and social barriers to HIV medication adherence in a triply diagnosed methadone population. *AIDS Patient Care and STDs, 17,* 635–644.

Preuss, U. W., Koller, G., Bondy, B., Bahlmann, M., & Soyka, M. (2001). Impulsive traits and 5-HT2A receptor promoter polymorphism in alcohol dependents: Possible association but no influence of personality disorders. *Neuropsychobiology, 43,* 186–191.

Putkonen, A., Kotilainen, I., Joyal, C. C., & Tiihonen, J. (2004). Comorbid personality disorders and substance use disorders of mentally ill homicide offenders: A structured clinical study on dual and triple diagnoses. *Schizophrenia Bulletin, 30,* 59–72.

Ralevski, E., Ball, S., Nich, C., Limoncelli, D., & Petrakis, I. (2007). The impact of personality disorders on alcohol-use outcomes in a pharmacotherapy trial for alcohol dependence and comorbid Axis I disorders. *American Journal on Addictions, 16,* 443–449.

Reback, C. J., Kamien, J. B., & Amass, L. (2007). Characteristics and HIV risk behaviors of homeless, substance-using men who have sex with men. *Addictive Behaviors, 32,* 647–654.

Regier, D. A., Narrow, W. E., & Rae, D. S. (1990). The epidemiology of anxiety disorders: The Epidemiologic Catchment Area (ECA) experience. *Journal of Psychiatric Research, 24,* 3–14.

Riihimäki, K., Vuorilehto, M., & Isometsä, E. (2013). Borderline personality disorder among primary care depressive patients: A five-year study. *Journal of Affective Disorders, 155,* 303–306.

Ross, J., Teesson, M., Darke, S., Lynskey, M., Ali, R., Ritter, A., et al. (2005). The characteristics of heroin users entering treatment: Findings from the Australian Treatment Outcome Study (ATOS). *Drug and Alcohol Review, 24,* 411–418.

Ross, S., Dermatis, H., Levounis, P., & Galanter, M. (2003). A comparison between dually diagnosed inpatients with and without Axis II comorbidity and the relationship to treatment outcome. *American Journal of Drug and Alcohol Abuse, 29,* 263–279.

Rubio, G., Jimenez, M., Rodriguez-Jimenez, R., Martinez, I., Iribarren, M. M., Jimenez-Arriero, M. A., et al. (2007). Varieties of impulsivity in males with alcohol dependence: The role of cluster-B personality disorder. *Alcoholism: Clinical and Experimental Research, 31,* 1826–1832.

Schiffman, J., Nakamura, B., Earleywine, M., & LaBrie, J. (2005). Symptoms of schizotypy precede cannabis use. *Psychiatry Research, 134,* 37–42.

Schmitz, J. M., Stotts, A. L., Averill, P. M., Rothfleisch, J. M., Bailley, S. E., Sayre, S. L., et al. (2000). Cocaine dependence with and without comorbid depression: A comparison of patient characteristics. *Drug and Alcohol Dependence, 60,* 189–198.

Schuckit, M. A., & Smith, T. L. (1996). An 8-year followup of 450 sons of alcoholic and control subjects. *Archives of General Psychiatry, 53,* 202–210.

Sher, K. J. (1991). *Children of alcoholics: A critical appraisal of theory and research.* Chicago: University of Chicago Press.

Sher, K. J., & Levenson, R. W. (1982). Risk for alcoholism and individual differences in the stress-response-dampening effect of alcohol. *Journal of Abnormal Psychology, 91,* 350–367.

Sher, K. J., & Trull, T. J. (1994). Personality and disinhibitory psychopathology: Alcoholism and antisocial personality disorder. *Journal of Abnormal Psychology, 103,* 92–102.

Sher, K. J., Trull, T. J., Bartholow, B. D., & Vieth, A. (1999). Personality and alcoholism: Issues, methods, and etiological processes. In K. E. Leonard & H. T. Blane (Eds.), *Psychological theories of drinking and alcoholism* (pp. 54–105). New York: Guilford.

Slutske, W. S., Heath, A. C., Dinwiddie, S. H., Madden, P. A., Bucholz, K. K., Dunne, M. P., Statham, D. J., & Martin, N. G. (1998). Common genetic risk factors for conduct disorder and alcohol dependence. *Journal of Abnormal Psychology, 107*, 363–374.

Slutske, W. S., Heath, A. C., Madden, P. A., Bucholz, K. K., Statham, D. J., & Martin, N. G. (2002). Personality and genetic risk for alcohol dependence. *Journal of Abnormal Psychology, 111*, 124–133.

Stinson, F. S., Dawson, D. A., Goldstein, R. B., Chou, S. P., Huang, B., Smith, S. M., et al. (2008). Prevalence, correlates, disability, and comorbidity of DSM-IV narcissistic personality disorder: Results from the wave 2 National Epidemiologic Study on Alcohol and Related Conditions. *Journal of Clinical Psychiatry, 69*, 1033–1045.

Tadić, A., Wagner, S., Hoch, J., Başkaya, Ö., von Cube, R., Skaletz, C., ... Dahmen, N. (2009). Gender differences in axis I and axis II comorbidity in patients with borderline personality disorder. *Psychopathology, 42*(4), 257–263.

Tang, Y., Kranzler, H. R., Gelernter, J., Farrer, L. A., & Cubells, J. F. (2007). Comorbid psychiatric diagnoses and their association with cocaine-induced psychosis in cocaine-dependent subjects. *American Journal on Addictions, 16*, 343–351.

Tomko, R. L., Trull, T. J., Wood, P. K., & Sher, K. J. (2014). Characteristics of borderline personality disorder in a community sample: Comorbidity, treatment utilization, and general functioning. *Journal of Personality Disorders, 28*, 734–750.

Torrens, M., Serrano, D., Astals, M., Perez-Dominguez, G., & Martin-Santos, R. (2004). Diagnosing comorbid psychiatric disorders in substance abusers: Validity of the Spanish versions of the Psychiatric Research Interview for Substance and Mental Disorders and the Structured Clinical Interview for DSM-IV. *American Journal of Psychiatry, 161*, 1231–1237.

Tragesser, S. L., Sher, K. J., Trull, T. J., & Park, A. (2007). Personality disorder symptoms, drinking motives, and alcohol use and consequences: Cross-sectional and prospective mediation. *Experimental and Clinical Psychopharmacology, 15*(3), 282–292.

Trathen, B., O'Gara, C., Sarkhel, A., Sessay, M., Rao, H., & Luty, J. (2007). Co-morbidity and cannabis use in a mental health trust in South East England. *Addictive Behaviors, 32*, 2164–2177.

Trull, T. J., Jahng, S., Tomko, R. L., Wood, P. K., & Sher, K. J. (2010). Revised NESARC personality disorder diagnoses: Gender, prevalence, and comorbidity with substance dependence disorders. *Journal of Personality Disorders, 24*(4), 412–426.

Trull, T. J., Sher, K. J., Minks-Brown, C., Durbin, J., & Burr, R. (2000). Borderline personality disorder and substance use disorders: A review and integration. *Clinical Psychology Review, 20*, 235–253.

Trull, T. J., Solhan, M. B., Tragesser, S. L., Jahng, S., Wood, P. K., Piasecki, T. M., & Watson, D. (2008). Affective instability: Measuring a core feature of borderline personality disorder with ecological momentary assessment. *Journal of Abnormal Psychology, 117*, 647–661.

Tull, M. T., Gratz, K. L., & Weiss, N. H. (2011). Exploring associations between borderline personality disorder, crack/cocaine dependence, gender, and risky sexual behavior among substance-dependent inpatients. *Personality Disorders: Theory, Research, and Treatment, 2*(3), 209.

Van Emmerik-van Oortmerssen, K., Glind, G., Koeter, M. W., Allsop, S., Auriacombe, M., Barta, C., ... Schoevers, R. A. (2014). Psychiatric comorbidity in treatment-seeking substance use disorder patients with and without attention deficit hyperactivity disorder: Results of the IASP study. *Addiction, 109*(2), 262–272.

Vergara-Moragues, E., González-Saiz, F., Lozano, O. M., & García, A. V. (2013). Psychiatric profile of three-month retention in cocaine-dependent patients treated in a therapeutic community. *Journal of Studies on Alcohol and Drugs, 74*(3), 452.

Verheul, R. (2001). Co-morbidity of personality disorders in individuals with substance use disorders. *European Psychiatry, 16*, 274–282.

Verheul, R., van den Bosch, L. M. C., & Ball, S. A. (2005). Substance abuse. In J. M. Oldham, A. E. Skodol, & D. S. Bender (Eds.), *Textbook of personality disorders* (pp. 463–476). Washington, DC: American Psychiatric Publishing.

Volavka, J., Czobor, P., Goodwin, D. W., Gabrielli, W. F., Penick, F. C., Mednick, S. A., et al. (1996). The electroencephalogram after alcohol administration in high-risk men and the development of alcohol use disorders 10 years later: Preliminary findings. *Archives of General Psychiatry, 53*, 258–263.

Walter, M., Gunderson, J. G., Zanarini, M. C., Sanislow, C. A., Grilo, C. M., McGlashan, T. H., ... Skodol, A. E. (2009). New onsets of substance use disorders in borderline personality disorder over 7 years of follow-ups: Findings from the Collaborative Longitudinal Personality Disorders Study. *Addiction, 104*(1), 97–103.

Weaver, T., Madden, P., Charles, V., Stimson, G., Renton, A., Tyrer, P., ... , Ford, C. (2003). Comorbidity of substance misuse and mental illness in community mental health and substance misuse services. *British Journal of Psychiatry, 183*, 304–313.

Wedig, M. M., Silverman, M. H., Frankenburg, F. R., Reich, D. B., Fitzmaurice, G., & Zanarini, M. C. (2012). Predictors of suicide attempts in patients with borderline personality disorder over 16 years of prospective follow-up. *Psychological Medicine, 42*(11), 2395–2404.

Weizman, T., Gelkopf, M., Melamed, Y., Adelson, M., & Bleich, A. (2003). Treatment of benzodiazepine dependence in methadone maintenance treatment patients: A comparison of two therapeutic modalities and the role of psychiatric comorbidity. *Australian and New Zealand Journal of Psychiatry, 37*, 458–463.

Welch, S. S., & Linehan, M. M. (2002). High-risk situations associated with parasuicide and drug use in borderline personality disorder. *Journal of Personality Disorders, 16*, 561–569.

Widiger, T. A., & Trull, T. J. (1993). Borderline and narcissistic personality disorders. In H. Adams & P. Sutker (Eds.), *Comprehensive handbook of psychopathology* (2nd ed., pp. 371–394). New York: Plenum.

Widom, C. S., Czaja, S. J., & Paris, J. (2009). A prospective investigation of borderline personality disorder in abused and neglected children followed up into adulthood. *Journal of Personality Disorders, 23*(5), 433–446.

Wilens, T. E., Kwon, A., Tanguay, S., Chase, R., Moore, H., Faraone, S. V., et al. (2005). Characteristics of adults with attention deficit hyperactivity disorder plus substance use disorder: The role of psychiatric comorbidity. *American Journal on Addiction, 14*, 319–327.

Wu, L., & Howard, M. O. (2007). Psychiatric disorders in inhalant users: Results from The National Epidemiologic Survey on Alcohol and Related Conditions. *Drug and Alcohol Dependence, 88*, 146–155.

Zanarini, M. C., Barison, L. K., Frankenburg, F. R., Reich, D. B., & Hudson, J. I. (2009). Family history study of the familial coaggregation of borderline personality disorder with Axis I and non-borderline dramatic cluster Axis II disorders. *Journal of Personality Disorders, 23*(4), 357.

Zanarini, M. C., & Frankenburg, F. R. (1997). Pathways to the development of borderline personality disorder. *Journal of Personality Disorders, 11*, 93–104.

Zikos, E., Gill, K. J., & Charney, D. A. (2010). Personality disorders among alcoholic outpatients: Prevalence and course in treatment. *Canadian Journal of Psychiatry, 55*(2), 65–73.

Zimmerman, M., Rothschild, L., & Chelminski, I. (2005). The prevalence of DSM-IV personality disorders in psychiatric outpatients. *American Journal of Psychiatry, 162*, 1911–1918.

Comorbidity of Anxiety and Depression with Substance Use Disorders

Sherry H. Stewart, Valerie V. Grant, Clare J. Mackie, *and* Patricia J. Conrod

Abstract

The comorbidity of substance use disorders (SUDs) with anxiety and depression is the focus of substantial research attention and approached from myriad perspectives. This chapter focuses on the resultant complex research literature, first providing an overview of epidemiologic studies that have examined the prevalence of co-occurrence of SUDs (including alcohol and other drug use disorders) with anxiety and depressive disorders, as well as clinical correlates of these forms of comorbidity. Next, theoretical models of the onset and maintenance of emotional disorder–SUD comorbidity are considered, followed by a review of various types of studies evaluating these theoretical models (studies focusing on order-of-onset, the independent versus substance-induced disorder distinction, self-reported motives for use, genetic epidemiology, and experimental studies). Distinctions and commonalities between anxiety–SUD associations and depression–SUD associations are examined throughout. The chapter concludes by examining treatment implications of this comorbidity and suggests future directions for this burgeoning field.

Key Words: Anxiety disorder, depressive disorder, comorbidity, self-medication, mutual maintenance, alcohol use disorder, drug use disorder

The comorbidity of substance use disorders (SUDs) with anxiety disorders and depressive disorders has been the focus of a great deal of research attention for many years. Researchers have approached the study of comorbidity from myriad perspectives, resulting in a very complex research literature. The focus of this chapter is to provide an overview of the prevalence of the co-occurrence of SUDs (including alcohol use disorders [AUDs] and other drug use disorders [DUDs]) with anxiety disorders and depressive disorders, theoretical models of the onset and maintenance of comorbidity, clinical correlates of comorbidity, and treatment implications of comorbidity. Distinctions and commonalities between anxiety–SUD associations and depression–SUD associations are examined. The majority of anxiety/depression–SUD comorbidity research has focused on AUDs, so our review focuses primarily on AUDs. However, literature on

comorbidity with other SUDs is discussed whenever possible. We exclude bipolar disorders in our review given their unique relationships with SUDs (e.g., see Merikangas et al., 2008; Preisig, Fenton, Stevens, & Merikangas, 2001) and the fact that they are now considered in a separate category from depressive disorders in the *Diagnostic and Statistical Manual of Mental Disorders, Fifth Edition* (DSM-5; American Psychiatric Association [APA], 2013).

Prevalence

A variety of methodologies have been used to measure the prevalence of comorbidity of anxiety disorders and depressive disorders with SUDs. Rates of anxiety disorders and depressive disorders (primarily major depressive disorder and persistent depressive disorder or "dysthymia") have been examined in clinical samples of individuals with AUDs and SUDs and vice versa (i.e., rates of AUDs and

SUDs in clinical samples of individuals with anxiety disorders and/or depressive disorders). However, because individuals with multiple disorders are more likely to present for treatment than those with a single disorder—a phenomenon known as "Berkson's bias" (Berkson, 1946)—comorbidity prevalence estimates derived in this fashion are likely to be exaggerated. Epidemiological studies in the general population are especially helpful in determining prevalence estimates of co-occurrence; thus, we focus our review on these studies. Typically, the co-occurrence of disorders is quantified in odds ratios (ORs), which reflect the relative odds that individuals with a certain first disorder will meet criteria for a second disorder relative to individuals without the first disorder. An OR of 1.0 indicates that the presence of the first disorder does not bear upon the likelihood of having the second disorder. Higher (>1.0) ORs suggest that the presence of the first disorder increases the odds of the second disorder, whereas lower ORs (<1.0) reflect a decreased odds of the second disorder if the first disorder is present (Zahradnik & Stewart, 2008). Comorbidity is typically measured either across the lifespan (i.e., both disorders occur within an individual's lifetime but not necessarily at the same time) or across a 12-month period (i.e., both disorders occur in the same person within the same 12-month period). Most of the literature reviewed presents information either about the change in likelihood of an SUD due to the presence of an anxiety disorder or depressive disorder, or vice versa, but not both.

Substance Use Disorder–Anxiety Comorbidity

Several large-scale community surveys have provided estimates of SUD–anxiety disorder comorbidity in adults, including the Epidemiologic Catchment Area (ECA) study (Regier et al., 1990), the National Comorbidity Survey (NCS; Kessler et al., 1996), the International Consortium in Psychiatric Epidemiology study (ICPE; Merikangas et al., 1998), the National Comorbidity Survey Replication (NSC-R; Kessler, Chiu, Demler, & Walters, 2005), the National Epidemiologic Survey on Alcohol and Related Conditions (NESARC; Grant et al., 2004), the National Survey of Mental Health and Well-Being (NSMHWB; Degenhardt, Hall, & Lynskey, 2001), and the Canadian Community Health Survey: Mental Health and Well-Being (CCHS 1.2; Rush et al., 2008). Studies in this area have often used aggregated anxiety disorders in their analyses, obscuring potential

differential relationships among distinct anxiety disorders and SUDs. Nonetheless, there are theoretical and empirical reasons to suggest that different anxiety disorders might have distinct relationships with SUDs (e.g., Kushner, Sher, & Beitman, 1990). In the same way, different SUDs might be expected to demonstrate different patterns of association with anxiety and depression (e.g., Stewart & Conrod, 2008). Thus, ORs are presented for individual disorders whenever possible.

It is important to note that the epidemiological studies reviewed herein have been conducted with previous versions of the DSM (i.e., the DSM-III [APA, 1980], DSM-III-R [APA, 1987], and DSM-IV [APA, 1994]) which made a distinction between substance abuse and substance dependence. These categories corresponded to the less and more severe forms of the disorder, respectively. However, in the current version of the DSM (i.e., the DSM-5 [APA, 2013]), no such distinction is made, and all symptoms are listed under a single diagnostic label of SUD (Straussner, 2013). Another change in the most recent version of the DSM (i.e., the DSM-5) is that the diagnoses of post-traumatic stress disorder (PTSD) and obsessive-compulsive disorder (OCD) are no longer considered part of the anxiety disorders category because they have been deemed sufficiently distinct to warrant placement in their own categories of "trauma- and stressor-related disorders" and "obsessive-compulsive and related disorders," respectively (APA, 2013). However, in much of the extant comorbidity literature, they have been grouped with the anxiety disorders due to the strong involvement of anxiety-related processes in their symptomatology and their placement in the anxiety disorders diagnostic category in previous versions of the DSM. For these reasons, these two anxiety disorders are included in our review in spite of their recent change in categorization in the DSM-5.

EPIDEMIOLOGIC CATCHMENT AREA

The results of the ECA (Regier et al., 1990), relying on DSM-III (APA, 1980) criteria, showed that the lifetime OR of any SUD for individuals with any anxiety disorder (vs. those without any anxiety disorder) was 1.7. A diagnosis of any anxiety disorder was associated with a significantly increased likelihood of alcohol dependence (OR = 1.8) but not alcohol abuse (OR = 1.0). A diagnosis of any anxiety disorder was related to an increased probability of experiencing both drug dependence (OR = 2.4) and drug abuse (OR = 2.3). Likewise, the diagnosis of any AUD was associated with a significantly increased chance of experiencing any anxiety disorder (OR = 1.5), as was the diagnosis of any drug use disorder (DUD; OR = 2.5).

The presence of each individual anxiety disorder studied conferred a significantly increased likelihood of alcohol dependence (phobia OR = 1.6, OCD OR = 2.5, and panic disorder OR = 3.3) and drug dependence (phobia OR = 1.6, OCD OR = 2.5, and panic disorder OR = 3.3) but not alcohol abuse or other drug abuse (Regier et al., 1990). An examination of specific DUDs indicated that the odds of having any anxiety disorder were significantly higher for individuals with a marijuana use disorder (OR = 2.3), an opiate use disorder (OR = 2.8), an amphetamine use disorder (OR = 2.9), a barbiturate use disorder (OR = 4.5), or a hallucinogen use disorder (OR = 5.0). The odds of having any anxiety disorder among individuals with a cocaine use disorder was higher than 1.0 (OR = 2.9) but nonsignificant, likely due to the low overall prevalence of cocaine use disorders. As noted by Kushner, Krueger, Frye, and Peterson (2008), this pattern defies a simple self-medication explanation since anxiety disorders are associated not only with abuse/dependence on depressant-type drugs that might be expected to reduce anxiety symptoms. In fact, the highest degree of association was between anxiety disorders and hallucinogens—drugs that do not have a calming effect on anxiety symptoms. There are at least two possible explanations for this pattern (Kushner et al., 2008). First, different mechanisms could explain the patterns of comorbidity for depressant/tranquilizing drugs (in this case, self-medication) versus stimulant drugs (in this case, substance-induced anxiety). Alternatively, consistent with the self-medication model, even the stimulant drugs such as cocaine or nicotine could have effects such as enhancing a sense of well-being that could be reinforcing to an anxious individual.

NATIONAL COMORBIDITY SURVEY

Using criteria from the revised DSM-III (DSM-III-R; APA, 1987), the NCS provided lifetime and 12-month ORs related to comorbidity of SUDs with other psychiatric disorders (Kessler et al., 1996). The presence of any lifetime anxiety disorder was associated with a significantly increased probability of having any lifetime SUD (OR = 2.1). Similarly, having any 12-month anxiety disorder was associated with more than twice the chance of experiencing any 12-month SUD (OR = 2.5). Examining SUD diagnoses separately showed that experiencing any lifetime anxiety

disorder significantly increased the likelihood of experiencing a lifetime diagnosis of alcohol dependence (OR = 2.1), drug dependence (OR = 3.3), and drug abuse (OR = 1.4) but not alcohol abuse (OR = 1.2). Having any 12-month anxiety disorder was significantly associated with alcohol abuse (OR = 1.7), alcohol dependence (OR = 2.6), and drug dependence (OR = 3.6) but not drug abuse (OR = 1.3).

All of the individual lifetime anxiety disorder diagnoses studied were associated with a significantly increased likelihood of having a lifetime diagnosis of alcohol dependence (generalized anxiety disorder [GAD], OR = 2.8; PTSD, OR = 2.6; social phobia, OR = 2.2; simple phobia, OR = 2.1; panic disorder, OR = 2.0; and agoraphobia with or without panic OR = 1.7; Kessler et al., 1996). None of the individual lifetime anxiety disorders was associated with significantly increased odds of lifetime alcohol abuse, however. Generally, individual lifetime anxiety disorders did not significantly increase the odds of experiencing lifetime drug abuse, with the exception of lifetime PTSD, which was associated with a significantly increased likelihood of experiencing lifetime drug abuse (OR = 1.6). However, specific lifetime anxiety disorders were each associated with significantly elevated rates of drug dependence (GAD, OR = 3.8; PTSD, OR = 4.0; social phobia, OR = 2.6; simple phobia, OR = 2.5; panic disorder, OR = 3.8; agoraphobia with or without panic OR = 2.8).

Results were generally similar for 12-month disorders. However, panic disorder was not significantly associated with an increased risk of alcohol dependence, despite an OR of 1.7. There was no evidence that individual anxiety disorders conferred additional risk for alcohol abuse, with the exception of 12-month social phobia (OR = 2.3). Although lifetime PTSD was associated with significantly increased odds of lifetime drug abuse (as mentioned), 12-month PTSD was not. The only other difference between the lifetime and 12-month ORs was that GAD was not associated with significantly elevated odds of experiencing drug dependence in the 12-month analyses.

Agosti, Nunes, and Levin (2002) used NCS data to specifically examine psychiatric comorbidity among individuals with a lifetime diagnosis of cannabis dependence. Individuals with lifetime cannabis dependence who had used cannabis during the month prior to the interview were more likely to have a current anxiety disorder compared to those without a history of cannabis dependence

(OR = 2.6). Lifetime cannabis dependence also increased the likelihood of experiencing lifetime agoraphobia (OR = 1.8), GAD (OR = 2.7), panic disorder (OR = 2.3), social phobia (OR = 3.3), PTSD (OR = 2.98), and simple phobia (OR = 1.8).

INTERNATIONAL CONSORTIUM IN PSYCHIATRIC EPIDEMIOLOGY STUDY

The ICPE study combined epidemiologic data sets from Canada, Germany, Mexico, the Netherlands, and the United States (including the NCS) to investigate lifetime comorbidity of substance dependence with depressive and anxiety disorders using DSM-III-R criteria (Merikangas et al., 1998). The presence of any anxiety disorder was associated with a significantly increased chance of experiencing alcohol dependence (ORs ranged from 1.8 to 3.2) at each site except Mexico, which had a large and positive yet nonsignificant OR of 2.7. Similarly, the presence of any anxiety disorder was associated with significantly increased odds of having drug dependence (ORs ranged from 3.3 to 5.2). The ICPE did not present data on alcohol abuse per se, just on alcohol-related problems. These latter results are not presented here because they may not be comparable to previous studies that have used alcohol abuse diagnoses as the criterion variable.

NATIONAL COMORBIDITY SURVEY REPLICATION

Kessler and colleagues (2005) reported on comorbidity among 12-month DSM-IV (APA, 1994) diagnoses captured by the NCS-R. ORs were not presented, but tetrachoric correlations between individual anxiety disorders and SUDs including alcohol abuse, alcohol dependence, drug abuse, and drug dependence were provided. Panic disorder, social phobia, GAD, PTSD, and OCD (but not agoraphobia, specific phobia, or separation anxiety disorder) were each significantly positively associated with alcohol abuse. Only specific phobia, social phobia, GAD, and PTSD were significantly positively associated with alcohol dependence. It should be noted that the method used to assess substance dependence in the NCS-R has been criticized because it deviated from DSM-IV criteria by essentially using abuse as a prerequisite for dependence, leading to underestimation of dependence prevalence (Grant, Compton et al., 2007). Social phobia and GAD were each significantly positively associated with drug abuse and dependence, but the other anxiety disorders were not. Separation anxiety

disorder was significantly negatively associated with drug dependence.

In a subsequent analysis of NCS-R data, Kessler et al. (2006) reported on the epidemiology of DSM-IV diagnoses of lifetime panic disorder and agoraphobia, including ORs quantifying comorbidity. Individuals with panic disorder without agoraphobia had significantly increased odds of experiencing any SUD (OR = 3.3). Respondents with panic disorder with agoraphobia had even greater odds of experiencing any SUD (OR = 4.8). Ruscio, Stein, Chiu, and Kessler (2010) later reported that individuals with lifetime OCD also had significantly increased odds of experiencing any lifetime SUD (OR = 4.1), including both AUDs (OR = 4.9) and DUDs (OR = 3.2), even while controlling for basic demographics (i.e., age, sex, and race/ethnicity).

NATIONAL EPIDEMIOLOGIC SURVEY ON ALCOHOL AND RELATED CONDITIONS

Like the NCS-R, the NESARC (Grant et al., 2004) used DSM-IV criteria but without using substance abuse as a precondition for substance dependence. Overall, the presence of any 12-month SUD increased the odds of having any 12-month anxiety disorder almost twofold (OR = 1.9). This pattern was present for substance dependence (OR = 2.8) but not for substance abuse (OR = 1.1). The presence of 12-month alcohol abuse did not significantly increase the odds of any of the specific 12-month anxiety disorder diagnoses (including panic disorder with agoraphobia, panic disorder without agoraphobia, social phobia, specific phobia, and GAD). Conversely, 12-month alcohol dependence significantly increased the chances of experiencing each of the 12-month anxiety disorders (panic disorder with agoraphobia, OR = 3.6; panic disorder without agoraphobia, OR = 3.4; GAD, OR = 3.1; social phobia, OR = 2.5; and specific phobia, OR = 2.2).

A subsequent analysis of NESARC data (Hasin, Stinson, Ogburn, & Grant, 2007) indicated that the presence of lifetime alcohol dependence was associated with significantly increased chances of having each of the lifetime anxiety disorders assessed, even controlling for sociodemographic characteristics (panic disorder with agoraphobia, OR = 3.5; panic disorder without agoraphobia, OR = 2.9; GAD, OR = 2.8; social phobia, OR = 2.7; and specific phobia, OR = 2.7). After adjustment for other psychiatric disorders (including other anxiety disorders, mood disorders, and personality disorders) in addition to sociodemographic characteristics, the presence of lifetime alcohol dependence signaled significantly increased risk for only panic disorder without agoraphobia (OR = 1.3) and specific phobia (OR = 1.4).

Similarly, Hasin and colleagues' (2007) examination of 12-month disorders revealed that the presence of 12-month alcohol dependence was associated with significantly higher odds of each of the 12-month anxiety disorders, even after adjusting for sociodemographic variables (panic disorder with agoraphobia, OR = 3.6; panic disorder without agoraphobia, OR = 3.4; GAD, OR = 3.0; social phobia, OR = 2.3; and specific phobia, OR = 2.3). After adjustment for other psychiatric disorders in addition to sociodemographic conditions, 12-month alcohol dependence still increased the odds of experiencing any anxiety disorder (OR = 1.5), but the ORs for the individual 12-month anxiety disorders were not significantly different from 1.0. The finding that unique disorder-specific associations tended to evaporate when analyses controlled for comorbidity suggests the possibility that much of the association of alcohol dependence with anxiety disorders may be due to factors common to the anxiety, mood, and personality disorders. Additional research is needed to identify what these common factors might be (e.g., common genetic factors and/ or common personality vulnerabilities such as neuroticism/negative affectivity or anxiety sensitivity).

In the NESARC, the differences between drug abuse and drug dependence ORs were not as pronounced as those between alcohol abuse and alcohol dependence ORs (Grant et al., 2004). Twelve-month drug abuse significantly increased the odds of having each of the individual anxiety disorders (panic disorder with agoraphobia OR, = 3.5; GAD, OR = 2.1; social phobia, OR = 2.0; and specific phobia, OR = 1.6), except panic disorder without agoraphobia (OR = 1.6, *ns*). Risk of 12-month anxiety disorders was even stronger for individuals with 12-month drug dependence (panic disorder with agoraphobia, OR = 10.5; panic disorder without agoraphobia, OR = 7.6; GAD, OR = 10.4; social phobia, OR = 5.4; and specific phobia, OR = 3.8). In another study of NESARC data, Huang et al. (2006) determined that lifetime nonmedical prescription drug use disorders significantly increased the odds of any lifetime anxiety disorder (sedative use disorder, OR = 3.7; tranquilizer use disorder, OR = 4.2; opioid use disorder, OR = 3.0; and amphetamine use disorder, OR = 3.3). Panic disorder with agoraphobia was the anxiety disorder with the strongest relationship to each nonmedical prescription drug use disorder (ORs ranged from 4.3 to 7.9).

NATIONAL SURVEY OF MENTAL HEALTH AND WELL-BEING

The NSMHWB examined comorbidity of DSM-IV anxiety disorders and cannabis use disorders in a representative sample of Australians (Degenhardt et al., 2001). Respondents with 12-month cannabis dependence were at significantly increased odds of having a 12-month anxiety disorder as compared to those without cannabis dependence (OR = 4.3). This relationship held even when adjustments were made for demographic variables (OR = 3.49) but not when other drug use and neuroticism were also controlled, suggesting these may be common third variables that could explain the association between anxiety and cannabis use disorders. Individuals with cannabis abuse were not at increased risk of anxiety disorders.

CANADIAN COMMUNITY HEALTH SURVEY

In a representative sample of Canadians, Rush and colleagues (2008) found that 12-month DSM-IV substance dependence significantly increased the likelihood of having a 12-month anxiety disorder (including panic disorder, agoraphobia, and social phobia; OR = 4.76).

SUMMARY OF EPIDEMIOLOGICAL STUDIES OF SUD–ANXIETY COMORBIDITY

The epidemiological data show that anxiety disorders increase the odds of SUDs and vice versa. In general, the comorbidity of anxiety disorders and SUDs is stronger for dependence than for abuse and stronger for (nonalcohol) DUDs than AUDs. We examine possible reasons for this pattern later in this chapter. Additionally, each of the individual anxiety disorders has been shown to co-occur with SUDs at a rate greater than chance, with the exception of separation anxiety disorder. In the one survey that examined this issue, only panic disorder without agoraphobia and specific phobia were found to have unique co-occurrence with alcohol dependence that remained after adjustment for sociodemographic variables and the presence of mood and personality disorders. Finally, although few studies have examined comorbidity of anxiety disorders with SUDs involving specific drugs of abuse, it appears from the ECA (Regier et al., 1990) that anxiety disorders are associated not only with abuse/dependence on drugs with tranquilizing or sedative effects, but also with abuse/dependence on stimulant and hallucinogenic drugs that would theoretically increase anxiety symptoms.

SUD–Depression Comorbidity

The ECA, the NCS, the National Longitudinal Alcohol Epidemiologic Survey (NLAES; Grant & Harford, 1995), the NCS-R, the NESARC, and the CCHS 1.2 (Currie et al., 2005) studied the comorbidity of SUDs with depressive disorders, including major depressive disorder (MDD) and dysthymic disorder. In the ICPE and NSMHWB analyses, all mood disorders, including bipolar disorders, were aggregated, so their results will not be presented here because our focus in this chapter is on SUD comorbidity with MDD and dysthymia (i.e., diagnoses in the depressive disorders category in the DSM-5 [APA], 2013).

EPIDEMIOLOGIC CATCHMENT AREA

The ECA study (Regier et al., 1990) revealed that the odds of any lifetime SUD were significantly increased for individuals with lifetime MDD and lifetime dysthymic disorder (respective ORs = 1.9 and 2.4). More specifically, dysthymia, but not MDD, significantly increased the odds of alcohol dependence (ORs = 2.3 and 1.6, respectively). Neither MDD nor dysthymia increased the odds of alcohol abuse. Nonetheless, both MDD and dysthymia were associated with significantly increased odds of drug dependence and drug abuse (for MDD, ORs = 3.7 and 3.3, respectively; for dysthymia, ORs = 3.6 and 3.6, respectively). Analyses of individual DUDs used "any affective disorder," including bipolar disorders, and thus are not presented here.

NATIONAL COMORBIDITY SURVEY

Kessler and colleagues (1996) reported that the presence of a lifetime major depressive episode (MDE) was associated with a significantly increased probability of having any lifetime SUD (OR = 2.3), as was the presence of lifetime dysthymia (OR = 1.9). Likewise, having 12-month MDE significantly increased the odds of having any 12-month SUD (OR = 3.0), as did having 12-month dysthymia (OR = 2.6). An examination of separate SUD diagnoses revealed that experiencing a lifetime MDE significantly increased the likelihood of experiencing a lifetime diagnosis of alcohol dependence (OR = 2.7), drug dependence (OR = 2.8), and drug abuse (OR = 1.7) but not alcohol abuse (OR = 1.0). It should be noted that the NCS examined MDEs, not MDD. Consequently,

individuals with bipolar disorder are included in the group of individuals who have experienced a MDE. Lifetime MDE and dysthymia each significantly increased the likelihood of experiencing lifetime drug dependence (ORs = 2.8 and 2.5, respectively), but only MDE significantly increased the likelihood of alcohol dependence (OR = 2.7) and drug abuse (OR = 1.7). The 12-month results were slightly different, with both MDE and dysthymia each significantly increasing the odds of having alcohol dependence (ORs = 3.7 and 3.9, respectively), only MDE significantly increasing the likelihood of drug dependence (OR = 3.6), and neither MDE nor dysthymia significantly raising the odds of alcohol or drug abuse. Using the same dataset, Agosti et al. (2002) found that lifetime cannabis dependence significantly increased the odds of experiencing lifetime MDE (OR = 2.42) and lifetime dysthymic disorder (OR = 2.3).

NATIONAL LONGITUDINAL ALCOHOL EPIDEMIOLOGIC SURVEY

The NLAES provided comorbidity estimates of DSM-IV AUDs and MDD (Grant & Harford, 1995). The presence of lifetime MDD significantly increased the odds of experiencing both alcohol dependence (OR = 3.8) and alcohol abuse (OR = 1.7). Similarly, the presence of past-year MDD significantly increased the chances of having past-year alcohol dependence (OR = 4.2) and alcohol abuse (OR = 2.2). An examination of DUD-MDD comorbidity in the NLAES showed that lifetime MDD significantly increased the odds of lifetime DUDs (OR = 5.24), including drug abuse (OR = 3.26) and drug dependence (OR = 6.87; Grant, 1995). The presence of lifetime MDD was associated with increased odds of lifetime prevalence of DUDs for each drug class studied, including cannabis use disorders (OR = 4.70), cocaine use disorders (OR = 4.96), sedative use disorders (OR = 6.06), amphetamine use disorders (OR = 6.19), hallucinogen use disorders (OR = 6.26), prescription drug use disorders (OR = 6.32), and tranquilizer use disorders (OR = 6.46). All ORs (for abuse and dependence in each drug class) were significant, but ORs were higher for dependence than abuse in each drug class. Because of low prevalences for many DUD classes, only cannabis and cocaine use disorders were subjected to past-year comorbidity analyses. MDD increased the odds of cannabis abuse (OR = 4.95), cannabis dependence (OR = 12. 15), cocaine abuse (OR = 4.38), and cocaine dependence (OR = 5.25).

NATIONAL COMORBIDITY SURVEY REPLICATION

Twelve-month MDE and dysthymia each had significantly positive tetrachoric correlations with each SUD (including alcohol abuse, alcohol dependence, drug abuse, and drug dependence; Kessler et al., 2005). Approximately 24% of respondents with lifetime MDD also met criteria for a lifetime SUD, whereas 27% of individuals with 12-month MDD also had 12-month SUD (Kessler et al., 2003).

NATIONAL EPIDEMIOLOGIC SURVEY ON ALCOHOL AND RELATED CONDITIONS

The presence of any 12-month SUD significantly increased the odds of having 12-month MDD (OR = 2.5) and 12-month dysthymia (OR = 2.2; Grant et al., 2004). For MDD, this pattern was present for alcohol dependence (OR = 3.7), drug dependence (OR = 9.0), and drug abuse (OR = 2.5) but not alcohol abuse (OR = 1.2). A similar pattern was seen for dysthymia, with alcohol dependence (OR = 2.8), drug dependence (OR = 11.3), and drug abuse (OR = 2.6) but not alcohol abuse (OR = 0.8) increasing the odds of experiencing dysthymia. The finding of significantly increased odds of 12-month MDD and 12-month dysthymia given the presence of 12-month alcohol dependence held even after adjustment for sociodemographic characteristics (ORs = 2.1 and 2.2, respectively) but not after adjustment for both sociodemographic characteristics and other psychiatric disorders (ORs = 1.3 and 0.9, respectively; Hasin et al., 2007). This suggests other psychiatric disorders as a possible common third variable to explain the associations of alcohol dependence with MDD and dysthymia. However, the lifetime NESARC data told a slightly different story (Hasin et al., 2007). The likelihood of MDD was increased given the presence of alcohol dependence (OR = 2.2) or alcohol abuse (OR = 1.2), even while controlling for sociodemographic characteristics. Only alcohol dependence significantly increased the odds of dysthymia (OR = 2.6). When adjustments were made for both sociodemographic characteristics and other psychiatric disorders, alcohol abuse no longer significantly increased the likelihood of MDD, but alcohol dependence was still associated with significantly higher odds of MDD (OR = 1.4).

Hasin, Goodwin, Stinson, and Grant (2005) examined the reverse relationship, that is, change in odds of SUDs given MDD, and found that the presence of 12-month MDD significantly increased the odds of alcohol dependence (OR = 2.1), alcohol abuse (OR = 1.3), drug dependence (OR = 3.7), and drug abuse (OR = 1.4), even after adjusting for sociodemographic variables. Similarly, lifetime MDD significantly increased the likelihood of having alcohol dependence (OR = 1.9), alcohol abuse (OR = 1.2), drug dependence (OR = 2.5), and drug abuse (OR = 1.7) even with adjustment for sociodemographic variables.

Using the same dataset, Huang et al. (2006) determined that lifetime nonmedical prescription drug use disorders significantly increased the odds of lifetime MDD (sedative use disorder, OR = 2.4; tranquilizer use disorder, OR = 2.4; opioid use disorder, OR = 2.4; and amphetamine use disorder, OR = 2.2) and lifetime dysthymia (sedative use disorder, OR = 3.9; tranquilizer use disorder, OR = 3.4; opioid use disorder, OR = 3.0; and amphetamine use disorder OR = 3.4).

CANADIAN COMMUNITY HEALTH SURVEY

Currie and colleagues (2005) found that 12-month alcohol dependence and 12-month illicit drug dependence were associated with significantly increased odds of having 12-month MDD (ORs = 2.3 and 4.3, respectively), controlling for basic demographic variables.

SUMMARY OF EPIDEMIOLOGICAL STUDIES OF SUD–DEPRESSION COMORBIDITY

In epidemiological studies, SUD–depression comorbidity shows a pattern of results similar to SUD–anxiety comorbidity. The presence of depression (both MDD and dysthymic disorder) increases the odds of experiencing an SUD and vice versa. Generally, as was seen for the anxiety disorders, the association between depression and SUDs is stronger and more consistent for dependence than for abuse and stronger/more consistent for DUDs than AUDs.

Kushner and colleagues (2008) have offered several explanations for this specific pattern of associations in the case of anxiety disorder–SUD comorbidity. Given that the same pattern is observed for depressive disorder–SUD comorbidity, these potential explanations can be extended to understanding the co-occurrence of SUDs with emotional disorders more generally. First, the stronger association of emotional disorders with substance dependence rather than substance abuse is consistent with an AUD subtyping scheme offered 25 years ago by Cloninger (1987). Specifically, abuse may be more associated with externalizing disorders such as antisocial personality disorder whereas dependence may be more associated with internalizing disorders like depression and anxiety. According to Cloninger (1987), internalizing characteristics promote a style of drinking that is more likely to result in substance dependence whereas externalizing characteristics promote a drinking style that is more likely to result in substance abuse. A second possibility is that much of the emotional disorder symptoms observed in comorbid cases are the result of processes associated with substance withdrawal—a symptom of dependence (see Schuckit, 2006). A third possibility was offered recently by Vergés, Steinley, Trull, and Sher (2010). They suggest that the stronger associations of the emotional disorders with substance dependence versus abuse is an artifact of the diagnostic algorithms used in the DSM-IV (APA, 1994) for making each SUD diagnosis (i.e., 3 of 7 criteria for dependence; 1 of 4 criteria for abuse without meeting criteria for dependence) rather than reflecting a stronger comorbidity of the emotional disorders with a more "severe" form of SUD, per se. Vergés et al. obtained evidence consistent with this possibility by applying the DSM-IV diagnostic algorithms to all possible sets of SUD symptoms from the NESARC data. They showed that psychiatric comorbidity was stronger for substance "dependence" than "abuse" regardless of the specific symptoms used in the algorithms.

It is more difficult to reach conclusions regarding the stronger relation of the emotional disorders with DUDs than with AUDs given a primary limitation of the epidemiologic literature to date. Specifically, the extant literature has tended to combine all types of DUD (e.g., cocaine, hallucinogens, nicotine) into a single category, separating them only from AUDs. This obviously adds noise to the DUD category and could obscure relations of emotional disorders to DUDs involving specific drug classes (Kushner et al., 2008).

Clinical Correlates of Emotional Disorder–SUD Comorbidity

There is substantial reason to be concerned about the comorbidity of emotional disorders with SUDs, over and above their sheer high prevalence. In this section, we look at the clinical correlates of comorbidity of anxiety and depressive disorders with SUDs.

Clinical correlates of anxiety disorder—SUD co-occurrence

Across a range variety of anxiety disorders, the presence of a co-occurring anxiety disorder–SUD is associated with poorer treatment outcome and a bleaker longer term prognosis for either disorder relative to those who have only one of these disorders (Stewart, 2010; Stewart & Conrod, 2008). Moreover, individuals with this form of comorbidity present with a more complex and severe clinical picture relative to individuals with only one of these disorders (Stewart & Conrod, 2008). For example, the presence of comorbid PTSD has been shown to lead to poorer short-term SUD treatment outcome (Ouimette, Ahrens, Moos, & Finney, 1997; 1998; Ouimette, Finney, & Moos, 1999) and a greater risk for SUD relapse in the longer term (Brown, Stout, & Mueller, 1996; Dansky, Brady, & Saladin, 1998; Ouimette, Moos, & Finney, 2003). Similarly, panic disorder comorbid with SUD has been shown to have a negative impact on prognosis (Burns, Teesson, & O'Neill, 2005; Willinger et al., 2002). Moreover, SUD patients with comorbid panic disorder experience more severe withdrawal symptoms (Breslau, Kilbey, & Andreski, 1991) and drop out of smoking cessation treatment (Covey, Hughes, Glassman, Blazer, & George, 1994) and AUD treatment (Labounty, Hatsukami, Morgon, & Nelson, 1992) at higher rates than do other SUD patients. In addition, panic disorder patients with comorbid SUD are at increased suicide risk relative to panic disorder patients with no SUD comorbidity (Hornig & McNally, 1995).

Clinical Correlates of Depression–SUD Co-occurrence

Individuals with depression–SUD comorbidity seem to share a poorer treatment outcome and prognosis and a more severe clinical presentation, similar to that previously described for comorbid anxiety disorder–SUDs. For example, addiction treatment studies suggest that the presence of comorbid depressive disorder is associated with higher rates of relapse to alcohol dependence following traditional AUD treatment (e.g., Glenn & Parsons, 1991; O'Sullivan et al. 1983; Rounsaville, Dolinsky, Babor, & Meyer, 1987; Schuckit, 1983). Moreover, among comorbid depressed–SUD patients, "independent depression" (which, as will be discussed in more detail in a later section, develops prior to the onset of the substance use or persists for a lengthy period—e.g., about a month—after the cessation of substance withdrawal or intoxication; APA, 2013) is associated with poorer outcomes, including more frequent relapses to substance misuse and higher suicide rates, than is substance-induced depressive disorder (Brown, Evans, Miller, Burgess, & Mueller, 1997; Ramsey, Kahler, Read, Stuart, & Brown, 2004; Sabourin & Stewart, 2009; Swendsen & Merikangas, 2000). Taken together, these findings suggest that understanding the relationship between emotional disorders and substance misuse is critical for developing more effective treatments and for individuals suffering from the devastating effects of these forms of comorbidity.

Theoretical Models of Comorbidity

Three primary models have been put forth to account for the onset of the comorbidity of SUDs with both anxiety disorders and depressive disorders. These are illustrated in panels A through C in Figure 6.1. The first two models posit direct causal associations between the two disorders. The first model of comorbidity, illustrated in Figure 6.1A, suggests that substance misuse causes anxiety or depression. This causation could occur directly, through physiological mechanisms. For example, a "neuro-kindling" process, brought on as a result of repeated substance withdrawal experiences, could result in anxiety pathology (see Kushner et al., 1990; 2008). Alternatively, substance-induced disturbances in stress responding could lead to the development of anxiety or depression (McNaughton, 2008). Koob and Le Moal (2005) have described a relevant process that they refer to as the "dark side" of drug

addiction: as substance dependence and withdrawal develop, dysregulation in the functioning of the hypothalamic-pituitary-adrenal (HPA) axis takes place, producing aversive, stress-like subjective states including anxiety and depression. This causation could also occur indirectly. For example, substance-related impairments in social, health, and occupational domains could ultimately result in a mood or anxiety disorder (e.g., see Swendsen & Merikangas, 2000).

Alternatively, a large body of research has examined the converse possibility, illustrated in Figure 6.1B, that the presence of anxiety or depression causes the development of SUDs. Several theories have been proposed to explain this possible causal pathway, including the self-medication hypothesis (Khantzian, 1985; 1997), the tension-reduction theory (see Greeley & Oei, 1999), the stress-response dampening model (Sher, 1987), and the adaptive orientation (Alexander & Hadaway, 1982). Although each is unique, these theories hold in common the idea that depressed or anxious individuals learn to use substances of abuse for their reinforcing effects and that heightened use for these reasons ultimately results in an SUD (Morris, Stewart, & Ham, 2005). For example, some drugs have negatively reinforcing effects in relieving pain (e.g., alcohol, opiates) that could be particularly rewarding to an individual suffering from a depressive disorder; other drugs have negatively reinforcing sedative, anxiolytic, or stress-response

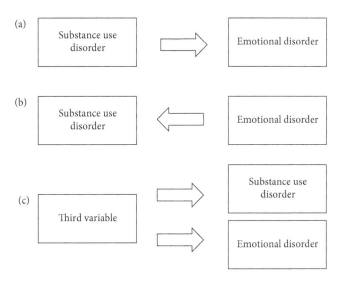

Figure 6.1. Three possible models of comorbidity onset. "Emotional disorder" refers to either an anxiety disorder or a depressive disorder.

"Substance use disorder" refers to either an alcohol or other drug use disorder. Panel A is consistent with a substance-induced induction of anxiety or depression model. Panel B is consistent with a self-medication model. Panel C is consistent with a common third-variable explanation. Adapted from Stewart and Conrod (2008).

dampening effects (e.g., alcohol, benzodiazepines) that could be particularly rewarding to an anxious individual (Stewart & Conrod, 2008). Drugs of abuse might also exert their rewarding effects through cognitive mechanisms. For example, alcohol could be rewarding to a depressed individual because of its effects in dampening cognitive biases that maintain depressed mood (Stephens & Curtin, 1995). Similarly, alcohol could be particularly reinforcing to panic-prone individuals due to its ability to dampen their tendency to catastrophize about the meaning of arousal-related bodily sensations (MacDonald, Baker, Stewart, & Skinner, 2000). Other drugs like cocaine and ecstasy could be used to self-medicate the anhedonia characteristic of depression by enhancing the user's sense of well-being (Stewart & Conrod, 2008) or by inducing positive emotional states (Brown & Stewart, 2008).

A third possible model of comorbidity, illustrated in Figure 6.1C, suggests that a common etiological variable or "third variable" (Stewart & Conrod, 2008) underlies SUD–anxiety comorbidity and SUD–depression comorbidity. In this case, there is no direct causal relation between the SUD and the emotional disorder themselves. Possible candidates for this third variable include common genetic factors that predispose to both types of disorders, common personality risk factors (e.g., anxiety sensitivity; see review by Stewart & Kushner, 2001), environmental risk factors (e.g., parental abuse or neglect, a disruptive family environment), or exposure to prenatal environmental factors (e.g., maternal alcohol use; Merikangas, Stevens, & Fenton, 1996; Stewart & Conrod, 2008), For example, family and twin studies have provided some evidence of a common genetic contribution to the association between alcohol consumption and anxiety disorder symptoms (e.g., Tambs, Harris, & Magnus, 1997).

A fourth possible model relates to comorbidity maintenance as opposed to onset. This model is illustrated in Figure 6.2. It is important to stress that the mechanisms involved in the maintenance of emotional disorder–SUD comorbidity are not necessarily the same as those involved in comorbidity onset (see Kushner et al., 2008; Stewart & Conrod, 2008). Independent of the initial pathway to the development of a comorbid emotional disorder–SUD, once the two disorders are present in a given individual, each disorder could serve to maintain or even exacerbate the other in a feed-forward cycle. For example, an individual

with comorbid MDD and AUD may use alcohol to cope with negative affect in the short term (Khantzian, 1985), but the physiological and/or psychological effects of his or her heavy alcohol use might accentuate depressed feelings in the longer run (Schuckit, 2006), thus creating more opportunity for continued self-medication, and so on. Thus, both self-medication processes and substance-induced intensification of negative affect processes are said to be operative in this model, creating a vicious cycle between symptoms of each disorder (see Figure 6.2).

Examination of Theoretical Models of SUD–Anxiety Comorbidity Onset
Order of Onset

Chilcoat and Breslau (1998) review several criteria that can be used to guide causal inference, including temporality, which they refer to as "the only undisputed criterion of causality" (p. 830). Of course, establishing temporality alone is not sufficient for determining causality. However, a necessary condition for causality is that the causal factor must occur prior to the effect. Typical order of onset studies use meeting full syndromal criteria as milestones for onset of each disorder in question. However, when reviewing this data, it is important to caution that there can be relations between emotional disturbance and substance use prior to any manifest "disorder." For example,

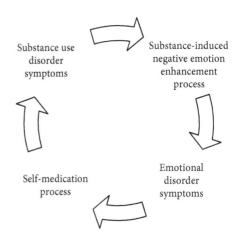

Figure 6.2. The mutual maintenance model.

"Emotional disorder" refers to either an anxiety disorder or a depressive disorder. "Substance use disorder" refers to either an alcohol or other drug use disorder. This model illustrates the vicious cycle that can be at play between symptoms of emotional disorders and substance use disorders such that each maintains the other, or even exacerbates the other, over time. Adapted from Stewart and Conrod (2008).

an individual might begin abusing substances to self-medicate emerging but subsyndromal anxiety symptoms. In this case, the substance use disorder would appear to have emerged first, even though the relevant etiologic process was self-medication of anxiety.

Several studies have examined the order of onset of SUDs versus anxiety disorders. Kushner and colleagues (2008) reviewed retrospective reports of order of onset of SUDs and anxiety disorders from several epidemiological studies, including the ECA, NCS, ICPE, and NCS-R and determined that, on average, anxiety predated SUDs in 77% of the sample of individuals with SUD–anxiety disorder comorbidity. These data support either a self-medication or third-variable explanation of comorbidity. Nonetheless, retrospective estimates of age of onset are limited in that bias may be introduced into the data (e.g., respondents may justify their current substance misuse to themselves and others by saying that they are using substances to cope with an antecedent anxiety disorder). Thus, prospective data are important in uncovering true order of onset of comorbid disorders.

A few studies have prospectively examined order of onset of SUDs and anxiety disorders. Most studies in this area have focused on the question of whether anxiety disorders prospectively predict SUD onset. Swendsen and colleagues (2010) presented 10-year follow-up data from the NCS. On the whole, the presence of any anxiety disorder at baseline significantly prospectively predicted first onset of alcohol dependence with abuse (OR = 3.2), controlling for sociodemographic variables. Specific anxiety disorders that significantly prospectively predicted first onset of alcohol dependence with abuse included panic disorder (OR = 3.2), social phobia (OR = 3.3), specific phobia (OR = 2.7), PTSD (OR = 3.2), and separation anxiety (OR = 2.7) but not GAD or agoraphobia. Overall, the presence of any anxiety disorder at baseline also significantly prospectively predicted the onset of illicit drug dependence with abuse (OR = 3.5), adjusted for sociodemographic variables. Individual anxiety disorders that significantly prospectively predicted first onset of illicit drug dependence with abuse included social phobia (OR = 2.8), PTSD (OR = 3.9), and separation anxiety (OR = 3.0) but not panic disorder, agoraphobia, specific phobia, or GAD.

Swendsen et al. (2010) also examined the impact of initial anxiety disorders on the transition from alcohol abuse at baseline to subsequent alcohol dependence with abuse. Overall, the presence of any anxiety disorder at baseline increased the odds of transitioning from alcohol abuse to alcohol dependence with abuse (OR = 2.7), controlling for sociodemographic factors. This relationship was significant for panic disorder (OR = 3.8), social phobia (OR = 2.9), PTSD (OR = 4.5), and separation anxiety (OR = 2.1) but not specific phobia, GAD, or agoraphobia. In contrast, initial anxiety disorders did not significantly prospectively predict increased odds of transitioning from illicit drug abuse to illicit drug dependence with abuse. Nonetheless, they did significantly increase the likelihood of transitioning from being a nonuser of illicit drugs to being a user and from being a user to developing drug abuse for panic disorder (OR = 3.1 and 3.4, respectively), social phobia (OR = 1.9 and 2.1, respectively), specific phobia (2.3 and 1.9, respectively), and separation anxiety (OR = 3.8 and 2.8, respectively).

In an approximately 13-year follow-up at the Baltimore site of the ECA, Crum and Pratt (2001) found that a diagnosis of social phobia at baseline did not predict subsequent onset of AUDs, although subclinical social phobia was associated with an increased risk of later AUDs (OR = 2.3). This study was limited by the fact that most respondents were older than the typical age of onset of SUDs at baseline, and the sample analyzed was limited to those without an SUD at baseline.

A smaller prospective study of a younger sample (prepubertal children) demonstrated that DSM-III-R anxiety disorders diagnosed prior to puberty significantly increased the odds of developing AUDs (OR = 2.3, adjusted for sociodemographic variables), but not DUDs, within 10–15 years of the initial anxiety disorder diagnosis (Weissman et al., 1999). In a large prospective community survey, Zimmermann and colleagues (2003) found that adolescents and young adults with DSM-IV anxiety disorders at baseline had a marginally significant increased risk of developing any AUD by the 4-year follow-up. Panic attacks significantly prospectively predicted alcohol abuse, and both panic attacks and social phobia prospectively predicted hazardous alcohol use (determined by amount of alcohol consumed). None of the other anxiety disorders studied (i.e., panic disorder with or without agoraphobia, specific phobia, phobia not otherwise specified, and GAD) prospectively predicted hazardous alcohol use or AUDs. In a longitudinal study of adolescents over the course of approximately 14 years, Buckner and colleagues (2008) found that baseline

DSM-III-R diagnoses of social anxiety disorder and panic disorder significantly prospectively predicted increased odds of DSM-IV alcohol dependence (ORs = 3.98 and 5.82, respectively), whereas OCD, overanxious disorder, specific phobia, and separation anxiety disorder did not. None of the anxiety disorders examined predicted alcohol abuse or cannabis abuse. Only social anxiety disorder significantly predicted later cannabis dependence (OR = 4.89). In a longitudinal study of community adolescents over the course of 10 years, Wittchen and colleagues (2007) examined the relationship between baseline DSM-IV psychological disorders and the cumulative lifetime incidence of cannabis use disorders, controlling for sex. Having any anxiety disorder at baseline significantly increased the odds of cumulative lifetime incidence of cannabis use disorders (OR = 1.7). When individual anxiety disorders were studied separately, only specific phobia (OR = 1.8) and GAD (OR = 3.9), but not panic attacks/panic disorder, social phobia, agoraphobia, or separation anxiety, significantly prospectively predicted increased odds of cannabis use disorders.

A minority of studies examined the possibility that SUDs might either precede *or* follow anxiety disorders. Costello, Mustillo, Erkanli, Keeler, and Angold (2003) followed a large representative sample of children who were 9–13 years at baseline until age 16 years and determined that anxiety disorders predicted onset of SUDs, but SUDs did not predict onset of anxiety disorders. A study by Mackie, Castellanos-Ryan, and Conrod (2011) followed adolescents at four separate time points over an 18-month period. They found that personality moderated the relationship between anxiety symptoms and alcohol use such that adolescents with higher levels of both anxiety symptoms and the personality risk factor (anxiety sensitivity) were more likely to show a faster rate of increase in alcohol use. Early alcohol use did not affect the rate of change in anxiety symptoms, however. A prospective study of college students (oversampled for a family history of AUDs) followed across 7 years, beginning in their freshman year, found that among individuals diagnosed with a DSM-III anxiety disorder (including GAD, social phobia, agoraphobia with a history of panic attacks, and panic attacks without agoraphobia) at baseline, the odds of developing a new diagnosis of alcohol dependence at year 7 were approximately 3.5 times higher compared to individuals without a baseline anxiety disorder diagnosis (Kushner, Sher, & Erikson, 1999). Conversely, students with a diagnosis of alcohol dependence at baseline were approximately 4.5 times more likely to develop an anxiety disorder at year 7 than those without an initial alcohol dependence diagnosis. A similar pattern of results was found when alcohol abuse was combined with dependence, although it was not as strong. Kushner and colleagues' (1999) findings point to a reciprocal relationship between anxiety disorders and alcohol dependence, with anxiety disorders operating as risk factors for alcohol dependence and vice versa.

In an epidemiological follow-up study, Grant and colleagues (2009) examined NESARC data and found that none of the individual anxiety disorders studied, including panic disorder, social phobia, specific phobia, GAD, and PTSD, was associated with a significantly increased likelihood of onset of alcohol abuse at 3-year follow-up, controlling for sociodemographic characteristics. Conversely, alcohol abuse at baseline did significantly increase the odds of GAD at follow-up (OR = 1.9, adjusted for sociodemographic characteristics). The incidence of alcohol dependence was prospectively predicted by baseline specific phobia (OR = 1.5), GAD (OR = 2.0), and PTSD (OR = 1.8), even with adjustment for sociodemographic characteristics, whereas panic disorder and social phobia did not prospectively predict alcohol dependence. Conversely, baseline alcohol dependence significantly prospectively increased the odds of having panic disorder (adjusted OR = 2.1), social phobia (OR = 2.1), and GAD (OR = 2.3) but not specific phobia at follow-up. (PTSD was not examined in these analyses.) Controlling for sociodemographic characteristics, the presence of panic disorder, specific phobia, GAD, and PTSD at baseline significantly increased the likelihood of drug abuse by follow-up (ORs = 4.3, 2.3, 3.7, 4.5, and 5.4, respectively), whereas social phobia did not. Examining the drug abuse–anxiety link in the opposite direction revealed that drug abuse at baseline only significantly prospectively predicted panic disorder (adjusted OR = 1.9) and GAD (adjusted OR = 1.8) but not social phobia or specific phobia. Also controlling for sociodemographic characteristics, panic disorder, social phobia, GAD, and PTSD each significantly increased the odds of incident (new onset) drug dependence at follow-up (ORs = 7.5, 3.4, 5.0, and 3.7, respectively), but specific phobia did not. Baseline drug dependence only significantly prospectively predicted incidence of GAD (adjusted OR = 2.3) but not panic disorder, social phobia, or specific phobia. When adjustments were made for other psychiatric disorders in addition to sociodemographic characteristics, the only significant relationship between baseline anxiety disorders and subsequent SUDs or vice versa was between baseline panic disorder and drug dependence at follow-up (OR = 3.7).

In summary, with some exceptions, anxiety disorders typically precede SUDs, which favors the self-medication model (see Figure 6.1B). Nonetheless, there is some evidence to suggest that SUDs may also precede anxiety disorders, which is consistent with the substance-induced anxiety model (see Figure 6.1A). However, which of these models is most supported does appear to depend on the specific anxiety disorder in question (see Stewart & Conrod, 2008). For example, GAD was found to follow SUDs in several studies, suggesting that this particular anxiety disorder may be more likely to be substance-induced. This may be linked to conceptualizations of GAD as a distress disorder (like MDD), rather than a fear disorder like panic disorder (e.g., Watson, 2005). One working hypothesis could be that fear disorders are more likely to precede SUDs whereas distress disorders are more likely to follow SUDs. It is also important to emphasize that emerging evidence is supportive of a reciprocal relation between the symptoms of anxiety and SUDs (e.g., Kushner et al., 1999), which is consistent with the mutual maintenance model illustrated in Figure 6.2.

Independent Versus Substance-Induced Anxiety Disorder Diagnoses

Beginning with the DSM-IV (APA, 1994) and continuing in the DSM-5 (APA, 2013), the diagnostic criteria explicitly emphasized that in comorbid anxiety–SUD cases, the diagnostician must assess whether the co-occurring anxiety disorder was "independent" or "substance-induced." The criteria required to make this determination were also provided more clearly and specifically in the DSM-IV and DSM-5. This distinction was emphasized because it was increasingly recognized that symptoms of substance withdrawal, for example, can mimic anxiety states, as can intoxication with certain substances (e.g., amphetamine). Herein, we briefly review epidemiologic research that has examined the comorbidity of anxiety disorders with SUDs in terms of the independent versus substance-induced anxiety disorder distinction as it has relevance for evaluating the various theories of comorbidity etiology depicted in Figure 6.1. According to the DSM-5, independent anxiety develops prior to the onset of the substance use, or it persists for a lengthy period of time (e.g., about a month) after the cessation of substance intoxication/withdrawal, or there is other evidence of an independent anxiety disorder (e.g., a history of recurrent non–substance-related anxiety episodes; APA, 2013). In contrast, substance-induced anxiety is defined as an anxiety disorder in which the symptoms emerge during or soon after intoxication or withdrawal from a substance capable of inducing anxiety symptoms (APA, 2013). It should be noted that the independent versus substance-induced emotional disorder distinction bears some resemblance to, but is broader than, its predecessor, the distinction between primary and secondary disorders. The latter is based only on the chronology of development of the symptoms (i.e., order of onset), with the primary disorder being the one that appeared first (e.g., Schuckit & Montiero, 1988).

Grant et al. (2004) examined the NESARC data to specifically focus on the association between SUDs and independent anxiety and depression. We review the results for independent anxiety here and cover those for independent depression in a later section. Grant et al. (2004) found that all independent anxiety disorders examined (i.e., panic disorder with and without agoraphobia, specific phobia, social phobia, and GAD) were strongly and consistently related to having any SUD (i.e., 12-month ORs = 1.6–3.1). Among the anxiety disorders, panic disorder with agoraphobia was most strongly related to SUDs (i.e., 12 month ORs = 1.9–10.5). Interestingly, substance-induced anxiety was quite rare: of those with a current anxiety disorder, only 0.2% were substance-induced. In fact, the relative rarity of substance-induced anxiety in the general population is recognized in the most recent edition of the DSM—the DSM-5—where its prevalence is estimated at only 0.002% (APA, 2013). Similar to the conclusions drawn on the basis of studies examining order of onset, the Grant et al. (2004) study results are more consistent with the notion that anxiety causes substance misuse (see Figure 6.1B) rather than the converse notion of substance misuse causing an anxiety disorder (see Figure 6.1A).

Self-Reported Motives for Use

Another approach to determine the source of anxiety–SUD comorbidity has been to directly ask individuals why they consume alcohol or other drugs. In the NCS sample, Bolton, Cox, Clara, and Sareen (2006) examined individuals' own perceptions of self-medication with alcohol or drugs among respondents who met criteria for any lifetime anxiety disorder. The prevalence of reported self-medication was 21.9% among individuals with any anxiety disorder. However, this tendency was shown to vary across the anxiety disorders. Those with GAD had the highest prevalence of self-medication (35.6%), whereas those with social phobia, public speaking subtype, had the lowest (7.9%). This latter finding is consistent with theoretical speculation that self-medication is unlikely for certain anxiety disorders in which using substances to cope is not socially acceptable (e.g., to cope with having to give a public speech; Kushner, Abrams, & Borchardt, 2000). The findings for GAD in this study point to self-medication as the likely mechanism to explain comorbidity, which is inconsistent with the findings on temporal precedence that favor the substance-induced anxiety model. The nature of the relationship between GAD and SUD is thus deserving of additional research attention (Stewart & Conrod, 2008).

Genetic Epidemiology

Genetic epidemiology, or the study of the genetic determinants of disorders in families and populations, provides another source of information that may help to determine the relative tenability of the three aforementioned possible models of comorbidity etiology outlined in Figure 6.1. Family studies, twin studies, and studies examining candidate genes can all provide important data bearing on the associations among comorbid disorders. These studies can also detect "third variables," such as common genetic or environmental influences that may underlie comorbidity. Unfortunately, many of the studies in this area have not adequately parsed out anxiety and depression, so it may be difficult to make conclusive comparisons between anxiety–SUD comorbidity and depression–SUD comorbidity with respect to genetic epidemiology.

FAMILY STUDIES

In family studies, if one disorder (e.g., an anxiety disorder) causes another disorder (e.g., an SUD), the relatives of probands with the causal disorder (anxiety disorder) would be expected to show an increased likelihood of exhibiting the pure form of the causal disorder (anxiety disorder with no SUD) and an increased risk of having both disorders (anxiety disorder and SUD) but no increased risk of the pure form of the second disorder (SUD), compared to the relatives of probands without these disorders (Merikangas et al., 1996). However, if a "third-variable" explanation accounts for the comorbidity of the two disorders, then the relatives of probands with the pure form of one disorder (e.g., anxiety disorder) would be expected to have increased rates of the pure form of the other disorder (e.g., SUD) and vice versa (Merikangas et al., 1996). Kushner et al. (2000) reviewed family studies of anxiety disorders and AUDs and found some evidence suggesting that either type of disorder could cause the other and also some limited evidence for shared etiology of these disorders. In a study not reviewed by Kushner et al. (2000), Merikangas et al. (1998) examined mechanisms of co-occurrence of anxiety disorders and AUDs in a sample of relatives of probands with AUDs and/or anxiety disorders and unaffected controls. Rates of alcohol dependence were elevated only among those relatives of probands with social phobia who also had social phobia, suggesting that social phobia and alcohol dependence are transmitted independently. Merikangas and colleagues concluded that their findings were more consistent with a self-medication model (i.e., in which social phobia leads to alcohol dependence). Conversely, they determined that the co-occurrence of panic disorder and alcohol dependence was at least partly attributable to shared vulnerability factors.

In another study, among a sample of treatment-seeking probands with AUDs and controls, Nurnberger and colleagues (2004) found that relatives of probands with alcohol dependence were at significantly elevated risk of experiencing OCD (OR = 4.00), panic disorder (OR = 1.90), and PTSD (OR = 2.77) but not social phobia, independent of whether the probands had an anxiety disorder or whether the relative experienced co-occurring alcohol dependence. In other words, the Nurnberger et al. findings indicate that the pure (non-comorbid) form of alcohol dependence is linked to the pure form of the anxiety disorders noted earlier, suggesting a common etiology underlying the comorbidity of these disorders. Marquenie and colleagues (2007) examined the etiology of anxiety disorder–alcohol dependence comorbidity using family history data from a representative general population study. They found partial support for a model in which anxiety disorders enhanced risk of developing alcohol dependence and a model in which alcohol dependence increased risk of anxiety disorders. A shared genetic/familial etiology model received no support, and neither did an alternative model in which comorbid disorders were considered to be a unique psychopathological entity. Unfortunately, this study was limited by the fact that information about relatives' psychopathology was collected by interviews with probands. Merikangas and colleagues (2009) determined that anxiety disorders aggregated independently from cannabis use disorders in families. This finding suggests that shared familial factors (i.e., third variables) do not underlie comorbidity of anxiety and cannabis use disorders.

TWIN STUDIES

Several twin studies have examined the comorbidity of anxiety disorders and SUDs. In a small sample of same-sex pairs of twins with a treatment-seeking alcohol dependent proband, Pickens, Svikis, McGue, and LaBuda (1995) studied genetic influences on the comorbidity of alcohol dependence with other disorders, including anxiety disorders, depressive disorders, and DUDs. Among men, but not women, genetic factors were marginally involved in the comorbidity of alcohol dependence with phobia but not with OCD or panic disorder. Although the results did not show a statistically significant genetic influence on comorbidity of alcohol dependence and panic disorder, results were suggestive of such an influence among men.

Kendler and colleagues (1995) conducted a multivariate twin analysis of genetic and environmental risk factors for several disorders, including phobia, GAD, panic disorder, MDD, and AUDs (including alcohol dependence and problem drinking) in a female twin sample. Two factors best explained genetic influences on these disorders, including one that loaded strongly on phobia and panic disorder, and one that loaded heavily on MDD and GAD. This is consistent with conceptualizations of mood and anxiety disorders that differentiate fear disorders (including panic and specific phobia) from distress disorders (including MDD and GAD; e.g., Watson, 2005). Genetic influences on AUDs were found to be primarily (76%) disorder-specific. Nonetheless, each of the two aforementioned major genetic factors contributed approximately 12% of the genetic variation for AUDs. Familial-environmental factors did not substantially influence AUDs or the anxiety disorders examined. Individual-specific environmental factors substantially influenced risk of anxiety disorders and AUDs. They consisted of both a common factor (especially for GAD and MDD), suggesting a set of environmental risk factors that heighten susceptibility to a wide range of psychiatric disorders, and disorder-specific influences (especially for phobias, panic disorder, and AUDs).

Using a similar modeling approach, Kendler, Prescott, Myers, and Neale (2003) examined the genetic and environmental risk factors responsible for comorbidity of SUDs and other common psychiatric disorders in same-sex twins. Two genetic common factors were found, including an "externalizing" one with high loadings on alcohol dependence, DUDs, antisocial behavior, and conduct disorder, and another "internalizing" one with high loadings on MDD, GAD, and phobia. Alcohol dependence and DUDs, but not the other disorders examined, also had considerable disorder-specific genetic loadings (accounting for 14% and 21% of variance in liability to alcohol dependence and DUDs, respectively). The internalizing genetic common factor accounted for a significant proportion of variance in liability to both alcohol dependence (34%) and DUDs (42%). Shared environmental factors accounted for a negligible proportion of variance in liability to alcohol dependence and DUDs. Unique environmental influences accounted for a substantial proportion of variance in liability to both alcohol dependence and DUDs and were mostly disorder-specific (36% and 23%, respectively), not related to common factors.

Nelson and colleagues (2000) examined the degree to which genetic and environmental risk factors were common across social phobia, MDD, and alcohol dependence by fitting a trivariate genetic factor model in a female twin sample. Neither common nor disorder-specific shared environmental components were retained in the best-fitting model. Common nonshared environmental components were not significant, but disorder-specific, nonshared environmental components were retained for each disorder. In addition, a common additive genetic component contributed significantly to each of the disorders studied. The common additive genetic factor accounted for 28% of the variance in social phobia risk and 18% of the variance in alcohol dependence risk. For alcohol dependence, but not social phobia or MDD, a disorder-specific additive genetic component was also retained, accounting for 46% of the variance in alcohol dependence risk.

Overall, the twin studies reviewed herein suggest that common genetic factors (i.e., a genetic "third variable") at least partially account for the comorbidity of anxiety disorders and SUDs. Conversely, neither common shared environmental factors nor common, nonshared environmental factors appear to account for much of this comorbidity.

CANDIDATE GENES

Emerging research is beginning to uncover specific candidate genes that may be responsible for comorbidity between anxiety disorders and SUDs. Cerdá, Sagdeo, Johnson, and Galea (2010) reviewed possible candidate genes for comorbidity between psychiatric disorders and SUDs, such as *5HTTLPR*, *MAOA*, and *DRD1–DRD4*. Only one of the studies they reviewed (i.e., Young et al., 2002) examined the comorbidity of alcohol misuse and anxiety without aggregating anxiety and depression. The results suggested that the A1 allele of the D_2 dopamine receptor gene is implicated in the co-occurrence of PTSD and harmful alcohol use.

It is important to caution here regarding some concerns that have been expressed about the ability of candidate gene studies to reliably identify specific gene effects for psychiatric diagnoses and SUDs (e.g., Kendler, 2005). Similarly, increasing doubts have been expressed about the utility of genome wide association studies (GWAS), at least as they are typically conducted using simple tests for the additive effects of single, relatively common genetic variants, to provide useful information in the case of psychiatric and SUDs (e.g., see Corvin, Craddock, & Sullivan, 2010). For example, meta-analyses of candidate gene studies suggest that the magnitude of the associations between individual genes and psychiatric diagnoses and SUDs have small ORs, rarely surpassing 1.3 (Kendler, 2005).

Experimental Studies

The majority of studies in the anxiety disorder–SUD comorbidity area have used epidemiological surveys and self-report questionnaires to investigate the association between emotional disorder symptoms and substance use/misuse. Although important and informative, such designs are limited in that they fail to identify potential causal mechanisms that may underlie the relationship between anxiety disorders and SUDs. Hence, the use of laboratory-based, experimental methods is crucial to enhancing our understanding of how substances of abuse affect emotional disorder symptoms and how emotional disorder symptoms affect substance use behaviors (Battista, Stewart, & Ham, 2010). The goal of this section of the chapter is to review studies that have tested the effects of various substances on anxiety disorder symptoms, or vice versa (i.e., the effects of anxiety disorder symptoms on substance intake), using a variety of laboratory-based paradigms. Furthermore, the studies covered in this section of the chapter include those designed to test the effects of substances on anxiety disorder symptoms, whether those effects be pharmacologically and/or cognitively mediated. In addition to

having a variety of pharmacological effects, alcohol and other drugs can also produce effects that are largely due to the user's expectations of what that substance should do (i.e., "expectancy" or "placebo" effects; e.g., Marlatt & Rohsenow, 1980; Wilson & Abrams, 1977). Substance abuse researchers often employ study designs that allow for the comparison of the pharmacological versus expectancy effects of a given substance of abuse; this study design compares those randomly assigned to an active drug condition to those randomized to a placebo control condition. An even more comprehensive design, the balanced-placebo design, consists of four cells of participants: (a) those who are led to believe they have received active drug and, in fact, they have (i.e., active drug); (b) those who are led to believe they have received active drug when, in fact, they have not (i.e., placebo); (c) those who are led to believe they have not received active drug when, in fact, they have (i.e., antiplacebo); and (d) those who are led to believe that they have not received active drug and, in fact, they have not (i.e., control). Researchers can also explicitly manipulate specific drug outcome expectancy dimensions by providing participants with information about putative drug effects (e.g., stressing that drug administration will lead to relaxation/anxiety reduction). Another method for looking at expectancy effects experimentally is to administer a self-report alcohol/drug outcome expectancy measure prior to administration of an active drug or placebo and to use scores on this measure as predictors of dampening of emotional responses to a stressor over-and-above assigned drug condition. In this section, we review studies examining the pharmacological effects of drugs of abuse (i.e., studies that involve active drug administration), those examining the expectancy effects of drugs of abuse (i.e., studies that involved placebo administration or administration of self-report expectancy questionnaires), and those using research designs to distinguish between pharmacological and expectancy effects.

As noted earlier, models such as the tension-reduction hypothesis posit that anxious individuals learn alcohol and drug use through its negatively reinforcing consequences. Specifically, such models hold that (a) alcohol and other substances of abuse are capable of reducing anxiety or tension, and (b) anxious individuals will be motivated to use substances for these anxiety-reducing effects. Studies designed to investigate the first hypothesis typically involve administration of a specified dose of the substance in question or a placeholder followed by a state anxiety induction procedure (e.g., giving a self-disclosing speech or going through a social interaction with a confederate for a socially phobic individual; inducing arousal sensations for a panic-prone individual). The purpose is to examine substance effects on anxious reactivity using subjective-emotional, physiological, cognitive, and/or behavioral measures. To test the second hypothesis, participants undergo a state anxiety induction procedure relevant to the anxiety pathology in question (e.g., exposure to trauma cues in the case of PTSD; engaging in a social interaction or giving a speech in social phobia) or are informed that they will be required to engage in such a task (to induce anticipatory anxiety) and then are offered the opportunity to consume the drug of abuse. The purpose is to determine whether anxious participants are motivated to consume the substance for its anxiety-reducing effects. Some studies of this second type examine craving or urges to use the drug, or behavioral intentions to use the drug, as the dependent/outcome variable of interest rather than substance use behavior per se. We review some examples of these types of study next.

A number of studies have examined whether alcohol and other drugs of abuse are capable of dampening reactivity to anxiety induction. For example, a balanced-placebo alcohol study by de Boer, Schippers, and van der Staak (1993) had a mixed gender sample of undergraduates take part in a social interaction with an opposite-gender confederate—a social phobia-relevant anxiety induction task. The study revealed a pharmacological anxiety-reducing effect of alcohol in both men and women, but an additional alcohol expectancy effect on anxiety reduction in women only. This study highlights the importance of looking at both pharmacological and expectancy drug effects and of examining the possible moderating effects of gender. However, this analogue study did not examine this issue among individuals with a clinical diagnosis (in this case, social phobia), so it remained to be determined if the results would apply to explaining the development of clinical forms of anxiety disorder–SUD comorbidity.

A study by Abrams, Kushner, Medina, and Voight (2001) had a sample of individuals with diagnosed social phobia take part in two speech tasks. First, all participants gave a self-disclosing speech while they were sober. Next, participants were randomly assigned to drink alcohol, placebo, or control beverages and then completed the speech task a second time. When considering levels of social

anxiety measured during the second speech, participants in the alcohol and placebo conditions experienced greater reductions in self-reported anxiety and greater increases in positive thoughts from the first to the second speech compared to participants in the control beverage condition; no differences were observed between those in the alcohol and placebo groups. This study indicates that among individuals with social phobia, alcohol-induced anxiety-reduction may be primarily due to an expectancy effect. These findings emphasize the importance of considering cognitive mechanisms when examining the effects of substances on state anxiety among individuals with syndrome-level anxiety disorders.

A more recent study by Battista, MacDonald, and Stewart (2012) examined the effects of alcohol on not only self-reported anxiety, but also on behavioral indices of anxiety, during a social interaction. Eighty-eight socially anxious participants were randomly assigned to an alcohol or nonalcoholic control beverage condition and participated in a videotaped social interaction. Videos were later coded for behavioral signs of social anxiety. Alcohol decreased self-reported anxious reactivity to the social interaction and increased the length of time participants spent speaking during the interaction. Thus, not only does alcohol decrease subjective anxiety among socially anxious individuals, but it may also decrease their anxiety-related avoidance behaviors that are observable to others.

One limitation of studies like the previous two are that they do not include a control group of individuals without the anxiety disorder or anxiety characteristic in question in order to determine whether individuals with the clinical anxiety disorder (or those at risk) are more sensitive than others to substance-induced anxiolytic effects.

A study by MacDonald et al. (2000) evaluated the hypothesis that individuals at risk for panic disorder should be more sensitive than others to alcohol's emotional reactivity dampening effects when they are experiencing feared arousal sensations. Undergraduates at high and low risk of panic (selected according to high and low scores on a measure of "anxiety sensitivity" or fear of arousal sensations) were randomly assigned to a placebo, low-dose alcohol, or high-dose alcohol beverage condition. After drinking their assigned beverage, participants underwent a voluntary hyperventilation challenge, designed to elicit arousal sensations. High-anxiety sensitive participants in the placebo beverage condition displayed greater affective and cognitive reactivity to the challenge than did low-anxiety sensitive participants in the placebo beverage condition. This indicated increased fear and negative thoughts during hyperventilation among sober panic-prone individuals. Alcohol dampening of affective and cognitive reactivity to hyperventilation was observed in a dose–response fashion only among the high-anxiety sensitive participants. The dose–response results are consistent with other findings (e.g., Donohue, Curtin, Patrick, & Lang, 2007) that anxiolytic drug effects are stronger and more consistent when pharmacologically significant drug doses are administered (e.g., producing blood alcohol concentrations of 0.08% or greater in the case of alcohol). Overall, the MacDonald et al. (2000) findings were consistent with the hypothesis that individuals at risk for panic disorder are particularly sensitive to alcohol-induced reductions in their degree of fear and negative thinking in response to physical arousal sensations, such as a racing heart or dizziness. This would theoretically lead to negative reinforcement of drinking, particularly of higher alcohol doses, in panic-prone individuals. A similar conclusion was reached by Conrod, Pihl, and Vassileva (1998) who conducted an alcohol challenge study comparing high-anxiety sensitive men to groups of men with high and low familial genetic risk for alcoholism. Sensitivity to the fear-dampening effects of a moderately intoxicating dose of alcohol was unique to the panic-prone group (i.e., high-anxiety sensitive men). Although these two analogue studies did show individual differences in sensitivity to alcohol's fear-dampening effects, they did not use individuals with diagnosed panic disorder as participants, again leaving the question open as to whether this mechanism is applicable to explaining the development of clinical forms of anxiety disorder–SUD comorbidity.

Kushner et al. (1996) tested whether alcohol intake reduces anxiety and panic symptoms associated with an arousal induction procedure among participants with diagnosed panic disorder. Participants were randomly assigned to consume either a moderate dose of alcohol or a placebo beverage. All participants were informed that they were consuming alcohol. Following beverage consumption and absorption, participants underwent an arousal induction challenge involving inhalation of 35% carbon dioxide. Anxiety and panic symptoms were assessed both before and after arousal induction. Participants in the alcohol group reported significantly less state anxiety both before and after arousal induction. Moreover, those who consumed

alcohol experienced fewer panic attacks than did those in the placebo condition. The researchers concluded that alcohol acts to reduce both panic and the anticipatory anxiety surrounding panic among panic disorder patients—effects that might negatively reinforce drinking in this diagnostic group.

A study by Lehman, Brown, Palfai, and Barlow (2002) extended this work by examining the effects of alcohol and alcohol outcome expectancies on panic symptoms and subjective anxiety in response to 35% carbon dioxide inhalation in a sample of patients with panic disorder. Participants were randomly assigned to either an alcohol or placebo beverage condition. A set of regressions were used to predict responses to the arousal induction challenge using assigned beverage condition, self-reported alcohol outcome expectancies, and level of anxiety sensitivity (or fear of anxiety sensations) as predictors. For severity of self-reported panic symptoms, participants with greater positive alcohol outcome expectancies at baseline reported fewer panic symptoms after the challenge, regardless of assigned beverage condition. For subjective anxiety, participants who drank alcohol (vs. placebo) reported less subjective anxiety both prior to and following the challenge, showing that alcohol reduced anxiety by dampening anticipatory anxiety about the arousal induction challenge. Thus, individual differences in alcohol outcome expectancies, as well as the pharmacological effects of alcohol, appear to influence the experience of anxiety and panic in response to arousal induction among individuals with panic disorder.

Some studies in the anxiety disorders–SUD area have begun to make use of cognitive paradigms to examine the impact of various drugs of abuse on information processing biases that might cause or maintain anxiety. For example, Gerlach, Schiller, Wild, and Rist (2006) used the emotional Stroop color-naming test (Stroop, 1935) and an implicit memory test to investigate whether alcohol hinders appraisal of and/or memory for social threat words among individuals diagnosed with social phobia. Groups of women with and without DSM-IV (APA, 1994) social phobia were randomly assigned to either a moderately intoxicating alcohol dose or to a nonalcoholic beverage control condition. Participants performed an emotional Stroop task (color naming of social threat and neutral words) followed by a word stem completion task to test their implicit memory for the words in the Stroop task. Socially phobic women color named social threat words more slowly than neutral words (the expected threat-related interference effect), but unexpectedly, this was true regardless of their assigned beverage condition. In contrast, controls color named social threat words more slowly than neutral words only in the nonalcoholic beverage condition but not after alcohol consumption—the pattern expected for the socially phobic patients. Results were more as expected for the memory task: in contrast to controls, the socially phobic individuals showed an implicit memory bias for social threat words, and this bias was dampened by alcohol. These results suggest that individuals with social phobia appraise social threat similarly with and without alcohol, but that they remember social threat less precisely later, after they have been drinking. This latter effect might reinforce the use of alcohol for self-medication in future.

A related alcohol challenge study by Battista, Pencer, and Stewart (2014) examined the effect of drinking alcohol at the time of a social event on later post-event processing of (i.e., rumination about) that social event among 84 socially anxious participants. Post-event processing was reduced in those initially randomized to the alcohol condition than those initially randomized to the nonalcoholic control beverage condition, but only among women, suggesting that socially anxious women may be particularly susceptible to this form of alcohol reinforcement.

Another set of studies has examined whether a relevant anxiety-induction manipulation can prompt drinking or drug use behavior, and/or urges, cravings, and intentions to use, among anxious participants. For example, Kidorf and Lang (1999) used a within-subjects design to investigate whether participants would drink more while anticipating a social anxiety-provoking task as compared to baseline (when they were not anticipating any task). Male and female undergraduates completed a measure of trait social anxiety at baseline and then took part in two lab-based sessions. During the first session, participants sat comfortably and were given unlimited access to their favorite alcoholic beverage. At the beginning of the second session, they were informed that they would have to give a self-disclosing speech. Then, they were again given unlimited access to their favorite alcoholic beverage. Participants consumed more alcohol when they were anticipating the speech than they had at baseline. This effect was particularly true for individuals with higher trait social anxiety. This suggests that highly trait anxious undergraduates are particularly

likely to use substances (alcohol in this case) in anticipation of a social stressor. However, because this analogue study did not make use of individuals with diagnosed social phobia, it remains unclear to what degree these findings are applicable to the motivation underlying the development of comorbid anxiety disorders–SUD.

Abrams, Kushner, Medina, and Voight (2002) extended the Kidorf and Lang (1999) study by recruiting a mixed-gender sample of individuals diagnosed with social phobia. All participants took part in two experimental sessions, the order of which was randomly determined. During one of the sessions, participants engaged in a social anxiety induction task: solving moral dilemmas with another participant. In the other session, participants engaged in a neutral task: reading magazines. Participants were also randomly assigned to conditions in which they could drink alcohol either *before* or *after* each of the sessions. Participants could choose to drink strong, moderate, or weak drinks in terms of alcoholic content. The strength of chosen drinks was the dependent variable of interest. Among socially phobic participants who were given the opportunity to drink *after* completing each task, *higher* strength drinks were chosen during the session involving the anxiety-provoking task compared to the session involving the neutral task, as hypothesized. In contrast, socially phobic men who were assigned to drink *before* each task, tended to drink *lower* strength drinks before the anxiety-provoking task compared to the neutral task. Thus, on the anticipatory drinking dependent variable, results in direct opposition to those predicted were observed, at least for socially phobic men. This pattern suggests that socially phobic individuals may drink *following* socially stressful situations (e.g., to deal with residual anxiety) rather than *in anticipation* of them (i.e., to avoid anxiety). An advantage of this study is that it used clinically diagnosed individuals from the community. However, a limitation is that no nonsocially phobic control group was included, so it is not possible to determine if socially phobic individuals are more motivated to drink to deal with anxiety following a social stressor than are others. Another limitation is that drinking was not permitted during the social anxiety induction task, so it is not possible to know if socially phobic individuals might chose stronger drinks *during* a social stressor.

A study by Buckner, Silgado, and Schmidt (2011) overcame these limitations in an experiment examining marijuana. More specifically, they examined marijuana craving in response to a social anxiety-provoking situation. Their study focused on the timing of marijuana craving in relation to the task to clarify whether urge to use increases when participants are anticipating the situation, during the situation, or afterward. The study also examined possible moderating effects of social phobia and gender (i.e., half the sample was female and one-third met diagnostic criteria for social phobia). Participants were randomly assigned to either a speech or a reading task. Participants completed ratings of urges to use marijuana at baseline (prior to being informed of task assignment), in anticipation of the task, during the task, and following the task. The speech task was associated with greater marijuana craving than the reading (control) task but only among participants with social phobia and female participants. The effect of task condition was particularly pronounced *during* the task.

Other studies have used similar lab-based experimental methods to examine the mechanisms underlying the comorbidity of PTSD with SUD. For example, Saladin et al. (2003) conducted a cue reactivity study in a sample of alcohol- and cocaine-dependent individuals, all of whom had a history of at least one prior sexual or physical assault. About half of the sample had current PTSD. Participants listened to four trials of a narrative script (description of the participant's worst trauma or a neutral scene) followed by the presentation of an in vivo drug cue (presentation of the participant's preferred drug or a neutral cue). Substance craving was assessed in response to the narrative and in response to presentation of the cues. PTSD symptom severity, assessed at baseline, significantly predicted both trauma cue-elicited and substance cue-elicited craving. Thus, exposure to trauma reminders can serve to trigger drug cravings in trauma survivors with substantial PTSD symptoms, demonstrating the motivational significance of trauma cue exposure in this form of anxiety disorder–SUD comorbidity.

In summary, a variety of paradigms and lab-based experimental methods have been used to investigate causal mechanisms underlying the comorbidity of anxiety disorders with SUDs. Although there are certainly data supportive of the hypotheses that substances reduce state anxiety and that the experience of anxiety motivates substance use, overall findings have been mixed (Battista et al., 2010; Buckner et al., 2013). Studies have varied on numerous factors such as sample type (e.g., unselected university students, analogue anxious, or diagnosed anxiety disorder),

sample gender composition, anxiety induction method (e.g., general stressor vs. disorder specific anxiety induction), drug dose (e.g., mildly vs. moderately intoxicating), whether or not expectancy effects are controlled or specifically investigated, the anxiety-related outcome variables employed (subjective-emotional, behavioral, cognitive, physiological), the timing of the anxiety measurement relative to the stressor (i.e., anticipatory anxiety vs. anxiety in response to the stressor), when substance cravings or substance ingestion is measured relative to the stressor (i.e., before, during, and/or after), the substance-related dependent measure (i.e., urges/cravings, behavioral intentions, actual substance intake), and, when applicable, how substance intake is measured (e.g., strength of alcohol chosen, total alcohol volume consumed). These variations may explain why findings have not always been supportive of predictions of the tension-reduction, self-medication, and related hypotheses.

Examination of Theoretical Models of SUD–Depression Comorbidity
Order of Onset

A number of epidemiological studies have examined retrospective reports of the order of onset of SUDs versus unipolar depressive disorders. Kessler et al. (1997) examined retrospectively reported temporal ordering of alcohol abuse and depression separately by sex in individuals who had a lifetime diagnosis of alcohol abuse in the NCS. Among individuals with lifetime alcohol abuse, primary alcohol abuse with secondary dysthymia was more common than alcohol abuse secondary to dysthymia (2.2% vs. 1.2% for men and 5.7% vs. 3.9% for women). For men, primary alcohol abuse with secondary depression was more common than the converse (6.8% vs. 1.9%), whereas for women, secondary alcohol abuse with primary depression was more common than the converse (18.2% vs. 10.5%). When individuals with lifetime alcohol dependence were considered, primary alcohol dependence with secondary dysthymia was more common than the converse (7.8% vs. 2.2% for men and 12.9% vs. 6.7% for women). Among respondents with lifetime alcohol dependence, alcohol dependence was more likely to occur prior to depression than the converse for men (15.3% vs. 6.2%) and less so for women (22.6% vs. 21.3%).

Similar to the overall findings for the NCS, retrospective age-of-onset reports from the NCS-R indicated that MDD occurred prior to SUDs in individuals with both disorders less than half the time (41.3% for lifetime diagnoses and 49.2% for 12-month diagnoses; Kessler et al., 2003). Retrospective order-of-onset data from the NLAES indicated that depression occurred prior to the AUD in 41.0% of respondents with both MDD and an AUD, and the AUD occurred prior to MDD in 42.5% of individuals with both disorders (Grant, Hasin, & Dawson, 1996).

Prospective research has also been conducted to determine the relative order of onset of SUDs versus depression. Similar to their findings pertaining to anxiety disorders, Weissman et al. (1999) found that MDD diagnosed in prepubertal children significantly increased the odds of developing AUDs (OR = 3.0, adjusted for demographic variables), but not DUDs, within 10–15 years of the baseline MDD diagnosis. Contrary to Costello and colleagues' (2003) finding that anxiety disorders predicted SUD onset, depression did not predict the development of SUDs. In the Zurich Cohort Study, involving six waves of data collection over a 20-year period, Merikangas et al. (2008) found that DSM-IV MDD did not prospectively predict the development of AUDs or cannabis use disorders. However, the presence of MDD did increase the odds of developing benzodiazepine use disorders (OR = 13.2). Wittchen and colleagues (2007) found that baseline MDEs or MDD significantly increased the likelihood of lifetime incidence of cannabis use disorders by follow-up (OR = 2.5), but dysthymia did not. The relationship between baseline depression and cannabis use disorders remained even after controlling for externalizing disorders. Marmorstein, Iacono, and Malone (2010) examined associations between DSM-III-R MDD and substance dependence in a longitudinal study (the Minnesota Twin Family Study) following adolescents through early adulthood. In a longitudinal cross-lag model, substance dependence between ages 17 and 20 years was associated with significantly increased risk of MDD between 20 and 24 years (OR = 2.32). MDD did not, however, significantly predict later substance dependence.

Several prospective investigations using epidemiological samples have been carried out to determine the temporal priority of depression versus SUDs. Gilman and Abraham (2001) examined prospective ECA data to determine the likelihood of baseline MDD or alcohol dependence being followed by the other disorder at 1-year follow-up. The presence of MDD at baseline did not significantly increase the risk of having alcohol dependence 1 year later, although the likelihood of developing alcohol dependence was elevated in individuals who had more depressive symptoms at baseline. Conversely, the presence of alcohol dependence at baseline significantly increased the odds of MDD after 1 year for both women (OR = 3.52) and men (OR = 1.77). Among individuals with both MDD and alcohol dependence, alcohol dependence was more likely to have preceded MDD than vice versa. Crum, Storr, and Chan (2005) examined follow-up data from the Baltimore site of the ECA after a median follow-up period length of 12.6 years. Latent class analysis of baseline depressive symptom criteria resulted in the identification of a depression syndrome class and a nondepression syndrome class. Relative to the nondepression syndrome class, participants in the depression syndrome class were at significantly higher risk of experiencing lifetime alcohol dependence. However, the two classes did not significantly differ with respect to the odds of new onset of alcohol dependence by follow-up. In another follow-up study of the Baltimore site of the ECA study, Bovasso (2001) found that the presence of baseline cannabis abuse significantly increased the odds of experiencing the onset of depressive symptoms over the nearly 15-year follow-up period (OR = 4.49) among respondents with no depressive symptoms at baseline. This relationship held even after potential confounding variables were controlled (e.g., sex, age, number of stressful life events, and chronic illnesses). Conversely, the incidence of cannabis abuse symptoms during the follow-up period was not prospectively predicted by baseline depressive symptoms.

In contrast to the NCS follow-up finding that baseline anxiety disorders significantly prospectively predicted first onset of alcohol dependence with abuse and illicit drug dependence with abuse, neither baseline dysthymia nor baseline MDD significantly predicted the onset of alcohol dependence with abuse or the onset of illicit drug dependence with abuse by the time of reinterview 10 years later (Swendsen et al., 2010). Dysthymia at baseline did, however, significantly prospectively predict an increased likelihood to transition from alcohol abuse to alcohol dependence with abuse at follow-up (OR = 5.2), but MDD did not. MDD at baseline significantly prospectively predicted increased odds of beginning illicit drug use at follow-up among individuals who did not use illicit drugs at baseline (OR = 1.9), but dysthymia did not.

Grant and colleagues (2009) examined the prospective associations between baseline unipolar mood disorders and SUDs and vice versa in the

NESARC. Controlling for sociodemographic characteristics, MDD at baseline significantly increased the prospective likelihood of alcohol dependence (OR = 1.6) and drug dependence (OR = 2.5) but not alcohol abuse or drug abuse. These relationships did not hold after controlling for the effects of other psychiatric disorders, including anxiety, in addition to sociodemographic characteristics. This suggests the possibility that comorbid anxiety disorders (or some factor common to anxiety disorders and MDD) might have actually been driving this effect. Conversely, baseline SUDs did not significantly prospectively increase the odds of MDD at follow-up. Baseline dysthymia did not significantly prospectively increase the odds of any SUD. Reciprocal relationships were not examined.

In a longitudinal study of a birth cohort of children from New Zealand, Fergusson, Boden, and Horwood (2009) examined interview data at three time points collected between ages 17 and 25 years. They used structural equation modeling to examine several possible models of association between DSM-IV AUDs and MDD, including a model assuming reciprocal associations between AUDs and MDD, a model presupposing a causal effect from AUDs to MDD, and a model assuming a causal effect from MDD to AUDs. The relationship between AUDs and MDD was best explained by a unidirectional causal model in which AUDs led to increased risk of MDD. In contrast, a recent four-wave longitudinal study of adolescents by Mackie et al. (2011) showed that elevated levels of depressive symptoms predicted faster rates of increase in alcohol use, whereas early alcohol use did not significantly influence the rate of change of depressive symptoms. Thus, the Mackie et al. study results are consistent with the perspective that there is a causal effect of depression on alcohol use; this has been demonstrated in other adolescent samples as well (e.g., Sihvola et al., 2008).

In summary, the findings of studies examining the order-of-onset of depression versus SUDs are fairly mixed (see reviews in Mackie et al., 2011; Mackie, Conrod, & Brady, 2012). The balance of the extant data from epidemiological studies with adults suggests that SUDs may be more likely to precede unipolar depressive disorders than vice versa in the majority of cases. However, potentially important gender differences appear to exist in the order of onset findings that favor self-medication for women and substance-induced depression in men (see reviews in Sabourin & Stewart, 2009; Stewart, Gavric, & Collins, 2009). Mackie et al. (2012) have

also noted that there appear to be important differences in which causal model is most supported based on the developmental stage of the sample. Specifically, the majority of studies that provide support for self-medication models of depression–SUD comorbidity tend to include adolescents or young adults who are at the onset of substance use. In contrast, the majority of evidence that supports the substance-induced depression model (Brown et al., 1995; Schuckit, 2006) has been obtained in samples of adults or university students in whom substance use has reached relatively more elevated levels, suggesting validity of a causal model of comorbidity at early stages of development and of a maintenance model of comorbidity at later stages of disorder onset or development.

Independent Versus Substance-Induced Mood Disorder Diagnoses

DSM-5 definitions for independent versus substance-induced mood disorders are analogous to those provided previously for this distinction with comorbid anxiety disorders–SUDs. As mentioned earlier, Grant et al. (2004) examined NESARC data to specifically focus on the association between SUDs and independent emotional disorders. As with comorbid anxiety disorders, both independent major depression and independent dysthymia were strongly related to having any SUD (i.e., 12-month ORs= 2.5 and 2.2, respectively). And, consistent with the findings for comorbid anxiety–SUD, substance-induced mood disorders were also quite rare; of those with a current mood disorder (including mania and hypomania; figures were not provided separately by specific mood disorder), only 1.0% were substance-induced. Thus, the results are more consistent with the notion that depression causes substance misuse (see Figure 6.1B) than with the possibility that substance misuse causes a mood disorder (see Figure 6.1A).

Self-Reported Motives for Use

Unfortunately, few studies have directly asked depressed individuals why they consume alcohol or other drugs as another approach to determining the nature of depression–SUD comorbidity. A study by Reyno, Stewart, Brown, Horvath, and Wiens (2006) examined motives for use indirectly by asking a sample of women receiving treatment for an AUD about their heavy drinking contexts. If a respondent indicates that her heavy drinking frequently occurs in situations involving conflict with others, for example, it is inferred that the motive underlying the heavy drinking is self-medication of negative affect emerging from the interpersonal conflict. Using this method, Reyno et al. (2006) showed that depression symptoms independently predicted frequency of drinking in response to interpersonal conflict situations, even after accounting for variance attributable to anxiety variables (anxiety symptoms and anxiety sensitivity). Thus, heavy drinking among AUD women with substantial depression symptoms appears related to drinking to manage negative affect emerging from interpersonal conflict. Because this was a correlational study, the direction of causality cannot be determined. It is also possible that interpersonal conflict is more likely to emerge from heavy drinking in AUD women with substantial depressive symptoms.

Genetic Epidemiology

Several of the same studies reviewed in the section examining genetic epidemiology of SUD–anxiety comorbidity also studied SUD–depression comorbidity. Those studies and others specifically pertaining to SUD–depression comorbidity are reviewed here.

FAMILY STUDIES

Swendsen and Merikangas (2000) reviewed family studies examining the comorbidity of depression and SUDs. At that time, they concluded that extant research findings had not necessarily ruled out a common etiology between depression and AUDs, but that, if present, this association was relatively weak. They further suggested that the familial association between depression and AUD may be partly attributable to the shared susceptibility between depression and anxiety disorders. They noted that there were few family studies examining depression–DUD comorbidity and that these studies were probably confounded by polysubstance (including alcohol) misuse. In addition to reviewing the research literature, Swendsen and Merikangas presented data from a family study showing that MDD was not associated with increased risk of alcohol dependence in relatives after controlling for comorbidity in the relatives, consistent with previous research suggesting independence of familial aggregation of depression and alcohol dependence.

In the decade and a half since the publication of the Swendsen and Merikangas (2000) review, new family studies of depression–SUD comorbidity have been published. In the study by Nurnberger and colleagues (2004) described earlier, relatives of probands with alcohol dependence were at significantly higher risk of experiencing MDD (OR = 1.35) even after controlling for comorbidity, suggesting a common etiology underlying the co-occurrence of these disorders. Odds of having dysthymia, on the other hand, were not significantly elevated in relatives of probands with alcohol dependence. In the aforementioned family study of cannabis use disorders by Merikangas et al. (2008), MDD was found to aggregate independently of cannabis use disorders in families. As with the findings pertaining to anxiety disorder–cannabis use disorder comorbidity, this result does not support the existence of common underlying risk factors for MDD and cannabis use disorders.

TWIN STUDIES

In the aforementioned study by Pickens and colleagues (1995), the results did not show a statistically significant genetic influence on comorbidity of alcohol dependence and MDD in the overall sample. Nonetheless, the pattern of results was suggestive of a genetic influence on this comorbidity in men. According to the study by Kendler and colleagues (1995) reviewed previously, AUD was, from a genetic perspective, most closely related to MDD as compared to the other disorders studied, including phobia, GAD, and panic disorder. As previously noted, Kendler and colleagues (2003) found that an internalizing genetic common factor with high loadings on MDD, GAD, and phobia accounted for a significant proportion of variance in susceptibility to alcohol dependence and DUDs. In the Nelson and colleagues (2000) study described earlier, the common additive genetic variance component accounted for 45% of the variance in MDD, which was substantially more than that seen in social phobia (i.e., 28%). Examining the same sample as Merikangas et al. (1998), Preisig and colleagues (2001) found no evidence of cross-aggregation of depressive disorders and alcohol dependence, suggesting that shared familial liability is not likely to account for the comorbidity between these disorders.

Several twin studies have specifically examined depression–SUD comorbidity. Kendler, Heath, Neale, Kessler, and Eaves (1993) conducted a twin study with females to examine possible causes of comorbidity between MDD and AUDs in women, using a variety of definitions of these disorders. The findings demonstrate that genetic factors that influence the risk of both MDD and AUDs account for the majority of the co-occurrence of these disorders. Nonetheless, the results show that MDD and AUDs are not the same disorder from a genetic point of view (i.e., the genetic correlation of these disorders is estimated between .50 and .60). In addition, individual-specific environmental factors played a role in the observed co-occurrence of MDD and AUDs, although their role was not as important as the genetic contribution.

Prescott, Aggen, and Kendler (2000) studied genetic influences on risk for lifetime co-occurrence of MDD and AUDs in a sample of twin pairs. They found that there are genetic and nonshared environmental factors that contribute to both MDD and AUDs, as well as disorder-specific factors. Common environmental factors were not found to contribute to MDD–AUD comorbidity. According to the authors, the overlap accounts for a relatively small proportion (9–14%) of the variation in susceptibility to these pathologies, suggesting that the familial transmission of MDD and AUDs is mostly disorder-specific. Of the overlap, approximately half (50–60%) is attributable to shared genetic factors, and the rest is due to specific environmental influences. Their results supported neither the self-medication model in which MDD causes the development of AUDs, nor the alcohol-induced depression model in which AUDs cause the development of MDD. However, they could not rule out less restrictive variants of the model in which AUD promotes MDD development. A common-liability model was not supported. They found that a correlated-liability model, in which MDD and AUD are posited to co-occur in families because the contributing influences are correlated, did fit the data well.

CANDIDATE GENES

Cerdá and colleagues (2010) reviewed research examining potential candidate genes underlying depression–SUD comorbidity. They found that several investigations have studied the role of dopamine receptor genes in the comorbidity of depression and AUDs with mixed results. In addition, they determined that there is some evidence to suggest a link between a high frequency of the S allele in the serotonin transporter gene and MDD–AUD comorbidity. Again, the previously noted concerns with candidate gene and GWAS studies (e.g., Corvin et al., 2010; Kendler, 2005) also apply here.

Experimental Studies

Although it is a common-held notion that "self-medication" is a process that explains the high comorbidity of depression with SUDs, the mechanisms by which alcohol and other drugs of abuse could produce symptom reduction for a depressed or depression-prone individual are not well understood. This is a particularly important line of investigation because previous investigations on other pathways to SUD have revealed personality-specific sensitivities to substance reinforcement (e.g., the specific sensitivity of high-anxiety sensitive individuals to alcohol-induced fear dampening mentioned earlier; Conrod et al., 1998).

One major hindrance to lab-based drug challenge work in this area has been the lack of experimental tasks that reliably differentiate depressed or depression-prone individuals from nondepressed or non–depression-prone individuals. The most consistent effect in the depression literature would be the diurnal cortisol patterns and cortisol responses to stress, with major depressive disorder being repeatedly associated with hyperactivity of the HPA axis (Pariante & Lightman, 2008). For example, a study by Heim et al. (2000) showed that women with a history of abuse in childhood and a current major depression diagnosis exhibited a sixfold greater adrenocorticotropic hormone (ACTH) response to stress than age-matched controls. Various drugs of abuse have been shown to alter HPA axis function. For example, acute administration of alcohol reduces cortisol responses to stress (Zimmerman et al., 2004). Individuals with a family history of alcoholism appear to be more sensitive to this stress response dampening effect of alcohol due to a preexisting hyperreactivity to stress (Zimmerman et al., 2004). Although we know of no experimental studies to date that have directly assessed the effects of substances of abuse on depressed patients' responses to stress, the experimental literature indirectly suggests a possible self-medication process through substance-induced dampening of the stress response in those prone to higher HPA-axis reactivity.

Another possible mechanism of depression self-medication involves substance effects on information processing biases that are thought to cause or maintain depression in cognitive models of depression. One study examining this possibility was conducted by Aramakis, Khamba, Macleod, Poulos, and Zack (2012) who used the Implicit Association Test (IAT; Greenwald, McGhee, & Schwartz, 1998) to measure the effects of alcohol on negative self-relevant associations. Their IAT version examined reaction time to classify positive attribute (e.g., CUTE) and negative attribute (e.g., UGLY) words when they were paired with self-relevant (e.g., ME) or non–self-relevant (e.g., THEM) object words. Undergraduate drinkers were randomly assigned to consume one of three beverage conditions: a moderately intoxicating dose of alcohol, a placebo condition, or a control beverage condition, then they performed a speech about their appearance (as a prime for negative self-referent associations) before they completed the IAT. Alcohol selectively slowed participant's negative self-relevant decisions. Preferential impairment of negative self-relevant associations by alcohol may be one cognitive mechanism underlying self-medication for depression that reinforces drinking behavior. This study did not, however, use depressed patients as participants nor did it examine whether depression levels or depression-proneness moderated these findings. One would expect this observed effect of alcohol preferentially impairing negative self-relevant associations to be strongest in depressed or depression-prone individuals.

Another study by Stephens and Curtin (1995) overcame this latter limitation by examining alcohol's effects on mood and processing of self-relevant information in a mixed-gender sample of undergraduates high and low in depression. Participants were randomly assigned to either an alcohol or placebo condition. Following beverage consumption and absorption, participants processed trait adjectives under self-relevant and semantic processing instructions, and recall was later tested. Results showed the expected biased recall of depressed content adjectives by depressed participants in the placebo condition; this effect was reversed in the alcohol condition. Moreover, reduced recall of negative self-referent information was significantly related to alcohol-induced mood enhancement in the high-depression participants. These effects of alcohol in reversing depression-relevant information processing biases might provide one potential reinforcement mechanism that could explain the high rates of overlap of depression with SUDs.

No lab-based experimental studies, to our knowledge, have examined whether depressed mood or other symptoms of depression can prompt substance craving or increase substance intake, particularly among depressed or depression-prone individuals. However, there is a relevant line of research involving lab-based mood induction that indirectly suggests that this may be the case. For example, a study by Birch, Stewart, Girling, and Berish (2006) used musical mood induction to bring on the mood states of interest in the lab and to examine their impact on drinking behavior. A mixed-gender sample of undergraduates was selected according to their drinking motives: half were selected for their status as coping-motivated drinkers (i.e., those reporting frequent drinking to manage negative emotional states like sadness), and the other half were selected for their status as enhancement-motivated drinkers (i.e., those reporting frequent drinking for excitement and stimulation). Half of the participants in each drinking motives group was randomly assigned to either a positive (cheerful) or negative (depressing) mood induction. Immediately following mood induction, participants were involved in an ostensibly unrelated task: rating a variety of beverages on various dimensions of taste. The real purpose of the task was to determine how much alcoholic (vs. nonalcoholic control) beverage they would consume. Consistent with hypothesis, coping-motivated drinkers (but not enhancement-motivated drinkers) assigned to the depressed mood induction showed a higher preference ratio for alcoholic to nonalcoholic beverage consumption; however, this effect was only seen among the women. In contrast, regardless of gender, coping-motivated drinkers did not show this alcohol preference following the positive mood induction. This study shows that the experience of depressed mood can motivate alcohol intake, at least among women who report frequent drinking to manage negative emotions such as sadness (Birch et al., 2006). Future studies could use this type of methodology to determine whether depressed individuals (or introverted/hopeless individuals who are at risk of depression) are particularly likely to increase their substance intake when experiencing depressed mood.

In summary, there is some emerging experimental data to suggest that depressed individuals may be particularly sensitive to substance effects on cortisol responses to stress and on cognitive biases that may maintain depression. These effects theoretically negatively reinforce substance use behaviors such that a depressed or depression-prone individual should be more likely to use substances for these desirable effects again in future. Indeed, recent findings suggest that the experience of a depressed mood state can prompt increased substance use behavior, at least among females who report frequent substance use to cope with negative emotions like sadness.

Treatment Considerations for Individuals with Comorbid Emotional Disorders–SUDs

We now turn to considering treatment for those with comorbid emotional disorders–SUDs. This section has two purposes—one theoretical and the other practical. First, treatment studies can provide an opportunity to understand theoretical mechanisms that maintain comorbidity. If an evidence-based intervention for a particular set of symptoms (e.g., relapse prevention for substance dependence) is shown to reduce the other set of symptoms (e.g., anxiety disorder symptoms), then findings could have implications for how we understand causal relationships between the two disorders (Kushner et al., 2005; Mackie et al., 2012). Second, an evaluation of the treatment literature can serve to guide clinical practice for those with co-occurring emotional disorders and SUDs.

Treatment Considerations for Anxiety Disorder–SUD Comorbidity

In the anxiety disorders area, which of the two causal hypotheses presented earlier (see 1A and 1B and) is best supported seems to depend on the specific anxiety disorder in question. For example, a study by Kushner et al. (2005) followed-up comorbid AUD treatment patients following alcoholism treatment. It was shown that GAD was likely to resolve following treatment for the AUD without the need for specific anxiety disorder treatment. This suggests that GAD is likely to be maintained by substance misuse among comorbid cases (Stewart & Conrod, 2008). In contrast, co-occurring PTSD and social phobia were unlikely to resolve with AUD treatment (Kushner et al., 2005). This pattern is inconsistent with the notion that substance misuse was maintaining these two particular anxiety disorders (Stewart & Conrod, 2008).

There have been mixed results concerning the impact of pharmacological treatment for anxiety on drinking outcomes, with some studies finding improvements in SUD outcomes and others finding more equivocal results (Kushner et al., 2000; Sabourin & Stewart, 2007). Randall et al. (2001a) found that treating individuals with comorbid AUD and social phobia with a selective serotonin reuptake inhibitor (SSRI; paroxetine) led to improvements in anxiety symptoms and a global index of severity of alcohol (i.e., Clinical Global Index). Conversely, paroxetine did not decrease drinking quantity and frequency (Randall et al., 2001a). Two studies have found that successful treatment of anxiety symptoms with buspirone also results in reduced alcohol use (i.e., Kranzler et al., 1994; Tollefson, Montague-Clouse, & Tollefson, 1992). In sum, there is some evidence that the successful pharmacological treatment of anxiety in comorbid individuals can lead to reductions in problematic alcohol use, consistent with the self-medication hypothesis (see Figure 6.1B) or the mutual maintenance model (see Figure 6.2), but the Randall et al. (2001a) findings indicate that there is more to the maintenance of problematic drinking in anxiety patients than simply self-medication (see Sabourin & Stewart, 2007).

It is also important to caution that using this form of study to examine the mechanisms to account for comorbidity has some inherent limitations. Specifically, it assumes that treatment for anxiety targets only the anxiety symptoms and that treatment for SUD targets only the SUD symptoms. But as Mackie et al. (2012) have noted, each therapy might contain some generic treatment components that could broadly impact on a variety of symptoms and problems. For example, an intervention designed to target SUD in comorbid anxious–SUD patients might be shown to have an impact on anxiety, but this effect might be achieved independent of any effect on substance use behavior. Thus, it is always important to consider the nature of the treatment modality in question and whether it might contain some generic treatment components that could account for change in symptoms of the comorbid disorder.

A small number of randomized controlled studies have been conducted assessing the additional benefit of treatments for an anxiety disorder over and above the benefits of treatment of the SUD in comorbid patients. These studies typically evaluate treatment outcome both in terms of benefits for the anxiety disorder and benefits for the SUD. Unfortunately, it is difficult to draw firm conclusions from the literature to date since the findings are mixed. We look at three sample trials to give a flavor for this emerging literature and then turn to the results of a meta-analysis (Hobbs, Kushner, Lee, Reardon, & Maurer, 2011) that helps us draw firmer conclusions from the extant treatment literature.

Kushner et al. (2006) compared two groups of patients with a comorbid diagnosis of panic disorder who were admitted for treatment of an AUD. The combined treatment group received 12 sessions of treatment for their panic disorder, in addition to alcohol-focused treatment. Their cognitive behavioral panic treatment consisted of psychoeducation, cue exposure, and cognitive restructuring. This combined treatment can be considered an "integrated" treatment for panic and alcohol dependence because it was specifically designed to address the interrelations between anxiety and alcohol use (Stewart & O'Connor, 2009). The control group received only an alcohol-focused treatment as usual. The combined treatment group was more effective than the treatment as usual control at 4-month follow-up on several outcome measures including diagnoses of panic disorder and alcohol dependence, number of heavy drinking episodes, total drinks, and severity of alcohol relapse (Kushner et al., 2006).

A randomized controlled trial by Schade et al. (2005) compared standard alcohol treatment alone to standard alcohol treatment with anxiety treatment among patients with a primary diagnosis of alcohol dependence and a comorbid diagnosis of social phobia, panic disorder, or agoraphobia. The anxiety treatment in the combined group consisted of anxiety-focused cognitive behavioral therapy (CBT) plus optional fluvoxamine (an SSRI). At a 32-week follow-up, the combined group showed improvements relative to the control group on anxiety outcomes. There were no differences between groups, however, in terms of alcohol outcomes. Sabourin and Stewart (2007) suggested that the improved anxiety outcomes might be important in the longer term by possibly serving as a protective factor for alcohol relapse in the combined treatment group. However, this possibility remains speculative in that the study did not examine longer term outcomes.

Another randomized controlled trial by Randall, Thomas, and Thevos (2001*b*) involved patients with comorbid social phobia and alcohol dependence who were randomized to one of two 12-week treatments: a combined cognitive behavioral treatment for the alcohol disorder (coping with urges to drink, drink refusal skills, problem solving) simultaneous with cognitive behavioral treatment for social phobia (relaxation training, discussion of social anxiety triggers, creation of anxiety hierarchy, graduated exposure exercises), or cognitive behavioral treatment for the alcohol disorder alone. In the combined treatment, established treatment protocols for each disorder were delivered at the same time, by the same therapist, and within the same treatment session—a "parallel" treatment approach. Contrary to expectations, both groups performed equally well on the social anxiety outcomes (both showing modest improvements). Moreover, the combined treatment unexpectedly resulted in increases in alcohol use relative to the alcohol-only treatment group. The authors suggested that the encouragement of exposure to feared social situations in the combined treatment may have led to increases in coping drinking (Randall et al., 2001*b*). Alternatively, Conrod and Stewart (2005) suggested that the parallel treatment approach used by Randall and colleagues may

have been to blame because it can be quite demanding for patients with complex problems to have to simultaneously undergo two distinct treatments. In contrast, integrated approaches such as that used by Kushner et al. (2006) can be employed more efficiently. Zahradnik and Stewart (2008) have further suggested that integrated treatments, but not parallel treatments, directly address the functional interrelations between the anxiety disorder and SUD symptoms. However, no studies to date have directly compared parallel versus integrated approaches to the treatment of comorbid anxiety and SUDs to test this speculation.

A meta-analysis by Hobbs et al. (2011) systematically reviewed the effects from the 15 published randomized controlled trials examining the impact of supplementing AUD treatment with a cognitive behavioral or pharmacologic treatment for a co-occurring emotional disorder (anxiety or depression). Although the trials examining co-occurring anxiety and depression were pooled for the main analyses, the authors also reported separate outcomes for the studies focused on anxiety–SUD comorbidity versus those focused on depression–SUD comorbidity. We report their meta-analytic results for anxiety in this section and for depression at the end of the next section of this chapter. Across the six trials that involved treatment of a co-occurring anxiety disorder, a pooled effect size of moderate magnitude (d = .52) was found for anxiety outcomes, and an effect of small magnitude (d = .27) was observed for a composite of alcohol outcomes. Collapsed across studies examining the treatment of co-occurring anxiety versus depression, a few other noteworthy patterns were observed. First, alcohol outcomes effect sizes were greater for some specific outcome domains than others (i.e., effects were larger for harm reduction than abstinence outcomes). Second, effect sizes for emotional disorder, but not alcohol, outcomes were greater for trials employing cognitive behavioral treatment of the emotional disorder than those employing pharmacological intervention. Finally, studies with larger effects on emotional disorder symptoms tended to have greater effects on the alcohol outcomes. The number of studies was not large enough to examine these latter issues separately for the studies focused on the treatment of comorbid anxiety versus depression, however. Overall, this meta-analytic review does support the additional treatment of anxiety disorders as a supplement to alcohol-focused treatment and suggests that one can expect moderate additional benefit to anxiety symptoms and some smaller but not insignificant benefit to alcohol outcomes by employing this dual-focus treatment approach for those with comorbid anxiety–AUDs. Additional reviews of this sort are required to summarize the emerging literature on the optimal treatment of anxiety disorders comorbid with SUDs other than AUD (e.g., benzodiazepine dependence, Otto et al., 1993; nicotine dependence, Zvolensky, Yartz, Gregor, Gonzalez, & Bernstein, 2008).

Another approach to the treatment of comorbid anxiety disorders–SUD is to target common factors thought to underlie both disorders. We conducted a study investigating the clinical utility of such an approach when personality factors were the common factor of interest. Specifically, we began by differentiating substance abusing women on the basis of personality factors that appear to be associated with risk for SUDs and then targeted treatments toward each personality type (Conrod, Pihl, Stewart, & Dongier, 2000a). Included in our list of personality dimensions to be examined was one that focused on fear of anxiety sensations (i.e., anxiety sensitivity) and another that combined introversion, neuroticism, and pessimism (i.e., introversion/hopelessness). These personality dimensions were shown to be statistically distinct from one another and from two other identified personality risk factors for substance abuse (i.e., impulsivity and sensation seeking; Conrod et al., 2000a). Our most exciting findings showed that statistically clustering substance abusing women into subgroups based on these four personality dimensions delineated personality-based subtypes of substance abuse that were associated with distinct patterns of substance dependence and comorbid psychopathology (Conrod et al., 2000a). We discuss the findings for the anxiety sensitive subtype in this section and those for the introverted/hopeless subtype in the next section on the treatment of comorbid depression–SUD. In particular, an anxiety-sensitive subtype demonstrated equivalent rates of alcohol dependence relative to an introverted/hopeless or impulsive/antisocial subtype but demonstrated uniquely elevated rates of anxiolytic dependence and comorbid anxiety-related psychopathology (Conrod et al., 2000a). We further tested the clinical validity of this newly derived typology by examining the differential outcome of brief cognitive behavioral interventions that differentially target each of these personality risk factors (Conrod et al., 2000b). Using a client–treatment matching design, we compared the 6-month outcome of substance abusing women who received an intervention that matched their personality profile to that of women who received an intervention that mismatched their personality profile or to that of women who received a motivational control intervention. Results favored outcome (e.g., greater number of days abstinent, greater reduction in dependence symptoms) for those who received the matched intervention relative to the mismatched and control interventions (Conrod et al., 2000b). Included in this study was an anxiety-sensitive subtype of substance abuser who received brief cognitive behavioral training focusing on skills that are specifically designed to reduce an anxiogenic thinking style and avoidant behavioral style (Conrod et al., 2000b). The finding that interventions that matched the individual's personality risk profile were more successful in facilitating reduction in substance dependence symptoms suggests that this personality factor might be etiologically involved in the maintenance of substance dependence behavior, particularly in women with comorbid anxiety-related psychopathology.

A recent trial by Olthuis, Stewart, Mackinnon, and Watt (2014) extended the use of the anxiety sensitivity matched intervention to a distance delivery format to increase its accessibility. Participants were 80 treatment-seeking, community-recruited middle-aged adults with high anxiety sensitivity. Participants were randomly assigned to either an 8-week telephone-delivered individual cognitive behavioral intervention targeting high anxiety sensitivity or to a waiting list control group. Participants were assessed at pretreatment baseline, immediate post-treatment, and at 1-month follow-up. Participants in the active treatment group showed greater decreases in anxiety sensitivity, anxiety disorder symptoms, coping-with-anxiety drinking motives, and physical and intrapersonal alcohol-related problems than wait list controls (Olthuis et al., 2014; Olthuis, Watt, MacKinnon, & Stewart, 2015). Mediation analyses suggested that the anxiety sensitivity matched intervention works in reducing alcohol-related problems by reducing fear of anxiety sensations, which in turn lessens the need to drink to manage anxiety (Olthuis et al., 2015).

More recently, we explored the role of anxiety sensitivity in earlier stages of the course of addiction by examining the extent to which this personality factor is associated with drinking and drug use behavior, substance problems, and risky motives for use in adolescents and young adults and whether it is a useful target for preventative interventions. Some general findings have resulted from such investigation. First, anxiety sensitivity can be reliably measured in young adults and adolescents and well discriminated from other personality risk factors for substance abuse, such as introversion/hopelessness (discussed later), impulsivity, and sensation seeking (Woicik, Conrod, Stewart, & Pihl, 2009). Second, anxiety sensitivity is associated with elevated substance use problems in young adulthood, although it is not reliably associated with increased substance use (Krank, Stewart, O'Connor, Woicik, Wall, & Conrod, 2011; Mackie et al., 2011; Woicik et al., 2009). Third, anxiety sensitivity has been uniquely associated with self-report reasons for alcohol use that reflected a desire to reduce negative emotional states and to reduce peer pressure (i.e., coping and conformity drinking motives, respectively; Woicik et al., 2009). Finally, targeting catastrophic thinking and anxiety sensitivity in youth at risk concurrently prevents onset of alcohol misuse, panic symptoms, and school avoidance in young adolescents (Castellanos & Conrod, 2006; O'Leary-Barrett, Mackie, Castellanos-Ryan, Al-Khudhairy, & Conrod, 2010), and reduces conformity drinking, relief alcohol outcome expectancies, and alcohol problems in young adults (Watt, Stewart, Birch, & Bernier, 2006). These prevention findings are consistent with a third-variable interpretation of the comorbidity of anxiety disorders with SUDs. However, they are also consistent with the possibility that anxiety sensitivity predisposes to anxiety psychopathology, which in turn increases risk for self-medication with various substances.

Treatment Considerations for Depression–SUD Comorbidity

A number of lines of investigation suggest that there are possible functional relations between depression and SUDs that deserve special clinical attention in treatment. For example, studies exploring the use of antidepressant medication in the treatment of alcohol dependence suggest that alcohol dependence in the absence of a comorbid mood disorder cannot be treated using antidepressant medication; however, in comorbid cases, antidepressant medication (compared to placebo) is associated with a reduction in depressive symptomatology that is accompanied by greater reductions in alcohol consumption and longer periods of abstinence (e.g., Cornelius et al., 1997; Mason, Kocsis, Ritvo, & Cutler, 1996). The results from these studies suggest that different treatment strategies are required for alcohol dependence that co-occurs with different patterns of psychopathology. These results hint at the possibility that alcohol dependence that

co-occurs with depression may be sustained by the depressive disorder or at least be mediated by etiologic mechanisms that differ from those involved in primary alcohol dependence.

Several well-controlled randomized trials focusing on the effects of dual psychosocial treatments show that concurrent treatment for depression is superior to traditional treatment for addiction in patients with concurrent depression and SUDs. One study with alcohol-dependent patients with elevated depressive symptom profiles showed that adding an eight-session CBT for depression (CBT-D) relative to adding a relaxation training control to their attendance at a partial-day hospitalization program for alcohol dependence was associated with more enhanced and sustained recovery from depressive symptoms, as well as with greater reductions in drinking (Brown et al., 1997). Similarly, a reanalysis of a randomized controlled trial of CBT and desipramine for cocaine-dependent individuals showed that in those patients with elevated levels of depression, CBT was associated with longer periods of abstinence and improved treatment retention (Carroll, Nich, & Rounsaville, 1995). A third study showed that CBT that included mood management strategies was significantly more effective than a 12-step treatment approach for cocaine-dependent patients with a history of major depression (Maude-Griffin et al., 1998). This is consistent with the notion that the depressive symptoms are maintaining the substance use in comorbid cases. Together, these findings suggest that depressive symptoms might play at least a partial causal role in substance-related behavior in these comorbid patients (see review by Mackie et al., 2012). They also provide clear suggestions regarding relatively more effective treatments for this form of comorbidity.

As mentioned in the previous section, a meta-analysis by Hobbs et al. (2011) systematically reviewed available published randomized controlled trials examining the impact of supplementing AUD treatment with a pharmacological or cognitive behavioral treatment for co-occurring depression. Across the nine trials that involved treatment of a co-occurring depressive disorder, a pooled effect size of $d = .21$ was found for depression outcomes, and a pooled effect size of $d = .17$ was observed for the alcohol outcome composite. Both of these effects were relatively small in magnitude but not inconsequential. The authors noted that the effect sizes of supplementary emotion disorder-focused treatment was significantly larger for those studies involving comorbid anxiety disorders (reviewed in an earlier section of this chapter) than for those involving comorbid depression in the case of emotional disorder outcomes (Hobbs et al., 2011). In the case of the alcohol outcome composite, supplementary depression-focused and supplementary anxiety-focused treatment performed similarly well. Overall, this meta-analytic review supports the additional treatment of depressive disorders as a supplement to alcohol-focused treatment and suggests that one can expect modest additional benefits to both depressive symptoms and alcohol outcomes for those with concurrent depression–AUD. Additional research is needed to understand why supplementary anxiety treatment yields larger effects than does supplementary depression treatment in terms of impacts on emotional disorder symptoms.

Studies examining alcoholism typologies further suggest that unique personality and symptom profiles are associated with an alcoholic subtype that co-occurs with primary depression—findings that may have important implications for treatment of this form of comorbidity. For example, Epstein, Ginsberg, Hesselbrock, and Schwarz (1994) demonstrated that a primary depressed subtype of alcoholic presents a unidimensional typology that differs from nondepressed and secondarily depressed subtypes on personality measures such as low harm avoidance, low gregariousness, histrionic traits, neurotic depression, and trait anxiety. A similar pattern of findings was reported by Martin and Sher (1994) who investigated the utility of the five-factor model of personality with respect characterizing alcoholic subtypes on the basis of comorbidity. Along with support for the roles of antisocial traits and anxiety in alcoholism, they found that alcoholism comorbid with mood disorders was associated with higher levels of neuroticism and introversion, and the latter characteristic was not implicated in the alcoholic subtype that co-occurred with anxiety disorders.

Our previously mentioned personality-matched treatment for SUDs comorbid with various mental health problems, such as anxiety and depressive disorders (Conrod et al., 2000b), was inspired by these previous findings of personality differences between alcoholic subtypes (Epstein et al., 1994; Martin & Sher, 1994). As mentioned earlier in the anxiety comorbidity treatment considerations section, one of the four distinct personality risk factors we identified combined introversion, neuroticism, and pessimism, and we referred to this as the "introversion/hopelessness" profile (Conrod et al., 2000a). Our results showed that the introverted/hopeless subtype of substance abuser demonstrated equivalent rates of alcohol dependence relative to an anxiety-sensitive or impulsive/antisocial subtype but demonstrated uniquely elevated rates of opioid dependence and comorbid depressive psychopathology (Conrod et al., 2000a). Included in the treatment matching portion of this study (Conrod et al., 2000b) was a treatment for the introverted/hopeless subtype of substance abuser that involved brief cognitive behavioral training focusing on skills that were specifically designed to reduce their depressogenic thinking style. The finding that interventions that matched the individual's personality risk profile were more successful in facilitating reduction in substance dependence symptoms (Conrod et al., 2000b) suggests that this personality factor might be involved in the etiology and/or maintenance of substance dependence behavior, particularly a form that co-occurs with depressive disorders.

More recently, the role of introversion/hopelessness in drinking and drug use behavior in adolescents and young adults has been investigated (e.g., Conrod, Stewart, Comeau, & Maclean, 2006; Mackie et al., 2011; Woicik et al., 2009), and several tentative conclusions can be offered. First, introversion/hopelessness can be reliably measured in adolescents and young adults and can be discriminated well from other personality risk factors for substance abuse, such as anxiety sensitivity (discussed earlier), impulsivity, and sensation seeking (Woicik et al., 2009). Second, introversion/hopelessness is associated with elevated substance use and more problematic use in young adulthood (Krank et al., 2011; Mackie et al., 2011; Woicik et al., 2009). Third, once scales were developed to assess the extent to which an individual uses alcohol to cope with depressive symptoms (Grant, Stewart, O'Connor, Blackwell, & Conrod, 2007), introversion/hopelessness was uniquely associated with self-report reasons for alcohol use that reflected a desire to reduce depressive symptoms and "numb pain" (Woicik et al., 2009). Other personality risk factors for substance use were shown to be related to different problematic motives for alcohol use, but coping with depressive symptoms was not among their self-reported reasons for drinking.

Finally, targeting negative thinking and hopelessness in youth at risk has been shown to concurrently prevent onset of both alcohol misuse and depression symptoms in young adolescents (Castellanos & Conrod, 2006; O'Leary-Barrett et al., 2010). Again, these prevention findings are consistent with a third-variable interpretation of the comorbidity of depression and SUDs. However, they may also be consistent with the possibility that introversion/hopelessness increases the risk for depressive disorders, which in turn increases risk for self-medication with substances and leads to an eventual SUD. These prevention findings are extremely encouraging because they show that there are ways to intervene early, before high-risk individuals become caught in the vicious cycle of emotional disorder symptoms fueling substance misuse and vice versa (see also review by O'Leary-Barrett, 2014).

Future Directions in the Study of Emotional Disorder–SUD Comorbidity

In this concluding section, we briefly explore some promising future directions for research in this area that may serve to move the field forward. We consider anxiety and depression together in this section.

As a new round of epidemiological studies is likely to be conducted following the recent release of the DSM-5, we have several suggestions for future comorbidity prevalence studies using the revised diagnostic criteria in the DSM-5. First, studies should examine comorbidity of specific anxiety and mood disorders with specific drugs of abuse (anxiolytics/sedatives vs. stimulants vs. hallucinogens vs. analgesics) as was done for the ECA (Regier et al., 1990). This type of design, when combined with examination of order of onset, would allow for testing of the hypotheses that stimulant use disorders contribute to the development of anxiety disorders, whereas anxiolytic/sedative and analgesic use disorders arise from attempts to self-medicate for anxiety disorders and depressive disorders, respectively (Conrod et al., 2000a).

Second, given that the distinction between substance abuse and dependence has been abolished in the DSM-5 (APA, 2013), it remains for future research to determine whether the association of anxiety disorders and depressive disorders with SUDs is stronger in the case of severe than mild SUDs—the terminology used in the DSM-5 to distinguish between SUD severity levels (see Straussner, 2013). Third, given the change in classification of OCD and PTSD in the DSM-5, as outlined earlier (i.e., no longer considered part of the anxiety disorders category), it would be interesting for a quantitative review to determine to what degree the SUD comorbidity patterns are similar or different for OCD and/or PTSD compared to those seen for the disorders retained as anxiety disorders

in the DSM-5. This would be helpful information for determining whether this change in categorization for OCD and PTSD is appropriate because comorbidity patterns are often considered a useful piece of evidence in determining whether disorders are similar (or distinct) enough to be placed in the same (or different) diagnostic categories.

Another area of future research interest is the recent addition of gambling disorder to the same diagnostic category as the SUDs in the DSM-5 (see Straussner, 2013), with both being considered addictive disorders (APA, 2013). The justification for this shift in diagnostic categorization is that accumulating evidence suggests substantial similarities between gambling disorder and SUDs in such aspects as clinical expression, underlying neural mechanisms, treatment, and comorbidity patterns (APA, 2013). In terms of patterns of comorbidity, there certainly do seem to be similarities in the patterns of anxiety disorder and depressive disorder comorbidity for both gambling disorder and the SUDs (Abdollahnejad, Delfabbro, & Denson, 2014; el-Guebaly et al., 2006; Lorains, Cowlishaw, & Thomas, 2011; Petry, Stinson, & Grant, 2005). Although it is clear that anxiety disorders and depressive disorders are highly comorbid with gambling disorder, it remains to be determined whether the underlying mechanisms to explain this comorbidity are similar to or distinct from those explored in this chapter to explain emotional disorder–SUD comorbidity.

Additionally, given distinctions made between fear- and distress-based emotional disorders (Watson, 2005), future epidemiologic studies examining relative order of onset specifically could test the working hypothesis suggested earlier that fear-based disorders are more likely to precede SUDs, whereas distress-based disorders are more likely to follow SUDs. Finally, future epidemiologic studies should also examine the relative order of emergence of key symptoms of each disorder (e.g., panic attacks in the case of panic disorder) rather than requiring that an individual meet full syndromal criteria. This would allow for examination of the idea that self-medication with alcohol/drugs may emerge in response to early symptoms of a given emotional disorder rather than in response to the full syndrome. Similarly, it would allow for examination of the possibility that anxiety or depressive disorders may develop in response to heavy substance use even prior to emergence of the serious negative consequences of substance use required for an SUD diagnosis.

There is also room for considerable additional work in the area of self-reported motives for use. Although there are numerous studies on the relations of motives for substance use to various risk characteristics for SUDs (e.g., anxiety sensitivity and introversion/hopelessness; Woicik et al., 2009) in young nonclinical samples, we need more studies that directly query comorbid patients on the reasons for their substance misuse. There are various methodologies that could be used here, such as self-report questionnaires like Cooper's (1994) Drinking Motives Questionnaire–Revised or a recent modification that separates drinking to cope with anxiety from drinking to cope with depression (Grant, Stewart, et al., 2007). To the degree that these questionnaires might not tap all domains of motives for use experienced by clinical cases, qualitative interviews could be very useful for exploring comorbid individuals' self-perceived reasons for alcohol and substance misuse. Studies that examine the degree to which comorbid anxiety disorder–SUD and depression–SUD individuals perceive the symptoms of their two disorders to be interrelated would also be helpful (see Brown et al., 1996, for sample study in the PTSD–SUD comorbidity area). Of course, this class of study is limited by virtue of the underlying assumption that comorbid individuals are aware of the reasons for their substance use and can accurately report on their motivational states.

We also need more research on the possible reciprocal relations of emotional disorder symptoms with SUD symptoms over time and at various stages of development. Such studies could evaluate more fully the model presented in Figure 6.2, which suggests that once the symptoms of both disorders (emotional and SUD) are established, they may mutually maintain one another or even exacerbate one another over time. Cross-lagged analyses (e.g., Marshall, Miles, & Stewart, 2010) could be applied to longitudinal datasets to examine this issue in more depth.

In future, genetic epidemiology studies need to more adequately parse out anxiety and depression to allow for more conclusive comparisons between the genetic contributions to depression–SUD comorbidity versus anxiety–SUD comorbidity. Candidate gene studies should go beyond simple tests for the additive effects of simple, relatively common genetic variants in terms of possible third-variable contributions to comorbid emotional disorders and SUDs (Kendler, 2005).

We have several suggestions for future experimental studies on the mechanisms underlying emotional disorder–SUD comorbidity. For research designed to test the hypothesis that substances of abuse reduce anxiety states, we recommend that future studies compare anxiety disorder patients or at-risk samples (e.g., high anxiety sensitivity, high trait social anxiety) to controls, examine gender as a possible moderator, employ stressors most relevant to the anxiety disorder/characteristic in question, use ecologically valid substance doses (Donohue et al., 2007), examine the anxiety response on multiple domains (i.e., not just self-report) and at multiple time points, and specifically manipulate or measure expectancy effects. Such methodological improvements would help us better understand under what circumstances and for whom alcohol and other drugs dampen the anxiety response. For research designed to test whether anxiety motivates substance misuse, in addition to relevant recommendations just given, we also suggest that future studies include a manipulation check to ensure that the anxiety induction technique is effective, measure substance intake unobtrusively (e.g., the "taste rating task"; Marlatt, Demming, & Reid, 1973) to avoid reactivity, and assess cravings and behavioral intentions whenever assessing substance intake is difficult or impossible. Such methodological improvements would help us better understand under what circumstances and for whom the experience of anxiety causes increases in substance ingestion.

In terms of directions for experimental research on the mechanisms underlying depression–SUD comorbidity, lab-based studies are needed to examine whether depressed mood can trigger substance craving or increase substance intake, particularly among depressed or depression-prone individuals. Lab-based mood induction methods, such as the musical mood induction procedure, could be used in such studies. We also require studies that directly assess the effects of substances of abuse on depressed individuals' (or those at risk) responses to stress to determine if they are more prone than others to substance-induced dampening of their HPA stress reactivity. Moreover, there are a rich set of experimental procedures (including physiological and cognitive paradigms) that could be used in future experimental work to better identify the mechanisms underlying self-medication for depression with various substances of abuse. Such work would be enormously helpful in advancing this area.

Finally, in terms of future directions in treatment, it will be important to conduct trials to directly compare parallel to integrated treatment approaches for assisting those with comorbid emotional disorders–SUDs. This would allow for a direct test of the possibility that parallel approaches may be too demanding for these often complex cases and that integrated treatments that provide a single treatment that addresses the interrelations between symptoms of the two disorders may be preferable in terms of both short- and longer term impacts on symptoms of both disorders. And although the results of the Hobbs et al. (2011) meta-analysis are encouraging in suggesting that patients with comorbid emotional disorders–AUDs should be provided with combined treatment rather than treatment focused on the AUD alone, we do not yet know if these results can be extended to the treatment of comorbid emotional disorders–SUDs more generally. Thus, the extant treatment literature in the DUD area should be subject to a meta-analysis like that provided within the AUD area by Hobbs et al. (2011). Finally, knowledge translation research is required to find ways to ensure that these findings regarding the most effective interventions for treating or even preventing emotional disorder–SUD comorbidity have appropriate uptake in the clinical practice context.

References

Abrams, K., Kushner, M., Medina, K. L., & Voight, A. (2001). The pharmacologic and expectancy effects of alcohol on social anxiety in individuals with social phobia. *Drug and Alcohol Dependence*, 64, 219–231.

Abrams, K., Kushner, M. G., Medina, K. L., & Voight, A. (2002). Self-administration of alcohol before and after a public speaking challenge by individuals with social phobia. *Psychology of Addictive Behaviors*, 16, 121–128.

Abdollahnejad, M. R., Delfabbro, P., & Denson, L. (2014). The clustering of psychiatric disorders in high-risk gambling populations. *Journal of Gambling Studies*, 30, 933–947.

Agosti, V., Nunes, E., & Levin, F. (2002). Rates of psychiatric comorbidity among U.S. residents with lifetime cannabis dependence. *American Journal of Drug and Alcohol Abuse*, 28, 643–652.

Alexander, B. K., & Hadaway, P. E. (1982). Opiate addiction: The case for an adaptive orientation. *Psychological Bulletin*, 92, 367–381.

American Psychiatric Association. (1980). *Diagnostic and statistical manual of mental disorders* (3rd ed.). Washington, DC: American Psychiatric Association.

American Psychiatric Association. (1987). *Diagnostic and statistical manual of mental disorders* (3rd ed., rev.). Washington, DC: American Psychiatric Association.

American Psychiatric Association. (1994). *Diagnostic and statistical manual of mental disorders* (4th ed.). Washington, DC: American Psychiatric Association.

American Psychiatric Association. (2013). *Diagnostic and statistical manual of mental disorders* (5th ed.). Washington, DC: American Psychiatric Association.

Aramakis, V. B., Khamba, B. K., Macleod, C. M., Poulos, C. X., & Zack, M. (2012). Alcohol selectively impairs negative self-relevant associations in young drinkers. *Journal of Psychopharmacology*, 26, 221–231.

Battista, S. R., MacDonald, D., & Stewart, S. H. (2012). The effects of alcohol on safety behaviors in socially anxious individuals. *Journal of Social and Clinical Psychology*, 31, 1074–1094.

Battista, S. R., Pencer, A., & Stewart, S. H. (2014). Drinking and thinking: Alcohol effects on post-event processing in socially anxious individuals. *Cognitive Therapy and Research*, 38, 33–42.

Battista, S. R., Stewart, S. H., & Ham, L. S. (2010). A critical review of laboratory-based studies examining the relationships of social anxiety and alcohol intake. *Current Drug Abuse Reviews*, 3, 3–22.

Berkson, J. (1946). Limitations of the application of fourfold table analysis to hospital data. *Biometrics Bulletin*, 2, 47–53.

Birch, C. D., Stewart, S. H., Girling, A. N., & Berish, M. J. (2006). The impact of mood, drinking motives, and gender on laboratory alcohol consumption. In A. V. Clark (Ed.), *Psychology of moods* (pp. 1–36). Hauppauge, NY: Nova Science.

Bolton, J., Cox, B., Clara, I., & Sareen, J. (2006). Use of alcohol and drugs to self- medicate anxiety disorders in a nationally representative sample. *Journal of Nervous and Mental Disease*, 194, 818–825.

Bovasso, G. B. (2001). Cannabis abuse as a risk factor for depressive symptoms. *American Journal of Psychiatry*, 158, 2033–2037.

Breslau, N., Kilbey, M., & Andreski, P. (1991). Nicotine dependence, major depression, and anxiety in young adults. *Archives of General Psychiatry*, 48, 1069–1074.

Brown, C. G., & Stewart, S. H. (2008). Exploring perceptions of alcohol use as self-medication for depression among women receiving community-based treatment for alcohol problems. *Journal of Prevention and Intervention in the Community*, 35, 33–47.

Brown, P. J., Stout, R. L., & Mueller, T. (1996). Posttraumatic stress disorder and substance abuse relapse among women: A pilot study. *Psychology of Addictive Behaviors*, 10, 124–128.

Brown, R. A., Evans, D. M., Miller, I. W., Burgess, E. S., & Mueller, T. I. (1997). Cognitive-behavioural treatment for depression in alcoholism. *Journal of Consulting and Clinical Psychology*, 65, 715–726.

Brown, S. A., Inaba, R. K., Gillin, J. C., Schuckit, M. A., Stewart, M. A., & Irwin, M. R. (1995). Alcoholism and affective disorder: Clinical course of depressive symptoms. *American Journal of Psychiatry*, 152, 45–52.

Buckner, J. D., Heimberg, R. G., Ecker, A. H., & Vinci, C. (2013). A biopsychosocial model of social anxiety and substance use. *Depression and Anxiety*, 30, 276–284.

Buckner, J. D., Schmidt, N. B., Lang, A. R., Small, J. W., Schlauch, R. C., & Lewinsohn, P. M. (2008). Specificity of social anxiety disorder as a risk factor for alcohol and cannabis dependence. *Journal of Psychiatric Research*, 42, 230–239.

Buckner, J. D., Silgado, J., & Schmidt, N. B. (2011). Marijuana craving during a public speaking challenge: Understanding marijuana use vulnerability among women and those with social anxiety disorder. *Journal of Behavior Therapy and Experimental Psychiatry*, 42, 104–110.

Burns, L., Teesson, M., & O'Neill, K. (2005). The impact of comorbid anxiety and depression on alcohol treatment outcomes. *Addiction*, 100, 787–796.

Carroll, K. M., Nich, C., & Rounsaville, B. J. (1995). Differential symptom reduction in depressed cocaine abusers treated with psychotherapy and pharmacotherapy. *Journal of Nervous and Mental Disease, 183*, 251–259.

Castellanos, N., & Conrod, P. J. (2006). Efficacy of brief personality-targeted cognitive behavioural interventions in reducing and preventing adolescent emotional and behavioural problems. *Journal of Mental Health, 15*, 1–14.

Cerdá, M., Sagdeo, A., Johnson, J., & Galea, S. (2010). Genetic and environmental influences on psychiatric comorbidity: A systematic review. *Journal of Affective Disorders, 126*, 14–38.

Chilcoat, H. D., & Breslau N. (1998). Investigations of causal pathways between PTSD and drug use disorders. *Addictive Behaviors, 23*, 827–840.

Cloninger, C. R. (1987). Neurogenetic adaptive mechanisms in alcoholism. *Science, 236*, 410–416.

Conrod, P. J., Pihl, R. O., Stewart, S. H., & Dongier, M. (2000*a*). Validation of a system of classifying female substance abusers based on personality and motivational risk factors for substance abuse. *Psychology of Addictive Behaviors, 14*, 243–256.

Conrod, P. J., Pihl, R. O., & Vassileva, J. (1998). Differential sensitivity to alcohol reinforcement in groups of men at risk for distinct alcoholism subtypes. *Alcoholism: Clinical and Experimental Research, 22*, 585–597.

Conrod, P. J., & Stewart, S. H. (2005). A critical look at dual focused cognitive-behavioral treatment for comorbid substance abuse and psychiatric disorders: Strengths, limitations and future directions. *Journal of Cognitive Psychotherapy, 19*, 265–289.

Conrod, P. J., Stewart, S. H., Comeau, M. N., & Maclean, M. (2006). Efficacy of cognitive behavioral interventions targeting personality risk factors for youth alcohol misuse. *Journal of Clinical Child and Adolescent Psychology, 35*, 550–563.

Conrod, P. J., Stewart, S. H., Pihl, R. O., Côté, S., Fontaine, V., & Dongier, M. (2000*b*). Efficacy of brief coping skills interventions that match different personality profiles of female substance abusers. *Psychology of Addictive Behaviors, 14*, 231–242.

Cooper, M. L. (1994). Motivations for alcohol use among adolescents: Development and validation of a four-factor model. *Psychological Assessment, 6*, 117–128.

Cornelius, J. R., Salloum, I. M., Ehler, J. G., Jarrett, P. J., Cornelius, M. D., Perel, J. M., et al. (1997). Fluoxetine in depressed alcoholics: A double-blind, placebo-controlled trial. *Archives of General Psychiatry, 54*, 700–705.

Corvin, A., Craddock, N., & Sullivan, P. F. (2010). Genome-wide association studies: A primer. *Psychological Medicine, 40*, 1063–1077.

Costello, E. J., Mustillo, S., Erkanli, A., Keeler, G., & Angold, A. (2003). Prevalence and development of psychiatric disorders in childhood and adolescence. *Archives of General Psychiatry, 60*, 837–844.

Covey, L. S., Hughes, D. C., Glassman, A. H., Blazer, D. G., & George, L. K. (1994). Ever-smoking, quitting, and psychiatric disorders: Evidence from the Durham, North Carolina, Epidemiologic Catchment Area. *Tobacco Control, 3*, 222–227.

Crum, R. M., & Pratt, L. A. (2001). Risk of heavy drinking and alcohol use disorders in social phobia: A prospective analysis. *American Journal of Psychiatry, 158*, 1693–1700.

Crum, R. M., Storr, C. L., Chan, Y. -F. (2005). Depression syndromes with risk of alcohol dependence in adulthood: A latent class analysis. *Drug and Alcohol Dependence, 79*, 71–81.

Currie, S. R., Patten, S. B., Williams, J. V. A., Wang, J., Beck, C. A., El-Guebaly, N., & Maxwell, C. (2005). Comorbidity of major depression with substance use disorders. *Canadian Journal of Psychiatry, 50*, 660–666.

Dansky, B. S., Brady, K. T., & Saladin, M. E. (1998). Untreated symptoms of PTSD among cocaine-dependent individuals: Changes over time. *Journal of Substance Abuse Treatment, 15*, 499–504.

De Boer, M. C., Schippers, G. M., & van der Staak, C. O. (1993). Alcohol and social anxiety in women and men: Pharmacology and expectancy. *Addictive Behaviors, 18*, 117–126.

Degenhardt, L., Hall, W., & Lynskey, M. (2001). The relationship between cannabis use, depression and anxiety among Australian adults: Findings from the National Survey of Mental Health and Well-Being. *Social Psychiatry and Psychiatric Epidemiology, 36*, 219–227.

Donohue, K. F., Curtin, J. J., Patrick, C. J., & Lang, A. R. (2007). Intoxication level and emotional response. *Emotion, 7*, 103–112.

el-Guebaly, N., Patten, S. B., Currie, S., Williams, J. V. A., Beck, C. A., Maxwell, C. J., & Wang, J. L. (2006). Epidemiological associations between gambling behavior, substance use and mood and anxiety disorders. *Journal of Gambling Studies, 22*, 275–287.

Epstein, E. E., Ginsburg, B. E., Hesselbrock, V. M., & Schwarz, J. C. (1994). Alcohol and drug abusers subtyped by antisocial personality and primary or secondary depressive disorders. *Annals of the New York Academy of Sciences, 108*, 187–201.

Fergusson, D. M., Boden, J. M., & Horwood, L. J. (2009). Tests of causal links between alcohol abuse or dependence and major depression. *Archives of General Psychiatry, 66*, 260–266.

Gerlach, A. L., Schiller, A., Wild, C., & Rist, F. (2006). Effects of alcohol on the processing of social threat-related stimuli in socially phobic women. *British Journal of Clinical Psychology, 45*, 279–295.

Gilman, S. E., & Abraham, H. D. (2001). A longitudinal study of the order of onset of alcohol dependence and major depression. *Drug and Alcohol Dependence, 63*, 277–286.

Glenn, S. W., & Parsons, O. A. (1991). Prediction of resumption of drinking in posttreatment alcoholics. *International Journal of Addictions, 26*, 237–254.

Grant, B. F. (1995). Comorbidity between DSM-IV drug use disorders and major depression: Results of a national survey of adults. *Journal of Substance Abuse, 7*, 481–497.

Grant, B. F., Compton, W. M., Crowley, T. J., Hasin, D. S., Helzer, J. E., Li, T. -K., . . . Woody, G. E. (2007). Errors in assessing *DSM-IV* substance use disorders. *Archives of General Psychiatry, 64*, 379–380.

Grant, B. F., Goldstein, R. B., Chou, S. P., Huang, B., Stinson, F. S., Dawson, D. A., . . . Compton, W. M. (2009). Sociodemographic and psychopathologic predictors of first incidence of DSM-IV substance use, mood and anxiety disorders: Results from the Wave 2 National Epidemiologic Survey on Alcohol and Related Conditions. *Molecular Psychiatry, 14*, 1051–1066.

Grant, B. F., & Harford, T. C. (1995). Comorbidity between DSM-IV alcohol use disorders and depression: Results of a national survey. *Drug and Alcohol Dependence, 39*, 197–206.

Grant, B. F., Hasin, D. S., & Dawson, D. A. (1996). The relationship between DSM-IV alcohol use disorders and DSM-IV major depression: Examination of the primary-secondary distinction in a general population sample. *Journal of Affective Disorders, 38,* 113–128.

Grant, B. F., Stinson, F. S., Dawson, D. A., Chou, P., Dufour, M. C., Compton, W., ... Kaplan, K. (2004). Prevalence and co-occurrence of substance use disorders and independent mood and anxiety disorders: Results from the National Epidemiologic Survey on Alcohol and Related Conditions. *Archives of General Psychiatry, 61,* 807–816.

Grant, V. V., Stewart, S. H., O'Connor, R. M., Blackwell, E., & Conrod, P. J. (2007). Psychometric evaluation of the five-factor Modified Drinking Motives Questionnaire—Revised in undergraduates. *Addictive Behaviors, 32,* 2611–2632.

Greeley, J., & Oei, T. (1999). Alcohol and tension reduction. In K. Leonard & H. Blane (Eds.), *Psychological theories of drinking and alcoholism* (2nd ed., pp. 14–53). New York: Guilford.

Greenwald, A. G., McGhee, D. E., & Schwartz, J. K. L. (1998). Measuring individual differences in implicit cognition: The Implicit Association Test. *Journal of Personality and Social Psychology, 74,* 1464–1480.

Hasin, D. S., Goodwin, R. D., Stinson, F. S., & Grant, B. F. (2005). Epidemiology of major depressive disorder. *Archives of General Psychiatry, 62,* 1097–1106.

Hasin, D. S., Stinson, F. S., Ogburn, E., & Grant, B. F. (2007). Prevalence, correlates, disability, and comorbidity of DSM-IV alcohol abuse and dependence in the United States. *Archives of General Psychiatry, 64,* 830–842.

Heim, C., Newport, D. J., Heit, S., Graham, Y. P., Wilcox, M., & Bonsall, R., ... Nemeroff, C. B. (2000). Pituitary-adrenal and autonomic responses to stress in women after sexual and physical abuse in childhood. *Journal of the American Medical Association, 284,* 592–597.

Hobbs, J. D. J., Kushner, M. G., Lee, S. S., Reardon, S. M., & Maurer, E. W. (2011). Meta-analysis of supplemental treatment for depressive and anxiety disorders in patients being treated for alcohol dependence. *The American Journal on Addictions, 20,* 319–329.

Hornig, C. D., & McNally, R. J. (1995). Panic disorder and suicide attempt: A reanalysis of data from the Epidemiologic Catchment Area study. *British Journal of Psychiatry, 167,* 76–79.

Huang, B., Dawson, D. A., Stinson, F. A., Hasin, D. S., Ruan, W. J., Saha, T. D., ... Grant, B. F. (2006). Prevalence, correlates, and comorbidity of nonmedical prescription drug use and drug use disorders in the United States: Results of the National Epidemiologic Survey on Alcohol and Related Conditions. *Journal of Clinical Psychiatry, 67,* 1067–1073.

Kendler, K. S. (2005). "A gene for ... ": The nature of gene action in psychiatric disorders. *American Journal of Psychiatry, 162,* 1243–1252.

Kendler, K. S., Heath, A. C., Neale, M. C., Kessler, R. C., & Eaves, L. J. (1993). Alcoholism and major depression in women: A twin study of the causes of comorbidity. *Archives of General Psychiatry, 50,* 690–698.

Kendler, K. S., Prescott, C. A., Myers, J., & Neale, M. C. (2003). The structure of genetic and environmental risk factors for common psychiatric and substance use disorders in men and women. *Archives of General Psychiatry, 60,* 929–937.

Kendler, K. S., Walters, E. E., Neale, M. C., Kessler, R. C., Heath, A. C., & Eaves, L. J. (1995). The structure of the genetic and environmental risk factors for six major

psychiatric disorders: Phobia, generalized anxiety disorders, panic disorder, bulimia, major depression, and alcoholism. *Archives of General Psychiatry, 52,* 374–383.

Kessler, R. C., Berglund, P., Demler, O., Jin, R., Koretz, D., Merikangas, K. R., ... Wang, P. S. (2003). The epidemiology of major depressive disorder: Results from the National Comorbidity Survey Replication (NCS-R). *Journal of the American Medical Association, 289,* 3095–3105.

Kessler, R. C., Chiu, W. T., Demler, O., & Walters, E. E. (2005). Prevalence, severity, and comorbidity of 12-month DSM-IV disorders in the National Comorbidity Survey Replication. *Archives of General Psychiatry, 62,* 617–627.

Kessler, R. C., Chiu, W. T., Jin, R., Ruscio, A. M., Shear, K., & Walters, E. E. (2006). The epidemiology of panic attacks, panic disorder, and agoraphobia in the National Comorbidity Survey Replication. *Archives of General Psychiatry, 63,* 415–424.

Kessler, R. C., Crum, R. M., Warner, L. A., Nelson, C. B., Schulenberg, J., & Anthony, J. C. (1997). Lifetime co-occurrence of DSM-III-R alcohol abuse and dependence with other psychiatric disorders in the National Comorbidity Survey. *Archives of General Psychiatry, 54,* 313–321.

Kessler, R. C., Nelson, C. B., McGonagle, K. A., Edlund, M. J., Frank, R. G., & Leaf, P. J. (1996). The epidemiology of co-occurring addictive and mental disorders: Implications for prevention and service utilization. *American Journal of Orthopsychiatry, 66,* 17–31.

Khantzian, E. J. (1985). The self-medication hypothesis of addictive disorders: Focus on heroin and cocaine dependence. *The American Journal of Psychiatry, 142,* 1259–1264.

Khantzian, E. J. (1997). The self-medication hypothesis of substance use disorders: A reconsideration and recent applications. *Harvard Review of Psychiatry, 4,* 231–244.

Kidorf, M., & Lang, A. R. (1999). Effects of social anxiety and alcohol expectancies on stress-induced drinking. *Psychology of Addictive Behaviors, 13,* 134–142.

Koob, G. F., & Le Moal, M. (2005). Plasticity of reward neurocircuitry and the "dark side" of drug addiction. *Nature Neuroscience, 8,* 1442–1444.

Krank, M. D., Stewart, S. H., O'Connor, R., Woicik, P. B., Wall, A. M., & Conrod, P. J. (2011). Structural, concurrent, and predictive validity of the Substance Use Risk Profile Scale in early adolescence. *Addictive Behaviors, 36,* 37–46.

Kranzler, H. R., Burleson, J. A., Del Boca, F. K., Babor, T. F., Korner, P., Brown, J., et al. (1994). Buspirone treatment of anxious alcoholics: A placebo-controlled trial. *Archives of General Psychiatry, 51,* 720–731.

Kushner, M. G., Abrams, K., & Borchardt, C. (2000). The relationship between anxiety disorders and alcohol use disorders: A review of major perspectives and findings. *Clinical Psychology Review, 20,* 149–171.

Kushner, M. G., Abrams, K., Thuras, P., Hanson, K. L., Brekke, M., & Sletten, S. (2005). Follow-up study of anxiety disorder and alcohol dependence in comorbid alcoholism treatment patients. *Alcoholism: Clinical and Experimental Research, 29,* 1432–1443.

Kushner, M. G., Donahue, C., Sletten, S., Thuras, P., Abrams, K., Peterson, J., et al. (2006). Cognitive-behavioral treatment of co-morbid anxiety disorder in alcoholism treatment patients: Presentation of a prototype program and future directions. *Journal of Mental Health, 15,* 697–707.

Kushner, M. G., Krueger, R., Frye, B., & Peterson, J. (2008). Epidemiological perspectives on co-occurring anxiety disorder and substance use disorder. In S. H. Stewart & P. J. Conrod (Eds.), *Anxiety and substance use disorders: The vicious cycle of comorbidity* (pp. 3–17). New York: Springer.

Kushner, M. G., Mackenzie, T. B., Fiszdon, J., Valentiner, D. P., Foa, E., Anderson, N., & Wangensteen, D. (1996). The effects of alcohol consumption on laboratory-induced panic and state anxiety. *Archives of General Psychiatry, 53,* 264–270.

Kushner, M. G., Sher, K. J., & Beitman, B. D. (1990). The relation between alcohol problems and the anxiety disorders. *The American Journal of Psychiatry, 147,* 685–695.

Kushner, M. G., Sher, K. J., & Erikson, D. J. (1999). Prospective analysis of the relation between DSM-III anxiety disorders and alcohol use disorders. *The American Journal of Psychiatry, 156,* 723–732.

Labounty, L. P., Hatsukami, D., Morgon, S. F., & Nelson, L. (1992). Relapse among alcoholics with phobic and panic symptoms. *Addictive Behaviors, 17,* 9–15.

Lehman, C. L., Brown, T. A., Palfai, T., & Barlow, D. H. (2002). The effects of alcohol outcome expectancy on a carbon-dioxide challenge in patients with panic disorder. *Behavior Therapy, 33,* 447–463.

Lorains, F. K., Cowlishaw, S., & Thomas, S. A. (2011). Prevalence of comorbid disorders in problem and pathological gambling: Systematic review and meta-analysis of population surveys. *Addiction, 106,* 490–498.

MacDonald, A. B., Baker, J. M., Stewart, S. H., & Skinner, M. (2000). Effects of alcohol on the response to hyperventilation of participants high and low in anxiety sensitivity. *Alcoholism: Clinical and Experimental Research, 24,* 1656–1665.

Mackie, C. J., Castellanos-Ryan, N., & Conrod, P. J. (2011). Personality moderates the longitudinal relationship between psychological symptoms and alcohol use in adolescents. *Alcoholism: Clinical and Experimental Research, 35,* 703–716.

Mackie, C. J., Conrod, P. J., & Brady, K. (2012). Depression and substance use. In J. C. Verster, K. Brady, M. Galanter, & P. J. Conrod (Eds.), *Drug abuse and addiction in medical illness: Causes, consequences, and treatment* (pp. 275–284). New York: Springer.

Marlatt, G. A., Demming, B., & Reid, J. B. (1973). Loss of control drinking in alcoholics: An experimental analogue. *Journal of Abnormal Psychology, 81,* 233–241.

Marlatt, G. A., & Rohsenow, D. J. (1980). Cognitive processes in alcohol use: Expectancy and the balanced placebo design. In N. K. Mello (Ed.), *Advances in substance abuse* (Vol. 1, pp. 159–199). Greenwich, CT: JAI Press.

Marmorstein, N. R., Iacono, W. G., & Malone S. M. (2010). Longitudinal associations between depression and substance dependence from adolescence through early adulthood. *Drug and Alcohol Dependence, 107,* 154–160.

Marshall, G. N., Miles, J. N., & Stewart, S. H. (2010). Anxiety sensitivity and PTSD symptom severity are reciprocally related: Evidence from a longitudinal study of physical trauma survivors. *Journal of Abnormal Psychology, 119,* 143–150.

Marquenie, L. A., Schadé, A., van Balkom, A. J., Comijs, H. C., de Graaf, R., Vollebergh, W., . . . , van den Brink, W. (2007). Origin of the comorbidity of anxiety disorders and alcohol dependence: Findings of a general population study. *European Addiction Research, 13,* 39–49.

Martin, E. D., & Sher, K. J. (1994). Family history of alcoholism, alcohol use disorders, and the five factor model of personality. *Journal of Studies on Alcohol, 55,* 81–90.

Mason, B. J., Kocsis, J. H., Ritvo, E. C., & Cutler, R. B. (1996). A double blind placebo-controlled trial of desipramine for primary alcohol dependence stratified on the presence or absence of major depression. *Journal of the American Medical Association, 275,* 761–767.

Maude-Griffin, P. M., Hohenstein, J. M., Humfleet, G. L., Reilly, P. M., Tusel, D. J., & Hall, S. M. (1998). Superior efficacy of cognitive-behavioural therapy for crack cocaine abusers: Main and matching effects. *Journal of Consulting and Clinical Psychology, 66,* 832–837.

McNaughton, N. (2008). The neurobiology of anxiety: Potential for co-morbidity of anxiety and substance use disorders. In S. H. Stewart & P. J. Conrod (Eds.), *Anxiety and substance use disorders: The vicious cycle of comorbidity* (pp. 19–33). New York: Springer.

Merikangas, K. R., Herrell, R., Swendsen, J., Rössler, W., Ajdacic-Gross, V., & Angst, J. (2008). Specificity of bipolar spectrum conditions in the comorbidity of mood and substance use disorders: Results from the Zurich Cohort Study. *Archives of General Psychiatry, 65,* 47–52.

Merikangas, K. R., Stevens, D., & Fenton, B. (1996). Comorbidity of alcoholism and anxiety disorders: The role of family studies. *Alcohol Health and Research World, 20,* 100–105.

Merikangas, K. R., Stevens, D. E., Fenton, B., Stolar, M., O'Malley, S., Woods, S. W., & Risch, N. (1998). Co-morbidity and familial aggregation of alcoholism and anxiety disorders. *Psychological Medicine, 28,* 773–788.

Merikangas, K. R., Li, J. J., Stipelman, B., Yu, K., Fucito, L., Swendsen, J., & Zhang, H. (2009). The familial aggregation of cannabis use disorders. *Addiction, 104,* 622–629.

Morris, E. P., Stewart, S. H., & Ham, L. S. (2005). The relationship between social anxiety disorder and alcohol use disorders: A critical review. *Clinical Psychology Review, 25,* 734–760.

Nelson, E. C., Grant, J. D., Bucholz, K. K., Glowinski, A., Madden, P. A., Reich, W., & Heath, A. C. (2000). Social phobia in a population-based female adolescent twin sample: Co-morbidity and associated suicide-related symptoms. *Psychological Medicine, 30,* 797–804.

Nurnberger, J. I., Jr., Wiegand, R., Bucholz, K., O'Connor, S., Meyer, E. T., Reich, T., . . . Porjesz, B. (2004). A family study of alcohol dependence: Coaggregation of multiple disorders in relatives of alcohol-dependent probands. *Archives of General Psychiatry, 61,* 1246–1256.

O'Leary-Barrett, M. (2014). The internalizing developmental pathway to substance use. In M. Leyton & S. H. Stewart (Eds.), *Substance abuse in Canada: Childhood and adolescent pathways to substance use disorders* (pp. 48–68). Ottawa, ON: Canadian Centre on Substance Abuse.

O'Leary-Barrett, M., Mackie, C. J., Castellanos-Ryan, N., Al-Khudhairy, N., & Conrod, P. J. (2010). Personality-targeted interventions delay uptake of drinking and decrease risk of alcohol-related problems when delivered by teachers. *Journal of the American Academy of Child and Adolescent Psychiatry, 49,* 954–963.

Olthuis, J. V., Stewart, S. H., Mackinnon, S. P., & Watt, M. C. (2014). Telephone-delivered CBT for high anxiety sensitivity: A randomized controlled trial. *Journal of Consulting and Clinical Psychology, 82,* 1005–1022.

Olthuis, J., Watt, M. C., MacKinnon, S. P. & Stewart, S. H. (2015). CBT for high anxiety sensitivity: Alcohol outcomes. *Addictive Behaviors*, *46*, 19–24.

O'Sullivan, K., Whillans, P., Daly, M., Carroll, B., Clare, A., & Cooney, J. (1983). A comparison of alcoholics with and without co-existing affective disorder. *British Journal of Psychiatry*, *143*, 133–138.

Otto, M. W., Pollack, M. H., Sachs, G. S., Reiter, S. R., Melzer-Brody, S., & Rosenbaum, J. F. (1993). Discontinuation of benzodiazepine treatment: Efficacy of a cognitive-behavior therapy for patients with panic disorder. *American Journal of Psychiatry*, *150*, 1485–1490.

Ouimette, P. C., Ahrens, C., Moos, R. H., & Finney, J. W. (1997). Posttraumatic stress disorder in substance abuse patients: Relationships to one-year posttreatment outcomes. *Psychology of Addictive Behaviors*, *11*, 34–47.

Ouimette, P. C., Ahrens, C., Moos, R. H., & Finney, J. W. (1998). During treatment changes in substance abuse patients with posttraumatic stress disorder: The influence of specific interventions and program environments. *Journal of Substance Abuse Treatment*, *15*, 555–564.

Ouimette, P. C., Finney, J. W., & Moos, R. H. (1999). Two-year posttreatment functioning and coping of substance abuse patients with posttraumatic stress disorder. *Psychology of Addictive Behaviors*, *13*, 105–114.

Ouimette, P. C., Moos, R. H., & Finney, J. W. (2003). PTSD treatment and five-year remission among patients with substance use and posttraumatic stress disorders. *Journal of Consulting and Clinical Psychology*, *71*, 410–414.

Pariante, C. M., & Lightman, S. L. (2008). The HPA axis in major depression: Classical theories and new developments. *Trends in Neurosciences*, *31*, 464–468.

Petry, N. M., Stinson, F. S., & Grant, B. F. (2005). Comorbidity of DSM-IV pathological gambling and other psychiatric disorders: Results from the National Epidemiologic Survey on Alcohol and Related Conditions. *Journal of Clinical Psychiatry*, *66*, 564–574.

Pickens, R. W., Svikis, D. S., McGue, M., & LaBuda, M. C. (1995). Common genetic mechanisms in alcohol, drug, and mental disorder comorbidity. *Drug and Alcohol Dependence*, *39*, 129–138.

Preisig, M., Fenton, B. T., Stevens, D. E., & Merikangas, K. R. (2001). Familial relationship between mood disorders and alcoholism. *Comprehensive Psychiatry*, *42*, 87–95.

Prescott, C. A., Aggen, S. H., & Kendler, K. S. (2000). Sex-specific genetic influences on the comorbidity of alcoholism and major depression in a population-based sample of US twins. *Archives of General Psychiatry*, *57*, 803–811.

Ramsey, S. E., Kahler, C. W., Read, J. P., Stuart, G. L., & Brown, R. A. (2004). Discriminating between substance-induced and independent depressive episodes in alcohol dependent patients. *Journal of Studies on Alcohol*, *65*, 672–676.

Randall, C. L., Thomas, S., & Thevos, A. K. (2001*b*). Concurrent alcoholism and social anxiety disorder: A first step toward developing effective treatments. *Alcoholism: Clinical and Experimental Research*, *25*, 210–220.

Randall, C. L., Johnson, M. R., Thevos, A. K., Sonne, S. C., Thomas, S. E., Willard, S. L., et al. (2001*a*). Paroxetine for social anxiety and alcohol use in dual diagnosed patients. *Depression and Anxiety*, *14*, 255–262.

Regier, D. A., Farmer, M. E., Rae, D. S., Locke, B. Z., Keith, S. J., Judd, L. L., & Goodwin, F. K. (1990). Comorbidity of mental disorders with alcohol and other drug abuse. *Journal of the American Medical Association*, *264*, 2511–2518.

Reyno, S. M., Stewart, S. H., Brown, C. G., Horvath, P., & Wiens, J. (2006). Anxiety sensitivity and situation-specific drinking in women with alcohol problems. *Brief Treatment and Crisis Intervention*, *6*, 268–282.

Rounsaville, B. J., Dolinsky, Z. S., Babor, T. F., & Meyer, R. E. (1987). Psychopathology as a predictor of treatment outcome in alcoholics. *Archives of General Psychiatry*, *44*, 505–513.

Ruscio, A. M., Stein, D. J., Chiu, W. T., & Kessler, R. C. (2010). The epidemiology of obsessive-compulsive disorder in the National Comorbidity Survey Replication. *Molecular Psychiatry*, *15*, 53–63.

Rush, B., Urbanoski, K., Bassani, D., Castel, S., Wild, T. C., Strike, C., . . . Somers, J. (2008). Prevalence of co-occurring substance use and other mental disorders in the Canadian population. *Canadian Journal of Psychiatry*, *53*, 800–809.

Sabourin, B. C., & Stewart, S. H. (2007). Alcohol use and anxiety disorders. In M. J. Zvolensky & J. A. J. Smits (Eds.), *Anxiety in health behaviors and physical illness* (pp. 29–54). New York: Springer.

Sabourin, B. C., & Stewart, S. H. (2009). Patterns of depression—substance use disorder comorbidity in women seeking addictions treatment. In J. Gallivan & S. Cooper (Eds.), *Pathways, bridges and havens: Psychosocial determinants of women's health* (pp. 160–177). Sydney, NS: Cape Breton University Press.

Saladin, M. E., Drobes, D. J., Coffey, S. F., Dansky, B. S., Brady, K. T., & Kilpatrick, D. G. (2003). PTSD symptom severity as a predictor of cue-elicited drug craving in victims of violent crime. *Addictive Behaviors*, *28*, 1611–1629.

Schade, A. Marquenie. L. A., Balkom, A. J., Koeter, M. W., de Ceurs, E., van den Brink, W., et al. (2005). The effectiveness of anxiety treatment on alcohol dependent patients with a comorbid phobic disorder: A randomized controlled trial. *Alcoholism: Clinical and Experimental Research*, *29*, 794–800.

Schuckit, M. A. (1983). Alcoholic patients with secondary depression. *American Journal of Psychiatry*, *140*, 711–714.

Schuckit, M. A. (2006). Comorbidity between substance use disorders and psychiatric conditions. *Addiction*, *101*, 76–88.

Schuckit, M. A., & Monteiro, M. G. (1988). Alcoholism, anxiety, and depression. *British Journal of Addiction*, *83*, 1373–1380.

Sher, K. J. (1987). Stress response dampening. In H. Blane & K. Leonard (Eds.), *Psychological theories of drinking and alcoholism* (pp. 227–271). New York: Guilford.

Sihvola, E., Rose, R. J., Dick, D. M., Pulkkinen, L., Marttunen, M., & Kaprio, J. (2008). Early onset depressive disorders predict the use of addictive substances in adolescence: A prospective study of adolescent Finnish twins. *Addiction*, *103*, 2045–2053.

Stephens, R. S., & Curtin, L. (1995). Alcohol and depression: Effects on mood and biased processing of self-relevant information. *Psychology of Addictive Behaviors*, *9*, 211–222.

Stewart, S. H. (2010). Concurrent anxiety disorders and substance use disorders. In F. Vaccarino (Ed.), *Substance abuse in Canada: Concurrent disorders* (pp. 22–29). Ottawa, ON: Canadian Centre on Substance Abuse.

Stewart, S. H., & Conrod, P. J. (2008). Anxiety disorder and substance use disorder co-morbidity: Common themes and future directions. In S. H. Stewart & P. J. Conrod (Eds.), *Anxiety and substance use disorders: The vicious cycle of comorbidity* (pp. 239–257). New York: Springer.

Stewart, S. H., Gavric, D., & Collins, P. (2009). Women, girls and alcohol. In K. Brady, S. Back, & S. Greenfield (Eds.), *Women and alcohol: A comprehensive handbook* (pp. 341–359). New York: Guilford.

Stewart, S. H., & Kushner, M. G. (2001). Introduction to the special issue on anxiety sensitivity and addictive behaviors. *Addictive Behaviors, 26*, 775–785.

Stewart, S. H., & O'Connor, R. M. (2009). Treating anxiety disorders in the context of concurrent substance misuse. In D. Sookman & R. Leahy (Eds.), *Treatment resistant anxiety disorders* (pp. 291–323). New York: Routledge.

Straussner, S. L. A. (2013). The *DSM-5* diagnostic criteria: What's new. *Journal of Social Work Practice in the Addictions, 13*, 448–453.

Stroop, J. R. (1935). Studies on interference in serial verbal reactions. *Journal of Experimental Psychology, 18*, 643–662.

Swendsen, J., Conway, K. P., Degenhardt, L., Glantz, M., Jin, R., Merikangas, K. R., ... Kessler, R. C. (2010). Mental disorders as risk factors for substance use, abuse and dependence: Results from the 10-year follow-up of the National Comorbidity Survey. *Addiction, 105*, 1117–1128.

Swendsen, J. D., & Merikangas, K. R. (2000). The comorbidity of depression and substance use disorders. *Clinical Psychology Review, 20*, 173–189.

Tambs, K., Harris, J. R., & Magnus, P. (1997). Genetic and environmental contributions to the correlation between alcohol consumption and symptoms of anxiety and depression: Results from a bivariate analysis of Norwegian twin data. *Behavior Genetics, 27*, 241–249.

Tollefson, G. D., Montague-Clouse, J., & Tollefson, S. L. (1992). Treatment of comorbid generalized anxiety in a recently detoxified alcohol population with a selective serotonergic drug (buspirone). *Journal of Clinical Psychopharmacology, 12*, 19–26.

Vergés, A., Steinley, D., Trull, T. J., & Sher, K. J. (2010). It's the algorithm! Why differential rates of chronicity and comorbidity are not evidence for the validity of the abuse-dependence distinction. *Journal of Abnormal Psychology, 119*, 650–661.

Watson, D. (2005). Rethinking the mood and anxiety disorders: A quantitative hierarchical model for DSM-V. *Journal of Abnormal Psychology, 114*, 522–536.

Watt, M. C., Stewart, S. H., Birch, C. D., & Bernier, D. (2006). Brief CBT for high anxiety sensitivity decreases drinking problems, relief alcohol outcome expectancies, and conformity drinking motives: Evidence from a randomized controlled trial. *Journal of Mental Health, 15*, 683–695.

Weissman, M. M., Wolk, S., Wickramaratne, P., Goldstein, R. B., Adams, P., Greenwald, S., ... Steinberg, D. (1999). Children with prepubertal-onset major depressive disorder and anxiety grown up. *Archives of General Psychiatry, 56*, 794–801.

Willinger, U., Lenzinger, E., Hornik, K., Fischer, G., Schonbeck, G., Aschauer, H. N., et al. (2002). Anxiety as a predictor of relapse in detoxified alcohol-dependent patients. *Alcohol and Alcoholism, 37*, 609–612.

Wilson, G. T., & Abrams, D. (1977). Effects of alcohol on social anxiety and physiological arousal: Cognitive versus pharmacological processes. *Cognitive Therapy and Research, 1*, 195–210.

Wittchen, H. -U., Fröhlich, C., Behrendt, S., Günther, A., Rehm, J., Zimmermann, P., ... Perkonigg, A. (2007). Cannabis use and cannabis use disorders and their relationship to mental disorders: A 10-year prospective-longitudinal community study in adolescents. *Drug and Alcohol Dependence, 88S*, S60–S70.

Woicik, P. A., Conrod, P. J., Stewart, S. H., & Pihl, R. O. (2009). The Substance Use Risk Profile Scale: A scale measuring traits linked to reinforcement specific substance use profiles. *Addictive Behaviors, 34*, 1042–1055.

Young, R. M., Lawford, B. R., Noble, E. P., Kann, B., Wilkie, A., Ritchie, T., ... Shadforth, S. (2002). Harmful drinking in military veterans with post-traumatic stress disorder: Association with the D2 dopamine receptor A1 allele. *Alcohol and Alcoholism, 37*, 451–456.

Zahradnik, M., & Stewart, S. H. (2008). Anxiety disorders and substance use disorder comorbidity. In M. Antony & M. Stein (Eds.), *Handbook of anxiety and the anxiety disorders* (pp. 565–576). Oxford, UK: Oxford University Press.

Zimmerman, U., Spring, K., Kunz-Ebrecht, S. R., Uhr, M., Wittchen, H. U., & Holsboer, F. (2004). Effect of ethanol on hypothalamic-pituitary-adrenal system response to psychosocial stress in sons of alcohol dependent fathers. *Neuropsychopharmacology, 29*, 1156–1165.

Zimmermann, P., Wittchen, H. -U., Höfler, M., Pfister, H., Kessler, R. C., & Lieb, R. (2003). Primary anxiety disorders and the development of subsequent alcohol use disorders: A 4-year community study of adolescents and young adults. *Psychological Medicine, 33*, 1211–1222.

Zvolensky, M. J., Yartz, A. R., Gregor, K., Gonzalez, A., & Bernstein, A. (2008). Interoceptive exposure based cessation intervention for smokers high in anxiety sensitivity: A case series. *Journal of Cognitive Psychotherapy, 22*, 346–365.

CHAPTER 7

An Integrative Common Liabilities Model for the Comorbidity of Substance Use Disorders with Externalizing and Internalizing Disorders

Erin C. Tully *and* William G. Iacono

Abstract

This chapter presents an integrative research-derived model to explain comorbidity among substance use disorders (SUDs), externalizing disorders, and internalizing disorders. This hierarchical model is based on phenotypic covariance among the disorders and latent common genetic liability. At the highest level of the hierarchy, general genetically influenced biological dispositions to negative emotionality and behavioral disinhibition each give rise to spectra of related personality traits, cognitive processes, behavioral tendencies, and psychopathology that account for the pattern of co-occurrence among mental disorders. At the lowest level of the hierarchy, disorder-specific genetic and environmental effects explain the presence of some and not other disorders associated with a given general liability. Interplay between the general liabilities and both other genes and environmental factors throughout development affect the likelihood of developing specific mental disorders.

Key Words: comorbidity, substance use disorders, externalizing disorders, internalizing disorders,

Comorbidity, or the tendency for disorders to co-occur at greater than chance rates (Clark, Watson, & Reynolds, 1995), is high among psychiatric disorders, with estimates that nearly 60% of individuals with a lifetime *Diagnostic and Statistical Manual of Mental Disorders* (DSM-IV) psychiatric disorder have diagnoses of more than one disorder (Kessler, Berglund, Demler, Jin, & Walters, 2005). Drug and alcohol use disorders are frequently comorbid with each other, and rates of substance use disorders (SUDs) are nearly three times as common among individuals with psychiatric disorders compared to individuals with no psychiatric disorder (Regier et al., 1990). Estimates from the National Comorbidity Survey-Replication (NCS-R) study indicate that SUDs are comorbid with antisocial disorders, mood disorders, and anxiety disorders. The likelihood of having a SUD was increased by six times among individuals with conduct disorder (CD; Nock, Kazdin, Hiripi, & Kessler, 2006), and last 12-month diagnoses of SUDs were about six to seven times more common among individuals with antisocial personality disorders (ASPD; Lenzenweger, Lane, Loranger, & Kessler, 2007). Twenty-four percent of individuals with lifetime major depressive disorder (MDD) had a lifetime SUD diagnosis (Kessler et al., 2003), compared to lifetime estimates of 14.6% for SUDs in the general population (Kessler et al., 2005). The likelihood of having a SUD was 2.2–4.8 times greater among individuals with panic disorders (PD) and/or agoraphobia (Kessler et al., 2006), and subsequent SUDs were about twice as likely for individuals with generalized anxiety disorder (GAD; Ruscio et al., 2007).

A great deal is known about the etiology of SUDs, including the typical developmental progression from behavioral and neurobiological predispositions to the emergence of SUDs during adolescence and early adulthood and the importance of both genetic and environmental influences on risk for SUDs. Considerably less is known about the origins of comorbidity with SUDs. This chapter provides a comprehensive review of the literature and describes an integrative model (Figure 7.1) to explain comorbidity among SUDs and other common mental disorders. The model is based on three central principles: (1) risk for psychopathology is multifactorial, reflecting cumulative effects of gene–environment interplay that begins in childhood and early adolescence, (2) covariance among common mental disorders is captured by two broad hierarchically organized dimensions characterized by externalizing and internalizing tendencies, and (3) the organization of this hierarchical system derives from genetically influenced biological dispositions to negative emotionality and, at a lower level of the hierarchy to behavioral disinhibition, negative thought processes, and physiological hyperarousal. Our main thesis is that comorbidity can largely be explained by genetic liabilities for biological processes that give rise to these externalizing and internalizing dimensions, each of which give rise to related personality traits, cognitive processes, behavioral tendencies, and symptoms of psychopathology. In the sections that follow, we review empirical and theoretical support for this model from a developmental perspective and then describe how the model explains the comorbidity of SUDs with other psychiatric disorders. We begin by reviewing research on the underlying covariance structure of psychopathology, which forms the basis for the hierarchical common liabilities model.

Common Genetic Liabilities

The high comorbidity among psychiatric disorders suggests that these disorders can be accounted for by a smaller number of higher order constructs. Multivariate twin studies have modeled the covariance of depression, anxiety, substance use, and antisocial disorders to identify the latent structure underlying comorbidity. In these studies, the amount of genetic influence shared among different disorders is calculated by comparing monozygotic and dizygotic twin pairs on the degree of association between a phenotype (e.g., alcohol dependence) in one twin and a different phenotype (e.g., ASPD) in the co-twin. Shared genetic influences can be inferred when monozygotic twins have greater cross-phenotype similarity than do dizygotic twins.

A meta-analysis of these multivariate studies (Krueger & Markon, 2006) revealed a best-fitting model with two correlated superordinate factors underlying two broad spectra of disorders: (a) an externalizing (EXT) spectrum/factor that encompasses antisocial deviance (i.e., CD and ASPD) and substance abuse/dependence and is described as the propensity to express distress outward, and (b) an internalizing (INT) spectrum/factor that encompasses depressive (MDD and dysthymia) and anxiety disorders (GAD, phobias, PD) and is described as a propensity to express distress inward. In the best-fitting model, this INT factor was further subdivided into two highly correlated but distinct subfactors. One INT factor, which we have labeled *anhedonia/misery* (INT-AM), underlies the covariance of MDD, persistent depressive disorder (formerly dysthymic disorder), and GAD; and the second INT factor, which we have labeled *fear/arousal* (INT-FA), underlies agoraphobia, social anxiety disorder, specific phobia, and panic disorder. PD had a modest loading on the INT-AM factor as well, and, given that other large multivariate twin studies (e.g., Kendler, Prescott, Myers, & Neale, 2003) find that PD loads more strongly onto a factor with MDD and GAD, PD is depicted with loadings on both INT subfactors in our common liabilities model.

Twin and adoption studies support the substantial role of genes in the etiology of mental disorders. In childhood and early adolescence, genes contribute to individual differences in traits like aggression, inattention, and fearfulness (Bartels et al., 2007; Hirata, Zai, Nowrouzi, Beitchman, & Kennedy; 2013; Trzaskowski, Zavos, Haworth, Plomin, & Eley, 2012; Zai et al., 2012), which are predictive of psychopathology later in adolescence and adulthood (e.g., Ormel et al., 2005; Pardini, Lochman, & Wells, 2004). Genetic factors contribute to disruptive behavior disorders, anxiety disorders, and depressive disorders in youth (Ehringer, Rhee, Young, Corley, & Hewitt, 2006), and, by adulthood, SUDs, antisocial behavior disorders, depressive disorders, and anxiety disorders are at least moderately heritable (Fu et al., 2002; Goldman, Oroszi, & Ducci, 2005; Hettema, Prescott, Myers, Neale, & Kendler, 2005; Sullivan, Neale, & Kendler, 2000; Tully, Iacono, McGue, 2010). The hierarchical INT/EXT structure suggests that disorders that load onto the same factor share common core processes, and research indicates that these shared processes are likely genetically influenced. Kendler et al.'s (2003) study showed that the distinction between the INT and

EXT factors was largely genetic rather than environmental in nature and that the two INT subfactors had distinct, although positively correlated, genetic loadings (Kendler, Prescott et al., 2003).

Disorders are most highly comorbid with other disorders that load highly onto the same factor (Kessler et al., 2005). However, disorders that load onto different factors are also comorbid, albeit to a lesser extent. This cross-factor comorbidity reflects the fact that the INT and EXT factors are moderately correlated ($r = .50$; Krueger & Markon, 2006) and suggests shared etiology of disorders across factors. In our common liabilities model, comorbidity of INT and EXT disorders is largely explained by a general liability that influences risk to INT and EXT disorders. The higher comorbidity of disorders loading on the same factor is explained by additional genetic liabilities shared only among disorders of the EXT factor, the INT-AM subfactor, or the INT-FA subfactor. Environmental factors are also proposed to contribute to the etiology of mental disorders, and some environmental factors (e.g., high levels of stress) increase risk for various mental disorders and thus contribute to comorbidity. In addition, unique genetic and environmental risks specific to each disorder account for multifinality (Cicchetti & Rogosch, 1996). In other words, they explain why individuals with the same general liability may experience different outcomes. We begin our discussion of common genetic liabilities with the highest order liability that accounts for comorbidity across the INT and EXT factors.

Negative Emotionality Liability

Although best-fitting models from multivariate analyses of covariance identify two higher order latent factors, the cross-factor comorbidity and correlation between the two factors suggest the possibility of a higher order liability that influences disorders in both the INT and EXT factors. We posit that comorbidity between SUDs and both externalizing and internalizing psychopathology is due in part to a general, genetically influenced liability, which we have labeled *negative emotionality* (NE). This general liability is expressed as a spectrum of neurobiological processes, personality traits, and behavioral tendencies common to both INT and EXT disorders, such as proneness to experiencing negative emotions like sadness and anger, propensities toward inadequate emotion regulation abilities, and maladaptive responses to negative emotions and stress.

Support for NE as a general liability is derived from findings of genetic influences on variables related to the NE construct and from studies of NE-related personality traits underlying both INT and EXT disorders. For example, neuroticism is a personality trait characterized by emotional instability, vulnerability to stress, and proneness to anxiety (Eysenck, Eysenck, & Barrett, 1985). Neuroticism is heritable (e.g., Birley et al., 2006) and has been associated with depression and anxiety (Gershuny & Sher, 1998; Hettema, Neale, Myers, Prescott, & Kendler, 2006; Kendler, Gardner, & Prescott, 2002; 2006; Kendler, Gatz, Gardner, & Pedersen, 2006; Klein, Kotov, & Bufferd, 2011), antisocial behavior (Derefinko & Lynam, 2006; Hicks & Patrick, 2006; Taylor, Reeves, James, & Bobadilla, 2006), and SUDs (Agrawal, Jacobson, Prescott, & Kendler, 2004; Elkins, King, McGue, & Iacono, 2006; Jackson & Sher, 2003; Hur, 2009; James & Taylor, 2007; Miller, Vogt, Mozley, Kaloupek, & Keane, 2006). It has also been found to account for a significant proportion of the comorbidity between INT and EXT disorders (Khan, Jacobson, Gardner, Prescott, & Kendler, 2005). In addition, Tellegen (1982) proposed a similar construct, also labeled *negative emotionality*, which is defined as a tendency to experience negative emotions and to become behaviorally dysregulated under stress. Negative emotionality prospectively predicts alcohol and marijuana dependence, CD, ASPD, depressive disorders, and anxiety disorders (Krueger, 1999a; Slutske et al., 2002; Tellegen, 1982).

Research on endophenotypes provides further support for shared NE-related genetic origins of INT and EXT disorders. Endophenotypes are attributes that are a product of genotypes that predispose to a disorder and are presumed to be more proximal to the genetic influences than clinical diagnoses themselves (Gottesman & Gould, 2003; Iacono & Malone, 2011). Disorders associated with the same endophenotypes likely share some of the same genetic influences (Yoon, Iacono, Malone, & McGue, 2006). Accurate identification of endophenotypes ultimately requires research at the molecular level, but indices of biological processes (e.g., psychophysiology measures, levels of hormones and neurotransmitters) that are correlated with clinically relevant phenotypes and genetically influenced are plausible endophenotypes. Many neurobiological systems associated with NE—in particular anger and responses to stress—are common to both INT and EXT disorders. Corticotropin-releasing factor

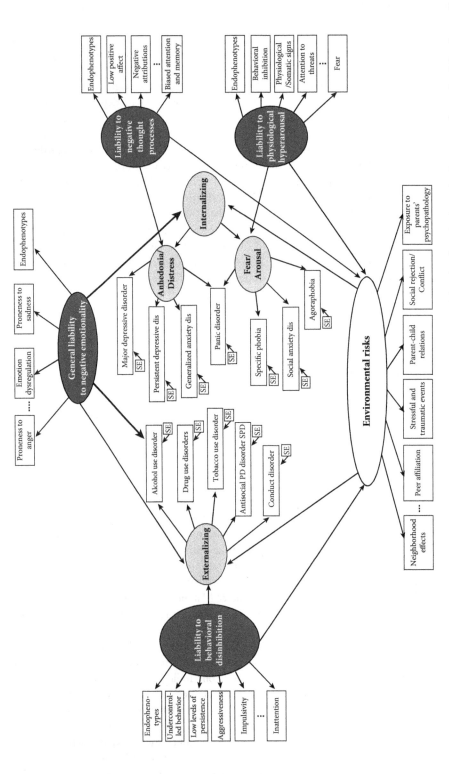

Figure 7.1. An integrative model that explains comorbidity among substance use disorders and other common mental disorders through a hierarchical structure of general and disorder-specific genetic and environmental effects.

A broad externalizing factor represents the covariance among conduct disorder, antisocial personality disorder, tobacco use disorder, drug use disorders, and alcohol use disorder, and a broad internalizing factor represents the covariance among depressive and anxiety disorders. The internalizing factor is further divided into two subfactors: (1) an anhedonia/misery factor that represents the covariance among major depressive disorder, persistent depressive disorder, and generalized anxiety disorder; and (2) a fear/arousal factor that represents the covariance among specific phobia, social anxiety disorder, and agoraphobia. Panic disorder loads onto both internalizing subfactors. These internalizing and externalizing factors derive from genetically influenced biological predispositions/liabilities, each of which is expressed as a spectrum of related personality traits, cognitive processes, and behavioral tendencies. At the highest level of the hierarchy, a liability to negative emotionality (NE; proneness to experiencing negative emotions, tendency toward dysregulation) influences risk for both externalizing and internalizing disorders. The NE liability has particularly strong loadings (bold lines) on the internalizing factor and on alcohol use disorders and thus is a substantial contributor to comorbidity among internalizing disorders, as

(continued on next page)

(CRF), the hypothalamic-pituitary-adrenal (HPA) axis, and noradrenergic pathways are involved in the body's stress response system and have been implicated in the pathophysiology of anxiety, mood, and addictive disorders (for review, see Brady & Sinha, 2005). Anger is largely regulated by dopaminergic and glutamate systems in the nucleus accumbens and prefrontal cortex, and neuroimaging and psychopharmacological treatment studies suggest that these systems also play a role in the neurobiology of depressive, anxiety, behavioral, and SUDs (for reviews, see Koob et al., 2004; Lara & Akiskal, 2006). Moreover, serotonin, dopamine, and CRF have been implicated in the etiology of substance-induced depression and anxiety (e.g., Markou, Kosten, & Koob, 1998; Rounsaville, 2004; Zoltgn et al., 1995), thus providing more evidence for common endophenotypes for INT disorders and SUDs. The genetic basis of these neurobiological substrates and systems is supported by association studies of candidate genes involved in the stress response, particularly functional polymorphisms related to monoaminergic neurotransmission (e.g., in the loci encoding the serotonin transporter, tyrosine hydroxylase, catechol-o-methyltransferase, glucocorticoid receptor; for review, see Levinson, 2006) and by research on phenotypic outcomes resulting from modifications of serotonin-related genes in rodents (for review, see Holmes, 2008). These studies link stress response polymorphisms to the neurobiology of neuroticism (Levinson, 2006), depression (Brouwer et al., 2006; Joensuu et al., 2010; Levinson, 2006; Sarosi et al., 2008), and alcohol-related disorders (Clarke et al., 2008; Florez et al., 2008; Merenäkk, 2011).

Understanding how NE liability contributes to high co-occurrence among disorders requires a developmental perspective. Trait negative emotionality is relatively stable from infancy through adulthood (Lonigan, Phillips, & Hooe, 2003; Pedlow, Sanson, Prior, & Oberklaid, 1993; Roberts & DelVecchio, 2000; Rothbart, Ahadi, & Evans, 2000), this stability is genetically mediated (e.g., Spengler, Gottschling, & Spinath, 2012), and associations between NE-related constructs and psychopathology begin early in development. Dispositional measures of negative emotions, such as tendencies toward sadness, anger, irritability, and frustration, have been associated with internalizing and externalizing problems in young children (Eisenberg et al., 2001), preadolescents (Anthony & Lonigan, 2002; Oldehinkel, Hartman, Winter, Veenstra, & Johan, 2004), and adolescents (Silk, Steinberg, & Morris, 2003). Measures of negative emotions early in childhood prospectively predict higher levels of psychopathology in late adolescence (Block, Gjerde, & Block, 1991) and young adulthood (Caspi, Moffitt, Newman, & Silva, 1996), and negative emotionality in late adolescence predicts subsequent development of major depression in adulthood (Wilson, DiRago, & Iacono, 2014). In one study, examiners rated children's behavior at age 3 in an unselected Dunedin birth cohort sample. Factor and cluster analyses of these ratings revealed five behaviorally and emotionally distinct groups of children that differed in psychiatric diagnoses at age 21. *Behaviorally inhibited* children were most likely to grow up to have depression diagnoses, and *behaviorally undercontrolled* children were most likely to have diagnoses of alcohol dependence and ASPD. Both of these groups were characterized by high negative emotions, including fear and stranger distress for the inhibited group and irritability and emotionally liability for the undercontrolled group. Importantly, the three groups with low levels of psychiatric problems at age 21 did not have high levels of negative emotions, including a

well as between internalizing disorders and alcohol use disorders. Negative emotionality has a smaller effect on comorbidity between INT disorders and other externalizing disorders. At the next level of the hierarchy, a liability to behavioral disinhibition (BD; undercontrolled behavior, low levels of persistence, aggressiveness, impulsivity, inattention) underlies risk for disorders in the externalizing factor. A liability to negative thought processes (NT processes; low positive affect, habitual negative attributions and expectations, biased attention and memory, worry, rumination) contributes to risk for the anhedonia/misery disorders. A liability to physiological arousal (PH; psychophysiological/somatic signs, fear, heightened attention to threats, behavioral inhibition) influences risk for fear/arousal disorders. Environmental risks are influenced by the genetic liabilities (e.g., BD contributes to affiliation with deviant peers) and also contribute to the etiology of internalizing and externalizing disorders. Some environmental factors (e.g., stressful and traumatic events, negative parent–child relations, exposure to parents' psychopathology) contribute to risk for both externalizing and internalizing disorders, whereas other environmental factors are likely to have a greater influence on either the externalizing factor (e.g., neighborhood crime and availability of substances, deviant peer affiliation) or the internalizing factor (e.g., social rejection, peer conflict). At the lowest level of the hierarchy, unique genetic and environmental risks specific to each disorder (SE; specific effects) explain why individuals with the same general liability do not all have the same outcomes. The cumulative effects of gene-environment interplay across development lead to the emergence of mental disorders, and the hierarchical structure of genetically influenced liabilities contributes to covariance among disorders and the observed pattern of comorbidity.

reserved group of children who were behaviorally comparable to the inhibited group but were not described as having fear and distress (Caspi et al., 1996). These findings implicate NE in early developmental pathways leading to psychopathology and also suggest a mediating role of inadequate strategies for regulating and processing negative emotions.

The common liabilities model proposes that the general NE liability influences risk for INT and EXT disorders both directly by predisposing individuals to experience and express negative emotions and indirectly through interactions with genes for lower order genetic liabilities specific to the INT and EXT factors, in particular liabilities related to the regulation of behavior, emotion, and thoughts. Regulation difficulties for individuals with EXT disorders lead them to express the NE liability as dysregulated external behaviors (e.g., aggression toward others, illicit substance use), whereas regulation difficulties for individuals with INT disorders lead them to experience the NE liability as internal dysregulation (e.g., rumination, excessive attention to negative information, persistent distress). In this way, the NE factor increases the likelihood that INT or EXT factor-specific genes will be expressed as INT or EXT disorders, thus contributing to the comorbidity of disorders falling into the INT or EXT spectra.

Regulation Liabilities

In the common liabilities model, the genetic liability for NE—the propensity to experience negative emotions—typically interacts with genetic liabilities underlying three types of emotion *regulation* difficulties to predict psychopathology. More specifically, the shared NE liability interacts with a liability to *behavioral disinhibition* (BD), which predisposes individuals to have difficulty regulating their behavioral responses to negative emotions and increases risk for externalizing disorders; and liabilities to *negative thinking* (NT) and *physiological hyperarousal* (PH), which predispose individuals to have difficulty internally regulating and processing negative emotions and increases risk for internalizing disorders. Theory and research from the developmental literature support this idea that internalizing and externalizing symptoms stem from a combination of propensities to experience negative emotions and propensities toward inadequate control of these emotions. Various models of child temperament propose both reactive traits (e.g., automatic behaviors and unregulated fear) and effortful or active

traits (e.g., self-regulation abilities and purposeful attentional focus) as components of developmental paths leading to psychopathology (Derryberry & Rothbart, 1988; 1997; Kochanska, Barry, Jimenez, Hollatz, & Woodard, 2009; Lonigan et al., 2004; Muris & Ollendick, 2005; Rothbart, 1989; Rothbart, Ahadi, & Hershey, 1994; Rothbart, Posner, & Hershey, 1995). A study involving a Dutch population-based sample of adolescents found that predispositions toward low effortful control (i.e., tendencies to voluntarily inhibit a dominant response in order to perform a subdominant but more adaptive response) magnified the effect of fearfulness on internalizing problems and the effect of frustration on externalizing problems in adolescents (Oldehinkel, Hartman, Ferdinand, Verhulst, & Ormel, 2007), and effortful control and negative affect were associated with familial loadings for both internalizing and externalizing psychopathology (Ormel et al., 2005). In the next two sections, we describe the regulation liabilities in greater detail from a developmental perspective.

Behavioral Disinhibition Liability for Externalizing Disorders

The EXT latent factor has been associated with low constraint in Tellegen's (1982) personality model (Krueger, McGue, & Iacono, 2001), indicating that individuals high in EXT tend to be impulsive and thrill-seeking and have low adherence to traditional moral values. The common liabilities model proposes that the high comorbidity among externalizing disorders is due to a common genetic liability for traits, behaviors, disorders, and endophenotypes that reflect a propensity toward *behavioral disinhibition* (BD), such as inattention, aggressiveness, impulsivity, and low persistence (for a complete review, see Iacono, Malone, & McGue, 2008).

Twin and adoption studies support shared genetic influences underlying the traits and disorders in the EXT spectrum. Multivariate studies indicate shared genetic influences underlying dependence on various licit substances (Agrawal et al., 2007; Lynskey et al., 2007; Swan, Carmelli, & Cardon, 1996; True, Xian et al., 1999), common genetic influences on different drugs in the illicit substance classes (Agrawal, Neale, Prescott, & Kendler, 2004a; Karkowski, Prescott, & Kendler, 2000; Kendler, Aggen, Tambs, & Reichborn-Kjennerud, 2006; Kendler, Jacobson, Prescott, & Neale, 2003; Tsuang et al., 1998), and either shared genetic influences on dependence across licit and illicit substances (Agrawal & Lynskey, 2006; Hopfer, Crowley, & Hewitt, 2003; True, Heath et al., 1999) or highly correlated genetic influences on licit and illicit factors ($r = .82$; Kendler, 2007). Other studies support significant genetic covariation between SUDs and disruptive behavior disorders in childhood (Burt, Krueger, McGue, & Iacono, 2001; Button et al., 2006; 2007; Dick, Viken, Kaprio, Pulkkinen, & Rose, 2005; Nadder, Rutter, Silberg, Maes, & Eaves, 2002; Silberg et al., 1996) and between SUDs and adult antisocial behavior disorders (Hicks, Foster, Iacono, & McGue, 2013; Hicks, Krueger, Iacono, McGue, & Patrick, 2004). Moreover, latent EXT factors comprised of SUDs and antisocial disorders are highly heritable (Hicks et al., 2007a; Hicks, Schalet, Malone, Iacono, & McGue, 2011; Kendler, Prescott et al., 2003). Finally, research supports shared genetic risks underlying EXT disorders and other behavioral disinhibition attributes, such as the personality traits of novelty seeking (Khan et al., 2005) and behavioral undercontrol (Krueger et al., 2001; Slutske et al., 2002), and early adolescent problem behaviors like substance experimentation and use, sexual intercourse, and police contact (Keyes, Iacono, & McGue, 2007; McGue, Iacono, & Krueger, 2006; Young, Stallings, Corley, Krauter, & Hewitt, 2000).

Research on biologically based endophenotypes provides further support for a common EXT genetic liability. Reduced amplitude of the P300 wave, a nonspecific index of brain activity, is a well-studied endophenotype that has been associated with childhood disruptive behavior disorders and antisocial personality disorder (Iacono, Carlson, Malone, & McGue, 2002), substance misuse and SUDs (Carlson, McLarnon, & Iacono, 2007; Iacono et al., 2002; Yoon et al., 2006), and the externalizing latent trait (Patrick, 2006). Although the biological systems underlying individual differences in the P300 wave are not well understood, the reduced P300 amplitude associated with externalizing may reflect a deficient neuromodulatory system leading to poor phase locking of the electrophysiological signals comprising the P300 wave (Burwell, Malone, Bernat, & Iacono, 2014). Individual differences in P300 amplitude predict subsequent development of EXT disorders (Iacono et al., 2002; Perlman, Markin, & Iacono, 2013) and are heritable (Perlman, Johnson, & Iacono, 2009; van Beijsterveldt & van Baal, 2002; Yoon et al., 2006, 2013). In addition, the association between attenuated P300 amplitude and

externalizing disorders is genetically mediated (Hicks et al., 2007a).

The midbrain dopamine reward system is a neurobiological mechanism involved in addiction to virtually all drugs of abuse (Kosten, George, & Kleber, 2005; Nestler, 2005) that has been proposed to underlie aggressive behavior as well (Patrick, 2006), which provides further support for genetic liability shared among SUDs and antisocial disorders. Consistent with this, Gray's model of motivational systems proposes two neurologically based personality systems: (a) the behavioral activation system (BAS), which is exhibited as sensitivity to rewards and motivation to engage in goal-directed efforts to experience positive feelings; and (b) the behavioral inhibition system (BIS), which refers to sensitivity to punishments and proneness to inhibit behavior that may lead to negative or painful outcomes (Gray, 1972; 1975; 1981). EXT disorders likely reflect increased BAS activation, in the form of midbrain reward system, and decreased BIS activation (Iacono et al., 2008), which is likely related to diminished prefrontal cortex functioning and difficulty regulating behavior and inhibiting inappropriate responses (Bechara, 2005; Miller & Cohen, 2001). BIS and BAS impairment across EXT disorders underlies high comorbidity among EXT disorders, whereas cross-disorder differences in BIS/BAS impairment is related to different outcomes among individuals with the BD liability. Individuals with SUDs tend to have more BAS problems, individuals with antisocial disorders tend to have more BIS problems, and individuals with comorbid SUDs and antisocial disorders tend to have problems with both systems.

Consideration of developmental research is again key to understanding how this genetic liability contributes to comorbidity. The BD liability is expressed as different phenotypes over the course of development with the same early temperament traits predicting various subsequent EXT disorders. Behavioral disinhibition traits, such as lack of inhibitory control, novelty seeking, and low harm avoidance, when expressed during early childhood, predict subsequent substance use and misuse during adolescence (Caspi, Henry, McGee, Moffitt, & Silva, 1995; Caspi et al., 1996; Masse & Tremblay, 1997; Wong et al., 2006), and the same traits assessed during late childhood, adolescence, and young adulthood predict tobacco, alcohol, and illicit drug symptoms and disorders in later in adulthood (Chassin, Fora, & King, 2004; Cloninger, Sigvardsson, & Bohman, 1988; Elkins et al., 2006; Grekin, Sher, & Wood, 2006; Krueger, 1999a; Sher, Bartholow, & Wood, 2000). These traits also manifest as disruptive behavior disorders (e.g., oppositional defiant disorder, CD) during childhood (Young et al., 2009), which are predictive of later SUDs (Kim-Cohen et al., 2003; Weinberg, Rahdert, Colliver, & Glantz, 1998), and as high-risk behaviors during early adolescence, such as antisocial behavior, experimentation with alcohol, precocious sexual activity, and academic difficulty, which in turn predict later SUDs and ASPD (Grant & Dawson, 1997; McGue & Iacono, 2005).

These early universal EXT traits become more differentiated across development. Caspi et al. (1995) found one latent factor for lack of control at ages 3 and 5 that became two distinct factors (an impulsive/undercontrolled factor and a fleeting attention/lack of persistence factor) by ages 7 and 9 (Caspi et al., 1995). Likewise, a longitudinal study investigating change in the underlying structure of the EXT factor from age 17 to 24 found a decrease in the amount of overlapping variance among externalizing disorders with age (Hicks et al., 2007b), reflecting decreased genetic influence on the covariation among disorders (Vrieze, Hicks, Iacono, & McGue, 2012). In addition, greater differentiation with age may be due to varied environmental risk exposure and age-related expression of genes that are specific to certain externalizing attributes (Agrawal, Neale, Prescott, & Kendler, 2004b; Grant et al., 2006; Hicks et al., 2004; Kendler, Prescott et al., 2003; Krueger et al., 2002; McGue et al., 2006; Young et al., 2000). These disorder-specific effects account for relative differences in the extent to which the shared liabilities contribute to the development of specific disorders and explain why only some and not other externalizing disorders appear in a given individual with the BD liability. For example, individuals with extreme antisocial tendencies are likely to be high in BD and relatively low in NE (Patrick, 2006).

Liability for Internalizing Disorders

Genetic risk factors associated with NE contribute substantially to the genetic overlap among internalizing disorders (Bienvenu, Hettema, Neale, Prescott, & Kendler, 2007; Fanous, Gardner, Prescott, Cancro, & Kendler, 2002; Fanous, Neale, Aggen, & Kendler, 2007; Gillespie & Martin, 2006; Hansell et al., 2012; Hettema, Neale et al., 2006; Hettema, Prescott, & Kendler, 2004; Kendler & Gardner, 2011; Levinson, 2006). Therefore, we do not propose a specific liability for the INT

factor but rather propose that the NE liability has a strong genetic influence on the internalizing factor and underlies all depressive and anxiety disorders. Consistent with the multivariate twin studies, we posit two subfactor-specific genetic liabilities. A liability to *physiological hyperarousal* (PH) underlies the disorders in the fear/arousal subfactor (i.e., agoraphobia, social phobia, specific phobia, and PD) and is expressed as psychophysiological/somatic signs, fear, heightened attention to threats, and behavioral inhibition. A liability to *negative thought processes* (NT), including worry, rumination, and negatively biased attention and interpretation, underlies disorders in the anhedonia/misery subfactor (i.e., MDD, persistent depressive disorder, GAD, and PD) and is expressed as habitual negative attributions and expectations and low positive affect.

This structure for a general NE liability and subfactor-specific PH and NT liabilities is similar to the tripartite model (Clark & Watson, 1991) and the integrative hierarchical model (Mineka, Watson, & Clark, 1998). The tripartite model proposes a general distress/negative affectivity dimension that is common to both depression and anxiety disorders, as well as an anhedonia (low positive affect) factor specific to depression and a physiological hyperarousal factor specific to anxiety. Our integrative hierarchical model combines elements of the tripartite model and Barlow's hierarchical organization of the anxiety disorders (Barlow, 1991; Zinbarg & Barlow, 1996) and posits that each anxiety and depressive disorder contains both a common component and a unique component. These models propose a general negative affectivity factor that accounts for a large proportion of variance in MDD and GAD and a much smaller proportion of the variance in most other anxiety disorders (e.g., social phobia, specific phobia) and that negative affectivity and low positive affectivity characterize many noninternalizing disorders. Watson (2005) further proposed a quantitative hierarchical model in which a general *emotion disorders* category can be subdivided into the bipolar disorders (bipolar I, bipolar II, cyclothymia), the distress disorders (MDD, dysthymic disorder, GAD, and PTSD), and the fear disorders (panic disorder, agoraphobia, social phobia, and specific phobia; Watson, 2005).

Analogous to the developmental progression of the BD liability, behavioral inhibition, specifically when it is characterized by poor autonomic regulation (Marshall & Stevenson-Hinde, 1998), typically appears during early childhood in individuals who will later develop anxiety (Hirshfeld-Becker et al.,

2007; McDermott et al., 2009), and anxiety may be an earlier expression of the common NE liability than depression. Anxiety is more likely than depression to onset during childhood, depression in child and adolescent samples is most often comorbid with anxiety (Anderson, Williams, McGee, & Silva, 1987; Angold, Costello, & Erkanli, 1999; Fleming, Offord, & Boyle, 1989), and the onset of anxiety tends to precede the onset of depression (Hettema, Kuhn et al., 2006; Kessler et al., 2005; Woodward & Fergusson, 2001). Twin studies of children and adolescents support significant genetic covariation between anxiety and subsequent depression that cannot be explained by genetic influences associated with earlier depression (Eaves et al., 2003; Rice et al., 2004), suggesting shared genetic etiology of childhood anxiety and later depression. Anxiety and depression do not always co-occur, and anxiety does not always precede depression, but these findings support a common liability underlying the two separate INT subfactors.

Research on associations between temperament/ personality traits and depressive and anxiety disorders supports the PH and NT liabilities. Many concurrent and a few prospective studies of children and adolescents support associations between high negative affect/neuroticism and both depression and anxiety, low positive affect/surgency and depression, and high physiological arousal and anxiety (e.g., Caspi et al., 1996; Chorpita & Daleiden, 2002; Compas, Conner-Smith, & Jaser, 2004; Lonigan, Carey, & Finch, 1994). Studies involving adult samples have similar findings. Internalizing factors defined by both depression and anxiety symptoms tend to have smaller correlations with positive emotionality than with negative emotionality (Krueger et al., 2001). Krueger (1999*b*) found a significant negative association between depressive disorders and the well-being dimension of Tellegen's Multidimensional Personality Questionnaire (which is described as cheerfulness, optimism, and proneness to enjoyment) and no association between well-being and anxiety disorders (Krueger, 1999*a*). In a similar way, constraint, a personality factor defined as a propensity for cautious and restrained behavior and endorsement of traditional values, does not typically correlate with the general INT factor (Krueger et al., 2001), and high constraint is characteristic of individuals with anxiety disorders but not depressive disorders (Krueger, 1999*a*). Consistent with the specificity of constraint to the PH liability, Gladstone et al. (2006) found that social anxiety mediated the relationship between childhood inhibition and later depression (Gladstone, Parker, Gladstone, & Parker, 2006).

Physiological Hyperarousal Liability

Some anxiety is normative, particularly in infancy and toddlerhood in response to separation from parents. This fear typically diminishes dramatically during early childhood (Muris, Meesters, Merckelbach, Sermon, & Zwakhalen, 1998), an age when fear-based anxiety disorders, such as separation anxiety disorder, social phobia, and specific phobias, are likely to onset (Kessler et al., 2005). Fear in these young children has significant genetic overlap with shyness/inhibition (62%) and negative mood (53%; Eley et al., 2003), suggesting developmental continuity with later internalizing disorders that share these traits, particularly disorders in the FA subfactor. These disorders are characterized by behavioral constraint (Krueger, 1999*a*) and intense physiological hyperarousal (PA), such as heart racing, sweating, and shortness of breath particularly in response to stressors (Cuthbert et al., 2003; Hofmann, Moscovitch, & Kim, 2006; Martin-Soelch, Stocklin, Dammann, Opwis, & Seifritz, 2006).

Turning to evidence of potential endophenotypes, research on psychophysiological characteristics of anxious and depressed individuals supports the distinction of the PH and NT liabilities within internalizing psychopathology. Anxiety disorders that load onto the FA factor are characterized by poor parasympathetic flexibility (Licht, de Geus, van Dyck, & Penninx, 2009; Sharma, Balhara, Sagar, Deepak, & Mehta, 2011) and exaggerated sympathetic arousal to affectively arousing stimuli, especially fear stimuli (Cuthbert et al., 2003; Larson, Nitschke, & Davidson, 2007). Cuthbert et al. (2003) found that individuals with PD were less physiologically responsive to the affective stimuli than individuals with specific phobias and social anxiety, a finding that is consistent with PD's relatively smaller genetic loading on the FA factor (Kendler, Prescott et al., 2003). Moreover, depressed individuals without anxiety disorders and anxious individuals with worry or anhedonic symptoms but not arousal symptoms do not show exaggerated physiological responses to these stimuli (Larson et al., 2007), and researchers have found blunted physiological responses to pleasant stimuli among individuals with depression (Forbes, Miller, Cohn, Fox, & Kovacs, 2005; Larson et al., 2007). A comprehensive review of this literature supports these conclusions (Vaidyanathan, Patrick, & Cuthbert, 2009) and links the differentiation of INT disorders to distinct underlying brain systems. Few studies have investigated the heritability of these psychophysiological indices. The extant literature supports modest genetic influences on conditioned eyeblink responses (Merrill, Steinmetz, Viken, & Rose, 1999) and on absolute startle reflex but not emotion-modulated startle reflex (Anokhin, Golosheykin, & Heath, 2007; see also Carlson, Katsanis, Iacono, & McGue, 1997). Research on the heritability of these psychophysiological indices is needed to establish their potential as endophenotypes for FA-INT disorders.

The amygdala is the primary brain structure for processing fear, and it has been linked to behavioral inhibition (Haas, Canli, Haas, & Canli, 2008; Kensinger & Corkin, 2004; Morgan & Morgan, 2006), suggesting neural substrates implicated in the functioning of the amygdala are also potential endophenotypes for FA-INT disorders and their precursors. Pharmacological studies indicate that blockage of receptors in the amygdala (e.g., N-methyl-D-aspartate [NMDA] receptors) inhibits fear responses and consolidation of fear memories, and NMDA antagonists successfully treat various anxiety disorders (Garakani, Mathew, & Charney, 2006). Impairment in amygdala functioning is also implicated in nonfear disorders (e.g., MDD), but genes associated with functioning of the amygdala receptors and neurotransmitters that bind to these receptors likely contribute considerably to the PH liability. Research showing associations between anxiety disorders and measures of heart rate variability and respiratory sinus arrhythmia in response to emotion-laden stimuli (e.g., Licht et al., 2009; Porges, 2011) suggest the physiological substrates underlying parasympathetic functioning may also be key endophenotypes.

Negative Thought Processes Liability

Twin studies have demonstrated substantial genetic covariance between MDD and GAD, and a significant proportion of that genetic overlap is due to the common genetic liability for NE (Hettema, Neale et al., 2006; Kendler, Gardner, Gatz, & Pedersen, 2007; Middeldorp, Cath, Van Dyck, & Boomsma, 2005). Nevertheless, Hettema et al. (2006) found a significant genetic factor shared among MDD, GAD, and PD that was independent from the genetic influences of neuroticism, and Kendler et al. (2007) found that only about 25% of the genetic correlation between MDD and GAD

was shared with neuroticism, leaving a considerable amount of shared genetic variation to be explained by other factors. We propose that the comorbidity among the disorders in the INT-AM subfactor are explained by a genetic predisposition for various interrelated *negative thought (NT) processes* that have empirical links to depression and anxiety, including attentional biases to threatening and sad stimuli, excessive contemplation of negative information, difficulty shifting attention away from negative information, and trouble suppressing pessimistic cognitions (e.g., Bradley, Mogg, White, Groom, & de Bono, 1999; Everaert, Koster, & Derakshan, 2012; Gotlib & Joormann, 2010; Hirsch, Clark, & Mathews, 2006; Mathews & MacLeod, 2005; Mogg, Philippot, & Bradley, 2004; Vanderhasselt et al., 2012; Zetsche, D'Avanzato, & Joormann, 2012). This predisposition underlies cognitive characteristics of these disorders, like worry, rumination, hopelessness, and negative attributions about the self and the future (e.g., Alloy et al., 2004; Nolen-Hoeksema, Wisco, & Lyubomirsky, 2008; Papageorgiou, 2006), as well as anhedonia and low levels of positive affect, which are also characteristics of these disorders (Krueger, 1999a; Watson, 2005). According to our model, individuals with an INT-AM disorder inherit both the NE liability and the NT liability and thus are prone to high levels of fear, anger, and sadness and to maladaptive cognitive processing and internal regulation of these negative emotions.

This cognitively based NT liability is consistent with the many cognitive theories of depression and anxiety, such as Beck's cognitive distortion model (Beck, 1967; 1976), the learned helplessness and hopelessness models (Abramson, Metalsky, & Alloy, 1989; Abramson, Seligman, & Teasdale, 1978; Seligman, 1974), Eysenck's hypervigilance theory of anxiety (Eysenck, 1992; 1997), and Beck's information processing model of anxiety (Beck & Clark, 1997). Furthermore, the combination of NE and NT liabilities is supported by transdiagnostic emotion regulation models that propose maladaptive cognitive regulation of negative emotions contribute to depression and anxiety (Aldao & Nolen-Hoeksema, 2010; Gross & Thompson, 2007; Hofmann, Sawyer, Fang, & Asnaani, 2012) and findings that cognitive processes, such as attentional biases toward threatening stimuli, moderate associations between behavioral inhibition and internalizing problems (e.g., Fox & Pine, 2012; Pérez-Edgar et al., 2011).

Although few studies have investigated the heritability of the many cognitive constructs associated with depression and anxiety, the few existing studies generally support moderate genetic influences on these constructs. Attributional style, a cognitive pattern characterized by internal, global, and stable attributions for negative events, was found to be moderately heritable (35%; Lau, Rijsdijk, & Eley, 2006) in a sample of adolescents, and anxiety sensitivity, which refers to misattributions regarding the harmful consequences of anxiety and intolerance of anxiety-related bodily sensations, was also moderately heritable in samples of adolescents (60%; Eley & Brown, 2004) and adults (45%; Stein, Jang, & Livesley, 1999). Eley and colleagues studied genetic influences on various simple cognitive variables in 8-year-old children. They found significant genetic influences on anxiety sensitivity (37%; Eley, Gregory, Clark, & Ehlers, 2007) but negligible genetic influences and significant shared environmental on negative interpretations of interpersonal relationships (Gregory et al., 2007). Genetic influences on anxiety sensitivity were highly correlated with genetic influences on panic/somatic symptoms of anxiety in children (Eley et al., 2007), and genetic influences on a measure of children's interpretations of situations as either negative or neutral were significantly correlated ($r = .65$) with genetic influences on children's depressive symptoms (Eley et al., 2008).

Like the BD and PH liabilities, the NT liability should be conceptualized in a developmental context as behavioral tendencies, temperament traits, and physiological processes begin to emerge in childhood and predispose individuals to develop INT-AM disorders. Although the ability to internally regulate emotions emerges in the first year of life (e.g., self-soothing), self-regulation abilities continue to develop rapidly through the critical preschool years and into childhood and adolescence (Cole, Michel, & Teti, 1994; Gralinski & Kopp, 1993; Kaler & Kopp, 1990; Rothbart, Posner, & Rosicky, 1994). Young children, who lack the cognitive abilities to develop stable expectancies and explanations for stress and negative emotions, express maladaptive internal regulation as behavioral restraint, shyness, and low attention regulation (Cicchetti & Tucker, 1994; Eisenberg et al., 2001; Nolen-Hoeksema, Girgus, & Seligman, 1992; Turner & Cole, 1994). Improved cognitive abilities during late childhood and adolescence allow for the development of more stable and pathological cognitive styles, such as pessimistic beliefs about causes and consequences of stressful events and hopelessness about the future (Kaslow, Adamson, & Collins, 2000; Nolen-Hoeksema et al., 1992). By early

adolescence, rumination, poor ability to shift attention away from aversive or negative stimuli when desired, high self-criticism, dysfunctional interpretation schemas, hopelessness about the future, and negative views of self, world, and future are associated with elevated internalizing problems (Bachanas & Kaslow, 2001; Murisa, Meesters, & Blijlevens, 2007; Oldehinkel et al., 2004; Silk et al., 2003).

With respect to endophenotypes, studies linking depression and anxiety to genes related to serotonergic modulation of the stress response (e.g., serotonin transporter gene; Holmes, 2008; Koller et al., 2008) and genes linked to HPA axis regulation (e.g., glucocorticoid receptor gene; Brouwer et al., 2006; Papiol et al., 2007) suggest that biological markers of HPA axis and serotonergic system functioning may be promising INT-AM disorder endophenotypes. Complex interactions between genetic susceptibility to serotonergic and noradrenergic system dysfunction and stress-related changes in the HPA axis have been implicated in the pathophysiology of depression (Firk, Markus, Firk, & Markus, 2007; Porter et al., 2004), and psychopharmacological treatment studies support the role of reduced neurotransmission of serotonin and norepinephrine in the pathophysiology of GAD (Nutt, Argyropoulos, Hood, & Potokar, 2006). Despite the extensive body of research linking corticotrophin-releasing factor and the HPA axis to depression (Hankin, Badanes, Abela, & Watamura, 2010; Nemeroff & Vale, 2005; Wardenaar et al., 2011), almost no research has focused on the role of the HPA axis in the etiology of GAD separate from the INT-FA anxiety disorders. Although findings of associations between the HPA axis functioning and anxiety disorders in general have been mixed (Risbrough & Stein, 2006), evidence from a study of HPA functioning in GAD patients showed significant changes in plasma cortisol following cognitive treatment (Tafet, Feder, Abulafia, & Roffman, 2005).

Molecular Genetics: Identifying Genes

At present, the specific genes associated with the NE, BD, PH, and NT liabilities are unknown, and thus we limit our discussion of candidate genes to a few brief comments. Interpreting research on candidate genes for psychiatric disorders and personality traits is complicated because effects are likely due to multiple genes, each of which has very small effects. Very large samples, replication across samples, and strong biologically informed a priori hypotheses are needed to place candidate gene findings on solid footings, and even then there is reason to be cautious regarding the likelihood that reported effects are not false-positive errors, especially when testing for gene × environment interactions (Duncan & Keller, 2011). Extreme caution is required before accepting as credible any reported association between a genetic variant and either a personality trait or a psychiatric disorder.

Against this cautionary backdrop, a sampling from molecular genetic studies supports overtransmission of the risk variants of various genes in individuals with different psychiatric disorders. For example, the muscarinic acetylcholine receptor M_2 gene (*CHRM2*) is involved in the stress response system among other functions (e.g., attention, learning, memory and cognition) and has been linked to alcohol and drug dependence (Wang et al., 2004), a general composite externalizing factor (Dick et al., 2008), and depression (Comings et al., 2002). In addition, findings regarding genes involved in SUDs (e.g., related to dopamine functioning) have also been implicated in BD traits like impulsivity and risk taking (Hiroi & Agatsuma, 2005; Kreek, Nielsen, Butelman, & LaForge, 2005) and the association between neuroticism and SUDs (Ellis et al., 2011).

Environmental Mediation and Moderation of Genetic Liabilities

Environmental factors are also important to the etiology of mental disorders and thus may contribute to comorbidity. In the common liabilities model, environmental risks are depicted as coalescing under a general factor that is influenced by the genetic liabilities and influences both INT and EXT psychopathology. By and large, environmental risks overlap extensively across disorders and EXT/INT factor groups. For example, low family support, conflict with peers, peer pressure, and broken relationships are associated with risk for substance use and depression in a sample of adolescents (e.g., Aseltine, Gore, & Colten, 1998). Nevertheless, some environmental risk factors are likely to influence certain disorders to a greater degree than other disorders and thus contribute to disorder-specific effects; for example, peer pressure may be a stronger predictor of substance use, and conflict with friends may be a stronger predictor of depression (Aseltine et al., 1998). Consistent with largely shared but some specific environmental effects, findings from a multivariate twin study suggest that factor-specific environmental risks do not distinguish INT disorders from EXT disorders, although some environmental influences are likely specific to smaller

subsets of disorders, such as CD and ASPD and MDD, GAD, and alcohol dependence (Kendler, Prescott et al., 2003).

The influence of environmental risk mechanisms on comorbidity is due in part to the tendency for multiple environmental risks to co-occur. For example, exposure to interparental conflict in the home is related to conflict with peers and peer rejection (Hipwell, Murray, Ducournau, & Stein, 2005; Kunz, 2001), and exposure to criminal and violent acts, deviant peers, and drug accessibility (all risk factors for both substance use and depression) tend to co-occur in the same neighborhoods (Curry et al., 2008; Stockdale et al., 2007; Valdez, Kaplan, & Curtis, 2007). "Environmental" risk factors, such as family conflict and affiliation with deviant peers, have been found to be genetically influenced (McGue, Elkins, Walden, & Iacono, 2005; Plomin & Bergeman, 1991; Tarantino et al., 2014), and thus genetic factors may also contribute the co-occurrence of multiple environment risks.

Research supports the "cumulative risk hypothesis" that added exposures to multiple risks across different stages of development convey greater risk than single exposure or exposure in a single developmental period. This repeated exposure to environmental risks also amplifies gene expression through gene-environment (G-E) interplay (Rutter & Silberg, 2002), which contributes to increased heritability of most mental disorders with age (Bergen et al., 2007). Gene-environment correlation is one mechanism of G-E interplay that contributes to comorbidity (Jaffee & Price, 2007). Genetic and environmental risks are correlated because parents transmit risk to offspring both by passing on genes to their offspring and by shaping their offspring's environment (contributing to "passive" G-E correlations) and because genetically influenced behavior directly influences the environment (contributing to "active" G-E correlations). For example, genetic liability to BD increases risk for both EXT disorders and exposure to environmental factors like parental conflict and affiliation with defiant peers (Keyes et al., 2007), which are nonspecific environmental factors that potentiate risk for EXT and INT disorders. Environmental factors also interact with genetic factors to increase or decrease risk for disorders. For example, genetic influences on substance use and deviant behaviors are amplified in urban settings where environmental risks (e.g., easy access to drugs, exposure to violence, and perhaps less parental monitoring) are more common than in rural environments (Legrand, Keyes, McGue,

Iacono, & Krueger, 2007; Rose, Dick, Viken, & Kaprio, 2001). As follows, environmental risks may also contribute to comorbidity by increasing the likelihood that common and disorder-specific genetic liabilities are expressed as mental disorders. Thus, genes and the environment influence each other and risk for disorders in a complex, reciprocal ways, and, importantly, because neither the genetic nor the environmental risk factors are disorder-specific, these G-E interplay mechanisms contribute to comorbidity of mental disorders.

Explaining Co-occurrence of SUDs and Other Disorders

Our common liabilities model explains comorbidity among mental disorders in general. In this section, we focus on how the model explains comorbidity with SUDs in particular and highlight some important assumptions of the model. The degree of influence of a given mechanism on the comorbidity of SUDs with another disorder varies from disorder to disorder. Likewise, the mechanism underlying the co-occurrence of two disorders in a given individual varies from person to person. Characteristics of the two disorders, such as age of onset and temporal order of emergence of the disorders, provide insight about the mechanisms underlying comorbidity.

Behavioral Disinhibition Liability: Link between SUDs and Antisocial Disorders

The model proposes that the BD genetic liability is the most likely factor underlying the comorbidity of SUDs with antisocial behavior disorders and that when SUDs are comorbid with antisocial disorders the age of initiation of substance use is typically during early adolescence. As we have previously discussed, the typical progression of externalizing problems related to the BD liability is (a) impulsivity, inattention, and aggressiveness during early childhood; (b) disruptive behavior disorders during childhood; (c) antisocial behaviors, initiation of substance use, precocious sexual activity, affiliation with deviant peers, and parent–child conflict during early to mid-adolescence; and, finally (d) the emergence of alcohol and drug abuse/dependence and ASPD in adulthood (Iacono et al., 2008).

In a review of comorbidity of SUDs in samples of youth, Armstrong and Costello (2002) report that approximately 60% of youth with an SUD have a comorbid disorder, and early-onset SUDs are most often comorbid with CD and oppositional defiant disorder (Armstrong & Costello, 2002). A longitudinal study of childhood internalizing

and externalizing disorders and early adolescent substance use supports this idea. King, Iacono, and McGue (2004) found that disruptive behavior disorders (CD, ODD, and, to a lesser extent, ADHD) in male and female 11-year-olds were robust predictors of age 14 substance use behaviors (e.g., use of alcohol, cigarette, and cannabis one or more times per month and being drunk; King et al., 2004). MDD and anxiety disorders were much less consistently predictive of substance use behaviors at age 14. Thus, through a developmental progression of expressed externalizing traits, behaviors, and environmental risks, the comorbidity of SUDs with CD and ASPD is most likely influenced through a general genetic liability to BD.

General NE Liability: Link between Alcohol Use Disorder and Anhedonia/Misery Disorder

In the model, the NE liability has its greatest influence on INT disorders, particularly the INT-AM disorders, and the model proposes that NE also has a strong effect on alcohol use disorder (AUD) and contributes to the high comorbidity between alcoholism and depression. Several lines of research support this idea. First, although alcohol dependence has a stronger loading on the EXT factor than the INT factor, there is evidence from twin studies that nevertheless suggests some shared latent covariance between alcohol dependence and the INT factor (Kendler, Prescott et al., 2003; King et al., 2004; Krueger et al., 2001). Second, twin studies have demonstrated that genetic factors underlie the comorbidity of depression and alcohol dependence (Kendler, Heath et al., 1993; Prescott, Aggen, & Kendler, 2000). Third, although high negative emotionality has been associated with substance dependence in general (Krueger, 1999a), it appears to have an especially strong association with AUD. McGue and colleagues (1997; 1999) found that alcohol dependence is particularly common among individuals who have high levels of both behavioral disinhibition *and* negative emotionality and that alcohol dependence is primarily associated with negative emotionality, while illicit drug use disorders are primarily associated with constraint (McGue, Slutske, & Iacono, 1999; McGue, Slutske, Taylor, & Iacono, 1997). Similarly, Elkins et al. (2004) found that adolescent offspring of parents with a history of alcohol dependence scored significantly higher on negative emotionality than adolescents with no parental history of alcohol dependence, and negative emotionality did not differ for offspring of parents with and without a drug abuse/dependence history (Elkins, McGue, Malone, & Iacono, 2004). They found that this pattern characterized both offspring with an SUD and those who had not yet developed an SUD, which supports negative emotionality as an indicator of familial risk for alcoholism.

Fourth, research suggests that understanding how the NE liability mechanism contributes to the comorbidity of SUDs and internalizing disorders requires studying specific negative emotions (e.g., Lara, Pinto, Akiskal, & Akiskal, 2006). Findings suggest that irritability and anger are associated with both alcohol use and depression but not with anxiety (Fava et al., 2010; Hussong & Chassin, 1994; Lara et al., 2006; Pardini et al., 2004; Tarter, Blacksona, Brighama, Mossa, & Caprarab, 1995). These findings suggest that NE-related proneness toward irritability and anger may underlie the comorbidity of alcohol dependence and internalizing disorders within the INT-AM factor specifically. The proneness toward irritability and anger is likely influenced by disorder-specific genetic and environmental factors and perhaps by the environmental factors that Kendler et al. (2003) found were shared among MDD, GAD, and alcohol dependence. The factors underlying the comorbidity of alcohol dependence with INT-FA disorders would likely be different and perhaps involve specific effects that remain to be identified.

Environmental Mechanisms

Environmental factors likely contribute to the comorbidity of SUDs with both INT and EXT disorders through shared environmental risk factors, the tendency for multiple environmental risks to co-occur, and G-E interplay. We expect, though, that environmental risk factors are relatively more influential than genetic factors when the co-occurring SUD has a late onset and that the relative influence of environmental factors to genetic factors is greater when SUDs co-occur with INT disorders than when SUDs co-occur with EXT disorders. Because the BD liability is likely to be expressed as substance use relatively early in adulthood or even in adolescence, SUDs with a late age of onset are not expected to be strongly influenced by this genetic liability. Although the NE liability contributes to comorbidity between INT disorders and SUDs, research also suggests that the experience of stressful events particularly chronic stressors over time, and the neurobiological effects of chronic stress response systems (e.g., on HPA system functioning) play an important role in the comorbidity of internalizing disorders and SUDs (Brady & Sinha, 2005).

Other Explanations for Comorbidity

Other explanations for the comorbidity of SUDs with other disorders are also supported by research. One commonly posited explanation is directional or reciprocal causality in which one disorder or the consequences of the disorder (e.g., neuroadaptations associated with chronic drug use) cause a second disorder, and these causal links may be reciprocal. Several lines of research support this explanation. First, internalizing (e.g., MDD, PD) and externalizing disorders (e.g., CD, ODD) have been found to prospectively predict SUDs and vice versa (Breslau, Novak, & Kessler, 2004; Fergusson, Boden, & Horwood, 2009; Goodman & Capitman, 2000; Greenfield et al., 1998; Kushner, Sher, & Erickson, 1999; Marmorstein & Iacono, 2011; Marmorstein, Iacono, & Malone, in press; Rao et al., 2000). These findings are consistent with directional causality, but findings of directionality do not necessarily imply causation and also do not rule out a common liability explanation for comorbidity.

Second, when depressive or anxiety disorders precede SUDs, a common explanation is the "self-medication" theory, which proposes that individuals begin using substances to "treat" symptoms of a primary disorder. For example, nicotine dependence co-occurs with depression, and smoking results in marked reductions in brain levels of monoamine oxidase A (MAO-A; Fowler et al., 1996), an enzyme that degrades serotonin and norepinephrine. MAO inhibitors are antidepressant drugs that block this process (Adli et al., 2008), suggesting that smoking, too, may have an antidepressant effect. The self-medication theory, though, is challenged by findings that SUDs often precede internalizing disorders (Fergusson et al., 2009; Marmorstein et al., 2010; Rao et al., 2000) and by a study that used biometric modeling to compare etiological models for the comorbidity of nicotine dependence and depression and found support for a correlated or shared familial liability (perhaps a common NE liability) rather than for one disorder leading to the other (Johnson, Rhee, Chase, & Breslau, 2004).

Third, longitudinal studies of adolescent and young adults have found that episodes of depression and substance use tend to occur in close temporal proximity (Fergusson et al., 2009; Rao et al., 2000). This research may indicate bidirectional influence of symptoms of the comorbid disorders but may also be explained by common environmental triggers, greater use of substances when feeling depressed among individuals who have a common genetic liability for both disorders, or negative consequences of one of the disorders (e.g., failing grades, strained interpersonal relationships) increasing symptoms of the other disorder. Fourth, when SUDs are comorbid with another condition, SUD symptoms tend to be more severe (Conway et al., 2006; Grant & Dawson, 1997), durations of remission and time to relapse are shorter (Greenfield et al., 1998; Hasin et al., 2002), and treatments are less effective unless there is conjunctive treatment for the comorbid disorder (Myrick & Brady, 2003). These findings may indicate that the comorbid disorder exacerbates (or is causally linked to) SUD symptoms, but these findings may also suggest a common genetic liability that underlies more severe, chronic, treatment-resistant symptoms of both disorders.

In summary, these lines of research are consistent with directional and reciprocal causality but are also compatible with a common liabilities model. These two explanations for comorbidity are not mutually exclusive, and both likely contribute to comorbidity in complex ways. To be more specific, the presence of a genetic liability does not determine that a disorder will develop but rather increases the likelihood that a disorder will develop given the presence of other genetic and environmental risk factors, which may include other psychiatric disorders. For example, a common genetic liability for NE increases the likelihood of developing both AUD and social anxiety disorder, and the liability may be expressed first as social anxiety symptoms which in turn casually contribute to the liability being expressed as alcohol dependence. The causality explanation is also likely complicated and mediated by changes in environmental risks (e.g., unemployment, strained interpersonal relationships, unhealthy compensatory strategies used to manage the primary disorder) and changes in the individual that are probably genetically influenced to some degree (e.g., changes in brain structures and functions, cognitive processes). Both common liabilities and causal relationships between comorbid disorders likely contribute to the noted strong correlations between the INT and EXT factors and the subfactors and among the individual disorders. Therefore, the hierarchical common liabilities model is not intended to be exhaustive or exclusive of other explanations for comorbidity but rather to integrate important findings about phenotypic covariance, genetics, environmental influences, biological systems, and developmental changes.

Conclusion

The etiology of mental disorders is increasingly understood to involve many interacting genetic and environmental factors. Individual pathways of risk begin with general genetic liabilities that, throughout development, interact with environmental factors and other genetic factors to increase the likelihood of developing certain mental disorders and decrease the likelihood of developing other disorders. This chapter provided a review of research on the comorbidity of INT and EXT disorders with SUDs and proposed an integrative hierarchical model based on phenotypic covariance and latent genetic liabilities to explain observed patterns of disorder co-occurrence. The highest order factor, NE, is associated with increased risk for all INT and EXT mental disorders included in Figure 7.1. In other words, individuals with these mental disorders are likely to share, to varying degrees, the genetic liability for NE, with the particular disorder they develop shaped by the presence of other genes genetic liabilities (e.g., genes affecting liability for disorders associated with BD) and environmental factors. The comorbidity of disorders increases as the number of shared genetic liabilities and shared environmental influences increases. Disorders that load onto the same INT/EXT spectra have high comorbidity because individuals with these disorders are likely to inherit not only the NE liability but also a more specific genetic liability that is shared by disorders in the spectrum.

Further differentiation occurs because each disorder in the model is also influenced by specific effects that are more specific (i.e., unique) to the disorder and account for the development of different disorders among individuals who share these higher order liabilities. These specific genetic and environmental effects differ in nature across the disorders, and the proportion of genetic to environmental influence unique to a disorder varies from one disorder to another. Using multivariate twin modeling, Kendler et al. (2003) found that disorder-specific loadings for unique environmental influences (i.e., not shared among family members) on these common mental disorders were substantial, whereas environmental influences shared among family members were very small. The magnitude of disorder-specific genetic loadings varied across disorders with substantial loadings found only for alcohol dependence and drug abuse/dependence, suggesting that these specific effects are largely environmental. As follows, genetic and environmental influences at the higher levels of the hierarchy explain comorbidity among different disorders, and specific genetic and environmental influences at the lowest level of the hierarchy account for multifinality and the etiology of individual disorders.

Limitations

Despite the breadth and comprehensiveness of this model, it does not attempt to account fully for mental disorder co-occurrence or to exclude other mechanisms that may also contribute to comorbidity (e.g., one disorder causing the other). The model focuses on common disorders that have typically been assessed in epidemiologic and behavior genetics investigations that examine the underlying structure of psychopathology and thus are known to have shared covariance with other INT or EXT disorders. Consequently, some disorders (e.g., posttraumatic stress disorder, personality disorders besides ASPD, psychotic disorders, bipolar disorders) are not included in the model. In addition, the model does not distinguish among different illicit drug use disorders. Further, relevant moderating variables, such as gender, ethnicity, and family history of psychopathology, are not included in the model but would improve the specificity of the model for understanding comorbidity in distinct groups and under various conditions. It is important to note, though, that although there are well-known gender differences in the mean level of EXT and INT attributes, many studies find no gender effects pointing to differences in the etiology of mental disorders, for example, in the hierarchical factor structures of psychopathology (Krueger, 1999b), the structure of genetic and environmental influences on externalizing disorders (e.g., Hicks et al., 2007b; Kendler, Prescott et al., 2003), heritability of disorders (Heath et al., 1997; Sullivan et al., 2000), and relationships between personality or temperament and psychopathology (Oldehinkel et al., 2004).

Implications and Future Directions

The goal of this chapter was to propose an integrative, research-derived model that provides an organizational framework for guiding future research on the origins of comorbid mental disorders. Although the structure and components of the model are all empirically derived, some components have more empirical support than others. The liability to persistent negative thinking, for example, is certainly consistent with theoretical models of

depression and anxiety and findings of characteristic negative thinking patterns in depressed and anxious individuals, but almost no research has investigated the genetic basis of these negative thinking patterns, the genetic covariation between these thinking patterns and internalizing psychopathology, or endophenotypes related to these constructs. Better phenotypic characterization of the behaviors, traits, and cognitive processes associated with these genetically influenced liabilities and research on the genetic covariation between these liabilities and psychopathology will advance our understanding of the structure underlying comorbidity of mental disorders. These broad phenotypes can then be used in the search for specific genes associated with psychopathology and, when studied in conjunction with specific disorders, will ultimately lead to delineation of the etiology and biological processes shared among comorbid disorders and biological processes that distinguish mental disorders. In addition, research on endophenotypes for the liabilities is lacking and is important for linking the neurobiological, genetic, and phenotypic findings to better understand the diverse, complex, interacting systems that contribute to comorbidity. Studies that use an interdisciplinary approach to investigating the interplay of genetics, neurobiological systems, and environmental factors will be key to understanding comorbidity.

This model can also be used to guide research on the genetic and environmental factors underlying psychopathology more broadly defined. Feinstein (1970), who coined the term comorbidity, originally described a broad construct that referred to comorbidity not just among medical disorders but also among symptoms of disorders and other clinical phenomena that do not meet criteria for disease status (Feinstein, 1970; Krueger & Markon, 2006). Krueger et al. (2002, 2005) and others have provided evidence that psychopathology is best conceptualized along continuous dimensions rather than as discrete entities (Krueger et al., 2005; Krueger & Piasecki, 2002). In fact, psychopathology researchers have debated use of the term "comorbidity" to describe mental disorders and how to best conceptualize the observed co-occurrence of mental disorders. Lilienfeld et al. (1994) and others discussed concerns that the term comorbidity inappropriately reifies psychopathology as defined by discrete, well-understood categorical diagnoses with distinct etiologies rather than conceptualizing it in a dimensional framework (Lilienfeld, Waldman, & Israel, 1994; Meehl,

2001), while others have argued that the concept of comorbidity is useful even when categories do not have clearly distinct etiologies (Spitzer, 1994). Krueger and Markon (2006) raise the related concern that co-occurrence of two legitimate diagnoses in a single individual should be distinguished from correlation or covariation of diagnoses in a group of people (Krueger & Markon, 2006). Regardless of whether or not the term "comorbidity" and discrete diagnostic categories are used, the empirical evidence and the proposed common liability model suggest that advancing our understanding of the origins of comorbidity (or "co-occurrence") requires broadening our conceptualization of this phenomenon to include not only diagnoses or dimensional measures of psychopathology but also related personality traits, behavioral tendencies, and neurobiological systems. It requires studying these broad factors from a developmental perspective in order to understand developmental differences in the expression of genetic liabilities, the progression of risk from early appearances of problems to impairing psychopathology, and how genetic and environmental interplay affects the course of comorbid disorder development. Finally, it implies that efforts to find genes for SUDs and related psychopathology would do well to capitalize on what we know about comorbidity. That is, rather than only trying to find genes for specific SUDs, efforts directed at finding genes associated with the covariance among disorders are also needed. Because behavior genetic studies have shown that the latent traits underlying this covariance are more heritable than the individual characteristics comprising it, gene finding approaches targeting the latent traits have strong payoff potential.

Acknowledgments

Preparation of this chapter was supported by the National Institutes on Drug Abuse (DA 13240, DA 05147, DA 024417), Alcohol Abuse and Alcoholism (AA 09367, AA 11886), and Mental Health (MH66140), and the National Cancer Institute (through DA 024417).

References

Abramson, L. Y., Metalsky, G. I., & Alloy, L. B. (1989). Hopelessness depression: A theory-based subtype of depression. *Psychological Review, 96*, 358–372.

Abramson, L. Y., Seligman, M. E. P., & Teasdale, J. (1978). Learned helplessness in humans: Critique and reformulation. *Journal of Abnormal Psychology, 87*, 49–74.

Adli, M., Pilhatsch, M., Bauer, M., Koberle, U., Ricken, R., Janssen, G., et al. (2008). Safety of high-intensity treatment with the irreversible monoamine oxidase inhibitor tranylcypromine in patients with treatment-resistant depression. *Pharmacopsychiatry, 41*, 252–257.

Agrawal, A., Jacobson, K., Prescott, C., & Kendler, K. S. (2004). A twin study of personality and illicit drug use and abuse/dependence. *Twin Research, 7*, 72–81.

Agrawal, A., & Lynskey, M. T. (2006). The genetic epidemiology of cannabis use, abuse, and dependence. *Addiction, 101*, 801–812.

Agrawal, A., Lynskey, M. T., Bucholz, K. K., Martin, N. G., Madden, P. A., & Heath, A. C. (2007). Contrasting models of genetic comorbidity for cannabis and other illicit drugs in adult Australian twins. *Psychological Medicine, 37*, 49–60.

Agrawal, A., Neale, M. C., Prescott, C. A., & Kendler, K. S. (2004a). Cannabis and other illicit drugs: Comorbid use and abuse/dependence in males and females. *Behavior Genetics, 34*, 217–228.

Agrawal, A., Neale, M. C., Prescott, C. A., & Kendler, K. S. (2004b). A twin study of early cannabis use and subsequent use and abuse/dependence of other illicit drugs. *Psychological Medicine, 34*, 1227–1237.

Aldao, A., & Nolen-Hoeksema, S. (2010). Specificity of cognitive emotion regulation strategies: A transdiagnostic examination. *Behaviour Research and Therapy, 48*(10), 974–983.

Alloy, L. B., Abramson, L. Y., Gibb, B. E., Crossfield, A. G., Pieracci, A. M., Spasojevic, J., et al. (2004). Developmental antecedents of cognitive vulnerability to depression: Review of findings from the cognitive vulnerability to depression project. *Journal of Cognitive Psychotherapy, 18*, 115–133.

Anderson, J. C., Williams, S., McGee, R., & Silva, P. A. (1987). DSM-III Disorders in preadolescent children. Prevalence in a large sample from the general population. *Archives of General Psychiatry, 44*, 69–76.

Angold, A., Costello, E. J., & Erkanli, A. (1999). Comorbidity. *Journal of Child Psychology and Psychiatry, 40*, 57–87.

Anokhin, A. P., Golosheykin, S., & Heath, A. C. (2007). Genetic and environmental influences on emotion-modulated startle reflex: A twin study. *Psychophysiology, 44*, 106–112.

Anthony, J. C., & Lonigan, C. J. (2002). An affect-based, hierarchical model of temperament and its relations with internalizing symptomatology. *Journal of Clinical Child & Adolescent Psychology, 31*, 480–490.

Armstrong, T. D., & Costello, J. (2002). Community studies on adolescent substance use, abuse, or dependence and psychiatric comorbidity. *Journal of Consulting and Clinical Psychology, 70*, 1224–1239.

Aseltine, R. H., Gore, S., & Colten, M. E. (1998). The co-occurrence of depression and substance abuse in late adolescence. *Development and Psychopathology, 10*, 549–570.

Bachanas, P. J., & Kaslow, N. J. (2001). Depressive disorders. In J. C. Conoley, A. M. LaGreca, & J. N. Hughes (Eds.), *Handbook of psychological services for children and adolescents* (pp. 323–352). New York: Oxford University Press.

Barlow, D. H. (1991). The nature of anxiety: Anxiety, depression, and emotional disorders. In R. M. Rapee & D. H. Barlow (Eds.), *Chronic anxiety: Generalized anxiety disorder and mixed anxiety-depression* (pp. 1–28). New York: Guilford.

Bartels, M., van Beijsterveldt, C., Derks, E. M., Stroet, T. M., Polderman, T. J., Hudziak, J. J., et al. (2007). Young Netherlands Twin Register (Y-NTR): A longitudinal multiple informant study of problem behavior. *Twin Research and Human Genetics, 10*, 3–11.

Bechara, A. (2005). Decision making, impulse control and loss of willpower to resist drugs: A neurocognitive perspective. *Nature Neuroscience, 8,* 1458–1463.

Beck, A. T. (1967). *Depression: Clinical, experimental, and theoretical aspects.* New York: Hoeber.

Beck, A. T. (1976). *Cognitive therapy and emotional disorders.* New York: International Universities Press.

Beck, A. T., & Clark, D. A. (1997). An information processing model of anxiety: Automatic and strategic processes. *Behaviour Research & Therapy, 35,* 49–58.

Bergen, S. E., Gardner, C. O., Kendler, K. S., Bergen, S. E., Gardner, C. O., & Kendler, K. S. (2007). Age-related changes in heritability of behavioral phenotypes over adolescence and young adulthood: A meta-analysis. *Twin Research & Human Genetics: The Official Journal of the International Society for Twin Studies, 10,* 423–433.

Bienvenu, O., Hettema, J. M., Neale, M. C., Prescott, C. A., & Kendler, K. S. (2007). Low extraversion and high neuroticism as indices of genetic and environmental risk for social phobia, agoraphobia, and animal phobia. *American Journal of Psychiatry, 164,* 1714–1721.

Birley, A. J., Gillespie, N. A., Heath, A. C., Sullivan, P. F., Boomsma, D. I., & Martin, N. G. (2006). Heritability and nineteen-year stability of long and short EPQ-R Neuroticism scales. *Personality and Individual Differences, 40,* 737–747.

Block, J. H., Gjerde, P. F., & Block, J. H. (1991). Personality antecedents of depressive tendencies in 18-year-olds: A prospective study. *Journal of Personality and Social Psychology, 60,* 726–738.

Bradley, B. P., Mogg, K., White, J., Groom, C., & de Bono, J. (1999). Attentional bias for emotional faces in generalized anxiety disorder. *British Journal of Clinical Psychology, 38*(3), 267–278.

Brady, K. T., & Sinha, R. (2005). Co-occurring mental and substance use disorders: The neurobiological effects of chronic stress. *American Journal of Psychiatry, 162,* 1483–1493.

Breslau, N., Novak, S. P., & Kessler, R. C. (2004). Psychiatric disorders and stages of smoking. *Biological Psychiatry, 55*(1), 69–76.

Brouwer, J. P., Appelhof, B. C., van Rossum, E. F., Koper, J. W., Fliers, E., Huyser, J., et al. (2006). Prediction of treatment response by HPA-axis and glucocorticoid receptor polymorphisms in major depression. *Psychoneuroendocrinology, 31,* 1154–1163.

Burt, S. A., Krueger, R. F., McGue, M., & Iacono, W. G. (2001). Sources of covariation among attention-deficit/hyperactivity disorder, oppositional defiant disorder, and conduct disorder: The importance of the shared environment. *Journal of Abnormal Psychology, 110,* 516–525.

Burwell, S. J., Malone, S. M., Bernat, E. M., & Iacono, W. G. (2014). Does electroencephalogram phase variability account for reduced P3 brain potential in externalizing disorders? *Clinical Neurophysiology.*

Button, T. M., Hewitt, J. K., Rhee, S. H., Young, S. E., Corley, R. P., & Stallings, M. C. (2006). Examination of the causes of covariation between conduct disorder symptoms and vulnerability to drug dependence. *Twin Research & Human Genetics, 9,* 38–45.

Button, T. M., Rhee, S. H., Hewitt, J. K., Young, S. E., Corley, R. P., & Stallings, M. C. (2007). The role of conduct disorder in explaining the comorbidity between alcohol and illicit drug dependence in adolescence. *Drug and Alcohol Dependence, 87,* 46–53.

Carlson, S. R., Katsanis, J. K., Iacono, W. G., & McGue, M. (1997). Emotional modulation of the startle reflex in twins: Preliminary findings. *Biological Psychology, 46,* 235–246.

Carlson, S. R., McLarnon, M. E., & Iacono, W. G. (2007). P300 amplitude, externalizing psychopathology, and earlier- versus later-onset substance-use disorder. *Journal of Abnormal Psychology, 116,* 565–577.

Caspi, A., Henry, B., McGee, R. O., Moffitt, T. E., & Silva, P. A. (1995). Temperamental origins of child and adolescent behavior problems: From age three to age fifteen. *Child Development, 66,* 55–68.

Caspi, A., Moffitt, T. E., Newman, D. L., & Silva, P. A. (1996). Behavioral observations at age 3 years predict adult psychiatric disorders. *Archives of General Psychiatry, 53,* 1033–1039.

Chassin, L., Fora, D. B., & King, K. M. (2004). Trajectories of alcohol and drug use and dependence from adolescence to adulthood: The effects of familial alcoholism and personality. *Journal of Abnormal Psychology, 113,* 483–498.

Chorpita, B. F., & Daleiden, E. L. (2002). Tripartite dimensions of emotion in a child clinical sample: Measurement strategies and implications for clinical utility. *Journal of Consulting and Clinical Psychology, 70,* 1150–1160.

Cicchetti, D., & Rogosch, F. (1996). Equifinality and multifinality in developmental psychopathology. *Development and Psychopathology, 8,* 597–600.

Cicchetti, D., & Tucker, D. (1994). Development and self-regulatory structures of the mind. *Development and Psychopathology, 6,* 533–550.

Clark, L. A., & Watson, D. (1991). Tripartite model of anxiety and depression: Psychometric evidence and taxonomic implications. *Journal of Abnormal Psychology, 103,* 103–116.

Clark, L. A., Watson, D., & Reynolds, S. (1995). Diagnosis and classification of psychopathology: Challenges to the current system and future directions. *Annual Review of Psychology, 46,* 121–153.

Clarke, T. K., Treutlein, J., Zimmermann, U. S., Kiefer, F., Skowronek, M. H., Rietschel, M., et al. (2008). HPA-axis activity in alcoholism: Examples for a gene-environment interaction. *Addiction Biology, 13,* 1–14.

Cloninger, C. R., Sigvardsson, S., & Bohman, M. (1988). Childhood personality predicts alcohol abuse in young adults. *Alcoholism, 12,* 494–505.

Cole, P. M., Michel, M. K., & Teti, L. O. (1994). The development of emotion regulation and dysregulation: A clinical perspective. *Monographs of the Society for Research in Child Development, 59,* 73–100.

Comings, D. E., Wu, S., Rostamkhani, M., McGue, M., Iacono, W. G., & MacMurray, J. P. (2002). Association of the Muscarinic Cholinergic 2 Receptor (CHRM2) gene with major depression in women. *American Journal of Medical Genetics, 114,* 527–529.

Compas, B. E., Conner-Smith, J., & Jaser, S. S. (2004). Temperament, stress reactivity, and coping: Implications for depression in childhood and adolescence. *Journal of Clinical Child & Adolescent Psychology, 33,* 21–31.

Conway, K. P., Compton, W., Stinson, F. S., & Grant, B. F. (2006). Lifetime Comorbidity of DSM-IV mood and anxiety disorders and specific drug use disorders: Results from the national epidemiologic survey on alcohol and related conditions. *Journal of Clinical Psychiatry, 67*(2), 247–257.

Curry, A., Latkin, C., Davey-Rothwell, M., Curry, A., Latkin, C., & Davey-Rothwell, M. (2008). Pathways to depression: The impact of neighborhood violent crime on inner-city residents in Baltimore, Maryland, USA. *Social Science & Medicine*, *67*, 23–30.

Cuthbert, B. N., Lang, P. J., Strauss, C., Drobes, D., Patrick, C. J., & Bradley, M. M. (2003). The psychophysiology of anxiety disorder: Fear memory imagery. *Psychophysiology*, *40*, 407–422.

Derefinko, K. J., & Lynam, D. R. (2006). Convergence and divergence among self-report psychopathy measures: A personality-based approach. *Journal of Personality Disorders*, *20*, 261–280.

Derryberry, D., & Rothbart, M. K. (1988). Affect, arousal, and attention as components of temperament. *Journal of Personality and Social Psychology*, *55*, 958–966.

Derryberry, D., & Rothbart, M. K. (1997). Reactive and effortful processes in the organization of temperament. *Development and Psychopathology*, *9*, 633–652.

Dick, D. M., Aliev, G., Wang, J. C., Grucza, R. A., Schuckit, M., et al. (2008). Using dimensional models of externalizing psychopathology to aid in gene identification. *Archives of General Psychiatry*, *65*, 310–318.

Dick, D. M., Viken, R. J., Kaprio, J., Pulkkinen, L., & Rose, R. J. (2005). Understanding the covariation among childhood externalizing symptoms: Genetic and environmental influences on conduct disorder, attention deficit hyperactivity disorder, and oppositional defiant disorder symptoms. *Journal of Abnormal Child Psychology*, *33*, 219–229.

Duncan, L. E., & Keller, M. C. (2011). A critical review of the first 10 years of candidate gene-by-environment interaction research in psychiatry. *American Journal of Psychiatry*, *168*, 1041–1049.

Eaves, L., Silberg, J., Erkanli, A., Eaves, L., Silberg, J., & Erkanli, A. (2003). Resolving multiple epigenetic pathways to adolescent depression. *Journal of Child Psychology & Psychiatry & Allied Disciplines*, *44*, 1006–1014.

Ehringer, M. A., Rhee, S. H., Young, S., Corley, R., & Hewitt, J. K. (2006). Genetic and environmental contributions to common psychopathologies of childhood and adolescence: A study of twins and their siblings. *Journal of Abnormal Child Psychology*, *34*, 1–17.

Eisenberg, N., Cumberland, A., Spinrad, T. L., Fabes, R. A., Shepard, S. A., Reiser, M., et al. (2001). The relations of regulation and emotionality to children's externalizing and internalizing problem behavior. *Child Development*, *72*, 1112–1134.

Eley, T. C., Bolton, D., O'Connor, T. G., Perrin, S., Smith, P., & Plomin, R. (2003). A twin study of anxiety-related behaviours in pre-school children. *Journal of Child Psychology and Psychiatry*, *44*, 945–960.

Eley, T. C., & Brown, T. A. (2004). Phenotypic and genetic/environmental structure of anxiety sensitivity in adolescents. *Behavior Genetics*, *34*, 637.

Eley, T. C., Gregory, A. M., Clark, D. M., & Ehlers, A. (2007). Feeling anxious: A twin study of panic/somatic ratings, anxiety sensitivity and heartbeat perception in children. *Journal of Child Psychology and Psychiatry*, *48*, 1184–1191.

Eley, T. C., Gregory, A. M., Lau, J. Y., McGuffin, P., Napolitano, M., Rijsdijk, F. V., et al. (2008). In the face of uncertainty: A twin study of ambiguous information, anxiety and depression in children. *Journal of Abnormal Child Psychology*, *36*, 55–65.

Elkins, I. J., King, S. M., McGue, M., & Iacono, W. G. (2006). Personality traits and the development of nicotine, alcohol, and illicit drug disorders: Prospective links from adolescence to young adulthood. *Journal of Abnormal Psychology*, *115*, 26–39.

Elkins, I. J., McGue, M., Malone, S., & Iacono, W. G. (2004). The effect of parental alcohol and drug disorders on adolescent personality. *American Journal of Psychiatry*, *161*, 670–676.

Ellis, J. A., Olsson, C. A., Moore, E., Greenwood, P., Van De Ven, M. O. M., & Patton, G. C. (2011). A role for the DRD4 Exon III VNTR in modifying the association between nicotine dependence and neuroticism. *Nicotine & Tobacco Research*, *13*(2), 64–69.

Everaert, J., Koster, E. H. W., & Derakshan, N. (2012). The combined cognitive bias hypothesis in depression. *Clinical Psychology Review*, *32*(5), 413–424.

Eysenck, M. W. (1992). *Anxiety: The cognitive perspective*. Hove, UK: Erlbaum.

Eysenck, M. W. (1997). *Anxiety and cognition: A unified theory*. Hove, UK: Erlbaum.

Eysenck, S. B. G., Eysenck, H. J., & Barrett, P. (1985). A revised version of the psychoticism scale. *Personality and Individual Differences*, *6*, 21–29.

Fanous, A., Gardner, C. O., Prescott, C. A., Cancro, R., & Kendler, K. S. (2002). Neuroticism, major depression and gender: A population-based twin study. *Psychological Medicine*, *32*, 719–728.

Fanous, A. H., Neale, M. C., Aggen, S. H., & Kendler, K. S. (2007). A longitudinal study of personality and major depression in a population-based sample of male twins. *Psychological Medicine*, *37*, 1163–1172.

Fava, M., Hwang, I., Rush, A. J., Sampson, N., Walters, E. E., & Kessler, R. C. (2010). The importance of irritability as a symptom of major depressive disorder: Results from the National Comorbidity Survey replication. *Molecular Psychiatry*, *15*(8), 856–867.

Feinstein, A. R. (1970). The pre-therapeutic classification of co-morbidity in chronic disease. *Journal of Chronic Diseases*, *23*, 455–468.

Fergusson, D. M., Boden, J. M., & Horwood, J. (2009). Tests of causal links between alcohol abuse or dependence and major depression. *Archives of General Psychiatry*, *66*, 206–266.

Firk, C., Markus, C. R., Firk, C., & Markus, C. R. (2007). Review: Serotonin by stress interaction: A susceptibility factor for the development of depression? *Journal of Psychopharmacology*, *21*, 538–544.

Fleming, J. E., Offord, D. R., & Boyle, M. H. (1989). Prevalence of childhood and adolescent depression in the community: Ontario Child Health Study. *British Journal of Psychology*, *28*, 647–654.

Florez, G., Saiz, P., Garcia-Portilla, P., Álvarez, S., Nogueíras, L., Morales, B., et al. (2008). Association between the Stin2 VNTR polymorphism of the serotonin transporter gene and treatment outcome in alcohol-dependent patients. *Alcohol and Alcoholism*, *43*, 516–522.

Forbes, E. E., Miller, A., Cohn, J. F., Fox, N. A., & Kovacs, M. (2005). Affect-modulated startle in adults with childhood-onset depression: Relations to bipolar course and number of lifetime depressive episodes. *Psychiatry Research*, *134*, 11–25.

Fowler, J. S., Volkow, N. D., Wang, G. J., Pappas, N., Logan, J., Shea, C., et al. (1996). Brain monoamine oxidase

A inhibition in cigarette smokers. *Proceedings of the National Academy of Sciences of the United States of America, 93,* 14065–14069.

Fox, N. A., & Pine, D. S. (2012). Temperament and the emergence of anxiety disorders. *Journal of the American Academy of Child & Adolescent Psychiatry, 51*(2), 125–128.

Fu, Q., Heath, A. C., Bucholz, K. K., Nelson, E., Goldberg, J., Lyons, M. J., et al. (2002). Shared genetic risk of major depression, alcohol dependence, and marijuana dependence: Contribution of antisocial personality disorder in men. *Archives of General Psychiatry, 59,* 1125–1132.

Garakani, A., Mathew, S. J., & Charney, D. S. (2006). Neurobiology of anxiety disorders and implications for treatment. *Mount Sinai Journal of Medicine, 73,* 941–949.

Gershuny, B. S., & Sher, K. J. (1998). The relation between personality and anxiety: Findings from a 3-year prospective study. *Journal of Abnormal Psychology, 107,* 252–262.

Gillespie, N. A., & Martin, N. G. (2006). Neuroticism as a genetic marker for mood and anxiety. In T. Canli (Ed.), *Biology of personality and individual differences* (pp. 225–250). New York: Guilford.

Gladstone, G. L., Parker, G. B., Gladstone, G. L., & Parker, G. B. (2006). Is behavioral inhibition a risk factor for depression? *Journal of Affective Disorders, 95,* 85–94.

Goldman, D., Oroszi, G., & Ducci, F. (2005). The genetics of addictions: Uncovering genes. *Nature Reviews Genetics, 6,* 521–532.

Goodman, E., & Capitman, J. (2000). Depressive symptoms and cigarette smoking among teens. *Pediatrics, 106,* 748–755.

Gotlib, I. H., & Joormann, J. (2010). Cognition and depression: Current status and future directions. *Annual Review of Clinical Psychology, 6,* 285–312.

Gottesman, I. I., & Gould, T. D. (2003). The endophenotype concept in psychiatry: Etymology and strategic intentions. *American Journal of Psychiatry, 160,* 636–645.

Gralinski, J. H., & Kopp, C. B. (1993). Everyday rules for behavior: Mothers' requests to young children. *Developmental Psychology, 29,* 573–584.

Grant, B. F., & Dawson, D. A. (1997). Age at onset of alcohol use and its association with DSM-IV alcohol abuse and dependence: Results from the national Longitudinal Alcohol Epidemiologic Survey. *Journal of Substance Abuse, 9,* 103–110.

Grant, J. D., Scherrer, J. F., Lynskey, M. T., Lyons, M. J., Eisen, S. A., et al. (2006). Adolescent alcohol use is a risk factor for adult alcohol and drug dependence: Evidence from a twin design. *Psychological Medicine, 36,* 109–118.

Gray, J. A. (1972). the psychophysiological basis of introversion-extraversion: A modification of Eysenck's theory. In V. D. Nebylitsyn & J. A. Gray (Eds.), *The biological basis of individual behaviour* (pp. 182–205). San Diego, CA: Academic Press.

Gray, J. A. (1975). *Elements of a two-process theory of learning.* New York: Academic.

Gray, J. A. (1981). A critique of Eysenck's theory of personality. In H. J. Eysenck (Ed.), *A model for personality* (pp. 246–276). Berlin: Springer-Verlag.

Greenfield, S., Weiss, R. Nuenz, L., Vagge, L., Kelly, J., Bellow, L., & Michael, J. (1998). The effect of depression on return to drinking: A prospective study. *Archives of General Psychiatry, 55,* 259–265.

Gregory, A. M., Rijsdijk, F. V., Lau, J. Y., Napolitano, M., McGuffin, P., Eley, T. C., et al. (2007). Genetic and environmental influences on interpersonal cognitions and associations with depressive symptoms in 8-year-old twins. *Journal of Abnormal Psychology, 116,* 762–775.

Grekin, E. R., Sher, K. J., & Wood, P. K. (2006). Personality and substance dependence symptoms: Modeling substance-specific traits. *Psychology of Addictive Behaviors, 20,* 415–424.

Gross, J. J., & Thompson, R. A. (2007). Emotion regulation: Conceptual foundations. In J. J. Gross (Ed.), *Handbook of emotion regulation.* (pp. 3–24). New York: Guilford.

Haas, B. W., Canli, T., Haas, B. W., & Canli, T. (2008). Emotional memory function, personality structure and psychopathology: A neural system approach to the identification of vulnerability markers. *Brain Research Reviews, 58,* 71–84.

Hankin, B. L., Badanes, L. S., Abela, J. R. Z., & Watamura, S. E. (2010). Hypothalamic–pituitary–adrenal axis dysregulation in dysphoric children and adolescents: Cortisol reactivity to psychosocial stress from preschool through middle adolescence. *Biological Psychiatry, 68*(5), 484–490.

Hansell, N. K., Wright, M. J., Medland, S. E., Davenport, T. A., Wray, N. R., Martin, N. G., et al. (2012). Genetic co-morbidity between neuroticism, anxiety/depression and somatic distress in a population sample of adolescent and young adult twins. *Psychological Medicine, 42*(6), 1249–1260.

Hasin, D. S., Liu, X., Nunes, E., McCloud, S., Samet, S., & Endicott, J. (2002). Effects of major depression on remission and relapse of substance dependence. *Archives of General Psychiatry, 59,* 375–380.

Heath, A. C., Bucholz, K. K., Madden, P. A., Dinwiddie, S. H., Slutske, W. S., Bierut, L. J., et al. (1997). Genetic and environmental contributions to alcohol dependence risk in a national twin sample: Consistency of findings in women and men. *Psychological Medicine, 27,* 1381–1396.

Hettema, J. M., Kuhn, J. W., Prescott, C. A., Kendler, K. S., Hettema, J. M., Kuhn, J. W., et al. (2006). The impact of generalized anxiety disorder and stressful life events on risk for major depressive episodes. *Psychological Medicine, 36,* 789–795.

Hettema, J. M., Neale, M. C., Myers, J. M., Prescott, C. A., & Kendler, K. S. (2006). A population-based twin study of the relationship between neuroticism and internalizing disorders. *American Journal of Psychiatry, 163,* 857–864.

Hettema, J. M., Prescott, C. A., & Kendler, K. S. (2004). Genetic and environmental sources of covariation between generalized anxiety disorder and neuroticism. *American Journal of Psychiatry, 161,* 1581–1587.

Hettema, J. M., Prescott, C. A., Myers, J. M., Neale, M. C., & Kendler, K. S. (2005). The structure of genetic and environmental risk factors for anxiety disorders in men and women. *Archives of General Psychiatry, 62,* 182–189.

Hicks, B. M., Bernat, E., Malone, S. M., Iacono, W. G., Patrick, C. J., Krueger, R. F., et al. (2007a). Genes mediate the association between P3 amplitude and externalizing disorders. *Psychophysiology, 44,* 98–105.

Hicks, B. M., Blonigen, D. M., Kramer, M. D., Krueger, R. F., Patrick, C. J., et al. (2007b). Gender differences and developmental change in externalizing disorders from late adolescence to early adulthood: A longitudinal twin study. *Journal of Abnormal Psychology, 116,* 433–447.

Hicks, B. M., Foster, K. T., Iacono, W. G., & McGue, M. (2013). Genetic and environmental influences on the familial trainsmission of externalizing disorders in adoptive and twin offspring. *JAMA Psychiatry.*

Hicks, B. M., Krueger, R. F., Iacono, W. G., McGue, M., & Patrick, C. J. (2004). Family transmission and heritability of externalizing disorders: A twin-family study. *Archives of General Psychiatry, 61*, 922–928.

Hicks, B. M., & Patrick, C. J. (2006). Psychopathy and negative emotionality: Analyses of suppressor effects reveal distinct relations with emotional distress, fearfulness, and anger-hostility. *Journal of Abnormal Psychology, 115*, 276–287.

Hicks, B. M., Schalet, B. D., Malone, S. M., Iacono, W. G., & McGue, M. (2011). Psychometric and genetic architecture of substance use disorder and behavioral disinhibition measures for gene association studies. *Behavior Genetics, 41*(4), 459–475.

Hipwell, A. E., Murray, L., Ducournau, P., & Stein, A. (2005). The effects of maternal depression and parental conflict on children's peer play. *Child: Care, Health and Development, 31*, 11–23.

Hirata, Y., Zai, C. C., Nowrouzi, B., Beitchman, J. H., & Kennedy, J. L. (2013). Study of the Catechol-O-Methyltransferase (COMT) gene with high aggression in children. *Aggressive Behavior, 39*(1), 45–51.

Hiroi, N., & Agatsuma, S. (2005). Genetic susceptibility to substance dependence. *Molecular Psychiatry, 10*, 336–344.

Hirsch, C. R., Clark, D. M., & Mathews, A. (2006). Imagery and interpretations in social phobia: Support for the combined cognitive biases hypothesis. *Behavior Therapy, 37*(3), 223–236.

Hirshfeld-Becker, D. R., Biederman, J., Henin, A., Faraone, S. V., Davis, S., Harrington, K., et al. (2007). Behavioral inhibition in preschool children at risk is a specific predictor of middle childhood social anxiety: A five-year follow-up. *Journal of Developmental and Behavioral Pediatrics, 28*(3), 225–233. doi: 10.1097/01.DBP.0000268559.34463.d0

Hofmann, S. G., Moscovitch, D. A., & Kim, H. J. (2006). Autonomic correlates of social anxiety and embarrassment in shy and non-shy individuals. *International Journal of Psychophysiology, 61*, 134–142.

Hofmann, S. G., Sawyer, A. T., Fang, A., & Asnaani, A. (2012). Emotion dysregulation model of mood and anxiety disorders. *Depression and Anxiety, 29*(5), 409–416.

Holmes, A. (2008). Genetic variation in cortico-amygdala serotonin function and risk for stress-related disease. *Neuroscience & Biobehavioral Reviews, 32*, 1293–1314.

Hopfer, C. J., Crowley, T. J., & Hewitt, J. K. (2003). Review of twin and adoption studies of adolescent substance use. *Journal of the American Academy of Child & Adolescent Psychiatry, 42*, 710–719.

Hur, Y. -M. (2009). Genetic and environmental covariations among obsessive–compulsive symptoms, neuroticism, and extraversion in South Korean adolescent and young adult twins. *Twin Research and Human Genetics, 12*(2), 142–149.

Hussong, A. M., & Chassin, L. (1994). The stress-negative affect model of adolescent substance use: Disaggregating negative affect. *Journal of Studies on Alcohol, 55*, 707–718.

Iacono, W. G., Carlson, S. R., Malone, S. M., & McGue, M. (2002). P3 event-related potential amplitude and the risk for disinhibitory disorders in adolescent boys. *Archives of General Psychiatry, 59*, 750–757.

Iacono, W. G., & Malone, S. M. (2011). Developmental endophenotypes: Indexing genetic risk for substance abuse with the P300 brain event-related potential. *Child Development Perspectives, 5*, 239–247.

Iacono, W. G., Malone, S. M., & McGue, M. (2008). Behavioral disinhibition and the development of early-onset addiction: Common and specific influences. *Annual Review of Clinical Psychology, 4*, 325–348.

Jackson, K. M., & Sher, K. J. (2003). Alcohol use disorders and psychological distress: A prospective state-trait analysis. *Journal of Abnormal Psychology, 112*, 599–613.

Jaffee, S. R., & Price, T. S. (2007). Gene-environment correlations: A review of the evidence and implications for prevention of mental illness. *Molecular Psychiatry, 12*, 432–442.

James, L. M., & Taylor, J. (2007). Impulsivity and negative emotionality associated with substance use problems and Cluster B personality in college students. *Addictive Behaviors, 32*, 714–727.

Joensuu, M., Lehto, S. M., Tolmunen, T., Saarinen, P. I., Valkonen-Korhonen, M., Vanninen, R., et al. (2010). Serotonin-transporter-linked promoter region polymorphism and serotonin transporter binding in drug-naïve patients with major depression. *Psychiatry and Clinical Neurosciences, 64*(4), 387–393.

Johnson, E. O., Rhee, S. H., Chase, G. A., & Breslau, N. (2004). Comorbidity of depression with levels of smoking: An exploration of the shared familial risk hypothesis. *Nicotine & Tobacco Research, 6*, 1029–1038.

Kaler, S. R., & Kopp, C. B. (1990). Compliance and comprehension in very young toddlers. *Child Development, 61*, 1997–2003.

Karkowski, L. M., Prescott, C. A., & Kendler, K. S. (2000). Multivariate assessment of factors influencing illicit substance use in twins from female-female pairs. *American Journal of Medical Genetics, 96*, 665–670.

Kaslow, N. J., Adamson, L. B., & Collins, M. H. (2000). A developmental psychopathology perspective on the cognitive components of child and adolescent depression. In A. J. Sameroff, M. Lewis, & S. M. Miller (Eds.), *Handbook of developmental psychopathology* (2nd ed., pp. 491–510). New York: Plenum.

Kendler, K. S., Aggen, S. H., Tambs, K., & Reichborn-Kjennerud, T. (2006). Illicit psychoactive substance use, abuse and dependence in population sample of Norwegian twins. *Psychological Medicine, 36*, 955–962.

Kendler, K. S., & Gardner, C. O. (2011). A longitudinal etiologic model for symptoms of anxiety and depression in women. *Psychological Medicine, 41*(10), 2035–2045.

Kendler, K. S., Gardner, C. O., Gatz, M., & Pedersen, N. L. (2007). The sources of co-morbidity between major depression and generalized anxiety disorder in a Swedish national twin sample. *Psychological Medicine, 37*, 453–462.

Kendler, K. S., Gardner, C. O., & Prescott, C. A. (2002). Toward a comprehensive developmental model for major depression in women. *American Journal of Psychiatry, 159*, 1133–1145.

Kendler, K. S., Gardner, C. O., & Prescott, C. A. (2006). Toward a comprehensive developmental model for major depression in men. *American Journal of Psychiatry, 163*, 115–124.

Kendler, K. S., Gatz, M., Gardner, C. O., & Pedersen, N. L. (2006). Personality and major depression: A Swedish longitudinal, population-based twin study. *Archives of General Psychiatry, 63*, 1113–1120.

Kendler, K. S., Heath, A. C., Neale, M. C., Kessler, R. C., & Eaves, L. J. (1993). Alcoholism and major depression in women: A twin study of the causes of comorbidity. *Archives of General Psychiatry, 50*, 690–698.

Kendler, K. S., Jacobson, K. C., Prescott, C. A., & Neale, M. C. (2003). Specificity of genetic and environmental risk factors for use and abuse/dependence of cannabis, cocaine, hallucinogens, sedatives, stimulants, and opiates in male twins. *American Journal of Psychiatry, 160*, 687–695.

Kendler, K. S., Myers, J., & Prescott, C. A. (2007). Specificity of genetic and environmental risk factors for symptoms of cannabis, cocaine, alcohol, caffeine, and nicotine dependence. *Archives of General Psychiatry, 64*, 1313–1320.

Kendler, K. S., Prescott, C. A., Myers, J., & Neale, M. C. (2003). The structure of genetic and environmental risk factors for common psychiatric and substance use disorders in men and women. *Archives of General Psychiatry, 60*, 929–937.

Kensinger, E. A., & Corkin, S. (2004). Two routes to emotional memory: Distinct neural processes for valence and arousal. *Proceedings of the National Academy of Sciences of the United States of America, 101*, 3310–3315.

Kessler, R. C., Berglund, P., Demler, O., Jin, R., Koretz, D., Merikangas, K. R., et al. (2003). The epidemiology of major depressive disorder: Results from the National Comorbidity Survey Replication (NCS-R). *Journal of the American Medical Association, 289*, 3095–3105.

Kessler, R. C., Berglund, P., Demler, O., Jin, R., & Walters, E. E. (2005). Lifetime prevalence and age-of-onset distributions of DSM-IV disorders in the National Comorbidity Survey Replication. *Archives of General Psychiatry, 62*, 593–602.

Kessler, R. C., Chiu, W. T., Jin, R., Ruscio, A. M., Shear, K., & Walters, E. E. (2006). The epidemiology of panic attacks, panic disorder, and agoraphobia in the national comorbidity survey replication. *Archives of General Psychiatry, 63*, 415–424.

Keyes, M., Iacono, W. G., & McGue, M. (2007). Early onset problem behavior, young adult psychopathology, and contextual risk. *Twin Research & Human Genetics, 10*, 45–53.

Khan, A. A., Jacobson, K. C., Gardner, C. O., Prescott, C. A., & Kendler, K. S. (2005). Personality and comorbidity of common psychiatric disorders. *British Journal of Clinical Psychology, 186*, 190–196.

Kim-Cohen, J., Caspi, A., Moffitt, T. E., Harrington, H., Milne, B. J., & Poulton, R. (2003). Prior juvenile diagnoses in adults with mental disorder: Developmental follow-back of a prospective-longitudinal cohort. *Archives of General Psychiatry, 60*, 709–717.

Klein, D. N., Kotov, R., & Bufferd, S. J. (2011). Personality and depression: Explanatory models and review of the evidence. *Annual Review of Clinical Psychology, 7*, 269–295.

King, S. M., Iacono, W. G., & McGue, M. (2004). Childhood externalizing and internalizing psychopathology in the prediction of early substance use. *Addiction Biology, 99*, 1548–1559.

Kochanska, G., Barry, R. A., Jimenez, N. B., Hollatz, A. L., & Woodard, J. (2009). Guilt and effortful control: Two mechanisms that prevent disruptive developmental trajectories. *Journal of Personality and Social Psychology, 97*(2), 322–333.

Koller, G., Zill, P., Skoruppa, T., Bondy, B., Preuss, U. W., & Soyka, M. (2008). Low level of harm avoidance is associated with serotonin transporter functional haplotype in alcohol-dependent individuals. *Psychiatric Genetics, 18*, 59–63.

Koob, G. F., Ahmed, S. H., Boutrel, B., Chen, S. A., Kenny, P. J., Markou, A., et al. (2004). Neurobiological mechanisms in the transition from drug use to drug dependence. *Neuroscience and Behavioral Review, 27*, 739–749.

Kosten, T. R., George, T. P., & Kleber, H. D. (2005). The neurobiology of substance dependence: Implications for treatment. In R. J. Frances, S. I. Miller & A. H. Mack (Eds.), *Clinical textbook of addictive disorders* (pp. 3–15). New York: Guilford.

Kreek, M. J., Nielsen, D. A., Butelman, E. R., & LaForge, K. S. (2005). Genetic influences on impulsivity, risk taking, stress responsivity and vulnerability to drug abuse and addiction. *Nature Neuroscience, 8*, 1450–1457.

Krueger, R. F. (1999a). Personality traits in late adolescence predict mental disorders in early adulthood: A prospective-epidemiological study. *Journal of Personality, 67*, 39–65.

Krueger, R. F. (1999b). The structure of common mental disorders. *Archives of General Psychiatry, 107*, 216–227.

Krueger, R. F., Hicks, B. M., Patrick, C. J., Carlson, S. R., Iacono, W. G., & McGue, M. (2002). Etiologic connections among substance dependence, antisocial behavior, and personality: Modeling the externalizing spectrum. *Journal of Abnormal Psychology, 111*, 411–424.

Krueger, R. F., & Markon, K. E. (2006). Reinterpreting comorbidity: A model-based approach to understanding and classifying psychopathology. *Annual Review of Clinical Psychology, 2*, 111–133.

Krueger, R. F., Markon, K. E., Patrick, C. J., & Iacono, W. G. (2005). Externalizing psychopathology in adulthood: A dimensional-spectrum conceptualization and its implications for DSM-V. *Journal of Abnormal Psychology, 114*, 537–550.

Krueger, R. F., McGue, M., & Iacono, W. G. (2001). The higher-order structure of common DSM mental disorders: Internalization, externalization, and their connection to personality. *Personality and Individual Differences, 30*, 1245–1259.

Krueger, R. F., & Piasecki, T. M. (2002). Toward a dimensional and psychometrically-informed approach to conceptualizing psychopathology. *Behaviour Research and Therapy, 40*, 485–500.

Kunz, J. (2001). Parental divorce and children's interpersonal relationships: A meta-analysis. *Journal of Divorce & Remarriage, 34*, 19–47.

Kushner, M. G., Sher, K. J., & Erickson, D. J. (1999). Prospective analysis of the relation between DSM-III anxiety disorders and alcohol use disorders. *American Journal of Psychiatry, 156*, 723–732.

Lara, D. R., & Akiskal, H. S. (2006). Toward an integrative model of the spectrum of mood, behavioral and personality disorders based on fear and anger traits: II. Implications for neurobiology, genetics and psychopharmacological treatment. *Journal of Affective Disorders, 94*, 89–103.

Lara, D. R., Pinto, O., Akiskal, K., & Akiskal, H. S. (2006). Toward an integrative model of the spectrum of mood, behavioral and personality disorders based on fear and anger traits: I. Clinical implications. *Journal of Affective Disorders, 94*, 67–87.

Larson, C. L., Nitschke, J. B., & Davidson, R. J. (2007). Common and distinct patterns of affective response in dimensions of anxiety and depression. *Emotion, 7*, 182–191.

Lau, J. Y., Rijsdijk, F., & Eley, T. C. (2006). I think, therefore I am: A twin study of attributional style in adolescents. *Journal of Child Psychology and Psychiatry, 47*, 696–703.

Legrand, L. N., Keyes, M., McGue, M., Iacono, W. G., & Krueger, R. F. (2007). Rural environments reduce the genetic influence on adolescent substance use and rule-breaking behavior. *Psychological Medicine*, *38*, 1–10.

Lenzenweger, M. F., Lane, M. C., Loranger, A. W., & Kessler, R. C. (2007). DSM-IV personality disorders in the national comorbidity survey replication. *Biological Psychiatry*, *62*, 553–564.

Levinson, D. F. (2006). The genetics of depression: A review. *Biological Psychiatry*, *60*, 84–92.

Licht, C. M. M., de Geus, E. J. C., van Dyck, R., & Penninx, B. W. J. H. (2009). Association between anxiety disorders and heart rate variability in the Netherlands Study of Depression and Anxiety (NESDA). *Psychosomatic Medicine*, *71*(5), 508–518.

Lilienfeld, S. O., Waldman, I. D., & Israel, A. C. (1994). A critical examination of the use of the term and concept of comorbidity in psychopathology research. *Clinical Psychology: Science and Practice*, *1*, 71–103.

Lonigan, C. J., Carey, M. P., & Finch, A. J., Jr. (1994). Anxiety and depression in children and adolescents: Negative affectivity and the utility of self-reports. *Journal of Consulting and Clinical Psychology*, *62*, 1000–1008.

Lonigan, C. J., Phillips, B. M., & Hooe, E. S. (2003). Relations of positive and negative affectivity to anxiety and depression in children: Evidence from a latent variable longitudinal study. *Journal of Consulting and Clinical Psychology*, *71*, 465–481.

Lonigan, C. J., Vasey, M. W., Phillips, B. M., Hazen, R. A., Lonigan, C. J., Vasey, M. W., et al. (2004). Temperament, anxiety, and the processing of threat-relevant stimuli. *Journal of Clinical Child & Adolescent Psychology*, *33*, 8–20.

Lynskey, M. T., Grant, J. D., Li, L., Nelson, E. C., Bucholz, K. K., et al. (2007). Stimulant use and symptoms of abuse/dependence: Epidemiology and associations with cannabis use: A twin study. *Drug and Alcohol Dependence*, *86*, 147–153.

Markou, A., Kosten, T. R., & Koob, G. F. (1998). Neurobiological similarities in depression and drug dependence: A self-medication hypothesis. *Neuropsychopharmacology*, *18*, 135–174.

Marmorstein, N. R., & Iacono, W. G. (2011). Explaining associations between cannabis use disorders in adolescence and later major depression: A test of the psychosocial failure model. *Addictive Behaviors*, *36*, 773–776.

Marmorstein, N. R., Iacono, W. G., & Malone, S. M. (2010). Longitudinal associations between depression and substance dependence from adolescence through early adulthood. *Drug & Alcohol Dependence*, *107*(2–3), 154–160.

Marshall, P. J., & Stevenson-Hinde, J. (1998). Behavioral inhibition, heart period, and respiratory sinus arrhythmia in young children. *Developmental Psychobiology*, *33*(3), 283–292. doi: 10.1002/(sici)1098–2302(199811)33:3<283::aid-dev8>3.0.co;2-n

Martin-Soelch, C., Stocklin, M., Dammann, G., Opwis, K., & Seifritz, E. (2006). Anxiety trait modulates psychophysiological reactions, but not habituation processes related to affective auditory stimuli. *International Journal of Psychophysiology*, *61*, 87–97.

Masse, L. C., & Tremblay, R. E. (1997). Behavior of boys in kindergarten and the onset of substance use during adolescence. *Archives of General Psychiatry*, *55*, 62–68.

Mathews, A., & MacLeod, C. (2005). Cognitive vulnerability to emotional disorders. *Annual Review of Clinical Psychology*, *1*(1), 167–195.

McDermott, J. M., Perez-Edgar, K., Henderson, H. A., Chronis-Tuscano, A., Pine, D. S., & Fox, N. A. (2009). A history of childhood behavioral inhibition and enhanced response monitoring in adolescence are linked to clinical anxiety. *Biological Psychiatry*, *65*(5), 445–448.

McGue, M., Elkins, I., Walden, B., & Iacono, W. G. (2005). Perceptions of the parent-adolescent relationship: A longitudinal investigation. *Developmental Psychology*, *41*, 971–984.

McGue, M., & Iacono, W. G. (2005). The association of early adolescent problem behavior with adult psychopathology. *American Journal of Psychiatry*, *162*, 1118–1124.

McGue, M., Iacono, W. G., & Krueger, R. F. (2006). The association of early adolescent problem behavior and adult psychopathology: A multivariate behavioral genetic perspective. *Behavior Genetics*, *36*, 591–602.

McGue, M., Slutske, W., & Iacono, W. G. (1999). Personality and substance use disorders: II. Alcoholism versus drug use disorders. *Journal of Consulting and Clinical Psychology*, *67*, 2.

McGue, M., Slutske, W., Taylor, J., & Iacono, W. G. (1997). Personality and substance use disorders: I. Effects of gender and alcoholism. *Alcoholism, Clinical, and Experimental Research*, *21*, 513–520.

Meehl, P. (2001). Comorbidity and taxometrics. *Clinical Psychology: Science and Practice*, *8*, 507–519.

Merenäkk, L., Mäestu, J., Nordquist, N., Parik, J., Oreland, L., Loit, H. -M., et al. (2011). Effects of the serotonin transporter (5-HTTLPR) and α$_{2A}$-adrenoceptor (C-1291G) genotypes on substance use in children and adolescents: A longitudinal study. *Psychopharmacology*, *215*(1), 13–22.

Merrill, K. A., Steinmetz, J. E., Viken, R. J., & Rose, R. J. (1999). Genetic influences on human conditionability: A twin study of the conditioned eyeblink response. *Behavior Genetics*, *29*, 95–102.

Middeldorp, C., Cath, D., Van Dyck, R., & Boomsma, D. (2005). The co-morbidity of anxiety and depression in the perspective of genetic epidemiology: A review of twin and family studies. *Psychological Medicine*, *35*, 611–624.

Miller, E. K., & Cohen, J. D. (2001). An integrative theory of prefrontal cortex function. *Annual Review of Neuroscience*, *24*, 167–202.

Miller, M. W., Vogt, D. S., Mozley, S. L., Kaloupek, D. G., & Keane, T. M. (2006). PTSD and substance-related problems: The mediating roles of disconstraint and negative emotionality. *Journal of Abnormal Psychology*, *115*, 369–379.

Mineka, S., Watson, D., & Clark, L. A. (1998). Comorbidity of anxiety and unipolar mood disorders. *Annual Review of Psychology*, *49*, 377–412.

Mogg, K., Philippot, P., & Bradley, B. P. (2004). Selective attention to angry faces in clinical social phobia. *Journal of Abnormal Psychology*, *113*(1), 160–165.

Morgan, B. E., & Morgan, B. E. (2006). Behavioral inhibition: A neurobiological perspective. *Current Psychiatry Reports*, *8*, 270–278.

Murisa, P., Meesters, C., & Blijlevens, P. (2007). Self-reported reactive and regulative temperament in early adolescence: Relations to internalizing and externalizing problem behavior and "Big Three" personality factors. *Journal of Adolescence*, *3*, 1035–1049.

Muris, P., Meesters, C., Merckelbach, H., Sermon, A., & Zwakhalen, S. (1998). Worry in normal children. *Journal of the American Academy of Child and Adolescent Psychiatry*, *37*, 703–710.

Muris, P., & Ollendick, T. H. (2005). The role of temperament in the etiology of child psychopathology. *Clinical Child and Family Psychology Review*, *8*, 271–289.

Myrick, H., & Brady, K. (2003). Current review of the comorbidity of affective, anxiety, and substance use disorders. *Current Opinions in Psychiatry*, *16*, 261–270.

Nadder, T. S., Rutter, M., Silberg, J. L., Maes, H. H., & Eaves, L. J. (2002). Genetic effects on the variation and covariation of attention deficit-hyperactivity disorder (ADHD) and oppositional-defiant disorder/conduct disorder (ODD/CD) symptomatologies across informant and occasion of measurement. *Psychological Medicine*, *32*, 39–53.

Nemeroff, C. B., & Vale, W. W. (2005). The neurobiology of depression: Inroads to treatment and new drug discovery. *Journal of Clinical Psychiatry*, *66*, 5–13.

Nestler, E. J. (2005). Is there a common molecular pathway for addiction? *Nature Neuroscience*, *8*, 1445–1449.

Nock, M. K., Kazdin, A. E., Hiripi, E., & Kessler, R. C. (2006). Prevalence, subtypes, and correlates of DSM-IV conduct disorder in the National Comorbidity Survey Replication. *Psychological Medicine*, *36*, 699–710.

Nolen-Hoeksema, S., Girgus, J. S., & Seligman, M. E. (1992). Predictors and consequences of childhood depressive symptoms: A 5-year longitudinal study. *Journal of Abnormal Psychology*, *101*, 405–422.

Nolen-Hoeksema, S., Wisco, B. E., & Lyubomirsky, S. (2008). Rethinking rumination. *Perspectives on Psychological Science*, *3*(5), 400–424.

Nutt, D., Argyropoulos, S., Hood, S., & Potokar, J. (2006). Generalized anxiety disorder: A comorbid disease. *European Neuropsychopharmacology*, *16*, S109–S118.

Oldehinkel, A. J., Hartman, C. A., Ferdinand, R. F., Verhulst, F. C., & Ormel, J. (2007). Effortful control as modifier of the association between negative emotionality and adolescents' mental health problems. *Development and Psychopathology*, *19*, 523–539.

Oldehinkel, A. J., Hartman, C. A., Winter, A. F., Veenstra, R., & Johan, O. (2004). Temperament profiles associated with internalizing and externalizing problems in preadolescence. *Development and Psychopathology*, *16*, 421–440.

Ormel, J., Oldehinkel, A. J., Ferdinand, R. F., Hartman, C. A., De Winter, A. F., Veenstra, R., et al. (2005). Internalizing and externalizing problems in adolescence: General and dimension-specific effects of familial loadings and pre-adolescent temperament traits. *Psychological Medicine*, *35*, 1825–1835.

Papageorgiou, C. (2006). Worry and rumination: Styles of persistent negative thinking in anxiety and depression. In G. C. L. Davey & A. Wells (Eds.), *Worry and its psychological disorders: Theory, assessment and treatment* (pp. 21–40). Hoboken, NJ: Wiley.

Papiol, S., Arias, B., Gasto, C., Gutierrez, B., Catalan, R., & Fananas, L. (2007). Genetic variability at HPA axis in major depression and clinical response to antidepressant treatment. *Journal of Affective Disorders*, *104*, 83–90.

Pardini, D., Lochman, J., & Wells, K. (2004). Negative emotions and alcohol use initiation in high-risk boys: The moderating effect of good inhibitory control. *Journal of Abnormal Child Psychology*, *32*, 505–518.

Patrick, C. J. (2006). The construct of emotion as a bridge between personality and psychopathology. In R. F. Krueger & J. Tackett (Eds.), *Personality and psychopathology* (pp. 174–209). New York: Guilford.

Pedlow, R., Sanson, A., Prior, M., & Oberklaid, F. (1993). Stability of maternally reported temperament from infancy to 8 years. *Developmental Psychology*, *29*, 998–1007.

Pérez-Edgar, K., Reeb-Sutherland, B. C., McDermott, J. M., White, L. K., Henderson, H. A., Degnan, K. A., et al. (2011). Attention biases to threat link behavioral inhibition to social withdrawal over time in very young children. *Journal of Abnormal Child Psychology*, *39*(6), 885–895.

Perlman, G., Johnson, W., & Iacono, W. G. (2009). The heritability of P300 amplitude in 18-year-olds is robust to adolescent alcohol use. *Psychophysiology*, *46*, 962–969.

Perlman, G., Markin, A., & Iacono, W. G. (2013). P300 amplitude reduction is associated with early-onset and late-onset pathological substance use in a prospectively studied cohort of 14 year-old adolescents. *Psychophysiology*, *50*, 974–982.

Plomin, R., & Bergeman, C. S. (1991). The nature of nurture: Genetic influence on "environmental" measures. *Behavior and Brain Sciences*, *14*, 373–427.

Porges, S. W. (2011). *The polyvagal theory: Neurophysiological foundations of emotions, attachment, communication, and self-regulation*. New York: W. W. Norton & Co.

Porter, R. J., Gallagher, P., Watson, S., Young, A. H., Porter, R. J., Gallagher, P., et al. (2004). Corticosteroid-serotonin interactions in depression: A review of the human evidence. *Psychopharmacology*, *173*, 1–17.

Prescott, C. A., Aggen, S. H., & Kendler, K. S. (2000). Sex-specific genetic influences on the comorbidity of alcoholism and major depression in a population-based sample of US twins. *Archives of General Psychiatry*, *57*, 803–811.

Rao, U., Daley, S. E., & Hammen, C. (2000). Relationship between depression and substance use disorders in adolescent women during the transition to adulthood. *Journal of the American Academy of Child & Adolescent Psychiatry*, *39*, 215–222.

Regier, D. A., Farmer, M. E., Rae, D. S., Locke, B. Z., Keith, S. J., Judd, L. L., et al. (1990). Comorbidity of mental disorders with alcohol and other drug abuse. Results from the Epidemiologic Catchment Area (ECA) Study. *Journal of the American Medical Association*, *264*, 2511–2518.

Rice, F., van den Bree, M. B., Thapar, A., Rice, F., van den Bree, M. B. M., & Thapar, A. (2004). A population-based study of anxiety as a precursor for depression in childhood and adolescence. *BMC Psychiatry*, *4*, 43.

Risbrough, V. B., & Stein, M. B. (2006). Role of corticotropin releasing factor in anxiety disorders: A translational research perspective. *Hormones and Behavior*, *50*, 550–561.

Roberts, B. W., & DelVecchio, W. F. (2000). The rank-order consistency of personality traits from childhood to old age: A quantitative review of longitudinal studies. *Psychological Bulletin*, *126*, 3–25.

Rose, R. J., Dick, D. M., Viken, R. J., & Kaprio, J. (2001). Gene-environment interaction in patterns of adolescent drinking: Regional residency moderates longitudinal influences on alcohol use. *Alcoholism: Clinical & Experimental Research*, *25*, 637–643.

Rothbart, M. K. (1989). Temperament and development. In J. E. Kohnstamm, J. E. Bates, & M. K. Rothbart (Eds.), *Temperament in childhood* (pp. 187–247). New York: Wiley.

Rothbart, M. K., Ahadi, S. A., & Evans, D. E. (2000). Temperament and personality: Origins and outcomes. *Journal of Personality and Social Psychology*, *78*, 122–135.

Rothbart, M. K., Ahadi, S. A., & Hershey, K. L. (1994). Temperament and social behavior in childhood. *Merrill-Palmer Quarterly*, *40*, 21–39.

Rothbart, M. K., Posner, M. I., & Hershey, K. L. (1995). Temperament, attention, and developmental psychology. In D. Cicchetti & D. J. Cohen (Eds.), *Developmental psychopathology: Vol. 1. Theory and methods* (pp. 315–340). New York: Wiley.

Rothbart, M. K., Posner, M. I., & Rosicky, J. (1994). Orienting in normal and pathological development. *Development and Psychopathology, 6*, 635–652.

Rounsaville, B. J. (2004). Treatment of cocaine dependence and depression. *Biological Psychiatry, 56*, 803–809.

Ruscio, A. M., Chiu, W. T., Roy-Byrne, P., Stang, P. E., Stein, D. J., Wittchen, H. U., et al. (2007). Broadening the definition of generalized anxiety disorder: Effects on prevalence and associations with other disorders in the National Comorbidity Survey Replication. *Journal of Anxiety Disorders, 21*, 662–676.

Rutter, M., & Silberg, J. (2002). Gene-environment interplay in relation to emotional and behavioral disturbance. *Annual Review of Clinical Psychology, 53*, 463–490.

Sarosi, A., Gonda, X., Balogh, G., Domotor, E., Szekely, A., Hejjas, K., et al. (2008). Association of the STin2 polymorphism of the serotonin transporter gene with a neurocognitive endophenotype in major depressive disorder. *Progress in Neuro-Psychopharmacology & Biological Psychiatry, 32*, 1667–1672.

Seligman, M. E. P. (1974). Depression and learned helplessness. In R. J. Friedman & M. Katz (Eds.), *The psychology of depression: Contemporary theory and research* (pp. 83–113). Washington, DC: Winston.

Sharma, R. K., Balhara, Y. P. S., Sagar, R., Deepak, K. K., & Mehta, M. (2011). Heart rate variability study of childhood anxiety disorders. *Journal of Cardiovascular Disease Research, 2*(2), 115–122.

Sher, K. J., Bartholow, B. D., & Wood, M. D. (2000). Personality and substance use disorders: A prospective study. *Journal of Consulting and Clinical Psychology, 68*, 818–829.

Silberg, J., Rutter, M., Meyer, J., Maes, H., Hewitt, J., & Simonoff, E. et al., (1996). Genetic and environmental influences on covariation between hyperactivity and conduct disturbance in juvenile twins. *Journal of Child Psychology & Psychiatry & Allied Disciplines, 37*, 803–816.

Silk, J. S., Steinberg, L., & Morris, A. S. (2003). Adolescents' emotion regulation in daily life: Links to depressive symptoms and problem behavior. *Child Development, 74*, 1869–1880.

Slutske, W. S., Heath, A. C., Madden, P. A., Bucholz, K. K., Statham, D. J., & Martin, N. G. (2002). Personality and the genetic risk for alcohol dependence. *Journal of Abnormal Psychology, 111*, 124–133.

Spengler, M., Gottschling, J., & Spinath, F. M. (2012). Personality in childhood—A longitudinal behavior genetic approach. *Personality and Individual Differences, 53*(4), 411–416.

Spitzer, R. L. (1994). Psychiatric "co-occurrence"? I'll stick with "comorbidity." *Clinical Psychology: Science and Practice, 1*, 88–92.

Stein, M. B., Jang, K. L., & Livesley, W. J. (1999). Heritability of anxiety sensitivity: A twin study. *American Journal of Psychiatry, 156*, 246–251.

Stockdale, S. E., Wells, K. B., Tang, L., Belin, T. R., Zhang, L., Sherbourne, C. D., et al. (2007). The importance of social context: Neighborhood stressors, stress-buffering mechanisms, and alcohol, drug, and mental health disorders. *Social Science & Medicine, 65*, 1867–1881.

Sullivan, P. F., Neale, M. C., & Kendler, K. S. (2000). Genetic epidemiology of major depression: Review and meta-analysis. *American Journal of Psychiatry, 157*, 1552–1562.

Swan, G. E., Carmelli, D., & Cardon, L. R. (1996). The consumption of tobacco, alcohol, and office in Caucasian male twins: A mulivariate genetic analysis. *Journal of Substance Abuse, 8*, 19–31.

Tafet, G. E., Feder, D. J., Abulafia, D. P., & Roffman, S. S. (2005). Regulation of hypothalamic-pituitary-adrenal activity in response to cognitive therapy in patients with generalized anxiety disorder. *Cognitive, Affective & Behavioral Neuroscience, 5*, 37–40.

Tarantino, N. Tully, E. C., Garcia, S., South, S., Iacono, W. G., & McGue, M. (2014). Genetic and environmental influences on affiliation with deviant peers during adolescence and early adulthood. *Developmental Psychology, 50*, 663–673.

Tarter, R. E., Blacksona, T., Brighama, J., Mossa, H., & Caprarab, G. V. (1995). The association between childhood irritability and liability to substance use in early adolescence: A 2-year follow-up study of boys at risk for substance abuse. *Drug and Alcohol Dependence 39*, 253–261.

Taylor, J., Reeves, M., James, L., & Bobadilla, L. (2006). Disinhibitory trait profile and its relation to cluster b personality disorder features and substance use problems. *European Journal of Personality, 20*, 271–284.

Tellegen, A. (1982). *Brief manual for the multidimensional personality questionnaire.* Unpublished manuscript, University of Minnesota, Minneapolis.

True, W. R., Heath, A. C., Scherrer, J. F., Xian, H., Lin, N., et al. (1999). Interrelationship of genetic and environmental influences on conduct disorder and alcohol and marijuana dependence symptoms. *American Journal of Medical Genetics, 88*, 391–397.

True, W. R., Xian, H., Scherrer, J. F., Madden, P. A., Bucholz, K. K., et al. (1999). Common genetic vulnerability for nicotine and alcohol dependence in men. *Archives of General Psychiatry, 56*, 655–661.

Tsuang, M. T., Lyons, M. J., Meyer, J. M., Doyle, T., Eisen, S. A., et al. (1998). Co-occurrence of abuse of different drugs in men: The role of drug-specific and shared vulnerabilities. *Archives of General Psychiatry, 55*, 967–972.

Tully, E. C., Iacono, W. G., & McGue, M. (2010). Changes in genetic and environmental influences on the development of nicotine dependence and major depressive disorder from middle adolescence to early adulthood. *Development and Psychopathology, 22*, 831–848.

Trzaskowski, M., Zavos, H. M. S., Haworth, C. M. A., Plomin, R., & Eley, T. C. (2012). Stable genetic influence on anxiety-related behaviours across middle childhood. *Journal of Abnormal Child Psychology, 40*(1), 85–94.

Turner, J. E., & Cole, D. A. (1994). Development differences in cognitive diatheses for child depression. *Journal of Abnormal Child Psychology, 22*, 15–32.

Vaidyanathan, U., Patrick, C. J., & Cuthbert, B. N. (2009). Linking dimensional models of internalizing psychopathology to neurobiological systems: Affect-modulated startle as an indicator of fear and distress disorders and affiliated traits. *Psychological Bulletin, 135*, 909–942.

Valdez, A., Kaplan, C. D., & Curtis, R. L., Jr. (2007). Aggressive crime, alcohol and drug use, and concentrated poverty in 24 U. S. urban areas. *American Journal of Drug and Alcohol Abuse, 33*, 595–603.

van Beijsterveldt, C. E., & van Baal, G. C. (2002). Twin and family studies of the human electroencephalogram: A review and a meta-analysis. *Bioligical Psychology*, *61*, 111–138.

Vanderhasselt, M. -A., De Raedt, R., Dillon, D. G., Dutra, S. J., Brooks, N., & Pizzagalli, D. A. (2012). Decreased cognitive control in response to negative information in patients with remitted depression: An event-related potential study. *Journal of Psychiatry & Neuroscience*, *37*(4), 250–258.

Vrieze, S., Hicks, B. M., Iacono, W. G., & McGue, M. (2012). Decline in genetic influence on the co-occurrence of alcohol, marijuana, and nicotine dependence symptoms from age 14 to 29. *American Journal of Psychiatry*, *169*, 1073–1081.

Wang, J. C., Hinrichs, A. L., Stock, H., Budde, J., Allen, R., Bertelsen, S., et al. (2004). Evidence of common and specific genetic effects: Association of the muscarinic acetylcholine receptor M2 (CHRM2) gene with alcohol dependence and major depressive syndrome. *Human Molecular Genetics*, *13*, 1903–1911.

Wardenaar, K. J., Vreeburg, S. A., van Veen, T., Giltay, E. J., Veen, G., Penninx, B. W. J. H., et al. (2011). Dimensions of depression and anxiety and the hypothalamo-pituitary-adrenal axis. *Biological Psychiatry*, *69*(4), 366–373.

Watson, D. (2005). Rethinking the mood and anxiety disorders: A quantitative hierarchical model for DSM-V. *Journal of Abnormal Psychology*, *114*, 522–536.

Weinberg, N. Z., Rahdert, E., Colliver, J. D., & Glantz, M. D. (1998). Adolescent substance abuse: A review of the past 10 years. *American Academy of Child and Adolescent Psychiatry*, *37*, 252–261.

Wilson, S., DiRago, A. C., & Iacono, W. G. (2014). Prospective inter-relationship between late adoelscent personality and major depressive disorder in early adulthood. *Psychological Medicine*, *44*(3), 567–577.

Wong, M. M., Nigg, J. T., Zucker, R. A., Puttler, L. I., Fitzgerald, H. E., et al. (2006). Behavioral control and resiliency in the onset of alcohol and illicit drug use: A prospective study from preschool to adolescence. *Child Development*, *77*, 1016–1033.

Woodward, L. J., & Fergusson, D. M. (2001). Life course outcomes of young people with anxiety disorders in adolescence. *Journal of the American Academy of Child Adolescent Psychiatry*, *40*, 1086–1093.

Yoon, H., Iacono, W. G., Malone, S., & McGue, M. (2006). Using the brain P300 response to identify novel phenotypes reflecting genetic vulnerability for adolescent substance misuse. *Addictive Behaviors*, *31*, 1067–1087.

Yoon, H. H., Malone, S. M., Burwell, S. J., Bernat, E. M., & Iacono, W. G. (2013). Association between P3 event-related potential amplitude and externalizing disorders: A time domain and time frequency investigation of 29 year-old adults. *Psychophysiology*, *50*, 595–609.

Young, S. E., Friedman, N. P., Miyake, A., Willcutt, E. G., Corley, R. P., Haberstick, B. C., et al. (2009). Behavioral disinhibition: Liability for externalizing spectrum disorders and its genetic and environmental relation to response inhibition across adolescence. *Journal of Abnormal Psychology*, *118*(1), 117–130.

Young, S. E., Stallings, M. C., Corley, R. P., Krauter, K. S., & Hewitt, J. K. (2000). Genetic and environmental influences on behavioral disinhibition. *American Journal of Medical Genetics*, *96*, 684–695.

Zai, C. C., Ehtesham, S., Choi, E., Nowrouzi, B., de Luca, V., Stankovich, L., et al. (2012). Dopaminergic system genes in childhood aggression: Possible role for DRD2. *World Journal of Biological Psychiatry*, *13*(1), 65–74.

Zetsche, U., D'Avanzato, C., & Joormann, J. (2012). Depression and rumination: Relation to components of inhibition. *Cognition and Emotion*, *26*(4), 758–767.

Zinbarg, R. E., & Barlow, D. H. (1996). Structure of anxiety and the anxiety disorders: A hierarchical model. *Journal of Abnormal Psychology*, *105*, 181–193.

Zoltgn, S., Biro, Eva, Gardi, J., Vecsernyds, M., Julesz, J., & Telegdy, G. (1995). Brain corticotropin-releasing factor mediates "anxiety-like" behavior induced by cocaine withdrawal in rats. *Brain Research*, *675*, 89–97.

PART 2

Effects of Substance Use on Health and Societal Problems Across the Life Span

Effects of Drug Exposure on Development

Alissa D. Bazinet, Lindsay Squeglia, Edward P. Riley, *and* Susan F. Tapert

Abstract

Exposure to alcohol or other drugs during the prenatal or adolescent stage of life is associated with harmful consequences to cognition, behavior, or brain structure and function of the developing child or adolescent. Resulting impairment, when it exists, can be subtle to severe depending on several moderating factors, such as dose, timing, and frequency of exposure, polysubstance exposure, environmental influences, and genetic predispositions. This chapter reviews the relevant literature to date on the neurodevelopmental effects of prenatal alcohol/drug exposure and adolescent substance use. Neuropsychological, neurobehavioral, and neuroimaging studies utilizing a variety of methodological designs are included to illustrate the wide-ranging impact of early substance exposure on subsequent developmental changes across childhood, adolescence, and young-adulthood.

Key Words: prenatal alcohol exposure, prenatal drug exposure, adolescent substance use, neuropsychological studies, neurodevelopment, neuroimaging

Exposure to alcohol and other drugs of abuse at an early age can have devastating and long-term consequences on an individual's physical and central nervous system (CNS) development, which in turn can result in neuropsychological impairment and/or an increased risk of adverse psychosocial outcomes throughout the life span. There are two primary routes through which a child may be prematurely exposed to alcohol or drugs: (1) during the prenatal period through maternal use of substances while pregnant and (2) through the child's own use of substances, most typically during adolescence. Maternal breastfeeding represents another possible route of exposure because alcohol and other psychoactive substances can be transferred to an infant through this mechanism. The range of outcomes possible from these exposures is diverse and depends on a multitude of other factors, such as type of substance used; frequency, dose, and timing of use; polysubstance exposure; and environmental and genetic factors. Some children may evidence

little to no abnormalities in physical characteristics (e.g., growth, brain structure), behavior, or cognition as the result of an exposure, whereas others may show alterations ranging from subtle deficits in one circumscribed area to global growth deficiency or significant impairments across cognitive domains. This chapter focuses on the influence of early exposure to commonly abused substances on physical, neuropsychological, and psychosocial development. It is divided into two main sections: Prenatal Exposure to Substances and Adolescent Substance Use. Each of these sections highlights the major drugs of abuse, including alcohol, marijuana, stimulants, opiates, and other psychoactive substances, and outlines the relevant research on developmental outcomes related to these exposures. Due to the greater volume of literature describing the effects of prenatal alcohol exposure and adolescent alcohol use on development (as compared to other drugs of abuse), there will be a heavier emphasis placed on alcohol throughout the chapter.

Prenatal Exposure to Substances
Methodological Considerations

A "teratogen" refers to any substance with the potential to disturb normal development in an embryo or fetus, and birth defects may result from exposure to such substances during the prenatal period. Drugs and alcohol are common teratogens that affect developmental outcomes. In general, the specific timing and dose of an exposure during embryogenesis has an impact on whether a particular teratogen will lead to a malformation or other adverse neurobehavioral outcome later in life. For alcohol in particular, animal models of prenatal alcohol exposure, as well as observations in human research, have suggested a general dose–response relationship to alcohol's teratogenic effects; that is, different levels of exposure are responsible for variations in outcomes (Meyer & Riley, 1986). Some teratogenic exposures have little risk of causing malformation or adverse effects if the level of exposure is below a certain threshold. In human populations, it is often difficult to identify a direct causal link between a teratogenic exposure and a given outcome (Davies & Bledsoe, 2005), given the commonality of multiple drug exposures and other factors related to drug use during pregnancy that may affect outcomes, such as mother's nutrition, demographic or genetic factors of the mother and fetus, and postnatal environmental characteristics (e.g., May et al., 2008). Another common limitation in research on prenatal drug exposures is that retrospective reporting is most often used to determine levels of exposures. These measures are notoriously unreliable (e.g., Jacobson, Chiodo, Sokol, & Jacobson, 2002), and information is not always available because many babies with heavy levels of exposures are taken from their birth mothers shortly after birth and placed into foster or adoptive care; thus, information about drug exposure in these cases must rely on a collateral source. Prospectively designed studies offer a way to collect information about maternal use of substances near the time of birth, but these types of studies often do not measure heavy exposures, and maternal report remains subjective no matter which method of reporting is used. Thus, in human studies, exact timing, frequency, and dose of a given teratogenic substance is most often not known. It is important to consider these confounds when interpreting results of prenatal drug exposure studies in humans.

Prenatal Alcohol Exposure

Alcohol is one of the most commonly used substances during pregnancy and is also more likely than many drugs of abuse to negatively impact fetal development, causing birth defects, growth deficiency, mental retardation, and neuropsychological impairment. A 2009 survey from the National Birth Defects Prevention Study revealed that 30.3% of all women in the United States reported drinking alcohol at some time during pregnancy, and 8.3% of pregnant women reported binge drinking at least once (defined as four or more drinks on one occasion). After the first month of pregnancy, drinking rates declined; although 22.5% of women reported drinking on at least one instance beyond the first month, and 8% of women reported drinking during the third trimester (Ethen et al., 2009). Drinking rates among pregnant women remain high despite a well-documented body of evidence linking prenatal alcohol exposure to adverse developmental outcomes. Perhaps the most well-known consequence of prenatal alcohol exposure is fetal alcohol syndrome (FAS), characterized by pre- and postnatal growth deficiencies, craniofacial anomalies (thin upper lip, indistinct philtrum, short palpebral fissures), and evidence of CNS damage or dysfunction (Hoyme et al., 2005). Although FAS was first recognized by the scientific community more than 35 years ago (Jones & Smith, 1973), it has become increasingly clear in recent decades that it represents a more severe outcome of drinking during pregnancy and that the effects of prenatal alcohol exposure are varied and lie on a continuum of physical anomalies and behavioral and cognitive deficits. Individuals with documented histories of prenatal alcohol exposure who lack the physical characteristics required for a diagnosis of FAS show similar neurobehavioral deficits compared to those with the full-blown disorder (Mattson, Riley, Gramling, Delis, & Jones, 1997; 1998). In light of this discovery, the umbrella term *fetal alcohol spectrum disorders* (FASD) has been adopted to describe the full range of effects possible as a result of prenatal alcohol exposure (Bertrand et al., 2004). It should be emphasized that this term is nondiagnostic and is used to describe all affected individuals, from those who meet full criteria for FAS to those with more subtle cognitive or behavioral difficulties. Historically, estimates of the prevalence of FAS in the United States have ranged from 0.5 to 2.0 cases per 1,000 live births with 1,000–6,000 new cases each year (Bertrand, Floyd, & Weber, 2005). The prevalence of FASD has been estimated to be much higher, at 1% of all births in the United States (May & Gossage, 2001; Sampson et al., 1997). More recently, May and Gossage (2009) reviewed the prevalence of FAS and FASD in school populations and concluded that the prevalence of FAS in typical, mixed-racial, and mixed-socioeconomic populations within the United States may be much higher than previously thought, at 2–7 cases per 1,000. They estimated that the current prevalence of FASD in populations of younger school children may be as high as 2–5% in the United States and some Western European countries.

PHYSICAL CHARACTERISTICS

Children with FASD are often born with physical growth deficiency. According to the Centers for Disease Control and Prevention (CDC; Bertrand et al., 2005) and the Institute on Medicine (IOM) guidelines as revised by Hoyme et al.(2005), "growth deficiency" is specified as falling in the 10th percentile or lower for growth, after adjusting for age, sex, gestational age, and race or ethnicity. Although growth deficiency is a criterion for a diagnosis of FAS, it is the least sensitive, and estimates suggest that only 40% of children who meet the other diagnostic criteria for FAS (craniofacial anomalies, CNS dysfunction, and evidence of prenatal exposure) are growth deficient (Davies & Bledsoe, 2005). It should also be noted that growth deficiency may result from other explanatory factors related to alcohol exposure, such as other drug exposures (e.g., tobacco exposure), malnutrition, or environmental deprivation.

Craniofacial abnormalities are the most sensitive and specific criteria for FAS diagnosis. The three facial features key to the FAS phenotype include a thin upper lip, a smooth philtrum (the vertical groove between the nose and upper lip), and small palpebral fissure lengths (the width of the eye openings). According to the CDC guidelines (Bertrand et al., 2005), all three of these features must be present for an individual to receive a diagnosis of FAS; the revised IOM guidelines (Hoyme et al., 2005) require only two of the three features to be present. Other facial features associated with FAS include epicanthal folds (skin fold of the upper eyelid), ptosis (drooping of the upper eyelid), a low and flat nasal bridge, strabismus ("lazy eye"), "clown eyebrows" (often associated with microcephaly), and prominent ears or ear abnormalities (see Figure 8.1). These features are more common in FAS than in the typically developing population but are not required for the diagnosis because they can also reflect variations in ethnicity, normal development, or other developmental disorders.

When the characteristic facial markers are subtle or absent, identification of FASD becomes more difficult and must rely on evidence of CNS dysfunction along with a confirmed history of prenatal alcohol exposure. CNS dysfunction in alcohol-exposed individuals is more loosely defined than are the physical criteria but can be determined using a variety of methods, including evidence of structural brain abnormalities, neurologic problems, or functional deficits demonstrated on neuropsychological testing. However, the revised IOM guidelines are more restrictive than those of the CDC in terms of the definition of "CNS dysfunction," requiring either structural brain abnormalities as evidenced by neuroimaging or head circumference at or below the 10th percentile; functional deficits are not included as possible diagnostic criteria (Hoyme et al., 2005). The IOM guidelines also include criteria for a diagnosis of partial FAS, alcohol-related birth defects, and alcohol-related neurodevelopmental disorder, in order to facilitate individuals with FASD who do not meet all diagnostic criteria for FAS (Hoyme et al., 2005).

STRUCTURAL BRAIN ABNORMALITIES

Prior to the advent of modern neuroimaging techniques, information regarding brain development and morphology in FASD was gleaned through autopsy studies. In an initial report, Jones and Smith (1973) described widespread damage to the brain of an infant with FAS, including microcephaly, errors in neuronal migration resulting in multiple structural displacements, agenesis of the corpus callosum and anterior commissure, and abnormalities in the cerebellum and brainstem. Subsequent reports confirmed these findings and ultimately concluded that brain abnormalities in FAS were heterogeneous and that no identifiable pattern existed (Clarren, Alvord, Sumi, Streissguth, & Smith, 1978; Coulter, Leech, Schaefer, Scheithauer, & Brumback, 1993; Jones & Smith, 1975; Peiffer, Majewski, Fischbach, Bierich, & Volk, 1979). However, these autopsy studies were unable to clarify brain abnormalities typical of those living with FASD because the individuals described died as a result of prenatal exposure to alcohol and thus are not representative cases.

Magnetic resonance imaging (MRI) is a noninvasive imaging technique that creates high-quality structural pictures of the brain through the use of a magnetic field and radio waves. MRI provides relevant information about patterns of structural strengths and weaknesses in the brains of individuals living with FASD, both with and without

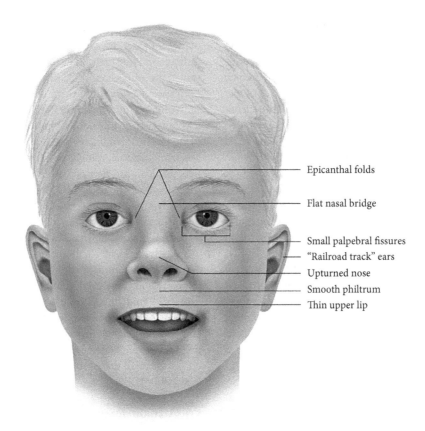

Epicanthal folds

Flat nasal bridge

Small palpebral fissures
"Railroad track" ears
Upturned nose
Smooth philtrum
Thin upper lip

Figure 8.1 Facial features associated with fetal alcohol syndrome (FAS).
Courtesy of Darryl Leja, NHGRI, NIH.

dysmorphic features. Consistent with autopsy studies, MRI investigations have reliably reported reductions in overall brain volume (Archibald et al., 2001; Astley et al., 2009a; Coles et al., 2011; Lebel et al., 2008; Nardelli, Lebel, Rasmussen, Andrew, & Beaulieu, 2011; Roussotte et al., 2011; Sowell, Thompson et al., 2001; Swayze et al., 1997; Willoughby, Sheard, Nash, & Rovet, 2008), cerebral volume (Archibald et al., 2001; Mattson et al., 1992; 1994; Mattson, Riley, Sowell et al., 1996), and cerebellar volume (Archibald et al., 2001; Astley et al., 2009a; Mattson et al., 1992; 1994; Mattson, Riley, Sowel et al., 1996; O'Hare et al., 2005; Riikonen, Salonen, Partanen, & Verho, 1999; Sowell et al., 1996). Importantly, although many MRI studies describe regional volumetric reductions in the frontal, temporal, parietal, and, to a lesser degree, occipital lobes in children with FASD relative to controls, a great number of these findings are confounded with the concomitant finding of smaller overall brain volumes. In studies where overall brain volume is statistically controlled for in analyses, the frontal and parietal lobes appear

to be especially sensitive to alcohol teratogenesis, although there is some evidence for relative abnormalities within the temporal lobes as well. Only the occipital lobe appears to be spared from alcohol's wide-ranging effects.

Several different imaging analysis techniques (i.e., traditional volumetric, voxel-based morphometric, and surface-based) have been used to uncover relative volumetric reductions (Archibald et al., 2001; Sowell, Thomson, Mattson et al., 2002) and decreased cerebral tissue density (Sowell, Thompson, Mattson et al., 2001) in the parietal lobes, as well as a narrowed size and appearance of bilateral temporal and parietal regions (particularly within the perisylvian cortices; Sowell, Thompson, Mattson et al., 2002). With regard to abnormalities in the frontal lobes, one study found decreases in the size of the left orbitofrontal cortex, such that children with FASD appeared to have a "blunted" shape to this brain region compared to their typically developing counterparts (Sowell, Thompson, Mattson et al., 2002). Another study found a progressive decrease in frontal lobe volumes across four alcohol-exposed groups categorized by severity (with the smallest volumes observed in the FAS/partial FAS group; Astley et al., 2009a). One study examined longitudinal changes in cortical volumes in a cohort of alcohol-exposed children and adolescents and their typically developing counterparts gathered from three separate sites in the United States and South Africa. Trajectories of cortical volume change across a 2-year period were found to differ between the alcohol-exposed subjects and unexposed controls in posterior brain regions, namely the parietal cortex. Specifically, control children showed a more plastic cortex with a prolonged pattern of cortical volume increases followed by vigorous volume loss during adolescence, whereas the alcohol-exposed participants showed primarily volume loss, suggesting decreased plasticity. Also, smaller changes in cortical volumes across scans were associated with lower intelligence and increased facial morphology in both groups and were related to the amount of prenatal alcohol exposure during each trimester of pregnancy in the exposed group (Lebel et al., 2012). These findings provide evidence that IQ scores and facial dysmorphology can predict, to some degree, the particular pattern of structural brain development that occurs in subsequent years.

The susceptibility of the frontal and parietal regions to the insult of prenatal alcohol exposure is further supported by studies examining the volumes and distribution of gray and white matter within the brains of individuals with FASD. Gray matter makes up the outer layer of the cerebral hemispheres and consists primarily of nerve cell bodies whereas white matter consists of bundles of myelinated nerve cell axons that connect gray matter areas. With regard to volumes of gray and white matter within the whole brain, studies have found reductions in cerebral white matter (Archibald et al., 2001), total gray matter (Nardelli et al., 2011), and cortical gray matter (Roussotte et al., 2011) in alcohol-exposed subjects, even after accounting for total brain volume. Similarly, relative white and gray matter volume decreases have been observed in lobar regions of alcohol-exposed subjects' brains, namely the frontal lobes (Astley et al., 2009a; Sowell, Thompson, Peterson et al., 2002) and parietal lobes (Archibald et al., 2001; Sowell, Thompson, Peterson et al., 2002). With regard to the temporal lobes, one study found relative white matter (but not gray matter) reductions associated with prenatal alcohol exposure (Sowell, Thompson, Peterson et al., 2002) whereas another study found decreases in both white and gray matter volumes in

the temporal-occipital regions of alcohol-exposed subjects' brains (Li et al., 2008). Increased gray matter density in parietal and temporal regions has also been observed in relation to alcohol exposure (Sowell, Thompson, Mattson et al., 2001; 2002). Notably, the just-reviewed abnormalities in gray and white matter occur in the very same areas where regional size differences are evident.

In typical development, decreases in gray matter volume occur over time as individuals mature (Giedd et al., 1999), while myelination stimulates an increase in white matter volume during adolescence and early adulthood, facilitating faster and more efficient neural transmission and cognitive processing (Yakovlev & Lecours, 1967). Thus, the findings of decreased white matter volumes and increased gray matter density in regions of the brain sensitive to alcohol teratogenesis imply an immature pattern of brain organization in FASD across childhood and adolescence. Further evidence of differential brain development related to early alcohol exposure is provided by studies of cortical thickness in the FASD population. Typically developing cortex tends to "thin out" (i.e., become more myelinated with fewer synapses) with increasing age (e.g., Huttenlocher, 1979; Yakovlev & Lecours, 1967). Two studies have reported increased cortical thickness in regions of the frontal, parietal, and temporal cortices in individuals with FASD relative to controls (Sowell, Mattson, et al., 2008; Yang et al., 2011). In addition, increased cortical thickness in inferior frontal regions has been associated with reduced palpebral fissure length, suggesting a link between severity of brain abnormalities and facial dysmorphology (Yang et al., 2011). In contrast to these reports, one study did not find evidence of increased cortical thickness in alcohol-exposed individuals; however, differential patterns of cortical thinning with age were observed within alcohol-exposed and nonexposed groups, suggesting that prenatal alcohol exposure is associated with atypical developmental pathways (Zhou et al., 2011).

Diffusion tensor imaging (DTI) is another structural imaging technique rapidly gaining popularity due to its ability to provide specialized information about the microstructure of white matter tissue and the integrity of white matter tracts within the brain. Specifically, DTI measures the diffusion of water molecules within white matter tissue, which provides an estimate of the tissue's overall maturity and organization. Two of the most common variables used in DTI research are fractional anisotropy (FA), which measures water diffusion along a single direction, and mean diffusivity (MD), an index of the overall displacement of water molecules (for review, see Basser & Jones, 2002; Lim & Helpern, 2002). In general, higher FA and lower MD signify a more organized pattern of white matter that, in turn, implies quicker neural processing. Whole fiber tractography DTI is a method that examines thick bundles of white matter fibers responsible for communicating across widespread brain regions, and it has been used in a few studies to investigate white matter pathways in alcohol-exposed individuals. Evidence from these investigations suggests that several of these pathways display more disorganization in FASD, specifically those with connections to temporal (Lebel et al., 2008), superior frontal (Fryer et al., 2009), and occipital to inferior frontal and parietal (Fryer et al., 2009) regions. These pathways are thought to play a role in language and visuospatial processing, executive function, and visual processing, respectively, and they represent cognitive functions that are consistently impaired in individuals with FASD. Findings of reduced white matter integrity along functional pathways in the brains of individuals with FASD complement previously described findings of decreased white matter density within specific regions of structural abnormality, providing further support for the notion that abnormal brain development and neuronal disorganization continues throughout development, long after the initial insult of prenatal alcohol exposure has passed.

In addition to the effects on global and lobar brain structure and organization as just described, prenatal exposure to alcohol has consistently been linked with morphological changes within specific brain structures. The corpus callosum, cerebellum, and areas of the basal ganglia appear to be particularly vulnerable. One of the most dramatic consequences that has been observed in the developing brain as a result of prenatal alcohol exposure is complete or partial agenesis (absence) of the corpus callosum, the thick white matter tract connecting the right and left cerebral hemispheres (e.g., Bhatara et al., 2002; Riley et al., 1995; Swayze et al., 1997). The corpus callosum is responsible for interhemispheric transfer and thus plays a role in the coordination of various functions, such as bimanual coordination in motor tasks, sustained attention, vision, and spatial and working memory (Devinsky & D'Esposito, 2004). Although complete agenesis of the corpus callosum occurs more frequently in FASD than in the typically developing population, it is still relatively rare, even among severe cases of FAS. Hypoplasia (underdevelopment) of the corpus callosum is a more common occurrence, as are size reductions (Astley et al., 2009a; Autti-Rämö et al., 2002; Riley et al., 1995; Sowell, Mattson, Thompson et al., 2001), increased shape variability (Bookstein, Sampson, Connor, & Streissguth, 2002; Bookstein, Streissguth, Sampson, Connor, & Barr, 2002), and displacement (Sowell, Mattson, Thompson et al., 2001) of the structure. The posterior region (termed the splenium) of the corpus callosum appears to be displaced more anteriorly and inferiorly in individuals with FASD as compared to controls, and the degree of displacement occurs to a lesser degree in nondysmorphic cases compared to those with FAS. Children with greater callosal displacement also exhibit more significant impairment on a verbal learning task, suggesting that this regional dysmorphology may be directly related to some of the functional deficits observed in this population (Sowell, Mattson, Thompson et al., 2001). DTI studies have found microstructural damage and disorganization in the white matter tissue of the corpus callosum related to prenatal alcohol exposure, with abnormalities consistently reported in posterior regions of the structure, including higher MD in the isthmus (Wozniak et al., 2006) and lower FA in the splenium (Lebel et al., 2008; Ma et al., 2005; Sowell, Johnson, et al., 2008; Wozniak et al., 2009) and isthmus (Wozniak et al., 2009). Investigations of anterior regions of the corpus callosum have reported increased MD (Lebel et al., 2008) and decreased FA (Ma et al., 2005) in the genu, or most frontal region of the structure. Additionally, one study has reported lower FA in the overall body of the corpus callosum (Fryer et al., 2009).

The cerebellum is another region implicated as vulnerable to the insult of prenatal alcohol exposure. The cerebellum is responsible for the integration of sensory perception, coordination, and motor control, and portions of this structure are thought to contribute to the development of attention (Devinsky & D'Esposito, 2004) and classical conditioning processes (Kim & Thompson, 1997). Reduced cerebellar volume (Archibald et al., 2001; Mattson et al., 1992) and surface area (Autti-Rämö et al., 2002) are common findings in individuals with FASD although it appears that the damage may be localized to the anterior vermis, an earlier developing portion of the cerebellum. Specifically, the anterior vermis (lobules I–V) has shown significant volume reductions whereas later developing regions of the cerebellum appear to be spared

(Autti-Rämö et al., 2002; Sowell et al., 1996). O'Hare et al. (2005) also demonstrated abnormal spatial displacement in the anterior vermis, such that the anterior and superior edges of the region appear to be shifted inferiorly and posteriorly in alcohol-exposed individuals as compared to controls. Furthermore, the degree of displacement was greater in those individuals with a diagnosis of FAS (1–3 mm displacement) compared to their non-dysmorphic counterparts (1.4 mm displacement). In the same study, cerebellar vermis displacement was negatively correlated with verbal learning and memory abilities (O'Hare et al., 2005). Findings of structural anomalies in the cerebellum may help to explain the deficits in motor functioning (Roebuck, Simmons, Mattson, & Riley, 1998; Roebuck-Spencer, Mattson, Marion, Brown, & Riley, 2004), attention regulation (Akshoomoff, Courchesne, & Townsend, 1997), and classical conditioning responding (Woodruff-Pak, Goldenberg, Downey-Lamb, Boyko, & Lemieux, 2000) that have been noted in individuals with FASD.

Deep gray matter structures within the brain (e.g., the basal ganglia and hippocampus) also demonstrate substantial changes associated with prenatal alcohol exposure. One structure that has shown consistent alcohol-related alterations is the basal ganglia, a group of deep subcortical nuclei that are heavily connected to cortical and subcortical motor areas and are involved in cognitive, affective, and motivational functions (Devinsky & D'Esposito, 2004). The basal ganglia consist of five separate nuclei: the caudate, putamen, globus pallidus, nucleus accumbens, and substantia nigra. Of these, studies have shown smaller relative volumes of the caudate (Archibald et al., 2001; Astley et al., 2009a; Mattson et al., 1992; Mattson, Riley, Sowell et al., 1996), globus pallidus (Nardelli et al., 2011; Roussotte et al., 2011), and putamen (Astley et al., 2009a; Nardelli et al., 2011; Riikkonen et al., 2005; Roussotte et al., 2011) in alcohol-exposed individuals. One study has also shown disproportionate gray matter volumes in the caudate region of alcohol-exposed children's brains after accounting for overall brain size (Mattson et al., 1992).

Evidence for abnormalities within the hippocampus, a region of the brain responsible for memory formation, storage, and organization, is mixed. Some studies have reported significantly smaller hippocampal volumes after accounting for total brain volume (Nardelli et al., 2011; Willoughby et al., 2008), whereas others have observed no differences in this region above and beyond differences in total brain volume (Archibald et al., 2001; Astley et al., 2009a; Coles et al., 2011; Riikonen et al., 2005; Roussotte et al., 2011). Other areas of the brain with mixed findings include the diencephalon and thalamus (regions responsible for relaying sensory information and controlling autonomic functions), with observations of either no change (Archibald et al., 2001; Mattson et al., 1994) or smaller volume or area (Autti-Rämö et al., 2002; Mattson, Riley, Sowell et al., 1996), and the amygdala (a region responsible for processing emotion), with only one study to date finding significant size differences (Nardelli et al., 2011). One study specifically measured cingulate gyrus morphology in subjects with prenatal alcohol exposure and found relative reductions in white matter volumes in this structure thought to be involved in mediating attention and cognitive control (Bjorkquist, Fryer, Reiss, Mattson, & Riley, 2010).

Importantly, structural brain anomalies may underlie deficits in neurocognitive functioning commonly observed in FASD populations. Studies of brain–behavior relationships in this population using quantitative measures gleaned from structural MRI or DTI in combination with neuropsychological testing are relatively few to date, but those that exist have shown relationships between cognitive performance and structural abnormalities in expected brain regions. With regard to the corpus callosum, correlations between callosal abnormalities and impaired verbal learning (Sowell, Mattson, Thompson et al., 2001), executive function and motor abilities (Bookstein, Streissguth et al., 2002), and finger localization (Roebuck, Mattson, & Riley, 2002) have been found. In addition, reduced hippocampal volume has been associated with poorer verbal recall (Coles et al., 2011; Willoughby et al., 2008) and worse performance on a nonverbal memory task (Coles et al., 2011). Other findings have included correlations among attention and working memory and cingulate gray matter volumes (Bjorkquist et al., 2010), full-scale IQ and putamen volumes (Roussotte et al., 2011), and verbal learning/memory and caudate volumes (Fryer et al., 2012).

FUNCTIONAL BRAIN ABNORMALITIES

Additional information about brain–behavior relationships can be gained through studies of functional neuroimaging. In contrast to the frequent and replicated findings of specific structural abnormalities in the brains of individuals with FASD, less is known about associated functional brain deficits in this population. Part of the reason for the paucity of information relates to rapidly changing methodology for studying brain functioning and the related difficulties in interpretation of such findings. To date, a handful of functional studies have been conducted with alcohol-exposed individuals using a variety of techniques such as positron emission tomography (PET), single photon emission computed tomography (SPECT), magnetic resonance spectroscopy (MRS), and functional MRI (fMRI).

The first studies of functional brain activity among individuals with FASD focused on the neurochemical makeup of the alcohol-exposed brain, examining such constructs as cerebral blood flow, neurotransmitter levels, and glucose metabolism. Using SPECT, studies have discovered reduced blood flow in the temporal, left parietal-occipital, and right frontal brain regions of alcohol-exposed individuals relative to controls (Bhatara et al., 2002; Riikonen et al., 1999). In addition, these same individuals demonstrated reduced serotonin levels in the medial frontal cortex and higher levels of dopamine transporter binding in the basal ganglia, which could be related to abnormalities in motor functioning, emotional dysregulation, and/or behavior problems often observed in individuals prenatally exposed to alcohol. One study using PET found a subtle reduction in glucose metabolism in the thalamus and caudate of young adults diagnosed with FAS (Clark, Li, Conry, Conry, & Loock, 2000). This finding is notable because glucose is the primary energy substrate for the brain, and a decreased glucose metabolism suggests a reduced amount of energy available for cognitive processing. MRS investigations provide further evidence of altered brain metabolism in FASD. These studies calculate ratios for the metabolites N-acetylaspartate/choline (NAA/Cho) and N-acetylaspartate/creatine (NAA/Cr), as well as absolute concentrations of NAA, choline, and creatine found in various brain regions. One study found lower NAA-to-Cho and NAA-to-Cr ratios in the parietal and frontal cortices, frontal white matter, corpus callosum, thalamus, and cerebellar dentate nucleus of alcohol-exposed individuals, and, furthermore, these individuals evidenced higher absolute concentrations of choline and creatine compared to controls but showed no difference in NAA levels. Because creatine and choline are markers of glial cell functioning and NAA is a marker of neuronal functioning, the authors speculated that the altered metabolite ratios were likely reflective of abnormalities in the glial cell population (responsible for supporting and protecting neurons) rather

than in the neuronal cell population (Fagerlund et al., 2006). Another MRS study showed a higher ratio of NAA-to-Cr in bilateral caudate regions in the brains of alcohol-exposed individuals relative to controls suggesting that neuronal functioning (as opposed to glial cell functioning) may be compromised in striatal regions within this population (Cortese et al., 2006).

Like DTI among structural studies of the brain, the popularity of fMRI for studying functional activity in the brain has skyrocketed over the past decade. This is likely due to fMRI's unique ability to directly measure brain functioning while participants engage in some cognitive task. The primary variable used within fMRI is the blood oxygen level-dependent (BOLD) signal, which is correlated with cerebral blood flow and thus serves as a proxy for a measure of brain activation. Stronger BOLD signals are thought to indicate increased activation in corresponding regions of the brain (Logothetis, Pauls, Augath, Trinath, & Oeltermann, 2001; Ogawa, Lee, Kay, & Tank, 1990). fMRI studies of individuals prenatally exposed to alcohol have uncovered BOLD response differences between individuals with FASD and typically developing controls during tasks of spatial working memory, attention, verbal learning and memory, arithmetic and number processing, and response inhibition.

The first of these studies used a spatial working memory task, and individuals with FASD showed increased functional activity during the task in the inferior and middle frontal cortices compared to matched controls. In addition, controls showed greater frontal lobe activity with increasing task difficulty, whereas alcohol-exposed participants did not show this pattern (Malisza et al., 2005). Another study of spatial working memory found that alcohol-exposed participants showed increased BOLD response in frontal, superior temporal and occipital gyri, insulae, and subcortical regions compared to their nonexposed counterparts (Spadoni et al., 2009). Similarly, O'Hare and colleagues (2009) found that, compared to controls, children and adolescents with FASD showed increased BOLD response in left dorsal frontal and inferior parietal cortices, as well as in bilateral posterior temporal regions during a verbal working memory task, while Li and colleagues (2008) found that young adults with FASD evidenced increased functional activation relative to controls in the occipital-temporal region of the brain during a sustained attention task. Similar patterns of increased BOLD response in widespread frontal regions were observed in alcohol-exposed subjects relative to controls during two studies of response inhibition and verbal paired associate learning (Fryer, Tapert et al., 2007; Sowell et al., 2007). However, in these studies, alcohol-exposed individuals also displayed a decreased BOLD response in the brain regions thought to mediate the relevant cognitive function (e.g., in the caudate during the response inhibition task and in the left medial and posterior temporal regions in the verbal learning task). One study examining working memory and facial recognition found the opposite pattern of the studies presented thus far, in that the alcohol-exposed participants had a decreased BOLD response in prefrontal and parietal regions relative to controls, particularly in the right hemisphere (Astley et al., 2009b). Two fMRI studies examined functional alterations associated with number processing ability in individuals with FASD because math has been implicated as an area of specific cognitive deficit in this population (e.g., Kable & Coles, 2004). The first of these used a subtraction task and observed lower activation in prenatally exposed young adults compared to controls in parietal and prefrontal regions thought to be involved in arithmetic processing (Santhanam Li, Hu, Lynch, & Coles, 2009). In the second of these, Meintjes and colleagues (2010) employed tasks of addition and proximity judgment and found generally more widespread activation across the whole brain in school-aged children with FASD; in contrast, the control children showed more specific activations in regions of the brain thought to subserve math processing skills. A recent study investigated the potential role of family history of alcoholism in the neural functioning abnormalities observed in individuals with prenatal alcohol exposure. Specifically, individuals with FASD and those with a confirmed family history of alcoholism but no prenatal alcohol exposure showed greater BOLD activation in the lentiform nucleus and insular regions relative to controls during a spatial working memory task, whereas only the FASD group showed increased BOLD activation in the left middle and superior frontal gyri in comparison to controls (Norman et al., 2013).

Although interpretation of fMRI findings can be controversial, many of these studies to date report increased activation in frontal regions associated with prenatal alcohol exposure. This can imply an "inefficient" neural network, in that individuals with FASD may be taxing their neural resources to a greater degree during cognitive tasks when compared to their typically developing peers.

Alternatively, increased activation in frontal regions paired with decreased activation in task-specific regions may imply that a "compensatory" mechanism is in place, in which neural resources are "reallocated" to help complete a task in spite of an inherent impairment in functioning. Whatever the interpretation, the collective findings from studies of brain functioning in alcohol-exposed individuals suggest that alterations do exist, and these initial studies pave the way for future understanding of the underlying mechanisms related to cognitive dysfunction in FASD.

NEUROPSYCHOLOGICAL STUDIES

Neuropsychological tests are tasks designed to measure an individual's peak level of performance on different cognitive domains (e.g., memory, attention, visuospatial skills, language, executive functioning) that are linked to certain brain regions or pathways (Lezak, Howieson, Loring, Hannay, & Fischer, 2004). Studies of neuropsychological performance in individuals with FASD complement findings of structural and functional brain abnormalities. Like neuroimaging, neuropsychological studies attempt to identify patterns of strengths and weaknesses in individuals with heavy prenatal alcohol histories in the hopes of defining a neurobehavioral profile to aid in diagnosis and treatment. Studies suggest impairment in overall intellectual functioning in alcohol-exposed individuals, along with specific deficits in learning, memory, language, attention, visuospatial abilities, fine and gross motor skills, executive functioning, and social and adaptive functioning.

Given the range of outcomes possible along the fetal alcohol spectrum, it is not surprising that estimates of general intellectual functioning among these individuals vary. One study indicated that children with FAS have mean IQ scores that are significantly lower than those with partial FAS or nondysmorphic alcohol-related neurodevelopmental disorders (Chasnoff, Wells, Telford, Schmidt, & Messer, 2010), whereas another reported a relation between general cognitive function and degree of facial dysmorphology and growth deficiency (Ervalahti et al., 2007). In FAS, IQs have been noted from 20 to 120, with averages in the low 70s (Mattson & Riley, 1998); the estimate for nondysmorphic individuals with FASD tends to be slightly higher, with average IQs falling somewhere around the mid-80s (Mattson, Riley, Gramling, Delis, & Jones 1997). Although it has been implicated as the leading cause of preventable mental retardation in the United States (Pulsifer, 1996) the majority of individuals with FAS are not mentally retarded. Although roughly 25% of alcohol-exposed individuals have IQs of less than 70, many have IQs that fall into the average range (Streissguth, Barr, Kogan, & Bookstein, 1996).

Children prenatally exposed to alcohol also have lower academic achievement and an increased rate of learning problems in both verbal and mathematical domains (e.g., Howell, Lynch, Platzman, Smith, & Coles, 2006; Rasmussen & Bisanz, 2010) compared to typically developing peers. One mechanism accounting for lower achievement may be deficits in verbal and nonverbal learning and memory that have consistently been demonstrated in individuals with FASD. On tests of memory for unstructured word lists, alcohol-exposed children recall fewer words than controls on both immediate free recall and recognition trials (e.g., Crocker, Vaurio, Riley, & Mattson, 2011; Mattson, Riley, Delis, Stern, & Jones, 1996). However, the two groups do not show any differences in retention of learned information over a delay (Mattson, Riley, Gramling, Delis, & Jones 1998; Mattson & Roebuck, 2002). This pattern of results suggests that deficits in verbal memory associated with prenatal alcohol exposure may be related to an encoding impairment, or difficulty in learning new information, rather than to a long-term storage or retrieval problem. However, on tasks that require learning structured material (i.e., stories), children with FASD have shown intact immediate and delayed recall of this material (i.e., Pei, Rinaldi, Rasmussen, Massey, & Massey, 2008), suggesting that encoding difficulties may be limited to unstructured verbal material. With regard to nonverbal memory, there is some evidence that individuals with FASD display impairment in both encoding and storage/retrieval of nonverbal information (Mattson & Roebuck, 2002; Willford, Richardson, Leech, & Day, 2004). Spatial recall, or the ability to remember the location of an object, appears to be most affected, while object recall, or ability to remember pictures of objects remains intact (e.g., Hamilton, Kodituwakku, Sutherland, & Savage, 2003; Uecker & Nadel, 1998).

In terms of language ability, individuals with FASD appear to have deficits in both expressive and receptive language (e.g., Church, Eldis, Blakley, & Bawle, 1997; Mattson et al., 1998), although expressive abilities may be relatively more affected. Alcohol-exposed children have also shown impairments in phonological processing (Streissguth et al., 1994), which may underlie verbal learning deficits

and translate to difficulty with reading and lower academic achievement.

Attention is a relatively well-studied neurocognitive domain in prenatal alcohol exposure, largely due to the observation that individuals with FASD frequently carry a comorbid diagnosis of attention deficit hyperactivity disorder (ADHD). Rates of ADHD in the alcohol-exposed population have been estimated at upward of 90% (Fryer, McGee, Matt, Riley, & Mattson, 2007). Performance on sustained attention tasks, in which individuals must respond to infrequent and randomly presented target stimuli over a long period of time, is especially compromised in alcohol-exposed individuals (Coles, Platzman, Lynch, & Freides, 2002; Mattson, Calarco, & Lang, 2006). There is some evidence that visual attention impairments are more prevalent than impairments in auditory attention, although difficulties with auditory sustained attention tasks may only be evident during periods of high task demand, such as instances when the length of the interval occurring between targets is lengthened (Mattson et al., 2006). One study found that alcohol-exposed children can be distinguished from controls with greater than 90% accuracy using common neuropsychological and parent-report measures of attention, such as the Wechsler Intelligence Scale for Children (WISC-III) Freedom from Distractibility index and the Attention Problems subscale of the Child Behavior Checklist (CBCL; see Lee, Mattson, & Riley, 2004).

Visuospatial functioning appears to be an area of relative weakness in individuals with FASD. Specifically, studies have uncovered local deficits (difficulties in copying and recalling detailed features of visually presented stimuli), whereas global perception (ability to copy and recall the configural features) remains intact (Mattson, Gramling, Delis, Jones, & Riley, 1996). In addition to these higher order visuospatial processing deficits, alcohol-exposed individuals also show basic visuospatial disabilities on simple drawing tasks from the Beery Developmental Test of Visual-Motor Integration (Conry, 1990; Janzen, Nanson, & Block, 1995; Mattson et al., 1998). It is important to note that visuospatial tasks most often require a motor component, and observed deficits in visuospatial processing may be partially accounted for by poor motor ability.

Prenatal alcohol exposure has been shown to affect both fine and gross motor function (Autti-Rämö & Granström, 1991; Connor, Sampson, Streissguth, Bookstein, & Barr, 2006). Specifically, delayed motor development and deficits such as tremors, weak grasp, and poor hand-eye coordination have been consistently reported (reviewed in Mattson & Riley, 1998). Postural stability is also affected, such that alcohol-exposed children are able to maintain balance under stable environmental conditions but display significant anterior-posterior body sway when somatosensory information is compromised and are unable to compensate by using available visual or vestibular information (Roebuck et al., 1998). These difficulties may be related to the cerebellar abnormalities that have been described in neuroimaging studies.

Executive function, which refers to a higher order set of skills responsible for overseeing and organizing many lower order cognitive tasks, is an area of recent focus and interest in the alcohol-exposed population. Specific deficits have been noted across several types of executive functioning abilities, including planning and problem solving (Kodituwakku, Handmaker, Cutler, Weathersby, & Handmaker, 1995), inhibitory control (e.g., Connor, Sampson, Bookstein, & Barr, & Streissguth, 2000; Mattson, Goodman, Caine, Delis, & Riley, 1999), concept formation and "set shifting" (e.g., Carmichael Olson, Feldman, Streissguth, Sampson, & Bookstein, 1998; McGee, Schonfeld, Roebuck-Spencer, Riley, & Mattson, 2008; Vaurio, Riley, & Mattson, 2008), and verbal fluency (e.g., Rasmussen & Bisanz, 2009; Vaurio et al., 2008). Studies have also found working memory deficits in children with FASD, which are thought to underlie many other executive control and attention skills (Green et al., 2009, Kodituwakku et al., 1995); these impairments appear to persist even after controlling for IQ (e.g., Burden, Jacobson, Sokol, & Jacobson, 2005).

Through examining findings from neuropsychological assessments in the alcohol-exposed population, a preliminary profile of relative strengths and weaknesses can be constructed. Recently, research has focused less on identifying specific areas of cognitive deficit associated with prenatal alcohol exposure and more on outlining a comprehensive neurobehavioral profile that can be used to accurately identify individuals afflicted with FASD and to target specific areas for intervention (Mattson, Crocker, & Nguyen, 2011). To summarize, the research to date suggests that prenatal exposure to alcohol is characterized by general deficits in intellectual ability, as well as in relative deficits in visual attention, verbal and nonverbal learning, executive function, motor function, and visuospatial processing. In addition, alcohol-exposed individuals often have comorbid ADHD diagnoses and may display increased levels of hyperactivity, externalizing behavior problems, and social skills deficits. Strengths have been identified in auditory attention, retention of verbal information, and basic language functioning. Two recent studies by Mattson and colleagues (2010; 2013) used latent profile analysis to test whether alcohol-exposed subjects could be accurately classified and distinguished from non-alcohol-exposed subjects on the basis of neuropsychological test performance. In the first of these, 22 neuropsychological variables were chosen based on each variable's ability to distinguish alcohol-exposed subjects from controls during univariate analyses. The resulting neurobehavioral profile was successful at distinguishing subjects with FAS from nonexposed controls with 92% accuracy; when this analysis was repeated in children with nondysmorphic FASD, the accuracy dropped to 84.7%; 68.4% of alcohol-exposed cases and 95% of controls were correctly classified (Mattson et al., 2010). In the second study, 11 neuropsychological test variables were selected for inclusion in the larger profile, and data from six sites in the United States and South Africa were examined in three separate classification analyses: (1) subjects with FAS versus controls, (2) alcohol-exposed subjects without FAS versus controls, and (3) all alcohol-exposed subjects (with and without FAS) versus non-alcohol-exposed subjects with ADHD. For the first analysis, overall classification accuracy was 76.1% (77.2% FAS, 75.7% controls), whereas accuracy was 71.5% in the second analysis (70.1% alcohol-exposed/non-FAS, 72.4% controls) and 73.9% (59.8% alcohol-exposed, 75.7% ADHD) for the third (Mattson et al., 2013). These data suggest that neuropsychological impairments associated with prenatal alcohol exposure are clinically meaningful, and performance on neuropsychological tests can be used to accurately distinguish alcohol-affected children from typically developing children and children with ADHD. The latter finding is particularly important because children with FASD are often misdiagnosed as having idiopathic ADHD, especially in the absence of information regarding maternal use of alcohol during pregnancy. Thus, understanding the specific cognitive and behavioral abilities that can aid in specificity of diagnosis is imperative. So far, investigations comparing neuropsychological performance between the two clinical groups have identified several similarities and differences. Specifically, children with FASD show greater impairment in general cognitive functioning (i.e., IQ scores), as well as on tasks of verbal fluency, problem-solving, shifting attention, verbal encoding, facial and emotional processing, and daily living skills, whereas children with idiopathic ADHD show greater impairments in basic motor control, focused and sustained attention, and retrieval memory. The two groups show similar impairments in set shifting, complex motor skills, static balance, social and communication skills, and parental report of behavior (Mattson, Crocker, & Nguyen, 2011).

BEHAVIORAL AND PSYCHOSOCIAL FUNCTIONING

In addition to impaired neuropsychological performance, individuals with FASD are more likely to have maladaptive and clinically significant behavioral characteristics compared to the general population. Children with FASD have high rates of parent-reported behavior problems (e.g., Mattson & Riley, 2000; Nash et al., 2006), and alcohol-exposed adolescents and adults are at increased risk for legal difficulties and incarceration (e.g., Fast & Conry, 2009). One study reported that 60% of 253 adolescents and adults with FASD (aged 12 and older) had experienced trouble with the law (Streissguth et al., 1996). Other studies show a disproportionately high rate of alcohol-exposed individuals detained in juvenile delinquency facilities (e.g., Boland, Burrill, Duwyn, & Karp, 1998; Fast, Conry, & Loock, 1999), and many more may be undiagnosed due to inadequate or nonexistent screening procedures in corrections facilities (Burd, Selfridge, Klug, & Bakko, 2004). Higher rates of drug and alcohol problems also tend to co-occur in adolescents and adults with FASD (Streissguth et al., 1996), as do psychiatric diagnoses (e.g., Burd, Klug, Martsolf, & Kerbeshian, 2003; Fryer, McGee et al., 2007; O'Connor & Paley 2006) and increased lifetime suicide attempts (e.g., Baldwin, 2007). Increases in adverse life outcomes may be related to the deficits in adaptive functioning (i.e., communication skills, daily living skills, and socialization) commonly observed from an early age in individuals with prenatal alcohol exposure (e.g., Crocker, Vaurio, Riley, & Mattson 2009; Jirikowic, Kartin, & Carmichael Olson, 2008; Thomas, Kelly, Mattson, & Riley, 1998). Socialization may be especially affected (e.g., Crocker et al., 2009; McGee, Bjorkquist, Price, Mattson, & Riley, 2009; McGee, Fryer, Bjorkquist, Mattson, & Riley, 2008; Thomas et al., 1998; Whaley, O'Connor, & Gunderson 2001) because these abilities fail to improve with increasing age, suggesting an arrest of these skills rather than a delay in development (e.g., Crocker et al., 2009). Behavioral and social disabilities may in fact be the most debilitating consequences of prenatal alcohol exposure due to the significant impact on not only the individual, but on interpersonal relationships and society as a whole.

Marijuana Exposure

Marijuana is one of the most widely used psychoactive substances in the United States, and use tends to peak between 15 and 30 years of age. This pattern of use can potentially expose the developing brain to the substance during both the prenatal period and during a critical period of adolescent brain development. Estimates of marijuana use during pregnancy vary from 2% in a sample of survey respondents using self-report (Ebrahim & Gfroerer, 2003) to 20–27% in high-risk populations using objective measures of use, such as urine screens (MacGregor, Sciarra, Keith, & Sciarra, 1990; Zuckerman et al., 1989). In a study of more than 1,600 expectant mothers across four urban sites in the United States, 6% of the sample endorsed smoking marijuana at some point throughout their pregnancies (Arria et al., 2006). The primary psychoactive substance in marijuana, Δ-9-tetrahydrocannabinol (THC), easily crosses the placenta and can remain in the mother's body for 30 days, prolonging potential fetal exposure. Marijuana smoking produces a higher level of carbon monoxide than does tobacco, which may be a potential mechanism leading to adverse effects on the developing fetus.

PHYSICAL CHARACTERISTICS AND BRAIN CHANGES

Studies have suggested a modest effect of marijuana on prenatal growth, although there are inconsistencies across studies. In general, marijuana-exposed infants have shown reduced birthweight (Fergusson, Horwood, & Northstone, 2002; Hatch & Bracken, 1986; Zuckerman et al., 1989), smaller head circumference (Fergusson et al., 2002), and decreased gestation length (e.g., Cornelius, Taylor, Geva, & Day, 1995; Fried, Watkinson, & Willan, 1984; Hatch & Bracken, 1986) compared to nonexposed infants. The weight effects that are found appear to be related to intrauterine growth retardation (IUGR) due to chronic oxygen deprivation in utero. This type of growth retardation has been linked with poorer neurodevelopmental outcomes (compared to normal-weight babies or babies with other types of

IUGR), especially if the head circumference is also small. The observed effects of marijuana on prenatal growth (e.g., birthweight) do not appear to persist into later growth deficiency during childhood and adolescence, although a couple of studies have suggested a persisting impact on height (Cornelius, Goldschmidt, Day, & Larkby, 2002), as well as on head circumference in the children of heavy marijuana users (Fried, Watkinson, & Gray, 1999).

Exposure to marijuana during critical periods of brain maturation is also linked to abnormal development of several neurotransmitter systems, including catecholaminergic, serotonergic, γ-aminobutyric acid (GABA)ergic, glutamatergic, and opioid systems (see Trezza, Cuomo, & Vanderschuren, 2008, for a summary). Most of this evidence comes from studies of animal populations, which demonstrate changes in the neuronal organization of adult rat brains following perinatal exposure to THC. Serotonin and glutamate systems appear to be most critically affected. Decreased serotonin levels in diencephalic brain regions important for memory have been observed in newly born rat pups, whereas reduced serotonin levels in the hypothalamus, neostriatum, hippocampus, septum nuclei, and midbrain raphe nuclei have been noted in the brains of adult rats prenatally exposed to THC (Molina-Holgado, Alvarez, Gonzalez, Antonio, & Leret, 1997; Molina-Holgado, Amaro, Gonzalez, Alvarez, & Leret, 1996). In addition, prenatal exposure to THC appears to increase the expression and functional activity of glutamate transporters in the prefrontal cortex of adolescent rats (Castaldo et al., 2007).

NEUROCOGNITIVE EFFECTS

Most of what is known about the neurobehavioral and cognitive effects of prenatal marijuana exposure in humans comes from two large longitudinal studies initiated in 1978 and 1982. The first of these, the Ottawa Prenatal Prospective Study (OPPS) examined the association between marijuana and other drug use during pregnancy and the effects on offspring in the areas of growth, cognition, and behavior. This study used a sample of predominantly low-risk, Caucasian, middle-class families and followed children up to the age of 18–22 years. The second study, the Maternal Health Practices and Child Development (MHPCD) Study, examined prenatal use of alcohol, cannabis, and cocaine in a higher risk cohort of low socioeconomic status families in Pittsburgh, Pennsylvania. Outcomes from this study have been

reported in offspring up to the age of 14 years. Both studies reported some evidence of abnormal autonomic nervous system functioning in newly born marijuana-exposed infants up to 1 month old. The OPPS study reported poorer habituation to visual but not auditory stimuli in marijuana-exposed infants at less than 1 week, 9 days, and 30 days of age, as well as increased tremors accompanied by exaggerated and prolonged startle responses (Fried & Makin, 1987; Tansley, Fried, & Mount, 1986). Similarly, studies have found altered sleep patterns in such infants (Scher, Richardson, Coble, Day, & Stoffer, 1988) and increased likelihood of exhibiting a high-pitched cry (Lester & Dreher, 1989). Past the neonatal period, there is limited to no evidence of delayed or abnormal cognitive development in marijuana-exposed children younger than 3 years of age. In the low-risk cohort, there was no association between prenatal marijuana exposure and cognitive and language development at 12 or 24 months of age (Fried & Watkinson, 1988). In the high-risk cohort, there was a dose-dependent association between marijuana use during the third trimester of pregnancy and a decrease in scores on the Bayley Scales of Infant Development at 9 months of age; however, this relation disappeared by 18 months of age (Richardson, Day, & Goldschmidt, 1995). In children 3 years of age and older, both the OPPS and MHPCD studies have uncovered similar findings of subtle cognitive impairments in marijuana-exposed children compared to nonexposed peers. Specifically, in utero exposure to marijuana was associated with impaired short-term memory as well as with verbal and visual abstract reasoning at a 3-year follow up (Day et al., 1994). In another investigation, 3-year-olds whose mothers used marijuana during pregnancy showed increased fearfulness, poorer motor skills, and had shorter lengths of play compared to nonexposed children (Faden & Graubard, 2000). At 4 years, children in the OPPS sample whose mothers used more than five joints a week during pregnancy showed poorer performance on verbal and memory outcome measures from the McCarthy Scales of Children's Abilities, and these associations remained after controlling for all confounding variables. At 5 and 6 years of age, maternal cannabis use was associated with increased omission errors on a vigilance task but not with global cognitive skills (Fried, O'Connell, & Watkinson, 1992; Leech, Richardson, Goldschmidt, & Day, 1999).

In a study of standardized intelligence test performance in 6-year-olds from the MHPCD cohort, Goldschmidt, Richardson, Willford, and

Day (2008) found that heavy prenatal marijuana exposure (i.e., one or more cigarettes per day) during the first trimester was associated with lower verbal reasoning scores on the Stanford-Binet Intelligence Scale, whereas heavy use during the second trimester predicted lower composite, short-term memory, and quantitative scores. Third trimester heavy use was also associated with lower quantitative scores. In comprehensive neuropsychological assessments of the OPPS school-aged children between 9 and 14 years of age, no association between global intelligence and prenatal marijuana exposure has been found; however, subtle differences have been uncovered between exposed children and controls. The primary variables that discriminated between marijuana-exposed and nonexposed children in these assessments were the Block Design and Picture Completion subtests of the WISC-III, as well as tests of impulse control, visuospatial processing, and problem solving. Also, neuroimaging studies of this cohort have noted altered neural functional response patterns during response inhibition and visuospatial working memory tasks (Smith, Fried, Hogan, & Cameron, 2004; 2006). Given these results, the authors argue that prenatal marijuana exposure primarily impacts aspects of higher level executive function and "top-down" performance, which leads to difficulty problem-solving in situations requiring visual integration, analysis, and sustained attention. In accordance with this view, the MHPCD cohort studies have found links between prenatal marijuana exposure, inattention, and impulsivity (Goldschmidt, Richardson, Cornelius, & Day, 2004), as well as with subtle deficits in memory and learning (Richardson, Ryan, Willford, Day, & Goldschmidt, 2002).

A recent study by Goldschmidt, Richardson, Willford, Severtson, and Day (2012) found a significant negative relationship between prenatal marijuana exposure and academic achievement in the MHPCD cohort at age 14, as assessed by the Wechsler Individual Achievement Test (WIAT) composite and reading scores. In addition, this relationship was mediated by the effects of prenatal marijuana exposure on children's intelligence test performance at age 6, attention problems and depression symptoms at age 10, and early initiation of their own marijuana use. The authors note that studies of the middle-class OPPS cohort have not found a relationship between prenatal marijuana exposure and academic achievement in childhood, suggesting that higher socioeconomic status may serve as a significant protective factor that lowers the risk for adverse effects (Goldschmidt et al., 2012).

PSYCHOSOCIAL OUTCOMES

In addition to subtle effects on cognition, particularly in the areas of executive functioning and visuospatial processing, prenatal marijuana exposure appears to have an effect on later psychosocial and psychiatric functioning of children and adolescents whose mothers smoked marijuana during pregnancy. In the MHPCD cohort, delinquent behavior, as measured by the CBCL and Teacher Report Form was increased in the cannabis- exposed group, and this relation was mediated by inattention difficulties. In addition, this group had an increased rate of self-reported depressive symptoms at 10 years of age, and this effect remained after controlling for other prenatal exposures (Gray, Day, Leech, & Richardson, 2005). There is also some evidence that prenatal marijuana exposure is related to an increased rate of substance use later in life. Specifically, in the OPPS study, greater cannabis and tobacco use was reported in 16- to 21-year-olds with prenatal marijuana exposure compared to their nonexposed peers, and this effect was more pronounced in males (Porath & Fried, 2005).

Stimulant Exposure
COCAINE

Cocaine use during pregnancy initially received an onslaught of attention in the 1980s, when "crack" cocaine use plagued urban centers throughout the United States. At that time, the popular belief was that babies born to crack-/cocaine-abusing women would suffer lifelong developmental and behavioral handicaps. Although rates of cocaine use have generally declined in the United States since the late 1980s, prenatal cocaine use remains a significant public health concern. Although effects do not appear as dramatic as once thought, research over the past 30 years has documented an array of subtler acute and long-term consequences of cocaine use during pregnancy on infant growth, health, and neurobehavior. Prevalence estimates of cocaine use among pregnant women range from 1% in a National Pregnancy and Health Survey to 18% in an inner-city sample from Boston (Zuckerman et al., 1989). Ten percent of mothers in the Maternal Lifestyle Study, a large multisite longitudinal study evaluating the effects of cocaine and opiate use on offspring development, reported using cocaine during pregnancy (Lester et al., 2001).

Physical Characteristics and Pregnancy Complications

Cocaine use among expectant mothers has been linked with a number of pregnancy complications, including spontaneous abortion, abruptio placenta (separation of the placenta from the site of uterine implantation before delivery of the fetus), stillbirths, fetal distress, and premature delivery (Chiriboga, Bateman, Brust, & Hauser, 1993). IUGR, low birthweight, and microcephaly are more common in cocaine-exposed infants; growth effects tend to show a dose–response relationship, and low levels of exposure or exposure exclusively during the first trimester may not negatively impact fetal growth (Chiriboga et al., 1993). Neonatal strokes, focal seizures, and abnormal electroencephalograms have also been described in clinical reports of heavily cocaine-exposed infants, although there are inconsistencies in the findings and these events may be mediated by other delivery complications linked to cocaine use, such as abruptio placenta or birth asphyxia. A direct mechanism of maternal cocaine use on neonatal strokes may be vasoconstriction and decreased blood flow in the fetal cerebrum. Other congenital malformations linked to heavy cocaine exposure include abnormalities of the reproductive tract and/or urinary system, absence of limbs or parts of limbs, narrowing or absence of portions of the intestines, single cardiac ventricle, brain malformations (e.g., skull defects, delayed ossification, agenesis of the corpus callosum), and ocular anomalies (e.g., strabismus, nystagmus, eyelid edema, delayed visual maturation; Chiriboga, 2003). Infants born to cocaine-abusing mothers also display abnormal neurologic functioning in the first few weeks of life, including poor feeding, insomnia and sleep disturbances, tremor, hypertonia, hyperreflexia, increased startle response, and difficulties with regulation of neonatal behavioral state (Bingol, Fuchs, Diaz, Stone, & Gromisch, 1987; Chasnoff, Lewis, Griffith, & Willey, 1989; Chiriboga, Brust, Bateman, & Hauser, 1999; Oro & Dixon, 1987).

Neurocognitive Effects

Long-term neurocognitive effects of prenatal cocaine exposure tend to manifest as specific neurobehavioral and/or learning problems, but studies have not found a relationship with global cognitive deficits in preschool or school-aged children (e.g., Azuma & Chasnoff, 1993; Chiriboga et al., 1995; Richardson, Conroy, & Day, 1996; Wasserman et al., 1998). However, studies have found that cocaine-exposed infants show poorer visual recognition memory and information processing abilities, as well as faster reaction times to visual stimuli on the Fagan Test of Infant Intelligence (Struthers & Hansen, 1992). Delays in motor development have also been noted in cocaine-exposed infants and toddlers (Arendt, Angelopoulos, Salvator, & Singer, 1999). One of the more consistent findings linked to prenatal cocaine exposure in infants and young children is that of behavior problems or a "difficult" temperament. Specifically, cocaine-exposed infants have been described as excessively excitable and irritable, and they tend to favor increased stimulation compared to nonexposed infants (e.g., Karmel & Gardner, 1996). At preschool age, increased fussiness, difficult temperament characterized by frequent and severe temper tantrums, impulsivity, aggression, and emotional lability have been observed (Faden & Graubard, 2000). These behaviors tend to diminish over time and may completely resolve by the time children reach school age or adolescence. In older children, prenatal cocaine exposure is associated with subtle deficits on some neurocognitive tasks, including delayed language (Bland-Stewart, Seymour, Beeghly, & Frank, 1998; Delaney-Black et al., 2000), attention deficits (Noland et al., 2005), poorer verbal and visual abstract reasoning (Bennett, Bendersky, & Lewis, 2008; Griffith, Azuma, & Chasnoff, 1994), and impaired visuospatial working memory (Mayes, Snyder, Langlois, & Hunter, 2007). Two recent longitudinal studies have examined the effects of prenatal cocaine exposure across development, with somewhat conflicting results. Betancourt and colleagues (2011) collected data from adolescents at ages 12, 14.5, and 17 years old and found no effects of prenatal cocaine exposure on measures of inhibitory control, working memory, or receptive language; however, adolescents prenatally exposed to cocaine performed more poorly on an incidental face memory task. On an incidental word memory task, adolescents with prenatal cocaine exposure improved more slowly with age (across the three time points) than did their nonexposed peers (Betancourt et al., 2011). In the second study, Bandstra and colleagues (2011) uncovered a dose-dependent negative relationship between level of prenatal cocaine exposure and performance on expressive and receptive language tasks at ages 3, 5, and 12 years, which persisted after controlling for age, sex, and other prenatal drug exposures. Neuroimaging studies provide some preliminary support for altered brain functioning associated with prenatal cocaine exposure, specifically during tasks of response inhibition (Sheinkopf et al., 2009) and emotional arousal and working memory (Li et al., 2009), as well as structural brain alterations, including decreased white matter organization (Warner et al., 2006), decreased white matter volume and area of the corpus callosum (Dow-Edwards et al., 2006), and alterations in striatal morphology (Roussotte et al., 2012).

METHAMPHETAMINE

Methamphetamine use has exceeded cocaine use in most regions of the United States and is now considered the dominant drug problem plaguing the Western and Midwestern states in the country (Rawson et al., 2000). Concern over the effects of prenatal exposure to methamphetamine in recent years now parallels the concern over prenatal cocaine exposure that prevailed in the 1980s. Because methamphetamine and amphetamine use during pregnancy has become prevalent only recently, there are few studies characterizing its effects on the developing fetus. Similar to findings reported in cocaine-exposed infants, increased rates of premature birth, fetal distress, and growth deficiency have been reported in the offspring of women who used methamphetamine during pregnancy (Eriksson, Larsson, Winbladh, & Zetterstrom, 1978). Instances of cleft lip and liver disease have also been reported in these infants (Plessinger, 1998). Longitudinal studies of the neurocognitive effects of prenatal methamphetamine use have recently been initiated. The Infant, Development, Environment, and Lifestyle (IDEAL) study is one such prospective study that follows methamphetamine-exposed children and neurobehavioral outcomes from birth to 36 months. An early report from this study found that prenatal exposure to methamphetamine was associated with lower arousal, more lethargy, increased physiological stress, and poor quality of movement within the first 5 days of life (Smith et al., 2008). In addition, effects showed a dose–response relationship, with higher levels of amphetamine metabolites in meconium (early infant stool) associated with increased CNS stress. One preliminary study of methamphetamine-exposed children and adolescents aged 3–16 found that such children performed more poorly than controls on tasks of visual motor integration, sustained attention, verbal memory, and long-term spatial memory. In addition, despite comparable whole-brain volumes across groups, methamphetamine-exposed children showed smaller hippocampal and striatal volumes (particularly within the bilateral putamen, left globus pallidus, and left hippocampal regions); volume size within these structures also correlated with

poorer performance on attention and verbal memory tasks (Chang et al., 2004).

Opiate Exposure

In the Maternal Lifestyle Study, 2.3% of women reported use of heroin or methadone during their pregnancies (Lester et al., 2001). Surprisingly, despite the negative effects of opiates on the user, there are few observed effects on the developing fetus. Low birthweight and symmetric IUGR have been described and are associated with prenatal heroin use; methadone does not appear to have an effect on fetal growth. Pregnant opiate users also have a significantly higher risk of miscarriage or premature delivery.

Neonatal abstinence syndrome (NAS) is a well-documented withdrawal syndrome often present in infants born to opiate-addicted mothers. Symptoms include gastrointestinal distress, respiratory distress, increased irritability, and CNS effects such as tremors, convulsions, hypertonicity, hyperreflexia, sleep disturbances, feeding difficulties, and occasional seizures. The onset of NAS varies from a few hours after birth to 2 weeks of age, and symptoms may persist up to a few months of age (Finnegan, 1985). Infants suffering from NAS may have "difficult" temperaments and be resistant to caretaker interactions such as cuddling and soothing. They are also likely to have a decreased ability to respond normally to auditory or visual stimuli. These early alterations in socialization may lead to decreased attention from caretakers and may have detrimental effects on children's development later in life (Finnegan, 1985).

Early reports of neurobehavior in opiate-exposed infants and young children have described increased hyperactivity, shorter attention span, sleep disturbances, and neuromotor abnormalities (Rosen & Johnson, 1985). Studies of older children aged 3–6 have suggested mild memory and perceptual difficulties compared to controls, but overall test scores remained within the normal range (Lifschitz & Wilson, 1991). In general, it is difficult to separate the impact of prenatal opiate exposure from the effects of a poor postnatal environment on children's long-term outcomes. One study found that the presence of a withdrawal syndrome at birth was the main mediating factor accounting for developmental delays and lower IQ scores in methadone-exposed children (Bauman & Levine, 1986). Another study noted that an impoverished early environment had a disproportionately adverse effect on the development of methadone-exposed children compared with nonexposed children (Marcus, Hans, & Jeremy, 1984). However, opiate-exposed infants adopted out at birth showed educational attainment and IQ equivalent to a group of matched controls, although the opiate-exposed group did have increased rates of depressive symptoms as adults (Lipman, Offord, Boyle, & Racine, 1993).

Prenatal Drug Exposure and Vulnerability to Future Substance Use

Research has identified a wide range of risk and protective factors related to the likelihood of engaging in drug use behavior or developing drug abuse or dependence disorders throughout an individual's lifetime. In general, the initiation of drug use is associated with social and environmental factors, whereas higher levels of drug involvement, abuse, and dependence are associated with biological and psychiatric factors (Glantz & Chambers, 2006). Major comorbidities associated with alcohol and drug use disorders include antisocial personality characteristics, psychopathology, and cognitive or behavioral dysregulation. Because prenatal drug exposure has been found to increase the likelihood of regulatory difficulties in arousal, emotion, attention, inhibition, and impulse control, as well as impaired cognition and externalizing behavior disorders, it naturally follows that individuals exposed to alcohol and/or drugs prenatally are more likely to develop these comorbidities at some point in their lifetimes. However, whether the increased vulnerability for drug abuse/dependence in these individuals is the result of the drug exposure itself or the combined result of associated genetic, familial, environmental, and parenting factors that go along with having a mother who abuses drugs during pregnancy is a difficult question to answer. Studies of animal populations are less complicated and provide some insight, suggesting that, compared to nonexposed rats, prenatally drug-exposed rats are more responsive to the drug to which they were exposed as well as to other psychoactive drugs in that they show increased self-administration of these drugs (e.g., Lidow, 2003; Malanga & Kosofsky, 2003). Thus, prenatal drug exposure, independent of familial behavior and environmental factors, may result in altered reward systems in the brain and consequently lead to increased rates of substance abuse problems later in life.

Adolescent Substance Use

Adolescence is a unique transitional period in human development between childhood and adulthood, one that is marked by significant biological, psychological, social, and role transformations. The specific age range encapsulating adolescence can vary across studies but for the purposes of this review, we use ages 12 through 18, unless otherwise noted. These dramatic changes correspond with substantial increases in alcohol and drug use. Although some experimentation with alcohol and drugs may be normative for this developmental period, adolescents may risk both acute (e.g., car accidents, risky sexual behavior) and long-term (e.g., neurocognitive impairment, development of substance use disorders [SUDs]) negative consequences. According to the National Institute of Drug Abuse Monitoring the Future Study, 30% of youth have used alcohol and 19% have used an illicit drug by eighth grade. These rates increase considerably during adolescence, with 69% of adolescents reporting alcohol use and 49% reporting illicit drug use by the time they graduate high school. Heavy episodic drinking is also common among youth, with 24% of 12th graders endorsing binge drinking (i.e., four or more drinks for females and five or more drinks for males) in the past two weeks and 28% admitting being drunk in the past 30 days. Rates of smoking also increase during this time, with 40% of 12th graders endorsing cigarette use and 17% reporting they are current smokers (Johnston, O'Malley, Bachman, & Schulenberg, 2013).

Although the adult literature has consistently shown an adverse impact of heavy substance use on physical and psychological well-being (Cunha-Oliveira, Rego, & Oliveira, 2008; Oscar-Berman & Marinkovic, 2003; 2007; Vik, Cellucci, Jarchow, & Hedt, 2004), research has only begun to explore the negative sequelae associated with substance use during adolescence. High rates of adolescent substance use have important public health and clinical implications. Substance use is related to a wide range of health and risk-taking behaviors (Miller, Naimi, Brewer, & Jones, 2007) and is associated with the three leading causes of death among youth: unintentional injury, homicide, and suicide (Prevention, 2009).

Developmental Changes in Adolescence Related to Substance Use

During adolescence, the human brain experiences rapid structural and functional alterations. Paradoxically, these developmental neural changes both contribute to adolescents' increased risky behaviors (such as substance use) while simultaneously heightening the vulnerability of the brain to the neurotoxic effects of substances. During adolescence, both gray and white matter components of the brain undergo significant developmental changes. Two major processes that contribute to brain maturation during adolescence are (1) synaptic refinement and (2) increased myelination (Giedd et al., 1999; Yakovlev & Lecours, 1967). Synaptic refinement refers to the pruning of unnecessary synaptic connections, resulting in gray matter reductions and cortical thinning. Myelination refers to the progressive increase in the fatty myelin sheath that covers neuronal axons. Together, these processes contribute to greater efficiency and specialization of adolescent brain regions. Synaptic pruning (Huttenlocher, 1990) occurs primarily in the prefrontal and temporal cortex (Giedd, 2004), beginning in the striatum and prefrontal regions of the brain (Jernigan, Trauner, Hesselink, & Tallal, 1991; Sowell, Thompson, Holmes, Jernigan, & Toga, 1999) and ending in the dorsolateral prefrontal cortex (Gogtay et al., 2004; Sowell, Trauner, Gamst, & Jernigan, 2002). In conjunction with gray matter reduction, white matter continues to increase linearly with age (Barnea-Goraly et al., 2005; Giedd et al., 1999; Pfefferbaum et al., 1994), particularly in the cerebellum (Keller et al., 2003) and the hippocampus (Jernigan & Gamst, 2005), an area critical to learning and memory. Continued neuromaturation with age underlies changes in affect regulation, reward sensitivity (Chambers, Taylor, & Potenza, 2003), and working memory (Jernigan & Gamst, 2005) and increases the speed of neuronal transmission between brain regions.

The dopaminergic system experiences significant reorganization during adolescence because dopamine activity decreases substantially in the nucleus accumbens throughout this period. Dopamine has been implicated as a primary mechanism involved in affective and motivational regulation. Spear (2002) hypothesized that the sudden drops in striatal dopamine levels that occur around puberty may contribute to adolescents' propensity to actively seek out novel and risky behaviors to compensate for a dopamine void. These greater motivational drives for novel experiences, coupled with underdeveloped frontal lobes and inhibitory control capacity, are suggested to influence an adolescent's susceptibility to engage in impulsive and risky behaviors like substance use (Chambers et al., 2003).

Although adolescents' predisposition for alcohol and drug use may be partially explained by neuromaturational phenomena, shifts in social and peer influence during adolescence also substantially contribute to the increase in substance-related behaviors during this time period (Baumrind, 1987; Cloninger, Sigvardsson, & Bohman, 1988). In 2012, 24% of 12th graders reported that most or all of their friends get drunk at least once a week, with only 23% reporting that none of their friends get drunk at least once a week (Johnston, O'Malley, Bachman, & Schulenberg, 2012). Twenty-four percent of 12th graders reported often being around peers who were using illicit drugs in the past year, and 82% reported having at least one friend who often uses illicit drugs (Johnston et al., 2012). Increased exposure to alcohol and drugs and the perceived easy accessibility to substances (Johnston et al., 2007) contributes to the greater prevalence of substance use during adolescence.

Alcohol Use

NEUROPSYCHOLOGICAL STUDIES

Cross-sectional studies of heavy-drinking adolescent populations have found differences in neurocognitive functioning among adolescents with alcohol use disorders (AUDs) compared to controls. Deficits associated with heavy alcohol use include significantly poorer visuospatial skills (Giancola, Mezzich, & Tarter, 1998; Tapert & Brown, 1999), sustained attention and perceptual efficiency (Tapert & Brown, 2000; Tarter, Mezzich, Hsieh, & Parks, 1995), and language abilities (Moss, Kirisci, Gordon, & Tarter, 1994; Tapert & Brown, 2000; Tarter et al., 1995). For female adolescent substance users, deficits have been found on tasks of executive functioning, specifically those involving planning, abstract reasoning, and generation of new solutions to problems (Giancola, Shoal, & Mezzich, 2001; Moss et al., 1994).

Longitudinal studies have also been conducted to determine whether neurocognitive deficits are premorbid factors or consequences of heavy alcohol use. Adolescents treated for SUDs who reported continued heavy drinking and greater alcohol hangover or withdrawal symptoms over the follow-up had decrements on tasks of attention and visuospatial functioning compared to nonusing adolescents (Tapert & Brown, 1999; Tapert, Granholm, Leedy, & Brown, 2002). These findings have been replicated in a prospective study that characterized at-risk adolescents prior to initiating alcohol use. For females, initiation of moderate to heavy alcohol use over the follow-up period was associated with relative worsening of visuospatial functioning, whereas greater hangover symptoms over the follow-up period predicted poorer sustained attention in males (Squeglia, Spadoni, Infante, Myers, & Tapert, 2009). These studies suggest that heavy drinking during adolescence may be associated with decrements in cognitive performance, possibly due to the vulnerability of the adolescent brain during ongoing neuromaturation. The longitudinal design of these studies lends support to the hypothesis that neurocognitive deficits may result from, rather than predate, adolescent alcohol use.

Examination of postdrinking symptoms (e.g., hangover and withdrawal) has been of particular interest because these symptoms indicate intense alcohol consumption, have been associated with brain changes (Parsons & Stevens, 1986), and are not dependent on quantity of alcohol consumed (Wiese, Shlipak, & Browner, 2000). Adult alcoholics with a greater history of withdrawal symptoms have exhibited greater deficits on tests of learning and memory (Glenn, Parsons, Sinha, and Stevens, 1988). This finding is supported in the animal literature, linking increased withdrawal episodes to poorer learning (Bond, 1979; Freund, 1970; Freund & Walker, 1971). In human adolescents, poorer visuospatial performance (Brown, Tapert, Granholm, & Delis, 2000; Tapert et al., 2002), attention (Tapert et al., 2002), verbal and nonverbal retention (Brown et al., 2000), memory (Tapert et al., 2001), and greater abnormalities in brain response to cognitive tasks (Tapert et al., 2004) have been found in adolescents who endorsed more alcohol withdrawal symptoms. Thus, the effects of alcohol withdrawal on adolescent cognitive functioning may be more detrimental than the actual frequency and quantity of alcohol consumed or may more accurately mark the extent of a heavy drinking episode than recollections of alcohol quantity.

Moderating variables like gender, comorbid psychopathology, and family history of alcohol use have also been examined to determine the extent of their influence on neurocognitive performance in adolescent alcohol users. Evidence has suggested that females may be more vulnerable to the deleterious impact of alcohol use (Caldwell et al., 2005; Medina et al., 2008; Moss et al., 1994; Schweinsburg et al., 2003; Squeglia, Schweinsburg, Pulido, & Tapert, 2011; Squeglia, Sorg, et al., 2012; Squeglia et al., 2009). Conduct, attention deficit hyperactivity, anxiety, and affective disorders (Brown & D'Amico, 2001; Myers, Stewart, & Brown, 1998; Tomlinson, Brown, & Abrantes, 2004) have also been found to moderate alcohol treatment outcomes. Positive family history of alcohol dependence has been shown to interact with substance use, predicting

worse language and attentional functioning (Tapert & Brown, 2000), as well as neural abnormalities (Tapert, Cheung, et al., 2003).

STRUCTURAL BRAIN ABNORMALITIES

Neuroimaging techniques have been used to study the impact of alcohol use on brain structure and function to better understand the principal regions and pathways that underlie observed cognitive deficits in adolescent users. Hippocampal volumes are one area of particular interest because this region of the brain is critical to memory functioning, including storage and recall, rote memory, memory for verbal material within context, and spatial memory. Preclinical research has shown that adolescence may be a particularly vulnerable period for hippocampal damage. Acute exposure to a relatively small amount of alcohol has been shown to disrupt N-methyl-D-aspartate (NMDA) receptor-mediated long-term potentiation in the hippocampus of adolescent rats while having little or no effect on the hippocampus of adult rats (Pyapali, Turner, Wilson, & Swartzwelder, 1999). Neurogenesis of the adolescent hippocampus may be impaired due to alcohol-related inhibition of neural stem cell growth (McClain et al., 2011; Morris, Eaves, Smith, & Nixon, 2009).

In clinical research, decreased bilateral hippocampal volumes have been found in adolescents who met criteria for AUDs compared to nonusing adolescents, with smaller hippocampi associated with earlier age of onset and longer duration of the disorder (De Bellis et al., 2000). Nagel, Schweinsburg, Phan, and Tapert (2005) and Medina, Schweinsburg, Cohen-Zion, Nagel, and Tapert (2007) found similar results, with smaller left hippocampal volumes observed in alcohol-using adolescents compared to controls, even after excluding teens with co-occurring conduct disorder. However, hippocampal volume did not correlate with alcohol use, suggesting possible premorbid differences between groups in hippocampal volume. Taken together, these studies suggest that the hippocampus plays a role in AUDs among adolescents. The degree to which the hippocampus is a predisposing factor for heavy alcohol use or a particularly vulnerable brain region to the effects of alcohol has yet to be determined, and therefore longitudinal studies examining this structure are needed.

The frontal lobe is an area of the brain that is associated with higher order executive functioning, emotional regulation, integration of novel stimuli, and cognitive flexibility. In adults, heavy alcohol use is associated with smaller prefrontal regions (Pfefferbaum, Sullivan, Mathalon, & Lim, 1997). Initial findings in adolescent populations have suggested that the prefrontal cortex may be more vulnerable to the effects of alcohol compared to other brain regions because this area of the brain continues to develop throughout adolescence and young adulthood. De Bellis et al. (2005) found significantly smaller prefrontal cortex volumes as well as decreased white matter in this region in adolescents with comorbid alcohol use and psychiatric disorders compared to demographically matched controls. These findings were replicated in a study examining adolescents who did not meet criteria for comorbid mood or attention disorders (Medina et al., 2008). A gender-by-alcohol interaction was present, with alcohol-dependent females having smaller prefrontal cortex and white matter volumes than controls, and alcohol-dependent males having larger prefrontal and white matter volumes than controls. These findings suggest that gender moderates the relationship between adolescent alcohol use on prefrontal neuromaturation, with females having more pronounced negative sequelae from continued drinking.

The cerebellum, which plays a crucial role in both motor and cognitive functions, has also been associated with alcohol-related damage (Pfefferbaum & Sullivan, 2005); however, the effect of alcohol use on adolescent cerebellar structure is less clear. In a group of healthy, non-alcohol use disordered teens, Lisdahl and colleagues (2011) found that greater binge drinking during adolescence was linked to smaller cerebellar volumes, above and beyond variability attributable to risk factors for binge drinking (Lisdahl, Thayer, Squeglia, McQueeny, & Tapert, 2011). De Bellis and colleagues (2005) found similar results, in which males with an AUD had smaller cerebellar volumes than did male controls (De Bellis et al., 2005).

Normal adolescent brain development involves substantial cortical thinning, which has been linked to elimination of weaker synaptic connections (Giedd, 2004; Stiles & Jernigan, 2010). Yet limited work has examined how alcohol impacts normal cortical thinning during this developmental period. Squeglia, Sorg, and colleagues (2012) examined how heavy episodic drinking in adolescents aged 16–19 related to indices of cortical thickness. Binge drinking-by-gender interactions were seen for cortical thickness in four left frontal brain regions, in which female bingers had thicker cortices than did female controls, and male bingers had thinner

cortices than did male controls. Thicker left frontal cortices (i.e., less mature cortices) corresponded with poorer visuospatial, inhibition, and attention performances for female bingers and worse attention for male bingers. The finding that female drinkers had thicker cortices than did male drinkers is particularly notable considering that female cortices begin thinning 1–2 years earlier than males on average (Giedd, 2004; Lenroot et al., 2007), and this could suggest an even greater deleterious effect of drinking on female brain maturation than statistical comparisons indicated. Longitudinal investigations are needed to elucidate the temporal sequence of events, as well as the underlying mechanism driving cortical thinning during adolescence.

DTI methodology has also been used to examine the integrity of white matter tracts throughout the brains of alcohol users. In adults, chronic alcohol use has been associated with more abnormal white matter volume and less organization of white matter tracts (Kril, Halliday, Svoboda, & Cartwright, 1997; Pfefferbaum, Adalsteinsson, & Sullivan, 2006; Pfefferbaum & Sullivan, 2005; Pfefferbaum et al., 2000). Tapert, Theilmann, and Schweinsburg (2003) reported that adolescents with AUDs had reduced white matter microstructural integrity in the corpus callosum as compared to demographically matched youth without AUDs, particularly in the posterior aspect (i.e., the splenium). Lower FA values in the body of the corpus callosum were significantly related to longer durations of heavy drinking and greater alcohol withdrawal symptoms, and lower FA in the splenium correlated with larger quantities of recent alcohol consumption. In a study by McQueeny et al. (2009), adolescents with histories of binge drinking who did not meet criteria for alcohol abuse or dependence showed less white matter integrity in 18 major fiber tract pathways, specifically in the frontal, cerebellar, temporal, and parietal regions, areas that underlie learning, memory, and executive functioning. Six of the 18 regions were significantly related to greater lifetime hangover symptoms and/or higher estimated peak blood alcohol levels. The microstructural changes in these areas could underlie neurocognitive deficits associated with alcohol use during adolescent brain maturation. However, longitudinal studies will help elucidate the nature of the relationship between white matter integrity and alcohol use.

Poorer white matter integrity may be both a precursor and a consequence of heavy drinking. In 11- to 15-year alcohol-naïve youth, Herting, Schwartz, Mitchell, and Nagel (2010) found that those youth with positive family history of AUDs had poorer white matter integrity in several brain regions, along with poorer performance on a task of delay discounting and reaction time, when compared to youth who had no family history of AUDs. These preexisting differences in white matter integrity may be a phenotypic marker of future substance use and risk-taking behaviors. Jacobus and colleagues found that white matter integrity measured in 16- to 19-year-old adolescents was related to more self-reported substance use and delinquency/aggression at an 18-month follow-up, highlighting the importance and potential clinical utility of the observed cross-sectional differences found by Herting and colleagues (Jacobus et al., 2013). In a prospective study by Bava, Jacobus, Thayer, and Tapert (2013), alcohol use from ages 18 to 20 predicted poorer white matter integrity at follow-up 1.5 years later in young adults, suggesting that regular heavy alcohol use over the course of development likely has deleterious effects on brain tissue above and beyond baseline differences that may relate to genetic predispositions. In sum, it appears that white matter abnormalities both precede and are a consequence of alcohol and other substance use during adolescence.

FUNCTIONAL BRAIN ABNORMALITIES

Recent fMRI studies have begun to examine the influence of alcohol use on adolescent brain functioning. In one study, adolescents who drank heavily for 1–2 years showed greater brain response during a spatial working memory task in bilateral parietal cortices (Tapert et al., 2004), with decreased response in other regions including the left precentral gyrus and bilateral cerebellar areas, despite no behavioral differences on task performance. This finding was more pronounced in adolescents who reported increased withdrawal and hangover symptoms and had greater lifetime alcohol consumption. These abnormalities, in spite of similar task performance, indicate that subtle neural reorganization might occur in heavy-drinking adolescents early in their drinking trajectory. In contrast to these findings, alcohol-dependent adolescent females with 4–5 years of drinking history exhibited significantly less BOLD response than controls during the same spatial working memory task in parietal and prefrontal regions of the brain (i.e., right superior and inferior parietal, right middle frontal, right postcentral, and left superior frontal cortex). The alcohol-dependent women also performed worse on spatial working memory trials, which was associated with greater alcohol withdrawal symptomatology, less spatial working memory response in the right parietal cortex, and lower scores on neuropsychological tests of memory and cognitive flexibility (Tapert et al., 2001). These results are consistent with previous findings that withdrawal symptoms are associated with poorer spatial functioning and memory (Brown et al., 2000; Tapert & Brown, 1999). Although adolescents with shorter drinking histories were able to perform similarly to controls on spatial working memory tasks despite differential neural activation, adolescents who had more long-term alcohol exposure showed greater behavioral deficits. This suggests that the brain is initially resilient to neural insults, whereas continued alcohol use may negatively interfere with normal neural functioning.

Differences between adolescent drinkers and controls on tasks of verbal encoding (i.e., learning of novel word pairs) have also been found. In a study comparing 16- to 18-year-old binge drinkers to controls, Schweinsburg et al. (2010) found that bingers showed more response in right superior frontal and bilateral posterior parietal cortices, but less response in occipital cortex during verbal encoding, suggesting greater engagement of working memory systems during this task. In addition, controls showed activation in the left hippocampus during novel encoding, whereas binge drinkers did not, which is suggestive of disadvantaged processing of novel verbal information for bingers. Binge drinkers also showed slightly worse word pair recall, suggesting subtle alterations in learning abilities (Schweinsburg, McQueeny, Nagel, Eyler, & Tapert, 2010). Similarly, a 2011 follow-up to this investigation found an increased dorsal frontal and parietal BOLD response among 16- to 18-year-old binge drinkers, with decreased inferior frontal response during verbal encoding (Schweinsburg, Schweinsburg, Nagel, Eyler, & Tapert, 2011). Taken together, these findings suggest that binge drinking is associated with aberrant neural activity during verbal working memory.

Binge drinkers also show differences in processing of affective information. Xiao and colleagues looked at more complex cognitive processing with a decision-making task (the Iowa Gambling Task) in binge drinkers aged 16–18. Binge drinkers showed increased BOLD activity in the limbic brain regions (i.e., amygdala and insula) compared to matched controls. Increased drinking severity was positively related to BOLD activity in the insula and negatively related to BOLD activity in the orbitofrontal cortex (Xiao et al., 2013). This suggests that hyper-reactivity in brain regions responsible for emotional and incentive-related behaviors are associated with risky behaviors like binge drinking.

Several recent prospective studies have shown preexisting differences in neural activation prior to adolescent engagement in substance use. Specifically, brain activation patterns have been able to predict future alcohol use, alcohol-related impairments (e.g., "blackouts"), and SUD symptomatology. In 12- to 14-year-old adolescents who were scanned prior to initiation of alcohol use, those adolescents who transitioned into heavy alcohol use by age 18 had less baseline BOLD activation in frontal, temporal, and parietal cortices in response to a go/no-go task of response inhibition than did matched controls (Norman et al., 2011). On the same go/no-go task in a different sample of 12- to 14-year-old substance-naïve adolescents, greater baseline activation during inhibitory processing was related to more alcohol-induced blackouts at a 5-year follow-up, suggesting a neurobiological vulnerability to alcohol-induced memory impairment (Wetherill, Castro, Squeglia, & Tapert, 2013). In a slightly older group of 16- to 19-year-old teens, less ventromedial prefrontal activation and greater left angular gyrus activation predicted greater substance use (both alcohol and marijuana) at an 18-month follow-up (Mahmood, Jacobus, Bava, Scarlett, & Tapert, 2010). Nees and colleagues (2012) found that reward-related brain activation (e.g., ventral striatum) aided in the prediction of early-onset drinking in adolescents, further supporting the notion that preexisting brain differences, along with personality and behavioral traits, may leave certain youth vulnerable to addictive behaviors (Nees et al., 2012).

To our knowledge, only one study exists that has two longitudinal fMRI data points examining adolescent alcohol use. In this study, 12- to 16-year-old adolescents were scanned before they ever used any alcohol or drugs and then were rescanned approximately 3 years later on the same scanner (Squeglia, Pulido et al., 2012). Those who transitioned into heavy use (n = 20) were matched to continuous nondrinkers (n = 20) over the follow-up on several risk factors for alcohol use, as well as on developmental factors. Adolescents who transitioned into heavy drinking over the follow-up showed less baseline BOLD response during a visual working memory task in frontal and parietal regions when compared to matched controls, which increased after the initiation of heavy alcohol use. In contrast, continuous nondrinkers showed decreasing activation in these regions, as would be expected with maturation. Lower baseline activation predicted future alcohol use above and beyond common predictors of substance use (e.g., family history, age, gender), consistent with previous findings suggesting that neural abnormalities predate initiation of heavy substance use (Mahmood et al., 2010; Norman et al., 2011; Wetherill et al., 2013). Taken together, these findings suggest that neural response patterns may be risk factors for future initiation of substance use and that heavy drinking during adolescence is associated with subtle alterations in brain functioning. Future longitudinal studies with more imaging time points and larger sample sizes are warranted to disentangle predisposing neural risks with alcohol-related cognitive impairments, as well as to increase our understanding of timing effects of these neural consequences.

Gender and comorbid substance use are important considerations when examining the effect of alcohol use on brain functioning. Squeglia and colleagues (2011) found binge drinking-by-gender interactions in BOLD activation to a spatial working memory task, with female binge drinkers showing less activation than female controls, and male binge drinkers exhibiting greater BOLD response than male controls. For female binge drinkers, less activation was associated with poorer neurocognitive performance; however, the opposite was found for male binge drinkers (Squeglia et al., 2011). These findings are consistent with previous work that suggests differences in brain activation between males and females and increased vulnerability of females to alcohol-related brain changes (Caldwell et al., 2005). In teens with co-occurring alcohol and marijuana use disorders, Schweinsburg et al. (2005) found less inferior frontal and temporal activation and increased medial frontal activation compared to controls in response to the spatial working memory task, suggesting altered neural processing in teens with comorbid alcohol and marijuana use (Schweinsburg et al., 2005). In sum, both gender and co-occurring substance use are important variables to consider in adolescent substance use research because they may interact with alcohol use.

Event-related potential (ERP) is a technique used to measure underlying cognitive functioning using electrophysiological response to a stimulus. Adolescent binge drinking has been associated with abnormal ERP response to a visual working memory task (Crego et al., 2009). Differential activation patterns to task subcomponents suggest that binge drinkers require greater attentional effort to perform the task and have a decreased ability to distinguish task-relevant information from unrelated stimuli, which may be associated with deficits in processes underlying working memory. These findings fit closely with results from fMRI studies (e.g., Tapert et al., 2004).

Insufficient cerebral blood flow can cause irreparable damage to brain regions and is, therefore, an important indicator of neuronal health. In the adult literature, chronic alcoholics have shown reduced blood flow to almost all regions of the brain (Suzuki, Oishi, Mizutani, & Sato, 2002). Using perfusion-weighted MRI, Clark et al. (2007) found that alcohol-dependent young women had less blood flow in the prefrontal and parietal regions (i.e., bilateral middle frontal gyri, left precuneus, right cingulate, and bilateral inferior parietal lobules) compared to nondrinkers, with no regions of the brain experiencing increased blood flow in alcohol-dependent females. Understanding cerebral blood flow patterns may help elucidate the metabolic changes behind observed differences in functional brain activity in alcohol-using adolescents compared to nonusers.

Alcohol use during adolescence may also put youth at risk for developing alcohol abuse or dependence disorders. A longitudinal study of more than 22,000 adolescents found that individuals who began drinking alcohol before age 15 were 38% more likely to develop alcohol dependence and 52% more likely to develop alcohol abuse at some point in their lifetime, as compared to youth who waited until age 18 to begin drinking, even after controlling for preexisting risk factors such as family history, adverse childhood experiences, and behavioral disorders (Dawson, Goldstein, Chou, Ruan, & Grant, 2008). Although the mechanism for this increased risk is unknown, alcohol-induced deficits in executive functioning incurred during adolescence may facilitate development of future AUDs (Goudriaan, Grekin, & Sher, 2007; Johnson et al., 2008).

Marijuana Use
NEUROPSYCHOLOGICAL STUDIES

Marijuana is the most common illicit drug of abuse among adolescents (Johnston et al., 2007). Studies have failed to show consistent negative consequences of marijuana use on neurocognitive functioning in samples of long-term, regularly marijuana-using adults, except in the domains of learning and forgetting, where subtle but discernible

harmful effects are present (Grant, Gonzalez, Carey, Wolfson, & Natarajan, 2003). Studies using neuropsychological assessments of adolescent marijuana users have found that heavy marijuana use is related to poorer learning and memory performance (Millsaps, Azrin, & Mittenberg, 1994; Schwartz, Gruenewald, Klitzner, & Fedio, 1989), as well as to worse attention and executive functioning (Thoma et al., 2011). Even after 4 weeks of monitored abstinence, adolescent marijuana users perform more poorly than nonusers on tasks of psychomotor speed, complex attention, story memory, and planning and sequencing abilities, even after controlling for lifetime alcohol use and depressive symptoms (Medina, Hansen et al., 2007). Dose-dependent relationships were observed between lifetime marijuana use in the above-mentioned cognitive domains after controlling for lifetime alcohol use (Medina, Hanson et al., 2007). In a prospective study by Tapert and colleagues (2002), frequent marijuana use over an 8-year follow-up period was associated with poorer attention, particularly in speeded psychomotor processing. These findings suggest that the adolescent brain may be more vulnerable to the deleterious effects of marijuana, above and beyond co-occurring alcohol use.

Longitudinal studies following at-risk samples of adolescent boys found that poor baseline (pre-substance use) executive functioning skills predicted greater adolescent-initiated marijuana use at follow-up (Aytaclar, Tarter, Kirisci, & Lu, 1999). These findings suggest that preexisting decrements in cognitive capacity may predispose adolescents to initiate marijuana use. Initiation of marijuana use during adolescence may also have long-lasting neurocognitive consequences (Meier et al., 2012), particularly in the areas of sustained attention, executive functioning (Fontes et al., 2011), impulse control (Gruber, Silveri, Dahlgren, & Yurgelun-Todd, 2011), and verbal memory (Solowij et al., 2011).

STRUCTURAL BRAIN ABNORMALITIES

Structural imaging studies of adolescent marijuana users have often focused on the hippocampus due to its important role in memory performance. Medina, Schweinsburg, and colleagues (2007) examined three groups of adolescents: (1) controls, (2) heavy alcohol users, and (3) heavy alcohol and marijuana users. Heavy-drinking adolescents showed greater right versus left asymmetry compared to both controls and heavy alcohol/marijuana adolescent users. This asymmetry was significantly associated with alcohol abuse/dependence severity, even after controlling for gender, conduct disorder, ethnicity, and age. Contrary to the alcohol findings, greater marijuana abuse/dependence was associated with larger left hippocampal volumes and greater left versus right asymmetry, but comorbid marijuana and alcohol users did not differ from controls on asymmetry or volume (Medina, Schweinsburg et al., 2007). The similarities between controls and comorbid alcohol and marijuana users, as opposed to adolescents who only used alcohol, could suggest neuroprotective properties of marijuana when used in combination with alcohol. Alternatively, alcohol and marijuana use may create conflicting mechanisms, such as neuroinflammation and myelin suppression, so that macromorphometric structures may appear normal. An additional explanation could be that heavy marijuana use during adolescence may interfere with synaptic pruning, leaving larger amounts of gray matter in the left hippocampus (Medina, Schweinsburg et al., 2007; Nagel et al., 2005). This study also found a functional relationship between hippocampal asymmetry and verbal learning, which was abnormal among both the heavy alcohol users and the heavy alcohol and marijuana users compared to the controls. Overall, alcohol and marijuana use during adolescence has been associated with abnormal hippocampal volumes, which may underlie learning and memory deficits.

In a preliminary comparison of prefrontal volumes of marijuana-using and control adolescents, few differences were found (Medina et al., 2008). Female marijuana-using adolescents had 4% larger posterior and prefrontal cortex volumes, with increased prefrontal volumes associated with poorer verbal memory. Overall, marijuana-using adolescents showed larger gray matter volumes, with more volume associated with poorer verbal mental set and attentional functioning, after controlling for intracranial size and alcohol history. These findings suggest that marijuana use may interrupt gray matter pruning in marijuana-using adolescents, a key process in neuromaturation and cognitive development.

The only existing longitudinal imaging study with pre- and post-marijuana use data found that smaller orbitofrontal volumes at age 12 predicted marijuana initiation by age 16 (Cheetham et al., 2012). Cross-sectional structural MRI studies have found thinner cortices in prefrontal and insular regions and thicker cortices in posterior regions (Lopez-Larson et al., 2011) in marijuana- and alcohol-using adolescents when compared to

healthy controls; however, it is unclear if differences existed prior to marijuana use.

DTI studies have had varied findings in regards to white matter integrity in marijuana-using adolescents, with most cross-sectional research showing poorer white matter integrity in marijuana users compared to controls and negative associations with neurocognitive performance (Bava et al., 2009; Jacobus, Bava, Cohen-Zion, Mahmood, & Tapert, 2009). Poorer white matter integrity has been predictive of future substance use and aggressive/delinquent behaviors, which suggests that some of these imaging biomarkers may have clinical utility in predicting future outcomes (Bava et al., 2013; Cheetham et al., 2012; Jacobus et al., 2013).

Medina, Nagel, Park, McQueeny, and Tapert (2007) found comparable white matter volumes between adolescent marijuana users and matched controls. However, marijuana users did exhibit more depressive symptoms than controls, and these symptoms were associated with white matter volumes. Specifically, smaller white matter volumes were associated with greater depressive symptoms in marijuana users only. These findings suggest that marijuana use may be associated with slight alterations in white matter tracts responsible for mood regulation. In a study of 72 adolescents, marijuana users showed significantly reduced white matter integrity as compared to matched nonusers in 10 brain regions, with three unexpected areas of higher integrity among users (Bava et al., 2009). These findings suggest that frontoparietal circuitry may be affected in adolescent users of marijuana in addition to alcohol, with possible abnormalities in axonal and myelin maturation. Another study found that heavy marijuana-using adolescents showed reduced white matter integrity in frontotemporal connections by means of the arcuate fasciculus, an area of the brain involved in the generation and understanding of language. However, this study did not control for alcohol use, and therefore the differences may be due to drinking frequency and quantity (Ashtari, Cervellione, Cottone, Ardekani, & Kumra, 2009). Furthermore, DeLisi and colleagues (2006) reported no differences in white matter integrity between adolescent marijuana users and controls. Continued research using longitudinal designs will be essential in teasing apart the relationship between white matter integrity and marijuana use.

FUNCTIONAL BRAIN ABNORMALITIES

Two recent studies have focused on brain functioning during tasks of working memory in adolescent marijuana users. Schweinsburg et al. (2008) found that marijuana-dependent adolescents had abnormal brain activation in response to a spatial working memory task compared to matched controls, despite similar task performance. Specifically, teens with comorbid alcohol and cannabis use disorders had less activation in the inferior frontal and temporal regions and greater dorsolateral prefrontal BOLD response compared to controls on tasks of working memory. However, this was conducted after only 48 hours or more of abstinence, and therefore abnormal brain response could be an artifact of acute or subacute marijuana withdrawal (Pope, Gruber, Hudson, Huestis, & Yurgelun-Todd, 2001). Jacobsen and colleagues examined three groups of demographically matched adolescents, including heavy marijuana users, heavy tobacco smokers, and nonusers after 1 month of abstinence. Marijuana users were less accurate on tasks of working memory and showed increased BOLD response in the right hippocampus relative to control and tobacco-smoking groups, suggesting cannabis users failed to inhibit hippocampal activity during the task. These effects were potentially mediated by cannabis-induced interference with inhibitory neurotransmission or apoptosis in the hippocampus (Jacobsen, Mencl, Westerveld, & Pugh, 2004).

Tapert et al. (2007) examined the effect of marijuana use on response inhibition using a go/no-go task in a sample of marijuana-dependent adolescents who had been abstinent for 4 weeks. Despite showing intact task performance, marijuana users exhibited more BOLD response than did nonusers during inhibition ("no-go") trials in the right dorsolateral prefrontal, bilateral medial frontal, bilateral inferior, and superior parietal lobules. On response selection ("go") trials, marijuana users had greater BOLD activation in the right prefrontal, insular, and parietal cortices. Both findings held after controlling for lifetime and recent alcohol use. Greater BOLD response during inhibition trials predicted greater decrements in neuropsychological performance, specifically more impulsivity, less complex attention, less cognitive flexibility, and poorer planning strategies. Taken together, these studies suggest some neural dysfunction and compensatory reorganization in the brains of adolescent cannabis users. However, longitudinal studies are needed to determine the extent to which these abnormalities predate regular marijuana use or are consequences of it.

Understanding the impact of marijuana use on the developing adolescent brain is essential because early-onset marijuana disorders have been associated with poorer adult brain health. Adult males who initiated heavy marijuana use before age 17 had smaller whole-brain volumes, smaller ratios of gray matter to white matter, and significantly greater cerebral blood flow than did males who initiated marijuana use after age 17 (Wilson et al., 2000). Brain ERP studies have also found that early-onset marijuana use disorders have been associated with adult attenuated electrophysiological response during selective attention tasks (Kempel, Lampe, Parnefjord, Hennig, & Kunert, 2003). Additionally, early-onset cannabis users performed more poorly on tasks of visual scanning and sustained attention (Ehrenreich et al., 1999) and had decreased vocabulary scores, suggesting preexisting inherent or educational disadvantages (Pope et al., 2003).

Marijuana use during adolescence has been implicated in the development of psychotic symptoms. In a longitudinal study, cannabis use was associated with an increased risk of experiencing schizophrenia symptoms even after controlling for pre-marijuana use psychotic symptoms, with marijuana use before age 15 associated with the greatest risk for schizophrenia (Arseneault et al., 2002). Further research examining the relationship between marijuana use and subsequent psychosis has been inconclusive but is likely moderated by genetic factors (Caspi et al., 2005), with carriers of the catechol-O-methyltransferase (COMT) valine 158 allele showing a substantially increased risk of future psychotic symptoms if cannabis was used during adolescence.

MDMA ("Ecstasy") Use

Methylenedioxymethamphetamine (MDMA, known as "ecstasy") is a synthetic psychoactive drug of increasing popularity; it has stimulant and mild hallucinogenic properties that produce feelings of euphoria, emotional warmth, and distortions in time perception and tactile experiences. Current rates of MDMA use in eighth graders are at 1.4%, which increases threefold to 4.1% by 12th grade (Johnston et al., 2007). The influence of MDMA on adolescent neuromaturation has not been clearly assessed; however, ecstasy use during adolescence has been associated with delayed reaction times during tests of selective attention and dysfunctional inhibitory circuitry in the hippocampus during tasks of verbal working memory load (Jacobsen, Mencl, Pugh, Skudlarski, & Krystal, 2004).

Because of the relatively lower prevalence of MDMA use among adolescents, most ecstasy studies have been with young adults. Studies have shown that greater MDMA use is related to increased volume in the globus pallidus (Reneman, Majoie, Habraken, & den Heeten, 2001), greater glial cell content (Chang, Ernst, Grob, & Poland, 1999), neuronal abnormalities in the frontal cortex (Reneman, Majoie, Flick, & den Heeten, 2002), and abnormalities in serotonergic (Buchert et al., 2003; McCann et al., 2005; McCann, Szabo, Scheffel, Dannals, & Ricaurte, 1998; Reneman, Booij et al., 2001; Reneman, Endert, et al., 2002; Semple, Ebmeier, Glabus, O'Carroll, & Johnstone, 1999) and dopaminergic (Reneman, Booij, et al., 2002) systems. For females, MDMA use has been associated with significantly less serotonin transporter density than controls, suggesting that females might be more vulnerable to the neurotoxic effects of MDMA (Reneman, Booij, et al., 2001).

In a study of MDMA users with minimal exposure to other drugs, MDMA users had significant deficits on measures of mental processing speed and impulsivity compared to controls (Halpern et al., 2004); however, these findings may pertain to co-occurring substance use and preexisting factors (Curran, 2000). Decrements in verbal recall, verbal memory, and sustained attention have also been found in more regular MDMA users (Parrott & Lasky, 1998; Verkes et al., 2001). Medina, Shear, and Corcoran (2005) found that MDMA use was associated with poorer verbal learning and memory in a dose-dependent manner, with no significant impairments on executive functioning or attention. Females had worse neuropsychological performance on tasks of design fluency, suggesting that gender may moderate the neurotoxic effects of MDMA use. In addition to cognitive decrements, MDMA has also been associated with sleep disorders, depression, anxiety, impulsivity, and hostile behavior (Morgan, 2000; Parrott, 2004; Parrott & Lasky, 1998).

Longitudinal studies have been utilized to determine whether the differences between MDMA users and nonusers are the cause rather than the consequence of ecstasy use. A prospective imaging study (de Win et al., 2008) has characterized individuals at risk for using MDMA prior to initiating ecstasy use. Over the follow-up period, individuals who initiated low-quantity MDMA use (6 ± 2 tablets, on average) showed decreased regional relative cerebral blood flow in the globus pallidus and the putamen, an area associated with learning, and poorer white matter integrity in the thalamus and frontoparietal regions. Compared to previous literature,

no changes in serotonin transporter densities and brain metabolites were observed. Another prospective study examining the neuropsychological consequences of MDMA use found that immediate and delayed verbal recall and verbal recognition were significantly lower in MDMA users compared to nonusers, despite initial equivalence on these tasks at baseline (Schilt et al., 2007). These findings suggest that even small doses of MDMA may negatively impact brain health and could lead to poorer neuropsychological functioning. Studies specifically examining the impact of ecstasy use on adolescent brain development are needed.

Stimulant Use

As with MDMA, there are few studies specifically examining the effects of adolescent stimulant (i.e., amphetamine, methamphetamine, and cocaine) use on brain functioning. In a longitudinal study of youth treated for SUDs (Tapert et al., 2002), more frequent stimulant (predominantly methamphetamine) use during adolescence was associated with poorer attention, speeded psychomotor processing, and impaired working memory functioning in young adulthood after controlling for baseline functioning on these tasks and demographic characteristics.

In the adult literature, cocaine (Jacobsen, Giedd, Gottschalk, Kosten, & Krystal, 2001) and methamphetamine (Jernigan et al., 2005) users have shown larger volumes of subcortical structures than have nonusers, yet smaller cortical and limbic (Bartzokis et al., 2000; Franklin et al., 2002) as well as overall white matter volumes (Thompson et al., 2004). Methamphetamine users also showed widespread neuronal damage in the basal ganglia and frontal white matter (Ernst, Chang, Leonido-Yee, & Speck, 2000) and orbitofrontal and dorsolateral prefrontal dysfunction associated with poorer decision-making abilities (Paulus et al., 2002).

Stimulant use has also been associated with abnormalities in dopaminergic and serotonergic system functioning. Stimulant-dependent adults consistently show a reduction in striatal dopamine transporters (Sekine et al., 2001; Volkow, Chang, Wang, Fowler, Ding et al., 2001; Volkow, Chang, Wang, Fowler, Franceschi et al., 2001; Volkow, Chang, Wang, Fowler, Leonido-Yee et al., 2001), which is associated with psychomotor and memory impairment and psychiatric symptomatology. Protracted methamphetamine use has been associated with widespread reductions in serotonin transporter binding sites, which was correlated with elevated aggressiveness (Sekine et al., 2006). Neurocognitive deficits on tasks of learning, working memory, set shifting, and inhibition (McKetin & Mattick, 1998; Nordahl, Salo, & Leamon, 2003; Ornstein et al., 2000; Salo et al., 2002; Simon et al., 2000) are frequently observed in stimulant users, consistent with dopamine depletion (Baunez & Robbins, 1999; Rogers et al., 1999) and serotonergic involvement (Coull et al., 1995; Harrison, Everitt, & Robbins, 1997).

Use of Other Psychoactive Substances

There has been minimal research examining neurocognitive sequelae associated with other psychoactive drugs and polydrug use during adolescence. Nicotine use during adolescence, more so than during adulthood, has been associated with deficits in attention and inhibition in the animal literature (Counotte et al., 2009). In a clinical longitudinal study by Fried, Watkinson, and Gray (2006), adolescents who smoked regularly showed deficits in auditory and verbal competence, including receptive and expressive vocabulary, arithmetic, and auditory memory compared to nonsmoking adolescents. Chronic heavy nicotine use in adolescence has also been associated with deficits in memory and attention (Jacobsen et al., 2005) and risk-taking propensity (Lejuez et al., 2003). Smoking cessation has been related to increased cognitive performance, suggesting that the brain is able to repair itself after heavy nicotine use (Fried et al., 2006). Although the effects of polydrug use have not been studied specifically in adolescents, Grant et al. (1978) found that young adults who were using four or more drugs (i.e., "polydrug users") had the greatest neuropsychological deficits, particularly when using prescription drugs in addition to heavy alcohol use.

Summary and Conclusions

Early exposure to alcohol and other drugs through prenatal exposure to substances or adolescent substance use can have long-term consequences on individuals' CNS development, which may lead to abnormal brain changes and/or impaired neurocognitive, social, and behavioral functioning throughout the life span. Prenatal exposure to alcohol and drugs is associated with certain physical characteristics in newly born offspring, such as growth deficiency, health complications, craniofacial abnormalities, or altered infant neurobehavior. Prenatal exposure to alcohol is associated with

structural brain abnormalities and immature neuronal organization in the frontal, parietal, and temporal lobes; corpus callosum; cerebellum; and basal ganglia, as well as decreased white matter integrity in the corpus callosum and in white matter tracts spanning widespread regions of the cerebrum. It is also associated with functional brain changes and impaired cognitive functioning in attention, verbal and spatial learning and memory, executive function, motor function, and visuospatial processing. Prenatal exposure to marijuana is associated with more subtle neurocognitive deficits in executive function, attention, and visuospatial processing, whereas prenatal cocaine exposure is associated with delayed language, impaired learning, and poorer visual processing and visuospatial working memory. Less is known about the long-term effects of other drug exposures, and interpretation of the effects of any one substance is often difficult due to the complications of polydrug exposures and the chaotic environment and parenting practices that tend to co-occur with mothers using alcohol and drugs during pregnancy. Prenatal drug exposures have also been associated with increased rates of externalizing behavior problems and psychiatric problems, including increased propensity for later substance abuse and dependence.

Adolescence is a critical transitional period between childhood and adulthood, one that involves extensive biological, psychological, and social changes that increase adolescents' propensity to use substances while concurrently contributing to a more vulnerable developing brain. Exposure to alcohol, marijuana, MDMA, stimulants, nicotine, and other psychoactive drugs during this period could have long-lasting implications on adolescents' neurodevelopmental trajectory.

Alcohol use during adolescence has been associated with abnormalities in the hippocampus and prefrontal lobes, diminished white matter quality, abnormal brain response, and decreased cerebral blood flow. Heavy marijuana use has been related to decrements in learning and memory, psychomotor speed, attention, and planning, as well as to abnormal hippocampal volumes and irregular brain activation on tasks of working memory and inhibition. Adolescent and young adult MDMA use has been associated with slower reaction times, abnormal brain activation on tasks of verbal working memory, and decrements in serotonergic and dopaminergic system functioning. For adolescent nicotine users, greater smoking has been linked to deficits in language, arithmetic abilities, attention, and auditory memory. The impact of stimulant and polydrug use during adolescence has been understudied, and therefore no conclusive evidence is reported.

These findings suggest that heavy alcohol and drug use during adolescence may interfere with normal adolescent brain development and could potentially have long-lasting psychological, academic, occupational, and social consequences. Additionally, because most substance treatment programs require active receiving, encoding, and integrating of material, as well as active listening and problem-solving skills, impaired learning and memory and executive abilities incurred from substance use during adolescence could preclude individuals from fully engaging and benefiting from treatment. Exploring moderating factors like gender, family history of substance use, and psychiatric comorbidity will be essential in understanding the differential impact of substance use on neurocognitive functioning.

Future Directions

In both the prenatal and adolescent literature, the vast majority of studies conducted utilize a cross-sectional design approach. Future studies should include longitudinal investigations to examine developmental changes in children's and adolescents' neurocognition or brain structure and function across time. Prospective studies are needed to ascertain the effects of adolescent substance use on brain development and functioning, ideally characterizing adolescents prior to the onset of substance use and following them over the course of adolescence and young adulthood. To capture sufficient numbers of youth who transition into substance use, high-risk samples will need to be identified. The factors associated with elevated risk for SUD in youth (i.e., family history of SUD, conduct disorder, first drinking episode before age 14) may be associated with unique neural traits that also require careful characterization. Although clinic-based prospective studies of prenatal alcohol and drug exposure are also valuable contributions to the literature, given the ability to exercise greater methodological control of moderating variables (e.g., dose and timing effects), they are often associated with lower overall levels of exposure. The highest risk cases are often missed because women engaging in high levels of alcohol and drug use during their pregnancies are less likely to utilize clinics, making these studies less generalizable to the entire population of exposed children.

One of the main difficulties in interpretation of both prenatal and adolescent studies is polysubstance use. Most pregnant women and adolescents who use drugs use more than one drug in combination, so ascertaining the unique influence of nicotine, alcohol, cannabis, or any other particular drug on neurodevelopment requires multivariate statistical approaches and considerable statistical power (i.e., large sample sizes). Using a variety of different tools to measure neural functioning (i.e., neuropsychological studies, MRI, fMRI, DTI, SPECT, PET, and gene expression methods) will eventually, in concert, provide a more complete understanding of the neural consequences of prenatal alcohol/drug exposure and adolescent substance use.

Ultimately, the goal of these lines of research should be (1) disseminating replicated findings to pregnant women, youth, parents, schools, and the public in general to help prevent harmful levels of prenatal alcohol/drug exposure and adolescent substance use and (2) tailoring prevention and intervention programs to appropriately engage pregnant women at risk of using alcohol/drugs during pregnancy and substance-involved adolescents. Ideal prevention and intervention programs should build motivation for behavior change, provide feasible alternatives to substance use, facilitate the recovery of any neural insults, and help to incorporate positive behavior changes into long-term health lifestyles.

References

Akshoomoff, N. A., Courchesne, E., & Townsend, J. P. (1997). Attention coordination and anticipatory control. *International Review of Neurobiology, 41*, 575–598.

Archibald, S. L., Fennema-Notestine, C., Gamst, A., Riley, E. P., Mattson, S. N., & Jernigan, T. L. (2001). Brain dysmorphology in individuals with severe prenatal alcohol exposure. *Developmental Medicine and Child Neurology, 43*, 148–154.

Arendt, R., Angelopoulos, J., Salvator, A., & Singer, L. (1999). Motor development of cocaine-exposed children at age two years. *Pediatrics, 103*, 86–92.

Arria, A. M., Derauf, C., LaGasse, L. L., Grant, P., Shah, R., Smith, L., . . . Lester, B. (2006). Methamphetamine and other substance use during pregnancy: Preliminary estimates from the Infant Development, Environment, and Lifestyle (IDEAL) study. *Maternal and Child Health Journal, 10*, 293–302.

Arseneault, L., Cannon, M., Poulton, R., Murray, R., Caspi, A., & Moffitt, T. E. (2002). Cannabis use in adolescence and risk for adult psychosis: Longitudinal prospective study. *British Medical Journal, 325*, 1212–1213.

Ashtari, M., Cervellione, K., Cottone, J., Ardekani, B. A., & Kumra, S. (2009). Diffusion abnormalities in adolescents and young adults with a history of heavy cannabis use. *Journal of Psychiatric Research, 43*, 189–204.

Astley, S. J., Aylward, E. H., Olson, H. C., Kerns, K., Brooks, A., Coggins, T. E., . . . Richards, T. (2009a). Magnetic resonance imaging outcomes from a comprehensive magnetic resonance study of children with fetal alcohol spectrum disorders. *Alcoholism, Clinical and Experimental Research, 33*, 1671–1689.

Astley, S. J., Aylward, E. H., Olson, H. C., Kerns, K., Brooks, A., Coggins, T. W., . . . Richards, T. (2009b). Functional magnetic resonance imaging outcomes from a comprehensive magnetic resonance study of children with fetal alcohol spectrum disorders. *Journal of Neurodevelopmental Disorders, 1*, 61–80.

Autti-Rämö, I., Autti, T., Korkman, M., Kettunen, S., Salonen, O., & Valanne, L. (2002). MRI findings in children with school problems who had been exposed prenatally to alcohol. *Developmental Medicine and Child Neurology, 44*(2), 98–106.

Autti-Rämö, I., & Granström, M. -L. (1991). The psychomotor development during the first year of life of infants exposed to intrauterine alcohol of various duration. *Neuropediatrics, 22*, 59–64.

Aytaclar, S., Tarter, R. E., Kirisci, L., & Lu, S. (1999). Association between hyperactivity and executive cognitive functioning in childhood and substance use in early adolescence. *Journal of the American Academy of Child & Adolescent Psychiatry, 38*, 172–178.

Azuma, S. D., & Chasnoff, I. J. (1993). Outcome of children prenatally exposed to cocaine and other drugs: A path analysis of three-year data. *Pediatrics, 92*, 396–402.

Baldwin, M. R. (2007). Fetal alcohol spectrum disorders and suicidality in a healthcare setting. *International Journal of Circumpolar Health, 66*, 54–60.

Bandstra, E., S., Morrow, C. E., Accornero, V. H., Mansoor, E., Xue, L., & Anthony, J. C. (2011). Estimated effects of in utero cocaine exposure on language development through early adolescence. *Neurotoxicology and Teratology, 33*, 25–35.

Barnea-Goraly, N., Menon, V., Eckert, M., Tamm, L., Bammer, R., Karchemskiy, A., . . . Reiss, A. L. (2005). White matter development during childhood and adolescence: A cross-sectional diffusion tensor imaging study. *Cerebral Cortex, 15*, 1848–1854.

Bartzokis, G., Beckson, M., Lu, P. H., Edwards, N., Rapoport, R., Wiseman, E., & Bridge, P. (2000). Age-related brain volume reductions in amphetamine and cocaine addicts and normal controls: Implications for addiction research. *Psychiatry Research: Neuroimaging, 98*(2), 93–102.

Basser, P. J., & Jones, D. K. (2002). Diffusion-tensor MRI: Theory, experimental design, and data analysis. *NMR in Biomedicine, 15*, 456–457.

Bauman, P. S., & Levine, S. A. (1986). The development of children of drug addicts. *International Journal of the Addictions, 21*, 849–863.

Baumrind, D. (1987). A developmental perspective on adolescent risk-taking behavior in contemporary America. In W. Damon (Ed.), *Adolescent social behavior and health* (pp. 93–126). San Francisco: Jossey-Bass.

Baunez, C., & Robbins, T. W. (1999). Effects of dopamine depletion of the dorsal striatum and further interaction with subthalamic nucleus lesions in an attentional task in the rat. *Neuroscience, 92*, 1343–1356.

Bava, S., Frank, L. R., McQueeny, T., Schweinsburg, B. C., Schweinsburg, A. D., & Tapert, S. F. (2009). Altered white matter microstructure in adolescent substance users. *Psychiatry Research: Neuroimaging, 173*, 228–237.

Bava, S., Jacobus, J., Thayer, R. E., & Tapert, S. F. (2013). Longitudinal changes in white matter integrity among adolescent substance users. *Alcoholism: Clinical & Experimental Research, 37*(Suppl. 1), E181–E189.

Bennett, D. S., Bendersky, M., & Lewis, M. (2008). Children's cognitive ability from 4 to 9 years old as a function of prenatal cocaine exposure, environmental risk, and maternal verbal intelligence. *Developmental Psychology, 44*, 919–928.

Bertrand, J., Floyd, R. L., & Weber, M. K. (2005). Guidelines for identifying and referring persons with fetal alcohol syndrome. *Morbidity and Mortality Weekly Report Recommendations and Reports, 54*(RR–11), 1–14.

Bertrand, J., Floyd, R. L., Weber, M. K., O'Connor, M., Riley, E. P., Johnson, K. A., & Cohen, D. E. (2004). *National task force on FAS/FAE: Guidelines for referral and diagnosis.* Atlanta, GA: Centers for Disease Control and Prevention.

Betancourt, L. M., Yang, W., Brodsky, N. L., Gallagher, P. R., Malmud, E. K., Gianetta, J. M., . . . Hurt, H. (2011). Adolescents with and without gestational cocaine exposure: Longitudinal analysis of inhibitory control, memory, and receptive language. *Neurotoxicology and Teratology, 33*, 36–46.

Bhatara, V. S., Lovrein, F., Kirkeby, J., Swayze, V., II, Unruh, E., & Johnson, V. (2002). Brain function in fetal alcohol syndrome assessed by single photon emission computed tomography. *South Dakota Journal of Medicine, 55*(2), 59–62.

Bingol, N., Fuchs, M., Diaz, V., Stone, R. K., & Gromisch, D. S. (1987). Teratogenicity of cocaine in humans. *Journal of Pediatrics, 110*, 93–96.

Bjorkquist, O. A., Fryer, S. L., Reiss, A. L., Mattson, S. N., & Riley, E. P. (2010). Cingulate gyrus morphology in children and adolescents with fetal alcohol spectrum disorders. *Psychiatry Research, 181*, 101–107.

Bland-Stewart, L. M., Seymour, H. N., Beeghly, M., & Frank, D. A. (1998). Semantic development of African-American children prenatally exposed to cocaine. *Seminars in Speech and Language, 19*, 167–187.

Boland, F. J., Burrill, R., Duwyn, M., & Karp, J. (1998). *Fetal alcohol syndrome: Implications for correctional service.* Ottawa: Correctional Service of Canada.

Bond, N. (1979). Impairment of shuttlebox avoidance learning following repeated alcohol withdrawal episodes in rats. *Pharmacology Biochemistry & Behavior, 11*, 589–591.

Bookstein, F. L., Sampson, P. D., Connor, P. D., & Streissguth, A. P. (2002). Midline corpus callosum is a neuroanatomical focus of fetal alcohol damage. *Anatomical Record Part B: New Anatomist, 269*, 162–174.

Bookstein, F. L., Streissguth, A. P., Sampson, P. D., Connor, P. D., & Barr, H. M. (2002). Corpus callosum shape and neuropsychological deficits in adult males with heavy fetal alcohol exposure. *NeuroImage, 15*, 233–251.

Brown, S. A., & D'Amico, E. J. (2001). Outcomes for alcohol treatment for adolescents. In M. Galanter (Ed.), *Recent developments in alcoholism* (Vol. XVI, pp. 307–327). New York: Plenum.

Brown, S. A., Tapert, S. F., Granholm, E., & Delis, D. C. (2000). Neurocognitive functioning of adolescents: Effects of protracted alcohol use. *Alcoholism: Clinical and Experimental Research, 24*, 164–171.

Buchert, R., Thomasius, R., Nebeling, B., Petersen, K., Obrocki, J., Jenicke, L., . . . Clausen, M. (2003). Long-term effects of "ecstasy" use on serotonin transporters of the brain investigated by PET. *Journal of Nuclear Medicine, 44*, 375–384.

Burd, L., Klug, M. G., Martsolf, J. T., & Kerbeshian, J. (2003). Fetal alcohol syndrome: Neuropsychiatric phenomics. *Neurotoxicology and Teratology, 25*, 697–705.

Burd, L., Selfridge, R. H., Klug, M. G., & Bakko, S. A. (2004). Fetal alcohol syndrome in the United States corrections system. *Addiction Biology, 9*, 169–176.

Burden, M. J., Jacobson, S. W., Sokol, R. J., & Jacobson, J. L. (2005). Effects of prenatal alcohol exposure on attention and working memory at 7.5 years of age. *Alcoholism: Clinical and Experimental Research, 29*, 443–452.

Caldwell, L. C., Schweinsburg, A. D., Nagel, B. J., Barlett, V. C., Brown, S. A., & Tapert, S. F. (2005). Gender and adolescent alcohol use disorders on BOLD (blood oxygen level dependent) response to spatial working memory. *Alcohol & Alcoholism, 40*, 194–200.

Carmichael Olson, H., Feldman, J. J., Streissguth, A. P., Sampson, P. D., & Bookstein, F. L. (1998). Neuropsychological deficits in adolescents with fetal alcohol syndrome: Clinical findings. *Alcoholism: Clinical and Experimental Research, 22*, 1998–2012.

Caspi, A., Moffitt, T. E., Cannon, M., McClay, J., Murray, R., Harrington, H., ... Craig, I., W. (2005). Moderation of the effect of adolescent-onset cannabis use on adult psychosis by a functional polymorphism in the catechol-O-methyltransferase gene: Longitudinal evidence of a gene X environment interaction. *Biological Psychiatry, 57*, 1117–1127.

Castaldo, P., Magi, S., Gaetani, S., Cassano, T., Ferraro, L., Antonelli, T., ... Cuomo, V. (2007). Prenatal exposure to the cannabinoid receptor agonist WIN 55,212-2 increases glutamate uptake through overexpression of GLT1 and EAAC1 glutamate transporter subtypes in rat frontal cerebral cortex. *Neuropharmacology, 53*, 369–378.

Chambers, R. A., Taylor, J. R., & Potenza, M. N. (2003). Developmental neurocircuitry of motivation in adolescence: A critical period of addiction vulnerability. *American Journal of Psychiatry, 160*, 1041–1052.

Chang, L., Ernst, T., Grob, C. S., & Poland, R. E. (1999). Cerebral (1)H MRS alterations in recreational 3, 4-methylenedioxymethamphetamine (MDMA, "ecstasy") users. *Journal of Magnetic Resonance Imaging, 10*, 521–526.

Chang, L., Smith, L. M., LoPresti, C., Yonekura, M. L., Kuo, J., Walot, I., & Ernst, T. (2004). Smaller subcortical volumes and cognitive deficits in children with prenatal methamphetamine exposure. *Psychiatry Research, 132*(2), 95–106.

Chasnoff, I. J., Lewis, D. E., Griffith, D. R., & Willey, S. (1989). Cocaine and pregnancy: Clinical and toxicological implications for the neonate. *Clinical Chemistry, 35*, 1276–1278.

Chasnoff, I. J., Wells, A. M., Telford, E., Schmidt, C., & Messer, G. (2010). Neurodevelopmental functioning in children with FAS, pFAS, and ARND. *Journal of Developmental and Behavioral Pediatrics, 31*, 192–201.

Cheetham, A., Allen, N. B., Whittle, S., Simmons, J. G., Yücel, M., & Lubman, D. I. (2012). Orbitofrontal volumes in early adolescence predict initiation of cannabis use: A 4-year longitudinal and prospective study. *Biological Psychiatry, 71*, 684–692.

Chiriboga, C. A. (2003). Fetal alcohol and drug effects. *Neurologist, 9*, 267–279.

Chiriboga, C. A., Bateman, D. A., Brust, J. C., & Hauser, W. A. (1993). Neurologic findings in neonates with intrauterine cocaine exposure. *Pediatric Neurology, 9*(2), 115–119.

Chiriboga, C. A., Brust, J. C., Bateman, D., & Hauser, W. A. (1999). Dose-response effect of fetal cocaine exposure on newborn neurologic function. *Pediatrics, 103*, 79–85.

Chiriboga, C. A., Vibbert, M., Malouf, R., Suarez, M. S., Abrams, E. J., Heagarty, M. C., ... Hauser, W. A. (1995). Neurological correlates of fetal cocaine exposure: Transient hypertonia of infancy and early childhood. *Pediatrics, 96*, 1070–1077.

Church, M. W., Eldis, F., Blakley, B. W., & Bawle, E. V. (1997). Hearing, language, speech, vestibular, and dentofacial disorders in fetal alcohol syndrome. *Alcoholism: Clinical and Experimental Research, 21*, 227–237.

Clark, C. M., Li, D., Conry, J., Conry, R., & Loock, C. (2000). Structural and functional brain integrity of fetal alcohol syndrome in nonretarded cases. *Pediatrics, 105*, 1096–1099.

Clark, C. P., Brown, G. G., Eyler, L. T., Drummond, S. P., Braun, D. R., & Tapert, S. F. (2007). Decreased perfusion in young alcohol-dependent women as compared with age-matched controls. *American Journal of Drug and Alcohol Abuse, 33*, 13–19.

Clarren, S. K., Alvord, E. C., Jr., Sumi, S. M., Streissguth, A. P., & Smith, D. W. (1978). Brain malformations related to prenatal exposure to ethanol. *Journal of Pediatrics, 92*, 64–67.

Cloninger, C. R., Sigvardsson, S., & Bohman, M. (1988). Childhood personality predicts alcohol abuse in young adults. *Alcoholism: Clinical & Experimental Research, 12*, 494–505.

Coles, C. D., Goldstein, F. C., Lynch, M. E., Chen, X., Kable, J. A., Johnson, K. C., & Hu, X. (2011). Memory and brain volume in adults prenatally exposed to alcohol. *Brain & Cognition, 75*, 67–77.

Coles, C. D., Platzman, K. A., Lynch, M. E., & Freides, D. (2002). Auditory and visual sustained attention in adolescents prenatally exposed to alcohol. *Alcoholism: Clinical and Experimental Research, 26*, 263–271.

Connor, P. D., Sampson, P. D., Bookstein, F. L., Barr, H. M., & Streissguth, A. P. (2000). Direct and indirect effects of prenatal alcohol damage on executive function. *Developmental Neuropsychology, 18*, 331–354.

Connor, P. D., Sampson, P. D., Streissguth, A. P., Bookstein, F. L., & Barr, H. M. (2006). Effects of prenatal alcohol exposure on fine motor coordination and balance: A study of two adult samples. *Neuropsychologia, 44*, 744–751.

Conry, J. (1990). Neuropsychological deficits in fetal alcohol syndrome and fetal alcohol effects. *Alcoholism: Clinical and Experimental Research, 14*, 650–655.

Cornelius, M. D., Goldschmidt, L., Day, N. L., & Larkby, C. (2002). Alcohol, tobacco and marijuana use among pregnant teenagers: 6-year follow-up of offspring growth effects. *Neurotoxicology and Teratology, 24*, 703–710.

Cornelius, M. D., Taylor, P. M., Geva, D., & Day, N. L. (1995). Prenatal tobacco and marijuana use among adolescents: Effects on offspring gestational age, growth and morphology. *Pediatrics, 95*, 738–743.

Cortese, B. M., Moore, G. J., Bailey, B. A., Jacobson, S. W., Delaney-Black, V., & Hannigan, J. H. (2006). Magnetic resonance and spectroscopic imaging in prenatal alcohol-exposed children: Preliminary findings in the caudate nucleus. *Neurotoxicology and Teratology, 28*, 597–606.

Coull, J. T., Sahakian, B. J., Middleton, H. C., Young, A. H., Park, S. B., McShane, R. H., ... Robbins, T. W. (1995). Differential effects of clonidine, haloperidol, diazepam and tryptophan depletion on focused attention and attentional search. *Psychopharmacology, 121*, 222–230.

Coulter, C. L., Leech, R. W., Schaefer, G. B., Scheithauer, B. W., & Brumback, R. A. (1993). Midline cerebral dysgenesis, dysfunction of the hypothalamic-pituitary axis, and fetal alcohol effects. *Archives of Neurology, 50*, 771–775.

Counotte, D. S., Spijker, S., Van de Burgwal, L. H., Hogenboom, F., Schoffelmeer, A. N., De Vries, T. J., ... Pattij, T. (2009). Long-lasting cognitive deficits resulting from adolescent nicotine exposure in rats. *Neuropsychopharmacology, 34*, 299–306.

Crego, A., Holguín, S. R., Parada, M., Mota, N., Corral, M., & Cadaveira, F. (2009). Binge drinking affects attentional and visual working memory processing in young university students. *Alcoholism: Clinical & Experimental Research, 33*, 1870–1879.

Crocker, N., Vaurio, L., Riley, E. P., & Mattson, S. N. (2009). Comparison of adaptive behavior in children with heavy prenatal alcohol exposure or attention-deficit/hyperactivity disorder. *Alcoholism: Clinical and Experimental Research, 33*, 2015–2023.

Crocker, N., Vaurio, L., Riley, E. P., & Mattson, S. N. (2011). Comparison of verbal learning and memory in children with heavy prenatal alcohol exposure or attention deficit/hyperactivity disorder. *Alcoholism: Clinical and Experimental Research, 35*, 1114–1121.

Cunha-Oliveira, T., Rego, A. C., & Oliveira, C. R. (2008). Cellular and molecular mechanisms involved in the neurotoxicity of opioid and psychostimulant drugs. *Brain Research Reviews, 58*, 192–208.

Curran, H. V. (2000). Is MDMA ("ecstasy") neurotoxic in humans? An overview of evidence and of methodological problems in research. *Neuropsychobiology, 42*, 34–41.

Davies, J. K., & Bledsoe, J. M. (2005). Prenatal alcohol and drug exposures in adoption. *Pediatric Clinics of North America, 52*, 1369–1393.

Dawson, D. A., Goldstein, R. B., Chou, S. P., Ruan, W. J., & Grant, B. F. (2008). Age at first drink and the first incidence of adult-onset DSM-IV alcohol use disorders. *Alcoholism: Clinical & Experimental Research, 32*, 2149–2160.

Day, N. L., Richardson, G. A., Goldschmidt, L., Robles, N., Taylor, P. M., Stoffer, D. S., ... Geva, D. (1994). Effect of prenatal marijuana exposure on the cognitive development of offspring at age three. *Neurotoxicology and Teratology, 16*, 169–175.

De Bellis, M. D., Clark, D. B., Beers, S. R., Soloff, P. H., Boring, A. M., Hall, J., ... Keshavan, M. S. (2000). Hippocampal volume in adolescent-onset alcohol use disorders. *American Journal of Psychiatry, 157*, 737–744.

De Bellis, M. D., Narasimhan, A., Thatcher, D. L., Keshavan, M. S., Soloff, P., & Clark, D. B. (2005). Prefrontal cortex, thalamus, and cerebellar volumes in adolescents and young adults with adolescent-onset alcohol use disorders and comorbid mental disorders. *Alcoholism: Clinical & Experimental Research, 29*, 1590–1600.

Delaney-Black, V., Covington, C., Templin, T., Kershaw, T., Nordstrom-Klee, B., Ager, J. W., Jr., ... Sokol, R. J. (2000). Prenatal exposures adversely affect childhood language development. *Pediatric Research, 47*(4 Pt. 2), 146A.

DeLisi, L. E., Bertisch, H. C., Szulc, K. U., Majcher, M., Brown, K., Bappal, A., & Ardekani, B. A. (2006). A preliminary DTI study showing no brain structural change associated with adolescent cannabis use. *Harm Reduction Journal, 3*(17).

Devinsky, O., & D'Esposito, M. (2004). *Neurology of cognitive and behavioral disorders.* New York: Oxford University Press.

de Win, M. M., Jager, G., Booij, J., Reneman, L., Schilt, T., Lavini, C., ... van den Brink, W. (2008). Sustained effects of ecstasy on the human brain: A prospective neuroimaging study in novel users. *Brain, 131*(Pt. 11), 2936–2945.

Dow-Edwards, D. L., Benveniste, H., Behnke, M., Bandstra, E. S., Singer, L. T., Hurd, Y. L., & Stanford, L. R. (2006). Neuroimaging of prenatal drug exposure. *Neurotoxicology and Teratology, 28*, 386–402.

Ebrahim, S. H., & Gfroerer, J. (2003). Pregnancy-related substance use in the United States during 1996-1998. *Obstetrics & Gynecology, 101*, 374–379.

Ehrenreich, H., Rinn, T., Kunert, H. J., Moeller, M. R., Poser, W., Schilling, L., ... Hoehe, M. R. (1999). Specific attentional dysfunction in adults following early start of cannabis use. *Psychopharmacology, 142*, 295–301.

Eriksson, M., Larsson, G., Winbladh, B., & Zetterstrom, R. (1978). The influence of amphetamine addiction on pregnancy and the newborn infant. *Acta Paediatrica Scandinavica, 67*, 95–99.

Ernst, T., Chang, L., Leonido-Yee, M., & Speck, O. (2000). Evidence for long-term neurotoxicity associated with methamphetamine abuse: A 1H MRS study. *Neurology, 54*, 1344–1349.

Ervalahti, N., Korkman, M., Fagerlund, A., Autti-Ramo, I., Loimu, L., & Hoyme, H. E. (2007). Relationship between dysmorphic features and general cognitive function in children with fetal alcohol spectrum disorders. *American Journal of Medical Genetics Part A, 143A*, 2916–2923.

Ethen, M. K., Ramadhani, T. A., Scheuerle, A. E., Canfield, M. A., Wyszynski, D. F., Druschel, C. M., & Romitti, P. A. (2009). Alcohol consumption by women before and during pregnancy. *Maternal and Child Health Journal, 13*, 274–285.

Faden, V. B., & Graubard, B. I. (2000). Maternal substance use during pregnancy and developmental outcome at age three. *Journal of Substance Abuse, 12*, 329–340.

Fagerlund, Å., Heikkinen, S., Autti-Rämö, I., Korkman, M., Timonen, M., Kuusi, T., ... Lundbom, N. (2006). Brain metabolic alterations in adolescents and young adults with fetal alcohol spectrum disorders. *Alcoholism: Clinical and Experimental Research, 30*, 2097–2104.

Fast, D. K., & Conry, J. (2009). Fetal alcohol spectrum disorders and the criminal justice system. *Developmental Disabilities Research Reviews, 15*, 250–257.

Fast, D. K., Conry, J., & Loock, C. A. (1999). Identifying fetal alcohol syndrome among youth in the criminal justice system. *Journal of Developmental and Behavioral Pediatrics, 20*, 370–372.

Fergusson, D. M., Horwood, L. J., & Northstone, K. (2002). Maternal use of cannabis and pregnancy outcome. *BJOG: An International Journal of Obstetrics & Gynecology, 109*, 21–27.

Finnegan, L. P. (1985). Effects of maternal opiate abuse on the newborn. *Federation Proceedings, 44*, 2314–2317.

Fontes, M. A., Bolla, K. I., Cunha, P. J., Almeida, P. P., Jungerman, F., Laranjeira, R. R., ... Lacerda, A. L. (2011). Cannabis use before age 15 and subsequent executive functioning. *British Journal of Psychiatry, 198*, 442–447.

Franklin, T. R., Acton, P. D., Maldjian, J. A., Gray, J. D., Croft, J. R., Dackis, C. A., ... Childress, A. R. (2002). Decreased gray matter concentration in the insular, orbitofrontal, cingulate, and temporal cortices of cocaine patients. *Biological Psychiatry, 51*, 134–142.

Freund, G. (1970). Alcohol, barbiturate, and bromide withdrawal syndrome in mice. In N. K. M. J. H. Mendelson (Ed.), *Recent advances in studies of alcoholism: An interdisciplinary symposium*. Rockville, MD: National Institute on Alcohol Abuse and Alcoholism.

Freund, G., & Walker, D. W. (1971). Impairment of avoidance learning by prolonged ethanol consumption in mice. *Journal of Pharmacology And Experimental Therapeutics, 179*, 284–292.

Fried, P. A., & Makin, J. E. (1987). Neonatal behavioural correlates of prenatal exposure to marihuana, cigarettes and alcohol in a low risk population. *Neurotoxicology and Teratology, 9*, 1–7.

Fried, P. A., O'Connell, C. M., & Watkinson, B. (1992). 60- and 72-month follow-up of children prenatally exposed to marijuana, cigarettes, and alcohol: Cognitive and language assessment. *Journal of Developmental and Behavioral Pediatrics, 13*, 383–391.

Fried, P. A., & Watkinson, B. (1988). 12- and 24-month neurobehavioural follow-up of children prenatally exposed to marihuana, cigarettes and alcohol. *Neurotoxicology and Teratology, 10*, 305–313.

Fried, P. A., Watkinson, B., & Gray, R. (1999). Growth from birth to early adolescence in offspring prenatally exposed to cigarettes and marijuana. *Neurotoxicology and Teratology, 21*, 513–525.

Fried, P. A., Watkinson, B., & Gray, R. (2006). Neurocognitive consequences of cigarette smoking in young adults—a comparison with pre-drug performance. *Neurotoxicology & Teratology, 28*, 517–525.

Fried, P. A., Watkinson, B., & Willan, A. (1984). Marijuana use during pregnancy and decreased length of gestation. *American Journal of Obstetrics and Gynecology, 150*, 23–27.

Fryer, S. F., Mattson, S. N., Jernigan, T. L., Archibald, S. L., Jones, K. L., & Riley, E. P. (2012). Caudate volume predicts neurocognitive performance in youth with heavy prenatal alcohol exposure. *Alcoholism: Clinical and Experimental Research, 36*, 1932–1941.

Fryer, S. L., McGee, C. L., Matt, G. E., Riley, E. P., & Mattson, S. N. (2007). Evaluation of psychopathological conditions in children with heavy prenatal alcohol exposure. *Pediatrics, 119*, e733–e741.

Fryer, S. L., Schweinsburg, B. C., Bjorkquist, O. A., Frank, L. R., Mattson, S. N., Spadoni, A. D., & Riley, E. P. (2009). Characterization of white matter microstructure in fetal alcohol spectrum disorders. *Alcoholism: Clinical and Experimental Research, 33*, 514–521.

Fryer, S. L., Tapert, S. F., Mattson, S. N., Paulus, M. P., Spadoni, A. D., & Riley, E. P. (2007). Prenatal alcohol exposure affects frontal-striatal BOLD response during inhibitory control. *Alcoholism: Clinical and Experimental Research, 31*, 1415–1424.

Giancola, P. R., Mezzich, A. C., & Tarter, R. E. (1998). Executive cognitive functioning, temperament, and antisocial behavior in conduct disordered adolescent females. *Journal of Abnormal Psychology, 107*, 629–641.

Giancola, P. R., Shoal, G. D., & Mezzich, A. C. (2001). Constructive thinking, executive functioning, antisocial behavior, and drug use involvement in adolescent females with a substance use disorder. *Experimental and Clinical Psychopharmacology, 9*, 215–227.

Giedd, J. N. (2004). Structural magnetic resonance imaging of the adolescent brain. *Annals of the New York Academy of Sciences, 1021*, 77–85.

Giedd, J. N., Blumenthal, J., Jeffries, N. O., Castellanos, F. X., Liu, L., Zijdenbos, A., . . . Rapoport, J. L. (1999). Brain development during childhood and adolescence: A longitudinal MRI study. *Nature Neuroscience, 2*, 861–863.

Glantz, M. D., & Chambers, J. C. (2006). Prenatal drug exposure effects on subsequent vulnerability to drug abuse. *Development and Psychopathology, 18*, 893–922.

Glenn, S., Parsons, O., Sinha, R., & Stevens, L. (1988). The effects of repeated withdrawals from alcohol on the memory of male and female alcoholics. *Alcohol & Alcoholism, 23*, 337–342.

Gogtay, N., Giedd, J. N., Lusk, L., Hayashi, K. M., Greenstein, D., Vaituzis, A. C., . . . Thompson, P. M. (2004). Dynamic mapping of human cortical development during childhood through early adulthood. *Proceedings of the National Academy of Sciences, 101*, 8174–8179.

Goldschmidt, L., Richardson, G. A., Cornelius, M. D., & Day, N. L. (2004). Prenatal marijuana and alcohol exposure and academic achievement at age 10. *Neurotoxicology and Teratology, 26*, 521–532.

Goldschmidt, L., Richardson, G. A., Willford, J., & Day, N. L. (2008). Prenatal marijuana exposure and intelligence test performance at age 6. *Journal of the American Academy of Child and Adolescent Psychiatry, 47*, 254–263.

Goldschmidt, L., Richardson, G. A., Willford, J., Severtson, S. G., & Day, N. L. (2012). School achievement in 14-year-old youths prenatally exposed to marijuana. *Nerotoxicology and Teratology, 34*, 161–167.

Goudriaan, A. E., Grekin, E. R., & Sher, K. J. (2007). Decision making and binge drinking: A longitudinal study. *Alcoholism: Clinical & Experimental Research, 31*, 928–938.

Grant, I., Adams, K. M., Carlin, A. S., Rennick, P. M., Judd, L. L., & Schooff, K. (1978). The collaborative neuropsychological study of polydrug users. *Archives of General Psychiatry, 35*, 1063–1074.

Grant, I., Gonzalez, R., Carey, C., Wolfson, T., & Natarajan, L. (2003). Non-acute (residual) neurocognitive consequences of marijuana: A meta-analytic study. *Journal of the International Neuropsychological Society, 9*, 679–689.

Gray, K. A., Day, N. L., Leech, S., & Richardson, G. A. (2005). Prenatal marijuana exposure: Effect on child depressive symptoms at ten years of age. *Neurotoxicology and Teratology, 27*, 439–448.

Green, C. R., Mihic, A. M., Nikkel, S. M., Stade, B. C., Rasmussen, C., Munoz, D. P., & Reynolds, J. N. (2009). Executive function deficits in children with fetal alcohol spectrum disorders (FASD) measured using the Cambridge Neuropsychological Tests Automated Battery (CANTAB). *Journal of Child Psychology and Psychiatry, 50*, 688–697.

Griffith, D. R., Azuma, S. D., & Chasnoff, I. J. (1994). Three-year outcome of children exposed prenatally to drugs. *Journal of the American Academy of Child and Adolescent Psychiatry, 33*, 20–27.

Gruber, S. A., Silveri, M. M., Dahlgren, M. K., & Yurgelun-Todd, D. (2011). Why so impulsive? White matter alterations are associated with impulsivity in chronic marijuana smokers. *Experimental and Clinical Psychopharmacology, 19*, 231–242.

Halpern, J. H., Pope, H. G., Jr., Sherwood, A. R., Barry, S., Hudson, J. I., & Yurgelun-Todd, D. (2004). Residual neuropsychological effects of illicit 3,4-methylenedioxymethamphetamine (MDMA) in individuals with minimal exposure to other drugs. *Drug and Alcohol Dependence, 75*, 135–147.

Hamilton, D. A., Kodituwakku, P., Sutherland, R. J., & Savage, D. D. (2003). Children with fetal alcohol syndrome are impaired at place learning but not cued-navigation in a virtual Morris water task. *Behavioural Brain Research*, *143*, 85–94.

Harrison, A. A., Everitt, B. J., & Robbins, T. W. (1997). Central 5-HT depletion enhances impulsive responding without affecting the accuracy of attentional performance: Interactions with dopaminergic mechanisms. *Psychopharmacology (Berl)*, *133*, 329–342.

Hatch, E. E., & Bracken, M. B. (1986). Effect of marijuana use in pregnancy on fetal growth. *American Journal of Epidemiology*, *124*, 986–993.

Herting, M. M., Schwartz, D., Mitchell, S. H., & Nagel, B. J. (2010). Delay discounting behavior and white matter microstructure abnormalities in youth with a family history of alcoholism. *Alcoholism: Clinical & Experimental Research*, *34*, 1590–1602.

Howell, K. K., Lynch, M. E., Platzman, K. A., Smith, G. H., & Coles, C. D. (2006). Prenatal alcohol exposure and ability, academic achievement, and school functioning in adolescence: A longitudinal follow-up. *Journal of Pediatric Psychology*, *31*, 116–126.

Hoyme, H. E., May, P.A., Kalberg, W.O., Kodituwakku, P., Gossage, J.P., Trujillo, P.M., ... Robinson, L.K. (2005). A practical clinical approach to diagnosis of fetal alcohol spectrum disorders: Clarification of the 1996 Institute of Medicine Criteria: In reply. *Pediatrics*, *115*, 1787–1788.

Huttenlocher, P. R. (1979). Synaptic density in human frontal cortex - developmental changes and effects of aging. *Brain Research*, *163*, 195–205.

Huttenlocher, P. R. (1990). Morphometric study of human cerebral cortex development. *Neuropsychologia*, *28*, 517–527.

Jacobsen, L. K., Giedd, J. N., Gottschalk, C., Kosten, T. R., & Krystal, J. H. (2001). Quantitative morphology of the caudate and putamen in patients with cocaine dependence. *American Journal of Psychiatry*, *158*, 486–489.

Jacobsen, L. K., Krystal, J. H., Mencl, W. E., Westerveld, M., Frost, S. J., & Pugh, K. R. (2005). Effects of smoking and smoking abstinence on cognition in adolescent tobacco smokers. *Biological Psychiatry*, *57*, 56–66.

Jacobsen, L. K., Mencl, W. E., Pugh, K. R., Skudlarski, P., & Krystal, J. H. (2004). Preliminary evidence of hippocampal dysfunction in adolescent MDMA ("ecstasy") users: Possible relationship to neurotoxic effects. *Psychopharmacology (Berl)*, *173*, 383–390.

Jacobsen, L. K., Mencl, W. E., Westerveld, M., & Pugh, K. R. (2004). Impact of cannabis use on brain function in adolescents. *Annals of New York Academy of Sciences*, *1021*, 384–390.

Jacobson, S. W., Chiodo, L. M., Sokol, R. J., & Jacobson, J. L. (2002). Validity of maternal report of prenatal alcohol, cocaine, and smoking in relation to neurobehavioral outcome. *Pediatrics*, *109*, 815–825.

Jacobus, J., Bava, S., Cohen-Zion, M., Mahmood, O., & Tapert, S. F. (2009). Functional consequences of marijuana use in adolescents. *Pharmacology Biochemistry & Behavior*, *92*, 559–565.

Jacobus, J., Thayer, R. E., Trim, R. S., Bava, S., Frank, L. R., & Tapert, S. F. (2013). White matter integrity, substance use, and risk taking in adolescence. *Psychology of Addictive Behaviors*.

Janzen, L. A., Nanson, J. L., & Block, G. W. (1995). Neuropsychological evaluation of preschoolers with fetal alcohol syndrome. *Neurotoxicology and Teratology*, *17*, 273–279.

Jernigan, T. L., & Gamst, A. C. (2005). Changes in volume with age–consistency and interpretation of observed effects. *Neurobiology of Aging*, *26*, 1271–1274 (discussion 1275–1278).

Jernigan, T. L., Gamst, A. C., Archibald, S. L., Fennema Notestine, C., Mindt, M. R., Marcotte, T. L., ... Grant, I. (2005). Effects of methamphetamine dependence and HIV infection on cerebral morphology. *American Journal of Psychiatry*, *162*, 1461–1472.

Jernigan, T. L., Trauner, D. A., Hesselink, J. R., & Tallal, P. A. (1991). Maturation of human cerebrum observed in vivo during adolescence. *Brain*, *114*, 2037–2049.

Jirikowic, T., Kartin, D., & Carmichael Olson, H. (2008). Children with fetal alcohol spectrum disorders: A descriptive profile of adaptive function. *Canadian Journal of Occupational Therapy*, *75*, 238–248.

Johnson, C. A., Xiao, L., Palmer, P., Sun, P., Wang, Q., Wei, Y., ... Bechara, A. (2008). Affective decision-making deficits, linked to a dysfunctional ventromedial prefrontal cortex, revealed in 10th grade Chinese adolescent binge drinkers. *Neuropsychologia*, *46*, 714–726.

Johnston, L. D., O'Malley, P. M., Bachman, J. G., & Schulenberg, J. E. (2007). *Monitoring the Future national results on adolescent drug use: Overview of key findings, 2006*. Bethesda, MD: National Institute on Drug Abuse.

Johnston, L. D., O'Malley, P. M., Bachman, J. G., & Schulenberg, J. E. (2012). *Monitoring the Future national survey results on drug use, 1975–2011: Vol. I. Secondary school students*. Ann Arbor: Institute for Social Research, The University of Michigan (pp. 81-92).

Johnston, L. D., O'Malley, P. M., Bachman, J. G., & Schulenberg, J. E. (2013). *Monitoring the Future national results on drug use: Overview, Key Findings on Adolescent Drug Use 2012*. Ann Arbor: Institute for Social Research, The University of Michigan.

Jones, K. L., & Smith, D. W. (1973). Recognition of the fetal alcohol syndrome in early infancy. *Lancet*, *302*, 999–1001.

Jones, K. L., & Smith, D. W. (1975). The fetal alcohol syndrome. *Teratology*, *12*, 1–10.

Kable, J. A., & Coles, C. D. (2004). Teratology of alcohol: Implications for school settings. In R. T. Brown (Ed.), *Handbook of pediatric psychology in school settings*. Mahwah, NJ: Lawrence Erlbaum.

Karmel, B. Z., & Gardner, J. M. (1996). Prenatal cocaine exposure effects on arousal-modulated attention during the neonatal period. *Developmental Psychobiology*, *29*, 463–480.

Keller, A., Castellanos, F. X., Vaituzis, A. C., Jeffries, N. O., Giedd, J. N., & Rapoport, J. L. (2003). Progressive loss of cerebellar volume in childhood onset schizophrenia. *American Journal of Psychiatry*, *160*, 128–133.

Kempel, P., Lampe, K., Parnefjord, R., Hennig, J., & Kunert, H. J. (2003). Auditory-evoked potentials and selective attention: Different ways of information processing in cannabis users and controls. *Neuropsychobiology*, *48*, 95–101.

Kim, J. J., & Thompson, R. F. (1997). Cerebellar circuits and synaptic mechanisms involved in classical eyeblink conditioning. *Trends in Neurosciences*, *20*, 177–181.

Kodituwakku, P. W., Adnams, C. M., Hay, A., Kitching, A. E., Burger, E., Kalberg, W. O., ... May, P. A. (2006). Letter and category fluency in children with fetal alcohol syndrome from a community in South Africa. *Journal of Studies on Alcohol, 67*, 502–509.

Kodituwakku, P. W., Handmaker, N. S., Cutler, S. K., Weathersby, E. K., & Handmaker, S. D. (1995). Specific impairments in self-regulation in children exposed to alcohol prenatally. *Alcoholism: Clinical and Experimental Research, 19*, 1558–1564.

Kril, J. J., Halliday, G. M., Svoboda, M. D., & Cartwright, H. (1997). The cerebral cortex is damaged in chronic alcoholics. *Neuroscience, 79*, 983–998.

Lebel, C., Mattson, S. N., Riley, E. P., Jones, K. L., Adnams, C. M., May, P. A., ... Sowell, E. R. (2012). A longitudinal study of the long-term consequences of drinking during pregnancy: Heavy in utero alcohol exposure disrupts the normal processes of brain development. *Journal of Neuroscience, 32*, 15243–15251.

Lebel, C., Rasmussen, C., Wyper, K., Walker, L., Andrew, G., Yager, J., & Beaulieu, C. (2008). Brain diffusion abnormalities in children with fetal alcohol spectrum disorder. *Alcoholism: Clinical and Experimental Research, 32*, 1732–1740.

Lee, K. T., Mattson, S. N., & Riley, E. P. (2004). Classifying children with heavy prenatal alcohol exposure using measures of attention. *Journal of the International Neuropsychological Society, 10*, 271–277.

Leech, S. L., Richardson, G. A., Goldschmidt, L., & Day, N. L. (1999). Prenatal substance exposure: Effects on attention and impulsivity of 6-year-olds. *Neurotoxicology and Teratology, 21*, 109–118.

Lejuez, C. W., Aklin, W. M., Jones, H. A., Richards, J. B., Strong, D. R., Kahler, C. W., & Read, J. P. (2003). The Balloon Analogue Risk Task (BART) differentiates smokers and nonsmokers. *Experimental and Clinical Psychopharmacology, 11*, 26–33.

Lenroot, R. K., Gogtay, N., Greenstein, D. K., Wells, E. M., Wallace, G. L., Clasen, L. S., ... Giedd, J. N. (2007). Sexual dimorphism of brain developmental trajectories during childhood and adolescence. *NeuroImage, 36*, 1065–1073.

Lester, B. M., & Dreher, M. (1989). Effects of marijuana use during pregnancy on newborn cry. *Child Development, 60*, 765–771.

Lester, B. M., ElSohly, M., Wright, L. L., Smeriglio, V. L., Verter, J., Bauer, C. R., ... Maza, P. L. (2001). The Maternal Lifestyle Study: Drug use by meconium toxicology and maternal self-report. *Pediatrics, 107*, 309–317.

Lezak, M. D., Howieson, D. B., Loring, D. W., Hannay, H. J., & Fischer, J. S. (2004). *Neuropsychological assessment* (4th ed.). New York: Oxford University Press.

Li, Z., Coles, C. D., Lynch, M. E., Hamann, S., Peltier, S., LaConte, S., & Hu, X. (2009). Prenatal cocaine exposure alters emotional arousal regulation and its effects on working memory. *Neurotoxicology and Teratology, 31*, 342–348.

Li, Z., Ma, X., Peltier, S., Hu, X., Coles, C. D., & Lynch, M. E. (2008). Occipital-temporal reduction and sustained visual attention deficit in prenatal alcohol exposed adults. *Brain Imaging and Behavior, 2*, 39–48.

Lidow, M. S. (2003). Consequences of prenatal cocaine exposure in nonhuman primates. *Developmental Brain Research, 147*(1–2), 23–36.

Lifschitz, M. H., & Wilson, G. S. (1991). Patterns of growth and development in narcotic-exposed children. In M. M. Kilbey & K. Asghar (Eds.), *Methodological issues in controlled studies on effects of prenatal exposure to drug abuse* (Vol. *114*, pp. 323–339). Rockville, MD: NIDA Research Monographs.

Lim, K. O., & Helpern, J. A. (2002). Neuropsychiatric applications of DTI—a review. *NMR in Biomedicine, 15*, 587–593.

Lipman, E. L., Offord, D. R., Boyle, M. H., & Racine, Y. A. (1993). Follow-up of psychiatric and educational morbidity among adopted children. *Journal of the American Academy of Child and Adolescent Psychiatry, 32*, 1007–1012.

Lisdahl, K. M., Thayer, R., Squeglia, L. M., McQueeny, T. M., & Tapert, S. F. (2011). Recent binge drinking predicts smaller cerebellar volumes in adolescents. *Psychiatry Research, 211*, 17–23.

Logothetis, N. K., Pauls, J., Augath, M., Trinath, T., & Oeltermann, A. (2001). Neurophysiological investigation of the basis of the fMRI signal. *Nature, 412*, 150–157.

Lopez-Larson, M. P., Bogorodzki, P., Rogowska, J., McGlade, E., King, J. B., Terry, J., & Yurgelun-Todd, D. (2011). Altered prefrontal and insular cortical thickness in adolescent marijuana users. *Behavioural Brain Research, 220*, 164–172.

Ma, X., Coles, C. D., Lynch, M. E., LaConte, S. M., Zurkiya, O., Wang, D., & Hu, X. (2005). Evaluation of corpus callosum anisotropy in young adults with fetal alcohol syndrome according to diffusion tensor imaging. *Alcoholism: Clinical and Experimental Research, 29*, 1214–1222.

MacGregor, S. N., Sciarra, J. C., Keith, L., & Sciarra, J. J. (1990). Prevalence of marijuana use during pregnancy. A pilot study. *Journal of Reproductive Medicine, 35*, 1147–1149.

Mahmood, O. M., Jacobus, J., Bava, S., Scarlett, A., & Tapert, S. F. (2010). Learning and memory performances in adolescent users of alcohol and marijuana: Interactive effects. *Journal of Studies on Alcohol and Drugs, 71*, 885–894.

Malanga, C. J., & Kosofsky, B. E. (2003). Does drug abuse beget drug abuse? Behavioral analysis of addiction liability in animal models of prenatal drug exposure. *Developmental Brain Research, 147*(1–2), 47–57.

Malisza, K. L., Allman, A. A., Shiloff, D., Jakobson, L., Longstaffe, S., & Chudley, A. E. (2005). Evaluation of spatial working memory function in children and adults with fetal alcohol spectrum disorders: A functional magnetic resonance imaging study. *Pediatric Research, 58*, 1150–1157.

Marcus, J., Hans, S. L., & Jeremy, R. J. (1984). A longitudinal study of offspring born to methadone-maintained women. III. Effects of multiple risk factors on development at 4, 8, and 12 months. *Am J Drug Alcohol Abuse, 10*, 195–207.

Mattson, S. N., Calarco, K. E., & Lang, A. R. (2006). Focused and shifting attention in children with heavy prenatal alcohol exposure. *Neuropsychology, 20*, 361–369.

Mattson, S. N., Crocker, N., & Nguyen, T. T. (2011). Fetal alcohol spectrum disorders: Neuropsychological and behavioral features. *Neuropsychology Review, 21*, 81–101.

Mattson, S. N., Goodman, A. M., Caine, C., Delis, D. C., & Riley, E. P. (1999). Executive functioning in children with heavy prenatal alcohol exposure. *Alcoholism: Clinical and Experimental Research, 23*, 1808–1815.

Mattson, S. N., Gramling, L., Delis, D., Jones, K. L., & Riley, E. P. (1996). Global-local processing in children prenatally exposed to alcohol. *Child Neuropsychology, 2*(3), 165–175.

Mattson, S. N., & Riley, E. P. (1998). A review of the neurobehavioral deficits in children with fetal alcohol syndrome or prenatal exposure to alcohol. *Alcoholism: Clinical and Experimental Research, 22*, 279–294.

Mattson, S. N., & Riley, E. P. (2000). Parent ratings of behavior in children with heavy prenatal alcohol exposure and

IQ-matched controls. *Alcoholism: Clinical and Experimental Research, 24,* 226–231.

Mattson, S. N., Riley, E. P., Delis, D. C., Stern, C., & Jones, K. L. (1996). Verbal learning and memory in children with fetal alcohol syndrome. *Alcoholism: Clinical and Experimental Research, 20,* 810–816.

Mattson, S. N., Riley, E. P., Gramling, L. J., Delis, D. C., & Jones, K. L. (1997). Heavy prenatal alcohol exposure with or without physical features of fetal alcohol syndrome leads to IQ deficits. *Journal of Pediatrics, 131,* 718–721.

Mattson, S. N., Riley, E. P., Gramling, L. J., Delis, D. C., & Jones, K. L. (1998). Neuropsychological comparison of alcohol-exposed children with or without physical features of fetal alcohol syndrome. *Neuropsychology, 12,* 146–153.

Mattson, S. N., Riley, E. P., Jernigan, T. L., Ehlers, C. L., Delis, D. C., Jones, K. L., ... Bellugi, U. (1992). Fetal alcohol syndrome: A case report of neuropsychological, MRI and EEG assessment of two children. *Alcoholism: Clinical and Experimental Research, 16,* 1001–1003.

Mattson, S. N., Riley, E. P., Jernigan, T. L., Garcia, A., Kaneko, W. M., Ehlers, C. L., & Jones, K. L. (1994). A decrease in the size of the basal ganglia following prenatal alcohol exposure: A preliminary report. *Neurotoxicology and Teratology, 16,* 283–289.

Mattson, S. N., Riley, E. P., Sowell, E. R., Jernigan, T. L., Sobel, D. F., & Jones, K. L. (1996). A decrease in the size of the basal ganglia in children with fetal alcohol syndrome. *Alcoholism: Clinical and Experimental Research, 20,* 1088–1093.

Mattson, S. N., & Roebuck, T. M. (2002). Acquisition and retention of verbal and nonverbal information in children with heavy prenatal alcohol exposure. *Alcoholism: Clinical and Experimental Research, 26,* 875–882.

Mattson, S. N., Roesch, S. C., Fagerlund, A., Autti-Ramo, I., Jones, K. L., May, P. A., ... the Collaborative Initiative on Fetal Alcohol Spectrum Disorders. (2010). Toward a neurobehavioral profile of fetal alcohol spectrum disorders. *Alcoholism: Clinical and Experimental Research, 34,* 1640–1650.

Mattson, S. N., Roesch, S. C., Glass, L., Deweese, B. N., Coles, C. D., Kable, J. A., ... the Collaborative Initiative on Fetal Alcohol Spectrum Disorders. (2013). Further development of a neurobehavioral profile of fetal alcohol spectrum disorders. *Alcoholism: Clinical and Experimental Research, 37,* 517–528.

May, P. A., & Gossage, J. P. (2001). Estimating the prevalence of fetal alcohol syndrome: A summary. *Alcohol Research and Health, 25*(3), 159–167.

May, P. A., & Gossage, J. P. (2009). Prevalence and epidemiologic characteristics of FASD from various research methods with an emphasis on recent in-school studies. *Developmental Disabilities Research Reviews, 15,* 176–192.

May, P. A., Gossage, J. P., Marais, A. S., Hendricks, L. S., Snell, C. L., Tabachnick, B. G., ... Viljoen, D. L. (2008). Maternal risk factors for fetal alcohol syndrome and partial fetal alcohol syndrome in South Africa: A third study. *Alcoholism: Clinical and Experimental Research, 32,* 738–753.

Mayes, L., Snyder, P. J., Langlois, E., & Hunter, N. (2007). Visuospatial working memory in school-aged children exposed in utero to cocaine. *Child Neuropsychology, 13*(3), 205–218.

McCann, U., Szabo, Z., Seckin, E., Rosenblatt, P., Mathews, W., Ravert, H., ... Ricaurte, G. (2005). Quantitative PET studies of the serotonin transporter in MDMA users and controls using [11C]McN5652 and [11C]DASB. *Neuropsychopharmacology, 30,* 1741–1750.

McCann, U. D., Szabo, Z., Scheffel, U., Dannals, R. F., & Ricaurte, G. A. (1998). Positron emission tomographic evidence of toxic effect of MDMA ("ecstasy") on brain serotonin neurons in human beings. *Lancet, 352,* 1433–1437.

McClain, J. A., Morris, S. A., Deeny, M. A., Marshall, S. A., Hayes, D. M., Kiser, Z. M., & Nixon, K. (2011). Adolescent binge alcohol exposure induces long-lasting partial activation of microglia. *Brain, Behavior, and Immunity, Suppl. 1,* S120–S128.

McGee, C. L., Bjorkquist, O. A., Price, J. M., Mattson, S. N., & Riley, E. P. (2009). Social information processing skills in children with histories of heavy prenatal alcohol exposure. *Journal of Abnormal Child Psychology, 37,* 817–830.

McGee, C. L., Fryer, S. L., Bjorkquist, O. A., Mattson, S. N., & Riley, E. P. (2008). Deficits in social problem solving in adolescents with prenatal exposure to alcohol. *American Journal of Drug and Alcohol Abuse, 34,* 423–431.

McGee, C. L., Schonfeld, A. M., Roebuck-Spencer, T. M., Riley, E. P., & Mattson, S. N. (2008). Children with heavy prenatal alcohol exposure demonstrate deficits on multiple measures of concept formation. *Alcoholism: Clinical and Experimental Research, 32,* 1388–1397.

McKetin, R., & Mattick, R. P. (1998). Attention and memory in illicit amphetamine users: Comparison with non-drug-using controls. *Drug and Alcohol Dependence, 5*(2), 181–184.

McQueeny, T., Schweinsburg, B.C., Schweinsburg, A.D., Jacobus, J., Bava, S., Frank, L. R., & Tapert, S.F. (2009). Altered white matter integrity in adolescent binge drinkers. *Alcoholism: Clinical & Experimental Research, 33,* 1278-1285.

Medina, K. L., Hanson, K. L., Schweinsburg, A. D., Cohen-Zion, M., Nagel, B. J., & Tapert, S. F. (2007). Neuropsychological functioning in adolescent marijuana users: Subtle deficits detectable after a month of abstinence. *Journal of International Neuropsychological Society, 13,* 807–820.

Medina, K. L., McQueeny, T., Nagel, B. J., Hanson, K. L., Schweinsburg, A. D., & Tapert, S. F. (2008). Prefrontal cortex volumes in adolescents with alcohol use disorders: Unique gender effects. *Alcoholism: Clinical & Experimental Research, 32,* 386–394.

Medina, K. L., Nagel, B. J., Park, A., McQueeny, T., & Tapert, S. F. (2007). Depressive symptoms in adolescents: Associations with white matter volume and marijuana use. *Journal of Child Psychology and Psychiatry and Allied Disciplines, 48,* 592–600.

Medina, K. L., Schweinsburg, A. D., Cohen-Zion, M., Nagel, B. J., & Tapert, S. F. (2007). Effects of alcohol and combined marijuana and alcohol use during adolescence on hippocampal volume and asymmetry. *Neurotoxicology & Teratology, 29,* 141–152.

Medina, K. L., Shear, P. K., & Corcoran, K. (2005). Ecstasy (MDMA) exposure and neuropsychological functioning: A polydrug perspective. *Journal of International Neuropsychological Society, 11,* 753–765.

Meier, M. H., Caspi, A., Ambler, A., Harrington, H., Houts, R., Keefe, R. S., ... Moffitt, T. E. (2012). Persistent cannabis users show neuropsychological decline from childhood to midlife. *Proceedings of the National Academy of Sciences of the United States of America, 109*(40), E2657–E2664.

Meintjes, E. M., Jacobson, J. L., Molteno, C. D., Gatenby, J., Warton, C., Cannistraci, C. J., ... Jacobson, S. W. (2010).

An fMRI study of number processing in children with fetal alcohol syndrome. *Alcoholism: Clinical and Experimental Research, 34*, 1450–1464.

Meyer, L. S., & Riley, E. P. (1986). Behavioral teratology of alcohol. In E. P. Riley & C. V. Vorhees (Eds.), *Handbook of behavioral teratology* (pp. 101–140). New York: Plenum.

Miller, J. W., Naimi, T. S., Brewer, R. D., & Jones, S. E. (2007). Binge drinking and associated health risk behaviors among high school students. *Pediatrics, 119*, 76–85.

Millsaps, C. L., Azrin, R. L., & Mittenberg, W. (1994). Neuropsychological effects of chronic cannabis use on the memory and intelligence of adolescents. *Journal of Child and Adolescent Substance Abuse, 3*, 47–55.

Molina-Holgado, F., Alvarez, F. J., Gonzalez, I., Antonio, M. T., & Leret, M. L. (1997). Maternal exposure to delta 9-tetrahydrocannabinol (delta 9-THC) alters indolamine levels and turnover in adult male and female rat brain regions. *Brain Research Bulletin, 43*(2), 173–178.

Molina-Holgado, F., Amaro, A., Gonzalez, M. I., Alvarez, F. J., & Leret, M. L. (1996). Effect of maternal delta 9-tetrahydrocannabinol on developing serotonergic system. *European Journal of Pharmacology, 316*, 39–42.

Morgan, M. J. (2000). Ecstasy (MDMA): A review of its possible persistent psychological effects. *Psychopharmacology (Berl), 153*, 230–248.

Morris, S. A., Eaves, D. W., Smith, A. R., & Nixon, K. (2009). Alcohol inhibition of neurogenesis: A mechanism of hippocampal neurodegeneration in an adolescent alcohol abuse model. *Hippocampus, 20*, 596–607.

Moss, H. B., Kirisci, L., Gordon, H. W., & Tarter, R. E. (1994). A neuropsychologic profile of adolescent alcoholics. *Alcoholism: Clinical & Experimental Research, 18*, 159–163.

Myers, M. G., Stewart, D. G., & Brown, S. A. (1998). Progression from conduct disorder to antisocial personality disorder following treatment for adolescent substance abuse. *American Journal of Psychiatry, 155*, 479–485.

Nagel, B. J., Schweinsburg, A. D., Phan, V., & Tapert, S. F. (2005). Reduced hippocampal volume among adolescents with alcohol use disorders without psychiatric comorbidity. *Psychiatry Research: Neuroimaging, 139*, 181–190.

Nardelli, A., Lebel, C., Rasmussen, C., Andrew, G., & Beaulieu, C. (2011). Extensive deep gray matter volume reductions in children and adolescents with fetal alcohol spectrum disorder. *Alcoholism: Clinical and Experimental Research, 35*, 1404–1417.

Nash, K., Rovet, J., Greenbaum, R., Fantus, E., Nulman, I., & Koren, G. (2006). Identifying the behavioural phenotype in fetal alcohol spectrum disorder: Sensitivity, specificity and screening potential. *Archives of Women's Mental Health, 9*, 181–186.

Nees, F., Tzschoppe, J., Patrick, C. J., Vollstädt-Klein, S., Steiner, S., Poustka, L., ... IMAGEN Consortium. (2012). Determinants of early alcohol use in healthy adolescents: The differential contribution of neuroimaging and psychological factors. *Neuropsychopharmacology, 37*, 986–995.

Noland, J. S., Singer, L. T., Short, E. J., Minnes, S., Arendt, R. E., Kirchner, H. L., & Bearer, C. (2005). Prenatal drug exposure and selective attention in preschoolers. *Neurotoxicology and Teratology, 27*, 429–438.

Nordahl, T. E., Salo, R., & Leamon, M. (2003). Neuropsychological effects of chronic methamphetamine use on neurotransmitters and cognition: A review. *Journal of Neuropsychiatry & Clinical Neuroscience, 15*, 317–325.

Norman, A. L., O'Brien, J. W., Spadoni, A. D., Tapert, S. F., Jones, K. J., Riley, E. P., & Mattson, S. N. (2013). A functional magnetic resonance imaging study of spatial working memory in children with prenatal alcohol exposure: Contribution of familial history of alcohol use disorders. *Alcoholism: Clinical and Experimental Research, 37*, 132–140.

Norman, A. L., Pulido, C., Squeglia, L. M., Spadoni, A. D., Paulus, M. P., & Tapert, S. F. (2011). Neural activation during inhibition predicts initiation of substance use in adolescence. *Drug and Alcohol Dependence, 119*, 216–223.

O'Connor, M. J., & Paley, B. (2006). The relationship of prenatal alcohol exposure and the postnatal environment to child depressive symptoms. *Journal of Pediatric Psychology, 31*, 50–64.

O'Hare, E. D., Kan, E., Yoshii, J., Mattson, S. N., Riley, E. P., Thompson, P. M., ... Sowell, E. R. (2005). Mapping cerebellar vermal morphology and cognitive correlates in prenatal alcohol exposure. *NeuroReport, 16*, 1285–1290.

O'Hare, E. D., Lu, L. H., Houston, S. M., Bookheimer, S. Y., Mattson, S. N., O'Connor, M. J., & Sowell, E. R. (2009). Altered frontal-parietal functioning during verbal working memory in children and adolescents with heavy prenatal alcohol exposure. *Human Brain Mapping, 30*, 3200–3208.

Ogawa, S., Lee, T. M., Kay, A. R., & Tank, D. W. (1990). Brain magnetic resonance imaging with contrast dependent on blood oxygenation. *Proceedings of the National Academy of Sciences of the United States of America, 87*, 9868–9872.

Ornstein, T. J., Iddon, J. L., Baldacchino, A. M., Sahakian, B. J., London, M., Everitt, B. J., & Robbins, T. W. (2000). Profiles of cognitive dysfunction in chronic amphetamine and heroin abusers. *Neuropsychopharmacology, 23*, 113–126.

Oro, A. S., & Dixon, S. D. (1987). Perinatal cocaine and methamphetamine exposure: Maternal and neonatal correlates. *Journal of Pediatrics, 111*, 571–578.

Oscar-Berman, M., & Marinkovic, K. (2003). Alcoholism and the brain: An overview. *Alcohol Research and Health, 27*, 125–133).

Oscar-Berman, M., & Marinkovic, K. (2007). Alcohol: Effects on neurobehavioral functions and the brain. *Neuropsychology Review, 17*, 239–257.

Parrott, A. C. (2004). MDMA (3,4-Methylenedioxymethamphetamine) or ecstasy: The neuropsychobiological implications of taking it at dances and raves. *Neuropsychobiology, 50*, 329–335.

Parrott, A. C., & Lasky, J. (1998). Ecstasy (MDMA) effects upon mood and cognition: Before, during and after a Saturday night dance. *Psychopharmacology (Berl), 139*, 261–268.

Parsons, O. A., & Stevens, L. (1986). Previous alcohol intake and residual cognitive deficits in detoxified alcoholics and animals. *Alcohol & Alcoholism, 21*, 137–157.

Paulus, M. P., Hozack, N. E., Zauscher, B. E., Frank, L., Brown, G. G., Braff, D. L., & Shuckit, M. A. (2002). Behavioral and functional neuroimaging evidence for prefrontal dysfunction in methamphetamine dependent subjects. *Neuropsychopharmacology, 26*, 53–63.

Pei, J. R., Rinaldi, C. M., Rasmussen, C., Massey, V., & Massey, D. (2008). Memory patterns of acquisition and retention of verbal and nonverbal information in children with fetal alcohol spectrum disorders. *Canadian Journal of Clinical Pharmacology, 15*, e44–e56.

Peiffer, J., Majewski, F., Fischbach, H., Bierich, J. R., & Volk, B. (1979). Alcohol embryo- and fetopathy: Neuropathology of

3 children and 3 fetuses. *Journal of the Neurological Sciences*, *41*, 125–137.

Pfefferbaum, A., Adalsteinsson, E., & Sullivan, E. V. (2006). Supratentorial profile of white matter microstructural integrity in recovering alcoholic men and women. *Biological Psychiatry*, *59*, 364–372.

Pfefferbaum, A., Mathalon, D. H., Sullivan, E. V., Rawles, J. M., Zipursky, R. B., & Lim, K. O. (1994). A quantitative magnetic resonance imaging study of changes in brain morphology from infancy to late adulthood. *Archives of Neurology*, *51*, 874–887.

Pfefferbaum, A., & Sullivan, E. V. (2005). Disruption of brain white matter microstructure by excessive intracellular and extracellular fluid in alcoholism: Evidence from diffusion tensor imaging. *Neuropsychopharmacology*, *30*, 423–432.

Pfefferbaum, A., Sullivan, E. V., Hedehus, M., Adalsteinsson, E., Lim, K. O., & Moseley, M. (2000). In vivo detection and functional correlates of white matter microstructural disruption in chronic alcoholism. *Alcoholism: Clinical & Experimental Research*, *24*, 1214–1221.

Pfefferbaum, A., Sullivan, E. V., Mathalon, D. H., & Lim, K. O. (1997). Frontal lobe volume loss observed with magnetic resonance imaging in older chronic alcoholics. *Alcoholism: Clinical & Experimental Research*, *21*, 521–529.

Plessinger, M. A. (1998). Prenatal exposure to amphetamines. Risks and adverse outcomes in pregnancy. *Obstetrics and Gynecology Clinics of North America*, *25*, 119–138.

Pope, H. G., Jr., Gruber, A. J., Hudson, J. I., Cohane, G., Huestis, M. A., & Yurgelun Todd, D. (2003). Early onset cannabis use and cognitive deficits: What is the nature of the association? *Drug and Alcohol Dependence*, *69*, 303–310.

Pope, H. G., Jr., Gruber, A. J., Hudson, J. I., Huestis, M. A., & Yurgelun-Todd, D. (2001). Neuropsychological performance in long term cannabis users. *Archives of General Psychiatry*, *58*, 909–915.

Porath, A. J., & Fried, P. A. (2005). Effects of prenatal cigarette and marijuana exposure on drug use among offspring. *Neurotoxicology and Teratology*, *27*, 267–277.

Prevention, CDC. (2009). *Web-based injury statistics query and reporting system*. Retrieved February 28, 2008, from www.cdc.gov/ncipc/wisqars

Pulsifer, M. B. (1996). The neuropsychology of mental retardation. *Journal of the International Neuropsychological Society*, *2*, 159–176.

Pyapali, G. K., Turner, D. A., Wilson, W. A., & Swartzwelder, H. S. (1999). Age and dose-dependent effects of ethanol on the induction of hippocampal long-term potentiation. *Alcohol*, *19*, 107–111.

Rassmussen, C., & Bisanz, J. (2009). Executive functioning in children with fetal alcohol spectrum disorders: Profiles and age-related differences. *Child Neuropsychology*, *15*, 201–215.

Rasmussen, C., & Bisanz, J. (2010). The relation between mathematics and working memory in young children with fetal alcohol spectrum disorders. *Journal of Special Education*, *45*, 184–191.

Rawson, R., Huber, A., Brethen, P., Obert, J., Gulati, V., Shoptaw, S., & Ling, W. (2000). Methamphetamine and cocaine users: Differences in characteristics and treatment retention. *Journal of Psychoactive Drugs*, *32*, 233–238.

Reneman, L., Booij, J., de Bruin, K., Reitsma, J. B., de Wolff, F. A., Gunning, W. B., . . . van den Brink, W. (2001). Effects of dose, sex, and long-term abstention from use on toxic effects of MDMA (ecstasy) on brain serotonin neurons. *Lancet*, *358*, 1864–1869.

Reneman, L., Booij, J., Lavalaye, J., de Bruin, K., Reitsma, J. B., Gunning, B., . . . van Den Brink, W. (2002). Use of amphetamine by recreational users of ecstasy (MDMA) is associated with reduced striatal dopamine transporter densities: A [123I]beta-CIT SPECT study: Preliminary report. *Psychopharmacology (Berl)*, *159*, 335–340.

Reneman, L., Endert, E., de Bruin, K., Lavalaye, J., Feenstra, M. G., de Wolff, F. A., & Booij, J. (2002). The acute and chronic effects of MDMA ("ecstasy") on cortical 5-HT2A receptors in rat and human brain. *Neuropsychopharmacology*, *26*, 387–396.

Reneman, L., Majoie, C. B., Flick, H., & den Heeten, G. J. (2002). Reduced N-acetylaspartate levels in the frontal cortex of 3,4-methylenedioxymethamphetamine (ecstasy) users: Preliminary results. *American Journal of Neuroradiology*, *23*, 231–237.

Reneman, L., Majoie, C. B., Habraken, J. B., & den Heeten, G. J. (2001). Effects of ecstasy (MDMA) on the brain in abstinent users: Initial observations with diffusion and perfusion MR imaging. *Radiology*, *220*, 611–617.

Richardson, G. A., Conroy, M. L., & Day, N. L. (1996). Prenatal cocaine exposure: Effects on the development of school-age children. *Neurotoxicology and Teratology*, *18*, 627–634.

Richardson, G. A., Day, N. L., & Goldschmidt, L. (1995). Prenatal alcohol, marijuana, and tobacco use: Infant mental and motor development. *Neurotoxicology and Teratology*, *17*, 479–487.

Richardson, G. A., Ryan, C., Willford, J., Day, N. L., & Goldschmidt, L. (2002). Prenatal alcohol and marijuana exposure: Effects on neuropsychological outcomes at 10 years. *Neurotoxicology and Teratology*, *24*, 309–320.

Riikonen, R. S., Nokelainen, P., Valkonen, K., Kolehmainen, A. I., Kumpulainen, K. I., Kononen, M., . . . Kuikka, J. T. (2005). Deep serotonergic and dopaminergic structures in fetal alcoholic syndrome: A study with nor-beta-CIT-single-photon emission computed tomography and magnetic resonance imaging volumetry. *Biological Psychiatry*, *57*, 1565–1572.

Riikonen, R., Salonen, I., Partanen, K., & Verho, S. (1999). Brain perfusion SPECT and MRI in foetal alcohol syndrome. *Developmental Medicine and Child Neurology*, *41*, 652–659.

Riley, E. P., Mattson, S. N., Sowell, E. R., Jernigan, T. L., Sobel, D. F., & Jones, K. L. (1995). Abnormalities of the corpus callosum in children prenatally exposed to alcohol. *Alcoholism: Clinical and Experimental Research*, *19*, 1198–1202.

Roebuck, T. M., Mattson, S. N., & Riley, E. P. (2002). Interhemispheric transfer in children with heavy prenatal alcohol exposure. *Alcoholism, Clinical and Experimental Research*, *26*, 1863–1871.

Roebuck, T. M., Simmons, R. W., Mattson, S. N., & Riley, E. P. (1998). Prenatal exposure to alcohol affects the ability to maintain postural balance. *Alcoholism: Clinical and Experimental Research*, *22*, 252–258.

Roebuck-Spencer, T. M., Mattson, S. N., Marion, S. D., Brown, W. S., & Riley, E. P. (2004). Bimanual coordination in alcohol-exposed children: Role of the corpus callosum. *Journal of the International Neuropsychological Society*, *10*, 536–548.

Rogers, R. D., Everitt, B. J., Baldacchino, A., Blackshaw, A. J., Swainson, R., Wynne, K., . . . Robbins, T. W. (1999).

Dissociable deficits in the decision-making cognition of chronic amphetamine abusers, opiate abusers, patients with focal damage to prefrontal cortex, and tryptophan-depleted normal volunteers: Evidence for monoaminergic mechanisms. *Neuropsychopharmacology, 20*, 322–339.

Rosen, T. S., & Johnson, H. L. (1985). Long-term effects of prenatal methadone maintenance. *NIDA Research Monograms, 59*, 73–83.

Roussotte, F., Soderberg, L., Warner, T., Narr, K., Lebel, C., Behnke, M., . . . Sowell, E. R. (2012). Adolescents with prenatal cocaine exposure show subtle alterations in striatal surface morphology and frontal cortical volumes. *Journal of Neurodevelopmental Disorders, 4*, 2–10.

Roussotte, F., Sulik, K., Mattson, S. N., Riley, E. P., Jones, K. L., Adnams, C., . . . Sowell, E. R. (2011). Regional brain volume reductions relate to facial dysmorphology and neurocognitive function in fetal alcohol spectrum disorders. *Human Brain Mapping, 33*, 920–937

Salo, R., Nordahl, T. E., Possin, K., Leamon, M., Gibson, D. R., Galloway, G. P., . . . Sullivan, E. V. (2002). Preliminary evidence of reduced cognitive inhibition in methamphetamine-dependent individuals. *Psychiatry Research: Neuroimaging, 111*, 65–74.

Sampson, P. D., Streissguth, A. P., Bookstein, F. L., Little, R. E., Clarren, S. K., Dehaene, P., . . . Graham, J. M., Jr. (1997). Incidence of fetal alcohol syndrome and prevalence of alcohol-related neurodevelopmental disorder. *Teratology, 56*, 317–326.

Santhanam, P., Li, Z., Hu, X., Lynch, M. E., & Coles, C. D. (2009). Effects of prenatal alcohol exposure on brain activation during an arithmetic task: An fMRI study. *Alcoholism: Clinical and Experimental Research, 33*, 1901–1908.

Scher, M. S., Richardson, G. A., Coble, P. A., Day, N. L., & Stoffer, D. S. (1988). The effects of prenatal alcohol and marijuana exposure: Disturbances in neonatal sleep cycling and arousal. *Pediatric Research, 24*, 101–105.

Schilt, T., de Win, M. M. L., Koeter, M., Jager, G., Korf, D. J., van den Brink, W., et al. (2007). Cognition in novice ecstasy users with minimal exposure to other drugs: A prospective cohort study. *Archives of General Psychiatry, 64*, 728–736.

Schwartz, R. H., Gruenewald, P. J., Klitzner, M., & Fedio, P. (1989). Short-term memory impairment in cannabis-dependent adolescents. *American Journal of Diseases in Children, 143*, 1214–1219.

Schweinsburg, A. D., McQueeny, T., Nagel, B. J., Eyler, L. T., & Tapert, S. F. (2010). A preliminary study of functional magnetic resonance imaging response during verbal encoding among adolescent binge drinkers. *Alcohol, 44*, 111–117.

Schweinsburg, A. D., Nagel, B. J., Schweinsburg, B. C., Park, A., Theilmann, R. J., & Tapert, S. F. (2008). Abstinent adolescent marijuana users show altered fMRI response during spatial working memory. *Psychiatry Research: Neuroimaging, 163*, 40–51.

Schweinsburg, A. D., Schweinsburg, B. C., Cheung, E. H., Brown, G. G., Brown, S. A., & Tapert, S. F. (2005). fMRI response to spatial working memory in adolescents with comorbid marijuana and alcohol use disorders. *Drug & Alcohol Dependence, 79*, 201–210.

Schweinsburg, A. D., Schweinsburg, B. C., Nagel, B. J., Eyler, L. T., & Tapert, S. F. (2011). Neural correlates of verbal learning in adolescent alcohol and marijuana users. *Addiction, 106*, 564–573.

Schweinsburg, B. C., Alhassoon, O. M., Taylor, M. J., Gonzalez, R., Videen, J. S., Brown, G. G., . . . Grant, I. (2003). Effects of alcoholism and gender on brain metabolism. *American Journal of Psychiatry, 160*, 1180–1183.

Sekine, Y., Iyo, M., Ouchi, Y., Matsunaga, T., Tsukada, H., Okada, H., . . . Mori, N. (2001). Methamphetamine-related psychiatric symptoms and reduced brain dopamine transporters studied with PET. *American Journal of Psychiatry, 158*, 1206–1214.

Sekine, Y., Ouchi, Y., Takei, N., Yoshikawa, E., Nakamura, K., Futatsubashi, M., . . . Mori, N. (2006). Brain serotonin transporter density and aggression in abstinent methamphetamine abusers. *Archives of General Psychiatry, 63*, 90–100.

Semple, D. M., Ebmeier, K. P., Glabus, M. F., O'Carroll, R. E., & Johnstone, E. C. (1999). Reduced in vivo binding to the serotonin transporter in the cerebral cortex of MDMA ("ecstasy") users. *British Journal of Psychiatry, 175*, 63–69.

Sheinkopf, S. J., Lester, B. M., Sanes, J. N., Eliassen, J. C., Hutchinson, E. R., Seifer, R., . . . Casey, B. J. (2009). Functional MRI and response inhibition in children exposed to cocaine in utero. Preliminary findings. *Developmental Neuroscience, 31*, 159–166.

Simon, S. L., Domier, C., Carnell, J., Brethen, P., Rawson, R., & Ling, W. (2000). Cognitive impairment in individuals currently using methamphetamine. *American Journal on Addictions, 9*, 222–231.

Smith, A. M., Fried, P. A., Hogan, M. J., & Cameron, I. (2004). Effects of prenatal marijuana on response inhibition: An fMRI study of young adults. *Neurotoxicology and Teratology, 26*, 533–542.

Smith, A. M., Fried, P. A., Hogan, M. J., & Cameron, I. (2006). Effects of prenatal marijuana on visuospatial working memory: An fMRI study in young adults. *Neurotoxicology and Teratology, 28*, 286–295.

Smith, L. M., Lagasse, L. L., Derauf, C., Grant, P., Shah, R., Arria, A., . . . Lester, B. M. (2008). Prenatal methamphetamine use and neonatal neurobehavioral outcome. *Neurotoxicology and Teratology, 30*, 20–28.

Solowij, N., Jones, K. A., Rozman, M. E., Davis, S. M., Ciarrochi, J., Heaven, P. C., . . . Yücel, M. (2011). Verbal learning and memory in adolescent cannabis users, alcohol users and non-users. *Psychopharmacology, 216*, 131–144.

Sowell, E. R., Jernigan, T. L., Mattson, S. N., Riley, E. P., Sobel, D. F., & Jones, K. L. (1996). Abnormal development of the cerebellar vermis in children prenatally exposed to alcohol: Size reduction in lobules I-V. *Alcoholism: Clinical and Experimental Research, 20*, 31–34.

Sowell, E. R., Johnson, A., Kan, E., Lu, L. H., Van Horn, J. D., Toga, A. W., . . . Bookheimer, S. Y. (2008). Mapping white matter integrity and neurobehavioral correlates in children with fetal alcohol spectrum disorders. *Journal of Neuroscience, 28*, 1313–1319.

Sowell, E. R., Lu, L. H., O'Hare, E. D., McCourt, S. T., Mattson, S. N., O'Connor, M. J., & Bookheimer, S. Y. (2007). Functional magnetic resonance imaging of verbal learning in children with heavy prenatal alcohol exposure. *NeuroReport, 18*, 635–639.

Sowell, E. R., Mattson, S. N., Kan, E., Thompson, P. M., Riley, E. P., & Toga, A. W. (2008). Abnormal cortical thickness and brain-behavior correlation patterns in individuals with heavy prenatal alcohol exposure. *Cerebral Cortex, 18*, 136–144.

Sowell, E. R., Mattson, S. N., Thompson, P. M., Jernigan, T. L., Riley, E. P., & Toga, A. W. (2001). Mapping callosal morphology and cognitive correlates: Effects of heavy prenatal alcohol exposure. *Neurology, 57*, 235–244.

Sowell, E. R., Thompson, P. M., Holmes, C. J., Jernigan, T. L., & Toga, A. W. (1999). In vivo evidence for post adolescent brain maturation in frontal and striatal regions. *Nature Neuroscience, 2*, 859–861.

Sowell, E. R., Thompson, P. M., Mattson, S. N., Tessner, K. D., Jernigan, T. L., Riley, E. P., & Toga, A. W. (2001). Voxel-based morphometric analyses of the brain in children and adolescents prenatally exposed to alcohol. *NeuroReport, 12*, 515–523.

Sowell, E. R., Thompson, P. M., Mattson, S. N., Tessner, K. D., Jernigan, T. L., Riley, E. P., & Toga, A. W. (2002). Regional brain shape abnormalities persist into adolescence after heavy prenatal alcohol exposure. *Cerebral Cortex, 12*, 856–865.

Sowell, E. R., Thompson, P. M., Peterson, B. S., Mattson, S. N., Welcome, S. E., Henkenius, A. L., ... Toga, A. W. (2002). Mapping cortical gray matter asymmetry patterns in adolescents with heavy prenatal alcohol exposure. *NeuroImage, 17*, 1807–1819.

Sowell, E. R., Trauner, D. A., Gamst, A., & Jernigan, T. L. (2002). Development of cortical and subcortical brain structures in childhood and adolescence: A structural MRI study. *Developmental Medicine and Child Neurology, 44*, 4–16.

Spadoni, A. D., Bazinet, A. D., Fryer, S. L., Tapert, S. F., Mattson, S. N., & Riley, E. P. (2009). BOLD response during spatial working memory in alcohol-exposed youth. *Alcoholism: Clinical and Experimental Research, 33*, 2067–2076.

Spear, L. P. (2002). The adolescent brain and the college drinker: Biological basis of propensity to use and misuse alcohol. *Journal of Studies on Alcohol, Suppl. 14*, 71–81.

Squeglia, L. M., Pulido, C., Wetherill, R. R., Jacobus, J., Brown, G. G., & Tapert, S. F. (2012). Brain response to working memory over three years of adolescence: Influence of initiating heavy drinking. *Journal of Studies on Alcohol and Drugs, 73*, 749–760.

Squeglia, L. M., Schweinsburg, A. D., Pulido, C., & Tapert, S. F. (2011). Adolescent binge drinking linked to abnormal spatial working memory brain activation: Differential gender effects. *Alcoholism: Clinical and Experimental Research, 35*, 1831–1841.

Squeglia, L. M., Sorg, S. F., Schweinsburg, A. D., Wetherill, R. R., Pulido, C., & Tapert, S. F. (2012). Binge drinking differentially affects adolescent male and female brain morphometry. *Psychopharmacology, 220*, 529–539.

Squeglia, L. M., Spadoni, A. D., Infante, M. A., Myers, M. G., & Tapert, S. F. (2009). Initiating moderate to heavy alcohol use predicts changes in neuropsychological functioning for adolescent girls and boys. *Psychology of Addictive Behaviors, 23*, 715–722.

Stiles, J., & Jernigan, T. L. (2010). The basics of brain development. *Neuropsychology Review, 20*, 327–348.

Streissguth, A. P., Barr, H. M., Kogan, J., & Bookstein, F. L. (1996). *Final report: Understanding the occurrence of secondary disabilities in clients with fetal alcohol syndrome (FAS) and fetal alcohol effects (FAE)*. Seattle, WA: University of Washington.

Streissguth, A. P., Barr, H. M., Olson, H. C., Sampson, P. D., Bookstein, F. L., & Burgess, D. M. (1994). Drinking during pregnancy decreases word attack and arithmetic scores on standardized tests: Adolescent data from a population-based prospective study. *Alcoholism: Clinical and Experimental Research, 18*, 248–254.

Struthers, J. M., & Hansen, R. L. (1992). Visual recognition memory in drug-exposed infants. *Journal of Developmental and Behavioral Pediatrics, 13*, 108–111.

Suzuki, Y., Oishi, M., Mizutani, T., & Sato, Y. (2002). Regional cerebral blood flow measured by the resting and vascular reserve (RVR) method in chronic alcoholics. *Alcoholism: Clinical & Experimental Research, 26*, 95S–99S.

Swayze, V. W., II, Johnson, V. P., Hanson, J. W., Piven, J., Sato, Y., Giedd, J. N., ... Andreasen, N. C. (1997). Magnetic resonance imaging of brain anomalies in fetal alcohol syndrome. *Pediatrics, 99*, 232–240.

Tansley, B. W., Fried, P. A., & Mount, H. T. (1986). Visual processing in children exposed prenatally to marihuana and nicotine: A preliminary report. *Canadian Journal of Public Health, 77*(Suppl. 1), 72–78.

Tapert, S. F., Brown, G. G., Kindermann, S. S., Cheung, E. H., Frank, L. R., & Brown, S. A. (2001). fMRI measurement of brain dysfunction in alcohol-dependent young women. *Alcoholism: Clinical & Experimental Research, 25*, 236–245.

Tapert, S. F., & Brown, S. A. (1999). Neuropsychological correlates of adolescent substance abuse: Four-year outcomes. *Journal of the International Neuropsychological Society, 5*, 481–493.

Tapert, S. F., & Brown, S. A. (2000). Substance dependence, family history of alcohol dependence and neuropsychological functioning in adolescence. *Addiction, 95*, 1043–1053.

Tapert, S. F., Cheung, E. H., Brown, G. G., Frank, L. R., Paulus, M. P., Schweinsburg, A. D., ... Brown, S. A. (2003). Neural response to alcohol stimuli in adolescents with alcohol use disorder. *Archives of General Psychiatry, 60*, 727–735.

Tapert, S. F., Granholm, E., Leedy, N. G., & Brown, S. A. (2002). Substance use and withdrawal: Neuropsychological functioning over 8 years in youth. *Journal of the International Neuropsychological Society, 8*, 873–883.

Tapert, S. F., Schweinsburg, A. D., Barlett, V. C., Brown, S. A., Frank, L. R., Brown, G. G., & Meloy, M. J. (2004). Blood oxygen level dependent response and spatial working memory in adolescents with alcohol use disorders. *Alcoholism: Clinical & Experimental Research, 28*, 1577–1586.

Tapert, S. F., Schweinsburg, A. D., Drummond, S. P. A., Paulus, M. P., Brown, S. A., Yang, T. T., & Frank, L. R. (2007). Functional MRI of inhibitory processing in abstinent adolescent marijuana users. *Psychopharmacology, 194*, 173–183.

Tapert, S. F., Theilmann, R. J., & Schweinsburg, A. D. (2003). Reduced fractional anisotropy in the splenium of adolescents with alcohol use disorder. *Proceedings of the International Society of Magnetic Resonance Medicine, 11*(p. 8217).

Tarter, R. E., Mezzich, A. C., Hsieh, Y. -C., & Parks, S. M. (1995). Cognitive capacity in female adolescent substance abusers. *Drug and Alcohol Dependence, 39*, 15–21.

Thoma, R. J., Monnig, M. A., Lysne, P. A., Ruhl, D. A., Pommy, J. A., Bogenschutz, M., ... Yeo, R. A. (2011). Adolescent substance abuse: The effects of alcohol and marijuana on neuropsychological performance. *Alcoholism: Clinical & Experimental Research, 35*, 39–46.

Thomas, S. E., Kelly, S. J., Mattson, S. N., & Riley, E. P. (1998). Comparison of social abilities of children with fetal alcohol syndrome to those of children with similar IQ scores and normal controls. *Alcoholism: Clinical and Experimental Research, 22*, 528–533.

Thompson, P. M., Hayashi, K. M., Simon, S. L., Geaga, J. A., Hong, M. S., Sui, Y., . . . London, E. D. (2004). Structural abnormalities in the brains of human subjects who use methamphetamine. *Journal of Neuroscience, 24,* 6028–6036.

Tomlinson, K. L., Brown, S. A., & Abrantes, A. (2004). Psychiatric comorbidity and substance use treatment outcomes of adolescents. *Psychology of Addictive Behaviors, 18,* 160–169.

Trezza, V., Cuomo, V., & Vanderschuren, L. J. (2008). Cannabis and the developing brain: Insights from behavior. *European Journal of Pharmacology, 585,* 441–452.

Uecker, A., & Nadel, L. (1998). Spatial but not object memory impairments in children with fetal alcohol syndrome. *American Journal on Mental Retardation, 103,* 12–18.

Vaurio, L., Riley, E. P., & Mattson, S. N. (2008). Differences in executive functioning in children with heavy prenatal alcohol exposure or attention-deficit/hyperactivity disorder. *Journal of the International Neuropsychological Society, 14,* 119–129.

Verkes, R. J., Gijsman, H. J., Pieters, M. S., Schoemaker, R. C., de Visser, S., Kuijpers, M. E. A., . . . Cohen, A. F. (2001). Cognitive performance and serotonergic function in users of ecstasy. *Psychopharmacology, 153,* 196–202.

Vik, P. W., Cellucci, T., Jarchow, A., & Hedt, J. (2004). Cognitive impairment in substance abuse. *Psychiatric Clinics of North America, 27,* 97–109.

Volkow, N. D., Chang, L., Wang, G. J., Fowler, J. S., Ding, Y. S., Sedler, M., . . . Pappas, N. (2001). Low level of brain dopamine D2 receptors in methamphetamine abusers: Association with metabolism in the orbitofrontal cortex. *American Journal of Psychiatry, 158,* 2015–2021.

Volkow, N. D., Chang, L., Wang, G. J., Fowler, J. S., Franceschi, D., Sedler, M., . . . Logan, J. (2001). Loss of dopamine transporters in methamphetamine abusers recovers with protracted abstinence. *Journal of Neuroscience, 21,* 9414–9418.

Volkow, N. D., Chang, L., Wang, G. J., Fowler, J. S., Leonido-Yee, M., Franceschi, D., . . . Miller, E. N. (2001). Association of dopamine transporter reduction with psychomotor impairment in methamphetamine abusers. *American Journal of Psychiatry, 158,* 377–382.

Warner, T. D., Behnke, M., Eyler, F., Padgett, K., Leonard, C., Hou, W., . . . Blackand, S. J. (2006). Diffusion tensor imaging of frontal white matter and executive functioning in cocaine-exposed children. *Pediatrics, 11,* 2014–2024.

Wasserman, G. A., Kline, J. K., Bateman, D. A., Chiriboga, C., Lumey, L. H., Friedlander, H., . . . Heagarty, M. C. (1998). Prenatal cocaine exposure and school-age intelligence. *Drug and Alcohol Dependence, 50,* 203–210.

Wetherill, R. R., Castro, N., Squeglia, L. M., & Tapert, S. F. (2013). Atypical neural activity during inhibitory processing in substance-naïve youth who later experience alcohol-induced blackouts. *Drug and Alcohol Dependence, 128,* 243–249.

Whaley, S. E., O'Connor, M. J., & Gunderson, B. (2001). Comparison of the adaptive functioning of children prenatally exposed to alcohol to a nonexposed clinical sample. *Alcoholism: Clinical and Experimental Research, 25,* 1018–1024.

Wiese, J., Shlipak, M., & Browner, W. (2000). The Alcohol Hangover. *Annals of Internal Medicine, 132,* 897–902.

Willford, J. A., Richardson, G. A., Leech, S. L., & Day, N. L. (2004). Verbal and visuospatial learning and memory function in children with moderate prenatal alcohol exposure. *Alcoholism: Clinical and Experimental Research, 28,* 497–507.

Willoughby, K. A., Sheard, E. D., Nash, K., & Rovet, J. (2008). Effects of prenatal alcohol exposure on hippocampal volume, verbal learning, and verbal and spatial recall in late childhood. *Journal of the International Neuropsychological Society, 14,* 1022–1033.

Wilson, W., Mathew, R., Turkington, T., Hawk, T., Coleman, R. E., & Provenzale, J. (2000). Brain morphological changes and early marijuana use: A magnetic resonance and positron emission tomography study. *Journal of Addictive Disorders, 19*(1), 1–22.

Woodruff-Pak, D. S., Goldenberg, G., Downey-Lamb, M. M., Boyko, O. B., & Lemieux, S. K. (2000). Cerebellar volume in humans related to magnitude of classical conditioning. *NeuroReport, 11,* 609–615.

Wozniak, J. R., Mueller, B. A., Chang, P. -N., Muetzel, R. L., Caros, L., & Lim, K. O. (2006). Diffusion tensor imaging in children with fetal alcohol spectrum disorders. *Alcoholism: Clinical and Experimental Research, 30,* 1799–1806.

Wozniak, J. R., Muetzel, R. L., Mueller, B. A., McGee, C. L., Freerks, M. A., Ward, E. E., . . . Lim, K. O. (2009). Microstructural corpus callosum anomalies in children with prenatal alcohol exposure: An extension of previous diffusion tensor imaging findings. *Alcoholism, Clinical and Experimental Research, 33,* 1825–1835.

Xiao, L., Bechara, A., Gong, Q., Huang, X., Li, X., Xue, G., . . . Johnson, C. A. (2013). Abnormal affective decision making revealed in adolescent binge drinkers using a functional magnetic resonance imaging study. *Psychology of Addictive Behaviors.*

Yakovlev, P. I., & Lecours, A. R. (1967). The myelogenetic cycles of regional maturation of the brain. In A. Minkowski (Ed.), *Regional Development of the Brain in Early Life* (pp. 3–70). Boston: Blackwell Scientific.

Yang, Y., Roussotte, F., Kan, E., Sulik., K., Mattson, S. N., Riley, E. P., . . . Sowell, E. R. (2011). Abnormal cortical thickness alterations in fetal alcohol spectrum disorders and their relationships with facial dysmorphology. *Cerebral Cortex, 22,* 1170–1179. doi: 10.1093/cercor/bhr193

Zhou, D., Lebel, C., Lepage, C., Rasmussen, C., Evans, A., Wyper, K., . . . Beaulieu, C. (2011). Developmental cortical thinning in fetal alcohol spectrum disorders. *NeuroImage, 58,* 16–25. doi: 10.1016/j.neuroimage.2011.06.026

Zuckerman, B., Frank, D. A., Hingson, R., Amaro, H., Levenson, S. M., Kayne, H., . . . Bauchner, H. (1989). Effects of maternal marijuana and cocaine use on fetal growth. *New England Journal of Medicine, 320*(12), 762–768.

Effects of Alcoholism on Neurological Function and Disease in Adulthood

Marlene Oscar-Berman, Trinity A. Urban, *and* Avram J. Holmes

Abstract

Alcoholism is associated with disparate and widespread negative consequences for brain anatomy and function. Consistent with a diffuse neurobiological profile, alcoholism is marked by a heterogeneous mix of cognitive and emotional abnormalities. Alcohol use disorders arise through diverse origins and follow an uncertain clinical course, with severity and consequences depending on many factors. The identification of specific alcoholism-related deficits is constrained both by methodological techniques employed and the distinct populations studied. To understand alcoholism-related alterations in brain structure and function, it is critical to consider the influence of contextual factors on clinical course. The optimal approach for understanding alcohol use disorders leverages a variety of scientific methodologies and clinical settings. The resulting confluence of data can provide evidence linking alterations in neurobiology with behavioral and neuropsychological effects of alcoholism. Critically, these data may help determine the degree to which abstinence and treatment facilitate the reversal of brain atrophy and dysfunction.

Key Words: alcoholism, cognition, emotion, neuroimaging, frontal brain systems, limbic systems, reward circuitry

Wine, beer, whiskey, and other alcoholic beverages contain ethanol, a psychoactive ingredient, and alcohol consumption has mental as well as physiological effects. Generally, consumption begins with a feeling of relaxation, which can turn to exuberance. However, at higher doses, intoxication or inebriation occur, and an individual's mental and physical faculties are noticeably changed. Common symptoms of excessive alcohol consumption include slurred speech, impaired balance and coordination, flushed skin, red eyes, reduced inhibitions, and heightened emotions. Acute consumption can result in exhaustion, vomiting, and loss of consciousness, as well as subsequent depression and hangover.

Individuals are considered to have an alcohol use disorder (AUD; American Psychiatric Association [APA], 2013) if they abuse alcohol or are alcohol-dependent. Alcohol *abuse*, as described by the American Psychiatric Association (APA, 1994), is a psychiatric condition whereby the consumption of alcoholic beverages continues despite negative repercussions for health, well-being, and interpersonal relationships. Alcohol *dependence* has additional physiological consequences such as drinking larger amounts or for longer periods than intended, increased alcohol tolerance, and withdrawal symptoms upon cessation of drinking. In addition to diminishing the quality of daily life, excessive drinking shortens life expectancies (Rehm, Gmel, Sempos, & Trevisan, 2003). AUDs also impose high costs on society for disability and health expenditures in terms of crime, fire destruction, motor vehicle crashes, increased health care, legal fees, decreased occupational productivity, and social welfare administration (Gmel & Rehm, 2003; Rehm et al., 2003).

Recently, with the release of DSM-5, the APA integrated alcohol abuse and alcohol dependence into a single disorder called AUD. In DSM-IV, the diagnostic criteria for abuse and dependence were distinct. In DSM-5, the abuse and dependence criteria are considered simultaneously. Anyone meeting two or more of the 11 possible criteria during the same 12-month period receives a diagnosis of AUD. Additionally, DSM-5 removes legal problems associated with diagnoses in DSM-IV, instead incorporating craving as a criterion. The severity of the AUD can be defined as mild (2–3 symptoms), moderate (4–5 symptoms), or severe (6 or more symptoms).

It is important to distinguish between the acute and the residual effects of alcohol use disorders (Crews et al., 2005). Acute effects are relatively short-lived, whereas residual effects can last from weeks to years. Residual effects of AUDs are those that remain despite a person's continued sobriety and abstinence. Among the long-term residual consequences of alcoholism are changes in neural gene expression, reduced brain volume, neuropsychological impairments, and reduced postural stability. Researchers interested in studying alcohol's residual effects usually restrict patient enrollment to alcoholics who have been abstinent for a minimum of 4 weeks; this is important for obtaining stable levels of performance after ethanol and its metabolites have been fully eliminated from the body. In studying the residual effects of chronic alcoholism, researchers also may choose to study individuals who have abused alcohol for a long period of time (e.g., a minimum of 5 years in their lifetime); this permits the measurement of cumulative effects (Oscar-Berman, Kirkley, Gansler, & Couture, 2004).

Criteria for classifying someone as an alcoholic can vary (Abel, Kruger, & Friedl, 1999; Eckardt et al., 1998), but it is thought that excessive alcohol use and alcoholism exist along a continuum of alcohol use behaviors (Helzer et al., 2006). Approximately half of the nearly 20 million people in the United States who are problem drinkers have residual neuropsychological difficulties that range from mild to very severe. For example, up to 2 million alcoholics have permanent and debilitating conditions that require lifetime custodial care (Rourke & Løberg, 1996). Such severe conditions include alcohol-induced persisting amnestic disorder (also called alcoholic Korsakoff's syndrome; Oscar-Berman & Evert, 1997) and alcohol-induced persisting dementia (APA, 1994), which seriously affects many

mental functions in addition to memory (e.g., language, reasoning, and problem-solving abilities).

Risky drinking patterns differ among individuals. Women and men often contrast in the consequences of excessive alcohol consumption (Ruiz & Oscar-Berman, 2013), and youngsters and the elderly generally are at increased risk for alcohol-related problems (Ely, Hardy, Longford, & Wadsworth, 1999). Thus, in men between the ages of 30 and 50, risky levels are more than 14 drinks per week or more than four drinks in a single day at least once a month; for women in the same age range, as well as for men and women over 65 years of age, the limits are more than seven drinks per week and three drinks per day (Dawson, Grant, Stinson, & Zhou, 2005). Additionally, the age of a drinker can affect the impact associated with alcohol consumption. For example, even when factors such as weight and other physical characteristics are accounted for, the physical, emotional, social, and psychological costs to a teen who drinks alcohol are potentially far more significant than the outcome for an adult who drinks the same amount but who may be able to better control his or her actions and emotional and social responses.

In this chapter, we review the brain systems that are most vulnerable to the effects of alcoholism, as well as some of the residual cognitive and emotional consequences. Throughout, it is important to remember that alcoholism is a complex and multidimensional disorder (Maltzman, 2008; Oscar-Berman & Marinković, 2007). Among the many factors influencing the expression and course of the disease are family history of alcoholism; an individual's prenatal and perinatal environments; gender; the social and ethnic surroundings during childhood; the age of onset of alcohol consumption; the type, amount, and frequency of alcohol consumed; the severity and duration of the dependency; nutritional status during periods of consumption; comorbid medical, neurological, and psychological conditions; and the use or abuse of other psychopharmacological substances. Additionally, the comorbid occurrence of alcoholism with other medical, neurological, and psychiatric conditions can interact to aggravate alcoholism's effects on the brain and behavior (Petrakis, Gonzalez, Rosenheck, & Krystal, 2002). Examples of common comorbid complications include medical conditions such as malnutrition and diseases of the liver and the cardiovascular system; neurological conditions such as head injury, inflammation of the brain (i.e., encephalopathy), and fetal alcohol syndrome or fetal alcohol effects; and psychiatric conditions such as depression, anxiety, post-traumatic stress disorder, schizophrenia, and the use of medicines or other drugs. Psychiatric conditions are known to contribute to further drinking, but the presence of a lifetime psychiatric diagnosis does not militate against achieving long-term abstinence (Di Sclafani, Finn, & Fein, 2007).

Alcohol and Brain Neurotransmitters

Alcohol's effects on neurological function and disease are carried out through the actions of a variety of brain neurotransmitters, where there is a complex interplay between excitatory and inhibitory systems. Alcohol, consistent with a variety of other drugs of abuse, increases dopamine levels. The dopamine system supports the mechanisms that attribute salience to events in the environment, playing a major role in reward-motivated behavior (Schultz, 1998). There is substantial evidence that alcohol co-opts the ventral striatal dopamine system that normally responds to reward and novelty seeking behaviors. Alcohol also increases serotonin, which can have both excitatory and inhibitory effects, depending on the affected receptor type. Differing brain serotonin levels may distinguish between anxious and aggressive alcohol users. Other alcohol-related neurotransmitter effects are increased excitement and activity through noradrenaline (norepinephrine), analgesic and stress-reducing functions through endogenous opioids, and reduced anxiety and slowed movement through an increase in neurotransmitter γ-aminobutyric acid (GABA; inhibitory) or a decrease in glutamate (excitatory). Some scientists believe that the main neurotransmitter involved in the brain's reward system is dopamine (Bowirrat & Oscar-Berman, 2005). When dopamine is released in response to alcohol ingestion, it then interacts with its receptors, beginning a cascade in which other neurotransmitters, especially GABA, glutamate, and serotonin, are affected. Alcohol also has a direct influence on the release of GABA, glutamate, and serotonin. Alcohol's interaction with GABA receptors inhibits its release onto dopaminergic neurons. Glutamate increases dopamine release. Serotonin stimulates enkephalin release, which then inhibits GABA, which fine-tunes dopamine release. Alcohol-induced activation of the endogenous enkephalinergic system and the associated occupation of δ opioid receptors are hypothesized to result in the maintenance of continued alcohol drinking (Froehlich, Zweifel, Harts, Lumeng, & Li, 1991). Dopamine alone and in harmony with the other

transmitters creates a resultant cascade, giving rise to our conscious perception of the rewarding effects of alcohol. The numerous transmitters involved in alcohol's action explain its diverse effects and complex interactions with other prescribed and illicit drugs. Moreover, prolonged alcoholism can result in permanent alterations in neurotransmitter systems.

Vulnerable Brain Regions

Alcoholism can result in damage to the brain in numerous ways. In addition to the direct effects of alcohol on neurotransmitter systems and cortical functioning, the brain can suffer the indirect effects of alcohol-related damage to other organs, including the liver, pancreas, and heart (Klatsky, Koplik, Gunderson, Kipp, & Friedman, 2006; Stranges et al., 2004). For example, chronic alcohol abuse can decrease the expression levels of genes necessary for the brain's adaptive cellular response to insulin and insulin-like growth factor. Eventually, this could result in neurodegeneration similar to that caused by type 2 diabetes mellitus (de la Monte et al., 2008). Brain damage also can result from head trauma due to falls or other accidents occurring under the influence of alcohol. Additionally, poor dietary habits accompanying chronic intoxication can result in vitamin deficiencies and associated damage to the bodily tissues, including the nervous system (Oscar-Berman & Evert, 1997).

The type and extent of structural damage to brain tissues associated with excessive alcohol consumption traditionally were studied through postmortem examination of neuropathological specimens (Victor, Adams, & Collins, 1971). Recent technical advances in neuroimaging techniques, such as magnetic resonance imaging (MRI) and diffusion tensor imaging (DTI) allow us to search for the presence of these shifts in neurobiological function in vivo, in a rapid and noninvasive manner across large numbers of participants. Other recent technological advances are sensitive to measures of brain function (Hurley & Taber, 2008). These methodologies, including functional MRI (fMRI) and positron emission tomography (PET), have the ability to detect shifts in brain blood flow and metabolism. Whereas fMRI measures changes in blood oxygenation in the brain, PET measures emissions from radioactively labeled metabolically active chemicals that have been injected into the bloodstream. Methods such as fMRI and PET rely on hemodynamic changes in brain activity, an indirect correlate of neural activity. In general, hemodynamic brain scanning techniques are highly sensitive to localization of brain function. They can provide millimeter spatial sampling of brain regions and reliably probe the location of alcohol-induced brain changes. Moreover, these techniques can be instrumental in the development of pharmacological treatments that will target brain areas impacted during inebriation, and they will be helpful in charting the course of recovery of brain functioning with abstinence. However, although they have numerous advantages, hemodynamic brain scanning techniques are limited with respect to precise temporal characteristics of brain activity.

In contrast, electrophysiological measures, such as event-related brain potentials (ERP) and magnetoencephalography (MEG), have tight temporal resolution. Consisting of scalp recordings of neural events within milliseconds of their occurrence, these techniques are sensitive to the electrical activity generated by the firing of nerve impulses within the brain. ERP and MEG recordings can be used to delineate alcohol-induced abnormalities through the observation of distinct surface waveforms, which are hypothesized to represent specific neural processes. Consequently, they can indicate alterations in temporally overlapping stages of processing. However, unlike fMRI and PET, the loci of the underlying neural generators contributing to the surface activity cannot be inferred unambiguously through either ERP or MEG recordings.

Overall, when applied to alcoholics, the various procedures—whether they rely on neuropathology, neuroradiology, hemodynamic responses, or electrophysiological recordings—have provided consistent evidence of brain abnormalities associated with alcoholism. These abnormalities are reflected in the form of brain shrinkage (as evidenced by widening of the sulci on the brain's surface or enlargement of the ventricles deep inside the brain), as well as structural damage to axons and abnormal brain activation patterns or neurophysiological activity.

Regions of the brain that are most vulnerable to the widespread effects of alcoholism are the mesocorticolimbic reward circuit and the frontocerebellar system (Harris et al., 2008; Makris et al., 2008; Sullivan et al., 2003; Volkow, Wang, Tomasi, & Baler, 2013).

Reward Circuitry

The mesocorticolimbic circuit is a complex multifunctional network that supports responses to rewards and punishments, motivation, impulsivity, and inhibition. It consists of the amygdala, hippocampus, nucleus accumbens (ventral striatum), and ventral diencephalon (basal forebrain, ventral tegmentum, and hypothalamus), as well as cortical areas with modulating and oversight functions, such as dorsolateral-prefrontal, orbitofrontal, temporal pole, subcallosal, and cingulate cortices, parahippocampal gyri, and the insula. These key brain regions can be seen in Figures 9.1 and 9.2. It has been theorized that alcoholism might affect neurogenesis, the incorporation of newly formed neurons, into specific regions (He, Nixon, Shetty, & Crews, 2005). Several studies have demonstrated alcoholism-related structural brain anomalies, including atrophy and white-matter damage within aspects of this circuitry (Agartz, Momenam, Rawlings, Kerich, & Hommer, 1999; Chanraud et al., 2007; Schneider et al., 2001; Sullivan, Marsh, Mathalon, Lim, & Pfefferbaum, 1995; Szabo et al., 2004). Persistent waves of alcohol-induced neurochemical stimulation are hypothesized to co-opt the ventral striatal circuits that mediate reward while disrupting the frontoparietal aspects of cortex that support self-control and the willful regulation of craving and impulsive drug consumption (Kober et al., 2010; Volkow et al., 2013).

To explore alcoholism-related abnormalities of the reward circuit as an interconnected system, one study examined the morphometry of the reward network in its entirety (Makris et al., 2008). This study revealed significant reductions in total reward network volume in alcoholics compared to nonalcoholic controls. Specific reward regions affected were the right dorsolateral-prefrontal cortex, right anterior insula, right nucleus accumbens, and left amygdala. Larger volumes of nucleus accumbens and anterior insula in alcoholic subjects were associated with increasing length-of-abstinence, suggesting some potential recovery of structural deficits. Global brain and gray matter measures did not differ between groups, nor did cortical (frontal pole, cuneus cortex) or subcortical (dorsal striatum) control regions, indicating that the observed deficits were specific to the reward network.

A related study used DT-MRI to measure pathological changes in white matter tracts that are critical to connectivity among structures in the reward circuitry (Harris et al., 2008). Compared to nonalcoholic control subjects, alcoholic subjects had white matter microstructure deficits in several tracts connecting limbic system structures with the frontal lobes (i.e., superior longitudinal fascicles II and III, orbitofrontal cortex white matter, and the cingulum bundle).

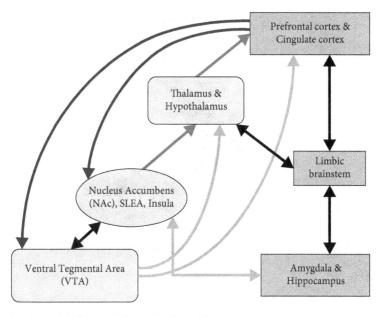

Figure 9.1. Brain regions involved in the extended reward and oversight system.

Prefrontal and cingulate regions connect to the nucleus accumbens (NAc) in the ventral striatum, the midbrain ventral tegmental area (VTA), and reciprocally with other limbic system structures (limbic brainstem, amygdala, and hippocampus). Limbic structures also interconnect with the NAc and to the basal forebrain (substantia innominata, or sublenticular extended amygdala: SLEA). The VTA projects to the NAc (reciprocally), to the thalamus and hypothalamus, and to prefrontal cortex. The NAc projects to the thalamus, which projects to prefrontal cortex.

Modeled after Figure 1 in Makris et al., 2008.

Studying groups of anatomical regions, which are components of structural circuits and functional networks (Fuster, 2008), is an important avenue in identifying biomarkers for a disease. This approach offers the potential to reduce the effects of diagnostic heterogeneity, identify new clinical subtypes, and accurately determine factors that lead to the development and continuation of maladaptive alcohol usage.

Frontocerebellar System

Frontocerebellar circuitry affected by alcoholism consists of a far-reaching neuronal network of brain structures and fiber tracts connecting portions of the frontal lobes with all of the other lobes of the brain, as well as with many subcortical structures and the cerebellum (Fuster, 2008; Sullivan et al., 2003). Information flows from the frontal cortex through the pons in the brainstem to the cerebellum, and from the cerebellum through the thalamus to frontal cortex. The posterior region of the frontal lobes controls motor functions, and the anterior region of the frontal lobes (prefrontal cortex) is hypothesized to serve a regulatory function within the brain (Goldberg, 2001; Lichter & Cummings, 2001).

Substance use disorders are characterized by deficits in the effortful regulation of impulsive responses

and cue-induced cravings (Chambers, Garavan, & Bellgrove, 2009; Dalley, Everitt, & Robbins, 2011; Everitt et al., 2008; Jentsch & Taylor, 1999; Kirby & Petry, 2004; Robinson & Berridge, 2003; Verdejo-García, Lawrence, & Clark, 2008; Volkow et al., 2013), whereas frontal and parietal aspects of cortex support the active resistance of temptation (Crockett et al., 2013; Kober et al., 2010). The shift from voluntary to habitual substance usage is reflected in a transition from cortical to striatal control of drug seeking/taking behaviors (Everitt & Robbins, 2005; Volkow et al., 2013) and decreased gray matter in frontoparietal regions associated with self-regulation (Ersche, Williams, Robbins, & Bullmore, 2013; Fein et al., 2002; Sullivan & Pfefferbaum, 2005).

Alcoholism-related damage to the frontal lobes has been repeatedly documented (Chanraud et al., 2007; Harris et al., 2008; Kubota et al., 2001; Oscar-Berman & Hutner, 1993; Ratti, Bo, Giardini, & Soragna, 2002). Postmortem studies of brain pathology have revealed decreased density of nearly a quarter of the neurons in the prefrontal cortex of alcoholics (Harper, 1998; Harper & Matsumoto, 2005). Structural MRI studies have confirmed frontal lobe volume loss in alcoholic subjects (Harris et al., 2008; Makris et al., 2008;

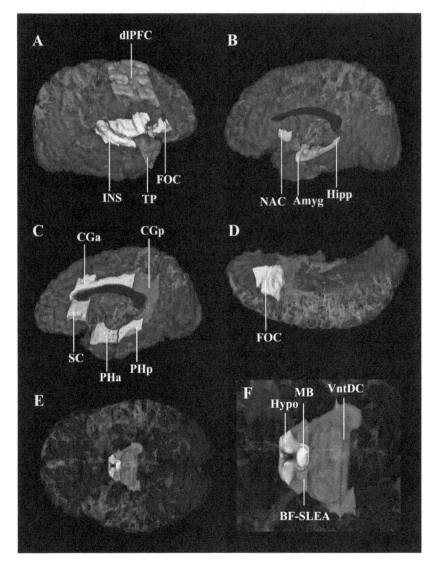

Figure 9.2. Three-dimensional representation of the cortical and subcortical structures composing the reward system in the human brain.

Image A shows a lateral view of the right hemisphere. Images B and C show a medial view of the right hemisphere; image D is an inferior view; images E and F are ventral views of both hemispheres showing the hypothalamus, mammillary bodies, sublenticular extended amygdala (SLEA), and ventral diencephalon. The latter structures are shown in image F in a zoomed view. Abbreviations: Amyg, amygdala; BF-SLEA, basal forebrain/sublenticular extended amygdala; CGa, anterior cingulate cortex; CGp, posterior cingulate gyrus; dlPFC, dorsolateral-prefrontal cortex; FOC, orbitofrontal cortex; Hipp, hippocampus; Hypo, hypothalamus; INS, insula; MB, mammillary body; NAC, nucleus accumbens area; PHa, anterior parahippocampal gyrus; PHp, posterior parahippocampal gyrus; SC, subcallosal cortex; TP, temporal pole; VDC, ventral diencephalon.

Modified from Makris et al., 2008.

Pfefferbaum, Sullivan, Mathalon, & Lim, 1997). Likewise, functional abnormalities of frontal brain systems have been identified with fMRI scans of abstinent alcoholics (Sullivan & Pfefferbaum, 2005; Tapert et al., 2001), as well as with PET scans measuring glucose metabolism during intoxication (Volkow et al., 1995). Frontal lobe blood flow and metabolism may serve as a precursor to the observed structural deficits, decreasing in alcoholics before

significant shrinkage or major cognitive problems become detectable (Nicolás et al., 1993; Wang et al., 1993).

Regions of the frontal lobes receive connections from the cerebellum (Schmahmann, 1997; 2000). Some of the connections are reciprocal and constitute cerebellar-prefrontal loops between the two structures. Other loops include basal ganglia structures and the thalamus. The various pathways contribute a different kind of feedback to the cortex for control of motor behavior, and the coordination of motor actions is hierarchically organized (Fuster, 2008). At the top of the hierarchy is prefrontal cortex, followed by premotor cortex, primary motor cortex, and then lower level structures, including parts of the spinal cord, pons, medulla, tectum, basal ganglia, and the cerebellum. The cerebellum, resting at the base of the brain, contains approximately half of the brain's neurons. It consists mainly of two large tightly folded lobes (joined at the middle by the vermis) and small flocculonodular lobes (flocculi). The cerebellum connects with the other brain structures through the cerebellar peduncles, located anteriorly. Atrophy of the cerebellum is commonly associated with alcoholism (Sullivan et al., 2003). White matter volume of the cerebellar vermis is significantly reduced, with vermian atrophy reported to occur in up to 40% of all alcoholics (Baker, Harding, Halliday, Kril, & Harper, 1999; Pentney, Mullan, Felong, & Dlugos, 2002).

The cerebellum coordinates movement of voluntary muscles, balance, and eye movements, and it is also believed to play a role in supporting cognitive and emotional processes (Buckner, 2013; Schmahmann, 1997; 2000). Damage to the cerebellum in alcoholics results in disruption of motor timing, postural stability, and coordination, as well as deficits consistent with the damage typically associated with frontal lobe lesions (i.e., attention shifting, cognitive planning, problem solving, word production, and verbal associative learning). Not surprisingly, frontocerebellar circuitry involves some of the same structures as those in the mesocorticolimbic reward circuit.

In the remainder of this chapter, the focus is on the cognitive and emotional impairments associated with alcoholism-related brain damage. Keep in mind that there are innumerable neuronal pathways connecting different areas of the brain with one another, including the regions implicated in alcohol-related neurological disease. In many instances, therefore, the consequences of damage to one structure or system can appear to be similar to the consequences of damage to another because of the vast and complexly interdigitated array of brain networks (Fuster, 2008). Additionally, some individuals with a long history of alcoholism can appear free from impairments in certain basic neuropsychological functions. This has led some researchers to hypothesize that the lack of detectable deficits in these individuals may reflect the compensatory recruitment of alternative brain regions, effectively masking the presence of cognitive impairments (Chanraud, Pitel, Muller-Oehring, Pfefferbaum, & Sullivan, 2013; Oscar-Berman & Marinković, 2007; Oscar-Berman et al., 2014). Accordingly, readers should note that at times it may be difficult to distinguish between functions that are spared in subpopulations of alcoholics and those that appear unimpaired due to the compensatory recruitment of other brain mechanisms.

Neurobehavioral Abnormalities in Alcoholism

Despite the complexity and multiplicity surrounding the neurological consequences of long-term chronic alcoholism, consistent patterns have emerged from the literature. Among the most readily observable deficits associated with alcoholism are cognitive changes (such as reduced visuospatial perceptual capabilities, memory loss, diminished ability to make plans and judgments, and increased rigidity in behavior) and emotional alterations (such as increased apathy and insensitivity to emotional cues; Clark, Oscar-Berman, Shagrin, & Pencina, 2007; Marczinski, Abroms, Van Selst, & Fillmore, 2005; Oscar-Berman et al., 2004; 2014; Sullivan & Pfefferbaum, 2005).

Traditionally, cognitive and emotional aspects of brain function were thought to be dissociable, with cognition occurring in cortical regions such as prefrontal cortex and dorsal aspects of cingulate gyrus, and emotion being generated in subcortical structures, including the amygdala and thalamus (Pessoa, 2008). It is important to note, however, that such a functional dissociation is no longer considered accurate. Instead, studies have shown that cognitive and emotional processes are tightly interwoven, acting together in a unified manner and jointly contributing to behavior (Northoff et al., 2000; 2004). Thus, it is likely that cognitive and emotional deficits are linked because alcoholism-related brain changes encompass widely distributed and partially overlapping brain networks.

Cognitive Impairments

One of the most severe neurological consequences of long-term alcoholism on mental functioning is alcoholic Korsakoff's syndrome (Oscar-Berman & Evert, 1997). This syndrome is marked by impairments in memory, in particular anterograde amnesia, the inability to remember new information for more than a few seconds. Other impairments, such as reduced visual perception and attention abilities, are present, but those difficulties are mild and not as obvious as the memory loss (Oscar-Berman & Evert, 1997). Despite the impairments, overall intelligence, as measured by standardized IQ tests, usually remains intact. This is because long-term memories formed prior to the onset of prolonged heavy drinking remain relatively preserved compared to recently acquired memories (Borsutzky, Fujiwara, Brand, & Markowitsch, 2008). Thus, general intelligence is spared because the types of information and abilities tapped by many IQ tests have been learned early in life (vocabulary, simple arithmetic, etc.). There is no single brain region affected by Korsakoff's disease, but areas that have been implicated in patients' severe memory loss are portions of the mesocorticolimbic reward circuit and the frontocerebellar system: the hippocampus and amygdala; parts of the diencephalon (e.g., the mammillary bodies of the hypothalamus, and the dorsomedial and anterior thalamic regions); the basal forebrain, located just in front of the diencephalon; prefrontal cortex; and the cerebellum (Fellgiebel, Scheurich, Siessmeier, Schmidt, & Bartenstein, 2003; Oscar-Berman, 2012; Reed et al., 2003).

Korsakoff's syndrome usually is preceded by a more acute, transient stage of neurological problems, which includes confusion, impairments of consciousness, difficulties moving eye muscles, and problems with gross muscle control (collectively referred to as Wernicke's encephalopathy); this stage usually disappears with abstinence and good nutrition. Other severe and permanent alcoholism-related conditions include alcohol-induced persisting dementia, Marchiafava-Bignami disease, and central pontine and extrapontine myelinolysis (nerve damage caused by the destruction of the myelin sheath of nerve cells; APA, 1994; Charness, 1993; Khaw & Heinrich, 2006; Martin, 2004; Sair et al., 2006; Staszewski, Macek, & Stepien, 2006). These disorders can have debilitating consequences for motor functioning, as well as for many mental functions in addition to memory (e.g., language, reasoning, and problem solving abilities), but these conditions are even more uncommon than Korsakoff's syndrome.

The once widely held view that alcoholics without evidence of Korsakoff's syndrome are cognitively intact has been abandoned in light of data revealing cognitive impairments and associated changes in brain structure in alcoholics lacking obvious clinical signs of anterograde amnesia (Oscar-Berman et al., 2004; Oscar-Berman & Marinković, 2007). Presently, clinical and experimental indications of neuropsychological dysfunction in alcoholic patients (with and without Korsakoff's syndrome) are known to include the cognitive domains of attention, perceptual processing, visuospatial abilities, learning, memory, and a variety of "executive functions" (Oscar-Berman & Marinković, 2007; Sullivan, 2000; Sullivan & Pfefferbaum, 2005). Thus, alcoholics can display limited attentional resources, process incoming information inefficiently, have difficulty dealing with objects in two- or three-dimensional space, learn slowly and remember poorly, and they may present with impaired judgment.

Compared to other alcoholism-related cognitive impairments, deficits in executive functions (which depend on many of our cognitive abilities, such as attention, perception, memory, and language) have eluded formal investigation until recently (Chanraud et al., 2007; Ratti et al., 2002; Royall et al., 2002; Sullivan & Pfefferbaum, 2005). Although theorists and researchers can differ in their definition of executive functions, most agree that they include self-awareness and other higher order cognitive processes, those aspects of cognition that allow us to be independent individuals with purpose and foresight about what we will do and how we will behave in response to changes in our environment. For example, executive abilities include judgment, abstraction, problem solving, decision making, planning, and social conduct. Adaptive executive functioning depends on the integrity of brain systems involving the frontal lobes (Fuster, 2008), as well as their connections within the mesocorticolimbic and the frontocerebellar systems (Chanraud et al., 2007; Sullivan & Pfefferbaum, 2005).

Deficits in executive function are associated with changes in personality and emotional abilities attributable to damage to the mesocorticolimbic and frontocerebellar circuits. In particular, frontoparietal aspects of cortex have been implicated in the presentation of disinhibitory personality traits. Disinhibition implies impulsivity and a lack of concern for the consequences of untoward behaviors (Miller & Cummings, 1999), and epidemiological and clinical studies have consistently found a strong association between alcoholism and lifetime history of antisocial personality traits and symptoms (Goldstein et al., 2007; Tragesser, Trull, Sher, & Park, 2008). Trait impulsivity covaries with striatal metabolism (Buckholtz et al., 2010) in the same regions co-opted by drugs of abuse (Robinson & Berridge, 1993; Schultz, 1998). Some aspects of frontoparietal cortex that support the inhibition of impulsive responses (Essex, Clinton, Wonderley, & Zald, 2012; Figner et al., 2010; Hare, Camerer, & Rangel, 2009) also support the active resistance of temptation and cue-induced craving (Crockett et al., 2013; Kober et al., 2010). Moreover, there is evidence of possible premorbid frontal abnormalities in individuals at risk for alcoholism, a subset of whom display impulsivity, rule breaking, insensitivity to reinforcement, poor response to social censure and punishment, and antisocial personality disorder (ASPD; Hesselbrock, 1991; Holdcraft, Iacono, & McGue, 1998; Pihl & Peterson, 1991). Accordingly, drug-induced striatal responses may be more likely to hijack behavior in individuals with decreased inhibitory control, leading them to prioritize and overvalue immediate goals (e.g., impulsive substance use; Bechara, 2005).

Compared to type I alcoholic personalities (late-onset, binge-drinkers; Cloninger, 1987), type II alcoholic personalities (early drinking onset, antisocial personality characteristics, and refractory to treatment) may be the most vulnerable to frontal system deficits (Laakso et al., 2002) as well as to emotional processing difficulties (Sperling et al., 2000). Functional and structural neuroimaging techniques have revealed frontal brain abnormalities in alcoholics and in individuals with ASPD (Oscar-Berman & Marinković, 2007; Raine, Buchsbaum, & LaCasse, 1997; Virkkunen et al., 1994). In the few studies that have specifically compared neurobehavioral functioning in alcoholics with and without ASPD (Ducci et al., 2007; Waldstein, Malloy, Stout, & Longabaugh, 1996), those with ASPD have evidenced greater impairments. Moreover, one study of alcoholics with and without antisocial personality symptoms found that alcoholism, duration of heavy drinking, and ASPD symptoms were significant predictors of frontal system dysfunction and negative affect (depression, anger, and tension; Oscar-Berman et al., 2009). Whether the presence of ASPD symptoms is a risk marker or a reflection of chronic alcoholism, both alcoholism (Oscar-Berman & Marinković, 2007; Ratti et al., 2002) and ASPD (Dolan & Park, 2002; Morgan & Lilienfeld, 2000) have been related to dysfunction of brain networks involving the frontal lobes.

Emotional Impairments

Alcoholics can present with impairments in a host of emotional processes including the accurate recognition of emotion in the prosody of other's speech and facial expressions (Kornreich et al., 2002; Maurage et al., 2009; Maurage, Campanella, Philippot, Martin, & de Timary, 2008; Oscar-Berman, Hancock, Mildworf, Hutner, & Weber, 1990; Philippot et al., 1999), as well as difficulties identifying, differentiating, and expressing their own emotional states (Maurage et al., 2011; Stasiewicz et al., 2012), a deficit that has been found to co-vary with the extent of alcohol use (Thorberg et al., 2011). It is generally agreed that alcohol can serve to regulate mood either by enhancing positive emotions or by making negative emotions more tolerable (Birch, Stewart, & Zack, 2006; Greeley & Oei, 1999; Sher, 1987; Sher & Grekin, 2007). Consistent with the possibility that some individuals may consume alcohol as an affect regulation strategy, alcoholics overestimate the intensity of emotional expressions (Philippot et al., 1999) and are particularly prone to misinterpreting negative facial expressions such as fear, anger, and sadness (Kornreich et al., 2013; Maurage et al., 2009; Oscar-Berman et al., 1990).

Emotional (Davis & Whalen, 2001; Devinsky et al., 1995; Milad & Quirk, 2012; Phelps & LeDoux, 2005) and social processes (Adolphs, 2001; Amodio & Frith, 2006; Phelps, 2006; Van Overwalle, 2009) reflect largely overlapping constructs, which are likely supported through a shared neural architecture. Dysregulated affect and impaired social cognition co-occur within healthy populations (Holmes et al., 2012). In line with evidence for emotional functioning deficits in alcoholics, researchers have observed impairments in the comprehension of conditional social rules as well as decreased emotional intelligence in this population (Kornreich et al., 2011). The emotional and social factors that contribute to alcohol consumption are a critical area for further study, particularly in the area of treatment response. Whereas abstinence associates with increased positive social relationships (Hibbert & Best, 2011), the presence of both negative affect and emotion regulation deficits are predictive of relapse (Berking et al., 2011; Witkiewitz & Marlatt, 2004).

Research on brain underpinnings of emotional functions has rapidly progressed following the development of neuroimaging techniques that allow for the disclosure of specific neural regions and brain systems that support the expression and regulation of emotional responses. Research in this area has demonstrated that the prefrontal cortex and the limbic system, including the hippocampus, amygdala, thalamus, hypothalamus, and cingulate gyrus, play an integral role in emotional and social, as well as cognitive functions (Adolphs, 2001; Amodio & Frith, 2006; Holmes et al., 2012; Marinković et al.,

2009; Phan, Wager, Taylor, & Liberzon, 2002; Phelps, 2006; Van Overwalle, 2009).

Emotional states can trigger thoughts about alcohol consumption and may initiate drinking behaviors (Birch et al., 2006). In attempting to understand cognitive-emotional interactions, it is important to consider the structural connectivity among the areas implicated in emotional and cognitive processes. For example, previous research suggests that brain regions such as the amygdala distribute information to the prefrontal cortex (Barbas, 2007; Swanson, 2003), and this relationship may emotionally bias judgment and decision making, leading to the over- or underestimation of risk (Bechara, 2003; Forgas, 1995; Loewenstein, Weber, Hsee, & Welch, 2001). Although nonalcoholic individuals typically display a strong response in the amygdala and hippocampus when viewing emotional expressions, alcoholics exhibit a blunted brain response (Marinković et al., 2009). In line with impairments in the recognition of facial expressions of fear, relative to healthy participants, alcoholics exhibit decreased activation in orbitofrontal and insular cortex when viewing emotional faces (O'Daly et al., 2012). In addition to these observed shifts in brain function, alcoholics also exhibit decreased brain volumes in prototypical emotional and social brain regions including aspects of orbitofrontal cortex, rostral anterior cingulate cortex, nucleus accumbens, amygdala, hippocampus, and insula (Makris et al., 2008; Wobrock et al., 2009).

Research findings from healthy adults, as well as from patients with brain lesions unrelated to alcoholism, have suggested that there is an asymmetry in the control of emotion regulation (Borod, 2000; Davidson, Scherer, & Goldsmith, 2003). The left cerebral hemisphere has been implicated in approach processes, demonstrating increased activation in the left caudate, putamen, superior temporal cortex, and dorsolateral prefrontal cortex in response to positively valenced emotional stimuli (Davidson & Irwin, 1999; Liberzon, Phan, Decker, & Taylor, 2003). Conversely, the right cerebral hemisphere is believed to be involved in withdrawal behavior, exhibiting potentiated activation to negative emotion in the right amygdala, hippocampus, caudate, and occipitotemporal gyrus (Hugdahl & Davidson, 2004; Wager, Phan, Liberzon, & Taylor, 2003). It is possible that deficient activation in the left hemispheric structures could underlie feelings of sadness or depression, whereas feelings of fear or anxiety could be associated with decreased activation in the right hemisphere.

Of interest, alcoholic individuals have difficulty on tasks resembling those on which patients with damage to the right hemisphere also encounter problems. In particular, patients with right hemisphere lesions, as well as alcoholics, show emotional abnormalities such as a diminished reaction to serious physical or psychological events, personal difficulties, or cognitive deficiencies (Gainotti, Caltagirone, & Zocolotti, 1993). Additionally, deficits in prosody (emotional intonations in speech) have been found in patients with right hemisphere frontal damage (Borod, 2000; Ross, 1984) and in alcoholics (Monnot, Lovallo, Nixon, & Ross, 2002), and deficits in recognition of emotional facial expressions have been linked to right hemisphere damage (Borod, 2000) and to alcoholism (Kornreich et al., 2001; Townshend & Duka, 2003).

Because of a similarity in deficits seen in alcoholics and patients with damage to the right hemisphere, it has been hypothesized that "right-brain" functions, including emotional functions, are more vulnerable to the effects of alcoholism than are left-brain functions (Oscar-Berman & Schendan, 2000). Studies of people with brain lesions have provided evidence that disruption of the integrity of the corpus callosum can contribute to right hemisphere functional deficits (Paul, Van Lancker-Sidtis, Schieffer, Dietrich, & Brown, 2003), and bilateral cortical atrophy can interfere with interhemispheric (cross-callosal) transfer efficiency (Brown & Sainsbury, 2000; Curran, Hills, Patterson, & Strauss, 2001). Diffusely distributed bilateral cortical atrophy and thinning of the corpus callosum might be interpreted as a selective right hemisphere functional deficit using conventional neuropsychological tests because right hemisphere functions may have less cortical representation than left hemisphere functions (possibly because left hemisphere functions are used more frequently) or bilateral damage could cause an interhemispheric collaboration dysfunction (e.g., excessive interhemispheric inhibition or a cross-callosal transfer dysfunction) that affects emotional functions more than linguistic functions.

To test these hypotheses, researchers examined the processing of visual information using redundant targets in alcoholics and healthy controls. Among the authors' predictions were (a) that interhemispheric parallel processing of information would be compromised in alcoholics relative to controls, (b) interhemispheric transfer time would be prolonged in alcoholics relative to controls, and (c) interhemispheric transfer time prolongation would be greater in older than younger subjects (Schulte, Sullivan, & Pfefferbaum, 2004). They observed that the effects of redundant targets were smaller in older alcoholics than in older subjects with or without history of alcoholism, suggesting reduced interhemispheric neural summation. Also, the level of performance was associated with callosal size in controls in contrast to alcoholics. A decrease in the size of the corpus callosum was related to prolonged interhemispheric transfer time, and thinning of the corpus callosum occurred in alcoholism and in old age.

Consistent with these findings are other reports of an interaction between alcoholism and aging for abnormalities of the corpus callosum (Pfefferbaum, Lim, Desmond, & Sullivan, 1996; Pfefferbaum, Rosenbloom, Serventi, & Sullivan, 2002). There also was an interaction observed between aging and alcoholism with regard to brain tissue volumes, with volume abnormalities greater in older than younger alcoholics relative to age norms. Finally, in vivo MRI (Pfefferbaum et al., 1996; Ruiz et al., 2013) and postmortem studies (Harper & Kril, 1988) have revealed significant callosal thinning in chronic alcoholics. In addition, in vivo studies based on DTI have shown compromise of callosal fiber coherence in alcoholic men (Pfefferbaum et al., 2000) and women (Pfefferbaum et al., 2002), the extent of which relates to the degree of attentional and working memory deficits. One might speculate that thinning of the corpus callosum may render alcoholics less able to inhibit negative affect in right hemisphere circuits.

In healthy populations, there are sex differences in the brain's hemodynamic responses to affective and social stimuli (Cahill, 2006; Koch et al., 2007; McRae et al., 2008; Thomas et al., 2001; but see, Wager et al., 2003). Wager and colleagues reported that although healthy control men exhibited more lateralized activation to emotional stimuli as compared to their female counterparts, there were no general differences in brain activation patterns (Wager et al., 2003). Additional studies examining gender differences in emotional processing demonstrated that men and women exhibit differences in amygdala activation when remembering negative or positive stimuli. However, the results of prior research in this area have not always been consistent. Research conducted by Canli and colleagues (Canli, Sivers, Whitfield, Gotlib, & Gabrieli, 2002) indicated that men display stronger right amygdala activation when remembering unpleasant pictures, whereas women activated the left amygdala more

strongly. In contrast, Wrase et al. (2003) found that although men and women activated the left amygdala to negative stimuli, only men activated the amygdala bilaterally to positive images. Although these findings reveal that women are more likely than men to use alcohol to cope with their emotions, they highlight the complex nature of the neural correlates of emotion regulation and demonstrate the need for more specific hypotheses regarding brain regions thought to underlie emotional responses (Brady & Randall, 1999; Gilman & Hommer, 2008). Furthermore, when presented with pictures of emotional stimuli, male alcoholics have shown blunted fMRI activation in regions implicated in the processing of emotional stimuli, including the middle frontal gyrus, anterior cingulate cortex, and amygdala (Marinković et al., 2009; Salloum et al., 2007). However, little is known about female alcoholics' neural responses to emotional stimuli.

Treatment and Recovery with Abstinence

Alcoholism can be difficult to treat, but when individuals are ready to change their behavior, there are a variety of treatment options (Maltzman, 2008; McCarthy, Edmundson, & Hartnett, 2006). These include medications, psychological therapies, and community-based services such as Alcoholics Anonymous. Although the neurological deficits that occur with excessive alcohol consumption are marked, research indicates that cognitive functions and motor coordination may improve at least partially within 3–4 weeks of abstinence, with the most notable improvement in short-term memory (Crews et al., 2005; Rosenbloom, Sullivan, & Pfefferbaum, 2003; Sullivan, Rosenbloom, Lim, & Pfefferbaum, 2000). Recovery is accompanied by at least partial reversal of brain shrinkage and metabolic functions in the frontal lobes and cerebellum (Bartsch et al., 2007; Crews et al., 2005; O'Neill, Cardenas, & Meyerhoff, 2001). However, the impact of abstinence on cognitive recovery is not straightforward, and research examining brain volumes in alcoholics compared to demographically matched healthy nonalcoholic controls has yielded inconsistent results.

Pfefferbaum and colleagues demonstrated that alcoholics showed an increase in cortical gray matter, sulcal, and lateral ventricular volumes early in abstinence (up to a month), as well as an improvement in third ventricular volume with continued abstinence (up to a year; Pfefferbaum et al., 1995). Yet another report noted baseline atrophy in abstinent alcoholics, which resolved following 8 months abstinence (Cardenas, Studholme, Gazdzinski, Durazzo, & Meyerhoff, 2007). Another study following alcoholics and controls over a 5-year period observed age-related changes in both groups (Pfefferbaum et al., 1995). However, within this sample, alcoholics showed a greater rate of gray matter volume loss than did controls, a result similar to the age-related brain changes observed in the current study. Makris and colleagues (Makris et al., 2008) observed both a negative correlation between cerebral cortex volume and years of heavy drinking and a positive correlation between length of abstinence and volume of cerebral cortex, nucleus accumbens, and anterior insula, thereby confirming both the deleterious cerebral effects of chronic alcoholism and the potential for improvement in brain structural deficits with abstinence.

Given these mixed findings, it is likely that the extent of recovery is obscured by patient characteristics such as age, sex, years of heavy drinking, motivation to change, and length of abstinence (Forsberg & Goldman, 1985; Le Berre et al., 2012; Pfefferbaum et al., 2002). For instance, there is evidence to suggest that the anatomical correlates of both alcoholism and abstinence can vary as a function of both the quantity of alcohol consumed as well as the sex of the individual in question (Ruiz et al., 2013). This is an area that warrants further study since the identification of behavioral, demographical, and psychological characteristics impacting the time course of recovery could facilitate the development of individually tailored rehabilitation plans, thereby increasing treatment efficacy.

Conclusion and Future Directions

Alcoholism can arise through heterogeneous origins, with symptom severity and illness course depending on variables such as family history, age, gender, and mental or physical health. Substantial demographic and contextual variability across populations and research studies can obscure the identification of discrete brain systems associated with pathological alcohol use. Additionally, the use of group, rather than dimensional analyses, and a reliance on small samples contribute to a number of inferential problems in studying substance use disorders. However, much progress has been made, and the evidence for impairments of neurobiological and neurobehavioral functions following years of chronic alcoholism is unequivocal.

For future research, there are important unanswered questions about the location and extent of damage that can be approached using a variety of neuroimaging and neurobehavioral methods. For example, multimodal imaging and analysis techniques can help to integrate results among structural MRI, DTI, and fMRI, which would then be linked to drinking histories and neuropsychological performance. The resulting confluence of data can provide evidence that informs hypotheses about neural structures and networks that are responsible for alcoholism-related abnormalities. Other refinements would follow for characterizing the time course and nature of recovery of function and for the contribution of individual differences associated with variables such as age, gender, and family history.

In sum, to advance our understanding of the links between (a) variability in brain function with (b) the risk for, consequences of, and recovery from chronic alcohol use, we must increase our knowledge of individual differences and the size of our samples while leveraging a variety of scientific methodologies and clinical settings. Additionally, through the use of high-throughput longitudinal studies and multiple neuroimaging methods, future research will help to improve our understanding of the relations between the extent of alcohol use and individual variability in neurobehavioral, cognitive, and emotional functions, as well as the degree to which abstinence and treatment could facilitate the reversal of brain atrophy and dysfunction. Ultimately, this will provide us with treatment and prevention strategies that can be tailored to the needs of individual patients.

Acknowledgments

The writing of this chapter was supported by funds from National Institute on Alcohol Abuse and Alcoholism grants R01–AA07112 and K05–AA00219, and by the Medical Research Service of the US Department of Veterans Affairs.

References

Abel, E. L., Kruger, M. L., & Friedl, J. (1999). How do physicians define "light," "moderate," and "heavy" drinking? *Alcoholism: Clinical and Experimental Research, 22*(5), 979–984.

Adolphs, R. (2001). The neurobiology of social cognition. *Current Opinion in Neurobiology, 11*(2), 231–239.

Agartz, I., Momenam, R., Rawlings, R. R., Kerich, M. J., & Hommer D. W. (1999). Hippocampal volume in patients with alcohol dependence. *Archives of General Psychiatry, 56*(4), 356–363.

American Psychiatric Association. (1994). Diagnostic and statistical manual of mental disorders (DSM-IV). Washington, DC: Author.

American Psychiatric Association. (2013). Diagnostic and statistical manual of mental disorders (5th ed.). Arlington, VA: Author.

Amodio, D. M., & Frith, C. D. (2006). Meeting of minds: The medial frontal cortex and social cognition. *Nature Reviews Neuroscience*, *7*(4), 268–277.

Baker, K. G., Harding, A. J., Halliday, G. M., Kril, J. J., & Harper, C. G. (1999). Neuronal loss in functional zones of the cerebellum of chronic alcoholics with and without Wernicke's encephalopathy. *Neuroscience*, *19*(2), 429–438.

Barbas, H. (2007). Flow of information for emotions through temporal and orbitofrontal pathways. *Journal of Anatomy*, *211*(2), 237–249.

Bartsch, A. J., Homola, G., Biller, A., Smith, S. M., Weijers, H. G., Wiesbeck, G. A., et al. (2007). Manifestations of early brain recovery associated with abstinence from alcoholism. *Brain*, *130*, 36–47.

Bechara, A. (2003). Risky business: Emotion, decision-making, and addiction. *Journal of Gambling Studies*, *19*, 23–51.

Bechara, A. (2005). Decision making, impulse control and loss of willpower to resist drugs: A neurocognitive perspective. *Nature Neuroscience*, *8*(11), 1458–1463.

Berking, M., Margraf, M., Ebert, D., Wupperman, P., Hofmann, S. G., Junghanns, K. (2011). Deficits in emotion-regulation skills predict alcohol use during and after cognitive-behavioral therapy for alcohol dependence. *Journal of Consulting and Clinical Psychology*, *79*(3), 307–318.

Birch, C. D., Stewart, S. H., & Zack, M. (2006). Emotion and motive effects on drug-related cognition. In R. W. Wiers & A. W. Stacy (Eds.), *Handbook of implicit cognition and addiction* (pp. 267–280). Thousand Oaks, CA: Sage.

Borod, J. C. (2000). *The neuropsychology of emotion*. New York: Oxford University Press.

Borsutzky, S., Fujiwara, E., Brand, M., & Markowitsch, H. J. (2008). Confabulations in alcoholic Korsakoff patients. *Neuropsychologia*, *46*(13), 3133–3143.

Bowirrat, A., & Oscar-Berman, M. (2005). Relationship between dopaminergic neurotransmission, alcoholism, and Reward Deficiency syndrome. *American Journal of Medical Genetics. Part B, Neuropsychiatric Genetics*, *132B*(1), 29–37.

Brady, K. T., & Randall, C. L. (1999). Gender differences in substance use disorders. *Psychiatric Clinics of North America*, *22*(2), 241–252.

Brown, L. N., & Sainsbury, R. S. (2000). Hemispheric equivalence and age-related differences in judgments of simultaneity to somatosensory stimuli. *Neuropsychology, Development, and Cognition. Section A, Journal of Clinical and Experimental Neuropsychology 22*(5), 587–598.

Buckholtz, J. W., Treadway, M. T., Cowan, R. L., Woodward, N. D., Li, R. A., Ansari, M. S., et al. (2010). Dopaminergic network differences in human impulsivity. *Science*, *329*(5991), 532.

Buckner, R. L. (2013). The cerebellum and cognitive function: 25 years of insight from anatomy and neuroimaging. *Neuron*, *80*(3), 807–815.

Cahill, L. (2006). Why sex matters for neuroscience. *Nature Reviews Neuroscience*, *7*(6), 477–484.

Canli, T., Sivers, H., Whitfield, S. L., Gotlib, I. H., & Gabrieli, J. D. (2002). Amygdala response to happy faces as a function of extraversion. *Science*, *296*(5576), 2191.

Cardenas, V. A., Studholme, C., Gazdzinski, S., Durazzo, T. C., & Meyerhoff, D. J. (2007). Deformation–based morphometry of brain changes in alcohol dependence and abstinence. *Neuroimage*, *34*(3), 879–887.

Chambers, C. D., Garavan, H., & Bellgrove, M. A. (2009). Insights into the neural basis of response inhibition from cognitive and clinical neuroscience. *Neuroscience & Biobehavioral Reviews*, *33*(5), 631–646.

Chanraud, S., Martelli, C., Delain, F., Kostogianni, N., Douaud, G., Aubin, H. J., et al. (2007). Brain morphometry and cognitive performance in detoxified alcohol-dependents with preserved psychosocial functioning. *Neuropsychopharmacology*, *32*(2), 429–438.

Chanraud, S., Pitel, A. L., Muller-Oehring, E. M., Pfefferbaum, A., & Sullivan, E. V. (2013). Remapping the brain to compensate for impairment in recovering alcoholics. *Cerebral Cortex*, *23*(1), 97–104.

Charness, M. E. (1993). Brain lesions in alcoholics. *Alcoholism: Clinical and Experimental Research*, *17*(1), 2–11.

Clark, U. S., Oscar-Berman, M., Shagrin, B., & Pencina, M. (2007). Alcoholism and judgments of affective stimuli. *Neuropsychology*, *21*(3), 346–362.

Cloninger, C. R. (1987). Neurogenetic adaptive mechanisms in alcoholism. *Science*, *236*(4800), 410–416.

Crews, F. T., Buckley, T., Dodd, P. R., Ende, G., Foley, N., Harper, C., et al. (2005). Alcoholic neurobiology: Changes in dependence and recovery. *Alcoholism: Clinical and Experimental Research*, *29*(8), 1504–1513.

Crockett, M. J., Braams, B. R., Clark, L., Tobler, P. N., Robbins, T. W., & Kalenscher, T. (2013). Restricting temptations: Neural mechanisms of precommitment. *Neuron*, *79*(2), 391–401.

Curran, T., Hills, A., Patterson, M. B., & Strauss, M. E. (2001). Effects of aging on visuospatial attention: An ERP study. *Neuropsychologia*, *39*, 288–301.

Dalley, J. W., Everitt, B. J., & Robbins, T. W. (2011). Impulsivity, compulsivity, and top-down cognitive control. *Neuron*, *69*(4), 680–694.

Davidson, R. J., & Irwin, W. (1999). The functional neuroanatomy of emotion and affective style. *Trends in Cognitive Science*, *3*(1), 11–21.

Davidson, R. J., Scherer, K. R., & Goldsmith, H. H. (Eds.). (2003). *Handbook of affective sciences*. New York: Oxford University Press.

Davis, M., & Whalen, P. J. (2001). The amygdala: Vigilance and emotion. *Molecular Psychiatry*, *6*(1), 13–34.

Dawson, D. A., Grant, B. F., Stinson, F. S., & Zhou, Y. (2005). Effectiveness of the derived Alcohol Use Disorders Identification Test (AUDIT-C) in screening for alcohol use disorders and risk drinking in the US general population. *Alcoholism: Clinical and Experimental Research*, *29*(5), 844–854.

de la Monte, S. M., Tong, M., Cohen, A. C., Sheedy, D., Harper, C., & Wands, J. R. (2008). Insulin and insulin-like growth factor resistance in alcoholic neurodegeneration. *Alcoholism: Clinical and Experimental Research*, *32*(9), 1630–1644.

Devinsky, O., Morrell, M. J., & Vogt, B. A. (1995). Contributions of anterior cingulate cortex to behaviour. *Brain*, *118* (Pt. 1), 279–306.

Di Sclafani, V., Finn, P., & Fein, G. (2007). Psychiatric comorbidity in long-term abstinent alcoholic individuals. *Alcoholism: Clinical and Experimental Research*, *31*(5), 795–803.

Dolan, M., & Park, I. (2002). The neuropsychology of antisocial personality disorder. *Psychological Medicine*, *32*(3), 417–427.

Ducci, F., Enoch, M. A., Funt, S., Virkkunen, M., Albaugh, B., & Goldman, D. (2007). Increased anxiety and other similarities in temperament of alcoholics with and without antisocial personality disorder across three diverse populations. *Alcohol*, *41*(1), 3–12.

Eckardt, M. J., File, S. E., Gessa, G. L., Grant, K. A., Guerri, C., Foffman, P. L., et al. (1998). Effects of moderate alcohol consumption on the central nervous system. *Alcoholism: Clinical and Experimental Research*, *22*, 998–1040.

Ely, M., Hardy, R., Longford, N. T., & Wadsworth, M. E. (1999). Gender differences in the relationship between alcohol consumption and drink problems are largely accounted for by body water. *Alcohol and Alcoholism*, *34*(6), 894–902.

Ersche, K. D., Williams, G. B., Robbins, T. W., & Bullmore, E. T. (2013). Meta-analysis of structural brain abnormalities associated with stimulant drug dependence and neuroimaging of addiction vulnerability and resilience. *Current Opinion in Neurobiology*, *23*(4), 615–624.

Essex, B. G., Clinton, S. A., Wonderley, L. R., & Zald, D. H. (2012). The impact of the posterior parietal and dorsolateral prefrontal cortices on the optimization of long-term versus immediate value. *Journal of Neuroscience*, *32*(44), 15403–15413.

Everitt, B. J., Belin, D., Economidou, D., Pelloux, Y., Dalley, J. W., & Robbins, T. W. (2008). Neural mechanisms underlying the vulnerability to develop compulsive drug-seeking habits and addiction. *Philosophical Transactions: Biological Sciences*, *363*(1507), 3125–3135.

Everitt, B. J., & Robbins, T. W. (2005). Neural systems of reinforcement for drug addiction: From actions to habits to compulsion. *Nature Neuroscience*, *8*(11), 1481–1489.

Fein, G., Di Sclafani, V., Cardenas, V. A., Goldmann, H., Tolou-Shams, M., & Meyerhoff, D. J. (2002). Cortical gray matter loss in treatment-naïve alcohol dependent individuals. *Alcoholism: Clinical and Experimental Research*, *26*(4), 558–564.

Fellgiebel, A., Scheurich, A., Siessmeier, T., Schmidt, L. G., & Bartenstein, P. (2003). Persistence of disturbed thalamic glucose metabolism in a case of Wernicke-Korsakoff syndrome. *Psychiatry Research*, *124*(2), 105–112.

Figner, B., Knoch, D., Johnson, E. J., Krosch, A. R., Lisanby, S. H., Fehr, E., & Weber, E. U. (2010). Lateral prefrontal cortex and self-control in intertemporal choice. *Nature Neuroscience*, *13*(5), 538–539.

Forgas, J. P. (1995). Mood and judgment: The affect infusion model (AIM). *Psychological Bulletin*, *117*(1), 39–66.

Forsberg, L. K., & Goldman, M. S. (1985). Experience-dependent cognitive recovery of visuospatial functioning in older alcoholic persons. *Journal of Abnormal Psychology*, *94*(4), 519–529.

Froehlich, J. C., Zweifel, M., Harts, J., Lumeng, L., & Li, T. K. (1991). Importance of delta opioid receptors in maintaining high alcohol drinking. *Psychopharmacology (Berl)*, *103*(4), 467–472.

Fuster, J. M. (2008). *The prefrontal cortex* (4th ed.). New York: Academic Press.

Gainotti, G., Caltagirone, C., & Zocolotti, P. (1993). Left/right and cortical/subcortical dichotomies in the neuropsychological study of human emotions. *Cognition and Emotion*, *7*, 71–93.

Gilman, J. M., & Hommer D. W. (2008). Modulation of brain response to emotional images by alcohol cues in alcohol-dependent patients. *Addiction Biology*, *13*(3–4), 423–434.

Gmel, G., & Rehm, J. (2003). Harmful alcohol use. *Alcohol Research & Health*, *27*(1), 52–62.

Goldberg, E. (2001). *The executive brain: Frontal lobes and the civilized mind.* New York: Oxford University Press.

Goldstein, R. B., Dawson, D. A., Saha, T. D., Ruan, W. J., Compton, W. M., & Grant, B. F. (2007). Antisocial behavioral syndromes and DSM-IV alcohol use disorders: Results from the National Epidemiologic Survey on Alcohol and Related Conditions. *Alcoholism Clinical and Experimental Research*, *31*(5), 814–828.

Greeley, J., & Oei, T. (1999). Alcohol and tension reduction. In K. E. Leonard & H. T. Blane (Eds.), *Psychological theories of drinking and alcoholism* (2nd ed., pp. 14–53). New York: Guilford.

Hare, T. A, Camerer, C. F., & Rangel, A. (2009). Self-control in decision-making involves modulation of the vmPFC valuation system. *Science*, *324*(5927), 646–648.

Harper, C. G. (1998). The neuropathology of alcohol-specific brain damage, or does alcohol damage the brain? *Journal of Neuropathology and Experimental Neurology*, *57*(2), 101–110.

Harper, C. G., & Kril, J. J. (1988). Corpus callosal thickness in alcoholics. *Addiction*, *83*(5), 577–580.

Harper, C. G., & Matsumoto, I. (2005). Ethanol and brain damage. *Current Opinion in Pharmacology*, *5*, 73–78.

Harris, G. J., Jaffin, S. K., Hodge, S. M., Kennedy, D., Caviness, V. S., Marinković, K., et al. (2008). Frontal white matter and cingulum diffusion tensor imaging deficits in alcoholism. *Alcoholism: Clinical and Experimental Research*, *32*(6), 1001–1013.

He, J., Nixon, K., Shetty, A. K., & Crews, F. T. (2005). Chronic alcohol exposure reduces hippocampal neurogenesis and dendritic growth of newborn neurons. *European Journal of Neuroscience*, *21*(10), 2711–2720.

Helzer, J. E., Bucholz, K. K., Bierut, L. J., Regier, D. A., Schuckit, M. A., & Guth, S. E. (2006). Should DSM-V include dimensional diagnostic criteria for alcohol use disorders? *Alcoholism: Clinical and Experimental Research*, *30*(2), 303–310.

Hesselbrock, M. N. (1991). Gender comparison of antisocial personality disorder and depression in alcoholism. *Journal of Substance Abuse*, *3*(2), 205–219.

Hibbert, L. J., & Best, D. W. (2011). Assessing recovery and functioning in former problem drinkers at different stages of their recovery journeys. *Drug and Alcohol Review*, *30*(1), 12–20.

Holdcraft, L. C., Iacono, W. G., & McGue, M. K. (1998). Antisocial personality disorder and depression in relation to alcoholism: A community-based sample. *Journal of Studies on Alcohol*, *59*(2), 222–226.

Holmes, A. J., Lee, P. H., Hollinshead, M. O., Bakst, L., Roffman, J. L., Smoller, J. W., & Buckner, R. L. (2012). Individual differences in amygdala-medial prefrontal anatomy link negative affect, impaired social functioning, and polygenic depression risk. *Journal of Neuroscience*, *32*(50), 18087–18100.

Hugdahl, K. L., & Davidson, R. J. (Eds.). (2004). *The asymmetrical brain.* Cambridge, MA: MIT.

Hurley, R. A., & Taber, K. H. (2008). *Windows to the brain: Insights from neuroimaging* (1st ed.). New York: American Psychiatric Publishing.

Jentsch, J. D., & Taylor, J. R. (1999). Impulsivity resulting from frontostriatal dysfunction in drug abuse: Implications for the control of behavior by reward-related stimuli. *Psychopharmacology*, *146*(4), 373–390.

Khaw, A. V., & Heinrich, A. (2006). Marchiafava-Bignami disease: Diffusion-weighted MRI in corpus callosum and cortical lesions. *Neurology*, *66*(8), 1286.

Kirby, K. N., & Petry, N. M. (2004). Heroin and cocaine abusers have higher discount rates for delayed rewards than alcoholics or non-drug-using controls. *Addiction*, *99*(4), 461–471.

Klatsky, A. L., Koplik, S., Gunderson, E., Kipp, H., & Friedman, G. D. (2006). Sequelae of systemic hypertension in alcohol abstainers, light drinkers, and heavy drinkers. *American Journal of Cardiology*, *98*, 1063–1068.

Kober, H., Mende-Siedlecki P., Kross, E. F., Weber, J., Mischel, W., Hart, C. L., & Ochsner K. N. (2010). Prefrontal-striatal pathway underlies cognitive regulation of craving. *Proceedings of the National Academy of Sciences*, *107*(33), 14811–14816.

Koch, K., Pauly, K., Kellermann, T., Seiferth, N. Y., Reske, M., Backes, V., et al. (2007). Gender differences in the cognitive control of emotion: An fMRI study. *Neuropsychologia*, *45*(12), 2744–2754.

Kornreich, C., Blairy, S., Philippot, P., Hess, U., Noel, X., Streel, E., et al. (2001). Deficits in recognition of emotional facial expression are still present in alcoholics after mid-to long-term abstinence. *Journal of Studies on Alcohol*, *62*(4), 533–542.

Kornreich, C., Brevers, D., Canivet, D., Ermer, E., Naranjo, C., Constant, E., et al. (2013). Impaired processing of emotion in music, faces and voices supports a generalized emotional decoding deficit in alcoholism. *Addiction*, *108*(1), 80–88.

Kornreich, C., Delle-Vigne, D., Knittel, J., Nerincx, A., Campanella, S., Noel, X., et al. (2011). Impaired conditional reasoning in alcoholics: A negative impact on social interactions and risky behaviors? *Addiction*, *106*(5), 951–959.

Kornreich, C., Philippot, P., Foisy, M. L., Blairy, S., Raynaud, E., Dan, B., et al. (2002). Impaired emotional facial expression recognition is associated with interpersonal problems in alcoholism. *Alcohol and Alcoholism*, *37*(4), 394–400.

Kubota, M., Nakazaki, S., Hirai, S., Saeki, N., Yamaura, A., & Kusaka, T. (2001). Alcohol consumption and frontal lobe shrinkage: Study of 1432 non-alcoholic subjects. *Journal of Neurology, Neurosurgery, and Psychiatry*, *71*(1), 104–106.

Laakso, M. P., Gunning-Dixon, F., Vaurio, O., Repo-Tiihonen, E., Soininen, H., & Tiihonen, J. (2002). Prefrontal volumes in habitually violent subjects with antisocial personality disorder and type 2 alcoholism. *Psychiatry Research*, *114*(2), 95–102.

Le Berre, A. P., Vabret, F., Cauvin, C., Pinon, K., Allain, P., Pitel, A.-L., Eustache, F., & Beaunieux, H. (2012). Cognitive barriers to readiness to change in alcohol-dependent patients. *Alcoholism: Clinical and Experimental Research*, *36*(9), 1542–1549.

Liberzon I., Phan, K. L., Decker, L. R., & Taylor, S. F. (2003). Extended amygdala and emotional salience: A PET activation study of positive and negative affect. *Neuropsychopharmacology*, *28*(4), 726–733.

Lichter, D. G., & Cummings, J. L. (Eds.). (2001). *Frontal-subcortical circuits in psychiatric and neurological disorders*. New York: Guilford.

Loewenstein, G. F., Weber, E. U., Hsee, C. K., & Welch N. (2001). Risk as feelings. *Psychological Bulletin*, *127*(2), 267–286.

Makris, N., Oscar-Berman, M., Jaffin, S. K., Hodge, S. M., Kennedy, D. N., Caviness, V. S., et al. (2008). Decreased volume of the brain reward system in alcoholism. *Biological Psychiatry*, *64*(3), 192–202.

Maltzman, I. (2008). Alcoholism: Its treatments and mistreatments. Hackensack, NJ: World Scientific Publishing.

Marczinski, C. A., Abroms, B. D., Van Selst, M., & Fillmore, M. T. (2005). Alcohol-induced impairment of behavioral control: Differential effects on engaging vs. disengaging responses. *Psychopharmacology (Berlin)*, *182*(3), 452–459.

Marinković, K., Oscar-Berman, M., Urban, T., O'Reilly, C. E., Howard, J. A., Sawyer, K., & Harris, G. J. (2009). Alcoholism and dampened temporal limbic activation to emotional faces. *Alcoholism: Clinical and Experimental Research*, *33*(11), 1880–1892.

Martin, R. J. (2004). Central pontine and extrapontine myelinolysis: The osmotic demyelination syndromes. *Journal of Neurology, Neurosurgery, and Psychiatry* *75*(Suppl.), iii22–iii28.

Maurage, P., Campanella, S., Philippot, P., Charest, I., Martin, S., & de Timary, P. (2009). Impaired emotional facial expression decoding in alcoholism is also present for emotional prosody and body postures. *Alcohol and Alcoholism*, *44*(5), 476–485.

Maurage, P., Campanella, S., Philippot, P., Martin, S., & de Timary, P. (2008). Face processing in chronic alcoholism: A specific deficit for emotional features. *Alcoholism: Clinical and Experimental Research*, *32*(4), 600–606.

Maurage, P., Grynberg, D., Noel, X., Joassin, F., Philippot, P., Hanak, C., et al. (2011). Dissociation between affective and cognitive empathy in alcoholism: A specific deficit for the emotional dimension. *Alcoholism-Clinical and Experimental Research*, *35*(9), 1662–1668.

McCarthy, D., Edmundson, E., & Hartnett, T. (2006). Charting a path between research and practice in alcoholism treatment. *Alcohol Research & Health*, *29*(1), 5–10.

McRae, K., Ochsner, K. N, Mauss, I. B, Gabrieli, J. D., & Gross, J. J. (2008). Gender differences in emotion regulation: An fMRI study of cognitive reappraisal. *Group Processes & Intergroup Relations*, *11*(2), 143–162.

Milad, M. R., & Quirk, G. J. (2012). Fear extinction as a model for translational neuroscience: Ten years of progress. *Annual Review of Psychology*, *63*(1), 129–151.

Miller, B. L., & Cummings, J. L. (1999). *The human frontal lobes: Functions and disorders*. New York: Guilford.

Monnot, M., Lovallo, W. R., Nixon, S. J., & Ross, E. (2002). Neurological basis of deficits in affective prosody comprehension among alcoholics and fetal alcohol-exposed adults. *Journal of Neuropsychiatry and Clinical Neuroscience*, *14*(3), 321–328.

Morgan, A. B., Lilienfeld, S. O. (2000). A meta-analytic review of the relation between antisocial behavior and neuropsychological measures of executive function. *Clinical Psychological Review*, *20*(1), 113–136.

Nicolás, J. M., Catafau, A. M., Estruch, R., Lomeña, F. J., Salamero, M., Herranz, R., et al. (1993). Regional cerebral blood flow-SPECT in chronic alcoholism: Relation to neuropsychological testing. *Journal of Nuclear Medicine*, *34*(9), 1452–1459.

Northoff, G., Heinzel, A., Bermpohl, F., Niese, R., Pfennig, A., Pascual-Leone, A., & Schlaug, G. (2004). Reciprocal modulation and attenuation in the prefrontal cortex: An fMRI study on emotional-cognitive interaction. *Human Brain Mapping*, *21*(3), 202–212.

Northoff, G., Richter, A., Gessner, M., Schlagenhauf, F., Fell, J., Baumgart, F., et al. (2000). Functional dissociation between medial and lateral prefrontal cortical spatiotemporal activation in negative and positive emotions: A combined fMRI/MEG study. *Cerebral Cortex*, 10(1), 93–107.

O'Daly, O. G., Trick, L., Scaife, J., Marshall, J., Ball, D., Phillips, M. L., et al. (2012). Withdrawal-associated increases and decreases in functional neural connectivity associated with altered emotional regulation in alcoholism. *Neuropsychopharmacology*, 37(10), 2267–2276.

O'Neill, J., Cardenas, V. A., & Meyerhoff, D. J. (2001). Effects of abstinence on the brain: Quantitative magnetic resonance imaging and magnetic resonance spectroscopic imaging in chronic alcohol abuse. *Alcoholism: Clinical and Experimental Research*, 25(11), 1673–1682.

Oscar-Berman, M. (2012). Function and dysfunction of prefrontal brain circuitry in alcoholic Korsakoff's syndrome. *Neuropsychology Review*, 22(2), 154–169.

Oscar-Berman, M., & Evert, D. L. (1997). Alcoholic Korsakoff's syndrome. In P. D. Nussbaum (Ed.), *Handbook of neuropsychology and aging* (pp. 201–215). New York: Plenum.

Oscar-Berman, M., Hancock, M., Mildworf, B., Hutner, N., & Weber, D. A. (1990). Emotional perception and memory in alcoholism and aging. *Alcoholism: Clinical and Experimental Research*, 14(3), 383–393.

Oscar-Berman, M., & Hutner, N. (1993). Frontal lobe changes after chronic alcohol ingestion. In W. A. Hunt & S. J. Nixon (Eds.), *Alcohol-induced brain damage* (Vol. Monograph No. 22, pp. 121–156). Rockville, MD: NIAAA.

Oscar-Berman, M., Kirkley, S. M., Gansler, D. A., Couture, A. (2004). Comparisons of Korsakoff and non-Korsakoff alcoholics on neuropsychological tests of prefrontal brain functioning. *Alcoholism: Clinical and Experimental Research*, 28(4), 667–675.

Oscar-Berman, M., & Marinković, K. (2007). Alcohol: Effects on neurobehavioral functions and the brain. *Neuropsychology Review*, 17(3), 239–257.

Oscar-Berman, M., & Schendan, H. E. (2000). Asymmetries of brain function in alcoholism: Relationship to aging. In L. Obler & L. T. Connor (Eds.), *Neurobehavior of language and cognition: Studies of normal aging and brain damage* (pp. 213–240). New York: Kluwer Academic.

Oscar-Berman, M., Valmas, M. M., Sawyer, K. S., Kirkley, S. M., Gansler, D. A., Merritt, D., Couture, A. (2009). Frontal brain dysfunction in alcoholism with and without antisocial personality disorder. *Neuropsychiatric Disease and Treatment*, 5, 309–326.

Oscar-Berman, M., Valmas, M., Sawyer, K. S., Ruiz, S. M., Luhar, R., & Gravitz, Z. (2014). Profiles of impaired, spared, and recovered neuropsychological processes in alcoholism. In A. Pfefferbaum & E. V. Sullivan (Eds.), *Handbook of clinical neurology: Alcohol and the nervous system*. Edinburgh: Elsevier.

Paul, L. K., Van Lancker-Sidtis, D., Schieffer, B., Dietrich, R., & Brown, W. S. (2003). Communicative deficits in agenesis of the corpus callosum: Nonliteral language and affective prosody. *Brain and Language*, 85(2), 313–324.

Pentney, R. J., Mullan, B. A., Felong, A. M., & Dlugos, C. A. (2002). The total numbers of cerebellar granule neurons in young and aged Fischer 344 and Wistar-Kyoto rats do not change as a result of lengthy ethanol treatment. *Cerebellum*, 1(1), 79–89.

Pessoa, L. (2008). On the relationship between emotion and cognition. *Nature Reviews Neuroscience*, 9(2), 148–158.

Petrakis, I. L., Gonzalez, G., Rosenheck, R., & Krystal, J. H. (2002). Comorbidity of alcoholism and psychiatric disorders. *Alcohol Research & Health*, 26(1), 81–89.

Pfefferbaum, A., Lim, K. O., Desmond, J. E., & Sullivan, E. V. (1996). Thinning of the corpus callosum in older alcoholic men: A magnetic resonance imaging study. *Alcoholism: Clinical and Experimental Research*, 20(4), 752–757.

Pfefferbaum, A., Rosenbloom, M., Serventi, K. L., & Sullivan, E. V. (2002). Corpus callosum, pons, and cortical white matter in alcoholic women. *Alcoholism: Clinical and Experimental Research*, 26(3), 400–406.

Pfefferbaum, A., Sullivan, E. V., Hedehus, M., Adalsteinsson, E., Lim, K. O., & Moseley, M. (2000). In vivo detection and functional correlates of white matter microstructural disruption in chronic alcoholism. *Alcoholism: Clinical and Experimental Research*, 24(8), 1214–1221.

Pfefferbaum, A., Sullivan, E. V., Mathalon, D. H., & Lim, K. O. (1997). Frontal lobe volume loss observed with magnetic resonance imaging in older chronic alcoholics. *Alcoholism: Clinical and Experimental Research*, 21(3), 521–529.

Pfefferbaum, A., Sullivan, E. V., Mathalon, D. H., Shear, P. K., Rosenbloom, M. J., Lim, & K. O. (1995). Longitudinal changes in magnetic resonance imaging brain volumes in abstinent and relapsed alcoholics. *Alcoholism: Clinical and Experimental Research*, 19(5), 1177–1191.

Phan, K. L., Wager, T., Taylor, S. F., & Liberzon, I. (2002). Functional neuroanatomy of emotion: A meta-analysis of emotion activation studies in PET and fMRI. *Neuroimage*, 16(2), 331–348.

Phelps, E. A. (2006). Emotion and cognition: Insights from studies of the human amygdala. *Annual Review of Psychology*, 57(1), 27–53.

Phelps, E. A., & LeDoux, J. E. (2005). Contributions of the amygdala to emotion processing: From animal models to human behavior. *Neuron*, 48(2), 175–187.

Philippot, P., Kornreich, C., Blairy, S., Baert, I., Den Dulk, A., Le Bon, O., et al. (1999). Alcoholics' deficits in the decoding of emotional facial expression. *Alcoholism: Clinical and Experimental Research*, 23(6), 1031–1038.

Pihl, R. O., & Peterson, J. B. (1991). A biobehavioural model for the inherited predisposition to alcoholism. *Alcohol and Alcoholism (Suppl.)*, 1, 151–156.

Raine, A., Buchsbaum, M., & LaCasse, L. (1997). Brain abnormalities in murderers indicated by positron emission tomography. *Biological Psychiatry*, 42(6), 495–508.

Ratti, M. T., Bo, P., Giardini, A., & Soragna, D. (2002). Chronic alcoholism and the frontal lobe: Which executive functions are impaired? *Acta Neurologica Scandinavica*, 105(4), 276–281.

Reed, L. J., Lasserson, D., Marsden, P., Stanhope, N., Stevens, T., Bello, F., et al. (2003). FDG-PET findings in the Wernicke-Korsakoff syndrome. *Cortex*, 39(4–5), 1027–1045.

Rehm, J., Gmel, G., Sempos, C. T., & Trevisan, M. (2003). Alcohol-related morbidity and mortality. *Alcohol Research & Health*, 27(1), 39–51.

Robinson, T. E., & Berridge, K. C. (1993). The neural basis of drug craving: An incentive-sensitization theory of addiction. *Brain Research Reviews*, 18(3), 247–291.

Robinson, T. E., & Berridge, K. C. (2003). Addiction. *Annual Review of Psychology*, 54(1), 25–53.

Rosenbloom, M., Sullivan, E. V., & Pfefferbaum, A. (2003). Using magnetic resonance imaging and diffusion tensor imaging to assess brain damage in alcoholics. *Alcohol Research & Health*, *27*(2), 146–152.

Ross, E. D. (1984). Right hemisphere's role in language, affective behavior and emotion. *Trends in Neuroscience*, *7*, 342–346.

Rourke, S. B., & Løberg, T. (1996). The neurobehavioral correlates of alcoholism. In I. Grant & S. J. Nixon (Eds.), *Neuropsychological assessment of neuropsychiatric disorders* (2nd ed., pp. 423–485). New York: Oxford University Press.

Royall, D. R., Lauterbach, E. C., Cummings, J. L., Reeve, A., Rummans, T. A., Kaufer, D. I., et al. (2002). Executive control function: A review of its promise and challenges for clinical research. A report from the Committee on Research of the American Neuropsychiatric Association. *Journal of Neuropsychiatry & Clinical Neurosciences*, *14*(4), 377–405.

Ruiz, S. M., & Oscar-Berman, M. (2013). Closing the gender gap: The case for gender-specific alcoholism research. *Journal of Alcoholism & Drug Dependence*, *1*(e6), 1–3. doi: 10.4172/2329-6488.1000e106

Ruiz, S. M., Oscar-Berman, M., Sawyer, K. S., Valmas, M. M., Urban, T., & Harris, G. J. (2013). Drinking history associations with regional white matter volumes in alcoholic men and women. *Alcoholism: Clinical and Experimental Research*, *37*(1), 110–122.

Sair, H. I., Mohamed, F. B., Patel, S., Kanamalla, U. S., Hershey, B., Hakma, Z., & Faro, S. H. (2006). Diffusion tensor imaging and fiber-tracking in Marchiafava-Bignami disease. *Journal of Neuroimaging*, *16*(3), 281–285.

Salloum, J. B., Ramchandani, V. A., Bodurka, J., Rawlings, R., Momenan, R., George, D., & Hommer, D. W. (2007). Blunted rostral anterior cingulate response during a simplified decoding task of negative emotional facial expressions in alcoholic patients. *Alcoholism: Clinical and Experimental Research*, *31*(9), 1490–1504.

Schmahmann, J. D. (Ed.). (1997). *The cerebellum and cognition* (Vol. *41*). San Diego: Academic Press.

Schmahmann, J. D. (2000). The role of the cerebellum in affect and psychosis. *Journal of Neurolinguistics*, *13*, 189–214.

Schneider, F., Habel, U., Wagner, M., Franke, P., Salloum, J. B., Shah, N. J., et al. (2001). Subcortical correlates of craving in recently abstinent alcoholic patients. *American Journal of Psychiatry*, *158*(7), 1075–1083.

Schulte, T., Sullivan, E. V., & Pfefferbaum, A. (2004). Parallel interhemispheric processing in aging and alcoholism: Relation to corpus callosum size. *Neuropsychologia*, *42*, 257–271.

Schultz, W. (1998). Predictive reward signal of dopamine neurons. *Journal of Neurophysiology*, *80*, 1–27.

Sher, K. J. (1987). Stress response dampening. In H. Blane & K. Leonard (Eds.), Psychological theories of drinking and alcoholism (pp. 227–271). New York: Guilford.

Sher, K. J., & Grekin, E. R. (2007). Alcohol and affect regulation. In J. Gross (Ed.), *Handbook of emotion regulation* (pp. 560–580). New York: Guilford.

Sperling, W., Frank, H., Martus, P., Mader, R., Barocka, A., Walter, H., & Lesch, M. (2000). The concept of abnormal hemispheric organization in addiction research. *Alcohol and Alcoholism*, *35*(4), 394–399.

Stasiewicz, P. R., Bradizza, C. M., Gudleski, G. D., Coffey, S. F., Schlauch, R. C., Bailey, S. T., et al. (2012). The relationship of alexithymia to emotional dysregulation within an alcohol dependent treatment sample. *Addictive Behaviors*, *37*(4), 469–476.

Staszewski, J., Macek, K., & Stepien, A. (2006). Reversible demyelinisation of corpus callosum in the course of Marchiafava-Bignami disease. *Neurologia i Neurochirurgia Polska*, *40*(2), 156–161.

Stranges, S., Freudenheim, J. L., Muti, P., Farinaro, E., Russell, M., Nochajski, T. H., Trevisan, M. (2004). Differential effects of alcohol drinking pattern on liver enzymes in men and women. *Alcoholism: Clinical and Experimental Research*, *28*(6), 949–956.

Sullivan, E. V. (2000). Neuropsychological vulnerability to alcoholism: Evidence from neuroimaging studies. In A. Noronha, M. Eckardt & K. Warren (Eds.), *Review of NIAAA's neuroscience and behavioral research* (Vol. Monograph No. 34, pp. 473–508). Bethesda, MD: NIAAA.

Sullivan, E. V., Harding, A. J., Pentney, R., Dlugos, C., Martin, P. R., Parks, M. H., et al. (2003). Disruption of frontocerebellar circuitry and function in alcoholism. *Alcoholism: Clinical and Experimental Research*, *27*(2), 301–309.

Sullivan, E. V., Marsh, L., Mathalon, D. H., Lim, K. O., & Pfefferbaum, A. (1995). Anterior hippocampal volume deficits in nonamnesic, aging chronic alcoholics. *Alcoholism: Clinical and Experimental Research*, *19*(1), 110–122.

Sullivan, E. V., & Pfefferbaum, A. (2005). Neurocircuitry in alcoholism: A substrate of disruption and repair. *Psychopharmacology (Berlin)*, *180*(4), 583–594.

Sullivan, E. V., Rosenbloom, M. J., Lim, K. O., & Pfefferbaum, A. (2000). Longitudinal changes in cognition, gait, and balance in abstinent and relapsed alcoholic men: Relationships to changes in brain structure. *Neuropsychology*, *14*(2), 178–188.

Sullivan, E. V., Pfefferbaum, A. (2005). Neurocircuitry in alcoholism: A substrate of disruption and repair. *Psychopharmacology*, *180*(4), 583–594.

Swanson, L. W. (2003). The amygdala and its place in the cerebral hemisphere. *Annals of the New York Academy of Sciences*, *985*, 174–184.

Szabo, Z., Owonikoko, T., Peyrot, M., Varga, J., Mathews, W. B., Ravert, H. T., et al. (2004). Positron emission tomography imaging of the serotonin transporter in subjects with a history of alcoholism. *Biological Psychiatry*, *55*(7), 766–771.

Tapert, S. F., Brown, G. G., Kindermann, S. S., Cheung, E. H., Frank, L. R., & Brown, S. A. (2001). fMRI measurement of brain dysfunction in alcohol-dependent young women. *Alcoholism: Clinical and Experimental Research*, *21*(2), 236–245.

Thomas, K. M., Drevets, W. C., Whalen, P. J., Eccard, C. H., Dahl, R. E., Ryan, N. D., & Casey, B. J. (2001). Amygdala response to facial expressions in children and adults. *Biological Psychiatry*, *49*(4), 309–316.

Thorberg, F. A., Young, R. M., Sullivan, K. A., Lyvers, M., Connor, J. P., Feeney, G. F. X. (2011). Alexithymia, craving and attachment in a heavy drinking population. *Addictive Behaviors*, *36*(4), 427–430.

Townshend, J. M., & Duka, T. (2003). Mixed emotions: Alcoholics' impairments in the recognition of specific emotional facial expressions. *Neuropsychologia*, *41*(7), 773–782.

Tragesser, S. L., Trull, T. J., Sher, K. J., & Park, A. (2008). Drinking motives as mediators in the relation between personality disorder symptoms and alcohol use disorder. *Journal of Personality Disorders*, *22*(5), 525–537.

Van Overwalle, F. (2009). Social cognition and the brain: A meta-analysis. *Human Brain Mapping, 30*(3), 829–858.

Verdejo-García, A., Lawrence, A. J., & Clark, L. (2008). Impulsivity as a vulnerability marker for substance-use disorders: Review of findings from high-risk research, problem gamblers and genetic association studies. *Neuroscience and Biobehavioral Reviews, 32*(4), 777–810.

Victor, M. A., Adams, R. D., & Collins, G. H. (1971). The Wernicke-Korsakoff syndrome. A clinical and pathological study of 245 patients, 82 with post-mortem examinations. *Contemporary Neurology Series, 7*, 1.

Virkkunen, M., Rawlings, R., Tokola, R., Poland, R. E., Guidotti, A., Nemeroff, C., et al. (1994). CSF biochemistries, glucose metabolism, and diurnal activity rhythms in alcoholic, violent offenders, fire setters, and healthy volunteers. *Archives of General Psychiatry, 51*(1), 20–27.

Volkow, N. D., Hitzemann, R., Wang, G. J., Fowler, J. S., Burr, G., Pascani, K., et al. (1995). Monitoring the brain's response to alcohol with positron emission tomography. *Alcohol Health and Research World, 19*, 296–299.

Volkow, N. D., Wang, G. -J., Tomasi, D., & Baler, R. D. (2013). Unbalanced neuronal circuits in addiction. *Current Opinion in Neurobiology, 23*(4), 639–648.

Wager, T. D., Phan, K. L., Liberzon, I., & Taylor, S. F. (2003). Valence, gender, and lateralization of functional brain anatomy in emotion: A meta-analysis of findings from neuroimaging. *NeuroImage, 19*(3), 513–531.

Waldstein, S. R., Malloy, P. F., Stout, R., Longabaugh, R. (1996). Predictors of neuropsychological impairment in alcoholics: Antisocial versus nonantisocial subtypes. *Addictive Behaviors, 21*(1), 21–27.

Wang, G. J., Volkow, N. D., Roque, C. T., Cestaro, V. L., Hitzemann, R. J., Cantos, E. L., et al. (1993). Functional importance of ventricular enlargement and cortical atrophy in healthy subjects and alcoholics as assessed with PET, MR imaging, and neuropsychologic testing. *Radiology, 186*(1), 59–65.

Witkiewitz, K., & Marlatt, G. A. (2004). Relapse prevention for alcohol and drug problems - That was Zen, this is Tao. *American Psychologist, 59*(4), 224–235.

Wobrock, T., Falkai, P., Schneider-Axmann, T., Frommann, N., Wolwer, W., & Gaebel, W. (2009). Effects of abstinence on brain morphology in alcoholism: A MRI study. *European Archives of Psychiatry and Clinical Neuroscience, 259*(3), 143–150.

Wrase, J., Klein, S., Gruesser, S. M., Hermann, D., Flor, H., Mann, K., et al. (2003). Gender differences in the processing of standardized emotional visual stimuli in humans: A functional magnetic resonance imaging study. *Neuroscience Letters, 348*(1), 41–45.

Substance Involvement and Physical Health: Unintentional Injury, Organ-Specific Diseases Including Cancer, and Infectious Diseases

Svetlana Popova *and* Jürgen Rehm

Abstract

Substance use, mainly defined as the consumption of alcohol, tobacco, and illegal drugs, is a major risk factor for disease, disability, and mortality. Alcohol consumption can cause a number of chronic diseases, including several types of cancer, diseases of the gastrointestinal tract, various cardiovascular diseases, alcohol use disorders and infectious diseases, such as tuberculosis and pneumonia. Certain patterns of light moderate drinking, without heavy drinking occasions, may incur a protective effect on ischemic disease categories and diabetes. Finally, alcohol has been established as a causal factor for unintentional and intentional injury. Illegal drug use has been mainly linked to four health outcomes: overdose and other injury, noncommunicable diseases, certain mental disorders, and infectious diseases. In the final section, a comprehensive list of diseases attributable to tobacco smoking is provided, and the most important selected medical conditions are described. These include lung cancer, chronic obstructive pulmonary disease, and ischemic heart disease.

Key Words: alcohol, tobacco, illegal drugs, morbidity, mortality, causality, unintentional injury, organ-specific diseases, HIV, cancer

Substance use, mainly defined as the consumption of alcohol, tobacco, and illegal drugs, is a major risk factor for disease, disability, and mortality. In 2012, the Institute of Health Metrics and Evaluation published analyses on the impact of various risk factors on the 2010 global burden of disease (GBD) using the comparative risk assessment (CRA) approach (Lim et al., 2012). Based on this study, tobacco, alcohol, and illegal drugs were the second, fifth, and nineteenth leading contributors to disability adjusted life years (DALYs) (6.3%, 3.9%, and 1.0%, respectively) in all countries for the year 2010.

In many developed countries, premature mortality and both short- and long-term disability attributable to substance use are responsible for immense health expenditures and costs (Anderson & Baumberg, 2006; Collins & Lapsley, 2008; Ezzati et al., 2002; Rehm et al., 2006, 2009a).

This chapter provides an overview of the health consequences of psychoactive substance use, including alcohol, illegal drugs, and tobacco, with current evidence on causal associations of different diseases. The most important selected medical conditions of morbidity and mortality attributable to substance use are also described.

Alcohol

There are more than 30 International Classification of Diseases (ICD-10) three- or four-digit codes that include alcohol in their name or definition (WHO, 2007) and indicate alcohol consumption as a necessary cause. Additionally, there are more than 200 ICD-10 three-digit disease codes in which alcohol is a component cause (Rothman, Greenland, & Lash, 2008). Depending on the pattern of consumption, alcohol may also be protective against some diseases; most notably is its observed cardioprotective effect; that is, the beneficial effect of alcohol on ischemic heart disease (IHD; Rehm, Sempos, & Trevisan, 2003*d*; Roerecke & Rehm, 2012). However, the net effect is overwhelmingly negative; therefore, alcohol constitutes a serious public health problem (Lim et al., 2012; Rehm, Shield, Rehm, Gmel, & Frick, 2013; Room, Babor, & Rehm, 2005). In general, it has been found that for many disease conditions associated with alcohol, risk increases as the average volume of consumption increases (Rehm, Room, Graham, Monteiro, Gmel, & Sempos, 2003*b*; 2004; 2010). In addition to the volume of alcohol, patterns of drinking have also been implicated in a number of health conditions, especially injury.

According to the 2010 CRA study estimates, 5.2% of all global deaths and 3.9% of global DALYs were attributable to alcohol in 2010 (Lim et al., 2012).

Definition of Alcohol as a Risk Factor

The relationship between alcohol consumption and health and social outcomes is complex and multidimensional. As shown in Figure 10.1, alcohol consumption is linked to acute and long-term health and social consequences through three intermediate mechanisms: intoxication, dependence (clinical disorder), and direct biological effects (such as the long-term toxic effect of excessive drinking on the liver or beneficial effect of moderate drinking on IHD; Babor et al., 2003; Rehm et al., 2003*b*).

The CRA defines alcohol exposure using two dimensions: (a) average volume of alcohol consumption and (b) patterns of drinking (Ezzati et al., 2002; Rehm et al., 2003*a*; 2004; 2010; WHO, 2002). The average volume of consumption has been the conventional measure of exposure in alcohol epidemiology (Bruun et al., 1975) and has been linked to many disease conditions (Corrao, Bagnardi, Zambon, & Arico, 1999; English et al., 1995; Rehm et al., 2003*b*; 2010; Schultz et al., 1991).

The CRA approach defined patterns of drinking traditionally in terms of (a) heavy drinking occasions, (b) drinking in public settings, and (c) the proportion of drinking that occurs outside of meals (for further details, see Rehm et al., 2004). However, for the 2010 study, it was restricted to frequency and level of heavy drinking occasions. Patterns of drinking have been primarily linked to two categories of disease outcomes: acute effects of alcohol (such as accidental or intentional injuries; see Shield, Gmel, Patra, & Rehm, 2012) and cardiovascular outcomes (IHD, see Roerecke & Rehm, 2010).

Alcohol affects almost every organ system of the body. At lower doses, women are more susceptible to its effects than men due to less first-pass alcohol metabolism and lower body weights on average (Bradley, Badrinath, Bush, Boyd-Wickizer, & Anawalt, 1998). The disease conditions related to alcohol can be grouped into three main

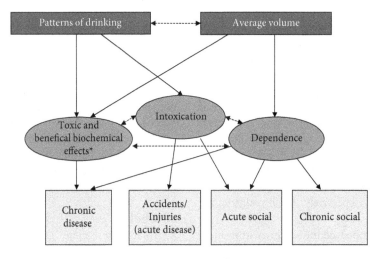

Figure 10.1. Conceptual model of alcohol consumption, intermediate mechanisms, and long-term consequences.
* Independent of intoxication or dependence.

categories, each of which reflects the nature of the conditions and the nature of the etiologic influence of alcohol on those conditions: (1) wholly alcohol-attributable, which, by definition, is a condition with 100% alcohol-attributable fractions (AAFs) and no statistical procedures necessary for estimating risk relationships; (2) chronic, and (3) acute, where alcohol is a contributory cause (i.e., with AAFs lower than 100%). Table 10.1 presents the major disease and injury categories attributable to alcohol.

Chronic Health Consequences

There are conditions that are not wholly attributable to alcohol, but consistent, sufficient evidence exists for a causal relationship, which is defined as (1) evidence of an association (positive or negative) between alcohol consumption and the disease or injury is documented; (2) chance, confounding variables, and other biases can be ruled out with reasonable confidence as factors in the association; and (3) evidence of a plausible mediating process exists (English et al., 1995). This judgment was made using the usual criteria for establishing causality in epidemiology (Hill, 1965; Rothman & Greenland, 1998), with the most weight placed on the following four criteria: consistency across several studies, established experimental biological evidence of mediating processes or at least physiological plausibility (biological mechanisms), strength of the association (effect size), and temporality (i.e., cause before effect).

As shown in Table 10.1, alcohol is related to many disease conditions and, in most cases, detrimentally. In addition, for most diseases, there is a dose–response relationship, with risk of the disease increasing with higher levels of alcohol consumption. Exceptions lie within the cardiovascular area, especially IHD, and with diabetes mellitus. For these diseases, the relationship with consumption is more J-shaped (i.e., higher risks for abstainers than for light drinkers, at least for some subgroups of the population). In addition, as described later (in section "Ischemic Heart Disease"), drinking patterns are also an important factor of risk for IHD. The main chronic disease conditions attributable to alcohol and described in this chapter are, in ascending order of ICD-10 codes, tuberculosis (TB), human immunodeficiency virus/acquired immune deficiency syndrome (HIV/AIDS), malignant neoplasms, diabetes mellitus, neuropsychiatric disorders, cardiovascular diseases, pneumonia, cirrhosis of the liver, cholelithiasis, pancreatitis, psoriasis, conditions arising during the perinatal period, and fetal alcohol syndrome (FAS).

TUBERCULOSIS

A technical meeting organized by World Health Organization (WHO) and co-sponsored by the South African Medical Research Council at Cape Town to review evidence relating to the links between alcohol consumption and selected infectious diseases determined sufficient evidence for a causal impact of alcohol on TB incidence and on worsening of the disease (Parry, Rehm, Poznyak, & Room, 2009). It has long been known that alcohol is associated with TB (Rush, 1785/2013) and that the association between heavy drinking and TB incidence is both strong and consistent (Lönnroth et al., 2008); however, the causality of this association was not clear (Rieder, 1999). Two plausible pathways have been identified and empirically established between heavy alcohol consumption and TB. First, alcohol affects the immune system thus facilitating infection and conversion to active TB in infected individuals (Friedman, Pros, & Klein, 2006; Szabo, 1997; Szabo & Mandrekar, 2009), and, second, alcohol leads to social environments that facilitate TB infection (Rehm et al., 2009b). Obviously, other factors impact the association and may lead to both heavy consumption of alcohol and TB in certain cases (e.g., poverty), but this does not invalidate the conclusion that alcohol is a contributory cause for incidence of TB in other cases (Rehm et al., 2009b). Regarding the course of the disease, there is sufficient evidence indicating that alcohol consumption, especially heavy consumption, affects help seeking and disrupts medication intake as well as treatment processes, leading to worse treatment outcomes than when compared to abstinence (Jakubowiak, Bogorodskaya, Borisov, Danilova, & Kourbatova, 2007; Parry et al., 2009; Rehm et al., 2009b).

HUMAN IMMUNODEFICIENCY VIRUS/ ACQUIRED IMMUNE DEFICIENCY SYNDROME

At the meeting held in Cape Town mentioned earlier, it was concluded that there is conclusive evidence of a causal linkage between heavy drinking patterns and/or alcohol use disorders (AUDs) and the exacerbation of the disease course of HIV/ AIDS. Alcohol use has also consistently been shown to be associated with the prevalence and incidence of HIV (Baliunas, Rehm, Irving, & Shuper, 2010; Fisher, Bang, & Kapiga, 2007; Shuper, Joharchi, Irving, & Rehm, 2009), but the conclusion at the

Table 10.1. Alcohol-attributable disease and injury categories

CONDITION	ICD-10	REFERENCE TO META-ANALYSES/ SYSTEMATIC REVIEWS	EFFECT
INFECTIOUS DISEASES			
Tuberculosis	A15–A19, B90	Lönnroth et al., 2008; Parry et al., 2009; Rehm et al., 2009*b*; Szabo, 1997 *Technical meeting 2008 concluded sufficient evidence for a causal impact (Parry et al., 2009).*	Detrimental
Human immunodeficiency virus/acquired immune deficiency syndrome (HIV/ AIDS)	B20–B24	Baliunas et al., 2010; Fisher et al., 2007; Kalichman et al., 2007; Parry et al., 2009; Rehm et al., 2012; Shuper et al., 2009; 2010 *There is not sufficient evidence to quantify the causal impact on incidence, but there is sufficient evidence of causal impact on course of disease, which can in part be modeled (Gmel et al., 2011; Shield et al., 2013).*	Detrimental
MALIGNANT NEOPLASMS			
Mouth, nasopharynx, other pharynx and oropharynx cancer	C00–C13	Baan et al., 2007; Bagnardi et al., 2001; Corrao et al., 2004; English et al., 1995; Gutjahr et al., 2001; IARC, 2010; Purdue et al., 2009; Rehm et al., 2003*b*; 2004; Ridolfo & Stevenson, 2001; Single et al., 1996; 1999; Sjögren et al., 2000; Tramacere et al., 2010; Turati et al., 2010; Zeka et al., 2003. *IARC confirmed cancers of the oral cavity and pharynx to be related causally to alcohol drinking in monograph meeting of February 2007 (Baan et al., 2007; IARC, 2010).*	Detrimental
Oesophagus cancer	C15	Baan et al., 2007; Corrao et al., 2004; English et al., 1995; Gutjahr et al., 2001; IARC, 2010; Islami et al., 2011; Lewis & Smith, 2005; Rehm et al., 2003*b*; 2004; Ridolfo & Stevenson, 2001; Single et al., 1996; 1999; Sjögren et al., 2000; Zeka et al., 2003 *IARC confirmed esophagus cancer to be related to alcohol drinking in monograph meeting of February 2007 (Baan et al., 2007; IARC, 2010).*	Detrimental
Stomach cancer	C16	Shimazu et al., 2008; Tramacere et al., 2012*a* *IARC concluded inadequate evidence that alcohol causes stomach cancer because of the inconsistency of the research evidence. Last IARC meeting concluded a possible relationship but confounding of smoking and dietary habits could not be excluded (Baan et al., 2007; IARC, 2010).*	Detrimental
Colon and rectal cancer	C18–C21	Baan et al., 2007; Bagnardi et al., 2001; Cho et al., 2004; Corrao et al., 2004; IARC, 2010; Fedirko et al., 2011; Mizuoe et al., 2008; Moskal et al., 2007; Rehm et al., 2003*b*; 2004 *IARC newly included colorectal cancer as related causally to alcohol drinking in monograph meeting of February 2007 (Baan et al., 2007; IARC, 2010).*	Detrimental

Table 10.1. Continued

CONDITION	ICD-10	REFERENCE TO META-ANALYSES/ SYSTEMATIC REVIEWS	EFFECT
Liver cancer	C22	Baan et al., 2007; Bagnardi et al., 2001; Corrao et al., 2004; English et al., 1995; Gutjahr et al., 2001; IARC, 2010; La Vecchia et al., 2008; Rehm et al., 2004; Ridolfo & Stevenson, 2001; Single et al., 1996; 1999; Sjögren et al., 2000 *IARC confirmed primary liver cancer as related causally to alcohol drinking in monograph meeting of February 2007 (Baan et al., 2007; IARC, 2010).*	Detrimental
Pancreas cancer	C25	Bagnardi et al., 2001 *Confounding of smoking could not be excluded, therefore, causality needs to be reassessed*	Detrimental
Larynx cancer	C32	Altieri et al., 2005; Baan et al., 2007; Bagnardi et al., 2001; Corrao et al., 2004; English et al., 1995; Gutjahr et al., 2001; IARC, 2010; Islami et al., 2010; Purdue et al., 2009; Rehm et al., 2003b; 2004; Ridolfo & Stevenson, 2001; Single et al., 1996; 1999; Sjögren et al., 2000; Zeka et al., 2003 *IARC confirmed larynx cancer to be causally related to alcohol drinking in monograph meeting of February 2007 (Baan et al., 2007; IARC, 2010).*	Detrimental
Trachea, bronchus, and lung cancer	C33–C34	*Was excluded from the list of outcomes related causally to alcohol by English et al. (1995). This decision has not been revised by any further meta-analysis. Meta-analyses on alcohol and lung cancer found mixed results (Bagnardi et al., 2001; Chao, 2007; Korte et al., 2002; Freudenheim et al., 2005), but even when RRs were elevated for heavy consumption, confounding by smoking could not be fully excluded (Korte et al., 2002). The substantive reviews found no sufficient support for a causal relation (Bandera et al., 2001; Wakai et al., 2007). Last IARC meeting concluded a possible relationship but confounding of smoking and dietary habits could not be excluded (Baan et al., 2007; IARC, 2010).*	Detrimental
Breast cancer (female)	C50	Baan et al., 2007; Bagnardi et al., 2001; Carrao et al., 2004; Ellison et al., 2001; Gutjahr et al., 2001; Hamajima et al., 2002; IARC, 2010; Key et al., 2006; Rehm et al., 2003b; 2004; Ridolfo & Stevenson, 2001; Single et al., 1996; 1999; Singletary, 2003; Singletary & Gapstur, 2001; Sjögren et al., 2000; Smith-Warner et al., 1998; Suzuki et al., 2008 *IARC newly included breast cancer as related causally to alcohol drinking in monograph meeting of February 2007 (Baan et al., 2007; IARC, 2010).*	Detrimental

(continued)

Table 10.1. Continued

CONDITION	ICD-10	REFERENCE TO META-ANALYSES/ SYSTEMATIC REVIEWS	EFFECT
Prostate cancer	C61	Dennis, 2000; Fillmore et al., 2009; Rota et al., 2012 *Insufficient causal evidence*	Detrimental
Other neoplasms	D00–D48 (except D09.9, D37.9, D38.6, D39.9, D40.9, D41.9, D48.9)	Rehm et al., 2004 *Mixed category, no assessment or quantification of causality possible*	Detrimental
Diabetes mellitus	E10–E13	Carlsson et al., 2005; English et al., 1995; Gutjahr et al., 2001; Howard et al., 2004; Koppes et al., 2005; Rehm et al., 2004, Single et al., 1996; 1999	Mainly beneficial
Alcohol-induced pseudo-Cushing syndrome	E24.4	100% AAF per definition	Detrimental

NEUROPSYCHIATRIC DISORDERS

CONDITION	ICD-10	REFERENCE TO META-ANALYSES/ SYSTEMATIC REVIEWS	EFFECT
Alzheimer disease and other dementias	F01–F03, G30, G31	Graves et al., 1991; Letenneur, 2007; Letenneur et al., 2004; Peters et al., 2008 *Overall, studies showed a beneficial effect, with the beneficial effects on the ischemic system being the main potential explanation (Panza et al., 2008). However, studies show substantial heterogeneity and confounding and other explanations could not be ruled out (Ashley et al., 2000; Letenneur, 2007; Tyas et al., 2001).*	Mainly beneficial
Mental and behavioral disorders due to use of alcohol	F10.0, F10.3–F10.9	100% AAF per definition	Detrimental
Alcohol abuse	F10.1	100% AAF per definition	Detrimental
Alcohol dependence syndrome	F10.2	100% AAF per definition	Detrimental
Unipolar depressive disorders	F32, F33, F34.1	Rehm et al., 2004 *No adequate quantification possible as there may be reverse causality or causation by a third variable.*	Detrimental
Degeneration of nervous system due to alcohol	G31.2	100% AAF per definition	Detrimental
Epilepsy	G40, G41	English et al., 1995; Gutjahr et al., 2001; Hillbom et al., 2003; Rehm et al., 2003b; 2004; Ridolfo & Stevenson, 2001; Samokhvalov et al., 2010a; Single et al., 1996; 1999; Sjören et al., 2000 *Meta-analyses did often not distinguish between primary epilepsy/unprovoked seizures and provoked seizures such as alcohol withdrawal-induced seizures.*	Detrimental
Alcoholic polyneuropathy	G62.1	100% AAF per definition	Detrimental

Table 10.1. Continued

CONDITION	ICD-10	REFERENCE TO META-ANALYSES/ SYSTEMATIC REVIEWS	EFFECT
Alcoholic myopathy	G72.1	100% AAF per definition	Detrimental
CARDIOVASCULAR DISEASES			
Hypertensive heart disease	I10–I13	Corrao et al., 2004; English et al., 1995; Gutjahr et al., 2001; Rehm et al., 2003*b*; 2003*d*; 2004; Ridolfo & Stevenson, 2001; Single et al., 1996; 1999; Sjören et al., 2000	Detrimental, seems to depend on patterns of drinking for low volume
Ischaemic heart disease	I20–I25	Corrao et al., 2000; 2004; Di Castelnuovo et al., 2002; English et al., 1995; Gutjahr et al., 2001; Koppes et al., 2005; McKee & Britton, 1998; Puddey et al., 1999; Rehm et al., 2003*b*; 2003*d*; 2004 Single et al., 1996; 1999; Sjören et al., 2000; Ridolfo & Stevenson, 2001	Beneficial or detrimental, depending on patterns of drinking for low to medium volume; detrimental effect for high volume
Cardiomyopathy	I42	George & Figueredo, 2011 *Not clear if alcohol has a relationship to cardiomyopathy over and beyond the subcategory of alcoholic cardiomyopathy I42.6.*	Detrimental
Alcoholic cardiomyopathy	I42.6	100% AAF per definition	Detrimental
Conduction disorders and other dysrhythmias	I47–I48	English et al., 1995; Gutjahr et al., 2001; Rehm et al., 2004; Ridolfo & Stevenson, 2001; Single et al., 1996; 1999; Sjören et al., 2000	Detrimental
Heart failure		English et al., 1995; Gutjahr et al., 2001; Rehm et al., 2004; Ridolfo & Stevenson, 2001; Single et al., 1996; 1999 *This is an unspecific category with no identification of underlying pathology. Therefore, the relationship between average volume of consumption and outcome was usually not determined by meta-analyses but indirectly from other circulatory diseases*	Detrimental
Ischaemic stroke	I63–I67, I69.3	Camargo, 1989; Carrao et al., 1999, 2004; English et al., 1995; Gutjahr et al., 2001; Mazzaglia et al., 2001; Rehm et al., 2003b, 2004; Reynolds et al., 2003; Ridolfo & Stevenson, 2001; Single et al., 1996, 1999; Sjören et al., 2000;	Beneficial or detrimental dependent on patterns of Drinking (similar to IHD).
Hemorrhagic and other nonischemic stroke	I60–I62, I69.0, I69.1, I69.2	Camargo, 1989; Carrao et al., 1999; 2004; English et al., 1995; Gutjahr et al., 2001; Mazzaglia et al., 2001; Rehm et al., 2004; Reynolds et al., 2003; Ridolfo & Stevenson, 2001; Single et al., 1996; 1999; Sjören et al., 2000; Teunissen et al., 1996	Mainly detrimental, except for low doses

(continued)

Table 10.1. Continued

CONDITION	ICD-10	REFERENCE TO META-ANALYSES/ SYSTEMATIC REVIEWS	EFFECT
Oesophageal varices	I85	English et al., 1995; Gutjahr et al., 2001; Rehm et al., 2003b; 2004; Ridolfo & Stevenson, 2001; Single et al., 1996; 1999; Sjören et al., 2000	Detrimental
Lower respiratory infections: pneumonia	J09–J22, J85, P23	Samokhvalov et al., 2010b	Detrimental
DIGESTIVE DISEASES			
Other digestive diseases	K20–K22, K28–K31, K38, K57–63, K75.2, K75.3, K75.4, K76–K77, K90–K91, K92.8	English et al., 1995; Gutjahr et al., 2001; Rehm et al., 2004; Ridolfo & Stevenson, 2001; Single et al., 1996; 1999; Sjören et al., 2000	Detrimental
Alcoholic gastritis	K29.2	100% AAF per definition	Detrimental
Cirrhosis of the liver	K70, K73, K74	Carrao et al., 2004; English et al., 1995; Gutjahr et al., 2001; Rehm et al., 2003b; 2004; 2009; Ridolfo & Stevenson, 2001; Single et al., 1996; 1999; Sjören et al., 2000	Detrimental
Gall bladder and bile duct disease	K80–K83	English et al., 1995; Gutjahr et al., 2001; Rehm et al., 2003b; Ridolfo & Stevenson, 2001; Single et al., 1996; 1999; Sjören et al., 2000 *Beneficial effect only found for K80 (cholelithiasis); the above references are limited to this.*	Beneficial
Pancreatitis	K85, 86	Corrao et al., 2004; English et al., 1995; Gutjahr et al., 2001; Irving et al., 2009; Rehm et al., 2003b; 2004; Ridolfo & Stevenson, 2001; Single et al., 1996; 1999; Sjören et al., 2000 *Often determined by clinical case studies (but see Corrao et al., 1999), but there is one recent meta-analysis (Irving et al., 2009). There are subcategories of alcohol-induced acute (K85.2) and chronic pancreatitis (K86.0).*	Detrimental
Alcohol-induced acute pancreatitis	K85.2	100% AAF per definition	Detrimental
Alcohol-induced chronic pancreatitis	K86.0	100% AAF per definition	Detrimental
Other digestive diseases	K20–K22, K28–K31, K38, K57–K63, K75.2, K75.3, K75.4, K76–K77, K90–K92 (except K92.0, K92.1, K92.2, K92.9)	English et al., 1995; Gutjahr et al., 2001; Rehm et al., 2004; Ridolfo & Stevenson, 2001; Single et al., 1996; 1999; Sjören et al., 2000 *Detrimental effect of alcohol has only been found for K22.6 (gastroesophageal hemorrhage). The above references are limited to K22.*	Detrimental

Table 10.1. Continued

CONDITION	ICD-10	REFERENCE TO META-ANALYSES/ SYSTEMATIC REVIEWS	EFFECT
SKIN DISEASES			
Psoriasis	L40, L41	Behnam et al., 2005; Corrao et al., 2004; Dika et al., 2007; English et al., 1995; Gutjahr et al., 2001; Naldi, 2004; Rehm et al., 2003*b*; 2004; Ridolfo & Stevenson, 2001; Schäfer, 2006; Single et al., 1996; 1999 *Overall insufficient evidence on the causal impact of alcohol on the association with psoriasis.*	Detrimental
CONDITIONS ARISING DURING THE PERINATAL PERIOD			
Pregnancy with abortive outcome	O00–O08	English et al., 1995; Gutjahr et al., 2001; Rehm et al., 2003*b*; 2004; Ridolfo & Stevenson, 2001; Single et al., 1996; 1999 *To be applied to the fraction of women with alcohol consumption during pregnancy*	Detrimental
Maternal care for (suspected) damage to foetus from alcohol	O35.4	100% AAF per definition	Detrimental
Foetus and newborn affected by maternal use of alcohol	P04.3	100% AAF per definition	Detrimental
Certain conditions originating in the perinatal period	P05–P07, P22, P25–P28, P77	Abel & Hannigan, 1995; English et al., 1995; Gutjahr et al., 2001; Henderson et al., 2007*a*; 2007*b*; Odendaal et al., 2009; Patra et al., 2011; Rehm et al., 2004; Ridolfo & Stevenson, 2001; Schäfer, 2006; Single et al., 1996; 1999; Zuckerman & Hingson, 1986 *To be applied to the fraction of women with alcohol consumption during pregnancy; English et al. (1995) concluded that for all birth defects combined (ICD-10: Q00–Q99) there was inadequate evidence for a causation of alcohol during pregnancy. Other reviews, based on the same criteria for causality as English et al. (1995), concluded sufficient evidence for a causal effect.*	Detrimental
Fetal alcohol syndrome	Q86.0	100% AAF per definition	Detrimental
UNINTENTIONAL INJURIES	V01–X59, Y40–Y89		Detrimental
Transport injuries (including road traffic accidents)	V01–V98, Y85.0	Taylor & Rehm, 2012; Taylor et al., 2010	Detrimental
Falls	W00–W19	Rehm et al., 2004; Taylor & Rehm, 2012; Taylor et al., 2010	Detrimental
Exposure to mechanical forces (including machinery accidents)	W20–W52	Taylor & Rehm, 2012; Taylor et al., 2010	Detrimental

(continued)

Table 10.1. Continued

CONDITION	ICD-10	REFERENCE TO META-ANALYSES/ SYSTEMATIC REVIEWS	EFFECT
Drowning	W65–W74	Rehm et al., 2004; Taylor & Rehm, 2012; Taylor et al., 2010	Detrimental
Fires, heat and hot substances	X00–X19	Taylor & Rehm, 2012; Taylor et al., 2010	Detrimental
Poisonings	X40–X44, X46–X49	Rehm et al., 2004; Taylor & Rehm, 2012; Taylor et al., 2010	Detrimental
Accidental poisoning & exposure to alcohol	X45, X45.0–X45.9	100% AAF per definition	Detrimental
Poisoning by exposure to alcohol, undetermined intent	Y15	100% AAF per definition	Detrimental
Other unintentional injuries	W75–W99, X30–X33, X50–X58	Rehm et al., 2004; Taylor & Rehm, 2012; Taylor et al., 2010	Detrimental
INTENTIONAL INJURIES	X60–Y09, Y35–Y36, Y87.0, Y87.1, Y89.0, Y89.1		Detrimental
Self-inflicted injuries	X60–X84, Y87.0	Rehm et al., 2004; Taylor & Rehm, 2012; Taylor et al., 2010	Detrimental
Intentional self-poisoning by & exposure to alcohol	X65	100% AAF per definition	Detrimental
Interpersonal violence	X85–Y09, Y87.1	Rehm et al., 2004; Taylor & Rehm, 2012; Taylor et al., 2010	Detrimental
Legal intervention	Y35, Y89.0	Rehm et al., 2004; Taylor & Rehm, 2012; Taylor et al., 2010	Detrimental
Problems related to lifestyle alcohol use	Z72.1	100% AAF per definition	Detrimental

AAF, alcohol-attributable fraction; CRA, comparative risk assessment; GBD, Global Burden of Disease and Injury; IARC, International Agency for Research on Cancer; ICD, International Classification of Diseases; IHD, ischemic heart disease; RR, relative risk
The shaded rows indicate conditions for which the current analyses concluded sufficient evidence for a causal relationship and sufficient data on outcomes and risk relations to be included in the CRA 2005/2010.

meeting was that, to substantiate causality, further research was needed (Shuper et al., 2010). Alcohol use, especially heavy use, weakens the immune system, which creates a more vulnerable system for infection. However, to become infected with HIV, there must be an additional active behavioral component (e.g., engaging in unprotected sex). Even though alcohol use in general has been associated with the act of partaking in unprotected sex (Halpern-Felsher, Millstein, & Ellen, 1996; Kalichman, Simbayi, Kaufman, Cain, & Jooste, 2007; Leigh & Stall, 1993; Rehm, Shield, Joharchi, & Shuper, 2012), when the relationship between alcohol consumption and unprotected sex is examined within event-level contexts (e.g., based on daily diary assessments), the relationship weakens and even disappears (Halpern-Felsher et al., 1996; Leigh, 2002; Leigh & Stall, 1993; Weinhardt & Carey, 2000; Woolf & Maisto, 2009). This has led to the interpretation that alcohol use may serve as a marker for other variables that might underlie the association between alcohol use and unprotected sex, such as personality characteristics like sexual compulsivity (Kalichman & Rompa, 1995), sensation seeking (Kalichman, Heckman, & Kelly, 1996; Zuckerman, 1994), and/or psychiatric conditions such as antisocial personality disorder (Golding & Perkins, 1996). However, another line of research could exclude personality variables as explaining the correlation between alcohol use and HIV incidence: experimental research with alcohol being manipulated clearly indicated that it is causally linked to intentions for unsafe sex (Rehm et al., 2012). Thus the causality has been established but, for now, there is no way to quantify this effect.

There is, however, enough evidence to conclude a causal impact of alcohol on the course of the disease (Parry et al., 2009) and to quantify this effect (Gmel, Shield, & Rehm, 2011; Shield, Shuper, Gmel, & Rehm, 2013). As seen with TB, alcohol use was shown to interfere with HIV treatment, demonstrated through much higher dropout rates, higher nonadherence to medication and more treatment failures when alcohol use is a factor (Hendershot, Stoner, Pantalone, & Simoni, 2009). There is also an indication of a dose–response relationship, in which problem drinking or AUDs interfere more strongly than alcohol exposure per se (Hendershot et al., 2009). Together with evidence that nonadherence to antiretroviral medication and treatment failure are linked to higher mortality, the effect of alcohol use on AIDS mortality can be quantified (Gmel et al., 2011; Shield et al., 2013).

MALIGNANT NEOPLASMS

Cancer Mortality and Morbidity Attributable to Alcohol Consumption

In 2004, malignant neoplasms attributable to alcohol consumption caused 345,300 deaths (96,400 female deaths and 248,900 male deaths), and 3,872,000 DALYs lost (1,129,000 female DALYs lost and 2,743,000 male DALYs lost). This burden represents 0.6% of all deaths (0.3% of all female deaths and 0.8% of all male deaths) and 0.3% of all DALYs lost (0.2% of all female DALYs lost and 0.3% of all male DALYs lost) in 2004 (Lim et al., 2012). It should be noted that alcohol-attributable cancer in 2004 reflects the level of drinking in the mid-1990s due to the long latency of cancer (Holmes, Meier, Booth, Guo, & Brennan, 2012).

Cancer's Contribution to the Total Alcohol-Attributable Burden of Disease

In 2004, alcohol consumption was responsible for 2,498,000 deaths (563,000 female deaths and 1,935,000 male deaths). Of the total number of deaths and DALYs lost that were attributable to alcohol consumption in 2004, alcohol-attributable cancers were responsible for 13.8% of all alcohol-attributable deaths (17.1% and 12.9% of all alcohol-attributable female and male deaths, respectively) and 6.0% of all alcohol-attributable DALYs lost (11.2% and 5.0% of all alcohol-attributable female and male DALYs lost, respectively; Lim et al., 2012).

In February 2007, the International Agency for Research on Cancer (IARC) Working Group (consisting of 26 scientists from 15 countries) confirmed that, based on the current research evidence, alcoholic beverages are *carcinogenic to humans* (Group 1). Specifically, the Working Group confirmed the causal relationship between alcohol consumption and the occurrence of malignant neoplasms of the oral cavity, pharynx, larynx, esophagus, liver, colon, rectum, and female breast (Baan et al., 2007; International Agency for Research on Cancer [IARC], 2008; 2010). Additionally, a *lack of carcinogenicity* was concluded for renal-cell carcinoma and non-Hodgkin lymphoma. For stomach and lung cancer, it was concluded that carcinogenicity was possible but not established. Evidence on causality between alcohol consumption and risks of other types of cancer was sparse or inconsistent (Baan et al., 2007; IARC, 2008; 2010). Furthermore, the Working Group concluded that there was "sufficient evidence" for the carcinogenicity of ethanol in animals and also classified ethanol in alcoholic beverages as carcinogenic to humans (Group 1; IARC http://monographs.iarc.fr/ENG/Preamble/CurrentPreamble.pdf).

Cancer of the Upper Digestive Tract: Oral Cavity, Pharynx, Larynx, and Esophagus

A causal relationship between alcohol consumption and cancer of the oral cavity, pharynx, larynx, and esophagus has been confirmed in numerous epidemiological studies. These studies have shown a neoplastic effect of heavy alcohol consumption and a linear correlation with both the duration and amount of consumption (IARC, 1988). Research has also demonstrated that daily consumption of approximately 50 g of ethanol increases the risk of developing these cancers by 2–3 times when compared to the risk of abstainers (Altieri, Garavallo, Boseti, Gallus, & Vecchia, 2005; Bagnardi, Blangiardo, La Vecchia, & Corrao, 2001; Corrao, Bagnardi, Zambon, & La Vecchia, 2004; Gutjahr, Gmel, & Rehm, 2001; Ridolfo & Stevenson, 2001;

Sjögren, Eriksson, Bronstrom, & Ahlm, 2000). First reported in 1961, the combined effect of drinking and smoking has been shown to be multiplicative (IARC, 1988).

Current systematic reviews and meta-analyses on alcohol consumption and the increased risk of developing cancer of the upper digestive tract have been published by Tramacere et al. (2010) and Turati et al. (2010) for oral and pharyngeal cancers, Islami et al. (2010) for laryngeal cancer, and Islami et al. (2011) for esophageal cancer.

Colon and Rectal Cancer

A causal relation between alcohol and colorectal cancer has been established by the IARC (Baan et al., 2007; IARC, 2010). Several meta-analyses have provided evidence for an increased relative risk (RR) for colorectal cancer of about 1.4 with regular consumption of approximately 50 g of alcohol per day, compared with that in abstainers (Cho et al., 2004; Moskal, Norat, Ferrari, & Riboli, 2007). This association is similar for both colon and rectal cancers (Cho et al., 2004; Moskal et al., 2007).

Moskal and colleagues (2007) estimated a 15% increase in the risk of developing colon or rectal cancer with an increased consumption of 100 g of alcohol per week. A potential mechanism is the action of alcohol through folate metabolism or synergistically with low folate intake (because low folate intake increases the risk of colorectal cancer); however, these effects may be moderate (Boffetta & Hashibe, 2006; Moskal et al., 2007). Moskal et al. (2007) suggested that the genotoxic effects of acetaldehyde, a metabolite of alcohol, and genetic polymorphisms are factors for increasing the risk of colorectal cancer.

A recent meta-analysis provided strong evidence for an association between light (≤1 drink/day) alcohol consumption and colorectal cancer risk (Fedirko et al., 2011).

Liver Cancer

The causal relationship between alcohol consumption and liver cancer was confirmed during the first IARC Monographs meeting on the evaluation of carcinogenic risks of alcohol to humans (IARC, 1988). The evidence suggested that the consumption of alcohol is an independent risk factor for primary liver cancer.

A meta-analysis by Corrao and colleagues (2004) demonstrated an increase in risk by a factor of 1.8 for hepatocellular carcinoma and an increase by a

factor of 27 for the risk of liver cirrhosis for heavy drinkers (i.e., 100 g of ethanol a day). The development of liver cirrhosis seems more likely to account for alcohol-related liver carcinogenicity, although changes in the hepatic metabolism of carcinogens might also contribute (Boffetta & Hashibe, 2006). Synergistic interactions between tobacco and alcohol and between hepatitis B virus (HBV) or hepatitis C virus (HCV) and alcohol may also affect the risk of developing liver cancer (IARC, 1988).

Breast Cancer (Female)

Numerous epidemiological studies have indicated a positive relationship between alcohol consumption and the incidence of breast cancer (Corrao et al., 2004; Hamajima et al., 2002; Key et al., 2006; Longnecker, 1994; Singletary & Gapstur, 2001; Smith-Warner et al., 1998). This heightened risk exists even at a moderate level of alcohol consumption (Singletary, 2003) and increases with higher levels of alcohol consumption (Corrao et al., 2004; Hamajima et al., 2002). Of note, no differences in risks have been observed between types of alcoholic drinks (Singletary & Gapstur, 2001). On the basis of several epidemiological studies, each additional 10 g of alcohol per day is associated with an increase of 7.1% in the RR of breast cancer (Hamajima et al., 2002) or possibly even higher (10% was estimated by Key et al., 2006).

Even for regular alcohol consumption of about 18 g of alcohol per day, the increase in RR has been found to be statistically significant (Hamajima et al., 2002). This same study reported that about 4% of female breast cancer cases in developed countries might be attributable to alcohol consumption. Moreover, the authors observed that the risk of breast cancer was the same for women who both drank and smoked and for those who drank but never smoked.

The mechanism of association between alcohol and breast cancer may involve increased levels of estrogen (Boffetta & Hashibe, 2006; Foster & Marriott, 2006) or increased levels of plasma insulin-like growth factor (IGF) produced by the liver due to moderate consumption of alcohol (Yu & Berkel, 1999; also see Key et al., 2006; Singletary & Gapstur, 2001).

Lung Cancer

A review of eight case–control and nine cohort studies did not find sufficient evidence on the causal relation between alcohol and lung cancer (Bandera, Freudenheim, & Vena, 2001). However, a meta-analysis by Korte and colleagues (2002) reported an association between alcohol and lung cancer risk in very high consumption groups based on cohort and hospital-based case–control studies. For lower consumption groups, the observed associations could be explained by smoking. However, one pooled analysis of seven prospective studies reported that alcohol consumption was strongly associated with a greater risk of lung cancer for men who had never smoked, although residual confounding from smoking (e.g., possible effect of a misreporting of smoking status, passive smoke exposure, and confounding due to the smoking of pipes and cigars) could not be excluded (Freudenheim et al., 2005).

Because evidence for the possible biological mechanisms was inconclusive, and residual confounding by smoking may explain part of observed relations, the IARC decided to exclude lung cancer from the list of diseases influenced by alcohol during their last meeting (IARC, 2008).

Prostate Cancer

Observational research has suggested that there is a significant positive dose–response association between the risk of developing prostate cancer and alcohol consumption. A recent meta-analysis indicated that alcohol consumption is significantly linked to an increased risk of developing prostate cancer in a dose-dependent manner (Rota et al., 2012). This observation is consistent with previous meta-analyses concluding that alcohol consumption and the risk for prostate cancer are significantly correlated (Dennis, 2000; Fillmore, Kerr, Stockwell, Chikritzhs, & Bostrom, 2006). The biological pathways that associate alcohol consumption with an increased risk of prostate cancer are currently unknown. Thus, additional research is needed to clarify whether there is a causal link.

Other Types of Cancer

A nonsignificant positive association has been observed between alcohol consumption and endometrial (Bagnardi et al., 2001; Rota et al., 2012), ovarian (Bagnardi et al., 2001), and pancreatic cancers (Bagnardi et al., 2001). However, because the relationship between alcohol consumption and endometrial and pancreatic cancer is modest (even at high levels of average daily alcohol consumption), additional studies with large numbers of participants are needed to accurately assess the relationship.

Conflicting epidemiological evidence exists for the association between alcohol consumption and bladder (Bagnardi et al., 2001; Pelucchi et al.,

2012) and stomach cancers (Shimazu et al., 2008; Tramacere et al., 2012a). Meta-analyses observe both significant and nonsignificant associations. The IARC Working Group suggested that alcohol consumption might be associated with an increased risk of stomach cancer, but confounding by smoking and dietary habits could not be ruled out (Baan et al., 2007; IARC, 2008; 2010).

Cohort and case–control studies demonstrated that increased alcohol consumption was associated with a significantly lower risk for renal-cell cancer in both men and women (Hsu et al., 2007; Hu et al., 2003). Prospective cohort studies and large case–control studies showed either an inverse association or no association between alcohol consumption and non-Hodgkin lymphoma (most of these studies showed a lower risk in drinkers than in nondrinkers; Besson et al., 2006; Morton et al., 2005). Therefore, the IARC Working Group concluded that for renal-cell cancer and non-Hodgkin lymphoma there is "evidence suggesting lack of carcinogenicity" for alcohol consumption (Baan et al., 2007; IARC, 2008; 2010). These results should be interpreted with caution because the biological mechanisms are not understood, and confounding and/or misclassification of abstainers within the observational studies may be responsible for the observed protective effect.

One recent meta-analysis reported the inverse association between alcohol consumption and Hodgkin lymphoma (Tramacere et al., 2012b). However, this inverse association was restricted to—or was observed to be greater in—case–control as compared with cohort studies, which prompts caution in the interpretation of results.

Associations between alcohol consumption and other cancers have also been observed; however, the evidence is generally sparse or inconsistent. Observational research and biological studies are needed to confirm previous study results and the mechanisms as to how alcohol affects the risk of developing these cancers.

DIABETES MELLITUS

Moderate alcohol consumption is associated with a reduced risk of type 2 diabetes. Several possible biological mechanisms may explain the observed relationship. Development of insulin resistance is a key factor in the pathogenesis of type 2 diabetes (Fujimoto, 2000), and the risk reduction may be explained by an increase in insulin sensitivity following moderate alcohol consumption (Hendriks, 2007). Increased insulin sensitivity has been found in observational studies (Kiechl et al., 1996; Lazarus, Sparrow, & Weiss, 1997; Mayer, Newman, Quesenberry, Friedman, & Selby, 1993), as well as in randomized controlled trials (Davies et al., 2002; Sierksma et al., 2004). Alternatively, ethanol oxidation produces measurable downstream metabolites, such as acetaldehyde and acetate (Sarkola, Iles, Kohlenberg-Mueller, & Eriksson, 2002), which may reduce the risk of type 2 diabetes. Moderate alcohol consumption is also known to increase high-density lipoprotein (HDL) cholesterol concentrations (Rimm, Williams, Fosher, Criqui, & Stampfer, 1999), although at higher levels of consumption body weight, triglyceride concentration, and blood pressure may increase (Wannamethee & Shaper, 2003a; Wannamethee et al., 2003b; see also the section on Ischemic Heart Disease). Another plausible protective mechanism is through the anti-inflammatory effect of alcohol (Imhof et al., 2001; Sierksma, van der Gaag, Kluft, & Hendriks, 2002). However, whether moderate alcohol intake is itself a protective factor for diabetes or whether it is a marker for other healthy lifestyle choices is not certain. Currently, the overall level of evidence for the causal impact of alcohol on diabetes is considered to border between sufficient and limited (Rehm et al., 2010).

NEUROPSYCHIATRIC DISORDERS

The consumption of alcohol has been implicated with the onset of psychiatric disorders (Bott, Meyer, Rumpf, Hapke, & John, 2005; Drake & Mueser, 1996; Marshall & Farrell, 2007; Petrakis, Gonzalez, Rosenheck, & Krystal, 2002; Sullivan, Fiellin, & O'Connor, 2005; Swendsen et al., 1998). Those who consume about 20–30 g of alcohol per day could have an increased risk of having a psychiatric disorder by two- to threefold when compared to abstainers or moderate drinkers (Bott et al., 2005; Swendsen et al., 1998). Women, when consuming the same amount of alcohol as men, are more likely to develop psychiatric disorders (Bott et al., 2005).

Alcohol use disorders and severe mental illness, such as schizophrenia and bipolar disorder, often occur simultaneously (Drake & Mueser, 1996). About 37% of individuals with AUD may have other psychiatric disorders, including antisocial personality disorder, mood disorder, and anxiety disorder (Marshall & Farrell, 2007). Individuals with both AUD and psychiatric disorders are prone to developing other symptoms, including psychological instability, relapse of psychological conditions, and disruptive behavior (Drake & Mueser, 1996).

Alcohol use disorders are also likely to worsen the state of depression, increase the risk for relapse to a state or period of depression, and decrease the chance of recovery from depression, thus increasing the risk of mortality (Sullivan et al., 2005). Alcohol-related symptoms of depression, anxiety, psychosis, and antisocial behavior have been shown to disappear after several days or weeks of abstinence (Shivani, Goldsmith, & Anthenelli, 2002), although these symptoms may also persist after long periods of abstinence (Kushner, Abrams, & Borchardt, 2000).

Although there is a common agreement about the comorbidity of AUD and psychiatric disorders, there are different hypotheses regarding primary causality. These include that (1) alcoholism is the primary problem giving rise to depression and other psychiatric disorders, (2) psychiatric disorders instigate alcoholism in individuals when they use alcohol to self-medicate, and (3) alcoholism and psychiatric disorders occur simultaneously (Kushner et al., 2000).

Alzheimer Disease and Other Dementias

A number of studies have suggested a beneficial effect of alcohol consumption, especially wine, on Alzheimer disease and dementia (Letenneur, Larrieu, & Barberger-Gateau, 2004; Lindsay et al., 2002; Luchsinger & Mayeux, 2004; Pinder & Sandler, 2004; Ruitenberg et al., 2002; Truelsen, Thudium, & Gronbaek, 2002). However, no clear biological pathway has been identified, nor can confounding be excluded. Thus, the overall evidence regarding a causal effect of alcohol consumption on Alzheimer disease and dementia has been considered insufficient by most reviews.

Epilepsy

Rehm and colleagues (2010) found a consistent relationship between alcohol consumption and increased risk of epilepsy, especially for higher doses of alcohol, as reported in several studies (Leone et al., 1994; 1997; 2002; Ng, Hauser, Brust, & Susser, 1988; Ogunniyi, Osuntokun, Bademosi, Adeuja, & Schoenberg, 1987; Samokhvalov, Irving, Mohapatra, & Rehm, 2010a; Zeng, Zhen, Mao-Sheng, & Mei-Hua, 2003).

The consistent dose–response relationship is rooted in plausible biological pathways. In particular, chronic alcohol consumption has diverse effects on the central nervous system (CNS), affecting its structure and function in many ways. There are several major theories explaining the effects of alcohol consumption on the development of epilepsy. One postulates a "kindling" effect (Ballenger & Post, 1978). According to this theory, repeated withdrawals, including natural withdrawal through sleep, over time may lead to the gradual lowering of the epileptogenic threshold (Ballenger & Post, 1978). Another theorizes that epileptogenesis in heavy alcohol users may also be explained by cerebral atrophy (Dam, Fuglsang-Frederikse, Svarre-Olsen, & Dam, 1985). It has also been hypothesized that the causes of epilepsy in alcohol users include cerebrovascular infarctions, lesions, head traumas (from alcohol-attributable injuries), changes in neurotransmitter systems, and ionic imbalances leading to the onset of seizures (Barclay, Barvour, Stewart, Day, & Gilvarry, 2008; Dam et al., 1985; Freedland & McMicken, 1993a; Rathlev, Ulrich, Delanty, D'Onofrio, & D'Onofrio, 2006). Analyses conducted by Rehm and colleagues (2010) indicated that the strongest evidence was for the "kindling" hypothesis, cerebral atrophy, and brain lesions, each directly linking irreversible CNS changes to chronic alcohol consumption and potentially triggering the onset of epilepsy or spontaneous seizures unrelated to immediate alcohol intake. Additionally, it has been shown that heavy alcohol consumption may worsen the clinical course of existing epilepsy via increased clearance of antiepileptic drugs and noncompliance with treatment regimen (Rathlev et al., 2006).

CARDIOVASCULAR DISEASES
Hypertensive Heart Disease

The relationship between alcohol consumption and hypertensive disease is relatively complex. On one hand, an overall consistently detrimental dose–response effect has been shown for men (Corrao et al., 2004), whereas moderate consumption of alcohol has, in some studies, shown to be protective for women. However, despite the consistent effect of chronic alcohol use on increasing blood pressure (Beilin & Puddey, 1992; Klatsky, 2007), the mechanism of action is unclear, yet a number of theories about potential pathways have been proposed (Klatsky, 2007). These include activation of the sympathetic nervous system to constrict blood vessels and increase the contractile force of the heart (Randin et al., 1995) or a possible role of the sensitivity of baroreceptors in vessel walls that results in a diminished ability to regulate blood pressure via arterial contraction and relaxation (el-Mas & Abdel-Rahman, 1993).

The protective effect, seen only in moderate doses and among women, may be explained in the same way that alcohol is protective for IHD, by changing concentrations of high- and low-density lipoproteins (HDL and LDL, respectively) in the blood or reducing platelet aggregation on vessel walls. The fact that the protective effect is not seen in men may be a result of their higher rates of binge drinking, resulting in an overall detrimental effect, but the literature is equivocal.

Ischemic Heart Disease

Ischemic heart disease is a major cause of death and global burden disease and is projected to increase in the future (Mathers & Loncar, 2006). The relationship of alcohol to IHD is complex. Light to moderate regular consumption of alcohol has been linked to favorable IHD outcomes, whereas heavy drinking occasions, even when coupled with average light or moderate consumption, have been related to an increase in IHD risk (McKee & Britton, 1998; Murray et al., 2002; Puddey, Rakic, Dimmitt, & Beilin, 1999; Rehm et al., 2003d). The epidemiological evidence that regular light to moderate average alcohol consumption protects against IHD is strengthened by growing and, in some instances, substantial evidence concerning the biological mechanisms by which a protective effect could be mediated (Mukamal & Rimm, 2001; Rankin, 1994; Renaud, Criqui, Farchi, & Veenstra, 1993; Rimm et al., 1999; Single, Robson, Rehm, & Xie, 1999; Svärdsudd, 1998). First, moderate alcohol intake has been clearly linked to favorable lipid profiles, especially with increases in HDLs; Baraona & Lieber, 1998; Rimm et al., 1999). It has been estimated that as much as 40–50% of the protective effect may be attributable to this mechanism (Criqui et al., 1987; Criqui & Ringel, 1994). Second, moderate alcohol intake favorably affects coagulation profiles (Rimm et al., 1999), particularly through its effects on platelet aggregation (McKenzie & Eisenberg, 1996) and fibrinolysis (Reeder, Aikens, Li, & Booyse, 1996). A meta-analysis of 42 published trials confirmed the influence of alcohol both on lipids and on blood-clotting factors (Rimm et al., 1999). Other mechanisms have also been discussed (Rehm et al., 2003d), but, based on current knowledge, they appear to play less prominent roles in explaining the beneficial effects of regular light to moderate drinking. A review by Fillmore and colleagues (2006) suggested that the cardiac protection afforded by alcohol may have been overestimated. According to the authors, most studies combined former drinkers with abstainers, and approximately half of these studies also combined occasional drinkers with abstainers. It is therefore likely that a significant number of individuals with some preexisting illness were included in the abstainer category. Moreover, regular light drinking may be a marker for good health among older people but not a cause of it (Fillmore et al., 2006). Other authors have also concluded that evidence for any cardioprotective effect from moderate alcohol consumption at the population level is insufficient (Norstrom & Ramstedt, 2005).

Reviews on patterns of drinking and IHD (McKee & Britton, 1998; Puddey et al., 1999; Rehm et al., 2003*d*) have revealed that irregular heavy drinking occasions may have detrimental effects, whereas heavy drinking occasions have been linked to adverse cardiovascular events for some time (Corrao, Rubbiati, Bagnardi, Zambron, & Poikolainen, 2000; Poikolainen, 1983; Rehm et al., 2003*d*). Several studies have been conducted with a methodologically rigorous assessment of IHD as an endpoint while controlling for average volume as a confounder and with lifetime abstention as a reference (McElduff & Dobson, 1997; Murray et al., 2002; Trevisan et al., 2001*a*; Trevisan, Schisterman, Mennotti, Farchi, & Conti, 2001*b*). All of these studies have found a protective effect for daily average light to moderate drinkers, but no, or detrimental effects, for people whose drinking patterns included heavy drinking occasions, even if their usual pattern was moderate. Studies by Agarwal (2002) and Mukamal et al. (2003) have also found that drinking patterns are an important determinant of the risk of IHD for a given amount of alcohol consumption. The detrimental effects of heavy drinking occasions on IHD are consistent with the physiological mechanisms of increased clotting and reduced threshold for ventricular fibrillation after heavy drinking occasions (see review by McKee & Britton, 1998). In summary, heavy drinking occasions are mainly associated with physiological mechanisms that increase the risk of sudden cardiac death and other cardiovascular outcomes, in contrast to the physiological mechanisms triggered by steady low to moderate consumption that are linked to favorable cardiac outcomes. Another pattern of drinking with relevance to IHD is drinking with meals. In particular, Trevisan and colleagues (2001*a*; 2001*b*) found consistently higher risks for people who drank outside of meals compared to those who drank mainly with meals and snacks, again

after adjustment for age, education, and volume of alcohol consumed.

Unfortunately, most cohort studies investigating the relationship between alcohol and IHD have been conducted on cohorts in which heavy drinking occasions were infrequent and some of the most detrimental patterns were not present. The reason for this is that cohorts have usually been selected to maximize follow-up rates. This selection bias has resulted in an overrepresentation of more health-conscious middle-class people who have relatively favorable patterns of drinking. To overcome this gap and to provide estimates for less favorable drinking patterns, Rehm and colleagues conducted a multilevel analysis on IHD mortality rates on data from 74 countries (Rehm et al., 2003*c*; 2004). The utilized data covered an average time span of 21 years with per capita consumption as an influencing factor and pattern of drinking as a moderator; gross national product (GNP) and year were used as controls for potential confounding variables. As predicted, they showed that per capita consumption had a differential impact when drinking patterns were included in the model. In countries with regular moderate drinking with meals (e.g., France, Italy, Spain), the influence of average volume was beneficial, whereas in countries where drinking tends to be characterized by irregular and heavy drinking, the influence of average volume on IHD mortality was found to be detrimental (e.g., Chile, India, Mexico, Russia, India; see Rehm et al., 2003*a*; Gmel, Rhem, & Frick, 2003).

The results from this study are consistent with the finding that the antialcohol campaign in the Gorbachev era had a beneficial impact on cardiovascular mortality in Russia: the 25% reduction in estimated per capita alcohol consumption between 1984 and 1987 (counting the unregistered alcohol supply; Shkolnikov & Nemtsov, 1997) was accompanied by a decreased death rate from cardiovascular diseases of 9% for males and 6% for females (Leon et al., 1997). After the campaign ended, there was a steep increase in cardiovascular mortality, although factors outside the increased rate of alcohol consumption were likely to have also played a role in this change, such as the change in the social system, the collapse of the medical treatment system, and increasing problems in food supply (Notzon et al., 1997).

Dysrhythmias

The association between alcohol consumption and cardiac rhythm disorders has been recognized for quite some time (Balbão, de Paola, & Fenelon, 2009). Alcohol has been identified as a cause of new-onset atrial fibrillation in 30–60% of patients in two separate studies (Lowenstein, Gbow, Cramer, Olivia, & Ratner, 1983; Rich, Siebold, & Campion, 1985). Several mechanisms explaining the development of dysrhythmias due to alcohol consumption have been proposed, including direct alcohol cardiotoxicity and hyperadrenergic activity during drinking, as well as withdrawal, impairment of vagal tone, and increased intra-atrial conduction time (Schoonderwoerd, Smit, Pen, & Van Gelder, 2008).

Estimations of the association between alcohol consumption and the onset of cardiac dysrhythmias vary in different studies, including several large-scale prospective studies (Benjamin et al., 1994; Krahn, Manfreda, Tate, Mathewson, & Cuddy, 1995; Wilhelmsen, Rosengren, & Lappas, 2001). The Framingham Heart Study (Benjamin et al., 1994) revealed a low association with moderate alcohol consumption, but the association became significant among individuals consuming more than 36 g of pure alcohol per day (about three drinks). In the Copenhagen City Heart Study (Mukamal, Tolstrup, Friberg, Jensen, & Gronbaek, 2005), an increase in the risk of atrial fibrillation was described for people consuming more than 35 drinks per week. In a study by Planas and colleagues (2006) an increased risk of the reoccurrence of atrial fibrillation was shown with moderate alcohol consumption. Overall, the existing studies show increased risk of the development of dysrhythmias related to heavy alcohol consumption, whereas the effects of light to moderate alcohol consumption are inconclusive.

Stroke

Meta-analyses (Corrao et al., 2004; Reynolds et al., 2003) have shown alcohol to both reduce and increase the risk of stroke, depending on the type of stroke, quantity of alcohol consumed, and drinking pattern. Both of these studies found a positive linear relation between alcohol consumption and hemorrhagic stroke but observed a positive association between heavy alcohol consumption and ischemic stroke. According to these meta-analyses, low to moderate alcohol consumption (i.e., 1–2 drinks per day) seems to have a protective effect on ischemic stroke.

Foster and Marriott (2006) have ascribed the variation in the effect of alcohol consumption to the difference in the causes of the incidence of hemorrhagic and ischemic strokes. Ischemic stroke is caused by a blockage in a blood vessel in the brain, commonly arising from a blood clot formed somewhere else, and therefore has a similar etiology to that of IHD. Conversely, a ruptured blood vessel that supplies brain, thus releasing blood into the brain, causes hemorrhagic stroke. Moderate alcohol consumption has anticoagulant effects through decreases in plasma fibrinogen (the precursor of the insoluble blood-clotting protein) and decreases in platelet adhesiveness, resulting in a decrease in platelet aggregation that reduces the risk of ischemic stroke; the same anticoagulant effects of alcohol increase the risk of hemorrhagic stroke. However, higher amounts of homocysteine in the blood present in individuals consuming high amounts of alcohol are associated with increased risk of stroke and IHD.

Reynolds and colleagues (2003) observed that the association between alcohol consumption and RR of stroke was similar in men and women; however, RR for 1–2 drinks per day was lower for women than for men. In contrast, RR for women consuming 5 or more drinks per day was much higher than for men consuming same amount of alcohol.

Several studies reported racial/ethnic disparities in stroke epidemiology, mortality, and hospitalization rates (Casper, Barnett, Williams, Halverson, & Braham, 2003; Chong & Sacco, 2005; Kittner et al., 1993; Stansbury, Huanguang, Williams, Vogel, & Duncan, 2005). Specifically, black–white disparities in stroke mortality were reported with RRs of 3.5 for ischemic stroke, 2.2 for subarachnoid hemorrhage, and 5.2 for intracerebral hemorrhage (Ayala et al., 2001). One study reported that age-adjusted stroke hospitalization rates for blacks were over three times higher than rates for whites, whereas rates for Hispanics were slightly higher than rates for whites (Pathak & Sloan, 2009).

PNEUMONIA

Community-acquired pneumonia (CAP) is defined as an acute infection of the lower respiratory tract occurring in a patient who has not resided in a hospital or a long-term care facility in the previous 14 days (Bartlett et al., 2000). Community-acquired pneumonia is a leading cause of morbidity and mortality worldwide (Luna et al., 2000; Mandell et al., 2007). The association between alcohol consumption and CAP has been long been recognized (Osler, 1905; Rush, 1785/2013). Currently, data about alcohol and the risk of CAP are derived primarily from case series of patients (Koivula, 2001). In case-series studies, it is not completely clear whether any apparent association between alcohol consumption and CAP was causal or related to the existence of confounding factors due to a lack of control groups. Evidence from epidemiologic studies using case–control or cohort designs is scarce. This is exemplified by systematic review of relevant studies (Kohlhammer, Schwartz, Raspe, & Schafer, 2005) that concluded that there was insufficient evidence to determine a causal link between alcohol consumption and CAP. However, emerging evidence in a recent meta-analysis including studies with alcoholics and with the general population, as well as with a gradient of alcohol consumption, suggests that alcohol has a causal impact on the incidence of CAP (Samokhvalov, Irving, & Rehm, 2010b). This study found that the RR of CAP increased linearly with increasing alcohol consumption. Individuals consuming 24, 60, and 120 g of alcohol daily had RRs of 1.12 (95% confidence interval [CI] 1.02–1.23), 1.33 (95% CI 1.06–1.67), and 1.77 (95% CI 1.13–2.78), respectively, relative to nondrinkers. Furthermore, alcoholics, as defined by clinical criteria, had an eightfold increased risk of CAP (RR 8.22, 95% CI 4.85–13.95) compared with nonalcoholics.

It is biologically plausible that alcohol consumption is an important risk factor for CAP. Heavy alcohol consumption can cause alterations of the immune system that increase host susceptibility to CAP. Also, high alcohol intake can facilitate the development of CAP due to its sedative properties, which lead to diminished oropharyngeal tones, an increased risk of aspiration, diminished cough reflex, and mucociliary clearance (Nelson & Kolls, 2002; Szabo & Mandrekar, 2009).

CIRRHOSIS OF THE LIVER

There is a strong correlation between alcohol consumption and the risk of liver cirrhosis (Bautista, 2005; Corrao et al., 1999; 2004; English et al., 1995; Gutjahr et al., 2001; Rehm et al., 2004; Ridolfo & Stevenson, 2001; Single et al., 1996; 1999; Sjögren et al., 2000).

About 20% of people with alcohol dependence develop liver cirrhosis (Seitz & Homan, 2001). The risk of mortality from liver cirrhosis increases from 5 per 100,000 among abstainers to 41 per 100,000 among people consuming four or more drinks per day (Thun et al., 1997). Hepatitis C virus (HCV) infection also increases the risk of liver cirrhosis at any level of alcohol consumption, as well as the severity of cirrhosis (Schiff, 1997; Schiff & Ozden, 2003). There is also an interaction with aliphatic

alcohol congeners from homemade spirits that are derived from fruit and imbibed without meals that increases the risk of cirrhosis (Bossetti et al., 2002; Ramstedt, 2007; Szucs, Sarvary, McKee, & Adany, 2005). Another threat is the use of surrogate alcohol or illegal alcohols, due to the presence of toxins (Lachenmeier, Rehm, & Gmel, 2007). Women, regardless of their level of alcohol consumption, are more likely develop liver cirrhosis than men (Mann, Smart, & Govoni, 2003).

Evidence suggests that alcohol consumption is linked more strongly to cirrhosis mortality than to morbidity. This is because drinking, especially heavily, has been shown to considerably worsen existing liver disease and to have detrimental effects on the immune system, thus negatively affecting the course of existing liver disease and increasing the likelihood of death (Lieber, 1988; Neuman, 2003; Szabo & Mandrekar, 2009). A meta-analysis conducted by Rehm and colleagues (2009c) confirmed that for both men and women the impact of alcohol was stronger on liver cirrhosis mortality compared to morbidity.

CHOLELITHIASIS (GALL STONES)

There is some evidence that alcohol may reduce the risk of cholelithiasis (gall stones; Ashley, Rehm, Bondy, Single, & Rankin, 2000; Leitzmann et al., 1998; Rehm et al., 2003b; Rehm et al., 2004). However, some studies did not observe a beneficial effect of alcohol on cholelithiasis (Kratzer et al., 1997; Sahi, Paffenbarger, Hsieh, & Lee, 1998).

PANCREATITIS

Alcohol consumption has been shown to be associated consistently with an increased risk of pancreatitis, and plausible biological mechanisms have been identified for the effect (see Irving, Samokhvalov, & Rehm, 2009). In particular, the metabolites of alcohol, such as acetaldehyde and fatty acid ethyl esters, may initiate and/or enhance pancreatic injury. Alcohol may also attenuate or augment inflammatory cell activation, leading to fibrosis in the pancreas (Lerch et al., 2003; Szabo, Mandrekar, Oak, & Mayerle, 2007, Szabo & Mandrekar, 2009; Tattersall, Apte, & Wilson, 2008; Vonlaufen, Wilson, Pirola, & Apte, 2007). All of these mechanisms come into play, particularly with heavy consumption. Thus, the meta-analysis of Irving and colleagues (2009) found that, compared with nondrinkers, alcohol consumption of two or fewer drinks per day (≤24 g pure alcohol/ day) was almost identical to the risk of nondrinkers

(RR = 1.0, 95% CI 0.8–1.2; P = 0.887). Drinking three to four drinks was associated only with marginally significant higher risk than for abstention (RR = 1.2, 95% CI 1.0–1.5, P = 0.059), but, overall, the dose–response relationship increased monotonically (Irving et al., 2009).

PSORIASIS

Medical literature for practitioners and patients describes alcohol as a psoriasis trigger. Most of the studies and reviews conducted in the past decades support a detrimental impact of alcohol consumption on psoriasis, especially in male patients (Behnam, Behnam, & Koo, 2005; Dika, Bardazzi, Balestri, & Maibach, 2007; English et al., 1995; Gutjahr et al., 2001; Higgins & du Vivier, 1994a; Kostovic & Lipozencic, 2004; Meyer, Viraben, & Paul, 2008; Poikolainen, Reunala, Karvonen, Lauharanta, & Karkkainen, 1990; Schäfer, 2006; Smith & Fenske, 2000).

In addition to the finding of a clear dose–response relationship (Meyer et al., 2008; Naldi, 2004; Schäfer et al., 1997), the prevalence of psoriasis among alcoholics has been reported to be between two and ten times higher than in the general population (Evstaff'ev & Levin, 1989; Higgins, Peters, & du Vivier, 1993; Lindegard, 1986; Poikolainen et al., 1990). In one study (Ginsburg & Link, 1993), between 17% and 30% of patients with psoriasis (depending on the measure of alcohol consumption) were classified as having difficulties with alcohol. However, part of the association between alcohol and psoriasis could, alternatively, be attributed to higher alcohol consumption as a consequence of the disease (Kirby et al., 2008; Poikolainen et al., 1990). It was found that abstinence from alcohol was related to psoriasis remission, whereas resuming consumption of alcohol was associated with the recurrence of psoriasis (Bolognia, Lorizzo, & Rapini, 2008; Vincenti & Blunden, 1987). Alcohol consumption is also associated with less favorable responses to the treatment of psoriasis and decreased compliance with the treatment (Gupta, Schork, Gupta, & Ellis, 1993; Zaghloul & Goodfield, 2004).

The mechanism by which the consumption of alcohol affects psoriasis has not yet been fully clarified. The majority of researchers suggest that alcohol affects psoriasis mainly by weakening the immune system and predisposing drinkers to infections (Cohen & Halevy, 1999; Farkas, Kemeny, Szell, Dobozy, & Bata-Csorgo, 2003; Higgins & du Vivier et al., 1994b). It has also been suggested that the stimulatory effect of ethanol and acetone (which exceeds its normal endogenous level in the blood of heavy drinkers) on keratinocytes causes epidermal hyperproliferation, which may be one of the reasons why psoriasis can be precipitated by alcohol use in genetically predisposed individuals (Cohen & Halevy, 1999; Farkas et al., 2003; Higgins & du Vivier, 1994b).

There appears to be a consistent association between alcohol consumption and psoriasis, but the overall level of evidence for causality is insufficient, especially with respect to the biological pathways (Rehm et al., 2010; Wolf, Wolf, & Ruocco, 1999).

PRETERM BIRTH COMPLICATIONS

Heavy alcohol consumption has been implicated in increasing the risk of preterm birth (Albertsen, Andersen, Olsen, & Gronbaek, 2004; Kesmodel, Olsen, & Secher, 2000; Larroque, Kaminski, Lelong, Subtil, & Dehaene, 1993; Lundsberg, Bracken, & Saftlas, 1997; Parazzini et al., 2003). However, some studies have reported modest inverse associations between low levels of alcohol consumption and preterm delivery with low birthweight (e.g., Lundsberg et al., 1997; McDonald, Armstrong, & Sloan, 1992), although this may be a result of a higher prevalence of such drinking patterns among women who are more socioeconomically advantaged (Albertsen et al., 2004; Kesmodel et al., 2000). In addition, the risks associated with different dimensions of drinking during the different phases of pregnancy are unclear. For instance, one study showed that moderate amounts of alcohol intake increased the risk for preterm delivery during late pregnancy but not during early pregnancy (Lundsberg et al., 1997). In contrast, another study found elevated risk of preterm birth complications with drinking in early pregnancy (Little, Asker, Sampson, & Renwick, 1986).

The biological mechanism responsible for the association between alcohol consumption and preterm birth complications may be explained in terms of elevated prostaglandin levels among drinkers because a rise in the level of prostaglandin can cause preterm birth (Cook & Randal, 1998). The hormone progesterone has been shown to suppress prostaglandin production (Chaud, Faletti, Beron de Estrada, Gimeno, & Gimeno, 1994; Mitchell & Smith, 1992; Pakrasi, Cheng, & Dey, 1983), which is an important regulator of prostaglandin synthesis during parturition. Heavy alcohol exposure decreases both the synthesis and level of progesterone (Ahluwalia, Smith, Adeyiga, Akbasak, & Rajguru, 1992; Wimalasena, 1994), resulting in the failure to control the level of prostaglandin and leading, eventually, to the onset of the physiological events associated with parturition (Challis & Olson, 1988; Cook & Randal, 1998).

FETAL ALCOHOL SYNDROME

Prenatal alcohol exposure (PAE) can lead to multiple adverse developmental outcomes and is recognized to be the most common, preventable cause of mental deficiency in the Western world. Fetal alcohol spectrum disorder (FASD) is a non-diagnostic term, which includes FAS, partial FAS (pFAS), alcohol-related neurodevelopmental disorder (ARND), and alcohol-related birth defects (ARBD). As of now, FAS is the only FASD-related diagnosis coded in the ICD-10. The effects of PAE may include physical, mental, behavioral, and learning disabilities that are likely to have lifelong implications.

It has been commonly accepted that alcohol is a powerful teratogen, and the link between heavy drinking (binge-like exposure: four or more drinks per occasion) during pregnancy and the risk of FAS is well established (Abel, 1998; Jacobson & Jacobson, 1994; 1999; Jones, Smith, Ulleland, & Streissguth, 1973; Kelly et al., 2009; Sood et al., 2001).

However, several studies have found no increased risk of behavioral and developmental problems in children born to women who drank low amounts of alcohol during pregnancy, defined as 1–2 drinks per week or per occasion (Gray & Henderson, 2006; Kelly et al., 2009; Linnet et al., 2003; Testa, Quigley, & Eiden, 2003). Notably, there is also evidence that low amounts of alcohol consumption (up to 3–4 drinks per week) during pregnancy may have adverse effects on child neurodevelopment (Sood et al., 2001).

Due to insufficient evidence regarding fetal safety or harm at low levels of alcohol consumption in pregnancy and insufficient evidence to define any threshold for low-level drinking in pregnancy, abstinence is the most prudent choice during pregnancy (Carson et al., 2010).

Acute Health Consequences: Accidental Injury and Poisoning, Suicide, Interpersonal Violence, and Assaults

Most researchers agree on causality between alcohol and the following conditions: road injuries (V87–V89); injuries from falls (W00–W19), fires (X00–X09), excessive cold (X31); drowning (W65–W74), occupational and machine injuries (W24–W31, W45, W60); suicide (X60–X84, Y87.0), and assault (X85–X99, Y00–Y09, Y87.1; English et al., 1995; Gutjahr et al., 2001; Rehm et al., 2004; Ridolfo & Stevenson, 2001; Single et al., 1996; 1999; Sjögren et al., 2000; Taylor & Rehm, 2012; Taylor et al., 2010; but see Gmel & Rehm, 2003). However, it should be noted that there is no general consensus regarding AAFs for these outcomes.

Alcohol use has been associated with increased risk of injury and death in a wide variety of settings, including vehicular crashes, bicycling accidents, incidents involving pedestrians, falls, fires, injuries related to sports and recreational activities, self-inflicted injuries, and injuries resulting from interpersonal violence (Cherpitel, 1992; Freedland & McMicken, 1993b; Hingson & Howland, 1987; 1993; Hurst, Harte, & Firth, 1994; Martin, 1982; USDHHS, 1997; 2000). There is also some evidence that the presence of alcohol in the body at the time of injury may be associated with greater severity of injury and less positive outcomes (Cherpitel, 1996; Traynor, 2005).

Studies relating average volume of drinking to risk of injury have found that the risk of injury is positively related to the average consumption of alcohol, and increased risk starts at relatively low volumes of consumption (e.g., Cherpitel et al., 1995). Several specific patterns of drinking have been related to injury risk. In particular, frequency of heavy drinking and perceived intoxication are both associated with injury in general (Cherpitel, 1996), as well as with death due to injury (Li, Smith, & Baker, 1994). In studies of the relationship between drinking patterns and risk of injury from drunk driving (Gruenewald & Nephew, 1994; Treno, Gruenewald, & Ponicki, 1997; Treno & Holder, 1997), the highest risk was found for individuals who consume relatively large amounts of alcohol on some occasions and whose highest amounts were markedly greater than their average amounts per occasion, after adjusting for other drinking pattern variables and characteristics of the drinker. This finding suggests that those who do not usually drink heavily may be most at risk for injury when they drink heavily. Hence, the risk of mortality in accidents is likely to be more for men than for women. A time-series study in Canada displayed higher risk for men compared to women, with an increase in per liter of alcohol consumption accompanied by an increase in accident mortality of 5.9 among males and 1.9 among females (Skog, 2003).

A long series of retrospective studies using a case–control design involved the comparison of blood alcohol concentration (BAC) levels in individuals who had experienced a collision or trauma with selected individuals not involved in trauma (Cherpitel, 1992; Freedland & McMicken, 1993b; Fuller, 1995; Hurst et al., 1994; Stoduto et al., 1993; USDHHS, 1997). These found increasing risk with increasing levels of BAC. One of the most influential case–control series was the Grand Rapids study of 5,985 collisions and 7,590 controls (Borkenstein, Crowther, Shumate, Ziel, & Zylman, 1964; Hurst et al., 1994). Reanalysis of this study using current, more sophisticated statistical techniques found that all levels of BAC were associated with an increased risk of crashes relative to a BAC of zero and that the risk curve was an accelerating slope in which the risk of crashes involving injury increased markedly with higher BACs (Hurst et al., 1994).

There are obvious reasons why alcohol is related to injury. Controlled experimental studies have demonstrated that even moderate doses of alcohol have cognitive and psychomotor effects such as increased reaction time, impaired cognitive processing, and reduced coordination and vigilance that are all relevant to the risk of injury (Eckardt et al., 1998; Krüger, Utzelmann, Berghaus, & Krog, 1993; Moskowitz & Robinson, 1988; USDHHS, 1997). A comprehensive review by Eckardt and colleagues (1998) concluded that the threshold dose for negative effects on psychomotor tasks is generally found around 40–50 mg% (equivalent to BACs of .04–.05%). This review also noted that injury could occur as a result of alcohol's disruption of psychomotor function in individuals with BACs at this level.

Overall, causality at least for traffic accidents can be established for the following reasons:

- Alcohol is clearly associated with the outcome.
- There is a dose–response relationship: the higher the BAC, the higher the risk of crashes involving injury.
- There is a biological explanation for the relationship based on the mediating effects of alcohol on cognitive and psychomotor performance.
- Where suitable interventions have been implemented to reduce alcohol in the situation, the outcome is reduced as well, as demonstrated by the meta-analysis of Shults et al. (2001), which found that random breath testing programs and selective breath testing checkpoints were effective

in reducing the mortality of traffic accidents by 20% and 18%, respectively.

The fact that alcohol is causally related to traffic accidents does not imply that the attributable fractions are constant across conditions or regions. Alcohol-attributable fractions for unintentional injuries vary by place and time, not only because of drinking patterns but also because of other interacting factors, such as conditions of roads and vehicles, seatbelt usage, availability of public transport, and more. Thus, the AAFs for injuries have wider confidence intervals than the risk relationships between alcohol and chronic diseases discussed earlier (see later discussion and Rehm et al., 2004).

Thus, acute consequences such as injuries and accidents are clearly linked to average volumes of alcohol consumption and patterns of drinking, especially heavy drinking occasions with intoxication. Therefore, in modeling the risk relationships, both dimensions have to be incorporated. This was achieved in the CRA by using a multilevel analysis similar to the analyses done for alcohol and IHD described earlier (see Rehm et al., 2004, for details). The results confirmed the hypotheses that alcohol has a detrimental effect on injury, with patterns of heavy drinking occasions potentiating the relationship between violence and average volume of alcohol consumption. Alcohol-attributable fractions vary widely by sex, age, condition, and different geographic regions (see Rehm et al., 2004).

Illegal Drugs

Although other risk factors contribute more to the global burden of disease, the overall burden of diseases attributable to illegal drug use is considerable. Globally, both smoking and alcohol use each cause about five times the burden compared to illegal drugs (4.1% and 4.0% vs. 0.8%, respectively; see Rehm & Room, 2005). Only in developed countries is illegal drug use among the 10 most burdensome risk factors for the burden of disease.

Illegal drug use is associated with many diseases and conditions. Here, four areas of morbidity due to illegal drug use are distinguished: overdose and other injury, noncommunicable diseases, mental disorders, and infectious diseases.

Morbidity
INJURY, ACCIDENTS, AND POISONINGS
The most acute forms of problems or consequences possibly associated with drug use—phenomena that

can occur with a single-occasion use—are possible injury, both intentional and unintentional. A number of different forms of "injury" have been shown to be associated with illegal drug use (Chermack & Blow, 2002; Degenhardt & Hall, 2012; Fergusson & Horwood, 2001; Hall & Degenhardt, 2009; Hall, Degenhardt, & Lynskey, 2001; Kelly, Darke, & Ross, 2004; Macdonald et al., 2003) and can occur as a form of harm independent of the length or regularity of drug use.

One main form of injury is drug poisoning or overdose. Several studies have documented that a large proportion of street drug users have experienced one or more episodes of drug poisonings or (nonfatal) overdoses in their lives. Thus, it has been estimated that between 35% and 50% of injection drug users (IDUs) experience an overdose in their lifetime (Darke & Zador, 1996; Darke, Ross, Zador, & Sunjic, 2000*a*; Fischer, Medved, Gliksman, & Rehm, 1999; Tobin & Latkin, 2003). Most of these overdoses are accidental and not attempted suicides, but rather result from the uncertainties regarding the potency of illegal products and the circumstances of use. For instance, in Australia, 5% of fatal heroin overdoses over 5 years were classified as suicides (Darke & Ross, 2001) whereas 92% of methadone maintenance patients reported that their most recent overdoses were accidental rather than intentional (Darke, Sims, McDonald, & Wickes, 2000*b*; Warner-Smith, Darke, Lynskey, & Hall, 2001). Furthermore, survivors of drug overdose may suffer from various physical complications, such as renal failure, cardiovascular complications, lung infections, and cognitive disorders (Hulse, English, Milne, & Holman, 1999).

Additional forms of injury associated with drug use are accidents experienced while under the influence of illegal drugs, such as motor vehicle accidents (MVAs) or other traffic accidents occurring with drivers under the influence of psychoactive drugs (other than or in addition to alcohol). Drugs typically subsumed under the rubric of "illegal drugs" influence a number of skills and abilities (e.g., cognition, vision, psychomotor control, reaction time) essential for the safe operation of motor vehicles and other machinery. On this basis, several studies have documented illegal drug users to be at a greater risk for MVA involvement, although there is a controversial debate about the causal role of illegal drug use in MVAs (Degenhardt & Hall, 2012; Hall et al., 2001; Hall & Degenhardt, 2009; Kelly et al., 2004). A meta-analysis found that the percentage of nonfatally injured drivers testing positive

for cannabis ranged from 5.0% to 16.9%, whereas those testing positive for cocaine ranged from 0.6% to 5.6%, with the corresponding percentages for fatally injured drivers being in the same broad range (Macdonald et al., 2003).

Two caveats should be considered in the interpretation of these numbers. First, the underlying studies were mainly from the United States and other developed countries during the 1990s, and thus the prevalences are based on the overall pattern of drug use in these countries at this time. Second, these rates may not be indicative of the rates of accidents *caused* by illegal drugs because the dose of drugs in the body must be above a certain level to cause cognitive and psychomotor impairments, and, even at such a level, some of the accidents may have occurred without the drug. However, the prevalence of injured drivers with a blood level above the threshold in the cited studies was generally higher when compared to the prevalence in the general population; therefore, some of the accidents with drug-positive drivers should be considered causally related to drug use.

The last category of injury related to drugs concerns intentional injuries. Drug users appear to be at an elevated risk of suicide when compared to the general population (Degenhardt & Hall, 2012; Degenhardt et al., 2011*a*; 2011*b*). A meta-analysis by Hallfors and colleagues (2004) indicated that suicide is 14 times greater among heroin users than non–drug dependent populations of the same age. Data from six study sites in five US cities has demonstrated that approximately 36% of IDUs have suicidal ideation, whereas 7% of the individuals surveyed attempted suicide in the 6 months prior to enrolment (Havens et al., 2004). One study also found that adolescents engaging in illegal drug use are at increased odds for depression, suicidal ideation, and suicide attempts (Fischer et al., 2005).

NONCOMMUNICABLE PHYSICAL DISEASE

Overall, illegal drug users display a disproportionately higher degree of morbidity and health problems as compared to the general population. A variety of noncommunicable physical health problems have been shown to be associated with illegal drug use. Yet these problems greatly depend on the kind(s) of drug used as well as the wider circumstances of use. Consequences of drug use include cardiovascular disease, pulmonary disease, cancer, and gastrointestinal problems due to neurological damage (Darke, Kaye, McKetin, & Duflou, 2008; Degenhardt & Hall, 2012; Degenhardt et al.,

2011*a*; 2011*b*; Karch, 2002; Randall et al., 2011). Street drug user populations, including IDUs and/ or oral crack, are likely to have one of the highest degrees of long-term health problems. For example, one comparable study on untreated illegal opioid users (half of the cohort lived in transitional housing or on the street) in the five most populous cities of Canada revealed that 50% of the participants rated their health status to be "fair" or "poor" (Peles, Schreiber, Gordon, & Adelson, 2005; Rosenblum et al., 2003), far below that of the general Canadian population, among whom only 12% report such status. Some of the most serious chronic health problems reported by the participants were hepatitis, pain, and mental issues.

Elevated levels of severe and/or chronic pain were found to be common complaints in illegal opioid users, in and out of treatment programs (Ives et al., 2006; Jamison, Kauffman, & Katz, 2000; Kahan, Srivastava, & Shen, 2006; Manchikanti, 2006). However, there is evidence that elevated pain (e.g., through injury) may have preceded illegal drug use, suggesting this use is a consequence of untreated or ineffectively treated pain problems. Severe pain in illegal opioid users may even be a result of ineffective treatment (Brooner, King, Kidorf, Schmidt, & Bigelow, 1997; Khantzian, 1985; Skodol, Oldham, & Gallaher, 1999).

MENTAL DISORDERS

Mental health problems are also more prevalent in illegal drug users, ranging throughout Axis I and Axis II of the *Diagnostic and Statistical Manual of Mental Disorders* (DSM). One consistent finding is that personality disorders are much more prevalent among those who use analgesics (e.g., opioids), whereas affective disorders have been found to be linked with stimulants (e.g., cocaine) in addition to analgesics (Brooner et al., 1997; Hall, Degenhardt, & Teeson, 2009; Khantzian, 1985; Marshall & Werb, 2010; Skodol et al., 1999).

"Drug dependence" is defined as a mental disorder under both DSM and ICD criteria. As such, drug use directly contributes to the mental health burden. However, it needs to be underscored that only a subfraction of illegal drug users—depending on which drug type is considered—are formally diagnosed as "dependent" or would be considered as fulfilling the criteria of "drug dependence."

Elevated rates of mental health disorders among illegal drug users have been widely documented in treatment samples (e.g., Frei & Rehm, 2002), street user samples (e.g., Fischer et al., 2005), and general population surveys (e.g., Degenhardt & Hall, 2012; Kessler, Chiu, Demier, & Walters, 2005; National Comorbidity Survey Replication, www.hcp.med. harvard.edu/ncs/index.php).

One pooled analysis found that 78% of opioid addicts had at least one comorbid mental condition, excluding other substance use disorders (Frei & Rehm, 2002). Personality disorders had an especially high prevalence among opiod addicts (42%), followed by mood disorders (31%) and anxiety disorders (8%). Comorbid psychiatric conditions are not restricted to opioids, but have been found in all drug users, including cannabis users (Hall et al., 2001). For cannabis use, an association with psychotic symptoms has been most discussed, especially in light of a potential causal role of cannabis use (Andreasson, Allebeck, & Rydberg, 1989; Hall & Degenhardt, 2009; Moore et al., 2007).

There is evidence that psychiatric comorbidity is also considerably elevated in users of cocaine or crack. Approximately 34% of cocaine-dependent users with depression also had antisocial personality disorder, and almost 28% had borderline personality disorder (Schmitz et al., 2000). One study found that the lifetime rate of psychiatric comorbidity in a community-sample of crack cocaine users was substantially elevated, with 36.4% of the sample indicating psychiatric comorbidity based on the DSM-IV (primarily antisocial personality disorder and depression; Falck et al., 2004). A sample of non-treatment-receiving crack cocaine users found substantially higher levels of depression (based on the Beck Depression Inventory): overall, 55% had symptoms of moderate to severe depression, suggesting that the prevalence of depression in cocaine users may be higher than previously reported (Falck et al., 2002).

The question of the direction of association between mental health disorders and drug use has been discussed frequently. Controversy remains, and no conclusive resolution has been widely accepted. Whereas one perspective suggests that mental health disorders are caused or triggered by illegal drug use, the reverse perspective proposes that illegal drug use may be a consequence of mental health problems (especially of those that are undiagnosed or ineffectively treated). It has been found that psychotic episodes are caused or triggered by cannabis use, whereas an illustration of the latter is drug use in the context of mental health problems subsumed under the paradigm of "self-medication," in which drug use is understood as an intended effort by the user to exploit the drug's experienced beneficial psychoactive effects in alleviation of mental health problems (e.g., the use of stimulants to counteract depressive symptoms; Khantzian, 1997). Whereas clear evidence exists for the association of drug use with other mental disorders, there is not much evidence supporting a clear causal role of illegal drug use in these associations.

INFECTIOUS DISEASE

Unsafe injection practices, unsafe sexual contacts, and multiple daily injections place IDUs at elevated risk for various infectious diseases, such as HBV, HCV and HIV (Degenhardt & Hall, 2012; Fischer et al., 2004; March, Ovideo-Joekes, & Romero, 2007; UNAIDS, 2002; Wylie, Shah, & Jolly, 2006). Although prevalence rates vary by country, in many developed countries, HCV rates are above 50% for IDUs. For example, the prevalence of HCV among IDUs in the United States varies from 80% to 95% (Edlin, 2002), in Canada from 16% to 88% (Bowker et al., 2004; Ford et al., 2000), in Australia from 50% to 60% (Doab, Treloar, & Dore, 2005), and in Europe it is more than 60% (EMCDDA, 2003). HIV rates tend to be lower and have larger intercountry variability. In addition to the elevated risks for infectious disease in IDUs, there is also a high prevalence rate of comorbidity between different infectious diseases. The role of illegal drug use in the transmission of infectious disease is also a strong example of how illegal drug use can affect people other than the drug users themselves.

HIV/AIDS is a global epidemic, in part fueled by drug use. For example, there was an emerging drug-related HIV epidemic in Russia, where, at the end of 2004, there were 3 million drug users and 300,000 cases of HIV (Luo & Cofrancesco, 2006). Seventy percent of all reported HIV cases were estimated to be associated with unsafe drug injection practices. The majority of the drug users in Russia have never been tested for HIV and lack basic information regarding the transmission of disease through unsafe drug use practices (Luo & Cofrancesco, 2006). A similar scenario occured in China (Liu, Lian, & Zhao, 2006), where, as of 2004, there were an estimated 1.14 million drug users, most of which were unemployed farmers (Liu et al., 2006). There were 840,000 reported cases of AIDS in China, 43% of which were IDUs (Liu et al., 2006).

MARIJUANA AND CANCER

In many countries, marijuana is considered to have the least risk among illegal drugs and is the second most commonly smoked substance after tobacco. There is concern that smoking marijuana may be a risk factor for tobacco smoking-attributable cancers because the smoke of marijuana contains a number of the same carcinogens found in tobacco. Smoking marijuana may be in fact more harmful than smoking tobacco because more tar is inhaled and retained.

Several studies support the biological plausibility of an association between marijuana smoking and lung cancer on the basis of molecular, cellular, and histopathologic findings (Berthiller et al., 2008; Voirin et al., 2006). However, the role of marijuana as a risk factor of lung cancer is difficult to assess because most marijuana smokers are also tobacco smokers. The epidemiologic evidence that marijuana smoking may lead to lung cancer is limited and inconsistent (Hashibe et al., 2005; 2006; Mehra, Moore, Crothers, Tetrault, & Fiellin, 2006).

An IARC study (Hashibe et al., 2005) reviewed several epidemiological studies that assessed the association of marijuana use and risk of cancers of the lung, head and neck, colorectal, non-Hodgkin's lymphoma, prostate, and cervix, and glioma (Efird et al., 2004; Holly, Lele, Bracci, & McGrath, 1999; Hsairi et al., 1993; Sidney, Quesenberry, Friedman, & Tekawa, 1997; Zhang et al., 1999). Due to methodological limitations of existing studies, including selection bias, possible underreporting where marijuana use is illegal, small sample sizes, limited generalizability, and too few heavy marijuana users in study samples, the authors concluded that the reviewed studies were insufficient for adequately evaluating the impact of marijuana on cancer risk. In light of the growing interest in medicinal marijuana, further epidemiologic studies are needed to clarify the true risks of regular marijuana smoking on cancer and other health conditions.

Mortality

In addition to various forms of morbidity, illegal drug use related mortality is another major problem (Degenhardt & Hall, 2012; Degenhardt et al, 2011a; 2011b; Karch, 2002; Singleton et al., 2009). There are different ways in which illegal drug use may be implicated in fatal outcomes, and this can be best described by *direct* and *indirect* effect paths. The most important direct effect path for mortality is that of fatal drug poisonings in the form of drug overdose deaths. Indirect pathways can be thought of as leading to the consequences of the disease categories just discussed (e.g., drug use leading to

HIV infections leading to AIDS and subsequently to death).

Although large categories of illegal drugs—for example, cannabis—present no evidence of a direct path for mortality, other populations of illegal drug users have been documented as having a higher elevated mortality risk compared to general populations. This has been demonstrated by several studies on so-called "high-risk" drug users (e.g., IDUs including but not limited to illegal opioid users; Degenhardt, Hall, Warner-Smith, & Lynskey, 2004), which have estimated the average annual death rate for problem drug users—defined mainly as drug injectors—of 1.12% (95% CI 0.78–1.46), with other studies identifying an annual mortality rate of 0.5–2.0% (Darke & Hall, 2003; Darke et al., 2007; Hser, Hoffman, Grella, & Anglin, 2001). Following a meta-analysis by English and colleagues (1995), the standardized mortality ratio of injection opiate drug users aged 15–34 years was 13.2 (95% CI 12.3–14.1). In other words, opiate injectors were found to have a mortality risk 13 times that of the general population when matched by age and sex.

Accidental overdose deaths can explain a large portion of these deaths. People who die from drug overdoses tend to be young adults with a mean age in the late 20s to early 30s, typically male, and usually have several years of drug use experience. Most are daily or almost daily drug users, and the majority administer drugs by injection (Darke, Degenhardt, & Mattik, 2007). In addition, poverty, homelessness, coadministration of alcohol and benzodiazepines with opioids, recent changes in patterns of use affecting tolerance to drug (e.g., recent release from prison, enforced or voluntary abstinence, other treatment), impaired physical health status of the user, depression, and history of drug overdose during lifetime are all factors associated with a greater risk for overdose death (Darke & Zador, 1996; Darke et al., 2007; O'Driscoll et al., 2001; Warner-Smith et al., 2001). It is also believed that some overdoses are related to the mental health status and subsequent attempts to alleviate depressive symptoms through increased drug use.

Particular attention has been given to increasing global numbers of overdose deaths related to opioids (Drummer, 2005). A challenging aspect within these toxicological observations is attributing causality for mortality to specific drugs found within the blood system, which in most instances is difficult. In this context, numerous jurisdictions have reported increases in mentions of methadone among drug overdose cases, although, in many instances, these increases likely reflect a greater exposure of drug users due to expanded treatment access, rather than an amplified role of methadone in causing deaths. Considerable concern has also been raised by greatly increased numbers of overdose deaths (especially in the United States) in which prescription opioids have been implicated, surpassing the overdose death numbers (for 2002) for both cocaine and heroin deaths, respectively (Paulozzi, Budnitz, & Xi, 2006).

Among several other wider risk factors documented as influencing fatal poisonings related to illegal drug use (see the section on "Risk Factors"), an important one to be mentioned here is polydrug use—especially that of co-occurring CNS stimulant and suppressant use, which has been identified as a significant predictor of drug overdose death incidents in numerous studies (Burns, Martyres, Clode, & Boldero, 2004; Steentoft et al., 2002; Wolf, Lavezzi, Sullivan, Middleberg, & Flannagan, 2005).

This discussion is summarized in the list of disease conditions found to be causally related to illegal drug use (see Table 10.2).

Risk Factors for Morbidity and Mortality Associated with Illegal Drug Use

In addition to drug use itself, studies have identified a large number of different risk factors on different levels (e.g., social, environmental or behavioral) that influence the likelihood in which morbidity or mortality associated with illegal drug use occurs. Although these factors can only be alluded to in an illustrative fashion here, these wider risk factors are important to consider specifically for the development of preventive or targeted interventions aimed at reducing morbidity and/or mortality as key harm consequences of illegal drug use.

One important social factor or determinant associated with elevated risk of morbidity or mortality has been identified as social integration, or, more specifically, housing status (e.g., homelessness). Street drug users without stable housing or who are living on the street have been found to be at a substantially higher risk for (fatal and nonfatal) drug overdose, risk behaviors for infectious disease transmission (e.g., needle sharing or unsafe injecting), and physical health problems associated with their drug use (Degenhardt & Hall, 2012; Fischer et al., 2004; Galea & Vlahov, 2002; Karch, 2002; Rhodes et al., 2003). For example, in a large multisite sample of HIV-infected persons in the United States, the odds of recent drug use, needle use, or sex exchange were

Table 10.2. Illegal drugs use-attributable disease and injury categories

CONDITION	ICD-10	REFERENCE TO META-ANALYSES OR OTHER INFORMATION FOR DETERMINING DAF
Viral Hepatitis B	B16, B18.0–B18.1	Relationship is usually not determined by prevalence of exposure and RR, but based on proportion in registry data in the respective country
Viral Hepatitis C	B17.1, B18.2	
HIV infection	B20–B24	
MENTAL & BEHAVIOURAL DISORDERS DUE TO USE OF		
Opioids	F11	100% DAF per definition
Cannabinoids	F12	100% DAF per definition
Cocaine	F14	100% DAF per definition
Other stimulants, including caffeine	F15	100% DAF per definition, but illegal drugs have to be separated out
Hallucinogens	F16	100% DAF per definition
Other psychoactive substances	F19	100% DAF per definition, but illegal drugs have to be separated out
Acute and subacute endocarditis	I33	Single et al., 1996, for RR
Pregnancy complications	O44–O46, O67, O35.5, O36.5	English et al., 1995, for RR
Neonatal conditions; low birthweight; and maternal opiate use	P02.0–P02.2, P04.8, P05–P07, P96.1	English et al., 1995, for RR
Foetus and newborn affected by maternal use of drugs of addiction	P04.4	English et al., 1995, for RR
POISONING BY		
Opium	T40.0	100% DAF per definition
Heroin	T40.1	100% DAF per definition
Other opioids	T40.2	100% DAF per definition
Methadone	T40.3	100% DAF per definition, but illegal drugs have to be separated out
Other synthetic narcotics	T40.4	100% DAF per definition
Cocaine	T40.5	100% DAF per definition
Cannabis	T40.7	100% DAF per definition
Local anesthetics (cocaine)	T41.3	100% DAF per definition
Cannabis-attributable traffic accidents	Specific codes V01–V89*	Macdonald et al., 2003, for meta-analysis on proportion
Cocaine-attributable traffic accidents	Specific codes V01–V89*	Macdonald et al., 2003, for meta-analysis on proportion

Table 10.2. Continued

CONDITION	ICD-10	REFERENCE TO META-ANALYSES OR OTHER INFORMATION FOR DETERMINING DAF
Accidental poisoning by and exposure to narcotics and psychodysleptics [hallucinogens], not elsewhere classified	X42	100% DAF per definition, but illegal drugs have to be separated out
Suicide, self-inflicted injuries	X60–X84, Y87.0	Relationship is usually not determined by prevalence of exposure and RR, but based on registry data such as coroners' reports
Homicide	X85–Y09, Y87.1	Macdonald et al., 2003, for meta-analysis on proportion
Opioids and related analgesics causing adverse effects in therapeutic use	Y45.0	100% DAF per definition
ALL-CAUSE MORTALITY		Degenhardt et al., 2004, for a meta-analysis

DAF, drug-attributable fraction; RR, relative risk

2–4 times higher among the homeless and unstably housed when compared to persons with stable housing; these risk behaviors changed at follow-up for those whose housing situation had improved (Aidala, Cross, Stall, Harre, & Sumartojo, 2005). Several studies have demonstrated the absence of stable housing to be a strong predictor of risk behavior for or actual seroconversion of HIV among IDUs (Corneil et al., 2006; Strathdee et al., 1997).

Further related socioenvironmental factors of drug use-related risks for morbidity or mortality refer to criminal justice interventions. For example, recent or lifetime incarceration history has been shown to predict infectious disease (e.g., HIV) status in IDUs as well as overdose mortality risk within a limited time period after release from detention (Galea & Vlahov, 2002; Hammett, Harmon, & Rhodes, 2002; Seaman, Brettle, & Gore, 1998). A retrospective cohort study of inmates released from correctional facilities in Washington State (1999–2003) indicated that during the first 2 weeks of release, the risk of death among former inmates was 12.7 (95% CI 9.2–17.4) times that among other state residents, with a markedly elevated RR of death from drug overdose of 129 (95% CI 89–186), making drug overdose the leading cause of death among former inmates (Binswanger et al., 2007). Similarly, aggressive policing tactics aimed at street drug users have been shown to be associated with elevated risk behaviors (e.g., "worrying and hurrying") associated

with possible morbidity and mortality consequences (Maher & Dixon, 1999; Small et al., 2006).

On a behavioral level, numerous studies have documented that patterns of illegal drug use—akin to, for example, alcohol use and its related harm—can be substantially related to morbidity or mortality consequences. For example, among female Aboriginal IDUs in Vancouver, frequent use of "speedballs" (combined heroin and cocaine injection; RR 3.1; 95% CI 1.4–7.1) and binges of injection drug use (2.3; 1.0–5.2) were found to be independent predictors of HIV seroconversion (Craib et al., 2003). Similarly speedball use associated with frequent and erratic injection behavior has been independently associated with recent overdose episodes (nonfatal) in several IDU populations in Canada and the United States (Kerr et al., 2007; Ochoa, Hahn, Seal, & Moss, 2001). Similarly, several key (e.g., physical or mental health) harm indicators associated with cannabis use have been documented to be associated with frequent and/or long-term use of cannabis (Hall et al., 2001).

Tobacco

The ultimate risk of death from smoking is high. It is estimated that about one-half to two-thirds of long-term smokers will eventually be killed by their addiction (Doll, Peto, Boreham, & Sutherland, 2004; Peto, Lopez, Boreham, & Thun, 2003). Worldwide, based on current consumption patterns, approximately

1 billion people in the 21st century will be killed by their addiction to tobacco (WHO, 2008). About half of these people will die between the ages of 35 and 69, resulting in the loss of about 20–25 years of life as compared to the life expectancy of nonsmokers (Doll et al., 2004; Peto et al., 2003; Jha, 2009).

In 2010, tobacco smoking, including second-hand smoke (6.3 million [5.4 million to 7.0 million deaths and 6.3% [5.5–7.0] DALYs) was the second leading risk factor after high blood pressure for global disease burden (Lim et al., 2012) in all countries. The risk causes a substantially lower burden in women than in men because fewer women smoke or they smoke for a shorter duration than men in most regions. In 2010, tobacco smoking, including second-hand smoke, accounted for 8.4% of worldwide disease burden among men (the leading risk factor) compared with 3.7% among women (fourth highest risk factor; Lim et al., 2012).

Evidence indicates that smoking cessation significantly reduces the risk of death from tobacco-related diseases (Crispo et al., 2004; Doll et al., 2004; Jha et al., 2006, 2013; Lam et al., 2002; Ikeda et al., 2012; Wu et al., 2013). Crispo and colleagues (2004) reported that the proportion of the risk of lung cancer avoided by quitting smoking before the age of 40 was at 80% in Italy and 91% in the United Kingdom, Germany, and Sweden.

The following discussion focuses on the consequences of smoking on morbidity and mortality. A list of malignant and nonmalignant health conditions related to tobacco, developed based on *Health Consequences of Smoking: A Report of the Surgeon General* (USDHHS, 2004), is presented in Table 10.3.

The 2004 US Surgeon General's report considered the following criteria in judging causality: consistency, strength of association, specificity, temporality, coherence, dose–response, and experimental evidence. The report implemented a standardized, hierarchical language to summarize conclusions about causality, the strongest of which is "evidence is sufficient to infer causality." Table 10.3 includes only those health outcomes for which this conclusion was reached.

Please also refer to the most recent 2010 Surgeon General's report, which describes in detail the ways that tobacco smoke damages every organ in the body and causes both disease and death (USDHHS, 2010).

MALIGNANT NEOPLASMS

The role of tobacco as a carcinogen is well established and described elsewhere. In 2004, the US Surgeon General (USDHHS, 2004) added several diseases to the list of those for which evidence is sufficient to conclude a causal relationship between smoking and disease: stomach cancer, renal cell carcinoma, uterine cervical cancer, pancreatic cancer, and pneumonia. For the full list of malignant neoplasms causally associated with tobacco please see Table 10.3.

CARDIOVASCULAR DISEASES
Atherosclerosis

A consistent positive association between smoking and atherosclerosis has been reported (O'Leary et al., 1992; Yataco & Gardner, 1999; Lee & Cooke, 2011). O'Leary et al. (1992) investigated the association between smoking and the presence of atherosclerosis using carotid intimal-medial thickness (IMT) as the marker for subclinical disease because of its strong association with IHD. A positive association was reported, with the highest thickness recorded for "current" smokers, even after adjusting for all other risk factors.

Intimal-medial thickness has also been used to investigate the relationship between fetal tobacco smoke exposure and vascular damage (Geerts, Bots, Grobbee, & Uiterwaal, 2008). Geerts and colleagues (2008) performed ultrasound IMT measurements on fetuses exposed to tobacco smoke and compared these to fetuses with no tobacco smoke exposure. Fetuses exposed to tobacco smoke displayed an IMT 13.4 µm thicker than offspring of mothers who did not smoke during their pregnancy.

Intimal-medial thickness and flow-mediated dilation (FMD) have been used to detect changes in the physical structure of blood vessel endothelium that contribute to the development of atherosclerosis. In a longitudinal study by Kallio and colleagues (2010) on healthy 13-year-olds, it was reported that high levels of tobacco exposure were related to increased IMT and decreased FMD when compared to low and medium exposure groups, signaling endothelial dysfunction.

Experimental data have also demonstrated the acute effects of smoking on atherosclerosis (Yataco & Gardner, 1999). Ankle-arm index (AAI) is the systolic blood pressure of the ankle divided by the systolic blood pressure of the arm and is an accepted index of subclinical peripheral arterial disease, with lower values indicating disease. Experimental evidence from Yataco and Gardner (1999) reported that smoking two cigarettes significantly decreases AAI compared with

Table 10.3. Smoking-attributable disease and injury categories

CONDITION	ICD-10	REFERENCE TO META-ANALYSES/REVIEW
Mental and behavioral disorders due to use of tobacco	F17	100% SAF per definition
Toxic effect of tobacco and nicotine	T65.2	100% SAF per definition
MALIGNANT NEOPLASMS		
Oropharyngeal cancer	C00–C14, D00.0	English et al., 1995
Esophageal cancer	C15, D00.1	English et al., 1995
Stomach cancer	C16, D00.2	Tredaniel et al., 1997
Pancreas cancer	C25, D01.9	English et al., 1995
Laryngeal cancer	C32, D02.0	English et al., 1995
Trachea, bronchus, and lung cancers	C33–C34	Simonato et al., 2001
Cervical cancer	C53, D06	Plummer et al., 2003
Urinary tract cancer	C64–C68	Zeegers et al., 2000
Renal cell carcinoma	C64	Hunt et al., 2005
Bladder cancer	C67, D09.0	Brennan et al., 2000; 2001
Acute myeloid leukemia	C92.0	Brownson et al., 1993
CARDIOVASCULAR DISEASES		
Ischemic heart disease	I20–I25	Law et al., 1997; Law & Wald, 2003
Pulmonary circulatory disease	I26–I28	English et al., 1995
Cardiac arrhythmias	I47–I49	Follow IHD
Heart failure; complications and ill-defined descriptions and of heart disease	I50–I51	Follow IHD
Cerebrovascular diseases	I60–I69	English et al., 1995
Atherosclerosis	I70–I79	English et al., 1995
RESPIRATORY DISEASES		
Influenza and pneumonia	J10–J18	English et al., 1995
Chronic obstructive pulmonary disease	J40–J44	Single et al., 1996
Ulcers	K25–K28	English et al., 1995
CONDITIONS ARISING DURING THE PERINATAL PERIOD		
Foetus and newborn affected by maternal use of tobacco	P04.2	100% SAF per definition

(continued)

Table 10.3. Continued

CONDITION	ICD-10	REFERENCE TO META-ANALYSES/REVIEW
Low birthweight & short gestation	P05–P07	English et al., 1995
Sudden infant death syndrome	R95	English et al., 1995
UNINTENTIONAL INJURIES		
Fires	X00–X09	Relationship is usually not determined by prevalence of exposure and RR, but based on proportion in registry data in the respective country

IHF, ischemic heart disease; RR, relative risk; SAF, smoking-attributable fraction

the AAI on days in which participants refrained from smoking. In addition, evidence of a statistically significant linear dose–response relationship between subclinical atherosclerosis and the amount smoked has been reported (Fine-Edelstein et al., 1994).

Smoking is not only related to an increased risk (i.e., incidence) of subclinical atherosclerosis, but it also affects disease prognosis and experienced symptoms. Zieske et al. (1999) assessed atherosclerotic lesions in 50 smokers and 50 nonsmokers and found that smokers were twice as likely to have advanced lesions compared to nonsmokers, leading to a conclusion that lesions progress more rapidly in smokers. Sanada and colleagues (2012) compared changes in atherosclerosis development by measuring IMT changes in never, past, and current smokers over the course of 2 years. They reported that current smokers had significantly higher maximum changes from baseline IMT values. It was concluded that current smokers' atherosclerosis development was accelerated. Current smokers also have a higher incidence of severe symptomatology (e.g., pain in the extremities; Smith et al., 1998).

Results from pooled analyses have indicated that smoking was strongly related to carotid atherosclerosis, regardless of age (Howard et al., 1997). Evidence from a pathology study in which data were drawn from a series of autopsies of young adults, regardless of cause of death, demonstrated clear and strong associations between a history of smoking and the presence of aortic and coronary atherosclerosis (Strong et al., 1999). However, the extent of atherosclerosis has been found to increase with age and active smoking behavior (McGill et al., 2001; Zieske et al., 1999; Hudson & Mannino, 2010).

Ischemic Heart Disease

Although smoking tobacco has been firmly established as a leading cause of IHD, several refinements have been made to this growing body of literature. Smoking has been identified as a strong risk factor for IHD in women younger than 50. Dunn and colleagues (1999) conducted a study of women 44 years of age or younger and found that odds ratios (OR) for IHD showed a strong dose–response relationship, with a risk of 2.47 for those smoking 1–5 cigarettes a day and increasing to 74.6 for those smoking 40 or more cigarettes per day, compared to nonsmokers. The reported attributable risk for tobacco use and IHD in this group was 73%. Additionally, the highest risk of IHD (6.8) has been reported for female smokers younger than 55 (Prescott, Hippe, Schnohr, Hein, & Vestbo, 1998).

As mentioned earlier, there exists a strong dose–response relationship between the number of cigarettes smoked per day and the risk of IHD (Stampfer, Hu, Manson, Rimm, & Willett, 2000). Specifically, adjusted RRs were reported for former smokers, individuals smoking 1–14 cigarettes a day, and those who smoke 15 or more cigarettes a day, as 1.55, 3.12, and 5.48, compared to lifetime nonsmokers, respectively. Compared to lifetime nonsmokers, the RR in smokers rises with the number of cigarettes smoked and falls after cessation.

It has also been documented that the risk of IHD is of a similar magnitude in other ethnic groups (for example, African Americans; Liao, McGee, Cooper, & Sutkowski, 1999; Rosenberg, 1999). Because most previous information was gathered using European Caucasians, it is important for a causal relationship to be supported across various racial and ethnic groups. A study by Wu et al. (2013) was the first to establish a link between current smoking and IHD mortality in the Southeast Asian community. This study found that there was an increased risk of death from IHD among both ever (hazard ratios 1.68, 0.94–2.99) and current cigarette/bidi (filterless locally produced cigarettes) smokers (hazard ratios 1.94, 1.08–3.49) in men, with a stronger association for current smokers. In addition, ever smokers who had smoked for more than 30 years or had accumulated more than 30 pack-years were two times more likely to die from IHD.

The common question is whether or not the type of cigarette smoked has any influence on IHD risk. It has been demonstrated that smoking low-yield cigarettes has lower influence on IHD risk when compared to medium-yield and high-yield cigarettes (Negri et al., 1993; Parish et al., 1995; Tang et al., 1995).

Cerebrovascular Disease

Smoking has been clearly identified as a major risk factor associated with an increase in both the incidence of and mortality from cerebrovascular disease. Cigarette smoking has been found to increase the risk of stroke by an estimated 50% (Shinton & Beevers, 1989) with a reported RR of 2.5 for overall stroke mortality (Kuller et al., 1991), although the effect differs according to the stroke subtype. An RR of 1.9 has been reported for ischemic stroke, with 2.9 for subarachnoid hemorrhage (Shinton & Beevers, 1989). In addition, Doll and colleagues (1994) found that, compared to lifetime nonsmokers, current smokers at baseline had RRs of 1.31 for thrombotic stroke, 1.37 for hemorrhagic stroke, and 2.14 for subarachnoid hemorrhage. Lawlor et al. (2008) reported that smoking at baseline was associated with substantial increases in risk of ischemic stroke (hazard ratio 1.58) and subarachnoid hemorrhage (hazard ratio 1.91).

A clear dose–response relationship between an increased risk of stroke and an increase in the average number of cigarettes smoked per day has also been reported (Bhat et al., 2008; Doll et al., 1994; Robbins, Manson, Lee, Satterfield, Hennekens, 1994; Shah & Cole, 2010). In general, data from a 10-year follow-up of more than 22,000 participants showed that, compared to lifetime nonsmokers, current smokers of 1–19 cigarettes per day had an age-adjusted RR for stroke incidence of 2.02, and smokers of 20 or more cigarettes a day had an adjusted RR of 2.52 (Robbins et al., 1994). The dose–response relationship has been found to be particularly strong for subarachnoid hemorrhage, specifically RR 1.43, 1.71, and 3.43 for smokers of

1–14, 15–24 and more than 24 cigarettes per day, respectively (Doll et al., 1994). In a study determining the presence of a dose–response between stroke and number of cigarettes smoked per day in women, Bhat and colleagues (2008) observed an increase in the ORs of stroke with increasing numbers of cigarettes per day (OR 2.2 for 1–10 cigs/day, OR 2.5 for 11–20 cigs/day, OR 4.3 for 21–39 cigs/day, and OR 9.1 for 40+ cigs/day).

Using estimates of prevalence and RR from the large Cancer Prevention Study II (CPS-II), it has been estimated that among persons younger than 65 years of age, smoking was responsible for 51% of cerebrovascular disease deaths in men and 55% in women (USDHHS, 1989). These estimations not only demonstrate the particularly elevated risk for individual smokers under the age of 65, but also document that the smoking-associated risk is relatively equal between men and women. To further support this assertion, Knekt et al. (1991) found that the RR for subarachnoid hemorrhage for men is 2.4 and for women, 2.5, which is reasonably comparable.

Wannamethee and colleagues (1995) investigated the notion that the risk of cerebrovascular disease decreases steadily after smoking cessation. They found that stroke risks for former smokers fell to the lowest levels around 5 years after smoking cessation; the remaining risk levels depended on the amount smoked: former heavy smokers fell to a similar level of that of light smokers, and former light smokers fell to a level similar to that of lifetime nonsmokers.

ACUTE RESPIRATORY ILLNESS

Sufficient evidence exists to support a causal relationship between smoking and acute respiratory illness (including influenza infections, pneumonia, and other acute upper and lower respiratory tract infections). Almirall and colleagues (1999*a*; 1999*b*) conducted a population-based matched (gender and age) case–control study to determine the contribution of tobacco smoking on community-acquired pneumonia. The investigators reported that the OR for pneumonia for former smokers compared with nonsmokers was 1.77 and 1.68 for current smokers. The effects of the number of cigarettes smoked per day (adjusted OR) compared with individuals who had never smoked were as follows: 1–9 cigarettes/day = 0.80; 10–20 cigarettes/day = 1.40; >20 cigarettes/day = 2.77 and former smokers = 1.58. As such, the results indicated not only a causal relationship, but also a dose–response relationship between smoking and acute lower respiratory tract infections and, in this case, specifically pneumonia. The population-based case–control study (Nuorti et al., 2000) demonstrated that smoking was the strongest independent risk factor for invasive pneumococcal pneumonia among otherwise health individuals. The ORs were 4.1 for active smokers and 2.5 for nonsmokers, while the attributable risks were 51% and 17%, respectively.

CHRONIC OBSTRUCTIVE PULMONARY DISEASE

Smoking affects the entire lung, including its structure and function. Smoking compromises lung defenses against infection and causes harmful biological processes (i.e., oxidant stress, inflammation, and a protease-antiprotease imbalance) that result in airway and alveolar injury and lead to chronic obstructive pulmonary disease (COPD; USDHHS, 2004). There is extensive evidence from previous Surgeon General's reports on COPD and smoking, such as the 1984 report that found 80–90% of chronic obstructive lung disease (COLD) in the United States was attributable to cigarette smoking (USDHHS, 1984). In 2001, it was reported that cigarette smoking is a primary cause of COPD among women in the United States, with risk increasing with the amounts and duration of smoking. Approximately 90% of mortality from COPD among women has been attributed to cigarette smoking (USDHHS, 2001, p. 14).

TUBERCULOSIS

Several studies have suggested a link between smoking and infection with *Mycobacterium tuberculosis* (Alcaide et al., 1996; Anderson, Sy, Thompson, & Addy, 1997; Buskin, Gale, Weiss, & Nolan, 1994; Gajalakshmi, Peto, Kanaka, & Jha, 2003; Liu et al., 1998; Ferrera et al., 2012). A large case–control study of 43,000 adult male deaths with 35,000 controls examined this relationship and found that the RR for death from tuberculosis was 4.5 (95% CI 4.0–5.0) for urban residents and 4.2 (95% CI 3.7–4.8) for rural residents (Gajalakshmi et al., 2003). The smoking-attributable fraction of deaths from tuberculosis was reported as 61%. Alcaide and colleagues (1996) found an estimated attributable risk of smoking for newly diagnosed tuberculosis of 48% (95% CI 13–69). However, causality has not been confirmed.

PREGNANCY COMPLICATIONS

Placenta previa, which is the implantation of the placenta over or near the internal os of the cervix, has consistently been found to be more frequent in smokers compared to nonsmokers. Kramer et al. (1991) found that maternal smoking approximately doubled the risk of placenta previa after adjusting for maternal age (OR 2.1). Handler and colleagues (1994), expanding on this work, found that pregnant women who smoked more than 20 cigarettes per day were more than two times more likely to experience placenta previa compared with nonsmokers (OR 2.3). Moreover, current cigarette smoking has been associated with a 2.6- to 4.4-fold increased risk of placental previa, and a dose–response relationship was demonstrated, with an OR of 2.2 for light smokers and 4.0 for heavy smokers compared with individuals who had never smoked (Chelmow, Andrew, & Baker, 1996).

Many studies have found an increased risk of placental abruption, the premature separation of a normally implanted placenta before delivery, associated with active smoking during pregnancy. Voigt and colleagues (1990) reported that pregnant smokers had an RR of 1.6 for placental abruption. It has been demonstrated that for each pack of cigarettes smoked per day the risk of placental abruption increases by 40% (OR 1.39; Raymon & Mills, 1993). In addition, Misra and Ananth (1999) found a 40% increased risk for placental abruption (OR 1.4; 95% CI 1.0–1.8) with each year of maternal smoking preceding the pregnancy.

Bouyer and colleagues (2003) reported an adjusted OR of 3.9 for risk of ectopic pregnancy in women smoking more than 20 cigarettes per day.

SUDDEN INFANT DEATH SYNDROME

Sudden infant death syndrome (SIDS) has been investigated in relation to fetal exposure to maternal smoking, as well as to the exposure of the infant to smoking by the mother and others during the postpartum period. A dose–response relationship has been documented by a number of researchers. Haglund and Cnattingius (1990) compared mothers who smoked 1–9 cigarettes during their pregnancy with those who smoked 10 or more cigarettes per day. Smoking 1–9 cigarettes per day doubled the risk of SIDS, and smoking more than 10 cigarettes per day tripled the risk of SIDS, compared with nonsmokers. Mitchell et al. (1991) reported the ORs associated with maternal cigarette smoking compared with no maternal smoking as follows: 1–9 cigarettes/day, OR 1.87; 10–19 cigarettes/day, OR 2.64; more than 20 cigarettes/day, OR 5.06. In a recent meta-analysis conducted by Zhang and Wang (2013), prenatal and postnatal maternal smoking was associated with a significantly increased risk of

SIDS (OR = 2.25, 95% CI = 2.03–2.50 for pre-natal maternal smoking analysis and OR = 1.97, 95% CI = 1.77–2.19 for postnatal maternal smoking analysis, respectively) by random effects model. The effects were dose-dependent. A literature review conducted by Mitchell and Mildred (2000) revealed a pooled RR of 1.5 for postnatal tobacco exposure and SIDS.

Fleming and colleagues (2000) investigated SIDS in relation to environmental tobacco exposure during the postpartum period and reported a dose–response relationship. There was a significant linear increase in risk with an increase in the number of individuals smoking within the infants' household. With one person smoking, the OR for SIDS was 4.7; two persons smoking yielded an OR of 11.3, and with three or more persons smoking, the OR was 16.9.

Similarly, Klonoff-Cohen (1997) reported a dose–response relationship for postpartum smoking exposures even after adjusting for prenatal smoking levels of the mother. With one person smoking in the infant's room, the OR for SIDS was 3.67; two to four persons smoking in the infant's room yielded an OR of 20.91.

REDUCED FEMALE FERTILITY

Augood et al. (1998) found that the overall OR for risk of infertility in female smokers compared to nonsmokers was 1.60. Alderete and colleagues (1995) found that smokers had about one-half the fertility (OR 0.5–0.6) of nonsmokers for conception times of 6 and 12 months. Cigarette smoking among women was associated with a significant decreased fecundability (fecundability ratio 0.90; Curtis, Savitz, & Arbuckle, 1997). A systematic literature review on the impact of cigarette smoking and smoke constituents on the different stages of reproductive function, including epidemiological, clinical, and experimental studies, is available from Dechanet and colleagues (2011).

Interactions Between Substances in the Etiology of Disease

So far, we have concentrated on the relationships between substance use and incidence of various disease and injury outcomes. There are also interactions between substances that cause disease. For example, alcohol and tobacco consumption both impact the development of esophageal cancer (see the classic study of Tuyns, Péquignot, & Jensen, 1977; for an overview, see Taylor & Rehm, 2006). Most studies found a multiplicative effect; that is, the combined

risk for drinking and smoking was higher than the addition of both effects combined. In other words, combining both risk factors led to an increased risk over and above the added risks of each risk factor. Other cancers of the upper aerodigestive tract showed the same multiplicative effects (Taylor & Rehm, 2006). Overall, however, not many other disease and injury categories have been found where such multiplicative effects of alcohol and tobacco use were evidenced (Taylor & Rehm, 2006).

A different kind of interaction on health outcomes are accidental overdose deaths. In most of these deaths, multiple substances contributed, and it is almost impossible to identify one of these substances as the main cause (Darke et al., 2007). Not only illegal drugs contribute to overdose deaths, but also legal substances such as alcohol or prescription pharmaceuticals. In a study in Ontario, more than 90% of the oxycodone-related deaths involved a nonopioid depressant of the CNS (e.g., alcohol, benzodiazepines, cyclic antidepressants, or a combination of these; see Dhalla et al., 2009).

In summary, there are clear instances in which the combination of substances has a causal role in the etiology of disease and injury. At this point, these effects seem to be the exception rather than the rule.

The Role of Substances in the Course of Disease

Substance use does not only impact on the incidence of disease, but also the course of a disease, regardless of the original cause. Two mechanisms are important in this respect:

• Substance use, especially heavy use, impacts the human immune system, both innate and acquired (Friedman, Newton, & Klein, 2003; Friedman et al., 2006).
• Alcohol and illegal drugs often disrupt medication schedules.

Although detailing these mechanisms is beyond the scope of this chapter, we would like to give just one example of the consequences of alcohol use on medication schedules. In a meta-analysis, Hendershot and colleagues (2009) found that alcohol drinkers were approximately half as likely to be classified as adherent to antiretroviral therapy for HIV/AIDS (OR 0.548; 95% CI 0.490–0.612) when compared to abstainers (or those who drank relatively less). Effect sizes for problem drinking, defined as meeting the National Institute on Alcohol Abuse and Alcoholism criteria for at-risk drinking or criteria for an AUD, were greater (OR 0.474; 95% CI 0.408–0.550) than those reflecting any or global drinking (OR 0.604; 95% CI 0.531–0.687). Because adherence to antiretroviral medication is an important factor in the survival of HIV/AIDS patients, the public health impact of alcohol on these treatment regimens is substantial, especially in countries with high HIV prevalence (e.g., Rehm & Parry, 2009).

Clearly, the impact of substance use on medication schedules is not always as severe as in the example given, but, overall, there is a substantial public health impact on the course of disease and injury.

Conclusion

As is evident from this chapter, substance use can have serious adverse health consequences. These adverse impacts can range from irreversible physical diseases, such as cirrhosis of the liver, to severe psychological problems, such as depression and suicide attempts, and to traumatic injuries. Adverse health consequences may be due to drug-specific effects, methods of administration, behavioral habits associated with substance use, or common comorbidities.

Morbidity and mortality attributable to substance use are avoidable. A large portion of this burden can be reduced considerably if known effective policies are implemented.

Future Directions

Future directions in the areas of substance use and physical health should focus on investigating the exact causal impact of alcohol, tobacco, and illicit drugs on infectious disease; their mechanisms on cancer development; the role they have on the incidence of other mental disorders; the causality; and the role of genetic vulnerability.

Further Reading

Corrao, G., Bagnardi, V., Zambon, A., & La Vecchia, C. (2004). A meta-analysis of alcohol consumption and the risk of 15 diseases. *Preventive Medicine, 38,* 613–619.

Degenhardt, L., & Hall, W. (2012). Extent of illicit drug use and dependence, and their contribution to the global burden of disease. *Lancet, 379*(9810), 55–70.

Lim, S. S., Vos, T., Flaxman, A. D., Danaei, G., Shibuya, K., Adair-Rohani, H., ... Memish, Z. A. (2012). A comparative risk assessment of burden of disease and injury attributable to 67 risk factors and risk factor clusters in 21 regions, 1990-2010: A systematic analysis for the Global Burden of Disease Study 2010. *Lancet, 380*(9859), 2224–2260. (Errata published 2013, in Lancet 381(9874), 1276; *Lancet 381*(9867), 628.).

Rehm, J., Baliunas, D., Borges, G. L. G., Graham, K., Irving, H. M., Kehoe, T., Parry, C. D., Patra, J., Popova, S., Poznyak,

V., Roerecke, M., Room, R., Samokhvalov, A. V., & Taylor, B. (2010). The relation between different dimensions of alcohol consumption and burden of disease - an overview. *Addiction, 105*(5), 817–843.

Room, R., Babor, T., & Rehm, J. (2005). Alcohol and public health: A review. *Lancet, 365,* 519–530.

US Department of Health and Human Services (USDHHS). (2004). *The health consequences of smoking: A report of the Surgeon General.* Atlanta, GA: US Department of Health and Human Services, Center for Chronic Disease Prevention and Health Promotion, Office of Smoking and Health.

US Department of Health and Human Services (USDHHS). (2010). *How tobacco smoke causes disease: The biology and behavioral basis for smoking-attributable disease: A report of the Surgeon General.* Atlanta, GA: US Department of Health and Human Services, Centers for Disease Control and Prevention, National Center for Chronic Disease Prevention and Health Promotion, Office on Smoking and Health.

Whiteford, H. A., Degenhardt, L., Rehm, J., Baxter, A. J., Ferrari, A. J., Erskine, H. E., Charlson, F. J., Norman, R. E., Flaxman, A. D., Johns, N., Burstein, R., Murray, C. J. L., & Vos, T. (2013). Global burden of disease attributable to mental and substance use disorders: findings from the Global Burden of Disease Study 2010. *Lancet, 382*(9904), 1575–1586. doi: 10.1016/S0140-6736(13)61611-6

World Health Organization (WHO). (2014). *Global status report on alcohol and health.* Geneva: WHO. Available from http://www.who.int/substance_abuse/publications/global_alcohol_report/en/

References

Abel, E. L. (1998). *Fetal alcohol abuse syndrome.* New York: Plenum Press.

Abel, E. L., & Hannigan, J. H. (1995). "J-shaped" relationship between drinking during pregnancy and birth weight: Reanalysis of prospective epidemiological data. *Alcohol & Alcoholism, 30,* 345–355.

Agarwal, D. P. (2002). Cardioprotective effects of light-moderate consumption of alcohol: A review of putative mechanisms. Review. *Alcohol and Alcoholism, 37*(5), 409–415.

Ahluwalia, B., Smith, D., Adeyiga, O., Akbasak, B., & Rajguru, S. (1992). Ethanol decreases progesterone synthesis in human placental cells: Mechanism of ethanol effect. *Alcohol, 9,* 395–401.

Aidala, A., Cross, J., Stall, R., Harre, D., & Sumartojo, E. (2005). Housing status and HIV risk behaviors: Implications for prevention and policy. *Archives of General Psychiatry, 9*(3), 251–265.

Albertsen, K., Andersen, A. N., Olsen, J., & Gronbaek, M. (2004). Alcohol consumption during pregnancy and the risk of preterm delivery. *American Journal of Epidemiology, 159,* 155–161.

Alcaide, J., Altet, M. N., Plans, P., Parrón, I., Folguera, L., Saltó, E., Domínguez, A., Pardell, H., & Salleras, L. (1996). Cigarette smoking as a risk factor for tuberculosis in young adults: A case-control study. *Tubercle and Lung Disease, 77*(2), 112–116.

Alderete, E., Eskenazi, B., & Sholtz, R. (1995). Effect of cigarette smoking and coffee drinking on time to conception. *Epidemiology, 6*(4), 403–408.

Almirall, J., Bolibar, I., Balanzo, X., & Gonzalez, C. A. (1999a). Risk factors for community-acquired pneumonia in adults: A population-based case-control study. *European Respirology Journal, 13*(2), 349–355.

Almirall, J., Gonzalez, C. A., Balanzo, X., & Bolibar, I. (1999*b*). Proportion of community-acquired pneumonia cases attributable to tobaccos smoking. *Chest, 116*(2), 375–379.

Altieri, A., Garavello, W., Boseti, C., Gallus, S., & Vecchia, C. L. (2005). Alcohol consumption and risk of laryngeal cancer. *Oral Oncology, 41*, 956–965.

Anderson, P., & Baumberg, B. (2006). *Alcohol in Europe. A report of the European Commission* London: Institute of Alcohol Studies.

Anderson, R. H., Sy, F. S., Thompson, S., & Addy, C. (1997). Cigarette smoking and tuberculin skin test conversion among incarcerated adults. *American Journal of Preventive Medicine, 13*(3), 175–181.

Andreasson, S., Allebeck, P., & Rydberg, U. (1989). Schizophrenia in users and nonusers of cannabis. *Acta Psychiatrica Scandinavica, 79*, 505–510.

Ashley, M., Rehm, J., Bondy, S., Single, E., & Rankin, J. (2000). Beyond ischaemic heart disease: Are there other health benefits from drinking alcohol? *Contemporary Drug Problems, 27*, 735–777.

Augood, C., Duckitt, K., & Templeton, A. A. (1998). Smoking and female infertility: A systematic review and meta-analysis. *Human Reproduction Update, 13*(1532), 1539.

Ayala, C., Greenlund, K. J., Croft, J. B., Keenan, N. L., Donehoo, R. S., Giles, W. H., Kittner, S. J., & Marks, J. S. (2001). Racial/ethnic disparities in mortality by stroke subtype in the United States, 1995–1998. *American Journal of Epidemiology, 154*, 1057–1063.

Baan, R., Straif, K., Grosse, Y., Secretan, B., El Ghissassi, F., Bouvard, V., Alteri, A., Cogliano, V., & on behalf of the WHO international agency for research on cancer monograph working group. (2007). Carcinogenicity of alcoholic beverages. *Lancet Oncology, 8*(4), 292–293.

Babor, T., Caetano, R., Casswell, S., Edwards, G., Giesbrecht, N., Graham, K., Grube, J., Gruenewald, P., Hill, L., Holder, H., Homel, R., Österberg, E., Rehm, J., Room, R., & Rossow, I. (2003). *Alcohol: No ordinary commodity. Research and public policy*. Oxford and London: Oxford University Press.

Bagnardi, V., Blangiardo, M., La Vecchia, C., & Corrao, G. (2001). Alcohol consumption and the risk of cancer: A meta-analysis. *Alcohol Research & Health, 25*(4), 263–270.

Balbão, C. E. B., de Paola, A. A. V., & Fenelon, G. (2009). Effects of alcohol on atrial fibrillation. *Therapeutic Advances in Cardiovascular Disease, 3*, 53–63.

Baliunas, D., Rehm, J., Irving, H. M., & Shuper, P. A. (2010). Alcohol consumption and risk of incident human immunodeficiency virus infection: A meta-analysis. *International Journal of Public Health, 55*(3), 159–166.

Ballenger, J. C., & Post, R. M. (1978). Kindling as a model for alcohol withdrawal syndromes. *British Journal of Psychiatry, 133*, 1–14.

Bandera, E., Freudenheim, J., & Vena, J. (2001). Alcohol and lung cancer: A review of the epidemiologic evidence. *Cancer Epidemiology, Biomarkers and Prevention, 10*, 813–821.

Baraona, E., & Lieber, C. (1998). Alcohol and lipids. In M. Galanter (Ed.), *Recent developments in alcoholism, Vol. 14: The consequences of alcoholism* (pp. 97–134). New York: Plenum Press.

Barclay, G. A., Barvour, J., Stewart, S., Day, C. P., & Gilvarry, E. (2008). Adverse physical effects of alcohol misuse. *Advances in Psychiatric Treatment, 14*, 139–151.

Bartlett, J. G., Dowell, S. F., Mandell, L. A., File, T. M. Jr., Musher, D. M., & Fine, M. J. (2000). Practice guidelines for the management of community-acquired pneumonia in adults. Infectious Diseases Society of America. *Clinical and Infectious Diseases, 31*(2), 347–382.

Bautista, A. P. (2005). Liver injury during alcohol use and withdrawal. In V. R. Preedy, R. R. Watson (Eds.), *Comprehensive handbook of alcohol related pathology* (pp. 491–500). London: Elsevier Academic Press.

Behnam, S. M., Behnam, S. E., & Koo, J. Y. (2005). Alcohol as a risk factor for plaque-type psoriasis. *Cutis, 76*, 181–185.

Beilin, L. J., & Puddey, I. B. (1992). Alcohol and hypertension. *Clinical and Experimental Hypertension, A14*, 119–138.

Benjamin, E. J., Levy, D., Vaziri, S. M., D'Agostino, R. B., Belanger, A. J., & Wolf, P. A. (1994). Independent risk factors for atrial fibrillation in a population-based cohort: The Framingham Heart Study. *Journal of the American Medical Association, 271*, 840–844.

Berthiller, J., Straif, K., Boniol, M., Voirin, N., Benhaim-Luzon, V., Ayoub, W. B., Dari, I., Laouamri, S., Hamdi-Cherif, M., Bertal, M., Ayed, F. B., & Sasco, A. J. (2008). Cannabis smoking and risk of lung cancer in men: A pooled analysis of three studies in Maghreb. *Journal of Thoracic Oncology, 3*(12), 1398–1403.

Besson, H., Brennan, P., Becker, N., Nieters, A., De Sanjosé, S., Font, R., Maynadié, M., Foretova, L., Cocco, P. L., Staines, A., Vornanen, M., & Boffetta, P. (2006). Tobacco smoking, alcohol drinking and non-Hodgkin's lymphoma: A European multicenter casecontrol study (Epilymph). *International Journal of Cancer, 119*, 901–908.

Bhat, V. M., Cole, J. W., Sorkin, J. D., Wozniak, M. A., Malarcher, A. M., Giles, W. H., Stern, B. J., & Kittner, S. J. (2008). Dose-response relationship between cigarette smoking and risk of ischemic stroke in young women. *Stroke, 39*, 2439–2443.

Binswanger, I., Stern, M., Deyo, R., Heagerty, P., Cheadle, A., Elmore, J., & Koepsell, T. (2007). Release from prison—a high risk of death for former inmates. *New England Journal of Medicine, 356*, 157–165.

Boffetta, P., & Hashibe, M. (2006). Alcohol and cancer. *Lancet Oncology, 7*(2), 149–156.

Bolognia, J. L., Lorizzo, J. L., & Rapini, R. P. (2008). *Psoriasis: Dermatology* (2nd ed.) St. Louis, MO: Mosby Elsevier.

Borkenstein, R., Crowther, R., Shumate, R., Ziel, W., & Zylman, R. (1964). *The role of the drinking driver in traffic accidents*. Bloomington, IN: Department of Police Administration, Indiana University.

Bossetti, C., Levi, F., Lucchini, F., Zatonski, W. A., Negri, E., & La Vecchia, C. (2002). Worldwide mortality from cirrhosis: An update to 2002. *Journal of Hepatology, 46*, 827–839.

Bott, K., Meyer, C., Rumpf, H., Hapke, U., & John, U. (2005). Psychiatric disorders among at-risk consumers of alcohol in the general population. *Journal of Studies on Alcohol, 66*, 246–253.

Bouyer, J., Coste, J., Shojaei, T., Pouly, J. L., Fernandez, H., Gerbaud, L., & Job-Spira, N. (2003). Risk factors for ectopic pregnancy: A comprehensive analysis based on a large case-control, population-based study in France. *American Journal of Epidemiology, 157*, 185–194.

Bowker, S. L., Soskolne, C. L., Houston, S. C., Newman, S. C., & Jhangri, G. S. (2004). Human immunodeficiency virus (HIV) and hepatitis C virus (HCV) in a Northern Alberta population. *Canadian Journal of Public Health, 95*, 188–192.

Bradley, K. A., Badrinath, S., Bush, K., Boyd-Wickizer, J., & Anawalt, B. (1998). Medical risks for women who drink alcohol. *Journal of General Internal Medicine, 13*(9), 627–639.

Brennan, P., Bogillot, O., Cordier, S., Greiser, E., Schill, W., & Vineis, P. (2000). Cigarette smoking and bladder cancer in men: A pooled analysis of 11 case-control studies. *International Journal of Cancer, 86*, 289–294.

Brennan, P., Bogillot, O., Greiser, E., Chang-Claude, J., Wahrendorf, J., & Cordier, S. (2001). The contribution of cigarette smoking to bladder cancer in women (pooled European data). *Cancer Causes & Control, 12*, 411–417.

Brooner, R., King, V., Kidorf, M., Schmidt, C. J., & Bigelow, G. (1997). Psychiatric and substance use comorbidity among treatment-seeking opioid abusers. *Archives of General Psychiatry, 54*, 71–80.

Brownson, R. C., Novotny, T. E., & Perry, M. C. (1993). Cigarette smoking and adult leukemia: A meta-analysis. *Archives of Internal Medicine, 153*, 469–475.

Bruun, K., Edwards, G., Lumio, M., Majeka, K., Pan, L., Popham, R. E., Room, R., Schmidt, W., Skog, O., Sulkunen, P., & Österberg, E. (1975). *Alcohol control policies in public health perspective.* Helsinki, Finland: Finnish Foundation for Alcohol Studies.

Burns, J. M., Martyres, R. F., Clode, D., & Boldero, J. M. (2004). Overdose in young people using heroin: Associations with mental health, prescription drug use and personal circumstances. *Medical Journal of Australia, 181*(Suppl.7), S25–S28.

Buskin, S. E., Gale, J. L., Weiss, N. S., & Nolan, C. M. (1994). Tuberculosis risk factors in adults in King County, Washington, 1988 through 1990. *American Journal of Public Health, 84*, 1750–1756.

Camargo C. A. (1989). Moderate alcohol consumption and stroke: The epidemiologic evidence. *Stroke, 20*, 1611–1626.

Carlsson, S., Hammar, N., & Grill, V. (2005). Alcohol consumption and type 2 diabetes meta-analysis of epidemiological studies indicates a U-shaped relationship. *Diabetologia, 48*, 1051–1054.

Carson, G., Cox, L. V., Crane, J., Croteau, P., Graves, L., Kluka, S., Koren, G., Martel, M. J., Midmer, D., Nulman, I., Poole, N., Senikas, V., Wood, R., & Society of Obstetricians and Gynaecologists of Canada. (2010). Alcohol use and pregnancy consensus clinical guidelines. *Journal of Obstetrics and Gynaecology Canada, 32*(8 Suppl. 3), S1–S31.

Casper, M. L., Barnett, E., Williams, I., Halverson, J. A., & Braham, V. E. (2003). *Atlas of stroke mortality: Racial, ethnic, and geographic disparities in the United States.* Atlanta, GA: Centers for Disease Control and Prevention.

Challis, J., & Olson, D. (1988). Parturition. In E. Knobil & J. Neill (Eds.), *The physiology of reproduction* (pp. 2177–2216). New York: Raven Press.

Chao, C. (2007). Associations between beer, wine, and liquor consumption and lung cancer risk: A meta-analysis. *Cancer Epidemiology, Biomarkers & Prevention, 16*, 2436–2447.

Chaud, M., Faletti, A., Beron de Estrada, M., Gimeno, A. L., & Gimeno, M. A. (1994). Synthesis and release of prostaglandins D2 and E2 by rat uterine tissue throughout the sex cycle. Effects of 17-beta-estradiol and progesterone. *Prostaglandins, Leukotrienes and Essential Fatty Acids, 51*, 47–50.

Chelmow, D., Andrew, D. E., & Baker, E. R. (1996). Maternal cigarette smoking and placenta previa. *Obstetrics and Gynecology, 87*(5 Pt. 1), 703–706.

Chermack, S. T., & Blow, F. C. (2002). Violence among individuals in substance abuse treatment: The role of alcohol and cocaine consumption. *Drug and Alcohol Dependence, 661*(1), 29–37.

Cherpitel, C. (1992). The epidemiology of alcohol-related trauma. *Alcohol Health and Research World, 16*, 191–196.

Cherpitel, C. (1996). Alcohol in fatal and nonfatal injuries: A comparison of coroner and emergency room data from the same country. *Alcoholism: Clinical and Experimental Research, 20*(2), 338–342.

Cherpitel, C. J., Tam, T., Midanik, L., et al. (1995). Alcohol and non-fatal injury in the US general population: A risk function analysis. *Accident Analysis Prevention, 27*, 651–661.

Cho, E., Smith-Warner, S., Ritz, J., van den Brandt, P., Colditz, G., & Folsom, A. (2004). Alcohol intake and colorectal cancer: A pooled analysis of 8 cohort studies. *Annals of Internal Medicine, 140*(8), 603–613.

Chong, J. Y., & Sacco, R. L. (2005). Epidemiology of stroke in young adults: Race/ethnic differences. *Journal of Thrombosis and Thrombolysis, 20*, 77–83.

Cohen, A. D., & Halevy, S. (1999). Alcohol intake, immune response, and the skin. *Clinics in Dermatology, 17*, 411–412.

Collins, D. J., & Lapsley, H. M. (2008). *The costs of tobacco, alcohol and illicit drug abuse to Australian society in 2004/05: Summary version.* Canberra, Australia: Department of Health and Ageing.

Cook, J. L., & Randal, C. L. (1998). Ethanol and parturition: A role for prostaglandins. *Prostaglandins, Leukotrienes and Essential Fatty Acids, 58*, 135–142.

Corneil, T., Kuyper, L., Shoveller, J., Hogg, R., Li, K., Spittal, P., Schechter, M., & Wood, E. (2006). Unstable housing, associated risk behaviour, and increased risk for HIV infection among injection drug users. *Health & Place, 12*, 79–85.

Corrao, G., Bagnardi, V., Zambon, A., & Arico, S. (1999). Exploring the dose-response relationship between alcohol consumption and the risk of several alcohol-related conditions: A meta-analysis. *Addiction, 94*, 1551–1573.

Corrao, G., Bagnardi, V., Zambon, A., & La Vecchia, C. (2004). A meta-analysis of alcohol consumption and the risk of 15 diseases. *Preventive Medicine, 38*, 613–619.

Corrao, G., Rubbiati, L., Bagnardi, V., Zambon, A., & Poikolainen, K. (2000). Alcohol and coronary heart disease: A meta-analysis. *Addiction, 95*(10), 1505–1523.

Craib, K. J. P., Spittal, P. M., Wood, E., Laliberte, N., Hogg, R. S., Li, K., Heath, K., Tyndall, M. W., O'Shaughnessy, M. V., & Schechter, M. T. (2003). Risk factors for elevated HIV incidence among Aboriginal injection drug users in Vancouver. *Canadian Medical Association Journal, 168*(1), 19–24.

Criqui, M., Cowan, L., Tyroler, J., Bangdiwala, S., Heiss, G., Wallace, R., & Cohn, R. (1987). Lipoprotein medicators for the effects of alcohol consumption and cigarette smoking on cardiovascular mortality. Results from the Lipid Research Clinics follow-up study. *American Journal of Epidemiology, 126*, 629–637.

Criqui, M., & Ringel, B. (1994). Does diet or alcohol explain the French paradox? *Lancet, 344*, 1719–1723.

Crispo, A., Brennan, P., Jockel, K. H., Rosario, A. S., Wichmann, H. E., & Nyberg, F. (2004). The cumulative risk of lung cancer among current, ex—and never-smokers in European men. *British Journal of Cancer, 91*(7), 1280–1286.

Curtis, K. M., Savitz, D. A., & Arbuckle, T. E. (1997). Effects of cigarette smoking, caffeine consumption, and alcohol intake on fecundability. *American Journal of Epidemiology*, *146*(1), 32–41.

Dam, A. M., Fuglsang-Frederikse, A., Svarre-Olsen, U., & Dam, M. (1985). Late-onset epilepsy: Etiologies, types of seizure, and value of clinical investigation, EEG, and computerized tomography scan. *Epilepsia*, *26*, 227–231.

Darke, S., Degenhardt, L., & Mattik, R. (2007). *Mortality amongst illicit drug users: Epidemiology, causes and intervention*. Cambridge: Cambridge University Press.

Darke, S., & Hall, W. (2003). Heroin overdose: Research and evidence-based intervention. *Journal of Urban Health*, *80*(2), 189–200.

Darke, S., Kaye, S., McKetin, R., & Duflou, J. (2008). Major physical and psychological harms of methamphetamine use. *Drug and Alcohol Review*, *27*, 253–262.

Darke, S., & Ross, J. (2001). The relationship between suicide and overdoes among methadone maintenance patients in Sydney, Australia. *Addiction*, *96*, 1443–1453.

Darke, S., Ross, J., Zador, D., & Sunjic, S. (2000*a*). Heroin-related deaths in New South Wales, Australia, 1992-1996. *Drug and Alcohol Dependence*, *60*, 141–150.

Darke, S., Sims, J., McDonald, S., & Wickes, W. (2000*b*). Cognitive impairment among methadone maintenance patients. *Addiction*, *95*, 687–695.

Darke, S., & Zador, D. (1996). Fatal heroin "overdose": A review. *Addiction*, *91*, 1764–1772.

Davies, M. J., Baer, D. J., Judd, J. T., Brown, E. D., Campbell, W. S., & Taylor, P. R. (2002). Effects of moderate alcohol intake on fasting insulin and glucose concentrations and insulin sensitivity in postmenopausal women: A randomized controlled trial. *Journal of the American Medical Association*, *287*, 2559–2562.

Dechanet, C., Anahory, T., Mathiue Daude, J. C., Quantin, X., Reyftmann, L., Hamamah, S., Hedon, B., & Dechaud, H. (2011). Effects of cigarette smoking on reproduction. *Human Reproductive Update*, *17*, 76–95.

Degenhardt, L., Bucello, C., Mathers, B., Ali, H., Hickman, M., & McLaren, J. (2011*b*). Mortality among dependent users of heroin and other opioids: A systematic review and meta-analysis of cohort studies. *Addiction*, *106*, 32–51.

Degenhardt, L., & Hall, W. (2012). Extent of illicit drug use and dependence, and their contribution to the global burden of disease. *Lancet*, *379*(9810), 55–70.

Degenhardt, L., Hall, W., Warner-Smith, M., & Lynskey, M. (2004). Illicit drug use. In M. Ezzati, A. Lopez, A. Rodgers, & C. J. L. Murray (Eds.), *Comparative quantification of health risks: Global and regional burden of disease attributable to selected major risk factors* (pp. 1109–1175). Geneva: World Health Organization.

Degenhardt, L., Singleton, J., Calabria, B., McLaren, J., Kerr, T., Mehta, S., Kirk, G., & Hall, W. D. (2011*a*). Mortality among cocaine users: A systematic review of cohort studies. *Drug and Alcohol Dependence*, *113*, 88–95.

Dennis, L. K. (2000). Meta-analysis for combining relative risks of alcohol consumption and prostate cancer. *Prostate*, *42*(1), 56–66.

Dhalla, I. A., Mamdani, M. M., Sivilotti, M. L., Kopp, A., Qureshi, O., & Juurlink, D. N. (2009). Prescribing of opioid analgesics and related mortality before and after the introduction of long-acting oxycodone. *Canadian Medical Association Journal*, *181*(12), 891–896.

Di Castelnuovo, A., Rotondo, S., Iacoviello, L., Donati, M. B., & de Gaetano, G. (2002). Meta-analysis of wine and beer consumption in relation to vascular risk. *Circulation*, *105*, 2836–2844.

Dika, E., Bardazzi, F., Balestri, R., & Maibach, H. I. (2007). Environmental factors and psoriasis. *Current Problems in Dermatology*, *35*, 118–135.

Doab, A., Treloar, C., & Dore, G. (2005). Knowledge and attitudes about treatment for hepatitis C virus infection and barriers to treatment among current injection drug users in Australia. *Clinical Infectious Diseases*, *Suppl.5*(40), S313–S320.

Doll, R., Peto, R., Boreham, J., & Sutherland, I. (2004). Mortality in relation to smoking: 50 years' observation on male British doctors. *British Medical Journal*, *328*, 1519–1533.

Doll, R., Peto, R., Hall, E., Wheatley, K., & Gray, R. (1994). Mortality in relation to consumption of alcohol: 13 years' observations on male British doctors. *British Medical Journal*, *309*, 911–918.

Drake, R. E., & Mueser, K. T. (1996). Alcohol-use disorder and severe mental illness. *Alcohol Health and Research World*, *20*, 86–93.

Drummer, O. (2005). Recent trends in narcotic deaths. *Therapeutic Drug Monitoring*, *27*(6), 738–740.

Dunn, N. R., Faragher, B., Thorogood, M., de Caestecker, L., MacDonald, T. M., McCollum, C., Thomas, S., & Mann, R. (1999). Risk of myocardial infraction in young female smokers. *Heart*, *82*(5), 581–583.

Eckardt, M., File, S., Gessa, G., Grant, K., Guerri, C., Hoffman, P., Kalant, H., Koop, G., Li, T., & Tabakoff, B. (1998). Effects of moderate alcohol consumption on the central nervous system. *Alcoholism: Clinical and Experimental Research*, *22*, 998–1040.

Edlin, B. R. (2002). Prevention and treatment of hepatitis C in injection drug users. *Hepatology*, *36*(5 Suppl.1), S210–S219.

Efird, J. T., Friedman, G. D., Sidney, S., Klatsky, A., Habel, L. A., Udaltsova, N. V., Van den Eeden, S., & Nelson, L. M. (2004). The risk for malignant primary adult-onset glioma in a large, multiethnic, managed-care cohort: Cigarette smoking and other lifestyle behaviors. *Journal of Neurooncology*, *68*, 57–69.

Ellison, R., Zhang, Y., McLennan, C., & Rothman, K. (2001). Exploring the relation of alcohol consumption to risk of breast cancer. *American Journal of Epidemiology*, *154*, 740–747.

el-Mas, M. M., & Abdel-Rahman, A. A. (1993). Direct evidence for selective involvement of aortic baroreceptors in ethanolinduced impairment of baroreflex control of heart rate. *Journal of Pharmacology and Experimental Therapeutics*, *264*, 1198–1205.

EMCDDA. (2003). *Annual report: State of the drugs problem in the European Union and Norway*. Lisboa: European Monitoring Centre for Drugs and Drug Addiction.

English, D., Holman, C., Milne, E., Winter, M., Hulse, G., Codde, G., Bower, G., Corti, B., de Klerk, N., Knuiman, M., Kurinczuk, J., Lewin, G., & Ryan, G. (1995). *The quantification of drug caused morbidity and mortality in Australia 1995*. Canberra, Australia: Commonwealth Department of Human Services and Health.

Evstaffev, V. V., & Levin, M. M. (1989). Dermatologic pathology in chronic alcoholics. *Vestnik Dermatologii i Venerologii*, *8*, 72–74.

Ezzati, M., Lopez, A., Rodgers, A., Vander Horn, S., Murray, C., & Comparative Risk Assessment Collaborating Group.

(2002). Selected major risk factors and global and regional burden of disease. *Lancet*, *36*, 1347–1360.

Falck, R. S., Wang, J., Carlson, R. G., Eddy, M., & Siegal, H. A. (2002). The prevalence and correlates of depressive symptomatology among a community sample of crack-cocaine smokers. *Journal of Psychoactive Drugs*, *34*(3), 281–288.

Falck, R. S., Wang, J., Siegal, H. A., & Carlson, R. G. (2004). The prevalence of psychiatric disorder among a community sample of crack cocaine users: An exploratory study with practical implications. *Journal of Nervous and Mental Disease*, *192*, 503–507.

Farkas, A., Kemeny, L., Szell, M., Dobozy, A., & Bata-Csorgo, Z. (2003). Ethanol and acetone stimulate the proliferation of HaCaT keratinocytes: The possible role of alcohol in exacerbating psoriasis. *Archives of Dermatological Research*, *295*, 56–62.

Fergusson, D., & Horwood, L. (2001). Cannabis use and traffic accidents in a birth cohort of young adults. *Accident Analysis and Prevention*, *33*, 703–711.

Ferrera, G., Murray, M., Winthrop, K., Centis, R., Sotgiu, G., Migliori, G. B., Maeurer, M., Zumla, A. (2012). Risk factors associated with pulmonary tuberculosis: Smoking, diabetes and anti-TNFa drugs. *Current Opinion in Pulmonary Medicine*, *18*, 233–240.

Fillmore, K. M., Kerr, W. C., Stockwell, T., Chikritzhs, T., & Bostrom, A. (2006). Moderate alcohol use and reduced mortality risk: Systematic error in prospective studies. *Addiction Research & Theory*, *14*(2), 101–132.

Fine-Edelstein, J. S., Wolf, P. A., O'Leary, D. H., Poehlman, H., Belanger, A. J., Kase, C. S., & D'Agostino, R. B. (1994). Precursors of extracranial carotid atherosclerosis in the Framingham Study. *Neurology*, *44*(6), 1046–1050.

Fischer, B., Haydon, E., Rehm, J., Krajden, M., & Reimer, J. (2004). Injection drug use and the hepatitis C virus: Considerations for a targeted treatment approach—the case study of Canada. *Journal of Urban Health*, *81*(3), 428–447.

Fischer, B., Medved, W., Gliksman, L., & Rehm, J. (1999). Illicit opiates in Toronto: A profile of current users. *Addiction Research*, *7*(5), 377–415.

Fischer, B., Rehm, J., Brissette, S., Brochu, S., Bruneau, J., el-Guebaly, N., Noël, L., Tyndall, M., Wild, C., Mun, P., & Baliunas, D. (2005). Illicit opioid use in Canada: Comparing social, health and drug use characteristics of untreated users in five cities (OPICAN study). *Journal of Urban Health*, *82*(2), 250–266.

Fisher, J. C., Bang, H., & Kapiga, S. H. (2007). The association between HIV infection and alcohol use: A systematic review and meta-analysis of African studies. *Sexually Transmitted Diseases*, *34*(11), 856–863.

Fleming, P. J., Blair, P. S., Bacon, C., & Berry, J. (2000). *Sudden unexpected death in infancy. The CESDI SUDI studies*. London: The Stationary Office.

Ford, P. M., Pearson, M., Sankar-Mistry, P., Stevenson, T., Bell, D., Austin, J., & Queen's University HIV Prison Study Group (2000). HIV, hepatitis C and risk behaviour in a Canadian medium security federal penitentiary. *Quarterly Journal of Medicine*, *93*(2), 113–119.

Foster, R. K., & Marriott, H. E. (2006). Alcohol consumption in the new millennium—weighing up risks and benefits for our youth. *Nutrition Bulletin*, *31*, 286–331.

Fedirko, V., Tramacere, I., Bagnardi, V., Rota, M., Scotti, L., Islami, F., Negri, E., Straif, K., Romieu, I., La Vecchia, C., Boffetta, P., & Jenab, M. (2011). Alcohol drinking and colorectal cancer risk: An overall and dose-response meta-analysis of published studies. *Annals of Oncology*, *22*(9), 1958–1972.

Freedland, E. S., & McMicken, D. B. (1993a). Alcohol-related seizures, part I: Pathophysiology, differential diagnosis and evaluation. *Journal of Emergency Medicine*. *11*, 463–473.

Freedland, E. S., & McMicken, D. B. (1993b). Alcohol and trauma. *Emergency Medicine Clinics of North America*, *11*, 225–239.

Frei, A., & Rehm, J. (2002). Die Prävalenz psychischer Komorbidität unter Opiatabhängigen: Eine Metaanalyse bisheriger Studien. *Psychiatrische Praxis*, *29*, 258–262.

Freudenheim, J. L., Ritz, J., Smith-Warner, S. A., Albanes, D., Bandera, E. V., van den Brandt, P. A., Colditz, G., Feskanich, D., Goldbohm, R. A., Harnack, L., Miller, A. B., Rimm, E., Rohan, T. E., Sellers, T. A., Virtamo, J., Willett, W. C., & Hunter, D. J. (2005). Alcohol consumption and risk of lung cancer: A pooled analysis of cohort studies. *American Journal of Clinical Nutrition*, *82*, 657–667.

Friedman, H., Newton, C., & Klein, T. W. (2003). Microbial infections, immunomodulation, and drugs of abuse. *Clinical Microbiology Reviews*, *16*, 209–219.

Friedman, H., Pros, S., & Klein, T. W. (2006). Addictive drugs and their relationships with infectious diseases. *FEMS Immunology and Medical Microbiology*, *47*, 330–342.

Fuller, M. (1995). Alcohol use and injury severity in trauma patients. *Journal of Addictive Diseases*, *14*, 47–53.

Fujimoto, W. Y. (2000). The importance of insulin resistance in the pathogenesis of type 2 diabetes mellitus. *American Journal of Medicine*, *108*, 9S–14S.

Gajalakshmi, V., Peto, R., Kanaka, T. S., & Jha, P. (2003). Smoking and mortality from tuberculosis and other diseases in India: Retrospective study of 43 000 adult male deaths and 35 000 controls. *Lancet*, *362*, 507–515.

Galea, S., & Vlahov, D. (2002). Social determinants and the health of drug users: Socioeconomic status, homelessness, and incarceration. *Public Health Reports*, *117*(Suppl 1), S135-S145.

Geerts, C. C., Bots, M. L., Grobbee, D. E., & Uiterwaal, C. S. P. M. (2008). Parental smoking and vascular damage in young adult offspring: Is early life exposure critical? The Atherosclerosis Risk in Young Adults study. *Arteriosclerosis, Thrombosis, and Vascular Biology*, *28*, 2296–2302.

George, A., & Figueredo, V. M. (2011). Alcoholic cardiomyopathy: A review. *Journal of Cardiac Failure*, *17*(10), 844–849.

Ginsburg, I. H., & Link, B. G. (1993). Psychosocial consequences of rejection and stigma feelings in psoriatic patients. *International Journal of Dermatology*, *32*, 587–591.

Gmel, G., & Rehm, J. (2003). Harmful alcohol use. *Alcohol Research & Health*, *27*(1), 52–62.

Gmel, G., Rehm, J., & Frick, U. (2003). Trinkmuster, Pro-Kopf-Konsum von Alkohol und koronare Mortalitat. *Sucht*, *49*(2), 95–104.

Gmel, G., Shield, K. D., & Rehm, J. (2011). Developing a method to derive alcohol-attributable fractions for HIV/AIDS mortality based on alcohol's impact on adherence to antiretroviral medication. *Population Health Metrics*, *9*(1), 5.

Golding, M., & Perkins, D. O. (1996). Personality disorder in HIV infection. *International Review of Psychiatry*, *8*, 253–258.

Graves A. B., van Duijn C. M., Chandra V., Fratiglioni L., Heyman A., Jorm A. F. Kokmen, E., Kondo, K.,

Mortimer, J. A., Rocca, W. A., Shalat, S. L., Soininen, H., & Hofman, A. for the Eurodem Risk Factors Research Group. (1991). Alcohol and tobacco consumption as risk factors for Alzheimer's disease: A collaborative re-analysis of case–control studies. *International Journal of Epidemiology, 20*, S48–S57.

Gray, R., & Henderson, J. (2006). *Review of the fetal effects of prenatal alcohol exposure.* Report to the Department of Health. Oxford, UK: National Perinatal Epidemiology Unit, University of Oxford.

Gruenewald, P., & Nephew, T. (1994). Drinking in California: Theoretical and empirical analyses of alcohol consumption patterns. *Addiction, 89*, 707–723.

Gupta, M. A., Schork, N. J., Gupta, A. K., & Ellis, C. N. (1993). Alcohol intake and treatment responsiveness of psoriasis: A prospective study. *Journal of the American Academy of Dermatology, 28*, 730–732.

Gutjahr, E., Gmel, G., & Rehm, J. (2001). The relation between average alcohol consumption and disease: An overview. *European Addiction Research, 7*(3), 117–127.

Haglund, B., & Cnattingius, S. (1990). Cigarette smoking as a risk factor for sudden infant death syndrome: A population-based study. *American Journal of Public Health, 80*(1), 29–32.

Hall, W., & Degenhardt, L. (2009). The adverse health and psychological effects of non-medical cannabis use. *Lancet, 374*, 1383–1391.

Hall, W., Degenhardt, L., & Lynskey, M. (2001). *The health and psychological effects of cannabis use.* Report No. 44. Canberra, Australia: Commonwealth Department of Health and Ageing.

Hall, W., Degenhardt, L., & Teesson, M. (2009). Understanding comorbidity between substance use, anxiety and affective disorders: Broadening the research base. *Addictive Behaviors, 34*, 526–530.

Hallfors, D. D., Waller, M. W., Ford, C. A., Halpern, C. T., Brodish, P. H., & Iritani, B. (2004). Adolescent depression and suicide risk association with sex and drug behavior. *American Journal of Preventive Medicine, 27*(3), 224–231.

Halpern-Felsher, B. L., Millstein, S. G., & Ellen, J. M. (1996). Relationship of alcohol use and risky sexual behavior: A review and analysis of findings. *Journal of Adolescent Health, 19*, 331–336.

Hamajima, N., Hirose, K., Tajima, K., Rohan, T., Calle, E., & Heath, C. (2002). Alcohol, tobacco and breast cancer—collaborative reanalysis of individual data from 53 epidemiological studies, including 58,515 women with breast cancer and 95,067 women without the disease. *British Journal of Cancer, 87*(11), 1234–1245.

Hammett, T., Harmon, M., & Rhodes, W. (2002). The burden of infectious disease among inmates of and releases from US correctional facilities, 1997. *American Journal of Public Health, 92*(11), 1789–1794.

Handler, A. S., Manson, E. D., Rosenberg, D. L., & Davis, F. G. (1994). The relationship between exposure during pregnancy to cigarette smoking and cocaine use and placenta previa. *American Journal of Obstetrics and Gynecology, 170*(3), 884–889.

Hashibe, M., Morgenstern, H., Cui, Y., Tashkin, D. P., Zhang, Z. F., Cozen, W., Mack, T. M., & Greenland, S. (2006). Marijuana use and the risk of lung and upper aerodigestive tract cancers: Results of a population-based case-control study. *Cancer Epidemiology, Biomarkers and Prevention, 15*(10), 1829–1834.

Hashibe, M., Straif, K., Tashkin, D. P., Morgenstern, H., Greenland, S., & Zhang, Z. F. (2005). Epidemiologic review of marijuana use and cancer risk. *Alcohol, 35*(3), 265–275.

Havens, J. R., Strathdee, S. A., Fuller, C. M., Ikeda, R., Friedman, S. R., Des Jarlais, D. C., Morseh, P. S., Baileyi, S., Kerndtj, P., Garfeink, R. S., & Collaborative Injection Drug User Study Group. (2004). Correlates of attempted suicide among young injection drug users in a multi-site cohort. *Drug and Alcohol Dependence, 75*, 261–269.

Hendershot, C. S., Stoner, S. A., Pantalone, D. W., & Simoni, J. M. (2009). Alcohol use and antiretroviral adherence: Review and meta-analysis. *Journal of Acquired Immune Deficiency Syndromes, 52*(2), 180–202.

Henderson, J., Gray, R., & Brocklehurst, P. (2007*a*). Systematic review of effects of low–moderate prenatal alcohol exposure on pregnancy outcome. *British Journal of Obstetrics & Gynaecology, 114*, 243–252.

Henderson, J., Kesmodel, U., & Gray, R. (2007*b*). Systematic review of the fetal effects of prenatal binge-drinking. *Journal of Epidemiology & Community Health, 61*, 1069–1073.

Hendriks, H. F. J. (2007). Moderate alcohol consumption and insulin sensitivity: Observations and possible mechanisms. *Annals of Epidemiology, 17*, S40–S42.

Higgins, E. M., & du Vivier, A. W. (1994*a*). Cutaneous disease and alcohol misuse. *British Medical Bulletin, 50*, 85–98.

Higgins, E. M., & du Vivier, A. W. (1994*b*). Alcohol abuse and treatment resistance in skin disease. *Journal of the American Academy of Dermatology, 30*, 1048.

Higgins, E. M., Peters, T. J., & du Vivier, A. W. (1993). Smoking, drinking and psoriasis. *British Journal of Dermatology, 129*, 749–750.

Hill, A. (1965). The environment and disease: Association or causation? *Proceedings of the Royal Society of Medicine, 58*, 295–300.

Hillbom, M., Pieninkeronen, I., & Leone, M. (2003). Seizures in alcohol-dependent patients. *CNS Drugs, 17*, 1013–1030.

Hingson, R., & Howland, J. (1987). Alcohol as a risk factor for injury or death resulting from accidental falls: A review of the literature. *Journal of Studies on Alcohol, 48*, 212–219.

Hingson, R., & Howland, J. (1993). Alcohol and non-traffic unintended injuries. *Addiction, 88*, 877–883.

Holly, E. A., Lele, C., Bracci, P. M., & McGrath, M. S. (1999). Case-control study of non-Hodgkin's lymphoma among women and heterosexual men in the San Francisco Bay Area, California. *American Journal of Epidemiology, 150*, 375–389.

Holmes, J., Meier, P. S., Booth, A., Guo, Y., & Brennan, A. (2012). The temporal relationship between per capita alcohol consumption and harm: A systematic review of time lag specifications in aggregate time series analyses. *Drug and Alcohol Dependence, 123*, 7–14.

Howard, A. A., Arnsten, J. H., & Gourevitch, M. N. (2004). Effect of alcohol consumption on diabetes mellitus: A systematic review. *Annals of Internal Medicine, 140*, 211–219.

Howard, G., Manolio, T. A., Burke, G. L., Wolfson, S. K., & O'Leary, D. H. (1997). Does the association of risk factors and atherosclerosis change with age? An analysis of the combined ARIC and CHS cohorts. *Stroke, 28*(9), 1693–1701.

Hsairi, M., Achour, N., Zourari, B., Romdhane, H., Achour, A., Maalej, M., & Nacef, T. (1993). Etiologic factors in primary bronchial carcinoma in Tunisia. *Tunisie Medicale, 71*, 265–268.

Hser, Y., Hoffman, V., Grella, C., & Anglin, M. (2001). A 33-year follow-up of narcotics addicts. *Archives of General Psychiatry*, 58(5), 503–508.

Hsu, C. C., Chow, W. H., Boffetta, P., Moore, L., Zaridze, D., Moukeria, A., Janout, V., Kollarova, H., Bencko, V., Navratilova, M., Szeszenia-Dabrowska, N., Mates, D., & Brennan, P. (2007). Dietary risk factors of kidney cancer in eastern and central Europe. *American Journal of Epidemiology*, 166(1), 62–70.

Hu, J., Mao, Y., White, K. (2003). Diet and vitamin or mineral supplements and risk of renal cell carcinoma in Canada. *Cancer Causes and Control*, 14, 705–714.

Hudson, N. L., & Mannino, D. M. (2010). Tobacco use: A chronic illness. *Journal of Community Health*, 35, 549–553.

Hulse, G., English, D., Milne, E., & Holman, C. (1999). The quantification of mortality resulting from the regular use of illicit opiates. *Addiction*, 94(2), 221–229.

Hunt, J. D., van der Hel, O. L., McMillan, G. P., Boffetta, P., & Brennan, P. (2005). Renal cell carcinoma in relation to cigarette smoking: Meta-analysis of 24 studies. *International Journal of Cancer*, 114, 101–108.

Hurst, P., Harte, W., & Firth, W. (1994). The Grand Rapids dip revisited. *Accident Analysis and Prevention*, 26, 647–654.

Ikeda, F., Ninomiya, T., Doi, T., Hata, J., Fukuhara, M., Matsumoto, T., & Kiyohara, Y. (2012). Smoking cessation improves mortality in men: The Hisayama study. *Tobacco Control*, 21, 416–421.

Imhof, A., Froehlich, M., Brenner, H., Boeing, H., Pepys, M. B., & Koenig, W. (2001). Effect of alcohol consumption on systemic markers of inflammation. *Lancet*, 357, 763–767.

International Agency for Research on Cancer (IARC). (1988). *Alcohol drinking*, Vol. 44: International Agency for Research on Cancer Monographs on the evaluation of carcinogenic risks to humans. Lyon, FR: Author.

International Agency for Research on Cancer (IARC). (2008). *Alcoholic beverage consumption and ethyl carbamate (urethane)*, Vol. 96: International Agency for Research on Cancer Monographs on the evaluation of carcinogenic risks to humans. Lyon, FR: Author.

International Agency for Research on Cancer (IARC). (2010). *Alcohol consumption and ethyl carbamate*. Monograph 96 on the evaluation of carcinogenic risks to humans. Lyon, FR: Author.

Irving H. M., Samokhvalov A., & Rehm J. (2009). Alcohol as a risk factor for pancreatitis. A systematic review and meta-analysis. *Journal of Oncology Practice*, 10, 387–392.

Islami, F., Fedirko, V., Tramacere, I., Bagnardi, V., Jenab, M., Scotti, L., Rota, M., Corrao, G., Garavello, W., Schüz, J., Straif, K., Negri, E., Boffetta, P., & La Vecchia, C. (2011). Alcohol drinking and esophageal squamous cell carcinoma with focus on light-drinkers and never-smokers: A systematic review and meta-analysis. *International Journal of Cancer*, 129(10), 2473–2484.

Islami, F., Tramacere, I., Rota, M., Bagnardi, V., Fedirko, V., Scotti, L., Garavello, W., Jenab, M., Corrao, G., Straif, K., Negri, E., Bofetta, P., & La Vecchia, C. (2010). Alcohol drinking and laryngeal cancer: Overall and dose-risk relation—a systematic review and meta-analysis. *Oral Oncology*, 46(11), 802–810.

Ives, T. J., Chelminski, P. R., Hammett-Stabler, C. A., Malone, R. M., Perhac, J. S., Potisek, N. M., Shilliday, B. B., Dewalt, D. A., & Pignone, M. P. (2006). Predictors of opioid misuse in patients with chronic pain: A prospective cohort study. *BMC Health Services Research*, 6(1), 46.

Jacobson, J. L., & Jacobson, S. W. (1994). Prenatal alcohol exposure and neurobehavioral development: Where is the threshold? *Alcohol Health & Research World*, 18, 30–36.

Jacobson, J. L., & Jacobson, S. W. (1999). Drinking moderately and pregnancy. Effects on child development. *Alcohol Research & Health*, 23(1), 25–30.

Jakubowiak, W. M., Bogorodskaya, E. M., Borisov, E. S., Danilova, D. I., & Kourbatova, E. K. (2007). Risk factors associated with default among new pulmonary TB patients and social support in six Russian regions. *International Journal of Tuberculosis and Lung Disease*, 11(1), 46–53.

Jamison, R. N., Kauffman, J., & Katz, N. P. (2000). Characteristics of methadone maintenance patients with chronic pain. *Journal of Pain and Symptom Management*, 19, 53–62.

Jha, P. (2009). Avoidable global cancer deaths and total deaths from smoking. *Nature Reviews: Cancer*, 9, 655–664.

Jha, P., Chaloupka, F. J., Moore, J., Gajalakshmi, V., Gupta, P. C., Peck, R., Asma, S., & Zatonski, W. (2006). Tobacco addiction. In D. T. Jamison, J. Breman, A. Measham, G. Alleyne, M. Claeson, D. Evans, P. Jha, A. Mills, & P. Musgrove (Eds.), *Disease control priorities in developing countries* (2nd ed., pp. 869–886). Oxford and New York: Oxford University Press.

Jha, P., Ramasundarahettige, C., Landsman, V., Rostron, B., Thun, M., Anderson, R. N., McAfee, T., & Peto, R. (2013). 21-st century hazards of smoking and benefits of cessation in the United States. *New England Journal of Medicine*, 368, 341–350.

Jones, K. L., Smith, D. W., Ulleland, C. N., & Streissguth, A. P. (1973). Pattern of malformation in offspring of chronic alcoholic mothers. *Lancet*, 1(7815), 1267–1271.

Kahan, M., Srivastava, A., & Shen, K. (2006). Why we object to NAOMI. Heroin maintenance in Canada. *Canadian Family Physician*, 52, 709–711.

Kalichman, S. C., & Rompa, D. (1995). Sexual sensation seeking and sexual compulsivity scales reliability, validity, and predicting HIV risk behavior. *Journal of Personality Assessment*, 65, 586–601.

Kalichman S. C., Heckman T., & Kelly J. A. (1996). Sensation seeking, substance use, and HIV-AIDS risk behavior: Directional relationships among gay men. *Archives of Sexual Behavior*, 25, 141–154.

Kalichman, S. C., Simbayi, L. C., Kaufman, M., Cain, D., & Jooste, S. (2007). Alcohol use and sexual risks for HIV/AIDS in sub-Saharan Africa: Systematic review of empirical findings. *Prevention Science*, 8(2), 141–151.

Kallio, K., Jokinen, E., Saarinen, M., Hämäläinen, M., Volanen, I., Kaitosaari, T., Rönnemaa, T., Viikari, J., Raitakari, O. T., & Simell, O. (2010). Arterial intima-media thickness, endothelial function, and apolipoproteins in adolescents frequently exposed to tobacco smoke. *Circulation: Cardiovascular Quality and Outcomes*, 3, 196–203.

Karch, S. B. (2002). *Karch's pathology of drug abuse* (3rd ed.). Boca Raton, FL: CRC Press.

Kelly, E., Darke, S., & Ross, J. (2004). A review of drug use and driving: Epidemiology, impairment, risk factors and risk perceptions. *Drug and Alcohol Review*, 23, 319–344.

Kelly, Y., Sacker, A., Gray, R., Kelly, J., Wolke, D., & Quigley, M. A. (2009). Light drinking in pregnancy, a risk for behavioural problems and cognitive deficits at 3 years of age? *International Journal of Epidemiology, 38*(1), 129–140.

Kerr, T., Fairbairn, N., Tyndall, M., Marsh, D., Li, K., Montaner, J., & Wood, E. (2007). Predictors of non-fatal overdose among a cohort of polysubstance-using injection drug users. *Drug and Alcohol Dependence, 87*, 39–45.

Kesmodel, U., Olsen, S. F., & Secher, N. J. (2000). Does alcohol increase the risk of preterm delivery? *Epidemiology, 11*, 512–518.

Kessler, R., Chiu, W. T., Demler, O., & Walters, E. (2005). Prevalence, severity, and comorbidity of 12-month DSM-IV disorders in the National Comorbidity Survey Replication. *Archives of General Psychiatry, 62*(6), 617–627.

Key, J., Hodgson, S., Omar, R. Z., Jensen, T. K., Thomson, S. G., Boobis, A. R., Davies, D. S., & Elliott, P. (2006). Meta-analysis of studies of alcohol and breast cancer with consideration of the methodological issues. *Cancer Causes and Control, 17*, 759–770.

Khantzian, E. (1985). The self-medication hypothesis of addictive disorders: Focus on heroin and cocaine dependence. *American Journal of Psychiatry, 142*, 1259–1264.

Khantzian, E. (1997). The self-medication hypothesis of substance use disorders: A reconsideration and recent applications. *Harvard Review of Psychiatry, 4*, 231–244.

Kiechl, S., Willeit, J., Poewe, W., Egger, G., Oberhollenzer, F., Muggeo M., & Bonora, E. (1996). Insulin sensitivity and regular alcohol consumption: Large, prospective, cross sectional population study (Bruneck study). *British Medical Journal, 313*, 1040–1044.

Kirby, B., Richards, H. L., Manson, D. L., Fortune, D. G., Main, C. J., & Griffiths, C. E. M. (2008). Alcohol consumption and psychological distress in patients with psoriasis. *British Journal of Dermatology, 158*, 138–140.

Kittner, S. J., McCarter, R. J., Sherwin, R. W., Sloan, M. A., Stern, B. J., Johnson, C. J., Buchholz, D., Seipp, M. J., & Price, T. R. (1993). Black-white differences in stroke risk among young adults. *Stroke, 24*(Suppl. 12), 13–15.

Klatsky, A. L. (2007). Alcohol, cardiovascular diseases and diabetes mellitus. *Pharmacological Research, 55*, 237–472.

Klonoff-Cohen, H. (1997). Sleep position and sudden infant death syndrome in the United States. *Epidemiology, 8*(3), 327–329.

Knekt, P., Reunanen, A., Aho, K., Heliovaara, M., Rissanen, A., Aroma, A., & Impivaara, O. (1991). Risk factors for subarachnoid hemorrhage in a longitudinal population study. *Journal of Clinical Epidemiology, 44*(9), 933–939.

Kohlhammer, Y., Schwartz, M., Raspe, H., & Schafer, T. (2005). Risk factors for community acquired pneumonia (CAP). A systematic review. *Deutsche Medizinische Wochenschrift, 130*(8), 381–386.

Koivula, I. H. (2001). Epidemiology of community-acquired pneumonia. In T. J. Marrie (Ed.), *Community-acquired pneumonia* (pp. 13–27). New York: Kluwer Academic Publishers.

Koppes, L. L. J., Bouter, L. M., Dekker, J. M., Heine, R. J., & Hendricks, H. F. J. (2005). Moderate alcohol consumption lowers the risk of type 2 diabetes. A meta-analysis of prospective observational studies. *Diabetes Care, 28*, 719–725.

Korte, J. E., Brennan, P., Henley, S. J., & Boffetta, P. (2002). Dose-specific meta-analysis and sensitivity analysis of the relation between alcohol consumption and lung cancer risk. *American Journal of Epidemiology, 155*, 496–506.

Kostovic, K., & Lipozencic, J. (2004). Skin diseases in alcoholics. *Acta Dermatovenerologica Croatica, 12*, 181–190.

Krahn, A. D., Manfreda, J., Tate, R. B., Mathewson, F. A. L., & Cuddy, T. E. (1995). The natural history of atrial fibrillation: I: I: Incidence, risk factors, and prognosis in the Manitoba follow-up study. *American Journal of Medicine, 98*, 476–484.

Kramer, M. D., Taylor, V., Hickok, D. E., Daling, J. R., Vaughan, T. L., & Hollenback, K. A. (1991). Maternal smoking and placenta previa. *Epidemiology, 2*(3), 221–223.

Kratzer, W., Kachele, R., Mason, A., Muche, R., Hay, B., Wiesneth, W., Hill, V., Beckh, K., & Adler, G. (1997). Gallstone prevalence in relation to smoking, alcohol, coffee consumption and nutrition: The Ulm Gallstone Study. *Scandinavian Journal of Gastroenterology, 32*, 953–958.

Krüger, H., Utzelmann, H., Berghaus, G., & Krog, G. (1993). Effects of low alcohol dosages: A review of the literature. In H. Krüger, H. Utzelmann, G. Berghaus, & G. Krog (Eds.), *Alcohol, drugs and traffic safety—T92* (pp. 763–778). Cologne, DE: Verlag TUV Rheinland.

Kuller, L. H., Ockene, J. K., Meilahn, E., Wentworth, D. N., Svendsen, K. H., & Neaton, J. D. (1991). Cigarette smoking and mortality: MRFIT Research Group. *Preventive Medicine, 20*(5), 638–654.

Kushner, M. G., Abrams, K., & Borchardt, C. (2000). The relationship between anxiety disorders and alcohol use disorders: A review of major perspectives and findings. *Clinical Psychology Review, 20*, 149–171.

Lachenmeier, D. W., Rehm, J., & Gmel, G. (2007). Surrogate alcohol: What do we know and where do we go? *Alcoholism: Clinical and Experimental Research, 31*(10), 1613–1624.

Lam, T. H., He, Y., Shi, Q. L., Huang, J. Y., Zhang, F., Wan, Z. H., Sun, C. S., & Shouli, L. (2002). Smoking, quitting, and mortality in a Chinese cohort of retired men. *Annals of Epidemiology, 12*(5), 316–320.

Larroque, B., Kaminski, M., Lelong, N., Subtil, D., & Dehaene P. (1993). Effects on birth weight of alcohol and caffeine consumption during pregnancy. *American Journal of Epidemiology, 137*, 941–950.

Law, M. R., Morris, J., & Wald, N. J. (1997). Environmental tobacco smoke exposure and ischaemic heart disease: An evaluation of the evidence. *British Medical Journal, 315*(7114), 973–980.

Law, M. R., & Wald, N. J. (2003). Environmental tobacco smoke and ischemic heart disease. *Progress in Cardiovascular Diseases, 46*, 31–38.

Lawlor, D. A., Song, Y. M., Sung, J., Ebrahim, S., & Smith, G. D. (2008). Association of smoking and cardiovascular disease in a population with low cholesterol levels: A study of 648 346 men from the Korean national health system prospective cohort study. *Stroke, 39*, 760–767.

La Vecchia C., Zhang Z. F., & Altieri A. (2008). Alcohol and laryngeal cancer: An update. *European Journal of Cancer Prevention, 17*, 116–124.

Lazarus, R., Sparrow, D., & Weiss S. T. (1997). Alcohol intake and insulin levels. The Normative Aging Study. *American Journal of Epidemiology, 145*, 909–916.

Lee, J., & Cooke, J. P. (2011). The role of nicotine in the pathogenesis of atherosclerosis. *Atherosclerosis, 215*, 281–283.

Leigh, B. C. (2002). Alcohol and condom use: A meta-analysis of event-level studies. *Sexually Transmitted Diseases, 29*, 476–482.

Leigh, B. C., & Stall, R. (1993). Substance use and risky sexual behavior for exposure to HIV. Issues in methodology, interpretation, and prevention. *American Psychologist, 48*(10), 1035–1045.

Leitzmann, M. F., Giovannucci, E. L., Rimm, E. B., Stampfer, M. J., Spiegelman, D., Wing, A. L., & Willett, W. C. (1998). The relation of physical activity to risk for symptomatic gallstone disease in men. *Annals of Internal Medicine, 128,* 417–425.

Leon, D., Chenet, L., Shkolnikov, V., Zakharov, S., Shapiro, J., Rakhmanova, G., Vassin, S., & McKee, M. (1997). Huge variation in Russian mortality rates 1984-1994: Artefact, alcohol, or what? *Lancet, 350,* 383–388.

Leone, M., Bottachi, E., Beghi, E., Morgando, E., Mutani, R., Amedeo, G., Cremo, R., Gianelli, M., & Ravaqli Ceroni, L. (1997). Alcohol use is a risk factor for a first generalized tonic-clonic seizure. *Neurology, 48,* 614–620.

Leone, M., Bottacchi, E., Beghi, E., Morgando, E., Mutani, R., Cremo, R. Ravaqli Ceroni L., Floriani, I., & Alcohol and Epilepsy Study Group. (2002). Risk factors for a first generalized tonic-clonic seizure in adult life. *Neurological Sciences, 23,* 99–106.

Leone, M., Bottacchi, E., Gionco, M., Nardozza, V., & Sironi L. (1994). Alcohol and epileptic seizures: A case control study. *Alcologia, 6,* 215–219.

Lerch, M. M., Albrecht, E., Ruthenburger, M., Mayerle, J., Halangk, W., & Kruger, B. (2003). Pathophysiology of alcohol induced pancreatitis. *Pancreas, 27,* 291–296.

Letenneur L. (2007). Moderate alcohol consumption and risk of developing dementia in the elderly: The contribution of prospective studies. *Annals of Epidemiology, 17,* S43–S45.

Letenneur, L., Larrieu, S., & Barberger-Gateau, P. (2004). Alcohol and tobacco consumption as risk factors of dementia: A review of epidemiological studies. *Biomedicine & Pharmacotherapy, 58,* 95–99.

Lewis, S. J., & Smith, D. G. (2005). Alcohol, ALDH2, and esophageal cancer: A meta-analysis which illustrates the potentials and limitations of a Mendelian randomization approach. *Cancer Epidemiology, Biomarkers & Prevention, 14,* 1967–1971.

Li, G., Smith, G. D., & Baker, S. P. (1994). Drinking behavior in relation to cause of death among US adults. *American Journal of Public Health, 84,* 1402–1406.

Liao, Y., McGee, D. L., Cooper, R. S., & Sutkowski, M. B. E. (1999). How generalizable are coronary risk prediction models? Comparison of Framingham and two national cohorts. *American Heart Journal, 137,* 837–845.

Lieber, C. S. (1988). Biochemical and molecular basis of alcohol-induced injury to liver and other tissues. *New England Journal of Medicine, 319,* 1639–1650.

Lim, S. S., Vos, T., Flaxman, A. D., Danaei, G., Shibuya, K., Adair-Rohani, H., … Memish, Z. A. (2012). A comparative risk assessment of burden of disease and injury attributable to 67 risk factors and risk factor clusters in 21 regions, 1990-2010: A systematic analysis for the Global Burden of Disease Study 2010. *Lancet, 380*(9859), 2224–2260. (Errata published 2013, in Lancet 381(9874), 1276; Lancet 381(9867), 628.)

Lindegard, B. (1986). Diseases associated with psoriasis in a general population of 159,200 middle-aged, urban, native Swedes. *Dermatologica, 172,* 298–304.

Lindsay, J., Laurin, D., Verreault, R., Hebert, R., Helliwell, B., Hill, G., & McDowell, I. (2002). Risk factors for Alzheimer's disease: A prospective analysis of the Canadian study of health and aging. *American Journal of Epidemiology, 156,* 445–453.

Linnet, K. M., Dalsgaard, S., Obel, C., Wisborg, K., Henriksen, T. B., Rodriguez, A., Kotimaa, A., Moilanen, I., Thomsen, P. H., Olsen, J., & Jarvelin, M. R. (2003). Maternal lifestyle factors in pregnancy risk of attention deficit hyperactivity disorder and associated behaviors: Review of the current evidence. *American Journal of Psychiatry, 160*(6), 1028–1040.

Little, R. E., Asker, R. L., Sampson, P. D., & Renwick, J. H. (1986). Fetal growth and moderate drinking in early pregnancy. *American Journal of Epidemiology, 123,* 270–278.

Liu, B. Q., Peto, R., Chen, Z. M., Boreham, J., Wu, Y. P., Li, J. Y., Campbell, T. C., & Chen, J. S. (1998). Emerging tobacco hazards in China: 1. Retrospective proportional mortality study of one million deaths. *British Medical Journal, 317*(7170), 1411–1422.

Liu, Z., Lian, Z., & Zhao, C. (2006). Drug use and HIV/AIDS in China. *Drug and Alcohol Review, 25,* 173–175.

Longnecker, M. (1994). Alcoholic beverage consumption in relation to risk of breast cancer: Meta-analysis and review. *Cancer Causes and Control, 5,* 73–82.

Lönnroth, K., Williams, B., Stadlin, S., Jaramillo, E., & Dye, C. (2008). Alcohol use as a risk factor for tuberculosis—a systematic review. *BMC Public Health, 8,* 289.

Lowenstein, S. R., Gbow, P., Cramer, J., Olivia, P. B., & Ratner, K. (1983). The role of alcohol in new-onset atrial fibrillation. *Archives of Internal Medicine, 143,* 1882–1885.

Luchsinger, J. A., & Mayeux, R. (2004). Dietary factors and Alzheimer's disease. *Lancet Neurology, 3,* 579–587.

Luna, C. M., Famiglietti, A., Absi, R., Videla, A. J., Nogueira, F. J., Fuenzalida, A. D., & Gene, R. J. (2000). Community-acquired pneumonia: Etiology, epidemiology, and outcome at a teaching hospital in Argentina. *Chest, 118*(5), 1344–1354.

Lundsberg, L. S., Bracken, M. B., & Saftlas, A. F. (1997). Low-to moderate gestational alcohol use and intrauterine growth retardation, low birthweight, and preterm delivery. *Annals of Epidemiology, 7,* 498–508.

Luo, R., & Cofrancesco, J. Jr., (2006). Injection drug use and HIV transmission in Russia. *AIDS, 20,* 935–936.

Macdonald, S., Anglin-Bodrug, K., Mann, R., Erickson, P., Hathaway, A., Chipman, M., & Rylett, M. (2003). Injury risk associated with cannabis and cocaine use. *Drug and Alcohol Dependence, 72*(2), 99–115.

Maher, L., & Dixon, D. (1999). Policing and public health: Law enforcement and harm minimization in a street-level. *British Journal of Criminology, 39,* 488–512.

Manchikanti, L. (2006). Prescription drug abuse: What is being done to address this new drug epidemic? *Pain Physician, 9,* 287–321.

Mandell, L. A., Wunderink, R. G., Anzueto, A., Bartlett, J. G., Campbell, G. D., Dean, N. C., Dowell, S. F., File, T. M., Jr., Musher, D. M., Niederman, M. S., Torres, A., & Whitney, G. C. (2007). Infectious Diseases Society of America/American Thoracic Society consensus guidelines on the management of community-acquired pneumonia in adults. *Clinical and Infectious Diseases, 44*(Suppl. 2), S27–S72.

Mann, R., Smart, R. G., & Govoni, R. (2003). The epidemiology of alcoholic liver disease. *Alcohol Research & Health, 27*(3), 209–219.

March, J., Oviedo-Joekes, E., & Romero, M. (2007). Factors associated with reported hepatitis C and HIV among injecting drug users in ten European cities. *Enfermedades infecciosas y microbiologi'a cli'nica, 25*(2), 91–97.

Marshall, B. D. L., & Werb, D. (2010). Health outcomes associated with methamphetamine use among young people: A systematic review. *Addiction, 105,* 991–1002.

Marshall, E. J., & Farrell, M. (2007). Substance use and psychiatric comorbidity. *Psychiatry, 6,* 23–26.

Martin, S. (1982). The epidemiology of alcohol-related interpersonal violence. *Alcohol Health and Research World, 16,* 230–237.

Mathers, C. D., & Loncar, D. (2006). Projections of global mortality and burden of disease from 2002 to 2030. *PLoS Medicine, 3,* e442.

Mayer, E. J., Newman, B., Quesenberry, C. P., Jr., Friedman, G. D., & Selby J. V. (1993). Alcohol consumption and insulin concentrations. Role of insulin in associations of alcohol intake with high-density lipoprotein cholesterol and triglycerides. *Circulation, 88,* 2190–2197.

Mazzaglia, G., Britton, R., Altmann, D. R., & Chenet, L. (2001). Exploring the relationship between alcohol consumption and non-fatal or fatal stroke: A systematic review. *Addiction, 96,* 1743–1756.

McDonald, A. D., Armstrong, B. G., & Sloan, M. (1992). Cigarette, alcohol, and coffee consumption and prematurity. *American Journal of Public Health, 82,* 87–90.

McElduff, P., & Dobson, A. (1997). How much alcohol and how often? Population based case-control study of alcohol consumption and risk of a major coronary event. *British Medical Journal, 314*(7088), 1159–1164.

McGill, H. C. J., McMahan, C. A., Zieske, A. W., Malcom, G. T., Tracy, R. E., & Strong, J. P. (2001). Effects of non-lipid risk factors on atherosclerosis in youth with a favorable lipoprotein profile. *Circulation, 103*(11), 1546–1550.

McKee, M., & Britton, A. (1998). The positive relationship between alcohol and heart disease in Eastern Europe: Potential physiological mechanisms. *Journal of the Royal Society of Medicine, 9,* 402–407.

McKenzie, C., & Eisenberg, P. (1996). Alcohol, coagulation, and arterial thrombosis. In S. Zakhari & M. Wassef (Eds.), *Alcohol and the cardiovascular system* (pp. 413–439). Bethesda, MD: National Institutes of Health, National Institute on Alcohol Abuse and Alcoholism.

Mehra, R., Moore, B. A., Crothers, K., Tetrault, J., & Fiellin, D. A. (2006). The association between marijuana smoking and lung cancer: A systematic review. *Archives of Internal Medicine, 166*(13), 1359–1367.

Meyer, N., Viraben, R., & Paul, C. (2008). Addictions and psoriasis: An example of the dermatologist's implication in preventive medicine? *Annales De Dermatologie Et De Venereologie, 135,* S259–S262.

Misra, D., & Ananth, C. V. (1999). Risk factor profiles of placental abruption in first and second pregnancies: H: Heterogeneous etiologies. *Journal of Clinical Epidemiology, 52,* 453–461.

Mitchell, E. A., & Mildred, J. (2000). Smoking and the sudden infant death syndrome. *Reviews on Environmental Health, 21*(2), 81–103.

Mitchell, E. A., Scragg, R., Stewart, A. W., Becroft, D. M., Taylor, B. J., Ford, R. P., Hassall, I. B., Barry, D. M., Allen, E. M., & Roberts, A. P. (1991). Results from the first year of the New Zealand cot death study. *New Zealand Medical Journal, 104*(906), 70–76.

Mitchell, S. N., & Smith S. K. (1992). The effect of progesterone and human interferon alpha-2 on the release of PGF2 alpha

and PGE from epithelial cells of human proliferative endometrium. *Prostaglandins, 44,* 457–470.

Mizoue, T., Inoue, M., Wakai K., Nagata C., Shimazu T., Tsuji I., Otani, T., Tanaka, K., Matsuo, K., Tamakoshi, A., Sasauki, S., Tsugane, S., & Research Group for Development and Evaluation of Cancer Prevention Strategies in Japan. (2008). Alcohol drinking and colorectal cancer in Japanese: A pooled analysis of results from five cohort studies. Meta-analysis. *American Journal of Epidemiology, 167,* 1397–1406.

Moore, T. H., Zammit, S., Lingford-Hughes, A., Barnes, T. R., Jones, P. B., Burke, M., & Lewis, G. (2007). Cannabis use and risk of psychotic or affective mental health outcomes: A systematic review. *Lancet, 370*(9584), 319–328.

Morton, L. M., Zheng, T., Holford, T. R., Holly, E. A., Chiu, B. C., Costantini, A. S., Stagnaro, E., Willett, E. V., Dal Maso, L., Serraino, D., Chang, E. T., Cozen, W., Davis, S., Severson, R. K., Bernstein, L., Maybe, S. T., Dee, F. R., Cerhan, J. R., Hartge, P., & InterLymph Consortium. (2005). Alcohol consumption and risk of non-Hodgkin lymphoma: A pooled analysis. *Lancet Oncology, 6,* 469–476.

Moskal, A., Norat, T., Ferrari, P., & Riboli, E. (2007). Alcohol intake and colorectal cancer risk: A dose-response meta-analysis of published cohort studies. *International Journal of Cancer, 120,* 664–671.

Moskowitz, H., & Robinson, C. (1988). *Effects of low doses of alcohol on driving-related skills: A review of the evidence.* Washington, DC: National Highway Traffic Safety Administration.

Mukamal, K. J., Tolstrup, J. S., Friberg, J., Jensen, G., & Gronbaek, M. (2005). Alcohol consumption and risk of atrial fibrillation in men and women—the Copenhagen City Heart Study. *Circulation, 112,* 1736–1742.

Mukamal, K., Conigrave, K., Mittleman, M., Camargo, C., Stampfer, M., Willett, W., & Rimm, E. (2003). Roles of drinking pattern and type of alcohol consumed in coronary heart disease in men. *New England Journal of Medicine, 348*(2), 109–118.

Mukamal, K., & Rimm, E. (2001). Alcohol's effects on the risk for coronary heart disease. *Alcohol Research & Health, 25,* 255–261.

Murray, R., Connett, J., Tyas, S., Bond, R., Ekuma, O., Silversides, C., & Barnes, G. (2002). Alcohol volume, drinking pattern, and cardiovascular disease morbidity and mortality: I: I: Is there a U-shaped function? *American Journal of Epidemiology, 155*(3), 242–248.

Naldi, L. (2004). Epidemiology of psoriasis. *Current Drug Targets—Inflammatory & Allergy, 3,* 121–128.

Negri, E., Franzosi, M. G., LaVecchia, C., Santoro, L., Nobili, A., & Tognoni, G. (1993). Tar yields of cigarettes and risk of myocardial infarction: GISSI-EFIRM Investigators. *British Medical Journal, 306*(6892), 1567–1570.

Nelson, S., & Kolls, J. K. (2002). Alcohol, host defense and society. *Nature Reviews Immunology, 2*(3), 205–209.

Neuman M. (2003). Cytokines—central factors in alcoholic liver disease. *Alcohol Research & Health, 27,* 307–316.

Ng, S. K. C., Hauser, A. W., Brust, J. C. M., & Susser, M. (1988). Alcohol consumption and withdrawal in new-onset seizures. *New England Journal of Medicine, 319,* 666–673.

Norstrom, T., & Ramstedt, M. (2005). Mortality and population drinking: A review of the literature. *Drug and Alcohol Review, 24*(6), 537–547.

Notzon, F. C., Komarov, Y. M., Ermakov, S. P., Sempos, C. T., Marks, J. S., & Sempos, E. V. (1997). Causes of declining life expectancy in Russia. *Journal of American Medical Association, 279*, 793–800.

Nuorti, J. P., Butler, J. C., Farley, M. M., Harrison, L. H., McGeer, A., Kolczak, M. S., & Brieman, R. F. (2000). Cigarette smoking and invasive pneumococcal disease. Active Bacterial Core Surveillance Team. *New England Journal of Medicine, 342*(10), 681–689.

Odendaal, H. J., Steyn, D. W., Elliott, A., & Burd, L. (2009). Combined effects of cigarette smoking and alcohol consumption on perinatal outcome. *Gynecologic and Obstetric Investigation, 67*, 1–8.

O'Driscoll, P., McGough, J., Hagan, H., Thiede, H., Critchlow, C., & Alexander, E. (2001). Predictors of accidental fatal drug overdose among a cohort of injection drug users. *American Journal of Public Health, 91*(6), 984–987.

Ogunniyi, A., Osuntokun, B. O., Bademosi, O., Adeuja, A. O. G., & Schoenberg, B. S. (1987). Risk factors for epilepsy: Case–control study in Nigerians. *Epilepsia, 28*, 280–285.

O'Leary, D. H., Polak, J. F., Kronmal, R. A., Kittner, S. J., Bond, M. G., Wolfson, S. K., Jr., Bommer, W., Price, T. R., Gardin, J. M., & Savage, P. J. (1992). Distribution and correlates of sonographically detected carotid artery disease in the Cardiovascular Health Study. The CHS Collaborative Research Group. *Stroke, 23*(12), 1752–1760.

Ochoa, K., Hahn, J., Seal, K., & Moss, A. (2001). Overdosing among young injection drug users in San Francisco. *Addictive Behaviors, 26*, 453–460.

Osler, W. (1905). *Principles and practice of medicine.* New York: Appleton & Co.

Pakrasi, P. L., Cheng, H. C., & Dey, S. K. (1983). Prostaglandins in the uterus: Modulation by steroid hormones. *Prostaglandins, 26*, 991–1009.

Panza F., Capurso C., D'Introno A., Colacicco A. M., Frisardi V., Santamato A., Ranieri, M., Fiore, P., Vendemiale, G., Seripa, D., Pilotto, A., Capurso, A., & Solfrizzi, V. (2008). Vascular risk factors, alcohol intake, and cognitive decline. *Journal of Nutrition, Health & Aging, 12*, 376–381.

Parazzini, F., Chatenoud, L., Surace, M., Tozzi, L., Salerio, B., Bettoni G., & Benzi, G. (2003). Moderate alcohol drinking and risk of preterm birth. *European Journal of Clinical Nutrition, 57*, 1345–1349.

Parish, S., Collins, R., Peto, R., Youngman, L., Barton, J., Jayne, K., Clarke, R., Appleby, P., Lyon, V., Cederholm-Williams, S., Marshall, J., & Sleight, P. (1995). Cigarette smoking, tar-yields, and non-fetal myocardial infarction: 14,000 cases and 32,000 controls in the United Kingdom. *British Medical Journal, 311*(7003), 471–477.

Parry, C. D. H., Rehm, J., Poznyak, V., & Room, R. (2009). Alcohol and infectious diseases: Are there causal linkages? *Addiction, 104*(3), 331–332.

Pathak, E. B., & Sloan, M. A. (2009). Recent racial/ethnic disparities in stroke hospitalizations and outcomes for young adults in Florida, 2001–2006. *Neuroepidemiology, 32*(4), 312.

Patra, J., Bakker, R., Irving, H., Jaddoe, V. W. V., Malini, S., & Rehm, J. (2011). Dose-response relationship between alcohol consumption before and during pregnancy and risk of low birth weight, preterm birth and small for gestational age (SGA)—A systematic review and meta-analyses. *BJOG: An International Journal of Obstetrics & Gynaecology, 118*(12), 1411–1421.

Paulozzi, L., Budnitz, D., & Xi, Y. (2006). Increasing deaths from opioid analgesics in the United States. *Pharmacoepidemiology and Drug Safety, 15*(9), 618–627.

Peles, E., Schreiber, S., Gordon, J., & Adelson, M. (2005). Significantly higher methadone dose for methadone maintenance treatment (MMT) patients with chronic pain. *Pain, 113*(3), 340–346.

Pelucchi, C., Galeone, C., Tramacere, I., Bagnardi, V., Negri1, E., Islami, F., Scotti, L., Bellocco, R., Corrao, G., Boffetta, P., & La Vecchia, C. (2012). Alcohol drinking and bladder cancer risk: A meta-analysis, *Annals of Oncology, 23*(6), 1586–1593.

Peters, R., Peters, J., Warner, J., Beckett, N., & Bulpitt, C. (2008). Alcohol, dementia and cognitive decline in the elderly: A systematic review. *Age and Ageing, 37*, 505–512.

Peto, R., Lopez, A. D., Boreham, J., & Thun, M. (2003). *Mortality from smoking in developed countries.* Oxford, UK: Oxford University Press.

Petrakis, I. L., Gonzalez, G., Rosenheck, R., & Krystal, J. H. (2002). Comorbidity of alcoholism and psychiatric disorders. *Alcohol Research and Health, 26*, 81–89.

Pinder, R. M., & Sandler, M. (2004). Alcohol, wine and mental health: Focus on dementia and health. *Journal of Psychopharmacology, 18*, 449–456.

Planas, F., Romero-Menor, C., Vasquez-Oliva, G., Poblet, T., & Navarro-López F. (2006). Historia natural y factores de riesgo de recurrencia de la fibrilación auricular primaria (Registro FAP) [Natural history of, and risk factors for, idiopathic atrial fibrillation recurrence (FAP Registry)]. *Revista Española de Cardiología, 59*, 1106–1112.

Plummer, M., Herrero, R., Franceschi, S., Meijer, C. J., Snijders, P., Bosch, F. X., De Sanjose, S., & Munoz, N. (2003). Smoking and cervical cancer: Pooled analysis of the IARC multi-centric case-control study. *Cancer Causes and Control, 14*, 805–814.

Poikolainen, K. (1983). Inebriation and mortality. *International Journal of Epidemiology, 12*, 151–155.

Poikolainen, K., Reunala, T., Karvonen, J., Lauharanta, J., & Karkkainen P. (1990). Alcohol intake: A risk factor for psoriasis in young and middle-aged men? *British Medical Journal, 300*, 780–783.

Prescott, E., Hippe, M., Schnohr, P., Hein, H. O., & Vestbo, J. (1998). Smoking and risk of myocardial infarction in women and men: Longitudinal population study. *British Medical Journal, 316*(7137), 1043–1047.

Puddey, I. B., Rakic, V., Dimmitt, S. B., & Beilin, L. J. (1999). Influence of pattern of drinking on cardiovascular disease and cardiovascular risk factors—A review. *Addiction, 94*, 649–663.

Purdue, M. P., Hashibe, M., Berthiller, J., La Vecchia, C. Dal Maso, L., Herreo, R., . . . Hayes, R. B. (2009). Type of alcohol beverage and risk of head and neck cancer. A pooled analysis within the INHANCE Consortium. Meta-analysis. *American Journal of Epidemiology, 169*, 132–142.

Ramstedt, M. (2007). Population drinking and liver cirrhosis mortality: Is there a link in Eastern Europe? *Addiction, 102*, 1212–1223.

Randall, D., Degenhardt, L., Vajdic, C. M., Burns, L., Hall, W., Law, M., & Butler, T. (2011). Increasing cancer mortality among opioid-dependent persons in Australia: A new public health challenge for a disadvantaged population. *Australian and New Zealand Journal of Public Health, 35*(3), 220–225.

Randin, D., Vollenweider, P., Tappy, L., Jequier, E., Nicod, P., & Scherrer U. (1995). Suppression of alcohol-induced hypertension by dexamethasone. *New England Journal of Medicine, 332,* 1733–1737.

Rankin, J. (1994). Biological mechanisms at moderate levels of alcohol consumption that may affect coronary heart disease. *Contemporary Drug Problems, 21,* 45–57.

Rathlev, N. K., Ulrich, A. S., Delanty, N., D'Onofrio, D., & D'Onofrio, G. (2006). Alcohol-related seizures. *Journal of Emergency Medicine, 31,* 157–163.

Raymon, E. G., & Mills, J. L. (1993). Placental abruption: Maternal risk factors and associated fetal conditions. *Acta Obstetricia et Gynecologica Scandinavia, 72*(8), 633–639.

Reeder, V., Aikens, M., Li, X., & Booyse, F. (1996). Alcohol and the fibrinolytic system. In S. Zakhari & M. Wassef (Eds.), *Alcohol and the cardiovascular system* (pp. 391–411). Bethesda, MD: National Institutes of Health, National Institute on Alcohol Abuse and Alcoholism.

Rehm, J., Baliunas, D., Brochu, S., Fischer, B., Gnam, W., Patra, J., Popova, S., Sarnocinska-Hart, A., & Taylor, B. (2006). *The costs of substance abuse in Canada 2002.* Ottawa, Canada: Canadian Centre on Substance Abuse. Retrieved from www.ccsa.ca.

Rehm, J., Baliunas, D., Borges, G. L. G., Graham, K., Irving, H., Kehoe, T., Parry, C. D., Patra, J., Popova, S., Poznyak, V., Roerecke, M., Room, R., Samokhvalov, A. V., & Taylor, B. (2010). The relation between different dimensions of alcohol consumption and burden of disease: An overview. *Addiction, 105,* 817–843.

Rehm, J., Mathers, C., Popova, S., Thavorncharoensap, M., Teerawattananon, Y., & Patra, J. (2009*a*). Global burden of disease and injury and economic cost attributable to alcohol use and alcohol-use disorders. Series: Alcohol and Global Health. *Lancet, 373,* 2223–2233.

Rehm, J., & Parry, C. D. (2009). Alcohol consumption and infectious diseases in South Africa. *Lancet, 374,* 2053.

Rehm, J., Rehn, N., Room, R., Monteiro, M., Gmel, G., Jernigan, D., & Frick, U. (2003*a*). The global distribution of average volume of alcohol consumption and patterns of drinking. *European Addiction Research, 9*(4), 147–156.

Rehm, J., & Room, R. (2005). The global burden of disease attributable to alcohol, tobacco and illicit drugs. In T. Stockwell, P. Gruenewald, T. Toumbourou, & W. Loxley (Eds.), *Preventing harmful substance use: The evidence base for policy and practise* (pp. 25–41). Chichester, UK: Wiley.

Rehm, J., Room, R., Graham, K., Monteiro, M., Gmel, G., & Sempos, C. (2003*b*). The relationship of average volume of alcohol consumption and patterns of drinking to burden of disease—An overview. *Addiction, 98*(10), 1209–1228.

Rehm, J., Room, R., Monteiro, M., Gmel, G., Graham, K., Rehn, N., Sempos, C., & Jernigan, D. (2003*c*). Alcohol as a risk factor for global burden of disease. *European Addiction Research, 9*(4), 157–164.

Rehm, J., Room, R., Monteiro, M., Gmel, G., Graham, K., Rehn, N., Sempos, C. T., Frick, U., & Jernigan, D. (2004). Alcohol Use. In M. Ezzati, A. D. Lopez, A. Rodgers, & C. J. L. Murray (Eds.), *Comparative quantification of health risks. Global and regional burden of disease attributable to selected major risk factors.* (Vol. 1, pp. 959–1109). Geneva: WHO.

Rehm, J., Samokhvalov, A. V., Neuman, M. G., Room, R., Parry, C. D., Lönnroth, K., Patra, J., Poznyak, V., & Popova, S. (2009*b*). The association between alcohol use, alcohol use disorders and tuberculosis (TB). A systematic review. *BMC Public Health, 9*(1), 450.

Rehm, J., Sempos, C., & Trevisan, M. (2003*d*). Average volume of alcohol consumption, patterns of drinking and risk of coronary heart disease—a review. *Journal of Cardiovascular Risk, 10*(1), 15–20.

Rehm J., Shield, K. D., Joharchi, N., & Shuper, P. A. (2012). Alcohol consumption and the intention to engage in unprotected sex: Systematic review and meta-analysis of experimental studies. *Addiction, 107*(1), 51–59.

Rehm, J., Shield, K. D., Rehm, M. X., Gmel, G., & Frick, U. (2013). Modelling the impact of alcohol dependence on mortality burden and the effect of available treatment interventions in the European Union. *European Neuropsychopharmacology, 23*(2), 89–97.

Rehm J., Taylor B., Mohapatra S., Irving H., Baliunas D., Patra J., & Roerecke, M. (2009*c*). Alcohol as a risk factor for liver cirrhosis—a systematic review and meta-analysis. *Drug and Alcohol Review, 29*(4), 437–445.

Renaud, S., Criqui, M., Farchi, G., & Veenstra, J. (1993). Alcohol drinking and coronary heart disease. In P. Verschuren (Ed.), *Health issues related to alcohol consumption,* pp 81–123. Washington, DC: International Life Sciences Institute Press.

Reynolds, K., Lewis, B., Nolen, J., Kinney, G., Sathya, B., & He, J. (2003). Alcohol consumption and risk of stroke: A meta-analysis. *Journal of the American Medical Association, 289*(5), 579–588.

Rhodes, T., Mikhailova, L., Sarang, A., Lowndes, C. M., Rylkov, A., Khutorskoy, M., & Renton, A. (2003). Situational factors influencing drug injecting, risk reduction and syringe exchange in Togliatti City, Russian Federation: A qualitative study of micro risk environment. *Social Science and Medicine, 57,* 39–54.

Rich, E. C., Siebold, C., & Campion, B. (1985). Alcohol-related acute atrial fibrillation, a case–control study and review of 40 patients. *Archives of Internal Medicine, 145,* 830–833.

Ridolfo, B., & Stevenson, C. (2001). *The quantification of drug-caused mortality and morbidity in Australia 1998.* Canberra: Australian Institute of Health and Welfare.

Rieder, H. L. (1999). *Epidemiologic basis of tuberculosis control.* Paris: International Union Against Tuberculosis and Lung Disease.

Rimm, E., Williams, P., Fosher, K., Criqui, M., & Stampfer, M. (1999). Moderate alcohol intake and lower risk of coronary heart disease: Meta-analysis of effects on lipids and haemostatic factors. *British Medical Journal, 19*(7224), 1523–1528.

Robbins, A. S., Manson, J. E., Lee, I. M., Satterfield, S., & Hennekens, C. H. (1994). Cigarette smoking and stroke in a cohort of US male physicians. *Annals of Internal Medicine, 120*(6), 458–462.

Roerecke, M., & Rehm, J. (2010). Irregular heavy drinking occasions and risk of ischemic heart disease: A systematic review and meta-analysis. *American Journal of Epidemiology, 171*(6), 633–644.

Roerecke, M., & Rehm, J. (2012). Alcohol intake revisited: Risks and benefits. *Current Atherosclerosis Reports, 14*(6), 556–562.

Room, R., Babor, T., & Rehm, J. (2005). Alcohol and public health: A review. *Lancet, 365,* 519–530.

Rosenberg, W. (1999). Sex and drugs and HCV? *Gut, 45*(1), 7–8.

Rosenblum, A., Joseph, H., Fong, C., Kipnis, S., Clement, N., & Portenoy, R. (2003). Prevalence and characteristics of chronic pain among chemically dependent patients in methadone maintenance and residential treatment facilities. *Journal of the American Medical Association, 289*(18), 2370–2378.

Rota, M., Scotti, L., Turati, F., Tramacere, I., Islami, F., Bellocco, R., Negri, E., Corrao, G., Boffetta, P., La Vecchia, C., & Bagnardi, V. (2012). Alcohol consumption and prostate cancer risk: A meta-analysis of the dose–risk relation. *European Journal of Cancer Prevention, 21*(4), 350–359.

Rothman, K., & Greenland, S. (1998). *Causation and casual inference* (2nd ed.). Philadelphia, PA: Lippincott-Raven Publishers.

Rothman, K. J., Greenland, S., & Lash, T. L. (2008). *Modern epidemiology* (3rd ed.). Philadelphia, PA: Lippincott Williams & Wilkins.

Ruitenberg, A., van Swieten, J. C., Witteman, J. C. M., Mehta, K. M., van Duijn, C. M., Hofman, A., & Breteler, M. (2002). Alcohol consumption and risk of dementia: The Rotterdam Study. *Lancet, 359,* 281–286.

Rush, B. (1785/2013). *An inquiry into the effects of ardent spirits upon the human body and mind: With an account of the means of preventing, and of the remedies for curing them. 8th edition.* Exeter, NH: Richardson. (Original work published 1785.)

Sahi, T., Paffenbarger, R. S. J., Hsieh, C. C., & Lee, I. M. (1998). Body mass index, cigarette smoking, and other characteristics as predictors of self-reported, physician-diagnosed gallbladder disease in male college alumni. *American Journal of Epidemiology, 147,* 644–651.

Samokhvalov, A. V., Irving, H., Mohapatra, S., & Rehm J. (2010a). Alcohol consumption, unprovoked seizures and epilepsy: A systematic review and meta-analysis. *Epilepsia, 51,* 1177–1184.

Samokhvalov, A. V., Irving, H. M., & Rehm, J. (2010b). Alcohol consumption as a risk factor for pneumonia: Systematic review and meta-analysis. *Epidemiology and Infection, 138*(12), 1789–1795.

Sanada, S., Nishida, M., Ishii, K., Moriyama, T., Komuro, I., & Yamauchi-Takihara, K. (2012). Smoking promotes subclinical atherosclerosis in apparently healthy men. *Circulation Journal, 76,* 2884–2891.

Sarkola, T., Iles, M. R., Kohlenberg-Mueller, K., & Eriksson, C. J. (2002). Ethanol, acetaldehyde, acetate, and lactate levels after alcohol intake in white men and women: Effect of 4-methylpyrazole. *Alcoholism: Clinical and Experimental Research, 26,* 239–245.

Schäfer, T. (2006). Epidemiology of psoriasis. Review and the German perspective. *Dermatology, 212,* 327–337.

Schäfer, T., Nienhaus, A., Haupt, G., Vieluf, D., Nagel, S., Berger, J., et al. (1997). Befunde der Hautuntersuchung und allergologischen Diagnostik [Results of the skin examination and allergological diagnostic]. In Behörde für Arbeit Gesundheit und Soziales der Freien und Hansestadt Hamburg (Ed.), *Epidemiologisches Untersuchungsprogramm Bille-Siedlung* (pp. 158–194). Frankfurt am Main: Peter Lang Verlag.

Schiff, E. R. (1997). Hepatitis C and alcohol. *Hepatology, 26*(3 Suppl. 1), 39S–42S.

Schiff, E. R., & Ozden, N. (2003). Hepatitis C and alcohol. *Alcohol Research & Health, 27,* 232–239.

Schmitz, J., Stotts, A., Averill, P., Rothfleisch, J., Bailley, S., Sayre, S., & Grabowski, J. (2000). Cocaine dependence with and without comorbid depression: A comparison of patient characteristics. *Drug and Alcohol Dependence, 60,* 189–198.

Schoonderwoerd, B. A., Smit, M. D., Pen, L., & Van Gelder, I. C. (2008). New risk factors for atrial fibrillation: Causes of "not-solone atrial fibrillation." *Europace, 10,* 668–673.

Schultz, J. M., Rice, D. P., Parker, D. L., Goodman, R. A., Stroh, G., & Chalmers, N. (1991). Quantifying the disease impact of alcohol with ARDI software. *Public Health Reports, 106,* 443–450.

Seaman, S., Brettle, R., & Gore, S. (1998). Mortality from overdose among injecting drug users recently released from prison: Database linkage study. *British Medical Journal, 316,* 426–428.

Seitz, H. K., & Homan, N. (2001). Effect of alcohol on the orogastrointestinal tract, the pancreas and the liver. In N. Heather, T. J. Peters, & T. Stockwell (Eds.), *International handbook of alcohol problems and dependence,* pp. 149–167. West Sussex, UK: John Wiley, & Sons, Ltd.

Shah, R. S., & Cole, J. W. (2010). Smoking and stoke: The more you smoke the more you stroke. *Expert Review of Cardiovascular Therapy, 8*(7), 917–932.

Shield, K., Gmel, G., Patra, J., & Rehm, J. (2012). Global burden of injuries attributable to alcohol consumption in 2004: A novel way of calculating the burden of injuries attributable to alcohol consumption. *Population Health Metrics, 10*(1), 9.

Shield, K. D., Shuper, P. A., Gmel, G., & Rehm, J. (2013). Global burden of HIV/AIDS in 2004 resulting from alcohol attributable non-adherence to medication regimes. *International Journal of Alcohol and Drug Research, 2*(1), 19–44.

Shimazu, T., Tsuji, I., Inoue, M., Wakai, K., Nagata, C., Mizoue, T., Tanaka, S., Tsugane, S., & Research Group for the Development and Evaluation of Cancer Prevention Strategies in Japan. (2008). Alcohol drinking and gastric cancer risk: An evaluation based on a systematic review of epidemiologic evidence among the Japanese population. *Japanese Journal of Clinical Oncology, 38,* 8–25.

Shinton, R., & Beevers, G. (1989). Meta-analysis of relation between cigarette smoking and stroke. *British Medical Journal, 298*(6676), 789–794.

Shivani, R., Goldsmith, R. J., & Anthenelli, R. M. (2002). Alcoholism and psychiatric disorders diagnostic challenges. *Alcohol Research and Health, 26,* 90–98.

Shkolnikov, V., & Nemtsov, A. (1997). The anti-alcohol campaign and variations in Russian mortality. In J. Bobadilla, C. Costello, & F. Mitchell (Eds.), *Premature death in the new independent states* (pp. 239–261). Washington, DC: National Academy Press.

Shults, R., Elder, R., Sleet, D., Nichols, J., Alao, M., Carande-Kulis, V., Zaza, S., Sosin, D., Thompson, R., & Task Force on Community Preventive Services. (2001). Reviews of evidence regarding interventions to reduce alcohol-impaired driving. *American Journal of Preventive Medicine, 21*(4 Suppl.), 66–88.

Shuper, P. A., Joharchi, N., Irving, H., & Rehm, J. (2009). Alcohol as a correlate of unprotected sexual behavior among people living with HIV/AIDS: Review and meta-analysis. *AIDS and Behavior, 13,* 1021–1036.

Shuper, P. A., Neuman, M., Kanteres, F., Baliunas, D., Joharchi, N., & Rehm, J. (2010). Causal considerations on alcohol and HIV/AIDS—a systematic review. *Alcohol and Alcoholism, 45*(2), 159–166.

Sidney, S., Quesenberry, C. P., Jr., Friedman, G. D., & Tekawa, I. S. (1997). Marijuana use and cancer incidence (California, United States). *Cancer Causes and Control, 8,* 722–728.

Sierksma, A., Patel, H., Ouchi, N., Kihara, S., Funahashi, T., Heine, R. J., Grobbee, D. E., Kluft, C., & Hendriks, H. F. (2004). Effect of moderate alcohol consumption on adiponectin, tumor necrosis factor-alpha, and insulin sensitivity. *Diabetes Care, 27*, 184–189.

Sierksma, A., van der Gaag, M. S., Kluft, C., & Hendriks, H. F. (2002). Moderate alcohol consumption reduces plasma C-reactive protein and fibrinogen levels: A randomized, diet-controlled intervention study. *European Journal of Clinical Nutrition, 56*, 1130–1136.

Simonato, L., Agudo, A., Anrens, W., Benhamou, E., Benhamou, S., Boffetta, P., . . . Zambon, P. (2001). Lung cancer and cigarette smoking in Europe: An update of risk estimates and an assessment of inter-country heterogeneity. *International Journal of Cancer, 91*, 876–887.

Single, E., Robson, L., Rehm, J., & Xie, X. (1999). Morbidity and mortality attributable to alcohol, tobacco, and illicit drug use in Canada. *American Journal of Public Health, 89*(3), 385–390.

Single, E., Robson, L., Xie, X., & Rehm, J. (1996). *The costs of substance abuse in Canada*. Ottawa: Canadian Centre on Substance Abuse.

Singletary, K., & Gapstur, S. (2001). Alcohol and breast cancer: Review of epidemiologic and experimental evidence and potential mechanisms. *Journal of the American Medical Association, 286*, 2143–2151.

Singletary, S. E. (2003). Rating the risk factors for breast cancer. *Annals of Surgery, 237*(4), 474–482.

Singleton, J., Degenhardt, L., Hall, W., & Zabransky, T. (2009). Mortality among people who use amphetamines: A systematic review of cohort studies. *Drug and Alcohol Dependence, 105*, 1–8.

Sjögren, H., Eriksson, A., Brostrom, G., & Ahlm, K. (2000). Quantification of alcohol-related mortality in Sweden. *Alcohol and Alcoholism, 35*, 601–611.

Skodol, A. E., Oldham, J. M., & Gallaher, P. E. (1999). Axis II comorbidity of substance use disorders among patients referred for treatment of personality disorders. *American Journal of Psychiatry, 156*, 733–738.

Skog, O. J. (2003). Alcohol consumption and fatal accidents in Canada, 1950-1998. *Addiction, 98*(7), 883–893.

Small, D., Drucker, E., & Editorial for Harm Reduction Journal. (2006). Policy makers ignoring science and scientists ignoring policy: The medical ethical challenges of heroin treatment. *Harm Reduction Journal, 3*, 16.

Smith, F. B., Lowe, G. D., Lee, A. J., Rumley, A., Leng, G. C., & Fowkes, F. G. (1998). Smoking, hemorheologic factors, and progression of peripheral arterial disease in patients with claudication. *Journal of Vascular Surgery, 28*(1), 129–135.

Smith, K. E., & Fenske, N. A. (2000). Cutaneous manifestations of alcohol abuse. *Journal of the American Academy of Dermatology, 43*, 1–16.

Smith-Warner, S. A., Spiegelman, D., Yaun, S. S., van den Brandt, P., Folsom, A. R., Goldbohm, R. A., Graham, S., Holmberg, L., Howe, G. R., Marshall, J. R., Miller, A. B., Potter, J. D., Speizer, F. E., Willett, W. C., Wolk, A., & Hunter, D. J. (1998). Alcohol and breast cancer in women: A pooled analysis of cohort studies. *Journal of the American Medical Association, 279*(7), 535–540.

Sood, B., Delaney-Black, V., Covington, C., Nordstrom-Klee, B., Ager, J., Templin, T., Janisse, J., Martier, S., & Sokol, R. J. (2001). Prenatal alcohol exposure and childhood behavior at age 6 to 7 years: I. Dose-response effect. *Pediatrics, 108*(2), 1–9.

Stampfer, M. J., Hu, F. B., Manson, J. E., Rimm, E. B., & Willett, W. C. (2000). Primary prevention of coronary heart disease in women through diet and lifestyle. *New England Journal of Medicine, 343*(1), 16–22.

Stansbury, J. P., Huanguang, J., Williams, L. S., Vogel, W. B., & Duncan, P. W. (2005). Ethnic disparities in stroke epidemiology, acute care, and postacute outcomes. *Stroke, 36*, 374–387.

Steentoft, A., Teige, B., Holmgren, P., Vuori, E., Kristinsson, J., Hansen, A. C., Ceder, G., Wethe, G., & Rollmann, D. (2002). Fatal poisoning in Nordic drug addicts in 2002. *Forensic Science International, 160*(2–3), 148–156.

Stoduto, G., Vingilis, E., Kapur, B., Sheu, W., McLellan, B., & Liban, C. (1993). Alcohol and drug use among motor vehicle collision victims admitted to a regional trauma unit: Demographic, injury, and crash characteristics. *Accident Analysis and Prevention, 25*(4), 411–420.

Strathdee, S., Patrick, D., Archibald, C. P., Ofner, M., Cornelisse, P., Rekart, M., Schechter, M. T., & O'Shaughnessy, M. V. (1997). Social determinants predict needle-sharing behaviour among injection drug users in Vancouver, Canada. *Addiction, 92*(10), 1339–1347.

Strong, J. P., Malcom, G. T., McMahan, C. A., Tracy, R. E., Newman, W. P., Herderick, E. E., & Cornhill, J. F. (1999). Prevalence and extent of atherosclerosis in adolescents and young adults: Implications for prevention from the Pathological Determinants of Atherosclerosis in Youth Study. *Journal of the American Medical Association, 281*(8), 727–735.

Sullivan, L. E., Fiellin, D. A., & O'Connor, P. G. (2005). The prevalence and impact of alcohol problems in major depression: A systematic review. *American Journal of Medicine, 118*, 330–341.

Suzuki, R., Orsini, N., Mignone, L., Saji, S., & Wolk, A. (2008). Alcohol intake and risk of breast cancer defined by estrogen and progesterone receptor status. A meta-analysis of epidemiological studies. *International Journal of Cancer, 122*, 1832–1841.

Svärdsudd, K. (1998). Moderate alcohol consumption and cardiovascular disease Is there evidence for a preventive effect? *Alcoholism: Clinical and Experimental Research, 22*(7), 307S–314S.

Swendsen, J., Merikangas, K., Canino, G., Kessler, R., Rubio-Stipec, M., & Angst, J. (1998). Comorbidity of alcoholism with anxiety and depressive disorders in four geographic communities. *Comprehensive Psychiatry, 39*(4), 176–184.

Szabo, G. (1997). Alcohol's contribution to compromised immunity. *Alcohol Health and Research World, 21*(1), 30–41.

Szabo, G., & Mandrekar, P. (2009). A recent perspective on alcohol, immunity, and host defense. *Alcoholism: Clinical and Experimental Research, 33*(2), 220–232.

Szabo, G., Mandrekar, P., Oak, S., & Mayerle, J. (2007). Effect of ethanol on inflammatory responses Implications for pancreatitis. *Pancreatology, 7*, 115–123.

Szucs, S., Sarvary, A., McKee, M., & Adany, R. (2005). Could the high level of cirrhosis in central and eastern Europe be due partly to the quality of alcohol consumed? An exploratory investigation. *Addiction, 100*(4), 536–542.

Tang, J. L., Morris, J. K., Wald, N. J., Hole, D., Shipley, M., & Tunstall-Pedoe, H. (1995). Mortality in relation to tar yield of cigarettes: A prospective study of four cohorts. *British Medical Journal, 311*(7019), 1530–1533.

Tattersall, S. J., Apte, M. V., & Wilson, J. S. (2008). A fire inside: Current concepts in chronic pancreatitis. *Journal of Internal Medicine, 38*, 592–598.

Taylor, B., Irving, H. M., Kanteres, F., Room, R., Borges, G., Cherpitel, C., Greenfield, T., & Rehm, J. (2010). The more you drink, the harder you fall: A systematic review and meta-analysis of how acute alcohol consumption and injury or collision risk increase together. *Drug and Alcohol Dependence, 110*(1–2), 108–116.

Taylor, B., & Rehm, J. (2006). When risk factors combine: The interaction between alcohol and smoking for aerodigestive cancer, coronary heart disease, and traffic and fire injury. *Addictive Behaviors, 31*(9), 1522–1535.

Taylor, B., & Rehm, J. (2012). The relationship between alcohol consumption and fatal motor vehicle injury: H: High risk at low alcohol levels. *Alcoholism: Clinical and Experimental Research, 36*(10), 1827–1834.

Testa, M., Quigley, B. M., & Eiden, R. D. (2003). The effects of prenatal alcohol exposure on infant mental development: A meta-analytical review. *Alcohol and Alcoholism, 38*, 295–304.

Teunissen, L. L., Rinkel, G. J. E., Algra, A., & van Gijn, J. (1996). Risk factors for subarachnoid hemorrhage: A systematic review. *Stroke, 27*, 544–549.

Thun, M. J., Peto, R., Lopez, A. D., Monaco, J. H., Henley, S. J., Heath, C. W., Jr., & Doll, R. (1997). Alcohol consumption and mortality among middle-aged and elderly US adults. *New England Journal of Medicine, 337*(24), 1705–1714.

Tobin, K., & Latkin, C. (2003). The relationship between depressive symptoms and nonfatal overdose among a sample of drug users in Baltimore, Maryland. *Journal of Urban Health, 80*(2), 220–229.

Tramacere, I., Negri, E., Bagnardi, V., Garavello, W., Rota, M., Scotti, L., Islami, F., Corrao, G., Goffetta, P., & La Vecchia, C. (2010). A meta-analysis of alcohol drinking and oral and pharyngeal cancers. Part 1: Overall results and dose-risk relation. *Oral Oncology, 46*(7), 497–503

Tramacere, I., Negri, E., Pelucchi, C., Bagnardi, V., Rota, M., Scotti, L., Islami, F., Corrao, G., La Vecchia, C., & Boffetta, P. (2012*a*). A meta-analysis on alcohol drinking and gastric cancer risk. *Annals of Oncology, 23*(1), 28–36.

Tramacere, I., Pelucchi, C., Bonifazi, M., Bagnardi, V., Rota, M., Bellocco, R., Scotti, L., Islami, F., Corrao, G., Boffetta, P., La Vecchia, C., & Negri, E. (2012*b*). A meta-analysis on alcohol drinking and the risk of Hodgkin lymphoma. *European Journal of Cancer Prevention, 21*, 268–273.

Traynor, T. L. (2005). The impact of driver alcohol use on crash severity: A crash specific analysis. *Transportation Research, Part E*(41), 421–437.

Tredaniel, J., Boffetta, P., Buiatti, E., Saracci, R., & Hirsch, A. (1997). Tobacco smoking and gastric cancer: Review and meta-analysis. *International Journal of Cancer, 72*, 573.

Treno, A., Gruenewald, P., & Ponicki, W. (1997). The contribution of drinking patterns to the relative risk of injury in six communities: A self-report based probability approach. *Journal of Studies on Alcohol, 58*, 372–381.

Treno, A., & Holder, H. D. (1997). Measurement of alcohol-involved injury in community prevention: The search for a surrogate III. *Alcoholism: Clinical and Experimental Research, 21*, 1695–1703.

Trevisan, M., Ram, M., Hovey, K., Russel, M., Freudenheim, J., Muti, P., Dorn, J., & Nochanjski, T. (2001*a*). Alcohol drinking patterns and myocardial infarction. *American Journal of Epidemiology, 153*, S97.

Trevisan, M., Schisterman, E., Mennotti, A., Farchi, G., & Conti, S. (2001*b*). Drinking pattern and mortality: The Italian risk factor and life expectancy pooling project. *Annals of Epidemiology, 11*, 312–319.

Truelsen, T., Thudium, D., & Gronbaek, M. (2002). Amount and type of alcohol and risk of dementia. *Neurology, 59*, 1313–1319.

Turati, F., Garavello, W., Tramacere, I., Bagnardi, V., Rota, M., Scotti, L., Islami, F., Corrao, G., Boffetta, P., La Vecchia, C., & Negri, E. (2010). A meta-analysis of alcohol drinking and oral and pharyngeal cancers. Part 2: Results by subsites. *Oral Oncology, 46*(10), 720–726.

Tuyns, A. J., Péquignot, G., & Jensen, O. M. (1977). Esophageal cancer in Ille-et-Vilaine in relation to levels of alcohol and tobacco consumption. Risks are multiplying. *Bulletin du Cancer, 64*(1), 45–60.

Tyas, S. L. (2001). Alcohol use and the risk of developing Alzheimer's disease. *Alcohol Research & Health, 25*, 299–306.

UNAIDS. (2002). *Report on the global HIV/AIDS epidemic 2002.* Geneva: UNAIDS.

USDHHS. (1984). *The health consequences of smoking: Chronic obstructive lung disease. A report of the surgeon general.* DHHS Publication No. (PHS) 84-50205. Rockville, MD: US Department of Health and Human Services, Public Health Service, Office on Smoking and Health.

USDHHS. (1989). *Reducing the health consequences of smoking: 25 Years of progress. A report of the surgeon general.* DHHS Publication No. (CDC) 89-8411. Rockville, MD: US Department of Health and Human Services, Public Health Center for Chronic Disease Prevention and Health Promotion, Office on Smoking and Health.

USDHHS. (1997). *Ninth special report to the US Congress on alcohol and health.* Report No. 97-4017. Rockville, MD: US Department of Health and Human Services, National Institute on Alcohol Abuse and Alcoholism (NIAAA).

USDHHS. (2000). *Tenth special report to the US Congress on alcohol and health: Highlights from current research.* Report No. 00-1583. Rockville, MD: US Department of Health and Human Services, National Institute on Alcohol Abuse and Alcoholism (NIAAA).

USDHHS. (2001). *Women and smoking. A report of the Surgeon General.* Rockville, MD: US Department of Health and Human Services, Public Health Service, Office of the Surgeon General.

USDHHS. (2004). *The health consequences of smoking: A report of the Surgeon General.* Atlanta, GA: Department of Health and Human Services, Center for Chronic Disease Prevention and Health Promotion, Office on Smoking and Health.

USDHHS. (2010). *How tobacco smoke causes disease: The biology and behavioral basis for smoking-attributable disease: A report of the Surgeon General.* Atlanta, GA: US Department of Health and Human Services, Centers for Disease Control and Prevention, National Center for Chronic Disease Prevention and Health Promotion, Office on Smoking and Health.

Vincenti, G. E., & Blunden, S. M. (1987). Psoriasis and alcohol abuse. *Journal of the Royal Army Medical Corps, 133*, 77–78.

Voigt, L. F., Hollenbach, K. A., Krohn, M. A., Daling, J. R., & Hickok, D. E. (1990). The relationship of abruptio placentae with maternal smoking and small for gestational age infants. *Obstetrics and Gynecology, 75*(5), 771–774.

Voirin, N., Berthiller, J., Benhaim-Luzon, V., Boniol, M., Straif, K., Ayoub, W. B., Ayed, F. B., & Sasco, A. J. (2006). Risk of lung cancer and past use of cannabis in Tunisia. *Journal of Thoracic Oncology, 1*(6), 577–579.

Vonlaufen, A., Wilson, J. S., Pirola, R. C., & Apte, M. V. (2007). Role of alcohol metabolism in chronic pancreatitis. *Alcohol Research & Health, 30*, 48–54.

Wakai, K., Nagata, C., Mizoue, T., Nishino, Y., Tsuji, I., Inoue, M. Tsigane, S., & Research Group for the Development and Evaluation of Cancer Prevention Strategies in Japan. (2007). Alcohol drinking and lung cancer risk: An evaluation based on a systematic review of epidemiologic evidence among the Japanese population. *Japanese Journal of Clinical Oncology, 37*, 168–174.

Wannamethee, S. G., Camargo, C. A., Jr., Manson, J. E., Willett, W. C., & Rimm, E. B. (2003*b*). Alcohol drinking patterns and risk of type 2 diabetes mellitus among younger women. *Archives of Internal Medicine, 163*, 1329–1336.

Wannamethee, S. G., & Shaper A. G. (2003*a*). Alcohol, body weight, and weight gain in middle-aged men. *American Journal of Clinical Nutrition, 77*, 1312–1317.

Wannamethee, S. G., Shaper, A. G., Whincup, P. H., & Walker, M. (1995). Smoking cessation and the risk of stroke in middle-aged men. *Journal of the American Medical Association, 274*(2), 155–160.

Warner-Smith, M., Darke, S., Lynskey, M., & Hall, W. (2001). Heroin overdose: Causes and consequences. *Addiction, 96*, 1113–1125.

Weinhardt, L., & Carey, M. (2000). Does alcohol lead to sexual risk behavior? Findings from event-level research. *Annual Review of Sex Research, 11*, 125–157.

WHO. (2002). *The world health report 2002: Reducing risks, promoting healthy life*. Geneva: WHO.

WHO. (2007). *International classification of diseases and related health problems, 10th revision (version for 2007)*. Geneva: WHO.

WHO. (2008). *WHO report on the global tobacco epidemic*. Geneva: WHO.

Wilhelmsen, L., Rosengren, A., & Lappas, G. (2001). Hospitalizations for atrial fibrillation in the general male population: Morbidity and risk factors. *Journal of Internal Medicine, 250*, 382–389.

Wimalasena, J. (1994). Ethanol has direct effects on human choriocarcinoma cell steroid hormone secretion. *Alcoholism: Clinical and Experimental Research, 18*, 369–374.

Wolf, B. C., Lavezzi, W. A., Sullivan, L. M., Middleberg, R. A., & Flannagan, L. M. (2005). Alprazolam-related deaths in Palm Beach County. *American Journal of Forensic Medicine and Pathology, 26*(1), 24–27.

Wolf, R., Wolf, D., & Ruocco, V. (1999). Alcohol intake and psoriasis. *Clinics in Dermatology, 17*, 423–430.

Woolf, S. E., & Maisto, S. A. (2009). Alcohol use and risk of HIV infection among men who have sex with men. *AIDS and Behavior, 13*, 757–782.

Wu, F., Chen, Y., Parvez, F., Segers, S., Argos, M., Islam, T., Ahmed, A., Rakibuz-Zaman, M., Hasan, R., Sarwar, G., & Ahsan, H. (2013). A prospective study of tobacco smoking and mortality in Bangladesh. *PLoS ONE, 8*(3), e58516.

Wylie, J., Shah, L., & Jolly, A. M. (2006). Demographic, risk behaviour and personal network variables associated with prevalent hepatitis C, hepatitis B, and HIV infection in injection drug users in Winnipeg, Canada. *BMC Public Health, 13*(6), 229.

Yataco, A. R., & Gardner, A. W. (1999). Acute reduction in ankle/brachial index following smoking in chronic smokers with peripheral arterial occlusive disease. *Angiology, 50*(5), 355–360.

Yu, H., & Berkel, H. (1999). Do insulin-like growth factors mediate the effect of alcohol on breast cancer risk? *Medical Hypotheses, 52*, 491–496.

Zaghloul S. S., & Goodfield, M. J. (2004). Objective assessment of compliance with psoriasis treatment. *Archives of Dermatology, 140*, 408–414.

Zeegers, M. P., Tan, F. E., Dorant, E., & van den Brandt, P. A. (2000). The impact of characteristics of cigarette smoking on urinary tract cancer risk: A meta-analysis of epidemiologic studies. *Cancer, 89*, 630–639.

Zeka, A., Gore, R., & Kriebel, D. (2003). Effects of alcohol and tobacco on aerodigestive cancer risks: A meta-regression analysis. *Cancer Causes and Control, 14*, 897–906.

Zeng, J., Zhen, H., Mao-Sheng, H., & Mei-Hua, J. (2003). A case–control study on the risk factors and other socio-psychological factors of epilepsy. *Chinese Journal of Epidemiology, 24*, 116–118.

Zhang, K., & Wang, X. (2013). Maternal smoking and increased risk of sudden infant death syndrome: A meta-analysis. *Legal Medicine, 15*, 115–121.

Zhang, Z. F., Morgenstern, H., Spitz, M. R., Tashkin, D. P., Yu, G. P., Marshall, J. R., Hsu, T. C., & Schantz, S. P. (1999). Marijuana use and increased risk of squamous cell carcinoma of the head and neck. *Cancer Epidemiology, Biomarkers and Prevention, 8*, 1071–1078.

Zieske, A. W., Takei, H., Fallon, K. B., & Strong, J. P. (1999). Smoking and atherosclerosis in youth. *Atherosclerosis, 144*(2), 403–408.

Zuckerman, M. (1994). *Biological Expression and Biological Bases of Sensation Seeking*. New York: Cambridge University Press.

Zuckerman, B. S., & Hingson, R. (1986). Alcohol consumption during pregnancy: A critical review. *Developmental Medicine & Child Neurology, 28*, 649–654.

Substance Use Disorders and Intentional Injury

S. Janet Kuramoto-Crawford *and* Holly C. Wilcox

Abstract

Intentional injuries affect millions of lives worldwide. The authors provide an overview of the epidemiological and preventive evidence on the relationship between substance use disorders (SUD) and intentional injuries. Emphasis is placed on suicide and intimate partner violence, as each area has received substantial research attention in relation to SUD. There is robust epidemiological evidence on the relationship between SUD, notably with alcohol use disorders, and most intentional injuries. Research has focused on the identification of factors that distinguish individuals with alcohol use disorders who are at particularly high risk for intentional injuries. Characterization of those with other drug use disorders who are at risk for engaging in intentional injuries and the role of SUD in intentional injuries has been less extensively investigated. The authors conclude with a discussion of public health approaches to the prevention of intentional injuries among individuals with SUD.

Key Words: substance-related disorders, suicide, self-injurious behavior, violence

Introduction

The first comprehensive worldwide report on violence and health highlighted intentional injury as a public health problem that affects millions of lives worldwide (Krug, Dahlberg, Mercy, Zwi, & Lozano, 2002). Intentional injury, commonly referred to as violence, is a manner of injury defined by the Centers for Disease Control and Prevention (CDC) as those that are fatal (homicide or suicide) and those that are nonfatal (assault, either sexual or other, and self-harm) (CDC, 2009; http://www.cdc.gov/ncipc/wisqars/). Intentional injury can be directed at either the self or others. Self-directed violence, often referred to as self-harm, includes suicide attempt and nonsuicidal injury, each of which may lead to death by suicide. *Suicide* is defined by the CDC as intentionally self-inflicted injury that results in death along with suicidal intent. *Suicide attempt* is a nonfatal behavior in which individuals with suicidal intent engage in, which may or may not result in injury (Crosby, Ortega, & Melanson,

2011; Silverman, Berman, Sanddal, & O'Carrol, 2007). *Suicide ideation*, or thoughts of killing oneself, is an important precursor for suicide attempt and death; however, this chapter will include only behavioral outcomes that are considered as intentional injuries, specifically suicide attempt and suicidal death. Nonsuicidal self-harm is the intentional infliction of harm upon one's own body in the absence of suicidal intent (Crosby et al., 2011; Silverman et al., 2007). Deliberate self-harm (DSH) is another related concept, which has been increasingly recognized as an important intentional injury (Haw & Hawton, 2008); however, the definition of this concept is ambiguous as to whether it includes suicidal intent (Mangnall & Yurkovich, 2008). Many prior studies have not clearly distinguished between suicide and nonsuicidal self-harm or DSH, and limited empirical evidence is still available on nonsuicidal self-harm and DSH in its relationship to SUD. Hence, the intentional injuries that will be discussed in this chapter are completed and attempted suicide, homicide, an assault, and intimate partner violence (IPV). A suicide act can either be considered active or passive, depending on how close the behavior is to death by suicide. Certain behaviors such as alcohol consumption, smoking, and drug use can be considered self-destructive or passive suicidal behaviors. The focus of this chapter is on the active form of suicidal behavior, which includes fatal and nonfatal suicide attempts.

Interpersonal violence is a type of violence directed at others such as homicide and assault. *Homicide* is defined by the CDC as fatal injuries inflicted by another person with intent to injure or kill, by any means. This category excludes injuries due to legal intervention and operations of war. Justifiable homicide is not included. *Assault* is defined by the CDC as confirmed or suspected injury from an act of violence where physical force by one or more persons is used with the intent of causing harm, injury, or death to another person; or an intentional poisoning by another person. This category includes perpetrators, as well as intended and unintended victims of violent acts (e.g., innocent bystanders). This category excludes unintentional shooting victims (other than those occurring during an act of violence), unintentional drug overdoses, and children or teenagers "horsing" around. Sexual assault includes rape, completed or attempted; sodomy, completed or attempted; and other sexual assaults with bodily force, completed or attempted. *Intimate partner violence* is broadly defined as violence toward an intimate partner (Nicolaidis & Paranjape, 2009).

Substance abuse and/or dependence (substance use disorder [SUD]) has received substantial attention in its role with intentional injury. SUD is defined as abuse or dependence of alcohol or drugs, as defined in the *Diagnostic and Statistical Manual of Mental Disorders* (DSM)-IV (American Psychiatric Association, 1994). Often, substance misuse may be used to indicate abuse or problem drinking that has not been formally assessed using the DSM. The majority of studies included in this chapter used DSM criteria for alcohol and drug abuse or dependence; studies that did not use such criteria are also included.

Although drug overdose can be a consequence of SUD, sorting out the intentionality behind drug overdose is often challenging for clinicians and researchers, and whether suicide lies in a continuum of overdose or is qualitatively distinct is still debated (Center for Substance Abuse Treatment, 2009). Deaths by overdose among illicit drug users

can be considered "hidden suicides" (Heale, Dietze, & Fry, 2003; Neale, 2000), but others suggest that drug overdoses among drug users are largely accidental (Kjelsberg, Winther, & Dahl, 1995; Rossow & Lauritzen, 1999; Wines, Saitz, Horton, Lloyd-Travaglini, & Samet, 2007). A review summarized fifteen studies in this area and compared and contrasted factors associated with suicide attempt and nonfatal accidental drug overdose. The review suggested that drug users who experienced both suicide attempt and accidental drug overdose are a high-risk group with extensive polydrug use and low psychosocial functioning (Bohnert, Roeder, & Ilgen, 2010).

This chapter comprises two components: self-directed violence (suicide and suicide attempt) and interpersonal violence (homicide and assault). We first examine the extent of the problem and describe the empirical findings on the relationship between each type of violence and SUD. The subsequent sections discuss the possible roles of SUD on intentional injuries and characterization of individuals with SUD who are at greatest risk for engaging in these behaviors. The chapter concludes with an overview of the public health model of intentional injury prevention and description of preventive interventions relevant to SUD. Whenever possible, SUD will be specified either as AUD or other DUD excluding caffeine and nicotine.

Epidemiology of Intentional Injuries
Fatal Intentional Injuries

Suicide. The world report on violence and health reported that, for approximately one-half of the estimated 1.6 million individuals who died from violence worldwide, the cause was suicide. However, this figure is most likely an underestimate given the high stigma associated with suicide (Krug et al., 2002). Suicide is a significant, preventable public health problem in the United States. In 2010, 38,364 Americans died from suicide, and it remains the tenth leading cause of death for all age groups and the third leading cause of death for youth (ages 10–14 and 15–24) (CDC, 2013).

Homicide. Nearly one-third of the estimated 1.6 million people who lost their lives to violence worldwide died as a result of a homicide in 2000 (Krug et al., 2002). In 2010, 16,259 Americans died from homicide. Homicide was the second leading cause of death among those 15–24 years old (CDC, 2013). The pervasiveness of violence has led to worldwide efforts to recognize, define, understand, and prevent this public health problem (Krug et al.).

Nonfatal Intentional Injuries

Suicide attempt. Nonfatal injuries such as self-harm (which includes both suicide attempt and self-harm) and assaults are much more common. For every one suicide, it is estimated there are 25 attempted suicides (Crosby, Han, Ortega, Parks, & Gfoerer, 2011). National surveillance data among youths report that approximately 7.8% of high school students reported a suicide attempt in the past year in 2011 (CDC, 2012). A systematic review conducted by Nock and colleagues (2008) suggested that anywhere from 0.2% to 2.0% of the general population had attempted suicide in the past year. The data from the Drug Abuse Warning Network (DAWN; https://dawninfo.samhsa.gov/data/), which provides statistics on drug-related suicide attempts that occurred in the U.S. emergency departments, estimated that 212,736 adults and adolescents had been admitted for attempts in 2010 (Substance Abuse and Mental Health Services Administration, 2012).

Interpersonal violence. Over 1.7 million assaults that resulted in nonfatal injuries have been reported to the CDC (2011). IPV is the leading cause of non-fatal injury in women, with between 10% and 69% of women reporting physical assault by an intimate male partner (WHO, 2000). Several data sources are available to estimate the prevalence of IPV, and these reported anywhere rates of IPV of 20% to 30% in the United States (Saltzman & Houry, 2009). More recently, the National Intimate Partner and Sexual Violence Survey (NISVS) in the United States estimated that approximately 12 million people are impacted by IPV each year (CDC, 2013).

Epidemiological Relationship between SUD and Intentional Injuries

The first step in the public health paradigm is to establish an association between the two constructs of interest, in this case, SUD and intentional injury (Center for Substance Abuse Treatment, 2008; IOM, 2002). This section will review epidemiological studies that have examined this relationship. While there are a number of studies that contribute to this knowledge base, preference was given to national surveys, meta-analyses, and systematic reviews. The distinction is made between AUD and non-AUD (DUD) for suicide only, because the field has mostly focused on AUD alone rather than DUD or comorbid AUD and DUD.

AUD and Suicide

National epidemiological surveys and psychological autopsy studies have established a strong link between AUD and suicidal behavior (death and attempt). A meta-analysis suggested that AUD is associated with a ten-fold greater risk for suicide, compared with the general population (Wilcox, Conner, & Caine, 2004). Using twenty-seven mortality studies, the lifetime risk for suicide in individuals with alcohol problems has been estimated to be 7%, which is much higher than the 0.4% risk for the general population (Inskip, Harris, & Barraclough, 1998).

In addition, a series of reviews that have examined the relationship between AUD and suicide attempt provide evidence of a strong relationship (Conner & Duberstein, 2004; Esposito-Smythers & Spirito, 2004; Hufford, 2001; Pirkola, Suominen, & Isometsa, 2004; Pompili et al., 2010; Schneider, 2009; Sher, 2006b). Those with AUD have an approximately six-fold increased risk for suicide attempt, according to estimates from the National Comorbidity Survey (NCS), a national survey conducted among U.S. households during 1990–1992 (Kessler, Borges, & Walters, 1999). The National Comorbidity Survey-Replication (NCS-R) study conducted in 2001–2003 found that 43% of suicide attempters had alcohol dependence and 35.9% had alcohol abuse (Nock & Kessler, 2006). Individuals with AUD were also noted to have greater risk for suicide attempt than alcohol users without AUD (Borges, Walters, & Kessler, 2000). Among a national probability sample of African Americans in the National Survey on American Life (NSAL), individuals with AUD had approximately five-fold increased odds for suicide attempt compared with those without AUD (Joe, Baser, Breeden, Neighbors, & Jackson, 2006).

DUD and Suicide

Although research on the relationship between DUD and suicide is more sparse than studies on the AUD–suicide link (Center for Substance Abuse Treatment, 2008), a meta-analysis suggests that individuals with DUD have 11.3 times higher risk for dying from suicide, at least with respect to opioid, mixed drugs, and injection drugs (Wilcox et al., 2004). According to the NCS-R study, the prevalence of drug abuse or dependence was 32.9% and 23.1%, respectively, in individuals who attempted suicide (Nock & Kessler, 2006). Drug abuse and dependence were also associated with five-fold and six-fold increased odds, respectively, for suicide attempt in a national survey conducted among African Americans, compared with those without DUD (Joe et al., 2006).

DUD is associated with attempted and completed suicide in both adolescent populations (Esposito-Smythers & Spirito, 2004; Pompili et al., 2012; Wilcox, 2004) and adults (Borges et al., 2000; Wilcox et al., 2004). Although not necessarily specific to those who meet the DSM-IV criteria for DUD, many studies have suggested that heroin users are at increased risk for suicide (Darke & Ross, 2002). The risk for suicide attempt appears to be higher among those dependent on alcohol, inhalants, or opioids after accounting for comorbid mental disorders (Borges et al., 2000). However, the severity of dependence (as indicated by a greater number of substance abuse/dependence DSM criteria) appears to be a more important risk factor for suicide attempt than dependence on specific drugs (Borges et al., 2000). As individuals who use drugs may use a number of drugs (Leri, Bruneau, & Stewart, 2003), it can be challenging to examine a link between specific drugs and suicidal behavior. The latter section discusses polydrug use as one of the important correlates for individuals with SUD at risk for suicidal behavior.

SUD and Interpersonal Violence

Several studies in European countries have examined the relationship between homicide and SUD. These studies overall found that homicide perpetrators have higher rates of SUD compared with those from the general population (Eronen, Hakola, & Tiihonen, 1996; Putkonen, Kotilainen, Joyal, & Tuhonen, 2004; Schanda et al., 2004). One study in England and Wales found that over 30% and 40% of the homicide cases involved perpetrators with AUD or DUD, respectively (Shaw et al., 2006). More recently, a large study conducted among U.S. veterans have noted those with AUD and/or DUD were more likely to die from homicide (Chermack, Bohnert, Price, Austin, & Ilgen, 2012). The findings suggest the importance of treating SUD to decrease the risk for both homicide perpetuation and victimization.

U.S. epidemiological studies from both the NCS and Epidemiological Catchment Area (ECA) have noted that those with SUD report more violent behaviors than those with other mental disorders (Corrigan & Watson, 2005; Swanson, Holzer, Ganju, & Jono, 1990). The ECA survey reported that, although those with psychosis were slightly more likely to engage in violence than those without any mental disorders, the rate was substantially higher in individuals with comorbid SUD (Swanson et al., 1990). A more recent longitudinal study in the U.S. household population using the National Epidemiological Survey on Alcohol-Related Conditions (NESARC) found that individuals with SUD and comorbid mental disorders were at increased risk for committing violent acts approximately 3 years later (Elbogen & Johnson, 2009). In their study, mental illness alone was not independently associated with violence. A review of fifteen studies also reported that those with comorbid mental disorders and substance abuse were at increased risk for committing violent acts, although many of the included studies were cross-sectional and did not attempt to sort out directionality (Maniglio, 2009). These studies have concluded or suggested that the link between SUD and violence perpetration is much stronger than that of nonaddictive mental disorders and violence perpetration.

A number of empirical studies have shown that both AUD and DUD are related to perpetration of IPV. A meta-analysis of 54 studies showed a modest association between alcohol use/abuse and IPV (Foran & O'Leary, 2008). Of these, only eight studies examined violence that females inflicted on males. Although both types of IPV were linked with alcohol use/abuse, the effect size for female-to-male aggression and alcohol use/abuse was somewhat smaller than that for male-to-female aggression (Foran & O'Leary, 2008). AUD has been associated with IPV for both genders (Madgol et al., 1997), and a meta-analysis suggested that AUD was more strongly associated with IPV aggression than other drinking measures such as frequency of alcohol consumption and binge drinking (Foran and O'Leary, 2008). A more recent meta-analysis of 28 studies conducted among youth aged 11–21 years suggested that frequency of alcohol use, frequency of heavy episodic drinking, and problematic use were all strongly associated with dating violence perpetuation (Rothman, McNaughton, Johnson, & LaValley, 2012).

A review of studies among illicit drug users also suggests that violence may be drug specific; there is slightly stronger evidence for cocaine, phencyclidine, amphetamines, but not necessarily for opiates (Boles & Miotto, 2003; Kuhns & Clodfelter, 2009; Parker & Auerhahn, 1998). A meta-analysis of drug abuse and IPV found the strongest evidence for cocaine abuse (Moore et al., 2008). Another review highlights the link between marijuana use and violence in epidemiological studies (Moore & Stuart, 2005). However, marijuana dependence and IPV may be associated more with withdrawal (Moore et al.), although the relationship between marijuana dependence and IPV remains slightly inconsistent (Fals-Stewart, Golden, & Schumacher, 2003). The potential role of SUD on IPV will be examined further in the next section. Another recent study using NESARC examined specific substance use disorders on IPV perpetuation and victimization; this study found that alcohol and cocaine use disorders increased the risk for IPV perpetration, whereas cannabis and opioid use disorders were more strongly associated with IPV victimization (Smith, Homish, Leonard, & Cornelius, 2012).

Section Summary

The epidemiological data and reviews establish a strong base of evidence in the relations between SUD and intentional injuries. The relationship between AUD and intentional injuries (both suicidal behavior and interpersonal injury) are consistent. Less consistent evidence exists for different types of DUD and intentional injuries. Epidemiological evidence suggests that in terms of risk for suicidal behavior, the number of drugs abused indicates higher risk for suicidal behavior. The risk for interpersonal violence appears to be specific to the type of drug used, but inconsistencies remain, especially for nonalcohol drugs. However, as individuals who use drugs may use multiple drugs, it may be challenging to sort out specific type of drugs in its relationship with intentional injuries. Polydrug use in general may be a marker for increased vulnerability to intentional injuries; patterns of polydrug use may be important to consider in the future to further sharpen the relationship between SUD and intentional injuries.

The Role of SUD in the Risk for Intentional Injury

The following section will review the literature on the possible causal roles of SUD on intentional injuries. There are at least three ways in which SUD can be related to intentional injuries: (a) SUD can cause intentional injuries, (b) SUD is an effect caused by intentional injuries, or (c) SUD and intentional injuries are related because they a share common cause. The directionality of the relationship, as well as identification of mediating factors, serves an important role to inform the development of preventive intervention.

In Mann's Stress-Diathesis model (1999), stressors represent contemporaneous, proximal variables, such as onset or worsening of depression or drug misuse, recent interpersonal loss, and difficulties in the financial and legal domains. Variables that represent the diathesis are more distal and may include genetic predispositions, chronic stressors, childhood trauma and adversity, enduring drug and alcohol misuse, aggressive traits, and gender (Mann, Waternaux, Haas, & Malone, 1999). As SUD may be related to intentional injuries via both pathways, by increasing the likelihood of engaging in stressors and by serving as a diathesis, we examine evidence from both possibilities in this section.

The Role of AUD in Suicidal Behavior

How AUD may increase the risk for suicidal behavior. The conceptual framework by Hufford (2001) and Conner and Duberstein (2004) considers AUD as a distal factor that may increase the risk for suicide (Conner & Duberstein, 2004; Hufford, 2001). In the framework by Conner and Duberstein (2004), risk of suicidal behavior is higher in individuals with alcoholism who have the following predisposing factors: impulsivity/aggression, severity of alcoholism, negative affect, and hopelessness. Alcohol can also decrease an individual's capability to cope effectively (Hufford, 2001), which may also increase their risk for suicidal behavior. Additionally, individuals with AUD may have more precipitating risk factors that increase their propensity to engage in suicidal behavior. Interpersonal disruptions and major depressive episodes are conceptualized as precipitating factors to suicide (Conner, Beautrais, & Conwell, 2003b). Alcoholism has been implicated to be an important factor in the stress-diathesis model for suicidal behavior, by increasing the probability of unintentional injury such as head injury (Mann et al., 1999). Damage to the brain may lead to neurobehavioral deficits, which may increase the risk for suicidal behavior (Sher, 2006a). However, no study to date has been identified that used mediational models to formally examine the indirect effect of AUD and suicidal behavior through these potential precipitating factors.

In addition to the increase in precipitating factors in individuals with AUD, alcohol consumption has been suggested to be the most prominent proximal factor for suicidal behavior (Hufford, 2001). The consumption of alcohol may distort cognitive functioning, may increase one's willingness to act on anger, aggression, and impulsivity, and may facilitate individuals to engage in suicidal behavior by disinhibiting the fear associated with dying or carrying out a suicide attempt (Brady, 2006; Hufford, 2001; Spirito & Esposito, 2006). The role of acute intoxication has been investigated in number of descriptive and epidemiological studies. This evidence suggests that individuals who died from suicide had higher concentrations of alcohol in their blood than those who did not (Cherpitel, Borges, & Wilcox, 2004). A recent study also found that the lethality of suicide attempt was associated with acute alcohol use at the time of attempt among a sample of mood disorder patients (Sher et al., 2009).

The frequent and chronic use of alcohol may induce psychological and physiological changes that may lead to increased risk for suicide (Brady, 2006). The chronic adaptation to alcohol may lead to low serotonergic function (Gorwood, Batel, Ades, Hamon, & Boni, 2000). Such low functioning of the serotonergic system may increase an individual's risk for thinking about suicide (Gorwood et al., 2000). Low serotonergic activity has been implicated to play a key role in the triangular relationship between alcohol, suicidal behavior, and impulsive/aggression (Gorwood et al.; Mann, 2003; Preuss, Koller, Soyka, & Bondy, 2001).

Nock and colleagues (2008) recommended examining factors associated with transitioning from different stages of suicide risk (e.g., ideation, plan, attempt) as a future direction for suicide research. At least one longitudinal study using the NCS sample found that presence of AUD increased suicide ideation but not attempt among ideators (Borges, Angst, Nock, Ruscio, & Kessler, 2008), suggesting that AUD may increase the risk for suicidal behavior through greater predisposition toward suicidal ideation. Likewise, in an epidemiological sample of African Americans, although AUD increased risk for suicide attempt and ideation, AUD was not significantly associated with attempt among ideators (Joe et al., 2006). Depression and impulsive aggression may relate to different aspect of suicidal behavior among those with AUDs as well. Individuals with mood disorders are more likely to experience suicidal ideation; however, a history of depression does not appear to increase the risk for transitioning to attempt among individuals with AUD (Conner et al., 2007). On the other hand, impulsivity among individuals with AUD has been implicated to be a strong factor for transitioning to an unplanned attempt or death by suicide (Conner et al.). These findings fit into the context of the two-hit hypothesis, which proposes that individuals with both mental disorders and impulsivity are at particularly high

risk for suicidal behavior (Brent & Mann, 2005). However, much work is still needed on the role of AUD in transitioning of suicide risk.

How suicidal behavior may increase risk for AUD. Surprisingly little empirical investigation has examined the role of suicidal behavior on the development of AUD. According to the escape theory of suicide, suicidal ideation and past attempt have been theorized to be a behavior driven to reduce and escape from the pain they are experiencing (Baumeister, 1990). Self-medication via alcohol may be one attempt to reduce this pain (Khantzian, 1997), which may enhance their risk for developing AUD. However, no study was identified that explicitly examined this directionality of the relationship.

How shared factors may account for the relationship between AUD and suicidal behavior. Not all suicide risk appears to be directly or indirectly related to the presence of AUD. Presence of mental disorder and impulsive aggression, if conceptualized as causing AUD, can be considered as shared/common factors that increase the risk for AUD and suicide independently. However, epidemiological studies have suggested that the association between AUD and suicide attempt remained even after adjusting for mental disorders, suggesting that the relationship between AUD and suicidal behavior is not entirely accounted for by shared factors (Borges et al., 2000).

The Role of DUD on Suicidal Behavior

Relatively few studies have examined the causal relationship between DUD and suicidal behavior (Erinoff et al., 2004; Wilcox, 2004) and, unlike the research on AUD and suicide, the conceptual framework for suicidal behavior among individuals with DUD is lacking. However, the scant evidence provides support for the importance of both a direct and a shared causal role of DUD on suicidal behavior.

How DUD may increase risk for suicidal behavior. Unlike the literature on AUD and suicide, surprisingly little research has been conducted to examine the direct association between DUD and suicidal behavior. One national longitudinal study found that lifetime diagnosis of DUD was associated with increased risk for suicidal ideation in the follow-up but did not increase the risk for plan or attempt among those who reported ideation (Borges et al., 2008). The finding suggested that the relationship between DUD and suicidal behavior was largely mediated by the increased risk for ideation, similar to the findings for AUD. No other study to date has examined how DUD may facilitate transitioning from one stage of suicidal behavior to another.

At least one study has found that the indicators of the severity of DUD (duration of SUD and early onset of SUD) are strong risk factors for suicide attempt, even after controlling for Axis I disorders (Landheim, Bakken, & Vaglum, 2006). However, this study did not distinguish alcohol dependence from other drug dependence. The use and abuse of substances may lead to several neurobiological changes, as well as environmental changes, that may increase the risk for suicidal behavior (Mack & Lightdale, 2006), although empirical evidence is scant. Examination of how removal or reduction of a risk factor may affect the outcome of interest can also suggest a possible causal pathway. Several studies have observed reduced suicide risk over time among individuals in drug treatment (Darke et al., 2007; Ramchand, Griffin, Harris, McCaffrey, & Morral, 2008), suggesting a possible causal role of drug use on suicidal behavior by reducing drug use. However, more studies are needed that specifically examine if drug treatment decreases risk for suicidal behavior.

How suicidal behavior may increase the risk for DUD. As described in the section for AUD, suicidal behavior may increase individual's propensity to use drugs, which may increase their risk for developing DUD. One study conducted among community-based youths has addressed this question. This study found that suicidal ideation, but not suicide attempt, predicted drug dependence nine years later, even after accounting for other factors such as baseline depression and demographic characteristics (MacDonald, Taylor, & Clarke, 2009). Further research may be needed to examine if this finding extends to the adult population as well.

How shared factors may account for the relationship between DUD and suicidal behavior. The relationship is also complicated since individuals at risk for DUD and suicidal behavior share similar risk factors (Goldston, 2004). Several studies provide evidence to support this hypothesis. One study suggests that the presence of opioid dependence does not appear to synergistically increase the risk for suicide above and beyond other risk factors (Maloney, Degenhardt, Darke, Mattick, & Nelson, 2007). This lends support to a hypothesis that, at least with respect to opiate drug users, substance abusers have greater risk for suicidal behavior because these individuals are more likely to experience other risk factors related to suicide such as family/social

dysfunctions and comorbidity with depression (Darke & Ross, 2002). Additionally, heroin users often use other drugs and may have higher risk for other substance use disorder such as alcohol and benzodiazepine (Darke & Ross, 1997).

The shared/common factor hypothesis may be particularly relevant for adolescents, for these individuals may have problem behaviors that place them at risk for developing SUD. The DUD may develop as a response to cope with psychological distress, which also places them at risk for suicidal behavior (Esposito-Smythers & Spirito, 2004). There are relatively few studies that examined the relationship between drugs other than alcohol on suicide attempt in adolescents. These studies have found that adolescents who used inhalants were at increased risk for suicide attempt compared with noninhalant users (Kelly, Cornelius, & Clark, 2004; Sakai, Hall, Mikulich-Gilbertson, & Crowley, 2004). The inhalant users and abusers also had high conduct disorder comorbidity, other comorbid DUD/AUD, major depression and abuse/neglect (Sakai et al., 2004). These factors may potentially serve as shared factors that increase both the risk for developing SUD and suicidal behavior among adolescents, yet research has been limited in this area.

Relatively few studies have also been conducted specifically among individuals with cannabis dependence, and the evidence remains inconsistent. Although a higher risk for suicide attempt has been found among those with cannabis abuse, this relationship appears to be largely mediated or confounded by psychiatric comorbidity, childhood abuse and social dysfunction (Beautrais, Joyce, & Mulder, 1999; Kelly et al., 2004). In contrast, one twin study noted that a twin with cannabis dependence had higher risk for suicide attempt than co-twin without cannabis dependence (Lynskey et al., 2004). A recent review that examined cannabis use and mortality risk found only four studies examining the relationship between cannabis use/abuse on suicide, and the evidence appears inconsistent (Calabria, Degenhardt, Hall, & Lynskey, 2010).

The Role of SUD in Interpersonal Violence

A number of models, hypotheses, and conceptual frameworks have been proposed to explain the relationship between drug use and interpersonal violence (Boles & Miotto, 2003; Kuhns & Clodfelter, 2009; Parker & Auerhahn, 1998; Stuart et al., 2008). In terms of IPV and AUD, alcohol use has been conceptualized as neither necessary nor sufficient cause of IPV (Cunradi, 2009). However, alcohol use can play an important role in the precipitation of IPV and its possibility will be explored here. Unlike the literature on suicide, however, to the best of knowledge, no conceptual framework was found that examined the role of SUD in pathways to violence perpetration.

How SUD may increase the risk for Interpersonal Violence. The increased risk for violence among individuals with SUD may be directly attributed to the use of drugs. Goldstein suggested three ways in which drug use can be related to violence (Boles & Miotto, 2003; Goldstein, 1985). First, *systemic violence* refers to violence that involves drug trade such as turf wars. Second, *economic compulsive violence* is a type of violence that is related to drug acquisition. Third, *psychopharmacological violence* is defined as a type of violence exacerbated under the influence of the drugs. Also referred to as the proximal effect model, pharmacological violence appears to have received most attention in Goldstein's tripartite framework. Both animal and human studies have supported that alcohol use increases aggressive behavior (Hoaken & Stewart, 2003). More recently, Hoaken and colleagues in an updated review consistently concluded that alcohol use increases aggressive behavior; they further added that aggressive behavior may be more likely to occur with alcohol use in those who are already predisposed to aggression and suggested the need to characterize these profiles (Hoaken, Hamill, Ross, Hancock, Lau, & Tapscott, 2012).

Several other studies support the proximal effect model in its relationship to IPV, as more IPV is inflicted on the days of consumption compared with days without (Fals-Stewart et al., 2003). A more recent study in the Netherlands also found that individuals with SUD were more likely to be under the influence of drugs and alcohol at the time of perpetration than were those without SUD (Kraanen, Scholing, & Emmelkamp, 2009). Alcohol consumptions affect an individual's physical and cognitive functioning, reduces self-control, and disinhibits violent constraint (Caetano, Schafer, & Cunradi, 2001). There is evidence that intoxication due to alcohol, but not necessarily the initiation of drinking, is an important predictor for IPV (Foran & O'Leary, 2008). A drinker's expectancies of the effects of alcohol and socioculturally grounded beliefs that intoxication will excuse the individual from blame may also exacerbate these behaviors (Collins & Messerschmidt, 1993), although this has been questioned in a more recent study among a sample of high school students (Stappenbeck &

Fromme, 2010). One study found a nonsignificant relationship between alcohol dependence and violence after accounting for intoxication at the time of incident; the finding suggested that the influence of intoxication is an important situational factor to youth violence (Arseneault, Moffitt, Caspi, Taylor, & Silva, 2000), perhaps more so than having an AUD.

A review also examined how decrease in substance use via alcohol or drug treatment is associated with decreased risk for IPV among individuals with AUD (Murphy et al., 2010). Such studies also help clarify the mechanism of the relationship by understanding how removal of a factor influences another outcome. This review of ten studies noted a moderate decrease in the IPV rate up to 2 years following substance abuse treatment. Of the ten studies examined, nine were studies on alcohol treatment. The decrease was more robust among individuals who had favorable treatment outcomes (Murphy & Ting, 2010).

The direct link between illicit drug use and violence remains inconclusive (Kuhns & Clodfelter, 2009). Unlike the role of alcohol on violence, the varying pharmacological properties of illicit drugs and the lack of evidence suggest that more research needs to be conducted. Hoaken et al. also suggested there are confounded and indirect relationship between many drugs and aggressive behavior, although they also concluded more research is still needed to better establish the relationship and how drug use increases risk for aggressive behavior (Hoaken et al., 2012). However, the methodology is complicated by the combined use of alcohol and drugs at the time of violence (Kuhns & Clodfelter, 2009). The only fairly consistent evidence appears to be with respect to heroin, which does not seem to increase the risk for violence (Boles & Miotto, 2003; Parker & Auerhahn, 1998). A longitudinal study in Norway also found crimes related to drug acquisition and selling were more commonly convicted crimes among heroin users three years prior to entering treatment for opioid maintenance (Bukten et al., 2011). A recent review also suggested opiate users are more likely to exhibit aggressive behavior to obtain drugs (Hoaken et al., 2012). Parker and Auerhahn (1998) suggest that if violence does occur, the most likely involved substance is alcohol. It is also important to consider the effect of withdraw and its tendency for violence. At least three reviews suggested that the association between marijuana dependence and violence are more likely due to withdrawal from the drug

(Hoaken et al., 2012; Hoaken & Stewart, 2003; Moore et al., 2008).

Another relatively less studied model is the indirect model, which suggests that a mediating factor plays a significant role in the relationship between SUD and IPV. The role of martial dissatisfaction has also been investigated as a mediator, but independent effects of alcohol have remained in the risk for IPV (Fals-Stewart et al., 2003). According to the structural conflict facilitation hypothesis, individuals are more likely to engage in violence after verbal insults that are exacerbated by situational contexts such as low SES and daily stress (Stalans & Ritchie, 2008). The insults appeared to mediate the relationship between marijuana dependence and IPV, but direct effects still remained for AUD (Stalans & Ritchie, 2008).

Antisocial personality traits have been shown to mediate the relationship between concurrent drug use and IPV among individuals with AUD (Murphy, O'Farrell, Fals-Stewart, & Feehan, 2001). Feingold et al. (2008) also noted that the relationship between alcohol problem and IPV was largely mediated by antisocial behavior and polydrug abuse, suggesting that the role of alcohol in IPV may not be as strong as previously suggested. However, the association between marijuana and hallucinogen dependence and IPV remained even after controlling for antisocial behavior in at least one study (Feingold, Kerr, & Capaldi, 2008). More research and conceptual clarity is needed on the role of SUD on interpersonal violence.

How shared factors may account for the relationship between SUD and violence. The general deviance/spurious effects model is slightly different from Goldstein's tripartite framework, which suggests that shared factors account for the relationship between SUD and violence (Stuart et al., 2008). Research has shown little support for this model, at least with respect to IPV. Even after controlling for a number of potential shared factors, the independent relationship between alcohol problems and IPV still remained (Coker, Smith, McKeown, & King, 2000). However, it is often possible for partners with SUD to have additional problems that increase their propensity to exert violence to their partners (Collins & Messerschmidt, 1993), although whether the problems are exacerbated by SUD or whether it caused both SUD and violence has not been rigorously investigated. A study using NESARC data also supported the association between crack cocaine compared with cocaine powder on violence were largely accounted by third factors such as demographic and

comorbid mood disorders (Vaughn, Fu, Perron, Bohnert, & Howard, 2010). Head injury and other neurobiological deficits also may be involved in the relationship between alcohol use and IPV; however, research is needed to examine how these factors are interrelated (for a review on the biology of IPV, see Pinto et al., 2010).

Similar to risk for suicide, aggression may be a common factor that increases risk for violence perpetration and SUD independently. Although the relationship between drug/alcohol use and youth violence is less clear (Dahlberg, 1998), this model may be particularly relevant for youth violence, as common risk factors such as impulsivity and aggression have been found to increase the risk for both SUD and violent behaviors. This review highlighted the neurobiological functions that are associated with drug abuse and violence and noted the important role of prefrontal cortex dysfunction on both factors (Fishbein, 2000). At least one prospective study found that substance intoxication, excessive threat perception, and comorbid conduct disorder accounted for the majority of the relationship between SUD and youth violence (Arseneault et al., 2000). In terms of illegal drugs, there is also a need to consider drug preference, as individuals with a greater tendency for violence may prefer one drug over the other (Hoaken & Stewart, 2003).

Section Summary

Unlike the literature on epidemiological evidence establishing the association between SUD and intentional injuries, those that examined the mechanism of its association are few. The literature suggests that the role of SUD on intentional injuries is a combination of both the presence of a shared factor and direct/indirect effect. However, this may also depend on if the population of interest is adults or adolescents. At least with respect to suicide, AUD has been conceptualized as a distal factor that increases risk for suicide-related risks, although alcohol use itself can potentially facilitate engaging in suicidal behavior. The role of DUD on suicidal behavior has been examined less frequently but more so for SUD and interpersonal violence. The evidence suggests that the mechanism is highly complex and multifactorial. How intentional injuries can be predictors for the development of SUD is understudied. Additionally, many of the identified shared factors focused on individual level factors such as comorbid mental disorders. The sociocontextual factors and risks associated with living in neighborhoods with high drug abuse and violence also has important implications but has not been rigorously examined in the relationship between SUD and intentional injuries. Many studies reviewed were cross-sectional; more methodological rigorous studies that use longitudinal designs, causal inference and mediation methods will be fruitful to further advance knowledge in this area.

Characterization of Individuals with SUD at Risk for Intentional Injuries

A more complete understanding of the interplay of risk and protective factors from biological, psychological, and social perspectives is an important step in building a public health paradigm that will inform suicide prevention (IOM, 2002). Risk and protective factors are correlates that either confer vulnerability or resilience toward certain behaviors (Rutter, 1989). Such knowledge will contribute to the more accurate identification of individuals at risk of engaging in intentional injuries. This section will focus on factors that have been associated with intentional injuries specifically among those with SUD. This section does not intend to be an exhaustive review. Rather, it will focus on a select few that have been noted across studies, albeit with some inconsistencies. Table 11.1 summarizes these risk factors. These factors are divided into broad categories of risk factors such as demographic, psychiatric disorders and SUD, personality traits, and interpersonal factors. A subsection on protective factors follows the risk factors. Although the majority of studies examined were cross-sectional, there were a limited number of longitudinal studies. These

longitudinal studies are discussed in a separate subsection titled "longitudinal predictors," following the subsections on risk and protective factors.

Characteristics of Individuals with AUD at Increased Risk for Suicidal Behavior

Demographics. Most studies compared individuals with AUD who have a history of suicide attempt with those without a history of suicide attempt and were conducted among treatment-seeking samples. These studies identified certain demographic factors that distinguish between the two groups. The most consistent factor for history of suicide attempt is female gender (Conner, Beautrais, & Conwell, 2003a; Preuss et al., 2002; Roy & Janal, 2007; Roy, Lamparski, DeJong, Moore, & Linnoila, 1990). A study suggested that men with alcohol dependence are more likely to die by suicide (Conner et al., 2003b). Another study also found a higher proportion of men with alcohol misuse problems among those who died by suicide (Pirkola, Isometsa, Heikkinen, & Lonnqvist, 2000). Several findings suggest that women with AUD also have a high risk for dying from suicide relative to women without AUD, and this difference was greater than men with and without AUD (Harris & Barraclough, 1997; Wilcox et al., 2004). These findings appear to suggest the relationship between AUD and intentional injury may be stronger in women. However, more men with AUD die by suicide than women with AUD, which is congruent with the literature that suggests that females have greater rates of suicide attempt than males,

Table 11.1. Featured Risk Factors for Suicidal Behavior and IPV among Individuals with SUD

	Suicidal Behavior	IPV
Demographic	• Family history of suicide • Female for attempt • Nonmarried status • Younger age	• Family history of violence • Nonmarried status • Younger age
Comorbidity/ Personality/drug use	• Comorbid psychiatric disorders such as mood, bipolar, borderline personality disorders • Drug and alcohol problem severity • History of suicidal behavior/violence • Impulsivity/aggression • Polydrug use	• Conduct problem • Drug and alcohol problem severity • History of violence/incarceration • Impulsivity/aggression • Types of drug used; polydrug use
Interpersonal	• Childhood maltreatment • Interpersonal loss • Social isolation • Unemployment/legal problem	• Childhood maltreatment • Family impairment

whereas males are more likely to die from suicide (Canetto & Sakinofsky, 1998).

Similarly, suicide attempt and death appear to be higher in younger alcoholics (Houston, Hawton, & Shepperd, 2001; Pirkola et al., 2000; Preuss et al., 2003), although at least one study noted that the relationship between alcohol dependence and suicide becomes stronger with increased age (Conner et al., 2003a). Nonmarried status (being single, widowed, divorced, or separated) has also been noted to distinguish attempters from nonattempters (Pirkola et al., 2000; Preuss et al., 2002, 2003), but this has not been found in another study (Roy & Janal, 2007). In the general population, Caucasians have higher risk for suicidal behavior, compared with any other racial/ethnic group (Loebel, 2005). However, racial differences have not been noted among treatment-seeking individuals with alcohol dependence (Preuss et al., 2003; Roy & Janal, 2007). A family history of suicide was also found more prevalent among alcohol dependent individuals with a history of suicidal behavior (Beautrais, 2000; Preuss et al., 2002, 2003; Roy & Janal, 2007).

Psychiatric disorders and SUD. Comorbid psychiatric disorders are common among individuals with AUD (Swendsen & Merikangas, 2000). Research has consistently shown that individuals with comorbid psychiatric disorders have much higher risk for suicide than those without comorbidity (Blow, Brockmann, & Barry, 2004) in adolescent population as well (Pompili et al., 2012), and comorbid mood disorders are particularly relevant to suicide risk (Center for Substance Abuse Treatment, 2009). The relationship between suicide and comorbid mood disorders also appears to differ depending on whether the mood disorder is substance-induced. Although both types of depression (substance induced and non–substance induced) have been associated with suicide attempt among alcohol-dependent individuals (Preuss et al., 2002), at least one study found that those with non–substance-induced depression are more likely to have an earlier onset of suicidal behavior (Preuss et al., 2003). This finding suggests that individuals with preexisting depression may have a more severe course of suicidal risks, compared with alcohol-dependent individuals with substance-induced depression (Preuss et al., 2002), and early major depression is a "candidate" endophenotype for suicidal behavior (Mann et al., 2009).

Individuals with alcohol dependence and bipolar disorder are also at increased risk for suicide attempt (Levin & Hennessy, 2004). The studies examining this relationship were mostly conducted among individuals with bipolar disorder (Dalton, Cate-Carter, Mundo, Parikh, & Kennedy, 2003; Potash et al., 2000). Schizophrenia (Limosin, Loze, Philippe, Casadebaig, & Rouillon, 2007), conduct disorder in adolescents (Illomaki, Rasanen, Viilo, & Hakko, 2006), and DUD (Hesselbrock, Hesselbrock, Syzmanski, & Weidmann, 1988; Preuss et al., 2002) are also associated with an increased risk for suicidal behavior among individuals with AUD.

Severity of AUD and consequences of AUD also differentiate the risk for suicidal behavior. Consequences of more severe AUD such as alcohol-related physical problems are higher in attempters than in nonattempters (Preuss et al., 2002). Even among those with AUD, the risk for suicide may greatly differ depending on the severity or chronicity of the disorder, such as younger age of onset and longer duration of alcohol problems (Kelly et al., 2004; Roy & Janal, 2007).

Personality traits. Impulsivity/aggression in the form of violent behavior has consistently been associated with suicidal behavior (Conner, Duberstein, Conwell, Seidlitz, & Caine, 2001; Mann et al., 1999) and has been conceptualized as one of the predisposing factors in the relationship between AUD and suicidal behavior (Conner & Duberstein, 2004). Koller and colleagues (2002) also found that impulsive aggression traits were associated with suicide attempt; this appeared to be independent of depression or personality disorders among alcohol dependent inpatients (Koller, Preuss, Bottlender, Wenzel, & Soyka, 2002). A recent study also found that impulsive suicide attempters had higher behavioral impulsivity than nonimpulsive attempters among individuals with alcohol dependence in treatment (Wojnar et al., 2009).

Hopelessness has been noted as an important psychosocial construct that increases risk for suicide attempt (Beck, Brown, Berchick, Stewart, & Steer, 2006). Although empirical evidence on the role of hopelessness and suicide is somewhat mixed in individuals with AUD (Conner et al., 2001), hopelessness has been conceptualized as increasing vulnerability for suicide in individuals with AUD (Conner & Duberstein, 2004).

Interpersonal. Interpersonal stressors can serve as proximal risk factors for suicide risk (Conner & Duberstein, 2004; Erinoff et al., 2004; Murphy, Wetzel, Robins, & McEvoy, 1992; Pirkola et al., 2004). Individuals with AUD may be particularly likely to experience interpersonal stressors, as these events may be exacerbated by, or even caused by, the heavy use of alcohol. Interpersonal loss has been considered an important precipitating factor for suicide among individuals with AUD (Conner & Duberstein, 2004; Conner et al., 2003). Among male alcoholics who died by suicide, the impact of interpersonal problems and unemployment were found to be greater in those between 21 and 34 years of age compared with those who are older (Conner, Duberstein, & Conwell, 1999). Unemployment and legal problems have been associated with higher suicide risk among this population as well (Murphy et al., 1992; Preuss et al., 2002; Roy et al., 1990). Social isolation and perceived loneliness are also important environmental factors associated with suicidal behavior (Murphy et al., 1992). Interpersonal factors can also serve as distal risk factors; for example, individuals with AUD who have a history of childhood abuse and victimization are consistently shown to be at increased risk for suicidal behavior (Makhija & Sher, 2007; Roy & Janal, 2007).

Protective factors. In contrast to the abundant literature on risk factors associated with suicidal behavior among individuals with AUD, less research has been conducted on protective factors for suicidal behavior. One study has found that moral objection to suicide was low in individuals with comorbid alcohol and depression compared with those without comorbid AUD (Richardson-Vejlgaard, Sher, Oquendo, Lizardi, & Stanley, 2009). Several studies have noted the protective effect of seeking social support on reducing the risk of suicide, but these studies were not necessarily conducted among individuals with AUD (Chioqueta & Stiles, 2007; Kaslow et al., 2005; Kaslow, Jacobs, Young, & Cook, 2006). Some studies report that problem-focused coping style is associated with lower suicidal risk, in addition to feelings of responsibility toward family, moral objectivity, fear of suicide, and social disapproval (Linehan, Goodstein, Nielsen, & Chiles, 1983; Malone et al., 2000). Getting treatment for AUD is also potentially a protective factor for suicidal behavior (Mann, Zalcman, Rush, Smart, & Rhodes, 2008) and is discussed further in the prevention section of this chapter.

Longitudinal predictors. One longitudinal study was identified among alcohol dependent individuals. Lifetime history of suicide attempt was a strong predictor for attempt 5 years later. This study also found that correlates that distinguished individuals with and without lifetime history of attempt also predict future attempt, such as younger age, other

drug dependence, and severity of psychiatric disorders. However, at least one longitudinal study noted that female gender and race did not predict suicide attempt 5 years later (Preuss et al., 2003), suggesting that although female gender may have higher rates of lifetime prevalence for suicide attempt, the development of suicide attempt may not differ by gender.

Risk Factors for Suicidal Behavior among Individuals with DUD

Most research on DUD and suicidal behavior has been conducted among individuals with opioid or cocaine use disorders or has combined individuals with varying DUDs. Overall, these studies suggest that those with DUD appear to share similar risk factors for suicidal risk, compared with the general population. However, the prevalence of these risk factors is higher in drug users (Darke & Ross, 2002; Maloney et al., 2007).

Demographics. Similar to the literature on AUD and suicide, many of these studies were cross-sectional and compared individuals with and without a history of lifetime suicide attempt. Being female has been associated with a history of attempt in a number of studies (Kelly et al., 2004; Maloney, Degenhardt, Darke, & Nelson, 2009; Roy, 2001, 2003a). Adult drug abusers who attempted suicide were somewhat younger than nonattempters (Roy, 2003b). Race does not appear to significantly differ between attempters and nonattempters in adolescent (Kelly et al., 2004) and adult substance abusers (Roy, 2003b). However, some racial differences were noted in comorbidity of substance abuse and mental illness among those who died from suicide. Using the National Violent Death Reporting System across the 13 states, Karch and colleagues (2006) found that non-Hispanic whites and blacks who died by suicide were more likely to have comorbid disorders, whereas Hispanics were more likely to have substance abuse but were not identified to have mental illness (Karch, Barker, & Strine, 2006). Family history of suicide has also been shown as a strong predictor for suicidal behavior in this population (Roy, 2003a; Tremeau et al., 2005).

Psychiatric disorders, SUD, and Personality Traits. Comorbid mental disorders also increase suicide risk in adults (Comtois, Russo, Roy-Byrne, & Ries, 2004; Darke et al., 2007; Ilgen, Harris, Moos, & Tiet, 2007; Kelly et al., 2004; Maloney et al., 2007; Moscicki, 2001; Roy, 2003a; Ilgen, Conner, Valenstein, Austin, & Blow, 2010a). The comorbidity of mental disorders was associated with increased risk for suicide and suicidal behavior among adolescents in a number of studies as well (Bridge, Goldstein, & Brent, 2006). Borderline personality disorder (BPD) and bipolar disorder (BD) are two psychiatric diagnoses that are highly comorbid with substance abuse. A more recent study noted that the SUD and suicide attempt relationship existed only in BD-I (Sublette et al., 2009), suggesting that this relationship may differ depending on the subtype of BD. Individuals with SUD who have these diagnoses have been shown to have particularly high risk for suicidal behavior (Dougherty, Mathias, Marsh, Moeller, & Swann, 2004). More recently, a study found that individuals in residential substance abuse treatment who have BPD in addition to high distress tolerance had greatest risk for suicidal attempt (Anestis, Gratz, Bagge, & Tull, 2012). Impulsivity is a key factor in both diagnoses (APA, 1994) and is gaining attention as one of the potential endophenotypes for suicidal behavior (Mann et al., 2009). Individuals who abuse drugs and have attempted suicide have high aggression/impulsivity (Tremeau et al., 2008). Impulsivity and screening positive for BPD have been associated with risk for suicide attempt among opiate-dependent individuals (Maloney et al., 2009). Although antisocial personality disorder (ASPD) is highly prevalent and comorbid with BPD among drug users, at least one study of heroin users noted that the association between ASPD and suicide attempt was largely accounted for by comorbid BPD (Darke, Williamson, Ross, Teesson, & Lynskey, 2004).

Other comorbidity such as posttraumatic stress disorder and other DUD was also found to increase risk for suicidal behavior among this population (Ilgen et al., 2010a; Maloney et al., 2007). Severity of the DUD (Borges et al., 2000), polydrug use (Darke et al., 2007; Ilgen et al., 2010a; Wines, Saitz, Horton, Lloyd-Travaglini, & Samet, 2004), in addition to comorbidity with AUD (Ilgen et al., 2007a; Maloney et al., 2007; Roy, 2003a) have also been associated with suicidal behavior. Additional factors associated with suicide attempt include alcohol intoxication and difficulty controlling violent behavior (Tiet, Illgen, Byrnes, & Moos, 2007). Ramchand and colleagues also noted that conduct disorder was a significant predictor for suicide attempt among an adolescent substance abusing sample (2008). Among a national sample of veterans who entered substance abuse treatment, prior violence has been associated with lifetime suicide attempt (Ilgen, Burnette, Conner, Czyz, Murray, & Chermack, 2010b).

Interpersonal. Several interpersonal factors have been found to discriminate suicide attempters from nonattempters as well. Parental psychopathology (Darke & Ross, 2002; Rossow & Lauritzen, 2001) and childhood trauma such as sexual abuse and maltreatment have been found in high prevalence among those with DUD and have been related to suicidal behavior (Benda, 2003; Maloney et al., 2007; Rossow & Lauritzen, 2001; Roy, 2003a; Wines et al., 2004). Interpersonal loss may also increase the risk for suicidal behavior among those with DUD (Darke et al., 2007; Johnsson & Fridell, 1997). Among those with opiate dependence, low perceived belonging also increased vulnerability to suicide attempt (Conner, Britton, Sworts, & Joiner, 2007).

Protective factors. Similar to the literature on AUD and suicide, the literature on protective factors for suicide among individuals with DUD is limited. In at least one study, criminal justice system contact and engagement in treatment for DUD has been associated with lower risk for suicide attempt (Ilgen et al., 2007a).

Longitudinal predictors. Several longitudinal studies among opiate users have examined predictors of future suicide attempt. All of these studies have shown past history of suicide ideation and attempt as one of the strongest predictors for future suicidal behavior (Britton & Conner, 2010; Darke, Williamson, Ross, & Teesson, 2005; Ilgen et al., 2007a; Tiet et al., 2007; Wines et al., 2004). Other potential predictors include social isolation (Darke et al., 2005), polydrug use (Darke et al., 2005; Ilgen et al., 2007a), and greater depressive symptoms/psychiatric problems (Britton et al., 2010; Ilgen et al., 2007a; Wines et al., 2004). Female gender predicted suicide attempt a year later in one study among a treatment-seeking sample (Britton et al., 2010) but not in another longitudinal study (Darke et al., 2005).

Risk Factors for Interpersonal Violence among Individuals with SUD

In comparison to a number of studies examining correlates associated with suicidal behavior among individuals with SUD (especially with respect to those with AUD), surprisingly few studies have characterized individuals with SUD who may be at risk for perpetrating interpersonal violence. However, because not all individuals who have SUD engage in violence (Schumacher, Fals-Stewart, & Leonard, 2003), identification of factors that distinguish individuals with SUD who are more prone to violence are important for targeted interventions. Batterer typology helps categorize perpetrators into subtypes, and SUD prevalence has been noted to vary across these subtypes. Specifically, the dysphoric or borderline (DB) batterers and generally violent and antisocial (GVA) batterers appears to have higher substance abuse problems compared with family-only batterers (Hamberger, 2009; Holtzworth-Munroe & Stuart, 1994).

Demographics. Several cross-sectional studies have examined characteristics of those who have engaged in violent behavior in treatment-seeking samples. There is some inconsistency as to whether IPV is more likely in females or males. One study noted that males were more likely to be involved in alcohol-related violence than females (Collins & Messerschmidt, 1993). This trend has been noted among individuals with SUDs as well (Macdonald, Erickson, Wells, Hathaway, & Pakula, 2008), although not without inconsistencies (Chermack & Blow, 2002). Whether males with SUD engaged in violence may be specific to the type of violence involved, as at least one study noted that both genders were likely to engage in IPV, but males with SUDs were more likely than females with SUDs to engage in nonpartner violence (Chermack, Fuller, & Blow, 2000; Macdonald et al., 2008). Younger age has consistently been associated with a higher prevalence of violence perpetration among those in substance abuse treatment (Burnette et al., 2008; Chermack et al., 2000). Partner aggression perpetrators have also been noted to be younger among individuals with SUD (Chermack et al., 2008). Additionally, history of incarceration and unmarried status have been associated with a history of violence (Burnette et al.). Family history of violence has also been implicated to play an important factor in violence among those with SUD and has been shown to be related to the risk of violence through childhood conduct problems (Chermack et al., 2000).

Other substance use and personality traits. Frequency of cocaine and alcohol use has been associated with violence among those with SUD (Macdonald et al., 2008), as well as drug problem severity (Chermack et al., 2000). Alcohol dependence severity has also been associated with IPV, although this association did not remain once other factors such as concurrent drug use and antisocial personality were accounted for (Murphy et al., 2001). Among fifty-four individuals with a history of violence, younger age of onset for substance abuse was also associated with violence recidivism

and aggression (Gustavson et al., 2007). In addition, situational factors such as the type of drug used and whether this was in combination with alcohol appear to distinguish those who engaged in violence (Chermack & Blow, 2002).

Individual and personality factors have also been found to distinguish those with SUDs who engaged in violence from those who did not engage. These factors include traits such as hostility, impulsivity, and aggression (Macdonald et al., 2008). A review also suggested that substance abusers who engaged in violent behavior tend to be more hostile and impulsive and have more neurobiological deficits (Fishbein, 2000). The role of antisocial personality traits has also received some attention as a predictor for IPV among individuals with SUD (Murphy et al., 2001).

Interpersonal. Childhood physical abuse in men and both childhood physical and sexual abuse in women were associated with history of violence perpetration among a sample of individuals in substance abuse treatment (Burnette et al., 2008). "Family impairment" such as a history of child abuse or dysfunctional family environment has also been associated with violence perpetration among psychoactive substance abusing female adolescents (Mezzich et al., 1997).

Protective factors and potential predictors. To the best of our knowledge, the literature is not available on protective factors for interpersonal violence among those with SUD, and longitudinal studies that examined potential predictors of violence perpetration among those with SUD were limited. In at least one longitudinal study, excessive drinking, in addition to high hostility and avoidant coping style also predicted IPV (Schumacher, Homish, Leonard, Quigley, & Kearns-Bodkin, 2008). This may be a future area of research.

Section Summary

Several key common features have been identified that distinguish individuals at risk for suicidal behavior and/or interpersonal violence among those with SUD: younger age, heavy substance abuse, impulsive/aggressive traits, and childhood stressors. The presence of common features suggests that there may be some overlap among those with SUD at risk for suicidal behavior and interpersonal violence such as IPV; however, no formal studies was identified that examined the extent of these overlaps. Other psychiatric disorders also increase risk for suicidal behavior among individuals with SUD, whereas research in interpersonal violence has focused more on the co-occurring use of other drugs and alcohol. Several longitudinal studies have examined suicide risk and SUD; these studies have consistently shown that history of suicide attempt is a strong predictor for subsequent suicide attempt. However, predictors for intentional injuries in general are limited among those with SUD. Literature on protective factors that distinguish individuals with and without a history of intentional injuries is lacking as well.

Prevention of Intentional Injury

The multifactorial nature of the link between suicide and interpersonal injuries on SUD calls for a public health approach to prevention that integrates a number of disciplines to reduce the burden of these problems. Developing, implementing, and testing interventions form the third step in the public health paradigm of prevention (IOM, 2002). Knox and colleagues suggest suicide prevention should follow the approach of heart disease prevention that integrates universal, selective, and indicative prevention strategies (Knox, Conwell, & Caine, 2004). A similar approach has been adapted for this framework to violence prevention, especially with youth violence (Webster-Stratton & Taylor, 2001). CDC's National Center for Injury Prevention and Control (http://www.cdc.gov/ViolencePrevention/overview/strategicdirections.html) also highlights strategic directions for violence prevention for child maltreatment, IPV and suicidal behavior. These efforts underscore the importance of integrating knowledge in both disciplines of intentional injuries to advance violence prevention. Substance Abuse and Mental Health Services Administration (SAMHSA) also promotes initiatives in prevention of suicidal behavior, mental health, and substance abuse (http://www.samhsa.gov/prevention/).

The distinction between universal, selective, and indicated prevention strategies primarily depends upon the population in which the prevention efforts take place (Gordon, 1987). *Universal prevention* approaches are geared toward the entire population, regardless of their baseline risk for suicide or violence perpetration. Not all individuals will respond to a universal preventive intervention, however. Although a number of universal prevention approaches are possible, we will highlight studies that focus on prevention of SUD in keeping with the context of this chapter. *Selective prevention* focuses on individuals known to be at risk for suicidal and violent behavior. Treatment of SUD will fit this context; the overview of literature

provided in previous sections underscore that those with SUD are particularly at risk for these behaviors. *Indicated prevention* strategies are similar to selective prevention in their focus on high-risk individuals. However, unlike selective prevention strategies, indicated strategies target individuals who have already expressed detectable risks. In terms of suicide and interpersonal violence prevention, prevention approaches among individuals who have a history of attempt or juvenile offenders, for example, will fall into this category. Table 11.2 summarizes these approaches and provides examples. A more recent review summarized the effectiveness of various drug policy initiatives aimed to prevent public problems related to drug use and abuse using a similar framework; interested readers are referred to this literature for a more extensive review on this topic (Strang, Babor, Caulkins, Fischer, Foxcroft, & Humphreys, 2012).

Prevention of Suicide and Suicidal Behavior

A systematic review of suicide prevention efforts highlighted the need for the evaluation of suicide prevention programs (Mann et al., 2005). The Evidence-Based Practices Project (EBPP) was created in 2002 to draw attention to and review evidence-based suicide prevention programs, and of the 24 programs reviewed, 8 were found to be effective and 12 to be promising (Rodgers, Sudak, Silverman, & Litts, 2007).

Universal prevention: There are several suicide prevention approaches that fall into this category such as school-based education, gatekeeper training, screening, media, and means restriction (Mann et al., 2005). Among these categories, only education, media, and means restriction have received some evaluation and have shown evidence of reducing suicide risk (Mann et al.). Restricting the availability of drugs and alcohol is one type of means restriction. Several studies have been conducted to examine whether alcohol and drug restriction have decreased the risk for suicide across countries (Mann et al.). A study conducted in Estonia found that the antialcohol campaign in 1986–1988 was associated with decreased suicide and decreased BAC level of suicide in both males and females (Varnik, Kolves, Vali, Tooding, & Wasserman, 2006), although this study could not directly attribute this decrease to restriction of alcohol. Restricting the pack size of analgesics by imposing and reducing the maximum number of tablets in a pack has also been associated with reduced suicide in the United Kingdom (Hawton et al., 2004), and this has been categorized as one of the effective evidence-based prevention programs based on the criteria of EBPP

Table 11.2. Overview of Public Health Approach to Prevention of Suicide and IPV

	Target Population	Example of the Target Population	Strategy Goal	Example of Prevention Strategies	
				Suicidal Behavior	IPV
Universal	Entire population	School-aged children	Prevent or delay the emergence of suicidal behavior and violence perpetration	• School-based programs to reduce drug abuse and increase mental health awareness • Screening of suicidal behavior • Restriction of alcohol and drug availability	• Family, individual, and classroom-based programs that address conduct problems in young children • Restriction of alcohol and drug availability
Selective	High risk groups with known risk factors	Individuals with SUD	Prevent or delay the emergence of suicidal behavior and violence perpetration among a high-risk group	• Treatment of mental disorders • Treatment of SUD	• Treatment of SUD
Indicated	Those who exhibit signs of intentional injuries	Individuals with SUD and history of suicide and/or violence	Prevent transitioning from suicide attempt to death and/or engage in multiple attempts; prevent recidivism	• Suicide risk management • Treatment of mental disorders • Treatment of SUD	• Multisystemic therapy in juvenile offenders • Behavioral Couples Therapy for IPV • Treatment of SUD

(Rodgers et al., 2007). In addition to means restriction, targeting known risk factors is another suicide prevention strategy considered to be a universal prevention approach. Such programs include prevention of drug use and onset of SUD, as well as disruptive behavior. The Good Behavior Game (GBG) is a classroom-based intervention that targeted behavioral regulation among first- and second-grade children (Dolan et al., 1993), which has been shown to be effective in reducing drug abuse (Kellam et al., 2008). This intervention was found to be associated with decreased ideation and attempts over a decade later as well (Wilcox et al., 2008).

Selective prevention: Mental health and addiction treatment among individuals with SUD will fall into this category, for individuals who abuse drugs are at particularly high risk for suicidal behavior than those who do not abuse drugs. The number of risk factors

discussed in this chapter among those with SUD further aids in distinguishing individuals with SUD who are particularly at risk for suicide. A multisite longitudinal evaluation of substance abuse treatment programs found that longer engagement in drug use treatment was associated with decreased suicidal risk 1 year later (Ilgen et al., 2007). Another study found a reduced suicide risk 3 years later among heroin users who entered treatment, although the rate was still higher than the general population (Darke et al., 2007). In a population-level study in Manitoba, Alcoholic Anonymous membership rate was also associated with decreased risk for suicide mortality rate, especially among female suicide (Mann et al., 2008). A study suggested that adolescents in substance abuse treatment have high suicide risk at treatment admittance, which still persisted somewhat even after treatment (Ramchand et al., 2008). The authors recommended that suicide prevention should start once they enter these treatment settings (Ramchand et al., 2008). At least one study suggested that individuals in remission from substance abuse are not necessarily without risk for suicide if mental health problem remains (Aharonovich, Liu, Nunes, & Hasin, 2002). Given the high comorbidity of mental disorders and SUD, a more integrative model of care for mental health and substance abuse is needed to better address suicide risk among this population. Additionally, treatment providers should be more aware of suicide risk assessment and management among this population. The majority of individuals who die from suicide are known to make contact with health care professionals within a year prior to their death (Andersen, Andersen, Rosholm, & Gram, 2000). Similar findings were more recently noted among over 3000 veterans with SUD who died from suicide; over half have received care from the Veterans Affairs health service within a month before their suicide and primarily in medical treatment settings (Ilgen, Conner, Roeder, Blow, Austin, & Valenstein, 2012). The Center for Substance Abuse Treatment (CSAT; 2009) published the Treatment Improvement Protocol, which provides a detailed guideline on assessment of suicide-related risks for substance abuse counselors. Several interventions have been conducted among individuals with AUD to specifically reduce the suicide risk (Cornelius, Clark, Salloum, Bukstein, & Kelly, 2004), but very few empirical studies are available for individuals with DUD.

Indicated prevention: The evidence for medication effectiveness on reducing suicide risk among individuals with SUD is scarce, especially since many controlled studies purposefully exclude individuals with active suicidal ideation (Cornelius et al., 2004). The treatment response of antidepressants among adolescents with SUD and suicidal ideation is particularly lacking (Cornelius et al.), and even less evidence is available among individuals with DUD who have thought about and engaged in suicidal behavior.

Prevention of Interpersonal Violence

The integration of substance use treatment for prevention of violence appears to be increasingly recognized in the field of IPV; in particular. Temple and colleagues (2009) briefly examine universal, selective, and indicated prevention of IPV among substance using individuals and found several prevention studies that may have implications for IPV prevention. However, most of these studies were focused on indicated prevention strategies.

Universal prevention: Similar to prevention efforts of suicide, universal prevention strategies for violence may include reduction in availability of drugs and alcohol and better screening of individuals at risk for SUD. Jewkes (2002) highlights decrease in alcohol consumption as one of a primary prevention effort to reduce the risks for IPV. Given the potentially shared etiology of drug abuse and violence, it is also important for programs that address early delinquent behaviors to prevent the development of both drug abuse and violence (Webster-Stratton et al., 2001). Many effective prevention programs are available, designed at varying levels (e.g. child, family, and classroom) that addresses conduct behavior in young children aged 0 to 8 years to prevent the development of substance abuse and violence (for a comprehensive review, see Webster-Stratton et al., 2001).

Selective interventions: Several studies have examined the impact of substance abuse treatment among individuals with SUD, which also included individuals who did not necessarily have a history of IPV (Klostermann et al., 2010). At least one study noted that among those with an alcohol problem, standard substance abuse treatment did reduce the IPV rate (O'Farrell, Fals-Stewart, Murphy, & Murphy, 2003). Treatment for AUD has been shown to decrease husband-to-wife IPV and wife-to-husband marital IPV at the sixth-month follow-up (Stuart et al., 2003). Alcohol treatment was related to reduction in IPV in other studies as well (O'Farrell, Hutton, & Murphy, 1999). SUD treatment has also been shown to reduce subsequent crimes that are not necessarily IPV (Hubbard, Craddock, & Anderson, 2003; Prendergast, Podus, Chang, & Urada, 2002). One longitudinal study in Norway found that those who were in opioid maintenance treatment (OMT) had lower rates of violent crime conviction than 3 years prior to OMT for both men and women (Havnes, Bukten, Gossop, Waal, Stangeland, & Clausen, 2012). Brackley, Williams, and Wei (2010) discuss IPV screening for treatment providers, in particular for nurses; they also introduced the Treatment Improvement Protocol 25, which was published in 1997 by CSAT to integrate substance abuse treatment with domestic violence response.

Indicated interventions aim to reduce future violence among those who have a history of violent behavior. Much of the literature on IPV prevention focused on substance abuse treatment among individuals with a history of IPV. Incorporating clients' needs, such as addressing the substance abuse problems of these clients, has been recognized as one of the theory-based approaches to improving batterer prevention programs (Stuart, Temple, & Moore, 2007). Treatment of SUD in perpetrators is especially important, for substance-abusing perpetrators have particularly low participation rates for domestic violence treatment and are more likely to drop out of treatment programs (DeMaris, 1989). At least three reviews have been published in recent years that examined different types of interventions among perpetrators of IPV. Klostermann et al. (2010) reviewed four types of treatments available for IPV among individuals with SUD: (a) standard substance abuse treatment, (b) referral to domestic violence intervention programs, (c) partner-involved conjoint therapy, and (d) Behavioral Couples Therapy for treatment of substance abuse. Behavioral Couples Therapy seemed to show most effectiveness among individuals with SUD (Klostermann, Kelley, Mignone, Pusateri, & Fals-Stewart). Another review found a moderate reduction of violence among those who received Behavioral Couples Therapy than individual substance abuse treatment (Murphy & Ting, 2010). Stover and colleagues (2009) also reviewed randomized controlled trials with over twenty participants per randomized group and suggested that combined treatment of IPV with substance abuse appeared to be promising approach for IPV perpetrators with substance abuse problems (Stover, Meadows, & Kaufman, 2009). These studies suggest the importance of integrating violence prevention in the context of substance abuse treatment (Fals-Stewart & Kennedy, 2005). Similarly, Stuart (2005) highlighted the importance of integrating alcohol abuse treatment in batterer intervention programs to reduce violence recidivism (Stuart, 2005). A randomized trial found that fluoxetine, in combination with CBT and alcohol treatment, reduced anger and irritability among sixty participants who were seeking treatment for alcohol dependence, but the study also encountered high dropout rates (George et al., 2011). A review focusing on prison setting noted mixed evidence on the association between OMT and reduction in criminal activity and reincarceration, although there were strong evidence on OMT and reduction in heroin use and injection risk behaviors (Hedrich, Alves, Farrell, Stöver, Møller, & Mayet, 2012).

Interventions among individuals with a past history of violence have been shown effective in reducing youth violence (Limbos et al., 2007). One of these programs is multisystemic therapy (MST), which is a community and family–based treatment intervention (Randall & Cunningham, 2003). The MST program has been conducted among juvenile offenders and has been shown effective in reducing aggressive crime in this population (Randall & Cunningham, 2003). This program also reduced aggressive crimes but not property crimes among juvenile offenders with DSM-III-R criteria for SUD in the fourth-year follow-up (Hennggeler, Clingempeel, Brondino, & Pickrel, 2002). Mental health and substance abuse treatment programs (Cuellar, Markowitz, & Libby, 2004) have also shown effective in reducing youth violence among juveniles.

Section Summary

Prevention efforts for suicidal behavior and interpersonal violence are being conducted across different levels of interventions, especially using universal approaches. Targeting risk factors for SUD and treatment of SUD are increasingly recognized as important aspects in the prevention of intentional injuries, for both suicidal behavior and interpersonal violence. However, it is clear that more prevention efforts are necessary across these settings, as well as evaluation of these efforts to better identify effective programs.

Conclusion and Future Directions

The epidemiological evidence suggests a strong relationship between SUD and intentional injuries, particularly with respect to suicidal behavior and IPV. Research on risk factors for suicidal behavior among individuals with AUD is relatively abundant compared with other areas examined in this chapter. However, empirical testing of causal relationships is limited in all areas, with many studies conducted cross-sectionally. With respect to AUD and suicide, more evidence supports a distal role of AUD in its relationship with suicidal behavior. Most literature on violence appears to focus on the direct relationship between the use of drugs and violent behavior; less effort has been placed on the role of SUD in violence perpetration. Currently prevention efforts on violence and suicide are conducted independently of each other. Given the number of common risk factors associated with suicide and violence, especially among youth, future prevention efforts may benefit from concerted efforts to target shared risk factors for both suicide and violence (Lubell & Vetter, 2006; Swahn et al., 2008). Based on the literature review conducted in this chapter, we make the following five recommendations for future research:

1. Examine social/contextual risk and protective factors for intentional injuries among substance abusers, especially among individuals with DUD;

2. Better characterization of individuals with SUD who are at risk of perpetrating violence;

3. Conduct longitudinal studies to test conceptual frameworks and causal relationships;

4. Identify mediating and potentially modifiable factors in the relationships between intentional injuries and SUD;

5. Further development and evaluation of prevention efforts for intentional injury alongside the dissemination of those shown to be effective in prior studies.

References

Aharonovich, E., Liu, X., Nunes, E., & Hasin, D. S. (2002). Suicide attempts in substance abusers: Effects of major depression in relation to substance use disorders. *American Journal of Psychiatry*, 159(9), 1600–1602.

American Psychiatric Association (APA). (1994). *Diagnostic and Statistical Manual of Mental Disorders [DSM-IV]* (4th ed.). Washington, DC: American Psychiatric Association.

Andersen, U. A., Andersen, M., Rosholm, J. U., & Gram, L. F. (2000). Contacts to the health care system prior to suicide: a comprehensive analysis using registers for general and psychiatric hospital admissions, contacts to general practitioners and practising specialists and drug prescriptions. *Acta Psychiatrica Scandinavica*, 102(2),126–134.

Anestis, M. D., Gratz, K. L., Bagge, C. L., & Tull, M. T. (2012). The interactive role of distress tolerance and borderline personality disorder in suicide attempts among substance users in residential treatment. *Comprehensive Psychiatry*, 53(8),1208–1216.

Arseneault, L., Moffitt, T. E., Caspi, A., Taylor, P., & Silva, P. A. (2000). Mental disorders and violence in a total birth cohort: Results from the Dunedin study. *Archives of General Psychiatry*, 57(10), 979–986.

Baumeister, R. F. (1990). Suicide as escape from self. *Psychological review*, 97(1), 90–113.

Beautrais, A. L. (2000). Risk factors for suicide and attempted suicide among young people. *The Australian and New Zealand Journal of Psychiatry*, 34(3), 420–436.

Beautrais, A. L., Joyce, P. R., & Mulder, R. T. (1999). Cannabis abuse and serious suicide attempts. *Addiction*, 94(8), 1155–1164.

Beck, A. T., Brown, G., Berchick, R. J., Stewart, B. L., & Steer, R. A. (2006). Relationship between hopelessness and ultimate suicide: A replication with psychiatric outpatients. *Focus*, 4(2), 291–296.

Benda, B. B. (2003). Discriminators of suicide thoughts and attempts among homeless veteran who abuse substances. *Suicide and Life-Threatening Behavior*, 33(4), 430–442.

Blow, F. C., Brockmann, L. M., & Barry, K. L. (2004). Role of alcohol in late-life suicide. *Alcoholism, Clinical and Experimental Research*, 28(5), 48S–56S.

Bohnert, A. S., Roeder, K., & Ilgen, M. A. (2010). Unintentional overdose and suicide among substance users: a review of overlap and risk factors. *Drug and Alcohol Dependence*, 110(3), 183–192

Boles, S. M., & Miotto, K. (2003). Substance abuse and violence: A review of the literature. *Aggression and Violent Behavior*, 8(2), 155–174.

Borges, G., Angst, J., Nock, M. K., Ruscio, A. M., & Kessler, R. C. (2008). Risk factors for the incidence and persistence of suicide-related outcomes: A 10-year follow-up study using the National Comorbidity Surveys. *Journal of Affective Disorders*, 105(1–3), 25–33.

Borges, G., Walters, E. E., & Kessler, R. C. (2000). Associations of substance use, abuse, and dependence with subsequent suicidal behavior. *American Journal of Epidemiology*, 151(8), 781–789.

Brackley, M. H., Williams, G. B., & Wei, C. C. (2010). Substance abuse interface with intimate partner violence: what treatment programs need to know. *Nursing Clinics of North America*, 45(4),581-589.

Brady, J. (2006). The association between alcohol misuse and suicidal behaviour. *Alcohol Alcohol.*, 41(5), 473–478.

Brent, D. A., & Mann, J. J. (2005). Family genetic studies, suicide, and suicidal behavior. *American Journal of Medical Genetics*, 133(C), 13–24.

Bridge, J. A., Goldstein, T. R., & Brent, D. A. (2006). Adolescent suicide and suicidal behavior. *Journal of Child Psychology & Psychiatry.* 47(3-4), 372-94

Britton, P. C., & Conner, K. R. (2010). Suicide attempts within 12 months of treatment for substance use disorders. *Suicide and Life-Threatening Behavior*, 40(1), 14–21.

Bukten, A., Skurtveit, S., Stangeland, P., Gossop, M., Willersrud, A.B., Waal, H., Havnes, I., Clausen, T. (2011). Criminal convictions among dependent heroin users during a 3-year period prior to opioid maintenance treatment: a longitudinal national cohort study. *Journal of Substance Abuse Treatment*, 41(4), 407–414.

Burnette, M. L., Ilgen, M., Frayne, S. M., Lucas, E., Mayo, J., & Weitlauf, J. C. (2008). Violence perpetration and childhood abuse among men and women in substance abuse treatment. *Journal of Substance Abuse Treatment*, 35(2), 217–222.

Caetano, R., Schafer, J., & Cunradi, C. B. (2001). Alcohol-related intimate partner violence among white, black, and hispanic couples in the United States. *Alcohol Research & Health*, 25(1), 58–65.

Calabria, B., Degenhardt, L., Hall, W., & Lynskey, M. (2010). Does cannabis use increase the risk of death? Systematic review of epidemiological evidence on adverse effects of cannabis use. *Drug and Alcohol Review*, 29(3), 318–330.

Canetto, S. S., & Sakinofsky, I. (1998). The gender paradox in suicide. *Suicide and Life-Threatening Behavior*, 28(1), 1–23.

Center for Substance Abuse Treatment. (2008). *Substance Abuse and Suicide Prevention: Evidence and Implications—A White Paper* (DHHS Pub No. SMA-08-4352). Rockville, MD.

Center for Substance Abuse Treatment. (2009). *Addressing Suicidal Thoughts and Behaviors in Substance Abuse Treatment* (HHS Publication No. (SMA) 09-4381). Rockville, MD: Substance Abuse and Mental Health Services Administration, Office of Applied Studies.

Centers for Disease Control and Prevention. (2013). The National Intimate Partner and Sexual Violence Survey (NISVS). Retrieved from http://www.cdc.gov/ViolencePrevention/NISVS/index.html

Centers for Disease Control and Prevention. (2013). Web-based Injury Statistics Query and Reporting System (WISQARS): Leading Causes of Death Report. Retrieved from http://webappa.cdc.gov/sasweb/ncipc/leadcaus10_us.html

Centers for Disease Control and Prevention. (2009). Web-based Injury Statistics Query and Reporting System (WISQARS): Nonfatal injuries report. Retrieved from http://webappa.cdc.gov/sasweb/ncipc/nfirates.html

Centers for Disease Control and Prevention. (2011). Web-based Injury Statistics Query and Reporting System (WISQARS): Nonfatal injuries report. Retrieved from http://webappa.cdc.gov/sasweb/ncipc/nfirates2001.html

Centers for Disease Control and Prevention. (2012). Youth risk behavior surveillance—United States, 2011. *MMWR, Surveillance Summaries, 61*(no. SS-4). Retrieved from www.cdc.gov/mmwr/pdf/ss/ss6104.pdf

Chermack, S. T., & Blow, F. C. (2002). Violence among individuals in substance abuse treatment: The role of alcohol and cocaine consumption. *Drug and Alcohol Dependence, 66*(1), 29–37.

Chermack, S. T., Fuller, B. E., & Blow, F. C. (2000). Predictors of expressed partner and non-partner violence among patients in substance abuse treatment. *Drug and alcohol dependence, 58*(1–2), 43–54.

Chermack, S. T., Murray, R. L., Walton, M. A., Booth, B. A., Wryobeck, J., & Blow, F. C. (2008). Partner aggression among men and women in substance use disorder treatment: Correlates of psychological and physical aggression and injury. *Drug and Alcohol Dependence, 98*(1–2), 35–44.

Chermack, S. T., Stoltenberg, S. F., Fuller, B. E., & Blow, F. C. (2000). Gender differences in the development of substance-related problems: The impact of family history of alcoholism, family history of violence and childhood conduct problems. *Journal of Studies on Alcohol, 61*(6), 845–852.

Chermack, S. T., Bohnert, A. S., Price, A. M., Austin, K., & Ilgen, M. A. (2012). Substance use disorders and homicide death in veterans. *Journal of Studies on Alcohol and Drugs, 73*(1), 10–14.

Cherpitel, C. J., Borges, G. L., & Wilcox, H. C. (2004). Acute alcohol use and suicidal behavior: A review of the literature. *Alcoholism, Clinical and Experimental Research, 28*(5 Suppl), 18S-28S.

Chioqueta, A. P., & Stiles, T. C. (2007). The relationship between psychological buffers, hopelessness, and suicidal ideation: Identification of protective factors. *Crisis, 28*(2), 67–73.

Coker, A. L., Smith, P. H., McKeown, R. E., & King, M. J. (2000). Frequency and correlates of intimate partner violence by type: Physical, sexual, and psychological battering. *American Journal of Public Health, 90*(4), 553–559.

Collins, J. J., & Messerschmidt, P. M. (1993). Epidemiology of alcohol-related violence. *Alcohol Health & Research World, 17*(2), 93–93.

Comtois, K. A., Russo, J. E., Roy-Byrne, P., & Ries, R. K. (2004). Clinicians' assessments of bipolar disorder and substance abuse as predictors of suicidal behavior in acutely hospitalized psychiatric inpatients. *Biological Psychiatry, 56*(10), 757–763.

Conner, K. R., Beautrais, A., & Conwell, Y. (2003a). Moderators of the relationship between alcohol dependence and suicide and medically serious suicide atttempts: Analyses of Canterbury Suicide Project Data. *Alcoholism, Clinical and Experimental Research, 27*(7), 1156–1161.

Conner, K. R., Beautrais, A., & Conwell, Y. (2003b). Risk factors for suicide and medically serious suicide attempt among alcoholics: Analyses of Canterbury suicide project data. *Journal of Studies on Alcohol, 64*(4), 551–554.

Conner, K. R., Britton, P. C., Sworts, L. M., & Joiner, J. T. E. (2007). Suicide attempts among individuals with opiate dependence: The critical role of belonging. *Addictive Behaviors, 32*(7), 1395–1404.

Conner, K. R., & Duberstein, P. (2004). Predisposing and precipitating factors for suicide among alcoholics: Empirical review and conceptual integration. *Alcoholism, Clinical and Experimental Research, 28*(5), 6S-17S.

Conner, K. R., Duberstein, P. R., & Conwell, Y. (1999). Age-related patterns of factors associated with completed suicide in men with alcohol dependence. *American Journal on Addictions, 8*(4), 312–318.

Conner, K. R., Duberstein, P. R., Conwell, Y., Seidlitz, L., & Caine, E. D. (2001). Psychological vulnerability to completed suicide: A review of empirical studies. *Suicide and Life-Threatening Behavior, 31*(4), 367–385.

Conner, K. R., Hesselbrock, V. M., Meldrum, S. C., Schuckit, M. A., Bucholz, K. K., Gamble, S. A., et al. (2007). Transitions to, and correlates of, suicidal ideation, plans, and unplanned and planned suicide attempts among 3,729 men and women with alcohol dependence. *Journal of Studies on Alcohol and Drugs, 68*(5), 654–662.

Cornelius, J. R., Clark, D. C., Salloum, I. M., Bukstein, O. G., & Kelly, T. M. (2004). Interventions in suicidal alcoholics. *Alcoholism, Clinical and Experimental Research, 28*(5), 89S–96S.

Corrigan, P. W., & Watson, A. C. (2005). Findings from the National Comorbidity Survey on the frequency of violent behavior in individuals with psychiatric disorders. *Psychiatric Research, 136*(2–3), 153–162.

Crosby, A. E., Han, B., Ortega, L. A. G., Parks, S. E., & Gfoerer, J. (2011). Suicidal thoughts and behaviors among adults aged ≥18 years–United States, 2008–2009. *MMWR Surveillance Summaries, 60*(no. SS-13). Retrieved from www.cdc.gov/mmwr/preview/mmwrhtml/ss6013a1.htm?s_cid=ss6013a1_e.

Crosby, A. E., Ortega, L., & Melanson, C. (2011). Self-directed violence surveillance: Uniform definitions and recommended data element, version 1.09. Atlanta, GA: Centers for Disease Control and Prevention, National Center for Injury Prevention and Control.

Cuellar, A. E., Markowitz, S., & Libby, A. M. (2004). Mental health and substance abuse treatment and juvenile crime. *Journal of Mental Health Policy and Economics, 7*(2), 59–68.

Cunradi, C. B. (2009). Substance abuse in intimate partner violence. In C. Mitchell & D. Anglin (Eds.), *Intimate partner violence: A health-based perspective* (pp. 173–182). New York, NY: Oxford University Press.

Dahlberg, L. L. (1998). Youth violence in the United States: Major trends, risk factors, and prevention approaches. *American Journal of Preventive Medicine, 14*(4), 259–272.

Dalton, E. J., Cate-Carter, T. D., Mundo, E., Parikh, S. V., & Kennedy, J. L. (2003). Suicide risk in bipolar patients: The role of co-morbid substance use disorders. *Bipolar Disorders, 5*(1), 58–61.

Darke, S., & Ross, J. (1997). Polydrug dependence and psychiatric comorbidity among heroin injectors. *Drug and Alcohol Dependence, 48*(2), 135–141.

Darke, S., & Ross, J. (2002). Suicide among heroin users: Rates, risk factors and methods. *Addiction*, *97*(11), 1383–1394.

Darke, S., Ross, J., Williamson, A., Mills, K. L., Havard, A., & Teesson, M. (2007). Patterns and correlates of attempted suicide by heroin users over a 3-year period: Findings from the Australian treatment outcome study. *Drug and Alcohol Dependence*, *87*(2–3), 146–152.

Darke, S., Williamson, A., Ross, J., & Teesson, M. (2005). Attempted suicide among heroin users: 12-month outcomes from the Australian Treatment Outcome Study (ATOS). *Drug and Alcohol Dependence*, *78*(2), 177–186.

Darke, S., Williamson, A., Ross, J., Teesson, M., & Lynskey, M. (2004). Borderline personality disorder, antisocial personality disorder and risk-taking among heroin users: Findings from the Australian Treatment Outcome Study (ATOS). *Drug and Alcohol Dependence*, *74*(1), 77–83.

DeMaris, A. (1989). Attrition in batterer's counseling: The role of social and demographic factors. *The Social Service Review*, *63*(1), 142–154.

Dolan, L. J., Kellam, S. G., Brown, C. H., Werthamer-Larsson, L., Rebok, G. W., Mayer, L. S., et al. (1993). The short-term impact of two classroom-based preventive interventions on aggressive and shy behaviors and poor achievement. *Journal of Applied Developmental Psychology*, *14*(3), 317–345.

Dougherty, D. M., Mathias, C. W., Marsh, D. M., Moeller, F. G., & Swann, A. C. (2004). Suicidal behaviors and drug abuse: Impulsivity and its assessment. *Drug and Alcohol Dependence*, *76*(Suppl. 1), S93–S105.

Elbogen, E. B., & Johnson, S. C. (2009). The intricate link between violence and mental disorder: Results from the National Epidemiologic Survey on Alcohol and Related Conditions. *Archives of General Psychiatry*, *66*(2), 152–161.

Erinoff, L., Anthony, J. C., Brown, G. K., Caine, E. D., Conner, K. R., Dougherty, D. M., et al. (2004). Overview of workshop on drug abuse and suicidal behavior. *Drug Abuse and Suicidal Behavior*, *76*(Suppl. 1), S3–S9.

Eronen, M., Hakola, P., & Tiihonen, J. (1996). Mental disorders and homicidal behavior in Finland. *Archives of General Psychiatry*, *53*(6), 497–501.

Esposito-Smythers, C., & Spirito, A. (2004). Adolescent substance use and suicidal behavior: A review with implications for treatment research. *Alcoholism, Clinical and Experimental Research*, *28*(5), 77S–88S.

Fals-Stewart, W., Golden, J., & Schumacher, J. A. (2003). Intimate partner violence and substance use: A longitudinal day-to-day examination. *Addictive Behaviors*, *28*(9), 1555–1574.

Fals-Stewart, W., & Kennedy, C. (2005). Addressing intimate partner violence in substance-abuse treatment. *Journal of Substance Abuse Treatment* *29*(1), 5–17.

Feingold, A., Kerr, D. C. R., & Capaldi, D. M. (2008). Associations of substance use problems with intimate partner violence for at-risk men in long-term relationships. *Journal of Family Psychology*, *22*(3), 429–438.

Fishbein, D. (2000). Neuropsychological function, drug abuse, and violence: A conceptual framework. *Criminal Justice and Behavior*, *27*(2), 139–159.

Foran, H. M., & O'Leary, K. D. (2008). Alcohol and intimate partner violence: A meta-analytic review. *Clinical Psychology Review*, *28*(7), 1222–1234.

George, D. T., Phillips, M. J., Lifshitz, M., Lionetti, T. A., Spero, D. E., Ghassemzadeh, N., et al. (2011). Fluoxetine treatment of alcoholic perpetrators of domestic violence: A 12-week, double-blind, randomized, placebo-controlled intervention study. *Journal of Clinical Psychiatry*, *72*(1), 60-65.

Goldstein, P. J. (1985). Drugs/violence nexus: A tripartite conceptual framework. *Journal of Drug Issues*, *39*, 143-174.

Goldston, D. B. (2004). Conceptual issues in understanding the relationship between suicidal behavior and substance use during adolescence. *Drug and Alcohol Dependence*, *76*(S1), S79-S91.

Gordon, R. (1987). An operational classification of disease prevention. In J. A. a. S. Steinberg, M. M. (Ed.), *Preventing mental disorders*. Rockville, MD: U.S. Department of Health and Human Services.

Gorwood, P., Batel, P., Ades, J., Hamon, M., & Boni, C. (2000). Serotonin transporter gene polymorphisms, alcoholism, and suicidal behavior. *Biological Psychiatry*, *48*(4), 259–264.

Gustavson, C., Ståhlberg, O., Sjödin, A., Forsman, A., Nilsson, T., & Anckarsäter, H. (2007). Age at onset of substance abuse: A crucial covariate of psychopathic traits and aggression in adult offenders. *Psychiatry Research*, *153*(4), 195–198.

Hamberger, L. K. (2009). Risk factors for intimate partner violence perpetration: Typologies and characteristics of batterers. In C. Mitchell & D. Anglin (Eds.), *Intimate partner violence: A health-based perspective* (pp. 115–132). New York, NY: Oxford University Press.

Harris, E. C., & Barraclough, B. (1997). Suicide as an outcome for mental disorders. A meta-analysis. *British Journal of Psychiatry*, *170*, 205–228.

Havnes, I., Bukten, A., Gossop, M., Waal, H., Stangeland, P., & Clausen, T. (2012). Reductions in convictions for violent crime during opioid maintenance treatment: A longitudinal national cohort study. *Drug and Alcohol Dependence*, *124*(3), 307–10.

Haw, C., & Hawton, K. (2008). Life problems and deliberate self-harm: Associations with gender, age, suicidal intent and psychiatric and personality disorder. *Journal of Affective Disorders*, *109*(1–2), 139–148.

Hawton, K., Simkin, S., Deeks, J., Cooper, J., Johnston, A., Waters, K., et al. (2004). UK legislation on analgesic packs: Before and after study of long term effect on poisonings. *BMJ*, *329*(7474), 1076–1080.

Heale, P., Dietze, P., & Fry, C. (2003). Intentional overdose among heroin overdose survivors. *Journal of Urban Health*, *80*(2), 230–237.

Hedrich, D., Alves, P., Farrell, M., Stöver, H., Møller, L., & Mayet S. (2012). The effectiveness of opioid maintenance treatment in prison settings: A systematic review. *Addiction*, *107*(3), 501–17.

Henggeler, S. W., Clingempeel, W. G., Brondino, M. J., & Pickrel, S. G. (2002). Four-year follow-up of multisystemic therapy with substance-abusing and substance-dependent juvenile offenders. *Journal of the American Academy of Child & Adolescent Psychiatry*, *41*(7), 868–874.

Hesselbrock, M. N., Hesselbrock, V., Syzmanski, K., & Weidmann, M. (1988). Suicide attempt and alcoholism. *Journal of Studies on Alcohol*, *49*(5), 436–442.

Hoaken, P. N. S., & Stewart, S. H. (2003). Drugs of abuse and the elicitation of human aggressive behavior. *Addictive Behaviors*, *28*(9), 1533–1554.

Hoaken, P. N. S., Hamill, V. L., Ross, E. H., Hancock, M., Lau, M. J., & Tapscott, J. L. (2012). Drug use & abuse and human aggressive behaviour. In J. Verster, K. Brady, E. Strain, M. Galanter, & P. Conrod (Eds.), *Drug abuse and* addiction in medical illness: Causes, consequences, and treatment (pp. 467–477). New York, NY: Springer.

Holtzworth-Munroe, A., & Stuart, G. L. (1994). Typologies of male batterers: Three subtypes and the differences among them. *Psychological Bulletin, 116*(3), 476–497.

Houston, K., Hawton, K., & Shepperd, R. (2001). Suicide in young people aged 15–24: A psychological autopsy study. *Journal of Affective Disorder, 63*(1-3), 159–170.

Hubbard, R. L., Craddock, S. G., & Anderson, J. (2003). Overview of 5-year followup outcomes in the Drug Abuse Treatment Outcome Studies (DATOS). *Journal of Substance Abuse Treatment, 25*(3), 125–134.

Hufford, M. R. (2001). Alcohol and suicidal behavior. *Clinical Psychology Review, 21*(5), 797–811.

Ilgen, M. A., Harris, A. H. S., Moos, R. H., & Tiet, Q. Q. (2007a). Predictors of a suicide attempt one year after entry into substance use disorder treatment. *Alcoholism, Clinical and Experimental Research, 31*(4), 635–642.

Ilgen, M. A., Jain, A., Lucas, E., & Moos, R. H. (2007b). Substance use-disorder treatment and a decline in attempted suicide during and after treatment. *Journal of Studies on Alcohol and Drugs, 68*(4), 503–509.

Ilgen, M. A., Burnette, M. L., Conner, K. R., Czyz, E., Murray, R., & Chermack, S. (2010b). The association between violence and lifetime suicidal thoughts and behaviors in individuals treated for substance use disorders. *Addictive Behaviors, 35*(2),111–115.

Ilgen, M. A., Conner, K. R., Valenstein, M., Austin, K., & Blow, F. C. (2010a). Violent and nonviolent suicide in veterans with substance-use disorders. *Journal of Studies on Alcohol and Drugs, 71*(4), 473–479.

Ilgen, M. A., Conner, K. R., Roeder, K. M., Blow, F. C., Austin, K., & Valenstein, M. (2012). Patterns of treatment utilization before suicide among male veterans with substance use disorders. *American Journal of Public Health, 102*(Suppl. 1), S88–S92.

Illomaki, E., Rasanen, P., Viilo, K., & Hakko, H. (2006). Suicidal behavior among adolescents with conduct disorder—The role of alcohol dependence. *Psychiatry Research, 150*(3), 305–311.

Inskip, H. M., Harris, E. C., & Barraclough, B. (1998). Lifetime risk of suicide for affective disorder, alcoholism and schizophrenia. *British of Journal Psychiatry, 172*, 35–37.

Institute of Medicine (IOM). (2002). *Reducing suicide: A national imperative. Committee on Pathophysiology and prevention of adolescent and adult suicide,*. Washington, DC: Board of Neuroscience and Behavioral Health.

Jewkes, R. (2002). Intimate partner violence: causes and prevention. *Lancet, 359*(9315), 1423–1429.

Joe, S., Baser, R. E., Breeden, G., Neighbors, H. W., & Jackson, J. S. (2006). Prevalence of and risk factors for lifetime suicide attempts among blacks in the United States. *JAMA: The Journal of the American Medical Association, 296*(17), 2112–2123.

Johnsson, E., & Fridell, M. (1997). Suicide attempts in a cohort of drug abusers: A 5-year follow-up study. *Acta Psychiatrica Scandinavica, 96*(5), 362–366.

Karch, D. L., Barker, L., & Strine, T. W. (2006). Race/ethnicity, substance abuse, and mental illness among suicide victims in 13 US states: 2004 Data from the National Violent Death Reporting System. *Injury Prevention, 12*(Suppl. 2), ii22–ii27.

Kaslow, N. J., Jacobs, C. H., Young, S. L., & Cook, S. (2006). Suicidal behavior among low-income African American women: A comparison of first-time and repeat suicide attempters. *Journal of Black Psychology, 32*(3), 349–365.

Kaslow, N. J., Sherry, A., Bethea, K., Wyckoff, S., Compton, M. T., Grall, M. B., et al. (2005). Social risk and protective factors for suicide attempts in low income African American men and women. *Suicide and Life-Threatening Behavior, 35*(4), 400–412.

Kellam, S. G., Brown, C. H., Poduska, J. M., Ialongo, N. S., Wang, W., Toyinbo, P., et al. (2008). Effects of a universal classroom behavior management program in first and second grades on young adult behavioral, psychiatric, and social outcomes. *Drug and Alcohol Dependence, 95*(Suppl. 1), S5–S28.

Kelly, T. M., Cornelius, J. R., & Clark, D. B. (2004). Psychiatric disorders and attempted suicide among adolescents with substance use disorders. *Drug and Alcohol Dependence, 73*(1), 87–97.

Kessler, R. C., Borges, G., & Walters, E. E. (1999). Prevalence of and risk factors for lifetime suicide attempts in the National Comorbidity Survey. *Archives of General Psychiatry, 56*(7), 617–626.

Khantzian, E. J. (1997). The self-medication hypothesis of substance use disorders: A reconsideration and recent applications. *Harvard Review of Psychiatry, 4*(5), 231–244.

Kjelsberg, E., Winther, M., & Dahl, A. A. (1995). Overdose deaths in young substance abusers: Accidents or hidden suicides? *Acta Psychiatrica Scandinavica, 91*(4), 236–242.

Klostermann, K. C., Kelley, M. L., Mignone, T., Pusateri, L., & Fals-Stewart, W. (2010). Partner violence and substance abuse: Treatment interventions. *Aggression and Violent Behavior, 15*(3), 162–166.

Knox, K. L., Conwell, Y., & Caine, E. D. (2004). If suicide is a public health problem, what are we doing to prevent it? *American Journal of Public Health, 94*(1),37-45.

Koller, G., Preuss, U. W., Bottlender, M., Wenzel, K., & Soyka, M. (2002). Impulsivity and aggression as predictors of suicide attempts in alcoholics. *European Archives of Psychiatry and Clinical Neuroscience, 252*(4), 155–160.

Kraanen. F. L., Scholing, A., & Emmelkamp, P. M. G. (2009). Substance use disorders in perpetrators of intimate partner violence in a forensic setting. *International Journal of Offender Therapy and Comparative Criminology. 54*(3):430-40.

Krug, E. G., Dahlberg, L. L., Mercy, J. A., Zwi, A. B., & Lozano, R. (2002). *World report on violence and health.* Geneva, Switzerland: World Health Organization.

Kuhns, J. B., & Clodfelter, T. A. (2009). Illicit drug-related psychopharmacological violence: The current understanding within a causal context. *Aggression and Violent Behavior, 14*(1), 69–78.

Landheim, A. S., Bakken, K., & Vaglum, P. (2006). What characterizes substance abusers who commit suicide attempts? Factors related to Axis I disorders and patterns of substance use disorders. *European Addiction Research, 12*(2), 102–108.

Leri, F., Bruneau, J., & Stewart, J. (2003). Understanding polydrug use: Review of heroin and cocaine co-use. *Addiction, 98*, 7.

Levin, F. R., & Hennessy, G. (2004). Bipolar disorder and substance abuse. *Biological Psychiatry, 56*(10), 738–748.

Limbos, M. A., Chan, L. S., Warf, C., Schneir, A., Iverson, E., Shekelle, P., et al. (2007). Effectiveness of interventions to prevent youth violence: A systematic review. *American Journal of Preventive Medicine, 33*(1), 65–74.

Limosin, F. d. r., Loze, J.-Y., Philippe, A., Casadebaig, F. o., & Rouillon, F. d. r. (2007). Ten-year prospective follow-up study of the mortality by suicide in schizophrenic patients. *Schizophrenia Research, 94*(1–3), 23–28.

Linehan, M. M., Goodstein, J. L., Nielsen, S. L., & Chiles, J. A. (1983). Reasons for staying alive whne you are thinking of killing yourself: The reasons for living inventory. *Journal of Consulting and Clinical Psychology, 51*(2), 276–286.

Loebel, J. P. (2005). Practical geriatrics: Completed suicide in late life. *Psychiatric Services, 56*(3), 260–262.

Lubell, K. M., & Vetter, J. B. (2006). Suicide and youth violence prevention: The promise of an integrated approach. *Violence Prevention: Expanding the Applied Science, 11*(2), 167–175.

Lynskey, M. T., Glowinski, A. L., Todorov, A. A., Bucholz, K. K., Madden, P. A. F., Nelson, E. C., et al. (2004). Major depressive disorder, suicidal ideation, and suicide attempt in twins discordant for cannabis dependence and early-onset cannabis use. *Archives of General Psychiatry, 61*(10), 1026–1032.

MacDonald, R., Taylor, J., & Clarke, D. (2009). The relationship between early suicide behaviors and mental health: Results from a nine-year panel study. *Journal of Adolescence, 32*(5), 1159–1172.

Macdonald, S., Erickson, P., Wells, S., Hathaway, A., & Pakula, B. (2008). Predicting violence among cocaine, cannabis, and alcohol treatment clients. *Addictive Behaviors, 33*(1), 201–205.

Mack, A. H., & Lightdale, H. A. (2006). Substance-related disorders. In R. I. Simon & R. E. Hales (Eds.), *Textbook of suicide assessment and management* (pp. 347–366): Washington DC, American Psychiatric Publishing.

Madgol, L., Moffitt, T. E., Caspi, A., Newman, D. L., Fagan, J., & Silva, P. A. (1997). Gender differences in partner violence in a birth cohort of 21-year-olds: Bridging the gap between clinical and epidemiological approaches. *Jouranl of Consulting and Clinical Psychology, 65*(1), 68–78.

Makhija, N., & Sher, L. (2007). Childhood abuse, adult alcohol use disorders and suicidal behaviour. *QJM, 100*(5), 305–309.

Malone, K. M., Oquendo, M. A., Haas, G. L., Ellis, S. P., Li, S., & Mann, J. J. (2000). Protective factors against suicidal acts in major depression: Reasons for living. *American Journal of Psychiatry, 157*(7), 1084–1088.

Maloney, E., Degenhardt, L., Darke, S., Mattick, R. P., & Nelson, E. C. (2007). Suicidal behaviour and associated risk factors among opioid-dependent individuals: A case-control study. *Addiction, 102*(12), 1933–1941.

Maloney, E., Degenhardt, L., Darke, S., & Nelson, E. C. (2009). Implusivity and borderline personality as risk factors for suicide attempts among opioid-dependent individuals. *Psychiatry Research, 169* (1), 16–21.

Mangnall, J., & Yurkovich, E. (2008). A literature review of deliberate self-harm. *Perspectives in Psychiatric Care, 44*(3), 175–184.

Maniglio, R. (2009). Severe mental illness and criminal victimization: A systematic review. *Acta Psychiatrica Scandinavica, 119*(3), 180–191.

Mann, J. J. (2003). Neurobiology of suicidal behaviour. *Nature Reviews Neuroscience, 4*(10), 819–828.

Mann, J. J., Apter, A., Bertolote, J., Beautrais, A., Currier, D., Haas, A., et al. (2005). Suicide prevention strategies: A systematic review. *JAMA: The Journal of the American Medical Association, 294*(16), 2064–2074.

Mann, J. J., Arango, V. A., Avenevoli, S., Brent, D. A., Champagne, F. A., Clayton, P., et al. (2009). Candidate endophenotypes for genetic studies of suicidal behavior. *Biological Psychiatry, 65*(7), 556–563.

Mann, J. J., Waternaux, C., Haas, G. L., & Malone, K. M. (1999). Toward a clinical model of suicidal behavior in psychiatric patients. *The American Journal of Psychiatry, 156*(2), 181–189.

Mann, R. E., Zalcman, R. F., Rush, B. R., Smart, R. G., & Rhodes, A. E. (2008). Alcohol factors in suicide mortality rates in Manitoba. *The Canadian Journal of Psychiatry, 53*(4), 243–251.

Mezzich, A. C., Giancola, P. R., Tarter, R. E., Lu, S., Parks, S. M., & Barrett, C. M. (1997). Violence, suicidality, and alcohol/drug use involvement in adolescent females with a psychoactive substance use disorder and controls. *Alcoholism: Clinical and Experimental Research, 21*(7), 1300–1307.

Moore, T. M., & Stuart, G. L. (2005). A review of the literature on marijuana and interpersonal violence. *Aggression and Violent Behavior, 10*(2), 171–192.

Moore, T. M., Stuart, G. L., Meehan, J. C., Rhatigan, D. L., Hellmuth, J. C., & Keen, S. M. (2008). Drug abuse and aggression between intimate partners: A meta-analytic review. *Clinical Psychology Review, 28*(2), 247–274.

Moscicki, E. K. (2001). Epidemiology of completed and attempted suicide: Toward a framework for prevention. *Clinical Neuroscience Research, 1*(5), 310–323.

Murphy, C. M., O'Farrell, T. J., Fals-Stewart, W., & Feehan, M. (2001). Correlates of intimate partner violence among male alcoholic patients. *Journal of Consulting and Clinical Psychology, 69*(3), 528–540.

Murphy, C. M., & Ting, L. A. (2010). The effects of treatment for substance use problems on intimate partner violence: A review of empirical data. *Aggression and Violent Behavior, 15*(5), 325–333.

Murphy, G. E., Wetzel, R. D., Robins, E., & McEvoy, L. (1992). Multiple risk factors predict suicide in alcoholism. *Archives of General Psychiatry, 49*(6), 459–463.

Neale, J. (2000). Suicidal intent in non-fatal illicit drug overdose. *Addiction, 95*(1), 85-93.

Nicolaidis, C., & Paranjape, A. (2009). Defining intimate partner violence: Controversies and implications. In C. Mitchell & D. Anglin (Eds.), *Intimate partner violence: A health-based perspective* (pp. 19–20). New York, NY: Oxford University Press.

Nock, M. K., Borges, G., Bromet, E. J., Alonso, J., Angermeyer, M., Beautrais, A., et al. (2008). Cross-national prevalence and risk factors for suicidal ideation, plans and attempts. *The British Journal of Psychiatry, 192*(2), 98–105.

Nock, M. K., & Kessler, R. C. (2006). Prevalence and risk factors for suicide attempts versus suicide gestures: Analysis of the National Comorbidity Survey. *Journal of Abnormal Psychology, 115*(3), 616–623.

O'Farrell, T.J., Fals-Stewart, W., Murphy, M., & Murphy, C.M. (2003). Partner violence before and after individually based alcoholism treatment for male alcoholic patients. *Journal of Consulting and Clinical Psychology, 71*(1), 92–102.

O'Farrell, T. J., Hutton, V. V., & Murphy, C. M. (1999). Domestic violence before and after alcoholism treatment: A two-year longitudinal study. *Journal of Studies on Alcohol, 60*(3), 317–321.

Parker, R. N., & Auerhahn, K. (1998). Alcohol, drugs, and violence. *Annual Review of Sociology, 24*(1), 291–311.

Pinto, L. A., Sullivan, E. L., Rosenbaum, A., Wyngarden, N., Umhau, J. C., Miller, M. W., et al. (2010). Biological correlates of intimate partner violence perpetration. *Aggression and Violent Behavior, 15*(5), 387–398.

Pirkola, S. P., Isometsa, E. T., Heikkinen, M. E., & Lonnqvist, J. K. (2000). Suicides of alcohol misusers and non-misusers in a nationwide population. *Alcohol and Alcoholism*, *35*(1), 70–75.

Pirkola, S. P., Suominen, K., & Isometsa, E. (2004). Suicide in alcohol-dependent individuals: Epidemiology and management. *CNS Drugs*, *18*(7), 423–436.

Pompili, M., Serafini, G., Innamorati, M., Dominici, G., Ferracuti, S., Kotzalidis, G. D., et al. (2010). Suicidal behavior and alcohol abuse. *International Journal of Environmental Research and Public Health*, *7*(4), 1392–1431.

Pompili, M., Serafini, G., Innamorati, M., Biondi, M., Siracusano, A., Giannantonia, M. D., et al. (2012). Substance abuse and suicide risk among adolescents. *European Archives of Psychiatry and Clinical Neuroscience*, *262*(6), 469–485

Potash, J. B., Kane, S., Chiu, Y., Simpson, S. G., MacKinnon, D. F., McInnis, M. G., et al. (2000). Attempted suicide and alcoholism in bipolar disorder: Clinical and familial relationships. *American Journal of Psychiatry*, *157*(12), 2048–2050.

Prendergast, M. L., Podus, D., Chang, E., & Urada, D. (2002). The effectiveness of drug abuse treatment: A meta-analysis of comparison group studies. *Drug and Alcohol Dependence*, *67*(1), 53–72.

Preuss, U. W., Koller, G., Soyka, M., & Bondy, B. (2001). Association between suicide attempts and 5-HTTLPR-S-allele in alcohol-dependent and control subjects: Further evidence from a German alcohol-dependent inpatient sample. *Biological Psychiatry*, *50*(8), 636–639.

Preuss, U. W., Schuckit, M., Smith, T. L., Danko, G. P., Hesselbrock, M. N., & Nurnberger, J. I., Jr. (2002). A comparison of alcohol-induced and independent depression in alcoholics with histories of suicide attempts. *Journal of Studies on Alcohol*, *63*(4), 498–502.

Preuss, U. W., Schuckit, M. A., Smith, T. L., Danko, G. P., Bucholz, K. K., Hesselbrock, M. N., et al. (2003). Predictors and correlates of suicide attempts over 5 years in 1,237 alcohol-dependent men and women. *American Journal of Psychiatry*, *160*(1), 56–63.

Preuss, U. W., Schuckit, M. A., Smith, T. L., Danko, G. P., Buckman, K., Bierut, L., et al. (2002). Comparison of 3190 alcohol-dependent individuals with and without suicide attempts. *Alcoholism, Clinical and Experimental Research*, *26*(4), 471–477.

Putkonen, A., Kotilainen, I., Joyal, C. C., & Tuhonen, J. (2004). Comorbid personality disorders and substance use disorders of mentally ill homicide offenders: A structured clinical study on dual and triple diagnoses. *Schizophrenia Bulletin*, *30*(1), 59–72.

Ramchand, R., Griffin, B. A., Harris, K. M., McCaffrey, D. F., & Morral, A. R. (2008). A prospective investigation of suicide ideation, attempts, and use of mental health service among adolescents in substance abuse treatment. *Psychology of Addictive Behaviors*, *22*(4), 524-32.

Randall, J., & Cunningham, P. B. (2003). Multisystemic therapy: A treatment for violent substance-abusing and substance-dependent juvenile offenders. *Interpersonal Violence and Substance Use*, *28*(9), 1731–1739.

Richardson-Vejlgaard, R., Sher, L., Oquendo, M. A., Lizardi, D., & Stanley, B. (2009). Objections to suicide among depressed patients with alcohol use disorders. *Journal of Affective Disorders*, *117*(3), 197–201.

Rodgers, P. L., Sudak, H. S., Silverman, M. M., & Litts, D. A. (2007). Evidence-based practices project for suicide prevention. *Suicide & Life—Threatening Behavior*, *37*(2), 154–164.

Rossow, I., & Lauritzen, G. (1999). Balancing on the edge of death: Suicide attempts and life-threatening overdoses among drug addicts. *Addiction*, *94*(2), 209–219.

Rossow, I., & Lauritzen, G. (2001). Shattered childhood: A key issue in suicidal behavior among drug addicts? *Addiction*, *96*(2), 227-40.

Rothman, E. F., McNaughton, R. L., Johnson, R. M., & LaValley, M. (2012). Does the alcohol make them do it? Dating violence perpetration and drinking among youth. *Epidemiologic Reviews*, *34*(1),103–119.

Roy, A. (2001). Characteristics of cocaine-dependent patients who attempt suicide. *American Journal of Psychiatry*, *158*(8), 1215–1219.

Roy, A. (2003a). Characteristics of drug addicts who attempt suicide. *Psychiatric Research*, *121*(1), 99–103.

Roy, A. (2003b). Characteristics of HIV patients who attempt suicide. *Acta Psychiatrica Scandinavica*, *107*(1), 41–44.

Roy, A., & Janal, M. N. (2007). Risk factors for suicide attempts among alcohol dependent patients. *Arch.Suicide Res.*, *11*(2), 211–217.

Roy, A., Lamparski, D., DeJong, J., Moore, V., & Linnoila, M. (1990). Characteristics of alcoholics who attempt suicide. *American Journal of Psychiatry*, *147*(6), 761–765.

Rutter, M. (1989). Pathways from childhood to adult life. *Journal of Child Psychology and Psychiatry*, *30*(1), 23–51.

Sakai, J. T., Hall, S. K., Mikulich-Gilbertson, S., & Crowley, T. J. (2004). Inhalant use, abuse, and dependence among adolescent patients: Commonly comorbid problems. *Journal of American Academy of Child and Adolescent Psychiatry*, *43*(9), 1080–1088.

Saltzman, L. E., & Houry, D. (2009). Prevalence of nonfatal and fatal intimate partner violence in the United States. In C. Mitchell & D. Anglin (Eds.), *Intimate partner violence: A health-based perspective* (pp. 31–38). New York, NY: Oxford University Press.

Schanda, H., Knecht, G., Schreinzer, D., Stompe, T., Ortwein-Swoboda, G., & Waldhoer, T. (2004). Homicide and major mental disorders: A 25-year study. *Acta Psychiatrica Scandinavica*, *110*(2), 98–107.

Schneider, B. (2009). Substance use disorders and risk for completed suicide. *Archives of Suicide Research*, *13*(4), 303–316.

Schumacher, J. A., Fals-Stewart, W., & Leonard, K. E. (2003). Domestic violence treatment referrals for men seeking alcohol treatment. *Journal of Substance Abuse Treatment*, *24*(3), 279–283.

Schumacher, J. A., Homish, G. G., Leonard, K. E., Quigley, B. M., & Kearns-Bodkin, J. (2008). Longitudinal moderators of the relationship between excessive drinking and intimate partner violence in the early years of marriage, *Journal of Family Psychology*, *22*(6), 894-904.

Shaw, J., Hunt, I. M., Flynn, S., Amos, T., Meehan, J., Robinson, J., et al. (2006). The role of alcohol and drugs in homicides in England and Wales. *Addiction*, *101*(8), 1117–1124.

Sher, L. (2006a). Alcohol and suicide: Neurobiological and clinical aspects. *ScientificWorldJournal*, *6*, 700–706.

Sher, L. (2006b). Alcoholism and suicidal behavior: A clinical overview. *Acta Psychiatrica Scandinavica*, *113*(1), 13–22.

Sher, L., Oquendo, M. A., Richardson-Vejlgaard, R., Makhija, N. M., Posner, K., Mann, J. J., et al. (2009). Effect of acute alcohol use on the lethality of suicide attempts in patients with mood disorders. *Journal of Psychiatric Research, 43*(10), 901–905.

Silverman, M. M., Berman, A. L., Sanddal, N. D., O'Carroll, P. W. (2007). Rebuilding the Tower of Babel: A revised nomenclature for the study of suicide and suicidal behaviors. Part 2: Suicide-related ideations, communications, and behaviors. *Suicide and Life-Threatening Behavior, 37*(3), 264–277.

Smith, P. H., Homish, G. G., Leonard, K. E., & Cornelius, J. R. (2012). Intimate partner violence and specific substance use disorders: Findings from the National Epidemiologic Survey on Alcohol and Related Conditions. *Psychology of Addictive Behaviors, 26*(2), 236–245. *Erratum in Psychology of Addictive Behaviors, 26*(2), 254.

Spirito, A., & Esposito, C. L. (2006). Attempted and completed suicide in adolescence. *Annual Review of Clinical Psychology, 2,* 237–266.

Stalans, L. J., & Ritchie, J. (2008). Relationship of substance use/abuse with psychological and physical intimate partner violence: Variations across living situations. *Journal of Family Violence, 23*(1), 9–24.

Stappenbeck, C. A., & Fromme, K. (2010). Alcohol use and perceived social and emotional consequences among perpetrators of general and sexual aggression. *Journal of Interpersonal Violence, 25*(4), 699–715.

Stover, C. S., Meadows, A. L., & Kaufman, J. (2009). Interventions for intimate partner violence: Review and implications for evidence-based practice. *Professional Psychology: Research and Practice, 40*(3), 223–233.

Strang, J., Babor, T., Caulkins, J., Fischer, B., Foxcroft, D., & Humphreys, K. (2012). Drug policy and the public good: Evidence for effective interventions. *Lancet, 379*(9810),71–83.

Stuart, G. L. (2005). Improving violence intervention outcomes by integrating alcohol treatment. *Journal of Interpersonal Violence, 20*(4), 388–393.

Stuart, G. L., Ramsey, S. E., Moore, T. M., Kahler, C. W., Farrell, L. E., Recupero, P. R., et al. (2003). Reductions in marital violence following treatment for alcohol dependence. *Journal of Interpersonal Violence, 18*(10), 1113–1131.

Stuart, G. L., Temple, J. R., Follansbee, K. W., Bucossi, M. M., Hellmuth, J. C., & Moore, T. M. (2008). The role of drug use in a conceptual model of intimate partner violence in men and women arrested for domestic violence. *Psychology of Addictive Behaviors, 22*(1), 12–24.

Stuart, G. L., Temple, J. R., & Moore, T. M. (2007). Improving batterer intervention programs through theory-based research. *Journal of American Medical Association, 298*(5), 560–562.

Sublette, E. M., Carballo, J. J., Moreno, C., Galfalvy, H. C., Brent, D. A., Birmaher, B., et al. (2009). Substance use disorders and suicide attempts in bipolar subtypes. *Journal of Psychiatric Research, 43*(3), 230–238.

Substance Abuse and Mental Health Services Administration, Drug Abuse Warning Network, 2010: National Estimates of Drug-Related Emergency Department Visits. HHS Publication No. (SMA) 12–4733, DAWN Series D-38. Rockville, MD: Substance Abuse and Mental Health Services Administration, 2012.

Swahn, M. H., Simon, T. R., Hertz, M. F., Arias, I., Bossarte, R. M., Ross, J. G., et al. (2008). Linking dating violence, peer violence, and suicidal behaviors among high-risk youth. *American Journal of Preventive Medicine, 34*(1), 30–38.

Swanson, J. M., Holzer, C. E., Ganju, V. K., & Jono, R. T. (1990). Violence and psychiatric disorder in the community: evidence from the Epidemiologic Catchment Area surveys. *Hospital and Community Psychiatry, 41*(761–770).

Swendsen, J. D., & Merikangas, K. R. (2000). The comorbidity of depression and substance use disorders. *Clinical Psychology Review, 20*(2), 173–189.

Temple, J. R., Stuart, G. L., & O'Farrell, T. J. (2009). Prevention of intimate partner violence in substance-using populations. *Substance Use and Misuse 44*(9–10), 1318–1328.

Tiet, Q. Q., Illgen, M. A., Byrnes, H. F., & Moos, R. H. (2007). Suicide attempts among substance use disorder patients: An initial step toward a decision tree for suicide management. *Alcoholism, Clinical and Experimental Research, 30*(6), 998–1005.

Tremeau, F., Darreye, A., Staner, Correa, H., Weibel, H., Khindichian, F., et al. (2008). Suicidality in opioid-dependent subjects. *American Journal on Addictions, 17*(3), 187–194.

Tremeau, F., Saner, L., Duval, F., Correa, H., Crocq, M., Darreye, A., et al. (2005). Suicide attempts and family history of suicide in three psychiatric populations. *Suicide & Life—Threatening Behavior, 35*(6), 702–713.

Varnik, A., Kolves, K., Vali, M., Tooding, L. M., & Wasserman, D. (2006). Do alcohol restrictions reduce suicide mortality? *Addiction, 102*(2), 251–256.

Vaughn, M. G., Fu, Q., Perron, B. E., Bohnert, A. S., & Howard, M. O. (2010). Is crack cocaine use associated with greater violence than powdered cocaine use? Results from a national sample. *American Journal of Drug and Alcohol Abuse, 36*(4), 181–186.

Webster-Stratton, C., & Taylor, T. (2001). Nipping early risk factors in the bud: Preventing substance abuse, delinquency, and violence in adolescence through interventions targeted at young children (0–8 years). *Prevention Science, 2*(3), 165–192.

Wilcox, H. C. (2004). Epidemiological evidence on the link between drug use and suicidal behaviors among adolescents. *Canadian Academy of Child and Adolescent Psychiatry, 13*(2), 27–30.

Wilcox, H. C., Conner, K. R., & Caine, E. D. (2004). Association of alcohol and drug use disorders and completed suicide: An empirical review of cohort studies. *Drug and Alcohol Dependence, 76*(1), S11–S19.

Wilcox, H. C., Kellam, S. G., Brown, C. H., Poduska, J. M., Ialongo, N. S., Wang, W., et al. (2008). The impact of two universal randomized first- and second-grade classroom interventions on young adult suicide ideation and attempt. *Drug and Alcohol Dependence, 95*(S1), S60–S73.

Wines, J. J. D., Saitz, R., Horton, N. J., Lloyd-Travaglini, C., & Samet, J. H. (2004). Suicidal behavior, drug use and depressive symptoms after detoxification: A 2-year prospective study. *Drug Abuse and Suicidal Behavior, 76*(Supplement 1), S21–S29.

Wines, J. J. D., Saitz, R., Horton, N. J., Lloyd-Travaglini, C., & Samet, J. H. (2007). Overdose after detoxification: A prospective study. *Drug and Alcohol Dependence, 89*(2–3), 161–169.

Wojnar, M., Ilgen, M. A., Czyz, E., Strobbe, S., Klimkiewicz, A., Jakubczyk, A., et al. (2009). Impulsive and non-impulsive suicide attempts in patients treated for alcohol dependence. *Journal of Affective Disorders, 115*(1–2), 131–139.

World Health Organization (WHO). (2000). World Health Report 2000. *Health system: Improving performance.* Geneva, Switzerland: WHO.

Substance Use and Crime

Helene Raskin White

Abstract

The author explores the associations between alcohol and drug use and crime. First, general theoretical models of the substance use–crime connection, including substance use causing crime, crime leading to substance use, and a common cause model, are presented. Next, the empirical research that examines situational and global associations between substance use and crime is reviewed, and this research is tied to the explanatory models. The review indicates that the substance-using/crime-committing population is heterogeneous and there are multiple paths that lead to substance use and crime. For some individuals, acute intoxication increases the risks of violent crime; for some, the need for expensive and addictive drugs increases the risks for income-generating crime; for some, exposure to drug cultures and drug markets increases all types of crime, especially violent crime; for some, the criminal lifestyle increases substance use; and, finally, for others, common underlying characteristics (e.g., family, personality, genetics, neighborhoods) increase the risks for both substance use and crime. The author concludes with a discussion of implications for treatment and prevention and suggestions for future research.

Key Words: criminal offending, victimization, crime-substance use relation, substance use, crime, developmental aspects

Introduction

One of the most reliable findings in criminology is the strong correlation between substance abuse and criminal offending (Welte, Barnes, Hoffman, Wieczorek, & Zhang, 2005). Substance users are more likely to commit crimes than nonusers and criminal offenders generally report heavier alcohol and drug use than nonoffenders (Bennett, Holloway, & Farrington, 2008; White & Gorman, 2000). Although it is clear that an important connection exists between substance use and crime, the precise nature of the relationship remains elusive and there are many plausible explanations for the associations between substance use and crime. In fact, the nature of the relationship between substance use and crime is multifaceted and differs depending on type of crime and type of substance

use as well as individual, situational, and cultural factors. As Anthony and Forman (2003, p. 12) note, "There is no single drug–crime relationship," but rather "there are drugs–crime relationships, most of which are complex." The purpose of this essay is to review the literature on the substance and crime.[1]

One problem with studying the associations between substance use and crime is that "substance use–related crime" means different things in different studies. For example, substance use–related homicide can include murders related to drug distribution, committed while using alcohol or drugs, or committed in the act of a crime to get money for drugs. Also, in some official statistics and research reports, alcohol is included as a drug when estimating the level of drug-related crimes, whereas in others it is not (see Anthony & Forman, 2003; Miczek, DeBold, Haney, Tidey, Vivian, & Weerts, 1994).

In addition, measurement of alcohol and drug use varies greatly across studies; some studies measure acute use while others measure chronic use, and some measure substance use–related problems while others measure dependence. Similarly, there is a lack of consistency in measures of crime across studies. (See Roizen, 1993; White, 1990; White & Gorman, 2000, for additional methodological issues related to definitions, measures, sampling, experimental designs, and analyses.)

Given this lack of agreement and consensus in definitions and measures, one must be cautious in making comparisons across studies and in evaluating the literature presented here. In this essay, alcohol and illicit drug (e.g., marijuana, cocaine, heroin, psychedelics, etc.) use are differentiated and collectively referred to as substance use. Crimes are separated into violent crimes including violent street crimes (e.g., homicide, physical assault, robbery), sexual assault, and intimate partner violence (IPV), and property crimes (e.g., burglary, motor vehicle theft, larceny theft).[2] Illicit drug use and drug possession, which are crimes in and of themselves, are not considered here as crimes unless as part of a set of research findings specifically linking them to the commission of other types of crime. In addition, drug dealing is not considered as a crime because it would inflate the drug–crime relationship, although its relationship to substance use and crime is discussed. Similarly, status crimes, such as minor in possession, as well as public intoxication and driving under the influence, are not included.

First, the various theoretical models that have been used to explain the substance use–crime association are discussed. Then, the empirical research on the nature and extent of the situational and global associations between substance use and crime is reviewed. The essay ends with the implications of the existing research for treatment and prevention and suggestions for future research.

Theoretical Models

There are three basic explanatory models for the relationship between substance use and crime: (1) substance use leads to crime; (2) crime leads to substance use; and (3) the relationship is either coincidental or explained by a set of common causes (see White, 1990). Each model may be applicable to different subgroups of the population of substance using criminals or to different

incidents of alcohol/drug-related crime. Note that these three basic models represent simplistic models, which can be expanded into reciprocal, mediational, moderational, and conditional models (see Pernanen, 1993). Next, the three basic models are briefly described.

Substance Use Leads to Crime

Substance use can lead to crime either because of the psychopharmacological properties of substances, the economic motivation to get drugs, or systemic crime associated with the illegal drug market (Goldstein, 1985).

THE PSYCHOPHARMACOLOGICAL MODEL

The psychopharmacological model proposes that the effects of intoxication (including disinhibition, cognitive-perceptual distortions, attention deficits, bad judgment, and neurochemical changes) cause criminal (especially violent and impulsive) behavior (Collins, 1981; Fagan, 1990). Chronic intoxication may also contribute to aggression and crime due to factors such as withdrawal, sleep deprivation, nutritional deficits, impairment of neuropsychological functioning, or enhancement of psychopathologic personality disorders (Virkkunen & Linnoila, 1993). In other words, chronic administration of alcohol or drugs (or withdrawal among those addicted) can lead to physiological or neuropsychological changes that result in changes in mood state, such as increased negative affect (Fagan, 1990; Miczek et al., 1994). Negative affect and other mood changes, in turn, can increase the risks for aggressive behavior.

Cognitive disruption models. Several models have been proposed to account for the acute pharmacological effects of intoxication on crime, and they apply mostly to the effects of alcohol on aggressive behavior. These models are based on the fact that alcohol causes changes within the person that increase the risks for aggressive behavior, such as reduced intellectual functioning, reduced self-awareness, reduced executive functioning (see later), reduced self-attention, reduced anxiety, reduced attention to situational cues, and inaccurate assessment of risks (Bushman, 1997; Leonard, 2008). In other words, intoxication causes cognitive disruption and impairs cognitive processes that would normally inhibit aggressive responding. One dominant model is the attention allocation model, known as the "alcohol myopia" model (Steele & Josephs, 1990). Alcohol interferes with information processing and disrupts an individual's ability to allocate attention to multiple aspects of a situation. Therefore, intoxicated individuals focus their attention on the most salient (i.e., instigatory) cues and ignore the other less salient (i.e., inhibitory) cues (see Giancola, 2002, p. 132). Steele and Josephs (1990) have argued that alcohol will only increase aggression in situations where individuals have inhibition conflict. That is, when behavior is controlled by instigatory and inhibitory cues that are nearly equal in strength, the effects of alcohol will be strongest (Cooper, 2002). In contrast, when instigatory cues are stronger than inhibitory cues, an individual will be likely to act aggressively regardless of alcohol consumption, whereas when inhibitory cues are stronger than instigatory cues, an individual will not be likely to act aggressively even under the influence of alcohol. Another psychopharmacological model, the anxiolytic model, assumes that alcohol reduces fear reactions by interfering with the recognition of threat (Pihl, Peterson, & Lau, 1993).

Giancola (2002) argued that all of these various cognitive effects models fit under an executive functioning impairment model. Executive functioning (also referred to by some researchers as executive cognitive functioning [ECF]) is "a higher order cognitive construct involved in planning, initiation and regulation of goal-directed" behavior, which subsumes "attentional control, previewing, informational appraisal, strategic goal planning, abstract reasoning, temporal response sequencing, self- and social monitoring, . . . cognitive flexibility, hypothesis generation and the ability to organize and adaptively utilize information contained in working memory" (Giancola, p. 133). Giancola argued that impairment in ECF caused by intoxication results in alcohol-related aggression (a mediation model). Furthermore, alcohol is more likely to lead to aggression in individuals with low compared with high ECF (a moderation model). (For greater detail on these psychopharmacological models, see Bushman, 1997; Chermack & Giancola, 1997; Giancola, 2002; Ito, Miller, & Pollock, 1996; and Parker & Rebhun, 1995.)

Expectancy models. In addition to pharmacological effects of alcohol, another broad explanation for the impact of alcohol on aggression focuses on beliefs and expectations of the drinker regarding alcohol (Leonard, 2008). MacAndrew and Edgerton's (1969) classic study on alcohol use and aggression in preliterate societies demonstrated that the disinhibiting effects of alcohol intoxication on aggression were not universal. Instead, MacAndrew and Edgerton argued that it is the cultural expectancies about the effects of alcohol that causes increased aggression in some societies. In other words, those individuals who believe that alcohol causes aggression will be more likely than those without such beliefs to become aggressive after drinking. Whereas some research suggests that alcohol expectancies may contribute to IPV (Field, Caetano, & Nelson, 2004; Leonard, 2008) and sexual assaults (Testa, 2002), laboratory studies do not provide strong support for a pure expectancy model for alcohol and physical aggression (see Experimental Studies).

Drug effects. The psychopharmacological model has been mostly attributed to alcohol and violent crime. Nevertheless, other drugs with similar psychoactive properties to alcohol (e.g., barbiturates and tranquilizers) may have similar effects on violence (Blanchard, Veniegas, Elloran, & Blanchard, 1993; Lundholm, Haggård, Möller, Hallqvist, & Thiblin, 2013). In addition, some studies suggest that stimulants (e.g., crack cocaine and amphetamines) and various steroids increase violence (Pihl & Sutton, 2009). Furthermore, the cognitive disruptions caused by alcohol and these other drugs may also influence decisions to commit property crimes, especially impulsive decisions (Fergusson & Horwood, 2000). More detail on psychopharmacological effects of specific substances is presented in Experimental Studies.

THE ECONOMIC MODEL

The economic model assumes that drug users need to generate illicit income to support their drug habit. Therefore, they engage in crimes such as robbery, burglary, prostitution, and shoplifting to get drugs or the money to buy drugs. This model appears to be applicable for certain drugs, especially those that are addictive and expensive (e.g., heroin and crack).

Early research on heroin addicts. Support for the economic motivation model originated from literature on heroin addicts, which indicated that raising or lowering the frequency of substance use among addicts raised or lowered their frequency of crime, especially property crime (e.g., Anglin & Perrochet, 1998; Chaiken & Chaiken, 1990). In addition, criminal activity was significantly greater following addiction to drugs than before addiction (Nurco, Hanlon, Kinlock, & Duszynski, 1988). While heroin use may not initiate crime, addiction is often a key point in the acceleration of an existing criminal career (Chaiken & Chaiken, 1990). Containment of heroin use through treatment and close supervision appeared to lead to dramatic reductions in both drug use and crime (Inciardi & Pottieger, 1998). Anglin and Perrochet (1998) argued that the fact that treatment reduces income-generating crimes rather than all crimes lends support for the economic motivation model.

However, some studies suggest that there are individual differences in the effects of treatment on reducing crime. For example, Nurco and colleagues (1988) found that a reduction only occurred for individuals with previously low levels of criminal activity. Those individuals with criminally derived incomes prior to addiction remained criminally active after treatment (see also Lipton & Johnson, 1998). Thus, the economic motivation model might explain the drug-crime connection for addicts with little prior criminal involvement, while for those with heavier criminal involvement a common cause model (see later) may be most relevant. Further, there are other individual factors, such as ethnicity/race and social class, which influence the effects of treatment on crime reduction (Nurco et al., 1988; Waldorf, 1998).

Drug use and property crime. Most economically motivated crimes are property (e.g., burglary, shoplifting) rather than violent crimes. McGolothin (1985) found that addicts commit more property crime but not more violent crime compared with those who use less drugs (see also Jofre-Bonet & Sindelar, 2001; Uggen & Thompson, 2003; Workowski, 2003). In a study of homicides in New York City, only 4% of all drug-related homicides were classified as economically motivated (Goldstein, Brownstein, Ryan, & Bellucci, 1989), and cocaine was the drug most often associated with economically motivated homicides (see also Lipton & Johnson, 1998).

Gottfredson, Kearley, and Bushway (2008) modeled within-subject change over an 11-month period in a sample of chronic drug-using offenders. They found that the use of heroin and/or cocaine had much stronger effects on income-generating than violent crime. Surprisingly, they found that alcohol use was also more strongly associated with income-generating than violent crime. In fact, none of the substances studied were significantly related to violent crime. Overall, they found that the effect of drug treatment on property crime was completely mediated through reductions in substance use (see also Longitudinal Studies). Gottfreson et al. concluded that the predominant effect of substance use on crime is to increase income-generating crime,

probably to pay for drugs (see also Thompson & Uggen, 2012).

Anglin and Perrochet (1998) argued that the association between drugs and property crime is not universal and suggested that in countries, such as the United Kingdom (U.K.) and the Netherlands, where drug maintenance and treatment were provided by the government, there are much lower levels of property crime attributed to narcotics use. In contrast, studies in the U.K. and Australia have found that economic motivation accounts for a substantial amount of criminal activity (Bennett & Holloway, 2006). For example, in a U.K. study, Bennett and Holloway (2006) found that a large majority (approximately 60%–80%) of drug-using offenders reported that there is a connection between their offending and their drug use. Among those who reported a connection, the most common explanations were economic and psychopharmacological. The reasons cited for the connection between substance use and crime depended on the type of substance use. Those criminals using heroin and cocaine generally claimed an economic connection, whereas alcohol, barbiturate, stimulant, and PCP use were most often associated with crime due to the pharmacological properties of these substances (see also Manzoni, Fischer, & Rehm, 2007).

In contrast, in the U.S., only about 16% of 2002 jail inmates, 17% of 2004 state prisoners, and 18% of 2004 federal prisoners reported having committed a crime in order to get money for drugs (Karberg & James, 2005; Mumola & Karberg, 2006). For jail and state inmates, more property (27% and 30%, respectively) than violent (8% and 10%, respectively) offenders reported committing their offense to get money for drugs, whereas for federal prisoners, there was not much difference between property and violent offenders (11% versus 15%, respectively).

Prostitution. Female addicts tend to commit primarily nonviolent income-generating crimes especially prostitution, drug selling, and shoplifting (Chaiken & Chaiken, 1990; Maher & Hudson, 2007), although female drug users engage in a variety of crimes (Baskin & Sommers, 1997; Erickson & Watson, 1990). There are high rates of drug use among prostitutes and high rates of prostitution among female drug abusers (Edwards, Halpern, Wechsberg, & Wendee, 2006; Maxwell & Maxwell, 2000). Not only do women engage in prostitution to get money for drugs, but they often barter sex for drugs (Goldstein, Ouellet, & Fendrich, 1992; Kwiatkowski & Booth, 2000). Male prostitutes also engage in a high amount of illicit drug use (Timpson, Ross, Williams, & Atkinson, 2007).

Yacoubian, Urbach, Larsen, Johnson, and Peters (2000) used data from the Arrestee Drug Abuse Monitoring (ADAM) program to compare female prostitutes to other offenders. They found that, with controls for sociodemographic characteristics, alcohol use, and injection drug use, females arrested for prostitution, compared with other female arrestees, were more likely to test positive for cocaine and to self report use of cocaine and crack. There were no other drug test results that were significantly different between the two groups.

Much of the research on prostitution, similar to research conducted on other criminal behavior engaged in by male and female drug abusers, suggests that many prostitutes committed crimes prior to becoming addicted to drugs and that prostitution served as a means of making a living not just a means of obtaining drugs. Even if these women had not previously engaged in prostitution, they had engaged in some types of criminal behavior prior to addiction, such as shoplifting, larceny, and burglary (Erickson & Watson, 1990). In other words, drug use does not cause prostitution; rather individuals who are prone to drug use are also prone to criminal behavior of all kinds (Inciardi, 1986). However, addiction then maintains or increases the frequency of prostitution for many women (Belcher & Herr, 2005; Cusick & Hickman, 2005).

Prostitutes are often victims of crime, especially violent crime and IPV (El-Bassel, Witte, Wada, Gilbert, & Wallace, 2001; Erickson, Butters, McGillicuddy, & Hallgren, 2000; Surratt, Inciardi, Kurtz, & Kiley, 2004). In fact, several researchers have suggested that the association between prostitution and drug use is reciprocal in that prostitutes who suffer from emotional trauma due to victimization or feelings of guilt and distress may turn to drugs to cope. In turn, the need for drugs increases the need for more frequent prostitution (Romero-Daza, Weeks, & Singer, 2003; Young, Boyd, & Hubbell, 2000). (See Erickson & Watson, 1990; Goldstein et al., 1992; Maxwell & Maxwell, 2000 for greater detail on prostitution and drug use.)

Adolescents. Whereas the literature supports an association of addictive drug use with property crime and prostitution among adults, most studies of adolescents do not support an economic motivation model (White, 1990). Based on self-report data from a nationally representative sample, Menard and Mihalic (2001) concluded that the economic motivation model is only applicable to a small number (about 2%) of drug-using adolescents and emerging adults,[3] which is unsurprising in a community sample of nonaddicted users.

Summary. In sum, the economic motivation model is more applicable for property than violent crimes. In addition, inconsistencies in findings regarding the relative strength of the economic model reflect differences in the age composition of the samples, the stage of substance use (e.g., recreational versus dependent), and type of substance used. Furthermore, historical, geographical, and social policy factors affect the need for income-generating crime. Many researchers feel that reductions in property crime that occurred during the 1980s and 1990s were due to increases in drug dealing during the crack epidemic (Harrison, 1992; Miczek et al., 1994), although not all agree (MacCoun, Kilmer, & Reuter, 2003). Next, drug dealing and the systemic model are discussed.

THE SYSTEMIC MODEL

The systemic model posits that the system of drug distribution and use is inherently connected with crime. Systemic types of crimes surrounding drug distribution include fights over organizational and territorial issues, enforcement of rules, punishments of and efforts to protect buyers and sellers, and transaction-related crimes (such as thefts or robberies of dealers or buyers, assaults to collect debts, and resolution of disputes over quality or amount) (Miczek et al., 1994). In addition, there is often third party violence, such as bystander shootings or assaults on prostitutes who sell drugs. Further, drug markets can create community disorganization, which, in turn, affects the norms and behaviors of individuals who live in the community. Such community disorganization may be associated with increases in crime that are not directly related to drug selling (see Blumstein, 1995; Fagan & Chin, 1990; Gorman, Zhu, & Horel, 2005).

Drug dealing. Studies in the 1990s consistently showed that crack users were heavily involved in dealing, but they were also involved in non-drug criminality (Johnson, Natarajan, Dunlap, & Elmoghazy, 1994; Inciardi & Pottieger, 1994). In a study of in-custody, inner-city male adolescents, researchers found that large percentages of dealers did not use cocaine or crack but that few crack or cocaine users did not also deal (Lipton & Johnson, 1998; see also Inciardi & Pottieger, 1998). Johnson and colleagues (1994) compared crack abusers to other drug users and found that, in general, crack abusers used drugs at a much higher rate, were more involved in drug dealing, and had higher frequencies of nondrug crimes (except compared with heroin users). Crack selling, however, was prevalent among cocaine snorters and marijuana users also. In fact, for all illicit drug users, crack selling was the most frequent crime and generated the largest cash income. Thompson and Uggen (2012) suggest that cocaine and heroin use are related to increases in all types of illegal earnings, and that dealing and other types of economically motivated crime share common determinants. In other words, most dealers do not specialize in dealing but rather engage in several types of income-generating crime.

Van Kammen and Loeber (1994) demonstrated that previous involvement in violent crime increased the risk of drug dealing for male adolescents, as did previous involvement in property crime. Individuals drawn to dealing were already violent and delinquent, and once involved in drug use or dealing their level of violent behavior (including weapons possession) increased (see also Fagan & Chin, 1990). Other studies have also found that crack use did not increase initiation rates for violent crimes and dealers were criminally involved prior to becoming crack dealers (Johnson et al., 1994; Inciardi & Pottieger, 1991). Johnson, Williams, Dei, and Sanabria (1990) argued that violence in the crack trade was a result of violent individuals selecting themselves into this work as well as being recruited. More recently, White, Loeber, and Farrington (2008) found, in a high-risk sample of young men, that among those who engaged in both behaviors, serious violent offending preceded drug dealing by about one year. Serious theft preceded dealing by one to three years depending on cohort. They also found that, controlling for earlier violent offending, drug dealing was significantly related to later violent offending during adolescence and emerging adulthood. Nevertheless, not all drug dealers are violent and levels of violence differ depending on types of drug markets, types of drugs, and regions of the country (Curtis & Windle, 2007; Sales & Murphy, 2007). In fact, after reviewing the literature, Desroches (2007) noted that, in developed countries, those individuals involved in higher levels of drug trafficking rarely engage in violence.

Although drug use is more often related to property than violent crime, drug dealing is more often associated with violent crime (De Li, Priu, & MacKenzie, 2000; White et al., 2008). In a study of probationers, De Li and colleagues (2000) examined the monthly associations among offending, dealing, and drug use controlling for lifestyle factors.

Overall, drug dealing was a stronger predictor than drug use of both property and violent crime and the interaction of the two was the strongest predictor. In a national study, Menard and Mihalic (2001) found evidence in support of the systemic model in a sample of adolescents and emerging adults. Dealing increased the odds of violent offending and victimization more than drug use did. Furthermore, involvement in dealing in adolescence (rather than drug use) was a strong predictor of violent offending in emerging adulthood. In contrast to studies of higher-risk samples, their results suggested that involvement in dealing led to violence rather than violence leading to dealing.

Summary. Overall, analyses of survey and ethnographic data on drug dealing and official records data suggest that the systemic model probably explains much of the violence related to illicit drug use in the U.S. in the past two to three decades (Curtis & Windle, 2007; Fagan & Chin, 1990; Goldstein et al., 1989). This conclusion is especially supported for drug-related homicides, which increased significantly with the appearance of crack in 1985, declined in the 1990s, and then increased again (Blumstein, 1995; Goldstein et al., 1989). Nonetheless, the systemic model may be too simplistic an explanatory model because the associations between drug markets and violence have been found to depend on individual, structural, cultural, contextual, and historical factors (Ousey & Lee, 2004). For example, Oser, Palmer, Staton-Tindall, and Leukfeld (2008) found no support for the systemic model among a sample of felony probationers in rural Appalachian Kentucky interviewed between 2001 and 2004. Furthermore, systemic violence is not universal and depends on national policies regarding drug control (White & Gorman, 2000). Most longitudinal studies suggest, at least among high-risk samples, that violent individuals are recruited or self select into dealing rather than dealing leading to violence. Therefore, these results lend support for a common cause model (see later).

Crime Leads to Substance Use

Rather than substance use "causing" crime, it is also possible that criminal behavior may lead to increased alcohol and drug use (Hagan & Forster, 2003; Welte et al., 2005). Criminal offenders may be more likely than nonoffenders to select (or be pushed into) social situations and subcultures in which heavy drinking and drug use are condoned or encouraged. Furthermore, offenders often choose peer groups and lifestyles that promote alcohol and drug use (Chaiken & Chaiken, 1990; Collins & Messerschmidt, 1993). For example, several aspects of the professional criminal lifestyle are conducive to heavy drinking and drug use, such as working periodically, partying between jobs, being unmarried, and being geographically mobile (Collins & Messerschmidt, 1993). Not only do lifestyle factors explain the strong association between drug use and offending, they may also account for the strong association between drug use and victimization and between offending and victimization (De Li et al., 2000). Thus, instead of the need for a drug compelling an individual to commit a robbery, the income generated from a robbery might provide the individual with extra money to buy drugs and place the individual in an environment that is supportive of drug use (Collins, Hubbard, & Rachal, 1985). In fact, using drugs to celebrate a successful crime is a common explanation reported by offenders for the link between substance use and crime (Bennett & Holloway, 2006). In addition, it has been proposed that deviant individuals may use drugs in order to self-medicate (Khantzian, 1985) or to give themselves an excuse to commit a criminal act (Collins, 1993; Zhang, Welte, & Wieczorek, 2002).

It is also possible that the relationship between substance use and crime is reciprocal (Mason & Windle, 2002; White, Loeber, Stouthamer-Loeber, & Farrington, 1999). That is, substance use and crime may be causally linked and mutually reinforcing, and, thus, drinking and drug use may lead to increased criminal behavior and criminal behavior may lead to increased drinking and drug use (Chaiken & Chaiken, 1990; Fagan & Chin, 1990; for research on the reciprocal model, see Longitudinal Studies).

The Relationship Is Due to Common Causes

The common cause model postulates that substance use and crime do not have a direct causal link. Rather, they are related because they share common causes, within the individual, family, and social structure (Friedman, 1998; White, 1990; White, Brick, & Hansell, 1993).

COMMON CAUSES

There are many risk factors for childhood and adolescent delinquency that are also risk factors for teenage drug use and for adult alcohol and drug problems. Some of the common risk factors include: hyperactivity, impulsivity, antisocial personality disorder, risk taking, inability to delay gratification, abuse or rejection in family, lack of parental nurturance, early school failure, peer rejection,

social disorganization, and availability of drugs and/or weapons (Hawkins, Catalano, & Miller, 1992; Reiss & Roth, 1993). Behavior-genetics research supports a common externalizing dimension that underlies substance dependence and antisocial behaviors (Krueger, Markon, Patrick, & Iacono, 2005; Zucker et al., 2006).

Subcultural norms may also reinforce both criminal behavior and substance use (Fagan, 1990). Besides individual and interpersonal-level influences, substance use and crime may share common environmental and situational causes. Research shows, for example, that rates of crime are high in neighborhoods that are poor, are densely populated, are racially segregated, and have a transient population (Gorman, Zhu, & Horel, 2005; Sampson, Raudenbush, & Earls, 1997). Drug exposure and use are also more common among residents of disadvantaged and disorganized neighborhoods, probably because of illicit drug market concentration in such communities (Ensminger, Anthony, & McCord, 1997; Freisthler, Lascala, Gruenewald, & Treno, 2005).

Certain types of places and situations also generate greater rates of both substance use and crime. For example, crime rates are high when and where people (especially young males) are drinking (e.g., at bars and sports stadiums) and at night and on weekends (Fagan, 1993). A perfect illustration is soccer matches in the U.K., where heavy drinking in a competitive environment with norms supportive of aggression contributes to high rates of crowd violence (Dunning, Murphy, & Williams, 1986). Proponents of the routine activities perspective argue that bars and sports stadiums are crime "hot spots" because they bring together motivated offenders and suitable targets in the absence of effective social control (Roncek & Maier, 1991). (For greater detail on contextual factors, see Situational Associations.)

GENERALITY VERSUS SPECIFICITY OF PROBLEM BEHAVIORS

Jessor and Jessor (1977) identified a problem behavior syndrome in which cigarette use, precocious sexual behavior, problem drinking, use of marijuana and other drugs, stealing, and aggression clustered together. They found that, among adolescences, this cluster of behaviors was explained by the same set of environmental and personality variables and was negatively related to conventional behavior. Other researchers have argued that problem behaviors in adolescence constitute several distinct factors rather than a single construct (for a review see White & Labouvie, 1994). Although common causes have been identified for substance use and criminal offending, several longitudinal studies have found unique predictors of substance use and abuse compared with violent and property offending demonstrating the importance of both common and specific contributions to each (e.g., Brook, Whiteman, & Cohen, 1995; McCord & Ensminger, 1997; White & Labouvie, 1994; White, Pandina, & LaGrange, 1987).

White and Labouvie (1994) claimed that there was little support for a generality of deviance hypothesis among adolescents because of the generally low correlations between substance use and delinquency, the fact that various behavior problems follow different developmental paths, the fact that substance use and crime do not cluster together for all adolescents, and the fact that there are several distinct influences on each behavior. Furthermore, the generality of problem behaviors depends on cultural context. For example, Little, Weaver, King, Liu, and Chassin (2008) found that there were historical changes in the strength of the association between marijuana use and deviance proneness suggesting that societal norms regarding the appropriateness of certain behaviors (e.g., marijuana use) influence the structure of the problem behavior syndrome.

Summary of Explanatory Models

The above models offer several alternative explanations for an association between substance use and crime. Keep in mind that each of these models may be relevant for certain individuals, types of substance use, and types of crimes. Next, the empirical research testing causal and spurious models is reviewed.

Empirical Research on the Association between Substance Use and Crime

Cooper (2002) distinguished situational associations between two behaviors from global associations. Situational associations are defined as associations in which the two behaviors co-occur at the same point in time or when engaging in one behavior is related to engaging in the other within a selected time period. In other words, situational associations are those in which specific instances of substance use are associated with the occurrence of a criminal event (also referred to as acute or proximal associations in the drug-crime literature or event-related in the alcohol literature; see also Leonard, 2008, p. 33). Global associations are defined as those

in which individuals who engage in one behavior are also more likely to engage in the other at some point in their lives (i.e., whether individuals displaying specific long-term patterns of substance use are more likely to commit crimes). Global associations have also been referred to as chronic or developmental associations in the drug-crime literature. Neither situational nor global associations prove causality, although situational associations provide stronger evidence for a direct proximal link. That is, in order to attribute violence to acute substance use intoxication, it must first be demonstrated that substance use and violence are reliably linked on a specific occasion (i.e., a situational association) (Cooper, 2002). Nevertheless, common causes, as well as directional influences, can occur at both the global and situational level.

Situational Associations

Situational level analyses include between-person and within-person designs. Compared to between-person designs, within-person designs (e.g., studying the same person's behavior when drinking compared with when sober) are better able to "rule out the possibility that stable individual differences cause people both to drink" and to become aggressive (Cooper, 2002, p. 109). However, laboratory studies with random assignment can also provide evidence in support of acute alcohol effects even when using a between-subjects design. Next, results from survey and epidemiological studies examining situational associations between substances use and crime are reviewed separately for alcohol and drugs. Then results from experimental studies on substance use and aggression are examined.

ALCOHOL AND CRIME

In general, studies find a stronger situational association between alcohol use and violent than property crime. For example, in 2004, 37% of state prisoners reported that they were under the influence of alcohol at the time of their violent offense, compared with 29% of property offenders (Rand, Sabol, Sinclair, & Snyder, 2010).

Alcohol and violent crime. While rates vary greatly across studies, they indicate that between 40% and 60% of all homicides and physical assaults are committed when the offender, victim, or both have been drinking (see Collins & Messerschmidt, 1993; Haggård-Grann, Hallqvist, Långström, & Möller, 2006; Karberg & James, 2005; Murdoch, Pihl, & Ross, 1990; Roizen, 1993). Rates of alcohol involvement in violent crime are fairly consistent in the U.S., Canada, and Australia, as well as countries in Europe, South American, and Central America, although absolute rates of violence vary substantially across countries (Keys Young, 1994; Kraanen, Scholing, & Emmelkamp, 2012; Murdoch et al., 1990; Room & Rossow, 2001).

There is a debate in the literature on whether acute use is responsible for criminal events or whether acute use simply represents a chronic pattern of use among offenders. That is, some offenders may drink all of the time and be under the influence of alcohol whether or not they are committing crimes. Thus, use at the time of committing a crime may only indicate that offenders use alcohol often, rather than that their use causes them to commit the violent act. In fact, studies indicate that violent offenders have much higher rates of daily drinking, heavy drinking and alcohol abuse than the general population (Greenfeld & Henneberg, 2001; Kraanen et al., 2012; White & Gorman, 2000; see Global Associations). Nevertheless, while more than half of the assault offenders in one study reported drinking at the time of their offense, more than half of those drinking did not think that drinking was relevant to the commission of the crime (Collins & Messerschmidt, 1993). In addition, perpetrators often drink to give themselves an excuse to justify their behavior (Abbey, 2002; Zhang et al., 2002).

Based on interviews with offenders and criminal justice records, Collins and Schlenger (1988) compared chronic (psychiatric diagnosis of alcohol abuse or dependence) and acute (drinking just prior to the violent event) effects of alcohol on violence among violent male offenders. They found that acute episodes of drinking, but not chronic patterns of alcohol use, were significantly related to violent offending. Leonard (2008) argued that chronic drinkers will simply have more occasions of acute intoxication and that observed global associations between alcohol and violence may simply represent greater occasions of situational use. In other words, chronic excessive drinkers "may simply be at risk for violence because each occasion of intoxication may facilitate the occurrence of violence" (Leonard, 2008, p. 38).

Much of the research on situational associations is based on offender reports of use, which could be inflated to justify their violent behavior. Nevertheless, surveys with victims also provide empirical support for the alcohol–crime relationship, although rates depend on victim perceptions (Greenfeld & Henneberg, 2001; Pernanen, 1991). In 1998, 37% of all violent crime victims (who

could make a judgment) reported that the offender had been drinking at the time of the offense (Greenfeld & Henneberg, 2001). Note also that victims are often using alcohol or drugs and actually may be the impetus for the violent encounter. In fact, it is difficult to separate the victim from the perpetrator in many instances (National Institute of Justice, 2003).

Felson, Burchfield, and Teasdale (2007) examined the associations between alcohol intoxication and various types of offending using data from the National Violence Against Women and Men survey. Across all assaults, they found that in 36% of the incidents the offender was using alcohol (and no other substance) and in 19% the victim was. They found that offenders who physically assaulted strangers were more likely to be drinking than those who assaulted people they knew. Felson et al. suggested that it is more dangerous and more unlikely for a person to physically assault a stranger than someone they know. Therefore, the researchers argued that the anxiolytic effects of alcohol may make stranger assaults more viable. Alternatively, impaired appraisal of victim's motives due to alcohol use by the perpetrator might also explain the higher rates of drinking in assaults against strangers, compared with people that are known. In contrast, victims were more likely to be drinking in incidents involving people they knew (especially partners) than strangers. Whereas there were no significant differences between offender drinking in physical compared with sexual assaults, alcohol played a greater role in sexual than physical victimization. Thus, alcohol's role in assaults differed by type of assault and relationship between offender and victim. Alcohol was most prevalent in physical assaults on strangers and least prevalent for assaults on partners (see also Pernanen, 1991). Similarly, using data from a large, nationally representative sample of inmates, Felson and Staff (2010) found that alcohol intoxication played its strongest role in crimes that involved personal confrontation. (For details on gender and race/ethnicity differences in the role of alcohol in offending, see Felson et al., 2007.)

Within-individual analyses have shown that individuals are violent more often on days when they are drinking than when they are not (Chermack & Blow, 2002; Felson, Teasdale, & Burchfield, 2008; Mulvey et al., 2006). In a study of barroom violence, Leonard, Collins, and Quigley (2003) found that the belief that alcohol causes aggression rather than alcohol use was associated with the occurrence of aggression but not the severity of aggression. In contrast, heavy drinking by the perpetrator was associated with severity of aggression. Using emergency room data from six different countries, Macdonald, Cherpitel, Borges, DeSouza, Giesbrecht, and Stockwell (2005) found a dose response relationship between blood alcohol concentration (until extreme intoxication) and violent injuries even after controlling for demographic and situational factors. The location of the drinking was even a stronger predictor than the amount of alcohol consumed, again supporting the importance of contextual factors. Wells, Thompson, Cherpitel, MacDonald, Marais, and Borges (2007) conducted a similar cross-national study and also found a relationship between drinking in the event and greater violent injury. Although men were more likely to be drinking heavier than women before a violent injury, compared with a nonviolent injury, when heavy drinking was controlled, there was no gender difference in the association between drinking in the event and violent injury. Data from the U.S. indicated that frequent heavy drinking was more strongly associated with a violent injury for women than men, suggesting that heavy drinking women are at greater risk of violent victimization (see Wells et al., 2007, for more information about gender differences in other studies).

Alcohol and aggression among adolescents. Several community studies of adolescents have also assessed self reports of drinking and using drugs at the time of committing various offenses. Menard and Mihalic (2001) found support for a situational association between alcohol use, but not drug use, and violent index offending during adolescence and emerging adulthood. Overall, alcohol's pharmacological effects were strongest for violent offenses, vandalism, and public disorder offenses but were not significant for most other offenses in both adolescence and emerging adulthood.

White, Tice, Loeber, and Stouthamer-Loeber (2002) examined self-reported proximal associations between alcohol and drug use and illegal activities for young men from age 16 through 19. Violent, compared with property, offenses were committed more often under the influence of alcohol and drugs. The researchers could not separate alcohol from drugs, although when they limited the analyses to only alcohol users, the results remained the same. White et al. also found that more adolescents reported an association between alcohol and fighting than between marijuana and fighting (see also White & Hansell, 1998).

A study of incarcerated youth in New South Wales reported that the most frequently used drug prior to committing a violent offense was alcohol followed by cocaine (Lennings, Copeland, & Howard, 2003). Using individual-level analyses, Felson and colleagues (2008) found support for a causal effect of alcohol intoxication on fighting among adolescents; however, the results indicated that alcohol had a greater effect on individuals with violent tendencies than those without, which is consistent with findings from experimental studies (see later).

Alcohol and sexual assault. About one-half of all sexual assaults involve drinking by the perpetrator and/or victim (Abbey, Zawacki, Buck, Clinton, & McAuslan, 2001; Home Office, 2004b; Ullman, Karabastos, & Koss, 1999). Across studies of offenders, rates of alcohol use by adult rapists vary from 13% to 63% and for juvenile sex offenders from 3% to 72% (Testa, 2002). However, data from victimization surveys indicate that about 60% to 65% of sexual assault incidents involve alcohol or drug use by the perpetrator and 35% to 55% involve use by the victim. There is a much stronger association between alcohol or drug use and sexual assault on a date than in other situations (Testa, 2002).

In a national study of college students, Koss (1988) found that about three-fourths of the rape perpetrators and over half of the victims had been drinking alcohol (with or without use of another drug). Most of the incidents of sexual assault among college students are perpetrated by someone the victim knows and about half occur on a date (Abbey, 2002). In college rape cases, it is most common that if one person is drinking then the other is also drinking. Sexual assaults involving alcohol, compared with those that do not, are more likely to occur between men and women who do not know each other well and tend to occur outside the home (Abbey et al., 2001). Data are conflicting as to whether alcohol affects the seriousness of the assault (i.e., completed rape compared with noncompleted rape or coercion) and the seriousness of injuries (Abbey, Zawacki, Buck, Clinton, & McAuslan, 2004); effects depend on who has been drinking, the nature of the relationship, and the amount of victim resistance (Brecklin & Ullman, 2002; Testa, 2002). Overall, it appears that drinking by victims may be a better predictor of sexual assault outcomes than drinking by perpetrators (Abbey et al., 2001). (For a discussion of methodological issues in studying the relationship between alcohol and sexual aggression, see Testa, 2002.)

Abbey (2002) developed a model to explain the situational effects of alcohol on sexual assaults. This model combines the cognitive disruption of alcohol on communication and attention to cues, the anxiolytic effects of alcohol, beliefs about the effects of alcohol, motor impairment due to alcohol, and peer norms that encourage heavy drinking and forced sex. In this model, alcohol use by both parties interacts with beliefs and situational factors to increase the likelihood of sexual assault.

Alcohol and IPV. Alcohol is also involved in about 25% to 50% of all incidents of IPV (Home Office, 2004a; Leonard, 2000, 2008; Sanmartin, Molina, & Garcia, 2003). One study of IPV found that husband drinking during the event was predictive of physical violence, whereas wife drinking was not predictive once husband drinking was controlled (Leonard & Quigley, 1999). This association held even with controls for sociodemographic characteristics, personality characteristics, chronic drinking patterns, and event characteristics. Drinking during the event was also predictive of more severe episodes of violence. Other studies have also found that drinking during an event is predictive of more serious forms of IPV and more serious injury (e.g., Murphy, Winters, O'Farrell, Fals-Stewart, & Murphy, 2005; Thompson & Kingree, 2006).

Thompson and Kingree (2006) compared IPV to nonIPV physical assaults using data from the National Survey of Violence Against Women. They found that, for women, alcohol use by the perpetrator was twice as likely in IPV compared with non-IPV assaults, whereas for men, alcohol use by the perpetrator was four times less likely in IPV than non-IPV incidents. Furthermore, for female victims, use was more common in non-IPV than IPV victimization, whereas for men there was no difference. (For greater detail on situational associations of alcohol and IPV, see Derrick & Leonard in this volume.)

Alcohol and property crime. Little research has focused on the role of alcohol in property offenses. Generally, robbery is considered a violent crime because it involves force. However, several researchers include it as a property crime because it involves income generation (e.g., Gottfredson et al., 2008). Situational use of alcohol is implicated in about one-third of robberies, as well as one-third of other income-generating crimes, such as burglary and theft. In the 2002 survey of jail inmates, 38% reported committing a robbery under the influence of alcohol, 29% a burglary, 29% larceny theft, and 35% motor vehicle theft (Karberg & James,

2005). In general, alcohol use occurs more often in income-generating crimes that are more, compared with less, impulsive and are committed in groups, compared with alone (Collins & Messerschmidt, 1993). In contrast, planned crimes by professional criminals who make a living from their criminal activities are less likely than unplanned crimes to be committed under the influence of alcohol. Drinking also increases the probability of a person being a victim of a robbery, possibly because the person is less likely to protect him/herself and his/her judgment may be disrupted (Collins & Messerschmidt, 1993).

Individual differences. Gender, age, and ethnicity differences in the situational association between alcohol and crime have been observed. Rates of alcohol-related violent offenses are higher for males than for females, and highest in the 20- to 30-year-old age group compared with younger or older samples (Collins & Messerschmidt, 1993). Although absolute rates of violent crime are lower for women, Martin and Bryant (2001) found that alcohol intoxication was a stronger predictor of violence for female, compared with male arrestees (see also Nunes-Dinis & Weisner, 1997). In 2002, more male (35%) than female (22%) jail inmates were under the influence of alcohol at the time of their offense. In that same survey, more whites (39%) than blacks (29%) or Hispanics (30%) were under the influence of alcohol at the time of their offense (Karberg & James, 2005). Generally, rates of violence under the influence of alcohol have been found to be somewhat higher for whites than blacks (Greenfeld & Henneberg, 2001; Swahn & Donovan, 2006). In contrast, Caetano, Cunradi, Schafer, and Clark (2000) found that drinking during an IPV event was more frequent among blacks than among whites, independent of gender and socioeconomic status (SES), and that rates of male-to-female IPV were higher among male binge drinkers than male abstainers, especially for blacks.

Besides demographic characteristics, individual personality and temperament have been found to be significant moderators of the effects of alcohol on violence. In fact, one of the most consistent findings is that individuals with aggressive tendencies (e.g., hostility, trait anger) are more likely than those without to act aggressively under the influence of alcohol (Leonard, 2008; Norström & Pape, 2010). Similarly, antisocial personality disorder increases the likelihood of behaving aggressively under the influence of alcohol (Moeller & Dougherty, 2001). It is possible that the interaction of these personality traits with alcohol is not linear. Instead, alcohol's influence on aggression may be a function of an individual's threshold for aggression (Leonard, 2001). Because alcohol increases the risks for violence by lowering aggression thresholds, individuals who are near the threshold would be pushed over the threshold when they drink. In contrast, those already over the threshold (e.g., highly aggressive individuals) would not be affected by alcohol. Those far from the threshold would also not be influenced by alcohol. Low ECF has also been shown to increase the effects of alcohol on violence (Giancola, 2004). (For greater detail on individual moderators see Chermack & Giancola, 1997, and Leonard, 2008.)

Environmental differences. Besides individual characteristics, environmental factors moderate the association between alcohol use and violence. For example, certain characteristics of bars (e.g., loud noise, inconvenient access routes, poor ventilation, overcrowding, permissive social environments, and aggressive staff) make them more conducive for fighting and aggression than other bars (Graham, Schmidt, & Gillis, 1995; Home Office, 2004c; Roberts, 2007). Drinking contexts may contribute to aggression directly in terms of the types of activities that occur (e.g., competitive games) and exposure to situations that trigger aggression (e.g., drunkenness in others), as well as indirectly by affecting the amount of alcohol that is consumed (e.g., bars differ in their norms regarding appropriate drinking levels) (Wells, Graham, Speechley, & Koval, 2005). Overall, the research suggests that alcohol-related aggression is most likely to occur at settings away from home where excessive drinking is normative, where fewer social guardians are available, and where there are fewer proscriptive norms about socially appropriate behavior (Wells et al., 2005), although findings differ somewhat for men and women (Quigley & Leonard, 2004/2005; Wells et al., 2007). In the U.K., violence occurs most often around pubs and clubs on weekend nights and rates of violence are especially high around pub closing times as crowds of intoxicated strangers (mostly young males) converge on the street at the same time (Home Office, 2004c; see also Brower & Carroll, 2007). In sum, situational factors, such as location, access, and type of clientele, can contribute to a situational relationship between alcohol use and violence (see Boles & Miotto, 2003; Fagan, 1993; Wells et al., 2005).

Summary. As stated earlier, alcohol is more often consumed when committing a violent crime than a property crime. In a meta-analysis of studies examining all types of alcohol-violence relationships, Lipsey, Wilson, Cohen, and Derzon (1997) reported significant, although very modest, effect sizes for situational associations (weighted mean correlation = .10). Furthermore, when studies controlled for confounding variables (including demographic characteristics, other drug use, and risk factors for violence, such as childhood abuse, childhood aggression, and criminal status), the alcohol–violence correlation was reduced substantially. Correlations were higher in samples of youth (under age 21) than in samples of adults. Lipsey et al. (1997) argued that the existing studies do not establish a causal relationship. In contrast, Room and Rossow (2001) claimed that there is enough empirical evidence to support a causal relationship between alcohol use and violence. They suggested that the relationship is neither necessary nor sufficient, but rather is conditional. In other words, drinking in combination with other factors causes incidents of violent behavior. More support for a situational association between alcohol and violence is presented later under Experimental Studies.

DRUG USE AND CRIME

Overall, the research supports a stronger situational association between drug use and property crime than drug use and violent crime. Likewise, data from adult arrestees and prisoners in the U.S. and abroad indicate that drug use is more strongly associated with property crime, whereas alcohol use is more strongly associated with violent crime (Dorsey, Zawitz, & Middleton, 2002; EMCDDA, 2004; Karberg & James, 2005; Martin & Bryant, 2001; Valdez, Yin, & Kaplan, 1997). Furthermore, some research suggests that situational use of certain drugs (e.g., cocaine) in combination with alcohol may increase risks for violence (Chermack & Blow, 2002; Martin & Bryant, 2001).

Crimes committed under the influence of drugs. About one-fourth to one-third of incarcerated individuals reported being under the influence of drugs at the time of committing their offense (32% of 2004 state prisoners, 26% of 2004 federal prisoners, and 29% of 2002 jail inmates) (Karberg & James, 2005; Mumola & Karberg, 2006). In 2002, jail inmates reported that they were under the influence of drugs in 20% of homicides, 13% of rapes, 18% of assaults, 39% of robberies, 32% of larcenies, 41% of burglaries, and 40% of motor vehicle thefts (Karberg & James, 2005). Rates for 2004 state prisoners were similar: 27% of homicides,

17% of rapes, 24% of assaults, 40% of robberies, 40% of larcenies, 41% of burglaries, and 39% of motor vehicle thefts, but slightly lower for most categories for 2004 federal prisoners: 17% of homicides, 14% of rapes, 20% of assaults, 29% of robberies, and 14% of all property crimes (Mumola & Karberg, 2006). Overall, jail (33% versus 22%, respectively) and state (39% versus 28%, respectively) inmates were more likely to commit property than violent crimes under the influence of drugs, although rates were somewhat lower for property than violent offenses among Federal prisoners (14% versus 26%, respectively) (Karberg & James, 2005; Mumola & Karberg, 2006). Marijuana and cocaine were the most often cited drugs. Among jail inmates in 2002, female inmates were more likely to have used drugs than alcohol at the time of their offense, whereas male inmates were more likely to have used alcohol. Whites compared with ethnic/racial minorities were more likely to have used both alcohol and drugs prior to their offense. Older inmates were more likely to have used alcohol before their offense, whereas younger inmates were more likely to have used drugs (Karberg & James, 2005).

Distinctions between alcohol and drugs and types of crimes are not as apparent for adolescent as adult offenders. In 1993, 8% and 10%, respectively, of all youth in custody in state institutions reported that they were under the influence of only alcohol when they committed a violent or a property crime (U.S. Department of Justice, 1994). Similarly, 12% committed a violent offense and 17% a property crime while under the influence of only drugs. Approximately one-fourth committed property or violent crimes while under the influence of both drugs and alcohol.

As stated before, use of drugs at the time of crime commission might simply reflect more frequent use of drugs among criminal offenders rather than a causal effect of drug use on crime commission. In fact, criminal justice statistics indicate that offenders are more frequent drug users than the rest of the population (Dorsey et al., 2002), and this finding holds for men and women (Graham & Wish, 1994), as well as for adolescents (Dembo et al., 1990; see Global Associations later).

Drug use and victimization. Drug use is also associated with being a victim of a violent crime. A study in the U.S. in the early 1990s found that about half of all victims of homicide had drugs (usually cocaine) in their system (U.S. Department of Justice, 1992). Similarly, a study of sexual assault victims in the U.K. found that sexual assault victims had much higher rates of cocaine, ecstasy, and amphetamines in their systems, compared with general population rates (Scott-Ham & Burton, 2005). The association between being drugged and being a victim of sexual assault has gained lot of attention in the media and certain "date-rape-drugs" (e.g., flunitrazepam [Rohypnol], gamma-hydroxybutyrate [GHB], and ketamine) have been implicated in a number of assaults. However, a recent review of the literature that included toxicology reports (of blood or urine) on sexual assault victims concluded that covert use of these drugs accounts for as little as 2% of all sexual assaults (Beynon, McVeigh, McVeigh, Leavey, & Bellis, 2008). Furthermore, in most instances, those who tested positive for date-rape-drugs also had other drugs in their systems such as alcohol and marijuana.

EXPERIMENTAL STUDIES

Much of the empirical evidence supporting a situational association between substance use (especially alcohol use) and aggression has come from laboratory studies of animals and humans. While studies of animals demonstrate that low to moderate doses of alcohol increase aggressive responding, there are many problems in generalizing from animal aggression to human violence (see Miczek et al., 1994). Studies of humans only are briefly discussed next.

Substance use and general aggression. Experimental studies typically use the Taylor Aggression Paradigm (TAP; Taylor, 1967) to examine the association between substance (usually alcohol) use and aggression. In the TAP, subjects compete against a fictitious opponent in a reaction time task. Subjects administer shocks to their "opponents" when they win and receive a shock from the fictitious opponent when they lose. The average shock level and duration of shocks are used as indicators of aggression. The effects of alcohol on aggression are assessed by comparing shock levels and duration of shocks administered between sober and intoxicated subjects or within subjects when they are sober compared with when they are intoxicated (Giancola, 2002; for a discussion of other experimental paradigms, see Chermack & Giancola, 1997; Gustafson, 1993). Although there are several methodological issues, which make it difficult to generalize from the laboratory to real world situations (for a review, see White & Gorman, 2000), the existing data provide support for the validity of the results from experimental studies (Giancola, 2002). In most studies, subjects are randomly assigned to either a control condition (in which they are given an nonalcoholic beverage to drink), a placebo condition (in which they are told that they drank alcohol but are given a nonalcoholic beverage to drink), and an alcohol condition (in which they are told that they drank alcohol and are given an alcoholic beverage to drink). A few studies use a fourth condition, anti-placebo, in which subjects are told that they drank a nonalcoholic beverage but are given an alcoholic beverage to drink.

Controlled experimental laboratory studies have consistently found that subjects in the alcohol condition react more aggressively than those in the control or placebo conditions especially when provoked (Bushman, 1997; Giancola, 2002). That is, subjects who drank alcohol administered higher shock intensity levels and longer shock durations compared with those in the placebo or control conditions. Thus, this experimental research clearly supports the fact that acute intoxication increases aggressive behavior. In contrast, experimental studies have not found strong placebo effects, suggesting that expectancies do not play a large role in causing aggressive responding in laboratory situations (Leonard, 2008).

Results from experimental studies indicate that the effects of alcohol use on aggression are moderated by subject characteristics, experimental design conditions, and beverage characteristics (e.g., dose, type) (Chermack & Giancola, 1997; Gustafson, 1993; Ito et al., 1996; Pihl et al., 1993). Design conditions that have been found to increase aggression include: aggressive cues, provocation, frustration, pain and discomfort, and incentives (Leonard, 2008). Subject characteristics that increase aggressive responding include anger proneness, irritability, aggressive attitudes, and poor ECF. In contrast, subject characteristics that mitigate against aggression include empathy and self-control (Leonard, 2008). Most laboratories studies have found a stronger effect of alcohol on aggression for men compared with women (Leonard, 2008). (For greater detail on experimental studies of alcohol and aggression, see Bushman, 1997; Giancola, 2002; Ito et al., 1996.)

Besides alcohol, other anxiolytic drugs such as benzodiazepines have been shown to increase aggressive responding in experimental studies (Blanchard et al., 1993; Lundholm et al., 2013). However, for the most part, common street drugs, such as marijuana, heroin, and cocaine have not, although the effects of specific drugs on violence often depend on dosage (Haggård-Grann et al., 2006; Miczek et al., 1994). In fact, laboratory studies indicate that marijuana and opiates have the opposite effect of alcohol in that moderate doses temporarily inhibit aggression and violence, although withdrawal from opiates increases aggression. (For a review of specific drug effects on aggression, see Anthony & Forman, 2003; Boles & Miotto, 2003; Miczek et al., 1994; Moore & Stuart, 2005; Parker & Auerhahn, 1998.) However, few laboratory studies of drug effects on aggression have been conducted with the sophisticated controls that alcohol studies have included (MacCoun et al., 2003).

Alcohol and sexual aggression. Several experimental studies have also assessed the role of alcohol in sexual aggression using various paradigms. These paradigms often involve watching pornography, reacting to vignettes about a sexual encounter between a man and woman, or observations of interactions between men and women. Most of this research has been conducted on college students. In general, the results show that both intoxication and expectancies of alcohol consumption affect outcomes (Abbey et al., 2001; Testa, 2002). This finding is interesting given that, for the most part, the experimental studies of alcohol effects on physical aggression have not found strong support for placebo effects. However, most laboratory studies of physical aggression have not examined the moderating effects of individually held alcohol aggression expectancies on the placebo condition. That is, it may be that the expectation of drinking alcohol in the laboratory only affects those individuals who have preexisting expectancies that alcohol increases aggression. For example in a laboratory study of placebo effects of alcohol on sexual behavior, George, Stoner, Norris, Lopez, and Lehman (2000) found strong placebo effects only among those who also held strong beliefs about alcohol's capacity to disinhibit or enhance sexual experience.

SUMMARY OF SITUATIONAL ASSOCIATIONS

In sum, survey and experimental research provide strong evidence of a situational relationship between alcohol use and violence, thus supporting a psychopharmacological model. Chermack and Giancola (1997) developed a conceptual model to explain the role of alcohol in situational violence. They proposed that alcohol-related aggression is a multidetermined phenomenon influenced by the interaction of developmental risk factors (temperament, ECF, family aggression, peer influences), alcohol-related factors (acute effects such as cognitive impairment), psychological factors (psychiatric symptoms, attitudes toward aggression, affective and motivation states), and contextual influences (provocation, setting, relationship type).

On the other hand, a psychopharmacological model cannot explain much of the relationship between most types of drug use and violent or property crime. Rather, the systemic model accounts for a great deal of drug-related violence and the economic motivation model accounts for some drug-related property crimes. At the individual level, systemic and economic explanations often depend on chronic use patterns and types of drugs being used; these global associations are reviewed next.

Global Associations

In this section data on the global associations between patterns of substance use and offending are discussed, first examining alcohol use and crime and then drug use and crime. Next, findings from longitudinal within-subject studies examining the developmental associations between substance use and crime over time are described. Finally, findings from studies that have examined these associations within larger contexts are summarized.

ALCOHOL USE AND CRIME

Alcohol use, alcohol use disorders, and criminal offending. As mentioned earlier, offenders are heavier drinkers than the rest of the population. In 1996, about one-third of jail inmates were daily drinkers (Greenfeld, 1998), compared with less than 5% of adults (19- to 28-years-old) in the community, surveyed at the same point in time (Johnston, O'Malley, Bachman, & Schulenberg, 2007). Almost half of jail inmates met the criteria for alcohol abuse or dependence in 2002 (Karberg & James, 2005). The highest rates of abuse and dependence were among those who committed assault (58%), burglary (54%), and robbery (53%). In contrast, across five national general population surveys, less than 10% of the participants met the criteria for current abuse or dependence on alcohol (Ross, 2008). White, compared with black, offenders reported higher rates of binge drinking and alcohol problems (Greenfeld & Henneberg, 2001). In a U.K. national sample, Coid et al. (2006) found that alcohol dependence was associated with the occurrence of violence, as well as with greater injury to the perpetrator and victim (see also Kraanen et al., 2012).

Alcohol use, sexual assaults, and intimate partner violence. Sexual assault is another type of violence that is associated with alcohol use patterns. In 2002,

a little over one-third of jail inmates who committed sexual assaults met the criteria for alcohol abuse or dependence, which, while higher than the general population, was much lower than all other types of offenders (Karberg & James, 2005; see also Kraanen et al., 2012). Young men and adult men who perpetrate sexual assault are more like to be heavy drinkers than those who do not perpetrate sexual assault (Abbey et al., 2001; Brown & Burton, 2010), although their rates of drinking problems are similar to those committing nonsexual violent offenses (Testa, 2002). Testa suggested that the higher rates of alcohol dependence among men who commit sexual assault might simply reflect higher levels of psychopathology and deviance. Victims of sexual assault also tend to be heavy drinkers. (For greater detail on alcohol and sexual assault, see Abbey, 2002; Abbey et al., 2001, 2004; Testa, 2002.)

There is also an association between drinking patterns and IPV. Specifically, excessive drinkers and alcoholics are more likely than lighter drinkers and nondrinkers to act violently toward their intimate partners (Leonard, 2000). Furthermore, a number of studies have found that heavy drinking predicts later domestic violence and that reductions in drinking among alcoholics are related to reductions in domestic violence (Leonard, 2000). In general, the association between drinking behavior and IPV appears to hold for men and women even when common risk factors are controlled (Leonard & Blane, 1992; Leonard & Senchak, 1996; White & Chen, 2002). Testa and colleagues (2012), however, found that both husbands' and wives' drinking had a stronger association with IPV perpetration by men than by women. Studies have also found that drinking problems among men and women are associated with increased risk of male-to-female IPV even with controls for sociodemographic and psychosocial variables (Cunradi, Caetano, & Schafer, 2002; Testa et al., 2012). Cunradi and colleagues (2002) suggested that drinking problems may elevate marital discord, fights, and verbal aggression, which, in turn, may increase the risks for IPV. However, Johnson (2000) found that when attitudes about the rightness of male degradation and control of women were controlled, heavy drinking was no longer a predictor of male-to-female IPV. Female victims of IPV are also heavy and problem drinkers and this relationship appears to be reciprocal. That is, problem drinking women are more likely to experience IPV than non–problem drinking women; however, being a victim of IPV increases the risks for developing alcohol and drug problems (Miller, Wilsnack, &

Cunradi, 2000; Waller Iritani, Christ et al., 2012). Heavier drinking males are also more likely to experience IPV (Waller, Iritani, Flewelling et al., 2012). (For greater detail on global associations between alcohol use and IPV, see Derrick & Leonard in this volume and Wekerle & Wall, 2002.)

Summary. There is strong evidence that offenders are heavier drinkers and report higher rates of alcohol dependence than community populations. As stated earlier, this global association between alcohol use and crime may simply reflect a higher risk for being intoxicated in a specific situation and, thereby, experiencing cognitive impairment, which increases aggressive and impulsive behavior (Leonard, 2008). Alternatively, the global association might reflect a general underlying deviance syndrome.

DRUG USE AND CRIME

High rates of drug use and abuse among offenders have been found in the U.S. and abroad (Boles & Miotto, 2003; EMCDDA, 2004; Kraanen et al., 2012). In general, heavier drug users are more likely to commit property than violent offenses, whereas heavier drinkers are more likely to commit violent than property offenses (Valdez et al., 1997).

Drug use and criminal offending. ADAM data from 2010 indicated that (depending on city) between 52% and 80% of male adult arrestees tested positive for any illicit drug (i.e., marijuana, crack or powder cocaine, opiates, methamphetamine, or PCP) at the time of their arrest (Office of National Drug Control Policy, 2011). These rates for men had not changed much since 2000 when rates for female adult arrestees testing positive for any illicit drug were between 38% and 81% (http://www.ncjrs.org/pdffiles1/nij/193013.pdf). (Note that rates at the time of the arrest do not necessarily indicate use at the time of the crime commission.) In comparison, in a recent national household survey, 17% of men and 11% of women aged 18 and older reported past year illicit drug use (http://www.oas.samhsa.gov/NSDUH/2k7NSDUH/tabs/LOTSect1pe.htm). Marijuana and cocaine are the drugs most often identified in arrestee urine; in 2003 rates were slightly higher for marijuana than cocaine among men, but higher for cocaine than marijuana among women (Zhang, 2003). For juvenile arrestees, marijuana was found to be the most commonly used drug with cocaine a distant second (U.S. Department of Justice, 2002).

Self reports from jail inmates also indicate very high rates of illicit drug use. In 2002, 82% reported ever using an illicit drug and two-thirds were regular users (i.e., used at least once a week for a month) (Karberg & James, 2005). In contrast, in a national household survey of adults 18 and older, 54% of the men and 44% of the women reported lifetime use of an illicit drug; only 10% of men and 5% of women reported past month illicit drug use (http://www.oas.samhsa.gov/NSDUH/2k7NSDUH/tabs/LOTSect1pe.htm).

Not only are there high rates of substance use among offenders, but there are also high rates of offending among substances users. The strength of these global associations, however, depends on the type of substance used. In a meta-analysis, Bennett and colleagues (2008) found that the odds of any type of offending were 3 to 4 times higher in drug users than nonusers and higher odds among drug users held for robbery (1.7 times the odds), burglary (2 to 3 times), prostitution (about 3 times), and shoplifting (4 to 6 times). Crack users, compared with nonusers of crack, had the highest odds of offending (6 times), followed by heroin (3.5 times) and cocaine (2.6 times) users. Marijuana users (1.5 times) and amphetamine users (1.9 times) had the lowest odds. Only a few studies identified in the meta-analysis directly compared men and women and found that the odds of committing a crime for drug users, compared with nonusers, were higher for women than men. In addition, the odds were higher for samples of adults than samples of juveniles. The analysis also indicated that the association between drug use and crime has been growing stronger over time from the 1980s until the 2000s. Bennett and Halloway (2005) found that multiple drug users committed more crimes than single drug users even among heroin, crack, and cocaine users. They attributed this finding to the cost of using many expensive drugs or to an excessive lifestyle.

Drug use disorders and criminal offending. Offenders also report higher rates of substance use disorders than nonoffenders. In 2002, more than half of jail inmates met the criteria for abuse or dependence on drugs (Karberg & James, 2005) compared with less than 4% of adults who met the criteria for a current diagnosis and less than 14% who met the criteria for a lifetime diagnosis of drug abuse or dependence across five U.S. national studies (Ross, 2008). Female jail inmates in the U.S. were significantly more likely to meet the criteria for drug (61%) than alcohol (39%) dependence or abuse, whereas male inmates were only slightly more likely (54% and 50%, respectively) (Karberg & James, 2005). In addition, whites were more likely to report substance use disorders than other ethnic/racial groups. Property offenders (62%) were more likely than violent offenders (48%) to meet the criteria for drug abuse or dependence. The highest rates of drug abuse or dependence were among those who committed burglary or robbery and the lowest rate was among sexual offenders. Abracen, Looman, and Anderson (2000) found that male sexual offenders were more likely to abuse alcohol, whereas nonsexual violent offenders were more likely to abuse illicit drugs. Data from the 2003 ADAM survey indicated that, across cities, a median of 39% of male and 41% of female arrestees were at risk for drug dependence (Zhang, 2003), compared with 4% of adults in a national household survey who reported dependence on illicit drugs in the past year (http://www.oas.samhsa.gov/NSDUH/2k7NSDUH/tabs/LOTSect1pe.htm). Similarly high rates of substance abuse have been found among juvenile offenders. In one study of juvenile detainees, almost half reported one or more substance use disorder and one in five reported two or more disorders (McClelland, Elkinton, Teplin, & Abram, 2004).

Whereas data on situational associations between marijuana use and violence are equivocal, there is strong evidence from correlational studies that marijuana users report higher rates of violence than nonusers and that marijuana-dependent persons report higher rates of violent crime than those not dependent even with controls for alcohol dependence, sex, and SES (Moore & Stuart, 2005). However, Macdonald, Erickson, Wells, Hathaway, and Pakula (2008) found that clients in treatment for cocaine reported the most involvement in violent incidents (57%) and those in treatment for marijuana reported the least (27%).

Drug use and IPV. There has been much less research linking drug use than alcohol use to IPV, although some studies have examined drug use among perpetrators and/or victims. Stuart, Temple, Follansbee, Bucossi, Hellmuth, and Moore (2008) examined the role of drug use in IPV among a sample of men and women who were arrested for IPV. They found that past year illicit drug use rates for victims and perpetrators were much higher than those in general population surveys. In multivariate models, illicit drug use was a significant predictor of perpetration even with controls for perpetrator and victim alcohol problems, personality factors known to predict violence, and marital discord. In fact, illicit drug use was a stronger predictor than alcohol problems for physical IPV. They found that

stimulant and marijuana use were significant for male perpetration, but found no differences among drugs for female perpetration.

Other research supports their findings. For example, Magdol, Moffitt, Caspi, and Silva (1997) found that emerging adults who perpetrated IPV against cohabiting or dating partners were more like to use more types of illicit drugs than nonperpetrators and Pan, Neidig, and O'Leary (1994) found that drug problems were associated with an increased risk of severe but not nonsevere IPV. Moore and Stuart's (2005) review indicated that marijuana use is highly prevalent among men who engage in IPV and Smith, Homish, Leonard, and Cornelius (2012) found that women with a marijuana use disorder, compared to those without, were more likely to perpetrate IPV. Finally, Logan, Walker, Staton, and Leukefeld (2001) found that regular and frequent use of cocaine was related to physical IPV among a sample of incarcerated substance abusers (see also Stuart et al., 2008, and Derrick & Leonard in this volume).

Use of illicit drugs (such as cocaine and opiates) among women has been related to IPV victimization (Testa, Livingston, & Leonard, 2003). In fact, women in drug treatment report higher rates of IPV victimization than those in the community (Miller et al., 2000). In a community study, Cunradi, Caetano, and Shafer (2002) found that male drug use was not associated with male perpetration of IPV but that female drug use was significantly related to being the victim of moderate and severe IPV and these results held after controls for demographic, psychosocial, and neighborhood variables. Stuart and colleagues (2008) demonstrated that stimulant use was related to IPV victimization for both men and women. (For greater detail on IPV and drug use see the chapter by Derrick & Leonard in this volume.)

Drug use and delinquency in adolescence. In adolescent samples, studies examining the association between various stages of drug use and delinquency have reported a high degree of synchrony in progression. Abstainers and alcohol-only users are most likely to be nondelinquents; those who use alcohol and marijuana, compared with only alcohol, are more likely to be delinquent; and those who progress to the use of other drugs, compared with those who do not, are most likely to have also progressed to involvement in more serious forms of delinquency (see Elliott, Huizinga, & Menard, 1989; Fagan, Weis, Cheng, & Watters, 1987; White, Johnson, & Garrison, 1985). Yet, these types of analyses have also indicated that there are several heterogeneous groups of adolescents; for some drug use and delinquency are closely related and for others they are independent of each other (see Fagan et al., 1987; White et al., 1987; White & Labouvie, 1994). In addition, the strength of the associations between substance use and delinquency depends on the severity of the delinquency and the types of substances used (Fagan Weis, & Cheng, 1988; White & Hansell, 1998), as well as the age, sex, and nature of the sample examined (Huizinga & Jakob-Chien, 1998).

LONGITUDINAL ASSOCIATIONS

Many studies have examined the global associations between substance use and crime using longitudinal data. In terms of temporal order, generally onset of aggressive behavior developmentally precedes onset of alcohol and drug use (Farrington, 1995; Robins, 1970; White et al., 1993; Windle, 1990) and onset of serious violent offending often precedes onset of illicit drug use (e.g., White et al., 2008).

Heavy drinking in adolescence has been predictive of both violent and property offending in later adolescence and adulthood (Fergusson & Horwood, 2000; Menard & Mihalic, 2001; Orlando, Tucker, Ellickson, & Klein, 2005; Swahn & Donovan, 2006). In general, trajectories of alcohol and marijuana use characterized by high use and early onset or increasing use over time are associated with young adult and adult antisocial and criminal behavior (Brook, Zhang & Brook, 2011; Hill, White, Chung, Hawkins, & Catalano, 2000; Lynne-Landsman, Bradshaw, & Ialongo, 2010; Tucker, Ellickson, Orlando, Martino, & Klein, 2005).

Similarly, results from several studies indicate that individuals, especially males, who were aggressive in childhood or adolescence, were more likely to be heavier drinkers in adolescence and adulthood (Farrington, 1995; White et al., 1993; White & Hansell, 1996). Hill, Chung, Herrenkohl, and Hawkins (2000, as cited in Weisner, Kim, & Capaldi, 2005) found that adolescent chronic property offenders, compared with nonoffenders, were more likely to exhibit drug, but not alcohol, dependence in emerging adulthood (age 21), whereas chronic violent offenders, compared with nonoffenders, were more likely to exhibit later alcohol dependence. Using the same data set, Mason, Hitch, Kosterman, McCarty, Herrenkohl, and Hawkins' (2010) results indicated that adolescent

delinquency was predictive of alcohol dependence in young adulthood, although the association was stronger for low-income, compared with middle-income, youth. Weisner and colleagues (2005) found that low-level and high-level chronic offenders (aged 12–24) reported higher rates of alcohol and drug use than nonoffenders and rare offenders at ages 23–26.

Thus, early drinking and drug use are predictive of later offending and early delinquency is predictive of later alcohol and drug problems. In fact, many studies support a reciprocal effect of substance use and criminal offending, especially during adolescence (Dembo, Williams, Wothke, & Schmeidler, 1994; Huang, White, Kosterman, Catalano, & Hawkins, 2001; Weisner et al., 2005; White et al., 1999). Mason and Windle (2002) tested a cross-lagged model of substance use (latent variable of alcohol, marijuana, and tobacco) on delinquency (latent variable of property damage, aggression, and theft) over four waves during adolescence. They found that substance use was more strongly related to later delinquency than delinquency was related to later substance use. However, the former relationship was only significant from wave 1 to wave 2, whereas the latter relationship was significant at all four waves. There were differences, however, by gender; the cross-lagged models were significant for boys but not for girls. Wei, Loeber, and White (2004) examined the associations between alcohol and marijuana use and violence among young men from ages 11 to 20. Frequent marijuana use, compared with frequent alcohol use, was more strongly related to later violence. When common risk factors, specifically race/ethnicity and hard drug use, were controlled, the relationship between frequent marijuana use and violence (and vice-versa) was no longer significant suggesting a spurious relationship. Therefore, the developmental associations between substance use and criminal offending, at least during adolescence, may simply reflect a common cause model, in which both behaviors are predicted by the same underlying risk factors.

Welte, Zhang, and Wieczorek (2001) found that early delinquency moderated the effects of substance use on crime. For those who reported early onset of delinquency, substance use was not related to later delinquency and early delinquency was not related to later substance use; however, for those who reported late onset of delinquency, there was a strong effect of earlier substance use on later delinquency and an effect of early delinquency on later substance use.

The strength of the developmental associations between alcohol and violence appear to depend on the age period studied, with the strongest association occurring during adolescence (Derzon & Lipsey, 1999; White, Mun, Lee, & Loeber, 2012). For example, White, Jackson, and Loeber (2009) found moderate associations between trajectories of drinking and violence during adolescence (aged 13–18), but no significant associations during emerging adulthood (aged 18–25). In addition, adolescent trajectories of violence did not predict emerging adult drinking and adolescent trajectories of drinking did not predict emerging adult violent offending (see also White et al., 2012).

Nevertheless, studies have shown that reductions in substance use in young adulthood may play a key role in de-escalation of offending (Hussong, Curran, Moffitt, Caspi, & Carrig, 2004; Kazemian, Farrington, & Le Blanc, 2009; Stoolmiller & Blechman, 2005) and that chronic use of substances impedes desistance from delinquency (e.g., Farrington & Hawkins, 1991; Kazemian et al., 2009). For example, Welte and colleagues (2005) found that drug use interfered with an early maturation out of delinquency and attributed this to involvement with deviant peers or involvement in drug dealing. In contrast, alcohol use and dependence were strongly related to an increasing trajectory of delinquency. Overall, the existing longitudinal research points to a reciprocal and complex relationship between substance use and crime over the life course, which is dependent on individual and environmental factors.

Furthermore, several within-subjects analyses have found that individuals commit more offenses at the same time in their lives when they are most involved with substances (Welte et al., 2005). For example, in a sample of male adolescents, White, Fite, Pardini, Mun, and Loeber (2013) found that, during adolescence, within-individual annual increases in alcohol use quantity from one's own typical levels of drinking were concurrently associated with within-individual increases in aggressive behavior, and vice versa. However, increases in alcohol were more strongly associated with increases in aggressive behavior among those with attitudes favoring violence and those who lived in high-crime neighborhoods. In contrast, within-individual increases in marijuana use were associated with decreases in aggressive behavior. Overall, their results indicated that the association between alcohol use and aggressive behavior varies depending on individual and contextual factors. The association

between alcohol and aggression did not differ for black and white young men. Similarly, White et al. (2012) found that, although patterns of drinking and violence differed for black and white young men, the association between heavy drinking and violent offending was similar for both races.

Mulvey, Odgers, Skeem, Gardner, Schubert, and Lidz (2006) conducted a within-subjects analysis of drug use and crime commission on a daily basis among a high-risk sample of adolescents and young adults recruited from the emergency department. Violent days were more likely to be substance-using days and vice versa, although the findings for marijuana use were weaker than for alcohol and other illicit drugs. In addition, there was no association between drug use (marijuana or other drug use) on one day and violence on the next, whereas drinking predicted next-day violence. In an adult offender population, Gottfredson and colleagues (2008) found that periods of reductions in cocaine/heroin and alcohol use were related to reductions in income-generating but not violent crime. In contrast, Horney, Osgood, and Marshall (1995) found that periods of illegal drug use were related to increases in drug dealing, property crime, and assault in a sample of male offenders. Consistent with Gottfredson et al., Horney et al. did not find a significant effect of periods of heavy drinking on violent crime.

In terms of IPV, longitudinal research has been inconsistent on whether drinking problems at one point in time predict IPV at a later point in time (Leonard, 2008). Nevertheless, men who remain sober after being treated for their alcohol dependence engage in less partner violence than men who return to drinking (Leonard, 2008). (See chapter by Derrick & Leonard in this volume for more detail.)

MACRO ASSOCIATIONS

Thus far in this chapter, the global associations between substance use and crime have been examined primarily at the individual or micro level (e.g., differences between offenders and nonoffenders or differences between drug users and nonusers). However, some researchers have examined these associations within larger contexts, such as neighborhood, cities, and countries (i.e., the macro level). Next, that research is briefly summarized.

Availability. One important environmental factor that affects the nature of the substance use-crime relationship is the availability of substances (see Golub & Johnson, 1999 and White & Gorman, 2000 for a discussion of drug epidemics and their effects on the drug-crime relationship). Rates of homicide and other forms of violence have been related to alcohol availability and per capita consumption at the societal and community level (Cook & Moore, 1993; Parker & Rebhun, 1995; Room & Rossow, 2001). Alcohol availability and per capita consumption have been found to predict violent crime in international, as well as in U.S. state, comparisons, although the strength of the relationship is reduced when other variables, such as poverty, are controlled (Parker, 1993). Studies conducted in Scandinavia have found reductions in interpersonal violence when alcohol availability and consumption have been reduced (Makela, Osterberg, & Sulkunen, 1981; Room & Rossow, 2001). Further, efforts to reduce drinking (e.g., by increasing the tax on alcohol) have been shown to decrease violent crime (Cook & Moore, 1993).

Several studies using city-level data in the U.S. have also demonstrated an association between alcohol availability and various forms of violence even after controlling for confounding factors (Gruenewald, Freisthler, Remer, LaScala, & Treno, 2006; Parker & Rebhun, 1995; Scribner, MacKinnon, & Dwyer, 1995). In addition, alcohol outlet density has been found to be a significant predictor of neighborhood variations in the level of violent crime in studies conducted in several U.S. cities (Alaniz, Cartmill, & Parker, 1998; Pridemore & Grubesic, 2013; Scribner, Cohen, Kaplan, & Allen, 1999; Speer, Gorman, Labouvie, & Ontkush, 1998; Toomey, Erickson, Carlin, Lenk, Quick, Jones, & Harwood, 2012). Furthermore, studies in the U.S. and abroad have demonstrated a positive association between offsite outlet density and IPV (Livingston, 2011; Roman & Reid, 2012). Thus, contextual factors play a major role in both situational and global associations between substance use and crime.

City trends. White and Gorman (2000) examined the associations between drug use and crime across U.S. cities by plotting annual crime rates (extracted from the Uniform Crime Reports) against drug-testing results from the ADAM data from 1989-1998. They found some evidence that cocaine use and violent crime were increasing and decreasing in the same years. The relationship between marijuana use and violence was primarily negative and relatively strong, whereas the relationship between violent crime and heroin use was weaker and less consistent. They also found that the association of property crime with cocaine use was mostly positive, with marijuana use mostly negative,

and with heroin use largely inconsistent. What was particularly noteworthy about their findings was the lack of consistency across cities. Thus, they concluded that that there was no uniform association between any type of drug use and any type of crime. Rather, the trends varied greatly from place to place. After conducting similar analyses, Martin, Maxwell, White, and Zhang (2004) found a much stronger association between alcohol and violent crime than alcohol and property crime, although they found no consistent association between either type of crime and cocaine use.

SUMMARY OF GLOBAL ASSOCIATIONS

There is clearly a strong association between being a substance user/abuser and being a criminal offender. Nevertheless, the strength of this association depends on individual and contextual factors, stage in the life cycle, type and stage of drug use, and type of crime.

Implications for Treatment and Prevention

This review suggests that there is a strong association between substance use and crime. Use of substances, like alcohol, increase individuals' propensity for acting aggressively and impulsively, which increases violent and impulsive crime. Use of illicit drugs, especially expensive and addictive drugs like heroin and cocaine, increases the need for income-generating crime and places individuals into situations within the illegal drug market that reinforce criminal behavior. Crime, especially violent crime, places a huge burden on society. Next, the costs of substance use-related crime are highlighted along with a brief discussion of intervention and prevention strategies to reduce substance use-related crime.

Societal Costs of Substance Use

Whereas property crimes account for a greater proportion of overall crime than violent crimes, violent crimes account for much higher comprehensive costs due to pain and suffering, lost quality of life, and lost future income (Miller, Levi, Cohen, & Cox, 2006). Other costs of violence are absorbed by social systems, including schools, the juvenile justice system, mental health agencies, and security systems in private, commercial, and educational premises. Miller and colleagues (2006) argued that the costs of crime attributed to drugs are half of that attributed to alcohol. They estimated that the costs attributed to the perpetrator's use of alcohol in 1999 were $83 billion, whereas those attributed to perpetrator drug use were $37 billion. In a press release following the publication of that study, Miller estimated that the costs for alcohol-related and drug-related crime in 2005 were $80 billion and $40 billion, respectively (Ponkshe, 2007). Note that these estimates do not include crimes in which the victim but not perpetrator was drinking or using drugs. Thus, heavy-drinking violent offenders and alcohol-related crimes place a large burden on the criminal justice system and on society.

Nevertheless, drug related-crimes also have a serious impact on society. Between 60% and 80% of all crime is drug related and 70%-80% of all released prisoners have drug-related problems (Deitch, Koutsenok, & Ruiz, 2000). French, McCollister, Alexandre, Chitwood, and McCoy (2004) found that the costs of crime were 3.5 times (11.5 times for perpetrators and 1.7 times for victims) greater for the average chronic drug user versus the average nonuser. Costs included victim costs, protection and enforcement costs, and lost productivity. In addition, French et al. noted there are psychological costs including fear and distress about becoming a victim in a crime. Thus, individuals who use drugs contribute a disproportion share of societal costs of crime.

Much of the costs of substance use-related crime can be attributed to individuals with substance abuse problems. As reported in the section on global associations, many offenders suffer from substance use disorders. Those inmates who meet the criteria for substance abuse or dependence are much more likely than other inmates to have a repetitive criminal record (Karberg & James, 2005). For example, in 2002, those inmates with abuse and dependence were twice as likely as other inmates to have had three or more prior probation or incarceration sentences. Although rates of inmates receiving treatment under correctional supervision have been increasing (Karberg & James, 2005), Belenko and Peugh (2005) estimated that about one-third of the men and one-half of the women in State prisons are in need of residential treatment. A survey in 2002 indicated that about two-thirds of jail inmates with substance abuse or dependence had received substance abuse treatment or participated in an alcohol or drug program in the past and many of them had participated while in jail or prison (Karberg & James, 2005). Given the higher rates of recidivism among substance-abusing inmates, it is obvious that current interventions are not working well. Therefore, it imperative that more effective treatment approaches are implemented.

Treatment Programs for Substance Abusing Offenders

There are several alternative treatment programs being used with offenders including therapeutic communities, counseling (psychosocial), supervision, twelve step programs (e.g., Alcoholics Anonymous [AA] and Narcotics Anonymous [NA]), drug courts, drug testing, narcotics maintenance or provision, and boot camps (for a description of the various treatment alternatives for offenders, see McBride, VanderWaal, & Terry-McElrath, 2003). Numerous evaluations of these programs and reviews of these evaluations have been published (e.g., Holloway, Bennett, & Farrington, 2008; Leukefeld & Tims, 1992; Mitchell, Wilson, & MacKenzie, 2007; see also the entire issue of the *Journal of Substance Abuse Treatment*, 2007, Vol. 32, no. 3). In general, the research indicates that one of the most effective interventions for offenders both within and outside the criminal justice system is therapeutic communities (TCs) (Halloway et al., 2008; Pearson & Lipton, 1999; Mitchell et al., 2007). TCs are "generally intensive, long-term, self-help-based, highly structure residential treatment programs" (McBride et al., 2003, p. 129). The least effective interventions are boot camps, which are highly structured programs modeled after military basic training in which participants engage in rigorous exercise regimens, drills, and challenge courses (Mitchell et al., 2007; Pearson & Lipton, 1999). Furthermore, although narcotics maintenance (e.g., methadone) programs may reduce substance use, there is little evidence to suggest that they reduce crime (Mitchell et al., 2007). In a large international (primarily U.S. studies) meta-analysis, Halloway et al. (2008) found that in more than two-thirds of all programs analyzed, the intervention group did better than the comparison group in terms of subsequent criminal offending, although not all of these differences were statistically significant. The mean effect size indicated a 26% reduction in criminal behavior. However, they found that only TCs and supervision produced significant reductions in crime (51% and 47%, respectively). Also, based on a narrative review (opposed to the meta-analysis), programs with some kind of psychosocial therapeutic method reported the best outcomes (Halloway et al., 2008). Overall, there is enough evidence to suggest that certain types of substance abuse treatment, especially TCs, are effective crime prevention strategies (Halloway et al., 2008; Lipton, Falkin, & Wexler, 1992). Therefore, greater effort should be made to provide evidence-based substance abuse treatment services to offenders.

Some people have questioned the ethics and effectiveness of mandatory treatment. However, studies have found that legally referred treatment is just as effective, if not more effective, than voluntary treatment (see Farabee, Prendergast, & Anglin, 1998 for a review). Further, Halloway et al.'s (2008) meta-analysis did not indicate any differences in outcomes between programs that were implemented within and outside the context of the criminal justice system.

Unfortunately, many offenders do not receive any treatment either within or outside of the criminal justice system; those who do most often receive substance abuse education/awareness or low-intensity (less than 4 hours per week) group counseling, all of which are not very effective (Taxman, Perdoni, & Harrison, 2007). Similarly, juveniles in corrections receive mostly educational services and these services are provided with little intensity or duration (Young, Dembo, & Henderson, 2007). In addition, because most aftercare programs vary in the quality of services and length of time, evaluation results on the added benefits of aftercare are equivocal (Pelissier, Jones, & Cadigan, 2007). Therefore, in order to reduce substance-related crime, it is not enough to simply provide services to offenders. Instead, services must use evidence-based practices, adhere to treatment fidelity, and be intensive enough to have an effect.

Prevention Strategies

Besides better treatment approaches for substance-abusing offenders, there is a need for better prevention programs to reduce substance use and crime. Research indicates that the earlier interventions are initiated, the better the outcomes (Young et al., 2007). Nevertheless, most of the substance use interventions for juvenile offenders are provided in long-term residential facilities rather than in detention or probation, where youth have their first contacts with the juvenile justice system (Young et al., 2007). It would be even better to intervene with youth prior to their first offense. For example, efforts to reduce alcohol consumption, especially among aggressive adolescents and adolescents with low ECF, could substantially reduce crime, especially violent crime (White et al., 1993). Furthermore, early prevention with aggressive children might reduce later violent crime (for a description of model programs for violence

prevention, see Tolan & Guerra, 1994 and the *Blue Prints for Violence Prevention* series at http://www.colorado.edu/cspv/infohouse/publications.html#blueprintspubs).

In addition to individual-focused interventions, there is a need for harm reduction strategies to change situational contexts that increase the risk for violence. Several effective strategies offer potential for reducing alcohol-related violence, such as replacing glass containers with plastic or shatter-proof glass, staggering bar closing hours, changing the environment of licensed establishments (e.g., reducing noise and crowding), modifying bar admission practices and staff behavior, and training bar staff in interpersonal conflict resolution and responsible beverage service. In addition, increasing social control (e.g., providing street guardians, more police patrols, and closed-circuit TVs in licensed establishments and their surrounding neighborhoods) would help to reduce alcohol-related violence. Some policy changes could also reduce alcohol-related violence (e.g., prohibiting the use of alcohol at sporting events and other large public events and prohibiting happy hours and other free drink offers (http://www.icap.org/portals/0/download/all_pdfs/blue_book/Module_07_Drinking_and_Violence.pdf). Several researchers have also suggested that implementing certain drug policy changes might reduce drug-related crime, such as marijuana decriminalization, lessening the powder and crack cocaine sentencing disparity, and getting rid of mandatory minimum sentences (see McBride et al. 2003 for a detailed discussion).

Finally, changes are needed to reduce societal factors that increase the risks for substance abuse and crime. These changes would entail providing youth with better paying jobs, better schools, and more opportunities, remedying community disorganization, and reducing economic hardships (White & Gorman, 2000, p. 198). For example, Welsh (2007) found that although TCs reduced recidivism, they did not necessarily reduce drug use (see also Mitchell et al., 2007). Instead, employment after incarceration reduced both drug use and reincarceration. In sum, by implementing various individual, situational, and societal strategies, the costs associated with substance use-related crime can be significantly reduced.

Future Research

The literature reviewed above indicates that substance use and crime are strongly related.

Nevertheless, the substance-using/crime-committing population is heterogeneous and there are multiple paths that lead to substance use and crime, as well as connect the two forms of behavior. For some individuals instances of acute intoxication increase the risks for violent and impulsive crime; for some the need for expensive and addictive drugs increases the risks for income-generating crime; for some individuals exposure to drug cultures and drug markets increases all types of crime, especially violent crime; for some the criminal lifestyle increases substance use; and, finally, for some common underlying characteristics (e.g., family, personality, genetics, neighborhoods) increase the risks for both substance use and crime. Not only do substance use and crime associations vary across individuals, they also vary across occasions, types of substance use, and types of crimes. Thus, it is possible that each of these explanations might be valid for the same individual under different circumstances and at different phases in the life course. As Faupel and Klockars (1987) suggested, the association between substance use and crime varies by stage of drug use: during the initial user stage, the association is spurious; during the more intense user stage, drug use is facilitated by criminal behavior; and during the street addict career stage, drug use directly causes crime (see also Keene, 2005).

The existing research has provided much insight into the nature of the substance use-crime connection, especially the link between alcohol and violence. In fact, Lipsey and colleagues (1997) suggested that the field needs to move beyond the question of whether alcohol causes violence and begin to identify the individual, moderator, and contextual variables that characterize situations in which alcohol use will potentiate violent behavior. Recent laboratory and survey research has begun to heed that suggestion and to unravel underlying processes. On the other hand, fewer well-controlled studies examining the interactions of individual, moderator, and situational variables have been conducted on the role of drug use in violent events. Therefore, there is a need to extend this multifaceted type of research from alcohol to other drugs (Moore & Stuart, 2005).

In addition, there are other gaps in knowledge regarding substance use and crime. For example, although there are ethnic/racial and gender differences in the nature and extent of the drug-crime relationship, more research is needed to explain these differences. In particular, longitudinal studies with larger populations of ethnic/racial minorities are needed to understand developmental changes in substance use and crime and to identify proximal and distal risk and protective factors (see White et al., 2012). More research is also needed on environmental contexts (e.g., societal norms towards specific drugs, availability, and laws prohibiting use of certain drugs) and how they influence the drug-crime association (MacCoun et al., 2003). Further, much of the research on drugs and crime has focused on lower class addicts and street crime. Little research has been conducted on the role of drugs in white collar crime (McBride et al., 2003). Also, it is well documented that many drug-using criminal offenders also have other comorbid mental health problems. Therefore, more research is needed on the relationships among drug use, mental illnesses, and crime and on appropriate interventions within the community and within the criminal justice system to deal with these co-existing problems. Most importantly, better-designed prevention and intervention research is needed to determine which components of which interventions work for which individuals under which conditions.

In summary, the studies reviewed above make it clear that situational and global associations between substance use and crime depend on drug type, crime type, contextual, cultural, and historical factors, and individual differences in gender, age, race/ethnicity, expectancies, reactions to drugs, and temperament. Researchers, therefore, need to collect data across multiple domains and use multidimensional models to examine mediators and moderators (Chermack & Giancola, 1997).

Acknowledgment

The writing of this chapter was supported in part by grants from the National Institute on Alcohol Abuse and Alcoholism (ARRA R01 AA16798), National Institute on Drug Abuse (R01 DA034608; P20 DA17552), and National Institute of Mental Health (P30 MH079920). Portions of this chapter were excerpted from White and Gorman (2000) and White (2005). I thank Judit Ward, Dan Calandro, James Cox, William Bejarano, Eric Yesner, and Jennifer Lugris for their help with the literature search and references. I am also indebted to Dennis Gorman, Stephen Hansell, Kristina Jackson, Rolf Loeber, Eun-Young Mun, Robert Pandina, Dustin Pardini, and Magda Stouthamer-Loeber for their intellectual contributions to my research and writing on drug use and crime.

Notes

1. All the relevant literature cannot be covered and the reader is referred to several excellent reviews for greater detail (e.g., Boles & Miotta, 2003; Chaiken & Chaiken, 1990; Fagan, 1990; Harrison, 1992; MacCoun, Kilmer, & Reuter, 2003; McBride, VanderWaal, & Terry-McElrath, 2003; Miczek, DeBold, Haney, Tidey, Vivian, & Weerts, 1994; Parker & Auerhahn, 1998; White, 1990, 1997a, 1997b; White & Gorman, 2000).

2. This essay does not include child abuse and neglect although it is a form of crime related to substance use. There are numerous studies that have examined the effects of parental substance use on child physical and sexual abuse and neglect, as well as the effects of child abuse and neglect on later substance use (for more information, see Miller & Mancuso, 2004; Simpson & Miller, 2002; Widom & Hiller-Sturmhöfel, 2001; Widom, Marmorstein, & White, 2006; Widom, White, Czaja, & Marmorstein, 2007).

3. Emerging adulthood is defined as a phase in the life cycle between adolescence and young adulthood. It encompasses the period from the end of high school to adoption of adult roles, such as marriage, parenthood, and career (approximately ages 18–25) (Arnett, 2000).

References

Abbey, A. (2002). Alcohol-related sexual assault: A common problem among college students. *Journal of Studies on Alcohol, Suppl. 14 Mar*, 118–128.

Abbey, A., Zawacki, T., Buck, P. O., Clinton, A. M., & McAuslan, P. (2001). Alcohol and sexual assault. *Alcohol Research & Health, 25*, 43–51.

Abbey, A., Zawacki, T., Buck, P. O., Clinton, A. M., & McAuslan, P. (2004). Sexual assault and alcohol consumption: What do we know about their relationship and what types of research are still needed? *Aggression and Violent Behavior, 9*(3), 271–303.

Abracen, J., Looman, J., & Anderson, D. (2000). Alcohol and drug abuse in sexual and nonsexual violent offenders. *Sexual Abuse: Journal of Research and Treatment, 12*(4), 263–274.

Alaniz, M. L., Cartmill, R. S., & Parker, R. N. (1998). Immigrants and violence: The importance of context. *Hispanic Journal of Behavioral Sciences, 20*, 155–174.

Anglin, M. D., & Perrochet, B. (1998). Drug use and crime: A historical review of research conducted by the UCLA drug abuse research center. *Substance Use & Misuse, 33*(9), 1871–1914.

Anthony, J. C., & Forman, V. (2003). At the intersection of public health and criminal justice research on drugs and crime. In National Institute of Justice, *Towards a drug and crime research agenda for the 21st century* (pp. 11–64). Washington, DC: U.S. Department of Justice, Office of Justice Programs.

Arnett, J. J. (2000). Emerging adulthood: A theory of development from the late teens through the twenties. *American Psychologist, 55*, 469–480.

Baskin, D. R. & Sommers, I. B. (1997). *Casualties of community disorder: Women's careers in violent crime*. Boulder, Co: Westview Press.

Belenko, S., & Peugh, J. (2005). Estimating drug treatment needs among state prison inmates. *Drug and Alcohol Dependency, 77*, 269–281.

Belcher, J. R., & Herr, S. (2005). Development of grounded theory: Moving towards a theory of the pathways into street prostitution among low-income women. *Journal of Addictions Nursing, 16*(3), 117–124.

Bennett, T., & Holloway, K. (2005). The association between multiple drug misuse and crime. *International Journal of Offender Therapy & Comparative Criminology, 49*, 63–81.

Bennett, T., & Holloway, K. (2006). Variations in drug users' accounts of the connection between drug misuse and crime. *Journal of Psychoactive Drugs, 38*(3), 243–254.

Bennett, T., Holloway, K., & Farrington, D. (2008). The statistical association between drug misuse and crime: A meta-analysis. *Aggression and Violent Behavior, 13*, 107–118.

Beynon, C. M., McVeigh, C., McVeigh, J., Leavey, C., & Bellis, M. A. (2008). The involvement of drugs and alcohol in drug-facilitated sexual assault: A systematic review of the evidence. *Trauma, Violence, & Abuse, 9*(3), 178–188.

Blanchard, D. C., Veniegas, R., Elloran, I., & Blanchard, R. J. (1993). Alcohol and anxiety: Effects on offensive and defensive aggression. *Journal of Studies on Alcohol, Suppl. 11 Sep*, 9–19.

Blue Prints for Violence Prevention series. http://www.colorado.edu/cspv/infohouse/publications.html#blueprintspubs

Blumstein, A. (1995). Youth violence, guns and the illicit-drug industry. In C. Block & R. Block (Eds.), *Trends, risks, and interventions in lethal violence* (pp. 3–15). Washington, DC: National Institute of Justice.

Boles, S. M., & Miotto, K. (2003). Substance abuse and violence. A review of the literature. *Aggression and Violent Behavior, 8*, 155–174.

Brecklin, L. R., & Ullman, S. E. (2002). The roles of victim and offender alcohol use in sexual assaults: Results from the national violence against women survey. *Journal of Studies on Alcohol, 63*(1), 57–63.

Brook, J. S., Whiteman, & Cohen, P. (1995). Stages of drug use, aggression, and theft/vandalism: Shared and unshared risks. In H. B. Kaplan (Ed.), *Drugs, crime, and other deviant adaptations: Longitudinal studies* (pp. 83–98). New York, NY: Plenum Press.

Brook, J. S., Zhang, C. S., & Brook D. W. (2011). Antisocial behavior at age 37: Developmental trajectories of marijuana use extending from adolescence to adulthood. *American Journal on Addiction, 20*(6), 509–515.

Brower, A. M., & Carroll, L. (2007). Spatial and temporal aspects of alcohol-related crime in a college town. *Journal of American College Health, 55*(5), 267–275.

Brown, A., & Burton, D. L. (2010). Exploring the overlap in male juvenile sexual offending and general delinquency: Trauma, alcohol use, and masculine beliefs. *Journal of Child Sexual Abuse: Research, Treatment, & Program Innovations for Victims, Survivors, & Offenders, 19*(4), 450–468.

Bushman, B. J. (1997). Effects of alcohol on human aggression: Validity of proposed explanations. In M. Galanter (Ed.), *Recent developments in alcoholism, Vol. 13: Alcohol and violence: Epidemiology, neurobiology, psychology, family issues* (pp. 227–243). New York, NY: Plenum Press.

Caetano, R., Cunradi, C., Schafer, J., & Clark, C. (2000). Intimate partner violence and drinking patterns among White, Black and Hispanic couples in the U.S. *Journal of Substance Abuse, 11*, 123–138.

Chaiken, J. M., & Chaiken, M. R. (1990). Drugs and predatory crime. In M. Tonry & J. Q. Wilson (Eds.), *Drugs and crime, 13* (pp. 203–239). Chicago: University of Chicago Press.

Chermack, S. T., & Blow, F. C. (2002). Violence among individuals in substance abuse treatment: The role of alcohol and cocaine consumption. *Drug and Alcohol Dependence,* *66*(1), 29–37.

Chermack, S. T., & Giancola, P. R. (1997). The relation between alcohol and aggression: An integrated biopsychosocial conceptualization. *Clinical Psychology Review, 17*(6), 621–649.

Coid, J., Yang, M., Roberts, A., Ullrich, S., Moran, P., Bebbington, P., Brugha, T., Jenkins, R., . . . Singleton, N. (2006). Violence and psychiatric morbidity in the national household population of Britain: Public health implications. *British Journal of Psychiatry, 189*(1), 12–19.

Collins, J. J. (1981). Alcohol careers and criminal careers. In J. J. Collins (Ed.), *Drinking and crime* (pp. 152–206). New York, NY: Guilford Press.

Collins, J. J. (1993). Drinking and violence: An individual offender focus. In S. E. Martin (Ed.), *Alcohol and interpersonal violence. Fostering multidisciplinary perspectives* (NIAAA Research Monograph No. 24, pp. 221–235). Rockville, MD: National Institute of Health.

Collins, J. J., Hubbard, R. L., & Rachal, J. V. (1985). Expensive drugs use and illegal income: A test of explanatory hypotheses. *Criminology, 23,* 743–764.

Collins, J. J., & Messerschmidt, P. M. (1993). Epidemiology of alcohol-related violence. *Alcohol Health & Research World, 17*(2), 93.

Collins, J. J., & Schlenger, W. E. (1988). Acute and chronic effects of alcohol use on violence. *Journal of Studies on Alcohol, 49,* 516–521.

Cook, P. J., & Moore, M. J. (1993). Economic perspectives on reducing alcohol related violence. In S. E. Martin (Ed.), *Alcohol and interpersonal violence. Fostering multidisciplinary perspectives* (NIAAA Research Monograph No. 24, pp. 193–212). Rockville, MD: National Institute of Health.

Cooper, M. L. (2002). Alcohol use and risky sexual behavior among college students and youth: Evaluating the evidence. *Journal of Studies on Alcohol, Suppl. 14 Mar,* 101–117.

Cunradi, C. B., Caetano, R., & Schafer, J. (2002). Alcohol-related problems, drug use, and male intimate partner violence severity among US couples. *Alcoholism: Clinical and Experimental Research, 26*(4), 493–500.

Curtis, R., & Windle, T. (2007). "You're always training the dog": Strategic interventions to reconfigure drug markets. *Journal of Drug Issues, 37,* 867–891.

Cusick, L., & Hickman, M. (2005). "Trapping" in drug use and sex work careers. *Drugs: Education, Prevention & Policy, 12*(5), 369–379.

De Li, S., Priu, H. D., & MacKenzie, D. L. (2000). Drug involvement, lifestyles and criminal activities among probationers. *Journal of Drug Issues, 30*(3), 593–620.

Deitch, D., Koutsenok, I., & Ruiz, A. (2000). The relationship between crime and drugs: What we have learned in recent decades. *Journal of Psychoactive Drugs, 32,* 391–397.

Dembo, R., Williams, L., Wish, E. D., Berry, E., Getreu, A., Washburn, M., & Schmeidler, J. (1990). Examination of the relationships among drug use, emotional/psychological problems, and crime among youths entering a juvenile detention center. *International Journal of the Addictions, 25,* 1301–1340.

Dembo, R., Williams, L., Wothke, W., & Schmeidler, J. (1994). The relationships among family problems, friends' troubled behavior, and high risk youths' alcohol/other drug use and delinquent behavior: A longitudinal study. *International Journal of the Addictions, 29*(11), 1419–1442.

Derzon, J. H., & Lipsey, M. W. (1999). A synthesis of the relationship of marijuana use with delinquent and problem behaviors. *School Psychology International, 20,* 57–68.

Desroches, F. (2007). Research on upper level drug trafficking: Review. *Journal of Drug Issues, 37,* 827–844.

Dorsey, T. L., Zawitz, M. W., & Middleton, P. (2002). Drugs and crime facts (NCJ165148), available online at http//www.ojp.usdoj.gov/bjs/pub/pdf/dcf.pdf.

Dunning, E., Murphy, P., & Williams, J. (1986). Spectator violence at football matches: Towards a sociological explanation. *British Journal of Sociology, 37*(2), 221–244.

Edwards, J. M., Halpern, C. T., & Wechsberg, W. M. (2006). Correlates of exchanging sex for drugs or money among women who use crack cocaine. *AIDS Education & Prevention, 18*(5), 420–429.

El-Bassel, N., Witte, S. S., Wada, T., Gilbert, L., & Wallace, J. (2001). Correlates of partner violence among female street-based sex workers: Substance abuse, history of childhood abuse, and HIV risks. *AIDS Patient Care and STDs, 15*(1), 41–51.

Elliott, D. S., Huizinga, D., & Menard, S. W. (1989). *Multiple problem youth: Delinquency, substance use, and mental health problems.* New York, NY: Springer-Verlag.

EMCDDA (European Monitoring Centre for Drugs and Drug Addiction) (2004). 2003 *annual report on the drug situation in the EU & Norway,* Lisbon: EMCDDA, available online at http//www.emcdda.eu.int.

Ensminger, M. E., Anthony, J. C., & McCord, J. (1997). The inner city and drug use: Initial findings from an epidemiological study. *Drug and Alcohol Dependence, 48*(3), 175–184.

Erickson, P. G., Butters, J., McGillicuddy, P., & Hallgren, A. (2000). Crack and prostitution: Gender, myths, and experiences. *Journal of Drug Issues, 30*(4), 767–788.

Erickson, P. G., & Watson, V. A. (1990). Women, illicit drugs, and crime. In L. T. Kozlowski, H. M. Annis, H. D. Cappell, F. B Glaser, M. S. Goodstadt, Y. Israel, & et al. (Eds.), *Research advances in alcohol and drug problems, 10* (pp. 251–272). New York, NY: Plenum.

Fagan, J. (1990). Intoxication and aggression. In M. Tonry & J. Q. Wilson (Eds.), *Drugs and crime* (pp. 241–320). Chicago: University of Chicago Press.

Fagan, J. (1993). Set and setting revisited. Influence of alcohol and illicit drugs on the social context of violent events. In S. E. Martin (Ed.), *Alcohol and interpersonal violence. Fostering multidisciplinary perspectives* (NIAAA Research Monograph No. 24, pp. 161–191). Rockville, MD: National Institute of Health.

Fagan, J., & Chin, K. (1990). Violence as regulation and social control in the distribution of crack. In M. De La Rosa, E. Y. Lambert & B. Gropper (Eds.), *Drugs and violence. Causes, correlates and consequences, NIDA Research Monograph 103* (pp. 8–43). Rockville, MD: National Institute on Drug Abuse.

Fagan J., Weis, J. G., & Cheng, Y. (1988). *Delinquency and substance use among inner city students.* New York, NY: New York City Criminal Justice Agency.

Fagan, J., Weis, J. G., Cheng, Y., & Watters, J. K. (1987). *Drug and alcohol use, violent delinquency and social bonding: Implications for theory and intervention.* San Francisco, CA: The URSA Institute.

Farabee, D., Prendergast, M., & Anglin, M. D. (1998). The effectiveness of coerced treatment for drug-abusing offenders. *Federal Probation, 62*(1), 3–10.

Farrington, D. P. (1995). The development of offending and antisocial behaviour from childhood: Key findings from the Cambridge Study in Delinquent Development. *Journal of Child Psychology and Psychiatry, 36*, 929–964.

Farrington, D. P., & Hawkins, J. D. (1991). Predicting participation, early onset and later persistence in officially recorded offending. *Criminal Behaviour and Mental Health, 1*(1), 1–33.

Faupel, C. E., & Klockars, C. B. (1987). Drugs-crime connections: Elaborations from life histories of hard-core heroin addicts. *Social Problems, 34*(1), 54–68.

Felson, R. B., Burchfield, K. B., & Teasdale, B. (2007). The impact of alcohol on different types of violent incidents. *Criminal Justice and Behavior, 34*(8), 1057–1068.

Felson, R. B., & Staff, J. (2010). The effects of alcohol intoxication on violent versus other offending. *Criminal Justice and Behavior 37*, 1343–1360.

Felson, R. B., Teasdale, B., & Burchfield, K. B. (2008). The influence of being under the influence: Alcohol effects on adolescent violence. *Journal of Research in Crime & Delinquency, 45*, 119–139.

Fergusson, D. M., & Horwood, L. J. (2000). Alcohol abuse and crime: A fixed-effects regression analysis. *Addiction, 95*(10), 1525–1536.

Field, C. A., Caetano, R. & Nelson, S. (2004). Alcohol and violence related cognitive risk factors associated with the perpetration of intimate partner violence. *Journal of Family Violence, 19*, 249–253.

Freisthler, B., Lascala, E. A., Gruenewald, P. J., & Treno, A. J. (2005). An examination of drug activity: Effects of neighborhood social organization on the development of drug distribution systems. *Substance Use & Misuse, 40*(5), 671–686.

French, M. T., McCollister, K. E., Alexandre, P. K., Chitwood, D. D., & McCoy, C. B. (2004). Revolving roles in drug-related crime: The cost of chronic drug users as victims and perpetrators. *Journal of Quantitative Criminology, 20*(3), 217–241.

Friedman, A. S. (1998). Substance use/abuse as a predictor to illegal and violent behavior: A review of the relevant literature. *Aggression and Violent Behavior, 3*(4), 339–355.

George, W. H., Stoner, S. A., Norris, J., Lopez, P. A. & Lehman, G. L. (2000). Alcohol expectancies and sexuality: A self-fulfilling prophecy analysis of dyadic perceptions and behavior. *Journal of Studies on Alcohol, 61*, 168–176.

Giancola, P. R. (2002). Alcohol-related aggression during the college years: Theories, risk factors, and policy implications. *Journal of Studies on Alcohol, Suppl. 14 Mar*, 129–139.

Giancola, P. R. (2004). Executive functioning and alcohol-related aggression. *Journal of Abnormal Psychology, 113*(4), 541–555.

Goldstein, P. J. (1985). The drugs/violence nexus: A tripartite conceptual framework. *Journal of Drug Issues, 15*(4), 493–506.

Goldstein, P. J., Ouellet, L. J., & Fendrich, M. (1992). From bag brides to skeezers: A historical perspective on sex-for-drugs behavior. *Journal of Psychoactive Drugs, 24*(4), 349–361.

Goldstein, P. J., Brownstein, H. H., Ryan, P. J., & Bellucci, P. A. (1989). Crack and homicide in New York City, 1988. A conceptually based event analysis. *Contemporary Drug Problems, 16*, 651–687.

Gorman, D. M., Zhu, L., & Horel, S. (2005). Drug "hot-spots," alcohol availability and violence. *Drug and Alcohol Review, 24*(6), 507–513.

Gottfredson, D. C., Kearley, B. W., & Bushway, S. D. (2008). Substance use, drug treatment, and crime: An examination of intra-individual variation a drug court population. *Journal of Drug Issues, 38*(2), 601–630.

Golub, A. L., & Johnson, B. D. (1999). Cohort changes in illegal drug use among arrestees in Manhattan: From the heroin injection generation to the blunts generation," *Substance Use & Misuse, 34*, 1733–1763.

Graham, K., Schmidt, G., & Gillis, K. (1995). Circumstances when drinking leads to aggression. An overview of research findings, Proceedings from *The International Conference on Social and Health Effects of Different Drinking Patterns*, Toronto, Canada.

Graham, N., & Wish, E. D. (1994). Drug use among female arrestees: Onset, patterns, and relationships to prostitution. *The Journal of Drug Issues, 24*, 315–329.

Greenfeld, L. A. (1998). *Alcohol and crime*. Washington, DC: U.S. Department of Justice, Bureau of Justice Statistics.

Greenfeld, L. A., & Henneberg, M. A. (2001). Victim and offender self-reports of alcohol involvement in crime. *Alcohol Research & Health, 25*(1), 20–31.

Gruenewald, P. J., Freisthler, B., Remer, L., LaScala, E. A., & Treno, A. (2006). Ecological models of alcohol outlets and violent assaults: Crime potentials and geospatial analysis. *Addiction, 101*(5), 666–677.

Gustafson, R. (1993). What do experimental paradigms tell us about alcohol-related aggressive responding? *Journal of Studies on Alcohol, Suppl. 11 Sep*, 20–29.

Hagan, J., & Foster, H. (2003). S/He's a rebel: Toward a sequential stress theory of delinquency and gendered pathways to disadvantage in emerging adulthood. *Social Forces, 82*(1), 53–86.

Haggård-Grann, U., Hallqvist, J., Långström, N., & Möller, J. (2006). The role of alcohol and drugs in triggering criminal violence: A case-crossover study. *Addiction, 101*(1), 100–108.

Harrison, L. D. (1992). The drug-crime nexus in the USA. *Contemporary Drug Problems, 19*, 203–245.

Hawkins, J. D., Catalano, R. F., & Miller, J. Y. (1992). Risk and protective factors for alcohol and other drug problems in adolescence and early adulthood. Implications for substance abuse prevention, *Psychological Bulletin, 112*, 64–105.

Hill, K. G., Chung I.-J., Herrenkohl T. I., & Hawkins J. D. (2000, November). *Consequences of trajectories of violent and non-violent offending*. Paper presented at the Annual Meeting of the American Society of Criminology, San Francisco, CA.

Hill, K., White, H. R., Chung, I.-J., Hawkins, J. D., & Catalano, R. F. (2000). Early adult outcomes of adolescent alcohol use: person- and variable-centered analyses of binge drinking trajectories. *Alcoholism: Clinical and Experimental Research, 24*, 892–901.

Holloway, K., Bennett, T. H., & Farrington, D. P. (2008). *Effectiveness of treatment in reducing drug-related crime: A systematic review*. Stockholm, Sweden: Swedish Council for Crime Prevention.

Home Office (2004a). *Alcohol and intimate partner violence. Key findings from the research*, Findings 216, London: Home Office.

Home Office (2004b). *Alcohol and sexual violence. Key findings from the research*, Findings 215, London: Home Office.

Home Office (2004c). *Violence in the night-time economy. Key findings from the research*, Findings 214, London: Home Office.

Horney, J., Osgood, D. W., & Marshall, I. H. (1995). Criminal careers in the short-term: Intra-individual variability in crime and its relation to local life circumstances. *American Sociological Review, 60*(5), 655–673.

Huang, B., White, H. R., Kosterman, R., Catalano, R. F., & Hawkins, J. D. (2001). Developmental associations between alcohol and interpersonal aggression during adolescence. *Journal of Research in Crime & Delinquency, 38*(1), 64–83.

Huizinga, D. & Jakob-Chien, C. (1998). The contemporaneous co-occurrence of serious violent juvenile offending and other problem behaviors. In Loeber, R. & Farrington, D. P. (Eds.), *Serious & violent juvenile offenders* (pp. 47–67). Thousand Oaks, CA: Sage Publications.

Hussong, A. M., Curran, P. J., Moffitt, T. E., Caspi, A., & Carrigm M. M. (2004). Substance abuse hinders desistance in young adults' antisocial behavior. *Development and Psychopathology, 16*, 1029–46.

Inciardi, J. A. (1986). *The war on drugs.* Palo Alto, CA: Mayfield.

Inciardi, J. A., & Pottieger, A. E. (1991). Crack, and crime. *Journal of Drug Issues, 21*, 257–270.

Inciardi, J. A. & Pottieger, A. E. (1994). Crack-cocaine use and street crime. *Journal of Drug Issues, 24*, 273–292.

Inciardi, J. A., & Pottieger, A. E. (1998). Drug use and street crime in Miami: An (almost) twenty-year retrospective. *Substance Use & Misuse, 33*(9), 1839–1870.

Ito, T. A., Miller, N., & Pollock, V. E. (1996). Alcohol and aggression. A meta-analysis on the moderating effects of inhibitory cues, triggering events, and self-focused attention. *Psychological Bulletin, 120*, 60–82.

Jessor, R., & Jessor, S. (1977). *Problem behavior and psychosocial development. A longitudinal study of youth,* New York, NY: Academic Press.

JofreBonet, M., & Sindelar, J. L. (2001). Drug treatment as a crime fighting tool. *Journal of Mental Health Policy and Economics, 4*(4), 175–188.

Johnson, B. D., Natarajan, M., Dunlap, E., & Elmoghazy, E. (1994). Crack abusers and noncrack abusers. Profiles of drug use, drug sales and nondrug criminality. *Journal of Drug Issues, 24*, 117–141.

Johnson, B. D., Williams, T., Dei, K. A., & Sanabria, H. (1990). Drug abuse in the inner city. Impact on hard-drug users and the community. In M. Tonry & J. Q. Wilson (Eds.), *Drugs and crime 13* (pp. 9–67). Chicago: University of Chicago Press.

Johnson, H. (2000). The role of alcohol in male partners' assaults on wives. *Journal of Drug Issues, 30*, 725–740.

Johnston, L. D., O'Malley, P. M., Bachman, J. G., & Schulenberg, J. E. (2007). *Monitoring the Future: National survey results on drug use,* 1975–2006. Bethesda, MD: National Institute on Drug Abuse.

Kazemian, L. Farrington, D. P., & Le Blanc, M. (2009). Can we make accurate long-term predictions about patterns of de-escalation in offending behavior? *Journal of Youth and Adolescence, 38*, 384–400.

Karberg, J. C., & James, D. J. (2005). *Substance dependence, abuse, and treatment of jail inmates, 2002.* Washington, DC: U.S. Department of Justice, Office of Justice Programs, Bureau of Justice Statistics.

Keene, J. (2005). A case-linkage study of the relationship between drug misuse, crime, and psychosocial problems in a total criminal justice population. *Addiction Research & Theory, 13*(5), 489–502.

Keys Young (1994). *Alcohol misuse and violence. The incidence and prevalence of alcohol use and violence in the Australian Community,* Canberra, Australia, Common Wealth of Australia.

Khantzian, E. J. (1985). The self-medication hypothesis of addictive disorders. Focus on heroin and cocaine dependence. *American Journal of Psychiatry, 142*, 1259–1264.

Koss, M. P. (1988). Hidden rape: Sexual aggression and victimization in a national sample of students in higher education. In A. W. Burgess (Ed.), *Rape and sexual assault,* 2 (pp. 3–25). New York, NY: Garland.

Kraanen, F. L., Scholing, A., & Emmelkamp, P. M. G. (2012). Substance use disorders in forensic psychiatry: Differences among different types of offenders. *International Journal of Offender Therapy & Comparative Criminology, 56*(8), 1201–1219.

Krueger, R. F., Markon, K. E., Patrick, C. J., & Iacono, W. G. (2005). Externalizing psychopathology in adulthood: A dimensional-spectrum conceptualization and its implications for DSM-V. *Journal of Abnormal Psychology, 114*, 537–550.

Kwiatkowski, C. F., & Booth, R. E. (2000). Differences in HIV risk behaviors among women who exchange sex for drugs, money, or both drugs and money. *AIDS and Behavior, 4*(3), 233–240.

Lennings, C. J., Copeland, J., & Howard, J. (2003). Substance use patterns of young offenders and violent crime. *Aggressive Behaviors, 29*(5), 414–422.

Leonard, K. E. (2000). *Domestic violence and alcohol. What is known and what do we need to know to encourage environmental interventions.* Paper presented at the meeting of the National Crime Prevention Council, Alcohol and Crime. Research and Practice for Prevention, Washington, DC

Leonard, K. E. (2001). Domestic violence and alcohol: What is known and what do we need to know to encourage environmental interventions? *Journal of Substance Use, 6*, 235–247.

Leonard, K. E. (2008). The role of drinking patterns and acute intoxication in violent interpersonal behaviors. In International Center for Alcohol Policies. *Alcohol and violence: Exploring patterns and responses* (pp. 29–55). Washington, DC: International Center for Alcohol Policies.

Leonard, K. E., & Blane, H. T. (1992). Alcohol and marital aggression in a national sample of young men. *Journal of Interpersonal Violence, 7*, 19–30.

Leonard, K. E., Collins, R. L., & Quigley, B. M. (2003). Alcohol consumption and the occurrence and severity of aggression. *Aggressive Behavior, 29*, 346–365.

Leonard, K. E., & Quigley, B. M. (1999). Drinking and marital aggression in newlyweds: An event-based analysis of drinking and the occurrence of husband marital aggression. *Journal of Studies on Alcohol, 60*, 537–545.

Leonard, K. E., & Senchak, M. (1996). Prospective prediction of husband marital aggression among newlywed couples. *Journal of Abnormal Psychology, 105*, 369–380.

Leukefeld, C. G. & Tims, F. M. (1992). Drug abuse treatments in prisons and jails. *National Institute on Drug Abuse Research Monograph Series, 118.* Rockville MD: U.S. Department of Health and Human Services.

Lipsey, M. W., Wilson, D. B., Cohen, M. A., & Derzon, J. H. (1997). Is there a causal relationship between alcohol use and violence? A synthesis of evidence. In M. Galanter (Ed.), *Recent developments in alcoholism, volume 13. Alcohol and violence* (pp. 245–282). New York, NY: Plenum Press,

Lipton, D. S., Falkin, G. P., & Wexler, H. K. (1992). Correctional drug abuse treatment in the united states: An overview. In C.

G. Leukefeld, & F. M. Tims (Eds.), *Drug abuse treatment in prisons and jails, National Institute on Drug Abuse Research Monograph Series, 118* (pp. 8–30). Rockville, MD: National Institute on Drug Abuse.

Lipton, D. S., & Johnson, B. D. (1998). Smack, crack, and score: Two decades of NIDA-funded drugs and crime research at NDRI 1974–1994. *Substance Use & Misuse, 33*(9), 1779–1815.

Little, M., Weaver, S., King, K., Liu, F., & Chassin, L. (2008). Historical change in the link between adolescent deviance proneness and marijuana use, 1979 to 2004. *Prevention Science, 9*(1), 4–16.

Livingston, M. (2011). A longitudinal analysis of alcohol outlet density and domestic violence. *Addiction, 106*(5), 919–925.

Logan, T. K., Walker, R., Staton, M., & Leukefeld, C. (2001). Substance use and intimate violence among incarcerated males. *Journal of Family Violence, 16*(2), 93–114.

Lundholm, L., Haggård, U., Möller, J., Hallqvist, J., & Thiblin, I. (2013). The triggering effect of alcohol and illicit drugs on violent crime in a remand prison population: A case cross-over study. *Drug & Alcohol Dependence, 129*(1), 110–115.

Lynne-Landsman, S. D., Bradshaw, C. P., & Ialongo, N. S. (2010). Testing a developmental cascade model of adolescent substance use trajectories and young adult adjustment. *Development and Psychopathology, 22*(4), 933–948.

MacAndrew, C., & Edgerton, R. B. (1969). *Drunken comportment: A social explanation.* Chicago: Aldine.

MacCoun, R., Kilmer, B., & Reuter, P. (2003). *Research on drugs-crime linkages. The next generation.* In National Institute of Justice, *Towards a drugs and crime research agenda for the 21st century* (pp. 65–90). Washington, DC: Department of Justice, Office of Justice Programs.

Macdonald, S., Cherpitel, C. J., Borges, G., DeSouza, A., Giesbrecht, N., & Stockwell, T. (2005). The criteria for causation of alcohol in violent injuries based on emergency room data from six countries. *Addictive Behaviors, 30*, 103–113.

Macdonald, S., Erickson, P., Wells, S., Hathaway, A., & Pakula, B. (2008). Predicting violence among cocaine, cannabis, and alcohol treatment clients. *Addictive Behaviors, 33*, 201–205.

Magdol, L., Moffitt, T. E., Caspi, A., & & Silva, P. A. (1997). Developmental antecedents of partner abuse: A prospective-longitudinal study. *Journal of Abnormal Psychology, 107*, 375–389.

Maher, L. & Hudson, S. L. (2007). Women in the drug economy: A metasynthesis of the qualitative literature. *Journal of Drug Issues, 37*, 805–826.

Makela, K., Osterberg, E., & Sulkunen, P. (1981). Drink in Finland. Increasing alcohol availability in a monopoly state. In Single, E., Morgan, P., & de Lint, J. (eds.) *Alcohol, society and the state. Vol. 2. The social history of control policy in seven countries* (pp. 31–60). Toronto: Addiction Research Foundation.

Manzoni, P., Fischer, B., & Rehm, J. (2007). Local drug–crime dynamics in a Canadian multi-site sample of untreated opioid users. *Canadian Journal of Criminology & Criminal Justice, 49*(3), 341–373.

Martin, S. E., & Bryant, K. (2001). Gender differences in the association of alcohol intoxication and illicit drug abuse among persons arrested for violent and property offenses. *Journal of Substance Abuse, 13*(4), 563–581.

Martin, S. E., Maxwell, C. D., White, H. R., & Zhang, Y. (2004). Trends in alcohol use, cocaine use, and crime: 1989–1998. *Journal of Drug Issues, 34*(2), 333–359.

Mason, W. A., Hitch, J. E., Kosterman, R., McCarty, C. A., Herrenkohl, T. I., & Hawkins, J. D. (2010). Growth in adolescent delinquency and alcohol use in relation to young adult crime, alcohol use disorders, and risky sex: A comparison of youth from low-versus middle-income backgrounds. *Journal of Child Psychology and Psychiatry, 51*(12), 1377–1385.

Mason, W. A, & Windle, M. (2002). Reciprocal relations between adolescent substance use and delinquency: A longitudinal latent variable analysis. *Journal of Abnormal Psychology, 111*, 63–76.

Maxwell, S. R., & Maxwell, C. D. (2000). Examining the "criminal careers" of prostitutes within the nexus of drug use, drug selling, and other illicit activities. *Criminology, 38*(3), 787–809.

McBride, D. C., VanderWaal, C. J., & Terry-McElrath, Y. M. (2003). The drug-crime wars: Past, present, and future directions in theory, policy, and program interventions. In National Institute of Justice, *Towards a drugs and crime Research agenda for the 21st century* (pp. 97–157). Washington, DC: U.S. Department of Justice, Office of Justice Programs.

McClelland, G. M., Elkington, K. S., Teplin, L. A., & Abram, K. M. (2004). Multiple substance use disorders in juvenile detainees. *Journal of the American Academy of Child Adolescent Psychiatry, 43*, 1215–1224.

McCord, J., & Ensminger, M. E. (1997). Multiple risks and co-morbidity in an African-American population. *Criminal Behavior and Mental Health, 7*, 339–352.

McGolothin, W. H. (1985). Distinguishing effects from concomitants of drug use: The case of crime. In L. N. Robins (Ed.), *Studying drug abuse: Series in psychosocial epidemiology, VI* (pp. 153–172). New Brunswick, NJ: Rutgers University Press.

Menard, S., & Mihalic, S. (2001). The tripartite conceptual framework in adolescence and adulthood. Evidence from a national sample. *Journal of Drug Issues, 31*, 905–940.

Miczek, K. A., DeBold, J. F., Haney, M., Tidey, J., Vivian, J., & Weerts, E. M. (1994). Alcohol, drugs of abuse, aggression, and violence. In A. J. Reiss, & J. A. Roth (Eds.), *Understanding and preventing violence, 3* (pp. 377–468). Washington, DC: National Academy Press.

Miller, B. A., & Mancuso, R. F. (2004). Connecting childhood victimization to later alcohol/drug problems: Implications for prevention. *Journal of Primary Prevention, 25*, 149–169.

Miller, B. A., Wilsnack, S. C., & Cunradi, C. B. (2000). Family violence and victimization: Treatment issues for women with alcohol problems. *Alcoholism: Clinical and Experimental Research, 24*(8), 1287–1297.

Miller, T. R., Levy, D. T., Cohen, M. A., & Cox, K. L. (2006). Costs of alcohol and drug-involved crime. *Prevention Science, 7*, 333–342.

Mitchell, O., Wilson, D. B., & MacKenzie, D. L. (2007). Does incarceration-based drug treatment reduce recidivism? A meta-analytic synthesis of the research. *Journal of Experimental Criminology, 3*(4), 353–375.

Moeller, F. G., & Dougherty, D. M. (2001). Antisocial Personality Disorder, Alcohol, and Aggression. *Alcohol Research & Health, 25*, 5–11.

Moore, T. M., & Stuart, G. L. (2005). A review of the literature on marijuana and interpersonal violence. *Aggression and Violent Behavior, 10*(2), 171–192.

Mulvey, E. P., Odgers, C., Skeem, J., Gardner, W., Schubert, C., & Lidz, C. (2006). Substance use and community violence: A test of the relation at the daily level. *Journal of Consulting and Clinical Psychology, 74*, 743–754.

Mumola, C. J., & Karberg, J. C. (2006). Drug use and dependence, state, and federal prisoners, 2004. In *Bureau of Justice Statistics: Special Report* (pp. 1–9). Washington DC: U.S. Department of Justice Office of Justice Programs.

Murdoch, D., Pihl, R. O., & Ross, D. (1990). Alcohol and crimes of violence. Present issues. *The International Journal of the Addictions, 25*, 1065–1081.

Murphy, C. M., Winters, J., O'Farrell, T. J., Fals-Stewart, W., & Murphy, M. (2005). Alcohol consumption and intimate partner violence by alcoholic men: Comparing violent and nonviolent conflicts. *Psychology of Addictive Behaviors, 19*, 35–42.

National Institute of Justice. (2003). *Towards a drug and crime research agenda for the 21st century*. Washington, DC: U.S. Department of Justice, Office of Justice Programs.

Norström, T., & Pape, H. 2010. Alcohol, suppressed anger, and violence." *Addiction 105*, 1580–1586.

Nunes-Dinis, M. C., & Weisner, C. (1997). The relationship of alcohol and drugs to violent behavior in a sample of arrestees: Gender differences. *The American Journal of Drug and Alcohol Abuse, 23*(1), 129–141.

Nurco, D. N., Hanlon, T. E., Kinlock, T. W., & Duszynski, K. R. (1988). Differential criminal patterns of narcotic addicts over an addiction career. *Criminology, 26*, 407–423.

Office of National Drug Control Policy (2011). *ADAM II 2010 annual report*. Washington, DC: Office of National Drug Control Policy, Executive Office of the President.

Orlando, M., Tucker, J. S., Ellickson, P. L., & Klein, D. J. (2005). Concurrent use of alcohol and cigarettes from adolescence to young adulthood: An examination of developmental trajectories and outcomes. *Substance Use & Misuse, 40*(8), 1051–1069.

Oser, C. B., Palmer, J. M., Staton-Tindall, M., & Leukfeld, C. G. (2008). The drugs-violence nexus among rural felony probationers. *Journal of Interpersonal Violence, 24*, 1285–1303.

Ousey, G. C., & Lee, M. R. (2004). Investigating the connections between race, illicit drug markets, and lethal violence, 1984–1997. *Journal of Research in Crime and Delinquency, 41*(4), 352–383.

Pan, H. S., Neidig, P. H., & O'Leary, K. D. (1994). Predicting mild and severe husband-to-wife physical aggression. *Journal of Consulting and Clinical Psychology, 62*(5), 975–981.

Parker, R. N. (1993). The effects of context on alcohol and violence. *Alcohol Health & Research World, 17*, 117–122.

Parker, R. N., & Auerhahn, K. (1998). Alcohol, drugs, and violence. *Annual Review of Sociology, 24*, 291–311.

Parker, R. N., & Rebhun, L. (1995). *Alcohol and homicide. A deadly combination of two American traditions*. Albany, NY: State University of New York Press.

Pearson, F. S., & Lipton, D. S. (1999). A meta-analytic review of the effectiveness of corrections-based treatments for drug abuse. *The Prison Journal, 79*(4), 384–410.

Pelissier, B., Jones, N., & Cadigan, T. (2007). Drug treatment aftercare in the criminal justice system: A systematic review. *Journal of Substance Abuse Treatment, 32*, 311–320.

Pernanen, K. (1991). *Alcohol in human violence*. New York, NY: Guilford.

Pernanen, K. (1993). Alcohol-related violence: Conceptual models and methodological issues. In S. E. Martin (Ed.), *Alcohol and interpersonal violence: Fostering multidisciplinary perspectives* (NIAAA Research Monograph No.

24, pp. 149–159). Rockville, MD: National Institute of Health.

Pihl, R. O., Peterson, J. B., & Lau, M. A. (1993). A biosocial model of the alcohol-aggression relationship. *Journal of Studies on Alcohol, Suppl. 11 Sep*, 128–139.

Pihl, R. O., & Sutton, R. (2009). Drugs and aggression readily mix; So what now? *Substance use & Misuse, 44*(9), 1188–1203.

Ponkshe, P. (January 9, 2007). "Cost of crimes attributed to alcohol double those attributed to drugs." Press release.

Pridemore, W. A., & Grubesic, T. H. (2013). Alcohol outlets and community levels of interpersonal violence: Spatial density, outlet type, and seriousness of assault. *Journal of Research in Crime and Delinquency, 50*(1), 132–159.

Quigley, B. M., & Leonard, K. E. (2004/2005) Alcohol use and violence among young adults. *Alcohol Research & Health, 28*, 191–194.

Rand, M, R., Sabol, W. J., Sinclair, M. M., & Snyder, H. N. (2010). *Alcohol and Crime: Data f rom 2002 to 2008*. Washington, DC: Bureau of Justice Statistics. Retrieved from http://bjs.ojp.usdoj.gov/index.cfm?ty=pbdetail&iid=2313.

Reiss, A. J., Jr., & Roth, J. A. (1993). *Understanding and preventing violence*. Washington, DC: National Academy Press.

Roberts, J. C. (2007). Barroom aggression in Hoboken, New Jersey: Don't blame the bouncers! *Journal of Drug Education, 37*(4), 429–445.

Robins, L. N. (1970). The adult development of the antisocial child. *Seminars in Psychiatry, 2*, 420–434.

Roizen, J. (1993). Issues in the epidemiology of alcohol and violence. In S. E. Martin (Ed.), *Alcohol and interpersonal violence fostering multidisciplinary perspectives* (NIAAA Research Monograph 24, pp. 3–36). Rockville, MD: National Institute of Health.

Roman, C. G., & Reid, S. E. (2012). Assessing the relationship between alcohol outlets and domestic violence: Routine activities and the neighborhood environment. *Violence and Victims, 27*(5), 811–828.

Romero-Daza, N., Weeks, M., & Singer, M. (2003). "Nobody gives a damn if I live or die": Violence, drugs, and street-level prostitution in inner-city Hartford, Connecticut. *Medical Anthropology, 22*(3), 233–259.

Roncek, D. W., & Maier, P. A. (1991). Bars, blocks, and crimes revisited: Linking the theory of routine activities to the empiricism of "hot spots". *Criminology, 29*, 725–753.

Room, R., & Rossow, I. (2001). The share of violence attributable to drinking. *Journal of Substance Use, 6*, 218–228.

Ross, S. (2008). The mentally ill substance abuser. In M. Galanter, & H. D. Kleber (Eds.), *Textbook of substance abuse treatment* (4th ed., pp. 537–554). Washington, DC: American Psychiatric Publishing Inc.

Sales, P. & Murphy, S. (2007). San Francisco's freelancing ecstasy dealers: Towards a sociological understanding of drug markets. *Journal of Drug Issues, 37*, 919–949.

Sampson, R. J., Raudenbush, S. W., & Earls, F. (1997). Neighborhoods and violent crime: A multilevel study of collective efficacy. *Science, 277*, 918–924.

Sanmartin, J., Molina, A., & Garcia, Y. (2003). *International report 2003: Partner violence against women. Statistics and legislation*. Valencia, Spain: Centro Reina Sofia.

Scott-Ham, M., & Burton, F. (2005). Toxicological findings in cases of alleged drug-facilitated sexual assault in the United Kingdom over a 3-year period. *Journal of Clinical Forensic Medicine, 12*, 175–186.

Scribner, R. A., MacKinnon, D. P., & Dwyer, J. H. (1995). The risk of assaultive violence and alcohol availability in Los Angeles County. *American Journal of Public Health, 85,* 335–340.

Scribner, R. A., Cohen, D. Kaplan, S. & Allen, S. (1999). Alcohol availability and homicide in New Orleans: Conceptual considerations for small area analysis of the effect of alcohol outlet density. *Journal of Studies on Alcohol, 60,* 310–316.

Simpson T. L., & Miller, W. R. (2002). Concomitance between childhood sexual and physical abuse and substance use problems: A review. *Clinical Psychology Review, 22,* 27–77.

Smith, P. H., Homish, G. G., Leonard, K. E., & Cornelius, J. R. (2012). Intimate partner violence and specific substance use disorders: Findings from the National Epidemiologic Survey on Alcohol and Related Conditions. *Psychology of Addictive Behaviors, 26*(2), 236–245.

Speer, P. W., Gorman, D. M., Labouvie, E. W. & Ontkush, M. J. (1998). Violent crime and alcohol availability: Relationships in an urban community. *Journal of Public Health Policy, 19,* 303–318.

Steele, C. M., & Josephs, R. A. (1990). Alcohol myopia: Its prized and dangerous effects. *American Psychologist, 45*(8), 921–933.

Stoolmiller, M., &. Blechman, E. A. (2005). Substance abuse is a robust predictor of adolescent recidivism. *Criminal Justice and Behavior, 32,* 302-28.

Stuart, G. L., Temple, J. R., Follansbee, K. W., Bucossi, M. M., Hellmuth, J. C., & Moore, T. M. (2008). The role of drug use in a conceptual model of intimate partner violence in men and women arrested for domestic violence. *Psychology of Addictive Behaviors, 22*(1), 12–24.

Surratt, H. L., Inciardi, J. A., Kurtz, S. P., & Kiley, M. C. (2004). Sex work and drug use in a subculture of violence. *Crime & Delinquency, 50*(1), 43–59.

Swahn, M. H., & Donovan, J. E. (2006). Alcohol and violence: Comparison of the psychosocial correlates of adolescent involvement in alcohol-related physical fighting versus other physical fighting. *Addictive Behaviors, 31,* 2014–2029.

Taxman, F. S., Perdoni, M. L., & Harrison, L. D. (2007). Drug treatment services for adult offenders: The state of the state. *Journal of Substance Abuse Treatment, 32*(3), 239–254.

Taylor, S. P. (1967). Aggressive behavior and physiological arousal as a function of provocation and the tendency to inhibit aggression. *Journal of Personality, 35*(2), 297–310.

Testa, M. (2002). The impact of men's alcohol consumption on perpetration of sexual aggression. *Clinical Psychology Review, 22*(8), 1239–1263.

Testa, M., Kubiak, A., Quigley, B. M., Houston, R. J., Derrick, J. L., Levitt, A., ... Leonard, K. E. (2012). Husband and wife alcohol use as independent or interactive predictors of intimate partner violence. *Journal of Studies on Alcohol and Drugs, 73*(2), 268–276.

Testa, M., Livingston, J. A., & Leonard, K. E. (2003). Women's substance use and experiences of intimate partner violence: A longitudinal investigation among a community sample. *Addictive Behaviors, 28*(9), 1649–1664.

Thompson, M. P., & Kingree, J. B. (2006). The roles of victim and perpetrator alcohol use in intimate partner violence outcomes. *Journal of Interpersonal Violence, 21*(2), 163–177.

Thompson, M., & Uggen, C. (2012). Dealers, thieves, and the common determinants of drug and nondrug illegal earnings. *Criminology, 50*(4), 1057–1087.

Timpson, S. C., Ross, M. W., Williams, M. L., & Atkinson, J. (2007). Characteristics, drug use, and sex partners of a sample of male sex workers. *The American Journal of Drug and Alcohol Abuse, 33*(1), 63–69.

Tolan, P. H. & Guerra, N. G. (1994). Prevention of delinquency: Current status and issues. *Applied & Preventive Psychology, 3*(4), 251–273.

Toomey, T. L., Erickson, D. J., Carlin, B. P., Lenk, K. M., Quick, H. S., Jones, A. M., & Harwood, E. M. (2012). The association between density of alcohol establishments and violent crime within urban neighborhoods. *Alcoholism: Clinical and Experimental Research, 36*(8), 1468–1473.

Tucker J. S., Ellickson P. L., Orlando M., Martino S. C., & Klein D. J. (2005). Substance use trajectories from early adolescence to emerging adulthood: A comparison of smoking, binge drinking, and marijuana use. *Journal of Drug Issues, 35*(2), 307–331.

Uggen, C. & Thompson, M. (2003). The socioeconomic determinants of ill-gotten gains: Within-person changes in drug use and illegal earnings. *American Journal of Sociology, 109,* 146–185.

Ullman, S. E., Karabatsos, G., & Koss, M. P. (1999). Alcohol and sexual assault in a national sample of college women. *Journal of Interpersonal Violence, 14,* 603–625.

U.S. Department of Justice, Bureau of Justice Statistics. (1992). *Drugs, crime, and the justice system: A national report,* NCJ 133652. Washington DC: U.S. Department of Justice.

U.S. Department of Justice, Bureau of Justice Statistics. (1994). *Fact sheet: Drug data summary,* NCJ 148213. Washington DC: U.S. Department of Justice.

U.S. Department of Justice, National Institute of Justice. (2002). *2000 annual report Arrestee Drug Abuse Monitoring.* Washington, DC: U.S. Department of Justice, Office of Justice Programs.

Valdez, A., Zenong Y., & Kaplan, C. D. (1997). A comparison of alcohol, drugs, and aggressive crime among Mexican-American, black, and white male arrestees in Texas," *American Journal of Drug and Alcohol Abuse, 23,* 249–265.

Van Kammen, W., & Loeber, R. (1994). Are fluctuations in delinquent activities related to the onset and offset in juvenile illegal drug use and drug dealing? *Journal of Drug Issues, 24,* 9–24.

Virkkunen, M., & Linnoila, M. (1993). Brain serotonin, type II alcoholism and impulsive violence. *Journal of Studies on Alcohol, Suppl. 11 Sep,* 163–169.

Waldorf, D. (1998). Misadventures in the drug trade. *Substance Use & Misuse, 33,* 957–1991.l7

Waller, M. W., Iritani, B. J., Flewelling, R. L., Christ, S. L., Halpern, C. T., & Moracco, K. E. (2012). Violence victimization of young men in heterosexual relationships: Does alcohol outlet density influence outcomes? *Violence and Victims, 27*(4), 527–547.

Waller, M. W., Iritani, B. J., Christ, S. L., Clark, H. K., Moracco, K. E., Halpern, C. T., & Flewelling, R. L. (2012). Relationships among alcohol outlet density, alcohol use, and intimate partner violence victimization among young women in the United States. *Journal of Interpersonal Violence, 27*(10), 2062–2086.

Wei, E. H., Loeber, R., & White, H. R. (2004). Teasing apart the developmental associations between alcohol and marijuana use and violence. *Journal of Contemporary Criminal Justice, 20*(2), 166–183.

Weisner, M., Kim, H. K., & Capaldi, D. M. (2005). Developmental trajectories of offending: Validation and prediction to young adult alcohol use, drug use, and depressive symptoms. *Development and Psychopathology, 17,* 251–270.

Wells, S., Graham, K., Speechley, M., & Koval, J. (2005). Drinking patterns, drinking contexts and alcohol-related aggression among late adolescent and young adult drinkers. *Addiction, 100*(7), 933–944.

Wells, S., Thompson, J. M., Cherpitel, C., MacDonald, S., Marais, S., & Borges, G. (2007). Gender differences in the relationship between alcohol and violent injury: An analysis of cross-national emergency department data. *Journal of Studies on Alcohol and Drugs, 68*(6), 824–833.

Welsh, W. N. (2007). A multisite evaluation of prison-based therapeutic community drug treatment. *Criminal Justice and Behavior, 34*(11), 1481–1498.

Welte, J., Barnes, G., Hoffman, J., Wieczorek, W., & Zhang, L. (2005). Substance involvement and the trajectory of criminal offending in young males. *The American Journal of Drug and Alcohol Abuse, 31*(2), 267–284.

Welte, J. W., Zhang, L., & Wieczorek, W. F. (2001). The effects of substance use on specific types of criminal offending in young men. *Journal of Research in Crime and Delinquency, 38,* 416–438.

Wekerle, C. & Wall, A. M. (Eds.) (2002). *The violence and addiction equation.* New York, NY: Brunner-Routledge.

White, H. R. (1990). The drug use-delinquency connection in adolescence. In Weisheit, R. A. (Ed.), *Drugs, crime and the criminal justice system* (pp. 215–256). Cincinnati, OH: Anderson Publishing Co.

White, H. R. (1997a). Alcohol, illicit drugs, and violence. In D. M. Stoff, J. Breiling, & J. D. Maser (Eds.), *Handbook of antisocial behavior* (pp. 511–523). New York, NY: John Wiley and Sons.

White, H. R. (1997b). Longitudinal perspective on alcohol use and aggression during adolescence. In M. Galanter (Ed.), *Recent developments in alcoholism (Vol. 13): Alcohol and violence* (pp. 81–103). New York, NY: Plenum Press.

White, H. R. (2005). A summary of research on drug-related violence. In M. A. Zahn, H. H. Brownstein, & S. L. Jackson (Eds.), *Violence: From theory to research* (pp. 195–211). Newark, NJ: LexisNexis-Anderson.

White, H. R., Brick, J., & Hansell, S. (1993). A longitudinal investigation of alcohol use and aggression in adolescence. *Journal of Studies on Alcohol, Suppl. 11,* 62–77.

White, H. R., & Chen, P. H. (2002). Problem drinking and intimate partner violence. *Journal of Studies on Alcohol, 63*(2), 205–214.

White, H. R., Fite, P., Pardini, D., Mun, E.-Y., & Loeber, R. (2013). Moderators of the dynamic link between alcohol and aggressive behavior among adolescent males. *Journal of Abnormal Child Psychology, 41,* 211–222.

White, H. R., & Gorman, D. M. (2000). Dynamics of the drug-crime relationship. In G. LaFree (Ed.), *Criminal justice 2000. The nature of crime. Continuity and change* (pp. 151–218). Washington, DC: U.S. Department of Justice.

White, H. R., & Hansell, S. (1996). The moderating effects of gender and hostility on the alcohol-aggression relationship. *Journal of Research on Crime and Delinquency, 33,* 451–472.

White, H. R., & Hansell, S. (1998). Acute and long-term effects of drug use on aggression from adolescence into adulthood. *Journal of Drug Issues, 28,* 837–858.

White, H. R., Jackson, K., & Loeber, R. (2009). Developmental sequences and comorbidity of substance use and violence. In M. Krohn, A. Lizotte, & G. P. Hall (Eds.), *Handbook of deviance and crime* (pp. 433–468). New York, NY: Springer Publications.

White, H. R., Johnson, V., & Garrison, C. G. (1985). The drug-crime nexus among adolescents and their peers. *Deviant Behavior, 6,* 183–204.

White, H. R., & Labouvie, E. W. (1994). Generality versus specificity of problem behavior. Psychological and functional differences. *Journal of Drug Issues, 24,* 55–74.

White, H. R., Loeber, R., & Farrington, D. P. (2008). Substance use, drug dealing, gang membership, and gun carrying and their predictive associations with serious violence and serious theft. In R. Loeber, D. P. Farrington, M. Stouthamer-Loeber & H. R. White (Eds.), *Violence and serious theft: Development and prediction from childhood to adulthood* (pp. 137–166). New York, NY: Routledge Taylor and Francis Group.

White, H. R., Loeber, R., Stouthamer-Loeber, M., & Farrington, D. P. (1999). Developmental associations between substance use and violence. *Development and Psychopathology, 11,* 785–803.

White, H. R., Mun, E.-Y., Lee, C., & Loeber, R. (2012). Developmental patterns of alcohol use in relation to persistence and desistance of serious violent offending among African American and Caucasian young men. *Criminology, 50,* 391–426.

White, H. R., Pandina, R. J., & LaGrange, R. L. (1987). Longitudinal predictors of serious substance use and delinquency. *Criminology, 25,* 715–740.

White, H. R., Tice, P., Loeber, R., & Stouthamer-Loeber, M. (2002). Illegal acts committed by adolescents under the influence of alcohol and drugs. *Journal of Research in Crime and Delinquency, 39,* 131–152.

Widom C. S., & Hiller-Sturmhöfel, S. H. (2001). Alcohol abuse as risk factor of and consequence of child abuse. *Alcohol Research & Health, 25,* 52–57.

Widom, C. S., Marmorstein, N. R., & White, H. R. (2006). Childhood victimization and illicit drug use in middle adulthood. *Psychology of Addictive Behavior, 20,* 394–403.

Widom, C. S., White, H. R., Czaja, S., & Marmorstein, N. (2007). Long-term effects of child abuse and neglect on alcohol use and excessive drinking in middle adulthood. *Journal of Studies on Alcohol and Drugs. 68,* 317–326.

Windle, M. (1990). A longitudinal study of antisocial behaviors in early adolescence as predictors of late adolescent substance use: Gender and ethnic group differences. *Journal of Abnormal Psychology, 99*(1), 86–91.

Workowski, E. J. (2003). Criminal violence and drug use: An exploratory study among substance abusers in residential treatment. *Journal of Offender Rehabilitation, 37,* 109–121.

Yacoubian Jr., G. S., Urbach, B. J., Larsen, K. L., Johnson, R. J., & Peters Jr., R. J. (2000). A comparison of drug use between prostitutes and other female arrestees. *Journal of Alcohol & Drug Education, 46*(2), 12.

Young, A. M., Boyd, C., & Hubbell, A. (2000). Prostitution, drug use, and coping with psychological distress. *Journal of Drug Issues, 30*(4), 789–800.

Young, D. W., Dembo, R., & Henderson, C. E. (2007). A national survey of substance abuse treatment for juvenile offenders. *Journal of Substance Abuse Treatment, 32*(3), 255–266.

Zhang, Z. (2003). *Drug and alcohol use and related matters among arrestees 2003*. Washington, DC: National Institute of Justice, Office of Justice Programs.

Zhang, L., Welte, J. W., & Wieczorek, W. W. (2002). The role of aggression-related alcohol expectancies in explaining the link between alcohol and violent behavior. *Substance Use & Misuse, 37*(4), 457–471.

Zucker, R. A., Wong, M. W., Clark, D. B., Leonard, K. E., Schulenberg, J. E., Cornelius, J. R., Fitzgerald, H. E., Homish, G. G., ... Puttler, L. I. (2006). Predicting risky drinking outcomes longitudinally: What kind of advance notice can we get? *Alcoholism: Clinical and Experimental Research, 30*, 243–252.

Substance Use and School and Occupational Performance

Ioana Popovici *and* Michael T. French

Abstract

Health economists have been actively investigating the relationships between substance use and educational achievement/labor market performance outcomes. Although researchers agree on the direction and magnitude of the relationships between substance use and some of these outcomes, many questions remain unanswered. For instance, the literature generally indicates that drug use has a negative impact on most academic outcomes. Less evidence exists, however, of a negative impact of alcohol use on education. Although results suggest that drinking is associated with lower grades, and most research shows that drinking negatively impacts the probability of graduating from high school, several studies have been unable to find significant relationships between alcohol consumption and the number of years of schooling completed. Similarly, although most studies find a wage premium for moderate alcohol users, results on the effect of problem drinking or the use of other drugs on the probability of employment are mixed.

Key Words: substance use, alcohol, other drugs, educational achievement, labor market performance, wages, employment

Introduction

Epidemiological studies have demonstrated an association between substance abuse (alcohol and other drugs) and a variety of medical consequences, such as cardiovascular disease (D'Onofrio, Becker, & Woolard, 2006; Murray et al., 2002; Nolen-Hoeksema, 2004; Perret et al., 2002; Rehm et al., 2003; Rehm, Greenfield, & Rogers, 2001; Rimm, 2000), psychiatric disorders (Chi & Weisner, 2008; Grant et al., 2004; Hasin & Nunes, 1997; McBride, Van Buren, Terry, & Goldstein, 2000; Wu & Howard, 2007;), and injuries (Cherpitel et al., 2003; Gutjahr, Gmel, & Rehm, 2001; MacDonald, Wells, Giesbrecht, & Cherpitel, 1999; Mertens, Flisher, Fleming, & Weisner, 2007; Miller, Lestina, & Smith, 2001; Vinson, Borges, & Cherpitel, 2003; Zavala & French, 2003). Many economists have contributed to this epidemiological literature, but far more have analyzed the relationships between substance use and educational

achievement (Chatterji & DeSimone, 2005; Renna, 2008; Roebuck, French, & Dennis, 2004; Wolaver, 2002), labor market performance (Alexandre & French, 2004; Feng, Zhou, Butler, Booth, & French, 2001; French & Zarkin, 1995; French, Zarkin, & Dunlap, 1998; Mullahy & Sindelar, 1996; Van Ours, 2007), criminal activity (French & Maclean, 2006; French, McCollister, Alexandre, Chitwood, & McCoy, 2004; Rajkumar & French, 1997), and health services utilization (French, McGeary, Chitwood, & McCoy, 2000; McGeary & French, 2000; Parthasarathy & Weisner, 2006).

Among these consequences, educational achievement and labor market performance have received the most attention from economists. Several studies have linked substance use with undesirable educational and labor market outcomes, such as lower educational achievement, truancy, lower earnings/wages, unemployment, and reduced labor supply. Competing explanations of these associations abound, however, and their complexity makes it difficult to determine causality. For example, a negative association between alcohol abuse and the probability of being employed does not necessarily imply that alcohol abuse causes a higher likelihood of unemployment. It is certainly plausible that losing a job will lead to increased alcohol consumption (reverse causality). Alternatively, heavy consumption of alcohol and the probability of unemployment may be jointly determined by a common attitude toward risk that was unintentionally omitted from the empirical model (omitted variables bias). As these examples demonstrate, establishing whether substance use has a direct negative effect on educational and labor market outcomes is not a straightforward task. Causality between substance use and its potential consequences remains a source of debate among economists (French & Popovici, 2009), and there is a great deal of inconsistency in findings across studies that attempt to uncover the causal mechanisms.

Understanding the nature, magnitude, and direction of the link between substance use and educational/occupational outcomes has critical policy implications. If substance use has a negative impact on educational achievement or labor market performance, public policy tools geared toward modifying substance use choices (e.g., alcohol taxation, purchasing age limits, penalties for illicit drug possession, stricter substance-use regulations) could have the added benefit of improving these outcomes. Moreover, finding a strong and stable association between substance use and educational/occupational outcomes has important implications for substance abuse prevention and treatment program funding (McLellan, Lewis, O'Brien, & Kleber, 2000). If a third factor, such as parental influence, affects both substance use and schooling, then policies directed at parental education and support could be another effective use of public resources.

Substance Use and Educational Achievement
Conceptual Framework/Motivation

Several theories have been posited to explain a possible link between substance use and academic performance. It should be noted that the theories presented below are not mutually exclusive, as one or more of these mechanisms might operate simultaneously. Clinical research has indicated that substance use can have harmful effects on the development of the human brain (Hannigan, Spear, Spear, & Goodlett, 1999) and that substance abuse

reduces cognitive functioning, impairs learning and memory, and has the potential to worsen existing mental conditions (Brook, Balka, & Whiteman, 1999; Brown, Tapert, Granhol, & Delis, 2000; Hawkins, Catalano, & Miller, 1992; Zeigler et al., 2005). Since the human brain continues to develop in the early 20s, alcohol and other drugs can have an even more severe effect when consumed in adolescence. Studies suggest that alcohol use disorders in college students are associated with deficits in cognitive and neuropsychological functioning (Sher, Martin, Wood, & Rutledge, 1997; Wood, Sher, & Bartholow, 2002). Given this medical evidence, along with the fact that cognitive skills are critical determinants of school performance, one would expect a direct negative effect of heavy drinking or other drug use on educational attainment.

Although Parsons (1986) found inconclusive evidence of a negative effect of "social" drinking (or low levels of "soft" drug use) on cognition, a more recent review suggests that alcohol consumption above certain thresholds can lead to brain changes and cognitive-perceptual inefficiencies (Parsons & Nixon, 1998). An indirect mechanism by which drinking might negatively affect school performance is through the allocation of time spent studying and attending class (Powell, Williams, & Wechsler, 2004; Williams, Powell, & Wechsler, 2003; Wolaver, 2002). Social drinking (or the consumption of soft drugs) might reduce the number of hours spent studying or going to class, hence negatively affecting academic performance. Martinez and colleagues (2008) found that heavy drinking predicts attrition from college.

A mechanism supporting a reverse hypothesis is that studying reduces the time available for leisure, including social drinking or recreational drug use. In other words, enhanced school performance might lead to a reduction in substance use through time constraints. In support of this hypothesis, Wood and colleagues (2007) found that scheduling college classes on Friday mornings reduces excessive drinking on Thursday nights. Some authors argue that drinking might be a means of coping with poor educational performance (Renna, 2008), drawing up on evidence that dropping out of high school is correlated with the probability of developing alcohol abuse/dependence later on in life (Crum, Helzer, & Anthony, 1993). Poor school performance may also be a risk factor for cannabis use (Hawkins et al., 1992).

Although a negative effect of substance use on schooling outcomes seems most plausible, some authors have proposed theories that support a positive relationship. According to Williams and colleagues (2003), the friendships, social networks, and camaraderie forged while drinking might help alleviate stress, thus having a positive effect on school performance.

Finally, adolescent substance use is highly correlated with a range of individual and family characteristics that might also affect educational attainment. Stated differently, substance use might be an endogenous determinant of school performance. Factors such as personal attitude toward risk, rate of time preference, parental supervision or substance use, parental attitudes toward substance use and education, or peer influences are difficult to measure and, many times, not sufficiently controlled for in empirical models. Omitting some of these important predictors might lead to the estimation of spurious or biased effects of substance use on educational attainment. In other words, the consumption of addictive substances and poor academic performance might be jointly determined by a specific attitude towards risk that was unintentionally omitted from the model. Research suggests that controlling for prior academic achievement results in a reduction in the magnitude of the association between alcohol consumption and educational outcomes in college (Wood, Sher, Erickson, & DeBord, 1997; Wood, Sher, & McGowan, 2000). Failing properly to address this omitted variables problem will lead to biased coefficient estimates. Indeed, omitted variables bias could help explain some inconsistencies (mainly in magnitude) found in the literature. Many studies recognize and employ statistical techniques to address the potential endogeneity of substance use, but these techniques are not standardized or uniformly applied (French & Popovici, 2009).

Some variation in the magnitude of the relationship found between substance use and educational achievement could also stem from diversity in measures and samples. A few studies focus on alcohol abuse or dependence, while others examine the quantity and/or frequency of alcohol consumption or the age of substance use onset. Similarly, schooling outcomes vary and include number of years of school completed, the probability of graduating high school/college, truancy, and grade point average (GPA). Some of these measures are self-reported, while others are abstracted. The following section presents an overview of the results of these studies.

Review of Studies
ALCOHOL USE

Initial studies in this area found large negative correlations between alcohol use and educational attainment outcomes. Benham and Benham (1982) used a sample of young individuals from the 1910s and 1920s who were followed after 30 years. They found that drinking problems reduce the level of education by 1.5 years. Mullahy and Sindelar (1989, 1994) explored the impact of early onset alcohol dependence on the number of years of schooling completed. They found that teenage onset of alcoholism is correlated with early termination of schooling. Using data from Wave 1 of the New Haven site of the Epidemiological Catchment Area survey, Mullahy and Sindelar (1994) found that onset of alcoholism symptoms by age 22 reduces educational attainment by 5%. The results of these early studies should be interpreted with caution, however, as few address the potential endogeneity of alcohol use. As mentioned earlier, single equation cross-sectional results do not necessarily imply causality.

The earliest study to recognize and attempt to address the endogeneity issue is Cook and Moore (1993). The authors used a sample of high-school seniors from the 1982 wave of the National Longitudinal Survey of Youth (NLSY). They estimated the effect of drinking on the number of years of post secondary school completed by 1988. Their results showed that frequent drinking reduces educational attainment by 2.3 years. Although large, their estimates were relatively imprecise.

Several other studies have also found a negative impact of alcohol consumption on educational attainment. Using a sample from the NLSY, Yamada, Kendrix, and Yamada (1996) focused on high school graduation as their dependent variable. Their results indicated that a 10% increase in alcohol consumption reduces the probability of graduation by 6.5%. Koch and McGeary (2005) found that alcohol initiation before the age of 14 lowers the probability of high-school completion by 7% to 22%. Analyzing data from the NLSY, Chatterji and DeSimone (2005) found that heavy alcohol use has a negative effect on the probability of graduating or remaining in school. Using the same survey, Renna (2007) found that heavy drinking in high school decreases the probability of graduating on schedule.

Other studies have uncovered little or no effect of alcohol use on education. Chatterji (1998) used the NLSY and could find no evidence of a significant relationship between weekly use of alcohol before the age of 17 and years of education attained by the age of 21. Using data on same-sex sibling pairs from the 1979–1990 panels of the NLSY, Koch and Ribar (2001) estimated the relationship between drinking onset and the number of years of schooling completed by the age of 25. They found that the older the age of initiation, the greater was the number of years of schooling completed. Nevertheless, their results were not robust to alternative specifications, and the authors concluded that the impact of drinking on education is probably small. Dee and Evans (2003) used pooled data from the Monitoring the Future surveys to analyze the relationship between minimum legal drinking age (MLDA) laws and alcohol consumption, and the Census Bureau's 1990 Public Use Sample to estimate the relationship between drinking ages and schooling. They used both sets of results to estimate more accurately the impact of alcohol use on educational outcomes. Their results indicated that teen drinking does not have a significant effect on the probability of completing high school, entering college, or completing college. The authors concluded that, according to their results, adolescent alcohol use does not independently affect educational achievement. Using data from the National Education Longitudinal Study, Chatterji's (2006a) results suggest a negative correlation between high school drinking and educational attainment around the age of 26. Despite the strong association, the author did not present any information to support a causal relationship.

Some researchers have argued that alcohol use may affect the quality of human capital stock accumulated, such as school performance per se rather than the numbers of years of schooling. A growing body of research has focused on the impact of alcohol consumption on measures of performance. The results found in DeSimone and Wolaver (2005) suggest that alcohol use is negatively correlated with the probability that a student will receive an "A" grade and positively correlated with the likelihood of receiving a grade lower than a "B." The estimated effect is stronger for binge drinking than for light drinking. Wolaver (2002) used data from the 1993 College Alcohol Study and found that drinking in college reduces college GPA and the number of study hours and also affects the choice of academic major, with drinkers less likely to choose majors that traditionally pay high salaries (e.g., engineering) and more likely to choose majors that command lower salaries (e.g., social sciences). Using data from the Harvard School of Public Health's College Alcohol Study, Williams and colleagues (2003) investigated the direct and indirect effects of drinking in college on educational attainment. They found that the quantity of alcohol consumed is negatively correlated with GPA and the number of hours spent studying. Renna (2008) used the NLSY and found that binge drinking in high school negatively affects the likelihood of receiving a high-school diploma and is positively associated with the probability of graduating with a general education development (GED) degree instead.

OTHER DRUG USE

Although alcohol is the most commonly used substance among adolescents (Substance Abuse and Mental Health Services Administration [SAMHSA], 2008), researchers have also focused on the impact of the use of other drugs (e.g., cannabis, cocaine, methamphetamine) on education. Some studies have found that drug use reduces the probability of high school completion. Chatterji (2006b) used data from the National Education Longitudinal Study to explore the relationship between marijuana and cocaine use during high school and the number of years of schooling completed. The results showed a negative relationship between drug use and educational outcomes. Using data on high school seniors from the NLSY, Yamada and colleagues (1996) found that monthly or more frequent marijuana consumption reduces the probability of high school completion. Bray, Zarkin, Ringwalt, and Qi (2000) analyzed data on students from a southeastern U.S. public school system. Their findings suggest that marijuana use initiation during high school more than doubles the probability of high school dropout. The effects were comparable for 16-, 17-, and 18-year-olds. Roebuck and colleagues (2004) explored the relationship between drug use and school attendance. The authors used pooled data on high school students from the 1997 and 1998 National Household Surveys on Drug Abuse. Their results indicated a positive relationship between marijuana use and both truancy and dropping out of high school. The results, however, were mainly attributed to chronic marijuana users.

Labor Market Performance
Conceptual Framework/Motivation

Following Grossman's seminal article (Grossman, 1972), economists often model labor market outcomes as a function of the individual's human and health capital. One would expect that better health and greater human capital would improve labor market performance. On the other hand, labor market success (e.g., occupational prestige, rewarding work, higher earnings) can positively influence overall physical and mental health status. Good health is partly determined by modifiable behavioral choices such as deciding to exercise, to drink in moderation, to eat a healthy diet, and not to smoke or use addictive substances (Davis et al., 1994; French, Popovici, & Maclean, 2009; McGinnis & Foege, 1993; Mokdad, Marks, Stroup, & Gerberding, 2000). Thus, a logical extension of the human capital model (Becker, 1975; Grossman, 1972) relates labor market performance to substance use. Given the background presented earlier, we would expect to find a significant negative association between substance use and productivity. In the short-run, substance use might directly affect productivity through a higher probability of injury, absenteeism, accidents, or overall job performance. In the long run, substance use might have an indirect effect on workers' productivity through educational capital or on-the-job training. Numerous studies have confirmed that education and experience are positively correlated with employment, earnings, and occupational prestige (Card, 1999; Dustmann & Meghir, 2005; Williams, 2009). Moreover, several studies have explored the causal relationship between education and labor market outcomes, finding that wages are a convex function of years of education (Card, 1999; Lemieux, 2006; Mincer, 1997). In a competitive labor market, differences in skill acquisition and productivity should emerge in the form of lower labor supply and earnings differentials.

Although a negative effect of substance use on labor market performance is most plausible based on theoretical considerations, a positive effect is also possible. The epidemiological, medical, and economics literatures report a variety of benefits (mainly through reduced stress and a lower risk of cardiovascular disease) related to moderate alcohol use (French & Zavala, 2007; Peele & Brodsky, 2000; Shaper, 1993). It is therefore possible that moderate alcohol use may enhance labor market productivity as well, thereby increasing earnings.

Several arguments can be made in support of a reverse effect, whereby labor market changes affect substance use. Individuals who lose their jobs are at a higher risk of misusing alcohol or consuming illegal substances due to the trauma and pressure associated with job loss. Job loss also lowers the opportunity costs associated with consuming alcohol and other drugs (Forcier, 1985). Alternatively, a decline in earnings or outright job loss will limit the

resources available to purchase alcohol and other drugs, which would imply a negative relationship between employment problems and substance use (Ruhm, 1995). This phenomenon is commonly referred to as an "income effect" in the economics literature.

Finally, just as school achievement and substance use could be simultaneously determined by a third factor that was unintentionally omitted from the model, substance use could be endogenous when studying labor market outcomes. Factors such as psychiatric problems, problems with family or friends, or underlying personality traits that could influence both substance use and occupational performance are difficult to observe and quantify. As mentioned earlier, failure to account for these factors could result in biased coefficient estimates. A large number of studies have used various methods to control for the potential endogeneity of substance use. Nevertheless, obtaining the data necessary to apply these methods is challenging, which has made the credibility of such findings a source of debate among researchers (French & Popovici, 2009).

A wide range of labor market outcomes have appeared in the literature, with some studies focusing on wages, earnings, or number of hours worked, while others explored the effect of substance use on the probability of employment, unemployment, or labor market participation. Measures for substance use also exhibit considerable variation, with some studies analyzing the effects of any substance use, moderate use, or heavy consumption, while others preferred to use indicators of abuse or dependence. The following section presents a review of studies that explore the relationship between substance use and labor market performance.

Review of Studies
ALCOHOL USE AND WAGES/EARNINGS

Early studies in the literature found a negative and significant correlation between heavy alcohol use and earnings (Mullahy & Sindelar, 1989, 1991, 1993; see Cook & Moore, 2000, for a review of this literature). Mullahy and Sindelar (1989) found that early-onset alcoholism negatively affects earnings through lower levels of education. Mullahy and Sindelar (1991, 1993) confirmed that alcoholism has a strong negative impact on earnings.

Although these studies found significant associations, their findings do not imply causality from substance use to earnings. A key limitation of these initial studies is a failure to address the potential endogeneity of alcohol use. In other words, one cannot infer that drinking leads to lower wages. Lower earnings might in fact lead to lower alcohol consumption if alcohol is a normal good. Another possibility is that variables unintentionally omitted from the model (such as time preference or unobserved personal characteristics) might affect both earnings and drinking.

Several recent studies have addressed the potential endogeneity of drinking in wages/earnings equations. Among these, some found that, compared with abstinence or heavy drinking, moderate alcohol use is associated with higher wages or earnings (Barrett, 2002; Bray, 2005; French & Zarkin, 1995; Hamilton & Hamilton, 1997; Heien, 1996; MacDonald & Shields, 2001). Using a company-based survey, French and Zarkin (1995) found a significant wage premium for moderate drinkers compared with abstainers or heavy drinkers. Heien (1996) found a 50% wage premium at the optimal level of alcohol consumption. Using Canadian data, Hamilton and Hamilton (1997) found a nonlinear relationship between alcohol use and wages. Their results indicate a wage premium for moderate drinking over abstinence as well as a substantial wage penalty for heavy drinking. These findings were confirmed by Barrett (2002) using the Australian National Health Survey for 1989–1990. In a model of wage determination where wages are affected by drinking through the formation and accumulation of human capital, Bray's (2005) findings suggest that moderate drinking is positively associated with the returns to education or experience relative to abstinence and heavy drinking. MacDonald and Shields (2001) found support for an inverted U-shaped relationship between alcohol use and wages in the United Kingdom, with moderate drinking generating the highest returns.

The fact that other studies have addressed the endogeneity issue and found no significant penalty for heavy drinking makes it difficult to interpret this literature. For example, using data from the 1991 and 1992 National Household Surveys on Drug Abuse, Zarkin and colleagues (1998) could not replicate the results found by French and Zarkin (1995) at the national level. They found instead that the wage premium endured above moderate levels of alcohol use. Moreover, the authors found no statistically significant wage premium for moderate-drinking women. Using data from the Netherlands, Van Ours (2004) showed that alcohol use generates a 10% wage premium for males but found no effect of drinking on wages for females. The author suggested that these findings might be

related to social networking. Relative to abstainers, Auld (2005) found a 10% income premium for moderate-drinking Canadian males and a 12% income premium for heavy drinkers.

Other studies have focused entirely on the impact of heavy drinking or alcohol abuse on wages and earnings. Using data from the U.S. NLSY, Kenkel and Ribar (1994) found a 12% earnings penalty for heavy drinking and a 30% penalty for alcohol abusing young males. They downplayed the findings for females, however, because they were not robust to sensitivity tests.

ALCOHOL USE AND EMPLOYMENT

According to a review of the early literature examining the relationship between alcohol consumption and employment (Cook & Moore, 2000), drinking per se has little to no effect on labor supply. Studies focused on alcohol dependency (Mullahy & Sindelar, 1991; 1993) showed evidence of a negative relationship between problem drinking and employment, where problem drinking referred to individuals who met the criteria for alcohol abuse or dependence.

Again, a major shortcoming of these earlier studies is the high likelihood of omitted variables bias. More recently, several studies have tried to address the potential endogeneity of alcohol use in their empirical specification (Feng et al., 2001; Kenkel & Ribar, 1994; Johansson, Alho, Kiiskinen, & Poikolainen, 2007; MacDonald & Shields, 2004 Mullahy & Sindelar, 1996), but the results are mixed.

The majority of studies suggest that heavy or problematic alcohol consumption negatively affects the probability of employment. Using data from the U.S. National Health Interview Survey, Mullahy and Sindelar (1996) were able to confirm their earlier results that alcohol abuse increases the probability of being unemployed and reduces the likelihood of being employed. Yet their results were not statistically significant. Terza (2002) reanalyzed the data in Mullahy and Sindelar (1996) by applying a new econometric estimation method, a multinomial choice regression specification (i.e., multinomial logit with an endogenous treatment effect) that allows for nonlinearity of the regression structure while accounting for the endogeneity of substance use (McFadden, 1973). Rather than treat the employment status variable as continuous, this new method allowed for the nonlinearity of the regression specification implied by the multinomial nature of the dependent variable (i.e., out of the labor force, unemployed, or employed). Although Terza's results are largely consistent with Mullahy and Sindelar (1996), in contrast to the latter study, problem drinking is found to have a statistically significant negative effect on the likelihood of employment. MacDonald and Shields (2004) analyzed data from the Health Survey of England and found a negative and statistically significant relationship between problem drinking and the likelihood of being employed. Johansson and colleagues (2007) found alcohol dependence to be negatively associated with the likelihood of being employed in Finland.

A few other studies contradicted the results presented above, raising questions about the true effect of drinking on labor supply. Feng and colleagues (2001) found that problem drinking (defined as having met the criteria for an alcohol abuse/dependence diagnosis) was positively and significantly associated with employment for men in a sample of prime-age individuals from six southern states in the United States. Yet the coefficients in this study changed signs and were not statistically significant for women. The authors presented several possible explanations for these conflicting results (i.e., problem drinkers might be able to mask their drinking, tight labor markets might force employers to overlook problem drinking when hiring, or employees might engage in problem drinking only outside the workplace). Kenkel and Ribar (1994) analyzed a sample of young adults from the NLSY and found contradictory results as well. Specifically, they found that alcohol abuse has a negative effect on hours worked for men and a positive effect for women. Only the results for women, however, were statistically significant. The authors cautioned that the relatively young age of the sample (younger than 31 years) should be considered when interpreting these results, as the harmful health effects of chronic heavy drinking often emerge later in life.

EXPLORING REVERSE CAUSALITY

As noted earlier, several mechanisms support a reverse effect of employment, labor supply, or earnings on alcohol consumption. A few studies use aggregate data to examine the effect of unemployment on overall alcohol consumption (Brenner, 1979; Freeman, 1999; Ruhm, 1995). These studies found that drinking varies procyclically (i.e., an increase in the unemployment rate reduces aggregate drinking). This result confirms the hypothesis that alcohol is a normal good and that when incomes shrink, alcohol consumption therefore decreases as

well. Nevertheless, macro data have several limitations, the most important being the inability to empirically determine the effect of unemployment across different categories of drinkers. Some of these shortcomings have been overcome in recent studies through the use of individual-level data, but the results have generally been mixed. Dee (2001) and Ruhm and Black (2002) examined the impact of macroeconomic conditions (proxied by the unemployment rate in state of residence) on individual-level drinking. Dee (2001) used the 1984–1995 cross sections of the Behavioral Risk Factor Surveillance System (BRFSS) and estimated state fixed-effects models. He found that although binge drinking is countercyclic, overall drinking decreases during economic downturns. Ruhm and Black (2002) used data from the 1987–1999 interview years of the BRFSS and found a procyclic variation in overall drinking (mostly concentrated among heavy drinkers). Ettner (1997) examined the impact of being unemployed on alcohol use and dependence. The author used cross-sectional data from the 1988 National Health Interview Survey and found that both alcohol consumption and dependence are procyclic (being unemployed lowers alcohol use and dependence) but that the effects of involuntary unemployment are mixed.

OTHER DRUGS AND WAGES/EARNINGS

Although one would expect a negative association between other (often illegal) drug use and wages, the results are inconsistent. Surprisingly, some studies report results showing that drug use is associated with a wage premium (Gill & Michaels, 1992; Kaestner, 1991; Register & Williams, 1992). Using the 1984 wave of the NLSY, Kaestner (1991) examined the wage effects of cannabis and cocaine use for young adults. He found a wage premium for marijuana and cocaine users. Moreover, the result was consistent across gender and age groups. The author states that illicit drug use may have a greater impact on labor supply and annual earnings than on wages per se. Gill and Michaels (1992) used the 1980 and 1984 waves of the same national survey. Their results also suggest that illicit drug users receive higher wages than nonusers. The authors surmise that individuals might consume illegal substances to deal with workplace stress and emotional difficulties, which might elevate their productivity, at least in the short term. Register and Williams (1992) found similar results. Using the 1984 wave of the NLSY, they found that young males who use cannabis earn higher wages than nonusers. Nevertheless, no statistically significant association was found between cocaine consumption and wages. Given differences in the recognition and treatment of endogeneity across studies, this limitation could be driving some of these surprising results.

Several other studies found evidence of a negative association between other drug use and wages, although the magnitude of the relationship varied widely across age groups and patterns of use (Buchmueller & Zuvekas, 1998; Burgess & Propper, 1998; Bryant, Sumaranayake, and Wilhite, 2000; Kaestner, 1994b; Kandel, Chen, & Gill, 1995; Van Ours, 2007). Kaestner (1994b) updated his earlier analysis by using a panel from the NLSY. He found negative wage effects of cannabis and cocaine use among men and negative associations between wages and lifetime cannabis use among women. The wage effects of recent cannabis and cocaine use, however, were positive among women. The author suggested that some drug users might intentionally select jobs in which their drug use does not affect their productivity. Kandel and colleagues (1995) analyzed the effect of illicit drug consumption on earnings using a cohort of the NLSY. Their results indicate that the sign and magnitude of the relationship between earnings and drug use vary across individuals' career stages. They found a positive relationship between wages and drug use in the early stages of an individual's career and a negative relationship later. Using the same data source, Burgess and Propper (1998) investigated the effects of adolescent illicit drug use on employment outcomes in adulthood. Their results suggest that soft drug use in adolescence has, at most, a very modest effect on the earnings of men in their late 20s or 30s. Nevertheless, they found that early "hard" drug use has a significant negative impact. These effects were substantial and affected both the earnings level and growth. Buchmueller and Zuvekas (1998) examined the relationship between wages and various categories of illicit drug use in a sample of young adults and prime age workers using the 1980–1984 Epidemiologic Catchment Area surveys. They found that young workers who reported daily illicit drug consumption were more likely to earn lower incomes than young workers who did not report such use. Among prime-age males, the authors found strong evidence that pathological use or dependence was negatively associated with earnings. Bryant and colleagues (2000) used the NLSY to examine past illicit drug use and found that a history of illicit drug use lowered expected wages. More recently, Van Ours (2007) explored the

wage effects of cannabis use for prime-age males in Amsterdam. He found that recent cannabis use has a negative effect on wages. Moreover, he found the wage loss to be greater for cannabis users who initiated consumption early in life.

Finally, French and colleagues (1998) used a dataset compiled from employees at six different workplaces. Using a range of lifetime and current indicators of illicit drug use, the authors identified predominantly nonsignificant relationships between various patterns of illicit drug use and wages after controlling for alcohol use.

OTHER DRUGS AND EMPLOYMENT

Research consensus has not been reached on the direction and magnitude of the effects of various patterns of illicit drug use on employment. Some studies report worse employment outcomes for illicit drug users. French, Roebuck, and Alexandre (2001) used the 1997 National Household Survey on Drug Abuse (NHSDA) to investigate the effect of both chronic and nonchronic illicit drug use on employment and labor force participation. Their results strongly indicated that chronic illicit drug use was associated with a lower probability of employment for males and females and a lower probability of labor force participation for males. Non-chronic illicit drug use was not significantly correlated with any of the selected employment indicators. MacDonald and Pudney (2000) used data from the British Crime Survey to estimate the effect of illicit drug use on occupational attainment and employment. They found little evidence to support a significant relationship between drug use and occupational attainment. Nevertheless, their findings suggest a strong positive correlation between drug use (particularly the use of opiates, cocaine, and crack cocaine) and the risk of unemployment. DeSimone (2002) analyzed the relationship between marijuana and cocaine use and employment among males using NLSY data (1984–1988). The results indicate that the use of either marijuana or cocaine significantly reduces the likelihood of employment among males. Cocaine use demonstrated an adverse employment effect that was 50% to 100% greater than that of marijuana use. Alexandre and French (2004) used unique data collected in low-income and high-crime neighborhoods in Miami, Florida, to examine the relationship between chronic illicit drug use and a range of employment indicators. The main finding of the research was that chronic illicit drug use significantly reduced the probability of employment regardless of specification or gender.

Other studies were not able to find robust support for the hypothesis that illicit drug use is detrimental to labor market success. Gill and Michaels (1992) found that drug use is correlated with a lower likelihood of being employed, but hard drug use is, surprisingly, not significantly related to employment. Register and Williams (1992) found that marijuana use in the past 30 days is negatively associated with employment, but having used marijuana on the job any time in the last year is positively associated with employment. Cocaine consumption showed a similar sign pattern, but the coefficients were not statistically significant. Kaestner (1994a) used data from the NLSY to estimate the effect of illicit drug use on the labor supply of young adults. Specifically, the author examined whether frequency and timing of marijuana and cocaine use were systematically associated with labor supply using both cross-sectional and panel data models. The cross-sectional estimates revealed that illicit drug use had a significant negative impact on labor supply while the longitudinal estimates indicated that consumption of these substances did not significantly affect labor supply. Zarkin and colleagues (1998) used cross-sectional data from the 1991 NHSDA and included several categories of substances such as marijuana, alcohol, cigarettes, cocaine, and other drugs. The authors found that illicit drug use has little effect on the number of hours worked by young men.

Discussion and Conclusion

During the past two to three decades, economists and other researchers have been actively investigating the relationships between substance use (alcohol and other drugs), educational attainment, and labor market outcomes. In general, the literature indicates that substance use (especially cannabis and cocaine) has a negative impact on most schooling outcomes, such as number of years of education completed, high school graduation, and grades. Moreover, results suggest that drinking is associated with lower grades, and most research shows a negative effect of drinking on the probability of graduating high school. Several studies, however, were unable to find evidence of a negative impact of alcohol use on educational achievement measured as number of years of schooling completed.

When it comes to the effect of substance use on labor market performance, most studies find a wage premium for moderate alcohol users relative to other drinking categories. Results are mixed, however, with respect to the effect of problem drinking or the use of other drugs on the probability of employment.

Future Directions

Reliably estimating the effects of substance use on individual and societal outcomes is important for policy makers, educators, employers, social service organizations, and other groups. The present review points to the need for future research in this area and particularly for studies employing quality data sets and rigorous research methods to address causality, direction, and magnitude.

Several questions remain to be addressed in future studies. For instance, is there a relationship between alcohol use and the number of years of schooling completed? What is the direction of the causality reflected by the negative associations found between cannabis and cocaine use and schooling outcomes? Does a wage penalty exist for alcohol abusers or users of other drugs? In addition, more research is needed on the relationship between substance use and employment outcomes. Finally, as mentioned above, the primary statistical challenge that must be addressed in this line of research is the potential endogeneity of substance use. Addressing the endogeneity issue and establishing causality is not an easy task, as demonstrated by the inconsistency of results across studies. This review clearly illustrates the need for future studies that use rigorous research methods to address this problem.

Acknowledgments

Financial assistance for this study was provided by research grants with the National Institute on Alcoholism and Alcohol Abuse (R01 AA015695) and the National Institute on Drug Abuse (R01 DA018645). We gratefully acknowledge William Russell and Carmen Martinez for editorial assistance.

References

Alexandre, P. K., & French, M. T. (2004). Further evidence on the labor market effects of addiction: Chronic drug use and employment in metropolitan Miami. *Contemporary Economic Policy, 22*, 382–393.

Auld, M. C. (2005). Smoking, drinking, and income. *The Journal of Human Resources, 15*, 504–518.

Barrett, G. F. (2002). The effect of alcohol consumption on earnings. *The Economic Record, 78*, 79–96.

Becker, G. S. (1975). *Human capital: A theoretical and empirical analysis with special reference to education* (2nd ed.). Chicago, IL: University of Chicago Press.

Benham, L., & Benham, A. (1982). Employment, earnings, and psychiatric diagnosis. In V. Fuchs (Ed.), *Economic aspects of health* (pp. 203–220). Chicago, IL: University of Chicago Press.

Bray, J. W. (2005). Alcohol use, human capital, and wages. *Journal of Labor Economics, 23*, 279–312.

Bray, J., Zarkin, G., Ringwalt, C., & Qi, J. (2000). The relationship between marijuana initiation and dropping out of high school. *Health Economics*, 9, 9–18.

Brenner, M. H. (1979, September). Mortality and the national economy. *Lancet*, 15, 568–573.

Brook, J. S., Balka, E. B., & Whiteman, M. (1999). The risks for late adolescence of early marijuana use. *American Journal of Public Health*, 89, 1549–1554.

Brown, S. A., Tapert, S. F., Granhol, E., & Delis, D. C. (2000). Neurocognitive functioning of adolescents: Effects of protracted alcohol use. *Alcoholism: Clinical and Experimental Research*, 24, 164–171.

Buchmueller, T. C., & Zuvekas, S. H. (1998). Drug use, drug abuse, and labor market outcomes. *Health Economics*, 7, 229–245.

Burgess, S. M., & Propper, C. (1998). Early health-related behaviours and their impact on later life chances: Evidence from the US. *Health Economics*, 7, 381–399.

Bryant, R. R., Sumaranayake, V. A., & Wilhite, A. (2000). The effect of drug use on wages: A human capital interpretation. *American Journal of Drug Alcohol Abuse*, 26, 659–682.

Card, D. E. (1999). The causal effect of education on earnings. In O. Ashenfelter and D. Card (Eds.) *Handbook of labor economics* (vol. 3, no. 3, 1st ed.) (pp. 1801–1863). Amsterdam: Elsevier Science North-Holland.

Chatterji, P. (1998). Does use of alcohol and illicit drugs during adolescence affect educational attainment? Results from three estimation methods. Working paper. Johns Hopkins University School of Hygiene and Public Health.

Chatterji, P. (2006a). Does alcohol use during high-school affect educational attainment?: Evidence from the National Education Longitudinal Study. *Economics of Education Review*, 25, 482–497.

Chatterji, P. (2006b). Illicit drug use and educational attainment. *Health Economics*, 15, 489–511.

Chatterji, P., & DeSimone, J. (2005). *Adolescent drinking and high-school dropout* (NBER Working Paper Series, No. 11337). Cambridge, MA: National Bureau of Economic Research.

Cherpitel, C. J., Bond, J., Ye, Y., Borges, G., MacDonald, S., Stockwell, T., et al. (2003). Alcohol-related injury in the ER: A cross-national meta-analysis from the Emergency Room Collaborative Alcohol Analysis Project (ERCAAP). *Journal of Studies on Alcohol*, 64, 641–649.

Chi, F. W., & Weisner, C. M. (2008). Nine-year psychiatric trajectories and substance use outcomes—an application of the group-based modeling approach, *Evaluation Review*, 32, 39–58.

Cook, P. J., & Moore, M. J. (1993). Drinking and schooling. *Journal of Health Economics*, 12, 411–429

Cook, P. J., & Moore, M. J. (2000). Alcohol. In A. Culyer and J. Newhouse (Eds.). *Handbook of health economics* (Vol. 1b), (pp. 629–674). Amsterdam: Elsevier.

Crum, R. M., Helzer, J. E., & Anthony, J. C. (1993). Level of education and alcohol abuse and dependence in adulthood: A further inquiry. *American Journal of Public Health*, 83, 830–837.

Davis, M. A., Neuhaus, J. M., Moritz, D. J., Lein, D., Barclay, J. D., & Murphy, S. P. (1994). Health behaviors and survival among middle-aged and older men and women in the NHANES I Epidemiologic Follow-up Study. *Preventive Medicine*, 23, 369–376.

Dee, T. S. (2001). Alcohol abuse and economic conditions: Evidence from repeated cross-sections of individual-level data. *Health economics*, 10, 257–270.

Dee, T. S., & Evans, W. N. (2003). Teen drinking and educational attainment: Evidence from two-sample instrumental variables estimates. *Journal of Labor Economics*, 21, 178–209.

DeSimone, J. (2002). Illicit drug use and employment. *Journal of Labor Economics*, 20, 952–977.

DeSimone, J., & Wolaver, A. (2005). *Drinking and academic performance in high school*. (NBER Working Paper Series, #11035). Cambridge, MA: National Bureau of Economic Research.

D'Onofrio, G., Becker, B., & Woolard, R. H. (2006). The impact of alcohol, tobacco, and other drug use and abuse in the emergency department. *Emergency Medicine Clinics of North America*, 24, 925–967.

Dustmann, C., & Meghir, C. (2005). Wages, experience and seniority. *Review of Economic Studies*, 72, 77–108.

Ettner, S. (1997). Measuring the human cost of a weak economy: Does unemployment lead to alcohol abuse? *Social Science and Medicine*, 44, 251–260.

Feng, W., Zhou, W., Butler, J. S., Booth, B. M., & French, M. T. (2001). The impact of problem drinking on employment. *Health Economics*, 10, 509–521.

Forcier, M. W. (1985). Labor force behavior of alcoholics: A review. *The International Journal of Addictions*, 20, 253–268.

Freeman, D. G. (1999). A note on economic conditions and alcohol problems. *Journal of Health Economics*, 18, 661–670.

French, M. T., & Maclean, J. C. (2006). Underage alcohol use, delinquency, and criminal activity. *Health Economics*, 15, 1261–1281.

French, M. T., McCollister, K. E., Alexandre, P. K., Chitwood, D. D., & McCoy, C. B. (2004). Revolving roles in drug-related crime: The cost of chronic drug users as victims and perpetrators. *Journal of Quantitative Criminology*, 20, 217–241.

French, M. T., McGeary, K. A., Chitwood, D. D., & McCoy, C. B. (2000). Chronic illicit drug use, health services utilization and the cost of medical care. *Social Science& Medicine*, 50, 1703–1713.

French, M. T., & Popovici, I. (2009). That instrument is lousy! In search of agreement when using instrumental variables estimation in substance use research. Working paper in review.

French, M. T., Popovici, I., & Maclean, J. C. (September-October, 2009). Do alcohol consumers exercise more? Findings from a national survey. *American Journal of Health Promotion*, 24, 2–10.

French, M. T., Roebuck, M. C., & Alexandre, P. K. (2001). Illicit drug use, employment, and labor force participation. *Southern Economic Journal*, 68, 349–368.

French, M. T., & Zarkin, G. A. (1995). Is moderate alcohol use related to wages? Evidence from four worksites. *Journal of Health Economics*, 14, 319–344.

French, M. T., Zarkin, G. A., & Dunlap, L. J. (1998). Illicit drug use, absenteeism, and earnings at six US worksites. *Contemporary Economic Policy*, 16, 334–346.

French, M. T., & Zavala, S. K. (2007). The health benefits of moderate drinking revisited: Alcohol use and self-reported health status. *American Journal of Health Promotion*, 21, 484–491.

Gill, A. M., & Michaels, R. J. (1992). Does drug use lower wages? *Industrial and Labor Relations Review*, 45, 419–434.

Grant, B. F., Dawson, D. A., Stinson, F. S., Chou, S. P., Dufour, M. C., & Pickering, R. P. (2004). The 12-month prevalence and trends in DSM-IV alcohol abuse and dependence: United States, 1991–1992 and 2001–2002. *Drug and Alcohol Dependence, 74*, 223–234.

Grossman, M. (1972). On the concept of health capital and the demand for health. *Journal of Political Economy, 80*, 223–255.

Gutjahr, E., Gmel, G., & Rehm, J. (2001). Relation between average alcohol consumption and disease: An overview. *European Addiction Research, 7*, 117–127.

Hamilton, V., & Hamilton, B. (1997). Alcohol and earnings: Does drinking yield a wage premium? *Canadian Journal of Economics, 30*, 135–151.

Hannigan, J. H., Spear, L. P., Spear, N. E., & Goodlett, C. R. (Eds.). (1999). *Alcohol and alcoholism: Effects on brain and development*. Mahwah, New Jersey: Lawrence Erlbaum Associates.

Hasin, D. S., & Nunes, E. (1997). Comorbidity of alcohol, drug, and psychiatric disorders: Epidemiology. In H. R. Kranzler and B. J. Rounsaville (Eds.), *Dual diagnosis and treatment: Substance abuse and comorbid mental and psychiatric disorders* (pp. 1–31). New York: Marcel Dekker, Inc.

Hawkins, J. D., Catalano, R. F., & Miller, J. Y. (1992). Risk and protective factors for alcohol and other drug problems in adolescence and early adulthood: Implications for substance use prevention. *Psychological Bulletin, 112*, 64–105.

Heien, D. M. (1996). Do drinkers earn less? *Southern Economic Journal, 60*, 63–68.

Johansson, E., Alho, H., Kiiskinen, U., & Poikolainen, K. (2007). The association of alcohol dependency with employment probability: Evidence from the population survey "Health 2000 in Finland." *Health Economics, 16*, 739–754.

Kaestner, R. (1991). The effect of illicit drug use on the wages of young adults. *Journal of Labor Economics, 9*, 381–412.

Kaestner, R. (1994a). The effect of illicit drug use on the labor supply of young adults. *The Journal of Human Resources, 29*, 126–155.

Kaestner, R. (1994b). New estimates of the effect of marijuana and cocaine use on wages. *Industrial and Labor Relations Review, 47*, 454–470.

Kandel, D., Chen, K., & Gill, A. (1995). The impact of drug use on earnings: A lifespan perspective. *Social Forces, 74*, 243–270.

Kenkel, D., & Ribar, D. (1994). Alcohol consumption and young adults' socio-economic status. *Brookings Paper on Economic Activity (Micro)*, 119–161.

Koch, S. F., & McGeary, K. A. (2005). The effect of youth alcohol initiation on high-school completion. *Economic Inquiry, 43*, 750–765.

Koch, S. F., & Ribar, D. C. (2001). A siblings analysis of the effects of alcohol consumption onset on educational attainment. *Contemporary Economic Policy, 19*, 162–174.

Lemieux, T. (2006). Postsecondary education and increasing wage inequality. *The American Economic Review, 96*, 195–199.

MacDonald, Z., & Pudney, S. (2000). Illicit drug use, unemployment, and occupational attainment. *Journal of Health Economics, 19*, 1089–1115

MacDonald, Z., & Shields, M. A. (2001). The impact of alcohol consumption on occupational attainment in England. *Economica, 68*, 427–453.

MacDonald, Z., & Shields, M. A. (2004). Does problem drinking affect employment? Evidence from England. *Health Economics, 13*, 139–155.

MacDonald, S., Wells, S., Giesbrecht, N., & Cherpitel, C. J. (1999). Demographic and substance use factors related to violent and accidental injuries: Results from an emergency room study. *Drug and Alcohol Dependence, 55*, 53–61.

Martinez, J. A., Sher, K. J., & Wood, P. K. (2008). Is heavy drinking really associated with attrition from college? The alcohol-attrition paradox. *Psychology of Addictive Behaviors, 22*, 450–456.

McBride, D. C., Van Buren, H., Terry, Y. M., & Goldstein, B. J. (2000). Depression, drug use and health services need, utilization and cost. In J. A. Levy (Series Ed.) and J. A. Levy, R. C. Stephens, & D. C. McBride (Vol. Eds.), *Advances in medical sociology (Vol. 7): Emergent issues of the field of drug abuse* (pp. 67–99). Stamford, CT: JAI Press.

McFadden, D. (1973). Conditional logit analysis of qualitative choice behavior. In P. Zarembka (Ed.), *Frontiers in econometrics* (pp.105–142). New York: Academic Press.

McGeary, K. A., & French, M. T. (2000). Illicit drug use and emergency room utilization. *Health Services Research, 35*(1 Pt 1), 153–169.

McGinnis, J. M., & Foege, W. H. (1993). Actual causes of death in the United States. *Journal of the American Medical Association, 270*, 2207–2212.

McLellan, A. T., Lewis, D. C., O'Brien, C. B., & Kleber, H. D. (2000). Drug dependence, a chronic medical illness: Implications for treatment, insurance, and outcomes evaluation. *Journal of the American Medical Association, 284*, 1689–1695.

Mertens, J. R., Flisher, A. J., Fleming, M. F., & Weisner, C. M. (2007). Medical conditions of adolescents in alcohol and drug treatment: Comparison with matched controls. *Journal of Adolescent Health, 40*, 173–179.

Miller, T. R., Lestina, D. C., & Smith, G. S. (2001). Injury risk among medically identified alcohol and drug abusers. *Alcoholism-Clinical and Experimental Research, 25*, 54–59.

Mincer, J. (1997). Changes in wage inequality, 1970–1990. In S. W. Polachek (Ed.), *Research in labor economics* (vol. 16) (pp. 1–18). Amsterdam: Elsevier Science North-Holland.

Mokdad, A. H., Marks, J. S., Stroup, D. F., & Gerberding, J. L. (2000). Actual causes of death in the United States. *Journal of the American Medical Association, 291*, 1238–1245.

Mullahy, J., & Sindelar, J. L. (1989). Life-cycle effects of alcoholism on education, earnings, and occupation. *Inquiry, 26*, 272–282.

Mullahy, J., & Sindelar, J. L. (1991). Gender differences on labor market effects of alcoholism. *American Economic Review, 81*, 161–165.

Mullahy, J., & Sindelar, J. L. (1993). Alcoholism, work, and income. *Journal of Labor Economics, 11*, 494–520.

Mullahy, J., & Sindelar, J. L. (1994). Alcoholism and income: The role of indirect effects. *The Milbank Quarterly, 72*, 359–375.

Mullahy, J., & Sindelar, J. L. (1996). Employment, unemployment, and problem drinking. *Journal of Health Economics, 15*, 409–434.

Murray, R. P., Connett, J. E., Tyas, S. L., Bond, R., Ekuma, O., Silversides, C. K., et al. (2002). Alcohol volume, drinking pattern, and cardiovascular disease morbidity and mortality: Is there a U-shaped function? *American Journal of Epidemiology, 155*, 242–248.

Nolen-Hoeksema, S. (2004). Gender differences in risk factors and consequences for alcohol use and problems. *Clinical Psychology Review, 24*, 981–1010.

Parsons, O. A. (1986). Cognitive functioning in sober social drinkers: A review and critique. *Journal of Studies on Alcohol, 47*, 101–114.

Parsons, O. A., & Nixon, S. J. (1998). Cognitive functioning in sober social drinkers: A review of the research since 1986. *Journal of Studies on Alcohol, 59*, 180–190.

Parthasarathy, S., & Weisner, C. (2006). Health care services use by adolescents with intakes into an outpatient alcohol and drug treatment program. *American Journal of Addictions, 15(S1)*, 113–121.

Peele, S., & Brodsky, A. (2000). Exploring psychological benefits associated with moderate alcohol use: A necessary corrective to assessments of drinking outcomes? *Drug and Alcohol Dependence, 60*, 249–250.

Perret, B., Ruidavets, J. B., CVieu, C., Jaspard, B., Cambou, J. P., Terce, F., et al. (2002). Alcohol consumption is associated with enrichment of high-density lipoprotein particles in polyunsaturated lipids and increased cholesterol esterification rate. *Alcoholism-Clinical and Experimental Research, 26*, 1134–1140.

Powell, L. M., Williams, J., & Weschler H. (2004). Study habits and the level of alcohol use among college students. *Education Economics, 12*, 135–149.

Rajkumar, A. S., & French, M. T. (1997). Drug abuse, crime costs, and the economic benefits of treatment. *Journal of Quantitative Criminology*, 13, 291–323.

Register, C. A., & Williams, D. R. (1992). Labor market effects of marijuana and cocaine use among young men. *Industrial and Labor Relations Review, 45*, 435–448.

Rehm, J., Greenfield, T. K., & Rogers, J. D. (2001). Average volume of alcohol consumption, patterns of drinking, and all-cause mortality: Results from the U.S. National Alcohol Survey. *American Journal of Epidemiology, 153*, 64–71.

Rehm, J., Room, R., Graham, K., Monteiro, M., Gmel, G., & Sempbs, C. T. (2003). The relationship of average volume of alcohol consumption and patterns of drinking to burden of disease: An overview. *Addiction, 98*, 1209–1228.

Renna, F. (2007). The economic cost of teen drinking: Late graduation and lowered earnings. *Health Economics, 16*, 407–419.

Renna, F. (2008). Teens' alcohol consumption and schooling. *Economics of Education, 27*, 69–78.

Rimm, E. (2000). Alcohol and cardiovascular disease. *Current Atherosclerosis Reports, 2*, 529–535.

Roebuck, M. C., French, M. T., & Dennis, M. L. (2004). Adolescent marijuana use and school attendance. *Economics of Education Review, 23*, 133–141.

Ruhm, C. J. (1995). Economic conditions and alcohol problems. *Journal of Health Economics, 14*, 583–603.

Ruhm, C. J., & Black, W. E. (2002). Does drinking really decrease in bad times? *Journal of Health Economics, 21*, 659–678.

Shaper, A. G. (1993). Editorial: Alcohol, the heart, and health. *American Journal of Public Health, 83*, 799–801.

Sher, K. J., Martin, E. D., Wood, P. K., & Rutledge, P. C. (1997). Alcohol use disorders and neuropsychological functioning in first-year undergraduates. *Experimental and Clinical Psychopharmacology, 5*, 304–315.

Substance Abuse and Mental Health Services Administration (SAMHSA), Office of Applied Studies. (2008). *Results from the 2007 National Survey on Drug Use and Health: National findings* (NSDUH Series H-34, DHHS Publication No. SMA 08–4343). Rockville, MD.

Terza, J. V. (2002). Alcohol abuse and employment: A second look. *Journal of Applied Econometrics, 17*, 393–404.

Van Ours, J. C. (2004). A pint a day raises a man's pay; but smoking blows that gain away. *Journal of Health Economics, 23*, 863–886.

Van Ours, J. C. (2007). The effects of cannabis use on wages of prime-age males. *Oxford Bulletin of Economics and Statistics, 69*, 619–634.

Vinson, D. C., Borges, G., & Cherpitel., C. J. (2003). The risk of intentional injury with acute and chronic alcohol exposures: A case-control and case-crossover study. *Journal of Studies on Alcohol, 64*, 350–357.

Williams, J., Powell, L. M., & Wechsler, H. (2003). Does alcohol consumption reduce human capital accumulation? Evidence from the College Alcohol Study. *Applied Economics, 35*, 1227–1239.

Williams, N. (2009). Seniority, experience, and wages in the UK. *Labour Economics, 16*, 272–283.

Wolaver, A. M. (2002). Effects of heavy drinking in college on study effort, grade point average, and major choice. *Contemporary Economic Policy, 20*, 415–428.

Wood, P. K., Sher, K. J., & Bartholow, B. D. (2002). Alcohol use disorder and cognitive abilities in young adulthood: A prospective study. *Journal of Consulting and Clinical Psychology, 70*, 897–907.

Wood, P. K., Sher, K. J., Erickson, D. A., & DeBord, K. A. (1997). Predicting academic problems in college from freshman alcohol involvement. *Journal of Studies on Alcohol, 58*, 200–210.

Wood, M. D., Sher, K. J., & McGowan, A. (2000). Collegiate alcohol involvement and role attainment in early adulthood: Findings from a prospective high-risk study. *Journal of Studies on Alcohol, 61*, 278–289.

Wood, P. K., Sher, K. J. & Rutledge, P.C. (2007). College student alcohol consumption, day of the week, and class schedule. *Alcoholism: Clinical and Experimental Research, 31*, 1195–1207.

Wu, L-T., & Howard, M. O. (2007). Psychiatric disorders in inhalant users: Results from the National Epidemiologic Survey on Alcohol and Related Conditions. *Drug and Alcohol Dependence, 88(2–3)*, 146–155.

Yamada, T., Kendrix, M., & Yamada, T. (1996). The impact of alcohol consumption and marijuana use on high-school graduation. *Health Economics, 5*, 77–92.

Zarkin, G. A., Mroz, T. A., Bray, J. W., & French, M. T. (1998). The relationship between drug use and labor supply for young men. *Labour Economics, 5*, 385–409.

Zavala, S. K., & French, M. T. (2003). Dangerous to your health: The role of chronic drug use in serious injuries and trauma. *Medical Care, 41*, 309–322.

Zeigler, D. W., Wang, C. C., Yoast, R. A., Dickinson, B. D., McCaffree, M. A., Robinowitz, C. B., et al.; Council on Scientific Affairs, & American Medical Association. (2005). The neurocognitive effects of alcohol on adolescents and college students. *Preventive Medicine, 40*, 23–32.

PART 3

Assessing Substance Use and Dependence

Biological Markers of Substance Use: Focus on the Objective Assessment of Alcohol Exposure

Lawrence D. Snell, Sanjiv V. Bhave, Laszlo Takacs, *and* Boris Tabakoff

Abstract

Ascertaining an individual's history of alcohol consumption is an important component in the proper treatment of accidental trauma or acute or chronic illness, as well as for matters of public health and safety, legal issues, insurance coverage, and the management of and recovery from hazardous/harmful levels of alcohol consumption. Although self-report of alcohol consumption in both research and clinical settings represents the most common mode of assessment, there is long-standing interest in developing objective measures of alcohol consumption that do not rely on the ability or willingness of a person to truthfully report consumption. Biologic diagnostic tests or biomarkers can provide information on current and past quantity and frequency of alcohol consumption. This chapter discusses and evaluates many of the biomarker candidates that have been investigated and provides insights into future searches for optimal diagnostic tools to provide biologic evidence of duration, quantity, and frequency of individual alcohol consumption. We have included a limited discussion of biomarkers for assessing cannabis use since cannabis and alcohol use many times are a concomitant feature of intoxication.

Key Words: biomarker, alcohol consumption, cannabis, hazardous, harmful, criteria, specificity, sensitivity

Introduction

The production and consumption of ethanol (beverage alcohol) by humans can easily be traced back to 4,000 B.C.—more than 6,000 years. The reasons for alcohol consumption have been explored extensively and although scientists are uncovering quite intricate neurobiologic determinants of why certain individuals consume more or less alcohol within the context of their daily activities, the common perceptions of alcohol's effects vary widely. Caddy and Block (1983) summarized the human perception of alcohol's effects as "an energizer, a tranquilizer, a superego solvent, a sacred symbol, a medicine, a food, a social leveler, a source of subjective feelings of power" and a host of other social and symbolic effects.

Perhaps surprising to those who do consume alcohol, not all adult humans consume alcoholic beverages. For instance, the 2012 National Survey on Drug Use and Health (NSDUH; http://www.samhsa.gov/data/NSDUH/2012SummNatFindDetTables/DetTabs/NSDUH-DetTabsSect2peTabs1to42-2012.htm#Tab2.15A), indicated that 52% of Americans 12 years of age or older reported imbibing at least one drink in the past 30 days. This statement also indicates that 48% of the group who were surveyed did not consume any ethanol (to their knowledge) during the past 30-day period. Of course, the skeptics among us may question one side or the other's ability to provide a truthful self-report on alcohol consumption.

What Is Wrong with Consuming Alcohol, and Why Is It Anyone's Business How Much I Consume?

Alcohol (ethanol) is a caloric substance and is considered a food in a number of societies. Additionally, "modest" levels of alcohol consumption have been reported to have beneficial effects in allaying coronary heart disease, stroke, breast cancer, and Alzheimer's disease (Baglietto, English, Gertig, Hopper, & Giles, 2005; Collins et al., 2009). However, it has been acknowledged by the vast majority of researchers that the beneficial effects of ethanol follow an inverted U- or J-shaped curve (Figure 14.1; Poikolainen, 1995; Thompson, 2013). Thus, as the amount of alcohol consumed is increased, the beneficial effects cease to be important for the overall health of the individual, and instead a plethora of adverse health effects become prominent: liver disease, cardiovascular disease, stroke, intestinal problems, propensity for cancer, reproductive problems, damage to the fetus, lowering of seizure thresholds, gout, pancreatitis, induction of abnormal metabolism of medications and resistance to anesthetics, memory deficits, and psychiatric disorders including anxiety and depression. The physical state of acute alcohol intoxication

Figure 14.1 A typical U- or J-shaped curve of relative risk for adverse health effect for alcohol or wine consumers compared with nondrinkers.

Nondrinkers are assigned a risk of 1, and drinkers are plotted according to level of consumption. The relative risk equals number of events (e.g., myocardial infarction) among drinkers divided by number of events among nondrinkers. Note that the relative risk of adverse health events for drinkers is lower than that for nondrinkers when consumption is between one and four drinks per day, whereas consumption exceeding four drinks results in an increased risk above that of nondrinkers.

From de Lorimier et al. (2000). *American Journal of Surgery, 180*, 357–361.

generates danger to the intoxicated individual and to those who come in contact with him or her. As noted in other chapters in this Handbook, alcohol intoxication is associated with violence and intentional and unintentional injury. Just as important is the realization that the negative effects of alcohol intoxication on performance (mental and physical) last well beyond the stage when alcohol is present in the body (hangover). Research has demonstrated significant deficits in cognition and reaction time up to 24 hours after individuals have fully metabolized consumed ethanol (Naranjo & Bremner, 1993; for recent reviews on hangover-related cognitive deficits, see Ling, Stephens, & Heffernan, 2010; Prat, Adan, Pérez-Pàmies, & Sànchez-Turet, 2008, Stephens, Ling, Heffernan, Heather, & Jones, 2008).

The relationship between quantity of alcohol consumed and the development of alcohol dependence has also been well investigated by Grant and her colleagues (Keyes, Geier, Grant, & Hasin, 2009) who determined a high correlation between the average number of drinks a person consumes per day and the likelihood of a positive diagnosis for alcohol dependence. Drinking more than an average of 4–5 drinks per day provides for a 50% chance of an individual demonstrating the signs of alcohol dependence, including tolerance to alcohol's actions; withdrawal signs, which can be as severe as life-threatening convulsions; an inability to abstain from drinking; an inability to stop once one begins drinking; drinking in spite of negative health and social consequences; and having one's daily activities become centered on obtaining alcohol, imbibing alcohol, or trying to recover from alcohol's actions.

The World Health Organization has provided guidelines for classifying alcohol consumption as nonhazardous, hazardous, and harmful (Edwards, Arif, & Hodgson, 1982) and has developed the Lexicon of Alcohol and Drug Terms (http://www.who.int/substance_abuse/terminology/who_ladt/en/index.html) for use by clinicians, administrators, and researchers to standardize verbiage when describing different patterns of alcohol intake (Table 14.1). These terms were generated from a careful survey of the literature (particularly epidemiologic studies) that indicated the chances of adverse consequences (health, social, etc.) at certain levels of alcohol consumption. For the purposes of this chapter, we utilize these terms to avoid describing levels of alcohol intake that may be ambiguous and vague. These guidelines also take into account the usual differences in body size between men and

Table 14.1. Phenotypes (WHO Lexicon of Alcohol and Drug Terms)

Abstinence	Refraining from drinking alcoholic beverages, whether as a matter of principle or for other reasons. Those who practice abstinence from alcohol are termed "abstainers," "total abstainers," or more colloquially, "teetotalers." The term "current abstainer" is usually defined as a person who has not consumed an alcoholic beverage in the preceding 12 months; this definition does not necessarily coincide with a respondent's self-description as an abstainer
Non-hazardous drinking* (Moderate drinking, social drinking, controlled drinking)	A pattern of drinking that is by implication contrasted with hazardous and harmful drinking. It denotes drinking that is moderate in amount and does not cause problems (personal, legal).
Hazardous drinking* (heavy drinking, risky drinking)	1. A pattern of alcohol use that increases the risk of harmful consequences for the user. In contrast to harmful use, hazardous use refers to patterns of alcohol intake that are of public health significance despite the absence of any current disorder in the individual user. 2. Drinking above medically recommended levels for low-risk consumption but without current evidence of concomitant alcohol-related harm.
Harmful drinking*	A pattern of alcohol use that is causing damage to health. The damage may be physical or mental. Harmful alcohol use commonly, but not invariably, has adverse social consequences
Alcohol abuse	An ambiguous term that applies to hazardous and harmful alcohol use that is not associated with dependence. DSM-IV alcohol abuse is defined as maladaptive patterns of drinking leading to clinically significant impairment or distress and is manifested by one or more of the following symptoms: recurrent drinking resulting in failure to fulfill major role obligations; recurrent drinking-related legal problems; and continued drinking despite recurrent social or interpersonal problems caused or exacerbated by drinking.
Alcohol dependence	The term implies a need for repeated doses of alcohol to feel good or avoid feeling bad and/or a pattern of compulsive use. In DSM-IV, alcohol dependence is defined by seven diagnostic criteria: tolerance; the withdrawal syndrome or drinking to relieve or avoid withdrawal symptoms; drinking larger amounts or for longer periods than intended; persistent desire or unsuccessful attempts to cut down on drinking; spending a great deal of time obtaining alcohol, drinking, or recovering from the effects of drinking; giving up important social, occupational, or recreational activities in favor of drinking; and continued drinking despite physical or psychological problem caused or exacerbated by drinking.
Alcohol Use Disorder	In previous versions of the DSM (III, III-R, and IV), alcohol use disorder referred to the presence of either alcohol abuse or alcohol dependence. In DSM-5 (American Psychiatric Association, 2013), the abuse/dependence distinction is abandoned and replaced by a unitary alcohol use disorder as indicated by ≥2 of 11 diagnostic criteria. DSM-5 explicitly grades severity by the number of criteria met (mild: 2–3; moderate: 4–5, and severe: 6 or more).

* For more detailed descriptions of this term, see text.

women and assign lower levels of consumption for categorizing women. To provide quantitative levels of alcohol consumption associated with these terms, we utilize the ethanol intake levels described by Saunders and Lee (2000):

• Nonhazardous drinking: males, less than 40 g of alcohol per day; females, less than 20 g of alcohol per day

• Hazardous drinking: males, more than 40 and up to 80 g of alcohol per day; females, more than 20 g and up to 40 g of alcohol per day

• Harmful drinking: males, more than 80 g of alcohol per day; females, more than 40 g of alcohol per day

However, we note that the United States Departments of Agriculture and Health and

Human Services have also published guidelines and definitions:

- Moderate drinking (one drink per day for women; two drinks per day for men)
- Heavy or high-risk drinking (more than three drinks on any day or more than seven drinks per week for women; more than four drinks per day on any day or more than 14 drinks per week for men)
- Binge drinking (within a 2-hour period, four or more drinks for women and five or more drinks for men; Dietary Guidelines for Americans, 2010)

It is important to note that these categories provide norms (average values), and there are many reasons why such norms may not apply in a particular situation (e.g., pregnancy) or cultural setting (Cherpitel, 1998; Floyd et al., 2008). One also has to realize that by referring to average daily or weekly intake, such guidelines do not provide license for binge drinking (i.e., drinking 14 drinks on one occasion during the week and dividing this number of drinks by 7 to arrive at an average of 2 drinks per day; Sheffield, Darkes, Del Boca, & Goldman, 2005), and this is one reason why the Dietary Guidelines for Americans (2010) describe moderate drinking patterns both with respect to daily and weekly limits.

Physicians are concerned with individual levels of alcohol intake because hazardous/harmful alcohol consumption predisposes to disease, results in negative outcomes in disease progression, and interferes significantly in the success of treatment (Dillie, Mundt, French, & Fleming, 2005; Spies et al., 1998). Alcohol treatment professionals need to have objective means of ascertaining success (Allen, Fertig, Litten, Sillanaukee, & Anton, 1997). The insurance industry is interested in ascertaining hazardous/harmful drinking for actuarial purposes and issuance of policies (Bean, Kleaver, Roberts, & Harasymiw, 2001). The judicial system is interested in hazardous/harmful drinking for making appropriate judgments and monitoring offenders (Marlowe, Festinger, Dugosh, Lee, & Benasutti, 2007), and the transportation industry is interested in ascertaining hazardous/harmful drinking to prevent the negative consequences not only of acute intoxication, but also of the cognitive or other deficits that may be a result of prior hazardous/harmful drinking (Gay Anderson & Riley, 2008). Additionally, most commercial entities are also interested in whether a current or past history of hazardous/harmful alcohol consumption contributes to workplace accidents or poor job performance. Finally, ethicists are interested in whether information regarding hazardous/harmful drinking should be collected, identified, and made available to those seeking such information (Klag, O'Callaghan, & Creed, 2005).

Ethanol Pharmacokinetics

Ethanol levels can be measured directly in serum, whole blood, and urine or through surrogate measures such as ethanol in breath, saliva, or sweat. However, many factors affect the interpretation of an isolated ethanol level in an acutely intoxicated individual. The detection of ethanol in any of these body constituents at a single time point depends on the amount of ethanol consumed, how long drinking has been maintained, and the time that has passed since the last drink was taken. An understanding of the dynamic process of ethanol absorption, distribution, metabolism, and elimination (ADME) is the single most important factor in interpreting a static ethanol level.

Passive absorption of ethanol starts immediately after ingestion. It has been suggested that about 20% of ethanol is absorbed through the stomach, and 80% of the ingested ethanol is absorbed through the small intestine (Norberg, Jones, Hahn, & Gabrielsson, 2003; Pizon, Becker, & Bikin, 2007). The rate of gastric emptying has been observed to influence the rate of uptake of ethanol in the blood stream—thus, factors that influence the rate of gastric emptying in turn modulate the rate of ethanol absorption (Norberg et al., 2001). Consumption of ethanol after meals decreases the rate of ethanol absorption, and, conversely, ethanol consumption on an empty stomach increases the rate of ethanol absorption. Similarly, the mode of administration, the dose of ethanol ingested, and the speed of ingestion add to the variability in the rate of ethanol absorption (Norberg et al., 2001).

Once absorbed, ethanol is distributed throughout the body. The rate of distribution of ethanol depends on the rate of peripheral blood flow (Norberg et al., 2003; Pizon et al., 2007), and the volume of distribution is influenced by factors such as total body water and body size, as well as body fat and gender (Norberg et al., 2003). It has been observed that differences in total body water between males and females influence the differences in the absorption and distribution of ethanol between males and females (Norberg et al., 2003; Pizon et al., 2007). As a result, women show higher peak concentrations of ethanol than men after drinking equivalent amounts (Ramchandani, Bosron, & Li, 2001). Other possible factors influencing this difference in peak concentration are differences in first-pass metabolism of ethanol in the gastrointestinal tract (Baraona et al., 2001; Frezza et al., 1990) and differences in liver mass (size) relative to sex (Norberg et al., 2003; Ramchandani et al., 2001).

The vast majority of ethanol (90–95%) is metabolized by liver alcohol dehydrogenase (ADH; Norberg et al., 2003). About 2–5% of the ethanol is eliminated in breath, urine, and sweat (Norberg et al., 2003), and a minor amount of ethanol (<5%) is metabolized by the microsomal P450 enzymes. In addition to these different routes of elimination, a small fraction of ingested ethanol is consumed by the glucuronidation pathway—ethanol conjugates with uridine diphosphate glucuronic acid to form ethyl glucuronide (EtG; Kissack, Bishop, & Roper, 2008).

The ADH family of enzymes catalyzes the conversion of ethanol, using NAD^+ as a coenzyme, to acetaldehyde. Differences in the levels of expression and/or polymorphisms in the members of ADH family of enzymes seem to contribute to the differences in ethanol sensitivity and metabolic rates in individuals (Edenberg, 2007).

Acetaldehyde is then oxidized to acetate by aldehyde dehydrogenase (ALDH). In humans, in addition to various isoforms of ADH, there are 19 members in the ALDH "superfamily" of enzymes. Members of this superfamily are involved in the metabolism of a wide range of endogenous and exogenous aldehydes (see ALDH database: http://www.aldh.org/). ALDH isoforms belonging to subfamily 1 and 2 (ALDH1A1 and ALDH2, respectively) play a major role in eliminating acetaldehyde derived from ethanol. ALDH1A1 is a cytosolic enzyme, a homotetramer, expressed widely in a number of tissues including brain, liver, retina, and gastrointestinal tract. ALDH2 is a mitochondrial enzyme with a high affinity for acetaldehyde (Chen, Peng, Wang, Tsao, & Yin, 2009). Thus, the end products of ethanol catabolism, as a result of oxidation of acetate via the Krebs (TCA) cycle, are CO_2 and H_2O.

Oxidation of ethanol via ADH explains a number of its metabolic effects but does not account for the metabolic tolerance and a number of associated events that develop in the alcoholic. After chronic ethanol consumption, the activity of the microsomal ethanol-oxidizing system (CYP2E1) increases (Lieber, 1999). CYP2E1 can be strikingly induced by a variety of substrates, especially ethanol (Lieber, 1997). CYP2E1 inducibility has been demonstrated in a variety of species including humans (Tsutsumi,

Lasker, Shimizu, Rosman, & Lieber, 1989), and it plays a major role in the increased rate of elimination of ethanol in ethanol-dependent individuals (Lieber, 1997; Lu & Cederbaum, 2008).

The increase in cytochrome P450 enzymes not only increases the metabolism of ethanol, but also increases metabolism of other drugs. CYP2E1 activates some commonly used drugs (such as acetaminophen) to their toxic metabolites and promotes carcinogenesis. In addition, catabolism of retinol is accelerated, thus resulting in its depletion. Contrasting with the stimulating effects of chronic consumption, acute ethanol intake inhibits the metabolism of other drugs. Moreover, metabolism by CYP2EI results in a significant release of free radicals that, in turn, diminish glutathione (GSH) and other defense systems against oxidative stress, and this plays a major pathogenic role in alcoholic liver disease (Lieber, 1997).

Initial studies of ethanol ADME demonstrated that once blood ethanol concentrations, after consumption of two "standard" drinks (http://pubs.niaaa.nih.gov/publications/Practitioner/CliniciansGuide2005/guide.pdf), have reached their peak values, the disappearance of ethanol is pseudo-linear and follows approximately zero-order kinetics (Figure 14.2; Mellanby, 1919; Widmark, 1933). Thus, the time it takes to reach half the blood ethanol concentration is completely dependent on its original level. A number of models have been developed to understand the distribution and elimination of ethanol. In some of these models, it was assumed that the ingested ethanol is distributed instantaneously into a single compartment (Widmark, 1933; Wilkinson et al., 1976). As early as 1919, single-compartment models were developed to estimate blood alcohol concentrations based on the assumption that elimination of ethanol

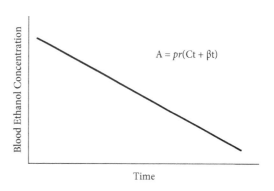

Figure 14.2. Zero kinetics of ethanol elimination as proposed by Widmark (1933; *Biochem Z, 267,* 128–134).

is a zero-order process (Mellanby, 1919; Widmark, 1933; Wilkinson et al., 1976). These models can be used to back-calculate the blood alcohol concentrations (amount of alcohol consumed) by taking the time delay between ingestion and obtaining a blood sample. Widmark (1933) used the equation $A = pr(C_t + \beta t)$, where A is the amount of ethanol ingested in grams, p is the body weight in kilograms, r is the apparent volume of distribution of alcohol expressed as a fraction of body weight (g/kg), C_t is the blood alcohol concentration (mg/g blood) at time t, β is the slope of apparent linear decline of alcohol concentration with time (mg ethanol/(g blood × minutes), and t is the time (minutes) after oral dosing (Widmark, 1933). This model assumes complete absorption and distribution of alcohol by the body independent of the amount of alcohol ingested.

Subsequent studies demonstrated that the value of β (the slope of linear decline of alcohol concentration with) in Widmark's equation was dependent on the amount of ethanol ingested (Haggard & Greenberg, 1934; Newman, Lehman, & Cutting, 1937). These observations did not support models based on zero-order kinetics of ethanol elimination. Nonlinear kinetic parameters to describe alcohol elimination/metabolism (Lundquist & Wolthers, 1958; Wagner, Wilkinson, Sedman, Kay, & Weidler, 1976) indicated that the profile of ethanol elimination was "hockey-stick"-like rather than a straight line: the ethanol elimination curve approached the zero level gradually. The majority of these studies also evidenced variability due to genetic and environmental factors in the elimination rate of ethanol in different individuals. Figure 14.3 shows a realistic potential range of ethanol concentrations over time when using the types of simulations introduced by Wagner et al. (1976) and illustrated in this case by Pizon and his coworkers (2007).

Several conclusions can be drawn from Figure 14.3. First, as discussed earlier, the blood ethanol levels are proportional to the amount of ethanol consumed over a particular (equivalent) time period (assuming you are measuring in individuals of identical physical characteristics). Second, the deviation from a pseudo-linear decline in ethanol elimination kinetics is evidenced primarily at lower concentrations of blood ethanol levels. Thus, it is more difficult to make any assumptions about the initial blood ethanol levels and level of drinking by extrapolation if the individual consumed modest levels of ethanol (e.g., the blood levels illustrated for the "standard"

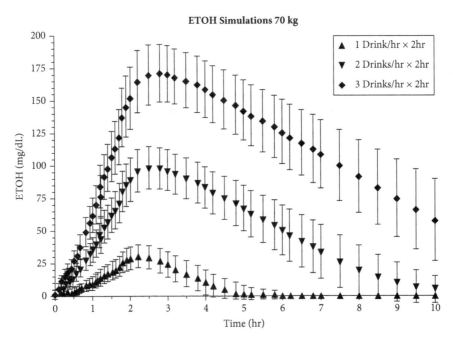

Figure 14.3. Simulation of serum ethanol concentrations over time for a 70 g adult after ingesting one, two, or three drinks per hour for 2 hours.

Concentrations were generated with the Monte Carlo function of Boomer v 3.3.1 software using literature values and ranges for distribution volume, Vmax and Km. One drink is equal to a 12 oz. beer (5% ethanol v/v), 1.5 oz of distilled liquor (40% v/v), or 5 oz wine glass (12% v/v).

From Pizon et al. (2007). *Journal of Medical Toxicology*, 3, 63.

individual drinking two drinks per hour over a 2-hour period when measured 8–10 hours after drinking). The pseudo-linear extrapolation works best in cases where larger quantities of ethanol are consumed over short periods and measures are made within 4–6 hours after the individual stops drinking. The forensic implications of linear versus nonlinear interpretations of blood ethanol decline continue to be debated in the literature (Norberg et al., 2003) and in the courts across the United States and other countries.

The other important issue to observe from Figure 14.3 is that blood levels of ethanol in the "standard" individual who consumes three drinks per hour over a 2-hour period are still at approximately 75 mg% 10 hours after the period of drinking. The threshold for accurate measurement of blood ethanol levels using standard methodology is 0.1 μg/mL (Tangerman, 1997). Therefore one can measure that this individual has imbibed ethanol by measuring blood ethanol levels for up to 20 hours after he stopped drinking. Clearly, the more that a person drinks on one occasion, the longer the period that his or her drinking can be ascertained by direct measure of blood ethanol levels. This measure will not guarantee how much ethanol was imbibed, but the longer the period after cessation of ethanol ingestion, the stronger the assumption that larger amounts were consumed.

Markers

The term "marker" has entered the common parlance as a substitute for "diagnostic test" because "diagnostic test" indicates a level of assurance regarding disease that sometimes is difficult to attain with any single biologic test. Thus, the term "marker" indicates the *probability* that a disease state exists or may at some point develop in an individual. In this chapter, we concentrate on *state markers*, markers that can indicate the level of exposure to disease-causing agents and/or the presence of a disease. State markers have a long history in medicine and drug development. Alcohol can be considered a "disease-causing agent" because its ingestion in certain cases can produce adverse effects. The classic use of state markers as related to drug use is to measure a drug per se (or its metabolites) in the course of ADME studies for safety assessment and, in a clinical setting, for establishing and maintaining a therapeutic dosing regimen. Clearly, the presence of the drug or characteristic metabolites in an animal can be considered a gold standard for indicating that drug exposure (although possibly not voluntary ingestion) has occurred. On the other hand, in many cases, one may wish to ascertain the history of drug use by an individual after all of the drug existing in the body at any given time has been metabolized and/or excreted. The search for *surrogate markers* that can indicate past drug use is the subject of the remainder of this chapter. In all cases in which one is asserting that a biologic test is demonstrating past drug use without the measure of the drug or its characteristic metabolites, there needs to be some accepted measure for past drug use that can form the standard against which the performance of the biologic test can be judged.

Timeline Followback

In a significant portion of work related to developing biologic state markers of alcohol use, the gold standard for assessing the quantity and frequency of an individual's past alcohol intake is the alcohol timeline followback (TLFB) method. The TFLB was originally designed as paper-and-pencil assessment tool using several memory aids including a calendar format to enhance recall. It has been evaluated in self-administered (including computer administration) and face-to-face settings. Alcohol abuser self-reports are generally verifiable when the interviews are conducted in a clinical or research setting, when clients are alcohol-free, and when they are given assurances of confidentiality (Sobell, 1990). However, despite having a general degree of confidence in alcohol abusers' self-reports, virtually all studies find that a small proportion of respondents' self-reports are inaccurate (Del Boca & Darkes, 2003; Sobell, Maisto, Sobell, & Cooper, 1979) and therefore other tests including biological markers of past alcohol use have been sought (see also Del Boca et al., this volume).

Physicians (and other health professionals) are frequently uncomfortable with or feel unprepared for asking their patients questions about alcohol consumption and would rather have biological testing to inform them of a patient's level of alcohol use (e.g., Friedmann, McCullough, & Saitz, 2001). An effective biomarker for alcohol intake would provide an objective confirmation of suspected hazardous/harmful drinking suggested by TFLB or other verbal questions in a subject unwilling or unable to give an accurate account of past use.

Ideal Biomarkers

The ideal postingestion biomarker for ethanol intake would have good sensitivity (i.e., have a meaningful quantitative association between incremental changes—increase or decrease—in alcohol intake) and good specificity (i.e., not be affected by other conditions, such as the use of other drugs or the presence of coexisting disorders; Allen et al., 1997). Thus, it would produce few false positives. For widespread clinical application, the biomarker should be easily and reliably measured. The search for accurate and inexpensive biologic measures that provide an objective measure of past alcohol consumption has been the focus of several decades of research and evaluation. However, alcohol consumption patterns, like most human behavior, are complex, consisting of various phenotypes over a wide range of quantity and frequency of alcohol intake. It is possible that a single ideal biomarker of alcohol consumption will never be identified.

Evaluating and Using Biomarkers

Potential biomarkers for alcohol use must be evaluated against several criteria. When treatment professionals evaluate a patient's history of alcohol consumption, they want to know not only about recent drinking patterns, but also about long-term drinking patterns and whether that drinking has been nonhazardous or hazardous/harmful (see Table 14.1 for definitions of these terms).

Screening For and Confirming Heavy Alcohol Use

The ability to screen for heavy or harmful alcohol use and syndromal alcohol use disorder (AUD) has many applications. A physician's awareness of a possible co-occurring alcohol problem can improve differential diagnosis and treatment (Dillie et al., 2005; Spies et al., 1998). Biomarkers can also assist in differential diagnosis by determining the possible role of alcohol use in a disease process (e.g., hypertension or diabetes; Sillanaukee, Strid, Jousilahti et al., 2001).

If the need for AUD intervention has been established, and the patient expresses the desire to reduce drinking, treatment can be designed to employ biomarkers to enhance the probability of a positive outcome. One of the more important uses of biomarkers is that the results can provide biological feedback to motivate patients to reduce or cease drinking. Giving feedback on and reviewing improvement in biomarker results provide objective evidence to the patient of the benefit of stopping or reducing alcohol use (Conigrave, Davies, Haber, & Whitfield, 2003; Kristenson, Trell, & Hood, 1981; O'Connor & Schottenfeld, 1998).

Biomarkers are also useful for evaluating new therapeutic interventions for alcohol-related conditions in clinical trials. Biomarkers provide objective outcome data on the efficacy of new medications or behavioral modification treatments (Allen, Litten, Strid, & Sillanaukee, 2001). Including the biomarker outcome data in study design reinforces the credibility of findings with audiences that may be skeptical of the validity of uncorroborated reports of abstinence or reduced drinking by alcoholics.

A substantial portion of alcoholic-dependent individuals who experience remission either with or without formal treatment are likely to experience relapse (Moos & Moos, 2006). A biomarker that can detect resumption of alcohol intake during treatment would help prevent the various complications often resulting from a return to escalating alcohol intake (Irwin, Baird, Smith, & Schuckit, 1988).

It is evident that a biomarker that reflects recent (days or weeks) levels, decreases, or increases in alcohol intake (i.e., relapse drinking) would be suitable for use in the treatment of alcohol problem drinking. A high specificity is a prerequisite to avoid the negative influence of alleging continued hazardous/harmful drinking when the patient has actually been compliant.

Criteria for Acceptance of a Biomarker

The probability that the biomarker will become a common component of the battery of tools used by treatment professionals is greatly enhanced by its ease of use. The biological and technical aspects of measuring the biomarker will impact significantly on its clinical utility. Even an ideal biomarker that requires laborious sample preparation and specialized equipment to obtain accurate results will have difficulty finding its way into common use.

To accurately evaluate a potential biomarker, one must recognize the planned use of the biomarker (screening, confirmation, treatment, monitoring) and be cognizant of the characteristics of the subject population in which the marker will be used. It has been relatively easy to differentiate those individuals considered harmful drinkers from abstainers using biomarkers, but much more difficulty has been encountered in identifying those drinking at nonhazardous versus hazardous levels (Korzec, Korzec, Conigrave, Gisolf, & Tabakoff, 2009), younger (<30 years old) individuals drinking at hazardous/harmful levels (Clark, Lynch, Donovan, & Block, 2001), women (Bernards, Graham, Demers, Kairouz, & Wells, 2007), and individuals suffering from nonalcoholic liver versus alcoholic liver disease (Nyblom, Berggren, Balldin, & Olsson, 2004).

State Markers of Alcohol Intake
Windows of Assessment: What Is the Goal?

Each biomarker has a distinctive window of utility comprising the duration of ethanol consumption and the quantity of ethanol that needs to be consumed before the baseline value of the biomarker is perturbed in an individual. The interval required before the biomarker returns to the reference value after the individual stops drinking alcohol and any possible variation in these parameters due to other variables (e.g., gender, age, other drugs used, and other diseases) are other components that characterize this window of utility. Figure 14.4 is a graphical representation of these windows of utility for several of the most commonly used markers and biomarkers under investigation. As can be seen, each biomarker will be more or less useful as a diagnostic for screening for AUD, confirming AUD, treating AUD, or monitoring alcohol consumption.

Specific Biomarkers

Here, biomarkers are reviewed with emphasis on the windows of utility and literature, reports of sensitivity and specificity, and practical application in a clinical setting.

Liver Enzymes
γ-GLUTAMYL TRANSFERASE

Serum γ-glutamyl transferase (GGT) is widely employed as a marker of alcohol consumption (Rosalki, 1975). GGT is a liver enzyme that transports amino acids across cellular membranes and assists in the synthesis of glutathione. Serum levels of GGT rise in response to hepatocellular damage. When a hazardous/harmful drinker remains abstinent for an extended period (2–4 weeks), the levels of GGT usually return to normal if hazardous/harmful alcohol use was the cause of the elevation. An elevated serum GGT level is not, by itself, sufficient to conclude that an individual is drinking excessive levels of alcohol because GGT is also raised in a variety of nonalcoholic liver diseases (Rosalki, 1975).

Serum GGT levels have been found to be elevated in about 75% of individuals who are "alcohol-dependent," with a range in sensitivity of 60–90% (Carlsson, Hiltunen, Beck, Stibler, & Borg, 1993; Helander & Carlsson, 1996; Rosalki & Rau, 1972; Stetter, Gaertner, Wiatr, Mann, & Breyer-Pfaff, 1991; Wu, Slavin, & Levi, 1976). The sensitivity is greatest when alcohol-dependent patients and chronic hazardous/harmful drinkers are compared to totally abstinent and infrequent nonhazardous drinkers (Carlsson et al., 1993; Helander

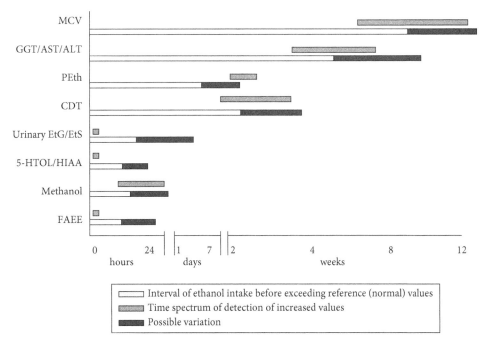

Figure 14.4. Windows of assessment for commonly used and proposed biomarkers of alcohol use-related disorders. From Wurst et al. (2003). *Addiction, 98* (Suppl. 2), 51–61.

& Carlsson, 1996; Scouller, Conigrave, Macaskill, Irwig, & Whitfield, 2000; Wu et al., 1976). In groups consuming hazardous amounts of alcohol but with no evidence of dependence, the sensitivities are much lower (20–50%; Carlsson et al., 1993; Helander, Beck, & Jones, 1996; Saunders, Aasland, Babor, & Grant, 1993; Wu et al., 1976), particularly in the primary care setting (Carlsson et al., 1993; Helander & Carlsson, 1996; Kristenson, Trell, Fex, & Hood, 1980; Nilssen & Forde, 1991; Wu et al., 1976). The increase in serum GGT in response to different amounts and duration of alcohol consumption varies considerably between individuals. In one study, a single dose of 1 g/kg ethanol after 4 weeks abstinence was enough to result in a doubling of GGT levels in "chronic alcoholics" (Nemesanszky, Lott, & Arato, 1988), whereas, in non-dependent, currently abstinent subjects, at least 60 g/d alcohol for a minimum of 5 weeks is required before any GGT increase occurs (Belfrage et al., 1973). GGT is rarely elevated in alcohol-consuming subjects under the age of 30 (Carlsson et al., 1993; Kristenson et al., 1980; Whitfield, Hensley, Bryden, & Gallagher, 1978).

ASPARTATE AMINOTRANSFERASE AND ALANINE AMINOTRANSFERASE

Serum aspartate aminotransferase (AST) and alanine aminotransferase (ALT) are hepatocellular enzymes involved in amino acid metabolism. They participate in gluconeogenesis by catalyzing the transfer of amino groups from aspartic acid or alanine to ketoglutaric acid to produce oxaloacetic acid and pyruvic acid, respectively (Pratt & Kaplan, 2000). AST is present in cytosolic and mitochondrial isoenzymes and is found in the liver, cardiac muscle, skeletal muscle, kidneys, brain, pancreas, lungs, leucocytes, and red cells. It is less sensitive and specific for the liver. ALT, a cytosolic enzyme, is found in its highest concentrations in the liver and is more specific to the liver (Pratt & Kaplan, 2000). Hepatocellular injury and not necessarily cell death is the trigger for release of these enzymes into the circulation.

Like GGT, serum aminotransferases are not increased by a single episode of hazardous/harmful alcohol consumption in non-dependent subjects (Devgun, Dunbar, Hagart, Martin, & Ogston, 1985). Serum levels depend markedly on the degree of past liver damage and how recently alcohol has been consumed. Alcohol intakes of 3–4 g/kg body weight per day for more than two days can lead to moderate transient increases in AST in healthy

subjects. Serum AST is often elevated in patients who are "alcohol-dependent" (Chan, Welte, & Whitney, 1987; Cohen & Kaplan, 1979), although generally not to more than 2–4 times upper normal limits.

Serum AST, which is released from the liver, consists of two isoenzymes: mitochondrial AST (mAST) and cytosolic AST (cAST; Chan et al., 1987; Cohen & Kaplan, 1979). In serum samples of normal healthy individuals, cAST makes up more than 90% of the total AST enzyme activity, but when excessive alcohol consumption selectively injures mitochondria in the liver, mAST is preferentially released (Ishii, Okuno, Shigeta, & Tsuchiya, 1979). mAST has been reported to have a sensitivity of approximately 90% in identifying alcohol-dependent patients (Nalpas et al., 1984; Okuno et al., 1988). The specificity of this liver enzyme is low. In one study, 79% of patients with nonalcoholic liver disease had elevated mAST levels (Nalpas, Vassault, Charpin, Lacour, & Berthelot, 1986). The literature indicates that the sensitivities for identifying harmful drinking levels are 25–60% for AST (depending on whether the patients are known alcoholic-dependents or are being screened for hazardous/harmful intake.

ALT is the more specific measure of alcohol-induced liver injury because it is found predominantly in the liver. Alcohol is the most common cause of ALT elevation in otherwise healthy people (>50%; Katkov et al., 1991). In patients with alcohol-induced liver disease, serum levels of ALT decrease due to an alcohol-related deficiency in pyridoxal 5-phosphate (Diehl et al., 1984).

The ratio of AST to ALT in serum may aid in the diagnosis of some liver diseases (e.g., nonalcoholic fatty liver disease, alcoholic liver disease, chronic hepatitis B and C, autoimmune liver disease, hemochromatosis, Wilson disease, α1-antitrypsin deficiency, and celiac disease). In most patients with acute liver injury the ratio is 1 or greater, whereas in alcoholic hepatitis it is generally about 2 (Cohen & Kaplan, 1979). Notably, however, AST levels of more than eight times normal and ALT levels more than five times normal are exceptionally rare in alcoholic liver disease (Cohen & Kaplan, 1979).

Serum levels of GGT, AST, and ALT are usual measures of the cumulative (weeks) intake of alcohol at hazardous/harmful levels and exhibit moderate sensitivities. As such, they can be and have been used to screen for a longer term pattern of alcohol intake. However, due to their low specificities and variability in human populations, liver enzyme levels appearing in serum, by themselves, are not reliable enough to support a diagnosis of harmful/hazardous alcohol intake or alcohol dependence (Neumann & Spies, 2003). They are most effectively used in conjunction with physical examination, alcohol-related clinical history, and verbal questionnaires. In monitoring treatment response, the return of these enzymes to normal serum levels, particularly GGT, may be a powerful patient-motivating factor (Hoeksema & de Bock, 1993). However, the extended period of time that liver enzymes can remain at abnormal levels (weeks) makes liver enzyme levels less powerful in detecting a termination of abstinence and a relapse into drinking.

Carbohydrate-Deficient Transferrin

Transferrin exists in serum in various forms containing 0–9 sialic acid residues. The predominant form of transferrin in non-alcohol consuming individuals is tetrasialotransferrin (80%; Allen, Litten, Anton, & Cross, 1994). Carbohydrate-deficient transferring (CDT), as the name implies, is an abnormally sialated form of serum transferrin consisting of the asialo, monosialo, and disialo isoforms (Marz, Hatton, Berry, & Regoeczi, 1982). Commercial methods to measure serum CDT include high-performance liquid chromatography (%CDT by HPLC™, Biorad, Hercules, California, USA), capillary zone electrophoresis (Capillarys™, SE-BIA; Evry, France), a two-antibody immunoassay (CDTect™, Axis-Shield, Oslo, Norway), and turbidometric immunoassays (%CDT-TIA™, Axis-Shield, Oslo, Norway).

Galβl,4GlcNAc α2,6-sialyltransferase (ST6GalI) mediates the glycosylation of proteins and lipids to form functionally important glycoproteins and glycolipids in the Golgi compartment (Harduin-Lepers et al., 2001). Clinical observations show that the down-regulation of the ST6GalI gene and consequent impaired activity of ST6GalI is the major cause for the appearance of asialo conjugates in the blood of long-term alcohol dependent individuals (Stibler & Borg, 1981; Tsutsumi, Wang, & Takada, 1994). It has been proposed that a down-regulation of ST6GalI protein synthesis associated with alcohol consumption is the basis for the appearance of CDT in the serum of hazardous/harmful alcohol drinkers (Gong, Garige, Hirsch, & Lakshman, 2007).

CDT levels have been reported to be elevated by consumption of 50–80 g/d ethanol for 1 or 2 weeks and to persist in an elevated state for 2 weeks or longer after the cessation of drinking (Stibler,

1991). The elevated levels have a half-life of about 15 days if an individual stops drinking ethanol. The main strength of CDT is its reported high specificity (75–90%; Anton, 2001; Bortolotti, De Paoli, & Tagliaro, 2006; Nystrom, Perasalo, & Salaspuro, 1992), with disialo-transferrin demonstrating the highest sensitivity (~82% in males and 93% in females) for distinguishing chronic hazardous/harmful alcohol drinkers from nonhazardous alcohol drinkers (Martensson, Harlin, Brandt, Seppa, & Sillanaukee, 1997). Asialo-transferrin was also able to distinguish hazardous/harmful alcohol from nonhazardous alcohol intake but with lower sensitivity in males (68%). The trisialo-transferrin has not been found to be correlated to chronic alcohol consumption.

Some of this variability in sensitivity is method dependent. Studies using HPLC and capillary zone electrophoresis (CZE) can yield separate measures of each of the transferrin glycoforms, including asialo- and disialo-transferrin, whereas the immunometric methods (CDTect and %CDT) report total CDT (carbohydrate deficient isoforms). In most reported studies that have evaluated CDT as a biomarker of alcohol use/abuse, CDT was determined using the immunometric methods. These studies have established that CDT is adequate at detecting hazardous/harmful alcohol use (>60 g/d) and alcohol-dependence (Allen et al., 1994; Conigrave et al., 2002) but shows poor sensitivities in less extreme drinking populations (e.g., women, general population sample, occasional heavy drinkers, healthy volunteers) of only 12–45%. Also, false positives have been reported with nonalcoholic liver disease, the genetic variant of transferrin known as D1 (found in 1% of the black population, <1% in the white US population, and in up to 2% of Northern Europeans), and in the rare carbohydrate-deficient glycoprotein syndrome (Allen et al., 1994; Conigrave et al., 2002; Sillanaukee, Strid, Allen, & Litten, 2001). Additionally, it has been shown that there are gender differences in the levels of the three CDT isoforms depending on the levels of alcohol consumption (Allen et al., 1994; Martensson et al., 1997). Higher baseline concentrations of CDT in females than in males have been observed in individuals with low alcohol consumption, indicating that at least some of the CDT isoforms are present in higher concentrations in women. Several meta-analyses indicate that CDT is no better than GGT as a screening test for hazardous/harmful alcohol intake (Allen et al., 1994; Conigrave et al., 2002; Scouller et al., 2000). Multifactorial analysis has revealed that CDT levels are also affected by age, body mass index, and smoking (Allen et al., 1994; Conigrave et al., 2002; Tabakoff et al., 2002). Another contributor to inconsistencies in clinical reports of the utility of CDT as a biomarker is a lack of consensus of the cutoff limits for "normal" (i.e., nonhazardous) and "hazardous" daily alcohol intake (Allen, Litten, Fertig, & Sillanaukee, 2001).

However, CDT is currently considered the most useful marker to screen for harmful alcohol intake. It has been recommended that immunoassays for CDT be used for initial screening, whereas HPLC and CZE are applied for confirmation. This is especially true in a forensic setting (Bortolotti et al., 2006). CDT appears to be a more sensitive marker than GGT in the detection of relapse in the detoxification treatment of alcohol-dependent patients (Salaspuro, 1999). A CDT "sensitization" effect has been observed in which, following a period of abstinence, lower levels of alcohol consumption are sufficient to again elevate CDT (Anton, Moak, & Latham, 1996). Across a set of four studies (Allen, Sillamaukee, & Anton, 1999; Mitchell, Simpson, & Chick, 1997; Rosman, Basu, Galvin, & Lieber, 1995; Schmidt et al., 1997) that computed the accuracy of CDT as an indicator of relapse (relapse defined as a return to drinking), the median sensitivity was 68% and the median specificity was 75%.

Mean Corpuscular Volume

Although the specific mechanisms of the ethanol effects on blood cells are poorly known, several studies have suggested direct toxic effects of alcohol and its metabolites on the production of hematologic precursor cells and on red cell morphology. Macrocytosis, or enlarged erythrocytes, is associated with heavy chronic drinking lasting for at least a few months (Tabakoff et al., 2002). Mean corpuscular volume (MCV) is an average estimate of the volume of erythrocytes and serves as an indicator of macrocytosis, which tends to exceed the average range in hazardous/harmful drinkers. MCV has low sensitivity (40–50%) and a high specificity (80–90% as a screen for alcohol dependence; Sillanaukee, Aalto, & Seppa, 1998).

MCV responds slowly to abstinence and remains high for up to 3 months after a person stops drinking (Hasselblatt, Martin, Maul, Ehrenreich, & Kernbach-Wighton, 2001), making this marker less useful clinically as a tool for follow-up purposes (i.e., termination of drinking and relapse). Furthermore, MCV has a poor specificity as an alcohol marker in patients with vitamin B_{12} or folic acid deficiency, liver diseases, hypothyroidism, or myelodysplastic syndromes, or when there is an elevated reticulocyte count (Niemela, 2007).

5-Hydroxytryptophol

5-Hydroxytryptophol (5-HTOL) was demonstrated as a minor metabolite of serotonin (5-HT) more than four decades ago (Davis, Cashaw, Huff, & Brown, 1966). Metabolism of 5-HT occurs mainly in the intestine, liver, and lung (Some & Helander, 2002), first by action of monoamine oxidase (MAO) to form the intermediate 5-hydroxyindole-3-acetaldehyde (5-HIAL); then, this intermediate aldehyde is either oxidized by an aldehyde dehydrogenase to 5-hydroxyindole acetic acid (5-HIAA) or reduced by an aldehyde reductase (aldehyde oxidoreductase; Beck & Helander, 2003; Tabakoff et al., 1970; Tabakoff, Groskopf, Anderson, & Alivisatos, 1974) to 5-HTOL. The most important enzyme for 5-HTOL formation is the aldehyde reductase, which is 30 times more active in the reduction of 5-HIAL than for oxidation of 5-HTOL (Svensson et al., 1999). This enzyme is highly dependent on the concentration of the cofactor NADH, and, under normal conditions, the redox state does not favor the pathway leading to 5-HTOL formation. Ethanol ingestion results in an increase in the NADH-to-NAD+ ratio, and this increase in the ratio then in turn dramatically favors formation of 5-HTOL by aldehyde reductase (Beck & Helander, 2003; Davis, Brown, Huff, & Cashaw, 1967).

The majority of 5-HTOL is removed from the body (mostly in urine) as a conjugated form, either as a sulfate or glucuronide (Beck & Helander, 2003), and it has been observed that almost 80% of 5-HTOL is removed as a conjugate of glucuronic acid (GTOL; Helander, Beck, & Boysen, 1995). The metabolites of 5-HT originate mainly from peripheral sources, and only to a small extent from the central nervous system (Aizenstein & Korf, 1979).

The increases in the formation of 5-HTOL in plasma and urine following ethanol intake can be assayed using gas chromatographic separation with mass spectrometric detection (GC-MS; Beck, Borg, Jonsson, Lundman, & Valverius, 1984), whereas the glucuronidated metabolite can be measured directly in urine using liquid chromatographic separation with tandem mass spectrometric detection (LC-MS/MS; Stephanson, Helander, & Beck, 2007). The ratios of 5-HTOL-to-5-HIAA or GTOL-to-5-HIAA are normally used to compensate for urine dilution and dietary intake of 5-HT (Helander et al., 1992).

When the effect of acute ethanol consumption (50–80 g ethanol over a 2 hour period) on serotonin metabolism was examined in healthy non-alcohol dependent volunteers, the plasma and urine levels of 5-HIAA were reduced by about 40% and 25%, whereas the 5-HTOL and GTOL levels were increased an average of 7- and 50-fold, respectively (Helander, Beck, & Jones, 1996). The maximal effect on both 5-HIAA and 5-HTOL levels was found 4–6 hours after drinking. Urine 5-HTOL and the 5-HTOL-to-5-HIAA ratio did not return to baseline until 19 hours after the start of the alcohol ingestion (i.e., about 10 hours after ethanol reached zero level).

Several validation studies for the use of 5-HTOL-to-5-HIAA ratio in urine have been performed involving alcohol-dependent patients undergoing detoxification. The performance and accuracy of this ratio as a marker of recent alcohol intake is best for a period of several hours after blood ethanol levels are no longer measurable (Bendtsen, Jones, & Helander, 1998; Hagan & Helander, 1997; Helander et al., 1996). 5-HTOL-to-5-HIAA ratios have also been found to correlate well ($r^2 = 0.84$) with alcohol intake self-reports, and the accuracy of the ratio is not influenced by age, gender, ethnic origin, or common diseases (Helander & Eriksson, 2002). A particular drawback with the 5HTOL-to-5HIAA ratio is that one treatment mode for alcohol dependence is the use of inhibitors of aldehyde dehydrogenase (e.g., disulfiram [Antabuse]), and these drugs may also elevate 5-HTOL values (Beck, Helander, Carlsson, & Borg, 1995; Helander, 1998).

Another possible confound investigated is the ingestion of foods that contain high amounts of 5-HT (e.g., bananas). After consumption of 3–4 bananas by healthy volunteers, urinary 5-HIAA and 5-HTOL increased markedly (15- to 30-fold) with the highest concentrations found in urine specimens collected after 2–4 hours. Urinary levels did not return to normal until after 8–10 hours. Of the banana-derived 5-HT ingested, 60–80% was recovered in the urine as 5-HIAA and only 0.3–0.5% as 5-HTOL (Helander, Wikstrom, Lowenmo, Jacobsson, & Beck, 1992). However, because both the time course and relative increase in 5-HTOL was similar to that of 5-HIAA, there was no effect on the urinary 5-HTOL-to-5-HIAA ratio. This contrasts with the elevation in the 5-HTOL-to-5-HIAA ratio produced by acute ethanol ingestion.

The window of assessment for ethanol consumption by an elevated 5-HTOL/5-to-HIAA ratio in urine is about 5–15 hours beyond the time that one can measure blood ethanol levels. The sensitivity of 5-HTOL is dependent on the dose of ethanol ingested. At doses of less than 50 g ethanol over a 1–2 hour period, 5-TOL is generally not detectable. The 5-HTOL-to-5-HIAA ratio can be considered a highly specific biomarker of recent (<24 hour) high ethanol intake, and the urine 5-HTOL-to-5-HIAA ratio has been utilized in a number of clinical and forensic settings (Carlsson et al., 1993; Helander et al., 1996; Voltaire, Beck, & Borg, 1992). From these studies, it can be concluded that the 5-HTOL-to-5-HIAA ratio would find utility as a tool for screening, confirmation, relapse, and monitoring of *recent* high alcohol consumption. However, the sophisticated methodology required for determination of 5-HTOL has hindered its clinical application.

Phosphatidylethanol

Phosphatidylethanol (PEth) is an abnormal phospholipid formed from phosphatidylcholine only in the presence of ethanol via the action of phospholipase-D (Gustavsson, 1995). PEth can be measured in blood using liquid chromatography electrospray mass spectrometric detection (HPLC–ELSD). The rate of degradation of PEth is slow compared to its formation. The half-life of PEth in blood has been calculated to be approximately 4 days. Therefore, in the case of individuals who drink daily at high levels, PEth can accumulate in erythrocytes and neutrophils and comprise up to 1–2% of the total cellular phospholipid pool (Hannuksela, Liisanantti, & Savolainen, 2002).

The relationship between blood PEth and alcohol use was based on the observation that chronic alcohol-dependent patients consuming 60–300 g of ethanol per day for at least 1 week before admission to a clinic for detoxification had mean PEth levels of 13.2 µmol/L on the first day, and levels remained detectable up to 14 days after admission (Hansson, Caron, Johnson, Gustavsson, & Alling, 1997). PEth is not expected to be present in individuals who do not consume ethanol, and this was confirmed in subjects who abstained from ethanol consumption for 4 days before measurement. Consequently, PEth measurements are a relatively specific marker for alcohol consumption.

Once PEth levels are raised by chronic alcohol consumption, they remain detectable up to 3 weeks after the beginning of an alcohol-free period

(Gunnarsson et al., 1998). This may be a result of the discovery that almost all PEth in blood is found in erythrocyte fraction. A study conducted on healthy volunteers revealed that a single dose of ethanol does not produce measurable amounts of PEth, whereas consumption of more than 1,000 g of ethanol during a 3 week period (~50 g/d) was sufficient to raise PEth levels to detectable levels (Varga & Alling, 2002).

PEth was recently evaluated for its ability to discriminate recently active drinking alcohol-dependent patients undergoing hospitalized detoxification (self-reported daily consumption of 224 g/d for the previous week—harmful levels of intake) from sober forensic psychiatric inpatients in a closed ward (i.e., current abstinence). Receiver operating characteristics (ROC) analysis was performed for drinkers against the sober patients with PEth as the test variable. At a cutoff of 0.36 μmol/L, the sensitivity of PEth was 94.5% with the expected specificity of 100%. The sensitivity of the assay may be somewhat inflated because the discrimination was based on two populations that are at opposite ends of the alcohol intake spectrum (Hartmann et al., 2007).

Based on these findings, PEth can be considered a sensitive and specific marker for *chronic* intake of higher (harmful) amounts of alcohol. PEth is similar to GGT in that it is a *cumulative* measure of ethanol intake requiring a longer period of consumption, but, unlike GGT, it is quite specific for ethanol intake. It can be distinguished in its marker characteristics from CDT and 5-HTOL in the requirement of a longer period of consumption of hazardous/harmful amounts of ethanol. PEth measurements should have utility in screening for periods of hazardous/harmful drinking that have persisted for weeks or months before assessment.

EtG and Ethyl Sulfate

EtG and ethyl sulfate (EtS) are nonvolatile, water-soluble metabolites of ethanol formed by the action of UDP-glucuronyltransferase and sulfotransferase (Schneider & Glatt, 2004; Wurst & Metzger, 2002), respectively. EtG and EtS are minor metabolites of ethanol, and each accounts for less than 0.05% of total ethanol metabolites (Dahl, Stephanson, Beck, & Helander, 2002; Helander & Beck, 2005). EtG and EtS are detectable in blood less than 1 hour after ethanol ingestion. After ethanol has been eliminated from the body, EtG and EtS remain measurable for 8–12 hours in serum and 80–120 hours in urine, and the levels and duration

of the presence of these metabolites depend on the quantity of ethanol consumed (Borucki et al., 2005; Schmitt, Droenner, Skopp, & Aderjan, 1997; Wurst, Seidl, Ladewig, Muller-Spahn, & Alt, 2002). Because of their low concentrations, measurement of EtG and EtS has required sensitive and accurate liquid chromatographic separation with mass spectrometric detection (LC-MS) methods for qualitative and quantitative determinations (Morini et al., 2008).

In perhaps the most comprehensive evaluation of its clinical utility, urine EtG testing was compared to other biomarkers in subject samples from the World Health Organization and International Society on Biomedical Research on Alcoholism (WHO-ISBRA) study of state and trait markers of alcohol abuse and dependence (Tabakoff et al., 2002). This subject sample contained individuals whose ethanol intake ranged from total abstinence to chronic hazardous/harmful drinking. Wurst et al. (2005) found that urine levels of EtG were negatively correlated with days of sobriety and positively correlated with total grams of ethanol consumed in the previous month. In a ROC analysis for nondrinkers and individuals sober for more than 4 days versus individuals drinking in the recent 4 days, EtG was able to discriminate these groups with a sensitivity of 85.5% and a specificity of 68.3%. However, when the groups comprised individuals with self-reported sobriety of less than 24 hours versus those with self-reported sobriety or more than 24 hours, EtG was able to discriminate these groups of individuals with a sensitivity of 90.8% and a specificity of 76.5%. EtG levels were not affected by race-ethnicity, smoking, body mass index, or cirrhosis of the liver. However, increased EtG levels were also found in patients who used marijuana (Wurst, Wiesbeck, Metzger, & Weinmann, 2004).

Incidental exposure to alcohol-containing products (e.g., hand sanitizer, cough syrup, and mouthwash) has led to false-positive reports (Costantino, Digregorio, Korn, Spayd, & Rieders, 2006; Rohrig, Huber, Goodson, & Ross, 2006). False-positive findings may also result from extended storage of urine samples at room temperature if the samples are contaminated with yeast (Saady, Poklis, & Dalton, 1993). The presence in urine samples of bacteria associated with urinary tract infections has been reported to generate false-negatives because these uropathogens have enzymes that can cleave glucuronide (Helander & Dahl, 2005).

False-negative findings have also been reported following fluid-induced diuresis. High water intake following ethanol ingestion was found to dilute EtG levels below the 100 ng/mL cutoff levels used as an indicator of alcohol intake (Dahl et al., 2002). The effect of urine dilution can, however, be rectified if urine creatinine levels are also measured and the ratio of EtG-to-creatinine is obtained (Goll, Schmitt, Ganssmann, & Aderjan, 2002).

Due to its extreme sensitivity and its extended window of detection compared to ethanol or 5-HTOL, measurement of EtG in plasma and urine have been proposed as a excellent candidate marker to monitor alcohol use (abstinence) and to detect relapse (confirm alcohol abstinence). Evaluation in forensic and clinical settings found that EtG was more effective in detecting clandestine alcohol consumption in psychiatric patients required to remain abstinent than were measurements of CDT or PEth (Wurst et al., 2003). When urine EtG levels were evaluated in a population with self-reported ethanol intake ranging from 0.5 to 445 g/d and also reporting sobriety for more than 4 days, more cases were positive for EtG than urine 5HTOL-to-5-HIAA ratio levels (Wurst & Metzger, 2002).

Equipment to run this assay (LC-MS/MS) is costly and only available in specialized laboratories. Because of this, widespread clinical use of this test has been hindered. The measurement of EtG has found utility in forensic and court settings where access to the equipment is more likely available. EtG has been tested primarily in one lab in Europe, and, in a 2012 advisory, the Federal Substance Abuse and Mental Health Services Administration (SAMSHA) stated that more research is needed on the use of urine EtG to detect hazardous/harmful alcohol drinking in order to determine how test results may be influenced by health status, ethnicity, gender, genetic variation, drug use and various chemical agents (Substance Abuse and Mental Health Services Administration, 2012).

Recently, Böttcher et al. (2008) reported the validation of an enzyme-linked immunosorbent assay (ELISA)-based assay for EtG in urine samples based on the development of a new monoclonal antibody for EtG. Comparison of the ELISA with the established LC-MS method showed very good agreement ($r^2 = 0.931$). Using a cutoff limit of 0.5 mg/mL EtG, the sensitivity of the ELISA was 98.7% with a specificity of 98.0%. Upon full validation of this assay, EtG may find utility in the monitoring of drinking status in individuals being treated clinically for alcohol misuse and/or dependence.

Fatty Acid Ethyl Esters

Nonoxidative metabolism of ethanol to fatty acid ethyl esters (FAEE) is an important pathway of ethanol disposition during hazardous/harmful alcohol use. FAEEs are formed via the esterification of ethanol with endogenous fatty acids or fatty acyl coenzyme A Measurement of FAEE involves the purification of FAEEs from plasma, serum, or tissue by solid-phase extraction and quantification by GC-MS (Bernhardt, Cannistraro, Bird, Doyle, & Laposata, 1996).

FAEEs have been implicated as possible mediators for at least some of the toxic effects associated with alcohol consumption (Haber, Wilson, Apte, & Pirola, 1993), as short term markers of ethanol intake in serum, and as long-term markers in liver, adipose tissue, and hair.

Elevated FAEE levels can be detected in serum and erythrocytes shortly after ethanol intake. In controlled drinking studies, blood ethanol concentrations and FAEE levels were found to follow very similar kinetics, although FAEE levels remained elevated for approximately 24 hour after alcohol was no longer detectable (Soderberg et al., 1999). Thus, FAEEs have been proposed as a marker for a recent intake of ethanol. A subsequent study, however, reported that FAEE serum levels of alcohol drinkers consuming at harmful levels (340 g/d) remain elevated for up to 99 hour (Borucki et al., 2005), indicating altered elimination kinetics. As a result, alcohol-dependent subjects positive for blood ethanol have higher serum FAEE levels compared to episodic drinkers (subjects who consume hazardous quantities of ethanol on occasion; "binge" drinkers; Soderberg, Salem, Best, Cluette-Brown, & Laposata, 2003). This discrimination may be important for clinicians contemplating detoxification protocols. An alcohol-dependent individual showing high FAEE levels would be carefully monitored for withdrawal complications, whereas an episodic drinker might require different treatment to prevent serious morbidity.

FAEEs are also formed in several tissues (liver, duodenum, pancreas, and adipose tissue), and, for this reason, FAEEs have been evaluated for use in forensic settings. FAEE levels were measured in adipose tissue obtained from individuals with detectable blood ethanol levels at autopsy, from alcohol-dependent victims with negative blood alcohol at autopsy, and from nonhazardous drinkers with negative blood alcohol at autopsy. The diagnostic value of FAEE concentrations in adipose tissue was found to correlate well (0.72) with blood alcohol levels in these individuals (Refaai et al., 2002). Measurement of FAEEs in tissues may find good utility in forensic settings when blood samples are limited or not available. The latter application is more likely because sample processing and methods for FAEE analysis are labor- and time-intensive and GC-MS technology is not available in many clinical settings.

Methanol

Methanol is normally present in the body in trace amounts. It is formed during the enzymatic conversion of S-adenylmethionine to S-adenylhomocyteine (Axelrod & Daly, 1965). Methanol is metabolized by the same hepatic enzymes as ethanol (i.e., ADH and ALDH). Although methanol and ethanol share the same metabolic pathway, methanol is metabolized at a much slower rate (about one-seventh; Gossel & Bricker, 1994). Normal serum concentrations of methanol range from 0.5 to 1.0 mg/L.

Following alcohol consumption, ethanol is preferentially metabolized, and methanol accumulates in the body (Leaf & Zatman, 1952; Majchrowicz & Mendelson, 1971). In healthy controls consuming 0.8 g/kg ethanol, urine concentrations of methanol reach a peak at 6 hours and remain increased for 2–6 hours after ethanol is no longer detectable (Helander et al., 1996; Jones & Sternebring, 1992). Therefore, elevated concentrations of methanol can be an indicator of alcohol consumption, and abnormally high concentrations of methanol in body fluids or breath have been suggested as an alternative biomarker of recent alcohol drinking (Jones, 1986). The fact that methanol remains elevated for some hours longer than ethanol is present in the body indicates that measurement of methanol can provide a wider window for ascertaining recent alcohol intake.

During chronic drinking, methanol accumulates gradually to reach much higher concentrations, and complete clearance after drinking cessation requires several days (Brinkmann et al., 2000; Majchrowicz & Mendelson, 1971). Several studies indicate that continuous hazardous/harmful alcohol consumption, such as that by alcohol-dependent subjects, results in very high plasma concentrations of methanol (>10 mg/L; Helander et al., 1996; Helander & Eriksson, 2002; Roine, Eriksson, Ylikahri, Penttila, & Salaspuro, 1989). In alcohol-dependent subjects who were not acutely intoxicated, plasma levels of methanol were still up to 10 times the normal range (Brinkmann et al., 2000). During ethanol withdrawal, the concentration of methanol in plasma

and urine remains steady until ethanol concentration falls below 0.2 g/kg (Haffner, Banger, Graw, Besserer, & Brink, 1997), and methanol returns to endogenous concentrations in the course of 2 days.

The ability of methanol to discriminate alcoholic-dependent subjects from subjects drinking less than 40 g/d (including currently abstinent individuals) is relatively poor (sensitivity and specificity <50%; Brinkmann et al., 2000) because the analysis of methanol alone is not completely specific as a screen for hazardous/harmful alcohol consumption. An elevated concentration of methanol in urine may originate partly from dietary sources (Davoli, Cappellini, Airoldi, & Fanelli, 1986; Lindinger, Taucher, Jordan, Hansel, & Vogel, 1997). Moreover, methanol is also present as a congener in certain alcoholic beverages, which augments the endogenous sources of methanol and leads to higher than expected levels when even small quantities of such beverages are consumed.

Acetaldehyde Adducts

Acetaldehyde, the initial metabolite of ethanol, usually appears at low levels in the circulation because it is rapidly metabolized to acetate in the liver (Di Padova, Worner, & Lieber, 1987). However, acetaldehyde is a very reactive molecule, and, by forming Schiff bases with amines, it readily binds to proteins, thus leading to an irreversible reaction that yields acetaldehyde-protein adducts (stable and unstable adducts; Hoffmann, Meyer, Sorrell, & Tuma, 1993). Reactive molecules are also formed when ethanol is metabolized by CYP-450 2E1 pathway, which generates reactive oxygen radicals. The reactive oxygen radicals in turn influence lipid peroxidation to generate reactive aldehyde species such as malondialdehyde (MDA) and 4-hydroxy-2-nonenal (HNE; Tuma & Casey, 2003). Acetaldehyde, along with the longer chain aldehydes MDA and HNE, have been observed to interact with certain proteins (albumin, hemoglobin, tubulin, and lipoproteins) and certain small molecules (biogenic amines; Tuma & Casey, 2003; Zakhari, 2006). It has been also been found that the human immune system generates antibodies against these aldehyde adducts of erythrocyte proteins.

WHOLE-BLOOD COMPONENTS THAT REACT WITH ACETALDEHYDE

Hemoglobin is a protein located in red blood cells that forms adducts with acetaldehyde (whole-blood associated acetaldehyde; WBAA) after ethanol ingestion (Niemela & Israel, 1992; Sillanaukee,

Seppa, Koivula, Israel, & Niemela, 1992). Both free and bound acetaldehyde in blood can be measured using HPLC methods with fluorescence detection. This assay is highly specific and has a sensitivity in the picomole range (Peterson & Polizzi, 1987). WBAA formation peaks 30 minutes after alcohol ingestion because the reactive acetaldehyde, which can also be generated nonenzymatically by the action of oxygenated hemoglobin on ethanol, initially forms a reversible adduct with erythrocyte hemoglobin (Chen, Lin, Ferguson, Scott, & Peterson, 1994; Peterson, Jovanovic-Peterson, & Schmid-Formby, 1988; Wickramasinghe, Thomas, & Hasan, 1994). These WBAA-reversible complexes, detectable in the blood stream for up to 48 hour after the last drink, are converted to irreversible WBAA (Wickramasinghe et al., 1994). The irreversible WBAA accumulates with time and remains detectable in the bloodstream for at least a month after alcohol consumption has ceased (Chen et al., 1994; Peterson et al., 1988).

WBAA levels in hazardous/harmful alcohol drinkers have been found to be significantly higher than levels found in totally abstinent individuals (Halvorson, Noffsinger, & Peterson, 1993; Peterson et al., 1988). WBAA increases significantly with alcohol ingestion, even after a single high dose of ethanol (2 g/kg), when the conventional markers (GGT and MCV) show no change, thus suggesting that increases in WBAA are not related to alcohol-induced liver damage. There are no gender differences in WBAA measurements when total hemoglobin levels are accounted for (Hazelett et al., 1998; Sillanaukee et al., 1992). Although the use of tobacco products will raise breath acetaldehyde sixfold within 15 minutes, this returns to baseline within 30 minutes; WBAA measurements remained unchanged in smokers throughout the experiment and were not different from those of nonsmokers (McLaughlin, Scott, & Peterson, 1990).

WBAA exhibits the highest specificity (>99%) using cutoff scores that discriminate individuals consuming more than six drinks per day (>80 g/d ethanol; harmful drinking) compared to subjects reporting six or fewer drinks per day. However, at these cutoff levels, WBAA has a low sensitivity (20%). Despite the low sensitivity, the insurance industry has used WBAA for more than a decade to screen for hazardous alcohol consumption (Peterson, 2004). The disappearance of WBAA follows the half-life of the hemoglobin and therefore is not useful in monitoring changes in drinking status.

SALSOLINOL

Adducts formed by the interaction of acetaldehyde with neurotransmitters belonging to the catecholamine and indoleamine family of molecules have also been observed (Quertemont & Didone, 2006; Zakhari, 2006), and these adducts have been suggested to mediate some of the behavioral effects of alcohol consumption (Quertemont & Didone, 2006; Zakhari, 2006).

Salsolinol (SAL) is a tetrahydroisoquinoline formed as a result of the condensation reaction of the neurotransmitter dopamine with acetaldehyde, and it can be measured in urine, plasma, and brain samples by GC-MS (Haber, Jahn, Ehrenreich, & Melzig, 2002). The amount of SAL found in bodily fluids can be elevated in individuals receiving high doses of dihydroxyphenylalanine (DOPA) as treatment for parkinsonism (Scholz, Klingemann, & Moser, 2004). SAL is also present in some foods such as cacao, cheese, banana, and soy sauce and in alcoholic beverages such as beer and wine. Therefore, elevated levels of SAL in blood or urine are not very specific for identifying hazardous/harmful ethanol consumption.

Reports on the direct relationship between alcohol intake and SAL formation have been contradictory. According to some reports, chronic alcohol consumption (Adachi et al., 1986; Collins, Nijm, Borge, Teas, & Goldfarb, 1979; Faraj, Camp, Davis, Lenton, & Kutner, 1989) is associated with increases in plasma and urine levels of SAL, whereas others have reported that urine SAL levels decrease following acute ethanol consumption (Haber et al., 1996). The variability in the reported levels of SAL in plasma and urine might be a result of variables including diet conditions and analytical problems associated with the detection of SAL (Haber et al., 2002). It has been shown, however, that peripheral blood mononuclear cells (lymphocytes) of non-alcohol consuming subjects have a SAL concentration much higher than that found in the plasma, which is less affected by nutritional factors (Haber, Stender, Mangholz, Ehrenreich, & Melzig, 1999). Measurement of this presumably *endogenous* SAL in lymphocytes indicated that, compared to nonhazardous drinkers, individuals drinking at hazardous/harmful levels who have been abstinent for as little as 1 week have *decreased* SAL levels in lymphocytes (Haber et al., 2002). After 13 weeks of abstinence, a further decrease in SAL levels is measured in the lymphocytes of alcohol-dependent (hazardous/harmful drinkers) subjects (Haber et al., 2002). Due to the great interindividual variations in both urine and plasma SAL levels, measurement of SAL in these bodily fluids is unlikely to provide a useful marker (Feest, Kemper, Nickel, Rabe, & Koalick, 1992) that will distinguish between hazardous/harmful and nonhazardous drinkers (Musshoff, 2002). The utility of lymphocyte measures of SAL as a biomarker for chronic alcohol consumption is still under investigation.

Acetaldehyde Antibodies

Antibodies against the acetaldehyde adducts of erythrocyte proteins have been measured in hazardous/harmful drinkers (Hietala, Koivisto, Latvala, Anttila, & Niemela, 2006), and these antibodies to acetaldehyde-modified proteins have been proposed as markers of recent alcohol intake (Israel, Orrego, & Niemela, 1988). In particular, the IgA response to acetaldehyde-modified proteins has been reported to be a specific marker of alcoholic liver disease (Worrall, de Jersey, Shanley, & Wilce, 1991). The highest plasma reactivity was found in alcohol-dependent subjects, especially those with steatosis and alcoholic hepatitis. Plasma from patients with nonalcoholic liver disease and from nonhazardous drinking subjects also reacted with the acetaldehyde conjugates to show the presence of antibodies, but to a lesser extent than plasma from alcoholics. The specificity of these antibodies as markers of hazardous/harmful alcohol drinking or alcoholic liver disease may not be high, but the utility of these acetaldehyde measurements may be in screening alcohol drinkers consuming at hazardous/harmful levels and alcohol-dependent drinkers at risk for alcohol-induced liver disease.

Other Blood Proteins

SIALIC ACID INDEX OF APOLIPOPROTEIN J

Apolipoprotein J (APO J) is a glycoprotein found in high-density lipoprotein complexes (HDLs) that are responsible for the transport of lipids from one lipoprotein to another (Burkey, deSilva, & Harmony, 1991; Trougakos & Gonos, 2002). APO J is highly sialated, containing 4–6 times more sialic acid residues than transferrin, and measuring the sialation of APO J has been proposed to provide a more sensitive marker for chronic alcohol consumption than CDT.

The measurement of the APO J sialation involves the immunoaffinity purification of plasma HDL-APO J followed by determination of the number of sialic acid residues by acid hydrolysis and spectrophotometric measurement of sialic acid. Most technicians in clinical laboratories can perform this assay. The values are then expressed as the ratio of the moles of sialic acid per mole of APO J (sialic-acid index of APO-J or SIJ). In human subjects, an intake of about 60 g of alcohol for 30 days leads to a 50% or greater depletion of sialic acid from plasma HDL-APO J in both male and female alcoholics compared to controls (sensitivity, 90–92%; Ghosh, Hale, & Lakshman, 1999). Furthermore, there is a positive correlation of alteration in SIJ with days of abstinence, with SIJ levels returning to control levels after 8 weeks. These data support the contention that loss or restoration of sialic acid molecules from Apo J protein is a direct reflection of alcohol consumption and can be monitored for a period covering weeks after the termination of consumption. Within this window, SIJ might serve as a screening marker for past or present hazardous/harmful alcohol consumption but would not be a sensitive marker of relapse drinking. Like GGT, APO J might also be a suitable marker to provide biological feedback to motivate patients to stop or reduce alcohol intake.

CHOLESTERYL ESTER TRANSFER PROTEIN

The cholesteryl ester transfer protein (CETP) is a plasma glycoprotein that transfers cholesteryl esters, triglycerides, and phospholipids between lipoproteins (Barter et al., 2003). The protein is posttranslationally modified in the liver by addition of four asparagine N-linked carbohydrates to which sialic acid residues are attached (Stevenson, Wang, Deng, & Tall, 1993). In abstainers and nonhazardous drinkers, CEPT transfers cholesteryl esters from HDL to very-low-density lipoproteins (VLDL) and low-density lipoproteins (LDL) in exchange for triglycerides.

Chronic hazardous/harmful alcohol consumption reduces the carbohydrate content of several N-linked glycoproteins (Gravel et al., 1996). Thus, CETP is analogous to CDT, and the defective glycosylation of CETP is associated with altered binding of lipoproteins (Liinamaa, Hannuksela, Kesaniemi, & Savolainen, 1997). Plasma CETP activity is determined using an assay independent of endogenous plasma lipoproteins. The assay detects the exchange of radioactive cholesteryl esters between labeled LDL and unlabeled HDL (Hannuksela, Kesaniemi, & Savolainen, 1992).

Plasma CETP activity is 26% lower in hazardous/harmful alcohol drinkers and is inversely correlated with alcohol intake (Hannuksela, Marcel, Kesaniemi, & Savolainen, 1992). CETP activity detects 63% of alcohol-dependent individuals from controls (nonhazardous drinkers) with a specificity of 82% if the cutoff point was set at the mean CETP activity of the controls (Hannuksela et al., 1992). The sensitivity and specificity of CETP activity are similar to those of GGT and AST. The results thus indicate that plasma CETP activity could be used as an additional method to detect hazardous/harmful drinking, although wide variation in the normal population and the elaborate analysis limit its usefulness.

TOTAL SERUM SIALIC ACID

As previously mentioned, alcohol consumption markedly inhibits the hepatic sialation process, with transferrin, APO J, and CETP being the prime examples. Therefore, it is not surprising that the measurement of total serum sialic acid (TSA) has been proposed to serve as a marker for excessive alcohol consumption (Romppanen et al., 2002). Because most of the sialic acid is conjugated at terminal positions on carbohydrate side chains (e.g., CDT, SIJ), measurement of TSA requires that sialic residues are first hydrolyzed from serum proteins and then purified. This can be accomplished by acidification or the use of the enzyme TSA neuraminidase and measurement of sialic acid by a spectrophotometric method similar to that described for SIJ. Alternatively, after liberation of sialic acid by acid hydrolysis and sample clean-up, sialic acid can be measured using HPLC separation on an anion exchange column with amperometric detection. Although these methods could be performed in most research laboratories, they are not commonly available in clinical laboratories.

There are only a few reports on the clinical utility of TSA as a marker of alcohol consumption. TSA was recently evaluated by Romppanen et al. (2002) who demonstrated that TSA levels are significantly elevated in alcoholics compared to healthy controls with good specificity (100%) but only moderate sensitivity (51%). Thus, TSA does not perform markedly better than the traditional serum markers MCV, GGT, and AST. However, unlike these markers, TSA level was not different between alcoholics with or without liver disease. Thus, TSA, CDT, CEPT, or SIJ may be of value in situations where one is trying to distinguish hazardous/harmful drinking from liver disease generated by non-alcohol related etiology.

N-ACETYL-β-HEXOSAMINIDASE

N-acetyl-β-hexosaminidase (also called beta hexosaminidase [β-Hex]) is a lysosomal hydrolase that exists in most cell types and is involved in the metabolism of carbohydrates and gangliosides in liver cells. The β-Hex molecule is composed of combinations of two polypeptide chains, α and β, which results in the existence of several isoforms of β-Hex (B, I, P, A, and S). Isoforms B, P, and I contain two β units; isoform A is composed of α and β subunits; whereas isoform S contains only α subunits (Isaksson & Hultberg, 1989). Isoforms B, I, and P are heat stable, whereas isoforms A and S are heat labile (Price & Dance, 1972).

β-Hex activity can be measured in serum and urine by fluorometric and spectrophotometric methods using inexpensive reagents. The activities of the major isoforms are distinguished by a simple heat treatment. This treatment allows the expression of β-Hex B levels as a percentage of the total β-Hex activity (% β-Hex B), which is more sensitive as a marker of alcohol consumption than the absolute levels of β-Hex B (Stowell, Stowell, Garrett, & Robinson, 1997).

After heavy alcohol consumption, lysosomes are damaged, and, subsequently, cells release β-Hex into the blood (Hultberg, Isaksson, & Tiderstrom, 1980; Stowell et al., 1997). It has been shown that β-Hex activities in the serum and urine of alcoholics are significantly increased in alcoholics as well as in healthy volunteers after drinking more than 60 g/d alcohol for at least 10 days (Hultberg et al., 1980; Karkkainen, Poikolainen, & Salaspuro, 1990). Stowell et al. (1997) compared %β-Hex with MCV, GGT, AST, ALT, and CDT measured in serum as a marker of alcohol drinking across a range of consumption that included alcohol-dependent drinkers, hazardous/harmful drinkers, nonhazardous drinkers, and nondrinkers. Using the established cutoff values for each of the above-mentioned markers for detecting more than 60 g/d alcohol consumption (hazardous/harmful drinking), %β-Hex activity had a higher sensitivity and specificity (94% and 91%) than all other markers. It must be noted, however, that at the time this study was performed, CDT was measured using the CDTect immunoassay. It is possible that recent improvements in CDT measurement (%CDT, %CDT by HPLC, CZE) could improve the performance of this marker (CDT).

Another drawback of β-Hex as a marker of hazardous/harmful drinking is that serum β-Hex can be increased by a number of conditions unrelated to alcohol use, such as hypertension, diabetes mellitus, liver cirrhosis, myocardial infarction, cerebral infarction, pregnancy, and possibly atherosclerosis (Hultberg, Isaksson, Lindgren, Israelsson, & Brattstrom, 1996; Hultberg, Isaksson, Nilsson, & Lindgarde, 1994; Isaksson & Hultberg, 1989; Pitkanen, Kyllastinen, Koivula, & Hormila, 1980). Thus, the specificity of β-Hex as a single marker of alcohol abuse is weakened if any of these conditions are evident in a subject.

MONOAMINE OXIDASE B

The platelet is the most intensively studied blood cell for biological markers of alcohol-dependence. One of the best researched platelet proteins is MAO-B. The activity of this enzyme has been reported to identify (1) hazardous alcohol use (state marker; Sandler, Reveley, & Glover, 1981) and/or (2) a predisposition to alcohol dependence (trait marker; Ferguson & Goldberg, 1997).

Researchers first detected the potential association between low platelet MAO-B enzyme activity levels and alcohol dependence in the 1970s (Fowler, Tipton, MacKay, & Youdim, 1982). Since then, many studies have demonstrated that alcohol-dependent individuals have lower platelet MAO activity levels than do nondependent sex-matched controls. However, these findings are not unanimous (Anthenelli, Smith, Craig, Tabakoff, & Schuckit, 1995; Tabakoff et al., 1988). One explanation for the discrepant results is that many other trait or state variables, some of which are correlated with alcoholism, also impact on platelet MAO activity. A number of intrinsic characteristics (e.g., gender and race, comorbid psychiatric illnesses, other medical illnesses, metabolic factors, personality traits) and extrinsic factors (e.g., tobacco smoking, medications, other drug use, and platelet sampling differences) appear to influence MAO activity. Three recent reports (Anthenelli et al., 1998; Snell, Glanz, & Tabakoff, 2002; Whitfield et al., 2000) found that after variations in smoking and gender were taken into account, alcohol dependence did not contribute any additional variance to the differences in MAO activity between alcoholics and controls.

However, a recent study found that, in a large study population (629 subjects), platelet MAO-B protein concentrations, as measured by quantitative immunoblot techniques, did not differ significantly between smokers and nonsmokers but were lower in subjects with a diagnosis of lifetime alcohol dependence (DSM-IV) compared to subjects who were never alcohol dependent (Snell et al., 2002). Most of the alcohol-dependent subjects in this study were still actively consuming ethanol. ROC analysis indicated a sensitivity of 71% and a specificity of 68% for detecting males consuming more than 40 g/d of ethanol (hazardous/harmful drinking). Based on these findings, a sensitive ELISA assay for MAO-B protein was developed, and preliminary studies in an alcoholic patient population undergoing detoxification indicate that low platelet MAO-B concentrations may serve as a biomarker for hazardous/harmful alcohol intake that returns to normal levels after 1–2 weeks of abstinence. (Snell, Herion, Helig, & Tabakoff, 2008). Further studies will establish whether this marker may also detect relapse drinking.

Markers in Nontraditional Tissues and Excreta

Blood and urine can be considered the "traditional" samples used for the analyses of licit and illicit drugs and their metabolites in the ADME studies, as well for monitoring medication compliance issues (Kraemer & Paul, 2007; Maurer, 2007; Musshoff, 2002). The advent of sensitive analytical methodologies (GC-MS, LC-MS, or LC-MS/MS) has made it possible to use as well small amounts of samples such as hair, breath, saliva, sweat, and meconium for these purposes. Compared to the "traditional" samples, one of the advantages of using these "nontraditional" samples is the noninvasive ways in which such samples can be obtained by comparison to obtaining samples of blood. Some of these nontraditional samples, such as hair, have also been used in monitoring alcohol and drug abuse (Koren, Hutson, & Gareri, 2008; Pragst & Balikova, 2006).

Breath

It has been suggested that about 5% of ethanol consumed is lost through breath (Swift, 2003). Breath alcohol analysis was first introduced almost 60 years ago as a test to monitor alcohol intoxication (Harger, 1948). These initial tests were based on oxidation of potassium permanganate using the Drunkometer (Harger, 1948). The technology used in breath alcohol monitoring has changed over the past 60 years. Some of the instruments, such as Alcotest 7410 (Drager Safety, Germany) and AlcoSensor IV (Intoximeter, USA), use fuel cell-based detectors, whereas Alcomat (Siemens, Germany) and Alkometer A2.0 (AWAT, Poland) use detectors based on infrared absorption technology. A recent study, similar to earlier reports (Bendtsen, Hultberg, Carlsson, & Jones, 1999), has demonstrated a good correlation between data obtained using these devices and the results of blood alcohol analysis (Zuba, 2008). The alcohol breath test has been widely used by law enforcement officials to monitor alcohol consumption due to the ease of obtaining samples. However, a number of biological variables, such as lung size, breathing pattern, and gender, have been observed to influence the results of alcohol breath tests (Hlastala, 1998; Hlastala & Anderson, 2007). Initial observations that breath alcohol concentrations were approximately 2,100-fold less compared to blood alcohol concentrations led to formulation of a conversion factor (the BBR: blood-to-breath ratio) to derive estimates of blood alcohol concentration from the breath alcohol measurements (Hlastala, 1998). Estimates of BBR have been observed to be sensitive to a number of variables such as equilibrium of ethanol between lungs and the upper airways and temperature and water contents of the air, as well as breathing pattern (Hlastala & Anderson, 2007). In addition to these variables, variations in breath alcohol measurements can also be introduced by differences in absorption and/or elimination (i.e., time elapsed after the last consumption of ethanol) at the time of measurement of the breath alcohol (Hlastala & Anderson, 2007; Lindberg et al., 2007), differences in the point of blood collection (Lindberg et al., 2007), and differences in blood alcohol concentrations (Pavlic, Grubwieser, Brandstatter, Libiseller, & Rabl, 2006). In addition to the use of breath to monitor ethanol, breath samples have also been used to analyze acetaldehyde contents (Jones, Skagerberg, Borg, & Anggard, 1984; Kamat et al., 2007; Turner, Spanel, & Smith, 2006). Breath acetaldehyde concentrations, although 2,000 times lower than blood ethanol concentrations, show good correlation with blood ethanol concentrations (Jones et al., 1984). Breath analysis can be used only for a limited duration of time, usually up to 6 hour after the last volume of ethanol was consumed.

Hair

Although obtaining hair samples for measures of alcohol use is comparatively easy, there are a number of caveats involved in interpreting the data obtained. Some of the difficulties in this interpretation arise due to the fact that hair is exposed to environmental factors that may influence the results of the test. Because even modest drinking or ethanol present in the environment can be absorbed by the hair, detection of alcohol in hair samples cannot be used as a definitive marker for hazardous/harmful alcohol use (Pragst et al., 2000). Use of hair in monitoring alcohol use is also complicated by certain genetic factors, such as individual differences in pigmentation, which may influence the absorption capacity of hair.

Detection (and quantitation) of FAEEs and EtG in hair samples has also been used to monitor chronic alcohol use. FAEEs can be detected in the blood for up to 24 hour after the cessation of alcohol consumption (Doyle et al., 1996; Laposata, 1997), but it is also deposited in hair, mostly in the sebum (Auwarter et al., 2001), and measures of FAEE in hair have been utilized for measuring alcohol consumption that may have taken place days before obtaining the sample. FAEEs have been detected at very low levels (0.06–.37 ng/mg of hair sample) in nondrinkers and in nonhazardous drinkers, whereas, in alcohol-dependent subjects with excessive alcohol consumption, the range of FAEEs in hair was 0.92–30 ng/mg (Auwarter et al., 2001; Hartwig, Auwarter, & Pragst, 2003).

EtG, similar to FAEEs, is incorporated into growing hair, thus making it a suitable marker for monitoring periods of past chronic alcohol consumption (Kissack et al., 2008; Pragst & Balikova, 2006; Pragst, Yegles, Swift, & Zuba, 2008). In general, higher EtG concentrations have been observed in hair samples from individuals with a history of hazardous/harmful alcohol use compared to the undetectable levels in controls (totally abstinent) and drinkers consuming nonhazardous levels of ethanol (Politi, Zucchella, Morini, Stramesi, & Polettini, 2007; Yegles et al., 2004).

It should be noted that whereas serum and urine measurements of FAEEs and EtG are suitable for monitoring abstinence and relapse drinking because of rapid changes in their levels, measurements of these biomarkers in hair can estimate cumulative alcohol intake; thus, these measurements are more suitable for screening for hazardous/harmful alcohol use over a past period of time versus a more instantaneous measure of an individual's drinking status.

Saliva

Oral fluids (saliva), similar to hair, offer the advantage of ease in obtaining samples to monitor alcohol use. A wide variety of devices are available for the collection of oral fluids, and these samples have been used in monitoring a range of licit/illicit drugs and their metabolites (Gallardo & Queiroz, 2008; Kidwell, Holland, & Athanaselis, 1998; Lillsunde, 2008). Saliva samples have been used to monitor ethanol consumption in clinical settings (Degutis, Rabinovici, Sabbaj, Mascia,

& D'Onofrio, 2004; Peredy & Powers, 1997). In the majority of these studies, a good correlation between ethanol levels in saliva and plasma (blood/serum) has been observed (Degutis et al., 2004; Jones, 1993). The time for blood and saliva ethanol concentrations to reach peak values was observed to be similar to that of peak breath ethanol concentrations (about 36–44 minutes; Jones, 1993). Similarly, after about 8 hours, ethanol could not be detected in either blood, saliva, or breath samples (Jones, 1993). A number of factors, such as mouth contamination due to ingestion of certain foods and/or biting nails or putting objects in the mouth, influence the results obtained using oral fluids to monitor licit/illicit drug use (Kidwell et al., 1998; Peredy & Powers, 1997). Oral ingestion of ethanol contained in over-the-counter drugs (or simply the use of mouthwash) can also result in a false-positive test when saliva is used to monitor ethanol levels (Kidwell et al., 1998).

However, saliva concentrations of ethanol follow a time course similar to that of blood and breath concentrations, and saliva can be utilized to detect very recent alcohol use in settings where the use of alcohol is contraindicated or illegal (i.e., emergency rooms, use of dangerous equipment, piloting airplanes).

Sweat

The use of sweat to monitor alcohol drug use also has certain advantages similar to other nontraditional samples. Sweat has been used to detect or monitor several illicit drugs (Kidwell et al., 1998; Peredy & Powers, 1997). Licit/illicit drugs can become incorporated into sweat via several different mechanisms, such as passive diffusion or transdermal passage (Gallardo & Queiroz, 2008). Recent studies have used sweat collected using a sweat patch to monitor ethanol consumption by analyzing EtG (Schummer, Appenzeller, & Wennig, 2008). Compared to undetectable levels in control subjects, the concentrations of EtG observed in subjects exposed to ethanol were 23 ±12.6 µg/L (Schummer et al., 2008). A number of drawbacks, such as difficulty in knowing the volume of sweat collected, possible contamination during application/removal of patch or due to bacteria, and losses due to evaporation, are associated with using sweat obtained from sweat patches to monitor licit/illicit drug use. Interpretation of data obtained in such studies utilizing sweat becomes difficult due to the lack of pharmacokinetic information about various licit/illicit drugs, including ethanol (Brown, 1985;

Phillips, Little, Hillman, Labbe, & Campbell, 1984; Schummer et al., 2008).

In addition to sweat patches, electronic alcohol sensors attached to the body have also been used to monitor alcohol consumption (Marques & McKnight, 2009; Sakai, Mikulich-Gilbertson, Long, & Crowley, 2006; Swift, Martin, Swette, LaConti, & Kackley, 1992). Two different types of transdermal sensors, one based on an electrochemical device (Giner TAS) and other based on a fuel cell sensor (AMS SCRAM), have been used in these studies. Such alcohol sensors, based on electrochemical technology, detect alcohol flux across the skin rather than the alcohol concentration. The sensor is placed over the skin surface, the accumulated transdermal ethanol (vapor) is oxidized, and the generated oxidation current is taken as a measure of ethanol concentration (Swift et al., 1992). In these preliminary studies, a good correlation between the transdermal ethanol concentrations detected by this sensor and blood alcohol concentrations was observed (Swift et al., 1992).

The transdermal alcohol monitoring system based on fuel cell technology monitors transdermal alcohol levels at time intervals and can store the data for about 140 such measurements. The results stored in an ankle monitor can be conveyed (using radio frequencies) to a secure database via modem (Sakai et al., 2006). A recent study comparing these two transdermal alcohol monitoring systems demonstrates the utility of such devices but also shows that product improvements are needed to get a good sensitivity and specificity (Marques & McKnight, 2009). In addition to the needed improvements in the sensitivity and accuracy of these devices, there are some other drawbacks in obtaining a high degree of accuracy; factors such as skin thickness, level of hydration, and temperature of the surface layer (stratum corneum) of the skin can affect ethanol transport, and, in turn, ethanol measurements by such devices (Anderson & Hlastala, 2006; Marques & McKnight, 2009). Use of such transdermal devices, which can provide semiquantitative measures of ethanol consumption, has shown that peak transdermal ethanol concentration occurs much later (about 120–180 minutes) compared to peak breath ethanol concentration (Barnett, Meade & Glynn, 2014; Leffingwell et al., 2013; Sakai et al., 2006).

The use of such transdermal devices does raise some right-to-privacy issues. Although there may be instances in which a court can mandate the wearing of such a device to assure total abstinence (e.g., pursuant to reissuing a driver's license after a drunk driving conviction), it is questionable whether individuals who are drinking alcohol at various levels will voluntarily choose to be continually monitored for alcohol intake.

Meconium

Meconium (fecal matter passed by neonates in the first few weeks postpartum) has also been used as a nontraditional sample to monitor licit/illicit drug use by the mother during pregnancy (Gallardo & Queiroz, 2008; Koren et al., 2008). Fetal swallowing has been suggested as one of the mechanisms for the presence of illicit/illicit drugs and their metabolites in the newborn (Gareri, Klein, & Koren, 2006). In addition to the ease of obtaining meconium samples, one of the major advantages is the fact that it is a repository of many compounds (licit/illicit drugs) that a fetus is exposed to during gestation. Meconium thus provides a history of fetal exposure and/or maternal consumption of various licit/illicit drugs and has been extensively used to monitor in utero exposure to a number of illicit drugs and ethanol (Gallardo & Queiroz, 2008; Gareri et al., 2006; Koren et al., 2008). A number of studies have demonstrated the presence of FAEEs in the meconium that correlated with maternal ethanol consumption derived from self-reports (Gareri et al., 2006). Although a good correlation between the time (trimester) and amount of maternal ethanol consumption and quantities of several individual species of FAEE has been observed (Bearer et al., 1999, 2003), a sum of the quantities of these FAEEs was shown to be a more reliable marker (Chan et al., 2003; Klein, Karaskov, & Korent, 1999).

Determinations of EtG and EtS levels in meconium samples have also been used to monitor fetal ethanol exposure (Morini et al., 2008). However, the levels of neither EtG or EtS correlated with reported levels of maternal alcohol consumption (Morini et al., 2008). In spite of the ease of obtaining meconium samples, a number of drawbacks are associated with its use to monitor fetal ethanol exposure (Burd & Hofer, 2008; Gallardo & Queiroz, 2008; Gareri et al., 2006). Due to its complex nature, analyses of meconium usually require very involved processes, which may influence the sensitivity and specificity of the analysis (Gallardo & Queiroz, 2008). Similarly, use of meconium to monitor fetal ethanol exposure becomes complicated because ethanol exposure prior to the formation of meconium may not be monitored using either FAEEs or EtG as biomarkers. Therefore, meconium can be used to monitor fetal ethanol exposure only during last trimester (the time period for the formation of meconium; Burd & Hofer, 2008).

Multifactor Measures and Analysis

Although each of the biomarkers discussed so far has individual value, each has differing strengths and weaknesses in terms of precision, accuracy, sensitivity, and specificity. As noted earlier, alcohol consumption patterns are complex, and no single biomarker has perfect sensitivity and specificity for all patterns of drinking. Acknowledging this fact, attention has turned toward the use of combinations of biomarkers, applied in parallel or sequentially, that detect all levels of alcohol consumption including complete abstinence, nonhazardous drinking, hazardous/harmful drinking, and alcohol dependence.

One combination that has been advanced is the use of a discriminant formula calculated from measures of CDT and GGT, termed γ-CDT (Sillanaukee & Olsson, 2001). This combination resulted in improved sensitivity (95%) over CDT and GGT alone (65% and 59%, respectively) for detecting subjects with alcohol consumption of more than 60 g/d compared to subjects drinking less than 60 g/d. A recent modification of this formula includes the physician's assessment of a patient's alcohol risk on a dichotomous scale (DOctor VERified; DOVER) or using the AUDIT questionnaire (QUestionnaire VERified [QUVER]; Bentele et al., 2007; Berner et al., 2006). Each of these combinations improved the diagnostic accuracy above the marker combinations alone. Finally, the combined use of CDT, MCV, and GGT measurements in blood samples from alcohol-dependent patients was found to lead to a significant elevation in sensitivity compared to the individual markers (Rinck et al., 2007).

The sequential use of CDT and GGT and computer learning has been applied to discriminate hazardous/harmful alcohol use from nonhazardous use and "alcohol abuse" from "alcohol dependence" (Schwan et al., 2004). Taken to its logical extreme, mathematical combinations of the laboratory variables albumin-to-globulin ratio, globulin, total protein, creatinine, blood urea nitrogen, blood urea nitrogen-to-creatinine ratio, alkaline phosphatase, triglycerides, total bilirubin, direct-reacting bilirubin, LDL, uric acid, neutrophils, monocytes, lymphocytes, and basophils have been used to calculate a mathematical model named the Early Detection of Alcohol Consumption (EDAC; Harasymiw, Vinson, & Bean, 2000). The EDAC has been reported to have a sensitivity of 88% when identifying hazardous/harmful drinking males and 98% specificity when assessing nonhazardous drinkers in the same population. When EDAC was analyzed in parallel with CDT, 92% of heavy drinkers showed abnormal EDAC and/or CDT tests, and 94% of nonhazardous drinkers were negative for both tests. When analyzed sequentially, the CDT test confirmed 61% of the hazardous/harmful drinkers identified by the EDAC test. Specificity rate for this testing strategy was 100% because the only false positives for EDAC tested negative for CDT (Harasymiw & Bean, 2001).

Biomarkers for monitoring abstinence that can be used in combination include urine alcohol, EtS, and EtG. When used together, these markers offer greater sensitivity to alcohol use than each biomarker alone (Wurst et al., 2006).

Proteomic Search for Markers of Hazardous/Harmful Alcohol Consumption

A new era in science emerged with the sequencing of the human genome. A considerable amount of effort is now being applied to the completion of a comprehensive transcriptome (messenger RNA) and proteome analysis to complement the already collected genetic information. The identification of novel proteomic markers of hazardous alcohol use and alcohol dependence has focused on proteins identified in the plasma, serum, and blood cells (e.g., erythrocytes, leukocytes, platelets). These approaches can be broadly divided into methods that utilize two-dimensional electrophoresis (2-DE) for separation of proteins and those using surface-enhanced laser desorption/ionization time of flight mass spectrometry (SELDI-TOF-MS) and liquid chromatography followed by mass spectrometry (LC-MS/MS).

Marshall and Williams (1991), using 2-DE, reported elevated levels of IgA, a1-chymotrysin, haptoglobins, and apo A1 lipoprotein in the serum of alcoholics. Although 2-DE is able to resolve thousands of proteins, it is labor intensive and suffers from reproducibility problems. The introduction of fluorescent 2-D differential gel electrophoresis (2D-DIGE) has increased reproducibility while simultaneously increasing sensitivity and the dynamic range of this technique (Unlu, Morgan, & Minden, 1997). In a recent report, 2D-DIGE technology was utilized to construct protein profiles of serum samples obtained from 12 subjects during a period when they were drinking hazardous/

harmful levels of alcohol and again 3 months after termination of alcohol drinking (Wu et al., 2007). Although, not identified, two protein spots on the gel increased in fluorescence intensity after the period of abstinence, and six protein spots decreased in fluorescence intensity after abstinence. This limited study supports the feasibility of applying proteomic technology to serum samples from hazardous/harmful alcohol drinkers to identify novel protein markers.

SELDI-TOF technology (ProteinChip array platform) has been used successfully to detect several disease-associated biomarkers and disease-related plasma protein fingerprints in complex biological matrices (Weinberger, Dalmasso, & Fung, 2002). Briefly, in this technology, a number of proteins contained in a serum sample are first retained in a solid-phase chromatographic surface. The retained proteins are subsequently ionized and detected by TOF MS. In the one application of SELDI-TOF to the area of excessive alcohol consumption, serum samples of alcohol-dependent subjects were obtained before and after a period of enforced abstinence (Nomura et al., 2004). A total of 11 potential biomarkers of excessive alcohol consumption were detected. Partial purification of three of these proteins and subsequent amino acid analysis identified them as the E chain of fibrinogen, apoprotein AI, and apoprotein AII.

Both the 2D-DIGE and the SELDI-TOF methods of proteomic profiling suffer from several limitations. Separation of proteins by 2D-DIGE is affected by poor solubilization of hydrophobic proteins, particularly membrane-bound proteins, and poor resolution of very-high and low-molecular weight proteins (Faber et al., 2006). SELDI-TOF is limited by low sensitivity for higher molecular weight proteins (Seibert, Wiesner, Buschmann, & Meuer, 2004). Both methods are relatively tedious and time-consuming. However, a high-throughput method for protein identification from complex biological samples has been demonstrated using an online coupling of 2-D LC-MS/MS. More specifically, the column peptide separation technology, coupled with quantitative MS (known as MudPIT) can be applied to blood constituents to assess relative levels of proteins in alcoholic and nonalcoholic subjects. Such technology can simultaneously provide information on relative levels of hundreds of proteins (Liu, Lin, & Yates, 2002), including membrane-bound proteins (Wu, MacCoss, Howell, & Yates, 2003). Although there are no published reports on the application of this method toward identification of protein biomarkers for alcohol intake, MudPIT has been used to measure differential expression of proteins in the blood platelets of alcoholics before and after treatment. Using spectral counts (the number of spectra representing identified peptides for a protein), MudPIT identified eight mitochondrial proteins that were expressed at lower levels in the platelets of patients upon admission compared to after 2 weeks of enforced abstinence (Tabakoff, B., personal communication). As more of the human proteome is uncovered through initiatives like the Human Plasma Proteome Project, application of proteomic methodology to the discovery of biomarkers for alcohol use and misuse is likely to yield many more novel candidates that will require validation.

Multidrug Markers

The recent legalization of cannabis use in certain states in the United States (Time: Colorado Washington Become First States to Legalize Marijuana (http://healthland.time.com/2012/11/07/two-u-s-states-become-first-to-legalize-marijuana/) and the common practice of using both licit and illicit drugs together with alcohol (NIAAA Publications, 2008 Alcohol Alert (http://pubs.niaaa.nih.gov/publications/AA76/AA76.htm) has brought to light a significant deficiency in forensic, medical, and workplace-related rapid, analytical techniques for measuring acute and chronic use of psychoactive substances. Clearly, there are currently in place sensitive and specific methods for measuring drugs like cannabinoid alkaloids in blood, urine, and tissues (Breidi, Barker, Petróczi, & Naughton, 2012; Zhang et al., 2014), but these methods have problems when dealing with individual specific metabolism and body distribution of the active ingredients and metabolites of marijuana.

Metabolic Biomarkers of Use and Abuse

The psychoactive component of marijuana is Δ^9-tertahydrocannabis (THC). THC binds to CB_1 and CB_2 cannabinoid receptors but its desired "high" is mediated by the CB_1 receptor pathway. During its metabolism, THC is first converted to 11-hydroxy-THC (11-OH-THC) by P-450 enzymes, 3A4, 2C9, and 2C19, and polymorphisms of these P-450 enzymes impact metabolic rates of THC (Jiang, Yamaori, Takeda, Yamamoto, & Watanabe, 2011). The first metabolite, 11-OH-THC is equipotent when compared to THC (Perez-Reyes, Timmons, Davis, & Wall, 1973). In the next metabolic step, 11-OH-THC is oxidized to 9-carboxy-THC (THCCOOH); this oxidized product is inactive at CB_1 receptors (Bland, Haining, Tracy, & Callery, 2005; Watanabe, Yamaori, Funahashi, Kimura, & Yamamoto, 2007). Smoked or ingested marijuana produces very different pharmacodynamic profiles; after smoking the ratio of THC-to-11-OH-THC is higher than following oral use. Half-life of THC is shorter than that of 11-OH-THC; however, the inactive metabolite THCCOOH, due to its water solubility, stays in the circulation for several days after use (Huestis, Henningfield, & Cone, 1992a, 1992b; Huestis, Mitchell, & Cone, 1996).

Cannabis metabolites, THC, 11-OH-THC, and THCOOH can be measured in blood, urine, and hair and are widely used for the diagnosis of acute and chronic use and overdose and, in retrospect, to infer cannabis use (i.e., postmortem). Although numerous reports indicate correlation of blood and urine THC and its metabolite levels with cognitive and psychomotor impairment (Ramaekers, Berghaus, van Laar, & Drummer, 2004; Hampson & Deadwyler, 1999), the correlation is weak. In addition there is sufficient evidence indicating that the pharmoacodynamics of THC and its metabolites are influenced by yet unidentified factors (e.g., neurohormonal status age and sex, with women appearing to metabolize THC slower; Karschner et al., 2009). Unreliability of assessment is suggested by data showing high day-to-day variability in test results in abstinent subjects. For example, Karschner et al. (2009) found that two patients from a group of 25 heavy users of cannabis produced alternate daily negative and positive blood and urine samples over a period of a week of abstinence in a controlled hospital setting. Such results generate caution about the use of THC and its immediate metabolites 11-OH-THC and THCCOOH as definitive measures of cannabis use both in the short term (i.e., 1–2 days after consumption) and in the longer term (2–10 days after consumption). Some countries in Europe and some states in the US have established 2–5 ng/mL as blood levels for THC that constitute the threshold for determining impairment while driving. However, the available data indicate that new tests are needed to provide more precise information. Reports indicate that some of the behavioral and cognitive effects of acute marijuana use may last 10 days or longer in some subjects, and this is even more pronounced in chronic users who clearly could have impaired cognitive and psychomotor function in the absence of detectable THC (Karschner et al., 2009).

The influence of use of other drugs such as marijuana, cocaine, heroin, and amphetamine on biological markers of alcohol use was noted by Chang et al. (1990). These authors noted that use of cocaine with alcohol resulted in lower mean corpuscular volume (MCV) as compared with subjects who were only consuming high levels of alcohol; marijuana use with alcohol was associated with lower AST levels than alcohol alone; heroin use with alcohol resulted in higher AST and γ-GGT than alcohol alone (Chang et al., 1990). Surprisingly, little work has been done more recently to build on these findings. A recent study did examine the effects of chronic ethanol use on markers of cocaine use as measured in samples of hair (Natekar et al., 2012). The increased levels of fatty acid ethylesters in hair as a result of ethanol consumption were associated with increased levels of cocaethylene (CE) in the hair of individuals using both cocaine and ethanol simultaneously. The proposed mechanism for this phenomenon was a metabolic interaction of ethanol with disposition of cocaine. It was demonstrated that, in the presence of circulating ethanol, the usual hydrolysis of cocaine to benzoylecgonine is shifted to transesterification to produce cocaethylene (Natekar et al., 2012). This demonstration, that the presence of ethanol in the body generates not only the ester derivatives of fatty acids indicative of alcohol use, but also ethyl esters of other psychoactive substances (when such reactions are structurally possible), led to investigation of other compounds that could be indicative of combined drug/alcohol use. Nadulski et al. (2010) used gas chromatography-negative chemical ionization MS (GC-NCI-MS) as well as tandem MS (GC-NHC-MS-MS) in an attempt to ascertain the presence of the ethyl ester of THC in plasma and hair of individuals who were simultaneously using cannabis and ethanol. Interestingly, these sensitive analytical techniques could not ascertain the presence of THC-COOEt above detection limits in any of the samples (Nadulski et al., 2010).

Future Directions

Physicians and clinicians have relied on patient self-report measures of ethanol intake (i.e., TLFB) for more than two decades to detect potential hazardous or harmful patterns of alcohol intake. Traditional biomarkers of excessive alcohol use (GGT, AST, and MCV) are useful only in screening or confirming chronic hazardous/harmful alcohol drinking. None of these markers alone is sensitive enough to determine the degree of hazardous/harmful alcohol drinking or specific enough to discriminate hazardous/harmful drinking from several other medical conditions (Niemela, 2007). An extensive effort has been expended to provide the clinical community with better objective measures of alcohol consumption to complement verbal assessments in the diagnosis and treatment of individuals at risk for hazardous/harmful alcohol use and alcohol dependence. With each advance in the ability to identify and quantitate the physiologic, biochemical, and chemical changes produced by or associated with alcohol use, new biomarkers have been discovered and evaluated.

As already indicated, a promising approach to diagnosing hazardous/harmful levels of alcohol consumption is the use of a combination of biochemical markers to increase the sensitivity of screening. Several blood tests have already been used as composite indices in the detection of hazardous alcohol consumption (Rinck et al., 2007), sometimes aided by computer algorithms (Sillanaukee & Olsson, 2001). Although these approaches provide higher sensitivity than any one test alone, they involve an increase in expense and complexity and have not become routine in clinical practice.

One solution to this drawback may lie in technological advances in the field of protein microarrays. Like their predecessor, the gene expression chip, for analysis of thousands of mRNAs at one time and the determination of whether mRNA expression is changed in disease states, protein microarrays or protein chips are spotted with thousands of known antibodies for the proteins of interest. Microarray-based sandwich immunoassays that start with the antibody-based chip are an attractive method for analyzing biological samples in normal and diseased states (Schweitzer et al., 2002). The biological sample (blood, serum, urine) is applied to the antibody-containing chip, and the chip is directly probed with a fluorescent molecule (e.g., a fluorescently labeled protein or small molecule tagged with biotin). The biotin binding to the chip can then be detected in a second step by using a fluorescently labeled affinity reagent (e.g., streptavidin). Another fluorescent labeling method for protein chips is *rolling circle amplification* (RCA). RCA indirect immunoassays use detection antibodies with covalently attached oligonucleotide primers that are then extended by DNA polymerase using hapten-labeled or fluorescently labeled nucleotides. The result is a highly localized and amplified signal (up to 1,000-fold; Kingsmore & Patel, 2003).

RCA-amplified protein chips can now profile up to 150 proteins in various substrates, including serum and plasma. Currently, this technology has not been applied to the use of multiple biomarkers for alcohol intake. With the potential identification of more protein biomarkers for alcohol intake using proteomic technologies, the feasibility of developing protein chips that can provide objective confirmation of multiple patterns of ethanol intake is on the horizon.

It should be noted that with the widespread use of smartphones and an emerging interest in mobile health applications, new devices for self-administered alcohol breath testing are being marketed that interface directly with individuals' smartphones to provide objective levels of breath alcohol concentration and allow for digital storing of data over time (e.g., the Breathomer; see breathometer.com). Although this technology is in its infancy, the development of body sensor networks (e.g., Lai et al., 2013) that integrate data from various physiological sensors (e.g., cardiovascular, physical activity) along with environmental variables (e.g., climate, geolocation) represents an exciting possibility for individuals and their health team to assess health-related parameters in real-time and generate temporally resolved characterizations of both alcohol exposures, physiological responses, and aspects of behavior. Indeed, whereas transdermal ethanol sensing is already being more widely employed in some settings, the potential to incorporate this standalone measure with other health-related real-time measures could provide new insights into the acute and cumulative effects of alcohol on the body.

Acknowledgments

This chapter was produced with support from NIAAA grants SBIR 5R44AA014531-05, U10 AA016663-01, and R24 AA013162-06A1 and the Banbury Fund.

Glossary

Biomarker	A chemical, biochemical, or physiologic feature that can be used to measure the progress of a disease or the effects of treatment
State marker	A biomarker that provides information about recent drinking activity
Trait marker	A biomarker that provides information about a person's genetic predisposition toward hazardous/harmful ethanol drinking
Sensitivity	A test's ability to detect small differences in concentration of the biomarker ("true positives")
Specificity	A test's ability to indicate the presence of the biomarker in a sample that is truly negative for that biomarker ("false positives")

References

Adachi, J., Mizoi, Y., Fukunaga, T., Kogame, M., Ninomiya, I., & Naito, T. (1986). Effect of acetaldehyde on urinary salsolinol in healthy man after ethanol intake. *Alcohol, 3*(3), 215–220.

Aizenstein, M. L., & Korf, J. (1979). On the elimination of centrally formed 5-hydroxyindoleacetic acid by cerebrospinal fluid and urine. *Journal of Neurochemistry, 32*(4), 1227–1233.

Allen, J. P., Fertig, J. B., Litten, R. Z., Sillanaukee, P., & Anton, R. F. (1997). Proposed recommendations for research on biochemical markers for problematic drinking. *Alcoholism: Clinical and Experimental Research, 21*, 244–247.

Allen, J. P., Litten, R. Z., Anton, R. F., & Cross, G. M. (1994). Carbohydrate-deficient transferrin as a measure of immoderate drinking: Remaining issues. *Alcoholism: Clinical and Experimental Research, 18*, 799–812.

Allen, J. P., Litten, R. Z., Fertig, J. B., & Sillanaukee, P. (2001). Carbohydrate-deficient transferrin: An aid to early recognition of alcohol relapse. *American Journal on Addictions, 10*(Suppl), 24–28.

Allen, J. P., Litten, R. Z., Strid, N., & Sillanaukee, P. (2001). The role of biomarkers in alcoholism medication trials. *Alcoholism: Clinical and Experimental Research, 25*, 1119–1125.

Allen, J. P., Sillamaukee, P., & Anton, R. (1999). Contribution of carbohydrate deficient transferrin to gamma glutamyl transpeptidase in evaluating progress of patients in treatment for alcoholism. *Alcoholism: Clinical and Experimental Research, 23*(1), 115–120.

American Psychiatric Association. (2013). *Diagnostic and statistical manual of mental disorders* (5th ed.). Arlington, VA: Author.

Anderson, J. C., & Hlastala, M. P. (2006). The kinetics of transdermal ethanol exchange. *Journal of Applied Physiology, 100*(2), 649–655.

Anthenelli, R. M., Smith, T. L., Craig, C. E., Tabakoff, B., & Schuckit, M. A. (1995). Platelet monoamine oxidase activity levels in subgroups of alcoholics: Diagnostic, temporal, and clinical correlates. *Biological Psychiatry, 38*, 361–368.

Anthenelli, R. M., Tipp, J., Li, T. K., Magnes, L., Schuckit, M. A., Rice, J., et al. (1998). Platelet monoamine oxidase activity in subgroups of alcoholics and controls: Results from the Collaborative Study on the Genetics of Alcoholism. *Alcoholism: Clinical and Experimental Research, 22*, 598–604.

Anton, R. F. (2001). Carbohydrate-deficient transferrin for detection and monitoring of sustained heavy drinking. What have we learned? Where do we go from here? *Alcohol, 25*, 185–188.

Anton, R. F., Moak, D. H., & Latham, P. (1996). Carbohydrate-deficient transferrin as an indicator of drinking status during a treatment outcome study. *Alcoholism: Clinical and Experimental Research, 20*(5), 841–846.

Auwarter, V., Sporkert, F., Hartwig, S., Pragst, F., Vater, H., & Diefenbacher, A. (2001). Fatty acid ethyl esters in hair as markers of alcohol consumption. Segmental hair analysis of alcoholics, social drinkers, and teetotalers. *Clinical Chemistry, 47*(12), 2114–2123.

Axelrod, J., & Daly, J. (1965). Pituitary gland: Enzymic formation of methanol from S-adenosylmethionine. *Science, 150*(698), 892–893.

Baglietto, L., English, D. R., Gertig, D. M., Hopper, J. L., & Giles, G. G. (2005). Does dietary folate intake modify effect of alcohol consumption on breast cancer risk? Prospective cohort study. *British Medical Journal, 331*(7520), 807.

Baraona, E., Abittan, C. S., Dohmen, K., Moretti, M., Pozzato, G., Chayes, Z. W., et al. (2001). Gender differences in pharmacokinetics of alcohol. *Alcoholism: Clinical and Experimental Research, 25*(4), 502–507.

Barnett, N. P., Meade, E. B., & Glynn, T. R. (2014). Predictors of detection of alcohol use episodes using a transdermal alcohol sensor. *Experimental and Clinical Psychopharmacology, 22*(1), 86.

Barter, P. J., Brewer, H. B., Jr., Chapman, M. J., Hennekens, C. H., Rader, D. J., & Tall, A. R. (2003). Cholesteryl ester transfer protein: A novel target for raising HDL and inhibiting atherosclerosis. *Arteriosclerosis, Thrombosis, and Vascular Biology, 23*(2), 160–167.

Bean, P., Kleaver, E., Roberts, B., & Harasymiw, J. (2001). A new century approach for alcohol screen in the insurance industry. *Journal of Insurance Medicine, 33*(2), 183–188.

Bearer, C. F., Jacobson, J. L., Jacobson, S. W., Barr, D., Croxford, J., Molteno, C. D., et al. (2003). Validation of a new biomarker of fetal exposure to alcohol. *The Journal of Pediatrics, 143*(4), 463–469.

Bearer, C. F., Lee, S., Salvator, A. E., Minnes, S., Swick, A., Yamashita, T., et al. (1999). Ethyl linoleate in meconium: A biomarker for prenatal ethanol exposure. *Alcoholism: Clinical and Experimental Research, 23*(3), 487–493.

Beck, O., Borg, S., Jonsson, G., Lundman, A., & Valverius, P. (1984). Measurement of 5-hydroxytryptophol and 5-hydroxyindoleacetic acid in human and rat brain and plasma. *Journal of Neural Transmission, 59*(1), 57–67.

Beck, O., & Helander, A. (2003). 5-hydroxytryptophol as a marker for recent alcohol intake. *Addiction, 98*(Suppl. 2), 63–72.

Beck, O., Helander, A., Carlsson, S., & Borg, S. (1995). Changes in serotonin metabolism during treatment with the aldehyde dehydrogenase inhibitors disulfiram and cyanamide. *Pharmacology & Toxicology, 77*(5), 323–326.

Belfrage, P., Berg, B., Cronholm, T., Elmqvist, D., Hagerstrand, I., Johansson, B., et al. (1973). Prolonged administration of ethanol to young, healthy volunteers: Effects on biochemical, morphological and neurophysiological parameters. *Acta Medica Scandinavica. Supplementum, 552*, 1–44.

Bendtsen, P., Hultberg, J., Carlsson, M., & Jones, A. W. (1999). Monitoring ethanol exposure in a clinical setting by analysis of blood, breath, saliva, and urine. *Alcoholism: Clinical and Experimental Research, 23*(9), 1446–1451.

Bendtsen, P., Jones, A. W., & Helander, A. (1998). Urinary excretion of methanol and 5-hydroxytryptophol as biochemical markers of recent drinking in the hangover state. *Alcohol & Alcoholism, 33*(4), 431–438.

Bentele, M., Kriston, L., Clement, H. W., Harter, M., Mundle, G., & Berner, M. M. (2007). The validity of the laboratory marker combinations DOVER and QUVER to detect physician's diagnosis of at-risk drinking. *Addiction Biology, 12*(1), 85–92.

Bernards, S., Graham, K., Demers, A., Kairouz, S., & Wells, S. (2007). Gender and the assessment of at-risk drinking: Evidence from the GENACIS Canada (2004-2005) telephone survey version of the AUDIT. *Drug and Alcohol Dependence, 88*(2–3), 282–290.

Berner, M. M., Bentele, M., Kriston, L., Manz, C., Clement, H. W., Harter, M., et al. (2006). DOVER and QUVER-new marker combinations to detect and monitor at-risk drinking. *Alcoholism: Clinical and Experimental Research, 30*(8), 1372–1380.

Bernhardt, T. G., Cannistraro, P. A., Bird, D. A., Doyle, K. M., & Laposata, M. (1996). Purification of fatty acid ethyl esters by solid-phase extraction and high-performance liquid chromatography. *Journal of Chromatography B: Biomedical Sciences and Applications, 675*(2), 189–196.

Bland, T. M., Haining, R. L., Tracy, T. S., & Callery, P. S. (2005). CYP2C-catalyzed delta (9)-tetrahydrocannabinol metabolism: Kinetics, pharmacogenetics and interaction with phenytoin. *Biochemical Pharmacology, 70*(7), 1096–1103.

Bortolotti, F., De Paoli, G., & Tagliaro, F. (2006). Carbohydrate-deficient transferrin (CDT) as a marker of alcohol abuse: A critical review of the literature 2001-2005. *Journal of Chromatography B, 841*(1–2), 96–109.

Borucki, K., Schreiner, R., Dierkes, J., Jachau, K., Krause, D., Westphal, S., et al. (2005). Detection of recent ethanol intake with new markers: Comparison of fatty acid ethyl esters in serum and of ethyl glucuronide and the ratio of 5-hydroxytryptophol to 5-hydroxyindole acetic acid in urine. *Alcoholism: Clinical and Experimental Research, 29*(5), 781–787.

Böttcher, M., Beck, O., & Helander, A. (2008). Evaluation of a new immunoassay for urinary ethyl glucuronide testing. *Alcohol and Alcoholism, 43*(1), 46–48.

Breidi, S. E., Barker, J., Petróczi, A., & Naughton, D. P. (2012). Enzymatic digestion and selective quantification of underivatised delta-9-tetrahydrocannabinol and cocaine in human hair using gas chromatography-mass spectrometry. *Journal of Analytical Methods in Chemistry, 2012*, 907893. doi: 10.1155/2012/907893.

Brinkmann, B., Kohler, H., Banaschak, S., Berg, A., Eikelmann, B., West, A., et al. (2000). ROC analysis of alcoholism markers—100% specificity. *International Journal of Legal Medicine, 113*(5), 293–299.

Brown, D. J. (1985). The pharmacokinetics of alcohol excretion in human perspiration. *Methods and Findings in Experimental and Clinical Pharmacology, 7*(10), 539–544.

Burd, L., & Hofer, R. (2008). Biomarkers for detection of prenatal alcohol exposure: A critical review of fatty acid ethyl esters in meconium. *Birth Defects Research Part A: Clinical and Molecular Teratology, 82*(7), 487–493.

Burkey, B. F., deSilva, H. V., & Harmony, J. A. (1991). Intracellular processing of apolipoprotein J precursor to the mature heterodimer. *Journal of Lipid Research, 32*(6), 1039–1048.

Caddy, G. R., & Block, T. (1983). Behavioral treatment methods for alcoholism. In *Genetics behavioral treatment social mediators and prevention: Current concepts in diagnosis* (pp. 139–165). New York: Plenum Press.

Carlsson, A. V., Hiltunen, A. J., Beck, O., Stibler, H., & Borg, S. (1993). Detection of relapses in alcohol-dependent patients: Comparison of carbohydrate-deficient transferrin in serum, 5-hydroxytryptophol in urine, and self-reports. *Alcoholism: Clinical and Experimental Research*, *17*(3), 703–708.

Chan, A. W., Welte, J. W., & Whitney, R. B. (1987). Identification of alcoholism in young adults by blood chemistries. *Alcohol*, *4*, 175–179.

Chan, D., Bar-Oz, B., Pellerin, B., Paciorek, C., Klein, J., Kapur, B., et al. (2003). Population baseline of meconium fatty acid ethyl esters among infants of nondrinking women in Jerusalem and Toronto. *Therapeutic Drug Monitoring*, *25*(3), 271–278.

Chang, M. M,. Kwon, J., Hamada, R. S., & Yahiku, P. (1990). Effect of combined substance use on laboratory markers of alcoholism. *Journal of Studies on Alcohol and Drugs*, *51*, 361–365.

Chen, H. M., Lin, W. W., Ferguson, K. H., Scott, B. K., & Peterson, C. M. (1994). Studies of the oxidation of ethanol to acetaldehyde by oxyhemoglobin using fluorigenic high-performance liquid chromatography. *Alcoholism: Clinical and Experimental Research*, *18*(5), 1202–1206.

Chen, Y. C., Peng, G. S., Wang, M. F., Tsao, T. P., & Yin, S. J. (2009). Polymorphism of ethanol-metabolism genes and alcoholism: Correlation of allelic variations with the pharmacokinetic and pharmacodynamic consequences. *Chemico-biological Interactions*, *178*(1–3), 2–7.

Cherpitel, C. J. (1998). Differences in performance of screening instruments for problem drinking among blacks, whites and Hispanics in an emergency room population. *Journal of Studies on Alcohol and Drugs*, *59*(4), 420–426.

Clark, D. B., Lynch, K. G., Donovan, J. E., & Block, G. D. (2001). Health problems in adolescents with alcohol use disorders: Self-report, liver injury, and physical examination findings and correlates. *Alcoholism: Clinical and Experimental Research*, *25*(9), 1350–1359.

Cohen, J. A., & Kaplan, M. M. (1979). The SGOT/SGPT ratio—an indicator of alcoholic liver disease. *Digestive Diseases and Sciences*, *24*(11), 835–838.

Collins, M. A., Neafsey, E. J., Mukamal, K. J., Gray, M. O., Parks, D. A., Das, D. K., & Korthuis, R. J. (2009). Alcohol in moderation, cardioprotection, and neuroprotection: Epidemiological considerations and mechanistic studies. *Alcoholism: Clinical and Experimental Research*, *33*(2), 206–219.

Collins, M. A., Nijm, W. P., Borge, G. F., Teas, G., & Goldfarb, C. (1979). Dopamine-related tetrahydroisoquinolines: Significant urinary excretion by alcoholics after alcohol consumption. *Science*, *206*(4423), 1184–1186.

Conigrave, K. M., Davies, P., Haber, P., & Whitfield, J. B. (2003). Traditional markers of excessive alcohol use. *Addiction*, *98*(Suppl 2), 31–43.

Conigrave, K. M., Degenhardt, L. J., Whitfield, J. B., Saunders, J. B., Helander, A., & Tabakoff, B. (2002). CDT, GGT, and AST as markers of alcohol use: The WHO/ISBRA collaborative project. *Alcoholism: Clinical and Experimental Research*, *26*, 332–339.

Costantino, A., Digregorio, E. J., Korn, W., Spayd, S., & Rieders, F. (2006). The effect of the use of mouthwash on ethyl-glucuronide concentrations in urine. *Journal of Analytical Toxicology*, *30*(9), 659–662.

Dahl, H., Stephanson, N., Beck, O., & Helander, A. (2002). Comparison of urinary excretion characteristics of ethanol and ethyl glucuronide. *Journal of Analytical Toxicology*, *26*(4), 201–204.

Davis, V. E., Brown, H., Huff, J. A., & Cashaw, J. L. (1967). The alteration of serotonin metabolism to 5-hydroxytryptophol by ethanol ingestion in man. *Journal of Laboratory and Clinical Medicine*, *69*(1), 132–140.

Davis, V. E., Cashaw, J. L., Huff, J. A., & Brown, H. (1966). Identification of 5-hydroxytryptophol as a serotonin metabolite in man. *Experimental Biology and Medicine*, *122*(3), 890–893.

Davoli, E., Cappellini, L., Airoldi, L., & Fanelli, R. (1986). Serum methanol concentrations in rats and in men after a single dose of aspartame. *Food and Chemical Toxicology*, *24*(3), 187–189.

Degutis, L. C., Rabinovici, R., Sabbaj, A., Mascia, R., & D'Onofrio, G. (2004). The saliva strip test is an accurate method to determine blood alcohol concentration in trauma patients. *Academic Emergency Medicine*, *11*(8), 885–887.

Del Boca, F. K., & Darkes, J. (2003). The validity of self-reports of alcohol consumption: State of the science and challenges for research. *Addiction*, *98*(S2), 1–12.

Del Boca, F. K., Darkes, J., & McRee, B. (this volume). Self-report Assessments of Psychoactive Substance Use and Dependence. In K. J. Sher, *The Oxford handbook of substance and substance use disorders*, Volume 2. New York: Oxford University Press.

Devgun, M. S., Dunbar, J. A., Hagart, J., Martin, B. T., & Ogston, S. A. (1985). Effects of acute and varying amounts of alcohol consumption on alkaline phosphatase, aspartate transaminase, and gamma-glutamyltransferase. *Alcoholism: Clinical and Experimental Research*, *9*(3), 235–237.

Diehl, A. M., Potter, J., Boitnott, J., Van Duyn, M. A., Herlong, H. F., & Mezey, E. (1984). Relationship between pyridoxal 5'-phosphate deficiency and aminotransferase levels in alcoholic hepatitis. *Gastroenterology*, *86*(4), 632–636.

Dietary Guidelines for Americans. (2010). United States' Departments of Agriculture and Health and Human Services. http://www.health.gov/dietaryguidelines/dga2010/DietaryGuidelines2010.pdf

Dillie, K. S., Mundt, M., French, M. T., & Fleming, M. F. (2005). Cost-benefit analysis of a new alcohol biomarker, carbohydrate deficient transferrin, in a chronic illness primary care sample. *Alcoholism: Clinical and Experimental Research*, *29*(11), 2008–2014.

Di Padova, C., Worner, T. M., & Lieber, C. S. (1987). Effect of abstinence on the blood acetaldehyde response to a test dose of alcohol in alcoholics. *Alcoholism: Clinical and Experimental Research*, *11*(6), 559–561.

Doyle, K. M., Cluette-Brown, J. E., Dube, D. M., Bernhardt, T. G., Morse, C. R., & Laposata, M. (1996). Fatty acid ethyl esters in the blood as markers for ethanol intake. *The Journal of the American Medical Association*, *276*(14), 1152–1156.

Edenberg, H. J. (2007). The genetics of alcohol metabolism: Role of alcohol dehydrogenase and aldehyde dehydrogenase variants. *Alcohol Research and Health*, *30*(1), 5–13.

Edwards, G., Arif, A., & Hodgson, R. (1982). Nomenclature and classification of drug- and alcohol-related problems: A shortened version of a WHO memorandum. *British Journal of Addiction*, *77*(1), 3–20.

Faber, M. J., Agnetti, G., Bezstarosti, K., Lankhuizen, I. M., Dalinghaus, M., Guarnieri, C., et al. (2006). Recent developments in proteomics: Implications for the study of cardiac hypertrophy and failure. *Cell Biochemistry and Biophysics*, *44*(1), 11–29.

Faraj, B. A., Camp, V. M., Davis, D. C., Lenton, J. D., & Kutner, M. (1989). Elevation of plasma salsolinol sulfate in chronic alcoholics as compared to nonalcoholics. *Alcoholism: Clinical and Experimental Research*, 13(2), 155–163.

Feest, U., Kemper, A., Nickel, B., Rabe, H., & Koalick, F. (1992). Comparison of salsolinol excretion in alcoholics and nonalcoholic controls. *Alcohol*, 9(1), 49–52.

Ferguson, R. A., & Goldberg, D. M. (1997). Genetic markers of alcohol abuse. *Clinica Chimica Acta*, *257*, 199–250.

Floyd, R. L., Jack, B. W., Cefalo, R., Atrash, H., Mahoney, J., Herron, A., & Sokol, R. J. (2008). The clinical content of preconception care: Alcohol, tobacco, and illicit drug exposures. *American Journal of Obstetrics and Gynecology*, 199(6), S333–S339.

Fowler, C. J., Tipton, K. F., MacKay, A. V., & Youdim, M. B. (1982). Human platelet monoamine oxidase—a useful enzyme in the study of psychiatric disorders? *Neuroscience*, 7, 1577–1594.

Frezza, M., di Padova, C., Pozzato, G., Terpin, M., Baraona, E., & Lieber, C. S. (1990). High blood alcohol levels in women. The role of decreased gastric alcohol dehydrogenase activity and first-pass metabolism. *New England Journal of Medicine*, 322(2), 95–99.

Friedmann, P. D., McCullough, D., & Saitz, R. (2001). Screening and intervention for illicit drug abuse: A national survey of primary care physicians and psychiatrists. *Archives of Internal Medicine*, 161(2), 248–251.

Gallardo, E., & Queiroz, J. A. (2008). The role of alternative specimens in toxicological analysis. *Biomedical Chromatography*, 22(8), 795–821.

Gareri, J., Klein, J., & Koren, G. (2006). Drugs of abuse testing in meconium. *Clinica Chimica Acta*, 366(1–2), 101–111.

Gay Anderson, D., & Riley, P. (2008). Determining standards of care for substance abuse and alcohol use in long-haul truck drivers. *Nursing Clinics of North America*, 43(3), 357–365, viii.

Ghosh, P., Hale, E. A., & Lakshman, R. (1999). Long-term ethanol exposure alters the sialylation index of plasma apolipoprotein J (Apo J) in rats. *Alcoholism: Clinical and Experimental Research*, 23(4), 720–725.

Goll, M., Schmitt, G., Ganssmann, B., & Aderjan, R. E. (2002). Excretion profiles of ethyl glucuronide in human urine after internal dilution. *Journal of Analytical Toxicology*, 26(5), 262–266.

Gong, M., Garige, M., Hirsch, K., & Lakshman, M. R. (2007). Liver Galbeta1,4GlcNAc alpha2,6-sialyltransferase is down-regulated in human alcoholics: Possible cause for the appearance of asialoconjugates. *Metabolism*, 56(9), 1241–1247.

Gossel, T. A., & Bricker, T. A. (1994). Alcohol, glycol and aldehyde. In *Principals of clinical toxicology* (Vol. 3, pp. 75–98). Chicago: CRC Press.

Gravel, P., Walzer, C., Aubry, C., Balant, L. P., Yersin, B., Hochstrasser, D. F., et al. (1996). New alterations of serum glycoproteins in alcoholic and cirrhotic patients revealed by high resolution two-dimensional gel electrophoresis. *Biochemical and Biophysical Research Communications*, 220(1), 78–85.

Gunnarsson, T., Karlsson, A., Hansson, P., Johnson, G., Alling, C., & Odham, G. (1998). Determination of phosphatidylethanol in blood from alcoholic males using high-performance liquid chromatography and evaporative light scattering or electrospray mass spectrometric detection. *Journal of Chromatography B: Biomedical Sciences and Applications*, 705(2), 243–249.

Gustavsson, L. (1995). ESBRA 1994 Award Lecture. Phosphatidylethanol formation: Specific effects of ethanol mediated via phospholipase D. *Alcohol & Alcoholism*, 30(4), 391–406.

Haber, H., Jahn, H., Ehrenreich, H., & Melzig, M. F. (2002). Assay of salsolinol in peripheral blood mononuclear cells of alcoholics and healthy subjects by gas chromatography-mass spectrometry. *Addiction Biology*, 7(4), 403–407.

Haber, H., Stender, N., Mangholz, A., Ehrenreich, H., & Melzig, M. F. (1999). Quantitative determination of endogenous tetrahydroisoquinoline salsolinol in peripheral blood mononuclear cells by gas chromatography-mass spectrometry. *Journal of Chromatography B: Biomedical Sciences and Applications*, 735(2), 299–303.

Haber, H., Winkler, A., Putscher, I., Henklein, P., Baeger, I., Georgi, M., et al. (1996). Plasma and urine salsolinol in humans: Effect of acute ethanol intake on the enantiomeric composition of salsolinol. *Alcoholism: Clinical and Experimental Research*, 20(1), 87–92.

Haber, P. S., Wilson, J. S., Apte, M. V., & Pirola, R. C. (1993). Fatty acid ethyl esters increase rat pancreatic lysosomal fragility. *Journal of Laboratory and Clinical Medicine*, 121(6), 759–764.

Haffner, H. T., Banger, M., Graw, M., Besserer, K., & Brink, T. (1997). The kinetics of methanol elimination in alcoholics and the influence of ethanol. *Forensic Science International*, 89(1–2), 129–136.

Hagan, R. L., & Helander, A. (1997). Urinary 5-hydroxytryptophol following acute ethanol consumption: Clinical evaluation and potential aviation applications. *Aviation, Space, and Environmental Medicine*, 68(1), 30–34.

Haggard, H. W., & Greenberg, L. A. (1934). Studies in absorption, distribution, and elimination of ethyl alcohol. III. Rate of oxidation in the body. *Journal of Pharmacology and Experimental Therapeutics*, 52, 167–178.

Halvorson, M. R., Noffsinger, J. K., & Peterson, C. M. (1993). Studies of whole blood-associated acetaldehyde levels in teetotalers. *Alcohol*, 10(5), 409–413.

Hampson, R. E., & Deadwyler, S. A. (1999). Cannabinoids, hippocampal function and memory. *Life Sciences*, 65(6), 715–723.

Hannuksela, M., Kesaniemi, Y. A., & Savolainen, M. J. (1992). Evaluation of plasma cholesteryl ester transfer protein (CETP) activity as a marker of alcoholism. *Alcohol and Alcoholism*, 27, 557–562.

Hannuksela, M., Marcel, Y. L., Kesaniemi, Y. A., & Savolainen, M. J. (1992). Reduction in the concentration and activity of plasma cholesteryl ester transfer protein by alcohol. *Journal of Lipid Research*, 33(5), 737–744.

Hannuksela, M. L., Liisanantti, M. K., & Savolainen, M. J. (2002). Effect of alcohol on lipids and lipoproteins in relation to atherosclerosis. *Critical Reviews in Clinical Laboratory Sciences*, 39(3), 225–283.

Hansson, P., Caron, M., Johnson, G., Gustavsson, L., & Alling, C. (1997). Blood phosphatidylethanol as a marker of alcohol abuse: Levels in alcoholic males during withdrawal. *Alcoholism: Clinical and Experimental Research*, 21(1), 108–110.

Harasymiw, J., & Bean, P. (2001). The combined use of the early detection of alcohol consumption (EDAC) test and carbohydrate-deficient transferrin to identify heavy drinking behaviour in males. *Alcohol and Alcoholism*, 36(4), 349–353.

Harasymiw, J. W., Vinson, D. C., & Bean, P. (2000). The early detection of alcohol consumption (EDAC) score in the identification of heavy and at-risk drinkers from routine blood tests. *Journal of Addiction Disease*, 19(3), 43–59.

Harduin-Lepers, A., Vallejo-Ruiz, V., Krzewinski-Recchi, M. A., Samyn-Petit, B., Julien, S., & Delannoy, P. (2001). The human sialyltransferase family. *Biochimie*, 83(8), 727–737.

Harger, R. N. (1948). Chemical tests for intoxication as an aid to traffic and industrial safety. *Industrial medicine & Surgery*, 17(2), 52–56.

Hartmann, S., Aradottir, S., Graf, M., Wiesbeck, G., Lesch, O., Ramskogler, K., Wolfersdorf, M., Alling, C., & Wurst, F. M. (2007). Phosphatidylethanol as a sensitive and specific biomarker—comparison with gamma-glutamyl transpeptidase, mean corpuscular volume and carbohydrate-deficient transferrin. *Addiction Biology*, 12(1), 81–84.

Hartwig, S., Auwarter, V., & Pragst, F. (2003). Fatty acid ethyl esters in scalp, pubic, axillary, beard and body hair as markers for alcohol misuse. *Alcohol and Alcoholism*, 38(2), 163–167.

Hasselblatt, M., Martin, F., Maul, O., Ehrenreich, H., & Kernbach-Wighton, G. (2001). Persistent macrocytosis following abstinence from chronic alcohol use. *Journal of the American Medical Association*, 286(23), 2946.

Hazelett, S. E., Liebelt, R. A., Brown, W. J., Androulakakis, V., Jarjoura, D., & Truitt, E. B., Jr. (1998). Evaluation of acetaldehyde-modified hemoglobin and other markers of chronic heavy alcohol use: Effects of gender and hemoglobin concentration. *Alcoholism: Clinical and Experimental Research*, 22(8), 1813–1819.

Helander, A. (1998). Monitoring relapse drinking during disulfiram therapy by assay of urinary 5-hydroxytryptophol. *Alcoholism: Clinical and Experimental Research*, 22(1), 111–114.

Helander, A., & Beck, O. (2005). Ethyl sulfate: A metabolite of ethanol in humans and a potential biomarker of acute alcohol intake. *Journal of Analytical Toxicology*, 29(5), 270–274.

Helander, A., Beck, O., & Boysen, L. (1995). 5-Hydroxytryptophol conjugation in man: Influence of alcohol consumption and altered serotonin turnover. *Life Sciences*, 56(18), 1529–1534.

Helander, A., Beck, O., & Jones, A. W. (1992). Urinary 5HTOL/5HIAA as biochemical marker of postmortem ethanol synthesis. *Lancet*, 340(8828), 1159.

Helander, A., Beck, O., & Jones, A. W. (1996). Laboratory testing for recent alcohol consumption: Comparison of ethanol, methanol, and 5-hydroxytryptophol. *Clinical Chemistry*, 42(4), 618–624.

Helander, A., & Carlsson, S. (1996). Carbohydrate-deficient transferrin and gamma-glutamyl transferase levels during disulfiram therapy. *Alcoholism: Clinical and Experimental Research*, 20, 1202–1205.

Helander, A., & Dahl, H. (2005). Urinary tract infection: A risk factor for false-negative urinary ethyl glucuronide but not ethyl sulfate in the detection of recent alcohol consumption. *Clinical Chemistry*, 51(9), 1728–1730.

Helander, A., & Eriksson, C. J. (2002). Laboratory tests for acute alcohol consumption: Results of the WHO/ISBRA study on state and trait markers of alcohol use and dependence. *Alcoholism: Clinical and Experimental Research*, 26(7), 1070–1077.

Helander, A., Wikstrom, T., Lowenmo, C., Jacobsson, G., & Beck, O. (1992). Urinary excretion of 5-hydroxyindole-3-acetic acid and 5-hydroxytryptophol after oral loading with serotonin. *Life Sciences*, 50(17), 1207–1213.

Hietala, J., Koivisto, H., Latvala, J., Anttila, P., & Niemela, O. (2006). IgAs against acetaldehyde-modified red cell protein as a marker of ethanol consumption in male alcoholic subjects, moderate drinkers, and abstainers. *Alcoholism: Clinical and Experimental Research*, 30(10), 1693–1698.

Hlastala, M. P. (1998). The alcohol breath test—a review. *Journal of Applied Physiology*, 84(2), 401–408.

Hlastala, M. P., & Anderson, J. C. (2007). The impact of breathing pattern and lung size on the alcohol breath test. *Annals of Biomedical Engineering*, 35(2), 264–272.

Hoeksema, H. L., & de Bock, G. H. (1993). The value of laboratory tests for the screening and recognition of alcohol abuse in primary care patients. *The Journal of Family Practice*, 37(3), 268–276.

Hoffmann, T., Meyer, R. J., Sorrell, M. F., & Tuma, D. J. (1993). Reaction of acetaldehyde with proteins: Formation of stable fluorescent adducts. *Alcoholism: Clinical and Experimental Research*, 17(1), 69–74.

Huestis, M. A., Henningfield, J. E., & Cone, E. J. (1992*a*). Blood cannabinoids. I. Absorption of THC and formation of 11-OH-THC and THCCOOH during and after smoking marijuana. *Journal of Analytical Toxicology*, 16(5), 276–282.

Huestis, M. A., Henningfield, J. E., & Cone, E. J. (1992*b*). Blood cannabinoids. II. Models for the prediction of time of marijuana exposure from plasma concentrations of Δ9-tetrahydrocannabinol (THC) and 11-nor-9-carboxy-delta 9-tetrahydrocannabinol (THCCOOH). *Journal of Analytical Toxicology*, 16(5), 283–290.

Huestis M. A., Mitchell J. M., & Cone E. J. (1996). Urinary excretion profiles of 11-nor-9-carboxy-delta 9-tetrahydrocannabinol in humans after single smoked doses of marijuana. *Journal of Analytical Toxicology*, 20(6), 441–452.

Hultberg, B., Isaksson, A., Lindgren, A., Israelsson, B., & Brattstrom, L. (1996). Plasma beta-hexosaminidase isoenzymes A and B in patients with cerebral infarction. *Clinica Chimica Acta*, 244(1), 35–44.

Hultberg, B., Isaksson, A., Nilsson, J. Å., & Lindgärde, F. (1994). Serum beta-hexosaminidase isoenzymes are related to risk factors for atherosclerosis in a large population of postmenopausal women. *Clinica Chimica Acta*, 227(1), 59–68.

Hultberg, B., Isaksson, A., & Tiderstrom, G. (1980). Beta-hexosaminidase, leucine aminopeptidase, cystidyl aminopeptidase, hepatic enzymes and bilirubin in serum of chronic alcoholics with acute ethanol intoxication. *Clinica Chimica Acta*, 105(3), 317–323.

Irwin, M., Baird, S., Smith, T. L., & Schuckit, M. (1988). Use of laboratory tests to monitor heavy drinking by alcoholic men discharged from a treatment program. *The American journal of psychiatry*, 145(5), 595–599.

Isaksson, A., & Hultberg, B. (1989). Immunoassay of beta-hexosaminidase isoenzymes in serum in patients with raised total activities. *Clinica Chimica Acta*, 183(2), 155–162.

Ishii, H., Okuno, F., Shigeta, Y., & Tsuchiya, M. (1979). Enhanced serum glutamic oxaloacetic transaminase activity of mitochondrial origin in chronic alcoholics. *Currents in Alcoholism*, 5, 101–108.

Israel, Y., Orrego, H., & Niemela, O. (1988). Immune responses to alcohol metabolites: Pathogenic and diagnostic implications. *Seminars in Liver Disease*, 8(1), 81–90.

Jiang, R., Yamaori, S., Takeda, S., Yamamoto, I., & Watanabe, K. (2011). Identification of cytochrome P450 enzymes responsible for metabolism of cannabidiol by human liver microsomes. *Life Sciences*, 89(5), 165–170.

Jones, A. W. (1986). Abnormally high concentrations of methanol in breath: A useful biochemical marker of recent heavy drinking. *Clinical Chemistry*, 32(6), 1241–1242.

Jones, A. W. (1993). Pharmacokinetics of ethanol in saliva: Comparison with blood and breath alcohol profiles, subjective feelings of intoxication, and diminished performance. *Clinical Chemistry*, 39(9), 1837–1844.

Jones, A. W., Skagerberg, S., Borg, S., & Anggard, E. (1984). Time course of breath acetaldehyde concentrations during intravenous infusions of ethanol in healthy men. *Drug and Alcohol Dependence*, 14(2), 113–119.

Jones, A. W., & Sternebring, B. (1992). Kinetics of ethanol and methanol in alcoholics during detoxification. *Alcohol and Alcoholism*, 27(6), 641–647.

Kamat, P. C., Roller, C. B., Namjou, K., Jeffers, J. D., Faramarzalian, A., Salas, R., et al. (2007). Measurement of acetaldehyde in exhaled breath using a laser absorption spectrometer. *Applied Optics*, 46(19), 3969–3975.

Karkkainen, P., Poikolainen, K., & Salaspuro, M. (1990). Serum beta-hexosaminidase as a marker of heavy drinking. *Alcoholism: Clinical and Experimental Research*, 14, 187–190.

Karschner, E. L., Schwilke, E. W., Lowe, R. H., Darwin, W. D., Pope, H. G., Herning, R.,. . . Huestis, M. A. (2009). Do delta9-tetrahydrocannabinol concentrations indicate recent use in chronic cannabis users? *Addiction*, 104(12), 2041–2048.

Katkov, W. N., Friedman, L. S., Cody, H., Evans, A., Kuo, G., Choo, Q. L., et al. (1991). Elevated serum alanine aminotransferase levels in blood donors: The contribution of hepatitis C virus. *Annals of Internal Medicine*, 115(11), 882–884.

Keyes, K. M., Geier, T., Grant, B. F., & Hasin, D. S. (2009). Influence of a drinking quantity and frequency measure on the prevalence and demographic correlates of DSM-IV alcohol dependence. *Alcoholism: Clinical and Experimental Research*, 33(5), 761–771.

Kidwell, D. A., Holland, J. C., & Athanaselis, S. (1998). Testing for drugs of abuse in saliva and sweat. *Journal of Chromatography B: Biomedical Sciences and Applications*, 713(1), 111–135.

Kingsmore, S. F., & Patel, D. D. (2003). Multiplexed protein profiling on antibody-based microarrays by rolling circle amplification. *Current Opinion in Biotechnology*, 14(1), 74–81.

Kissack, J. C., Bishop, J., & Roper, A. L. (2008). Ethylglucuronide as a biomarker for ethanol detection. *Pharmacotherapy*, 28(6), 769–781.

Klag, S., O'Callaghan, F., & Creed, P. (2005). The use of legal coercion in the treatment of substance abusers: An overview and critical analysis of thirty years of research. *Substance Use & Misuse*, 40(12), 1777–1795.

Klein, J., Karaskov, T., & Korent, G. (1999). Fatty acid ethyl esters: A novel biologic marker for heavy in utero ethanol exposure: A case report. *Therapeutic Drug Monitoring*, 21(6), 644–646.

Koren, G., Hutson, J., & Gareri, J. (2008). Novel methods for the detection of drug and alcohol exposure during pregnancy: Implications for maternal and child health. *Clinical Pharmacology & Therapeutics*, 83(4), 631–634.

Korzec, S., Korzec, A., Conigrave, K., Gisolf, J., & Tabakoff, B. (2009). Validation of the Bayesian Alcoholism Test compared to single biomarkers in detecting harmful drinking. *Alcohol and Alcoholism*, 44(4), 398–402.

Kraemer, T., & Paul, L. D. (2007). Bioanalytical procedures for determination of drugs of abuse in blood. *Analytical and Bioanalytical Chemistry*, 388(7), 1415–1435.

Kristensen, H., Trell, E., Fex, G., & Hood, B. (1980). Serum gamma-glutamyltransferase: Statistical distribution in a middle-aged male population and evaluation of alcohol habits in individuals with elevated levels. *Preventive Medicine*, 9, 108–119.

Kristenson, H., Trell, E., & Hood, B. (1981). Serum-gamma-glutamyltransferase in screening and continuous control of heavy drinking in middle-aged men. *American Journal of Epidemiology*, 114, 862–872.

Lai, X., Liu, Q., Wei, X., Wang, W., Zhou, G, & Han, G. (2013). A survey of body sensor networks. *Sensors*, 13, 5406–5447.

Laposata, M. (1997). Fatty acid ethyl esters: Short-term and long-term serum markers of ethanol intake. *Clinical Chemistry*, 43(8 Pt 2), 1527–1534.

Leaf, G., & Zatman, L. J. (1952). A study of the conditions under which methanol may exert a toxic hazard in industry. *British Journal of Industrial Medicine*, 9(1), 19–31.

Leffingwell, T. R., Cooney, N. J., Murphy, J. G., Luczak, S., Rosen, G., Dougherty, D. M., & Barnett, N. P. (2013). Continuous objective monitoring of alcohol use: Twenty-first century measurement using transdermal sensors. *Alcoholism: Clinical and Experimental Research*, 37, 16–22.

Lieber, C. S. (1997). Cytochrome P-4502E1: Its physiological and pathological role. *Physiological reviews*, 77(2), 517–544.

Lieber, C. S. (1999). Microsomal ethanol-oxidizing system (MEOS): The first 30 years (1968-1998)—a review. *Alcoholism: Clinical and Experimental Research*, 23(6), 991–1007.

Liinamaa, M. J., Hannuksela, M. L., Kesaniemi, Y. A., & Savolainen, M. J. (1997). Altered transfer of cholesteryl esters and phospholipids in plasma from alcohol abusers. *Arteriosclerosis, Thrombosis, and Vascular Biology*, 17(11), 2940–2947.

Lillsunde, P. (2008). Analytical techniques for drug detection in oral fluid. *Therapeutic Drug Monitoring*, 30(2), 181–187.

Lindberg, L., Brauer, S., Wollmer, P., Goldberg, L., Jones, A. W., & Olsson, S. G. (2007). Breath alcohol concentration determined with a new analyzer using free exhalation predicts almost precisely the arterial blood alcohol concentration. *Forensic Science International*, 168(2–3), 200–207.

Lindinger, W., Taucher, J., Jordan, A., Hansel, A., & Vogel, W. (1997). Endogenous production of methanol after the consumption of fruit. *Alcoholism: Clinical and Experimental Research*, 21(5), 939–943.

Ling, J., Stephens, R., & Heffernan, T. M. (2010). Cognitive and psychomotor performance during alcohol hangover. *Current Drug Abuse Reviews*, 3(2), 80–87.

Liu, H., Lin, D., & Yates, J. R., III. (2002). Multidimensional separations for protein/peptide analysis in the post-genomic era. *Biotechniques*, 32(4), 898–911.

Lu, Y., & Cederbaum, A. I. (2008). CYP2E1 and oxidative liver injury by alcohol. *Free Radical Biology and Medicine*, 44(5), 723–738.

Lundquist, F., & Wolthers, H. (1958). The kinetics of alcohol elimination in man. *Acta Pharmacologica et Toxicologica*, *14*(3), 265–289.

Majchrowicz, E. & Mendelson, J.H. (1971). Blood methanol concentrations during experimentally induced ethanol intoxication in alcoholics. *The Journal of Pharmacology and Experimental Therapeutics*, *179*(2), 293–300.

Marlowe, D. B., Festinger, D. S., Dugosh, K. L., Lee, P. A., & Benasutti, K. M. (2007). Adapting judicial supervision to the risk level of drug offenders: Discharge and 6-month outcomes from a prospective matching study. *Drug and Alcohol Dependence*, *88*(Suppl. 2), S4–S13.

Marques, P. R., & McKnight, A. S. (2009). Field and laboratory alcohol detection with 2 types of transdermal devices. *Alcoholism: Clinical and Experimental Research*, *33*(4), 703–711.

Marshall, T., & Williams, K. M. (1991). The simplified technique of high resolution two-dimensional polyacrylamide gel electrophoresis: Biomedical applications in health and disease. *Electrophoresis*, *12*(7–8), 461–471.

Martensson, O., Harlin, A., Brandt, R., Seppa, K., & Sillanaukee, P. (1997). Transferrin isoform distribution: Gender and alcohol consumption. *Alcoholism: Clinical and Experimental Research*, *21*, 1710–1715.

Marz, L., Hatton, M. W., Berry, L. R., & Regoeczi, E. (1982). The structural heterogeneity of the carbohydrate moiety of desialylated human transferrin. *Canadian Journal of Biochemistry*, *60*, 624–630.

Maurer, H. H. (2007). Current role of liquid chromatography-mass spectrometry in clinical and forensic toxicology. *Analytical and Bioanalytical Chemistry*, *388*(7), 1315–1325.

McLaughlin, S. D., Scott, B. K., & Peterson, C. M. (1990). The effect of cigarette smoking on breath and whole blood-associated acetaldehyde. *Alcohol*, *7*(4), 285–287.

Mellanby, E. (1919). Alcohol: Its absorption into and disappearance from blood under different conditions. *Medical Research Committee Special Report Series*, *31*, 1–48.

Mitchell, C., Simpson, D., & Chick, J. (1997). Carbohydrate deficient transferrin in detecting relapse in alcohol dependence. *Drug and Alcohol Dependence*, *48*(2), 97–103.

Moos, R. H., & Moos, B. S. (2006). Rates and predictors of relapse after natural and treated remission from alcohol use disorders. *Addiction*, *101*(2), 212–222.

Morini, L., Marchei, E., Pellegrini, M., Groppi, A., Stramesi, C., Vagnarelli, F., et al. (2008). Liquid chromatography with tandem mass spectrometric detection for the measurement of ethyl glucuronide and ethyl sulfate in meconium: New biomarkers of gestational ethanol exposure? *Therapeutic Drug Monitoring*, *30*(6), 725–732.

Musshoff, F. (2002). Chromatographic methods for the determination of markers of chronic and acute alcohol consumption. *Journal of Chromatography B*, *781*, 457–480.

Nadulski, T., Bleeck, S., Schrader, J., Bork, W. R., & Pragst, F. (2010). 11-nor-Delta9-tetrahydrocannabinol-9-carboxylic acid ethyl ester (THC-COOEt): Unsuccessful search for a marker of combined cannabis and alcohol consumption. *Forensic Science International*, *196*, 78–84.

Nalpas, B., Vassault, A., Charpin, S., Lacour, B., & Berthelot, P. (1986). Serum mitochondrial aspartate aminotransferase as a marker of chronic alcoholism: Diagnostic value and interpretation in a liver unit. *Hepatology*, *6*, 608–614.

Nalpas, B., Vassault, A., Le Guillou, A., Lesgourgues, B., Ferry, N., Lacour, B., et al. (1984). Serum activity of mitochondrial aspartate aminotransferase: A sensitive marker of alcoholism with or without alcoholic hepatitis. *Hepatology*, *4*, 893–896.

Naranjo, C. A., & Bremner, K. E. (1993). Behavioural correlates of alcohol intoxication. *Addiction*, *88*(1), 25–35.

Natekar, A., Motok, I., Walasek, P., Rao, C., Clare-Fasullo, G., & Koren, G. (2012). Cocaethylene as a biomarker to predict heavy alcohol exposure among cocaine users. *Journal of Population Therapeutics and Clinical Pharmacology*, *19*(3), e466–e472.

Nemesanszky, E., Lott, J. A., & Arato, M. (1988). Changes in serum enzymes in moderate drinkers after an alcohol challenge. *Clinical Chemistry*, *34*(3), 525–527.

Neumann, T., & Spies, C. (2003). Use of biomarkers for alcohol use disorders in clinical practice. *Addiction*, *98*(Suppl. 2), 81–91.

Newman, H. W., Lehman, A. J., & Cutting, W. C. (1937). Effect of dosage on rate of disappearance of alcohol from the blood stream. *Journal of Pharmacology and Experimental Therapeutics*, *61*, 58–61.

Niemela, O. (2007). Biomarkers in alcoholism. *Clinica Chimica Acta*, *377*(1–2), 39–49.

Nilssen, O., & Forde, O. H. (1991). The Tromso Study: The positive predictive value of gamma- glutamyltransferase and an alcohol questionnaire in the detection of early-stage risk drinkers. *Journal of Internal Medicine*, *229*, 497–500.

Niemela, O., & Israel, Y. (1992). Hemoglobin-acetaldehyde adducts in human alcohol abusers. *A Journal of Technical Methods and Pathology*, *67*(2), 246–252.

Nomura, F., Tomonaga, T., Sogawa, K., Ohashi, T., Nezu, M., Sunaga, M., et al. (2004). Identification of novel and down-regulated biomarkers for alcoholism by surface enhanced laser desorption/ionization-mass spectrometry. *Proteomics*, *4*(4), 1187–1194.

Norberg, A., Jones, A. W., Hahn, R. G., & Gabrielsson, J. L. (2003). Role of variability in explaining ethanol pharmacokinetics: Research and forensic applications. *Clinical pharmacokinetics*, *42*(1), 1–31.

Norberg, A., Sandhagen, B., Bratteby, L. E., Gabrielsson, J., Jones, A. W., Fan, H., et al. (2001). Do ethanol and deuterium oxide distribute into the same water space in healthy volunteers? *Alcoholism: Clinical and Experimental Research*, *25*(10), 1423–1430.

Nyblom, H., Berggren, U., Balldin, J., & Olsson, R. (2004). High AST/ALT ratio may indicate advanced alcoholic liver disease rather than heavy drinking. *Alcohol and Alcoholism*, *39*(4), 336–339.

Nystrom, M., Perasalo, J., & Salaspuro, M. (1992). Carbohydrate-deficient transferrin (CDT) in serum as a possible indicator of heavy drinking in young university students. *Alcoholism: Clinical and Experimental Research*, *16*, 93–97.

O'Connor, P. G., & Schottenfeld, R. S. (1998). Patients with alcohol problems. *New England Journal of Medicine*, *338*, 592–602.

Okuno, F., Ishii, H., Kashiwazaki, K., Takagi, S., Shigeta, Y., Arai, M., et al. (1988). Increase in mitochondrial GOT (m-GOT) activity after chronic alcohol consumption: Clinical and experimental observations. *Alcohol*, *5*, 49–53.

Pavlic, M., Grubwieser, P., Brandstatter, A., Libiseller, K., & Rabl, W. (2006). A study concerning the blood/breath alcohol conversion factor Q: Concentration dependency and its applicability in daily routine. *Forensic Science International, 158*(2–3), 149–156.

Peredy, T. R., & Powers, R. D. (1997). Bedside diagnostic testing of body fluids. *The American Journal of Emergency Medicine, 15*(4), 400–407.

Perez-Reyes, M., Timmons, M. C., Davis, K. H., & Wall, E. M. (1973). A comparison of the pharmacological activity in man of intravenously administered delta9-tetrahydrocannabinol, cannabinol, and cannabidiol. *Experientia 29*(11), 1368–1369.

Peterson, C. M., Jovanovic-Peterson, L., & Schmid-Formby, F. (1988). Rapid association of acetaldehyde with hemoglobin in human volunteers after low dose ethanol. *Alcohol, 5*(5), 371–374.

Peterson, C. M., & Polizzi, C. M. (1987). Improved method for acetaldehyde in plasma and hemoglobin-associated acetaldehyde: Results in teetotalers and alcoholics reporting for treatment. *Alcohol, 4*(6), 477–480.

Peterson, K. (2004). Biomarkers for alcohol use and abuse—a summary. *Alcohol Research and Health, 28*(1), 30–37.

Phillips, E. L., Little, R. E., Hillman, R. S., Labbe, R. F., & Campbell, C. (1984). A field test of the sweat patch. *Alcoholism: Clinical and Experimental Research, 8*(2), 233–237.

Pitkanen, E., Kyllastinen, M., Koivula, T., & Hormila, P. (1980). beta-N-acetylglucosaminidase and beta-glucuronidase activities in insulin-dependent diabetic subjects with retinopathy. *Diabetologia, 18*(4), 275–278.

Pizon, A. F., Becker, C. E., & Bikin, D. (2007). The clinical significance of variations in ethanol toxicokinetics. *Journal of Medical Toxicology, 3*(2), 63–72.

Poikolainen, K. (1995). Alcohol and mortality: A review. *Journal of clinical epidemiology, 48*(4), 455–465.

Politi, L., Zucchella, A., Stramesi, C., & Polettini, A. (2007). Markers of chronic alcohol use in hair: comparison of ethyl glucuronide and cocaethylene in cocaine users. *Forensic Science International, 172*(1), 23–27.

Pragst, F., & Balikova, M. A. (2006). State of the art in hair analysis for detection of drug and alcohol abuse. *Clinica Chimica Acta, 370*(1–2), 17–49.

Pragst, F., Spiegel, K., Sporkert, F., Bohnenkamp, M., Pragst, F., Yegles, M., et al. (2000). Are there possibilities for the detection of chronically elevated alcohol consumption by hair analysis? A report about the state of investigation. *Forensic Science International, 107*(1–3), 201–223.

Pragst, F., Yegles, M., Swift, R., & Zuba, D. (2008). Determination of fatty acid ethyl esters (FAEE) and ethyl glucuronide (EtG) in hair: A promising way for retrospective detection of alcohol abuse during pregnancy? *Therapeutic Drug Monitoring, 30*(2), 255–263.

Prat, G., Adan, A., Pérez-Pàmies, M., & Sànchez-Turet, M. (2008). Neurocognitive effects of alcohol hangover. *Addictive Behaviors, 33*(1), 15–23.

Pratt, D. S., & Kaplan, M. M. (2000). Evaluation of abnormal liver-enzyme results in asymptomatic patients. *New England Journal of Medicine, 342*(17), 1266–1271.

Price, R. G., & Dance, N. (1972). The demonstration of multiple heat stable forms of N-acetyl-β-glucosaminidase in normal human serum. *Biochimica et Biophysica Acta (BBA)-Protein Structure, 271*(1), 145–153.

Quertemont, E., & Didone, V. (2006). Role of acetaldehyde in mediating the pharmacological and behavioral effects of alcohol. *Alcohol Research & Health: The Journal of the National Institute on Alcohol Abuse & Alcoholism, 29*(4), 258–265.

Ramaekers, J. G., Berghaus, G., van Laar, M., & Drummer, O. H. (2004). Dose related risk of motor vehicle crashes after cannabis use. *Drug and Alcohol Dependence, 73*(2), 109.

Ramchandani, V. A., Bosron, W. F., & Li, T. K. (2001). Research advances in ethanol metabolism. *Pathologie Biologie, 49*(9), 676–682.

Refaai, M. A., Nguyen, P. N., Steffensen, T. S., Evans, R. J., Cluette-Brown, J. E., & Laposata, M. (2002). Liver and adipose tissue fatty acid ethyl esters obtained at autopsy are postmortem markers for premortem ethanol intake. *Clinical Chemistry, 48*(1), 77–83.

Rinck, D., Frieling, H., Freitag, A., Hillemacher, T., Bayerlein, K., Kornhuber, J., et al. (2007). Combinations of carbohydrate-deficient transferrin, mean corpuscular erythrocyte volume, gamma-glutamyltransferase, homocysteine and folate increase the significance of biological markers in alcohol dependent patients. *Drug and Alcohol Dependence, 89*(1), 60–65.

Rohrig, T. P., Huber, C., Goodson, L., & Ross, W. (2006). Detection of ethylglucuronide in urine following the application of Germ-X. *Journal of Analytical Toxicology, 30*(9), 703–704.

Roine, R. P., Eriksson, C. J., Ylikahri, R., Penttila, A., & Salaspuro, M. (1989). Methanol as a marker of alcohol abuse. *Alcoholism: Clinical and Experimental Research, 13*(2), 172–175.

Romppanen, J., Punnonen, K., Anttila, P., Jakobsson, T., Blake, J., & Niemela, O. (2002). Serum sialic acid as a marker of alcohol consumption: Effect of liver disease and heavy drinking. *Alcoholism: Clinical and Experimental Research, 26*(8), 1234–1238.

Rosalki, S. B. (1975). Gamma-glutamyl transpeptidase. *Advances in Clinical Chemistry, 17*, 53–107.

Rosalki, S. B., & Rau, D. (1972). Serum γ-glutamyl transpeptidase activity in alcoholism. *Clinica Chimica Acta, 39*, 41–47.

Rosman, A. S., Basu, P., Galvin, K., & Lieber, C. S. (1995). Utility of carbohydrate-deficient transferrin as a marker of relapse in alcoholic patients. *Alcoholism: Clinical and Experimental Research, 19*(3), 611–616.

Saady, J. J., Poklis, A., & Dalton, H. P. (1993). Production of urinary ethanol after sample collection. *Journal of Forensic Sciences, 38*(6), 1467–1471.

Sakai, J. T., Mikulich-Gilbertson, S. K., Long, R. J., & Crowley, T. J. (2006). Validity of transdermal alcohol monitoring: Fixed and self-regulated dosing. *Alcoholism: Clinical and Experimental Research, 30*(1), 26–33.

Salaspuro, M. (1999). Carbohydrate-deficient transferrin as compared to other markers of alcoholism: A systematic review. *Alcohol, 19*(3), 261–271.

Sandler, M., Reveley, M. A., & Glover, V. (1981). Human platelet monoamine oxidase activity in health and disease: A review. *Journal of Clinical Pathology, 34*, 292–302.

Saunders, J. B., Aasland, O. G., Babor, T. F., & Grant, M. (1993). Development of the alcohol use disorders identification test (AUDIT): WHO collaborative project on early detection of persons with harmful alcohol consumption-II. *Addiction, 88*(6), 791–804.

Saunders, J. B., & Lee, N. K. (2000). Hazardous alcohol use: Its delineation as a subthreshold disorder, and approaches to its diagnosis and management. *Comprehensive psychiatry, 41*(2 Suppl. 1), 95–103.

Schmidt, L. G., Schmidt, K., Dufeu, P., Ohse, A., Rommelspacher, H., & Muller, C. (1997). Superiority of carbohydrate-deficient transferrin to gamma-glutamyltransferase in detecting relapse in alcoholism. *American Journal of Psychiatry*, *154*(1), 75–80.

Schmitt, G., Droenner, P., Skopp, G., & Aderjan, R. (1997). Ethyl glucuronide concentration in serum of human volunteers, teetotalers, and suspected drinking drivers. *Journal of Forensic Sciences*, *42*(6), 1099–1102.

Schneider, H., & Glatt, H. (2004). Sulpho-conjugation of ethanol in humans in vivo and by individual sulphotransferase forms in vitro. *Biochemical Journal*, *383*(Pt. 3), 543–549.

Scholz, J., Klingemann, I., & Moser, A. (2004). Increased systemic levels of norsalsolinol derivatives are induced by levodopa treatment and do not represent biological markers of Parkinson's disease. *Journal of Neurology, Neurosurgery & Psychiatry*, *75*(4), 634–636.

Schummer, C., Appenzeller, B. M., & Wennig, R. (2008). Quantitative determination of ethyl glucuronide in sweat. *Therapeutic Drug Monitoring*, *30*(4), 536–539.

Schwan, R., Albuisson, E., Malet, L., Loiseaux, M. N., Reynaud, M., Schellenberg, F., et al. (2004). The use of biological laboratory markers in the diagnosis of alcohol misuse: An evidence-based approach. *Drug and Alcohol Dependence*, *74*(3), 273–279.

Schweitzer, B., Roberts, S., Grimwade, B., Shao, W., Wang, M., Fu, Q., et al. (2002). Multiplexed protein profiling on microarrays by rolling-circle amplification. *Nature Biotechnology*, *20*(4), 359–365.

Scouller, K., Conigrave, K. M., Macaskill, P., Irwig, L., & Whitfield, J. B. (2000). Should we use carbohydrate-deficient transferrin instead of γ-glutamyltransferase for detecting problem drinkers? A systematic review and meta-analysis. *Clinical Chemistry*, *46*, 1894–1902.

Seibert, V., Wiesner, A., Buschmann, T., & Meuer, J. (2004). Surface-enhanced laser desorption ionization time-of-flight mass spectrometry (SELDI TOF-MS) and ProteinChip ® technology in proteomics research. *Pathology-Research and Practice*, 200(2), 83–94.

Sheffield, F. D., Darkes, J., Del Boca, F. K., & Goldman, M. S. (2005). Binge drinking and alcohol-related problems among community college students: Implications for prevention policy. *Journal of American College Health*, *54*(3), 137–141.

Sillanaukee, P., Aalto, M., & Seppa, K. (1998). Carbohydrate-deficient transferrin and conventional alcohol markers as indicators for brief intervention among heavy drinkers in primary health care. *Alcoholism: Clinical and Experimental Research*, *22*, 892–896.

Sillanaukee, P. & Olsson, U. (2001). Improved diagnostic classification of alcohol abusers by combining carbohydrate-deficient transferrin and gamma-glutamyltransferase. *Chemical Chemistry*, *47*(4), 681–685.

Sillanaukee, P., Seppa, K., Koivula, T., Israel, Y., & Niemela, O. (1992). Acetaldehyde-modified hemoglobin as a marker of alcohol consumption: Comparison of two new methods. *Journal of Laboratory and Clinical Medicine*, *120*, 42–47.

Sillanaukee, P., Strid, N., Allen, J. P., & Litten, R. Z. (2001). Possible reasons why heavy drinking increases carbohydrate-deficient transferrin. *Alcoholism: Clinical and Experimental Research*, *25*, 34–40.

Sillanaukee, P., Strid, N., Jousilahti, P., Vartiainen, E., Poikolainen, K., Nikkari, S., et al. (2001). Association of self-reported diseases and health care use with commonly used laboratory markers for alcohol consumption. *Alcohol & Alcoholism*, *36*, 339–345.

Snell, L. D., Glanz, J., & Tabakoff, B. (2002). Relationships between effects of smoking, gender, and alcohol dependence on platelet monoamine oxidase-B: Activity, affinity labeling, and protein measurements. *Alcoholism: Clinical and Experimental Research*, *26*, 1105–1113.

Snell, L. D., Herion, D, Helig, M., & Tabakoff, B. (2008). The mysteries of MAO: Is it really a marker for marker for alcoholism? *Alcohol, Clinical and Experimental Research*, *32*, 228.

Sobell, L. C., Maisto, S. A., Sobell, M. B., & Cooper, A. M. (1979). Reliability of alcohol abusers' self-reports of drinking behavior. *Behaviour Research and Therapy*, *17*(2), 157–160.

Sobell, M. B. (1990). Self-report issues in alcohol abuse: State of the art and future directions. *Behavioral Assessment*, *12*, 91–106.

Soderberg, B. L., Salem, R. O., Best, C. A., Cluette-Brown, J. E., & Laposata, M. (2003). Fatty acid ethyl esters ethanol metabolites that reflect ethanol intake. *American Journal of Clinical Pathology. Pathology Patterns Reviews*, *119*(Suppl. 1), S94–S99.

Soderberg, B. L., Sicinska, E. T., Blodget, E., Cluette-Brown, J. E., Suter, P. M., Schuppisser, T., et al. (1999). Preanalytical variables affecting the quantification of fatty acid ethyl esters in plasma and serum samples. *Clinical Chemistry*, *45*(12), 2183–2190.

Some, M., & Helander, A. (2002). Urinary excretion patterns of 5-hydroxyindole-3-acetic acid and 5-hydroxytryptophol in various animal species: Implications for studies on serotonin metabolism and turnover rate. *Life Sciences*, *71*(20), 2341–2349.

Spies, C. D., Kissner, M., Neumann, T., BLUM, S., Voigt, C., Funk, T.,. . . Pragst, F. (1998). Elevated carbohydrate-deficient transferrin predicts prolonged intensive care unit stay in traumatized men. *Alcohol and Alcoholism*, *33*(6), 661–669.

Stephanson, N., Helander, A., & Beck, O. (2007). Alcohol biomarker analysis: Simultaneous determination of 5-hydroxytryptophol glucuronide and 5-hydroxyindoleacetic acid by direct injection of urine using ultra-performance liquid chromatography-tandem mass spectrometry. *Journal of Mass Spectrometry*, *42*(7), 940–949.

Stephens, R., Ling, J., Heffernan, T. M., Heather, N., & Jones, K. (2008). A review of the literature on the cognitive effects of alcohol hangover. *Alcohol and Alcoholism*, *43*(2), 163–170.

Stetter, F., Gaertner, H. J., Wiatr, G., Mann, K., & Breyer-Pfaff, U. (1991). Urinary dolichol—a doubtful marker of alcoholism. *Alcoholism: Clinical and Experimental Research*, *15*, 938–941.

Stevenson, S. C., Wang, S., Deng, L., & Tall, A. R. (1993). Human plasma cholesteryl ester transfer protein consists of a mixture of two forms reflecting variable glycosylation at asparagine 341. *Biochemistry*, *32*(19), 5121–5126.

Stibler, H. (1991). Carbohydrate-deficient transferrin in serum: A new marker of potentially harmful alcohol consumption reviewed. *Clinical Chemistry*, 37, 2029–3037.

Stibler, H., & Borg, S. (1981). Evidence of a reduced sialic acid content in serum transferrin in male alcoholics. *Alcoholism: Clinical and Experimental Research*, *5*(4), 545–549.

Stowell, L., Stowell, A., Garrett, N., & Robinson, G. (1997). Comparison of serum beta-hexosaminidase isoenzyme B activity with serum carbohydrate-deficient transferrin and other markers of alcohol abuse. *Alcohol & Alcoholism, 32*(6), 703–714.

Substance Abuse and Mental Health Services Administration. (2012). The role of biomarkers in the treatment of alcohol use disorders, 2012 revision. *Advisory, 11*(2).

Svensson, S., Some, M., Lundsjo, A., Helander, A., Cronholm, T., & Hoog, J. O. (1999). Activities of human alcohol dehydrogenases in the metabolic pathways of ethanol and serotonin. *European Journal of Biochemistry, 262*(2), 324–329.

Swift, R. (2003). Direct measurement of alcohol and its metabolites. *Addiction, 98*(Suppl. 2)(2–3), 73–80.

Swift, R. M., Martin, C. S., Swette, L., LaConti, A., & Kackley, N. (1992). Studies on a wearable, electronic, transdermal alcohol sensor. *Alcoholism: Clinical and Experimental Research, 16*(4), 721–725.

Tabakoff, B., Erwin, V. G., Tabakoff, B., Groskopf, W., Anderson, R., & Alivisatos, S. G. (1970). Purification and characterization of a reduced nicotinamide adenine dinucleotide phosphate-linked aldehyde reductase from brain. *Journal of Biological Chemistry, 245*(12), 3263–3268.

Tabakoff, B., Groskopf, W., Anderson, R., & Alivisatos, S. G. (1974). "Biogenic" aldehyde metabolism relation to pentose shunt activity in brain. *Biochemical pharmacology, 23*(12), 1707–1719.

Tabakoff, B., Helander, A., Conigrave, K. M., Martinez, L., Hoffman, P. L., Whitfield, J., et al. (2002). WHO/ISBRA study on state and trait markers in alcoholism. *Alcoholism: Clinical and Experimental Research, 25*, 99S–103S.

Tabakoff, B., Hoffman, P. L., Lee, J. M., Saito, T., Willard, B., & De Leon-Jones, F. (1988). Differences in platelet enzyme activity between alcoholics and nonalcoholics. *New England Journal of Medicine, 318*, 134–139.

Tangerman, A. (1997). Highly sensitive gas chromatographic analysis of ethanol in whole blood, serum, urine, and fecal supernatants by the direct injection method. *Clinical Chemistry, 43*(6 Pt 1), 1003–1009.

Thompson, P. L (2013). J-curve revisited: Cardiovascular benefits of moderate alcohol use cannot be dismissed. *Medical Journal of Australia, 198*, 419–422.

Trougakos, I. P., & Gonos, E. S. (2002). Clusterin/apolipoprotein J in human aging and cancer. *The International Journal of Biochemistry & Cell Biology, 34*(11), 1430–1448.

Tsutsumi, M., Lasker, J. M., Shimizu, M., Rosman, A. S., & Lieber, C. S. (1989). The intralobular distribution of ethanol-inducible P450IIE1 in rat and human liver. *Hepatology, 10*(4), 437–446.

Tsutsumi, M., Wang, J. S., & Takada, A. (1994). Microheterogeneity of serum glycoproteins in alcoholics: Is desialo-transferrin the marker of chronic alcohol drinking or alcoholic liver injury? *Alcoholism: Clinical and Experimental Research, 18*(2), 392–397.

Tuma, D. J., & Casey, C. A. (2003). Dangerous byproducts of alcohol breakdown—focus on adducts. *Alcohol Res Health, 27*(4), 285–290.

Turner, C., Spanel, P., & Smith, D. (2006). A longitudinal study of ethanol and acetaldehyde in the exhaled breath of healthy volunteers using selected-ion flow-tube mass spectrometry. *Rapid Communication Mass Spectrometry, 20*(1), 61–68.

Unlu, M., Morgan, M. E., & Minden, J. S. (1997). Difference gel electrophoresis: A single gel method for detecting changes in protein extracts. *Electrophoresis, 18*(11), 2071–2077.

Varga, A., & Alling, C. (2002). Formation of phosphatidylethanol in vitro in red blood cells from healthy volunteers and chronic alcoholics. *Journal of Laboratory and Clinical Medicine, 140*, 79–83.

Voltaire, A., Beck, O., & Borg, S. (1992). Urinary 5-hydroxytryptophol: A possible marker of recent alcohol consumption. *Alcoholism: Clinical and Experimental Research, 16*(2), 281–285.

Wagner, J. G., Wilkinson, P. K., Sedman, A. J., Kay, D. R., & Weidler, D. J. (1976). Elimination of alcohol from human blood. *Journal of Pharmaceutical Sciences, 65*(1), 152–154.

Watanabe, K., Yamaori, S., Funahashi, T., Kimura, T., & Yamamoto, I. (2007). Cytochrome P450 enzymes involved in the metabolism of tetrahydrocannabinols and cannabinol by human hepatic microsomes. *Life Sciences, 80*(15), 1415–1419.

Weinberger, S. R., Dalmasso, E. A., & Fung, E. T. (2002). Current achievements using ProteinChip array technology. *Current Opinion in Chemical Biology, 6*(1), 86–91.

Whitfield, J. B., Hensley, W. J., Bryden, D., & Gallagher, H. (1978). Effects of age and sex on biochemical responses to drinking habits. *Medical Journal of Australia, 2*, 629–632.

Whitfield, J. B., Pang, D., Bucholz, K. K., Madden, P. A., Heath, A. C., Statham, D. J., et al. (2000). Monoamine oxidase: Associations with alcohol dependence, smoking and other measures of psychopathology. *Psychological Medicine, 30*, 443–454.

Wickramasinghe, S. N., Thomas, S., & Hasan, R. (1994). Reaction of 14C-acetaldehyde with whole blood in vitro: Further evidence for the formation of unstable complexes with plasma proteins and red cells. *Alcohol & Alcoholism, 29*(1), 51–57.

Widmark, E. (1933). Verteilung und unwandltung des athyl alkohols in organimus des hundes. *Biochemische Zeitschift, 267*, 128–134.

Wilkinson, P. K., Sedman, A. J., Sakmar, E., Earhart, R. H., Weidler, D. J., & Wagner, J. G. (1976). Blood ethanol concentrations during and following constant-rate intravenous infusion of alcohol. *Clinical Pharmacology and Therapeutics, 19*(2), 213–223.

Worrall, S., de Jersey, J., Shanley, B. C., & Wilce, P. A. (1991). Antibodies against acetaldehyde-modified epitopes: An elevated IgA response in alcoholics. *European Journal of Clinical Investigation, 21*(1), 90–95.

Wu, A., Slavin, G., & Levi, A. J. (1976). Elevated serum gamma-glutamyl-transferase (transpeptidase) and histological liver damage in alcoholism. *American Journal of Gastroenterology, 65*, 318–323.

Wu, C. C., MacCoss, M. J., Howell, K. E., & Yates, J. R., III. (2003). A method for the comprehensive proteomic analysis of membrane proteins. *Nature Biotechnology, 21*(5), 532–538.

Wu, D., Tomonaga, T., Sogawa, K., Satoh, M., Sunaga, M., Nezu, M.,... Nomura, F. (2007). Detection of biomarkers for alcoholism by two-dimensional differential gel electrophoresis. *Alcoholism: Clinical and Experimental Research, 31*(1 Suppl), S67–S71.

Wurst, F. M., Dresen, S., Allen, J. P., Wiesbeck, G., Graf, M., & Weinmann, W. (2006). Ethyl sulphate: A direct ethanol metabolite reflecting recent alcohol consumption. *Addiction, 101*(2), 204–211.

Wurst, F. M., & Metzger, J. (2002). The ethanol conjugate ethyl glucuronide is a useful marker of recent alcohol consumption. *Alcoholism: Clinical and Experimental Research,* *26*(7), 1114–1119.

Wurst, F. M., Seidl, S., Ladewig, D., Muller-Spahn, F., & Alt, A. (2002). Ethyl glucuronide: On the time course of excretion in urine during detoxification. *Addiction Biology, 7*(4), 427–434.

Wurst, F. M., Tabakoff, B., Alling, C., Aradottir, S., Wiesbeck, G. A., Muller-Spahn, F.,. . . Hoffman, P. L. (2005). World Health Organization/International Society for Biomedical Research on Alcoholism study on state and trait markers of alcohol use and dependence: Back to the future. *Alcoholism: Clinical and Experimental Research, 29*(7), 1268–1275.

Wurst, F. M., Vogel, R., Jachau, K., Varga, A., Alling, C., Alt, A., & Skipper, G. E. (2003). Ethyl glucuronide discloses recent covert alcohol use not detected by standard testing in forensic psychiatric inpatients. *Alcoholism: Clinical and Experimental Research, 27*(3), 471–476.

Wurst, F. M., Wiesbeck, G. A., Metzger, J. W., & Weinmann, W. (2004). On sensitivity, specificity, and the influence of various parameters on ethyl glucuronide levels in urine—results from the WHO/ISBRA study. *Alcoholism: Clinical and Experimental Research,* 28(8), 1220–1228.

Yegles, M., Labarthe, A., Auwarter, V., Hartwig, S., Vater, H., Wennig, R., et al. (2004). Comparison of ethyl glucuronide and fatty acid ethyl ester concentrations in hair of alcoholics, social drinkers and teetotallers. *Forensic Science International, 145*(2–3), 167–173.

Zakhari, S. (2006). Overview: How is alcohol metabolized by the body? *Alcohol Research & Health, 29*(4), 245–254.

Zhang, L., Wang, Z. H., Li, H., Liu, Y., Zhao, M., Jiang, Y., & Zhao, W. S. (2014). Simultaneous determination of 12 illicit drugs in whole blood and urine by solid phase extraction and UPLC–MS/MS. *Journal of Chromatography B, 955,* 10–19.

Zuba, D. (2008). Accuracy and reliability of breath alcohol testing by handheld electrochemical analysers. *Forensic Science International, 178*(2–3), e29–e33.

Self-report Assessments of Psychoactive Substance Use and Dependence

Frances K. Del Boca, Jack Darkes, *and* Bonnie McRee

Abstract

Accurate assessment is critical to clinical interventions for problems associated with the use of alcohol and other drugs, and it is essential for research on the causes, consequences, and treatment of addiction. Verbal report is the most common method of assessing substance use behavior, diagnosing alcohol and drug use disorders, and measuring dependence severity. The authors describe self-report methods for the assessment of substance use and related constructs, together with the factors that influence their validity and utility. First, assessment procedures are described in terms of the characteristics and dimensions on which they vary. Guidelines for selecting specific types of instruments for clinical and research purposes are then provided, and the strengths and limitations of major assessment approaches are discussed. Finally, a social-psychological framework for understanding the question-answering process is presented, and assessment methods are evaluated in relation to the model. The authors conclude by identifying relevant areas of research.

Key Words: substance use assessment, alcohol measurement, clinical assessment, research assessment, screening and diagnosis, self-report validity, question-answering process

Introduction

Accurate assessment of clients and study participants is fundamental to clinical intervention for problems related to the use of psychoactive substances, as well as to research on the causes, consequences, and treatment of dependence (Allen, 2003a). The most common method of assessing alcohol and other drug use behavior, diagnosing substance use disorders (SUDs), and measuring severity of dependence is individual verbal report (Del Boca & Darkes, 2003; Del Boca & Noll, 2000; Large et al., 2012). A very large number of specific self-report instruments have been developed for clinical and research purposes. This essay describes these myriad methods and the factors that influence their validity and utility.

Instruments used to assess substance use behavior and related constructs vary in terms of a wide range of factors, including purpose, target population, substance of interest, content, administration mode, temporal frame, and response options. With respect to alcohol alone, a compilation of assessment devices published by the National Institute on Alcohol Abuse and Alcoholism more than a decade ago (NIAAA, 2003) included 78 instruments, many with multiple sections and/or subscales, and these were culled from a larger set of 250 candidates for inclusion. Thus, rather than focusing on specific instruments, this essay examines particular methods of assessment, together with their strengths and limitations.

Although our observations apply to assessments regarding most psychoactive substances with abuse potential, this review focuses primarily on instruments that measure alcohol consumption and dependence. These are far more plentiful; further, many measurement tools that pertain to illicit drugs are adaptations of instruments originally designed to assess drinking and its consequences (e.g., the *Form 90D* for assessing drug use [e.g., Westerberg, Tonigan, & Miller, 1998] is based on the *Form 90,* which measures alcohol consumption [e.g., Miller, 1996]; the *Cannabis Use Disorder Identification Test* [*CUDIT:* Adamson & Sellman, 2003] was adapted from the *Alcohol Use Disorders Identification Test* [*AUDIT:* Saunders et al., 1993; Babor et al., 2001]). (For assessment considerations relating to specific substances, see Shadel & Shiffman, 2008 [tobacco]; Carroll & Ball, 2008 [cocaine]; Rawson, Sodano, & Hillhouse, 2008 [amphetamines]; Westfall et al., 2008 [opioids]; Stephens & Roffman, 2008 [cannabis]; and Kilmer, Palmer, & Cronce, 2008 [club drugs, hallucinogens, inhalants, steroids]. See also Hjorthoj, Hjorthoj, & Nordentoft, 2012; Robinson et al., 2014).

We begin by categorizing the types of assessment procedures most often used in clinical and research settings and describing the characteristics and dimensions on which they vary. We then present guidelines for choosing assessment instruments for specific situations. More detailed descriptions of the major methods for assessing alcohol and illicit drug use, SUDs, and dependence severity follow. Next, we introduce a social-psychological framework that we have used in previous work to explicate the interacting influences that affect the accuracy of verbal reports, and we evaluate major assessment methods in terms of these factors. In so doing, we draw on research and theory in disciplines usually not associated with substance use assessment, and we refer readers to related resources for enhancing the veracity and utility of verbal reports. We conclude by identifying directions for future research that can enhance understanding of the question-answering process and maximize the validity of self-report assessments relating to substance use.

Types of Assessment Instruments

Instruments used to assess psychoactive substance use, SUDs, and related constructs may be grouped in a variety of ways. Table 15.1 presents four cross-cutting approaches to categorizing assessment procedures: purpose; referent or construct measured; general approach or method; and task variables. This framework is intended to illustrate the complexity involved in comparing methods and to place the many single instruments that measure substance use behavior, SUDs, and dependence severity within a broader context of assessment issues.

Purpose of Assessment

The purpose of assessment is the most important element in categorizing instruments, as the goal of measurement should determine the choice of approach in any specific situation. In terms of purpose, clinical evaluation is often distinguished from research assessment (see Allen, 2003a) (see Table 15.1). Clinical evaluation is uniquely client-centered, focusing on case finding via screening and diagnosis and the appraisal of individual treatment needs. Historically, most clinical assessment was subjective and impressionistic. However, with the advent of cognitive-behavioral and motivational intervention frameworks, clinical evaluation has become a more formal and structured component of treatment planning and delivery (cf. Donovan, 2003, 2008).

As suggested in Table 15.1, the primary aims of assessment are to determine whether an individual meets criteria for a diagnosis of substance abuse or dependence; the nature and degree of substance involvement and its consequences, including withdrawal symptoms; the presence of co-occurring psychopathology (which disproportionately affects abusers of psychoactive substances [e.g., Milby, Schumacher, & Stainback, 1997; Ross, 2008; SAMHSA, 2010]); levels of psychosocial functioning and social support; personal and environmental factors that contribute to problematic consumption; and the specific emotional, cognitive, and contextual stimuli that trigger occasions of use. Assessment results are used to refer clients to appropriate types and levels of care and, ideally, to monitor and evaluate the effects of treatment (Babor et al., 1994; Del Boca & Darkes, 2007a; Stout, 2003; Tonigan, 2003). Indeed, the review of assessment findings (individualized client feedback) has become an integral part of interventions for substance use problems, often used to enhance motivation to change and actively involve participants in setting treatment goals (e.g., Miller & Rollnick, 1991, 2002; see Donovan, 2003, 2008, for a fuller discussion of the role of assessment in clinical decision-making and treatment).

Research suggests that clients regard assessment favorably (Sobell, 1993) and that treatment programs that use formal assessment procedures are more successful in retaining clients (Institute of Medicine, 1990). Apart from the benefits that accrue to individuals, assessment results pooled across clients in treatment can identify gaps in service, as well as facilitate program evaluation (Allen, 2003a).

Table 15.1. Major Categories of Self-report Assessments of Substance Use and Dependence

Purpose of Assessment	Measured Construct	Major Approaches/Methods	Task Variables
Clinical Assessment	**Substance use behavior (specific substances, categories of substances; generic drug use)**	**Substance use behavior**	**Content (e.g., specific substances; consequences)**
Screening	**Quantity, frequency of use; frequency of heavy use; ingestion mode (e.g., oral, injection)**	Summary estimates of consumption (e.g., quantity, frequency of use)	**Administration format**
Diagnosis		Daily estimation of consumption	Interview (structured; semi-structured)
Clinical evaluation for treatment planning and client feedback	Ecology of substance use (e.g., drinking situations; social support)	Retrospective reports of use	Questionnaire
(e.g., substance use behavior; dependence severity; adverse consequences, problems; with-drawal risk; co-morbid psycho- pathology; psychosocial functioning; social support; expectancies; read ness to change; high-risk situations; coping skills; self-efficacy)		Prospective reports of use	**Mode of administration**
	Dependence syndrome	Ecological momentary assessment	Personal interview (face-to-face; telephonic)
Evaluation of client progress and outcome	**Formal SUD diagnoses**	**Substance use diagnoses; dependence severity; adverse consequences/problems**	Self-administered
Significant other assessment	**Hazardous, harmful use**	Screening tools	Paper-and-pencil
	Severity of dependence	Diagnostic interviews	Computer-assisted
	Adverse consequences; substance-related problems; severity of substance involvement	Psychometric scales	Computer-administered
Research Assessment	Family, social relations; employment problems; legal issues; physical/medical complaints; emotional/psychological problems; aggression/violence; cognitive consequences		Web-based
Evaluation of participant eligibility	Craving		**Response formats**
Characterization of research samples	Risk/vulnerability/propensity for addiction		Open-ended
(e.g., substance use behavior; dependence severity; adverse consequences, problems; other intake variables)	Psychosocial functioning		Multiple choice (including forced choice; true-false)
	Cognitive/affective constructs (e.g., Craving; expectancies; self-efficacy; readiness to change)		Likert-type rating scales
Verification of self-report **(e.g., collateral informant reports)**	Treatment processes		**Time frame**
Test intervention/treatment efficacy			Life-time
Assess treatment process			Specific time window (e.g., past year, 30 days, week)
Measure compliance/treatment exposure			Contemporaneous
Investigate mediators/moderators			(e.g., typical or usual behavior)
Examine risk/vulnerability/ propensity for addiction, etiology of dependence, etc.			
Estimate prevalence			
Examine relationships between substances use and disease, impairment, other harms			

Table entries in bold typeface are the primary focus of this essay.

Whereas the practitioner uses assessment to tailor treatment to individual client needs, the clinical researcher assesses participants to test systematically the efficacy of therapeutic approaches. As indicated in Table 15.1, assessment allows for careful specification of research populations via inclusion/exclusion criteria; permits investigators to describe study samples in detail; and provides a baseline characterization of participant status at intake that can serve as a benchmark for measuring change. Assessment is also important for addressing a broad range of research questions regarding the mechanisms of change involved in efficacious treatments; the causes of substance use; the etiology of dependence; the effects of substance use on physical and mental well-being; and the effectiveness of policy initiatives designed to curb use or its harmful effects (Del Boca & Darkes, 2007a). For all of these research purposes, standardized, rather than customized, assessment is essential (Allen, 2003a).

Despite differences in focus, there are many shared features of assessments performed in clinical and research situations. In both settings, assessment is not likely to be restricted to a single instrument or a single session. Rather, administration of a particular instrument usually occurs within the context of a larger assessment battery intended to measure a variety of substance-related constructs (e.g., other substance use, drinking situations, expectancies, motivation to change); comorbid conditions (e.g., affective disorders); and traits or skills related to treatment goals (e.g., self-efficacy, coping skills) (Del Boca & Darkes, 2007a; Donovan, 2003, 2008). In both settings, assessments may be conducted at multiple time points to monitor the progress of clients or research participants and, ultimately, to assess the outcomes of treatment or other experimental manipulations.

Measured Constructs

A second, logical, approach to categorizing assessment instruments is in terms of the entity or construct measured. As shown in Table 15.1, there are obvious parallels between assessment purposes and instrument content; however, the fulfillment of a single goal may require the measurement of multiple constructs, and assessments of particular content domains can be used to achieve multiple aims. Although many constructs, directly or indirectly related to actual substance use, are measured in clinical and research settings, patterns of consumption, SUDs, and severity of dependence or involvement are essential elements in virtually all assessment batteries. Issues related to the accurate assessment of these behaviors and constructs are printed in boldface type in Table 15.1 and are the major focus of this essay. (See Cooney, Kadden, & Steinberg, 2005; Donovan, 2003, 2008; Donovan & Marlatt, 2008; Kavanagh et al., 2013; Rohsenow, 2008, regarding the assessment of other substance-related constructs.)

Major Assessment Approaches

The third column in Table 15.1 lists the major methods of assessment used in clinical practice and research studies. As shown, there are several different approaches to measuring consumption, including summary questions regarding the quantity and frequency of use and daily estimation approaches that attempt to ascertain the amount consumed on each day during a specified reference period (e.g., the 90 days prior to the assessment). SUDs are most often assessed via structured or semistructured interviews that determine whether individuals meet criteria for assigning lifetime and/or current diagnoses. Other measures are based on a conceptualization of severity as a continuum; these instruments typically contain items regarding symptoms of dependence or problems that have developed as a consequence of use. The ultimate result is one or more scale scores reflecting dependence severity, substance involvement, or adverse consequences, either in general or in different domains (e.g., physical consequences, psychosocial problems).

Task Variables

In addition to content, instruments for assessing substance-related behavior and constructs differ in terms of the task or procedural variables that are listed in the fourth column of Table 15.1. Regarding format and administration mode, interviews (in-person and telephone) and self-administered, paper-and-pencil questionnaires predominate; however, many additional technologies have become available, including computerized (e.g., Couper & Rowe, 1996; Newman et al., 2002) and web-based (e.g., Couper, Traugott, & Lamias, 2001; Fricker & Schonlau, 2002) instruments; automated voice response systems (e.g., Kranzler et al., 2004); text messaging approaches (e.g., Kuntsche & Cooper, 2010); and hand-held electronic diaries that prompt participants for responses in real time (e.g., Hufford & Shields, 2002). (See Del Boca & Darkes, 2003, regarding many of these alternatives; see Neal et al., 2006, regarding technologies for assessing daily events; see Shiffman, 2016, regarding ecological momentary assessments.) Instruments also differ in how individuals provide requested information (e.g., open-ended responses vs. preselected options) and in the time frame under consideration, which may be contemporaneous (i.e., typical or usual behavior) or reflect a specific reference period (e.g., lifetime, past year, past 30 days, past week). Variations in how the assessment task is structured should influence the selection of instruments, in part, because they affect the ease of, and time required for, administration. As discussed more fully below, task variables can also affect the accuracy of the information collected.

Guidelines for Instrument Selection

Table 15.2 lists factors that should be considered in choosing measurement tools; it includes guidelines common to both clinical and research situations, as well as those specific to each domain (see also Allen, 2003a). As the table indicates, the two realms are more similar than different in terms of selection criteria.

Criteria Relevant Across Clinical and Research Situations

The most important qualities required for assessments performed for any purpose are *reliability* and *validity* (see Table 15.2). Although frequently thought to be more relevant to research than to clinical decision-making, these two measurement properties are as applicable to effective clinical assessment as they are to research (Allen, 2003a; Rotgers, 2002). Reliability describes the extent to which measurements are replicable or consistent across time, different sets of equivalent items, evaluators, or other variable conditions of instrument administration (Anastasi, 1988). In very general terms, validity refers to the ability of a device to measure what is intended. In classic test theory, reliability is characterized as primarily subject to random sources of error, whereas validity is said to be additionally influenced by systematic bias. Reliability does not guarantee validity; however, it is generally regarded

Table 15.2. Considerations for Choosing an Assessment Instrument

Research and Clinical Situations	Clinical Settings	Research Investigations
Psychometric Properties Reliability Validity Sensitivity and specificity (screening instruments)	Relevance for intervention/ treatment planning Utility for personal feedback Availability of normative information, especially regarding relevant subgroups Utility for monitoring client progress and outcomes	Relevant to investigational goals (e.g., intervening variables, outcomes) Sensitivity for distinguishing participants and measuring change Comparability to measures used in the other studies Multi-dimensional assessment Clinical relevance Precision of measurement Appropriate statistical properties
Respondent Issues Easily understood, conducive to accurate responses Considers target population characteristics, circumstances Culturally, linguistically, developmentally appropriate Acceptable, relevant to clients/ participants		
Administration Issues Available assessment resources Specialized training, credentials, supervision required Mode of administration Complexity of administration and scoring Cost and copyright issues Supporting materials (e.g., manuals, websites) Sequencing and fit within the larger assessment process/battery Length and time needed for completion Potential order effects and reactivity of measurement		

as a necessary, although not sufficient, condition. Reliability and validity are not absolute properties of a measuring device: Assessment tools may provide consistent and accurate measurements in some circumstances, with some types of individuals, but not in other situations or with different respondent groups (e.g., Haynes, Mumma, & Pinson, 2009; Hunsley & Marsh, 2008). (For perspectives regarding reliability and validity of measurement, see Allen, 2003a; Carmines & Zeller, 1979; Cicchetti, 1994; Del Boca & Brown, 1996; Nunnally & Bernstein, 1994; Tonigan, 2003.) Sensitivity and specificity of measurement are most applicable to screening instruments and are discussed more fully below.

As indicated in Table 15.2, assessment instruments should be evaluated in light of the capabilities, developmental issues, and cultural sensitivities of the clients and/or research participants who are asked to complete them (Allen, 2003a; Blume, Morera, & de la Cruz, 2008). Substance users are usually in distress when they begin treatment and may evidence some degree of cognitive impairment. Thus, it is advisable to choose instruments that are easily understood and avoid technical terminology; for paper-and-pencil questionnaires or other assessments that require respondents to read, items should be phrased at a reading level appropriate to the target population. Many instruments are available in multiple languages (e.g., the *Addiction Severity Index* has been translated into 17 languages, including a computerized Spanish-language version, see Butler et al., 2009); if translated versions are used, clinical staff and investigators should assure that these are appropriate for their purposes (e.g., a particular Spanish language questionnaire may be better suited for respondents with a Mexican, than a Cuban, heritage). Because patterns and consequences of use, as well as cognitive capabilities, often differ for adult and younger respondents, a number of instruments have been developed specifically for college students and adolescents, and, to a lesser degree, young children. Finally, instruments should be chosen that respondents themselves find acceptable and meaningful.

Table 15.2 lists several practical and logistical considerations in choosing assessment instruments. Although funded research studies often have more resources to support assessment than specialty substance abuse treatment programs, these issues apply to both clinical and investigational settings (Allen, Litten, & Anton, 1992). Assessment can be a very costly enterprise; personnel are needed for administration, and specialized training and/or credentials

may be required. Some complex instruments (e.g., those with extensive decision trees) can often be more easily administered via computer. Although this mode of administration may decrease the amount of staff time needed for assessment, it may be expensive or inappropriate for some populations (Del Boca & Darkes, 2003). There are often costs associated with the procurement or duplication of copies and supporting materials and, depending on the instrument, copyright and/or scoring fees. Because the administration, scoring, and interpretation of some measurement tools can be complicated, the availability of user support (e.g., dedicated websites, Help Lines) is also a consideration in instrument selection. (See also Rotgers, 2002.)

Finally, because single instruments are often embedded within larger assessment batteries, clinicians and researchers need to evaluate how well each measurement tool fits within the larger set. Within this context, the length of the instrument and the time required for its completion become salient concerns. The design of any assessment battery should also consider the possibility that order effects (e.g., Weinberger et al., 2006) and/or reactivity (e.g., Gastfriend et al., 2005) may contaminate responses, as these constitute threats to validity of measurement. The influence of these artifacts can often be assessed or controlled, if not eliminated entirely. To minimize order effects, it is generally advisable to administer open-ended instruments early in the assessment sequence, and, in research settings, to counterbalance or randomize the order of self-administered questionnaires across participants (Del Boca & Darkes, 2007a).

Reactivity occurs when the act of measurement itself affects the behavior that is assessed; it happens most often in circumstances where assessment sessions are lengthy or when repeated measurements serve to direct the respondent's attention to problematic behavior. Evidence of reactivity in substance abuse research has been found in self-monitoring studies of alcohol consumption (e.g., Miller, Gribskov, & Mortell, 1981; see also Clifford & Maisto, 2000; Helzer et al., 2002, Kypri et al., 2007). In research situations, reactivity can affect treatment outcomes, interact with intervention manipulations, and mask treatment response (Gastfriend et al., 2005; Schrimsher & Filtz, 2011). The potential for reactivity can be lessened by maintaining a nonjudgmental stance in response to respondents' reports, by embedding sensitive questions within instruments that include a range of different topics, and by decreasing the length and frequency of assessment sessions. Statistical techniques that uncover trending in data sequences may be useful in detecting measurement reactivity. (See Schrimsher & Filtz, 2011, for a fuller discussion of assessment reactivity and its potential for reducing alcohol use and related problems; see Del Boca & Darkes, 2007a; Gastfriend et al., 2005; Connors et al., 1994, 2003; Tonigan, 2003, regarding assessment issues in substance use research.)

Clinicians and researchers are advised to pretest all candidate instruments with members of the target population to assure that they are well understood, relevant, and acceptable, and that the amount of time needed for completion falls within an acceptable range. Additionally, feasibility testing provides an opportunity to monitor the assessment performance of clinical and research staff. For instruments that involve personal interviews (e.g., diagnostic assessments), researchers should systematically evaluate interrater reliability (e.g., Del Boca, Babor, & McRee, 1994; Del Boca & Brown, 1996); if found to be inadequate, additional training should be provided until a performance criterion is achieved. (See Del Boca & Darkes, 2007a; O'Malley et al., 2005, regarding the conduct of feasibility studies.)

Clinical Assessment

Due to the individualized nature of assessment in treatment settings, some instrument selection criteria are more relevant to clinical than to research situations. As indicated in Table 15.2, the potential utility of instruments for clinical decision-making, and for the provision of clear and meaningful personal feedback, is particularly important in constructing an assessment battery for use in clinical settings (see Donovan, 2003, 2008).

Normative data for assessment tools are also helpful to the clinician, because they provide a context for judging the severity of the client's problems. Unfortunately, most normative data reference relatively broad groups; such information is most useful when it permits more fine-grained comparisons (e.g., in terms of gender, age group, racial/ethnic identification), as the implications of substance use often vary for subgroups of the general population (Allen, 2003a; Grant et al., 2012). For example, drinking typically affects women and the elderly somewhat differently than men, with lower quantities of alcohol often producing higher blood alcohol concentrations (Gunzerath et al., 2004; Lucey et al., 1999).

To assess specific client needs, support clinical decision-making, and monitor progress, relevant measures ideally should be administered before, during, and following treatment (Donovan, 1988). Although specialty substance abuse treatment programs increasingly perform comprehensive assessment at intake, few conduct systematic follow-up evaluations during or after treatment participation (Rotgers, 2002), despite the emphasis placed on assessment by accrediting agencies (TJC, 2013). Nevertheless, specific instruments should be selected with the prospect that multiple administrations may occur, and that later assessments are likely to be conducted under circumstances different from those at intake (e.g., change in mode of administration from personal to telephone interview, shifts in client motivation or perspective). Given the relatively limited resources available to many treatment facilities and the nature of the populations served, the use of standardized, research-validated, paper-and-pencil questionnaires—rather than personal interviews or computerized assessments—has been advocated for these clinical settings (Rotgers, 2002).

Research Assessment

The primary consideration in selecting assessment instruments for investigational use is their relevance to the specific research questions under investigation. Often these concern the efficacy or effectiveness of interventions or treatments intended to reduce substance use and concomitant problems. As indicated in Table 15.2, outcome variables used to evaluate treatment approaches should be reflective of intervention goals; capable of registering changes in the condition under study; permit comparisons with other investigations; and be both multidimensional and clinically meaningful (Del Boca & Darkes, 2007a; see also Donovan et al., 2012; Tiffany et al., 2012).

Although researchers usually examine a range of variables, a small number, most often measures of substance use behavior, are commonly designated *a priori* as *primary outcome measures*. A number of different variables have been used in research (Finney, Moyer & Swearington, 2003). For treatments of alcohol dependence, frequency (e.g., proportion of abstinent days) and intensity (e.g., drinks per drinking day) of consumption have served as primary outcomes in several landmark studies (e.g., Project MATCH, see Babor & Del Boca, 2003). To enable cross-study comparisons, some researchers have recommended that these two variables, together with drinking consequences or problems, be more widely adopted (e.g., Kadden & Litt, 2004). Percent days of heavy drinking (often operationalized as six or more standard drinks for men, four or more for women) was endorsed as the optimal outcome measure at a conference held by the NIAAA in the United States (Allen, 2003b; Sobell et al., 2003).

With respect to illicit drug use, several expert panels have been convened in efforts to establish a standard, primary outcome measure for use in treatment research. Rather than endorsing a single measure that might be used across studies, these panels have recommended that the selection of primary outcome variables be based on the specific aims of particular investigations (e.g., Van den Brink, et al., 2006). Most recently, a panel sponsored by the National Institute of Drug Abuse (NIDA) agreed that no single index is applicable for all or most clinical trials but that the most appropriate proximal outcome measure should be consumptive behavior, preferably determined by toxicological, as well as verbal report, methods (Donovan et al., 2012).

Consistent with the NIDA panel's recommendations, researchers should consider treatment goals and hypothesized mechanisms of action in choosing primary outcome measures (Stout, 2003). For example, sustained sobriety may be an appropriate measure of outcome for abstinence-oriented programs, whereas reductions in heavy use occasions and substance-related problems may be more relevant for harm-reduction interventions. Similarly, pharmacological interventions are often expected to produce their effects via different influences on brain chemistry, and primary outcome variables should be selected to reflect these different mechanisms (Anton & Randall, 2005; COMBINE Study Research Group, 2003). An added benefit of choosing patient outcome measures that are tailored to the hypothesized effects of treatment may be a significant improvement in statistical power (Stout, 2003).

The consensus among investigators is that assessment of treatment efficacy should be multidimensional (Carroll, 1997; Cisler et al., 2005; Babor et al., 1994; Borkovec, 1993) and clinically meaningful. Thus, in addition to measures of substance involvement, indicators of quality of life (Donovan et al., 2005), and mechanisms of change (e.g., improved coping skills, increases in self-efficacy) should be assessed (Del Boca & Darkes, 2007a).

Regarding relevance, *statistically* significant mean differences in substance use, in and of themselves, are not generally regarded as meaningful in clinical settings. To address this issue, investigators have sometimes defined *a priori* criteria to differentiate treatment "responders" from "non-responders"

(Borkovec, 1993) or examined change in the at-risk status of intervention/treatment recipients (e.g., from "harmful" to "hazardous" patterns of use; see later). Additionally, composite indicators have been constructed that combine consumption status with substance-related problems to produce a set of mutually exclusive categories that are progressively more negative in terms of outcome (e.g., abstinent, using, using heavily, using heavily with consequences) (e.g., Zweben & Cisler, 1996, 2003; see also Rothwell, 2005).

Additionally, investigators should consider the degree of precision of measurement required to address adequately the research questions under investigation. Whereas treatment outcome studies may only require that participants be reliably and accurately ordered along a continuum of substance use, other types of research may necessitate more precise estimates. For example, epidemiological studies that examine the disease burden associated with substance use often attempt to determine the specific levels or patterns of consumption that produce different types or levels of harm (e.g., Rehm et al., 2003, 2010). Finally, regardless of the type of investigation, assessment instruments should be chosen that produce data compatible with the distributional and other assumptions of planned statistical analyses.

Major Methods of Self-report Assessment
Substance Use Behavior

Unlike hypothetical constructs such as dependence, there is relatively little debate about the conceptual nature of the phenomena intended to be assessed by instruments that measure consumption. The objective is to accurately assess *behavior*, that is, the act of drinking or ingesting some other psychoactive substance and the amount consumed in the process (Del Boca & Noll, 2000). Nevertheless, a large number of measurement tools have been developed for this purpose. Despite the diversity among these instruments, most can be grouped within two broad categories: (a) summary measures, often termed quantity-frequency (Q/F) measures, and (b) daily estimation (DE) procedures.

SUMMARY MEASURES OF CONSUMPTION

Within this category are sets of questions that ask respondents to estimate the quantity of alcohol or drug consumed per occasion and to summarize their frequency of use. When assessing alcohol use, a brief definition of "standard drink" (i.e., 5 oz. glass of wine, 12 oz. can of beer, 1.5 oz. shot of hard liquor; see Donovan, 2009) is usually provided to ensure that a common metric is used in reporting amounts consumed. Estimates may describe the "typical" or "usual" pattern of use or refer to a specific time interval (e.g., past year, past month, past week); response options are most often (although not always) presented as multiple choice options that are ordinal, but not interval, scaled. For example (Saunders et al., 1993):

"How many drinks containing alcohol do you have on a typical day when you are drinking?"

(0) 1 or 2
(1) 3 or 4
(2) 5 or 6
(3) 7, 8, or 9
(4) 10 or more

"How often do you have a drink containing alcohol?"

(0) Never
(1) Monthly or less
(2) 2 to 4 times a month
(3) 2 to 3 times a week
(4) 4 or more times a week

Variants on the basic Q/F approach have been used in clinical, as well as epidemiological, investigations. Although questions remain about the cognitive and motivational processes that underlie respondents' replies to Q/F items, the general reliability, validity, and utility of these measures is not in dispute. The obvious advantages of this method are efficiency and versatility: Large numbers of individuals can be assessed quickly via interviews or questionnaires, using whatever time frames and response options are of interest. However, because Q/F measures are widely used in sample surveys that are repeated over time, an overriding consideration in choosing a particular item set is often comparability with prior research.

One of the more enduring validity issues regarding most Q/F measures concerns the within-person variability that characterizes patterns of use, especially for individuals who tend to consume large quantities (Greenfield, 2000). Regarding alcohol use, one solution to this potential problem has been to add questions that ask specifically about the frequency of heavy use (e.g., how often the respondent consumes "5 or more drinks per occasion," or "drinks to intoxication"; see also Calahan, Cisin, & Crossley, 1969). Another approach is the *graduated frequency* (GF) method, which comprises a series of questions referring to graded quantities (e.g., the

number or proportion of occasions when 1–2 drinks were consumed, when 3–4 drinks were consumed, etc.). In general, GF measures tend to yield higher volume estimates than conventional Q/F questions (e.g., Midanik, 1994) and may overestimate consumption (Poikolainen, Podkeltnova, & Alho, 2002), possibly as a result of asking more questions or of unintended overlap (Dawson, 1998a). Nevertheless, the GF method has become widely used in sample surveys, and the study of its validity is an active area of research (e.g., Gmel et al., 2006; Greenfield et al., 2009; Midanik et al., 2013; see also Gmel, Shield, & Rehm, 2013).

Q/F approaches assess both the quantity and frequency of substance use; however, responses regarding how often use occurs are likely to be more valid than estimates of the amounts consumed. Respondents can generally recall whether or not they used alcohol or some other drug, and patterns of consumption are often somewhat routinized (e.g., occurring most weekends or associated with specific occasions such as football games). With respect to quantities of alcohol consumed, it has been suggested, "that the variation contributed by this source of measurement may be of equal importance to all the other influences" (Greenfield & Kerr, 2008, p. 1090). The adoption of the standard drink metric is complicated by differing standards across, and sometimes even within, countries (World Health Organization [WHO], 2000). Further, regardless of the extent to which the ethanol content of various beverages is predefined for respondents, research indicates that their reports regarding "number of drinks consumed" are based on the serving amounts that they themselves typically imbibe (Kaskutas & Graves, 2000), and that these may vary substantially (Kerr et al., 2005). Such variations are particularly problematic for research that attempts to relate alcohol consumption patterns to physical harms and, from a policy perspective, for efforts aimed at establishing guidelines regarding "sensible drinking limits." (See Greenfield & Kerr, 2008, for a more detailed consideration of this issue.) With respect to other substances, it is clear that potency and units of consumption (e.g., "lines" of cocaine, "joints" of marijuana) can vary widely, limiting the ability of respondents to provide precise estimates of quantities consumed.

With respect to the frequency of use, one important decision in the use of Q/F measures concerns assessment time frame. Short reference periods (e.g., past week, past 30 days) are more easily recalled, but may not be representative of the respondent's general drinking pattern (Greenfield & Kerr, 2008). Additionally, there is often a requirement to match reference periods with other measures, especially instruments that assess substance-related problems or adverse consequences. Due to the infrequent occurrence of many events included in these instruments (e.g., arrests, fights), assessment time windows tend to be relatively long (cf. Dawson, 1998b).

DAILY ESTIMATION METHODS

Daily estimation approaches to assessing psychoactive substance use may be retrospective or prospective; only the former are considered here (see Del Boca & Darkes, 2003; Leigh, 2000; Schiffman, 2013, regarding ecological momentary assessments). By far the most widely used instrument is the *Timeline Followback* (*TLFB*: e.g., Sobell & Sobell, 1992, 1995a, 2000), developed initially for assessing alcohol consumption. A number of variations on the basic TLFB procedure are available (e.g., *Form 90*: Miller, 1996; Miller & Del Boca, 1994), including adaptations for measuring illegal drug use, both for adults (e.g., Robinson et al., 2014; Westerberg et al., 1998) and for adolescents (Slesnick & Tonigan, 2004).

The basic administration procedure is similar across retrospective DE instruments. Respondents are presented with a calendar that covers a specified time window (ranging from 7 days to an entire year) and, in the case of alcohol use, are instructed to estimate, using aided-recall techniques, the number of standard drinks (or to describe beverage content and precise quantity consumed) for every day in the period. The task is most often administered within the context of a personal interview, although there are versions available for telephone (e.g., *Form 90-T*: Miller, 1996) and for computer-assisted (e.g., *Timeline Followback*: Sobell & Sobell, 1995b) and online (Pederson et al., 2012) assessment. DE procedures clearly require more resources (e.g., interviewer time, training, etc.; for computer-assisted versions, specialized equipment) and impose a much greater burden on respondents than Q/F measures.

Because respondents are thought to retrieve actual episodes of alcohol or other substance use from memory using aided-recall techniques, DE procedures have greater face validity than Q/F methods. By sampling behavior over a period of time in which substance use may have been quite variable, consumption occasions are incorporated that do not match the typical or usual occurrences of use queried by many Q/F measures (Sobell & Sobell, 2003). Moreover, *patterns* of consumption

are discernible. With some instruments (e.g., *Form 90:* Miller, 1996), additional information is obtained (gender, body weight, duration of drinking episode) that permits calculation of blood alcohol concentration (BAC) estimates. However, because of large individual variation in pharmacokinetics, such estimates should be regarded as rough approximations rather than precise indicators of BAC. (See Gmel et al., 2008, and Posey & Mozayan, 2007, for discussions of the pharmacokinetics of alcohol and their implications for estimating BAC by means of verbal report.) DE methods also offer the opportunity to track other events over time, so that, for example, immediate precipitants or triggers of substance use can be identified. However, the collection of additional data can increase respondent burden substantially.

There is considerable evidence supporting the reliability and validity of retrospective DE methods based on research with a variety of different respondent populations (e.g., Pedersen et al., 2012; Robinson et al., in press; Sobell et al., 1979, 1986, 1988; see Sobell & Sobell, 2003). Although at least one study has shown acceptable levels of reliability for assessment windows as long as 1 year, most investigations have examined shorter time frames, reporting very good reliability for summary measures based on calendars up to 90 days in length for alcohol consumption (e.g., Tonigan, Miller, & Brown, 1997) and 6 months for cocaine and heroin use (Ehrman & Robbins, 1994). A large number of studies have compared the drinking data produced by retrospective daily estimation procedures and prospective daily report methods, which require participants to describe their alcohol use each day (via diaries, daily logs, or telephone calls) during an assessment period (see Leigh, 2000, for a review). Although subject to some of the same sources of bias, prospective DE methods should be less prone to memory errors than retrospective approaches. Correlations between summary measures (total volume consumed, drinks per occasion, and number of drinking days) are generally high, although prospective procedures tend to produce more drinking occasions, and higher estimated consumption amounts, than retrospective methods (Leigh, 2000).

Daily estimation procedures are recommended for assessing patient outcomes in treatment efficacy research (Del Boca & Darkes, 2007a). Although they involve added time and expense, these methods have several advantages over Q/F measures. First, available research suggests that they produce more valid consumption estimates than Q/F measures (e.g., Sobell & Sobell, 1995c; see Sobell & Sobell, 2003). Second, DE methods generate raw data that permit the creation of numerous summary drinking measures (e.g., drinks per drinking day; percent days abstinent). Third, variables created from daily estimation records can be computed over differing time intervals (e.g., total volume per month; mean drinks per occasion; percent heavy drinking days in the last 3 months) to facilitate comparisons across investigations with different follow-up durations. Fourth, the DE approach generates data records that are suitable for many different statistical analysis procedures, including survival and time-series analyses, as well as traditional ANOVA and regression models. The raw data allow computation of time-to-event and event-duration measures, which have revealed treatment effects in some studies when other summary outcome measures have not (Babor & Del Boca, 2003). DE procedures also produce data that can be used to model statistically all or parts of the continuous record of substance use (e.g., latent growth curve modeling; see Muthén & Muthén, 2007; Nagin, 1999). These statistical approaches, which compare treatment groups in terms of model parameters indicative of individual change over time (e.g., slope), are more congruent than traditional methods (e.g., ANOVA) with evolving conceptualizations of recovery as a dynamic, temporal process, rather than a static end point (e.g., Dennis, Scott, & Funk, 2003; McClellan et al., 2005; Moos, 2003; Orford, 2008; Simpson, 2004; Tucker & Roth, 2006).

Despite these advantages, most studies in the literature that have used daily estimation procedures have failed to capitalize on their potential; most often, summary consumption indices are calculated across time, suggesting that less burdensome assessment methods may be adequate for many purposes. A second caveat regarding the use of retrospective daily estimation procedures concerns precision of measurement. Because DE methods appear to quantify consumption accurately, there may be a tendency to view reported amounts in absolute terms, rather than as estimates or approximations. As already noted, the difficulties involved in reporting precise quantities consumed on any specific occasion are many. In terms of alcohol use, drinks vary in size; specific recipes for mixed drinks or cocktails may differ; beverage brands and proofs are frequently unknown; and conversion to the standard drink metric may be problematic (e.g., college students often drink from pitchers, kegs, and other nonstandard containers) (Greenfield & Kerr, 2008; Kaskutas & Graves, 2000; Leigh, 2000). Other substances pose similar challenges. Units of consumption are also not standard for many illicit drugs (e.g., "joints" or "pipe bowls" of marijuana; "lines" of cocaine); substances can vary widely in potency, and, in many instances, consumption is a group experience (e.g., "joints" or "bongs" are passed among users). Additionally, heavy drinking and/or illicit substance use may impair memory for beverages/units consumed late during an occasion of use. Finally, even with the assistance of aided-recall techniques, individuals are limited in their ability to remember drinking episodes that are temporally distant. As noted by the developers of the basic technique (see Sobell & Sobell, 1995c), there are reasons to question the degree to which these instruments consistently yield valid reports for *specific days* in the calendar, although this may not be an important limitation in many, if not most, clinical or research contexts.

SUD and Dependence Severity Assessment

As shown in the third column in Table 15.1, there are three major types of measures that are used to diagnose SUDs and assess the severity of dependence: screening instruments, diagnostic interviews, and psychometric questionnaires.

SCREENING INSTRUMENTS

Routine screening for problems related to psychoactive substance use is a relatively recent phenomenon, resulting in part from the adoption of a public health perspective in the addictions field. The assumption that underlies broad-based screening in this domain is that individuals potentially in need of intervention or treatment can be successfully identified by asking a relatively small number of questions regarding patterns of use and/or adverse consequences. Originally developed as a means of identifying individuals with probable alcohol dependence, screening tools for less severely involved drinkers and for users of other substances have been developed and are now widely used in settings such as hospital emergency departments and trauma centers, where presenting injuries are often the result of alcohol or illicit drug use (Higgins-Biddle et al., 2009; SAMHSA, 2013; WHO, 2007).

The primary purpose of screening instruments is to identify individuals who are likely to have a particular disorder, as well as those who are at risk for developing the disorder, so that appropriate levels of intervention or treatment can be provided to ameliorate the condition or prevent its progression. From a public health perspective, screening should be restricted to disorders with the following characteristics: (a) the disorder should cause substantial morbidity or mortality; (b) efficacious treatments should be available to address the condition; (c) early intervention delivered after a positive screening result should produce a more favorable outcome than treatment delivered at a later point in the disorder's progression; and (d) the condition should be sufficiently prevalent to justify the cost of widespread screening of individuals without obvious symptoms (Stewart & Connors, 2004/2005). Alcohol use disorders clearly fit these criteria: Excessive drinking is a known contributor to many health problems (Rehm et al., 2003, 2010); an array of treatment approaches have been found to be efficacious; brief interventions delivered to those at the lower end of the severity spectrum have been shown consistently to reduce consumption and level of risk for dependence (see Babor et al., 2007, for a review); and the prevalence of alcohol-related problems is high relative to other disorders for which widespread screening is advised (Stewart & Connors, 2004/2005). With the passage of the Affordable Care Act (ACA) in 2010, early identification and intervention for substance use disorders have moved front and center as part of the effort to transform the country's health care system from an acute care model to a prevention-oriented approach (JBS International, Inc. et al., 2012).

Although the associated disorders are less common, illicit drug screening programs hold considerable promise. Because users of illicit substances tend also to consume alcohol, programs that combine *s*creening, *b*rief *i*ntervention, and *r*eferral to *t*reatment (SBIRT) for both risk factors (and for tobacco use) potentially provide economies of scale for service delivery and improved outcomes for service recipients (Babor et al., 2007). An international multi-site trial showed reductions in total illicit substance involvement scores for cannabis, cocaine, amphetamine-type stimulants, and opioids (Humeniuk, et al., 2012). In other investigations, reductions in use have been observed for cocaine and heroin (Bernstein et al., 2005), cannabis (Stephens et al., 2007; Bernstein et al., 2009), amphetamines (Baker et al., 2006), and benzodiazepines (e.g., Heather et al., 2004; Mugunthan, McGuire, & Glasziou, 2011). Decreases in both drinking and illegal drug use were reported for a large-scale, federally-funded SBIRT initiative that combines screening for alcohol and other substance use (Madras et al., 2008). However, the results of other, more recent, studies have called into question the efficacy of screening and brief invention for illicit drugusers (see Hingston & Compton, 2014).

Ideally, screening for at-risk psychoactive substance use should be conducted in locations, such as criminal justice settings, hospital emergency departments, and trauma centers, where the probability of identifying users is high. It is estimated that approximately two-thirds of the adult incarcerated population used psychoactive substances prior to confinement (Young et al., 2009), and frequent users of illicit drugs are almost twice as likely to report emergency department visits than those who use less often or not at all (Cherpitel & Ye, 2008).

In addition to the criteria already listed, screening instruments should, of course, predict the conditions they are designed to identify. In practical application, there are cutoff points for screening scores that indicate levels of risk. Several yardsticks are used to evaluate the accuracy of screening devices in relation to these thresholds. *Sensitivity* represents the probability that a screening test will produce a positive result when an individual actually has the disorder, whereas *specificity* indicates the ability of the test to identify correctly those individuals who do *not* have the condition. The more sensitive the instrument, the fewer are the number of false negatives; the more specific the test, the fewer are the false positives. Test sensitivity can be increased by lowering the cutoff point; however, this typically results in a corresponding decrease in specificity. Because of the inevitable tradeoffs between these two properties, the relative desirability of reducing false negatives or false positives within the screening situation should be weighed in selecting a screening tool for use in a particular clinical or research situation. Related statistical indices for the evaluation of screening instruments include positive and negative predictive value. Note that these estimates are all calculated in relation to a specific criterion (e.g., diagnosis of substance use disorder), with values changing depending on the target condition. (See Connors & Volk, 2003, and Stewart & Connors, 2004/2005, for a more detailed discussion of the criteria for evaluating screening instruments.)

There are a number of different criteria against which screening measures have been evaluated. These include the *Diagnostic and Statistical Manual of Mental Disorders* (DSM) and the *International Classification of Diseases* (ICD) criteria for SUDs, which are described more fully in the next section. Until recently (with the advent of DSM-5), both systems included nondependent substance use categories representing less severe conditions. In DSM-IV-TR, substance *abuse* was generally characterized by recurrent use that leads to and persists despite potential hazards, personal, social, and/or legal problems. A WHO expert committee has delineated four nondependent conditions: (a) *unsanctioned use,* or ingestion of a substance that is not socially approved; (b) *dysfunctional use,* which leads to impaired psychological or social functioning; (c) *hazardous use,* a pattern of consumption that increases the risk of harmful consequences; and (d) *harmful use,* which causes damage to health. Although these less severe conditions perform less well psychometrically than the dependence criterion (Saunders, 2006), screening for problematic patterns of substance involvement is congruent with the public health objective of early identification of, and intervention with, at-risk users of alcohol and other psychoactive substances (Babor et al., 2007).

Screening instruments for alcohol and illicit drugs have evolved over time. Early screening tools (e.g., the *Michigan Alcoholism Screening Test, [MAST]*, Selzer, 1971, and shorter variants, the *Brief MAST*, Pokorny, Miller, & Kaplan, 1972, and the *Short MAST [SMAST]*, Selzer, Vinokur, & van Rooijen, 1975; the *CAGE*, Ewing, 1984) focused on identifying alcohol-dependent individuals rather than those at risk for developing the disorder. In an effort to broaden the range of individuals captured, as well as increase the cultural and linguistic generalizability of alcohol screening results, the WHO developed the *Alcohol Use Disorders Test (AUDIT;* Babor et al., 2001; Saunders et al., 1993), which identifies hazardous drinking patterns, as well as probable alcohol use disorders. The *AUDIT* has been validated across ethnic and cultural groups in numerous countries (e.g., Volk et al., 1997; cf. Allen et al., 1997). Shorter versions have also been tested (e.g., *AUDIT-PC, AUDIT-FAST, AUDIT-C*; Aertgeerts et al., 2000; Canagasaby & Vinson, 2005), and a parallel screening instrument for problems associated with drug use, the *Drug Use Disorders Identification Test (DUDIT)* has also been developed (e.g., Voluse et al., 2012).

Very brief screening tools, including several single-item tests, typically focus on drinking behavior rather than adverse consequences. For example, Williams and Vinson (2005) found that one question regarding the most recent episode of heavy drinking had good sensitivity and specificity in detecting hazardous drinking and alcohol use

disorders. Johnson, Sobell, and Sobell (2010) found that a single binge-drinking item was effective in identifying women at risk for an alcohol-exposed pregnancy. Similarly, recent efforts have focused on the development and validation of single-item screening tests for illicit drug and prescription drug abuse (e.g., Smith et al., 2010). Such screening tools may best be regarded as "prescreening" questions that can be embedded within larger intake protocols to facilitate efficient broad-based screening within general health care settings. Prescreen results identify individuals to whom a "full screen" should be administered; these longer instruments have the added value of providing information that can serve as the immediate point of departure for the delivery of a brief intervention (Vinson et al., 2004).

Screening tools have been developed for use with special populations, including women and the elderly (Chan & Pristach, 1993; Moore et al., 2002; Russell, 1994). For adolescents, screening instruments specific to substance use (e.g., *Substance Abuse Subtle Screening Inventory [SASSI]*, Miller, 1997; *Drug and Alcohol Problem [DAP]*, Klitzner et al., 1987; *CRAFFT* [Car, Relax, Alone, Friends, Forget, Trouble], Knight et al., 1999), as well as omnibus instruments that screen for problems in a variety of additional domains (e.g., mental health or family issues) (instruments include *Problem Oriented Screening Instrument for Teenagers [POSIT]*, Rahdert, 1991; and *Personal Experience Screening Questionnaire [PESQ]*, Winters, 1990), have been developed. Tools are also available for screening users of specific substances other than alcohol. For example, as noted earlier, the *Cannabis Use Disorders Identification Test*, or *CUDIT*, is an adaptation of the *AUDIT* that screens for cannabis abuse and dependence disorders (Adamson & Sellman, 2003).

Although many users of illicit substances are polydrug users, there has been less attention devoted to the construction of instruments that screen for multiple substances in adults. To fill this gap, the *Alcohol, Smoking and Substance Involvement Screening Test (ASSIST;* WHO *ASSIST* Working Group, 2002) was developed to screen for at-risk use of psychoactive substances, as well as related problems. The test uses a common format to screen for 11 substances, as well as injection drug use, and the scoring procedure estimates the relative importance of these different risk behaviors for the purpose of prioritizing counseling interventions.

Diagnostic assessment serves many purposes. Its most frequent clinical function is to identify those who meet formal diagnostic criteria for an SUD. In so doing, it both indicates the need for, and justifies, treatment. Conversely, there are those who, while accepting the utility of current psychiatric diagnoses, question their validity (e.g., Kendell & Jablensky, 2003). Nonetheless, it is a reality of modern health care that, regardless of validity concerns, formal diagnosis of substance abuse or dependence is often a clinical necessity that facilitates the treatment of patients in need of services and secures third-party payment for those services. Beyond the formal assignment of an SUD diagnosis, assessment in the treatment venue is also useful in identifying patterns of symptoms that might indicate specific lifestyle or behavioral areas of concern and suggest specific targets for intervention.

Diagnosis also has clear application to research venues where accurate identification and description of participants in both epidemiological and treatment studies are essential, as is the ability to generalize the results of randomized clinical trials to applied settings (e.g., Del Boca & Darkes, 2007b). For the research literature to accurately inform clinical application, common instrumentation must be used. In turn, outcome evaluation in clinical practice must be able to inform research on the effectiveness of practice alternatives. The utility of both research and applied findings is predicated on reliable and valid assessment.

Diagnostic criteria. The most frequently used classification system for SUDs in the United States, until the recent release of the DSM-5 (American Psychiatric Association [APA], 2013), was the *Diagnostic and Statistical Manual of the American Psychiatric Association, Fourth Edition, Text Revision (DSM-IV-TR*; APA, 2000). The DSM system is the product of a long history of iterations and modifications, culminating in the DSM-5 (APA, 2013). The *International Classification of Diseases—Tenth Edition (ICD-10*; WHO, 1992) is the primary system used outside of the United States.

Before the release of DSM-5, both U.S. and European experts used the *alcohol dependence syndrome* (Edwards, 1986; Edwards & Gross, 1976) as the basis for substance abuse and dependence criteria. The dependence syndrome incorporates behaviors and symptoms related to the repetitive use of alcohol and other psychoactive substances that cluster in time and occur repeatedly. Interestingly, although the symptoms comprised by the syndrome are most often *associated* with heavy use (e.g., tolerance, withdrawal), excessive consumption per se has not been an explicit component of classification systems.

DSM-5 represents a change in conceptual and diagnostic approach, having eliminated separate abuse and dependence categorizations in favor of a single set of criteria for the categorical diagnosis of Substance Use Disorders and an indicator of severity based on the number of symptoms endorsed. As indicated in Tables 15.3 and 15.4, the criteria retained in DSM-5 are largely the same as those in DSM-IV-TR, with the exception of the deletion of a criterion under the former Substance Abuse diagnosis addressing recurrent legal problems and the addition of a criterion regarding craving. Thus, although reflecting a marked conceptual shift in the understanding of substance use disorders, changes in the diagnostic criteria are relatively minor and somewhat transferrable.

Due to collaborative efforts to enhance the reliability and validity of diagnosis (e.g., Babor, 1992), the current version of ICD and the previous DSM (IV) system were largely compatible. The primary conceptual difference between the two classification systems was that the ICD-10 dependence includes craving, whereas DSM-IV did not. Additionally, ICD-10 refers to *harmful use* instead of *abuse* as in DSM-IV-TR (although the criteria used are similar), and the systems do not always agree on the dependence-producing potential of given categories of drugs. For example, androgenic-anabolic steroids (AAS) are explicitly listed as non–dependence-producing substances in the ICD-10, whereas researchers in the United States have suggested adaptations of the DSM-IV-TR criteria for the diagnosis of AAS dependence (e.g., Kanayama, Hudson, & Pope, 2009). After many years of development and debate, with the recent release of DSM-5, the underlying conceptual models of the ICD and DSM systems have become somewhat incompatible. Given the relative newness of the DSM-5 conceptualization, and some uncertainty regarding its future acceptance (an emerging issue across many diagnostic categories; e.g., Pull, 2013; Wakefield, 2013), the present review focuses on SUD diagnostic criteria as reflected in the DSM-IV-TR (APA, 2000).

Ultimately, diagnostic schemes are inventions: "all diagnostic instruments and practices construct their objects rather than describe an existing reality" (Keane, Moore, & Fraser, 2011, p. 875).

Table 15.3. Substance Use Disorder Criteria for DSM IV-TR

Substance Dependence	Substance Abuse
• A maladaptive pattern of substance use leading to clinically significant impairment or distress, as manifested by three (or more) of the following, occurring at any time in the same 12-month period:	• A maladaptive pattern of substance use leading to clinically significant impairment or distress, as manifested by one or more of the following occurring at any time in the same 12-month period:
1. Tolerance (as evidenced by diminished effects of the substance unless dose is markedly increased) 2. Withdrawal (evidenced by a characteristic withdrawal syndrome or substance use to avoid it) 3. Substance often taken in larger amounts or over periods longer than intended 4. Persistent desire or unsuccessful efforts to cut down or control substance use 5. A great deal of time spent in obtaining the substance, using the substance, or recovering from use of the substance 6. Important social, work, or recreational activities given up because of use of the substance 7. Continued use of the substance despite knowledge of problems caused or exacerbated by the substance — With physiological dependence if number 1 or 2 is present. — Without physiological dependence if neither 1 or 2 is present	1. Recurrent substance use resulting in failure to fulfill major role obligations at work, school, or home 2. Recurrent substance use in situations in which is it physically hazardous 3. Recurrent legal problems related to substance use 4. Continued use of substances despite persistent or recurrent social or interpersonal problems caused or exacerbated by the effects of the substance — Requires that the symptoms have never met the criteria for dependence on the same class of substance

These constructions are meant to reflect the best understanding of the phenomenon of interest at the time, with the explicit acknowledgement that such understanding evolves as a function of the interaction of research and practice. Hence, diagnostic instruments are best viewed as tools that are fluid and changeable as knowledge increases; "[it] would be unfortunate if our concept of dependence was shaped more by the limitations of our measurement tools than by the clinical and epidemiological realities we are trying to understand" (Babor, 2007, p. 1535). Consistent with this understanding of diagnostic criteria as today's "best guesses" regarding the nature of dependence or addiction, the DSM system has evolved from its first publication in 1952 (DSM -I) through DSM-IV TR (APA, 2000), to the more substantial conceptual shift represented by the DSM-5 (APA, 2013). As knowledge and conceptualizations have changed over time, so has the categorization of substance use disorders. Each is a hypothesis that bears the testing of time. As noted above, it remains to be seen how the conceptual shift reflected in the DSM-5 will fare in that test.

The DSM I (APA, 1952) referred to addiction (subsuming both alcoholism and drug addiction;

for a discussion regarding a return to the use of the term addiction see O'Brien, 2011; O'Brien, Volkow, & Li, 2006), classifying it as a sub-category of Sociopathic Personality Disturbance, a categorization largely continued in DSM II (APA, 1968), where alcoholism and drug dependence were subsumed under personality disorders and certain other nonpsychotic mental disorders. The perceived limitations of these criteria led to the development of more detailed alternatives (e.g., Feighner et al., 1972; *Research Diagnostic Criteria [RDC]*, e.g., Spitzer, Endicott & Robins, 1978) that ultimately served as progenitors of the SUD criteria in later editions of the DSM.

The DSM criteria changed drastically with the release of the 3rd edition (DSM III; APA, 1980), which took a much more detailed and symptom-based approach, and wherein a section for Substance Use Disorders, separate from personality disorders, was specified. In addition, diagnoses for both substance abuse (behavioral indicators) and dependence (physiological indicators; tolerance and withdrawal) were included. The revised 3rd edition (DSM III-R; APA, 1987) further refined these criteria, expanding dependence to include both physiological and behavioral indicators, and formally

Table 15.4. Substance Use Disorder Criteria for DSM-5

• A maladaptive pattern of substance use leading to clinically significant impairment or distress, as manifested by three (or more) of the following, occurring at any time in the same 12-month period:

1. recurrent substance use resulting in a failure to fulfill major role obligations at work, school, or home (e.g., repeated absences or poor work performance related to substance use; substance-related absences, suspensions, or expulsions from school; neglect of children or household)
2. recurrent substance use in situations in which it is physically hazardous (e.g., driving an automobile or operating a machine when impaired by substance use)
3. continued substance use despite having persistent or recurrent social or interpersonal problems caused or exacerbated by the effects of the substance (e.g., arguments with spouse about consequences of intoxication, physical fights)
4. tolerance, as defined by either of the following:
   a. a need for markedly increased amounts of the substance to achieve intoxication or desired effect
   b. markedly diminished effect with continued use of the same amount of the substance (Note: Tolerance is not counted for those taking medications under medical supervision such as analgesics, antidepressants, ant-anxiety medications or beta-blockers.)
5. withdrawal, as manifested by either of the following:
   a. the characteristic withdrawal syndrome for the substance (refer to Criteria A and B of the criteria sets for Withdrawal from the specific substances)
   b. the same (or a closely related) substance is taken to relieve or avoid withdrawal symptoms (Note: Withdrawal is not counted for those taking medications under medical supervision such as analgesics, antidepressants, anti-anxiety medications or beta-blockers.)

6. the substance is often taken in larger amounts or over a longer period than was intended
7. there is a persistent desire or unsuccessful efforts to cut down or control substance use
8. a great deal of time is spent in activities necessary to obtain the substance, use the substance, or recover from its effects
9. important social, occupational, or recreational activities are given up or reduced because of substance use
10. the substance use is continued despite knowledge of having a persistent or recurrent physical or psychological problem that is likely to have been caused or exacerbated by the substance
11. Craving or a strong desire or urge to use a specific substance.
    1. *Severity specifiers:*
    2. Moderate: 2–3 criteria positive
    3. Severe: 4 or more criteria positive
    4. *Specify if:*
       a. *With Physiological Dependence*: evidence of tolerance or withdrawal (i.e., either Item 4 or 5 is present)
       b. *Without Physiological Dependence*: no evidence of tolerance or
       c. withdrawal (i.e., neither Item 4 nor 5 is present)

---

establishing a hierarchical structure for SUDs. Substance abuse became a residual category representing substance-related disruption, the diagnosis of which was precluded by a diagnosis of dependence within the same drug class. Such an approach facilitated the identification of patterns of hazardous or injurious behavior that might occur in the absence of dependence (e.g., Babor, 1995). The *DSM IV-TR* (APA, 2000) largely continued this structure for the diagnosis of SUDs; dependence and abuse criteria are listed in Table 15.3.

In keeping with the tradition of evolving diagnostic criteria, there has been a long running discussion in the literature regarding the categorical nature of SUD criteria (e.g., Nathan, 1993) and how they might be modified (e.g., Helzer, Bucholz, & Gossop, 2007; Martin, Chung, & Langebucher,

2008). The utility of the polythetic (defining disorders by multiple symptoms of which only a given number are required to infer a disorder) and categorical (binary assignment of diagnosis) nature of the existing diagnostic systems has been questioned (e.g., Krueger & Bezdjian, 2009). Under such a structure, a wide range of symptom patterns can result in a similar diagnosis, potentially producing considerable heterogeneity among those receiving similar diagnoses. This, in turn, has an impact on the utility of diagnostic information for case conceptualization, treatment planning, and outcome evaluation.

During the development of DSM-5, numerous suggestions mere made, from the semantic—a return to the term "addiction" (O'Brien, 2011)—to the inclusion of a category of non-consumptive addictive behaviors (e.g., Musalek, 2007). Perhaps the most substantive change is the incorporation of hybrid criteria that provide both categorical diagnosis (diagnostic threshold defined by the presence of a given number of symptoms within a given time frame) and dimensional indications of severity based on the number of criteria exhibited (e.g., Helzer et al., 2007; Martin et al., 2008). The appropriate number of symptoms required to meet severity criteria was a matter of some debate (e.g., Babor, 2011). Statistical modeling of categorical (binary) and dimensional (continuous) data has also highlighted the potential utility of such changes (e.g., Muthén, 2006; Slade, Grove, & Teeson, 2009).

Thus, DSM-5, while making minimal changes to diagnostic criteria, combines the categories of abuse and dependence from the DSM IV into a single substance use disorder that can be diagnosed when 2 or more criteria (see Table 15.4) are manifested within a 12-month period, with severity described as a function of the number of criteria met (2–3 for moderate, 4 or more for severe). In addition, a Substance Use Disorder can be diagnosed with or without physiological dependence based on whether tolerance or withdrawal is observed. It remains to be seen how this new conceptualization is accepted in the field, how it affects those diagnosed under the previous system, and how quickly it results in updated structured measures for diagnosis. Thus, our description and discussion of diagnostic instruments addresses those in existence at the time of this review. It is unclear how or when existing tools might be adapted for obtaining data consistent with the DSM-5 model.

Diagnostic instruments. A wide range of instruments is available for diagnostic assessment, and there are a number of comprehensive reviews of these measures in the literature (e.g., Cooney, Kadden, & Steinberg, 2005; Donovan & Marlatt, 2005; NIAAA, 2003; Rohsenow, 2008). The major instruments provide systematic methods for obtaining self-reports of the occurrence of diagnostic symptoms based on a range of existing criteria, most often the *DSM*. However, it is useful to consider measures that address severity of symptoms as well.

Most diagnostic instruments are administered via semistructured interviews. A brief description of representative devices gives some indications of the ways in which these instruments vary. Perhaps the most structured among the more widely used assessments is the *Diagnostic Interview Schedule-IV* (DIS

IV), which was originally developed for use with the DSM III (hence, the DIS III) in 1980 (Robins et al., 1981) and subsequently updated to assess *DSM III-R* and *DSM-IV* criteria. The *DIS III-R* was shown to have excellent psychometric properties; data regarding the current version are less available (Rohsenow, 2008; see, however, Horton, Compton, & Cottler, 1998, regarding reliability). Because it is highly structured, trained technicians are required for administration; however, little or no formal clinical training is needed. A computerized version, the CDIS-IV, is available; however, cost may be prohibitive in some settings (Carroll & Rounsaville, 2002). Although designed for use in epidemiological research (Robins et al., 2000), the DIS also has clear clinical research and practice applications. (For more information, visit http://epi.wustl.edu/dis/Dishome.htm.)

The *Composite International Diagnostic Interview—Substance Abuse Module* (CIDI-SAM; Robins, Cotler, & Babor, 1995) assesses diagnostic criteria in accordance with both the DSM IV and the ICD-10 classification systems. The CIDI-SAM is brief with demonstrated reliability in a number of populations (Carroll & Rounsaville, 2002); the CIDI Core interview, although highly valid for diagnosing Axis I disorders (Rohsenow, 2008), is a lengthy assessment. Both instruments necessitate formal training for administration and scoring, and clinicians and researchers should consider the time and personnel required, given the availability of other instruments. The CIDI does, however, offer a reliable no-cost computerized version. (Descriptive information, including training and other resources can be found at http://www.hcp.med.harvard.edu/wmhcidi/.)

The *Semi-Structured Assessment for the Genetics of Alcoholism* (SSAGA-II) was developed specifically for use in the Collaborative Study on the Genetics of Alcoholism (COGA). It is a reliable and valid (e.g., Hesselbrock et al., 1999), highly structured interview that can be administered by well-trained clinicians (Cooney et al., 2005). Diagnoses can be determined for *DSM* and *ICD* criteria, as well as the Feighner and *RDC* systems, facilitating comparisons with studies in the research literature. Child and adolescent versions, as well as instrument forms, are available at minimal cost (visit http://zork.wustl.edu/niaaa/form.htm).

The *Structured Clinical Interview for the DSM (SCID)* offers several different versions (e.g.,

Research Version, Clinician's Version) that vary in length and complexity, but are all intended to assist in the assignment of formal diagnoses under the DSM criteria. Its structure allows for administration by those with minimal clinical training. The SCID exhibited "good" validity for current and life-time SUD diagnosis among adult patients (e.g., Kranzler et al., 1996) and high interrater reliabilities for both individual criteria and overall diagnosis among adolescent drinkers (Martin et al., 2000). A wide range of information regarding the SCID is provided at http://www.scid4.org/index.html, where the instrument is also available for purchase.

The *Alcohol Use Disorder and Associated Disabilities Interview Schedule-IV* (AUDADIS-IV) provides a structured interview format for assessing both SUD and mental disorders in both clinical (e.g., Hasin et al., 1997) and general (Grant et al., 1995, 2003) populations using DSM criteria. It can be administered by nonclinicians and has exhibited high reliabilities for alcohol and tobacco use (e.g., Grant et al., 2003). The instrument can be accessed at http://pubs.niaaa.nih.gov/publications/audadis.pdf.

Severity of substance involvement. Dimensional measures of severity are useful in both clinical and research settings. These include simple counts of symptoms (i.e., the number of diagnostic criteria met) as assessed by diagnostic instruments, as well as self-administered questionnaires that address a broader range of adverse consequences and/or problems associated with psychoactive substance use. As with diagnostic interviews, a description of representative instruments provides an indication of the types of instruments available. Symptom counts can reportedly serve adequately as barometers of severity. In the absence of the complete amelioration of the disorder noted at intake, such information can provide an indication of change in a patient's SUD status, for example, from more to less severely dependent.

The *Substance Dependence Severity* Scale (SDSS; Miele et al., 2000a, 2000b) offers information regarding DSM and ICD diagnoses of substance dependence and abuse/harmful use among adults and adolescents over age 16. Assessment is keyed to relative short periods of time (30 days), and frequency and severity of symptoms, in addition to presence, are measured, providing an index of recent severity of abuse or dependence across a variety of substances. This instrument does, however, require a trained clinician for administration and can be relatively time consuming (up to

40 minutes) (Carroll & Rounsaville, 2002). The similarly titled *Severity of Dependence Scale* (SDS) provides a brief, five-item alternative that assesses severity of dependence across a range of substances (Gossop et al., 1995; Martin et al., 2006). The five items represent a pattern of symptoms reflecting dependence (e.g., perceptions of control, desire to quit, perceived difficulty of cessation), each scored on a scale with higher scores indicating more severe dependence.

In addition to instruments that attempt to measure the severity of dependence, there are numerous measures of variables that are somewhat similar in content, assessing adverse consequences and problems related to alcohol and other drug use (e.g., the *Drinker Inventory of Consequences*, DrInC, Miller, Tonigan, & Longabaugh, 1995; the *Inventory of Drug Use Consequences,* InDUC, Tonigan & Miller, 2002), as well as constructs such as craving. As in other domains, there are brief adaptations (e.g., the SIP, a short form of the DrInC) and instruments tailored specifically to adolescents and college students.

The *Addiction Severity Index* (ASI; McClellan et al. 1992; 1980) deserves special mention, as it has been described as, "one of the most useful assessment tools in planning and assessing treatment outcome for drug-abusing populations" (Carroll & Rounsaville, 2002, p. 1332). History of use, patterns of consumption, and adverse consequences are assessed within a semi-structured interview. Because co-existing disorders are common in those who have problems with psychoactive substance use, five additional life domains that might logically be affected by substance use are assessed: medical, legal, employment, social/family, and psychological functioning. Scores across these domains can be profiled to highlight assets or deficits and to support treatment. Although research indicates that reductions in substance use occur in concert with improvements in other domains (e.g., Carroll et al., 1993; Kosten, Rounsaville, & Kleber, 1986), it has also been suggested that treatments that target other areas of dysfunction can facilitate improved outcomes (e.g., McClellan et al., 1997). A number of different versions, including those developed for use with different populations, are available (see http://www.tresearch.org/resources/instruments.htm).

Assessment of adolescents and children. There is broad agreement that any use of psychoactive substance by adolescents is a major concern (e.g., Brown et al., 2008). Early involvement with alcohol or illicit drugs has been shown to predict increased risk for later problems; for example, studies suggest that binge drinking in adolescence increases risk for negative outcomes later in life (e.g., Chassin, Pitts, & Prost, 2002; Monti et al., 2005; Bagge & Sher, 2008). Hence, accurate assessment of important elements in the expression of SUDs in adolescents is crucial.

Existing models of adult substance use and SUDs cannot be straightforwardly applied to adolescents as symptoms manifest themselves differently in younger users (e.g., Chung & Martin, 2005; Tarter, 1990; Winters, 2003). Diagnosing adolescent SUDs requires an appreciation for the developmental issues that differentiate adolescents from their adult counterparts. For instance, the symptom "drinking more or longer than intended" includes the embedded assumption that a limit on use had been set; however, rather than intending to limit consumption, adolescents typically become intoxicated by design. Several comprehensive reviews of the measures developed specifically for use in the diagnosis of SUDs in adolescents, as well as the conceptual and practical issues that must be addressed in assessment, are available (e.g., Winters, 2003; Winters & Kaminer, 2008; Winters & Fahnhorst, 2005). It is beyond the scope of this essay to provide an extensive review; hence, as with adult instruments, a small number of widely used exemplars are described here.

The *Diagnostic Interview Schedule for Children* (DISC; Costello, Edelbrook & Costello, 1985; Shaffer et al., 2000) includes forms for both the child and parent; it is a highly structured interview intended for administration by trained non-clinicians. The DISC IV (based on the DSM IV) has demonstrated sensitivity in the identification of adolescents hospitalized with an SUD (Fisher et al., 1993); details on the history and psychometric properties of the DISC-IV are reviewed by Shaffer et al., 2000.

The *Adolescent Diagnostic Interview* (ADI; Winters & Henly, 1993) provides an assessment of DSM SUD criteria, as well as several clinically-significant domains of functioning (e.g., use history, psychosocial stressors, and other psychiatric disorders; Winters, 2003). Psychometric data are available (Winters & Henly, 1993; Winters et al., 1999). The *Personal Experience Inventory* (PEI; Winters & Henly, 1989) is comprised of scales assessing problem severity, psychosocial risk, and veracity (response bias or distortion). It includes several additional supplemental screens for eating disorders, suicide risk, physical/sexual abuse, and parental history of SUD. The PEI has good psychometric properties; additionally, a customized, computer-generated report (narrative summary, as well as scale scores) is produced for each client to assist in treatment planning (Winters & Henly, 1989).

A Cognitive Social-Psychological Model of the Question-Answering Process

Historically, self-reports regarding alcohol and illicit drug use were widely regarded with suspicion. However, with the increase in recognition that reliability and validity are matters of degree rather than absolute (e.g., Babor et al., 1990; Langenbucher & Merrill, 2001; Leigh, 2000; Midanik, 1982, 1988; Mieczkowski, 1991; Sobell & Sobell, 1995a), attempts have been made to structure assessment situations in ways that encourage accurate responding. To facilitate this process, we have proposed a framework that specifies the major potential sources of error in the question-answering process (Babor et al., 1987; Babor et al., 1990; Babor & Del Boca, 1992; Del Boca & Noll, 2000).

Our organizing framework (see Figure 15.1) shares features with other models of the response process (e.g., Cannell, Marquis, & Laurent, 1977; Cannell, Miller, & Oksenberg, 1981; Schwarz, Groves, & Schuman, 1998; Strack & Martin, 1987; Sudman, Bradburn, & Schwarz, 1996; Tourangeau, 1984; Tourangeau, Rips, & Rasinski, 2000). An important assumption is that verbal reports are governed by the same principles as other forms of behavior and are shaped by multiple, interacting influences. Accordingly, response behavior can be understood in terms of theory and research in domains of basic science such as human perception, cognition and memory; language comprehension; motivation and judgment; and social influence processes; as well as applied areas such as communication, consumer research, and survey methods.

Relevant Research Traditions

There are three primary sources of relevant theory and research on self-report methods: studies conducted by addictions researchers; work by survey researchers and epidemiologists; and a subspecialty of survey research that has sought to apply cognitive theory and methods to understanding response processes.

Investigators in the addictions field have produced a large and widely dispersed literature comparing different self-report methods of assessing

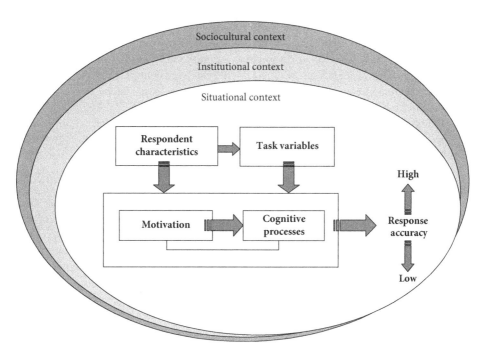

Figure 15.1. A framework for understanding the question-answering process: classes of factors that influence the accuracy of verbal responses.

Adapted from Babor, T. F., Brown, J., & Del Boca, F. K. (1990). Validity of self-reports in applied research on addictive behaviors: Fact or fiction? *Behavioral Assessment, 12,* 5–31.

substance use with each other, as well as to alternative data sources (e.g., biochemical measures). Most often, researchers have conducted secondary analyses of data initially collected for other purposes (e.g., evaluations of treatment efficacy). Most studies have been atheoretical, and they have varied considerably in their ability to isolate different sources of variation. Further, investigators have often been guided by assumptions that may not always be valid.

The notion that drinking is regarded as socially undesirable behavior, coupled with the observation that alcohol sales consistently exceed self-report consumption estimates (e.g., Midanik, 1982), has contributed to the conclusion that methods that produce higher estimates of use are more accurate (e.g., Leigh, 2000; Schwarz et al., 1998). This assumption may not be valid in many assessment circumstances. For example, clients entering treatment have been shown to exaggerate consumption (Midanik, 1988), and it has been suggested that college students (who often view heavy drinking as socially desirable) tend to over-report quantities of alcohol consumed (e.g., Schwarz et al., 1998). Nevertheless, despite contradictory data (e.g., Del Boca & Noll, 2000), the "more is better" criterion has become somewhat of a gold standard.

It is also commonly assumed that alternative data sources are more valid than self-reports, in part, because they are regarded as less vulnerable to intentional distortion (Del Boca & Noll, 2000). Although the quality of biological markers for alcohol and other substances has improved substantially in recent years (Wish, Hoffman, & Nemes, 1997), each candidate measure has limitations in sensitivity and/or specificity (cf. Carroll, 1995; Del Boca & Noll, 2000). Collateral informant reports about the behaviors of associates are potentially subject to many of the same sources of error as self-reports of one's own behavior (cf. Del Boca & Noll, 2000). Reviews of the literature have generally concluded that, for most clinical and research purposes, self-reports regarding alcohol and other psychoactive substance use are reasonably reliable and valid when the data-gathering situation is constructed to minimize bias (e.g., Babor et al., 1990; Del Boca & Noll, 2000; Midanik, 1982; 1988). Nevertheless, the issue remains controversial, and some form of corroborating evidence continues to be collected in both clinical and research settings. (See Del Boca & Darkes, 2003, for a fuller discussion of this issue.)

In contrast to investigators in the addictions field, epidemiological and survey researchers have conducted numerous methodological studies on a variety of factors related to study capture rates and sources of response error. This research has demonstrated relatively high rates of logical and estimation errors in survey responses (e.g., Fendrich & Vaughn, 1994) and shown that minor variations in question phrasing and formatting can strongly influence responses, even for seemingly innocuous topics (cf. Schwarz et al., 1998). Although methodologically rigorous, most studies have not been grounded in theory. The extensive literature conducted within this tradition is summarized in several resources (e.g., Bradburn & Sudman, 1981; Bradburn, Sudman, & Associates, 1979; Dillman, 1978, 2000), including some useful websites (e.g., http://survey.sesrc.wsu.edu/dillman/).

A third source of relevant theory and research is work on the "cognitive and communication aspects of survey research" (cf. Schwarz, 1999), a field of inquiry that has developed over the past two decades. There are a number of volumes that summarize findings in this area (e.g., Hippler, Schwarz, & Sudman, 1987; Jabine et al., 1984; Jobe & Loftus, 1991; Schwarz et al., 1998; Schwarz & Sudman, 1992, 1994, 1996; Stone et al., 2000; Tanur, 1992; Tourangeau et al., 2000). Work has been guided explicitly by theory and research on language comprehension, memory, and judgment; thus, the findings are thought to have relevance beyond survey studies to any situation that involves verbal reports (Schwarz, 1999). Investigators have also focused attention on the role that conversational norms might play when respondents interpret the meaning of questions that are asked in assessment situations. Study designs include tightly controlled laboratory experiments, as well as sample surveys. Although the literature pertaining to the assessment of substance use and related constructs is not large, several studies of alcohol consumption measures have been guided by this general framework (see Greenfield & Kerr, 2008, for an overview).

Components of the Framework
SOCIAL CONTEXT

As depicted in Figure 15.1, the question-answering process occurs within a multi-layered context that is influenced by broad sociocultural norms, subcultural pre- and proscriptions, and the more local assessment setting (e.g., household survey, treatment facility, emergency department), as well as by the immediate interpersonal situation, which may involve research personnel, treatment staff, additional respondents, family members, or other bystanders. Very importantly, the social context influences the perceived role of the respondent in the question-answering process and the nature of the perceived contingencies associated with particular responses (e.g., Babor et al., 1990; Bradburn, 1983; Del Boca & Noll, 2000). Because perceptions of social desirability vary depending on subcultural norms, response bias is likely to vary across locations, settings, and population subgroups.

Conversational norms that govern human discourse also influence response behavior. Questions posed by researchers and clinicians are thought to be comprehended on a *pragmatic* (inferential), as well as a *literal* (semantic), level. Pragmatic understanding of communication is most often described in terms of the conversational maxims originally postulated by Grice (1975). These maxims refer to assumptions that are held by individuals during social discourse; they are based on a general principle of cooperation and enable listeners to infer the intentions of the speaker. For example, the maxim of *relation* specifies that a speaker intends what he or she says to relate to the ongoing exchange. Accordingly, respondents expect each item in a questionnaire or interview to relate to an overall topic, and they will make inferences regarding the intended meaning of queries on that basis (see also Schwarz, 1999; Schwarz et al., 1998). Research has confirmed that the positioning of questions or sets of items within a questionnaire can alter responses, very likely because interpretations of content changed as a function of context (e.g., Weinberger et al., 2006).

RESPONDENT CHARACTERISTICS

Respondent variables include enduring attributes such as demographic identifications (e.g., gender, race/ethnicity, religious preference); reference groups (e.g., fraternities and sororities); personality traits (e.g., need for approval, sociopathy); intelligence (or cognitive impairment); longstanding attitudes, values, and beliefs (e.g., perceived norms regarding drinking; mistrust of medical researchers); personal circumstances (e.g., involvement in the criminal justice system); and transitory states such as sobriety, physical condition (e.g., fatigue, alcohol withdrawal), and affective state (e.g., depression, anxiety). Instruments that query respondents about potentially sensitive topics, such as substance use, are often thought to be particularly susceptible to individual differences in social desirability response set. However, this has been more often assumed than directly tested (cf. Bradburn, 1983; Schwarz, 1999), and high concordance between self-reports of drinking and biochemical indicators has been found in respondents with high social desirability scores (Yoshino & Kato, 1995).

Although often regarded as less significant than other factors affecting verbal reports (cf. Schwarz et al., 1998), available research suggests that respondent variables may play an important role in research on alcohol and illicit drug use. Dependence severity (e.g., Babor et al., 2000), recovery stage, and sobriety or withdrawal state have all been shown to influence responses (e.g., Brown, Kranzler, & Del Boca, 1992; Sobell & Sobell, 1990; Sobell, Toneatto, & Sobell, 1994). In substance use surveys, age, gender, and, in particular, race/ethnicity, have been associated with response bias (e.g., Connors, Watson, & Maisto, 1985). There are indications in the literature that African American respondents tend to underreport use of many substances (e.g., Bauman & Ennett, 1994; Falck et al., 1992), but the generality of these findings is not conclusive (Langenbucher & Merrill, 2001). Finally, and very importantly for the assessment of substance use, the actual pattern of behavior enactment itself (its frequency and distribution over time) may affect the ability of the respondent to answer questions accurately and completely. Studies comparing prospective and retrospective DE methods of assessing alcohol use have found that frequent drinkers tend to underestimate their drinking, whereas infrequent imbibers overreport consumption, and that data are more accurate for individuals whose consumption patterns are stable or at the extremes of the drinking distribution (very infrequent or almost daily) (e.g., Lemmens, Tan, & Knibbe, 1992).

TASK VARIABLES

Survey research suggests that task attributes (see Table 15.1) account for more of the variance in response accuracy than any other general factor (Schwarz et al., 1998). As indicated in Figure 15.1, task variables primarily influence the veracity of self-reports through their effects on the respondent's willingness (motivation) and/or ability (cognitive processes) to provide accurate information. For example, the degree of confidentiality implied by procedures, and the perceived likelihood of independent confirmation, may influence willingness to respond truthfully; similarly, task difficulty (describing drinking behavior in the distant past) may tax the ability to respond accurately.

Probably the most obvious task variable affecting response behavior is question content. Not surprisingly, investigators have found that topic sensitivity influences response veracity. In general, the more stigmatized the behavior, the greater is the probability of underreporting (Langenbucher & Merrill, 2001). Underreporting is more common in response to questions regarding opiates and cocaine than to queries regarding marijuana use (e.g., Harrison, 1992). Perceptions of alcohol use appear to be particularly variable, depending on the level of use that is queried (any alcohol use versus drinking to intoxication) and the subculture of the respondent.

Assuming that alcohol consumption and other illicit drug use may be sensitive topics for many respondents, administration mode, because of its implications for perceived anonymity and confidentiality, is likely to influence response veracity (Del Boca & Darkes, 2003). Higher levels of socially undesirable or pathological behavior have been reported on self-administered and computer-assisted assessments, as compared with personal interviews (cf. Langenbucher & Merrill, 2001; see, however, Skinner & Allen, 1983). Although it is commonly assumed that the greater sense of privacy or perceived anonymity of such assessments accounts for this difference, it may be due, at least in part, to other factors (e.g., the ability to work at one's own pace).

Although not always considered an important factor in survey research (cf. Schwarz et al., 1998), interviewer variables may contribute to response bias in substance use research (e.g., Connors et al., 1985; Magura et al., 1987). Interviewer attitudes and expectations, as well as training and skill, personal characteristics (gender, race/ethnicity, age), and perceived role can influence the accuracy of responses (e.g., Johnson et al., 2000). For example, in treatment or program evaluation studies, data collection by a treating clinician may result in underreports of consumption during outcome evaluations (Babor et al., 1990; Del Boca & Noll, 2000).

Apart from administration procedures and content, numerous aspects of instrument design influence response behavior. Question modules often begin by asking respondents whether they have ever consumed alcohol or drugs or experienced particular consequences of use. Depending on the response, more specific questions are posed regarding particular drugs, the quantity and frequency of use, or more recent time periods. While these "skip patterns" increase assessment efficiency and reduce respondent burden, they are also associated with relatively high rates of nonresponse (e.g., Featherston & Moy, 1990) and with inconsistent responding across questionnaire items (e.g., Zuckerman & Hess, 1996). There is a growing literature on the use of skip patterns in survey research. Based on knowledge about perceptual processes, such studies have identified methods for defining a clear, "navigational path through the questionnaire" (Redline et al., 1999, p. 1). Readers are referred to several studies by Dillman and associates (available at http://survey/sesrc/wsu.edu/dillman/papers/htm) that indicate how the physical layout of skip pattern items in self-administered questionnaires, in combination with written instructions, can potentially increase rates of response and reduce errors (e.g., Dillman, Carley-Baxter, & Jackson, 1999; Dillman, Redline, & Carley-Baxter, 1999; Redline et al., 1999).

Although less common, skip patterns can also produce errors in interviews. One method of capturing respondents who may incorrectly deny lifetime use or symptoms of dependence is to add one or more additional gateway questions to the instrument. For example, a follow-up question that rephrases the original item, or asks about another aspect of substance use (e.g., age of first use), might be directed to all respondents rather than the subset who initially answered affirmatively. This approach retains much of the efficiency associated with skip patterns but, at the same time, has the potential to capture respondents who may otherwise have been lost as a consequence of inattention or misunderstanding of the initial question's intent.

Research has consistently shown that the specification of response options can have a significant impact on how questions are interpreted (cf. Schwarz, 1999). In alcohol research, it is common to present participants with categories that specify different quantities consumed (e.g., ranging from 1 to 10 or more standard drinks) and scaled frequencies of use (e.g., ranging from "never" to "daily or almost daily"). The range of alternatives presented defines for the respondent the range of normative behavior, particularly at the upper end of the distribution. In an attempt to normalize more extreme behavior patterns, response options for alcohol consumption questions sometimes include large quantities (16 or more drinks) and high frequencies (e.g., more than once per day). It is generally assumed that allowing for more extreme responses will produce more accurate data, under the assumption that "more is better." However, this practice may instead produce exaggerated reports, especially in some populations. Relatively little of the considerable amount of research that has been conducted on response options (see Schwarz & Sudman,

1996, Chapter 5; Schwarz, 1999) has focused on self-reports of drinking or other substance use. Because response options can alter the meaning of questions and cause shifts in the definition and distribution of reported behaviors, it can be problematic to compare the results for respondents who have answered identical questions with differing response formats (Schwarz & Oyserman, 2001), a practice not uncommon in research. Studies are needed to examine how response options for questions about substance use affect the accuracy of self-reports, and to determine the extent to which comparisons that involve items with differing alternatives may produce erroneous findings.

As indicated above, questions about psychoactive substance use vary in terms of assessment time frame. Respondents are sometimes instructed to describe their typical pattern; more often they are asked to consider a particular time period. Numerous studies have attempted to examine how question phrasing influences response strategies and affects accuracy. In general, specific questions (e.g., those with a defined time frame) have been shown to produce more accurate responses than global questions (e.g., queries about usual or typical behavior) (e.g., Belson, 1981; Greenfield & Kerr, 2008). At the same time, however, it has been suggested that specific reference periods are susceptible to misinterpretation. The phrase, "during the last 12 months," may be viewed as the last calendar year, or as including or excluding the current month (Bradburn, Rips, & Shevell, 1987). In the realm of drinking assessment, several investigators have suggested that answers to quantity/frequency questions tend to describe *modal* rather than *average* behavior (e.g., Midanik, 1991; Poikolainen & Karkkainen, 1983), and there is some evidence that respondents exclude abstinent periods in their responses regarding "the last 12 months" (Weisner et al., 1999).

MOTIVATION

Willingness to respond accurately can be influenced by the physical and psychological state of the respondent. Sobriety, fatigue, withdrawal symptoms, and negative psychological states such as depression or anxiety, may decrease cooperation and adversely affect response accuracy, either because of diminished effort or because such states influence perceptions regarding the purpose of the assessment. Motivation is most likely to be affected by the perceived contingencies in the situation, including the degree of threat or embarrassment associated with a particular topic, and thus response validity should vary as a function of the degree of perceived anonymity or confidentiality of the assessment.

Because they reduce the perceived probability of negative consequences, the important role of anonymity and confidentiality in enhancing self-report validity is regarded as axiomatic in addictions research (Langenbucher & Merrill, 2001). The available evidence indicates that perceived anonymity may lead to increased response rates, but that reports of alcohol use do not largely differ based on guarantees of anonymity as compared with confidentially (e.g., Malvin & Moskowitz, 1983; Murray & Perry, 1987; Werch, 1990). Although some differences have been reported (e.g., Bjarnason & Adalbjarmnardottir, 2000), their practical significance appears limited. Nevertheless, selection bias based on differential willingness to respond may be an issue, depending on the situation.

Motivation is most often discussed in terms of the disincentives that compromise self-report validity. In many situations, however, benefits can accrue for completing assessments. For example, participants are often paid for the time and effort involved in research. Dillman (2000) has characterized the interaction between those collecting and those providing self-reports in terms of social exchange theory. Accordingly, respondent motivation can be enhanced in ways that go beyond financial compensation. An environment in which respondents are afforded positive regard, receive open expressions of appreciation, have input into the process and their values respected, are provided an interesting experience, and receive social validation for their contributions, can tip the balance in favor of rewards, enhancing respondent motivation and the validity of self-reports.

COGNITIVE PROCESSES

Several interacting cognitive processes are involved in the production of a response to a question regarding psychoactive substance use: The respondent must attend to the request for information *(attention)*, interpret the question *(comprehension)*, recall from memory pertinent behaviors *(retrieval)*, integrate information via comparative, inferential, or attribution processes *(integration)*, and then decide (not necessarily in a deliberate or conscious manner) how to respond *(response selection)* (cf. Babor et al., 1990). The effects of these cognitive processes on response accuracy have been extensively investigated during the last two decades (cf. Schwarz et al., 1998).

Cognitive processes that are assumed to be related to clients' motivational states—attention, comprehension, and response selection—are frequently addressed in clinical settings and in research. It is recognized that attention can be compromised by fatigue, depression, or intoxication, and that respondents evaluate the psychological meaning of the response (integration) in relation to personal goals, such as fear of being labeled, avoiding arrest, or admission to treatment. Although the interplay of motivational and cognitive factors is an important determinant of self-report veracity, the more purely cognitive processes of retrieval and integration are also susceptible to bias.

With respect to information retrieval, the limitations of memory have long been recognized in addictions research. Research indicates, however, that the limits of human information processing extend beyond the failure to remember specific events from the distant past (Del Boca & Noll, 2000). In recent years the understanding of factors that influence retrieval processes in behavioral assessments has increased greatly (cf. Bradburn, 2000; Menon & Yorkson, 2000; Schwarz, 1990; Schwarz et al., 1998; Schwarz & Oyserman, 2001; Tourangeau, 2000), providing a frame of reference for evaluating current methods for the measurement of substance use. Rather than using a "recall-and-count" strategy to answer questions regarding the frequency of a particular behavior (as queried by quantity/frequency items, for example), individuals use a variety of cognitive short cuts (heuristics or inference rules) (e.g., Bradburn et al., 1987; Pearson, Ross, & Dawes, 1992; Schwarz & Sudman, 1994; Sudman et al., 1996). For example, information retrieval is strongly influenced by the recency and saliency of past events (cf. Loftus, 1979). Additionally, respondents often use current behavior as a standard when answering questions about past behavior and may invoke an implicit theory of self in assessing whether, and how much, change has occurred (Schwarz et al., 1998).

One method that has been used in efforts to improve behavioral frequency estimates is the decomposition of general questions into a series of more specific items (e.g., rather than asking how many times alcohol was consumed, separate questions are asked about beer, wine, and liquor). The decomposed items are intended to assist respondents in recalling episodes that they may have otherwise forgotten. This approach to phrasing questions consistently results in higher behavioral estimates than more global items (e.g., Blair & Burton, 1987;

Sudman & Schwarz, 1989). Although the "more is better" criterion would suggest that decomposition enhances self-report accuracy, research indicates that it may instead exaggerate actual behavior frequency (Belli et al., 2000), possibly due to a change in the method of cognitive processing (Schwarz and Oyserman, 2001). There is a general tendency to overestimate rare events and to underestimate high-frequency occurrences (Fiedler & Armbruster, 1994). Compared to specific items, global questions necessarily refer to behaviors that occur more frequently, and they consequently produce underestimates. The relatively infrequent events assessed by decomposed questions are likely overreported, and summing responses across the item series can produce sizeable overestimates of behavior. Thus, the use of this strategy with frequent users should be approached with caution.

Although they overcome some of the limitations of Q/F measures, retrospective DE procedures are not immune to retrieval biases. For behaviors that are frequently enacted, individuals typically do not store all concrete instances in memory; rather, episodes of alcohol or other substance use may be assimilated to more global representations (Linton, 1982; Neisser, 1986), which may distort the descriptions of specific occasions (cf. Schwarz et al., 1998). Respondents, particularly heavier users, may respond to questions regarding specific days in terms of heuristics (e.g., my typical behavior at fraternity parties, the usual amount I drink on Fridays) (Linton, 1982; Neisser, 1986; cf. Schwarz et al. 1998). Further, because calendar dating is generally not a good cue for accessing specific events from memory, accurate retrieval may require the use of multiple cues that are relevant to the individual respondent (e.g., going to parties, spending time with a particular friend) (cf. Schwarz, 1990; Schwarz & Oyserman, 2001). In addition to their implications for the accuracy of daily drinking estimates, these considerations suggest that the validity of retrospective daily estimation procedures is likely to be dependent on both the skill of the interviewer and the active cooperation of the respondent. As a consequence, adaptations of this assessment approach for self-administration or for telephone interviewing, and for assessment periods that involve lengthy time windows, may be difficult to implement successfully.

There are many more specific issues with respect to memory retrieval than those briefly considered here. For example, studies indicate that recall can be enhanced by allowing sufficient time to search

events in memory. Accordingly, explicit directions to respondents to, "take all the time you need" have been found to improve recall (Cannell et al., 1981). Similarly, research indicates that longer questions may improve accuracy because respondents take more time to consider their answers (Cannell et al., 1981). Strategies such as these, which address cognitive processes in our framework, also need to be considered in terms of motivation. The potential increase in accuracy produced by more time-intensive assessment may be offset by a resulting decrease in motivation to cooperate (Schwarz & Oyserman, 2001).

One final aspect of information processing merits mention. The *attribution* of causality is an important component of cognitive integration processes that is potentially problematic for diagnostic interviews and instruments that assess adverse consequences or problems associated with substance use. Respondents are frequently asked to make judgments as to whether negative emotional states or events are or are not a result of substance use. The study of attribution processes has a long history in social psychology, and a variety of biases in assigning causality have been identified. For example, in reference to self, positive outcomes are more likely to be attributed to personal causes such as effort, whereas negative events are more likely to be attributed to external causes, such as the behavior of others or bad luck (e.g., Mezulis et al., 2004). Further, this pattern varies somewhat by respondent characteristics, such as gender (e.g., Grubb & Harrower, 2009) and culture (e.g., Kuendig et al., 2008). The extent to which alcohol or other substances themselves are seen as causal agents that diminish feelings of personal responsibility (e.g., "it's not really me, but the drug that made me do it") has received limited research attention. Nevertheless, it seems likely that attribution biases may influence respondents' judgments regarding the symptoms, consequences, and problems associated with alcohol and illicit drug use.

Conclusions and Future Directions

We have described the important methodological features of the major methods used in assessing substance use, SUDs, and dependence severity, and presented guidelines for selecting appropriate instruments for clinical and investigational purposes. Additionally, we have introduced a framework that draws attention to the factors that influence the validity of self-reports. Much is known about the sources of error that potentially influence the accuracy of verbal responses. However, a great deal more work is needed to understand fully how contextual factors and task variations affect the cognitive and motivational processes involved in response behavior, especially with respect to questions regarding substance use and dependence. Much of the research conducted on self-report methods in the addictions literature has made use of data collected for other purposes. We advocate research that focuses specifically on self-report assessment approaches in their own right, conducted by investigators schooled in addiction science and familiar with the vagaries involved in measuring psychoactive substance use and related constructs.

The following general questions remain high priorities for research: What cognitive strategies do respondents use to access, retrieve, and integrate relevant information in responding to queries regarding substance use and its consequences? How do these vary as a function of respondent characteristics? In particular, how are cognitive strategies in the question-answering process affected by the consumption patterns of respondents? What approaches can assist individuals in estimating behavioral and event frequencies, on the one hand, and consumption quantities, on the other? How can the assessment process, in general, and task elements, in particular, be modified to enhance the respondent's *ability* to understand the intent of the clinician/investigator and to recall and integrate the information needed for an accurate response? What incentives and disincentives can be manipulated within the assessment situation to *motivate* respondents to cooperate fully and to provide accurate answers to questions regarding substance use and its consequences?

Studies that borrow methods from cognitive psychology to investigate how respondents retrieve and process information when asked to estimate behavioral frequencies can serve as a model for research designed to address some of these questions (e.g., Conrad, Brown, & Cashman, 1998; cf. Schwarz, 1990; Schwarz & Oyserman, 2001). Survey researchers also offer a number of different approaches that can assist clinicians and investigators in understanding the meaning of respondents' answers to questions in commonly used assessment instruments (see Schwarz et al., 1998). These include asking respondents to paraphrase questions (Schuman, 1966), verbal protocols in the form of retrospective or (preferably) concurrent "thinking aloud" protocols (e.g., Groves, Fultz, & Martin, 1992; Willis, Royston, & Bercini, 1991), and

behavior coding of taped responses for clarification requests, interruptions, and the like (see Bolton & Bronkhorst, 1996). Although alcohol researchers have capitalized on some of these paradigms to examine the processes used by respondents to estimate consumption in epidemiological studies (cf. Greenfield & Kerr, 2008), more work is needed.

As described above, conceptualizations of addiction are likely to continue to evolve over time as research evidence accumulates, and assessment approaches must keep pace with both theoretical and empirical advances. Research is needed to develop methods of measurement that can explicate the ramifications of different patterns of consumption; tap the multi-faceted nature of the dependence construct, and, in particular, its neurobiological aspects; enhance understanding of the heterogeneity among those afflicted with SUDs; and assess individual differences in dependence liability. From a clinical perspective, methods are needed that capture the phenomenology of experiences such as craving (cf. Allen, 2003a); assist the clinician in the therapeutic process; illuminate the processes involved in recovery; assist in defining the point at which a lapse becomes a relapse (cf. Donovan, 2008); examine the role of assessment itself in behavior change; and evaluate the efficacy and effectiveness of different approaches to prevention, intervention, and treatment. Even if supplemented by measurement methods other than self-report, it seems likely that, given their ease of administration and apparent validity, new assessment tools will continue to rely also on individual verbal responses.

Thus, despite their limitations, self-report methods are likely to remain a major source of information used to aid substance-involved individuals in the recovery process and to investigate the important research questions that challenge the field. Fortunately, available evidence indicates that self-report methods produce reasonably accurate and useful data in situations that are structured to enhance the veracity of response. Additional research will further improve our understanding of the question-answering process, increase our ability to obtain valid self-reports, and, consequently, maximize the utility of our instruments.

References

Aertgeerts, B., Buntinx, F., Bande-Knops, J., Vandermeulen, C., Roelants, M., Ansoms, S., & Fevery, J. (2000). The value of CAGE, CUGE and AUDIT in screening for alcohol abuse and dependence among college freshman. *Alcoholism: Clinical and Experimental Research, 24*, 53–57.

Adamson, S. J., & Sellman, J. D., (2003). A prototype screening instrument for cannabis use disorder: The Cannabis Use Disorders Identification Test (CUDIT) in an alcohol-dependent clinical sample. *Drug and Alcohol Review, 22*, 309–315.

Allen, J. A. (2003a). Assessment of alcohol problems: An overview. In National Institute on Alcohol Abuse and Alcoholism (NIAAA), *Assessing alcohol problems: A guide for clinicians and researchers* (2nd ed., pp. 1–12). U.S. NIH Publication No. 03-3745. Washington, DC: Department of Health and Human Services.

Allen, J. A. (2003b). Measuring outcome in interventions for alcohol dependence and problem drinking: Executive summary of a conference sponsored by the National Institute on Alcohol Abuse and Alcoholism. *Alcoholism: Clinical and Experimental Research, 53*, 1657–1660.

Allen, J. P., Litten, R. Z., & Anton, R. (1992). Measures of alcohol consumption in perspective. In R. Z. Litten & J. P. Allen (Eds.), *Measuring alcohol consumption: Psychosocial and biochemical methods* (pp. 205–226). Totowa, NJ: Humana Press.

Allen, J. P., Litten, R. Z., Fertig, J. B., & Babor, T. F. (1997). A review of research on the Alcohol Use Disorders Test (AUDIT). *Alcoholism: Clinical and Experimental Research, 21*, 613–619.

American Psychiatric Association. (APA). (1952). *Diagnostic and statistical manual of mental disorders.* Washington, DC: APA.

American Psychiatric Association. (APA). (1968). *Diagnostic and statistical manual of mental disorders* (2nd ed). Washington, DC: APA.

American Psychiatric Association. (APA). (1980). *Diagnostic and statistical manual of mental disorders* (3rd ed). Washington, DC: American Psychiatric Press.

American Psychiatric Association. (APA). (1987): *Diagnostic and statistical manual of mental disorders* (3rd ed., revised). Washington, DC; American Psychiatric Press.

American Psychiatric Association. (APA). (2000). *Diagnostic and statistical manual of mental disorders* (4th ed., text revision). Washington, DC; American Psychiatric Press.

American Psychiatric Association. (APA). (2013). *Diagnostic and statistical manual of mental disorders* (5th ed.). Washington, DC; American Psychiatric Press.

Anastasi, A. (1988). *Psychological testing* (6th ed.). New York: MacMillan.

Anton, R. F., & Randall, C. L. (2005). Measurement and choice of drinking outcome variables in the COMBINE study. *Journal of Studies on Alcohol, S15,* 104–109.

Babor, T. F. (1992). Substance-related problems in the context of international classificatory systems. In M. Lader, G. Edwards, & D. C. Drummond (Eds.), *The nature of alcohol and drug related problems* (pp. 83–97). New York: Oxford University Press.

Babor, T. F. (1995). The road to DSM-IV: Confessions of an erstwhile nosologist. Commentary No. 2. *Drug and Alcohol Dependence, 38,* 75–79.

Babor, T. F. (2007). We shape our tools, and thereafter our tools shape us: Psychiatric epidemiology and the alcohol dependence syndrome concept. *Addiction, 102,* 1534–1535.

Babor, T. F. (2011). Substance, not semantics, is the issue: Comments on the proposed addiction criteria for DSM V. *Addiction, 106,* 870–872.

Babor, T. F., Brown, J., & Del Boca, F. K. (1990). Validity of self-reports in applied research on addictive behaviors: Fact or fiction? *Behavioral Assessment, 12,* 5–31.

Babor, T. F., & Del Boca, F. K. (1992). Just the facts: Enhancing measurement of alcohol consumption using self-reports methods. In R. Z. Litten & J. P. Allen (Eds.), *Measuring alcohol consumption: Psychosocial and biochemical methods* (pp. 3–19). Totowa, NJ: Humana Press.

Babor, T. F., & Del Boca, F. K. (Eds.) (2003). *Treatment matching in alcoholism.* Cambridge: Cambridge University Press.

Babor, T. F., Higgins-Biddle, J. C., Saunders, J. B., & Monteiro, M. G. (2001). *AUDIT The alcohol use disorders identification test: Guideline for use in primary care* (2nd ed.) Geneva: World Health Organization.

Babor, T. F., Longabaugh, R., Zweben, A., Fuller, R. K., Stout, R. L., Anton, R. F., et al. (1994). Issues in the definition and measurement of drinking outcomes in alcoholism treatment research. *Journal of Studies on Alcohol, S12,* 101–111.

Babor, T., McRee, B., Kassebaum, P., Grimaldi, P., Ahmed, K., & Bray, J. W. (2007). Screening, Brief Intervention, and Referral to Treatment (SBIRT): Toward a public health approach to the management of substance abuse. *Substance Abuse, 28,* 7–30.

Babor, T. F., Steinberg, K., Anton, R., & Del Boca, F. K. (2000). Talk is cheap: Measuring drinking outcomes in clinical trials. *Journal of Studies in Alcohol, 61,* 55–63.

Babor, T. F., Stephens, R. S., & Marlatt, G. A. (1987). Verbal report methods in clinical research on alcoholism: Response bias and its minimization. *Journal of Studies on Alcohol, 48,* 410–424.

Bagge, C. L., & Sher, K. J. (2008). Adolescent alcohol involvement and suicide attempts: Toward the development of a conceptual framework. *Clinical Psychology Review, 28,* 1283–1296.

Baker, A., Bucci, S., Lewin, T. J., Kay-Lambkin, F., Constable, P. M., & Carr, V. J. (2006). Cognitive-behavioural therapy for substance use disorders in people with psychotic disorders: Randomised controlled trial. *British Journal of Psychiatry, 188,* 439–448.

Bauman, K., & Ennett, S. E. (1994). Tobacco use by Black and White adolescents: The validity of self-reports. *American Journal of Public Health, 84,* 394–398.

Belli, R. F., Schwarz, N., Singer, E., & Talarico, J. (2000). Decomposition can harm the accuracy of retrospective behavioral reports. *Applied Cognitive Psychology, 14,* 295–308.

Belson, W. A. (1981). *The design and understanding of survey questions.* Aldershot, UK: Gower.

Bernstein, J., Bernstein, E., Tassiopoulos, K., Heeren, T., Levenson, S., & Hingson, R. (2005). Brief motivational intervention at a clinic visit reduces cocaine and heroin use. *Drug and Alcohol Dependence, 7,* 49–59.

Bernstein, E., Edwards, E., Dorfman, D., Heeren, T., Bliss, C., & Bernstein, J. (2009). Screening and brief intervention to reduce marijuana use among youth and young adults in a pediatric emergency department. *Academic Emergency Medicine, 16,* 1174–1185.

Bjarnason, T., & Adalbjarmnardottir, S. (2000). Anonymity and confidentiality in school surveys on alcohol, tobacco, and cannabis use. *Journal of Drug Issues, 30,* 335–343.

Blair, E., & Burton, S. (1987). Cognitive processes used by survey respondents to answer behavioral frequency questions. *Journal of Consumer Research, 14,* 280–288.

Blume, A. W., Morera, O. F., & de la Cruz, B. G. (2008). Assessment of addictive behaviors in ethnic-minority cultures. In D. M. Donovan & G. A. Marlatt (Eds.),

Assessment of addictive behaviors (2nd ed., pp. 49–70). New York: Guilford Press.

Bolton, R. N., & Bronkhorst, T. M. (1996). Questionnaire pretesting: Computer assisted coding of concurrent protocols. In N. Schwarz & S. Sudman (Eds.), *Answering questions: Methodology for determining cognitive and communicative processes in survey research*. San Francisco: Jossey-Bass.

Borkovec, T. D. (1993). Between-group therapy outcome research: Design and methodology. In L. S. Onken, J. D. Blaine, & J. J. Boren (Eds.), *Behavioral treatments for drug abuse and dependence* (pp. 249–289). NIDA Monograph No.137. Bethesda, MD: National Institute on Drug Abuse.

Bradburn, N. M. (1983). Response effects. In P. E. Rossi & J. D. Wright (Eds.), *Handbook of survey research* (pp. 289–328). New York: Academic Press.

Bradburn, N. M. (2000). Temporal representation and event dating. In A. Stone, J. S. Turkkan, C. A. Bachrach, J. B. Jobe, H. S. Kurtzman, & V. S. Cain (Eds.), *The science of self-report: Implications for research and practice* (pp. 49–62). Mahwah, NJ: Erlbaum.

Bradburn, N. M., Rips, L. J., & Shevell, S. K. (1987). Answering autobiographical questions: The impact of memory and inference on surveys. *Science, 236*, 157–161.

Bradburn, N. M., & Sudman, S. (Eds.). (1981). *Improving interview method and questionnaire design*. San Francisco: Josscy-Bass.

Bradburn, N. M., Sudman, S., & Associates. (1979). *Improving interview method and questionnaire design: Response effects to threatening questions in survey research*. San Francisco: Jossey-Bass.

Brown, J., Kranzler, H. R., & Del Boca, F. K. (1992). Self-reports of alcohol and drug abuse inpatients: Factors affecting reliability and validity. *British Journal of Addiction, 87*, 207–218.

Brown, S. A., McGue, M., Maggs, J., Schulenberg, J., Hingson, R., Swartzwelder, S., et al. (2008). A developmental perspective on alcohol and youths 16 to 20 years of age. *Pediatrics, 121*, S290–S310.

Butler, S. F., Redondo, J. P., Fernandez, K. C., & Villapiano, A. (2009). Validation of the Spanish Addiction Severity Index Multimedia Version (S-ASI-MV). *Drug and Alcohol Dependence, 1*, 18–27.

Cahalan, D., Cisin, I. H., & Crossley, H. M. (1969). *American Drinking Practices, a national study of drinking behavior and attitudes*. New Brunswick, NJ: Rutgers Center of Alcohol Studies.

Canagasaby, A., & Vinson, D. C. (2005). Screening for hazardous or harmful drinking using one or two quantity-frequency questions. *Alcohol and Alcoholism, 40*, 208–213.

Cannell, C. F., Marquis, K. H., & Laurent, A. (1977). A summary of studies of interviewing methodology. *Vital and Health Statistics, Series 2, No. 69*. DHEW Publication (HRA 77-1343), Washington, DC: Government Printing Office.

Cannell, C. F., Miller, P. V., & Oksenberg, L. (1981). Research on interviewing techniques. In J. Leinhardt (Ed.), *Sociological methodology* (pp. 389–437). San Francisco: Jossey-Bass.

Carmines, E. G., & Zeller, R. A. (1979). *Reliability and validity assessment*. Thousand Oaks, CA: Sage.

Carroll, K. M. (1995). Methodological issues and problems in assessment of substance use. *Psychological Assessment, 7*, 349–358.

Carroll, K. M. (1997). New methods of treatment efficacy research: Bridging clinical research and clinical practice. *Alcohol Health and Research World, 21*, 352–359.

Carroll, K. M., & Ball, S. A. (2008). Assessment of cocaine abuse and dependence. In D. M. Donovan & G. A. Marlatt (Eds.), *Assessment of addictive behaviors* (2nd ed., pp. 155–184). New York: Guilford Press.

Carroll, K. M., Power, M. D., Bryant, K. J., & Rounsaville, B. J. (1993). A one-year follow-up status of treatment-seeking cocaine abusers: Psychopathology and dependence severity as predictors of outcome. *Journal of Nervous and Mental Disease, 181*, 71–79.

Carroll, K. M., & Rounsaville, B. J. (2002). On beyond urine: Clinically useful instruments in the treatment of drug dependence. *Behaviour Research and Therapy, 40*, 1329–1344.

Chan, A. W., & Pristach, E. A. (1993). Use of the TWEAK test in screening for alcoholism/heavy drinking in three populations. *Alcoholism: Clinical and Experimental Research, 17*, 1188–1192.

Chassin, L., Pitts, S. C., & Prost, J. (2002). Binge drinking trajectories from adolescence to emerging adulthood in a high-risk sample: Predictors and substance use outcomes. *Journal of Consulting and Clinical Psychology, 70*, 67–78.

Cherpitel, C. J., & Ye, Y. (2008). Drug use and problem drinking associated with primary care and emergency room utilization in the U.S. general population: Data from the 2005 national alcohol survey. *Drug and Alcohol Dependence, 92*, 226–230.

Chung, T., & Martin, C. S. (2005). What were they thinking? Adolescents' interpretations of DSM-IV alcohol dependence symptom queries and implications for diagnostic validity. *Drug and Alcohol Dependence, 80*, 191–200.

Cicchetti, D. V. (1994). Guidelines, criteria, and rules of thumb for evaluating normed and standardizaed assessment instruments in psychology. *Psychological Assessment, 6*, 284–290.

Cisler, R. A., Kivlahan, D. R., Donovan, D., & Mattson, M. E. (2005). Assessing non-drinking outcomes in combined pharmacotherapy and psychotherapy clinical trials for the treatment of alcohol dependence. *Journal of Studies on Alcohol, S15*, 110–118.

Clifford, P. R., & Maisto, S. A. (2000). Subject reactivity effects in alcohol treatment outcome research. *Journal of Studies on Alcohol, 61*, 787–793.

COMBINE Study Research Group. (2003). Testing combined pharmacotherapies and behavioral interventions in alcohol dependence (The COMBINE Study): A pilot feasibility study. *Alcoholism: Clinical and Experimental Research, 27*, 1123–1131.

Connors, G. J., Allen, J. P., Cooney, N. L., DiClemente, C. C., Tonigan, J. S., & Anton, R. F. (1994). Assessment issues and strategies in alcoholism treatment matching research. *Journal of Studies on Alcohol, S12*, 92–100.

Connors, G. J., Miller, W. R., Anton, R. F., & Tonigan, J. S. (2003). Clinical assessment: Measuring matching characteristics and treatment outcomes. In T. F. Babor & F. K. Del Boca (Eds.), *Treatment matching in alcoholism* (pp. 29–41). Cambridge: Cambridge University Press.

Connors, G. J., & Volk, R. J. (2003). Self-report screening for alcohol problems among adults. In National Institute on Alcohol Abuse and Alcoholism (NIAAA), *Assessing alcohol problems: A guide for clinicians and researchers* (2nd ed., pp. 21–35). U.S. NIH Publication No. 03-3745. Washington, DC: Department of Health and Human Services.

Connors, G. J., Watson, D. W., & Maisto, S. A. (1985). The influence of subject and interviewer characteristics on the reliability of young adults' self-reports of drinking. *Journal of Psychopathology and Behavioral Assessment, 7*, 365–374.

Conrad, F. G., Brown, N. R., & Cashman, E. R. (1998). Strategies for estimating behavioral frequency in survey interviews. *Memory, 6*, 339–366.

Cooney, N. L., Kadden, R. M., & Steinberg, H. R. (2005). Assessment of alcohol problems. In D. M. Donovan & G. A. Marlatt (Eds.) *Assessment of addictive behaviors* (2nd ed., pp. 71–112). New York: Guilford.

Costello, E. J., Edelbrook, C., & Costello, A. J. (1985). Validity of the NIMH Diagnostic Interview Schedule for Children: A comparison between psychiatric and pediatric referrals. *Journal of Abnormal Child Psychology, 13*, 579–595.

Couper, M. P., & Rowe, B. (1996). Evaluation of a computer-assisted self-interview component in a computer-assisted personal interview survey. *Public Opinion Quarterly, 60*, 89–106.

Couper, M. P., Traugott, M. W., & Lamias, M. J. (2001). Web survey design and administration. *Public Opinion Quarterly, 65*, 230–253.

Dawson, D. A. (1998a). Volume of ethanol consumption: Effects of different approaches to measurement. *Journal of Studies on Alcohol, 59*, 191–197.

Dawson, D. A. (1998b). Measuring alcohol consumption: Limitations and prospects for improvement. *Addiction, 93*, 965–968.

Del Boca, F. K., Babor, T. F., & McRee, B. (1994). Reliability enhancement and estimation in multisite clinical trials. *Journal of Studies on Alcohol, S12*, 130–136.

Del Boca, F. K., & Brown, J. (1996). Reliability of self-administered questionnaires in alcohol treatment questionnaires. *Psychology of Addictive Behaviors, 10*, 7–29.

Del Boca, F. K., & Darkes, J. (2003). The validity of self-reports of alcohol consumption: State of the science and challenges for research. *Addiction; 98S2*, 1–12.

Del Boca, F. K., & Darkes, J. (2007a). Enhancing the validity and utility of randomized clinical trials in addictions treatment research: II. Participant samples and assessment. *Addiction, 102*, 1194–1203.

Del Boca, F. K., & Darkes, J. (2007b). Enhancing the validity and utility of randomized clinical trials in addictions treatment research: I. Treatment implementation and research design. *Addiction, 102*, 1047–1056.

Del Boca, F. K., & Noll, J. A. (2000). Truth or consequences: The validity of self-report data in health services research. *Addiction, 95*, S3, S347–S360.

Dennis, M. L., Scott, C. K., & Funk, R. (2003). An experimental evaluation of recovery management checkups (RMC) for people with chronic substance use disorders. *Evaluation and Program Planning, 26*, 339–352.

Dillman, D. A. (2000). *Mail and Internet surveys: The tailored design method.* New York: Wiley.

Dillman, D. A., Carley-Baxter, L. R., & Jackson, A. (1999). *Skip pattern compliance in three test forms: Theoretical and empirical evaluation* (Technical report No. 99-01). Pullman, WA, Washington State University, Social & Economic Sciences Research Center.

Dillman, D. A., Redline, C. D., & Carley-Baxter, L. R. (1999). *Influence of type of question on skip pattern compliance in self-administered questionnaires.* Paper presented at the meeting of the American Statistical Association, Baltimore, MD.

Donovan, D. M. (1988). Assessment of addictive behaviors: Implications of an emerging biopsychosocial model. In

D. M. Donovan & G. A. Marlatt (Eds.), *Assessment of addictive behaviors* (pp. 3–48). New York: Guilford Press.

Donovan, D. M. (2003). Assessments to aid in the treatment planning process. In National Institute on Alcohol Abuse and Alcoholism (NIAAA), *Assessing alcohol problems: A guide for clinicians and researchers* (2nd ed., pp. 125–188). U.S. NIH Publication No. 03-3745. Washington, DC: Department of Health and Human Services.

Donovan, D. M. (2008). Assessment of addictive behaviors for relapse prevention. In D. M. Donovan & G. A. Marlatt (Eds.), *Assessment of addictive behaviors* (2nd ed., pp. 1–48). New York: Guilford Press.

Donovan, D. M., Bigelow, G. E., Brigham, G. S., Carroll. K. M., Cohen, A. J., et al. (2012). Primary outcome indices in illicit drug dependence treatment research: Systematic approach to selection and measurement of drug use endpoints in clinical trials. *Addiction, 107*, 694–708.

Donovan, D. M., & Marlatt, G. A. (Eds.) (2005). *Assessment of addictive behaviors* (2nd ed.). New York: Guilford Press.

Donovan, D., Mattson, M. E., Cisler, R. A., Longabaugh, R., & Zweben, A. (2005). Quality of life as an outcome measure in alcoholism treatment research. *Journal of Studies on Alcohol, S15*, 119–139.

Donovan, J. (2009). Estimated blood alcohol concentrations for child and adolescent drinking and their implications for screening instruments. *Pediatrics, 123*, e975–e981.

Edwards, G. (1986). The alcohol dependence syndrome: A concept as stimulus to enquiry. *British Journal of Addiction, 81*, 171–183.

Edwards, G., & Gross, M. M. (1976). Alcohol dependence: Provisional description of a clinical syndrome. *British Medical Journal, 1*, 1058–1061.

Ehrman, R. N., & Robbins, S. J. (1994). Reliability and validity of 6-month timeline reports of cocaine and heroin use in a methadone population. *Journal of Consulting and Clinical Psychology, 62*, 843–850.

Ewing, J. A. (1984). Detecting alcoholism: The CAGE questionnaire. *Journal of the American Medical Association, 252*, 1905–1907.

Falck, R., Siegal, H. A., Forney, M. A., Wang, J., & Carlson, R. G. (1992). The validity of injection drug users self-reported use of opiates and cocaine. *Journal of Drug Issues, 22*, 8223–8232.

Featherston, F., & Moy, L. (1990). *Item nonresponse in mail surveys.* Paper presented at the International Conference of Measurement Errors in Surveys, Tucson, Arizona.

Fiedler, K., & Armbruster, T. (1994). Two halves may be more than one whole: Category split effects on frequency illusions. *Journal of Personality and Social Psychology, 66*, 633–645.

Feighner, J. P., Robins, E., Guze, S. B., Woodruff, R. A., Winokur, G., & Muinoz, R. (1972). Diagnostic criteria for psychiatric research. *Archives of General Psychiatry, 26*, 57–63.

Fendrich, M., & Vaughn, C. M. (1994). Diminished lifetime substance use over time: An inquiry into differential underreporting. *Public Opinion Quarterly, 58*, 96–123.

Finney, J. W., Moyer, A., & Swearington, C. E. (2003). Outcome variables and their assessment in alcohol treatment studies: 1968-1998. *Alcoholism: Clinical and Experimental Research, 27*, 1671–1679.

Fisher, P., Shaffer, D., Piacentini, J. C., Lapkin J., Kafantaris, V., Leonard, H., & Herzog, D. B. (1993). Sensitivity of the Diagnostic Interview Schedule for Children, 2nd edition (DISC 2.1) for specific diagnoses of children and adolescents. *Journal of the American Academy of Child and Adolescent Psychiatry, 32*, 666–673.

Fricker, R. D., & Schonlau, M. (2002). Advantages and disadvantages of internet research surveys: Evidence from the literature. *Field Methods, 14*, 347–367.

Gastfriend, D. R., Donovan, D., Lefebvre, R., & Murray, K. T. (2005). Developing a baseline assessment battery: Balancing patient time burden with essential clinical and research monitoring. *Journal of Studies on Alcohol, S15*, 94–103.

Gmel, G., Graham, K., Kuendig, H., & Kuntsche, S. (2006). Measuring alcohol consumption—should the "graduated frequency" approach become the norm in survey research? *Addiction, 101*, 16–30.

Gmel, G., Kuendig, H., Augsburger, M., Schreyer, N., & Daeppen, J. (2008). Do objective measures of blood alcohol concentrations make more sense than self-reports in emergency department studies? *Journal of Addiction Medicine, 2*, 96–102.

Gmel, G., Shield, K. D., & Rehm, J. (2013). Tools for estimating alcohol consumption. In P. Boyle (Ed.), *Alcohol: Science, policy and public health*. New York: Oxford University Press.

Gossop, M., Darke, S., Griffiths, P., Hando, J., Powis, B., Hall, W., & Strang, J. (1995). The Severity of Dependence Scale (SDS): Psychometric properties of the SDS in English and Australian samples of heroin, cocaine and amphetamine users. *Addiction, 90*, 607–614.

Grant, B. F., Harford, T. C., Dawson, D. A., Chou, P. S., & Pickering, R. (1995). The Alcohol Use Disorder and Associated Disabilities Interview Schedule (AUDADIS): Reliability of alcohol and drug modules in a general population sample. *Drug and Alcohol Dependence, 39*, 37–44.

Grant, B. F., Dawson, D. A., Stinson, F. S., Chou, P. S., Kay, W., & Pickering, R. (2003). The Alcohol Use Disorder and Associated Disabilities Interview Schedule-IV (AUDADIS-IV): Reliability of alcohol consumption, tobacco use, family history of depression and psychiatric diagnostic modules in a general population sample. *Drug and Alcohol Dependence, 71*, 7–16.

Grant, J. D., Verges, A. J., Jackson, K. M., Trull, T. J., Sher, K. J., & Bucholz, K. K. (2012). Age and ethnic differences in the onset, persistence and recurrence of alcohol use disorder. *Addiction, 107*, 756–765.

Greenfield, T. K. (2000). Ways of measuring drinking patterns and the differences they make: Experience with graduated frequencies. *Journal of Substance Abuse, 12*, 33–49.

Greenfield, T. K., & Kerr, W. C. (2008). Alcohol measurement methodology in epidemiology: Recent advances and opportunities. *Addiction, 103*, 1082–1099.

Greenfield, T. K., Kerr, W. C., Bond, J., & Ye, Y. (2009). Improving graduated frequencies alcohol measures for monitoring consumption patterns: Results from an Australian national survey and a US diary validity study. *Contemporary Drug Problems, 36*, 705.

Grice, H. P. (1975). Logic and conversation. In P. Cole & J. L. Morgan (Eds.), *Syntax and semantics: Vol. 3. Speech acts* (pp. 41–58). New York: Academic Press.

Groves, R. M., Fultz, N. H., & Martin, E. (1992). Direct questioning about comprehension in a survey setting. In J. M. Tanur (Ed.), *Questions about questions* (pp. 49–61). New York: Russell Sage.

Grubb, A. R., & Harrower, J. (2009). Understanding attribution of blame in cases of rape: An analysis of participant gender, type of rape and perceived similarity to the victim. *Journal of Sexual Aggression, 15*, 63–81.

Gunzerath, L., Faden, V., Zakhari, S., & Warren, K. (2004). National Institute on Alcohol Abuse and Alcoholism report on moderate drinking. *Alcoholism: Clinical and Experimental Research, 28*, 829–847.

Harrison, L. D. (1992). Trends in illicit drug use in the USA: Conflicting results from national surveys. *International Journal of the Addictions, 27*, 817–847.

Hasin, D., Carpenter, K. M., McCloud, S., Smith, M., & Grant, B. F. (1997). The Alcohol Use Disorder and Associated Disabilities Interview Schedule (AUDADIS): Reliability of alcohol and drug modules in a clinical sample. *Drug and Alcohol Dependence, 44*, 133–141.

Haynes, S. N., Mumma, G. H., & Pinson, C. (2009). Idiographic assessment: Conceptual and psychometric foundations of individualized behavioral assessment. *Clinical Psychology Review, 29*, 179–191.

Heather, N., Bowie, A., Ashton, H., McAvoy, B., Spencer, I., Brodie, J., et al. (2004). Randomised controlled trial of two brief interventions against long-term benzodiazepine use: Outcome of intervention. *Addiction Research and Theory 12*, 141–154.

Helzer, J. E., Badger, G. J., Rose, G. L., Mongeon, J. A., & Searles, J. S. (2002). Decline in alcohol consumption during two years of daily reporting. *Journal of Studies on Alcohol, 63*, 551–558.

Helzer, J. E., Bucholz, K. K., & Gossop, M. (2007). A dimensional option for the diagnosis of substance dependence in DSM-V. *International Journal of Methods in Psychiatric Research, 16*, S24–S33.

Hesselbrock, M., Easton, C., Bucholtz, K. K., Schuckit, M., & Hesselbrock, V. (1999). A validity study of the SSAGA—a comparison with the SCAN. *Addiction, 94*, 1361–1370.

Higgins-Biddle, J., Hungerford, D., & Cates-Wessel, K. (2009). *Screening and brief interventions for unhealthy alcohol use: A step-by-step implementation guide for trauma centers*. Atlanta, GA: Centers for Disease Control and Prevention, National Center for Injury Prevention and Control.

Hingston, R., & Compton, W.M. (2014). Screening and brief intervention and referral to treatment for drug use in primary care: Back to the drawing board. *Journal of the American Medical Association, 312*, 488–489.

Hippler, H. J., Schwarz, N., & Sudman, S. (1987). *Social information processing and survey methodology*, New York: Springer Verlag.

Hjorthoj, C., Hjorthoj, A., & Nordentoft, M. (2012). Validity of Timeline Follow-back for self-reported use of cannabis and other illicit substances—Systematic review and meta-analysis. *Addictive Behaviors, 37*, 226–230.

Horton, J., Compton, W. M., & Cottler, L. B. (1998). Assessing psychiatric disorders among drug users: Reliability of the revised DIS-IV. In L. Harris (Ed.), *NIDA Research Monograph: Problems of drug dependence*. Washington, DC: NIH. Publication No. 99-4395.

Hufford, M. R., & Shields, A. L. (2002). Electronic diaries: Applications and what works in the field. *Applied Clinical Trials, April*, 46–59.

Humeniuk, R., Ali, R., Babor, T., Souza-Formigoni, M., de Lacerda, R., Ling, W., . . . Vendetti, J. (2012). A randomized controlled trial of a brief intervention for illicit drugs linked to the Alcohol, Smoking and Substance Involvement Screening Test (ASSIST) in clients recruited from primary health-care settings in four countries. *Addiction, 107*, 957–966.

Hunsley, J., & Marsh, E. J. (2008). Developing criteria for evidence-based assessment: An introduction to assessments that work. In J. Hunsley & E. J. Mash (Eds.). *A guide to assessments that work* (pp. 1–14). New York: Oxford.

Institute of Medicine. (1990). *Broadening the base of treatment for alcohol problems.* Washington, DC: National Academies Press.

Jabine, T. B., Straf, M. L., Tanur, J. M., & Tourangeau, R. (Eds.). (1984). *Cognitive aspects of survey methodology,* New York: Springer Verlag.

JBS International, Inc., Bartlett, J., Klemanski, J., McCorry, F., & Wasner, D. (2012). *Sustaining SBIRT: Tactics for transformational change.* Rockville, MD: Report prepared for the Department of Health and Human Services, Substance Abuse and Mental Health Services Administration, Center for Substance Abuse Treatment.

Jobe, J., & Loftus, E. (Eds.). (1991). Cognitive aspects of survey methodology. *Applied Cognitive Psychology, 5*(Spec Issue).

Johnson, K. E., Sobell, M. B., & Sobell, L. C. (2010). Using one question to identify women at risk for an alcohol-exposed pregnancy. *Journal of the American Osteopathic Association, 110,* 381–384.

Johnson, T. P., Fendrich, M., Shaligram, C., Garcy, A., & Gillespie, S. (2000). An evaluation of the effects of interviewer characteristics in and RDD telephone survey of drug use. *Journal of Drug Issues, 30,* 77–102.

Kadden, R. M., & Litt, M. D. (2004). Searching for treatment outcome measures across trials. *Journal of Studies on Alcohol, 65,* 145–152.

Kanayama, G., Hudson, J. I., & Pope, H. G. (2009). Features of men with anabolic-androgenic steroid dependence: A comparison with nondependent AAS users and with AAS nonusers. *Drug and Alcohol Dependence, 102,* 130–137.

Kaskutas, L. A., & Graves, K. (2000). An alternative to standard drinks as a measure to alcohol consumption. *Journal of Substance Abuse, 12,* 1267–1278.

Kavanagh, D. J., Statham, D. J., Feeney, G. F. X., Young, R. M., May, J., et al. (2013). Measurement of craving. *Addictive Behaviors, 38,* 1572–1584.

Keane, H., Moore, D., & Fraser, S. (2011). Addiction and dependence: Making realities in the DSM. *Addiction, 106,* 875–877.

Kendell, R., & Jablensky, A. (2003). Distinguishing between the validity and utility of psychiatric diagnoses. *American Journal of Psychiatry, 160,* 4–12.

Kerr, W. C., Greenfield, T. K., Tujague, J., & Brown, S. (2005). A drink is a drink? Variation in the alcohol content of beer, wine, and spirits drinks in a U.S. methodological sample. *Alcoholism: Clinical and Experimental Research, 29,* 2015–2015.

Kilmer, J. R., Palmer, R. S., & Cronce, J. M. (2008). Assessment of club drug, hallucinogen, inhalant, and steroid use and misuse. In D. M. Donovan & G. A. Marlatt (Eds.), *Assessment of addictive behaviors* (2nd ed., pp. 274–304). New York: Guilford Press.

Klitzner, M., Schwartz, R. H., Gruenewald, P., & Blasinsky, M. (1987). Screening for risk factors for adolescent alcohol and drug use. *American Journal of Diseases of Children, 141,* 45–49.

Knight, J. R., Shrier, L. A., Bravender, T. D., Farrell, M., Vanderbilt, J., & Shaffer, H. J. (1999). A new brief screen for adolescent substance abuse. *Archives of Pediatric Adolescent Medicine, 153,* 591–596.

Kosten, T. R., Rounsaville, B. J., & Kleber, H. D. (1986). A 2.5 year follow-up of depression, life events and treatment effects on abstinence among opioid addicts. *Archives of General Psychiatry, 43,* 733–738.

Kranzler, H. R., Kadden, R. M., Babor, T. F., Tennen, H., & Rounsaville, B. J. (1996). Validity of the SCID in substance abuse patients. *Addiction, 91,* 859–868.

Kranzler, H. R., Khamis, A.-H., Tennen, H., Feinn, R., & Young, K. (2004). Using daily interactive voice response technology to measure drinking and related behaviors in a pharmacotherapy study. *Alcoholism: Clinical and Experimental Research, 28,* 1060–1064.

Krueger, R. R., & Bezdjian, S. (2009). Enhancing research and treatment of mental disorders with dimensional concepts: Toward DSM-V and ICD-11. *World Psychiatry, 8,* 3–6.

Kuendig, H., Plant, M. A., Plant, M. L., Miller, P., Kuntsche, S., & Gmel, G. (2008). Alcohol-related adverse consequences: Cross-cultural variations in attribution process among young adults. *European Journal of Public Health, 18,* 386–391.

Kuntsche, E., & Cooper, M. L. (2010). Drinking to have fun and get drunk: Motives as predictors of weekend drinking over and above usual drinking habits. *Drug and Alcohol Dependence, 110,* 259–262.

Kypri, K., Langley, J. D., Saunders, J. B., & Cashell-Smith, M. L. (2007). Assessment may conceal benefit: Findings from a randomized controlled trial for hazardous drinking. *Addiction, 102,* 62–70.

Langenbucher, J., & Merrill, J. (2001). The validity of self-reported cost events by substances abusers: Limits, liabilities, and future directions. *Evaluation Review, 25,* 184–210.

Large, M. M., Smith, G., Sara, G., Paton, M. B., Kedzior, K. K., & Nielssen, O. B. (2012). Meta-analysis of self-reported substance use compared with laboratory substance assay in general adult mental health settings. *International Journal of Methods in Psychiatric Research, 21,* 134–148.

Leigh, B. C. (2000). Using daily reports to measure drinking and drinking patterns. *Journal of Substance Abuse, 12,* 51–65.

Lemmens, P., Tan, E. S., & Knibbe, R. A. (1992). Measuring quantity and frequency of drinking in a general population survey: A comparison of five indices. *Journal of Studies on Alcohol, 53,* 476–486.

Linton, M. (1982). Transformations of memory in everyday life. In U. Neisser (Ed.), *Memory observed: Remembering in natural context* (pp. 77–91). San Francisco: Freeman.

Loftus, E. F. (1979). *Eyewitness testimony.* Cambridge, MA: Harvard University Press.

Lucey, M. R., Hill, E. M., Young, J. P., Demo-Dananberg, L., & Beresford, T. P. (1999). The influences of age and gender on blood ethanol concentrations in healthy humans. *Journal of Studies on Alcohol, 60,* 103–110.

Madras, B. K., Compton, W. M., Avula, D., Stegbauer, T., Stein, J. B., & Clark, H. W. (2008). Screening, brief intervention, referral to treatment (SBIRT) for illicit drug and alcohol use at multiple healthcare sites: Comparison at intake and 6 months later. *Drug and Alcohol Dependence. 99,* 280–295.

Magura, S., Goldsmith, D., Casriel, C., Goldstein, R. J., & Lipton, D. S. (1987). The validity of methadone clients' self-reported drug use. *International Journal of the Addictions, 22,* 727–749.

Malvin, J. H., & Moskowitz, J. M. (1983). Anonymous versus identifiable self-reports of adolescent drug attitudes, intentions, and use. *Public Opinion Quarter, 47,* 557–566.

Martin C. S., Chung, T., & Langenbucher, J. W. (2008). How should we revise diagnostic criteria for substance use disorders in DSM-V? *Journal of Abnormal Psychology, 117,* 561–575.

Martin, C. S., Pollock, K. S., Bukstein, N. K., & Lynch, K. G. (2000). Inter-rater reliability of the SCID alcohol and substance use disorders section among adolescents. *Drug and Alcohol Dependence, 59,* 173–176.

Martin, G., Copeland, J., Gates, P., & Gilmore, S. (2006). The Severity of Dependence Scale (SDS) in an adolescent population of cannabis users: Reliability, validity, and diagnostic cut-off. *Drug and Alcohol Dependence, 83,* 90–93.

McClellan, A. T., Grissom, G. R., Zanis, D., & Randall, M. (1997). Problem-service matching in addiction treatment: A prospective study of four programs. *Archives of General Psychiatry, 54,* 730–735.

McClellan, A. T., Kushner, H., Metzger, D., Peters, R., Smith, I., Grissom, G., et al. (1992). The fifth edition of the Addiction Severity Index. *Journal of Substance Abuse Treatment, 9,* 199–213.

McClellan, A. T., Luborsky, L., O'Brien, C. P., & Woody, G. E. (1980). An improved diagnostic instrument for substance abuse patients: The Addiction Severity Index. *Journal of Nervous and Mental Disease, 168,* 26–33.

McClellan, A. T., McKay, J. R., Forman, R., Cacciola, J., & Kemp, J. (2005). Reconsidering the evaluation of addiction treatment: From retrospective follow-up to concurrent recovery monitoring. *Addiction, 100,* 447–458.

Menon, G., & Yorkson, E. A. (2000). The use of memory and contextual cues in the formation of behavioral frequency judgments. In A. Stone, J. S. Turkkan, C. A. Bachrach, J. B. Jobe, H. S. Kurtzman, & V. S. Cain (2000). *The science of self-report: Implications for research and practice* (pp. 63–80). Mahwah, NJ: Erlbaum.

Mezulis, A. H., Abramson, L. Y., Hyde, J. S., & Hankin, B. L. (2004). Is there a universal positivity bias in attributions? A meta-analytic review of individual, developmental, and cultural differences in the self-serving attributional bias. *Psychological Bulletin, 130,* 711–747.

Midanik, L. (1982). The validity of self-reported alcohol consumption and alcohol problems. A literature review. *British Journal of Addiction, 77,* 357–382.

Midanik, L. (1988). Validity of self-reported alcohol use. A literature review and assessment. *British Journal of Addiction, 83,* 1019–1029.

Midanik, L. (1991). "Unstandard" ways of answering standard questions: Protocol analysis in alcohol survey research. *Drug and Alcohol Dependence, 27,* 245–252.

Midanik, L. (1994). Comparing usual quantity/frequency and graduated frequency scales to assess yearly alcohol consumption. Results from the 1990 U. S. National Alcohol Survey. *Addiction, 89,* 407–412.

Midanik, L. T., Ye, Y., Greenfield, T. K., & Kerr, W. (2013). Missed and inconsistent classification of current drinkers: Results from the 2005 U.S. National Alcohol Survey. *Addiction, 108,* 348–355.

Mieczkowski, T. (1991). The accuracy of self-reported drug use: An evaluation and analysis of new data. In R. Weisheit (Ed.), *Drugs, crime, and the criminal justice system.* Cincinnati: Anderson Publishing.

Miele, G. M., Carpenter, K. M., Cockerham, M. S., Trautman, K. D., Blaine, J., & Hasin, D. S. (2000a). Substance Dependence Severity Scale (SDSS): Reliability and validity of a clinician-administered interview for DSM IV substance use disorders. *Drug and Alcohol Dependence, 59,* 63–75.

Miele, G. M., Carpenter, K. M., Cockerham, M. S., Trautman, K. D., Blaine, J., & Hasin, D. S. (2000b). Concurrent and predictive validity of the Substance Dependence Severity Scale (SDSS). *Drug and Alcohol Dependence, 59,* 77–88.

Milby, J. B., Schumacher, J. E., & Stainback, R. D. (1997). Substance use-related disorders. In S. M. Turner and M. Hersen (Eds.), *Adult psychopathology and diagnosis* (3rd ed., pp. 159–202). New York: John Wiley.

Miller, F. G. (1997). SASSI: application and assessment for substance-related problems. *Journal of Substance Misuse, 2,* 163–166.

Miller, W. R. (1996). *Manual for Form 90: A structured assessment interview for drinking and related behaviors.* Project MATCH Monograph Series, Vol. 5, NIH Publication No. 96-4004. Bethesda, MD: National Institute on Alcohol Abuse and Alcoholism.

Miller, W. R., & Del Boca, F. K. (1994). Measurement of drinking behavior using the Form 90 family of instruments. *Journal of Studies on Alcohol, S12,* 112–118.

Miller, W. R., Gribskov, C. J., & Mortell, R. L. (1981). Effectiveness of a self-control manual for problem drinkers with and without therapist contact. *International Journal of Addiction, 16,* 1247–1254.

Miller, W. R., & Rollnick, S. (1991). Using assessment results. In W. R. Miller & S. Rollnick (Eds.), *Motivational interviewing* (pp. 89–99). New York: Guilford Press.

Miller, W. R., & Rollnick, S. (2002). *Motivational interviewing: Preparing people for change* (2nd ed.). New York: Guilford Press.

Miller, W. R., Tonigan, J. S., & Longabaugh, R. (1995). *The Drinker Inventory of Consequences (DrInC): An Instrument for Assessing Adverse Consequences of Alcohol Abuse.* Project MATCH Monograph Series, Vol. 4. DHHS Publication No. 95-3911. Rockville, MD: National Institute on Alcohol Abuse and Alcoholism.

Monti, P. M., Miranda, R., Jr., Nixon, K., Sher, K. J., Swartzwelder, H. S., Tapert, S. F., . . . Crews, F. T. (2005). Adolescence: Booze, brains, and behavior. *Alcoholism: Clinical and Experimental Research, 29,* 207–220.

Moore, A. A., Beck, J. C., Babor, T. F., Hays, R. D., & Reuben, D. B. (2002). Beyond alcoholism: Identifying older, at-risk drinkers in primary care. *Journal of Studies on Alcohol, 63,* 316–324.

Moos, R. H. (2003). Addictive disorders in context: Principles and puzzles of effective treatment and recovery. *Psychology of Addictive Behavior, 17,* 3–12.

Mugunthan, K., McGuire, T., & Glaszious, P. (2011). Minimal interventions to decrease long-term use of benzodiazepines in primary care: A systematic review and meta-analysis. *The British Journal of General Practice, 61,* 573–578.

Murray, D. M., & Perry, C. L. (1987). The measurement of substance use among adolescents: When is the "bogus pipeline" method needed? *Addictive Behaviors, 12,* 225–233.

Musalek, M. (2007). Pathological gambling: Addition or impulse disorder? *European Psychiatry, 22,* S1, S37.

Muthén, B. (2006). Should substance use disorders be considered as categorical or dimensional? *Addiction, 10,* S1, 6–16.

Muthén, L. K., & Muthén, B. O. (2007). *Mplus user's guide* (5th ed.). Los Angeles, CA: Muthén & Muthén.

Nagin, D. S. (1999). Analyzing developmental trajectories: A semiparametric, group-based approach. *Psychological Methods, 4*, 139–157.

Nathan, P. E. (1993). Can alcohol abuse and dependence be dimensionalized—and should they be? *Psychological Inquiry, 4*, 113–115.

National Institute on Alcohol Abuse and Alcoholism (NIAAA). (2003). *Assessing alcohol problems: A guide for clinicians and researchers* (2nd ed.) U.S. NIH Publication No. 03-3745. Washington, DC: Department of Health and Human Services.

Neal, D. J., Fromme, K., Del Boca, F. K., Parks, K. A., King, L. P., Pardi, A. M., Collins, R. L., ... Corbin, W. R. (2006). Capturing the moment: Innovative approaches to daily alcohol assessment. *Alcoholism: Clinical and Experimental Research, 30*, 282–291.

Neisser, U. (1986). Nested structure in autobiographical memory. In D. C. Rubin (Ed.), *Autobiographical memory* (pp. 71–88). Cambridge: Cambridge University Press.

Newman, J. C., Des Jarlais, D. C., Turner, C. F., Gribble, J., Cooley, P., & Paone, D. (2002). The differential effects of face-to-face and computer interview modes. *American Journal of Public Health, 92*, 294–297.

Nunnally, J. C., & Bernstein, I. H. (1994). *Psychometric theory* (3rd ed.). New York: McGraw-Hill.

O'Brien, C. P. (2011). Addiction and dependence in DSM-V. *Addiction, 106*, 866–867.

O'Brien, C. P., Volkow, N., & Li, T.-K. (2006). What's in a word? Addiction versus dependence in DSM-V. *American Journal of Psychiatry, 163*, 764–765.

O'Malley, S. S., Martin, D. J., Hosking, J. D., & Mason, B. J. (2005). How pilot studies improve large-scale clinical trials: Lessons learned from the COMBINE study. *Journal of Studies on Alcohol, S15*, 66–71.

Orford, J. (2008). Asking the right questions in the right way: The need for a shift in research on psychological treatments for addiction. *Addiction, 103*, 875–885.

Pearson, R. W., Ross, M., & Dawes, R. M. (1992). Personal recall and limits of retrospective questions in surveys. In J. Tanur (Ed.), *Questions about questions* (pp. 65–94). New York: Russell Sage.

Pedersen, E. R., Grow, J., Duncan, S., Neighbors, C., & Larimer, M. E. (2012). Concurrent validity of an online version of the Timeline Followback assessment. *Psychology of Addictive Behaviors, 26*, 672–677.

Poikolainen, K., & Karkkainen, P. (1983). Diary gives more accurate information about alcohol consumption than questionnaire. *Drug and Alcohol Dependence, 11*, 209–216.

Poikolainen, K., Podkeltnova, I., & Alho, H. (2002). Accuracy of quantity-frequency and graduated frequency questionnaires in measuring alcohol intake: Comparison with daily diary and commonly used laboratory markers. *Alcohol & Alcoholism, 37*, 573–576.

Pokorny, A. D., Miller, B. A., & Kaplan, H. B. (1972). The brief MAST: A shortened version of the Michigan Screening Test (MAST). *American Journal of Psychiatry, 129*, 342–345.

Pull, C. B. (2013). Too few or too many? Reactions to removing versus retaining specific personality disorders in DSM-5. *Current Opinion in Psychiatry, 26*, 73–78.

Posey, D., & Mozayan, A. (2007). The estimation of blood alcohol concentration: Widmark revisited. *Forensic Science, Medicine, and Pathology, 3*, 33–39.

Rahdert, E. (1991). *The adolescent assessment and referral manual*. DHHS Publication No. ADM-91-1735. Rockville, MD: National Institute on Drug Abuse.

Rawson, R. A., Sodano, R., & Hillhouse, M. (2008). Assessment of amphetamine use disorders. In D. M. Donovan & G. A. Marlatt (Eds.), *Assessment of addictive behaviors* (2nd ed., pp. 185–214). New York: Guilford Press.

Redline, C., Dillman, D., Smiley, R., & Carley-Baxter, L. (1999). Making the visible invisible: An experiment with skip instructions. Paper presented at the Annual Association of Public Opinion Research, St. Petersburg, FL.

Rehm, J., Baliunas, D., Borgas, G. L. G., Graham, K., Irving, H., Kehoe, T., ... Taylor, B. (2010). The relation between different dimensions of alcohol consumption and burden of disease: An overview. *Addiction, 105*, 817–843.

Rehm, J., Room, R., Graham, K., Monteiro, M., Gmel, G., & Sempos, C. (2003). The relationship of average volume of alcohol consumption and patterns of drinking to burden of disease—an overview. *Addiction, 98*, 1209–1228.

Robins, L. N., Cotler, L. B., & Babor, T. (1995). *CIDI substance abuse module*. St. Louis, MO: Washington University School of Medicine.

Robins, L. N., Cotler, L. B., Bucholz, K. K., Compton, W. M., North, C. S., & Rourke, K. M. (2000). *Diagnostic Interview Schedule for the DSM IV (DIS-IV)*. St. Louis, MO: Washington University School of Medicine.

Robins, L. N., Helzer, J. E., Croughan, J., & Radcliff, K. S. (1981). National Institute of Mental Health diagnostic interview schedule. *Archives of General Psychiatry, 38*, 381–389.

Robinson, S. M., Sobell, L. C., Sobell, M. B., & Leo, G. I. (2014). Reliability of the Timeline Followback for cocaine, cannabis, and cigarette use. *Psychology of Addictive Behaviors, 28*, 154–162.

Rohsenow, D. J. (2008). Substance use disorders. In J. Hunsley & E. J. Mash (Eds.) *A guide to assessments that work* (pp. 319–338). New York: Oxford.

Ross, S. (2008). The mentally ill substance abuser. In M. Galanter & H. D. Kleber (Eds) *American Psychiatric Publishing textbook of substance abuse treatment* (4th ed., pp. 537–554). Arlington, VA: American Psychiatric Publishing.

Rotgers, F. (2002). Clinically useful, research validated assessment of persons with alcohol problems. *Behaviour Research and Therapy, 40*, 1425–1441.

Rothwell, P. M. (2005). External validity of randomised controlled trials: "To whom do the results of this trial apply?" *Lancet, 365*, 82–93.

Russell, M. (1994). New assessment tools for risk drinking during pregnancy: T-ACE, TWEAK, and other. *Alcohol Research and Health 18*, 55–61.

Saunders, J. B. (2006). Substance dependence and non-dependence in the Diagnostic and Statistical Manual of Mental Disorders (DSM) and the International Classification of Diseases (ICD): Can an identical conceptualization be achieved? *Addiction, 101, S1*, 48–58.

Saunders, J. B., Aasland, O. G., Babor, T. F., de la Fuente, J. R., & Grant, M. (1993). Development of the Alcohol Use Disorders Identification Test (AUDIT): WHO collaborative project on early detection of persons with harmful alcohol consumption. II. *Addiction, 88*, 791–804.

Schrimsher, G. W., & Filtz, K. (2011). Assessment reactivity: Can assessment of alcohol use during research be an active treatment? *Alcoholism Treatment Quarterly, 29*, 108–115.

Schuman, H. (1966). The random probe. A technique for evaluating the validity of closed questions. *American Sociological Review, 31*, 218–222.

Schwarz, N. (1990). Assessing frequency reports of mundane behaviors: Contributions of cognitive psychology to questionnaire development. In C. Hendrick & M. S. Clark (Eds.), *Research methods in personality and social psychology (Review of Personality and Social Psychology. Vol. 11)*, (pp. 98–119). Beverly Hills: Sage Publications.

Schwarz, N. (1999). Self-report: How the questions shape the answers. *American Psychologist, 54*, 93–105.

Schwarz, N., Groves, R. M., & Schuman, H. (1998). Survey methods. In D. T. Gilbert, S. T. Fiske, & G. Lindzey (Eds.), *Handbook of social psychology* (Vol. 1, 4th ed., pp. 143–179). New York: McGraw-Hill.

Schwarz, N., & Oyserman. (2001). Asking questions about behavior: Cognition, communication, and questionnaire construction. *American Journal of Evaluation, 22*, 127–160.

Schwarz, N., & Sudman, S. (Eds.). (1992). *Context effects in social and psychological research.* New York: Springer Verlag.

Schwarz, N., & Sudman, S. (1994). *Autobiographical memory and the validity of self-reports.* New York: Springer Verlag.

Schwarz, N., & Sudman, S. (1996). *Answering questions: Methodology for determining cognitive and communicative processes in survey research.* San Francisco: Jossey-Bass.

Selzer, M. L. (1971). The Michigan Alcohol Screening Test (MAST): The quest for a new diagnostic instrument. *American Journal of Psychiatry, 127*, 1653–1658.

Selzer, M. L., Vinokur, A., & Van Rooijen, L. (1975). A self-administered Short Michigan Alcoholism Screening Test (SMAST). *Journal of Studies on Alcohol, 36*, 117–126.

Shadel, W. G., & Shiffman, S. (2008). Assessment of smoking behavior. In D. M. Donovan & G. A. Marlatt (Eds.), *Assessment of addictive behaviors* (2nd ed., pp. 113–154). New York: Guilford Press.

Shaffer, D., Fisher, P., Lucas, C. P., Dulcan, M. K., & Schwab-Stone, M. E. (2000). NIMH Diagnostic Interview Schedule for Children Version IV (NIMH DISC-IV): Description, differences from previous versions, and reliability of some common diagnoses. *Journal of the American Academy of Child & Adolescent Psychiatry, 39*, 28–38.

Shiffman, S. (2016). Ecological momentary assessment. In K. J. Sher (Ed.), *Oxford handbook of substance use and substance use disorders* (Vol. 2, pp. 466–510). New York: Oxford University Press.

Simpson, D. D. (2004). A conceptual framework for drug treatment process and outcome. *Journal of Substance Abuse Treatment, 27*, 99–121.

Skinner, H. A., & Allen, B. A. (1983). Does the computer make a difference? Computerized versus face-to-face versus self-report assessments of alcohol, drug, and tobacco use. *Journal of Consulting and Clinical Psychology, 51*, 267–275.

Slade, T., Grove, R., & Teeson, M. (2009). A taxometric study of alcohol abuse and dependence in a general population sample: Evidence of dimensional latent structure and implications for DSM-V. *Addiction, 104*, 742–751.

Slesnick, N., & Tonigan, J. S. (2004). Assessment of alcohol and other drug use by runaway youths: A test-retest study of the Form 90. *Alcoholism Treatment Quarterly, 22*, 21–34.

Smith, P. C., Schmidt, S. M., Allensworth-Davies, D., & Saitz, R. (2010). A single-question screening test for drug use in primary care. *Archives of Internal Medicine, 170*, 1155–1160.

Sobell, L. C. (1993). *Motivational interventions with problem drinkers.* Paper presented at the Sixth Meeting of the International Conference on Treatment for Addictive Behaviors, Sante Fe, NM.

Sobell, L. C., & Sobell, M. B. (1990). Self-report issues in alcohol abuse: State of the art and future directions. *Behavioral Assessment, 12*, 91–106.

Sobell, L. C., & Sobell, M. B. (1992). Timeline Followback: A technique for assessing self-reported ethanol consumption. In J. Allen & R. Z. Litten (Eds.), *Measuring alcohol consumption: Psychosocial and biological methods* (pp. 41–72). Totowa, NJ: Humana Press.

Sobell, L. C., & Sobell, M. B. (1995a). *Alcohol Timeline Followback users' manual.* Toronto: Addiction Research Foundation.

Sobell, L. C., & Sobell, M. B. (1995b). *Alcohol Timeline Followback computer software,* Toronto: Addiction Research Foundation.

Sobell, L. C., & Sobell, M. B. (1995c). Alcohol consumption measures. J. P. Allen & M. Columbus (Eds.) *Assessing alcohol problems: A guide for clinicians and researchers* (pp. 55–73). Bethesda, MD: National Institute on Alcohol Abuse and Alcoholism.

Sobell, L. C., & Sobell, M. B. (2000). Alcohol Timeline Followback (TLFB). *Handbook of psychiatric measures* (pp. 477–479). Washington, DC: American Psychiatric Association.

Sobell, L. C., & Sobell, M. B. (2003). Alcohol consumption measures. In National Institute on Alcohol Abuse and Alcoholism (NIAAA), *Assessing alcohol problems: A guide for clinicians and researchers* (2nd ed., pp. 75–99). U.S. NIH Publication No. 03-3745. Washington, DC: Department of Health and Human Services.

Sobell, L. C., Sobell, M. B., Connors, G. J., & Agrawal, S. (2003). Assessing drinking outcomes in alcohol treatment efficacy studies: A yardstick of success. *Alcoholism: Clinical and Experimental Research, 27*, 1661–1666.

Sobell, M. B., Sobell, L. C., Klajner, F., Pavan, D., & Basian, E. (1986). The reliability of a timeline method for assessing normal drinker college students' recent drinking history: Utility for alcohol research. *Addictive Behavior, 11*, 149–162.

Sobell, L. C., Sobell. M. B., Leo, G. I., & Cancilla, A. (1988). Reliability of a timeline method: Assessing normal drinkers' reports of recent drinking and a comparative evaluation across several populations. *British Journal of Addiction, 83*, 393–402.

Sobell, M. B., Sobell, L. C., & VanderSpek, R. (1979). Relationships between clinical judgment, self-report and breath analysis measures of intoxication. *Journal of Consulting and Clinical Psychology, 47*, 204–206.

Sobell, L. C., Toneatto, T., & Sobell, M. B. (1994). Behavioral assessment and treatment planning for alcohol, tobacco, and other drug problems—Current status with an emphasis on clinical applications. *Behavior Therapist, 25*, 533–580.

Spitzer, R. L., Endicott, J., & Robins, E. (1978). Research diagnostic criteria: rationale and reliability. *Archives of General Psychiatry, 35*, 773–782.

Stephens, R. S., & Roffman, R. A. (2008). Assessment of cannabis uses disorders. In D. M. Donovan & G. A. Marlatt (Eds.), *Assessment of addictive behaviors* (2nd ed., pp. 248–273). New York: Guilford Press.

Stephens, R. S., Roffman, R. A., Fearer, S. A., Williams, C., & Burke, R. S. (2007). The marijuana check-up: Promoting change in ambivalent marijuana users. *Addiction, 102*, 947–957.

Strack, F., & Martin, L. (1987). Thinking, judging, and communicating: A process account of context effects in attitude surveys. In H. J. Hippler, N. Schwarz, & S. Sudman (Eds.), *Social information processing and survey methodology* (pp. 123–148). New York: Springer Verlag.

Stewart, S. H., & Connors, G. J. (2004/2005). Screening for alcohol problems: What makes a test effective? *Alcohol Research and Health, 28,* 5–16.

Stone, A. A., Turkkan, J. S., Bachrach, C. A., Jobe, J. B., Kurtzman, H. S., & Cain, V. S. (2000). *The science of self-report: Implications for research and practice,* Mahwah, NJ: Erlbaum.

Stout, R. L. (2003). Methodological and statistical considerations in measuring alcohol treatment effects. *Alcoholism: Clinical and Experimental Research, 27,* 1686–1691.

Substance Abuse and Mental Health Services Administration (SAMHSA). (2010). *Results from the 2009 National Survey on Drug Use and Health: Mental Health Findings.* NSDUH Series H-39, No. SMA 10-4609. Rockville, MD: Department of Health and Human Services.

Substance Abuse and Mental Health Services Administration (SAMHSA). (2013). *Systems-level implementation of screening, brief intervention, and referral to treatment.* Technical Assistance Publication (TAP) Series 33. Publication No. SMA 13-4741. Rockville, MD: Department of Health and Human Services.

Sudman, S., Bradburn, N. M., & Schwarz, N. (1996). *Thinking about answers: The application of cognitive processes to survey methodology,* San Francisco: Jossey-Bass.

Sudman, S., & Schwarz, N. (1989). Contributions of cognitive psychology to advertising research. *Journal of Advertising Research, 29,* 43–53.

Tanur, J. M. (Ed.). (1992). *Questions about questions,* New York: Russell Sage.

Tarter, R. E. (1990). Evaluation and treatment of adolescent substance abuse: A decision tree model. *American Journal of Drug and Alcohl Abuse, 16,* 1–46.

The Joint Commission (TJC). (2013). *Standards for behavioral health care.* Oakbrook Terrance, IL: Joint Commission Resources.

Tiffany, S. T., Friedman, L. Greenfield, S. F., Hasin, D. S., & Jackson, R. (2012). Beyond drug use: A systematic consideration of other outcomes in evaluations of treatment for substance use disorders. *Addiction, 107,* 709–718.

Tonigan, J. S. (2003). In National Institute on Alcohol Abuse and Alcoholism (NIAAA), *Assessing alcohol problems: A guide for clinicians and researchers* (2nd ed., pp. 1–12). U.S. NIH Publication No. 03-3745. Washington, DC: Department of Health and Human Services.

Tonigan, J. S., & Miller, W. R. (2002). The Inventory of Drug Use Consequences (InDUC): Test-retest stability and sensitivity to change. *Psychology of Addictive Behaviors, 16,* 165–168.

Tonigan, J. S., Miller, W. R., & Brown, J. M. (1997). The reliability of Form 90: An instrument for assessing alcohol treatment outcome. *Journal of Studies on Alcohol, 58,* 358–364.

Tourangeau, R. (1984). Cognitive science and survey methods: A cognitive perspective. In T. B. Jabine, M. L. Straf, J. M Tanur, & R. Tourangeau (Eds.), *Cognitive aspects of survey methodology* (pp. 25–50). New York: Springer Verlag.

Tourangeau, R. (2000). Remembering what happened: memory errors and survey reports. In A. Stone, J. S. Turkkan, C. A. Bachrach, J. B. Jobe, H. S. Kurtzman, & V. S. Cain (2000).

The science of self-report: Implications for research and practice (pp. 29–48). Mahwah, NJ: Erlbaum.

Tourangeau, R., Rips, L. J., & Rasinski, K. A. (2000). *The psychology of survey response.* Cambridge: Cambridge University Press.

Tucker, J. A., & Roth, D. L. (2006). Extending the evidence hierarchy to enhance evidence-based practice for substance use disorders. *Addiction, 101,* 918–932.

Van den Brink, W., Montgomery, S. A., Van Ree, J. M., & van Zwieten-Boot, B. J., on behalf of the Consensus Committee. (2006). ECNP Consensus Meeting March 2003: Guidelines for the investigation of efficacy in substance use disorders. *European Neuropsychopharmacology. 16,* 224–230.

Vinson, D. C., Galliher, J. M., Reidinger, C., & Kappus, J. A. (2004). Comfortably engaging: Which approach to alcohol screening should we use? *Annals of Family Medicine, 2,* 398–404.

Volk, R. J., Steinbauer, J. R., Cantor, S. B., & Holzer, C. E. (1997). The Alcohol Use Disorders Identification Test (AUDIT) as a screen for at-risk drinking in primary care patients of different ethnic/racial backgrounds. *Addiction, 92,* 197–206.

Voluse, A. C., Giola, C. J., Sobell, L. C., Dum, M., Sobell, M. B., & Simco, E. R. (2012). Psychometric properties of the Drug Use Disorders Identification Test (DUDIT) with substance abusers in outpatient and residential treatment. *Addictive Behaviors, 37,* 36–41.

Wakefield, J. C. (2013). DSM-5: An overview of changes and controversies. *Clinical Social Work Journal, 41,* 139–154.

Weinberger, A. H., Darkes, J., Del Boca, F. K., & Goldman, M. S. (2006). Items as context: The effect of item order on factor structure and predictive validity. *Basic and Applied Social Psychology, 28,* 17–26.

Weisner, C., Kaskutas, L. A., Hilton, M. E., & Barile, A. L. (1999). "When you were drinking" vs. "in the past 12 months": the impact of using different time frames in clinical and general populations. *Addiction, 94,* 731–736.

Werch, C. E. (1990). Two procedures to reduce response bias in reports of alcohol consumption. *Journal of Studies on Alcohol, 51,* 327–330.

Westerberg, V. S., Tonigan, J. S., & Miller, W. R. (1998). Reliability of the Form 90D: An instrument for quantifying drug use. *Substance Abuse, 19,* 179–189.

Westfall, J., Wasserman, D. A., Masson, C. L., & Sorensen, J. L. (2008). Assessment of opioid use. In D. M. Donovan & G. A. Marlatt (Eds.), *Assessment of addictive behaviors* (2nd ed., pp. 215–247). New York: Guilford Press.

Williams, R., & Vinson, D. (2005). Validation of a single screening question for problem drinking. *The Journal of Family Practice, 50,* 307–312.

Willis, G., Royson, P., & Bercini, D. (1991). The use of verbal report methods in the development and testing of survey questions. *Applied Cognitive Psychology, 5,* 251–267.

Winters, K. C. (1990). *Manual for the Personal Experience Screening Questionnaire.* Los Angeles, CA: Western Psychological Services.

Winters, K. C. (2003). *Assessment of alcohol and other drug use behaviors among adolescents.* NIH Publication No. 03-3745. Bethesda, MD: NIH.

Winters, K. C., & Fahnhorst, T. (2005). Assessment issues in adolescent drug abuse treatment research. In M. Galanter, C. Lowman, G. M. Boyd, V. B. Faden, E. Witt, & D. Lagressa

(Eds.), *Recent developments in alcoholism: Alcohol problems in adolescents and young adults.* New York: Springer.

Winters, K. C., & Henly, G. A. (1989). *Personal Experiences Inventory and Manual.* Los Angeles: Western Psychiatric Services.

Winters, K. C., & Henly, G. A. (1993). *Adolescent Diagnostic Interview Schedule and Manual.* Los Angeles: Western Psychological Services.

Winters, K. C., & Kaminer, Y. (2008). Screening and assessing adolescent substance use disorders in clinical populations. *Journal of the American Academy of Child and Adolescent Psychiatry, 47,* 740–744.

Winters, K. C., Latimer, W. W., Stinchfield, R. D., & Henly, G. A. (1999). Examining psychosocial correlates of drug involvement among drug clinic-referred youth. *Journal of Child and Adolescent Substance Abuse, 9,* 1–17.

Wish, E. D., Hoffman, J. A., & Nemes, S. (1997). The validity of self-reports of drug use at treatment admission and at follow-up: Comparisons with urinalysis and hair assays. In L. Harrison & A. Hughes (Eds.), *The Validity of self-reported drug use: Improving the accuracy of survey estimates* pp. 200–226. NIDA Research Monograph No. 167. Rockville, MD: National Institute on Drug Abuse.

WHO ASSIST Working Group. (2002). The Alcohol, Smoking and Substance Involvement Screening Test (ASSIST): Development, reliability and feasibility. *Addiction. 97,* 1183–1194.

WHO Technical Report Series 944. (2007). *WHO Expert Committee on Problems Related to Alchol Consumption, Second Report.* Geneva, Switzerland: World Health Organization.

World Health Organization (WHO). (1992). *The International Statistical Classification of Diseases and related health problems (10th revision).* Geneva: World Health Organization.

World Health Organization (WHO). (2000). *International guide for monitoring alcohol consumption and related harm.* Copenhagen: World Health Organization, Department of Mental Health and Substance Dependence, Noncommunicable Diseases and Mental Health Cluster.

Yoshino, A., & Kato, M. (1995). Influence of social desirability response set for assessing the outcome of treated alcoholics. *American Journal of Community Psychology, 25,* 887–891.

Young, D. W., Farrell, J. L., Henderson, C. E., & Taxman, F. S. (2009). Filling service gaps: Providing intensive treatment services for offenders. *Drug and Alcohol Dependence, 103S,* S33–S42.

Zweben, A., & Cisler, R. (1996). Composite outcome measures in alcoholism treatment research: Problems and potentialities. *Substance Use and Misuse; 31,* 1783–1805.

Zweben, A., & Cisler, R. A. (2003). Clinical and methodological utility of a composite outcome measure for alcohol treatment research. *Alcoholism: Clinical and experimental research, 27,* 1680–1685.

Ecological Momentary Assessment

Saul Shiffman

Abstract

Ecological momentary assessment (EMA) is a method for collecting data in real time and in real-world settings in order to avoid retrospective biases, collect ecologically valid data, and study behavioral processes over time. EMA is particularly suited for studying substance use because use is episodic and related to contextual factors like mood, setting, and cues. This chapter addresses the application of EMA to substance use research, describing important elements of EMA design and analysis and illustrating them with examples from substance use research. It discusses and reviews data on methodological issues such as compliance and reactivity and covers considerations in designing EMA studies of substance use. Data on the associations between EMA data on substance use and more traditional self-report data are reviewed. EMA methods reveal substance use patterns not captured by questionnaires or retrospective data and hold promise for substance use research and treatment.

Key Words: ecological momentary assessment, diary methods, ecological validity, assessment, self-monitoring, substance use, relapse, electronic diary, reactivity, compliance

Valid measurement is central to any field of research and treatment, and substance use is no exception. Researchers and clinicians who study or treat substance use and abuse must rely on accurate measures of substance use itself, as well as on the antecedents and drivers of substance use and the symptoms that may emerge as a consequence. Almost universally, these are assessed by self-report: we ask substance users to tell us how much and how often they used drugs, what contexts they used them in, how stressed they were before or after use, and so on. This inquiry usually takes place in research labs and clinics—that is, in settings far removed from the substance use itself. Thus, assessment of substance use largely consists of users telling us about then-and-there. But such reports are subject to many biases due to recall and context, and there are advantages to be gained by instead understanding substance use from users' reports in the here-and-now. Collection of such real-time, real-world data is the province of *ecological momentary*

assessment (EMA; Shiffman, 2007; Shiffman, Stone, & Hufford, 2008; Stone & Shiffman, 1994), a group of data-collection methods that seems particularly suitable for studies of substance use and abuse. The application of EMA methods to studies of substance use is the focus of this chapter.

The chapter begins by describing EMA methods and the rationale for their adoption. To illustrate EMA substance use research concretely, the description begins with a couple of examples from the author's research on smoking. The chapter then proceeds to discuss core principles of EMA methods. After considering the historical roots and antecedents of EMA, the chapter proceeds to a discussion of the limitations of autobiographical memory because this provides one key rationale for EMA's focus on momentary assessment. The next section discusses why EMA methods may be particularly suitable for studying substance use. With this as background, the chapter reviews a range of EMA designs, using studies of substance use to illustrate each. The review is not focused on substantive findings, but rather on using the studies to illustrate diverse approaches to EMA research on substance use. This is followed by discussion of methodological issues and concerns, some of which are particular to research on substance use. After reviewing empirical comparisons between EMA data and data from other sources, the chapter discusses some of the practical issues in carrying out EMA studies and touches on statistical analysis of EMA data. Although the chapter is primarily concerned with the use of EMA methods for collection of research data, a brief section addresses the potential use of EMA methods in clinical assessment and treatment.

Ecological Momentary Assessment Principles

EMA methods are designed to help substance use researchers get ecologically valid data about behavior, thoughts, and feelings over time while avoiding the pitfalls of retrospective recall. Thus, EMA studies consist of repeated assessments of subjects' real-time states, in subjects' real-world natural environments. Before elaborating these points in the abstract, it will be helpful to begin with examples from the author's own work to concretely illustrate the use of EMA in substance use research.

Examples of Ecological Momentary Assessment Substance Use Research

SITUATIONAL ANTECEDENTS OF SMOKING

Although primarily motivated by the need for regular nicotine self-administration (US Department of Health and Human Services [USDHHS], 1988), smoking is thought to also be influenced by the smoker's situation and state. For example, laboratory studies suggest that smoking cues, such as the sight of another smoker, can trigger craving and smoking (Carter & Tiffany, 2001). The role of affective distress in promoting smoking is thought to be particularly important (Kassel, Stroud, & Paronis, 2003). Indeed, on questionnaires, most smokers say they smoke when stressed and to relieve distress (Shiffman, 1993). Thus, understanding the situational correlates of smoking can shed light on how smoking is cued and perpetuated.

To gain insight into smoking occasions, we (Shiffman, 2009; Shiffman et al., 2002) asked smokers to monitor their smoking for 2 weeks while they went about the business of their daily lives. Smokers were given an electronic diary (ED)—a palmtop computer programmed to perform the requisite functions—and were instructed to record each cigarette they smoked. The ED assessed the context of

smoking by administering questions about the setting (where subjects were, what they were doing, whom they were with, whether anyone was smoking) and about their subjective state (mood, craving). Over the course of 2 weeks, the average subject recorded 303 cigarettes and reported the details of a subset of these smoking occasions (about five occasions per day were selected for assessment). These data described the characteristics of smoking settings. To put these in the context of the smoker's overall experience (more on this later), the ED also "beeped" the smokers at random nonsmoking moments throughout the day, about five times a day, at which time it administered the same assessment of setting and subjective state. Thus, over the course of a day, as they went about their lives, smokers completed 10 assessments: on five smoking and five nonsmoking occasions. Briefly, analyses contrasting the two contexts showed that particular situational characteristics were, indeed, associated with smoking. For example, smoking was more likely after meals and when the smoker was with others who were smoking. Contrary to the global retrospective reports of smokers, though, there was no relationship between negative affect and smoking—affect was similar in smoking and nonsmoking situations. These findings, since replicated in similar studies (Carter et al., 2008; Shiffman, Paty, Gwaltney, & Dang, 2004), confirmed the findings of laboratory research on smoking cues while also suggesting that smokers' reports of the link between smoking and mood might be invalid.

THE ROLE OF SELF-EFFICACY IN LAPSES AND PROGRESSION TO RELAPSE

Both theory (Bandura, 1977) and research (Gwaltney, Metrik, Kahler, & Shiffman, 2009) have implicated abstinence self-efficacy (ASE)—the belief that one is capable of succeeding in the task of quitting—in the success of smokers' quit efforts. ASE has generally been assessed statically—usually just once at the outset of a quit effort—even though theory suggests that ASE is likely to be modified by ongoing experience (e.g., Marlatt & Gordon, 1985).

To better understand the role of ASE in the processes leading up to initial lapses and in the processes that drive progression from an initial lapse toward relapse, we (Shiffman, Balabanis et al., 2000) used EMA methods to track dynamic changes in ASE. Smokers who had achieved abstinence carried an ED as they tried to maintain abstinence. Their ASE was assessed five times per day, at randomly selected times, and aggregated to estimate an average ASE for each day. Subjects who lapsed also used ED to record any smoking. Following a lapse, analysis found that today's smoking affected tomorrow's ASE. But even after accounting for smoking, a time-to-event or survival analysis showed that variations in today's ASE affected the risk of relapsing tomorrow. This suggested a reciprocal process in which smoking decreased ASE and increased smoking in a downward spiral toward relapse. These analyses confirmed the importance of ASE in the relapse process but suggested that the dynamics of ASE were most important after a lapse as the smoker struggles to avoid the downhill slide toward relapse.

Ecological Momentary Assessment in Summary

These studies illustrate, in particular applications, some core features of EMA methods:

• Data are collected in subjects' real-world environments, as subjects go about their lives. This is the "ecological" aspect of EMA. By collecting data in real-world settings, EMA takes advantage of naturally occuring variations in experience and exposures and ensures the generalizability of the findings to the subjects' real lives (i.e., ecological validity).

• Assessments focus on subjects' *current* state and situation; for example, self-reports ask about current affect, rather than asking for recall or summary over long periods. This is the "momentary" aspect of EMA, and it aims to avoid the error and bias associated with retrospection.

• Moments are strategically selected for assessment, for example, based on particular features or events of interest (e.g., occasions when subjects smoked) or by random sampling (to achieve representative sampling of subjects' experiences).

• Subjects complete multiple assessments over time, providing a picture of how their experiences and behaviors vary over time and across situations.

• The repeated series of EMA assessments allow the analysis to focus on within-subject variability over time and context, whether contasting different kinds of settings (e.g., smoking vs. nonsmoking), analyzing the trajectory of experience over time (e.g., day-to-day changes in ASE), or analyzing the relationship beween different variables over time (e.g., relationship between smoking and ASE).

It is important to emphasize that EMA is not a single research method or technology; it encompasses a range of methods. The particular design, assessment schedule, assessment content, and technology will vary across studies depending on the goals of the research. What EMA studies have in common is the collection of assessments of subjects' current or recent states, sampled repeatedly over time, in their natural environments.

MOMENTARY, REAL-TIME ASSESSMENT

Perhaps the most unique characteristic of EMA methods is their focus on capturing data close to the moment of experience. This focus on the moment derives from an awareness of the limitations of retrospective recall, as discussed later. Modern research on autobiographical memory (our memories of our own experience) shows that memory can be quite unreliable (Bradburn, Rips, & Shevell, 1987, Tourangeau, 2000). Importantly, recall is not just inaccurate. Introducing inaccuracy would be serious enough, but this would only introduce "noise"— random error that would undermine study power but could be overcome by collecting more data. Worse, recall is often systematically biased. That is, the errors made in recalling information change the data in systematic ways that can lead to erroneous conclusions.

REAL-WORLD DATA

Substance use often occurs in particular settings and contexts—critically, outside the research environment. Therefore, if one is interested in substance use, it is best assessed in real-world settings. We often do not know what aspects of the social, physical, and subjective environment are important, so we cannot really model them in the lab. We must go where they are found—in subjects' natural environments. Stated more simply, EMA emphasizes ecologically valid observations. EMA does not rely on analogue representations of the environment in the lab or on subjects' recollection of their behavior, nor on their generalizations about their behavior, but actually collects its data in real-world, real-life settings. The aim is that observations will then be generalizable to real-world substance use, enabling researchers to assess the linkages between substance use and the events, environments, and internal states subjects actually experience.

REPEATED ASSESSMENT

EMA methods are typically deployed when the behavior of interest is dynamic (i.e., varies over time). (One could assess height by EMA, but it would not be a good use of the method.) If the target of assessment varies over time, and if we are assessing it in a momentary way, it follows that we must assess it repeatedly in order to capture these variations. The frequency and duration of assessment varies widely, from 65 assessments per day for 2 days (Shapiro, Jamner, Davtdov, & James, 2002), to daily for as long as a year (Jamison et al., 2001), but EMA studies almost always include repeated assessments over time. EMA studies typically use the temporal resolution afforded by multiple measures to focus on the within-subject changes in behavior and experience over time and across contexts, addressing how symptoms vary over time or how behavior is influenced by situational antecedents.

In summary, EMA aims to assess the ebb and flow of experience and behavior over time, capturing life as it is lived, moment to moment, hour to hour, day to day, as a way of faithfully characterizing individuals and of capturing the dynamics of experience and behavior over time and across settings.

Ecological Momentary Assessment Scope and History

EMA is sometimes mistakenly associated narrowly with particular designs, such as the use of randomly scheduled prompts to collect assessments, or with certain technologies, such as the use of palmtop computers or mobile phones. However, EMA encompasses a broad range of particular methods that share the characteristics just described. It encompasses data collected using paper-and-pencil diaries or palmtop computers, with prompting by the clock, by a beeper, a programmed watch, or a palmtop computer, and with data collected by self-report, by devices for physiological monitoring, or by other instruments and devices. The methods are united by their common methodological and conceptual underpinnings, not by technology or design.

EMA aims to encompass and unify a variety of historical traditions that share common—but often unarticulated—foundations and assumptions. This includes diary methodology (Verbrugge, 1980), social interaction records (Reis & Wheeler, 1991), self-monitoring methods (McFall, 1977), experience sampling methods (DeVries, 1992; Hektner, Schmidt, & Csikszentmihalyi, 2007), ambulatory physiological monitoring (e.g., Kamarck et al., 1998), and a broad array of monitoring approaches enabled by the recent development of sophisticated electronic sensors (Intille, 2007). The object of EMA is to attempt to encompass all of these and unify them under a common methodological framework.

Autobiographical Memory and Limitations of Recall

A major factor in motivating the use of EMA methods is recognition of the limitations of autobiographical memory (Hammersley, 1994). Although it is natural for all of us to trust our own memories and regard them as a faithful playback of events, modern cognitive research on memory suggests that memory is better regarded as reconstruction than simple retrieval. Much of the information we and researchers are looking for is not explicitly encoded in memory and, if it is, is very difficult to retrieve. We do not store and remember things so that they can later serve the research investigator. Whether particular experiences are attended to and stored depends substantially on their salience and on their links to other events in a web of memory. Experiences are particularly likely to be encoded and retrieved if they are emotionally salient or unique; routine experience (such as ongoing substance use!) is less likely to be encoded and harder to retrieve.

A key implication of the modern view of autobiographical memory is that the faults in recall do not just introduce random error, but actually bias the contents of the recalled data. This is largely a consequence of the shortcuts or "heuristics" our memory system uses to reconstruct "memory." It is important to keep in mind that these cognitive processes are unconscious and involuntary. Particularly in the substance use field, we are often concerned with subjects' deliberate and motivated distortions. But these distortions are neither; they occur even among well-meaning subjects trying to be accurate and believing that they are. (Subjective estimates of accuracy and certainty correlate poorly with actual accuracy, e.g., Harsch & Neisser, 1989; Shiffman, Hufford et al., 1997.) Although review of autobiographical memory is beyond the scope of this chapter, a few key points are worth emphasis.

• The operation of heuristics generally gives information that is most easily retrieved. So, for example, salient events (e.g., extreme affect) color recall of entire periods and estimates of event frequency (Tversky & Kahneman, 1974). Recent events or experiences also exercise disproportionate influence. This has the potential to introduce very significant bias.
• It is not just distant recall that is biased; biases in recall can appear very quickly. In studies by Redelmeier (Redelmeier, Katz, & Kahneman, 2003), recall of pain was substantially distorted

by undue influence of the most extreme and most recent pain only 20 minutes after the experience.

• The potential for bias is further multiplied when subjects are asked to summarize or aggregate their experiences, which is typically what questionnaires demand ("How often do you use cocaine?" "How depressed do you typically feel 2 hours after using?"). Subjects do not respond to these queries by recalling and summarizing specifically recalled experiences but rather by drawing on heuristics to estimate an answer.

• What we "recall" is heavily influenced by what we believe. We unconsciously reorganize our "memories" to make them fit a coherent script or theory of events or to reconcile past events with subsequent developments (Ross, 1989). These biases are particularly troubling because they tend to produce coherent and systematic accounts of the past that tend to confirm the investigator's theories, which are often consistent with subjects' theories (e.g., that people use drugs when emotionally distressed).

• One of the most profound biases is due to the fact that what is recalled is influenced by the subject's psychological state at the time of recall—for example, how much pain someone is in biases their recall of past pain (Eich, Reeves, Jaeger, & Graff-Radford, 1985), and subjects in negative moods tend to retrieve negatively valenced content (Kihlstrom, Eich, Sandbrand, & Tobias, 2000). State-dependent memory is an example of this (Lowe, 1982; Peters & McGee, 1982).

This last point has profound implications for data collection because it implies that *what* is reported is dependent on *when* it is reported. So, collecting data in the investigator's research setting, which is quite unrepresentative, sets up potential for bias. But so also does collecting field data at unrepresentative times: for example, having subjects complete daily diaries at the end of the day, when subjects are typically relaxed and at rest, may bias their recall of tension and arousal. Similarly, allowing subjects to select when they provide reports may introduce bias because they may select unrepresentative times (e.g., when stress or substance use reminds them to report, or when the absence of stress makes it easy to report). This further motivates EMA's focus on collecting data close to the point of experience and emphasizes the importance of sampling a representative sample of moments for assessment.

Ecological Momentary Assessment Designs and Approaches

Conducting an EMA study requires consideration of the EMA design—that is, how the EMA data are to be collected and, in particular, how assessments are distributed over time. (See discussion of temporal design in a broader context in Collins & Graham, 2002.) The time of assessment is often not considered crucial when investigators believe they are getting a global view of a subject's behavior (e.g., by global questionnaires). However, because EMA is based on sampling subjects' behavior over time and recognizes that subjects' states at the time of reporting can influence the data, it becomes crucial to consider the timing of assessments.

Roughly, one can think of EMA assessment and sampling schemes in two classes: event-based sampling and time-based sampling (Wheeler & Reis, 1991). Event-based schemes do not aim to characterize subjects' entire experience but rather to focus on particular discrete events or episodes in subjects' lives—for example, episodes of substance use—and organize the data collection around these events. Time-based sampling typically aims to characterize experience more broadly and inclusively—for example, observing how mood varies over time—without a predefined focus on discrete events.

Table 16.1 outlines some of the decisions EMA investigators must make in designing a protocol, discussing each issue, and providing published examples illustrating such decisions and designs.

Event-Based Monitoring

Event-based sampling is particularly important for studies of substance use because substance use itself is often an event (usually *the* event) of interest. In event-based monitoring, subjects are asked to make a recording and/or complete an assessment each time the target event occurs. Obviously, this requires that the event be well-defined and that subjects be in a position to detect when it occurs. Events may be very simple and objective—any smoking, consuming five or more drinks in a day—or they may be complex or subjective—drinking "to intoxication" or experiencing "a strong temptation" to use opiates. Event-based monitoring relies on the subject to initiate a recording (except in rare cases where an instrument can detect an event). This requires cooperation, and compliance with this instruction can be hard to verify, as discussed subsequently. For some research questions, just having a record of the events may suffice: one may be interested in how many events there have been (e.g.,

Table 16.1. Design Decisions in Ecological Momentary Assessment Design

Decision/issue	Explanation	Considerations	Citations to examples, where available
Event recording			
Defining event	What constitutes an event?	If subject-initiated, must be unambiguous definition, understood by subject; may require training. Subjective definitions (e.g., "intense craving") most difficult, and subject to variations across subjects and time. Some "events" (e.g., "relapse") may be defined after-the-fact for analysis.	Collins et al. (1998), Shiffman, Paty et al. (1996)
Timing of recording	Is recording to be made at initiation or termination of the event?	Recording at initiation may enhance reactivity. Recording at termination may be influenced by the event itself (e.g., effects of substance use), but is also able to capture more information about the event	Collins et al. (1998), Shiffman, Paty et al. (1996), Shiffman et al. (2002)
Assessment	Is an assessment administered at event entries?	May just need to record that event occurred, without collecting additional data, which adds to burden and may increase reactivity	Shiffman et al. (2009)
Universal assessment	Are all events assessed?	If events are frequent, assessing all events may be too burdensome	Shiffman et al. (2002); Tidey et al. (2008)
Assessment frequency	If not, what proportion or number of events are assessed?	May aim for a certain number or certain proportion. May be important to equalize assessment burden across subjects differing in event frequency	Shiffman & Paty (2006)
Event sampling	How are events selected for assessment?	Random selection minimizes bias. May select events based on theoretical importance (e.g., *first* drink)	Shiffman & Paty (2006); Tidey et al. (2008)
How triggered	If event is detected automatically, how will subject be prompted to record?	For assessment of events detected automatically (e.g., exercise, via actigraphy), must have method of prompting subject for assessment	?

(continued)

Table 16.1. Continued

Decision/issue	Explanation	Considerations	Citations to examples, where available
Confessional assessment	Can subjects report after-the-fact on events not recorded in real time?	Gathering such data allows for more accurate event counting and numbering, but subjects may get the impression that retrospective reporting is acceptable	Shiffman, Paty et al. (1996)
Time-based recording			
Frequency	How often will assessments be scheduled?	Frequency should be determined by expected rate of relevant change, but must be balanced with subject burden.	Delfino et al. (2001); Shiffman & Waters (2004)
Scheduling	How will assessments be scheduled?	Schedule should be determined by theoretical considerations and by plans for analysis.	
Fixed/random	Will assessments be scheduled at fixed intervals? Random intervals? Other schedule?	Random schedules minimize bias. Fixed schedules can be anticipated, which may lead to reactivity.	Kamarck et al. (1998); Shiffman et al. (2002)
Precision	How precisely is the timing of assessment defined?	Broad specifications for timing of assessment (e.g., "evening") allow for subject convenience, but also give subjects discretion over timing, which can introduce bias.	Perrine et al. (1995)
Stratification	Will the schedule be stratified to ensure sampling of various time blocks?	Simple randomization can lead to uneven coverage of time in a given day. Stratification ensures more even coverage, but is more complex to program.	Armeli et al. (2005)
Oversampling	Will any time blocks have an increased frequency/ probability of assessment?	Coverage need not be even—may oversample certain times of day if they are of special interest (e.g., evening for social drinking).	Shiffman, Elash et al. (2000)
Relation to events	If event sampling is also implemented, is there a relationship between event entries and time-based prompting?	Time sampling scheme may need to be contingent on events, e.g., avoiding prompting soon after events, or deliberately prompting after events to collect post-event data.	Shiffman et al. (2002); Carter et al. (2008)

Table 16.1. Continued

Decision/issue	Explanation	Considerations	Citations to examples, where available
Prompting	How will subjects be prompted for assessment?	More forceful physical means of notifying subject for assessment may be more effective in difficult environments (e.g., noise), but may be more intrusive (e.g., allow "vibration" instead of sound?). Prompting based on milestone events (e.g., "bedtime") is imprecise and likely to select a biased sample of occasions.	
Time window	When subjects are prompted, how long will they have to respond?	Prompting for a longer time gives subjects more time to respond to alarm, but may be intrusive, or run down batteries on promoting device.	
Back-filling	Can subjects back-fill a missed assessment?	Allowing subjects to respond after prompt has lapsed may gather more data, but may introduce more retrospection and diminish subjects' urgency about responding to prompts.	
Coverage of time	During what part of the day can assessment prompts be delivered? How will this be determined?	If time available for prompting/assessment is limited, may obtain biased sample. Setting a fixed period of daily coverage for all subjects is easiest but may not accommodate some subjects' schedules. Setting individual start/stop times may not accommodate day-to-day variation in schedules. Setting start/stop times in real time allows for flexible coverage, but depends on subject's faithful compliance.	Shiffman et al. (2002); Todd (2004)
Time-out provisions	Will there be a provision for subjects to suspend prompting?	Subjects may need to be protected from intrusion at certain times (e.g., driving), but such voluntary time-outs are subject to abuse.	Shiffman et al. (2002)

(continued)

Table 16.1. Continued

Decision/issue	Explanation	Considerations	Citations to examples, where available
Recall period/ coverage	What time period is covered by the assessment?	Time frame of assessments must be defined. Shorter time-frames (e.g., "right now") minimize recall but increase variability and minimize coverage. Longer time frames introduce recall bias and may make unrealistic demands on subjects' ability to track timing of events and experiences. Full coverage ("since last assessment") can be used to retrospectively assess event occurrence or frequency.	Mohr et al. (2001)
Analysis			
Aggregation / Unit of analysis	How will scores be aggregated (if at all over observations)? What is the unit of analysis?	These decisions are sometimes made at the analysis stage, but it is important to think them through at the design stage. Individual observations are sometimes aggregated to create day-level summaries, but other units at smaller (e.g., morning, afternoon, evening) or larger (e.g., weekly) levels are also useful.	Shiffman, Engberg et al. (1997); Shiffman & Waters (2004)

to see if frequency of use has decreased with treatment) or in the timing of the events (e.g., how soon after a stressor does the person use drugs). More often, one is interested in the characteristics of the events—their duration, the situation they occurred in, the subject's mood preceding the event—which requires that an assessment be administered when the event is reported. Issues related to assessment of events are discussed subsequently.

Time-Based Assessments

Time-based designs do not key on a target event but rather schedule assessments by the clock in order to sample subjects' states over time. For example, one might assess subjects every 4 hours to ascertain their mood, and thus be able to characterize their typical mood and also the trajectory of their mood over a particular interval. Some phenomena can be captured continuously—for example, physical movement through actigraphy—but most have to be sampled intermittently on some schedule. The schedule may be fixed, either by the clock at fixed intervals (e.g., every 4 hours), by milestone events (e.g., meals), or periods (e.g., morning, evening) that are not truly fixed in time. (Daily diaries are a special case discussed later.)

Fixed assessment schedules have some limitations. If assessment always occurs in connection with particular milestone events, they may not represent broader experience outside those events. Scheduling assessments in broad time periods (e.g., "evening") gives subjects considerable discretion about when to complete assessments and risks introducing bias related to subjects' states (e.g., subjects may attend to assessments when things are calm and avoid them when stressed). Assessments may occur on an arbitrary fixed schedule, but this means that subjects can anticipate the assessment, which might affect their responses, and it also presents a risk that the assessment schedule becomes entrained to a natural rhythm in the person's life (e.g., hourly assessments getting linked to a teacher's regular change of classes).

The limitations of fixed assessments are largely remedied by scheduling assessments at random. Like drawing a random sample from a population of people, sampling moments at random ensures that the resulting sample is representative and unbiased. As in population sampling, the sampling scheme for momentary EMA assessments can be modified to improve the design's efficiency. For example, the randomized assessment schedule can be stratified within time blocks to ensure even coverage of the day (e.g., Armeli, Todd, & Mohr, 2005, sampled at random within blocks of 10:00–11:30, 15:00–16:30, and 20:00–21:30; see also McCarthy, Piasecki, Fiore, & Baker, 2006), and certain parts of the day can be oversampled if particular statistical precision is needed (e.g., Shiffman, Elash et al., 2000).

Unlike event-based monitoring, where the event itself provides a cue to make a recording, time-based schedules require a separate cue to trigger assessment. With some kinds of schedules, it is left to the subject to recognize a natural milestone (e.g., a meal), a socially recognized interval (e.g., morning), or a particular time by the clock (e.g., record at 1 p.m.). However, randomly scheduled assessments require a device that is controlled by the randomized schedule and signals the subject when an assessment is to be completed. Investigators have used personal digital assistants (PDAs, palmtop computers), programmed watches, beepers, and mobile phones for the purpose. (See a later section, as well as Hufford, 2007; Shiffman, 2007, for a discussion of devices.)

The investigator must determine the frequency of time-based assessments based on considerations of how rapidly the target phenomenon is expected to vary and how the analysis will use the assessments (Collins & Graham, 2002). EMA studies of substance use have used widely varying frequencies ranging from three assessments per day to 50 or more (Delfino, Jamner, & Whalen, 2001). Obviously, consideration of subject burden also must enter into decisions about assessment frequency. Issues of compliance will be discussed in a later section.

Variations
ASSESSING TIME-BASED MILESTONES
There is a special case of time-based assessment in which the scheduling is not based on sampling

of moments to represent subjects' overall experience but rather on interest in that particular time of day or time milestone. For example, Muraven, Collins, Morsheimer, Shiffman, and Paty (2005) arranged to assess drinkers each morning to capture how they felt "the morning after" a drinking episode (including hangover symptoms). Consistent with counterintuitive hypotheses from the *limit violation model*, when subjects were more distressed about the previous days' drinking, they actually drank more the following day. See also Epler et al. (2014). Studies have also used morning assessments soon after waking to assess sleep quality (e.g., Kos, Hasenfratz, & Battig, 1997; Shiffman, Engberg et al., 1997) with minimal need for recall.

USE OF RECALL IN ECOLOGICAL MOMENTARY ASSESSMENT
Some EMA studies of substance use truly focus on the moment, but assessments often involve some degree of retrospection. For example, McCarthy et al. (2006) and Piasecki, Richardson, and Smith (2007) both asked smokers about their smoking in the preceding 15 minutes. Shiffman et al. (2002; 2004) asked about mood at the moment but asked about drinking in the previous 15 minutes. In a coverage strategy, Mohr et al. (2001) and Todd et al. (2009) asked drinkers about interpersonal stresses experienced since the previous assessment, which occurred an average of 5 hours earlier. Debriefing completed drinking episodes (Collins et al., 1998) or lapse episodes (O'Connell, Schwartz, Gerkovich, Bott, & Shiffman, 2004; Shiffman, Paty, et al., 1996) necessarily involves some retrospection. Thus, the focus on momentary experience is not absolute; it might more liberally be thought of as a focus on "recent" experience. There are no robust data to suggest how much retrospection is problematic. It is likely that this varies based on the information to be recalled (e.g., salience, concreteness, variability), as well as on experiences in the interval between the target event and recall (e.g., further substance use). However, since recall can be biased over even a short interval (Redelmeier et al., 2003), investigators should ideally minimize the use of recall, even over short intervals.

SAMPLING VERSUS COVERAGE STRATEGIES
Time-based assessments have been conceptualized as drawing a time-sample of representative moments from the subject's life in order to project to the whole. However, time-based assessments are sometimes used not to sample subjects' current

states but to try to capture summaries that cover the entire day by asking subjects, at each assessment, to summarize their experience for the entire time since the previous assessment. Such "coverage" strategies (Shiffman et al., 2008) can be used to capture information about substance use. Todd (2004) assessed smokers four times each day, each time asking subjects to estimate how many cigarettes they had smoked since the last assessment or about its antecedents. Armeli et al. (2007) asked subjects to report on interpersonal problems experienced since the previous assessment. A coverage approach may be seen as providing two benefits: first, it provides more comprehensive assessment; after all, a sampling plan might miss important events/experiences. Second, for assessment of drug-use episodes, it can reduce subject burden because each episode need not be entered separately. However, the approach may introduce substantial retrospective bias. Added to the usual considerations of recall, the coverage approach implicitly requires that subjects maintain an accurate mental timeline of prior assessments and intermediate events and experiences. Yet, research suggests that people are particularly poor at keeping track of time and identifying when events took place (Sudman & Bradburn, 1973) and tend to "telescope" the timing of events (i.e., bring them closer to the present), often resulting in double-counting of events. This suggests that coverage strategies be regarded with caution.

Daily Diaries: A Special Case of Ecological Momentary Assessment

Whereas EMA emphasizes *real-time* assessments throughout the day, daily diaries have been used very frequently in substance use research to gather field data. This seems particularly common in research on alcohol (e.g., Armeli, Todd, Conner, & Tennen, 2008; Mohr, Brannan, Mohr, Armeli, & Tennen, 2008; Park, Armeli, & Tennen, 2004; Toll, Cooney, McKee, & O'Malley, 2006), perhaps because alcohol is often consumed in the evening, making it more plausible that subjects may be able to recall and accurately record their behavior. Within the framework that we have been discussing, daily diaries can be categorized as fixed-interval assessments with an assessment frequency of once per day, employing a retrospective coverage strategy (i.e., asking about the whole day). Daily diaries fall within the ambit of EMA in that the method involves repeated assessments over time, in the field, with a focus on within-subject variability over time. However, daily diaries lack the "real-time" aspect of modern EMA work and obviously rely on considerable retrospection. For variables like mood, where subjects are asked to summarize an entire day's experience even though mood may vary considerably, true recall is likely to stretch the capabilities of autobiographical memory, introducing considerable risk of bias. Moreover, since mood is likely to be different in the evening than during the rest of the day, bias may be introduced due to subjects' states at the time of recall (i.e., in repose at the end of the day, the day's trials and tribulations may lose their sting). Recalling that biases due to heuristic recall strategies operate even over short time frames, recall of drug or alcohol consumption may be subject to bias. Comparisons of daily diary data to real-time data will enable researchers to determine whether the former is a reasonable proxy for the latter. Research is needed to shed light on those periods when accurate recall is and is not likely. Thus, use of daily diaries requires a cautious approach.

Even if one considered recall within-a-day valid, daily diaries also have limited temporal resolution, allowing study of between-day but not within-day phenomena. The importance of this will vary with the target behavior and with assumptions about the influences upon it. Substance use in particular may be substantially influenced by more proximal within-day factors, such as exposure to drug cues and opportunities or immediate mood. For example, Shiffman and Waters (2004) found that daily measures of mood did not predict the incidence of smoking lapses, but relapse risk *was* related to within-day mood changes in the hours leading up to the lapse event itself. Thus, day-level data may miss important sources of dynamic variation that drive substance use. This review emphasizes real-time EMA data, but touches on daily diary studies as well when they are particularly appropriate to particular points.

Suitability of Ecological Momentary Assessment for Substance Use Research

Having defined EMA and introduced basic design concepts, we can now appreciate why EMA methods are particularly well-suited to studying substance use. Substance use itself is a discrete, episodic behavior that lends itself to event-oriented recording, making EMA a useful method for tracking its frequency and distribution over time. Furthermore, other constructs emphasized in theories of drug abuse also lend themselves to EMA assessment. For example, the immediate situation in which substance use occurs is thought to be important, both because it may expose users to conditioned cues for substance use (e.g., other users) or because it may provide motives or incentives for use (e.g., negative affect the user seeks to relieve). Beyond the immediate situation, theory has emphasized the role of broader dynamic background influences in the person's life (e.g., stress, coping) that also lend themselves to momentary measurement in the person's real-life environment. Furthermore, theory has also emphasized the role of the acute effects of drugs (i.e., euphoria, relief of stress), which also lend themselves to momentary assessment. This makes EMA particularly well-suited to the study of substance use.

A further impetus to studying substance use in real-world settings is that the factors that influence substance use can be hard to simulate in the laboratory. That difficulty is likely magnified when studying illicit substance use because subjects may be reluctant to display such socially disapproved behavior while under observation. Because of its complex interactions with the environmental context, substance use antecedents and effects may need to be studied in the real world (Moskowitz & Young, 2006).

Ecological Momentary Assessment Designs with Applications to Studies of Substance Use

This section discusses and illustrates different EMA designs—that is, the use of different schedules and combinations of event- and time-based assessments. The diverse approaches are illustrated with EMA studies of substance use. Table 16.2 outlines many of these designs, touching on the kind of research questions each can answer and providing citations that illustrate each approach. These are reviewed not with the intent of covering the whole EMA–drug-use literature nor with the intent of discussing the studies' substantive findings and insights into substance use but rather with the intent of illustrating the EMA designs, protocols, and analyses that have been applied to answering questions about substance use. Accordingly, this section is organized by design elements—that is, event- and time-based assessments, in various combinations and relationships—rather than by drug or theoretical focus. (Because EMA studies are subject to different forms of analysis, the examples highlight particular analyses and may cite a single study more than once if different analyses illustrate different points.) The diverse designs and objectives of EMA studies of substance use are also mirrored in diverse approaches to data analysis, as illustrated here and discussed elsewhere (Shiffman, 2014).

The reader will note that most of the studies reviewed focus on tobacco and alcohol use; this simply reflects the fact that this is where EMA methods have been most widely applied, for reasons discussed subsequently. The review begins with the simplest possible EMA study—one that merely collects records of substance use events.

Analyses Restricted to Data on Event Occurrence

Some studies have used data consisting solely of records of event occurrence. For example, Shiffman, Kirchner, Ferguson, Scharf, and Gitomer (2008) described the smoking patterns of nondaily smokers, relying on event records to describe the number and timing of smoking events. The *absence of* event records can also be meaningful. In a randomized trial of high-dose nicotine patches, Shiffman, Scharf et al. (2006) assessed whether active treatment could help smokers achieve initial smoking cessation (as distinct from maintenance), which was defined by the absence of smoking records for 24 hours. The timing of substance use events can also serve as an important outcome. For example, in the same trial of nicotine patch, Shiffman, Scharf et al. (2006) asked smokers who had quit smoking to record any episodes of smoking. A survival analysis then examined the time from quitting to the first lapse as a measure of treatment efficacy; active treatment increased time to first lapse.

The distribution of substance use events over time can also be fruitfully analyzed. Just using event records entered on a watch-like device, Hopper et al. (2006) provided the first detailed description of patterns of ecstasy use by day of week and time of day. Ecstasy use was concentrated in weekend nights. In a different vein, Shiffman, Kirchner et al. (2009) used simple event records of smoking to determine how often cigarettes were clustered together in bouts of smoking (within 60 minutes of each other). Social smokers were found to be particularly likely to smoke in bouts. Chandra, Shiffman, Scharf, Dang, and Shadel (2007) analyzed how the rate of smoking varied over time of day. Each subject's smoking rate (cigarettes per hour) was summarized into 2-hour blocks over the day, and the data yielded a typology of daily smoking patterns that were related to smokers' degrees of nicotine dependence and were significant predictors of lapse risk.

When multiple events are recorded, the clustering and sequencing of events can be informative.

Table 16.2. Varieties of Ecological Momentary Assessment Designs

Approach	EMA data required	Logical/Analytic approach	Questions the approach can address (examples)	Considerations
Event occurrence or counts	Event records	Analysis simply notes whether an event occurred, or how many events occurred	• What percent of subjects on nicotine patch vs. placebo resume smoking after treatment? (Shiffman, Scharf, et al., 2006) • How many cigarettes do subjects smoke? (Shiffman, 2009) • Does naltrexone reduce the frequency of drinking occasions? (Tidey et al., 2008)	Does not require assessment beyond event records. If event frequency is low and recall bias is not a concern, may be obtained via end-of-day reports
Time to event	Time-tagged event records	Analysis focuses on the timing of a key event, in relation to some non-EMA milestone starting point	• Do smokers remain abstinent longer before lapsing when treated with nicotine patch (vs. placebo)? (Shiffman, Scharf, et al., 2006)	Precision needed will depend on the particular setting. Survival analysis or time-to-event methods typically used. This assumes covariates/predictors are static factors such as treatment or stable subject characteristics and are not time-varying.
Time distribution of events	Time-tagged event records	Analysis focuses on how events are distributed over time in relation to the clock or calendar	• Is ecstasy use more likely in the evening than the morning? On weekends vs. weekdays? (Hopper et al., 2006) • Are there meaningful variations in smoking patterns over the day? (Chandra et al., 2007)	Requires appropriately precise determination and documentation of time
Timing relationships among events	Time-tagged event records	Analysis focuses on the timing of events in relation to each other	• Are cigarettes smoked in "binges" or at even intervals? (Shiffman, Kirchner et al., 2009)	Requires appropriately precise determination and documentation of time
Situational attributes of events	Assessments of events	Analysis focuses descriptively on attributes (e.g., mood) of events, with no contrasting group of nonevent records	• Are smokers typically drinking when they lapse? (Shiffman Paty, et al., 1996)	Useful for describing the *prevalence* of attributes in events, but the lack of contrasting nonevent observations makes valid inference difficult (Paty et al., 1992).
Subject average states	Time-based assessments	Characterizes subjects' states descriptively or compares across intervention groups (with no reference to events)	• How does nicotine patch affect withdrawal symptom intensity? (Shiffman, 2008) • What is the typical mood state of smokers? How does it compare to nonsmokers?	Benefits from the increased reliability obtained by aggregating multiple assessments but is fundamentally a between-subjects analysis

Table 16.2. Continued

Approach	EMA data required	Logical/Analytic approach	Questions the approach can address (examples)	Considerations
Variability in subject states	Time-based assessments	These analyses focus on within-subject variability (rather than mean) as an index of a behavioral process	• Are teens with more volatile (variable) mood more susceptible to taking up smoking? (Weinstein et al., 2008)	Statistical methods for analyzing variability are relatively new
Temporal trajectories in subject states	Time-based assessments	The focus is on change in mean level over time to trace the natural history of states (with no reference to events)	• How long does nicotine withdrawal-related mood disturbance last? (Shiffman, Patten et al., 2006) • Do nicotine withdrawal symptoms decline monotonically over time? (Piasecki et al., 2003)	Time, as defined by an anchoring event (e.g., cessation, substance use), is the independent variable.
Association of situational attributes with event risk	Assessments of events + nonevent assessments (time-based sampling)	Using case–control logic, analysis contrasts events and nonevents without reference to the timing of either.	• Are smokers *more likely than usual* to be drinking alcohol when they smoke? (Shiffman et al., 2002)	Assess *association* of attributes with events (vs. nonevents), so overcomes interpretive limitation of event-only data, but establishes only an atemporal association, not sequence, much less causality.
Antecedents or sequelae of events	Event records + nonevent assessments (time-based sampling)	Uses single time-based assessments falling before or after index events to examine subject states prior to or following the event	• How does mood change after smoking? (Carter et al., 2008) • How does self-efficacy change after a smoking lapse? (Shiffman et al., 1997)	Time is not explicitly referenced in the analysis, but sequence (observations falling before and after the event) is the key analytic construct.
Block-to-block prediction	Mix of event records/ assessments or nonevent assessments (time-based sampling)	Uses data about subject states or events during one block of time to predict subject state or events in a subsequent block	• Does stress during the weekdays predict amount of alcohol consumed on the subsequent weekend? (Hussong et al., 2001)	Such analyses typically require aggregation blocks of time, which may not necessarily be of similar duration. Analyses are prospective, but observed relationships may not be causal.
Temporal trajectories leading up to or following events	Event records + nonevent assessments (time-based sampling)	Uses a series time-based assessments falling before or after index events to trace trends in subject states prior to the event or after the event	• What is the trajectory of mood in the days and hours before a smoking relapse? (Shiffman & Waters, 2004)	Time is the key independent variable and is anchored by an index event. The analyses are not "predictive" of events because they only examine series that start with or terminate in an event.

(*continued*)

Table 16.2. Continued

Approach	EMA data required	Logical/Analytic approach	Questions the approach can address (examples)	Considerations
Time between events	Event assessments	Uses the characteristics of an initial event to predict the latency or risk over time of a subsequent repeat event. Both the starting point and the end-point of the time line are EMA-recorded events.	• Are smokers more likely to progress (or progress more quickly) to relapse following smoking lapses that produce greater hedonic satisfaction? (Shiffman, Ferguson et al., 2006)	This approach can be extended to encompass a series multiple events (e.g., lapses) in subjects.
Time-to-event, with time varying covariates	Event records + nonevent assessments (time-based sampling) or event assessments	Uses a moving series of assessments (usually time-based) to predict the risk of an event occurring	• How do day-to-day variations in self-efficacy affect the risk of lapsing? (Shiffman, Balabanis et al., 2000)	Such analyses often require aggregation of the series into evenly spaced units of time. This approach can be extended to encompass a series multiple events (e.g., lapses) in subjects.

Note: See also Shiffman, 2014, for discussion and illustration of analytic approaches

Hopper at al. (2006) asked ecstasy users to make event records not only of ecstasy use, but also of alcohol and other drug consumption, hypothesizing that ecstasy use would promote subsequent use of other drugs. They found the opposite: on nights when ecstasy was used, alcohol use was actually *less* likely and was more likely to occur *before* (rather than after) ecstasy use. Thus, even the very simplest EMA records—time-tagged records of events with no other assessment—can support meaningful analyses of substance use.

Analyzing Characteristics of Events (Events with Data)

When subjects not only record events, but also answer questions about the event, additional analyses become possible. For example, Dunbar, Scharf, Kirchner, and Shiffman (2010) used data in which smokers had reported their cravings and the settings for cigarettes smoked to characterize variation in craving and its associations with situational variables. The most craved cigarettes included those smoked when subjects were eating or drinking and with other smokers. Event data that include quantity of use can also be used to construct an outcome indicator. Shiffman, Scharf et al. (2006) asked smokers to track lapse episodes after quitting and had them record how much they had smoked

on each occasion, which allowed the investigators to construct a definition of relapse (smoking at least five cigarettes per day on 3 consecutive days). Survival analysis showed that, compared to smokers on active nicotine patch, smokers on placebo progressed faster from an initial lapse to relapse.

Event data also become more informative when different kinds of events are tracked and can then be contrasted. For example, a study done by O'Connell, Schwartz, Gerkovich, Bott, and Shiffman (2004) had smokers who had quit smoking record two different events: episodes of smoking (lapses) and occasions when they experienced peaks of craving and came close to lapsing but didn't (temptations). Analysis contrasting lapses and temptations revealed that lapses were likely to occur when subjects failed to cope and when they were feeling rebellious. In this instance, the two contrasting events had been defined a priori and were explicit in subjects' event-monitoring task. Contrasts between event classes can also be based on distinctions defined after the fact. For example, Collins et al. (1998) asked heavy drinkers who were trying to cut back, to record all episodes of drinking as well as to assess their mood and setting and how much they drank. The investigators subsequently defined "excessive drinking" as consumption of more than five drinks in an episode, finding that episodes of excessive drinking (in contrast to episodes of moderate drinking) were marked by more positive mood at the start of the episode. Thus, data about substance use events can be very useful in characterizing substance use.

Analyses Restricted to Time-Based Assessments

Some analyses address meaningful questions about substance use without analyzing data in substance use events at all (although in each of the following analyses event data were used to assess patterns of substance use so that researchers could determine which subjects were qualified to remain in the analysis). Examples often involve examination of symptoms, such as withdrawal symptoms. For example, in a randomized trial, Shiffman, Elash et al. (2000) compared craving relief achieved by a 24-hour nicotine patch (worn overnight and replaced on waking) versus a 16-hour nicotine patch (taken off at bedtime and replaced on waking) using randomly scheduled time-based assessments to assess craving throughout the day. An interesting twist was that the random sampling schedule was designed to oversample the morning hours, when the differences between the patch formulations were expected to be greatest. As hypothesized, the 24-hour formulation proved to produce lower craving in the morning (and the rest of the day, too).

In another example, Kos, Hasenfratz, and Battig (1997) randomized smokers to smoke ad lib or abstain for two 4-day periods, while administering six assessments per day at various milestone times (e.g., waking, before dinner, etc.). The assessments included subjective ratings of withdrawal symptoms and also objective performance on a cognitive (Stroop) task (MacLeod, 1991). Abstinence increased craving and withdrawal. Contrary to expectations, there was no effect on Stroop performance, although older subjects performed worse than younger subjects. (This study also illustrates the implementation of an objective non–self-report assessment in an EMA design.)

Time-based assessments are not just useful in the context of randomized or comparative studies, but can also be useful in describing the natural history or trajectory of relevant phenomena. For example, Shiffman, Patten et al. (2006) explored the natural history (trajectory, duration) of nicotine withdrawal symptoms using data collected by random time-sampling of smokers after they quit without pharmacotherapy. In this study, time-sampled data collected while subjects were still smoking was used not only to estimate the average level of baseline symptoms, but also the between-day variability of symptoms, which was then used statistically to interpret the post-quit data. This study suggested that withdrawal symptoms typically resolved within a week. In contrast, Piasecki et al. (2003), who used data from daily withdrawal symptoms to assess the trajectory of symptoms in different groups of smokers identified by cluster-analysis concluded that many smokers' symptoms stayed relatively constant or even rose over an 8-week period.

Combining Event- and Time-Based Assessments

CASE CROSS-OVER DESIGNS
Limitations of Event-Only Data

An earlier section described how data restricted to events could shed light on substance use patterns. However, contrary to some older diary studies (Shiffman & Prange, 1988; Surawy & Cox, 1987), data limited to the context of drug-use events cannot be used to determine the association between substance use and particular settings or to validly assess individual differences in such associations (Paty, Kassel, & Shiffman, 1992). Without a contrasting set of data from situations that were *not* associated with substance use, data on substance use occasions can be misleading, much as epidemiological data about the correlates of a disease require data from both diseased and nondiseased individuals to construct a case–control design (Paty et al., 1992). However, coupled with data on nonuse occasions collected using time-based sampling, such data can support a powerful case–control case cross-over design (the latter being a designation for within-subjects controls; Maclure & Mittleman, 2000).

The importance of interpreting event data in the context of control data on nonuse occasions is illustrated in Figure 16.1, which shows data from three individual smokers who monitored their smoking and its antecedents (Shiffman, Dunbar, et al., 2014). The graph shows data relevant to evaluating whether coffee drinking is associated with smoking (Matarazzo & Saslow, 1960). Notice first the data from smoking observations obtained from event-based assessments. It is evident that Subject A more often reports that he's drinking coffee when he's smoking, compared to the other two subjects (20% vs. 14% each for the others). This might lead one to think that coffee is a more important stimulus to smoking for this

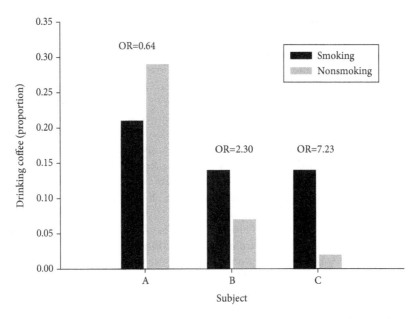

Figure 16.1. Importance of base-rates for evaluating association with drug use comparison of three subjects coffee drinking and smoking.

subject compared to the other two. But adding in the "control" data from situations assessed when subjects are *not* smoking (collected via random time-based assessments) changes the picture completely. With the perspective of these additional data, we see that A very frequently drinks coffee and is actually *even more* likely to report drinking coffee when *not* smoking (29% of observations) than when smoking (20%). In other words, for this subject, there is actually a *negative* association between smoking and coffee consumption (odds ratio [OR] = 0.64). In contrast, both of the other two subjects are more likely to report drinking coffee when smoking than when not smoking, demonstrating positive associations. Furthermore, even though the proportion of cigarettes smoked for which coffee drinking was reported is identical for the two subjects (14%), the *association* between coffee and cigarettes differs substantially: it is considerably greater for C, who is rarely found to be drinking coffee when not smoking (2% of the time), such that the odds of drinking coffee while smoking are more than seven times greater (OR = 7.23). This illustrates how essential it is to consider control data on non–drug-use settings if one is to understand the setting contexts of substance use (see Paty et al., 1992). Thus, nonuse or nonevent data constitute an essential control for event-based data when evaluating associations with situational context.

The Case Cross-Over Design

A number of studies have combined event-based and time–based data in a case-control (cases = drug events, controls = time-based nondrug) or case cross-over design (e.g., Carter et al., 2008; Delfino et al., 2001; Moghaddam & Ferguson, 2007; Shiffman et al., 2002; Shiffman & Paty, 2006; Shiffman et al., 2004). For example, Carter et al. (2008) explored the situational antecedents of smoking by comparing reports of mood when subjects were just about to smoke versus the same characteristics sampled at random in nonsmoking settings. Contrary to expectations from questionnaire data, smoking was not systematically preceded by negative moods. Other studies have also reported a null effect (Shiffman et al., 2002; 2004).

A similar case cross-over study by Shiffman et al. (2002) illustrates the importance of controls for situational confounds in such studies. The data showed that being in a bar was strongly associated with smoking. However, controlling for alcohol consumption, the presence of other smokers, engagement in leisure activity, and lax smoking regulations—all associated with smoking and more likely to occur in bars—completely accounted for the effect of being in a bar. This case is obvious, but illustrates that real-world situations have their own ecology and seldom allow for clean evaluation of any one influence, making such statistical controls essential. Investigators pursuing such analyses are advised to include measures of confounding factors in their assessments to enable better inferences. With the potential for measured and unmeasured confounding in mind, the case cross-over design, combining event- and time-based assessments, offers a powerful way to assess situational correlates of substance use.

PRE–POST DESIGNS

An important variation that also combines event-based, subject-initiated recording with protocol-driven, prompted, time-based recording is the pre–post or follow-up design. For example, Carter et al. (2008) were interested in the effect of smoking on mood. They provided smokers with a PDA and asked them to record each cigarette. On a random subset of these event occasions, the PDA administered an assessment of the setting preceding smoking. So far, this is just event-based sampling. However, on a random subset of smoking occasions, the PDA followed up on the recording of a cigarette by initiating prompting of the subject for assessment 20 minutes later, when the effects of smoking could presumably be discerned. (In this study, few individual cigarettes were assessed both pre and post, so there were separate samples of both occasions.) Carter et al. (2008) found small but significant reductions in negative mood following smoking, which is consistent with smokers' (and theorists') claims that nicotine relieves emotional distress. However, both Delfino, Jamner, and Whalen (2001) and Moghaddam and Ferguson (2007) also used pre–post designs, and neither study found consistent mood changes following smoking. In a similar design for assessing alcohol, R. L. Collins et al. (1998) collected mood data at the outset and at the end of drinking episodes. While episodes of excessive drinking (>5 drinks) tended to start with particularly positive mood, excessive drinking was associated with a shift toward negative mood by the end of the episode. In any case, the pre–post design is a powerful way to assess the effects of substance use in real-world settings.

PROSPECTIVE CASE CROSS-OVER DESIGNS

The case cross-over designs just discussed largely ignore time (with the exception of the pre–post design): that is, consistent with the case–control approach, they compare one collection of case observations (substance use events) with controls (time-based assessments), without any reference to their temporal ordering. The approach is essentially cross-sectional. But, given that EMA data are naturally ordered in time, they provide a platform for prospective analyses of substance use—analyses that very much take time and temporal ordering into account. For example, Delfino et al. (2001) performed a prospective analysis of the effect of mood on smoking using a very intense schedule of assessment every 20 minutes. Their analysis modeled the influence of mood at a given assessment on the probability of smoking at the next assessment approximately 10–20 minutes later. They found no consistent influence of prior mood on subsequent smoking (at the next assessment). (It is important to note that temporal priority of the putative cause over the effect is compatible with a causal relationship but doesn't prove it. For example, even if mood predicted smoking, it might be because subjects who anticipated smoking therefore experienced mood changes or because withdrawal affected both mood and motivation to smoke.)

In another example of prospective analysis, Armeli, Dehart, Tennen, Todd, and Affleck (2007) administered three time-based assessments per day—morning, afternoon, and evening—and used afternoon (3:00–4:30 p.m.) reports of interpersonal stress and negative affect predicted subsequent drinking (captured by event entries). (Because drinking tends to be concentrated in the evening, a number of studies focus on evening drinking.) There was no main effect of prior stress on later drinking, but subjects who expected drinking to make them feel carefree did drink more after a high-stress day. Todd et al. (2005) provides valuable perspective on prospective analyses because he performed both cross-sectional and prospective analyses on the same dataset of assessments collected four times a day. Although associations between negative events and smoking were seen in both concurrent and prospective analyses, the concurrent associations between perceived stress and smoking disappeared in the prospective analyses. These analyses suggest the utility of using an EMA data stream to gain a prospective perspective.

One important issue in constructing prospective analyses is how data are aggregated and how time is treated in the analysis (see Collins & Graham, 2002; Shiffman, 2014). An analysis by Hussong, Hicks, Levy, and Curran (2001) illustrates how data from momentary assessments can be aggregated and analyzed in ways that impose strong, if implicit, assumptions on how effects are mediated over time. Hussong et al. collected mood and drinking data at random 2-hour intervals over 28 days. The data were aggregated into daily summaries, which they then further aggregated into two blocks—one representing weekday (M–Th) and one representing weekend (F–Su) experience. The analysis examined how weekday mood predicted weekend drinking (and vice versa). Weekday mood did not predict weekend drinking. What is notable is the way that time is treated in this analysis. The only variation in time or influence of time that appears in the analysis is at the boundary between weekdays and weekends. Not only is within-day variation across the 2-hourly assessments collapsed, but time within weekdays and weekends is also collapsed, so that any variability and any influence of mood on drinking *within* each block (weekdays, weekends) is ignored. The analysis does not allow Monday's mood to influence Tuesday's drinking, and it also implicitly assumes that Monday's mood influences Sunday's drinking as much as Thursday's mood influences Friday's drinking. Thus, even within prospective designs, the organization and analysis of data determine what time-bound effects can be detected. The next section examines a different approach to prospective analysis that treats temporal effects very differently.

TIME-TO-EVENT ANALYSES

Another way in which EMA investigators have addressed the influence of time in their analyses is through survival or time-to-event analyses. These analyses estimate the risk of substance use occurring over time by attending to how much time passes until a substance use event occurs, modeling this as a function of covariate predictors. This is in contrast to approaches that set up a fixed time-point at which the dependent variable is assessed. The fixed time-frame approach is illustrated in Hussong et al.'s (2001) analysis, which defines drinking on the weekend as the end-point, to be predicted from mood during the weekdays (treated as a single block). In contrast, Armeli, Todd, Conner, and Tennen (2008), who were also interested in how mood affected the occurrence of drinking over the week, modeled the risk of drinking on each successive day, using a cumulative, moving average of mood to predict on which day of the week subjects would start drinking. They found that subjects who said they engaged in drinking to cope started drinking a day earlier during high-anxiety periods than low-anxiety periods.

Similarly, using within-day data, Swendsen et al. (2000) used the fixed-block approach, using evening (8:00–9:30) mood data to predict the volume of later drinking (regardless of its timing), finding that both happiness and nervousness predicted more

drinking. In contrast, Todd et al. (2009) collected data in an identical way, but used morning mood (10:00–11:30 a.m.) to predict the time of onset of later drinking (regardless of amount), finding that morning nervousness and anger were associated with earlier onset of drinking (e.g., around 5 p.m. in high-nervous days, 9 p.m. on low-nervous days).

The time-to-event approach not only treats time differently than the traditional longitudinal approach—it also treats substance use differently. In the time-to-event approach, substance use is a discrete "binary" event that either occurs or not (regardless of quantity), whereas the time-block approach usually looks at the quantity of substance use but ignores timing within blocks. However, it is possible to analyze a discrete outcome in the fixed-block approach, as in Delfino et al.'s analysis of how mood at a particular assessment affected the probability (not quantity) of use in the next assessment. Conversely, one can bring quantity of use into the definition of events, as in Shiffman, Scharf et al.'s (2006) analysis of "relapse," which was defined as smoking at least five cigarettes per day, for 3 consecutive days. A key difference is that, in the time-to-event approach, time is (relatively) continuous; in the block approach, time is discrete (i.e., baseline, follow-up). The time-to-event approach explicitly examines the passage of time without an event as an indicator of the risk of an event. This risk-over-time can be modeled from static predictors at the beginning of an interval (as exemplified in Todd et al.'s use of morning mood to predict onset of drinking for the rest of the day) or can vary dynamically over the interval (as exemplified by Armeli et al.'s cumulative mood index, which changed over days leading up to initiation of drinking). EMA data provide multiple ways to examine influences over time and thereby challenge the investigator to formulate clear, theory-based models of how the variables in the analysis influence each other over time. This point is elaborated further in a subsequent discussion of modes of analysis for EMA drug-use data.

TRAJECTORY OF ANTECEDENTS ANALYSES

Another approach that has been used to prospectively assess antecedents of substance use events has been to use time-based assessments to examine the trajectory or trend in variables during a period leading up to substance use. For example, to demonstrate that smoking lapses attributed to distress really were preceded by distress, Shiffman and Waters (2004) examined trends in negative affect in the hours preceding subjects' first lapses and found significant increases in negative affect over the preceding 6 hours. Examination of a prior (nonlapse) day revealed no similar trend in affect, suggesting that the observed time trends were not spurious variation. Similarly, Epstein et al. (2009) found that episodes of cocaine use in treated users were preceded by steeply rising likelihood of seeing the drug and by increasing positive and negative mood indicators in the 5 hours preceding use. Similarly, increasing negative mood preceded episodes of craving for heroin, but, surprisingly, not heroin use itself. In a separate control analysis, Epstein et al. showed that the observed trends were not seen in the hours preceding a nonuse control observation. These analyses don't "predict" the episode of use because they are deliberately selected from the period preceding a known episode of use, but they interpret the observed trends in relation to the target episode. Thus, the trajectory of experience, documented by time-based assessments preceding significant episodes, can be the focus of informative prospective analyses.

Individual Difference Moderators

The discussion of EMA studies of substance use has emphasized within-subject effects, which are EMA's greatest strength. But EMA studies can also be used to examine between-subject effects, particularly in interaction with within-subject effects. One example is the substantial literature on *drinking to cope* (DTC; Cooper, Russell, Skinner, Frone, & Mudar, 1992), which is conceptualized as an individual difference in drinking motives and patterns, such that some people consume alcohol in order to cope with stress or emotional distress. Thus, DTC is conceptualized as a between-person moderator of within-subject effects: individuals high on DTC motives (between-person, assessed by questionnaire) are expected to show a stronger association between antecedent stress or mood and drinking (a within-subject effect, assessed by EMA). This has been subject to many empirical tests using different EMA designs and analyses, with very mixed and complex results. For example, Todd, Armeli, Tennen, Carney, and Affleck (2003) examined within-day relationships between stress and negative affect and drinking and found that the drinking of high-DTC drinkers was generally unaffected; instead, low-DTC drinkers were observed to reduce their drinking under high stress. In a later study, Todd, Armeli, and Tennen (2009) explored whether morning mood affected the time at which drinking

was initiated later, on weekday and weekends: they found that morning negative affect did accelerate onset of drinking more for high-DTC drinkers, but only on weekdays. Many other analyses have examined the moderating effects of DTC with inconsistent and often negative results varying by EMA design, analytic approach, and the particular moods examined (e.g., Armeli et al., 2000; Carney, Armeli, Tennen, Affleck, & O'Neil, 2000; Hussong, Galloway, & Feagans, 2005; Todd et al., 2005), but, in any case, the studies illustrate analysis of individual difference moderators of within-subject associations between mood and drinking. Aside from DTC expectancies, Armeli, Dehart, Tennen, Todd, and Affleck (2007) report that other drinking expectancies moderated the relationship between daily stress and evening drinking.

Other examples of individual difference moderators of within-subject associations with substance use abound. Beckham et al. (2008) showed that the association between stress and smoking was stronger in subjects with post-traumatic stress disorder. Shiffman and Paty (2006) showed that the association between drinking and smoking was stronger among nondependent smokers (vs. heavier, dependent smokers). This analysis also illustrated the use of within-subjects regression analyses to idiographically assess the strength of association between smoking and situational antecedents for each subject, as indexed by statistics analogous to R^2, abstracting from associations with particular stimuli to demonstrate greater stimulus control among the nondependent smokers. EMA data can allow for strong inferences about within-subjects effects, which can, in turn, be tested for between-group differences.

Ecological Momentary Assessment for Outcome Analyses

EMA methods have unique advantages for process analyses, so it is not surprising that most of the studies reviewed have been observational studies with a process focus. However, EMA methods can also be useful for outcome analyses. Event monitoring can be used to capture the quantity or distribution of substance use after treatment. For example, Tidey et al. (2008) used electronic diary EMA reports of drinking events to assess drinking in heavy drinkers treated with naltrexone or placebo: naltrexone resulted in significantly fewer drinking days, although it had no effect on how much drinking took place on those days, suggesting the importance of distinguishing different aspects of drinking behavior. In a randomized trial of combinations of bupropion and counseling, McCarthy et al. (2008) used EMA records of individual smoking occasions to assess abstinence; bupropion increased abstinence, but counseling had no effect. EMA measures of smoking have also been used in survival analyses to precisely estimate the time of milestones in smoking cessation in order to evaluate the effects of nicotine patch on quitting, lapsing, and relapsing (Shiffman, Scharf, et al., 2006). As discussed earlier, time-based EMA monitoring has also been used to examine the effects of treatment on symptoms, such as craving and withdrawal, which are often regarded as outcomes in themselves. For example, McCarthy et al. (2008) assessed the effects of bupropion on cigarette craving, finding that treatment caused craving to decline more quickly over time. Thus, EMA analyses are useful for a variety of outcome analyses.

Assessing Mediation

EMA data can be very useful in mediation analyses, which can help us understand how treatment works. Theoretical models often posit intermediate effects of treatment, measurable during the treatment phase, that are supposed to be the active ingredient in efficacy. For example, bupropion was hypothesized to help smokers quit by reducing craving. In a randomized trial of bupropion versus placebo for smoking cessation, McCarthy et al. (2008) used data collected during three random assessments per day to estimate both the level of craving when subjects quit and also the rate at which craving declined over days. Bupropion did not affect the initial level of post-quit craving but did increase its rate of decline, and this effect partially mediated the effect of bupropion on enhancing abstinence, thus confirming the model. Ferguson, Shiffman, and Gwaltney (2006) tested the widely accepted conjecture that nicotine patch lowers the risk of lapsing primarily by reducing craving and withdrawal. A day-level model in which craving and withdrawal were treated as time-varying covariates (i.e., each days' symptoms predicting the next day's lapse risk) showed that symptom reduction only accounted for part, but not all, of the effects of patch treatment.

In a more complex model, Armeli, Feinn, Tennen, Kranzler et al. (2006), building on findings suggesting that positive and negative affect promote drinking, examined the effect of naltrexone on the association between affect and heavy drinking in a group of heavy drinkers. Using daily diaries, they found that naltrexone buffered drinkers from the effects of both positive and negative affect: for subjects on placebo, both positive and negative affect were associated with heavy drinking; for subjects on naltrexone, affect did not influence heavy drinking. (It is not clear from the data reported whether naltrexone treatment simply reduced the relationship between affect and drinking or if it actually blunted affective experience, but the EMA data would be capable of distinguishing the two processes.) A later analysis (Armeli et al., 2006), concentrating specifically on positive or negative social interactions, produced more complex results (e.g., subjects on naltrexone were *more* likely to drink and to drink heavily on days with celebratory social occasions, perhaps to overcome naltrexone's blunting effect on alcohol reinforcement). In any case, these analyses illustrate how EMA data can be used not only to evaluate *whether* a treatment works, but also *how* it works. Thus, EMA methods have considerable utility in drug treatment trials, not only for assessing outcome, but also for assessing processes that may mediate or moderate treatment effects.

EMA data are also useful for assessing mediation of naturally occurring processes outside of treatment. For example, Armeli et al. (2007) present analyses suggesting that the influence of daily interpersonal problems on subsequent drinking (moderated by drinking expectancies) may be mediated by negative affect in the afternoon, which is related to both interpersonal stress and subsequent drinking. Thus, naturalistic process studies also lend themselves to mediational analyses.

Statistical Analysis of EMA Data

These cited studies amply illustrate that no one analysis fits all EMA studies. Indeed, the EMA literature, including the literature on EMA and substance use, demonstrates a notable diversity and creativity in framing and structuring data and analyses to best address the researcher's particular questions (see Shiffman, 2014). So, for example, many studies of drinking have collected data on drinking and its putative antecedents (e.g., mood). Some have analyzed the data cross-sectionally within day, whereas others have analyzed them prospectively with lags to the previous day, and yet others focused on the week as a unit, predicting weekend drinking from weekday experience or using survival analysis to examine how soon into the week subjects began drinking. Similarly, in analyses of relapse, momentary data have been analyzed at the momentary level to describe lapse episodes or analyzed over time to explore the processes leading up to lapses, either while maintaining the precise time-line or after collapsing the momentary data into day-level aggregates. Each of these approaches uses the same underlying data but sets up different data structures and analytic approaches to answer different questions, or at least different slants on the same question. As discussed, a key issue, discussed at length elsewhere (Shiffman, 2014) is how the analysis represents or deals with time—whether the passage of time is ignored (e.g., when time-independent collections of events are analyzed in case cross-over designs), becomes the dependent variable (e.g., in time-to-event analyses), or is treated as a dimension along which other factors vary (e.g., as time-varying covariates).

Analyses of Abstinence Self-Efficacy: Illustrating Variations in Conception, Data Organization, and Analysis

As a way of illustrating how diverse approaches to data structure and analysis can address different questions within the same EMA data stream, the following section reviews a series of analyses of the influence of ASE on relapse risk based on a study in which smokers completed event-based assessments of each lapse, including their ASE after the lapse, and also were assessed at random times by time-based assessments. However, the analyses differ in which parts of this data stream they use, if/how they aggregate data, and what they take as the end-point of the time-to-event analysis.

The first, simplest, and most traditional analysis (Gwaltney, Shiffman, Balabanis, & Paty, 2005) used EMA data only to determine who had lapsed and found that questionnaire-assessed baseline ASE only marginally predicted lapse risk and did not predict progression to relapse (but see Shiffman, Balabanis et al., 2000). A further analysis moved away from global assessment of ASE to using EMA to assess ASE in the real world during a critical transition—the first day of abstinence—and found that quit-day ASE predicted lapse risk. Note that this analysis uses EMA data on ASE, but only from a fixed and limited time period immediately after quitting.

A further analysis moved away from such static prediction, based on a single time block, to dynamic prediction from day-to-day levels of ASE (i.e., daily average ASE, treated as a time-varying covariate). Daily variations in ASE predicted the occurrence of a lapse and, once subjects lapsed, daily ASE predicted the progression to relapse, even after accounting for concomitant smoking (cf. Shiffman, Balabanis et al., 2000).

These analyses aggregated ASE ratings to daily averages, rather than considering ASE ratings during specific critical moments, such as lapse events. Yet theory suggests that these moments are pivotal for understanding ASE dynamics and their influence on relapse (Marlatt & Gordon, 1985). Indeed, in an earlier study, Shiffman et al. (1997) showed that initial lapses did indeed result in a drop in ASE (comparing post-event reports with pre-event time-based assessments). Relapse theory posited that the degree to which the initial lapse decreased ASE would predict progression to relapse. Shiffman, Hickcox et al. (1996) tested this hypothesis, but found that reductions in ASE following the very first lapse (assessed at the event) did not predict the rate of progression to a second lapse or relapse (captured via further events).

These analyses of lapse nature were limited because they only considered the very first lapse and thus failed to consider what might happen over a series of lapses. Kirchner, Shiffman, and Cheong (2007) examined instead multiple lapses and how ASE after each successive lapse predicted progression to the next lapse. This analysis allowed ASE to vary dynamically, but over lapse events rather than over time per se (in contrast to Gwaltney et al., 2005, described earlier). As posited by theory, lower post-lapse ASE predicted progression to a subsequent lapse. Moreover, the process was also affected by the dynamics of ASE across successive lapse events: at any given lapse, within-subject *decreases* in post-lapse ASE from the previous lapse to the present one further predicted progression over and above the simple ASE level at the present lapse. In this analysis, lapse events generate both the predictors (post-lapse ASE) and the end-point (next lapse). Notably, this analysis used only event-based (lapse) data, with no aggregation over time and no use of time-based assessments, in contrast to Gwaltney et al., who used aggregated (daily) ASE ratings from time-based assessments and did not use ASE ratings collected at lapse events. Each approach answers a different question about ASE by framing the data and the analysis differently.

Nor do these analyses exhaust what one might fruitfully ask about ASE and relapse using these same EMA data streams. For example, one might ask whether the substantial drop in ASE seen after the initial lapse (observed in Shiffman et al., 1997a) continues to be seen after later lapses, as lapses proliferate and perhaps come to be accepted. Does

ASE fall progressively lower? Is the rate of decline related to progression to relapse? Conversely, one might assess whether the drop in ASE following a lapse is transient: does it recover? Over what period? Does it recover faster or better if the smoker successfully overcomes a situational temptation? One might also ask whether within-day variability in ASE—implying a certain fragility in the smoker's confidence—might predict relapse over and above the mean daily ASE. These examples illustrate the flexibility of EMA data, which provide a detailed natural history of behavior and experience (e.g., temptations, lapses, and ASE) to be organized and analyzed in different ways to answer different research questions about process-over-time.

Thus, a well-designed EMA study can provide the investigator with a stream of data that can then be conceptualized, filtered, organized, and analyzed in different ways to yield insights about different aspects of the underlying processes. Table 16.2 summarizes a range of approaches to conceptualization and analysis of EMA data, relating the kind of data needed for each approach and linking each approach to the kind of research questions it can answer (with examples in each case, most actually represented in the literature). The richness and flexibility of EMA data and its ability to be framed and analyzed in different ways to address different research questions makes EMA highly productive but also place special demand on EMA investigators to consider the fit between their research questions and the form of the data structure and analysis.

Statistical Models for Ecological Momentary Assessment Data

Despite this plethora of approaches, which mostly turn on nonstatistical, conceptual issues, EMA data do share certain statistical challenges and requirements by virtue of the extensive repeated measurement of individuals. Unlike traditional "repeated measures" designs, the number of assessment occasions in EMA datasets is often very numerous. Moreover, individuals typically vary in the number of assessments, and the assessments may not be evenly spaced in time, making both traditional between-subjects analyses and traditional repeated-measures approaches poor fits. The analysis must take into account the nesting of multiple observations within each subject and the autocorrelation among observations. It is beyond the scope of this chapter to address statistical approaches in detail. However, a number of different methods (many grouped under the rubric of "hierarchical" methods that recognize the hierarchy of observation units—i.e., person and observation) are available and are discussed in other sources (Schwartz & Stone, 1998; Walls & Schafer, 2006). A developing approach to EMA data analysis exploits the fact that the probability of sampling events and moments in EMA studies is known to enhance the power of the analyses (Rathbun, Shiffman, & Gwaltney, 2007). Furthermore, as illustrated by some of the reviewed EMA studies, hierarchical linear regression approaches are not the only option; for example, survival, or time-to-event analyses, including recurrent-event analyses (Wileyto et al., 2004), may often be suited to studies of substance use episodes. The scope of possible analyses is very broad: Walls and Schafer (2006) introduce a very wide array of methods, many likely unfamiliar to substance use researchers.

Methodological Issues in Ecological Momentary Assessment

Having introduced EMA concepts and designs and illustrated them, we move next to discussing methodological issues in EMA research. Table 16.2 summarizes some of the key decisions an EMA investigator must make, noting the considerations for each and citing examples of how these decisions have been dealt with in the literature.

Event-Based Assessments
EVENT AND ASSESSMENT FREQUENCY

Event-monitoring can present a substantial subject burden. For event monitoring, the recording frequency is not set by the investigator but is a function of the frequency of events, such as substance use. Most substance use is relatively sparse. However, it can be frequent, as in the example of cigarette smoking, which typically occurs 15–40 times per day in clinical populations, with frequencies of 60 per day or more not unknown. At these frequencies, even just recording the event imposes a burden, but completing assessments on each of these occasions quickly escalates the burden and provides a disincentive to recording events. A further complication is that the assessment burden varies across subjects based on frequency of use, particularly so when the study's aim is to compare light and heavy users (Shiffman & Paty, 2006). One solution has been to ask subjects to record all events but only administer assessments on a more modest and fixed number of occasions selected at random. For example, several studies (Beckham et al., 2008; Shiffman et al., 2002; 2004; Shiffman & Paty, 2006) have randomly sampled about five smoking occasions per day. Having the EMA computer sample events at random ensures that the resulting assessments are representative of all smoking occasions. Other studies have selected occasions in other ways: for example, Cooney et al. (2007) only assessed the first cigarette reported in each of four daily assessment intervals, and Tidey et al. (2008) assessed only the first two drinks each day. This ensures that some assessments fall into each time block or day, but it is not clear whether this sample of use occasions is representative. In the case of alcohol and other substances where cumulative dose is important, this may not sample subjects across the full range of intoxication. Moreover, because of differences in body mass, alcohol tolerance, and clearance, even the fixed number of drinks may have vastly different impact for different people.

Just as frequent substance use can present a challenge to EMA study design, so can rare events. Relapse investigators have been particularly interested in the *very first* lapse to substance use because it represents a pivotal transition from abstinence back to use. Even though lapses, per se, are all too frequent, the initial lapse episode is a unique and therefore rare event whose timing cannot be known in advance. As exemplified in EMA relapse studies (Cooney et al., 2007; Shiffman, Paty, Gnys, Kassel, & Hickcox, 1996) the strategy in EMA studies is to engage subjects in ongoing monitoring, so that they are poised to record the first lapse if and when it does occur. This process is by no means foolproof: for example, despite overall good compliance in that study, 16% of subjects in Shiffman, Paty et al. failed to record their first lapse in real time and thus could not be used in analyses of first lapses.

TIMING OF EVENT RECORDING

When subjects are asked to record events, such as substance use, we must also tell them *when* to initiate their recording. Having subjects record the event at its outset (i.e., when the subject is just starting to smoke, drink, etc.) has the advantage that the subject's state has not yet been affected by the substance use itself so is prospective with respect to use. However, it has several disadvantages. It may be more reactive. Research on self-monitoring suggests that prospective recording may maximize reactivity (McFall, 1977; Rozensky, 1974) likely because it makes the subject aware of his behavior while he is in a position to stop it. Relatedly, when the subject is in an appetitive "approach" state moving toward the gratification of substance use,

he may not be willing or even able to interrupt for recording. Finally, some important data are simply not available at the outset of the substance use episode: for example, subjects do not yet know how much they will ingest or how it will make them feel. For those reasons, most EMA studies have collected event data retrospectively after the substance use has occurred (Cooney et al., 2007; O'Connell et al., 2004; Shiffman, Paty et al., 1996) but there are exceptions (Shiffman et al., 2002). Ideally, the interval between the event and the recording should be kept to a minimum to avoid bias. Smokers in Shiffman, Paty et al. reported that they initiated reports about initial lapses to smoking an average of 8.4 minutes after the event, and drinkers in Collins et al. (1998) reported recording drinking episodes within 1 minute of their conclusion. Particularly when events have substantial impact, as a lapse might be expected to have, retrospective recording carries some risk of bias even when the interval is short.

Rather than choosing between gathering data at the outset or the end of a substance use episode, some investigators have gathered data on both occasions. Collins et al. (1998) asked subjects to initiate an assessment when they started drinking (which captured the drinking setting and predrink mood) and then another one when the drinking episode ended (which captured the number of drinks and postdrink mood and regret). Compliance was very high, with subjects reporting initiating the predrinking assessment within 1 minute of starting to drink 87% of the time and about half of the post-episode assessments within 1 minute of ceasing to drink.

As discussed subsequently, it seems inevitable that subjects will sometimes fail to record an episode of use in a timely way. On the assumption that knowing this has occurred is better than not, some investigators (e.g., Armeli et al., 2007; Shiffman, 2009; Shiffman, Paty et al., 1996) have periodically asked subjects to "confess" to these monitoring failures. For example, Shiffman, Paty et al. asked subjects daily whether they had failed to record a smoking lapse that occurred on that day; other than enumerating them, no other data were collected about these missed episodes. However, knowing that these episodes had occurred, and when, allowed these investigators to identify which lapses recorded in real time were truly the first lapses after quitting (84% of them) and also to construct a more accurate record of smoking over time for time-to-event analyses (Shiffman, Scharf, et al., 2006) and for analysis of quantity consumed (Armeli et al., 2007).

Studies with such "confessionals" must strike a delicate balance in soliciting such retrospective data while avoiding the message that such retrospective recording is an acceptable substitute for real-time recording.

DEFINING TARGET EVENTS

It is obvious that event monitoring requires that the subject have a clear understanding of what constitutes an event. Even when the focus is on occasions of substance use as events, very explicit definitions are necessary. Does one puff on a cigarette constitute "smoking"? What about inhaling someone else's side-stream smoke? Although studies have sometimes focused on individual units of drug-taking (a single drink, a single cigarette, a single pill), some drugs do not come conveniently quantified this way. Furthermore, investigators may wish to capture a more naturalistic unit, such as an "episode" of use, which may involve multiple units (e.g., having three drinks with dinner; e.g., Collins et al., 1998). Such definitions of target events obviously add some complexity and ambiguity, but they may be deemed more naturalistic or less reactive by allowing the subject to complete the "episode" without interrupting to record it.

The burden of definition becomes even greater if events are subjective; for example, deciding when an increase in craving constitutes a "temptation" to relapse. Training of subjects in preparation for the study, which is necessary in any case, provides an opportunity to communicate these definitions, and, in my experience, regular debriefing while the subjects are monitoring is also very helpful to perfecting and maintaining the definitions.

As discussed, for analysis, the investigator can define more complex "events" based on the data while keeping the subject's monitoring task simple. So, for example, Collins et al. (1998) directed subjects to record any drinking, no matter the quantity, but then subsequently categorized some episodes as "excessive" drinking based on the quantity of alcohol consumed.

Time-Based Assessments

ASSESSMENT FREQUENCY/DENSITY

EMA investigators implementing time-based assessments have to decide on the frequency of assessment. Studies have varied widely in the frequency of time-based assessments. Whereas several studies prompted subjects about five times a day (O'Connell et al., 2004; Shiffman et al., 2002; 2004), Delfino et al. (2001) prompted subjects as often as every 20 minutes, resulting in 50 or more assessments per day. The frequency of assessment clearly is a big factor in subject burden, and studies with more frequent assessments typically are restricted to shorter durations (e.g., a few days).

Clearly, in addition to sensitivity to subject burden, the assessment density should be dictated by conceptual and empirical considerations, particularly with respect to the expected rate of change or fluctuation in the phenomena of interest—both substance use and its putative drivers (see Collins & Graham, 2002). Different research questions and analyses may call for different data densities. The schedule of five time-based assessments per day in Shiffman et al.'s study of smoking and relapse was more than adequate for evaluating situational correlates of smoking during ad lib smoking, where it produced 70 nonsmoking observations per smoker during the 2-week baseline period (Shiffman et al., 2002). Conversely, the same frequency seemed rather sparse when Shiffman and Waters (2004) were analyzing the day of the very first smoking lapse episode to detect shifts in mood in the hours preceding the lapse: more than a third of subjects had no time-based assessments preceding the lapse, and the remainder averaged only three assessments in the hours preceding the lapse. Thus, the investigator has to consider the range of research questions and analyses contemplated and the assessment density needed for each.

TIME COVERAGE OF ASSESSMENTS

EMA prompts are intrusive, and the intrusion must be managed. Unrestricted prompting is illustrated in a protocol by Freedman, Lester, McNamara, Milby, and Schumacher (2006), which rang subjects' study-issued cell phone all through the day and night, without regard for subjects' sleep schedules. (The author reports that many of the homeless crack-cocaine addicts were conscientious enough to wake up to take the calls in the middle of the night!) Conversely, investigators sometimes arbitrarily restrict the hours during which the EMA protocol is active in order to avoid "beeping" subjects when they are asleep (e.g., stopping beeping subjects after 10 p.m.; Cooney et al., 2007; Hussong et al., 2001). The obvious concern is that this can yield an unrepresentative sample because it fails to sample an important part of the day: much substance use occurs late in the day (e.g., Shiffman, Paty et al., 1996). Moreover, mood, activity, and social setting also vary by time, and very late hours are distinctly different from the rest of the day. One solution has been to provide a way for subjects to turn off the computer when they are going to sleep, essentially treating it like an alarm clock (e.g., Shiffman et al., 2002). This requires appropriate software programming. Some studies have tried to address the issue by having the protocol active during the subject's predesignated "typical waking hours" (McCarthy et al., 2006; Todd, 2004). However, because a subject's bedtime and wake time varies, particularly on the days the subject is using drugs, this may not be a complete solution. It is not just sleep that may need to be protected from the intrusion of prompting. Subjects may have other times—worship services, meetings, intimate times—during which being beeped can be very intrusive and even, as when driving, when responding to a prompt may be dangerous. Some investigators have allowed subjects to suspend prompting for limited times. It appears that this abuse of such a facility can be avoided: even among adolescent smokers, subjects only suspended prompting about once a day (slightly more on school days, which makes sense) for an average of 80 minutes (Mermelstein, Hedeker, Flay, & Shiffman, 2007). Adult smokers only suspended prompting 2–3 times per week for less than a half hour per day (Shiffman et al., 2002), and heavy drinkers were reported to have made similar prudent use of such software features (Collins et al., 1998; Tidey et al., 2008). That having been said, it is not known how such time-outs may affect the representativeness of the acquired data.

Additional Issues

DURATION OF STUDY

Like decisions about assessment density, decisions about the duration of EMA monitoring must be sensitive to subject burden but ultimately be informed by theoretical and empirical expectations of the phenomenon under study. If the phenomenon under study is thought to be at steady state (e.g., ongoing, ad lib substance use), then the main consideration may be how long it takes to collect the number of observations and the degree of variability needed for the intended analysis. Assuming substance use is being measured as a key variable, one would need to see enough substance use episodes, and enough within-subject variability in substance use, to support the planned within-subject analyses. Similarly, empirical knowledge or theoretical predictions about the natural history of other variables under study informs the decision: if one is going to analyze the effect of marital spats on substance use, one needs to estimate how often such spats will

occur in order to know how long to monitor. In studies of relapse, one needs to know the likelihood of lapse events (first and otherwise) over time.

If one is studying a process that is expected to change over time, the data collection period must obviously encompass the developments of interest. Relapse curves tend to flatten out after 3–6 months, so studies of relapse (Cooney et al., 2007; O'Connell et al., 2004; Shiffman, Paty et al., 1996) would gain little from continuing any further. In fact, studies of relapse tend to focus on the first few weeks of abstinence, where the highest yield is expected, because this is when lapses are most likely.

Developmental processes, such as the development of dependence, may take place over intervals that are unrealistic for continuous intensive monitoring. One strategy for assessing development is to plan multiple brief periods of monitoring spaced at intervals that are thought to capture the developmental process. For example, Weinstein, Mermelstein, Shiffman, and Flay (2008) engaged teen smokers in three rounds of intensive EMA monitoring for a week at a time, every 6 months over a 1-year period. The longitudinal analysis showed that mood variability, which was elevated at baseline in those who adopted smoking, declined among those who escalated smoking over the observation period, suggesting that smoking had stabilized their mood.

The obvious limit to lengthy monitoring is subject burden and its expected effect on subject compliance and retention. Compliance issues and findings are addressed subsequently. Here, suffice it to say that although it seems reasonable to expect that compliance would decrease over time and that long study durations would increase attrition, the literature contains no empirical analyses of these questions. It seems prudent to reasonably limit study burden as a product of assessment density and study duration, but parametric data on the effect of these parameters are wanting.

DATA AGGREGATION

In organizing their data for analysis, EMA investigators face decisions about whether and how to aggregate their data. In momentary EMA protocols (i.e., other than daily dairies), individual moments, events, or blocks of time are the unit of data collection. However, as the literature cited here suggests, the unit of data collection need not be the unit of analysis. It is common for momentary data to be aggregated to larger units, such as days (e.g., Hussong et al., 2001;

Shiffman, Balabanis et al., 2000). This has the virtue of using what seems like a natural unit of time and yielding more "orderly" data with equally spaced units of equal duration. Also, aggregating data over multiple observations has the effect of yielding a more reliable score. Personality psychologists have shown that measures of a person's behavior that are aggregated over time or multiple observations are more robust predictors of future behavior (Epstein, 1986). One can think of each assessment as consisting of the "true score"—the person's true tendency or true feelings, mixed in with "noise," which might be due to errors of measurement or (in the case of assessing personality or personal tendencies) with situation-specific variations in behavior. When observations are aggregated and averaged, the random variations due to "noise," which vary in different directions, tend to cancel out, such that the score becomes more stable and more reflective of the true score or the person's true tendency. (This is very similar to the way in which reliability of a questionnaire scale rises as more questions are added.) The most important consideration for decisions about aggregation is the investigator's question and theoretical model. If the question is properly framed as one relating to progression (of mood, or use, or whatever) over days or other summary units, aggregation may be helpful and carries the benefits noted.

Conversely, there will clearly be cases where aggregation is not appropriate. For example, if one is concerned with the characteristics of particular episodes, such as lapses or occasions of use, such data must be analyzed at a disaggregate level of individual events. Aggregation also carries the cost of ignoring within-day (or week, etc.) variance and thus assuming that the important or meaningful variation occurs over larger time frames. Caution is called for in these judgments. In part because a good deal of theory in substance use focuses on stable individual differences, and because the field has not had access to finer level data, investigators may overestimate the stability of important variables and underestimate the importance of proximal or volatile influences. So, for example, to understand how mood relates to use of cocaine, assessing how the user felt, on average, on days she used cocaine may not be informative—one may need to understand how she felt just at the time she initiated use. Particularly because emotions are volatile and subject to sudden and even dramatic changes within a day, averaged data

may be uninformative and even misleading and highly likely to miss important influences on substance use.

Two empirical findings illustrate the importance of finer level data. First, Shiffman and Waters (2004) explored the influence of negative mood on first lapses to smoking. They first examined day-level averages in the days leading up to the initial lapse. Daily average negative mood or stress did not predict the risk of lapsing on a subsequent day. In contrast, mood assessments within the lapse day, in the hours leading up to the lapse, showed a clear pattern of escalating distress leading up to lapses (that were attributed to distress). The second cautionary finding concerned variations in smokers' ASE, which is often regarded as relatively stable and, indeed, often treated as a trait-like individual difference (Gwaltney et al., 2009). However, using momentary ratings of ASE in time-based assessments, Gwaltney, Shiffman, and Sayette (2005) showed that ASE varies meaningfully according to the immediate situation; for example, ASE was lower in moments when smokers were emotionally distressed. Variations were particularly notable among those with lower "trait" ASE, assessed by questionnaire at baseline. Thus, there is often more variation in variables of interest than assumed, and behavior may be more influenced by proximal experiences than assumed. Aggregation can mask important and relevant variation and therefore should be undertaken cautiously.

Concerns Regarding Ecological Momentary Assessment in Substance Use Research

Although EMA may be particularly suited to substance use research, substance use research also raises particular and sometimes unique challenges and issues for the application of EMA.

Cooperation of Substance Users

Application of EMA to studying substance use and abuse poses special challenges. Substance use may be illegal or, even if legal, frowned upon. Furthermore, substance users and abusers often suffer from multiple personal and social pathologies and are not considered particularly cooperative or conscientious subjects. Accordingly, substance use investigators have often been concerned that substance users would be unwilling or unable to comply with EMA protocols and have also worried that subjects would lose or steal devices issued to them. These concerns have impeded adoption of EMA methods in studies of substance use, particularly for illicit drugs. (In contrast, there has been substantial adoption in tobacco and alcohol research.)

However, the empirical evidence is reassuring. In a compelling demonstration, Freedman et al. (2006) were able to get good compliance from homeless crack-cocaine addicts enrolled in a study using cell phones. Not only was the population challenging, but so was the protocol: subjects were called every 3 hours all through the day and night for 14 days. Compliance was good: subjects responded to 77% of calls between 6 a.m. and midnight (which probably still included hours when subjects were sleeping). Study retention was also excellent, and only 1 of 30 phones was lost. Similarly, Epstein et al. (2009) gave Palm Pilot PDAs to cocaine and heroin addicts who carried them for about 4 months; these researchers report reasonable compliance and no extraordinary difficulties with devices. Other investigators have also recently reported good results with challenging substance use populations such as female opiate addicts (Johnson, Barrault, Nadeau, & Swendsen, 2009) and ecstasy users who were also engaged in use of alcohol, marijuana, cocaine, and hallucinogens (Hopper et al., 2006).

The reader will have noticed the preponderance of studies of alcohol and tobacco use in this review. In contrast to the multiple studies of these users of legal drugs, there are few EMA studies of illicit substance use, some of which are focused on simply demonstrating feasibility. Concerns about cooperation and compliance among illicit substance users probably account for the dearth of studies in these populations. The demonstrations of feasibility now making their way into the literature will likely encourage greater use of EMA methods among illicit drug users.

Reporting While Intoxicated

A further challenge in collecting data about episodes of psychotropic substance use is the concern that subjects' intoxication might make it difficult for subjects to complete data entry or to do so in a valid way. I know of no published study that addresses this question. However, in an unpublished study, Lorraine Collins and I collected data on PDAs from subjects who had consumed enough alcohol to be intoxicated and demonstrated that their PDA entries matched almost perfectly to data provided by interview around the same time. However, the question of whether perceptions are blurred or biased by intoxication with alcohol or other drugs remains. This question is not unique to EMA, but also arises

in laboratory studies where subjects are studied in intoxicated states, which could affect their response to psychometric scales or even their ability to record their responses accurately.

Intoxication may not only impair subjects' ability to report EMA data but also their willingness to do so. Intoxication itself, and the settings and psychological states associated with it, may undermine subjects' motivation to engage in this instrumental task. Thus, some of the states and behaviors that may be of most interest to researchers—for example, the peak of a drinking binge—may be rendered invisible in the data.

Reactivity

One concern that applies to all EMA studies but is particularly sharp for studies of substance use is *reactivity*—the possibility that the research methods themselves affect the behavior under study and thus distort the findings. EMA methods seem particularly vulnerable to reactivity because the assessments are completed repeatedly and in close proximity to the behavior of interest. Event recording of substance use episodes would seem to have particular reactive potential because it could make subjects aware of their substance use at a time when they have an opportunity to change it. Moreover, substance use is typically considered undesirable, even by the drug-using subject, and thus more vulnerable to reactivity. Research has shown that self-monitoring of behavior is most reactive when subjects are motivated to change their behavior (McFall, 1977). Reactivity is also maximized when subjects are asked to record undesirable target events before they are completed (Rozensky, 1974), probably because this gives subjects a chance to reconsider the behavior. (This suggests that event recording could be scheduled to occur *after* an episode to minimize reactivity; see Shiffman, Paty et al., 1996). Thus, EMA seems to have great potential for reactivity.

Thus far, studies assessing reactivity of drug-user recording have not demonstrated strong reactivity. In a study (Shiffman et al., 2002) of smokers who were asked to record each cigarette smoked as they prepared to quit smoking—which should maximize reactivity—found only a modest decrease in cigarette consumption (a reduction of 0.3 cigarettes per day) and no change on carbon monoxide levels, suggesting any changes in consumption were modest. Rowan et al. (2007) reported some changes in smoking-related cognitions due to monitoring, but their monitoring protocol included a specific intervention (suggesting appropriate coping), so this would seem to be an effect of intervention, not just monitoring.

In the alcohol literature, Collins et al. (1998) reported a significant decrease in drinking over 8 weeks of monitoring among treatment-seeking heavy drinkers. In contrast, Simpson et al. (2005) reported a study on daily monitoring of drinking that incorporated a no-monitoring control group; monitoring had no effect on drinking despite subjects' impressions that it had. Hufford et al. (2002) found no significant change in drinking in 2 weeks of monitoring drink-by-drink, and, surprisingly, found the least change in drinking among those who were trying to change their drinking. Hufford observed that subjects' interest in changing their drinking decreased after the monitoring period. Carney, Tennen, Affleck, Del Boca, and Kranzler (1998) reported no change in drinking over 2 weeks of monitoring. The absence of robust changes in substance use due to monitoring seems surprising. Moos (2008) speculates that the very intensity of EMA assessment may blunt reactivity by causing habituation. However, reactivity could vary by context and EMA protocol, and the issue is by no means settled. Inclusion of no-monitoring control groups in studies can help assess reactivity. Investigators need to be alert to the potential for reactivity in designing EMA protocols.

The sheer burden of EMA assessment could also conceivably affect subjects' behavior and experience. If responding to EMA prompts imposes a burden or stress, this could conceivably promote increased substance use or undermine attempts to quit. Litt, Cooney, and Morse (1998) reported that EMA monitoring did not appear to affect drinking outcomes among treated alcoholics (compared to a group that did not monitor), despite the subjects' verbal reports that monitoring had suppressed their urges and drinking. Repeated EMA assessments are also likely to make subjects more self-aware, which could change behavior in ways that could exacerbate existing trends ("Boy, I really *am* depressed") or ameliorate them ("I seem to be tired; I'd better plan to get more sleep"). However, studies have not found any change in symptoms due to momentary (e.g., Hufford et al., 2002) or daily (e.g., Simpson et al., 2005) monitoring. Outside the substance use area, Stone et al. (2003) reported a randomized trial in which the burden of EMA was systematically varied. There were no systematic changes in pain ratings when the frequency of EMA pain assessments was increased from 3 to 12 times per day. Thus, although reactivity remains a concern, the literature to date has not indicated strong reactivity effects.

Compliance

EMA methods make severe demands of participating subjects. Subjects are expected to carry an assessment device, respond to randomly scheduled prompts and assessments, and record target behaviors. Moreover, the strength of the method depends on subject compliance. Noncompliance—failure to record data when prompted or to record events—can lead to significant bias. When subjects choose when they do or do not record substance use or do or do not respond to time-based assessment prompts, they may complete assessments only when they are not stressed or only when their craving is not intense, thus biasing the analyses. Thus, compliance is critical.

COMPLIANCE WITH TIME-BASED RECORDING

Compliance with time-based assessments implemented via prompts issued under the investigator's control is readily assessed because one can track when a prompt was issued and whether it received a response. Although it is unrealistic to expect perfect compliance—subjects may not be able to hear the prompt or be indisposed (e.g., in the shower) when it comes—good compliance has been demonstrated in some studies. Compliance has varied widely across studies, ranging from more than 90% in some studies (Armeli et al., 2007; Litt, Cooney, & Morse, 2000; Shiffman et al., 2002; Todd et al., 2009), with many studies reporting compliance rates around 75–80% (e.g., Carter et al., 2008; McCarthy et al., 2008; Tidey et al., 2008), and others as low as 50% (Litt et al., 1998; Otsuki, Tinsley, Chao, & Unger, 2008; Shapiro et al., 2002). It is not completely clear what causes this variation. Some may be due to the nature of the subjects and the settings they inhabit (e.g., noisy environments can make it hard to hear assessment prompts; see Hopper et al, 2006), some to the degree of subject burden, and some due to subject training and management. To the last point, Beckham et al. (2008) report that compliance improved from 67% to 78% when an incentive for completing assessments was introduced, suggesting that incentives can help boost compliance. Achieving and maintaining high compliance is critical to an EMA study's validity.

The means available for assessing timely compliance vary with the tools used in data collection. Many studies of drinking have used electronic diaries in which a palmtop computer handled all the field tasks: presenting and recording assessments and prompting subjects at scheduled assessment times, and creating time-stamped records that verify timely completion. However, the timeliness of paper diaries is impossible to judge, and concerns have been raised about records on paper diaries. A study that covertly instrumented paper diaries (Stone, Shiffman, Schwartz, Broderick, & Hufford, 2002) found that subjects falsified the timing information on the majority of entries, and hoarded and back-filled (or forward-filled!) the entries at another time, thus undermining the very purpose of using diary methods. Strikingly, only 11% of the returned paper diaries that seemed timely, based on subjects' recorded date and time, could actually have been completed in a timely way. A few studies have used an electronic device (such as a programmable watch or blood pressure cuff) to prompt subjects, who then recorded the assessments in a paper diary (e.g., Delfino et al., 2001; Litt et al., 1998). In that instance, returned diaries are sometimes used as evidence of compliance. However, both Broderick, Schwartz, Shiffman, Hufford, and Stone (2003) and Litt et al. (1998) have demonstrated that such back-filling and falsification occurs even when subjects are beeped electronically (subjects apparently record the time of the beep, then complete the diary later). Some studies have used methods such as checking postmarks on mailed diaries to avoid or detect back-filling, and some investigators have claimed that they achieve superior paper diary compliance (Green, Rafaeli, Bolger, Shrout, & Reis, 2006). However, electronic diaries, now widely available, are the most robust method of time-stamping data and avoiding falsification. Electronic diaries also have other advantages, such as handling of prompting schedules and management of branching and other contingencies in assessment (see Hufford, 2007; Shiffman et al., 2008).

COMPLIANCE WITH RECORDING
OF SUBSTANCE USE

Assessing compliance with recording of events (e.g., substance use) is much more challenging than assessing compliance with prompted assessments because we usually have no way of knowing how many events there truly were or when they occurred. If a subject records no heroin use on Wednesday, we usually cannot know whether the subject was truly abstinent or simply failed to record one or more drug-use events. There is no "gold standard" measure against which subject reports can be compared. It is tempting to use subject retrospective reports of use as the comparator, but, as discussed in a later section, such reports are suspect. Nevertheless, although compliance data are often not explicitly reported (cf. Stone & Shiffman, 2002), one can often compare rates of EMA event recording to subjects' global estimates of consumption. Like the data on compliance with prompts, imputed compliance with event entries also seems to vary across studies. For example, the proportion of cigarettes estimated to have been entered ranges from 22% (Rowan et al., 2007) to 50% (Delfino et al., 2001; Shapiro et al., 2002) and up to 90% (Shiffman, 2009).

Compliance may be lower, more variable, and even harder to estimate when subjects who are abstinent and trying to maintain abstinence are asked to record lapses. For example, Litt et al. (1998) report that their recovering alcoholic subjects only recorded a minority of their lapses (but this study was marked by poor compliance on all measures). Later, the same group (Litt et al., 2000) noted that a different sample of recovering alcoholics recorded much *more* drinking on EMA than on a later retrospective assessment. Thus, compliance with alcohol lapse recording remains uncertain, but studies including biochemical markers (discussed subsequently) indicate that some lapses are not recorded. A further related concern is that about a third of alcoholics seem to suspend recording for a few days after a lapse (Litt et al., 1998; 2000), which would interfere with collection of data about further lapses and about the sequelae of lapses. Similar phenomena might occur within a single drinking episode: subjects may fail to enter later drinks as the number of drinks mounts and subjects become more intoxicated. In any case, compliance with event entries is critical to EMA and seems particularly problematic during abstinence, but it is difficult to assess.

Comparisons with Time-Line Follow-Back Measures

One way to try to address whether subjects comply with EMA event entries reporting substance use is to compare the amount or frequency of use reported by EMA to the amount reported by retrospective self-reports collected using the time-line follow-back (TLFB) method (Sobell, 1995). In TLFB, subjects are asked to recall their substance use for a past period (usually 7–30 days) employing a calendar structure and with the use of anchors (e.g., special events on particular days) to aid memory. Investigators typically regard the EMA data as more likely to be valid, but these studies are also meant to address questions about whether subjects can be relied on to accurately record their use with EMA methods.

In examining TLFB data, it is important to recognize its limitations. A study of 232 smokers analyzed 2 weeks' worth of TLFB data (Shiffman, 2009) and found that the TLFB reports of daily cigarette consumption showed very substantial digit bias or "heaping"—the rounding of reported quantities. Almost half of daily TLFB records were rounded to even multiples of 10, suggesting that TLFB data need to be treated with some skepticism. In contrast, the contemporaneous cigarette counts from EMA recording showed no digit bias.

In the same study, the EMA records showed an average of 2.6 fewer cigarettes per day (11% of total) than subjects later recalled on TLFB, suggesting that subjects sometimes failed to record some cigarettes. However, on about one-third of days, subjects later recalled smoking *fewer* cigarettes than they had actually entered. This suggests that subjects sometimes failed to record all cigarettes, but it also suggests that failure to record could not consistently account for discrepancies between EMA and TLFB, which likely also reflect error in TLFB measures.

In addition to looking for correspondence in the absolute number of drug-use events recorded, studies have also examined the correlation between the two measures. The correlation between EMA and TLFB was examined on two levels: the correlation between the averages, which reflects individual differences in smoking rate, and correlations across days within subjects, which reflect the patterns that both methods aim to capture. In Shiffman (2009) the overall average cigarette consumption (aggregated across all days) was highly correlated between methods, $\beta = 0.77$. In other words, both sources identify the same people as light or heavy smokers. However, the within-subject correlation across days (i.e., the day-by-day match) was modest, $\beta = 0.29$. In other words, the patterns of variation in cigarette consumption over days did not match very well. (Very similar figures have been reported for EMA vs. recalled pain; Broderick et al., 2008). This suggests that for estimating smokers' relative overall consumption, TLFB is adequate. However, when estimating patterns or changes in consumption, EMA may be necessary.

In a similar study of drinking, Carney et al. (1998) report that the between-subjects correlation for drinks per day (aggregated across days) was 0.89 (see also Hufford et al., 2002), whereas the average within-subject cross-day correlation dropped to 0.44, suggesting that less than 20% of the variance in TLFB overlapped with EMA records. As was the case in other studies (Carney et al., 1998; Perrine, Mundt, Searles, & Lester, 1995; Toll et al., 2006), the individual EMA-TLFB correlations for each subject varied very widely, with correlations ranging from 0.32 to 0.90. The causes and correlates of this variability are unknown, suggesting the potential for bias due to individual differences.

The studies reviewed so far have examined reports during ad lib use. Studies that examined the correlation between EMA and TLFB data during treatment have a different dynamic, in part because abstinence is dominant and may artificially inflate agreement. Also, in the context of abstinence, occasions of use may be more salient and memorable, although also more embarrassing. Toll, Cooney, McKee, and O'Malley (2005) studied smokers who completed daily sessions with an interactive voice response system (IVRS; i.e., reporting to an automated phone system) and weekly TLFB during the first week of quitting; these researchers report that more smoking was reported on IVRS than on TLFB, but with discrepancies in both directions. Litt et al. (2000) report that alcoholics just discharged from treatment recorded much more drinking on EMA than on TLFB. Tucker, Foushee, Black, and Roth (2007) examined daily IVRS records and TLFB during recovery from drinking in 37 subjects. Aggregate measures of drinking days showed excellent agreement ($r = 0.98$). More detailed day-by-day agreement was lower; on weeks when drinking was reported, perfect agreement was achieved only 17% of the time. Again, there was wide variation in the degree of agreement. This suggests again that retrospective measures may distort patterns of drinking even when they capture the overall level.

Comparisons with Biochemical Markers

Although we lack a true gold standard, substance use, more than other behaviors studied with EMA, may lend itself to objective verification because it leaves biological traces. Several studies have related EMA data on use to biochemical markers. In Freedman, Lester, McNamara, Milby, and Schumacher's (2006) study of homeless crack addicts, 7% of participants showed positive urine tests while failing to report cocaine use in their EMA data, suggesting perhaps reasonable but imperfect compliance. As is the case with many biochemical markers, the drug tests could not verify or contradict exact quantities or timing of substance use. A study by Perrine, Mundt, Searles, and Lester (1995) used daily measures of blood alcohol concentration (BAC) in the evening to validate daily IVRS entries over 28 days. Although BAC provided a crude indicator of alcohol consumption, the evening BAC would not reflect either earlier morning or later night-time drinking. Nevertheless, across subjects, IVRS reports of drinks consumed, averaged over days, correlated 0.72 with observed BAC. Within-subject correlations across days were still high (r = 0.61) but varied considerably across subjects (–0.07–0.92).

Smoking elevates carbon monoxide (CO), but cigarette consumption correlates only weakly with CO for multiple reasons: CO absorption from cigarettes varies considerably, CO can be absorbed from other sources, and CO clearance is rapid and variable. Nevertheless, in a study of smokers over 2 weeks (Shiffman, 2009), EMA records of cigarette consumption correlated reasonably well with observed levels of CO. A more compelling analysis examined *changes* in CO across multiple measurement occasions and found good correlations between EMA-recorded cigarettes and CO levels, particularly among subjects whose CO levels varied (r = 0.69). Because CO has a short half-life, it particularly reflects *recent* smoking, and this was used to assess whether cigarettes were recorded in a timely way. CO levels correlated specifically with the number of cigarette entries made in the preceding 2 hours (the half-life of CO), even when controlling for the total number of cigarettes consumed that day, suggesting that subjects had recorded cigarettes in a timely way. Chandra et al.'s (2007) finding that the time distribution of cigarette entries predicted success in quitting also suggests that cigarettes were recorded in a timely way.

As was the case for analyses of TLFB measures, indices of compliance with recording of lapses after treatment was less encouraging. Toll et al. (2006) report that smokers' daily IVRS reports of claimed abstinence were contradicted by CO measures 9% of the time. Non-EMA claims of abstinence are also often contradicted by CO measures, particularly in treatment samples (Benowitz et al., 2002). Smokers are reluctant to admit to lapses, whether by EMA or other self-report methods. This may be true of all substance users in treatment.

Although analyses of biochemical markers are informative, most markers are limited in that they cannot verify or contradict consumption of a particular amount of drug or its timing due to the imprecision of current biochemical measures. The development of devices capable of recording biomarkers nearly in real time (e.g., ethanol sensors on the skin; Venugopal et al., 2008) may help resolve this problem, making objective verification of EMA event recordings possible. In the interim, investigators can use current biological tests as a crude check against EMA records of substance use.

Ecological Momentary Assessment Data in Relation to Other Measures
Comparing Ecological Momentary Assessment Data to Questionnaire Data

EMA data have often been used to assess situational patterns of substance use, which are seen as being relevant to motives for substance use. Such patterns have traditionally been assessed through global reports on questionnaires ("Do you smoke more when stressed?"). The question arises whether the patterns captured in detail via EMA might also be captured by such questionnaires, which are far easier to administer. Data on smoking patterns suggest that questionnaires do not adequately capture variations in smoking settings and moments. Among heavy smokers in a clinic, correlations between EMA-assessed patterns and questionnaire-reported patterns were near zero, even when identical items were used in both assessments (Shiffman, 1993). Similarly, in a study of light-smoking Asian college students, Otsuki, Tinsley, Chou, and Unger (2008) found no correlation between questionnaire-assessed social motives and coping motives and the patterns assessed via EMA.

Although the recently cited studies examined circumstances of smoking, rather than the motives, Piasecki, Richardson, and Smith (2007) asked college student smokers in an EMA protocol to directly report their motives for smoking each cigarette as they reported it. Associations between monitored motives and questionnaire-assessed motives were modest (median OR = 1.07), and the majority were not significantly different than 0—a devastating finding for such validity coefficients. Some of the most striking discrepancies occurred for motives related to negative-affect reduction, where questionnaire measures of negative affect were unrelated to real-time reports. Further, whereas smoking to reduce negative affect is typically cited as the leading motive for smoking in questionnaire measures (Shiffman, 1993), it was the *least* often cited motive when motives were tracked by EMA. Questionnaires do not seem to validly capture smoking patterns or motives as assessed by EMA.

Much of the literature on drinking has focused on a similar set of hypotheses about individual differences in drinking motives, focusing on drinkers who score high on DTC (Cooper et al., 1992)—that is, those who report drinking to reduce affective distress. Many studies have used EMA data or daily diaries to test whether smokers who report DTC motives demonstrate a stronger link between stress and drinking. The results have been mixed and complex. One of the more positive findings emerges from the study cited earlier (Armeli et al., 2008), in which cumulative daily stress ratings were used to predict on what day of the week subjects started drinking. The data showed that for subjects with high DTC, accumulating anxiety during the week led to earlier onset of drinking; among those low in DTC, higher anxiety led to later drinking onset. However, the relationship was not consistent: anger showed reverse effects. In another study, Todd, Armelli, and Tennen (2009) found that DTC did not moderate the relationship between mood and the onset of drinking throughout the week, but did do so during the work week, but only for some negative moods and not others. Another study showed that there was no relationship between stress and drinking among high-DTC subjects, although stress may reduce drinking among low DTC subjects (Todd, Armeli, Tennen, Carney, & Affleck, 2003). In sum, the results suggest that DTC questionnaires may tap some individual differences in smoking motives but that the relationships, as revealed by EMA, are far more complex than is captured in the DTC questionnaires.

Comparing Ecological Momentary Assessment Recording of a Single Episode to Later Recall

In contrast to those studies in which subjects are asked to characterize their general pattern of use, relapse researchers have been interested in the details of a single particular occasion—the very first lapse after subjects achieve abstinence. Data on first lapses have typically been collected by debriefing subjects months after the episode (e.g., Marlatt & Gordon, 1985; Shiffman, Hufford et al., 1997). Shiffman, Hufford et al. evaluated the accuracy of such retrospective recall by comparing data gathered that way to EMA data recorded in real time by subjects using a PDA to record lapses. The analysis revealed that recall accuracy was quite poor, with κ statistics for agreement in the .20s. Moreover, the retrospective reports appeared to be influenced by subjects' current smoking status, which could introduce substantial bias: for example, it is natural for subjects who know they have since resumed smoking to attribute the lapse, in retrospect, to internal and stable causes, given the outcome. Finally, Shiffman, Hufford et al. suggested that much of what passed for "recall" might actually be based on declarative knowledge about typical lapse situations. (This became evident when people who had never smoked could characterize the typical lapse situation about as well as the actual smokers could do retrospectively, suggesting that retrospective accounts of lapse episodes may have been produced from general knowledge about lapse episodes rather than from specific autobiographical recall of a particular lapse episode.) Moreover, the use of EMA methods made a substantive difference in conclusions about relapse process. Whereas retrospective data made it appear that subjects' feelings about their first lapse was associated with subsequent relapse (Curry, Marlatt, & Gordon, 1987)—probably because subjects' smoking status at the time of recall and their beliefs about relapse influenced their recall—prospective analyses from real-time data found little support for this notion (Shiffman, Hickcox et al., 1996). This illustrates how EMA data can provide new insights that go beyond those from recall methods.

Predictive and Construct Validity

Another way to assess the incremental construct validity of EMA assessment methods versus traditional questionnaires is to allow the two measurement types to "compete" in predicting an outcome of interest. Two analyses compared the ability of questionnaire- and EMA-based measures of smoking patterns to predict outcomes. On theoretical grounds, smokers who smoke to relieve negative affect are expected to fare poorly at quitting. In a direct comparison, Shiffman et al. (2007) tested the ability of a questionnaire measure of "negative affect smoking" and an EMA measure of negative affect smoking (the difference in negative affect between smoking and nonsmoking moments) to predict subsequent relapse. Only the EMA-based measure (the individual subject's correlation between mood and smoking) predicted individual differences in relapse risk. In another analysis (Shiffman, Hickcox et al., 1997b), questionnaire-based measures of association of smoking and drinking failed to predict who would lapse while drinking, but EMA-based measures significantly predicted lapsing while drinking. More comparisons of predictive and construct validity of questionnaire and EMA methods would be useful.

Ecological Momentary Assessment Measures

Most EMA studies use structured psychometric self-report scales much like those used in non-EMA psychometric assessment. There are special considerations in selecting and adapting questions for EMA, but these are not addressed here. However, EMA self-report need not be limited to such structured responses. A study by O'Connell et al. (1998) illustrated the use of a tape recorder to collect open-ended narrative data. O'Connell et al. were interested in the particular coping strategies subjects used to avoid lapsing but were concerned that a structured "checklist" assessment of coping strategies would be particularly reactive—it would essentially teach coping. So, instead, O'Connell et al. had subjects describe in their own words what they did or thought to avoid relapse, and their responses were later transcribed and coded. O'Connell et al.'s data confirmed the role of coping in preventing temptations from turning into lapses and identified responses that were more effective. This illustrates collecting self-report data without the structure of scaled responses.

Although EMA studies tend to rely on simple self-report, the EMA approach can incorporate a variety of other measures, particularly with the use of PDAs to enable sophisticated stimulus presentation and response assessment. Measurement of simple reaction-time can be useful. For example, Lukasiewicz, Benyamina, Reynaud, and Falissard (2005) tested the hypothesis that alcohol craving would slow reaction time by competing for cognitive resources. PDA-based EMA methods can also be used to implement cognitive performance tests, in which the PDA presents cognitive tasks on-screen to assess both correctness in responding and reaction time. In one study (Shiffman, Gnys, Paty, Kassel, & Hickcox, 1995), we demonstrated on several cognitive tasks that tobacco abstinence impaired cognitive performance among heavy daily smokers but not among "chippers"—light "casual" smokers who are not dependent. Kos et al. (1997) implemented a Stroop task (MacLeod, 1991), which tests ability to reject distraction from a task, but were unable to detect effects of abstinence, which is thought to impair concentration. Cognitive performance measures could also be used to assess acute intoxication with other drugs, although I am not aware of a published report of such use.

More complex tasks can also be administered. Waters and Li (2008) have implemented several "emotional Stroop" tasks on a PDA. Emotional Stroop tasks measure the degree to which a topic, such as smoking or anxiety, captures the subject's attention to a degree that interferes with cognitive performance. It assesses the degree to which individuals demonstrate "attentional bias"—that is, the tendency to preferentially attend to certain stimuli, such as those associated with substance use. The study demonstrated validity on an anxiety task (anxious subjects were more distracted by anxiety-relevant words), although it did not demonstrate any differences between smokers and nonsmokers in the degree to which they were distracted by smoking-related words. Warthen and Tiffany (2009) have extended EMA to assessment of cue reactivity, which is usually assessed in the laboratory (Carter & Tiffany, 2001), by using a PDA to present smokers with smoking-related and neutral photos. They showed reliable effects on craving, which could allow assessment of reactivity under various contexts. Thus, PDAs can be used to present a variety of stimuli and assess a variety of responses.

Technological developments increasingly allow data to be collected without any active subject response at all. For example, accelerometers can measure activity continuously or even detect certain kinds of motion, such as walking (Intille, 2007). PDA-based devices can be set to record ambient sound (Mehl, Pennebaker, Crow, Dabbs, & Price, 2001) and thus capture snippets of conversation or other sound (e.g., music) that can indicate the social and physical context. There is a large body of work on ambulatory assessment of psychophysiological responses (mostly cardiovascular; e.g., Kos et al., 1997). Other examples more directly related to studying substance use include the use of a sensor taped to the skin that measures blood alcohol levels (Davidson, Camara, & Swift, 1997; Venugopal et al., 2008) and thus provides a real-time, passive, and objective indicator of alcohol consumption and an indirect indicator of intoxication. Saito et al. (2005) have described the use of a sensor worn by the subject that samples and chemically analyzes ambient air; such sensors could conceivably be used, for example, to measure the subject's exposure to environmental tobacco smoke, which may be an important cue for smoking. Global positioning satellite (GPS) technology, now in widespread use, can passively track subject movements and location to aid in understanding the geographical context of substance use. For example, Kirchner et al. (2013) has demonstrated that proximity to tobacco retail outlets (assessed from passively sensed GPS signals mapped against geocoding of outlets) was related to risk of relapse among smokers who were quitting (see also Epstein et al., 2014). Instruments can also aid in event recording. For example, Brue, Karlson, and Escamilla (2001) have described a cigarette case that makes a time-stamped record each time it is opened to withdraw a cigarette. Researchers are also demonstrating integrated systems of sensors and technologies to capture behavior automatically (Stone, Shiffman, Atienza, & Nebeling, 2007). The Internet and growing wireless connectivity also provide increasing potential for real-time collection of data of all kinds, both from self-report and from connected devices. Thus, there is ever-growing potential for technology to enhance the richness of self-report EMA data with data that assess other aspects of subject functioning and data that passively capture the subject's location, movement, environment, and physiological state. Such multimodality assessments will undoubtedly enhance our understanding of substance use in the future.

Practical Issues in Ecological Momentary Assessment Research

The implementation of EMA places unique demands on both researchers and subjects. A detailed discussion of the practical aspects of implementing EMA is beyond the scope of this review, but is well covered in Hufford (2007). Here, I touch briefly on considerations of hardware and software and management of subjects and data.

Ecological Momentary Assessment Hardware and Software

Collection of EMA data requires devices to support data collection in the field. The "device" may be as simple as paper and pencil or as high-tech as a sophisticated and highly connected mobile phone. No matter what the technology, certain functions, listed here, must be provided for. Table 16.3 shows a range of devices and their support of various functions (see Shiffman, 2007). The functions include:

1. Presenting assessment content such as questions and response options if self-report data are being collected. This is obviously possible with everything from printed paper to palmtop computers. Meta-analysis suggests that verbal measures presented on-screen are psychometrically equivalent to their paper versions (Gwaltney, Shields, & Shiffman, 2008). IVRSs differ in that the assessment content is presented aurally and serially, which can challenge subjects' cognitive capacity (e.g., forgetting the first response option by the time they get to the seventh).

2. Recording the data for later retrieval. This is a basic function served by a variety of devices. Some devices (e.g., IVRS) store data centrally, which can have some security advantages (e.g., data are safe if the device is lost); most electronic devices currently used for EMA periodically send their data to a central store. Privacy can also be an issue for local storage, particularly with paper: subjects may not want a spouse or child to see their records.

3. Managing the logic of the assessment (e.g., enforcing skip patterns, testing data for validity of the responses, etc.). This is a major shortfall of paper diaries: subjects often enter out of range or invalid answers, skip questions, and violate skip patterns (Quinn, Goka, & Richardson, 2003).

4. Time-stamping the record to document time of completion; on paper diaries, this relies on subjects' recorded completion times. However, these records are not valid (Broderick et al., 2003; Litt et al., 1998; Stone et al., 2002). Some studies have had subjects return paper diaries daily by mail and used postmark to verify timeliness within limits, but this only establishes timing within 1–2 days.

5. Managing the schedule of assessments (e.g., determining when a time-based assessment is to be made). This can be handled by a device separate from the recording device (e.g., a programmed watch or a phone call to prompt an entry on paper) or be integrated with the data recording device.

    a. When the assessment schedule can be determined in advance, it can be programmed into a separate device, such as a programmable wristwatch.

    b. When the assessment schedule needs to change in response to events, either in the data (e.g., scheduling an assessment for x minutes after an occasion of substance use) or outside the data (e.g., adapting to subjects' varying wake-up time and bedtime), the scheduling device needs to be more flexible and programmable, and able to be integrated with the data stream. Computers, smartphones, and IVRS can provide such facilities.

6. Prompting the subject, if the protocol involves active prompting. Studies with paper recording have used separate devices such as pagers. More sophisticated computerized devices can integrate prompting with scheduling and data functions and can take an action when a subject fails to respond to prompting, such as recording the event or repeating the prompt at another time.

This discussion focuses on devices for self-report. Devices that gather physiological data (e.g., ambulatory heart rate and blood pressure) or that automatically record physical events (e.g.,

Table 16.3. Devices for Ecological Momentary Assessment Studies

Device / technology	Self-report device	Presenting assessment content	Prompting[1]	Recording data	Time-stamping[2]	Managing assessment logic[3]	Scheduling; pre-defined[4]	Scheduling; responsive[5]
Paper and pencil	Y	✓	✗	✓	✗	✗	✗	✗
Tape recorder	Y	✓	✗	✓	✗	✗	✗	✗
Smartphone	Y	✓	✓	✓	✓	✓	✗	✓
Palmtop computer or mobile phone	Y	✓	✓	✓	✓	✓	✓	✓
Interactive voice response (IVR)	Y	✓	✓/✗[6]	✓	✓	✓	✓	✓
Beeper/watch	N[7]	✗	✓	✗	✗	—	✓	✗
Physiological monitor	N	—[8]	✗	✓	✓	✓	✓/✗[9]	✗
Event recorder[10]	N	—	✗	✓	✓	—	—	—

✓ supported ✗ not supported — Not applicable

1. Ability to proactively prompt the user (e.g., by "beeping")
2. Data records are associated with a date and time of completion
3. Includes managing and enforcing skip patterns and ensuring in-range and formally correct data
4. For example, random scheduling or other arbitrary schedule that can be predefined
5. Allowing for change in scheduling in response to data received or to subject events such as indicating bedtime
6. Although IVRS is usually implemented as an in-bound call technology, some systems can execute outbound calls on a programmed schedule
7. These devices are used solely to issue prompts
8. No "content" needs to be presented for psychophysiological assessment or event recording. Some physiological monitors are appearing that are integrated with devices capable of collecting self-report data
9. Many devices handle only fixed intervals
10. For example, instrumented medication containers

opening of a cigarette case) need a subset of this functionality. When biological samples are collected in EMA studies, time-stamping may be important, but there is no standard method for doing this.

Portability is an essential feature of EMA devices when the aim is to capture data at representative moments because the device should travel with the subject in the environments he typically inhabits. This limits the applicability of otherwise capable devices like laptops and web-based systems. To state the obvious, cost and logistics weigh into selecting a method for data collection. Each investigator must decide the appropriate trade-off of cost and burden for capability, data quality, and validity. Cost considerations need to encompass the entire research process. The cost of devices and of software development is often a key consideration, but investigators should avoid being overly influenced by initial start-up costs and should also consider downstream costs, such as the cost of cell phone service or of data entry from paper diaries. Unfortunately, high fixed costs of technological solutions can make it very hard to initiate small or pilot studies.

When electronic devices are used, software is even more important than hardware. A variety of software and services is available, both from commercial sources and via freeware (e.g., Conner, 2013; Le, Choi, & Beal, 2006; Runyan et al., 2013). The task of programming for an EMA study for a specific protocol, even reprogramming freeware packages, should not be underestimated. Keep in mind that minor software errors can be disastrous and that limited functionality can substantially affect the scientific value of the data. Developing software de novo is even more challenging, and investigators are well advised to use existing software or services. The technological burden associated with EMA studies remains a substantial barrier to adoption.

Other Practical Considerations

EMA studies also demand considerable resources and administrative effort related to managing study subjects and data. Training of subjects on the protocol, the assessment, and any device used is an essential—and time-consuming—aspect of EMA studies. Data management for EMA studies can be quite demanding. EMA studies often yield huge datasets with hundreds of thousands of diverse observations (e.g., events, momentary, daily assessments) whose temporal relationships must be carefully maintained. These datasets also often include records that do not have self-report data at all but record other transactions of some importance (e.g., records of missed assessment prompts); these also have to be maintained within the database. Furthermore, preparation of datasets for particular analytic approaches may require substantial processing (e.g., aggregating to create a day-level dataset, finding observations preceding or succeeding events of interest, counting or characterizing events to create derived endpoints). Data management facilities for maintaining these databases and producing analytical datasets are an essential resource for EMA studies and should be planned into the study. EMA studies produce very rich datasets but also demand a substantial commitment of resources and attention.

Use of Ecological Momentary Assessment Methods for Drug Abuse Treatment

Many of the same factors that make EMA attractive for assessment in research also make it attractive for use in *ecological momentary intervention* (EMI; Beckjord & Shiffman, 2014; Heron & Smyth, 2010). Even simple event recording without any assessment or time-based data collection can be important as a way to track and then modify the frequency of substance use. Cinciripini, Wetter, and McClure (1997) showed that smokers could be helped to quit by imposing a structured schedule of reduced smoking frequency. In a series of studies, Riley, Jerome, Behar, and Weil (2002) piloted the use of a simple computer to implement such scheduled gradual reduction. Subjects first used the computer to record all smoking episodes; the computer subsequently took control of their smoking, signaled them when to smoke, and gradually increased the interval between cigarettes. Riley et al. also demonstrated a similar approach to scheduling use of nicotine medications to achieve cessation (Riley, Pici, Forman, & Behar, 2003). With collection of richer data, EMA methods have potential as richer adjuncts to treatment (see Carter, Day, Cinciripini, & Wetter, 2007; Reitzel et al., 2011). EMA can provide valid and up-to-date assessments of the antecedents of substance use, which provides a natural link to treatment based on stimulus control or self-control methods: the patient can be guided to avoid triggering stimuli or prepare coping strategies for use when encountering high-risk situations. Furthermore, going beyond assessment to intervention, real-time interventions seem to have great potential—for example, a device could be programmed to note trends in the data (e.g., craving rising, affect getting worse, exposure to drug stimuli) and warn patients when they are at risk and/or suggest a productive course of action. Thus, EMA-based treatment could provide on-the-spot intervention just when it's needed, any time of the day or night. Dozens of apps claiming to help people quit smoking are available, for example, but these typically do not use an evidence-based approach and lack data on efficacy (Abroms, Padmanabhan, Thaweethai, & Phillips, 2011). One early but very complex and sophisticated intervention program showed no benefit over standard treatment, but the control group was exposed to many of the benefits of the EMI (Wetter et al., 2011). Thus, the promise of highly tailored EMI interventions has yet to be definitively demonstrated. However, studies of simpler scheduled and on-demand SMS (mobile phone text) messages have demonstrated some effects (Rodgers et al., 2005; Weitzel, Bernhardt, Usdan, Mays, & Glanz, 2007), suggesting that EMI still holds promise.

Conclusion

EMA methods, which focus on studying real-world behavior in real time and on the relation of behavior to its settings, are well-suited to studying substance use in all its phases: initiation, ongoing use, cessation, and relapse. EMA studies have contributed detailed analyses of the relationship of mood to substance use and of the details of relapse process that would not have been possible with other methods. As EMA methods are further developed and more broadly applied, they are likely to offer even more detailed insight into substance use and abuse, perhaps laying foundations for new treatment paradigms. Furthermore, the application of EMA approaches to on-the-spot intervention with substance users holds the potential to revolutionize treatment delivery.

Future Directions

• Some developments in EMA methods and their applications to substance use will be driven by developments in technology. As mobile technology creates smaller, more capable, even-better-connected, easier to use, and more universal devices, EMA and EMI applications will become more sophisticated and capable. The increasing sophistication and ubiquity of mobile phones heralds the day when EMA won't need a separate device; it will just run on the subject's cell phone and link to the investigator through the communications "net."

• Further technology drivers will come from the proliferation of small, smart, communicative sensors that will track subject movement, physical and physiological state, and drug intake, and may also assess the environment—all without requiring active response from the subject—and supplementing self-report. Technology evolution will be the easy part; the challenge will be to meaningfully integrate the mass of multichannel data. New statistical and conceptual models and development of new analytics and theories to explain substance use on a more microlevel will be required.

• Data collection based on recall will continue to be a research tool for the foreseeable future. Research that helps define the circumstances under which recall yields reliable and valid data would help recall find its proper role, as would research on assessment methods that may minimize the distortions introduced by recall.

• EMI approaches to intervention using smart algorithms that track the client's behavior, thoughts, and feelings and deliver an intervention ideally suited for the immediate circumstance will emerge as powerful approaches to treatment. Development of such protocols will raise many questions about how to assess the client's needs, how to select the right intervention, how to decide when to intervene, and how to learn what works and what doesn't. Such highly fluid and customized interventions will also be a challenge to evaluate, but methods of development and evaluation are evolving along with technology and methodology (see https://community.isr.umich.edu/public/Default.aspx?alias=community.isr.umich.edu/public/jitai&).

EMA and EMI have a bright future to help us understand and change drug abuse.

Further reading

Hektner, J. M., Schmidt, J. A., & Csikszentmihalyi, M. (2007). *Experience sampling method: Measuring the quality of everyday life*. Thousand Oaks, CA: Sage Publications.

Shiffman, S. (2005). Dynamic influences on smoking relapse process. *Journal of Personality*, *73*(6), 1715–1748.

Shiffman, S. (2014). Conceptualizing analyses of ecological momentary assessment data. *Nicotine and Tobacco Research*, *16*(Suppl. 2), S76–S87. doi: 10.1093/ntr/ntt195

Shiffman, S., Stone, A. A., & Hufford, M. R. (2008). Ecological momentary assessment. *Annual Review of Clinical Psychology*, 4, 1–32.

Stone, A. A., Shiffman, S., Atienza, A., & Nebeling, L. (Eds.). (2007). *The science of real-time data capture: Self-reports in health research*. New York: Oxford University Press.

References

Abroms, L. C., Padmanabhan, N., Thaweethai, L., & Phillips, T. (2011). iPhone apps for smoking cessation: A content analysis. *American Journal of Preventive Medicine, 40*(3), 279–285. doi: 10.1016/j.amepre.2010.10.032

Armeli, S., Carney, M. A., Tennen, H., Affleck, G., & O'Neil, T. P. (2000). Stress and alcohol use: A daily process examination of the stressor-vulnerability model. *Journal of Personality and Social Psychology, 78*(5), 979–994.

Armeli, S., Dehart, T., Tennen, H., Todd, M., & Affleck, G. (2007). Daily interpersonal stress and the stressor—vulnerability model of alcohol use. *Journal of Social and Clinical Psychology, 26*, 896–921.

Armeli, S., Feinn, R., Tennen, H., & Kranzler, H. R. (2006). The effects of naltrexone on alcohol consumption and affect reactivity to daily interpersonal events among heavy drinkers. *Experimental and Clinical Psychopharmacology, 14*(2), 199–208.

Armeli, S., Todd, M., Conner, T. S., & Tennen, H. (2008). Drinking to cope with negative moods and the immediacy of drinking within the weekly cycle among college students. *Journal of Studies on Alcohol and Drugs, 69*(2), 313–322.

Armeli, S., Todd, M., & Mohr, C. (2005). A daily process approach to individual differences in stress-related alcohol use. *Journal of Personality, 73*(6), 1657–1658.

Bandura, A. (1977). Self-efficacy: Toward a unifying theory of behavioral change. *Psychological Review, 84*, 191–215.

Beckham, J. C., Wiley, M. T., Miller, S. C., Dennis, M. F., Wilson, S. M., McClernon, F. J., et al. (2008). Ad lib smoking in post-traumatic stress disorder: An electronic diary study. *Nicotine & Tobacco Research, 10*(7), 1149–1157.

Beckjord, E., & Shiffman, S. (2014). *Theoretical background for real-time monitoring and intervention related to alcohol use.* Manuscript submitted for publication.

Benowitz, N. L., Jacob, P., III, Ahijevych, K., Jarvis, M. J., Hall, S., LeHouezec, J., et al. (2002). Biochemical verification of tobacco use and cessation. *Nicotine & Tobacco Research, 4*(2), 149–159.

Bradburn, N., Rips, L., & Shevell, J. E. (1987). Answering autobiographical questions: The impact of memory and inference on surveys. *Science, 236*(4798), 157–161.

Broderick, J. E., Schwartz, J. E., Shiffman, S., Hufford, M. R., & Stone, A. A. (2003). Signaling does not adequately improve diary compliance. *Annals of Behavioral Medicine, 26* (2), 139–148.

Broderick, J. E., Schwartz, J. E., Vikingstad, G., Pribbernow, M., Grossman, S., & Stone, A. A. (2008). The accuracy of pain and fatigue items across different reporting periods. *Pain, 139*(1), 146–157.

Brue, V., Karlson, K., & Escamilla, G. (2001, March). *Utility of a computerized device in scheduled, reduced smoking.* Poster presented at the Seventh Annual Meeting of the Society for Research on Nicotine and Tobacco, Seattle, Washington.

Carney, M. A., Armeli, S., Tennen, H., Affleck, G., & O'Neil, T. P. (2000). Positive and negative daily events, perceived stress, and alcohol use: A diary study. *Journal of Consulting and Clinical Psychology, 68*(5), 788–798.

Carney, M. A., Tennen, H., Affleck, G., Del Boca, F. K., & Kranzler, H. R. (1998). Levels and patterns of alcohol consumption using timeline follow-back, daily diaries and real-time "electronic interviews." *Journal of Studies on Alcohol and Drugs, 59*(4), 447–454.

Carter, B. L., Day, S. X., Cinciripini, P. M., & Wetter, D. W. (2007). Momentary health interventions: Where are we and where are we going? In A. A. Stone, et al. (Ed.), *The science of real-time data capture: Self-reports in health research* (pp. 289–307). New York: Oxford University Press.

Carter, B. L., Lam, C. Y., Robinson, J. D., Paris, M. M., Waters, A. J., Wetter, D. W., et al. (2008). Real-time craving and mood assessments before and after smoking. *Nicotine & Tobacco Research, 10*(7), 1165–1169.

Carter, B. L., & Tiffany, S. T. (2001). The cue-availability paradigm: The effects of cigarette availability on cue reactivity in smokers. *Experimental Clinical Psychopharmacology, 9*(2), 183–190.

Chandra, S., Shiffman, S., Scharf, D. M., Dang, Q., & Shadel, W. G. (2007). Daily smoking patterns, their determinants, and implications for quitting. *Experimental and Clinical Psychopharmacology, 15*, 67–80.

Cinciripini, P. M., Wetter, D. W., & McClure, J. B. (1997). Scheduled reduced smoking: Effects on smoking abstinence and potential mechanisms of action. *Addictive Behaviors, 22*(6), 759–767.

Collins, L. M., & Graham, J. W. (2002). The effect of the timing and spacing of observations in longitudinal studies of tobacco and other substance use: Temporal design considerations. *Drug and Alcohol Dependence, 68*(Suppl. 1), S85–S96.

Collins, R. L., Morsheimer, E. T., Shiffman, S., Paty, J. A., Gnys, M., & Papandonatos, G. D. (1998). Ecological momentary assessment in a behavioral drinking moderation training program. *Experimental and Clinical Psychopharmacology, 6*, 306–315.

Conner, T. S. (2013). *Experience sampling and ecological momentary assessment with mobile phones.* Retrieved from http://www.otago.ac.nz/psychology/otago047475.pdf

Cooney, N. L., Litt, M. D., Cooney, J. L., Pilkey, D. T., Steinberg, H. R., & Oncken, C. A. (2007). Alcohol and tobacco cessation in alcohol-dependent smokers: Analysis of real-time reports. *Psychology of Addictive Behaviors, 21*(3), 277–286.

Cooper, M. L., Russell, M., Skinner, J. B., Frone, M. R., & Mudar, P. (1992). Stress and alcohol use: Moderating effects of gender, coping, and alcohol expectancies. *Journal of Abnormal Psychology, 101*(1), 139–152.

Curry, S., Marlatt, G. A., & Gordon, J. R. (1987). Abstinence violation effect: Validation of an attributional construct with smoking cessation. *Journal of Consulting and Clinical Psychology, 55*(2), 145–149.

Davidson, D., Camara, P., & Swift, R. (1997). Behavioral effects and pharmacokinetics of low-dose intravenous alcohol in humans. *Alcoholism: Clinical and Experimental Research, 21*(7), 1294–1299.

Delfino, R. J., Jamner, L. D., & Whalen, C. K. (2001). Temporal analysis of the relationship of smoking behavior and urges to mood states in men versus women. *Nicotine & Tobacco Research*, *3*(3), 235–248.

DeVries, M. (Ed.). (1992). *The experience of psychopathology: Investigating mental disorders in their natural settings*. Cambridge, UK: Cambridge University Press.

Dunbar, M. S., Scharf, D., Kirchner, T., & Shiffman, S. (2010). Do smokers crave some cigarettes more than others? Situational correlates of craving when smoking. *Nicotine & Tobacco Research*, *12*, 226.

Eich, E., Reeves, J., Jaeger, B., & Graff-Radford, S. (1985). Memory for pain: Relation between past and present pain intensity. *Pain*, *223*, 375–379.

Epler, A. J., Tomko, R. L., Piasecki, T. M., Wood, P. K., Sher, K. J., Shiffman, S., & Heath, A. C. (2014). Does hangover influence the time to next drink? An investigation using Ecological Momentary Assessment. *Alcoholism: Clinical and Experimental Research*. doi: 10.1111/acer.12386

Epstein, S. (1986). Does aggregation produce spuriously high estimates of behavior stability? *Journal of Personality and Social Psychology*, *50*(6), 1199–1210.

Epstein, D. H., Tyburski, M., Craig, I. M., Phillips, K. A., Jobes, M. L., Vahabzadeh, M., . . . Preston, K. L. (2014). Real-time tracking of neighborhood surroundings and mood in urban drug misusers: Application of a new method to study behavior in its geographical context. *Drug and Alcohol Dependence*, *134*, 22–29. doi: 10.1016/j.drugalcdep.2013.09.007

Epstein, D. H., Willner-Reid, J., Vahabzadeh, M., Mezghanni, M., Lin, J. L., & Preston, K. L. (2009). Real-time electronic diary reports of cue exposure and mood in the hours before cocaine and heroine craving and use. *Archives of General Psychiatry*, *66*(1), 88–94.

Ferguson, S., Shiffman, S., & Gwaltney, C. J. (2006). Do reductions in nicotine withdrawal symptoms and craving mediate treatment outcome in nicotine replacement therapy for smoking cessation? *Journal of Consulting and Clinical Psychology*, *74*, 1153–1161.

Freedman, M., Lester, K., McNamara, C., Milby, J., & Schumacher, J. (2006). Cell phones for Ecological Momentary Assessment with cocaine-addicted homeless patients in treatment. *Journal of Substance Abuse Treatment*, *30*, 105–111.

Green, A. S., Rafaeli, E., Bolger, N., Shrout, P. E., & Reis, H. T. (2006). Paper or plastic? Data equivalence in paper and electronic diaries. *Psychological Methods*, *11*, 87–105.

Gwaltney, C. J., Metrik, J., Kahler, C. W., & Shiffman, S. (2009). Self-efficacy and smoking cessation: A meta-analysis. *Psychology of Addictive Behaviors*, *23*, 56–66.

Gwaltney, C. J., Shields, A. S., & Shiffman, S. (2008). Equivalence of electronic and paper-and-pencil administration of patient reported outcome measures: A meta-analytic review. *Value in Health*, *11*, 322–333.

Gwaltney, C. J., Shiffman, S., Balabanis, M. H., & Paty, J. A. (2005). Dynamic self-efficacy and outcome expectancies: Prediction of smoking lapse and relapse. *Journal of Abnormal Psychology*, *114*, 661–675.

Gwaltney, C. J., Shiffman, S., & Sayette, M. A. (2005). Situational correlates of abstinence self-efficacy. *Journal of Abnormal Psychology*, *114*, 649–660.

Hammersley, R. (1994). A digest of memory phenomena for addiction research. *Addiction*, *89*, 283–293.

Harsch, N., & Neisser, U. (1989, November). *Substantial and irreversible errors in flashbulb memories of the Challenger explosion*. Poster presented at the annual meeting of the Psychonomic Society, Atlanta, GA.

Hektner, J. M., Schmidt, J. A., & Csikszentmihalyi, M. (2007). *Experience sampling method: Measuring the quality of everyday life*. Thousand Oaks, CA: Sage.

Heron, K. E., & Smyth, J. M. (2010). Ecological momentary interventions: Incorporating mobile technology into psychosocial and health behaviour treatments. *British Journal of Health Psychology*, *15*, 1–39. doi: 10.1348/135910709x466063

Hopper, J. W., Su, Z., Looby, A. R., Ryan, E. T., Penetar, D. M., Palmer, C. M., et al. (2006). Incidence and patterns of polydrug use and craving for ecstasy in regular ecstasy users: An ecological momentary assessment study. *Drug and Alcohol Dependence*, *85*(3), 221–235.

Hufford, M. R. (2007). Special methodological challenges and opportunities in Ecological Momentary Assessment. In A. A. Stone, S. Shiffman, A. Atienza & L. Nebeling (Eds.), *Science of real-time data capture: Self-reports in health research* (pp. 54–75). New York: Oxford University Press.

Hufford, M. R., Shields, A. L., Shiffman, S., Paty, & Balabanis, M. (2002). Reactivity to ecological momentary assessment: An example using undergraduate problem drinkers. *Psychology of Addictive Behaviors*, *16*(3), 205–211.

Hussong, A. M., Galloway, C. A., & Feagans, L. A. (2005). Drinking motives moderate daily mood-drinking covariation. *Journal of Studies on Alcohol*, *66*, 344–353.

Hussong, A. M., Hicks, R. E., Levy, S. A., & Curran, P. J. (2001). Specifying the relations between affect and heavy alcohol use among young adults. *Journal of Abnormal Psychology*, *110*(3), 449–461.

Intille, S. (2007). Technological innovations enabling automatic, context-sensitive Ecological Momentary Assessment. In A. A. Stone, S. Shiffman, A. Atienza & L. Nebeling (Eds.), *Science of real-time data capture: Self-reports in health research* (pp. 308–337). New York: Oxford University Press.

Jamison, R. N., Raymond, S. A., Levine, J. G., Slawsby, E. A., Nedeljkovic, S. S., & Katz, N. P. (2001). Electronic diaries for monitoring chronic pain: One-year validation study. *Pain*, *91*(3), 277–285.

Johnson, E. I., Barrault, M., Nadeau, L., & Swendsen, J. (2009). Feasibility and validity of computerized ambulatory monitoring in drug-dependent women. *Drug and Alcohol Dependence*, *99*(1–3), 322–326.

Kamarck, T. W., Shiffman, S., Smithline, L., Goodie, J. L., Thompson, H. S., Ituarte, J. J., et al. (1998). The diary of ambulatory behavioral states: A new approach to the assessment of psychosocial influences on ambulatory cardiovascular activity. In D. S. Krantz & A. Baum (Eds.) *Technology and methods in behavioral medicine* (pp. 163–194). Mahwah, NJ: Lawrence Erlbaum Associates.

Kassel, J. D., Stroud, L. R., & Paronis, C. A. (2003). Smoking, stress, and negative affect: Correlation, causation, and context across stages of smoking. *Psychological Bulletin*, *129*, 270–304.

Kihlstrom, J., Eich, E., Sandbrand, D., & Tobias, B. (2000). Emotion and memory: Implications for self-report. In A. A. Stone, J. Turkkan, C. Bachrach, J. Jobe, H. Kurtzman, & V. Cain (Eds.), *The science of self-report: Implication for research and practice* (pp. 81–99). Mahwah, NJ: Lawrence Erlbaum Associates.

Kirchner, T. R., Cantrell, J., Anesetti-Rothermel, A., Ganz, O., Vallone, D. M., & Abrams, D. B. (2013). Geospatial exposure to point-of-sale tobacco: Real-time craving and smoking-cessation outcomes. *American Journal of*

Preventive Medicine, 45(4), 379–385. doi: 10.1016/j. amepre.2013.05.016

Kirchner, T. R., Shiffman, S., & Cheong, J. (2007, February). *Modeling the abstinence-violation effect during smoking cessation.* Paper presented at the Annual meeting of the Society for Research on Nicotine and Tobacco, Austin, TX.

Kos, J., Hasenfratz, M., & Battig, K. (1997). Effects of a 2-day abstinence from smoking on dietary, cognitive, subjective, and physiologic parameters among younger and older female smokers. *Physiology & Behavior, 61*(5), 671–678.

Le, B., Choi, H. N., & Beal, D. J. (2006). Pocket-sized psychology studies: Exploring daily diary software for Palm Pilots. *Behavior Research Methods, 38*(2), 325–332.

Litt, M. D., Cooney, N. L., & Morse, P. (1998). Ecological Momentary Assessment (EMA) with treated alcoholics: Methodological problems and potential solutions. *Health Psychology, 17*(1), 48–52.

Litt, M. D., Cooney, N. L., & Morse, P. (2000). Reactivity to alcohol-related stimuli in the laboratory and in the field: Predictors of craving in treated alcoholics. *Addiction, 95*(6), 889–900.

Lowe, G. (1982). Alcohol-induced state-dependent learning: Differentiating stimulus and storage hypothesis. *Current Psychological Research, 2,* 215–222.

Lukasiewicz, M., Benyamina, A., Reynaud, M., & Falissard, B. (2005). An in vivo study of the relationship between craving and reaction time during alcohol detoxification using the ecological momentary assessment. *Alcoholism: Clinical and Experimental Research, 29*(12), 2135–2143.

Maclure, M., & Mittleman, M. A. (2000). Should we use a case-cross-over design? *Annual Review of Public Health, 21*(1), 193–221.

Marlatt, G. A., & Gordon, J. R. (1985). *Relapse prevention.* New York: Guilford.

Matarazzo, J. D., & Saslow, G. (1960). Psychological and related characteristics of smokers and nonsmokers. *Psychological Bulletin, 57,* 493–513.

MacLeod, C. M. (1991). Half a century of research on the Stroop effect: An integrative review. *Psychological Bulletin, 109*(2), 163–203.

McCarthy, D. E., Piasecki, T. M., Fiore, M. C., & Baker, T. B. (2006). Life before and after quitting smoking: An electronic diary study. *Journal of Abnormal Psychology, 115*(3), 454–466.

McCarthy, D. E., Piasecki, T. M., Lawrence, D. L., Jorenby, D. E., Shiffman, S., & Baker, T. B. (2008). Psychological mediators of bupropion sustained-release treatment for smoking cessation. *Addiction, 103*(9), 1521–1533.

McFall, R. M. (1977). Parameters of self-monitoring. In R. B. Stuart (Ed.), *Behavioral self-management: Strategies, techniques, and outcome* (pp. 196–214). New York: Brunner/ Mazel.

Mehl, M. R., Pennebaker, J. W., Crow, D. M., Dabbs, J., & Price, J. H. (2001). The Electronically Activated Recorder (EAR): A device for sampling naturalistic daily activities and conversations. *Behavior Research Methods, Instruments & Computers, 33*(4), 517–523.

Mermelstein, R., Hedeker, D., Flay, B., & Shiffman, S. (2007). Real-time data capture and adolescent cigarette smoking: Moods and smoking. In A. A. Stone, S. Shiffman, A. Atienza & L. Nebeling (Eds.), *The science of real-time data capture: Self-reports in health research* (pp. 117–135). New York: Oxford University Press.

Moghaddam, N. G., & Ferguson, E. (2007). Smoking, mood regulation, and personality: An event-sampling exploration of potential models and moderation. *Journal of Personality, 75*(3), 451–478.

Mohr, C. D., Armeli, S., Tennen, H., Carney, M. A., Affleck, G., & Hromi, A. (2001). Daily interpersonal experiences, context, and alcohol consumption: Crying in your beer and toasting good times. *Journal of Personal and Social Psychology, 80*(3), 489–500.

Mohr, C. D., Brannan, D., Mohr, J., Armeli, S., & Tennen, H. (2008). Evidence for positive mood buffering among college student drinkers. *Personality and Social Psychology Bulletin, 34*(9), 1249–1259.

Moos, R. H. (2008). Context and mechanisms of reactivity to assessment and treatment. *Addiction, 103*(2), 249–250.

Moskowitz, D., & Young, S. N. (2006). Ecological Momentary Assessment: What it is and why it is a method of the future in clinical psychopharmacology. *Journal of Psychiatry & Neuroscience, 31,* 13–20.

Muraven, M., Collins, R. L., Morsheimer, E. T., Shiffman, S., & Paty, J. A. (2005). The morning after: Limit violations and the self-regulation of alcohol consumption. *Psychology of Addictive Behaviors, 19,* 253–262.

O'Connell, K. A., Gerkovich, M. M., Cook, M. R., Shiffman, S., Hickcox, M., & Kakolewski, K. E. (1998). Coping in real time: Using Ecological Momentary Assessment techniques to assess coping with the urge to smoke. *Research in Nursing & Health, 21*(6), 487–497.

O'Connell, K. A., Schwartz, J. E., Gerkovich, M. M., Bott, M. J., & Shiffman, S. (2004). Playful and rebellious states vs. negative affect in explaining the occurrence of temptations and lapses during smoking cessation. *Nicotine & Tobacco Research, 6,* 661–674.

Otsuki, M., Tinsley, B. J., Chao, R. K., & Unger, J. B. (2008). An ecological perspective on smoking among Asian American college students: The roles of social smoking and smoking motives. *Psychology of Addictive Behaviors, 22*(4), 514–523.

Park, C. L., Armeli, S., & Tennen, H. (2004). The daily stress and coping process and alcohol use among college students. *Journal of Studies on Alcohol, 65*(1), 126–135.

Paty, J. A., Kassel, J. D., & Shiffman, S. (1992). The importance of assessing base rates for clinical studies: An example of stimulus control of smoking. In M. W. deVries (Ed.), *The Experience of Psychopathology: Investigating Mental Disorders in their Natural Settings* (pp. 347–352). New York: Cambridge University Press.

Perrine, M. W., Mundt, J. C., Searles, J. S., & Lester, L. S. (1995). Validation of daily self-reported alcohol consumption using interactive voice response (IVR) technology. *Journal of Studies on Alcohol, 56*(5), 487–490.

Peters, R., & McGee, R. (1982). Cigarette smoking and state-dependent memory. *Psychopharmacology 76*(3), 232–235.

Piasecki, T. M., Jorenby, D. E., Smith, S. S., Fiore, M. C., & Baker, T. B. (2003). Smoking withdrawal dynamics: III. Correlates of withdrawal heterogeneity. *Experimental and Clinical Psychopharmacology, 11*(4), 276–285.

Piasecki, T. M., Richardson, A. E., & Smith, S. M. (2007). Self-monitored motives for smoking among college students. *Psychology of Addictive Behaviors, 21*(3), 328–337.

Quinn, P., Goka, J., & Richardson, H. (2003). Assessment of an electronic daily diary in patients with overactive bladder. *British Journal of Urology, 91*(7), 647.

Rathbun, S. L., Shiffman, S., & Gwaltney, C. J. (2007). Modeling the effects of partially observed covariates on Poisson process intensity. *Biometrika, 94*, 153–165.

Redelmeier, D. A., Katz, J., & Kahneman, D. (2003). Memories of colonoscopy: A randomized trial. *Pain, 104*, 187–194.

Reis, H., & Wheeler, L. (1991). Studying social interaction with the Rochester Interaction Record. In M. Zanna (Ed.), *Advances in experimental social psychology* (Vol. 24, pp. 270–318). San Diego, CA: Academic.

Reitzel, L. R., McClure, J. B., Cofta-Woerpel, L., Mazas, C. A., Cao, Y., Cinciripini, P. M., . . . Wetter, D. W. (2011). The efficacy of computer-delivered treatment for smoking cessation. *Cancer Epidemiology, Biomarkers, & Prevention, 20*(7), 1555–1557. doi: 10.1158/1055-9965.EPI-11-0390

Riley, W. T., Jerome, A., Behar, A., & Weil, J. (2002). Computer and manual self-help behavioral strategies for smoking reduction: Initial feasibility and one year follow-up. *Nicotine and Tobacco Research, 4*(Supplement 2), S183–S188.

Riley, W. T., Pici, M., Forman, V. L., & Behar, A. (2003). *Computerized dosing of nicotine inhalers: Effects on use and quit rates.* Paper presented at the 9th Annual meeting of the Society for Research on Nicotine and Tobacco, New Orleans, LA.

Rodgers, A., Corbett, T., Bramley, D., Riddell, T., Wills, M., Lin, R. B., et al. (2005). Do u smoke after txt? Results of a randomised trial of smoking cessation using mobile phone text messaging. *Tobacco Control, 14*(4), 255–261.

Ross, M. (1989). Relation of implicit theories to the construction of personal histories. *Psychological Review, 96*(2), 341–357.

Rowan, P. J., Cofta-Woerpel, L., Mazas, C. A., Vidrine, J. I., Reitzel, L. R., Cinciripini, P. M., et al. (2007). Evaluating reactivity to ecological momentary assessment during smoking cessation. *Experimental and Clinical Psychopharmacology, 15*(4), 382–389.

Rozensky, R. H. (1974). The effect of timing of self-monitoring behavior on reducing cigarette consumption. *Journal of Behavior Therapy and Experimental Psychiatry, 5*, 301–303.

Runyan, J. D., Steenbergh, T. A., Bainbridge, C., Daugherty, D. A., Oke, L., & Fry, B. N. (2013). A smartphone ecological momentary assessment/intervention "app" for collecting real-time data and promoting self-awareness. *PLoS ONE, 8*(8), e71325. doi: 10.1371/journal.pone.0071325

Saito, M., Kumano, H., Yoshiuchi, K., Kokubo, K., Yamamoto, Y., Shimohara, N., et al. (2005). Symptom profile of multiple chemical sensitivity in actual life. *Psychosomatic Medicine, 67*, 318–325.

Schwartz, J. E., & Stone, A. A. (1998). Data analysis for EMA studies. *Health Psychology, 17*, 6–16.

Shapiro, D., Jamner, L. D., Davtdov, D. M., & James, W. (2002). Situations and moods associated with smoking in everyday life. *Psychology of Addictive Behavior, 16*(4), 342–345.

Shiffman, S. (1993). Assessing smoking patterns and motives. *Journal of Consulting and Clinical Psychology, 61*, 732–742.

Shiffman, S. (2007). Designing protocols for Ecological Momentary Assessment. In A. A. Stone, S. Shiffman, A. Atienza & L. Nebeling (Eds.), *The science of real-time data capture: Self-reports in health research* (pp. 27–53). New York: Oxford University Press.

Shiffman, S. (2008). Effect of nicotine lozenges on affective smoking withdrawal symptoms: Secondary analysis of a randomized, double-blind, placebo-controlled clinical trial. *Clinical Therapeutics, 30*, 1461–1475.

Shiffman, S. (2009). How many cigarettes did you smoke? Assessing cigarette consumption by global report, time-line follow-back, and ecological momentary assessment. *Health Psychology, 28*, 519–526.

Shiffman, S. (2014). Conceptualizing analyses of ecological momentary assessment data. *Nicotine and Tobacco Research, 16*(Suppl. 2), S76–S87. doi: 10.1093/ntr/ntt195

Shiffman, S., Balabanis, M. H., Gwaltney, C. J., Paty, J. A., Gnys, M., Kassel, J. D., et al. (2007). Prediction of lapse from associations between smoking and situational antecedents assessed by Ecological Momentary Assessment. *Drug and Alcohol Dependence, 91*, 159–168.

Shiffman, S., Balabanis, M. H., Paty, J. A., Engberg, J., Gwaltney, C. J., Liu, K., et al. (2000). Dynamic effects of self-efficacy on smoking lapse and relapse. *Health Psychology, 19*(4), 315–323.

Shiffman, S., Dunbar, M. S., Li, X., Scholl, S. M., Tindle, H. A., Anderson, S. J., & Ferguson, S. G. (2014). Smoking patterns and stimulus control in intermittent and daily smokers. *PLoS ONE, 9*(3), e89911. doi: 10.1371/journal.pone.0089911

Shiffman, S., Elash, C. A., Paton, S. M., Gwaltney, C. J., Paty, J. A., Clark, D. B., et al. (2000). Comparative efficacy of 24-hour and 16-hour transdermal nicotine patches for relief of morning craving. *Addiction, 95*(8), 1185–1195.

Shiffman, S., Engberg, J., Paty, J. A., Perz, W., Gnys, M., Kassel, J. D., et al. (1997). A day at a time: Predicting smoking lapse from daily urge. *Journal of Abnormal Psychology, 106*, 104–116.

Shiffman, S., Ferguson, S. G., & Gwaltney, C. J. (2006). Immediate hedonic response to smoking lapses: Relationship to smoking relapse, and effects of nicotine replacement therapy. *Psychopharmacology, 184*, 608–614.

Shiffman, S., Gwaltney, C. J., Balabanis, M., Liu, K. S., Paty, J. A., Kassel, J. D., et al. (2002). Immediate antecedents of cigarette smoking: An analysis from Ecological Momentary Assessment. *Journal of Abnormal Psychology, 111*(4), 531–545.

Shiffman, S., Hickcox, M., Paty, J. A., Gnys, M., Kassel, J. D., & Richards, T. (1996). Progression from a smoking lapse to relapse: Prediction from abstinence violation effects, nicotine dependence, and lapse characteristics. *Journal of Consulting and Clinical Psychology, 64*, 993–1002.

Shiffman, S., Hickcox, M., Paty, J. A., Gnys, M., Kassel, J. D., & Richards, T. (1997a). The Abstinence Violation Effect following smoking lapses and temptations. *Cognitive Therapy and Research, 21*(5), 497–523.

Shiffman, S., Hickcox, M., Paty, J. A., Gnys, M., Richards, T., & Kassel, J. D. (1997b). Individual differences in the context of smoking lapse episodes. *Addictive Behaviors, 22*(6), 797–811.

Shiffman, S., Hufford, M., Hickcox, M., Paty, J. A., Gnys, M., & Kassel, J. D. (1997). Remember that? A comparison of real-time versus retrospective recall of smoking lapses. *Journal of Consulting and Clinical Psychology, 65*(2), 292–300.

Shiffman, S., Kirchner, T. R., Ferguson, S. G., & Scharf, D. N. (2009). Patterns of intermittent smoking: An analysis using Ecological Momentary Assessment. *Addictive Behaviors, 34*, 514–519.

Shiffman, S., Kirchner, T., Ferguson, S., Scharf, D., & Gitomer, A. (2008, February). Efficacy of cellular phones for monitoring intermittent smoking patterns. Poster presented at the Annual Meeting of the Society for Research on Nicotine and Tobacco, Portland, OR.

Shiffman, S., Patten, C. A., Gwaltney, C. J., Paty, J. A., Gnys, M., Kassel, J. D., et al. (2006). Natural history of nicotine withdrawal. *Addiction, 101*, 1822–1832.

Shiffman, S., & Paty, J. A. (2006). Smoking patterns and dependence: Contrasting chippers and heavy smokers. *Journal of Abnormal Psychology, 115*(3), 509–523.

Shiffman, S., Paty, J. A., Gnys, M., Kassel, J. D., & Elash, C. (1995). Nicotine withdrawal in chippers and regular smokers: Subjective and cognitive effects. *Health Psychology, 14*, 301–309.

Shiffman, S., Paty, J. A., Gnys, M., Kassel, J. D., & Hickcox, M. (1996). First lapses to smoking: Within-subjects analyses of real-time reports. *Journal of Consulting and Clinical Psychology, 64*, 366–379.

Shiffman, S., Paty, J. A., Gwaltney, C. J., & Dang, Q. (2004). Immediate antecedents of cigarette smoking: An analysis of unrestricted smoking patterns. *Journal of Abnormal Psychology, 113*(1), 166–171.

Shiffman, S., & Prange, M. (1988). Self-reported and self-monitored smoking patterns. *Addictive Behaviors, 13*, 201–204.

Shiffman, S., Scharf, D. M., Shadel, W. G., Gwaltney, C. J., Dang, Q., Paton, S. M., et al. (2006). Analyzing milestones in smoking cessation: Illustration in a nicotine patch trial in adult smokers. *Journal of Consulting and Clinical Psychology, 74*(2), 276–285.

Shiffman, S., Stone, A. A., & Hufford, M. (2008). Ecological momentary assessment. *Annual Review of Clinical Psychology, 4*, 1–32.

Shiffman, S., & Waters, A. J. (2004). Negative affect and smoking lapses: A prospective analysis. *Journal of Consulting and Clinical Psychology, 72*(2), 192–201.

Simpson, T. L., Kivlahan, D. R., Bush, K. R., & McFall, M. E. (2005). Telephone self-monitoring among alcohol use disorder patients in early recovery: A randomized study of feasibility and measurement reactivity. *Drug and Alcohol Dependence, 79*(2), 241–250.

Sobell, L. S. M. (1995). *Alcohol timeline followback users' manual.* Toronto: Addiction Research Foundation.

Stone, A. A., Broderick, J. E., Schwartz, J. E., Shiffman, S., Litcher-Kelly, L., & Calvanese, P. (2003). Intensive momentary reporting of pain with an electronic diary: Reactivity, compliance, and patient satisfaction. *Pain, 104*, 343–351.

Stone, A. A., & Shiffman, S. (1994). Ecological momentary assessment (EMA) in behavioral medicine. *Annals of Behavioral Medicine, 16*(3), 199–202.

Stone, A. A., & Shiffman, S. (2002). Capturing momentary, self-report data: A proposal for reporting guidelines. *Annals of Behavioral Medicine, 24*, 236–243.

Stone, A. A., Shiffman, S., Atienza, A., & Nebeling, L. (Eds.). (2007). *The science of real-time data capture: Self-reports in health research.* New York: Oxford University Press.

Stone, A. A., Shiffman, S., Schwartz, J. E., Broderick, J. E., & Hufford, M. R. (2002). Patient non-compliance with paper diaries. *British Medical Journal, 324*, 1193–1194.

Sudman, S., & Bradburn, N. M. (1973). Effects of time and memory factors on response in surveys. *Journal of the American Statistical Association, 68*(344), 805–815.

Surawy, C., & Cox, T. (1987). Smoking under natural conditions: A diary study. *Personality and Individual Differences, 8*(1), 33–41.

Swendsen, J. D., Tennen, H., Carney, M. A., Affleck, G., Willard, A., & Hromi, A. (2000). Mood and alcohol consumption: An experience sampling test of the self-medication hypothesis. *Journal of Abnormal Psychology, 109*(2), 198–204.

Tidey, J. W., Monti, P. M., Rohsenow, D. J., Gwaltney, C. J., Miranda, R., McGeary, J. E., et al. (2008). Moderators of naltrexone's effects on drinking, urge and alcohol effects in non-treatment-seeking heavy drinkers in the natural environment. *Alcohol: Clinical and Experimental Research, 32*, 58–66.

Todd, M. (2004). Daily processes in stress and smoking: Effects of negative events, nicotine dependence, and gender. *Psychology of Addictive Behaviors, 18*(1), 31–39.

Todd, M., Armeli, S., & Tennen, H. (2009). Interpersonal problems and negative mood as predictors of within-day time to drinking. *Psychology of Addictive Behaviors, 23*(2), 205–215.

Todd, M., Armeli, S., Tennen, H., Carney, M., & Affleck, G. (2003). A daily diary validity test of drinking to cope measures. *Psychology of Addictive Behaviors, 17*(4), 303–311.

Todd, M., Armeli, S., Tennen, H., Carney, M. A., Ball, S. A., Kranzler, H. R., et al. (2005). Drinking to cope: A comparison of questionnaire and electronic diary reports. *Journal of Studies on Alcohol, 66*, 121–129.

Toll, B. A., Cooney, N. L., McKee, S. A., & O'Malley, S. S. (2005). Do daily interactive voice response reports of smoking behavior correspond with retrospective reports? *Psychology of Addictive Behaviors, 19*(3), 291–295.

Toll, B. A., Cooney, N. L., McKee, S. A., & O'Malley, S. S. (2006). Correspondence between Interactive Voice Response (IVR) and Timeline Followback (TLFB) reports of drinking behavior. *Addictive Behaviors, 31*(4), 726–731.

Tourangeau, R. (2000). Remembering what happened: memory errors and survey reports. In A. A. Stone, C. A. Bachrach, J. B. Jobe, H. S. Kurtzman & V. S. Cain (Eds.), The Science of Self Report: Implications for Research and Practice (pp. 29–48). Mahwah, NJ: Lawrence Erlbaum Associates.

Tucker, J. A., Foushee, H. R., Black, B. C., & Roth, D. L. (2007). Agreement between prospective interactive voice response self-monitoring and structured retrospective reports of drinking and contextual variables during natural resolution attempts. *Journal of Studies on Alcohol and Drugs, 68*(4), 538–542.

Tversky, A., & Kahneman, D. (1974). Judgment under uncertainty: Heuristics and biases. *Science, 185*(4157), 1124–1131.

US Department of Health and Human Services. (1988). *The health consequences of smoking: Nicotine addiction.* A report of the surgeon general. Washington, DC: US Government Printing Office.

Venugopal, M., Feuvrel, K. E., Mongin, D., Bambot, S., Faupel, M., Panangadan, A., Talukder, A., & Pidva, R. (2008). Clinical evaluation of a novel interstitial fluid sensor system for remote continuous alcohol monitoring. *Sensors Journal, IEEE, 8*, 71–80.

Verbrugge, L. M. (1980). Health diaries. *Medical Care, 18*(1), 73–95.

Walls, T. A., & Schafer, J. L. (Eds.). (2006). *Models for intensive longitudinal data.* New York: Oxford University Press.

Warthen, M. W., & Tiffany, S. T. (2009). Evaluation of cue reactivity in the natural environment of smokers using ecological momentary assessment. *Experimental and Clinical Psychopharmacology, 17*(2), 70–77.

Waters, A. J., & Li, Y. (2008). Evaluating the utility of administering a reaction time task in an ecological momentary assessment study. *Psychopharmacology, 197*(1), 25–35.

Weinstein, S. M., Mermelstein, R., Shiffman, S., & Flay, B. (2008). Mood variability and cigarette smoking escalation among adolescents. *Psychology of Addictive Behaviors, 22*(4), 504–513.

Weitzel, J. A., Bernhardt, J. M., Usdan, S., Mays, D., & Glanz, K. (2007). Using wireless handheld computers and tailored text messaging to reduce negative consequences of drinking alcohol. *Journal of Studies on Alcohol and Drugs, 68*(4), 534–537.

Wetter, D. W., McClure, J. B., Cofta-Woerpel, L., Costello, T. J., Reitzel, L. R., Businelle, M. S., & Cinciripini, P. M. (2011). A randomized clinical trial of a palmtop computer-delivered treatment for smoking relapse prevention among women. *Psychology of Addictive Behaviors, 25*(2), 365–371. doi: 10.1037/a0022797

Wheeler, L., & Reis, H. (1991). Self-recording of everyday life events: Origins, types, and uses. *Journal of Personality, 59,* 339–354.

Wileyto, P., Patterson, F., Niaura, R., Epstein, L., Brown, R., Audrain-McGovern, J., et al. (2004). Do small lapses predict relapse to smoking behavior under bupropion treatment? *Nicotine & Tobacco Research, 6*(2), 357–366.

PART 4

Substance Use Treatment

Brief Interventions and Motivational Interviewing

Jennifer E. Hettema, Christopher C. Wagner, Karen S. Ingersoll, *and* Jennifer M. Russo

Abstract

This chapter focuses on the use of brief interventions for the treatment of alcohol and other substance use disorders and risky use. The authors provide definitions of brief interventions and a rationale for their use. They review the evidence base for brief interventions across primary care, emergency medical, college, and correctional settings, and include analysis of the impact of brief intervention on drinking and drug use and the relative costs of such services. They also describe several widely used frameworks or organizing structures for brief interventions including FRAMES (provide *feedback*, emphasize *responsibility*, give *advice*, *menu* of options, express *empathy*, support *self-efficacy*), SBIRT (screening, brief intervention, and referral to treatment), and the five As (ask, assess, advise, assist, arrange). Finally, the authors discuss the therapeutic approach of motivational interviewing as an interaction style that can be used within the context of many brief intervention structures.

Key Words: brief intervention, brief treatment, motivational interviewing

Introduction

Brief interventions provide a viable means to prevent the development and progression of substance use problems, treat a range of severities of use, and facilitate referral-making for those for whom more intensive treatment may be appropriate. Alcohol use disorders occur among more than 76 million people internationally (WHO, 2004) and rates of illicit substance use reach similar numbers (UNODC, 2009), indicating that the need for effective, efficient treatment is profound. Alcohol and substance use increase the risk for physical, mental health, and social problems (Rehm, 2003) and brief interventions within opportunistic settings promote significant, long-term reductions in use, associated problems, and cost (Fleming, 2002). Motivational interviewing (MI) is an evidence-based practice that is highly applicable to brief interventions and compatible with many recommended brief intervention approaches. This chapter provides an overview of the rationale, definition, and evidence base

of brief interventions within different settings, and describes the MI model and its applicability to brief intervention approaches.

Overview of Brief Interventions
Definition

Many terms are used to describe brief interventions, including "simple advice," "minimal interventions," "brief counseling," or "short-term counseling" (Barry, 1999). The definition of "brief" varies widely across settings and even within the context of empirical research. On the continuum of substance abuse care, brief interventions can fill the gap between primary prevention and intensive or specialized treatment and can be implemented with a variety of settings and populations by specialists and nonspecialists. Although brief interventions are often associated with opportunistic settings like primary care, they can also be implemented in specialty treatment settings for alcohol and substance use disorders. Furthermore, brief interventions can be applied to the full range of severities of use, from risky to dependent, though evidence seems to suggest that they may be most effective with less severe populations. Targeted behavioral outcomes of brief interventions vary from treatment engagement to direct reduction of use. Some have differentiated brief interventions from brief therapies. From this perspective, brief interventions are approaches to help clients change one particular behavior or action, such as treatment attendance, while brief therapies address larger goals, such as maintaining abstinence or longer-term treatment adherence (Barry, 1999).

Brief interventions may also vary considerably in the communication style and underlying modality or theory being used to encourage change. In many ways, brief interventions can be seen as shells that can hold a variety of treatment modalities. Although brief intervention types vary, many have an emphasis on targeting and increasing motivation and rely on the principles and techniques of MI (Libby, 2008).

While formal definitions vary widely, most agree that brief interventions are a body of practices that share the common elements of being time-limited, structured, and goal-oriented. In addition, brief interventions often share certain characteristics, including (a) a focus on reduced drinking or harm reduction versus abstinence, (b) delivery by someone who is not an addictions specialist, (c) being directed at risky or nondependent versus dependent substance users, and (d) attention to the construct of motivation (Moyer et al., 2002). While the diversity of brief intervention formats increases availability and accessibility, variability in definitions creates a methodological challenge to summarizing the literature.

Rationale

Several factors provide a rationale for continuing to develop, investigate and implement brief interventions in the area of substance use (Saitz, 2005). For one, while rates of alcohol and other substance misuse and diagnoses are high, most individuals do not receive specialty treatment. The NIAAA (2005) estimates that 16% (40 million) of adults in the United States are drinking at risky levels and 7.5% (19 million) meet criteria for alcohol abuse or dependence. These results are similar to those reported in the National Survey on Drug Use and Health (SAMHSA, 2010), which estimates that over 23 million Americans meet criteria for a substance use disorder. Despite these high rates, the NSDUH reports that only 2.3 million Americans with an alcohol or drug use diagnosis have received specialty treatment for their substance use disorder in the last year.

This low rate of participation in specialty treatment relates to many factors. Most important, perhaps, is the fact that many individuals are not interested in receiving such services. Of the nearly 21 million people with a diagnosable substance use disorder who did not receive specialty treatment in 2008, fewer than 5% indicated a perceived need for treatment (SAMHSA, 2010). Individuals report disinterest in specialty treatment because of many factors, including not being ready to stop using, not having health coverage or ability to pay, possible negative effects on work or employment, and lack of information about where to go for treatment (SAMHSA, 2010). Stigma also contributes to disinterest in specialty treatment. Individuals are concerned that receiving such treatment might cause their neighbors or community to have a negative opinion of them (Copeland, 1997). Much of this fear of stigmatization is well grounded, as some forms of treatment such as methadone maintenance have been linked to discrimination (Hettema et al., 2009). Brief interventions in non-specialty settings may provide a viable alternative for individuals who are not interested in participating in specialty treatment. Such treatments are also more acceptable to individuals, particularly those with less severe use levels or consequences (Moyer et al., 2002).

In addition to individual barriers that reduce participation in specialty treatment, systemic factors also play a role. For one, specialty substance abuse treatment programs have limited capacity and are only able to accommodate a fraction of those individuals with substance use disorder diagnoses. While the capacity of outpatient treatment programs is hard to estimate, residential and inpatient substance abuse programs have a limited capacity of barely 100,000 beds and exceed a 90% utilization rate, leaving little room for additional patients (SAMHSA, 2006). In fact, long waiting lists are commonly cited as a barrier to treatment entry for substance use disorders (MacMaster et al., 2005). Limited capacity also appears to affect some groups more than others. For example, access to specialty treatment may be especially problematic for those individuals living in rural areas (Fortney & Booth 2001).

Professionals in health care encounter a large number of individuals who are using substances in a risky manner or who meet criteria for substance use disorders. With rates of risky use approaching 16% of the general population (NIAAA, 2005), a primary care physician with a patient panel size of 2000 encounters 320 patients with potentially harmful alcohol use annually. These rates would be even higher when including individuals with risky drug use. While opportunistic treatment within medical settings may be a viable alternative to specialty treatment, less than 16% report every discussing alcohol use with a health professional (McKnight-Eily et al., 2014) and, unfortunately, problematic use often goes undetected in these settings. For example, primary care physicians may intervene in only one of 10 cases of alcohol dependence (McGlynn et al., 2003) and may be even less likely to intervene with risky users.

Despite high rates of alcohol and substance misuse internationally, and evidence to support the effectiveness of brief interventions, most providers do not use brief interventions. Alcohol and substance use contribute to many other problems that are commonly encountered within settings in which brief interventions can be administered, increasing the benefits that can be realized by addressing this important need. For example, in medical settings, health problems such as liver cirrhosis, coronary artery disease, cancer, injury, suicide, and psychiatric problems can be negatively affected by or even caused by alcohol and substance misuse. Providing interventions in different time limited professional settings to individuals who would not otherwise participate in specialized treatment could have significant public health benefits.

Evidence Base

Although the concept of brief interventions is increasing in popularity, this approach is not a new idea in the treatment of alcohol and substance use disorders. Bien et al. (1993) cite an early salient example of the promise of brief intervention in a study from Edwards et al. (1983), in which a single session of "sympathetic and constructive" advice was found to be comparable to an extensive treatment package consisting of Alcoholics Anonymous facilitation, medications, and extensive treatment that could include inpatient treatment for non-responders. Since that time, brief interventions have been the focus of considerable research efforts, particularly in the area of alcohol use in health care settings. Overall, research supports the effectiveness of brief interventions, which generally outperform comparison conditions and perform equally as well as extended treatment.

Evidence from Primary Care Settings

The World Health Organization conducted a large international trial into the effectiveness of brief interventions in primary care settings (Babor & Grant, 1992). Investigators randomly assigned at-risk drinkers to a control condition, a 5-minute advice condition, or a condition that included advice plus 15 minutes of counseling and a self-help manual. Both intervention conditions led to significant reductions in alcohol use compared with the control condition. Several recent meta-analyses have found similar results regarding brief interventions within primary care settings. In a meta-analysis of 56 studies, brief interventions (four or fewer sessions) produced significant effect sizes for alcohol consumption and other drinking-related outcome variables among non–treatment-seeking populations for up to 1 year (Moyer et al., 2002). Whitlock et al. (2004) found that brief interventions in primary care reduced alcohol consumption anywhere from three to nine drinks per week, or an overall reduction in consumption of 13% to 34%. In a meta-analysis of 22 randomized controlled trials with more stringent acceptance criteria, Kaner and colleagues (2009) found a reduction in consumption by two to four drinks at 1-year follow-up, with greater effects on men than women. Also using fairly narrow selection criteria, Jonas et al. (2012) found that among brief interventions conducted with nondependent alcohol misusers, consumption decreased by 2.4 to 4.8 drinks per week.

Brief interventions often have benefits that exceed reduction in consumption. One recent meta-analysis of brief interventions for problem drinking found a decrease in the relative risk of mortality by about half compared with control conditions (Cuijpers et al., 2004). Maciosek (2006) found that the practice of alcohol screening and brief intervention was as effective as widely accepted prevention practices such as cervical and colorectal screening and influenza immunization in reducing clinically preventable burden (CPB). CPB estimates how much disease, injury, and death would be prevented if services were delivered to all targeted individuals. In another review, Solberg et al. (2008) found that screening and brief intervention for alcohol disorders were among the highest ranked preventive services in cost-effectiveness, return on investment, and how many dollars would be saved for each dollar spent. In fact, brief interventions for alcohol disorders were more cost-effective than cervical and colorectal screening, influenza immunization, and even hypertension screening and treatment. Overall, brief interventions for risky drinking in primary care may save $4 in cost for every $1 invested (Fleming, 2002).

While the evidence in favor of brief interventions for alcohol use is strong, brief interventions for substance use within primary care settings have a smaller, but growing, evidence base. For example, Bernstein et al. (2005) found that a one-session peer-led intervention for cocaine and heroin users identified by screening during routine medical care produced increased abstinence for both substances at 6-month follow-up point. Similar results have been found with regular marijuana users (Copeland et al., 2001; Stephens et al., 2000).

Another general finding is that, when it comes to substance abuse treatment, more is not necessarily better, and effects diminish over time. In the Moyer review (2002), differences between brief interventions and more extended treatments in treatment seeking were negligible. Wutzke et al. (2002) and Kaner et al. (2009) similarly found that the intensity of the intervention was not related to outcome. In their review, Bien et al. (1993) also concluded that extensive treatments do not tend to outperform brief interventions. While the above studies support the effectiveness of BI compared with more extensive treatments, some evidence suggests that longer treatment duration is beneficial in some cases, particularly when investigated using community

or noncontrolled trials (Hubbard et al., 2003; McKay, 2005). As is the case with many substance use interventions, effects of brief interventions tend to diminish over time. Another brief intervention study found that participants who showed significant reductions in alcohol consumption at early follow-up points no longer differed from comparison participants on alcohol consumption, mortality, or alcohol-related diagnoses after 10 years (Wutzke et al., 2002).

When thinking about brief interventions, it is helpful to highlight that there is a spectrum of severity when it comes to alcohol and substance misuse. While the alcohol or substance dependent individual is perhaps the first to come to mind, this group actually constitutes a small minority of the population of substance users. There is a much larger proportion of individuals who are drinking at risky levels (see Figure 17.1). Brief intervention with these risky drinkers could perhaps produce some of the largest payoffs by reducing personal and societal costs of substance misuse. Evidence from meta-analysis also suggests that the effects of brief intervention may be stronger for those with risky use or less severe alcohol problems (Moyer, 2002).

EVIDENCE FROM EMERGENCY SETTINGS

Of the 115 million visits to U.S. emergency departments (EDs) and trauma centers annually

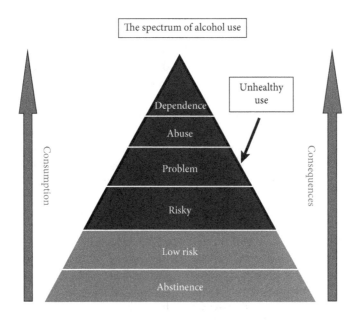

Figure 17.1. The spectrum of alcohol use. Adapted from Saitz, 2005.

(USDHHS, 2007), an estimated 29% are alcohol related (McDonald, 2004) and as many as 50% of presenting patients are drinking at risky levels (Desy, 2010). These settings create great promise for SBIRT implementation because of the high base rate of risky drinkers, the presence of a potential "teachable moment" that may result from alcohol-related injuries or medical complications, and the presence of highly skilled medical professionals as potential interventionists. Some studies suggest that brief interventions conducted in emergency settings have beneficial effects; they reduce reinjury rates by as much as 50% (Gentilello et al., 1999), prevent one DWI arrest for every nine brief interventions administered (Schermer et al., 2006), and save four times their cost in subsequent health care expenses (Gentilello et al., 2005).

In response to these impressive statistics and the contrasting evidence that emergency physicians do not routinely offer brief interventions to patients presenting with alcohol-related injuries (Lowenstein et al., 1990), in 2005 the American College of Surgeons (the primary organization responsible for developing trauma center requirements) enacted a landmark resolution that mandates Level I trauma centers screen injured patients for an alcohol use disorder and provide brief interventions to those who screen positive. More recently, the American College of Emergency Physicians (ACEP) has endorsed the use of SBIRT in ED settings (ACEP, 2011).

Despite the enthusiasm, some worry that ardency over ED SBIRT has outpaced the evidence (Saitz, 2009). While there is strong evidence that SBIRT targeting risky alcohol use is effective in primary care settings (Moyer, 2002; Whitlock, 2004) evidence specifically from ED settings is more mixed (Saitz, 2009). Meta-analyses reveal that there have been several negative trials of SBIRT in ED settings (Nilsen, 2008) resulting in questionable evidence of the impact of SBIRT on consumption (Havard, 2008). Critics point out (Saitz, 2009) that the most methodologically sound of available controlled trials do not find significant between-group differences favoring SBIRT over control (Daeppen et al., 2007; D'Onofrio, 2008). Of the positive trials of SBIRT in ED settings, many have methodological limitations including high rates of follow-up attrition (Gentilello, 1999), debatable analytic techniques (Schermer et al., 2006), or lack of a control group (Vaca, 2011). Several of these single arm studies have found significant drinking improvements, including a six-site national single arm study that found 50% reductions in consumption (Madras, 2009),

but it is difficult to make causal inferences without a control group. A 14-site nationwide assessment of real-world ED SBIRT implementation considering 3-, 6-, and 12-month effects showed short-term reductions of at-risk drinking but insignificant differences between subjects and control patients at 6 and 12 months (Bernstein & Bernstein, 2010). Additional methodologically sound controlled trials of SBIRT with ED populations are desperately needed.

EVIDENCE FROM COLLEGE SETTINGS

Rates of risky drinking and negative consequences are high in college populations (Larimer et al., 2004). College campuses have several opportunistic settings in which brief interventions for substance abuse can occur, including student health clinics, student organizations, and judicial systems that deal with alcohol and drug-related policy violations. Overall, efforts to screen and provide brief intervention with college samples have produced positive results (Larimer et al., 2004). For example, Schaus (2009) found that up to one quarter of college students seen in a primary care clinic at a public university were drinking at risky levels and that a two session intervention based on motivational interviewing significantly reduced drinking within this population.

Although the evidence is fairly strong for many college brief interventions, there is mixed evidence for mandated college samples. For example, Cimini et al. (2009), found no significant pre-post differences in drinking variables among public university students mandated to participate in treatment because of a school alcohol policy violation. Results were poor for all three intervention styles, including small motivational interviewing classes, interactive-educational groups, and peer-facilitated brief interventions. Similarly, Amaro et al. (2009) found that college students mandated to participate in a brief intervention based on employee assistance program models showed few improvements in primary drinking outcomes relative to control participants. However, another series of studies found improvements in drinking among college students adjudicated for drinking offenses when they underwent brief motivational interventions in small, interactive groups (LaBrie, Lamb, Pedersen, & Quinlan, 2006; Labrie, Thompson, Huchting, Lac, & Buckley, 2007).

Another factor impacting the effectiveness of brief interventions among college students is intervention style. All brief intervention styles do not appear to have equivalent effects. For example, educational strategies have generally been found to be ineffective at reducing risky alcohol use among college samples; in contrast, brief motivational interventions tend to have favorable results (Larimer & Cronce, 2002). Specifically, motivational enhancement therapy sessions, combining assessment feedback and MI, have shown promise among college individuals (Baer et al., 2001; Marlatt et al., 1998; Murphy et al., 2001) and groups (LaBrie et al., 2008; LaBrie, Pedersen, Lamb, & Quinlan, 2007).

Assessment and feedback results may also be a particularly effective component of other brief interventions for college student samples, and several studies indicate that normative feedback alone, even when given by mail, may be an effective intervention among this population (Murphy et al., 2004). Butler & Correia (2009) found that such feedback may be equally effective when administered electronically versus face to face. In fact, even assessment without normative feedback has been found to significantly affect some aspects of risky drinking (Walters et al., 2009).

EVIDENCE FROM CORRECTIONAL SETTINGS

Alcohol and substance use are associated with criminal behavior, and a significant proportion of the criminal justice population have histories of alcohol or drug abuse (Lapham, 2004). This fact, in combination with the regularity and frequency with which corrections staff and officers typically interact with individuals involved in the correctional system, has led the substance abuse field to focus on the feasibility of conducting brief interventions within such settings. While most states require screening of individuals convicted for driving while intoxicated, screening of individuals who committed other crimes is much more variable, despite generally high rates of use among this population (Lapham, 2004). However, criminal justice settings often refer offenders to specialized treatment programs. In fact, a large proportion of public system referrals for substance abuse treatment come from criminal justice settings. While brief interventions within correctional settings seem promising, evidence of the effectiveness of brief interventions with this population is sparse. Davis et al. (2003) found that brief MI increased the treatment engagement rate of substance abusing veterans following incarceration. However, Wells-Parker and Williams (2002) found less favorable results when testing the impact of a group discussion intervention on recidivism for DWI.

Frameworks and Organizing Structures for Delivering Brief Interventions

Several frameworks and organizing structures are available for the delivery of brief interventions. Most of these frameworks recommend specific steps that can be seen as shells filled with different interaction techniques or styles. This section will provide an overview of the rationale, procedures, and evidence base for a variety of brief intervention frameworks, including screening, brief intervention, and referral to treatment (SBIRT), FRAMES, the 5 As, and the Stages of Change.

Screening, Brief Intervention, and Referral to Treatment

SBIRT is a public health initiative designed to screen individuals for risky substance use or substance use disorders, conduct brief interventions that target individuals with risky alcohol use who do not need specialized treatment, and refer those with more severe use to specialized treatment (http://sbirt.samhsa.gov/about.htm). SBIRT typically takes place in community or medical settings where professionals have opportunities to screen individuals for substance use disorders and determine the appropriate level of intervention.

The first step in SBIRT involves screening individuals for risky or problematic use. Positive screens may then be followed with more intensive assessment to determine the presence of substance use disorders or other relevant substance-related consequences. As can be seen in Figure 17.1, substance use and related consequences among individuals occur on a continuum, ranging from abstinence to dependence. Epidemiologic research suggests that men who regularly drink more than four standard drinks in a day (or more than 14 per week) and women who regularly drink more than three in a day (or more than seven per week) are at increased risk for alcohol-related problems (Dawson et al., 2005). Because of this, the NIAAA recommends a single screening question querying the presence of use that exceeds these levels to identify individuals who are at risk for alcohol-related problems (NIAAA, 2005).

Other screening instruments for alcohol and drug use are also available and each has its own individual benefits and drawbacks in terms of sensitivity, specificity, and ease of administration. For example, the CAGE questionnaire (Ewing et al., 1984) is a four-question screening tool that is easy to use and remember because of its acronym: Have you ever felt you should cut down on your drinking? Have people *a*nnoyed you by criticizing your drinking? Have you ever felt bad or *g*uilty about your drinking? Have you ever had a drink first thing in the morning to steady your nerves or to get rid of a hangover (*e*ye–opener)? The instrument generally has good psychometric characteristics (Fiellin, 2000) including internal consistency reliability (Mischke & Venneri, 1987). Endorsement of three or more items has been found to be strongly predictive of an alcohol use disorder, with good levels of sensitivity and specificity, but the cut-off score of 1 for identification of risky drinkers has been criticized for poor sensitivity or high rates of false positives (MacKenzie et al., 1996). The Alcohol Use Disorders Identification Test (AUDIT; Saunders et al., 1993) screens for the quantity and frequency of alcohol use, binge drinking, symptoms of dependence, and alcohol-related consequences. The instrument can be self-administered and may be particularly appropriate for brief intervention studies because of its ability to identify people who have problems with alcohol but who may not be dependent (Feillin, 2000). The Michigan Alcoholism Screening Test (MAST; Selzer, 1971) includes questions about drinking and alcohol-related problems. This instrument can be particularly helpful in identifying alcohol dependence (Reid et al., 1999). The Drug Abuse Screening Test (DAST; Gavin, Ross, & Skinner, 1989) is a similar instrument that is available for detecting drug use disorders. Additionally, the World Health Organization (WHO) developed the Alcohol, Smoking and Substance Involvement Screening Test (ASSIST) to screen for problematic or risky use (WHO, 2008: http://www.who.int/substance_abuse/activities/assist_technicalreport_phase3_final.pdf). The instrument yields a risk category for nicotine, alcohol, and a range of drugs that can be used to inform the appropriate level of brief intervention. While NIAAA recommends universal screening of all patients seen in primary care settings, the approach may be particularly applicable or important during physical examinations, when prescribing a medication that interacts with alcohol, with women who are pregnant or trying to conceive, with patients who are likely to drink heavily (such as smokers, adolescents, and young adults and those who have health problems that might be alcohol related), or patients who have chronic illnesses that are not responding to treatment as expected (NIAAA, 2005).

Within the SBIRT model, following screening, providers determine the level of intervention that may be appropriate for a particular individual. Several tools and processes can be used to make this determination. For providers who use the ASSIST, the instrument yields a risk category of "low," "moderate," or "high" that corresponds to recommended intervention types, including no intervention, brief intervention, or brief intervention plus referral (WHO, 2008). For individuals with no use or low risk use, reinforcement of healthy behaviors is typically recommended, but intervention is not. For those who screen positive for at-risk use, additional assessment to determine the presence of dependence, degree of negative consequences, or presence of family history may be appropriate. Based on these responses, individuals with risky drinking alone may be appropriate for brief intervention, while those with signs of dependence or a positive family history of dependence may be most appropriate for brief treatment (treatment or intervention?) with referral to specialty treatment. Providers continue working and intervening with people who are not initially interested in referral to treatment.

One example of an SBIRT protocol was developed by the NIAAA (2005) as a guide for health care practitioners to screen and intervene with patients at risk for alcohol problems. The guide includes four steps. The first step involves asking about alcohol use, including the presence or absence of use and, in the presence of use, the presence of heavy drinking (five or more drinks for men; four or more drinks for women) or an elevated AUDIT score (8 or higher for men; 4 or higher for women). For those who are at risk, step two involves a more thorough assessment of alcohol use, including the diagnosis of alcohol abuse or dependence. Step three involves giving advice and assistance based on the drinking levels of the patient. This advice may include abstinence and specialty treatment for those with alcohol use disorders and cutting down for those with risky use. NIAAA recommends that the nature of assistance or brief intervention should be dependent on the readiness level of the patient. For those with low readiness to change, providers are encouraged to help patients explore ambivalence to change, while those who are high in readiness may benefit from setting a goal, developing a change plan, and receiving educational resources. At step four, providers are encouraged to acknowledge that change is difficult and support any positive changes in those who were unable to reduce drinking, as well as reinforce progress in those who were able to eliminate risky use. Rescreening at least annually is encouraged.

The SBIRT model has a strong evidence base for reducing rates of alcohol and substance use within medical settings. For example, the Substance Abuse and Mental Health Administration (SAMHSA) implemented and evaluated an SBIRT initiative across a variety of inpatient, outpatient, and emergency medical settings (Madras et al., 2009). The six sites in the study had some flexibility regarding the specific components of their SBIRT protocol, but generally screened patients using the DAST, AUDIT, quantity/frequency measures of consumption or some combination of the above. Nearly 460,000 individuals were screened within the trial. Risky use, defined as drinking more than five drinks in one sitting or using illicit substances in the past 30 days, was identified in 23% of patients and these individuals were provided with brief interventions that included site-customized adaptations of feedback, FRAMES (see description later), and MI. In addition, 3% of individuals with higher levels of use received more intensive brief treatment ranging from one to eight sessions across sites and 4% of individuals who indicated symptoms of substance dependence were referred for specialty treatment. Overall, the study revealed very positive results for the effects of SBIRT; those who received brief intervention reduced their drug use by 67.7% and their alcohol use by 38.6%.

FRAMES

In a review of brief treatment for alcohol interventions, Miller and Sanchez (1993) identified several key characteristics of effective brief interventions (Bien et al., 1993). These components corresponded to the acronym FRAMES, which refers to *f*eedback of personal risks, emphasizing that *r*esponsibility for change lies with the individual, *a*dvice-giving, providing a *m*enu of change options, an *e*mpathic interaction style, and the enhancement of *s*elf-efficacy. While many of these components, such as the emphasis on empathy and enhancement of self-efficacy, are consistent with MI (Miller & Rollnick, 2002), others, such as advice giving, are not.

Feedback of personal risks involves providing individuals with objective feedback about their alcohol or substance use. This could take the form of normative feedback on standardized assessment results, as is done in motivational enhancement therapy, or simply providing information about the presence or absence of risky or dependent use

or the impact of use on other medical or psychosocial issues. Clinicians emphasize the importance of personal responsibility to encourage the individual's sense of degree of personal control and interest in initiating behavioral change. Advice to change involves recommending that individuals stop or reduce use, with clear guidance about how to get started, and with an offer of support. Providing a menu of options gives individuals choices on drinking or substance use goals or specific treatment options. For example, the person may be presented with the choice of whether to cut down or eliminate their use, or offered various treatment options such as self-change, community support groups, or formal treatment. Using an empathic and reflective interaction style has been empirically demonstrated to be more effective than confrontational approaches (Miller & Rollnick, 2002) and is highly consistent with the MI style. Finally, the value of enhancing self-efficacy is based on decades of research on social cognitive theory (Bandura, 1986) that individuals' beliefs that they can effectively change increases the probability that they will attempt to and succeed at change. Fortunately, self-efficacy can be dramatically influenced by clinicians' actions, and clinicians' belief in their clients' ability to change has been found to be predictive of treatment engagement and ultimate outcome (Leake & King, 1977).

Five As

The 5 As is an intervention strategy, drawn originally from the smoking cessation literature, that provides recommended sequential steps for interventionists working with behavioral health issues such as substance use (Fiore et al., 2000). Within the model, providers are encouraged to: *a*sk about use, *a*ssess severity and readiness to change, *a*dvise cutting down or abstinence, *a*ssist in goal setting and further treatment if necessary, *a*rrange to monitor progress, and, in a recent addition of a sixth A, *a*ssure cross-cultural efficacy of practices (NIAAA, 2005). Other versions of the model vary slightly. For example, Whitlock et al. (2002) use the format: *a*ssess, *a*dvise, *a*gree, *a*ssist, *a*rrange. Assess involves completing validated screening or assessment instruments and questions to determine the presence or absence of a problem. Assess can also involve determining an individual's knowledge about substance use behavior and related consequences, motivations to change, and perceived barriers. Within this model, assessment results are used to inform interventions and are often relayed back to the individual in the form of feedback. Advise involves providing the individual with personally relevant and specific information about recommendations for change. The interpersonal style with which advice is given can vary dramatically across interventionists. Agree refers to the use of collaborative discussion and decision-making to help the individual develop a goal. Here, too, interventionists are often encouraged to provide a menu of options for individuals, involve significant others, and develop a goal that is specific and measurable. Assist involves helping the individual to develop a specific change plan or strategies to achieve their goal. Such strategies may include referral to specialized treatment. Last, arrange involves follow-up to reinforce change, assure cross-cultural appropriateness, revise goals, or address barriers.

The 5 As have a strong evidence base across a variety of health behaviors, including substance use, and are consistent with intervention elements found to be associated with improved outcomes in review and meta-analyses (Goldstein et al., 2004). In addition, providers report satisfaction with the 5 As approach, which they perceive as requiring little training, having a strong evidence base, and being simple and flexible (Grandes et al., 2008).

The Transtheoretical Model

The transtheoretical model (TTM; DiClemente et al., 1985; Prochaska & DiClemente, 2005) is a model of behavioral change that focuses on how people make deliberate, purposeful changes. The model largely focuses on behavioral changes that involve eliminating problem behaviors and beginning new, healthier behaviors. The most well-known aspect of the TTM is the "stages of change" (SOC) model, which views behavior change as a process that progresses from low problem awareness and readiness to change through high awareness and active efforts to initiate or maintain change. The model has five stages: precontemplation (individuals may not recognize their behavior as problematic and are not planning to change), contemplation (individuals are considering change but remain ambivalent about whether the benefits of behavior change outweigh the costs), preparation (individuals have decided to make a change and are making plans to change), action (individuals are actively taking steps to change), and maintenance (individuals are integrating behavior change into their ongoing lifestyle). While progression through the stages of change is sometimes linear, the developers emphasize that individuals can move from any stage

to another and cycle through the stages multiple times before achieving sustained change.

In addition to the stages of change, the TTM model focuses on change processes. Different experiences and activities are hypothesized to facilitate progression through the various stages of change, with some evidence supporting these hypotheses (DiClemente, 2003; Perz, DiClemente, & Carbonari, 1996). Experiential processes may be most relevant to progressing through the precontemplation and contemplation stages. Consciousness raising about the problem behavior and solutions, becoming more attuned to emotional aspects of change, considering how the problem affects others, and clarification of values in relation to the behavior are all thought to contribute to progress through the early stages. Behavioral processes are believed to facilitate progress through action and maintenance stages. These include making a choice and commitment to change, controlling temptations and triggers, avoiding risks, substituting and reinforcing alternative behaviors, and using available supports to help achieve and maintain change.

The TTM recognizes that a person's beliefs about the benefits and drawbacks of change, self-efficacy in the ability to change, environmental temptations, and individual biopsychosocial characteristics can influence progression toward change (Prochaska & DiClemente, 2005). The model has been used to help match individuals to appropriate levels and styles of treatment and such applications have been found to lower relapse rates and improve treatment engagement among individuals (Dempsey, 2008). It should be noted that the SOC model has received some criticism as an inappropriate assessment of readiness (West, 2005) and as having limited application to addiction in general (Sutton, 2001). However, it is an influential model of the stages and processes of change.

Brief Interventions and Interaction Style

As Bien et al. (1993) describe in their review of brief interventions for alcohol problems, the clinician's interaction style can have a significant impact on outcome. These authors cite early studies by Chafetz (1961, 1962, 1968), which demonstrate the importance of interaction style when making referrals to specialty treatment. In these studies, standard referral procedures used to encourage specialty treatment for patients presenting to emergency departments with alcohol-related problems were compared with a standardized brief intervention that used an empathic communication style.

The empathic approach improved attendance rates at a subsequent appointment for specialty treatment by up to 72%. In contrast, an intervention focused on advice giving, persuasiveness, and the authority of the physician, designed to increase engagement in specialty treatment for actively drinking patients with gastrointestinal disease, did not increase rates of follow-up care beyond those of the control condition (Kuchipudi et al., 1990).

Several therapeutic styles or intervention techniques can be used to form the basis of brief interventions. However, we will focus on the use of motivational interviewing as an interaction style that can be used in isolation or to fill the steps in the frameworks described above.

Motivational Interviewing
Overview of the Approach

MI is a therapeutic approach used to explore and resolve ambivalence about behavior change. MI has a strong evidence base for reducing substance use and related problems and has been applied extensively in brief interactions within medical and other opportunistic settings (Hettema et al., 2009). The approach has been defined as "a person-centered counseling style for addressing the common problem of ambivalence about change" (Miller & Rollnick, 2013, p. 21), as "a client-centered, directive method for enhancing intrinsic motivation to change by exploring and resolving ambivalence" (Miller & Rollnick, 2002) or, similarly, as a "collaborative, person-centered form of guiding to elicit and strengthen motivation for change" (Rollnick et al., 2008). The person-centered aspect of the approach refers to the assumption that the perceptions and goals of the individual versus those of the interventionists should be at the forefront of the interaction. Person-centered approaches also tend to focus on the expression of empathy and acceptance through techniques such as reflective listening. However, in addition to the person-centered aspects of MI, clinicians use directive or guiding strategies to intentionally pursue the resolution of ambivalence, elicit and strengthen motivation to change, and reduce substance use or related consequences. Thus, while focusing on and eliciting the client's perceptions, the MI interventionist strategically seeks to help the client develop an awareness of any discrepancy between substance use and personal goals and values.

MI was first described as an approach to help people with drinking problems (Miller, 1983) and

has been most commonly used with substance using populations, including tobacco, alcohol, and other illicit substances such as cocaine, marijuana, and opiates (Hettema et al., 2009). Ambivalence is common among people with substance use problems and disorders, as they often have mixed feelings about their use. For example, while an individual may perceive some negative consequences of their use, such as hangovers, work, or relationship problems, he or she may also enjoy some of the positive outcomes of use such as intoxication, reduction of negative emotions, or associated socialization. A person in this ambivalent state is likely to remain conflicted and refrain from change unless the balance of the pros and cons of continued use shifts.

MI practitioners view the spirit of the underlying approach as necessary for the successful implementation of specific skills. MI practitioners assume that individuals have within them prosocial and healthy values and that they should be treated as partners in the change exploration process versus recipients of expert advice (Miller & Rollnick, 2005). The MI spirit encourages collaboration, where the individual is seen as an expert on his or her own circumstances and the interventionist is the expert on skills for effectively managing a constructive conversation about change. The relational stance of collaboration assumes that individuals are capable of making sound decisions and often have the resources and information necessary to implement them. In fact, many individuals using substance use at risky levels are often aware of the potential risks of their behavior, effective strategies to reduce use, and resources to assist them, and mere listing of these facts is unlikely to promote change. Rather, MI interventionists avoid providing unneeded or unwanted information, and elicit more information than they provide. From the MI perspective, it is more important that the interventionist develop a supportive relationship with the individual and draw out the person's own motivations than give information, educate, or persuade, all of which may lead to resistance and potentially decrease the person's willingness to change.

The spirit of MI is also based on an implicit and explicit respect of the client's autonomy. It encourages the acknowledgement and support of the individual's ability and responsibility to consider options, make decisions, and take action. However, while the spirit of MI is evocative, it also allows and even encourages interventionists to provide opportunities for individuals to gain new perspectives on their substance use behaviors by thinking about and discussing issues related to their behavior in an organized and supportive environment.

Core Skills

MI practice builds on its spirit using a set of key skills that can be summarized using the acronym OARS: *o*pen-ended questions that elicit that individual's perspective or consideration of a topic, *a*ffirmations which can help to develop rapport and reinforce strengths or positive changes, *r*eflections that indicate interest, acceptance, and understanding of the client, and *s*ummaries that can be used to capture themes within interactions and transition between topics. These techniques are used to build rapport and therapeutic alliance, encourage consideration and exploration of change, and increase commitment to change.

Therapeutic Processes

In addition to the emphasis on using OARS as a basic communication style, the MI therapist uses broader therapeutic processes: engaging, focusing, evoking and planning (Miller & Rollnick, 2013). The first key process is *engaging*. Engagement in MI involves developing a deep trust between practitioner and client that allows for the development of client-centered goals. When clients are not deeply engaged, they tend to be more passive. While MI practitioners may have a clinical investment in a particular direction for client change (such as reducing use or harm), MI develops a collaborative relationship between client and practitioner, as it is not focused on knowledge or skill development. The second key process is *focusing*. Once clients are sufficiently engaged in therapeutic conversation, MI practitioners begin to narrow the focus to the issue of client change. What does the client not like about his or her life? What might be different, better? What might the client like to keep while moving forward, and what can be left behind? The third central MI process is *evoking* client perspectives and ideas about change rather than providing ideas and perspectives. At its core, MI is based on the idea that people motivate themselves to change, and that an effective way to elicit client change is to structure conversations so that clients identify and discuss the reasons, desires and needs they have to make changes. This is distinct from a more persuasive approach, in which the interventionist persuades or tells the individual how and why he or she should change. In MI, discrepancies thought to motivate behavioral change are developed by drawing out the individual's own ideas and feelings about substance use and perceptions about how the behavior fits in with personal goals and values. Given that ambivalent people have both sides of the argument about making changes vs. holding to the current course already internalized, MI practitioners evoke clients' own thoughts about change and are careful to avoid extolling the virtues of change due to the risk of motivating clients to make "yes, but" arguments defending the status quo. The fourth therapeutic process is *planning*. At some point, clients' focus of attention shifts from whether and why to change to how. The shift may be sudden, with a client who has been pondering possibilities who declares "I've got to change" or "I can't go on like this anymore." Other times, the shift may be gradual, almost unnoticeable, as the client goes back and forth between changing one way or another, or staying the same, considering hypothetical possibilities, then talking about how each possibility might work and what he could do toward that end. But however the conversation occurs, when clients tilt toward favoring change, MI practitioners shift to helping clients develop change plans and put them into action.

Strategies of MI

The core skills and principles of MI form the basis for many specific strategies or intervention techniques that can be used to implement motivational interviewing in practice. Whereas the core skills are micro-level interactional techniques, and the principles are macro-level guides, MI strategies are intermediate methods to structure conversations to maximize the emergence of motivation for change. Several of these strategies that are particularly applicable to brief applications of MI and examples of how to use them follow.

1. Agenda setting involves prioritizing tasks and topics for an interaction. Examples include: *How would you like to spend our time together today?* Or, *Which of these issues would you like to discuss first?* Or, *I'd like to figure out what's going on with your sore throat and then spend a few minutes following up on discussion of alcohol use from last time.*

2. Importance and confidence scaling can be used to assess motivation and also as a tool to elicit talk about change. *I'd like to understand more about how you view your drinking. On a scale of 0 to 10, with 0 being not at all important, and 10 being extremely important, how important is it for you to change your drinking now?* This question (and the similar question about confidence) can be followed by asking the individual why their score was not

something lower than what they indicated and what it would take to move to a higher number, both of which strategically elicit talk about change.

3. Providing information in an MI consistent way can involve asking permission or providing a menu of options. *I have some information about strategies for reducing drinking. Would it be all right if I shared them with you?* Or, *You talked about wanting to get some more information about managing your drinking. We offer several options here including meeting with a therapist to do a kind of "check up" about drinking, enrolling in our drinkers' support group, or discussing your health further with the nurse or with me. There are additional resources I can point you to, including written materials and interactive programs on the internet. Which, if any of these, are of interest to you?*

4. Elicit-Provide-Elicit involves increasing the collaborative nature of information provision by eliciting what an individual already knows about a topic, providing additional or corrective information in a tailored way, and then eliciting a response to the information. *What do you know about levels of safe drinking? . . . It has been found that women who drink more than 3 drinks a day or 7 drinks in a week are at an increased risk for a variety of health and other problems. What do you make of that?*

5. Exploring strengths can be used to help identify resources and develop plans as well as increase self-efficacy. *What are some personal qualities that you are proud of?* Or, *Which strengths did you use to overcome that challenge?*

6. Exploring values can be used to help individuals develop a discrepancy between harmful substance use and what is most important to them. *What things are most important to you in your life right now?* Or, *Take a look at this list of values. Take a minute to pick your top three and tell me what they mean to you.* Or, *You've mentioned how important your children are to you. What impact, if any, does your marijuana use have on your children?*

7. Looking backward gives individuals an opportunity to think about a time in their lives when substance use was not an issue and identify benefits of this way of being and also effective strategies for maintaining this behavior. *Let's talk about a time before you started using. What were you doing then? How did you feel?*

8. Looking forward involves asking individuals to think about their life down the road considering if they were or weren't able to make changes. A variation is to ask individuals to envision a future that they desire. *Where do you think you're going with your drinking if you look ahead a few years? What are some of the worst things that will likely happen if you maintain your current habits? What are some of the best things that might happen if you made some changes?*

9. Considering hypothetical changes helps individuals to identify important steps towards change and gives them an opportunity to foresee a different future without being forced to make a commitment. *If you were to make a change in your drinking, how might you go about it in order to succeed? What would be challenging? What would be rewarding?*

In addition to defining what strategies MI includes, it is also useful to define what it does not include. For example, unsolicited advice is not offered without first obtaining permission from the individual. Similarly, practitioners avoid confronting or warning clients with their own concerns about drinking or drug use choices. MI strategies or techniques are not simply added into interactions that are hierarchical in nature; rather, the MI style prescribes that the therapeutic relationship is inherently nonhierarchical and collaborative.

Evidence Base

Some of the first empirical evidence in support of the MI model came from an early study of MI in a Drinker's Check-up that involved assessing individuals for drinking behavior and related consequences and providing them with feedback in an MI consistent manner (Miller et al., 1988). This study showed early positive findings that brief interventions could significantly reduce drinking for up to 1 year and a follow-up study further demonstrated that MI-consistent interaction style predicted the degree of client success (Miller et al., 1993). Following these studies, a four-session adaptation of MI that included personalized feedback called Motivational Enhancement Therapy (MET) was tested within Project MATCH, a large multi-site randomized clinical trial, and was found to perform equally well at reducing drinking as more extensive cognitive behavioral therapy and 12-Step facilitation approaches (Project MATCH Research Group, 1997).

Since these early studies, there has been an explosion of interest in and studies of MI, with more than 200 clinical trials conducted to date, and the subsequent development of a nascent model of some of the mechanisms of MI (Miller & Rose, 2009). MI and its most common adaptation, MET, have been listed as evidence-based practices on the National Registry of Evidence-based Programs and Practices, which is an organization that facilitates the review and rating of substance abuse treatment modalities.

Several meta-analyses of MI have been conducted to date. In one early review, 30 randomized controlled trials of adaptations of motivational interviewing (AMIs) were included (Burke et al., 2003). The majority of included studies investigated the impact of MI on alcohol or drug use. The mean dose of the intervention is generally considered to be brief in nature, ranging from 15 to 240 minutes, and averaging 99 minutes. The authors found small to medium between group effect sizes for drinking and medium effect sizes for drug use. In these areas, AMIs doubled abstinence rates from 1:5 to 2:5. Overall the authors concluded that AMIs are effective and efficient, as they can produce similar results in two sessions to those achieved by other interventions styles in 8 sessions.

A more recent, larger meta-analysis of MI included 72 studies covering a range of problem behaviors. Again, the majority of studies focused on alcohol or drug use or engagement in substance use treatment. Hettema and colleagues (2005) found small to medium effect sizes for alcohol and drug use and much larger effects for engagement in substance abuse treatment. This meta-analysis also found that, similar to other behavioral treatments, effects of MI appear early and tend to diminish somewhat over time, except in studies in which MI is added to some other form of treatment. They found that the average effect size of MI was d = 0.77 at post-treatment, d = 0.31 at 4 to 6 months, and d = 0.30 at 6 to 12 months.

Another meta-analysis compared the effectiveness of MI to brief advice on a variety of health behaviors (Rubak, 2005). Seventy-two trials were included and those addressing alcohol use found that MI outperformed brief advice-based intervention on objective outcome variables such as blood alcohol concentration and standard ethanol content. MI demonstrated an effect in 74% of the RCTs assessed and likelihood of an effect increased with increases in the number of minutes per session and the number of encounters per patient. The authors concluded that MI is more beneficial than brief advice for a broad range of target behaviors, including substance use.

Most recently, Lundahl et al (2009) conducted a meta-analysis of 119 experimental and quasi-experimental studies across substance use, health behaviors, and treatment engagement domains. Lundahl estimated an effect size for MI of g = 0.28 against weak comparison groups and a nonsignificant effect of g = 0.09 against competing active treatments. While they question the results of the Hettema and Miller (2005) meta-analysis due to inclusion of a strongly positive outlier sample, their analysis may be unduly influenced by several negative studies of MI for smoking. In contrast, they report that approximately 75% of all participants in MI studies experience positive gains, with approximately 25% experiencing moderate to large gains. Lundahl and colleagues offer answers to several component questions in secondary analyses, including:—Does MI work? (Yes)

-Should I, or my agency, consider learning or adopting MI? (Yes)

Is MI only indicated for substance use problems? (No)

Is MI successful in motivating clients to change? (Yes)

-Is MI successful only with clients who have minor problems? (No)

-Is MI as successful as other interventions? (Yes, except with tobacco use and some miscellaneous drug problems, and often MI is as successful in lesser doses)

Are MI effects durable? (Yes, at least up to 1 to 2 years)

-Should practitioners learn "basic MI" or "MET"? (Learn MI to integrate with other approaches; learn MET to target specific behavior changes)

Is manual-guided MI superior to the alternative? (No)

-Does the format of MI influence outcomes? (No)

-Does professional background influence success of MI? (No)

-Does MI dosage matter? (Yes—in discrete delivery forms, more MI is related to better effects)

-Does MI work for most clients? (Uncertain)

-Does MI work in group formats? (Uncertain).

We note that the most recent review of the evidence for MI in group formats indicates that they show considerable promise (Wagner & Ingersoll, 2013).

In the area of substance abuse, a broad range of populations have been treated with MI in clinical and research settings. Treated populations range from youth experimenting with drinking through adults with severe alcohol and drug dependence problems, including those whose addiction problems have resulted in criminal justice system involvement. Studies have shown the efficacy of MI to reduce drinking, increase abstinence from drinking, reduce heavy drinking days, facilitate participation in harm reduction strategies such as using needle exchange programs, and reduce drug use. In addition, MI has been used to help patients with a number of medical diagnoses and related health conditions, some of which have less obvious relationships with substance abuse. In the domain of mental health, there is much growth in applications of MI (Arkowitz et al., 2008). Relating to substance use problems, MI has been used clinically and tested in research as a dual disorder intervention, targeting both substance use and mental illness. The U.S. Department of Justice has adopted MI as a preferred practice for those who are imprisoned or involved in community corrections settings related to substance abuse issues. Applications in child protective services and domestic violence prevention and treatment services provide further opportunity to use MI with those involved in the legal system. Additionally, MI is being increasingly applied to simultaneous behavior change initiatives. For example, promising projects show benefits of MI reducing the risk of alcohol-exposed pregnancy by targeting both drinking and contraception (Floyd et al., 2007). There are many possible behavioral targets of MI and a variety of settings in which the intervention can be delivered. Though MI began as an outpatient intervention for alcohol problems, involving meeting with a therapist for up to an hour, applications in briefer medical consultations are becoming increasingly common.

Summary & Conclusions

Overall, brief interventions show a great deal of promise for addressing alcohol and substance abuse issues. They can be effectively applied within a variety of settings through several frameworks developed to guide their applications. While many of these frameworks recommend MI-consistent strategies, a variety of therapeutic interaction techniques could be used to populate them. For example, the advise strategy that is present in both FRAMES and the 5 As would present differently depending on the interventionists' interaction style. Aspects of MI that involve attempting to elicit the individual's perspective on an advisable course of action, such as asking permission before giving advice and emphasizing personal choice, may or may not be used to enhance this step within these frameworks, making them more or less consistent with the MI model. Similarly, while distinct, the SOC model and MI "grew up together" and complement one another (DiClemente & Velasquez, 2002). Developers of the SOC model cite MI as a valuable approach to use when people are in the earlier stages of change,

to build interest in and motivation for change. However, within MI the concept of stages is seen more as a heuristic than as a reflection of reality. MI emphasizes that readiness to change is a byproduct of interpersonal interactions and can fluctuate from moment to moment.

When considering interaction techniques that may be used within brief intervention frameworks, MI seems to be a logical first choice and, within the literature, MI skills and principles are commonly overlaid on frameworks such as SBIRT and the 5 As. MI is an efficacious method to facilitate behavior change with strong evidence for its positive impact on addictive behavior. It often achieves good outcomes with fewer sessions and in less time than other substance abuse treatment methods. It has become a popular approach and is used around the world for the treatment of substance abuse as well as other behavioral change challenges. While the clinical methods have been detailed thoroughly, using MI in various brief intervention frameworks has not been thoroughly researched. Rollnick and colleagues (2008) advise that MI should only be applied when there is a primary focus on increasing readiness for change and the principles and spirit described above have been intentionally implemented. However, they note that it is still unresolved whether the spirit of motivational interviewing can, in fact, be captured in brief interactions of as little as 5 to 10 minutes. As MI expands into new areas of application beyond its individual substance abuse counseling roots, such as brief intervention in primary care, there is a need to develop innovative methods of delivery, measure outcomes, and provide effective training for practitioners, agencies, and trainers.

Priorities for Future Research

While research has shown promising results through application of SBIRT, further research is needed in a number of areas. To start, brief interventions should be studied in additional care settings and with other patient groups. As noted, the enthusiasm for SBIRT that prompted the American College of Surgeons to mandate Level I trauma centers to screen injured patients for an alcohol use disorders, and provide brief interventions to those who screen positive, was based largely on the strength of evidence collected in primary care settings. Further study of the efficacy of SBIRT specifically in emergency department settings is needed (Saitz, 2009). Additionally, the bulk of evidence supporting the use of SBIRT surrounds the screening and treatment of alcohol-related problems; studies addressing how brief interventions might effectively impact other substance abuse would be helpful.

It should also be noted that the Brief Intervention component of SBIRT refers to a range of different therapies. In other studies, different approaches to therapy yielded very different results. The efficacy of Motivational Interviewing has been demonstrated with both drinking and substance-using patients (Hettema et al., 2005). A study distinguishing between MI and other brief interventions, such as simple advice, could offer guidance on which approach(es) would be most useful and effective.

Training in effective application of SBIRT is another direction for future research. While brief interventions can improve patients' reduction in alcohol and substance use, there is an investment in staff training required. A study of how the length of an SBIRT training program impacts implementation could guide organizations on what amount of time and training resources would be required to effect a change in patient outcomes. For primary care physicians, an assessment of their current use of screening to detect alcohol or substance use in patients could provide a springboard to compare such practices with the potential improvements in detection and treatment through SBIRT. It would also be interesting to apply MI with primary care physicians to assess what issues they face with the implementation of SBIRT and MI with their patients. Allowing them to explore the challenges and potential benefits of implementing SBIRT in a supportive counseling session might illuminate the obstacles faced by other practitioners in a variety of settings.

References

Amaro, H., Ahl, M., Matsumoto, A., Prado, G., Mulé, C., Kemmemer, A., ... & Mantella, P. (2009). Trial of the university assistance program for alcohol use among mandated students. *Journal of Studies on Alcohol Drugs, Suppl.,* 45–56.

American College of Emergency Physicians (ACEP). [Accessed July 14th, 2014]. Clinical practice and management policy statement: Alcohol screening in emergency department. Available at: http://www.acep.org/Clinical—-Practice-Management/Alcohol-Screening-in-the-Emergency-Department/.

Arkowitz, H., Westra, H. A., Miller, W. R., & Rollnick, S. (2008). *Motivational interviewing in the treatment of psychological problems.* New York: Guilford Press.

Babor, T. F., & Grant, M. (Eds.). (1992). *Project on identification and management of alcohol-related problems. Report on phase II: A randomized clinical trial of brief interventions in primary health care.* Geneva, Switzerland: World Health Organization.

Baer, J. S., Kivlahan, D. R., & Blume, A. W. (2001). Brief intervention for heavy-drinking college students: 4-year follow-up

and natural history. *American Journal of Public Health 91,* 1310–1316.

Bandura, A. (1986). *Social foundations of thought and action: A social cognitive theory.* Englewood Cliffs, NJ: Prentice Hall.

Barry, K. L. (Ed.) (1999). *TIP 34: Brief interventions and brief therapies for substance abuse.* DHHS Publication No. (SMA) 99-3353. *Drug and Alcohol Dependence, 2005 77,* 49–59.

Bernstein, J., Bernstein, E., Tassiopoulos, K., Heeren, T., Levenson, S., & Hingson, R. (2005). Brief motivational intervention at a clinic visit reduces cocaine and heroin use. *Drug and Alcohol Dependence, 77,* 49–59.

Bernstein, E., Bernstein, J., et al. (2010) The impact of screening, brief intervention and referral for treatment in emergency department patients' alcohol use: A 3-, 6- and 12-month follow-up. *Alcohol & Alcoholism, 45,* 514–519. Epub 2010 Sep 27.

Bien, T. H., Miller, W. R., & Tonigan, J. S. (1993). Brief interventions for alcohol problems: A review. *Addiction, 88,* 315–335.

Burke, B. L., Arkowitz, H., & Menchola, M. (2003). The efficacy of motivational interviewing: A meta-analysis of controlled clinical trials. *Journal of Consulting and Clinical Psychology, 71*(5), 843–861.

Butler, L. H., & Correia, C. J. (2009). Brief alcohol intervention with college student drinkers: Face-to-face versus computerized feedback. *Psychology of Addictive Behaviors, 23,* 163–167.

Chafetz, M. E. (1961) A procedure for establishing therapeutic contact with the alcoholic. *Quarterly Journal of Studies on Alcohol, 22,* 325–328.

Chaftez, M. E., Blane, H. T., Abram, H. S., Golner, J., Lacy, E., McCourt, W. F., ... & Meyers, W. (1962). Establishing treatment relations with alcoholics. *Journal of Nervous and Mental Diseases, 134,* 395–409.

Chafetz, M. E. (1968) Research in the alcohol clinic: An around-the-clock psychiatric service of the Massachusetts General Hospital. *American Journal of Psychiatry, 124,* 1674–1679.

Cimini, M. D., Martens, M. P., Larimer, M. E., Kilmer, J. R., Neighbors, C., & Monserrat, J. M. (2009). Assessing the effectiveness of peer-facilitated interventions addressing high-risk drinking among judicially mandated college students. *Journal of Studies on Alcohol and Drugs, 16,* 57–66.

Copeland, J. (1997). Barriers to formal treatment among women who self-managed change in addictive behaviors. *Journal of Substance Abuse Treatment, 14,* 183–190.

Copeland, J., Swift, W., Roffman, R., & Stephens, R. (2001). A randomized controlled trial of brief cognitive-behavioral interventions for cannabis use disorder. *Journal of Substance Abuse Treatment, 21,* 55–64.

Cuijpers, P., Riper, H., & Lemmers, L. (2004). The effects on mortality of brief interventions for problem drinking: A meta-analysis. *Addiction, 99,* 839–845.

Daeppen, J. B., Gaume, J., Bady, P., et al. (2007). Brief alcohol intervention and alcohol assessment do not influence alcohol use in injured patients treated in the emergency department: A randomized controlled clinical trial. *Addiction, 102,* 1224–1233.

Dawson, D. A., Grant, B. F., & Li, T. K. (2005). Quantifying the risks associated with exceeding recommended drinking limits. *Alcoholism: Clinical and Experimental Research, 29,* 902–908.

Dempsey, C. L. (2008). *Stages of change model. Encyclopedia of substance abuse prevention, treatment, and recovery.* SAGE.

Desy, P. M., Howard, P. K., Perhats, C., & Li, S. (2010). Alcohol screening, brief intervention, and referral to treatment conducted by emergency nurses: An impact evaluation. *Journal of Emergency Nursing, 36*, 538–545.

DiClemente, C. C. (2003). *Addiction and change: how addictions develop and addicted people recover.* New York: Guilford Press.

DiClemente, C. C., & Prochaska, J. O. (1985). Processes and stages of self-change: Coping and competence in smoking behavior change. In S. Shiffman & T. A. Wills (Eds.), *Coping and substance use.* New York: Academic Press.

DiClemente, C. C., & Velasquez, M. (2002) Motivational interviewing and the stages of change. In W. R. Miller & S. Rollnick (Eds.), *Motivational interviewing, second edition: Preparing people for change.* New York: Guilford.

D'Onofrio, G., Pantalon, M. V., Degutis, L. C., et al. (2008). Brief intervention for hazardous and harmful drinkers in the emergency department. *Annals of Emergency Medicine, 51*, 742–750.

Edwards, G., Duckitt, A., Oppenheimer, E., Sheehan, M., & Taylor, C. (1983). What happens to alcoholics? *Lancet, 2*, 269–271.

Ewing, J. A. (1984). Detecting alcoholism: The CAGE questionnaire. *Journal of the American Medical Association, 252*, 1905–1907.

Fiellin, D. A., Reid, M. C., & O'Connor, P. G. (2000). Screening for alcohol problems in primary care: A systematic review. *Archives of Internal Medicine, 160*, 1977–1989.

Fiore, M. C., Bailey, W. C., Cohen, S. J., et al. (October 2000). *Treating tobacco use and dependence. Quick reference guide for clinicians.* Rockville, MD: US Department of Health and Human Services, Public Health Service.

Fleming, M. F., Mundt, M. P., French, M. T., Manwell, L. B., Staauffacher, E. A., & Barry, K. L. (2002). Brief physician advice for problem drinkers: Long-term efficacy and cost-benefit analysis. *Alcoholism Clinical and Experimental Research, 26*, 36–43.

Floyd, R. L., Sobell, M., Velasquez, M. M., Ingersill, K., Nettleman, M., Sobell, L., . . . Nagaraja, J. (2007). Preventing alcohol-exposed pregnancies: A randomized controlled trial. *American Journal of Preventive Medicine, 32*, 1–10.

Fortney, J., & Booth, B. M. (2001). Access to substance abuse services in rural areas. *Recent Developments in Alcoholism, 15*, 177–197.

Gavin, D. R., Ross, H. E., & Skinner, H. A. (1989). Diagnostic validity of the Drug Abuse Screening Test in the assessment of DSM-III drug disorders. *British Journal of Addiction, 84*, 301–307.

Gentilello, L. M., Rivara, F. P., & Donovan, D. M. (1999). Alcohol interventions in a trauma center as a means of reducing the risk of injury recurrence. *Annals of Surgery, 230*, 473–483.

Gentilello, L. M., Ebel, B. E., Wickizer, T. M., Salkever, D. S., & Rivara, F. P. (2005). Alcohol interventions for trauma patients treated in emergency departments and hospitals: a cost benefit analysis. *Annals of Surgery, 241*, 541–550.

Goldstein, M. G., Whitlock, E. P., & DePue, J. (2004). Multiple behavioral risk factor interventions in primary care: Summary of research evidence. *American Journal of Preventive Medicine, 27*(2S): 61–70.

Grandes, G., Sanchez, A., Cortada, J. M., Balague, L., Calderon, C., Arrazola, A., . . . Millan, E. (2008). Is integration of healthy lifestyle promotion into primary care feasible? Discussion and consensus sessions between clinicians and researchers. *BMC Health Services Research, 8*, 213–225.

Havard, A., Shakeshaft, A., & Sanson-Fisher, R. (2008). Systematic review and meta-analyses of strategies targeting alcohol problems in emergency departments: Interventions reduce alcohol-related injuries. *Addiction, 103*, 368–376.

Hettema, J., Steele, J., & Miller, W. R. (2005). Motivational interviewing. *Annual Review of Clinical Psychology, 1*, 91–111.

Hettema, J. E., & Sorensen, J. S. (2009). Access to care for methadone maintenance patients in the United States. *International Journal of Mental Health and Addictions, 6*, 407–420.

Hubbard, R. L., Craddock, S. G., & Anderson, J. (2003). Overview of 5-year follow-up outcomes in the Drug Abuse Treatment Outcome Studies (DATOS). *Journal of Substance Abuse Treatment, 25*, 125–134.

Jonas, D. E., Garbutt, J. C., Amick, H. R., Brown, J. M., Brownles, K. A., Council, C. L., . . . Harris, R. P. (2012). Behavioral counseling after careening for alcohol misuse in primary care: A systematic review and meta-analysis for the U.S. Preventive Services Task Force. *Annals of Internal Medicine.* http://annals.org/ on 10/09-2012

Kaner, E. F., Dickinson, H. O., Beyer, F., Plenaar, E., Schelesinger, C., Campbell, F., . . . Heather, N. (2009). The effectiveness of brief alcohol interventions in primary care populations: A systematic review. *Drug and Alcohol Review, 28*(3), 301–323.

Kristenson, H., Ohlin, H., Hulten-Nosslin, M. B., Trell, E., & Hood, B. (1983). Identification and intervention of heavy drinking in middle-aged men: Results and follow-up of 24-60 months of long-term study with randomized controls. *Alcoholism: Clinical and Experimental Research, 7*, 203–209.

Kuchipudi, V., Hobein, K., Fleckinger, A., & Iber, F. L. (1990). Failure of a 2-hour motivational intervention to alter recurrent drinking behavior in alcoholics with gastrointestinal disease. *Journal of Studies on Alcohol, 51*, 356–360.

LaBrie, J. W., Huchting, K., Tawalbeh, S., Pedersen, E. R., Thompson, A. D., Shelesky, K., et al. (2008). A randomized motivational enhancement prevention group reduces drinking and alcohol consequences in first-year college women. *Psychology of Addictive Behaviors: Journal of the Society of Psychologists in Addictive Behaviors, 22*, 149–155.

LaBrie, J. W., Lamb, T. F., Pedersen, E. R., & Quinlan, T. (2006). A group motivational interviewing intervention reduces drinking and alcohol-related consequences in adjudicated college students. *Journal of College Student Development, 47*, 267–280.

LaBrie, J. W., Pedersen, E. R., Lamb, T. F., & Quinlan, T. (2007). A campus-based motivational enhancement group intervention reduces problematic drinking in freshmen male college students. *Addictive Behaviors, 32*, 889–901.

Labrie, J. W., Thompson, A. D., Huchting, K., Lac, A., & Buckley, K. (2007). A group motivational interviewing intervention reduces drinking and alcohol-related negative consequences in adjudicated college women. *Addictive Behaviors, 32*, 2549–2562.

Larimer, M. E., Cronce, J. M., Lee, C. M., & Kilmer, J. R. (2004–2005). Brief intervention in college settings. *Alcohol Res Health, 28*, 94–104.

Larimer, M. E., & Cronce, J. M. (2002). Identification, prevention, and treatment: A review of individual-focused strategies to reduce problematic alcohol consumption by college students. *Journal of Studies on Alcohol, Suppl. 14*, 148–163.

Leake, G. J., & King, A. S. (1977). Effect of counselor expectations on alcoholic recovery. *Alcohol Health & Research World, 11*, 16–22.

Libby, T. A. (2008). Brief Interventions. In G. Fisher & N. Roget (Eds.), *Encyclopedia of substance abuse prevention, treatment, and recovery.* SAGE.

Lowenstein, S. R., Weissberg, M., & Terry, D. (1990). Alcohol intoxication, injuries and dangerous behaviors—and the revolving emergency department door. *Journal of Trauma, 30*, 1252–1257.

Lundahl, B. W., Tollefson, E., Kunz, C., Brownell, C., & Burke, B. L. (2009). A meta-analysis of motivational interviewing: Twenty five years of empirical studies. *Research on Social Work Practice, 65*, 1232–1245.

MacMaster, S. (2005). Experiences with, and perceptions of, barriers to substance abuse and HIV services among African-American women who use crack cocaine. *Journal of Ethnicity in Substance Abuse, 4*, 53–75.

Maciosek, M. V., Coffield, A. B., Edwards, N. M., Flottemesch, T. J., Goodman, M. J., & Solberg, L. I. (2006). Priorities among effective clinical preventive services: Results of a systematic review and analysis. *American Journal of Preventive Medicine, 31*, 52–61.

MacKenzie, D. M., Langa, A., & Brown, T. M. (1996). Identifying hazardous or harmful alcohol use in medical admissions: A comparison of AUDIT, CAGE and brief MAST. *Alcohol and Alcoholism, 31*(6), 591–599.

Madras, B. K., Compton, W. M., Avula, D., Stegbauer, T., Stein, J. B., & Clark, H. W. (2009). Screening, brief interventions, referral to treatment (SBIRT) for illicit drug and alcohol use at multiple healthcare sites: Comparison at intake and 6 months later. *Drug and Alcohol Dependence, 99*, 280–295.

Marlatt, G. A., Baer, J. S., & Kivlahan, D. R. (1998). Screening and brief intervention for high-risk college student drinkers: Results from a 2-year follow-up assessment. *Journal of Consulting and Clinical Psychology, 66*, 604–615.

McDonald, A. J., Wang, N., & Camargo, C. A. (2004). US emergency department visits for alcohol-related diseases and injuries between 1992 and 2000. *Archives of Internal Medicine, 164*, 531–537.

McGlynn, E. A., Asch, S. M., & Adams, J. (2003). The quality of health care delivered to adults in the United States. *New England Journal of Medicine, 348*, 2635–2645.

McKay, J. R. (2005). Is there evidence for extended interventions for alcohol and drug use disorders? *Addiction, 11*, 1594–1610.

McKnight-Eily, L. R., Liu, Y., Brewer, R. D., Kanny, D., Lu, H., Denny, C. H., Balluz, L., Collins, J. (2014) Vital signs: Communication between health professionals and their patients about alcohol use—44 states and District of Columbia, 2011. *Morbidity and Mortality Weekly, 63*, 16–23.

Miller, W. R. (1983). Motivational interviewing with problem drinkers. *Behavioural Psychotherapy 11*, 147–172.

Miller, W. R., Sovereign, R. G., & Krege, B. (1988). Motivational interviewing with problem drinkers: II. The Drinker's Check-up as a preventive intervention. *Behavioural Psychotherapy, 16*, 251–268.

Miller, W. R., Benefield, R. G., & Tonigan, J. S. (1993). Enhancing motivation for change in problem drinking: A controlled comparison of two therapist styles. *Journal of Consulting and Clinical Psychology, 61*, 455–461.

Miller, W. R., & Sanchez, V. C. (1993). Motivating young adults for treatment and lifestyle change. In G. Howard (Ed.), *Issues in alcohol use and misuse in young adults.* Notre Dame, IN: University of Notre Dame Press.

Miller, W. R., & Rollnick, S. (2013). *Motivational interviewing: Helping people change.* New York: Guilford.

Miller, W. R., & Rose, G. S. (2009). Toward a theory of motivational interviewing. *American Psychologist, 64*, 527–537.

Mischke, H. D., & Venneri, R. L. (1987). Reliability and validity of the MAST, Mortimer Filkins questionnaire and CAGE in DWI assessment. *Journal of Studies on Alcohol, 48,* 492–501.

Moyer, A., Finney, J. W., Swearingen, C. E., & Vergun, P (2002). Brief interventions for alcohol problems: A meta-analytic review of controlled investigations in treatment seeking and non-treatment seeking populations. *Addiction, 97*, 279–292.

Murphy, J. G., Duchnick, J. J., & Vuchinich, R. E. (2001). Relative efficacy of a brief motivational intervention for college student drinkers. *Psychology of Addictive Behaviors, 15*, 373–379.

Murphy, J. G., Benson, T. A., & Vuchinich, R. E. (2004). A comparison of personalized feedback for college student drinkers delivered with and without a motivational interview. *Journal of Studies on Alcohol, 65*, 200–203.

National Institute on Alcohol Abuse and Alcoholism. (2005). *Helping patients who drink too much: A clinician's guide.* NIH Publication No. 05–3769. Bethesda, MD: NIH.

Nilsen, P., Baird, J., Mello, M. J., et al. (2008). A systematic review of emergency care brief alcohol interventions for injury patients. *Journal of Substance Abuse Treatment, 35*(2), 184–201. Epub 2008 Feb 20.

Perz, C. A., DiClemente, C. C., & Carbonari, J. P. (1996). Doing the right thing at the right time: The intersection of stages and processes of change in successful smoking cessation. *Health Psychology, 15*, 462–468.

Prochaska, J. O., & DiClemente, C. C. (2005). The transtheoretical approach. In J. C. Norcross & M. R. Goldfried (Eds.), *Handbook of psychotherapy integration* (2nd ed., pp. 147–171). New York: Oxford University Press.

Project MATCH Research Group. (1997). Matching alcoholism treatments to client heterogeneity: Project MATCH post-treatment drinking outcomes. *Journal of Studies on Alcohol, 58*, 7–29.

Rehm, J., Room, R., Graham, K., Monteiro, M., Gmel, G., & Sempos, C. T. (2003). The relationship of average volume of alcohol consumption and patterns of drinking to burden of disease: An overview. *Addiction, 98*, 1209–1228.

Rollnick, S., & Miller, W. R. (1995). What is motivational interviewing? *Behavioural and Cognitive Psychotherapy, 23*, 325–334.

Rollnick, S., Miller, W. R., & Butler, C. C. (2008). *Motivational interviewing in health care.* New York: Guilford Press.

Rubak, S., Sandbaek, A., Lauritzen, T., & Christensen, B. (2005). Motivational interviewing: A systematic review and meta-analysis. *The British Journal of General Practice, 55*(513), 305–312.

Saitz, R. (2005). Unhealty alcohol use. *New England Journal of Medicine, 352*, 596–607.

Saitz, R. SBIRT: Has the enthusiasm outpaced the evidence? Yes! (2009). In E. Bernstein, J. A. Bernstein, J. B. Stein, & R. Saitz (Eds.), SBIRT in emergency care settings: Are we ready to take it to scale? *Academic Emergency Medicine, 16*(11), 1072–1077.

SAMHSA. (2006). National Survey of Substance Abuse Treatment Services (N-SSATS). http://wwwdasis.samhsa.gov/webt/state_data/US06.pdf

Saunders, J. B., Aasland, O. G., Babor, T. F., de la Fuente, J. R., & Grant, M. (1993). Development of the Alcohol Use Disorders Identification Test (AUDIT): WHO collaborative project on early detection of persons with harmful alcohol consumption. II. *Addiction, 88,* 791–804.

Schaus, J. F., Sole, M. L., McCoy, T. P., Mullett, N., & O'Brien, M. C. (2009). Alcohol screening and brief intervention in a college student health center: A randomized controlled trial. *Journal of Studies on Alcohol and Drugs, Suppl.,* 131–141.

Schermer, C. R., Moyers, T. B., Miller, W. R., & Bloomfield, L. A. (2006). Trauma center brief interventions for alcohol disorders decrease subsequent driving under the influence arrests. *Journal of Trauma, 60,* 29–34.

Selzer, M. L. (1971). The Michigan Alcoholism Screening Test: The quest for a new diagnostic instrument. *American Journal of Psychiatry, 127,* 1653–1658.

Solberg, L. I., Maciosek, M. V., & Edwards, N. M. (2008). Primary care intervention to reduce alcohol misuse ranking its health impact and cost effectiveness. *American Journal of Preventive Medicine, 34,* 143–152.

Stephens, R. S., Roffman, R. A., & Curtin L. (2000). Comparison of extended versus brief treatments for marijuana use. *Journal of Consulting and Clinical Psychology, 68,* 898–908.

Substance Abuse and Mental Health Services Administration. (2009). *Results from the 2008 National Survey on Drug Use and Health: National findings.* Rockville, MD: Office of Applied Studies, NSDUH Series H-36, HHS Publication No. SMA 09-4434.

Substance Abuse and Mental Health Services Administration. (2010). *Results from the 2009 National Survey on Drug Use and Health: Volume I. Summary of National Findings* Rockville, MD: Office of Applied Studies, NSDUH Series H-38A, HHS Publication No. SMA 10-4856.

Sutton, S. (2001). Back to the drawing board? A review of applications of the transtheoretical model to substance use. *Addiction, 96,* 175–186.

United Nations Office on Drugs and Crime. (UNODC). (2009). *World Drug Report.* http://www.unodc.org/documents/wdr/WDR_2009/WDR2009_eng_web.pdf

U.S. Department of Health and Human Services, Centers for Disease Control and Prevention. (2007). *National Hospital Ambulatory Medical Care Survey: 2005 emergency department summary.* Washington, DC: National Center for Health Statistics, 386.

Vaca, F., Winn, D., Anderson, C., Kim, D., & Arclia, M. (2011). Six-month follow-up of computerized alcohol screening, brief intervention, and referral to treatment in the emergency department. *Substance Abuse, 32*(11), 144–152.

Walters, S. T., Vader, A. M., Harris, T. R., & Jouriles, E. N. (2009). Reactivity to alcohol assessment measures: An experimental test. *Addiction, 104,* 1305–1310.

Wagner, C. C., & Ingersoll, K. S. (2013). The evidence for MI groups. In C. C. Wagner & K. S. Ingersoll (Eds.), *Motivational interviewing in groups* (pp. 70–86). New York: Guilford Press.

Wells-Parker, E., & Williams, M. (2002). Enhancing the effectiveness of traditional intervention with drinking drivers by adding brief individual intervention components. *Social Science Research, 63,* 655–664.

West, R. (2005). Time for a change: Putting the transtheoretical (stages of change) model to rest. *Addiction, 100,* 1036–1039.

Whitlock, E. P., Orleans, C. T., Pender, N., & Allan, J. (2002). Evaluating primary care behavioral counseling interventions: An evidence-based approach. *American Journal of Preventive Medicine, 22,* 267–284.

Whitlock, E. P., Polen, M. R., Green, C. A., Orleans, T., & Klein, J. (2004). Behavioral counseling interventions in primary care to reduce risky/harmful alcohol use by adults: A summary of the evidence for the U.S. Preventive Services Task Force. *Annals of Internal Medicine, 140,* 557–568.

World Health Organization. (2004). *Global status report on alcohol.* Geneva: World Health Organization.

Wutzke, S. E., Conigrave, K. M., Saunders, J. B., & Hall, W. D. (2002). The long-term effectiveness of brief interventions for unsafe alcohol consumption: A 10 year follow-up. *Addiction, 97,* 665–675.

Cognitive-Behavioral Approaches

Damaris J. Rohsenow *and* Megan M. Pinkston-Camp

Abstract

Cognitive-behavioral approaches to treatment are derived from learning principles underlying behavioral and/or cognitive therapy. Only evidence-based approaches are recommended for practice. Support for different approaches varies across substance use disorders. For alcohol use disorders, cognitive-behavioral coping skills training and cue-exposure treatment are beneficial when added to an integrated treatment program. For cocaine dependence, contingency management combined with coping skills training or community reinforcement, and coping skills training added to a full treatment program, produce increased abstinence. For marijuana abuse, contingency management or coping skills training improve outcomes. For opiate dependence, contingency management decreases use of other drugs while on methadone. For smoking, aversive conditioning produces good results and key elements of coping skills training are supported, best when medication is also used. Recent advances include Web-based coping skills training, virtual reality to present cues during cue exposure, and text-messaging to remind clients to use coping skills in the natural environment.

Key Words: behavior therapy, cognitive-behavioral therapy, cognitive therapy, contingency management, coping skills treatment, cue-exposure treatment, financial incentives, operant learning, respondent learning, social learning theory

Introduction

The past two decades saw major changes in theoretical approaches and treatment strategies for people with substance use disorders (SUDs). Recognition grew that medical or pharmacological treatments, when available, are not sufficient and that SUDs involve learned behaviors more than psychological inadequacies (Onken, Blaine, & Boren, 1993). For some substances (e.g., cocaine or marijuana), no pharmacotherapy has yet received approval so that only "talking" approaches are available. When medications are available, they are more effective against a backdrop of pharmacotherapy (Onken et al., 1993). Psychosocial approaches not based on learning theory principles usually either failed to improve abstinence from substances (e.g., Kang et al., 1991) or have not systematically been tested with scientific standards for evidence (e.g., Rawson et al., 1991). This set the stage for developing evidence-based cognitive and behavioral methods. Behavioral treatments to help people with SUDs change their life styles and learn alternative ways to handle relapse precipitants ("triggers") are now seen as important for success (e.g., Onken et al., 1993).

This essay covers cognitive-behavioral approaches in the broad sense: the focus is on evidence-based treatment approaches that use principles of behavior therapy and/or cognitive therapy (e.g., Beck, Wright, Newman, & Liese, 1993; Monti, Kadden, Rohsenow, Cooney, & Abrams, 2002). Behavioral approaches include relaxation training and aversion therapy. Contingency management (CM) (also called financial incentives) is a behavioral approach that has been conducted alone or combined with other cognitive and behavioral treatments (Higgins, Silverman, & Heil, 2008). When cognitive and behavioral principles are combined, the approach is called cognitive-behavioral treatment or therapy (CBT), particularly for approaches that focus on coping skills training (CST) for handling emotions or high-risk situations for relapse or interpersonal situations more effectively. Some forms of CST are called relapse prevention training (RPT), but in a sense this refers to the goal of the treatment rather than a separate set of methods (Miller, Willbourne, & Hettema, 2003). Cue exposure with response prevention, a behavioral approach, has a foundation in behavioral principles of habituation and/or extinction, and as practiced by some groups (e.g., Rohsenow et al., 2002) integrates coping skills practice to become a CBT. Acceptance and commitment therapy (ACT) is a cognitive approach focused on decreasing escape from key symptoms.

We could not evaluate some approaches that combined many of these different elements into the same program such as one by Hall et al. (1984); that combined aversion therapy, relaxation training, feedback on physical tests and costs, and skills training to cope with expected relapse situations; the Matrix Model (e.g., Rawson & Obert, 2002) that combines CBT with many other types of treatment elements not derived from the learning theories; or an approach that combined motivational interviewing, skills training, and case management that is not a CBT (MTP Research group, 2004). We also did not evaluate programs for adolescents, as the developmental needs of this population require special consideration.

This essay will not review other approaches that could be considered cognitive in nature. Brief interventions, motivational interviewing, and behavioral couples therapy are covered in other essays. There is evidence for consistent lack of effectiveness for insight-oriented psychotherapies, confrontational approaches, general alcoholism counseling, and educational approaches such as lectures and films (Miller et al., 2003), and these approaches are not based in the learning theories. CBTs focused primarily on comorbid psychopathologies (e.g., dialectical behavioral therapy) will not be covered except that comorbid depression will be touched on briefly because this was part of the history of developing the CBT approaches and because depressed affect is a common relapse precipitant addressed in CBT. We will only include dependencies that involve ingestion of a drug (alcohol, drugs of abuse, and nicotine) while excluding caffeine and behaviors such as gambling or sex, which are sometimes referred to as addictions. When we review evidence for approaches, we will omit studies that were uncontrolled or had other serious methodological flaws, except when there are few studies and the less controlled ones provide suggestive evidence of promise for an approach.

The CBT and CM approaches can be used as stand-alone treatments for people with early stage SUDs. However, in general, the treatment of people with more extensive SUDs is considered to require a comprehensive approach that may include social services, medical care, medications for comorbidities, case management, job training, 12-Step involvement, etc. For this reason, the CBTs are often used and evaluated as part of a comprehensive treatment program for drug and alcohol dependence. Finally, for tobacco dependence, the clinical practice guidelines recommend that one of the tobacco pharmacotherapies be recommended unless medical conditions contraindicate it (USDHHS, 2000), so CBT is now used in combination with such medications for helping smokers to quit smoking.

Relapse Prevention versus Abstinence Initiation: What's in the Name?

Relapse prevention as a treatment goal. Some treatment programs accept clients who are still using drugs, alcohol, or tobacco and focus on abstinence initiation as the first target before working on maintenance or relapse prevention. Other programs require abstinence for treatment entry, so all of their treatment is geared toward keeping the clients abstinent, and thus toward relapse prevention. For some problem drinkers, programs may be focused just on reducing drinking to non-problematic levels, such as in many college interventions. Thus, "relapse prevention" is essentially a treatment goal rather than a specific approach. Most of the approaches we cover are designed for relapse prevention when applied to dependence on illicit drugs or alcohol and for both abstinence initiation and relapse prevention when applied to tobacco dependence. Motivational interviewing (not covered) is one of the few treatments designed specifically for abstinence initiation (although also applied to consolidating motivation among the abstinent), and the brief physician advice to quit smoking using National Cancer Institute's guidelines (ask, assess, advise, assist, arrange follow-up) is another (Glynn & Manly, 1995). Aversive conditioning could have both goals, but since one would want to avoid drug experiences with positive reinforcement between sessions, it is probably best applied to relapse prevention. Since cue-exposure treatment (CET) requires response prevention for efficacy, it is designed only for relapse prevention goals. Contingency management is ideally suited to both abstinence initiation and relapse prevention goals.

Relapse Prevention as a Type of CBT. There are also some specific CBT treatments for alcohol or drug dependence named "relapse prevention treatment (RPT)"; these are essentially a subset of CSTs for SUDs. The treatments formally called RPT (except for one by Gorski [1996], never empirically evaluated) are all based on formal learning theory and founded in using cognitive and behavioral skills-training techniques, as described by Marlatt in the first chapter of his book on the topic (e.g., Marlatt & Donovan, 2005). Marlatt first coined the name after adapting CST to address specific relapse precipitants in separate modules (Chaney, O'Leary, & Marlatt, 1978) based on the first systematic categorization of situations that triggered relapse for people with alcohol use disorders (AUDs) (Marlatt & Gordon, 1985). While the CBTs derived from this model are often called RPT, these are not essentially different in methods from many other cognitive-behavioral CSTs because they are derived from the same background in social learning theory (e.g., Abrams & Niaura, 1987) and decision theory (Edwards, 1954). Some use identical techniques but were not called RPT (e.g., McCrady et al., 1985; Rohsenow et al., 2000). The Communication Skills Training of Monti et al. (1990; also adapted for Project MATCH), while not called RPT, is designed to teach lifestyle change skills that will keep the person from relapsing, using CST. For this reason, the approaches called RPT will be covered with other coping skills training approaches rather than as though they were a separate type of approach. Historically, the coining of the term did produce somewhat of a paradigm shift in the way clinicians in practice settings conceptualized the purpose of treatments for smoking, AUDs, and SUDs, largely by shifting the emphasis of these treatments away from interpersonal psychotherapy and psychotherapy based on the supportive/psychodynamic model toward building skills designed to directly decrease the probability of relapse.

From Theoretical Model to Practice Principles

The cognitive-behavioral approaches encompass evidence-based treatments built on social learning theory predominantly (Bandura, 1977, 1997), particularly respondent conditioning, operant conditioning, social learning principles, and cognitive therapy principles. It is beyond the scope of this essay to give a full overview of the cognitive social learning theories (see Abrams & Niaura, 1987; chapter 1 of Monti et al., 2002; or chapter 1 of Marlatt & Gordon, 1985, for fuller descriptions of the theory as applied to SUDs). A very brief overview of some basic principles involved in promoting behavior change in these approaches can be helpful to provide a context for the CBTs. A common conceptualization underlying the treatments is that the client lacks important coping skills for handling daily life without using substances. These skills include skills for handling internal states (moods, cravings, stress, pain), interpersonal situations (e.g., family, conflicts, building positive relationships), and employment situations effectively. Certain external situations and/or internal states have developed individualized learned associations with substance use and therefore pose a higher risk for relapse than other situations. Even when the client has some appropriate skills, the client may expect more positive outcomes from substance use than from applying the skills to stay/become abstinent (outcome expectancies) or may doubt his/ability to apply the skills effectively (self-efficacy expectancies).

Parts of early decision theory (Edwards, 1954) provide another basis for the cognitive-behavioral approaches, stating that a behavioral choice is the function of the possible negative and positive consequences of behavior, the value of each consequence to the individual, and the perceived likelihood of occurrence of each consequence. Research based on this theory showed that a decision to seek help is associated with expecting more disadvantages than advantages to the behavior and with more negative consequences of substance use (Hingson et al., 1982; Kanfer, 1986; Prochaska et al., 1994). Helping clients weigh personally relevant consequences of behavioral choices also underlies functional analyses of relapse episodes to help guide decisions to use more adaptive responses (Rohsenow et al., 2000).

Some aspects of social learning theory that apply to building abstinence or preventing relapse involve client and therapist identifying situations (environmental and internal) which often trigger substance use (via operant or respondent conditioning principles), cognitions (automatic thoughts, beliefs, expected consequences of various behavioral choices, self-efficacy about one's ability to use alternative behaviors) that are elicited by these situations, and probable consequences (pleasurable and unpleasant, immediate and delayed) of the substance use and of nonsubstance alternative to use. "Functional analysis" is the term used for this analysis of the cognitions and emotions that arise in specific situations, the role of cognitions in emotions, the behaviors that follow those cognitions and emotions, and the consequences of the behavioral choices (Kanfer & Phillips, 1970; McCrady et al., 1985). This approach is particularly useful for analyzing situations that pose a high risk for relapse (McCrady et al., 1985; Rohsenow et al., 2000). Theoretical social learning principles guiding the intervention methods include that people learn through direct instruction (by other clients, therapists, family, friends); through modeling of alternatives (by other clients and therapists); by learning to counter automatic thoughts/beliefs with adaptive alternative thoughts through a combination of instruction, experiments to test the validity of certain beliefs, and practice using alternative thoughts; by practice using a variety of new skills with corrective feedback; by changing the environment to reduce encounters with situations that trigger relapse and to increase contact with positive reinforcement for not using substances; and by changing the social and/or employment or living environment to increase positive reinforcement and support for alternatives to substance use. The approaches are sometimes called "skills training" approaches because a variety of adaptive cognitive and behavioral skills are taught and practiced in role plays and in home work. The approaches are all primarily oriented toward the present and future (e.g., current and near future urges to use), rather than focusing on childhood or other developmental issues, and on the client actively learning new ways to deal with life.

Relaxation or Meditation Training
OVERVIEW OF APPROACH

Early models of SUDs focused on stress as an emotional state being considered to be a primary contributor to substance use and relapse. This led to a focus on relaxation or meditation as an early behavioral approach. Clients were typically taught guided relaxation techniques using progressive muscle relaxation (tensing and releasing muscle groups), autogenic training (focusing on noticing sensations in various body groups), guided breathing, meditation (focus on a repeated stimulus such as a sound or visual pattern), or hypnosis, with recommendations to practice the relaxation twice a day (see review by Klajner, Hartman, & Sobell, 1984).

SUMMARY OF EVIDENCE

While such training may make a person feel more relaxed, reviews across a great many studies found no evidence that these approaches, as either stand-alone or adjunctive treatment, had any significant effect on substance use outcomes (Klajner et al., 1984; Miller et al., 2003) or smoking abstinence (Fiore et al., 2000). Finally, a review of hypnotherapy trials by the Cochrane Group did not support hypnosis as a treatment for smoking cessation (Abbott, Stead, White, & Ernst, 1999). The behavioral field moved away from this simplistic approach so as to address more of the complexities of SUDs.

Aversive Conditioning Approaches
OVERVIEW OF APPROACH

Some approaches to treating SUDs focused on aversive operant or respondent learning. The therapist most commonly induces nausea via ingestion of an agent like apomorphine, emetine hydrochloride, or lithium hydrochloride, then the client is exposed to or ingests the addictive substance (Miller & Hester, 1986). More rarely, apnea was induced by injecting succinycholine to paralyze the person for about 60 seconds (inducing terror) while letting them taste alcohol (Clancy et al., 1967). Electrical aversion (e.g., Vogler et al., 1971) was also used in some studies by pairing electrical shocks with tasting the substance. Finally, covert sensitization involved imagining aversive scenes while drinking small amounts of alcohol (e.g., Ashem & Donner, 1968).

Drug Dependence Applications. Chemical aversion therapy in various studies (e.g., Frawley & Smith, 1990) paired exposure to the sight, smell, and taste of a cocaine-substitute chemical with chemically induced nausea in a repeated series of sessions over days.

Alcohol Dependence Applications. The nausea-based approaches have had the client ingest an emetic and then drink some of his or her preferred beverage, while electric conditioning provides shocks to a neutral part of the body each time the person starts to drink the beverage (e.g., Cannon,

Baker, & Wehl, 1981). Covert images included plausible negative consequences of drinking to excess (Elkins, 1980).

Tobacco Dependence. The most common method of conducting aversive conditioning for smoking cessation involves rapid smoking or rapid puffing procedures. In rapid smoking, nausea occurs from toxic levels of nicotine and smoke constituents so that nausea is directly associated with smoking. The original treatment approach involves three sessions per week for the first 2 or 3 weeks starting with the quit day (Lichtenstein et al., 1973; Schmahl et al., 1972). In each session, clients smoke three consecutive cigarettes by inhaling cigarette puffs once every 6 seconds, followed by a 5-minute break, then they repeat the procedure up to two more times (maximum of nine cigarettes) until the client refuses to smoke anymore and reports nausea (e.g., Hall et al., 1984). Rapid puffing is similar but without inhaling as much per puff.

Summary of Evidence

Evidence for Use with AUD or SUD Treatment. A systematic meta-analysis of treatment approaches for AUDs (Miller et al., 2003) concluded that aversion therapy strategies based on nausea have modestly positive success across studies in reducing drinking, but results were inconsistent across the various studies, there was often considerable refusal to participate, and attrition was sometimes high. Results for electrical aversion and covert sensitization were less encouraging, with no consistent results seen (Miller & Hester, 1986; Miller et al., 2003). Lack of success with using apnea as an approach (Clancy et al., 1967; Laverty, 1966) led to its discontinuation in the 1960s. Adequately controlled published studies for drug use disorders were not found.

Evidence for Use in Smoking Treatment. For treating tobacco dependence, aversive smoking using either rapid smoking or other aversion techniques) has the highest levels of success of all nonpharmacological treatments (Piasecki & Baker, 2001; USDHHS, 2000). In many studies, initial quit rates close to 100% and 6 month or more quit rates of 50% to 60% were reported (Brandon et al., 1987; Hall et al., 1984; Poole et al., 1981; Tiffany et al., 1986), with 50% still abstinent at 2 years (Hall et al., 1984). In a more recent meta-analysis, rapid smoking and other aversive smoking methods produced estimated point-prevalence abstinence rates at outcome (5 or more months after start) of 17% to 20%, with odds ratios of 1.7 to 2.0 compared with control treatments (Piasecki & Baker, 2001; USDHHS, 2000). However, the aversive approaches have reduced acceptance with clients and therapists alike. Also, most of the evidence comes from studies published in the 1970s and 1980s with small numbers of subjects and without biochemical verification, so how well it would do with current smokers (who are more dependent than smokers in the 1970s) and pitted against other current treatment approaches is unknown (Piasecki & Baker, 2001). Still, this may be the best approach for some resistant smokers. The clinical practice guidelines for smoking indicate that this procedure should only be conducted under medical supervision because there may be a health risk despite initial safety trials with healthy smokers (USDHHS, 2000). For these reasons, recent years have shown more focus on CBTs and on CM approaches that use positive incentives for change.

Cognitive Therapy
Overview of Approach

Because principles and practices of cognitive therapy are incorporated into most other CBT approaches, it is best to start with an overview of cognitive therapy as applied to treating SUDs. Cognitive therapy of substance abuse as described by Beck et al. (1993) was developed primarily from two sources: the cognitive therapy method developed for depression (Beck et al., 1979) and the model of relapse prevention developed by Marlatt and Gordon (1985). While a conceptualization of the development of the SUD is included in these sources (e.g., Beck et al., 2005), we will focus on the intervention methods.

The basic cognitive model of a high-risk situation for drug use starts with activating stimuli (internal or external cues associated with drug use in the past, such as moods or the sight of drugs). When leading to drug use or relapse, the stimuli activate the client's drug-related beliefs, both anticipatory and relief-oriented (expected consequences of using/not using), leading to automatic thoughts (thoughts that seem to occur spontaneously, often with little awareness), such as "I have to use or everyone will think I'm a jerk." These lead to urges and cravings to use as well as other emotions. Facilitating beliefs may also come into play (e.g., "I'll just test my control, one drink can't hurt"; "She thinks I use drugs anyway so I'll show her!"). Core beliefs the individual has about him/herself, such as "I'm worthless" or "I'm unlovable" or "I'll never be any good no matter what I do," may interact with the drug-related beliefs and automatic thoughts. These thoughts and beliefs lead to an action plan to seek the drugs or alcohol.

The therapist's approach is to modify both the core and drug-related beliefs and the automatic thoughts elicited by high-risk situations and to help the client learn new behaviors to replace the maladaptive ones. Case conceptualization starts with analyzing the specific client's personal situational antecedents of substance use, the thoughts and emotions that are triggered by these situations, the core dysfunctional beliefs they have about themselves, other people, and substance use, and the patterns of behavior the client uses in response to these beliefs. The therapist works with the clients to help them learn to identify the automatic thoughts and to begin to counteract them. One step involves listing both the advantages and disadvantages of both drug use and of abstinence. Second, through Socratic questioning and modeling, the therapist helps the client learn to develop alternative more adaptive thoughts to replace the maladaptive ones with. The client practices countering the automatic maladaptive thoughts with more adaptive alternatives that are more likely to lead to abstinence. For example, a client might learn to counter "I feel so lousy, I might as well use cocaine and get high—I'll feel better" with "I'll feel better briefly, but then I'll crash, I'll lose my job, my kids will be taken away again, and I'll end up back in treatment. It's not worth it." The automatic thought might be valid "I'll feel high," but helping the client to investigate all the consequences of the first reaction can help lead to a more adaptive solution. Specific attention is paid to helping the person learn alternative ways to handles urges/cravings, by analyzing the antecedents that lead to these feelings (which could be prevented, if possible), alternative thoughts (especially reminding oneself of the consequences of giving in to them), and alternative behaviors (e.g., engaging in a distracting activity).

This approach is used to deal with situations that trigger drug use (ongoing or relapse). However, it is also used to help the person learn more effective ways to handle anger, depression, anxiety, and other emotions without using drugs (cognitive-behavioral mood management training). Thus, it involves both drug-specific situations and more general life skills to promote a more sober lifestyle.

Summary of Evidence

We could find no research that evaluated effectiveness of purely cognitive therapy for drug, alcohol or tobacco use disorders. Rather, cognitive therapy has been used as an aspect of CBT in clinical trials.

Cognitive-Behavioral Skills Training
Overview of Approach

Cognitive-behavioral skills training, usually abbreviated as either CBT or CST, combines cognitive therapy with other behavioral methods (e.g., escape, avoidance, alternative activities, conflict resolution skills) derived from learning theory. (We will mostly use the abbreviation CST to avoid confusion with the broader sense of the essay title.) This approach was derived from behavioral treatments for depression and anxiety (Kanfer & Phillips, 1970) and then the core elements were extended to SUDs. The most common application to SUDs is using CST to teach clients with SUDs coping skills to help them become or remain abstinent. The core elements are designed to address the underlying conceptualization that the client lacks important adaptive coping skills for daily life. These can include lack of adequate skills to regulate positive and negative mood states and to cope with interpersonal situations (work, intimate relationships, friendships, parenting). Coping difficulties can involve the interaction of underlying biological predisposing factors with stressful environmental demands and having learned maladaptive ways to handle these demands. Therefore, the major domains addressed by cognitive-behavioral CST are (a) interpersonal skills for building better relationships, (b) cognitive and behavioral emotion-coping skills for regulating moods more effectively, (c) general coping skills for improving daily living (increase general level of positive events, decrease probability and intensity of negative events, provide sources of social support), (d) skills for coping with sudden stressful events without using substances, and (e) coping with substance use cues without using. The skills training helps to increase clients' sense of self-efficacy about handling situations without using substances by providing practice with feedback. Feedback from group members and therapists helps to develop the client's outcome expectancies about positive results occurring from use of the new skills. Underlying biological vulnerabilities (e.g., comorbid psychiatric conditions, neurological conditions, medical illnesses) may need to be addressed through appropriate other treatments so that these do not impede learning in CST.

CST is conducted in either group or individual sessions. Individual sessions have the advantage of privacy since we have found that some clients are quite reluctant to become vulnerable by disclosing their illegal activities in front of other clients; these people open up more readily one on one. Group sessions have the advantage of lower cost, making role plays more realistic by involving other clients, specific skills suggestions coming from clients, and modeling of solutions by other clients. CST has been conducted as part of an intensive SUD treatment program or as stand-alone outpatient care. CST as described in most studies is usually structured around topics, one of which is covered in each session with a client or clients, with topic choice adaptable to the specific needs of individual clients.

In general, CST session topics are structured in one of two ways: skill-focused or situation focused. Either each session is designed to teach a skill useful in recovery (e.g., drug refusal or assertiveness) and has the client apply it to a variety of personal situations, or each session identifies a high-risk situation for relapse (e.g., receiving money or depression) and provides a menu of coping skills for the client to learn and practice in the context of his or her individual examples of that situation. The situation-based approach, sometimes called RPT, commonly involves functional analysis of the situations as the basis for teaching and practicing coping skills. The therapist manual includes a list of anticipatory cognitive and behavioral coping skills (e.g., taking a sober support with them to a party or arranging direct deposit of paychecks), immediate cognitive coping (including cognitive restructuring and thinking of positive consequences of sobriety), and immediate behavioral coping skills (e.g., assertive refusal or going to a safe location) (Rohsenow et al., 2000). The skills-focused approach can cover both high-risk situations (e.g., seeing drugs) and changes in life style design to promote being clean and sober (e.g., developing sober support networks; learning healthy forms of recreation; conversation skills; giving and receiving positive feedback) (Monti et al., 2002). Each approach has merits and may differ in acceptability to clients depending on the type of clientele in the program. Our cocaine-dependent clients rejected the idea that they needed skills training but accepted the idea that they needed to learn to handle trigger situations.

Alcohol Dependence Applications. This approach was developed and applied to the AUDs before other SUDs. The first CST approaches for AUDs were structured around high-risk situations (Chaney, et al., 1978). An analysis of high risk situations for relapsing to alcohol was conducted (Marlatt & Gordon, 1985). Then an eight session CST was developed that focused each session on methods of coping with each of these categories of situations, with four interpersonal situations and four intrapersonal ones covered (Chaney et al., 1978). In groups, clients described their own personal examples of the high-risk situation that was the topic for the day (e.g., interpersonal conflict, anger or frustration, intrapersonal negative emotional states such as depression, urges/temptations, social pressure to drink, wanting to enhance positive states, and testing personal control over alcohol), then iteratively role-played alternative methods of handling the situations, with coaching instructions and feedback. While the initial treatment that was empirically tested was structured around these eight situations, use of the broader principles with less structure was described in the subsequent book on relapse prevention (Marlatt & Gordon, 1985).

The second major approach to CST with AUDs, called Communication Skills Training, is focused on developing social skills designed to promote a lifestyle that encourages sobriety (Monti et al., 1990; 2002; Monti & Rohsenow, 2003). The underlying premise is that the client lacks skills to build a positive life while sober as well as lacking skills for handling specific high-risk situations. Without a supportive and rewarding life while sober, the client will be less likely to maintain sobriety. Therefore, "communication skills training" focuses each session on a category of skill that can be applied across a variety of situations to prevent relapse or to promote a more positive lifestyle to increase the odds of sobriety (Monti et al., 2002; Monti & Rohsenow, 2003). The higher-priority modules (for shorter lengths of stay) are on drink refusal skills, giving constructive criticism, receiving criticism about suspected drinking/drug use, listening skills, conversation skills for developing new sober friendships, developing social support networks, and resolving relationship problems. Additional optional modules involve skills that can be covered separately or integrated into the high-priority modules: nonverbal language, assertiveness, refusing requests, and receiving criticism in general. Specific guidelines are provided about specific types of skills that would be most useful in each of these situations (e.g., "be specific," "state feedback in terms of your own feeling rather than just facts"), and most of each session is spent in role-plays of applications of these skills to personal situations with coaching and feedback. Analyses have shown that the use of both situation-specific skills for coping with urges to drink in high-risk situations (e.g., "go to a meeting when I have an urge; "shoot hoops") and general lifestyle change skills that do not involve high-risk situations (e.g., "go to meetings on a regular basis," "get more exercise") correlate with less drinking during the year after treatment (Rohsenow et al., 2001).

A third major approach is to conduct cognitive-behavioral mood management training (CBMMT) (Monti et al., 1990; 2002; Monti & Rohsenow, 2003). The underlying premise is that interpersonal or intrapersonal negative mood states and urges/cravings (conceptualized in this case as a type of affect) are causes of the majority of relapse situations (Marlatt & Gordon, 1985). The final common pathway to the drinking decision may involve the emotional reactions to lifestyle situations and to high-risk situations, so that these emotional reactions may serve as drinking triggers. Strong emotional states disrupt attentional processes, ability to apply situational coping skills, and self-efficacy. CBMMT is designed to slow down the process of reacting to events to (a) help the client do a functional analysis of the chain of events, thoughts, feeling, and physical reactions that lead to a decision to drink or to resist drinking; (b) become aware of and challenge maladaptive thoughts; (c) teach cognitive coping to counteract negative thinking; and (d) help the client learn alternative ways to cope with unpleasant emotions that may involve either underarousal (e.g., boredom, loneliness, lethargy) or overarousal (e.g., thrill seeking, frustration, risk-taking). The coping skills in this approach can be divided into two categories: (a) coping with specific mood states (managing urges, negative moods and emergencies), and (b) lifestyle changes (learning problem-solving skills in general, decision making skills, and the importance of balance in life). The seven higher-priority modules are on managing urges to drink, solving problems that arise in life, increasing pleasant activities, anger management, managing negative thinking, seemingly irrelevant decisions, and planning for emotional emergencies (Monti et al., 2002; Monti & Rohsenow 2003). Specific guidelines for specific types of skills that

would be most useful vary depending on the topic from functional analysis to formal problem-solving methods to cognitive restructuring and behavioral retraining. Again, most of each session is spent in role-plays of applications of these skills to personal situations. The skills training approach used in Project MATCH combined some of the CBMMT modules with a few of the Communication Skills Training modules (see Project MATCH Research Group, 1998).

The Problem Drinker Program by McCrady et al. (1985) is a mixture of the above three approaches in that some group sessions focus on identifying antecedents that trigger drinking or temptations, with functional analysis conducted of these situations, other group sessions focus on emotional reactions and conduct CBMMT via functional analysis, and yet other group sessions focus on particular skills that can be used across a variety of situations (e.g., alternative behaviors, drink refusal skills, assertiveness) but applied within functional analyses of each client's own situations.

A fourth approach targeted moderate drinking goals for problem drinkers who had not sought abstinence-oriented treatment (Miller, Taylor, & West, 1980). This approach taught behavioral self-control training designed to teach moderation in alcohol consumption, including calculating the number of drinks to stay below a certain blood alcohol level along with techniques for spacing out the drinks and making contracts to stay within their agreed limits.

Drug Dependence Applications. The first CST to be developed and used with cocaine-dependent patients in randomized controlled clinical trials was the RPT developed by Carroll and her colleagues for cocaine use disorders (Carroll, Nich, & Rounsaville, 1995, Carroll, Rounsaville, & Gawin, 1991). Over 12 to 24 weeks, clients learned to identify situations likely to result in craving or cocaine use (social emotional, environmental, thoughts), then used functional analyses in which they were taught and rehearsed coping skills to handle these situations, including taking steps to reduce availability of cocaine, practicing handling an initial slip (episode of initial use), managing thoughts about drug use, along with learning improved decision-making skills and problem solving (Carroll, Rounsaville, & Keller, 1991; see Carroll & Rawson, 2005, for fuller treatment guidelines). Also included were discussions of ambivalence (expected pros and cons of continuing or stopping use) and of apparently irrelevant decisions that lead to relapse, and lifestyle modification to increase non–drug-rewarding activities. The initial studies showed CST that for cocaine abusers produced more abstinence than did interpersonal psychotherapy (Carroll, Rounsaville, & Gawin, 1991; Carroll et al. 1994a, 1994b, 1995). A CST used for aftercare for cocaine abusers provided up to 42 group and individual sessions for coping with current, past, and future risky situations (McKay et al., 1997).

Another CST based on teaching skills within the context of high-risk situations is the cocaine-specific coping skills training of Rohsenow's group (Monti et al., 1997; Rohsenow et al., 2000, 2005). Investigations identified the common categories of high-risk situations (interpersonal, intrapersonal, and environmental) to use as the focus of sessions (Michalec et al., 1992; Rohsenow et al., 2000). For example, unlike alcohol-dependent patients, cocaine abusers report money as a compelling trigger of use, alcohol use but not marijuana use was a relapse precipitant, and when negative emotion preceded relapse it was virtually always anger/irritation and not depression/sadness or anxious/tense (Rohsenow et al., 2000, 2005). Functional analyses of individual situations within the session's topic provided the basis for training anticipatory and immediate cognitive and behavioral coping skills. An advantage with managed care is that this approach required only six or eight sessions on consecutive days for efficacy.

While Hall's group based their CST for cocaine abusers on the cognitive theories of Beck et al. (1993), both behavioral and cognitive techniques were used to strengthen commitment to abstinence, manage irrational thoughts and negative moods, and learn to cope with high-risk situations and urges to use, along with life-style changes to increase positive mood and social support (Maude-Griffin et al., 1998). Thus, it is very similar to the RPT of Carroll's group.

CST for marijuana dependence has been developed by a few groups. Carroll adapted their CST to marijuana abuse while adding motivational enhancement up front (Carroll et al., 2006). Stephens' group (e.g., Stephens, Roffman, & Curtin, 2000) applied a model based on the RPT writings to abstinence initiation. Up to 18 sessions build motivation by discussing pros and cons of change, identify high-risk situations via self-monitoring, build coping skills with planned exercises (e.g., relaxation and assertion training) and role plays (stress and anger coping, urge coping, self-reward, enlisting social support, lifestyle

modification to increase pleasurable activities), and identify and use cognitive restructuring to address rationalizations. The 14 weekly sessions of CST by Budney's group (e.g., Budney, Higgins, Radonovich, & Novy, 2000) was adapted from Project MATCH. In this CST, a motivational counseling session is followed by drug-related coping skills training (e.g., drug refusal practice, dealing with urges, planning for high-risk situations) followed by lifestyle coping skills training selected from a menu of choices (including mood management, enhancing social networks, communication training). While CST is used in studies by other groups as well, the CST methods are subsets of the ones described here.

Computerized CST is the most exciting new development in this approach. A seven-module computerized CST called CBT4CBT (Carroll et al., 2008, 2009) is based on NIDA's treatment manual for CBT (http://www.drugabuse.gov/txmanual/cbt/cbt1.html). Each module focuses on a different skill such as dealing with cravings, identifying and handling high-risk situations, and negotiating difficult decisions. It uses films clips of situations with requests for the clients to think about what they could do, interactive graphics, games, assignments, and practice exercises. No experience with computers is needed, and there is hardly any written material to read, making it easy for low-income and low-educated people to use, and they enjoy using it.

Tobacco Dependence Applications. A great number of different smoking-cessation studies have used behavioral counseling (Piasecki & Baker, 2001; USDHHS, 2000). Some of the common elements in behavioral treatments for smoking include providing information about the expected course of withdrawal, information and recommendations about effects of medications, teaching behavioral methods for coping with withdrawal and urges when quitting smoking (e.g., alternative behaviors for coping with the anxiety of withdrawal such as exercise or relaxation and eliciting support from family members), anticipating high-risk situations for relapse and providing problem-solving skills for these situations, and arranging extra-treatment support. A variety of public sources (e.g., American Lung Association) provide handouts with such information.

Several of the more effective aspects identified in the meta-analyses of smoking cessation treatments (Piasecki & Baker, 2001; USDHHS, 2000) are particularly central to CBT-based CST. One is skills training for solving practical problems involved in smoking cessation. These include skills for arranging the environment to make it more difficult to smoke, planning exactly what to do on one's quit day, planning how to cope with withdrawal, analyses of barriers to smoking cessation and skills to overcome such barriers, functional analysis of situations that pose a high risk for relapse, and coping with a lapse that occurs. Another is arranging extra-treatment support: instructing family members and friends in ways to best be supportive, teaching interpersonal skills for the client to use in communicating with others about his/her smoking cessation, teaching the client to seek out support from others, and in some cases providing a cessation partner.

The smoking treatment approaches called cognitive-behavioral CST or RPT focus on identifying personal high-risk situations (common ones are the end of a meal, on awakening, or when drinking alcohol), then conducting functional analyses of these situations. Identifying the situations can be done in an open-ended discussion, by questionnaires, or through self-monitoring diaries (Shiffman et al., 1985). Assessment of existing coping skills by self-report, self-monitoring or role plays provides information about existing skills to draw on and areas that can be improved. Skills that are taught are designed to foster avoidance or escape from these situations (anticipatory coping), methods of coping with immediate temptations without smoking (immediate coping), and coping with a lapse to smoking (restorative coping) (e.g., Shiffman et al., 2005). A number of specific behavioral and cognitive coping skills have been identified that are associated with successful response to relapse crises (and some maladaptive ones to avoid) (Shiffman, 1984). However, the largest effect on success in relapse crises comes from using any of the coping methods versus not coping at all, indicating that learning a few coping responses that are likely to be used is more important than learning many different skills (Shiffman et al., 1985). CBMMT has been developed for smokers with major depression (e.g., Hall, Muñoz, & Reus, 1994). Finally, lifestyle changes can be taught so as to provide better ongoing support of a nonsmoking life, by developing a more satisfying life to meet needs and provide ongoing positive and negative reinforcement through healthy means (Shiffman et al., 1985). Smoking cessation treatments based on this model are recommended by the clinical practice guidelines and other

sources (National Institute on Drug Abuse, 1999; USDHHS, 2000).

Summary of Evidence

Evidence for Use with AUD Treatment. CBTs for the AUDs have received strong support in many studies, but outcomes vary depending on the type of social skills training, mood management training or relapse-prevention training employed, according to a systematic quantitative review (Miller et al., 2003). Not all types of CSTs are alike, and settings and populations vary considerably. The RPT and interpersonal approaches described above and studies with similar CSTs have shown good results (see reviews by Monti et al., 2002; Monti & Rohsenow, 2003). These reviews and analyses by Morganstern and Longabaugh (2000) illustrate some of the conditions under which these approaches show better results: as an adjunct to a comprehensive SUD treatment program rather than as the sole treatment (which could possibly also mean it works better for people who need more comprehensive treatment than for less impaired drinkers), when measures of effective treatment implementation were included, and when the CST focused on interpersonal skills training rather than mood management training. Project MATCH (1997), like some earlier studies, only provided skills training as aftercare or stand-alone outpatient treatment and found it equally effective compared with motivational interviewing or 12-Step facilitation. However, most of their CST included only CBMMT with most clients receiving only one of the interpersonal communication skills sessions. On the other hand, the communication skills training approach used as a component of a full treatment program (Monti et al., 1990, 2001; Rohsenow et al., 2001) showed lasting effects on drinking outcomes with demonstrated effects on coping skills during the treatment, even when managed care reduced the mean number of sessions received to 4 to 6 sessions. Thus, it is important to focus on interpersonal skills and to provide comprehensive treatment as a backdrop for the CST. Several studies have shown which specific types of coping skills are or are not associated with reduced drinking (e.g., Dolan et al., 2013; Monti et al., 1993; Rohsenow et al., 2001), so that treatments can focus on just the specific skills associated with better outcomes. A comparison of CST tailored to individual coping skills needs was more effective than group coping skills training in increasing abstinent days (Litt et al., 2009). Overall,

CST using CBT principles deserves a solid place in a comprehensive treatment program for people with AUDs.

Patient-treatment matching analyses help to identify who will benefit more from CST. For example, while CBMMT and communication skills training had been equally effective in the original study (Monti et al., 1990), the CBMMT was ineffective for the patients with lower education or greater initial levels of anxiety or urge to drink in high-risk role plays while effectiveness of the communication skills training was not affected by patient characteristics (Rohsenow et al., 1991). Thus, for better educated people with less disruptive moods, it may be that many forms of treatment will work while people with lower education or stronger emotional reactions cannot use the cognitive techniques as well and do better with behavioral rehearsal of social skills. In Project MATCH, people with more alcohol dependence symptoms benefitted more from 12-Step facilitation than from skills training. Analyses of treatment matching by level of sociopathy, psychopathology, or cognitive impairment have shown inconsistent results across different studies (Cooney et al., 1991; Kadden et al., 1989, 2001; Kalman et al., 2000; Project MATCH, 1997).

Evidence for Use in SUD Treatment. CSTs for cocaine, opiate, cannabis and polysubstance use disorders were investigated in a recent meta-analysis that included 34 well-controlled studies of general CBT (usually CST), RPT-based CST, CM, or some combination of these (Dutra et al., 2008). Across all studies, these psychosocial treatments produced better outcomes than their control groups (e.g., ranging from treatment as usual to wait list) with moderate sized statistical effects, and with lower dropout rates for the CST and/or CM treatments than for the control treatments. While the effect sizes were larger for self-reported outcomes than for biological measures (e.g., urine drug screens), the 12 studies that included both self-report and biological measures found no significant difference between these types of measures, as is usual when calendar-assisted timeline methods are used (Ehrman & Robbins, 1994) with a set and setting or confidentiality (Sobell & Sobell, 1986). Across all treatment types, on average 31% of people achieved abstinence compared with 13% of people in control conditions. The approaches were most effective for cannabis use, next most effective for cocaine use, then for opiate use, with the lowest effect sizes when the treatments targeted mixed

polysubstance use. CST and/or RPT was second only to CM for beneficial effects of treatment. While there has been variability across studies, CST appears to have a particular advantage in having durable effects (Carroll, Rounsaville, Nich, et al., 1994) and being in beneficial for the more severely dependent people with cocaine use disorders (Carroll et al., 1991, 1994). However, CBT4CBT resulted in improved coping skills and substance use outcomes more for higher IQ than lower IQ substance abusers (Kiluk et al., 2011). CST that targeted substance use and suicidality in comorbid teens was better than enhanced treatment as usual in reducing heavy drinking days and marijuana use along with fewer suicide attempts and hospital visits (Esposito-Smythers et al., 2011).

Studies of processes by which the treatments may work have been informative. Amount of homework completion within CST correlates with better skills and predicts less cocaine use during the year following treatment, indicating that active involvement in the coping skills training mediates outcome (Carroll, Nich, & Ball, 2005). A study investigated whether patients acquire the skills taught them in CST. Indeed, clients in different types of treatment responded in a role-play test with the types of coping skills that were congruent with the type of treatment they were assigned to (Carroll, Nich, Frankforter, & Bisighini, 1999). Recently, an analysis was conducted of the specific types of lifestyle or relapse coping skills, both behavioral and cognitive, that are associated with reduced cocaine use after cocaine-specific coping skills training (Rohsenow et al., 2005). The results can be used to improve treatment approaches by focusing only on the most effective ones and eliminating the skills found unrelated to outcome.

In terms of the specific drugs of abuse with the best results (marijuana and cocaine), the RPT developed by Carroll's group has repeatedly shown better cocaine use outcomes compared with interpersonal psychotherapy (Carroll et al., 1991, 1994a, 1995, 2004). The six- to eight-session cocaine-specific coping skill training based on functional analysis of known high-risk situations also produced significantly less cocaine use in either group or individual format compared with control treatment (Rohsenow et al., 2000, 2004). The CST developed by Hall's group (Maude-Griffin et al., 1998) produced greater abstinence compared with manualized 12-Step facilitation. However, the approach developed by Wells et al. (1994) was not successful. The RPT used as aftercare by McKay et al (1997) resulted in less abstinence than standard care during the aftercare treatment. The CST approaches appear particularly effective with heavier cocaine users or those with comorbid disorders (e.g., Carroll et al., 1991, 1994a; Maude-Griffin et al., 1998; McKay et al., 1997). It is important that to note that clients treated with CST (RPT) often continue to reduce their cocaine use after they have completed treatment (Carroll et al., 1994b; Rohsenow et al., 2000), including less cocaine or alcohol use for RPT than standard care 6 to 24 months after starting aftercare for those who were not abstinent from these at the start of aftercare (McKay et al., 1999). Similarly, a sleeper effect was found for CST targeting cocaine use among methadone-maintained patients, where CM produced better within-treatment results while CST produced better outcomes than CM at the 26- and 52-week follow-ups (Rawson et al., 2002). Thus, CST often produces enduring effects.

For marijuana applications, the approach developed by Stephens' group found equivalent results for CST and social support discussion groups (Stephens et al., 1994) so these two treatments were combined for the next study. However, the 14-session combined treatment was no more effective than a 2-session motivational interview over 16 months, although both were better than a waiting-list control (Stephens et al., 2000). On the other hand, the combined CST with motivational enhancement approach by Carroll et al. (2006) was more effective than drug counseling for attendance and urines free from marijuana. While motivational enhancement with or without CST produced equivalent marijuana abstinence (Budney et al., 2000), CM with CST was superior to CM without CST in producing abstinence during 12 months post-treatment (Budney et al., 2006), indicating that CST can add to the effectiveness of CM.

The computerized approach, CBT4CBT (Carroll et al., 2008, 2009), is also successful. Substance-dependent patients were randomized to standard treatment with or without biweekly access to CBT4CBT (Carroll et al., 2008). The CBT4CBT resulted in similar retention, positive evaluations, and significantly more urines negative for drugs within treatment with a trend for longer continuous abstinence. Completion of homework assignments correlated with better outcomes. In the 6-month follow-up (Carroll et al., 2009), those who received standard care alone increased their drug use over time while those who also received CBT4CBT tended to improve somewhat in drug use. Thus, the brief computerized CST produced enduring improvements in outcome.

Evidence for Use in Smoking Treatment. According to the meta-analyses in the clinical practice guidelines (USDHHS, 2000), some behavioral counseling is better than no counseling, and format (individual, proactive telephone, self-help, group) mostly did not affect the odds of quitting (USDHHS, 2000) except for somewhat increased odds of abstinence with individual face-to-face counseling (Piasecki & Baker, 2001). The optimal total number of minutes of counseling was 31 to 90 minutes with no additional benefit from longer counseling, but more than eight sessions produced the best benefit, suggesting that many brief contacts are optimal (Piasecki & Baker, 2001; USDHHS, 2000). The most effective types of behavioral content (after aversive smoking) included practical problem solving/skills training, intra-treatment social support, and arranging extra-treatment social support (Piasecki & Baker, 2001; USDHHS, 2000). A focus only on mood management was sometimes but not necessarily better than health education, even for smokers with major depression (Hall et al., 1996; Hall, Muñoz & Reus, 1994), while clients with major depression fared better with CST (Brown et al., 2001; Haas et al., 2004; Kapson & Haaga, 2010). While intra-treatment support (encouragement, showing caring, fostering discussion, and sharing personal disclosures) were evaluated across a great many different types of counseling, practical problem solving and arranging extra-treatment support are central features of most CST so these results provide support for the skills training model. While these skills-training treatments are superior to no counseling, CST for tobacco dependence does not have clearly different results from counseling not formally based on learning theories, partly because so many counseling approaches include overlapping elements these days so it is difficult to find a control condition that is truly different from CST (Piasecki & Baker, 2001). Piasecki and Baker (2001) also noted that the meta-analysis inherently needs to combine studies with a range of sample sizes and methodological problems, and that the most convincing evidence in support of the CST approach comes from the large-scale methodologically rigorous trial by Stevens and Hollis (1989). Thus, smoking treatments that contain CST-based skills training are as or more effective than any other nonpharmacological treatment approaches except aversion therapy and are applicable to a wider range of smokers than aversion therapy.

A few studies compared CST with and against pharmacotherapy. In primary care, CST alone produced lower one-year abstinence rates than bupropion or nicotine replacement alone or motivational interviewing (Wittchen et al., 2011). After 12 weeks of counseling with buproprion and nicotine replacement, an additional 11 weeks of CST alone was as effective as 11 additional weeks of bupropion with or without the CST in increasing long-term abstinence compared with no extra treatment (Hall et al., 2011).

Summary of Evidence

Overall, CST has excellent support for use with alcohol and cocaine dependence, and good support for marijuana dependence although based on little research. CST elements are some of the best supported aspects of counseling for smoking treatment. A particular benefit of CST is the persistence of gains long after the treatment has ended, an advantage also evident when CST is added to CM. Thus, CST should be included in any treatment program for these disorders.

Contingency Management
Overview of Approach

CM, also called financial incentives, is based on operant conditioning principles, in which patients who abstain from drug use are provided with financial (monetary or prize) incentives using methods based on behavioral principles that are designed to increase their abstinence. The landmark controlled studies were implemented by Higgins & Silverman (1991), Liebson, Tommasello, and Bigelow (1978) and Stitzer and Bigelow (1982). The target behavior that clinicians seek to eliminate by using CM is use of one of more substances. As such, CM requires objective measures of clients' abstinence from the substance(s) (e.g., urine toxicology screens). Contingent on proof of abstinence, the clients receive immediate reinforcement for the positive behavior in the form of money, vouchers redeemable for approved merchandise, or other incentives. Unlike simple reward systems, the methods involved must be employed in a precise manner to ensure learning, using the following key principles.

One of the key principles is the timing of reinforcement. After a response, such as providing a drug-free urine sample, how immediately a consequence then occurs determines the effectiveness of the consequence (Griffith et al., 2000). If a client provides a urine sample that is sent to a lab for analysis and the client does not receive the incentive for a drug-free urine sample until days later, the

effectiveness of the reinforcement will be decreased and most likely will not reinforce the behavior of abstinence (e.g., Schwartz et al., 1987). Since it is often problematic to give cash to people with SUD out of concern that they may spend it on drugs, a voucher for a certain monetary amount of goods or to a merchant that is actually redeemed later has been found to act as immediate reinforcement, however.

A second key principle is the contingency component. If the incentive does not follow the target behavior (e.g., abstinence) contingently or consistently, the effectiveness of the conditioning will be decreased, while if the incentive follows the response consistently over time, its ability to modify the response is increased. An immediate and consistent schedule of reinforcement leads to faster learning. After a behavior has been learned via consistent reinforcement, then reinforcing it on an intermittent schedule will increase the likelihood that the behavior will be maintained for the long term. The importance of the incentives being contingent was shown when participants were randomized to receive noncontingent vouchers or vouchers contingent on abstinence from cocaine use. While both groups received similar amounts of vouchers, the condition in which the participants received contingent vouchers maintained a longer duration of abstinence from cocaine than did the noncontingent arm (Higgins et al., 1994; Higgins et al., 2000).

A third key principle is reinforcing the actual behavior you wish to change. In a comparison of CM that reinforced negative urine drug screens versus CM that reinforced completing activities congruent with treatment goals, the CM that reinforced drug abstinence resulted in more within-treatment abstinence, although outcomes did not differ at 6- and 9-month follow-ups (Petry et al., 2006). Although the ultimate goal would be complete abstinence for the lifetime, starting by shaping successive approximations of the target is another key principle and a way CM differs from simplistic "reward" systems. Providing a single large reward for being abstinent for a whole month involves setting the bar too high and usually fails. The client must be able to "contact the reinforcer"—the initial behavior change must be easy enough for the client to accomplish without too much effort. For this reason, clients ideally would only need a single day of abstinence to earn an incentive, nonabstinence does not result in loss of incentives already earned, and incentives can be earned again as soon as another day of abstinence is achieved. However, for many people, even a full day of abstinence is asking too much at first (e.g., Peirce et al., 2006). In some CM programs, initially incentives can be earned for reductions in cocaine metabolites or in evidence of smoking, increasing the likelihood that clients will go on to have abstinence days after the reduction period (e.g., Lamb et al., 2004b; Preston et al., 2001. Thus, rewarding very small changes in behavior is necessary at first while providing additional incentives for continuous abstinence. After continuous abstinence has been achieved for some time, then the reinforcement schedule can be thinned out to require longer abstinence to receive an incentive, to decrease the odds of relapse.

A fourth key principle is detecting the abstinence correctly. With accurate breath, saliva or urine tests, this problem is reduced, but there can be problems in implementing each of these effectively. With urine drug screens, the substance may be excreted for days to weeks after abstinence is initiated. Therefore, some programs provide some days of free incentives just for providing urine samples before requiring that they show no drug use (Budney & Stanger, 2008). It is possible but very expensive to conduct on-site quantitative testing to show a decrease in the amount excreted each day and clinics cannot afford quantitative testing on-site. Using expired carbon monoxide (CO) to detect smoking is inexpensive but requires three times a day testing seven days a week to completely detect any nonabstinence (Lamb et al., 2004), posing an excessive burden. Cotinine detects more nicotine use over a longer period of time so is preferred after initial abstinence, although more costly. For alcohol, the detection period for alcohol in the breath is fairly short making it difficult to detect accurately; the development of transdermal alcohol sensors will provide more lasting detection of alcohol use. Web-cameras can also allow someone to blow into a breath alcohol or CO detector and display the results (e.g., Meredith & Dallery, 2013), eliminating a travel burden that could interfere with compliance.

A fifth key principle is choosing an incentive that is personally valued by the target individual and is large enough to promote the targeted change. Some "reward" programs not based on these principles use rewards that staff think would work or that would be healthy, but these rewards may not be valued by clients. The type of incentive given can vary but money and a wide choice of merchandise are the two

incentives that are most universally valued. Within CM for substance abuse treatment, the rewards for abstinence have ranged from money (Shaner et al., 1997), to escalating amounts of vouchers that could be exchanged for merchandise items that are consistent with drug-free lifestyles (Higgins et al., 1994), to the opportunity to win prizes of varying magnitudes (Petry et al., 2000, 2005). Access to clinic privileges such as ability to receive take-home methadone privileges contingent on the client's ability to produce clean urine samples for a period of time have been effective (Stitzer et al., 1992) but have been less effective because these are less valued than money (Chutuape, Silverman, & Stitzer, 1998). Finally, access to social services and work opportunities have been made contingent on decreases in alcohol use (e.g., Donlin, Knealing, & Silverman, 2008; Miller, 1975). Additionally, larger incentives generally produce more abstinence than do smaller incentives (Stitzer & Bigelow, 1983, 1984, 1986), but income level does not affect the efficacy of a given level of payment (Rash, Olmstead, & Petry, 2009). However, "fishbowl" methods reduce the amount of money these programs cost without reducing effectiveness (Petry et al., 2000). With a fishbowl, each abstinent reading allows a person to draw one or more slips from a bowl where each slip has a certain probability of resulting in a low value, medium value, or large value prize, or no prize; with successive abstinences, the person can draw more slips with each abstinent reading.

Inducing abstinence at the very start of treatment is important for longer term success since abstinence during the first weeks of treatment predicts longer term abstinence (e.g., Petry et al., 2012; Preston et al., 1998). CM is particularly useful for inducing initial abstinence.

Drug Dependence Applications. Probably the earliest attempt to do CM was a pilot study in which patients in cocaine clinics were offered an option to sign a contingency contract agreeing to urine monitoring with personalized aversive consequences for positive or missing samples (Anker & Crowley, 1982). Potential consequences involved letters they signed to legal or professional authorities admitting nonabstinence, letters that could result in serious consequences if mailed. While 31 of the 32 who agreed to such contracts stayed cocaine-free, 52% of those approached refused participation because the method was unacceptably harsh and involved too large a change in behavior.

Since the earliest attempts, CM interventions have come a long way. The most extensive work has been done with developing CM for cocaine-dependent patients who have sought treatment (for treatment manual, see Budney & Higgins, 1998). Over time, Higgins and his colleagues determined that an escalating schedule of reinforcement for consecutive clean urines, with resets after a lapse, combined with drug counseling that includes community reinforcement is the most effective procedure (for review of development, see Higgins & Wong, 1998). In this approach, CM over 24 weeks allows patients to earn vouchers; the vouchers are redeemable for goods chosen by agreement between therapist and patient as congruent with a drug-free lifestyle and purchased by the staff for the patient. Urines are collected and tested for cocaine metabolites three times a week for weeks 1 to 2 and twice a week thereafter. A negative (clean) urine earns a voucher for $2.50, with each successive clean urine earning $1.25 more, with a $10 bonus after every three consecutive clean specimens in a week (these rates were used in the 1990s and early 2000s and might need to be adjusted upward). With a clean specimen only, the staff member engages in pleasant conversation with the patient for a few minutes as well. A positive (dirty) or missing urine earns no voucher and resets the value of the next vouchers back to the initial $2.50 level. However, after five consecutive clean urines, the specimen after that can earn the next higher value that would have been available before the reset occurred. Points or vouchers can never be taken away once earned since punishment approaches decrease effectiveness by increasing dropouts (Budney & Higgins, 1998). During weeks 13 to 24, the magnitude of the incentive is reduced to one state lottery ticket for each cocaine-negative specimen. Because a person's urine can test positive for cocaine for 2 days to 2 weeks after ceasing use, patients are warned of this fact and may be given $1 just for submitting a urine sample during this time. Even more effective is conducting quantitative analyses the first three weeks and letting patients earn vouchers for any specimens that show a 25% or more decrease in cocaine metabolite (Preston, Umbricht, Wong, & Epstein, 2001). This shaping procedure results in more patients abstinent in the subsequent weeks when only complete abstinence is reinforced. Patients who are nonabstinent at the start of treatment required about twice the rate of payment as their abstinent compatriots to achieve success (Petry et al., 2012).

An important aspect of this program for cocaine-dependent patients is engaging the patient in at least twice weekly counseling using the *community reinforcement approach* (CRA) since it is designed to alter the patient's environment to increase reinforcement from nondrug sources. The typical components included are an assessment of needs and goals, disulfiram therapy for the majority who also abuse alcohol, couples therapy to teach how to give positive interactions for pro-sober behaviors while reducing aversive interactions (withdrawing reinforcement) for pro-drug behaviors, a job-finding intervention for those who wish it, social skills training, training in finding sober sources of social and recreational activities, and functional analysis based CST to handle high-risk situations. The disulfiram is important because alcohol ingestion shifts reinforcer preference from money to cocaine (Higgins, Roll, & Bickel, 1996).

Methadone-maintained opiate-dependent patients need to have opiate abstinence induced initially but also tend to have considerable other drug use so either opiate use or other drug use has been the target of CM programs, using similar procedures (Carroll et al., 2001; Higgins & Silverman, 1999; Kirby et al., 1998; Piatrowski et al., 1999; Preston, Umbricht, & Epstein, 2000; Silverman et al., 1996, 1998; Stitzer & Petry, 2006). However, some studies have used take-home methadone privileges instead of vouchers for merchandise as a low cost incentive (e.g., Kidorf & Stitzer, 1996; McCaul et al., 1984; Stitzer et al., 1992), reinforcing because patients do not like to have to travel to the clinic 7 days a week. A few other studies used as incentives payments toward drug-free housing, recreational activities and job-skills training (Gruber, Chutuape, & Stitzer, 2000; Jones et al., 2005; Katz et al., 2001). The "fishbowl" method has been used where methadone patients draw chances at receiving prizes for cocaine-free urine samples (Petry et al., 2005). To help to prevent relapse after abstinence has been successful produced using, the monetary reinforcer schedule can change to flat payments during maintenance (Preston, Umbricht, & Epstein, 2002).

For cannabis dependence, some considerations are that cannabinoids will appear in the urine at the 50 or 100 ng/ml detection levels for 1 to 3 weeks after cannabis used is stopped, and that it is important to provide a test of excessive dilution of the urine (creatinine level) to prevent false negatives (Budney & Stanger, 2008). The voucher schedule has been adapted to allow for the delay before abstinence can be detected. Clients are given warning of this fact and the vouchers not started until after 2 weeks have passed. During the initial 2 weeks, a voucher for $5 worth of goods is provided for every valid urine specimen to reinforce providing urine, prime the reinforcer, and reinforce abstinence in those whose urine shows abstinence earlier than 2 weeks. Because of the long time cannabinoids stay in the system, urine testing is done only two times per week because it is sufficient to detect use while minimizing positive results carrying over to subsequent samples. Finally, the overall magnitude of incentives that can be earned has been lower in initial studies ($590 for 12 weeks) than was used for cocaine ($1030 and up), for practical reasons. All other aspects of the voucher program are the same as for cocaine.

One other use of CM within the context of SUD treatment is to increase use of medications by reinforcing use of either medications for the substance use itself or of other medications such as antiretrovirals for HIV/AIDS (Carroll & Rounsaville, 2007).

Alcohol Dependence Applications. CM techniques were first used in the treatment of alcohol dependence by rewarding individuals who were abstinent from drinking with rewards (Miller, 1975). Despite the early attempts to decrease alcohol use by using CM techniques, few studies or clinical applications of CM have been implemented in the treatment of alcohol dependence due to the lack of reliable and feasible methods for verifying abstinence. Alcohol use has been measured objectively through the use of breath analyzer tests, urine tests, and transdermal patches. Despite these measurements, alcohol is expelled from the body quickly. Thus, a urine or breath sample may show that there is no alcohol present when the individual has consumed alcohol within the last 24 hours and it already had metabolized out of his or her system. The transdermal alcohol sensor, when available, will offer an advantage for objective measurements of alcohol use for CM interventions. The transdermal patch or alcohol dosimeter, when applied to the skin absorbs alcohol in perspiration over a 7- to 10-day period (Phillips & McAloon, 1980; Swift, 1993). The alcohol that is absorbed in the patch is then analyzed with an electrochemical analyzer to determine a cumulative amount of alcohol consumed. The patch has shown high sensitivity and specificity for detecting alcohol in perspiration with high correlations with blood alcohol levels (Swift, 1993). Utilization of the transdermal alcohol sensor in future CM interventions may provide the objective measurement necessary for the appropriate application of CM in alcohol treatment.

Given the lack of a reliable measurement tool to test for the presence of alcohol, CM techniques have been applied to the treatment of alcohol use by rewarding attendance at outpatient treatment sessions, access to paid employment, and adherence to disulfiram, a medication that negatively reinforces alcohol consumption but that is usually no more effective than placebo due to nonadherence to the medication (Fuller et al., 1986). An early combined approach required participants to ingest disulfiram given by a nurse at the treatment program; every 2 weeks a letter was sent to the employer saying whether the participant had complied with treatment (Robichaud, Strickler, Bigelow, & Liebson, 1979).

Tobacco Dependence Applications. CM has been used to facilitate initiation of smoking cessation. It is particularly important for people to maintain abstinence during the first 2 weeks of their quit attempt because abstinence during this period strongly predicts long-term smoking abstinence (e.g., Garvey et al., 1992; Gourlay et al., 1994; Kenford et al., 1994; Westman et al., 1997). CM can bolster this period in particular. The tricky part about applying CM to smoking cessation is choosing the method and timing of verification of abstinence. Expired carbon monoxide (CO) levels give immediate accurate feedback, but unless administered three times per day, some smoking could occur without detection. However, requiring thrice daily meetings every day for many weeks to check CO poses a high burden on both client and staff, and low-income or adolescent smokers may not have their own transportation. When using CO levels, counting 4 to 5 ppm or less as abstinent is necessary to minimize false-negative readings (Javors, Hatch, & Lamb, 2005). Saliva or urine cotinine levels have a longer detection window so that three times per week is sufficient to detect all smoking, but these typically require sending clients to a facility that can conduct gas chromatography or enzyme-multiplied immunoassay testing. Many cotinine test strips have not been sufficiently valid, but a newer semiquantitative urine cotinine immunoassay test strip was reported to have high sensitivity and moderate specificity in detecting tobacco abstinence after a few days of abstinence (Schepis et al., 2008). Several days of continuous abstinence is required before cotinine levels fall into the abstinent range (Hughes et al., 2003), so CO is needed to bridge that gap both initially and after a lapse. Finally, any nicotine replacement treatment will cause elevated cotinine levels so only CO can be used to monitor abstinence. A number of interventions use once or twice a day CO levels as the compromise assessment method (e.g., Rohsenow et al., 2002; Sigmon, Lamb, & Dallery, 2008). A study with pregnant women (not using nicotine replacement) thinned the schedule of testing from daily CO in the first week to cotinine testing twice a week, then once a week, then on alternate weeks throughout pregnancy (Higgins et al., 2004).

The other procedures that are best with smoking include an escalating schedule of payments with successive abstinence and resets for nonabstinent or missing readings, bonuses for three consecutive abstinent readings, starting with a 5-day shaping period when payments are contingent on cutting down by a percentage of their baseline CO reading, and providing payments or vouchers for payments immediately after the reading (Amodei & Lamb, 2005; Lamb, 2004b; Lamb et al., 2004a; Roll & Higgins, 2000). Higher payments allow more people to achieve the abstinence criterion than do lower payments (Stitzer & Bigelow, 1983, 1984, 1986). When reinforcement is linked to continuous abstinence, relapse is less likely (Roll et al., 1996).

Summary of Evidence

Evidence for Use in SUD Treatment. CM has been particularly successful in the treatment of SUD. In reviews and a meta-analysis, the strongest effects were seen for CM or CM with CST over all other treatment types (Carroll & Onken, 2005; Dutra et al., 2008). CM has been shown as efficacious across different drug using populations, including cocaine- (e.g., Higgins et al., 1994), opiate- (Higgins et al., 1986), and marijuana- (Budney et al., 2000) dependent patients. It is less effective to date for methamphetamine (Rawson et al., 2006) but almost no studies have been done with this population. CM has been found effective in both individual and group therapy environments (Petry, Martin, & Simcic, 2005). For posttreatment and/or clinically significant abstinence, abstinence rates of 27% were found for CST with CM and 31% for CM alone across studies (Dutra et al., 2008).

The strongest track record exists for treating cocaine dependence. Over a series of studies, the 24-week voucher-based CM with CRA was found to improve treatment retention, abstinence, and quality of life, with the contingent voucher component specifically increasing these effects (e.g., Higgins et al., 1991, 1993, 1994, 1999, 2000a; Kirby et al., 1998; Petry, Alessi, & Hanson, 2007; for review,

see Higgins, Heil, Rogers, & Chivers, 2008). Those in the CM condition also had longer continuous abstinence and more improvement in drug problems than those not receiving vouchers (Higgins et al., 1994; Silverman et al., 1996). Importantly, subsequent studies showed that people in the CM condition continued to have greater abstinence 6 and 15 months after treatment (Higgins et al., 1995, 2000b). Duration of continuous abstinence achieved during the initial treatment period is the best predictor of long-term abstinence (Higgins, Badger, & Budney, 2000).

To see if CST or CRA assists cocaine-dependent people with abstinence, CM intervention with and without CRA or CBT (using CST) were compared. CRA with CM was more effective than CM without other treatment during the 12-week CM period and the CRA resulted in better retention, less heavy drinking, more days employed, and fewer other problems during treatment and follow-up (Higgins et al., 2003). When CM alone or with CST or CST without CM were compared, cocaine use during active treatment was reduced by CM and not by CBT but CBT led to a slowly emerging post-treatment reduction in cocaine use (Epstein, Hawkins, Covi, Umbricht, & Preston, 2003).

CM with opiate-dependent patients in methadone treatment shows small to medium effect sizes in meta analyses and qualitative reviews, with better results with more rapid delivery of the reinforcer, more frequent urine screens, longer duration of treatment, higher methadone dose, targeting one drug for abstinence rather than abstinence from more than one drug, and higher incentive values (Epstein & Preston, 2008; Griffith et al., 2000; Lussier et al., 2006). Although effective incentive magnitudes require about $1,000 to $2,000 over 12 weeks to increase cocaine abstinence among methadone-maintained patients (e.g., Epstein et al., 2003; Rawson et al., 2002; Silverman et al., 1996, 1998) or, for failures at that level, $3,500 over 9 weeks (Silverman et al., 1999), similar effectiveness has been shown using only $117 in prizes using the "fishbowl" method of drawing chances for a prize (Petry, Alessi, Hanson, & Sierra, 2007; Petry, Martin, & Simcic, 2005). CM is more effective for opioid-dependent patients not on opioid agonist therapy than for those on methadone maintenance (Petry & Carroll, 2013). After opiate abstinence was achieved during an 8-week induction phase with an escalating schedule of incentives, patients who were randomized to receive 12 weeks of nonescalating vouchers and take-home methadone doses as incentives for drug-free urines had more abstinence than those randomized to receive noncontingent incentives (Preston, Umbricht, & Epstein, 2002), supporting the value of extending the CM without requiring continued escalation during maintenance. Finally, CM was also used to reinforce medication adherence for naltrexone treatment of opiate dependence, with effective results (Carroll et al., 2001).

Only a few studies have targeted use of marijuana specifically so far. A CM intervention was found to be significantly more effective than either a motivational enhancement intervention or a combination of both motivational enhancement and CBT (Budney et al., 2000). However, in another study of young adults with marijuana dependence, the combination of motivational enhancement treatment and CST with CM was more effective in reducing drug use than either CM with drug counseling or the Motivational enhancement plus CST without CM (Carroll et al., 2006). In a third study, while CST did not add to the effectiveness of CM for marijuana abstinence during the CM period, the CST enhanced the posttreatment maintenance of the initial positive effects of CM (Budney et al., 2006). Reinforcing attendance instead of marijuana abstinence increased attendance without increasing abstinence (Sinha et al., 2003).

CM has been shown to be an effective treatment in populations viewed as difficult to treat, such as in participants diagnosed with antisocial personality disorder (Messina, Farabee, & Rawson, 2003). In a pilot study, homeless people who have co-occurring psychiatric conditions, individuals assigned to CM reduced their cocaine and alcohol use more than those who were only assessed, suggesting that the low-cost CM procedures are feasible and may be efficacious in this population (Tracy et al., 2007). Thus, CM can be useful with populations often difficult to treat.

Thus, there is good evidence for effectiveness of all of these CBTs for treating SUDs, especially when individual substances of abuse are targeted in the treatment. CM has the best record for inducing abstinence during the first 3 months or so of treatment, gains are maintained when CM is combined with other counseling such as CST or community reinforcement (which includes CST). While CM has the greatest effectiveness for cocaine dependence of all treatments, many programs do not yet have the resources for such a treatment approach.

Evidence for Use in AUD Treatment. As early as 1975, Miller demonstrated that by providing reinforcers (i.e., shelter, employment, food, and clothing) to public inebriates contingent on negative breath-alcohol tests, researchers could effectively reduce public inebriation. One group received social service support regardless of their alcohol consumption while individuals in the contingent group had their social services support was suspended for 5 days each time they used alcohol. The number of arrests for public drunkenness decreased only in the contingent group, and the members of the contingent group increased the amount of hours of employment as compared with the noncontingent group (Miller, 1975).

In meta-analysis, CM has a significant but only modest effect size for AUD treatment (Miller et al., 2003), but few reasonably powered randomized trials were found. Alcoholics in outpatient treatment were randomized to receive CM or not; in CM, negative breath alcohol tests every weekday and performing treatment-related activities earned draws of slips indicating prizes worth between $1 and $100, in a lottery-like "fishbowl" procedure (Petry, Martin, Cooney, & Kranzler, 2000). The CM significantly increased treatment retention but with limited evidence that it may have increased abstinence. Homeless, unemployed alcohol-dependent people could work in a sheltered workplace for pay 4 hours per day, continent on negative breath alcohol at the start of each day and at random intervals 7 days a week (Wong, Kolodner, Fingerhood, Bigelow, & Silverman, 2005). People whose work access depended on alcohol abstinence had more alcohol abstinence and work attendance than the two control groups. Newer work using the transdermal alcohol sensor to remotely and continuously monitor alcohol through the skin showed significant reductions in alcohol use in a pilot study (Barnett et al., 2011), indicating that this is a viable way to conduct CM for alcohol use.

CM has been used successfully to reduce alcohol use among opiate-dependent patients by providing methadone contingent upon their adherence to disulfiram (Bickel et al., 1988; Liebson, Tommasello, & Bigelow, 1978). A study in which the employer was told if the person complied with disulfiram resulted in less absenteeism but was not designed to show direct effects on alcohol use (Robichaud et al., 1979).

Overall, few clinical trials have investigated the efficacy of CM to reduce alcohol use days and many studies have serious methodological shortcomings, so it is difficult to evaluate its effectiveness in this population. The newest studies show the most promise for an approach, but these need more evaluation.

Evidence for Use in Smoking Treatment. Most of the studies have been designed to demonstrate immediate effects in people who had not sought treatment and were not intending to quit. CM methods were found effective in promoting initial smoking reductions and abstinence (Roll et al., 1996, 1998; Stitzer & Bigelow, 1982, 1983, 1984, 1985; Stitzer et al., 1986). CM for smoking even promotes initial tobacco abstinence in people diagnosed with schizophrenia or who are pregnant, two other populations with high smoking rates considered difficult to treat (Higgins et al., 2004; Roll et al., 1998; Tidey et al., 2002). Generally subjects return to regular smoking when contingent reinforcers are withdrawn in studies relying on CM without counseling (Robles et al., 2005; Stitzer & Bigelow, 1982, 1983, 1985; Stitzer et al., 1986). The strong yet temporary effect of CM in smokers so far demonstrates the value of experimental investigations of paid abstinence rather than true clinical intervention (Rand et al., 1989). However, some studies with smokers motivated to quit did not show differential abstinence after the contingencies ended (Rand et al., 1989; Shoptaw et al., 2002). Unlike studies of CM for cocaine use, the CM methods for smoking cessation were not part of comprehensive smoking cessation programs where on-going abstinence was the goal. Such work is mostly still to be done.

A few studies used CM in a population who had not sought smoking treatment but who had a stronger motivation to quit smoking—pregnant women. When the women could receive a lump sum for continuous abstinence throughout pregnancy and 2 months postpartum and all in CM also had a social support person who was paid for the pregnant woman's abstinence, more were abstinent at the end of CM (34%) than in the control group (9%) (Donatelle et al., 2000). When CM was given throughout pregnancy and the first 12 weeks postpartum along with an educational pamphlet on quitting methods for pregnant women, abstinence was greater at end of pregnancy (37 versus 9%) and 12 weeks (33 versus 0%), compared with monitoring only, with gains maintained at 24 weeks post-partum (27 versus 0%) assessments (Higgins et al., 2004). To date, results from six controlled trials have found CM to increase smoking abstinence rates before and after birth in economically disadvantaged smokers (Higgins et al., 2012).

A few studies investigated CM for smoking among substance-dependent patients with mixed results. One study with methadone maintenance patients reported significantly reduced CO levels and smoking rate during treatment (Shoptaw et al., 1996). The second study reported no statistically significant treatment effects with methadone patients (Schmitz et al., 1995) which may be related to differences in the CM parameters used. In a third study CM for smoking combined with 77 minutes of smoking skills training with women substance abusers produced substantial reductions maintained for 2 weeks after CM ended but with return to baseline smoking thereafter (Robles et al., 2005). CM for smokers crossed with relapse prevention training for methadone patients showed within-treatment effects of CM but no effects during follow-up (Shoptaw et al., 2002). These studies are limited by lack of control groups (three studies), small sample sizes (three studies), no counseling to increase motivation (all studies), reverse shaping (Robles et al., 2005), and low reinforcement payments (first two studies). Despite these limitations, CM was found to be an acceptable form of smoking treatment and achieved smoking reductions among drug abusers in three of the four studies, but more work needs to be done combining CM with smoking counseling for use with smokers seeking smoking cessation.

Thus, at this time there is not sufficient evidence that CM will result in smoking cessation that lasts after the CM period is over, mostly because studies investigating it as a part of a combined treatment for treatment seekers have not been done. However, the evidence for decreasing smoking in pregnant women during pregnancy through the first months after birth is now compelling.

Summary of Evidence

CM is the most effective treatment approach for cocaine dependence, with efficacy also shown for opiate and marijuana dependence, particularly when combined with CST or with community reinforcement that includes CST. While the few studies using CM for AUD have shown beneficial results, more work is needed to effectively monitor alcohol use and more controlled trials are needed before it can be recommended for practice settings. Most of the studies of CM with smokers have not been conducted with treatment seekers and have not included additional counseling to motivate or assist cessation so results have not lasted beyond the CM period. The exception is its use with pregnant smokers, where there was some intrinsic motivation to stop smoking at least perinatally and increased rates of smoking cessation persisted at least 3 months after the end of CM.

Concerns Raised about CM. One concern raised about CM approaches has been that the high costs of the financial incentives (e.g., about $1200) would limit the ability of community organizations to utilize the approach. However, in recent years highly effective and lower cost contingency management procedures have also been developed (Bride & Humble, 2008; Petry et al., 2000; Petry, Alessi, Hanson, & Sierra, 2007; Petry & Martin, 2002). When using prize based incentives, although the CM intervention cost more than usual substance abuse care, the intervention lead to better patient outcomes and longer durations of abstinence (Olmstead, Sindelar, & Petry, 2007). Moreover, after initially escalating monetary incentives to create behavior change (i.e., abstinence), reducing the value of the voucher over time and during periods of abstinence not only decreases the cost of the intervention, but abstinence is still maintained despite the decrease in rewards (Stitzer & Petry, 2006). Finally, research has shown that the rates of abstinence do not decline when less valuable incentives, such as lottery tickets, are substituted for the voucher system later in treatment (Higgins et al., 1993) and prizes have been donated by community businesses.

Another question regarding the effectiveness of CM is in regarding to its long term durability. Results have been mixed; whereas some studies have found that participants were able to maintain their abstinence after the intervention others have found the opposite effect. When looking across studies, best results are obtained when the CM is conducted with people who have sought treatment for the substance that is targeted, when additional effective counseling is provided (especially CST or community reinforcement with CST), and when incentive levels are high (or a fishbowl lottery is used) and a longer period of CM is used.

A third concern had been raised as to whether CM would undermine intrinsic motivation to change. Fortunately, CM does not undermine motivation: its effect on behavior occurs in the absence of any measurable effect on self-reported motivation to change (Ledgerwood & Petry, 2006).

Finally, the success of CM could be affected by the findings of a recent functional magnetic resonance imaging study (fMRI). In the study, sensitivity to monetary rewards was compromised in light of cocaine addiction (Goldstein et al., 2007). This deficit, which needs to be replicated in larger samples of people with currently active versus abstaining cocaine use disorders, may underlie the compromised ability to advantageously modify behavior in response to changing inner motivations and environmental contingencies. Coupled with the positive outcomes in Petry's controlled studies, the fMRI study suggests that abstinent drug users are able to respond to reinforcers in well-structured and constrained environments that also incorporate treatment programs. However, these behaviors may not generalize to the everyday environments of drug-addicted individuals, where external or predictable reinforcement for advantageous behaviors are not readily available (Goldstein, Alia-Klein et al., 2007; Goldstein, Tamasi, Alia-Klein, Cottone, et al., 2007). In light of these findings, further studies are necessary for understanding the long term effectiveness of CM and if the addition of CBT or other behavioral strategies can assist with the generalizability of CM after the intervention has ceased to exist.

Acceptance and Commitment Therapy
Overview of Approach

Acceptance and commitment therapy (ACT) (Hayes & Strosahl, 2004) was created as a descendent of Skinner's radical behaviorism and a challenge of CST (Hayes, Strosahl, & Wilson, 1999). Some of the concepts were first proposed by Marlatt's (1985) prescription that "the client should simply allow the urge to occur without giving in to it . . . to assume an objective stance of detached awareness, and to "let it be" without reacting to it" (pp. 240–241). Cognitive behavioral therapies teach clients how to reduce or eliminate negative thoughts because the negative thoughts or emotions can lead to negative behaviors (e.g., thinking "I'm no good" leads to abusing substances). From an ACT perspective, the negative thoughts and emotions may, but need not, produce bad behavioral outcomes. In ACT, the attempts to reduce, eliminate, or decrease the likelihood of negative thoughts and emotions, may in the short term reduce negative behaviors, yet over the long term, worsen the potential outcomes. Proponents of ACT purport that especially in western society, we are taught from an early age that negative thoughts and emotions should be controlled or stopped (Wilson, Hayes, & Byrd, 2000). For instance, if an individual was fired from a job, he may feel poorly about himself. His friends may tell him to stop thinking so negatively, to forget about the old job and move on to another job and more positive feelings. Thus, the individual is told to not only stop thinking negatively, but also to ignore the reactions he or she is having about the loss of the job. This avoidance and attempt to eliminate negative thoughts is known as experiential avoidance (Wilson et al., 2000). Culminating evidence supports the notion that avoiding or changing negative thoughts does in fact support emotional health in the short term, yet in the long term, thought suppression predicts poorer long-term outcomes (Wilson et al., 2000), such as development of substance abuse. Substance abuse may be a form of experiential avoidance in that it aids individuals in suppressing or avoiding negative thoughts (Chaney, 1989; Wilson et al., 2000).

Drug Dependence Applications. ACT has emphases on acceptance, spirituality, mindfulness, and behavior change (Hayes, Strosahl, & Wilson, 1999). Only recently have researchers implemented its use in substance abusing populations. From an ACT theoretical viewpoint, substance use may be motivated by an attempt to regulate negative private experiences through experiential avoidance. ACT for substance abuse treatment focuses on helping clients to realize the breadth of their psychological difficulties and to overcome the cognitive and emotional barriers to stopping destructive drug use patterns. There are five main treatment phases that are implemented in the treatment of substance abuse in ACT (Wilson et al., 2000, p. 213) including:

1. Creative Hopelessness: Making contact with the scope of the problem and the effort expended to solve it;
2. Values Assessment: Exploration of the client's personal values to direct and dignify the treatment;
3. Control as the Problem: Identifying ineffective control strategies;
4. Defusing Language: Making room for acceptance;
5. Applied Willingness: Putting values into action.

Another variant uses ACT principles to target shame (Luoma et al., 2012).

Hayes and colleagues have manualized much of the ACT therapy protocols based on their research. Most ACT protocols require that patients participate in both individual and group based ACT treatment (Wilson et al., 2000).

Tobacco Dependence Applications. Using ACT in tobacco dependence interventions has focused on the identification and treatment of distress tolerance. Accordingly, clients are taught skills that assist with nicotine withdrawal, negative affect, and feelings associated with smoking, based on the idea that teaching smokers to minimize efforts to avoid or escape these aversive internal states will strengthen their ability to persist in attempts at smoking cessation.

Evidence for Use in SUD Treatment. Hayes & Strosahl (2004) examined the efficacy of Intensive Twelve Step Facilitation Therapy (ITSF) and ACT when combined with methadone maintenance as compared with methadone maintenance alone for polysubstance-abusing opiate addicts. Despite decreased power due to high attrition, participants in the ACT study arm had significantly lower rates of opiate and total drug use at follow-up as compared with participants in the control group. Unfortunately, the researchers were unable to determine whether it was the ACT or the ITSF that accounted for the results since these were confounded. There are now two unconfounded controlled studies. When comparing 12 sessions of ACT versus cognitive-behavioral therapy for methamphetamine users, equivalent attendance (about 3 sessions) and improvements in substance use and substance use consequences were seen in both treatment conditions (Smout et al., 2010). As an adjunct to a residential SUD treatment program, group ACT-based intervention targeting shame resulted in fewer days of substance use at 4-month follow-up compared with a similar number of extra sessions of treatment as usual alone (Luoma et al., 2012).

Evidence for Use in Smoking Treatment. When smokers were taught to either suppress or accept their urges to smoke in laboratory exposure to smoking cues, then to quit smoking for 3 days, there was no difference in number of cigarettes smoked during that time (Litvin, Kovacs, Hayes & Brandon, 2012). In a pilot study, investigators implemented an ACT based intervention with a sample of regular smokers demonstrated that the participants were able to achieve a median of 24 days of continuous abstinence from smoking (Brown et al., 2008). This is an encouraging finding given that these participants had difficulty maintaining abstinence for more than 3 days in the past. This provides support that the distress tolerance skills taught in the intervention may have assisted the participants with coping with the negative affect and thoughts that they experienced during their abstinence. However, a number of other coping skills were taught together with ACT so results cannot be attributed to ACT itself. Another pilot study comparing ACT to cognitive-behavioral therapy found 12-month confirmed smoking abstinence to be 2.3 times greater after ACT than the comparison treatment (Hernández-López et al., 2009). The one uncontrolled study that deserves mention is one that used ACT in a telephone-delivered intervention and compared it to historical results for standard coping-skills based telephone counseling; after ACT, 29% said they did not smoke at all (without biological confirmation) in the 12 months following intervention compared with 12% historically (Bricker et al., 2010). All these results are preliminary and a fully powered well-controlled study is still needed with biologically confirmed abstinence. However, these pilot studies show initial promise that is worth following up.

Summary of Evidence

ACT is still an emerging method with very few controlled comparisons against a comparison treatment, and no fully powered controlled studies for smoking. One unconfounded study shows good initial promise for the value of this approach for substance dependence, and controlled pilot studies show some promise for smoking, with no studies yet for alcohol use disorders. Future research is needed to determine to what extent this approach will be supported compared with other established treatments in methodologically sound studies.

Cue-Exposure with Response Prevention
Overview of Approach

CET is designed to reduce respondent conditioning to stimuli that have been repeatedly associated with drug use in the past (Rohsenow et al., 1990). This is done by repeatedly presenting the sight, sounds, and/or smells associated with drug use ("cues") while the person is in a safe environment with no access to the drug, so that these become unreinforced trials of exposure. The purpose is to make clients less reactive and therefore less susceptible to these cues when the clients encounter the cues on their own after treatment.

There are three different mechanisms by which cues are believed to pose a risk for relapse for abstinent people after treatment. First is by means of classical (respondent) conditioned responses, in which the cues elicit a variety of physiological and emotional reactions that lead to an urge (desire) to use the substance (Rohsenow et al., 1990). (Consistent with the recommendations of Kozlowski et al. [1989], we use the term "urge" or "desire" rather than "craving" because urge is less ambiguous and covers a broader continuum of degree of desire to use.) Second, these reactions then interfere with a client's ability to use coping skills effectively (see Monti, Rohsenow, & Hutchison, 2000). This may possibly occur by tying up allocation of attentional resources, leading fewer resources available to remember and engage in coping skills (Sayette et al., 1994), consistent with the way stress responses generally can interfere with ability to use coping (Abrams & Niaura, 1987). Third, the cues and the internal responses to the cues lead to operant behavior (substance use) that reinforce the behavior by reducing the aversive aspects of the response (and of the cues when the cues include unpleasant situational antecedents); the operant behavior can occur quite rapidly and automatically, outside of awareness (Tiffany, 1990).

For these reasons, CET is believed to work through one or both of two mechanisms: (a) breaking the conditioned association between the cues associated with substance use and substance use behavior (habituation), so that the cues no longer elicit conditioned reactions (or elicit weak ones), thereby not automatically leading to the operant behavior (substance use), and (b) providing the opportunity to practice coping with urges to use so that urges will be less likely to disrupt the client's ability to apply coping skills when in the presence of cues after treatment. The implications of this model include that (a) exposure should occur long enough for responses to habituate within-session; (b) a wide variety of different cues should be used in exposure sessions; and (c) urge coping practice should occur early in the exposure when elicited reactions are at a peak. While it is not entirely clear whether CET works more via habituation or more via the urge coping practice, the urge coping practice both makes the sessions more acceptable to clients and provide a useful set of tools while not interfering with the exposure *per se*. Thus, pragmatically it makes sense to use both aspects in treatment.

Some notes about the natures of cues to use are important across CET approaches. Since it is not practical to conduct the exposure in the natural environment in most cases, and since many cues that trigger relapse or urges involve interpersonal or emotional situations (e.g., ex-spouse calls on the telephone; at home alone on the weekend feeling bored and lonely), two methods are commonly used: presenting the sight, smell, and feel of the substance itself since it is the final common pathway to use, and using imaginal or scripted imagery of more complex situations. The use of virtual reality (VR) as a vehicle is in its early stages (Kuntze et al., 2001; Lee et al., 2003), and photographs of teens using alcohol have been investigated with adolescents where the real beverage should not be used (Curtin et al., 2005). However, studies comparing standardized sets of cues to personalized cues have consistently found that personalized cues are far more effective in eliciting urges and psychophysiological reactions (Niaura et al., 1998; Staiger & White, 1991), so the sets of photographs and VR programs are likely to be weaker methods as well as not being able to present emotional cues or intimate conflicts particularly well.

Drug Dependence Applications. In the CET approach developed with opiate-dependent or with cocaine-dependent clients separately, a gradated series of cues is presented over a series of separate days, with the cues matching the client's own route of administration (see Childress et al., 1992, 1993). Audiotapes of people making drug buys and/or using are followed by videos of such situations, with the final cue being a mock shooting up ritual with a blunt empty needle (see Childress et al., 1992, for a fuller description). Each session starts with brief psychotherapy, then 10 minutes of cue exposure, followed by deep relaxation, with up to 35 sessions provided. In addition to provoking self-reported craving, these cues elicit physiological responses that are not consistently in either the drug-consistent or the drug-opposite direction, but rather generally indicate increased arousal, supportive of the appetitive-motivational theory of such conditioning (see Niaura et al., 1988, and Rohsenow et al., 1990, for a comprehensive discussion of the competing theories and their support).

Alcohol Dependence Applications. In a major CET approach used in several studies (see full description in Monti et al., 2002), each CET session starts with up to 15 minutes of holding and sniffing one's customary alcoholic beverage (the length of time determined by time for self-reported urge to fall to a low level), followed by imaginal exposure to individualized high-risk situations (guided imagery to have the client imagine being in the high-risk situation while not drinking). The first session starts with pure exposure, then subsequent exposures also teach and have the client practice using a series of urge-specific coping skills, focusing on the ones that have been found to be associated with drinking reductions (see Rohsenow et al., 2001, for details). The coping skills with the best support (Rohsenow et al., 2000) include telling themselves they can wait out the urge and it will go down (the first skill taught, drawing on their experiences with pure exposure in the first session), thinking about negative consequences that would happen if they drank (staying future oriented), thinking about positive consequences that would happen if they drank, imagining eating or drinking something else, and imagining engaging in an alternative activity (distracting or supportive). Skills that did not correlate with outcome included cognitive mastery statements, cognitive distraction, and Marlatt's (1985) urge-reduction imagery (Rohsenow et al., 2000). The client is then provided with a personalized list of the skills incorporating their own personal details to take home. A second approach to CET involves clients holding and smelling their usual alcoholic beverage without asking them to use coping skills (Drummond & Glautier, 1994). A third approach, used for clients with moderate drinking goals, involves consuming a moderate dose of alcohol than holding and sniffing another drink without drinking it (Heather et al., 2000; Sitharthan et al., 1997).

Tobacco Dependence Applications. The cues used in CET for tobacco dependence have included lighting and holding a lit cigarette without inhaling it, laboratory analogues to common situations (e.g., a staff member smoking in the presence of the client), and imagery (imagining a stressful or upsetting situation, e.g. Shadel et al., 1998). Exposure to cues has been conducted combined with having the clients practice coping skills in the situation (Niaura et al., 1999). Virtual reality programs include standardized smoking environments (e.g., a bar and alcohol drink) as well as cigarette cues (Bordnick et al., 2005; Lee et al., 2004). Newer VR applications try to individualize the smoking cues more to the objects and locations most associated with smoking for any one client, and include avatars that appear to be smoking (Culbertson et al., 2012).

Summary of Evidence

Evidence for Use in SUD Treatment. Few studies have been published investigating CET for opiate- or cocaine-dependent clients. While the study with methadone-maintained opiate-dependent clients found CET to produce significant reduction in craving but not withdrawal symptoms, the group that received psychotherapy without CET did equivalently well in terms of abstinence at follow up (McLellan et al., 1986). Another small study found no differences between clients receiving CET and controls in craving, withdrawal, or drug use (Dawe et al., 1993). When used for cocaine dependence with recently detoxified clients, craving and withdrawal ratings both decreased over 15 sessions, with craving ratings at or near zero by the seventh session (O'Brien et al., 1990). While the majority of clients dropped out of post-CET outpatient treatment quickly and usually relapsed to cocaine use, time to drop out and self-reported amount of cocaine use was lower for clients who received CET compared with control groups (O'Brien et al., 1990). However, the CET did not appear to have an appreciable effect on drug use at follow-up (Childress et al., 1992). Therefore, there is little evidence for using CET for people with opiate or cocaine dependence.

Evidence for Use in Smoking Treatment. Few controlled treatment trials of CET for smoking have been done, probably because the first large randomized controlled trial found no benefit to adding CET to cognitive-behavioral skills training and nicotine gum (Niaura et al., 1999). Some smaller early studies (e.g., Corty & McFall, 1984; Gotestam & Melin, 1983; Lowe et al., 1980; Raw & Russell, 1980) also failed to show beneficial results. The first CET using VR did not investigate effects on smoking outside the sessions (Lee et al., 2004). However, a controlled study providing all with up to 16 sessions of CBT plus CET using individualized cues presented via VR (20 minutes of exposure per session) or placebo exposure (VR without smoking cues) found a significantly higher quit rate (biologically confirmed) and fewer cigarettes per day at end of treatment for those who received the smoking cues via VR (Culbertson et al., 2012).

Thus, while there is clearly room for more study, currently it is not indicated for clinical use for smokers at this time. However, the VR-based CET shows initial promise in one study. Future studies will need to show significant effects on abstinence rates reported over at least 6 months of follow-up,

Evidence for Use in AUD Treatment. Evidence supports CET's effectiveness with clients with AUD when CET is used as a part of a comprehensive treatment program (see Monti et al., 2002). Studies using exposure to the alcoholic beverage without coping skill training in the presence of cues have shown beneficial results in several studies. An initial small trial (n = 35) of ten 40-minute sessions of CET using sight and smell of the usual drinks compared with relaxation treatment (both as adjuncts to inpatient programs) found the alcohol-dependent clients receiving CET drank significantly less alcohol and had longer time to relapse to heavy drinking. Another study randomized 42 nondependent problem drinkers with goals of moderate drinking to CET or CBT, with the CET involving consuming a moderate dose of alcohol than holding and sniffing another drink without drinking it, both in the clinic and in homework (Sitharthan et al., 1997). They also self-monitored drinking and learned strategies for moderate drinking. Those who received CET drank less often and had fewer drinks during the next 6 months than those who received CBT. A larger study with a similar CET approach assigned alcoholics with moderate drinking goals to either CET or behavioral self-control training (Heather et al., 2000). In the CET, clients drank one drink then resisted further drinking in eight 90-minute sessions and in homework. Both treatment approaches were equally effective in reducing drinking during the next 6 months.

The studies using exposure to the alcoholic beverage with embedded urge coping skills training have also shown beneficial results in several studies. The initial small-scale study (n = 34) with this CET method (six 1-h sessions on consecutive days) for people with AUDs in abstinence-oriented inpatient treatment found that while both CET and control patients did equally well during the first 3 months, 3 to 6 months after treatment clients receiving CET had a significantly lower number of drinking days and tended to have fewer drinks per day than did alcoholics in standard care (Monti et al., 1993b). In particular, among the majority subset of clients who initially reacted to cues with increased urge to drink, those in CET reduced their urges more, were more likely to use coping skills after treatment, and had higher abstinence rates 6 months later. In the next larger study (n = 100 people with AUD in an intensive treatment program), CST (communication skills training) versus a control procedure (alcohol education) was crossed with individual sessions of the CET approach (versus relaxation training control) in a 2 × 2 randomized controlled design (Rohsenow et al., 2001). Those receiving CET had fewer heavy drinking days if they lapsed during the 12-month follow-up than those who received no CET. Furthermore, those receiving both CET and CST had significantly fewer drinks on days that they drank from 6 to 12 months out than did those in the other conditions. Clients who received CET also reported more use of the urge-specific coping strategies during the 12 months of follow-up, and use of many of these strategies correlated with reduced drinking. Thus, receiving an average of eight CET sessions during intensive substance treatment had beneficial effects lasting out to at least 12 months. The third study from this group randomized 165 clients with AUD (enrolled in an intensive treatment program) to group CET combined with CST (2-hour sessions, with the alcohol present the whole time) or relaxation and alcohol education sessions (Monti et al., 2001). Clients who received the CET plus CST were less likely to relapse and reported fewer heavy drinking days over the next 12 months than did patients in the control condition, even though they received only four to five sessions of the experimental treatment against the background of a strong intensive treatment program. These patients also reported using more of the skills they were taught over the 12 months and less urge to drink in response to a post-treatment cue assessment sessions.

Summary of Evidence. In summary, while CET for opiate- or cocaine-dependent clients has not been successful, and there is no evidence of an effect after treatment ends for smokers, the controlled studies of CET for people with alcohol use disorders show consistently beneficial effects on alcohol treatment outcomes. These studies show effects lasting throughout the 12 months of follow-up despite the fact that only four to eight sessions were received within the context of a full standard treatment program. The studies using exposure to beverage cues without concomitant urge coping training but, in some cases, with practice drinking moderate amounts of alcohol within a moderation framework also showed significant reductions in drinking during the 6 months these clients were followed. CET with or without urge coping skills training at the same time had beneficial results. The embedded urge coping skills training allows clients to safely practice coping with a variety of drinking triggers in a safe place and results in increased use of skills that correlate with reduced drinking during the subsequent year, and thus may provide an advantage over exposure without skills training, with no disadvantages.

Conclusion

Strong support is seen for many of the CBTs, but the support varies for each type of CBT across substance of abuse.

• For alcohol use disorders, CST (including RPT) has strong support especially when focused on interpersonal skills more than on mood management, and when adjunctive to an integrated treatment program. Relatively few sessions have been seen to produce lasting effects. CST significantly improves alcohol use and problems compared with standard treatment without CST. CET for AUDs, with or without embedded urge copings skills training, has strong support with fewer studies. CM for AUDs is in its infancy (due to difficulty assessing alcohol use frequently enough) but shows promise.

• For cocaine use disorders, CM combined with CST or the community reinforcement approach (with CST embedded) has the best abstinence rates, with emerging evidence of benefits persisting after CM ends and with improved quality of life. CST without CM is the other approach with the best evidence of effectiveness.

• For marijuana use, there is a shorter history of controlled research using CBTs. There is evidence that CM improves outcomes, that the CST of Carroll's group (2006) is better than drug counseling, and that CM has better long-term results when combined with CST than when not.

• For opiate dependence, most studies have targeted reducing use of other drugs during methadone maintenance. CM shows modest but significant beneficial effects on drug use, particularly when targeting use of only one other drug. High payments are needed, and are more effective than using take-home methadone doses as the incentive, but the "fishbowl" method can reduce the costs without reducing efficacy. Little work has been done on CST for opiate use.

• For smoking treatment, any counseling should be adjunctive to pharmacotherapy when medically possible. The strongest effects on outcome are found with aversion therapy, but this treatment is unappealing to clients and therapists and it needs to be conducted under medical supervision. Evidence supports some key elements of CST including coping skills training and arranging for social support, but does not consistently support mood management training. CM has not been evaluated with smokers who have sought treatment and with adjunctive counseling, the way it was found effective for cocaine dependence. However, CM did considerably increase smoking abstinence in pregnant smokers, with effects persisting after CM ended. CET was not effective in the one controlled trial with real cues but was effective within-treatment in one study using VR to present smoking environments.

• Relaxation or meditation training is ineffective for any substance treatment. Aversion therapy has been abandoned for substances other than smoking. CET does not appear beneficial except for treating AUDs. ACT is largely untested.

Thus, overall CST and CM have strong support and warrant being included in comprehensive treatment programs for SUDs as indicated above.

Future Directions

Dissemination. Although a number of effective and diverse treatment approaches have been studied and demonstrate effectiveness in decreasing substance abuse, cognitive behavioral approaches are underutilized in treatment settings (McLellan, Carise, & Kleber, 2003; Rawson et al., 2002; Roman & Blum, 1997). Although 80% of substance abuse treatment providers report interest in implementing research-based interventions, many are specifically interested in research based treatments that emphasize spirituality and 12-Step programs, for which there is a paucity of empirical support (Forman, Bovasso, & Woody, 2001). However, the movement in publicly funded centers toward using evidence-based treatments will encourage more use of treatment approaches with a foundation in research evidence. Therefore, dissemination and training for clinical staff remain key. Most (90%) substance abuse counselors can be trained to conduct manualized CBT with at least adequate skill levels (Morgenstern et al., 2001). The Substance Abuse and Mental Health Services Administration (SAMSHA)'s Center for Substance Abuse Treatment (CSAT) has developed a Web-based National Registry of Evidence-Based Treatments (NREPP) so that clinicians can easily

find out about treatments that have a good evidence base with information about how to obtain treatment manuals and training. The National Institute on Drug Abuse has also placed evidence-based treatment manuals on the Web for use (e.g., www.drugabuse.gov/txmanual/cbt/). Another program that more directly addresses the implementation of evidence-based interventions is the Addiction Technology Transfer Center Network (ATTC). The ATTCs increase dissemination of evidence-based treatments to clinicians by providing a range of training and technical assistance activities, with 14 regional offices around the country. ATTCs have been successfully working out the various problems involved in getting acceptance from the clinical community in implementing these treatments in real-world settings (for their guidelines on how to do this, see ATTC, 2004).

Using Medications to Increase Effectiveness. Many medications may result in an additive effect by focusing on independent mechanisms of effects (e.g., Monti et al., 2001). More exciting is when medications can increase the effects of a behavioral intervention. For CET, there is some animal evidence that drugs that target glutamatergic nerve transmission can facilitate extinction learning, so should be tried in human cue exposure treatment (Cleva, Gass, Widholm, & Olive, 2010). Similarly, propranolol (a beta-adrenergic antagonist) administered during cue exposure may disrupt the reconsolidation of retrieved memories of a cue paired with pain in animals and humans (Deblec & Ledoux, 2004; Kindt et al., 2009), and this medication shows already promise as an adjunct to exposure therapy for trauma victims (Brunet et al., 2008). This medication needs to be investigated as an adjunct to substance CET in people so see if the memory disruption effects assist with such exposure treatments as well.

Using Technology to Overcome Problems. Reaching rural populations without large population centers or people with various other barriers to coming in to treatment programs (e.g., shift work) provides other challenges. The development of computer-based CBT indicates the role that new media can have in reaching more scattered populations. As use of the internet increases, such computer-based programs could be adapted for Web-based dissemination so as to overcome barriers of transportation, excessive distance, child care, and shift work—all of which can interfere with receiving treatment in centers. The anonymity can lessen barriers of stigma and lead to more honest disclosure (Hester & Miller, 2006). Currently, Web-based treatments have been developed and initially tested for college drinking interventions primarily (see Elliott, Carey, & Bolles, 2008, for review). Of the studies using electronic-based interventions, many used the Web to administer one or more arms of the trials, usually involving motivational interviewing with personalized feedback or alcohol education. Some advantages to adapting CBT to the Web could include the ability to personalize the approach by selecting skills training modules that apply to their own situations while skipping ones with less relevance, to go at one's own pace, and to use Web cameras to observe people taking breath tests or engaging in role plays for later feedback. A disadvantage is losing the feedback from the group of participants, but it is possible that online chat rooms with Web cameras could overcome this hurdle. While economically disadvantaged people still may not have access to the Web, these can be installed in community locations, and many people with AUDs report having access to the internet and showed interest in engaging in Web-based treatment (Cunningham et al., 2006; Saitz et al., 2004). This intriguing idea needs further development. In addition, text messaging is increasingly being investigated as a way to deliver reminders to use coping skills in the natural environment after initial treatment as well as to assess effects on drinking in the environment (e.g., Cohn et al., 2011; Preziosa et al., 2009).

Virtual reality (VR) equipment provides another tool designed to provide an array of visual and auditory stimuli that are commonly associated with urges to use substances. The VR for alcohol cues has even begun to incorporate olfactory cues, and drinkers reported that the scenes were realistic and compelling, and that they evoked craving (Bordnick et al., 2008). While in its early development stage for smoking (e.g., Bordnick et al., 2005; Culbertson et al., 2012; Lee et al., 2004) and alcohol (Bordnick et al., 2008; Cho et al., 2008), it is possible that this can provide another way to conduct not only CET but also coping skills training in the context of high-risk situations. While initially limited to standardized cues, increasing personalization of these cues and environments is under way, both to preferred brands of cigarette or drink and to actual environments (e.g., Culbertson et al., 2012).

Innovations Under Way. Cost is often cited as a barrier to implementing the most effective approach to treating drug dependence, contingency management. Already, nonmonetary contingencies such as take-home methadone and access to work settings have been used to find less costly effective methods. The work on using "fishbowls" to draw chances for a reward has been found to greatly reduce cost without reducing efficacy. Continued work on finding methods to make the costs of this approach reachable to all programs is needed. Some innovative ways to deal with the problem of determining alcohol use and smoking without overly frequent transportation will probably include using Web cameras to watch as a person self-administers breath tests for detecting smoking or alcohol use (Dallery, Glenn, & Raiff, 2007), and wearable transdermal alcohol monitors with automatic Internet uploads of data on a regular basis (Barnett et al., 2011).

Final Comment. While the basic work of determining treatment approaches with immediate and/or lasting efficacy has been done, ways to make the work more easily disseminable are now the key questions. Program directors and staff ratings of the effectiveness of types of treatment do not necessarily correspond to the actual evidence in many cases; adoption of evidence-based treatments by substance abuse treatment practitioners, rather than being determined by evidence, has been shown to be related to organizational training and information resources (Herbeck, Hser, & Teruya, 2008). Focusing on ways to disseminate the most effective treatments is the key challenge.

References

Abbott, N., Stead, L., White, A. R., & Barnes, J. (1999). Hypnotherapy for smoking cessation (Cochrane Review). *The Cochrane Library, 2.* doi: 10.1002/14651858. CD001008

Abrams, D. B., & Niaura, R. S. (1987). Social learning theory. In H. T. Blane & K. E. Leonard (Eds.), *Psychological theories of drinking and alcoholism* (pp. 131–178). New York: Guilford Press.

Addiction Technology Transfer Centers. (2004). *The change book: A blueprint for technology transfer* (2nd ed.) Kansas City, MO: Author.

Amodei, N., & Lamb, R. J. (2005). Predictors of initial abstinence in smokers enrolled in a smoking cessation program. *Substance Use and Misuse, 40,* 141–149.

Anker, A. L., & Crowley, T. J. (1982). Use of contingency contracts in specialty clinics for cocaine abuse. In L. Harris (Ed.), *Committee on the Problems of Drug Dependence 1982.* Research Monograph 41 (pp. 452–459), National Institute on Drug Abuse.

Ashem, B., & Donner, L. (1968). Covert sensitization with alcoholics: A controlled replication. *Behaviour Research & Therapy*, 6, 7–12.

Bandura, A. (1977). *Social learning theory*. Englewood Cliffs, NJ: Prentice-Hall.

Bandura, A. (1997). *Self-efficacy: The exercise of control*. New York: Freeman.

Barnett, N. P., Tidey, J., Murphy, J. G., Swift, R., Colby, S. M. (2011). Contingency management for alcohol use reduction: A pilot study using a transdermal alcohol sensor. *Drug and Alcohol Dependence*, 118, 391–399.

Beck, A. T., Rush, A. J., Shaw, B. F., & Emery, G. (1979). *Cognitive therapy of depression*. New York: Guilford.

Beck, A. T., Wright, F. D., Newman, C. F., & Liese, B. S. (1993). *Cognitive therapy of substance abuse*. New York: Guilford.

Beck, J. S., Liese, B. S., & Najavits, L. M. (2005). Cognitive therapy. In R. J. Frances, S. I. Miller, & A. H. Mack (Eds.), *Clinical textbook of addictive disorders* (3rd ed., pp. 474–501). New York: Guilford.

Bickel, W. K., Rizzuto, P., Zielony, R. D., Klobas, J., Pangiosonlis, P., et al., (1988). Combined behavioral and pharmacological treatment of alcoholic methadone patients. *Journal of Substance Abuse*, 1, 161–171.

Bordnick, P. S., Graap, K. M., Copp, H. L., Brooks, J., & Ferrer, M. (2005). Virtual reality cue reactivity assessment in cigarette smokers. *CyberPsychology & Behavior*, 8, 487–492.

Bordnick, P. S., Traylor, A. C., Copp, H. L., Graap, K. M., Carter, B., Ferrer, M., & Walton, A. P. (2008). Assessing reactivity to virtual reality alcohol based cues. *Addictive Behaviors*, 33, 743–756.

Brandon, T. H., Zelman, D. C., & Baker, T. B. (1987). Effects of maintenance sessions on smoking relapse: Delaying the inevitable? *Journal of Consulting and Clinical Psychology*, 55, 780–782.

Bricker, J. B., Mann, S. L., Marek, P. M., Liu, J., & Peterson, A. V. (2010). Telephone-delivered Acceptance and Commitment Therapy for adult smoking cessation: A feasibility study. *Nicotine & Tobacco Research*, 12, 454–458.

Bride, B. E., & Humble, M. N. (2008). Increasing retention of african-american women on welfare in outpatient substance user treatment using low-magnitude incentives. *Substance Use & Misuse*, 43, 1016–1026.

Brown, R. A., Kahler, C. W., Niaura, R., Abrams, D. B., Sales, S. D., Ramsey, S. E., et al., (2001). Cognitive-behavioral treatment for depression in smoking cessation. *Journal of Consulting and Clinical Psychology*, 69, 471–480.

Brown, R. A., Palm, K. M., Strong, D. R., Lejuez, C. W., Kahler, C. W., Zvolensky, M. J., Hayes, S. C., Wilson, K. G., & Gifford, E. V. (2008). Distress tolerance treatment for early-lapse smokers: Rationale, program description, and preliminary findings. *Behavior Modification*, 32, 302–332.

Brunet, A., Orr, S. P., Tremblay, J., Nader, K., & Pitman, R. K. (2008). Effects of post-retrieval propranolol on psychophysiological responding during subsequent script-driven traumatic injury in post-traumatic stress disorder. *Journal of Psychiatric Research*, 42, 503–506.

Budney, A. J., & Higgins, S. T. (1998). *A community reinforcement plus vouchers approach: Treating cocaine addiction*. Rockville, MD: United States Department of Health and Human Services.

Budney, A. J., Higgins, S. T., Radonovich, K. J., & Novy, P. L. (2000). Adding voucher-based incentives to coping skills and motivational enhancement improves outcomes during treatment for marijuana dependence. *Journal of Consulting and Clinical Psychology*, 68, 1051–1061.

Budney, A. J., Moore, B. A., Rocha, H. L., & Higgins, S. T. (2006). Clinical trial of abstinence-based vouchers and cognitive-behavioral therapy for cannabis dependence. *Journal of Consulting and Clinical Psychology*, 74, 307–316.

Budney, A. J., & Stanger, C. (2008). Marijuana. In Higgins, S. T., Silverman, K., & Heil, S. H. (Eds.), *Contingency management in substance abuse treatment* (pp. 61–79). New York: Guilford.

Cannon, D. S., Baker, T. B., & Wehl, C. K. (1981). Emetic and electric shock alcohol aversion therapy: Six- and twelve-month follow-up. *Journal of Consulting and Clinical Psychology*, 49, 360–369.

Carroll, K. M., Ball, S. A., Martino, S., Nich, C., Babuscio, T. A., & Rounsaville, B. J. (2009). Enduring effects of a computer-assisted training program for cognitive behavioral therapy: A 6-month follow-up of CBT4CBT. *Drug and Alcohol Dependence*, 100, 178–181.

Carroll, K. M., Ball, S. A., Martino, S., Nich, C., Babuscio, T. A., Nuro, K. F., Gordon, M. A., Portnoy, G. A., & Rounsaville, B. J. (2008). Computer-assisted delivery of cognitive-behavioral therapy for addiction: A randomized trial of CBT4CBT. *American Journal of Psychiatry*, 165, 881–888.

Carroll, K. M., Ball, S. A., Nich, C., O'Connor, P. G., Eagan, D. A., Frankforter, T. L., . . . Rounsaville, B. J. (2001). Targeting behavioral therapies to enhance naltrexone treatment of opioid dependence. *Archives of General Psychiatry*, 58, 755–761.

Carroll, K. M., Easton, C. J., Nich, C., Hunkele, K. A., Neavins, T. M., Sinha, R., . . . Rounsaville, B. J. (2006). The use of contingency management and motivational/skills-building therapy to treat young adults with marijuana dependence. *Journal of Consulting and Clinical Psychology*, 74, 955–966.

Carroll, K. M., Fenton, L. R., Ball, S. A., Nich, C., Frankforter, T. L., Shi, J., & Rounsaville, B. J. (2004). Efficacy of disulfiram and cognitive behavior therapy in cocaine-dependent outpatients. *Archives of General Psychiatry*, 61, 264–272.

Carroll, K. M., Nich, C., & Ball, S. A. (2005). Practice makes progress? Homework assignments and outcome in treatment of cocaine dependence. *Journal of Consulting and Clinical Psychology*, 73, 749–755.

Carroll, K. M., Nich, C., Frankforter, T. L., & Bisighini, R. M. (1999). Do patients change in the ways we intend? Assessing acquisition of coping skills among cocaine-dependent patients. *Psychological Assessment*, 11, 77–85.

Carroll, K. M., Nich, C., & Rounsaville, B. J. (1995). Differential symptom reduction in depressed cocaine abusers treated with psychotherapy and pharmacotherapy. *Journal of Nervous and Mental Disease*, 183, 251–259.

Carroll, K. M., & Onken, L. S. (2005). Behavioral therapies for drug abuse. *American journal of Psychiatry*, 162, 1452–1460.

Carroll, K. M., & Rounsaville, B. J. (2007). A perfect platform: Combining contingency management with medications for drug abuse. *American Journal of Drug and Alcohol Abuse*, 33, 343–365.

Carroll, K. M., Rounsaville, B. J., & Gawin, F. H. (1991). A comparative trial of psychotherapies for ambulatory cocaine abusers: Relapse prevention and interpersonal psychotherapy. *American Journal of Drug and Alcohol Abuse*, 17, 229–247.

Carroll, K. M., Rounsaville, B. J., Gordon, L. T., Nich, C., Jatlow, P. M., Bisighini, R. M., & Gawin, F. H. (1994a).

Psychotherapy and pharmacotherapy for ambulatory cocaine abusers. *Archives of General Psychiatry, 51*, 177–187.

Carroll, K. M., Rounsaville, B. J., Nich, C., Gordon, L. T., Wirtz, P. W., & Gawin, F. H. (1994b). One year follow-up of psychotherapy and pharmacotherapy for cocaine dependence: Delayed emergence of psychotherapy effects. *Archives of General Psychiatry, 51*, 989–997.

Carroll, K. M., Rounsaville, B. J., & Keller, D. S. (1991). Relapse prevention strategies for the treatment of cocaine abuse. *American Journal of Drug and Alcohol Abuse, 17*, 249–265.

Carroll, K. M., Rounsaville, B. J., Nich, C., Gordon, L. T., Wirtz, P. W., & Gawin, F. H. (1994). One-year follow-up of psychotherapy and pharmacotherapy for cocaine dependence: Delayed emergence of psychotherapy effects. *Archives of General Psychiatry, 51*, 989–997.

Carroll, K. M., Rounsaville, B. J., Nich, C., Gordon, L., & Gawin, F. (1995). Integrating psychotherapy and pharmacotherapy for cocaine dependence: Results from a randomized clinical trial. In L. S. Onken, J. D. Blaine, & J. J. Boren (Eds.), *Integrating behavioral therapies with medications in the treatment of drug dependence.* Research Monograph 150, National Institute on Drug Abuse.

Chaney, E. F. (1989). Social skills training. In R. K. Hester & W. R. Miller (Eds.), *Handbook of alcoholism treatment approaches: Effective alternatives.* New York: Pergamon.

Chaney, E. F., O'Leary, M. R., & Marlatt, G. A. (1978). Skill training with alcoholics. *Journal of Consulting and Clinical Psychology, 46*, 1092–1104.

Childress, A. R., Ehrman, R. N., Rohsenow, D. J., Robbins, S. J., & O'Brien, C. P. (1992). Classically conditioned factors in drug dependence: Understanding and modifying the response to drug signals. In J. H. Lowinson, P. Ruiz, & R. Milman (Eds.), *Substance abuse: A comprehensive textbook* (pp. 56–69). Baltimore: Williams and Wilkins.

Childress, A. R., Hole, A. V., Ehrman, R. N., Robbins, S. J., McLellan, A. T., & O'Brien, C. P. (1993). Cue reactivity and cue reactivity interventions in drug dependence. In L. S. Onken, J. D. Blaine, & J. J. Boren (Eds.), *Behavioral treatments for drug abuse and dependence* (pp. 73–95). Research Monograph 137, National Institute on Drug Abuse.

Cho, S., Ku, J., Park, J., Han, K, Lee, H., Choi, Y. K., . . . Shen, D. F. (2008). Development and verification of an alcohol craving–induction tool using virtual reality: Craving characteristics in social pressure situation. *CyberPsychology & Behavior, 11*, 302–309.

Chutuape, M. A., Silverman, K., & Stitzer, M. L. (1998). Survey assessment of methadone treatment services as reinforcers. *American Journal of Drug and Alcohol Abuse, 24*, 1–16.

Clancy, J., Vanderhoof, E., & Campbell, P. (1967). Evaluation of an aversive technique as a treatment for alcoholism. *Quarterly Journal of Studies on Alcoholism, 28*, 476–485.

Cleva, R. M., Gass, J. T., Widholm, J. J., & Olive, M. F. (2010). Glutamatergic targets for enhancing extinction learning in drug addiction. *Current Neuropharmacology, 8*, 394.

Cohn, A. M., Hunter-Reel, D., Hagman, B. T., & Mitchell, J. (2011). Promoting behavior change from alcohol use through mobile technology: The future of ecological momentary assessment. *Alcoholism: Clinical and Experimental Research, 35*, 2209–2215.

Cooney. N. L., Kadden, R. M., Litt, M. D., & Gerter, H. (1991). Matching alcoholics to coping skills or interactional therapies: Two-year follow-up results. *Journal of Consulting and Clinical Psychology, 59*, 598–601.

Corty, E., & McFall, R. M. (1984). Response prevention in the treatment of cigarette smoking. *Addictive Behaviors, 9*, 405–408.

Culbertson, C. S., Shulenberger, S., De La Garza, R., Newton, T. F., & Brody, A. L. (2012). Virtual reality cue exposure therapy for the treatment of tobacco dependence. *Journal of Cybertherapy and Rehabilitation, 5*, 57–64.

Cunningham, J. A., Selby, P., Kypri, K., & Humphreys, K. (2006). Access to the Internet among drinkers, smokers and illicit drug users: Is it a barrier to the provision of interventions on the World Wide Web? *Medical Informatics and the Internet in Medicine, 31*, 53–58.

Curtin, J. J., Barnett, N. P., Colby, S. M., Rohsenow, D. J., & Monti, P. M. (2005). Cue reactivity in adolescents: Measurement of separate approach and avoidance reactions. *Journal of Studies on Alcohol, 66*, 332–343.

Dallery, J., Glenn, I. M., & Raiff, B. R. (2007). An Internet-based abstinence reinforcement treatment for cigarette smoking. *Drug and Alcohol Dependence, 86*, 230–238.

Dawe, S., Powell, J., Richards, D. Gossop, M., Marks, I., Strang, J., & Gray, J. A. (1993). *Addiction, 88*, 1233–1245.

Deblec, J., & Ledoux, J. (2004). Disruption of reconsolidation but not consolidation of auditory fear conditioning by noradrenergic blockade in the amygdala. *Neuroscience, 129*, 267–272.

Dolan, S. L., Rohsenow, D. J., Martin, R. A., & Monti, P. M. (2013). Urge-specific and lifestyle coping strategies of alcoholics: Relationships of specific strategies to treatment outcome. *Drug and Alcohol Dependence, 128*, 8–14.

Donatelle, R. J., Prows, S. L., Champeau, D., & Hudson, D. (2000). Randomized controlled trial using social support and financial incentives for high risk pregnant smokers: Significant other supporter (SOS) program. *Tobacco Control, 9*(Suppl. III), iii67–iii69.

Donlin, W. D., Knealing, T., & Silverman, K. (2008). Employment-based reinforcement in the treatment of drug addiction. In S. T. Higgins, K. Silverman, & S. H. Heil (Eds.), *Contingency management in substance abuse treatment* (pp. 314–333). New York: Guilford.

Drummond, D. C., & Glautier, S. P. (1994). A controlled trial of cue exposure treatment in alcohol dependence, *Journal of Consulting and Clinical Psychology, 62*, 809–817.

Dutra, L., Stathopoulou, G., Basden, S. L., Leyro, T. M., Powers, M. B., & Otto, M. W. (2008) A meta-analytic review of psychosocial interventions for substance use disorders. *American Journal of Psychiatry, 165*, 179–187.

Edwards, W. (1954). The theory of decision making. *Psychological Bulletin, 51*, 380–417.

Ehrman, R. N., & Robbins, S. J. (1994). Reliability and validity of six-month timeline reports of cocaine and heroin use in a methadone population. *Journal of Consulting and Clinical Psychology, 62*, 843–850.

Elkins, R. L. (1980). Covert sensitization treatment of alcoholism: Contributions of successful conditioning to subsequent abstinence maintenance. *Addictive Behaviors, 5*, 67–89.

Elliot, J. C., Carey, K. B., & Bolles, J. R. (2008). Computer-based interventions for college drinking: A qualitative review. *Addictive Behaviors, 33*, 994–1005.

Epstein, D. H., Hawkins, W. E., Covi, L., Umbricht, A., & Preston, K. L. (2003). Cognitive-behavioral therapy plus contingency management for cocaine use: Findings during treatment and across 12-month follow-up. *Psychology of Addictive Behaviors, 17*, 73–82.

Epstein, D. H., & Preston, K. L. (2008). Opioids. In S. T. Higgins, K. Silverman, & S. H. Heil (Eds.), *Contingency management in substance abuse treatment* (pp. 42–60). New York: Guilford.

Esposito-Smythers, C., Spirito, A., Kahler, C. W., Hunt, J., & Monti, P. (2011). Treatment of co-occurring substance abuse and suicidality among adolescents: A randomized trial. *Journal of Consulting and Clinical Psychology, 79*, 728–739.

Fiore, M. C., Bailey, W. C., Cohen, S. J., Dorfman, S. F., Goldstein, M. G., Gritz, E. R., … Wewers, M. E. (2000). *Treating Tobacco Use and Dependence: Clinical Practice Guideline*. Public Health Service: USDHHS, Washington, DC.

Forman, R. F., Bovasso, G., & Woody, G. (2001). Staff beliefs about addiction treatment. *Journal of Substance Abuse Treatment, 21*, 1–9.

Frawley, P. J., & Smith, J. W. (1990). Chemical counter conditioning in the treatment of cocaine dependence as part of a multimodal treatment program: Treatment outcome. *Journal of Substance Abuse Treatment, 7*, 21–29.

Fuller, R. K., Branchey, L., Brightwell, D. R., Derman, R. M., Emrick, C. D., Iber, F. L., et al., (1986). Disulfiram treatment of alcoholism: A Veterans Administration cooperative study. *Journal of the American Medical Association, 256*, 1449–1455.

Garvey, A. J., Bliss, R. E., Hitchcock, J. L., Heinold, J. W., & Rosner, B. (1992). Predictors of smoking relapse among self-quitters: A report from the Normative Aging Study. *Addictive Behaviors, 17*, 367–377.

Glynn, T. J., & Manly, M. W. (1995). *How to help your patients stop smoking: A National Cancer Institute manual for physicians*. Washington, DC: National Cancer Institute, DHHS Publication #89-3064.

Goldstein, R. Z., Alia-Klein, N., Tomasi, D., Zhang, L., Cottone, L. A., Maloney, T., et al. (2007). Is decreased prefrontal cortical sensitivity to monetary reward associated with impaired motivation and self-control in cocaine addiction? *American Journal of Psychiatry, 164*, 43–51.

Goldstein, R. Z., Tomasi, D., Alia-Klein, N., Cottone, L. A., Zhang, L., Telang, F., et al. (2007). Subjective sensitivity to monetary gradients is associated with frontolimbic activation to reward in cocaine abusers. *Drug and Alcohol dependence, 87*, 233–240.

Gorski, T. T. (1996, June). The high cost of relapse. *Professional Counselor, xvi*, 29–30.

Gotestam, K. G., & Melin, L. (1983). An experimental study of covert extinction on smoking cessation. *Addictive Behaviors, 8*, 27–31.

Gourlay, S. G., Forbes, A., Marriner, T., Pethica, D., & McNeil, J. J. (1994). Prospective study of factors predicting outcome of transdermal nicotine treatment in smoking cessation. *British Medical Journal, 309*, 842–846.

Griffith, J. D., Rowan-Szal, G. A., Roark, R. R., & Simpson, D. D. (2000). Contingency management in outpatient methadone treatment: A meta-analysis. *Drug and Alcohol Dependence, 58*, 55–66.

Gruber, K., Chutuape, M. A., & Stitzer, M. L. (2000) Reinforcement-based intensive outpatient treatment for inner city opiate abusers: A short-term evaluation. *Drug and Alcohol Dependence, 57*, 211–223.

Haas, A. L., Muñoz, R. F., Humfleet, G. L., Reus, V. I., & Hall, S. M. (2004). Influences of mood, depression history, and treatment modality on outcomes in smoking cessation. *Journal of Consulting and Clinical Psychology, 72*, 563–570.

Hall, S. M., Humfleet, G. L., Muñoz, R. F., Reus, V. I., Prochaska, J. J., & Robbins, J. A. (2011). Using extended cognitive behavioral treatment and medication to treat dependent smokers. *American Journal of Public Health, 101*, 2349–2356.

Hall, S. M., Muñoz, R. F., & Reus, V. I. (1994). Cognitive-behavioral intervention increases abstinence rates for depressive-history smokers. *Journal of Consulting and Clinical Psychology, 62*, 141–146.

Hall, S. M., Muñoz, R. F., Reus, V. I., Sees, K. L., Duncan, C., Humfleet, G. L., & Hartz, D. T. (1996). Mood management and nicotine gum in smoking treatment: A therapeutic contact and placebo-controlled study. *Journal of Consulting and Clinical Psychology, 64*, 1003–1009.

Hall, S. M., Rugg, D., Tunstall, C., & Jones, R. T. (1984). *Journal of Consulting and Clinical Psychology, 52*, 372–382.

Hall, R. G., Sachs, D. P. L., Hall, S. M., & Benowitz, N. L. (1984). Two-year efficacy and safety of rapid smoking therapy in patients with cardiac and pulmonary disease. *Journal of Consulting and Clinical Psychology, 52*, 574–581.

Hayes, S. C., & Strosahl, K. D. (2004). *A practical guide to acceptance and commitment therapy*. New York: Springer.

Hayes, S. C., Strosahl, K. D., & Wilson, K. G. (1999). Acceptance and commitment therapy: An experiential approach to behavior change. New York: Guilford.

Heather, N., Brodie, J., Wale, S., Wilkinson, G., Luce, A., Webb, E., & McCarthy, S. (2000). A randomized controlled trial of moderation-oriented cue exposure. *Journal of Studies on Alcohol, 61*, 561–570.

Herbeck, D. M., Hser, Y. I., & Teruya, C. (2008). Empirically supported substance abuse treatment approaches: A survey of treatment providers' perspectives and practices. *Addictive Behaviors, 33*, 699–712.

Hernández-López, M., Luciano, C. M., Bricker, J. B., Roales-Nieto, J. G., & Montesinos, F. (2009). Acceptance and commitment therapy for smoking cessation: A preliminary study of its effectiveness in comparison with cognitive behavioral therapy. *Psychology of Addictive Behaviors, 23*, 723–730.

Hester, R. K., & Miller, J. H. (2006). Economic perspectives: Screening and intervention: Computer-based tools for diagnosis and treatment of alcohol problems. *Alcohol Health and Research, 29*, 36–40.

Higgins, S. T., Badger, G. J., & Budney, A. J. (2000a). Initial abstinence and success in achieving longer term cocaine abstinence. *Experimental and Clinical Psychopharmacology, 8, 377–386*.

Higgins, S. T., & Budney, A. J. (1993). Treatment of cocaine dependence via the principles of behavior analysis and behavioral pharmacology. In L. S. Onken, J. D. Blaine, & J. J. Boren (Eds.), *Behavioral treatments for drug abuse and dependence* (pp. 97–121). Research Monograph 137, National Institute on Drug Abuse.

Higgins, S. T., Budney, A. J., Bickel, W. K., Foerg, F. E., Donham, R., & Badger, G. J. (1994). Incentives improve outcome in outpatient behavioral treatment of cocaine dependence. *Archives of General Psychiatry, 51*, 568–576.

Higgins, S. T., Delaney, D. D., Budney, A. J., Bickel, W. K., Hughes, J. R., Foerg, F. E., & Fenwick, J. W. (1991). A behavioral approach to achieving initial cocaine abstinence. *American Journal of Psychiatry, 148*, 1218–1224.

Higgins, S. T., Heil, S. H., Rogers, R. E., & Chivers, L. (2008). Cocaine. In S. T. Higgins, K. Silverman, & S. H. Heil (Eds.),

Contingency management in substance abuse treatment (pp. 19–41). New York: Guilford.

Higgins, S. T., Heil, S. H., Solomon, L. J., Lussier, J. P., Abel, R. L., Lynch, M. E., & Badger, G. J. (2004). A pilot study on voucher-based incentives to promote abstinence from cigarette smoking during pregnancy and postpartum. *Nicotine and Tobacco Research, 6,* 1015–1020.

Higgins, S. T., Roll, J. M., & Bickel, W. K. (1996). Alcohol pretreatment increases preference for cocaine over monetary reinforcement. *Psychopharmacology, 123,* 1–8.

Higgins, S. T., Roll, J. M., Wong, C. J., Tidey, J. W., & Dantona, R. (1999). Clinic and laboratory studies on the use of incentives to decrease cocaine and other substance use. In S. T. Higgins & K. Silverman (Eds.), *Motivating behavior change among illicit-drug abusers* (pp. 35–56). Washington, DC: American Psychological Association.

Higgins, S. T., Sigmon, S. C., Wong, C. J., Heil, S. H., Badger, G. J., Donham, R., et al. (2003). Community reinforcement therapy for cocaine-dependent outpatients. *Archives of General Psychiatry, 60,* 1043–1052.

Higgins, S. T., & Silverman, K. (Eds.) (1999). *Motivating behavior change among illicit-drug abusers.* Washington, DC: American Psychological Association.

Higgins, S. T., Silverman, K., & Heil, S. H. (2008). *Contingency management in substance abuse treatment.* New York: Guilford.

Higgins, S. T., Washio, Y., Heil, S. H., Solomon, L. J., Gaalema, D. E., Higgins, T. M., & Bernstein, I. M. (2012). Financial incentives for smoking cessation among pregnant and newly postpartum women. *Preventive medicine, 55,* S33–S40.

Higgins, S. T., & Wong, C. J. (1998). Treating cocaine abuse: What does research tell us? In S. T. Higgins & J. L. Katz (Eds.), *Cocaine abuse: Behavior, pharmacology, and clinical applications* (pp. 343–361). New York: Academic Press.

Higgins, S. T., Wong, C. J., Badger, G. J., Haug Ogden, D. E., & Dantona, R. L. (2000). Contingent reinforcement increases cocaine abstinence during outpatient treatment and 1 year of follow-up. *Journal of Consulting and Clinical Psychology, 68,* 64–72.

Higgins, S. T., Wong, C. J., Badger, G. J., Ogden, D. E., & Dantona, R. L. (2000b). Contingent reinforcement increases cocaine abstinence during outpatient treatment and 1 year of follow-up. *Journal of Consulting and Clinical Psychology, 68,* 64–72.

Hingson, R., Mangione, T., Meyers, A., & Scotch, N. (1982). Seeking help for drinking problems: A study in the Boston metropolitan area. *Journal of Studies on Alcohol, 43,* 273–288.

Hughes, J. R., Keely, J. P., Niaura, R. S., Ossip-Klein, D. J., Richmond, R. L, & Swan, G. E. (2003). Measures of abstinence in clinical trials: Issues and recommendations. *Nicotine & Tobacco Research, 5,* 13–25.

Javors, M. A., Hatch, J. P., & Lamb, R. J. (2005). Evaluation of cut-off levels for breath carbon monoxide as a marker for cigarette smoking over the past 24 hours. *Addiction, 100,* 159–167.

Jones, H. E., Wong, C. J., Tuten, M., & Stitzer, M. L. (2005). Reinforcement-based therapy: 12-month evaluation of an outpatient drug-free treatment for heroin abusers. *Drug and Alcohol Dependence, 79,* 119–128.

Kadden, R. M., Cooney. N. L., Gerter, H., & Litt, M. D. (1989). Matching alcoholics to coping skills or interactional therapies: Post-treatment results. *Journal of Consulting and Clinical Psychology, 57,* 698–704.

Kadden, R. M., Litt, M. D., Cooney. N. L., Kabela, E., & Gerter, H. (2001). Prospective matching of alcoholic clients to cognitive-behavioral or interactional group therapy. *Journal of Studies on Alcohol, 62,* 359–369.

Kalman, D., Longabaugh, R., Clifford, P. R., Beattie, M., & Maisto, S. A. (2000). Matching alcoholics to treatment: Failure to replicate finding of an earlier study. *Journal of Substance Abuse Treatment, 19,* 183–187.

Kanfer, F. H. (1986). Implications of a self-regulation model of therapy for treatment of addictive behaviors. In W. R. Miller & N. Heather (Eds.), *Treating addictive behaviors: Processes of change* (pp. 29–47). New York: Plenum Press.

Kanfer, F. H., & Phillips, J. S. (1970). *Learning foundations of behavior therapy.* New York: John Wiley & Sons.

Kang, S., Kleinman, P. H., Woody, G. E., Milman, R. B., Todd, T. C., Kemp, J., & Lipton, D. S. (1991). Outcomes for cocaine abusers after once-a-week psychosocial therapy. *American Journal of Psychiatry, 148,* 630–635.

Kapson, H. S., & Haaga, D. A. (2010). Depression vulnerability moderates the effects of cognitive behavior therapy in a randomized controlled trial for smoking cessation. *Behavior Therapy, 41,* 447–460.

Katz, E. C., Chutuape, M. A., & Stitzer, M. L. (2001). Voucher reinforcement for heroin and cocaines abstinence in an outpatient drug-free program. *Experimental and Clinical Psychopharmacology, 10,* 136–143.

Kenford, S. L., Fiore, M. C., Jorenby, D. E., Smith, S. S., Wetter, D., & Baker, T. B. (1994). Predicting smoking cessation: Who will quit with and without the nicotine patch. *Journal of the American Medical Association, 271,* 589–594.

Kiluk, B. D., Nich, C., & Carroll, K. M. (2011). Relationship of cognitive function and the acquisition of coping skills in computer assisted treatment for substance use disorders. *Drug and Alcohol Dependence, 114,* 169–176.

Kindt, M., Soeter, M., & Vervliet, B. (2009). Beyond extinction: Erasing human fear responses and preventing the return of fear. *Nature Neuroscience, 12,* 256–258.

Klajner, F., Hartman, L. M., & Sobell, M. B. (1984). Treatment of substance abuse by relaxation training: A review of its rationale, efficacy and mechanisms. *Addictive Behaviors, 9,* 41–55.

Kidorf, M., & Stitzer, M. L. (1996). Contingent use of take-home and split-dosing to reduce illicit drug use of methadone patients. *Behavior Therapy, 27,* 41–51.

Kirby, K. C., Marlowe, D. B., Festinger, D. S., Lamb, R. J., & Platt, J. J. (1998). Schedule of voucher delivery influences cocaine abstinence. *Journal of Consulting and Clinical Psychology, 66,* 761–767.

Kozlowski, L. T., Mann, R. E., Wilkinson, D. A., & Poulos, C. X. (1989). "Cravings" are ambiguous: Ask about urges or desires. *Addictive Behaviors, 14,* 443–445.

Kuntze, M. F., Stoermer, R., Mager, R., Roessler, A., Mueller-Spahn, F., Bullinger, A. H. (2001). Immersive virtual environments in cue exposure. *Cyberpsychology & Behavior, 4,* 497–501.

Lamb, R. J. (2004, June). *Pre-contingency behavior predicts success of smokers in contingency management treatment.* Poster presented at the annual meeting of the College on Problems in Drug Dependence, San Juan, Puerto Rico, USA.

Lamb, R. J., Kirby, K. C., Morral, A. R., Galbick, G., & Iguchi, M. Y. (2004a). Improving contingency management programs for addiction. *Addictive Behaviors, 29,* 507–523.

Lamb, R. J., Morral, A. R., Kirby, K. C., Iguchi, M. Y., & Galibicka, G. (2004b). Shaping smoking cessation using percentile schedules. *Drug and Alcohol Dependence, 76,* 247–259.

Laverty, S. G. (1966). Aversion therapies in the treatment of alcoholism. *Psychosomatic Medicine, 28,* 651–666.

Ledgerwood, D. M., & Petry, N. M. (2006). Does contingency management affect motivation to change substance use? *Drug and Alcohol Dependence, 83,* 65–72.

Lee, J. H., Ku, J., Kim, K., Kim, B., Kim, I. Y., Yang, B. H., . . . Kim, S. I. (2003). Experimental application of virtual reality for nicotine craving through cue exposure. *CyberPsychology & Behavior, 6,* 275–280.

Lee, J. H., Lim, Y., Graham, S. J., Kim, G., Wiederhold, B. K., Wiederhold, M. D., Kim, I. Y., Kim, S. I. (2004). Nicotine craving and cue exposure therapy by using virtual environments. *CyberPsychology & Behavior, 7,* 705–713.

Lichtenstein, E., Harris, D. E., Birchler, G. R., Wahl, J. M., & Schmahl, D. P. (1973). Comparison of rapid smoking, warm smoky air, and attention placebo in the modification of smoking behavior. *Journal of Consulting and Clinical Psychology, 40,* 92–98.

Liebson, I. A., Tommasello, A., & Bigelow, G. E. (1978). A behavioral treatment of alcoholic methadone patients. *Annals of Internal Medicine, 89,* 342–344.

Litt, M. D., Kadden, R. M., & Kabela-Cormier, E. (2009). Individualized assessment and treatment program for alcohol dependence: Results of an initial study to train coping skills. *Addiction, 104,* 1837–1838.

Litvin, E. B., Kovacs, M. A., Hayes, P. L., & Brandon, T. H. (2012). Responding to tobacco craving: Experimental test of acceptance versus suppression. *Psychology of Addictive Behaviors, 26,* 830–837.

Lowe, M. R., Green, L., Kurtz, S. M., Ashenberg, Z. S., & Fisher, E. B., Jr. (1980). Self-initiated, cue-extinction, and covert sensitization procedures in smoking cessation. *Journal of Behavioral Medicine, 3,* 357–372.

Luoma, J. B., Kohlenberg, B. S., Hayes, S. C., & Fletcher, L. (2012). Slow and steady wins the race: A randomized clinical trial of acceptance and commitment therapy targeting shame in substance use disorders. *Journal of Consulting and Clinical Psychology, 80,* 43–53.

Lussier, J. P., Heil, S. H., Mongeon, J. A., Badger, G. J., & Higgins, S. T. (2006). A meta-analysis of voucher-based reinforcement therapy for substance use disorders. *Addiction, 101,* 192–203.

Marlatt, G. A. (1985). Cognitive assessment and intervention procedures for relapse prevention. In G. A. Marlatt & J. R. Gordon (Eds.), *Relapse prevention: Maintenance strategies in the treatment of addictive behaviors* (pp. 201–279). New York: Guilford Press.

Marlatt, G. A., & Gordon, J. R. (Eds.) (1985). *Relapse prevention: Maintenance strategies in the treatment of addictive behaviors.* New York: Guilford Press.

Marlatt, G. A., & Donovan, D. M. (Eds.) (2005). *Relapse prevention: Maintenance strategies in the treatment of addictive behaviors* (2nd ed.). New York: Guilford Press.

Maude-Griffin, P. M., Hohenstein, J. M., Humfleet, G. L., Reilly, P. M., Tusel, D. J., & Hall, S. M. (1998). Superior efficacy of cognitive-behavioral therapy for urban crack cocaine abusers: Main and matching effects. *Journal of Consulting and Clinical Psychology, 66,* 832–837.

McCaul, M. E., Stitzer, M. L., Bigelow, G. E., & Liebson, I. A. (1984). Contingency management interventions: Effects on treatment outcome during methadone detoxification. *Journal of Applied Behavior Analysis, 17,* 35–43.

McCrady, B. S., Dean, L., Dubreuh, E., & Swanson, S. (1985). The problem drinkers' project: A programmatic application of social-learning-based treatment. In G. A. Marlatt & J. R. Gordon (Eds.), *Relapse prevention: Maintenance strategies in the treatment of addictive behaviors* (pp. 417–471). New York: Guilford Press.

McKay, J. R., Alterman, A. I., Cacciola, J. S., Rutherford, M. J., O'Brien, C. P., & Koppenhaver, J. (1997). Group counseling versus individualized relapse prevention aftercare following intensive outpatient treatment for cocaine dependence. *Journal of Consulting and Clinical Psychology, 65,* 778–788.

McKay, J. R., Alterman, A. I., Cacciola, J. S., O'Brien, C. P., Koppenhaver, J., & Shepard, D. S. (1999). Continuing care for cocaine dependence: Comprehensive 2-year outcomes. *Journal of Consulting and Clinical Psychology, 67,* 420–427.

McLellan, A. T., Carise, D., & Kleber, H. D. (2003). Can the national addiction treatment infrastructure support the public's demand for quality care? *Journal of Substance Abuse Treatment, 25,* 117–121.

McLellan, A. T., Childress, A. R., O'Brien, C. P., & Ehrman, R. N. (1986). Extinguishing conditioned responses during treatment for opiate dependence: Turning laboratory findings into clinical procedures. *Journal of Substance Abuse Treatment, 3,* 33–40.

Meredith, S. E., & Dallery, J. (2013). Investigating group contingencies to promote brief abstinence from cigarette smoking. *Experimental and Clinical Psychopharmacology, 21,* 144–154.

Messina, N., Farabee, D., & Rawson, R. (2003). Treatment responsivity of cocaine-dependent patients with antisocial personality disorder to cognitive-behavioral and contingency management interventions. *Journal of Consulting and Clinical Psychology, 71,* 320–329.

Michalec, E., Zwick, W. R., Monti, P. M., Rohsenow, D. J., Varney, S., Niaura, R. S., & Abrams, D. B. (1992). A cocaine high-risk situations questionnaire: Development and psychometric properties. *Journal of Substance Abuse, 4,* 377–391.

Miller, P. (1975). A behavioral intervention program for public drunkenness offenders. *Archives of General Psychiatry, 32,* 915–918.

Miller, W. R., & Hester, R. K. (1986). The effectiveness of alcoholism treatment: What research reveals. In W. R. Miller & N. Heather (Eds.), *Treating addictive behaviors: Processes of change* (pp. 121–174). New York: Plenum Press.

Miller, W. R., Willbourne, P. L., & Hettema, J. E. (2003). What works? A summary of alcohol treatment outcome research. In R. K. Hester & W. R. Miller (Eds.), *Handbook of alcoholism treatment approaches: Effective alternatives* (3nd ed., pp. 13–63). Boston: Allyn & Bacon.

Monti, P. M., Abrams, D. B., Binkoff, J. A., Zwick, W. R., Liepman, M. R., Nirenberg, T. D., & Rohsenow, D. R. (1990). Communication skills training, communication skills training with family, and cognitive behavioral mood management training for alcoholics. *Journal of Studies on Alcohol, 51,* 263–270.

Monti, P. M., Kadden, R., Rohsenow, D. J., Cooney, N., & Abrams, D. B. (2002). *Treating alcohol dependence: A coping skills training guide* (2nd ed.). New York: Guilford Press.

Monti, P. M., & Rohsenow, D. J. (2003). Coping skills training and cue exposure treatment. In R. K. Hester & W. R. Miller (Eds.), *Handbook of alcoholism treatment approaches: Effective alternatives* (3nd ed., pp. 213–236). Boston: Allyn & Bacon.

Monti, P. M., Rohsenow, D. J., & Hutchison, K. E. (2000). Toward bridging the gap between biological, psychobiological, and psychosocial models of alcohol craving. *Addiction*, 95 (Supplement 2), S229–S236.

Monti, P. M., Rohsenow, D. J., Michalec, E., Martin, R. A., & Abrams, D. B. (1997). Brief coping skills treatment for cocaine abuse: Substance use outcomes at 3 months. *Addiction*, 92, 1717–1728.

Monti, P. M., Rohsenow, D. J., Rubonis, A., Niaura, R., Sirota, A., Colby, S., Goddard, P., & Abrams, D. B. (1993b). Cue exposure with coping skills treatment for male alcoholics: A preliminary investigation. *Journal of Consulting and Clinical Psychology*, 61, 1011–1019.

Monti, P. M., Rohsenow, D. J., Swift, R. M, Gulliver, S. B., Colby, S. M., Mueller, T. I., ... & Asher, M. K. (2001). Naltrexone and cue exposure with coping and communication skills training for alcoholics: Treatment process and one-year outcomes. *Alcoholism: Clinical and Experimental Research*, 25, 1634–1647.

Morgenstern, J., Morgan, T. J., McCrady, B. S., Keller, D. S., & Carroll, K. M. (2001). Manual-guided cognitive-behavioral therapy training: A promising method for disseminating empirically supported substance abuse treatments to the practice community. *Psychology of Addictive Behaviors*, 15, 83–88.

MTP Research Group. (2004). Brief treatments for cannabis dependence: Findings from a randomized multi-site trial. *Journal of Consulting and Clinical Psychology*, 72, 455–466.

National Institute on Drug Abuse. (1999). *Principles of drug addiction treatment*. National Institute on Drug Abuse, National Institute of Health, NIH Publication No. 99, 99-4280.

Niaura, R. S., Abrams, D. B., Shadel, W. G., Rohsenow, D. J., Monti, P. M., & Sirota, A. D. (1999). Cue exposure treatment for smoking relapse prevention: A controlled clinical trial. *Addiction*, 94, 685–695.

Niaura, R. S., Rohsenow, D. J., Binkoff, J. A., Monti, P. M., Abrams, D. A., & Pedraza, M. (1988). The relevance of cue reactivity to understanding alcohol and smoking relapse. *Journal of Abnormal Psychology*, 97, 133–152.

Niaura, R. S., Shadel, W. G., Abrams, D. B., Monti, P. M., Rohsenow, D. J., & Sirota, A. (1998). Individual differences in cue reactivity among smokers trying to quit: Effects of gender and cue type. *Addictive Behaviors*, 23, 209–224.

O'Brien, C. P., Childress, A. R., McLellan, A. T., & Ehrman, R. N. (1990). Integrating systematic cue exposure with standard treatment in recovering drug dependent patients. *Addictive Behaviors*, 15, 355–365.

Olmstead, T. A., Sindelar, J. L., & Petry, N. M. (2007). Cost-effectiveness of prize-based incentives for stimulant abusers in outpatient psychosocial treatment programs. *Drug and Alcohol Dependence*, 87, 175–182.

Onken, L. S., Blaine, J. D., & Boren, J. J. (1993). Behavioral treatments of drug abuse and dependence: Progress, potential, and promise. In L. S. Onken, J. D. Blaine, & J. J. Boren (Eds.), *Behavioral treatments for drug abuse and dependence* (pp. 1–4). Research Monograph 137, National Institute on Drug Abuse.

Petry, N. M. (2000). A comprehensive guide to the application of contingency management procedures in general clinic settings. *Drug and Alcohol Dependence*, 58, 9–25.

Petry, N. M., Alessi, S. M., Carroll, K. M., Hanson, T., MacKinnon, S., Rounsaville, B., & Sierra, S. (2006). Contingency management treatments: Reinforcing abstinence versus adherence with goal-related activities. *Journal of Consulting and Clinical Psychology*, 74, 592–601.

Petry, N. M., Alessi, S. M., & Hanson, T. (2007). Contingency management improves abstinence and quality of life in cocaine abusers. *Journal of Consulting and Clinical Psychology*, 75, 307–315.

Petry, N. M., Alessi, S. M., Hanson, T., & Sierra, S. (2007). Randomized trial of contingent prizes versus vouchers in cocaine-using methadone patients. *Journal of Consulting and Clinical Psychology*, 75, 983–991.

Petry, N. M., Barry, D., Alessi, S. M., Rounsaville, B. J., & Carroll, K. M. (2012). A randomized trial adapting contingency management targets based on initial abstinence status of cocaine-dependent patients. *Journal of Consulting and Clinical Psychology*, 80, 276–285.

Petry, N. M., & Carroll, K. M. (2013). Contingency management is efficacious in opioid-dependent outpatients not maintained on agonist pharmacotherapy. *Psychology of Addictive Behaviors*, 27, 1036–1043.

Petry, N. M., Martin, B., Cooney, J. L., & Kranzler, H. R. (2000). Give them prizes, and they will come: Contingency management for treatment of alcohol dependence. *Journal of Consulting and Clinical Psychology*, 68, 250–257.

Petry, N. M., Martin, B., & Simcic, F. (2005). Prize reinforcement contingency management for cocaine dependence: Integration with group therapy in a methadone clinic. *Journal of Consulting and Clinical Psychology*, 73, 354–359.

Petry, N. M., Pierce, J., Stitzer, M. L., Blaine, J., Roll, J. M., et al. (2005). Prize-based incentives improve outcomes of stimulant abusers in outpatient psychosocial treatment programs: A National Drug Abuse Treatment Clinical Trials Network Study. *Archives of General Psychiatry*, 62, 1148–1156.

Phillips, M., & McAloon, M. H. (1980). A sweat-patch test for alcohol consumption: Evaluation in continuous and episodic drinkers. *Alcoholism: Clinical and Experimental Research*, 4, 391–395.

Piasecki, T. M., & Baker, T. B. (2001). Any further progress in smoking cessation treatment? *Nicotine and Tobacco Research*, 3, 311–323.

Piatrowski, N. A., Tusel, D. J., Sees, K. L., Reilly, P. M., Banys, P., Meek, P., & Hall, S. M. (1999). Contingency contracting with monetary reinforcers for abstinence from multiple drugs in a methadone program. *Experimental and Clinical Psychopharmacology*, 7, 399–411.

Peirce, J. M., Petry, N. M., Stitzer, M. L., Blaine, J., Kellogg, S. H., Satterfield, F., et al. (2006). Effects of lower-cost incentives on stimulant abstinence in methadone maintenance treatment: A national Drug Abuse Clinical Trials Network multi-site study. *Archives of General Psychiatry*, 63, 201–208.

Poole, A. D., Sanson-Fisher, G. A., & German, G. A. (1981). The rapid smoking technique: therapeutic effectiveness. *Behaviour Research & Therapy*, 19, 389–397.

Preston, K. L., Silverman, K., Higgins, S. T., Brooner, R. K., Montoya, I., Schuster, C. R., & Cone, E. J. (1998). Cocaine use early in treatment predicts outcome in a behavioral treatment program. *Journal of Consulting and Clinical Psychology*, 66, 691–696.

Preston, K. L., Umbricht, A., & Epstein, D. H. (2002). Abstinence reinforcement maintenance contingency and one-year follow-up. *Drug and Alcohol Dependence*, 67, 125–137.

Preston, K. L., Umbricht, A., & Epstein, D. H. (2000). Methadone dose increase and abstinence reinforcement for treatment of continued heroin use in methadone maintenance patients. *Archives of General Psychiatry, 57*, 395–404.

Preston, K. L., Umbricht, A., Wong, C. J., & Epstein, D. H. (2001). Shaping cocaine abstinence by successive approximation. *Journal of Consulting and Clinical Psychology, 69*, 643–654.

Preziosa, A., Grassi, A., Gaggioli, A., & Riva, G. (2009). Therapeutic applications of the mobile phone. *British Journal of Guidance and Counseling, 37*, 313–325.

Prochaska, J. O., Velicer, W. F., Rossi, J. S., Goldstein, M. G., Marcus, B. H., Rakowski, W., . . . & Rossi, S. R. (1994). Stages of change and decisional balance for twelve problem behaviors. *Health Psychology, 13*, 39–46.

Project MATCH Research Group. (1997). Matching alcoholism treatments to client heterogeneity: Project MATCH post-treatment drinking outcomes. *Journal of Studies on Alcohol, 58*, 7–29.

Project MATCH Research Group. (1998). Project MATCH: Matching alcoholism treatments to client heterogeneity: Treatment main effects and matching effects on drinking during treatment. *Journal of Studies on Alcohol, 59*, 631–639.

Rash, C. J., Olmstead, T. A., & Petry, N. M. (2009). Income does not affect response to contingency management treatments among community substance abuse treatment-seekers. *Drug and alcohol dependence, 104*, 249–253.

Rand, C. S., Stitzer, M. L., Bigelow, G. E., & Mead, A. M. (1989). The effects of contingent payment and frequent workplace monitoring on smoking abstinence. *Addictive Behaviors, 14*, 121–128.

Raw, M., & Russell, M. A. H. (1980). Rapid smoking, cue exposure and support in the modification of smoking. *Behaviour Research & Therapy, 18*, 363–372.

Rawson, R. A., Huber, A., McCann, M. J., Shoptaw, S., Farabee, D., Reiber, C., et al. (2002). A comparison of contingency management and cognitive-behavioral approaches during methadone maintenance for cocaine dependence. *Archives of General Psychiatry, 59*, 817–824.

Rawson, R. A., McCann, M. J., Flammino, F., Shoptaw, S., Miotto, K., Reiber, C., & Ling, W. (2006). A comparison of contingency management and cognitive-behavioral approaches for stimulant dependent individuals. *Addiction, 101*, 267–274.

Rawson, R. A., & Obert, J. L. (2002). Relapse prevention groups. In D. W. Brooks & H. I. Spitz (Eds.), *Group psychotherapy of substance abuse* (pp. 322–348). Washington, DC: American Psychological Association.

Rawson, R. A., Obert, J. L., McCann, M. J., Castro, F. G., & Ling, W. (1991). Cocaine abuse treatment: A review of current strategies. *Journal of Substance Abuse, 3*, 457–491.

Robichaud, C., Strickler, D., Bigelow, G., & Liebson, I. (1979). Disulfiram maintenance employee alcoholism treatment: A three-phase evaluation. *Behavioral Research and Therapy, 17*, 618–621.

Robles, E., Crone, C. C., Whiteside-Mansell, L., Conners, N. A., Bokony, P. A., Worley, L. L. M., & McMillan, D. E. (2005). Voucher-based incentives for cigarette smoking reduction in a women's residential treatment program. *Nicotine & Tobacco Research, 7*, 111–117.

Rohsenow, D. J., Martin, R. A., & Monti, P. M. (2005). Urge-specific and lifestyle coping strategies of cocaine abusers: Relationships to treatment outcomes. *Drug and Alcohol Dependence, 78*, 211–219.

Rohsenow, D. J., Monti, P. M., Binkoff, J. A., Liepman, M. R., Nirenberg, T. D., & Abrams, D. B. (1991). Patient-treatment matching for alcoholic men in communication skills versus cognitive-behavioral mood management training. *Addictive Behaviors, 16*, 63–69.

Rohsenow, D. J., Monti, P. M., Colby, S. M., & Martin, R. A. (2002). Brief interventions for smoking cessation in alcoholic smokers. *Alcoholism: Clinical and Experimental Research, 26*, 1950–1951.

Rohsenow, D. J., Monti, P. M., Martin, R. A., Colby, S. M., Myers, M. G., Gulliver, S. B., . . . & Abrams, D. B. (2004). Motivational enhancement and coping skills training for cocaine abusers: Effects on substance use outcomes. *Addiction, 99*, 862–874.

Rohsenow, D. J., Monti, P. M., Martin, R. A., Michalec, E., & Abrams, D. B. (2000). Brief coping skills treatment for cocaine abuse: 12-month substance use outcomes. *Journal of Consulting and Clinical Psychology, 68*, 515–520.

Rohsenow, D. J., Monti, P. M., Rubonis, A. V., Gulliver, S. B., Colby, S. M., Binkoff, J. A., & Abrams, D. B. (2001). Cue exposure with coping skills training and communication skills training for alcohol dependence: Six and twelve month outcomes. *Addiction, 96*, 1161–1174.

Rohsenow, D. J., Niaura, R. S., Childress, A. R., Abrams, D. B., & Monti, P. M. (1990). Cue reactivity in addictive behaviors: Theoretical and treatment implications. *International Journal of the Addictions, 25* (7A & 8A), 957–993.

Rohsenow, D. J., Sirota, A. D., Martin, R. A., & Monti, P. M. (2004). The Cocaine Effects Questionnaire for patient populations: Development and psychometric properties. *Addictive Behaviors, 29*, 537–553.

Roll, J. M., & Higgins, S. T. (2000). A within-subject comparison of three different schedules of reinforcement of drug abstinence using cigarette smoking as an exemplar. *Drug and Alcohol Dependence, 58*, 103–109.

Roll, J. M., Higgins, S. T., Budney, A. J., Bickel, W. K., & Badger, G. J. (1996). A comparison of cocaine-dependent cigarette smokers and non-smokers on demographic, drug use and other characteristics. *Drug and Alcohol Dependence. 40*, 195–201.

Roll, J. M., Higgins, S. T., Steingard, S., & McGinley, M. (1998). Use of monetary reinforcement to reduce the cigarette smoking of persons with schizophrenia: A feasibility study. *Experimental Clinical Psychopharmacology, 6*, 157–161.

Roman, P. M., & Blum, T. C. (1997). National treatment center study. Athens, GA: Institute of Behavioral Research, University of Georgia.

SAMHSA (1997, February). National admissions to substance abuse treatment services: The treatment episode data set (TEDS) 1992-1995 (Advance Report No. 12). Rockville, MD: Substance Abuse and Mental Health Services Administration, Office of Applied Studies.

Saitz, R., Helmuth, E. D., Aromaa, S. E., Guard, M. S., Belanger, M., & Rosenbloom, D. L. (2004). Web-based screening and brief intervention for the spectrum of alcohol problems. *Preventive Medicine, 39*, 969–975.

Sayette, M. A., Monti, P. M., Rohsenow, D. J., Gulliver, S. B., Colby, S. M., Sirota, A. D., . . . & Abrams, D. B. (1994). The effects of cue exposure on reaction time in male alcoholics. *Journal of Studies on Alcohol, 55*, 629–633.

Schepis, T. S., Duhig, A. M., Liss, T., McFetridge, A., Wu, R., Cavallo, D. A., . . . & Krishnan-Sarin, S. (2008). Contingency management for smoking cessation: Enhancing feasibility through use of immunoassay test strips measuring cotinine. *Nicotine & Tobacco Research*, *10*, 1495–1501.

Schmahl, D. P., Lichtenstein, E., & Harris, D. E. (1972). Successful treatment of habitual smokers with warm, smoky air and rapid smoking. *Journal of Consulting and Clinical Psychology*, *38*, 105–111.

Schwartz, B., Lauderdale, R. M., Montgomery, M. L., Burch, E. A., & Gallant, D. M. (1987). Immediate versus delayed feedback on urinalysis reports for methadone maintenance patients. *Addictive Behaviors*, *12*, 293–295.

Shadel, W. G., Niaura, R., Abrams, D. B., Goldstein, M. G., Rohsenow, D. J., Sirota, A. D., & Monti, P. M. (1998). Scripted imagery manipulations and smoking cue reactivity in a clinical sample of self-quitters. *Experimental and Clinical Psychopharmacology*, *6*, 179–186.

Shaner, A., Roberts, L. J., Eckman, T. A., Tucker, D. E., Tsuang, J. W., et al. (1997). Monetary reinforcement of abstinence from cocaine abmong mentally ill patients with cocaine dependence. *Psychiatric Services*, *48*, 807–810.

Shiffman, S. (1984). Coping with temptations to smoke. *Journal of Consulting and Clinical Psychology*, *52*, 261–267.

Shiffman, S., Kassel, J., Gwaltney, C., & McChargue, D. (2005). Relapse prevention for smoking. In G. A. Marlatt & D. M. Donovan (Eds.), *Relapse prevention: Maintenance strategies in the treatment of addictive behaviors* (2nd ed., pp. 92–129). New York: Guilford Press.

Shiffman, S., Read, L., Maltese, J., Rapkin, D., & Jarvik, M. E. (1985). Preventing relapse in ex-smokers: A self-management approach. In G. A. Marlatt & J. R. Gordon (Eds.), *Relapse prevention: Maintenance strategies in the treatment of addictive behaviors* (pp. 472–520). New York: Guilford Press.

Shoptaw, S., Rotheram-Fuller, E., Yang, X., Frosch, D., Nahom, D., Jarvik, M. E., . . . & Ling, W. (2002). Smoking cessation in methadone maintenance. *Addiction*, *97*, 1317–1328.

Sigmon, S. C., Lamb, R. J., & Dallery, J. (2008). Tobacco. In S. T. Higgins, K. Silverman, & S. H. Heil (Eds.), *Contingency management in substance abuse treatment*. New York: Guilford.

Silverman, K., Chutuape, M. A., Bigelow, G. A., & Stitzer, M. L. (1999). Voucher-based reinforcement of cocaine abstinence in treatment-resistant methadone patients: Effects of reinforcement magnitude. *Psychopharmacology*, *146*, 128–138.

Silverman, K., Higgins, S., Brooner, R., Montoya, I., Cone, E., Schuster, C., & Preston, K. (1996). Sustained cocaine abstinence in methadone maintenance patients through voucher-based reinforcement therapy. *Archives of General Psychiatry*, *53*, 409–415.

Silverman, K., Wong, C. J., Umbricht-Schneiter, A., Montoya, I. D., Schuster, C. R., & Preston, K. L. (1998). Broad beneficial effects of cocaine abstinence reinforcement among methadone patients. *Journal of Consulting and Clinical Psychology*, *66*, 811–824.

Sinha, R., Easton, C., Renee-Aubin, L., & Carroll, K. M. (2003). Engaging young probation-referred marijuana-abusing individuals in treatment: A pilot trial. *American Journal on Addictions*, *12*, 314–323.

Sitharthan, T., Sitharthan, G., Hough, M. J., & Kavanagh, D. J. (1997). Cue exposure in moderation drinking: A comparison with cognitive-behavior therapy, *Journal of Consulting and Clinical Psychology*, *65*, 878–882.

Smout, M. F., Longo, M., Harrison, S., Minniti, R., Wickes, W., & White, J. M. (2010). Psychosocial treatment for methamphetamine use disorders: A preliminary randomized controlled trial of cognitive behavior therapy and acceptance and commitment therapy. *Substance Abuse*, *31*, 98–107.

Stephens, R. S., Roffman, R. A., & Curtin, L. (2000). Comparison of extended versus brief treatments for marijuana use. *Journal of Consulting and Clinical Psychology*, *68*, 898–908.

Stephens, R. S., Roffman, R. A., & Simpson, E. E. (1994), Treating adult marijuana dependence: A test of the relapse prevention model. *Journal of Consulting and Clinical Psychology*, *62*, 92–99.

Sobell, L. C., & Sobell, M. B. (1986). Can we do without alcohol abusers' self-reports? *The Behavior Therapist*, *7*, 141–146.

Staiger, P. K., & White, J. M. (1991). Cue reactivity in alcohol abusers: Stimulus specificity and extinction of the responses. *Addictive Behaviors*, *16*, 211–221.

Stephens, R. S., Roffman, R. A., & Curtin, L. (2000). Comparison of extended versus brief treatments for marijuana use. *Journal of Consulting and Clinical Psychology*, *68*, 898–908.

Stevens, V. J., & Hollis, J. F. (1989). Preventing smoking relapse using an individually tailored skills-training technique. *Journal of Consulting and Clinical Psychology*, *57*, 420–424.

Stitzer, M. L., & Bigelow, G. E. (1982). Contingent reinforcement for reduced carbon monoxide levels in cigarette smokers. *Addictive Behaviors*, *7*, 403–412.

Stitzer, M. L., & Bigelow, G. E. (1983). Contingent payment for carbon monoxide reduction: Effects of pay amount. *Behavior Therapy*, *14*, 647–656.

Stitzer, M. L., & Bigelow, G. E. (1985). Contingent reinforcement for reduced breath carbon monoxide levels: Target-specific effects on cigarette smoking. *Addictive Behaviors*, *10*, 345–349.

Stitzer, M. L., & Bigelow, G. E. (1986). Contingent payment procedures for smoking reduction and cessation. *Journal of Applied Behavior Analysis*, *19*, 197–202.

Stitzer, M. L., & Bigelow, G. E. (1984). Contingent reinforcement for carbon monoxide reduction: Within subject effects of pay amount. *Journal of Applied Behavior Analysis.* *17*, 477–483.

Stitzer, M. L., Iguchi, M. Y., & Felch, L. J. (1992). Contingent take-home incentive: Effects on drug use of methadone maintenance patients. *Journal of Consulting and Clinical Psychology*, *60*, 927–934.

Stitzer, M., & Petry, N. (2006). Contingency management for treatment of substance use. *Annual Review of Clinical Psychology*, *2*, 411–434.

Stitzer, M. L., Rand, C. S., Bigelow, G. E., & Mead, A. M. (1986). Contingent payment procedures for smoking reduction and cessation. *Journal of Applied Behavioral Analysis*, *19*, 197–202.

Swift, R. M. (1993). Transdermal measurement of alcohol consumption. *Addiction*, *88*, 1037–1039.

Tidey, J. W., O'Neill, S. C., & Higgins, S. T. (2002). Contingent monetary reinforcement of smoking reductions, with and without transdermal nicotine, in outpatients with schizophrenia. *Experimental and Clinical Psychopharmacology*, *10*, 241–247.

Tiffany, S. T. (1990). A cognitive model of drug urges and drug-use behavior: Role of automatic and nonautomatic processes, *Psychological Review*, *97*, 147–168.

Tiffany, S. T., Martin, E. M., & Baker, T. B. (1986). Treatments for cigarette smoking: An evaluation of the contributions of aversion and counseling procedures. *Behaviour Research & Therapy, 24*, 437–452.

Tracy, K., Babuscio, T., Nich, C., Kiluk, B., Carroll, K. M., Petry, N. M., & Rounsaville, B. J. (2007). Contingency management to reduce substance use in individuals who are homeless with co-occurring psychiatric disorders. *The American Journal of Drug and Alcohol Abuse, 33*, 253–258.

United States Department of Health and Human Services (USDHHS). (2000). *Treating tobacco use and dependence: Clinical practice guideline.* Washington, DC: Public Health Service, USDHHS.

Vogler, R. E., Lunde, S. E., & Martin, P. L. (1971). Electrical aversion conditioning with chronic alcoholics: Follow-up and suggestions for research. *Journal of Consulting and Clinical Psychology, 36*, 450.

Westman, E. C., Behm, F. M., Simel, D. L., & Rose, J. E. (1997). Smoking behavior on the first day of a quit attempt predicts long-term abstinence. *Archives of Internal Medicine, 157*, 335–340.

Wells, E. A., Peterson, P. L., Gainey, R. R., Hawkins, D. J., & Catalano, R. F. (1994). Outpatient treatment for cocaine abuse: A controlled comparison of relapse prevention and Twelve-Step approaches. *American Journal of Drug and Alcohol Abuse, 20*, 1–17.

Wilson, K. G., Hayes, S. C., & Byrd, M. (2000). Exploring compatibilities between acceptance and commitment therapy and 12-Step treatment for substance abuse. *Journal of Rational-Emotive and Cognitive-Behavior Therapy, 18*, 209–234.

Wittchen, H. U., Hoch, E., Klotsche, J., & Muehlig, S. (2011). Smoking cessation in primary care: A randomized controlled trial of bupropione, nicotine replacements, CBT and a minimal intervention. *International Journal of Methods in Psychiatric Research, 20*, 28–39.

Wong, C. J., Kolodner, K., Fingerhood, M., Bigelow, G. E., & Silverman, K. (2005). *A therapeutic workplace for homeless alcohol-dependent individuals.* Paper presented at the College on Problems of Drug Dependence, Orlando, FL.

Further Readings

Abrams, D. B., Niaura, R. S., Brown, R. A., Emmons, K. M., Goldstein, M. G., & Monti, P. M. (2003). *The tobacco dependence treatment handbook: A guide to best practices.* New York: Guilford.

Beck, A. T., Wright, F. D., Newman, C. F., & Liese, B. S. (1993). *Cognitive therapy of substance abuse.* New York: Guilford.

Carroll, K. M. (1998). A cognitive-behavioral approach: Treating cocaine addiction. National Institute on Drug Abuse.

Higgins, S. T., Silverman, K., & Heil, S. H. (2008). *Contingency management in substance abuse treatment.* New York: Guilford.

Monti, P. M., Kadden, R., Rohsenow, D. J., Cooney, N., & Abrams, D. B. (2002). *Treating alcohol dependence: A coping skills training guide* (2nd ed.). New York: Guilford Press.

Petry, N. M. (2000). A comprehensive guide to the application of contingency management procedures in general clinic settings. *Drug and Alcohol Dependence, 58*, 9–25.

Marital and Family Approaches

Keith Klostermann

Abstract

Traditionally, alcohol use disorders and other substance use disorders have been viewed by the majority of treatment providers and researchers, as well as by the public at large, as problems of the "individual" that were most effectively treated by focusing on the diagnosed individual. More recently, this individual-focused conceptualization has slowly given way to a greater awareness of family members' crucial roles in the etiology, maintenance, and long-term course of substance use and addictive behavior. As a result, clinicians and researchers alike have placed renewed emphasis on understanding substance misuse from a systemic perspective and on exploring how partner- and family-involved interventions may be used to address individuals' substance abuse. Available evidence reveals that marital and family therapy approaches are among the most efficacious available in terms of prevention, initiating change, and treating substance use disorders.

Key Words: family, treatment, alcoholism, drug abuse, substance abuse

Historically, substance use disorders have been considered personal problems, perhaps best captured in the long-held and often stated axiom among treatment providers, "Alcoholism and drug abuse are individual problems best treated on an individual basis." This viewpoint has held sway in the substance abuse treatment community for much of the past half-century (e.g., Jellinek, 1960). More recently, however, staunch adherence to this individual-focused conceptualization of alcoholism and drug abuse has slowly given way to a greater acceptance and acknowledgment of the family's critical role in the development and maintenance of drug and alcohol abuse. As a result, an increasing number of treatment providers and the programs in which they work are intervening with the family as a way to reduce or eliminate substance abuse by one or more of its members.

During the past three decades, the results of numerous clinical studies have demonstrated the efficacy of family-based treatment approaches for substance use disorders. Meta-analytic reviews of randomized clinical trials have concluded that partner- and family-involved treatments produce better outcomes across several domains of functioning (e.g., reduced substance use, improved marital and family functioning) compared to individual-based interventions that focus exclusively on the substance-abusing client (e.g., Stanton & Shadish, 1997). In response to these findings, the Joint Commission on Accreditation of Health Care Organizations (JCAHO) standards for accrediting substance abuse treatment programs in the United States now requires that an adult family member who lives with an identified substance-abusing patient be included, at minimum, in the initial assessment of the treatment process (Brown, O'Farrell, Maisto, Boies, & Suchinski, 1997).

Enthusiasm for understanding the role that family members may play in the development, maintenance, and treatment of alcoholism and drug abuse has not been limited to researchers or even the broader professional community; the sheer volume of texts that have appeared on the topics of co-dependency, adult children of alcoholics, addictive personality, enabling, and so forth is voluminous. For example, an Internet search of a large online book retailer revealed that more than 400 books were available presently for purchase on the topic of co-dependency alone. Moreover, self-help support groups for family members of alcoholics and drugs abusers (e.g., Al-Anon) are present in virtually every community. Because relationship problems and substance use disorders so frequently co-occur, it would be very difficult to find clinicians who specialize in the treatment of substance use disorders or relationship problems who have not had to address both sets of issues concurrently (either with the client individually or in the context of the client's larger family system).

The purpose of this chapter is to (a) discuss how substance abuse affects the family and how providers can draw on fundamental principles of marital and family therapy to improve interactions among family members; (b) present the models, techniques, and principles of marital and family therapy that have been used with substance-abusing clients, their partners, and extended family members; (c) discuss various partner- and family-involved approaches for substance use that focus on prevention, initiation of change, and active treatment; and (d) explore possible future directions with respect to partner- and family-involved therapies with substance-abusing clients.

Substance Use and Family Functioning: Practical and Conceptual Considerations
Definitions: Marriage and Family

Throughout history, there has been a lack of consensus regarding the definition of *family* or *marriage*. Given that different societal norms and attitudes influence definitions of such cultural constructions, coupled with the fact that cultures and beliefs change over time, the definition of what is meant by marriage and family continues to evolve. Yet, in an effort to operationalize these terms for the purposes of identifying an "intervention unit," it seems possible to identify qualities and characteristics of these institutions that are somewhat consistent under a variety of circumstances and conditions. In the most inclusive sense, family or marriage (or at least an intimate relationship—marriage carries legal elements as well as sociocultural ones) implies an enduring involvement on an emotional level with other people. Thus, family may be defined according to the individual's closest emotional connections, of which marriage is a subset. In other words, an individual constructs his or her family or his or her partner(s), which is not to be confused,

of course, with those persons the individual "likes." This interpretation moves beyond the pure genetic, biological, or legal definitions by also including emotional and behavioral connections defined by the individual who identifies "partner" and "family." Typically, providers consider a romantic partner as one with whom the client is married or cohabiting for at least 1 year. Moreover, broader family systems are often partially defined by those with whom the client current lives (e.g., married partner, children) or lived with while growing up (e.g., family of origin members, such as parents and siblings). Consequently, the family unit can take many different forms, including, but not limited to (a) a traditional nuclear family in which members are cohabiting in the household (in which either one or both parents are working); (b) a household or family headed by a single parent; (c) a "blended" family resulting from divorce, separation, or remarriage; (d) a same-sex couple with or without custodial children; (e) a multigenerational household including grandparents, parents, and children; or even (e) long-term cohabiting partners who are not romantically linked but define themselves as a family (McCrady, 2006). Depending on the presenting needs of the client, any one of these family constellations can ultimately become the unit of intervention.

Prevalence of Substance Use Disorders and Comorbidity with Family Problems

Previous studies support the assertion that substance abuse and family problems very often coexist. For example, O'Farrell and Birchler (1987) found that levels of relationship distress among alcoholic and drug-abusing dyads are typically high, and these couples are more likely to divorce (Lebow, 2005) compared to the general population. Moreover, relationship dysfunction has been found to be predictive of worse prognosis in alcohol and drug abuse treatment (Vanicelli, Gingerich, & Ryback, 1983), and poor response to substance abuse treatment seems to be predictive of ongoing marital difficulty (e.g., Billings & Moos, 1983; Collins, Ellickson, & Klein, 2007).

Unfortunately, as the individual's substance problem progresses, he or she may become increasingly isolated from other family members, which may make it difficult to engage them later in the treatment process (Halford & Osgarby, 1993). Relatedly, other family members may experience a wide array of emotions (e.g., anger, guilt, fear, embarrassment) as a result of the patient's drinking or drug use and, consequently, reduce or eliminate contact altogether with the substance-abusing person (Collins et al., 2007). The therapeutic implications of this type of isolation is mixed; while some family approaches might consider this type of avoidance to be appropriate and therapeutic, other models might view this behavior as corrosive.

The Interplay Between Substance Use and Marital/Family Maladjustment

The interconnection between substance use and relationship distress appears to be marked by what can be best described as "reciprocal causality." Alcoholism and drug abuse by a family member appear to contribute causally to the many relationship problems observed in these families. Families characterized by substance abuse may experience high levels of relationship dissatisfaction, instability, conflict, sexual dissatisfaction, or psychological distress. A number of studies have also found that relationship dysfunction is strongly linked to substance use and appears to be a major contributing factor to relapse among alcoholics and drug abusers after treatment (e.g., Epstein & McCrady, 1998; Halford & Osgarby, 1993; Lemke, Brennan, & Schutte, 2007). Thus, the link between substance use and relationship problems is not unidirectional, with one consistently causing the other; rather, each can serve as a precursor to the other, creating a "vicious cycle" from which couples that include a partner who abuses drugs or alcohol often have difficulty escaping.

There are several family environmental antecedent conditions and reinforcing consequences of substance use. In particular, marital and family problems (e.g., poor communication and problem-solving, arguing, financial stressors) often serve as precursors to excessive drinking or drug use (Klostermann, 2006). Unfortunately, the resulting family response may have an unintended effect and inadvertently facilitate continued drinking or drug use once these problematic behaviors have developed. For example, substance abuse often provides more subtle adaptive consequences for the family members, such as eliciting the expression of emotion and affection (e.g., caretaking when a parent or partner is suffering from a hangover). Moreover, even when recovery from the alcohol or drug problem has begun, marital and family conflicts can, and very often do, precipitate relapses (Halford & Osgarby, 1996; Rotunda, West, & O'Farrell, 2004).

Although the misuse of alcohol and other psychoactive substances by adults often has serious physical, emotional, behavioral, and economic consequences, the ancillary short- and long-term negative effects on those who live with these adults are often no less destructive or traumatic. In general, children who live with parents who abuse alcohol and other drugs often are victimized by the deleterious environments these caregivers frequently create. Stress and negative affect, which are comparatively high in families with an alcoholic family member, are associated with alcohol use in adolescents (Chassin, Curran, Hussong, & Colder, 1996). Thus, it appears that alcohol-abusing parents are less likely than nonalcoholic parents to monitor what their children are doing, which, in turn, may lead to unhealthy associations of their adolescent children with substance-using peers (Connors, Donovan, & DiClemente, 2001).

The strong interrelationship between substance use and family interaction suggests interventions that treat the dyadic or larger family systems (versus an exclusive focus on the substance-abusing patient) hold much promise for being effective. Although marital and family therapy approaches take many different forms, they share two overarching objectives that evolve from a recognition of the nature and degree of interrelationship between substance use and family member interaction: (a) harness the power of the family and/or dyadic system to positively support the patient's efforts to eliminate abusive drinking and drug use and, relatedly, (b) alter dyadic and family interaction patterns to promote an environment in the home that is conducive to long-term stable abstinence for the substance-abusing individual.

Foundational Frameworks of Partner- and Family-Involved Approaches for Alcoholism and Drug Abuse

Given the finding that marital and family treatments have been shown to be clinically effective for a variety of health problems (Snyder & Whisman, 2003), many different marital and family therapy approaches have been developed (or at least modified) for use with substance-abusing patients including strategic family therapy, structural family therapy, cognitive behavioral family therapy, behavioral couples therapy, and solution-focused family therapy. Of these, three theoretical perspectives have come to dominate family-based conceptualizations and are thus viewed as the foundation for the family-based treatment strategies most often used with substance-abusing clients: (1) family disease approach, (2) family systems perspective, and

(3) behavioral models (Gondoli & Jacob, 1990). Each of these frameworks is reviewed in more detail here, with an emphasis on some of the hallmark therapy techniques identified with each approach.

Family Disease Approach

The best known and most widely used paradigm is the *family disease approach*. From this vantage, alcoholism and other drug abuse are viewed as an illness of the entire family, suffered not only by the substance user, but also by the other family members. Consequently, as the term implies, alcoholism and drug abuse are thought of or viewed as a "family disease," one that affects all (or nearly all) family members. In particular, family members of substance users are viewed as suffering from the disease of "co-dependence," which describes the process underlying the various problems observed in the families of individuals who abuse psychoactive substances. Schaef (1986) argues that co-dependence is a disease that parallels the addiction disease process and is marked by characteristic family symptoms such as external referencing, caretaking, self-centeredness, control issues, dishonesty, frozen feelings, perfectionism, and fear. The cornerstone of co-dependency theory is *enabling*, which, as the term implies, is described as any set of behaviors that perpetuates the psychoactive substance use (Koffinke, 1991) and may include activities such as making it easier for the alcoholic or drug abuser to engage in substance use or shielding the substance user from the negative consequences often resulting from substance misuse. However, there is much debate about the use of this term, with definitions ranging from its use as a shorthand label for affected family members to it being perceived as a personality disorder that some have argued should be included in the American Psychiatric Association's *Diagnostic and Statistical Manual* (Kinney, 2009).

Given that the family disease model argues that the entire family unit is believed to be sick, the solution is for each family member to recognize that he or she has a disease, detach from the substance user, and engage in his or her own program of recovery (e.g., Al-Anon, Al-Ateen, or Adult Children of Alcoholics groups). Family members are taught that there is nothing they can do to help the substance user to stop using other than to cease enabling and to detach and focus on reducing their own emotional distress and improving coping behaviors. However, in a recent review of studies of alcoholism treatments conducted between 1966 and 2005,

the Cochrane Library concluded, "No experimental studies unequivocally demonstrated the effectiveness of AA [Alcoholics Anonymous] or TSF [12-step facilitation] approaches for reducing alcohol dependence or problems" (Johnson, 2010, p. B3). Given AA's emphasis on anonymity, researchers have had a difficult time determining the effectiveness of these types of programs. Furthermore, although AA has revealed its success rates at times, the majority of data have come from people who have experienced success in the program and still maintain ties to the organization, rather than from representative samples; thus, these results must be considered within this context, which may have implications for the generalizability of the findings.

Family Systems Approach

The family systems model views the misuse of alcohol or other drugs as a major organizing principle for patterns of interactional behavior within the family system. A reciprocal relationship exists between family functioning and substance use, with an individual's drug and alcohol use being best understood in the context of the entire family's functioning. According to family systems theory, substance abuse in either adults or adolescents often evolves during periods in which the individual family member is having difficulty addressing an important developmental issue (e.g., leaving the home) or when the family is facing a significant crisis (e.g., job loss, marital discord). During these periods, substance abuse can serve to (a) distract family members from their central problem or (b) slow down or stop a transition to a different developmental stage that is being resisted by the family as a whole or by one of its members (Stanton, Todd et al., 1982).

From the family systems perspective, substance use represents an unhealthy attempt to manage difficulties, one that, over time, become homeostatic and regulates family transactions. Because the substance use serves an important function, the therapist seeks to understand its role in the family and explain how the behavior has come about and the purpose it serves. Thus, the primary objective of treatment involves restructuring the interaction patterns associated with the substance use, thereby making the drinking or drug use unnecessary in maintaining more healthy systemic functioning.

Several studies have been conducted to evaluate different forms of family systems therapy including outpatient marital therapy (Corder, Corder,

& Laidlaw, 1972; Zweben, Perlman, & Li, 1988), conjoint hospitalization (McCrady, Paolino, Longabaugh, & Rosi, 1979), and multicouple group therapy (Cadogan, 1973). Results of these studies consistently revealed family systems treatment yielded higher rates of abstinence compared to individual treatment or no treatment at all. However, these improvements did not hold up over time because the average effect size for the follow-up periods (i.e., 18 months or 4 years) was nonsignificant (Edwards & Steinglass, 1995).

Behavioral Approach

Behavioral family therapy models are heavily influenced by operant and social learning theories in their conceptualization of the substance user within the family context. Simply stated, behavioral approaches assume that family interactions serve to reinforce alcohol- and drug-using behavior. From this vantage, substance-using behavior is learned in the context of social interactions (e.g., observing peers, parents, role models in the media) and reinforced by contingencies in the individual's environment. Thus, from a behavioral perspective, substance use is maintained, in part, from the antecedents and consequences that are operating in the family environment. Three general reinforcement patterns are typically observed in substance-abusing families: (a) reinforcement for substance using behavior in the form of attention or caretaking, (b) shielding the substance user from experiencing negative consequences related to his or her drinking or drug use, and (c) punishing drinking behavior (e.g., McCrady, 1986).

Consistent with the tenets of operant and social learning approaches, treatment emphasizes contingency management designed to reward sobriety, reduce negative reinforcement of drinking or drug use, and increase prosocial behaviors that may be incompatible with substance use. More specifically, the substance user and involved family members are taught techniques to increase positive interactions, improve problem solving, and enhance communication skills. Behaviorists believe that the use of these newly developed skills serves to reduce the likelihood of continued drinking or drug use by the substance-using family member.

A number of studies have been conducted to assess the efficacy and effectiveness of family-involved behavioral treatment. Hedberg and Campbell (1974) examined four types of behavioral treatment. This particular investigation is novel in that one study condition included the identified patient's entire nuclear family, and subjects were allowed to choose their preferred treatment goal (i.e., abstinence or controlled drinking). In addition, Azrin and colleagues (1982) conducted a series of studies examining the effectiveness of a community reinforcement approach (CRA) in increasing the quality, frequency, and variety of social reinforcers as a way of reducing alcohol-abusing behaviors. McCrady, Noel, and Adams (1986) compared the effectiveness of behavioral treatments to various types of couples treatments in terms of drinking behavior, marital satisfaction, and psychosocial functioning. O'Farrell, Cutter, and Floyd (1985) compared behavioral marital therapy to systemic marital therapy and standard individual treatment in terms of alcohol use and relationship satisfaction. Taken as whole, the results of these investigations are mixed. More specifically, findings from the Hedberg and O'Farrell et al. investigations revealed that behavioral family treatment was no more effective on the outcomes of interest than was individual treatment. Moreover, the McCrady et al. study did not find significant differences in spouse-involved treatments. However, CRA consistently outperformed traditional individual-based treatment.

Partner- and Family-Involved Therapies for Substance Abuse: Intervention Approaches

As noted previously, an extensive body of research evidence supports the effectiveness of partner- and family-involved interventions to treat alcoholism and drug abuse. Indeed, a large number of intervention approaches that integrate treatment for substance abuse and the family have been discussed in the empirical and clinical literatures including (a) structural/strategic family therapy, (b) multidimensional family therapy, (c) multiple family therapy, (d) multisystemic/multidimensional family therapy, (e) behavioral and cognitive behavioral family therapy (f) network therapy, (g) Bowen family systems therapy, and (h) solution-focused brief therapy. Whereas in some cases some of these models may be perceived as minor variants of other more established approaches, many would argue that these nuanced differences strongly influence treatment response and outcomes for a given client and his or her family.

Regardless of the family-involved model under consideration, it is helpful to understand the overarching therapeutic goals from the stance of levels of recovery (e.g., Heath & Stanton, 1998), which are:

- *Attainment of sobriety.* The dyad- or family system has elements and components that are dysfunctional, but healthy change is possible.
- *Adjustment to sobriety.* The family system is reorganized and incorporates new healthful behaviors by the substance-abusing client and other family members.
- *Long-term maintenance.* The family system supports and maintains a healthy lifestyle conducive to sobriety that does not incorporate drinking or drug use.

For reasons that are more pragmatic than conceptual or theoretical, family-involved therapeutic interventions for substance use disorders have been thought of as either *marital approaches* (that include intimate partners as part of the intervention) or *family approaches* (that address larger family systems that may or may not include the dyadic system). Of course, in practice and research, this distinction often becomes blurry (e.g., some partner-involved therapies for substance abuse have also incorporated substantial elements of parent training to improve children's adjustment; see Kelley et al., 2010), but it has some utility in terms of organizing any discussion of various intervention methods. As an example, multisystemic therapy is a comprehensive family treatment approach that focuses not only on adolescents, but also on their homes and families, teachers and schools, neighborhoods, and friends.

Marital Approaches

A marital approach that has received extensive empirical support for the treatment of alcoholism and substance abuse is Behavioral Couples Therapy (BCT; Emmelkamp & Vedel, 2006), which has also been referred to as Behavioral Marital Therapy and Learning Sobriety Together. During the past three decades, couples therapy for substance abuse has received extensive empirical scrutiny, with most research focusing on BCT. In general, these studies have compared BCT to some form of traditional individual-based treatment for substance abuse (e.g., coping skills therapy, TSF). Findings from these studies have consistently found that participants who received BCT (a) experienced higher rates of abstinence and fewer drug- or alcohol-related problems (e.g., Epstein, McCrady, & Morgan, 2007; Walitzer & Derman, 2004), (b) have happier relationships (Emmelkamp & Vedel, 2006),

and (c) experienced a lower risk of relationship dissolution (e.g., separation, divorce; see Powers, Vedel, & Emmelkamp, 2008) compared to those in the individual treatment condition.

PRIMARY BCT TREATMENT ELEMENTS

In the early stages of treatment, therapists attempt to shift the focus from negative feelings and interactions about past and possible future substance use to positive behavioral exchanges between partners. In later sessions, emphasis is placed on communication skills training, problem-solving strategies, negotiating behavior change agreements, and continuing recovery strategies.

When using BCT as part of a general intervention package, a therapist treats the substance-abusing patient and his or her intimate partner with the goal of building support for abstinence from within the dyadic system. With the help of the therapist, the partners develop a "recovery contract" (also referred to as a "sobriety contract") in which the couple agrees to engage in a daily "sobriety trust discussion." In this brief exchange, the substance-abusing partner states his or her intent not to drink or use drugs that day. In turn, the partner verbally expresses positive support for the patient's efforts to remain sober. For substance-abusing patients who are medically cleared and willing, daily ingestion of medications designed to support abstinence (e.g., naltrexone, Antabuse), witnessed and verbally reinforced by the patient's partner, may also be included as part of the sobriety trust discussion. The patient's partner tracks each time the sobriety trust discussion is completed on a daily calendar provided by the therapist and is asked to bring it to each session. Ultimately, the purpose of this ritual is to begin the process of restoring trust between partners. In particular, by the time many couples decide to enter couples treatment, the relationship may be characterized by a lack of trust as a result of the client's lies, deceit, and manipulation regarding the extent of alcohol or drug use.

Importantly, as a condition of the recovery contract, both partners agree not to discuss past drinking or drug use or fears of future substance use when at home (i.e., between scheduled couple therapy sessions) over the course of couples treatment. Instead, partners are asked to reserve such potentially emotionally charged discussions for their weekly couple therapy sessions, which can then be monitored and, if needed, mediated by the therapist. Many contracts also include specific provisions for sober support activities including partners' regular attendance at self-help meetings (e.g., AA, Al-Anon) and community activities (e.g., church groups), which are also marked on a calendar provided during the course of treatment.

At the start of a typical BCT session, the therapist reviews the recovery calendar to ascertain overall compliance with the different aspects of the contract. The calendar provides an ongoing record of progress that is reviewed by the therapist and clients at each session and provides a visual (and temporal) record of problems with adherence to home practice assignments that can be addressed by the therapist and couple. For couples that have difficulty maintaining the calendar, the therapist works with the partners to identify potential barriers, as well as strategies that may be implemented to overcome any obstacles. In an effort to ensure that between-session activities are performed correctly, at each session the therapist asks the couple to perform the previously assigned tasks and abstinence trust discussion and provides corrective feedback as needed. This in-session modeling is critical in that if couples are incorrectly performing the assigned tasks (e.g., including a negative component to the abstinence trust discussion), it may diminish one or both partners' enthusiasm or willingness to perform the assigned tasks and reduce the likelihood of weekly progress and, ultimately, goal attainment.

BCT METHODS USED TO ENHANCE RELATIONSHIP FUNCTIONING

In addition to eliminating substance use, BCT also seeks to concurrently improve relationship functioning through the use of standard couple-based behavioral assignments that are aimed at increasing positive feelings, increasing the number of shared activities, and improving communication; these relationship factors are viewed as conducive to sobriety. In the "catch your partner doing something nice" (Turner, 1972) activity, each partner is asked to notice and acknowledge one pleasing behavior performed by the other each day. The "caring day" assignment (e.g., Liberman, Wheeler, deVisser, Kuehnel, & Kuehnel, 1980) asks each partner to surprise their significant other with a day of special things that show care for their partner (a specific activity the partner will enjoy and not vice versa). Planning and engaging in mutually agreed-upon "shared rewarding activities" (e.g., O'Farrell & Cutter, 1984) is believed to be important because years of alcohol and drug abuse may have resulted in the cessation of conjoint shared, pleasing activities. Thus, this activity must involve both partners, either as a dyad or with their children

or other adults, and can be performed at or away from home. Teaching communication skills (e.g., Gottman, Notarius, Gonso, & Markman, 1976) such as paraphrasing, empathizing, and validating, can help the substance-abusing patient and his or her partner better address stressors in the relationship and in their lives as they arise, which also is viewed as reducing the risk of relapses.

COUPLES-BASED RELAPSE PREVENTION AND PLANNING

Relapse prevention occurs during the final stages of BCT. More specifically, the partners are asked to develop a written plan (i.e., continuing recovery plan) designed to promote stable abstinence (e.g., continuation of a daily abstinence trust discussion, attending self-help support meetings) and list contingency plans in the event a relapse occurs (e.g., contacting the therapist, re-engaging in self-help support meetings, contacting a sponsor; Klostermann & Fals-Stewart, 2008). A key element for many couples in creating the continuing recovery plan is the negotiation of the posttreatment duration of the skills and techniques learned during treatment. Couples often have difficulty agreeing on a timeframe for the cessation of the contract activities. Upon completion of BCT, the substance-abusing partner typically wants a life that does not involve structured exercises, whereas the non-substance-abusing partner is often apprehensive and mistrustful about progress made in treatment (i.e., relationship improvement, abstinence) and thus advocates for continued involvement with certain activities (e.g., self-help meeting attendance, abstinence trust discussions). As an example, the substance-abusing partner may express a desire to forgo the daily abstinence trust discussion since treatment is over and he or she has been sober and feels confident about the progress made in treatment. In this situation, partners develop a mutually agreed-to, long-term gradual reduction of the frequency of the activity until it is eliminated (e.g., for the first month, the couple performs the daily abstinence trust discussion, as was done during active treatment; for the second month, the abstinence trust discussion is performed three times per week; for the third month, the abstinence trust discussion is performed once per week, and so forth). If problems arise with any of the planned transitions, partners are encouraged to contact their BCT counselor to discuss the best way to proceed.

SESSION STRUCTURE AND TREATMENT DURATION

BCT sessions tend to be moderately to highly structured, consisting of three main components: (1) review/check-in on previous weeks substance use (if any), relationship issues, and compliance with home practice assigned the previous week; (2) introduction of new material; and (3) assignment of home practice. For example, a typical BCT session begins with an update on any drinking or drug use that has occurred since the prior session. Compliance with different aspects of the recovery contract is reviewed, and any difficulties completing the agreed-upon tasks are discussed and addressed. Relationship or other difficulties that may have arisen during the past week are then addressed during the session, with the goal being problem resolution. The session then transitions to a review of any homework from the previous session. Next, new material is introduced and modeled by the therapist; clients are then asked to rehearse these skills in session because they will be assigned as home practice between sessions. At the end of each session, partners are given specific homework assignments to complete before the next scheduled session.

Traditionally, the substance-abusing patient and his or her partner are seen together in BCT, typically for 15–20 outpatient couple sessions over the course of 5–6 months. Appropriate candidates for BCT are (a) couples in which partners are married or cohabiting for at least 1 year, (b) couples in which neither partner has a co-occurring psychiatric condition that may significantly interfere with participation in BCT (e.g., schizophrenia, psychosis), and (c) dyads in which only one member of the couple has a current problem with alcoholism or drug abuse. In those cases in which the identified patient is unwilling to engage in treatment, unilateral family therapy (UFT) may be an effective alternative. In UFT, the therapist works exclusively with the non-substance-using partner in helping to engage the identified client in treatment (Edwards & Steinglass, 1995). This approach is described in detail later in this chapter.

During the past 3 decades, couples therapy for substance abuse has received extensive empirical scrutiny, with most research focusing on BCT. In general, these studies have compared BCT to some form of traditional individual-based treatment for substance abuse (e.g., coping skills therapy, TSF). Findings from these studies have been consistent; compared to those who receive individual treatment, those participants assigned to receive BCT (a) experience higher rates of abstinence and fewer drug- or alcohol-related problems (e.g., Epstein et al., 2007; Walitzer & Dermen, 2004), (b) have happier relationships (Emmelkamp & Vedel, 2006), and (c) experience a lower risk of relationship dissolution (e.g., separation, divorce; see Powers et al., 2008).

Family Approaches

As previously noted, a wide array of family-involved approaches to treat substance abuse have been developed for use with a variety of presenting problems. Given the multiple forms of family-based approaches to address substance abuse coupled with the very large range of outcomes that have been of interest to both treatment providers and investigators, it is well beyond the scope of this chapter to discuss them all. Yet it is nonetheless instructive and important to provide an overview of the family therapy literature for the treatment of alcoholism and drug abuse in terms of overarching areas of emphasis. For the purpose of this overview, the discussion is organized in terms of three general areas: (a) prevention, (b) initiating change, and (c) treatment.

PREVENTION

There are several antecedents to the initiation of drug use and problematic drinking, many of which relate to risk or protective factors in the family. Given that protection is a primary function of a family unit, it is very often the first and most important line of defense in terms of helping the individual develop the psychological infrastructures (e.g., self-esteem) and resilience to reduce or prevent vulnerability to substance abuse. Unfortunately, many unhealthy families create an environment conducive to the development of substance use disorders. As such, family therapy is often used to strengthen the entire system in an effort to reduce familial risk factors and foster protective ones.

Most family-oriented prevention/intervention systems focus on strengthening the family's role in the positive socialization of children; the overarching goal of these programs is the prevention of future alcohol or drug abuse in children who are not currently abusers (DeMarsh & Kumpfer, 1985). Family prevention approaches represent a variety of interventions including parent–child interactions, communication and affective skill building, child management principles, and parent training. Investigations conducted over the past 20 years (e.g., Dishion & Kavanaugh, 2005; Dishion, Reid, & Patterson, 1988) reveal that parent and peer training interventions are viable methods for preventing premature drug use.

Controlled studies for family prevention/intervention models that have had positive results include the Focus on Families Project (Catalano et al., 1992), Preparing for the Drug-Free Years (Hawkins et al., 1988), Family Effectiveness Training (Szapocznik et al., 1989), and the Strengthening Families Program (Kumpfer & Alvarado, 2003). The targeted children for these models range in age from 3 to 14 years of age.

INITIATING CHANGE

Specific partner- and family-involved treatments have been developed to help substance-using individuals recognize problem behavior and seek help to change. The Community Reinforcement Training (CRT) approach is based on an assumption that changes in reinforcement and contingencies can be used to change an alcohol abuser's behavior (e.g., Sisson & Azrin, 1993). Along these lines, Community Reinforcement and Family Training (CRAFT; Smith & Meyers, 2009) is an approach to teach family members (e.g., spouses of substance abusers) how to (a) encourage the substance abuser to evaluate whether or not drinking or drug use is problematic, (b) support sobriety, (c) seek out and encourage treatment for substance abuse, and (d) engage in treatment in a way that is most beneficial. A more direct approach, the Johnson Institute Intervention, commonly referred to as the "intervention," involves training family and significant others to confront the substance abuser, request that he or she seek treatment, and impose consequences for not seeking help (Johnson, 1986). The goal of this program is treatment engagement by the alcohol abuser. However, this approach is controversial (on practical and ethical bases), and there is limited evidence of effectiveness among the widely diverse population of individuals with substance use disorders (Connors, Donovan, & DiClemente, 2001). The goals of UFT involve helping family members develop or strengthen coping skills, improve family functioning, and create a family environment conducive to sobriety or at least reduced drinking and drug use. In the UFT approach, families engage in a series of guided steps prior to initiating any sort of confrontation of the substance abuser about

his or her problem and seeking formal treatment. A small-scale study of the efficacy of this approach revealed that participation in UFT was associated with significantly greater likelihood that individuals with drinking problems would enter treatment or reduce their drinking (Thomas, Santa, Bronson, & Oyserman, 1987).

It is also important to mention certain related approaches that, rather than focusing on initiating change, emphasize self-healing. For example, Dittrich (1993) has developed a group treatment program for wives of treatment-resistant substance abusers designed to help partners cope with their own emotional distress rather than try to motivate the substance-abusing partner to seek help or otherwise change. Following closely in the tradition of Al-Anon, this particular approach advocates that family members detach from the substance abuser in a loving way, accept that they are powerless to control the substance abuser, and seek support from other Al-Anon members.

Results of randomized clinical trials have compared some of these approaches in terms of their efficacy in engaging clients in treatment. In a National Institute on Alcohol Abuse and Alcoholism (NIAAA)-funded investigation, Miller, Meyers, and Tonigan (1999) compared the CRAFT approach, Al-Anon, and Johnson Institute Intervention approaches for their effectiveness in engaging individuals with drinking problems in formal treatment. The highest overall treatment rate for the alcoholic family members was associated with the CRAFT therapy (64%). The majority of families in the Johnson Institute condition chose not to complete the intervention; in fact, only 30% followed-up with the critical confrontation session. Because Al-Anon is not designed to facilitate entry into treatment, it is not surprising that this was not a common outcome (Miller et al., 1999).

TREATMENT

Some of the more common family therapy approaches utilized with substance-abusing patients are described here. It is important to note that the diverse suppositions of the mechanisms of action underlying family treatment for substance abuse are not mutually exclusive; simply stated, each of these approaches includes elements of one or more of the others in its conceptualization of how familial problems evolve. However, key differences exist in the way each paradigm explains the variety of pernicious factors that influence negative family outcomes.

Although there is much agreement among the various theories that substance abuse has a serious deleterious impact on family functioning, the role of alcohol and drug is viewed differently depending on the manner in which these behaviors are conceptualized and the degree to which they are emphasized.

In Behavioral Contracting (Steinglass, Bennett, Wolin, & Reiss, 1987), it is believed that substance abuse creates stress on the entire family system and becomes the dominant organizing construct for the family. Through the use of behavioral techniques (e.g., enactments, rehearsals) and written contracts, the therapist works to address the presenting issues or concerns in the context of the family unit. In addition, the therapist also helps the family to cope with any potential emotional distress (i.e., emotional desert) resulting from the elimination of the substance-abusing behavior. In one of the only controlled outcome studies of family systems approaches, Zweben, Perlman, and Li (1988) found no significant group differences on any of the outcomes under investigation between alcohol abusers assigned to either eight sessions of conjunct therapy focused on a communication-interactional approach or a control group that received a single session of "advice giving."

Multisystemic Family Therapy (MFT; Cunningham & Henggeler, 1999) aims to understand the substance-abusing behavior within a more extended and authentic context. MFT assumes that substance abuse is influenced by variables from multiple systems. Thus, one of the goals of treatment is to assess the strengths and needs of each system and their relationship to the presenting problem. Family members play a large role in establishing treatments goals. MFT focuses on the here-and-now, rather than on past behaviors, and it targets specific and well-defined problems through the use of daily and weekly assignments. The therapist is responsible for addressing and overcoming any barriers that may result during the course of treatment. MFT is a well-studied treatment approach and is supported by 16 published outcomes studies, which cover clients with a range of presenting issues or concerns (e.g., violent and chronic juvenile offenders, substance-abusing juveniles, sexual offenders, maltreating families). Results of the Missouri Delinquency Project showed individuals involved in MST experienced 59% fewer arrests, 68% fewer drug-related arrests, 57% fewer days in adult confinement, and 43% fewer days on adult probation compared to individuals assigned to the control group over the 14-year post-treatment follow-up period (http://mstservices.com/files/outcomes_1a.pdf).

The central goal of Network Therapy (Galanter, 1993) is to create balance in the family system. As such, family members work to support the identified patient in his or her recovery by creating a stable, substance-free environment, and encouraging the client to avoid situations that might promote substance use (e.g., people, places, things, etc.). Self-help attendance is also strongly promoted in this approach. In a randomized trial of buprenorphine maintenance, Galanter et al. (2004) examined 33 clients receiving network therapy plus buprenorphine maintenance to 33 clients who received individual counseling plus buprenorphine maintenance. Results indicated that 64.5% of network therapy clients submitted negative weekly urine samples for opioids compared to 45.3% of those clients assigned to the individual condition. Moreover, results indicated a positive relationship between the number of network therapy sessions attended and opiate-free samples.

Solution-Focused Therapy (SFT; Berg & Miller, 1992) primarily emphasizes solutions to presenting issues or concerns, rather than on the origins of the problem; in other words, the focus is on solutions, not problems. The goals of SFT are client-generated, and the role of the therapist is to emphasize exceptions (i.e., those times when the problem does not occur) and identify small achievable goals that may enhance optimism for further behavioral change. Unfortunately, there is a dearth of research examining the efficacy of SFT with substance-abusing clients (Smock, Trepper, Wetchler, McCollum, Ray, & Price, 2008). In their review of SFT outcome studies, Gingerich and Eisengart (2000) found that of the 15 efficacy studies identified, only two included substance-abusing samples. Of these, one study found 36% of participants assigned to SFT only used two sessions to meet the study's recovery threshold compared to only 2% of participants assigned to the control group (Lambert et al., 1998). In the other study, using a case study design with an alcohol-abusing male participant, Polk (1996) reported the client worked more and drank less over the course of treatment.

In Stanton's Therapeutic Techniques (Stanton et al., 1982), substance-abusing behavior is believed to originate in adolescence as part of an attempt at achieving a developmental milestone (i.e., individuation) and is conceptualized as a cyclical process between people from intimate relationships. From this viewpoint, the family system seeks to maintain homeostasis, thereby indirectly reinforcing the substance-abusing behavior. According to Stanton, the primary goals for clients are to (1) abstinence, (2) employment or attendance in school or a training program, and (3) maintenance of independent living arrangements. The role of the therapist is to join with the family and maintain an active stance in directing the course of treatment. Along these lines, one of Stanton's primary therapeutic objectives is to alter repetitive behavioral sequences. Thus, the therapist aims to disrupt the family's unhealthy pattern of functioning in an effort to promote change. In a landmark study on the use of family therapy with heroin-abusing clients, Stanton and colleagues (1982), reported that two-thirds of the participants assigned to the 10-session family therapy condition experienced what was described as a good outcome. More specifically, adult male opiate addicts reported significant changes in drug-taking behaviors (Liddle & Dakof, 1995). This investigation was important in that it was the first of its kind to empirically test the use of family therapy in treating drug-abusing clients.

Wegscheider-Cruse's Theory (Wegscheider, 1981) posits that members of substance-abusing families take on behavioral roles (i.e., substance abuser, enabler, hero, scapegoat, lost child, or mascot) within the family in an effort to maintain balance within the system and as a way to cope with the addicted individual's behavior. The primary goal of treatment is to reduce or eliminate the rigidity of each role, resulting in increased flexibility within the system. The basic assumption underlying this approach is that change in one part of the family system will lead to changes in other problematic areas as well. The role of the therapist is to educate the family about addiction, confront denial, and offer concrete suggestions for help, which may include additional forms of self-help activities.

The preponderance of controlled substance abuse treatment clinical trials that include a family component examine adults with partners and possibly the children of adult alcohol abusers. However, it is also important to recognize the role of family and significant others in the treatment of adolescents who struggle with alcohol problems. In addition to the models just listed, two other approaches have been developed for use predominately with substance-abusing adolescents and their families: (a) Brief Strategic Family Therapy and (b) Multidimensional Family Therapy.

In Brief Strategic Family Therapy (BSFT; Szapocznik, Hervis, & Schwartz, 2003), substance-abusing behavior is believed to develop in response to unsuccessful attempts at dealing with developmental challenges. Rigid family structures are also thought to contribute to the onset of adolescent substance abuse. The BSFT therapist attempts to intervene in the system through the parents by changing parenting practices, improving the parent–adolescent relationship, and teaching conflict resolution skills. Santisteban et al. (2003) compared marijuana-abusing adolescents assigned to either BFST or a participatory learning group intervention and found adolescents assigned to the BSFT condition reported significantly greater reductions in marijuana use than those assigned to the control condition.

Multidimensional Family Therapy (MDFT; Liddle & Hogue, 2001) considers adolescent substance abuse the result of multiple interacting factors, which may include failure to meet developmental challenges as well as other forms of abuse or trauma. The primary goals of MDFT are to improve adolescent, parental, and overall family functioning, which, in turn, will impact the substance abusing and other problematic behaviors. MDFT is a very flexible approach; treatment length is determined collaboratively by the provider, setting, and family, and may include a combination of individual and family sessions. The MDFT process begins with a thorough multisystem assessment of both developmental ecological risk and protective factors. Using this information, a case conceptualization is developed that identifies the strengths and weaknesses in the adolescent's multiple systems and becomes the basis of treatment. Liddle and colleagues (2001) randomly assigned marijuana- and alcohol-abusing adolescents to MDFT, adolescent group therapy (AGT), or a multifamily educational intervention (MEI). Findings revealed participants assigned to MDFT reported lower ratings for severity of drug use at treatment termination and 12-month follow-up compared to participants assigned to the other two conditions.

Barriers to Effective Partner- and Family-Involved Interventions

There are several clinically significant barriers unique to family interventions with substance-abusing patients and their families. One that is commonly found among couples and families with a substance-abusing member is partner violence. In situations where there is a risk of severe violence (i.e., aggression that has the potential to result in serious injury or is life-threatening), the immediate intervention goal is safety; in these situations, partner and family therapy is contraindicated (e.g., Klostermann, Kelley, Milletich, & Mignone, 2011. For some families, there may be legal restrictions (i.e., restraining orders, no contact orders) that preclude conjoint family sessions.

Another barrier is the presence of more than one actively substance-abusing family member in the family; particularly if these individuals have formed a drinking or drug use partnership of some type (Klostermann & Fals-Stewart, 2008). These dual-using family systems may support continued use versus abstinence since the shared recreational activity typically involves substance use. Research on family-based approaches for these family configurations is lacking, and it is often recommended that individual therapy be used prior to engaging family members in treatment. Another demonstrated barrier to family interventions to treat substance abuse is the existence of high levels of blame and rumination from family members (usually the partner) toward the substance-abusing individual (O'Farrell & Fals-Stewart, 2006. Interestingly, there are also important practical and logistical barriers to partner or family intervention; these include (a) geographical distances among family members or among family members and the treatment provider; (b) family members who are divorced, incarcerated, or otherwise separated; (c) coordination of family members' and treatment providers' schedules; and (d) securing reimbursement for services delivered to multiple individuals in the context of formal treatment (Kennedy, Klostermann, Gorman, & Fals-Stewart, 2005).

Future Directions

Although there is a growing awareness of the efficacy of partner- and family-involved approaches to the treatment of alcoholism and drug abuse, there are several important gaps in both the research literature and clinical practice that reflect the next generation of research in this area. More specifically, the following four areas seem most pressing: (a) dissemination of evidence-based marital and family treatments to community-based treatment programs, (b) application of these approaches with specific populations, (c) examination of the mechanisms of action underlying the positive effects observed, and (d) exploring the use of partner- and family-involved models as part of a stepped care approach.

• *Dissemination.* Although a number of marital and family approaches have demonstrated

research support for their efficacy, many have yet to be widely adopted in community-based alcoholism and drug abuse treatment. McGovern, Fox, Xie, and Drake (2004) examined community addiction providers (i.e., directors [$n = 21$] and clinicians [$n = 89$]) experiences, beliefs, and readiness to implement a variety of evidence-based practices. Results were mixed; providers reported more readiness to adopt TSF, cognitive behavioral therapy, motivational interviewing, and relapse prevention, while less ready to implement contingency management, BCT, and pharmacotherapies. McGovern and colleagues concluded that in order for treatments to be successfully disseminated, investigators must clearly demonstrate the relevance of the treatment to clinicians and staff, even if empirical support is already established. Other factors to consider include degree of difficulty in implementation, how closely (or not) the treatment is aligned with the therapist's preferred theoretical orientation or agency counseling approach, cost of providing treatment, and whether or not the treatment fills a perceived area of need for the clinic. Each of these areas may serve as a potential barrier to successful dissemination of the treatment.

• *Specific populations.* Although the body of empirical literature supporting the use of marital and family therapy for substance abuse is substantial, it is critical to also recognize its limitations. Among these are the types of families that are typically the subject of such studies, which usually include largely white, male substance-abusing patients. Studies on the efficacy of marital and family therapy approaches for women with substance use disorders are far less common, although available evidence does suggest that they are efficacious (McCrady, Epstein, Cook, Jensen, & Hildebrandt, 2009). Even fewer studies have examined partner- and family-involved interventions with same-sex couples (Klostermann et al., 2011). Future studies are needed to examine gender orientation-specific factors as well as non-gender orientation-specific factors that may increase substance misuse among gay and lesbian individuals.

Furthermore, a great deal of research has been conducted related to both family therapy and culture and ethnicity, but very little of this has appeared in the family therapy literature on substance abuse. This represents what is likely the most important gap in the extant empirical literature to date. Among major life experiences that must be accounted for when treating families in which a member has a problem with drinking or drug use is how factors such as acculturation and ethnic identity influence the treatment process.

• *Mechanisms of action.* We now have confidence that many treatments are effective (Miller & Wilbourne, 2002), but despite the successful efforts of substance abuse treatment researchers to conduct rigorous clinical trials and spell out in treatment manuals what the treatments consist of, little research has actually investigated what the active ingredients of these treatments are (Longabaugh, 2007). In other words, what are the mechanisms of action that make certain partner- and family-involved approaches curative? If these factors can be identified, then these approaches can be modified to optimize their efficiency and effectiveness.

• *Partner- and family-involved treatment in the context of stepped care.* Despite the demonstrated efficacy of manualized marital and family approaches, there are large individual differences in patient response to treatment. As noted by McKay (2009), even for the most efficacious treatments, there are a certain number of people who do not respond to treatment; yet, in an effort to tightly control the intervention, nonresponding patients receive the same amount of manualized treatment as those who respond well. Research on standardized interventions to treat substance abuse disorders is beginning to shift away from a "one-size-fits-all" perspective and move toward adaptive interventions. Adaptive interventions, although standardized, call for different dosages of treatment to be employed strategically with patients and families across time. Given the heterogeneity in familial characteristics and response to treatment, future studies are needed to develop tailored interventions based on treatment algorithms that dictate treatment modifications triggered by the patient's initial response and changes in symptom severity. Thus, more flexible versions of marital and family treatments may be more easily disseminated to community providers and more palatable to patients receiving the intervention.

Conclusion

As has been well-documented in scholarly journals and popular media, the emotional, economic, and societal toll of alcoholism and drug abuse is incalculable. The effects of substance use disorders affect not only the clients, but those around them; in fact, those emotionally closest to the substance-abusing client often suffer the most. Partner- and family-involved approaches have had well-documented success because these methods examine outcomes across multiple domains of functioning that go well beyond frequency of substance use (e.g., child and family adjustment, family violence, relationship quality). By seeking to foster family environments conducive to abstinence, marital and family approaches have great potential to help individuals and families maintain long-term and even multigenerational healthful change.

References

Azrin, N. H., Sisson, R. W., Meyers, R., & Godley, M. (1982). Alcoholism treatment by disulfiram and community reinforcement therapy. *Journal of Behavior Therapy and Experimental Psychiatry, 13,* 105–112.

Berg, I. K., & Miller, S. D. (1992). *Working with the problem drinker: A solution-focused approach.* New York: W.W. Norton.

Billings, A. G., & Moos, R. H. (1983). Comparisons of children of depressed and non-depressed parents: A social environmental perspective. *Journal of Abnormal Child Psychology, 11,* 463–485.

Brown, E. D., O'Farrell, T. J., Maisto, S. A., Boies, K., & Suchinsky, R. (Eds.). (1997). *Accreditation guide for substance abuse treatment programs.* Newbury Park, CA: Sage.

Cadogan, D. A. (1973). Marital group therapy in the treatment of alcoholism. *Quarterly Journal of the Study of Alcohol, 34,* 1187–1194.

Catalano, R. F., Morrison, D. M., Wells, E. A., Gillmore, M. R., Iritani, B., & Hawkins, J. D. (1992). Ethnic differences in family factors related to early drug initiation. *Journal of Studies on Alcohol, 53,* 208–217.

Chassin, L., Curran, P. J., Hussong, A. M., & Colder, C. R. (1996). The relation of parent alcoholism to adolescent substance use: A longitudinal follow-up study. *Journal of Abnormal Psychology, 105,* 70–80.

Collins, R. L., Ellickson, P. L., & Klein, D. J. (2007). The role of substance use in young adult divorce. *Addiction, 102*(5), 786–794.

Connors, G., Donovan, D., & DiClemente, C. C. (2001) Substance Abuse Treatment and the Stages of Change: Selecting and Planning Interventions. New York: Guilford Press.

Corder, B. F., Corder, R. F., & Laidlaw, N. C. (1972). An intensive treatment program for alcoholics and their wives. *Quarterly Journal of the Study of Alcohol, 33,* 1144–1146.

Cunningham P. B., & Henggeler S. W. (1999). Engaging multiproblem families in treatment: Lessons learned throughout the development of multisystemic therapy. *Family Process, 38,* 265–281.

DeMarsh, J. K., & Kumpfer, K. L. (1985). Family, environmental, and genetic influences on children's future chemical dependency. *Journal of Children in Contemporary Society: Advances in Theory and Applied Research, 18,* 117–152.

Dishion, T. J., & Kavanaugh, K. (2005). *Intervening in adolescent problem behavior: A family-centered approach.* New York: Guilford Press.

Dishion, T. J., Reid, J. B., & Patterson, G. R. (1988). Empirical guidelines for a family intervention for adolescent drug use. In R. E. Coombs (Ed.), *The family context of adolescent drug use* (pp. 189–224). New York: Haworth.

Dittrich, J. E. (1993). A group program for wives of treatment resistant alcoholics. In T. J. O'Farrell (Ed.), *Treating alcohol problems: Marital and family interventions* (pp. 78–114). New York: Guilford.

Edwards, M. E., & Steinglass, P. (1995). Family therapy treatment outcomes for alcoholism. *Journal of Marital and Family Therapy, 21,* 475–509.

Emmelkamp, P. M., & Vedel, E. (2006). *Evidence-based treatment for drug and alcohol abuse.* New York: Taylor and Francis Group.

Epstein, E. E., & McCrady, B. S. (1998). Behavioral couples treatment of alcohol and drug use disorders: Current status and innovations. *Clinical Psychology Review, 18,* 689–711.

Epstein, E. E., McCrady, B. S., & Morgan, T. J. (2007). Couples treatment for drug-dependent males: Preliminary efficacy of a stand alone outpatient model. *Addictive Disorders & Their Treatment, 6,* 21–37.

Galanter, M. (1993). Network therapy for addiction: A model for office practice. *American Journal of Psychiatry, 150,* 28–36.

Galanter, M., Dermatis, H., Glickman, L., Maslansky, R., Sellers, M. B., Neumann, E., et al. (2004). Network therapy: Decreased secondary opioid use during buprenorphine maintenance. *Journal of Substance Abuse Treatment, 26,* 313–318.

Gingerich, W. J., & Eisengart, S. (2000). Solution-focused brief therapy: A review of the outcome research. *Family Process, 39,* 477–498.

Gondoli, D. M., & Jacob, T. (1990). Family treatment of alcoholism. In R. Watson (Ed.), *Drug and alcohol abuse reviews: Vol. 1. Prevention and treatment of drug and alcohol abuse* (pp. 245–262). New York: Humana Press.

Gottman, J. M., Notarius, C., Gonso, J., & Markman, H. (1976). *A couples guide to communication.* Champaign, IL: Research Press.

Halford, W. K., & Osgarby, S. M. (1993). Alcohol abuse in clients presenting with marital problems. *Journal of Family Psychology, 6*(3), 245–254.

Halford, W. K., & Osgarby, K. A. (1996). Brief behavioural couples therapy: A preliminary evaluation. *Behavioural and Cognitive Psychotherapy, 24* (03), 263-273

Hawkins, J. D., Catalano, R. F., Brown, E. O., Vadasy, P. F., Roberts, C., Fitzmahan, D., Starkman, N., & Randsell, M. (1988). *Preparing for the Drug (Free) Years: A family activity book.* Seattle, WA: Comprehensive Health Education Foundation.

Heath, A. W., & Stanton, M. D. (1998). Family-based treatment: Stages and outcomes. In R. J. Frances & S. I. Miller (Eds.), *Clinical textbook of addictive disorders* (2nd ed., pp. 496–520). New York: Guilford.

Hedberg, A. G., & Campbell, L. (1974). A comparison of four behavioral treatments of alcoholism. *Journal of Behavior Therapy and Experimental Psychiatry, 5,* 251–256.

Jellinek, E. M. (1960). *The disease concept of alcoholism.* New Haven, CT: Hillhouse.

Johnson, B. A. (2010, August 8). *12 steps to nowhere.* The Washington Post, p. B3.

Johnson, V. E. (1986). *Intervention: How to help someone who doesn't want help.* Center City, MN: Hazelden.

Kelley, M., Klostermann, K., Doane, A. N., Mignone, T., Lam, K. K., Fals-Stewart, W., & Padilla, M. A. (2010). The case for examining and treating the combined effects of parental drug use and intimate parental violence on children in their homes. *Aggression and Violent Behavior, 15,* 76–82.

Kennedy, C., Klostermann, K., Gorman, C., & Fals-Stewart, W. (2005). Treating substance abuse and intimate partner violence: Implications for addiction professionals. *Counselor Magazine, 6*(1), 28–34.

Kinney, J. (2009). *Loosening the grip* (9th ed.). New York: McGraw-Hill.

Klostermann, K. (2006). Substance abuse and intimate partner violence: Treatment considerations. *Substance Abuse Treatment, Prevention, and Policy, 1,* 1–24.

Klostermann, K., & Fals-Stewart, W. (2008). Behavioral couples therapy for substance abuse. *Journal of Behavior Analysis of Offender and Victim, 1*(4), 81–93.

Klostermann, K., Kelley, M. L., Milletich, R. J., & Mignone. (2011). Alcoholism and partner aggression among gay, lesbian, and bisexual couples. *Aggression and Violent Behavior, 16,* 115–119.

Koffinke, C. (1991). Family recovery issues and treatment resources. In D. C. Daley & M. S. Raskin (Eds.), *Treating the chemically dependent and their families.* Newbury Park, CA: Sage.

Kumpfer, K. L., & Alvarado, R. (2003). Family interventions for the prevention of drug abuse. *American Psychologist, 58,* 457–465.

Lambert, M. J., Burlingame, G. M., Umphress, V., Hansen, N. B., Vermeersch, D. A., Clouse, G. C., et al. (1998). The reliability and validity of the Outcome Questionnaire. *Clinical Psychology and Psychotherapy, 3,* 249–258.

Lebow, J. (2005). Family therapy at the beginning of the twenty-first century. In J. Lebow (Ed.), *Handbook of clinical family therapy* (pp. 1–16). Hoboken, NJ: John Wiley & Sons.

Lemke, S., Brennan, P. L., & Schutte, K. K. (2007). Upward pressures on drinking: Exposure and reactivity in adulthood. *Journal of Studies on Alcohol and Drugs, 68,* 437–445.

Liddle, H. A., & Dakof, G. A. (1995). Family-based treatment for adolescent drug use: State of the science. *National Institute on Drug Abuse: Research Monograph Series, 156,* 218–255.

Liddle, H. A., Dakof, G. A., Parker, K., Diamond, G. S., Barrett, K., & Tejada, M. (2001). Multidimensional family therapy for adolescent drug abuse: Results of a randomized clinical trial. *American Journal of Drug and Alcohol Abuse, 27,* 651–688.

Liddle, H. A., & Hogue, A. (2001). Multidimensional family therapy for adolescent substance abuse. In E. F. Wagner & H. B. Waldron (Eds.), *Innovations in adolescent substance abuse interventions* (pp. 229–261). New York: Pergamon.

Liberman, R. P., Wheeler, E. G., deVisser, L. A., Kuehnel, J., & Kuehnel, T. (1980). *Handbook of marital therapy: A positive approach to helping troubled relationships.* New York: Plenum Press.

Longabaugh, R. (2007). The search for mechanisms of change in behavioral treatments for alcohol use disorders: A commentary. *Alcoholism: Clinical & Experimental Research, Special Issue, 31,* S1.

McCrady, B. S. (1986). Implications for behavior therapy of the changing alcoholism health care delivery system. *Behavior Therapist, 9,* 171–174.

McCrady, B. S. (2006). Family and other close relationships. In W. R. Miller, & K. M. Carroll (Eds.), *Rethinking substance abuse: What the science shows and what we should do about it* (pp. 161–181). New York: Guilford Press.

McCrady, B. S., Epstein, E. E., Cook, S., Jensen, N., & Hildebrandt, T. (2009). A randomized trial of individual and couple behavioral alcohol treatment for women. *Journal of Consulting and Clinical Psychology*, 77(2), 243-256.

McCrady, B. S., Noel, N. E., & Adams, D. B. (1986). Comparative effectiveness of three types of spouse involvement in outpatient behavioral alcoholism treatment. *Journal of Studies on Alcoholism*, 47, 459–467.

McCrady, B. S., Paolino, T. E, Longabaugh, R., & Rosi, J. (1979). Effects of joint hospital admission and couples treatment for hospitalized alcoholics: A pilot study. *Addictive Behaviors*, 4, 155–165.

McGovern, M. P., Fox, T. S., Xie, H., & Drake, R. E. (2004). A survey of clinical practices and readiness to adopt evidence-based practices: Dissemination research in an addiction treatment system. *Journal of Substance Abuse Treatment*, 26, 305–312.

McKay, J. R. (2009). *Treating substance use disorders with adaptive continuing care*. Washington, DC: American Psychological Association.

Miller, W. R., Meyers, R. J., & Tonigan, J. S. (1999). Engaging the unmotivated in treatment for alcohol problems: A comparison of three strategies for intervention through family members. *Journal of Consulting and Clinical Psychology*, 67, 688–697.

Miller, W. R., & Wilbourne, P. L. (2002). Mesa grande: A methodological analysis of clinical trials of treatments for alcohol use disorders. *Addiction*, 97, 265–277.

O'Farrell, T. J., & Birchler, G. R. (1987). Marital relationships of alcoholic, conflicted, and nonconflicted couples. *Journal of Marital and Family Therapy*, 13, 259–274.

O'Farrell, T. J., & Cutter, H. S. G. (1984). Behavioral marital therapy couples groups for male alcoholics and their wives. *Journal of Substance Abuse Treatment*, 1, 191–204.

O'Farrell, T. J., Cutter, H. S. G., & Floyd, F. J. (1985). Evaluating behavioral marital therapy for male alcoholics: Effects on marital adjustment and communication from before to after treatment. *Behavior Therapy*, 16, 147–167.

O'Farrell, T. J., & Fals-Stewart, W. (2006). Behavioral couples therapy for alcoholism and drug abuse. New York: Guilford Press.

Polk, G. W. (1996). Treatment of problem drinking behavior using solution-focused therapy: A single subject design. *Crisis Intervention*, 3, 13–24.

Powers, M. B., Vedel, E., & Emmelkamp, P. M. (2008). Behavioral couples therapy (BCT) for alcohol and drug use disorders: A meta-analysis. *Clinical Psychology Review*, 28, 952–962.

Rotunda, R. J, West L., O'Farrell T. J. (2004). Enabling behavior in a clinical sample of alcohol-dependent clients and their partners. *Journal of Substance Abuse Treatment*, 26, 269–276.

Santisteban, D. A., Coatsworth, J. D., Perez-Vidal, A., Kurtines, W. M., Schwartz, S., LaPerriere, A., et al. (2003). The efficacy of brief strategic family therapy in modifying Hispanic adolescent behavior problems and substance abuse. *Journal of Family Psychology*, 17, 121–133.

Schaef, A. W. (1986). *Co-dependence: Misunderstood—mistreated*. San Francisco: Harper & Row.

Smock, S. A., Trepper, T. S., Wetchler, J. L., McCollum, E. E., Ray, R., & Pierce, K. (2008). Solution-focused group therapy for level 1 substance abusers. *Journal of Marital and Family Therapy*, 34, 107–120.

Sisson, R. W., & Azrin, N. H. (1993). Family member involvement to initiate and promote treatment of problem drinking. *Journal of Behavior Therapy and Experimental Psychiatry*, 17, 15–21.

Smith, J. E., & Meyers, R. J. (2009). Community reinforcement and family training. In G. L. Fisher & N. A. Roget (Eds.), *Encyclopedia of substance abuse prevention, treatment, and recovery*. Thousand Oaks, CA: Sage.

Snyder, D. K., & Whisman, M. A. (2003). *Treating difficult couples: Helping clients with coexisting mental and relationship disorders*. New York: Guilford Press.

Stanton, M. D., Todd, T. C., & Associates. (1982). *The family therapy of drug abuse and addiction*. New York: Guilford.

Stanton, M. D., & Shadish, W. R. (1997). Outcome, attrition, and family-couple treatment for drug abuse: A meta-analysis and review of the controlled, comparative studies. *Psychological Bulletin*, 122, 170–191.

Steinglass, P., Bennett, L. A., Wolin, S. J., & Reiss, D. (1987). *The alcoholic family*. New York: BasicBooks.

Szapocznik, J., Hervis, O., & Schwartz, S. (2003). *Therapy manuals for drug addiction: Brief strategic family therapy for adolescent drug abuse*. Bethesda, MD: National Institute on Drug Abuse.

Szapocznik, J., Santisteban, D., Rio, A., Perez-Vidal, A., Santisteban, D., & Kurtines, W. M. (1989). Family effectiveness training: An intervention to prevent drug abuse and problem behaviors in Hispanic adolescents. *Hispanic Journal of Behavioral Sciences*, 11, 4–27.

Thomas, E. J., Santa, C., Bronson, D., & Oyserman, D. (1987). Unilateral family therapy with spouses of alcoholics. *Journal of Social Service Research*, 10, 145–162.

Turner, J. (1972, October). *Couple and group treatment of marital discord*. Paper presented at the sixth annual meeting of the Association for Advancement of Behavior Therapy, New York.

Vanicelli, M. Gingerich, S., & Ryback, R. (1983). Family problems related to the treatment and outcome of alcoholic patients. *British Journal of Addiction*, 78, 193–204.

Walitzer, K. S., & Derman, K. H. (2004). Alcohol-focused spouse involvement and behavioral couples therapy: Evolution of enhancements to drinking reduction treatment for male problem drinkers. *Journal of Consulting and Clinical Psychology*, 72, 944–955.

Wegscheider, S. (1981). *Another chance: Hope and health for the alcoholic family*. Palo Alto, CA: Science and Behavior Books.

Zweben, A., Pearlman, S., & Li, S. (1988). A comparison of brief advice and conjoint therapy in the treatment of alcohol abuse: The results of the marital systems study. *British Journal of Addiction*, 83, 899–916.

Self-Help Organizations for Substance Use Disorders

Anna Lembke *and* Keith Humphreys

Abstract

Self-help groups for substance use disorders have been active for decades, and notions of self-help have been prevalent for centuries. After presenting universal features of self-help organizations, the authors focus on Alcoholics Anonymous (AA) and Moderation Management (MM), discussing the origins, membership, and philosophy of AA and MM and highlighting important differences between these organizations. AA's emphasis on spirituality, interpersonal conduct, and abstinence as the only goal contrasts sharply with MM's emphasis on personal autonomy, rational cognitions, and setting drinking limits. The chapter discusses scientific evidence of the effectiveness of AA and MM on substance use outcomes and potential social and psychological mechanisms of change. More research is needed in the area of self-help organizations. In the meantime, AA is proven effective for alcohol-dependent individuals who embrace its philosophy, and MM may fill an important niche for nondependent drinkers or those in the precontemplation stages of change.

Key Words: Alcoholics Anonymous, Moderation Management, mutual help groups, self-help, philosophy, abstinence, 12-steps, spirituality, higher power

In this chapter, we discuss the definition and historical origins of self-help, a concept that harkens back to Luther and the 16th century, but probably derives primordially from the striving and flexibility inherent to human beings. We then focus specifically on self-help groups for substance use disorders (SUDs), which are distinct from books on self-improvement or other self-help modalities. We describe universal features that characterize all self-help organizations and then focus on two different self-help organizations for problem drinking: Alcoholics Anonymous (AA) and Moderation Management (MM). We choose these two organizations because AA represents one of the earliest and most popular self-help organizations for SUDs, whereas MM demonstrates the evolution of a new form of self-help group and thereby provides a foil for AA's program of recovery. We cover the origins, membership, and philosophy of each organization and then discuss scientific evidence on the

efficacy of each. We close with a section describing the social, psychological, and spiritual mechanisms of change in each group and how these different mechanisms are compelling to some members but create an obstacle to participation for others.

Definition and Historical Origins of Self-Help

The term *self-help* probably came into popular usage in 1859, when Samuel Smiles (1859) published *Self-Help, with Illustrations of Character and Conduct* (and the second edition of this book which added *Perseverance* in 1866). Its opening sentence, "Heaven helps those who help themselves," is a frequently quoted but seldom referenced homily. *Self-help* was classically defined as any positive transformation in feeling, thought, action, religious insight, or social standing in an individual that is accomplished through personal initiative and without reliance on a trained professional or other authority figure.

The practice of self-help has much earlier origins and can be traced at least as far back as 1543, when Martin Luther translated the New Testament from Latin into the German vernacular. With Luther's completed translation of the Latin Bible, the text became directly available to anyone who could read German. This event radically altered religious development, which no longer required the mediation of an anointed clergyman or other religious authority. Spiritual transformation could occur through reading, reflection, and through direct supplication of God without an intermediary. The German humanist Johann Cochlaeus analyzed the impact of Martin Luther's translation:

> Luther's New Testament was so much multiplied and spread by printers that even tailors and shoemakers, yea, even women and ignorant persons who had accepted this new Lutheran gospel, and could read a little German, studied it with the greatest avidity as the fountain of all truth. Some committed it to memory, and carried it about in their bosom. In a few months such people deemed themselves so learned that they were not ashamed to dispute about faith and the gospel not only with Catholic laymen, but even with priests and monks and doctors of divinity.
>
> *(cited in Schaff, 1910)*

By emphasizing the individual's active participation in his or her betterment and de-emphasizing the role of experts in galvanizing change, Luther's Bible may well be hailed as the very first self-help book, to be followed by a veritable avalanche of self-help modalities in the centuries to come. The subsequent self-help initiatives were not limited to individuals but also comprised groups of peers who met to address treating problems previously treated by professionals. Indeed, because so many self-help initiatives involve groups working together, *mutual help* is often a more accurate descriptor (although those who found such organizations almost always prefer the term *self-help*). In the developed world, self-help may be the rule rather than the exception as a means by which people attempt personal change, including for SUDs (Miller & McCrady, 1993). Modern self-help practices come in many forms, from inspirational books and other written media, to radio shows, television programs, and now the blogosphere as well. Today, mutual help organizations exist for almost any problem humans share, with nearly every major contributor to morbidity and mortality represented (Humphreys & Ribisl, 1999).

In this chapter, we focus on *self-help groups*. Self-help groups are similar to other self-help modalities in that they have as their goal positive change in the life of the individual, accomplished through personal initiative and without the influence of an authoritative intermediary. But self-help groups are distinct from other types of self-help approaches in that the group dynamic itself is fundamental to the transformative process. Core beliefs of self-help groups are that the individual cannot achieve transformation without the aid of others in the group, and giving help is as critical as receiving help in the path toward change.

All self-help organizations have certain features: (1) members who share a common problem or status; (2) self-directed nonprofessional leadership; (3) an emphasis on knowledge gained from experience rather than book learning; (4) a credo of reciprocal helping; (5) specific goals for personal change, often outlined in some kind of written document; and (6) no payment for participation or membership. Self-help organizations also differ in some important ways. Some organizations provide only support and fellowship (e.g., many of those organizations dedicated to chronic or terminal illness), whereas others specifically outline a program for change (e.g., Alcoholics Anonymous). Some groups are secular (e.g., SMART Recovery), whereas others have an explicit spiritual or religious emphasis (e.g., *Christ-centered* self-help groups). Some organizations advocate for political involvement (e.g., *Vie Libre*) and accept external funds, whereas others specifically argue against these activities. (For a review, see *Circles of Recovery*, Humphreys, 2004, pp. 17–21.)

Seventy percent of all self-help group meeting visits per year in the United States are to groups targeting addiction to alcohol or drugs (Humphreys, 2004). In the pages that follow, we focus specifically on two self-help organizations designed to target addiction to alcohol; namely, Alcoholics Anonymous (AA) and Moderation Management (MM). We compare and contrast these two organizations for a number of reasons. Alcoholics Anonymous is the precursor for almost all self-help groups that exist today. Moderation Management differs from AA in its core philosophy, thus providing an important counterpoint in the evolution of self-help groups.

Alcoholics Anonymous: Origins, Membership, Core Philosophy

Founded in 1935 by two alcoholics, William Griffith Wilson (*Bill W*) and Dr. Robert Holbrook Smith (*Dr. Bob*), AA was strongly influenced it its early days by the Oxford Group, a 1920s American evangelical movement (Humphreys, 2004). The Oxford Group, whose membership was not limited to alcoholics, preached that sin could be completely overcome through spiritual transformation. Members of the Oxford Group who were struggling with alcoholism reached out to Bill W., who was an alcoholic who had tried repeatedly and unsuccessfully to quit drinking.

Bill W. underwent a spiritual transformation during an emergency detoxification, in which he saw a bright light and felt that he was fundamentally changed from his prior self. He was abstinent for several months thereafter, a longer period of sobriety than he had ever achieved. But the spiritual transformation was not in itself sufficient, and Bill W. began again to feel vulnerable to relapse. It was at that time that he made contact with Dr. Bob, another alcoholic whom he knew through the Oxford Group. The men met and talked for several hours at a house in Akron, Ohio, in what has come to be known as the first Alcoholics Anonymous meeting. The encounter had a life-changing effect on both Bill W. and Dr. Bob, as they gained hope through sharing their stories and became convinced that the way to overcome their addiction to alcohol was for them to help other alcoholics. The basic format of AA meetings today still consists primarily of members' sharing their personal narratives, with an opening and closing ritual on either end.

Soon thereafter the two began working together with other alcoholics. By August 1936, Alcoholics Anonymous meetings within an Oxford Group context were being held both in Akron and New York City. Both men decided to sever their relationship with the Oxford Groups, primarily to move the organization out of a strictly Protestant religious framework that limited the appeal of AA to many alcoholics. The small AA groups were then on their own. By 1939, AA had several hundred members. By 1940, their newly formed board of trustees listed 22 cities in which groups were well established and holding weekly meetings. When Dr. Bob died in 1950, AA had 50,000 members (Humphreys, 2004). Alcoholics Anonymous has since grown into a worldwide organization with perhaps 5 million members (Humphreys, 2004). Along the way, it inspired similar organizations such as Narcotics Anonymous, Gamblers Anonymous, Overeaters Anonymous, and many more.

Alcoholics Anonymous membership is entirely voluntary, free of charge, and open to anyone who attends with a desire to stop drinking. A prospective member need not be abstinent from alcohol to attend AA. This succinct yet profound requirement for membership communicates that AA is welcoming to anyone who suffers from the problem of alcohol addiction, while also communicating the core philosophy of AA, which is that the goal for all alcoholics is to stop drinking, not merely cut back or otherwise change one's pattern of alcohol use. According to AA, alcoholics fundamentally lack the ability to control their alcohol use, making abstinence the only viable alternative. This philosophy is in sharp contrast to that promulgated by the self-help organization Moderation Management, as we will later describe.

Alcoholics Anonymous has several important texts that delineate the steps toward change. The first is known informally as *The Big Book* (actual title *Alcoholics Anonymous*), which was published in 1939 and increased public awareness about AA (Alcoholics Anonymous, 1939). *The Big Book* consists largely of testimonials of alcoholics in recovery, describing their varied paths of getting and staying sober through the help of AA. The second book, *Twelve Steps and Twelve Traditions* (Alcoholics Anonymous, 1952–1953), outlines in detail the specific steps that a member can follow to achieve change, stop drinking, and recover from the disease of alcoholism. The distinction between cessation of alcohol use and recovery is critical in AA, as the desired end point of *sobriety* involves personal transformation beyond drinking. There are 12 steps in all, which is why AA is often referred to as a *12-step* organization, setting the stage for many self-help organizations to follow, many of which use nearly identical steps in their recovery programs. The 12 steps of AA are as follows:

1. We admitted we were powerless over alcohol—that our lives had become unmanageable.

2. Came to believe that a Power greater than ourselves could restore us to sanity.

3. Made a decision to turn our will and our lives over to the care of God as we understood Him.

4. Made a searching and fearless moral inventory of ourselves.

5. Admitted to God, to ourselves, and to another human being the exact nature of our wrongs.

6. Were entirely ready to have God remove all these defects of character.

7. Humbly asked Him to remove our shortcomings.

8. Made a list of all persons we had harmed, and became willing to make amends to them all.

9. Made direct amends to such people wherever possible, except when to do so would injure them or others.

10. Continued to take personal inventory and when we were wrong promptly admit it.

11. Sought through prayer and meditation to improve our conscious contact with God as we understood Him, praying only for knowledge of His will for us and power to carry that out.

12. Having had a spiritual awakening as the result of these steps, we tried to carry this message to alcoholics and to practice these principles in all our affairs.

The word *power* or its derivative appears three times in the steps. The notion that power does not reside inside the individual, but rather somewhere outside the individual, is fundamental to the AA philosophy. The road to recovery demands that the individual acknowledge his or her lack of self-efficacy and give up his or her sense of self-centeredness. The *Higher Power* of Alcoholics Anonymous is very loosely defined and can consist of anything from a Christ-like deity, to the ineffable mystery of nature, to the awe-inspiring support of the group fellowship. What is essential to the AA philosophy is not how members conceptualize the Higher Power, but rather that they are willing to give themselves over to that Higher Power, no longer relying exclusively on personal resources for the answer to problems. This is consistent with AA's view that grandiosity and self-centeredness are character flaws that undergird alcoholism. Alcoholism is viewed as a chronic disease from which one is never cured, but only in recovery; but stopping drinking alone is not sufficient for recovery (*dry-drunk* and *so-driety*). Alcoholics Anonymous believes that the alcoholic must tackle core narcissism, or *self-will run riot*, that fuels the disease of alcoholism. The individual may be abstinent and yet still engaging in a narcissistic selfishness that is antithetical to sobriety. According to AA, true recovery can only happen when stopping drinking is combined with giving the self over to something outside the self, and, conversely, sustained abstinence is only possible when one has acknowledged his or her lack of being in control. This view has strong links to Protestant concepts of sin, but also resonates well with the Freudian ideas that were widespread when the organization came of age after World War II. According to Stephanie Brown, who has written extensively on the therapeutic processes of AA, "Alcoholism and other addictions are fundamentally related to power … characterized by a distorted and faulty belief in the power of self" (Brown, 1993). The well-known psychiatrists Harry Tiebout (1949) and Gregory

Bateson (1971) have also written extensively on the importance of surrender and the myth of self-power as fundamental to the philosophy of AA.

Alcoholic Anonymous's 12 steps also provide guidance on interpersonal relationships. The AA philosophy describes not merely the reciprocal helping that is a core of many self-help groups, but also how members should interact with important people in their lives. Alcoholic Anonymous has formalized the role of the *sponsor* as a more senior member of the group who provides support to newer members. Every new member is expected to identify a sponsor and to actively seek out that person's help in the process of recovery. More senior members are encouraged to become sponsors as a way to help fellow members and also as a way to promote their own sobriety. When members feel their recovery is at risk, one of the first things they are encouraged to do is call their sponsor. Steps 5, 8, 9, and 12 speak directly toward how members need to be vigilant about the ways in which they may have harmed others and be ready to take responsibility for this harm by expressing regret to the victim. Alcoholic Anonymous is quite detailed about how this process of making amends should occur and encourages honesty in all interpersonal and intrapersonal dealings. According to AA, a stance of humility and responsibility underscores all healthy relationships, including one's relationship with one's Higher Power.

In addition to its emphasis on spirituality, ethics, interpersonal conduct, and humility, AA relies heavily on behavioral models of change to directly target drinking behavior. Behavioral models that are represented in AA include counterconditioning (changing the response to a stimulus; e.g., calling one's sponsor instead of drinking), stimulus control (changing the problematic stimulus; e.g., avoiding alcoholic peers), and reinforcement/contingency management (rewards and punishment; e.g., the use of chips and tokens as reward techniques for days of sobriety). Examples of all of these behavioral strategies abound in AA. DiClemente (1993) argues that individuals who are in the active and maintenance phases of sobriety benefit more from behavioral strategies in AA than those in the precontemplation and contemplation stages. DiClemente (1993) provides an excellent discussion of behavioral therapeutical techniques in AA, as well as AA as it applies to the Transtheoretical Model of Change (Precontemplation, Contemplation, Preparation, Action, and Maintenance).

The path to change in AA can be difficult for some members to follow. A common obstacle to participation in AA includes discomfort with the concept and language of a Higher Power. Some members object to declaring themselves lifelong *alcoholics* and want someday to engage in moderate drinking. Some members disagree up front with abstinence as the only goal. Other members want to achieve abstinence but not make the other changes in character and interpersonal conduct deemed by AA so vital to recovery. An alternative self-help organization for problem drinking, which was born of these and other obstacles to participation in AA, is an organization called Moderation Management.

Moderation Management: Origins, Membership, Core Philosophy

Moderation Management is a self-help organization that was founded in 1994 by Audrey Kishline. It is unique among the various self-help organizations for SUDs in that it advocates for reduced substance use and reduced harm from substance use, rather than mandating abstinence. Moderation Management was intentionally founded as a counterpoint to AA, its goal at inception being to help *nondependent* problem drinkers whose drinking was not adequately targeted by AA or other similar 12-step programs. Thus, although some think of MM as an alternative to AA for alcoholics, the organization itself rejects this role, recommending that *alcoholics* (those with alcohol dependence) seek other forms of help.

Audrey Kishline had a drinking problem and partook in traditional 12-step programs like AA. She strongly felt that the central message of AA did not speak to her subjective experience and also undermined her core sense of confidence and self-efficacy. She did not feel that she was powerless over alcohol, as described by AA's first step, but that with the right kind of fellowship, she could drink in moderation without negative consequences. She also resisted the notion that alcoholism was a core part of her identity or an incurable disease from which she might only be in recovery. She founded MM to help others like herself who acknowledged a problem with alcohol but did not embrace the ideas of powerlessness, incurability, and abstinence as the only goal for alcohol consumption.

Moderation Management possesses the universal features of self-help organizations, namely, members who share a common problem or status, an emphasis on knowledge gained from experience, a credo of reciprocal helping, specific goals for personal change outlined in a written document, in this case *Moderate Drinking: The Moderation Management Guide for People Who Want to Reduce Their Drinking* (Kishline, 1994), and no payment for participation

or membership. Like other self-help groups, MM meetings occur in member-led face-to-face (F2F) gatherings, although unlike AA, MM does allow for treatment professionals to help start MM groups. Many more MM meetings occur online. Probably due to the era in which it developed, MM was the first alcohol self-help organization to be accessed as much online as in person (Klaw, Huebsch, & Humphreys, 2000).

Membership in MM is not openly accepting of any kind of problem drinker. Moderation Management has specific criteria for membership, and even has something akin to a screening test that prospective members are asked to undergo before joining. Prospective members are supposed to be nondependent problem drinkers. In other words, MM caters to a population of individuals with less severe drinking problems than might typically be encountered at an AA meeting. To test eligibility, prospective members are asked to complete a 30-day abstinence period prior to joining. If unable to do so, MM may not be for them. After the abstinence period, MM members are asked to limit drinking to guidelines influenced by the research of Sanchez-Craig and colleagues (Sanchez-Craig, Wilkinson, & Davila, 1995); that is, no more than nine drinks per week or three per day for women; no more than 14 per week or four per day for men; and both men and women are to have 3–4 nondrinking days per week.

Just as AA's criterion for membership communicates a core aspect of its philosophy, so do the membership requirements for MM communicate its philosophy, which is fundamentally different from that of AA. Moderation Management espouses the belief that problem drinkers have the power to control their drinking and can rely on their own judgment and self-agency to return to moderate drinking. In other words, abstinence is not the only solution. This belief has broader implications for the MM philosophy, particularly as it compares to the core philosophies of AA. Moderation Management members can essentially do away with AA steps 1 through 3: *We admitted we were powerless over alcohol—that our lives had become unmanageable, we came to believe that a Power greater than ourselves could restore us to sanity,* and *we made a decision to turn our will and our lives over to the care of God as we understood Him* (Alcoholics Anonymous, 1952–1953). In doing away with the first three step of AA, MM rejects the need for a Higher Power or spiritual transformation in the path toward change, beliefs that are central to AA's path for recovery. Moderation Management also rejects AA's idea that narcissism or "self-will run riot" is a core aspect of the disease of alcoholism. Although MM obviously does not encourage narcissism in a pathological sense, it does put an emphasis on self-agency and personal will.

Moderation Management has a nine-step cognitive behavioral change program (Kishline, 1994):

1. Attend meetings or online groups and learn about the program of Moderation Management.
2. Abstain from alcoholic beverages for 30 days and complete steps three through six during this time.
3. Examine how drinking has affected your life.
4. Write down your life priorities.
5. Take a look at how much, how often, and under what circumstances you had been drinking.
6. Learn the MM guidelines and limits for moderate drinking.
7. Set moderate drinking limits and start weekly "small steps" toward balance and moderation in other areas of your life.
8. Review your progress and update your goals.
9. Continue to make positive lifestyle changes and attend meetings whenever you need ongoing support or would like to help newcomers.

The nine steps of MM do not describe limits on power or locus of control, or of giving oneself over to something outside oneself. Even the ethos of reciprocal helping is only briefly mentioned in the ninth step, as an optional function, *whenever you need ongoing support or would like to help newcomers* (Kishline, 1994), rather than as the central role that interpersonal ethics and reciprocal helping plays in AA. Moderation Management's nine steps present a measured, rational, logical approach, with an absence of spiritual content and almost no appeal to the emotional self. For some individuals, the absence of spirituality, the emphasis on self-efficacy, and the overall logical approach is precisely what draws them to MM and away from AA.

Moderation Management is a hotly debated topic in the addiction field, in part because it challenges some of the primary tenets of AA, but more because Audrey Kishline ultimately killed two people while driving drunk. Moderation Management is built on the premise that individuals can accurately self-select for a group like MM, which excludes those with alcohol dependence but welcomes those with less severe forms of problem drinking. Opponents of MM argue that the alcoholic will never appropriately self-select because denial and "self-will run riot" are part of the disease of addiction, and the alcoholic will always consider his or her drinking to be under better control than

it is. Opponents of MM put forth the sad history of Audrey Kishline herself, who left MM to join AA and shortly thereafter was driving while intoxicated and killed two people in a horrific car accident. Proponents of MM argue that the fact that Kishline recognized that she had become alcohol-dependent and left MM to join AA prior to the accident is evidence that their selection process is well-founded.

Although both AA and MM share the universal features of all self-help organizations, they differ in significant ways, most importantly their target population (all problem drinkers in AA vs. nondependent drinkers only in MM) and their goals for change (abstinence in AA vs. harm reduction through moderate drinking or abstinence in MM). The two organizations also differ greatly in their emphasis on spirituality, with AA highlighting the importance of giving oneself over to a Higher Power and MM promulgating self-control and rational cognitions as the cornerstone of non-harmful alcohol consumption. Proponents of MM argue that their group fills a niche that is not filled by AA or other self-help organizations targeting alcohol use problems, whereas AA argues that all problem drinkers are potentially well-served by AA, thus making MM superfluous or even harmful. The effectiveness of AA versus MM has not been directly compared, which might be a contrived comparison in any event because they intend to serve different populations. Alcoholics Anonymous is a vastly larger organization than MM and has been around for many more decades. However, AA and MM have been studied separately, with abundant data on the effectiveness of AA in combating alcohol addiction and some preliminary data on MM's effectiveness in attracting nondependent problem drinkers.

Effectiveness of Self-Help Groups for Substance Use Disorders

The vast majority of the data on self-help groups is from studies of AA and other 12-step organizations that promote abstinence as the means of recovery. As we discuss here, AA is effective at reducing substance use and improving the lives of its members and is as effective as professional outpatient treatments, such as cognitive behavioral therapy (CBT), at a fraction of the financial cost.

Project MATCH compared the outcome of 12-step facilitation counseling with two other forms of professional treatment for alcohol use disorders: Motivational interviewing (MI) and CBT. Twelve-step facilitation counseling is professionally guided treatment that uses the 12 steps of

AA as a template for recovery. Across these conditions, patients who attended AA more often in the 3-month interval after treatment had better abstinence rates than did patients who did not (Tonigan, 2001). In another study, patients with alcohol use disorders who attended AA at least weekly, versus those who did not attend, had more reduction in alcohol use and more abstinent days (Gossop et al., 2003). Likewise, in patients with alcohol and/or drug use disorders who participated in AA or Narcotics Anonymous (NA), a group similar to AA but specifically targeting the use of illicit drugs, abstinence rates at 12 months were all higher than rates for those not participating in AA or NA (Crape, Latkin, Caris, & Knowlton, 2002). The data suggest that the longer individuals attend AA groups, the longer they will remain abstinent. Moos and Moos showed that longer duration of attendance in AA in the first year after seeking help was associated with higher abstinence rates 1, 8, and 16 years later (Moos, & Moos, 2006), as well as lower 15-year mortality (Timko, DeBenedetti, Moos, & Moos, 2006).

Historically, studies assessing the impact of AA involvement on substance use are not randomized and are therefore limited by self-selection bias. However, in recent trials, randomized designs have become more common. A randomized controlled trial in which patients in treatment were actively recruited to AA (intensive referral; counselors linking patients to 12-step volunteers, and using 12-step journals to check on meeting attendance) compared to those who received a standard referral to AA (standard referral, patients receiving a schedule for local 12-step Self-help Group [SHG] meetings) had better drug and alcohol use outcomes in the following 6 months (Timko, Debenedetti, & Billow, 2006).

Subsequently, in a randomized trial with 169 alcohol-dependent outpatients, Walitzer, Dermen, and Barrick (2009) found that motivational enhancement to attend AA had no positive effect. However, directive counseling to attend AA resulted in higher meeting attendance and a higher percentage of days abstinent than did a comparison condition with no emphasis on AA. Although it was focused on expanding social network support for sobriety from all sources (not just AA), a randomized trial by Litt and colleagues (2007) also yielded important results. Alcohol-dependent individuals randomized to a social network support condition had more AA involvement and less alcohol consumption than did those randomized to case management.

Substance use outcomes from participation in AA and other similar organizations appear to be on par with professionally administered outpatient treatment. Humphreys and Moos (2007) have shown that outcomes for drinking and psychosocial markers are comparable between 12-step groups and professionally administered CBT for outcomes except abstinence, for which 12-step groups are associated with higher rates at 1- and 2-year follow-ups. Individuals who enter AA have less income, less education, and have experienced more bad outcomes from their drinking than individuals who initially obtain professional outpatient care (Humphreys & Moos, 1996). Moreover, AA members expend 45% less on alcohol-related health care than do comparable individuals seeking professional treatments over 3 years (Humphreys & Moos, 1996).

Alcoholics Anonymous and similar 12-step groups may be most effective for those who are more severely addicted, perhaps because such individuals can more easily embrace the 12-step philosophy (Moos & Timko, 2008). Heavier substance users and those with less control over substances are more likely to have better attendance for longer durations than are less impaired users (Tonigan & Bogenschutz, 2006). In terms of alcoholics who have psychiatric comorbidities, the evidence for efficacy is mixed. Ritsher, Moos, and Finney (2002) found that alcoholics with co-occurring psychiatric disorders are as likely to attend and benefit from AA as are alcoholics without co-occurring psychiatric disorders. However, Kelly, McKellar, and Moos (2003) have shown that those with major depressive disorder (MDD) are less likely to affiliate with AA than are those without co-occurring MDD and also appear to have poorer abstinence outcomes at 2-year follow-up despite affiliating. These data are difficult to interpret, given the overlap in symptom phenotype between depression and SUDs (Mueser, Drake, & Wallach, 1998). Alcoholics Anonymous appears to be effective for individuals with severe alcohol dependence, and co-occurring psychiatric illness may or may not be an obstacle to participation. More data are needed on this subpopulation of drinkers with co-occurring disorders.

Religious individuals are slightly more likely than nonreligious individuals to affiliate with AA initially, but once affiliated (Kaskutas, Turk, Bond, & Weisner, 2003), less religious individuals benefit from AA as much as more religious ones do (Winzelberg & Humphreys, 1999). Individuals court-mandated to attend AA are less likely to benefit as non–court mandated; mandated patients as compared with nonmandated patients attended more meetings and were more likely to endorse a spiritual awakening (Humphreys, Kaskutas, & Weisner, 1998).

There are no prospective studies examining the efficacy of MM on substance use or other markers of well-being. The number of meetings of MM available at any given place or time is a mere fraction of the number of meetings of AA groups, which makes researching it more challenging. There are two cross-sectional studies examining the types of drinkers attracted to MM and how members differ if they access the group in F2F meetings, online, or both (Humphreys & Klaw, 2001; Kosok, 2006). These studies surveyed members to assess drinking patterns and basic sociodemographic variables. The effectiveness of MM depends, by its own description, on its ability to attract nondependent drinkers. Moderation Management outlines drinking amounts that should not be exceeded in order to qualify for participation in its groups.

Humphreys and Klaw (2001) reported that of 177 surveyed MM participants, 62 attended F2F meetings, 73 participated only over the Internet (online; OL), and 42 did both. The majority of MM members are white, middle-aged, college-educated, and employed. Gender is equally split. In terms of drinking days, 61.7% of MM members who attend F2F meetings drink 4 or more days per week; 87.1% of MM members who participate in MM online drink 4 or more days per week, and 85.4% of drinkers who both attend F2F meetings and participate OL drink 4 or more days per week.

This finding is significant in a number of respects. The majority of members in all three groups appear to drink on more days than MM recommends for moderate nondependent drinkers. Those who participate online appear to drink on more days than those who do not, which may speak indirectly to differences in efficacy between F2F meetings and OL meetings, although this has yet to be studied to establish cause and effect. Humphreys and Klaw also find that 49.1% of F2F members drink five or more drinks per drinking day, 70.6% of OL members drink five or more drinks per drinking day, and 53.8% of members who participate in both drink five or more drinks per drinking day. Moderation Management recommends no more than four drinks per day for men and no more than three drinks per day for women. At least half of the members in all three groups are exceeding MM guidelines for moderate drinking. This study does not directly assess criteria for current alcohol dependence among MM members (Humphreys & Klaw, 2001).

The Kosok (2006) study essentially replicates the Humphreys and Klaw study, with a similar survey analysis of MM members completed 5 years later,

after the organization had grown and expanded its Internet use in particular. Of the 272 MM members surveyed, 45 participated in the F2F group only, 172 in the OL group only, and 55 in the both groups. Like Humphreys and Klaw, Kosok finds the majority of MM members are white, middle-aged, college-educated, and employed. However, in Kosok's study, women made up 66% of members. Also like Humphreys and Klaw, the Kosok study finds that MM members are regular, heavy drinkers, with the majority exceeding MM mandates for moderate drinking. In the Kosok study, 61% of members drink on a daily basis, not the 3–4 days recommended by MM, and the average number of drinks on a drinking day is six, not the 3–4 drinks recommended. Kosok also finds that members participating in F2F groups drink less than those in online options (Kosok, 2006).

Both the Humphreys and Klaw (2001) and Kosok (2006) studies found that the majority of MM members drink in excess of what is mandated by MM guidelines, and drinking amounts and frequency are higher among members who participate online than in those who attend F2F meetings. Nonetheless, many members do follow the guidelines, and, on measures of alcohol-related problem severity and perceived severity of drinking, members of MM scored about one standard deviation lower than members of AA, measuring in the low dependency range (30). This suggests that MM members overall have less severe drinking problems than AA members; but another possibility is that MM members are not perceiving their drinking as problematic, whereas AA members are encouraged to do so. Kosok, by contrast, finds that MM members measure in the medium dependency range, which may represent a difference in methodology or a change over the interceding years in the membership of MM to a population of drinkers with more significant alcohol-related problems.

It is interesting to observe that the majority of MM members do not adhere to the moderate drinking guidelines outlined by the MM literature. This does not prove that the organization is without value: many people speed when driving, yet speed limits promote public safety by anchoring what is considered *fast*. Some evidence suggests that individuals with more severe drinking problems are more likely than those with less severe problems to actively participate in MM after an initial inquiry (Klaw, Horst, & Humphreys, 2006), although on average members' levels of severity of drinking in MM are below those of AA members. To extend the speed limit analogy, MM may be a helpful guide for individuals who are habitually exceeding the speed limit but have not yet crashed. More research is needed to determine whether MM's majority population of heavy, regular drinkers is able to achieve the goals of moderation espoused by MM, although they do not appear to meet MM's own guidelines for moderation when they join. It is also interesting to note that those who attend F2F meetings of MM drink less than their counterparts who participate online. Given the ubiquity of online interaction of humans today, it will also be important to establish whether meetings in cyberspace can have the same impact as F2F meetings.

Although there are no longitudinal efficacy data for MM, there is a growing literature on the positive impact of brief interventions by health care professionals that emphasize reducing drinking in those with hazardous nondependent use. It is also true that the numbers of problem drinkers far exceed alcohol-dependent drinkers, and this population is seldom receptive to an abstinence goal but may be receptive to decreasing use. In other words, there is a reasonable target population for MM—a group of individuals who may indeed be receptive to and benefit from a goal of substance use reduction and who may not be appropriate for AA or abstinence. It will be interesting to see if MM can build up the kind of momentum that AA has over its lifetime and attract the kinds of members who might really benefit from participation.

Social and Psychological Mechanisms of Change in Self-Help Groups

Self-help groups promote change through mechanisms also found in behavior therapy (counterconditioning, stimulus control, and reinforcement, as briefly described in previous sections). Change is also facilitated by social-interpersonal and intrapersonal psychological mechanisms, which can be loosely grouped into the following five categories: (1) providing structure, (2) teaching specific coping strategies, (3) enhancing social networks, (4) increasing self-efficacy, and (5) fostering a new identity. Spiritual transformation is considered by many as fundamental to the change mechanism in AA, and so we will also discuss how this is thought to occur.

Self-help groups promote change by providing structure. They provide a specific time and place where meetings are held, usually in person, but in the case of MM, often on the Internet. On a very basic level, meetings fill a member's time with activity incompatible with drinking and demand that member's presence and attention. Heavy substance use takes up an inordinate amount of time in a person's life, and giving up substances creates a vacuum that can contribute to boredom and profound feelings of sadness and hopelessness, not to mention craving for substances. Self-help group meetings fill time and structure a day, replacing the prior dominant structure (i.e., seeking, using, and recovering from substance use). Self-help groups also provide structure through predictable meeting formats, such as an opening ritual, sharing stories, and a closing ritual. These predictable formats mitigate social anxiety, combat the social isolation inherent in SUDs, and keep members focused on the goals of the group. Moderation Management members who attend F2F meetings drink on average less than those who attend meetings online, which suggests that the inherent structure of F2F meetings contributes to recovery in a way that cannot be matched by the individually regulated style of participation afforded by the Internet.

Self-help groups promote change by teaching specific strategies for coping; for example, how to challenge destructive thoughts and avoid use triggers. These specific strategies are disseminated in various ways. They are communicated from one member to another at meeting time and also take shape in the group's literature in the form of homilies (e.g. *The Serenity Prayer* in AA), catch-phrases (e.g. *stinkin' thinkin', one day at a time* in AA, and *balance and moderation in all areas of life* in MM), and, of course, in *The Steps. The Steps* provide an organized roadmap for recovery and embody the well-known learning principle of *chaining* (i.e., breaking a complex process down into well-defined segments). Snow et al. has shown that individuals who are actively involved in AA are more likely to use certain coping strategies over others to avoid substance (Snow, Prochaska, & Rossi, 1994). For example, members of AA, when faced with the impulse to use substances, are more likely to talk to someone about their drinking problem (e.g., call their sponsor), seek out the company of non–substance using peers (e.g., go to meeting), and give themselves positive rewards for not drinking (Snow et al., 1994). Although a similar study has yet to be conducted for MM, one could imagine MM members utilizing similar coping skills when faced with the challenge of drinking in moderation.

Self-help groups also promote change by enhancing social networks. In self-help groups focused on abstinence, the group provides a social circle in which substance use is prohibited, giving members the opportunity to learn how to spend time with and create bonds with other people without relying on substances as a form of entertainment or a means of social lubrication. In self-help groups focused on harm reduction, a similar mechanism comes into play, whereby the group provides a social circle in which moderate drinking is acceptable while excessive harmful drinking is frowned on. Many addicted persons who want to quit using substances report that the influence of substance-using friends creates a major obstacle to recovery. Self-help groups foster a new social milieu that, in many cases of strong affiliation, comes to completely supplant the individual's former social circle. Studies have shown that individuals who attend 12-step groups develop new friends who are more likely to abstain from substances and who provide more support for recovery and that nearly half of the association of self-help group involvement and substance use at 1-year is related to the strength of these new social networks (Humphreys & Noke, 1997).

Self-help groups promote change by increasing self-efficacy. *Self-efficacy* can be defined as the sense of confidence one has that one can meet chosen goals. It differs from motivation per se in that motivation is *I want to do it*, and efficacy is *I can do it*. Self-help groups increase self-efficacy in a number of important ways, one of which is the sharing of personal narratives by members at all different stages of recovery. These narratives serve as a constant reminder of what life was like while using/abusing substances, what life has become since stopping or decreasing use, and what life might be like again should substance use/abuse resume. Members in the later stages of recovery can look at new members and realize how far they have come, and members in the early stages of recovery can look at long-term members and realize what is possible. Both these perspectives enhance the sense of *I can do it*. By instilling hope through this mechanism of mirroring, members experience change. In Project MATCH, AA attendance 6 months after receiving the acute treatment (12-step vs. CBT vs. MI) predicted self-efficacy at 9 months, which in turn predicted abstinence at 15 months (Connors, Tonigan, & Miller, 2001).

Self-help groups promote change by fostering a new identity. First of all, to affiliate with a given self-help group, prospective members must self-identify with having the problem shared by other members of the group. For many individuals with addiction, this is not an easy task.

Acknowledging that one has the problem of addiction is a major shift in identity. In AA, members are asked early to embrace the new identity of being an *alcoholic*. This new identity is promoted in AA by a common ritual in which members state: "My name is Jane and I am an alcoholic." Along with this identity as an alcoholic, members in AA are also asked to let go of their own sense of being in control of their lives and to give this control over to something outside of themselves. Changing one's internal sense of locus of control is also a major change in identity. Although members of MM are not asked to give up a sense of being in control, they, too, experience a shift in identity by admitting that their drinking is problematic and joining with others to publicly embrace a desire for change. The ethos of reciprocal helping also contributes to identity change. By acting as a sponsor or provider of emotional support to another member, one begins to view oneself as having begun to achieve a way of being in the world that is radically different from the way one was. Finally, working the fourth step of AA and admitting one's own contribution to problematic interpersonal relationships encourages members to view themselves and others differently, thereby further shaping a new sense of identity. Identity change allows closer affiliation with the group, which in turn has been shown to improve attendance at meetings and substance use outcomes (Blonigen et al., 2009).

Brown, Tiebout, Bateson, and others have written extensively on the spiritual path that is taken in AA and how this path is at the core of change. All three argue that the process of recovery is related to power and surrender of that power to something outside oneself, as described in detail in earlier sections. In AA, *hitting bottom* is a term used to describe that point of surrender when the illusion of control can no longer be maintained in the face of stark reality (e.g., job loss, marriage dissolution, illness, etc.). Once the alcoholic has surrendered the sense of being in control, he or she is then ready to make the shift into recovery. The acceptance of lack of control over one's own destiny is a fundamentally spiritual orientation that is arguably at the heart of all religions. Fowler has detailed the progression from spiritual surrender, or *hitting bottom*, through the different phases of spiritual transformation (Fowler, 1993) and linked them to Brown's trajectory of recovery, from the transition phase, to the early recovery phase, to the ongoing recovery phase (Brown, 1993).

The transition phase of recovery (Brown, 1993) is marked by affiliation with and dependency on the group and a following of the rules and steps in a somewhat blinded fashion. This phase corresponds to an early stage in faith-based development that is characterized by magical-imitative dependency and rule-grounded affiliation (Fowler, 1993). Next comes the early recovery phase, in which members begin to integrate new attitudes and behaviors, attend to their subjective experience, and face life issues, including layers of guilt and shame. This corresponds to the synthetic-convention stage of faith development, in which the individual begins to experience a shift in identity and a personal relationship with the Higher Power, but still relies heavily on the group for self-reflection and core identity. The phase of ongoing recovery is one in which the individual can identify character defects and take real ownership and responsibility for life actions, learning to use the steps as tools to achieve serenity. The ongoing recovery phase corresponds to the reflective stage of faith, in which persons can think critically about beliefs and practices and apply them in real time as a guide, not a mandate, and in which humility and selflessness become a vehicle for grace, not a sacrifice to surrender.

Conclusion

In reflecting on the differences between AA and MM, the contrast between these organizations is brought into greatest relief by the notion of surrendering control to a Higher Power. Surrendering existential control is probably easier when alcohol use has led to serious adverse consequences (i.e., "hitting bottom"). Drinkers with more drinking-related problems may find it easier to embrace the notion that their lives have *become unmanageable* (AA Step 1), and that a Power greater than themselves can restore them *to sanity* (AA Step 2). The MM organization, by contrast, is subscribed to by predominantly white, employed, educated persons: in other words, the dominant social class. Despite regular, heavy alcohol consumption, many MM members have been able to maintain significant control in some domains of life. Although potentially less receptive to the spiritual mechanism of change in AA, MM members are able to acknowledge that drinking is problematic and to look for solutions. It remains to be seen whether MM provides an effective mechanism of change; but if indeed DiClemente is correct and drinkers in the precontemplation and contemplation stages of change are not well-served by AA, MM might fill an important niche not only

for nondependent problem drinkers, but also for alcoholics who are contemplating change but not yet ready to take that leap and haven't yet—through life circumstances—been forced to. The limited research on MM suggests that some portion of its members, based on amounts alone, may not be able to follow MM guidelines. But we do not, as some other critics have, necessarily consider this a liability, particularly if MM is able to either modify the course of a drinking problem or move members from a stage of precontemplation to one of action, which might possibly include joining AA.

Acknowledgments

Dr. Humphreys's work on this chapter was supported in part by a research career scientist award from the Department of Veterans Affairs.

References

Alcoholics Anonymous. (1939). *Alcoholics Anonymous: The story of how many thousands of men and women have recovered from alcoholism.* New York: Alcoholics Anonymous World Services.

Alcoholics Anonymous. (1952–1953). *Twelve steps and twelve traditions.* New York: Alcoholics Anonymous World Services.

Bateson, G. (1971). The cybernetics of "self": A theory of alcoholism. *Psychiatry: Journal for the Study of Interpersonal Processes, 34,* 1–18.

Blonigen, D. M., Timko, C., Moos, B. S., & Moos, R. H. (2009). Treatment, alcoholics anonymous, and 16-year changes in impulsivity and legal problems among men and women with alcohol use disorders. *Journal of Studies on Alcohol and Drugs, 70*(5): 714–725.

Brown, S. (1993). Therapeutic processes in Alcoholics Anonymous. In B. S. McCrady & W. R. Miller (Eds.), *Research on Alcoholics Anonymous: Opportunities and alternatives* (pp. 137–152). New Brunswick, NJ: Alcohol Research Documentation, Inc., Rutgers University.

Connors, G. J., Tonigan, J. S., & Miller, W. R. (2001). A longitudinal model of intake symptomatology, AA participation and outcome: Retrospective study of the project MATCH outpatient and aftercare samples. *Journal of Studies on Alcohol and Drugs, 62*(6), 817–825.

Crape, B. L., Latkin, C. A., Laris, A. S., & Knowlton, A. R. (2002). The effects of sponsorship in 12-step treatment of injection drug users. *Drug and Alcohol Dependence, 65*(3), 291–301.

DiClemente, C. C. (1993). Alcoholics Anonymous and the structure of change. In B. S. McCrady & W. R. Miller (Eds.), *Research on Alcoholics Anonymous: Opportunities and alternatives* (pp. 79–97). New Brunswick, NJ: Alcohol Research Documentation, Inc., Rutgers University.

Fowler, J. W. (1993). Alcoholics Anonymous and faith development. In B. S. McCrady & W. R Miller (Eds.), *Research on Alcoholics Anonymous: Opportunities and alternatives* (pp. 113–135). New Brunswick, NJ: Alcohol Research Documentation, Inc., Rutgers University.

Gossop, M., Harris, J., Best, D., Man, L. H., Manning, V., Marshall, J., & Strang, J. (2003). Is attendance at Alcoholics

Anonymous meetings after inpatient treatment related to improved outcomes? A 6-month follow-up study. *Alcohol and Alcoholism*, *38*(5), 421–426.

Humphreys, K. (2004). *Circles of recovery: Self-help organizations for addictions*. Cambridge, UK: Cambridge University Press.

Humphreys, K., Kaskutas, L. A., & Weisner, C. (1998). The relationship of pre-treatment Alcoholics Anonymous affiliation with problem severity, social resources and treatment history. *Drug and Alcohol Dependence*, *49*(2), 123–131.

Humphreys, K., & Klaw, E. (2001). Can targeting nondependent problem drinkers and providing internet-based services expand access to assistance for alcohol problems? A study of the moderation management self-help/mutual aid organization. *Journal of Studies on Alcohol and Drugs*, *62*(4), 528.

Humphreys, K., & Moos, R. H. (1996). Reduced substance-abuse-related health care costs among voluntary participants in Alcoholics Anonymous. *Psychiatric Services*, *47*(7), 709–713.

Humphreys, K., & Moos, R. H. (2007). Encouraging posttreatment self-help group involvement to reduce demand for continuing care services: Two-year clinical and utilization outcomes. *Alcoholism: Clinical and Experimental Research*, *31*, 64–68.

Humphreys, K., & Noke, J. M. (1997). The influence of post-treatment mutual help group participation on the friendship networks of substance abuse patients. *American Journal of Community Psychology*, *25*(1), 1–16.

Humphreys, K., & Ribisl, K. (1999). The case for a partnership with self-help groups. *Public Health Reports*, *114*, 322–329.

Kaskutas, L. A., Turk, N., Bond, J., & Weisner, C. (2003). The role of religion, spirituality and Alcoholics Anonymous in sustained sobriety. *Alcoholism Treatment Quarterly*, *21*(1), 1–16.

Kelly, J. F., McKellar, J. D., & Moos, R. (2003). Major depression in patients with substance use disorders: Relationship to 12-step self-help involvement and substance use outcomes. *Addiction*, *98*(4), 499–508.

Kishline, A. (1994). *Moderate drinking: The moderation management guide for people who want to reduce their drinking*. New York: Crown.

Klaw, E., Horst, D., & Humphreys, K. (2006). Inquirers, triers, and buyers of an alcohol harm reduction self-help organization. *Addiction Research & Theory*, *14*(5), 527–553.

Klaw, E., Huebsch, P. D., & Humphreys, K. (2000). Communication patterns in an on-line mutual help group for problem drinkers. *Journal of Community Psychology*, *28*, 535–546.

Kosok, A. (2006). The Moderation Management programme in 2004: What type of drinker seeks controlled drinking? *International Journal of Drug Policy*, *17*(4), 295–303.

Litt, M. D., Kadden, R. M., Kabela-Cormier, E., & Petry, N. (2007). Changing network support for drinking: Initial findings from the Network Support Project. *Journal of Consulting and Clinical Psychology*, *75*, 542–555.

Miller, W. R., & McCrady, B. S. (1993). The importance of research on Alcoholics Anonymous. In B. S. McCrady & W. R. Miller (Eds.), *Research on Alcoholics Anonymous: Opportunities and alternatives* (pp. 3–11). New Brunswick, NJ: Rutgers Center on Alcohol Studies.

Moos, R. H., & Moos, B. S. (2006). Participation in treatment and Alcoholics Anonymous: A 16-year follow-up of initially untreated individuals. *Journal of Clinical Psychology*, *62*(6), 735–750.

Moos, R. H., & Timko, C. (2008). Outcome research on 12-step and other self-help programs. In Galanter & H. D. Kleber (Eds.), *Textbook of substance abuse treatment* (4th ed., pp. 511–521). Washington, DC: American Psychiatric Press.

Mueser, K. T., Drake, R. E., & Wallach, M. A. (1998). Dual diagnosis: A review of etiological theories. *Addictive Behaviors*, *23*(6), 717–734.

Ritsher, J. B., Moos, R. H., & Finney, J. W. (2002). Relationship of treatment orientation and continuing care to remission among substance abuse patients. *Psychiatric Services*, *53* (5), 595–601.

Sanchez-Craig, M., Wilkinson, D. A., & Davila, R. (1995). Empirically based guidelines for moderate drinking: 1-year results from three studies with problem drinkers. *American Journal of Public Health*, *85*, 823–828.

Schaff, P. (1910). *History of the Christian church v. III. Modern Christianity: The Swiss Reformation*. New York: Charles Scribner's Sons.

Smiles, S. (1859). *Self-help; with illustrations of character and conduct*. London: S. W. Partridge & Company.

Smiles, S. (1866). *Self-help; with illustrations of character, conduct, and perseverance* (2nd ed.). Boston: Ticknor & Fields.

Snow, M. G., Prochaska, J. O., & Rossi, J. S. (1994). Processes of change in Alcoholics Anonymous: Maintenance factors in long-term sobriety. *Journal of Studies on Alcohol and Drugs*, *55*(3), 362.

Tiebout, H. M. (1949). The act of surrender in the psychotherapeutic process with special reference to alcoholism. *Quarterly Journal of Studies on Alcohol*, *10*, 48–58.

Timko, C., DeBenedetti, A., & Billow, R. (2006). Intensive referral to 12-Step self-help groups and 6-month substance use disorder outcomes. *Addiction*, *101*(5), 678–88.

Timko, C., DeBenedetti, A., Moos, B. S., & Moos, R. H. (2006). Predictors of 16-year mortality among individuals initiating help-seeking for an alcoholic use disorder. *Alcoholism: Clinical and Experimental Research*, *30*(10), 1711–1720.

Tonigan, J. S. (2001). Benefits of Alcoholics Anonymous attendance: Replication of findings between clinical research sites in Project MATCH. *Alcoholism Treatment Quarterly*, *19*, 67–78.

Tonigan, J. S., Bogenschutz, M. P., & Miller, W. R. (2006). Is alcoholism typology a predictor of both Alcoholics Anonymous affiliation and disaffiliation after treatment? *Journal of Substance Abuse Treatment*, *30*(4), 323–330.

Walitzer, K. S., Dermen, K. H., & Barrick, C. (2009). Facilitating involvement in Alcoholics Anonymous during outpatient treatment: A randomized clinical trial. *Addiction*, *104*, 391–401.

Winzelberg, A., & Humphreys, K. (1999). Should patients' religiosity influence clinicians' referral to 12-step self-help groups? Evidence from a study of 3,018 male substance abuse patients. *Journal of Consulting and Clinical Psychology*, *67*(5), 790–794.

Pharmacotherapy of Substance Use, Craving, and Acute Abstinence Syndromes

Robert M. Swift

Abstract

Advances in the understanding of the neurobiological basis of addiction have led to a better understanding of the causes of drug and alcohol dependence, as well as to new alternatives in the treatment of these disorders. By addressing some of the underlying neurobiological changes that cause and maintain drug and alcohol dependence, pharmacotherapies can provide an important adjunctive treatment for alcohol- and drug-dependent and behaviorally addicted patients. During detoxification, pharmacotherapies can reduce the severity of withdrawal. After detoxification, pharmacotherapies can be useful as an adjunct to psychosocial treatments to help maintain abstinence or reduced addictive behaviors by reducing craving, reducing the rewarding effects of drugs, and improving the allostasis that accompanies abstinence. This chapter describes the neurobiology of drugs and alcohol, how chronic use leads to brain adaptations that result in addiction, and the actions of medications used to treat addictive disorders.

Key Words: pharmacotherapy, withdrawal, medications, craving, adjunctive treatment, disulfiram, naltrexone, acamprosate, buprenorphine, varenicline, methadone

The Neurobiology of Addiction

In the past several decades, we have learned much about why persons develop addictions—that is, why they use psychoactive substances or engage in repeated harmful behaviors, such as compulsive gambling to excess or in an uncontrolled fashion. The causes of addiction are complex and include both environmental (social and cultural) and biological (genetic and physiological) factors. Drugs, alcohol, and rewarding behaviors, such as gambling, share common brain mechanisms that produce pleasure (reward) and relieve distress (Koob & Volkow, 2010; Probst & van Eimeren, 2013). However, over time, the frequent exposure of the brain to psychoactive substances or rewarding behaviors causes long-term adaptations in neurotransmitter release, receptors, and other aspects of neuronal signal transduction. It is these adaptations that lead to addiction. This chapter discusses

some of the neurobiological changes that occur in response to acute and chronic drug and alcohol use and how some of these changes can be ameliorated through the use of medications that target this neurobiology.

The behavioral effect of most drugs starts with a pharmacological effect that alters the activity in a specific neurotransmitter system. For example, nicotine interferes with the action of acetylcholine at the nicotinic acetylcholine receptor, cocaine interferes with the activity of certain transporters that remove dopamine (DA) from the synapse, and opiates mimic the action of endorphin neurotransmitters at opioid receptors. Other drugs, notably alcohol and inhalant solvents, can affect several different neurotransmitters acting through more nonspecific effects on cell membranes and by binding to hydrophobic areas on membrane proteins. Table 21.1 shows the most commonly abused

Table 21.1. Psychoactive Substances and Their Mechanisms of Action

Drug	Mechanism of Action
Alcohol (Ethanol)	Affects membrane bound ion channel and G-protein receptors (dopamine, norepinephrine, serotonin, GABA, NMDA, etc.); "binds" to hydrophobic pockets in proteins and alters protein structure and function
Amphetamines and similar stimulants	Potentiates the action of neurotransmitters DA and norepinephrine by binding to transporters; also release neurotransmitters
Caffeine	Binds to adenosine receptors; inhibits a phosphodiesterase enzyme leading to increased levels of the second-messenger cyclic AMP
Cannabis	Cannabinoids bind to G protein-linked cannabinoid receptors for endogenous lipid signaling ligands (anandamide, 2-arachidonyl glycerol)
Cocaine	Binds to DA, norepinephrine, and serotonin transporters, blocking neurotransmitter reuptake into neurons; also releases neurotransmitters
Hallucinogens (LSD, Hallucinogenic amphetamines)	Antagonists at 5-HT_{1A} and 5-HT_2 serotonin receptors; may also release serotonin
Inhalants (organic solvents)	Solvents act similarly to ethanol, disrupt membranes and membrane-bound proteins
Inhalants (nitrites)	Mimic the action of nitric oxide at its receptors
Nicotine	Binds to nicotinic acetylcholine receptors; low doses stimulate the receptors, high doses block the receptors
Opioids	Binds to opioid receptors for endorphins (μ receptors), enkephalins (δ receptors), dynorphins (κ receptors)
Phencyclidine and ketamine	Binds to NMDA glutamate receptors, decreasing glutamate excitation
Sedatives, hypnotics, and benzodiazepine anxiolytics	Binds to $GABA_A$ receptor-chloride channel complex, increasing chloride conductance and inhibiting neuronal firing

5-HT, serotonin; AMP, adenosine monophosphate; DA, dopamine; GABA, γ-aminobutyric acid; NMDA, N-methyl-D-aspartate.

psychoactive substances, and the neurotransmitter systems affected.

Although each class of psychoactive substances typically targets a single, main neurotransmitter system, a common action of all drugs is to affect the neurotransmitter DA. The stimulant and rewarding effects of psychoactive substances (including alcohol, cannabis, nicotine, sedatives, and stimulants) and rewarding behaviors, such as gambling, are mediated through activation of the neurotransmitter DA in the ventral tegmentum and nucleus accumbens (Wise & Borarth, 1987). A mesolimbic DA pathway and related limbic circuits, including the hippocampus, amygdala, and prefrontal cortex, are part of the motivational system that regulates responses to natural reinforcers, such as food and water, sex, and social interaction (Koob & Volkow, 2010). Activation of the mesolimbic pathway increases the activity of DA neurons in the ventral tegmental area (VTA) of the midbrain and increases the release of DA into the nucleus accumbens (NAcc) and other areas of the limbic forebrain, such as the amygdala and prefrontal cortex (Brodie, Shefner, & Dunwiddie, 1990; Weiss, Lorang, Bloom, & Koob, 1993). Some substances, including amphetamines and cocaine, activate the DA pathway directly; other substances, including alcohol, cannabis nicotine, opiates, and rewarding behaviors activate the pathway indirectly through the action of other neurotransmitters (Figure 21.1). Repeated activation of this motivation–reward system by drugs, alcohol, or rewarding behaviors sensitizes the system, resulting in an increased salience or importance of the drug, an increased motivation

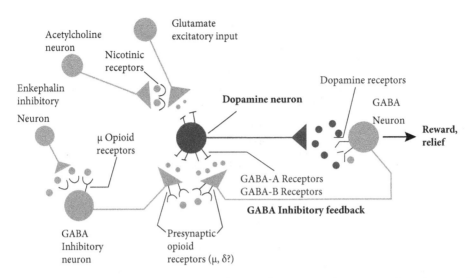

Figure 21.1 A dopamine (DA) neuron originating in the ventral tegmental area (VTA) and projecting to the nucleus accumbens. Dopamine neurons are regulated by a variety of neurotransmitter systems, several of which are shown. Drugs and alcohol activate the DA neurons, leading to reward and/or relief. Some drugs, such as amphetamines and cocaine, influence DA directly; drugs such as alcohol, nicotine, and opioids affect DA function indirectly.

to use addictive substances/activities, and the development of craving in response to stimuli associated with substance use (Nestler, 2001).

The neuronal adaptations due to repeated psychoactive substance use also can lead to withdrawal, an adaptive state characterized by unpleasant, punishing symptoms that occur whenever the substance is not present. The most common neurobiological mechanism for withdrawal is a change in the number of postsynaptic neurotransmitter receptors or in receptor sensitivity that occurs with chronic drug use. Withdrawal is not specific to addictive substances/activities because a withdrawal syndrome often results from the discontinuation of nonaddictive medications such as β-adrenergic blockers, antihistamines, antiarrhythmics, and antidepressants.

Typically, withdrawal symptoms are behaviorally and physiologically opposite to the drug effects. Thus, sedatives such as alcohol, barbiturates, or benzodiazepines produce a withdrawal syndrome characterized by excitation and can include symptoms of insomnia, anxiety, hallucinations, and seizures. Stimulants such as cocaine or amphetamines produce a withdrawal characterized by sedation, lethargy, fatigue, and depressed mood. The withdrawal from most substances has two phases: an acute, intense withdrawal beginning within hours after the cessation of drug or alcohol use and lasting several days to a few weeks, and a chronic or protracted and more indolent withdrawal that can last weeks to months. The duration and intensity

of acute and chronic withdrawal symptoms depends on the pharmacokinetics and pharmacodynamics of the drug, the amount and duration of drug use, and individual differences in vulnerability to experiencing withdrawal.

How chronic substance use and its associated neuroadaptations lead to acute withdrawal is well described for alcohol. The alcohol withdrawal syndrome is characterized by generalized central nervous system (CNS) excitation, anxiety, tremors, insomnia, and, in severe cases, seizures and hallucinations (delirium tremens; Swift, 1999a). Many of the symptoms of alcohol withdrawal can be explained by alcohol's actions on two brain ion channel neurotransmitters: γ-aminobutyric acid (GABA) and glutamate. GABA is the major inhibitory neurotransmitter in the brain and exerts its inhibitory effect on neurons by binding to the GABA_A receptor and opening an inhibitory chloride channel in nerve cell membranes. Glutamate is the major excitatory neurotransmitter in the CNS and exerts its excitatory activity by binding to glutamate N-methyl-D-aspartate (NMDA) receptors and opening an excitatory calcium ion channel. Acutely, alcohol facilitates the inhibitory effects of GABA at the GABA_A receptor and inhibits the excitatory effects of glutamate at the glutamate NMDA receptor. With repeated and chronic alcohol administration, the brain adapts to downregulate the inhibitory GABA_A receptors and upregulate the excitatory glutamate NMDA receptors, effectively increasing neuronal excitation to balance the sedative effects of alcohol. Then, if an alcohol-dependent person abruptly stops drinking, the sedative effects of alcohol can no longer balance the excitatory state and withdrawal symptoms emerge. Because re-exposure to alcohol produces an almost immediate cessation of withdrawal symptoms, withdrawal is an important factor in maintaining drug use.

After acute withdrawal symptoms have abated, abstinent drug- and alcohol-dependent individuals continue to experience a protracted, distressing state known as *allostasis*, characterized by increased anxiety, dysphoria, and difficulty coping with stress. Allostasis can last for weeks or months after the cessation of drug use (Bowirrat & Oscar-Berman, 2005; Comings & Blum, 2000; Koob, 2006). There appear to be two components to allostasis: abnormalities in the stress response system and abnormalities in reward system. The stress response system consists of nervous system (limbic system, hypothalamus, autonomic nervous system) and endocrine (pituitary gland, adrenal gland) systems that help the organism adapt to physiological and/or emotional stress. In the brain, the neurotransmitters corticotrophin-releasing factor (CRF), neuropeptide Y (NPY), dynorphins, and norepinephrine are important to the stress response; in the periphery, norepinephrine, epinephrine, and the adrenal hormone cortisol are the main mediators of the stress response. Acutely, the stress response is adaptive and important to survival; however, when stress is chronic and persistent, the response is maladaptive and unpleasant. A hyperactive stress response system can be innate or acquired. In animal models of addiction and in populations of human drug users, variation in the genes that control CRF, NPY, and other neurotransmitters involved in stress response have been shown to be associated with increased use of alcohol and drugs (Colombo, 1997; Lappalainen et al., 2002). The fact that many addictive substances/activities temporarily relieve stress and tension promotes the use of these substances (Brownell et al., 1986); however, with chronic alcohol and drug use, the stress response system adapts, becoming hyperresponsive whenever alcohol and drugs are not present. The hyperactive stress response is unpleasant and leads to a cycle of continued drug use to reduce the stress response, which leads to continued hyperactivity of stress response, and so on.

The other component of allostasis is reduced reward and pleasure. Persons with alcohol and drug dependence find that naturally rewarding stimuli, such as money, good food, and social status become less rewarding and less important than the drug. The reduced reward is thought to result from a decrement in dopaminergic function and from activation of the habenula, which occurs when reward is expected, but does not occur. Activation of the habenula may induce disappointment or sadness. In animals, the cessation of chronic alcohol use is followed by a decrement in DA release (Diana, Pistis, Carboni, Gessa, & Rossetti, 1993). In humans, neuroimaging studies show that chronic drug and alcohol use is associated with decreased DA function, as evidenced by reductions in D_2 DA receptors and decreased DA release in the striatum (Volkow, Fowler, Wang, Swanson, & Telang, 2007). In addition to causing reduced reward, the reduced mesolimbic dopaminergic activity affects limbic and cortical regions of the brain that are involved with decision making, behavioral integration, and behavioral inhibition. The decreased DA activity is thought to impair the orbitofrontal cortex, the cingulate gyrus, and the insula, leading to the loss of control over alcohol use and the impulsive and compulsive alcohol intake that characterizes alcohol dependence.

Craving is a behavior that is a component of reward, withdrawal, and allostasis (Swift, 1999b). "Craving" or "urge" to drink or to use drugs may be thought of as a phenomenon integrating a desire to increase a positive feeling and/or to overcome one that is negative. Craving is now included as one of the criteria for the diagnosis of addiction in the *Diagnostic and Statistical Manual of Mental Disorders* (DSM-V; APA, 2013). If craving is intense, the need to use alcohol or drugs can become a preoccupation or obsession. Craving is associated with increased relapse, particularly early in abstinence period (Anton, 1999; Rohsenow & Monti, 1992). Craving can be triggered by various stimuli, including the active use of a substance, experiencing withdrawal from a substance, or by experiencing internal or external cues associated with past substance use. Craving has been associated with sensitization of DA systems. Imaging studies show that alcohol and drug cues activate DA in limbic and memory circuits (amygdala, dorsal striatum, and hippocampus; Volkow et al., 2002). Furthermore, the administration of DA agonists and antagonists such as modafinil, haloperidol, tiapride, and olanzapine has been shown to moderate craving for drugs and alcohol (Swift, 2010). However, other neurotransmitter systems are also associated with craving, particularly serotonin (5-HT) systems, opioids, and glutamate.

Addictive disorders are particularly common in certain psychiatric disorders, especially schizophrenia, bipolar disorder, panic disorder, post-traumatic stress disorder, and certain personality disorders (Regier et al., 1990). The reasons for the high comorbidity of addictive disorders with certain psychiatric disorders are unknown. One hypothesis suggests that alcohol and drugs are used as self-medication to reduce psychological distress or psychiatric symptoms (Khantzian, 1985). Related to the self-medication hypothesis is the idea that psychiatric patients may abuse substances to relieve side effects of neuroleptic medications, including motor side effects and sedation (Schneier & Siris, 1987). Another hypothesis suggests that certain psychiatric disorders and addictive disorders may share a common neurobiological etiology. For example, alcohol and drug abuse may precipitate psychosis in individuals genetically vulnerable to schizophrenia or bipolar disorder (Tien & Anthony 1990; Turner & Tsuang 1990). Research on the etiology of psychiatric disorders and substance use disorders suggests that the disorders share a common neuroanatomy, with involvement of the limbic system and prefrontal cortex, and a common neurochemistry, with dysfunction in several common neurotransmitter systems, notably DA.

As with most complex behavioral disorders, there is a genetic contribution to the risk that an individual will develop an addictive disorder. In the case of alcohol dependence, for which the genetics has been best studied, approximately 40–50% of the risk for an individual developing the disorder is inherited (Heath, 1995). The risk of developing tobacco dependence is slightly lower, closer to 30–40%. However, the inheritance of addictive disorders is complex; there is no single gene that explains the genetic risk for dependence; rather, a number of genes interact with each other and with the environment. The best-studied gene that affects the risk of developing substance dependence is the gene that codes for the alcohol metabolizing enzyme aldehyde dehydrogenase (ALDH). Approximately 40% of individuals of Asian ancestry carry a variant of the ALDH gene (ALDH2*2) that results in altered alcohol metabolism and the accumulation of acetaldehyde, a toxic intermediate of alcohol metabolism. Whenever alcohol is consumed by individuals who carry this variant gene, they produce excess acetaldehyde, resulting in nausea, vomiting, sweating, and dizziness. At a population level, having this gene variant is protective against developing alcohol dependence (Crabb, Edenberg, Bosron, & Li,

1989; Higuchi, Matsushita, Murayama, Takagi, & Hayashida, 1995). Other genes may increase the risk of developing alcohol dependence. For example, a variant of the gene that codes for a subunit of the GABA receptor reduces the sedative effects of alcohol and may permit persons who carry the gene to drink larger quantities of alcohol (Das, Harel, Dey, Covault, & Kranzler, 2010). Researchers have so far identified more than 100 gene variants that can either increase or decrease the risk of developing alcoholism or other addictive disorders, and many more genes will no doubt be discovered (Goldman, Oroszi, & Ducci, 2005; Strat, Ramoz, Schumann, & Gorwood, 2008).

The Treatment of Addictive Disorders

One way to reduce the impact of addictive disorders is through treatment. Treatment consists of medical, psychological, and social interventions to reduce or eliminate the harmful effects of the addictive substances/activities or behaviors on the individual, his or her family and associates, and others in society. Currently, most treatments for addiction are psychosocially based. There are many evidence-based treatments for addictive disorders that have been shown to be effective, including cognitive behavioral therapy, motivational interviewing, and community reinforcement (Miller & Wilbourne, 2002; National Institute on Drug Abuse [NIDA], 2009). Although psychosocial treatments for addictive disorders can be effective in reducing substance use and increasing health and well-being, psychosocial treatments are not always completely successful for all patients Addictive disorders are chronic, relapsing disorders and frequently require repeated treatment episodes (McLellan, Lewis, O'Brien, & Kleber, 2000). In some studies, the proportion of newly abstinent substance-dependent patients who return to drug or alcohol use within the year following treatment can be 60% or greater (Brownell et al., 1986).

As knowledge of a neurobiological basis for addiction has increased, there has been increasing interest in the use of medications to improve the effectiveness of existing psychosocial treatments for addictive disorders. Certainly, medications are widely used for the treatment of other behavioral disorders, such as depression, anxiety, and psychosis. Medications are commonly used in the initial detoxification treatment for substance use and less commonly used for long-term maintenance treatment.

Mechanisms of Action of Pharmacotherapies

The main goals of addiction treatment are to help addicts avoid psychoactive substances and/or compulsive behaviors, to develop better methods of coping with life stresses, and to improve self-esteem and self-efficacy. Medications are increasingly used as part of an interdisciplinary addiction treatment program that also includes psychosocial therapies, such as counseling and self-help groups. The initial phase of treatment for most patients is detoxification to achieve a drug-free state and to minimize any withdrawal-associated morbidity. Pharmacotherapies are commonly used as part of detoxification treatment to ameliorate withdrawal symptoms, particularly when symptoms are severe. Because withdrawal treatment alone is usually insufficient to provide sustained abstinence from the use of alcohol or drugs, additional treatment is necessary to prevent relapse. Pharmacotherapies can be used along with psychosocial therapies to prevent relapse to drugs and alcohol. By modifying processes such as reinforcement, motivation, craving, and allostasis, medications can potentially alter the development and maintenance of dependence.

The following sections of this review discuss the neuropharmacology of the most common substances of abuse, focusing on how medications can be used to improve treatment. The sections discuss the mechanisms of action of the medications and the evidence for their efficacy.

Alcohol

Alcohol (ethanol) is a small molecule that can affect many different cells and organs in the body. In the brain, alcohol affects many neurotransmitters and other components of signal transduction by binding to receptors and other membrane proteins and altering the function of these proteins. Alcohol can directly affect chemical neurotransmission in nicotinic acetylcholine, DA, cannabinoid, GABA, glutamate, opioids, 5-HT, and many other signaling systems. Although the multiple actions of alcohol adds to the complexity of understanding alcohol's behavioral effects, it also makes possible multiple potential targets for pharmacological treatment (see Table 21.2).

Table 21.2. Medications Commonly Used for the Treatment of Alcohol Dependence

FDA-Approved Medication	Mechanism of Action
Disulfiram (Antabuse)	Aldehyde dehydrogenase inhibitor When taken with alcohol, leads to nausea, dizziness, headache, flushing, and acts as a deterrent to alcohol use
Naltrexone (ReVia) and generics	μ-Receptor opioid antagonist Binds to opioid receptors, blocking alcohol reward pathways and alcohol craving
Acamprosate (Campral)	Glutamate receptor modulator; helps reduce glutamate hyperactivity during postacute withdrawal period
Sustained Release Naltrexone (Vivitrol)	μ-Receptor opioid antagonist; long-acting (up to 30 days) after intramuscular injection
Non-FDA-Approved Medication	**Mechanism of Action**
Topiramate (Topamax)	Blocks glutamate AMPA receptors, increases GABA; originally marketed as antiepileptic, analgesic; reduces pleasurable effects of alcohol
Baclofen (Lioresal)	Binds to $GABA_B$ receptors, reducing DA and alcohol reward; originally marketed as muscle relaxant, antispastic Gabapentin and γ-hydroxy butyrate (GHB) may also work through $GABA_B$ receptor mechanisms.
SSRI antidepressants (fluoxetine, sertraline, etc.)	Blocks serotonin reuptake; reduces drinking in type A (later onset) alcoholics
Atypical antipsychotics	Dopamine blockers (e.g., olanzapine, quetiapine, tiapride)

AMPA, α-amino-3-hydroxy-5-methyl-4-isoxazolepropionic acid; GABA, γ-aminobutyric acid

Treatment of Alcohol Withdrawal Syndrome

The alcohol withdrawal syndrome is due to compensatory CNS changes in response to a chronically administered depressant substance (ethanol). The behavioral manifestations of alcohol withdrawal are primarily excitatory and consist of hyperarousal from central and sympathetic stimulation (Littleton, 1998). Physical signs of alcohol withdrawal are hand and body tremors, diaphoresis, tachycardia and hypertension, dilated pupils, increase in temperature, seizures, restlessness, behavioral hyperactivity, agitation, ataxia, and clouding of consciousness. Symptoms of alcohol withdrawal are anxiety, panic attacks, paranoid delusions or ideation, illusions, disorientation, visual hallucinations (often of animals), and auditory hallucinations.

Alcohol withdrawal signs and symptoms can range from mild to severe. They typically peak from 1 to 3 days after withdrawal and last for 5 to 7 days. Approximately 5% of alcohol-dependent individuals in withdrawal develop severe withdrawal delirium (delirium tremens). However, for most alcoholics, alcohol withdrawal is mild and requires minimal medical intervention. The best predictor of severe alcohol withdrawal is a previous history of seizures or delirium tremens.

In pharmacological treatment of the alcohol withdrawal syndrome, a medication is administered to prevent the emergence of excitatory withdrawal signs and symptoms while allowing brain to readapt to an alcohol-free state. Administration of depressant substances markedly attenuates the signs and symptoms of withdrawal and may decrease medical morbidity and mortality (Leggio, Kenna, & Swift, 2008). It has been proposed that treating alcohol withdrawal may prevent the worsening of withdrawal signs and symptoms over time, Patients presenting for detoxification treatment are frequently poorly nourished, so treatment also should include correction of physiological abnormalities, hydration, and nutritional support, including vitamins and parenteral thiamine.

Benzodiazepines are the most widely used medications to treat alcohol and sedative withdrawal because of their low toxicity and anticonvulsant activity (Mayo-Smith, 1997). Their safety and effectiveness have been well established by double-blind, controlled studies. Benzodiazepines are frequently administered using a symptom-triggered detoxification paradigm, in which doses of medication are matched to a patient's tolerance and symptoms; this method avoids both over- and undermedication. Antiepileptic medications, such as carbamazepine

and valproic acid, effectively reduce most signs and symptoms of alcohol withdrawal and are widely used in some European countries. In using antiepileptics, patients are rapidly titrated to blood levels that are therapeutic for seizures. Additional benzodiazepines are administered for breakthrough symptoms. β-Adrenergic blocking drugs are particularly useful as secondary agents for controlling tachycardia and hypertension in patients with coronary disease. Medications such as propranolol hydrochloride and atenolol have been used as primary agents in treating alcohol withdrawal. However, β-blockers are most effective in reducing peripheral autonomic signs of withdrawal and are less effective for CNS signs such as delirium. Antipsychotics, such as haloperidol, are useful for treating hallucinosis and paranoid symptoms sometimes associated with withdrawal.

Some patients do not require pharmacological intervention. Nonmedically oriented treatment facilities use a nondrug method known as social-setting detoxification, which relies on peer and group support for patients. This behavioral method reduces withdrawal signs and symptoms without an increased incidence of medical complications. However, some patients do require careful monitoring and pharmacological treatment during the withdrawal process. In particular, a history of delirium tremens or seizures or the presence of medical or psychiatric comorbidities increases the need for inpatient detoxification. Some experts have expressed concern that repeated, untreated alcohol withdrawal might worsen subsequent withdrawal episodes due to kindling effects; they have suggested that any symptomatic withdrawing patient receive pharmacological treatment.

Medications to Treatment Alcohol Dependence

After detoxification, patients require ongoing maintenance or rehabilitation treatment for their alcohol abuse and dependence. The mainstay of maintenance treatment traditionally has been psychosocial, usually consisting of counseling (therapy) and attendance at self-help groups. New guidelines recommend the use of pharmacotherapy along with psychosocial therapies. Agencies, including the National Institute on Alcohol Abuse and Alcoholism (NIAAA) and the Center for Substance Abuse Treatment (CSAT) recommend consideration of the approved pharmacotherapies in the treatment of all patients (NIAAA, 2008; CSAT, 2009). Currently, three medications are approved by the US Food and Drug Administration (FDA) for the maintenance treatment of alcohol dependence: disulfiram, naltrexone (oral and intramuscular formulations), and acamprosate. Several other medications are not FDA approved but have shown efficacy in controlled studies and are used for adjunctive treatment off-label. The pharmacology of these medications and the evidence for their effectiveness is discussed in the next sections.

DISULFIRAM

Disulfiram (Antabuse®) increases the unpleasant, punishing effects of alcohol by inhibiting the alcohol metabolizing enzyme ALDH, the same enzyme with the genetic variant that is protective against developing alcoholism. Disulfiram causes an accumulation of acetaldehyde whenever alcohol is consumed. High levels of acetaldehyde in the body result in skin flushing, rapid pulse, sweating, shortness of breath, nausea, and vomiting. Cardiac problems and death may occur if large amounts of alcohol are consumed. The possibility of experiencing this unpleasant reaction provides a strong deterrent to the consumption of alcohol for some patients (Brewer, 1993).

Although disulfiram has been used for alcoholism treatment for more than 50 years, there have been few well-controlled studies on its treatment effectiveness. A large, multicenter double-blind treatment study that compared 1 year of 250 mg/d disulfiram, 1 mg disulfiram (placebo), and a multivitamin in 605 male alcohol-dependent subjects found the disulfiram to be no more effective than placebo (Fuller et al., 1986). More recent studies suggest that direct supervision of disulfiram ingestion and involvement in psychosocial treatment can increase the medication's effectiveness. A 6-month, double-blind study in 126 British patients found that those who received 200 mg/d disulfiram had more total days abstinent, reduced weekly drinking, and lower levels of γ-glutamyltransferase compared with those who received a vitamin placebo (Chick, Gough, & Falkowski, 1992). The combination of disulfiram with a behavioral contract in the context of marital therapy has been shown to be effective in reducing relapse to alcohol (O'Farrell, Allen, & Litten, 1995).

The usual disulfiram dose is 250 mg/day, with a range of 125–500 mg. In spite of its potential toxicity and questions about its effectiveness, many patients and clinicians feel disulfiram can be a useful adjunct to treatment. Some patients use disulfiram episodically during periods of high risk for relapse; others use the medication continuously for years. Patients who take disulfiram must be committed to complete abstinence because drinking alcohol can produce a dangerous disulfiram-alcohol reaction. Disulfiram also has a number of side effects, including hepatitis and psychosis.

OPIOID ANTAGONISTS: NALTREXONE AND NALMEFENE

Opiate medications, such as morphine, heroin, and methadone have behavioral effects because they mimic the action of naturally occurring opioid neurotransmitters in the brain. Certain medications can block the action of both opiate medications and opioid neurotransmitters; these medications are called opioid antagonists. It was observed that when opioid antagonists were administered to animals trained to consume alcohol, the animals consumed less alcohol (Myers, Borg, & Mossberg, 1986; Reid & Hubbell, 1987; Volpicelli, Davis, & Olgin, 1986). Subsequently, two 12-week, randomized, placebo-controlled clinical trials in 70 and 97 alcohol-dependent humans demonstrated that treatment with the opioid antagonist medication naltrexone reduced drinking and prolonged abstinence in alcohol-dependent patients (O'Malley et al., 1992; Volpicelli, Alterman, Hayashida, & O'Brien, 1992). Based on these studies, the FDA approved naltrexone as an adjunct to psychosocial therapies in the treatment of alcoholism in 1994. Evidence suggests that opioid antagonists may have a dual mechanism of action to reduce alcohol consumption: blockade of rewarding effects of alcohol and suppression of craving.

Since the approval of naltrexone, there have been many controlled clinical trials of naltrexone. Most, but not all of these trials have shown efficacy of naltrexone compared to placebo. Several meta-analyses of the naltrexone clinical trials have been published. The large US multisite COMBINE Study involving 1,380 alcohol-dependent patients found naltrexone, compared to placebo, to produce small but significant reductions in relapse to heavy drinking in patients receiving a medically oriented behavioral intervention (Anton et al., 2006).

Several meta-analyses of published randomized, controlled clinical trials assessing oral naltrexone in alcohol dependence found that naltrexone reduced the relapse rate to heavy drinking significantly, but with a small effect size (Rösner, Leucht, Lehert, & Soyka, 2008; Maisel, Blodgett, Wilbourne, et al., 2013). There was a

nonsignificant trend in reduction of the abstinence rate (Bouza, Angeles, Munoz, & Amate,
2004; Srisurapanont & Jarusuraisin, 2005).

Several patient characteristics are associated with
a positive response to naltrexone. Medication adherence is particularly important for naltrexone effectiveness. In three different clinical trials, naltrexone
had a positive effect on drinking outcomes only in
patients showing high medication adherence (Chick
et al., 2000; Monti et al., 2001; Volpicelli, Rhines,
Rhines, Volpicelli, & Alterman, 1997. Other predictors of a positive response to naltrexone include
a high level of craving, a positive family history of
alcoholism (Rubio et al., 2005) and possessing a
specific genetic polymorphism (Asn40Asp) in the
μ opioid receptor gene (Anton et al., 2008; Oslin
et al., 2003).

Oral naltrexone is recommended for use in the
first 90 days of abstinence, when the risk of relapse
is highest; however, it has been shown to be generally safe and well tolerated by alcoholic patients
for periods of up to a year. In a large study of its
safety in alcoholism treatment, the most common
side effects are anxiety, sedation, and nausea in
approximately 10% of patients (Croop, Faulkne,
& Labriola, 1997). Patients taking naltrexone will
be insensitive to opioid effects, including analgesia,
although this effect will dissipate within 72 hours
of drug discontinuation. If opiate analgesics are
needed in an emergency, opiate blockade can be
reversed with carefully monitored high-dose opiates. Although high doses of naltrexone (300 mg/d)
have been associated with the development of liver
toxicity, liver problems are rarely observed with 50
mg/d doses. A Treatment Improvement Protocol
(TIPS) published by CSAT and a medication guide
published by NIAAA provide comprehensive information and treatment guidelines for naltrexone
(CSAT, 2009; NIAAA, 2008).

Because the effectiveness of naltrexone depends
on a high rate of medication adherence, a sustained
release, once-monthly injectable formulation of
naltrexone was developed. A sustained-released
naltrexone preparation, marketed as Vivitrol®, was
FDA approved for the treatment of alcohol dependence in 2004. A 6-month, multicenter, randomized controlled trial of placebo and two doses
of sustained-release naltrexone in 627 actively
drinking alcohol-dependent adults showed a significant dose-dependent decrease in the rate of
heavy drinking (26% at the highest dose) compared with placebo (Garbutt et al., 2005). The
most common adverse events associated with

extended-release naltrexone are injection site ten-
derness, nausea (which affected 33%), headache,
and fatigue. Occasionally, abscesses occur at the
injection site and have engendered an FDA warning letter. In addition to improved adherence,
sustained-release naltrexone may produce less
hepatotoxicity than oral naltrexone because the
injected sustained-release drug does not undergo
first-pass metabolism in the liver.

Nalmefene is a μ-opioid antagonist approved for
the reversal of acute opioid intoxication. It differs
from naltrexone in having partial agonist activity
at the κ-opioid receptor and less hepatotoxicity.
Two placebo-controlled clinical trials, conducted
in the United States by Mason and colleagues
in 21 and 105 alcohol-dependent participants
(Mason et al., 1994) found nalmefene combined
with psychosocial treatment to be superior to
placebo and psychosocial treatment in reducing
heavy drinking. In contrast, a multisite, 12-week
controlled clinical trial in which 270 abstinent
alcohol-dependent participants were randomized to placebo or nalmefene, with all participants
receiving motivational enhancement therapy, did
not find any efficacy for nalmefene (Anton et al.,
2004). A recent European double-blind placebo
controlled trial in which 598 alcohol-dependent
drinkers were randomized to nalmefene or placebo in a targeted or "as needed fashion" (i.e., on
days when participants perceived that they were at
high risk for drinking) found that nalmefene was
efficacious in reducing number of drinking days
and total amounts of alcohol consumed (Mann,
Bladström, Torup, Gual, & van den Brink, 2013).
Nalmefene is approved for alcoholism treatment in
several European countries, although not currently
approved in the United States.

ACAMPROSATE

Acamprosate (calcium acetylhomotaurine) is a
structural analogue of the brain chemical taurine,
which was found to reduce alcohol consumption in
several animal models of alcoholism. Its mechanism
of action is not completely understood but most
likely involves a functional antagonism or modulation of the glutamate NMDA receptor, which is
upregulated in chronic alcoholism (Littleton, 1995).
In several European studies with alcohol-dependent
patients, acamprosate reduced relapse drinking and
craving for alcohol and had minimal side effects
(Paille et al., 1995; Pelc et al., 1997; Sass, Soyka,
Mann, & Zieglgänsberger, 1996). In most studies,
twice as many patients receiving acamprosate were

totally abstinent from alcohol at the end of treatment compared to those receiving placebo. Meta-analyses that compare acamprosate statistically across several studies have supported the efficacy of acamprosate in improving rates of abstinence and increasing time to first drink, although with small effect sizes. (Bouza et al., 2004; Mann, Lehert, & Morgan, 2004). Interestingly, the efficacy of acamprosate seems strongest in those trials conducted prior to the year 2000. Two US trials, a 6-month multisite study (Mason, Goodman, Chabac, & Lehert, 2006) and the COMBINE Study (Anton et al., 2006) and a recent multisite German trial (Mann et al., 2013) failed to find similar efficacy. The reasons for the differences in effectiveness may relate to differences in the severity of alcoholism, typologies of patients, and the use of inpatient detoxification in early studies.

OTHER MEDICATIONS FOR ALCOHOL DEPENDENCE

In addition to disulfiram, naltrexone, and acamprosate, there is evidence that several other medications may be effective in reducing drinking or other aspects of alcohol dependence. These medications are not FDA approved but are sometimes prescribed off-label. This review will discuss gabapentin, topiramate, baclofen, and γ-hydroxybutyrate (GHB).

Antiepileptic medications such as gabapentin have been used successfully to treat alcohol withdrawal (Malcolm, Ballenger, Sturgis, & Anton, 1989; Myrick et al., 2009). Gabapentin is reported also to reduce alcohol consumption, improve sleep, and decrease alcohol craving in alcohol-dependent subjects (Brower et al., 2008; Mason, Light, Williams, & Drobes, 2009). The antiepileptic medication topiramate represents a particularly promising medication for the treatment of alcohol dependence, although it is not approved by the FDA. In a 12-week, randomized controlled trial in 150 patients with alcohol dependence receiving medication adherence therapy, topiramate treatment significantly decreased the numbers of drinks per day, drinks per drinking day, and drinking days and increased the number of days of abstinence compared to placebo (Johnson et al., 2003). A subsequent US multisite trial (Johnson et al., 2007) demonstrated the efficacy of a 300 mg/d dose of topiramate to reduce heavy drinking. Topiramate causes a number of dose-dependent neurological side effects, and further studies are required to determine optimal dosing. Currently, topiramate is not approved by the FDA for the treatment of alcohol dependence, but it is endorsed by NIAAA and other groups.

The antiepileptic medication gabapentin, which blocks calcium channels and stimulates $GABA_B$ receptors, has been shown to be effective in treating both alcohol withdrawal and alcohol dependence and sleep disturbances in alcoholic patients (Brower et al., 2008). Gabapentin was recently found to significantly reduce drinking in a 12-week duration clinical trial conducted with 150 alcohol-dependent recently abstinent outpatients (Mason et al., 2013). A high dose of gabapentin (1,800 mg) reduced heavy drinking and craving and improved sleep more than a low dose of gabapentin or placebo.

SEROTONERGIC AND DOPAMINERGIC MEDICATIONS

Given the importance of DA and 5-HT neurobiology on alcohol dependence, there is interest in dopaminergic and serotonergic medications for adjunctive treatment of alcohol dependence. In two placebo controlled trials, olanzapine reduced alcohol craving and consumption in a 12-week trial of patients with alcohol dependence (Hutchison et al., 2006), and quetiapine reduced heavy drinking (Kampman et al., 2007). However, a multisite placebo-controlled trial of quetiapine in heavy drinkers did not show efficacy in reducing drinking (Litten et al., 2012).

Selective serotonin reuptake inhibitors (SSRIs), which augment serotonergic function, appear to reduce alcohol consumption in some studies. In heavy-drinking humans, SSRIs were found to reduce alcohol consumption by 15–20% (Naranjo & Bremner, 1993). Further studies failed to replicate these results. A double-blind, placebo controlled study of fluoxetine found no difference in drinking in nondepressed patients (Kranzler et al., 1995). However, two subsequent studies suggested that SSRIs may have efficacy in a subtype of alcoholic characterized by later age of drinking onset and less severe psychopathology.

Ondansetron, a $5\text{-}HT_3$ receptor antagonist used for nausea, was found efficacious in alcohol-dependent subjects with an early onset of alcoholism prior to age 25 (Johnson et al., 2000). A more recent efficacy study demonstrated effectiveness in patients with specific polymorphisms that affect the 5-HT transporter or the binding of 5-HT to the $5\text{-}HT_3$ receptor subtype (Johnson, 2013).

The $GABA_B$ agonist medication baclofen, marketed as an antispasmodic, reduces alcohol consumption in several animal models of alcoholism (Colombo et al., 2003). A small randomized double-blind controlled study found baclofen to reduce alcohol drinking in alcohol-dependent persons (Addolorato et al., 2002). More recently, baclofen was shown to reduce drinking and enhance abstinence in a larger randomized double-blind controlled study in alcohol-dependent patients with liver cirrhosis (Addolorato et al., 2007). Although animal research suggests that baclofen can reduce reinforcement, baclofen was not found to attenuate alcohol reward in humans (Evans & Bisaga, 2009). Recently, several European studies have suggested that the medication GHB, used clinically for the treatment of narcolepsy, may be useful for the treatment of alcohol withdrawal (Addolorato et al., 1999) and alcohol dependence (Addolorato, Caputo, Capristo, Stefanini, & Gasbarrini, 2000; Addolorato & Gasbarrini, 2005). γ-Hydroxybutyrate has agonist effects at $GABA_B$ receptors, but also binds to $GABA_A$ receptors. However, in the United States, GHB is frequently abused as a date rape drug. The $GABA_A$ effects may explain the sedation and the ability of GHB to cause dependence.

Nicotine

Nicotine is an alkaloid drug present in the leaves of the tobacco plant, *Nicotiana tabacum*. Native Americans used the plant for centuries in ceremonies, rituals, and as a medicinal herb. Since its discovery by Europeans, tobacco use has spread worldwide, and today nicotine is the most prevalent psychoactive drug in use. Approximately 42 million persons in the United States (about 25% of the population) are daily users of cigarettes, with another 10 million using another form of tobacco. Nicotine appears to activate the mesolimbic DA system through activation of cholinergic systems in the ventral tegmental area (Corrigall, Coen, & Adamson, 1994). See Figure 21.1.

Tobacco use is a major public health problem, and the morbidity and mortality resulting from the use of nicotine includes cardiovascular and respiratory disease and cancers, particularly of the lung and head and neck. Many deleterious effects of tobacco are not due to nicotine but to other toxic and carcinogenic compounds present in tobacco extract or smoke. Patients who are unable to quit smoking on their own and to remain abstinent may be helped by pharmacotherapies including nicotine replacement therapy and antidepressants.

The successful treatment of nicotine dependence occurs with interventions that combine pharmacologic and behavioral therapies (Hughes, Goldstein, Hurt, & Shiffman, 1999). According to the clinical practice guidelines review (US Department of Health and Human Services [USDHHS], 2008), all nicotine-dependent patients should be offered some form of pharmacotherapy unless medical conditions contraindicate it.

Three types of pharmacotherapy have demonstrated their efficacy for smoking cessation: nicotine replacement therapy (NRT), bupropion, and varenicline. The goal of NRT is to reduce withdrawal symptoms associated with smoking cessation, thus helping the smoker resist the urge to smoke cigarettes (Silagy, Lancaster, Stead, Mant, & Fowler, 2004). Nicotine replacement therapy is the most widely recommended approach, with cessation rates for NRT plus counseling ranging between 20% and 30% at 1-year follow-up. Several forms of NRT are commercially available (e.g., gum, transdermal patch, nasal spray, oral inhaled nicotine [electronic cigarette], and sublingual tablets/lozenges). Although nicotine replacement has been used primarily for detoxification and relief of withdrawal symptoms during smoking cessation, some patients use nicotine replacement in a maintenance fashion.

Bupropion is an antidepressant with a dopaminergic–noradrenergic profile and may also bind to nicotinic receptors (Le Foll & George, 2007). A 7-week double-blind controlled trial of sustained-release bupropion enrolling 615 smokers showed that the drug was effective for smoking cessation (Hurt et al., 1997). A successive study enrolled healthy community volunteers motivated to quit smoking. After an open-label treatment with sustained-release bupropion, subjects ($n = 784$) were randomized to receive sustained-release bupropion or placebo for 45 weeks. The results showed that sustained-release bupropion for 12 months delayed smoking relapse (Hays et al., 2001). A double-blind controlled trial also showed that treatment with sustained-release bupropion alone or in combination with a nicotine patch resulted in significantly higher long-term rates of smoking cessation than either nicotine patch alone or placebo (Jorenby et al., 1999).

Varenicline is a novel medication available for the treatment of tobacco dependence. The drug is a partial agonist at the $\alpha_4\beta_2$ subtype of the nicotinic receptor and also binds weakly to other nicotinic receptor subtypes. Acting as an agonist, varenicline mimics the action of nicotine, binds to the $\alpha_4\beta_2$ receptors, and stimulates the release of mesolimbic DA. However, in the presence of nicotine, varenicline acts as an antagonist, blocking the ability of nicotine to stimulate the DA system and reducing the pleasure of smoking. A large multicenter randomized study demonstrated that varenicline was effective in the treatment of tobacco dependence and was well tolerated by patients (Nides et al., 2006; Oncken et al. 2006). Interestingly, a recent meta-analysis has also suggested that varenicline is more efficacious than bupropion (Eisenberg et al., 2008). Concerns about mood changes and suicidality in patients receiving varenicline led to the FDA imposing a "black box" warning on varenicline's labeling. However, recent studies that compared varenicline with other smoking cessation treatment did not demonstrate significant suicidality (Kuehn, 2012).

Other smoking cessation therapies are currently under investigation. One of the most promising is rimonabant, a specific antagonist at cannabinoid CB_1 receptors. A recent meta-analysis of three placebo-controlled studies showed that 20 mg of rimonabant, combined with behavioral treatment, increased the odds of smoking cessation and prevented weight gain (Cahill & Ussher, 2007). However, there are concerns that cannabinoid antagonists may increase depression and suicidality; therefore the medication is not available in the United States and was removed from the market in Britain.

Opioids

Opiates drugs produce euphoria, decreases in stress and anxiety, and analgesia because they bind to neuronal opioid receptors and mimic the action of the endogenous opioid peptide neurotransmitters enkephalin, endorphin, and dynorphin. Recent evidence suggests that there exist at least four distinct types of opioid receptors, three of which are designated by the Greek letters μ, δ, and κ; the forth is known is the *nociceptin receptor* (Girdlestone, 2000). Endorphins are the main ligand for the μ receptor, enkephalins are the main ligands for δ receptor, dynorphins are the main ligands for the κ receptor, and nociceptin (orphanin FQ) is the main ligand for the nociceptin receptor. Drugs that act primarily through the μ receptor include heroin, morphine, and methadone; such drugs produce analgesia, euphoria, and respiratory depression. Drugs that are mediated through the κ receptor include the so-called mixed agonist-antagonists, butorphanol and pentazocine, which produce analgesia but less respiratory depression. The δ receptor appears to bind endogenous opioid peptides. Several opioid drugs, including etorphine and buprenorphine, bind weakly to nociceptin receptors. At high doses, opioid drugs may lose receptor specificity and have agonist or antagonist properties at multiple receptor subtypes.

Most of the opioid medications used clinically and most of those abused have their predominant effects at the μ opioid receptors. With regular use of a μ-opioid agonist, μ-opioid receptors downregulate and other neuronal systems adapt, so that chronic opiate users develop tolerance and dependence. Then, cessation of opiate use results in an unpleasant withdrawal syndrome.

Opioid Withdrawal

The opioid withdrawal syndrome is characterized by sympathetic hyperactivity, anxiety, agitation, pain, and intense craving for opioids. These symptoms are extremely distressing and often lead to reinstitution of opioid use. Reduction of withdrawal signs and symptoms is usually accomplished through slow taper of opiates (usually methadone) or the use of α2 agonist agents, such as clonidine or lofexidine. α2 agonists act at presynaptic noradrenergic neurons in the locus coeruleus, block the activation of central norepinephrine systems in the brain that occurs during opioid withdrawal, and ameliorate the agitation and anxiety of withdrawal (Aghajanian, 1976; Gold, Redmond, & Kleber, 1979). The time course of withdrawal depends on the pharmacokinetics of the opiate drug that causes the dependence. Withdrawal from short half-life drugs, such as heroin or oxycodone, begins within hours of stopping drug use and usually lasts for 5–7 days. Withdrawal from long half-life drugs, such as methadone, begins 24–48 hours after stopping drug use and can last from 10–14 days.

Opioid Substitution Therapies

The concept of opioid substitution is to provide patients with a medically monitored opiate substitute to maintain opioid dependence, thereby preventing withdrawal and increasing tolerance to diminish the effects of illicit opiates. In this "harm reduction" paradigm, patients remain opioid dependent but typically stop the use of illicit opioids. Two medications are FDA approved for substitution: methadone and buprenorphine. All of these medications are required to be used in the setting of a structured maintenance treatment program, which includes monitored medication administration, periodic random urine toxicological screening to assess compliance, and the provision of psychological, medical, and vocational services.

METHADONE MAINTENANCE

Methadone is a synthetic opiate that is orally active, possesses a long-duration of action, produces minimal sedation or "high," and has few side effects at therapeutic doses. Methadone was first shown to be an effective treatment in an open-label study of 22 patients in New York City (Dole & Nyswander, 1965), and it is now used worldwide. Over the past 40 years, studies consistently have shown methadone maintenance to be effective in the treatment of addicts who are dependent on heroin and other opiates (O'Brien, 2005; Senay, 1985). A meta-analysis of studies comparing methadone maintenance to placebo or drug-free treatment found methadone maintenance to be significantly better than nonpharmacologic therapy in reducing heroin use and improving program retention (Mattick, Breen, Kimber, & Davoli, 2003). In addition, methadone maintenance has been shown to reduce opiate-related mortality and morbidity, reduce HIV transmission, decrease criminal activity, and increase employment (Vocci, Acri, & Elkashef, 2005). A longitudinal study that compared more than 100 representative methadone maintenance programs found that the most effective programs provided intensive psychosocial and medical services, flexibility in methadone dosing, and allowed higher doses of methadone, in excess of 80 mg/d (D'Aunno & Pollack, 2002).

Methadone treatment is integrated with a comprehensive psychosocial treatment program. Long-standing program participants are allowed to "take home" some doses of methadone under a contingency contract that permits take-home doses as long as treatment compliance is maintained. Counseling sessions are held weekly with a counselor trained and certified in addiction treatment. Medical care, employment counseling, and other rehabilitative services are provided on a regular basis. Urine toxicological screening is performed randomly and periodically to assess compliance with treatment.

Methadone is administered to patients daily, under observation. Long-standing program participants using "take-home" doses of methadone may self-administer. Daily doses usually range from 20 mg/d to more than 100 mg/d. Higher doses are shown to be generally associated with better treatment retention. Urine toxicological screening is performed randomly and periodically to assess compliance with treatment. Counseling and other rehabilitative services are provided on a regular basis.

BUPRENORPHINE

In 2002, the FDA approved sublingual buprenorphine tablets (Subutex) and buprenorphine/naloxone tablets (Suboxone) for the management of opiate dependence (Ling et al., 1994; Vocci et al., 2005). Buprenorphine is a partial μ- and κ-agonist opiate that was used medically as an analgesic. Importantly, the drug's agonist properties predominate at lower doses and antagonist properties predominate at higher doses. These properties have led to its increasing use as an adjunctive substitution/maintenance treatment for opioid dependence. A randomized trial comparing buprenorphine maintenance to methadone maintenance for 16 weeks in 164 newly treated opiate users showed similar reductions in illicit drug use and similar retention in treatment (Strain, Stitzer, Liebson, & Bigelow, 1994). A 6-month study comparing methadone maintenance with a stepped-care approach to buprenorphine found identical rates of treatment retention (Kakko et al., 2007). Possible advantages of buprenorphine compared to methadone include a less intense withdrawal syndrome upon discontinuation and less potential for abuse because agonist effects diminish at higher doses.

Federal law now permits individual physicians who are certified in buprenorphine use and possess a special license from the Drug Enforcement Administration to prescribe buprenorphine and buprenorphine/naloxone to up to 100 opioid-dependent patients who are also receiving psychosocial treatment. In the setting of a structured treatment program, daily buprenorphine dosing has been shown to be an effective maintenance treatment. Medication doses usually range from 4 mg/d to up to 16 mg/d, administered sublingually, since the medication is not effective orally.

In spite of the demonstrated evidence of effectiveness of maintenance treatment with methadone and buprenorphine, the concept of opioid substitution therapy remains extremely controversial. Indeed, opioid substitution therapies are among the most highly regulated treatments and must follow strict guidelines described in the Code of Federal Regulations (CFR 42, section 8).

NALTREXONE

Another pharmacological adjunctive treatment for the treatment of opioid dependence is antagonist therapy with naltrexone (also FDA-approved for the treatment of alcohol dependence). Naltrexone is an pure opioid antagonist at μ-, κ-, and δ-opioid receptors. When taken regularly, an oral daily dose of 50 mg naltrexone completely blocks the euphoric, analgesic, and sedative properties of opiates (Resnick, Schuyten-Resnick, & Washton, 1980). Patients receiving naltrexone first must be completely detoxified from opiates or risk experiencing opioid withdrawal. In spite of its potential, studies with oral naltrexone as an adjunctive treatment have shown high treatment dropout and poor medication compliance, particularly in poorly motivated individuals with poor social supports (Capone et al., 1986). Naltrexone was most effective in highly motivated individuals, such as impaired professionals and parolees (Kosten & Kleber, 1984).

To address poor medication adherence with oral naltrexone, several sustained release, injectable forms of naltrexone have been developed. Sixty detoxified opioid-dependent patients receiving once monthly injections of a sustained release naltrexone preparation in conjunction with twice weekly counseling showed dose-dependent reductions in illicit drug use and improvements in treatment retention (Comer, et al., 2006). A sustained release naltrexone preparation (Vivitrol), originally marketed for the treatment of alcohol dependence, is now FDA approved for opioid dependence treatment. A study on detoxified opioid-dependent patients receiving once monthly injections of sustained release naltrexone in conjunction with twice weekly counseling showed dose-dependent reductions in illicit drug use and improvements in treatment retention compared to a placebo injection (Krupitsky et al., 2011).

Cocaine

Cocaine is a potent stimulant of the CNS, potentiating the action of the central catecholamine neurotransmitters norepinephrine and DA. Cocaine binds to monoamine neurotransmitter transporters, the function of which is to inactivate monoamine neurotransmitters by moving the transmitter back into neurons and away from receptors. Cocaine is most potent at blocking the DA transporter; thus, its behavioral effects are consistent with increased DA activity and include increased arousal, euphoria, a sense of creativity, grandiosity, excitement, and motor activation. At high doses or with escalating use, the effects can include anxiety, agitation, irritability, apprehension, and paranoia. Chronic use of cocaine results in neuroadaptations that include decreased function of the transporters,

decreased sensitivity of receptors, and depletion of DA. Cessation of chronic cocaine use produces a withdrawal syndrome characterized by dysphoria, depression, and intense drug craving.

The treatment of cocaine dependence has been primarily psychosocial and includes individual and group counseling, group therapy, and cognitive behavioral therapy and contingency contracting, all of which have been shown to be effective in maintaining abstinence (Higgins, 1996; Rounsaville, Gawin, & Kleber, 1985). So far, there are no FDA-approved medications for the adjunctive treatment of cocaine dependence, although there has been considerable research focused on discovering a "magic bullet" for cocaine use (Vocci et al., 2005). Initially, the norepinephrine reuptake blocking antidepressant desipramine and the DA agonist bromocriptine were reported to be efficacious, but these effects were not replicated. Recently, several compounds have shown some evidence of efficacy in preliminary studies. Disulfiram, used for treating alcohol dependence, may also have efficacy in cocaine treatment through an inhibitory effect on the brain enzyme, DA-β-hydroxylase. A clinical trial in 121 cocaine-dependent patients randomized to placebo or disulfiram and also receiving one of two types of behavioral therapy showed a significant reduction in cocaine use in the disulfiram group (Carroll, 2000). Preliminary evidence suggests the utility of GABAergic medications such as baclofen, vigabatrin, and tiagabine for the treatment of cocaine dependence (O'Brien, 2005). A clinical trial comparing the GABA$_B$ agonist baclofen to placebo in 70 cocaine-dependent outpatients found reduced cocaine use in baclofen-treated patients, particularly heavy users (Shoptaw et al., 2003). Interestingly, a pilot trial tested topiramate in cocaine dependence and showed that topiramate-treated subjects were more likely to be abstinent from cocaine compared to placebo-treated subjects (Kampman et al., 2004). However, perhaps the most promising compound is represented by modafinil (O'Brien, 2005; Vocci et al., 2005). Modafinil is a stimulant that increases daytime alertness in narcoleptic patients. Although its mechanism of action is unknown, modafinil, like cocaine, binds to norepinephrine and DA transporters. A clinical trial comparing placebo to 400 mg modafinil in 62 cocaine-dependent subjects also undergoing twice-weekly cognitive behavioral therapy found significant decreases in cocaine use (Dackis et al., 2005). Modafinil appears to reduce the craving, anergia, and anhedonia associated with cocaine withdrawal. However, a more recent placebo-controlled trial in 210 cocaine-dependent subjects failed to reproduce these results (Dackis et al., 2012).

Recently, the indole alkaloid ibogaine has been shown to decrease stimulant use in animals and is being tested in cocaine-dependent persons (Sershen, Hashim, & Lajtha, 1997).

Amphetamines

The amphetamines are a group of drugs structurally related to the catecholamine neurotransmitters norepinephrine, epinephrine, and DA. Amphetamines have similar effects to cocaine in that both drugs release catecholamines from nerve endings and act as catecholamine agonists at receptors in the peripheral autonomic and central nervous systems. Amphetamines are not naturally occurring compounds, but some, including methamphetamine, are easily synthesized from commonly available chemicals; this has led to increasing availability and widespread use. Recently, interdiction and knowledge of the dangers of the drugs have reduced availability and use, so that the estimated number of persons who are current users of methamphetamine dropped by more than half from 731,000 in 2006 to 314,000 in 2008.

Intoxication with stimulants such as amphetamines, methylphenidate, or other sympathomimetics produces a clinical picture of sympathetic and behavioral hyperactivity. Hypertensive crises, cerebral bleeds, and vasculitis have resulted from the use of these drugs. Many chronic amphetamine users progressively increase drug doses for periods of several days to weeks, followed by a period of abstinence. An "amphetamine psychosis" with manifestations of agitation, paranoia, delusions, and hallucinosis mimicking paranoid schizophrenia or a manic syndrome may follow chronic high-dose use of these drugs (Ellinwood, 1969). Chronic use of amphetamine causes a depletion of DA and other catecholamine from brain neurons, causing marked dysphoria and fatigue whenever amphetamines are not present. Neuroimaging studies find that chronic users show dysregulation of corticolimbic connections. This results in chronic users experiencing poor executive functioning, impulsivity, and deficits in information processing (Aron & Paulus, 2007).

The current treatment of stimulant dependence is predominantly psychosocially based; pharmacologically based treatments that can address the underlying neurobiology of amphetamine dependence are lacking. There are ongoing clinical trials of modafinil, topiramate, and other medications that have been shown to be effective for other substances. One small, single-site trial using d-amphetamine as a substitution treatment for methamphetamine found reductions in methamphetamine use and better retention than placebo (Longo et al., 2010).

Caffeine

Caffeine and the related methylxanthines theophylline and theobromine are among the most commonly used drugs in our society. These agents occur in coffee, tea, cola, and other carbonated drinks, and are consumed by more than 80% of the population (Dews, 1982). Caffeine is present in chocolate and in many prescribed and over-the-counter medications, including stimulants (NoDoze), and appetite suppressants (Dexatrim), analgesics (Anacin, APC tablets), and cold and sinus preparations (Dristan, Contac).

The CNS effects of caffeine include psychomotor stimulation, increased attention and concentration, and suppression of the need for sleep. Even at low or moderate doses, caffeine can exacerbate symptoms of anxiety disorders and may increase requirements for neuroleptic or sedative medications (Charney, Henninger, & Jatlow, 1985). At high doses and in sensitive individuals, methylxanthines may produce tolerance and behavioral symptoms of tremor, insomnia, jitteriness, and agitation. In moderate to heavy users, a withdrawal syndrome characterized by lethargy, hypersomnia, irritability, and severe headache follows cessation of use. Clinically significant caffeine withdrawal symptoms are commonly observed in even low to moderate users of caffeine (Hughes et al., 1991) and may occur with reduced caffeine intake during a medical or psychiatric hospitalization. The signs and symptoms of caffeine intoxication or caffeine withdrawal may complicate medical or psychiatric treatment by increasing patient distress and by leading to an unnecessary work-up for other disorders.

Methylxanthines produce physiological effects through actions at the cellular level. They produce cardiac stimulation, diuresis, bronchodilation, and CNS stimulation through several mechanisms. They inhibit the enzyme cyclic adenosine monophosphate (cAMP) phosphodiesterase and increase intracellular levels of this second-messenger, thereby augmenting the action of many hormones and neurotransmitters such as norepinephrine. They also have a direct inhibitory effect on adenosine receptors and may have other neurotransmitter effects as well.

Treatment of caffeine dependence limits consumption of caffeine-containing foods, medications, and beverages. Beverages such as coffee or cola may be substituted with decaffeinated forms. Often, patients are unaware of the extent of their caffeine consumption and of the caffeine content of consumables. They require education about the caffeine content of these substances. Withdrawal symptoms such as headache and lethargy may be treated with a caffeine taper or symptomatically with analgesics and rest.

Cannabis

Cannabis, also called marijuana or hemp, is a plant indigenous to India but now grown worldwide. The leaves, flowers, and seeds of the plant contain many biologically active compounds, the most important of which are the lipophilic cannabinoids, especially Δ-9-tetrahydrocannabinol (THC) and cannabidiol (CBD). Cannabinoids have behavioral effects because they mimic the action of naturally occurring lipid signaling molecules anandamide and 2-arachidonyl glycerol (2-AG) at brain cannabinoid receptors (Mackie, 2008). The mechanism of action of cannabidiol is more complex. Cannabidiol may bind to other receptors, including the nociceptin opioid receptor and the $5HT_{1A}$ subtype of the 5-HT receptor. The two main types of cannabinoid receptors, CB_1 and CB_2, are widely distributed in the body. In the brain, the CB_1 receptor is concentrated in the hypothalamus and limbic system and other areas that control mood and appetitive behaviors, including the consumption of food, drugs, and alcohol. The CB_2 receptors are present in liver and cells of the immune system and may control inflammation and immune responses.

The biologically active substances are administered by smoking or ingesting dried plant parts (marijuana, bhang, ganga), the resin from the plant (hashish), or extracts of the resin. After inhalation or ingestion, the cannabinoids rapidly enter the CNS. THC has biphasic elimination with a short initial half-life (1–2 hours) reflecting redistribution and a second half-life of days to weeks.

Cannabis intoxication is characterized by tachycardia, muscle relaxation, euphoria, and a sense of well-being. Time sense is altered, and emotional lability, particularly inappropriate laughter, occurs. Performance on psychomotor tasks, including driving, is impaired (Klonoff, 1974). Marijuana has antiemetic effects, analgesic effects, and reduces intraocular pressure. THC is extremely reinforcing in animal models of drug dependence. THC is also anxiogenic and, with high doses of drug, depersonalization, paranoia, and anxiety reactions occur. In contrast, CBD is anxiolytic and antipsychotic and has fewer psychotropic effects (Mechoulam, Peters, Murillo-Rodriguez, 2007). Tolerance to the effects of cannabis occurs with chronic use, and cessation of use can produce a withdrawal syndrome characterized by craving, anxiety, and restlessness and insomnia, particularly in heavy users (Cooper & Haney, 2009). Chronic use of cannabis has been associated with an apathetic amotivational state and cognitive impairments that improve upon discontinuation of the drug (Pope et al., 2001).

After many years of being classified as Schedule 1 drug and available only illicitly in the United States, cannabis preparations are becoming increasingly available as "medical marijuana" and are being used to treat medical conditions such as multiple sclerosis, glaucoma, and chronic pain. Marijuana is now legal in some states. In Canada, an oral/nasal spray composed of 50% THC and 50% CBD is commercially available under the trade name Sativex and is marketed for relief of neuropathic pain in multiple sclerosis and other conditions. Because the concentration of CBD in Sativex is much higher than CBD in smoked marijuana (usually less than 5% of the cannabinoids), this preparation may have improved analgesic and anxiolytic effects. However, the use of medical marijuana is poorly controlled, so that it is being used for indications without much evidence for effectiveness.

Currently, the treatment of cannabis dependence is psychosocial. There is interest in using dronabinol (Δ-9-tetrahydrocannabinol), a commercially available pharmaceutical preparation, as a potential substitution treatment in cannabis dependence. Dronabinol has been shown to block some of the intoxicating effects of marijuana and to reduce cannabis withdrawal symptoms. Other medications, including the α2 agonist lofexidine and lithium are currently being studied as potential treatments.

Barbiturates or Other Sedative Hypnotics and Anxiolytics

Sedative medications include barbiturates, benzodiazepines, nonbenzodiazepine hypnotics (e.g., zolpidem), chloral derivatives, propofol, GHB, ethchlorvynol (Placidyl), and methaqualone (Quaaludes). Sedatives are used clinically for their anxiolytic and hypnotic effects and to induce anesthesia and conscious sedation for medical procedures. Sedatives are among the most commonly prescribed drugs and a major source of adverse drug interactions and drug emergencies, including overdoses (Coben et al., 2010).

Most of the medications in this group derive their pharmacological activity by inhibiting neuronal activity through the chloride channel–GABA$_A$ receptor complex in brain (Seeman, 1972). Specific binding sites exist for benzodiazepines, barbiturates, and other drugs on this receptor complex. The binding of a sedative drug may directly or indirectly (acting through GABA) increase chloride conductance, leading to hyperpolarization (and inhibition) of neurons (Costa & Guidotti, 1979; Schulz & MacDonald, 1981) and resulting in sedation. Because alcohol also has inhibitory effects at the GABA$_A$ receptor, alcohol and sedatives can interact to significantly enhance sedation. Chronic use of sedative medications causes the brain receptors to adapt to the sedative medication by becoming less sensitive to inhibition and produces tolerance.

The withdrawal syndrome that follows cessation of sedative drug use is characterized by extreme stimulation of the CNS and can include seizures, cardiac arrhythmias, and death. The need for detoxification depends on the duration and amount of sedative drug abuse, which can be estimated by means of a pentobarbital challenge test (Smith & Wesson, 1970). Pentobarbital 200 mg is administered orally, and the patient observed 1 hour later. If the patient develops drowsiness or nystagmus on a 200 mg dose, the patient is not barbiturate dependent. If 200 mg lacks effect, the dose should be repeated hourly until nystagmus or drowsiness develops. The total dosage administered at this end point approximates the patient's daily sedative habit and may be used as a starting point for detoxification. The barbiturate dose should be tapered over 10 days, with approximately a 10% reduction each day. Alternatively, the patient can be loaded with a long-acting benzodiazepine such as diazepam or clonazepam, and this medication tapered over 7–10 days and discontinued (Patterson, 1990). There are no studies that have been conducted that use pharmacological treatment as a maintenance treatment for sedative abuse and dependence, and there are no medications approved for this purpose.

Hallucinogens

Some drugs are used for hallucinogenic or psychotomimetic effects. This diverse group of drugs include psychedelics such as lysergic acid diethylamide (LSD), mescaline, psilocybin, and dimethyltryptamine (DMT); hallucinogenic amphetamines such as methylenedioxyamphetamine (MDA),

methylenedioxymethamphetamine (MDMA or ecstasy), phencyclidine (PCP), ketamine, and similarly acting arylcyclohexylamines; and anticholinergics, such as scopolamine. All cause a state of intoxication characterized by hallucinosis, affective changes, and delusional states. The mechanisms by which these drugs induce hallucinations and cognitive and mood changes is not well understood and varies according to the drug (Nichols, 2004). Hallucinogens of the LSD class act on serotonergic brain systems, binding to 5HT$_{2A}$ receptors in the cortex. Hallucinogenic amphetamines are able to release 5-HT and DA from neurons and are also associated with serotonergic neurotoxicity (Ricaurte, Bryan, Strauss, Seiden, & Schuster, 1985). Dissociative hallucinogens related to PCP probably act at NMDA glutamate receptors. Anticholinergics act at muscarinic cholinergic receptors. There is some evidence that hallucinogenic drug use may precipitate psychotic illnesses in certain individuals predisposed to the development of such illnesses (Bowers & Swigar, 1983).

Medications to Treat Gambling Addiction

The DSM-V recognizes one behavioral addiction: pathological gambling. Despite the societal and financial burden of pathological gambling, there are no FDA-approved treatments at this point. Treatments using opioid receptor antagonists result in the most positive outcomes. The mechanism is thought to be due to blockade of endorphins, which reduces mesolimbic dopaminergic activity. A double-blind placebo-controlled trial of naltrexone efficacy at doses as high as 250 mg/d in 45 subjects over 11 weeks showed significant improvements on all gambling symptom measures (Kim, Grant, Adson, & Shin, 2001). These results were later replicated in an 18-week double-blind placebo-controlled trial of 77 subjects, and no outcome differences were noted between doses of 50, 100 or 150 mg/d (Grant, Kim, & Hartman, 2008). Similarly, nalmefene has shown to be significantly superior to placebo in reducing symptoms and severity of behaviors in gambling addiction in two double-blind placebo-controlled trials (Grant et al., 2006; 2010). Reductions in gambling from opioid antagonists are greatest in persons with a family history positive for alcohol dependence (Grant, 2009).

Although DA plays a central role in gambling reward, DA receptor antagonists have not been shown efficacious in the treatment of gambling disorders. Two double-blind placebo-controlled trials of olanzapine for the treatment of pathological gambling in 21 subjects over 7 weeks and in 42 subjects over 12 weeks did not reveal any reductions in gambling behaviors (Fong, Kalechstein, Bernhard, Rosenthal, & Rugle, 2008; McElroy, Nelson, Welge, Kaehler, & Keck, 2008). More recently, an open label proof-of-concept study in 24 subjects with gambling addiction using tolcapone, an inhibitor of catechol-O-methyl transferase (COMT), the enzyme responsible for DA degradation, showed a reduction in symptoms that was even more pronounced in a subset of the population with the specific val/val COMT polymorphism (Grant et al., 2013).

Mood stabilizers have been evaluated in double-blind placebo-controlled trials. Lithium was found to be superior to placebo in reducing craving and gambling behaviors in a study of 40 pathological gamblers over 10 weeks (Hollander, Pallanti, Allen, Sood, & Baldini Rossi, 2005). Topiramate did not prove to be a useful treatment in a 14-week study of 42 subjects (Berlin et al., 2013).

Considering all medications, Pallesen et al. (2007) conducted a meta-analysis that looked at 16 randomized controlled trials found that either pharmacological treatment of pathological gambling is consistently superior to placebo and that effect sizes were negatively related to the number of male subjects assessed in the study; however, no significant outcome differences were found between the different classes of medications evaluated. A more recent meta-analysis showed a small but significant benefit to the use of opioid antagonists over placebo, but not with other classes of medications (Bartley & Bloch, 2013).

Conclusion

This chapter has summarized the neurobiology of addiction and discussed the mechanisms of action of pharmacotherapies in the treatment of alcohol, drug, and behavioral addictions. There exists considerable evidence that adding adjunctive pharmacological treatment to traditional psychosocial treatments can significantly improve treatment success. Effective, FDA-approved pharmacotherapies currently exist for alcohol, opiate, and nicotine dependence (see Table 21.3). In the future, new pharmacotherapies will be developed that are even more effective, are demonstrated to be cost-effective, are matched to treatment based on patient characteristics, and can be utilized outside of specialty settings (e.g., in primary care). However, pharmacotherapies will only be effective to the extent that they are accepted by clinicians and patients. There exists a perception

Table 21.3. Types of Medications used for Addiction Treatment

1. Medications that block withdrawal the signs and symptoms
   Example: Clonidine, lofexidine in opioid withdrawal/opioid detoxification, carbamazepine for sedative withdrawal
2. Medications with similar properties that can substitute for the abused substance
   Example: Methadone maintenance treatment for opioid dependence, nicotine patch or nicotine gum for nicotine dependence
3. Medications that block the drug "high"
   Example: Naltrexone for opioid dependence and alcohol dependence
4. Medications that produce aversive effects when the substance is used
   Example: Disulfiram treatment in alcoholism
5. Medications that reduce craving
   Example: Naltrexone and topiramate in alcohol dependence
6. Medications that treat comorbid psychiatric disorders
   Example: Antidepressants in comorbid depression and anxiety disorders

among some patients and treatment providers that medication use is incompatible with abstinence or with 12-step treatment philosophy. This is clearly not the case; although Alcoholics Anonymous (AA) does not endorse medication use, a pamphlet distributed by AA Central Services supports the use of appropriately prescribed, nonaddictive medications (Alcoholics Anonymous [AA], 1984).

Medications should probably never be used as a sole treatment but rather as part of a comprehensive treatment program that addresses the psychological, social, and spiritual needs of the patient. Adherence with medication dosing is a major factor in the effectiveness all medications. Therefore, techniques to enhance adherence are key in the use of medications. Adequate clinician and patient education about indications, optimal dosing, and the risks and benefits of medications are necessary to promote compliance. The use of compliance-enhancing injectable depot forms of medication is available for naltrexone. It is possible that multiple medications administered together or in sequence may be required to obtain optimal treatment effectiveness. Finally, the cost-effectiveness of medication compared to other forms of therapy will be an important factor in the decision of third-party payers to accept the use of medications.

References

Addolorato, G., Balducci, G., Capristo, E., Attilia, M. L., Taggi, F., Gasbarrini, G., & Ceccanti, M. (1999). Gamma-hydroxybutyric acid (GHB) in the treatment of alcohol withdrawal syndrome: A randomized comparative study versus benzodiazepine. *Alcoholism: Clinical and Experimental Research, 23*(10), 1596–1604.

Addolorato, G., Caputo, F., Capristo, E., Domenicali, M., Bernardi, M., Janiri, L., Agabio, R., Colombo, G., Gessa, G. L., & Gasbarrini, G. (2002). Baclofen efficacy in reducing alcohol craving and intake: A preliminary double-blind randomized controlled study. *Alcohol and Alcoholism, 37*(5), 504–508.

Addolorato, G., Caputo, F., Capristo, E., Stefanini, G. F., & Gasbarrini, G. (2000). Gammahydroxybutyric acid efficacy, potential abuse, and dependence in the treatment of alcohol addiction. *Alcohol, 20*, 217–222.

Addolorato, G., & Gasbarrini, G. (2005). Gamma-hydroxybutyric acid. *New England Journal of Medicine, 353*, 1632–1633.

Addolorato, G., Leggio, L., Ferrulli, A., Cardone, S., Vonghia, L., Mirijello, A., Abenavoli, L., D'Angelo, C., Caputo, F., Zambon, A., Haber, P. S., & Gasbarrini, G. (2007). Effectiveness and safety of baclofen for maintenance of alcohol abstinence in alcohol-dependent patients with liver cirrhosis: Randomised, double-blind controlled study. *Lancet, 370*(9603), 1915–1922.

Aghajanian, G. K. (1976). Tolerance of locus ceruleus neurons to morphine and inhibition of withdrawal response by clonidine. *Nature, 276*, 186–188.

Alcoholics Anonymous (AA). (1984). The A. A. member—medications and other drugs. AA General Service Conference. Available at http://www.aa.org/assets/en_US/aa-literature/p-11-the-aa-membermedications-and-other-drugs

American Psychiatric Association. (2013). *Diagnostic and Statistical Manual of mental Disorders* (5th ed.). Washington, DC: APA Press.

Anton, R. F. (1999). What is craving? Models and implications for treatment. *Alcohol Research and Health, 23*(3), 165–173.

Anton, R. F., O'Malley, S. S., Ciraulo, D. A., Cisler, R. A., Couper, D., Donovan, D. M.,... COMBINE Study Research Group. (2006). Combined pharmacotherapies and behavioral interventions for alcohol dependence: The COMBINE study: A randomized controlled trial. *Journal of the American Medical Association, 295*, 2003–2017.

Anton, R. F., Oroszi, G., O'Malley, S. S., Couper, D., Swift, R., Pettinati, H., & Goldman, G. (2008). Mu—opiate receptor (OPRM1) 118 allele variant and naltrexone response: Results from the COMBINE study. *Archives of General Psychiatry, 65*(2), 135–144.

Anton, R. F., Pettinati, H., Zweben, A., Kranzler, H. R., Johnson, B., Bohn, M. J., McCaul, M. E., Anthenelli, R., Salloum, I., Galloway, G., Garbutt, J., Swift, R., Gastfriend, D., Kallio, A., & Karhuvaara, S. (2004). A multi-site dose ranging study of nalmefene in the treatment of alcohol dependence. *Journal of Clinical Psychopharmacology, 24*(4), 421–428.

Aron, J. L., & Paulus, M. P. (2007). Location, location: Using functional magnetic resonance imaging to pinpoint brain differences relevant to stimulant use. *Addiction, 102* (Suppl. 1), 33–43.

Bartley, C. A., & Bloch, M. H. (2013). Meta-analysis: Pharmacological treatment of pathological gambling. *Expert Review of Neurotherapeutics, 13*(8), 887–894.

Berlin, H. A., Braun, A., Simeon, D., Koran, L. M., Potenza, M. N., McElroy, S. L., Fong, T., Pallanti, S., & Hollander, E. (2013). A double-blind, placebo-controlled trial of topiramate for pathological gambling. *World Journal of Biological Psychiatry, 14*(2), 121–128.

Bouza, C., Angeles, M., Munoz, A., & Amate, J. M. (2004). Efficacy and safety of naltrexone and acamprosate in the treatment of alcohol dependence: A systematic review. *Addiction, 99*, 811–828.

Bowers, M. B., & Swigar, M. E. (1983). Vulnerability to psychosis associated with hallucinogen use. *Psychiatry Research, 9*, 91–97.

Bowirrat, A., & Oscar-Berman, M. (2005). Relationship between dopaminergic neurotransmission, alcoholism, and Reward Deficiency syndrome. *American Journal of Medical Genetics B: Neuropsychiatric Genetics, 132B*(1), 29–37.

Brewer, C. (1993). Recent developments in disulfiram treatment. *Alcohol and Alcoholism, 28*, 383–395.

Brodie, M. S., Shefner, S. A., & Dunwiddie, T. V. (1990). Ethanol increases the firing rate of dopamine neurons of the rat ventral tegmental area in vitro. *Brain Research, 508*, 65–69.

Brower, K. J., Myra Kim, H., Strobbe, S., Karam-Hage, M. A., Consens, F., & Zucker, R. A. (2008). A randomized double-blind pilot trial of gabapentin versus placebo to treat alcohol dependence and comorbid insomnia. *Alcoholism: Clinical and Experimental Research, 32*(8), 1429–1438.

Brownell, K. D., Marlatt, G. A., Lichtenstein, E., & Wilson, G. T. (1986). Understanding and preventing relapse. *American Psychologist, 41*, 765–782.

Cahill, K., & Ussher M. (2007). Cannabinoid type 1 receptor antagonists (rimonabant) for smoking cessation. *Cochrane Database of Systematic Reviews*, Issue 4. Art. No. CD005353. doi: 10.1002/14651858.CD005353.pub3

Capone, T., Brahen, L., Condren, R., Kordal, N., Melchionda, R., & Peterson, M. (1986). Retention and outcome in a narcotic antagonist treatment program. *Journal of Clinical Psychology, 42*, 825–833.

Carroll, K. M., Nich, C., Ball, S. A., McCance, E., Frankforter, T. L., & Rounsaville, B. J. (2000). One-year follow-up of disulfiram and psychotherapy for cocaine-alcohol users: Sustained effects of treatment. *Addiction, 95*, 1335–1349.

Center for Substance Abuse Treatment (CSAT). (2009). *Incorporating Alcohol Pharmacotherapies Into Medical Practice.* Rockville (MD): Substance Abuse and Mental Health Services Administration (US). (Treatment Improvement Protocol (TIP) Series, No. 49.) Available from: http://www.ncbi.nlm.nih.gov/books/NBK64041/

Charney, D. S., Henninger, G. R., & Jatlow, P. I. (1985). Increased anxiogenic effects of caffeine in panic disorders. *Archives of General Psychiatry, 42*, 233–243.

Chick, J., Anton, R., Checinski, K., Croop, R., Drummond, D. C., Farmer, R., et al. (2000). A multicentre, randomized, double-blind, placebo-controlled trial of naltrexone in the treatment of alcohol dependence or abuse. *Alcohol and Alcoholism, 35*, 587–593.

Chick, J., Gough, K., & Falkowski, W. (1992). Disulfiram treatment of alcoholism. *British Journal of Psychiatry, 161*, 84–89.

Coben, J. H., Davis, S. M., Furbee, P. M., Sikora, R. D., Tillotson, R. D., & Bossarte, R. M. (2010). Hospitalizations for poisoning by prescription opioids, sedatives, and tranquilizers. *American Journal of Preventive Medicine, 38*(5) 517–524.

Code of Federal Regulations (42 CFR, Part 8). Certification of Opioid Treatment Programs. Available at: http://www.gpo.gov/fdsys/granule/CFR-2007-title42-vol1/CFR-2007-title42-vol1-part8

Colombo, G. (1997). ESBRA-Nordmann 1996 Award Lecture: Ethanol drinking behaviour in Sardinian alcohol-preferring rats. *Alcohol and Alcoholism, 32,* 443–453.

Colombo, G., Vacca, G., Serra, S., Brunetti, G., Carai, M. A. M., & Gessa, G. L. (2003). Baclofen suppresses motivation to consume alcohol in rats. *Psychopharmacology, 167,* 221–224.

Comer, S. D., Sullivan, M. A., Yu, E., Rothenberg, J. L., Kleber H. D., Kampman, K., Dackis, C., & O'Brien, C. P. (2006). Injectable, sustained-release naltrexone for the treatment of opioid dependence: A randomized, placebo-controlled trial. *Archives of General Psychiatry, 63,* 210–218.

Comings, D. E., & Blum, K. (2000). Reward deficiency syndrome: Genetic aspects of behavioral disorders. *Progress in Brain Research, 126,* 325–341.

Cooper, Z. D., & Haney, M. (2009). Actions of delta-9-tetrahydrocannabinol in cannabis: Relation to use, abuse, dependence. *International Review of Psychiatry, 21*(20), 104–112.

Corrigall, W. A., Coen, K. M., & Adamson, K. L. (1994). Self-administered nicotine activates the mesolimbic dopamine system through the ventral tegmental area. *Brain Research, 653,* 278–284.

Costa, E., & Guidotti, A. (1979). Molecular mechanisms in the receptor action of benzodiazepines. *Annual Review of Pharmacology and Toxicology, 19,* 531–545.

Crabb, D. W., Edenberg, H. J., Bosron, W. F., & Li, T. K. (1989). Genotypes for aldehyde dehydrogenase deficiency and alcohol sensitivity. The inactive ALDH2*2 allele is dominant. *Journal of Clinical Investigation, 83,* 314–316.

Croop, R. S., Faulkner, E. B., & Labriola, D. F. (1997). The safety profile of naltrexone in the treatment of alcoholism. Results from a multicenter usage study. *Archives of General Psychiatry, 54,* 1130–1135.

Dackis, C. A., Kampman, K. M., Lynch, K. G., Pettinati, H. M., O'Brien, C, P. (2005). A double-blind, placebo-controlled trial of modafinil for cocaine dependence. *Neuropsychopharmacology, 30*(1), 205–211.

Dackis, C. A., Kampman, K. M., Lynch, K. G., Plebani, J. G., Pettinati, H. M., Sparkman, T., O'Brien, C. P. (2012). A double-blind, placebo-controlled trial of modafinil for cocaine dependence. *Journal of Substance Abuse Treatment, 43*(3), 303–312.

Das, S., Harel, O., Dey, D. K., Covault, J., & Kranzler, H. R. (2010). Analysis of extreme drinking in patients with alcohol dependence using Pareto regression. *Statistics in Medicine, 29*(11), 1250–1258.

D'Aunno, T., & Pollack, H. A. (2002). Changes in methadone treatment practices: Results from a national panel study, 1988-2000. *Journal of the American Medical Association, 288,* 850–856.

Dews, P. B. (1982). Caffeine. *Annual Review of Nutrition, 2,* 323–341.

Diana, M., Pistis, M., Carboni, S., Gessa, G. L., & Rossetti, Z. L. (1993). Profound decrement of mesolimbic dopaminergic neuronal activity during ethanol withdrawal syndrome in rats: Electrophysiological and biochemical evidence. *Proceedings of the National Academy of Sciences USA, 90,* 7966–7969.

Dole, V. P., & Nyswander, M. (1965). A medical treatment for diacetylmorphine (heroin) addiction: Clinical trial with methadone hydrochloride. *Journal of the American Medical Association, 193,* 646–650.

Eisenberg, M. J., Filion, K. B., Yavin, D., Bélisle, P., Mottillo, S., Joseph, L., Gervais, A., O'Loughlin, J., Paradis, G., Rinfret, S., & Pilote, L. (2008). Pharmacotherapies for smoking cessation: A meta-analysis of randomized controlled trials. *Canadian Medical Association Journal, 179,* 135–144.

Ellinwood, E. H. (1969). Amphetamine psychosis: A multidimensional process. *Seminars in Psychiatry, 1,* 208–226.

Evans, S. M., & Bisaga, A. (2009). Acute interaction of baclofen in combination with alcohol in heavy social drinkers. *Alcoholism: Clinical and Experimental Research, 33*(1), 19–30.

Fong, T., Kalechstein, A., Bernhard, B., Rosenthal, R., & Rugle, L. (2008). A double-blind, placebo-controlled trial of olanzapine for the treatment of video poker pathological gamblers. *Pharmacology, Biochemistry and Behavior, 89*(3), 298–303.

Fuller, R.K., Branchey, L., Brightwell, D.R., Derman, R.M., Emrick, C.D., Iber, F.L.,. . . Lowenstam, I. (1986). Disulfiram treatment of alcoholism. A Veterans Administration cooperative study. *Journal of the American Medical Association, 256,* 1449–1455.

Garbutt, J. C., Kranzler, H. R., O'Malley, S. S., Gastfriend, D. R., Pettinati, H. M., Silverman, B. L., et al. (2005). Efficacy and tolerability of long-acting injectable naltrexone for alcohol dependence: A randomized controlled trial. *Journal of the American Medical Association, 293,* 1617–1625.

Girdlestone, D. (2000). Opioid receptors. In B. M. Cox, C. Chavkin, M. J. Christie, O. Civelli, C. Evans, M. D. Hamon, et al. (Eds.), *The IUPHAR compendium of receptor characterization and classification* (2nd ed., pp. 321–333). London: IUPHAR Media.

Gold, M. S., Redmond, D. E. Jr., & Kleber, H. D. (1979). Noradrenergic hyperactivity in opiate withdrawal suppressed by clonidine. *American Journal of Psychiatry, 136,* 100–102.

Goldman, D., Oroszi, G., & Ducci, F. (2005). The genetics of addictions: Uncovering the genes. *Nature Reviews Genetics, 6,* 521–532.

Grant, J. E. (2009). *Opioid antagonists in the treatment of pathological gambling and kleptomania. Opiate receptors and antagonists.* New York: Humana.

Grant, J. E., Kim, S. W., & Hartman, B. K. (2008). A double-blind, placebo-controlled study of the opiate antagonist naltrexone in the treatment of pathological gambling urges. *Journal of Clinical Psychiatry, 69*(5), 783–789.

Grant, J. E., Potenza, M. N., Hollander, E., Cunningham-Williams, R., Nurminen, T., Smits, G., & Kallio, A. (2006). Multicenter investigation of the opioid antagonist nalmefene in the treatment of pathological gambling. *American Journal of Psychiatry, 163*(2), 303–312.

Grant, J. E., Odlaug, B. L., Potenza, M. N., Hollander, E., & Kim, S. W. (2010). Nalmefene in the treatment of pathological gambling: Multicentre, double-blind, placebo-controlled study. *British Journal of Psychiatry,. 197*(4), 330–331.

Grant, J. E., Odlaug, B. L., Chamberlain, S. R., Hampshire, A., Schreiber, L. R., & Kim, S. W. (2013). A proof of concept study of tolcapone for pathological gambling: Relationships with COMT genotype and brain activation. *European Neuropsychopharmacology, 23*(11), 1587–1596.

Hays, J. T., Hurt, R. D., Rigotti, N. A., Niaura, R., Gonzales, D., Durcan, M. J., Sachs, D. P., Wolter, T. D., Buist, A. S.,

Johnston, J. A., & White, J. D. (2001). Sustained-release bupropion for pharmacologic relapse prevention after smoking cessation: A randomized, controlled trial. *Annals of Internal Medicine, 135,* 423–433.

Heath, A. C. (1995). Genetic influences on alcoholism risk. A review on adoption and twin studies. *Alcohol Health and Research World, 19*(3), 166–171.

Higgins, S. T. (1996). Some potential contributions of reinforcement and consumer-demand theory to reducing cocaine use. *Addictive Behaviors, 21,* 803–816.

Higuchi, S., Matsushita, S., Murayama, M., Takagi, T., & Hayashida, M. (1995). Alcohol and aldehyde dehydrogenase polymorphisms and the risk for alcoholism. *American Journal of Psychiatry, 152,* 1219–1221.

Hollander, E., Pallanti, S., Allen, A., Sood, E., & Baldini Rossi, N. (2005). Does sustained-release lithium reduce impulsive gambling and affective instability versus placebo in pathological gamblers with bipolar spectrum disorders? *American Journal of Psychiatry, 162*(1), 137–145.

Hughes, J. R., Higgins, S. T., Bickel, W. K., Hunt, W. K., & Gulliver, S. (1991). Caffeine self-administration, withdrawal and adverse effects among coffee drinkers. *Archives of General Psychiatry, 48*(7), 611–617.

Hughes, J. R., Goldstein, M. G., Hurt, R. D., & Shiffman, S. (1999). Recent advances in the pharmacology of smoking. *Journal of the American Medical Association, 281*(1), 72–76.

Hurt, R. D., Sachs, D. P., Glover, E. D., Offord, K. P., Johnston, J. A., Dale, L. C., Khayrallah, M. A., Schroeder, D. R., Glover, P. N., Sullivan, C. R., Croghan, I. T., & Sullivan, P. M. (1997). A comparison of sustained-release bupropion and placebo for smoking cessation. *New England Journal of Medicine, 337,* 1195–1202.

Hutchison, K. E., Ray, L., Sandman, E., Rutter, M. C., Peters, A., Davidson, D., & Swift, R. (2006). The effect of olanzapine on craving and alcohol consumption. *Neuropsychopharmacology, 31*(6), 1310–1317.

Johnson, B. A., Ait-Daoud, N., Bowden, C. L., DiClemente, C. C., Roache, J. D., Lawson, K., Javors, M. A., & Ma, J. Z. (2003). Oral topiramate for treatment of alcohol dependence: A randomised controlled trial. *Lancet, 361*(9370), 1677–1685.

Johnson, B. A., Roache, J. D., Javors, M. A., DiClemente, C. C., Cloninger, C. R., Prihoda, T. J., Bordnick, P. S., Ait-Daoud, N., & Hensler, J. (2000). Ondansetron for reduction of drinking among biologically predisposed alcoholic patients: A randomized controlled trial. *Journal of the American Medical Association, 284*(8), 963–971.

Johnson, B. A., Rosenthal, N., Capece, J. A., Wiegand, F., Mao, L., Beyers, K., McKay, A., Ait-Daoud, N., Anton, R. F., Ciraulo, D. A., Kranzler, H. R., Mann, K., O'Malley, S. S., Swift, R. M., Topiramate for Alcoholism Advisory Board, & Topiramate for Alcoholism Study Group. (2007). Topiramate for treating alcohol dependence: a randomized controlled trial. *JAMA, 298*(14), 1641–1651.

Johnson, B. A., Seneviratne, C., Wang, X. Q., Ait-Daoud, N., & Li, M. D. (2013). Determination of genotype combinations that can predict the outcome of the treatment of alcohol dependence using the 5-HT(3) antagonist ondansetron. *American Journal of Psychiatry, 170*(9), 1020–1031.

Jorenby, D. E., Leischow, S. J., Nides, M. A., Rennard, S. I., Johnston, A., Hughes, A. R., Smith, S. S., Muramoto, M. L., Daughton, D. M., Doan, K., Fiore, M. C., & Baker, T. B. (1999). A controlled trial of sustained-release bupropion, a

nicotine patch, or both for smoking cessation. *New England Journal of Medicine, 340,* 685–691.

Kakko, J., Grönbladh, L., Svanborg, K. D., von Wachenfeldt, J., Rück, C., Rawlings, B., Nilsson, L. -H., & Heilig, M. (2007). A stepped care strategy using buprenorphine and methadone versus conventional methadone maintenance in heroin dependence: A randomized controlled trial. *American Journal of Psychiatry, 164,* 797–803.

Kampman, K. M., Pettinati, H., Lynch, K. G., Dackis, C., Sparkman, T., Weigley, C., & O'Brien, C. P. (2004). A pilot trial of topiramate for the treatment of cocaine dependence. *Drug and Alcohol Dependence, 75*(3), 233–240.

Kampman, K. M., Pettinati, H. M., Lynch, K. G., Whittingham, T., Macfadden, W., Dackis, C., Tirado, C., Oslin, D. W., Sparkman, T., & O'Brien, C. P. (2007). A double-blind, placebo-controlled pilot trial of quetiapine for the treatment of Type A and Type B alcoholism. *Journal of Clinical Psychopharmacology, 27*(4), 344–351.

Khantzian, E. J. (1985). The self-medication hypothesis of addictive disorders. Focus on heroin and cocaine dependence. *American Journal of Psychiatry, 142,* 1259–1264.

Kim, S. W., Grant, J. E., Adson, D. E., & Shin, Y. C. (2001). Double-blind naltrexone and placebo comparison study in the treatment of pathological gambling. *Biological Psychiatry, 49*(11), 914–921.

Klonoff, H. (1974). Marihuana and driving in real-life situations. *Science, 186,* 317–324.

Koob, G. F. (2006). Alcoholism: Allostasis and beyond. *Alcoholism: Clinical and Experimental Research, 27,* 232–243.

Koob, G. F., & Volkow, N. D. (2010). Neurocircuitry of addiction. *Neuropsychopharmacology, 35*(1), 217–238.

Kosten, T. R., & Kleber, H. D. (1984). Strategies to improve compliance with narcotic antagonists. *American Journal of Drug and Alcohol Abuse, 10,* 249–266.

Kranzler, H. R., Burleson, J. A., Korner, P., Del Boca, F. K., Bohn, M. J., Brown, J., & Liebowitz, N. (1995). Placebo-controlled trial of fluoxetine as an adjunct to relapse prevention in alcoholics. *American Journal of Psychiatry, 152*(3), 391–397.

Krupitsky, E., Nunes, E. V., Ling, W., Illeperuma, A., Gastfriend, D. R., & Silverman, B. L. (2011). Injectable extended-release naltrexone for opioid dependence: A double-blind, placebo-controlled, multicentre randomised trial. *Lancet, 377*(9776), 1506–1513.

Kuehn, B. M. (2012). New reports examine psychiatric risks of varenicline for smoking cessation. *Journal of the American Medical Association, 307*(2), 129–130.

Lappalainen, J., Kranzler, H. R., Malison, R., Price, L. H., Van Dyck, C., Rosenheck, R. A., Cramer, J., Southwick, S., Charney, D., Krystal, J., & Gelernter, J. (2002). A functional neuropeptide Y Leu7Pro polymorphism associated with alcohol dependence in a large population sample from the United States. *Archives of General Psychiatry, 59,* 825–831.

Le Foll, B., & George, T. P. (2007). Treatment of tobacco dependence: Integrating recent progress into practice. *Canadian Medical Association Journal, 177,* 1373–1380.

Leggio, L., Kenna, G. A., & Swift, R. M. (2008). New developments for the pharmacological treatment of alcohol withdrawal syndrome: A focus on non-benzodiazepine GABAergic medications. *Progress in Neuropsychopharmacology and Biological Psychiatry, 32,* 1106–1117.

Ling, W., Rawson, R. A., Compton, M. A., (1994). Substitution pharmacotherapies for opioid addiction: from methadone to LAAM and buprenorphine. *Journal of Psychoactive Drugs, 26*(2), 119–128.

Littleton, J. (1995). Acamprosate in alcohol dependence: How does it work? *Addiction, 90,* 1179–1188.

Littleton, J. (1998). Neurochemical mechanisms underlying alcohol withdrawal. *Alcohol Health and Research World, 22*(1), 13–24.

Litten, R. Z., Fertig, J. B., Falk, D. E., Ryan, M. L., Mattson, M. E., Collins, J. F., Murtaugh, C., Ciraulo, D., Green, A. I., Johnson, B., Pettinati, H., Swift, R., Afshar, M., Brunette, M. F., Tiouririne, N. A., Kampman, K., & Stout, R. (2012). NCIG 001 study group. A double-blind, placebo-controlled trial to assess the efficacy of quetiapine fumarate XR in very heavy-drinking alcohol-dependent patients. *Alcoholism: Clinical and Experimental Research, 36*(3), 406–416.

Longo, M., Wickes, W., Smout, M., Harrison, S., Cahill, S., White, J. M. (2010). Randomized controlled trial of dexamphetamine maintenance for the treatment of methamphetamine dependence. *Addiction, 105*(1), 146–154.

Mackie. K. (2008). Cannabinoid receptors: Where they are and what they do. *Journal of Neuroendocrinology, 20*(Suppl. 1), 10–14.

Maisel, N. C., Blodgett, J. C., Wilbourne P. L., Humphreys, K., & Finney, J. W. (2013). Meta-analysis of naltrexone and acamprosate for treating alcohol use disorders: When are these medications most helpful? *Addiction, 108*(2), 275–293.

Malcolm, R., Ballenger, J. C., Sturgis, E. T., & Anton, R. (1989). Double blind controlled trial comparing carbamazepine to oxazepam treatment of alcohol withdrawal. *American Journal of Psychiatry, 146,* 617–621.

Mann, K., Lehert, P., & Morgan, M. Y. (2004). The efficacy of acamprosate in the maintenance of abstinence in alcohol-dependent individuals: Results of a meta-analysis. *Alcoholism: Clinical and Experimental Research, 28,* 51–63.

Mann, K., Bladström, A., Torup, L., Gual, A., & van den Brink, W. (2013). Extending the treatment options in alcohol dependence: A randomized controlled study of as-needed nalmefene. *Biological Psychiatry, 73*(8), 706–713.

Mann, K., Lemenager, T., Hoffmann, S., Reinhard, I., Hermann, D., Batra, A., Berner, M., Wodarz, N., Heinz, A., Smolka, M. N., Zimmermann, U. S., Wellek, S., Kiefer, F., & Anton, R. F. (2013). The PREDICT study team. Results of a double-blind, placebo-controlled pharmacotherapy trial in alcoholism conducted in Germany and comparison with the US COMBINE study. *Addiction Biology, 18*(6), 937–946.

Mason, B. J., Light, J. M., Williams, L. D., & Drobes, D. J. (2009). Proof-of-concept human laboratory study for protracted abstinence in alcohol dependence: Effects of gabapentin. *Addiction Biology, 14*(1), 73–83.

Mason, B. J., Goodman, A. M., Chabac, S., & Lehert, P. (2006). Effect of oral acamprosate on abstinence in patients with alcohol dependence in a double-blind, placebo-controlled trial: The role of patient motivation. *Journal of Psychiatric Research, 40,* 383–393.

Mason, B. J., Ritvo, E. C., Morgan, R. O., Salvato, F. R., Goldberg, G., Welch, B., & Mantero-Atienza, E. (1994). A double-blind, placebo-controlled pilot study to evaluate the efficacy and safety of oral nalmefene HCl for alcohol dependence. *Alcoholism: Clinical and Experimental Research, 18*(5), 1162–1167.

Mason, B. J., Quello, S., Goodell, V., Shadan, F., Kyle, M., & Begovic, A. (2013). Gabapentin treatment for alcohol dependence: A randomized clinical trial. *JAMA Internal Medicine, 174*(1), 70–77. doi: 10.1001/jamainternmed.2013.11950

Mattick, R. P., Breen, C., Kimber, J., & Davoli, M. (2003). Methadone maintenance therapy versus no opiate replacement therapy for opiate dependence. *Cochrane Database Systematic Review, 2,* CD002209.

Mayo-Smith, M. F. (1997). Pharmacological management of alcohol withdrawal: A metaanalysis and evidence-based practice guideline. American Society of Addiction Medicine working group on pharmacological management of alcohol withdrawal. *Journal of the American Medical Association, 278,* 144–151.

McElroy, S. L., Nelson, E. B., Welge, J. A., Kaehler, L., & Keck, P. E. Jr. (2008). Olanzapine in the treatment of pathological gambling: A negative randomized placebo-controlled trial. *Journal of Clinical Psychiatry, 69*(3), 433–440.

McLellan, A. T., Lewis, D. C., O'Brien, C. P., & Kleber, H. D. (2000). Drug dependence–a chronic medical illness. Implications for treatment, insurance and outcomes evaluation. *Journal of the American Medical Association, 284*(13), 1689–1695.

Mechoulam, R., Peters, M., Murillo-Rodriguez, E., & Hanus, L. O. (2007). Cannabidiol—recent advances. *Chemistry & Biodiversity, 4*(8), 1678–1692.

Miller, W. R., & Wilbourne, P. L. (2002). Mesa Grande: A methodological analysis of clinical trials of treatments for alcohol use disorders. *Addiction, 97*(3), 265–277.

Monti, P. M., Rohsenow, D. J., Swift, R., Gulliver, S. B., Colby, S. M., Mueller, T. I., et al. (2001). Naltrexone and cue-exposure with coping and communications skills training for alcoholics: Treatment process and one-year outcomes. *Alcoholism: Clinical and Experimental Research, 25,* 1634–1647.

Myers, R. D., Borg, S., & Mossberg, R. (1986). Antagonism by naltrexone of voluntary alcohol selection in the chronically drinking macaque monkey. *Alcohol, 3*(6), 383–388.

Myrick, H., Malcolm, R., Randall, P. K., Boyle, E., Anton, R. F., Becker, H. C., & Randall, C. L. (2009). A double-blind trial of gabapentin versus lorazepam in the treatment of alcohol withdrawal. *Alcoholism: Clinical and Experimental Research, 33*(9), 1582–1588.

Naranjo, C. A., & Bremner, K. E. (1993). Clinical pharmacology of serotonin-altering medications for decreasing alcohol consumption. *Alcohol and Alcoholism (Suppl.), 2,* 221–229.

National Institute on Alcohol Abuse and Alcoholism (NIAAA). (2008). Prescribing medications for alcohol dependence. In USDHHS, *Helping patients who drink too much: A clinician's guide."* NIH Publication 07–3769. Available at www.niaaa.nih.gov/guide

National Institute on Drug Abuse (NIDA). (2009). Principles of drug addiction treatment: A research based guide (2nd ed.). NIH Publication No. 09-4180. (Original work published 1999)

Nestler, E. J. (2001). Molecular basis of long-term plasticity underlying addiction. *Nature Reviews Neuroscience, 2,* 119–128.

Nichols, D. E. (2004). Hallucinogens. *Pharmacological Therapeutics, 101,* 131–181.

Nides, M., Oncken, C., Gonzales, D., Rennard, S., Watsky, E. J., Anziano, R., & Reeves, K. R. (2006). Smoking cessation with varenicline, a selective alpha4beta2 nicotinic receptor partial agonist: Results from a 7-week, randomized, placebo- and bupropion-controlled trial with 1-year follow-up. *Archives of Internal Medicine, 166*, 1561–1568.

O'Brien, C. P. (2005). Anticraving medications for relapse prevention: A possible new class of psychoactive medications. *American Journal of Psychiatry, 162*(8), 1423–1431.

O'Farrell, T. J., Allen, J. P., & Litten, R. Z. (1995). Disulfiram (Antabuse) contracts in treatment of alcoholism. *NIDA Research Monograph, 150*, 65–91.

O'Malley, S. S., Jaffe, A. J., Chang, G., Schottenfeld, R. S., Meyer, R. E., & Rounsaville, B. (1992). Naltrexone and coping skills therapy for alcohol dependence. *Archives of General Psychiatry, 49*, 881–887.

Oncken, C., Gonzales, D., Nides, M., Rennard, S., Watsky, E., Billing, C. B., Anziano, R., & Reeves, K. (2006). Efficacy and safety of the novel selective nicotinic acetylcholine receptor partial agonist, varenicline, for smoking cessation. *Archives of Internal Medicine, 166*, 1571–1577.

Oslin, D. W., Berrettini, W., Kranzler, H. R., Pettinati, H., Gelernter, J., Volpicelli, J. R., & O'Brien, C. P. (2003). A functional polymorphism of the mu-opioid receptor gene is associated with naltrexone response in alcohol-dependent patients. *Neuropsychopharmacology, 28*(8), 1546–1552.

Paille, F. M., Guelfi, J. D., Perkins, A. C., Roye, R. J., Steru, L., & Parot, P. (1995). Double-blind randomized multicentre trial of acamprosate in maintaining abstinence from alcohol. *Alcohol and Alcoholism, 30*, 239–247.

Pallesen, S., Molde, H., Arnestad, H. M., Laberg, J. C., Skutle, A., Iversen, E., Støylen, I. J., Kvale, G., & Holsten, F. (2007). Outcome of pharmacological treatments of pathological gambling: A review and meta-analysis. *Journal of Clinical Psychopharmacology, 27*(4), 357–364.

Patterson, J. F. (1990). Withdrawal from alprazolam using clonazepam: Clinical observations. *Journal of Clinical Psychiatry (Suppl.), 51*(5), 47–49.

Pelc, I., Verbanck, P., LeBon, O., Gavrilovic, M., Lion, K., & Lehert, P. (1997). Efficacy and safety of acamprosate in the treatment of detoxified alcohol-dependent patients. A 90-day placebo-controlled dose finding study. *British Journal of Psychiatry, 171*, 73–77.

Pope, H. G., Gruber, A. J., Hudson, J. I., Huestis, M. A., & Yurgelun-Todd, D. (2001). Neuropsychological performance in long-term cannabis users. *Archives of General Psychiatry, 58*, 909–915.

Probst, C. C., & van Eimeren, T. (2013). The functional anatomy of impulse control disorders. *Current Neurology and Neuroscience Report, 13*(10), 386.

Regier, D. A., Farmer, M. E., Rae, D. S., Locke, B. Z., Keith, S. J., Judd, L. L., & Goodwin, F. K. (1990). Comorbidity of mental disorders with alcohol and other drug abuse results from the Epidemiologic Catchment Area (ECA) study *Journal of the American Medical Association, 19*, 2511–2518.

Reid, L. D., & Hubbell, C. L. (1987). Excess of drinking related to excess activity of opioid systems. *Alcohol, 4*, 149–168.

Resnick, R. B., Schuyten-Resnick, E., & Washton, A. M. (1980). Assessment of narcotic antagonists in the treatment of opioid dependence. *Annual Review of Pharmacology and Toxicology, 20*, 463–474.

Ricaurte, G., Bryan, G., Strauss, L., Seiden, L., & Schuster, C. (1985). Hallucinogenic amphetamine selectively destroys brain serotonin nerve terminals. *Science, 229*(4717), 986–988.

Rohsenow, D., & Monti, P. (1992). Cue elicited urge to drink and salivation in alcoholics: Relationship to individual differences and relapse. *Advances in Behavioral Research and Therapy, 14*, 195–210.

Rösner S, Leucht S, Lehert P, Soyka M. (2008). Acamprosate supports abstinence, naltrexone prevents excessive drinking: evidence from a meta-analysis with unreported outcomes. *Journal of Psychopharmacology, 22*(1), 11–23.

Rounsaville, B. J., Gawin, F. H., & Kleber, H. D. (1985). Interpersonal psychotherapy adapted for ambulatory cocaine users. *American Journal of Drug and Alcohol Abuse, 11*, 171.

Rubio, G., Ponce, G., Rodriguez-Jimenez, R., Jimenez-Arriero, M. A., Hoenicka, J., & Palomo, T. (2005). Clinical predictors of response to naltrexone in alcoholic patients: Who benefits most from treatment with naltrexone? *Alcohol and Alcoholism, 40*(3), 227–233.

Sass, H., Soyka, M., Mann, K., & Zieglgänsberger, W. (1996). Relapse prevention by acamprosate. Results from a placebo controlled study on alcohol dependence. *Archives of General Psychiatry, 53*, 673–680.

Schneier, F. R., & Siris, S. G. (1987). A review of psychoactive substance use and abuse in schizophrenia-Patterns of drug choice. *Journal of Nervous and Mental Disease, 175*, 641–652.

Schulz, D. W., & Macdonald, R. L. (1981). Barbiturate enhancement of GABA-mediated inhibition and activation of chloride channel conductance: Correlation with anticonvulsant and anesthetic actions. *Brain Research, 209*, 177–188.

Seeman, P. (1972). Membrane effects of anesthetics and tranquilizers. *Pharmacological Reviews, 24*, 583–655.

Senay, E. C. (1985). Methadone maintenance treatment. *International Journal of Addiction, 20*, 803–821.

Sershen, H., Hashim, A., & Lajtha, A. (1997). Ibogaine and cocaine abuse: Pharmacological interactions at dopamine and serotonin receptors. *Brain Research Bulletin, 42*(3), 161–168.

Shoptaw, S., Yang, X., Rotheram-Fuller, E. J., Hsieh, Y. -C., Kintaudie, P. C., Charuvastra, V. C., & Ling, W. (2003). Randomized placebo-controlled trial of baclofen for cocaine dependence: Preliminary effects for Individuals with chronic patterns of cocaine use. *Journal of Clinical Psychiatry, 64*, 1440–1448.

Silagy, C., Lancaster, T., Stead, L., Mant, D., & Fowler, G. (2004). Nicotine replacement therapy for smoking cessation. *Cochrane Database Systematic Reviews, 3*, CD000146.

Smith, D. E. & Wesson, D. R. (1970). A New Method for Treatment of Barbiturate Dependence. *Journal of the American Medical Association, 213*(2), 294–295.

Srisurapanont, M., & Jarusuraisin, N. (2005). Naltrexone for the treatment of alcoholism: A meta-analysis of randomized controlled trials. *International Journal of Neuropsychopharmacology, 8*, 267–280.

Strain, E. C., Stitzer, M. L., Liebson, I. A., & Bigelow, G. E. (1994). Comparison of buprenorphine and methadone in the treatment of opioid dependence. *American Journal of Psychiatry, 151*, 1025–1030.

Strat, Y. L., Ramoz, N., Schumann, G., & Gorwood, P. (2008). Molecular genetics of alcohol dependence and related endophenotypes. *Current Genomics, 9*(7), 444–451.

Swift, R. (2010). Medications acting on the dopaminergic system in the treatment of alcoholic patients. *Current Pharmaceutical Design, 16*, 2136–2140.

Swift, R. M. (1999a). Drug therapy for alcohol dependence. *New England Journal of Medicine, 340*, 1482–1490.

Swift, R. M. (1999b). Medications for alcohol craving. *Alcohol Health and Research, 23*(3), 207–213.

Tien, A. Y., & Anthony, J. C. (1990). Epidemiological analysis of alcohol and drug use as risk factors for psychotic experiences. *Journal of Nervous and Mental Disease, 178,* 473–480.

Turner, W. M., & Tsuang, M. T. (1990). Impact of substance abuse on the course and outcome of schizophrenia. *Schizophrenia Bulletin, 16,* 87–95.

United States Department of Health and Human Services (USDHHS). (2008). Treating tobacco use and dependence: 2008 Update. Clinical Practice Guideline. Rockville, MD: U.S. Department of Health and Human Services. Public Health Service. May 2008. Available at: http://www.ahrq.gov/professionals/clinicians-providers/guidelines-recommendations/tobacco/clinicians/update/treating_tobacco_use08.pdf

Vocci, F. J., Acri, J., & Elkashef, A. (2005). Medication development for addictive disorders: The state of the science. *American Journal of Psychiatry,. 162,* 1432–1440.

Volkow, N. D., Fowler, J. S., Wang, G. -J., Swanson, J. M., & Telang, F. (2007). Dopamine in drug abuse and addiction: Results of imaging studies and treatment implications. *Archives of Neurology, 64*(11), 1575–1579.

Volpicelli, J., Davis, M., & Olgin, J. (1986). Naltrexone blocks the post-shock increase of alcohol consumption. *Life Sciences, 38,* 841–847.

Volpicelli, J. R., Alterman, A. I., Hayashida, M., & O'Brien, C. P. (1992). Naltrexone in the treatment of alcohol dependence. *Archives of General Psychiatry, 49,* 876–880.

Volpicelli, J. R., Rhines, K. C., Rhines, J. S., Volpicelli, L. A, Alterman, A. I, & O'Brien CP (1997). Naltrexone and alcohol dependence: Role of subject compliance. *Archives of General Psychiatry, 54,* 737–742.

Weiss, F., Lorang, M. T., Bloom, F. E., & Koob, G. F. (1993). Oral alcohol self-administration stimulates dopamine release in the rat nucleus accumbens: Genetic and motivational determinants. *Journal of Pharmacology and Experimental Therapeutics, 267,* 250–258.

Wise, R. A., & Bozarth, M. A. (1987). A psychomotor stimulant theory of addiction. *Psychological Review, 94,* 469–492.

PART 5

Prevention and Policy

Programs and Policies Designed to Reduce Impaired Driving

Robert B. Voas *and* James C. Fell

Abstract

Alcohol has been associated with traffic crashes for more than 100 years, as indicated by the publication of the first scientific report on the effect of drinking by operators of "motorized wagons" in 1904. This chapter presents an overview of the status of policies and programs designed to reduce highway crashes involving alcohol-impaired drivers. Alcohol safety programs are reviewed under three headings: primary prevention, secondary prevention, and tertiary prevention. Primary prevention covers programs directed at reducing the high-risk drinking that leads to impaired driving, including programs directed at preventing drinking by youths aged 20 and younger and at preventing service to obviously intoxicated individuals. Secondary prevention covers programs directed at separating drinking from driving through law enforcement, public information programs, and driver licensing regulations. Finally, tertiary prevention focuses on programs directed at preventing identified drinking drivers from future impaired driving through license sanctions, vehicle actions, treatment programs, and monitoring systems

Key Words: alcohol availability, impaired driving laws, enforcement, breath testing, alcohol ignition interlocks, technology, monitoring, blood alcohol concentration limit, sobriety checkpoints

Motor vehicle crashes became a public safety problem in the United States at the beginning of the 20th century. Alcohol has been associated with traffic crashes for more than 100 years, as indicated by the publication of the first scientific report on the effect of drinking by operators of "motorized wagons" in 1904 (Editorial, 1904). The Federal Highway Administration (FHWA) estimated that 172 people died in motorized vehicle crashes in 1904 (National Center for Statistics and Analysis [NCSA], 2004). The number of those crashes that were alcohol related would be purely speculative, but current relatively accurate records indicate that, in 2011, 9,876 (31%) of the 32,367 US traffic fatalities were alcohol related (e.g., resulted from a crash involving a driver with an illegal blood alcohol concentration [BAC] of .08 or higher; National Center for Statistics and Analysis, 2012). Currently, alcohol-related crashes cost US society $129.7 billion annually (Zaloshnja & Miller, 2009). Formal

state and national efforts to prevent impaired driving began in the second decade of the 20th century when the state of New York passed the first law criminalizing impaired driving in 1910. For the first half of that century, efforts to reduce impaired driving centered on traffic safety programs and the criminal justice system, focusing on deterrence through the apprehension and sanctioning of impaired drivers. However, since the founding of the federal agencies dealing with highway safety (e.g., the National Highway Traffic Safety Administration [NHTSA]) and with alcoholism (e.g., National Institute on Alcohol Abuse and Alcoholism [NIAAA]) in the late 1960s, concern for the impaired driving problem has expanded to include the field of public health. This brought in a new focus on programs aimed at controlling high-risk drinking, such as the establishment of a minimum drinking age law, the promotion of responsible alcohol sales and service programs, and methods for identifying and treating those drivers convicted of driving under the influence (DUI) of alcohol who have drinking problems.

The objective of this chapter is to present an overview of the status of policies and programs designed to reduce highway crashes involving impaired drivers. It is designed for readers with a special interest in promoting, developing, and implementing safety programs. It grows out of a program conducted by the Pacific Institute for Research and Evaluation (PIRE) to produce tools for communities to use in planning and implementing alcohol safety programs (Birckmayer, Boothroyd, Friend, Holder, & Voas, 2008; Birckmayer, Holder, Yacoubian, & Friend, 2004). Readers interested in promoting impaired driving programs and policies should augment this review by reading Birckmayer et al. (2008), which provides a more complete description of some of the topics covered here. Because impaired driving programs involve a wide range of topics, it is difficult to cover them within the limits of a single chapter. It is impossible to provide a complete review of the literature on the more than 50 programs described herein. Rather, the most important recent articles on each topic are included to provide the reader with a method of pursuing more information in the literature. Aside from the Birckmayer article, readers with an interest in this area should consult the report published by NHTSA (2008) on "Countermeasures That Work," which lists 104 traffic safety programs covering all areas of road user safety. This chapter differs from that report in that it is limited to alcohol safety programs and includes more coverage of public health programs related to reducing high-risk drinking and treatment programs for drinking drivers. The reader will also want to review "Effectiveness of Behavioral Highway Safety Countermeasures" (Preusser, Williams, Nichols, Tison, & Chaudhary, 2008), which reviews the evidence for the programs listed in "Countermeasures That Work" and "Impaired Driving: Opportunities and Problems" (Voas & Fell, 2011).

This chapter does not attempt to cover driver behavior in general or theories of crash causation. For that information, the recent text by Shinar (2007) would be a useful initial source. Those interested in the body's absorption and elimination of alcohol in relation to impairment should consult Jones (2000) and Jones and Pounder (1998). Those interested in the broader issues presented by the distribution and sales of alcohol should consult Babor et al. (2003) and Voas and Fell (2011). Finally, those most interested in the treatment of impaired drivers may wish to consult Cavaiola and Wuth (2002).

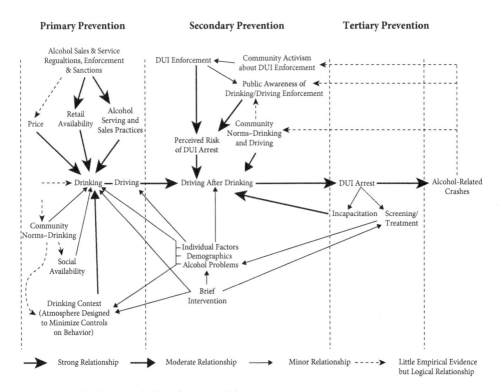

Figure 22.1. Alcohol-related motor vehicle crash causal model.

In this chapter, alcohol safety programs are reviewed under three headings: primary prevention, secondary prevention, and tertiary prevention, as shown in Figure 22.1, taken from Birckmayer and colleagues' (2008, p. 8) crash causation model. Primary prevention covers those programs directed at reducing the high-risk drinking that leads to impaired driving. It includes programs directed at preventing drinking by high-risk groups, such as youths aged 20 and younger, and at preventing service to obviously intoxicated individuals. Secondary prevention covers programs directed at separating drinking from driving through law enforcement, public information programs, and driver licensing regulations. Finally, tertiary prevention focuses on programs directed at preventing identified drinking drivers from future impaired driving through license actions, treatment programs, and monitoring systems. The interactions among the programs are shown by the directional arrows, and the relative importance of the various programs is indicated with lines.

Primary Prevention: Reducing High-Risk Drinking

Preventing Sales to High-Risk Groups

The ultimate method for preventing impaired driving would be to prevent the sale of alcohol. This proved to be impractical, as was demonstrated by the failure of the government to control sales during the Prohibition Era (http://www.niaaa.nih.gov/AboutNIAAA/OrganizationalInformation/History.html). Nevertheless, many states and communities maintain laws prohibiting sales to individuals viewed to be at high risk for alcohol dependence or alcohol use disorders following the repeal of Prohibition. Sales bans were retained for two high-risk groups: for youths, up to age 18 or 21, and for visibly intoxicated patrons of bars or liquor stores.

Minimum Drinking Age Laws

Among the more important holdovers from the Prohibition period were minimum drinking age laws that, in some states, prohibited purchases by or sales to those younger than 18 through 20, and in other states, those younger than 21. The significance of drinking age did not manifest itself until the Vietnam war when the voting age was lowered to 18, and some states with drinking ages set at 21 lowered the drinking age to 18, resulting in an increase in crashes involving 18- to 20-year-olds. This led to a policy reversal, with some states

initially raising the drinking age to 21, ultimately leading to congressional action in 1984 requiring all states to enact minimum legal drinking age (MLDA) laws set at 21 or face a reduction in the federal funds they receive for highway construction (O'Malley & Wagenaar, 1991; Wagenaar, 1982; Wagenaar & Toomey, 2002; Williams & Lillis, 1986). The staff at the General Accounting Office (US General Account Office [GAO], 1987) reviewed 32 published research studies, both before and after the law changed. The GAO concluded that there was solid scientific evidence that increasing the minimum age for purchasing alcohol reduced the number of alcohol-involved traffic crashes for those aged 20 and younger. More recent studies (Klepp, Schmid, & Murray, 1996; O'Malley & Wagenaar, 1991; Yu, Varone, & Shacket, 1997; Voas, Tippetts, & Fell, 1999a), including a comprehensive review of literature from 1960 to 1999 by Wagenaar and Toomey (2002), uniformly showed that increasing the minimum drinking age significantly decreased self-reported drinking by young people, the number of fatal traffic crashes, and the number of arrests for DUI involving youths aged 20 and younger. Shults et al. (2001) conducted a meta-analysis of 33 studies of the MLDA. They reported that the MLDA resulted in changes of 10–16% in fatal crashes: increasing if the minimum age were lowered and decreasing if the MLDA were increased. Kypri et al. (2006) found that when New Zealand lowered its drinking age from 20 to 18, crash injuries among 15- to 19-year-olds increased. Although effective methods for enforcing MLDA laws have been demonstrated using police-supervised underage decoys (Michigan State Police, 1989; Preusser, Williams, & Weinstein, 1994), weak enforcement appears to be the norm; consequently, youth can easily access alcohol (Forster, Murray, Wolfson, & Wagenaar, 1995; Jones-Webb et al., 1997; Radecki & Strohl, 1991; Wagenaar, 1993; Wagenaar & Wolfson, 1994). For example, Forster et al. (1995) found that buyers who were aged 21 but looked underage could buy alcohol about 50% of the time. "Cops in Shops," another method for enforcing underage drinking laws, places undercover officers as cashiers in liquor stores. This procedure has not been adequately evaluated. Wagenaar and Wolfson (1994) found that, without adequate penalties for owners of outlets, attempts to reduce underage retail sales were likely to be ineffective. They reported that only 2 of every 1,000 occurrences of underage drinking resulted in an arrest. Recently,

Wagenaar, Toomey, and Erickson (2005) reported on a community trial featuring the enforcement of the MLDA law through police checks of outlets. They found that the enforcement effort was primarily effective against those locations actually checked by the police and that the effect wore off after 3 months, suggesting that a long-term intermittent effort is required to produce lasting results.

Laws Associated with MLDA

The MLDA laws provide the foundation for 16 supporting measures that would likely be undermined if the basic MLDA legislation were to be repealed by a state (Fell, Fisher, Voas, Blackman, & Tippetts, 2008*a*). Some of those provisions are (a) underage individuals who attempt to use false identification (ID) to obtain alcohol will have their driver's licenses suspended, (b) adult provision of alcohol to underage youths is illegal, (c) the production of false IDs is prohibited, (d) underage youths selling or serving alcohol in commercial establishments is illegal, and (e) underage individuals driving with any alcohol in their bodies is illegal.

A recent study of the effects of MLDA-21 found that the rate of drinking drivers aged 20 and younger in fatal crashes decreased significantly when laws making it illegal to possess or purchase alcohol were raised to age 21 (by 16%), when laws suspending driver's licenses for underage alcohol violations (called "use and lose" laws) were adopted (by 5%), and when laws prohibiting any alcohol for drivers aged 20 and younger (called "zero-tolerance" laws) went into effect (by 5%; Fell, Fisher, Voas, Blackman, & Tippetts, 2009*a*).

Laws Against Serving Obviously Intoxicated Patrons

Currently, 47 states and the District of Columbia prohibit sales to obviously intoxicated persons (Florida, Nevada, and Wyoming are the only exceptions; NIAAA's Alcohol Policy Information System [2005], NHTSA, 1998). Nevertheless, alcohol sales to intoxicated patrons in bars occur frequently. This is a matter of considerable concern because an estimated 50% of impaired drivers had their last drink at a licensed establishment (Anglin, Caverson, Fennel, Giesbrecht, & Mann, 1997; Eby, 1995; Foss, Perrine, Meyers, Musty, & Voas, 1990; O'Donnell, 1985; Palmer, 1986). These laws are often not enforced by the police and are ignored by bar and liquor store owners. For example, Toomey et al. (2004) used trained actors who tried to buy alcohol while appearing intoxicated. The research team found 79% of the 372 establishments studied sold alcohol to these "pretend" drunks. McKnight and Streff (1994) demonstrated that undercover visits by officers to bars looking for instances of illegal service followed by a citation or a warning letter to the owner resulted in a reduction of service to intoxicated patrons and in the percentage of arrested DUI offenders who reported having their last drink in a bar.

Limiting Alcohol Availability

Clearly, making alcohol less available should limit consumption and thus reduce impaired driving. Availability is generally viewed as how accessible or convenient it is for individuals to obtain alcohol. A broader definition would include price, in which the effort to obtain alcohol can be considered as an element of the cost. In general, when alcohol purchases are convenient and easily accessible in a given community, people drink more and the rates of alcohol problems are higher. Aside from outright prohibition of sales, as occurred during the Prohibition Era in the United States and in some states following the repeal of the Volstead Act, state and local governments can influence the availability of alcohol in many ways. These include increasing the price through excise taxes, controlling the number and locations of alcohol outlets, and controlling the type of service (i.e., on-premises [bars and restaurants] or off-premises [liquor stores]). There is substantial evidence that such regulations can reduce alcohol problems, including impaired driving.

PRICE: ALCOHOL EXCISE TAXES

Most research indicates that the price of alcohol is inversely related to alcohol consumption. As with most commodities, as alcohol prices rise, consumption decreases, leading to a reduction in alcohol-related problems. Conversely, when prices drop, use and related problems rise. Several studies have shown that increased alcohol costs are associated with reductions in both violent and nonviolent crime (Cook & Moore, 1993; Grossman & Markowitz, 2001; Markowitz, 2000; Markowitz & Grossman, 1998; 2000; Saffer, 2001). Impaired driving is no exception. Higher excise taxes on alcohol (a surrogate measure for price) reduce alcohol-associated public health problems, including traffic crashes (Chaloupka, Saffer, & Grossman, 1993; Cook, Motha, McKirgan, & O'Holloran,

1992). Cook (1981) studied the effect of 39 changes in state taxes on distilled spirits between 1960 and 1975. In 30 of the 39 instances, sales of distilled spirits and traffic fatalities fell after the tax increase.

Several researchers (Chaloupka et al., 1993; Cook, 1981; Mast, Benson, & Rasmussen, 1999) reported that increased taxes were related to fewer alcohol-related crashes (see recent reviews by Adrian, Ferguson, & Her, 2001; Birckmayer et al., 2004; Chaloupka, Grossman, & Saffer, 2002). It appears that price differentials may affect some drivers more than others. Kenkel (1993) estimated that a 10% increase in the price of alcohol would result in 7% less drinking and driving among men and an 8% reduction among women, and these percentages were even greater for young men and women (13% and 21%, respectively). This is not surprising because the effect of a price differential would be expected to be a function of income, with women and young people generally earning less than their male and older counterparts do.

Although raising excise taxes is a potential countermeasure for impaired driving, tax hikes have not been widely used to influence drinking in the United States. Chaloupka et al. (2002) reported that alcohol prices remained stable during the last quarter of the 20th century; this price stability, combined with inflation, has produced real price reductions over time. Between 1975 and 1990, the real price of distilled spirits dropped by 32%, wine by 28%, and beer by 20% (Chaloupka et al., 2002).

Wagenaar, Salois, and Komro (2009) conducted a meta-analysis on studies of the effects of alcohol price and tax levels on alcohol consumption. They found highly significant relationships ($p < .001$) between alcohol tax or price measures and indices of alcohol consumption ($r = -0.17$ for beer; -0.30 for wine; -0.29 for distilled spirits; and -0.44 for total alcohol). In a later study, Maldonado-Molina and Wagenaar (2010) found that increased alcohol taxes in Florida were associated with significant and sizable reductions in alcohol-attributable mortality. They concluded that 600–800 lives per year could be saved in Florida alone if real tax rates returned to 1983 levels.

HOURS OF SALE

Several studies have shown that changing either the hours or the days of alcohol sales can redistribute the times at which alcohol-related crashes and alcohol-related violence occur (e.g.,

see Hauge & Nordlie, 1984; Ligon & Thyer, 1993; Nordlund, 1984; 1985; Österberg & Säilä, 1991; Smith, 1988a; Vingilis et al., 2006; Voas et al., 2002b; 2006a). Smith (1988a), for example, found that the introduction of Sunday alcohol sales in the city of Brisbane, Australia, was related to casualties and property damage caused by traffic crashes. Chikritzhs and Stockwell (2006) examined the effect of longer hours of sales for licensed hotels (i.e., bars) in Perth, Western Australia, on impaired driver road crashes and driver BACs. They documented a significant increase in monthly crash rates for patrons of the hotels.

Voas et al. (2002b; 2006a) studied a naturally occurring experiment that occurred on January 1, 1999, in Juárez, Mexico, across the border from El Paso, Texas, when the Mexican government implemented a requirement that bars, previously open all night, close at 2 a.m. For their study, they conducted quarterly breath-test surveys of drinkers returning to El Paso from a night of drinking in Juárez and found that the number returning after 3 a.m. dropped almost to zero. Furthermore, for 2 years following the 2 a.m. closing policy, the number of drinkers crossing into Mexico was reduced by 50% overall. Vingilis et al. (2006) found that when the bars in Ontario, Canada, were allowed to remain open for an extra hour, there was an increase in alcohol-related fatal crashes in US communities bordering Windsor, which attracts a large number of young Americans who patronize its bars on weekends.

LIMITS ON ALCOHOL OUTLETS

Retail availability of alcohol is shaped by state and local regulations that determine the number, location, types, and serving and selling practices of alcohol retailers. There is great variation in how states and localities regulate retail availability. Some are very restrictive, whereas others have only limited controls. Whether in a formal or an informal market, alcoholic beverages are sold to the retail customer in two forms. One form is off-premise sales (liquor stores and grocery stores), where alcohol is purchased for consumption elsewhere. The opportunities to affect these off-premise retail outlets are generally limited to regulations on the time, cost, and place of the alcohol sales. The other form of alcoholic beverage sales is by the individual drink in on-premise outlets, such as bars or restaurants. Because the drinking location is known, there is a greater opportunity to influence directly what happens at the time of purchase and during the consumption of the beverage. Regulations may specify drink sizes; disallow discounted drinks, such as during "happy hours"; and require responsible beverage service (RBS) training (described hereafter) and provide programs such as Safe Rides for drinking drivers. Furthermore, regulations may specify the amount of income from food service (to encourage restaurants rather than bars), availability of entertainment, and other non–alcohol-specific matters.

DENSITIES OF RETAIL OUTLETS

Several longitudinal studies have demonstrated that a change in the number of outlets is related to a change in alcohol use. When overall availability is low, the addition of a few outlets can have noticeable effects on drinking. Gruenewald, Ponicki, and Holder (1993) conducted a time-series cross-sectional analysis of alcohol consumption and density of alcohol outlets across 50 US states. The results suggested that a 10% reduction in the density of alcohol outlets would reduce consumption of spirits by 1–3% and consumption of wine by 4%. Limiting the number of outlets for alcoholic beverages increases the effort required to find and travel to a liquor store, known in economic terms as "opportunity cost" for obtaining alcohol. Thus, limiting the number of outlets may raise the "full price" effect of obtaining alcohol (Grossman, Coate, & Arluck, 1987; Gruenewald, 1993). The number of outlets may be restricted through state policies that make licenses more difficult to obtain, such as increasing the cost of a license. Furthermore, the density of outlets may also be limited by requiring a minimum distance between them.

Campbell et al. (2009), in a Guide to Community Preventive Services by the Centers for Disease Control and Prevention, found that greater outlet density was associated with increased alcohol consumption and related harms, including medical conditions, injury, crime, and violence.

OUTLET LOCATIONS

The location of alcohol sales outlets may be limited by local, state, or national provisions. For instance, an outlet typically cannot be located in violation of local zoning laws that limit the outlet locations to particular kinds of commercial sites. A common provision used by many US states forbids location of an alcohol sales outlet near a school or place of worship. Alcohol sales may also be forbidden at locations such as highway rest stops.

These laws and regulations serve to restrict the availability of alcohol within specific neighborhoods. There is little evidence on the extent to which these provisions influence alcohol consumption or alcohol-related problems, although one study suggested that locating an outlet near a highway system may affect alcohol-related crashes more than locating the same outlet in a dense downtown area (Gruenewald & Treno, 2000).

STATE RETAIL MONOPOLIES

One method for restricting and regulating alcohol availability is for the state government to monopolize the ownership of one or more types of alcohol outlets (e.g., outlets that sell hard liquor). A government monopoly typically greatly reduces the number of outlets, limits the hours of sale, and removes the private profit motive for increasing sales. Miller, Snowden, Birckmayer, and Hendrie (2006) determined that state retail alcohol monopolies are associated with reduced underage drinking and a 9.3% reduction in the impaired driving death rate of drivers younger than 21. In contrast, evidence suggests that elimination of government monopolies and privatization of alcohol sales increased the number of alcohol outlets and alcohol sales (Holder & Wagenaar, 1990; Wagenaar & Holder, 1995; 1996). Thus, government monopolies of liquor outlets reduce alcohol consumption because the network of stores in a government-operated system is sparse and the hours of operation are limited.

Norström et al. (2010) found that replacing Sweden's current alcohol retail monopoly with private licensed stores yielded an increase in alcohol consumption, causing an additional 770 deaths, 8,500 assaults, 2,700 drinking-driving offenses, and 4.5 million sick days for Swedish citizens each year. A Community Guide by the CDC (Centers for Disease Control and Prevention, 2011) recommended against further privatization of alcohol sales in states with current control of retail sales based on strong evidence that privatization results in increased per capita alcohol consumption, a well-established proxy for excessive drinking.

LIQUOR BY THE DRINK

Following the repeal of Prohibition to limit alcohol problems, one method used by 20 or more states was to prohibit on-premise establishments, such as hotels and restaurants, from selling liquor by the individual drink. This allowed off-premise outlets to sell liquor in bottles but prevented the operation of bars that sell by the drink. Over the years, several states have repealed their "liquor-by-the-drink" laws. Holder and Blose (1987) conducted a study in North Carolina where, in 1979, individual counties were allowed to sell by the individual drink. They found that in counties that chose to sell liquor by the drink, spirits sales rose between 6% and 7.4% and police-reported alcohol-related crashes increased by 16% to 24%. No change in alcohol-related crashes was found for counties continuing to ban liquor-by-the-drink sales. Thus, there is evidence that limiting sales to off-premise outlets reduces alcohol-related problems by reducing alcohol availability.

RESPONSIBLE BEVERAGE SERVICE PROGRAMS

An important opportunity to reduce impaired driving by patrons of drinking establishments lies in the prevention of sales or service of alcohol to underage or intoxicated individuals through the enforcement of state Alcohol Beverage Control (ABC) laws. Recent studies have indicated that illegal sales to underage individuals are down from the 44–97% range to the 26–39% range; however, sales to the obviously intoxicated appear to be in the 58–79% range (Toomey, Erickson, Lenk, & Kilian, 2008). This has placed a focus on the RBS policies of outlet owners and on the training of servers. Interventions by servers and managers are more likely to reduce alcohol-involved crashes than driver-oriented prevention efforts (e.g., "don't drink and drive") because such programs do not rely on the judgment of those who have been drinking and may be impaired by alcohol. Several states and many municipalities have enacted laws that either mandate server education directly or create strong incentives (e.g., providing some shelter from dram shop litigation) for outlet managers to send their serving staffs to training programs.

Intervention training programs for servers can include teaching servers about ABC laws, identifying intoxicated patrons, offering patrons food with drinks, delaying service to rapid drinkers, refusing service to intoxicated or underage patrons, and discouraging intoxicated patrons from driving (see Rydon & Stockwell, 1997, for a summary of the RBS strategies for licensed establishments). RBS can be implemented at both on- (Saltz & Stanghetta, 1997) and off-premise establishments (Grube, 1997).

Evaluations of server training programs have shown some significant shifts toward more responsible service by both servers and managers of licensed establishments (Gliksman & Single, 1988; Howard-Pitney, Johnson, Altman, Hopkins,

& Hammond, 1991; McKnight, 1988; Mosher, Delewski, Saltz, & Hennessey, 1989; Molof & Kimball, 1994; Russ & Geller, 1986; Saltz, 1987; Saltz & Hennessy, 1990a; Saltz & Stanghetta, 1997; Shults et al., 2001; Stockwell, Lang, & Rydon, 1993). Favorable outcomes, however, have been largely limited to efforts aimed at preventing patrons from becoming intoxicated rather than those directed at refusing service to those who are already impaired by alcohol. McKnight (1991) examined the effects of server education programs on service to pseudopatrons who simulated signs of visible intoxication. Observations of 1,500 cases of service were extremely discouraging. Service was refused only 5% of the time before training and 7% after training. Stockwell et al. (1993) found refusal rates of only 10% both before and after training.

Although several studies have demonstrated that RBS programs that incorporate server training reduce the number of intoxicated patrons leaving a bar (e.g., see Dresser & Gliksman, 1998; Gliksman et al., 1993; Lapham, Skipper, Chang, Barton, & Kennedy, 1998; Saltz, 1987; Saltz & Hennessy, 1990b), the impact of server training alone is limited. It is most effective when coupled with a change in the actual serving policy and practices of a bar or restaurant. Saltz and Hennessy (1990a) concluded that server training alone was unlikely to affect patron intoxication significantly, so management must be prepared to alter policies that lead to overdrinking. Experience has shown that, to refuse service, servers must have the strong support of management, as demonstrated by actions such as the manager taking over when a patron becomes angry and reimbursing waitstaffs' tips when unhappy patrons fail to provide a gratuity. Producing such management support is generally accomplished by creating the perception that ABC laws are being strongly enforced and that illegal service will be detected, potentially resulting in the suspension of the establishment's liquor license. Without this enforcement pressure on management, training of servers will have little effect (Wagenaar et al., 2005).

In a recent systematic review of interventions designed to reduce alcohol use and related harms in drinking environments, Jones, Hughes, Atkinson, and Bellis (2011) included seven studies that evaluated server training interventions to increase RBS practices. Three of the seven studies specifically examined the impact of server training on RBS intervention practices by servers. One found no impact, and the other two found some increases in server intervention. Both studies, however, indicated a low frequency of intervention among the trained servers. Effects of server intervention programs on patrons' alcohol consumption were also mixed. One study of statewide mandated server training already discussed (Holder & Wagenaar, 1994) showed that such training had a statistically significant effect on single-vehicle nighttime crashes. Another study (Graham et al., 2004) found that an intervention designed to reduce aggression among bar patrons (better lighting, visible presence of bouncers) had a modest impact on severe and moderate patron aggression (reduction in verbal arguments and physical fights).

Research on RBS programs has shown that RBS practices can be a valuable tool in lowering the rates of high-risk alcohol consumption and impaired driving. For example, Johnsson and Berglund (2003) suggested that server training programs can help reduce the level of intoxication of bar patrons. In this study, the average BACs of patrons of intervention bars (the bars given a server training program) were reduced more than in the patrons at the control bars at a 1-month follow-up survey. Toomey et al. (2001) found a similar result in their study. In this project, the owners and managers of five bars in Minnesota received information on risk level, policies to prevent illegal sales, legal issues, and communication. The result of underage and pseudointoxicated purchase attempts conducted before and after the intervention showed that underage sales decreased by 11.5%, and pseudointoxicated sales fell by 46% compared to the control bars. Due to the small sample size, these results were not statistically significant, but they were in the desired direction.

LAWS THAT SUPPORT RESPONSIBLE BEVERAGE SERVICE

The laws that motivate owners and managers to adopt and support server training, in addition to the already-mentioned state ABC and server training laws, include dram shop laws and tort liability. Dram shop laws allow individuals injured by an adult or a minor who is under the influence of alcohol to recover damages from the alcohol retailer who served or sold alcohol to the person causing the injury (Holder et al., 1993; Mosher, 1979; Mosher, Toomey, Good, Harwood, & Wagenaar, 2002; Sloan, Stout, Whetten-Goldstein, & Liang, 2000). In some jurisdictions, the retailer can also be liable for the damages the minor or drinker causes to him- or herself. Owners and licensees can be held liable

for their employees' actions under most or all dram shop liability laws (Mosher et al., 2002). Research suggests that implementation of dram shop liability may lead to significant increases in checking age identification and to greater care in serving practices (e.g., Sloan et al., 2000). The available studies also indicate that dram shop liability laws can significantly reduce alcohol-related traffic crash deaths and total traffic crash deaths among minors (Chaloupka et al., 1993; Sloan, Reilly, & Schenzler, 1994; Sloan et al., 2000). Furthermore, these laws reduce alcohol-related traffic crashes, total traffic crashes, homicides, and other unintentional injuries in the general population (Chaloupka et al., 1993; Sloan et al., 1994; 2000). Overall, dram shop liability has been estimated to reduce alcohol-related traffic fatalities among underage drivers by 3–4% (Chaloupka et al., 1993).

Tort liability provides for court action against owners of outlets or social hosts who are found responsible for illegally providing alcohol to minors or obviously intoxicated individuals who then go on to harm third parties (see discussion by Sloan et al., 2000). The rationale for third-party liability is that drunks or minors who were served alcohol may lack the ability to make appropriate compliance decisions (Kraakman, 1998). Evidence of the relationship between alcohol regulations and alcohol-related motor vehicle crashes was provided by Sloan et al. (2000). They analyzed traffic fatalities across all states and examined the potential effect of several fatality factors over time and across states and found that imposing tort liability on commercial services resulted in reduced fatality rates for drivers aged 15–20.

Limiting Alcohol Advertising

Although Atkin (1990) noted that alcohol commercials have a slight effect on alcohol misuse and on drinking and driving, empirical evidence for the direct effect of alcohol advertising on aggregate drinking levels is limited. Research does suggest that young persons are influenced by media portrayals of alcoholic beverages (see Casswell, 1995; Grube, 1995). Kuo, Weschler, Greenberg, and Lee (2003) analyzed the 2001 College Alcohol Study, in which more than 10,000 college students were surveyed, as well as 830 on-premise and 1,684 off-premise venues at 118 colleges. Results showed that low price, heavy advertising, and other promotional activities were associated with increased heavy drinking among college students. The alcohol industry, showing some concern about the effect of alcohol advertising on youth, has adopted a voluntary code of not advertising in venues that attract a youthful audience of 30% or more and of sponsoring "responsibility" ads. Young people aged 12–20, however, were 12 times more likely to see an alcohol advertisement than a responsibility message (Center on Alcohol Marketing and Youth, 2008).

Aside from its effects on youth, the rationale for a restriction on advertising is based on its indirect effects on the social climate surrounding alcohol (Casswell, 1995; Hill & Casswell, 2001; Partanen & Montonen, 1988). Alcohol advertising communicates the message that society approves of drinking (Postman, Nystrom, Strate, & Weingartner, 1988) and may reduce the likelihood of implementing public policies directed at reducing high-risk drinking (Casswell, 1995; Farrell, 1985; Van Iwaarden, 1985). Studies of natural experiments on partial advertising bans have shown conflicting results regarding their effectiveness in reducing consumption levels (Montonen, 1996). Studies by several researchers failed to show clear effects (Ogborne & Smart, 1980; Simpson, Beirness, Mayhew, & Donelson, 1985; Smart & Cutler, 1976). In contrast, a major cross-national time-series study of advertising bans implemented in European countries during the 1970s showed significant effects, including lower levels of consumption and alcohol-related problems, as indicated by motor vehicle fatality rates (Edwards et al., 1994; Saffer, 1991; 1993).

COUNTERADVERTISING

Given the lack of government authority in the United States to restrict advertising, counteradvertising provides a method for reducing harmful use of a legal product. Counteradvertising can take the form of health warning labels on product packaging, media literacy efforts to raise public awareness of industry tactics, and a module in community or school prevention programs (e.g., Giesbrecht & Douglas, 1990; Greenfield & Zimmerman, 1993). Some states also require posted warnings of alcohol risks in establishments that serve or sell alcohol. Research on such media campaigns thus far has been limited primarily to evaluations of the federally mandated warnings on alcoholic beverage containers. Federal warning label legislation, implemented in November 1989, included (a) birth defect risks during pregnancy, (b) impairment when driving, (c) impairment when operating machinery, and (d) health problems. Evaluations have shown that a significant proportion of the population reports having seen the warning labels (Graves, 1993; Kaskutas & Greenfield, 1992). Studies of warning labels have shown that those exposed to them report more

precautionary behaviors, including increased caution regarding drinking and driving and drinking during pregnancy (Greenfield, 1997; Greenfield, Graves, & Kaskutas, 1999; Greenfield & Kaskutas, 1998; Kaskutas & Greenfield, 1992). However, no direct effects of warning labels on alcohol-related problems have been reported (MacKinnon, Pentz, & Stacy, 1993).

Community Norms and Citizen Activism

Community norms about heavy drinking or drunkenness can be powerful determinants of social policies, including laws and other strategies designed to reduce alcohol problems. These values and norms are part of the broader culture, but they can vary within a given community, social group, or subculture. At the community level, values and norms may be reflected in a well-publicized enforcement campaign to reduce sales of alcohol to minors. Such campaigns not only reduce underage access to alcohol, but also affirm the value the community places on protecting its young people. Community norms may also be expressed through bans on alcohol use in parks and other public places or by establishing regulations to restrict "happy hours" and other price promotions of alcohol. Typically, communities that become concerned with drinking and drinking-driving problems develop consortiums of local organizational leaders (Holder, 1996) that organize and support programs to reduce risky consumption. Such organizations can develop a comprehensive program to reduce dangerous alcohol consumption by using existing laws (which are often poorly enforced) and passing local ordinances. In the early 1980s, the public's attitude toward drinking and driving was substantially transformed by the victim activist movement marked by the founding and growth of Mothers Against Drunk Driving (MADD). Media coverage of drinking and driving increased (Clark & Hilton, 1991; Moulden & Russell, 1994). Most observers (McCarthy, Wolfson, & Harvey, 1987) credit victim activist groups, particularly MADD, for this sudden increase in press coverage. The sanctions for impaired driving also increased. Hence, Merki and Lingg (1987) concluded that MADD has been a major force behind the adoption by the states and communities of eight effective impaired driving strategies. Only one study (McCarthy & Ziliak, 1990) has attempted to measure directly the contribution of an activist organization to crash reduction. In their study of California communities, these researchers found that the presence of a

MADD chapter significantly reduced the number of DUI injury crashes. For a review of the history of MADD and its influence on impaired driving, see Fell and Voas (2006a).

College Programs

Universities have a major problem with heavy drinking by students (Hingson, Heeren, Winter, & Wechsler, 2005b; Wechsler, Davenport, Dowdall, Moeykens, & Castillo, 1994; Wechsler, Lee, Kuo, & Lee, 2000). States, communities, and university administrators can create special regulations to control drinking by students. These local regulations can limit the locations of bars relative to the university or control the noise and nuisances surrounding off-campus student housing. Universities may have policies prohibiting alcohol on campus or at school activities or restrict alcohol advertising on campus (Wechsler et al., 2000). Grimes and Swisher (1989) found that students report such policies are barriers to drinking, but there are few controlled evaluations of such policies (Cohen & Rogers, 1997; Odo, McQuiller, & Stretsky, 1999; Voas et al., 2008a) from which to draw a conclusion regarding their effectiveness.

An online survey of college administrators at 351 randomly sampled 4-year colleges was conducted in 2008. The prevalence of 31 alcohol policies at these colleges was assessed. Most colleges reported implementing some of these policies, but only two of every five colleges reported adopting many alcohol policies (Lenk, Erickson, Nelson, Winters, & Toomey, 2012). A Study to Prevent Alcohol-Related Consequences (SPARC) recently assessed the efficacy of a comprehensive intervention that used a community-organizing approach to implement environmental strategies in and around college campuses. The objective of the program was to reduce high-risk drinking and alcohol-related consequences among college students. The researchers found significant decreases in the five intervention colleges relative to the five comparison colleges in severe consequences due to students' own drinking and alcohol-related injuries caused to others. The authors concluded that a community-organizing approach that promotes the implementation of environmental interventions can significantly affect high-risk drinking and its consequences among college students (Wolfson et al., 2012).

Social Availability

Social availability involves access to alcohol through noncommercial sources (e.g., receiving, stealing, or buying alcohol from friends, relatives, or strangers). Social sources for youths aged 20 and younger who cannot purchase alcohol legally have received considerable research attention. One of the most common means by which adolescents obtain alcohol is by asking an adult aged 21 or older to purchase alcohol for them (Jones-Webb et al., 1997; Smart, Adlaf, & Walsh, 1996; Wagenaar et al., 1993). Youths also cite their parents as a common source of alcohol, either using the alcohol that is present in the home or obtaining and drinking alcohol with the permission of their parents (Smart et al., 1996; Wagenaar et al., 1993). Younger youths rely on social sources much more than older youths (Harrison, Fulkerson, & Park, 2000; Schwartz, Farrow, Banks, & Giesel, 1998; Wagenaar et al., 1996). Youths appear to have ready access to alcohol. Most 12th graders report that it is "fairly" easy or "very" easy to obtain alcohol (Johnson, O'Malley, & Bachman, 2003; Swahn, Hamming, & Ikeda, 2002). Underage youths typically procure alcohol from social sources through adults or at parties where parents and other adults are not present (Jones-Webb et al., 1997; Wagenaar et al., 1993). Wagenaar et al. (1996) found that 46% of 9th graders, 60% of 12th graders, and 68% of youth aged 18–20 obtained alcoholic beverages from an adult on their last drinking occasion. Students in the 9th grade rely on home sources of alcohol much more than older students. The reliance on home supply declines significantly by the end of high school, but social sources continue to remain an important means of access across all ages. This suggests the importance of involving parents in school and community programs to reduce underage drinking.

Drinking at local bars and restaurants, particularly by those younger than 21, is constrained by MLDA laws and by state alcohol control laws and local ordinances, as well as by the owner's need to maintain a premise that attracts clients. Conversely, drinking that occurs in locations away from public view (e.g., in homes or parks) can be relatively unconstrained, often produces a large number of impaired drinkers, and is more difficult to control. Local authorities, however, exercise some control through keg registration laws and social host laws, backed up by party patrol programs. Keg registration laws require the purchaser of a keg of beer to complete a form that links his or her name to a number on the keg; consequently, an individual who supplies alcohol to a party can be identified. In a study of 97 US communities, Cohen, Mason, and Scribner (2001) found that requiring keg registration was significantly and negatively correlated ($r = -.29$) with traffic fatality rates. Parties are frequently cited as one of the settings at highest risk for youth alcohol consumption and related problems and have been linked to impaired driving, sexual assaults, violence, property damage, and the initiation of alcohol use by younger adolescents at the instigation of older adolescents (Mayer, Forster, Murray, & Wagenaar, 1998; Schwartz & Little, 1997; Wagenaar et al., 1993). One method for controlling high-risk drinking locations are party patrols, which involve police searching out and entering parties that are in progress. The police can use noise or nuisance ordinances as a basis for entering a party. When underage drinking is discovered, the drinkers and the persons supplying the alcohol can be cited.

Brief Interventions to Reduce Risky Consumption

Brief interventions that can be administered in a short time in conjunction with educational, administrative, or general health programs lend themselves to delivering messages directed at influencing the drinking of individuals who may be at risk from their drinking but are unaware of their problem or at least not actively seeking a solution. This individually oriented technique generally involves providing personal feedback to individuals on the relation of their drinking to the drinking of their peers or general normative behavior, together with the potential health consequences of continuing to overconsume (Barnett, Monti, & Wood, 2001; Ritson, 2005). Such brief interventions should be distinguished from school-based efforts to influence drinking and drug use that, although successful in providing information, have limited effectiveness in changing drinking or drinking-problem behavior (Larimer & Cronce, 2002; see Shope, Elliott, Raghunathan, & Waller, 2001, for a recent review of high school drinking and drinking and driving educational programs). Brief interventions are generally directed at high-risk drinkers who have yet to suffer harm from their drinking and are not actively seeking help. To date, brief interventions directed at such risky drinkers (heavy drinkers and binge drinkers) have primarily been offered through college student health programs and in primary care facilities.

Although programs administered to groups have generally not been successful, one group intervention with college students that has shown some promise is "social marketing" (Haines, 1996; Haines & Spear, 1996). This type of intervention is directed at changing students' perceptions of the typical drinking behavior of their peers because evidence indicates that students misperceive the amount of drinking by others. Social marketing theory proposes that if students' overestimates of the amount of drinking of other students can be corrected, they will reduce their own drinking (Perkins, 2002). Although many "social marketing" studies report positive results, most have been dependent on self-reports of drinking as an outcome measure and have not involved control groups (Clapp, Lange, Russell, Shillington, & Voas, 2003). However, Foss, Diekman, Bartley, and Goodman (2004) reported a reduction in measured BACs of students.

One-on-one counseling sessions (e.g., programs described by Marlatt et al., 1998, and Roberts, Neal, Kivlahan, Baer, & Marlatt, 2000) have proven effective in significantly decreasing the alcohol-related problems of college freshmen identified as at high risk for negative consequences from heavy drinking. Such programs have involved assisting the participants in understanding their current drinking levels in relation to their peers and in recognizing the negative consequences of heavy drinking, as well as in developing personal programs to reduce consumption (Lange et al., 2002). One method of delivering such programs to individuals without individualized instruction is through computerized systems. Several researchers have implemented brief motivational enhancement interventions in waiting rooms at student health care centers (Dimeff, 1997; Dimeff, Baer, Kivhahan, & Marlatt, 1999; Kypri et al., 2004; Monti et al., 1999). Students awaiting service at the health center can use these programs to self-diagnose their drinking problems, and the program then provides suggestions to gain control over their drinking.

Perhaps the most important underused opportunity to treat people with alcohol abuse problems typically rests with their primary care physician or related nursing staff (Gentilello, 2005; Solberg, Maciosek, & Edwards, 2008). Historically, physicians have not routinely provided screening and brief interventions due to limited time, resources, and information on effectiveness. In addition, restrictions set on reimbursement by health insurance providers and the limited training of physicians in alcohol counseling methods tend to minimize brief interventions on drinking practices by physicians. This may change because Medicare, the federal health insurance program for seniors, changed its rules as of 2007 regarding payment for such counseling. Primary care facilities offer a particularly good opportunity because less expensive, skilled medical support personnel may be more available for conducting interventions. Nurses are ideal service providers because they are highly skilled, have a higher level of contact with potential brief intervention recipients (Dyehouse & Sommers, 1995), and are less costly than physicians.

Brief interventions have decreased problem drinking across many settings and populations (Sommers, Dyehouse, & Howe, 2001). These include medical settings for nonacute care, such as primary care offices (Bien, Miller, & Tonigan, 1993; Fleming, Barry, Manwell, Johnson, & London, 1997). Controlled studies in primary care settings have shown that brief interventions can effectively decrease alcohol use (Bien et al., 1993), alcohol-related problems (Israel et al., 1996), health care utilization, and overall consumption (Fleming et al., 1997; Israel et al., 1996). Solberg et al. (2008) conducted a meta-analysis of 10 evaluation reports of brief intervention programs by primary physicians and found that they were effective in reducing heavy drinking by an average of 17.3% and hazardous drinking by a comparable 17.6%.

Summary of Opportunities to Reduce Risky Drinking

This primary prevention section has focused on policies and programs that can reduce risky drinking and lead to a reduction of impaired driving and other drinking problems. The evidence suggests the following strategies can reduce risky drinking.

- Restrictions on who may purchase alcohol (the MLDA law)
- Retail compliance checks by the police designed to enforce the MLDA and ABC laws against service to the obviously intoxicated
- State control of alcohol sales—unfortunately, a disappearing policy
- Alcohol outlet density restrictions
- Restrictions on location of outlets in sensitive areas such as schools
- Restrictions on hours and days of sale
- Increased alcohol taxes
- Retail price controls
- Media and awareness programs
- Brief interventions, with college students and in physicians' offices

Unfortunately, the research evidence supporting the effectiveness of these policies is limited to a handful of studies, not all of which agree. Furthermore, although the public supports the MLDA law, they show less support for laws or policies limiting adult drinking. Instead, they support the alcohol industry's strong resistance to any measure that limits alcohol availability to adults. Still, controls over drinking do provide an important opportunity to reduce high-risk drinking and the resulting impaired driving.

Secondary Prevention

Despite the primary prevention programs directed at reducing high-risk drinking that leads to a BAC of .08 or higher—which is illegal for driving—a substantial number of drinkers with high BACs are operating vehicles on US roadways, although this number has been decreasing over the past four decades. National Roadside Surveys were conducted in the United States in 1973, 1986, 1996, and 2007. Over that period, the percentage of weekend nighttime drivers with positive BACs fell from 36% in 1973 to 12% in 2007. However, in 2007, 2.2% of the drivers on the road had BACs at or above the illegal level of .08% (Lacey, Kelley-Baker, Brainard, Tippetts, & Lyakhovich, 2008; Lacey et al., 2009a; 2009b).

In this section on secondary prevention, we provide an overview of the programs and policies that separate high-risk drinking from driving. We begin with the programs that ensure an individual has the basic skills to operate a motor vehicle—driver education and licensing—with a focus on the impaired driving elements of such programs. Of particular interest is the current movement to adopt graduated driver licensing (GDL) laws that partially protect novice drivers from exposure to impaired driving while they gain their initial driving skills. Included in this discussion of young and novice drivers is a review of the zero-tolerance law applicable to drivers younger than 21. We examine the relationship of impaired driving to a major traffic safety effort devoted to persuading drivers to use safety belts. Next, we review the evidence for the effectiveness of current impaired driving laws in reducing alcohol-related crashes, specifically focusing on enforcement technology. Finally, methods for publicizing laws and enforcement programs are described, as are community safety programs designed to support enforcement programs.

Traffic Safety Education

DRIVER EDUCATION

The high crash rate of young novice drivers, including their involvement in alcohol-related crashes, has been recognized for the past 50 years. Initially, school-based driver education programs, a prerequisite for high school sophomores, were adopted to develop driving skills and promote safety behavior that would help avoid impaired driving. As enthusiasm for such courses grew, however, states passed legislation to require these programs as a prerequisite for licensing. This had the unintended effect of encouraging early licensing because obtaining a driver's license became the objective of taking the course. Consequently, many high school youths who would normally have waited until they were in college or in the workforce began driving at age 15 or 16. Whatever the benefits of the driver education program, it could not compensate for the increased exposure produced by the larger number of youthful drivers on the road. Thus, experience demonstrated that universal driver education in the public schools, although providing some driving skills, was not effective in reducing crashes (Mayhew, Simpson, Williams, & Ferguson, 1998; Williams, 1996; Williams & Ferguson, 2004).

GRADUATED DRIVER LICENSING

Over the past decade, the alternative to relying on driver education programs has been an extended period of supervised driving required as part of the licensing process. This approach provides an opportunity for skill development while limiting the novice driver's exposure to higher risk conditions, such as nighttime driving. Research has shown that the first few months of licensure for young novice drivers entail the highest crash risk (Mayhew, Simpson, & Pak, 2003; McCartt, Shabanova, & Leaf, 2003; Sagberg, 1998). To address this issue, many states have recently adopted GDL laws that require a staged progression to full license privileges (National Center for Statistics and Analysis [NCSA], 2003). GDL is the opposite of historic licensing systems that, in most states, generally offer a quick and easy path to full driving privileges at a young age, resulting in extremely high crash rates for beginning drivers. Evaluations of state programs in Florida (Ulmer, Preusser, Williams, Ferguson, & Farmer, 2000), North Carolina (Foss, Feaganes, & Roggman, 2001; Foss & Goodwin, 2003), and Michigan (Shope & Molnar, 2004; Shope, Molnar, Elliott, & Waller, 2001), where reductions in crashes involving 16- and 17-year-olds have ranged up to 26%, clearly show the benefits of adopting the GDL law. Chen, Baker, and Li (2006) found that GDL programs appeared to be associated with an 11% reduction in fatal crashes involving 16-year-olds in the states that had implemented them.

GDL laws now exist in all 50 states and the District of Columbia. These laws generally require three-staged licensing for novice drivers: (a) a learner's permit period—practice driving with a licensed driver aged 21 or older, (b) an intermediate or provisional stage—drive solo only under certain conditions (e.g., restricts late-night driving and limits teen passengers), and (3) a full license with no restrictions (minimum age of 18 in some states). The young driver must meet certain requirements to "graduate" to each stage. Several national studies of GDL systems have indicated they help reduce the crash rates of young novice drivers aged 15 to 17 (Dee, Grabowski, & Morrisey, 2005; McCartt, Teoh, Fields, Braitman, & Hellinga, 2009; Vanlaar et al., 2009).

RESTRICTIONS ON TEEN DRIVING

The potential effectiveness of extending the restrictions on teen driving by raising the legal driving age or passing nighttime curfew laws has been explored. Williams (1985) and Williams, Karpf, and Zador (1983) compared US states with differing ages of licensing and concluded that 65–85% reductions in fatal crash involvements by 16-year-old drivers could be achieved by raising the legal age of driving to 17. The long delay, however, proved to be unpopular, and most GDL laws allow learner's permits at age 15 or 16. Williams and his colleagues (1985) and Preusser, Williams, Zador, and Blomberg (1984) explored the influence of nighttime curfew policies by comparing crash rates for young teenagers (aged 15, 16, or 17, depending on the state) in states with and without curfew laws. These researchers estimated reductions in the crash involvement of 16-year-old drivers during curfew hours ranging from 25% to 69% and concluded that the laws were beneficial relative to their costs. However, later work by Williams, Ferguson, and Wells (2005) challenged this evidence. They examined fatal crashes involving 16-year-olds in the United States from 1993 to 2003, a period when many states enacted GDL laws that delayed nighttime driving, and found that the proportion of crashes occurring between midnight and 5 a.m. had remained at 11%. A possible explanation is the tendency for GDL laws to limit the prohibition against driving to very late nighttime hours only.

Fell, Jones, Romano, and Voas (2011) found that the adoption of a GDL law of average strength was associated with a significant decrease in fatal crash involvements of 16- and 17-year-old drivers relative to fatal crash involvements of older drivers. GDL laws rated as "good" by the Insurance Institute for Highway Safety showed stronger relationships to fatal crash reductions, and laws rated as "less than good" showed no reductions in crash involvements relative to the older driver comparison groups. The authors concluded that states adopting a basic GDL law can expect a decrease of 8 to 14% in the proportion of 16- and 17-year-old drivers involved in fatal crashes (relative to 21- to 25-year-old drivers), depending on their other existing laws that affect novice drivers.

However, Romano, Fell, and Voas (2011) found differential effects of GDL laws depending on the young driver's race and ethnicity. The analysis of states with GDL laws enacted between 2000 and 2007 showed no change for young (aged 16–17) Hispanic drivers in fatal crashes before and after a GDL law was adopted. Overall, GDL reductions were largest and significant for young white drivers, followed by African Americans, and then Asians, with no significant reductions for young Hispanics. GDL laws also had no apparent effect on speeding-related fatal crashes for any of these novice drivers.

The nighttime and passenger restrictions of the GDL laws were recently evaluated for their effectiveness (Fell, Todd, & Voas, 2011). Nighttime restrictions were found to reduce 16- and 17-year-old driver involvements in nighttime fatal crashes by an estimated 10% and 16- and 17-year-old drinking drivers in nighttime fatal crashes by 13%. Passenger restrictions were found to reduce 16- and 17-year-old driver involvements in fatal crashes with teen passengers by an estimated 9%. These results confirm the effectiveness of these provisions in GDL systems.

In a recent study of GDL laws by Masten, Foss, and Marshall (2011), they found substantial reductions in fatal crashes for 16-year-old drivers associated with the adoption of strong GDL laws (down 26%), but for 18-year-olds, they found increases in fatal crashes in those same states (up 12%). The authors suggested that strong GDL laws might have delayed licensure of many youth until they were aged 18 to avoid all the GDL provisions and requirements. An analysis by Fell, Romano,

and Voas (2013) indicated similar results. Using the findings for each age that was significant ($p <$ .05), associated with GDL laws in general, 1,945 lives were saved by the reductions in fatal crashes involving drivers aged 16. For the "good" GDL laws, there was a net increase in fatalities of 377 due to the increase in fatal crashes by drivers aged 18, with an additional increase of 855 fatalities if the 19-year-old increase is included. "Good" GDL laws resulted in 2,347 lives saved due to the reduction of drivers aged 16 in fatal crashes but were associated with an increase of 2,724 fatalities from fatal crash involvements of drivers aged 18.

The outcome of this study indicates once more that GDL laws save the lives of the population they target: novice drivers aged 15–17. This favorable impact is even larger for the better GDL programs (i.e., the enacted GDL is "good"). These results also indicate that the lives of some drivers aged 15–17 saved by GDL laws are offset among the associated increases in fatal crashes by drivers aged 18–19. The reasons for the conflict in GDL benefits are unclear. They could be caused by (a) drivers aged 18–19 skipping the GDL phases and beginning to drive at a later age, thus reducing their driving experience; (b) drivers aged 18–19 exhibiting more risk-taking behaviors (e.g., impaired driving, lack of safety belt use, distracted driving) than younger drivers; (c) drivers aged 18–19 having increased exposure to risk for a fatal crash (e.g., more late-night driving; more driving on high-speed roads); and/or (d) drivers aged 18–19 who have gone through the two phases of GDL lacking driving experience under risky conditions because of all the restrictions in the GDL laws. Whatever the reasons, this finding suggests that GDL laws should be applied to protect novice drivers older than ages 16–17, perhaps up to age 21. Further research to clarify this finding is needed.

SAFE RIDE AND DESIGNATED DRIVER PROGRAMS

Among the most popular methods for separating drinking and driving is the designated driver concept in which one member of a group traveling to a drinking location agrees to drive and not to drink. Merchants can support such efforts by providing free nonalcoholic drinks to the individual acting as the designated driver. A complementary concept to the Designated Driver program that does not require planning by individuals patronizing drinking establishments is the Safe Ride program, in which the proprietor or community organization provides a sober driver for individuals too impaired to drive safely. Safe Ride and Designated Driver programs have been studied with some promising results (Caudill, Harding, & Moore, 2000; Meier, Brigham, & Gilbert, 1998; Simons-Morton & Cummings, 1997). The designated driver concept has gained momentum in the United States, with most Americans endorsing it as a strategy to reduce driving under the influence (Winsten, 1994). Additionally, many community and national organizations have vigorously promoted the use of Designated Driver programs (Apsler, Harding, & Goldfein, 1987; Caudill, Harding, & Moore, 2001; DeJong & Wallack, 1992; Harding, Caudill, & Moore, 1998).

Both the safe ride and designated driver strategies may produce unintended consequences for groups of drinkers. Individuals who become passengers rather than drivers may feel freer to drink heavily. This may increase their risk of non–traffic-related trauma (e.g., falls, fires, or violence). Telephone and barroom surveys of drinkers who had been transported by a designated driver have shown small but significantly elevated drinking outside the home when a designated driver was available (Harding & Caudill, 1997). In addition, implementation of the concept may be incomplete or inappropriate. For instance, groups of drinkers may designate a driver after drinking has commenced or at the end of a night of drinking (Fell, Voas, & Lange, 1997; Lange, Voas, & O'Rourke, 1998). Despite these limitations, the designated driver concept appears to hold substantial promise for reducing the incidences of impaired driving. It is simple, inexpensive, almost universally recognized, and, as shown in several national polls, has overwhelming acceptance by most Americans. There is evidence that simply raising the issue of having a designated driver with young adults heading to bars reduces the BACs of drivers when they return from a night of drinking (Lange, Reed, Johnson, & Voas, 2006; Voas, Johnson, & Miller, 2013).

An alternative transportation program called the "Road Crew" was initiated in three communities in Wisconsin in 2003. It was developed using new product development techniques and implemented by establishing broad coalitions within the communities. A key feature of the program is rides home and between home and bars or taverns in older luxury vehicles subsidized via fares and tavern contributions. An evaluation showed a significant shift in riding/driving behavior among 21- to 34-year-olds

and a projected 17% decline in alcohol-related crashes in the first year of operation (Rothschild, Mastin, & Miller, 2006).

PRIMARY SAFETY BELT LAWS

NHTSA estimates that safety belts, when worn in a passenger car involved in a serious crash, are 45% effective in preventing fatalities (Klein & Walz, 1998). Klein and Walz (1998) also tracked vehicle safety belt use in the Fatality Analysis Reporting System (FARS) from 1982 through 1995 and found nonuse to be positively correlated with BAC levels for every year. In 1995, 75% of drivers at .10 BAC did not use safety belts compared to 34% of the drivers at zero BACs. There are two types of state laws regarding safety belt use: secondary laws, which allow officers to cite unbelted drivers only if they are stopped for some other traffic offense, and primary laws, which permit stopping the vehicle of an unbelted user. Lange and Voas (1998) found that when California moved from a secondary to a primary law, safety belt use increased from 70% to 90% among nondrinking drivers. In contrast, the usage rate among drivers with BACs of .10 or higher increased from 50% to 90%. Aside from their direct effect in reducing the severity of injuries, primary safety belt laws may be particularly effective in deterring impaired drivers because they allow the officer to stop the car, leading to the detection of drinking. Further evidence for the potential effectiveness of primary belt laws in reducing impaired driving crashes was provided by Voas, Fell, Tippetts, Blackman, and Nichols (2007). In a study of five states that passed primary safety belt laws, four states experienced a decline in alcohol-related fatal crashes compared to non–alcohol-related fatal crashes.

Drinking and Driving

Throughout most of the industrialized world, DUI laws are based on illegal per se laws, which make it an offense to operate a vehicle with a BAC at or higher than a specified level—.05 in most European countries and Australia, and .08 in New Zealand, Canada, and the United States (Wren & Drive & Stay Alive Inc., 2003). There is, however, a substantial difference in the specific provisions of these laws in Europe and Australia compared to the United States. Outside the United States, most countries' laws are modeled on what Ross (1982a) called the "Scandinavian System," which allows a motorist to be stopped, both on suspicion of impaired driving and at random,

Table 22.1. Key Driving-under-the-Influence (DUI) Laws

DUI Law	Description
Impaired driving law	The traditional law against drinking and driving that depends on the officer presenting observations of the suspect's behavior that demonstrates the driver was under the influence of alcohol. It does not depend on the presentation of a blood alcohol content (BAC) test result, but if the BAC level is available, it becomes presumptive evidence of intoxication.
Per se law	Operating a vehicle with a BAC at or higher than a specified illegal limit. When a BAC level is not available, the prosecution must be conducted under the impaired driving law.
Zero-tolerance law (a "status" law based on age)	Based on the minimum legal drinking age law, the zero-tolerance law makes it an offense for a person younger than age 21 to operate a motor vehicle with any measurable amount of alcohol in his or her body; generally specified as a BAC of .02 or greater.
Implied-consent law	Establishes that, by accepting a driver's license, a driver agrees to submit to a chemical test if an officer has probable cause to make an arrest for impaired driving. In the event of a refusal, most statutes provide that no test will be given, but the suspect's license will be suspended. Alternatively, the officer can seek a warrant to require a blood test.
Administrative license revocation law	Provides that a DUI suspect whose chemical test result is higher than the illegal limit (currently .08) is subject to an immediate license suspension. A provision must be made for a hearing if requested by the offender.
High BAC laws	Provides for increased sanctions for a convicted DUI offender whose BAC level is .15 or greater.
Test refusal law	Provides for increased sanctions for DUI suspects who refuse the chemical test.
Anticonsumption, open container law	Prohibits consumption of alcohol by the driver while in charge of a vehicle or more commonly prohibits an open alcohol container in the passenger compartment of a vehicle. Passengers in commercial vehicles, such as buses, are normally exempted.

and breath tested at the roadside, followed by a mandatory evidential blood test. In the United States, random stops are allowed under limited conditions: an officer cannot require the driver to provide a roadside breath test, and an arrest must be based on observed impairment. Finally, in Europe, Australia, and Canada, refusing the evidential breath test carries the same penalties as conviction for DUI; in the United States, the driver is subject to license suspension if the test is refused, but refusal may result in avoiding a court trial and more severe penalties due to lack of evidence. Because of these limitations, based on the Fourth Amendment of the US Constitution, the DUI criminal justice system in the United States is complex. The complexity of the system has been well described in a set of four volumes on the US DUI enforcement, prosecution, sanctioning, and monitoring system published by the Traffic Injury Research Foundation of Canada

(Robertson & Simpson, 2002a; 2002b; 2002c; Simpson & Robertson, 2001).

Over the past quarter century, much of the research in traffic safety has focused on the evaluation of proposed new laws and the development of tools for use by the police and courts in the enforcement of DUI laws. The most significant laws are listed in Table 22.1, and recent research on key DUI laws is described in the following sections.

Impaired Driving Laws

Before implementation of BAC testing, all DUI prosecutions were brought under impaired driving laws that required the state to provide behavioral evidence of impairment. Evidence generally consisted of the officer's observations of aberrant driving or the failure of the suspect to perform sobriety tests. These laws remained in place following the passage of illegal per se laws because of the offender's right to refuse the evidential test.

ILLEGAL PER SE LAWS

A basic problem with relying on the officer's observations is that they are necessarily subjective. This can be an important issue when determining the level of intoxication, given that heavy drinking leads to alcohol tolerance that may reduce the common signs of intoxication available to police (e.g., slurred speech, lack of manual dexterity, bloodshot eyes) resulting in failure to detect over-the-limit drivers. There is considerable evidence that officers do fail to arrest a substantial number of legally impaired drivers with whom they come in contact, particularly when contact time is limited as it is in sobriety checkpoint operations (see Enforcement Programs).

Case-controlled relative risk studies, such as Borkenstein et al.'s (1974) and Blomberg et al.'s (Blomberg, Peck, Moskowitz, Burns, & Fiorentino, 2005; Blomberg, Peck, Moskowitz, Burns, & Fiorentino, 2009; Voas, Torres, Romano, & Lacey, 2012; Zador, Krawchuk, & Voas, 2000), provide the basis for defining impaired driving in terms of BAC. Initially set at .15 BAC in the 1950s, state per se limits in the United States were generally lowered to .10 BAC by the 1980s. The strong evidence that BACs as low as .05 increased crash risk motivated several states to lower their limit to .08 in the 1990s. By 2000, the US Congress passed legislation encouraging all states to adopt .08 BAC laws by threatening to withhold a portion of a state's federal highway funds for noncompliance. This movement stimulated many research studies of the crash reductions associated with lowering the BAC limit from .10 to .08. Most of these studies found sizeable decreases in alcohol-related crashes associated with the .08 BAC limit. Between 1991 and 2000, nine evaluations of .08 laws involving 11 states were conducted in the United States (Apsler, Char, Harding, & Klein, 1999; Foss, Stewart, & Reinfurt, 1998; Hingson, Heeren, & Winter, 1996; 2000; Johnson & Fell, 1995; Research and Evaluation Associates [REA], 1991; Rogers, 1995; Voas, Taylor, Kelley Baker, & Tippetts, 2000; Voas, Tippetts, & Fell, 2000). A meta-analysis by Schults et al. (2001) of 25 studies on the enactment of the .08 law found that the median crash reduction among the studies they reviewed was 7%.

Fell and Voas (2006b) conducted a general review of studies of the effect of lowering the BAC limit in foreign countries and the United States and concluded that lowering the BAC limit to .05 would be likely to reduce alcohol-related crashes. In 1988, the illegal BAC limit was lowered from .08 to .05 g/dL in Austria. A study of the law found that there was an overall 9.4% decrease in alcohol-related crashes relative to the total number of crashes (Bartl & Esberger, 2000). However, they noted that intense media and enforcement campaigns also occurred around the time that the limit was lowered, making it nearly impossible to attribute the reductions to any one of these factors, at least in the short term. Bartl and Esberger (2000) concluded that "lowering the [il]legal BAC limit from .08 to .05 g/dL in combination with intensive police enforcement and reporting in the media leads to a positive short-term effect." This provided support for the view that a .05 g/dL BAC illegal limit, as part of a comprehensive approach to fighting impaired driving, can have beneficial effects.

Homel (1994) found that lowering the BAC limit from .08 to .05 g/dL in New South Wales, Australia, significantly reduced fatal crashes on Saturdays by 13%. Henstridge, Homel, and Mackay (1995) conducted a rigorous time-series analysis of random breath testing (RBT) and .05 BAC laws in Australia, controlling for many factors including seasonal effects, weather, economic trends, road use, alcohol consumption, and day of the week. Although the primary focus of the Australian study was the impact of RBT, the findings on the effect of .05 BAC laws were also significant. The study statistically accounted for the effect of other alcohol countermeasures to determine the specific values of the declines that were attributable directly to either RBT or the lower .05 BAC limit. The study analyzed traffic data for periods ranging from 13 to 17 years and found Australian states that lowered their BAC limits from .08 to .05 g/dL experienced meaningful declines in alcohol-related crash measures. After Queensland, Australia, reduced its per se BAC limit to .05 g/dL in 1982, it experienced an 18% reduction in fatal collisions and a 14% reduction in serious collisions. These results were not confounded by the effects of RBT because it was not introduced until 8 years later. Similarly, the .05 g/dL BAC limit in New South Wales was estimated to have reduced serious collisions by 7%, fatal collisions by 8%, and single-vehicle nighttime collisions by 11%. This translated into the averting of an estimated 605 serious, 75 fatal, and 296 single-vehicle nighttime collisions per year. Although the .05 g/dL

BAC limit was introduced only 2 years before RBT in New South Wales, the authors accounted for this in their analyses and attempted to determine the crash reductions specifically attributable to each of the interventions.

Smith (1988b) specifically evaluated the effects of lowering the BAC limit in Queensland from .08 to .05 g/dL BAC. The proxy measure of changes in nighttime crashes as compared to daytime crashes was used. There was a significant 8.2% reduction in nighttime serious injury crashes (requiring hospitalization) and a 5.5% reduction in nighttime property damage crashes associated with the .05 g/dL BAC limit in the first year. Smith partially attributes some of the crash reductions in the second and third years after the adoption of .05 g/dL BAC to increased enforcement. When lowering the illegal BAC limit stimulates increased enforcement, it should be considered a benefit of the law, not a drawback, as concluded by Smith.

ZERO-TOLERANCE LAWS FOR UNDERAGE DRIVERS

By 1988, all states had enacted MLDA laws making it illegal for those younger than 21 to purchase or possess alcohol. This provided a basis for implementing a zero BAC limit for drivers aged 20 and younger. In 1995, the US Congress passed a law creating a financial penalty (a reduction in their highway construction funds) for states that did not adopt zero-tolerance laws for drivers younger than 21. By 1998, all states and the District of Columbia had passed laws making it illegal for any driver younger than 21 to have a positive BAC (generally defined as a BAC of .02 or greater). These zero-tolerance laws for youth have proven effective in reducing fatal crashes involving underage drinking drivers (Blomberg, 1992; Fell, Fisher, Voas, Blackman, & Tippetts, 2009b; Fell & Voas, 2006b; Hingson, Heeren, & Winter, 1994; Hingson, Howland, Heeren, & Winter, 1992; Voas, Tippetts, & Fell, 2003; Zwerling & Jones, 1999). Shults et al. (2001) conducted a meta-analysis of the studies of zero-tolerance laws and found reductions of 9–24% in fatal crashes. Despite this evidence that zero-tolerance laws are associated with crash reductions, their impact has been limited because of conflicts in the law that have made enforcement less effective (Ferguson, Fields, & Voas, 2000) and because of a tendency for zero-tolerance arrests to be accompanied by a reduction in DUI arrests (Blackman, Voas, Gullberg, & Tippetts, 2001; McCartt, Blackman, & Voas, 2007; Voas, Lange, & Tippetts, 1998).

IMPLIED-CONSENT LAWS

Although the US Supreme court ruled in *Smerber v. California* (1966, 384 US 757) that validly arrested DUI offenders can be forced to provide a blood sample for alcohol analysis, most states are unwilling to adopt a practice that would require restraining DUI offenders to draw a blood sample forcibly. As a compromise, states passed implied-consent legislation, which held that the driver, by seeking a license, had agreed to provide a sample and refusal was a basis for the motor vehicle department to suspend the license. Although this provides a strong motivation for a DUI suspect to comply with the test, according to Simpson and Robertson (2001), most defense attorneys advise their clients to refuse the test because an over-the-limit BAC results in an immediate license suspension under an administrative license suspension law (see hereafter) and makes DUI conviction much more certain. This problem is likely to be exacerbated by the growth of high BAC laws (described hereafter) that are based on the offender's BAC level. Initially, implied-consent laws appeared to be effective in motivating most offenders to comply with the evidential test requirement. Recent studies, however, suggest a substantial number of those arrested for DUI refuse the test. Zwicker, Hedlund, and Northrup (2005) reported refusal rates as high as 80% in 40 of the 50 states for which they could obtain data. Ross, Simon, Cleary, Lewis, and Storkamp (1995) reported a 50% rate. Simpson and Robertson (2001), in their survey of 2,731 police officers, found that, about a third of the time, officers experienced some type of refusal to cooperate in a DUI investigation, and multiple offenders were more likely than first offenders to refuse the chemical test.

ENHANCED TEST REFUSAL LAWS

Robertson and Simpson (2002c) noted that the availability of a BAC measurement is important to the prosecutor's decision to file a charge, as well as to the outcome of the case itself. Moreover, the absence of a BAC level may preclude prosecuting an offender under a high BAC law in the 32 states that provide more severe sanctions for offenders with BACs of .15 or higher (see next paragraph). Although there is some evidence that the lack of a BAC measure is associated with a lower probability of conviction and higher recidivism (Kelley-Baker et al., 2008; McCartt et al., 2007), to date there have been no studies on the influence of test refusal on crash involvement. Based on their survey of police officers, Simpson and Robertson (2001) described several options for reducing chemical test refusals by making the consequences of refusal more severe than taking the test. For example, the suspension period for refusal could be longer than for taking and failing the test, or refusing to take the test could be a criminal offense. They also suggested forcing the blood test, an option adopted by some police departments that has been allowed by the Supreme Court, providing the officer obtains a warrant. The basic requirement is either to make refusal impossible by forcing the test (Jones, Lacey, & Wiliszowski, 1998) or to ensure that the penalty for refusal is at least as severe as for failing the test. As of 2001, nine states have criminalized refusal (Zwicker et al., 2005).

ADMINISTRATIVE LICENSE REVOCATION

Administrative license suspension (ALS) or revocation (ALR) laws provide for the arresting officer to seize the driver's license when an offender is arrested for DUI. The confiscated license is sent to the motor vehicle department, which then suspends the driving privileges of the offender shortly after apprehension. Thus, the penalty follows rapidly on the offense, which, based on deterrence theory (described hereafter), should have a specific deterrent effect on the offending driver. The significance of ALR laws is enhanced by the evidence that, in addition to their specific effect on offenders, they may have a general deterrent effect on the driving public as a whole. Zador (1991), in an early study of the states implementing ALR laws, found that a reduction in fatal crashes could be attributed to such laws. Voas et al. (2003) conducted a panel study of the 50 states and the District of Columbia from 1982 to 1997 and found that ALR laws were associated with a 19% decline in alcohol-related fatal crashes. A meta-analysis of 46 studies of state laws, which included 12 evaluations of ALR laws by Zobeck and Williams (1994), found an average reduction of 5% in alcohol-related crashes and a reduction of 26% in fatal crashes associated with ALR. Miller, Galbraith, and Lawrence (1998) concluded that the benefit-to-cost ratio for ALR was $11 for each dollar invested when violators received a 6-month license suspension. Wagenaar and Maldonado-Molina (2007) studied the impact of driver licenses suspension policies in 49 states and came to the conclusion that the speed with which the license penalty followed on apprehension was more significant than the severity of the penalty. As

of 2005, 41 states have enacted ALR laws (NHTSA, 1998; NIAAA, 2005).

HIGH BAC LAWS

A BAC of .15 or higher at the time of arrest has been considered a sign that the offender has a drinking problem since the federal government began to support community alcohol programs with the initiation of the Alcohol Safety Action Projects (ASAPs) in 1969 (Levy, Voas, Johnson, & Klein, 1977; Nichols, Ellingstad, & Struckman-Johnson, 1978; Voas, 1972; 1981). This focus on high BAC levels as a drinking problem indicator has increased with the recent emphasis on the role of the "hardcore drinking driver" as the major contributor to alcohol-related crashes (Simpson, Mayhew, & Beirness, 1996). Despite some conflicting evidence regarding the significance of BAC as a predictor of problem drinking, Wieczorek, Miller, and Nochajski (1992) found only a small association between the BAC level and alcohol-related problems as measured on the Mortimer-Filkins test. As of July 2005, 32 states and the District of Columbia have enacted high BAC laws (Hedlund, 2006) that provide for longer suspensions and more severe penalties for drivers with high BACs. So far, there has been only one study of their implementation. McCartt and Northrup (2004), in a study of Minnesota's high BAC law applicable to offenders with BACs of .20 or higher, detected a short-term increase in the severity of penalties for that target group but did not have evidence of a reduction in recidivism or crashes. Despite the wide adoption of high BAC statutes, so far, there is no evidence that such laws reduce crashes.

OPEN CONTAINER LAWS

Because underage youths cannot drink legally in licensed establishments and at social events supervised by adults, their drinking frequently occurs in parks or on beaches, often in private vehicles. Private vehicles are also a somewhat frequent location for adult drinking. It would therefore appear obvious that discouraging drinking in a motor vehicle is important to reduce impaired driving. Public support for banning open containers is high (Stuster, Burns, & Fiorentino, 2002). This has led to federal legislation encouraging states to enact open container laws; consequently, 38 states had adopted such laws as of July 2005 (Hedlund, 2006). Stuster et al. (2002) evaluated the influence of open container laws on fatal crashes in four states and found no evidence of a reduction in the 6 months following enactment of the law. Although the evidence to support such laws is weak, the logical face validity of banning open containers in cars may express a societal negative attitude toward impaired driving, which could make these laws an important part of the overall effort to reduce alcohol-related crashes.

Enforcement of Alcohol Safety Laws

The effectiveness of traffic laws related to impaired driving depends on deterring vehicle operators from driving after drinking. The principal factor in creating deterrence is how effectively the laws are enforced. Classical deterrence theory is a psychological model designed to explain the influence of punishment on personal behavior. It holds that three factors—risk of detection, severity of the sanction, and the speed with which the sanction is applied—determine the response to laws. Ross (1982*b*) provided perhaps the clearest explanation of deterrence, emphasizing that it is the perception of each of the three factors—rather than the actual risk of detection, the sanction severity, and sanction celerity—that controls the behavior of offenders. The basic theoretical concept has been demonstrated in many evaluations of traffic safety programs conducted in the past half century. The relative influence of each element of the theory, however, has been studied less. Ross and Klette (1995), based on their studies of Scandinavian laws, concluded that the perceived probability of arrest was a more significant factor than the severity of the penalty (Ross, 1992*a*). Some evidence for this position was developed from studies of DUI enforcement in the United States (Ross, McCleary, & LaFree, 1990; Ross & Voas, 1990). The relative effectiveness of enforcement compared to sanctions in creating deterrence is a significant issue; much of the cost of sanctions (fines, treatment, and vehicle sanctions) is borne by offenders, making them relatively low cost to the state. Conversely, the full cost of enforcement is born by the state.

The actual risk of arrest for DUI in the United States is quite small. Estimates have varied from 1 in 2,000, based on an analysis of average annual officer arrest rates (2 per year per officer; Borkenstein, 1975), to about 1 in 88, based on responses to a national telephone survey and FBI crime statistics (Zador, Krawchuck, & Moore, 2001). The most carefully developed risk estimates were those reported by Beitel, Sharp, and Glauz (2000) and by Hause, Voas, and Chavez (1982), based on field

researchers riding with police. They found a probability of arrest for 6 in 1,000 drivers with BACs of .10 or higher. The swiftness in applying a sanction has substantially increased with the adoption of ALR laws, and high BAC laws have increased the severity of sanctions for DUI. Although the technology for apprehending impaired drivers has improved, much of its potential is underused, leaving enforcement as the element in deterrence with the most potential for further progress.

SOBRIETY CHECKPOINTS

Sobriety checkpoints provide US police departments with the closest approximation to the highly successful RBT enforcement procedure used in Australia, Sweden, and other countries. RBT, as implemented in Australia, allows officers to stop any vehicle on the road at random and to take a breath test from the driver. Operators with BACs higher than .05, the illegal limit, are transported to the police station for an evidential test. In contrast, in the United States, vehicles can only be stopped at random at specially designed "checkpoints," and the drivers cannot be required to take a breath test. Rather, the officer must conduct an interview to determine whether the driver is impaired, and, if there is evidence of impairment, the officer must require the driver to perform a set of field sobriety tests to establish impairment before transporting the offender to the police station.

Henstridge, Homel, and Mackay (1997), in a time-series analysis of four Australian states, found that RBT was twice as effective as "selective" checkpoints similar to those conducted in the United States. Sherman (1990) found that in Queensland, Australia, RBT resulted in a 35% reduction in fatal crashes, compared with 15% for checkpoints. They estimated that every increase of 1,000 in the daily RBT testing rate corresponded to a decline of 6% in all serious crashes and 19% in single-vehicle nighttime crashes. Moreover, analyses revealed a measurable continuing deterrent effect of RBT on the motorist population after the program had been in place for 10 years. Homel (1988) showed that the deterrent influence of RBT also provided heavy drinkers with a legitimate excuse to drink less when drinking with friends.

Studies of the US sobriety checkpoint procedure found that they are associated with significant decreases in alcohol-related crashes (Epperlein, 1987; Lacey, Rudisill, Popkin, & Stewart, 1986; Levy, Asch, & Shea, 1990; Levy, Shea, & Asch, 1988; Voas, 2008; Voas, Rhodenizer, & Lynn, 1985;

Wells, Preusser, & Williams, 1992). Four reviews of checkpoint programs have been published. Peek-Asa (1999) reviewed six studies occurring between 1983 and 1996 and reported reductions of 17–75% in alcohol-related fatalities. Two related meta-analyses studies of 15 US checkpoint programs occurring between 1985 and 1999 were conducted by Shults et al. (2001) and Elder and Shults (2002). Elder and Shults (2002) found that the median reduction in crashes associated with checkpoints was 20%. A survey of state checkpoint operations by Fell and colleagues (2004) reported effectiveness figures similar to those of Elder and Shults (2002). A cost–benefit study of sobriety checkpoints indicated that, for every $1 invested in the checkpoint strategy, the community conducting the checkpoint saved $6 (Miller et al., 1998). In a recent report published by the Transportation Research Board of the National Academies of Science (Transportation Research Board, 2010), the lessons from other nations indicate that frequent and sustained use of sobriety checkpoints could save up to 3,000 lives annually if similarly used in the United States.

Despite these positive results, a recent survey of states that use checkpoints (Fell, Ferguson, Williams, & Fields, 2003) showed that only 12 of the 37 states conducted checkpoints weekly. Their survey found four main reasons for their infrequent use: (1) lack of local police resources and funding, (2) lack of support by state task forces and citizen activists, (3) checkpoints not efficient for producing DUI arrests, and (4) checkpoints not cost-effective in reducing crashes. Other investigators have reported similar reasons (Ross, 1992b; 1992c). There are counterarguments available to each of these issues:

1. Police departments generally use larger numbers of officers and vehicles in checkpoint operations than is required by the courts. This increases their expense, thus making checkpoint operations dependent on receiving additional outside funds. Recent studies have shown that low-manpower checkpoints staffed by relatively few (four to six) officers can be effective. The Stuster and Blowers (1995) study demonstrated that checkpoints with as few as three to five officers could be as effective as a much larger staff of officers. Recently, a "mini-checkpoint" program was undertaken by Lacey, Kelley-Baker, Ferguson, and Rider (2006) in West Virginia. Low-staff checkpoints (with three to five officers) were conducted weekly in two experimental counties in the state (106 in one year). The low-staff checkpoints were relatively inexpensive to conduct, costing from $350 to $400 per checkpoint.

2. Local support by community action groups can significantly encourage strong enforcement, as described hereafter.

3. Many checkpoint operations limit the interviews with motorist to a minute or less in order to contact as many drivers as possible and avoid traffic delays. The short interview time is inadequate for officers to assess the drivers' appearance and behavior to determine whether they are impaired. Consequently, half of the over-the-limit drivers escape detection (discussed hereafter). It is possible, as Voas (2008) found with a low-staff checkpoint program in Charlottesville, Virginia, for officers to produce DUI arrests as efficiently at a checkpoint as on regular patrol, particularly if passive alcohol sensors (PAS) are used.

4. As described, there is ample evidence that well-publicized checkpoint programs effectively reduce alcohol-related crashes. Much of this benefit is attributable to their general deterrent effect, independent of the extent to which they apprehend over-the-limit drivers. This has encouraged the view that it is not important for checkpoints to produce arrests because their primary purpose is deterrence. However, no one has examined the effect that checkpoints have on the impaired driving of over-the-limit motorists who escape detection at checkpoints. Are they encouraged to drink and drive more frequently?

A benefit of checkpoint operations not been fully evaluated is the suppression of crime beyond impaired driving. Elder et al. (2002), in their review of sobriety checkpoints, noted that checkpoint operations resulted in the apprehension of suspended DUI offenders driving illicitly and individuals carrying weapons (p. 273), outcomes that provide benefits in addition to their influence on impaired driving crashes. Other reports on checkpoint operations have noted this serendipitous benefit (Fell, Langston, Lacey, Tippetts, & Cotton, 2008b; Lacey, Jones, & Smith, 1999; Voas, 2008; Voas et al., 1985). Particularly important from a traffic safety viewpoint are the citations for safety belt nonuse, which is a particular problem with impaired drivers (Voas et al., 2007).

Between 2000 and 2003, the US Department of Transportation funded demonstration projects designed to reduce impaired driving through well-publicized and frequent enforcement in seven states: Georgia, Indiana, Louisiana, Michigan, Pennsylvania, Tennessee, and Texas. Significant reductions in fatal crashes in the intervention states relative to surrounding states were obtained in Georgia, Indiana, Michigan, and Tennessee when comparing the ratio of drinking to nondrinking drivers in fatal crashes (Fell, Tippetts, & Levy, 2008d). Significant reductions in a second measure—alcohol-related fatalities per 100 million vehicle miles traveled— were also obtained in Indiana and Michigan. The other three states showed only marginal, nonsignificant changes relative to their comparison jurisdictions or states. As compared to surrounding states, fatal crash reductions in Georgia, Indiana, Michigan, and Tennessee, ranged from 11% to 20%. In these four states, the programs were estimated to have saved lives ranging from 25 to 60: Indiana, 23; Tennessee, 43; Michigan, 57; and Georgia, 60. Some common features of the programs that provided significant reductions were the use of paid media to publicize the enforcement (in three states), the use of a statewide model rather than selected portions of the state (all four states), and the use of highly visible and frequent sobriety checkpoints (in three states). The authors concluded that a variety of media and enforcement procedures that supplement ongoing statewide efforts can yield meaningful crash reduction effects among alcohol-impaired drivers.

TRADITIONAL DUI ENFORCEMENT

Procedures for enforcing laws against impaired driving have grown out of the standard traffic enforcement responsibilities of police departments. Traffic officers have many responsibilities, some of which include directing traffic, responding to crash scenes, and enforcing traffic regulations related to high-risk driving (such as speeding and red-light running). In addition, they may be called to crime scenes or tasked with security responsibilities for government officials. Police departments have limited resources that must cover competing responsibilities for traffic general enforcement, crime suppression, and security operations. DUI arrest activity must compete with other high-priority functions for the same limited resources. In a classic study of DUI enforcement for NHTSA, Borkenstein (1975) analyzed the enforcement activities in urban areas in the United States. He noted that, "In a typical American city, 10% of police resources are allocated to traffic law enforcement, but included in the violations are such

mundane offenses as blocking driveways and parking violations" (p. 659). Because the typical patrol officers have a wide range of activities, Borkenstein estimated that they made only two DUI arrests a year. Based on surveys of the number of drinking drivers on the roads, he further estimated that the probability of being arrested with a BAC of .10, the illegal limit at that time, was 1 in 2,000.

DEDICATED PATROLS

Since Borkenstein's study in 1975, state BAC limits have been reduced from .10 to .08, federal funding for DUI enforcement has increased, and many police departments have established special DUI patrols. Such patrols dedicated only to DUI enforcement can significantly increase DUI arrests. Dedicated patrols generally operate on weekends when the prevalence of impaired driving is greatest. Experience in the 35 NHTSA ASAP community programs in the 1970s indicated that two or three dedicated patrols operating on weekends could double the annual number of DUI arrests (Levy, Voas, Johnson, & Klein, 1978; Voas, 1981).

SATURATION PATROLS

Saturation patrols are dedicated patrols that generally involve larger than normal numbers of officers frequently achieved by more than one jurisdiction participating in the activity. They provide a high-visibility alternative to checkpoints that are particularly suitable for those states with constitutional limitations on the use of sobriety checkpoints (Fell et al., 2003). The large number of police vehicles is intended to attract public and media attention to the enhanced enforcement effort. Saturation patrols appear to be effective in reducing impaired driving if they are highly publicized, but recent research on this strategy is much more limited and is not as extensive or as convincing as that on sobriety checkpoints. The one direct comparison of the checkpoint and saturation methods in California conducted by Stuster and Blowers (1995) favored checkpoints. In addition, saturation patrols may have the same major limitation as checkpoints in that they require a substantial number of officers.

Enforcement Technology

During the past 30 years, considerable effort has been expended in the development of technological methods and devices to increase the effectiveness of DUI enforcement. Research has been conducted on each phase of the arrest process

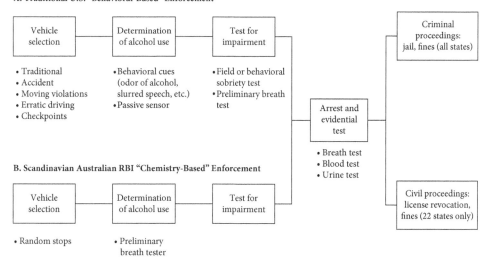

A. Traditional U.S. "Behavioral-Based" Enforcement

| Vehicle selection | Determination of alcohol use | Test for impairment |

- Traditional
- Accident
- Moving violations
- Erratic driving
- Checkpoints

- Behavioral cues (odor of alcohol, slurred speech, etc.)
- Passive sensor

- Field or behavioral sobriety test
- Preliminary breath test

Arrest and evidential test

- Breath test
- Blood test
- Urine test

Criminal proceedings: jail, fines (all states)

B. Scandinavian Australian RBI "Chemistry-Based" Enforcement

| Vehicle selection | Determination of alcohol use | Test for impairment |

- Random stops

- Preliminary breath tester

Civil proceedings: license revocation, fines (22 states only)

Figure 22.2. Model comparing chemistry-based random breath-test programs with US behavioral-based DUI enforcement system.

shown in Figure 22.2. The model shown in Figure 22.2 (revised from Voas & Lacey, 1990) contrasts the "chemistry-based" enforcement system (bottom line) typical of Australia and Sweden (which involves stopping vehicles at random and requiring a preliminary breath test, followed by an evidential test at the police station) with the US "behavioral-based" enforcement system (top line). Step 1 of that procedure is to identify and stop vehicles in the traffic stream likely to be driven by impaired drivers. The next step is to detect those drivers who have been drinking heavily and then (step 3) to ask the driver to participate in sobriety testing. Each of these three steps has received some research attention directed at producing methods and equipment that will increase the officer's efficiency in apprehending impaired drivers.

DETECTION OF VEHICLES DRIVEN BY DUI OFFENDERS

For detection of vehicles driven by impaired drivers (step 1), the federal government has funded several studies of the vehicle maneuvers that suggest the driver is impaired (Harris, Dick, Casey, & Jarosz, 1980; Stuster, 1993). These signs provide the officers with probable cause to stop the vehicle to determine whether the driver has been drinking. To develop these cues, research assistants rode with the police and recorded their observations of the cues that led to stopping a motorist. The BACs for all motorists stopped were obtained: they were either arrested for DUI or volunteered after being

dismissed by the officer. Based on these data, a manual containing a cue list for police use was assembled and field tested (Stuster, 1997).

Step 2 is the identification of a driver who has been drinking heavily. Because a breath test is generally viewed as a search under the Fourth Amendment of the US Constitution, officers must have a "reason to believe" the suspect is impaired before proceeding with a DUI investigation. Typically, officers use a set of signs—such as bloodshot eyes, odor of alcohol on the breath, fumbling with the driver's license—as indicators of impairment (Stuster, 1997). Perhaps the most frequently occurring indicator appearing on police reports is the odor of alcohol. Moskowitz, Burns, and Ferguson (1999) found, however, that when individuals were limited to detecting drinking only through their sense of smell, they were unable to identify impaired drivers with any regularity. Thus, officers have limited and relatively unreliable cues when interviewing a driver at the left window of a vehicle. The utility of the random test system in Australia does not depend on observations of the driver's appearance and behavior.

Step 3 involves a sobriety test. In the United States, drivers cannot be required to take a preliminary breath test; therefore, officers must rely on observations of the driver's behavior that demonstrate impairment. To provide a standardized (or standard) set of observations for use in court, Burns and Moskowitz (1977) developed a set of three Standardized Field Sobriety Tests (SFSTs): a one-leg stand, the walk and turn, and the horizontal

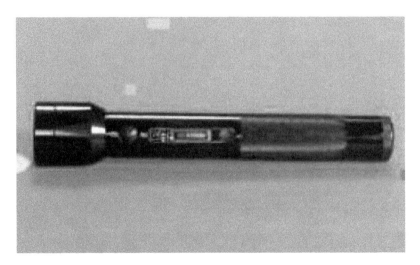

Figure 22.3. PAS III, a standard police flashlight with a built-in passive alcohol sensor.

gaze nystagmus tests. Several field evaluations demonstrated that the battery of tests has substantial validity for identifying drivers with BACs of .10 or higher (Burns & Anderson, 1995; Stuster & Burns, 1998; Tharp, Burns, & Moskowitz, 1981). Stuster and Burns (1998) and Burns and Dioquino (1997) demonstrated that the three-test battery was equally accurate for identification of drivers at BACs of .08. McKnight et al. (2002) and Stuster and Burns (1998) found that, by modifying the scoring of the horizontal gaze nystagmus test, it was useful for identifying drivers with BACs as low as .04. However, Burns and Anderson (1995) found that, when breath tests were collected after the officer released the driver because the officer believed he or she was not over the limit, 36% of those released had BACs that exceeded the illegal limit (see Burns, 2003, for a review of the development of the SFSTs).

PASSIVE BREATH TESTERS

As noted, police departments have resisted implementing checkpoints partly because few DUI arrests are made in checkpoint operations (Fell et al., 2004). An important factor in this limitation in arrests is the fact that officers cannot test every driver stopped, as they do in Australia, but must first determine that the individual has been drinking and may be impaired. A device designed to aid the officer in detecting drinking is the PAS III, a standard police flashlight with a built-in PAS. The sensor device draws in a mix of expired and environmental air from in front of a person's face and is not considered a search prohibited by the Fourth Amendment. These sensors (Figure 22.3) can provide a good estimate of the driver's BAC (Farmer, Wells, Ferguson, & Voas, 1999; Voas, Romano, & Peck, 2006b). The PAS is particularly effective when observation time is short, as it is in checkpoints. However, efforts to persuade officers to make greater use of passive sensors have generally failed (Fell, Compton, & Voas, 2008c). A series of studies has demonstrated that when officers use passive sensors at a checkpoint, more drinking drivers are detected and the arrest rate increases by approximately 50% (Ferguson, Wells, & Lund, 1995; Lestina & Lund, 1989; Lund & Jones, 1987; Lund, Kiger, Lestina, & Blackwell, 1991). Aside from its effectiveness in increasing the detection of drinking drivers, the most important effect of the PAS on impaired driving may be its potential to increase the perceived risk of being apprehended for DUI if driving after drinking. If police use of the PAS is well publicized, it should increase general deterrence to impaired driving. Heavy drinkers who count on their increased tolerance to alcohol to avoid detection (Ross & Gonzales, 1988) might be deterred by the police's ability to detect drinking in an otherwise sober-appearing driver. Furthermore, making underage drivers aware that even very small amounts of alcohol in the blood can be detected should increase their concern about being cited under the zero-tolerance law. Although the PAS has been used in many enforcement programs, relatively few (Voas, Holder, & Gruenewald, 1997; Wells et al., 1992) have actively publicized its use. More comprehensive research on the effects of publicizing PAS use in DUI enforcement is needed.

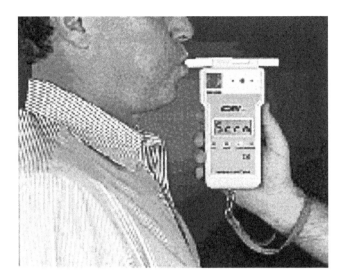

Figure 22.4. SD-4 preliminary breath test device.

PRELIMINARY BREATH TESTERS

In the United States, when the police have been provided with handheld preliminary breath test (PBT) devices (see Figure 22.4) for use in testing motorists at the roadside, DUI arrests have increased (Cleary & Rodgers, 1986; Saffer & Chaloupka, 1989). Tests conducted by NHTSA indicate that, when properly used, these handheld devices are as accurate as the large desktop evidential units used in police stations (Frank & Flores, 1989). Currently, many, if not most, police departments have some handheld PBT units (Simpson & Robertson, 2001). These units are legislatively authorized in 29 states and the District of Columbia. Simpson and Robertson (2001) found that most officers in their survey reported that PBT devices were very useful for detecting intoxication, and 69% indicated that they would like to see an increase in their availability. Current operational practices limit their effectiveness, however, because they are normally used only after the officer has conducted the SFSTs.

Publicizing Enforcement Programs

Because deterrence depends on the perceived rather than the actual probability of being arrested, it is generally accepted that enforcement programs must be well publicized to be effective. General safety publicity without a related enforcement program is usually ineffective in reducing crashes. For example, publicizing general safety messages, such as *If You Drink Don't Drive*, without an associated law or enforcement effort have generally failed to demonstrate an effect on a highway safety measure (Wilde, Hoste, Sheppard, & Wind, 1971). However, Ross (1973) and Voas and Hause (1987) documented crash reductions produced by publicity in advance of program application, such as a new law (Ross) or enforcement effort (Voas and Hause). Sometimes, an enforcement program by itself produces enough public visibility and media attention to make the public aware of the program without a special media program (e.g., Voas, 2008; Voas & Hause, 1987). Aside from free media provided by the press because of an ongoing enforcement effort, three types of information campaigns help educate the public on impaired driving laws and enforcement: (a) public service announcements (PSAs), (b) paid media campaigns, and (c) media advocacy programs. Each program has its strengths and limitations. Few media campaigns of any type have been adequately evaluated.

PUBLIC SERVICE ANNOUNCEMENTS

PSAs, which local television stations must air as a part of their continued licensing requirements from the Federal Communications Commission in the United States, have been a major method for warning the public about the danger of impaired driving and for promoting safety behaviors, such as the *Friends Don't Let Friends Drive Drunk* campaign. Because PSAs are usually funded by the communications industry, they are attractive, high-quality products based on standard industry focus group research procedures. Although local TV stations provide free airtime, they are likely to air the PSAs during nonprime time when other paying advertisements are not being aired (e.g., late-night or early-morning hours). Studies have indicated that PSAs can familiarize the public with safety slogans, but no studies have demonstrated a reduction in impaired driving or risky drinking based on a program of PSAs (Holder & Treno, 1997). Giesbrecht and Grube (2003) reviewed research on the effects of media designed to reduce alcohol use or its related problems. They cited only a single study of the effects of PSAs about drinking during pregnancy that showed an increased awareness of the dangers of drinking while pregnant.

PAID MEDIA CAMPAIGNS

In relation to alcohol safety, paid media campaigns have been used most frequently in national, annual *Click It or Ticket* campaigns to increase the use of safety belts or campaigns directed at impaired driving during holidays, such as Labor Day and Christmas, when many local police departments receive funding to implement special enforcement efforts (Tison et al., 2008). Holder and Treno (1997) concluded that planned mass media campaigns are most effective as reinforcers of efforts to reduce high-risk drinking in general and drunk driving in particular. Mass media efforts alone are insufficient, however. Friend and Levy (2002) conducted a comprehensive review of mass media campaigns on tobacco. Results suggested that well-funded and implemented mass media campaigns targeted at smokers, with a comprehensive tobacco control program, were associated with reduced smoking rates among both adults and youths. Similar strong effects of paid media on impaired driving remain to be demonstrated.

MEDIA ADVOCACY

Media advocacy refers to the strategic use of news media by those seeking to advance a social or public policy initiative. Unlike specifically designed public information campaigns, media advocacy works directly with the local news outlets (radio, television, newspapers, and magazines) to increase local news attention to a specific public health problem or program. Media advocacy encompasses a range of strategies aimed at reframing public debate of issues (Wallack, Dorfman, Jernigan, & Themba, 1993; Wallack, Grube, Madden, & Breed, 1990). In this context, mass media can bring attention to a specific alcohol problem, advance the importance of one or more specific policies to reduce the problem, put pressure on decision makers who can make new policies or change existing policies, and

help organize a community effort to bring about a desired policy change.

Media advocacy generally does not target offenders or potential offenders; rather, it appeals to community members to support local agencies (e.g., the police and city council) that support enforcement and educational efforts. As such, media advocacy is a major component of the community programs described hereafter. Media advocacy involves carefully planned news events that attract press attention and cover an important community issue, program, or organization. Such events are usually based on research data that have uncovered an important problem for the community, such as a growing number of teenage fatalities in alcohol-related crashes. A community leader reports the information in a TV interview or at a press conference. The message projected is that local citizens have a problem in their community that requires attention and about which local leaders are concerned. This local relevance of the message is an important feature that differentiates media advocacy programs from national mass media efforts, which avoid being community specific so they can be used broadly throughout the country (Treno & Holder, 1997).

Community Alcohol Safety Programs

Although national laws and publicity programs have an important influence on impaired driving, DUI enforcement is primarily an activity of local police departments, which are generally overburdened with broad responsibilities for law enforcement. Consequently, drinking and driving may receive relatively low priority among the department's activities. Maintaining a sufficient level of enforcement activity to create strong deterrence to impaired driving requires support from the local government and community residents. Moreover, publicizing enforcement activities requires support from the local news media. Thus, effective DUI enforcement involves a complex community system (Holder, Saltz, Treno, Grube, & Voas, 1997; Voas, Lange, & Treno, 1997). An effective system creates and maintains the public's concern with the impaired driving problem and supports the police programs directed at reducing impaired driving.

This recognition of the community as the locus of impaired driving prevention has led to broad support by federal agencies (such as NHTSA and NIAAA) and private foundations (such as the Robert Wood Johnson Foundation) for alcohol problem reduction programs in communities.

Relatively few of the many community alcohol and other drugs (AOD) reduction efforts have been adequately evaluated. Four comprehensive programs directed at drinking and drinking-driving within the community have received relatively extensive evaluations: the *Saving Lives Program* (Hingson et al., 1996), the *Communities Mobilizing for Change Program* (Wagenaar et al., 2000*a*; Wagenaar, Murray, & Toomey, 2000*b*), the *Community Trials Program* (Holder et al., 2000), and the *Fighting Back Community Program* (Hingson et al., 2005*a*). In addition, three community efforts in specialized settings have been evaluated, two of which relate to community/college campus programs—the *Matter of Degree Program* (Nelson, Weitzman, & Wechsler, 2005) and the *College Community Environmental Prevention Program* (Clapp, Johnson, Voas, & Lange, 2005)—and a third related to a border community, *Operation Safe Crossing* (Voas et al., 2002*b*).

The Communities Mobilizing for Change Program (Wagenaar et al., 2000*a*) was directed at changing the liquor sales environment to reduce underage drinking and impaired driving by enforcing MLDA laws prohibiting sales to those aged 20 and younger. Fifteen communities were randomly assigned to the intervention or control condition for 2.5 years. The treated communities, compared with the untreated communities, demonstrated reduced sales to underage youth, as well as reduced alcohol consumption and DUI arrests among 15- to 20-year-olds.

The Community Trials Program (Holder et al., 2000) was a multifaceted environmental program designed to reduce alcohol-involved injuries and fatalities among all age groups. The program, which was implemented in three communities (with three comparison sites), featured five mutually reinforcing environmental strategies: (a) community mobilization, (b) responsible beverage service, (c) drinking-and-driving enforcement, (d) underage drinking enforcement, and (e) limiting alcohol access. This national community prevention trial presented clear evidence that the use of local environmental strategies not only reduced alcohol-involved traffic crashes, but also reduced the violence associated with alcohol. Heavy drinking was reduced by 13%, alcohol-related assaults appearing in emergency rooms were reduced by 43%, nighttime injuries from crashes were reduced by 10%, and DUI crashes were reduced by 6% (Holder et al., 1998; 2000). In the treated communities, self-reported driving after drinking too much decreased significantly.

The Saving Lives Project (Hingson et al., 1996), conducted in six communities in Massachusetts, was designed to reduce alcohol-impaired driving and related problems (such as speeding, red-light running, and low safety belt use) by applying a broad range of traditional traffic safety program activities. The activities involved media campaigns, business information programs, speeding and drinking-driving awareness days, speed-watch telephone hotlines, police training, high school peer-led education, Students Against Destructive Decisions chapters, college prevention programs, and a host of other activities. Results of the evaluation indicated that, during its 5 years in operation, cities with the Saving Lives intervention had a 25% greater decline in fatal crashes than cities in the rest of Massachusetts.

The Fighting Back Community Program awarded grants to 12 communities from 1992 to 1997. Five of the 12 communities that displayed the most concentrated effort to expand substance abuse treatment and reduce alcohol availability were selected for evaluation by Hingson et al. (2005*a*). Sites established consortiums to conduct problem assessments and develop programs to reduce alcohol availability and increase substance abuse treatment. The programs supported both individually oriented traditional treatment programs and environmental initiatives to reduce alcohol availability. The results indicated that the Fighting Back communities experienced a 22% lower ratio of drinking drivers (BAC > .00) in fatal crashes than the control communities.

The Matter of Degree Program (Nelson et al., 2005) was directed at changing the student drinking environment by bringing together "key stakeholders" in the university and in the surrounding community to implement a variety of programs, including RBS training, keg registration, parental notification of alcohol-related offenses, increased supervision of Greek organization-sponsored social events, substance-free residence halls, and increased alcohol-free campus activities. Self-reported drinking and drinking-driving data were collected from 1997 to 2001 through student telephone surveys at 10 program sites. No significant reductions in driving after drinking were obtained.

Operation Safe Crossing (Voas et al., 2002*b*) involved the organization of a community coalition to reduce cross-border binge drinking in Mexico by young Americans. The coalition (a) used media advocacy to support the planned increased enforcement efforts at the border and in the Tijuana bars, (b) pressured bar owners to train staff on RBS strategies, (c) educated the public on the risks of cross-border binge drinking, and (d) supported college and military efforts to limit underage-targeted advertising of cross-border bars on campuses and military bases (Baker, 1997; Lange, Lauer, & Voas, 1999). This environmental strategy led to three significant outcomes: (a) a 31.6% reduction in late-night weekend border crossers, (b) a 39.8% reduction in underage pedestrian crossers who were legally intoxicated (BAC > .08), and (c) a 45% reduction in the number of 16- to 20-year-old drivers in alcohol-related crashes (Voas et al., 2002b).

The College Community Environmental Prevention Program (Clapp et al., 2005) was derived from the community trials model (Clapp, Segars, & Voas, 2002) and applied to a college campus. During the program, five interventions were implemented: (a) a reduction in alcohol promotion, (b) a social norms program designed to correct misperceptions regarding student drinking, (c) a DUI enforcement program, (d) a retail sales-and-availability program to train owners and servers of outlets catering to students, and (e) a program to discourage students from crossing into Mexico to binge drink. Reported drinking and driving was significantly reduced at the program campus relative to the control campus (Clapp et al., 2005; 2003b).

Summary of Secondary Prevention

In the 15 years between 1980 and 1995, several effective laws and programs—particularly the .08 illegal per se laws, administrative license revocation laws, and graduated licensing laws—were developed and implemented to deter impaired driving. Effective enforcement methods were also implemented: checkpoints, saturation patrols, SFSTs, and better enforcement tools (e.g., preliminary and evidential breath testers and passive sensors). During those 15 years, alcohol-related crashes declined substantially, partially reflecting the application of new laws and technologies (e.g., Fell et al., 2008a; Tippetts, Voas, Fell, & Nichols, 2005). However, little progress was made in the following decade to reduce impaired driving crashes (Sweedler et al., 2004), perhaps partially because DUI enforcement and criminal justice procedures in the United States are more constrained than in other industrialized nations that use random breath testing.

Tertiary Prevention Area

This section covers programs directed at individuals who continue to drive after drinking, that is, impaired drivers. It reviews issues involving the criminal justice system related to the prosecution and conviction of arrested DUI suspects and the effectiveness of traditional sanctions—fines, jail, license suspension, and probation—in reducing recidivism and alcohol-related crashes. It includes methods for screening individuals to determine the treatment and types of intervention programs most typically applied to DUI offenders. Also included are actions against the DUI offender's vehicle to prevent impaired driving. The chapter concludes with a description of developing technological approaches to monitoring DUI offenders to prevent their driving while impaired.

Background

The role of sanctions in the criminal justice system was most clearly described by Ross (1982a, p. 7). He identified retribution, incapacitation, and rehabilitation as the principal functions of simple deterrence. Voas (1999) provided a set of functions based specifically on drinking-driving laws. He suggested that the three functions of sanctions for DUI offenses involved the "three Rs"—Restriction, Rehabilitation, and Restitution. Restriction prevents future impaired driving through incapacitation. Rehabilitation focuses on treatment to support recovery of the offenders from their drinking problems. Restitution, generally fees or fines, means the DUI offender contributes to the support of the criminal justice system so that it is, at least partially, self-supporting (McKnight & Voas, 1982). Although funding enforcement and court expenses through restitution remains a goal of the DUI sanctioning system, the two primary objectives of the sanctions for impaired driving offenders are (a) to restrict their driving to protect the public and (b) to ensure they have assistance in overcoming their demonstrated inability to control their drinking. (Voas & Fisher, 2001, p. 33).

Restriction of the offender's driving is achieved through incapacitation for some specified period by creating a barrier to impaired driving. Logically, three possibilities are available: (a) prevent drinking, (b) prevent driving, or (c) prevent the combination of drinking followed by driving. Until recently, prevention of drinking has taken the form of supervision through intensive probation with regular chemical tests and surprise home inspections with breath tests or, infrequently, the use of mandatory Antabuse™ (disulfiram). Due to the high cost of intensive probation programs, electronic monitoring of BAC tests with home confinement systems has been widely used to ensure abstinence. New technological advances in continuous monitoring of the BAC from the surface of the skin show promise for monitoring abstinence 24/7 (Marques & McKnight, 2007).

Traditionally, prevention of driving by DUI offenders has been achieved through suspension of the driver's license. Jail also provides a method of denying access to a vehicle but is rarely imposed for a sufficient time span to have a significant effect on driving exposure (Voas & Fisher, 2001, p. 33). In the past decade, interest has increased in the separation of offenders from their vehicles through impoundment, immobilization, or forfeiture (Voas & DeYoung, 2002; Voas et al., 2008b).

Finally, over the past two decades, a technology for separating offender drinking from driving through vehicle alcohol interlocks has evolved so that it now prevents an offender from driving while impaired by requiring a breath test when starting the vehicle (Beirness & Marques, 2004).

Programs related to the second primary objective of sanction programs—to promote recovery—fall into three broad classes. The first is 10–12 hours of educational classes covering drinking and drinking-driving facts with the development of an action plan to avoid future DUI problems (Rider, Voas, Kelley-Baker, Grosz, & Murphy, 2007; Stewart & Malfetti, 1970). Second are the brief intervention programs with criminal justice processing (Lapham, 2004/2005). Third are the treatment programs involving one-on-one or group therapy, generally lasting 3–6 months, designed to deal with the underlying drinking problem and associated comorbidities (Dill & Wells-Parker, 2006).

Prosecution of DUI Offenders

The complexities of state DUI laws and the US criminal justice system have presented a significant impediment to the efficient handling of DUI offenders (Voas & Fisher, 2001). NHTSA and NIAAA have jointly issued *A Guide to Sentencing DUI Offenders* (2nd edition, 2006) to assist judges in sentencing DUI offenders. Robertson and Simpson (2002c) surveyed 390 prosecutors from 35 states to collect information on the problems encountered in the prosecution of DUI cases. They identified 10 problem areas, some of which were already discussed, such as complexity of state impaired driving laws and refusal of the breath test. They also reported that the prosecutors they surveyed estimated that 44% of defendants plead guilty, and, of those, 67%

negotiated an agreement that generally resulted in a reduced penalty. These agreements allow some offenders to plead to a non–alcohol-related offense, such as reckless driving, or allow some multiple offenders to plead to a first DUI offense. Such sanction reductions not only reduce the power of the court to apply control measures on the defendant, but also result in not recording the actual offense on the driver's record. Consequently, a subsequent offense will be treated at a lower level than if the original charge had appeared on the record (Voas & Fisher, 2001, p. 33).

Traditional Sanctions

DUI offenders have typically been subject to five traditional sanctions—jail, fines, licenses suspension, community service, and probation:

1. One problem in evaluating the utility of confinement in jail is that it potentially has both a general and specific deterrent effect, so it can be evaluated in two ways: by its overall effect on alcohol-related crashes and by its specific effect on the crashes of DUI offenders. Voas (1986) reviewed studies of the deterrent effect of jail sentences and concluded that they did not reduce recidivism following release from jail. Wagenaar, Zobeck, Hingson, and Williams (1995) and Zobeck and Williams (1994) reviewed 87 evaluation studies of laws providing mandatory jail and minimum fines covering 30 years from 1960 to 1991 and found only limited evidence for the effectiveness of those sanctions.

2. Like jail, fines can play a role in both general and specific deterrence. Wagenaar et al. (2007) recently produced some evidence that fines may affect alcohol-related crashes. They studied 26 states that implemented minimum fine policies between 1976 and 2002 and reported that six of those states demonstrated a significant reduction in single-vehicle nighttime fatal crashes. In four of those six states, however, the increase in fines was implemented simultaneously with other important DUI laws, so the changes could not be attributed solely to the increased fines.

3. License suspension, an effective specific deterrent, reduces the recidivism and crash involvement of DUI offenders because it decreases, but does not eliminate, their driving exposure (Coppin & Oldenbeek, 1965; McKnight & Voas, 1991; Peck, 1991; Peck, Sadler, & Perrine, 1985; Williams, Hagen, & McConnell, 1984). Unfortunately, up to 83% of suspended DUI offenders continue to drive illicitly somewhat (McCartt, Geary,

& Nissen, 2002; Ross & Gonzales, 1988). Suspended and revoked offenders who continue to drive are high-risk road users. Peck and Helander (2001) calculated that drivers with one or more DUI offenses were 1.7 more likely than the average driver to be in a crash in the next 3 years but were 14 times more likely to be in an alcohol-related crash. Hedlund and Fell (1995) reported that DUI offenders were 4.1 times more likely than the average driver to be the drinking driver in a fatal alcohol-related crash. Based on data from the FARS, suspended drivers account for 7.4% of all drivers in fatal crashes (Griffin III & DeLaZerda, 2000).

4. Community service programs in which offenders perform unpaid work for community organizations have been used primarily as a substitute for incarceration when jails are overcrowded or for indigent offenders who cannot pay fines. Their effect on recidivism and crash involvement is unknown (Voas & Fisher, 2001).

5. Probation can vary substantially in the severity of the restriction applied to the DUI offender. For most first offenders, it is a formality involving two meetings with a probation officer: one at the beginning of the probation period to receive assignments to sanction programs and one at the end of the probation period to ensure all the court requirements have been fulfilled. Recently, however, there has been increasing interest in sanctions (such as interlock programs and DUI/drug court programs discussed hereafter) that require closer monitoring of the offender and increased contact between the probation officer and the offender.

Overview of Court-Mandated Treatment/ Education Programs

The general model for court-mandated treatment programs in the United States grew out of the federal ASAP initiated in the early 1970s (Nichols, Weinstein, Ellingstad, & Struckman-Johnson, 1978; Voas & Fisher, 2001). The model recognizes two levels of alcohol involvement among drivers arrested for DUI: "problem drinkers" for whom drinking is at least partially out of their control and "social drinkers" who lack the necessary knowledge or motivation to separate drinking from driving. The model uses brief tests, interviews, and driving records to separate offenders into two groups: problem or social drinkers. Problem drinkers are assigned to group or individual therapy programs, generally requiring weekly sessions for 3–6 months, whereas social drinkers are assigned to 12-hour educational programs conducted in four weekly 3-hour sessions.

DUI OFFENDER SCREENING

Treatment programs determine the underlying problems that led to the impaired driving behavior so that the most effective remedies can be applied. Screening is the frontline triage system normally used in DUI prosecutions by court presentence investigators to determine at the time of sentencing whether offenders should be assigned to a brief educational program or to a more intensive treatment program. The specific treatment needs of each offender are then assessed at the treatment agency.

Most states mandate screening of DUI offenders to determine their need for treatment (Chang, Gregory, & Lapham, 2002). Federal guidelines for sentencing DUI offenders recommend that all offenders be screened for alcohol- and drug-use problems and recidivism risk (NHTSA, 2005). Screening instruments number in the hundreds; the major ones are documented in *Assessing Alcohol Problems: A Guide for Clinicians and Researchers* (Allen & Wilson, 2003). The challenges of screening in the court adjudication process have recently been summarized by Lapham (2004/2005) and Chang et al. (2002). Lapham notes that the coercive nature of the court process may motivate offenders to resist the process by understating their drinking symptoms, both to minimize the length and the intensity of the treatment to which they will be mandated and to avoid the costs of lengthier, more intense treatment. She suggests that well-trained interviewers are required to deal with this problem; however, many, if not most, courts cannot afford highly skilled staff (Knight et al., 2002, in Lapham, 2004/2005). Lacey, Jones, and Wiliszowski (1999) and Chang et al. (2002) have reviewed the available instruments and identified those that appear to be the most useful with criminal justice offenders. Given the relatively poor sensitivity and specificity of current measures, they suggest additional development and evaluation of predictive instruments, with particular attention paid to those instruments that are currently widely used but inadequately tested. They note that other more objective measures that may be useful adjuncts to screening include the use of collateral interviews in addition to self-report measures, routine breath-alcohol testing at screening appointments, and the requirement that offenders submit to biochemical tests to identify excessive or illegal alcohol or drug use.

Once assigned to treatment, the diagnostic process begun within the court setting is extended to a more in-depth assessment involving an intensive, systematic collection and analysis of data to inform the treatment staff of the special needs of the client. The assessment is designed to uncover alcohol dependency or abuse problems, as well as problems with substances other than alcohol and psychiatric comorbidities that will require attention as part of the recovery treatment. Many DUI offenders have co-occurring disorders, most commonly other drug abuse or dependence, depression, post-traumatic stress disorder, and antisocial personality disorder (Cavaiola & Wuth, 2002; Lapham, C'de Baca, McMillan, & Hunt, 2004). An assessment should reveal the intensity and length of treatment required for recovery; however, treatment lengths are usually set by legislation and limited because the offender must bear the cost. Although courts generally rely on treatment providers to report on the offender's satisfactory completion of the program, inflexible treatment lengths may limit the effectiveness of the programs.

OFFENDER TREATMENT

Although license suspension is the most effective single DUI sanction, recent evaluation studies have found remedial interventions (treatment and educational programs) to be more effective than traditional punitive sanctions, such as jail terms and fines when combined with license restriction, for reducing recidivism and alcohol-related crashes (DeYoung, 1997a; Green, French, Haberman, & Holland, 1991; Jones & Lacey, 1998; Jones, Wiliszowski, & Lacey, 1996; Kunitz et al., 2002; Martell, Stewart, & Jamburajan, 1998; Nochajski, Miller, Wieczorek, & Whitney, 1993; Tashima & Helander, 2000). Wells-Parker et al. (1995) conducted a meta-analysis of 215 evaluations of drink-driving remediation (treatment) programs. They concluded that the best designed studies indicated that treatment can produce an additional 7–9% reduction in drinking-driving recidivism and alcohol-related crashes when compared with control groups that largely received license restrictions only (sometimes more severe than for the treatment groups). The 7–9% reduction in recidivism may be conservative because several of the less well-designed studies produced larger reductions. Wells-Parker and Williams (2002), commenting on their review of court-mandated treatment, noted that, "In general, research has consistently shown that treatment has a modest effect on reducing drinking-driving and alcohol-impaired crashes among offenders who

are mandated to attend and who actually receive the intervention." Dill and Wells-Parker (2006), in their review of mandated treatment for DUI offenders, indicated that such programs have shown less effectiveness in reducing the severity of alcohol-related problems other than impaired driving. A notable exception, however, was the study by Mann et al. (1994): the offenders who received treatment had lower mortality rates compared with similar members of a comparison group.

POST-TREATMENT PROGRAMS

Relapse is a major problem in the treatment of addictions, and most therapeutic programs have made provisions for some continued support for clients following the treatment program. Traditionally, this may involve a continuing outpatient program and/or efforts to enroll the client in a self-help support group in the community. Continued participation in such groups during post-treatment is associated with a lower relapse rate. Alcoholics Anonymous affiliation alone, absent collateral professional treatment, has not resulted in routinely improved outcomes (Emrick, Tonigan, Montgomery, & Little, 1993; Kownacki & Shadish, 1999; Wells-Parker et al., 1995). Court sanctioning of DUI offenders can provide an important system for supporting offenders following the completion of a treatment program. Most multiple offenders are placed on probation and usually must be abstinent during that period. Thus, they are subject to monitoring during and potentially following treatment, depending on the length of probation. This can both increase attendance at treatment and reduce relapses following treatment. Unfortunately, the probation staff does not usually have the resources to meet regularly with offenders, but, when they do, they can support recovery by monitoring drinking and by assisting the offender in dealing with driving, family, and employment problems.

EDUCATIONAL PROGRAMS

As noted, social drinkers among DUI offenders, whose screening results indicate that they do not have an alcohol use disorder (AUD) problem, are generally assigned to a short (8- to 10-hour) educational program (Voas & Fisher, 2001). These programs are usually modeled on the "DUI Phoenix" program developed by Stewart and Malfetti (1970). Results indicate that such programs may successfully increase intermediate goals, such as readiness to change, but have limited effect on DUI recidivism (Stewart & Ellingstad, 1989; Wells-Parker et al., 1995). Recently, however, Rider et al. (2007) tested a novel educational curriculum on 10,000 first DUI offenders that was based on motivating offenders to avoid driving to any drinking event rather than focusing on controlling drinking at the event. The results indicated that offenders exposed to the new curriculum experienced a 42% reduction (p = .019) in recidivism when compared with the traditional DUI Phoenix curriculum. Evidence for the effectiveness of DUI educational programs is very limited, however.

INTENSIVE SUPERVISION PROBATION

Offenders who receive probation from intensive supervision programs (ISPs) have more contact with probation officers, a judge, or other designated authorities compared to standard (nonintensive) probation programs. Furthermore, these offenders participate in various educational, vocational, and therapeutic programs in the community (Harding, 1989; Transportation Research Board, 1995). According to the American Probation and Parole Association (APPA), an "intensive" program should consist of a smaller caseload and possibly a specialized caseload for probation officers so they can spend adequate time supervising and monitoring offenders assigned to them, but this is not possible in every community. Research on DUI sanctions strongly suggests that extended contact with sanctioning agencies, such as that imposed by an ISP, is important to reducing DUI recidivism (Jones et al., 1996; Wiliszowski, Murphy, Jones, & Lacey, 1996). Offenders usually assigned to intensive supervised probation are nonviolent, repeat offenders (typically with two or more DUI convictions in the past) who have served some time in jail.

There are many variations of supervision and probation programs for DUI offenders. These programs include case-specific restrictions (e.g., individualized conditions to probation), unsupervised probation, basic supervision probation (e.g., regularly scheduled visits to probation services with varying frequency), and intensive supervision probation (which may involve many program components and close monitoring). Three ISPs were evaluated by Wiliszowski, Fell, McKnight, Tippetts, and Ciccel (2010): the Minnesota Staggered Sentencing Program, the Westchester County New York DUI Enforcement Program, and the Oregon Driving Under the Influence of Intoxicants (DUII) Intensive Supervision Program (DISP). The Minnesota program appeared to be successful in reducing offender recidivism in a relatively small ISP (n = 200 offenders in the program). Compared to a similar matched group of DUI offenders, the staggered sentencing offenders had a significant (30.6%) lower recidivism rate (p = .017) up to 4 years postoffense. The program prevented an estimated 15–23 rearrests for DUI. Compared to a matched group of offenders, the Westchester County program appeared to be effective in the short term (18.1% lower recidivism in 5 years postoffense [p < .001]) but not in the long term (only 5.4% [p = .171] lower recidivism in 15 years postoffense). This program resulted in an estimated 78 fewer rearrests for DUI in the first 5 years. The Oregon DISP intervention group had 54.1% lower recidivism up to 8 years post index offense than both of the stratified matched-sample comparison groups, adjusting for the demographic covariates (Wald statistic = 51.50; p > .001). The program prevented 67 rearrests for DUI in the first 8 years. The cost–benefit of ISPs appears to be very good for the prevention of rearrests.

DUI/DRUG COURTS

A popular movement for handling drug offenders has been the establishment of drug courts that provide a program in which the threat of jail is used to motivate treatment compliance. Offenders facing lengthy jail sentences (6–12 months) are offered the alternative of entering a drug court program involving an intensive regimen of substance abuse treatment, case management, drug testing, probation supervision, and consistent monitoring. They report to regularly scheduled meetings with the judge who has special expertise in the drug court model and the authority to revoke probation and send noncooperating offenders to jail or, alternatively, the authority to reduce the length of the jail sentence (Fox & Huddleston, 2003). In a critical review of 120 evaluations of numerous drug court programs, the National Center on Addiction and Substance Abuse at Columbia University concluded that drug courts lower recidivism, reduce drug use, and reduce both direct and indirect costs of investigating and adjudicating drug-related crimes (Belenko, 1998; 2001).

Based on the effectiveness of drug courts, DUI courts have been established to provide intensive supervision of offenders by judges and other court officials who closely monitor compliance with court-ordered sanctions coupled with treatment. DUI courts generally involve frequent interaction between the offender and the DUI court judge, intensive supervision by probation officers, an appropriate level of treatment, random alcohol and other drug testing, community service, life-style changes, positive reinforcement for successful performance in the program, and jail time for noncompliance. Mostly nonviolent offenders who have had two or more prior DUI convictions are assigned to a DUI court, if one exists in the jurisdiction (Freeman-Wilson & Wilkosz, 2002; Tauber & Huddleston, 1999). Several studies have reported favorable results for DUI/drug courts (Breckenridge, Winfree, Maupin, & Clason, 2000; Frank & Jones, 2004; Fuller, Carey, & Kissick, 2007; Guerin & Pitts, 2002); however, additional evaluation is required, particularly in the area of cost-effectiveness because of the heavy use of court resources. Three DUI courts in Georgia were recently evaluated qualitatively and quantitatively (Fell, Tippetts, & Ciccel, 2011). After 4 years of exposure, the evaluation showed that when the DUI court graduates were combined with the DUI court-terminated offenders (intent-to-treat group), the DUI court offenders had significantly lower recidivism rates: 38% lower than a contemporary group of offenders and 65% lower than a retrospective group of offenders. The DUI court intent-to-treat group had a significantly lower recidivism rate: 15% compared to 24% for a group of matched offenders from three similar counties in Georgia (contemporary group) and a 35% rate for matched offenders from the same counties as the DUI court who would have been eligible for the DUI court had it been in existence (retrospective group). Offenders who were terminated from the DUI courts for various reasons had a recidivism rate of 26%. The overall finding from this analysis greatly supported the DUI court concept for reducing recidivism. These reductions in recidivism rates ranged from 38% to 79%, depending on the comparison group used. The DUI court program prevented between 47 and 112 repeat DUI arrests over the 4-year period analyzed, for a substantial cost savings to the state in terms of jail confinement, treatment, and probation.

VICTIM IMPACT PANELS

A widely used DUI offender program—the victim impact panel (VIP)—is designed to increase the DUI offender's appreciation for the damage that impaired driving can cause. At the VIP, victims of impaired drivers describe their injuries and the problems they have experienced due to their involvement in an alcohol-related crash (Shinar & Compton, 1995). MADD chapters in the United States provide VIPs to an estimated 400,000 DUI offenders per year. The empirical evidence regarding the effectiveness of VIPs is mixed and inconclusive. Anecdotal reports indicated that DUI offenders are often moved by victims' stories and vow to reform their ways. Some empirical studies also support this assertion (Fors & Rojeck, 1999; Shinar & Compton, 1995). Other studies, however, contradict those findings. Polacsek et al. (2001); Wheeler, Rogers, Tonigan, and Woodall (2004); and C'de Baca, Lapham, Liang, and Skipper (2001) examined rearrest rates of 6,702 first and repeat offenders in New Mexico between 1989 and 1994 following referral to VIPs. Results showed that, after controlling for multiple risk factors, VIP referral was not statistically associated with recidivism for female or male first offenders.

Screening and Brief Interventions in Emergency Rooms

When all three levels of prevention—primary, secondary, and tertiary—fail, many drivers become involved in crashes and wind up in hospital emergency rooms or regional trauma centers. This provides an opportunity outside the criminal justice system for the private health care system to intervene with high-risk drivers. The trauma of being involved in a crash is viewed as providing a "teachable moment," when individuals may be open to undertaking a behavioral change that will reduce their risk of future crashes and injuries. Research suggests that 30–50% of injured, crash-involved drivers admitted to emergency departments or trauma centers have BAC levels higher than the illegal limit for driving (Cornwell et al., 1998; Maio, Waller, Blow, Hill, & Singer, 1997; NHTSA, 2002; Soderstrom, 2001). Some of these offenders may receive a treatment intervention because of a DUI arrest; however, many are not charged because they are taken to the hospital before police officers have an opportunity to examine them for impairment. Furthermore, hospital staff rarely notify the police when they receive a high-BAC driver. When screened for AUDs, an estimated 27% of injured patients admitted to the emergency department or a trauma center test positive for alcohol abuse or dependence, indicating a large number of people entering emergency rooms who are potential DUI offenders (Gentilello, Ebel, Wickizer, Salkever, & Rivara, 2005). Thus, emergency rooms and trauma centers have an important opportunity to intervene with high-risk individuals who need treatment for alcohol problems—problems that may well lead to impaired driving and alcohol-related crashes.

In 2006, NHTSA funded a comprehensive review of brief intervention programs, which has yet to be published. A typical finding was that brief interventions decrease alcohol use (Fleming et al., 2002; Gentilello et al., 1999), including excessive and binge-drinking occasions. Other alcohol-related problems and negative consequences also decreased following such interventions (Mello et al., 2005; Monti et al., 1999). Most importantly, brief interventions effectively improve consequences related to driving, such as moving traffic violations (Gentilello et al., 1999; Monti et al., 1999), drinking-driving violations (Gentilello et al., 1999; Monti et al., 1999; Schermer, Moyers, Miller, & Bloomfield, 2006), motor vehicle crash involvement (Runge, Garrison, Hall, Waller, & Shen, 2002), crash-sustained injuries (Fleming et al., 2002), and motor vehicle fatalities (Fleming et al., 2002). Schermer et al. (2006) demonstrated that one rearrest for DUI could be prevented for every 10 cases needing treatment who are treated. Other studies have also found that brief interventions reduce alcohol-related arrests (Fleming et al., 2002; Gentilello et al., 1999), as well as other types of arrests (Fleming et al., 2002) and general legal involvement (Fleming et al., 2002).

Controlling Impaired Driving by DUI Offenders

Motorists convicted of DUI offenses are high-risk drivers who present a risk to themselves and the public until their drinking-driving behavior is modified. The public needs protection from these high-risk drivers while they are receiving treatment. Although specific deterrence programs, such as the threat of more severe penalties for a repeat offense, play a role in discouraging impaired driving by DUI offenders, the most effective sanctions are those that involve incapacitation. Aside from the traditional license suspension sanction, several more recent laws and programs have been implemented that limit driving in order to reduce recidivism. These laws provide for seizing and impounding, immobilizing, or forfeiting the offender's vehicle, and programs for interlock-equipped vehicles prevent a drinking driver from starting a vehicle. The alternate approach of controlling or preventing drinking is the court programs that provide for monitoring abstinence through surprise breath or urine test programs, remote electronically monitored in-home tests, or sensors worn on the body. The status of each of these preventive approaches is briefly discussed in the following paragraphs.

VEHICLE SANCTION LAWS

Because of the large number of suspended DUI offenders driving illegally and the limited enforcement resources available to deal with the problem, many states have enacted legislation to limit their illicit driving by seizing vehicles owned by DUI offenders. Such policies fall into two broad categories: (a) programs that confiscate or impound the vehicle and (b) programs that confiscate the vehicle plates and vehicle registration and/or require special plates on the vehicles of DUI offenders. Impounding the vehicle has been shown to reduce recidivism while the vehicle is being held. Cancelling the vehicle registration and seizing the plates has been less studied (Voas, Tippetts, & Lange, 1997; Voas et al., 2008b).

None of these vehicle controls is foolproof; each can be circumvented if the offender drives another vehicle registered in someone else's name. Nevertheless, vehicle sanctions have a specific deterrent effect that reduces the recidivism of DUI offenders (DeYoung, 1997b; DeYoung, 2000; Beck, Rauch, Baker, & Williams, 1999; Voas & DeYoung, 2002; Voas, 1992; Voas & Tippetts, 1995; Voas, Tippetts, & Taylor, 1997; 1998; Voas et al., 2008b). Overall, existing studies suggest that impoundment is an effective method of reducing the recidivism of DUI and driving-while-suspended (DWS) offenders. For vehicle impoundment to be effective, the vehicle must be impounded when the offender is arrested, and a procedure must be devised to deal with nonoffender owners. Most offenders do not retrieve their vehicles; therefore, some localities will be liable for storage and towing expenses if the sale of the offenders' vehicles does not raise sufficient funds to cover the expenses (Peck & Voas, 2002; Voas & DeYoung, 2002). License plate forfeiture appears to have considerable promise but has received limited evaluation (Voas et al., 2008b).

MONITORING BAC

An alternative to controlling the driving of DUI offenders is to control their drinking (Voas, 2010). Judges frequently admonish offenders to remain abstinent while on probation, but unless a program exists that monitors the BAC, this action has little force other than allowing the judge to impose more severe penalties if the offender returns to court during the probation period. In the past, offender abstinence has been monitored in several ways. Some courts have implemented closely supervised Antabuse administration. Others have implemented intensive supervision programs in which probation officers make surprise visits to the homes of offenders and conduct breath tests. As noted, DUI/drug courts generally provide for intensive monitoring of abstinence. Such systems are labor intensive and expensive for the courts. In the past couple of decades, innovative technological methods for collecting BAC data have received considerable attention. One of these systems, using electronically supervised, home-confinement programs, has been used for some time. This program involves telephone-monitored electronic remote breath-test systems that allow frequent monitoring of the BAC level while the offender is at home. There is limited evidence, however, for the effectiveness of such programs (Jones et al., 1996).

The South Dakota 24/7 Sobriety Program is a sobriety monitoring program aimed toward repeat DUI offenders, first DUI offenders with very high BACs, and similar offenders who have had repeated convictions related to alcohol abuse. Offenders report to the sheriff's office twice a day (at about 7 a.m. and 7 p.m.) for alcohol breath testing. If the offenders have any positive BACs or they miss a scheduled test, they go to jail for 12–36 hours. South Dakota adopted legislation in 2007 that established the 24/7 program statewide. The program is now operating in 60 of the 66 counties in South Dakota. Depending on the circumstances, judges may also require these offenders to undergo treatment, attend VIPs, and/or perform a certain number of hours of community service. Some offenders (because of their working hours, the distance they must travel in rural counties, and other legitimate reasons) agree to wear a transdermal alcohol monitoring (TAM) ankle bracelet instead of the twice per day breath testing. The TAM system records any alcohol use via sweat vapor every 30 minutes. From February 2005 through December 2011, 20,483 offenders provided twice-a-day breath tests. Of the 4,390,000 breath tests administered, the pass rate has been 99.3%. Between 2007 and the end of 2011, there were 15,582 no-shows (0.4%) out of 3,547,099 tests. From November 2005 through December 2011, 3,659 offenders were on TAM (524,516 days monitored). There were 77.2% who were fully compliant (no drinking events detected; no tampering) while on the bracelet. There were 337 confirmed drinking events and 1,185 confirmed tampering events. In 2009, more than half (54.5%) of the offenders passed all of their breath tests. Of the 45.5% who had failures, 19% failed

one test, 12% failed two tests, 5% failed three tests, and 9% failed four or more tests.

According to the Mountain Plains Evaluation report (Loudenburg, Drube, & Leonardson, 2010), the DUI recidivism rates after 3 years for 24/7 first offenders (with BACs > .17 on arrest) was 14.3% compared to 14.8% for similar offenders not on 24/7 (no difference). However, there was a significant 74% reduction in recidivism after 3 years for DUI second offenders (13.7% for comparison offenders vs. 3.6% for the 24/7 offenders), a 44% reduction in recidivism for DUI third offenders (15.3% vs. 8.6%), and a 31% reduction in recidivism for DUI fourth offenders (15.5% vs. 10.7%). Although assumed to be a contributing factor, no direct association between the 24/7 program and reductions in impaired driving fatal crashes or crashes in general have been found to date. According to the 24/7 Program Coordinator, South Dakota's campaign to reduce fatal crashes has included numerous approaches: increased DUI patrols, sobriety checkpoints, and an extensive DUI public education and information program, in addition to the 24/7 Program.

The Rand Corporation conducted an independent evaluation of the South Dakota 24/7 program. Specific results have been published in the *American Journal of Public Health*. According to Kilmer, Nicosia, Heaton, and Midgette (2013), there was a 12% reduction in repeat DUI arrests and a 9% reduction in domestic violence arrests associated with the adoption of the 24/7 program.

More direct transdermal monitoring systems that are worn on the body and monitor the BAC level 24 hours a day/7 days a week are just beginning to be used by the judicial system (Swift, 2003). Two devices have been studied—the SCRAM™ ankle bracelet and the WrisTAS™, which is about the size of a large wrist watch. Introduced about 10 years ago, the SCRAM device is currently being used in 48 states and the District of Columbia (excluding Hawaii and Massachusetts) in the United States. The company that produces the SCRAM bracelet reports that it works with more than 200 service providers in more than 1,800 courts and agencies around the United States and that close to 250,000 offenders have been monitored to date. Thirty-four states have had more than 1,000 offenders on SCRAM, and eight states have had more than 10,000 offenders using SCRAM over the years. The SCRAM incorporates a system for detecting circumvention (Marques & McKnight, 2009). Although laboratory evidence indicates that SCRAM is reasonably accurate in detecting a significant BAC, no adequate evaluation of the SCRAM unit has been conducted with DUI offenders to determine its effectiveness in maintaining abstinence.

A method for monitoring drinking that is just emerging in the United States but is more widely used in Europe is to analyze the biomarkers in blood, urine, or hair that result from consumption of alcohol. Although alcohol is cleared relatively rapidly from the body, usually within 8–12 hours even after heavy drinking, alcohol biomarkers persist in circulation, in hair, and in urine long after alcohol levels have fallen to zero in the blood. These biomarkers provide a way to measure total consumption over an extended time span. Longer lasting blood markers reflecting alcohol use, such as urinary ethylglucuronide (EtG), offer a window of detection of 36 hours or more following drinking (Borucki et al., 2005; Helander & Beck, 2005; Wurst et al., 2003). These blood markers are currently being used in Europe to manage the drinking of offenders. Tests for such blood markers can be required on a regular schedule, with the probability that they will detect illicit drinking because they are present in the blood for an extended period following drinking. Hair EtG is being used in Germany as a relicensing criterion for participants in the driver's license restitution processes following conviction for impaired driving. To be eligible for reinstatement, a person's hair EtG level must be below 3 picograms/milligram, which is known to reflect abstinence.

VEHICLE IGNITION INTERLOCKS

The most parsimonious approach to the control of DUI offenders' impaired driving is the ignition interlock, which requires the driver to provide a breath sample when starting the car and at random times while driving. The units have four basic elements: (1) a breath-alcohol sensor that records the driver's BAC level and can be set to provide a warning if any alcohol is detected and that will prevent starting the vehicle if the BAC is .03 or higher; (2) a rolling retest system that requires a new breath test every few minutes while driving to prevent someone else from starting the vehicle for a person who has been drinking; (3) a tamper-proof system for mounting the unit in the vehicle that is inspected every 30–60 days; and (4) a data logging system that records both the BAC tests and engine operation, thus ensuring that the offender is actually using the vehicle and not simply parking it while driving another vehicle. In 1992, NHTSA issued "Model Specifications for Breath Alcohol Ignition Interlock Devices" (Voas & Marques, 1992) that recommended standards for sensitivity and reliability and provided for the incorporation of rolling retests and data recording systems on ignition interlocks to make circumvention difficult. State-licensed service providers install the unit, inspect it regularly (generally, every 30–60 days), and provide a report on any attempt to circumvent the device to a court probation officer or a driver analyst at the department of motor vehicles. Such monitoring systems, with substantial consequences for tampering with the device, are essential for ensuring that offenders cannot drive the interlock-equipped vehicle while impaired. There is strong evidence that the recidivism of DUI offenders is substantially reduced while interlocks are on their vehicles (Coben & Larkin, 1999; Elder et al., 2011; Voas, Marques, Tippetts, & Beirness, 1999b; Willis, Lybrand, & Bellamy, 2004). This is true of both first and multiple offenders (Roth, Voas, & Marques, 2007), opening the possibility that a mandatory interlock program could have general deterrent effect on the public as a whole, as well as a specific deterrent effect on DUI offenders. The offenders who have installed interlocks have 36–90% lower DUI recidivism rates while the interlock is on their vehicles than do similar DUI offenders who remain suspended. Once the interlock is removed, however, their recidivism rate does not differ from fully suspended offenders.

Initially, the courts or the department of motor vehicles offered the interlock to suspended offenders as an option for driving legally for a portion of their suspension period. Several studies of such optional programs in West Virginia (Tippetts & Voas, 1998); California (DeYoung, Tashima, & Maston, 2005); Alberta, Canada (Voas et al., 1999b); and Quebec, Canada (Vézina, 2002) revealed that only about 10% of the eligible offenders installed an interlock.

The low penetration of optional interlock programs has led states to enact laws requiring judges to mandate the offender to install an interlock. To date, laws mandating interlocks have, with some exceptions (Marques, Voas, Roth, & Tippetts, 2008), not been markedly more successful in motivating offenders to install interlocks (Voas & Marques, 2003). The reasons for this are not entirely clear. Most interlock legislation exempts offenders who can prove they do not own a vehicle or who agree not to drive. Some courts are not well informed about the mandatory legislation, and some have no local interlock providers. Courts have also found the cost of the interlock program to be a barrier for low-income offenders, even though most interlock providers will reduce the price of the program for indigent offenders. There is evidence, however, from studies in Indiana (Voas, Blackman, Tippetts, & Marques, 2002*a*) and New Mexico (Voas et al., 2008*b*) that a larger proportion of DUI offenders can be pressured into installing units if the alternative is more unpleasant, such as electronically monitored house arrest. Thus, it appears that increasing the proportion of DUI offenders in interlock programs will require states to pass legislation that requires DUI offenders to accept a less desirable alternative if they reject the interlock. An alternative method of coercing the installation of an interlock is to make it a requirement for reinstatement of the driver's license for DUI offenders who have had their licenses suspended. Two studies of this procedure found that it successfully ensures that all offenders whose licenses are restored do install interlocks for a specified period; only half of all drivers convicted of DUI apply for reinstatement so that they remain fully suspended but potentially drive illicitly (Voas, Tippetts, Fisher, & Grosz, 2010, Voas, Tippetts, & Grosz, 2013). The interlock data recorder also provides important information for predicting future recidivism (Marques, Tippetts, & Voas, 2003*a*; 2003*b*; Marques, Voas, & Tippetts, 2003), particularly when combined with the prior record of the offender. This opens up the possibility that, rather than assigning interlock requirements for fixed periods, the offender would be required to have the interlock on the motor vehicle for a period determined by the interlock breath-test record. For example, offenders might be required to maintain the interlock on the vehicle until they have driven for 6 months without recording a positive breath test. Therapists can use the status of the interlock BAC record to assist them in determining how long DUI offenders should remain in treatment. The interlock record of all breath tests associated with driving can provide the treatment specialist with important information for use in evaluating the status of participating offenders, and the information can also be used in therapy sessions to help the offenders confront their drinking problems (Beirness, Marques, Voas, & Tippetts, 2003; Marques & Voas, 1995). Timken and Marques (2001*a*; 2001*b*) developed a *Support for Interlock Program* (SIP) that uses the data from the interlock recorder in therapy sessions for DUI offenders. A preliminary test of the SIP program was conducted and evaluated in Texas (Marques, Voas, & Timken, 2004; Marques, Voas, Timken, & Field, 2004).

Participants in the SIP program demonstrated large decreases in self-reported drinking and driving.

Summary of Tertiary Prevention Program Opportunities

Although convicted drinking drivers represent only 1% of the driving population, they are up to 14 times more likely to be in an alcohol-related crash. Thus, their apprehension and conviction, which brings them under the authority of the court system, provides an important opportunity to conduct interventions that can prevent them from driving impaired while participating in treatment that will assist with their recovery from the AUD that led to the impaired driving. The major laws and programs that appear to be effective in reducing impaired driving by DUI offenders include license suspension (even though offenders continue to drive, they drive less and more carefully), vehicle impoundment (while the vehicle is held), and vehicle interlocks (while the devices are on the offenders' vehicles). BAC monitoring systems, which ensure abstinence, also appear to be effective in preventing impaired driving, but these systems have not been adequately tested.

Treatment programs have been demonstrated to promote recovery from AUDs and to increase the effectiveness of traditional DUI sanctions in reducing recidivism. Particularly promising are DUI court programs that combine treatment with close monitoring of the offenders' drinking. These programs are expensive, however, and relatively few offenders are currently in such programs. A general limitation in court-mandated treatment programs is that many offenders avoid the requirement through plea bargains or failure to complete the programs.

Conclusion

Unfortunately, there is no silver bullet to eliminate alcohol-related crashes. Research and evaluation studies over the past 40 years have produced many effective programs to reduce high-risk drinking and the frequency of combining heavy drinking with driving, thus preventing identified impaired drivers from endangering other road users and assisting DUI offenders to overcome their drinking problem. For the most part, the legislation required for implementation of the most effective of those programs is in place; however, resources for enforcing the laws have been limited. Consequently, alcohol continues to play a role in nearly a third of all fatal crashes. Unless public concern about impaired driving results in a willingness to support increased enforcement of laws relating to alcohol sales and service and DUI, it is likely that future progress will primarily result from technological advances in monitoring DUI offenders.

Future Directions

The programs and policies that appear to provide the greatest opportunities for preventing alcohol-related crashes in the future are listed in the following paragraphs.

Opportunities in Primary Prevention

• *Strengthen enforcement of MLDA.* There is clear evidence that the MLDA law reduces alcohol-related crashes involving underage drivers. Although there are effective measures for enforcing the MLDA law, they are not widely and consistently used. Increased enforcement is needed.

• *Strengthen enforcement of service to obviously intoxicated.* Bars are a major source of impaired drivers. Laws making it illegal to serve obviously intoxicated patrons are poorly enforced. Research suggests that refusal of service can be greatly increased through increased enforcement. This opportunity to reduce the number of impaired drivers on the road should be exploited.

Opportunities in Secondary Prevention

• *Increase use of low-staff checkpoints.* Sobriety checkpoints, when well-publicized, are highly effective in reducing alcohol-related crashes but are underused because of staffing requirements. Research has shown that checkpoints with a smaller number of officers can be equally successful, particularly if the officers use passive sensors to detect drinking. Low-staff checkpoints equipped with passive sensors should be implemented each week in most communities.

• *Legalize use of PBTs.* Checking motorists at the roadside with PBTs, as is done in most industrialized countries, would greatly increase the efficiency of DUI enforcement while protecting the public against false arrest. In the United States, officers must have reason to believe that the driver was drinking before they can ask for a breath test. The Supreme Court ruled in *Spits v. Michigan* (Supreme Court of the US, 1990) that an exception to the Fourth Amendment of the US Constitution could be made to allow random stops at sobriety checkpoints because of the serious problem presented by impaired driving. The court has not been asked to rule on the use of PBTs. A ruling similar to that of *Spitz v. Michigan* would permit officers to use the same technological tools as most of the industrialized world.

• *Increase the number of community alcohol safety programs.* To enforce effectively the DUI laws, police departments need the support of an active alcohol safety activist group, such as MADD. Local community groups can assist in publicizing enforcement programs and support programs to reduce underage drinking through increased enforcement of MLDA laws and laws against service to the obviously intoxicated. Community programs have been effective in reducing alcohol-related crashes.

• *Reduce the illegal BAC to .05.* Fell and Voas (2006*b*) summarized the arguments for lowering the current illegal per se BAC to .05, a proposal endorsed recently by the National Transportation Safety Board (NTSB, 2013) and in 1999 by the American Medical Association. It is the limit most common in the world, with more than 100 countries using .05 BAC or lower for driving. At a .05 BAC, virtually all drivers are impaired in some driving performance measures. The risk of being involved in a crash increases significantly at .05 BAC and above. The relative risk of being killed in a single-vehicle crash with BACs of .05–.079 is 7–21 times higher than for drivers with a .00 BAC. Lowering the BAC limit from .08 to .05 has been a proven effective countermeasure in numerous countries around the world. Most Americans do not believe a person should drive after having two or three drinks in 2 hours. It takes at least four drinks for the average 170-pound male to exceed .05 BAC in 2 hours (three drinks for a 137-pound female). Most industrialized nations have established a .05 BAC limit or lower for driving. Progress in reducing impaired driving has stalled over the past 15 years. Lowering the BAC limit for driving from the current .08 to .05 could serve as a general deterrent to all those who drink and drive in the United States.

Opportunities in Tertiary Prevention

• *Interlock alternative programs.* Ignition interlocks are highly effective in reducing offender recidivism, but only a small portion of eligible DUI offenders can be motivated to install them. An alternative to the interlock program is needed for those offenders without cars or who are willing to take the risk of driving illicitly rather than installing the interlock because experience shows that offenders do continue to drive and become involved in crashes. Monitoring offenders' BACs appears to be an effective alternative to the interlock. On the horizon is a developing technology that detects driving via an ankle bracelet with accelerometers that measure the foot movements required to operate a vehicle. When perfected, this will allow the court to monitor offenders to ensure they are not driving. This could be offered as an alternative to the interlock. Programs need to be created that require electronically monitored abstinence or electronically monitored driving as alternatives to the interlock.

• *Coordinated interlock treatment programs.* The breath-test data recorded on the interlock unit provides important information for gauging recovery and predicting recidivism. Courts need to enlist treatment providers who can build recovery programs around the use of the interlock data-recorder information, similar to the SIP program implemented in Texas.

• *Silver bullet: cars that drunks can't drive.* A long-term development program was recently inaugurated by NHTSA, automobile manufacturers, and MADD to develop a system for all cars that can passively sense the BAC of the driver and prevent ignition of the vehicle's motor if the driver is over the BAC illegal limit. The program is called Driver Alcohol Detection System for Safety (DADSS) and is currently being funded by NHTSA and most of the motor vehicle manufacturers. If such a vehicle can be produced, it would finally fulfill the objective enunciated 40 years ago—to build "Cars that Drunks Can't Drive" (Voas, 1969). One of these monitors passively detects alcohol in the breath of the driver, making it unnecessary for the driver to blow into an interlock breath tube (Lambert et al., 2006). Another developing technology measures BAC passively through the skin, providing a substitute for blowing into the interlock (Ennis, 2006). These systems may have value as a method for activating a driver interlock system only when there is evidence of a drinking driver in the vehicle. Thus, the not-too-distant future offers the possibility of equipping all new vehicles with a system that would make impaired driving unlikely.

Acknowledgments

Work on this chapter was funded in part by NHTSA (Contract No. DTNH22-02-D-95121) and by NIAAA (Grant No. K05 AA014260). Harold Holder and Joel Grube of the Pacific Institute for Research and Evaluation provided substantial assistance in preparing the document.

This chapter is based on updated information described in two previous unpublished papers.

Birckmayer, J. D., Boothroyd, Renee I., Friend, K. B., Holder, Harold D., & Voas, Robert B. (2008). Prevention of Alcohol-Related Motor Vehicle Crashes: Logic Model Documentation Retrieved December 11, 2008, from http://www.pire.org/documents/Alc_rel_MV_crashes.doc

Voas, Robert B., & Lacey, J. (2011). *Alcohol and highway safety 2006: A review of the state of knowledge.* (Report No. DOT HS 811 374). Washington, DC: U.S. Department of Transportation, National Highway Traffic Safety Administration Retrieved from http://www.nhtsa.gov/staticfiles/nti/pdf/811374.pdf.

References

Adrian, M., Ferguson, B. S., & Her, M. (2001). Can alcohol price policies be used to reduce drunk driving? Evidence from Canada. *Substance Use and Misuse, 36*(13), 1923–1957.

Allen, J. P., & Wilson, V. (2003). *Assessing alcohol problems: A guide for researchers and clinicians* (2nd ed.). Washington, DC: National Institute on Alcohol Abuse and Alcoholism.

Anglin, L., Caverson, R., Fennel, R., Giesbrecht, N., & Mann, R. E. (1997). *A study of impaired drivers stopped by police in Sudbury, Ontario.* Toronto: Addiction Research Foundation.

Apsler, R., Char, A. R., Harding, W. M., & Klein, T. M. (1999). *The effects of .08 BAC laws.* Washington, DC: US Department of Transportation, National Highway Traffic Safety Administration.

Apsler, R., Harding, W., & Goldfein, J. (1987). *The review and assessment of designated driver programs as an alcohol countermeasure approach.* Washington, DC: US Department of Transportation, National Highway Traffic Administration.

Atkin, C. K. (1990). Effects of televised alcohol messages on teenage drinking patterns. *Journal of Adolescent Health Care, 11*(1), 10–24.

Babor, T., Caetano, R., Casswell, S., Edwards, G., Giesbrecht, N., Graham, K., Grube, J., Gruenewald, P., Hill, L., Holder, H., Homel, R., Osterberg, E., Rehm, J., Room, R., & Rossow, I. (2003). *Alcohol: No ordinary commodity—research and public policy.* New York: Oxford University Press.

Baker, J. (1997). US teen drinking in Tijuana. *Prevention File, 12*(3), 2–6.

Barnett, N. P., Monti, P. M., & Wood, M. D. (2001). Motivational interviewing for alcohol-involved adolescents in the emergency room. In *Innovations in adolescent substance abuse interventions.* Elsevier. Retrieved September, 2006, from http://www.elsevier.com/wps/find/bookdescription.cws_home/622189/descriptiondescription

Bartl, G., & Esberger, R. (2000). Effects of lowering the legal BAC limit in Austria. In H. Laurell & F. Schlyter (Eds.), *Proceedings of the 15th International Conference on Alcohol, Drugs and Traffic Safety—T'2000; May 22–26, 2000.* Stockholm, Sweden: International Council on Alcohol, Drugs and Traffic Safety (ICADTS).

Beck, K., Rauch, W., Baker, E., & Williams, A. (1999). Effects of ignition interlock license restrictions on drivers with multiple alcohol offenses: A random trial in Maryland. *American Journal of Public Health, 89*(11), 1696–1700.

Beirness, D., & Marques, P. (2004). Alcohol ignition interlock programs. *Traffic Injury Prevention, 5*(3), 299–308.

Beirness, D. J., Marques, P. R., Voas, R. B., & Tippetts, A. S. (2003). The impact of mandatory versus voluntary participation in the Alberta Ignition Interlock Program. *Traffic Injury Prevention, 4*(1), 24–27.

Beitel, G. A., Sharp, M. C., & Glauz, W. D. (2000). Probability of arrest while driving under the influence of alcohol. *Injury Prevention, 6*(2), 158–161.

Belenko, S. (1998). Research on drug courts: A critical review. *National Drug Court Institute Review, 1*(1), 1–42.

Belenko, S. (2001). Research on drug courts: A critical review. New York: The National Center on Addiction and Substance Abuse, Columbia University.

Bien, T. H., Miller, W. R., & Tonigan, J. S. (1993). Brief interventions for alcohol problems. A review. *Addiction, 88*(3), 315–336.

Birckmayer, J. D., Boothroyd, R. I., Friend, K. B., Holder, H. D., & Voas, R. B. (2008). Prevention of alcohol-related motor vehicle crashes: Logic model documentation. Calverton, MD: Pacific Institute for Research and Evaluation (PIRE). Retrieved December 11, 2008, from http://www.pire.org/documents/Alc_rel_MV_crashes.doc L:\ALMA\ENDNOTE\additions.enl

Birckmayer, J. D., Holder, H. D., Yacoubian, G. S., & Friend, K. B. (2004). A general causal model to guide alcohol, tobacco, and illicit drug prevention: Assessing the research evidence. *Journal of Drug Education, 34*(2), 121–153.

Blackman, K. O., Voas, R. B., Gullberg, R. G., & Tippetts, A. S. (2001). Enforcement of zero tolerance in the state of Washington—evidence from breath-test records. *Forensic Science Review, 13*(2), 77–86.

Blomberg, R. D. (1992). *Lower BAC limits for youth: Evaluation of the Maryland .02 law.* Washington, DC: US Department of Transportation, National Highway Traffic Safety Administration.

Blomberg, R. D., Peck, R. C., Moskowitz, H., Burns, M., & Fiorentino, D. (2005). *Crash risk of alcohol involved driving: A case-control study.* Stamford, CT: Dunlap & Associates,. Retrieved from http://www.dunlapandassociatesinc.com/crashriskofalcoholinvolveddriving.pdf

Blomberg, R. D., Peck, R. C., Moskowitz, H., Burns, M., & Fiorentino, D. (2009). The Long Beach/Fort Lauderdale relative risk study. *Journal of Safety Research, 40*(4), 285–292. doi: 10.1016/j.jsr.2009.07.002

Borkenstein, R. F. (1975). Problems of enforcement, adjudication and sanctioning. In S. Israelstam & S. Lambert (Eds.), *Alcohol, drugs and traffic safety: Proceedings of the 6th International Conference on Alcohol, Drugs and Traffic Safety, September 8–13, 1974* (pp. 655–662). Toronto: Addiction Research Foundation of Ontario.

Borkenstein, R. F., Crowther, R. F., Shumate, R. P., Ziel, W. B., & Zylman, R. (1974). The role of the drinking driver in traffic accidents. *Blutalkohol, 11*(Suppl. 1), 1–132.

Borucki, K., Schreiner, R., Dierkes, J., Jachau, K., Krause, D., Westphal, S., Wurst, F. M., Luley, C., & Schmidt–Gayk, H. (2005). Detection of recent ethanol intake with new markers: Comparison of fatty acid ethyl esters in serum and of ethyl glucuronide and the ration if 5–hydroxytryptophol to 5-hydroxyindole acetic acid in urine. *Alcoholism: Clinical and Experimental Research, 29*(5), 781–787.

Breckenridge, J. F., Winfree, L. T., Maupin, J. R., & Clason, D. L. (2000). Drunk drivers, DWI "drug court" treatment, and recidivism: Who fails? *Justice Research and Policy, 2*(1), 87–105.

Burns, M. (2003). An overview of field sobriety test research. *Perceptual and Motor Skills, 97*, 1189–1199.

Burns, M., & Anderson, E. W. (1995). *Field evaluation study of the standardized field sobriety test (SFST) battery* (Final report). Denver: Colorado Department of Transportation.

Burns, M., & Moskowitz, H. (1977). *Psychophysical tests for DWI arrest.* Springfield, VA: National Technical Information Service.

Burns, M. M., & Dioquino, T. (1997). *A Florida validation study of the standardized field sobriety test (SFST) battery.* Washington, DC: National Highway Traffic Safety Administration.

C'de Baca, J. C., Lapham, S. C., Liang, H. C., & Skipper, B. J. (2001). Victim impact panels: Do they impact drunk drivers? A follow-up of female and male first-time and repeat offenders. *Journal of Studies on Alcohol, 62*(5), 615–620.

Campbell, C. A., Hahn, R. A., Elder, R. W., Brewer, R. D., Chattopadhyay, S., Fielding, J., Naimi, T. S., Toomey, T., Lawrence, B., Middleton, J. C., & Services, Task Force on Community Preventive. (2009). The effectiveness of limiting alcohol outlet density as a means of reducing excessive alcohol consumption and alcohol-related harms. *American Journal of Preventive Medicine, 37*(6), 556–569. doi: 10.1016/j.amepre.2009.09.028

Casswell, S. (1995). Does alcohol advertising have an impact on the public health? *Drug and Alcohol Review, 14*(4), 395–403.

Caudill, B. D., Harding, W. M., & Moore, B. A. (2000). At–risk drinkers use safe ride services to avoid drinking and driving. *Journal of Substance Abuse, 11*(2), 149–160.

Caudill, B. D., Harding, W. M., & Moore, B. A. (2001). DWI prevention: Profiles of drinkers who use designated drivers. *Addictive Behaviors, 26*(2), 155–166.

Cavaiola, A., & Wuth, C. (2002). *Assessment and treatment of the DWI offender.* Binghamton, NY: The Haworth Press.

Center on Alcohol Marketing and Youth. (2008). *Youth exposure to alcohol advertising on television, 2001 to 2007.* Washington, DC: Georgetown University.

Centers for Disease Control and Prevention. (2011). *The community guide: Preventing excessive alcohol consumption: Privatization of retail alcohol sales.* Atlanta, GA: Author. Retrieved May 10, 2011, from http://www.thecommunityguide.org/alcohol/RRprivatization.html

Chaloupka, F. J., Grossman, M., & Saffer, H. (2002). The effects of price on alcohol consumption and alcohol-related problems. *Alcohol Research and Health, 26*(1), 22–34.

Chaloupka, F., Saffer, H., & Grossman, M. (1993). Alcohol-control policies and motor-vehicle fatalities. *Journal of Legal Studies, 22*(1), 161–186.

Chang, I., Gregory, C., & Lapham, S. C. (2002). *Reviews of screening instruments and procedures for evaluating DWI offenders.* Washington, DC: AAA Foundation for Traffic Safety. Retrieved from http://www.aaafoundation.org/pdf/DWIScreeningReport.pdf

Chen, L. H., Baker, S. P., & Li, G. (2006). Graduated driver licensing programs and fatal crashes of 16-year-old drivers: A national evaluation. *Pediatrics, 118*(1), 56–62.

Chikritzhs, T., & Stockwell, T. (2006). The impact of later trading hours for hotels on levels of impaired driver road crashes and driver breath alcohol levels. *Addiction*, *101*(9), 1254–1264.

Clapp, J., Lange, J. E., Russell, C., Shillington, A., & Voas, R. B. (2003a). A failed norms social marketing campaign. *Journal of Studies on Alcohol*, *64*(3), 409–414.

Clapp, J. D., Johnson, M., Voas, R. B., & Lange, J. E. (2005). Reducing DUI among college students: Results of an environmental prevention trial. *Addiction*, *100*(3), 327–334.

Clapp, J. D., Lange, J., Min, J. W., Shillington, A., Johnson, M. B., & Voas, R. (2003b). Two studies examining environmental predictors of heavy drinking by college students. *Prevention Science*, *4*(2), 99–108.

Clapp, J. D., Segars, L., & Voas, R. (2002). A conceptual model of the alcohol environment of college students. *Journal of Human Behavior and Social Environment*, *5*(1), 73–90.

Clark, W. B., & Hilton, M. E. (1991). *Alcohol in America: Drinking practices and problems.* Albany, NY: State University of New York Press.

Cleary, J., & Rodgers, A. (1986). *Analysis of the effects of recent changes in Minnesota's DWI laws: Part III. Longitudinal analysis of policy impacts.* St. Paul: Minnesota House of Representatives, Research Department.

Coben, J. H., & Larkin, G. L. (1999). Effectiveness of ignition interlock devices in reducing drunk driving recidivism. *American Journal of Preventive Medicine*, *16*(1S), 81–87.

Cohen, D., Mason, K., & Scribner, R. (2001). The population consumption model, alcohol control practices, and alcohol-related traffic fatalities. *Preventive Medicine*, *34*, 187–197.

Cohen, F., & Rogers, D. (1997). Effects of alcohol policy change. *Journal of Alcohol and Drug Education*, *42*, 69–82.

Cook, M., Motha, J., McKirgan, J., & O'Holloran, M. (1992). *Social cost of transport accidents in Australia.* Canberra: Bureau of Transport and Communication Economics.

Cook, P. J. (1981). The effect of liquor taxes on drinking, cirrhosis, and auto accidents. In M. Moore & D. Gerstein (Eds.), *Alcohol and public policy: Beyond the shadow of prohibition* (pp. 255–285). Washington, DC: National Academy Press.

Cook, P. J., & Moore, M. J. (1993). Violence reduction through restrictions on alcohol availability. *Alcohol Health and Research World*, *17*, 151–156.

Coppin, R. S., & Oldenbeek, G. (1965). *Driving under suspension and revocation: A study of suspended and revoked drivers classified as negligent operators* (Division of Research No. 18). Sacramento, CA: California Department of Motor Vehicles.

Cornwell, E. E., Belzberg, H., Velmahos, G., Chan, L. S., Demetriades, D., Stewart, B. M., Oder, D. B., Kahaku, D., Asensio, J. A., & Berne, T. V. (1998). The prevalence and effect of alcohol and drug abuse on cohort-matched critically injured patients. *American Surgeon*, *64*(5), 461–465.

Dee, T. S., Grabowski, D. C., & Morrisey, M. A. (2005). Graduated driver licensing and teen traffic fatalities. *Journal of Health Economics*, *24*(3), 571–589.

DeJong, W., & Wallack, L. (1992). The role of designated driver programs in the prevention of alcohol-impaired driving: A critical reassessment. *Health Education Quarterly*, *19*(4), 429–442.

DeYoung, D. J. (1997a). An evaluation of the effectiveness of alcohol treatment driver license actions and jail terms in reducing drunk driving recidivism in California. *Addiction*, *92*(8), 989–997.

DeYoung, D. J. (1997b). *An evaluation of the specific deterrent effect on vehicle impoundment on suspended, revoked, and unlicensed drivers in California.* Washington, DC: Department of Transportation, National Highway Traffic Safety Administration.

DeYoung, D. J. (2000). An evaluation of the general deterrent effects of vehicle impoundment on suspended and revoked drivers in California. *Journal of Safety Research*, *31*(2), 51–59.

DeYoung, D. J., Tashima, H. N., & Maston, S. V. (2005). An evaluation of the effectiveness of ignition interlock in California. In P. R. Marques (Ed.), *Alcohol ignition interlock devices. Vol. II: Research, policy, and program status 2005* (pp. 42–52). Oosterhout, The Netherlands: International Council on Alcohol, Drugs and Traffic Safety.

Dill, P. L., & Wells-Parker, E. (2006). Court-mandated treatment for convicted drinking drivers. *Alcohol Research and Health*, *29*(1), 41–48.

Dimeff, L. A. (1997). *Brief intervention for heavy and hazardous college drinkers in a student primary health care setting.* Ph.D. dissertation, University of Washington, Seattle.

Dimeff, L. A., Baer, J. S., Kivhahan, D. R., & Marlatt, G. A. (1999). *Brief alcohol screening and intervention for college students (BASICS): A harm reduction approach.* New York: Guilford Press.

Dresser, J., & Gliksman, L. (1998). Comparing statewide alcohol server training systems. *Pharmacology, Biochemistry, and Behavior*, *61*, 150.

Dyehouse, J. M., & Sommers, M. S. (1995). Brief intervention as an advanced practice strategy for seriously injured victims of multiple trauma. *AACN Advanced Critical Care*, *6*(1), 53–62.

Eby, D. W. (1995). The convicted drunk driver in Michigan: A profile of offenders. *UMTRI Research Review*, *25*(52), 1-11.

Editorial. (1904). *The Quarterly Journal of Inebriety*, *26*, 308–309.

Edwards, G., Anderson, P., Babor, T. F., Casswell, S., Ferrence, R., Giesbrecht, N., Godfrey, C., Holder, H. D., Lemmens, P., Mäkelä, K., Midanik, L. T., Norström, T., Österberg, E. Romelsjö, A., Room, R., Simpura, J., & Skog, O. -J. (Eds.). (1994). *Alcohol policy and the public good.* New York: Oxford University Press.

Elder, R. W., & Shults, R. A. (2002). Involvement by young drivers in fatal alcohol-related motor vehicle crashes—United States, 1982–2001. *Morbidity and Mortality Weekly Report*, *51*(48), 1089–1091.

Elder, R. W., Shults, R. A., Sleet, D. A., Nichols, J. L., Zaza, S., & Thompson, R. S. (2002). Effectiveness of sobriety checkpoints for reducing alcohol-involved crashes. *Traffic Injury Prevention*, *3*, 266–274.

Elder, R. W., Voas, R., Beirness, D., Shults, R. A., Sleet, D. A., Nichols, J. L., Compton, R., & Task Force on Community Preventive Services. (2011). Effectiveness of ignition interlocks for preventing alcohol-related crashes: A community guide systematic review. *American Journal of Preventive Medicine*, *40*(3), 362–376.

Emrick, C. D., Tonigan, J. S., Montgomery, H., & Little, L. (1993). Alcoholics Anonymous: What is currently known? In B. S. McCrady & W. R. Miller (Eds.), *Research on Alcoholics Anonymous: Opportunities and alternatives* (pp. 41–76). New Brunswick, NJ: Rutgers Center of Alcohol Studies.

Ennis, M. (2006, June 19). *Impairment detection of Lumidigm's biometric platform.* MADD Technology Symposium, Albuquerque, NM.

Epperlein, T. (1987). Initial deterrent effects of the crackdown on drunken drivers in the state of Arizona. *Accident Analysis and Prevention, 19*(4), 271–283.

Farmer, C. M., Wells, J. K., Ferguson, S. A., & Voas, R. B. (1999). Field evaluation of the PAS III passive alcohol sensor. *Traffic Injury Prevention, 1*(1), 55–61.

Farrell, S. (1985). Review of national policy measures to prevent alcohol-related problems. Geneva: World Health Organization.

Fell, J. C., Compton, C., & Voas, R. B. (2008c). A note on the use of passive alcohol sensors during routine traffic stops. *Traffic Injury Prevention, 9*(6), 534–538.

Fell, J. C., Ferguson, S. A., Williams, A. F., & Fields, M. (2003). Why are sobriety checkpoints not widely adopted as an enforcement strategy in the United States? *Accident Analysis and Prevention, 35*(6), 897–902.

Fell, J. C., Fisher, D. A., Voas, R. B., Blackman, K., & Tippetts, A. S. (2009a, June). The impact of underage drinking and related laws on youth alcohol-related fatal crashes. In *Transportation Research Circular No. E–C132: Young impaired drivers: The nature of the problem and possible solutions (A Workshop)*. Woods Hole, MA: Transportation Research Board of the National Academies.

Fell, J. C., Fisher, D. A., Voas, R. B., Blackman, K., & Tippetts, A. S. (2009b). The impact of underage drinking laws on alcohol-related fatal crashes of young drivers. *Alcoholism: Clinical and Experimental Research, 33*(7), 1208–1219.

Fell, J. C., Fisher, D. A., Voas, R. B., Blackman, K., & Tippetts, A. S. (2008a). The relationship of underage drinking laws to reductions in drinking drivers in fatal crashes in the United States. *Accident Analysis and Prevention, 40,* 1430–1440.

Fell, J. C., Jones, K., Romano, E., & Voas, R. B. (2011). An evaluation of graduated driver licensing effects on fatal crash involvements of young drivers in the United States. *Traffic Injury Prevention, 12*(5), 423–431. doi: Http://dx.doi.org/1 0.1080/15389588.2011.588296

Fell, J. C., Lacey, J. H., & Voas, R. B. (2004). Sobriety checkpoints: Evidence of effectiveness is strong, but use is limited. *Traffic Injury Prevention, 5*(3), 220–227.

Fell, J. C., Langston, E. A., Lacey, J. H., Tippetts, A. S., & Cotton, R. (2008b). *Evaluation of seven publicized enforcement programs to reduce impaired driving: Georgia, Louisiana, Pennsylvania, Tennessee, Indiana, Michigan, and Texas* (DOT HS 810 941). Washington, DC: National Highway Traffic Safety Administration.

Fell, J. C., Romano, E., & Voas, R. B. (2013). A national evaluation of graduated driver licensing laws in the United States. *T2013: International Council on Alcohol, Drugs and Traffic Safety (ICADTS) Conference, 25th to 28th August 2013.* Brisbane, QLD, Australia: ICADTS.

Fell, J. C., Tippetts, A. S., & Ciccel, J. D. (2011). An evaluation of three driving-under-the-influence courts in Georgia. *Annals of Advances in Automotive Medicine, 55,* 301–312.

Fell, J. C., Tippetts, A. S., & Levy, M. (2008d, October 5–8). Evaluation of seven publicized enforcement demonstration programs to reduce impaired driving: Georgia, Louisiana, Pennsylvania, Tennessee, Texas, Indiana, and Michigan. *52nd AAAM Annual Proceedings* (pp. 23–38). Evanston, IL: Association for the Advancement of Automotive Medicine.

Fell, J. C., Todd, M., & Voas, R. (2011). A national evaluation of the nighttime and passenger restriction components of graduated driver licensing. *Journal of Safety Research, 42*(4), 283–290. doi: Http://dx.doi.org/10.1016/j.jsr.2011.06.001

Fell, J. C., & Voas, R. B. (2006a). Mothers Against Drunk Driving (MADD): The first 25 years. *Traffic Injury Prevention, 7*(3), 195–212. doi: Http://dx.doi.org/10.1080/15389580802335273

Fell, J. C., & Voas, R. B. (2006b). The effectiveness of reducing illegal blood alcohol concentration limits for driving: Evidence for lowering the limit to .05 BAC. *Journal of Safety Research, 37*(3), 233–243.

Fell, J. C., Voas, R. B., & Lange, J. E. (1997). Designated driver concept: Extent of use in the USA. *Journal of Traffic Medicine, 25*(3–4), 109–114.

Ferguson, S. A., Fields, M., & Voas, R. B. (2000). Enforcement of zero tolerance laws in the US—prevention section. In H. Laurell & F. Schlyter (Eds.), *Alcohol, drugs and traffic safety—T 2000: Proceedings of the 15th International Conference on Alcohol, Drugs and Traffic Safety, May 22–26, 2000* (Vol. 2, pp. 713–718). Stockholm, Sweden: ICADTS.

Ferguson, S. A., Wells, J. K., & Lund, A. K. (1995). The role of passive alcohol sensors in detecting alcohol-impaired drivers at sobriety checkpoints. *Alcohol, Drugs, and Driving, 11,* 23–30.

Fleming, M. F., Barry, K. L., Manwell, L. B., Johnson, K., & London, R. (1997). Brief physician advice for problem drinkers: A randomized controlled trial in community-based primary care practices. *Journal of the American Medical Association, 277*(13), 1039–1045.

Fleming, M. F., Mundt, M. P., French, M. T., Manwell, L. B., Stauffacher, E. A., & Barry, K. L. (2002). Brief physician advice for problem drinkers: Long-term efficacy and benefit–cost analysis. *Alcoholism: Clinical and Experimental Research, 26*(1), 36–43.

Fors, S., & Rojeck, D. (1999). The effect of victim impact panels on DUI/DWI re-arrest rates: A twelve month follow-up. *Journal of Studies on Alcohol, 60*(4), 514–520.

Forster, J. L., Murray, D. M., Wolfson, M., & Wagenaar, A. (1995). Commercial availability of alcohol to young people: Results of alcohol purchase attempts. *Preventative Medicine, 24,* 324–347.

Foss, R., Diekman, S., Bartley, C., & Goodman, A. (2004). *Social norms program reduces measured and self-reported drinking at UNC-CH: The report on social norms, working paper 14.* Little Falls, NJ: PaperClip Communications.

Foss, R., & Goodwin, A. (2003). Enhancing the effectiveness of graduate driver licensing legislation. *Journal of Safety Research, 34,* 79–84.

Foss, R. D., Feaganes, J. R., & Roggman, L. A. (2001). Initial effects of graduated driver licensing on 16-year-old driver crashes in North Carolina. *Journal of the American Medical Association, 286*(13), 1631–1632.

Foss, R. D., Perrine, M. W., Meyers, A. M., Musty, R. E., & Voas, R. B. (1990). A roadside survey in the computer age. In M. W. Perrine (Ed.), *Proceedings of the 11th International Conference on Alcohol, Drugs and Traffic Safety, October 24–27, 1989, Chicago, Illinois.* (pp. 920–929). Chicago: National Safety Council.

Foss, R. D., Stewart, J. R., & Reinfurt, D. W. (1998). *Evaluation of the effects of North Carolina's 0.08% BAC law.* Washington, DC: US Department of Transportation, National Highway Traffic Safety Administration.

Fox, C., & Huddleston, W. (2003). Drugs in the US *Issues of Democracy, 8*(1), 13–19.

Frank, J. F., & Flores, A. L. (1989). *The accuracy of evidential breath testers at low BACs*. Washington, DC: National Highway Traffic Safety Administration.

Frank, J. F., & Jones, R. K. (2004). *Random assignment evaluation of the DUI court in Maricopa County (Phoenix), Arizona, USA*. Paper presented at the 17th International Conference on Alcohol, Drugs and Traffic Safety, Glasgow, Scotland.

Freeman–Wilson, K., & Wilkosz, M. P. (2002). *Drug court publications resource guide* (4th ed.). Alexandria, VA: National Drug Court Institute.

Friend, K., & Levy, D. T. (2002). Reductions in smoking prevalence and cigarette consumption associated with mass-media campaigns. *Health Education Research, 17*(1), 85–98.

Fuller, B., Carey, S. M., & Kissick, K. (2007). *Michigan DUI courts outcome evaluation*. Portland, OR: NPC Research.

Gentilello, L. M. (2005). Alcohol intervention in trauma centers: The opportunity and the challenge. *The Journal of Trauma, 59*, S18–20.

Gentilello, L. M., Ebel, B. E., Wickizer, T. M., Salkever, D. S., & Rivara, F. P. (2005). Alcohol interventions for trauma patients treated in emergency departments and hospitals: A cost benefit analysis. *Annals of Surgery, 241*, 541–550.

Gentilello, L. M., Rivara, F. P., Donovan, D. M., Jurkovich, G. J., Daranciang, E., Dunn, C. W., Villaveces, A., Copass, M., & Ries, R. R. (1999). Alcohol interventions in a trauma center as a means of reducing the risk of injury recurrence. *Annals of Surgery, 230*(4), 473–483.

Giesbrecht, N., & Douglas, R. R. (1990). *The demonstration project and comprehensive community programming: Dilemmas in preventing alcohol-related problems*. International Conference on Evaluating Community Prevention Strategies: Alcohol and Other Drugs, San Diego, CA.

Giesbrecht, N., & Grube, J. W. (2003). Education and persuasion strategies. In T. Babor, R. Caetano, S. Casswell, G. Edwards, N. Giesbrecht, K. Graham, J. Grube, P. Gruenewald, L. Hill, H. Holder, R. Homel, E. Österberg, J. Rehm, R. Room, & I. Rossow (Eds.), *Alcohol: No ordinary commodity: Research and public policy* (pp. 189–207). New York: Oxford University Press.

Gliksman, L., McKenzie, D., Single, E., Douglas, R., Brunet, S., & Moffatt, K. (1993). The role of alcohol providers in prevention: An evaluation of a server intervention programme. *Addiction, 88*(9), 1195–1203.

Gliksman, L., & Single, E. (1988). *A field evaluation of server intervention programs: Accommodating reality*. Paper presented at the Canadian Evaluation Society Meetings, Montreal, Quebec.

Graham, K., Osgood, D. W., Zibrowski, E., Purcell, J., Gliksman, L., Leonard, K., Pemanen, K., Saltz, R. F., & Toomey, T. L. (2004). The effect of the Safer Bars programme on physical aggression in bars: Results of a randomized controlled trial. *Drug and Alcohol Review, 23*(1), 31–41.

Graves, K. (1993). Evaluation of the alcohol warning label: A comparison of the United States and Ontario, Canada in 1990 and 1991. *Journal of Public Policy and Marketing, 12*(1), 19–29.

Green, R. E., French, J. F., Haberman, P. W., & Holland, P. W. (1991). The effects of combining sanctions and rehabilitation for driving under the influence: An evaluation of the New Jersey Alcohol Countermeasures Program. *Accident Analysis and Prevention, 23*(6), 543–555.

Greenfield, T. K. (1997). Warning labels: Evidence of harm-reduction from long-term American surveys. In M.

Plant, E. Single, & T. Stockwell (Eds.), *Alcohol: Minimizing the harm* (pp. 105–125). London: Free Association Books.

Greenfield, T. K., Graves, K. L., & Kaskutas, L. A. (1999). Long-term effects of alcohol warning labels: Findings from a comparison of the United States and Ontario, Canada. *Psychology and Marketing, 16*(3), 261–282.

Greenfield, T. K., & Kaskutas, L. A. (1998). Five years' exposure to alcohol warning label messages and their impacts: Evidence from diffusion analysis. *Applied Behavioral Science Review, 6*, 39–68.

Greenfield, T. K., & Zimmerman, R. S. (Eds.). (1993). *CSAP Prevention Monograph–14: Second international research symposium on experiences with community action projects for the prevention of alcohol and other drug problems*. Washington, DC: US Department of Health and Human Services.

Griffin, L. I., III, & DeLaZerda, S. (2000). *Unlicensed to kill*. Washington, DC: AAA Foundation for Traffic Safety.

Grimes, J. D., & Swisher, J. D. (1989). Educational factors influencing adolescent decision making regarding use of alcohol and drugs. *Journal of Alcohol and Drug Education, 35*, 1–15.

Grossman, M., Coate, D., & Arluck, G. M. (1987). Price sensitivity of alcoholic beverages in the United States. In H. D. Holder (Ed.), *Control issues in alcohol abuse prevention: Strategies for states and communities* (pp. 169–198). Greenwich, CT: JAI Press.

Grossman, M., & Markowitz, S. (2001). Alcohol regulation and violence on college campuses. In M. Grossman & C. R. Hsieh (Eds.), *The economic analysis of substance use and abuse: The experience of developed countries and lessons for developing countries* (pp. 257-289). Cheltenham, United Kingdom: Edward Elgar.

Grube, J. W. (1995). Television alcohol portrayals, alcohol advertising, and alcohol expectancies among children and adolescents. In S. Martin (Ed.), *The effects of mass media on the use and abuse of alcohol* (pp. 105–121). Rockville, MD: NIAAA.

Grube, J. W. (1997). Preventing sales of alcohol to minors: Results from a community trial. *Addiction, 92*(Suppl. 2), S251–S260.

Gruenewald, P. J. (1993). Alcohol problems and the control of availability: Theoretical and empirical issues. In M. E. Hilton & G. Bloss (Eds.), *Economics and the prevention of alcohol-related problems* (Vol. Research Monograph No. 25, pp. 59–90). (NIH Pub. No. 93–3513). Bethesda, MD: The Institute: National Institute on Alcohol Abuse and Alcoholism.

Gruenewald, P. J., Ponicki, W. R., & Holder, H. (1993). The relationship of outlet densities to alcohol consumption: A time series cross-sectional analysis. *Alcoholism: Clinical and Experimental Research, 17*(1), 38–47.

Gruenewald, P. J., & Treno, A. J. (2000). Local and global alcohol supply: Economic and geographic models of community systems. *Addiction, 95*(Suppl. 4), S537–S549.

Guerin, P., & Pitts, W. J. (2002). *Evaluation of the Bernalillo County Metropolitan DWI/Drug Court* (Final report). Albuquerque: University of New Mexico, Center for Applied Research and Analysis.

Haines, M., & Spear, S. (1996). Changing the norm: A strategy to decrease heavy episodic drinking among college students. *American Journal of College Health, 45*(2), 134–140.

Haines, M. P. (1996). *A social norms approach to preventing binge drinking at colleges and universities* (Monograph). Newton, MA: Higher Education Center for Alcohol and Other Drug Prevention.

Harding, W. M. (1989). *User's guide to new approaches and sanctions for multiple DWI offenders.* Springfield, VA: National Highway Safety Administration/National Technical Information Service.

Harding, W. M., & Caudill, B. D. (1997). Does the use of designated drivers promote excessive alcohol consumption? In C. Mercier-Guyon (Ed.), *Proceedings of the 14th Annual Conference on Alcohol, Drugs and Traffic Safety* Vol. 3. (pp. 1359–1364). Annecy, France: Centre d'Etudes et de Recherches en Médecine du Traffic.

Harding, W. M., Caudill, B. D., & Moore, B. A. (1998, June 20–25). *Do drivers drink more when they use a safe ride?* Paper presented at the annual meeting of the Research Society on Alcoholism, Hilton Head Island, SC.

Harris, D. H., Dick, R. A., Casey, S. M., & Jarosz, C. (1980). *The visual detection of driving while intoxicated.* Washington, DC: National Highway Traffic Safety Administration.

Harrison, P. A., Fulkerson, J. A., & Park, E. (2000). The relative importance of social versus commercial sources in youth access to tobacco, alcohol, and other drugs. *Preventive Medicine, 31*(1), 39–48.

Hauge, R., & Nordlie, O. (1984). Pa jakt etter virkeligheten [Chasing the reality]. *Nordisk Tidsskrift for Kriminalvidenskab, 71,* 70–75.

Hause, J. M., Voas, R. B., & Chavez, E. (1982). Conducting voluntary roadside surveys: The Stockton experience. In M. R. Valverius (Ed.), *Proceedings of the Satellite Conference to the 8th International Conference on Alcohol, Drugs and Traffic Safety, June 23–25, 1980, Umea, Sweden* (pp. 104–113). Stockholm: The Swedish Council for Information on Alcohol and Other Drugs.

Hedlund, J. (2006). *Countermeasures that work: A highway safety countermeasure guide for state highway safety offices.* Washington, DC: US Department of Transportation, National Highway Traffic Safety Administration.

Hedlund, J., & Fell, J. (1995). Persistent drinking drivers in the US *Annals of Advances in Automotive Medicine, 39,* 1–12.

Helander, A., & Beck, O. (2005). Ethyl sulfate: A metabolite of ethanol in humans and a potential biomarker of acute alcohol intake. *Journal of Analytic Toxicology, 29*(5), 270–274.

Henstridge, J., Homel, R., & Mackay, P. (1995). The long-term effects of random breath testing in Adelaide. In C. N. Kloeden & A. J. McLean (Eds.), *Proceedings of the 13th International Conference on Alcohol, Drugs and Traffic Safety—T'95,* August 13–18, 1995. Adelaide, Australia: International Council on Alcohol, Drugs and Traffic Safety (ICADTS).

Henstridge, J., Homel, R., & Mackay, P. (1997). *The long-term effects of random breath testing in four Australian states: A time series analysis.* Canberra, Australia: Federal Office of Road Safety.

Hill, L., & Casswell, S. (2001). Alcohol advertising and sponsorship: Commercial freedom or control in the public interest? In N. Heather, T. J. Peters, & T. Stockwell (Eds.), *International handbook of alcohol dependence and problems* (pp. 823–846). New York: John Wiley & Sons.

Hingson, R., Heeren, T., & Winter, M. (1994). Lower legal blood alcohol limits for young drivers. *Public Health Reports, 109*(6), 739–744.

Hingson, R., Heeren, T., & Winter, M. (1996). Lowering state legal blood alcohol limits to 0.08 %: The effect on fatal motor vehicle crashes. *American Journal of Public Health, 86*(9), 1297–1299.

Hingson, R., Heeren, T., & Winter, M. (2000). Effects of recent 0.08% legal blood alcohol limits on fatal crash involvement. *Injury Prevention, 6*(2), 109–114.

Hingson, R., Heeren, T., Winter, M., & Wechsler, H. (2005*b*). Magnitude of alcohol-related mortality and morbidity among US college students ages 18–24: Changes from 1998 to 2001. *Annual Review of Public Health, 26,* 259–279.

Hingson, R., Howland, J., Heeren, T., & Winter, M. (1992). Reduced BAC limits for young people (impact on night fatal) crashes. *Alcohol, Drugs and Driving, 7*(2), 117–127.

Hingson, R., McGovern, T., Howland, J., Heeren, T., Winter, M., & Zakocs, R. (1996b). Reducing alcohol-impaired driving in Massachusetts: The Saving Lives Program. *American Journal of Public Health, 86*(6), 791–797.

Hingson, R. W., Zakocs, R. C., Heeren, T., Winter, M. R., Rosenbloom, D., & DeJong, W. (2005*a*). Effects on alcohol related fatal crashes of a community based initiative to increase substance abuse treatment and reduce alcohol availability. *Injury Prevention, 11*(2), 84–90.

Holder, H., & Treno, A. J. (1997). Media advocacy in community prevention: News as a means to advance policy change. *Addiction, 92*(Suppl 2), S189–S199.

Holder, H. D. (1996). *Alcohol and the community: A systems approach to prevention.* Cambridge, UK: Cambridge University Press.

Holder, H. D., & Blose, J. O. (1987). Impact of changes in distilled spirits availability on apparent consumption: A time series analysis of liquor-by-the-drink. *British Journal of Addiction, 82*(6), 623–631.

Holder, H. D., Gruenewald, P. J., Ponicki, W., Grube, J. W., Saltz, R. F., Voas, R. B., Reynolds, R., Davis, J., Sanchez, L., Gaumont, G., Roeper, P., & Treno, A. J. (1998). *Prevention of alcohol-involved injuries and violence: Results from a six-year three-community prevention trial.* Berkeley, CA: Prevention Research Center.

Holder, H. D., Gruenewald, P. J., Ponicki, W. R., Treno, A. J., Grube, J. W., Saltz, R. F., Voas, R. B., Reynolds, R., Davis, J., Sanchez, L., Gaumont, G., & Roeper, P. (2000). Effect of community-based interventions on high-risk drinking and alcohol-related injuries. *Journal of the American Medical Association, 284*(18), 2341–2347.

Holder, H. D., Janes, K., Mosher, J., Saltz, R. F., Spurr, S., & Wagenaar, A. C. (1993). Alcoholic beverage server liability and the reduction of alcohol-involved problems. *Journal of Studies on Alcohol, 54*(1), 23–26.

Holder, H. D., Saltz, R. F., Treno, A. J., Grube, J. W., & Voas, R. B. (1997). Evaluation design for a community prevention trial: An environmental approach to reduce alcohol-involved trauma. *Evaluation Review, 21*(2), 140–165.

Holder, H. D., & Wagenaar, A. C. (1990). Effects of the elimination of a state monopoly on distilled spirits' retail sales: A time-series analysis of Iowa. *British Journal of Addiction, 85,* 1615–1625.

Holder, H. D., & Wagenaar, A, C. (1994). Mandated server training and reduced alcohol-involved traffic crashes: A time series analysis of the Oregon experience. *Accident Analysis and Prevention, 26*(1), 89–98.

Homel, R. (1994). Drink-driving law enforcement and the legal blood alcohol limit in New South Wales. *Accident Analysis and Prevention, 26*(2), 147–155.

Homel, R. (1988). *Policing and punishing the drinking driver. A study of general and specific deterrence.* New York: Springer-Verlag.

Howard-Pitney, B., Johnson, M. D., Altman, D. G., Hopkins, R., & Hammond, N. (1991). Responsible alcohol service: A study of server, manager, and environmental impact. *American Journal of Public Health, 81*(2), 197–198.

Israel, Y., Hollander, O., Sanchez-Craig, M., Booker, S., Miller, V., Gingrich, R., & Rankin, J. G. (1996). Screening for problem drinking and counseling by the primary care physician-nurse team. *Alcoholism: Clinical and Experimental Research, 20*(8), 1443–1450.

Johnson, D., & Fell, J. C. (1995). The impact of lowering the illegal BAC limit to .08 in five states in the US *Annals of Advances in Automotive Medicine, 39,* 45–64.

Johnson, L. D., O'Malley, P. M., & Bachman, J. G. (2003). *Monitoring the Future national survey results on drug use, 1975–2002. Volume 1: Secondary school students.* Bethesda, MD: National Institute on Drug Abuse.

Johnsson, K. O., & Berglund, M. (2003). Education of key personnel in student pubs leads to a decrease in alcohol consumption among the patrons: A randomized controlled trial. *Addiction, 98*(5), 627–633.

Jones, A. W. (2000). Measuring alcohol in blood and breath for forensic purposes—A historical review. *Forensic Science Review, 12*(1/2), 151–182.

Jones, A. W., & Pounder, D. J. (1998). *Measuring blood-alcohol concentration for clinical and forensic purposes.* Boca Raton, FL: CRC Press.

Jones, L., Hughes, K., Atkinson, A. M., & Bellis, M. A. (2011). Reducing harm in drinking environments: A systematic review of effective approaches. *Health & Place, 17*(2), 508–518.

Jones, R. K., & Lacey, J. H. (1998). *Evaluation of an individualized sanctioning program for DWI offenders.* Washington, DC: National Highway Traffic Safety Administration.

Jones, R. K., Lacey, J. H., & Wiliszowski, C. H. (1998). *Problems and solutions in DWI enforcement systems* (Final report, September 1995–March 1997). Washington, DC: US Department of Transportation, National Highway Traffic Safety Administration.

Jones, R. K., Wiliszowski, C. H., & Lacey, J. H. (1996). *Evaluation of alternative programs for repeat DWI offenders.* Washington, DC: National Highway Traffic Safety Administration, Office of Program Development and Evaluation.

Jones-Webb, R., Toomey, T., Miner, K., Wagenaar, A. C., Wolfson, M., & Poon, R. (1997). Why and in what context adolescents obtain alcohol from adults: A pilot study. *Substance Use & Misuse, 32*(2), 219–228.

Kaskutas, L., & Greenfield, T. K. (1992). First effects of warning labels on alcoholic beverage containers. *Drug and Alcohol Dependence, 31*(1), 1–14.

Kelley-Baker, T., Blackman, K., Vishnuvajjala, R., Romano, E., Tippetts, A. S., Voas, R., & Lacey, J. (2008, June 28–July 3). BAC refusals and recidivism. In *Proceedings of the 32nd annual meeting of the Research Society on Alcoholism.* Washington, DC: Research Society on Alcoholism.

Kenkel, D. S. (1993). Drinking, driving and deterrence: The effectiveness and social costs of alternative policies. *Journal of Law and Economics, 36*(2), 877–913.

Kilmer, B., Nicosia, N., Heaton, P., & Midgette, G. (2013). Efficacy of frequent monitoring with swift, certain, and modest sanctions for violations: Insights from South Dakota's 24/7 Sobriety Project. *American Journal of Public Health, 103*(1), e37–43. doi: 10.2105/AJPH.2012.300989

Klein, T. M., & Walz, M. C. (1998). *Estimating alcohol involvement in fatal crashes in light of increases in restraint use.* Washington, DC: National Highway Traffic Safety Administration, National Center for Statistics and Analysis. Retrieved from http://www-nrd.nhtsa.dot.gov/pdf/nrd-30/NCSA/Rpts/1998/Alc_Belt.pdf

Klepp, K. I., Schmid, L. A., & Murray, D. M. (1996). Effects of the increased minimum drinking age law on drinking and driving behavior among adolescents. *Addiction Research, 4*(3), 237–244.

Knight, J. R., Wechsler, H., Kuo, M., Seibring, M., Weitzman, E. R., & Schuckit, M. A. (2002). Alcohol abuse and dependence among US college students. *Journal of Studies on Alcohol, 63*(3), 263–270.

Kownacki, R. J., & Shadish, W. R. (1999). Does Alcoholics Anonymous work? The results from a meta-analysis of controlled experiments. *Substance Abuse and Misuse, 34*(13), 897–916.

Kraakman, R. (1998). Third-party liability. In P. Newman (Ed.), *The new Palgrave dictionary of economics and the law* (Vol. 3, pp. 583–587). London: Macmillian Reference.

Kunitz, S. J., Woodall, W. G., Zhao, H., Wheeler, D. R., Lillis, R., & Rogers, E. (2002). Rearrest rates after incarceration for DWI: A comparative study in a southwestern US county. *American Journal of Public Health, 92*(11), 1826–1831.

Kuo, M., Weschler, H., Greenberg, P., & Lee, H. (2003). The marketing of alcohol to college students: The role of low prices and special promotions. *American Journal of Preventive Medicine, 25,* 204–211.

Kypri, K., Saunders, J. B., Williams, M., McGee, R. O., Langley, J., Cashell-Smith, M. L., & Gallagher, S. J. (2004). Web-based screening and brief intervention for hazardous drinking: A double-blind randomized controlled trial. *Addiction, 99,* 1410–1417.

Kypri, K., Voas, R. B., Langley, J. D., Stephenson, S. C. R., Begg, D. J., Tippetts, A. S., & Davie, G. S. (2006). Minimum purchasing age for alcohol and traffic crash injuries among 15- to 19- year-olds in New Zealand. *American Journal of Public Health, 96*(1), 126–131.

Lacey, J., Kelley-Baker, T., Brainard, K., Tippetts, A. S., & Lyakhovich, M. (2008). *Evaluation of the checkpoint strikeforce program.* Washington, DC: National Highway Traffic Safety Administration.

Lacey, J., Kelley-Baker, T., Furr-Holden, C. D. M., Voas, R., Romano, E., Torres, P., Tippetts, A. S., Ramirez, A., Brainard, K., & Berning, A. (2009a). *2007 national roadside survey of alcohol and drug use by drivers: Alcohol results.* (DOT HS 811 248). Washington, DC: US Department of Transportation, National Highway Traffic Safety Administration. Retrieved from http://www.nhtsa.gov/Driving+Safety/Research+&+Evaluation/2007+National+Roadside+Survey+of+Alcohol+and+Drug+Use+by+Drivers.

Lacey, J. H., Jones, R. K., & Smith, R. G. (1999). *An evaluation of Checkpoint Tennessee: Tennessee's statewide sobriety checkpoint program* (DOT HS 808 841). Washington, DC: National Highway Traffic Safety Administration. Retrieved from http://www.nhtsa.dot.gov/people/injury/research/ChekTenn/ChkptTN.html

Lacey, J. H., Jones, R. K., & Wiliszowski, C. H. (1999). *Validation of problem drinking screening instruments for DWI offenders.* Washington, DC: National Highway Traffic Safety Administration.

Lacey, J. H., Kelley-Baker, T., Ferguson, S. A., & Rider, R. P. (2006). Low-manpower checkpoints: Can they provide effective DUI enforcement for small communities? *Traffic Injury Prevention, 7*(3), 213–218.

Lacey, J. H., Kelley-Baker, T., Furr-Holden, D., Voas, R. B., Moore, C., Brainard, K., Tippetts, A. S., Romano, E., Torres, P., & Berning, A. (2009*b*). *2007 national roadside survey of alcohol and drug use by drivers: Methodology* (Report No. DOT HS 811 237). Washington, DC: US Department of Transportation, National Highway Traffic Safety Administration. Retrieved from http://www.nhtsa.gov/Driving+Safety/Research+&+Evaluation/2007+National+Roadside+Survey+of+Alcohol+and+Drug+Use+by+Drivers.

Lacey, J. H., Rudisill, L. C., Popkin, C. L., & Stewart, J. R. (1986). Education for drunk drivers: How well has it worked in North Carolina? *Popular Government, 51*(3), 44–48.

Lambert, D. K., Myers, M. E., Jr., Oberdier, L., Sultan, M. F., Thrush, C. M., & Li, T. (2006). *Passive sensing of driver intoxication.* Warrendale, PA: SAE International.

Lange, J. E., Clapp, J. D., Turrisi, R., Taki, R., Jaccard, J., Johnson, M. B., Voas, R. B., & Larimer, M. (2002). College binge drinking: What is it? Who does it? *Alcoholism: Clinical and Experimental Research, 26*(5), 723–730.

Lange, J. E., Lauer, E., & Voas, R. B. (1999). A survey of the San Diego-Tijuana cross-border binging: Methods and analysis. *Evaluation Review, 23*(4), 378–398.

Lange, J. E., Reed, M. B., Johnson, M. B., & Voas, R. B. (2006). The efficacy of experimental interventions designed to reduce drinking among designated drivers. *Journal of Studies on Alcohol, 67*(2), 261–268.

Lange, J. E., & Voas, R. B., (1998). Patterns of border crossings associated with Tijuana binge drinking by US young people. *Alcoholism Clinical & Experimental Research. 22*(3 Abstr. Suppl.): 83a.

Lange, J. E., Voas, R. B., & O'Rourke, P. (1998). What is a designated driver anyway? Results of a California survey on definitions and use of designated drivers. *Journal of Traffic Medicine, 26*(3–4), 101–108.

Lapham, S. (2004/2005). Screening and brief intervention in the criminal justice system. *Alcohol Research and Health, 28*(2), 85–93.

Lapham, S. C., C'de Baca, J., McMillan, G., & Hunt, W. C. (2004). Accuracy of alcohol diagnosis among DWI offenders referred for screening. *Drug and Alcohol Dependence, 76*(2), 135–142.

Lapham, S. C., Skipper, B. J., Chang, I., Barton, K., & Kennedy, R. (1998). Factors related to miles driven between drinking and arrest locations among convicted drunk drivers. *Accident Analysis and Prevention, 30*(2), 201–206.

Larimer, M. E., & Cronce, J. M. (2002). Identification, prevention and treatment: A review of individual-focused strategies to reduce problematic alcohol consumption by college students. *Journal of Studies on Alcohol, 14*(Suppl.), 148–163.

Lenk, K. M., Erickson, D. J., Nelson, T. F., Winters, K. C., & Toomey, T. L. (2012). Alcohol policies and practices among four-year colleges in the United States: Prevalence and patterns. *Journal of Studies on Alcohol and Drugs, 73*, 361–367.

Lestina, D. C., & Lund, A. K. (1989). *Laboratory evaluation of two passive alcohol sensors.* Arlington, VA: Insurance Institute for Highway Safety.

Levy, D., Asch, P., & Shea, D. (1990). An assessment of county programs to reduce driving while intoxicated. *Health Education Research, 5*, 247–255.

Levy, D., Shea, D., & Asch, P. (1988). Traffic safety effects of sobriety checkpoints and other local DWI programs in New Jersey. *American Journal of Public Health, 79*, 291–293.

Levy, P., Voas, R. B., Johnson, P., & Klein, T. (1977). Evaluation of the ASAPs. *Journal of Safety Research, 10*, 162–176.

Levy, P., Voas, R. B., Johnson, P., & Klein, T. M. (1978). An evaluation of the Department of Transportation's alcohol safety action projects. *Journal of Safety Research, 10*(4), 162–176.

Ligon, J., & Thyer, B. A. (1993). The effects of a Sunday liquor sales ban on DUI arrests. *Journal of Alcohol and Drug Education, 38*(2), 33–40.

Loudenburg, R., Drube, G., & Leonardson, G. (2010). *South Dakota 24-7 sobriety program: Evaluation findings report.* Salem, SD: Mountain Plains Evaluation.

Lund, A. F., & Jones, I. S. (1987). Detection of impaired drivers with a passive alcohol sensor. In P. C. Noordzij & R. Roszbach (Eds.), *Alcohol, drugs and traffic safety '86* (pp. 379–382). New York: Excerpta Medica.

Lund, A. K., Kiger, S., Lestina, D., & Blackwell, T. (1991, January 15). *Using passive alcohol sensors during police traffic stops.* Paper presented at the 70th annual meeting of Transportation Research Board, Washington, DC.

MacKinnon, D. P., Pentz, M. A., & Stacy, A. W. (1993). The alcohol warning label and adolescents: The first year. *American Journal of Public Health, 83*, 585–587.

Maio, R. F., Waller, P. F., Blow, F. C., Hill, F. M., & Singer, K. M. (1997). Alcohol abuse/dependence in motor vehicle crash victims presenting to the emergency department. *Academic Emergency Medicine, 4*(4), 256–262.

Maldonado–Molina, M., & Wagenaar, A. (2010). Effects of alcohol taxes on alcohol–related mortality in Florida: Time-series analyses from 1969 to 2004. *Alcoholism: Clinical and Experimental Research, 34*(11), 1915–1921.

Mann, R. E., Anglin, L., Wilkins, K., Vingilis, E. R., MacDonald, S., & Sheu, W. J. (1994). Rehabilitation for convicted drinking drivers (second offenders): Effects on morality. *Journal of Studies on Alcohol, 55*(3), 372–374.

Markowitz, S. (2000). The price of alcohol, wife abuse and husband abuse. *Southern Economic Journal, 67*(2), 279–303.

Markowitz, S., & Grossman, M. (1998). Alcohol regulation and domestic violence towards children. *Contemporary Economic Policy, 16*(3), 309–320.

Markowitz, S., & Grossman, M. (2000). The effects of beer taxes on physical child abuse. *Journal of Health Economics, 19*(2), 271–282.

Marlatt, G. A., Baer, J. S., Kivlahan, D. R., Dimeff, L. A., Larimer, M. E., Quigley, L. A., Somers, J. M., & Williams, E. (1998). Screening and brief intervention for high-risk college student drinkers: Results from a two-year follow-up assessment. *Journal of Consulting and Clinical Psychology, 66*(4), 604–615.

Marques, P., & McKnight, A. S. (2009). Field and laboratory alcohol detection with two types of transdermal devices. *Alcoholism: Clinical and Experimental Research, 33*(4), 703–711.

Marques, P., Voas, R., Timken, D. S., & Field, C. A. (2004). *Motivational enhancement of interlock offenders to reduce DUI: Preliminary findings.* Paper presented at the 27th annual scientific meeting of the Research Society on Alcoholism, Vancouver, BC.

Marques, P. R., & McKnight, A. S. (2007). *Evaluating transdermal alcohol measuring devices.* Washington, DC: National Highway Traffic Safety Administration.

Marques, P. R., & McKnight, A. S. (2009). Field and laboratory alcohol detection with two types of transdermal devices. *Alcoholism: Clinical and Experimental Research, 33*(4), 703–711.

Marques, P. R., Tippetts, A. S., & Voas, R. B. (2003*a*). The alcohol interlock: An underutilized resource for predicting and controlling drunk drivers. *Traffic Injury Prevention, 4*(3), 188–194.

Marques, P. R., Tippetts, A. S., & Voas, R. B. (2003*b*). Comparative and joint prediction of DUI recidivism from alcohol ignition interlock and driver records. *Journal of Studies on Alcohol, 64*(1), 83–92.

Marques, P. R., & Voas, R. B. (1995). Case–managed alcohol interlock programs: A bridge between the criminal and health systems. *Journal of Traffic Medicine, 23*(2), 77–85.

Marques, P. R., Voas, R. B., Roth, R., & Tippetts, A. S. (2008). *Evaluation of the New Mexico Ignition Interlock Program.* Washington, DC: National Highway Traffic Safety Administration.

Marques, P. R., Voas, R. B., & Timken, D. S. (2004). Preliminary outcomes from a Texas manual-based group motivational intervention supplement for court-stipulated interlock DUI offenders. In J. Oliver, P. Williams & A. Clayton (Eds.), *Proceedings of the 17th International Conference on Alcohol, Drugs and Traffic Safety, August 8–13, 2004.* Glasgow, UK: X–CD Technologies.

Marques, P. R., Voas, R., Timken, D. S., & Field, C. A. (2004). *Motivational enhancement of interlock offenders to reduce DUI: Preliminary findings.* Paper presented at the 27th annual scientific meeting of the Research Society on Alcoholism, Vancouver, BC.

Marques, P. R., Voas, R. B., & Tippetts, A. S. (2003). Behavioral measures of drinking: Patterns in the interlock record. *Addiction, 98*(Suppl. 2), 13–19.

Martell, C. A., Stewart, J. R., & Jamburajan, S. (1998). *DWI evaluation and query system* (Final report). Chapel Hill: University of North Carolina Highway Safety Research Center.

Mast, B. D., Benson, B. L., & Rasmussen, D. W. (1999). Beer taxation and alcohol-related traffic fatalities. *Southern Economic Journal, 66*(2), 214–249.

Masten, S. V., Foss, R. D., & Marshall, S. W. (2011). Graduated driver licensing and fatal crashes involving 16- to 19-year-old drivers. *Journal of the American Medical Association, 306*(10), 1098–1103.

Mayer, R. R., Forster, J. L., Murray, D. M., & Wagenaar, A. C. (1998). Social settings and situations of underage drinking. *Journal of Studies on Alcohol, 59*(2), 207–215.

Mayhew, D. R., Simpson, H. M., & Pak, A. (2003). Changes in collision rates among novice drivers during the first months of driving. *Accident Analysis and Prevention, 35*, 683–691.

Mayhew, D. R., Simpson, H. M., Williams, A. F., & Ferguson, S. A. (1998). Effectiveness and role of driver education and training in a graduated licensing system. *Journal of Public Health Policy, 19*(1), 51–67.

McCarthy, J. D., Wolfson, M., & Harvey, D. S. (1987). *survey report of the project on the Citizens' Movement Against Drunk Driving.* Washington, DC: Center for the Study of Youth Development, The Catholic University of America.

McCarthy, P. S., & Ziliak, J. (1990). Effect of MADD on drinking-driving activities: An empirical study. *Applied Economics, 22*(9), 1215–1227.

McCartt, A. T., Blackman, K., & Voas, R. B. (2007). Implementation of Washington state's zero tolerance law: Patterns of arrests, dispositions, and recidivism. *Traffic Injury Prevention, 8*(4), 339–345.

McCartt, A. T., Geary, L. L., & Nissen, W. J. (2002). *Observational study of the extent of driving while suspended for alcohol-impaired driving.* Washington, DC: National Highway Traffic Safety Administration.

McCartt, A. T., & Northrup, V. S. (2004). *Enhanced sanctions for higher BACs: Evaluation of Minnesota's High BAC Law.* Washington, DC: National Highway Traffic Safety Administration.

McCartt, A. T., Shabanova, V. I., & Leaf, W. A. (2003). Driving experience, crashes and traffic citations of teenage beginning drivers. *Accident Analysis and Prevention, 35*, 311–320.

McCartt, A. T., Teoh, E. R., Fields, M., Braitman, K. A., & Hellinga, L. A. (2009). *Graduated licensing laws and fatal crashes of teenage drivers: A national study.* Arlington, VA: Insurance Institute for Highway Safety.

McKnight, A. J. (1988). *Development and field test of a responsible alcohol service program.* Washington, DC: US Department of Transportation, National Highway Traffic Safety Administration.

McKnight, A. J. (1991). Factors influencing the effectiveness of server-intervention education. *Journal of Studies on Alcohol, 52*(5), 389–397.

McKnight, A. J., Langston, E., McKnight, A. S., & Lange, J. (2002). Sobriety tests for low blood alcohol concentrations. *Accident Analysis and Prevention, 34*(3), 305–311.

McKnight, A. J., & Streff, F. M. (1994). The effect of enforcement upon service of alcohol to intoxicated patrons of bars and restaurants. *Accident Analysis and Prevention, 26*(1), 79–88.

McKnight, A. J., & Voas, R. B. (1982). *A guide to self-sufficient funding of alcohol traffic safety programs.* Washington, DC: US Department of Transportation, National Highway Traffic Safety Administration.

McKnight, A. J., & Voas, R. B. (1991). The effect of license suspension upon DWI recidivism. *Alcohol, Drugs and Driving, 7*(1), 43–54.

Meier, S. E., Brigham, T. A., & Gilbert, J. B. (1998). Analyzing methods for increasing designated driving. *Journal of Prevention & Intervention in the Community, 17*(1), 1–14.

Mello, M. J., Nirenberg, T. D., Longabaugh, R., Woolard, R., Minugh, A. P., Becker, B., Baird, J., & Stein, L. (2005). Emergency department brief motivational interventions for alcohol with motor vehicle crash patients. *Annals of Emergency Medicine, 45*(6), 620–625.

Merki, D., & Lingg, M. (1987). Combating the drunk driving problem through community action: A proposal. *Journal of Alcohol and Drug Education, 32*(3), 42–46.

Michigan State Police. (1989). *Surveillance of alcohol vending establishments: Michigan SAVE Program.* Lansing: Michigan State Police.

Miller, T. R., Galbraith, M., & Lawrence, B. A. (1998). Costs and benefits of a community sobriety checkpoint program. *Journal of Studies on Alcohol, 59*(4), 465–468. [Reprinted in A. N. Link & J. T. Scott (Eds.), *The economics of evaluation in public programs, international library of critical writings in economics*. Cheltenham, UK: Edward Elgar, 2011].

Miller, T. R., Snowden, C. B., Birckmayer, J., & Hendrie, D. (2006). Retail alcohol monopolies, underage drinking, and youth impaired driving deaths. *Accident Analysis and Prevention, 38*(6), 1162–1167.

Molof, M. J., & Kimball, C. (1994). *A study of the implementation and effects of Oregon's mandatory alcohol server training program*. Eugene: Oregon Research Services Inc.

Monti, P. M., Colby, S. M., Barnett, N. P., Spirito, A., Rhsenow, D. J., Myers, M., Woolard, R., & Lewander, W. (1999). Brief intervention for harm reduction with alcohol-positive older adolescents in a hospital emergency department. *Journal of Consulting and Clinical Psychology, 67*(6), 989–994.

Montonen, M. (1996). *Alcohol and the media*. Copenhagen, Denmark: World Health Organization, Regional Office for Europe.

Mosher, J. (1979). Dram Shop Law and the prevention of alcohol-related problems. *Journal of Studies on Alcohol, 40*(9), 773–798.

Mosher, J. F., Delewski, C., Saltz, R. F., & Hennessey, M. (1989). *Monterey/Santa Cruz responsible beverage project: Final report*. San Rafael, CA: Marin Institute for the Prevention of Alcohol and other Drug Problems.

Mosher, J. F., Toomey, T. L., Good, C., Harwood, E., & Wagenaar, A. C. (2002). State laws mandating or promoting training programs for alcohol servers and establishment managers: An assessment of statutory and administrative procedures. *Journal of Public Health Policy, 23*(1), 90–113.

Moskowitz, H., Burns, M., & Ferguson, S. (1999). Police officers' detection of breath odors from alcohol ingestion. *Accident Analysis and Prevention, 31*(3), 175–180.

Moulden, J. V., & Russell, A. (1994). Is it MADD trying to rate the states? A citizen activist approach to DWI prevention. *Alcohol, Drugs and Driving, 10*, 317–326.

National Center for Statistics and Analysis (NCSA). (2003). *Fatality Analysis Reporting System (FARS)*. Washington, DC: US Department of Transportation, National Highway Traffic Safety Administration. Retrieved April, 2003, from http://www-nrd.nhtsa.dot.gov/departments/nrd-30/ncsa//fars.html

National Center for Statistics and Analysis (NCSA). (2004). *Fact sheet. Motor vehicle traffic fatalities and fatality rate: 1899–2003*. Washington, DC: National Highway Traffic Safety Administration.

National Center for Statistics and Analysis (NCSA). (2012). *Traffic safety facts, 2011 data: Alcohol-impaired driving*. Washington, DC: US Department of Transportation, National Highway Traffic Safety Administration.

National Highway Traffic Safety Administration (NHTSA). (1998). *Alcohol-highway safety: A compendium of state alcohol-highway safety related legislation*. Washington, DC: Department of Transportation, National Highway Traffic Safety Administration (NHTSA).

National Highway Traffic Safety Administration (NHTSA). (2005). *A guide to sentencing DUI offenders*. Washington, DC: Author.

National Highway Traffic Safety Administration (NHTSA). (2008). *Countermeasures that work: A highway safety countermeasure guide for state highway safety offices* (3rd ed.). Washington, DC: US Department of Transportation, National Highway Traffic Safety Administration. Retrieved from http://www.nhtsa.gov/staticfiles/DOT/ NHTSA/Traffic%20Injury%20Control/Articles/ Associated%20Files/HS810891.pdf

National Highway Traffic Safety Administration, & American College of Emergency Physicians. (2002). *Alcohol screening and brief intervention in the medical setting*. Washington, DC: US Department of Transportation. Retrieved from http://www.nhtsa.dot.gov/people/injury/ems/alcohol_ screening/Overview.html

National Highway Traffic Safety Administration, & National Institute on Alcohol Abuse and Alcoholism. (2006). *A guide to sentencing DUI offenders* (2nd ed.). Washington, DC: Author.

National Institute on Alcohol Abuse and Alcoholism (NIAAA). (2005). *Alcohol Policy Information System (APIS)*. Retrieved December 19, 2008, from http://alcoholpolicy.niaaa.nih.gov

National Transportation Safety Board. (2013). *Reaching zero: Actions to eliminate alcohol-impaired driving*. Washington, DC: National Transportation Safety Board.

Nelson, T. F., Weitzman, E. R., & Wechsler, H. (2005). The effect of a campus-community environmental alcohol prevention initiative on student drinking and driving: Results from the "A Matter of Degree" program evaluation. *Traffic Injury Prevention, 6*, 323–330.

Nichols, J., Ellingstad, V., & Struckman-Johnson, D. (1978). An experimental evaluation of the effectiveness of short term education and rehabilitation programs for convicted drinking drivers. In *Proceedings of the National Council on Alcoholism annual forum, St. Louis, Missouri*. Washington, DC: National Highway Traffic Safety Administration.

Nichols, J. L., Weinstein, E. B., Ellingstad, V. S., & Struckman-Johnson, D. L. (1978). The specific deterrent effectiveness of ASAP education and rehabilitation programs. *Journal of Safety Research, 10*(4), 177–187.

Nochajski, T. H., Miller, B. A., Wieczorek, W. F., & Whitney, R. (1993). The effect of a drinker-driver treatment program: Does criminal history make a difference? *Criminal Justice and Behavior, 20*(2), 174–189.

Nordlund, S. (1984). Effekten av lørdagsstengningen ved Vinmonopolets butikker [Effects of Saturday closing of the wine/liquor monopoly outlets]. *Alkoholpolitik-Tidsskrift for Nordisk Alkoholforskning, 1*, 221–229.

Nordlund, S. (1985, June 2–7). *Effects of Saturday closing of wine and spirits shops in Norway*. Paper presented at the 31st International Institute on the Prevention and Treatment of Alcoholism, Rome, Italy.

Norström, T., Miller, T., Holder, H., Österberg, E., Ranstedt, M., Rossow, I., & Stockwell, T. (2010). Potential consequences of replacing a retail alcohol monopoly with a private license system: Results from Sweden. *Addiction, 105*(112), 2113–2119. doi: 10.1111/j.1360–0443.2010.03091.x

O'Donnell, M. A. (1985). Research on drinking locations of alcohol-impaired drivers: Implications for prevention policies. *Journal of Public Health Policy, 6*(4), 510–525.

Odo, J., McQuiller, L., & Stretsky, P. (1999). An empirical assessment of the impact of RIT's student alcohol policy on drinking and binge drinking behavior. *Journal of Alcohol and Drug Education, 44*, 49–67.

Ogborne, A. C., & Smart, R. G. (1980). Will restrictions on alcohol advertising reduce alcohol consumption? *British Journal of Addiction, 75*(3), 293–296.

O'Malley, P. M., & Wagenaar, A. C. (1991). Effects of minimum drinking age laws on alcohol use, related behaviors and traffic crash involvement among American youth: 1976–1987. *Journal of Studies on Alcohol, 52*(5), 478–491.

Österberg, E., & Säilä, S. -L. (Eds.). (1991). *Natural experiments with decreased availability of alcoholic beverages. Finnish alcohol strikes in 1972 and 1985* (Vol. *40*). Helsinki, Finland: The Finnish Foundation for Alcohol Studies.

Palmer, J. W. (1986). *Minnesota roadside survey: Alcohol positive drivers*. Saint Cloud, MN: Saint Cloud University.

Partanen, J., & Montonen, M. (1988). Alcohol and the mass media. *EURO Reports and Studies, 108*, 1–73.

Peck, R. C. (1991). General and specific deterrent effects of DUI sanctions: A review of California's experience. *Alcohol, Drugs and Driving, 7*(1), 13–42.

Peck, R. C., & Helander, C. J. (2001). *Repeat DUI offenders—an analysis of research needs and countermeasure development strategies*. Paper presented at the Transportation Research Board midyear meeting and workshop of the Committee on Alcohol, Other Drugs, and Transportation, Irvine, California.

Peck, R. C., Sadler, D. D., & Perrine, M. W. (1985). The comparative effectiveness of alcohol rehabilitation and licensing control actions for drunk driving offenders: A review of the literature. *Alcohol, Drugs and Driving: Abstracts and Reviews, 1*(4), 15–40.

Peck, R. C., & Voas, R. B. (2002). Forfeiture programs in California: Why so few? *Journal of Safety Research, 33*(2), 245–258.

Peek-Asa, C. (1999). The effect of random alcohol screening in reducing motor vehicle crash injuries. *American Journal of Preventive Medicine, 16*(1S), 57–67.

Perkins, H. W. (2002). Social norms and the prevention of alcohol misuse in collegiate contexts. *Journals of Studies on Alcohol, Suppl*(14), 164–172.

Polacsek, M., Rogers, E. M., Woodall, W. G., Delaney, H., Wheeler, D., & Nagesh, R. (2001). MADD victim impact panels and stages–of–change in drunk-driving prevention. *Journal of Studies on Alcohol, 62*(3), 344–350.

Postman, N., Nystrom, C., Strate, L., & Weingartner, C. (1988). *Myths, men, and beer: An analysis of beer commercials on broadcast television, 1987*. Washington, DC: AAA Foundation for Traffic Safety.

Preusser, D. F., Williams, A., Nichols, J., Tison, J., & Chaudhary, N. (2008). *National Cooperative Highway Research Program: Effectiveness of behavioral highway safety countermeasures*. Washington, DC: Transportation Research Board.

Preusser, D. F., Williams, A. F., & Weinstein, H. B. (1994). Policing underage alcohol sales. *Journal of Safety Research, 25*, 127–133.

Preusser, D. F., Williams, A. F., Zador, P. L., & Blomberg, R. D. (1984). The effect of curfew laws on motor vehicle crashes. *Law and Policy, 6*, 115–128.

Radecki, T. E., & Strohl, J. (1991). Survey of underage youth and alcohol purchase habits in 17 midwest and eastern states. *Drug Free Youth News*, 1–8.

Research and Evaluation Associates (REA). (1991). *The effects following the implementation of an 0.08 BAC limit and an administrative per se law in California*. Washington, DC: National Highway Traffic Safety Administration.

Rider, R. P., Voas, R. B., Kelley-Baker, T., Grosz, M., & Murphy, B. (2007). Preventing alcohol-related convictions: The impact of a novel curriculum for first-time offenders on DUI recidivism. *Traffic Injury Prevention, 8*(2), 147–152.

Ritson, B. (2005). Treatment for alcohol-related problems. *British Medical Journal, 330*, 139–141. Retrieved June 22, 2006, from http://bmj.bmjjournals.com/cgi/content/full/330/7483/139

Roberts, L. J., Neal, D. J., Kivlahan, D. R., Baer, J. S., & Marlatt, G. A. (2000). Individual drinking changes following a brief intervention among college students: Clinical significance in an indicated preventive context. *Journal of Consulting and Clinical Psychology, 68*(3), 500–505.

Robertson, R. D., & Simpson, H. M. (2002a). *DWI system improvements for dealing with hard core drinking drivers: Adjudication & sanctioning*. Ottawa, Ontario, Canada: Traffic Injury Research Foundation.

Robertson, R. D., & Simpson, H. M. (2002b). *DWI system improvements for dealing with hard core drinking drivers: Monitoring*. Ottawa, Ontario, Canada: Traffic Injury Research Foundation.

Robertson, R. D., & Simpson, H. M. (2002c). *DWI system improvements for dealing with hard core drinking drivers: Prosecution*. Ottawa, Ontario, Canada: Traffic Injury Research Foundation.

Rogers, P. (1995). *The general deterrent impact of California's 0.08% blood alcohol concentration limit and administrative per se license suspension laws*. Sacramento, CA: California Department of Motor Vehicles.

Romano, E., Fell, J., & Voas, R. B. (2011). The role of race and ethnicity on the effect of graduated driver licensing laws in the United States. *Annals of Advances in Automotive Medicine, 55*, 51–61.

Ross, H., & Gonzales, P. (1988). The effect of license revocation on drunk-driving offenders. *Accident Analysis and Prevention, 20*(5), 379–391.

Ross, H. L. (1973). Law, science and accidents: The British Road Safety Act of 1967. *The Journal of Legal Studies, 2*, 1–78.

Ross, H. L. (1982a). *Deterring the drinking driver: Legal policy and social control* (2nd ed.). Lexington, MA: D. C. Heath.

Ross, H. L. (1982b). Prevention and deterrence: The international experience. *Alcohol Health and Research World, 7*(1), 26–30, 39–43.

Ross, H. L. (1992a). Are DWI sanctions effective? *Alcohol, Drugs and Driving, 8*(1), 61–69.

Ross, H. L. (1992b). *The deterrent capability of sobriety checkpoints: Summary of the American literature* (Final report DOT HS 807 862). Washington, DC: National Highway Traffic Safety Administration.

Ross, H. L. (1992c). Reasons for non-use of sobriety checkpoints. *Police Chief, 59*, 58–63.

Ross, H. L., & Klette, H. (1995). Abandonment of mandatory jail for impaired drivers in Norway and Sweden. *Accident Analysis and Prevention, 27*(2), 151–157.

Ross, H. L., McCleary, R., & LaFree, G. (1990). Can mandatory jail laws deter drunk driving? The Arizona case. *Journal of Criminal Law and Criminology, 81*(1), 156–170.

Ross, H. L., Simon, S., Cleary, J., Lewis, R., & Storkamp, D. (1995). Causes and consequences of implied consent test refusal. *Alcohol, Drugs and Driving, 11*(1), 57–72.

Ross, H. L., & Voas, R. B. (1990). The new Philadelphia story: The effects of severe punishment for drunk driving. *Law and Policy, 12*(1), 51–79.

Roth, R., Voas, R. B., & Marques, P. R. (2007). Interlocks for first offenders: Effective? *Traffic Injury Prevention, 8*(4), 346–352.

Rothschild, M. L., Mastin, B., & Miller, T. W. (2006). Reducing alcohol-impaired driving crashes through the use of social marketing. *Accident Analysis and Prevention, 38*(6), 1218–1230. doi: 10.1016/j.aap.2006.05.010

Runge, J., Garrison, H., Hall, W., Waller, A., & Shen, G. (2002). *Identification and referral of impaired drivers through emergency department protocols.* Washington, DC: National Highway Traffic Safety Administration. Retrieved from http://www.nhtsa.dot.gov/people/injury/research/Idemergency/index.htm

Russ, N. W., & Geller, E. S. (1986). *Evaluation of a server intervention program for preventing drunk driving.* Blacksburg, VA: Virginia Polytechnic Institute and State University, Department of Psychology.

Rydon, P., & Stockwell, T. (1997). Local regulation and enforcement strategies for licensed premises. In M. Plant, E. Single, & T. Stockwell (Eds.), *Alcohol: Minimizing the harm. What Works?* (pp. 211–229). New York: Free Association Books.

Saffer, H. (1991). Alcohol advertising bans and alcohol abuse: An international perspective. *Journal of Health Economics, 10*(1), 65–79.

Saffer, H. (1993). Alcohol advertising bans and alcohol abuses: Reply. *Journal of Health Economics, 12*(2), 229–234.

Saffer, H. (2001). Substance abuse control and crime: Evidence from the National Survey of Drug Abuse. In M. Grossman & C. R. Hsieh (Eds.), *Economic analysis of substance use and abuse: The experience of developed countries and lessons for developing countries* (pp. 291–307). Cheltenham, United Kingdom: Edward Elgar.

Saffer, H., & Chaloupka, F. (1989). Breath testing and highway fatality rates. *Applied Economics, 21*(7), 901–912.

Sagberg, F. (1998). *Month-by-month changes in accident risk among novice drivers.* Paper presented at the proceedings of the 14th International Congress of Applied Psychology, Washington, DC.

Saltz, R. F. (1987). The roles of bars and restaurants in preventing alcohol-impaired driving: An evaluation of server intervention. *Evaluation and the Health Professions, 10*(1), 5–27.

Saltz, R. F. (1988). Server intervention and responsible beverage service programs. In *Surgeon General's workshop on drunk driving–Background papers* (pp. 169–179). Rockville, MD: US Department of Health and Human Services, Office of the Surgeon General.

Saltz, R. F. (1989). Research needs and opportunities for health educators in server intervention programs. *Health Education Quarterly, 16,* 429–438.

Saltz, R. F., & Hennessy, M. (1990*a*). *Reducing intoxication in commercial establishments: An evaluation of responsible beverage service practices.* Berkeley, CA: Prevention Research Center.

Saltz, R. F., & Hennessy, M. (1990*b*). The situational riskiness of alcoholic beverages. *Journal of Studies on Alcohol, 51*(5), 422–427.

Saltz, R. F., & Stanghetta, P. (1997). A community-wide responsible beverage service program in three communities: Early findings. *Addiction, 92*(Suppl. 2), S237–S249.

Schermer, C. R., Moyers, T. B., Miller, W. R., & Bloomfield, L. A. (2006). Trauma center brief interventions for alcohol disorders decrease subsequent driving under the influence arrests. *Journal of Trauma, 60*(1), 29–34.

Schwartz, R. H., Farrow, J. A., Banks, B., & Giesel, A. E. (1998). Use of false ID cards and other deceptive methods to purchase alcoholic beverages during high school. *Journal of Addictive Diseases, 17,* 25–34.

Schwartz, R. H., & Little, D. L. (1997). Let's party tonight: Drinking patterns and breath alcohol values at high school parties. *Family Medicine, 29*(5), 326–331.

Sherman, L. W. (1990). Police crackdowns: Initial and residual deterrence. In M. Tonry & N. Morris (Eds.), *Crime and justice: An annual review of research* (pp. 1–48). Chicago: University of Chicago Press.

Shinar, D. (2007). *Traffic safety and human behavior* (1st ed.). Kidlington, Oxford: Elsevier.

Shinar, D., & Compton, R. (1995). Victim impact panels: Their impact on DWI recidivism. *Alcohol, Drugs and Driving, 11*(1), 73–87.

Shope, J. T., Elliott, M. R., Raghunathan, T. E., & Waller, P. F. (2001). Long-term follow-up of a high school alcohol misuse prevention program's effect on students' subsequent driving. *Alcoholism: Clinical and Experimental Research, 25*(3), 403–410.

Shope, J. T., & Molnar, L. J. (2004). Michigan's graduated driver licensing program: Evaluation of the first four years. *Journal of Safety Research, 35*(3), 337–344.

Shope, J. T., Molnar, L. J., Elliott, M. R., & Waller, P. F. (2001). Graduated driver licensing in Michigan: Early impact on motor vehicle crashes among 16 year-old drivers. *Journal of the American Medical Association, 286*(13), 1593–1598.

Shults, R. A., Elder, R. W., Sleet, D. A., Nichols, J. L., Alao, M. O., Carande–Kulis, V. G., Zaza, S., Sosin, D. M., & Thompson, R. S. (2001). Reviews of evidence regarding interventions to reduce alcohol-impaired driving. *American Journal of Preventive Medicine, 21*(4 Suppl.), 66–88.

Simons–Morton, B. G., & Cummings, S. S. (1997). Evaluation of a local designated driver and responsible server program to prevent drinking and driving. *Journal of Drug Education, 27*(4), 321–333.

Simpson, H., Beirness, D., Mayhew, D., & Donelson, A. (1985). *Alcohol specific controls: Implications for road safety.* Ottawa, ON: Traffic Injury Research Foundation of Canada.

Simpson, H. M., Mayhew, D. R., & Beirness, D. J. (1996). *Dealing with the hard core drinking driver.* Ottawa, Canada: Traffic Injury Research Foundation.

Simpson, H. M., & Robertson, R. D. (2001). *DWI system improvements for dealing with hard core drinking drivers: Enforcement.* Ottawa, Ontario, Canada: Traffic Injury Research Foundation.

Sloan, F. A., Reilly, B. A., & Schenzler, C. (1994). Effects of prices, civil, and criminal sanctions, and law enforcement on alcohol-related mortality. *Journal of Studies on Alcohol, 55,* 454–465.

Sloan, F. A., Stout, E. M., Whetten-Goldstein, K., & Liang, L. (2000). *Drinkers, drivers, and bartenders: Balancing private choices and public accountability.* Chicago: University of Chicago Press.

Smart, R. G., Adlaf, E. M., & Walsh, G. W. (1996). Procurement of alcohol and underage drinking among adolescents in Ontario. *Journal of Studies on Alcohol, 57*(4), 419–424.

Smart, R. G., & Cutler, R. E. (1976). The alcohol advertising ban in British Columbia: Problems and effects of beverage consumption. *British Journal of Addiction, 71*(1), 13–21.

Smith, D. I. (1988*a*). Effect on traffic accidents of introducing Sunday alcohol sales in Brisbane, Australia. *International Journal of the Addictions, 23*(10), 1091–1099.

Smith, D. I. (1988*b*). Effect on traffic safety of introducing a 0.05% blood alcohol level in Queensland, Australia. *Medicine, Science and Law, 28*(2), 165–170.

Soderstrom, C. A., Dischinger, P. C., Kerns, T. J., Kufera, J. A., Mitchell, K. A., & Scalea, T. M. (2001). Epidemic increases in cocaine and opiate use by trauma center patients: Documentation with a large clinical toxicology database. *Journal of Trauma, 51*, 557–564.

Solberg, L. I., Maciosek, M., & Edwards, N. M. (2008). Primary care intervention to reduce alcohol misuse: Ranking its health impact and cost effectiveness. *American Journal of Preventive Medicine, 34*(2), 143–152.

Sommers, M. S., Dyehouse, J. M., & Howe, S. R. (2001). Binge drinking, sensible drinking, and abstinence after alcohol-related vehicular crashes: The role of intervention versus screening. *Annual Proceedings of the Association for Advanced Automotive Medicine, 45*, 317–328.

Stewart, E. I., & Malfetti, J. L. (1970). *Rehabilitation of the drunken driver: A corrective course in Phoenix, Arizona, for persons convicted of driving under the influence of alcohol.* New York: Teachers College Press.

Stewart, K., & Ellingstad, V. S. (1989). Rehabilitation counter-measures for drinking drivers. In *Background papers, Surgeon General's Workshop on drunken driving* (pp. 234–246). Washington, DC: Public Health Service.

Stockwell, T., Lang, E., & Rydon, P. (1993). High risk drinking settings: The association of serving and promotional practices with harmful drinking. *Addiction, 88*(11), 1519–1526.

Stuster, J., & Burns, M. (1998). *Validation of the standardized field sobriety test battery at BACs below 0.10 %.* Washington, DC: Department of Transportation, National Highway Traffic Safety Administration.

Stuster, J. W. (1993). *The detection of DWI motorcyclists.* Washington, DC: National Highway Traffic Safety Administration.

Stuster, J. W. (1997). *The detection of DWI at BACs below 0.10* (Final report). Washington, DC: US Department of Transportation, National Highway Traffic Safety Administration. Retrieved from http://www.popcenter.org/problems/drunk_driving/PDFs/NHTSA_1997.pdf

Stuster, J. W., & Blowers, M. A. (1995). *Experimental evaluation of sobriety checkpoint programs* (DOT HS 808 287). Washington, DC: US Department of Transportation, National Highway Safety Administration. Retrieved from http://ntl.bts.gov/lib/25000/25900/25932/DOT-HS-808-287.pdf

Stuster, J. W., Burns, M., & Fiorentino, D. (2002). *Open container laws and alcohol involved crashes: Some preliminary data.* Washington, DC: National Highway Traffic Safety Administration. Retrieved from http://www.nhtsa.dot.gov/people/injury/research/opencontainer/index.htm

Supreme Court of the US (1990). *Michigan Department of State Police et al. v. Sitz et al.* 429 N. W. 2d 190 (Mich. App. 1988).

Swahn, M. H., Hamming, B. J., & Ikeda, R. M. (2002). Prevalence of youth access to alcohol or a gun in the home. *Injury Prevention, 8*(3), 227–230.

Sweedler, B. M., Biecheler, M. B., Laurell, H., Kroj, G., Lerner, M., Mathijssen, M. P., Mayhew, D., & Tunbridge, R. J. (2004). Worldwide trends in alcohol and drug impaired driving. *Traffic Injury Prevention, 5*(3), 175–184.

Swift, R. M. (2003). Direct measurement of alcohol and its metabolites. *Addiction, 98*(Suppl. 2), 73.

Tashima, H. N., & Helander, C. J. (2000). *Annual report of the California DUI management information system.* Sacramento, CA: California Department of Motor Vehicles.

Tauber, J., & Huddleston, C. W. (1999). *DUI/drug courts: Defining a national strategy.* Alexandria, VA: National Drug Court Institute.

Tharp, V. K., Burns, M., & Moskowitz, H. (1981). *Development and field test of psychophysical tests for DWI arrests.* Washington,

DC: Department of Transportation, National Highway Traffic Safety Administration.

Timken, D., & Marques, P. R. (2001a). Support for Interlock Planning (SIP): Participants workbook. Calverton, MD: Pacific Institute for Research and Evaluation. Retrieved April 20, 2009, from www.pire.org/sip/sipmanuals.htm

Timken, D., & Marques, P. R. (2001b). Support for Interlock Planning (SIP): Providers manual. Calverton, MD: Pacific Institute for Research and Evaluation. Retrieved April 20, 2009, from www.pire.org/sip/sipmanuals.htm

Tippetts, A. S., & Voas, R. B. (1998). The effectiveness of the West Virginia interlock program. *Journal of Traffic Medicine, 26*(1–2), 19–24.

Tippetts, A. S., Voas, R. B., Fell, J. C., & Nichols, J. L. (2005). A meta-analysis of .08 BAC laws in 19 jurisdictions in the United States. *Accident Analysis and Prevention, 37*(1), 149–161.

Tison, J., Solomon, M. G., Nichols, J., Gilbert, S. H., Siegler, J. N., & Cosgrove, L. A. (2008). *May 2006 "Click It or Ticket" seat belt mobilization evaluation.* Washington, DC: National Highway Traffic Safety Administration.

Toomey, T., Wagenaar, A. C., Erickson, D. J., Fletcher, L. A., Patrek, W., & Lenk, K. M. (2004). Illegal alcohol sales to obviously intoxicated patrons at licensed establishments. *Alcohol: Clinical and Experimental Research, 28*(5), 769–774.

Toomey, T. L., Erickson, D. J., Lenk, K. M., & Kilian, G. R. (2008). Likelihood of illegal alcohol sales at professional sport stadiums. *Alcoholism: Clinical and Experimental Research, 32*(11), 1859–1864.

Toomey, T. L., Wagenaar, A. C., Gehan, J. P., Kilian, G., Murray, D. B., & Perry, C. L. (2001). Project Arm: Alcohol risk management to prevent sales to underage and intoxicated patrons. *Health Education & Behavior, 28*(2), 186–199.

Transportation Research Board. (1995). *Strategies for dealing with the persistent drinking driver* (Transportation Research Circular 437). Washington, DC: National Research Council.

Transportation Research Board. (2010). *Achieving traffic safety goals in the United States: Lessons from other nations* (Special report 300). Washington, DC: Transportation Research Board of the National Academies of Science, Committee for the Study of Traffic Safety Lessons from Benchmark Nations.

Treno, A. J., & Holder, H. D. (1997). Community mobilization, organizing, and media advocacy: A discussion of methodological issues. *Evaluation Review, 21*(2), 166–190.

Ulmer, R. G., Preusser, D. F., Williams, A. F., Ferguson, S. A., & Farmer, C. M. (2000). Graduated licensing program on the crash rate of teenage drivers. *Accident Analysis and Prevention, 32*(4), 527–532.

US General Accounting Office (GAO). (1987). *Drinking-age-laws: An evaluation synthesis of their impact on highway safety* (Report to the Chairman, Subcommittee on Investigations and Oversight, Committee on Public Works and Transportation, House of Representatives). Washington, DC: USGAO/US Superintendent of Documents.

Van Iwaarden, M. J. (1985). Public health aspects of the marketing of alcoholic drinks. In M. Grant (Ed.), *Alcohol policies* (pp. 45–55). Copenhagen, Denmark: World Health Organization.

Vanlaar, W., Mayhew, D., Marcoux, K., Wets, G., Brijs, T., & Shope, J. (2009). *An evaluation of graduated driver licensing programs in North America.* Ottawa, ON: Traffic Injury Research Foundation.

Vézina, L. (2002). The Quebec alcohol interlock program: Impact on recidivism and crashes. In D. Mayhew & C. Dussault (Eds.), *Proceedings of Alcohol, Drugs & Traffic Safety—T 2002: 16th International Conference on Alcohol, Drugs & Traffic Safety, August 4–9, 2002* (Vol. 1, pp. 97–104). Québec City: Société de l'assurance automobile du Québec.

Vingilis, E., McLeod, A. I., Seeley, J., Mann, R., Voas, R., & Compton, C. (2006). The impact of Ontario's extended drinking hours on cross-border cities of Windsor and Detroit. *Accident Analysis and Prevention, 38*(1), 63–70.

Voas, R. B. (1969). *Cars that drunks can't drive.* Washington, DC: National Highway Safety Research Center.

Voas, R. B. (1972). *ASAP program evaluation methodology and overall program impact.* Washington, DC: National Highway Traffic Safety Administration.

Voas, R. B. (1981). Results and implications of the ASAPs. In Leonard Goldberg (Ed.), *Alcohol, drugs and traffic safety—T80. Proceedings of the 8th International Conference on Alcohol, Drugs and Traffic Safety, June 15–19, 1980, Stockholm, Sweden* (Vol. 3, pp. 1129–1144). Göteborg: Graphic Systems.

Voas, R. B. (1986). Evaluation of jail as a penalty for drunken driving. *Alcohol, Drugs and Driving: Abstracts and Reviews, 2*(2), 47–70.

Voas, R. B. (1992). *Assessment of impoundment and forfeiture laws for drivers convicted of DWI.* Phase I report: *Review of state laws and their application.* Washington, DC: Department of Transportation, National Highway Traffic Safety Administration.

Voas, R. B. (1999). The three Rs for controlling the hardcore drinking driver: MADD's program for the repeat DWI offender. *The Prevention Pipeline, 12*(3), 1–6.

Voas, R. B. (2008). A new look at NHTSA's evaluation of the 1984 Charlottesville Sobriety Checkpoint Program: Implications for current checkpoint issues. *Traffic Injury Prevention, 9*(1), 22–30.

Voas, R. B. (2010). Monitoring drinking: Alternative to suspending license to control impaired drivers? *Transportation Research Record: Journal of the Transportation Research Board, 2182,* 1–7.

Voas, R. B., Blackman, K. O., Tippetts, A. S., & Marques, P. R. (2002a). Evaluation of a program to motivate impaired driving offenders to install ignition interlocks. *Accident Analysis and Prevention, 34*(4), 449–455.

Voas, R. B., & DeYoung, D. J. (2002). Vehicle action: Effective policy for controlling drunk and other high-risk drivers? *Accident Analysis and Prevention, 34*(3), 263–270.

Voas, R. B., & Fell, J. C. (2011). Preventing impaired driving: Opportunities and problems. *Alcohol Research and Health, 34*(2), 225–235.

Voas, R. B., Fell, J. C., Tippetts, A. S., Blackman, K., & Nichols, J. (2007). Impact of primary safety belt laws on alcohol-related front-seat occupant fatalities: Five case studies. *Traffic Injury Prevention, 8*(3), 232–243.

Voas, R. B., & Fisher, D. A. (2001). Court procedures for handling intoxicated drivers. *Alcohol Research and Health, 25*(1), 32–42.

Voas, R. B., & Hause, J. M. (1987). Deterring the drinking driver: The Stockton experience. *Accident Analysis and Prevention, 19*(2), 81–90.

Voas, R. B., Holder, H. D., & Gruenewald, P. J. (1997). The effect of drinking and driving interventions on alcohol-involved traffic crashes within a comprehensive community trial. *Addiction, 92*(Suppl. 2), S221–S236.

Voas, R. B., Johnson, M. B., & Miller, B. A. (2013). Alcohol and drug use among young adults driving to a drinking location. *Drug and Alcohol Dependence.* doi: Http://dx.doi.org/10.1016/j.drugalcdep.2013.01.014

Voas, R. B., Johnson, M. B., Turrisi, R. J., Taylor, D., Honts, C. R., & Nelsen, L. (2008a). Bringing alcohol on campus to raise money: Impact on student drinking and drinking problems. *Addiction, 103,* 940–950.

Voas, R. B., & Lacey, J. H. (1990). Drunk driving enforcement, adjudication, and sanctions in the United States. In R. J. Wilson & R. E. Mann (Eds.), *Drinking and driving: Advances in research and prevention* (pp. 116–158). New York: Guilford.

Voas, R. B., Lange, J. E., & Tippetts, A. S. (1998). Enforcement of the zero tolerance law in California: A missed opportunity? In *42nd annual proceedings of the Association for the Advancement of Automotive Medicine, Charlottesville, VA, October 5–7, 1998* (Vol. 42, pp. 369–383). Des Plaines, IL: Association for the Advancement of Automotive Medicine.

Voas, R. B., Lange, J., & Treno, A. J. (1997). Documenting community-level outcomes: Lessons from drinking and driving. *Evaluation Review, 21*(2), 191–208.

Voas, R. B., & Marques, P. R. (1992). Model specifications for breath alcohol ignition interlock devices (BAIIDs). *The Federal Register, 57*(67), 11772–11787.

Voas, R. B., & Marques, P. R. (2003). Commentary: Barriers to interlock implementation. *Traffic Injury Prevention, 4*(3), 183–187.

Voas, R. B., Marques, P. R., Tippetts, A. S., & Beirness, D. J. (1999b). The Alberta Interlock Program: The evaluation of a province-wide program on DUI recidivism. *Addiction, 94*(12), 1849–1859.

Voas, R. B., McKnight, A. S., Falb, T., Fell, J. C., Stewart, K., & Sweedler, B. (2008b). *Update of vehicle sanction laws and their application: Volume I—Summary* (DOT HS 811 028A). Washington, DC: National Highway Traffic Safety Administration. Retrieved from http://www.nhtsa.gov/Driving+Safety/Research+&+Evaluation/Update+of+Vehicle+Sanction+Laws+and+Their+Application

Voas, R. B., Rhodenizer, A. E., & Lynn, C. (1985). *Evaluation of Charlottesville checkpoint operations.* Washington, DC: National Highway Traffic Safety Administration. (Available in hard copy format only from the National Technical Information Service, Springfield, VA.)

Voas, R. B., Romano, E. O., Kelley-Baker, R., & Tippetts, A. S. (2006a). A partial ban on sales to reduce high-risk drinking south of the border: Seven years later. *Journal of Studies on Alcohol, 67*(5), 746–753.

Voas, R. B., Romano, E., & Peck, R. (2006b). Validity of the passive sensor for identifying high BAC drivers at the crash scene. *Journal of Studies on Alcohol, 67*(5), 714–721.

Voas, R. B., Taylor, E. P., Kelley-Baker, T., & Tippetts, A. S. (2000). *Effectiveness of the Illinois .08 law.* Washington, DC: National Highway Traffic Safety Administration.

Voas, R. B., & Tippetts, A. S. (1995). Evaluation of Washington and Oregon license plate sticker laws. In *39th annual proceedings of the Association for the Advancement of Automotive Medicine (AAAM)* (pp. 29–44). Des Plaines, IL: Association for the Advancement of Automotive Medicine.

Voas, R. B., Tippetts, A. S., & Fell, J. C. (1999a). The United States limits drinking by youth under age 21: Does this reduce fatal crash involvements? In *43rd annual proceedings*

of the Association for the Advancement of Automotive Medicine,
September 20-21, 1999, Barcelona (Sitges), Spain (vol. 43, pp.
265–278). Des Plaines, IL: Association for the Advancement
of Automotive Medicine.

Voas, R. B., Tippetts, A. S., & Fell, J. C. (2000). The relationship of alcohol safety laws to drinking drivers in fatal crashes.
Accident Analysis and Prevention, 32(4), 483–492.

Voas, R. B., Tippetts, A. S., & Fell, J. C. (2003). Assessing the
effectiveness of minimum legal drinking age and zero tolerance laws in the United States. Accident Analysis and
Prevention, 35(4), 579–587.

Voas, R. B., Tippetts, A. S., Fisher, D. A., & Grosz, M.
(2010). Requiring suspended drunk drivers to install
alcohol interlocks to reinstate their licenses: Effective?
Addiction, 105(8), 1422–1428. doi: Http://dx.doi.
org/10.1111/j.1360-0443.2010.02987.x

Voas, R. B., Tippetts, A. S., & Grosz, M. (2013). Administrative
reinstatement interlock programs: Florida, a 10-year study
of success. Alcoholism: Clinical and Experimental Research,
37(7), 1243-1251. doi: 10.1111/acer.12078

Voas, R. B., Tippetts, A. S., Johnson, M. B., Lange, J. E., &
Baker, J. (2002b). Operation Safe Crossing: Using science within a community intervention. Addiction, 97(9),
1205–1214.

Voas, R. B., Tippetts, A. S., & Lange, J. E. (1997). Evaluation of
a method for reducing unlicensed driving: The Washington
and Oregon license plate sticker laws. Accident Analysis and
Prevention, 29(5), 627–634.

Voas, R. B., Tippetts, A. S., & Taylor, E. P. (1997). Temporary
vehicle immobilization: Evaluation of a program in Ohio.
Accident Analysis and Prevention, 29(5), 635–642.

Voas, R. B., Tippetts, A. S., & Taylor, E. P. (1998). Temporary
vehicle impoundment in Ohio: A replication and confirmation. Accident Analysis and Prevention, 30(5), 651–655.

Voas, R. B., Torres, P., Romano, E., & Lacey, J. H. (2012).
Alcohol-related risk of driver fatalities: An update using 2007
data. Journal of Studies on Alcohol and Drugs, 73(3), 341–350.

Wagenaar, A., & Wolfson, M. (1994). Enforcement of the legal
minimum drinking age. Journal of Public Health Policy,
15, 37–53.

Wagenaar, A. C. (1982). Preventing highway crashes by raising
the legal minimum age for drinking: An empirical confirmation. Journal of Safety Research, 13, 57–71.

Wagenaar, A. C. (1993). Minimum drinking age and alco-
hol availability to youth: Issues and research needs. In M.
E. Hilton & G. Bloss (Eds.), Economics and the preven-
tion of alcohol–related problems (pp. 175–200). (Research
Monograph No. 25, NIH Pub. No. 93–3513). Bethesda,
MD: National Institute on Alcohol Abuse and Alcoholism.

Wagenaar, A. C., Finnegan, J. R., Wolfson, M., Anstine, P. S.,
Williams, C. L., & Perry, C. L. (1993). Where and how
adolescents obtain alcoholic beverages. Public Health Reports,
108(4), 459–464.

Wagenaar, A. C., & Holder, H. D. (1995). Changes in alcohol
consumption resulting from the elimination of retail wine
monopolies: Results from five US states. Journal of Studies on
Alcohol, 56(5), 566–572.

Wagenaar, A. C., & Holder, H. D. (1996). The scientific process
works: Seven replications now show significant wine sales
increases after privatization. Journal of Studies on Alcohol, 57,
575–576.

Wagenaar, A. C., & Maldonado–Molina, M. M. (2007). Effects
of drivers' license suspension policies on alcohol-related

crash involvement: Long-term follow-up in forty-six states.
Alcoholism: Clinical and Experimental Research, 31(8),
1399–1406.

Wagenaar, A. C., Maldonado–Molina, M. M., Erickson, D.
J., Ma, L., Tobler, A. L., & Komro, K. A. (2007). General
deterrence effects of US statutory DUI fine and jail penalties: Long-term follow-up in 32 states. Accident Analysis and
Prevention, 39(5), 982–994.

Wagenaar, A. C., Murray, D. M., Gehan, J. P., Wolfson, M.,
Forster, J. L., Toomey, T. L., Perry, C. L., & Jones-Webb,
R. (2000a). Communities mobilizing for change on alcohol: Outcomes from a randomized community trail. Journal
of Studies on Alcohol, 61(1), 85–94.

Wagenaar, A. C., Murray, D. M., & Toomey, T. L. (2000b).
Communities mobilizing for change on alcohol
(CMCA): Effects of a randomized trial on arrest and traffic
crashes. Addiction, 95, 209–217.

Wagenaar, A. C., Salois, M. J., & Komro, K. A. (2009).
Effects of beverage alcohol price and tax levels on drink-
ing: A meta-analysis of 1003 estimates from 112 studies.
Addiction, 104, 179–190.

Wagenaar, A. C., & Toomey, T. L. (2002). Effects of minimum
drinking age laws: Review and analyses of the literature from
1960 to 2000. Journal of Studies on Alcohol(Supplement No.
14), 206–225.

Wagenaar, A. C., Toomey, T. L., & Erickson, D. J. (2005).
Complying with the minimum drinking age: Effects of
enforcement and training interventions. Alcoholism: Clinical
and Experimental Research, 29(3), 255–262.

Wagenaar, A. C., Toomey, T. L., Murray, D. M., Short, B. J.,
Wolfson, M., & Jones-Webb, R. (1996). Sources of alcohol for
underage drinkers. Journal of Studies on Alcohol, 57(3), 325–333.

Wagenaar, A. C., Zobeck, T. S., Hingson, R., & Williams,
G. D. (1995). Studies of control efforts: A meta-analysis
from 1960 through 1991. Accident Analysis and Prevention,
27, 1–16.

Wallack, L., Dorfman, L., Jernigan, D., & Themba, M. (1993).
Media advocacy and public health: Power for prevention.
Newbury Park, CA: Sage.

Wallack, L., Grube, J. W., Madden, P. A., & Breed, W. (1990).
Portrayals of alcohol on prime-time television. Journal of
Studies on Alcohol, 51, 428–437.

Wechsler, H., Davenport, A., Dowdall, G., Moeykens, B., &
Castillo, S. (1994). Health and behavioral consequences of
binge drinking in college: A national survey of students at
140 campuses. Journal of the American Medical Association,
272(21), 1672–1677.

Wechsler, H., Lee, J. E., Kuo, M., & Lee, H. (2000).
College binge drinking in the 1990s: A continuing problem: Results of the Harvard School of Public Health 1999
College Alcohol Study. Journal of American College Health,
48, 199–210.

Wells, J. K., Preusser, D. F., & Williams, A. F. (1992). Enforcing
alcohol-impaired driving and seat belt use laws, Binghamton,
New York. Journal of Safety Research, 23, 63–71.

Wells-Parker, E., Bangert-Drowns, R., McMillen, R., &
Williams, M. (1995). Final results from a meta–analysis of
remedial interventions with drink/drive offenders. Addiction,
90(7), 907–926.

Wells-Parker, E., & Williams, M. (2002). Enhancing the effectiveness of traditional interventions with drinking drivers by
adding brief individual intervention components. Journal of
Studies on Alcohol, 63(6), 655–664.

Wheeler, D. R., Rogers, E. M., Tonigan, J. S., & Woodall, W. G. (2004). Effectiveness of customized Victim Impact Panels on first-time DWI offender inmates. *Accident Analysis and Prevention, 36*(1), 29–35.

Wieczorek, W. F., Miller, B. A., & Nochajski, T. H. (1992). The limited utility of BAC for identifying alcohol-related problems among DWI offenders. *Journal of Studies on Alcohol, 53*(5), 415–419.

Wilde, C. J. S., Hoste, J. L., Sheppard, D., & Wind, G. (1971). Road safety campaigns: Design and evaluation. In *Organization for economic co–operation and development* (pp. 75). Paris, France.

Wiliszowski, C., Murphy, P., Jones, R., & Lacey, J. (1996). *Determine reasons for repeat drinking and driving* (Final report). Washington, DC: Department of Transportation, National Highway Traffic Safety Administration (NHTSA).

Wiliszowski, C. H., Fell, J. C., McKnight, A. S., Tippetts, A. S., & Ciccel, J. D. (2010). An evaluation of three intensive supervision programs for serious DWI offenders. *Annals of Advances in Automotive Medicine, 54,* 375–387.

Williams, A. F. (1985). Young driver accidents: In search of solutions. In D. R. Mayhew, H. M. Simpson & A. C. Donalsen (Eds.), *Laws and regulations applicable to teenagers or new drivers: Their potential for reducing motor vehicle injuries.* (pp. 43–62). Ottawa, Canada: The Traffic Injury Research Foundation.

Williams, A. F. (1996). Magnitude and characteristics of the young driver crash problem in the United States. In H. M. Simpson (Ed.), *New to the road: Reducing the risks for young motorists* (pp. 19–25). Los Angeles, CA: Youth Enhancement Service, Brain Information Service, UCLA School of Medicine.

Williams, A. F., & Ferguson, S. A. (2004). Driver education renaissance? *Injury Prevention, 10*(1), 4–7.

Williams, A. F., Ferguson, S. A., & Wells, J. K. (2005). Sixteen-year-old drivers in fatal crashes, United States, 2003. *Traffic Injury Prevention, 6*(3), 202–206.

Williams, A. F., Karpf, R. S., & Zador, P. L. (1983). Variations in minimum licensing age and fatal motor vehicle crashes. *American Journal of Public Health, 73*(12), 1401–1403.

Williams, R. L., Hagen, R. E., & McConnell, E. J. (1984). A survey of suspension and revocation effects on the drinking-driver offender. *Accident Analysis and Prevention, 16*(5/6), 339–350.

Williams, T. P., & Lillis, R. P. (1986). Changes in alcohol consumption by 18-year-olds following an increase in New York State's purchase age to 19. *Journal of Studies on Alcohol, 47,* 290–296.

Willis, C., Lybrand, S., & Bellamy, N. (2004). Alcohol ignition interlock programmes for reducing drink driving recidivism. *Cochran Database of Systematic Reviews, 18*(4), CD004168.

Winsten, J. A. (1994). Promoting designated drivers: The Harvard Alcohol Project. *American Journal of Preventive Medicine, 10*(Suppl. 1), 11–14.

Wolfson, M., Champion, H., McCoy, T. P., Rhodes, S. D., Ip, E. H., Blocker, J. N., Martin, B. A., Wagoner, K. G., O'Brien, M. C., Sutfin, E. L., Mitra, A., & DuRant, R. H. (2012). Impact of a randomized campus/community trial to prevent high-risk drinking among college students. *Alcoholism: Clinical and Experimental Research, 36*(10), 1767–1778. doi: 10.1111/j.1530–0277.2012.01786.x

Wren, E., & Drive & Stay Alive Inc. (2003). *Drunk driving blood alcohol limits: International blood alcohol limits.* DSA. Retrieved December 19, 2008, from http://www.drive-andstayalive.com/articles%20and%20topics/drunk%20driving/artcl-drunk-driving-0005-global-BAC-limits.htm

Wurst, F. M., Vogel, R., Jachau, K., Varga, A., Alling, C., Alt, A., & Skipper, G. E. (2003). Ethyl glucuronide discloses recent covert alcohol use not detected by standard testing in forensic psychiatric inpatients. *Alcoholism: Clinical and Experimental Research, 27*(3), 471–476.

Yu, J., Varone, R., & Shacket, R. W. (1997). *Fifteen-year review of drinking age laws: Preliminary findings of the 1996 New York State Youth Alcohol Survey.* New York: Office of Alcoholism and Substance Abuse.

Zador, P., Krawchuck, S., & Moore, B. (2001). *Drinking and driving trips, stops by police, and arrests: Analyses of the 1995 national survey of drinking and driving attitudes and behavior.* Washington, DC: National Highway Traffic Safety Administration.

Zador, P. L. (1991). Alcohol-related relative risk of fatal driver injuries in relation to driver age and sex. *Journal of Studies on Alcohol, 52*(4), 302–310.

Zador, P. L., Krawchuck, S. A., & Voas, R. B. (2000). Alcohol-related relative risk of driver fatalities and driver involvement in fatal crashes in relation to driver age and gender: An update using 1996 data. *Journal of Studies on Alcohol, 61*(3), 387–395.

Zaloshnja, E., & Miller, T. R. (2009). Costs of crashes related to road conditions, United States, 2006. In *53rd annual proceedings of the Association for the Advancement of Automotive Medicine* (Vol. 53, pp. 141–153). Barrington, IL: Association for the Advancement of Automotive Medicine.

Zobeck, T. S., & Williams, G. D. (1994). *Evaluation synthesis of the impacts of DWI laws and enforcement methods* (Final report). Rockville, MD: Office of Policy Analysis, National Institute on Alcohol Abuse and Alcoholism.

Zwerling, C., & Jones, M. P. (1999). Evaluation of the effectiveness of low blood alcohol concentration laws for younger drivers. *American Journal of Preventive Medicine, 16*(1 Suppl.), 76–80.

Zwicker, T. J., Hedlund, J., & Northrup, V. S. (2005). *Breath test refusals in DWI enforcement: An interim report* (DOT HS 809 876). Washington, DC: US Department of Transportation, National Highway Traffic Safety Administration.

CHAPTER
23

Prevention and Intervention
in the School Setting

Elizabeth J. D'Amico, Karen Chan Osilla, *and* Stefanie A. Stern

Abstract

It is well known that the prevalence of alcohol and other drug (AOD) use in the United States increases during the middle school and high school years. The current chapter focuses on the effects of AOD use on youth, and risk and protective factors that may contribute to initiation and escalation of AOD use during this developmental period. The chapter also discusses the importance of creating developmentally appropriate prevention and intervention programming for this age group. The authors provide data on several middle school and high school prevention and intervention programs that have delivered curricula in the school setting to attempt to decrease AOD use. They focus on programs that had a student-only component for their program and had also published at least a 1-year follow-up. They also discuss potential future directions for prevention and intervention for this age group.

Key Words: adolescents, alcohol and drug use, prevention, intervention, school

Prevalence and Consequences of Alcohol and Other Drug Use

It is well known that the prevalence of alcohol and other drug (AOD) use in the United States increases during the middle school and high school years (Donovan, 2007; Johnston, O'Malley, Bachman, & Schulenberg, 2013). Specifically, from 6th to 8th grade, alcohol and marijuana use triples (D'Amico et al., 2005), and by the time teens reach 12th grade, 22.9% report using marijuana in the past 30 days, 8.4% report using other drugs, and 41.5% report drinking, with 28.1% reporting being drunk in the previous 30 days (Johnston et al., 2013). Using AOD during adolescence can affect risk of injury and later dependence. For example, youth who begin drinking in their teenage years are more likely during late adolescence and adulthood to experience alcohol-related unintentional injuries (e.g., motor vehicle crashes, falls, burns, and drownings; Hingson, Heeren, Jamanka, & Howland, 2000). In addition, AOD use is a risk

factor for violent behaviors as teens who report peer and dating violence are more likely to also report heavy drinking and marijuana use (Walton et al., 2009). Further, among adults in 2010 who first tried marijuana before age 14, 12.7% developed abuse or dependence of illicit drugs compared with 2.0% of adults who first tried marijuana after age 18. Similarly, 13.8% of adults who first drank alcohol before age 21 developed alcohol abuse or dependence compared with 1.8% who initiated use after age 21 (SAMHSA, 2012a).

There is evidence that some experimentation with alcohol and/or drugs is considered to be normal during adolescence (Chassin & DeLucia, 1996; Guilamo-Ramos, Turrisi, Jaccard, & Gonzalez, 2004; Hurrelmann, 1990). For example, popularity among youth is associated with minor levels of substance use and delinquency (Allen, Porter, McFarland, McElhaney, & Marsh, 2005). There is stronger evidence, however, that abstaining youth have better health outcomes and fewer alcohol and drug problems in young adulthood than youth who experiment with substances during this time (e.g., Ellickson, Martino, & Collins, 2004; Juon, Fothergill, Green, Doherty, & Ensminger, 2011; Tucker, Ellickson, Collins, & Klein, 2006; Tucker, Ellickson, Orlando, Martino, & Klein, 2005).

Because adolescents' brains and bodies are still developing, AOD use during this time period can adversely affect functioning across several different areas and can have serious consequences during adolescence and into early and late adulthood. For example, AOD use may disrupt the brain maturation process and impair brain function over the long term (Chambers, Taylor, & Potenza, 2003; Tapert, Caldwell, & Burke, 2004; White, 2009). Tapert and colleagues have consistently found that adolescents who use alcohol and marijuana regularly may process information differently compared with adolescents who do not use these substances (Padula, Schweinsburg, & Tapert, 2007; Tapert et al., 2007); these youth may also exhibit modest but significant neurocognitive deficits by late adolescence (Jacobus et al., 2009; Schweinsburg et al., 2005; Tapert & Brown, 2000).

AOD use during this time period can also affect interpersonal, occupational, and educational functioning whereby youth who use AOD more regularly have lower functioning in all three areas compared with youth who do not use AOD (Anderson, Ramo, Cummins, & Brown, 2010; Brown, D'Amico, McCarthy, & Tapert, 2001). For example, use of alcohol in adolescence has been associated with interpersonal consequences such as physical fights and injuries (Anderson et al., 2010; Bonomo et al., 2001) and more problems with school and employment (Ellickson, Tucker, & Klein, 2003; Patton et al., 2007). Use of marijuana during adolescence is associated with lower educational achievement (Broman, 2009), including school dropout and poorer school performance (Lynskey & Hall, 2000; Patton et al., 2007). Furthermore, use of alcohol and drugs in early adolescence has been associated with increased risk of major depression and psychiatric disorders in late adolescence (Brook, Brook, Zhang, Cohen, & Whiteman, 2002; Griffith-Lendering et al., 2013) and suicide attempts, and crime during both adolescence and adulthood (Fergusson, Horwood, & Swain-Campbell, 2002; Juon et al., 2011; Popovici, Homer, & French, 2012).

Finally, there are substantial economic costs to society from AOD use, including early mortality, lost productivity, legal costs, and health costs.

Underage drinking is a leading contributor to death from injuries for people under age 21. In 2008, 5,864 young people aged 15–20 died in motor vehicle crashes. Alcohol was involved in 31% of these deaths, and 25% of these drivers were legally drunk at the time of the crash (National Highway Traffic Safety Administration, 2008).

In terms of financial costs, heavy drinking costs the U.S. economy $223.5 billion a year, and the government pays more than 60% of health care costs (Bouchery, Harwood, Sacks, Simon, & Brewer, 2011). In 2010, underage drinking in the United States cost about $62 billion (Office of Juvenile Justice and Delinquency Prevention, 2013). Illicit substance use adds to these costs. Specifically, the Office of National Drug Control Policy estimated the cost of illicit substance use in the United States to be $193 billion in 2007, and approximately 62% of these costs were associated with lost productivity (National Drug Intelligence Center, 2011). There are also significant health costs from AOD use. For example, alcohol is causally related to more than 60 different medical conditions, and across the world, 4% of the global burden of disease is attributable to alcohol, which accounts for about as much death and disability globally as tobacco and hypertension. Use of other drugs is also associated with health problems, such as HIV/AIDS and hepatitis C (NIDA, 2012; Office of National Drug Control Policy, 2004).

In sum, AOD use during this important developmental period is associated with a wide range of problems that can last into young adulthood and adulthood. Prevention and intervention programs must address both initiation of use, particularly early initiation of use, and escalation of use that can occur as youth transition from early adolescence to middle and late adolescence.

Alcohol and Drug Use in School Settings and Associated Problems

Alcohol and drug use is prevalent within school settings across the United States, and the availability of alcohol and drugs at schools has substantially increased since the 1990s (Dinkes, Cataldi, Lin-Kelly, & Snyder, 2007). Nationally, 25% of high school students report that drugs were made available to them on school property (Dinkes et al., 2007). In 2012, 78% of 10th graders and 91% of 12th graders reported that alcohol was easy to obtain, and 69% of 10th graders and 82% of 12th graders reported it would be easy to obtain marijuana (Johnston et al., 2013). The National Household Education Survey collected data in telephone interviews with 6,504 students in 6th through 12th grade and assessed exposure to AOD. Findings indicated that about one-third of these students (33%) reported seeing other students at their schools under the influence of alcohol, and about one-quarter (27%) reported that other students were high on drugs other than alcohol during school hours (Nolin, Vaden-Kiernan, Feibus, & Chandler, 1997). Data from the Youth Risk Behavior Survey found that 23% of 9th through 12th graders reported that drugs were made available to them on school property (Robers, Zhang, Truman, & Snyder, 2012). Thus, many students are exposed to alcohol and drug use in the school setting, particularly as they transition from middle school to high school.

Youth in the United States also report that they are under the influence of alcohol or drugs during school hours. For example, data from the Youth Risk Behavior Survey show that about 5.1% of high school youth report drinking on school property and 5.9% report smoking marijuana on school property in the past 30 days (Eaton et al., 2011). Among substance users, these numbers are substantially higher. Among teens who drink alcohol, 18% report drinking at school, and among teens who use marijuana, 47% report smoking marijuana at school (Finn, 2006). These percentages highlight the importance of providing prevention and intervention services in the school setting.

Many problems in the school setting can be attributed to alcohol and drug use. For example, youth who report current cigarette smoking are more likely to be disengaged from school, which is evident in both lower attendance at school and lower grades (Austin, McCarthy, Slade, & Bailey, 2007; Tucker, Martinez, Ellickson, & Edelen, 2008). Teens who use marijuana during high school are more likely to be truant (Maynard, Salas-Wright, Vaughn, & Peters, 2012; Roebuck, French, & Dennis, 2004) and to dropout of school compared with teens who do not initiate use during this period (Bray, Zarkin, Ringwalt, & Junfeng, 2000). Furthermore, use of alcohol, marijuana and/or cocaine during high school is associated with higher risk of academic failure (Farhat, Simons-Morton, & Luk, 2011; Finn, 2012; Jeynes, 2002; McLeod, Uemura, & Rohrman, 2012) and completion of fewer years of postsecondary education (Chatterji, 2006; King, Meehan, Trim, & Chassin, 2006), which can have serious implications for adolescents' prospects later in life in terms of employment and being productive members of society.

The availability and use of AOD in school settings also affect the school environment. Specifically, schools with large numbers of students who report using substances or being intoxicated at school exhibited smaller gains in test scores compared with schools in which AOD use was not as prevalent (Hanson, Austin, & Bayha, 2003). In addition, when AOD use is part of the school context (e.g., there is a subculture in which drug-use-supportive values seem pervasive), when school rules are not clear, or when youth perceive peer consumption and/or population consumption as high, students in these schools are at increased risk for substance use (Piontek, Kraus, Bjarnason, Demetrovics, & Ramstedt, 2013; Rountree & Clayton, 1999; Sznitman, Dunlop, Nalkur, Khurana, & Romer, 2012) and academic problems (Hanson et al., 2003). Thus, in addition to individual-level consequences, such as dropout, the overall school environment may also be significantly affected by adolescents' AOD use.

Although the school environment may offer youth opportunities to engage in risk behaviors, such as AOD use, this environment can also be an opportunistic setting in which to reach adolescents. School-based programs are a popular way to provide prevention and intervention services to youth as there are fewer barriers, and adolescents in need of services may be more likely to access these services (Wagner, Tubman, & Gil, 2004). Schools offer a systematic way of reaching a large proportion of youth every year (Faggiano et al., 2009b). By implementing programs at school, common barriers to treatment utilization are reduced because students are already at school. These barriers include lack of transportation and time to travel to another location and concerns and distrust with an unfamiliar facility. School-based programs can also offer parents and adolescents a familiar environment that may be less stigmatizing, which can promote "buy-in" and higher utilization of services (Wagner et al., 2004).

Risk and Protective Factors That May Contribute to Adolescent AOD Use

There are many theories (see Table 23.1) that attempt to explain adolescent alcohol and drug use and focus on biological, behavioral, psychological, and demographic reasons for why adolescents may initiate AOD use or become problem users (e.g., Frisher, Crome, Macleod, Bloor, & Hickman, 2007; Petraitis, Flay, & Miller, 1995; Sher, Grekin, & Williams, 2005; Weinberg, 2001; World Health Organization, 2004-2005). For example, biological

Table 23.1. Risk and Protective Factors for Alcohol and Other Drug (AOD) Use

Domain	Risk Factors	Protective Factors
Individual	• Biological and psychological dispositions • Positive beliefs about alcohol and other drug (AOD) use • Early initiation of AOD use • Negative relationships with adults • Risk-taking propensity/impulsivity	• Opportunities for prosocial involvement • Rewards/recognition for prosocial involvement • Healthy beliefs and clear standards for behavior • Positive sense of self • Negative beliefs about AOD • Positive relationships with adults
Peer	• Association with peers who use or value AOD use • Association with peers who reject mainstream activities and pursuits • Susceptibility to negative peer pressure • Easily influenced by peers	• Association with peers who are involved in school, recreation service, religion, or other organized activities • Resistance to negative peer pressure • Not easily influenced by peers
Family	• Family history of AOD use • Family management problems • Family conflict • Parental beliefs about AOD	• Bonding (positive attachments) • Healthy beliefs and clear standards for behavior • High parental expectations • A sense of basic trust • Positive family dynamics
School	• Academic failure beginning in elementary school • Low commitment to school	• Opportunities for prosocial involvement • Rewards/recognition for prosocial involvement • Healthy beliefs and clear standards for behavior • Caring and support from teachers and staff • Positive instructional climate
Community	• Availability of AOD • Community laws, norms favorable toward AOD • Extreme economic and social deprivation • Transition and mobility • Low neighborhood attachment and community disorganization	• Opportunities for participation as active members of the community • Decreasing AOD accessibility • Cultural norms that set high expectations for youth • Social networks and support systems within the community
Society	• Impoverishment • Unemployment and underemployment • Discrimination • Pro–AOD-use messages in the media	• Media literacy (resistance to pro-use messages) • Decreased accessibility • Increased pricing through taxation • Raised purchasing age and enforcement • Stricter driving-under-the-influence laws

Table 23.1 is adapted from:
1. SAMHSA (2001). *Science-based substance abuse prevention: A guide*. DMMS Publication No. (SMA)d-3505. Rockville: MD.
2. Chinman. M; Imm, P; & Wandersman A. (2004) *Getting to outcomes 2004: Promoting accountability through methods and tools for planning, implementation, and evaluation*. Santa Monica, CA: RAND Corporation, TR-TR101. Available at http://www.rand.org/publications/TR/TR101/.

factors, such as increased tolerance to the negative effects and sensitivity to the positive effects of alcohol, are strongly associated with youth alcohol use (Spear, 2000; Spear & Varlinskaya, 2005). Other biological factors associated with both alcohol and drug use include inherent personality traits such as hyperactivity, aggression, depression, withdrawal, anxiety (Chan, Dennis, & Funk, 2008; Ensminger, Juon, & Fothergill, 2002; Zucker, Wong, Puttler, & Fitzgerald, 2003), rebelliousness (Ellickson, Tucker, Klein, & McGuigan, 2001; Voelkl & Frone, 2000), difficulty avoiding harm or harmful situations (Sussman, McCuller, & Dent, 2003), and disinhibition (Colder & O Connor, 2002; Wills, Walker, Mendoza, & Ainette, 2006; World Health Organization, 2004-2005). Being biologically related to first-degree relatives who have an alcohol use disorder (Carlson, Iacono, & McGue, 2002;

Chassin, Fora, & King, 2004; Donovan, 2004; Hartman, Lessem, Hopfer, Crowley, & Stallings, 2006; Sher, Walitzer, Wood, & Brent, 1991) or relatives with a drug use disorder (Gil, Vega, & Turner, 2002; Hopfer, Stallings, Hewitt, & Crowley, 2004) are also associated with adolescent AOD use.

Despite the strong association of many of these factors to AOD use during adolescence, biological factors are challenging to target through interventions because they are less amenable to change than psychosocial factors. Thus, for the current chapter, we will focus on prevention or intervention programs with adolescents that target psychosocial factors, such as coping with peer pressure and challenging misperceptions of peer AOD use.

One important factor that is associated with AOD use is the school environment. For example, recent research has shown that youth who attend schools where drugs are available or sold are three times more likely to report cigarette smoking and marijuana use (Califano, 2008; Hanson et al., 2003). One study followed youth from primary school (age 11) into secondary school (ages 13 and 15) to examine how AOD use rates might change based on school environment. They found that rates of AOD use within a school, along with disengagement and poor teacher-student relationships all contributed to more regular smoking and drinking at ages 13 and 15 (West, Sweeting, & Leyland, 2004).

Employment during the school year has also been associated with AOD use. Work intensity, or the number of work hours, may be an important characteristic to monitor among adolescents. Studies evaluating work intensity have shown both positive and negative associations with behavior (Mortimer, 2010). Employment may help adolescents sharpen their responsibility, time management skills, and resilience to stress (Mortimer & Staff, 2004; Steinberg & Cauffman, 1995). However, increased work intensity (working 20+hours/week during the school year) has been linked with heavy alcohol, tobacco, and drug use (McMorris & Uggen, 2000; Osilla et al., 2012; Ramchand, Ialongo, & Chilcoat, 2007; Wu, Hoven, & Fuller, 2003). Researchers have speculated that teens who work more hours may also receive less parental monitoring, have more income to spend on AOD, work in riskier environments, have greater opportunities to use AOD, and have greater exposure to older teens and adults who use AOD (Godley, Passetti, & White, 2006; Mortimer & Staff, 2004; Staff & Uggen, 2003; Wu et al., 2003).

Another factor that can contribute to AOD use during this developmental period is peer influence. Peer influence has been shown to increase substantially during middle school and high school (Steinberg & Monahan, 2007) and is often associated with adolescent AOD use. For example, it is well known that adolescents who associate with AOD-using peers are more likely to initiate AOD use (Geels, Vink, van Beijsterveldt, Bartels, & Boomsma, 2013; Maxwell, 2002; Poelen, Engels, Vorst, Scholte, & Vermulst, 2007; Van Ryzin, Fosco, & Dishion, 2012). In addition, adolescents' perceptions of their peers AOD use can also affect whether they initiate AOD or escalate their use of AOD (Brooks-Russell, Simons-Morton, Haynie, Farhat, & Wang, 2012; D'Amico & McCarthy, 2006; Fowler et al., 2007; Piontek et al., 2013).

One important question that has been examined over the past decade is whether peers or parents may play a stronger role in an adolescent's choice to initiate or escalate AOD use. Some research has shown that peer influence (both positive and negative) may play a larger role than parental influence in initiation and escalation of AOD use during adolescence (Beal, Ausiello, & Perrin, 2001; Crawford & Novak, 2002; Petraitis, Flay, Miller, Torpy, & Greiner, 1998; van den Bree & Pickworth, 2005; Windle, 2000; Wood, Read, Mitchell, & Brand, 2004). For example, one cross-sectional study found that peer disapproval of tobacco and marijuana was the only measure independently associated with abstinence from tobacco and marijuana use (Beal et al., 2001). Recent longitudinal work has also shown the importance of peer disapproval. Specifically, Mrug and McCay (2012) found that among youth aged 11–19, a one-unit increase in perceived disapproval was associated with an 80% greater likelihood of abstinence for peer disapproval compared with a 12% greater likelihood of abstinence for parental disapproval (Mrug & McCay, 2012). In addition, other work in this area has shown that modeling of alcohol and cigarette use by best friends and perceived prevalence of use among same aged peers are more strongly related to initiation and experimentation with alcohol (Jackson, 1997) and cigarettes (Scherrer et al., 2012) than parental modeling of AOD use. Longitudinal work has supported these cross-sectional findings and shown that use of alcohol by an adolescent's peers is more strongly related to use than parental factors (Windle, 2000; Zhang, Welte, & Wieczorek, 1997).

These findings fit with Social Learning Theory, which suggests that people tend to make assumptions about their environment based on their perceptions of the behavior and attitudes of others (Bandura, 1977, 1986; Maisto, Carey, & Bradizza, 1999). Social Learning Theory also suggests that people learn vicariously (Bandura, 1977; Maisto et al., 1999). For example, middle school youth who have strong positive expectancies about alcohol's effects on social behavior tend to drink more heavily (Tomlinson & Brown, 2012). Many youth tend to overestimate the percentage of peers who drink, smoke cigarettes, or use marijuana (e.g., D'Amico & Fromme, 2002; Ellickson, Bird, Orlando, Klein, & McCaffrey, 2003; McNeal, Hansen, Harrington, & Giles, 2004) and these overestimates are associated with heavier use and AOD-related consequences (Clark, Ringwalt, & Shamblen, 2011; Fulton, Krank, & Stewart, 2012; Kristjansson, Agrawal, Lynskey, & Chassin, 2012; Pedersen et al., 2013). Thus, school-based prevention and intervention efforts for this age group must focus on external and internal peer pressure to use AOD. Programs should also provide normative feedback to help youth gain a more realistic perspective of the AOD use among their age group (e.g., Brown, Anderson, Schulte, Sintov, & Frissell, 2005; D'Amico & Edelen, 2007; D'Amico, Tucker, et al., 2012; Schulte, Monreal, & Brown, 2010; Walker et al., 2011; Wynn, Schulenberg, Maggs, & Zucker, 2000).

It is important to note that although peers can influence both initiation and escalation of AOD use during adolescence, parents still play a significant role in whether or not a teen chooses to use AOD. For example, family factors, such as family supervision, parent approval, and family attachment are strongly associated with younger adolescents' AOD use compared with older adolescents' AOD use (Cleveland, Bontempo, & Greenberg, 2008; Sawyer & Stevenson, 2008); thus, parents may have more influence over an adolescent's initial use of AOD. In addition, other studies have shown that parental monitoring, involvement, and disapproval of AOD use are associated with a lower likelihood of drinking (SAMHSA, 2012a; Vermeulen-Smit, Ter Bogt, Verdurmen, Van Dorsselaer, & Vollebergh, 2012; Wood et al., 2004), smoking cigarettes (Simons-Morton, Abroms, Haynie, & Chen, 2004; Tobler & Komro, 2010), and using marijuana (Clark, Shamblen, Ringwalt, & Hanley, 2012; Lac, Alvaro, Crano, & Siegel, 2009; Van Ryzin et al., 2012). For example, Simons-Morton and colleagues found that parental involvement, monitoring, and expectations were associated with less drinking.

Specifically, these parental behaviors decreased the adolescent's exposure to alcohol-using peers during a time period when peer drinking tends to increase (Simons-Morton & Chen, 2005). Other studies have shown that parental monitoring in high school can decrease the likelihood of being exposed to marijuana in college (Pinchevsky et al., 2012), and that parental monitoring for at-risk youth at alternative schools is predictive of less marijuana use and less heavy drinking 1 year later (Clark et al., 2012).

Parents' use of AOD is also an important predictor of whether or not youth may choose to use AOD (Johnson & Johnson, 2001; Li, Pentz, & Chou, 2002; Mason & Spoth, 2012). Teens who have nonusing parents are less likely to smoke cigarettes or use AOD (Li et al., 2002; Miller, Siegel, Hohman, & Crano, 2013; Peterson, Leroux, et al., 2006; Schuck, Otten, & Engels, 2012; Schuck, Otten, Engels, Barker, & Kleinjan, 2012); thus nonuse appears to be protective. In contrast, parental drinking is strongly associated with adolescent drinking (Latendresse et al., 2008; Tobler & Komro, 2010; Vermeulen-Smit, Koning, et al., 2012), and youth who report that their parents use marijuana are more likely to initiate marijuana (Miller et al., 2013) and are twice as likely to smoke cigarettes, drink alcohol, and use marijuana (Li et al., 2002). Other family members, such as siblings can also play a role in adolescent AOD use. When older siblings report higher willingness to use AOD, younger siblings are more likely to report use of AOD (Pomery et al., 2005). Work in this area has also consistently shown that both actual use of older siblings (Fagan & Najman, 2005; Fisher, Miles, Austin, Camargo, & Colditz, 2007; Fulton et al., 2012; Kristjansson et al., 2012; Whiteman, Jensen, & Maggs, 2013) and perception of sibling alcohol and drug use (Ary, Tildesley, Hops, & Andrews, 1993; D'Amico & Fromme, 1997; Windle, 2000) are strongly associated with drinking behavior and positive beliefs about drugs. In addition, some work has shown that alcohol use (East & Khoo, 2005; Pomery et al., 2005; Slomkowski, Rende, Conger, Simons, & Conger, 2001) and cigarette smoking by older siblings (Bajan et al., 2003) are both more strongly related to adolescent use than parental use of these substances. Thus, school-based prevention or intervention programs should also focus on the influence of older siblings on adolescents' AOD use.

Attitudes and beliefs about AOD have also been examined as predictors of adolescent AOD use in numerous cross-sectional and longitudinal studies over the past three decades (Brown, 1993;

Fromme & D'Amico, 2000; Goldman, Brown, & Christiansen, 1987; McCarthy & Thompsen, 2006; Schell, Martino, Ellickson, Collins, & McCaffrey, 2005; Torrealday et al., 2008). Outcome expectancies, or the positive and negative beliefs that one holds about the effects of alcohol or drugs, are one type of belief that has been extensively examined and shown to be consistently and strongly associated with adolescent cigarette, alcohol, and marijuana use (Brown, 1990; Fromme, Katz, & Rivet, 1997; McCarthy, Pedersen, & D'Amico, 2009; Shih, Miles, Tucker, Zhou, & D'Amico, 2012; Skenderian, Siegel, Crano, Alvaro, & Lac, 2008; Torrealday et al., 2008). Some examples of positive expectancies are: "I will be more social" or "I will be brave and daring" (Fromme, Stroot, & Kaplan, 1993). Some examples of negative expectancies are, "I would feel dizzy" or "I would act aggressively" (Fromme et al., 1993). Cross-sectional and longitudinal work has indicated that adolescents with strong positive outcomes expectancies for alcohol or drugs are more likely to use these substances compared with youth who do not hold these strong positive beliefs (Fisher et al., 2007; Fulton et al., 2012; Skenderian et al., 2008; Smith, Goldman, Greenbaum, & Christiansen, 1995). In contrast, youth with stronger negative expectancies typically drink less (Cludius, Stevens, Bantin, Gerlach, & Hermann, 2013; Jones & McMahon, 1993) and report less drug use (Aarons, Brown, Stice, & Coe, 2001; Alfonso & Dunn, 2009; Galen & Henderson, 1999; Kristjansson et al., 2012; Torrealday et al., 2008).

Martino and colleagues (Martino, Collins, Ellickson, Schell, & McCaffrey, 2006) examined drinkers and nondrinkers as they transitioned from 8th grade to 9th grade. They found that for both drinkers and nondrinkers, youth who had greater exposure to pro-drinking peers and adults reported more positive alcohol expectancies compared with adolescents with less exposure to these influences (Martino et al., 2006). Because outcome expectancies and subsequent drinking and drug use are so strongly linked, prevention programs often spend time discussing these beliefs and how beliefs may influence both drinking and drug use (Brown et al., 2005; D'Amico & Edelen, 2007; D'Amico & Fromme, 2002; Fromme & Corbin, 2004; Metrik et al., 2009; Scott-Sheldon, Terry, Carey, Garey, & Carey, 2012; Walker et al., 2011).

In sum, there are many factors that can influence whether an adolescent chooses to initiate or escalate AOD use. Prevention programs for this age group

have created successful strategies to address these factors, such as focusing on misperceptions of use and discussing peer influence.

Developing Prevention and Intervention Programs for Adolescents

Decreasing barriers so that youth feel more comfortable accessing prevention and intervention services is crucial. Most youth do not seek out help or treatment if they have AOD-related problems (Office of Applied Studies, 2009). This underutilization may be due to many issues, including stigma (Corrigan, 2004), concerns about confidentiality (Rickwood, Deane, & Wison, 2007), feeling disconnected from the person implementing the service (D'Amico, 2005) or having difficulties articulating the problems associated with their substance use (Feldstein Ewing, Hendrickson, & Payne, 2008). Another reason that adolescents may not seek out services is because traditional intervention approaches are not well suited for this age group (D'Amico et al., 2005; D'Amico, Feldstein Ewing, et al., 2010; Deas, Riggs, Langenbucher, Goldman, & Brown, 2000). In fact, many intervention efforts for adolescents have been developed from adult or child models (Lonigan, Elbert, & Johnson, 1998; Weisz & Hawley, 2002). Because adolescence is a unique time in which many biological, social, and cognitive changes take place, prevention programming content for youth must address these developmental changes in order to be effective (D'Amico & Stern, 2008). Youth should be involved in the planning of the prevention and intervention curricula (D'Amico et al., 2005; Dusenbury, Falco, & Lake, 1995; McBride, Midford, Farringdon, & Phillips, 2000). Unfortunately, many program evaluations tend to occur *after* the curriculum is developed instead of while it is being developed (Donaldson, 2001; Sussman, Petosa, & Clarke, 1996). Thus, program content and/or materials may not be developmentally appropriate for youth and their specific adolescent problems and concerns may not be addressed. Successful prevention strategies for this age group must address adolescents' concerns proactively rather than adapting programs that are used for other age groups (Holmbeck, Devine, & Bruno, 2010; Weisz & Hawley, 2002).

One way to create developmentally appropriate programs for adolescents is to create curriculum content and materials with collaboration and input. Involving adolescents in the curriculum development increases the likelihood that the program will be developmentally appropriate, feasible, and acceptable as evidenced by several successful AOD interventions (Brown, 2001; D'Amico et al., 2005; D'Amico, Osilla, & Hunter, 2010; McBride et al., 2000; Stern, Meredith, Gholson, Gore, & D'Amico, 2007; Sussman et al., 1996). For example, when pilot testing curricula with middle school youth, D'Amico and colleagues found that younger adolescents preferred learning the materials through role play type scenarios (D'Amico et al., 2005). Other pilot tests of curricula have shown that adolescents are more likely to discuss their AOD use and problems with someone if they do not feel judged and can relate to the person providing the service (D'Amico, Miles, Stern, & Meredith, 2008; D'Amico, Osilla, et al., 2010; Stern et al., 2007). Thus, teens can play an important role in developing appropriate and effective programs.

Peer relationships are another important part of this developmental period. There are many successful ways to address peer influence in prevention programming for adolescents. Peer influence can involve several factors, including perceived prevalence or normative expectations of AOD use, friends' approval or social acceptability of use, and peers' respect for refusing AOD use. Work in this area has shown that decreases in alcohol, cigarette, or drug use due to prevention programs are often mediated by changes in peer influence (e.g., Botvin, Dusenbury, Baker, Orliz-Jarncs, & Botvin, 1992; Donaldson, Graham, & Hansen, 1994; Komro et al., 2001; Liu & Flay, 2009; Orlando, Ellickson, McCaffrey, & Longshore, 2005; Wynn et al., 2000). For example, in Project ALERT, a middle-school prevention program, peer influence to smoke cigarettes was the strongest mediator between the program and past month cigarette use 1 year later (Orlando et al., 2005). In addition, several studies have shown that perceived peer use of alcohol and drugs mediates the effects between the prevention program and drinking (Komro et al., 2001; Wynn et al., 2000) and drug use (Liu & Flay, 2009). Given the substantial increase in peer influence during this time period (Simons-Morton et al., 2004; Steinberg & Monahan, 2007) and younger adolescents' susceptibility to peer influence (Kelly et al., 2012), many prevention programs for this age group discuss peer pressure and/or provide normative information on AOD use for this age group (e.g., Brown et al., 2005; D'Amico, Hunter, Miles, Ewing, & Osilla, 2013; D'Amico, Tucker et al., 2012; Ellickson, McCaffrey, Ghosh-Dastidar, & Longshore, 2003; Perry et al., 2002).

Peer influence may also be addressed by providing the prevention information in a group setting. Studies have shown that the group context is an effective way to reach youth and provides an opportunity for teens to receive feedback from their peers (D'Amico, Feldstein Ewing, et al., 2010; Feldstein Ewing, Walters, & Baer, 2012). For example, adolescents are more likely to give credence to negative consequences voiced by peers than negative consequences suggested by the group leader (D'Amico, Feldstein Ewing, et al., 2010). Some research has suggested that this group feedback can sometimes be iatrogenic or "backfire" such that adolescents' deviant behavior may increase (Arnold & Hughes, 1999; Dishion, McCord, & Poulin, 1999; Dodge, Dishion, & Lansford, 2006). Other researchers have found that working with at-risk youth in a group setting is safe, effective and comparable to working with youth individually (Burleson, Kaminer, & Dennis, 2006; Burleson, Kaminer, & Dennis, 2006; Kaminer, 2005; Lee & Thompson, 2009; Vaughn & Howard, 2004; Waldron & Turner, 2008), and a meta-analytic review of over 66 studies of adolescent group programs targeting substance use found little evidence to support the iatrogenic hypothesis (Weiss et al., 2005). The group context is a cost-effective approach to reach youth, and the majority of adolescent prevention programs in the school setting provide the curriculum to students in a group during class time.

Successful programs also tend to focus on social influences and comprehensive life skills (Brody, Yu, Chen, Kogan, & Smith, 2012; Caria, Faggiano, Bellocco, & Galanti, 2011; Cuijpers, 2002; Faggiano et al., 2009a, 2009b; Lemstra et al., 2010; Tobler et al., 2000). Between childhood and adolescence, important changes occur in brain structure (Sowell et al., 2004), with the latest changes typically involving the maturation of the prefrontal cortex and the parietal cortex (Giedd, Shaw, Wallace, Gogtay, & Lenroot, 2006). Both of these structures are associated with decision making and evaluating short- versus long-term consequences (Cohen, Heller, & Ranganath, 2005; Galvan et al., 2005). Because the frontal lobes are still developing, along with emotional regulation, planning, and organization, adolescents may be less likely to focus on long-term negative consequences of risk behaviors (Galvan, Hare, Voss, Glover, & Casy, 2007; Luna, Paulsen, Padmanabhan, & Geier, 2013) and therefore may need help in planning ahead more effectively so that they can make healthier choices. Therefore, skills-focused programs that help youth with their decision-making skills tend to have a positive effect on both mediating variables (drug knowledge, decision making, self-esteem and peer pressure resistance) and AOD outcomes, compared with the usual curricula that may be provided. Specifically, these skills-based programs are more likely to reduce incidence of first time usage, frequency and amount of illicit substances used, and prevalence of users among primary or secondary school students (Faggiano et al., 2009b; Lemstra et al., 2010). Both the social influence and comprehensive life skills programs focus on interpersonal refusal skills, discussing the short- and long-term consequences of drug use, providing normative information (discussed above), and examining the influence of the media on AOD use. Comprehensive life skills programs include information taught in social influence programs and also focus on teaching other skills, such as assertiveness, problem solving, decision making, coping, communicating, and goal setting (Caria et al., 2011; Lemstra et al., 2010; Tobler et al., 2000). Several studies and reviews have shown that teaching these types of life skills can have positive outcomes on youth by reducing their AOD use (Botvin & Griffin, 2004; Buhler, Schroder, & Silbereisen, 2008; Coggans, 2006; Cuijpers, 2002; Lemstra et al., 2010; Tobler et al., 2000).

Meta-analytic research and reviews in this area have also shown that successful programs for this age group typically use an interactive method (Cuijpers, 2002; Faggiano et al., 2009b; Tobler et al., 2000) and therefore emphasize an active exchange among teens (Ennett et al., 2003; Jensen et al., 2011) and encourage the learning of drug refusal skills (Tobler et al., 2000). These types of methods have been successful in decreasing alcohol, cigarette and marijuana use among youth.

One way of increasing interaction between adolescents and the leader is through the use of motivational interviewing (Miller & Rollnick, 2012). Motivational interviewing (MI) is an inherently collaborative approach, which can work to increase adolescents' confidence in their abilities to cope (Resnicow et al., 2002) and help them to overcome difficulties that may have originally seemed insurmountable (Feldstein & Ginsburg, 2007). Described as a guiding approach, therapists conducting MI actively elicit client participation, with the goal of highlighting ambivalence about a target behavior, and eliciting change talk and commitment language (Miller & Rollnick, 2012). The style of MI is nonjudgmental and encouraging and is well suited to adolescents as it is a nonconfrontational approach and emphasizes self-responsibility and autonomy in decision making (Resnicow et al., 2002). Because MI emphasizes an interactive process in which facilitators and participants are active collaborators, this approach increases the probability that program materials will be both culturally appropriate and acceptable to this age group (D'Amico, Feldstein Ewing, et al., 2010). Further, the effectiveness of MI interventions for adolescent substance use behavior change is supported by a recent meta-analytic review (Jensen et al., 2011). Motivational interviewing is discussed more thoroughly in the chapter by Hettema, Wagner, Ingersoll, & Russo (Chapter 17, Vol. 2).

In sum, there are many effective strategies that can be used with adolescents to prevent initiation or decrease escalation of AOD use. Many of these strategies have been packaged into evidence-based programs that can be disseminated into school settings; however, communities often face difficulty in implementing these strategies with quality and achieving outcomes demonstrated by prevention researchers (D'Amico, Chinman, Stern, & Wandersman, 2009).

Implementing Evidence-Based Practices in the School Setting

The gap between research and practice (e.g., Green, 2001; Wandersman & Florin, 2003) is often the result of limited resources in real world settings. For example, although there are numerous evidence-based AOD prevention programs that are available to schools, schools can face challenges in implementing these programs. Schools must first be aware of the available programs and then navigate through the information and determine what program will work best in their setting with their available resources. The Substance Abuse and Mental Health Administration National Registry of Evidence Based Programs and Practices provides detailed information on evidence based programs that are available for youth (SAMHSA, 2012b). Schools must determine which program they want to use, the costs of the program, time needed to train staff, and availability of staff to implement the program. Additionally, as most programs are provided during class time, they must determine how this programming will fit into their already packed curricula. These types of community settings are often faced with limited resources to receive training and implement new programs, which can make it difficult to implement these evidence-based protocols with fidelity (D'Amico et al., 2009). Thus, schools may need additional support and guidance as they choose the prevention programming for their specific site.

Successful School-Based Programs

Overview. This section of the chapter will review many of the school-based programs in the United States, Australia, and Europe and discuss outcomes for these programs. In the field of prevention, drug and alcohol programs are typically classified as *universal*, designed for the general population; *selective*, designed for subgroups at risk for substance use, such as youth who have parents or older siblings who use substances; or *indicated*, designed for youth who are engaging in AOD use behavior and have an increased vulnerability for continued use (Griffin & Botvin, 2010; Institute of Medicine, 1994; National Institute on Drug Abuse, 1997). Universal or primary prevention oriented activities remain the most frequently used approach with young people, particularly in schools. Thus, the majority of programs that we will be discussing in the current chapter are universal programs, designed for the general population.

The programs we will focus on in this chapter occur in middle school and high school settings; some were designed to reach all youth whereas others were designed to reach at-risk adolescents. We focus on the school-based programs that conducted a trial of the program, published results in a peer-reviewed journal and had at least a 1-year follow-up of the program. The chapter also focuses on school-based programs that only had a student component. We do not focus on school-based programs that may have also involved the community, such as school-wide interventions that may have introduced policy changes, programs that included teacher and parenting interventions, or programs that involved coalitions to create changes in the neighborhood context as other chapters in this book discuss these issues. Examples of multi-component programs that also have a school-based focus are the "Healthy School and Drugs" project (Cuijpers, Jonkers, de Weerdt, & de Jong, 2002), the Gatehouse Project (Bond et al., 2004; Patton, Bond, Butler, & Glover, 2003), and Project SUCCESS (Schools Using Coordinated Community Efforts to Strengthen Students (Morehouse & Tobler, 2000; Vaughan & Johnson, 2007).

Table 23.2 provides information on several school-based prevention programs that focused on a student-only component for their intervention and have published *at least* a 1-year follow-up. We highlight some of these programs below.

It should be noted that the majority of the studies that we will review in this chapter measured alcohol and drug use by self-report. The limitations of self-report in general are well known, although these may be exaggerated (Chan, 2008). Many self-report methodologies have been validated and are the best available measurement of substance use over long periods of time. Under appropriate conditions, adolescents will self-report their substance use with high reliability (D'Amico & McCarthy, 2006; Dennis et al., 2002; Shillington & Clapp, 2000). Minimizing social desirability is important. For example, adolescent self-report obtained by a teacher, parent, school counselor, parole officer, or treating clinician should not be considered reliable because youth may feel pressured to report favorable behavior, or there may be consequences tied to their responses. Assessment must also be conducted privately and with strict confidentiality.

Drug testing, although objective, is a poor measure of substance use in nondrug dependent populations. Drug screening methods generally only detect substance use that has occurred in the last 1–3 days at best. Therefore, drug testing only reliably detects substance use that occurs every day, such as in substance dependent individuals (Goldstein & Brown, 2003). Drug testing methodologies will not detect the vast majority of sporadic use and thus they are of little value in prevention trials, where detection of initiation, experimentation, and occasional binge use of alcohol and drugs is important.

Middle school programs. Project ALERT is a school-based prevention program that was developed for middle school youth in the 1990s. This program focuses on helping youth understand how drug use affects them, identify pro-drug use pressures, and acquire skills for resisting those pressures (Ellickson & Bell, 1990). The program was delivered in eleven 45-minute sessions across both 7th (eight sessions) and 8th grade (three sessions). The first study involved a multi-site, longitudinal test of the program for 7th- and 8th-grade students (Ellickson & Bell, 1990). Thirty control and treatment schools from California and Oregon were chosen to reflect a diverse range of school and community environments, including urban, suburban, and rural areas. Nine of the schools had a minority population of 50% or more and 18 drew from neighborhoods with household incomes below the median for their state. At 15-month follow-up, students who had

Table 23.2. School-Based Prevention and Intervention Programs With Student-Only Components (Listed Alphabetically)[a]

Study Name	Study Type and Population	Intervention Description	Major Outcomes

A Stop Smoking in Schools Trial (ASSIST)

| Campbell et al., 2008 | 12- and 13-year-old students across 59 secondary schools in England and Wales (N = 10,70) | Influential students identified by the student population were trained to be peer supporters. The 2-day training included how to talk with peers about the effects of smoking and the benefits of not smoking, and other communication and leadership activities. During a 10-week intervention period, peer supporters had informal conversations about smoking with their peers in a variety of situations outside of the classroom (e.g., lunchtime, breaks, to and from school). | *1-year follow-up and 2-year follow-up*
The odds ratio for smoking among all students was lower for intervention schools compared with control schools 1 and 2 years after the intervention.
Adjusted odds ratio (95% CI) for being a smoker |

				1-year follow-up	*2-year follow-up*
			Smoking	.77 (.59–.99)*	.85 (.72–1.01)
			* p<.05		

Adolescent Alcohol Prevention Trial

| Hansen & Graham, 1991 | 7th-grade students in 12 junior high schools in Los Angeles and Orange Counties, California (N = 3,011) | Four intervention programs were implemented:
1) *Information only:* four lessons about the social and health consequences of using alcohol and drugs.
2) *Information and Resistance Training:* four information lessons and five lessons focused on helping youth identify and resist peer and advertising pressure
3) *Information and Normative Education:* four information lessons and five lessons correcting erroneous perceptions on prevalence and acceptability.
4) *Combined Information, Resistance Training and Normative Education:* three information lessons, 3 ½ lessons on resistance skills; and 3 ½ lessons on normative education. | *1-year follow-up*
Reduced use of alcohol, marijuana, and cigarettes for all students who received normative education (NE) (e.g., information and NE; information, resistance training and NE) compared with students who did not receive NE (e.g., information; information and resistance training).
Incidence of drunkenness increased only 4.2% in the two groups that received NE compared with 11.1% in non-NE groups.
No effects for resistance skills training. |

(continued)

Table 23.2. Continued

Study Name	Study Type and Population	Intervention Description	Major Outcomes		

Adolescent Alcohol Prevention Trial (continued)

| Donaldson et al., 1995 | Public and private elementary and junior high school students across 130 schools in Los Angeles and San Diego Counties (N = 11,995) | Students received one of four interventions similar to 1991 study in 5th grade or 7th grade. | Students in the 5th- and 7th-grade intervention groups who had higher refusal skills and viewed drinking as unacceptable were less likely to report 8th-grade alcohol use. In addition, for teens that attended the intervention during 5th grade, there was an interaction between refusal skills and whether teens viewed drinking as acceptable. |

8th-grade alcohol use for students attending the intervention in 5th vs. 7th grade (t-values)

	8th-grade alcohol use	
	5th-grade intervention	7th-grade intervention
Viewed drinking as acceptable	1.10	0.01
Viewed drinking as not acceptable	−2.04*	−2.52**
Refusal skills × drinking is acceptable	2.23*	0.55

* $p<.05$; ** $p<.01$

| Taylor et al., 2000 | Follow up with Los Angeles area 11th graders (N = 3,027) | Same curriculum as 1991 study. | *4-year follow-up* Rate of growth of lifetime and recent cigarette smoking, alcohol use, and lifetime drunkenness were all lower for the NE group compared with the information only group. |

Adolescent Alcohol Prevention Trial (continued)

Donaldson et al., 2000	Same sample as 1995 study.	Same curriculum as 1995 study.	Public school students who received normative education (NE) reported less lifetime drinking and cigarette use in the 8th to 10th grades compared with students who received the other interventions. Public school students who received resistance training (RT) reported using alcohol significantly more than other interventions.

Lifetime alcohol use at 1-, 2-, and 3-year follow-up (%)

	NE	Other
8th grade	47.1**	57.3
9th grade	72.3**	82.9
10th grade	81.5*	89.0

Lifetime cigarette use at 1-, 2-, and 3-year follow-up (%)

	NE	Other
8th grade	28.4*	34.1
9th grade	19.4***	33.2
10th grade	32.9	39.6

* $p<.05$; ** $p<.01$, *** $p<.001$

Alcohol Misuse Prevention Study (AMPS)

Shope et al., 1992	5th- and 6th-grade students at 49 schools in southeastern Michigan (N = 5,356)	AMPS program of 4 sessions and 3 booster sessions of 45 minutes each emphasizing social pressures resistance training, immediate effects of alcohol, risks of alcohol misuse and social pressures to misuse alcohol.	*26-month follow-up* The program did not affect overall rates of change in alcohol use or alcohol misuse. However, 6th-grade students that reported unsupervised or supervised drinking at baseline had less alcohol misuse at follow-up.

(continued)

Table 23.2. Continued

Study Name	Study Type and Population	Intervention Description	Major Outcomes

Alcohol Misuse Prevention Study (AMPS) (continued)

Means (SD) for alcohol use and misuse among 5th-grade students at follow-up

	Intervention + Booster	Intervention	Control
Alcohol use	0.62 (1.04)	0.59 (1.03)	0.68 (1.25)
Alcohol misuse	0.85 (1.50)	0.79 (1.47)	0.80 (1.52)

Means (SD) for alcohol use and misuse among 6th-grade students at follow-up

	Intervention	Control
Alcohol use	0.89 (1.28)	0.94 (1.45)
Alcohol misuse	1.17 (1.71)	1.27 (1.87)

Study Name	Study Type and Population	Intervention Description	Major Outcomes
Wynn et al., 2000	6th–10th grade students N = 232 (6th–7th) N = 332 (7th–8th) N = 371 (8th–10th)	Same curriculum as 1992 study.	AMPS contributed to increased refusal skills and knowledge of appropriate norms. From 8th to 10th grade, knowledge of appropriate norms mediated the effects of AMPS on alcohol misuse such that youth who reported more accurate norms were less likely to misuse alcohol.
Shope et al., 2001	10th-grade students in 6 school districts in southeastern Michigan were surveyed after receiving their driver's license. (N = 4,635)	Same curriculum as 1992 study.	Tested the effectiveness of AMPS on 10th-grade students 7.6 years after they received their driver's license (approximately at age 24 years). For the whole sample, no significant treatment effects were found for crash outcomes. Rates of 1st year serious offenses (e.g., involved use of alcohol, resulted in 3 or more points assigned to driver) were reduced slightly among students in the intervention group who consumed less than 1 drink per week; however, the treatment effects disappeared after the first year of licensure.

CHOICE

D'Amico & Edelen, 2007	Middle school students in two schools in southern California N = 1,527	A brief, voluntary, after-school program consisting of 5 sessions that repeated throughout the year. Sessions focused on providing normative feedback, challenging unrealistic positive expectancies, role playing pressure situations, and discussing coping strategies and planning for high-risk situations. Sessions were delivered using a motivational interviewing style.	Individual attendees reported less alcohol use and lower perceptions of alcohol, marijuana, and cigarette use than a matched sample of control students. In addition, school-wide effects showed that self-use and perceptions of friends' use of alcohol and marijuana increased more at the control school compared with the intervention school regardless of participation in the program.

Weighted mean (SD) 30-day use and perception of use rates at 1 year for participants in the intervention compared with a matched sample of control students

	Intervention	Control	SE
30-day alcohol use	.14 (.04)	.29 (.04)	.06**
30-day marijuana use	.09 (.04)	.13 (.03)	.04
% schoolmates who use alcohol (0–6)	1.91 (.26)	2.63 (.18)	.32*
% schoolmates who smoke marijuana (0–6)	1.34 (.25)	2.31 (.17)	.27**

* p<.05, ** p<.01

D'Amico et al., 2012	Middle school students in 16 schools in southern California N = 9,528	Same curriculum as in pilot test of CHOICE in 2007	African American and multiethnic students were more likely to attend. Past month alcohol users were more likely to initially attend, and marijuana users were more likely to continue attendance. Thus, CHOICE reached students of different racial/ethnic groups and attracted higher risk youth who may not typically obtain prevention services. Lifetime alcohol use in the ITT analysis (i.e., school level) achieved statistical significance, with an odds ratio (OR) of 0.70 and a number needed to treat (NNT) of 14.8. The NNT suggests that in a school where PC was offered, 1 adolescent out of 15 was prevented from initiating alcohol use during this time period.

(continued)

Table 23.2. Continued

Study Name	Study Type and Population	Intervention Description	Major Outcomes
CHOICE (continued)			
			Although not statistically significant (p = .20), results indicate that past month alcohol use was also lower in PC schools (OR = 0.81; NNT = 45). Comparisons of attenders versus matched controls yielded results for lifetime use similar to school-wide effects (OR = 0.74 and NNT = 17.6)
keepin' it REAL			
Hecht et al., 2003	7th- and 8th-grade urban middle school students in 35 schools in Arizona (N = 6,035)	keepin' it R.E.A.L. The resistance strategy forms the acronym **R**efuse/Rechasa, **E**xplain/Explica, **A**void/Apártate, and **L**eave/Levántate 10-lesson culturally grounded school-based prevention intervention promoting anti-drug norms and attitudes; teaching life skills to combat negative peer and other influences; and developing risk assessment, decision making, and resistance skills. Sessions were bolstered by booster activities and a media campaign. Three parallel versions were delivered: Mexican American, combined African American and European American, and Multicultural.	*14-month follow-up* While both the intervention and control groups increased consumption of alcohol and marijuana over time, the control group demonstrated a significantly greater increase. Little support for matching the content of the program to the culture/ethnicity of the student.
(Hecht et al., 2008)	5th-grade students who attended 1 of 23 middle schools in Phoenix, Arizona N = 1,566)	Adapted curriculum for 5th graders	*One-year follow-up* The adapted 5th-grade curriculum was no more effective than the control's school programming in changing students' resistance or decision-making skills, substance use intentions, expectancies, or normative beliefs, or lifetime and recent substance use.
Kulis et al., 2005	Mexican American middle school students from the 2003 study (N = 3,402)	Same curriculum as 2003 study.	Students in the Latino and multicultural intervention programs had slightly more positive outcomes in reduced alcohol and marijuana use compared with control schools. For example, at 14-month follow-up, students in any of the interventions had .22 fewer days of alcohol use in the past month compared with students in the control schools.

keepin' it REAL (continued)

The Latino and multicultural intervention participants did not differ in their substance use outcomes from participants in the non-Latino version.

14-month follow-up (mean difference between intervention and control in days used in the past month)

| | All | | | |
	Intervention vs. control	Latino vs. control	Non-Latino vs. control	MC vs. control
Alcohol use	−0.22**	−0.24	−0.17	−0.24**
Marijuana use	−0.18*	−0.24*	−0.15	−0.16*

* $p<.05$; ** $p<.01$

Kulis et al., 2007

Current substance using teens from 2003 study (N = 1,364)

Same curriculum as 2003 study.

A greater percentage of students in the intervention group that reported using alcohol at baseline reduced their past month alcohol use at 2, 8, or 14-month follow-up compared with students who reported drinking at baseline in the control group. No effects were found for cigarettes or marijuana.

Odds ratios of reduced or discontinued alcohol use

	Alcohol	Cigarettes	Marijuana
Reduced use	1.72*	1.05	1.19
Discontinued use	1.66	1.30	1.31

* $p<.05$

(continued)

Table 23.2. Continued

Study Name	Study Type and Population	Intervention Description	Major Outcomes
keepin' it REAL (continued)			
Marsiglia et al., 2011	Elementary and middle school students of Mexican heritage from 29 schools (N = 1,670)	Multiple versions including the same curriculum as 2003 study and an "acculturated enhanced" version that had two additional lessons on how to recognize and deal with acculturation challenges.	*Follow-up during 8th grade* Students who received the curriculum in 7th grade had similar reductions in marijuana and inhalants compared with students who received the curriculum in both 5th grade and 7th grade. In addition, students who received the intervention only in 7th grade also had reductions in cigarettes and alcohol. Students who received the curriculum in 5th grade did not benefit unless they also received the curriculum in 7th grade.
Life Skills Training Program (LST)			
Botvin et al., 1990	7th-grade students in 56 schools (suburban and rural) in New York state (N = 4,466)	15 class sessions of 12 curriculum units designed for 7th grade; 10 booster sessions in 8th grade; 5 booster sessions in 9th grade. Two prevention conditions: teacher training by workshop and feedback (E1) or teacher training via videotape and no feedback (E2). Focus on drug resistance skills, norms against substance use, and development of personal and social skills.	*3-year follow-up* Reduced cigarette use and marijuana use in both treatment conditions compared with control group. No significant effects for drinking frequency or amount of drinking. The frequency of getting drunk was significantly less in the E2 condition. *Univariate F values and adjusted follow-up substance use means and standard errors (SE) for prevention and control conditions*

	E1	E2	Control
Smoking	1.46	1.50	1.63**
	(0.04)	(0.04)	(0.03)
Drinking frequency	3.17	3.10	3.15
	(0.05)	(0.05)	(0.05)
Drinking amount	2.65	2.55	2.65
	(0.05)	(0.05)	(0.04)
Drunkenness	2.31	2.19	2.32*
	(0.04)	(0.04)	(0.04)
Marijuana Use	1.51	1.54	1.66*
	(0.04)	(0.04)	(0.04)

$* \; p<.05; \; ** \; p<.01$

Life Skills Training Program (LST) (continued)

Botvin et al., 1995	Follow up with 12th graders in 56 schools (N = 3,597)	Same curriculum as 1990 study.		

6-year follow-up
Reduced cigarette, alcohol, and marijuana use in both treatment conditions compared with control group for individuals who received at least 60% of the intervention. Follow up means were adjusted for baseline prevalence.

Botvin et al., 2001b	7th-grade students in 29 schools (urban, public) in New York City (N = 3,621)	LST for *minority youth* which included new graphics, language, and role-play scenarios appropriate for target population, adjusting the reading level for youth. The overall prevention strategy remained the same with 15 sessions in the 7th grade; 10 booster sessions in the 8th grade, taught by a classroom teacher. Teachers were taught via video material and a 1-day workshop.

1-year follow-up
LST participants reduced cigarette, alcohol, marijuana, polydrug use compared with control group.

Adjusted means and standard errors (SE) at 1-year follow up for substance use

	Intervention	Control
Smoking frequency	1.73 (.04)	1.94 (.05)**
Smoking quantity	1.19 (.02)	1.32 (.02)**
Drinking frequency	1.77 (.03)	1.99 (.04)**
Drunkenness frequency	1.17 (.02)	1.26 (.03)**
Drinking quantity	1.51 (.02)	1.68 (.03)**
Marijuana frequency	1.41 (.03)	1.51 (.04)*
Getting "high" frequency	1.26 (.03)	1.34 (.04)*
Lifetime polydrug use	0.78 (.02)	0.96 (.03)**
Current polydrug use	0.24 (.02)	0.33 (.02)**

Note: GLM *p*-value. * *p*<.05, ** *p*<.01

(continued)

Table 23.2. Continued

Study Name	Study Type and Population	Intervention Description	Major Outcomes

Life Skills Training Program (LST) (continued)

| Griffin et al., 2003 | 7th- and 8th-grade students identified as high risk either socially (e.g., had friends that smoked or drank) or academically (grades of C or less) from 29 inner-city middle schools (N = 802) | Same curriculum as 2001 study. | *1-year follow-up*
LST students reported less cigarette, alcohol, inhalant and polydrug use compared with control condition. There were no effects for marijuana use.

Adjusted substance use means and standard errors (SE) at 1-year follow-up |

		Intervention	Control
Smoking		1.79 (.08)	2.13 (.09)**
Drinking		1.82 (.08)	2.11 (.08)**
Marijuana		1.69 (.10)	1.87 (.11)
Polydrug use		0.42 (.05)	0.61 (.05)**

Note: GEE *p*-value; ** *p*<.01

| Spoth et al., 2013 | 7th-grade students from 24 schools in districts where over 20% qualified for free or reduced lunch | LST+Iowa Strengthening Families Program: For Parents and Youth 10–14 (SFP 10-14) | Follow-up when students were 21, 22, and 25 years of age LST+SFP 10-14 students reported lower rates of lifetime prescription drug misuse and prescription opioid misuse compared with a control condition across all ages, with the strongest effects for participants who were at highest risk. |

Lions-Quest "Skills for Adolescence" (SFA)

| Eisen et al., 2002 | 6th-grade middle school students in 34 schools in the Los Angeles, Detroit, and Washington-Baltimore areas (N = 7,426) | SFA is a 40-session (35–45 minute per session) curriculum focusing on teen pressures (3 sessions), self-efficacy and communication (4 sessions), peer relationships (8 sessions), coping with emotions (5 sessions), and drug-free living (20 sessions). | *1-year post-test follow-up*
For pre-test nonsmokers, past 30-day smoking was significantly lower for SFA schools than control schools. Hispanic students in SFA were more likely than control Hispanic students to have positive outcomes in drinking. No substance use differences were found between non-Hispanic youth who participated in SFA and non-Hispanic youth in the control group. |

Lions-Quest "Skills for Adolescence" (SFA) (continued)

Prevalence of drinking outcomes for Hispanics and non-Hispanics at 1-year follow-up (%)

	Intervention		Control	
	Hispanic	Non-H	Hispanic	Non-H
Past month drinking	6.92*	7.18	10.36*	5.59
Binge drinking	3.21**	2.92	6.23**	2.31

*$p<.05$; ** $p<.01$

Eisen et al., 2003 — Same sample as 2002 study (N = 7,426) — Same curriculum as 2002 study.

1-year post-intervention follow-up

Across gender and ethnicity, students in the SFA schools reported significantly less lifetime and 30-day marijuana use than control schools. For students who reported baseline binge drinking, students receiving the intervention reported less binge drinking at follow-up compared with control.

Adjusted prevalence rates (95% CI) at follow-up (%)

	Intervention	Control	CI
Lifetime marijuana use	27.24*	30.50	-6.55, -0.0
30-day marijuana use	11.32*	13.79	-4.70, -0.23
Binge drinking	27.0**	37.0	Not reported

*$p \leq .05$; ** $p \leq .01$

Menrath et al., 2012 — 31 randomly assigned schools (N = 1,370 students) — SFA or "Fit and Strong for Life"

1-year follow-up (at the end of the school year and 6-months later)

Students receiving either intervention had lower rates of smoking and higher life skills compared with a control group.

(continued)

Table 23.2. Continued

Study Name	Study Type and Population	Intervention Description	Major Outcomes
Project ALERT			
Ellickson & Bell, 1990	7th-grade students in 30 schools (urban, suburban, and rural) in California and Oregon (N = 6,527)	Eight sessions in 7th grade and 3 lessons in 8th grade. Half of the treatment schools were taught solely by health educators; the other half also used teen leaders. Focus on reasons not to use drugs, identifying pressures to use drugs, counter pro-drug messages, learn how to say no to external and internal pressures, understand that most people do not use drugs, and recognize the benefits of resistance.	*15-month follow-up* Effects for three levels of users were examined: Nonusers, experimenters, and users. No effects on alcohol use. Decreased smoking among baseline experimenters. For baseline smokers, negative results were found, with smokers in the Project ALERT teen leader program increasing use by 20%. Project ALERT curbed marijuana initiation rates by one-third. Both marijuana and cigarette abstainers had lower rates of initiation and current marijuana use compared with the control group. There were early significant reductions in drinking levels amongst nonusers, experimenters, and users, but effects were not sustained over time.
Ellickson et al., 2003	7th- and 8th-grade students at 55 South Dakota middle schools (N = 4,276)	Revised Project ALERT curriculum to address alcohol misuse: 11 lessons in 7th grade (3 new lessons) and 3 lessons in 8th grade. The additional sessions focused on smoking cessation and alcohol use via a video of former teenage smokers talking about why and how they quit. New home learning opportunities included parents in prevention activities.	*18-month follow-up* Three levels: low risk, moderate risk, and high risk. Reduced proportion of new smokers by 19%. Reduced proportion of new marijuana users by 39%; however, no effects on current marijuana use. High-risk participants had lower alcohol misuse scores compared with control students; however, there were no effects on alcohol initiation or current alcohol use.

Effects for low-risk group, 18 months after baseline

	Intervention	Control
Past month cigarette use	8.6	11.1
Marijuana initiation	5.0	8.0**
Alcohol overall misuse (mean score)	0.22	0.30

Project ALERT (continued)

Effects for moderate-risk group, 18 months after baseline

	Intervention	Control
Past month cigarette use	28.9	36.6*
Marijuana initiation	27.2	36.8*
Alcohol overall misuse (mean score)	0.64	0.65

Effects for high-risk group, 18 months after baseline

	Intervention	Control
Past month cigarette use	56.8	70.8*
Marijuana initiation	N/A	N/A
Alcohol overall misuse (mean score)	1.78	2.23*

Note: Numbers are percentages.
* p<.05; ** p<.01

St. Pierre et al., 2005

7th-grade students in 8 Pennsylvania schools (N = 1,649)

Used the revised curriculum of Project ALERT with 11 original lessons in 7th grade and 3 added lessons in 8th grade

HLM analysis found no differences between the ALERT programs and the control condition. The Teen assisted ALERT showed greater use of past year marijuana; however, this results could be due to chance given the number of tests that were conducted.

	Adult-led		Teen-assisted	
	b	S.E.	b	S.E.
Past month alcohol	.076	.241	.037	.239
Past year alcohol	−.156	.180	.015	.178
Binge drinking	−.003	.299	.0004	.296

(continued)

Table 23.2. Continued

Study Name	Study Type and Population	Intervention Description	Major Outcomes

Project ALERT (continued)

	Adult-led		Teen-assisted	
	b	S.E.	b	S.E.
Past month cigarette	.186	.255	.069	.253
Past year cigarette	.157	.221	.033	.217
Past month marijuana	.346	.322	.486	.349
Past year marijuana	.335	.283	.914**	.317

b is the logistic coefficient for the interaction of the treatment condition with the pre–post contrast, and S.E. is its standard error.

Study Name	Study Type and Population	Intervention Description	Major Outcomes
Longshore et al., 2007	At-risk youth from the original South Dakota evaluation who reported lifetime use of either tobacco or marijuana before the 7th grade evaluation (N = 1383)	ALERT and ALERT plus (booster lessons in 9th grade)	(see table below)

	Girls			Boys		
	Con	ALERT Plus	ALERT Only	Con	ALERT Plus	ALERT Only
Weekly Alcohol	39.6	26.8*	37.7	44.6	39.7	43.6
Weekly Tobacco	46.6	39.1	45.0	44.2	46.3	46.0
Weekly Marijuana	22.3	11.4*	20.3	23.6	19.1	26.1

Con = Control; % = p<.05

Study Name	Study Type and Population	Intervention Description	Major Outcomes
Ringwalt et al., 2009	Thirty-four schools with grades 6–8 in 11 states	Used the revised curriculum of Project ALERT with 11 original lessons in 7th grade and 3 added lessons in 8th grade	Examined lifetime and 30-day substance use for cigarettes, alcohol, marijuana and inhalants. The time × intervention interactions were not significant. They found that use increased over time for all four substances examined with no differential changes in substance use behaviors for intervention relative to control students.

Project Options

Brown et al., 2005	High school students at 3 schools in San Diego County, California (N = 1,254)	A voluntary intervention delivered at lunch or after school in 3 formats (students choose): 1) Individual (four sessions) 2) Group (six sessions) 3) Website (unlimited access) Curriculum focused on increasing readiness to change alcohol use and risk behaviors, communication skills, outcome expectancies, and normative feedback.	*One-semester follow-up* Eighteen percent of drinkers volunteered to attend the school-based intervention. Students who reported the greatest number of lifetime drinking episodes and had attended at least one session of the intervention were more likely to stop or cut down alcohol use than heavy drinkers who did not attend the program.

Odds ratios (95% CI) of cutting down or stopping alcohol use by the number of lifetime drinking episodes

	Odds ratio	CI
Limited number of lifetime drinking episodes		
Cutting down	0.69	0.35–1.34
Stopping use	0.85	0.46–1.56
High number of lifetime drinking episodes		
Cutting down	1.84*	1.05–3.21
Stopping use	2.42*	1.18–4.95

* $p \leq .05$

Schulte et al., 2010	High school students at 3 schools in San Diego County; Project Options participants (n = 327); comparison youth (n = 1,728)	Same curriculum	Project Options participants reported more accurate estimates of peer use; however, there was no effect of the intervention on adolescents' actual alcohol use

(*continued*)

Table 23.2. Continued

Study Name	Study Type and Population	Intervention Description	Major Outcomes
Project Towards No Drug Abuse (Project TND)			
Sussman et al., 1998	Continuation high school students in 21 schools in southern California N = 1,074	9 lessons covered in 3 sessions per week for 3 consecutive weeks. Two experimental conditions were tested: classroom program and classroom program plus school-as-community component. Classroom sessions provided motivation-skills-decision-making material targeting the use of cigarettes, alcohol, marijuana, hard drug, and violence-related behavior. School-as-community events included job training, field trips, and sports competitions.	*1-year follow-up* Reductions in alcohol use and hard drug use among users in the two experimental conditions compared with control students. No effects on cigarette or marijuana use. *Mean levels of use in the past 30 days, 1-year follow-up* |	Intervention (class)	Intervention (class plus school as community)	Control
Cigarettes	34.53	33.08	30.71
Alcohol	8.15	7.16	8.61*
Marijuana	12.31	13.02	11.21
Hard drugs	2.74	2.87	5.03*** | * $p<.05$, *** $p<.001$
Sussman, Sun et al., 2003; Sussman, Yang et al., 2003	Continuation high school students in 18 schools in southern California N = 1,037	Comparison of a health educator delivered program and a self-instruction curriculum.	*2-year follow-up* The health educator condition significantly lowered the probability of 30-day tobacco and hard drug use. No effects were found for the self-instruction curriculum.
Sun et al., 2006	Same sample as 1998 study N = 725 (46% of baseline subjects)	Same curriculum as 1998 study.	*5-year follow-up* Fewer students in the intervention groups reported 30-day hard drug use (cocaine, hallucinogens, stimulants, inhalants and other drugs; $p = .02$) than students in the control group.
Sun et al. 2008	Students in 18 high schools in Southern California (n = 2734)	Examine different parts of the TND curriculum. The three conditions were 1) cognitive perception information curriculum, 2) cognitive perception information+behavioral skills curriculum, or 3) standard care (control).	*1-year follow-up* Across all TND schools, the two different curricula did not significantly reduce cigarette, alcohol, marijuana, or hard drug use.

Project Towards No Drug Abuse (Project TND) (continued)

Rohrbach et al., 2010	Students from 65 high schools from 14 school districts (N = 2,538)	Curriculum delivered by physical health and health teachers who received comprehensive TND support (workshop, coaching, web-based support, and technical assistance) or workshop TND training only.	*1-year follow-up* There were no significant differences between the two TND schools and control school on cigarettes, alcohol, and hard drug use. There were marginal TND program effects on marijuana use ($p < .10$).

School Health and Alcohol Harm Reduction Project (SHAHRP)

McBride et al., 2000	8th-grade students in 14 schools in Perth, Western Australia (N = 2,343)	Conducted in two phases over a 2-year period: phase I conducted when students were 13 years old comprised 17 skills based activities conducted over 8–10 lessons (40–60 minutes each); Phase II conducted when youth were 14 years old comprised 12 activities delivered over 5–7 weeks. Activities included delivery of developmentally appropriate information, skill rehearsal, individual and small group decision making, and discussions based on scenarios suggested by students.	*Immediately after phase I* While both the intervention and control groups increased consumption of alcohol over this time, the control group demonstrated a significantly greater increase than the SHAHRP students (Mann-Whitney: $p = .0087$). SHAHRP students reported significantly greater alcohol knowledge scores as well as attitudes more supportive of safe alcohol use and harm minimization than control students.
McBride et al., 2004	Same sample as 2000 study	Same curriculum as 2000 study.	*32-month follow-up* Students who reported no baseline alcohol use were less likely to drink in a risky manner than students in their corresponding control groups at 8-, 20-, and 32-month follow-up time points. Students who received the intervention and were unsupervised drinkers at baseline had safer alcohol-related attitudes throughout all follow-up time points compared with the control group.
McKay et al., 2012	14–16 year-olds in Northern Ireland	Adapted SHAHRP to strengthen cultural competency of curriculum for Northern Ireland context	SHAHRP students reported greater knowledge about alcohol and its effects, safer alcohol-related attitudes, less harm from alcohol, and less alcohol use over the 11 month period when there was no intervention implementation.

(continued)

Table 23.2. Continued

Study Name	Study Type and Population	Intervention Description	Major Outcomes		

Start Taking Alcohol Risks Seriously (STARS)

| Werch et al., 2003 | 6th-grade students from two urban middle schools in Jacksonville, Florida (N = 650) | 2-year multicomponent intervention: brief 20 minute one-on-one health consultation from nurse in 6th grade and prevention postcards to parents; follow up nurse consultation in 7th grade with 4 take home lessons. | *1-year follow-up* STARS students reported fewer intentions to drink in the future, greater motivation to avoid alcohol use, and fewer total risk factors than control students. No significant differences were found between groups for actual alcohol use. | | |

Mean (SD) for alcohol use and risk factor measures at 1-year follow-up

	Intervention	Control
Intentions	5.56 (2.75)	6.70 (3.77)**
Alcohol frequency	0.37 (1.13)	0.57(1.62)
Alcohol quantity	0.27 (0.92)	0.47 (1.26)
Heavy alcohol use	0.11 (.60)	0.17 (.58)
Motivation to avoid	2.49 (1.17)	3.00 (1.79)**
Total alcohol risk	7.73 (1.83)	8.26 (1.96)**

** *p*<.01

Stay SMART

| St. Pierre et al., 1992 | Youth aged 13 years from ten Boys & Girls Clubs across the nation; results reported only for youth who participated in all four testing occasions (N = 161) | Lessons based on Botvin's LST (see above) plus additional lessons discussing sexual activity; 2 booster sessions were provided which reinforced knowledge and skills that were taught in the initial program. Youth voluntarily enrolled in program, but were then required to complete 9 of 12 sessions. | *27-month follow-up* Less recent marijuana use among youth who participated in the Stay SMART program and Stay SMART with boosters. Marginally significant results for reduced alcohol and cigarette use among program participants. | | |

Stay SMART (continued)

Adjusted means for prevention and control conditions at the 27-month follow-up

	Stay SMART only	Stay SMART + Boosters	Control
Alcohol behavior	1.89	1.87	2.04
Marijuana behavior	1.22	1.25	1.38*
Cigarette behavior	1.46	1.48	1.63

* $p \leq .05$

[a] Note: This table focuses on programs with student-specific prevention or intervention curricula. We do not include multicomponent school studies that may have provided a parent program or included changes in school policy. When possible, we provided means and standard deviations, t-tests, and/or odds ratios associated with the findings that are reported in each study. Portions of this table were taken from D'Amico, E. J., & Stern, S. A. (2008). Alcohol and drug use among youth: Advances in prevention. In J. A. Trafton & W. T. Gordon (Eds.).*Best practices in the behavioral management of health from preconception to adolescence* (Vol. 3, pp. 341–401). Los Altos, CA: Institute for Disease Management.

participated in Project ALERT were less likely to initiate cigarette and marijuana use, and had lower current use of these substances than students in the control schools. Although intervention effects were found for alcohol use at the 3-month follow-up, these were no longer significant at the 15-month follow-up (Ellickson & Bell, 1990).

The ALERT curriculum was revised to put more emphasis on curbing alcohol misuse and was tested in a large-scale, randomized trial with 55 schools in South Dakota (Ellickson, McCaffrey et al., 2003). Three additional lessons were added in 7th grade. The program continued to curb marijuana and cigarette use. It also decreased alcohol misuse and alcohol-related problems at 18-month follow-up (Ellickson, McCaffrey, et al., 2003). The authors also examined to what extent the program curriculum achieved these positive results through modification of four substance specific mediators that were targeted by the Project ALERT: low resistance self-efficacy, high positive beliefs, low negative beliefs, and positive peer influence. Similar to previous work in this area, they found that the peer influence construct, which was comprised of both perceived prevalence of substance use and perceived peer attitudes, was the strongest mediator for cigarette use. They also found that the program's effects for cigarettes were mediated by positive and negative cigarette expectancies. In contrast, for alcohol, they found that the program had small effects on the proposed mediators. The authors suggested that the program could be improved in this area by focusing more on adolescents' perception of peers' attitudes toward alcohol and the prevalence of alcohol use (Orlando et al., 2005).

In 2007, Longshore and colleagues (Longshore, Ellickson, McCaffrey, & St. Clair, 2007) examined the effects of Project ALERT and ALERT Plus, which included Project ALERT in middle school and additional booster lessons in 9th grade, on outcomes for at-risk youth. They defined at-risk youth as those who had reported lifetime use of either tobacco or marijuana prior to the baseline survey in 7th grade. They found that the ALERT Plus curriculum was effective for at-risk girls. Specifically, 27% of at-risk girls who received ALERT Plus reported weekly alcohol use and 11% reported weekly marijuana use, compared with 40% and 22% of at-risk girls in the control schools. The authors also replicated mediation effects found for Project ALERT indicating that the program works by modifying prodrug social influences and self-efficacy to resist these influences. There were no effects of ALERT Plus on at-risk boys, and no effects of Project ALERT on at-risk boys or girls (Longshore et al., 2007).

St. Pierre and colleagues (St Pierre, Osgood, Mincemoyer, Kaltreider, & Kauh, 2005) conducted an independent evaluation of Project ALERT in eight Pennsylvania middle schools and conducted four waves of posttests over the 2-year program and 1-year follow-up. They did not find any effects of ALERT on AOD use or on any of the mediators at any time point. Despite some differences in the research design from the original study of ALERT, the authors conclude that their null findings were not due to modifications in research design, sample size or data analysis approaches (St Pierre et al., 2005). In 2009, Ringwalt and colleagues (Ringwalt, Clark, Hanley, Shamblen, & Flewelling, 2010) tested the Project ALERT curriculum in a randomized controlled trial in 34 schools in grades 6 to 8 across 11 states. They implemented ALERT in 6th grade and examined effects on 30-day use of cigarettes, alcohol, marijuana, and inhalants 1 year after curriculum implementation. They found that substance use increased over time for all substances and did not support the long-term effectiveness of ALERT when delivered to 6th graders (Ringwalt et al., 2010). Overall, it appears that additional effectiveness studies are needed to assess this program in different contexts (Gorman & Conde, 2010).

The Life Skills Training Program (LST) was developed to target drug-related expectancies, teach skills to resist influences to use drugs, and promote the development of self-management and social skills for middle school students (Botvin, 1996). LST consists of fifteen 45-minute sessions. In addition, there are 10 booster sessions in 8th grade and five booster sessions in 9th grade. Several studies have examined the long-term effects of this program. Among mostly white students, there were fewer smokers, drinkers, and marijuana users by 12th grade among those who had received the LST curriculum relative to control students (Botvin, Baker, Dusenbury, Botvin, & Diaz, 1995). The program was also successful among minority youth: at 1-year follow-up, those youth who had received LST reported less smoking, drinking, and polydrug use relative to those in the control group (Botvin, Griffin, Diaz, & Ifill-Williams, 2001a). Studies on the LST have also shown that at a 1- and 2-year follow-up that the proportion of heavy drinkers was 50% lower in the LST group compared with the control group (Botvin, Griffin, Diaz, & Ifill-Williams, 2001b). The program has also been effective for higher risk youth. Griffin and colleagues assessed a subsample of youth who were identified as high risk based on their exposure to substance-using peers and low academic achievement. They found that at the 1-year follow-up, the high risk students who received the LST were less likely to report use of cigarettes, inhalants, alcohol, and other drugs compared with high-risk youth in the control group (Griffin, Botvin, Nichols, & Doyle, 2003). A longitudinal study that administered LST *combined with* the "Strengthening Families Program" in 7th grade found that youth in their early 20s reported lower rates of lifetime prescription drug misuse and prescription opioid use compared with those not receiving these interventions (Spoth et al., 2013). Although the LST program has shown some effectiveness for other drugs of abuse, studies have found less evidence for the effectiveness of LST on marijuana use and abuse (Gorman, 2011).

The Adolescent Alcohol Prevention Trial (AAPT) (Hansen & Graham, 1991) was designed to examine how different intervention components may impact subsequent alcohol and drug use. The AAPT included an information only group, a resistance training plus information group, a normative education plus information group, and a group that combined resistance training, normative education, and information (Taylor, Graham, Cumsille, & Hansen, 2000). Information only included four lessons about the social and health consequences of using alcohol and other drugs. Normative education provided four information sessions and five lessons that corrected misperceptions concerning the prevalence and acceptability of AOD use among peers and established conservative norms. Resistance skills training prepared the adolescent for rejecting potential pressure for alcohol and drug use in five lessons in addition to four information sessions (Taylor et al., 2000). An assessment of the efficacy of the AAPT used five waves of longitudinal data. Students were in the 7th grade when they received the program and final follow-up took place in the 11th grade. Findings indicated that only the normative education program had consistent beneficial effects on alcohol and drug use when compared with the information only program. Specifically, average use levels over the 4 years were lower for youth in the normative education program. In addition, the rate of growth of drug use for adolescents who received the normative education program was significantly slower compared with youth who received the information only program (Taylor et al., 2000). Donaldson and colleagues extended this finding by examining both self-report and best

friends' report of substance use. They found that the adolescents who received normative education had a delayed onset of alcohol use across the 8th, 9th, and 10th grades (Donaldson, Thomas, Graham, Au, & Hansen, 2000).

The Lions-Quest "Skills for Adolescence" (SFA) drug education program is a multicomponent life skills education program. SFA focuses on strategies to teach social competency and refusal skills, specifically teaching cognitive behavioral skills to help build self-esteem and personal responsibility, effective communication and decision making, resisting social influences and asserting rights, and increasing drug use knowledge and consequences (Eisen, Zellman, & Murray, 2003). Eisen and colleagues report that the SFA program curriculum promotes a "zero-tolerance" perspective to substance use and therefore the curriculum does not include discussion of norms related to substance use or a component to modify students' beliefs regarding the prevalence of peer use (Eisen et al., 2003). The Lions-Quest SFA evaluation included 34 schools from four school districts across three metropolitan areas. It was a group randomized trial with schools as the unit of assignment. The 17 intervention schools received only SFA as their 7th-grade drug education during the 1998–1999 school year and the control schools received their usual drug prevention programming, which ranged from school assemblies to local teacher-devised classroom activities to DARE exposure (Eisen, Zellman, Massett, & Murray, 2002). The curriculum was 40 sessions (35–40 minutes per session); however, 8 of the 40 were determined to be "key" sessions and teachers were required to conduct these 8 sessions. Surveys were conducted annually from 6th grade to 8th grade and the intervention was implemented over the 7th-grade year. At the end of 7th grade, 30-day cigarette use was lower for students at the SFA schools who did not use cigarettes at baseline compared with the control schools (Eisen et al., 2002). No significant effects were found for alcohol or illicit substances (Eisen et al., 2002). For users, they found that relative to students in control schools, students in SFA schools demonstrated significantly less progression to use of more advanced substances in the 7th grade (Eisen et al., 2002). At the end of 8th grade, they found that the SFA schools reported lower lifetime and 30-day marijuana use compared with the control schools. They also found that students in the SFA schools who reported heavy drinking at baseline were less likely to report heavy drinking in 8th grade compared with students in the control schools

(Eisen et al., 2003). Another study delivering SFA or "Fit and Strong for Life" among high-risk students in Germany found that students receiving either intervention at the beginning of the school year had reductions in smoking and increases in life skills compared with the control group at the end of the school year and six months later (Menrath et al., 2012).

The Start Taking Alcohol Risks Seriously (STARS) for families program is different from other school-based programs in that it is very brief. The program provides a single 20-minute one-on-one health consultation by a nurse for youth in the 6th grade. During 6th grade, these youth also receive a series of prevention postcards that are mailed to parents/guardians and provide key facts about alcohol and tips on how to discuss these facts with their children. In the 7th grade, STARS youth receive a follow-up nurse consultation and four family take-home lessons to encourage parent-child communication about prevention skills and knowledge (Werch et al., 2003). At 1-year follow-up, students who received the STARS intervention reported weaker intentions to drink in the future and greater motivation to avoid alcohol use than control students. Alcohol use was lower for STARS youth compared with control students; however, these differences were not statistically significant (Werch et al., 2003).

One of the few culturally grounded, school-based prevention programs is keepin' it REAL (Gosin, Marsiglia, & Hecht, 2003), a drug resistance curriculum tailored for Mexican-American youth in the southwest. Keepin' it REAL is composed of ten 40–45 minute lessons with five videos. The program teaches cognitive and communication skills for use with four "REAL" resistance strategies: Refuse, Explain, Avoid, and Leave (Gosin et al., 2003). Three curriculum versions were developed: one targeting Latino students (Mexican-American version), another targeting non-Latino students (African American and European version), and a multicultural version combining the previous two versions. The program was effective such that increases in alcohol, marijuana, and cigarette use were less substantial among intervention students compared with control students. The Latino version of the program generated more positive outcomes overall; however, there was little evidence that matching the message to the ethnicity of participants enhanced the program's effectiveness. Specifically, when analyses limited the sample to those youth

who reported Mexican/Mexican American ethnic identity, the Latino version did not generate better outcomes than the non-Latino version, suggesting that it may not be necessary to tailor prevention messages to each specific cultural group (Hecht et al., 2003; Kulis et al., 2005). A recent study examined the effects of this universal prevention program on adolescent substance users. They found that among youth who reported using alcohol at baseline, the reduction rate for program participants was 72% higher compared with the rate among control students. In addition, the rate of discontinuing alcohol use was 66% higher than the rate for control youth. Program participation was not associated with reductions in cigarette or marijuana use (Kulis, Nieri, Yabiku, Stromwall, & Marsiglia, 2007). Another recent study compared the effects of keepin' it REAL delivered to students of Mexican heritage during 5th, 7th, or both grades, and found that delivering the intervention in both grades was as effective at reducing marijuana and inhalants when the intervention was delivered in 7th grade alone (Marsiglia, Kulis, Yabiku, Nieri, & Coleman, 2011). Of note, the adapted curriculum for 5th graders was no more effective than traditional school substance use programming (Hecht et al., 2008).

High school programs. ASSIST (A Stop Smoking in Schools Trial) is a peer-led program for high school youth. For this program, peers were trained over two days on how to provide information to other students about the short-term risks of smoking, and the health, environmental, and economic benefits of remaining smoke free. The training also focused on developing communication skills, listening skills, ways of giving and receiving information, conflict resolution, attitudes toward risk-taking and exploration of personal values (Campbell et al., 2008). The intervention took place over 10 weeks during which peer leaders had informal conversations about smoking with their peers in a variety of situations (e.g., lunchtime, breaks, to and from school) and a record of these conversations was logged into a diary. The evaluation involved a cluster randomized trial of 10,730 students aged 12–13 years in 59 schools in England and Wales. Data were gathered at baseline, immediately following the intervention, and at 1-year and 2-year follow-up. Examination of baseline characteristics between the intervention and control schools indicated that more students at the control school reported smoking every week compared with students in the intervention schools. After controlling for all baseline differences, results indicated that prevalence of smoking was lower in the intervention schools compared with the control schools at all three follow-up time points, with some attenuation of these effects over time (Campbell et al., 2008). ASSIST was reanalyzed as part of the European Union-funded TEENAGE project to examine the effects on smoking for different socioeconomic categories. ASSIST showed the strongest results for youth in the lowest socioeconomic category (Mercken et al., 2012). An important part of the ASSIST intervention is choosing peer leaders, who are nominated by fellow students. The peer nomination process in the 2008 study resulted in a mix of students, with both genders and different ethnicities represented. Despite some student and teacher misgivings about the process, results from the trial suggest that the intervention was effective, indicating that the broad range of youth who were nominated as peer supporters and delivered the intervention contributed to the success of the program (Starkey, Audrey, Holliday, Moore, & Campbell, 2009). A cost-effectiveness analysis of ASSIST indicated that the cost of the program per student was modest at approximately 32 GBP or $50 (Hollingworth et al., 2013).

The School Health and Alcohol Harm Reduction Project (SHAHRP) is a program that took place in Australia. SHAHRP targeted students in secondary schools (aged 13–17) and was incorporated into the health education curriculum of each school. SHAHRP took place over a 2-year period and provided eight initial lessons when youth were 13 years old and five booster lessons the following year when youth were 14 years old. The overall goal of the program was to reduce alcohol-related harm by strengthening students' abilities to identify and cope with high-risk drinking situations. Program activities included skill rehearsal, individual and group decision making and discussions of risk scenarios suggested by students, emphasizing identifying alcohol-related harm and strategies to reduce harm. The study took place in 14 intervention and control schools and included over 2,300 youth. At the end of the first year, youth who participated in SHAHRP reported higher knowledge scores and more supportive attitudes toward using alcohol safely and a harm minimization approach. Both SHAHRP and control schools reported increases in alcohol consumption; however, the increase in consumption was greater for students at the control schools. Control school youth also reported more unsupervised drinking and greater alcohol-related harms (McBride et al., 2000). At the final follow-up, 17 months after completion of the five booster sessions, SHAHRP youth were less likely to consume alcohol at risky levels, had more nondrinkers than the control group, and reported less harm associated with their alcohol use than the control group (McBride, Farringdon, Midford, Meuleners, & Phillips, 2004). McKay and colleagues adapted SHAHRP and conducted a nonrandomized control longitudinal design with youth from 29 post-primary schools aged 14–16 in Northern Ireland. They modified both content and context of the curriculum to strengthen the cultural competency of the program for use in Northern Ireland. They assessed youth after each implementation phase and approximately 11 months after the intervention ended. SHAHRP students were more likely to report increased knowledge of alcohol, safer attitudes regarding alcohol, less harm from alcohol use, and less alcohol use (McKay, Mcbride, Sumnall, & Cole, 2012). McKay and colleagues are currently conducting a large randomized controlled trial with 11,500 youth to examine the effects of the adapted SHAHRP further (trial number ISRCTN47028486).

Successful selective prevention approaches also exist for high school aged youth (SAMHSA, 2012b), although there are far fewer of these types of programs than programs targeting the general population (Brown & D'Amico, 2003). Sussman and colleagues developed Project Towards No Drug Abuse (TND), which was tailored for high-risk youth in continuation high school settings (Sussman, 1996). Curriculum content was developed with the input of high-risk youth (Sussman, Dent, & Stacy, 2002; Sussman, Dent, Stacy, & Craig, 1998) and includes lessons which focus on active listening, stereotyping, confronting myths about substance use, providing information on chemical dependency, understanding the negative consequences of drug abuse, providing alternatives, learning self-control, and decision making (Sussman, 1996). In comparison to previous prevention programs, which focus on providing normative information, Sussman found that normative information was not well-received by high-risk youth and was not associated with any change in perceptions of use (Sussman, 1996). Instead, the TND curriculum focuses on how stereotyping may impact behavior. For example, many of these high-risk teens felt that others perceived them as deviant and as drug abusers. Thus, instead of focusing on providing normative feedback, one of the lessons focuses on how these students may be more at risk if they give into this self-fulfilling prophecy that others think they are drug abusers.

TND is taught in either a 9- or 12-session curriculum with each lesson lasting approximately 50 minutes (Sussman et al., 1998, 2002). Studies of the curriculum have indicated that the same types of lessons are applicable to both Latino and non-Latino white adolescents (Sussman, Yang, Baezconde-Garbanati, & Dent, 2003). In one study, high-risk youth who participated in TND decreased their hard drug use by 25% at a 1-year follow-up compared with a control group, but no reductions were found for tobacco and marijuana use (Sussman et al., 1998). In another study that implemented a 12-session curriculum led by health educators, reductions were seen for involvement with hard drugs and alcohol compared with a control condition at 1-year follow-up (Sussman et al., 2002). A 2-year follow-up indicated positive effects for tobacco and hard drug use (Sussman, Sun, McCuller, & Dent, 2003). In 2006, 5-year post program follow-up was conducted. The follow-up rate was 47% at this time point. Findings indicated that youth who received the classroom only intervention and the classroom plus school-as-community intervention reported less hard drug use in the past 30 days than the control group. No effects were found for alcohol, marijuana or cigarettes (Sun, Skara, Sun, Dent, & Sussman, 2006).

Two studies evaluated TND delivered by teachers (Sun, Sussman, Dent, & Rohrbach, 2008; Rohrbach, Sun, & Sussman, 2010). The 2008 study assigned 18 schools in Southern California to deliver different components of the TND program to understand the relative contribution of each component to the effectiveness of the program. The three conditions were (1) cognitive perception information curriculum, (2) cognitive perception information + behavioral skills curriculum, or (3) standard care (control). Across all TND schools, the two different curricula did not significantly reduce cigarette, alcohol, marijuana, or hard drug use at 1-year follow-up (Sun et al., 2008). The 2010 study involved teacher delivery of TND in 65 high schools in 14 school districts across the United States. Results for the 1-year follow-up showed marginal reductions in marijuana use for TND schools compared with standard care curricula schools ($p <$ .10); there were no significant differences between TND schools and control schools for alcohol, cigarettes or illicit drugs (Rohrbach et al., 2010). Overall, results suggest that this school-based

curriculum is effective in reaching this higher risk population in efficacy trials, but effects are weakened when implemented in the real world.

All of the programs discussed above take place in the school setting during school time. Most programs, with the exception of STARS, take approximately nine or more weeks to complete; some take as many 40 sessions. Typically, youth who receive the program have parental permission. In addition, the program is part of the classroom curriculum and therefore required, and the majority of youth in the school receive the program. We note, however, that the need for parental permission may cause differences between the populations that do and do not receive the program (e.g., Frissell et al., 2004), and this caveat should be considered when interpreting results.

Voluntary school-based programs. In contrast to the many mandated classroom programs for adolescent alcohol and drug use, there are few voluntary programs available for youth, for example, programs that may take place outside of class time (Little & Harris, 2003). Developing brief voluntary intervention programs is important because there is increased pressure on schools related to academic performance, which can leave less classroom time for prevention-related activities. In addition, curricula need to be developed that better match adolescents' needs so they will be more motivated to attend and obtain prevention-related information (D'Amico et al., 2006). Voluntary programs may also be more appealing to teens because they can *choose* to attend sessions that interest them. Teens who choose to attend intervention programs may therefore be more motivated to utilize this information and make changes in their AOD use.

The voluntary nature of these programs puts a premium on features that enhance student and community involvement, such as including program content that captures the attention of youth (who have other activities that compete for their "out-of-school time" such as sports, other school activities, or simply being with friends), providing a limited number of sessions, and collaborating with school staff, students and parents in the development of the program (Brown, 2001; D'Amico et al., 2005; Masterman & Kelly, 2003; Wagner et al., 2004). Perhaps because of these challenges, voluntary school-based intervention programs are relatively rare and few studies have evaluated their effectiveness in curbing subsequent alcohol and drug use. To date, only three studies have examined the effects of a voluntary intervention program on adolescent alcohol and drug use; thus, we report on all three even though the follow-up period may have been less than 1 year.

The first study used a voluntary intervention strategy for teens who participated in Boys and Girls Clubs by extending an invitation to all youth to participate in the Stay SMART program (St. Pierre, Kaltreider, Mark, & Aikin, 1992). Once youth voluntarily enrolled, however, they were required to attend 9 of the 12 sessions. Thus, initial involvement was voluntary, but subsequent attendance at these sessions was mandated. The Stay SMART program is a component of SMART Moves, which is the national prevention program adapted for Boys and Girls Clubs from Botvin's LST (Botvin, 1996). It includes the original topics discussed in the LST curriculum, with the additional topics designed to address early sexual activity (St. Pierre et al., 1992). The program also includes booster sessions that are designed to build upon the skills and knowledge presented in Stay SMART. At a 27-month post-test, youth who continued their participation in the Stay SMART program and booster sessions reported less involvement with marijuana compared with a control group (St. Pierre et al., 1992).

The second study evaluated the effects of a voluntary intervention implemented in several high schools on self-change efforts (e.g., cut down or quit attempts) for alcohol use (Brown et al., 2005). Project Options was available via individual (four sessions), group (six sessions) or website (unlimited access) format (Brown, 2001). Individual and group sessions took place either during lunch or after school. Curriculum content across all three options focused on coping, behavioral management, communication, outcome expectancies, and normative feedback. One important component of this research was to better understand which students would voluntarily choose the different intervention formats. Findings indicated that five of six participants chose the group format for participation and that youth from minority populations and mixed racial/ethnic backgrounds disproportionately sought the individual context for services (D'Amico et al., 2006). An article examining satisfaction with the program found that overall, students reported greater satisfaction with the group and individual formats compared with the website format (Kia-Keating, Brown, Schulte, & Monreal, 2008). Brown and colleagues (Brown et al., 2005) conducted a one-semester follow-up of Project Options

and focused on adolescents' efforts to change their drinking. They found that the heaviest drinking students who reported attending at least one session of the intervention (individual, group, or web format) also reported more attempts to cut down or quit drinking compared with heavy drinking adolescents who did not attend the program. This article did not examine changes in the actual drinking rates of these students (Brown et al., 2005). In 2010, Schulte and colleagues examined the effects of Project Options for youth in three high schools (N = 327) who reported lifetime drinking by comparing them to a matched sample of control youth from these schools who also reported lifetime drinking (N = 1,728). They measured perceptions of peer drinking and alcohol use in the fall and spring. Project Options youth reported more accurate estimates of peer alcohol use; however, there was no effect of the intervention on adolescents' actual alcohol use (Schulte et al., 2010). A cross-sectional examination of youth who self-selected into Project Options in the second semester of the 2006–2007 school year (6.3%) found that, compared with youth who did not attend, attendees were more likely to be male, report heavier drinking, and were more likely to report experiences of victimization or bullying, suggesting that this program attracted youth with some risk characteristics (McGee, Valentine, Schulte, & Brown, 2011).

The third trial involves middle school youth and a program called CHOICE. CHOICE takes place for a half hour after school once a week. There are five sessions, which repeat throughout the course of the school year. These sessions focus on providing normative feedback, discussing unrealistic positive beliefs about substances, helping teens deal with pressure to use substances through the use of role plays, discussion of the potential benefits of both continuing use and cutting down or stopping use, and discussion of risky situations and coping strategies, such as getting social support or learning how to avoid certain high-risk situations (D'Amico et al., 2005). CHOICE used a motivational interviewing approach focused on nonjudgmental and nonconfrontational communication (Miller & Rollnick, 2012). Specifically, sessions were collaborative and interactive and discussion focused on how students could make healthier choices.

D'Amico and colleagues conducted a small pilot test of CHOICE in 2005 in one middle school that did not have any other school prevention programming occurring at the time of this study (D'Amico & Edelen, 2007). Approximately 13% of students in the intervention school chose to attend CHOICE over an academic year and participants did not differ from nonparticipants on demographic characteristics, deviance, and self-esteem. Longitudinal evaluation of CHOICE examined whether this voluntary program would affect both individual *and* school-wide alcohol and drug use, even though not all students had attended (D'Amico & Edelen, 2007). Findings indicated that teens who attended CHOICE reported less alcohol use and lower perceptions of alcohol, marijuana, and cigarette use than a matched sample of control students from another school. In addition, comparison of all youth at the CHOICE school to all youth at a control school over a 2-year period indicated that alcohol and marijuana use, and perceptions of friends' use of alcohol and marijuana, increased more sharply among students in the control school relative to students in the CHOICE school. Effect sizes ranged from 0.21 to 0.52 (small to moderate) (D'Amico & Edelen, 2007). D'Amico and colleagues conducted a large randomized controlled trial of CHOICE in 16 middle schools and replicated results from this smaller pilot. In schools where CHOICE was offered, 1 adolescent out of 15 was prevented from initiating alcohol use during the academic year (D'Amico, Tucker et al., 2012). At the eight intervention schools, 15% (n = 703) of consented students voluntarily attended CHOICE during the year, which is similar to other after-school programs (Afterschool Alliance, 2009). In addition, in contrast to other after-school programs for this younger population, CHOICE reached a diverse and at-risk population of youth who typically do not obtain services (Harvard Family Research Project, 2007; Sterling, Weisner, Hinman, & Parthasarathy, 2010; Wu, Hoven, Tiet, Kovalenko, & Wicks, 2002), including nonwhite youth and youth who reported regular use of alcohol and marijuana (D'Amico, Green, et al., 2012). A cost analysis of the CHOICE program found that the median cost per enrolled student was approximately $21 per student (Kilmer, Burgdorf, D'Amico, Tucker, & Miles, 2011).

Summary

Our understanding of what contributes to adolescent AOD use and how to prevent initiation and escalation during this important developmental period has increased significantly over the past 20 years. Research consistently shows that the prevalence of AOD use increases during middle school and high school and that substance use during this time period can lead to severe consequences, such as school dropout, motor vehicle crashes, decreased chances of employment and substance use disorders. Of note, recent advances using fMRI suggest that alcohol and drug use can be particularly dangerous during the adolescent years when the brain is still developing. This research has also shown that AOD use can have significant effects on the brain even after AOD use has stopped. Additional longitudinal research in this area is needed to better understand the long-term effects of AOD use during adolescence on the brain.

Youth in the 21st century have to cope with substantial external and internal pressures to use AOD. For example, the availability of alcohol and drugs on school property has significantly increased over the past 10 years. Students are exposed to AOD use in the school setting through offers of AOD, increased discussion with peers about AOD use, and seeing fellow students under the influence of AOD during school hours. All of these factors likely affect students' ability to make healthy choices and highlight the importance of providing services for youth in the school setting.

Over the past 15 years, a substantial amount of research has been conducted on school-based prevention and intervention programs. By locating programs on school premises, many barriers, such as lack of transportation, mistrust of other organizations, and potential stigma of attending a treatment center are decreased. Thus, teens can access services more easily, making it more likely that they will obtain information or help when they need it. Typically, services are provided in a group format in this setting, which can be helpful as it encourages group communication and collaboration. In addition, it is more meaningful for youth when the strategies to make healthier choices are generated by their peers rather than by group leaders (D'Amico, Osilla, et al., 2010).

The work in this area has led to several promising strategies that are effective in reducing adolescent AOD use. Of note, these strategies address many of the developmental changes that occur during this time period. For example, there are notable increases in peer pressure during adolescence, thus, discussion of normative information and provision of skills training to help youth anticipate and plan for high-risk situations have both been successful in helping youth make healthier choices. In addition, the most effective interventions in this area have high levels of interaction and collaboration (Jensen et al., 2011) and are skills-focused (Griffin & Botvin, 2010). For example, using a motivational interviewing style is developmentally appropriate during adolescence because it emphasizes collaboration and the teen's autonomy in decision making and uses a nonconfrontational approach. The brevity and transportability of MI interventions are ideal in reaching youth across a variety of settings, including juvenile justice, medical clinics, homeless shelters, and schools (Baer, Garrett, Beadnell, Wells, & Peterson, 2007; D'Amico et al., 2008; Feldstein & Ginsburg, 2006; Martin & Copeland, 2008; McCambridge, Slym, & Strang, 2008; Peterson, Baer, Wells, Ginzler, & Garrett, 2006; Spirito et al., 2004; Stein et al., 2011; Walker, Roffman, Stephens, Wakana, & Berghuis, 2006). In the last few years, several studies have been published using motivational interviewing in the group setting with adolescents (D'Amico, Feldstein Ewing, et al., 2010; D'Amico et al., 2013; Feldstein Ewing, et al., 2012).

Future Directions

Despite the advantages of implementing prevention and intervention programs in schools, these settings are increasingly faced with challenges that limit their ability to provide these types of services. For example, community-based settings, like schools, often lack resources (i.e., tools or funding) or capacity (i.e., knowledge, attitudes, skills) to adapt and implement strategies that have been developed in resource-intense research settings (D'Amico et al., 2009). More specifically, schools must constantly cope with budget cuts, pressures to complete more intensive mandated curricula and obtain high test scores, and the increased workload for teachers and administrators. All of these factors contribute to the school's ability to provide programming and to implement the programming as it was intended. For example, it may be difficult for many schools to provide 40 hours of class time for AOD prevention programming and so their choices for programming may be limited. In addition, budget and time constraints may also affect the fidelity with which programs are implemented. Teachers may not have the time to be sufficiently trained or be able to conduct each session completely within the class time provided. Thus, there is often a large gap between research and practice (e.g., Green, 2001; Wandersman & Florin, 2003). Schools need support to implement the programs described above. This involves providing the knowledge and skills needed to conduct the steps required, such as needs assessment, setting priorities and program delivery. This also involves helping communities

obtain buy-in from stakeholders, school administration and parents (D'Amico et al., 2009).

Some ways to reduce time and cost barriers may be to provide programming after school or to use technology to reach adolescents. Recent work in this area has shown that teens will voluntarily attend after-school programs to obtain information on AOD (Brown et al., 2005; D'Amico & Edelen, 2007; D'Amico, Green, et al., 2012; D'Amico, Tucker, et al., 2012), and that these types of voluntary programs can reach at-risk youth (D'Amico, Green, et al., 2012; McGee, et al., 2011). Out-of-school-time programs can benefit youth in many ways by encouraging positive social development, reducing risk-taking behavior, and encouraging better school behavior (Lauver, Little, & Weiss, 2004). These programs can also be a cost-effective way for schools to reach adolescents who may have questions about AOD or want to make a change in their AOD use without having to utilize class time.

Future research should also consider the use of technology in outreaching to teens, parents, and teachers, such as accessing information on the Internet. The National Institute of Drug Abuse has a web-program called "NIDA for Teens" that provides resources about AOD use to teens, parents, and educators (NIDA, 2009). This website allows teens to individually find out information on the effects of drugs (e.g., the dangers of prescription drug use, learning the link between drugs and HIV) and also provides resources to parents and educators to share with teens (e.g., lesson plans, curricula, classroom activities). Teachers can access various teaching tools including a high school curriculum content called "The brain: Understanding neurobiology through the study of addiction," which describes the effects of addiction and drug abuse on the brain (NIDA, 2010). By making these resources available for free and at the convenience of the user, this type of information can be easily accessed and taught.

There are also several promising and successful web-based interventions that have been used with older adolescents, mainly college students (e.g., Kypri et al., 2004; Neighbors, Larimer, & Lewis, 2004). More recently, some web-based interventions have been tested with younger adolescents, aged 13–18. For example, one of the voluntary prevention programs discussed in the current chapter, Project Options, offered a web-based intervention option to high school aged teens, but found that these teens preferred accessing the information via group or individual formats versus the web

(Kia-Keating et al., 2008). Two studies examined the effects of using the Internet to provide prevention programming to adolescents. An Australian study compared a web-based prevention program to standard health classes. They found that 13-year-old youth who completed the web-based program reduced their weekly alcohol use and frequency of marijuana use at a 6-month follow-up compared with youth who only completed standard health classes (Newton, Andrews, Teesson, & Vogl, 2009). Woodruff and colleagues examined the effectiveness of an Internet virtual world chat room on cigarette smoking and found that 1 year later, adolescents who participated in the program reported more quit attempts (Woodruff, Conway, Edwards, Elliott, & Crittenden, 2007). Buller and colleagues (2008) found that for youth in 6th to 9th grades in Australia and the United States, a web-based program on smoking reduced smoking for teens in Australia but not the United States. They indicated that the amount of program exposure was low in many of the grades and that there was a dose-response relationship with reduced smoking prevalence (Buller et al., 2008). Another Internet, home-based intervention for cigarette smoking was available for 24 weeks to youth aged 11–18. Patten and colleagues (2006) compared Stomp Out Smokes (SOS) to a clinic-based, brief office intervention. Smoking abstinence at week 24 and week 36 did not significantly differ between the groups (Patten et al., 2006). Additional research is needed in this area to identify the types of adolescents who will access AOD prevention information via the web and how this type of intervention may affect their subsequent drinking and drug use behavior.

Recently, studies have begun to use smart phone technology to deliver interventions to youth, for example to help adolescents adhere to taking medication for HIV/AIDS (Puccio et al., 2006) or asthma (Seid et al., 2012), or providing help for smoking cessation (Haug, Meyer, Schorr, Bauer, & Ulrich, 2009; Obermayer, Riley, Asif, & Jean-Mary, 2004b; Riley, Obermayer, & Jean-Mary, 2008b; Rodgers et al., 2005). A recent study examined the feasibility of text messaging screening among adolescents in primary care and found that 87% of teens participated in the survey and 28% of them reported alcohol use (Ríos-Bedoya & Hay, 2013). Other studies have used text messaging with college students to effectively reduce cigarette smoking (Obermayer, Riley, Asif, & Jean-Mary, 2004a; Riley, Obermayer, & Jean-Mary, 2008a). Additional research is needed to identify whether the use of smart phone

technology can prevent initiation and escalation of AOD use among an adolescent population.

Finally, more research is needed to clarify the potential mechanisms of change that may affect reductions in AOD use (Clingempeel & Henggeler, 2002; Kazdin & Nock, 2003). Several recent studies have begun to examine this question. Understanding how changes in risk factors occur is important because the mechanism of change is not well understood for many programs that find reductions in AOD use (e.g., was the reduction in use related to youth making more self-change efforts, decreasing their association with peers who use, or other factors?). A better understanding of the mechanism(s) of change can help clarify factors most likely to affect AOD use, perhaps highlighting components of an intervention that are particularly significant for the targeted population (e.g., peer influence, Liu & Flay, 2009; Orlando et al., 2005).

Policy Recommendations

In order for school-based prevention programs to be successfully implemented, several policy changes are recommended. First, because these programs may be contingent on the financial resources available, stronger support is needed so that schools have the appropriate tools to provide services. This support may take the form of training teachers or other educators to integrate evidence-based prevention strategies and lessons into their curricula, providing ongoing support to teachers or educators so that successful prevention programs are delivered with fidelity, hiring staff to operate after-school programs on school premises, or providing resources to parents.

Resources are also needed to evaluate these prevention programs. As programs are disseminated to the public and delivered outside of the research context, it is crucial to evaluate whether programs continue to be effective and helpful for teens, and what changes may need to be made so that the program remains effective. It is also important to disseminate programs that are developmentally appropriate. These include interactive group-based programs that focus on psychosocial factors such as coping with peer pressure. Traditional programs that are purely educational, focus on the long-term consequences of AOD use, or are more didactic and confrontational are less likely to be successful with this age group.

Finally, programs need to reinforce prevention messages throughout middle school and high school. AOD use increases substantially during this time and it is imperative that adolescents receive prevention messages throughout this developmental period. Prevention programs must also continue to evolve as the adolescent world continues to change. Development of new curricula must include the input of adolescents, school officials, parents, and educators so that programs are accessible and developmentally appropriate. Schools will continue to be a popular setting to reach adolescents, and continued success of prevention programming with this age group is dependent on sustaining the involvement of all of the different players in these settings.

References

Aarons, G., Brown, S. A., Stice, E., & Coe, M. (2001). Psychometric evaluation of the marijuana and stimulant effect expectancy questionnaire for youth. *Addictive Behaviors, 26*, 219–236.

Afterschool Alliance. (2009). American after 3pm: The most in-depth study of how America's children spend their afternoons. Retrieved from http://www.afterschoolalliance.org/AA3_Full_Report.pdf

Alfonso, J., & Dunn, M. E. (2009). Differences in the marijuana expectancies of adolescents in relation to marijuana use. *Substance Use & Misuse, 42*, 1009–1025.

Allen, J. P., Porter, M. R., McFarland, F. C., McElhaney, K. B., & Marsh, P. (2005). The two faces of adolescents' success with peers: Adolescent popularity, social adaptation, and deviant behavior. *Child Development, 76*, 747–760.

Anderson, K. G., Ramo, D. E., Cummins, K. M., & Brown, S. A. (2010). Alcohol and drug involvement after adolescent treatment and functioning during emerging adulthood. *Drug and Alcohol Dependence, 107*(2–3), 171–181.

Arnold, M. E., & Hughes, J. N. (1999). First do no harm: Adverse effects of grouping deviant youth for skills training. *Journal of School Psychology, 37*, 99–115.

Ary, D. V., Tildesley, E., Hops, H., & Andrews, J. (1993). The influence of parent, sibling, and peer modeling and attitudes on adolescent use of alcohol. *The International Journal of the Addictions, 28*, 853–880.

Austin, G., McCarthy, W., Slade, S., & Bailey, J. (2007). *Links between smoking and substance use, violence, and school problems*. Los Alamitos, CA: West Ed.

Baer, J. S., Garrett, S. B., Beadnell, B., Wells, E. A., & Peterson, P. L. (2007). Brief motivational intervention with homeless adolescents: Evaluating effects on substance use and service utilization. *Psychology of Addictive Behaviors, 21*, 582–586.

Bajan, K. B., Leroux, B. G., Peterson, A. V., Jr, Bricker, J. B., Andersen, M. R., Kealey, K. A., et al. (2003). Nine-year prospective association between older siblings' smoking and children's daily smoking. *Journal of Adolescent Health, 33*(1), 25–30.

Bandura, A. (1977). *Social learning theory*. Englewood Cliffs, NJ: Prentice Hall.

Bandura, A. (1986). *Social foundations of thought and action: A social cognitive theory*. Upper Saddle River, NJ: Prentice-Hall.

Beal, A. C., Ausiello, J., & Perrin, J. M. (2001). Social influences on health risk behaviors among minority middle school students. *Journal of Adolescent Health, 28*, 474–480.

Bond, L., Patton, G., Glover, S., Carlin, J. B., Butler, C. C., Thomas, L., et al. (2004). The Gatehouse Project: Can a multilevel school intervention affect emotional wellbeing and health risk behaviours? *Journal of Epidemiology and Community Health, 58*, 997–1003.

Bonomo, Y., Coffey, C., Wolfe, R., Lynskey, M., Bowes, G., & Patton, G. (2001). Adverse outcomes of alcohol use in adolescents. *Addiction, 96*(10), 1485–1496.

Botvin, G. J. (1996). Substance abuse prevention through life skills training. In R. D. Peters & R. J. McMahon (Eds.), *Preventing childhood disorders, substance abuse, and delinquency* (pp. 215–240). Newbury Park, CA: Sage.

Botvin, G. J., Baker, E., Dusenbury, L., Botvin, E. M., & Diaz, T. (1995). Long-term follow-up results of a randomized drug abuse prevention trial in a White middle-class population. *Journal of the American Medical Association, 273*, 1106–1112.

Botvin, G. J., Baker, E., Dusenbury, L., Tortu, S., & Botvin, E. M. (1990). Preventing adolescent drug abuse through a multimodal cognitive-behavioral approach: Results of a three year study. *Journal of Consulting and Clinical Psychology, 58*, 437–446.

Botvin, G. J., Dusenbury, L., Baker, E., Orliz-Jarncs, S., & Botvin, E. M. (1992). Smoking prevention among urban minority youth: Assessing effects on outcome and mediating variables *Health Psychology, 11*, 290–299.

Botvin, G. J., & Griffin, K. W. (2004). Life Skills Training: Empirical findings and future directions. *Journal of Primary Prevention, 25*(2), 211–232.

Botvin, G. J., Griffin, K. W., Diaz, T., & Ifill-Williams, M. (2001a). Drug abuse prevention among minority adolescents: posttest and one-year follow-up of a school based preventive intervention. *Prevention Science, 2*, 1–13.

Botvin, G. J., Griffin, K. W., Diaz, T., & Ifill-Williams, M. (2001b). Preventing binge drinking during early adolescence: One- and two-year follow-up of a school-based preventive intervention. *Psychology of Addictive Behaviors, 15*, 360–365.

Bouchery, E. E., Harwood, H. J., Sacks, J. J., Simon, C. J., & Brewer, R. D. (2011). Economic costs of excessive alcohol consumption in the U.S., 2006. *American Journal of Preventive Medicine, 41*(5), 516–524.

Bray, J. W., Zarkin, G. A., Ringwalt, C., & Junfeng, Q. (2000). The relationship between marijuana initiation and dropping out of high school. *Health Economics, 9*, 9–18.

Brody, G. H., Yu, T., Chen, Y.-f., Kogan, S. M., & Smith, K. (2012). The Adults in the Making program: Long-term protective stabilizing effects on alcohol use and substance use problems for rural African American emerging adults. *Journal of Consulting and Clinical Psychology, 80*(1), 17–28.

Broman, C. L. (2009). The longitudinal impact of adolescent drug use on socioeconomic outcomes in young adulthood. *Journal of Child & Adolescent Substance Abuse, 18*, 131–143.

Brook, D. W., Brook, J. S., Zhang, C., Cohen, P., & Whiteman, M. (2002). Drug use and the risk of major depressive disorder, alcohol dependence, and substance use disorders. *Archives of General Psychiatry, 59*, 1039–1044.

Brooks-Russell, A., Simons-Morton, B., Haynie, D., Farhat, T., & Wang, J. (2012). Longitudinal relationship between drinking with peers, descriptive norms, and adolescent alcohol use. *Prevention Science*, electronic publication 2013-12459-001.

Brown, S. A. (1990). Adolescent alcohol expectancies and risk for alcohol abuse. *Addiction and Recovery, 10*, 16–19.

Brown, S. A. (1993). Drug effect expectancies and addictive behavior change. *Experimental and Clinical Psychopharmacology, 1*(1–4), 55–67.

Brown, S. A. (2001). Facilitating change for adolescent alcohol problems: A multiple options approach. In E. F. Wagner & H. B. Waldron (Eds.), *Innovations in adolescent substance abuse intervention* (pp. 169–187). Oxford: Elsevier Science.

Brown, S. A., Anderson, K., Schulte, M. T., Sintov, N. D., & Frissell, K. C. (2005). Facilitating youth self-change through school-based intervention. *Addictive Behaviors, 30,* 1797–1810.

Brown, S. A., & D'Amico, E. J. (2003). Outcomes of alcohol treatment for adolescents. In M. Galanter (Ed.), *Recent developments in alcoholism: Volume XVI: Selected treatment topics* (Vol. XVI, pp. 289–312). New York: Kluwer Academic/ Plenum Publishers.

Brown, S. A., D'Amico, E. J., McCarthy, D. M., & Tapert, S. F. (2001). Four year outcomes from adolescent alcohol and drug treatment. *Journal of Studies on Alcohol, 62,* 381–388.

Buhler, A., Schroder, E., & Silbereisen, R. K. (2008). The role of life skills promotion in substance abuse prevention: A mediation analysis. *Health Education Research, 23,* 621–632.

Buller, D., Borland, R., Woodall, W., Hall, J., Hines, J., Burris-Woodall, P., et al. (2008). Randomized trials on consider this, a tailored, Internet-delivered smoking prevention program for adolescents. *Health Education & Behavior, 35*(2), 260–281.

Burleson, J. A., Kaminer, Y., & Dennis, M. L. (2006). Absence of iatrogenic or contagion effects in adolescent group therapy: Findings from the Cannabis Youth Treatment (CYT) Study. *The American Journal on Addictions, 15,* 4–15.

Califano, J. A. (2008). *National survey of American attitudes on substance use. XIII: Teens and parents.* Columbia University, NY: The National Center on Addiction and Substance Use (CASA) at Columbia University.

Campbell, R., Starkey, F., Holliday, J., Audrey, S., Bloor, M., Parry-Langdon, N., et al. (2008). An informal school-based peer-led intervention for smoking prevention in adolescence (ASSIST): A cluster randomized trial. *Lancet, 371,* 1595–1602.

Caria, M. P., Faggiano, F., Bellocco, R., & Galanti, M. R. (2011). Effects of a school-based prevention program on European adolescents' patterns of alcohol use. *Journal of Adolescent Health Care, 48*(2), 182–188.

Carlson, S. R., Iacono, W. G., & McGue, M. (2002). P300 amplitude in adolescent twins discordant and concordant for alcohol use disorders. *Biological Psychology, 61,* 203–227.

Chambers, R. A., Taylor, J. R., & Potenza, M. N. (2003). Developmental neurocircuitry of motivation in adolescence: A critical period of addiction vulnerability. *American Journal of Psychiatry, 160,* 1041–1052.

Chan, D. (2008). So why ask me? Are self-report data really that bad? In C. E. Lance & R. J. Vandenberg (Eds.), *Statistical and methodological myths and urban legends: Doctrine, verity and fable in the organizational and social sciences* (pp. 309–336). New York: Psychology Press.

Chan, Y. F., Dennis, M. L., & Funk, R. R. (2008). Prevalence and comorbidity of major internalizing and externalizing problems among adolescents and adults presenting to substance abuse treatment. *Journal of Substance Abuse Treatment, 34,* 14–24.

Chassin, L., & DeLucia, C. (1996). Drinking during adolescence. *Alcohol Health & Research, 20,* 175–180.

Chassin, L., Fora, D. B., & King, K. M. (2004). Trajectories of alcohol and drug use and dependence from adolescence to adulthood: The effects of familial alcoholism and personality. *Journal of Abnormal Psychology, 113,* 483–498.

Chatterji, P. (2006). Illicit drug use and educational attainment. *Health Economics, 15,* 489–511.

Clark, H. K., Ringwalt, C. L., & Shamblen, S. R. (2011). Predicting adolescent substance use: The effects of depressed mood and positive expectancies. *Addictive Behaviors, 36*(5), 488–493.

Clark, H. K., Shamblen, S. R., Ringwalt, C. L., & Hanley, S. (2012). Predicting high risk adolescents' substance use over time: The role of parental monitoring. *The Journal of Primary Prevention, 33*(2–3), 67–77.

Cleveland, M. J., Bontempo, D. E., & Greenberg, M. T. (2008). The role of risk and protective factors in substance use across adolescence. *Journal of Adolescent Health, 43,* 157–164.

Clingempeel, W. G., & Henggeler, S. W. (2002). Randomized clinical trials, developmental theory, and antisocial youth: Guidelines for research. *Development and Psychopathology, 14,* 695–711.

Cludius, B., Stevens, S., Bantin, T., Gerlach, A. L., & Hermann, C. (2013). The motive to drink due to social anxiety and its relation to hazardous alcohol use. *Psychology of Addictive Behaviors, 27*(3), 806–813.

Coggans, N. (2006). Drug education and prevention: Has progress been made? *Drugs, Education, Prevention, and Policy, 13,* 417–422.

Cohen, M. X., Heller, A. S., & Ranganath, C. (2005). Functional connectivity with anterior cingulate and orbitofrontal cortices during decision making. *Cognitive Brain Research, 45,* 255–262.

Colder, C. R., & O'Connor, R. (2002). Attention biases and disinhibited behavior as predictors of alcohol use and enhancement reasons for drinking. *Psychology of Addictive Behaviors, 16*(Part 4), 325–332.

Corrigan, P. (2004). How stigma interferes with mental health care. *American Psychologist, 59,* 614–625.

Crawford, L. A., & Novak, K. B. (2002). Parental and peer influences on adolescent drinking: The relative impact of attachment and opportunity. *Journal of Child & Adolescent Substance Abuse, 12,* 1–26.

Cuijpers, P. (2002). Effective ingredients of school-based drug prevention programs: A systematic review. *Addictive Behaviors, 27,* 1009–1023.

Cuijpers, P., Jonkers, R., de Weerdt, I., & de Jong, A. (2002). The effects of drug abuse prevention at school: The "Healthy School and Drugs" project. *Addiction, 97,* 67–73.

D'Amico, E. J. (2005). Factors that impact adolescents' intentions to utilize alcohol-related prevention services. *Journal of Behavioral Health Services & Research, 32,* 332–340.

D'Amico, E. J., Anderson, K. G., Metrik, J., Frissell, K. C., Ellingstad, T., & Brown, S. A. (2006). Adolescent self-selection of service formats: Implications for secondary interventions targeting alcohol use. *American Journal on Addictions, 15,* 58–66.

D'Amico, E. J., & Edelen, M. (2007). Pilot test of Project CHOICE: A voluntary after school intervention for middle school youth. *Psychology of Addictive Behaviors, 21*(4), 592–598.

D'Amico, E. J., Ellickson, P. L., Wagner, E. F., Turrisi, R., Fromme, K., Ghosh-Dastidar, B., et al. (2005). Developmental considerations for substance use interventions from middle school through college. *Alcoholism: Clinical and Experimental Research, 29,* 474–483.

D'Amico, E. J., Feldstein Ewing, S. W., Engle, B., Hunter, S. B., Osilla, K. C., & Bryan, A. (2010). Group alcohol and drug treatment. In S. Naar-King & M. Suarez (Eds.), *Motivational interviewing with adolescents and young adults* (pp. 151–157). New York, NY: The Guilford Press.

D'Amico, E. J., & Fromme, K. (1997). Health risk behaviors of adolescent and young adult siblings. *Health Psychology, 16*(5), 426–432.

D'Amico, E. J., & Fromme, K. (2002). Brief prevention for adolescent risk-taking behavior. *Addiction, 97,* 563–574.

D'Amico, E. J., Green, H. D. J., Miles, J. N. V., Zhou, A. J., Tucker, J. A., & Shih, R. A. (2012). Voluntary after school alcohol and drug programs: If you build it right, they will come. *Journal of Research on Adolescence, 22*(3), 571–582.

D'Amico, E. J., Hunter, S. B., Miles, J. N. V., Ewing, B. A., & Osilla, K. C. (2013). A randomized controlled trial of a group motivational interviewing intervention for adolescents with a first time alcohol or drug offense. *Journal of Substance Abuse Treatment, 45*(5), 400–408.

D'Amico, E. J., Miles, J. N. V., Stern, S. A., & Meredith, L. S. (2008). Brief motivational interviewing for teens at risk of substance use consequences: A randomized pilot study in a primary care clinic. *Journal of Substance Abuse Treatment, 35,* 53–61.

D'Amico, E. J., Osilla, K. C., & Hunter, S. B. (2010). Developing a group motivational interviewing intervention for adolescents at-risk for developing an alcohol or drug use disorder. *Alcoholism Treatment Quarterly, 28,* 417–436.

D'Amico, E. J., Tucker, J. S., Miles, J. N. V., Zhou, A. J., Shih, R. A., & Green, H. D. J. (2012). Preventing alcohol use with a voluntary after school program for middle school students: Results from a cluster randomized controlled trial of CHOICE. *Prevention Science, 13*(4), 415–425.

D'Amico, E. J., Chinman, M., Stern, A., & Wandersman, A. (2009). Community prevention handbook on adolescent substance abuse prevention and treatment. In C. Leukefeld, T. Gullotta & M. S. Tindall (Eds.), *Adolescent substance abuse: Evidence-based approaches to prevention and treatment* (pp. 73–96). New York: Springer Science + Business Media.

D'Amico, E. J., & McCarthy, D. M. (2006). Escalation and initiation of younger adolescents' substance use: The impact of perceived peer use. *Journal of Adolescent Health, 39,* 481–487.

Deas, D., Riggs, P., Langenbucher, J., Goldman, M., & Brown, S. (2000). Adolescents are not adults: Developmental considerations in alcohol users. *Alcoholism: Clinical and Experimental Research, 24,* 232–237.

Dennis, M., Titus, J. C., Diamond, G., Donaldson, J., Godley, S. H., Tims, F. M., et al. (2002). The Cannabis Youth Treatment (CYT) experiment: Rationale, study design and analysis plans. *Addiction, 97*(Suppl 1), 16–34.

Dinkes, R., Cataldi, E. F., Lin-Kelly, W., & Snyder, T. D. (2007). *Indicators of crime and safety: 2007.* Washington, DC: U.S. Departments of Education and Justice.

Dishion, T. J., McCord, J., & Poulin, F. (1999). When interventions harm: Peer groups and problem behavior. *American Psychologist, 54,* 755–764.

Dodge, K., Dishion, T. J., & Lansford, J. E. (2006). *Deviant peer influences in programs for youth.* New York: The Guilford Press.

Donaldson, S. I. (2001). Mediator and moderator analysis in program development. In S. Sussman (Ed.), *Handbook of program development for behavior research and practice* (pp. 470–500). Thousand Oaks, CA: Sage Publications.

Donaldson, S. I., Graham, J. W., & Hansen, W. B. (1994). Testing the generalizability of intervening mechanism theories: Understanding the effects of adolescent drug use prevention interventions. *Journal of Behavioral Medicine, 17*(2), 195–216.

Donaldson, S. I., Piccinin, A. M., Graham, J. W., & Hansen, W. B. (1995). Resistance-skills training and onset of alcohol use: Evidence for beneficial and potentially harmful effects in public schools and in private catholic schools. *Health Psychology, 14,* 291–300.

Donaldson, S. I., Thomas, C. W., Graham, J. W., Au, J. G., & Hansen, W. B. (2000). Verifying drug abuse prevention program effects using reciprocal best friend reports. *Journal of Behavioral Medicine, 23,* 585–601.

Donovan, J. E. (2004). Adolescent alcohol initiation: A review of psychosocial risk factors. *Journal of Adolescent Health, 35*(6), e527–e518.

Donovan, J. E. (2007). Really underage drinkers: The epidemiology of children's alcohol use in the United States. *Prevention Science, 8,* 192–205.

Dusenbury, L., Falco, M., & Lake, A. (1995). Eleven components of effective drug abuse prevention curricula. *Journal of School Health, 67,* 127–133.

East, P. L., & Khoo, S. (2005). Longitudinal pathways linking family factors and sibling relationship qualities to adolescent substance use and sexual risk behaviors. *Journal of Family Psychology, 19*(4), 571–580.

Eaton, D. K., Kann, L., Kinchen, S., Shanklin, S., Flint, K. H., Hawkins, J., et al. (2011). *Youth Risk Behavior Surveillance—United States, 2011.* Atlanta, GA: Centers for Disease Control and Prevention and U.S. Department of Health and Human Services.

Eisen, M., Zellman, G. L., Massett, H. A., & Murray, D. M. (2002). Evaluating the Lions-Quest "Skills for Adolescence" drug education program: First-year behavior outcomes. *Addictive Behaviors 27,* 619–632.

Eisen, M., Zellman, G. L., & Murray, D. M. (2003). Evaluating the Lions-Quest "Skills for Adolescence" drug education program: Second-year behavior outcomes. *Addictive Behaviors, 28,* 883–897.

Ellickson, P. L., & Bell, R. M. (1990). Drug prevention in junior high: A multi-site, longitudinal test. *Science, 247,* 1299–1305.

Ellickson, P. L., Bird, C. E., Orlando, M., Klein, D. J., & McCaffrey, D. F. (2003). Social context and adolescent health behavior: Does school-level smoking prevalence affect students' subsequent smoking behavior? *Journal of Health and Social Behavior, 44,* 525–535.

Ellickson, P. L., Martino, S. C., & Collins, R. L. (2004). Marijuana use from adolescence to young adulthood: Multiple developmental trajectories and their associated outcomes. *Health Psychology, 23,* 299–307.

Ellickson, P. L., McCaffrey, D. F., Ghosh-Dastidar, B., & Longshore, D. L. (2003). New inroads in preventing adolescent drug use: Results from a large-scale trial of project ALERT in middle schools. *American Journal of Public Health, 93,* 1830–1836.

Ellickson, P. L., Tucker, J. S., & Klein, D. J. (2003). Ten-year prospective study of public health problems associated with early drinking. *Pediatrics, 111,* 949–955.

Ellickson, P. L., Tucker, J. S., Klein, D. J., & McGuigan, K. A. (2001). Prospective risk factors for alcohol misuse in late adolescence. *Journal of Studies on Alcohol, 62*, 773–782.

Ennett, S. T., Ringwalt, C. L., Thorne, J., Rohrbach, L. A., Vincus, A., Simons-Rudolph, A., et al. (2003). A comparison of current practice in school-based substance use prevention programs with meta-analysis findings. *Prevention Science, 4*(1), 1–14.

Ensminger, M. E., Juon, H. S., & Fothergill, K. E. (2002). Childhood and adolescent antecedents of substance use in adulthood. *Addiction, 97*, 833–844.

Fagan, A. A., & Najman, J. M. (2005). The relative contributions of parental and sibling substance use to adolescent tobacco, alcohol, and other drug use. *Journal of Drug Issues, 35*, 869–883.

Faggiano, F., Vigna-Taglianti, F., Versino, E., Zambon, A., Borraccino, A., & Lemma, P. (2009a). School-based prevention for illicit drug use: A systematic review. *Preventive Medicine, 46*, 385–396.

Faggiano, F., Vigna-Taglianti, F., Versino, E., Zambon, A., Borraccino, A., & Lemma, P. (2009b). School-based prevention for illicit drugs' use. *Cochrane Database of Systematic Reviews, 1*, 1–99.

Farhat, T. P., Simons-Morton, B., & Luk, J. W. (2011). Psychosocial correlates of adolescent marijuana use: Variations by status of marijuana use. *Addictive Behaviors, 36*(4), 404–407.

Feldstein Ewing, S. W., Hendrickson, S., & Payne, N. (2008). The validity of the desired effects of drinking scale with a late adolescent sample. *Motivational Interviewing in Groups, 22*(4), 587–591.

Feldstein Ewing, S. W., Walters, S., & Baer, J. S. (2012). Approaching group MI with adolescents and young adults: Strengthening the developmental fit. In C. C. I. Wagner & K. S. Ingersoll (Eds.), *Motivational interviewing in groups.* New York: The Guilford Press.

Feldstein, S. W., & Ginsburg, J. I. D. (2006). Motivational interviewing with dually diagnosed adolescents in juvenile justice settings *Brief Treatment and Crisis Intervention, 6*(3), 218–233.

Fergusson, D. M., Horwood, L. J., & Swain-Campbell, N. (2002). Cannabis use and psychosocial adjustment in adolescence and young adulthood. *Addiction, 97*, 1123–1135.

Finn, K. V. (2006). Patterns of alcohol and marijuana use at school. *Journal of Research on Adolescence, 16*, 69–77.

Finn, K. V. (2012). Marijuana use at school and achievement-linked behaviors. *The High School Journal, 95*(3), 3–13.

Fisher, L. B., Miles, I. W., Austin, S. B, Camargo, C. A., & Colditz, G. A. (2007). Predictors of initiation of alcohol use among US adolescents: Findings from a prospective cohort study. *Archives of Pediatric & Adolescent Medicine, 161*, 959–966.

Fowler, T., Shelton, K., Lifford, K., Rice, F., McBride, A., Nikolov, I., et al. (2007). Genetic and environmental influences on the relationship between peer alcohol use and own alcohol use in adolescents. *Addiction, 102*, 894–903.

Frisher, M., Crome, I., Macleod, J., Bloor, R., & Hickman, M. (2007). *Predictive factors for illicit drug use among young people: A literature review*, Great Britian Home Office Online Report http://dera.ioe.ac.uk/6903/1/rdsolr0507.pdf (pp. 1–49).

Frissell, K. C., McCarthy, D. M., D'Amico, E. J., Metrik, J., Ellingstad, T. P., & Brown, S. A. (2004). The impact of consent procedures on reported levels of adolescent alcohol use. *Psychology of Addictive Behaviors, 14*, 307–315.

Fromme, K., & Corbin, W. (2004). Prevention of heavy drinking and associated negative consequences among mandated and voluntary college students. *Journal of Consulting and Clinical Psychology 72*, 1038–1049

Fromme, K., & D'Amico, E. J. (2000). Measuring adolescent alcohol outcome expectancies. *Psychology of Addictive Behaviors, 14*, 206–212.

Fromme, K., Katz, E. C., & Rivet, K. (1997). Outcome expectancies and risk-taking behavior. *Cognitive and Therapy Research, 21*, 421–442.

Fromme, K., Stroot, E., & Kaplan, D. (1993). Comprehensive effects of alcohol: Development and psychometric assessment of a new expectancy questionnaire. *Psychological Assessment, 5*(1), 19–26.

Fulton, H. G., Krank, M. D., & Stewart, S. H. (2012). Outcome expectancy liking: A self-generated, self-coded measure predicts adolescent substance use trajectories. *Psychology of Addictive Behaviors, 26*, 870–879.

Galen, L. W., & Henderson, M. J. (1999). Validation of cocaine and marijuana effect expectancies in a treatment setting. *Addictive Behaviors, 24*, 719–724.

Galvan, A., Hare, T. A., Davidson, M., Spicer, J., Glover, G., & Casy, B. J. (2005). The role of ventral frontostriatal circuitry in reward-based learning in humans. *Journal of Neuroscience, 25*, 8650–8656.

Galvan, A., Hare, T. A., Voss, H., Glover, G., & Casy, B. J. (2007). Risk-taking and the adolescent brain: Who is at risk. *Developmental Science, 10*, F8–F14.

Geels, L. M., Vink, J. M., van Beijsterveldt, C. E. M., Bartels, M., & Boomsma, D. I. (2013). Developmental prediction model for early alcohol initiation in Dutch adolescents. *Journal of Studies on Alcohol and Drugs, 74*(1), 59–70.

Giedd, J. N., Shaw, P., Wallace, G., Gogtay, N., & Lenroot, R. K. (2006). Anatomic brain imaging studies of normal and abnormal brain development in children and adolescents. In D. Cicchetti & D. J. Cohen (Eds.), *Developmental psychopathology, Vol 2: Developmental neuroscience* (2nd ed., pp. 127–196). Hoboken, NJ: John Wiley & Sons.

Gil, A. G., Vega, W. A., & Turner, R. J. (2002). Early and mid-adolescence risk factors for later substance abuse by African Americans and European Americans. *Public Health Reports, 117*(Suppl 1), S15–S29.

Godley, S. H., Passetti, L. L., & White, M. K. (2006). Employment and adolescent alcohol and drug treatment and recovery: An exploratory study. *The American Journal on Addictions, 15*, 137–143.

Goldman, M. S., Brown, S. A., & Christiansen, B. A. (1987). Expectancy theory: Thinking about drinking. In H. T. Blane & K. E. Leonard (Eds.), *Psychological Theories of Drinking and Alcoholism* (pp. 181–266). New York: Guilford Publications.

Goldstein, A., & Brown, B. W. (2003). Urine testing in methadone maintenance treatment: Applications and limitations. *Journal of Substance Abuse Treatment, 25*, 61–63.

Gorman, D. (2011). Does the Life Skills Training program reduce use of marijuana? *Addiction Research & Theory, 19*(5), 470–481.

Gorman, D. M., & Conde, E. (2010). The making of evidence-based practice: The case of Project ALERT. *Children and Youth Services Review, 32*(2), 214–222.

Gosin, M., Marsiglia, F. F., & Hecht, M. L. (2003). Keepin' it R.E.A.L.: A drug resistance curriculum tailored to the strengths and needs of pre-adolescents of the southwest. *Journal of Drug Education, 33*, 119–142.

Green, L. W. (2001). From research to "best practices" in other settings and populations. *American Journal of Health Behavior, 25*(3), 165–178.

Griffin, K. W., & Botvin, G. J. (2010). Evidence-based interventions for preventing substance use disorders in adoelscents. *Child & Adolescent Psychiatric Clinics of North America, 19*(3), 505–526.

Griffin, K. W., Botvin, G. J., Nichols, T. R., & Doyle, M. M. (2003). Effectiveness of a universal drug abuse prevention approach for youth at high risk for substance use initiation. *Preventive Medicine, 36*(1), 1–7.

Griffith-Lendering, M. F. H., Wigman, J. T. W., van Leeuwen, A. P., Huijbregts, S. C. J., Huizink, A. C., Ormel, J., et al. (2013). Cannabis use and vulnerability for psychosis in early adolescence—A TRAILS study. *Addiction, 108*(4), 733–740.

Guilamo-Ramos, V., Turrisi, R., Jaccard, J., & Gonzalez, B. (2004). Progressing from light experimentation to heavy episodic drinking in early and middle adolescence. *Journal of Studies on Alcohol, 65*, 494–500.

Hansen, W. B., & Graham, J. W. (1991). Preventing alcohol, marijuana, and cigarette use among adolescents: Peer pressure resistance training versus establishing conservative norms. *Preventive Medicine, 20,* 414–430.

Hanson, T. L., Austin, G. A., & Bayha, J. L. (2003). *Are student health risks and low resilience assets an impediment to the academic progress of schools?* Los Alamitos, CA: West Ed.

Hartman, C. A., Lessem, J. M., Hopfer, C. J., Crowley, T. J., & Stallings, M. C. (2006). The family transmission of adolescent alcohol abuse and dependence. *Journal of Studies on Alcohol, 67*, 657–664.

Harvard Family Research Project. (2007). *Findings from HFRP's study of predictors of participation in out-of-school time activities: Fact sheet.* Cambridge, MA: Harvard Graduate School of Education.

Haug, S., Meyer, C., Schorr, G., Bauer, S., & Ulrich, J. (2009). Continuous individual support of smoking cessation using text messaging: A pilot experimental study. *Nicotine & Tobacco Research, 11*(8), 915–923.

Hecht, M. L., Elek, E., Wagstaff, D. A., Kam, J. A., Marsiglia, F., Dustman, P., et al. (2008). Immediate and short-term effects of the 5th grade version of the keepin' it REAL substance use prevention intervention. *Journal of Drug Education, 38*(3), 225–251.

Hecht, M. L., Marsiglia, F. F., Elek, E., Wagstaff, D. A., Kulis, S., Dustman, P., et al. (2003). Culturally grounded substance use prevention: An evaluation of the keepin' it R.E.A.L. curriculum. *Prevention Science, 4*, 233–248.

Hingson, R. W., Heeren, T., Jamanka, A., & Howland, J. (2000). Age of drinking onset and unintentional injury involvement after drinking. *Journal of the American Medical Association, 284*, 1527–1533.

Hollingworth, W., Cohen, D., Hawkins, J., Hughes, R., Moore, L., Holliday, J., et al. (2013). Reducing smoking in adolescents: Cost-effectiveness results from the cluster randomized ASSIST (A Stop Smoking In Schools Trial). *Nicotine & Tobacco Research, 14*(2), 161–168.

Holmbeck, G. N., Devine, K. A., & Bruno, E. F. (2010). Developmental issues and considerations in research and practice. In J. R. Weisz & A. E. Kazdin (Eds.), *Evidence-based psychotherapies for children and adolescents* (2nd ed., pp. 28–39). New York: Guilford Press.

Hopfer, C. J., Stallings, M. C., Hewitt, J. K., & Crowley, T. J. (2004). Family transmission of marijuana use, abuse, and dependence. *Journal of the American Academy of Child & Adolescent Psychiatry, 42*, 834–841.

Hurrelmann, K. (1990). Health promotion for adolescents: Preventive and corrective strategies against problem behavior. *Journal of Adolescence, 13*(3), 231–250.

Institute of Medicine. (1994). *Reducing risks for mental disorders: Frontiers for preventive intervention research.* Washington, DC: National Academies Press.

Jackson, C. (1997). Initial and experimental stages of tobacco and alcohol use during late childhood: relation to peer, parent, and personal risk factors. *Addictive Behaviors, 22*(5), 685–698.

Jacobus, J., McQueeny, T., Bava, S., Schweinsburg, B. C., Frank, L. R., Yang, T. T., et al. (2009). White matter integrity in adolescents with histories of marijuana use and binge drinking. *Neurotoxicology and Teratology, 31*(6), 349–355. doi: 10.1016/j.ntt.2009.07.006

Jensen, C. D., Cushing, C. C., Aylward, B. S., Craig, J. T., Sorell, D. M., & Steele, R. G. (2011). Effectiveness of motivational interviewing interventions for adolescent substance use behavior change: A meta-analytic review. *Journal of Consulting and Clinical Psychology, 79*(4), 433–440. doi: 10.1037/a0023992

Jeynes, W. H. (2002). The relationship between the consumption of various drugs by adolescents and their academic achievement. *American Journal of Drug and Alcohol Abuse, 28*, 15–35.

Johnson, P. B., & Johnson, H. L. (2001). Reaffirming the power of parental influence on adolescent smoking and drinking decisions. *Adolescent & Family Health, 2*, 37–43.

Johnston, L. D., O'Malley, P. M., Bachman, J. G., & Schulenberg, J. E. (2013). *Monitoring the Future national results on drug use: 2012 overview, key findings on adolescent drug use.* Ann Arbor, MI: Institute for Social Research, The University of Michigan.

Jones, B. T., & McMahon, J. (1993). Alcohol motivations as outcome expectancies. In W. R. Miller & N. Heather (Eds.), *Treating addictive behaviors* (pp. 75–91). New York: Plenum Press.

Juon, H.-S., Fothergill, K. E., Green, K. M., Doherty, E. E., & Ensminger, M. E. (2011). Antecedents and consequences of marijuana use trajectories over the life course in an African American population. *Drug and Alcohol Dependence, 118*(2–3), 216–223.

Kaminer, Y. (2005). Challenges and opportunities of group therapy for adolescent substance abuse: A critical review. *Addictive Behaviors, 30*(9), 1765–1774.

Kazdin, A. E., & Nock, M. K. (2003). Delineating mechanisms of change in child and adolescent therapy: Methodological issues and research recommendations. *Journal of Child Psychology and Psychiatry, 44*, 1116–1129.

Kelly, A. B., Chan, G. C. K., Toumbourou, J. W., O'Flaherty, M., Homel, R., Patton, G. C., et al. (2012). Very young adolescents and alcohol: Evidence of a unique susceptibility to peer alcohol use. *Addictive Behaviors, 37*(4), 414–419.

Kia-Keating, M., Brown, S. A., Schulte, M. T., & Monreal, T. K. (2008). Adolescent satisfaction with brief motivational enhancement for alcohol abuse. *Journal of Behavioral Health Services & Research, 36*, 385–395.

Kilmer, B., Burgdorf, J., D'Amico, E. J., Tucker, J. S., & Miles, J. N. V. (2011). A multi-site cost analysis of a school-based voluntary alcohol and drug prevention program. *Journal of Studies on Alcohol and Drugs, 72*(5), 823–832.

King, K. M., Meehan, B. T., Trim, R. S., & Chassin, L. (2006). Marker or mediator? The effects of adolescent substance use on young adult educational attainment. *Addiction, 101*(12), 1730–1740.

Komro, K. A., Perry, C. L., Williams, C. L., Stigler, M. H., Farbakhsh, K., & Veblen-Mortenson, S. (2001). How did Project Northland reduce alcohol use among young adolescents? Analysis of mediating variables. *Health Education Research, 16*, 59–70.

Kristjansson, S. D., Agrawal, A., Lynskey, M. T., & Chassin, L. A. (2012). Marijuana expectancies and relationships with adolescent and adult marijuana use. *Drug and Alcohol Dependence, 126*(1–2), 102–110.

Kulis, S., Marsiglia, F. F., Elek, E., Dustman, P., Wagstaff, D. A., & Hecht, M. L. (2005). Mexican/Mexican American adolescents and keepin' it REAL: An evidence-based substance use prevention program. *Children and Schools, 27*(3), 133–145.

Kulis, S., Nieri, T., Yabiku, S., Stromwall, L. K., & Marsiglia, F. F. (2007). Promoting reduced and discontinued substance use among adolescent substance users: Effectiveness of a universal prevention program. *Prevention Science, 8*, 35–49.

Kypri, K., Saunders, J. B., Williams, S., McGee, R. O., Langley, J. D., Cashell-Smith, M. L., et al. (2004). Web-based screening and brief intervention for hazardous drinking: A randomized controlled trial. *Addiction, 99*, 1410–1417.

Lac, A., Alvaro, E. M., Crano, W. T., & Siegel, J. T. (2009). Pathways from parental knowledge and warmth to adolescent marijuana use: An extension to the theory of planned behavior. *Prevention Science, 10*, 22–32.

Latendresse, S. J., Rose, R. J., Viken, R. J., Pulkkinen, L., Kaprio, J., & Dick, D. M. (2008). Parenting mechanisms in links between parents' and adolescents' alcohol use behaviors. *Alcoholism: Clinical and Experimental Research, 32*, 322–330.

Lauver, S., Little, P. M. D., & Weiss, H. (2004). Moving beyond the barriers: Attracting and sustaining youth participation in out-of-school time programs. In Harvard Family Research Project (Ed.), *Issues and opportunities in out-of-school time evaluation* (Vol. 6, pp. 1–16). Cambridge, MA: Harvard Graduate School of Education.

Lee, B. R., & Thompson, R. (2009). Examining externalizing behavior trajectories of youth in group homes: Is there evidence for peer contagion? *Journal of Abnormal Child Psychology, 37*(1), 31–44.

Lemstra, M., Bennett, N., Nannapaneni, U., Neudorf, C., Warren, L., Kershaw, T., et al. (2010). A systematic review of school-based marijuana and alcohol prevention programs targeting adolescents aged 10–15. *Addiction Research & Theory, 18*(1), 84–96.

Li, C., Pentz, M. A., & Chou, C.-P. (2002). Parental substance use as a modifier of adolescent substance use risk. *Addiction, 97*, 1537–1550.

Little, P. M. D., & Harris, E. (2003). A review of out-of-school time program quasi-experimental and experimental evaluation results. In Harvard Family Research Project (Ed.), *Out-of-school time evaluation snapshot* (Vol. 1, pp. 1–12). Cambridge, MA: Harvard Graduate School of Education.

Liu, L. C., & Flay, B. R. (2009). Evaluating mediation in longitudinal multivariate data: Mediation effects for the Aban Aya Youth Project drug prevention program. *Prevention Science, 10*(3), 197–207.

Longshore, D., Ellickson, P. L., McCaffrey, D. F., & St. Clair, P. A. (2007). School-based drug prevention among at-risk adolescents: Effects of ALERT Plus. *Health Education & Behavior, 34*(4), 651–668.

Lonigan, C. J., Elbert, J. C., & Johnson, S. B. (1998). Empirically supported psychosocial interventions for children: An overview. *Journal of Clinical Child Psychology, 27*, 138–145.

Luna, B., Paulsen, D. J., Padmanabhan, A., & Geier, C. (2013). The teenage brain: Cognitive control and motivation. *Current Directions in Psychological Science, 22*(2), 94–100.

Lynskey, M., & Hall, W. (2000). The effects of adolescent cannabis use on educational attainment: A review. *Addiction, 95*, 1621–1630.

Maisto, S. A., Carey, K. B., & Bradizza, C. M. (1999). Social learning theory. In K. E. Leonard & H. T. Blane (Eds.), *Psychological theories of drinking and alcoholism* (pp. 106–163). New York: Guilford Press.

Marsiglia, F., Kulis, S., Yabiku, S., Nieri, T., & Coleman, E. (2011). When to intervene: elementary school, middle school or both? Effects of Keepin' it Real on substance use trajectories of Mexican heritage youth. *Prevention Science, 12*(1), 48–62.

Martin, G., & Copeland, J. (2008). The adolescent cannabis check-up: Randomized trial of a brief intervention for young cannabis users. *Journal of Substance Abuse Treatment, 34*(4), 407–414.

Martino, S. C., Collins, L. M., Ellickson, P. L., Schell, T. L., & McCaffrey, D. (2006). Socio-environmental influences on adolescents' alcohol outcome expectancies: A prospective analysis. *Addiction, 101*, 971–983.

Mason, W. A., & Spoth, R. L. (2012). Sequence of alcohol involvement from early onset to young adult alcohol abuse: Differential predictors and moderation by family-focused preventive intervention. *Addiction, 107*(12), 2137–2148.

Masterman, P. W., & Kelly, A. B. (2003). Reaching adolescents who drink harmfully: Fitting intervention to developmental reality. *Journal of Substance Abuse Treatment, 24*(4), 347–355.

Maxwell, K. A. (2002). Friends: The role of peer influence across adolescent risk behaviors. *Journal of Youth and Adolescence, 31*, 267–277.

Maynard, B. R., Salas-Wright, C. P., Vaughn, M. G., & Peters, K. E. (2012). Who are truant youth? Examining distinctive profiles of truant youth using latent profile analysis. *Journal of Youth and Adolescence, 41*(12), 1671–1684.

McBride, N., Farringdon, F., Midford, R., Meuleners, L., & Phillips, M. (2004). Harm minimization in school drug education: Final results of the School Health and Alcohol Harm Reduction Project (SHAHRP). *Addiction, 99*, 278–291.

McBride, N., Midford, R., Farringdon, F., & Phillips, M. (2000). Early results from a school alcohol harm minimization study: The School Health and Alcohol Harm Reduction Project. *Addiction, 95*, 1021–1042.

McCambridge, J., Slym, R. L., & Strang, J. (2008). Randomized controlled trial of motivational interviewing compared with drug information and advice for early intervention among young cannabis users. *Addiction, 103*(11), 1809–1818.

McCarthy, D. M., Pedersen, S. L., & D'Amico, E. J. (2009). Analysis of item response and differential item functioning of alcohol expectancies in middle school youth. *Psychological Assessment, 23*, 444–449.

McCarthy, D. M., & Thompsen, D. M. (2006). Implicit and explicit measures of alcohol and smoking cognitions. *Psychology of Addictive Behaviors, 20*, 436–444.

McGee, E., Valentine, E., Schulte, M. T., & Brown, S. A. (2011). Peer victimization and alcohol involvement among adolescents self-selecting into a school-based alcohol intervention. *Journal of Child & Adolescent Substance Abuse, 20*, 253–269.

McKay, M. T., Mcbride, N. T., Sumnall, H. R., & Cole, J. C. (2012). Reducing the harm from adolescent alcohol consumption: Results from an adapted version of SHAHRP in Northern Ireland. *Journal of Substance Use, 17*(2), 98–121.

McLeod, J. D., Uemura, R., & Rohrman, S. (2012). Adolescent mental health, behavior problems, and academic achievement. *Journal of Health and Social Behavior, 53*(4), 482–497.

McMorris, B. J., & Uggen, C. (2000). Alcohol and employment in the transition to adulthood *Journal of Health & Social Behavior, 41*, 276–294.

McNeal, R. B., Jr., Hansen, W. B., Harrington, N. G., & Giles, S. M. (2004). How All Stars Works: An examination of program effects on mediating variables. *Health Education & Behavior, 31*(2), 165–178.

Menrath, I., Mueller-Godeffroy, E., Pruessmann, C., Ravens-Sieberer, U., Ottova, V., Pruessmann, M., et al. (2012). Evaluation of school-based life skills programmes in a high-risk sample: A controlled longitudinal multi-centre study. *Journal of Public Health, 20*(2), 159–170.

Mercken, L., Moore, L., Crone, M., De Vries, H., De Bourdeaudhuij, I., Lien, N., et al. (2012). The effectiveness of school-based smoking prevention interventions among low- and high-SES European teenagers. *Health Education Research, 27*(3), 459–469.

Metrik, J., Rohsenow, D. J., Monti, P., McGeary, J., Cook, T. A. R., de Wit, H., et al. (2009). Effectiveness of a marijuana expectancy manipulation: Piloting the balanced-placebo design for marijuana. *Experimental Clinical Psychopharmacology, 17*, 217–225.

Miller, S. M., Siegel, J. T., Hohman, Z., & Crano, W. D. (2013). Factors mediating the association of the recency of parent's marijuana use and their adolescent children's subsequent initiation. *Psychology of Addictive Behaviors, 27*(3), 848–853.

Miller, W. R., & Rollnick, S. (2012). *Motivational interviewing: Helping people change* (3rd ed.). New York: Guilford Press.

Morehouse, E. R., & Tobler, N. S. (2000). *Project SUCCESS final report* (grant No. 4 HD1 SP07240) (pp. 1–80). Rockville, MD: Center for Substance Abuse Prevention.

Mortimer, J. T. (2010). The benefits and risks of adolescent employment. *The Prevention Researcher, 17*(2), 8–11.

Mortimer, J. T., & Staff, J. (2004). Early work as a source of developmental discontinuity during the transition to adulthood. *Development and Psychopathology, 16*, 1047–1070.

Mrug, S., & McCay, R. (2012). Parental and peer disapproval of alcohol use and its relationship to adolescent drinking: Age, gender, and racial differences. *Psychology of Addictive Behaviors, 27*(3), 604–614.

National Drug Intelligence Center. (2011). *The economic impact of illicit drug use on American society*. Washington, DC: United States Department of Justice.

National Highway Traffic Safety Administration. (2008). *Traffic safety facts 2008*. http://www-nrd.nhtsa.dot.gov/ Pubs/811170.pdf. Washington, DC: National Center for Statistics and Analysis, U.S. Department of Transportation.

National Institute on Drug Abuse. (1997). *Drug abuse prevention for at risk groups*. Rockville, MD: DHHS: National Institutes of Health, National Institute on Drug Abuse, Office of Science Policy and Communications.

Neighbors, C., Larimer, M. E., & Lewis, M. A. (2004). Targeting misperceptions of descriptive drinking norms: Efficacy of a computer-delivered personalized normative feedback intervention. *Journal of Consulting and Clinical Psychology, 72*, 434–447.

Newton, N. C., Andrews, G., Teesson, M., & Vogl, L. E. (2009). Delivering prevention for alcohol and cannabis using the Internet: A cluster randomised controlled trial. *Preventive Medicine, 48*, 579–584.

NIDA. (2009). NIDA for teens: The science behind drug abuse. http://teens.drugabuse.gov/

NIDA. (2010). The brain: Understanding neurobiology through the study of addiction. http://science.education.nih.gov/ supplements/nih2/addiction/default.htm

NIDA. (2012). Drug abuse and HIV. NIH Publication No. 12-5760; NIDA Research Report Series: U.S. Department of Health and Human Services.

Nolin, M. J., Vaden-Kiernan, N., Feibus, M. L., & Chandler, K. (1997). *Student reports of availability, peer approval, and use of alcohol, marijuana, and other drugs at school: 1993*. Washington, DC: U.S. Department of Education, National Center for Education Statistics.

Obermayer, J., Riley, W., Asif, O., & Jean-Mary, J. (2004a). College smoking-cessation using cell phone text messaging. *Journal of American College Health, 53*(2), 71–78.

Obermayer, J. L., Riley, W. T., Asif, O., & Jean-Mary, J. (2004b). College smoking-cessation using cell phone text messaging. *Journal of American College Health, 53*, 71–78.

Office of Applied Studies. (2009). *Young adults' need for and receipt of alcohol and illicit drug use treatment: 2007*. Rockville, MD: Substance Abuse and Mental Health Services Administration.

Office of Juvenile Justice and Delinquency Prevention. (2013). Underage drinking costs http://www.udetc.org/ UnderageDrinkingCosts.asp (Vol. 2013): Pacific Institute for Research and Evaluation (PIRE).

Office of National Drug Control Policy. (2004). *The economic costs of drug abuse in the United States, 1992-2002*. Washington, DC: Executive Office of the President (Publication No. 207303).

Orlando, M., Ellickson, P. L., McCaffrey, D. F., & Longshore, D. L. (2005). Mediation analysis of a school-based drug prevention program: Effects of Project ALERT. *Prevention Science, 6*, 35–46.

Osilla, K. C., Hunter, S. B., Ewing, B. A., Ramchand, R., Miles, J. N. V., & D'Amico, E. J. (2012). The effects of employment among adolescents at-risk for future substance use. *Addictive Behaviors, 38*(3), 1616–1619.

Padula, C. B., Schweinsburg, A. D., & Tapert, S. F. (2007). Spatial working memory performance and fMRI activation interaction in abstinent adolescent marijuana users. *Psychology of Addictive Behaviors, 21*, 478–487.

Patten, C. A., Croghanb, I. T., Meisc, T. M., Deckerb, P. A., Pingreec, S., Colligana, R. C., et al. (2006). Randomized clinical trial of an Internet-based versus brief office intervention for adolescent smoking cessation. *Patient Education and Counseling, 64*(1–3), 249–258.

Patton, G., Bond, L., Butler, H., & Glover, S. (2003). Changing schools, changing health? Design and implementation of the Gatehouse Project. *Journal of Adolescent Health, 33*, 231–239.

Patton, G. C., Coffey, C., Lynskey, M. T., Reid, S., Hemphill, S., Carlin, J. B., et al. (2007). Trajectories of adolescent alcohol and cannabis use into young adulthood. *Addiction, 102*(4), 607–615.

Pedersen, E. R., Miles, J. N. V., Hunter, S. B., Osilla, K. C., Ewing, B. A., & D'Amico, E. J. (2013). Perceived norms moderate the association between mental health symptoms and drinking outcomes among at-risk adolescents. *Journal of Studies on Alcohol and Drugs, 74*(5), 736–745.

Perry, C. L., Williams, C. L., Komro, K. A., Veblen-Mortenson, S., Stigler, M. H., Munson, K. A., et al. (2002). Project Northland: Long-term outcomes of community action to reduce adolescent alcohol use. *Health Education Research, 17,* 117–132.

Peterson, A. V. J., Leroux, B. G., Bricker, J., Kealey, K. A., Marek, P. M., Sarason, I. G., et al. (2006). Nine-year prediction of adolescent smoking by number of smoking parents. *Addictive Behaviors, 31,* 788–801.

Peterson, P. L., Baer, J. S., Wells, E. A., Ginzler, J. A., & Garrett, S. B. (2006). Short-term effects of a brief motivational intervention to reduce alcohol and drug risk among homeless adolescents. *Psychology of Addictive Behaviors, 20,* 254–264

Petraitis, J., Flay, B. R., & Miller, T. Q. (1995). Reviewing theories of adolescent substance use: organizing pieces in the puzzle. *Psychological Bulletin, 117*(1), 67–86.

Petraitis, J., Flay, B. R., Miller, T. Q., Torpy, E. J., & Greiner, B. (1998). Illicit substance use among adolescents: A matrix of prospective predictors. *Substance Use & Misuse, 33,* 2561–2604.

Pinchevsky, G., Arria, A., Caldeira, K., Garnier-Dykstra, L., Vincent, K., & O'Grady, K. (2012). Marijuana exposure opportunity and initiation during college: Parent and peer influences. *Prevention Science, 13*(1), 43–54.

Piontek, D., Kraus, L., Bjarnason, T., Demetrovics, Z., & Ramstedt, M. (2013). Individual and country-level effects of cannabis-related perceptions on cannabis use. A multilevel study among adolescents in 32 European countries. *Journal of Adolescent Health, 52*(4), 473–479.

Poelen, E. A. P., Engels, R. C. M. E., Vorst, H. V. D., Scholte, R. H. J., & Vermulst, A. A. (2007). Best friends and alcohol consumption in adolescence: A within-family analysis. *Drug and Alcohol Dependence, 88,* 163–173.

Pomery, E. A., Gibbons, F. X., Gerrard, M., Cleveland, M. J., Brody, G. H., & Wills, T. A. (2005). Families and risk: Prospective analyses of familial and social influences on adolescent substance use. *Journal of Family Psychology, 19*(4), 560–570.

Popovici, I., Homer, J. F., Fang, H., & French, M. T. (2012). Alcohol use and crime: Findings from a longitudinal sample of U.S. adolescents and young adults. *Alcoholism: Clinical and Experimental Research, 36*(3), 532–543.

Puccio, J. A., Belzer, M., Olson, J., Salata, C., Tanaka, D., Tucker, D., et al. (2006). The use of cell phone reminder calls for assisting HIV-infected adolescents and young adults to adhere to highly active antiretroviral therapy: A pilot study. *AIDS Patient Care and STDs, 20,* 438–444.

Ramchand, R., Ialongo, N. S., & Chilcoat, H. D. (2007). The effect of working for pay on adolescent tobacco use. *The American Journal of Public Health, 97*(11), 2056–2062.

Resnicow, K., DiIorio, C., Soet, J. E., Borrelli, B., Hecht, J., & Ernst, D. (2002). Motivational interviewing in health promotion: It sounds like something is changing. *Health Psychology, 21,* 444–451.

Rickwood, D. J., Deane, F. P., & Wison, C. J. (2007). When and how do young people seek professional help for mental health problems? *Medical Journal of Australia, 187,* S35–S39.

Riley, W., Obermayer, J., & Jean-Mary, J. (2008a). Internet and mobile phone text messaging intervention for college smokers. *Journal of American College Health, 57*(2), 245–248.

Riley, W. T., Obermayer, J. L., & Jean-Mary, J. (2008b). Internet and mobile phone text messaging intervention for college smokers. *Journal of American College Health, 57,* 245–248.

Ringwalt, C., Clark, H., Hanley, S., Shamblen, S., & Flewelling, R. (2010). The effects of Project ALERT one year past curriculum completion. *Prevention Science, 11*(2), 172–184.

Ríos-Bedoya, C. F., & Hay, C. (2013). Feasibility of using text messaging for unhealthy behaviors screening in a clinical setting: A case study on adolescent hazardous alcohol use. *Journal of the American Medical Informatics Association, 20*(2), 373–376.

Robers, S., Zhang, J., Truman, J., & Snyder, T. D. (2012). *Indicators of School Crime and Safety: 2011* (NCES 2012-002/NCJ 236021). Washington, DC: National Center for Education Statistics, U.S. Department of Education, and Bureau of Justice Statistics, Office of Justice Programs, U.S. Department of Justice.

Rodgers, A., Corbett, T., Bramley, D., Riddell, T., Wills, M., Lin, R.B, & Jones, M. (2005). Do u smoke after txt? Results of a randomised trial of smoking cessation using mobile phone text messaging. *Tobacco Control, 14,* 255–261.

Roebuck, M. C., French, M. T., & Dennis, M. L. (2004). Adolescent marijuana use and school attendance. *Economics of Education Review, 23,* 133–141.

Rohrbach, L. A., Sun, P., & Sussman, S. (2010). One-year follow-up evaluation of the Project Towards No Drug Abuse (TND) dissemination trial. *Preventive Medicine, 51*(3–14), 313–319.

Rountree, P. W., & Clayton, R. R. (1999). A contextual model of adolescent alcohol use across the rural-urban community. *Substance Use and Misuse, 43,* 495–519.

SAMHSA. (2012a). *Results from the 2011 National Survey on Drug Use and Health: Summary of national findings.* Rockville, MD: Substance Abuse and Mental Health Services Administration,.

SAMHSA. (2012b). SAMHSA's national registry of evidence based programs and practices, http://www.nrepp.samhsa.gov/

Sawyer, T. M., & Stevenson, J. F. (2008). Perceived parental and peer disapproval toward substances: Influences on adolescent decision-making. *The Journal of Primary Prevention, 29*(6), 465–477.

Schell, T. L., Martino, S. C., Ellickson, P. L., Collins, R. L., & McCaffrey, D. (2005). Measuring developmental changes in alcohol expectancies. *Psychology of Addictive Behaviors, 19,* 217–220.

Scherrer, J. F., Xian, H., Pan, H., Pergadia, M. L., Madden, P. A. F., Grant, J. D., et al. (2012). Parent, sibling and peer influences on smoking initiation, regular smoking and nicotine dependence. Results from a genetically informative design. *Addictive Behaviors, 37*(3), 240–247.

Schuck, K., Otten, R., & Engels, R. C. M. E. (2012). The role of environmental smoking in smoking-related cognitions and susceptibility to smoking in never-smoking 9–12year-old children. *Addictive Behaviors, 37*(12), 1400–1405.

Schuck, K., Otten, R., Engels, R. C. M. E., Barker, E. D., & Kleinjan, M. (2012). Bidirectional influences between parents and children in smoking behavior: A longitudinal full-family model. *Nicotine & Tobacco Research, 15*(1), 44–51.

Schulte, M. T., Monreal, T. K., Kia-Keating, M., & Brown, S. A. (2010). Influencing adolescent social perceptions of alcohol use to facilitate change through a school-based intervention. *Journal of Child & Adolescent Substance Abuse*, *19*(5), 371–390.

Schweinsburg, A. D., Schweinsburg, B. C., Cheung, E. H., Brown, G. G., Brown, S. A., & Tapert, S. F. (2005). fMRI response to spatial working memory in adolescents with comorbid marijuana and alcohol use disorders. *Drug and Alcohol Dependence*, *79*, 201–210.

Scott-Sheldon, L. A. J., Terry, D. L., Carey, K. B., Garey, L., & Carey, M. P. (2012). Efficacy of expectancy challenge interventions to reduce college student drinking: A meta-analytic review. *Psychology of Addictive Behaviors*, *26*(3), 393–405.

Seid, M., D'Amico, E. J., Varni, J. W., Munafo, J. K., Britto, M. T., Kercsmar, C. M., et al. (2012). The in vivo adherence intervention for at risk adolescents with asthma: Report of a randomized pilot trial. *Journal of Pediatric Psychology*, *37*(4), 390–403.

Sher, K. J., Grekin, E. R., & Williams, N. A. (2005). The development of alcohol use disorders. *Annual Review of Clinical Psychology*, *1*, 493–523.

Sher, K. J., Walitzer, K. S., Wood, P. K., & Brent, E. E. (1991). Characteristics of children of alcoholics: Putative risk factors, substance use and abuse, and psychopathology. *Journal of Abnormal Psychology*, *100*, 427–448.

Shih, R. A., Miles, J. N. V., Tucker, J. S., Zhou, A. J., & D'Amico, E. J. (2012). Racial/ethnic differences in the influence of cultural values, alcohol resistance self-efficacy and expectancies on risk for alcohol initiation. *Psychology of Addictive Behaviors*, *26*(3), 460–470.

Shillington, A. M., & Clapp, J. D. (2000). Self-report stability of adolescent substance use: Are there differences for gender, ethnicity and age? *Drug Alcohol Depend*, *60*(1), 19–27.

Shope, J. T., Dielman, T. E., Butchart, A. T., & Campanelli, P. C. (1992). An elementary school-based alcohol misuse prevention program: A follow-up evaluation. *Journal of Studies on Alcohol*, *53*, 106–121.

Shope, J. T., Elliott, M. R., Raghunathan, T. E., & Waller, P. F. (2001). Long-term follow-up of a high school alcohol misuse prevention program's effect on students' subsequent driving. *Alcoholism: Clinical and Experimental Research*, *25*(3), 403–410.

Simons-Morton, B., Abroms, L., Haynie, D. L., & Chen, R. (2004). Latent growth curve analyses of peer and parent influences on smoking progression among early adolescents. *Health Psychology*, *23*, 612–621.

Simons-Morton, B., & Chen, R. (2005). Latent growth curve analyses of parent influences on drinking progression among early adolescents. *Journal of Studies on Alcohol 66*, 5–13.

Skenderian, J. J., Siegel, J. T., Crano, W. D., Alvaro, E. E., & Lac, A. (2008). Expectancy change and adolescents' intentions to use marijuana. *Psychology of Addictive Behaviors*, *22*, 563–569.

Slomkowski, C., Rende, R., Conger, K. J., Simons, R. L., & Conger, R. D. (2001). Sisters, brothers, and delinquency: Evaluating social influence during early and middle adolescence. *Child Development*, *72*(1), 271–283.

Smith, G. T., Goldman, M. S., Greenbaum, P. E., & Christiansen, B. A. (1995). Expectancy for social facilitation from drinking: The divergent paths of high-expectancy and low-expectancy adolescents. *Journal of Abnormal Psychology*, *104*, 32–40.

Sowell, E. R., Thompson, P. M., Leonard, C. M., Welcome, S. E., Kan, E., & Toga, A. W. (2004). Longitudinal mapping of cortical thickness and brain growth in normal children. *Journal of Neuroscience*, *24*, 8223–8231.

Spear, L. P. (2000). The adolescent brain and age-related behavioral manifestations. *Neuroscience & Biobehavioral Reviews*, *24*, 417–463.

Spear, L. P., & Varlinskaya, E. I. (2005). Adolescence. Alcohol sensitivity, tolerance, and intake. In *Recent developments in alcoholism: Alcohol problems in adolescents and young adults: Epidemiology, neurobiology, prevention, treatment* (Vol. 17, pp. 143–159). New York: Springer.

Spirito, A., Monti, P. M., Barnett, N. P., Colby, S. M., Sindelar, H., Rohsenow, D., et al. (2004). A randomized clinical trial of a brief motivational intervention for alcohol-positive adolescents treated in an emergency department. *Journal of Pediatrics*, *145*, 396–402.

Spoth, R., Trudeau, L., Shin, C., Ralston, E., Redmond, C., Greenberg, M., et al. (2013). Longitudinal effects of universal preventive intervention on prescription drug misuse: Three randomized controlled trials with late adolescents and young adults. *American Journal of Public Health*, *103*(4), 665–672.

St Pierre, T., Osgood, D., Mincemoyer, C., Kaltreider, D., & Kauh, T. (2005). Results of an independent evaluation of Project ALERT delivered in schools by Cooperative Extension. *Prevention Science*, *6*(4), 305–317.

St. Pierre, T. L., Kaltreider, D. L., Mark, M. M., & Aikin, K. J. (1992). Drug prevention in a community setting: A longitudinal study of the relative effectiveness of a three-year primary prevention program in Boys & Girls Clubs across the nation. *American Journal of Community Psychology*, *20*, 673–706.

Staff, J., & Uggen, C. (2003). The fruits of good work: Early work experiences and adolescent deviance. *Journal of Research in Crime and Delinquency*, *40*, 263–290.

Starkey, F., Audrey, S., Holliday, J., Moore, L., & Campbell, R. (2009). Identifying influential young people to undertake effective peer-led health promotion: the example of A Stop Smoking In Schools Trial (ASSIST). *Health Education Research*, *24*(6), 977–988.

Stein, L. A., Clair, M., Lebeau, R., Colby, S. M., Barnett, N. P., Golembeske, C., et al. (2011). Motivational interviewing to reduce substance-related consequences: Effects for incarcerated adolescents with depressed mood. *Drug and Alcohol Dependence*, *118*(2–3), 475–478.

Steinberg, L., & Monahan, K. C. (2007). Age differences in resistance to peer influence. *Developmental Psychology*, *43*, 1531–1543.

Steinberg, L. D., & Cauffman, E. (1995). The impact of employment on adolescent development. *Annals of Child Development*, *11*, 131–166.

Sterling, S., Weisner, C., Hinman, A., & Parthasarathy, S. (2010). Access to treatment for adolescents with substance use and co-occurring disorders: Challenges and opportunities. *Journal of the American Academy of Child & Adolescent Psychiatry*, *49*, 637–646.

Stern, S. A., Meredith, L. S., Gholson, J., Gore, P., & D'Amico, E. J. (2007). Project CHAT: A brief motivational substance abuse intervention for teens in primary care. *Journal of Substance Abuse Treatment*, *32*(153–165).

Sun, P., Sussman, S., Dent, C. W., & Rohrbach, L. A. (2008). One year follow-up evaluation of Project Towards No Drug Abuse (TND-4). *Preventive Medicine*, *47*(4), 438–442.

Sun, W., Skara, S., Sun, P., Dent, C. W., & Sussman, S. (2006). Project towards no drug abuse: Long-term substance use outcomes evaluation. *Preventive Medicine, 42,* 188–192.

Sussman, S. (1996). Development of a school-based curriculum for high-risk youths. *Journal of Psychoactive Drugs, 28,* 169–182.

Sussman, S., Dent, C. W., & Stacy, A. W. (2002). Project Towards No Drug Abuse: A review of the findings and future directions. *American Journal of Health Behavior, 26,* 354–364.

Sussman, S., Dent, C. W., Stacy, A. W., & Craig, S. (1998). One-year outcomes of Project Towards No Drug Abuse. *Preventive Medicine, 27,* 632–642.

Sussman, S., McCuller, W. J., & Dent, C. W. (2003). The associations of social self-control, personality disorders, and demographics with drug use among high-risk youth. *Addictive Behaviors, 28,* 1159–1166.

Sussman, S., Petosa, R., & Clarke, P. (1996). The use of empirical curriculum development to improve prevention research. *American Behavioral Scientist, 39,* 838–852.

Sussman, S., Sun, P., McCuller, W. J., & Dent, C. W. (2003). Project Towards No Drug Abuse: Two-year outcomes of a trial that compares health educator delivery to self-instruction. *Preventive Medicine, 37,* 155–162.

Sussman, S., Yang, D., Baezconde-Garbanati, L., & Dent, C. W. (2003). Drug abuse prevention program development: Results among Latino and non-Latino white adolescents. *Evaluation & the Health Professions, 26*(4), 355–379.

Sznitman, S. R., Dunlop, S. M., Nalkur, P., Khurana, A., & Romer, D. (2012). Student drug testing in the context of positive and negative school climates: Results from a national survey. *Journal of Youth and Adolescence, 41*(2), 146–155.

Tapert, S. F., & Brown, S. A. (2000). Substance dependence, family history of alcohol dependence and neuropsychological functioning in adolescence. *Addiction, 95*(7), 1043–1053.

Tapert, S. F., Caldwell, L., & Burke, M. A. (2004). Alcohol and the adolescent brain: Human studies. *Alcohol Research & Health, 28,* 205–212.

Tapert, S. F., Schweinsburg, A. D., Drummond, S. P. A., Paulus, M. P., Brown, S. A., Yang, T. A., et al. (2007). Functional MRI of inhibitory processing in abstinent adolescent marijuana users. *Psychopharmacology, 194,* 173–183.

Taylor, B. J., Graham, J. W., Cumsille, P., & Hansen, W. B. (2000). Modeling prevention program effects on growth in substance use: Analysis of five years of data from the Adolescent Alcohol Prevention Trial. *Prevention Science, 1*(4), 183–197.

Tobler, A. L., & Komro, K. A. (2010). Trajectories of parental monitoring and communication and effects on drug use among urban young adolescents. *Journal of Adolescent Health, 46*(6), 560–568.

Tobler, N. S., Roona, M. R., Ochshorn, P., Marshall, D. G., Streke, A. V., & Stackpole, K. M. (2000). School-based adolescent drug prevention programs: 1998 meta-analysis. *The Journal of Primary Prevention, 20,* 275–336.

Tomlinson, K. L., & Brown, S. A. (2012). Self-medication or social learning? A comparison of models to predict early adolescent drinking. *Addictive Behaviors, 37*(2), 179–186.

Torrealday, O., Stein, L. A., Barnett, N., Golembeske, C., Lebeau, R., Colby, S. M., et al. (2008). Validation of the marijuana effect expectancy questionnaire-brief. *Journal of Child & Adolescent Substance Abuse, 17*(4), 1–17.

Tucker, J. S., Ellickson, P. L., Collins, R. L., & Klein, D. J. (2006). Are drug experimenters better adjusted than abstainers and users? A longitudinal study of adolescent marijuana use. *Journal of Adolescent Health, 39,* 488–494.

Tucker, J. S., Ellickson, P. L., Orlando, M., Martino, S. C., & Klein, D. J. (2005). Substance use trajectories from early adolescence to emerging adulthood: A comparison of smoking, binge drinking, and marijuana use. *Journal of Drug Issues 35,* 307–332.

Tucker, J. S., Martinez, J. F., Ellickson, P. L., & Edelen, M. O. (2008). Temporal associations of cigarette smoking with social influences, academic performance, and delinquency: A four-wave longitudinal study from ages 13 to 25. *Psychology of Addictive Behaviors, 22,* 1–11.

van den Bree, M. B. M., & Pickworth, W. B. (2005). Risk factors predicting changes in marijuana involvement in teenagers. *Archives of General Psychiatry, 62,* 311–319.

Van Ryzin, M. J., Fosco, G. M., & Dishion, T. J. (2012). Family and peer predictors of substance use from early adolescence to early adulthood: An 11-year prospective analysis. *Addictive Behaviors, 37*(12), 1314–1324.

Vaughan, R., & Johnson, P. (2007). The effectiveness of Project SUCCESS (Schools Using Coordinated Community Efforts to Strengthen Students) in a regular secondary school setting. Unpublished manuscript. http://www.nrepp.samhsa.gov/ViewIntervention.aspx?id=71

Vaughn, M. G., & Howard, M. O. (2004). Adolescent substance abuse treatment: A synthesis of controlled evaluations. *Research on Social Work Practice, 14*(5), 325–335.

Vermeulen-Smit, E., Koning, I. M., Verdurmen, J. E. E., Van der Vorst, H., Engels, R. C. M. E., & Vollebergh, W. A. M. (2012). The influence of paternal and maternal drinking patterns within two-partner families on the initiation and development of adolescent drinking. *Addictive Behaviors, 37*(11), 1248–1256.

Vermeulen-Smit, E., Ter Bogt, T. F. M., Verdurmen, J. E. E., Van Dorsselaer, S. A. F. M., & Vollebergh, W. A. M. (2012). The role of education, parents and peers in adolescent heavy episodic drinking. *Drugs: Education, Prevention & Policy, 19*(3), 223–226.

Voelkl, K., & Frone, M. (2000). Predictors of substance use at school among high school students. *Journal of Educational Psychology, 92,* 583–592.

Wagner, E. F., Tubman, J. G., & Gil, A. G. (2004). Implementing school-based substance abuse interventions: Methodological dilemmas and recommended solutions. *Addiction, 99*(Suppl 2), 106–119.

Waldron, H. B., & Turner, C. W. (2008). Evidence-based psychosocial treatments for adolescent substance abuse. *Journal of Clinical Child and Adolescent Psychology, 37*(1), 238–261.

Walker, D. D., Roffman, R. A., Stephens, R. S., Wakana, K., & Berghuis, J. (2006). Motivational enhancement therapy for adolescent marijuana users: A preliminary randomized controlled trial. *Journal of Consulting and Clinical Psychology, 74*(3), 628–632.

Walker, D. D., Stephens, R., Roffman, R., DeMarce, J., Lozano, B., Towe, S., et al. (2011). Randomized controlled trial of motivational enhancement therapy with nontreatment-seeking adolescent cannabis users: A further test of the teen marijuana check-up. *Psychology of Addictive Behaviors, 25*(3), 474–484. doi: 10.1037/a0024076

Walton, M. A., Cunningham, R. M., Goldstein, A. L., Chermack, S. T., Zimmerman, M. A., Bingham, C. R., et al. (2009). Rates and correlates of violent behaviors among adolescents treated in an urban emergency department. *Journal of Adolescent Health, 45*(1), 77–83.

Wandersman, A., & Florin, P. (2003). Community interventions and effective prevention. *American Psychologist, 58,* 441–448.

Weinberg, N. Z. (2001). Risk factors for adolescent substance abuse. *Journal of Learning Disabilities, 34,* 342–351.

Weiss, B., Caron, A., Ball, S., Tapp, J., Johnson, M., & Weisz, J. R. (2005). Iatrogenic effects of group treatment for anti-social youth. *Journal of Consulting and Clinical Psychology, 73,* 1036–1044.

Weisz, J. R., & Hawley, K. M. (2002). Developmental factors in the treatment on adolescents. *Journal of Consulting and Clinical Psychology, 70,* 21–43.

Werch, C. E., Owen, D. M., Carlson, J. M., DiClemente, C. C., Edgemon, P., & Moore, M. (2003). One-year follow-up results of the STARS for families alcohol prevention program. *Health Education Research, 18,* 74–87.

West, P., Sweeting, H., & Leyland, A. (2004). School effects on pupils' health behaviours: Evidence in support of the health promoting school. *Research Papers in Education, 19,* 261–291.

White, A. (2009). Understanding adolescent brain development and its implications for the clinician. *Adolescent Medicine, 20,* 73–90.

Whiteman, S. D., Jensen, A. C., & Maggs, J. L. (2013). Similarities in adolescent siblings' substance use: Testing competing pathways of influence. *Journal of Studies on Alcohol and Drugs, 74*(1), 104–113.

Wills, T. A., Walker, C., Mendoza, D., & Ainette, M. G. (2006). Behavioral and emotional self-control: Relations to substance use in samples of middle and high school students. *Psychology of Addictive Behaviors, 20,* 265–278.

Windle, M. (2000). Parental, sibling, and peer influences on adolescent substance use and alcohol problems. *Applied Developmental Science Special Issue: Familial and Peer Influences on Adolescent Substance Use, 4,* 98–110.

Wood, M. D., Read, J. P., Mitchell, R. E., & Brand, N. H. (2004). Do parents still matter? Parent and peer influences on alcohol involvement among recent high school graduates. *Psychology of Addictive Behaviors, 18,* 19–30.

Woodruff, S. I., Conway, T. L., Edwards, C. C., Elliott, S. P., & Crittenden, J. (2007). Evaluation of an Internet virtual world chat room for adolescent smoking cessation. *Addictive Behaviors, 32,* 1769–1786.

World Health Organization. (2004–2005). Psychosocial processes and mechanisms of risk and protection. *Alcohol, Health & Research World, 28,* 143–154.

Wu, P., Hoven, C. W., & Fuller, C. J. (2003). Factors associated with adolescents receiving drug treatment: Findings from the National Household Survey on Drug Abuse. *Journal of Behavioral Health Services & Research, 30*(2), 190–201.

Wu, P., Hoven, C. W., Tiet, Q., Kovalenko, P., & Wicks, J. (2002). Factors associated with adolescent utilization of alcohol treatment services. *American Journal of Drug & Alcohol Abuse, 28,* 353–369.

Wynn, S. R., Schulenberg, J., Maggs, J. L., & Zucker, R. A. (2000). Preventing alcohol misuse: The impact of refusal skills and norms. *Psychology of Addictive Behaviors, 14*(1), 36–47.

Zhang, L., Welte, J. W., & Wieczorek, W. F. (1997). Peer and parental influences on male adolescent drinking. *Substance Use and Misuse, 32*(14), 2121–2136.

Zucker, R. A., Wong, M. A., Puttler, L. I., & Fitzgerald, H. E. (2003). Resilience and vulnerability among sons of alcoholics: Relationships to developmental outcomes between early childhood and adolescence. In S. S. Luthar (Ed.), *Resilience and Vulnerability: Adaptation in the Context of Childhood Adversities* (pp. 76–103). New York: Cambridge University Press.

PART 6

Concluding
Commentary

Anticipating the Future of Research on Substance Use and Substance Use Disorders

Kenneth J. Sher *and* Alvaro Vergés

Abstract

An increasing understanding of the etiology, course, prevention, and treatment of substance use disorders and their related harms continues apace, aided by multidisciplinary research efforts and new discoveries and technologies in a range of allied scientific disciplines. In this concluding chapter of *The Oxford Handbook of Substance Use and Substance Use Disorders,* the authors highlight a range of opportunities and challenges facing those interested in gaining a basic understanding of the nature of these phenomena and the novel approaches emerging to assess, prevent, and treat these conditions with the goal of reducing the enormous burden these problems place on individuals, families, communities, and our global society as a whole.

Key Words: addiction, assessment, treatment, prevention, public health

It is difficult, if not impossible to anticipate what substance use research will look like in 10 years and what new knowledge will be generated by research in the near and intermediate future. However, a review of some of the current challenges and emerging trends could provide a glimpse into what the next generation of research might look like. In this final chapter of the *Handbook*, we would like to highlight a few of these emerging issues.

Many of the chapters in this *Handbook* underscore a range of challenges facing investigation of various causes and consequences in the study of substance use and related phenomena. Some of those challenges are shared with the broader areas of psychology, biomedical research, and psychopathology, such as the replicability crisis that needs urgently to be addressed by the scientific community (e.g., Collins & Tabak, 2014; Ioannidis, 2012; Nosek et al., 2015; Pashler & Harris, 2012) and the missing heritability of complex diseases (e.g., Manolio et al., 2009; Wang, Kapoor, & Goate, 2012). Additionally, at least in the United States, the infrastructure for conducting research in substance

use and substance use disorders (SUDs), as well as health-related research more generally, is experiencing a crisis of sorts due to a variety of confluences that have resulted in a continually increasing population of researchers competing for diminishing research dollars and a questioning of whether the system that has generated many of the research findings reviewed in this *Handbook* is sustainable (Alberts, Kirschner, Tilghman, & Varmus, 2014).

In this concluding chapter, however, we will first consider four challenges that are specific to the substance use field: (1) characterizing the fundamental nature of addiction, (2) distinguishing the consequences of substance use from the characteristics of the user, and addressing the challenges posed by (3) new designer drugs and (4) new ways of delivering more "traditional" substances.

Future Challenges
Conceptualization of Addiction

A major challenge for the field has to do with the best way to conceptualize addictive behaviors. Although the exact nature of addiction has been a matter of debate for decades, the emergence of non-substance addictions has led to the need for a major conceptual change to understand the core of addictive processes. For example, research on pathological gambling has revealed a number of phenomenological and etiological similarities with SUDs (e.g., Blanco, Myers, & Kendler, 2012; Lesieur & Rosenthal, 1991; Lopez Viets, 1998; Potenza, 2006; van Holst, van den Brink, Veltman, & Goudriaan, 2010). Although chasing losses (i.e., returning to a gambling activity in an attempt to win back losses) constitutes a prominent feature of pathological gambling that is not shared with SUDs (Lesieur, 1988), the extent of the similarities has led to the reclassification of pathological gambling (now referred to as "gambling disorder") from impulse control disorders in the *Diagnostic and Statistical Manual* (DSM-IV; American Psychiatric Association [APA], 1994) to addictive disorders in DSM-5 (APA, 2013; Petry & O'Brien, 2013).

The inclusion of pathological gambling in the same category as SUDs has led to consideration of other non-substance addictions, including food addiction (e.g., Avena, Gold, Kroll, & Gold, 2012; Hebebrand et al., 2014; Volkow, Wang, Tomasi, & Baler, 2013), sexual addiction (e.g., Bancroft & Vukadinovic, 2004; Gold & Heffner, 1998; Rosenberg, Carnes, & O'Connor, 2014), exercise addiction (Berczik et al., 2012), Internet addiction (e.g., Block, 2008; Tao et al., 2010; Young, 1998), hair pulling addiction (Grant, Odlaug, & Potenza, 2007), and other so-called impulse control disorders that can be conceptualized as addictions (Grant & Potenza, 2005).

The case of food addiction is particularly illustrative of the complexity of the conceptual issues involved. Although there is evidence suggesting that food addiction and drug addiction might share a common underlying neurocircuitry (Saunders & Robinson, 2013; Smith & Robbins, 2013; Stice, Figlewicz, Gosnell, Levine, & Pratt, 2013; Volkow et al., 2013; Wise, 2013), some authors reject the idea of conceptualizing binge eating and obesity as reflecting an addictive process, given the current evidence (e.g., Harb & Almeida, 2014; Ziauddeen, Farooqi, & Fletcher, 2012; Ziauddeen & Fletcher, 2013). An important source of disagreement is the extent to which differences between food addiction and drug addiction can be tolerated within the same conceptual model. For instance, a major difference between the two is that food is necessary for survival whereas psychoactive drugs are not (Smith & Robbins, 2013; Volkow & Wise, 2005). In any case,

the notion that food can be addictive under some circumstances opens the possibility that any rewarding activity can be considered as potentially addictive (Schmitz, 2005). A significant implication of this debate is that, if a number of non-substance-related behaviors are capable of becoming addictive, then there is nothing unique about substances of abuse with regard to their addictive potential. If this is true, then the concept of addiction needs to be reframed by downplaying the role of pharmacological influences of specific substances and highlighting the role of desire and pleasure (e.g., Foddy & Savulescu, 2010; Orford, 2001).

In future years, more theoretical and empirical work will be needed to clarify the commonalities and differences among several types of addictive behaviors. As with food addiction, these developments might not only help to advance our understanding of non-substance addictions but of SUDs as well (Volkow & Wise, 2005). Indeed, most of the major theoretical approaches to understanding addiction, including incentive sensitization (Robinson & Berridge, 1993), allostasis (Koob & Le Moal, 2001) (and its forebear opponent-process theory, Solomon & Corbit, 1974), habit learning (Everitt & Robbins, 2005), classical conditioning (Siegel, Baptista, Kim, McDonald, & Weise-Kelly, 2000), and behavioral economic and neuroeconomic principles such as temporal discounting (Hamilton et al., 2015) represent general theories and mechanisms of behavior (see Bickel, Mueller, MacKillop, & Yi, Chap. 12, Vol. 1). Thus, a legitimate question, at least with respect to etiology, is "what makes addictive behaviors different from non-addictive behaviors?" Whereas we can point to specific addictive phenomena such as compulsive use of a substance as suggesting that there is a point of transition from non-addiction to addiction, the extent to which our existing theories resolve this transition remains an area of debate and a fertile area for advancing our science.

Hand-in-hand with refining and integrating models of addictive behavior at a theoretical level is developing approaches to directly assess these processes. This is critical not just for advancing the basic science of addiction but for understanding the heterogeneity of SUDs, characterizing the nature and degree of these processes in affected individuals, and identifying existing and novel treatments for targeting these processes. The proposed movement away from traditional diagnosis to more process or endophenotypic approaches in characterizing mental disorders (i.e., the Research Domain Criteria

[RDoC]; e.g., Cuthbert, 2015) has been proposed for addictive disorders (Litten et al., 2015) and holds promise for providing a closer integration of scientific understanding and clinical practice.

Distinguishing Consequences of Substance Use from the Behavior of Substance Users

To a very large degree, SUDs are defined on the basis of the ostensible consequences of substance use. That is, a substance user who reports sufficient problems with a given substance is diagnosed with a SUD. However, determining whether or not a given "problem" or "consequence" is truly a function of the substance use itself is not always easy to determine. Hervey Cleckley (1941) noted that the psychopath is prone to exhibit "fantastic and uninviting behavior with drink . . . *and sometimes without*" (emphasis added). That is, we tend to assume that when problem behaviors arise in an individual using substances, these problems are due to the substance. Sorting out whether or not a given behavior is actually caused by the acute or chronic effects of a drug of abuse is not a straightforward enterprise, as illustrated in many of the chapters in this *Handbook*, and in any individual case, it might be impossible to determine. Nevertheless, perhaps because we can easily query individuals as to whether or not their substance use resulted in various consequences, we often rely on those reports as prima facie evidence of a substance problem. Martin, Langenbucher, Chung, and Sher (2014) note that drug consequences are problematic in that (1) they are defined on the basis of a range of contextual factors, (2) substance use cannot always be shown to have a causal or even exacerbating role, and (3) they can be multivariately determined. Moreover, even if a given consequence can be shown to have a high likelihood of being caused by a drug, it is not easy to assign it to a single class of consequences, thus leading to the problem of double counting. For example, a given consequence could be viewed as suggesting both role impairment and reduced social activities . . . is this one or two consequences?

It should be emphasized that many approaches to ameliorating consequences of the impairing acute or chronic effects of substances do not necessarily have to tackle basic use patterns or SUDs but can address consequences directly at a program or policy level, as is often done in the area of traffic safety and addressing impaired driving (e.g., Voas & Fell, Chap. 22, Vol. 2). That is, consequences can be viewed as conceptually distinct from dependence or addiction and can be targeted separately. The DSM-5 approach to viewing consequences and dependence as part of a single continuum of "disorder" might contribute to conceptual fuzziness that obscures distinct targets for interventions.

Many of the chapters in this *Handbook* addressing comorbid psychopathology, including psychosis (Mueser, Noordsy, & Drake, Chap. 4, Vol. 2), mood and anxiety disorders (Stewart, Grant, Mackie, & Conrod, Chap. 6, Vol. 2), personality disorder (Trull et al., Chap. 5, Vol. 2), ADHD (Derefinko & Pelham, Chap 3, Vol. 2), and other consequences including crime (White, Chap. 12, Vol. 2), and human capital (Popovici & French, Chap. 13, Vol. 2) address this issue with respect to each of these specific domains. This is not to say that what we call drug consequences are not important, but, rather, they are often difficult to isolate with respect to any single causal factor. Approaches for diagnosing SUDs could benefit from a broader transdiagnostic approach that incorporates a more sophisticated view of the nature of ostensible drug consequences and, perhaps, focuses more on core features of addiction.

Designer Drugs

A major challenge for the future is the increasing number of newly developed recreational drugs that have legal status in most countries (Baumann et al., 2014; Brennan & Van Hout, 2012; Carroll, Lewin, Mascarella, Seltzman, & Reddy, 2012; Fattore & Fratta, 2011; Misselbrook & Hamilton, 2012; Uchiyama, Shimokawa, Kawamura, Kikura-Hanajiri, & Hakamatsuka, 2014). These so-called "designer drugs" or "legal highs" are usually synthesized through modification of the molecular structure of pre-existing illegal drugs (Buchanan & Brown, 1988; Hill & Thomas, 2011). Although this has been a concern since the late 1970s (Carroll et al., 2012), their ready availability through the Internet represents a new challenge for control and public health agencies (Fattore & Fratta, 2011). As stated by Corazza et al. (2011):

> Most of the novel psychoactive compounds available online . . . share a number of characteristics that may constitute a public health challenge, including: (a) not being approved for human consumption; (b) their intake possibly being associated with a number of unknown side effects/adverse reactions; (c) very few related pharmacological/toxicological data being available in the peer reviewed, scientific, literature, with the limited knowledge being mostly restricted to

pre-clinical studies; (d) rapidly appearing in always more sophisticated forms and remaining unregulated for a long period of time; (e) being most often synthesized in underground laboratories simply modifying the molecular structure of remaining controlled drugs . . ., hence raising further concerns in terms of presence of contaminating agents; (f) being largely available online and thus "just a click" away from our homes and potentially available to everyone; (h) being increasingly accepted as part of a "trendy" lifestyle, because the internet may arguably act as an enabler for niche activities to develop into social norms. (p. 128)

In the next decades, we will probably witness a proliferation of new, more refined designer drugs that will easily reach potential consumers in a number of countries simultaneously. Effective strategies to deal with this challenge will require international coordinated efforts and constantly updated sources of information available for policy-makers, researchers, and clinicians.

Old Wine in New Bottles

Although designer drugs pose a major challenge for public health, law enforcement, and treatment providers, new delivery systems for long-established substances of abuse represent both new challenges and opportunities. For example, electronic cigarettes (e-cigarettes), devices that deliver vaporized nicotine without combusting tobacco, have been hailed as a potential harm reduction strategy for those with tobacco dependence in that they are presumed to carry with them less harm (e.g., Cahn & Siegel, 2011) and may be used as a treatment approach to achieve smoking cessation (e.g., Bullen et al., 2013; Siegel, Tanwar, & Wood, 2011). Despite what appears to be a substantially better harm profile than combustible cigarettes, the introduction of e-cigarettes could potentially dissuade current smokers from quitting and lead to increased acceptance of smoking behavior (Benowitz & Goniewicz, 2013). Careful assessment on a population-wide basis of the costs and benefits of electronic cigarettes will ultimate help determine whether this innovation represents a major tool for improving public health or whether unintended consequences undermine these perceived benefits.

Although oral consumption of noncombusted marijuana is not new, legalization in some areas appears to be associated with increased accidental poisonings, especially in young children (Wang et al., 2014). As recently reviewed, edible marijuana is "responsible for the majority of health care visits due to marijuana intoxication for all ages" (p. 241) and reflects challenges of variability in packaging and dosing and difficulties in self-regulating the consumption of some product units (e.g., small fractions of a cookie; Monte, Zane, & Heard, 2015). As the case of e-cigarettes and edible marijuana illustrates, innovation in the sale and marketing of novel delivery systems represents potential opportunities and risks and requires careful assessment in order to evaluate public health impact.

Future Developments

Just as the Red Queen in *Through the Looking Glass and What Alice Found There* (Carroll, 1872) noted "it takes all the running you can do, to keep in the same place," cultural changes in norms surrounding substance use and its related problems and effective prevention programs could result in the need to constantly upgrade the efficacy of treatments just to maintain the success rates of treatments today. Breslau, Johnson, Hiripi, and Kessler (2001) found that individuals from more recent birth cohorts were less likely to use tobacco products than those from earlier birth cohorts, but the risk of tobacco dependence among smokers was substantially higher in the more recent cohorts. In attempting to explain this phenomenon, the authors speculated that "The growing awareness of the addictive potential of smoking and its adverse health effects has resulted in declining numbers who take up smoking. Those in recent cohorts who do take up smoking might be more deviant than smokers in earlier cohorts with respect to personality traits that influence smoking and the progression to nicotine dependence (e.g., risk taking, impulsivity)" (p. 815). Based on this type of explanation, it is a reasonable hypothesis that the average severity of dependence among those using is likely to be higher when public health efforts or cultural change alter the distribution of severity (or comorbid psychopathology or interest in behavior change) so that there is relatively little "low-hanging fruit" with respect to treatment. Although it is not clear if cessation rates among treatment-seeking individuals have gone down overall in recent years, some subpopulations of tobacco-dependent individuals (e.g., chronically mentally ill) may represent "hardened" populations that are less treatment responsive and represent a growing percentage of the population (see also Hughes & Brandon, 2003; Warner & Burns, 2003). The major point here is that substance-dependent individuals in the future may differ from those being treated today. As we increase our ability to prevent and successfully treat an increasing proportion of affected individuals, the remaining population of treatment-resistant individuals can present new challenges and highlight the need for continuing innovation in assessment and intervention. In this section, we review some of the promising developments that might help to deal with these and other challenges.

We note, however, that legalization or decriminalization of substances that are currently legal or controlled could have the opposite function. That is, it can be posited that as drug use becomes legal, its association with deviance (e.g., antisociality, comorbid psychopathology) might decrease, potentially having two effects. One is an increased use of currently illicit substances but another is a lower conditional probability of users becoming dependent or addicted. It will be critical to carefully evaluate the effects of drug legalization and decriminalization not just on the basis of changes in use patterns and likelihood of developing SUDs, but also the complementary effects on the use and consequences of other illicit and legal substances (e.g., alcohol; e.g., Anderson & Rees, 2014).

Classification

The diagnosis and classification of SUD continues to evolve, albeit ever so slightly. In the DSM-5 (APA, 2013), the distinction between substance abuse and dependence was abandoned in favor of a single SUD diagnosis. However, the 11-item criteria set for DSM-5 remained largely the same as in DSM-IV (APA, 1994) with the exception that one criterion (craving) was added and one was dropped (legal problems). Although the newest edition of the International Classification of Diseases (ICD-11) is still being finalized, interim reports (e.g., International Union of Psychological Science, 2015) suggest little change, with the major distinction of substance dependence and harmful use remaining largely unchanged. As noted earlier, the traditional approach to diagnosis as exemplified in the DSM and ICD is being actively challenged by more endophenotypic approaches such as RDoC (Litten et al., 2015), although it may be some time before an RDoC-inspired addiction classification meets the standards necessary for clinical decision-making (Sher, 2015).

Etiology

The past decades have seen impressive advances in our understanding of the developmental psychopathology of substance use and SUDs. Much has been learned about the early antecedents and cascading processes of risk that set the stage for later substance-related problems, and one future direction that emerges from this work is the need to understand the ways in which early adversity and maltreatment influence the later development of risk for SUDs. Moreover, although the past 25 years have seen an expansion of a developmental psychopathology approach as applied to SUDs in adolescence and emerging adulthood, there has been less application of a developmental psychopathology perspective in terms of understanding substance use outcomes in mid- and later life. Age-specific etiological factors in mid- and late-life (including the effects of role transitions) are in need of future study. Future research on aging samples is warranted, particularly because higher alcohol use among the Baby Boom cohort forecasts increases in alcohol problems among older individuals (National Institute on Alcohol Abuse and Alcoholism, 2000). These alcohol outcomes are not only important in their own right, but are also of potential significance in influencing alcohol use in offspring and grandchildren. Thus, future research should continue to expand the study of risk and resilience processes across the life span and across generations.

Much has been learned about the importance of adolescence and emerging adulthood as developmental stages for the initiation and decline in alcohol use and alcohol problems, and these recent advances illuminate areas of desirable future research. Much needed large-sample, prospective studies to identify potential neurotoxic effects of adolescent substance exposure and their effects on cognitive functioning are currently being fielded, and more are about to be launched. These studies require multiple levels of measurement (including neuropsychological assessment and imaging studies of underlying neurocircuitry) and should be able to clarify the dose–response relation between adolescent substance use and potential cognitive sequelae and also should specify the roles of individual substances alone and in combination. Moreover, research is needed to illuminate the influence of adolescent exposure to psychoactive substances on the normative development of cognitive control from adolescence to adulthood. For example, although there appears to be complex, bidirectional relations between alcohol use and personality development (e.g., Littlefield, Sher, & Wood, 2009; Littlefield, Vergés, Wood, & Sher, 2012; Quinn, Stappenbeck, & Fromme, 2011), little is known about the dosage and duration of alcohol intake that might influence the development of cognitive control and psychosocial maturity at these ages and how different substances may exert similar or different types of relations. In addition, further research is needed to clarify the nature of sensitivity to various substances' rewarding and aversive effects during adolescence and the ways in which such developmentally specific alterations in sensitivity may influence trajectories of substance use.

In terms of methodological issues, the increasing sophistication of quantitative methods requires continuing improvement both in measurement methods and in understanding measurement equivalence across developmental periods. Such a developmental approach to measurement will be important in assessing the performance of the new DSM-5. Moreover, although assessments of SUDs are currently based on self-report, in the future it may be possible to incorporate the use of behavioral and psychophysiological methods that tap into underlying processes of addiction. Finally, given the growing interest in gene–environment interaction, it is important for future studies to adopt strategies that provide sufficient statistical power to detect interactions, use appropriate methods to probe the form of interactions, and minimize spurious findings through replication and controls for multiple testing. Studies of gene–environment interaction also need to test hypotheses within a developmental context (e.g., Park, Sher, Todorov, & Heath, 2011) and within the context of gene–environment correlation (i.e., passive, active, and evocative effects).

The literature on the etiology of SUDs has identified distinct, non–mutually exclusive pathways underlying the development of these disorders (see Chassin, Sher, Hussong, & Curran, 2013; Sher, Grekin, & Williams, 2004, for reviews). These main etiological pathways have been called "externalizing" or "deviance proneness" (involving a genetic susceptibility to develop disorders from the externalizing spectrum—including SUDs—that share a core predisposition to "behavioral undercontrol"), "internalizing" or "stress and negative affect" (involving regulation of acute or chronic negative affect—due to genetic factors and stressful or traumatic experiences—through substance use), and "pharmacological vulnerability" (involving individual differences in heightened reward or decreased sensitivity to punishment derived from substance use). In terms of etiological pathways, both the deviance proneness pathway and the stress and negative affect pathway are in need of studies that provide greater specificity in terms of the facets of "behavioral undercontrol" and "negative affect" that predict SUD outcomes. Understanding these facets on multiple levels (e.g., behavioral tasks, psychophysiological measures) is a particularly important and challenging task. Applying process models that illuminate the multiple processes underlying behavioral task performance may be particularly helpful in achieving this goal. Moreover, future studies should identify potential contextual influences (such as parenting and family influences) that affect the development of behavioral undercontrol and affect regulation. Identifying these potentially modifiable contextual factors is particularly important because they are potential targets for preventive and treatment interventions. In this regard, it will be important to study SUDs in terms of their boundaries with other forms of internalizing and externalizing psychopathology (see Tully & Iacono, Chap. 7, Vol. 2 in this *Handbook*, for an integrative model of the comorbidity of SUDs and other externalizing and internalizing disorders). Moreover, although we have made substantial progress in understanding the deviance proneness, stress and negative affect, and pharmacological vulnerability models, these models are not meant to be considered in isolation, but instead are systematically interrelated. For example, individuals with high levels of behavioral undercontrol may experience greater stress response-dampening benefits of alcohol and thus be more likely to use alcohol to cope with stress. Moreover, early trauma exposure may also be a common antecedent with important implications for both emotional and behavioral dysregulation. These mechanisms integrate all three hypothesized pathways, and future studies should examine such integrative effects.

Finally, future research should also continue to test these questions on multiple levels. We have already described the increasing number of genetically informative studies with specific suggestions for future methods, but other multiple-level studies are needed that include identifying underlying neural mechanisms, social network influences, and neighborhood and social policy influences. It is particularly important to continue to develop theory and empirical evidence to identify the ways in which developmental pathways of risk and resilience to SUDs might be influenced by varying cultural values across demographic groups (race, ethnicity, socioeconomic status, and gender). McKinney and Caetano (Chap. 14, Vol. 1) review the complex associations of substance use and outcomes with race and ethnicity and how these vary across gender, age, and level of acculturation.

Assessment

At present, an abundance of useful tools are available for clinicians and researchers interested in assessing substance use and dependence. These include structured diagnostic interviews for assessing SUDs and related psychopathology (Cottler et al., 1997); clinician and patient rating scales for assessing various aspects of dependence (Heatherton, Kozlowski, Frecker, & Fagerström, 1991; McLellan, Luborsky, Woody, & O'Brien, 1980; Horn, Wanberg, & Foster, 1990); timeline follow-back interviews (Sobell & Sobell, 1992) for taking detailed retrospective assessments of substance use; measures of constructs related to substance use motivations, such as explicit outcome expectancies (Fromme & D'Amico, 2000; Wetter et al., 1994) for different substances and "reasons" for use (Cooper, Russell, Skinner, & Windle, 1992); and specialized measures of dependence-related concepts such as "restraint" (Collins & Lapp, 1992) and craving (Sayette et al., 2000). Most of these assessments are based on traditional approaches to test/measure development via self-report or observation.

In attempting to identify new assessment approaches that are likely candidates for wider use in the future, three emerging technologies that represent a break with tradition stand out. These include the use of electronic diaries for assessing individuals in their natural environments in real time (e.g., Shiffman, Chap. 16, Vol. 2), the use of implicit measures of cognition to capture substance-relevant motivation that is automatic and possibly outside of one's awareness (e.g., Wiers, Field & Stacy, Chap. 9, Vol. 1), and transdermal real-time monitoring of substance use (e.g., Snell, Bhave, Takacs, & Tabakoff, Chap. 14, Vol. 2).

Each of these three innovations holds promise for assessment that extends far beyond the common current-day approach of using questionnaires and interviews to assess classical symptoms of SUDs and related phenomena. For example, traditionally, most substance use and dependence assessments have been "explicit," meaning that patients are asked to provide voluntary self-reports on their substance use and related variables. In contrast, implicit measurement approaches refer to a range of indirect measures that assesses automatic cognitive processes that might be outside of one's awareness. There are a number of different definitions as to what constitutes an implicit measure, although, as a group, they

tend to have certain characteristics in common to varying degrees. According to De Houwer (2006), these include (1) the individual being assessed is unaware of what she is being assessed for, (2) the individual does not have conscious access to the cognition that is being assessed, and (3) the individual has limited control over the outcome being assessed. As noted by Wiers and Stacy (2006), these approaches have great potential for supplementing traditional approaches because they "assess cognitive processes that are unavailable to introspection, are less sensitive to self-justification and social desirability, explain unique variance or different aspects of behavior [than explicit measures . . . and provide] . . . a new important bridge between diverse disciplines as well as human and animal research on addiction" (p. 1). Indeed, implicit measures can be used to assess what are possibly core features of dependence, such as incentive salience (Robinson & Berridge, 1993), by objectively assessing the extent that substance-related stimuli can "grab" one's attention or are positively or negatively valenced. Indeed, as we have argued elsewhere (Sher, Wolf, & Martinez, 2009), these measures might be particularly useful for tracking the course of dependence, even in individuals who are abstinent and "recovering" from substance dependence.

One type of implicit measure involves assessing the tendency to approach or avoid a given stimulus. In general, this research is based on the theory that approach or avoidance behaviors are automatically activated by appraisals of the valence of a stimulus. In contrast to research on attentional bias and word association, research on the relation between action tendencies and addiction has not as yet received as much attention. Although some paradigms use association tests like the Implicit Association Test (IAT) to gauge approach or withdrawal (e.g., attributes such as "approach" words or "avoidance" words are used instead of more valenced words), the most clearly prototypic tasks entail having the subject perform an action that either involves moving an object toward or away from drug-relevant or control stimuli—as in the stimulus response compatibility test (De Houwer, Crombez, Baeyens, & Hermans, 2001)—or having subjects either pull toward or push away a stimulus (e.g., using a joystick) that varies in its drug-relevance (e.g., Wiers, Rinck, Dictus, & van den Wildenberg, 2009). As noted by Wiers and colleagues in this *Handbook* (Chap. 9, Vol. 1), to date, these methods have been used successfully with alcohol, tobacco, and marijuana users, and they provide another potential novel assessment of the motivational significance of drugs. Additionally, to the extent that approach to drug stimuli is a learned phenomenon, it raises the possibility that treatments can be developed that can help individuals "unlearn" these acquired tendencies (Wiers, Gladwin, Hofmann, Salemink, & Ridderinkhof, 2013; see the later Treatment section for more details).

Although the implicit measurement approach is compelling on a theoretical level, at present, these measures have not met the psychometric standards that are expected in clinical assessment instruments (Buchner & Wippich, 2000; Cunningham, Preacher, & Banaji, 2001), and most practicing substance abuse clinicians and counselors are not accustomed to employing cognitive measures in their practice (neuropsychologists being an obvious exception to this generalization). However, if the promise of implicit measurement is fulfilled, then it seems likely that clinicians will find supplementation of explicit measures with implicit ones to be clinically highly useful.

There is a long history of using biomarkers from urine, blood, and expired air for assessing baseline levels of substance use and treatment compliance (Allen, Litten, Strid, & Sillanaukee, 2001; Benowitz et al., 2002; Conigrave, Davies, Haber, & Whitfield, 2003; Lakshman et al., 2001; McClure, 2002), and biomarker research remains an active area of clinical research. However, traditionally, biomarker assessments are conducted at the clinic during patient visits and are therefore not useful for characterizing the timing pattern of substance use. Indeed, because most biomarkers are used for screening and assessing compliance or abstinence, they ideally have a fairly long half-life so that recent use can be detected over a period of days. Although still in its infancy, real-time objective assessment of substance use has proved feasible. For example, Swift (2000) and Sakai, Mikulich-Gilbertson, Long, and Crowley (2006; see also Hawthorne & Wojcik, 2006) have shown that transdermal ethanol sensors (i.e., wearable electrochemical devices that sample the concentration of alcohol in sweat) are a valid means of measuring blood alcohol concentrations (BAC), aligning well with breath measures of BAC; additionally, they can easily be worn in drinking environments and can continuously sample the BAC over time. These devices can store data over days and thus provide a quantitative, continuous measure of BAC levels over an extended time frame. Further development of this technique to make it robust enough for clinical practice and extension of real-time, objective, in vivo assessment of substance use or exposure to other substances could represent an extraordinary leap forward in the assessment of substance use.

Treatment

DRUG DEVELOPMENT AND CORTICAL STIMULATION

One type of treatment that is under investigation involves medications that prevent drugs of abuse from entering the brain. For example, one strategy that has been attempted is to develop nicotine vaccines that bind antibodies to nicotine in the blood, thus preventing it from crossing the blood–brain barrier and acting on nicotinic receptors in the brain. Although randomized controlled trials have yet to show the efficacy of this approach (Hartmann-Boyce, Cahill, Hatsukami, & Cornuz, 2012), researchers believe that this type of strategy warrants further investigation (Fahim, Kessler, & Kalnik, 2013). Similar efforts are also being investigated for treating cocaine and methamphetamine dependence (Kosten, Domingo, Orson, & Kinsey, 2014).

A number of other treatments—some approved, some experimental—also exist and include drugs that work on multiple neurotransmitter systems and multiple addictive behaviors. For example, the antiepileptic drug topiramate has been used to treat alcohol dependence, obesity, and binge eating disorder (Johnson et al., 2007; Marazziti, Corsi, Baroni, Consoli, & Catena-Dell'Osso, 2012).

However, there have been fewer drugs developed to address the generalized changes that occur with chronic adaptation to drugs as described earlier with respect to Koob and Le Moal's (2001) allostatic perspective (as well as negative affect theory; Baker, Piper, McCarthy, Majeskie, & Fiore, 2004). These changes in the brain are thought to be attributable to overactivation of the hypothalamic-pituitary-adrenal (HPA) axis. Consequently, drugs that could restore normal function to this system and prevent the "negative downward spiral" of inducing further allostatic derangement by self-medicating with the drug of abuse would be of great value clinically. For example, drugs that could antagonize corticotropin-releasing factor might be helpful in "unstressing" the addicted brain (Koob, 2010). Clearly, the more we know about the underlying neurocircuitry of drug reinforcement and dependence, the more we can identify potential targets for novel therapies.

A recent study suggested that cortical stimulation might be a promising intervention for cocaine dependence. Chen et al. (2013) identified a group of rats that was resistant to foot shock contingent on cocaine self-administration. Electrophysiological examination revealed that shock-resistant rats exhibited prelimbic cortex hypoactivity. Moreover, in vivo optogenetic prelimbic cortex stimulation significantly decreased compulsive cocaine-seeking in these rats. Although translational research needs to be conducted, these results suggest that transcranial magnetic stimulation (Fraser & Rosen, 2012) might be an effective intervention to reduce compulsive cocaine use in humans.

SELF-REGULATION ENHANCEMENT

If we take the viewpoint that much of the underlying pathology of SUDs is attributable to externalizing psychopathology, an important target for treatment becomes strengthening self-regulation or self-control. Although traditionally self-regulation has been viewed as a relatively stable individual trait and measured by traditional personality traits measures such as "constraint" (Tellegen, 1991) and "conscientiousness" (e.g., Costa & McCrae, 1992), recent research suggests that there are highly mutable aspects of self-control. Indeed, Muraven and Baumeister (2000; see also Baumeister, Vohs, & Tice, 2007; and see Hagger, Wood, Stiff, & Chatzisarantis, 2010, for a meta-analysis) argue that self-control is "like a muscle" and, analogously, can be strengthened through regular use, decreases with lack of use, and exhibits short-term fatigue after recent use. This somewhat optimistic view of self-control provides novel approaches for training or rehabilitating self-control in persons suffering from SUDs and holds out the promise for highly generalized treatments across a range of externalizing problems and impediments to healthy functioning in school, the labor market, interpersonal relationships, and the more general pursuit of long-term goals. Some examples of self-control "exercises" that have led to improvements in other self-regulatory behaviors, such as smoking fewer cigarettes and drinking less alcohol, include regular physical exercise, dietary monitoring, money management planning, working on improving study habits, squeezing and holding a handgrip, and avoiding sweets (Baumeister, Gailliot, DeWall, & Oaten, 2006; Muraven, 2010). Additionally, it has been shown that self-control behaviors, including smoking cessation, are improved by restoring individuals' blood glucose to a sufficient level (Gailliot

& Baumeister, 2007). It seems likely that we will continue to see the development of a wide range of approaches that target self-control as a general treatment strategy for successful and healthy living. For instance, it has been suggested that self-control exercises might focus not only on strengthening self-regulation but also on better managing the limited self-control resources available (Baumeister & Alquist, 2009). These interventions could span the range of current treatments including behavioral approaches, cognitive-behavioral approaches, mindfulness training (Baer, 2003), and pharmacological interventions that target neural circuitry involved in self-regulation (Vohs & Baumeister, 2004).

TREATMENTS FOR INDIVIDUALS AT VARIOUS STAGES OF DEPENDENCE

Extending treatment to "less severe" cases requires not only developing new treatment approaches, such as brief intervention and motivational interviewing (Dunn, Deroo, & Rivara, 2001; Moyer, Finney, Swearingen, & Vergun, 2002), but also suggests the utility of innovative modifications to existing treatments. For example, naltrexone, which was originally approved for treatment for alcohol dependence (O'Malley et al., 1992), has been reformulated in a long-acting, injectable form (Garbutt et al., 2005) that might be useful for treating severe levels of dependence characterized by poor compliance. At the other end of the scale, there have been studies documenting the viability of using "targeted" (i.e., situational) dosing of naltrexone for "early problem drinkers" (Kranzler et al., 2003; O'Malley et al., 2015). Thus, with respect to broadening the base of treatment to a wider spectrum of the substance-using population, we can envision innovations that are both wider (i.e., bringing in new approaches) and deeper (i.e., tailoring existing approaches to a more diverse range of clients).

PATIENT-TREATMENT MATCHING REVISITED

Although empirical evidence in support of patient-treatment matching has been equivocal (e.g., Project MATCH Research Group, 1998), this does not mean that the general strategy is flawed and further efforts should be abandoned. A potential limitation of major efforts such as Project Match (Project MATCH Research Group, 1997) is that the designers of these studies examined previously established treatments and then hypothesized individual differences in treatment responsiveness conditional upon treatment strategy. Although a reasonable strategy to explore, other more etiologically relevant approaches to patient-treatment matching may be more useful. For example, rather than taking previously established treatments as a starting point and then assessing relevant individual differences that may moderate treatment effects, the reverse strategy could be employed. For example, one could look at important individual differences (e.g., personality, motives for substance use) and develop treatments targeted at predominant substance use motivations. Such an approach has been explored by Conrod, Pihl, Stewart, and Dongier (2000), who have suggested that classifying individuals by differences in factors such as anxiety sensitivity and sensation seeking tends to reveal groups that are also different in terms of addictive psychopathology and coping skills deficits and that these differences may be used as specific targets for intervention. That is, interventions that target individuals' particular underlying motivations for use might be more effective than interventions that do not target such underlying motivations (Conrod, Castellanos, & Mackie, 2008; Conrod et al., 2000).

Perhaps nowhere is the promise of patient-treatment matching more exciting than in the area of pharmacogenomics. A vision of the National Institute of Health is *personalized medicine*, in which preventive and treatment efforts are tailored to an individual's unique health profile informed by genomics, proteomics, and other relevant fields (Culliton, 2006; Zerhouni, 2006). Pharmacogenomics represents one facet of personalized medicine and is the field that addresses how specific pharmacological treatments interact in unique ways with an individual's genotype (Hutchison, 2010).

Because SUDs arise from the use of specific drugs, and there is genetic variation in susceptibility to different drugs of abuse, pharmacogenomics plays an increasingly important part in our understanding of SUD etiology, holding out hope that we will be able to profile risk based on an individual's genomic profile. Thus, a long-term goal of modern health care research is not only to make health care in the future more personalized but also to make it *predictive* (i.e., anticipating the health risks before manifest disorder based on individual characteristics) and *preemptive* (i.e., intervening to prevent the development of specific diseases; Zerhouni, 2006). At present, such models for medicine, as exemplified in the new "precision medicine" initiative (Collins & Varmus, 2015) for cancer, are aspirational for SUD treatment, but, as we know more about how specific genes work to promote the development of SUDs,

we will have a rational guide for devising pharmacological strategies to preemptively intervene early in the course of disorder (e.g., Edenberg & Kranzler, 2005). However, given the relatively small effect sizes associated with vulnerability genes for most mental disorders (including SUDs; Kendler, Myers, & Prescott, 2007; Wang et al., 2012), it is not clear how effective pre-emptive interventions based on genotype alone are likely to be.

However, data are beginning to accrue that indicate that there are important, genetically based individual differences in response to medications used to treat substance dependence. Among the most discussed of these is a report by Oslin et al. (2003; see also Oslin, Berrettini, & O'Brien, 2006) that found that allelic variation in the μ-opioid receptor moderated treatment response to naltrexone in alcohol-dependent individuals. In this study, the treatment effect for naltrexone varied as a function of genotype which, in turn, was unrelated to outcome in the placebo arm of the study. This result was later replicated in the multisite COMBINE Study (Anton et al., 2008). Moreover, recent evidence suggests that genetic moderation of treatment outcome is not limited to pharmacotherapy but also plays a role in psychosocial interventions such as motivational enhancement therapy (Feldstein, Ewing, LaChance, Bryan, & Hutchison, 2009). Given the range of neuronal systems targeted by existing treatments and rapidly increasing knowledge concerning functional polymorphisms associated with these systems, we can expect rapid accumulation of findings concerning the extent to which relevant genotypes are important etiologically with respect to moderating reinforcing effects of psychoactive substances and with respect to moderating treatment effects (e.g., Edenberg & Kranzler, 2005; Hutchison, 2010; Kenna, McGeary, & Swift, 2004*a*, 2004*b*; Lichtermann, Franke, Maier, & Rao, 2000). These findings will have to be evaluated in terms of their clinical significance, and issues such as variations in allele frequencies among ethnic groups will need to be considered before disseminating pharmacogenomic approaches into clinical practice (Ray & Hutchison, 2011).

RE-EXAMINING EXISTING TREATMENTS IN LIGHT OF EVOLVING SCIENCE

As science progresses, theories are revised in light of new data and new insights. Even some of the most basic notions of behavioral science are revised in light of continuing research. For example, principles of learning (especially operant and Pavlovian conditioning) have guided the development of treatments for SUDs for many years, including aversion therapies (e.g., emetic and covert conditioning for alcohol dependence; Howard & Howard, 2001) and extinction-based procedures such as cue-exposure treatments (Heather & Bradley, 1990). Although such approaches are well motivated theoretically, to date they have not been shown to be a highly effective strategy and produce inconsistent results (Martin, LaRowe, & Malcolm, 2010).

However, in recent years, our views of what takes place in both acquiring and retrieving conditioned associations and during extinction has changed considerably. For example, the great importance of context on learning (especially for later learning that would be important in changing problematic behaviors) is being increasingly recognized (Bouton, 2000, 2002). Perhaps more important, the notion that extinction and counterconditioning procedures "destroy" prior learning is most likely incorrect, and extinction, rather than causing "unlearning," most likely lays down alternative learning that competes with what was learned previously (Bouton, 2002; Todd, Vurbic, & Bouton, 2014). Conklin and Tiffany (2002) describe a number of ways that we can use new knowledge regarding the nature of conditioning to develop more effective exposure-based treatments that have greater potential to be durable and show clinically necessary generalization. More recently, Laborda, McConnell, and Miller (2011) review newly developed techniques that aim at deepening extinction (e.g., massive extinction trials), linking extinction and test context (e.g., use of retrieval cues) and achieving both through the same procedure (e.g., extinction in multiple contexts). Although promising, the use of these techniques needs to be further investigated in clinical trials.

Additionally, as the neurobiology of learning continues to unfold, we can hope to develop various pharmacological interventions to facilitate the degree of learning that occurs. For example, recent research has shown promising effects of D-cycloserine (a partial NMDA receptor agonist) on facilitating extinction learning in the treatment of phobias in humans (Ressler et al., 2004), and preclinical work suggests that certain compounds can modulate the nature of drug-related associations in rodents (Feltenstein & See, 2007; Schroeder & Packard, 2004). To date, the findings have been promising in laboratory models of substance use but not with human patients, although this remains an active area of research (Kiefer et al., 2015; Myers & Carlezon, 2012).

Novel learning approaches have been inspired by recent research on implicit cognition in addiction. If automatic approach tendencies are learned, it seems reasonable to see if these can be retrained into avoidance tendencies. The same basic laboratory paradigms that are used to assess approach and avoidance tendencies in substance users (e.g., pulling or pushing a joystick) can be used to retrain these tendencies by arranging contingencies so that a patient's task is to, without explicit awareness, push drug cues away and pull nondrug cues toward oneself. Such an approach was employed by Wiers, Eberl, Rinck, Becker, and Lindenmeyer (2011), who found this to be an effective, adjunctive strategy in a controlled trial with a 1-year follow-up (this approach was subsequently replicated in a new sample; see Eberl et al., 2013). Similarly, experimental treatments aimed at retraining attention away from drug cues have been developed (e.g., Schoenmakers, Wiers, Jones, Bruce, & Jansen, 2007; Schoenmakers et al., 2010) and show initial promise. One of the potentially exciting aspects of these new approaches based on implicit cognition is that they hold promise for being used in less-motivated participants, and they increase the range of treatment options available to those seeking help.

DISSEMINATING AND PAYING FOR NEW TREATMENTS

Regardless of the efficacy of new and existing treatments, their effectiveness in dealing with the burden of substance-related disorder and disability will be limited if they are not employed by "real-world" providers with treatment-seeking populations. Unfortunately, the area of SUD treatment has historically been slow to adopt evidence-based treatments, and, at least with respect to alcohol use disorders, it has been claimed that "the most effective treatments . . . are least often used . . . whereas the least effective treatments are most often used" (Gotham, 2004, p. 160). Barriers to successful diffusion of SUD treatments from research settings to community settings occur at each step of the dissemination process, including the level of patients, counselors, supervisors, administrators, and the treatment delivery system (Fals-Stewart, Logsdon, & Birchler, 2004). Developing and evaluating strategies for successful implementation of evidence-based practices should be a major focus of treatment-related research in the future. Models of technology transfer (e.g., Rogers, 2003) may represent one useful approach to conceptualizing diffusion of innovation and actively seeding new treatments in appropriate settings (see Gotham, 2004), but until there are major changes in our ability to successfully diffuse new treatments into the clinic, the possibility of improving "real-world" treatment outcomes will be severely limited.

Clearly, the future of SUD treatment requires not only the continued development of efficacious treatments but concerted efforts by treatment developers, treatment providers, and other stakeholders to disseminate these into practice. Thoughtful implementation plans, perhaps coordinated by government agencies (e.g., Saxon & McCarty, 2005), are probably necessary when the nature of treatments and how they are delivered require systemic changes of provider networks and treatment systems. Implementation of costly treatments, especially to drug abusers who are often dependent on public treatment systems, will require careful cost-benefit analyses if public and private payers of treatment will be persuaded of the value of providing and paying for expensive new treatments (Cartwright, 2000; Cartwright & Solano, 2003).

DELIVERING ADDICTION SERVICES OVER THE INTERNET

The development of the Internet, especially over the past 10 years, has changed the way in which a number of human activities are conducted (e.g., delivery of news and entertainment, shopping, information retrieval, and forming and maintaining interpersonal relations, to name just a few). The Internet's ability to engage individuals who are widely dispersed geographically efficiently, at low cost, and with a degree of anonymity represents just a few features that make it attractive as a means for delivering services to persons with SUDs. Internet interventions for nicotine and alcohol use disorders have been proliferating for several years and, although varying in form and content, often include screening tools, informational resources and links, online journals, and discussion forums (Copeland & Martin, 2004). Those interventions can be easily disseminated, are conveniently available at all hours of the day (making them particularly useful for some subpopulations such as college students, Escoffery et al., 2005), are readily accessible to a large proportion of substance users at present (Cunningham, Selby, Kypri, & Humphreys, 2006), can provide rapid questionnaire feedback, and may be less expensive than traditional therapy involving on-site face-to-face contact with a therapist or even telephone-based treatments (Walker, Roffman, Picciano, & Stephens, 2007).

The potential reach of the Internet for various forms of social networking is almost limitless, and online affiliation with a wide range of different substance recovery groups (e.g., Alcoholics Anonymous, Narcotics Anonymous, and Smart Recovery) has gained popularity among recovering substance users throughout the world (Hall & Tidwell, 2003). It seems likely that the Internet's ability to foster virtual communities of individuals with common interests could provide new opportunities for various social support and recovery groups.

To date, little is known concerning the relative effectiveness of Internet-based interventions compared to more traditionally administered interventions. The few existing studies examining the efficacy of these types of interventions suggest that Internet-based treatments are effective (Gainsbury & Blaszczynski, 2011), but little is known at present about the precise mechanisms that would make these types of interventions work most effectively (Bewick et al., 2008). Consequently, we do not yet know how to optimize Internet-based services, for whom they are most appropriate (Copeland & Martin, 2004), and how best to integrate these services into the broader health care system.

In predicting the future of treatment for SUDs, one prediction seems almost certain: the Internet will become an increasing presence in our lives and come to serve increasing functions, including those related to substance use treatment. As the portability of the Web continues to increase (i.e., the "mobile web") with smartphones on high-speed data networks, each individual has increased opportunity to access some forms of services at a time and place that is convenient for him or her.

Along with these opportunities come new challenges, such as ensuring the quality of services provided, confidentiality of "patient" data, continuum of care, licensing of providers, and legal and administrative issues related to the geographic location of service delivery. It is anticipated that, over time, market and cultural forces coupled with provider concerns will likely goad integration of the Internet into the larger health care delivery system (Cunningham, 2007).

References

Alberts, B., Kirschner, M. W., Tilghman, S., & Varmus, H. (2014). Rescuing US biomedical research from its systemic flaws. *Proceedings of the National Academy of Sciences*, *111*(16), 5773–5777.

Allen, J. P., Litten, R. Z., Strid, N., & Sillanaukee, P. (2001). The role of biomarkers in alcoholism medication trials. *Alcoholism: Clinical and Experimental Research*, *25*(8), 1119–1125.

American Psychiatric Association (APA). (1994). *Diagnostic and statistical manual of mental disorders* (4th ed.). Washington, DC: Author.

American Psychiatric Association (APA). (2013). *Diagnostic and statistical manual of mental disorders* (5th ed.). Washington, DC: Author.

Anderson, D. M., & Rees, D. I. (2014). The legalization of recreational marijuana: How likely is the worst-case scenario? *Journal of Policy Analysis and Management*, *33*(1), 221–232.

Anton, R. F., Oroszi, G., O'Malley, S., Couper, D., Swift, R., Pettinati, H., & Goldman, D. (2008). An evaluation of μ-opioid receptor (OPRM1) as a predictor of naltrexone response in the treatment of alcohol dependence: Results from the Combined Pharmacotherapies and Behavioral Interventions for Alcohol Dependence (COMBINE) study. *Archives of General Psychiatry*, *65*(2), 135–144.

Avena, N. M., Gold, J. A., Kroll, C., & Gold, M. S. (2012). Further developments in the neurobiology of food and addiction: Update on the state of the science. *Nutrition*, *28*(4), 341–343.

Baer, R. A. (2003). Mindfulness training as a clinical intervention: A conceptual and empirical review. *Clinical Psychology: Science and Practice*, *10*(2), 125–143.

Baker, T. B., Piper, M. E., McCarthy, D. E., Majeskie, M. R., & Fiore, M. C. (2004). Addiction motivation reformulated: An affective processing model of negative reinforcement. *Psychological Review*, *111*(1), 33–51.

Bancroft, J., & Vukadinovic, Z. (2004). Sexual addiction, sexual compulsivity, sexual impulsivity, or what? Toward a theoretical model. *Journal of Sex Research*, *41*(3), 225–234.

Baumann, M. H., Solis, E., Watterson, L. R., Marusich, J. A., Fantegrossi, W. E., & Wiley, J. L. (2014). Baths salts, spice, and related designer drugs: The science behind the headlines. *Journal of Neuroscience*, *34*(46), 15150–15158.

Baumeister, R. F., & Alquist, J. L. (2009). Self-regulation as a limited resource: Strength model of control and depletion. In J. P. Forgas, R. F. Baumeister, & D. M. Tice (Eds.), *Psychology of self-regulation: Cognitive, affective, and motivational processes* (pp. 21–35). New York: Taylor & Francis.

Baumeister, R. F., Gailliot, M., DeWall, C. N., & Oaten, M. (2006). Self-regulation and personality: How interventions increase regulatory success, and how depletion moderates the effects of traits on behavior. *Journal of Personality*, *74*(6), 1773–1802.

Baumeister, R. F., Vohs, K. D., & Tice, D. M. (2007). The strength model of self-control. *Current Directions in Psychological Science*, *16*(6), 351–355.

Benowitz, N. L., & Goniewicz, M. L. (2013). The regulatory challenge of electronic cigarettes. *Journal of the American Medical Association*, *310*(7), 685–686.

Benowitz, N. L., Jacob, P., Hall, S., Tsoh, J., Ahijevych, K., Jarvis, M. J., . . . Velicer, W. (2002). Biochemical verification of tobacco use and cessation. *Nicotine and Tobacco Research*, *4*(2), 149–159.

Berczik, K., Szabó, A., Griffiths, M. D., Kurimay, T., Kun, B., Urbán, R., & Demetrovics, Z. (2012). Exercise addiction: Symptoms, diagnosis, epidemiology, and etiology. *Substance Use & Misuse*, *47*(4), 403–417.

Bewick, B. M., Trusler, K., Barkham, M., Hill, A. J., Cahill, J., & Mulhern, B. (2008). The effectiveness of web-based interventions designed to decrease alcohol consumption—a systematic review. *Preventive Medicine*, *47*(1), 17–26.

Bickel, W., Mueller, E. T., MacKillop, J., & Yi, R. (2016). Behavioral-economic and neuroeconomic perspectives on addiction. In K. J. Sher (Ed.), *The Oxford Handbook of Substance Use and Substance Use Disorders* (Vol. 1, pp. 422–446). New York: Oxford University Press. doi:10.1093/oxfordhb/9780199381708.013.005

Blanco, C., Myers, J., & Kendler, K. S. (2012). Gambling, disordered gambling and their association with major depression and substance use: A web-based cohort and twin-sibling study. *Psychological Medicine*, *42*(03), 497–508.

Block, J. J. (2008). Issues for DSM-V: Internet addiction. *American Journal of Psychiatry*, *165*, 306–307.

Bouton, M. E. (2000). A learning theory perspective on lapse, relapse, and the maintenance of behavior change. *Health Psychology*, *19*(1S), 57–63.

Bouton, M. E. (2002). Context, ambiguity, and unlearning: Sources of relapse after behavioral extinction. *Biological Psychiatry*, *52*(10), 976–986.

Brennan, R., & Van Hout, M. C. (2012). Miaow miaow: A review of the new psychoactive drug mephedrone. *Drugs and Alcohol Today*, *12*(4), 241–253.

Breslau, N., Johnson, E. O., Hiripi, E., & Kessler, R. (2001). Nicotine dependence in the United States: Prevalence, trends, and smoking persistence. *Archives of General Psychiatry*, *58*(9), 810–816.

Buchanan, J. F., & Brown, C. R. (1988). Designer drugs. *Medical Toxicology and Adverse Drug Experience*, *3*(1), 1–17.

Buchner, A., & Wippich, W. (2000). On the reliability of implicit and explicit memory measures. *Cognitive Psychology*, *40*(3), 227–259.

Bullen, C., Howe, C., Laugesen, M., McRobbie, H., Parag, V., Williman, J., & Walker, N. (2013). Electronic cigarettes for smoking cessation: A randomized controlled trial. *Lancet*, *382*(9905), 1629–1637.

Cahn, Z., & Siegel, M. (2011). Electronic cigarettes as a harm reduction strategy for tobacco control: A step forward or a repeat of past mistakes? *Journal of Public Health Policy*, *32*(1), 16–31.

Carroll, F., Lewin, A. H., Mascarella, S. W., Seltzman, H. H., & Reddy, P. A. (2012). Designer drugs: A medicinal chemistry perspective. *Annals of the New York Academy of Sciences*, *1248*(1), 18–38.

Carroll, L. (1872). *Through the looking glass and what Alice found there*. London: MacMillian.

Cartwright, W. S. (2000). Cost–benefit analysis of drug treatment services: Review of the literature. *Journal of Mental Health Policy and Economics*, *3*(1), 11–26.

Cartwright, W. S., & Solano, P. L. (2003). The economics of public health: Financing drug abuse treatment services. *Health Policy*, *66*(3), 247–260.

Chassin, L., Sher, K. J., Hussong, A., & Curran, P. (2013). The developmental psychopathology of alcohol use and alcohol disorders: Research achievements and future directions. *Development and Psychopathology*, *25*(4pt2), 1567–1584.

Chen, B. T., Yau, H. J., Hatch, C., Kusumoto-Yoshida, I., Cho, S. L., Hopf, F. W., & Bonci, A. (2013). Rescuing cocaine-induced prefrontal cortex hypoactivity prevents compulsive cocaine seeking. *Nature*, *496*(7445), 359–362.

Cleckley, H. M. (1941). *The mask of sanity*. St. Louis, MO: Mosby.

Collins, F. S., & Tabak, L. A. (2014). NIH plans to enhance reproducibility. *Nature, 505*(7485), 612–613.

Collins, F. S., & Varmus, H. (2015). A new initiative on precision medicine. *New England Journal of Medicine, 372*(9), 793–795.

Collins, R. L., & Lapp, W. M. (1992). The Temptation and Restraint Inventory for measuring drinking restraint. *British Journal of Addiction, 87*(4), 625–633.

Conigrave, K. M., Davies, P., Haber, P., & Whitfield, J. B. (2003). Traditional markers of excessive alcohol use. *Addiction, 98*(s2), 31–43.

Conklin, C. A., & Tiffany, S. T. (2002). Applying extinction research and theory to cue-exposure addiction treatments. *Addiction, 97*(2), 155–167.

Conrod, P. J., Castellanos, N., & Mackie, C. (2008). Personality-targeted interventions delay the growth of adolescent drinking and binge drinking. *Journal of Child Psychology and Psychiatry, 49*(2), 181–190.

Conrod, P. J., Pihl, R. O., Stewart, S. H., & Dongier, M. (2000). Validation of a system of classifying female substance abusers on the basis of personality and motivational risk factors for substance abuse. *Psychology of Addictive Behaviors, 14*(3), 243–256.

Cooper, M. L., Russell, M., Skinner, J. B., & Windle, M. (1992). Development and validation of a three-dimensional measure of drinking motives. *Psychological Assessment, 4*(2), 123–132.

Copeland, J., & Martin, G. (2004). Web-based interventions for substance use disorders: A qualitative review. *Journal of Substance Abuse Treatment, 26*(2), 109–116.

Corazza, O., Schifano, F., Farre, M., Deluca, P., Davey, Z., Drummond, C., . . . Scherbaum, N. (2011). Designer drugs on the internet: A phenomenon out-of-control? The emergence of hallucinogenic drug Bromo-Dragonfly. *Current Clinical Pharmacology, 6*(2), 125–129.

Costa, P. T., & McCrae, R. R. (1992). Four ways five factors are basic. *Personality and Individual Differences, 13*(6), 653–665.

Cottler, L. B., Grant, B. F., Blaine, J., Mavreas, V., Pull, C., Hasin, D., . . . Mager, D. (1997). Concordance of DSM-IV alcohol and drug use disorder criteria and diagnoses as measured by AUDADIS-ADR, CIDI and SCAN. *Drug and Alcohol Dependence, 47*(3), 195–205.

Culliton, B. J. (2006). Extracting knowledge from science: A conversation with Elias Zerhouni. *Health Affairs, 25*(3), w94–w103.

Cunningham, J. A. (2007). Internet-based interventions for alcohol, tobacco and other substances of abuse. In P. M. Miller & D. Kavanagh (Eds.), *Translation of addictions science into practice* (pp. 399–416). San Diego, CA: Elsevier.

Cunningham, J. A., Selby, P. L., Kypri, K., & Humphreys, K. N. (2006). Access to the Internet among drinkers, smokers and illicit drug users: Is it a barrier to the provision of interventions on the World Wide Web? *Informatics for Health and Social Care, 31*(1), 53–58.

Cunningham, W. A., Preacher, K. J., & Banaji, M. R. (2001). Implicit attitude measures: Consistency, stability, and convergent validity. *Psychological Science, 12*(2), 163–170.

Cuthbert, B. N. (2015). Research Domain Criteria: toward future psychiatric nosologies. *Dialogues in Clinical Neuroscience, 17*(1), 89–97.

De Houwer, J. (2006). What are implicit measures and why are we using them. In R. W. Wiers & A. W. Stacy (Eds.), *The handbook of implicit cognition and addiction* (pp. 11–28). Thousand Oaks, CA: Sage.

De Houwer, J., Crombez, G., Baeyens, F., & Hermans, D. (2001). On the generality of the affective Simon effect. *Cognition & Emotion, 15*(2), 189–206.

Derefinko, K. J., & Pelham, W. E. (2016). ADHD and substance use. In K. J. Sher (Ed.), *The Oxford Handbook of Substance Use and Substance Use Disorders* (Vol. 2, pp. 60–87). New York: Oxford University Press. doi: 10.1093/oxfordhb/9780199381708.013.18

Dunn, C., Deroo, L., & Rivara, F. P. (2001). The use of brief interventions adapted from motivational interviewing across behavioral domains: A systematic review. *Addiction, 96*(12), 1725–1742.

Eberl, C., Wiers, R. W., Pawelczack, S., Rinck, M., Becker, E. S., & Lindenmeyer, J. (2013). Approach bias modification in alcohol dependence: Do clinical effects replicate and for whom does it work best? *Developmental Cognitive Neuroscience, 4*, 38–51.

Edenberg, H. J., & Kranzler, H. R. (2005). The contribution of genetics to addiction therapy approaches. *Pharmacology & Therapeutics, 108*(1), 86–93.

Escoffery, C., Miner, K. R., Adame, D. D., Butler, S., McCormick, L., & Mendell, E. (2005). Internet use for health information among college students. *Journal of American College Health, 53*(4), 183–188.

Everitt, B. J., & Robbins, T. W. (2005). Neural systems of reinforcement for drug addiction: From actions to habits to compulsion. *Nature Neuroscience, 8*(11), 1481–1489.

Fahim, R. E., Kessler, P. D., & Kalnik, M. W. (2013). Therapeutic vaccines against tobacco addiction. *Expert Review of Vaccines, 12*, 333–342.

Fals-Stewart, W., Logsdon, T., & Birchler, G. R. (2004). Diffusion of an empirically supported treatment for substance abuse: An organizational autopsy of technology transfer success and failure. *Clinical Psychology: Science and Practice, 11*(2), 177–182.

Fattore, L., & Fratta, W. (2011). Beyond THC: The new generation of cannabinoid designer drugs. *Frontiers in Behavioral Neuroscience, 5*, 60.

Feldstein, M. W., Ewing, S. W., LaChance, H. A., Bryan, A., & Hutchison, K. E. (2009). Do genetic and individual risk factors moderate the efficacy of motivational enhancement therapy? Drinking outcomes with an emerging adult sample. *Addiction Biology, 14*(3), 356–365.

Feltenstein, M. W., & See, R. E. (2007). NMDA receptor blockade in the basolateral amygdala disrupts consolidation of stimulus-reward memory and extinction learning during reinstatement of cocaine-seeking in an animal model of relapse. *Neurobiology of Learning and Memory, 88*(4), 435–444.

Foddy, B., & Savulescu, J. (2010). A liberal account of addiction. *Philosophy, Psychiatry, & Psychology, 17*(1), 1–22.

Fraser, P. E., & Rosen, A. C. (2012). Transcranial direct current stimulation and behavioral models of smoking addiction. *Frontiers in Psychiatry, 3*, 79.

Fromme, K., & D'Amico, E. J. (2000). Measuring adolescent alcohol outcome expectancies. *Psychology of Addictive Behaviors, 14*(2), 206–212.

Gailliot, M. T., & Baumeister, R. F. (2007). The physiology of willpower: Linking blood glucose to self-control. *Personality and Social Psychology Review, 11*(4), 303–327.

Gainsbury, S., & Blaszczynski, A. (2011). A systematic review of Internet-based therapy for the treatment of addictions. *Clinical Psychology Review, 31*(3), 490–498.

Garbutt, J. C., Kranzler, H. R., O'Malley, S. S., Gastfriend, D. R., Pettinati, H. M., Silverman, B. L., … Vivitrex Study Group. (2005). Efficacy and tolerability of long-acting injectable naltrexone for alcohol dependence: A randomized controlled trial. *Journal of the American Medical Association*, *293*(13), 1617–1625.

Gold, S. N., & Heffner, C. L. (1998). Sexual addiction: Many conceptions, minimal data. *Clinical Psychology Review*, *18*(3), 367–381.

Gotham, H. J. (2004). Diffusion of mental health and substance abuse treatments: Development, dissemination, and implementation. *Clinical Psychology: Science and Practice*, *11*(2), 160–176.

Grant, J. E., Odlaug, B. L., & Potenza, M. N. (2007). Addicted to hair pulling? How an alternate model of trichotillomania may improve treatment outcome. *Harvard Review of Psychiatry*, *15*(2), 80–85.

Grant, J. E., & Potenza, M. N. (2005). Pathological gambling and other "behavioral" addictions. In R. J. Frances, S. I. Miller, & A. H. Mack (Eds.), *Clinical textbook of addictive disorders* (3rd ed., pp. 303–320). New York: Guilford.

Hagger, M. S., Wood, C., Stiff, C., & Chatzisarantis, N. L. (2010). Ego depletion and the strength model of self-control: A meta-analysis. *Psychological Bulletin*, *136*(4), 495–525.

Hall, M. J., & Tidwell, W. C. (2003). Internet recovery for substance abuse and alcoholism: An exploratory study of service users. *Journal of Substance Abuse Treatment*, *24*(2), 161–167.

Hamilton, K. R., Mitchell, M. R., Wing, V. C., Balodis, I. M., Bickel, W. K., Fillmore, M., … Moeller, F. G. (2015). Choice impulsivity: Definitions, measurement issues, and clinical implications. *Personality Disorders: Theory, Research, and Treatment*, *6*(2), 182–198.

Harb, M. R., & Almeida, O. F. X. (2014). Pavlovian conditioning and cross-sensitization studies raise challenges to the hypothesis that overeating is an addictive behavior. *Translational Psychiatry*, *4*(4), e387.

Hartmann-Boyce, J., Cahill, K., Hatsukami, D., & Cornuz, J. (2012). Nicotine vaccines for smoking cessation. *Cochrane Database of Systematic Reviews*, *8*, CD007072.

Hawthorne, J. S., & Wojcik, M. H. (2006). Transdermal alcohol measurement: A review of the literature. *Canadian Society of Forensic Science Journal*, *39*(2), 65–71.

Heather, N., & Bradley, B. P. (1990). Cue exposure as a practical treatment for addictive disorders: Why are we waiting? *Addictive Behaviors*, *15*(4), 335–337.

Heatherton, T. F., Kozlowski, L. T., Frecker, R. C., & Fagerström, K. O. (1991). The Fagerström test for nicotine dependence: A revision of the Fagerstrom Tolerance Questionnaire. *British Journal of Addiction*, *86*(9), 1119–1127.

Hebebrand, J., Albayrak, Ö., Adan, R., Antel, J., Dieguez, C., de Jong, J., … Dickson, S. L. (2014). "Eating addiction," rather than "food addiction," better captures addictive-like eating behavior. *Neuroscience & Biobehavioral Reviews*, *47*, 295–306.

Hill, S. L., & Thomas, S. H. (2011). Clinical toxicology of newer recreational drugs. *Clinical Toxicology*, *49*(8), 705–719.

Horn, J. L., Wanberg, K., & Foster, F. M. (1990). *Guide to the alcohol use inventory (AUI)*. Minneapolis, MN: NCS Pearson.

Howard, M. O., & Howard, M. O. (2001). Pharmacological aversion treatment of alcohol dependence. I. Production and prediction of conditioned alcohol aversion. *American Journal of Drug and Alcohol Abuse*, *27*(3), 561–585.

Hughes, J. R., & Brandon, T. H. (2003). A softer view of hardening. *Nicotine & Tobacco*, *5*(6) 961–962.

Hutchison, K. E. (2010). Substance use disorders: Realizing the promise of pharmacogenomics and personalized medicine. *Annual Review of Clinical Psychology*, *6*, 577–589.

International Union of Psychological Science. (2015). *2014 Annual report of the International Union of Psychological Science to the American Psychological Association: Revision of World Health Organization's ICD-10 mental and behavioural disorders*. Geneva: World Health Organization.

Ioannidis, J. P. (2012). Why science is not necessarily self-correcting. *Perspectives on Psychological Science*, *7*(6), 645–654.

Johnson, B. A., Rosenthal, N., Capece, J. A., Wiegand, F., Mao, L., Beyers, K., … Swift, R. M. (2007). Topiramate for treating alcohol dependence: A randomized controlled trial. *Journal of the American Medical Association*, *298*(14), 1641–1651.

Kendler, K. S., Myers, J., & Prescott, C. A. (2007). Specificity of genetic and environmental risk factors for symptoms of cannabis, cocaine, alcohol, caffeine, and nicotine dependence. *Archives of General Psychiatry*, *64*(11), 1313–1320.

Kenna, G. A., McGeary, J. E., & Swift, R. M. (2004a). Pharmacotherapy, pharmacogenomics, and the future of alcohol dependence treatment, part 1. *American Journal of Health-System Pharmacy*, *61*(21), 2272–2279.

Kenna, G. A., McGeary, J. E., & Swift, R. M. (2004b). Pharmacotherapy, pharmacogenomics, and the future of alcohol dependence treatment, Part 2. *American Journal of Health System Pharmacy*, *61*(22), 2380–2388.

Kiefer, F., Kirsch, M., Bach, P., Hoffmann, S., Reinhard, I., Jorde, A., … Vollstädt-Klein, S. (2015). Effects of d-cycloserine on extinction of mesolimbic cue reactivity in alcoholism: A randomized placebo-controlled trial. *Psychopharmacology*, *232*, 2353–2362.

Koob, G. F. (2010). The role of CRF and CRF-related peptides in the dark side of addiction. *Brain Research*, *1314*, 3–14.

Koob, G. F., & Le Moal, M. (2001). Drug addiction, dysregulation of reward, and allostasis. *Neuropsychopharmacology*, *24*(2), 97–129.

Kosten, T., Domingo, C., Orson, F., & Kinsey, B. (2014). Vaccines against stimulants: Cocaine and MA. *British Journal of Clinical Pharmacology*, *77*(2), 368–374.

Kranzler, H. R., Armeli, S., Tennen, H., Blomqvist, O., Oncken, C., Petry, N., & Feinn, R. (2003). Targeted naltrexone for early problem drinkers. *Journal of Clinical Psychopharmacology*, *23*(3), 294–304.

Laborda, M. A., McConnell, B. L., & Miller, R. R. (2011). Behavioral techniques to reduce relapse after exposure therapy. In T. R. Schachtman & S. Reilly (Eds.), *Associative learning and conditioning theory: Human and non-human applications* (pp. 79–103). New York: Oxford University Press.

Lakshman, R., Tsutsumi, M., Ghosh, P., Takase, S., Anni, H., Nikolaeva, O., … Rao, M. N. (2001). Alcohol biomarkers: Clinical significance and biochemical basis. *Alcoholism: Clinical and Experimental Research*, *25*(s1), 67S–70S.

Lesieur, H. R. (1988). Altering the DSM-III criteria for pathological gambling. *Journal of Gambling Behavior*, *4*(1), 38–47.

Lesieur, H. R., & Rosenthal, R. J. (1991). Pathological gambling: A review of the literature (prepared for the American Psychiatric Association task force on DSM-IV committee on disorders of impulse control not elsewhere classified). *Journal of Gambling Studies, 7*(1), 5–39.

Lichtermann, D., Franke, P., Maier, W., & Rao, M. L. (2000). Pharmacogenomics and addiction to opiates. *European Journal of Pharmacology, 410*(2), 269–279.

Litten, R. Z., Ryan, M. L., Falk, D. E., Reilly, M., Fertig, J. B., & Koob, G. F. (2015). Heterogeneity of alcohol use disorder: Understanding mechanisms to advance personalized treatment. *Alcoholism: Clinical and Experimental Research, 39*(4), 579–584.

Littlefield, A. K., Sher, K. J., & Wood, P. K. (2009). Is "maturing out" of problematic alcohol involvement related to personality change? *Journal of Abnormal Psychology, 118*(2), 360–374.

Littlefield, A. K., Vergés, A., Wood, P. K., & Sher, K. J. (2012). Transactional models between personality and alcohol involvement: A further examination. *Journal of Abnormal Psychology, 121*(3), 778–783.

Lopez Viets, V. C. (1998). Treating pathological gambling. In W. R. Miller & N. Heather (Eds.), *Treating addictive behaviors* (2nd ed., pp. 259–270). New York: Plenum.

Manolio, T. A., Collins, F. S., Cox, N. J., Goldstein, D. B., Hindorff, L. A., Hunter, D. J., . . . Visscher, P. M. (2009). Finding the missing heritability of complex diseases. *Nature, 461*(7265), 747–753.

Marazziti, D., Corsi, M., Baroni, S., Consoli, G., & Catena-Dell'Osso, M. (2012). Latest advancements in the pharmacological treatment of binge eating disorder. *European Review for Medical and Pharmacological Sciences, 16*(15), 2102–2107.

Martin, C. S., Langenbucher, J. W., Chung, T., & Sher, K. J. (2014). Truth or consequences in the diagnosis of substance use disorders. *Addiction, 109*(11), 1773–1778.

Martin, T., LaRowe, S., & Malcolm, R. (2010). Progress in cue exposure therapy for the treatment of addictive disorders: A review update. *Open Addiction Journal, 3*, 92–101.

McClure, J. B. (2002). Are biomarkers useful treatment aids for promoting health behavior change? An empirical review. *American Journal of Preventive Medicine, 22*(3), 200–207.

McKinney, C., & Caetano, R. (2016). Substance use and race and ethnicity. In K. J. Sher (Ed.), *The Oxford Handbook of Substance Use and Substance Use Disorders* (Vol. 1, pp. 483–525). New York: Oxford University Press. doi: 10.1093/oxfordhb/9780199381678.013.011

McLellan, A. T., Luborsky, L., Woody, G. E., & O'Brien, C. P. (1980). An improved diagnostic evaluation instrument for substance abuse patients: The Addiction Severity Index. *Journal of Nervous and Mental Disease, 168*(1), 26–33.

Misselbrook, G. P., & Hamilton, E. J. (2012). Out with the old, in with the new? Case reports of the clinical features and acute management of two novel designer drugs. *Acute Medicine, 11*(3), 157–160.

Monte, A. A., Zane, R. D., & Heard, K. J. (2015). The implications of marijuana legalization in Colorado. *Journal of the American Medical Association, 313*(3), 241–242.

Moyer, A., Finney, J. W., Swearingen, C. E., & Vergun, P. (2002). Brief interventions for alcohol problems: A meta-analytic review of controlled investigations in treatment-seeking and non-treatment-seeking populations. *Addiction, 97*(3), 279–292.

Mueser, K. T., Noordsy, d. L., Drake, R. E. (2016). Serious mental illness. In K. J. Sher (Ed.), *The Oxford Handbook of Substance Use and Substance Use Disorders* (Vol. 2, pp. 88–115). New York: Oxford University Press. doi:10.1093/oxfordhb/9780199381708.013.005

Muraven, M. (2010). Practicing self-control lowers the risk of smoking lapse. *Psychology of Addictive Behaviors, 24*(3), 446–452.

Muraven, M., & Baumeister, R. F. (2000). Self-regulation and depletion of limited resources: Does self-control resemble a muscle? *Psychological Bulletin, 126*(2), 247–259.

Myers, K. M., & Carlezon, W. A. (2012). D-cycloserine effects on extinction of conditioned responses to drug-related cues. *Biological Psychiatry, 71*(11), 947–955.

National Institute on Alcohol Abuse and Alcoholism. (2000). 10th special report to the US Congress on alcohol and health. Washington, DC: US Department of Health and Human Services.

Nosek, B. A., Alter, G., Banks, G. C., Borsboom, D., Bowman, S. D., Breckler, S. J., . . . Yarkoni, T. (2015). Promoting an open research culture. *Science, 348*(6242), 1422–1425.

O'Malley, S. S., Corbin, W. R., Leeman, R. F., DeMartini, K. S., Fucito, L. M., Ikomi, J., . . . Kranzler, H. R. (2015). Reduction of alcohol drinking in young adults by naltrexone: A double-blind, placebo-controlled, randomized clinical trial of efficacy and safety. *Journal of Clinical Psychiatry, 76*(2), e207–e213.

O'Malley, S. S., Jaffe, A. J., Chang, G., Schottenfeld, R. S., Meyer, R. E., & Rounsaville, B. (1992). Naltrexone and coping skills therapy for alcohol dependence: A controlled study. *Archives of General Psychiatry, 49*(11), 881–887.

Orford, J. (2001). *Excessive appetites: A psychological view of addictions.* New York: Wiley.

Oslin, D. W., Berrettini, W., Kranzler, H. R., Pettinati, H., Gelernter, J., Volpicelli, J. R., & O'Brien, C. P. (2003). A functional polymorphism of the μ-opioid receptor gene is associated with naltrexone response in alcohol-dependent patients. *Neuropsychopharmacology, 28*, 1546–1552.

Oslin, D. W., Berrettini, W. H., & O'Brien, C. P. (2006). Targeting treatments for alcohol dependence: The pharmacogenetics of naltrexone. *Addiction Biology, 11*(3–4), 397–403.

Park, A., Sher, K. J., Todorov, A. A., & Heath, A. C. (2011). Interaction between the DRD4 VNTR polymorphism and proximal and distal environments in alcohol dependence during emerging and young adulthood. *Journal of Abnormal Psychology, 120*(3), 585–595.

Pashler, H., & Harris, C. R. (2012). Is the replicability crisis overblown? Three arguments examined. *Perspectives on Psychological Science, 7*(6), 531–536

Petry, N. M., & O'Brien, C. P. (2013). Internet gaming disorder and the DSM-5. *Addiction, 108*(7), 1186–1187.

Popovici, I., & French, M. T. (2016). Substance use and school and occupational performance. In K. J. Sher (Ed.), *The Oxford Handbook of Substance Use and Substance Use Disorders* (Vol. 2, pp. 379–390). New York: Oxford University Press. doi:10.1093/oxfordhb/9780199381708.013.005

Potenza, M. N. (2006). Should addictive disorders include non-substance-related conditions? *Addiction, 101*(s1), 142–151.

Project MATCH Research Group. (1997). Matching alcoholism treatments to client heterogeneity: Project MATCH post-treatment drinking outcomes. *Journal of Studies on Alcohol, 58*, 7–29.

Project MATCH Research Group. (1998). Matching patients with alcohol disorders to treatments: Clinical implications from Project MATCH. *Journal of Mental Health*, *7*(6), 589–602.

Quinn, P. D., Stappenbeck, C. A., & Fromme, K. (2011). Collegiate heavy drinking prospectively predicts change in sensation seeking and impulsivity. *Journal of Abnormal Psychology*, *120*(3), 543–556.

Ray, L. A., & Hutchison, K. E. (2011). Molecular genetics and the treatment of addiction. In B. A. Johnson (Ed.), *Addiction medicine* (pp. 1101–1114). New York: Springer.

Ressler, K. J., Rothbaum, B. O., Tannenbaum, L., Anderson, P., Graap, K., Zimand, E., . . . Davis, M. (2004). Cognitive enhancers as adjuncts to psychotherapy: Use of D-cycloserine in phobic individuals to facilitate extinction of fear. *Archives of General Psychiatry*, *61*(11), 1136–1144.

Robinson, T. E., & Berridge, K. C. (1993). The neural basis of drug craving: An incentive-sensitization theory of addiction. *Brain Research Reviews*, *18*(3), 247–291.

Rogers, E. M. (2003). *Diffusion of innovations* (5th ed.) New York: Free Press.

Rosenberg, K. P., Carnes, P., & O'Connor, S. (2014). Evaluation and treatment of sex addiction. *Journal of Sex & Marital Therapy*, *40*(2), 77–91.

Sakai, J. T., Mikulich-Gilbertson, S. K., Long, R. J., & Crowley, T. J. (2006). Validity of transdermal alcohol monitoring: Fixed and self-regulated dosing. *Alcoholism: Clinical and Experimental Research*, *30*(1), 26–33.

Saunders, B. T., & Robinson, T. E. (2013). Individual variation in resisting temptation: Implications for addiction. *Neuroscience & Biobehavioral Reviews*, *37*(9), 1955–1975.

Saxon, A. J., & McCarty, D. (2005). Challenges in the adoption of new pharmacotherapeutics for addiction to alcohol and other drugs. *Pharmacology & Therapeutics*, *108*(1), 119–128.

Sayette, M. A., Shiffman, S., Tiffany, S. T., Niaura, R. S., Martin, C. S., & Shadel, W. G. (2000). The measurement of drug craving. *Addiction*, *95*(Suppl 2), S189–S210.

Schmitz, J. M. (2005). The interface between impulse-control disorders and addictions: Are pleasure pathway responses shared neurobiological substrates? *Sexual Addiction & Compulsivity*, *12*(2–3), 149–168.

Schoenmakers, T., Wiers, R. W., Jones, B. T., Bruce, G., & Jansen, A. (2007). Attentional re-training decreases attentional bias in heavy drinkers without generalization. *Addiction*, *102*(3), 399–405.

Schoenmakers, T. M., de Bruin, M., Lux, I. F., Goertz, A. G., Van Kerkhof, D. H., & Wiers, R. W. (2010). Clinical effectiveness of attentional bias modification training in abstinent alcoholic patients. *Drug and Alcohol Dependence*, *109*(1), 30–36.

Schroeder, J. P., & Packard, M. G. (2004). Facilitation of memory for extinction of drug-induced conditioned reward: Role of amygdala and acetylcholine. *Learning & Memory*, *11*(5), 641–647.

Sher, K. J. (2015). Moving the alcohol addiction RDoC forward. *Alcoholism: Clinical and Experimental Research*, *39*(4), 591–591.

Sher, K. J., Grekin, E. R., & Williams, N. A. (2004). The development of alcohol use disorders. *Annual Review of Clinical Psychology*, *1*, 493–523.

Sher, K. J., Wolf, S. T., & Martinez, J. A. (2009). How can etiological research inform the distinction between normal drinking and disordered drinking? In L. M. Scheier (Ed.), *Handbook of drug use etiology (pp. 225–246)*. Washington, DC: American Psychological Association.

Shiffman, S. (2016). 16. Ecological momentary assessment. In K. J. Sher (Ed.), *The Oxford Handbook of Substance Use and Substance Use Disorders* (Vol. 2, pp. 466–510). New York: Oxford University Press. doi:10.1093/oxfordhb/9780199381708.013.005

Siegel, M. B., Tanwar, K. L., & Wood, K. S. (2011). Electronic cigarettes as a smoking-cessation tool: Results from an online survey. *American Journal of Preventive Medicine*, *40*(4), 472–475.

Siegel, S., Baptista, M. A., Kim, J. A., McDonald, R. V., & Weise-Kelly, L. (2000). Pavlovian psychopharmacology: The associative basis of tolerance. *Experimental and Clinical Psychopharmacology*, *8*(3), 276–293.

Smith, D. G., & Robbins, T. W. (2013). The neurobiological underpinnings of obesity and binge eating: A rationale for adopting the food addiction model. *Biological Psychiatry*, *73*(9), 804–810.

Snell, L. D. Bhave, S. V., Takacs, L, & Tabakoff (2016). Biological markers of substance use: Focus on the objective assessment of alcohol exposure. In K. J. Sher (Ed.), *The Oxford Handbook of Substance Use and Substance Use Disorders* (Vol. 2, pp. 393–429). New York: Oxford University Press. doi:10.1093/oxfordhb/9780199381708.013.005

Sobell, L. C., & Sobell, M. B. (1992). Timeline follow-back. In R. Z. Litten & J. P Allen (Eds.), *Measuring alcohol consumption: Psychosocial and biochemical methods* (pp. 41–72). Totowa, NJ: Humana.

Solomon, R. L., & Corbit, J. D. (1974). An opponent-process theory of motivation: I. Temporal dynamics of affect. *Psychological Review*, *81*(2), 119–145.

Stewart, S., Grant, V. V., Mackie, C. J., & Conrod, P. J. (2016). Comorbidity of anxiety and depression with substance use disorders. In K. J. Sher (Ed.), *The Oxford Handbook of Substance Use and Substance Use Disorders* (Vol. 2, pp. 149–186). New York: Oxford University Press. doi:10.1093/oxfordhb/9780199381708.013.005

Stice, E., Figlewicz, D. P., Gosnell, B. A., Levine, A. S., & Pratt, W. E. (2013). The contribution of brain reward circuits to the obesity epidemic. *Neuroscience & Biobehavioral Reviews*, *37*(9), 2047–2058.

Swift, R. (2000). Transdermal alcohol measurement for estimation of blood alcohol concentration. *Alcoholism: Clinical and Experimental Research*, *24*(4), 422–423.

Tao, R., Huang, X., Wang, J., Zhang, H., Zhang, Y., & Li, M. (2010). Proposed diagnostic criteria for internet addiction. *Addiction*, *105*(3), 556–564.

Tellegen, A. (1991). Personality traits: Issues of definition, evidence, and assessment. In D. Cicchetti & W. M. Grove (Eds.), *Essays in honor of Paul E. Meehl: Vol. 1. Matters of public interest; Vol. 2. Personality and psychopathology.* (pp. 10–35). Minneapolis: University of Minnesota Press.

Todd, T. P., Vurbic, D., & Bouton, M. E. (2014). Behavioral and neurobiological mechanisms of extinction in Pavlovian and instrumental learning. *Neurobiology of Learning and Memory*, *108*, 52–64.

Trull, T. J., Solhan, M. B., Brown, W. C., Tomko, R. L., Schaefer, L., McLaughlin, D. D., & Jahng, S. (2016). Substance use disorders and personality disorders. In K. J. Sher (Ed.), *The Oxford Handbook of Substance Use and Substance Use Disorders* (Vol. 2, pp. 116–148). New York: Oxford University Press. doi:10.1093/oxfordhb/9780199381708.013.005

Tully, E. C., & Iacono, W. (2016). An integrative common liabilities model for the comorbidity of substance use disorders with externalizing and internalizing disorders. In K. J. Sher (Ed.), *The Oxford Handbook of Substance Use and Substance Use Disorders* (Vol. 1, pp. 187–212). New York: Oxford University Press. doi: 10.1093/oxfordhb/9780199381708.013.20

Uchiyama, N., Shimokawa, Y., Kawamura, M., Kikura-Hanajiri, R., & Hakamatsuka, T. (2014). Chemical analysis of a benzofuran derivative, 2-(2-ethylaminopropyl) benzofuran (2-EAPB), eight synthetic cannabinoids, five cathinone derivatives, and five other designer drugs newly detected in illegal products. *Forensic Toxicology, 32*(2), 266–281.

van Holst, R. J., van den Brink, W., Veltman, D. J., & Goudriaan, A. E. (2010). Why gamblers fail to win: A review of cognitive and neuroimaging findings in pathological gambling. *Neuroscience & Biobehavioral Reviews, 34*(1), 87–107.

Voas, R., & Fell, J. C. (2016). Programs and policies designed to reduce impaired driving. In K. J. Sher (Ed.), *The Oxford Handbook of Substance Use and Substance Use Disorders* (Vol. 1, pp. 621–676). New York: Oxford University Press.

Vohs, K. D., & Baumeister, R. F. (2004). Understanding self-regulation: An introduction. In R. F. Baumeister & K. D. Vohs (Eds.), *Handbook of self-regulation: Research, theory, and applications* (pp. 1–9). New York: Guilford.

Volkow, N. D., Wang, G. J., Tomasi, D., & Baler, R. D. (2013). Obesity and addiction: Neurobiological overlaps. *Obesity Reviews, 14*(1), 2–18.

Volkow, N. D., & Wise, R. A. (2005). How can drug addiction help us understand obesity? *Nature Neuroscience, 8*(5), 555–560.

Walker, D. D., Roffman, R. A., Picciano, J. F., & Stephens, R. S. (2007). The check-up: In-person, computerized, and telephone adaptations of motivational enhancement treatment to elicit voluntary participation by the contemplator. *Substance Abuse Treatment, Prevention, and Policy, 2*, 2.

Wang, G. S., Roosevelt, G., Le Lait, M. C., Martinez, E. M., Bucher-Bartelson, B., Bronstein, A. C., & Heard, K. (2014). Association of unintentional pediatric exposures with decriminalization of marijuana in the United States. *Annals of Emergency Medicine, 63*(6), 684–689.

Wang, J. C., Kapoor, M., & Goate, A. M. (2012). The genetics of substance dependence. *Annual Review of Genomics and Human Genetics, 13*, 241–261.

Warner, K. E., & Burns, D. M. (2003). Hardening and the hard-core smoker: Concepts, evidence, and implications. *Nicotine & Tobacco Research, 5*(1), 37–48.

Wetter, D. W., Smith, S. S., Kenford, S. L., Jorenby, D. E., Fiore, M. C., Hurt, R. D., . . . Baker, T. B. (1994). Smoking outcome expectancies: Factor structure, predictive validity, and discriminant validity. *Journal of Abnormal Psychology, 103*(4), 801–811.

White, H. R. (2016). Substance use and crime. In K. J. Sher (Ed.), *The Oxford Handbook of Substance Use and Substance Use Disorders* (Vol. 2, pp. 347–378). New York: Oxford University Press. doi:10.1093/oxfordhb/9780199381708.013.005

Wiers, R. W., Eberl, C., Rinck, M., Becker, E. S., & Lindenmeyer, J. (2011). Retraining automatic action tendencies changes alcoholic patients' approach bias for alcohol and improves treatment outcome. *Psychological Science, 22*(4), 490–497.

Wiers, R. W., Field, M., & Stacy, A. W. (2016). Passion's slave? Conscious and unconscious cognitive processes in alcohol and drug abuse. In K. J. Sher (Ed.), *The Oxford Handbook of Substance Use and Substance Use Disorders* (Vol. 1, pp. 311–350). New York: Oxford University Press. doi:10.1093/oxfordhb/9780199381708.013.005

Wiers, R. W., Gladwin, T. E., Hofmann, W., Salemink, E., & Ridderinkhof, K. R. (2013). Cognitive bias modification and cognitive control training in addiction and related psychopathology mechanisms, clinical perspectives, and ways forward. *Clinical Psychological Science, 1*, 192–212.

Wiers, R. W., Rinck, M., Dictus, M., & van den Wildenberg, E. (2009). Relatively strong automatic appetitive action-tendencies in male carriers of the OPRM1 G-allele. *Genes, Brain and Behavior, 8*(1), 101–106.

Wiers, R. W., & Stacy, A. W. (2006). Implicit cognition and addiction. *Current Directions in Psychological Science, 15*(6), 292–296.

Wise, R. A. (2013). Dual roles of dopamine in food and drug seeking: The drive-reward paradox. *Biological Psychiatry, 73*(9), 819–826.

Young, K. S. (1998). Internet addiction: The emergence of a new clinical disorder. *CyberPsychology & Behavior, 1*(3), 237–244.

Zerhouni, E. A. (2006). Clinical research at a crossroads: The NIH roadmap. *Journal of Investigative Medicine, 54*(4), 171–173.

Ziauddeen, H., Farooqi, I. S., & Fletcher, P. C. (2012). Obesity and the brain: How convincing is the addiction model? *Nature Reviews Neuroscience, 13*(4), 279–286.

Ziauddeen, H., & Fletcher, P. C. (2013). Is food addiction a valid and useful concept? *Obesity Reviews, 14*(1), 19–28.

INDEX